CW01011093

COUNTER-ATTACK

BUSINESS
STRATEGIES
FOR
EXPLOSIVE
GROWTH
IN THE
NEW ECONOMY

Published by CelebrityPress™, Orlando, FL
A division of The Celebrity Branding Agency®

Celebrity Branding® is a registered trademark
Printed in the United States of America.

LCCN: 2010940882
ISBN: 978-0-9829083-4-1

This publication is designed to provide accurate and authoritative information with regard to the subject matter covered. It is sold with the understanding that the publisher is not engaged in rendering legal, accounting, or other professional advice. If legal advice or other expert assistance is required, the services of a competent professional should be sought. The opinions expressed by the authors in this book are not endorsed by CelebrityPress™ and are the sole responsibility of the author rendering the opinion.

Most CelebrityPress™ titles are available at special quantity discounts for bulk purchases for sales promotions, premiums, fundraising, and educational use. Special versions or book excerpts can also be created to fit specific needs.

For more information, please write:

CelebrityPress™,
520 N. Orlando Ave, #44,
Winter Park, FL 32789

or call 1.877.261.4930

Visit us online at www.**CelebrityPressPublishing**.com

COUNTER-ATTACK

BUSINESS STRATEGIES FOR EXPLOSIVE GROWTH IN THE NEW ECONOMY

TABLE OF CONTENTS:

CHAPTER 1

THE POWER OF PERSUASION

BY BRIAN TRACY

Persuasion power can help you get more of the things you want faster than anything else you do. It can mean the difference between success and failure. It can guarantee your progress and enable you to use all of your other skills and abilities at the very highest level. Your persuasion power will earn you the support and respect of your customers, bosses, co-workers, colleagues and friends. The ability to persuade others to do what you want them to do can make you one of the most important people in your community.

Fortunately, persuasion is a skill, like riding a bicycle, that you can learn through study and practice. Your job is to become absolutely excellent at influencing and motivating others to support and assist you in the achievement of your goals and the accomplishment of your business objectives.

You can either persuade others to help you or be persuaded to help them. It is one or the other. Most people are not aware that every human interaction involves a complex process of persuasion and influence. And being unaware, they are usually the ones being persuaded to help others rather than the ones who are doing the persuading.

THE POWER OF MOTIVATION

The key to persuasion is motivation. Every human action is motivated by something. Your job is to find out what motivates other people and then to provide that motivation. People have two major motivations: the desire for gain and the fear of loss. The desire for gain motivates people to want more of the things they value in life. They want more money, more success, more health, more influence, more respect, more love and more happiness. Individual wants are limited only by individual imagination. No matter how much a person has, he or she still wants more and more. When you can show a person how he or she can get more of the things he or she wants by helping you achieve your goals, you can motivate them to act on your behalf.

President Eisenhower once said that, "Persuasion is the art of getting people to do what you want them to do, and to like it." You need always to be thinking about how you can get people to want to do the things that you need them to do to attain your objectives.

THE POWER OF FEAR

People are also motivated to act by the fear of loss. This fear, in all its various forms, is often stronger than the desire for gain. People fear financial loss, loss of health, anger or disapproval of others, loss of the love of someone and the loss of anything they have worked hard to accomplish. They fear change, risk and uncertainty, because these threaten them with potential losses.

Whenever you can show a person that by doing what you want them to do, they can avoid a loss of some kind, you can influence them to take a particular action. The very best appeals are those where you offer an opportunity to gain and an opportunity to avoid loss at the same time.

There are two ways to get the things you want in life. First, you can work by yourself and for yourself in your own best interests. You can be a "Robinson Crusoe" of modern life, relying on yourself for the satisfaction of your needs. By doing this, you can accomplish a little, but not a lot. The person who looks to himself or herself completely is limited in his or her capacities. He or she will never be rich or successful.

THE POWER OF LEVERAGE

The second way to get the things you want is by gaining and using *leverage*. Leverage allows you to multiply yourself and get far more out of the hours you put in, rather than doing everything yourself.

There are three forms of leverage you must develop to fulfill your full potential in our society: other people's efforts, other people's knowledge, and other people's money.

(1): OTHER PEOPLE'S EFFORTS

You leverage yourself through other people's efforts by getting other people to work with you and for you in the accomplishment of your objectives. Sometimes you can ask them to help you voluntarily, although people won't work for very long without some personal reward. At other times you can hire them to help you, thereby freeing you up to do higher-value work.

One of the most important laws of economics is called "Ricardo's Law." It is also called the Law of Comparative Advantage. This law states that when someone can accomplish a part of your task at a lower hourly rate than you would earn for accomplishing more valuable parts of your task, you should delegate or outsource that part of the task.

For example, if you want to earn $100,000 a year, in a 250 day year, you need to make $50.00 per hour. That means you must be doing work that is worth $50.00 per hour, eight hours per day, 250 days per year. Therefore, if there is any part of your work⎯like making photocopies, filing information, typing letters, or filling out expense forms⎯that is not valued at $50.00 per hour, you should stop doing it. You should persuade someone else who works at a lower hourly rate to do it for you. The more lower level tasks you can persuade others to do, the more time you will have to do tasks that pay you higher amounts of money. This is one of the essential keys to getting the leverage you need to become one of the higher paid people in your profession.

Management can be defined as "getting things done through others." To be a manager you must be an expert at persuading and influencing others to work in a common direction. This is why all excellent managers are also excellent low-pressure salespeople. They do not order people to do things; instead, they persuade them to accept certain responsibilities, with specific deadlines and agreed-upon standards of performance. When a person has been persuaded that he or she has a vested interest in doing a job well, he or she accepts ownership of the job and the result. Once a person accepts ownership and responsibility, the manager can step aside confidently, knowing the job will be done on schedule.

In every part of your life, you have a choice of either doing it yourself or delegating it to others. Your ability to get someone else to take on the job with the same enthusiasm that you would have is an exercise in personal persuasion. It may seem to take a little longer at the beginning, but it saves you an enormous amount of time in the completion of the task.

(2): OTHER PEOPLE'S KNOWLEDGE

The second form of leverage that you must develop for success in America is other people's knowledge. You must be able to tap into the brain power of many other people if you want to accomplish worthwhile goals. Successful people are not those who know everything needed to accomplish a particular task, but more often than not, they are people who know how to *find* the knowledge they need.

What is the knowledge that you need to achieve your most important goals? Of the knowledge required, what knowledge must you have personally in order to control your situation, and what knowledge can you borrow, buy, or rent from others?

It has been said that, in our information-based society, you are never more than one book or two phone calls away from any piece of knowledge in the country. With on-line computer services that access huge data bases all over the country, you can usually get the precise information you require in a few minutes by using a personal computer. Whenever you need information and expertise from another person in order to achieve your goals, the very best way to persuade them to help you is to ask them for their assistance.

Almost everyone who is knowledgeable in a particular area is proud of their accomplishments. By asking a person for their expert advice, you compliment them and motivate them to want to help you. So don't be afraid to ask, even if you don't know the individual personally.

(3): OTHER PEOPLE'S MONEY

The third key to leverage, which is very much based on your persuasive abilities, is other people's money. Your ability to use other people's money and resources to leverage your talents is the key to financial success. Your ability to buy and defer payment, to sell and collect payment in advance, to borrow, rent or lease furniture, fixtures and machinery, and to borrow money from people to help you multiply your opportunities is one of the most important of all skills that you can develop. And these all depend on your ability to persuade others to cooperate with you financially so that you can develop the leverage you need to move onward and upward in your field.

THE FOUR P'S OF PERSUASION

There are four "Ps" that will enhance your ability to persuade others in both your work and personal life. They are power, positioning, performance, and politeness. And they are all based on perception.

1. **Power:** The more power and influence that a person perceives that you have, whether real or not, the more likely it is that that person will be persuaded by you to do the things you want them to do. For example, if you appear to be a senior executive, or a wealthy person, people will be much more likely to help you and serve you than they would be if you were perceived to be a lower level employee.

2. **Positioning:** This refers to the way that other people think about you and talk about you when you are not there, your reputation. Your positioning in the minds and hearts of other people largely determines how open they are to being influenced by you.

    In everything you do involving other people, you are shaping and influencing their perceptions of you and your positioning in their minds. Think about how you could change the things you say and do so that people think about you in such a way that they are more open to your requests and to helping you achieve your goals.

3. **Performance:** This refers to your level of competence and expertise in your area. A person who is highly respected for his or her ability to get results is far more persuasive and influential than

a person who only does an average job.

The perception that people have of your performance capabilities exerts an inordinate influence on how they think and feel about you. You should commit yourself to being the very best in your field. Sometimes, a reputation for being excellent at what you do can be so powerful that it alone can make you an extremely persuasive individual in all of your interactions with the people around you. They will accept your advice, be open to your influence and agree with your requests.

4. **Politeness:** People do things for two reasons, because they *want* to and because they *have* to. When you treat people with kindness, courtesy and respect, you make them want to do things for you. They are motivated to go out of their way to help you solve your problems and accomplish your goals. Being nice to other people satisfies one of the deepest of all subconscious needs, the need to feel important and respected. Whenever you convey this to another person in your conversation, your attitude and your treatment of that person, he or she will be 'wide open' to being persuaded and influenced by you in almost anything you need.

THE POWER OF PERCEPTION

Remember, perception is everything. The perception of an individual is his or her reality. People act on the basis of their perceptions of you. If you change their perceptions, you change the way they think and feel about you, and you change the things that they will do for you.

You can become an expert at personal persuasion. You can develop your personal power by always remembering that there are only two ways to get the things you want in life, you can do it all yourself, or you can get most of it done by others. Your ability to communicate, persuade, negotiate, influence, delegate and interact effectively with other people will enable you to develop leverage using other people's efforts, other people's knowledge and other people's money. The development of your persuasion power will enable you to become one of the most powerful and influential people in your organization. It will open up doors for you in every area of your life.

ABOUT BRIAN

Brian Tracy is Chairman and CEO of Brian Tracy International, a company specializing in the training and development of individuals and organizations. Brian's goal is to help people achieve their personal and business goals faster and easier than they ever imagined.

Brian Tracy has consulted for more than 1,000 companies and addressed more than 5,000,000 people in 5,000 talks and seminars throughout the US, Canada and 55 other countries worldwide. As a Keynote speaker and seminar leader, he addresses more than 250,000 people each year.

He has studied, researched, written and spoken for 30 years in the fields of economics, history, business, philosophy and psychology. He is the top selling author of over 50 books that have been translated into 36 languages.

He has written and produced more than 300 audio and video learning programs, including the worldwide, best-selling Psychology of Achievement, which has been translated into more than 20 languages.

He speaks to corporate and public audiences on the subjects of Personal and Professional Development, including the executives and staff of many of America's largest corporations. His exciting talks and seminars on Leadership, Selling, Self-Esteem, Goals, Strategy, Creativity and Success Psychology bring about immediate changes and long-term results.

Prior to founding his company, Brian Tracy International, Brian was the Chief Operating Officer of a $265 million dollar development company. He has had successful careers in sales and marketing, investments, real estate development and syndication, importation, distribution and management consulting. He has conducted high level consulting assignments with several billion-dollar plus corporations in strategic planning and organizational development.

He has traveled and worked in over 80 countries on six continents, and speaks four languages. Brian is happily married and has four children. He is active in community and national affairs, and is the President of three companies headquartered in Solana Beach, California.

For more information on Brian Tracy programs, go to: www.briantracy.com

CHAPTER 2

FINDING SUCCESS IN SERVICE TO MY PATIENTS

BY DR. BARBARA TODD

Opportunities do not come with their values stamped upon them
~ Maltbie Babcock

I didn't just wake up one morning and have a successful dental practice. But I did wake up.

In 1987 when I received my dental degree, I was required—due to my South Carolina loan program guidelines – to set up practice in an area that was underserved. My choices were Aynor in Horry County or Murrells Inlet in Georgetown County. I opened my practice in Murrells Inlet after a failed attempt in Aynor. God works in mysterious ways. Closing the door on one practice opened a bigger window for me.

I had opened my practice with a single treatment room, one hygiene room - one of everything - in 1987. With borrowed money from a private lender and a dental company, I set up shop for one day a week to start. After working a four day week in a clinic-type setting doing restorative dentistry, I would work my own practice one day a week as I built up my patients and added more days each year. But I knew nothing about running a business. Day-to-day operations were a struggle. The first time that I had to fire a team member I thought I was going to pass out!

Dental school doesn't teach you the business side of running a success-ful practice. A single business class in dental school was not enough to bring success. Success came with learning to recognize opportunities. By 1989 I was stressed. My business wasn't growing as quickly as I had hoped. I didn't seem to have the right people working in my office. I had had many business books come across my desk and one of them was from Linda Miles, a former dental hygienist who now coached oth-ers on the finer points of running a successful dental office.

My first 'wake up call' was when I recognized that to be successful, I needed a business coach. Most successful people have some sort of coach to help them achieve greatness; whether it's Michael Jordan with Phil Jackson, or Sandra Bullock and her stylists and publicist, or even the President and his cabinet, there is always someone helping to get the best for them. I was tired of flying 'by the seat of my pants', so I hired Linda Miles & Associates to help coach me to be playoff or academy award-ready in my industry. When a business isn't thriving, a natural reaction would be to assume you can't afford a business coach, but what I realized is that this is exactly when you can't afford not to have one! Linda Miles came in and offered suggestions on how to hire people who would be assets to our organization, where to look for new business, and how to cultivate more business from our existing customer base.

For several years, a local pastor had been begging me to come on his radio show and answer call-in questions pertaining to dentistry. I re-sisted at first because I was afraid of being on the radio. When I finally agreed to be on his show, I couldn't believe how easy it was! I also couldn't believe that I had waited years to accept this free advertising for my practice. This is probably the second biggest 'wake-up call' of my career. Free advertising – the kind you get from 'word of mouth' of happy patients and friends or from people hearing your name on the radio-- is worth more than any advertising you might pay for.

The rest of what I learned came a little more slowly over the past 20 years. You won't have to wait that long though, because I want you to have the knowledge *today* that I took years to acquire.

KNOW YOUR TEAM

Today our practice has grown from three staff members to an eight member team. We have grown to be a homogenous team that runs as smoothly as possible while having as much fun as possible. No one person is better than or more important than the others in the office. We operate as a cohesive unit: we pray together, gather at a huddle each morning, have a staff meeting each month. Each person contributes ideas and plays an essential role. We play our parts consistently and strive daily to improve our performance.

KNOW YOUR CUSTOMER

Take fifteen minutes every morning before patient treatment to review what your chart audits indicate. Look at each patient as an individual. Are there any concerns or needs for this patient which have not been addressed? Any concerns in their families, marriages, graduations, new babies or sicknesses? *People are not interested in what you know so much as how much you care.*

At our monthly meetings, we discuss who we might choose as a patient that is having financial difficulties, and we plan on completing their necessary dental treatment at no charge. You may consider annual, semi annual or quarterly *gratis* treatments depending on the time and cost. Patients who understand that you care about their well being are patients who will tell their friends and family about their happy experiences.

LET EVERYONE BE PART OF YOUR VISION

 Your vision for the business should be known to all and agreed to by all. Employees who cannot agree to the vision for the practice might be the wrong people for the team. When your staff is a part of the process and understands the vision, they have a greater sense of ownership. This results in huge, positive growth for your practice! You should consider a one hour meeting per month where you review the marketing numbers for external and internal marketing with your staff. Take the time to talk about what they notice is happening with patients or in your practice.

Encourage staff to become part of your team by offering them referral bonuses. Our staff members get $20 for each new patient they refer and $50 if the new patient treatment if over $2000. I offered a paid trip for two to the staff member who refers ten new patients to the practice in a one-year period.

Make sure your staff understands and agrees that treating patients like you would want to be treated is of the utmost importance. And even though in a busy practice it can be the most challenging thing to do, LISTEN to your patients. It is all about your customer, patient, or client. Excellence is doing the right thing over and over when you don't feel like doing it. The staff can create and sprinkle seeds of love, patience and caring, but they can also kill patient relationships. Don't be afraid to terminate someone who isn't a good fit for your vision.

Always find out where customers heard about you. When a patient is extremely happy and they let us know, we ask immediately for a testimony that we can publish on our website. We ask if we can take a snap video and place on our website. Try other avenues for free advertising too - such as networking sites Facebook, LinkedIn or Twitter.

THINKING OUTSIDE THE ~~BOX~~ OFFICE

Something that's both fun and beneficial is throwing a Patient Appreciation Day. My practice has had three so far, and our patients have asked when they can expect to see another one. Consider some good entertainment such as a D.J., band or Karaoke - combined with some barbecue, 'chicken bog', or simple hot dogs and hamburgers. We had music, a massage therapist and 'chicken bog' with barbecue. It was set up under a large tent to offer some protection for those who cannot take the heat and in case of rain. All this was advertised at the office (at virtually no cost) six months before the party, with all the details. Our office team filled a table with homemade desserts, cakes, etc. This was the first table to become empty -- imagine that? All this took place on the lawn in the front of the office. Patients were invited to bring family and friends. For the next step, you want to think beyond those who are already patients.

Becoming a strong community supporter will help spread your office's good name 'faster than wildfire'. Have a Community Day where you give back something to all of your community, but especially for those who cannot afford your services. We recently held a Community Day where all our team plus several other Doctors donated their time and expertise to complete dental work for select patients who could not afford the treatment. We were able to service our community with approximately $15,500.00 worth of dentistry *gratis*. The patients we saw were in need and very appreciative, and all the staff donated that time because they felt better about helping those in need in their community. We donate our time annually to this event because it makes us feel happy and connected to the community we serve. As a bonus, our community better knows who we are and how we work.

Look for opportunities in your area where your presence is the advertising. Remember that these opportunities, like my experience participating on a radio call-in show, may be outside your current comfort zone. Maybe hosting an event isn't your *forte*, but it may be something that a member of your office team enjoys doing and excels at. This is where knowing your team and working as a cohesive unit will make you less stressed, and your practice more productive and prosperous.

TRACK IT

If you don't track what you do, you won't know what is working. When you have a person or patient who is singing your praises, have your staff offer them three business cards to share with friends or family. These cards offer a new patient $50.00 off any new patient examination, emergency visit or any other treatment they may want. The person giving the card will also get $50.00 off future treatment - after their referral comes to the office for their treatment. Unlike advertising in a local print ad, the business cards are easily trackable. You know exactly which patient the referral came from and how many people are taking advantage of your offer.

DON'T OVERLOOK THE SMALL STUFF

Little things such as giving a warm wipe when a procedure is finished can go a long way to making a patient feel comfortable and cared for. If it has been a long appointment, give the patient a drink like Ensure, water or juice -- something to give them a little energy. This is especially important if they have any health issues, or they seem worn out from the long appointment. Everyone likes refreshments and something to eat if the appointment is a very long one. There are so many different things you can offer free of charge. On holidays, flowers are great to give when the patient's treatment is completed: green carnations on April first, red carnations are a favorite for Mother's Day. You might even offer 'laughing gas' to make an appointment more relaxing. The key is to go above and beyond what your competitors would normally do, so you can set your practice apart.

Try having a senior citizens' drawing each month for a gift card to a nice local restaurant (with several restaurants from which to choose) so people can have a reason to look forward to hearing from their dentist's office. You can make the cards anywhere from 25.00 to 50.00+ dollars. Most patients will be so thrilled that they will drive to the office that day to pick up their gift card!

BE PROACTIVE

God helps those who help themselves to continue to take steps to grow. If you stop improving, you stop growing! Continue to learn how to make your customers' experiences even better. Do the right thing even though no one is watching and work with 'the cream of the crop' - people of excellence.

Join Toastmasters or some other club that will allow you to grow as a person while you grow your business. Step out of your comfort zone!

Opportunities to grow your business are endless, but you have to recognize the opportunities that come to you. If you think you and your business aren't exactly playoff-ready, don't worry. Seek out support. Remember, even Michael Jordan needed a coach.

Dr. Barbara A. Todd can be contacted at: Batodddmd@aol.com, or www. MurrellsInletDentistry.com 843-651-5557.

ABOUT BARBARA

Dr. Barbara A. Todd is a native of Conway, South Carolina. She maintains a private practice in Murrells Inlet, South Carolina and has enjoyed growing the practice since 1987. Barbara began her career as a dental assistant for a local dentist and was so influenced that she decided to pursue a dental hygiene degree. After practicing hygiene for several years, her heart was set on getting a dental degree at the Medical University of South Carolina in Charleston, S.C. rather than an Art degree she had considered earlier. She now uses those talents within the profession of dentistry. She finds it to be loads of fun and very gratifying.

Dr. Todd maintains memberships in numerous professional organizations, including the South Carolina Dental Association, American Dental Association, Academy of General Dentistry, American Academy of Implant Dentistry, Association of Oral Implantology, Grand Toastmasters Group and The Spears Study Group. She enjoys learning and continuing education is a constant endeavor to keep up with all the new and exciting developments. At present, she has accumulated over 1900 hours of continuing education. Barbara also enjoys a variety of activities and new challenges. Time with family and friends begin with boating, bicycling or just playing on the sand pile created for the nieces and nephews. She has spent time learning to motorcycle, fly (single engine Piper and Cherokee, helicopter, Schweitzer), and is now learning guitar and drums. Her thoughts are that life is a Smorgasbord of exploration. A favorite quote: Give the World the best you have and the best will come back to you~*Madeline Bridges.*

Barbara can be contacted at:
BaTodddmd@aol.com,
www.MurrellsInletDentistry@aol.com
or 843-651-5557

CHAPTER 3

MOTIVATION... AS A COMPETITIVE ADVANTAGE!

BY BASEM AL ATTAR

In a downward economy, people easily become de-motivated.

They're very concerned about their future, about their ability to meet their mortgage payments, and their ability to simply make ends meet.

Right about that time, the average boss would make things worse by dropping hints of layoffs, budget cuts and project suspensions.

He or she would sound and look worried, anxious or even irritated. At every meeting, in every email, there would be mention of the "tough times ahead" and what "has to be done" in order to "survive". This makes people even more nervous and uncertain.

Now here's the big secret:

People don't do their best when they are worried, uncertain and de-motivated. And at tough times, you really need your people to be doing their very best.

That's why you've got to be better than the average boss. You've got to know how to motivate your team, especially in times of crisis. In fact, throughout history, that's been a quality common to all great leaders who have managed to lead their teams to victory despite unbelievable odds.

I am not suggesting that you line up everyone and get on top of a horse to give a speech, although it could certainly cheer them up if you fell off.

Instead, you need to pay close attention to how your people feel and know how to keep them focused, high spirited and motivated.

If you can, don't just maintain, but rocket your team's motivation and enthusiasm in times of crisis, that in itself becomes a huge competitive advantage.

Think about it, while your competitors are busy slashing budgets, suspending projects and downsizing, you'd have a superior team that has the energy and drive to go out there and create business opportunities the doomsayers just can't see.

SO JUST HOW DO YOU BECOME A MASTER MOTIVATOR?

Most managers think that motivation is simply a matter of applying the 'carrot and stick' principle. You can get a mule to move in the direction you want by either dangling a carrot under it's nose or beating it with a stick! Or so the theory goes.

In real life, people (and even mules) are actually far more complex than that.

It's true that motivation is based on pain and pleasure, but one person's pain is another person's pleasure.

Not everyone desires the corner office or wants to avoid the night shift. Not all employees are motivated by a pay raise or promotion, and similarly not everyone is concerned with a pay cut or loss of benefits or privileges.

David McClelland, an American psychologist asked the smart question: what do people want? And he came up with a simple but profoundly effective answer. McClelland found that there are three categories for motivating people:

1. Need for Power

2. Need for Achievement and
3. Need for Relationships

POWER PEOPLE:

Power-motivated people enjoy being in charge. They want to have a sense of control over their environment. They enjoy making decisions and don't mind stepping up to difficult tasks and responsibilities.

You can easily identify a power-motivated employee when they come asking you for more authority or responsibility.

These people are sensitive to meddling in their domain or area of expertise and if you step in and make a decision for them, they could either sulk quietly for days or make sure you know your help isn't appreciated.

These individuals are highly motivated by promotion and indirect signs of power, including close proximity to the boss. A power-motivated person will always appreciate it when you ask their opinion, confide in them or even just take them out to lunch.

Give your power-motivated people room to make decisions, feel in control and exercise authority over their work.

A word of caution, make sure they don't become too authoritarian with other team members or that may create resistance and resentment.

ACHIEVEMENT PEOPLE:

Achievement-motivated people are 'turned on' by major goals. They enjoy working hard towards specific targets and feel a rush of success when they achieve them, very similar to an athlete crossing the finish line.

They love having a sense of mission and purpose.

Challenges on the road to achievement are the icing on the cake. They pride themselves on overcoming hurdles and so become very valuable in times of crisis.

Give them a clear mission, the resources they need to achieve it and watch them go!

Don't switch them among projects or tasks before they've had the chance to complete what they're doing and get the satisfaction of crossing that finish line.

Praise their achievements publicly and when they come up against a wall they can't climb, help them over it. Never give them a sense that your power as a boss is being used to limit their ability to achieve.

Naturally, achievement-motivated people dislike delays, indecision or anything that may decrease their ability to achieve.

They may not care for policy and procedures either. To them these are things that slow them down or distract them from their goal. This could strain their relationship with power-motivated supervisors who want to keep a firm hand on things.

On the other hand, they may not care to compete for promotions or positions of authority, preferring to be out there in the field scoring the goals rather than planning and managing. They often don't care who's in charge, as long as they're given the resources to achieve their targets.

Be ready to be surprised, every once in a while as the achievement-motivated employee achieves something beyond your expectations.

But be careful they don't disrupt team relations along the way.

RELATIONSHIP PEOPLE:

Relationship-motivated people want everyone to get along with everyone else. They want others to like and respect them.

They dislike conflict and attempt to avoid it whenever possible. When a conflict does arise (often between Power and Achievement people), relationship people work hard – sometimes too hard – to resolve it.

They just like having everyone get along as one big happy family. They will know who's birthday it is this month and be the driving force behind office celebrations. To the Relationship-type people, it's never just business.

Relationship-motivated people are the glue that keeps teams together. They put in extra effort to avoid miscommunication and patch up misunderstandings. They mediate and make sure everyone is comfortable and happy.

Although sometimes their input may not be as quantifiable as Power and

Achievement people, make no mistake, Relationship team members are essential for the continuity of performance and for avoiding negative vibes.

You need to make sure they don't neglect their core duties because of relationships or conflicts, and that they aren't playing favorites either.

THE THREE MOTIVATORS IN ACTION:

As a smart boss you first need to identify the main motivator for each of your team members. That could be tricky since all human beings are motivated by all three, to some degree.

But in each individual you can usually identify a dominant motivator, the one that really moves him or her to action.

Keep in mind that these motivators tell you the reasons why people will do things, not what they actually do.

For example, an Achievement-motivated person may be very eager to resolve a conflict. It's not necessarily to preserve the relationship. Instead it could be because they foresee the conflict slowing down productivity or causing them to under-achieve now or in the future.

Similarly, your Relationship employee may be a continuous top achiever, but his real reason may be to gain the respect of his peers rather than the achievement itself.

After identifying your team members' motivators, you can revisit the old concept of 'the carrot and stick', but in a far more effective way.

You see, some people will have "Away From" motivation. They move away from pain (the stick). Others will have "Towards" motivation. They move towards pleasure (the carrot). Both move, but for different reasons.

Power, achievement and relationships are, if you like, 'the carrots and sticks'. For example, some people will be moved to action by a possible loss of power, while others would be motivated by possible gain of power.

The smart manager (that's you) tests and uses both "Away" and "Towards" motivation with power, achievement and relationship people, each to their individual preference. You need to experiment, find out what works with whom and stick to it.

Pay particular attention to your own preferences. Are you motivated by 'carrots' or 'sticks'? Which is your favorite 'carrot'? …power, achievement or relationships?

You see, your natural tendency would be to motivate others exactly as you'd like to be motivated.

As an example, suppose you are achievement motivated and happen to move "Away from" pain rather than "towards" pleasure.

You might be singing the *"lets not miss the deadline"* tune, with none of your team humming along. Why?

Your power-motivated people only care about the deadline as long as they have some degree of control, while your relationship folks are more interested in the respect, reputation and admiration that could be won or lost by meeting the deadline. Even your fellow achievement-motivated people, who would rather move "towards" pleasure, prefer to hear you talk about *meeting the deadline* instead of *not missing it*.

With a few days practice, you'll be amazed at how fast you can craft your communications with your team members into customized messages designed to motivate each into action, despite the tough times, the downwards economy or whatever other hardships they face.

WHAT ABOUT GROUP MOTIVATION?

If you ever need to address a large audience, make sure your speech includes something for everyone.

You need to tell your audience exactly what relationships, achievements and power they're likely to gain or lose, if they do or do not act in accordance with your recommendations.

And by the way, that's exactly how you rally the troops when you're on top of a horse too!

So the general would tell his soldiers about the *love and respect* they would gain (or lose) when they go home – provided they are victorious. And he'd clarify what they can strategically *achieve* (or not) from today's battle, and finally the amount of *power or control* they would gain (or lose) depending on the outcome.

By the end of that speech, everyone would feel ready for action, each for their own reasons.

UNDERSTANDING FEEDBACK:

Just moving your people to action isn't quite enough though, because sometimes they will energetically move in the wrong direction.

So you've also got to master the art of giving feedback.

Feedback that doesn't de-motivate them!

Here are the two golden rules of feedback:

I - Always exaggerate the good and downplay the bad!

II - Always praise in public and correct in private!

A job well done would be described as excellent, great or wonderful!! Publically.

A mistake would be described as "a temporary slip, requiring further attention". Privately.

If you're doubtful about this approach, just try reversing it. Describe every success as "okay" or "not bad" and every mistake as a "disaster" or a "crisis". It won't take long before you find yourself working alone.

People don't like making mistakes and they don't like the boss drawing attention to them. So whenever someone is doing something wrong, draw attention to the mistake indirectly and privately. Give people the chance to correct their own mistakes whenever possible and praise them for doing so.

BE HONEST AND TRANSPARENT:

Funnily enough, a large part of motivation is not about the pep talk at all. It's about trust.

Never lie to your people. Keep them informed about what's going on as much as you possibly can.

If there is bad news, it's better that they hear it from you first. Don't let them pick it up from corridor gossip, often exaggerated and distorted.

Give them a chance to voice their questions and make sure you answer them to the best of your knowledge. If you don't have all the answers, admit that you honestly don't know and promise to find out if you can.

Watch out for decisions that may demoralize the team. If you have to lay off or fire someone, cut a budget or suspend a project, call a team meeting and make sure everyone understands, why you took your decision and how it may affect them personally.

In summary, your team should consider you the most reliable source of information. When faced with doubts, they should feel comfortable coming to you for clarification. That way you can always put things in perspective for them and keep them focused and motivated.

Finally, remember that people's feelings matter.

The average boss is grumpy, hard to please and usually doesn't care less for people's feelings.

Don't be an average boss, be a motivating leader.

If you're reading this book you know you want to be one. And you can be. If you take these ideas and concepts and practice them, you will be able to motivate your people to do amazing things. In return they will give you amazing results, even when the economy is down and the market is in havoc. Because people do amazing things when they are really motivated.

By the way, addressing an audience while sitting on top of a horse is a terrific experience. Just make sure you get the audience jumping up and down, not the horse!

ABOUT BASEM

Basem Al Attar is a Training and Development Consultant, NLP Trainer and Master Hypnotherapist.

He is the founder of Better Training - a company that specializes in skills development, and training. He's the author of many self-development programs on State Management, Creative Thinking, Communication, Leadership, Sales, Strategy, Productivity, Stress Management and NLP.

Over the past decade, thousands of people from 35 different countries have attended his training workshops. People often describe these events as "a life changing experience".

He also coaches executives from different countries around the globe, working with them on both personal and career development. With specific experience in the Middle East, Basem has worked with many multinationals in the region to help organizations create cultural change. His ability to help people create a positive mindset coupled with his sound business background has made him one of the most in-demand consultants working in the Middle East today.

For more information on Basem Al Attar and to receive your free report "10 Ways to Improve Your Collection", go to: www.bettertraining.net

CHAPTER 4

SEVEN STEPS TO THRIVE IN ANY ECONOMY

BY ALEX NOTTINGHAM, J.D., M.B.A.

According to the U.S. Small Business Administration, 50% of businesses fail within the first year, 80% within five years, and 96% within 10 years. This assumes the economy is stable.

In the 1990s, the economy was exploding. One of the nation's premier dentists was profiting greatly. The dentist created a center where people from all over the world could experience the finest in dentistry and service.

However, with the introduction of HMO insurance policies, this dental practice saw its client base evaporate. The vision was abandoned and the practice lost hundreds of thousands of dollars. Management was haphazard, employee talent was poor, motivation was lacking, and direction was missing.

Patients saw little or no value in associating themselves with the office. They frequently found excuses to cancel their appointments and sought out cheaper dental care. Referrals were nonexistent and bankruptcy was approaching. To make matters worse, the economic crisis hit a few years ago, the worst since the Great Depression.

In 2008, my company was brought in to re-engineer the dental practice. We used the steps you will learn in a moment to restore the practice not only to viability, but also to abundance. Strong internal and external marketing strategies were implemented. A former Bloomingdale's sales manager was brought in to reform customer service and training. Staff positions and roles were assigned. The good employees were challenged to become superb employees and the employees who could not rise to the occasion were quickly let go. As a result, revenue doubled in two years, and today the practice is up 125% from the previous year.

In a challenged economy, new economy, or growth economy, there are principles that hold true throughout time.

HERE ARE THE SEVEN STEPS TO THRIVE IN ANY ECONOMY!

1. GET MOTIVATED

"Whatever the mind can conceive and believe,
the mind can achieve."
~ *Napoleon Hill,* author of *Think And Grow Rich*

Think back to a moment when you exceeded your own expectations. Was it a game-winning hit, an 'A' on a test, an unexpected relationship, a raise or job promotion, or any accomplishment in life you value? How did it feel? I'm sure it felt great! This is what Dr. Maxwell Maltz refers to as that "winning feeling."

Your body cannot tell the difference between what is real and what is imagined. The mind dictates reality. Biofeedback studies show us that athletes cannot differentiate a real game from an imagined one. When they visualize a movement, the same nerves fire as if the game was real.

Once you evoke the feeling of success or that "winning feeling," you will feel good and start to attract people and circumstances that correspond to your feelings.

Here is how you create that "winning feeling":

- recall prior experiences where you felt that "winning feeling" and play it back in your mind

- apply that feeling to the present moment or some future activity
- assume a positive result will happen
- substitute negative emotions with positive ones
- make these changes gradually and
- observe the cause and effect

Your "winning feeling" and improved outlook will give you the motivation to pursue the next step.

2. GET AND SET GOALS

"Your ability to set goals is the master skill of success."
~ *Brian Tracy,* International Best Selling Author and Speaker

Your subconscious mind responds to whatever you consistently think about or set as a goal. It is automatic. Your subconscious does not differentiate or question. It just serves. Like a computer server obeys the user's request, your subconscious obeys your conscious mind. Therefore, it is vital that you feed your mind quality material.

Like a sea vessel, your subconscious mind is the ship, while your conscious mind is you, the captain of the ship. The only thing missing is a map.

Without a map, you may have great intentions, great energy, and motivation, but you will be wandering aimlessly. This is actually how most people go through life. They have grand ideas, but never specify how they will achieve them. They experience inconsistent results.

Setting goals with action steps is your map to success. Become an expert at goal setting.

Here are the steps in setting and achieving goals:

- Write them down
- Review them frequently
- Post pictures of them on your wall
- Think about what you are going to give for them (i.e. hard work, time, less TV)
- Be grateful for what you already have
- Feel as if you have already achieved them
- Think and talk about them all the time

You will be amazed how fast you start achieving what you want!

You may be motivated with goals, but you can't get there alone.

3. GET TALENT

"Get the right people on the bus...."
~ *Jim Collins,* author of *Good To Great*

Without hiring and keeping the right people, your business goals will fail.

Hiring the wrong people will not only prevent you from reaching your goals, but it can also have a disastrous effect on your business. The wrong people will disturb team chemistry, diminish team performance and attitudes, set a negative precedent, affect the experiences of your clients, and ultimately cost you a lot more money than the value the employee brings. Studies show that the wrong employee can cost you, on average, three times their salary!

The tolerance employers have for the "wrong" employee is astonishing. One of our clients had a litigious employee. The employee was let go for consistent improper documentation of hours. That employee ended up suing the company. The attorney's fees added up to over $30,000! A business can go bankrupt from the wrong employee, and now you can see why.

Do not be afraid to let someone go. It is not easy, but your company will benefit greatly for it. Not only that, you are doing the person you are letting go a favor. They can always find employment where they can contribute properly and make progress in their career.

Amazing things will happen when you dismiss the "wrong" employee. There are obvious benefits: staff is happier and more responsive, business is more productive, the replacement employee is substantially better, and you are relieved. There are also indirect benefits: an influx of clients, positive press, and new opportunities.

Remember, the "wrong" employee will cost you three times their salary, the average employee will pay for themselves, but the superior employee will produce 10 times their wage!

You are more motivated and have goals for the right people - to help execute those goals.

4. GET OFFENSIVE

"The best defense is a good offense."
~ *Jack Dempsey,* Heavyweight Fighter

You will often see sports teams that are ahead by several points start playing "prevent defense." This is where the team plays not to lose, rather than continuing the level of effort that got them the lead. It seems that nine times out of ten, the team ends up losing by being tentative.

No matter where you are in your business or situated in an economy, fight... fight... fight! Do not settle for the status quo. Do not settle for success. Keep pushing. Your greatest enemy is your comfort zone.

Ensure that you have a solid marketing strategy. Continue to try new things through creativity and innovation.

5. GET UNFAIR

"The secret of business, especially these days, is to focus relentlessly on your unfair advantage – the thing you do that others don't."
~ *John Rollwagen,* Executive

Your "unfair advantage" refers to your "competitive advantage."

A competitive advantage is something that you and your business excel in. It is not easily copied by competitors and the profit margins are very high. What is your competitive advantage? Is there a sufficient market to utilize this product or service?

Examples of a competitive advantage are Microsoft's operating systems, Apple's iPhone, and Google's search engine. Other companies compete, but are substantially inferior in function and marketing.

Once you locate your competitive advantage, you need to consistently exploit it! Talk about it, have your staff promote it, put it on all your marketing materials, and advertise.

Your unfair advantage may change over time; therefore, it is important to continually test for the marketing activity with the highest yield. Doesn't it make sense to put money only in activities that provide significant results?

6. GET RESULTS

"Insanity: doing the same thing over and over again
and expecting different results."
~ Albert Einstein

It is obvious that some marketing activities provide more than others. In 1897, an Italian professor of economics, Vilfredo Pareto studied the unequal patterns between the wealthy and the poor. His discovery led to the Pareto's Principle, which states that 80 percent of results arise from only 20 percent of energy.

In the book, The Breakthrough Principle of 16x, Richard Koch demonstrates the 16x rule with the 80/20 rule. If your big customers give you 80% of your sales, you get a payback factor of 4 by dividing 80 by 20. However, your small customers may give you 20% of sales with 80% of energy. You divide 20 units of reward with 80 units of effort and you get .25 payback factor.

If you compare the payback factor of the big customer (4) with the payback factor of the small customer (.25) by dividing .25 into 4, you get 16. This means by going after the 20% that provides 80% of the results, rather than the 80% that produces 20% of the results, you are increasing your results by 16x!

Once you discover what gets results, get unfair by focusing narrowly on it! Continually test and measure to determine your 20% and 16x results.

There are two types of marketing: internal and external. One of them is much more expensive than the other. Do you know which is which?

7. GET PERSONAL

"The purpose of business is to create and keep the customer."
~ Peter F. Drucker

According to customer retention studies, acquiring new customers costs five to six times more than retaining current ones. Therefore, most of your marketing efforts should be directed towards internal marketing—communicating offerings and value to the existing client base. The objectives are to retain clients, get clients to purchase more goods and services, and derive new client referrals.

There are several internal marketing techniques, such as email lists, direct mail, and phone calls. The pervasive expression for internal marketing is customer service. The aim of customer service is to create a personalized environment and enhanced experience for clients that support your internal marketing objectives.

Here are four ways to improve customer service:

- Make customer service your mission. Express it in everything you do, such as in your marketing materials and internal policy documents.
- Cultivate excitement and enthusiasm with your staff through team building exercises, seminars, workshops, and involvement in business practices. The energy created will positively affect your clients.
- Get your clients involved. Let them share in your fun.
- Observe and learn from the great customer service companies, such as the Ritz Carlton, Starbucks, and Disney.

If a dental office can excel in customer service, any business can!

CONCLUSION

Economies will change, customers will change, your company will change, but principles will not change. Therefore, use that which is unwavering as your center and guide. This way, you will thrive in any economy!

ABOUT ALEX

Alex Nottingham, J.D., M.B.A. is the President of Nottingham Consulting Group, LLC ("NCG"). Alex is a business consultant, executive coach, attorney, and author. He consults and coaches many clients, from dental and medical organizations to musicians and business professionals. With the implementation of powerful marketing strategies, upgrading and training of staff members, and executive coaching, his clients have witnessed breakthrough success in the millions.

Alex is the former CEO of inVIZION Media, LLC, an international digital signage marketing company whose client list included Avianca Airlines. In less than four months, he helped the company raise investor startup capital and develop relationships with business entities in Mexico, Peru, and Columbia.

Alex is involved in many projects that benefit both his clients and the community. Alex and his company created Ultimate Makeovers. This project is a collection of the finest doctors and health practitioners in Florida that perform makeovers for less fortunate members of the community and raise money for charity.

Alex received his Juris Doctor (JD) and Masters of Business Administration (MBA) from Florida International University. He was featured in the FIU Business Magazine as the first joint JD/MBA degree from FIU. Alex received his bachelor's degree in Management Information Systems (MIS) from the University of Central Florida where he graduated *Summa Cum Laude*. Alex received his coaching certification from Business Breakthroughs International, a Tony Robbins and Chet Holmes company.

About Nottingham Consulting Group

Nottingham Consulting Group (NCG) is a business consulting firm specializing in business management, coaching, and marketing strategies. NCG's award-winning team members use modern marketing techniques coupled with strategic planning to provide clients with breakthrough results.

To learn more about Alex Nottingham and how NCG can revitalize your business, visit www.nottinghamconsult.com or call 954-323-2220.

CHAPTER 5

LEGACY

BY DUSTIN & MARIYA OLDFATHER

"Give me beauty in the inward soul; may the outward and the inward man be at one"
~ Socrates

His skin tingled with excitement. The electricity was palpable, as though lightning might burst crackling through the auditorium at any moment. As John looked over the auditorium he watched them trickle in, meandering to their seats. He was struck by what he saw. The well-appointed guests were jovial and familiar, as if they had all known each other for years. There was a festive air, but he could sense there was a consequential occasion.

Peering deeper into the gathering crowd he recognized distinguished peers. A senator, his favorite old school teacher, and even the mayor were here chatting with his friends. "How did we get all of these people into the same room?" he thought. His heart warmed as he watched his family making their way past the collective. As they passed down to the front, he enjoyed their softly lit vignettes as they received long heart-felt embraces, and enjoyed brief misty-eyed chats. How beautiful they were…the most beautiful things alive.

As the din began to rise from the collecting crowd, he thought back to a time when he could not have imagined anything beautiful. It was the tail end of the first decade of 2000, and the news was all bad. Institutions were collapsing. Business was shrinking. It was a dismal scene. Everyone was losing big; losing their homes, losing their money, losing their retirement, losing their dignity. It all came gushing back in a violent flood of emotion.

If the clouds be full of rain, they empty themselves on the Earth; and if the tree fall toward the south, or toward the north, in the place where the tree falls it shall be. He who observes the wind shall not sow; and he who regards the clouds shall not reap.
~ Ecclesiastes 11:3-4

"Here I am, back in the office," he thought to himself, "Another unsatisfying night, trying to keep up." Piles of unfinished work, invoices and charts laid in all corners. He flipped on the lights and glanced at his phone on the charger, the battery spent from a day at war. The project binders simmered next to his desk. Emails, text messages and important voice mails still demanded his attention. His wife sent him an instant message asking if he would be home in time to have dinner, but he was too ashamed to respond.

What had once been his proudest vision, his business, had become a sentence. Everyone was depending on him, but he was failing them all in some way, no one more than himself. His pride and confidence had been amputated and replaced with anxiety and doubt. The office was a string of interruptions, ambushes of complaints, and blame.

Although he gave his best, he feebly attempted to be with his family with a soul worn thin. The dreams he had for his business were steadily evaporating. He resented everyone around him, including the clients he had been killing himself to get. It felt like sand was filling his lungs a little more each day. There was no way he could sustain this.

As the darkness settled in, John felt dizzy. The office started spinning and his stomach churned. The heavy gravity of failure fell on him like a massive planet. As he sat paralyzed and overwhelmed, a tear streamed down his face. He leaned over his wooden executive desk, crumpled his face into his hands, and he began to weep.

It is during our darkest moments that we must focus to see the light.
~ Aristotle Onassis

Thunder clapped and jolted him awake. As he gathered his consciousness, he wondered how long he had been out. "How am I going to get out of this?" He thought, as his mind began to race. Then he slowly reached his hand to his chin and began to think, deeply. "I am spread in so many directions, for more than I can physically handle," he thought "I can't possibly do more. Where do I even start?" His eyes lifted to the window and out of his sullen thoughts, the reflection of his face came into focus. In an innocent moment, he understood. He gave himself a gentle smile, stood up and headed out the door.

John burst through his front door, "Sweetheart…sweetheart, where are you? We need to talk." His wife was taken aback. "What's going on? What's wrong?" she said with alarm. John looked at his beautiful wife with love, regret, and hope and the world slowed down. "Please sit down on the couch for a moment I need to talk to you," he said. Kneeling down next to her he gathered himself, fighting back tears, and began in a somber tone, "I owe you an apology. You see, I have been lost. The weight of the business has been crushing me. As much as I have tried, I could not keep up. I wanted to be better for all of you. I wanted to be better for myself. I wanted to fulfill all of our dreams. I have fallen short. But tonight, I realized that everything that I need is right here, in our home , with you. I promise you, I will never fail you again. Please, forgive me."

John's wife took his hand, rested her head against his and they whispered softly to each other. As the night drifted on, they continued for hours confronting years of frustration that had built up between them. They had found each other again.

Resting his head on his pillow, the day began to steadily evaporate. His mind drifted into peace. It was time to let go starting at the center. Dreaming, he passed into sleep.

"If you are distressed by anything external, the pain is not due to the thing itself but to your own estimate of it; and this you have the power to revoke at any moment."
~ Marcus Aurelius

Arriving an hour early, he found his things exactly as he had left them. The technology in the room hummed and begged for his attention. Each step he made with a purpose, one by one, through his office. He turned off his computer, shutdown his cell phone, unplugged his phone jack, shut his door, locked it, and stripped everything from his desk. Then, he sat in silence.

After some time he came back to his thoughts of the night before. "It all starts with *me*," he thought, "there is only so much I can do." Out of his short exasperation he chuckled at his own silly flailing. He knew he controlled the gates to his own happiness. "From now on," he thought "I will do everything I can, and that will be good enough." In that instant he resolved to forgive himself for the years of self-neglect and over-commitment. His life, saturated with endless work, was now being wrung dry. He resolved to do his best, but to keep forgiving himself. This way, his spirit could be in the present, and so could he.

System Reset Ego – *Resolve, right now, to forgive yourself. Write down 3 things you have been feeling guilty about. Write down one action for each. Take one action on each of these items, right now. Say, you are sorry, and let these things go, right now. Yes, Right now. Stop trying to be perfect. We live in an imperfect world. You are an imperfect being. Let it be okay. Acknowledge your soul, and be kind to yourself, you deserve it.*

"In every man's heart there is a sleeping lion."
~ *Armenian Proverb*

Awaking to his centered mind he swelled with excitement. It was like the first day of school. His eyes lifted to the window and the blue sky sent his mind reeling in controlled chaos. The universe was filled with possibility. Why couldn't he see this, before?

The drive in was exhilarating as the morning sun lit nature's canvas. The clouds danced across the sky. He was alive, surging with energy, and glowing with enlightenment. He was the commander back at the helm. He wanted to smash everything and stamp out a new order.

System Reset Mindset – *Imagine that you are the great Jack Welch and that you were taking over your business. You are the general. You are the admiral. You are the greatest CEO of all time. What principles would you embody? How would you carry yourself? How would you conduct yourself? How would you allocate your time? What would you do more of? What would you no longer do? Return to Your Commander*

Mentality. You can no longer be asleep at the wheel.

"Such an attitude stems from a tragic misconception of time, from the strangely rational notion that there is something in the very flow of time that will inevitably cure all ills. Actually, time itself is neutral; it can be used either destructively or constructively...We must use time creatively, in the knowledge that the time is always ripe to do right. Now is the time…"
~ MLK Letter from a Birmingham Jail

He grabbed the blank journal that he had never bothered to open and picked up an expensive pen. "So, what am I living for?" Innocently, words streamed from the tip of the pen like water down a mountain, and it became crystal clear. He cherished his family. He wanted to be the best in his business, and he wanted to live in vibrant health.

"What is it that only I can do that means the most to my business?" he considered, as he dissected his own activities. Surprisingly, he discovered that there were three functions he performed that contributed the most. Of those, one was far more important than the others. He concluded that this was his primary function in the business. "What if I could just do the most important thing all day?" John's thought hung in his sub-conscious, "our business would explode!"

Only through focus can you do world-class things, no matter how capable you are.
~ Bill Gates

System Reset Primary – *Train everyday to be the best at your "primary function." Make performing your primary function an Olympic Event for the day. Imagine yourself at the center of a great sporting coliseum surrounded by millions of people, including your family. They are there to watch you at your work. Your performance will be written in the history books and read about for centuries. How would you perform? Strive to bring that level of focus to your work. Work as if your life and reputation depended on it, because, they do.*

Every gun that is made, every warship launched, every rocket fired signifies, in the final sense, a theft from those who hunger and are not fed, those who are cold and not clothed.
~ Dwight D. Eisenhower

In a blinding flash of the obvious, John understood that anytime he was wasting time at work or not serving his most important role, he was being negligent. So, he evaluated every task that arose. If a task was not in his top three functions and had no impact on the business, he deleted it. If a task had value to the business but was not in his specialties, he would assign it to the most qualified person available, then set a date for completion and review. And, for items that might have value in the future, he wrote them onto a "Someday List" for periodic review, or until the tasks became obsolete. In which case, he deleted those items also.

System Reset Waste – *Write down the 3 things you do each day that are a complete waste of your time. Write down why you do each item. Decide to delete, delegate or defer each item. Put yourself on the clock. Get a stopwatch and keep track of how much time you spend on task. (You will be surprised.)*

__Darwin Smith was diagnosed with cancer shortly after becoming CEO of Kimberly – Clark. He shared with his wife what he'd learned, "If you have a cancer in your arm, you've got to have the guts to cut off your arm. I've made a decision. We're going to sell the mills."__

John attacked everything that he once dreaded with clinical control and sophistication. If it weren't for the sprinkler system, he would have started a bonfire in his office and thrown it all in. He felt like a gladiator in the ring, begging for another contest. He ripped through everything and kept only the important. Everything non-essential was thrown away, or stowed for reference. He was in harmony, synchronized in his efficient space. He had transcended the familiar. He was burning to launch.

System Reset Strategy – *Allow a new approach to emerge. Evaluate each area that you currently allocate your resources. Can you afford to compete and win in each area? If not. Get out of it. Determine which areas you can win and concentrate your forces. Go dominate. Treat your time and resources as if your life depended on it. It does.*

Each new day he found a new focus, ever on the attack, with power, love and a sound mind. Each day he conquered a new dimension of himself and his business. At each new level he created more time, more life, and more love for those around him. He shimmered in vibrant health, mentally, spiritually and physically.

"I am certain of nothing but the holiness of the heart's affections and the truth of imagination."
~ J.Keats

The room swirled back into focus and he was back in the great hall decades later. Now, he understood why all of these people had come. This congregation would never be assembled again. It was the culmination of lives affected by him, a man they all admired. They were here to see him and celebrate his life.

He now appreciated the gift of The Depression he had lived through. That dark pressure had crystallized pure integrity. That pressure had forged him into granite for the trials ahead. Without it, he would have stumbled. With it, he transcended.

John took the podium and his warm words filled the hall, highlighting humorous moments and joyful memories, reminiscing through his amazing journey. His grace and eloquence artfully enlightened all present, as he sifted through wisdom mined from years of struggle.

Then, he brought his talk to a close. "Thank you all for coming tonight," he paused, "This moment is much different than I imagined. As a young man, I dreamed of a legacy of accomplishment and riches. Yet, as I stand here in realization of those dreams, I realize the real legacy is the manner in which we live. And so, I leave you with a challenge. And, my challenge to you is this, 'Take the best of who you are, become the person you know you can be, and create your extraordinary legacy.'"

"We must be the change we wish to create"
~ Gandhi

ABOUT DUSTIN AND MARIYA

Even before the day they met on Second Street in Rehoboth Beach, Delaware, **Dustin and Mariya Oldfather's** lives traveled similar paths. They were both committed to higher education and pursued extremely rigorous studies. While Dustin trained at the Florida Naval Base and studied molecular biology and nuclear physics, Mariya completed a challenging curriculum of math, language and computers, obtaining her degree in accounting from the prestigious University of National and World Economy in Sofia, Bulgaria. From the beginning, they respected each other's intellect, wit, and core values. They also abided by a shared philosophy of living life to the fullest. But more importantly, they were inspired by their mutual desire to embrace a coastal lifestyle.

It's no surprise that Dustin and Mariya have been able to turn their fondness for the Delaware shore into highly successful real estate careers. In fact, they have carved a name for themselves as the experts to consult when buying or selling a coveted oceanfront property. Specializing in Southern Delaware's extraordinary coastal communities, they offer extensive credentials and genuine enthusiasm for the lifestyle, along with a desire to help their clients make the most of it.

Combining Dustin's innovative thinking and thorough knowledge of mortgage programs with Mariya's strong analytical, financial and organization skills, their clients always experience a noticeable advantage in today's complex marketplace. Using the most current technology and their marketing prowess, Dustin and Mariya remain on the cutting edge of the real estate industry.

Dustin and Mariya are also certified Senior Housing Specialists and work closely with many local builders, enabling them to assist clients in every stage of their investment portfolio, from new construction to downsizing.

To learn more about Dustin and Mariya, visit: www.TheOldfatherGroup.com or www.ExtraordinaryCoastalProperties.com or call them toll free at: 866-612-6278.

CHAPTER 6

CREATING SUCCESS THROUGH ACCOUNTABILITY

BY BILL BANNER

LIVING ABOVE THE LINE

Accountability sometimes takes on a negative connotation – i.e. who is to blame (to be held accountable) when something goes wrong? The truth is, we are all accountable for our own success. Only through embracing our accountability can we become masters of our own future. While it is easy to "fall below the line" and look for the person, or the institution, or the "system", that caused us to be unhappy about a certain outcome or situation, more often than not the real reason that we are where we are is because we failed to plan, anticipate or consider the possible results. When we are in "negative mode", we tend to view problems around us as the result of the actions of others, rather than consider what we could do to succeed in spite of, or *as a result of,* the situation at hand. We can choose to be victims of our environment, or we can choose to be proactive, take ownership of our success and create our own future.

Truly successful people accept that they are accountable for what happens in their lives. They recognize that in order to achieve the results that they want, they need to take responsibility for making a plan and doing everything in their power to follow it. When things don't go quite right, rather than assigning blame, successful people ask themselves what could they have done differently to have avoided the outcome and how could they prevent it from happening again in the future. What additional planning could they have done or action could they have taken, to have had a better outcome? If an employee makes a mistake that has a negative impact on the business, the accountable leader does not ask "who's fault is this?", but rather asks themselves "how could I have trained this person better", or "what systems could I have put in place" to have avoided the situation or stopped the error 'from getting out the door'? Formal problem solving techniques used in manufacturing and other industries from around the world begin with one simple statement: "it's never the worker's fault". The accountability for the problem has to rest with the company and the leaders that put a process in place that allowed an error to occur. If we take this philosophy and apply it to every part of our careers and lives, we begin to take control of our future and success.

IF IT IS TO BE, IT'S UP TO ME

Taking ownership is the key to driving our careers. The simple saying "if it is to be, it's up to me" puts the concept of personal accountability into context. Personal accountability is about making a commitment to ourselves to achieve a certain goal. If for example, you want to get fit and trim, you need to make a commitment to yourself to follow an exercise and diet regime. No one else can do it for you. It's OK to enlist the help of a Nutritionist and a Personal Trainer, but the commitment to get started on a plan and to seek out the help is up to you. If you are in sales and your goal is to double your income in the next 12 months, you can't just wish it to happen. You need to develop a plan as to how you are going to increase the effectiveness of your prospecting so that you meet at least twice as many potential clients. Then you need to be sure that your selling techniques are solid, so that you convert a higher percentage of presentations and meetings into actual sales.

When we know what we want, we have only ourselves to rely upon to get us there. There are 4 steps to personal accountability:

1. First and foremost, you must a have a clearly defined **goal** that meets the S.M.A.R.T. criteria (Specific, Measureable, Aligned with your value system, Realistic and Time-bound)
2. You must take complete **personal responsibility** for the actions necessary to make it happen. Even if you need some outside help, you need to take charge and ownership of the goal and its outcome.
3. You need to seek out the **ideal solution.** This might be where you enlist the help of experts. There is nothing wrong with leveraging the experience of others to help you come to a faster or better conclusion, but taking responsibility for finding the solution remains with you no matter what.
4. Finally, you must **execute** the plan. All the best of intentions do no one any good unless **we put the plan in place and make our success happen.**

This approach is not just for major career and life goals. It is just as important for dealing with life's challenges along the way. When we learn that a major project we are working on is going to be delayed because of the performance of one of our team members or suppliers, we can sit back and resign ourselves to the fact that it is going to be late due to no fault of our own. Or, we can **step up** and take ownership of the situation and find a solution to mitigate the problem. We are often not measured by our ability to avoid problems, but rather on how well we perform to solve them.

ACCOUNTABILITY AS A MANAGEMENT TOOL

While we must drive our careers through our own accountability to ourselves first and foremost, accountability also provides a great framework within which to lead others. Using accountability as a management tool creates a work environment where employees are aligned with the company's values and priorities, and they are motivated to support others within the organization.

One of the issues that many managers have trouble dealing with is conflict in the workplace. Too often poor or mediocre performance is tolerated in an effort to avoid conflict or confrontation with employees.

While the performance may not be terrible, it is not up to the standard that the manager would have liked. The manager may or may not confront the individual on the quality of the work - depending on their personal style. The performance of the department or company suffers as a result due to poor execution. The question is, though, who is really at fault? Did the employee know the standard that was expected of them? Did they have the time, skills and tools to do the job the way the manager wanted?

Accountability really works in management situations when it is understood that the manager and employee are co-dependent on each other. The manager is every bit as accountable to the employee to provide the necessary resources to do the job as the employee is to the manager for getting it done.

The manager needs to be very clear on what outcome is expected of the employee, what specific timeframes are required and what standards are expected to be met. Before the employee accepts these requirements of accountability, both need to agree that they are achievable in the time frame allotted and that they have the skills and resources to accomplish them. If they are being asked to take on a new additional task, they are accountable to the manager to tell them if it will conflict with other priorities or assignments they already have. The manager is then accountable to reset the priorities or adjust the resources available to get the work done. Once the accountability factors are agreed to, the employee has an obligation to come forward as soon as they recognize that there is a problem. This enables the manager to adjust priorities and resources to best satisfy the overall goals.

The manager must also be sure that they are assigning tasks to people who have the appropriate level of task maturity to accomplish them. This determines the level of detail required in describing the task and what is expected to be accomplished. When, for example, a task is being assigned to a person who is relatively new or in a new role, a lot more detail is going to be required along with verification that the employee understands the requirements. In the case of a senior experienced employee, the accountability requirements can be described in a much more general fashion, just outlining the expectations for the end-goal.

One of the great side benefits of having an agreement on accountability is that the emotion and discomfort of discussing sub-par performance with employees is greatly reduced. When expectations are not met, the employee knows where they stand, and their performance can be discussed in a very straight forward and business-like manner – there are no surprises. Jack Welch, the former CEO of General Electric described in one of his books a conversation with one of his senior executives. The executive's business unit had been struggling and had not met the financial performance expectation for the last number of periods. They had been colleagues for many years, but at their meeting, the executive said "we've worked together a long time Jack, but if I don't get my numbers up, I know you are not going to be able to keep me". Accountability was strongly rooted in G.E.'s management philosophy.

FORMAL ACCOUNTABILITY AGREEMENTS

When I was running a manufacturing facility for a multi-national automotive supplier, I had accountability agreements with each of my department heads. Together we established an agreed to list that formed the basis of how the performance of each department and its manager was to be evaluated. As an example, here is the Accountability Agreement List for the Finance Department Manager:

- To ensure that appropriate systems and controls are in place to provide accurate and timely financial transactions and reports and to ensure that there are no material misrepresentations in financial reports
- To spearhead the annual Budget/Business Plan activity and maintain a regularly scheduled and accurate forecasting mechanism
- To implement and provide input for improvement of the ERP system. (a new initiative that year)
- To develop subordinates capable of succession into management of systems and people
- To review and improve department methodologies to enhance productivity and optimize resource allocation
- To maintain an active Business Plan document with periodic updates with respect to progress (Management Review)
- To support special assignments in a timely fashion as requested by the Division/Manufacturing Group/Corporate

- To be accountable for the output and behaviours of all Finance Department Employees
- To systematically provide support, information, and feedback to all other departments within the facility in pursuit of the common goals of the company.

While the above list might look to some like a job description (which in a way it is), it also encompasses explicit accountability for the behaviour of the department members and for co-operation with other departments. With an agreement like this in place, there really isn't any excuse for one department not supporting another. Also, once this manager had agreed to be responsible for the behaviour of his department, how long do you think it was before he had established similar agreements with everyone in his department? The agreement can be used to support training and development initiatives as well, so that the department manager is not only focussed on his or her personal and departmental performance, but also on succession planning - ensuring that qualified candidates are in the system and being developed to assume greater responsibility in time.

At annual review time, each department manager referred to their agreements and supporting documents to show how well they had done on each item. Where they might have missed the mark, they showed a plan for how they intended to improve in that area. While the onus was, of course, still on me to conduct my own evaluation of their performance, there certainly were no surprises for anyone, and the conversations went very smoothly even if the performance wasn't quite 'up to par'.

Aside from supporting the "regular" departmental functions, using an agreement like this is a great way to ensure that everyone in the company is aligned with the company goals and that all employees are focussed on what really matters for the success of the company. Having accountability for improving departmental productivity and resource allocation meant that we were always looking at how we could do more with less – and it wasn't driven by "the front office says we have to make some cuts around here". The manager was always working with his people to find new and better ways of doing things.

These agreements were developed to support **my accountability to my senior management**. I had overall responsibility for the profitability of my business unit. I was measured on business growth, Employee, and Customer satisfaction, strict adherence to all appropriate health, safety and corporate governance rules and regulations and on my succession plan - which would enable me, my team and my facility to grow and take on new and additional responsibilities – a key consideration for any business focussed on growth. Through these accountability agreements with my staff, I was able to ensure that they had the same focus that I did in their various departments, and collectively we were all working toward a common goal. Furthermore, I knew that if we were getting 'off track', they would use the agreement to come to me to get things re-aligned to ensure the best possible outcome.

Embracing accountability enables us to drive our own success by taking ownership of our future and the road to get us there. In a management environment, it enables us to share common goals and really enable everyone to recognize their part in achieving that success for the company and themselves.

ABOUT BILL

Bill Banner is an author, world-class business coach and leader with an extraordinary range of business expertise to achieve unprecedented performance. Having built his coaching practice upon 30 years of corporate experience, he is often called up to apply his results-based approach to operational excellence, team performance, marketing and business development.

Bill has written for BusinessLink Newspaper on enhancing business performance and coaches business owners and professionals on "how to get everything they truly want out of business ownership". Having grown and run successful multi-million business units himself, Bill mentors his clients with focus on business growth strategies, increasing profitability, igniting employee performance and satisfaction, and creating customer loyalty.

Formally trained first as a mechanical engineer, Bill has always enjoyed building things. What he is passionate about is building businesses and careers. In addition to 'one on one' coaching, Bill also specializes in Group Coaching, Workshops, and In-House Training and Development.

Bill is a graduate of the University of Toronto and the Michael De Groote School of Business at McMaster University

His business coaching practice is located in Hamilton, Ontario, part of the Canada's Golden Horseshoe.

To learn more about Bill Banner, visit:
www.billbanner.ca or http://billbanner.focalpointcoaching.com.
Bill can be reached at bbanner@focalpointcoaching.com or at 905-627-9285.

CHAPTER 7

IMPERATIVES FOR BUSINESS SUCCESS

BY MICHAEL CLAYTON

Titles indicate you are successful, and that you are in a position of influence! At least that is what I thought when I was younger in my professional career.

More than once I used my title within an organization believing it would bring quick response and decision from others, but I soon discovered they were not impressed or motivated by who I was or what my title indicated.

When I was in elementary school, my teacher would instruct our class to line up to go to the restroom. I always ran to get ahead of the other students. Why? I thought if I was at the front of the line that made me the leader. No so!

Much too late in my professional career, I came to understand that titles or other credentials do not motivate people, inspire greatness in others, or allow me to successfully lead a business organization. I learned true business success depends upon a person's ability to impact the thinking and actions of others. Thus, the greater the impact I desire to make, the greater my ability to influence others to share my dreams, adopt my goals, and move an organization forward at a successful pace.

Over the years I have discovered and learned many qualities that are imperatives for business success, but none are more important than these three:

1. INTEGRITY -- GAINS OUR INFLUENCE

Titles, position, wealth, credentials or whether you are chairman, director, or chief executive, the most important imperative to business success is integrity. It is that quality that permits a person to gain the influence necessary to lead an organization to success.

One of the many lessons I have learned is that when I have integrity, there is complete agreement between the words I express and the actions I perform. In other words, I am who I am; no matter where I am or who I may be with.

Integrity is extremely important for many reasons. Allow me to share two that I believe greatly enhance our business success:

First, integrity gives us creditability. The foundation of integrity is trust, and trust is the foundation for relationships, both personal and professional. It is imperative that business associates, customers, and those close to us know that we can be trusted. They must know that we are people of our word; that we can be depended upon to do what we say we will do, when we say we will do it, and when we make a mistake, that we will correct it.

Cavett Roberts, a successful business leader and founder of the National Speakers Association, once said, "If my people understand me, I'll get their attention. If my people trust me, I'll get their action." I translate that to business success confidently knowing that when customers trust us, they will buy from us. When employees trust us, they are more committed and dedicated to the success of the business, and will model that same trust to customers and clients.

Second, integrity builds for us a creditable reputation. Every person and organization has a perceived image. In other words, it is what people think we are and what we are like. On the other hand, integrity is what we really are and is a true picture of who we genuinely are as a person and leader. Our ability to influence others is not about our image, but it is about our integrity, which should be the bedrock of our reputation.

Mount Rushmore National Memorial is carved in the granite above Keystone, South Dakota. The sculpture began in 1927 and took 14 years to complete at a cost of one million dollars. It reveals the images of four great Presidents – George Washington, Thomas Jefferson, Theodore Roosevelt, and Abraham Lincoln.

Daily maintenance on the mountainside helps to prevent deterioration of the four images. Every September workers scale the sculpture removing bird nests, pulling shrubs and weeds, and filling the hundreds of natural cracks that crisscross the faces on the mountain. They fill the cracks with a mixture of white granite dust, linseed oil and white lead. If the cracks were unattended, the rains and melting snows would creep into the cracks and freeze, thus shattering the image of the Presidents.

As I have discovered, our lives are like that. We must constantly keep our cracks repaired or our image -- our reputation -- will be shattered and more importantly, our integrity will be marred.

True business success comes when we choose integrity over our image, embrace truth over that which often seems most convenient, and uphold honor above any potential personal or professional gain.

Without question, I have learned that integrity gains our influence and leads to business success.

2. CHARACTER -- SUSTAINS OUR INFLUENCE

Integrity is that quality that allows a business leader the right to impact and influence the thinking and responses of others. Second, is the development of an impeccable character. That is the quality that allows us to sustain our influence with others over the long term.

Character is that quality that cannot be purchased. You can't touch it, you don't inherit it, and you can't weigh it. It is the characteristic of an individual that can only be built, as it is the fundamental foundation of a truly successful life.

Norman Schwartzkopf said, "Leadership is a potent combination of strategy and character. But, if you must be without one, be without strategy."

In ancient days, brick makers, engravers, and other artisans used a symbol to mark those items they made. The symbol was soon known as their "character." The value of their work was in proportion to the skill with which the specific object was made. And only if the quality of the work was exceptional was the character valued and respected.

In other words, the quality of the person and their work gave value to their credentials. If the work was good, so was the character. If the work was bad, then the character was viewed and considered as poor.

Realistically a business or organization has both character and reputation. The fact is they are nothing more than the attitudes and actions of those who lead them. Character is that which comes from within who we are. Again, it is not about titles, credentials, position or wealth. None of those can ever accomplish what character can do.

A few lessons I have learned concerning character can greatly enhance our ability to experience business success. Let me share a few with you:

Character separates us from our competition. It is a quality or characteristic that either limits or enhances our potential to influence and impact others. John Morley said, "No man can climb out beyond the limitations of his own character."

Life and business success is based on relationships. Customers, employees, and other people with whom we come into contact are like Superman, they have x-ray vision. They soon come to know and experience the "real us." They see beyond the surface and discover who and what we really are. In others words, our character is exposed. That discovery truly does limit or enhance our ability to make a positive difference in their life and business decisions.

Character adds time to our influence. People know when they are treated right and they never forget it. A person with right character is not forgotten. Neither is a business relationship that is conducted with the same commitment and passion.

J.R Miller said, "The only thing that walks back from the tomb with the mourners and refuses to be buried, is the character of a man. What a man is, survives him. It can never be buried."

Great men and women are not necessarily remembered for the physical contribution they leave behind, but for the character for which they lived. That is the legacy most admired and most remembered.

Character is the foundation of our reputation. When I was growing up in Dallas it was always important to me, and most of my classmates, that we have a good reputation. Never is that more important than in the business marketplace. It has been said that, "we live and die by our reputation." Our success is often measured by the reputation we have established.

A good, positive reputation exists simply because it is a reflection of a person's character. William Hersey Davis said it well when he wrote these words:

"The circumstances amid which you live determine your reputation; the truth you believe determines your character. Reputation is what you are supposed to be; character is what you are. Reputation is the photograph; character is the face. Reputation comes over one from without; character grows up from within. Reputation is what you have when you come to a new community; character is what you have when you go away. Your reputation is made in a moment; your character is built in a lifetime. Your reputation is learned in an hour; your character does not come to light for a year. Reputation grows like a mushroom; character lasts like eternity. Reputation makes you rich or makes you poor; character makes you happy or makes you miserable. Reputation is what men say about you on your tombstone; character is what the angels say about you at the throne of God."

Without question, integrity gains our ability to influence and character grants us the ability to sustain our influence. With both we make a positive impact in the heads and hearts of people.

3. EXCELLENCE -- RETAINS OUR INFLUENCE

Integrity will gain you opportunity to impact and influence in all arenas of relationship. Character will sustain your ability to make a positive difference in the lives of people. It is a commitment to excellence that allows you to retain your opportunity to secure continued favor in those relationships, whether they are personal or professional.

My dad always told me, "Do your very best in everything you do." He was a living testament to that philosophy and business success principle. Though not formally educated, he could do just about anything. And, when he did it, he always did it exceptionally well. His dedication to excellence magnified to me the importance of doing what we do, better than what others expect.

Aristotle said, "We are what we repeatedly do. Excellence then is not a skill, but a habit." It is not something that happens by accident, but it is a goal set and reinforced with earnest effort, deliberate focus, and competent implementation.

A habit is formed when there is a connection between our head, hand and heart. The head is the "what to do and why." The hand represents the "how to do." The heart is the "want to do." Nothing becomes a habit until you know what to do and why, how to do it, and then WANT to make it happen. Thus, we will never achieve excellence until we "want" to engage that quality into our lives and business.

I once heard Michael Krasny, founder of CDW Computers say, " Perfection is unattainable, but if you strive for perfection you will obtain excellence." Excellence then is a decision; a choice that you and I make as business leaders each and every day.

My wife Dee and I recently returned to Disney World, the place of our honeymoon, to celebrate our 35th wedding anniversary. Though we had been back a few times before with our three children Chris, Kim and Kendal, this trip was uniquely special. Again, I was reminded of the philosophy of its founder Walt Disney. He said decades ago, "Do what you do so well that people want to come and watch you do it. And when they do, they will want to come back. And when they come back they will want to bring someone with them."

If you have ever been to a Disney Resort, you know that commitment to excellence is a foundation to their success. And, people just keep going back again and again, and inviting friends and family to go with them!

Integrity gains our influence. Character sustains our influence. Excellence retains our influence. I have learned these three qualities to be imperatives for business success. And I am reminded of the words of Elbert Hubbard, "Some men succeed by what they know; some by what they do; and a few by what they are."

ABOUT MICHAEL

Michael Clayton, known to many as *"The Cheerleader for TRUST,"* has spoken to more than 5,000 audiences across the United States and on three continents over the last forty plus years. A professional member of the National Speakers Association, and a Certified Seminar Leader (CSL), Michael has conducted keynote addresses and/or training seminars for State Farm Insurance, Social Security Administration, ExxonMobil, Coldwell Banker, AT&T, and hundreds of other for-profit and non-profit organizations.

Zig Ziglar has said, *"Michael Clayton is a multi-talented, integrity based individual with an outstanding reputation for his effectiveness in whatever he does. I am impressed with his spirit, his ability, and his commitment to excellence. He gives a solid presentation, has great speaking and people skills, and not only has something to say, but says it well. He is a seasoned communicator with a passion for positively impacting lives."*

Since 1996 Michael has served as the President/CEO of the Better Business Bureau serving southeast Texas, and is the only recipient of the "Award for Distinction for Special Communications" from the International Assemblies of Better Business Bureaus. He is called upon regularly by the international BBB to promote its message of "advancing trust in the marketplace," engaging audiences with the principles that are the foundation for business success.

To learn more about Michael Clayton, *"The Cheerleader for TRUST,"* and how he can impact your next corporate gathering, visit: www.michaelclayton.biz or call: (877) 494-3225.

CHAPTER 8

6 EASY STEPS ON HOW TO BECOME A SUCCESSFUL 21ST CENTURY PIONEER: A SERIAL IDEA CREATOR AND INNOVATOR

BY JON BJARNASON

Those of us who choose to go into business for ourselves are the new pioneers of this millennium. Pioneers of old 'searched for' continents – harvested new lands – battled nature. Today there is little of that going on – at least for most of us. The spirit of the Pioneers is still there – dormant – waiting for something to conquer. Humans need new 'continents' to conquer – finding our inner, though sometimes dormant entrepreneurial spirit, and forge ahead and claim new lands – or its modern version – starting a successful company.

If this applies to you, which I would think is a reasonable guess, since you are reading this book – then you should read on. If you are a business owner or are wondering whether you should start one – please take into consideration that the odds are stacked against you. All the numbers indicate it is a futile venture, and so massively so that I sometimes can't imagine why anyone in their right minds would want to try it. Only 1 in 10 gets by, 1 in 100 hits gold, 1 in 1,000 strikes the mother lode, and 1 in 100,000 becomes a modern version of Alexander the Great, Napoleon, Caesar or Columbus.

The truth, however, is that humans are at their greatest strength when the odds are stacked against them. The human spirit does not cave in to fear – unless we allow it to – and if we choose to believe that we are better, even when the odds are stacked against us – the human spirit can conquer anything.

OUR BELIEFS

I was always curious as to what it was that allowed one person in a room full of people – all hearing the same lecture – to walk out of that lecture with a brewing idea that created a fortune for them. Why that person? What made them tick? What was their secret?

If our beliefs can win – even when the odds are against us – why don't all of us believe we can tackle anything. What makes those who win against odds different? Luck? Or was it just that they did not believe they could fail – even when failure occurred?

Could it be that the two were connected – winning against the odds – getting million dollar ideas out of thin air? Could their beliefs have made a difference? And if so…can anyone win? Can anyone get ideas?

Well, you might believe that I am very simple in thinking so, but…yes; I do believe that anyone can. I do believe that we all have an entrepreneurial spirit within us that some of us manage to make better use of than others. Some repress their spirit because of fear – fear of failure or poverty. Because their beliefs do not allow them to think that they can battle the odds.

THE SOLUTION

What if we could lower the odds a bit? What would happen to our beliefs then? But how can we lower the odds in business? What is the answer? The solution is simple and people have been doing it for decades. We need to build systems. Create systems that allow even the business novice to awaken his entrepreneurial spirit – and become a 21st century pioneer. One simple – yet hugely attractive form of a business system – is a franchise, now available in all sizes and shapes.

One book on business systems that clearly showed me the importance of systems is *The E-Myth Revisited,* by Michael E. Gerbers. In it, the author takes us on a journey to show us why systems help us lower the odds of business creation, and how anybody can create freedom within their business.

THE TOOLS

Idea Diary:
>   Low tech:
>   ⇒ A small notebook

>   High tech:
>   ⇒ Phone/PDA

Central gathering and processing place:
>   Low tech:
>   ⇒ Blank white paper
>   ⇒ White paper with lines to write onto
>   ⇒ Folder

>   High tech:
>   ⇒ Own Computer or access to a computer
>   ⇒ Word processing software
>   ⇒ Mindmapping software (Very highly advised – but optional)

Library:
>   ⇒ Library card
>   ⇒ Build your own library of books

Time:
>   ⇒ Recurring appointments to read/learn
>   ⇒ Recurring appointments to process ideas

THE SYSTEM

The system is a few basic rules that you need to make a habit of reaffirming over the next 21 days. And through those 21 days – affirm the belief that Idea Creation and Innovation is a trainable habit – that gets easier with time.

~ Get into the habit

In one of the best habit-molding books ever written, *The New Psycho-Cybernetics*, edited and updated so expertly by Mr. Take-the-Bull–by-the-Horns himself – Dan S.(Superman) Kennedy, the author Maxwell Maltz talks frequently of the 21 days that we, as humans, need to change a habit and replace it with a new, better and more productive habit.

Upon reading this book, I realized that bad habits could never again interfere with my future progress in life. If it only takes 21 days of daily use of new and better habits – there was simply no excuse anymore in saying: "Well – that's just me – I have always been this way and done these things this way." Nope - sorry pal – not anymore.

Ever since then, I try to find those habits that are creating stress and trouble in my life and read up on the ways others have successfully conquered them. Since none of us is truly unique – I simply know that someone out there has 'gone down this road' before – and written books about their experience.

The habit that you want to create here is the one where you begin molding your dreams – taking your ideas and insights into the field that you love – work with it – and simply allow the magic to happen.

Be alert to your surroundings – your work habits. Where does friction occur? Where are people experiencing problems? (Always a good indication of where innovation is needed.) We can train ourselves to be more open to possibilities and opportunities – on how to be the one in a room full of people who walks away with a life-changing idea.

STEP 1
MAKE IDEA CREATION AND INNOVATION A HABIT

Ideas and insights come usually when you least expect them. Just read Richard Wiseman's *"Did You Spot The Gorilla?"*, and you will see how you can cultivate the habit of idea creation. The real dilemma for us is building the habit of being attuned – trusting our feelings when the ideas/solutions appear. Affirming the belief is important so that we can train ourselves to see the Gorilla.

Having a small notebook on hand, or Phone/PDA, allows you to immediately capture the idea and even begin processing the main points immediately. If you have no book on hand – you need to rely on memory – possibly stifling the creative side of the brain that is feeding you the idea.

STEP 2
ALWAYS HAVE YOUR NOTEBOOK/PHONE/PDA WITH YOU TO MAKE NOTES OF NEW IDEAS

Think of your ideas as your children that you need to feed and nurture to adulthood. The feeding and nurturing of ideas stem from the books that you read and the learning experience you amass through the years. If you work within a certain field – build a library of books that apply to that field – go to the local library and research books on subjects connected directly or even indirectly to that field. Find biographies of people that worked that field and find what helped them. Don't bother reinventing the wheel.

When you read them - stay focused and alert – have a specific goal in mind – questions you want answered – solutions you want to find. Have a target time set to finish the book – but with the intent of re-reading the interesting parts (those that you bookmark) more closely afterwards.

Make your mark in the book – circling the word with a pencil when you see something interesting – writing comments/ideas/questions on the margin when they come to mind. Skim through the uninteresting parts – the parts that you don't feel helpful to take you to your goal – but remember skimming is not just paging through without reading – but reading with the intent of finding keywords that could be helpful to you.

Remember to read books indirectly connected to the field or even have nothing whatsoever to do with it. You never know where the 'pot of gold' is. I have on numerous occasions reached for a book – that gave me answers – answers I did not even know I was looking for, or that I needed at the time. Each time it happened - my life got better. I can do this because I have become skilled in trusting myself when to pick a certain book. You can too.

STEP 3
BECOME A SERIAL READER AND MAKE CONTINUOUS LEARNING A LIFELONG HABIT.

What is your Most Valuable Activity? Find your MVAs - what is it that you do within the company – that create the income for your company to keep its doors open? This is a term coined by Dave Crenshaw in the book *Invaluable* – where he goes through the specific rules on how you can increase your value within the company. What is that special thing that you do, that if you would stop doing it – income would stop? It is usually selling or marketing. But it can be different/other things, and you need to find them and take control of your time and give your MVAs a recurring appointment in your schedule – preferably each and every day.

STEP 4
FIND YOUR MVA

With your MVAs in mind, make a schedule that incorporates all the different things you need to do within a business day – allotting time for each task. Be more productive by mastering your time – with a set of specific rules – allotting those 168 hours per week – but giving you time for your family, interests – or whatever gives your life meaning. Always keep in mind – the reason WHY you do the things that you do -- find your WHY, and give it the time it deserves.

STEP 5
BECOME A MASTER OF TIME INSTEAD OF ITS SLAVE

When you make an appointment with someone, you wouldn't break it for anything, would you? - Especially if you knew that the future of your company depended on it? If you create an appointment in your schedule every day to work on your MVAs – you will avoid slumps – because you are always working on the activities that bring in the money.

But don't stop there – create recurring appointments with your books and ideas – because these books and ideas will help you to become more productive within your MVAs and allow you to create new products and services. Choose books pertaining to your MVAs. It is very easy to ignore these in the busy schedule of a 'new economy' business owner or executive – and that is why it is very important that you allot time over the course of each week and create appointments that you will keep, because your future livelihood depends on it.

Create recurring appointments with your books

Get into the habit of reading a book a day – yes, a whole book through each day. When you get to the place where you can read a book a day – nothing compares to it. There are a lot of good books out there that can help you. But you should also get in the habit of re-reading them – especially the really good ones.

When you read books the second and third time over – now a little wiser and with a little more experience – you will emerge wiser still, because you distill the material in a different way. Words that held no clear meaning for you before are 'crystal clear' to you now.

Create recurring appointments with your ideas

You need to find a time during the week where you are able to disconnect entirely – no phone – no mail – nothing. Where you have 45 to 90 minutes or even 240 minutes of pure daydreaming. Reaching into your folder – packed with ideas – and working through an idea of yours. If you don't make the appointment beforehand – a set time during the week, it can be very easy to get sidetracked. But the habit – of working with your ideas – week after week - will have life changing affects on you. This habit allows you to become an Idea Creator and Innovator.

STEP 6
CREATE RECURRING APPOINTMENTS WITH YOUR BOOKS AND IDEAS

With these 6 steps in place the only thing you need to do is to reaffirm this habit for at least 21 days – day after day – and then keep going forever or for as long as you want.

~ Stay on target

In one of the key scenes of the first Star Wars movie: *A New Hope*, when Luke is flying down the ravine-like tunnel on the Death Star – with shots being fired, explosions all around him and a voice repeating over and over "Stay on target, Stay on target". It is memorable to me, because of the simple message it involves – *not to veer off track – to stay on target – no matter what.*

There might not be many explosions or shots fired at your business – if there are you might want to reconsider your line of work – but there are constant fires in our daily business life. Fires that need our attention – NOW! These fires however, are only one of many aspects that can bother us – making us veer off track.

The lesson here is to <u>stay on target</u>. Our business needs our ideas to grow and prosper. It needs innovation and idea creation as an integral part of its business system. Without it, we, as company owners, burn out handling fires that won't stop, until we take charge or admit defeat and close the door. The only person capable of controlling this process is the business owner him/herself - the Pioneer – the Entrepreneur – You!

THE CONCLUSION

My sincere hope for this chapter is for you to use it to make a map of the road less travelled, so that you do not have to make the same mistakes as those that have travelled that road before. What I did not know until late in my own life is that <u>the map was there for me to find all along</u> – others had left it on the roadside. Business moguls of the past and present, sensible men and women, authors of the various books – have all given us advice on the 'potholes' to avoid.

I have taken the road less travelled and so can you. Don't be afraid of the mistakes you will make along the way. They are a reminder that you are leaving your comfort zone and that is always a good thing. The system is one that has allowed me freedom to be a <u>21st Century Pioneer</u> – to awaken my dormant Entrepreneur - that I believed I had lost forever, as a shy, introverted bookkeeper, at the age of 25.

Use the system – work your ideas – create freedom and prosperity for you and your family – get yourself to Nirvana where Million Dollar ideas are like apples in a tree – where you just reach out and pluck them 'out of the ether'…helping you along the way to become a successful <u>21st Century Pioneer</u> – an Idea Creator and Innovator. Allowing you to boldly go where none have gone before.

For more information on the 6 steps, a more comprehensive list of what books you should read, and what courses to take and stories on the process in action – go to the website that accompanies this chapter – visit: www.theLearningBoss.com/CounterAttack

ABOUT JON

Jon Bjarnason, the Learning Boss, is a 4th generation Entrepreneur from Iceland – and founder of the Learning Boss Program where he has incorporated his knowledge and experience as an Entrepreneur, Small Business Owner, Speed Reading Instructor, Productivity Coach and iMindMap Master Trainer in helping other Entrepreneurs, Small Business Owners and Executives to achieve more success, freedom, time and focus in their daily life.

A small business owner himself for the past 15 years, he found his calling teaching Speed Reading and as a Business Coach while studying Corporate Law. He has been a guest at various Radio and TV programs and a 'sought after' Guest Speaker in Iceland at seminars for various companies and institutions.

In recent years he has been turning his spotlight on Productivity in the New Economy and making better use of our most valuable commodity – TIME – as a founding member of IAPC or the International Association of Productivity Coaches – and using his skills with Mind Maps and Speed Reading as a lifetime student and Serial Reader – he is constantly working on systems that allow individual Entrepreneurs, Small Business Owners and Executives to make time – for the tasks that matter most.

Jon's program, The Learning Boss Program, is a program dedicated to giving you the tools to help you become smarter, sharper, more progressive, aggressive, goal-oriented, organized and productive on your journey to the top of your field in the New Economy - through continuous learning and hands-on coaching. For more information and to learn more about how the program achieves it's goals with individual clients, you can visit: www.theLearningBoss.com/CounterAttack and get more details.

www.theLearningBoss.com

CHAPTER 9

USING QR CODES IN HIGH SPEED CROSS-MEDIA MARKETING

BY EDMOND MAUZER

"The future's already here. It's just not evenly distributed yet"
~ William Gibson

This is a printed QR code. Your customers' mobile phones scan it and they immediately land on your mobile webpage. It's a free technology.

I research, educate and consult in Japan, for the past 9 years now. Usually my friends in various businesses are interested in internet marketing strategies used outside of Japan, but this time I'll give you an insight on how QR codes impacted marketing strategies in Japan. I'll show you how we use QR codes in our daily lives and in marketing. I'll also show you in simple steps how to start using QR codes and benefit immediately.

As we and our machines evolve together, we got to a stage when we feel almost naked if we leave home without a mobile phone. It's already proven that mobile phones are the fastest expanding medium in human history. Everyone has a mobile phone. Where you see a mobile phone, there is a potential customer. They can reach you everywhere, at any time and from any context.

Internet went mobile, membership sites went mobile. Do you have a mobile site? How big is your list? A fast food chain (guess which) has a mobile site in Japan and their subscriber list built up to 16 million members. These customers have already used more than 4.5 million electronic coupons in the last two years, while offering statistical data in real time at a lower cost than ever.

What makes QR codes vital for you is that they are the tangible links printed on whatever support that connect the users to the internet. Bridging the real world to virtual space, QR codes are well integrated into our lives in Japan since more than five years ago. QR codes act as immediate calls to action, and as we carry our phones everywhere, we can click instantly and marketers can catch this "active moment".

WHAT EXACTLY IS A QR CODE?

Q(quick)R(response) codes contain text information coded into an image like those in this chapter. They look much the same but each lands you on a different web page. In fact they may contain any type of text, not just a URL. I have a QR code with my contact info on my business card and I also have a QR code on my Japanese visa.

HOW DO I GET MY QR CODE?

You make one for yourself for free! You access any of the online QR code generators, type in the URL you want to encode, submit it on the page and get the code instantly generated for you. Save it, print it.

HOW DO I ACCESS A WEB PAGE WITH A QR CODE?

Launch your QR code reader on your phone, take a picture with the square centered. The reader software decodes it and launches the URL in your phone's browser.

There was a time when we had to download a reader to the phone but all my phones less than five years old came with it preinstalled. In the US you may need to download a reader and the exact steps may vary, but essentially QR codes are your way to access web pages from printed links without any keyboard. These pages may be deeply hidden in the site, having longer URLs than you would normally type or even print.

WHY IS THIS TAKING OFF IN THE US RIGHT NOW?

Some say that QR codes may be useful only as this year's gimmicks, or that they are a solution looking for a problem, or that you should use them only with early adopters as a target, or that Japanese cell phones are too evolved to survive outside Japan. Before you listen to these 'expert' opinions, let me show you some signs that QR codes are entering the US.

In a recent campaign, Google produced and distributed 100,000 (different) QR codes to 100,000 local businesses in the US. When you scan them you get taken to the business' mobile Place Page where you can read reviews or get coupons etc. YouTube also adds a QR code generator besides the existing URL embedding capability. Go ahead, make an online search and get familiar with how everybody from brands to citics start using QR codes all over the world. Just try to be aware of them and I am sure you will see QR codes appearing everywhere.

HOW DO WE USE QR CODES IN JAPAN?

Let me give you a few random examples. Yesterday, in the bullet train I scanned the QR code on my beer to check something I read in a blog about the beer maker's mobile page. The gasoline station invites me to subscribe to their mobile service to get gasoline discount alerts. On the receipt from the restaurant, there is a QR code and a rectangle to fill in a coupon number. My phone reads the code, I answer a short multi-choice questionnaire on the restaurant's mobile site, and I get a coupon number. I write that in the rectangle on the receipt. Next time when I go to that restaurant I give them the receipt and I get 10% discount.

I register peoples contact info into my phones address book by scanning the QR code on their business card. My daughter watched the Alice trailer on her mobile (soon in 3D on mobile screens, no glasses needed...), scanning from a poster. My son finds out what the cow ate before ending up in his hamburger. People play games, download chaku-uta (music ringtones), machiuke (standby screens) or kisekae (mobile phone themes). These are usually branded...

For more illustrated examples read:

HOW SOME BUSINESSES USE THEM IN THEIR MARKETING?

1. A HEALTH PRODUCT MAKER

They use a mobile site to encourage the continuous use of a health product - a hair growth stimulant. On the mobile site there is a game, a *dojo* where each time you buy, you register your product and your belt level goes up like in martial arts. To promote this site they used QR codes on different media and mobile opt-ins, which are done by sending a blank mail from your mobile.

They went to the stores already selling their product and they pasted seals with QR codes on the boxes. They attached QR codes to their magazine ads. They also put QR codes on their website. QR codes look the same, but for analytical purposes they embedded different URL's for the different media: magazine, pc website. In three months they got more than 2000 new users for their mobile dojo, meaning continuous buyers of their product. As they had different URL's embedded in each different media, they could easily determine how much client flow originated from each of the means used. The breakdown of the client acquisition using QR codes is as follows: 30% from QR codes in magazines, 28% from QR codes on the pc website, 20% from QR codes on the products and leaflets in the shops. Blank mail opt-ins, an already traditional means in Japan yielded 3% and mobile search engines 2%.

2. AN EDUCATION JOURNAL

They publish details about foreign exchange programs four times a year and let users take action with their mobile phones. The main conversion directions are into counseling appointments, mail consultations, information requests and the study-abroad fair organized twice a year. They do landing page optimization by using different URL's each and every time they put a QR code in a new place. On a page about an upcoming event there will be a QR code leading to the subscription page of that event. They get 30% of their leads from QR codes in the journal, 25% from QR codes on their pc site, 20% from QR codes on posters and flyers, 15% from QR codes on brochures.

3. THE BEEF BOWL

A Japanese style *gyudon* (beef bowl) fast food chain, consisting of about 40 stores. They feel the tough economy, and the competition on prices. Solution: an area marketing strategy using QR codes. Concentrating on the loyalty of existing customers, developing specific menus based on area research, coupon codes for list members. All stores have their own QR codes, printed on POP ads which you can get at the restaurant tables and they are distributed in the neighborhood. They also tie-in twice a year with movie theaters and amusement centers and on these occasions the QR code access to their mobile site goes up dramatically.

4. CROSSWORD PUZZLE

A paid membership site. They participate in mobile carriers paid official directory menus - which are yielding less and less access. For sponsored search links and affiliate programs there is too much competition for such content providers, so they decided to do some cross media marketing. They publish monthly a one page free paper with 3 crossword puzzles and a QR code on it. For distribution they use a result-driven affiliate service. The QR code leads to a free membership site where you can submit your solution to a crossword puzzle for a sweepstakes entry. On the same page there is subscription link to their paid site where you can enjoy unlimited puzzles for JPY99 per month, with 200 puzzles added each month. They got 70,000 subscribers by using QR codes printed on free papers.

For more examples read:

HOW TO START ENGAGING THE GREATEST NUMBER OF PEOPLE USING QR CODES?

Understand that…

Mobile marketing is growing faster than PC marketing. The phones are switched on and connected to the internet. Your customers are near the phones and they often look to the screen. With QR codes they can click on catalogues, posters, t-shirts, business cards, sandwich wrappers, tattoos, big screens, etc.

1. Prepare your mobile site to fit on mobile screens, make sure it loads correctly in the phone's browser. You also should carefully think about the special opportunities presented by mobile, and not only copy and paste content from your existing site. And don't forget to offer some value! (Well, if you just want to have your first QR code, any URL or other text will do for a test ride.)

For some ideas on viral mobile content read:

2. Generate your QR code on a free QR code generator site, like qrcode.kaywa.com. As you refine your campaign, you may

generate several different codes for the same page according to the different tracking purposes.

Before generating QR codes, you may consider using shorter URLs. The more data goes into the code, the more pixels it needs. Some companies register shorter domain names, some use URL shortening services.

For more practical advice on generating QR codes read:

3. Print out your QR code in the sizes and on the supports desired and test it with several devices. In Japan the codes are usually around one inch wide. If you don't have a reader on your phone, search for and download one.
4. Distribute the QR codes in print and online (pc sites), monitor your campaign and refine it. Explore other options for using QR codes, like contact information coded on business cards.
5. Get ready for the influx of visitors!

From now on: Continue paying attention to how people's habits change with the evolution of the mobile phones and tagging systems like the QR codes. Make sure your marketing efforts respond to those changes. Good luck!

The story continues...for updated examples, info on who clicks what etc:

ABOUT EDMOND

Edmond Mauzer – known in Japan as Edi Sensei - helps universities and companies to expand online and transition into information businesses. He is the guru behind the internet service company fujii-family.co.jp which together with its sister company prothrive.co.jp are involved in producing, marketing and delivering information products for the health, food, entertainment, education and publishing industries. Edi Sensei founded the Internet Media Laboratory at Souzou Gakuen University where right now his team of intrapreneurs works on reinventing the university as an information business. He also works closely with the major Japanese mobile phone carriers on mobile e-learning projects.

Edi Sensei grew up in Transylvania, and he was part of the core team of the National Curriculum Council – which led to creation of a new competency-based education system in Romania. For two years, he trained extensively on this topic, and his audience included the education departments of all major universities. Nine years ago, he was awarded a research grant by the Japanese government. One year later, after passing the highest level of the Japanese Language Proficiency Test, he began teaching and consulting in Japanese. In a couple of years, he went from being a lecturer and associate professor to a senior tenured professor. He has twenty years of experience in educational and business settings as a seminar leader, consultant, business owner and professor.

CHAPTER 10

MARKETING MECHANISMS AND CHANGE
THE MICRO BUSINESS PLAN MODEL

BY ERNEST BASOCO

Image courtesy NASA/JPL-Caltech

START WITH MEGA

More than ever, change today is happening in ways that are not only unthinkable from the previous century or previous decade, things are developing in a more varied contradictory way, including the perception of value and price in the marketplace.

If selling is the process of persuading a person that your product or service is of greater value than the price being asked, to some degree there is usually a customized micro business plan or model for presenting this value.

Both in business and academia, business plans - particularly the technical marketing portion has been of great interest for me - even before the 90's working as a technical marketing manager for early stage development companies.

As a youth playing sports and attending school, I still remember the title to the cover of a New York Times Best Seller at an 80's book store called Megatrends by John Naisbitt. I was curious at the time, especially about the tag line, "Ten new directions transforming our lives." So I asked my mother at the time what this book was all about right there in the book store.

Together we looked at the cover, back, and inside flaps of the book. I remember my mother telling me this does look like an interesting subject. After setting the book back on its shelf I quickly moved over to the magazine rack, not thinking much of it afterward.

But the funny thing that happened back then was that a few weeks later that very book was sitting on the upright of our piano in the living room. Nothing was ever said to me about it again. I don't know if my mom actually ever read the book herself.

We never talked on the subject from then on. She must have known how much I liked the artwork from the cover of the book, with the dissecting vortex comprised of all colors of the rainbow. I remember thinking this image was just as cool as the vinyl record artwork cover for the Pink Floyd album Dark Side of the Moon, with the single ray of light coming into the prism before releasing as a rainbow through the other side.

Music and sports took a front row to reading back then, so I didn't get around to reading Megatrends myself until I had to write a college essay on the subject of an emerging global economy and the auto industry.

It wasn't until many years later that I had to recall the significance of Megatrends working in the real estate industry in Northern California. As fortune would have it, I was asked to be responsible for a higher profile project if I could precisely demonstrate how to perceive the client's own world. In no way was this world about selling traditional real estate in a traditional market.

This quickly became a world of special meetings, new research, and huge possibilities. A world where it felt like being on the cutting edge of something. That's when the picture of the Megatrends dissecting rainbow vortex came back into mind, along with the tag line, "...transforming our lives."

Many questions were posed at the initial meetings, some like "Have you ever been to a place that has transformed you in some way? A special trip to an inspiring destination such as Italy, the islands of Greece, or Paris?" I didn't know what to think at first about all this.

So the reflexive question I posed back was, "You mean did I have a very memorable new experience? Something so new that I remember it like a first love or a favorite song?" The answer that came right back was a big definite "yes." I was then asked to place a value on this because that's the world we are all being placed in now with this project.

Or in other words, not just looking at luxury architecture as real estate, but feeling its presence or its soul as functional art that can be transformational. Instantly I knew I had to add about 7 books on the subject of architects, artists, and architecture to my own individual library just before moving up to the next step: Developing a creative plan (the micro business plan model) to demonstrate the product being offered is of greater value than the price being asked.

How far do you think we can go with this? Take the design of this product and keep in mind the heart of it is equivalent to that very first love or very memorable experience in a timeless manner. Do not ever attempt to compete on the basis of price with it. From then on I had to think wow, are things really developing in a more contradictory way today - in the present? What about yesterday's Megatrends that were supposed to be so transformational back then?

GOING FROM MEGA TO MICRO TO NANO

Microtrends started as a philosophy first introduced by Microtrends author Mark J. Penn in 2007 where the basic concept is the era of Megatrends is dead, so the ten new directions transforming our lives is all but history. The most important trends now are not at all the big trends. Microtrends, these small 'one-percent of the population' trends really are the things that are driving changes according to Penn.

I wondered if there was at least one-percent of all the business people in real estate who had some belief that unique sales could be based on never competing around price. Maybe this is a Microtrend? To partially answer this question, I did take a statistical poll by calling a group of real estate business people.

The results were phenomenal because out of this group nobody said it was possible to compete with listing architectural residential real estate for sale without some consideration for price. Quickly I realized the challenge was not starting from a Microtrend but quite possibly from a Nanotrend.

Even with a qualified Microtrend already out there, it doesn't mean that people know about it according to American political pollster Penn. He suggests people do not get together about it until somebody significantly crystallizes it. From there, people recognize it as an 'ah-ha moment' before identifying themselves as being part of this Microtrend.

Can there be a newer model to take the standard paradigm and turn it upside down when it comes to competing on the basis of price? For decades, several luxury retailers never attempted to compete on the basis of price, some with success such as Bentley and some with much less like Lamborghini.

Selling unique luxury estates of architectural command still called for a great value proposition with some formulation of not totally competing on the basis of traditional pricing for this project. How do we beckon this customer or buyer for this very kind of real estate product and value? In effect the purpose was to create and satisfy a customer for this, beckoning a customer from a place somewhere between a Microtrend and a Nanotrend.

THE MARKETING MECHANISM: MICRO BUSINESS PLAN MODEL

The marketing mechanism then became essentially more of a sniper firearm than a shotgun approach, a micro business plan model. The marketing mechanism for this project was to create a luxury buyer fulfilled by the product being offered. The product is of value in the same way art dealers and luxury retailers such as Bentley and Maserati have been fulfilling value for years.

This micro business plan model was then derived from the marketing-mix industry standard large and small businesses have been using over decades of change. The basic term marketing-mix was introduced half a century ago in 1960 when a prominent marketer E. Jerome McCarthy reduced the marketing-mix recipe into 4 basic elements (the 4P's): product, price, placement and promotion.

The 4P's elements also evolved from a general mass marketing scope to a mass customization or niche customer focused approach, giving way to the 4C's elements as: capable (product), cost (price), convenience (placement), and communication (promotion). In today's era, 3 more elements have been added to the marketing-mix (the extended 3P's): people, process, physical evidence. Well thought out designs for a strong marketing mechanism, either mass-consumer or niche-focused, are mainly constructed from a combination of the 4P's and extended 3P elements.

So in our design, we learned the sales and marketing elements of beckoning a customer from a place somewhere between a Microtrend and a Nanotrend focus around the following seven micro-model elements, illustrated within the very right column below as the seven Micro C's:

GENERAL ELEMENTS: 4P'S AND 3P'S	CONSUMER/ CUSTOMER FOCUSED: 4C'S	MICRO MODEL ELEMENTS: THE 7 MICRO C'S
Product	Capable	1. Customer Specifications
Price	Cost	2. Customer Benefits
Placement	Convenience	3. Channeled Environment
Promotion	Communication	4. Combined Story and Branding
People		5. Coalition
Process		6. Customer Experience
Physical Evidence		7. Credibility

These seven micro model elements were the key ingredients to our micro business plan for marketing a limited one-of-a-kind architectural estate to a high-end consumer. What we summoned as buyer motivations, sales and marketing strategies, customer practices and everything it takes to walk through the residential estate and into the closing escrow office all were reduced into our custom roadmap of the 7 Micro-C's. Our 7 Micro-C's had the following considerations:

1. Customer Specifications: The product itself specified by an expert from works that balance special consumer wants with architecture, engineering, luxury finish and an experience of timeless beauty (timeless expression).

2. Customer Benefits: Price is what a capable buyer is willing to pay. Exceptional value is perceived from benefits that are tacit as well as benefits that are explicit. Tacit benefits include one-of-a-kind limited works, architectural or engineering genius, transforming function, and a moving experience. Explicit benefits include design, technology, and luxury. Demonstrating the product being offered is of exceptional value is related to the tacit benefits. Tacit benefits related to the customer's vision are the point of emphasis.

3. Channeled Environment: Create the environment to support and enhance the experience in which the product is marketed and sold.

4. Combined Story and Branding Promotion: Combine the personal story of development and history behind the product with the customer's vision with personalized branding. The customer's vision is very important to understand.

5. Coalition: Organize around channels of supporting people and supporting thought to form a coalition. Utilize joint marketing efforts, ad agencies, and other supporting professionals or experts--inside and outside the industry.

6. Customer Experience: Create an experience with the design, product, and service that anchors into past consumer experiences of significance and excellence. These are the elusive experiences of ultimate satisfaction, significance and fond memory. Tying into these anchors of experience with the one-of-a-kind product or service is the art of making the experience transformational. This is the soul of the product or service.

7. Credibility: Highlight existing factors of proof where like-kind sales have been conducted based on similar choices made by people considered to be as similar as the unique special Nanotrend or Microtrend buyer.

MARKET FORCES QUALIFY MICROTRENDS

All of the following brands below have something very important in common:

- Post Ranch Inn - Big Sur, California
- The Fat Duck Restaurant - London
- The French Laundry Restaurant - Yountville, California
- Maserati - Modena, Italy

It can be argued that all of the above brands made dramatic breakthroughs, originating from at one time either a Nanotrend or a Microtrend. Post Ranch Inn located in Big Sur, California is the ultimate organic architectural resort experience that does not compete on the basis of price. Price is only a question if you want the $900 room or the $2,500 room for one night. The $2,500 room equates to a $27 million estate in relative rent versus purchase terms. There is only one Post Ranch Inn across the globe and the $900 room equates to a $9.7 million estate.

Dining at either The French Laundry in Yountville, California or The Fat Duck in London create the once-in-a-lifetime dining experience. Here the transformational experience is valued as the soul of the product and service. With Maserati, all the automotive engineering genius is packed into head-turning elegance - which channels the user's environment from ultimate styling. For each of these brands, market forces and Microtrend elements qualified these dramatic breakthroughs.

There is recent evidence that the current Nanotrend is growing for select architectural estates and unique residential properties. In April of 2010, Boot Jack Ranch in Colorado became the largest residential transaction of the year, recording a sale of $46.5 million. Less than 7 weeks later, a French chateau in California on 2.2 acres located in Bel-Air jump-started this trend, by recording the highest price of any U.S. residence so far in 2010. The 7C's may be just a glimpse of the chasm between this Nanotrend and what the market ultimately qualifies as Microtrend. Somewhere in between, this very special consumer is still looking to be beckoned with the right touch.

Bibliography – selected sources

Penn, Mark. "Microtrends Interview - MSNBC Morning Joe" http://www.msnbc.msn.com/id/3036789/#29463841, March 2, 2009.

Penn, Mark. "Authors@Google: Mark Penn" http://www.youtube.com/watch?v=hifihRzPevE, October 5, 2007.

ABOUT ERNEST

Ernest Basoco's experience ranges from innovative early-stage corporate positions in marketing and sales to high-touch appointments handling all aspects of sales for architectural estates and luxury properties in Northern California Markets. For each real estate transaction, he believes in supporting the vision and creativity of people to implement a personalized plan for success, **with a focus on quality over quantity.** He was awarded the Certified Luxury Home Marketing Specialist designation, including a special membership to the Million Dollar Guild, reserved for professionals who perform in the top 10 percent tier of sales throughout the marketplace. He is a graduate of both the school of Engineering at Cal Poly - San Luis Obispo and the Graziadio School of Business at Pepperdine University in Malibu, CA.

CHAPTER 11

SUCCESS COMES FROM FILLING NEEDS

BY DR. INGA ZEMITE

While writing these lines, I am sitting on an airplane headed to Australia to attend an international congress in my field. I am going there as one of the leading specialists in my profession, the best in my country. I may be one of the leaders there, but I still have a lot to learn. It is my Tao of life.

I sometimes wonder why my life turned out the way it did. Most likely it's the way I think that has brought me here. I always believe that EVERYTHING is possible.

I was raised on a little ranch in the Gulbenes district in Latvia. It seemed to be the middle of nowhere, but it really doesn't matter where you are from. The only thing that matters is how that place makes you feel. Nature's beauty and a stress-free environment surrounded me.

When I was a little girl, I grew up in a very natural environment. My parents were poor agricultural workers, but that was not unusual where I lived and people were generally content with this. Moreover, we were constantly told by the mass media how happy we all should be that we got to live here and how dramatic people's lives were outside the Soviet

Union. I was a little girl, so I really trusted these stories. This TRUST gave me two very important things – safety and gratitude. I felt safe and thankful that I had the privilege to be here. I have never doubted the fact that I am very happy. This attitude has multiplied the happiness in my life. If only my father had not been ill…

To be honest, he was an alcoholic. Where I grew up, many people drank too much. What I know now, and I am sure about this, is that alcoholics feel deeply dissatisfied with their lives. Based on my experiences, I believe unfulfilled ambitions and low expectations from life are root causes of alcoholism. It's the Law of Expectations, the Law of the Universe as described by Brian Tracy in his work **Maximal Achievement** — *what we expect is what we receive.* Having low expectations caused my father to make poor decisions. By making these poor decisions he received what he expected. As a result, his life was full of suffering, and he tried to 'dull' this suffering by drinking. That is the worst story of my life. It is sad, because at the time I did not understand and I couldn't help my father. Of course, I now know that it is almost impossible to help, but at the very least, bringing some positive experiences to his life may have been a step in right direction.

Really, that is not what I would like to focus on here, because it is only one part of my world. There are always a plethora of good and bad things surrounding us. *It is up to each one of us to choose our own path and thus direct our own result.*

When I started school, I had very good teachers and excelled particularly in math. I did not have any academic problems at school, but when I think back on this period of my life, I realize that my greatest difficulty was to form relationships. As my parents moved frequently, I often changed schools and had to adapt to new situations, interact with different people, and constantly find new friends. As a child, it is not always easy to make new friends in a new class every two years, especially if you are not from a very wealthy family. I often noticed that some of my classmates had bad attitudes towards me. What I gained from this experience was the desire to be wealthy when I grew older. I learned patience and willpower. My bad experiences were in part due to a lack of self-confidence. But there is a positive side here as well! If you lack self-confidence, you can definitely improve yourself until you become confident. There will always be positive consequences from personal improvement.

My teenage years taught me that there are people in the world who go through difficult times, and it is worth it to stand up for them and help them. I have learned the greatest things about myself from helping others – and for me it is a necessity to help people. Really, that is the main factor guiding my life and my work. I would even say it is my success factor that I would like to share with the readers of this book.

After my early years, I studied hard and learned much from both academic endeavors and everyday life. I continued my learning by studying medicine. I started at the bottom in the medical field. First as a sanitary worker in a hospital, then as a nurse, followed by ten years on an ambulance, and finally graduating from medical school with a specialty in hair diseases. I have seen a lot of suffering and serious diseases along the way. I knew that I would not like to choose a very emotionally-trying field in medicine. The proposal for me to specialize in hair diseases came quite unexpectedly from the director of the health center where I worked.

As you can imagine, I was shocked by such a proposal, after all I was studying to save lives not hair! But at the time, it was very difficult for a young doctor to find a job in a good field, so this really presented me with an excellent opportunity. At the time, such medical help for hair problems did not exist. I would be the first in the field. I had to think about it, but I decided quickly that I would do it. <u>I DECIDED QUICKLY.</u> You know how important it is to be the first in any business?? It really was a great opportunity, but I only realized how great it was with time. This area of specialization fit my interests and imagination of what I wanted perfectly.

There was one very important aspect of this job. There was a NEED for such a specialist, but there were none available. People suffer from many hair problems – ranging from *androgenic alopecia* and diffuse hair loss to infections of the skin and *alopecia areata*. The understanding of these conditions was, I would say, quite vague. There are so many false myths about hair. One of the most absurd myths is the belief that if hair falls out, there isn't a thing you can do about it. To me this sounds ludicrous. The unfortunate thing is that many people believe this myth, so they do not even look for help when a problem appears.

There really was a great need for such a specialist, and I seized the opportunity. I read a lot and used all available media to gather knowledge on this topic. As I found useful and practical information, my confidence in this area grew steadily. Then the mass media started to show an interest in me as a competent medical adviser and consultant in this popular area. At the same time, pharmaceutical companies that produce products to reverse hair loss invited me to speak about hair diseases at local conferences for doctors and pharmacists. I was even invited to teach a course about hair diseases at the Medical Academy. All these events came one after another and strengthened my position as a leader in the field.

The thing I like most about my career is treating my patients. I have given so many consultations that they seem to take up all my time. Men, women, and children came with very different problems concerning their hair. Very often they were exhausted by the problem. They had tried all possible treatments they knew of, or found available, and often had no visible results. After an appropriate investigation, we were able to find the root of the problem and decide what would be the best treatment. The first step is usually to stop further hair loss - and then comes the treatments for improved hair growth. What is extremely important though, is that to treat this condition, you have to know principles of treatment.

Even if it seems to be easy (and it is not), it is really not possible to maintain your hair if you do the wrong things. If someone thinks they have a problem with their hair – it suddenly falls out in large amounts, or the volume of hair diminishes, or hairless patches appear on the scalp, or if the skin is itching and painful – a visit to the doctor is needed. If help is received in a timely manner, a person can keep their hair, regardless of genetics.

What can I say about hair? I have been involved in this specialty for 12 years now, and I have seen how difficult hair problems can be for people. A disease like *alopecia areata*, when hair falls out suddenly in patches, can be very emotionally upsetting. It really changes a person's life. I have seen cases where women lose their jobs and families because of it.

By the way, one of the reasons I decided to participate in the writing of this book was *to inform people that there are possible treatments for hair loss*. My inner desire to help people is being fulfilled again.

The best business lesson from my experience is that you can become successful if you offer people a product or service that they really need! Very often, businesses are constructed around the idea that a business makes a "GOOD PRODUCT" and then sales revolve around that product. Sometimes that product is only good in the minds of those selling it. In reality if you develop a product or service that people really need, like I have, you are always a winner.

If you work to help people, you will always have enough customers. If you satisfy your customers, you will become a celebrity in your field sooner or later.

I recommend you keep the following ideas from my personal experience in mind:

1. Be conscious! The mind is a like a little child at about 18 months – he can hear all but understand nothing. If you do not recognize this, it can cause problems – so pay attention to your mind – BE conscious!
2. Find something you really like to do! If something in my story touched your heart, try to understand what it was and why. Make it work for YOU.
3. Find something that you like that can be good for others!
4. Work on it! Make a plan. Learn the necessary methods and gather information to make it happen.
5. Get started!
6. Be decisive! Make decisions quickly and seize opportunities!
7. Know that everything is possible! There is nothing impossible in the world.
8. Examine your life! Try to identify the good that has come from your bad experiences. You can rid yourself of that pain.
9. Above all else, remember that you choose your attitude! That is the most important thing I would like you to take away from this – *we are in control of our own lives*. Our choices are based on our understanding, attitude, values and experience.
10. Finally, if you have hair problems – contact me!!

Many other experiences are described in this book. Although it would be valuable to read and contemplate all of them, no one will be able to use all of these experiences as a recipe for success, as we all differ in our values and experiences. Even the most successful practices of one person can be completely wrong for another. *What makes reading a book like this worthwhile is to put yourself in the situations described and try to imagine what you would do in the same situation.* Does it address your feelings? Do you think things were done right or would another way have been even better? Maybe you don't even understand why it is a success story... Make it yours!

ABOUT INGA

Dr. Inga Zemite is a medical doctor specializing in the treatment of scalp skin and hair diseases. She is a leading and well-known specialist in her field in Latvia. Since starting her practice in 1997, she has become a leading expert in her country as well as for patients from other European countries that seek out her advice. She is also a general practitioner and often appears on national TV, radio, and in different publications to give advice about hair treatments, healthy living and explaining the course of diseases. She is the founder and a leading member of the Latvian Hair Doctors Association and is highly regarded by other specialists in her field.

She founded a practice for hair patients in the center of Riga, Latvia. Patients coming to her clinic are carefully evaluated using a combination of questionnaires, clinical examination and appropriate medical investigation. This scientific system leads to an accurate understanding of the reason for the hair loss and thus leads to suitable treatment for each patient.

Dr. Zemite is constantly looking for new and updated treatment methods. She introduced well-known methods such as treatment of *alopecia areata* with contact allergens and mesotherapy for hair growth in Latvia. Natural treatments and even *ayurvedic* medicines are used in appropriate ways in her practice as well. The mix of traditional and nontraditional medicines makes treatment more and more effective..

To learn more about Inga Zemite,MD or to seek a consultation about your hair problem you can contact her through www.skype.com (JUMED (Latvia, Riga)) or call her in Latvia at +371 67 277887.

CHAPTER 12

THE SECRET TO SUCCESSFUL BRANDING

BY HOLT VAUGHN

DANG!

T his needed to be a good quarter! Cash flow has been tight, profits tighter. Pamela needed serious sales—and needed them now. But as she reviewed her ninety-day sales projections and dug into current operations, reality sank in. Pam had an "aha!" moment realizing why things were not working. Her fine organization was misfiring, not operating with all cylinders in sync. In fact, it could burn out fast.

THE SCENARIO

- Pam's salespeople are selling one product line while her marketing people are championing another.
- Her latest flyer (a half million copies) is pretty good, but it has her old logo and slogan on it, and the fonts used seem a bit too formal.
- The marketing video Pam just spent $75,000 on is impressive. It projects an industry giant with the 'hot shot' look of a multinational tech company. The trouble is, Pam runs a franchise of locally owned children's apparel stores!

As Pam's epiphany continues, her eyes are opened further.

- The language, photos, and videos on her Web site don't really match those used in the expensive social media campaign she's working on.
- The colors in the extensive e-mail blast she just sent out are bright reds and purples, but her other marketing pieces feature warm earth tones.

The more she looks, the more she's seeing this confusion and inconsistency in many places. No wonder sales are sagging; even she and her own people seem confused about the message they're sending. *They're communicating the wrong signals to the marketplace, and that is revealing itself in the bottom line.*

REALITY SETS IN

Pam should be thrilled, actually. She's coming to grips with the fact that the inconsistencies she's presenting to the world are stalling her success. She won't be winning any races against the competition. Worse yet, in today's *uber*-competitive brand-obsessed culture, she could 'blow a couple of rods' and be sidelined permanently. Pam sees that her organization must become a well-oiled machine consistently presenting a strong, unified message. It hits her that *in the new economy, messaging is instantaneous—and with more channels of communication than ever.* Everything that is not well integrated betrays and dilutes her ability to capture the hearts and minds of her audience.

What's more, Pam has noticed that one competitor seems to stand out in the crowded marketplace, collecting satisfied customers from their consistently strong campaigns. They always communicate with the same clear voice, reaching increased numbers through many well-integrated sales and marketing channels. Their value proposition (things customers will highly value) and market differentiation (the thing that makes their company, products, and services stand out as different, better, and unique among the competition) are concise, catchy and...*consistent.* It draws you in to buy *and sticks with you until the next time you need to buy.*

"We know our message too," Pam exclaims, "and we have a stronger product with higher value and a great organization with great people! When we get that message out, people see our value and respond. Yet [back to the aha! moment] we don't seem to build serious momentum. Our different departments (seemingly) work toward the same goals, but they are rarely effective at presenting a consistently cohesive message. We too want to be 'sticky'—to 'stick' in people's hearts and minds so they think of *us* and not the competition when they have a need. *What are we missing?*"

Two words: *brand manual* (also at times called corporate identity manual or style guide).

Do you have one?

Read on and get ready to GROW YOUR BUSINESS, OWN YOUR CATEGORY, and BUILD YOUR BRAND…in short, fix the above problem and make serious progress toward MORE SUCCESS IN THE NEW ECONOMY!

WORK HARD, WORK SMART! GROW OR DIE! YOUR BRAND IS EVERYTHING! …AND OTHER BUSINESS TRUISMS…

You've put forth tremendous effort investing in your organization. You've labored over the concepts, ideas, language, logos, images, and slogans you use to narrate your story to the world. When it is done right, communicated well, you know it works. You have registered trademarks, licenses, and copyrights. The products, services, people, Web site, flyers, videos, blogs, tweets, brochures, ads, marketing campaigns, building architecture and signage, and a million more details express all you are to the public. *Who is going to protect the integrity of all that, making sure it CONSISTENTLY SAYS THE RIGHT THING?* How are you going to ensure it all comes together and then STAYS TOGETHER as a cohesive powerful brand propelling you to success in the crowded marketplace of an often confusing new economy?

May I drive the point home? Your hard work…your brand…is everything. **You put loads of effort and resources into creating a strong bond between you and your customers. Fail with your core message—mess with your brand—and you fool with your lifeblood. Who is going to make certain:**

- That **the language** in your sales and marketing efforts is uniform, saying exactly what you know you need to say for success?

- That your in-house or outsourced **graphic** designers and **advertising** people will respect your **logos** and **company artwork**? That they will **UNDERSTAND your brand** well enough to do things right? Or will you be doing the worst thing possible: spending money that actually LOWERS your sales by sending the wrong message to the masses? Communication today is instantaneous! In the fog of confusion, people gravitate to the focused beam of a good message and instinctively avoid anything they can't define. You could spend millions on marketing, but even the smallest inconsistencies are a repellent, driving wary customers away. What if someone asked you to invest in a deal that would hurt your sales, decrease your brand equity, and ultimately put you out of business? You'd show them the door! But that is what you do when you spend your money on communications that confuse. You pay good money to actually undermine your efforts—like putting sugar in your gas tank and expecting your engine to take you to victory.
- That the **video production company, photographers, printers, and e-mail** marketers are held accountable to *accurately* portray your image, telling your story so your products and services are sold effectively?
- That the people creating your all-important **Web site** use the **correct words, colors, photos and graphics**, **search engine optimization,** and ease of navigation that you need to be perfectly consistent with all of your other efforts? For example, consider a company that prides itself on accessibility, only to have a Web site that buries the "Contact Us" button in an obscure corner. Then again, how would the Web designer even know that accessibility was one of your brand values?
- That **press releases** and **social media** campaigns are consistent with your organization's vision?
- **THAT *ALL OF* YOUR COMMUNICATIONS ARE ACCURATELY, CONSISTENTLY TELLING YOUR BRAND STORY, GROWING YOUR BUSINESS THE WAY YOU KNOW THINGS MUST BE DONE?**

Seem overwhelming and exhausting? Not at all! *Your brand manual does it for you!*

WHAT IS A BRAND MANUAL?

A brand manual is your organization's communications bible. It is the standard plumb line, go-to reference from which all your communications proceed. It's a control mechanism for all details outlined above. It demands that all varied visual and language elements be brought into harmony, creating a unified whole that gains *momentum* for your brand. It is capable of generating *geometric growth* because you'll have all sales, marketing, and distribution channels *saying the same thing and working together simultaneously* in the marketplace. *It becomes a very valuable company asset* and essential sales/marketing/communications tool. It greatly helps establish your corporate identity (who you are and what you do)—both internally (to your employees, staff, and advisors) and externally to the public (your customers, constituents, investors, the media and press). *It gets everyone from top to bottom on the same page quickly with relatively little effort considering the return on investment!*

7 SIMPLE STEPS TO CREATING YOUR BRAND MANUAL

1. **Write a complete description of your brand.** If you haven't already, you need to. And you need to labor over it until it's just right and very articulate. In essence *you are simply telling who you are and what you stand for.*

    If you are unsure about brands in general, there are great books and other resources available to get you started. Hopefully you created your Values Statement and Mission Statement when you first began your company. If so, they are a good place to start. Utilize company resources too; don't just go it alone. Outside perspectives from your people on the front lines are invaluable. Whether you have a large organization or are a sole proprietor, get people involved to help put your vision into words that inspire and clearly instruct. It is a good practice to include business associates, sharp friends, board of advisors, marketing department, sales people, etc. Keep things moving as you do this; don't get bogged down. Lead the process, make the tough decisions, listen well, and get it written.

2. **Include your brand strategy and vision:** a basic or very detailed version, or one of each in short form and a longer

reference work. If you need help, the same note applies here as in #1 above. Consider hiring an agency. There are some great branding, marketing, and communications companies out there. Helping with things like this is why we exist.

3. **Include your rules and guidelines for using all company logos, trademarks, copyrights, etc.** Cite specific examples and situations of how and where these symbols can and can't be used.

4. **Include rules and guidelines not only for symbols, but also for ALL visual elements used in your communications materials**: artwork and layout styles, color choices (e.g., primary colors or earth tones or a mix, CMYK vs. pantones, etc.), guidelines for using custom and stock photos, Web, video, e-mail and social networking guidelines, and so forth. Cite specific examples and situations.

5. **Include exact specifications of typographical elements** (fonts, sizes, dimensions, etc.). Cite specific examples and situations.

6. **Include a language style guide**. Do you use technical language or a conversational style? Is your verbiage to be poetic and whimsical or straightforward and earthy? Are there certain buzzwords or jargon that helps define you? What words or phrases should never be used in your communications? Cite specific examples and situations.

7. **Include rules and quality standards for all production and reproduction**. These include standards for the benefit of the advertising agencies, printers, video production companies, photographers, Web designers, and copywriters you will employ.

For a sample of a style guide go to
www.eastcoworldwide.com/counterattack

THE TURNAROUND: A LAST WORD

Your brand manual is one of your best employees!

Once created and properly managed, your brand manual acts as a control to ensure the all-important accuracy and consistency of your company messaging in all forms of communication! Your sales, advertising, and marketing are ruled by the guidelines you put into place. Just hand it off to those creating and executing your materials, and with little or no meeting time you can let them run with it. *Be sure to enforce its use and keep it updated on a regular basis via written company pro-cesses and policies!*

That little problem—that's costing you millions—where your sales-people and marketing are communicating two different things? Gone. Why? Because your brand manual ensures your copywriters and graph-ics people, advertisers and marketers are all getting (and using) the same message. Your one-half million flyers printed with the wrong logo, slogan, and fonts? Not a chance, because the designers who cre-ated it would have been using your brand manual, which contained the updated logo and slogan. The video you dropped $75,000 on wouldn't be a waste either, because the production company followed your brand manual and grasped the intangibles of your corporate spirit. The lan-guage, photos, and all else on your Web site now perfectly match the elements being used in your expensive social media campaign, so that is also creating momentum and geometric growth. The words, logos, pictures, and colors in your e-mail blasts and (hallelujah!) ALL of your marketing pieces match perfectly, **consistently sending the same pow-erful message to your now ever increasing loyal audience!**

Gone is confusion about the message you're sending. People inside your company and outside are beginning to truly understand who you are and what you provide. They perceive the value you bring and are forming a strong bond, an attachment to your products, services…your brand. *You're now consistently communicating the right signals to the marketplace, and that is revealing itself in a positive bottom line.*

ABOUT HOLT

Holt Vaughn is the founder and president of The Eastco Group. The award-winning group of media companies can be found at www.theeastcogroup.com and includes Eastco Worldwide, a full-service branding, marketing, and communications agency; Eastco's California Road Studios, a world-class audio, video, TV, and film production and post facility featured among *Mix Magazine*'s class of world's hottest new studios; and Vaughn Street, LLC, which works with some of the world's leading faith-based organizations. Holt is known for his ability to get great things done and is a sought-after strategist, producer, writer, and speaker. In addition, he has worked with world-class leaders and executives, international best-selling authors and artists, and organizations large and small, helping them go to the next level.

The innovative and big ideas, creative concepts, strategic plans, product development, audio/video/film productions, marketing, branding, and public relations/media strategies Holt and his team provide for clients have sold many millions of dollars of products and services and have effectively reached millions of people around the globe.

From projects featuring rock stars and pop phenoms, best-selling authors to Fortune 500 companies, and local and regional clients to publishers, educational and government institutions, Holt has overseen countless projects. As well as being a published writer who has developed leading works for international best-selling authors, Holt has served on college advisory committees and corporate boards, and his work has been covered in local and national publications and television within the entertainment industry, the business world, and the Christian community.

Holt can be contacted at: EastcoWorldwide.com, or by emailing Jon La Porta, Director of Sales and Marketing: jlaporta@eastcoworldwide.com

CHAPTER 13

KEY THINGS LEARNED BY THE WORLD'S BEST SALES TRAINERS

BY JOHN JOCHEM

B rian Tracy mentored me for a year. The goal was to double my income and double my time off. In this section, I'll touch upon Tracy's ideas, which worked for me.

The 80/20 Rule states that 20% of the salespeople sell or make 80% of the sales or income. 20% of the products or customers make up 80% of the sales. Focus on the 20% and increase the time you spend on the 20%. This includes 20% of the process or prospecting techniques that make up 80% of the sales. It is about your Hip National Bank.

You will need to start delegating actions which are below your income level to maximize your income. You will need to fire clients who are taking up too much of your time and not generating enough income. You will need to add more clients that are part of the 20%.

During my master's, I wrote about Tracy's process, which allowed me to double my income and double my time off. First, write your top 10 goals in present tense every day, e.g., 'I am a bestselling author'. Second, find the top goal, which when achieved, would have the biggest impact on your life. Third, list 20 things which can prevent you from achieving the top goal. Fourth, take the biggest obstacle and list 20 actions which you can take to overcome the obstacle. Finally, list 10 things you need to do today.

Tracy said to find out your weakness and then make your weakness one of your strengths. This process can take six month or it can take a year. My biggest weakness, when doing acquisitions, was prospecting. In two months, prospecting became a major strength for me. For some salespeople, it could be closing and for others, it might be follow up.

Tracy said that the more time you took off from work, that your production would increase. I didn't believe Tracy, but I followed his advice. My production per hour increased. You are better rested and more creative. The fun time goes up, which forces you to use hours smarter when you are at work and delegate more.

You are not in the business which you think you are in. My father was a Chevrolet dealer for virtually 40 years. He cared about gross profit for used cars. Reality was the quicker the used cars were sold, the higher the gross profit. Turn time for used cars or days in inventory for used cars was the business my father was in. I worked with the largest diabetic supply company, which sold diabetic testing strips covered by Medicare Part B. Each salesperson had to look at the pay plan and determine the business they were in by how they were getting compensated. Some had great volume and the number of shipments was how they got paid. Others sold more than testing strips and the other products were how they were getting paid. Some salespeople made their money from referrals at a higher dollar amount. Some businesses have a niche with the frequency of re-order or short ownership time. Other businesses might be add-on products. Find out your pay plan and how you really get paid and maximize your income.

TOM HOPKINS

Tom Hopkins has trained 3,000,000 salespeople and stated that you needed to listen to CD's. The goal should be six figures. The action, which put me over the top for the six figures wasn't CD's, but DVD's. Watching a DVD everyday is the discipline, which made all of the difference.

After reaching six figures, I was attending Tom Hopkins' three day Sales Mastery Boot Camp. A person decided to sit next to me, after seeing me for years at the same seminar. The salesperson wanted to reach the six figures and I was encouraging him and telling him that he could. After a few minutes of encouragement, I found out the person meant he wanted to have six figures each month. The income I earned in 365 days, he was earning in about 40 days. The point is there are always better ways and higher levels to rise to.

The best thing I learned from Tom Hopkins was how to use post cards. Every time I left town, I would mail my 'cash flow people' post cards. I was with Zig Ziglar in Dallas and mailed 200 post cards and the following week with Tom Hopkins in Scottsdale, AZ and mailed 200 postcards. I would fill out the post cards before arriving in Dallas and Scottsdale. From the postcards, my phone would ring off the hock when I got back to the office. People knew I cared about them; I was in touch with them and they wanted to talk with me. They saw how much I traveled and business came from those postcards. I always put my cell phone number on the postcard and a P.S. I always signed my name clearly. Millions of dollars in transactions happened as a result of postcards. People know me from postcards. John is at Disney World this week. John is at a seminar in Boston... Send the postcards and people will send you money.

Hopkins taught me a magical phrase, which when used, the person listening to you will forget everything before the phrase. The phrase "Oh, by the way ..." will save objections and conflicts with clients. I told the president of a company about the phrase 'Oh, by the way ...' and he and his partner didn't believe me. I informed the two of them, that I could say the worst possible thing about a person's mother and say 'oh, by the way' and the person would forget the comments about their mother. This was done at a meeting in front of the entire company. The president of the company and his partner became believers. 'Oh, by the way ...' can save you transactions and interrupt people's thought patterns. Use 'Oh, by the way ...' and watch your income increase.

Hopkins says to embrace failure and be persistent, and that selling is a numbers game. When I was with the world's largest diabetic mail order company in the sales department, the assistant to the vice president of sales grabbed me by her office. She said that a customer said I was rude to her and asked me if I was rude to a customer. My response was if the customer said I was rude then I was rude. The assistant to the vice president then asked what she should say to me, as people were gathering. My response was, "Tell me congratulations and to be rude to another customer." The assistant to the vice president was confused. I responded, "You monitor all my phone calls. You know it is not my intent to be rude to a person or to offend a person. You get paid on my volume. If somebody complains, it means I have volume and the company is making money. You want the company to make more money. So say congratulations for offending a person and to offend another person." The assistant to the vice president said 'congratulations for offending somebody and to offend another customer' with her mouth dropped. If you are not making mistakes, then you do not have volume. The more errors you make the higher your activity and the more transactions you will complete.

ZIG ZIGLAR AND KRISH DHANAM

I am a certified Zig Ziglar speaker and trainer and Krish Dhanam got me certified. Zig gave me the Banana Close. "If this applies to you, then you will have a grin from ear to ear so wide that you will be able to eat a banana sideways." The Banana Close makes the prospect smile, laugh, and relieves tension, while getting them to want to listen to you.

Krish says that you want to do something 'because' of a person and not 'for' the person. It took me a long time to understand this. On the PhD level, I got to be doing things 'because' of my loved ones 'because' if I didn't accomplish my work early, then I could not play. I did not do the PhD 'for' them. You want to do things 'because' of your loved ones.

If it is not right at home, then the salesperson cannot sell. As a manager, I focused on my salesperson's home life to maximize their work production. I got the most out of a salesperson by making sure their home life is working, but I do not place judgment on the salesperson or on my personal values.

Zig said that you will increase your income 10% by tracking your production and activity. You get paid for result. If you don't add value, then you will be added to the unemployment line. Find out the correlation of your results to certain activities. I found out that when I didn't eat lunch my sales increased; this is due to the food slowing me down. I found out when I prospected internally with other departments, my sales increased. I found out that when I left the office that my sales increased, even though most of my work was done over the phone.

JIM ROHN

Jim Rohn said success is a few disciplines practiced everyday and failure is a few errors in judgment repeated every day. Rohn also said that every discipline affects the rest of the disciplines. When you start focusing on your personal life and not your work life, that is when your work life will improve. Based upon Rohn, I went out and acquired new disciplines every six months. I lost 50 pound and started to exercise 35 miles a week. I had a date night and said 'I love you'. I went for my master's degree and then my PhD. I focused on giving compliments, saying 'please', 'thank you' and 'you're welcome'. Find one new discipline and practice the discipline for six months. An apple a day can be a good start.

JACK DOWNS

'I guess I must have bumped my head' or 'I guess we must have bumped our heads' are the phrases you use when you 'mess up' and accept responsibility. You always want to be accountable and retain rapport. The customer will release their emotions and the tension will decrease and the customer usually continues the relationship.

The Pepsi Close is when a (potential) client is offered food or a drink. The client will be obligated to you and more likely to move forward. If the prospect offers you a drink or food, always accept the food or drink. Never go into a meeting with a coffee or a drink. The goal is to be offered something in order to increase rapport, extend the meeting and increase the commitment level of the prospect.

Time = Obligation for a customer. In life, time is worth more than money. With love, time=love.

JACK CANFIELD

Canfield wrote The Success Principles and was mentored by W. Clement Stone. From this, you should first look for a mentor and add positive people into your life. Second, you should eliminate the negative people in your life. Third, you should learn to say no and value your time more. Fourth, you need to master delegating.

TONY ROBBINS

Tony Robbins teaches Neuro Associated Conditioning, which is also known as NLP (Neuro-Linguistic Programming). This is also known as VAK (visual, auditory, kinesthetic). The goal is to increase your closing ratio by 30%. The process is simple. People basically communicate in three different 'languages': visual, auditory and kinesthetic. First, find out which preferred 'language' the person uses. Second, use the same 'language' or type of words: i.e., if a person is using visual words, then use visual words.

Visual people use visual words when talking. Visual people can look up when thinking. Visual people talk the fastest. People from New York are usually visual people; remember the phrase… 'in a New York minute'. When you talk to a visual, you will talk as fast as they do. You will use words like see, visualize, colors, saw. The visual person will be connected to you and your closing ratio will drastically increase. If you talk too slow it will drive the visual person nuts.

Auditory people use auditory words or phrases: it rings a bell; I hear what you are saying; heard; sound; A visual will look right to left when thinking. The auditory will talk slower than the visual. Instead of the feel, felt, found, you will do it in an auditory way: I understand what you are saying. Others have told me the same thing. What they are now telling their friend who they found is…

The kinesthetic person should be called the feeling person. They look down when thinking. The kinesthetic or feeling person talks the slowest and represents the lowest percentage of people. If you talk too fast to a kinesthetic, then they will run from you and not trust you. The kinesthetic will use 'touchy-feely' words like feel, touch, firm, hard, rough, and smooth. You will use the feel, felt, found on this person.

SUMMARY OF KEY THOUGHTS

1. Do the Tracy Lists every day and increase your income
2. Work less and get more
3. 80/20 Rule
4. Know your pay plan and what business you are in
5. Watch a DVD a day to go to the next level
6. Send Post Cards
7. Say 'Oh, By The Way…'
8. Write your activities and increase your production by 10%
9. Make mistakes, increase your activity and volume
10. Develop one new discipline every six months
11. Say "I guess we must have bumped our head" and be accountable
12. Give away something to drink or eat and they will be obligated to you
13. Time = Obligation
14. Delegate and say no
15. Increase your closing ratio by 33% by mastering NLP

ABOUT JOHN

John Jochem teaches business principles on-line to college students; he has virtually completed all of his PhD courses and does some business consulting. John's area of expertise is Medicare Part B, sales and motivation. He has about a decade of experience with Medicare Part B companies, including: doing corporate acquisition for 3 out of the top 4 diabetic supply companies, working with 5 of the top 10 diabetic companies, helping to establish America's #2 respiratory wholesale medication company and working with America's #2 power wheel chair company. His best month in sales was 1,250 individual transactions with 1,250 people and his biggest corporate acquisition was about $25,000,000. John Jochem is a certified Zig Ziglar trainer and speaker; was named #1 out of 100,000 students Tom Hopkins trained in 2000. Tom Hopkins also authored *How to Master the Art of Selling*. John spent about two months on the road with Tony Robbins, who wrote *Unlimited Power*. He was on the National Dean's List as an undergraduate, which is the top 0.5% in the nation in grades. His majors were finance and marketing. He has a Master in Business Administration and shortly will complete his PhD. courses.

CHAPTER 14

THE SECRET TO PROFITS: PEOPLE!

BY GUNTARS STIKOVS

"An ounce of appreciation is worth a pound of money."
~ Sir Ian Bancroft

"I love my work."

Yes, I love my work, I enjoy working for my boss, and I'm proud to be a part of my company. As a matter of fact, it doesn't even feel like a company – it feels like a family. We all work together, make each other better and 'pull together' so we can reach our highest ambitions. We care about what we do and it shows in everything that we do, every single day.

I couldn't ask for a better work experience."

Sound familiar? Probably not. To most people, I am willing to wager that the above conversation sounds like a fairy tale. Instead, what frequently goes through many of their heads is…

"I hate my job."

"I don't like what I am doing. I hate my boss and he couldn't care less about me. I don't get paid nearly enough, I am forced to live paycheck to paycheck, and my requests for raises are consistently refused. No one listens to me or values my ideas or opinions and I don't feel like anyone respects me. I constantly feel insecure and stressed out at work – and my happiest moment is the moment when I know the business day is over.

I don't care what happens to this company."

If you run your own business and you suspect the people who work for you are thinking that way, you are bound to have problems not only with your employees, but with your all-important customer service. People are often the missing piece of the puzzle when any entrepreneur is trying to put together a successful business with lasting profit power.

APPRECIATING YOUR STAFF

You no doubt invest a lot of time, energy and money in your staff. But how much *appreciation* do you invest?

And your answer might be, "Well, I pay them. That's enough appreciation."

It may be enough for you – but it's probably not enough for them. And it could end up really hurting your brand.

The people who work for you are the face of your company. If they feel bitter or angry about their treatment by you, that negativity is going to be conveyed to the outside world. Even if someone who works for you doesn't directly deal with the public, they will still talk about how they feel about your business with friends and family. And that's how bad reputations are born.

How do you feel about your staff? Do you view them as an inconvenient necessity or an important asset? If it's more the former than the latter, then that resentment is bound to feed down to them.

Technology, products and services are often interchangeable from company to company. What usually makes the difference is the people – they convey what your brand is and what it's about. Again, if they're in a bad frame of mind about your company, then they will put that frame around your brand and 'douse it' with that negativity.

That's why you need to care for and nurture your employees – and treat them as individuals, not cogs in your enterprise. Every person is unique

– every person wants to be recognized for who they are, not who you think they should be. This isn't to say they don't have to fulfill their job requirements or can treat you with disrespect – if someone isn't working out because of their attitude, it's better to let them go. Just make sure the problem isn't at your end.

By providing the proper encouragement and attention to your employees, you make them feel appreciated and, crucially for your company, you motivate them to do their best for you. They become a living advertisement for how wonderful you and your business are – and that's much better than a surly staffer who carries around so much resentment that they actually think of ways to sabotage you.

This is especially true with your employees who directly interact with your customers. If they have no investment in you or your business, if they feel like it doesn't matter how well they do, they will communicate that dissatisfaction to your clients. An unhappy staff can easily lead to unhappy customers.

IMPLEMENTING THE "PEOPLE" FACTOR

What's the lifeblood of any company?

Sales. And customer care has a direct and profound effect on sales – if your customer service isn't up to par, your company could have difficulty surviving. The University of Michigan researched the American Customer Satisfaction Index – and found that 27% of all customers were not happy with the product or service they purchased. Think about that – over a quarter of consumers left with a negative feeling about buying from a company. Do you think they would patronize that company again?

Bad customer service drives away sales – it's a one-way ticket to losses, not profits. It's true that everything starts with a good business model – offering an in-demand product or service and marketing it in an effective, memorable way. That, to many business owners, is all they need to create the complete success story. Unfortunately, at the crucial point when the sale is actually made, that success story can suddenly have an unhappy ending.

Apple is a good example of what can happen with bad customer service. Recently, they released the newest model of the iPhone, an incredibly popular product. With the success of the earlier models, as well as the iPod and the iPad, this is a company that thought they could do no wrong.

But there was a problem – you had to hold the new iPhone *the exact right way* or you would have a weak or disrupted signal. Apple CEO Steve Jobs' first reaction to customer complaints? Instructing them on how to hold the phone and basically telling them it was their problem. But nobody wants to continually think about how they're holding a cell phone – they want it to function correctly on *their* terms, not the company's.

To make matters worse, Apple actually began charging customers to fix the problem with *their* product – all of which is, at the time of this writing, resulting in a class action suit by customers against Apple for releasing an inferior product. This is one of the few companies that could get away with this kind of behavior – their products are so unique and so in demand, that, in 2010, they can survive and even prosper while treating their customers this poorly. The overwhelming majority of our businesses, however, are not in that fortunate position.

Witness Toyota, a company with an amazing decades-long record of safety and customer satisfaction – now fighting for their lives because they refused to own up to dangerous defects in their vehicles until it was too late and the media had turned against them. Similarly, most of the American car companies actually had to go bankrupt before they saw that they had to increase their quality and customer care standards.

When company management is overly arrogant, treats its workers badly and also feels it knows better than their customers, they've lost touch with the all-important "people" factor – and, in time, that will result in many, many difficulties with their operation and their ability to make profits. Especially in a difficult economy such as today's, keeping a current customer happy is much easier and more cost-effective than trying to get new ones.

STRENGTHENING THE EMPLOYEE-CUSTOMER LINK

For your business to really work optimally, your employees should be happy – and, of course, so should your customers. That creates a positive energy that feeds directly back into your business brand, reputation and, ultimately, revenue streams.

The first step to making sure the employee-customers link is as strong as possible is to look at how your employees are approaching customers. Do they provide celebrity-quality support services? Do they make the customer aware of the value the company is providing to them? And is that value satisfactory to your customers? Are both employees and customers loyal to you and your organization? If not, how can you create that loyalty? Although loyalty and appreciation are not tangible qualities, they will translate into tangible benefits for your company's bottom line.

How do you answer these questions? Begin by systematically collecting and analyzing customer and employee feedback on a consistent basis. If there's a problem with either your products or services, or with your employees' attitudes, a pattern will emerge by surveying them.

Getting this kind of feedback also helps you to meet rapidly changing market needs. Things can change fast in volatile economic times, and those factors influence customers' choices and behavior to a large degree. As a matter of fact, involving your employees in this process can help get them invested in meeting your customers' needs as much as possible – and they may come up with some innovative ideas that could help your profit potential.

Also, inform your employees about the current challenges of the company in meeting customers' needs. The more they know, the more they can offer in the way of ideas you may not have thought of. Keeping everyone in the loop enables everyone to work together in a more tightly-knit way – they all look out for each other and try to solve problems that affect everyone. That both motivates people and boosts morale.

And just as you show your employees your appreciation, you should also show your customers their appreciation. Loyalty should be rewarded – it encourages more loyalty and gives your customers a reason to continue choosing you for their needs rather than the competition. Again, customer retention is a critical issue for these tough times – and loyalty programs help keep your buying base intact.

Any great enterprise really requires "the people factor" to lift it to lofty heights. The rules are simple, but require constant vigilance in order to keep them in effect.

- Work together to ensure that the company meets the market and customer needs.
- Appreciate people for everything they do. Pay attention when they talk.
- Create a positive work environment.
- Encourage risk-taking, allow the freedom to experiment, fail, and restart.
- Empower people, delegate authority, be open to ideas, have faith in the creativity of others.
- Remove anything that makes people less excited about doing their job. Celebrate success. Celebration is a great way to energize your company's staff.
- Love what you do and you will try to do it the best way you can.
- Reward collective, not individual successes, but value each individual and allow them a high profile.
- Inspire, challenge, encourage your staff to do great things - help them feel part of something genuine, important, and special and you will inspire real passion and loyalty.

Finally, remember that everyone's opinion counts. Keep people informed on everything that affects their particular job. Your staff must feel that they are "insiders" that are aware of everything that's going on – and that they make an important contribution to the company's success. Your employees must know where your company is going and must be able to influence this path.

The future belongs to individuals and companies that meet the highest standards of customer service. Work together to focus on your customers. In the end, it's their opinion – not yours or your employees' – that matters the most.

ABOUT GUNTARS

Guntars Stikovs is a graduate physiotherapist. He has been working in Ireland since 2004 in Beechfield Manor Senior House, where he provides basic personal care, social care and emotional support to elderly people who need help with day-to-day tasks. His role is to enable elderly people to keep as much of their independence as possible, and to be as socially and physically active as they can.

Guntars has also been actively self-employed as a free-lance physiotherapist. As such, he has been able to establish long-lasting business relationships with his customers even during this recession. He would like to add his appreciation for Mary Clear, Dir. Of Nursing, G.M. Ciaran Larmer, and Sally Rowland (one of the owners), at Beechfield Manor Nursing Home, and is thankful to the very dedicated staff there for their help.

People want to live a long time to see their family grow and make the most of it. Most people feel really lost when it comes to living a healthy lifestyle. They don't know where to start, where to go, what to do. That's why Guntars is here to help with the right kind of information.

To get more information, suggestions and tips to help you live a more healthy lifestyle, contact Guntars by visiting: www.Guntars-Stikovs.com

CHAPTER 15

THE BEST VIEW IS UP FRONT

FIVE KEY SKILLS FOR POSITIONING IN *YOUR* MARKET

BY STEVE ROSEBAUGH

Nothing can bring faster success in business than having a compelling position in your chosen market. Establishing a winning position involves a complex set of variables and has proven elusive to some of the most well known companies. But there are some proven skills to establishing a winning position and then keeping your position as the competition scrambles after you.

M y wife is a huge Elton John fan, so when he recently played a concert in town, we were ready and eager! Tickets were to go on sale beginning at 10:00 on a Saturday morning. Imagine my surprise when I logged into the website right at 10:00 and couldn't get through. I kept trying and got through a few minutes later. I was disappointed when I found that all of the prime seats were already taken! We settled for a well-positioned "value" pair of tickets and days later enjoyed a great concert.

It was apparent that my position was pretty common to most who were seeking tickets to the concert. But where were those prime seats going to so quickly? Clearly some people had inside knowledge, techniques, or technology that I was lacking. Now we could have certainly bought our way into some front row tickets, but at a tremendous price. If I wasn't able or willing to buy my way into front row tickets, I needed some uncommon knowledge about gaining access – or some well-placed friends.

It is usually NOT the best quality or lowest cost provider that becomes the leader in their market. It is usually the one who has positioned themselves best with their target customers. So how do you approach positioning for your product or service? Quality, price, service, distribution, and packaging are critical elements. But these are often reduced to "tickets to play". How do you stand out? What inside knowledge, techniques, or technology do you have? What is your unique selling proposition?

When I work with clients, this is a common discussion and it gets revisited regularly. It's that important! In my experience, this involves a complex set of variables, but there are some proven skills to establishing your position and then *keeping* your position. It will take time to practice and master these five skills, but they are guaranteed to provide incredible results for your business. Commit yourself to becoming a student of these disciplines.

SKILL 1
DILIGENTLY SEEK UNCOMMON KNOWLEDGE

You have a product or service in mind for your business, and you even have a lot of hard-earned experience in the market or industry. But what do you know that sets you apart from the rest? If you don't have a distinctive offer, how will you develop one? If you have one, how will you validate and protect it? Would you like to have a wellspring of valuable insights that put and keep you in a leadership position? While insights are everywhere and you should always have your antenna up, key relationships are where **uncommon knowledge is usually found**.

Developing high-trust relationships with leading customers and with key industry people is essential to your long-term success. Who do you know that is a leader in the market you want to serve? What can you offer them in exchange for their valuable time and insights? Hint: If it's money you have to offer, they are called "consultants". Hiring a consultant can certainly be part of a successful planning strategy, but your success should not be primarily resting on them.

Make a list of the key people you already know who might be in a position to help you form your strategy. List out the knowledge, expertise, and value they might be able to offer you. Next to that, list what knowledge, expertise, and value you can offer to each of them. Then discipline yourself to arrange meetings with each of them. Work to develop long-term relationships where appropriate and possible.

When you meet with them, be sure to keep the relationship as the primary objective, and don't dominate the time with only your interests. Be sure to seek out ways to help them, too. Plan your meetings with clear intentions and careful preparation. Don't ever fly seat-of-the-pants if you want to work with the truly accomplished. The objectivity of different viewpoints can be vital to your strategy. This ties very closely to the next skill.

SKILL 2
ASK GREAT QUESTIONS

One of the most proven and powerful ways to build trust and respect in a relationship is to ask great questions. When I was a young professional, I was always ready with a couple of carefully considered questions for when the big boss was around. It really helped me build a high-trust relationship quickly. This was key in helping me land an international assignment just a few years later. This is so critical that I could write a whole chapter just on great questioning.

Every successful business, no matter what it is, provides something of value to its customers. But how do you determine where the best opportunities are? It is critical that you develop a strong talent for asking questions, listening to their responses, and probing for details. You have to carefully consider what your best questions are. You have the potential to unveil a gold mine, if you're willing to dig in the right place long enough.

As you carefully listen to them, you must be patient and intent on hearing their complete responses. You continue to probe deeper until you find the gems you are seeking. Done well, you build trust in the relationship. You build a desire in the other person to help you. Remember, one great question that is thoroughly examined and explored can be far more valuable than ten good questions that fail to probe below the surface.

It is essential that you establish great clarity in understanding their responses. Work to determine the impacts associated with the problem or challenge they face. How much would it be worth if the problem could be addressed? Don't overlook the value of lost opportunity in their efforts to address current problems. Relentlessly pursue areas of high value.

Most new breakthroughs in markets are seldom due to something that is actually new. Some of the most successful breakthroughs in both business and technology usually involve a new *combination* of existing ideas. As you seek your unique opportunities, don't let industry insiders over-prescribe HOW their problem needs to be solved. Instead focus on WHAT the problem is and what impacts a solution would have. Your ability to envision new applications within their industry could be the most valuable skill you can offer them.

Customers may have different ideas about the scope of the "solution" they need, but it is up to you to define that scope carefully and not let one customer drag you into areas that later erode profits and keep you from taking a leadership position overall. This leads to our next skill, thinking strategically.

SKILL 3
THINK STRATEGICALLY ABOUT YOUR APPROACH

You have already begun to think strategically about your position, but now let's add a few other vital elements. These need to include your driving purpose, your personal goals, market directions, and an honest gap analysis on what it will take to get the solution ready for market.

Whatever solution or approach you have, it is critical in the long term that it is well aligned with your passion and values. You have to feel great about being the driving force behind your offer to the marketplace. What about this idea gets you up in the morning each day? Are there any elements that are inconsistent with your core values? For example, if you grew up in the home of an alcoholic, you may want to avoid businesses involved in the production, distribution, and sale of alcoholic beverages.

You also need to put the goals of the business venture in alignment with your own personal goals. Write them down. Study and develop the goals so they become compelling to you. Be sure to make them S.M.A.R.T. goals (Specific, Measurable, Aligned, Realistic, Time-bound), but also make sure they are personal, present tense, and stated in a positive manner.

As you review your key goals, develop an honest assessment of your needs to accomplish them. Take your time on this. Write down absolutely everything you need to do to achieve your goals and be very specific and thorough in completing your list. Organize the work into strategies you will need to employ. Begin to develop actual plans for each with increasing clarity. Look carefully at task concurrencies, dependencies, and resourcing. Outsource help whenever you can, especially if it's not your strength or if it involves tasks that are in the critical path to completing the work.

As you examine the market you will be entering, look for who the leaders are. How long have they been established in that market? What has made them successful? What are they doing that's new? Are there any new businesses entering the market? Where might competition arise? As you begin to see the market direction, ask yourself if your solution is consistent or different than the others. If it's different, congratulations. You have the potential to be a trend-setter and highly successful. Otherwise, you are likely to become just another "me, too" solution.

As you approach completion of your first prototype product or service, be sure to check it against previously defined requirements. Yes, continue to refine it, but be careful about creeping elegance at this point. It can be very tempting to add new features or variations that were not originally envisioned. If it's truly needed by your ideal customers, consider how it impacts the overall plan. Otherwise, save the refinements for future announcements and product launches. Getting to market on time is incredibly important to business success.

SKILL 4
TESTING FOR VALUE

Finding great customers to test your concepts before the actual launch can be incredibly valuable. You may already have some ideal customers in mind, and it is probably valuable for you to include one of them in your pre-market testing. You might also want to include a few customers on the fringe of your perceived market, but focus on the sweet spot. These kinds of customers are often referred to as "beta customers".

I said it's *probably* valuable for you to include an ideal customer. But for this to be absolutely true, you must honestly face your own responsibilities in this process. There may be cases where your ideal customer is telling you something you just don't believe. It seems inconsistent with your current strategy and what you know. You may be tempted to discount their feedback. Be careful! As long as there are competitors and alternatives in the market, you need to respect their opinions. There is at least a nugget of truth here worth understanding thoroughly, and there may be a nugget of insight you hadn't seen before.

In exchange for their valuable feedback on your new product or service, you offer them something in return. This might be special pricing or services, or it might be something more subjective, like the opportunity for influencing the final design. In any case, you must set an expectation of what you need from them in this process and not let them drop the ball just because they wanted the special price, service, access, etc. Honor the *quid pro quo*.

While it's troublesome to make major changes to your product or service, it's certainly better than launching something to market that no one will buy. More likely, you will learn new ideas for your marketing launch plans. A few small changes in your pricing, perceptions, and positioning can be quick to make and can have a huge impact on your initial launch results.

SKILL 5
MOVING QUICKLY

The impact of moving quickly is what often distinguishes a company as being the leader instead of just part of the pack. Some of the best profits are usually seen early in the life cycle of a new product or service. So by all means move quickly. But there is really more involved than just moving quickly.

It is critical that you hit published schedules to maintain market credibility. For years, IBM was rarely first to market with a new product or service. However, they developed a reputation for delivering an incredibly high quality solution on schedule. This allowed them to attract powerful and lucrative clients over the long term, even though they were not usually first to market. So be sure to under-promise and over-deliver on your product or service quality, and be sure to hit your schedules.

The disappointment of a late product launch is especially damaging when you are part of a larger supply chain to your customer. Your inability to deliver on time greatly complicates their lives and they will not forget those feelings of frustration and anger. So definitely make a big deal about your announced launch date, building excitement in your target market, and then *hit that date*.

STAY THE COURSE

You must truly believe in your strategy, and then stick with it long enough for it to succeed. If you fall victim to questioning your strategy and adjusting it too often, you will never establish yourself as an industry leader. You will end up looking like your competition and end up competing on cost, draining your potential for great profits. So do the hard work up front. Look at your business in all aspects *over time*, adjust your tactics as needed, and stay the course on your winning position.

ABOUT STEVE

Well-tuned and motivating coaches guide successful, high performing teams. Steve Rosebaugh has managed and led high performance teams for more than 20 years, guiding his organizations through transition and challenge while bringing results during the most difficult of times.

With a strong diversity of business experience within the complex semiconductor industry, Steve's background includes design, product engineering, manufacturing, quality, product management, and marketing. Steve also has international experience having spent three years in a large manufacturing center in Kuala Lumpur, Malaysia.

Working in both small and large companies, Steve has been successful in many functions, including: key account management, project management, conflict resolution, and operations management. He has won awards from leading customers and has also been published internationally in well-known industry publications.

As a Certified Business Performance Coach with FocalPoint International, Steve is providing customized coaching services to a variety of small businesses in the central Texas area. Steve lives in Austin with his wife of 30 years and has three grown children.

Steve Rosebaugh
Certified Business Performance Coach
http://steverosebaugh.com

CHAPTER 16

HOW TO INCREASE TRAFFIC TO YOUR WEBSITE AND SELL MORE THAN EVER BEFORE!

BY KHOA BUI

MY STORY

I remember the night I was driving down a hill, it was raining heavily, the roads were very slippery, I couldn't see very far because of the heavy rain and the window wipers were damaged, making it very hard to see what was ahead of me. The only thing I could see were the approaching red traffic lights all the way at the bottom of the hill and the many car lights that were passing through.

I began thinking about my life and how it was going. I realized that I spent over 10 years in school and 6 years in university – all to follow my dream of providing quality website services to the world. All those years of study, late nights of building websites in my room and reading books, I finally got my dream and started my first part time business in web design.

Two years later, I ended up being frustrated with the number of problems

I had with my website and my business. I realized the years I've spent in my website business had failed. I couldn't get any clients, I couldn't generate any traffic, I couldn't make any online sales, I couldn't market my site. The scariest truth was that I only made $200 profit in 2 years of having my business. How come I was so passionate about websites, but I had only made a very small income from it? (Especially considering I had invested years into my career.). Have you ever had the thought that you've wasted your entire life and wished you could just start over again?

As I got closer to the traffic lights, cars were still driving by. Normally, you'll begin to slow down, but this time I didn't even bother to lift my foot to hit the brakes, I just wanted to end it right there and start over again. I was hoping for a crash. There are times in your life you have really dark moments and forget everyone else around you, that night was my dark moment. Then all of a sudden, it hit me like a car crash, fortunately, it wasn't a car crash, it was an epiphany.

The epiphany was that I realized that I was doing the wrong things in my business, I was reading the wrong books, I was doing the wrong activities, I was spending time on the wrong aspects of the business. That night, I hit the brakes and started my life over again. I remember one of the best pieces of advice I received from Brian Tracy was the ability to set goals and work every day to achieve them. My goal was to start over again and focus on generating better results from my website.

A few months later, I made huge breakthroughs. I was able to generate a lot of traffic to my website and also convert that traffic to massive sales (making me thousands of dollars). As a result of that, the income I generated from my website enabled me to travel around the world and visit my dream destinations: such as Italy, France, Austria, Germany, Hong Kong, New York, Hawaii and more. I was also able to purchase my dream home by the river which looked surprisingly similar to the homes and locations I admired in home magazines. I was only 26 years old and my dreams had already come true! I've always dreamt of travelling the world and somehow, I achieved my dream.

I would never forget the day when I was white water rafting in Austria. The water was crystal clear. You could even see fish swimming alongside the boat and on the bottom of the river. We continued paddling to move faster and then we stopped and rested while the boat drifted along the river. As we drifted along the beautiful river, there were 6 of us and every single one of us just sat there in silence and enjoyed the view. There were no clouds in the sky, the sun was directly over us where you could also see the rays in the distance as well. We were drifting between the Austrian mountains where you could see both snow at the top of the mountains and many trees. In the distance, I saw small homes that looked like cabins and few cows and animals in the fields. As we went under a small bridge, we saw a few local people waving hello to us in the distance. It was a magical moment that really made an impact on my life. I realized that my work in the past had paid off and put me on this boat on the other side of the world. The work that I put into my website had generated enough income for me to experience that moment.

If you want to learn how I managed to turn my website around, increase more traffic to your website, help you make more money online, sell more of your products and services, travel more to your dream destinations, create a better lifestyle for you and your family; then this chapter maybe just what you're looking for. The strategies and techniques I will cover in this chapter have worked for me and I sincerely hope they will work for you too. I predict success if you do.

THE CASH WEBSITE TRIANGLE

After years of experimenting and testing, I have discovered it really takes only a few areas of your website to generate the best results. I have put it into a triangle diagram and I call it **The Cash Website Triangle;** it's simple yet profound in generating great results from your site. I will quickly describe it in a nutshell.

KHOA BUI'S
THE CASH WEBSITE TRIANGLE

141

There are three factors that are absolutely necessary to exist in order for a website to be generating income. One cannot exist without the other and they all depend on each other. If you were to remove one side, the triangle begins to weaken. They are:

- Traffic
- Marketing
- Product/Service

TRAFFIC

Traffic is simply getting qualified traffic to your website. For example, if your website sells air conditioners and you receive 1 million visitors to your website but that traffic was comprised of people only looking for dog training services, then there is no chance of you selling your products or services. You need to have the right quality traffic going to the right marketing and product on your website.

MARKETING

Marketing is where you convert your traffic to sales. Let's say that you have the right product/service and the right traffic going to your website; people wanting air conditioners for their cars – but your marketing says that you provide air conditioning services for homes not cars, then once again, you will not be able to sell your products/services since they are after air conditioning services for their cars. You need to match your website marketing to the right quality traffic and product / services.

PRODUCT OR SERVICE

Product or Service is where you make sure you deliver what you promise. Let's say that you've got the right traffic, people wanting air conditioning services for their cars, and you have the right marketing saying that you offer that service and they become a customer. However, when you deliver your service, it's not what they wanted. Your product/service had failed; so you will lose customers and struggle in your business.

THE RULE OF THUMB

Therefore, when looking at your website, you need to make sure you have the right traffic going to it, the right marketing converting that traffic to sales and the right product/service to provide to the customer.

HOW TO INCREASE TRAFFIC TO YOUR WEBSITE

To achieve massive traffic to your website, you want to aim for multiple strategies of generating traffic to your website. So here are my ultimate 11 strategies to easily generate massive traffic to your website.

THE ULTIMATE 11 STRATEGIES
TO GENERATE MORE TRAFFIC TO YOUR WEBSITE

1. CREATE VIDEOS AND SUBMIT THEM TO VIDEO SITES

Videos are not only a great traffic-generation tool, it's also a great way to build trust with your visitors. You can easily put together a video by simply using a digital camera, recording a quick video, download it onto your computer, edit it using easy-to-use editing software and then upload it to video sites such as YouTube. YouTube receives millions of visitors each day and having quality videos that contain a link back to your website produces great quality traffic to your website.

2. SETUP A BLOG SITE OR INTEGRATE ONE INTO YOUR OWN WEBSITE

Search engines love quality content and blog sites are recognized as a great source of information for visitors. You can easily create a free blog account by going to wordress.com or blogger.com or setup one with your existing website. By frequently writing on your blog site, more people will find you on the different blog articles you've written – also sending you heavy traffic.

3. USE SOCIAL NETWORKING TOOLS TO BUILD RELATIONSHIPS WITH YOUR VISITORS

Social networking sites such as Twitter, Facebook, MySpace, etc., are becoming a popular way to generate free traffic. The strategy behind social networking is to build a massive fan base and build a long term relationship with them by offering useful information and services. When you build a strong relationship with your fan base, you can instantly send them to your website by providing a link to your site.

4. WRITE QUALITY AND 'CONTENT RICH' ARTICLES

Writing 'content rich' articles is one of the best ways to generate traffic to your website. If you write your articles that contain keyword rich content, for example a dog training service business based in New York would have keywords such as "dog training new york" in the article, which would help people find your article. Make sure you provide a lot of value in your articles and educate your target market instead of just pitching your services. You can use your articles in your website, blog sites, press releases, ebooks etc.

5. SUBMIT YOUR ARTICLES TO POPULAR ARTICLE DIRECTORIES

Once you've written your article, you can begin to submit them to high traffic article directories such as ezine articles. Article directories are full of 'content rich' articles and search engines love searching through them. Popular article directories are usually more popular than brand new websites, therefore a great strategy is if search engines can't find your new website, then most likely they will find your article in article directories which point back to your website.

6. GET FREE PUBLICITY AND EXPOSURE

Getting free publicity is easier than you think. If you have something interesting to say to the public and have credible experience and knowledge, then publicity can generate a 'ton' of traffic to your website. Start off by writing a great story about your product or service and you can submit it to press release websites such as prlog.org. You can also submit your story to various media, who would love to feature your business or services in their newspapers, magazines, radio etc. You can also ask permission to contribute to online and offline newsletters by writing quality articles for their readers.

7. BUILD LINKS TO YOUR WEBSITE THROUGH WEBSITE LINKING

Website linking is simply having a link to your website on a popular high traffic website. Website linking works in two ways. One way is that it can generate great targeted traffic to your website and the second way is that is helps boost your websites popularity. If you had 100 websites linking to you, search engines would view your website as popular because 100 websites have voted for you and you would be ranked higher than the website with only 2 votes. You can measure your website popularly by installing Google Page Rank onto your web browser bar.

8. SEARCH ENGINE OPTIMIZE YOUR WEBSITE

Search Engine Optimization is the ability to tweak your website so that you can rise higher in the search engines. 80% of people click on the first link on the first page, and then the remaining 20% is dispersed throughout the last 19 results. By optimizing your website so it reaches the first page, you can enjoy the prestige and also the traffic it will bring you.

9. MAKE JOINT VENTURE DEALS WITH BUSINESSES AND PEOPLE

You can make deals with businesses or people with huge databases that match your target audience. For example, if you were a dog training company based in New York, you could do a joint venture with all the pet stores in New York by advertising your services in their newsletters and stores. You could also exchange services instead of money by offering cross promotions.

10. ADVERTISE ONLINE

There are many great sources of online advertising such as Google Adwords, Banner Advertising, Website advertising, Email advertising etc. All advertising can either be an investment or an expense. Therefore, it's important to ask yourself a few questions: Will your advertisement match your target audience? If you generate a very low response, will your advertisement pay for itself? Will your advertisement receive a suitable amount of traffic that gives it a better chance of success? Online advertising is a great way to attract huge amounts of traffic by replacing time with money.

11. ADVERTISE OFFLINE

Don't forget you can also generate traffic to your website by using offline methods such as signage, flyers, brochures, networking events, business cards, email signatures and word-of-mouth marketing. By using both online and offline advertising, you double your results and generate even more traffic to your website.

HOW TO CONVERT YOUR WEBSITE TRAFFIC TO SALES

Once you've successfully generated traffic to your website, you are now in a great position to start converting that traffic to sales. Here are my top 7 strategies to help you convert your website traffic to sales so you can sell more than ever before.

THE ULTIMATE 7 STRATEGIES
TO CONVERT YOUR WEBSITE TRAFFIC TO SALES

1. OVERLOAD YOUR WEBSITE WITH SOCIAL PROOF

People will pay more attention to what other people have to say about you than what you have to say, therefore it's important to include as many testimonials as you can on your website. The different types of testimonials include: written testimonials, picture testimonials such as 'before and after' shots and finally, video testimonials.

2. INCREASE YOUR RESPONSE RATE USING DIRECT RESPONSE COPY

Direct response copy is the art of writing that enables people to take action. When writing, make sure you use the principle of "WIIFM" – "What's In It For Me?" There are also special keywords that have a greater response in your copy such as "Free", "Add to Cart" and "Now". You also need to match your website copy so it communicates the right language to your target market.

3. INCLUDE A STRONG GUARANTEE

Do you have a guarantee with your product or service? What would happen if your product / service were to fail, would the customer be covered? Your customers are usually thinking of those questions before they buy from you, therefore you must be able to answer those objections first, in order to make the sale.

4. USE BENEFITS NOT FEATURES

Remember that people buy benefits not features. If you were selling gym equipment to home users, what would be more important to the customer? Would it be the size and dimensions of the gym equipment or the ability to easily lose weight, look more attractive to the opposite sex and increase their fitness levels from the comfort of their own home?

5. HELP YOUR VISITORS FIRST

When people reach your website, don't send them straight to your order page, many people will find that offensive since they don't know much about you. You have to build trust first before you ask for the sale, therefore, always focus on giving as much value to your customers first and then ask for their business. Genuinely help your visitors first and they will help you in return. You can do this by offering free information, knowledge and resources.

6. HAVE ATTRACTIVE BONUSES

Have you ever bought something just to get the free bonus item that comes with your purchase? Having an attractive bonus helps you increase your sale especially if it's what the customer wants, These can be music players, holiday tickets, gift cards for shopping sprees, massages, etc.

7. USE PAYMENT INSTALLMENTS

If you have a high-priced ticket item, it's a great idea to make it easier for your customers to pay you by breaking the cost down into monthly installments. Most of the time, customers want to purchase your product but don't have the entire amount. If you're selling to businesses, multi payments are an attractive option because it helps them control their spending and cash flow.

A FINAL WORD FROM KHOA BUI

I would like to say that it's a privilege for me to share my knowledge and experience with you. **Therefore, the last thing I would like to share with you is: to simply get out there and just do it.** Don't be afraid of failure, or worry about future events not working out, the things you feared 10 years ago – you've forgotten them already. *Always remember that life is short and that we will always make mistakes in the process.* Use the business strategies I've shared with you in this chapter and prosper in the new economy.

ABOUT KHOA

Khoa Bui was born in Vietnam in 1981. During that time, war was raging between North and South Vietnam. His family then immigrated to Perth, Western Australia by boat ,where they began to build their future from scratch.

Khoa started working with computers during the mid 1990's where he started to learn how to design his own websites on his own. After graduating from Edith Cowan University with a Masters of Science in Software Engineering in 2003, he started working for various software development companies in both the education and private sectors as a software developer. Two years later, he followed his dream and started his own web design and development firm "River Designs". Only three years later, Khoa had successfully generated thousands of dollars for his clients through effective traffic generation strategies and Internet Marketing.

Khoa also won the TS Design Award 10/10 for Best Design and Best Development in 2009 amongst thousands of web design firms. He has also appeared as a host on a computer TV series called "Byte Me". He was featured on the popular "Life Hacker" productivity site, is an Expert Author on eZineArticles, and writes for the National Speakers Association.

Khoa is the CEO and founder of Khoa Bui International and regularly consults with multi-million dollar clients by building their online brand and making their websites more successful. He has clients in Government, Mining, Education and the Private Sector and also contributes to various charities including the Starlight Children's Foundation and Juvenile Diabetes Research Foundation.

Khoa is also an international speaker and enjoys sharing his knowledge and expertise with his audiences. Finally, Khoa enjoys travelling around the world, writing and building projects that contribute to the world in some way.

If you wish to find out more about Khoa Bui, or to hire him as a speaker for your event, simply go to: www.khoa-bui.com . You can also sign up for his free "online success" weekly newsletter and receive the latest tips and strategies on increasing traffic to your website, increasing your online revenue and your business profits at www.khoa-bui.com

CHAPTER 17

LIVE YOUR VISION

BY MATT LINKLATER

A few years ago, I took a four-day trip to South Beach. The weather was fantastic. It was sunny and 80 degrees every day. I had intentions of just relaxing and hanging out by the pool, but one day I decided to plan an excursion, and selected an enjoyable snorkeling trip – or so I thought. The day started out great. I boarded the boat and had a relaxing ride. The sun was beating down on my face and the wind was in my hair.

Then, the terror ensued.

The boat stopped. We began to rock back and forth so violently that when the right side of the boat swayed we couldn't see the shore, and when the left side rocked up you couldn't see the horizon. I started to get ill. To add to my situation, the skipper happened to be a guy I played football against in college. Not only did he beat me on the field, but now I was getting sick on his boat!

In the end, I was so ill that I couldn't snorkel and I had to just sit on the boat in misery until the expedition was done. They told me that if I looked at the horizon or the shore that it would help me feel better. This proved not to be 100 percent true. What really helped was staring at the shore knowing that in just an hour I would be back safely on dry land. Finally, we arrived back on the shore. Eventually, my stomach calmed down and I was able to enjoy the rest of the day and the balance of my vacation.

This experience is what most of us face from time to time or have increasingly faced over the past couple of years. We face times like these whether in business or our personal lives. When we hit the rough patch or the rough waters, we need to increasingly become more focused on our dreams and aspirations. We need to live a life of possibility and passion. Do not focus on the rough patch, but focus on your clearly-defined goals, your horizon.

We may have had some rough times in the economy over the past two years. I know I have not been immune to the tough times. In the past two years, my fiancé and I had an immediate family member pass away, a serious illness with another immediate family member, we both have been laid off, she moved across the country, the list goes on. We have found the horizon for us is in clearly-defined goals. The more we focus on our dreams, desires and vision, the less we wallow in the rough waters.

Your thoughts are like laser beams. Your thoughts are so precise that you will manifest what your prevailing thoughts are. I recently heard that our nervous systems are bombarded with 2,000,000 bits of information per second. Our systems can only handle about 134 bits per second. An analogy would be if I handed you 134 toothpicks per second, could you handle them? Sure! Now imagine I was handing you 2,000,000 toothpicks per second, could you handle them? No! You would grab the 134 bits per second that you focused on. So the question is, where is your focus? Are you looking at the swelling waves of life's circumstances? Watch out! You may get sick and unable to fulfill your dream of swimming with the fish!

First, I say start by empowering yourself. We have approximately 60,000 thoughts in a day and 80% of them are negative! Start by changing these disempowering thoughts.

I WILL...

Take the statement 'I will _____ do something.' The very word 'will' instills that whatever you want to do is off into the never-ending future. How many of you have kids? Have you ever asked them to do something and the answer was I will? I ask you, did they ever do it? Not without you having to nag or ask again. In my coaching, many people say I will be this… or I will have this. By putting the word **will** in the statement you put whatever you are trying to accomplish into the infinite future. For instance maybe you say **I will** become profitable next month. Well, next month becomes next month and then the next month, on and on. Another disempowering statement is, **I will** start dieting on Monday. How many start the diet on Monday? I think we get the picture. **I will** is just a disempowering statement.

STOP "SHOULDING" ON YOURSELF

How many times have you said I should have done this or that? That is wasted time and effort. Sure we can learn from the past, but let it go. Nothing good happens when we focus on the past. As a matter of fact, in most situations you would make the exact same decision given the information you had at the moment you made the decision. A couple months back my fiancé left a company that she had been employed at for over 10 years. The company that she went to decided after her first 15 days of employment to close the business. Do you think that she was **"shoulding"** on herself? Absolutely! But nothing good comes from **"shoulding"**. Do not wallow in the rough waters, instead focus on your dreams, look at the shore, the goal, the true desire. Focus.

TRY

The word try is also disempowering. Just say the word try and see how it feels on the inside. The word is weak. The very word when put in a sentence such as, "I'll try" insinuates that we are not going to do something. Go ahead and try and do something. How did it work out? Start using empowering and definitive statements.

Saying disempowering words to ourselves is like providing the rough waves to get sea sick. We communicate with ourselves in many more ways than just the words we say. We have pictures, sounds, tastes, smells and feelings behind those words. The empowering words we use lead to more empowering pictures, sounds, sights, tastes and smells. Stop saying, "why can't I" and start saying, "I can". If you CAN'T, you MUST, and if you MUST, you CAN!

If you CAN, then lets start being "IRRATIONAL" with our goals. I recently was watching a news program with a segment on motivation. The newscaster said that people need to have goals that are within their reach. I agree that a goal of playing in the NBA is unrealistic if you've never played basketball. However, I propose that "realistic" goals are usually comfortable and easily attainable. Are you truly going to reach your potential if a goal is within your comfort zone? I'm not sure it is really a goal if it doesn't give you that slightly uncomfortable feeling of 'butterflies in your gut'. The issue is the strategy for hitting our goals. We are where we are in life because we have the strategies to be there, we created our life. The key is to have clearly-defined goals and then seek out the strategies on how to reach the new distant shore line of your life.

The most straightforward goal-setting process I've seen and used is the **S.M.A.R.T.** process.

SPECIFIC

The more specific you are in what you want, the more you will manifest what you want… also, the more exact your outcome will be, compared to what you originally wanted. My fiancé wrote down 27 attributes that she wanted in her future spouse. Although I came up short by missing one of those attributes, I guess at 5'8" I didn't fit the "tall" attribute, she was very specific about what she wanted in a life partner.

MEASUREABLE

Your goal has to be measurable. Instead of "I want" say "I have". You need to have a measurable quantity. Measurable would be a certain dollar amount, a certain position, or a certain type of person.

AS IF NOW

This means your goals have to be written in present tense. 'As if' you already possess the goal.

REALISTIC

A goal has to be realistic in the sense that you may not be able to become a concert pianist. To become a concert pianist one has to spend 20 years and 10,000 hours practicing at a piano. Therefore, becoming a concert pianist is not realistic, but we need to be IRRA-TIONAL! Push beyond where we are now to where we want to be. I propose the only difference from who we are and who we want to be are our strategies and quality of our thoughts.

TIMED

What is the exact date that you want to accomplish your goal?

To put it all together I use the following sentence structure:

It is now_____ and I have / am_____!
        Insert date   Insert goal

You also have keys to making your goal and your success the most achievable. Ask yourself the following questions.

1. Positive – Is my goal stated in positive terms?
2. Specify Present Situation – Where are you now?
3. Specify Outcome – What will you see, hear, and feel when you have it?
4. Evidence Procedure – How will you know when you have it?
5. Is it congruent – What will this outcome allow you to do?
6. Is it self initiated and self maintained? - Is it only for you?
7. Appropriately Contextualized – Where, when, how and with whom do you want it?
8. What resources or resourcefulness is/are needed – What do you have now and what do you need to get your outcome?
9. Is it ecological – For what purpose do you want this? What will you gain or lose?

This procedure is most important to your visualization of your horizon and most important for you to make an internal representation for your goal.

We have to put the goal precisely in your future. In my coaching practice, we use techniques as certified practitioners / coaches of Time Line Therapy™, by Tad James, to drop goals in our future. The first process is the elicitation of your time line - a Nuero Linguistic Programming technique. You will want a partner to read you the following paragraph.

"If I were to ask you, your unconscious mind, where is your past and where is your future, I have an idea you might say, "It's from right to left, or front to back, or up to down, or in some direction from you in relation to your body. And it's not your conscious concept that I'm interested in, it's your unconscious. So if I were to ask you where your future is and where your past is, what direction would you point? And your future, what direction would you point if I asked your unconscious mind, where's your future?"

Have your partner also read you the following first test of your time line.

Now, would you bring to mind the directions that you pointed to. Do you notice that they imply a line?

     If no: "Well, could you notice?"

(This process can be visual, auditory, or kinesthetic)

"Good, now, when I say line, I don't mean to imply only visual, because in a moment I am going to ask you to float up above that line, and by float, I also mean as the sounds of wind, the feeling of water, or visually. However you do this is perfect.

"Make sure you are looking through your own eyes. "

"Now, floating above your time line, float back into the past (pause). Are you there?"

"Now, float back to now, and stop there (pause). Are you there?"

"Now, float into the future (pause). Are you there?"

"Now, come back into the room."

How was that?

Great, now we have the steps to take your S.M.A.R.T. goal and place it precisely in your future. Again, you are going to need a partner to read you the next steps to maximize your goal setting process.

1. What is the last step that needs to happen so you know you got the goal?
2. Make a picture inside your head of the goal. Get a visual, notice the sounds, and feelings.
3. Step into the picture – Looking through your own eyes.
4. Adjust the picture for the most real representation. Make the colors the most real, the sounds the most sharp and the feelings the most intense.
5. Step out of the picture.
6. Take the picture and float above your time line.
7. Energize the picture with 4 deep breaths. In through your nose and out through your mouth.
8. Take the picture and float out into the future.
9. Insert the picture into your time line. "Let go of any internal feelings, sounds, or pictures and let it float right down in your time line."
10. Notice all the events between now and then align to support you in accomplishing your goal.
11. Float back to now.

At this point you are going to notice that your goal feels as real and as certain as ever and your horizon seems closer than ever. The best thing I can tell you is that you do not need all the answers to accomplish your goal. The best way to accomplish your goal is to not need it. You should surrender to your goal. As you review your goal, you will need to take action. Ask yourself this simple question every day, "How can I take a step closer to my goal today while enjoying the process?" The answers will open up to you each and every day on your journey to accomplishing your goal. Soon your feet will be firmly planted on the shore and every desire you have will be fulfilled!

ABOUT MATTHEW

Matthew Linklater is an entrepreneur and a former Vice President of three Fortune 100 companies. Matt is an accomplished motivational speaker, sales guru, personal coach and life-changer. Matt is the author of 3 books: (i) *Quick Witted - Saying The Right Thing To Win Big*; (ii) *Basic Training - Sales Boot Camp*, and now (iii) *Counter Attack* with the legendary Brian Tracy. He combines extensive business experience with expertise as a certified master practitioner, trainer, and coach of Neuro-Linguistic Programming — in conjunction with Time Line Therapy™ — to help you exceed your sales and life goals.

Matt prides himself on his congruent lifestyle, excelling both personally and professionally and living the healthiest life possible. He knows that when you point the mind, body and spirit in the right direction, you will manifest exactly what you desire.

Matt, along with his fiancée Denise, can help reach your dreams through their Live Your Vision coaching process. They believe strongly that the only thing holding us back is the quality of our thoughts. Matt and his beautiful fiancée reside in Chicago. When they're not inspiring people around the globe they can usually be found reading, learning and experiencing life to the fullest.

TheLinklater.com
www.linkedin.com/in/linklater
twitter.com/thelinklater

CHAPTER 18

KNOW WHERE YOU ARE – KNOW WHERE YOU'RE GOING:

SUSTAINING YOUR BUSINESS IN DIFFICULT TIMES

BY ONG WHATT KIM

"Success is simple. Do what's right, the right way, at the right time."
~ Arnold H. Glasgow

From my over thirty-seven years of experience in sales, marketing, training and consulting, I've learned more than a few things about what makes a business work at an optimum level and enables it to be a long-term survivor. In 1980 I began my first business, and today I run three companies that I take a hands-on approach to managing. (I also continue to be a much-in-demand Sales and Business Coach.)

I stay heavily involved in running my businesses because moving in a continuous direction towards future success is vital. There are two major components to ensuring that success – first, factually analyzing your place in your current industry sector, and second, taking the same rigorous analytical approach to planning on how to improve that position and achieve your long term goals and objectives.

While you can't predict everything that might happen in business, you can evaluate your current strengths and weaknesses, as well as that of your competition. Only then can you create a realistic plan to move forward – which needs to be continually reviewed, so that you won't be left behind.

I have managed to keep my businesses healthy and profitable through both good times and bad during the past three decades. How? With two processes I use in my businesses and that I also advocate in my business consulting – ICCP and COIL. They are two collections of letters than don't mean much on their own – but they can mean all the difference in determining a company's success and failure.

ICCP: DISCOVERING WHERE YOUR BUSINESS IS

ICCP stands for **Industry, Company, Competitor** and **Product** – the main elements that will affect your position in the marketplace. By using the ICCP system, your company can gather current information about your business by answering key questions revealed below that will shed light on your business standing.

We can understand the ICCP system a little better by looking at the flow chart below:

Industry ⟶ Company ⟶ Competitor ⟶ Product

By starting with the broadest category, the industry in which our business is located, and working our way down to the most specific, the products we create to serve that industry, we can see how well we function in the current economic climate.

Let's begin with the "I" in ICCP – **"Industry."** Only by researching and answering the important questions below as thoroughly and truthfully as possible can you understand how well you're functioning and meeting the needs of customers in your business sector.

- What segments of the industry are you in?
- What segment are you strongest in?
- Which segment gives you the most revenue?
- Describe your typical customer in a Customer Organization

Profile that includes demographic and geographic information, as well as their thinking and buying patterns.
- Also complete a Customer Buyer Profile, describing your typical buyer.
- What are the new emerging segments in your industry?
- What existing segments have you not yet explored? Should you?
- What are the latest challenges that your industry faces? What economic, international or regulatory issues are coming into play?
- What changes are taking place in your industry? What trends are affecting your market?
- What are the current practices of other businesses in the industry?

By fully exploring these questions, you will have a basis for understanding what's going on in your business sector and what issues and adjustments you might have to address in the near future, or, possibly immediately.

Now, we move on to the first "C" of ICCP – **"Company."** Do you really understand what's going on in your own business? If you don't, you could be in trouble down the line.

In order to create an accurate snapshot of your company, I strongly suggest you employ another group of letters – **SWOT**. SWOT stands for **Strengths, Weaknesses, Opportunities** and **Threats** – and the SWOT analysis is an important strategic planning method for any business venture.

With that in mind, take a good, hard look at your company's…

- **S**trengths: Attributes your company possesses that are helpful to achieving business success. These attributes could involve employees, management, capitalization, marketing, location or any number of factors.
- **W**eaknesses: Attributes your company possesses that are *harmful* to achieving the objectives.
- **O**pportunities: Outside business conditions that could be helpful to achieving success. These could include a need in the market that's not being met, a failing competitor, growing consumer prosperity or seeing a new customer demographic that's growing and can easily be targeted with marketing.
- **T**hreats: Outside conditions which could do damage to your company's success. For example, a new and strong competitor,

159

a weak economy, producing a product that's becoming irrelevant or outdated, or a shrinking industry.

Identifying the elements of your company's SWOT is essential to subsequent steps in the process of planning for achievement of business objectives. If you don't understand your strengths and weaknesses, both externally and internally, you could be missing a vital piece of the puzzle.

There are two more important questions to ask before you leave the analysis of your Company:

1. Why do customers want to do business with us?
2. What would prevent them from doing business with us?

To properly answer those questions, you have to put yourself into your customer's shoes – and be aware of why someone might or might not buy from you. The reasons could involve price, quality, availability, reputation or some other factor you're not taking into account. Remember, the negative as well as the positive always has to be closely examined.

Let's now look at the second "C" of ICCP – **"Competition."** As noted above, you have to understand why a customer would – or would not – choose to buy from your company. An important step towards that understanding is looking at your competitors and what they have to offer as opposed to what *you* have to offer.

Answer these three questions to begin your scrutiny of the competition:

1. Who are your competitors?
2. What is their strength?
3. What is their main mode of operation?

It's also helpful to do a SWOT analysis of your main opposition, so you can understand their strengths and weaknesses as well as you do your own. Much as a sporting team watches video of their future opponents to determine how to play against them, you need to know where you can successfully challenge them – and where you simply can't beat them – in order to effectively plan your business objectives. You don't get into a game you can't win – you, instead, look for your opening and take advantage of it.

Now, we reach the final "ICCP" letter – "P" for **"Product."** Keeping everything else in mind that you've learned through the ICCP process so far, answer the following questions:

1. Does your current range of products fulfill the needs of your customers?
2. What's your **USP** (**U**nique **S**elling **P**roposition)? This is something you need to be able to articulate in a simple, memorable way that differentiates yourself from your competition and gives your customers a solid reason to patronize your company.
3. What are your customers *really* buying? Often, people buy for emotional reasons, not practical ones. Look for the intangible as well as the tangible motives of your customers.

Obviously, the ICCP process is something that must be updated on a regular basis – the business world does not stand still and you must always take into account new information and new conditions as you move forward.

COIL: TAKING YOUR BUSINESS WHERE IT NEEDS TO GO

If you've thoroughly gone through the steps necessary to successfully complete the ICCP process, you've laid the groundwork for determining a direction for significant achievement in terms of your company's future.

To determine that direction, you must now switch from the ICCP process to the COIL process. Using the COIL process, you'll be able to strategically plan, design and execute the goals and objectives of your business – in a step-by-step fashion that allows you to monitor the different stages of that execution.

COIL stands for Create, Operate, Innovate and Lead – and, like ICCP, there is a natural flow to these elements, as seen below:

Create $\longrightarrow$ Operate $\longrightarrow$ Innovate $\longrightarrow$ Lead

We begin with "**Create**." Based on what you learned about your company and the marketplace through the ICCP, you must create strategies for your products and services that meet two basic criteria: (1) your company must be able to successfully provide/manufacture them and (2) there must be a need in the marketplace for these products and services that is not being met by your competition. In this mix, there must also be the all-important factor of marketing – how will you effectively sell what you plan to create?

Everyone's ideas are important in the creation phase – and so is final consensus. Having all management on board means they will be unified in backing these ideas and putting forth the full effort necessary for success.

Next, we move on to **"Operate."** How will your company execute these strategies? Are you properly staffed and equipped to do the job? Are you addressing your weak points – and taking proper advantage of your strengths in your plans? Creation means nothing unless that creation is properly implemented. You must create the systems necessary to fully realize your plans.

That takes us to **"Innovate."** How can you change your current practices to maximize your profits and your impact in the marketplace? How can you run your business more efficiently as you put into effect your new strategies? Is restructuring needed? Is the chain of command working properly or is there a great deal of miscommunication?

It is often difficult to shed the established ways of doing things – and, at the same time, sometimes we're over-eager to fix what's not at all broken. The innovation phase must include careful consideration of any proposed radical changes.

Once all these decisions have been made, you can move on to the final stage of COIL – **"Lead."** By zealously monitoring the execution of the decisions made by your team, you insure the success of your strategies. This naturally will entail reviewing your company's results frequently on an ongoing basis and making necessary adjustments and tweaking when necessary. A successful plan is a living thing, not something written in stone – and as life and business always surprises us with unexpected twists and turns, your plan must address those twists and turns, and adapt to them in order to prevail over them.

As I said at the beginning of this chapter, implementing the ICCP and COIL processes have helped me steer my businesses successfully through recessions as well as economic booms. In addition, these processes give me the necessary foundation as a sales and business coach to advise other companies on how best to find sustainable success.

It all begins with compiling verifiable information. By doing your home-work and honestly evaluating both your own internal issues inside your company as well as external conditions involving both the marketplace and your competition, you'll gain a broad perspective that will lead you to logical, commonsense approaches to your future business moves.

From this information-based perspective, you must then access the kind of creativity and innovation that will take your company to the next level. Information is not enough to run a business – and neither is inspiration. Rather, the proper combination of both are needed for any company to rise above the pack.

I wish you and your business continued success and I sincerely hope the ideas I've put forth in this chapter will aid in that success.

ABOUT ONG

Ong Whatt Kim has over 37 years of experience in sales, marketing, training and consulting. He has a well-rounded training background providing one-on-one sales performance coaching as well as conducting public and in-house training for corporate clients. As an Associate Trainer and Examiner with the PSB Academy for the Certificate in Salesmanship and Marketing, he is actively involved in the training of those embarking into, or currently in, the sales profession.

An entrepreneur, Ong Whatt Kim has over the years established a group of 3 companies. He is not only the owner of these businesses, but also a hands-on practitioner in directing and managing his companies. In business, he strongly believes the sales function plays a vital role in achieving success, and one must stay constantly in tune with the ever-changing landscape.

He is also engaged as an Associate Consultant by the Business Excellence Centre, PSB Corporation. He had lectured in Salesmanship and Marketing for the Extramural Studies Department of the National University of Singapore, Export Sales Techniques and the Advanced Program in Export Market Development for the Export Institute of Singapore, a division of the Trade Development Board.

In his role as the Regional Representative for the UK-based Managing and Marketing Sales Association (MAMSA) Examination Board, he is responsible for preparing candidates for international sales certification. He has also gained certification from US-based Sales Training International, Inc to conduct their courses and their Train-The-Trainers programs.

Ong Whatt Kim is constantly looking for strategic partners in the US who are keen to establish their presence in the Far East. Interested parties, please visit: www.mamsa.com.sg or you can email him at: whattkim@mamsa.com.sg

164

CHAPTER 19

GET OUT OF THE BUSINESS YOU'RE IN!

8 WAYS TO DISPLAY YOUR EXPERTISE, LOCK OUT YOUR COMPETITION & INCREASE PROFITS.

BY NICK NANTON ESQ., J.W. DICKS ESQ. & LINDSAY DICKS

I f you want to fight the adverse scenarios that plague every business, and survive and thrive in the new economy, you've got to stand out from the crowd. There are so many choices, both online and offline, for your prospects to pick from—you have to give them a reason to choose you. You've got to make them realize that even though there are many choices, you are the only one for them.

The most effective way to do this is to 'get out of the business you're in', and become an expert in your field.

Let's take an example. Let's say you were in the corporate video production business. If you were like most corporate video production companies, you would do all the standard things that any good business would do to market themselves. You would attend marketing meetings, join some associations, start a website, use some pay per click ads, set

165

up Facebook ads and maybe even do some direct mail. And there's nothing fundamentally wrong with any of that; actually, it's probably more than many businesses do, but the real problem is *you'll only ever get paid as much as people are willing to pay a corporate video production company.*

It's because you're in the wrong business. You shouldn't be in the business of video production, you should be in the business of being an expert on using video to convey your client's message and build their business. That's a business that brings real value to the client, and you could charge a "value-based" fee, not just what everyone else is charging for video production.

If you are in the printing business, you're only ever going to make a limited amount of money printing paper. But, if you can become an expert on how to print the paper, or more importantly how to create mailing campaigns that help people maximize their return on investment, you're always going to get paid more money. So you have to become an expert.

This same exercise works for every business. If you're trying to do business with other businesses, you have to add value to your offering by demonstrating to them how your product or service helps them grow their business as opposed to just supplying a product or service— that is, you've got to go deeper to really provide value. If you're trying to do business direct with consumers, you have to help them achieve whatever it is they really want, not just provide a service to them, if you want to be able to maximize your market value and your income.

But how do you become an expert? Most likely you are already an expert in multiple fields, but in order to be seen by your marketplace as an expert, you've got to build your expert status. The big mistake that most people make is they make a wrong assumption: that people know you're an expert. Even if your clients and prospects know you're an expert, they don't know how much of an expert you really are.

Which leads us to the secret that everyone misses. We all think that our clients and prospects can see inside of our heads, and they know exactly what we're thinking. Obviously, that's not true. So, here's what you've got to do, *you've got to display your expertise.* How can you do that? Here are 8 ways to display your expertise:

1. Get into social media. To get started, you can utilize what I call "the Napoleon Hill factor". Many of you have read the great and popular book "Think and Grow Rich" by Napoleon Hill. By reading that book alone, I know he has other works, but by reading that book alone we don't really know if Napoleon Hill is good at anything other than interviewing other experts and finding out what they're good at and sharing their secrets.

NOTE: they aren't Napoleon Hill's secrets, they are the secrets of others!

So you can do the same thing. Through social media you can start out by simply passing along great information from other people. You can quickly and easily become a "curator" of the best content that you can find and pass it along. That's one of the fastest and easiest ways to start displaying your expertise and start building a following.

2. Start a blog. The next thing you need to do is to start blogging. Blogs are awesome. There's practically a blog for every subject you could ever think of, and people 'went nuts' for a while thinking every blog would be profitable, which we now can see is not true. But again, it's another way for you to lay out your expertise so that anyone who wants to follow along can see that you really know what you're talking about. If by nothing else other than the fact that they can see "wow! this guy's got a hundred blogs" or 20 blogs or 30 blogs on the same subject. The other thing is that putting out those blogs will be great for search engine optimization, SEO. If you use the keywords that your customers are searching for, you'll figure out some "long tail" search terms that you weren't expecting or didn't think of. For example, one of the sentences that you write in your blog, not expecting it to be the superstar sentence, can end up delivering traffic to you. And there's another secret, but it relates to articles too, so let's talk about articles.

3. Write articles. Articles are usually just a little bit longer than blogs. The secret is that you're able to syndicate them in a different way. Syndication is the key--you can think of syndicating articles much like the old concept of syndicating radio shows or newspaper columns. *It's the concept of taking your content and pushing it out over someone else's network that already has readers or listeners*

There are Web sites that handle article syndication and blog syndication through rss feeds. Articles have to be just over 500 words to qualify for syndication on many of the article syndication sites. Blogs can be under 500 words. That's the main distinction, but the key is once you write them you don't just want to put them on your Web site or your own blogs. You have to syndicate them and put them out there for hundreds of thousands of Web sites to see. And a crucial step for maximum return from your blogs and articles is to include a byline about you that has a link back to your Web site, which not only drives SEO, it also drives traffic to your Web site if someone reads your syndicated content and wants to go back to your Web site to learn more. A great secret is to offer a free report, or something else of value, to the reader for coming back to your Web site. Again, articles and blogs are a great strategy, but you've got to make sure you get them onto the syndication sites. You can find great syndication sites by searching for "article syndication", "article marketing", "social bookmarking" and "blog syndication" on your favorite search engine.

4. Press releases. Press releases are awesome because they look like someone else is talking about you. Fortune 500 companies have been guarding this secret for years. The words we hear on the news about the newest car, or the newest products that launch usually come out of press releases that were written by the company that is responsible for the product or serve. So, you can use press releases as a way to build third party credibility for you and your business. When someone searches for you and they find a press release that you just signed a new deal with a client, or you were named as one of the top business people in your city, or anything else that is happening in your business that would be interesting to your ideal prospects, and it looks like someone else wrote about you, you're going to get a bump in credibility. So, use press releases to build your expertise.

Again you want to syndicate your press releases. There's a bunch of places to do it. One of our absolute favorites is PRLog.org and it's free. We think you're going to love it. As I mentioned before, it's free, and it SEO's really well.

5. Newsletters. There's two forms of newsletters: online newsletters (often called Ezines) and offline newsletters. Ezines and online newsletters are great. They're easy to set up and you should absolutely have one of those and use it to communicate with your clients and prospects on a regular basis to stay in front of them.

While we're discussing newsletters, here is a key point: most businesspeople make the huge mistake of letting their prospects control the communication flow between the business and the prospect. I can't tell you what a mistake this is. You've got to capture leads from business cards from the people you meet as well as the contact info of visitors to your Web site, so that you can control the communication. It's a huge advantage.

So send out those e-zines to remind them you exist and incite them to action with interesting, valid, concise content that's relevant to your prospects and clients today.

Now, let's talk about offline newsletters. Most businesses don't pay attention to this concept, and I (Nick) didn't either for quite some time. Jack convinced me several years ago we needed to create a physical newsletter. I said to Jack, "Why? No one reads the mail anymore." But he convinced me to give it a try and here's the real secret I found out by doing it: As much as we try to make our e-zines and our e-mails personal, it's never going to be the same as getting e-mail from your mother or from your best friend or from the guy in the office next door, or worse yet the next client. In the email inbox, an Ezine is one of the most impersonal pieces of communication we get because it's competing with hundreds of one to one messages a day. This makes the perceived value of the content go down, which is not what we're after.

But a physical newsletter in someone's mailbox, that's written like my friend, Dan Kennedy, suggests, and I quote "as if you're sitting down to have a cup of coffee with your prospects and clients each and every month." The key here is you have to write conversationally and you've got to be interesting. A good newsletter includes content about your life and your lifestyle but always leads back to informative and educational content. That's always going to be the most valuable piece of content most people get in their mailboxes, because it's one of the more personalized pieces of content that your client or prospect is getting in their mailbox. Their mailbox in front of their house, or their mail bin at the office, are usually full of flyers and bills.

Most people send personal correspondence now through e-mail, so we take our newsletter to a different playing field, out of the inbox and into the mailbox, where it immediately increases in value based on the competition: in the mailbox you're mostly competing against junk so it's a much easier battle to win. The other secret is you have to introduce your newsletter correctly. When sending out the first copy of our physical newsletter to a prospect or client, we put ours in an 8 by 10 inch canvas envelope that is solid black with our law firm logo on the outside of it in silver foil. We can assure you it gets opened! That's how they get the first one.

There's also a customized welcome letter in there. Look, if you send us something that says, "Dear Valued Prospect or Customer," we're not going to read it nor is anyone else. The people sending messages like that make it feel like they didn't even take the time to know who you are. We have mail merge at our finger tips now, use it! Make your message look customized. We send a customized letter that welcomes them, tells them the value of our newsletter, that some people even pay for it, but we'd like to gift it to them free, and here's what they can expect and we welcome their feedback. That's the setup. That way it's not 'just another rag' in the mail. Then when they get it every month and it's not in any special packaging, they know what it is and they value it more than 'just another rag' in the mail.

Another great strategy is to put your picture on the front of it because people associate that with you, and even if they don't read it they'll see you every month and they'll remember who you are. I (Nick) often tell of the first time I went to this annual industry convention and no one knew who I was. Then, Jack encouraged me to send our newsletter to 100 of the most influential people that attended. Can you guess what happened? I couldn't! The next year, when I went back to that same convention, people were walking up to me saying, "Hey Nick how's it going?" Wanting to tell me their side of the stories and comments I'd been writing about in the newsletter. It blew my mind. One guy even walked up and said, "Hey, my business coach circled this and told me I need to talk to you about it." And the guy actually wanted to hire me based on the recommendation. There's not much that you can do as inexpensively as a physical newsletter that will have the same impact.

6. Books. Books are the trump card in credibility. Many people dream of writing a book but most don't know where to begin or they think it's too hard. You get the ultimate respect from having a hardcover book out in the marketplace. Simply put, a book is a physical, tangible expression of how much you know. If you're competing with someone else for the same client, a book practically says, "Hey I know this much. How much does the other guy know?"

We also like the "thud factor,"-- that you can drop a book on a desk and it makes a loud thud. That's always kind of fun too. So, books are absolutely the trump card.

The easiest way to begin writing a book is to make an outline of 20 things you want to talk about surrounding your subject matter and write about 10 pages on each one. It's really not that hard!

7. Special reports. These are underutilized but can be a great tool. You can take any blog or article your write, or take a chapter from a book you previously wrote, or write a specific special report that will interest the people who want to do business with you. For example, if I were a real estate agent in today's market, I might write a special report on the top 10 ways to move your house in 10 days or less for top dollar. If you were trying to sell your house, don't you think you'd be interested in that? Absolutely. So, a special report on that subject, that you design and print and give to people, instead of giving everyone a business card at a networking meeting--or better yet, if you take that special report, put it in the mail and send it out to your prospects and clients, is so much more engaging than a business card. It reveals your expertise and it's something that they're going to look through and possibly even pass on to a friend. It's just much more engaging than a business card.

8. Information products. Information products are great because they allow you to take information that you already know, package it up in the form of a product, and sell it. You could give it away, but most people associate an information product, or "info-product" for short, with an item that is sold. If you want to leverage one of our previous strategies to make this process go even faster, you could take that special report we talked about, the '10 secrets for selling your house for top dollar', and you could turn each of the tips into a question. Now, you've got 10 questions, you can give them to a friend, you both call into FreeConferenceCall.com and your friend can interview you and ask you the questions. You can record the call, download it, you can have it transcribed or you can use the special report which you already wrote, and you can make that an information product. Bundle the audio and the transcripts or the audio and the special report and create a product you can sell.

But, don't make this one mistake that most people make: whenever you create something like this, whether it's a physical product or a virtual product, whether you're giving it away for free or not - put a price on it. By doing this, your clients and prospects will value it more. If you sell it they'll know the real value, and it's also a great tool to give away to your top prospects and say, "Take some time to review my product, I normally sell this but I'm going to give you a copy of it, because I know it will help you take the next step."

It's also a neat way to get paid to teach people why they should hire you. It's a great strategy.

There you have it, 8 strategies for displaying your expertise. Use these 8 strategies to "get out of the business you're in" and get into the "expert business." It's the fastest, easiest way to lock out your competition and increase your profits… lines of counter attack we can use in all economic times to boost our businesses!

ABOUT NICK

Nick Nanton, Esq. is known as The Celebrity Lawyer and Agent to the top Celebrity Experts for his role in developing and marketing business and professional experts, through personal branding, to help them gain credibility and recognition for their accomplishments. Nick is recognized as the nation's leading expert on personal branding as Fast Company Magazine's Expert Blogger on the subject and lectures regularly on the topic at the University of Central Florida. His book Celebrity Branding You® has been selected as the textbook on personal branding at the University.

Nick is an award winning songwriter and television producer and has worked on everything from large scale events to television shows with the likes of Bill Cosby, President George H.W. Bush, Brian Tracy and many more.

Nick is recognized as one of the top thought leaders in the business world and has co-authored five best-selling books, including the breakthrough hit Celebrity Branding You!®.

Nick serves as editor and publisher of Celebrity Press™, a publishing company that produces and releases books by top Business Experts. CelebrityPress has published books by Brian Tracy, Mari Smith, Ron Legrand and many other celebrity experts and Nick has led the marketing and PR campaigns that have driven more than 100 authors to Best-Seller status. Nick has been seen in USA Today, The Wall St. Journal, Newsweek, The New York Times, Entrepreneur® Magazine, FastCompany.com. The Huffington Post and has appeared on ABC, NBC, CBS, and FOX television affiliates speaking on subjects ranging from branding, marketing and law, to American Idol.

Nick is a member of the Florida Bar, holds a JD from the University of Florida Levin College of Law, as well as a BSBA in Finance from the University of Florida's Warrington College of Business. Nick is a voting member of The National Academy of Recording Arts & Sciences (NARAS, Home to The GRAMMYs), a 4-time Telly Award winner, and spends his spare time working with Young Life, Florida Hospital and rooting for the Florida Gators with his wife Kristina, and their two sons, Brock and Bowen.

To connect with Nick:
800-980-1626 • Nick@CelebrityBrandingAgency.com
Twitter.com/NickNanton • Facebook.com/NickNanton

ABOUT J.W.

JW Dicks is an attorney, best-selling author of 15 books, entrepreneur and personal branding business strategist. He has spent his entire 38-year career building successful businesses for himself

173

and his clients producing sales of over $500 million worth of products and services.

Today, JW serves as a consultant to business professionals and entrepreneurs to position their business and grow it through the power of personal branding, a concept he has developed and pioneered.

Through the use of proprietary methods , JW works with a client to create a vision and branding position for their business that is centered upon the client as the expert in their field. Once the branding position is set, JW helps the client develop a step by step business development system designed to reach their monetary and lifestyle goals.

JW is co-founder of Dicks & Nanton Agency, a new media, marketing, and branding company which implements online and offline business growth strategies for clients to help them get more new clients while increasing the value of the ones they have. The company uses its patent-pending formulas to get their clients guaranteed mass media credentials such as being quoted in major publications like USA Today, Newsweek and the Wall Street Journal, appearances on television shows created for ABC, FOX, NBC, and CBS along with becoming Best Selling authors in their field.

Although technically proficient in several disciplines, JW's clients consider his greatest attributes to be his business vision, creativity and ability to design and implement multi-layered profit centers for their businesses.

JW's business address is Orlando and his play address is his beach house where he spends as much time as he can with his wife, Linda, of 38 years, two daughters, son-in-law, and two Yorkies. His major hobby is fishing-- although the fish are rumored to be safe.

J.W. can be reached at 800-980-1626 or Jack@CelebrityBrandingAgency.com.

ABOUT LINDSAY

Lindsay Dicks helps her clients tell their stories in the online world. Being brought up around a family of marketers, but a product of Generation Y, Lindsay naturally gravitated to the new world of online marketing. Lindsay began freelance writing in 2000 and soon after launched her own PR firm that thrived by offering an in-your-face "Guaranteed PR" that was one of the first of its type in the nation.

Lindsay's new media career is centered on her philosophy that "people buy people." Her goal is to help her clients build a relationship with their prospects and customers. Once that relationship is built and they learn to trust them as the expert in their field then they will do business with them. Using Social Media and Search Engine Optimization, Lindsay takes that concept and builds upon it by working with her clients to create online "buzz" about them to convey their business and personal story. Lindsay's clientele span the entire business map and range from doctors and small business owners to Inc 500 CEOs.

Lindsay is a graduate of the University of Florida with a Bachelors Degree in Marketing. She is the CEO of CelebritySites™, an online marketing company specializing in social media and online personal branding. Lindsay is also co-author of the best-selling books, "Big Ideas for Your Business" and "Shift Happens," as well as the best-selling book "Power Principles for Success" with Brian Tracy. She was also selected as one of America's PremierExperts™ and has been quoted in Newsweek, the Wall Street Journal and USA Today, as well as featured on NBC, ABC, FOX and CBS television affiliates speaking on social media, search engine optimization and making more money online.

To connect with Lindsay:
Lindsay@CelebritySites.com
www.twitter.com/LindsayMDicks
www.facebook.com/LindsayDicks

CHAPTER 20

WHY SALESPEOPLE FAIL TO CLOSE

BY MICHAEL V. MICHALSKI –
SALES GENIUS INCORPORATED

I have been in direct sales, sales management and sales training and consulting for over 30 years. In that time I have been lucky to have been coached, mentored and trained by many individuals, corporations and other sales training consultants. I have learned and implemented many of the methodologies that I was taught and have had award winning success for several years.

When I worked for a major international corporation as the Northeast Regional Sales Manager, I had to manage multi-line distributors and their sales people. I was not only responsible for training the sales people on products but on how to sell effectively. I also had to work with their sales manager or the business owner. One question that I often got from management was why the sales people had such a hard time closing the deal.

I have given a lot of thought to this particular question and have some insights that I would like to share with your organization. I do not profess to have all the answers, but I feel that I have uncovered several that

177

can greatly diminish the salesperson's ability to close the deal.

The first thing that managers and salespeople need to understand is that failure to close or win a deal is a natural part of the sales process. The general 'rule of thumb' is that salespeople close one out of every four sales opportunities. That's the average. Obviously, if you are a professional, average is unacceptable. Following some of the suggestions below will definitely improve your closing rate. How much improvement depends on you and the methods you apply to the sales process.

Although I will attempt to list these in order - from the most important to those of lesser importance, you may disagree with how I rank them. That is OK. The main point is that you look at your sales approach and try to eliminate as many of these issues as possible. After all, I am just trying to share with you some strategies that have worked not only for me, but for many successful sales people.

In my humble opinion the biggest reason salespeople fail to close a qualified prospect is *the failure to form a relationship of trust and mutual respect with the decision makers*. It is critical that you show them that you are a valuable resource to their company, that you fully understand their problems and that your main objective is not to sell them a product, but instead you are there to provide solutions that resolve their problems. The key is to ask as many questions as necessary to fully understand their needs and that means you need to be a good listener and problem solver. With the information you gain, you can better position your product or service to specifically meet their needs.

The second reason that salespeople fail to close is related to the first reason. To earn their trust and respect, *you must be an expert in the industry or industries you are serving*. This means staying up on trends that affect the directions your clients may be moving towards, so you can position yourself to better meet their future needs. It is absolutely necessary to fully understand your products or services and that of your competitors. Knowing your competitors strengths and weaknesses allows you to present your product or service in the best possible light. It also gives you the ability to point out major advantages of your product or service over the competition.

In addition to knowing the above, you must also understand the processes and the integration of your product or service into the client's mode of operation. In other words, you need to customize your solution so that it fits seamlessly with the client.

The third reason for failing to close is due to *the failure of the salesperson to adapt their style of selling to the style of the buyer*. Companies don't buy from other companies. People buy from people. In a recent study, it was shown that the main impact on a client's decision to buy was based on their personal interaction with the salesperson. The brand name, reputation and price scored significantly lower. So learn about the different buying personalities and adjust yours to match theirs.

Another reason for failing to close is *not fully understanding the decision-making process*. Many salespeople waste their time trying to sell to someone who may be an influencer but may not be the decision maker. Try your best to uncover all the decision makers and influencers and discover their reasons to buy your product or service, and then make sure they are copied on your proposal. Keep in mind that the proposal should be a sales tool, and used to highlight all of the advantages that your solution will bring to the client. Spec. sheets, lengthy descriptions and prices do not make a good proposal by themselves. You must include your advantages and solutions. If possible, always try to include a Return on Investment (ROI) with the proposal.

The fifth reason salespeople fail to close is *because they try to oversell the product to the prospect*. People hate to be sold but they love to buy. The path to closure should be one in which the customer ASKS to buy! You get to this point when you've established your expertise and credibility, have established trust between yourself and the prospect, you fully understand their needs and have provided a solution that meets those needs. In this best case scenario, the close is just a natural progression of your sales process.

Conversely, there is another reason why salespeople fail to close. *This is due to the fact that many salespeople never ask for the order*; if the customer doesn't 'Ask' to buy then you need to ask for the order. The reason salespeople don't ask is due to the fear of failure. The salesperson would rather leave with the hope of getting a call from the prospect saying they want to buy, rather than hearing the prospect say no. Asking the customer if they are satisfied with your solution and asking them if they are willing to make a purchase decision gives you the opportunity to uncover some objections that you can quickly address on the spot. For myself, I would rather get a "yes" or a "no" and not a "maybe". This gives me another chance at closing the deal or allows me to put closure to this prospect for now, so I can focus on new opportunities that may be more likely to say "yes".

There is another type of fear of failure that can prevent a sale, only this time it is on the prospect's side. *Salespeople must be aware of the prospect's concern about making the wrong choice in products or services.* The fear that the prospect has is real and should not be underestimated. If the prospect makes the wrong choice, it could end up costing the company a lot of money and the buyer could lose his or her job. You must do absolutely everything you can to assure the prospect that they are making the right decision.

Similar to the fear of failure is the fear of change. Some salespeople fail to include the employees in their sales process. These employees are afraid that they may not be able to use the new product or service, and if they can't, they are afraid that they could lose their job. *Showing the employees how easy it is to use your new product or service and how this will make their jobs easier, is essential for winning the hearts and minds of those affected by change.*

Yet another reason salespeople fail to close is that *they fail to get the prospect emotionally involved.* People buy on emotion and then justify it with logic. Once you have uncovered the prospects pains, needs or wants, you need to keep digging down with your questions to uncover the emotional reason for buying. Maybe the prospect's boss said "fix this or find a new job". Now you have the prospect emotionally vested in finding a solution and you can use this information to change your sales approach.

Over the years I have worked with hundreds of salespeople. Unfortunately, another reason salespeople fail to close is that they are not very good salespeople to begin with. *Some employers do not do a good job of screening out bad candidates.* I have met too many salespeople that should not be in sales. When I tell an employer that a particular individual doesn't have what it takes to be successful, I can see the frustration on the employer's face. Hiring one poor performer can cost a company hundreds of thousands of dollars in lost wages, lost training costs, lost sales and lost clients. Employers should use professional staffing services that will 'screen out' poor performers. At a minimum, employers should take advantage of the many online tools, such as profile evaluations, in order to reduce poor hiring decisions.

One of the most overlooked and underused tools available to companies is training. Most companies do a good job with training their employees with the job skills that they need. However, many companies fall short when it comes to customer relationship training. *All employees that affect the customer's buying experience should be trained to consistently adhere to the company's mission statement and value proposition. They must be made to understand the role that each of them plays when dealing with customers and how this affects the sales process.* Every interaction with the customer, no matter how trivial it may seem, affects the salesperson's ability to close and keep clients

The lack of an effective sales training program for everyone in sales, regardless of their experience, is another reason why salespeople fail to close. Sales training must be ongoing in order to be effective. The training must focus on the entire sales process. The training program must be monitored and adjusted for maximum effectiveness. The most successful companies do this. They have a system that is proven to get results and their closing rates are almost double that of companies that do not perform ongoing training. It is an investment that will lead to higher closing rates and more profits. Studies have shown that companies that invest in ongoing training have higher employee morale, higher employee retention rates and the employees are more productive.

Another reason salespeople fail to close is because *they fail to fully qualify a prospect before going to see them*. Some salespeople are happy to fill their schedule up with appointments to show the boss how hard they are working. However, they fail to fully qualify the suspect. A suspect is not a prospect until they are qualified. Many suspects can be eliminated by asking key questions without the expense or the loss of time from driving to see the suspect. This leaves the salesperson more time to find qualified prospects!

Qualifying your suspects turns them into one of 2 groups. Either they become a real prospect or you soon discover that they would be a waste of time. I am not ignoring the fact that sometimes you get lucky and a suspect actually turns into a client. However, the better job you do of qualifying your suspects, the more likely you will be to get good prospects. Which will increase your chances of closing. Qualifying will weed out the "time wasters", "the tire kickers", the " I am not ready to change" and the "I don't have the money" suspects from real prospects. The more time you spend on qualifying, the more time you will have for closing.

In closing, I would just like to point out one other reason salespeople fail to close, and *this is due to poor prospecting methods*. Cold calling is a one-in-a-hundred close rate according to various sources. Salespeople will have a better chance of closing if they spend more time on the phone and computer researching targeted companies that fit their customer profile. There are many resources available online such as Hoovers, Google and Zoominfo. These are just a few of the sites where you can find and research suspects. There are literally hundreds of sites where you can gain invaluable information including key contacts.

After identifying prospects, use Facebook and Linkedin to make social network connections with people on the inside of the companies you are targeting, and establish a relationship with these people. They can get you invited into your prospects rather than you banging your head to get in the front door. Establish relationships with the other vendors at the companies you are targeting. They may also be able to get you invited in. Making more cold calls is not the answer in today's economy. Making laser beamed, focused calls on "qualified, targeted prospects" is the key to higher closing rates and lowering sales cost in today's economic environment.

ABOUT MICHAEL

Michael V. Michalski is a native of New Jersey. After completing school, he joined a US Corporation as a customer service representative. He quickly learned the products and the industry and was quickly promoted to outside sales representative. Michael excelled in this capacity and became the top producer in the Northeast. Within a few short years, he was promoted to the position of Western Regional Sales Manager at the age of 24. He was responsible for managing and growing a multi-line distribution network from California to Washington State. He worked with and managed 50 distributor sales representatives.

After successfully growing the company's business to all time new highs, Mr. Michalski left the organization when it was sold. He then joined a major competitor as a Marketing Specialist where he doubled their sales in the first 2 years. After a number of years, he was offered a position back on the East coast with an international corporation in the capacity of Northeast Regional Sales Manager. Within 4 years, Michael completely reorganized the distribution network from the ground up and turned the worst performing territory into the best performing territory. He won the President's Award for Top Regional Manager of the Year for four consecutive years.

Mr. Michalski decided to leave the company as a direct employee and became an Independent Manufacturers Representative for this company, and added several additional lines to his business. He ran the business for 17 years and enjoyed the success and satisfaction of owning his own business. During that time, Michael also worked as an independent consultant to the Electrotechnology Applications Center at the Northampton Community College where he co-developed a training program for the Pennsylvania Department of Environmental Protection on how new regulations would impact the wood finishing industry. He then trained over 200 DEP personnel over a two-year period, while still operating his own business.

Recognizing the value of the course that Mr. Michalski had developed for the DEP, he completely reworked the program on his own and developed the training program for the wood finishing industry. He offered this service to the industry and was soon training major wood finishing manufacturers with his program. During this time, he was approached by a colleague and was asked to join him as a partner in starting the first professional wood finishing training school in the US. Michael agreed and became the Vice President of Sales. After just a few short years, the business took off and is now a well known and highly respected resource in the industry.

Through this experience, Mr. Michalski discovered that he had a passion for training and consulting and decided to sell off his other businesses and devote his efforts to a Sales Training and Consulting career. During his many years of sales, management, business ownership, training and consulting, Michael amassed a wealth of knowledge in the entire sales process, which he now shares with other companies.

Mr. Michalski's sales training background includes Miller Heiman Strategic & Conceptual Selling, Xerox Professional Selling Skills I & II, Sales Dynamics, the Sandler Selling System and the Dale Carnegie Sales Course where he received the Highest Award for Achievement. He has published numerous articles in trade magazines and was the guest speaker at numerous regional trade shows. In 2005, Michael was invited to be the guest speaker at the International Wood Expo in Las Vegas.

CHAPTER 21

OVERCOMING TECHNICAL SALES OBJECTIONS

BY BRION JOHNSON

1. USE POSITIVE WORDS

"The pessimist complains about the wind; the optimist expects it to change; the realist adjusts the sails."
~ William Arthur Ward (1921-1994)

Early in my career I said "no" in a factual and conversational manner when a potential customer asked if our solution had a particular feature. The CEO of our company was present and after the meeting, he pulled me aside and said to never, ever, ever use "no" and for that matter, any negative words when talking with customers. At the time I did not fully comprehend why, but I understand now. Negative words and phrases have a way of making us feel uncomfortable about the product or service. Sometimes the only information a customer writes down or remembers are the "no" and "yes" statements. When tempted to say "no", even if true, think of ways to say "yes" to it and make it sound positive! How is that accomplished? Take out a piece of paper and write down two or three situations where saying "no" seemed like the right thing to say. Now, see if there are alternative ways it would be possible to say

185

"yes". Here are some examples that I've used.

If I have heard of the request or question before, I would say something like "that is something we have looked into and here is what we think that would look like". Even better, if it were something that will be available soon, I would say "that will be available in the next quarter." If I haven't thought about it or heard the question before I would say "that is a great idea, please describe how that would work." This exercise may give some insight to what the customer is really asking for. Listening attentively and thinking positively, a solution can usually be found, even if it requires outside help. The goal should be to gain a customers trust and to always say "yes". The alternative statements communicate that the product or solution is not capable of that particular feature or function at the present time, but the conversation is kept positive.

There may be times when a customers needs are beyond the scope and capabilities of the products and services you are offering within your organization. This is a great time to keep developing the customers trust and to discuss other partners or solutions if you know of some alternatives. People buy from people and if you can win a customers trust by being positive and looking for solutions for them, you will definitely gain them as a customer at some point and they will likely refer others to you.

2. USE THE BEST NUMBERS

"That action is best which procures the greatest happiness for the greatest numbers."
~ *Francis Hutcheson (1694-1746)*

Whether we realize it or not, we have feelings about numbers. Children love to say their age proudly like "I'm 5 and three quarters". In retail stores items are often $9.99 instead of $10.00. Why is that? Because $9.99 is less expensive than $10.00, and we can tell ourselves "it's under $10!" We like the feeling of buying at a lower price even by a penny, so why not take the same perspective to improve business discussions? Take a few minutes to write down some numbers that you use when describing your product or service. How much something costs, how long a project will take, or how many people or resources are required to accomplish a task. Now, consider writing some different values from what is usually stated and see how it sounds, and imagine how a customer might feel. Here are some examples to compare.

Compare "this project is going to take 2 months to complete" to "this project can be done in 8 weeks." How about "it would only take 60 days." In another example, which one sounds better? "The 3 year cost is $100,000" or "It's less than $2,800 a month for a 3 year agreement." The point is that the comparative amounts are the same, but each one conveys a different impression. This can be important when discussing costs, time and resources with potential customers. Of course, this is subjective, so use the phrase that you feel confident will help the customer agree you are offering a good value. When asked a challenging commitment question such as "how quickly can this project be completed?" or …"what is the total cost?" communicating a range is important. You might say "there are a number of factors and typically the cost is between $10,000 and $30,000 annually", or "the project usually takes 10-30 business days." In this manner you can discuss all the factors before the customer has made any commitments and gives both of you room to negotiate.

3. PERCEPTION IS REALITY

"The young man knows the rules, but the old man knows the exceptions."
~ *Oliver Wendell Holmes (1841-1935)*

Does your company have a solid reputation? Do you know how your customers really feel about your organization? Sometimes to achieve a customers business there is a need to overcome a negative opinion about your corporation. There are several ways to overcome negative perceptions. One way is to have existing customers speak on your behalf with your potential customers. Another way is to develop joint webinars and podcasts to showcase your solution in action. It may also be valuable to develop white papers and case studies and have outsiders blog about your solution. I have found that having an internal champion at your prospective customer's organization is invaluable. They can be your greatest supporters and sometimes the deal winner. In one case, we had convinced someone that had no buying authority for our solution, that our product and services were the best for their organizations need. This person became a powerful advocate and over a short amount of time, they were able to convince their co-workers and superiors that doing business with us was the ideal solution. They had spent many hours preparing an internal ROI (Return on Investment), as well as researched other possible solutions. While other solutions were comparable to meet the general needs, the buying authority considered doing business with us the priority because our internal sponsor held the view that we had the best solution to their most pressing need.

4. USE YOUR IMAGINATION

"Everything is simpler than you think and at the same time more complex than you imagine."
~ Goethe (1749-1832)

Sometimes overcoming obstacles requires much more time and thought than originally anticipated. Take a few minutes and write down a few imagined or even standard obstacles that a potential customer may have to overcome to do business with your organization. Once you have this list, try to visualize how the objections can be overcome and challenge yourself to see the issues from the customer's point of view. Do not assume that the solutions are easy or hard, just try to understand how the stumbling blocks can become stepping stones. In some cases role playing and rehearsing the conversations with other successful associates can have a huge impact on your business discussions. Feelings play an important role in conversations and should be considered. Many people are loyal to certain brands or ways of doing business. The better you understand the customer's ideas and thoughts, the better chance of overcoming the barriers you will have. While doing some research for a customer project, I was having a difficult time coming up with an effective solution. I imagined a few "what ifs" and discussed some options with a few co-workers. It suddenly occurred to us that we were trying to solve the wrong problem! We changed the question that we thought we were being asked and came to a completely different starting point. Suddenly the solution was clearly defined and extremely effective. If you can use your imagination effectively considering the "what ifs", the answer might come quicker than you realize!

5. EDUCATE

"A single conversation across the table with a wise man is worth a month's study of books."
~ Proverb

Once when I was meeting with a marketing group, they kept using an acronym I thought I was familiar with. At one point, someone stated the meaning of the acronym and that it was an internally defined acronym! I discovered that my whole thought process and therefore, solution, had to change because I was not informed about the meaning of the acronym. I learned that I needed to educate myself first and verify information while in discussions. Educating does not mean you talk down to anyone, or make anyone feel inferior. It means that you take the time to make sure everyone has a clear understanding of what you are talking about. It is of critical importance that you explain things in detail when there is room for misunderstanding. Many of us are in new businesses and in some cases the markets we are in are undeveloped. If you are one of these early pioneers it is essential that you help educate the people in the market. Attend and participate in any seminars, webinars, and conferences as you are able to. Even if you are in a very established market, there are innovations every day that you need to help your customers understand. If you and your company are somewhere in between an established company and a brand new company, then you have both advantages!

6. BUILD TRUST

To build trust with customers, understand that every time a customer is agreeing to something, they are taking a risk. Each step with a customer is taking a bit of their career into your hands. The results of the project could lead to a promotion and acclaim at best, or cost them their job at worst. Every email, call, and in-person meeting is a "moment of truth" that the customer is using to understand how you and the organization work. In some cases, you are typically the only person the customer will meet to evaluate the philosophy and values of the company. While the prospect may make a big deal of price and capabilities, the reason that companies need people and not just brochures and websites to sell their products, is because people buy from "people" as much as they buy products and services.

7. FIND THE REASON

Finding the main reason a customer will listen to you and do business with you should be your goal. It may take a lot of time, but it will be worth it. For as long as a potential or existing customer is willing to listen to you and your ideas, you should attempt to uncover the reason that you do not have their business yet, or why you do not have more of it! How many reasons can you think of that someone buys your product or service? Do you have the "best in class" product? Is your solution so unique that no one else has it? Are you the first to the market? Does your company have the lion's share of the business in your industry? Start digging deep and see how many reasons you can come up with. Whatever business you are in, there are probably a large number of reasons that someone buys from you and your company. In some cases even more importantly, they should understand what they are not receiving. I once met with a potential customer that seemed like a perfect fit. They loved the product and moved ahead with the purchase extremely fast. Unfortunately, it soon became apparent that the reason they bought the product was not clearly defined in their workflow and when they tried to fit it into their system, it did not work like they anticipated. In other words, the reason they bought the product had been misunderstood and they thought they were getting something different than what they bought. On the surface it seemed like the perfect solution. However, the reason for the requirement was undefined and the point was missed entirely. State the reason for the business early and often and refer to it as many times as possible so everyone has a clear picture of the solution.

8. SET HIGH EXPECTATIONS

"If you shoot for the stars and hit the moon, it's OK. But you've got to shoot for something. A lot of people don't even shoot."
~ *Confucius (551-479 BC)*

When asked how any potentially disastrous meeting went, an optimistic mentor of mine would reply with "It went as well as I expected." In other words, he set very high expectations and he seemed to always have difficult and challenging situations go his way. Can you say that about your conversations? If not, then keep working at it until the standard is set so high that it's difficult to reach! If you can set your mind on the best possible outcome of any situation, you will most likely start to experience it. Even if the situation does not play out the best possible way, it will most likely be significantly better than what you first thought. As the saying goes "Good, better, best; never let it rest 'til your good is better and your better is best."

If you can be positive, present the best numbers, ask questions, imagine new possibilities, educate your market and customers to build trust, and find the reason for the purpose, then set high expectations and enjoy the results of overcoming objections!

ABOUT BRION

Brion Johnson is currently Director, Global Business Development, Energy for MetaCarta, Inc., a Cambridge, MA based Geographic Search and Referencing Platform. He has worked for and with many corporations from startups to Fortune 50 companies. Over the last two decades he has participated in more than 20 mergers and acquisitions as an employee as well as a co-founder. He lives in Snohomish, Washington with his wife and 3 children.

http://www.brionjohnson.com

CHAPTER 22

WEALTH MINDSET

BY MORRIS NUTT

I am so honored that Brian Tracy asked me to be a part of this wonderful project. Brian has done such a masterful job over the decades in teaching us how to properly set goals and how to take action in attaining them. He is one of my mentors and heroes in life. In taking his courses and having achieved some measure of success, my discoveries both with myself and in talking with others has led me to believe that, other than goal-oriented processes, what leads anyone to achieving their goals is their mindset.

You may have heard the saying, "the most important six inches of real estate in the world is between your ears." I believe that saying to be very true! How we think about things, ideas and ourselves pre-determines our success far more than how we go about achieving a goal. The reason I believe this to be true is the process or processes we end up using in our lives are the result of how we originally thought about them in the first place. So what determines our mindset and how can we change our mindset to help us attain more of what we are after?

Obviously, we are affected by our experiences and our education. However you perceive your life up to this point will dictate your choices and your results. These patterns either lead to much success and happiness or their opposite. When recognizing these patterns, you may then duplicate them, if they are having the desired result you wish. You may also require a change or break in the patterns so you may begin having new results. Recognizing a pattern is the easy part. Changing is the key and the most challenging component to success that most of us face.

My goal is to help you recognize those patterns in your life that may be holding you back, address how to begin the process of creating healthy patterns and how to continue creating and maintaining healthy patterns into the future. First, I would like to tell you a story.

A little girl once sat down with a pad and pen and began to write a song. She had no idea what she was doing would eventually lead to anything other than the immense fun she was having at that moment. Writing helped her daydream and made her feel she was creating and contributing to life. She felt more alive and she felt more connected and more special. When she put her thoughts down on paper some magical force leapt into her body and took over like someone or something adding power to her, plugging her in. This little girl continued to enjoy this activity. Over and over she would write and write and then write some more.

Being the daughter of a teacher and a high school principal gave her upbringing a sense of discipline and focused direction. It also contributed to her taking piano at age six and then writing her first song at the tender age of ten. Her song actually was released but received very little airplay. But Nadine didn't give up. She kept writing and working hard at her passion, eventually landing a role as a regular on the Canadian television version of Nickelodeon. One year later Nadine entered some amateur talent competitions. She was looking for a big break. She eventually landed a spot on *Star Search* via a New York audition. Nadine flew to Los Angeles to appear on the show, but lost after one round. Humbled yet remaining upbeat and hopeful, Nadine soon signed a publishing deal with MCA Publishing at the age of fourteen.

She continued to work hard and in 1991 her first album was released in Canada only. She had co-written every track on the album. It went platinum. Three hit singles from the album led many to compare her to then popular music artists, Debbie Gibson and Tiffany. But Nadine was different. She had a different mindset. She had a wealth mindset. Nadine was so laser focused on her dreams of making it big and leaving a mark that she would not settle for the "bubble gum" pop moniker. One year later she released a second album. Again in Canada only. Again three songs were hits. This album was said to be more thoughtful in lyrics. Nadine was changing. Nadine also decided to change her name. She graduated from high school, moved out on her own and found that life would continue to challenge her. Living in Toronto and then Nashville, she would seek out and work with many songwriters. Nothing was working for her and an eventual move to Los Angeles led her to meet songwriter, Glen Ballard. The two collaborated and wrote together their first internationally-released album, *Jagged Little Pill.*

Alanis Nadine became Alanis Morissette and is known today by most people as just Alanis. She has sold more than 60 million records. She has won twelve Juno Awards and seven Grammys. Alanis has appeared in plays, television and film. But what was it that this little Canadian girl had that gave her such a wealth mindset? Why didn't she just give up when all of the different obstacles and challenges reared their ugly heads? How was she able to do what so many before her were unable to do? More importantly, what can we learn from her story so that we may learn and apply these success principles and wealth mindset to our own lives?

What is wealth mindset? In my opinion, a wealth mindset has very little to do with money and more to do with positive attitude and a bright outlook on life. A wealth mindset can be so much more than material attainment. Wealth mindset is being rich in attitude and outlook! You can be wealthy without having any material possessions. Having purpose and clarity in your life is a good amount of wealth. Being healthy in body, mind and spirit is an abundance of wealth. Helping others from a place of integrity may make you the wealthiest person on the planet. Everyone must have some means however, to be able to help as many people as possible.

The first person you need to be able to help is you. You are the greatest investment in the world! You need to be successful so you may reach your potential. So where do we start to get you going in the right direction? First we must recognize having a love for what one does. Through Alanis's story we come to realize that she simply worked hard at what she loved. What about you? Are you absolutely in love with what you do? Do you have an incredible passion for helping others through your work or service? If not, then why not do what comes natural for you? It might make a huge difference in your performance. After all, aren't we all performers? We perform each day as brothers, sisters, children, parents, bosses, employees, mates and friends. Each performance we offer either contains our best and most fun sides or it does not. But each performance definitely leaves a trail of patterns.

Another lesson from Alanis's story is the fact she was having fun. Fun is such a small word that it is thrown around a lot these days. In advertisements, it is a trigger word to encourage us to consume or desire something. It has been perhaps overused to such a degree that its true meaning gets lost in translation. Fun is more than a smile, a giggle, or a big dip on the roller coaster of life. Fun should be for us a state of bliss. Fun should endure even during challenging moments. When we do what we love for a living it no longer becomes work. It is just fun. Sir Richard Branson, billionaire and owner of Virgin Records, has such a wonderful quote about this. He said, *"I don't think of work as work and play as play. It's all living."*

Make no mistake there will be challenges. We have all been challenged at one time or another. We have all attempted and failed at something in our lives. People who have not failed have not attempted anything worthy. Alanis attempted and failed many times. She lost in competitions. She lost at producing hits right away. She lost at many challenges that faced her. Alanis never lost at working. She kept on trying. She kept on improving. She kept on loving what she did. She endured at having fun at what she had a passion for! And because of all the failures, she succeeded! You can too! Look at each challenge as nothing more than an opportunity. Your opportunity to learn, to grow, adapt and overcome.

One of the great lessons for me in reading about Alanis was her confidence and willingness to change. Most people have the hardest time with change. Getting out of your comfort zone will be one of the greatest rewards you ever experience. You just have to make the effort. When she graduated from high school she moved out on her own and then began searching from city to city for the best songwriters. How committed are you to your goals? Are you willing to move somewhere else to fulfill your dreams? Will you go out searching for whomever or whatever it takes to make sure your dreams and goals come true? It truly takes a wealth mindset to make it happen. Courage is the ability to take action when you are not in a safe place. <u>Getting out of your comfort zone is the first step towards realizing your goals.</u> Doing and being something different will offer you richer results than you have experienced.

So when you recognize your life patterns, choose to do what you love, have fun doing what you love and have fun enduring the challenges that come your way. What is the next big risk? I am about to share with you an idea that I believe is the most powerful lesson we can learn in life: **Your results in life will be determined more by who you choose to spend time with than the power of your own goals.**

As powerful as we each are in life, we find that our success is dependent upon others. As we learned in Alanis's story, her career really exploded when she went out on her journey searching for the best songwriters. *Jagged Little Pill,* one of the most commercially successful albums of all time, exists today from the collaboration between Alanis and Glen Ballard. You see Glen Ballard is just as important in this tale as Alanis. Without Glen there is no famous album and perhaps no Alanis as we know her today. Alanis succeeded because she surrounded herself with people that were passionate in their pursuit of excellence.

So how is your group? You know, the people with whom you spend the most time. Are they supportive of you and your goals? Do they encourage you? Do they hold you back? Do they hold you accountable and make you better? It is said that a true friend is someone who can make us do what we can. Guard your time with all of your might and share your friendship only with others that help you grow and support you to be your best. For all of the individual goal setting and planning you may be doing, ***you will always be the average of the five people you spend the most time with.***

Do you need to average up? Do you need to make changes on who you are spending time with? Like Alanis, you may even need to move so you can pursue new people with new ideas to help you along your path to success. Change is what you make it. Change will get you different results. Breaking old patterns and surrounding yourself with new people who pull you in the direction of your goals will definitely help you create and maintain a Wealthy Mindset.

With many challenges today facing us and even attacking us, my Counter-attack ideas restated are:

1. Have clarity and focus in doing what you love for others.
2. Enjoy the journey. Have fun even during the challenging moments.
3. Be willing to change and break out of old patterns.
4. Make sure the five people you spend the most time with have your best interests at heart. Make sure they pull you up in every way or you must change this Mastermind group. Do whatever it takes to remove any negative influences or people from your life, even if you have to move away to find the right support group.
5. Finally, I want you to know how special you really are. You have every tool now to accomplish anything you want to accomplish. Your ability to think and take action today will create the life you want. So face your fears and move forward. There is a whole new world and life awaiting you. Thank you for taking a great step today in reading Brian's book. He is one of many teachers you have in your life that are here to help you. God bless you on your miraculous journey! You are already a great success!

Much love,

Morris

ABOUT MORRIS

Morris Nutt is an independent financial planner, author, speaker and thought-leader living in Memphis, TN. He is Co-Author of *The Laws of Financial Success*. He loves helping others. He especially loves his family and spending time with his wife, Kelly, and his children. For more information, please visit thelawsoffinancialsuccess.com or morrisnuttfinancial.com.

CHAPTER 23

21 GREAT BUSINESS AND PERSONAL LESSONS I HAVE LEARNED IN MY 38 YEARS AS A SMALL BUSINESS OWNER

BY DAVID LEOPOLD

(Brian Tracy, My Greatest Business Mentor, Didn't Change My Life. He Just Set Me in the Right Direction, and I Changed My Life ~ Thank You Brian!)

Most of my "best lessons learned" are a result of direct interactions with key people in my life. Other lessons were simply results of actual business experiences from the last 38 years. Let's begin that discussion and journey.

GOD: The greatest lesson that I ever learned came from God. God is my author of life and death. God was there when I was conceived. God was watching over me very closely during four genetic heart surgeries and one brain surgery that I've had in the last 15 years of my life. So very clearly, five different times God has said, "David, this small business stuff isn't done yet."

(The remaining Lessons Learned are not in any prioritized order)

GRANDFATHER: My Grandfather (maternal) was my first Entrepreneur role model. He clearly demonstrated to me that focused hard work would make a return on a time investment. Folks wanted to work hard for "Harry" to gain his respect. When you gained his respect, he would do anything for you. I even remember when my Grandfather was in his late seventies and travelled almost 1500 miles to help my younger brother start a business. He taught me that if you treated folks fairly you could accomplish _any_ business goals… with their support.

DAD: My father was a very 'low key' Entrepreneur; he always put his family first, business second. His dream was to own and publish his own publication. As a high school student, I was present for three meetings he had to discuss his purchasing of a publication from the Publisher and several of his advisors. (Sorry, Dad, you paid 5 times as much for the publication as Mom did, but we did keep it in the family!) I was blessed to be able to continue Dad's Dream. Less than a year after he died, I bought his publication for $10,000 from my Mom, in a deal brokered by my Grandfather (maternal). I was 24 years old at the time. I've tried to make it a good investment for Mom over the years. For me, that investment was returned thousands of times and I thank Dad for planting that seed.

MOM: My Mother has been the only business partner that I have ever had and I thank her very much for accepting my offer to buy the business from her. I have enjoyed being her oldest son; we would not have made great business partners. Just three days ago, my 87-year old Mother said to me, "David, how is it again that you make money?" We both had fun with that one, didn't we Mom? An easier question from Mom has always been "Are you making any money?" That's relative…

MY SIBLINGS: My siblings have not always been 100 supportive of the things that I've done in life, and that's okay. However, I think they probably all have said, at some point in their life, "Somehow, David will figure it out."

JORDAN: (my son) Three years ago when Jordan was 20, he said to me, "Dad I don't think you're branding yourself properly. I don't think you're positioning yourself properly. Therefore, I don't think you're

Marketing yourself properly." And I said, "Great." So we spent that summer starting to fix things. I am very grateful that I made a decision to invest in Jordan's Marketing career in college. I have already realized more return on my $55,000 investment and I thank Jordan for that.

SAM: (my son) Sam, age 22, and I have engaged in many philosophical "life" discussions in the last several years. The discussion I have absolutely enjoyed the most, is direct marketing; Sam and his wife, Kimberly, (my "daughter"), are demonstrating that they are very outstanding direct marketers. In my "twenties", it took me more than three years to generate as much revenue as they have done in two years!

MY ANGEL FROM GOD, ANNETTE: I think the most important thing that my angel from God has taught me is that tough love is a positive aspect in one's life, demonstrating perhaps, the highest level of caring.

I. D. BLUMENTHAL: My first journey into serious entrepreneurship was when I accepted an offer from a gentleman, (by the name of I.D. Blumenthal) to "partner" with him (his investment) to publish a magazine he owned. "Mr. I.D." taught me that when you have a dream, and you are very passionate with that dream, and you are persistent with that dream, with patience, some day that dream will come true.

KEVIN MCKENNA: In the 1990's, Kevin (as a client) and I did some of the most successful direct marketing campaigns in the 90's. We even launched Kevin's business as "partners" together, in the '90's. Kevin has taught me much about Direct Marketing, (Insurance Direct Marketing and Consumer Direct Marketing). Direct Marketing has been the most important business aspect of my 38 years.

GLENN WILLIAMS: Glenn has taught me everything that I know about direct mail. It has been wonderful learning from an individual who might make more direct mail decisions than any other person in the universe.

1000+ CUSTOMERS: My 1000+ Customers (lifetime) with whom I have had direct interaction, have taught me to listen to the challenge and understand the problem. Never assume you have the solution until you totally, TOTALLY, understand the situation.

TRUST AND CONFIDENCE: Business will not work unless there is trust and confidence on both sides of the business table. Lacking ultimate trust and confidence, that business relationship should not proceed collaboratively.

BUSINESS STRATEGY: I constantly ask myself, perhaps the most important question when it comes to develop and execute a business strategy. Very simply, "Why am I doing what I am doing?" If can answer that question satisfactorily to myself, I will proceed with that business strategy.

MARKET STRATEGY: Market Strategy is being able to clearly articulate your value proposition fully integrated with sales results. All too often, marketing is not integrated with selling; they exist for one another and must exist with one another, in an integrated effort to take the message of the business to the marketplace. (I speak from the perspective of generating over $100MM of sales---with a very focused Marketing Strategy.)

MONEY MATTERS: It really wasn't until I started to think in "realistic big numbers" (thank you Michael Gerber for your "Rule of 10,000"!) that money matters became a much different mindset for myself and the growth and development of my company. There is money available someplace to work with you to help you achieve your dream(s). Be very clear however, that there must be a return on investment that is clearly defined.

TECHNOLOGY: Here I am, 61 years old and "starting" a new business. Predicated upon 38 years of Marketing and Sales experience, I have chosen a 23 year old "Technology Whiz Kid" as my business partner. Together, we are creating a very strong Community with "best of class" practices in marketing and the very best "State of the Art" application platforms in technology. We are fully integrating the two disciplines to build our community.

SOCIAL MEDIA: Too much has probably already been said and written about social media. It is absolutely the most addressed two words I have ever seen in my 38 years as a small business owner. Social media is a means of communication, with an Entrepreneur employing a certain technology unique to that particular community, where those "social media" discussions take place. That is, pure and simple, what it is all about, and it is the major way folks communicate with one another today. Social Media is not Community Business2Business.

SUCCESS: Success is relative and can only be measured and focused when personal goals and objectives are established. We determine for ourselves how success is measured; then set goals, objectives, and accountability to achieve that success.

BRIAN TRACY: What can I say about Brian Tracy? As an individual, he has had more impact than anyone on my thinking, in many times on my personal life and almost always in my business thinking. He is my greatest business mentor and doesn't even know it! But that doesn't matter. Brian Tracy communicates with clarity and simplicity, and writes it better than anybody I have ever listened to or read. His concepts are really very simple—read, learn from your reading, and then react to what it is that you have learned from your reading. Strive to be the best at what you do. That's a wonderful path, a goal to take in life. But always keep in mind, that in our life's journeys, there will be times when people's attitudes, other than your own, or their behaviors, will have to be addressed; that is not an overnight change. Behavioral changes take time. I read… and re-read Brian's: _The 100 Absolutely Unbreakable Laws of Business Success._

ENTREPRENEURSHIP: I've read many definitions. I've heard a lot of people philosophize about it. The most impactful statement or interaction that I have ever had about entrepreneurship, is with an organization called the Kauffman Foundation, "The Foundation of Entrepreneurship." I strongly urge any "Entrepreneur" to visit their website: www.BuildAStrongerAmerica.com – and take "The Entrepreneurs Pledge." I'm sure you will then understand why you have chosen the journey that you have…

THE DREAM: I once heard a motivational speaker mention (and it's had an impact on my thinking ever since), that perhaps the greatest gift we can give our children is the importance of the dream. And I hope, in fact, I have given Jordan and Sam the dream - so they can set goals and objectives in their lives, so that they each will achieve that dream.

It was indeed an honor to participate with other entrepreneurs in this collaborative publishing project. I have realized another dream. Thank you Nick Nanton. Thank you Brian Tracy for helping me make that dream come true.

ABOUT DAVID

Being born into a family of Entrepreneurs, David Leopold really did not put his Dream in place until his father's death, when he was 23. Publishing was the pre-chosen field, as his Father lived most of his own life before he realized his own dream of owning a publication. David personally struggled having his mother as a business partner. He did what any Entrepreneur would do; he bought the business from his Mother, in a deal brokered by his maternal Grandfather, a successful businessman.

That was in the 1970's. Prior to his first business investment, David had displayed an interest in Publishing, but his college journey actually took him in a different direction. He has never taken a business or marketing class, but has had numerous classroom experiences with college and high school students who have!

While being involved in three different publishing businesses in the 70's, he chose to pursue other marketing efforts in the 1980's. He was involved in at least six separate Direct Marketing/Direct Mail endeavors. It was in that decade that he developed his keen understanding of Return on Marketing Investment.

In the 1990's, he spent most of his time in "partnership" with a Fortune 500 company. The marketing discipline was Teleservices. He established a national reputation in Insurance Direct Marketing and was asked to participate in numerous speaking opportunities while interacting with 19 of the largest 52 Insurance Companies, generating approximately $41MM in revenue with his business "partner".

On January 1, 2000, he began to learn how to effectively use the Internet as a Marketing tool. Privately, he worked with three international service providers in the Insurance industry. In 2004, he began to develop his Small Business Model embracing the Business2Business discipline under his "Dreaming With Entrepreneurs" brand. Two years ago, he began to build The David Leopold Network Community. Small Businesses could realize unlimited business opportunities on the websites he developed with a 23 year old Applications Developer.

(i): www.OurSmallBusinessTV.com;
(ii): www.DavidsBarter.com; and
(iii): www.SmallBusinessBookPublishing.com)

Ultimately, The David Leopold Network Community will become a non-profit Foundation, with the mission to assist other Entrepreneurs with David's Marketing expertise.

CHAPTER 24

THE SERVICE STATION

BY ROB LIANO

A nyone can prosper in a good economy, but can you afford to be just anyone? Are you achieving *all* of the results you desire? I want to offer you a simple, easy to use, absolutely foolproof formula for success.

Take a moment and listen to this story:

It's late 1968. You've been eating up the road mile by mile in a faded blue 1954 Cadillac Eldorado. It's a car with a perfect pedigree for a road trip - low, sleek body; power assisted steering and brakes and a leather-trimmed interior. Even if your road warrior's best days are behind it, you're cruising in style. You glance down at the fuel gauge and notice it's thirsty. There's a green and white sign up ahead, and as you get closer it says exactly what you hoped: "Gas - 2 miles."

As you pull into the service station a man strolls over. Tall and lanky with dark hair and tanned weathered skin, the lines in his face are like a road map of his life. He's dressed in faded blue jeans and an unbuttoned grey work shirt. Oil seems permanently fixed under his fingernails. You can see his name in red letters on the right pocket of the shirt. "Harry".

Harry reaches your window. "Fill'er up?"

"Yep" you answer.

Walking to the back of the car, he lifts up the driver's side tail light to access the gas tank, and puts the nozzle in. Then he heads to the front of the car. "Pop the hood for me," he says.

You see a rag magically appear as Harry pulls out the dipstick, wipes it off, dips it again, and checks the level. "She's good," he says. He closes the hood, grabs a squeegee, sloshes it around in the soapy water and carries it to the front of the car. The grime and bugs, the memories of your journey simply vanish from the windshield, then you hear a click . . . the tank is full.

After putting the nozzle back on the pump, Harry walks up to your window and says "That'll be eight bucks." You hand him a ten, "keep the change, Harry. Thanks."

You just paid for service!

You allowed Harry to keep the change because of the great service he provided. He checked the oil, cleaned the windshield, and did his job well. That's why you rewarded him.

Harry knew a winning formula: Service = Success. What does this have to do with you? Everything - it's your key to success too.

Point to ponder: Have you ever spent a little extra because you received better service?

Consider this quote from Henry Ford:

"A business absolutely devoted to service will have only one worry about profits. They will be embarrassingly large."

Ford was right. No matter what you're marketing or selling, unless you have a monopoly or other competitive advantage, you WILL have direct competition from other people selling an equivalent product. That means the only thing that can possibly set you apart from the other guy is the level of service that you provide to your customers.

Now it does go a bit deeper than that, of course. But first, to establish the credibility of this concept, let's look at some real world examples of service and reward.

Example 1: A tip for a restaurant server after a meal is not usually given for the quality of the food, is it? It's based on the level of service provided. Was our water refilled promptly? Did we wait forever to order? Was the server cheerful and accommodating? We've learned to pay extra for better service even though we've already paid for the meal itself.

Example 2: You're shopping for a DVD player and you encounter a salesperson that offers to assist you. After a few minutes you get the impression that this sales representative doesn't really know as much as they should and that you're not really getting answers to your questions. You may even know more than they do. This usually leads to frustration and you think to yourself or even come right out and say "is there's someone else I can speak to?" You feel like you should take your business elsewhere, either to another store or to someone else who can truly help. You no longer trust that the person you first encountered will be able to guide you in the right direction and you're not about to risk doing business with them.

Example 3: If you go shopping for a car, who would you be more likely to buy from?

A: The salesperson that answers your questions by fumbling through a brochure, searching the Internet, or asking others for help to explain the details about the car.

B: The salesperson that doesn't bother listening to you, but instead wants you to listen to them. Someone who's more interested in what he wants to sell than what you want to buy.

OR

C: A sales professional that asks questions to determine exactly what you're looking for and when they find out, they know details about the car by heart, all of its features and how the competition compares. Someone who is prepared to provide you with what *you're* looking for.

My guess is that you'd choose salesperson C and that your buying decision, whether conscious or not, is based on the fact that they provided you with better service.

In all of the examples above, everyone is rewarded for the service they provide. Now let's expand the formula.

Great service = great reward. Poor service = poor reward.

It's not enough to simply provide service. In order to set yourself apart you must provide *expert* service. The difference between expert service and poor service means all the difference in the world to business owners, salespeople, and clients. Clients seek help and guidance and they'd rather give their business (and money) to an expert. If they didn't need an expert, they wouldn't really need anyone to assist them at all, would they?

Let's assume that you offer a product or service which you wholeheartedly believe in and it also provides great value to the client, both elements that are crucial to your success. All you need now is to add expert service to really expand your potential.

HOW DO YOU BECOME AN EXPERT?
HERE ARE 7 WAYS.

1. PRODUCT-IVITY

If you take your career seriously, you must know your products and services inside and out. Yes, this may take time and you may not always get sufficient training from your superiors. But by learning everything about your product or service you'll spare yourself frustration, feelings of inferiority, discouragement and lost business. Take a little time every day to learn about your industry. The morning paper can wait – your career cannot.

2. BRING IT ON.

Most every business always has some form of competition, so if a potential client asks you how your product or service stacks up against the other guy and you don't know the answer, guess what? They'll go to your competition to find out for themselves, and if they run into an expert there, you've probably lost that client's business to somebody who's better than you.

3. GETTING TO KNOW YOU.

You must know your clients. Learn their needs, their wants, their problems, and their budgets. That's the only way you'll be able to serve them properly. When you research the etymology of the word "client," you get an incredible understanding of how important your role is when dealing with customers. The basic understanding is "one who leans on another for protection." So it's literally your job and your responsibility to take care of customers and guide them toward making the right decision. You will protect them from bad products, higher prices, and unscrupulous sales people - you know, the ones with those really tacky ties. And think about this from the client's perspective, if you were *your* client, would YOU buy from YOU?

4. ASK – DON'T TELL.

This may sound obvious but don't tell a client what you can do for them. Ask them what they need you to do. Humans are conditioned to respond to questions, so one key to providing better service is to simply ask your client what their needs are. You must have heard someone say "It was nice talking to you". But have you ever heard someone say, "It was nice *listening* to you?" People want to be heard and acknowledged, and we can acknowledge clients by asking them questions. Another benefit to asking questions is if you ask people what they want and confirm it with them before proceeding, the client will feel confident that you are trying to find the right solution for them. This will maintain their desire to buy.

5. SHUT UP!

Listening is positioning. After you ask a question, be quiet. When you stop talking and start listening to your client, they will tell you everything you need to know in order to help them. I often jokingly say, "anything a client says can and will be held against them at the close." Secondly, shutting up also means not talking too much. Telling is not selling. Don't talk for 5 minutes straight; interact with the client instead. Think dialogue; not monologue. Think engaged or they'll be thinking divorce. Finally, don't talk when it's decision time. Instead, when you make your offer or close the sale be quiet and wait for your client to respond. It may feel uncomfortable at first, but just sweat it out, let them speak and then determine what your next move is.

6. KISS YOUR CLIENTS.

You've probably heard the expression – Keep It Simple, Stupid. I think that's dated and there's no need to add an insult just to make a point, so I've created another KISS acronym. "Keep Interest, Sell Simply." You cannot overwhelm a client with technical terms because it could actually interfere with their ability to make a decision. Just because you understand it, doesn't mean that they will. Have you ever had a doctor, attorney, or mechanic blurt out a bunch of technical jargon that leaves you wondering what the heck it means in English? Just explain the benefits in layman's terms. Overloading your clients with facts they don't need to know or want to know gives them a perfect excuse to "think about it," and we know what happens then, don't we? You can usually kiss that sale goodbye.

7. HELP!

Your customer is seeking help, so you may want to take a lesson from a "customer service" department. What happens when you call customer service with a problem and that person doesn't acknowledge your situation? You get even more frustrated, right? You aren't being listened to and they don't really seem to care about your problem. But what happens when you find a courteous, caring representative who takes the time to listen, understand the problem and work with you to fix it? You can't thank them enough. Sadly, the reason we appreciate them so much is because we've become accustomed to bad service, day in and day out. We're so used to people who don't get it, don't care, and won't help, that when we actually find a responsive professional, it's a significant event.

Use these 7 methods to become a true expert. Scripture says: *"give, and it shall be given to you. For whatever measure you deal out to others, it will be dealt to you in return."* It's sowing and reaping. So again, your reward, whether it's your income, a bonus, or otherwise, is equal to your service. And if you're an expert at what you do, you'll keep your job, get more referrals, receive testimonials, get a raise, maintain a successful business or get a promotion.

I urge you to continue your growth once you finish this book. What can you do to better serve your customers? What are your weaknesses? Figure out exactly what's necessary for you to have a more successful career and then take action today and open the door to closing more business!

ABOUT ROB

Rob Liano, the Rock Star Sales Trainer ™ is a published author and nationally renowned sales coach whose most recent accomplishments have been in the insurance field. Rob led two agencies to Top Producer status within 45 days, he was the featured speaker on the Success and Marketing Tour where his sessions: Objection Overruled and One Call Closing brought the house down. He also launched his own insurance agency in the midst of the recession and became a multi-million dollar producer within just a few months.

Rob has forged new techniques to create an innovative and non-failing system of selling. His effectiveness is not a secret and he wishes to share it with the world, whether on stage or a single phone call. Once you realize that in this technological era of instant gratification, many 'old school' techniques just don't cut it any more, you'll realize that Rob Liano's modern, cutting edge, easy to implement sales insights will simplify your sales life and take your career to the next level!

Contact Rob Liano today to bring Rock Star Sales Training ™ to a theater near you and start to enjoy the accolades that you deserve, because you have nothing to lose . . . except sales.

And don't forget to get your free copy of Rob's "7 Deadly Sales Sins" by visiting: www.rockstarsalestraining.com or call 1-888-379-8315

.

CHAPTER 25

WHO DO YOU NEED TO BE?

BY SALLY RAINBOW-OCKWELL

When I was younger, I was fortunate enough to work for a number of great entrepreneurs. They had built fantastic businesses from the ground up, and taken them to Stock Market listings. I joined these businesses during key stages of their growth, often as the very first IT Director the business had appointed. Exciting times – with charismatic and passionate leaders who were focussed on the next stage of growth.

Sounds great, huh? Well, what if I told you that none of these entrepreneurs was in control of their business within 2-3 years after our story began. Well, that's OK, you may say – they might have planned this, sold out for millions and gone on to live the jet-set lifestyle or create new businesses.

Well, rest assured, they are doing fine – but they're not where they really wanted to be. They're not leading their brainchild to even greater success. So they didn't maximise the huge potential.

Make no mistake, these are great men – but they could have been even greater. So, what held them back? I've pondered this question for many years – and as a Business Coach, it's a key question for many of my clients.

You see, these great men actually followed the "text book" program.

As their businesses grew, they brought on board key individuals with the skills and experience they lacked. So far, so good? Well, no actually! It's all very well having the right people, but you need to trust them, delegate effectively and inspire them to greater things. Hmm…. that's not quite so easy when you're a control freak, as many successful entrepreneurs are. So, to get it right, YOU actually need to change. Of course you still need to get the right people with the right skills, but unless YOU change to suit the stage of growth of your business, you won't get the best from them.

As a Business Coach, I work with my business owner clients on 3 key areas:

- Skills transfer – helping them and their team to gain new skills
- Accountability – Keeping them focussed on achieving the goals they set
- Mindset – how to BE the owner of the business of their dreams

The most important of these is Mindset. After all, the owner sets the tone for the team. If they aren't BEing the owner of a £50m revenue business, then the team won't **get** the business to £50m revenue.

OK, so what are these key behaviours? Well it all depends what stage your business is at. You need to recognize this and make the changes accordingly. Let's take a look at the key stages in a business and who you need to BE in order to be successful at that stage.

1. **Start-up**

    This calls for you to be the Visionary Entrepreneur, a Risk-Taker, a Passionate Workaholic. Above everything else you need to eat, sleep (sorry, did I say 'sleep'…forget that one!), drink and breathe *The Brand*. In short, **you need to BE The Brand!**

2. **Growth**

    Wow! This is exciting isn't it? Now you need to BE an Inspiring Leader, a Brilliant Networker & Influencer, still a Risk-Taker, and a Market Eagle – creatively seeking out new markets and new opportunities. That last bit sounds a bit like being the Captain of the Starship Enterprise doesn't it?! That's no coincidence – if you imagine you're Captain

Janeway with her crew stranded in the Delta quadrant, you'll BE the right person! The crew just **knew** she would get them home. Her drive and determination, together with her ability to take calculated risks, not to mention seeking out the new opportunities, made her a fantastic leader in this context.

3. Streamlining – maximising Profit

Whoa there! Time to steady the horses. It's no use being Janeway at this stage – or even worse, Captain Kirk! Being Captain Kirk at Stage 1 though would be great! This is the toughest time for most Entrepreneurs, and because of that, it's the time when most businesses either fail or get sold. If they do get sold, they've usually started to fail a little first too, so they're rarely sold for the best price.

If you don't master the changes in who you need to BE at this stage – guess what? You're leaving all the juicy morsels on the table for someone else to grab. Why would you **do** that? You've done all the hard work – why should they get all the benefits for so little effort? In case that didn't sink in, I'll say it again FOR SO LITTLE EFFORT. This stage isn't about working hard, it's about working smart. It's about you getting outside your comfort zone and BEing some of those people you secretly don't respect. Yes, it's time to bring out your inner Accountant. You see I know he's in there somewhere. He's the guy who helped you set up the business 'on a wing and a prayer' in the first place, keeping costs low at the start and watching every penny. It's time for him to wake up again and start paying attention to the details – of the numbers, processes and people. Think Mr Spock, Dr McCoy, Scotty! That doesn't mean you need to DO this stuff – heck no, that'd be a crazy use of your time! What it **does** mean is that you have to WANT it to get done and you have to make sure it gets done properly.

The good news is that this stage also needs a couple of things you're probably great at. Get *Creative* with thinking, "how can we do this better?" Play *'hard-ball'* with your suppliers to get the best prices. Get *Confident* and put your prices up. You can do all that stuff, right? Well you **could**, I know, but what about all those great people you recruited? How many of their ideas have you asked for? This is the time to reach out to the team and to motivate and reward them. It's about fully engaging with them, and BEing the Coach and Mentor, so that they become the best that they can be. It's a bit like raising a child to be a great adult – I know it's frustrating that they aren't YOU, but that's OK! With the right mix of people, and everyone BEing the best they can be, the sky's the limit.

4. Changing direction

So, you've got a thriving business selling video players. Then some bright spark invents the DVD. Did you see it coming? Were you keeping abreast of all the changes in your industry? Do you already have a key partnership to start distributing the new players? Well let's hope so, or else you'll be playing catch-up – or, even worse, you'll be out of business. Keeping ahead of the curve is critical – so do you even know where the curve is?-!-!

The good news is that this stage needs you to BE a lot of the people who helped create the great business in the first place – as well as a few you became along the way. Start reading and researching – BE Curious. Let your Creative side run free and welcome back the Risk Taker. What new products/services could you provide? What new Partnerships should you be forging?

Keep a little of the Accountant present though. Ask him to see what you don't see and ask the questions you don't ask – "What are the changes we need to make internally to survive and thrive?"

5. Moving on

I ask all my new clients a question which surprises them - "When will you be finished with this business?" Since most people start their business just as a JOB, to avoid working for someone else, that question 'kinda' throws them off balance a bit!

It's a fact though – at some stage you **will** finish. You could sell the business to a stranger or through a Management Buy-out, you could hand it down to your children and retire......or if you carry on, at some point it will go to your children when you die. Whatever happens, at some point you **will** finish. So, who do you need to BE at that stage?

(a). Handing over

Whether you're handing over to a family member or an existing manager, you'll need to BE the same – a great Coach and Mentor. This is like being a parent to young adults. Being Calm, Considered and Wise without interfering is tricky. I <u>know</u> you can see all the mistakes they're about to make! Sometimes if it's really serious, you may have to step in. Most times, you just need to offer your help, give it if it's wanted, and be there with help and support if it doesn't work out.

(b). Selling

Selling sounds a lot easier than handing over, doesn't it? After all, you don't have to pick up the pieces! Well, maybe – but the bad news is that unless you've done some form of handover, you won't get the best price when you <u>do</u> sell. So you really need to go through that stage first. Otherwise, if we take you out of the equation, then "Poof" ....the business doesn't work so well, so it's not worth so much.

OK, so you've been through the handing over stage. Now's the time to BE the Seller. That means BEing an Expert in your market – as it is now and how it will be in the coming years. It also means BEing an expert Negotiator and Innovative Deal Maker. That way, you'll find the best buyer and get the best deal.

So that's all there is to it!

If a business stayed the same throughout its life, it would be easy. My mother always said that she wished that her children had stayed under the age of 12 all their lives. She loved that time with us, but hated the teenage and young adult years. Many business owners feel the same way about their businesses – but it doesn't have to be that way. In order to get the best out of a business or a child – what if we recognised that **our role** needs to change as it grows? What if we understood and embraced the PURPOSE of our role – which is to create a separate and sustainable new 'life'? What if we wanted to be sure that new 'life' had purpose and direction, and delivered value to all who encountered it? If we approached the stages of our business like that, then we'd know that in order for the business to change, first **we** must change.

> *"If you do what you've always done,*
> *you'll get what you've always got."*

Awareness is the first step in any change – think about which stage your business is at and who you are BEing. Does it fit? What's the gap? Some people are very self-aware and can spot the changes that are needed. Others need help from a friend, mentor or coach. If you need that help, make sure you get it. Ask for feedback and listen to it!

Once you're aware of the gaps, how do you fix them? First start learning – read books, listen to CD's, attend seminars. Learn from the very best experts in that field. Then start **applying** your learning. Until that point there will be no change. The ancient Chinese proverb says "To know and not to do is not yet to know." So take some action! Make a few mistakes. Change the strategy a bit and try again. Take some more action.

It's tough to do all this on your own. All top sports people know this – which is why they all have coaches. Someone who keeps them outside their comfort zone and helps them to BE the performer they dream they can be. Business owners need one too – someone who gets them to BE the very best they can BE.

So, who's your coach?

ABOUT SALLY

Sally is a Global Award-winning ActionCoach Business Coach – and her results speak for themselves. Her clients have achieved increases in profits of up to 600%.

Sally has over 30 years of business experience in Distribution, Information Technology, Customer Service and Process Management. She has worked with all sizes of businesses, from large multi-nationals to small owner-managed businesses. She has delivered cost-saving process changes to increase profits by over £1m pa and has coached teams of up to 100 people. In addition to her Coaching business, Sally has been the Finance Director of another successful company. She has a unique ability to identify opportunities for improvement and to develop action plans to deliver results.

Sally's expertise includes marketing, sales, financial management, strategic leadership, recruitment and team planning.

To learn more, receive your free Business Growth tools, or to book your FREE Business Growth consultation, visit: www.actioncoach.com/sallyrainbow-ockwell or call **0044 (0)1793 783715**

Because being in business should give you more life!

CHAPTER 26

THE TWO WORST MISTAKES IN A RECESSION

BY MICHAEL JOYCE

When Brian told me the title of this new book would be COUN-TER ATTACK, I couldn't help but be reminded of the four years I spent in military school, and all the time we spent studying successful battle tactics, including counter attacks.

Counter attacks were always more successful when they were not expected by the enemy, and I think in today's economy, it is safe for you to assume that your key competitors are expecting anything and everything from you. Hopefully you in turn have your organization on "High Alert" to respond to any sudden shifts or movements by your competitors. At the end of this battle, there will be some real winners and real losers, and the decisions you make over the next 12 months will probably determine which side of that coin you are on.

At the end of the day, it's possible that your best counterattack opportunities will be within your own organization, analyzing the problems you have now, and assessing how many of those problems you are facing have your fingerprints all over them. Your best ROI will probably come from attacking there first, before committing your limited man-

225

power and resources to any external objectives.

The reality is that some businesses today are dealing with a recession, having dropped 20% or 30% in revenues, and are no longer able to make a profit, while other companies are operating in the midst of a full blown depression having lost 60%, 80% or 100% of their revenues. Those companies are hemorrhaging cash every month, as the owners frantically try to decide whether to just shut down their company, or commit all their cash reserves and try to fight their way through.

The wide gap between those two scenarios reminds me of the old joke, "What's the difference between a recession and a depression?" ...to which the answer is, "A recession is when you neighbor loses his job and a depression is when you lose your job."

One of the laws of nature is that for every action there is an equal and opposite reaction, and hopefully that law will apply in the case of this unprecedented financial downturn. I believe that it will, and that's the positive ray of hope I think we are all banking on, as we make critical decisions every day to get through this mess.

The bad news is that the clouds ahead look really bumpy and a lot of smart people say this is not going to be anything like a normal V-shaped recession. One of the great financial minds of our generation is California based Dr. Mohamed El-Erian, CEO of global investment powerhouse PIMCO. He advised all his clients that this unending cycle of uncertainty and flare-ups in countries around the world, including the United States, is the new normal, and that this cycle of upheaval will probably be with us for five years. Not exactly good news for a lot of us, and safe to say, this is definitely not your father's recession.

I have always been fascinated by what caused some great companies to fail during major recessions. Some even had strong brands with growth histories, and yet, when hard times came, they seemed to have made fatal mistakes. I believe we can often learn more about how to survive difficult times by analyzing those kinds of case studies, than we will by studying what successful companies did to get through a downturn.

I have a list of what I jokingly call "The Seven Cardinal Sins" that seem to cause most companies to go under during steep recessions. However, I'll focus today only on my top two picks, because after any fiscal au-

226

topsy they are always listed as the number one or two cause of death.

1. RUNNING OUT OF MONEY

Of all the sins to commit during a steep recession, running out of cash is the absolute worst because it is always fatal. Interestingly enough, those companies that failed almost always had a previous history of running out of cash, only to be rescued by banks or investors at the last moment, except of course for the last time.

Forty years ago, I was in the midst of my first major financial crisis; and Edward Rosen, who ran the RCA and Whirlpool distributorship based in Philadelphia, was acting as my mentor. He told me to bring all my financial data down from New York and he would see what he could do, to help me. Eddie's first and only request was, "Let me see your cash flow projections for the next twelve months." I explained that I had brought current P&L statements, an updated balance sheet, sales projections, inventory statements, payables, and receivables, but I did not have an accurate cash flow projection. He looked stunned and told me something that day that I never forgot. He said, "Always remember one thing Mike - a lousy business with great cash flow can survive indefinitely, but a great business with lousy cash flow will go under regardless of what all those financial statements in your hand say."

I notice that Wall Street analysts frequently identify a certain company as being a great takeover target because they are sitting on millions or billions in cash. Even in privately held companies, it can be pretty heady stuff to look at your cash on hand and think of all the brilliant moves you could make with that money - expansions, acquisitions, and new ventures, all of them great ideas accompanied by dazzling "cocktail math" projections to support the investments.

The reality is your cash should always be segregated into two accounts – emergency cash reserves and available cash. In my own business I know that in a steep V-shaped recession we will need two full years of operating capital to get through it. In your business what is the absolute worst case scenario you can envision? How much cash do you think you will need to get through it? Now double that figure and you are probably close to what you will actually need.

What I finally had to do in my own business to avoid those overpowering temptations to invest the money was to take the emergency cash reserves off the table completely, and make it disappear. That cash does not show on our operating statements anymore, and in fact, we don't even keep it in our main bank. I find that for me, using the "out of sight out of mind" technique works well, in the same way that setting my watch ahead fifteen minutes keeps me on schedule throughout the day.

Managing cash for the long term interests of the business is probably your single most important job as a CEO in my opinion. Look at how many times the fastest car on a NASCAR track mismanaged their fuel just a little bit and not only failed to win, but did not even cross the finish line. In business, if you want to win you have to first finish the race, and to do that you need enough cash on hand to power your company through the down cycles that <u>always</u> come after boom times. When things are going really well in your company, and you begin to think this euphoria will never end – get ready, it's just around the corner.

2. RUNNING OUT OF TIME

One of the toughest decisions any airline pilot will ever have to make during his career is deciding when to give up trying to keep the plane in the air, and instead prepare for a controlled crash landing. If he hesitates too long, he knows that option will disappear quite suddenly, and it is the fatal mistake usually made by 'low time' pilots with little or no experience.

In reality, you never know when all the alarms will suddenly go off in your business and the gauges will all begin to signal imminent disaster. In commercial aviation the entire crew is trained to evaluate a whole series of life or death options in a matter of seconds and then pick the best option. For the pilots, they do this in a simulator, so that both the pilot and copilot can get comfortable with being in those alarming situations and make their mistakes in a training session instead of in the air, so that when that rare and always unexpected emergency does appear, their recurrent training and cockpit experience help them to avoid making any fatal mistakes.

In business we tend not to talk about business disasters, as if just bringing up the subject might be contagious, and anyone on our team who does keep broaching this subject is usually labeled "negative" and gradually weeded out of future executive meetings. Instead, we are conditioned to studying success strategies, reminding each other to stay positive at all costs.

Andy Gove, the former CEO of Intel, told a great story of how his company was riding high in the world of computer chips enjoying total dominance of the industry in their niche. It seemed the company could do no wrong and just went from one incredible success to another. And then, without any warning, a Japanese company showed up in the marketplace with a new super chip that ran circles around their best selling product and the entire industry could see that Intel had been blindsided. Questions about their future began to surface and many said that Intel's days of glory were behind it.

The story of how Intel managed to hang onto their key accounts and work their way out of this near death experience was a great success story in itself and made for interesting reading, but what really struck me was that Gove was burned so badly by this event that he made the decision to never let it happen again. He set up a department inside of Intel whose sole mission was to figure out how to put Intel out of business. They examined every aspect of Intel - strengths, weaknesses, the products, the competition, and they even talked to Intel's customers looking for that one crack in the wall that might allow a competitor to break through the Intel defenses and deliver a fatal blow.

Instead, most of the companies I looked at had no real Plan B, or even worse, failed to make the decision to switch to Plan B soon enough. They kept hoping they could power through the downturn using their old tried-and-true techniques. When they went out of business, the frustration of everyone involved was extremely high, because all the facts and figures confirmed the company was finally heading in the right direction, they just ran out of time.

Have you seriously thought about exactly when you would make the decision to switch to your Plan B, assuming you even have one? Is it written down on paper? Are others in your company aware of it and in agreement with your benchmarks so that if you hesitate to pull the trigger they can, like a great co-pilot, warn you that the critical numbers say you have reached the point of no return?

I have a sign in my office that reads, "The secret to success in life depends on how well you handle Plan B" and in today's volatile world I think that is more true than ever.

CONCLUSION

Am I a pessimist? Of course not, only a tried and true optimist could be in the marine industry for over forty years and succeed. The future will always be better that the past, and it always has been since the beginning of recorded history.

After the Bay of Pigs Invasion fiasco in Cuba back in the 1960's President John F. Kennedy wryly observed, "Success has many fathers, but failure is an orphan." My only advice to you is if you want to avoid being blindsided, keep one eye on failure and you'll be a lot better prepared when all the alarms suddenly go off in your business.

ABOUT MICHAEL

Michael Joyce
Chairman / Chief Executive
Hargrave Custom Yachts, Inc. / Fort Lauderdale, Florida

Born in Philadelphia and raised in Haddonfield and Spring Lake, N.J., Mike and his wife Jan currently reside in Ft. Lauderdale, Florida along with their five dogs and enjoy spending their summers on a small island in the 1,000 Islands region in Ontario, Canada.

Career Overview - He began his business career in the music industry in the 1960's when he signed a recording contract with MGM Records and went on to produce records for RCA, Cameo Parkway, and Diamond Records. In 1969 he owned and operated a New York based marina and service operation before moving to Florida in 1977 to work for legendary yacht designer Jack Hargrave in West Palm Beach. In 1981 he opened a yacht importing business in Fort Lauderdale, distributing several leading brands of yachts before returning to take over the Hargrave Company in 1997 upon the death of the founder. Since taking over the company he has led Hargrave to become the number one builder of custom yachts in the 70'-135' size range in the US market.

Education - Attended St. Francis Prep in Spring Grove, Pa.; Bordentown Military Institute in Bordentown, N.J.; and Temple University in Philadelphia, Pa. where he majored in English. He is a graduate of the Dale Carnegie Course, Dale Carnegie Sales Program, and numerous American Management Association programs.

Service Organizations – Past Director of Rotary Club, Ft. Lauderdale, Past Director of Florida Yacht Brokers Association, Marine Industries of South Florida, Aircraft Owners & Pilots Association.

Charitable Activities – Supports numerous local and regional charities including the Humane Society of Broward Country, Jason Taylor Foundation, Love Thy Neighbor Homeless Feeding Program, Salvation Army, Ft. Lauderdale; Crystal Cathedral, Garden Grove, California.

Clubs and Associations – Ocean Reef Club, Key Largo, Florida; Coral Ridge Yacht Club, Ft. Lauderdale; Antique & Classic Boat Society and Antique Boat Museum, Clayton, New York.

Michael Joyce
mjoyce@hargrave.org

CHAPTER 27

BUSINESS STRATEGIES FOR EXPLOSIVE GROWTH IN THE NEW ECONOMY

BY TAMMY HOLYFIELD

STRATEGIC LEADERSHIP

T ime was running out as the vast enemy approached from the other side of the sea. Fear and terror tried to overwhelm the people with thoughts and feelings of hopelessness. Alarmed by the report, King Jehoshaphat resolved to seek the Lord as he proclaimed a fast for all Judah. A nation came together to face disaster, seemingly paralyzed by the impasse with no battle plan or obvious escape. As they assembled at the temple, Jehoshaphat stood up and said, "O LORD, God of our fathers, are you not the God who is in heaven? You rule over all the kingdoms of the nations. Power and might are in your hand, and no one can withstand you." He continued to cry out to God, recounting past victories, praising God and asking for help. He said, "For we have no power to face this vast army attacking us. We do not know what to do, but our eyes are upon you."

As a country, an organization or individually, all of us at some point experience seemingly overwhelming circumstances. It may look like you are surrounded and facing opposition from every angle – with no way out. As our nation faced a huge economic downturn, corporate scandals, terrorist threats, moral failure and fear dominating the media, our organization begin to experience the effects of the less-than-favorable market place. Like the people of Judah, our environment was plagued with rumors of hopelessness. There were many opinions, great ideas and strategic plans to launch our counter-attack, but one of the greatest drivers to victory was when I humbled myself and asked God for help. Similar to the words of King Jehoshaphat, I pleaded with God, saying, "I have tried everything and I don't know what else to do, but my eyes are upon you." Trusting in God and following His Spirit-inspired strategy gave us the confidence to refuse to accept defeat.

"True faith believes only one outcome – We Win!"
~ *Tammy Holyfield*

I believe the greatest strategy for explosive growth and success is the relentless determination to overcome life's challenges. As leaders, we have a great responsibility not only to create vision, but to communicate that vision in a manner that will inspire those around us into profitable action that produces sustainable results. Here are the nine essentials of strategic leadership that lead us to explosive results:

"Success is a process that equals profitable action producing sustainable results."

#1 CHANGE YOUR ANGLE AND INCREASE YOUR VISION

The sun is always shinning. That was a revelation to me. That's like saying opportunity is always available. It depends on where you are as to what you can see. Think of when an aircraft ascends, there is only so much you can see from the ground, but as you change your position of altitude there is an increase in ability to see from a new perspective. There are opportunities all around us, but when we are 'flat on our face' wallowing in the status of current conditions we can fail to see the possibilities. I have heard it said, "Change your angle and create your vision from a place of victory." Instead of dwelling on where we are or even on how to get out… try changing your angle and increasing your vision.

"Knowledge of what is possible is the beginning of success!"
~ Anonymous

#2 CONNECT YOUR VISION TO A GREATER PURPOSE AND CORE VALUES

Why continue? What keeps you in the game when it gets tough? Connecting your vision to a greater purpose will inspire and encourage you not to give up. I have found it takes a greater purpose than money to motivate during times of extreme challenge… it takes a mission being connected to core values.

For example, take Coca-Cola's corporate mission…

OUR MISSION

Our Roadmap starts with our mission, which is enduring. It declares our purpose as a company and serves as the standard against which we weigh our actions and decisions.

- To refresh the world...
- To inspire moments of optimism and happiness...
- To create value and make a difference.

P&G states this purpose: "We will provide branded products and services of superior quality and value that improve the lives of the world's consumers, now and for generations to come. As a result, consumers will reward us with leadership sales, profit and value creation, allowing our people, our shareholders and the communities in which we live and work to prosper."

In each instance, the company is built around its mission, purpose and core values. Changes in the market and the economy – as well as lucrative business opportunities – can complicate the ability of an organization to stay true to its identity. A solid connection to a greater purpose and core values sounds as a battle cry, bringing unity to all levels of an organization.

"Without vision the people perish."
~ Proverb

235

#3 COMMUNICATE THE VISION… CLEAR AND SIMPLE

Here is the truth, when we gathered our entire organization in one room to unveil the strategies and brilliant plans we had spent the last 60 days and sleepless nights to create, only about half even heard what we said. The other half was dialed into and focused on their own work, the endless whirlwind of e-mails, voice mails and everyday stuff.

Gallup Poll did a survey and asked 1.4 million people if they knew the goals of their company. The results were eye opening, less than 30% polled even knew what the goals were. I used to think I was over-communicating until I heard a member of our staff explaining to another a policy that I had communicated at a meeting. I was shocked and amazed as I heard a version of what I said and it wasn't at all what I said. It is vitally important to communicate in a way that is clear and simple.

I recently read a story about Roberto Goizueta, the former CEO of Coca-Cola. Roberto's success was attributed to his strategic leadership and the way he shared vision. He said, "Each of the six billion people on this planet consumes on average sixty-four ounces of fluids daily, of which only two ounces are Coca-Cola." Closing the sixty-two ounce gap became the centerpiece of inspiration and motivation within the company. Simple message, extraordinary results.

#4 TRANSLATE THE VISION INTO DAILY ACTION

Some people are often paralyzed by the scope of the corporate vision and that's why we need to translate or break it down into daily action. Translation is the ART of KNOWING YOUR PART. Making sure everyone knows how their efforts, each department, and the individual/area goals make the corporate goals reachable. Possibly the most powerful question we ask is this… "What are we doing this week, in the next seven days, to move the overall corporate goals forward?"

#5 EXECUTION

I like the saying, "Honey Bees get praised while mosquitoes get swatted." It is easy to look busy but what is actually being produced is a good question. Often the missing link between plans and results is execution. Strategy cannot be effectively planned without taking into account how to execute. Surprisingly the inability to execute is common in organizations of all sizes. We get side tracked with the day-to-day activities and miss the strategic mark. Or on the other end of the scale, there are those high level thinkers who are not interested in the "how" of getting things done. There is a balance between strategic thinking and execution of results.

According to Dun and Bradstreet, businesses in America fail due to lack of execution of the most important goals. We need to work toward the "right goals" that net the "right results".

As we grow in our leadership skills it is important to develop our instinct for execution, not only to see the big picture, but also to think through step-by-step what needs to happen to hit the mark. Unfortunately that instinct has not been cultivated in many organizations. For example, when leaders are detached from subordinates their expectations may tend to be unrealistic. Leaders may not think to involve them with the plan of execution. As a result they are not equipped to deal with unexpected issues, and strategies commonly fail. The solution is to establish a culture of execution that includes communication and accountability at all levels. Execution produces results when it is woven into the business. It becomes the driving force of the reward system and becomes the behavior that is practiced.

In the New York Times Bestseller, *Execution*, by Larry Bossidy and Ram Charan, they define execution as a systematic process of rigorously discussing "hows" and "whats", questioning, tenaciously following through, and ensuring accountability.

Creating an Execution Culture involves alignment. Alignment is essential to creating the framework for execution. It is the ability to clearly define priorities to maximize results as well as inter-relate people, strategy and operations. Some organizations have no idea if what they do day-to-day are the activities that really drive the bottom line in a positive way. These companies are gambling with their future prosperity. Long term success comes from alignment of realistic goals and priorities, as well as having the right people doing the right job.

#6 KEEP SCORE

Are we there yet? We need to keep track of where we are and how far to the GOAL line. Knowing how we are doing gives us renewed energy to press on. Have you ever seen a group of people on a basketball court or a football field? You can tell by the level of intensity if they are playing for fun or keeping score? The same holds true in business. Our organization has developed a two-week goal status reporting process that is our scoreboard, as well as our performance evaluation process, that aligns rewards with the execution of highest priorities.

#7 DEVELOP A CONTINUOUS IMPROVEMENT CULTURE

We are better than me, is a recipe for success. The result of this collaborative culture is a source of competitive advantage. It creates a place that is constantly improving and inspiring ordinary people to do extraordinary things.

When your people are collaborating and learning together, they are constantly discovering new ways to exceed expectations, new ways to develop products and services, and new ways to deliver those products and services.

In an annual survey, it has been established that the world's elite organizations share one thing: corporate cultures that value people and how they learn. These companies don't just claim they care about the development of their people, they behave that way. They offer world-class, intensive leadership and development programs that bridge the knowledge gap and align with the organizations highest strategic goals. These organizations balance the value of people and the importance of financial results.

#8 BE ACCOUNTABLE TO SOMEONE... NEVER COMPROMISE CHARACTER!

Every good leader needs a leader! Accountability works because it relies on one of the most powerful forces in the world: the power of the social contract and commitment. We try harder to keep goals and objectives when we have shared them with others. This increases the execution factor as you allow a trusted advisor to reveal any blind-spots. There must also be a healthy, transparent and trusting environment in which we hold each other accountable within the organization for honoring our commitments and keeping our promises.

"Your talent will never take you where your character can't keep you!"

In Stephen M.R. Covey's book "The Speed of Trust" he says, "There is one thing that changes everything. That one thing is common to every individual, relationship, team, family, organization, economy and civilization throughout the world – one thing if removed, will destroy the most powerful government, the most successful business, the most thriving economy, the most influential leadership, the strongest character, the deepest love. On the other hand, if developed and leveraged, that one thing has the potential to create unparalleled success and prosperity in every dimension of life. That one thing is – TRUST." It is true there is a speed in every area that directly equates to how much we trust each other. Be accountable and develop great character and you will experience new levels of success!

#9 GIVE THANKS AND CELEBRATE SUCCESS!

A great weapon of warfare is the ability to give thanks in the middle of the battle. That was the key to King Jehoshaphat's victory. King Jehoshaphat and the people of Judah walked away winning a battle they never had to fight. Not to mention it took them three days to collect all the wealth that was transferred to them. Giving thanks and celebrating success unites people and inspires greatness.

In conclusion, strategic leadership and business strategies are essential to explosive growth and organizational success, but it doesn't have to be so complex that it gets left out of our day-to-day operations. It is not something that is done once a year and the two inch thick document gets tucked away in a desk drawer. If executed with excellence, strategic planning and thinking becomes a culture that improves communication and clarifies direction, while establishing a common and shared vision for the organization to pursue. Keeping it simple, communicating and translating the plan into daily action, developing your character and giving thanks… *that's where the power lives.*

ABOUT TAMMY

TAMMY HOLYFIELD, CEO/HOLYFIELD CONSULTING

Leadership Expert, Author and Speaker.

Tammy Holyfield is an accomplished professional speaker, leadership expert, author and consultant, on a mission to teach and inspire people to improve their everyday life!

Using the methods and principles she teaches, Tammy has overcome great obstacles. Her message is dynamic, encouraging people to succeed and inspiring them to act!

Holyfield began her professional career in marketing and served as the Director of Marketing for Summit Pet Product Distributors, the IAMs Pet Food (Proctor and Gamble) regional distribution center. Today, she is the founder and CEO of Holyfield Consulting, a personal and business development company. Holyfield Consulting specializes in organizational development, strategic planning, communication, building trust, strengthening teams, leadership development, increasing accountability and executing results. Each week she writes a column entitled "Ask the Coach"® which provides readers a fresh perspective on current challenges facing the business world.

Tammy addresses thousands of people each year from diverse Fortune 500 companies and has consulted, and trained entrepreneurs, CEO's, professionals and individuals from all walks of life. Her ideas are proven, practical and get results. And clients say that working with Tammy created an increase in moral, solidified corporate culture, and bridged the communication gap from vision to results. Her audiences and clients agree Tammy teaches techniques and strategies that are easy to understand, and, can be put to use immediately to achieve greater results in their lives and careers. Tammy and her family make their home in High Point, NC.

www.TammyHolyfield.com

CHAPTER 28

A SUCCESSFUL FRANCHISE STORY: ACTED LIKE A FRANCHISE FROM DAY ONE

BY MATTHEW E. ALLEYNE

My story starts when I was a teenager. I walked down the city streets in my home town, Christchurch in New Zealand, looking at outlets like KFC, McDonald, Pizza Hut, and Shell, and asked myself, how are they able to do this? They have outlets everywhere? I started dreaming of owning my own franchise system. I was so inspired by this puzzle that I started consciously and unconsciously gathering information about the companies. I think the one thing that was most impressive was the brand consistency through all the shops. I noticed this as one key to their success, and I wanted to do the same… make a global business success!

At 18, I opened my first "want-to-be" franchise system. It was a mobile car cleaning business. No big surprise, it was a failure almost from the start. It had no system, no structure and worst of all, only one franchisee… myself.

After this, I spent the next decade learning all aspects of business - sales, marketing, accounting, development, customer relations, right down to self-promotion, and much, much more.

In 1999, I once again tried to open a franchise concept, but after my partners got hold of it, the concept was changed. I was squeezed into accepting it as being a Multi Level Marketing (MLM) system and not a franchise concept. The company was an overnight success.

Even though I was on the wrong path, I learned a lot from dealing with many thousands of distributors, in particular how to be a great motivational leader. As with all small MLM systems, it died a natural death 3 years later.

Do you think I stopped there? No way!

The next 5 years I spent educating myself further and gathering as much practical knowledge as possible. Now I focused on systems, structure and franchising.

And guess what, it paid off! Now, together with my wife, I own and operate Norway's fastest growing furniture franchise chain, ROCKA. We have the lowest break-even turnover in the industry, and achieved brand name status in just 3 years. ROCKA as a brand name is well placed in the mid-upper part of the market. We do not want to compete with IKEA.

Based on my experience, I have created a 21 time-proven steps-to-success system. Here I will share the 3 steps that rate highest in my system. If you would like to learn the remaining 18 steps, make contact and I will willingly share these with you.

1. BRAND IDENTITY AND MARKETING PROFILE (BIMP)

One of the most important elements in this business is how you want to brand yourself. Where do you want to be positioned in the market place? How do you want to be seen by your customers? *Your brand is your self-image!*

To me, branding is more than just the brand name, slogan or company logo. It is the business concept wrapped up into one big package.

Here is a quick list of some very important things to think about when you are planning your brand and building your business.

- What is your company profile?
- What colors suit your business best?
- How do you want people to perceive your business?
- What is your Unique Selling Point – USP?
- Are my potential customers using similar products or services today?
- Is your product or service in a niche market you can capture?
- Why is your business better than your competitors?
- Who are your competitors?
- Who is your ideal customer?
- Where do your customers live?
- How does your customer dress?
- What is the age demographic of your customers?
- What are your customers' professions?
- What are your customers' income levels?

The above are just a few of many questions you need to ask yourself to identify your brand, and to help position yourself with the correct profile to the market place from 'day one'.

I really recommend that you write down on paper the answers to the questions above, and all your ideas and thoughts you have for your business. This will help you focus on where you are going, and also help you to find or decide on your company name and corporate profile.

Fake it before you make it! This is a very old and true saying. To be a successful franchise business, you need to be perceived as a franchise from day one.

I remember when we opened our very first small showroom to supplement our website, people were always asking me how many shops we had. I had to answer, "Just this one for now, but ...we have clients from all over Norway." I laughed and said *"we have showrooms in every customers home"*. This was actually correct, as we only sell products exposing our brand, which are unique and 'on the cutting edge'. We use our products as in-house marketing billboards, showing everyone who comes in contact with a ROCKA product what we offer and stand for.

To become successful, you need to be branding constantly and consistently. My ROCKA recipe includes having our logo printed on our products, brand tags sewn in seams on furniture, leaving a service sticker after delivery, and sending out a box of branded chocolates every holiday season. Our favorite giveaway is high hotel-quality towels with our name embossed and embroided at the ends.

Our customers' love these towels. I have even seen photos of customers on Facebook using them on the beach. My motto is: *Be positively remembered by your existing customers and seen by your future customers!*

Branding and profiling is a very complex and strategic part of your business. You can spend millions of dollars on this with limited results. Branding and marketing can be a bottomless pit for money if you are not careful.

I highly recommend you make contact with a company specializing in this area to help you meet your goals and budget. This is an ongoing process. Choose a company that you really enjoy working with, and who understands what you want to achieve. And who understands you.

#2. COMPANY NAME (CN- PRONOUNCED SEEN)

As they say, what's in a name… in fact **a lot**! Your company name is the single most important part of your company; a good name will make or break your company.

Create a name that has meaning to you, a name you can be proud of. This is like naming a child, you must live with the name and be proud every time you read your name and hear it spoken.

When deciding on a name, do not be short sighted. You must think of where you want to go with your company in 10, or even 20 years time.

If you are thinking about franchising, I suggest you use a name that can be easily associated with your product or service. My wife came up with a word used in daily slang language in Norway, "ROCKA".

In Norway this means; hip, cool, trendy, edgy and unique. The name does not inform our clients what our business sells. It simply informs them of our business concept instead. We sell the coolest, most edgy and unique furniture, and we market in the same hip way. Our unique name helps us get away with a lot more than our competitors - as people expect us being a bit *ROCKA*. When our customers promote us to their friends they ask, *"Do you have a ROCKA sofa at home? I do…"* instead of, where did you buy your sofa? This is a big difference when it comes to marketing and branding

The main point here is that *your name must be in alignment with your brand identity*. It needs to tell your customers who you are and what you are offering in a direct way.

The best and most successful company names are short and sweet. Your name needs to be easy to remember, easy to say and must roll off the tongue.

How does your name sound, speak it out loud a few times. If it is too hard to understand or say, people will forget it quickly. Opt for a catchy rhyming name. Two syllable words are highly recommended. Some famous brand names I really like are; Yahoo *yaa-hoo*, Mobil *mo-bil*, Facebook *face-book*, Google *goo-gull*.

The greatness with these brand names is they do not even tell you what they are selling or offering their customers. However, the branding of these names has been so successfully achieved that everyone knows who they are and what they stand for. *I'm lovin' it!*

Another key factor is *extendibility*. Can your name be used to promote other products or services as well?

Our name, for example, can be used for many new companies if we want, e.g., ROCKA Café, ROCKA Clothing, ROCKA Travel and Brand ROCKA. The options are endless. Keep these points in mind when deciding on your name, think BIG!

Before committing 100% to a company name, check it is also an available domain name. If the *.com* version is not available, go for your countries domain extension. If then your name is still not available, go for an alternative domain name that will work for you. Try adding your business service. For example you can add that to the end of your name, e.g. ROCKA + Furniture. If you search www.rockafurniture.com I am sure a domain name will be available for registration. This will also be good for Search Engine Optimization (SEO).

There are many great domain name providers online where you can search and investigate this. You can use any search engine to instantly find a provider. A professional domain company can also provide you with cost efficient web hosting for your upcoming website.

To conclude, do you need any help on the creative side to come up with the ultimate name for your company? Contact an advertising agency; alternatively you can make contact with me. I have created many great names for both companies and myself over the years.

3. COMPANY LOGO (CL)

Your company logo is the result of your company name and brand identity. Sketch your initial design idea on a piece of paper and then write down a description of what you want to incorporate in this logo. *Your logo must scream out your vision!*

When it comes to logo design there are literally millions of design possibilities. Thousands of companies out there can help you create this important asset.

Do yourself a big favor – Do not let your young kids design your logo, and neither should your local printing shop. I know it is great fun to have your family involved with this process, but it can backfire. Just think for yourself how many times you have seen homemade logos, thinking… ooh man! that was ugly and unprofessional. *Don't let people think this about you!*

Less is more, remember to keep the design simple, and use colors that match your brand identity. Do some research on the Internet about the meaning of colors. This is very interesting reading.

I have personally used knowledge about colors to create my own logos in the past. The correct use of colors will actually influence your customers' feelings, emotions, buying habits and cultural perception of you. It must not be forgotten that colors can be culturally dependent, for example black is normally associated with death, but in China it is white. I have read that McDonald's apparently uses red and yellow there because of the significance of red=fast and yellow=hunger (hence fast food!).

Once you have an idea of the message you want to communicate, make contact with a professional designer to create your logo. Ask for a minimum of 3 different designs. Do not accept any design until you are completely satisfied.

I recommend that once you have received the first samples, sit on them for a few days before answering the designer. You may initially get a *wow* feeling, but this can go away very quickly. Take your time. Alternatively, you can create the logo yourself as I did with ROCKA, as I had experience, knowledge and our business idea clear in my mind. The ROCKA logo has been a big success in our market. Check it out at www.MrROCKA.com and decide for yourself.

Once your logo has been created and you are 110% happy with the profile's look and feel, 'nail it down' and commit to it. If you feel the slightest regret related to the design, go back to the drawing board and start again. It is really hard to live with something that is your profile to the market if you are not satisfied. Do not set yourself up for any regrets. If you are not sure about the design, go into a shopping centre. Take a random survey of 50 people who fit your brand profile, and get them to rate the company logo from one to ten. Then analyze the results and make your final decision.

Apply for a trademark to protect your company logo immediately from copycats. Include TM on your logo design, this means Trademark and is free for all to use. TM also shows your customers that you are serious.

Most people do not know the difference between TM and ® Registered Trademark. You can read all about trademarks at WIPO, World Intellectual Property Organization.

I always try to protect my logos under text and logo classifications. It usually takes around 6 months for a registered trademark to be approved, if it is approved at all.

The big ®. Registering your company name has great financial value. Your customers and competitors see that you are a serious brand name. Owning a registered trademark is a financial asset that you can sell or even rent for royalties in the future. Contact your local trademark or patent attorney for help with registration. It is a cheap, inexpensive and easy process that later can become worth millions.

THE FIRST 3 STEPS OF A 21 STEP PROCESS

As mentioned earlier, the information I provided you with now just scratches the surface of the 21 steps I used to succeed in franchising. I am constantly learning and growing and changing my business tactics like a chameleon, to suit the ever-changing market.

My 21-step process is a living dynamic system under ongoing development and improvement. Your business will be the same. Be prepared for change, even expect it... then nothing that comes your way will surprise or deter you.

Feel free to contact me: Mr ROCKA, at anytime, if you would like to learn more about my franchise systems and my 21-step business process.

Take it all with you now; and my blessings for you to succeed!

ABOUT MATTHEW

Matthew E. Alleyne is nothing short of a serial entrepreneur. Born in New Zealand and currently residing in Norway. Mr. Alleyne these days is more often called Mr. ROCKA. Starting his first business venture at the age of 9, a pick and packing service for his mother's home party business; while she was out selling, he was at home fulfilling the orders.

Mr. Alleyne's relentless passion as a serial entrepreneur has thrived for over 20 years, resulting in many successful business ventures. Currently Matthew Alleyne is building, with his wife and soul mate Mrs. ROCKA, Siw- Helen, Norway's fastest growing furniture franchise, ROCKA Furniture. After successfully dominating the domestic market the aim is to expand this proven franchise business model into international markets. Interested in learning about the furniture business? Contact Matthew directly for more information.

When not growing ROCKA into Norway's top furniture franchise, Mr. Alleyne operates numerous other companies that are involved in production, distribution and sales. His constant hands-on approach, and total dedication to business have made him the revered businessman he is today.

When not operating his businesses Matthew enjoys sharing his vast business knowledge and life experience with others. To date Matthew Alleyne has mentored hundreds of people onto personal and business success.

"Serial Entrepreneur": the starter of successive companies who makes a living by starting up companies and operating them until they are competitive, then selling them.

For more information, you contact Matthew on email: matthew@mrrocka.com

www.MrROCKA.com

CHAPTER 29

THE MISSING LINK TO SOLVING YOUR CLIENT'S PROBLEMS:

SPEAKING THE LANGUAGE OF EVERY LEVEL IN A COMPANY

BY RON MORRIS

Today's sales mantra states that if you want to sell to a company, you have to understand how your product or service solves that company's problems. You have to then talk to the company in those terms and discuss solving their problems and reaching their goals. Selling into a company more than ever requires that a company sees you as a trusted consultant to be turned to for solutions.

But people selling in the trenches know that is not enough. Depending on who you are talking to in the company — the CEO, HR, procurement, middle manager, or project manager — you will find each of these people speak a different language and have unique priorities no matter what the stated company-wide goals are.

NO SINGLE DECISION MAKER CAN CREATE THE CONSULTATIVE RELATIONSHIP YOU WANT

The days of one top figure handing down a decision are long gone. In today's sales environment it is not possible to develop the consultative sales relationship you want by simply trying to find the decision maker and getting him to say "yes."

If you have a single message based on some company-wide goals set at the highest level, it is likely that at many levels of the company your message will not be heard and you will be seen as just another salesperson knocking at their door. If you want to be heard, you need to tailor your solution and consultative message to fit the job position of the person you are dealing with.

HOW DOES THIS HELP?

Leveraging the special needs and mindset of individuals within an organization according to their position can greatly increase your rapport. If you bring up issues — even company-wide directives — that arc not a primary concern for the person you are talking with, you will at best not capture his interest and at worst be dismissed as a one-tone salesperson.

This issue has increasingly become apparent in recent years, as salespeople attempt to implement the trend of speaking to a company's overall strategic goals when approaching a client. As an example, a top-notch salesperson under my direction had all the tools to sell. He knew his product well and knew his industry inside and out. He had formulated his own opinions on the industry and its direction in the future. He had Google alerts running for the companies he was interested in selling to, so he could understand and keep abreast of the company's direction and goals – which in this case were to strive for innovation and to move into new markets. He had researched company directives from press releases found on the net, so he knew what the CEO was emphasizing for the coming year, and the challenges the company faced.

However, when he approached the company, he was directed to a middle manager who had been tasked with evaluating vendors. This manager knew about the company goals, but was relatively uninterested in the CEO's call for innovation and new markets. He seemed distracted and curt as a deadline was looming for several projects under his care.

Later, my salesman ended up talking to a person in the procurement department. This person had never heard of the company wide directive, and simply told him to fill in an online form – which clearly was designed to root out the very lowest price.

My salesman then had a chance to meet one of the company's regional sales managers at a conference. This sales manager knew of the company directives, but was really only interested in the immediate sales performance of the team he managed.

In an ideal world, a company's key goals and initiatives would filter down into all positions to be acted on. But the reality is that most of these grand directives and yearly goals exist only as press releases and never trickle down in a real way to the rank and file. Even when staff are made aware of these company priorities, the immediate requirements and concerns of any particular worker's job supersedes grandiose directives for growth, creativity and innovation from above.

The solution we worked out for our salespeople was to first be aware of the necessity to appeal to the needs and problems of the specific job type we are contacting. Often these priorities conflict or supersede the company's, and the only way to get people to hear you is to understand their day-to-day problems and concerns.

THE DIFFERENT LEVELS IN A COMPANY

Each level in a company has a different language based on their goals, concerns, pressures, etc. It is essential that you to learn to talk on the appropriate level when approaching a person in a certain position. However, in all cases, the following applies:

- You should be talking in terms of how their problem or concern can be solved. It should never be about the features or characteristics of your company or the solutions and products you are trying to sell.
- An effective salesperson in today's marketplace has to know their products, services and industry as a whole — inside and out. The definition of what that means in practical terms is that you must have opinions about how things are now in

your industry and how they will go in the future. You have to know your competitors, the markets they appeal to and why, the strengths and weaknesses of their offerings and prospects for the future. This is perspective. Perspective on a situation is what defines an expert and makes people want to turn to you for opinions and solutions to solve their problems.

- You need people at all levels in your customer company contributing to your sale. In some cases while a person in a certain position may not be able to say "yes" to your product or service (such as a project manager), that person's opinion may be key to pushing your service toward approval. It is important that you can relate to him on his level.

CHIEF-LEVEL PEOPLE (CEO, COO, ETC.)

Chief-level people (CEO, COO, etc.) receive their goals and direction from the company's board of directors and shareholders. These are people focused on growing the business and returning value to the company owners.

That means they can be focused on a variety of high-level goals: developing growth strategies for the company as a whole, expanding into new markets, spearheading new initiatives, creating greater market share, being quicker to market, re-allocating company wide resources for new initiatives, profitability, return on investment, and creating an end game for company investors (mergers, sales, and acquisitions which allow investors to recoup their investment).

In times of financial distress, a "turnaround CEO" can be appointed – especially after money is pumped into a company with a strategy to get it out of economic difficulty. These turnaround CEOs can be focused on cost-cutting efforts or secret initiatives that make a company's books look better and improve cash positions for a merger or acquisition. They can be tasked with quickly expanding into new markets or finding new avenues for quick sales.

HOW TO APPROACH CHIEF-LEVEL PEOPLE

You have to know company priorities before meeting these people. Chief-level positions are all about looking at a company from a strategic perspective. You do not want to talk about process, the vagaries of production, or how your product or service does a specific task.

If you are pushing the specifics of your product or service to these people, you will be seen as offering a cost to the company and your ideas will be rejected. Instead you need to start thinking like CEOs and consider what it really takes to achieve their objectives. Understand the challenges they are facing and talk about the steps needed to solve them--keeping in mind that eventually your product or service will be an essential part of a solution.

The discussion has to be about what it takes for the company to fulfill the goals the CEO has set. It has to make the chief-level person appreciate the value of getting to market more quickly or effectively. Or the ways top-line or bottom-line growth can be achieved. Everything has to be in service of their goals and not about your product or service.

It is important to note that most career salespeople do not normally think in a chief-level way. They naturally become fixated on the details of their product or service or on the specifics of "getting the job done."

If you go to a chief-level person and talk about the specifics of your product you will be seen as merely a salesperson trying to get a "yes" decision from the ultimate decider. The most impactful thing that any salesperson can do is learn to shift gears and operate in the world of concern of the chief-level person.

MEETING CHIEF-LEVEL PEOPLE IS NOT THE GOAL

Considering how hard it is to reach chief-level people in the U.S., many think that getting to them is the primary goal as they are seen as the ultimate decision-makers. Nothing could be further from reality. Talking to any one level of a company, even a chief-level person, is not enough to be seen as a trusted expert for the company and for developing your long-term presence.

Meeting with a chief-level person is not even the best person to sell to depending on the company. If you can get a chief-level person to commit to you, great, but often the results of chief-level meetings are useful only for a recommendation or referral to one of the lower levels of the company. This is where you will have to begin talking about the problems on another level to close the sale and build the relationship. Many chief-level people will approve of you and your product or service, but properly defer to people in other areas to make the decisions in evaluating supplier or vendors.

THE HR DEPARTMENT

HR people are usually anxious to make sure they have done something about the company-wide goals coming from chief-level people. HR is typically tasked with implementing whatever plans the chief-level people have defined.

HOW TO APPROACH HR

- HR wants to point to initiatives that they have started toward the implementation of company-wide goals. Any specific solution that an HR person can point to that is directly fulfilling goals handed down from chief-level people will be of interest.
- HR is responsive to advice from other managers in the company who speak highly of your solution or recommend you.
- They will be alarmed to hear that a rival company is doing something different and better in solving the same problems. If you know what the competition are doing, you will build credibility with HR.

MANAGERS

Managers bear the burden for the results of those beneath them while having to justify the existence of their own positions in the company. Managers are about leading teams who get things done. This means a focus on efficiency, productivity, and getting things done faster. They are squeezed between the demands of the people above them for results and from those below for creating an efficient workspace for getting things done.

Managers these days are under extremely high pressure. Many are dismissive and curt. They will only see you in terms of how you appreciate and understand their problems. There will be no tolerance to hear about your company or any of its features. We have all seen emails or PowerPoint presentations that simply tell about a company, when it was founded, etc. This approach does not work at all in modern sales and managers especially have no patience for it. They need their problems solved so they can leave the office on time.

Managers in large corporations exist in a sea of backstabbing and fear of being fired for messing up. The quickest way to develop a reputation as an expert and specialist is to solve the problems of a manager – which usually means giving them someone or something they can trust that makes their jobs easier and will make them look good in the company.

THE MOST OVERLOOKED FACT ABOUT MANAGERS

The most overlooked fact about managers is that they are constantly explaining themselves to others. That means your explanation of the way you solve their problem must be presented in such a way that the manager can turn around and explain the solution to others in the company. They need to have explanations they can present and use to lobby others. Write up relevant material designed so that the manager can use it in their presentations or explanations – and be sure to remind the manager the information is to be used for this purpose. They will greatly appreciate it.

Too many salespeople are presenting themselves as an expert or trusted consultant solely to the person they talking to. Be aware of who the person you speak to will need to explain themselves to others. Make sure your arguments are clear and can move around the company internally.

PROJECT MANAGERS

Dealing with a person designated as project manager is one of the best ways to get a person in a company lobbying for your solution. Project managers are concerned about getting things done, making deadlines, removing problems from their hands, sticking to budgets and then being able to take the credit for it all.

Project managers will roll over everyone and everything to get their project done on time. Initiatives from the company and company procedures usually will take a distant back seat to getting the resources they need for their project and getting their project done by their deadline and within budget.

These days project managers, team leaders, and project coordinators are often appointed *ad hoc* from other positions to complete specific projects.

They are often tasked with evaluating vendors related to their projects, but not with a final decision. Even if they are not a decision maker, they are part of the process, so if they consider you as a trusted consultant, your name will come up in meetings where solutions to problems are discussed. They can be key to pushing you as a solution within the company.

Project managers especially appreciate information that makes them think ... 'I didn't know about that. I am glad this person contacted me.'

THE DEATH OF
THE PROFESSIONAL PROJECT MANAGER

Once upon a time professional project managers were employed who were skilled in the science of organizing projects. They were accomplished and could decide decisively. These are now a dying breed as companies seek to reduce costs. Even companies with the need for dedicated project managers now hire the youngest, cheapest and least experienced people they can find to fill these roles.

The demise of the professional PM has lcd to an interesting side effect and benefit – novice project managers who are more concerned with getting the job done than focusing on price. Historically, project managers were in charge of budgets. However, in the era of the novice project manager, these people are often only tangentially concerned with the price of a product or solution – they are simply tasked with managing a project or process set up or envisioned by others.

This phenomenon represents another opportunity to understand the psychology of a novice project manager and focus on the aspects they value – just getting the process done. Once a project manager is in your corner with the belief you can make their like easier, they will push hard for you.

As with all managers, once you are known as a successful resource for solving project problems, project managers will quickly spread your fame through the company – because you can help them get things done.

HOW TO APPROACH
MANAGERS AND PROJECT MANAGERS

While it could be said that managers deal with people and project managers with projects, in modern pressure-cooker companies, the pressure they are under is relatively similar – the pressure to make things happen now, and do more with much less.

- Managers will only tolerate listening to you if you are solving their problem or making their lives easier. It is unlikely that they will have heard of or care about company-wide initiatives coming from the highest levels of the company.
- Show how you are solving their problems while they sleep. In other words, they can leave the office on-time.
- People at this level of job position are afraid of being blamed for mistakes so they often have many, many questions to assuage their fears. They need to feel confident you really know what you are doing.
- Be aware that the manager will have to share and explain what you tell them to others. Write explanations for them to use with their own explanations and presentations.
- Provide information or advice they do not already know that will assist them. You are trying to make them think about you: "wow, I am glad this guy contacted me." It gives the manager confidence that you are doing things to back them up and they will not end up making a mistake and being blamed. The project managers can report this information to others in the company and look like a hero.

SPEAKING THE LANGUAGE OF EACH LEVEL OF A COMPANY

The missing link in sales today is understanding that the immediate needs or goals of a person in a certain position will outweigh lofty company goals and initiatives.

Express your solution in terms that speak to each area's immediate priorities, regardless of a company's overall initiatives. Doing this allows you to relate to each position as an expert who understands and can offer solutions to the problems they are facing.

This will build your credibility and reputation at every level as a person others want to turn to for help. Know the priorities of those you talk to, listen to them, deliver information they will value, and you will succeed in becoming a trusted and valued sales consultant.

ABOUT RON

Ron Morris is an author, CEO, and political consultant. As a founder of both SaaS (Software as a Service) and localization companies, he is a recognized expert on doing business in Asia and international outsourcing.

As creator of Intelligence Guidance, a political consulting firm, Ron is also an acclaimed analyst covering Southeast Asian politics, security and business issues. He is a regular contributor and onscreen analyst for news agencies in Asia, Europe, and the U.S. and advises clients worldwide.

His latest book, *Never Work For Anyone Again*, explains the practicalities of being your own boss — the critical secrets of thinking that have to be mastered, before one can find the money-making idea of a lifetime.

To learn more about Ron Morris and how his insights can change your future, visit:

NeverWorkForAnyoneAgain.com

CHAPTER 30

STREET TEAM **PROMOTIONS**

BY PAUL EDGEWATER

The word "promotion" is from Latin and means to put forward. Whether it's promoting our own goods and services, or the goods and services of our clients, we are putting those goods and services forward (in front of the competition or general buyer apathy), so as to make our clients and customers aware of them. The goal of this chapter is to cover the salient points of executing successful street team promotions, sometimes called *guerrilla marketing*.

If your business card says "John Doe, Attorney at Law," people know a lot about what you do the instant they read the card. They may not know in which area you practice law, but everyone has seen and heard enough about lawyers that they already know quite a bit about your profession from the word go. When I give my card to someone and/ or tell them the name of our company, "Busy Bee Promotions," I'm often asked what exactly it is that we do.. Everyone has heard the word "promotions," but outside of our industry, the word garners a nebulous response at best. It would be fair to say that even *in* our industry, people often look back with a blank stare when told the name of our company, unable to even offer up the wonted smile and/or knowing nod that accompanies these types of polite acknowledgements. We're including marketing, advertising, sales, public relations and more in that category.

If there is familiarity with the term at all, it is usually with regard to *street team* promotions, i.e. a group of upbeat, smiling "brand ambassadors" passing out 'tchotchkes' or samples of some new product on a busy downtown street in a bustling commercial corridor, or at a special event of some kind. This is by no means the only aspect of the promotions industry, but it is a major one and is what I will be highlighting in this chapter.

At the beginning of this chapter we discussed the historical Latin etymology of the word "promotion(s)," but what is today's definition and how does it differ (if at all) from its original meaning? Although the definition is still the same now as it was in the time of Augustus, it connotes a lot more nowadays.

It would also be logical to ask what the difference is between promotions and marketing and sales. Marketing can be called a passive method of introducing the market to, or reminding the market of, your *unique selling proposition*, via (but not limited to) online channels, social media, print, billboard, television or radio advertising, etc. Sales, on the other hand, is a structured, face-to-face interaction that elaborates on your *unique selling proposition* that builds to a close. Promotions is when you convey your *unique selling proposition* via a face-to-face interaction with very *high-touch* tactics, by a "brand ambassador" who isn't necessarily there to close the sale at the time of the interaction. Additionally, they encounter strangers who may never have been exposed to your traditional channels of marketing. This ambassador is there to give your product, service, company and brand a face and a pulse. Promotions puts someone in front of your customer or potential customer who can interface with them, without the customer being put on the defensive (if they are not in a position to make a commitment). Think of a promotions initiative as a "human commercial." More often than not, the potential customer will be given a sample, coupon, a flier, or branded 'tchotchke' with your company contact information emblazoned on it after the interaction. If a favorable impression has been made, these strangers will become clients and customers. At my company, we aptly call our brand ambassadors "Bees" and what follows are some basic rules of the road for effective street team promotions.

I'm not an anthropologist, sociologist or psychologist. I'm a business man, so take what you are about to read with that disclaimer in mind. Over many years of executing street team promotions, I have made some observations about human behavior that you may find useful in your promotions endeavors. For instance, if you think that standing on a busy sidewalk passing out free goodies is a simple proposition, you'd be correct; it's not difficult to do. It is a little more difficult to do it *well,* however. The difficulty lies in understanding the psychology behind why some people will gladly accept your offer one day and give you the cold shoulder on another. Without getting into variables that can influence behavior (people being in a bad mood or in a hurry, etc. — things we have no control over), we can establish protocol with regard to your approach for getting your message out to as many people as possible, in the shortest amount of time.

I don't like saying this, but most people are followers. I'd like to think that people are self-motivated and will make decisions based on what's right for them and not because of what they observe other people doing. But that's not the case. I may be closer to being correct if we looked at people as individuals acting alone; but, as a collective (as in a crowd), all the rules change. I strongly suggest you read the timeless work of French author Gustav Le Bon, *The Crowd – A Study of the Popular Mind (*Dover Publications). It's the last word on the subject, even though it was originally published in 1895.

People will do things when they are a part of a crowd that they would never consider doing as individuals. People find security as an incognito cog of the collective. It gives them *carte blanche* to act the fool in public with their friends, or to participate in an all-out smash-and-grab after a hurricane destroys a commercial district. Here's an example you may relate to – Did you go to a bar to celebrate your 21st birthday with your friends? Did you conduct yourself in a manner that you would not have considered had you walked into the same bar, at the same time by yourself? Did you find comfort knowing your friends were there to back you up if you yelled and acted the fool?

Yes, the environment plays a part; you're supposed to cut loose and be less restrained in a bar than you would on the job or on a bus or train, but the amount of familiar or like-minded people you find yourself in the company of, plays an even bigger part in determining your behavior. Even when you're in an unfamiliar group. A good example of this is when looting takes place. Most of the people in those mobs don't know one another, yet there they are; smashing out windows and stealing things together as if they had planned it out together. What does all this have to do with street promotions, you ask? Plenty.

BODY LANGUAGE IN PROMOTIONS

Let's go back to the example of standing on the busy sidewalk and passing out tchotchkes. If people see other people taking something from you, more often than not, they too will take something from you. If on the other hand they see the person in front of them decline your offer, it makes it very likely that they too will decline your offer. In fact, if you keep your hand extended with your offer after having it be declined several times, it's very likely that everyone in that cluster of people will walk right past you. Here is what you do if you are in this situation; if a cluster of people are all declining your offer, they are almost invariably following the lead of the person in front of them. You need to immediately change your approach.

For instance, if you have your hand outstretched with a tchotchke and people are walking around your outstretched hand, *don't keep your hand outstretched!* All the people behind the person who just walked past you will do the same. They are all thinking that you have cooties because the person in front of them acted as if you did. Always keep your hands moving. A great tactic is to let a few people walk past you and not offer any of them anything. After enough people have gone by to ensure that no one else coming saw someone in front of them decline your offer, start up again. It works like a charm.

If you are pulling your giveaways out of a duffle bag or a box, make a presentation. Be a showperson. Don't just pass things out willy-nilly. You are, after all, there to make a favorable and lasting impression. Make eye contact, speak clearly, project with authority and assume people want what you have to offer. Don't ever ask someone if they would like whatever it is you're offering in the form of a closed ended question. Given a choice in these situations (and most situations for that matter), people will choose "no" as a default reaction. That said, when doing street promotions, you don't have a lot of time for a conversation that starts with an open ended question either. I suggest you take a different tack; proclaim instead, "this one's for YOU," or "check this out, it has YOUR name on it." Just be creative, whimsical and assertive. Assume that everyone is going to clamor to get one of your goodies from your goodie bag. If someone declines your offer, remember to stall on the next few people behind that person and then resume your activity.

ABOUT EYE CONTACT

All promotional activity starts with eye contact, but prolonged eye contact with strangers can be uncomfortable to some people. While making then quickly *breaking* eye contact is disarming and gets the ball rolling by drawing people towards you. It seems counterintuitive on the surface, but let's dig a little deeper. In 1966, anthropologist Edward T. Hall expanded on the 1955 works of German zoologist Heini Hediger, with regard to distance between animals and their social activity. Hall applied it to humans and called it "proxemics" and it is very applicable to the world of street promotions and helps us determine what tactic to take with passersby based on how far they are from us. For instance, if you're executing your promotion outside of a store or a train station where people can see you from a distance, you start to interact with people when they are in what Hall called "public distance" (about 12-25 feet away from you). At this distance, it's best to initially establish eye contact, as it is a bit too far to start conversing with someone (especially if you are in a crowded and loud area). If you don't make and then quickly *break* eye contact, people may still walk right past you.

Allow me to explain. It has been said that up to 90 percent of communication is non-verbal. With strangers though, it's mostly *all* non-verbal since they often don't want to speak with us when we are promoting. Example: You've gotten the attention of a passerby. You both make eye contact to acknowledge one another. If you don't break that eye contact, they can shoot you a polite smile and be on their merry way. If someone is within your public distance (from 12-25 feet away), they have anywhere from three to nine seconds (depending on how fast they are walking, etc.) as they approach you to politely decline your offer with just body language, since they are a bit too far for verbal communication without raising their voice. They don't want to verbalize a "no thanks" at that distance. They prefer to convey that message with their body language. A polite smile and a hand raised in the international "no thanks" gesture is all it takes. That's too much to surmount in the tiny window of time available to you.

So if we break eye contact, what do we do then to get compliance? After making eye contact, saying hello or using some other polite greeting, then make a call to action like "check this out" or "you really need to see this" or "I have something for you." Then immediately look down at your hands (either tearing off a coupon or reaching for a tchotchke in a duffle bag, etc.) as if it's *understood* that this person *will* approach you and take you up on your offer. More often than not, they will indeed approach you and come within Hall's social distance (4-7 feet away), then personal space (2.5-4 feet away), where you can now communicate with normal conversational speech. Why does this work? Because most people are inherently friendly and don't want to disappoint others. When you break eye contact and gesticulate that it is understood that this person is now approaching you for your offer, they don't want to disappoint you. Sounds silly, doesn't it? Try it; it works.

SPEAK CLEARLY AND LOUDLY

If you are not projecting your voice, people cannot hear you. Your normal conversational voice will not cut it in promotions. If you think you have a weak voice, there are plenty of excellent home study courses for maximizing the output and throw of your voice. I personally suggest courses designed by Roger Love. Even if you have good pipes, you'll be amazed at how under-utilized they are. You need a powerful voice when doing street promotions.

NEVER SIT

Unless you are confined to a wheelchair or you live with another disability that keeps you from standing, never sit when promoting. Those of us blessed to have the use of our legs must use them. There is no reason to sit during a promotions gig...ever!

KEEP YOUR PITCH AS SHORT AS POSSIBLE

Ten seconds is an eternity when speaking to someone on the street. Invest your time before hitting the street figuring out ways to streamline your spiel so as not to waste the time of potential clients and customers, or your own time for that matter. You need to interact with as many people per hour as possible to make your promotion a success.

DECIDE ON A BRAND-APPROPRIATE GIVEAWAYS

Recently one of my "Bees" returned to our office from a street festival with something given to him by an Energizer Bunny mascot; a backup battery pack for mobile devices powered by Energizer batteries. What a perfect tchotchke. Everyone can use something like this. Not only does it promote the batteries, it demonstrates how well they work and it encourages the user to become a customer of additional batteries as they are needed. How elegant and clever. Spend the time to research a brand-appropriate giveaway for your product and service. Don't settle for the ubiquitous branded-pen. Check with a reputable promotions company to see the plentiful array of options available to you.

CHOOSE YOUR PROMOTIONAL VENUES WITH CARE

Make sure that wherever you have your team promoting your products or services is where they will likely encounter your target market. For instance, passing out sample-size packets of sunscreen at the beach would be a no brainer and the people you promote to will love you. Conversely, be sure to *avoid* venues where your product or services may offend. For instance, don't promote Styrofoam products at an Earth Day festival. You'll only be making enemies. Keep the time of day or night in mind too. If you're passing out samples of coffee, the hours between 6:00 a.m. and 9:00 a.m. will be much more effective than between 6:00 p.m. and 9:00 p.m. Always have a backup location in case you are asked to leave a venue, especially if you're *guerrilla marketing* and haven't secured permission to do a promotion there.

DON'T EXECUTE A STREET PROMOTION SOLO

Work in a team. Strangers you meet on the street will trust the integrity of a team. If they see you working by yourself, you are suspect.

USE THE RIGHT PEOPLE FOR YOUR TEAM

After reading this, you'll either want to do your own promotions, or you may decide to delegate. This means hiring intelligent, resourceful, highly energetic and enthusiastic people. It should go without saying that anyone you've appointed to execute your street promotions, should be the best person for the job. Beyond the obvious criteria that your promotions team be comprised of professional, high-quality, business-savvy people, make sure that the makeup of your team is brand appropriate. For instance, if you are promoting a gym, your team should be made up of physically fit people, etc. Also keep your team as diverse as possible, with regard to age, race and gender. Never forget that you are trying to make a connection and establish rapport with potential customers and clients from as many walks of life as possible. As when hiring or contracting for any other position, take your time hiring and waste no time firing. Your brand ambassadors need to nail it and do it fast. They hold your company and reputation in their hands. The consummate promotions pro is a rare breed of person and not easy to find. Often they are hired guns and are difficult to hold on to as well. When you have a good team, keep them and keep them busy. In return, they will keep you very busy with new business!

The result of a successful street promotion will invariably be higher sales, which of course will strengthen our respective businesses. A robust *private sector* is not only the best *counter attack* to the tough times we find ourselves in, it's the only one that will pull the world back from financial ruin. If our goals be worthy, honorable and based on a sound economic, scientific and spiritual foundation, if we are here to serve our clients and customers needs before our own, then the very successes we reap will indeed be what saves the world. Earl Nightingale used to call it "getting rich by enriching others." It's a marketing version of the golden rule and it's good business no matter what industry you're in.

ABOUT PAUL

Paul Edgewater is co-founder of Chicago, IL-based, Busy Bee Promotions, Inc. and is Chief Operations Officer in charge of marketing and client relations. Busy Bee opened its doors in 1998 and conducts an average of 400 events monthly coast-to-coast. Paul has been featured in Promo Magazine and on FOX, ABC and NBC news affiliates promoting products and services for clients such as Starbucks Coffee, Verizon Wireless, Groupon, Whole Foods Market, AT&T, Venturing & Emerging Brands of Coca-Cola and many more. His specialty is in maximizing his clients' exposure in and out of their respective market places by executing very unconventional, attention-getting tactics including an acclaimed, free-20-second spot he garnered for Starbucks Coffee on Fox News by rattling off talking points while doing "360s" on a branded Segway Personal Transporter!

Paul is the author of "The Book On Promotions - *How The Free Market Will Save The World, One Tchotchke At A Time*" (available at: www.PaulEdgewater.com). He has more than 30 years of sales, marketing and promotions experience and is motivated by his intense love of the private sector and the free market system, and takes great pleasure in connecting his clients with new customers. In addition to his business pursuits, he is a weekend athlete with three marathons under his belt and also an accomplished singer, bass player, drummer and animal lover.

Paul lives steps off the Magnificent Mile in beautiful downtown Chicago and is available for speaking engagements and consultations.

For booking information or to contact Paul directly, visit:
www.BusyBeePromotions.com
or call Toll-Free 1-888-438-9995

CHAPTER 31

EXPLOSIVE GROWTH MUST BE EARNED THRU BETTER LEADERSHIP

BY ALEX RODRIGUEZ

- **The Faster You Sharpen Your Leadership Edge, The Faster You Will Accelerate Financial Success**

- **Raising Your Leadership Effectiveness after the Great Recession is an Absolute Must (Job #1) For Success in the New Economy**

- **Make Yourself a Leader's Leader Who Drives Outstanding Results**

"The quality of leadership, more than any other single factor, determines the success or failure of an organization."
~ By Fred Fiedler and Martin Chemers in
Improving Leadership Effectiveness

Explosive growth in the post-recession economy will be earned by businesses and individuals who practice and understand that *'better business leadership'* is the one vital comparative advantage under prevailing and emerging market conditions. The quicker you and your organization sharpen your leadership edge over the competition, the faster you will accelerate financial and lifetime success for your business, your family and your career. This chapter explores the 'how' and the 'why,' and also provides ideas for improving, your own leadership effectiveness.

THE GREAT RECESSION AND ITS AFTERMATH

The facts are in and they are staggering. Millions of jobs lost. Hundreds of thousands of businesses closed down permanently. Corporate valuations and personal portfolio stock values decimated lifetime fortunes. Millions of homes in foreclosure. Dreams of retirement deferred. Low income families forced to chose between buying food or medicine. It is no exaggeration to say that lives lost were directly attributable to the economic abyss the global economy spiraled into, in the years following December 2007 (month the recession began).

And sadly, it is not over yet. For some, it will never be over, due to the lasting problems they endured. The aftermath and recovery will take years to undo the harm and regain ground. Did we have to live through this? Not everyone was on the losing side. Some even prospered. Why? How? More importantly, why not you or your business?

BUSINESS LEADERSHIP
IN THE CURRENT ECONOMIC CLIMATE

It is said that times of crisis reveal true character and authentic leadership traits in each of us. Certainly the Great Recession spun the nation and business sector into a crisis unseen in generations. Executives in business leadership have been tested, some more than others of course, through the economic devastation of the last 24 to 36 months. Some rose to the occasion, others simply crumbled and continue to struggle; most of us muddled along as best we could trying our best to hold on to what we have. But now it's time to fight back. It is time for a strategic business counter-attack to overcome all obstacles and achieve success even in the most difficult economies. This brings us to the topic of leadership effectiveness.

HOW WILL YOU ACCELERATE THE FINANCIAL RESULTS OF YOUR BUSINESS IN LIGHT OF ANY PREVAILING EXTERNAL ECONOMIC CONDITIONS?

Because of the challenges you've encountered over the last three years, what are you doing now **<u>from a leadership perspective,</u>** that is *significantly different* to what you were doing prior to the market downturn? The effective leadership of your organization and its growth potential lie in large part on how you respond to this crucial question. Do not accept anything less than 'straight up' candor from yourself in answering this question. What are you doing differently when it comes to leadership? Your growth depends on it.

To be sure, most of us are handling our businesses differently, given that conditions have changed. However, the vast majority of business leaders continue to lead as they have led in the past. Therein lies the problem. This chapter's thesis is simple, yet profound: leaders who commit to lead through more effective leadership will be leaps and bounds ahead of others who do not. Effective leadership now more than ever is the most important business development – yes, even ahead of cash flow, market share and stock value. Without effective leadership, all else is at risk of loss.

Despite the lackluster economy and sluggish rebound, why is it that some businesses and individuals are doing remarkably better than most even in this environment? Why is it that those same folks are well positioned to 'make out like bandits' as the economy continues to improve? And most importantly, how will you make yourself one of them, the ultra-successful, despite any external economic factors?

As we enter 2011, it is imperative to dust ourselves off and look within first, to position ourselves for maximum financial success in the months and years ahead. This chapter focuses on improving *your business leadership effectiveness today* so that you can thrive in today's economy and accelerate your dreams of financial, business and personal lifetime success.

As Fiedler and Chemers have revealed through their intensive academic research on success and failure of organizations, leadership effectiveness is Task #1 for achieving success. Effective leadership is paramount for success and to thrive in an uncertain world. Conversely, a lack of effective leadership stresses any organization to eventual collapse.

LEADERS SET THE TONE / CLARITY / FOCUS OF ORGANIZATIONS

During my observation of leadership effectiveness learned through mid-management jobs within three Fortune 500 companies, through direct access to some of the keenest senior political and military leaders of our time, and in my own 'school of hard knocks' in leadership roles in business, government and the non-profit sectors, I have witnessed both excellent and effective leadership as well as ineffective leadership. Leadership effectiveness has been and continues to be my primary fascination and professional interest as a practioner 'in the arena.' Leadership effectiveness in short means progress, or risk of failure followed by eventual failure. If an organization is not progressing toward specific measureable goals, it is inching closer and closer to failure. It is, after all, simply not good enough to accept the *status quo* while competitors are leaping ahead of your organization.

WHY LEADERSHIP BY THREAT HAS BECOME A DISADVANTAGE

Leadership by threat as a human resource business strategy is ineffective and outdated.

While leadership by threat motivates people to do what is needed for fear of job loss, this approach also falls short of maximizing the full potential that employees possess. Leadership by threat shuts people down. They will typically do only what they are instructed to do vs. rising above and going the extra mile and delivering results that exceed expectations. Most organizations have a far-reaching vision statement. Yet seldom do employees truly know or care what the vision is. Why? It comes back to threat-based leadership and a lack of a mission-oriented environment.

WHY LEADERSHIP BY EXAMPLE AND INSPIRATION YIELDS BETTER RESULTS

Employees must feel their opinion matters, that their contributions are valued and that they are part of a bigger mission. Under this leadership approach, a leader or manager uses leadership techniques and tactics that make employees feel like they are genuinely valued by management, and that their contributions truly matter. Leadership by example

creates an "all hands on deck" mentality that every employee will es-
pouse, so long as they are included and consulted by management in
their business strategies.

HOW TO MAKE YOURSELF A LEADER'S LEADER IN THE NEW / EMERGING ECONOMY

In order to protect what you have, continue to grow and stay on offense
in this economic environment, YOU, as a leader's leader, will raise the
bar not only for yourself but for everyone on your team. The time tested
strategies below will help create better results for your organization by
you becoming a more effective "leader's leader."

I. EARNING EXPLOSIVE GROWTH THROUGH PRACTICING SERVICE-CENTERED LEADERSHIP;

A service orientation *uncovers true intentions / frames future market
opportunities*.

- The quicker you realize that your own success is not about
  you, that it is about service to others, the quicker your success
  will come to life.
- Genuinely placing the needs, wants and aspirations of
  others, especially your subordinates, ahead of your own will
  accelerate your success.

II. LEAD OR BE LED.... DO NOT SIMPLY 'MANAGE' OTHERS OR EXPECT THEM TO BRING YOU GOLD;

- Conventional wisdom tells us that "managing" means your
  work is mostly 're-active' in nature and not at all proactive.
- Leading means your work is mostly spent on offense where your
  customers will go and the money will flow too in due course.
- The higher you are in the organization, the less you should
  micro-manage.
  - o Instead of trying to 'control' things, lead by asking vital
    open-ended questions that empower everyone in your
    organization, especially subordinates. They are hungry to
    surprise you with their ingenuity!

III. COMMIT TO MASTER YOURSELF FIRST:

- Have you mastered the specific skill-sets demanded by your industry?
- Have you mastered the art of influencing others to accomplish the job without telling them what to do or how to do it?
- Have you mastered the soft inter-personal relationship building skills that inspire trust and confidence of subordinates and peers alike?
- What are the new or emerging trends, new rules, new demands by customers that require adjustments to your thinking and leading in your industry?

Why is making yourself a Leader's Leader relevant to your business? The single most important outcome of this entire book is to help you, the business leader, accelerate financial results. Countless studies indicate that better led teams always perform better than teams that lack effective leadership.

SO WHO IS A LEADER'S LEADER ANYWAY?

Any discussion regarding how to make yourself a leader's leader must first begin by describing exactly what a leader's leader is to begin with.

I am defining a leader's leader as:

A **Leader's Leader** is one who has *mastered* the art of leadership, *earned* the respect of fellow leaders / followers and whose *action* and *example* leads to *extra-ordinary results* in their business, their career and their life…

At the heart of becoming a leader's leader, are specific actions you must take:

A) Give Power Away: Result will be that Others Empower YOU

- Learn to 'let go' and trust your subordinates
- Manage down and challenge up more
- Cost of turf wars / ego trips is way too high among leaders
- Turf wars dampen collaboration down the food chain
- Model what you expect subordinates to do

Your followers will climb any mountain for you so long as what you do elicits pride in their work. Give them a greater purpose, a sense of dignity and better self-worth. You will notice that in return they will give you gold.

B) Discover/Re-discover/Nurture and Lead with Your Strengths

- Put Your Best Foot Forward
- Leverage others strengths

C) Lead Excelling Teams by Building Trust as Authentic Leader

- Do What You Promise, Always
- Place Team Success Objective Clearly Above All Else

LEAD OR BE LED

Live a deliberate life at work. Are you just working for a paycheck or are you helping achieve a greater vision and company mission? Decide now how you will tackle 'work' in the future. Will you truly add new and more value to your customers, the organization and your colleagues or are you satisfied by simply getting by? It is a choice. And millions of people who under-achieve and never realize their full potential, make the choice to simply coast, just survive, live reactively and complain all day long about everything. Not you… Not anymore. To lack a deliberate career plan is to live at the whim of external factors you cannot control... The choice is yours to lead or be led. Choose to lead.

WALK A DAY IN YOUR CUSTOMER'S SHOES

- Have you ever wondered or really cared about what truly motivates your customers? And I mean genuinely, not just 'bumper sticker' talk about how the customer comes first. Odds are that if you have, you are succeeding. If you have not uncovered what truly motivates your customers, you have not hit your optimal successes…
- Discover their true intentions, goals, desires, fears and unmet wants

- Uncover opportunities to serve the customers' current gaps
- Position yourself as the customer advocate in all situations
- If you stop understanding your customers true needs and wants, their need for you will lessen over time and eventually you will be replaced

MOVE WITH A PURPOSE OR THE WORLD WILL MOVE YOU

- Far too many people lost their home, are in foreclosure today, or will take years to make up the financial losses of the market over the last three years.
- At the heart of their loss is a lack of clarity and purpose in their lives
- They left at risk their most important job: financial soundness
- The point I want to crystallize is that it is vital to move with a purpose, to get your financial house in order first, or risk losing it all when things go bad.
- The things that we can control and should work to control today are often left to chance by too many. Naturally, when things go bad, people find themselves wondering what went wrong and complain all day long.
- Those who move with a purpose in life will reap more benefits and will leave less to chance through their meticulous preparation, whether in personal finances, career goals and aspirations or life in general. A great place to start would be to define what your life purpose is to begin with. That is, what do you want most out of life, followed by a deliberate plan to achieve that desired purpose.

Moving with a purpose in the world of business where the stakes are high and competition is relentless, is a vital task to work at daily... CEO's and leaders at every level must move with a clearer purpose than anyone else, if they are to achieve their desired financial results and lifetime dreams...

WHY PURSUE MORE EFFECTIVE LEADERSHIP NOW?

Failure to improve makes us completely vulnerable to the prevailing 'economic storms' that can negatively impact our business plans. The competition will eventually squash you if you do not take continuous leadership improvement seriously. And your life dreams will be shelved or discarded because of a lack of clarity around why you must be a better business leader in the post-recession or newly-emerging economy …one that continues to be fraught with risk and uncertainty.

CHAPTER HIGHLIGHTS REVIEW AND ACTION STEPS ROADMAP:

Raising Your Leadership Effectiveness after the Great Recession is an Absolute Must For Success in the New Economy!

To become successful in any economic environment, you must commit to:

- Lead by example in business vs. leading by threat.
- Run your business as lean as possible in the good times and create a rainy day fund for the inevitable downturns.
- Give Power Away – gain stakeholder buy-in to your vision.
- Move With a Purpose or the World Will Move You.
- Provide people with the vision, dignity and respect, plus the tools they need, then trust them to realize your vision.
- Create appropriate leadership incentives and measure performance along the way for course corrections.
- At the heart of these suggestions is to put a premium on leading people more effectively.

In summary, the future economic climate that we live in is up to us to create. Becoming a much more effective leader through some of the strategies we discussed will help you achieve the success you desire. Commit to becoming a "Leader's Leader" and see your career and financial success soar to new heights.

ABOUT ALEX

Alex Rodriguez is Founder and Managing Director of *Exit Strategy Advisors, LLC*, a strategy consulting firm committed to accelerating the financial results of its clients. Alex is a leading authority in *business leadership effectiveness* with Fortune 500 experience in strategic planning and business development. Alex earned degrees from Harvard University, the University of Arizona and New Mexico Military Institute.

Alex served as Presidential Management Fellow at the Office of the Secretary of Defense at the Pentagon. As former President and Board Member of the Tucson Unified School District Governing Board, Candidate for U.S. Congress and U.S. Army Captain with service in war-torn Bosnia, Alex is well versed in leadership effectiveness through 'in the trenches' experience as practitioner, and as a student of the art and science of leadership development. A recipient of the prestigious **"40 Under 40"** accolade by the *Arizona Daily Star*, Alex earned his voice in business leadership effectiveness and motivational speaking through the school of hard knocks.

Alex is currently working on his forthcoming book entitled **Influential Power! How to Give Power Away and Achieve Explosive Growth**. The book will lay out compelling new ways that help improve personal and business leadership success in today's uncertain economic environment. To reserve your copy, please visit: www.givepoweraway.com.

Alex was raised as the youngest of ten children in a first generation immigrant working class family. He was the first child with the privilege to graduate from college. Alex is an avid reader, enjoys playing racquetball and playing drums. Alex and his wife Claudia are the proud parents of Emi Sofia, their 2 year old daughter, and have a highly energetic Labrador Retriever named "Kasper."

Please visit www.exitstrategyadvisors.net to retain Alex Rodriguez for strategy consulting engagements, motivational speaking, joint ventures or strategic alliances.

CHAPTER 32

VISIONARY THINKING: HOW TO EXPAND YOUR BUSINESS IDEA

BY TUOMO VIITAJYLHA

'm glad that you found your way to this chapter. It's devoted to those of you who want to enhance your own potential to manifest greater visions and plans!

I'd like to ask you to question everything I'm saying here. Don't believe everything outright. Instead, use your own understanding and consider each of the points and ideas I'm presenting. This will expand your own thinking, giving you more clarity, and empower you to reach even further than by simply skimming quickly through this chapter.

Do that, and I'm sure that this short chapter will reach you, forming within you a clarified recognition of that which will truly empower you to keep expanding your business visions.

THE NEED

First I would like to point something out to you about the New Economy we are currently living in. The services and products out there are becoming more and more precise concepts that cause people to recognize and fulfill the increasingly specific needs in their lives.

For example, people no longer buy shoes that are several sizes too big, as they did a century ago. Today, these people demand products and services that are tailored to their lives.

You see, all of the successful concepts, companies and business ideas have their basis in creating or filling the needs and wants of people. **The more exact an *answer* you have for the need, the more exact product or service you can provide.**

Simple, right?

Consider this: At the height of the 2009 economic recession, American consumers spent approximately 900 billion US dollars on non-essential leisure activities and services, according to the Euromonitor business database's 2010 report on consumer lifestyles in the US. They spent this money on services that they felt they needed, despite the fact that the country was in a recession. You feel the same need to buy something each time you encounter something for sale. In some cases the need is weak, yet you go ahead and purchase the product, and in others it can be nearly overwhelming so you feel a strong urge to buy that product.

Then there are the essential needs that are so totally integrated into our economy/society that we don't even question their necessity. These are the fundamental needs, like electricity, food, health insurance, or water. The strongest business concepts are those working towards becoming fundamental needs. Google, for example, ranks at number one for 2009's overall web traffic. It accounted for 44.5 percent of all web traffic by the beginning of 2010, according to Alexa Internet, a web traffic monitoring consultant company.

Google, Facebook, Amazon and other large online and offline brands began their success stories by first fulfilling a relatively small need. As people used them, that need expanded, the companies grew, and they ultimately became fundamental. I believe that this is how all business concepts grow into large successful entities.

HOW DID THEY DO IT?
WHAT HAPPENED? HOW DID IT START?

First, they recognized a need. It could have simply started as a need in one person's mind, but when it was recognized by others, that need became empowered. As the need grew, it became more clarified until, eventually a solution to fulfill this need became apparent. The rest, as they say, is history. You need only follow this path of expanding a vision into a need, then have that need become recognized by many people so that it can become empowered.

To expand these business ideas, we must think about being creative.

Thinking about being creative may sound too logical, since many people feel that creativity is more intuitive than anything. I'm not claiming that creativity cannot be intuitive, such as for those that are artistically talented, I'm merely saying that there are logical approaches that can lead to similar results. Writers don't all wait for inspiration to strike before they jump into writing a novel. Sometimes you have to work at it, using tried and true methods to fashion a jumble of words into a coherent story. Similarly, you can apply purely mental and logical steps towards being creative in your business ideas.

So, are you willing to expand your business idea? Great!

Now lets have a closer look at what we're dealing with.

ARE YOU WILLING TO EXPAND?

True willingness to expand your business or business idea is, in fact, the vital first stepping stone in this process. It is truly the aspect that will kickoff the countdown for your new and amazing business idea to become a reality.

This willingness to expand is the result of the interplay between three key factors: your personal motives, desires and reasons, colored by your true alignment – your values resonating within your unique direction.

Everyone has needs and wants, but how conscious we are of them varies greatly.

Why are you willing to do something?

283

Well, think about this:

The more you want something, the more willing you are to get it.

The more reasons you have to do something, the more willing you are to do it.

The more you desire something, the more you are willing to work for it.

Willingness is the driving force.

The greater your willingness to create an amazing business idea and the greater in line it is with your values, the more empowered you are to go for it.

When you have found the best reasons and the best motives for you as an individual, you will notice that those values and reasons are also closely connected to your life purpose.

The reason I offer this idea so strongly is so that your willingness to expand your business idea forms the *essential starting point* of this creative process, and simultaneously, because it holds the key to unleashing the full power of your creativity.

Here are a couple of examples of how a *lack* of driving force or willingness manifests itself:

1. INSTANT STOP

It's easy to think "Yes, I want to create an amazing new business vision," but suddenly you are left thinking, "Well, what next? Where should I start?" Your business plan has come to an abrupt end before it truly began.

2. NO CONSISTENCY

You manage to start working with a new business idea, but then you become distracted by the first idea to come along and are prematurely diverted away from the creative process. You don't give yourself enough time to fully develop ideas and instead accept weaker, half-formed ideas. While created quickly, your first idea will lack the unique feature or twist that will differentiate it from all the rest and make it a world-class phenomenon. This is particularly important at the beginning of the creative process. You need to have a strong driving force in order to meet and overcome the intellectual challenges in your path without giving up or downgrading your thinking. When you clarify your reasons, you become emotionally involved and generate a greater driving force. You make your work meaningful and important to you, empowering it, and gaining a greater ability to focus, clarify and maintain consistency.

EXPANSION OF IDEAS

Imagine that the creative process involved in expanding a business idea is like a pipe. The entrance to the pipe is your starting point, the other end is your expanded business idea. Your ability to use your creativity and focus is the key component that will carry you through the pipe. This is powered by your willingness – your driving force.

When forming new ideas, we use our creativity. Ideas do not stand alone. They are made up of smaller concepts that, when combined, form that idea. So when you think of a dog, for example, you are actually thinking of the combination of the "furry," "animal," and "pet" concepts. You can also gather many ideas and combine them to form an even more complex idea. So "dog" is combined with the concepts of "service" and "blind people" and voila! You have the greater idea of a seeing eye dog. You probably aren't aware of it on a conscious level, but you do it all the time.

So, in other words, when you are using this logical process to expand your business idea you are taking smaller business ideas and merging them into greater business ventures. This process will generate some so-called "Aha!" moments, when you realize that several ideas that you are already very familiar with, can merge to create a totally new, meaningful idea. That is what I mean by expansion.

Don't break out of that pipe too early and get stuck with a limited and half-formed idea. Keep your focus and willingness clear, stick with it to the end, and unfold that new vision. You will become able to explore and unleash more of your own potential. Always have a clarified driving-force in you because, without it, you'll never get through the creative process pipe. This driving force is the same thing that will propel you through the execution of your new plan.

APPLY THE POWER OF CLARIFICATION

When I ask you to clarify an idea, I mean that you should observe and question the idea. Examine it from different angles and perspectives, illuminating special characteristics or flaws that might be present. You should aim to fully understand it's purpose and meaning.

Clarification is always a mental process. You might use a pen and paper, or a computer to support this process, but the process itself occurs primarily in your mind. You follow the threads of thought from your idea, in ever-increasing detail. Keep your focus and direction when examining your idea. You don't want your understanding to become muddled before the idea is clarified.

With full scale clarification, you will reveal the complete understanding and recognition of any idea. You will also recognize its finest details. If you get stuck while clarifying your idea, try to form questions about your idea, or even just a part of it. Ask these questions from different perspectives, attacking it from every angle. Even relatively simple questions can grant you an increased understanding of the subject. You carry quite a few answers in your mind, they just need the right questions to bring them to the surface.

FROM CLARIFIED FRAGMENTS TO GREATER VISIONS

When building these ideas, it's best to work step-by-step. Clarify and combine lesser ideas to form more complex greater ideas, then expand these greater ideas. Well done clarification will result in an extremely detailed and powerful vision as an overall outcome.

Note that a greater idea does not necessarily mean it has to be a big idea. It can be an amazingly in-depth understanding of how something works, or a particularly well defined idea of what a key need is for a certain group of people.

This also applies to lesser ideas. I don't mean that they need to be small in scale. With the word "lesser", I'm referring to it's essence or basic substance. For example, the idea to spread your product through every computer retailer on the globe can be a "lesser" idea. So in essence, greater and lesser ideas aren't actually separate concepts, it's just that a greater idea has more substance than a lesser idea.

GROUND THE EXPANDED VISION

Once you have clarified and expanded your business idea, you need to place it into the context of the physical world. You need to find ways to manifest even a single detail of your idea, then the next, and the next. With simple steps, you will begin to clearly see how your whole business idea is grounded and shaping into a concrete and executable plan.

It may seem daunting at first, but if you focus on each individual piece, one at a time, you will eventually see the whole puzzle coming together. As the pieces continue to fall into place, the whole idea will become clarified, clear, and ready to be executed.

New ideas, challenges and opportunities will emerge. You will gain a competitive edge by consciously applying this creative process in your business.

I cannot express enough the importance of having a clear answer to the question:

"Why are you willing to expand your business idea?"

The answer to that question is a reflection of your values, what is important for you. In other words the answer to that question is also a reflection of you.

But don't misunderstand what I mean - the answer is not you, nor is it your business or idea. It is, however, the perfect reflection of your present perspective, the combination of your values as an individual or group.

For example, if you were to borrow an idea from others during a brainstorming session, you will have altered their idea with your own perspective. The result of that session will be a unique mixture reflecting the values of you and your group, discrete and apart from simply a collection of everyone's ideas.

Always strive towards clarity in your ideas. Clarified ideas are the key to success, particularly in business. As the great American author, Napoleon Hill, once said, "More gold has been mined from the thoughts of men than has been taken from the earth."

SUMMARY/RECAP

1. Understand the importance of willingness in you.
2. Clarify what is meaningful and important for you regarding this business idea.
3. Direct your focus to clarify your ideas.
4. Become inspired by the essence of your ideas.
5. Play with the clarified fragments of ideas to form a greater vision.
6. Drill down to the master plan.

So, what is your next visionary business idea and plan?

Get to it!

ABOUT TUOMO

Tuomo Viitajylha is an out of the ordinary business consultant. He is a visionary thinker and consciousness explorer whose passion has always been seeking out the most truthful solutions. He goes beyond regular limitations to open the mind to new insights and reveal new opportunities for others and their companies.

He specializes in concrete knowledge and guidelines for expansion, new business strategies, and the mental process of understanding. He also teaches business professionals how to scale new insights and perspectives into broader, more powerful forms.

His focus is in the creation of powerful guidelines and tools that make it easier for people to become aware of their own overall potential and to act accordingly. He teaches how to use these tools to open visionary ideas, gain personal insight and inner clarity. These tools trigger untapped potential in the mind and allow people to step boldly in their unique direction in life.

In his mind, there exists strict laws governing how understanding and clarity work. These laws are key in the expansion of any idea, whether abstract or infinite.

Tuomo Viitajylha is also a keynote speaker. In his presentations, listeners experience what he refers to as "AHA!" moments. These are instances where understanding suddenly clicks into place. They also gain insightful perspectives about consciousness, and how to live their lives through the amazing reservoirs of wisdom, compassion and creativity – that are hidden in people.

To learn more about Tuomo Viitajylha and how you can unleash more of the potential in you or your business, as well expand your visionary thinking, visit: http://www.TuomoTapio.com

21 Great Ways to Build a High Profit Business

Believe it or not, profitability in any market is predictable. In this 1-hour audio program, I'll show you the techniques and strategies in order for you to boost profits, increase cash flow, reduce costs, and stay ahead of your competition. When you apply these strategies you'll immediately drive more sales and increase revenue!

The Power of Persuasion

The development of your persuasion power will enable you to become one of the most powerful and influential people in your organization. It can mean the difference between success and failure. It will open up doors for you in every area of your life. In this PDF report, you'll learn the tips and techniques to mastering the art of persuasion to get you more of the things you want faster than anything else you do.

Build A Great Business!
BRIAN TRACY'S TOTAL BUSINESS MASTERY

Learn the practical, proven skills and techniques you need to survive, thrive and grow in any business and in any market...

Did you know that all business skills are *learnable*? You can learn any skill you need, to accomplish any business or financial goal you can set for yourself.

And, not only are these essential skills learnable, but you *must* learn them if you are going to survive, thrive and grow in an increasingly competitive economy.

At Brian Tracy's "Build a Great Business! Total Business Mastery" seminar, you learn how to create a great business, in any industry, faster and easier than you ever thought possible.

This event is not only aimed at people who are already in business and who want to grow faster, it is also ideal for anyone thinking about starting a business for the first time.

Brian Tracy covers the 10 essential areas of business that you must master to make your business successful and achieve all your financial goals.

You will learn how to:

- Become a Great Businessperson
- Create a Great Business
- Produce a Great Product or Service
- Create a Great Customer Experience
- Create a Great Marketing Plan
- Create and Perfect a Great Sales Process
- Generate Great Numbers
- Become a Great Leader and an Excellent Manager
- Attract, Keep, and Develop Great People
- Live a Great Life in Every Area

In this 2 ½ day, live, interactive workshop setting, you will learn some of the very best strategies, methods, and techniques ever discovered have been brought together in one program to help you start, build, manage or turn around any business, in any industry.

For more information, go to
www.briantracy.com/TBMCA or call 858-436-7300.

WANTED

Lager drinkers.

Previous experience essential.

Club Carling is your chance to get even more out of the country's favourite lager. Four times a year, the Club Carling magazine will bring you interesting and unusual views of life, pub humour, exclusive interviews and features that you won't find anywhere else. And on top of all that there are stories from the Carling Premiership.

Win free Carling for a year.

You'll also get regular offers and freebies with all kinds of chances to win major prizes. Join now and we'll put you in a free draw where 10 lucky winners could win a year's supply *(that's 365 cans)* of Carling. Call now on **0345 00 1966** quoting the number on the football shirt below.

GET IT FREE FOUR TIMES A YEAR.

If you want to join the club and you're over 18, call us now on

0345 00 1966

Calls charged at local rate and should last about 3 minutes.

The Ultimate Guide To
The Ultimate Game

FOREWORD BY MIKE FLYNN
HEAD OF SPONSORSHIP, BASS BREWERS

On behalf of Carling, I welcome you to the 1999 edition of 'The Ultimate Football Guide'. We are once again delighted to be associated with a publication that is widely used by managers, players, media and fans alike.

A quick look through the book shows why it's such an essential source of information. It contains all you need to know (and more!) about each of the 92 league clubs - statistics, records, ground details and a breakdown of how all the teams performed last season. It's got the lot!

As sponsors of the Carling Premiership we have a comprehensive set of initiatives in place designed to enhance fans' enjoyment of the world's most exciting club competition.

If you're one of the growing number of fans with access to the internet, then the CarlingNet (www.fa-carling.com) will keep you up to date with all the action from the Carling Premiership almost the second it happens.

Keep an eye out for the winners of the Carling Player and Manager of the Month and the Carling Player and Manager of the Year Awards as well as the Carling No.1 Award, which recognises the select few that have made an outstanding contribution to the national game.

Derby fixtures are unique occasions, so we will once again be running the Carling Challenge - three regional leagues that monitor the performance of local rivals in the North-West, Midlands and London. Only games between teams in these regions count and whichever teams win their respective leagues will receive £10,000 to donate to a charity of their choice. All the other teams will be given £1,000 to donate to their chosen charity.

Carling Opta is the official supplier of player performance statistics to the Carling Premiership and their stats are widely used in the regional and national media. The statisticians at Carling Opta will once again be analysing every second of every Carling Premiership game so that managers and fans can be kept right up to date with the performances of all the Carling Premiership players.

As always, we will be making sure that fans have the opportunity to win tickets to Carling Premiership games through the hundreds of competitions we are running in the media.

What a year 1998 has been for football. Arsenal took the Carling Premiership crown to Highbury, we witnessed a thrilling play-off final between Sunderland and Charlton, and Macclesfield gained promotion in their first season in the Football League. The close season was lit-up by the World Cup and now another feast of football is upon us.

Let's hope 1999 is as good!

Cheers

Mike Flynn

CARLING

e panel that judges the Carling Awards
:resents all the game's key groups, including
s, making it the most representative judging
el ever assembled in football. The panel
sides over five awards, the Carling Manager
Player of the Month, the Carling Manager and
yer of the Year and the Carling No.1 Award.

e 1998/99 Carling Award Panel

nn Hoddle, **England Coach**
er Leaver, **FA Premier League**
rdon Taylor, **Professional Footballers' Association**
an Barnwell, **League Managers' Association**
b Shennan, **BBC Sport**
ıll Sloane, **BBC Sport**
ıan Barwick, **ITV Sport**
ıT Farmer, **ITV Sport**
: Wakeling, **Sky Sports**
:vor East, **Sky Sports**
an Green, **BBC Radio Sport**
nathan Pearce, **Capital Radio**
e Melling, **Football Writers' Association**
ex Montgomery, **Football Writers' Association**
ıristopher Davies, **Football Writers' Association**
:il Midgley, **Referees' Association**
aham Kelly, **Football Association**
aham Bean, **Football Supporters' Association**
ı Todd MBE, **The National Federation of**
otball Supporters' Clubs
:ith Pinner, **Arena International**
ark Hunter, **Bass Brewers**
:ve Goodger, **Bass Brewers**
ike Flynn, **Bass Brewers**

Carling Manager of the Month - 1993/94*

August	Alex Ferguson
September	Joe Kinnear
October	Mike Walker
November	Kevin Keegan
December	Trevor Francis
January	Kenny Dalglish
February	Joe Royle
March	Joe Kinnear
April	Joe Kinnear

Carling Manager of the Year

Alex Ferguson

*The Carling Player of the Month was introduced at the start of the 1994/95 season

Carling Manager & Player Awards - 1994/95

August	Kevin Keegan	Jurgen Klinsmann
September	Frank Clark	Robert Lee
October	Alex Ferguson	Paul Ince
November	Kenny Dalglish	Chris Sutton/Alan Shearer
December	Gerry Francis	Matt Le Tissier
January	Brian Little	Chris Waddle
February	Kevin Keegan	Duncan Ferguson
March	Ron Atkinson	Tony Yeboah
April	Howard Wilkinson	David Seaman

Carling Player of the Year — *Alan Shearer*
Carling Manager of the Year — *Kenny Dalglish*

Carling Manager & Player Awards - 1995/96

August	Kevin Keegan	David Ginola
September	Kevin Keegan	Tony Yeboah
October	Frank Clark	Trevor Sinclair
November	Alan Ball	Robert Lee
December	Roy Evans	Robbie Fowler
January	Roy Evans	Robbie Fowler/Stan Collymore
February	Alex Ferguson	Dwight Yorke
March	Alex Ferguson	Eric Cantona
April	Dave Merrington	Andrei Kanchelskis

Carling Player of the Year — *Peter Schmeichel*
Carling Manager of the Year — *Alex Ferguson*

arling Manager & Player Awards - 1997/98

ıugust	David Pleat	David Beckham
:ptember	Joe Kinnear	Patrik Berger
ctober	Graeme Souness	Matt Le Tissier
ovember	Jim Smith	Ian Wright
ecember	Gordon Strachan	Gianfranco Zola
ınuary	Stuart Pearce	Tim Flowers
:bruary	Alex Ferguson	Robbie Earle
ıarch	Bryan Robson	Juninho
pril	Graeme Souness	Mickey Evans

arling Player of the Year — *Juninho*
arling Manager of the Year — *Alex Ferguson*

arling Manager & Player Awards - 1997/98

ıugust	Roy Hodgson	Dennis Bergkamp
:ptember	Martin O'Neill	Dennis Bergkamp
ctober	Alex Ferguson	Paulo Wanchope
ovember	George Graham	Andy Cole/Kevin Davies
ecember	Roy Hodgson	Steve McManaman
ınuary	Howard Kendall	Dion Dublin
:bruary	Gordon Strachan	Chris Sutton
ıarch	Arsene Wenger	Alex Manninger
pril	Arsene Wenger	Emmanuel Petit

arling Player of the Year — *Michael Owen*
arling Manager of the Year — *Arsene Wenger*

Carling Manager & Player Awards - 1998/99 (to date)

August	Alan Curbishley	Michael Owen
September	John Gregory	Alan Shearer

Carling No.1 Awards

The Carling No.1 Award is awarded for outstanding contributions to the national game.

Carling No.1 Awards - 1994/95

Match of the Day - In celebration of the programme's 30th anniversary

Chelsea Independent Supporters Association - For organising a trip for one of its fans to Canada

Sir Stanley Matthews - In celebration of his 80th birthday

Carling No.1 Awards - 1995/96

Eric Harrison - Manchester United's youth coach was recognised for his role in the club's incredibly successful youth policy.

Alan Shearer - Alan picked up two Carling No.1 Awards, firstly for being the first player to score 100 goals in the Carling Premiership and secondly for scoring at least 30 Carling Premiership goals for the past three seasons - a feat not achieved since the Second World War

Carling No.1 Awards - 1996/97

John Motson - In recognition of his twenty five years as a BBC football commentator

Peter Shilton - In acknowledgement of his 1,000th league game

Tony Parkes - Recognising his achievement in helping to maintain Blackburn's position in the Carling Premiership

Carling No.1 Awards - 1997/98

Ian Wright - In recognition of his achievement in breaking Cliff Bastin's Arsenal goal-scoring record of 178 goals

Jim Smith - Awarded for his services to football, and specifically his tremendous league managerial career which spans 25 years

It's Fact Not Fantasy

Ask a group of fans who the best Carling Premiership striker was last season and you can guarantee several players would get a mention. Ask Carling Opta's statisticians and they'll give you only one name - Dennis Bergkamp.

As the official supplier of player performance statistics to the Carling Premiership you can certainly trust their selection. Carling Opta's statisticians analyse every second of every Carling Premiership game and produce the Carling Opta Run-Down based on each touch of the ball a player makes.

The run-down is an objective way of monitoring player performance. There are over 90 ways in which points are awarded or deducted, ranging from gaining 500 for scoring a goal outside the penalty area, to losing 300 for a red card.

Based on a six game rolling average, league tables are produced showing the 'form' players for five different categories: goalkeeper, defender, midfielder, attacking midfielder and striker.

Watch out for the run-down and Carling Opta player profiles in match-day programmes and in a host of regional and national newspapers.

CARLING OPTA RUN-DOWN TABLE-TOPPERS - 97/98

Here are the players who topped their class last season.

Strikers

1	Dennis Bergkamp	Arsenal	942
2	Paul Scholes	Man United	853
3	Dwight Yorke	Aston Villa (now Man Utd)	820
4	Michael Owen	Liverpool	791
5	Paolo Di Canio	Sheffield Wednesday	781

Attacking Midfielders

1	David Ginola	Tottenham Hotspur	1315
2	Steve McManaman	Liverpool	1274
3	David Beckham	Man United	1083
4	Neil Redfearn	Barnsley (now Charlton)	935
5	Mark Draper	Aston Villa	913

Midfielders

1	Jamie Redknapp	Liverpool	1108
2	Paul Ince	Liverpool	1075
3	David Batty	Newcastle	1073
4	Patrick Vieira	Arsenal	935
5	Dennis Wise	Chelsea	915

Defenders

1	Frank Leboeuf	Chelsea	1099
2	Tony Adams	Arsenal	1025
3	Steve Staunton	Aston Villa (now Liverpool)	1015
4	Gary Neville	Man United	850
5	Matt Elliott	Leicester City	848

Goalkeepers

1	Peter Schmeichel	Man United	617
2	Neil Sullivan	Wimbledon	592
3	Mart Poom	Derby County	508
4	Nigel Martyn	Leeds United	504
5	Paul Jones	Southampton	501

THE ULTIMATE FOOTBALL GUIDE 1999

Published by: SKY BLUE PUBLICATIONS

Sponsored by: Carling
Publisher: Bryan A Richardson
Editor: Mike Williams
Editorial Assistants: Ramona Bryson and Tony Matthews.

ISBN 0-9526904-3-8

Ultimate Football Guide
PO Box 1379
Coventry
CV2 4ZR
Publishers Telephone No.: 01203 234000
Fax: 01203 234015
Editorial Telephone No.: 07970 922 086

CLUB PAGES
INTRODUCTION

To help you understand the notations used within this book and to give you a brief idea of the information that can be found within the club section, the following notes should be read.

FIRST PAGE: Includes a review of the 1997-98 season; Senior club personnel; 1998-99 (where available) Playing squad photograph plus caption.

SECOND &
THIRD PAGES   Complete match by match details of the 1997-98 season.
This year an 'X' has been used to denote a player's appearance in a match throughout the four divisions. In the case of a substitution being made the following applies:
X1 (off) - S1 (on); X2 - S2; X3-S3; S - non-playing sub.

RECORDS PAGE(S)   Carling Premier and First Division clubs' records and statistics cover two complete pages.
Second and Third Division clubs' records and statistics are covered on one page with details of their Manager also included.

PLAYERS PAGE   This page is always left to the last minute so to include the summer signings, thus giving a list of players that are contracted to the club for the beginning of the **1998-99** season.
Details include - Height, Weight, Birth Date and Contract Date as well as League, FA Cup, League Cup and 'other'* appearances and goals.
*All European competitions and any other domestic competition, such as The Associate Members Cup, Play-offs and alike, come under the heading of 'Other' Appearances and goals.

SEVENTH PAGE
(Prem. & Div.1)   Overspill from the players page is then followed by details on the team manager.

GROUNDS PAGE   Contains matchday ticket prices along with details on the ground and easy to read directions, plus useful telephone numbers.
Also included on this page are details of the clubs' matchday programme.

F.A. CARLING PREMIERSHIP...

...1998-99

F.A. CARLING PREMIERSHIP 1997-98

FINAL LEAGUE TABLE

		P	W	D	L	F	A	W	D	L	F	A	Pts
			HOME						**AWAY**				
1	ARSENAL (+2)	38	15	2	2	43	10	8	7	4	25	23	78
2	MANCHESTER UNITED (-1)	38	13	4	2	42	9	10	4	5	31	17	77
3	LIVERPOOL (+1)	38	13	2	4	42	16	5	9	5	26	26	65
4	CHELSEA (+2)	38	13	2	4	37	14	7	1	11	34	29	63
5	LEEDS UNITED (+6)	38	9	5	5	31	21	8	3	8	26	25	59
6	BLACKBURN ROVERS (+7)	38	11	4	4	40	26	5	6	8	17	26	58
7	ASTON VILLA (-2)	38	9	3	7	26	24	8	3	8	23	24	57

INTO EUROPE -

		P	W	D	L	F	A	W	D	L	F	A	Pts
8	WEST HAM UNITED (+6)	38	13	4	2	40	18	3	4	12	16	39	56
9	DERBY COUNTY (+2)	38	12	3	4	33	18	4	4	11	19	31	55
10	LEICESTER CITY (-1)	38	8	10	3	21	15	7	4	8	30	26	53
11	COVENTRY CITY (+6)	38	8	9	2	26	17	4	7	8	20	27	52
12	SOUTHAMPTON (+4)	38	10	1	8	28	23	4	5	10	22	32	48
13	NEWCASTLE UNITED (-11)	38	8	5	6	22	20	3	6	10	13	24	44
14	Tottenham Hotspur (-4)	38	7	8	4	23	22	4	3	12	21	34	44
15	WIMBLEDON (-7)	38	5	6	8	18	25	5	8	6	16	22	44
16	SHEFFIELD WEDNESDAY (-9)	38	9	5	5	30	26	3	3	13	22	41	44
17	EVERTON (-2)	38	7	5	7	25	27	2	8	9	16	29	40

RELEGATED -

		P	W	D	L	F	A	W	D	L	F	A	Pts
18	BOLTON WANDERERS (DIV.1)	38	7	8	4	25	22	2	5	12	16	39	40
19	BARNSLEY (DIV.1)	38	7	4	8	25	35	3	1	15	12	47	35
20	CRYSTAL PALACE (DIV.1)	38	2	5	12	15	39	6	4	9	22	32	33

The figure in brackets denotes the number of places lost or gained on the clubs' 1996-97 final position.

European Qualification: Champions League - Arsenal & Manchester United.
UEFA Cup - Liverpool, Leeds United, Blackburn & Aston Villa.   ECWC - Chelsea (Holders), Newcastle United.

FA CARLING PREMERSHIP 1998-99

ARSENAL
(The Gunners)
F.A. CARLING PREMIERSHIP
SPONSORED BY: JVC (UK) LTD.

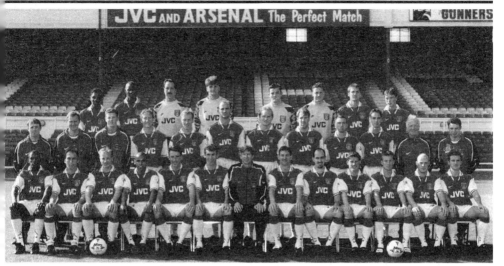

Back Row L-R: Gavin McGowan, Patrick Vieira, David Seaman, John Lukic, Lee Harper, Vince Bartram, Scott Marshall, Stephen Hughes.
Middle Row: Bobby Armitt (Kit Manager), Gary Lewin (Physiotherapist), Colin Lewin (Reserve Team Physiotherapist), Ray Parlour, Lee Dixon, John Hartson, Paul Merson, Nigel Winterburn, Matthew Rose, George Armstrong (Reserve Team Coach), Mark James (Masseur). **Front Row:** Ian Wright, David Platt, Dennis Bergkamp, Andy Linighan, Martin Keown, Arsene Wenger (Manager), Tony Adams, Steve Morrow, Adrian Clarke, Ian Selley, Paul Shaw, Remi Garde.

ARSENAL
FORMED IN 1886
TURNED PROFESSIONAL IN 1891
PLC IN 1990

CHAIRMAN: P D Hill-Wood
DIRECTORS:
D Dein (Vice-Chairman)
Sir R G Gibbs, C E B L Carr,
R C L Carr, K J Friar(managering), D Fiszman.
LIFE PRESIDENT
Sir Robert Bellinger CBE, DSO
SECRETARY/Managing Director:
Ken J Friar (0171 226 0304)
Assistant Secretary
David Miles
COMMERCIAL MANAGER
John Hazell (0171 359 0808)

MANAGER: Arsene Wenger
ASSISTANT: Pat Rice

RESERVE TEAM MANAGER
George Armstrong
YOUTH TEAM MANAGER
Tom Walley
PHYSIOTHERAPIST
Gary Lewin MCSP, SRP

CLUB STATISTICIAN FOR THE DIRECTORY
Chris Thompson

If your name happens to be Emmanuel Petit or Patrick Vieira, season 1997/98 will go down in your book as a vintage year. For not many players can boast to have been part of a domestic League and Cup double winning team as well as winning the greatest prize of all, the World Cup!

However, signs that Arsenal could win any trophy, let alone the 'double' ,were not evident in the first half of the season and only qualification for the Coca-Cola Cup quarter-finals gave the fans any real hope of silverware. Afterall Manchester United were top of the Carling Premiership with a lead of 13 points, over the 'Gunners', and Arsenal's European campaign had finished early with a first round exit against PAOK Salonika.

Come the New Year, and Arsene Wenger's team began to metamorphosis into a team that could have challenged the champions for their title, but it was too late now if only they had had a good start to the season. However, undaunted by United's lead Arsenal put together a run that saw them drop points only twice in ten games, and conceding only three goals. Included in this run was the result that probably swung the 'title pendulum' towards North London, a 1-0 victory at the home of the champions.

Arsenal still had it all to do though and quotes like "yes they've got games in hand, but I'd much rather have the points in the bag and be sitting on top of the Carling Premiership", made sure that the pressure was entirely on Arsenal. However, the 'Gunners' were unstoppable and a 4-1 win (3-0 after only 14 minutes) against Blackburn followed by a 5-0 thrashing of Wimbledon proved the point as Arsenal claimed the top spot, and they still had games in hand!

The games in hand were played and won, and Arsenal were crowned champions after another impressive display, this time against Everton - 4-0. They could be forgiven for switching off in the remaining two matches, as consecutive defeats by Liverpool (0-4 - the only club to do the double over the Gunners) and Aston Villa (0-1) gave the illusion that with Arsenal finishing only two points above United, the Carling Premiership title race must have been close, in reality Arsenal were leagues ahead.

To complete the double they had a date with below par Newcastle United at Wembley Stadium, and taking into account that yes it was the FA Cup, and yes it is 'a funny old game' nobody really gave the 'Magpies' a chance of stopping Arsenal from collecting their second double. It could have been a treble if they had held on to their 2-1 semi-final first leg win in the Coca-Cola Cup, but Chelsea under new management came back to win 4-3 on aggregate to claim a place in final.

Can the 'Gunners' retain their new crown?

Well, if their french duo maintain their drive and passion to win, if their defence, although maybe ageing, can hold firm and if Bergkamp, Overmars and the every improving Anelka are on song...would you back against them?

ARSENAL

M	DATE	COMP.	VEN	OPPONENTS	RESULT	H/T	LP	GOAL SCORERS/GOAL TIMES	ATT.
1	A 09	CP	A	Leeds United	D 1-1	1-1	11	Wright 35	(37993)
2	11	CP	H	Coventry City	W 2-0	1-0	1	Wright 29, 47	37324
3	23	CP	A	Southampton	W 3-1	1-1	2	Overmars 19, Bergkamp 57, 78	(15246)
4	27	CP	A	Leicester City	D 3-3	1-0	3	Bergkamp 9, 62, 88	(21089)
5	30	CP	H	Tottenham Hotspur	D 0-0	0-0	5		38102
6	S 13	CP	H	Bolton Wanderers	W 4-1	3-1	4	Wright 20, 25, 81, Parlour 44	38138
7	16	UEFA 1/1	A	PAOK Salonika	D 0-1	0-0			(42000)
8	21	CP	A	Chelsea	W 3-2	1-1	2	Bergkamp 45, 59, Winterburn 89	(33012)
9	24	CP	H	West Ham United	W 4-0	4-0	1	Bergkamp 12, Overmars 39, 44, Wright 42 (pen)	38012
10	27	CP	A	Everton	D 2-2	2-0	1	Wright 32, Overmars 41	(35457)
11	O 30	UEFA 1/2	H	PAOK Salonika	D 1-1	1-0		Bergkamp 22	37982
12	O 04	CP	H	Barnsley	W 5-0	3-0	1	Bergkamp 25, 31, Parlour 44, Platt 63, Wright 76	38049
13	14	CC 3	H	Birmingham City	W 4-1	0-1		Boa Morte 63, 108, Platt 99 (pen), Mendes-Rodriguez 113	27097
14	18	CP	A	Crystal Palace	D 0-0	0-0	1		(26180)
15	26	CP	H	Aston Villa	D 0-0	0-0	2		38061
16	N 01	CP	A	Derby County	L 0-3	0-0	2		(30004)
17	09	CP	H	Manchester United	W 3-2	2-2	2	Anelka 9, Vieira 26, Platt 83	38203
18	18	CC 4	H	Coventry City	W 1-0	0-0		Bergkamp 99	30199
19	22	CP	A	Sheffield Wednesday	L 0-2	0-1	3		(34373)
20	30	CP	H	Liverpool	L 0-1	0-0	5		38094
21	D 06	CP	A	Newcastle United	W 1-0	1-0	4	Wright 36	(36751)
22	13	CP	H	Blackburn Rovers	L 1-3	1-0	5	Overmars 18	38147
23	26	CP	H	Leicester City	W 2-1	1-0	6	Platt 36, Walsh 56 (OG)	38023
24	28	CP	A	Tottenham Hotspur	D 1-1	0-1	6	Parlour 62	(29610)
25	J 03	FAC 3	H	Port Vale	D 0-0	0-0			37471
26	06	CC QF	A	West Ham United	W 2-1	1-0		Wright 24, Overmars 52	(24770)
27	10	CP	A	Leeds United	W 2-1	0-0	5	Overmars 60, 72	38018
28	14	FAC 3R	A	Port Vale	D 1-1	0-0		Bergkamp 100	(14964)
29	16	CP	A	Coventry City	D 2-2	0-1	5	Bergkamp 50, Anelka 57	(22864)
30	24	FAC 4	A	Middlesbrough	W 2-1	2-0		Overmars 1, Parlour 19	(28264)
31	28	CC SF1	H	Chelsea	W 2-1	1-0		Overmars 23, Hughes 47	38114
32	31	CP	H	Southampton	W 3-0	0-0	5	Bergkamp 62, Adams 67, Anelka 68	38056
33	F 08	CP	H	Chelsea	W 2-0	2-0	5	Hughes 4, 42	38083
34	15	FAC 5	H	Crystal Palace	D 0-0	0-0			37164
35	18	CC SF2	A	Chelsea	L 1-3	0-1		Bergkamp 81 (pen)	(34330)
36	21	CP	H	Crystal Palace	W 1-0	0-0	3	Grimandi 49	38094
37	25	FAC 5R	H	Crystal Palace	W 2-1	2-1		Anelka 2, Bergkamp 28	(15674)
38	M 02	CP	A	West Ham United	D 0-0	0-0	3		(25717)
39	08	FAC QF	H	West Ham United	D 1-1	1-1		Bergkamp 26 (pen)	38077
40	11	CP	A	Wimbledon	W 1-0	1-0	2	Wreh 21	(22291)
41	14	CP	H	Manchester United	W 1-0	0-0	2	Overmars 79	(55174)
42	17	FAC QFR	A	West Ham United	D 1-1	1-0		Anelka 45	(25859)
43	28	CP	H	Sheffield Wednesday	W 1-0	1-0	2	Bergkamp 35	38087
44	31	CP	A	Bolton Wanderers	W 1-0	0-0	2	Wreh 47	(25000)
45	A 05	FAC SF	N	Wolverhampton Wand	W 1-0	1-0		Wreh 12	(39372)
46	11	CP	H	Newcastle United	W 3-1	1-0	2	Anelka 41, 64, Vieira 72	38102
47	13	CP	A	Blackburn Rovers	W 4-1	4-0	2	Bergkamp 2, Parlour 7, 14, Anelka 42	(28212)
48	18	CP	H	Wimbledon	W 5-0	3-0	1	Adams 11, Overmars 17, Bergkamp 19, Petit 54, Wreh 88	38024
49	25	CP	A	Barnsley	W 2-0	1-0	1	Bergkamp 23, Overmars 76	(18691)
50	29	CP	H	Derby County	W 1-0	1-0	1	Petit 34	38121
51	M 03	CP	H	Everton	W 4-0	2-0	1	Overmars 28, 57, Adams 89, Bilic 6 (OG)	38269
52	06	CP	A	Liverpool	L 0-4	0-3	1		(44417)
53	10	CP	A	Aston Villa	L 0-1	0-1	1		(39372)
54	16	FAC F	N	Newcastle United	W 2-0	1-0		Overmars 23, Anelka 69	79183

Best Home League Attendance: 38269 V Everton   **Smallest :37324 V Coventry City**   **Average :38053**

Goal Scorers:

CP	(68)	Bergkamp 16, Overmars 12, Wright 10, Anelka 6, Parlour 5, Adams 3, Platt 3, Wreh 3, Hughes 2, Petit 2, Vieira 2, Grimandi 1, Winterburn 1, Opponents 2
CC	(10)	Bergkamp 2, Boa Morte 2, Overmars 2, Hughes 1, Mendes-Rodriguez 1, Platt 1, Wright 1
FAC	(10)	Anelka 3, Bergkamp 3, Overmars 2, Parlour 1, Wreh 1
UEFA	(1)	Bergkamp 1

(D) Adams	(F) Anelka	(F) Bergkamp	(F) Boa Morte	(D) Bould	(M) Crowe	(D) Dixon	(M) Garde	(D) Grimandi	(M) Hughes	(D) Keown	(G) Lukic	(G) Manninger	(D) Marshall	(M) McGowan	(M) Mendes-Rodriguez	(M) Muntasser	(M) Overmars	(M) Parlour	(M) Petit	(M) Platt	(G) Rankin	(G) Seaman	(D) Upson	(F) Vernazza	(M) Vieira	(D) Winterburn	(F) Wreh	(F) Wright		
	S	X		X		X	X	S2		S			S				X	X	X	S1		X			X	X		X	D.J. Gallagher	1
	S	X				X	X	S2		S			X				X	X	X	S1		X	S		X	X		X	K W Burge	2
	S	X	S3	X		X	X			S			S2				X	X	X	S1		X			X	X		X	D R Elleray	3
	S1	X		X	X	X	S3			S			S				X	X	X	S2		X			X	X		X	G P Barber	4
	S2	X		X	X	S	X			S			S				X	X	X	S1		X			X	X			G S Willard	5
	S3	X	S2	X		X	X				S		S				X	X	X	S1		X			X	X		X	N S Barry	6
X	X3	X	S2	X		X	S				S		S				X2	X1	X	S1		X	S		X	X	S3	X	M Diaz	7
X	S	X	S1	X		X		S2			S		S				X	X	X			X			X	X		X	DJ Gallagher	8
X	S3	X	S	X		X		S1					S				X	X	X	S2		X			X	X		X	P E Alcock	9
X	S	X	S1	X			S3	X					S				X	X	X	S2		X			X	X		X	A B Wilkie	10
X	S2	X	S	X		X	S		S				S	S			X1	X2	X	S1		X			X	X		X	M Piraux	11
X	S1	X	S3	X		X		S					S				X	X	X	S2		X			X	X		X	P Jones	12
		X		S1	X		X	X		X	X		X	S2				X		X			X	X				X	U D Rennie	13
X		X	X	X						S	S	S2					X	X	S1			X			X	X	S		S W Dunn	14
X	S2	X	X	X		X		S	S		S						X	X	S1			X			X	X		X	P A Durkin	15
X	X		S2	X		X		S	S		S						X	X	X			X			X	X	S1	X	P E Alcock	16
X	X		S	S1		X		X	S		S						X	X	X			X			X	X	S2	X	M J Bodenham	17
	X	X		X		X			X	X	S	X	S2		X		X		X			X			X			S1	G R Ashby	18
X				X		X		X	S1	X		S	S2		X		X	X	X			X			X	S		S3	K W Burge	19
X		X	S			X		S2	X1	X		S					X			X2		X			X	S1		X	G Poll	20
X		X				X		X		X		S		S	S		X		X			X			X	X		X	S W Dunn	21
X	S	X	S2	S		X				X		S					X	X1	X	X2		X			X	X		X	G Willard	22
	S2	X		X		X		X		X		S		S			X	X	X1			X			X	X		X2	D R Elleray	23
	X3	X2		X		X1		S1	S2	X		S					X	X	X		S3	X	S		X	X			M A Riley	24
	X2	X	S3	X				X	S1	X		S					X	X3	X1			X	S		X	X	S2		P E Alcock	25
	X		X					X	S2	X		S					X2	X	X			X			X	X	S1	X1	G P Barber	26
	S	S	X	X		X		S	S	X		S					X	X	X			X			X	X		X	G R Ashby	27
	S2	X	S3	X		X		S1	X	X		S					S	X	X			X	S		X1	X		X2	N S Barry	28
	X2	X	S2	X		X		S1	S1	X1		S					X	X	X			X			X	X	S		S J Lodge	29
X	X	X	S	X			X1		S1	S		S	X				X	X	X			X			X	X	S		M A Riley	30
X	X	X	S	X				X1	X		S	X					X	X	X	S1			X			X			M J Bodenham	31
X	X2	X	S	X				S	S	X1		S					X	X	X	S1			X			X		S2	P Jones	32
X	X1	X	S	X		S2		X2	X		S						X3	X	X	S3			X			X		S1	D J Gallagher	33
	X3	X		X1		X	S	X	X2	S		X					X	X	X	S2					S1	X	S3		M J Bodenham	34
X	X	X				X		S2	S	X		S					X	X1	X	S1			X			X	X2		G Poll	35
	X		X		S	X		X	X	X		S		S1				X		S			X	X1		X			J T Winter	36
X	X	X1	X		S2	X			X	X	X	S					S1		X	S		X2	S		X				M J Bodenham	37
X	X		S2			X		S	X	X	S	X					X		X	X2	S		X1		X	S1			P A Durkin	38
X	X1	X				X	S		X	X	X	S					X	X	X			S			X	X	S1		M D Reed	39
X	S	X	S3			X	S1		X	X		S2					X2	X1	X				X		X	X	X3		D J Gallagher	40
X	S1	X				X	S2	S	X	X		S					X	X2	X				X		X	X	X1		A B Wilkie	41
X	X2	X	S3			X		X1	S1	X		S					X1		X3				X		X	X	S2		M D Reed	42
X	S2	X		S2		X1	S1	S3	X	X		S					X	X3		S			X		X	X	X2		S W Dunn	43
X	X3	X		S2			S	X	S1	X		S					X1	X	X	S3			X		X	X	X2		K W Burge	44
X	X3	X	S	S1			X	S2	X1	X		S					X	X	X	S3			X		X	X	X2		S J Lodge	45
X	X3	X	S3	X			X		S2	X		S					X2	X	S1			X	S		X	X	X1		G S Willard	46
X	X1	X		X	S		X		S2	X		S					X2	X	X				X		X	X	S		J Bodenham	47
X	X3	X	S			S1	X1			X		S				S	X	X	X				X		X2	X	S3		P Jones	48
X	X1	X		S			X			X		S	S				X	X	X				X		X	X		S1	M A Riley	49
X	X2	X1		S			X			S		X					X	X	X	S2			X		X	X		S1	N S Barry	50
X	X2			S3			S			X		S					X	X	X1	X					X	X	X3	S2	G R Ashby	51
	S2		X	X		X		X	X		S		X	S		S3		X2		X					S1		X3	X1	A B Wilkie	52
X	X		S				X	S	X								X	X1	X	S2					X	X	S1	X2	G Poll	53
X	X		S			X		S		X			S				X	X	X	S1		X			X	X	X1	S	P A Durkin	54

26	16	28	4	21		26	6	15	7	18			7	1		1	32	33	32	11		31	5	1	31	34	7	21	CP Appearances	
	10		11	3		2	4	6	10						2	1	2			20	1				2	1	9	2	CP Sub Appearances	
2	3	1	3	0+1	3		4	3+2	2			4	1+1		2		+1	3	4	2+2		2	1	2	3	1+2	1		CC Appearances	
6	8+1	7	1+3	4+1	0+1	7	1	3+2	3+3	7		5			7+1	7	7	1+3		4	1		8+1	8	2+4	1			FAC Appearances	
2	1+1	1	0+1	2		2									2	2	2	0+2		2		2	2	0+1	2				UEFA Appearances	

Also Played: Bartram S(13). Day S(36).

ARSENAL

CLUB RECORDS

BIGGEST VICTORIES
League: 12-0 v Loughborough Town, Division 2, 12.3.1900.
F.A. Cup: 11-1 v Darwen, 3rd Round, 9.1.1932.
League Cup: 7-0 v Leeds United, 2nd Round, 4.9.1979.
Europe: (ECWC) 7-0 v Standard Liege, 2n Round 3.11.93.
(UEFA) 7-1 v Staevnet, 1st Round, 25.9.1963.
(Fairs Cup) 7-1 v Dinamo Bacau, Q/Final, 18.3.1970.

BIGGEST DEFEATS
League: 0-8 v Loughborough Town, Division 2, 12.12.1896.
F.A. Cup: 0-6 v Sunderland, 1st Round, 21.1.1893.
0-6 v Derby County, 1st Round, 28.1.1899.
0-6 v West Ham, 3rd Round, 5.1.1946.
League Cup: 2-6 v Manchester United, 4th Round,28.11.90.
0-3 v Liverpool, 4th Round, 8.12.1981.
Europe: (UEFA) 2-5 v Spartak Moscow, 1st Round, 29.9.82.

MOST POINTS
3 points a win: 83, 1990-91.
2 points a win: 66, 1930-31.

MOST GOALS SCORED
127, Division 1, 1930-31.
Lambert 38, Jack 31, Bastin 28, Hulme 14, James 5, Brain 4, John 2, Williams 2, Johnson 1, Roberts 1, Jones 1.

MOST GOALS CONCEDED
86, Division 1, 1926-27; Division 1, 1927-28.

MOST FIRST CLASS MATCHES IN A SEASON
70 - 1979-80 (League 42, FA Cup 11, League Cup 7, Charity Shield 1, ECWC 9).

MOST LEAGUE WINS
29, Division 1, 1970-71.

MOST LEAGUE DRAWS
18, Division 1, 1969-70.

MOST LEAGUE DEFEATS
23, Division 1, 1912-13; Division 1, 1924-25.

INDIVIDUAL CLUB RECORDS

MOST GOALS IN A SEASON
Ted Drake - 42, 1934-35.

MOST GOALS IN A MATCH
7. Ted Drake v Aston Villa, Division 1, 14.12.1935 (7-1).

OLDEST PLAYER
Jock Rutherford, 41 years 236 days v Manchester City, 20.3.1926.

YOUNGEST PLAYER
Gerry Ward, 16 years 321 days v Huddersfield, 22.8.1953.

MOST CAPPED PLAYER
Kenny Sansom (England) 77 1981-86.

BEST PERFORMANCES

League: 1930-31: Played 42, Won 29, Drawn 10, Lost 4, Goals for 127, Goals against 59, Points 66. First in Division 1.
Highest Position: Division 1 Champions.
F.A. Cup: Winners in 1929-30 v Huddersfield 2-0.
Winners in 1935-36 v Sheffield United 1-0.
Winners in 1949-50 v Liverpool 2-0.
Winners in 1970-71 v Liverpool 2-1.
Winners in 1978-79 v Manchester Utd 3-2.
Winners in 1992-93 v Sheffield Wednesday 1-1 (aet), 1-1 (2-1 aet)
Most Recent Success: 1997/98: 3rd Rnd; 4th Rnd; 5th Rnd; 6th Rnd; Semi-Final v Wolverhampton W. 1-0; Final v Newcastle United 2-0.
League Cup: Winners in 1986-87 v Liverpool 2-1.
Most Recent Success: 1992-93: 2nd Rnd Millwall (h) 1-1, (a) 1-1 (won 3-1 on pens.); 3rd Rnd, Derby County (a) 1-1, (h) 2-1; 4th Rnd, Scarborough (a) 1-0; 5th Rnd Nottingham Forest (h) 2-0; Semi-final, Crystal Palace (a) 3-1 (h) 2-0; Final Sheffield Wednesday 2-1.
Europe: (UEFA) 1969-70: 1st Rnd, Glentoran 5-0,0-1; 2nd Rnd Sp.ch.de Port 0-0,3-0; 3rd Rnd, Rouen 0-0,1-0; 4th Round Dinemo Bacau 2-0,7-1; Semi-final, Ajax 3-0,0-1; Final , Anderlect 1-3,3-0.
(ECWC) 1993-94: 1st Round Odense 2-1,1-1; 2nd Round Standard Leige 3-0,7-0; 2nd Round Torino 0-0,1-0; Semi-Final Paris St. Girman 1-1,1-0; Final Parma 1-0.

DIVISIONAL RECORD

	Played	Won	Drawn	Lost	For	Against	Points
Division 1/P	3,336	1,426	869	1041	5,344	4,379	4,040
Division 2	428	216	73	139	825	550	505
Total	**3,764**	**1,642**	**942**	**1,180**	**6,159**	**4,929**	**4,545**

ADDITIONAL INFORMATION
PREVIOUS NAME
None.

PREVIOUS LEAGUES
None.

Club Colours: Red with white sleeve shirts, white shorts, red and white stockings.
Change Colours: Yellow shirts with navy blue band, navy blue shorts, blue & yellow stockings.

Reserve League: Football Combination.
Youth League: South Eastern Counties.

RECORDS AND STATISTICS

COMPETITIONS

Div 1/P	Div.2	Euro C	ECWC	UEFA
1904-13	1893-04	1971-72	1979-80	1963-64
1919-	1913-19	1991-92	1993-94	1969-70
			1994-95	1970-71
				1978-79
				1981-82
				1982-83
				1996-97

HONOURS

Div 1/P	FAC	Lge Cup	UEFA	ECWC	C/Sh'ld
1930-31	1929-30	1986-87	1969-70	1993-94	1930
1932-33	1935-36	1992-93			1931
1933-34	1949-50				1933
1934-35	**1970-71**				1934
1937-38	1978-79				1938
1947-48	1992-93				1948
1952-53	**1997/98**				1953
1970-71					1992
1988-89					shared
1990-91					
1997-98					

MOST APPEARANCES

David O'Leary 682+40 (1975-93)
(Including 3 Charity Shield & 2 Others)

Year	League	FA Cup	Lge Cup	Europe
1975-76	27	1	2	
1976-77	33	3	4	
1977-78	41	6	6	
1978-79	37	11	1	5
1979-80	34	9	6	9
1980-81	24	1	2	
1981-82	40	1	5	4
1982-83	36	5	7	2
1983-84	36	1	4	
1984-85	36	3	3	
1985-86	35	5	7	
1986-87	39	4	9	
1987-88	23	4	6	
1988-89	26	2		
1989-90	28+6	3	4	
1990-91	11+10	5+1	0+1	
1991-92	11+14	1	0+1	1
1992-93	5+5	1+3	2	
	522+35	66+4	68+2	21

MOST GOALS IN A CAREER

Ian Wright - 185 (1991-98)

Year	League	FA Cup	Lge Cup	Other
1991-92	24	-	2	-
1992-93	15	10	5	-
1993-94	23	1	6	5
1994-95	18	-	3	9
1995-96	15	1	7	-
1996-97	23	-	5	2
1997-98	10	1	-	-
Total	**128**	**13**	**28**	**16**

Current top goalscorer: Dennis Bergkamp - 52 (1995-98)

RECORD TRANSFER FEE RECEIVED

Amount	Club	Player	Date
£5,000,000	Middlesbrough	Paul Merson	07/97
£2,000,000	Leeds United	David Rocastle	07/92
£1,500,000	Liverpool	Michael Thomas	12/91
£1,250,000	Crystal Palace	Clive Allen	08/80

RECORD TRANSFER FEE PAID

Amount	Club	Player	Date
£8,500,000	Inter Milan	Dennis Bergkamp	06/95
£4,750,000	Sampdoria	David Platt	07/95
£2,500,000	Luton Town	Jon Hartson	01/95
£2,500,000	Crystal Palace	Ian Wright	09/91

MANAGERS

Name	Seasons	Best	Worst
T E Mitchell	1897-98	5(2)	5(2)
George Excoat	1898-99	7(2)	7(2)
Harry Bradshaw	1899-04	2(2)	8(2)
Phil Kelso	1904-08	7(1)	15(1)
George Morrell	1908-15	6(1)	15(1)
Leslie Knighton	1919-25	9(1)	20(1)
Herbert Chapman	1925-34	1(1)	14(1)
George Allison	1934-47	1(1)	6(1)
Tom Whittaker	1947-56	1(1)	6(1)
Jack Crayston	1956-58	5(1)	12(1)
George Swindin	1958-62	3(1)	15(1)
Billy Wright	1962-66	8(1)	17(1)
Bertie Mee	1966-76	1(1)	17(1)
Terry Neill	1976-83	3(1)	17(1)
Don Howe	1983-86	6(1)	7(1)
George Graham	1986-95	1(1)	6(1)
Bruce Rioch	1995-96	5(P)	5(P)
Arsene Wenger	1996-	1(P)	3(P)

LONGEST LEAGUE RUNS

of undefeated matches:	26 (28.4.1990 - 19.1.1991)	of league matches w/out a win:	23 (28.9.1912 - 1.3.1913)
of undefeated home matches:	33 (1.10.1902-22.10.1904)	of undefeated away matches:	13 (5.51990 - 12.1.1991)
without home win:	16 (23.4.1912 - 1.3.1913)	without an away win:	15 (7.1.1928 - 6.10.1928)
of league wins:	10 (12.9.1987 - 14.11.1987)	of home wins:	15 (5.9.1903 - 4.4.1904)
of league defeats:	7 (12.21977 - 12.3.1977)	of away wins:	6 (22.10.1977 - 27.12.1977)

Arsenal

PLAYERS NAME / Honours	Ht	Wt	Birthdate	Birthplace / Transfers	Contract Date	Clubs	League	L/Cup	FA Cup	Other	Lge	L/C	FAC	Oth
GOALKEEPER														
Manninger Alexander			04/06/77	Salzburg (Austria)		Cazino Salzburg								
Austrian u21. Prem'98. FAC'98				£500000	17/06/97	Arsenal	7	4	5					
Seaman David	6.2	13	10/09/63	Rotherham	22/09/81	Leeds United								
E:44,B.6,u21.10. Div.1'91.LC'93.				£4000	13/08/82	Peterborough Utd	91	10	5					
FAC'93'98. ECWC'94. FlgXl1				£100000	05/10/84	Birmingham City	75	4	5					
Prem'98.				£225000	07/08/86	Q.P.R.	141	13	17	4				
				£1300000	18/05/90	Arsenal	280	31	36	30				
DEFENCE														
Adams Tony	6.1	12.1	10/10/66	Romford	30/01/84	Arsenal	417+4	58+1	40+1	31	30	5	5	3
E: 55,B.4,u21.5,Y.5,S. CT'89 Div.1'89'91.LC'87'93.FAC'93'98. ECWC'94. Prem'98.														
Bould Steve	6.2	11.13	16/11/62	Stoke	15/11/80	Stoke City	179+4	13	10	5	6	1		
E:2,B.1. CT'89 Div.1'89.91. ECWC'94.				Loan	19/10/82	Torquay United	9		2					
Prem'98. FAC'98.				£390000	13/06/88	Arsenal	257+11	33	24+1	16+4	5	1		2
Dixon Lee	5.9	10.12	17/03/64	Manchester	21/07/82	Burnley	4	1						
E:21,B.4. CT'89 Div.1'89'91.				Free	16/02/84	Chester City	56+1	2	1	3	1			
FAC'93'98. ECWC'94. FLgXl.1. Prem'98.				Free	15/07/85	Bury	45	4	8	1	6		1	
				£40000	18/07/86	Stoke City	71	6	7	4	5			
				£400000	29/01/88	Arsenal	346+6	45	36	31	20		1	
David Grodin						Saint Etienne								
				£500000	19/06/98	Arsenal								
Keown Martin	6.1	12.4	24/07/66	Oxford	02/02/84	Arsenal	22		5					
E:18,B.1,u21.8,Y.4. Prem'98 FAC'98				Loan	15/02/85	Brighton & H.A.	21+2	2		2	1	1		1
				£200000	09/06/86	Aston Villa	109+3	12+1	6	2	3			
				£750000	07/08/89	Everton	92+4	11	12+1	6				
				£2000000	04/02/93	Arsenal	147+18	16+2	15+2	11+5	2	1		
Upson Matthew J	6.1	11.5	18/04/79	Eye	24/04/96	Luton Town (T)	0+1			1				
				£1000000	14/05/97	Arsenal	5	2	1					
Vivas Nelson						Boca Juniors								
Argentine Int.				£1600000		Arsenal								
Winterburn Nigel	5.1	10.7	11/12/63	Nuneaton	14/08/81	Birmingham City								
E:2,B.3,u21.1,Y.1. Div.1'89'91 CT'89.				Free	22/09/83	Wimbledon	164+1	13	12	2	8			
LC'93. FAC'93'98. ECWC'94. Prem'98				£407000	26/05/87	Arsenal	380+2	48	41	34	8	3		
MIDFIELD														
Black Michael J	5.8	11.8	06/10/76	Chigwell	31/05/97	Arsenal (T)								
Crowe Jason	5.9	10.9	30/09/78	Sidcup	13/05/96	Arsenal (T)		0+1	0+1					
Day James R			03/07/97			Arsenal								
Grimandi Gilles			11/11/70	Gap (France)		Monaco								
French championship'97. Prem'98. FAC'98.				£1500000	25/06/97	Arsenal	16+6	4	3+2	1				
Hughes Steve	6	12.12	18/09/76	Reading	01/08/94	Arsenal	17+16	3+3	5+3	2	1	1		
E: u21.4, Y. FAYC'94. Prem'98.														
MacDonald James	6	12.5	2/21/79	Inverness		Arsenal (T)								
Mendes-Rodriguez A			24/10/74	Nuremburg		FC Feucht								
				£250000	21/07/97	Arsenal	1+2	2			1			
Parlour Raymond	5.1	11.12	07/03/73	Romford	06/03/91	Arsenal	135+25	17+3	19	10+3	11		2	
E: B.1, u21.12, S. FLC'93. FAC'93'98. ECWC'94. Prem'98														
Pereira Luis Boa Morte			04/08/77	Lisbon		Sporting Lisbon								
Portuguese u21. Prem'98				£1750000	25/06/97	Arsenal	4+11	1	1+3	0+1	2			
Petit Emmanuel			22/10/70	Dieppe (France)		Monaco								
French Int. World Cup winner'98.				£3500000	25/06/97	Arsenal	32	3	7	2	2			
French Cup'91. Championship'97. Prem'98. FAC'98.														
Vieira Patrick	6.4	13	23/06/76	France		AC Milan								
French Int. World Cup winner'98				£3500000	14/08/96	Arsenal	61+3	5	11+1	3	4			
Prem'98. FAC'98.														

FORWARDS														
Anelka Nicolas 6.0 12 14/03/79			Versailles		Paris St Germain									
French Youth Int. Prem'98 FAC'98			£500000	06/03/97	Arsenal	16+14	3	8+1	1+1	6		3		
Bergkamp Dennis 6 12.05 18/05/69			Amsterdam		Inter Milan	52				11				
Dutch Int. Prem'98.					Ajax	185				103				
			£7500000	01/07/95	Arsenal	89+1	13	10	2	39	8	4	1	
Overmars Marc 29/03/73			Ernst (Holland)		Ajax									
Dutch Int. EC'95. WCC'95. Dutch league'94'95'96			£7000000	10/07/97	Arsenal	32	3	8+1	2	12	2	2		
Prem'98. FAC'98.														
Rankin Isaiah 5.10 11 22/05/78			London	12/09/95	Arsenal (T)	0+1								
Vernazza Paulo 6 11.10 11/1/79			London	11/18/97	Arsenal (T)	1	1							
Wreh Christopher 14/05/75			Monrovia (Liberia)		Monaco									
Prem'98. FAC'98				01/07/95	Arsenal	7+9	1+2	2+4	0+1	3		1		

MANAGER
ARSENE WENGER

Date of Birth . . . . 22nd September 1949.
Place of Birth . . . . Strasbourg.
Date of Appointment . . . . October 1996.

PREVIOUS CLUBS
As Manager. . . . . Nancy, Monaco, Grampus Eight.
As Asst/Coach . . . . Cannes.

HONOURS
As a Manager
Monaco: French Championship 1987/88.
Grampus Eight: Emperor's Cup 1995.
Arsenal: Carling Premiership 1997/98. FA Cup 1997/98.

Arsenal Stadium

Highbury, London N5 1BU

Capacity ....39,000.
First game..v Leicester Fosse, Division 2, 6.9.1913.
First floodlit game..v Glasgow Rangers, 1951.

ATTENDANCES
Highest ....73,295 v Sunderland, Div.1, 9.3.1935.
Lowest..600v Loughborough Town, Div.2, 12.3.1900.

OTHER GROUNDS ....Plumstead Common 1886-1887. Sportsman's Ground 1887-1888.
..................Manor Road 1888-1890/1893-1913. Invicta Ground 1890-1893. Highbury 1913 to date.

HOW TO GET TO THE GROUND

From the North
Leave Motorway M1 at junction 2 and follow signs to the City. In 6.2 miles pass Holloway Road Station and then take 3rd turning on left into Drayton Park Road. In 0.7 miles turn right into Avenell Road for Arsenal FC.

From the South
From London Bridge follow signs, to Bank of England, then follow signs to Angel (Islington). At traffic signals turn right (S.P. The North) and in 1 mile at Highbury roundabout forward into Holloway Road. Then take 3rd turning on right into Drayton Park Road. In 0.7 miles turn right into Avenell Road for Arsenal FC.

From the West
Leave motorway M4 at junction 1, Chiswick, and followed A315 (S.P. Chiswick). In 0.9 miles turn left A40 then follow signs to City to join motorway M41, then A40(M) at end forward into Ring Road A501. At Angel (Islington) turn left to Highbury roundabout, keep forward into Holloway Road. Then take 3rd turning on right into Drayton Park Road. In 0.7 miles turn right into Avenell Road for Arsenal FC.

Car Parking: Parking is permitted in adjacent streets with restrictions.
Nearest Railway Station: Finsbury Park and Highbury & Islington.

USEFUL TELEPHONE NUMBERS

Club switchboard 0171 704 4000
Club fax number.......................0171 704 4001
Club shop 0171 404 4120
Ticket Office..............................0171 404 4040

Marketing Department ....0171 704 4100 (fax 704 4101)
Internet address ....www.arsenal.co.uk
Clubcall 0891 20 20 20*
*Calls cost 50p per minute at all times. Call costings correct at time of going to press.

MATCHDAY PROGRAMME

Programme Editor .... Kevin Connolly.

Number of pages................. 48

Price £2

Subscriptions
. . Subscription price on application to club
.... shop.

Local Newspapers
.... Islington Gazette.

Local Radio Stations
...... Capital Radio, BBC Radio London.

MATCHDAY TICKET PRICES

Centre Blocks - East & West Upper Tier............... £34.00
Next to Centre Blocks - East & West U.T.............. £25.00
Wing blocks - East & West Upper Tier £22.50
Lower Tiers - East & West £17.50
Lower Tiers - East & West Wing Blocks £16.50
North Bank - Upper Tier............................ £26.50
North Bank - Upper Tier Wing £21.00
North Bank - Lower Tier............................ £21.00
North Bank - Lower Tier Wing £16.50
North Bank - Lower Tier Outer Wing £14.00
Clock End Stand £16.00

Family Enclosure - Members Only
Adult - Lower Tier £17.50
Adult - Lower Tier Wing Block £16.50
Senior Citizen & Cannon Club...................... £9.00
Junior Gunners £8.00

ASTON VILLA
(The Villa)
F.A. CARLING PREMIERSHIP
SPONSORED BY: LDV VANS

Aston Villa 1998-1999

ASTON VILLA
FORMED IN 1874
TURNED PROFESSIONAL IN 1885
LTD COMPANY IN 1896

PRESIDENT: J A Alderson
CHAIRMAN: Doug Ellis
DIRECTORS:
P D Ellis, S Stride,
M J Ansell, D M Owen, A J Hales
SECRETARY: Steven Stride
(0121 327 2299)
COMMERCIAL MANAGER
Abdul Rashid (0121 327 5399)

MANAGER: John Gregory
ASSISTANT: Allan Evans

RESERVE TEAM MANAGER
Malcolm Beard
YOUTH TEAM MANAGER
Tony McAndrew
PHYSIOTHERAPIST
Jim Walker

**CLUB STATISTICIAN/STATISTICIAN FOR
THE DIRECTORY**
David Bridgewater/Dave Hodges

Until the arrival as manager of the club's former 1970s midfield player John Gregory in early March - soon after they had been knocked out of the F.A. Cup by Coventry City - Aston Villa had not had the greatest of seasons in the Carling Premiership. Under Brian Little they had risen above halfway just once (early October) and, indeed, were situated nearer the relegation zone than they were to a top eight finish when Gregory first took over the reins. But after a dismal run of seven defeats in eleven starts under Little and then Gregory, slowly but surely the latter began to get the team playing organised, competitive and positive football, and in less than two months in charge he had seen his team climb to eighth in the table, to get within striking distance of a UEFA Cup place. Thereafter generally performances from March to the season's end were extremely good and, in fact, under Gregory Villa lost only two of their final 10 Carling Premiership matches and in doing so clinched a UEFA Cup place for 1998-99 by claiming seventh place in the final table.

Trinidad and Tobago international Dwight Yorke, Villa's top-scorer, had a fine season, as did the the lithe and exciting Lee Hendrie. Aussie goalkeeper Mark Bosnich also had a good campaign, along with central defenders Gareth Southgate (who went to France with England) and Ugo Ehiogu (absent only once), while the industrious Mark Draper, the versatile Simon Grayson and the hard-working Ian Taylor all grafted well in midfield. Two left-sided players - Alan Wright (who missed only two games) and Steve Staunton - both performed with credit, likewise forward Julian Joachim, who was used late in the season. Unfortunately Villa had hoped that their two main strikers - Stan Collymore and the Yugoslavian Savo Milosevic, who jointly cost the club over £10 million - would produce the goods, but sadly neither player scored sufficient goals (only 13 between them in the Carling Premiership)......and Milosevic was even dropped and fined by the club for spitting at fans during Villa's embarrassing 5-0 defeat at Blackburn. He was eventually transferred to the Spanish club, Real Zaragoza - and still went to the World Cup finals with his country.

League form apart, Villa looked, at one stage, to be going well in the UEFA Cup before losing out on the away goal rule to Atletico Madrid. This term they could produce a sound bet for European glory - and perhaps win one of the major domestic Cup competitions, if they can avoid injuries and suspensions and Gregory can field a settled side. Villa averaged over 36,000 at home games in 1997-98, having full houses on five occasions, and there's no doubt that the support will be there again.....if the results are forthcoming.

Tony Matthews.

ASTON VILLA

M	DATE	COMP.	VEN	OPPONENTS	RESULT	H/T	LP	GOAL SCORERS/GOAL TIMES	ATT.
1	A 09	CP	A	Leicester City	L 0-1	0-1	19		(20304)
2	12	CP	H	Blackburn Rovers	L 0-4	0-3	20		37112
3	23	CP	A	Newcastle United	L 0-1	0-1	20		(36783)
4	27	CP	A	Tottenham Hotspur	L 2-3	1-1	20	Yorke 27, Collymore 57	(26317)
5	30	CP	H	Leeds United	W 1-0	0-0	19	Yorke 67	39027
6	S 13	CP	A	Barnsley	W 3-0	1-0	12	Ehiogu 25, Draper 50, Taylor 72	(18649)
7	16	UEFA 1/1	A	Bordeaux (France)	D 0-0	0-0			(16000)
8	20	CP	H	Derby County	W 2-1	0-1	9	Yorke 73, Joachim 75	35444
9	22	CP	A	Liverpool	L 0-3	0-0	11		(34843)
10	27	CP	H	Sheffield Wednesday	D 2-2	1-2	14	Staunton 31, Taylor 49	32044
11	30	UEFA 1/2	H	Bordeaux (France)	W 1-0*	0-0		Milosevic 111	33072
12	O 04	CP	A	Bolton Wanderers	W 1-0	1-0	8	Milosevic 12	(24196)
13	15	CC 3	A	West Ham United	L 0-3	0-2			(20360)
14	18	CP	A	Wimbledon	L 1-2	1-1	11	Taylor 44	32087
15	21	UEFA 2/1	A	Athletico Bilbao	D 0-0	0-0			(46000)
16	26	CP	A	Arsenal	D 0-0	0-0	13		(38061)
17	N 01	CP	H	Chelsea	L 0-2	0-1	14		39372
18	04	UEFA 2/2	H	Athletico Bilbao	W 2-1	1-0		Taylor 28, Yorke 50	35915
19	08	CP	A	Crystal Palace	D 1-1	0-1	15	Joachim 86	(21097)
20	22	CP	H	Everton	W 2-1	1-1	11	Milosevic 38, Ehiogu 56	36389
21	25	UEFA 3/1	A	Steaua Bucharest	L 1-2	0-2		Yorke 54	(25000)
22	29	CP	A	West Ham United	L 1-2	0-1	13	Yorke 46	(24976)
23	D 06	CP	H	Coventry City	W 3-0	1-0	11	Collymore 21, Hendrie 71, Joachim 84	33250
24	09	UEFA 3/2	H	Steaua Bucharest	W 2-0	0-0		Milosevic 71, Taylor 85	35102
25	15	CP	A	Manchester United	L 0-1	0-0	12		(55151)
26	20	CP	H	Southampton	D 1-1	0-0	12	Taylor 64	29343
27	26	CP	H	Tottenham Hotspur	W 4-1	1-0	11	Draper 38, 68, Collymore 81, 88	38644
28	28	CP	A	Leeds United	D 1-1	0-0	10	Milosevic 85	(36287)
29	J 03	FAC 3	A	Portsmouth	D 2-2	1-2		Staunton 42, Grayson 88	(16013)
30	10	CP	A	Leicester City	D 1-1	1-0	10	Joachim 87	36429
31	14	FAC 3R	H	Portsmouth	W 1-0	1-0		Milosevic 21	23355
32	17	CP	A	Blackburn Rovers	L 0-5	0-2	12		(24834)
33	24	FAC 4	H	West Bromwich Albion	W 4-0	1-0		Grayson 4, Yorke 61, 64, Collymore 71	39372
34	F 01	CP	H	Newcastle United	L 0-1	0-0	15		38266
35	06	CP	A	Derby County	W 1-0	0-0	13	Yorke 90	(30251)
36	14	FAC 5	H	Coventry City	L 0-1	0-0			36979
37	18	CP	H	Manchester United	L 0-2	0-0	14		39372
38	21	CP	A	Wimbledon	L 1-2	1-2	15	Milosevic 41	(13131)
39	28	CP	H	Liverpool	W 2-1	1-1	14	Collymore 10, 64	39377
40	M 03	UEFA QF1	A	Athletico Madrid	L 0-1	0-1			(47000)
41	08	CP	A	Chelsea	W 1-0	0-0	13	Joachim 50	(33018)
42	11	CP	H	Barnsley	L 0-1	0-1	13		29519
43	14	CP	H	Crystal Palace	W 3-1	3-0	11	Taylor 1, Milosevic 14 (pen), 36	33781
44	17	UEFA QF2	H	Athletico Madrid	W 2-1	0-1		Taylor 72, Collymore 74	39163
45	28	CP	A	Everton	W 4-1	1-1	11	Joachim 11, Charles 62, Yorke 72 (pen), 81	(36471)
46	A 04	CP	H	West Ham United	W 2-0	0-0	9	Joachim 75, Milosevic 83	39372
47	11	CP	A	Coventry City	W 2-1	1-0	8	Yorke 5, 48	(22792)
48	18	CP	A	Southampton	W 2-1	1-1	8	Hendrie 6, Yorke 60	(15238)
49	25	CP	H	Bolton Wanderers	L 1-3	0-2	8	Taylor 57	38392
50	M 02	CP	A	Sheffield Wednesday	W 3-1	2-0	7	Yorke 21, Hendrie 25, Joachim 50	(34177)
51	10	CP	H	Arsenal	W 1-0	1-0	7	Yorke 37 (pen)	39372

Best Home League Attendance: 39377 V Liverpool   **Smallest :29343 V Southampton**   **Average :36136**

Goal Scorers:

CP	(49)	Yorke 12, Joachim 8, Milosevic 7, Collymore 6, Taylor 6, Draper 3, Hendrie 3, Ehiogu 2, Charles 1, Staunton 1
CC	(0)	
FAC	(7)	Grayson 2, Yorke 2, Collymore 1, Milosevic 1, Staunton 1
UEFA	(8)	Taylor 3, Milosevic 2, Yorke 2, Collymore 1

*AET.

(M) Barry	(G) Bosnich	(F) Byfield	(D) Charles	(D) Collins	(F) Collymore	(F) Curcic	(F) Davis	(M) Draper	(D) Ehiogu	(G) Ghent	(M) Grayson	(F) Hendrie	(M) Hughes	(F) Joachim	(F) Milosevic	(F) Murray	(D) Nelson	(G) Oakes	(G) Rachel	(D) Scimeca	(D) Southgate	(D) Staunton	(M) Taylor	(M) Townsend	(M) Vassell	(F) Walker	(D) Wright	(F) Yorke	Referee	No
		S		X		X	X	S							S	X		X	X		S	X		X	X		X	X	S J Lodge	1
		S		X		X	X	X							S2	X		X	X		S	X		S1	X		X	X	P E Alcock	2
X		X	X			X	X	X							S1	S		S2	S		X	X	X	X			S3	X	G S Willard	3
X		X	X	S1		X	X									S		S	S		X	X	X	X	X		S	X	M A Riley	4
X		X	X	S		X	X	X								S		S1	S		S	X	X				X	X	P Jones	5
X			X	S2		X	X	X							S	S		X	S		S1	X	X	X			X	X	G P Barber	6
X	S		X	S1		X	X	X1						S	S		S	X	S		S		X	X			X	X	A Ancion	7
X			X	X	X		X	S							S1	S3		X	S		S2	X	X	X			X	X	J T Winter	8
X			X	S		X	X	X							S1			X	S		S	X	X	X			X	X	M J Bodenham	9
X	S2		X	S		X	X								S	S1		X			S	X	X	X			X	X	N S Barry	10
X	S1		X	S			X	X						S	S	X	S	X1	S		S	X	X	X			X	X	K E Fisker	11
X	S2		X	S3	S	X	X								X			X	S		S1	X	X	X			X	X	G Poll	12
X	S2		X	S3	X	X	S1								X			X			X	X	X	X			X	X	S J Lodge	13
X	X		X			X	X	X							S2	X		S	S		X	X	X	X			S1	X	K W Burge	14
X	S		X	S	X	S	S1	S					S	S	X		X	S		X	X	X	X1			X	X	Hartmut Strampe	15
X	X			S		X	X	X	S	S	S	X			S	X		S	X		X						X	X	P A Durkin	16
			X			S	X	X				X	S2		X	X		X	X		X	S	S1				X	X	S W Dunn	17
X	X			S	S	X	S	S1				S	S	S	X1	S		X	X		X	X	X				X	X	Piller	18
X	X			S		X	S					S	S1	X	X	S		X			X	X	X				X	X	J T Winter	19
			X	X		X	X	S	S		S	S	X	S	X	S	S	X	X	S	X		X				X	X	U D Rennie	20
	S1		X			X	X					X	X		X			X1	X				X	X			X	X	Lubos Michel	21
	X		X	S		X	X					S1	S		S	X		X	X	S	X1		X				X	X	P E Alcock	22
X			X	S	X3	S3	X	X				X	S1		S2	X2		S			X	X					X	X1	G P Barber	23
X			X	S	S	S	X2	X				X1	S1		S	X		S2	S		S	X	X	X			X		B Heyneman	24
			X		X	X	X	X		S		X1	S1		S2	X2		S	X		S	X	X	X			X		P A Durkin	25
			X		X	X	X	X		S		X1	S1		S	S		S	X		S	X	X	X			X		D R Elleray	26
X	S	S	S	X		X	X	X				X	S		X			X	X		X	X	X				X		A B Wilkie	27
X	X1	S	S			X	X	X				X	S		X			X	X		X	X	X		S1			X		D J Gallagher	28
X	S		X2			X	X	X				X	S3		S2	X		X	S		S1	X1	X	X3			X		U D Rennie	29
X	S		X			X	X	X				X	S		S1	X		X1	X		X	X	X				X	X	M A Riley	30
X	S		X			X	X1	X				X	S1		S	S	S	S	X		X		X	X			X	X	U D Rennie	31
X	S		X			X	X	X				X	S		X	S		S	X		X	X	X				X	X	K W Burge	32
X	S1		X			X	X	X				X	S	S	S		S	S			X	X1	X				X	X	N S Barry	33
X	S	S	X			X	X	X				X	X		S1			S	S		X	X	X				X1	X	S J Lodge	34
X	S2	S	X			X	X	X	X1		S	X			S	X		S1	S		X	X	X				X	X2	P E Alcock	35
X	S1	S	X	X		X1	X	X				X	X		X			S	S		X	X	X			S	S	X	G S Willard	36
X	S	S	X			X	X	X				X	X		X			X	X		X		X			S	S	X	M J Bodenham	37
X	S2	S	X			X	X	X				X	S1		X	X1		X2	S		X	X	X			S	S	X	G R Ashby	38
X	S1	S	X1	S		X	X	X				X	X		X			S	S		X	X	X				X	X	G Poll	39
X	S	S	X2	S	S	X	X	X				X	X		S2			S	S		X1	X	S1	X			X	X	Stefano Braschi	40
X	S	S	S			X	X	X				X	X		X			S	S		X	X	X				X	X	S J Lodge	41
X	S	S1	S			X	X	X1				X	X		X			S2	S		X	X	X				X2	X	P Jones	42
X	S	S2	S			X	X	X1				S1	X		X			X2	S		X	X	X				X		G P Barber	43
X	S3	S	S2	S	X1	X	X	S				X	X		X	X2		S1	S		X	X	X				X	X	M Dan der Enee	44
X	S2	X				X	X	X				X1	X		X2			X	X		X	X	X				X	X	N S Barry	45
S	X	X1				X2	X	S2	X			X	X		X	S1	S	S		S1	X	X	X				X	X	S W Dunn	46
X		X	S			X	X	X1				X	X		X	X1	S	S		S1	X	X	X			S	X	X	D J Gallagher	47
X	S	S1				X	X	X1				X	X		S		S	X		S	X	X	X			S	X	X	A B Wilkie	48
X			S3			X	X	S2				X	X		X	X3		S	S		S1	X2	X1	X			X	X	D R Elleray	49
S1		S2		S			X	X				X	X2		X	S		X	X	S		X		X1			X	X	M J Bodenham	50
X	X	S				S1		X	X			X	X		S	X1	S		X	S		X					X	X	G Poll	51
1	30	1	14	23	3	31	37	28	13			16	19	21	8	16	32	27	30	3							35	30	CP Appearances	
1		6	4		2	4						5	4		10	4		4			5				2		1	2	CP Sub Appearances	
	1	0+1	0+1	4		1	0+1		1			0+1	1		1	1		1			2+1	3	4	3			1	1	CC Appearances	
4	0+1	0+1	4			4	4		4	2+2		1+1	2		1			2+1	3		4	3					4	2	FAC Appearances	
7	2+3	6+1	0+1			7	6		4+2	2+1		1+1	6		5+2	1		4	7		7+1	8					8	7	UEFA Appearances	

Also Played: (M) Crichton S(1,2).

ASTON VILLA

CLUB RECORDS

BIGGEST VICTORIES
League: 12-2 v Accrington, Division 1, 12.3.1892.
11-1 v Charlton Athletic, Division 2, 24.11.1959.
10-0 v Sheffield Wednesday, Division 1, 5.10.1912.
10-0 v Burnley, Division 1, 29.8.1925.
7-1 v Wimbledon, Premier Division, 11.2.1995.
F.A. Cup: 13-0 v Wednesday Old Athletic, 1st Rnd, 3.10.1886
League Cup: 8-1 v Exeter City, Round 2 2nd leg, 7.10.1985.
Europe: 5-0 v Valur, Round 1, 16.9.1981.

BIGGEST DEFEATS
League: 0-7 v Blackburn Rovers, Division 1, 19.10.1989.
0-7 v Everton, Division 1, 4.1.1890.
0-7 v West Bromwich Albion, Division 1, 19.10.1935.
0-7 v Manchester United, Division 1, 8.3.1950.
0-7 v Manchester United, Division 1, 24.10.1964.
F.A. Cup: 1-8 v Blackburn Rovers, Round 3, 16.2.1889.
League Cup: 1-6 v West Bromwich Albion, Round 2, 14.9.1966.
Europe: (UEFA) 1-4 v Antwerp, Round 2, 17.9.1975.
0-3 v Inter Milan, Round 2, 17.11.1990.

MOST POINTS
3 points a win: 78, Division 2, 1987-88.
2 points a win: 70, Division 3, 1971-72. (Division 3 record)

MOST GOALS
128, 1930/31 (Division 1 record).
Waring 49, Houghton 30, Walker 15, Beresford 14, Mandley 8, Brown 5, Chester 3, Gibson 2, Talbot 1, Tate 1.

MOST LEAGUE GOALS CONCEDED
110, Division 1, 1935-36.

MOST FIRST CLASS MATCHES IN A SEASON
61 (42 League, 3FA Cup, 6 League Cup, 1 Charity Shield, 9 European Cup) 1981-82.

MOST LEAGUE WINS
32, Division 3, 1971-72.

MOST LEAGUE DRAWS
17, Division 1, 1975-76.

MOST LEAGUE DEFEATS
24, Division 1, 1966-67.

INDIVIDUAL CLUB RECORDS

MOST GOALS IN A SEASON
Tom 'Pongo' Waring, 50 (49 League, 1 FA Cup) 1930-31.

MOST GOALS IN A MATCH
5, Harry Hampton v Sheffield Wednesday 10-0, 5.10.1912.
5, Harold Halse v Derby County 5-1, 19.10.1912.
5, Len Capwell v Burnley 10-0, 29.8.1925.
5, George Brown v Leicester 8-3, 2.1.1932.
5, Gerry Hitchens v Charlton Athletic 11-1, 18.11.1959.

OLDEST PLAYER
Ernie Callaghan, 39 years 257 days v Grimsby Town, Division 1, 12.4.1947.

YOUNGEST PLAYER
Jimmy Brown, 15 years 349 days v Bolton (a), 17.9.1969.

MOST CAPPED PLAYER
Paul McGrath (Republic of Ireland) 82. (51 while at Villa)
David Platt (England) 22.

BEST PERFORMANCES

League: Division 3 Champions 1971-72: Matches played 46, Won 32, Drawn 6, Lost 8, Goals for 88, Goals against 32, Points 70.
Highest: Division 1 Champions.

F.A. Cup: Winners in 1886-87 v West Bromwich Albion 2-0.
1894-95 v West Bromwich Albion 1-0.
1896-97 v Everton 3-2.
1904-05 v Newcastle United 2-0.
1912-13 v Sunderland 1-0.
1919-20 v Huddersfield Town 1-0.
Most recent success: 1956-57: 3rd Rnd. Luton Town 2-2, 2-0; 4th Rnd. Middlesbrough 3-2; 5th Rnd. Bristol City 2-1; 6th Rnd. Burnley 1-1, 2-0; Semi-Final West Bromwich Albion 2-2, 1-0; Final Manchester United 2-1.

League Cup: Winners in 1960-61 v Rotherham 0-2, 3-0.
1974-75 v Norwich City 1-0.
1976-77 v Everton 0-0, 1-1, 3-2.
1993-94 v Manchester United 3-1.
Most recent success: 1995-96: 2nd Rnd Peterborough Utd 6-0,1-1 3rd Rnd Stockport Co. 2-0. 4th Rnd QPR 1-0. 5th Rnd Wolves 1-0. Semi-Final Arsenal 2-2, 0-0. Final Leeds United 3-0.

Europe: (EC) 1981-82: 1st Rnd. Valur 5-0, 2-0; 2nd Rnd. Dynamo Berlin 2-1, 0-1; 3rd Rnd. Dynamo Kiev 0-0, 2-0; Semi-Final Anderlecht 1-0, 0-0; Final Bayern Munich 1-0.

DIVISIONAL RECORD

	Played	Won	Drawn	Lost	For	Against	Points
Division 1/P	3,386	1,426	756	1,204	5,746	5,216	3,849
Division 2	422	179	111	132	617	487	491
Division 3	92	51	21	20	139	78	123
Total	3,900	1,656	888	1,356	6,502	5,781	4,463

ADDITIONAL INFORMATION
PREVIOUS NAME
None.

PREVIOUS LEAGUES
None

Club Colours: Claret shirts with light blue sleeves, light blue & yellow trim, white shorts claret & blue trim, claret socks light blue trim.
Change Colours: Blue & claret shirt with white sections, white shorts & white socks. White shirt with claret & blue trim, claret shorts, white socks with claret & blue hoop.

Reserve League: Pontins Central League Premier Division.
Youth League: Melville Youth League.

RECORDS AND STATISTICS

COMPETITIONS

Div 1/P	Div.2	Div.3	Euro C.	UEFA	W.C.C.
1888-36	1936-38	1970-72	1981-82	1975-76	1982-83
1938-59	1959-60		1982-83	1977-78	
1960-67	1967-70			1983-84	
1975-87	1972-75		E S Cup	1990-91	
1988-	1987-88		1982-83	1993-94	
				1994-95	
				1996-97	

HONOURS

Div 1/P	Div.2	Div.3	FAC	Lge Cup	Euro C.
1893-94	1937-38	1971-72	1887	1961	1981-82
1895-96	1959-60		1895	1975	
1896-97			1897	1977	E.S.C.
1898-99			1905	1994	1982-83
1899-00			1913	1996	
1909-10			1920	C/Sh'ld	
1980-81			1957	1981	

MOST APPEARANCES

CHARLIE AITKEN 656+3 (1960-76)

Year	League	FA Cup	Lge Cup	Europe
1960-61	1			
1961-62	35	4	3	
1962-63	42	3	8	
1963-64	34	2	1	
1964-65	42	5	6	
1965-66	42	1	5	
1966-67	39	2	1	
1967-68	30+2	2	1	
1968-69	42	4	1	
1969-70	31	1	2	
1970-71	44	1	10	
1971-72	43	1	6	
1972-73	33	1	4	
1973-74	38	4	1	
1974-75	42	3	10	
1975-76	21	0+1	2	2
	559+2	34+1	61	2

MOST GOALS IN A CAREER

BILLY WALKER - 244 (1919-1934)

YEAR	LEAGUE	FA CUP
1919-20	8	5
1920-21	27	4
1921-22	21	6
1922-23	23	0
1923-24	14	3
1924-25	19	6
1925-26	21	1
1926-27	15	0
1927-28	10	1
1928-29	19	3
1929-30	8	1
1930-31	15	1
1931-32	9	0
1932-33	5	0
1933-34	0	0
Total	214	30

Current top goalscorer: Dwight Yorke - 99 (1990-98)

RECORD TRANSFER FEE RECEIVED

AMOUNT	CLUB	PLAYER	DATE
£5,500,000	Bari	David Platt	7/91
£1,750,000	Wolves	Andy Gray	9/79
£1,600,000	Everton	Earl Barrett	1/95
£1,500,000	Blackburn R.	Graham Fenton	11/95

RECORD TRANSFER FEE PAID

AMOUNT	CLUB	PLAYER	DATE
£7,000,000	Liverpool	Stan Collymore	05/97
£3,500,000	Partizen Belgrade	Savo Milosevic	7/95
£3,250,000	Leicester	Mark Draper	8/95
£2,500,000	Crystal Palace	Gareth Southgate	7/95

MANAGERS

NAME	SEASONS	BEST	WORST
Jim McMullen	1934-36	13(1)	21(1)
Jim Hogan	1936-39	12(1)	9(2)
Alex Massie	1945-50	6(1)	12(1)
George Martin	1950-53	6(1)	15(1)
Eric Houghton	1953-58	6(1)	20(1)
Joe Mercer	1958-64	7(1)	1(2)
Dick Taylor	1964-67	16(1)	21(1)
Tony Cummings	1967-68	16(2)	16(2)
Arthur Cox (CT)	1968		
Tommy Docherty	1968-70	18(2)	21(2)
Vic Crowe	1970-74	3(2)	4(3)
Ron Saunders	1974-82	1(1)	2(2)
Tony Barton	1982-84	6(1)	11(1)
Graham Turner	1984-86	10(1)	16(1)
Billy McNeil	1986-87		
Graham Taylor	1987-90	2(1)	2(2)
Jozef Venglos	1990-91	17(1)	17(1)
Ron Atkinson	1991-94	2(P)	10(P)
Brian Little	1994-98	4(P)	18(P)
John Gregory	1998-	7(P)	7(P)

LONGEST LEAGUE RUNS

of undefeated matches:	15 (16.1.1897 - 18.9.1897)	of league matches w/out a win:	12 (10.11.73 - 2.2.74)
	(18.12.1890 - 26.3.1910. 12.3.1949 - 27.8.1949)		(27.12. 1986 - 25.3.1987)
of undefeated home matches:	37 (24.4.1909 - 22.4.1911)	of undefeated away matches:	13 (5.9.1987 - 23.1.1988)
without home win:	8 (11.12.1920 - 28.3.1921)	without an away win:	27 (21.9. 1963 - 26.12.1964)
of league wins:	9 (22.3. - 18.9.1897. 15.10. - 10.12.1910)	of home wins:	14 (10.1.1903 - 25.11.1903)
of league defeats:	11 (22.3. 1963 - 4.4. 1963)	of away wins:	6 (6.2.1897 - 11.9. 1897)

ASTON VILLA

PLAYERS NAME / Honours	Ht	Wt	Birthdate	Birthplace / Transfers	Contract Date	Clubs	League	L/Cup	FA Cup	Other	Lge	L/C	FAC	Oth
G O A L K E E P E R														
Bosnich Mark	6.2	13.7	13/01/72	Sydney (Aus)		Sydney Croatia								
Australian Int. LC'94'96.				Free	05/06/89	Manchester United	3							
					01/01/90	Sydney Croatia								
				Free	28/02/92	Aston Villa	164	20+1	17	9				
Ghent Matthew			10/5/80	Burton		Aston Villa (T)								
Oakes Michael	6.1	12.6	30/10/73	Northwich	16/07/91	Aston Villa	26+2	2		3				
E: u21.6. LC'96.				Loan	26/11/93	Scarborough	1			1				
Rachel Adam	5.11	12.8	10/12/76	Birmingham	15/08/96	Aston Villa (T)								
D E F E N C E														
Barry Gareth			23/02/81	Hastings	23/02/98	Aston Villa (T)	1+1							
Charles Gary	5.9	11.2	13/04/70	Newham	07/11/87	Nottingham Forest	54+2	9	8+2	4+2	1		1	
E: 2,u21.6. FMC'92. LC'96.				Loan	16/03/89	Leicester City	5+3							
				£750000	29/07/93	Derby County	61	5+1	1	9	3			
				£1450000	06/01/95	Aston Villa	62+6	8+1	5+1	2+3	2			
Collins Lee David	6.1	12.6	10/09/77	Birmingham	05/07/96	Aston Villa (T)								
Ehiogu Ugochuku	6.1	12	03/11/72	Hackney	13/07/89	W.B.A.	0+2							
E:1B.1,u21.15. LC'96.				£40000	12/07/91	Aston Villa	168+11	15+1	14+2	13	9	1	1	1
Hughes Robert David	6.4	13.6	01/02/78	Wrexham	01/07/96	Aston Villa (T)	4+3							
W: u21.6. Y				Loan		Carlisle United	1							
Jaszczun Antony	5.10	10.10	16/09/77	Kettering	05/07/96	Aston Villa (T)								
Petty Ben J	6	12.5	22/03/77	Solihull	31/05/97	Aston Villa (T)								
Ridley Martin			3/30/80	Leicester		Aston Villa (T)								
Scimeca Riccardo	6.1	12.09	13/06/75	Leamington	07/07/93	Aston Villa	24+21	3+3	7+1	4				
E: B.1, u21.9. LC'96.														
Southgate Gareth	5.10	12.03	03/09/70	Watford	17/01/89	Crystal Palace	148+4	23+1	9	6	15	7		
E:27. Div.1'94. LC'96.				£2500000	23/06/95	Aston Villa	91	10	10	9	2	1		
Wright Alan	5.4	9.4	28/09/71	Ashton-u-Lyne	13/04/89	Blackpool	91+7	10+2	8	11+2				
E: u21.2,Y,S. LC'96.				£400000	25/10/91	Blackburn Rovers	67+7	8+1	5	3	1			
				£1000000	10/04/95	Aston Villa	119+2	11	12	10	3			
M I D F I E L D														
Curtolo David			9/30/80	Stockholm		Vastras								
					11/1/97	Aston Villa								
Draper Mark	5.11	11	11/11/70	Long Eaton	12/12/88	Notts County	206+16	14+1	10	21+2	40	2	2	5
E: u21.3. LC'96.				£1250000	22/07/94	Leicester City	39	2	2		5			
				£3250000	05/07/95	Aston Villa	95+1	10+1	9	9	5	1	2	
Ferraresi Fabio						Cesana								
				Free	23/06/98	Aston Villa								
Grayson Simon N	5.11	10.7	16/12/69	Ripon	13/06/88	Leeds United	2		1+1					
LC 96/97				£50000	13/03/92	Leicester City	175+13	16+2	9	13+1	4	2		
					01/07/97	Aston Villa	28+5	0+1	4	4+2			2	
Hazell Reuben			24/04/79	Brimingham	31/05/97	Aston Villa (T)								
Lescott Aaron	5.8	10.9	11/12/78	Birmingham	05/07/96	Aston Villa (T)								
Standing Michael			3/20/81	Shoreham		Aston Villa (T)								
Taylor Ian K	6.1	12.4	04/06/68	Birmingham		Moor Green								
AGT'93. LC'96.				£15000	13/07/92	Port Vale	83	4	6	13	28	2	1	4
				£1000000	12/07/94	Sheffield Wed.								
				£1000000	21/12/94	Aston Villa	105+8	8+1	7+1	9	12	2	1	3

Name			DOB	Birthplace	Date	Club	Lge		FAC	LC		Gls			
Thompson Alan	6	12.5	22/12/73	Newcastle	11/03/91	Newcastle United	13+3		1	3					
E: u21.2,Y.11. Div.1'97.					£250000	22/07/93	Bolton Wanderers	143+14	24+1	6+2	7+1	34	5	2	1
					£4500000	05/06/98	Aston Villa								

F O R W A R D

Name			DOB	Birthplace	Date	Club									
Blackwood Michael			9/30/79	Birmingham		Aston Villa (T)									
Byfield Darren	5.11	11	29/09/76	Birmingham	01/08/93	Aston Villa (T)	1+6		0+1						
Collymore Stan V	6.2	12.2	22/01/71	Stone	13/07/89	Wolverhampton W.									
E: 2					£100000	04/01/91	Crystal Palace	4+16	2+3			1	1		
					£100000	20/11/92	Southend United	30		3		15		3	
					£2000000	05/07/93	Nottingham Forest	64+1	9	2	2	41	7	2	
					£8500000	03/07/95	Liverpool	55+6	2+2	9	5+2	26		7	2
					£7000000	16/05/97	Aston Villa	23+2	1	4	6+1	6		1	1
Hendrie Lee	5.9	10.3	18/05/77	Birmingham	01/08/93	Aston Villa	15+9		3+4	2+1	3				
E: B.1, u21.2,Y.															
Joachim Julian	5.6	11.11	20/09/74	Peterborough	15/09/92	Leicester City	63+14	5+1	3	4+2	24	2	1	2	
E: u21.9,Y.8. UEFA Yth'93.					£1500000	24/02/96	Aston Villa	23+29	1	2+1	1+1	13			
Lee Alan D	6.2	13.9	21/08/78	Galway	21/08/95	Aston Villa (T)									
Middleton Darren	6	11.5	28/12/78	Lichfield	31/05/97	Aston Villa (T)									
Vassell Darius			13/06/80	Bimringham	30/03/98	Aston Villa (T)									
Walker Richard M	6	12	08/11/77	Bimringham	31/05/97	Aston Villa (T)	0+1								
Yorke Dwight	5.10	11.12	03/11/71	Canaan (Tobago)		Signal Hill									
T&T Int. LC'96.					£120000	19/12/89	Aston Villa	194+36	20+2	22+2	10	75	8	13	3

THE MANAGER
JOHN GREGORY

Date of Birth . . . . 11th May 1954.
Place of Birth . . . . Scunthorpe.
Date of Appointment. . . . . February 1998.

PREVIOUS CLUBS
As Manager . . . . Wycombe Wanderers.
As Coach . . . . Portsmouth, Leicester City, Aston Villa.
As a Player . . . . Northampton, Aston Villa, Brighton, QPR, Derby, Portsmouth,
. . . . Plymouth, Bolton.
HONOURS
As a Manager
None.

As a Player
International: 6 full caps for England.

Villa Park

Trinity Road, Birmingham B6 6HE

Capacity 39,339
First game..v Blackburn, Div.1, 17.4.1897 (3-0).
First floodlit game..v Portsmouth, Div.1, 25.8.1958 (3-2).
Internationals played at Villa Park..England v Scotland 8.4.1899, 3.5.1902, 8.4.1922.
v Wales 10.11.1948, 26.11.1958. v Ireland 14.11.1951. Argentina v Spain 13.7.1966. v W.Germany 16.7.1966.
............................Spain v W.Germany 20.7.1966. Brazil v Sweden 4.6.95. **Euro'96:** Holland v Scotland 10.6.96.
Switzerland v Holland 13.6.96. Scotland v Switzerland 18.6.96. Czech Republic v Portugal 23.6.96 (QF).

ATTENDANCES
Highest ....76,588 v Derby Co. FAC 6th Rnd, 2.3.1946.
Lowest ....2,900 v Bradford City, Div.1. 13.2.1915 (0-0).

OTHER GROUNDS..Aston Park 1874-76. Perry Barr 1876-1897.Villa Park 1897-

HOW TO GET TO THE GROUND

From North, East, South and West
Use Motorway, M6, junction 6.
Leave motorway and follow signs to Birmingham (NE). Shortly at roundabout take fourth exit, A38 (Sign posted Aston).
In half a mile turn right into Aston Hall Road for Aston Villa FC.

Car Parking
Asda Park in Aston Hall Road, a Park & Ride. Street Parking also available.

Nearest Railway Station: Witton or Aston

USEFUL TELEPHONE NUMBERS

Club switchboard 0121 327 2299
Club fax number 0121 322 2107
Club shop 0121 327 2800
Ticket Office. 0121 327 5353
Marketing Department 0121 327 5399

Internet address. . . . . . www.astonvilla-fc.co.uk

Clubcall 0891 12 11 48
Calls cost 50p per at all times.
Call costings correct at time of going to press.

MATCHDAY PROGRAMME

Programme Editor . . . . Sports Projects Ltd.

Number of pages 48

Price. £2

Subscriptions . . . . Apply to club.

Local Newspapers
. . . . Birmingham Post & Mail, Sports Argus,
. . Express & Star, Sporting Star, Sunday Mercury.

Local Radio Stations:
. . . . Xtra. AM, BRMB, BBC Radio W.M.

MATCHDAY TICKET PRICES

North Stand £19
Juv/OAP £9.50

Holte End Upper. £19
Juv/OAP £9.50
Lower £17
Juv/OAP £8.50

Trinity Road Upper £22
Juv/OAP £11
Trinity Road Lower Tier £18
Juv/OAP £9

Doug Ellis Stand Upper. £22
Juv/OAP £11
Doug Ellis Stand Lower. £18
Juv/OAP £9

BLACKBURN ROVERS
(The Rovers)
F.A. CARLING PREMIERSHIP
SPONSORED BY: CIS CO-OPERATIVE INSURANCE

1998-99 - Back Row L-R: David Worrell, Jeff Kenna, James Thomas, Tore Pedersen, John Filan, Tim Flowers, Alan Fettis, Darren Peacock, Stephane Henchoz, Jason Wilcox, Gary Croft. **Middle Row:** Alan Whitehead (Kit manager), Terry Darracott (Res. Team Manager), David Dunn, Marlon Broomes, Martin Dahlin, Chris Sutton, Martin Taylor, Tim Sherwood, Garry Flitcroft, Kevin Davies, Jimmy Corbett, Sebastien Perez, Arnoldo Longaretti (Fitness coach), Colin Lancaster (Masseur). **Front Row:** Roy Tunks (goalkeeping coach), Derek Fazackerley (First team coach), Anders Andersson, Callum Davidson, Roy Hodgson (Manager), Tony Parkes (Assistant Manager), Damien Duff, Damien Johnson, Kevin Gallacher, Mark Taylor (Physio), Alan Smith (Physio). Gary Croft, Damien Duff, Billy McKinlay.

BLACKBURN ROVERS
FORMED IN 1875
TURNED PROFESSIONAL IN 1880
LTD COMPANY IN 1897

PRESIDENT: W H Bancroft
SENIOR VICE PRESIDENT: J Walker
CHAIRMAN: R D Coar, BSC

DIRECTORS
R L Matthewman(Vice-Chairman),
John William (Chief Executive)
K C Lee, I R Stanners, G A Root FCMA

SECRETARY
Tom Finn (Director)
COMMERCIAL MANAGER
Ken Beamish

MANAGER: Roy Hodgson
ASSISTANT MANAGER
Tony Parkes
FIRST TEAM COACH
Derek Fazackerley
RESERVE TEAM MANAGER
Terry Darracott
PHYSIOS
Mark Taylor & Alan Smith

STATISTICIAN FOR THE DIRECTORY
Harry Berry

When Roy Hodgson was appointed he set himself the target of a place in Europe as his goal for the season. This was achieved with two minutes of the season remaining, when Chris Sutton's free kick finally breached Newcastle's defence and earned a UEFA Cup spot. This was a face saver for a team who in the first half of the season had appeared likely to gain a place in the Champions' competition but were brought down too earth when they could take only eighteen points from the final twenty games of the season.

The season had started with outgoing transfers, as Hodgson declined to keep unhappy players no matter the quality. The sale of Graeme Le Saux and Henning Berg brought in over ten million pounds and with other departures Hodgson was able to bring in new players and still have a surplus of twelve million pounds on transfers, the second year in succession this had happened to the club. Unhappily the new blood contained no instant successes. Only Stephane Henchoz became a first team regular and by the end of the season his partnership with Hendry was looking suspect.

That despite this lack of impetus the club commenced the season in such form was due to Hodgson's overhaul of the club's training methods, his influence on tactics and the admission by several of the experienced players that they had been under-achieving. Chris Sutton finished joint leading Carling Premiership goalscorer with Kevin Gallacher close behind, a real achievement since both men are not just goalscorers. Sutton is an old fashioned leader of the line, holding the ball and bringing other players into the play. Gallacher roams freely, interspersing his play with quick feints and darts, shooting unexpectedly and playing energetically throughout the season. Unhappily weaknesses could not be hidden. Le Saux was never replaced. Ripley had an Indian Summer that earned him an international call during which he was injured. After that he was never the same player. Wilcox had a mixed season, sometimes filling in at left back and losing his starting place to the highly promising Damien Duff. The midfield three of Sherwood, Flitcroft and McKinlay never lacked bite and effort but none are a playmaker. The defending in the last weeks was woeful with Kenna unexpectedly emerging as the most consistent player. The goalkeeping was varied with new man John Filan looking promising until he received a dreadful injury, Flowers was troubled by a shoulder problem which reduced his consistency and the less said about Alan Fettis's season , the better.

The team left both cup competitions after losing penalty shoot-outs but had better fortune in the FA Youth Cup where they reached the final and in Martin Taylor and David Dunn may have unearthed two youngsters for the future. Doubts remain about what a small town club like Blackburn, located in a quiet area of the North-West of England, can achieve on the European stage. The inability to attract top European stars is a problem and it is imperative that in their latest venture into Europe the club achieves some credibility.

Harry Berry.

BLACKBURN ROVERS

Carling Prem.   :5th   **FA CUP: 5th Round**   **LC CUP: 3rd Round**

M	DATE	COMP.	VEN	OPPONENTS	RESULT	H/T	LP	GOAL SCORERS/GOAL TIMES	ATT.
1	A 09	CP	H	Derby County	W 1-0	1-0	5	Gallacher 21	23557
2	12	CP	A	Aston Villa	W 4-0	3-0	1	Sutton 21, 25, 41, Gallacher 71	(37112)
3	23	CP	H	Liverpool	D 1-1	0-0	1	Dahlin 84	30187
4	25	CP	H	Sheffield Wednesday	W 7-2	5-1	1	Gallacher 2, 6, Wilcox 19, Sutton 23, 74, Bohinen 53, Hyde 10 (OG)	19618
5	30	CP	A	Crystal Palace	W 2-1	2-0	1	Sutton 23, Gallacher 32	(20849)
6	S 14	CP	H	Leeds United	L 3-4	3-4	2	Gallacher 8, Sutton 16 (pen), Dahlin 33	21956
7	17	CC 2/1	H	**Preston North End**	W 6-0	2-0		Dahlin 26, 54, Sutton 29, Gallacher 78, Andersson 84, Bohinen 89	22564
8	20	CP	A	Tottenham Hotspur	D 0-0	0-0	2		(26573)
9	24	CP	A	Leicester City	D 1-1	1-1	3	Sutton 36	(19921)
10	28	CP	H	Coventry City	D 0-0	0-0	5		19086
11	30	CC 2/2	A	**Preston North End**	L 0-1	0-1			(11472)
12	O 04	CP	A	Wimbledon	W 1-0	1-0	3	Sutton 6	(15600)
13	15	CC 3	A	**Chelsea**	D 1-1	0-0		**McKinlay 46**	(18671)
14	18	CP	H	Southampton	W 1-0	1-0	2	Sherwood 26	24130
15	25	CP	A	Newcastle United	D 1-1	0-1	3	Sutton 57	(36716)
16	N 01	CP	A	Barnsley	D 1-1	1-0	3	Sherwood 30	(18665)
17	08	CP	H	Everton	W 3-2	1-1	2	Gallacher 37, Duff 81, Sherwood 85	25397
18	22	CP	H	Chelsea	W 1-0	1-0	2	Croft 11	27683
19	30	CP	A	Manchester United	L 0-4	0-1	3		(55175)
20	D 06	CP	H	Bolton Wanderers	W 3-1	2-0	3	Gallacher 3, Sutton 20, Wilcox 90	25503
21	13	CP	A	Arsenal	W 3-1	0-1	2	Wilcox 57, Gallacher 65, Sherwood 90	(38147)
22	20	CP	H	West Ham United	W 3-0	1-0	2	Ripley 22, Duff 50, 72	21653
23	26	CP	A	Sheffield Wednesday	D 0-0	0-0	2		(33502)
24	28	CP	H	Crystal Palace	D 2-2	1-1	2	Gallacher 26, Sutton 77	23872
25	J 03	FAC 3	H	**Wigan Athletic**	W 4-2	2-0		**Gallacher 38, 60, Sherwood 49, McGibbon 21 (OG)**	22402
26	11	CP	A	Derby County	L 1-3	0-2	3	Sutton 87	(27823)
27	17	CP	H	Aston Villa	W 5-0	2-0	2	Sherwood 22, Gallacher 30, 54, 69, Ripley 81	24834
28	26	FAC 4	A	**Sheffield Wednesday**	W 3-0	2-0	2	Sutton 6, Sherwood 38, Duff 88	(15940)
29	31	CP	A	Liverpool	D 0-0	0-0	2		(43890)
30	F 06	CP	H	Tottenham Hotspur	L 0-3	0-1	2		30388
31	14	FAC 5	A	**West Ham United**	D 2-2	1-2		**Gallacher 2, Sutton 61**	(25729)
32	21	CP	A	Southampton	L 0-3	0-1	2		(15162)
33	25	FAC 5R	H	**West Ham United**	D 1-1	0-0		**Ripley 115**	21972
34	28	CP	H	Leicester City	W 5-3	3-0	2	Dahlin 11, Sutton 25, 45, 47, Hendry 63	24854
35	M 11	CP	A	Leeds United	L 0-4	0-0	3		(32933)
36	14	CP	A	Everton	L 0-1	0-0	4		(33423)
37	31	CP	H	Barnsley	W 2-1	1-0	4	Dahlin 9, Gallacher 87	24179
38	A 06	CP	H	Manchester United	L 1-3	1-0	4	Sutton 32 (pen)	30547
39	11	CP	A	Bolton Wanderers	L 1-2	0-1	6	Duff 51	(25000)
40	13	CP	H	Arsenal	L 1-4	0-4	6	Gallacher 51	28212
41	18	CP	A	West Ham United	L 1-2	1-2	6	Wilcox 44	(24733)
42	25	CP	H	Wimbledon	D 0-0	0-0	6		24848
43	29	CP	A	Chelsea	W 1-0	0-0	6	Gallacher 48	(33311)
44	M 02	CP	A	Coventry City	L 0-2	0-2	6		(18794)
45	10	CP	H	Newcastle United	W 1-0	0-0	5	Sutton 88	29300

Best Home League Attendance: 30547 V Manchester United   **Smallest :19086 V Coventry City**   Average :25253

Goal Scorers:

CP	(57)	Sutton 18, Gallacher 16, Sherwood 5, Dahlin 4, Duff 4, Wilcox 4, Ripley 2, Bohinen 1, Croft 1, Hendry 1, Opponents 1
CC	(7)	Dahlin 2, Andersson 1, Bohinen 1, Gallacher 1, McKinlay 1, Sutton 1
FAC	(10)	Gallacher 3, Sherwood 2, Sutton 2, Duff 1, Ripley 1, Opponents 1

(M) Andersson	(F) Beattie	(M) Bohinen	(D) Broomes	(D) Coleman	(D) Croft	(D) Dahlin	(M) Davidson	(F) Duff	(G) Fettis	(G) Filan	(M) Flitcroft	(G) Flowers	(F) Gallacher	(D) Henchoz	(D) Hendry	(M) Johnson	(D) Kenna	(M) McKinlay	(M) Pearce	(D) Pedersen T	(F) Pedersen P	(M) Ripley	(M) Sherwood	(F) Sutton	(D) Valery	(M) Watts	(F) Wilcox	(G) Williams		
S3		S						S1				X	X		X	X	X			X	X	S1			X2		X1	X	X	D.R. Elleray	1
S		S3						S2				X	X		X	X	X			X	X	S1			X		X	X	S	P E Alcock	2
		S3			S			S2				X	X		X	X	X			X	X	S1			X		X	X	S	S J Lodge	3
S		S1	S					S2				X	X	S3	X		X			X	X	X			X		X	X	S	J T Winter	4
S2		X			S	X		S				X	X		X	X	X			X	X	S1			X		X	X	S	K W Burge	5
S3		X1	S			X			S2	S		X	X	X	X	X		X				S1		X	X3		X2			S W Dunn	6
X		X	X		X	X		X				X	S3	X	S1		X			X	S2	X	X							S J Lodge	7
		X			S1	X			S			X	X	X	X	X		X	S2	S	S		X	X	X		X			G P Barber	8
		S1				X		S	S			X	X	X	X	X		X	S2	S			X	X	X		X			N S Barry	9
		S2				X		S1	S			X	X	X	X	X		X	S	S			X	X	X		X			P Jones	10
X	X			X	X			S1				X			X		X		X	X	X				X		X			M A Riley	11
		X			X	S		S	S			X	X	X	X	X		X	X				X	X				S		D J Gallagher	12
X		S2			X	X		X				X	X		S3	X		X			X			S1	X	X				K W Burge	13
		X			X	S		X	S			S	X	X	X	X		X	S1		S		X	X	X					G S Willard	14
		X			X	S		S1	S			S2	X	X	X	X		X			S		X	X	X	X				J T Winter	15
		S			X			X	S			S	X	X	X	X		X	X		S1		X	X	X		S2			G Poll	16
		S	S		X			S1	S			X	X	X	X			X	X		X		X	X	X		S2			P E Alcock	17
		S	S		X			S	S			X	X	X	X			X	X		X		X	X	X		S1			S J Lodge	18
		S2	S		X			S3	S			X	X	S1	X			X	X1		X		X2	X	X		X3			A B Wilkie	19
		S2			X			X1	S			S3	X	X	X	X		X	X		S		X2	X3	X		S1			M A Riley	20
S					X							S1	X	X	X	X		X			S	X1	X	X	S		X			G Willard	21
	S3	S2			X			X2	S			S1	X	X3	X	X		X	X		S		X1	X			X			G R Ashby	22
		S			X			X2	X			S1		X	X	X		X	X				X1	X	X		S2		S	J T Winter	23
		S	S		X2			X	S			X	X	X	X	X	X1	X			S1		X	X	X		S2			P Jones	24
	S3	S1						X	S			X	X	X2	X	X		X			S		X1	X	X	X	S2			N S Barry	25
					X1			X				X	X	X	X	X		X	S		S		X	X	X	S	S1		S	G Poll	26
		S			X			S1				X	X1	X2	X	X		X	S2		X		X	X	X		X			K W Burge	27
S2		S						X2	S			S1	X		X	X	X	X			S		X1	X	X	S1	X			J T Winter	28
		S			X			S1	S			X	X1	X	X	X		X	X			S	X	X	X		X			P A Durkin	29
		S2	S		X1	S1		X	S			S1	X		X	X		X	X2			X	X	X			X			G P Barber	30
		S	S		X1	S		S1	X			X	X		X	X		X				X	X	X			X			P Jones	31
	S2				X			X	X2			X	S		X1	X		X	X			S1	X		S		S			H D Rennie	32
					X			X2	S3			S1			X	X		X	X1			X3	X		X		S2			P Jones	33
S		S	S2	S1				X	X2			X	X		X		X1	X					X	X			X		S	N S Barry	34
					S			X1	X			X	X	X	X	S		X	X			S1	X	X	S		X			D R Elleray	35
		S			S	S		X	X			X	X	X	X	X		X	X			X1	X	X			X			G S Willard	36
					S			X3	S		S1	S2		X	X2	S3	X	X				X1	X	X			X		S	M D Reed	37
					S			S	S		X	X		X		X	X2	X	X			S	X	X			X		S	G R Ashby	38
					S			S1	S		X	X		X		X2	X	X				S2	X1	X	X		X		S	M A Riley	39
	S3				S			X3	X1			X	S		X	X		X	X2			S2	X		S1		X			J Bodenham	40
S								S	S2			X	S		X		X	X				X2	S1	X	X1		X			P A Durkin	41
X1	S				X			S1	S1			X			X		S	X				X	X	X			X			G Poll	42
S					S2			S1	S			X2			X	X	S	X						X1	X	X			S	P E Alcock	43
					S			X	S2			S1			X	X	S	X				S		X	X1		X			S J Lodge	44
S					S			S1	S2			X			S	X	X	X				X1		X			X			D R Elleray	45
1		6	2		19	11	1	17	7	7	28	24	31	36	34		37	26	1	3		25	29	35	14		24			CP Appearances	
3	3	10	2		4	10		9	1		5	1	2							4	4	2		4	2		1		7	CP Sub Appearances	
3	1	1+1	1	1	3	2		2+1			1+1	3	0+1	0+1	1		1	1	2			3	1+1	1+1	2	2	1			CC Appearances	
0+1	0+1	0+1			2	0+1		3+1	1		2+1	3	4	4	4		4	3				3	4	3	1+1		2+2			FAC Appearances	

Also Played: (M) Gill S(11). (D) Reed S(11). (M) Stewart S(33).

BLACKBURN ROVERS

CLUB RECORDS

BIGGEST VICTORIES
League: 9-0 v Middlesbrough, Division 2, 6.11.1954.
F.A. Cup: 11-0 v Rossendale, Round 1, 13.10.1884.
League Cup: 6-1 v Watford, Round 4, 9.12.1992.

BIGGEST DEFEATS
League: 0-8 v Arsenal, Division 1, 25.2.1933.
0-8 v Lincoln City, Division 2, 29.8.1953.
F.A. Cup: 0-6 v Nottingham Forest, Round 3, 1879-80.
1-6 v Manchester United, 1908-09.
1-6 v Luton Town, Round 3, 1952-53.
League Cup: 0-5 v Wimbledon, 24.9.1985.
1-6 v Nottingham Forest, 15.9.1979.
Europe: (UEFA) 0-1 v Trelleborgs, 27.9.1994.

MOST POINTS
3 points a win: 89, Premiership, 1994-95.
2 points a win: 60, Division 3, 1974-75.

MOST GOALS SCORED
114, 1954-55, Division 2.
Briggs 33, Quigley 28, Crossan 18, Mooney 16, Langton 13, Clayton 2, Bell 1, og 3.

MOST GOALS CONCEDED
102, Division 1, 1932-33.

MOST FIRST CLASS MATCHES IN A SEASON
60 - 1979-80 (League 46, FA Cup 7, League Cup 4, Anglo-Scottish Cup 3).
60 - 1988-89 (League 46, FA Cup 3, League Cup 4, Simod Cup 3, League Play-offs 4).

MOST LEAGUE WINS
27, Premiership, 1994-95.

MOST LEAGUE DRAWS
18, Division 2, 1980-81.

MOST LEAGUE DEFEATS
30, Division 1, 1980-81.

INDIVIDUAL CLUB RECORDS

MOST GOALS IN A SEASON
Ted Harper - 45, 1925-26 (League 43, FAC 2).

MOST GOALS IN A MATCH
7, Tommy Briggs v Bristol Rovers, Division 2, 5.2.1953.

OLDEST PLAYER
Bob Crompton, 40 years 151 days, 23.2.1920.

YOUNGEST PLAYER
Harry Dennison, 16 years 155 days, 8.4.1911.

MOST CAPPED PLAYER
Bob Crompton (England) 41.

BEST PERFORMANCES

League: 1994-95: Played 42, Won 27, Drawn 8, Lost 7, Goals for 80, Goals against 39, Points 89. Premiership Champions.
Highest Position: 1994-95 Premiership Champions.
F.A. Cup: Winners in 1884 v Queens Park, 2-1.
Winners in 1885 v Queens Park, 2-0.
Winners in 1886 v West Bromwich 0-0,2-0.
Winners in 1890 v Sheffield Wednesday 6-1.
Winners in 1891 v Notts County 3-1.
Most Recent Success: (1928) 3rd Rnd. Newcastle United 4-1; 4th Rnd. Exeter City 2-2,3-1; 5th Rnd. Port Vale 2-1; 6th Rnd. Manchester United 2-0; Semi-Final Arsenal 1-0; Final Huddersfield Town 3-1.
League Cup: Semi-Finalists in 1961-62 v Rochdale, 1-3.
Most Recent Success: (1992-93) 2nd Rnd. Huddersfield Town (a) 1-1, (h) 4-3 aet; 3rd Rnd. Norwich City 2-0; 4th Rnd. Watford (h) 6-1; 5th Rnd. Cambridge United (h) 3-2; Semi-Final Sheffield Wednesday (h) 2-4, (a) 1-2.
Europe: (UEFA) 1st Rnd. Trelleborg (h) 0-1, (a) 2-2.

ADDITIONAL INFORMATION
PREVIOUS NAME
None.
PREVIOUS LEAGUES
None.

Club Colours: Blue & white halved shirts, white shorts, white socks with blue trim.
Change Colours:

Reserve League: Pontins Central League Division 1.

DIVISIONAL RECORD

	Played	Won	Drawn	Lost	For	Against	Points
Division 1/P	2222	843	519	860	3670	3665	2293
Division 2	1446	583	364	499	2134	1981	1723
Division 3	230	104	59	67	299	249	267
Total	**3898**	**1530**	**942**	**1426**	**6103**	**5895**	**4283**

RECORDS AND STATISTICS

COMPETITIONS

Div 1/P	Div.2	Div.3	A/Scot
1888-1936	1936-39	1971-75	1975-76
1939-47	1947-57	1979-80	1976-77
1957-66	1966-71		1977-78
1992-	1975-79		1978-79
	1980-92	E.C.	1979-80
		1995-96	1980-81

HONOURS

Div 1/P	Div.2	Div.3	FAC	FMC	C/Sh'ld
1911-12	1938-39	1974-75	1884	1986-87	1912
1913-14			1885		
1994-95			1886		
			1890		
			1891		
			1928		

MOST APPEARANCES

D Fazackerley 689+3 (1970-87)

Year	League	FA Cup	Lge Cup	A/Scottish
1970-71	14			
1971-72	39	2	2	
1972-73	46	3	1	
1973-74	46	5	3	
1974-75	22+1	1	2	
1975-76	42	1	2	
1976-77	37+1	4	3	
1977-78	28	2	2	
1978-79	37	2	1	
1979-80	46	7	4	
1980-81	38	1	5	
1981-82	39	1	3	
1982-83	38	1	2	
1983-84	39	3	2	
1984-85	39	4	2	
1985-86	36+1	3	2	
1986-87	7		2	
	593+3	40	38	18

MOST GOALS IN A CAREER

Simon Garner - 192 (1978-92)

Year	League	FA Cup	Lge Cup	Others
1978-79	8			
1979-80	6			
1980-81	7		1	
1981-82	14	2	2	
1982-83	22	1		
1983-84	19	1	3	
1984-85	12		2	
1985-86	12			
1986-87	10		1	4
1987-88	14	1		
1988-89	20	1	2	
1989-90	18			2
1990-91	1	1		
1991-92	5			
Total	168	7	11	6

Current leading goalscorer: Chris Sutton 55 (1994-98)

RECORD TRANSFER FEE RECEIVED

Amount	Club	Player	Date
£15,000,000	Newcastle United	Alan Shearer	07/96
£3,750,000	Newcastle United	David Batty	05/94
£1,250,000	Manchester Utd	David May	05/94
£700,000	Manchester City	Colin Hendry	11/89

RECORD TRANSFER FEE PAID

Amount	Club	Player	Date
£7,250,000	Southampton	Kevin Davies	06/98
£5,000,000	Norwich City	Chris Sutton	07/94
£3,300,000	Southampton	Alan Shearer	07/92
£2,750,000	Leeds United	David Batty	10/93

MANAGERS

Name	Seasons	Best	Worst
Eddie Hapgood	1946-48	17(1)	21(1)
Will Scott	1948-50	14(2)	16(2)
Jack Bruton	1950-52	6(2)	14(2)
Jackie Bestall	1952-53	9(2)	9(2)
John Carey	1953-58	2(2)	9(2)
Dally Duncan	1958-61	8(1)	17(1)
Jack Marshall	1961-69	7(1)	19(2)
Eddie Quigley	1969-71	8(2)	21(2)
John Carey	1971-72	10(3)	10(3)
Ken Furphy	1972-74	3(3)	13(3)
Gordon Lee	1974-75	1(3)	1(3)
Jim Smith	1975-78	5(2)	11(2)
Jim Iley	1978-79	22(2)	22(2)
Howard Kendall	1979-81	4(2)	2(3)
Bobby Saxton	1981-86	6(2)	19(2)
Don Mackay	1986-91		
Kenny Dalglish	1991-95	1(P)	6(2/1)
Ray Harford	1995-97	7(P)	7(P)
Tony Parkes (Caretaker)	1997	13(P)	13(P)
Roy Hodgson	1997-	6(P)	6(P)

LONGEST LEAGUE RUNS

of undefeated matches:	23 (30.9.1987-27.2.1988)	of league matches w/out a win:	16 (25.11.1978-28.3.1979)
of undefeated home matches:	30 (14.4.1911-21.12.1912)	of undefeated away matches:	11(15.2.1912-1.11.1913)
			(30.9.1987-27.2.1988)
without home win:	11 (16.9.1978 - 24.3.1979)	without an away win:	24 (12.2.1910 - 27.2.1911)
of league wins:	8 (1.3.1980 - 7.4.1980)	of home wins:	13 (12.2.1954 - 20.11.1954)
of league defeats:	7 (12.3.1966 - 16.4.1966)	of away wins:	7 (12.1.1980 - 12.4.1980)

BLACKBURN ROVERS

PLAYERS NAME Honours	Ht	Wt	Birthdate	Birthplace Transfers	Contract Date	Clubs	League	L/Cup	FA Cup	Other	Lge	L/C	FAC	Oth
G O A L K E E P E R														
Fettis Alan	6.1	11.04	01/02/71	Belfast		Ards								
NI: 18, B.2, Y, S.				£50000	14/08/91	Hull City	127+1	7	5	6				
				£250000	13/01/96	Nottingham Forest	4		1+1					
				£300000	12/09/97	Blackburn Rovers	7+1		1					
Filan John	6.2	12.1	08/02/70	Sydney (Aus)		Sydney B'pest								
Australian u21 Int.				£40000	12/03/93	Cambridge United	52	4	3	1				
				Loan	23/12/94	Nottingham Forest								
				Loan	02/03/95	Coventry City								
				£350000	17/03/95	Coventry City	15+1	2						
				£750000	10/07/97	Blackburn Rovers	7							
Flowers Tim	6.2	14	03/02/67	Kenilworth	28/08/84	Wolverhampton W.	63	5	2	2				
E: 8,u21.3,Y.1. Prem'95.				£70000	13/06/86	Southampton	192	26	16	8				
				Loan	23/03/87	Swindon Town	2							
				Loan	13/11/87	Swindon Town	5							
				£2400000	04/11/93	Blackburn Rovers	165+1	13	13	10				
Stewart Gareth J	6	12.8	03/02/80	Preston	31/05/97	Blackburn R. (T)								
Williams Anthony S.			20/09/77		04/07/96	Blackburn R. (T)								
D E F E N C E														
Broomes Marlon	6	12.7	28/11/77	Birmingham	01/08/94	Blackburn Rovers	2+2	1						
E: u21.2, Y.				Loan	22/01/97	Swindon Town	12				1			
Coughlan Graham	6.2	13.4	18/11/74	Dublin	14/10/95	Blackburn Rovers								
				Loan	25/03/97	Swindon Town	3							
Croft Gary	5.9	10.8	17/02/74	Burton-on-Trent	07/07/92	Grimsby Town	103+10	5	3+2	3	2	1		
E: u21.4.				£1000000	29/03/96	Blackburn Rovers	23+5	5	2		1			
Davidson Callum	5.10	11	25/06/76	Sterling		St Johnstone								
				£1750000	12/02/98	Blackburn Rovers	1							
Henchoz Stephane	6.1	12.8	07/09/74	Billens		Hamburg								
				£3000000	14/07/97	Blackburn Rovers	36		0+1	4				
Kenna Jeff	5.11	11.7	27/08/70	Dublin	25/04/89	Southampton	82+4	2	5+1	3	4			
Ei:17,B.1,u21.8.				£1500000	15/03/95	Blackburn Rovers	115	8	8	6	1			
Peacock Darren	6.2	12.6	03/02/68	Bristol	11/02/86	Newport County	24+4	2	1	1+1				
WFAC'90				Free	23/03/89	Hereford United	56+3	6	6	6	4		1	
				£200000	22/12/90	Q.P.R.	123+3	12	3	2	6	1		
				£2700000	24/03/94	Newcastle United	131+2	13+1	11	17+1	2	2		
				Free	11/06/98	Blackburn Rovers								
Pedersen Tore	6	12.6	29/09/69	Norway		St Pauli								
Norway Int.				£500000	15/09/97	Blackburn Rovers	3+2	3						
Richards Ian	5.8	11.4	05/10/79	Barnsley	11/07/97	Blackburn R. (T)								
Richardson Leam N			19/11/79	Leeds		Blackburn R. (T)								
Ryan Ciaran			03/09/79	Dublin	31/05/97	Blackburn R. (T)								
Taylor Martin			09/11/79	Northumberland		Blackburn R. (T)								
Valery Patrick	5.11	11.5	03/07/69	France		Bastia								
				£450000	25/06/97	Blackburn Rovers	14+1	2	1+1					
Worrell David	5.9	11	12/01/78	Dublin	01/08/94	Blackburn Rovers								
M I D F I E L D														
Andersson Anders Per	5.9	11.5	15/03/74	Sweden		Malmo								
Swedish Int.				£500000	11/07/97	Blackburn Rovers	1+3	3	0+1		1			
Brown John K	6	11	24/12/79	Edinburgh	31/05/97	Blackburn Rovers								
Connolly Patrick J			03/03/80	Preston		Blackburn R (T)								
Dunn David J			27/12/79	Blackburn		Blackburn R. (T)								
Fitzpatrick Lee G.	5.10	11.7	31/10/78	Manchester	02/07/96	Blackburn R. (T)								
Flitcroft Gary	5.1	11	06/11/72	Bolton	02/07/91	Manchester City	84+6	10+1	10		13		1	
E: u21.10,Y1,S.				Loan	05/03/92	Bury	12							
				£3200000	26/03/96	Blackburn Rovers	58+6	3+1	3+1		3	1		
Gill Wayne	5.1	11.3	28/11/75	Chorley	01/08/94	Blackburn Rovers								
				Loan	01/04/98	Dundee								
Johnson Damien	5.9	10	18/11/78	Blackburn		Blackburn Rovers		1						
McAvoy Andrew D	6	12	28/08/79	Middlesbrough	14/07/97	Blackburn R. (T)								
McKinlay Billy	5.9	9.13	22/04/69	Glasgow		Dundee United								
S: 21, B.1, u21.6, Y, S.				£1750000	14/10/95	Blackburn Rovers	62+12	3	6+1		3	1		
Perez Sebastien	5.10	11.7	24/11/73	Saint-Chamond		SC Bastia								
French u21 Int.				£3000000	29/06/98	Blackburn Rovers								
Scates Garth			27/08/79	Dundonald		Blackburn R. (T)								

Name			DOB	Birthplace	Date	Club								
Sherwood Tim	6	11.6	06/02/69	St.Albans	07/02/87	Watford	23+9	4+1	9	4+1	2			
E: B.1,u21.4,u19.2. Prem'95.					18/07/89	Norwich City	66+5	7	4	5+1	10	1		2
				£175000	12/02/92	Blackburn Rovers	220+7	22+1	15+2	10	22	1	4	
				£500000										
Staton Luke	5.7	9.10	10/03/79	Doncaster		Blackburn Rovers								
Woodfield Craig M			04/09/79	Coventry		Blackburn R. (T)								
F O R W A R D														
Corbett Jimmy	5.9	10.12	06/07/80	Hackney	13/01/98	Gillingham (T)	8+8	0+1		0+1	2			
				£525000	22/05/98	Blackburn Rovers								
Dahlin Martin	6.1	13.3	16/04/68	Lund		Roma								
Swedish Int.				£2500000	23/07/97	Blackburn Rovers	11+10	2	0+1		4	2		
Davies Kevin	6	12.12	26/03/77	Sheffield	18/04/94	Chesterfield	113+16	7+2	10	9+2	22	1	6	1
E: Y.				£750000	14/05/97	Southampton	20+5	3+1	1		9	3		
				£7250000	01/06/98	Blackburn Rovers								
Duff Damien	5.10	9.7	02/03/79	Bally Boden	05/03/96	Blackburn Rovers	18+9	2+1	3+1		4		1	
E: Y,S.														
Gallacher Kevin	5.8	10.1	23/11/66	Clydebank		Dundee United								
S:31,B.2,u21.7,Y.				£900000	29/01/90	Coventry City	99+1	11	4	2	28	7		
				£1500000	23/03/93	Blackburn Rovers	116+5	7+1	12	1+1	41	2	4	
Hamilton Gary I			06/10/80	Bambridge		Blackburn R. (T)								
Hawe Steven J			23/12/80	Machbrafelt		Blackburn R. (T)								
Sutton Chris	6.3	12.1	10/03/73	Nottingham	02/07/91	Norwich City	89+13	8+1	10	6	35	3	5	
E: B.2,u21.13. Prem'95.				£5000000	13/07/94	Blackburn Rovers	108+5	10+1	8	6+3	44	6	4	1
Thomas James A.			16/01/79	Swansea	02/07/96	Blackburn R (T)								
Topley Jonathan W			12/07/80	Craigavon		Blackburn R. (T) F								
Wilcox Jason	5.1	11.6	15/07/71	Farnworth	13/06/89	Blackburn Rovers	198+21	16+1	13	7+2	28	1	1	
E:2, B.1. Prem'95.														

THE MANAGER
ROY HODGSON

Date of Birth . . . . 9th August 1947.
Place of Birth . . . . Croydon.
Date of Appointment . . . . June 1997

PREVIOUS CLUBS
As Manager . . . . . . Halmstad (Swed), Bristol City, Orebro, Malmo (both Swed),
. . . . Neuchatel Xamax (Switz), Switzerland National Team, Inter Milan.
As Coach/Assistant . . . . Bristol City.
As a Player . . . . Crystal Palace, South Africa.

HONOURS
As a Manager
Halmsted: The Swedish Championship (x2).
Malmo: The Swedish Championship (5 times consecutively). Swedish Cup (x2) - including League &
Cup double in 1986.
Switzerland National Record: P 40 W 21 D 10 L 10. Qualified for WC'84 & Euro'96.

As a Player
None.

Ewood Park

Blackburn, Lancashire BB2 4JF

Capacity . . . . .31,141.
First game . . . . .v Accrington, (Friendly), 13.9.1890.
First floodlit game . . . . .v Werder (Friendly), 1958-59.
Second set . . . . .v Aberdeen (Friendly), 7.12.1976.

Internationals played at Ewood . . . . .England v Scotland, 6.4.1891. England v Wales, 3.3.1924.

ATTENDANCES
Highest . . . . .61,783 v Bolton Wanderers, FA Cup, 2.3.1929.
Lowest . . . . .1,200 v West Bromwich Albion, Div.1, 22.12.1894.

OTHER GROUNDS . . . . .Brookhouse Ground 1875-76. Alexandra Meadow 1876-81.
. . . . .Leamington Road 1881-1890. Ewood Park 1890 to date.

HOW TO GET TO THE GROUND

From the North and West
M6 to junction 31 or A666 into Blackburn. A666 into Bolton Road, left into Kidder Street for Ewood Park.

From the South
M6 to junction 31 as from North or A666 via Bolton. After Darwen turn right into Kidder Street for Ewood Park.

From the East
A679 or A677 to Blackburn then A666 toward Bolton into Bolton Road. Left into Kidder Street for Ewood Park.

Car Parking
Ewood car park within walking distance.

Nearest Railway Station
Blackburn Central (01254 662 537/8).

USEFUL TELEPHONE NUMBERS

Club switchboard. 01254 698 888
Club fax number 01254 671 042
Club shop . . . . 01254 698 888 Ext. 2275
Ticket Office 0321 10 10 10

Marketing Department. . . 01254 698 888 Ext. 2202
Internet address . . . . http::/www.Rovers.co.uk
Clubcall 0898 12 11 79*
*Calls cost 50p per minute at all time.
Call costings correct at time of going to press.

MATCHDAY PROGRAMME

Programme Editor . . . . Peter White.

Number of pages 32

Price £1.70

Subscriptions £75 home & away, £40 home.

Local Newspapers
. . . . Lancashire Evening Telegraph.

Local Radio Stations
. . Red Rose Radio, BBC Radio Lancashire.

MATCHDAY TICKET PRICES

Jack Walker Stand - 'B' matches

Upper Tier Central £20

Upper Tier Outer (Adult/Juv&OAP) . . . . £19/£10

Lower Tier Central . . . . £19/£10

Lower Tier Outer . . . . £16/£10

Walker Steel Stand. . . . . £16/£10

Darwen Stand Upper & Lower Tier . . . . £16/£10

Blackburn End Lower. . . . . £16/£10

Family Stand . . . . £16/£10

For 'A' matches add £3 to the adult prices.

CHARLTON ATHLETIC
(The Addicks)
F.A. CARLING PREMIERSHIP
SPONSORED BY: MESH COMPUTERS PLC

1997-98 - Back Row L-R: Kevin Lisbie, Steve Jones, Gary Poole, Mike Salmon, Phil Chapple, Andy Petterson, Carl Leaburn, Matt Lee, Jason Tindall.
Middle Row: Keith Peacock (reserve team coach), Steve Watts (youth dev. officer), Dwayne Minors, Jamie Stuart, Brendon O'Connell (now at Wigan), Kevin Nicholls, Paul Emblem, Matt Holmes, Shaun Newton, Terry Westley (youth team coach), Jimmy Hendry (physio).
Front Row: Mark Kinsella, Clive Mendonca, Anthony Barness, Paul Mortimer, Stuart Balmer, Alan Curbishley (manager), Les Reed (first team coach), Keith Jones, Richard Rufus, Bradley Allen, Steve Brown, John Robinson.

CHARLTON ATHLETIC
FORMED IN 1905
TURNED PROFESSIONAL IN 1920
LTD COMPANY IN 1919

CHAIRMAN: M A Simons
VICE- CHAIRMAN & MANAGING DIRECTOR
R A Murray
DIRECTORS
R N Alwen, G P Bone, N E Capelin,
R D Collins, M A Gebbett, D J Hughes
R D King, M C Stevens, D C Sumners,
D G Ufton, R C Whitehead
C G Benford (Associate Director)
SECRETARY
Chris Parkes
COMMERCIAL MANAGER
Steve Dixon
MANAGER: Alan Curbishley
ASSISTANT MANAGER: Keith Peacock
FIRST TEAM COACH: Mervyn Day.
RESERVE TEAM MANAGER
Keith Peacock
YOUTH TEAM MANAGER
Terry Westley
PHYSIOTHERAPIST
Jimmy Hendry
STATISTICIAN FOR THE DIRECTORY
Paul Clayton

A fantastic season for the Addicks, culminating in promotion to the Carling Premiership via the play-offs. Their total of 88 points would normally have been enough to gain automatic promotion, but they finished in fourth place behind Sunderland, who they beat in a penalty shoot-out at the end of a thrilling play-off final at Wembley. Clive Mendonca, who was signed for a club record £700,000 from Grimsby Town in the Summer, scored a hat-trick in the game bringing his total for the season to 28, the best for a Charlton player since Derek Hales in 1975-76. The Addicks' total of 80 league goals was the best for 37 years.

Charlton's other Summer signing, Matty Holmes, was less fortunate, missing the early part of the season after suffering an injury in a pre-season game, and then breaking a leg in the Cup tie at Wolverhampton, forcing him to miss the remainder of the season. The experienced Mark Bowen joined on a free transfer from Japanese club Shimizu-S-Pulse, and two 16-year-olds, Paul Konchecky and Scott Parker were given debuts early in the season, Goalkeeper Sasa Ilic came into the side in February, and kept 12 clean sheets in his 17 appearances, 9 of them coming in consecutive games. Further signings, Danny Mills from Norwich and Eddie Youds from Bradford City were made in March to bolster the Addicks defence, and both have yet to play in a losing Charlton side. Winger Neil Heaney was also signed on loan from Manchester City just before transfer deadline.

Charlton's form at the Valley was remarkably consistent with only one league defeat all season, and nine wins were recorded on opponents grounds. The Cup form was not so impressive with an early exit from the Coca-Cola Cup at the hands of Ipswich Town, and a fourth round exit from the FA Cup at Molineux in a replay after Charlton had drawn with Wolverhampton Wanderers at The Valley. Nottingham Forest had earlier been well beaten, 4-1, in the third round.

Mark Kinsella was voted 'Supporters Player of the Year', to round off a superb season that saw him take on the captain's job at Charlton and win his first full International Cap for the Republic of Ireland. Keith Jones and Shaun Newton also had excellent seasons in the Charlton Athletic. Average league gates were up again to 13,275, and the new stand extension together with Carling Premiership football should ensure another rise next season.

With money available for new signings, manager Alan Curbishley will bring in new players to strengthen the squad, and The Addicks might surprise a few teams next season and retain their place in the top flight.

PAUL CLAYTON

CHARLTON ATHLETIC

Division 1 :4th   FA CUP: 4th Round   LC CUP: 1st Round

M	DATE	COMP.	VEN	OPPONENTS	RESULT	H/T	LP	GOAL SCORERS/GOAL TIMES	ATT.
1	A 09	FL	A	Middlesbrough	L 1-2	1-0	16	Jones S 9	(22414)
2	12	CC 1/1	H	Ipswich Town	L 0-1	0-1			6598
3	15	FL	H	Oxford United	W 3-2	1-0	8	Jones S 20, Mendonca 57, Lisbie 90	10230
4	23	FL	A	Bury	D 0-0	0-0	9		(4657)
5	26	CC 1/2	A	Ipswich Town	L 1-3	0-2		Mendonca 89	(10989)
6	30	FL	H	Manchester City	W 2-1	0-1	8	Jones K 69, Van 67 (OG)	14009
7	S 13	FL	A	Wolverhampton Wand	L 1-3	0-3	14	Chapple 72	(22683)
8	17	FL	A	Norwich City	W 4-0	3-0	9	Mendonca 7, 22, 28, Chapple 84	(10157)
9	21	FL	H	Bradford City	W 4-1	3-1	7	Mendonca 8, 69, Mortimer 18, Brown 23	11583
10	27	FL	H	Stockport County	L 1-3	1-0	9	Mortimer 41	12083
11	O 04	FL	A	Queens Park Rangers	W 4-2	2-1	5	Robinson 16, 59, Jones S 42, Chapple 62	(14825)
12	14	FL	A	Huddersfield Town	W 3-0	1-0	3	Mendonca 14, Brown 69, Robinson 75	(9596)
13	19	FL	H	Stoke City	D 1-1	0-0	4	Kinsella 79	12345
14	22	FL	H	Birmingham City	D 1-1	0-0	4	Mendonca 62	10072
15	25	FL	A	Tranmere Rovers	D 2-2	0-1	5	Kinsella 57, Leaburn 59	(5911)
16	N 01	FL	H	Ipswich Town	W 3-0	2-0	3	Mendonca 10, Chapple 34, Leaburn 90	12627
17	04	FL	A	Sunderland	D 0-0	0-0	5		(25455)
18	08	FL	A	West Bromwich Albion	L 0-1	0-1	6		(16124)
19	15	FL	H	Crewe Alexandra	W 3-2	2-1	6	Jones K 6, Allen 27, Holmes 76	14091
20	22	FL	A	Nottingham Forest	L 2-5	0-1	7	Allen 60, Woan 79 (OG)	(18532)
21	28	FL	H	Swindon Town	W 3-0	2-0	5	Jones K 9, Mendonca 42 (pen), 56	13769
22	D 06	FL	A	Reading	L 0-2	0-2	8		(8076)
23	09	FL	H	Sheffield United	W 2-1	1-0	6	Mendonca 44 (pen), 75	9868
24	13	FL	H	Port Vale	W 1-0	0-0	5	Newton 85	11077
25	20	FL	A	Portsmouth	W 2-0	1-0	3	Robinson 44, Leaburn 52	(8581)
26	26	FL	H	Norwich City	W 2-1	0-0	3	Kinsella 59, Robinson 62	14472
27	28	FL	A	Sheffield United	L 1-4	0-2	4	Bright 89	(18677)
28	J 03	FAC 3	H	Nottingham Forest	W 4-1	2-0		Robinson 38, Brown 42, Leaburn 64, Mendonca 74	13827
29	10	FL	H	Middlesbrough	W 3-0	2-0	3	Newton 20, 59, Bright 36	15742
30	17	FL	A	Oxford United	W 2-1	1-0	3	Mendonca 81, Robinson 87	(7234)
31	24	FAC 4	H	Wolverhampton Wand	D 1-1	0-0		Jones K 64	15540
32	28	FL	A	Manchester City	D 2-2	0-1	3	Jones S 74, 90	(24058)
33	31	FL	H	Bury	D 0-0	0-0	2		15312
34	F 03	FAC 4R	A	Wolverhampton Wand	L 0-3	0-1			(20429)
35	06	FL	A	Bradford City	L 0-1	0-1	5		(14851)
36	17	FL	H	Queens Park Rangers	D 1-1	1-1	4	Robinson 42	15555
37	21	FL	A	Stockport County	L 0-3	0-1	4		(7705)
38	25	FL	A	Stoke City	W 2-1	1-1	4	Robinson 17, Barness 73	(10027)
39	28	FL	H	Huddersfield Town	W 1-0	0-0	4	Bright 79	12908
40	M 03	FL	H	West Bromwich Albion	W 5-0	1-0	3	Bright 43, Newton 53, Mendonca 70 (pen), 79, Kinsella 73	10893
41	07	FL	A	Ipswich Town	L 1-3	1-0	4	Mendonca 22	(19831)
42	15	FL	H	Sunderland	D 1-1	0-1	4	Bright 55	15355
43	21	FL	A	Crewe Alexandra	W 3-0	2-0	4	Mills 3, Newton 44, Kinsella 76	(5252)
44	28	FL	H	Nottingham Forest	W 4-2	1-1	4	Bright 14, Mortimer 60, Mendonca 88 (pen), Kinsella 90	15815
45	A 04	FL	A	Swindon Town	W 1-0	0-0	4	Jones S 80	(7845)
46	07	FL	H	Wolverhampton Wand	W 1-0	1-0	3	Mendonca 8	13743
47	10	FL	H	Reading	W 3-0	1-0	3	Mendonca 6, Mortimer 43, Bright 79	14220
48	13	FL	A	Port Vale	W 1-0	0-0	4	Mendonca 73	(9973)
49	18	FL	H	Portsmouth	W 1-0	0-0	3	Jones S 57	14082
50	25	FL	H	Tranmere Rovers	W 2-0	1-0	3	Mendonca 10, 63 (pen)	15393
51	M 03	FL	A	Birmingham City	D 0-0	0-0	4		(25677)
52	10	PO SF1	A	Ipswich Town	W 1-0	1-0		Clapham 12 (OG)	(21681)
53	13	PO SF2	H	Ipswich Town	W 1-0	1-0		Newton 36	15585
54	25	PO F	H	Sunderland	D 4-4	1-0		Mendonca 24, 72, 104, Rufus 86	77739

Best Home League Attendance: 15815 V Nottingham Forest   Smallest :9868 V Sheffield United   Average :13271

Goal Scorers:

FL	(80)	Mendonca 23, Robinson 8, Bright 7, Jones S 7, Kinsella 6, Newton 5, Chapple 4, Mortimer 4, Jones K 3, Leaburn 3, Allen 2, Brown 2, Barness 1, Holmes 1, Lisbie 1, Mills 1, Opponents 2
CC	(1)	Mendonca 1
FAC	(5)	Brown 1, Jones K 1, Leaburn 1, Mendonca 1, Robinson 1
PO	(6)	Mendonca 3, Newton 1, Rufus 1, Opponents 1

1997-98

(F) Allen	(D) Balmer	(D) Barness	(M) Bowen	(F) Bright	(D) Brown	(D) Chapple	(F) Emblen	(F) Heaney	(F) Holmes	(G) Ilic	(F) Jones S	(M) Jones K	(M) Kinsella	(M) Konchesky	(F) Leaburn	(F) Lisbie	(F) Mendonca	(M) Mills	(M) Mortimer	(M) Newton	(M) Nicholls	(M) Parker	(G) Petterson	(M) Robinson	(D) Rufus	(G) Salmon	(D) Stuart	(D) Youds	Referee	No.
X	X		S2	X							X	X	X				X			X	S1		X	X	X				A.R. Leake	1
X	X		S2	X	S						X	X	X				X			X	S1		X	X	X				D Orr	2
X				X	S3						X	X	X	X		S2	X			X	S1		X	X	X				C T Finch	3
X				X	S1						X	X	X			S2	X			X	X	S3	X	X	X				G B Frankland	4
X			S2	X	X						X		X	X	S1	X			X	X			X	X	X		S2		S G Bennett	5
S		X			X	X					X	X	X			S	X			X	S		X	X	X				R J Harris	6
X	X			X	X						X	X	X	S1	S2	X		X		S3			X	X	X				K M Lynch	7
X	X	S2		X	X						X	X	X			S3	X		X		S1		X	X	X				A P D'Urso	8
X	X			X	S2						X	X	X			S	X		X		S1		X	X	X				A R Leake	9
X	X			X	S2	S1					X	X	X				X			X	S3		X	X	X				J A Kirkby	10
X	X	S2		X	S1						X	X	X			S3	X		X				X	X	X				P Taylor	11
	X	S		X	X				S1		X	X	X			S2	X		X				X	X	X				M Fletcher	12
S2	X	X			X				S1		X	X	X				X		X				X	X	X		S		R D Furnandiz	13
S		X	X		X				S2		X	X	X				X		X				X	X	X		S1		C R Wilkes	14
S		X	X		X				S			X	X	X			X		X				X	X	X		S		A G Wiley	15
S		S	X		X	X			S1			X	X				X		X				X	X	X				P Rejer	16
S		S2	X		X	X			X			X	X	X			X		S1				X	X	X				G Cain	17
X		S	X		X	X			X		S2	X	X	X			X		S1				X	X	X				S J Baines	18
X		S	X		X	X			X		S	X	X	X			X		S1				X	X	X				M E Pierce	19
X		S3	X		X	X			X		S2	X	X	X			X		S1				X	X	X				C J Foy	20
S		S1	X		X	X			X		X	X	X			X		S				X	X	X				A P D'Urso	21
S3	S1	X1			X				X		X	X	X	X3		X		S2				X	X2	X				S W Mathieson	22
S		S	X			X			X		X	X	X			X		S				X	X	X				M C Bailey	23
S		X	X		S	X			X1		X	X	X			X		S1				X	X	X				M R Halsey	24
		S	X	S	X	X					X	X	X	X	S1	X		X				X1	X	X				A Bates	25
S		S	X		X	X					X	X	X	X	S	X		X				X	X	X				P S Danson	26
		S1	X	S2	X	X					X	X3	X	X2		X		X		S3		X1	X	X				G Laws	27
S		S	X	S1	X	X					X2	X	X	X1		X		X		S2	S	X	X	X				R Pearson	28
S2		S	X	X2	X	X			S1			X	X			X		X1				X	X	X				R J Harris	29
S2		S3	X	X3	X				S1		X1	X	X			X		X2				X	X	X				A N Butler	30
S3	S	S2	X2	X	X	X			S1			X3	X			X		X				S	X1	X	X				G Poll	31
X	S	S1	X	X	X				X		X	X2	X			X		X1					X	X	X2				P R Richards	32
X1		S	X	X	X				X2		S1	X	X			X		X				X	S2	X					A G Wiley	33
S3	S2	S	X2	X	X	X			X1	S	X	S1	X			X		X				X	X	X3				G Poll	34
S2		S3	X3	X	X2	X					X		X					X1		X	S1	X	X	X				D Pugh	35
X1		S	X	X	X						X1	X		S1		X		S1	X				X	X	X				D Orr	36
X2	S3	S1	X3		X1	X						X	X	S2		X		X				X	X	X				G B Frankland	37
S	X	X	X		X	X			X			X	X	X1		X		S1		S		X						R D Furnandiz	38
	X	X	X1	X	S1	S			X			X	X	S2	X2		X					X	X					M J Brandwood	39
	X	X	X	X3	S2	S1			X			X	X	S3		X		X				X2	X1					R Styles	40
	X1	X	X	S	S				X			X	X	S1		X		X				X	X					P R Richards	41
	S	X1	X		X				X			X	X	S2	X	X	S1					X2	X					C R Wilkes	42
	X	X	X		X				X		X2	X	S3	S2	X	X3	S1	X1				X1						W C Burns	43
	S	X	X			S2			X	X	X	X	X	S1	X1	X1				X2	X				X		K M Lynch	44
		X	S	S	S	X	X	X	X	X3	X	X	X	X	X	X	X			X				X		X		R D Furnandiz	45
		X1		S1	S3	S2	X	X3	X	X	X	X	X	X2	X	X					X				X		F G Stretton	46
	X		S1	S3		S2	X	X1	X	X3	X	X	X	X2	X	X					X				X		M E Pierce	47
	X		S1		S3	X2	X	X	X	X	X1	X	X	X	X	X					X1				X		E K Wolstenholme	48
	S	X		S1	S	X	X1	X	X	X	X	X	X	X	X					X				X		J A Kirkby	49
S3		X	X	S1	X3	X	X1	X	X1	X	S2	X	X	X2	X					X				X		P Rejer	50
S		X	X1	X2	X	S2	X	S1	X3	X	S1	X	X	X						X				X		R J Harris	51
	S2	X	X1	S3	X2	S1	X3	X	X	X	X	X							X				X		M Fletcher	52
S		X	X	S	X	X1	X	X	X	S1	X								S2	X				X		E K Wolstenholme	53
	X	X3	S3	X1	X	S1	X	X	X2	X									S2	X				X		E K Wolstenholme	54
7	13	21	34	13	27	29		4	10	14	18	44	46	2	13	1	40	9	8	33	1		23	37	42	9		8	FL Appearances	
5	3	8	2	3	7	6	4	2	6		5			1	1	16		5	8	5	3		1			1		1	FL Sub Appearances	
2	1		0+2	2							2	1	2	1		0+1		2	1+1	2	1+1		2	2	1		0+1		CC Appearances	
0+2	0+1	0+1	3	2+1	3	3			1+1		1	2+1	3		1		2			3		0+1	1	3	3	2			FAC Appearances	
		1+1	3	3	0+2			3		3	1+2	3	3				2	2	0+1	3				0+1	3	3		3	PO Appearances	

Also Played: (D) Kearley S2(47). (M) Kerslake S(1).

CHARLTON ATHLETIC

CLUB RECORDS

BIGGEST VICTORIES
League: 8-1 v Middlesbrough, Division 1, 12.9.1953.
F.A. Cup: 7-0 v Burton Albion, Round 3, 7.1.1956.
League Cup: 5-0 v Brentford, Round 1, 12.8.1980.

BIGGEST DEFEATS
League: 1-11 v Aston Villa, Division 2, 14.11.1959.
F.A. Cup: 0-6 v Wrexham, Round 3, 5.1.1980.
League Cup: 1-7 v Blackpool, Round 2, 25.9.1963.

MOST POINTS
3 points a win: 88, Division 1, 1997-98.
2 points a win: 61, Division 3(S), 1934-35.

MOST GOALS SCORED
107, Division 2, 1957-58.
Summers 28, Leary 17, Ayre 11, Ryan 10, Kierman 8, Hewie 6, Werge 6, Lucas 6, White 2, Firmani 2, Lawrie 2, Jago 1, Allen 1, Opponents 7.

MOST GOALS CONCEDED
120, Division 1, 1956-57.

MOST FIRST CLASS MATCHES IN A SEASON
60 - 1993-94 (League 46, FA Cup 6, League Cup 2, Anglo-Italian Cup 6).

MOST LEAGUE WINS
27, Division 3(S), 1934-35.

MOST LEAGUE DRAWS
17, Division 2, 1969-70, 1990-91.

MOST LEAGUE DEFEATS
29, Division 1, 1956-57.

INDIVIDUAL CLUB RECORDS

MOST GOALS IN A SEASON
Ralph Allen: 33 goals in 1934-35 (League 32, FA Cup 1).

MOST GOALS IN A MATCH
5. Wilson Lennox v Exeter (a), Division 3(S), 2.2.1929 (5-2).
5. Eddie Firmani v Aston Villa, Division 1, 5.2.1955 (6-1).
5. John Summers v Huddersfield, Division 2, 21.12.1957 (7-6).
5. John Summers v Portsmouth, Division 2, 1.10.1960 (7-4).

OLDEST PLAYER
Sam Bartram, 42 years 48 days v Arsenal, Division 1, 10.3.1956.

YOUNGEST PLAYER
Paul Konchesky, 16 years 93 days v Oxford Utd, Div.1, August 1997.

MOST CAPPED PLAYER
John Hewie (Scotland) 19.
League: 1934-35: Matches Played 42, Won 27, Drawn 7, Lost 8,

BEST PERFORMANCES

Goals for 103, Goals against 52, Points 61. First in Division 3(S).
Highest Position: 2nd in Division 1, 1936-37.
F.A. Cup: 1946-47: 3rd Round Rochdale 3-1; 4th round West Bromwich Albion 2-1; 5th round Blackburn Rovers 1-0; 6th Round Preston North End 2-1; Semi-Final Newcastle United 4-0; Final Burnley 1-0.
League Cup: 4th round in 1962-63, 1964-65, 1978-79.
Most Recent Success: 1986-87: 2nd Round Lincoln City 3-1,1-0; 3rd Round Queens Park Rangers 1-0; 4th Round Arsenal 0-2.
Full Members Cup: 1986-87: 2nd Round Birmingham City 3-2; 3rd round Bradford City 2-0; 4th Round Everton 2-2 aet (won 6-5 on penalties); Semi-Final Norwich City 2-1 aet, Final Blackburn Rovers 0-1.

ADDITIONAL INFORMATION
PREVIOUS NAMES
None.
PREVIOUS LEAGUES
Southern League.

Club colours: Red shirts with white under-arm, white shorts, red socks.
Change colours: White shirts, green shorts, white socks.
Third strip: Green shirts with white & red hoop, green shorts & socks.
Reserves League: Avon Insurance Football Combination.

DIVISIONAL RECORD

	Played	Won	Drawn	Lost	For	Against	Points
Division 1	746	262	171	313	1,082	1,209	732
Division 2/1	1,628	576	425	627	2,395	2,583	1,795
Division 3	184	83	39	62	274	245	205
Division 3(S)	420	165	109	146	622	567	439
Total	2,978	1,086	744	1,148	4,373	4,604	3,171

RECORDS AND STATISTICS

COMPETITIONS

Div 1/P	Div.2/1	Div.3	Div 3(S)
1936-57	1929-33	1972-75	1921-29
1986-90	1935-36	1980-81	1933-35
1998-	1957-72		
	1975-80		
	1981-86		
	1990-98		

HONOURS

FA Cup	Div 3(S)
1947	1928-29
	1934-35

MOST APPEARANCES

Sam Bartram 623 (1934-56)

Year	League	FA Cup
1934-35	18	
1935-36	39	1
1936-37	42	1
1937-38	41	5
1938-39	42	1
1945-46	-	10
1946-47	41	6
1947-48	42	3
1948-49	41	1
1949-50	42	4
1950-51	37	2
1951-52	41	1
1952-53	38	1
1953-54	40	2
1954-55	42	3
1955-56	33	3
	579	44

MOST GOALS IN A CAREER

Derek Hales - 168 (1973-76 & 1978-85)

Year	League	FA Cup	Lge Cup
1973-74	8	-	-
1974-75	20	-	1
1975-76	28	-	3
1976-77	16	-	2
1978-79	8	-	1
1979-80	8	-	1
1980-81	17	4	2
1981-82	11	-	2
1982-83	14	1	2
1983-84	10	-	1
1984-85	8	-	-
Total	148	5	15

Current leading goalscorer: Clive Mendonca - 28 (1997-98)

Stuart Leary scored most League goals (153) 1951-62.
(League 153, FA Cup 8, League Cup 2) Total 163.

RECORD TRANSFER FEE RECEIVED

Amount	Club	Player	Date
£2,600,000	Leeds Utd	Lee Bowyer	7/96
£775,000	Chelsea	Scott Minto	5/94
£700,000	Newcastle Utd	Robert Lee	9/92
£650,000	Crystal Palace	Mike Flanagan	8/79

RECORD TRANSFER FEE PAID

Amount	Club	Player	Date
£700,000	Grimsby	Clive Mendonca	05/97
£600,000	Chelsea	Joe McLaughlin	8/89
£430,000	Chelsea	Colin Pates	10/88
£350,000	Port Vale	Andy Jones	9/87

MANAGERS

Name	Seasons	Best	Worst
Walter Rayner	1920-25	12(3S)	16(3S)
Alex McFarlane	1925-28	13(3S)	21(3S)
Albert Lindon	1928	11(3S)	11(3S)
Alex McFarlane	1928-32	10(2)	1(3S)
Albert Lindon	1932-33	22(2)	22(2)
Jimmy Seed	1933-56	2(1)	5(3S)
Jimmy Trotter	1956-61	22(1)	10(2)
Frank Hill	1961-65	4(2)	20(2)
Bob Stokoe	1965-67	16(2)	19(2)
Eddie Firmani	1967-70	3(2)	20(2)
Theo Foley	1970-74	20(2)	14(3)
Andy Nelson	1974-80	7(2)	3(3)
Mike Bailey	1980-81	3(3)	3(3)
Alan Mullery	1981-82	13(2)	13(2)
Ken Craggs	1982	17(2)	17(2)
Lennie Lawrence	1982-91	5(1)	17(2)
A Curbishley/ S Gritt	1991-95	7(2)	15 (2/1)
A Curbishley	1995-	4(1)	15(1)

LONGEST LEAGUE RUNS

of undefeated matches:	15 (4.10.80 - 20.12.80)	of league matches w/out a win:	16 (26.2.1955 - 22.8.1955)
of undefeated home matches:	28 (13.4.1935 - 3.10.1936)	of undefeated away matches:7 (4.10.80-6.12.80 & 29.12.90- 1.4.91, 2.12.95 - 24.2.96)	
without home win:	9 (5.3.1955 - 20.8.1955)	without an away win:	33 (29.3.1969 - 14.11.1970)
of league wins:	7 (7.10.1980 - 1.11.1980)	of home wins:	11 (4.12.1937 - 18.4.1938)
of league defeats:	10 (11.4.1990 - 15.9.1990)	of away wins:	5 (26.1.1935 - 23.3.1935, 2.12.95 - 10.2.96)

CHARLTON ATHLETIC

PLAYERS NAME / Honours	Ht	Wt	Birthdate	Birthplace / Transfers	Contract Date	Clubs	League	L/Cup	FA Cup	Other	Lge	L/C	FAC	Oth
G O A L K E E P E R														
Ilic Sasa	6.2	14	18/07/72	Melbourne		St Leonards Stamcroft								
Macedonian Int.					01/01/98	Charlton Athletic	14			3				
Petterson Andrew	6.2	14.2	26/09/69	Freemantle	30/12/88	Luton Town	16+3	2		2				
				Loan	26/03/93	Ipswich Town	1							
				£85000	15/07/94	Charlton Athletic	61+1	5	3	2				
Loan 08/12/94 Bradford City	3 Lge apps.			Loan	26/09/95	Ipswich Town	1							
Loan 23/01/96 Plymouth Argyle	6 Lge apps.			Loan	08/03/96	Colchester United	5							
Royce Simon	6.1	12	09/09/71	Forest Gate		Heybridge Swifts								
				£10000	15/10/91	Southend United	147+2	9	4	3				
				Free	26/06/98	Charlton Athletic								
Salmon Michael	6.2	12.12	14/07/64	Leyland	16/10/81	Blackburn Rovers	1							
				Loan	18/10/82	Chester City	16		2					
				Free	03/08/83	Stockport County	118	10	3	3				
				Free	31/07/86	Bolton Wanderers	26	2	4	4				
				£18000	07/03/87	Wrexham	100	4	4	9				
				£100000	06/07/89	Charlton Athletic	148	11	10	6				
D E F E N C E														
Balmer Stuart	6.1	12.4	20/06/69	Falkirk		Celtic								
S: Y.				£120000	24/08/90	Charlton Athletic	201+26	15	9+1	11+1	8		1	
Barness Anthony	5.1	10.12	25/03/73	Lewisham	06/03/91	Charlton Athletic	21+6	2	3	1+1	1		1	
				£350000	08/09/92	Chelsea	12+2	2		2+1				
				Loan	12/08/93	Middlesbrough				1				
				Loan	02/02/96	Southend United	5							
				£165000	15/08/96	Charlton Athletic	66+8	5	2+1	1+1	3			
Bowen Mark	5.8	11.6	07/12/63	Neath	01/12/81	Tottenham Hotspur	14+3		3	0+1	2			
W: 41, u21,Y,S.				£97000	23/07/87	Norwich City	285+4	28	27	17	22	1	1	1
					04/07/96	West Ham United								
via Shimizu (Japan) - Free 01/03/97				Free	15/09/97	Charlton Athletic	34+2		3	3				
Brown Steven B	6.1	12	13/05/72	Brighton	03/07/90	Charlton Athletic (T)	126+16	7	13	3+2	5		1	
Ifejiagwa Emeka				Nigeria		Lagos								
				£20000	01/06/98	Charlton Athletic								
Konchesky Paul	5.9	10.12	15/05/81	Barking		Charlton Athletic (T)	2+1	1						
E: Y.														
Lee Matthew A	5.11	11	13/05/69	Farnborough	02/07/97	Charlton Athletic (T)								
Mills Daniel J	5.11	11.09	18/05/77	Norwich	01/11/94	Norwich City	46+20	3+2	2				1	
E: Y.				£350,000	17/03/98	Charlton Athletic	9		2	1	1			
Poole Gary	6	11	11/09/67	Stratford	15/07/85	Tottenham Hotspur								
GMVC'91. Div.2'95. AMC'95.				Free	14/08/87	Cambridge United	42+1	2	2	3				
				£3000	01/03/89	Barnet	39+1	2	7	6	2			1
				Free	05/06/92	Plymouth Argyle	39	6	2	+1	5	2		
				£350000	09/07/93	Southend United	38		1	6	2			
				£50000	16/09/94	Birmingham City	70+2	13	7	10	1		1	2
				£250000	12/11/96	Charlton Athletic	14+2				1			
Powell Chris	5.1	11.07	08/09/69	Lambeth	24/12/87	Crystal Palace	2+1	0+1		0+1				
				Loan	11/01/90	Aldershot	11							
				Free	30/08/90	Southend United	219+2	11	7	17	3			
				£750000	01/06/95	Derby County	89+2	5	5		1		1	
				£825000	22/06/98	Charlton Athletic								
Rufus Richard R	6.1	11.2	12/01/75	Lewisham	01/07/93	Charlton Athletic	142+3	8	7	5				1
E: u21.6.														
Youds Edward	6	10.1	03/05/70	Liverpool	10/06/88	Everton	5+3	+1		1				
				Loan	29/12/89	Cardiff City	+1		+1					
				Loan	08/02/90	Wrexham	20				2			
				£250000	15/11/91	Ipswich Town	38+12	1+2	5+1		1			
Loan 20/01/95 Bradford City				£150000	17/03/95	Bradford City	85	7	3	4	8	2		
				£550000	26/03/98	Charlton Athletic	8			3				
M I D F I E L D														
Jones Keith	5.9	10.11	14/10/65	Dulwich	16/08/83	Chelsea	43+9	9+2	1	4+1	7	3		
E: Y2, S				£40000	03/09/87	Brentford	167+12	15	13	16	13	2	4	1
				£175000	21/10/91	Southend United	81+2	2	5	9	11			1
				£150000	16/09/94	Charlton Athletic	113+6	3+1	4+2	3	4		1	
Kinsella Mark A	5.9	11.8	12/08/72	Dublin		Home Farm								
Ei: u21.8, Y. GMVC'92. FAT'92.				Free	18/08/89	Colchester United	174+6	11	11	9+1	27	3	1	5
				£150000	27/09/96	Charlton Athletic	83	2	4	3	12		1	
Mortimer Paul H	5.11	11.3	08/05/68	Kensington		Fulham								
E: u21.2				Free		Farnborough								
				Free	22/09/87	Charlton Athletic	108+5	4+1	8	3+1	17			
				£350000	24/07/91	Aston Villa	10+2	2			1			
				£500000	18/10/91	Crystal Palace	18+4	1	1	3	2			
				Loan	22/01/93	Brentford	6			2				
				PE	05/07/94	Charlton Athletic	57+12	2	3	0+1	14		1	
Newton Shaun	5.8	10.4	20/08/75	Camberwell	01/07/93	Charlton Athletic	134+38	14	7+2	7+1	15	2		2
Nicholls Kevin J R	6	11.7	02/01/79	Newham	31/05/96	Charlton Athletic (T)	4+8	2+2			1			
Parker Scott	5.9	11	13/10/80	Lambeth	01/08/97	Charlton Athletic	0+3		0+1					

34

Player	Ht	Wt	DOB	Fee / From	Date	Club	Lg Ap	FA Ap	FL Ap	Ot Ap	Lg Gl	FA Gl	FL Gl	Ot Gl
Redfearn Neil Div.2'91.	5.1	12.4	20/06/65	Dewsbury		Nottingham Forest								
				Free	23/06/82	Bolton Wanderers	35	2	4		1			
				£8250	23/03/84	Lincoln City	96+4	4	3	7	13	1		
					22/08/86	Doncaster Rovers	46	2	3	2	14	1		
				£100000	31/07/87	Crystal Palace	57	6	1	1	10			
				£150000	21/11/88	Watford	22+2	1	6	5	3		3	1
				£150000	12/01/90	Oldham Athletic	56+6	3	7+1	1	16	1	3	
				£150000	05/09/91	Barnsley	289+3	21	20	5	72	6	6	
				£1045000	25/06/98	Charlton Athletic								
Robinson John R W: 8, u21.5.	5.1	11.2	29/08/71	Bulawayo	21/04/89	Brighton & H.A.	57+5	5	2+1	1+1	6	1		2
				£75000	15/09/92	Charlton Athletic	179+8	11+2	10+2	5+1	23	4	2	

F O R W A R D

Player	Ht	Wt	DOB	Fee / From	Date	Club	Lg Ap	FA Ap	FL Ap	Ot Ap	Lg Gl	FA Gl	FL Gl	Ot Gl
Allen Bradley E: u21.8, Y.8.	5.7	10	13/09/71	Romford	30/09/88	Q.P.R.	56+25	5+2	3+2	1	27	5		
				£400000	28/03/96	Charlton Athletic	30+10	3		1+3	9	2		
Bright Mark FMC'91	6	11	06/06/62	Stoke		Leek Town								
				Free	15/10/81	Port Vale	18+11	1+1	0+1	2	10		1	
				£33000	19/07/84	Leicester City	26+16	3+1	1		6			
				£75000	13/11/86	Crystal Palace	224+3	22	13+1	23	90	11	2	9
				£1375000	11/09/92	Sheffield Wednesday	112+21	20+1	13		48	11	7	
via Sion - Free 27/01/97				Loan	13/12/96	Millwall	3		1		1			
				Free	27/03/97	Charlton Athletic	17+5	0+2	2+1	3	9			
Emblen Paul D	5.10		03/04/77	Bromley		Tonbridge A.								
				£7500	03/05/97	Charlton Athletic	0+4							
Holmes Matthew J E	5.7	10.7	01/08/69	Luton	22/08/88	Bournemouth	105+9	7	8+2	5	8			
				Loan	23/03/89	Cardiff City	0+1							
				£40000	19/08/92	West Ham United	63+13	4	6	3	5			1
				£1200000	15/08/95	Blackburn Rovers	8+1			2+1	1			
				£2500000	29/07/97	Charlton Athletic	10+6		1+1		1			
Hunt Andrew	6	12	09/06/70	Grays		Kings Lynn								
				Free		Kettering Town								
				£150000	29/01/91	Newcastle United	34+9	3	2	3	11	1	2	
				£100000	25/03/93	W.B.A.	201+11	12	7	8+1	76	3	3	3
				Free	23/06/98	Charlton Athletic								
Jones Stephen G	6	12.12	17/03/70	Cambridge		Billericay Town								
				£22000	16/11/92	West Ham United	8+8		2+2	1+1	4		1	
Loan 27/01/95 Bournemouth				Free	25/04/95	Bournemouth	71+3	4	3	3	26	3	1	
					01/06/96	West Ham United	5+3		0+1	2				
					14/02/97	Charlton Athletic	20+5	2	1	1+2	7			
				Loan	24/12/97	Bournemouth	5		1		4			1
Lisbie Kevin A	5.10	11	17/10/78	Hackney	24/05/96	Charlton Athletic (T)	5+37	0+4	0+1		2			
Mendonça Clive P	5.1	10.7	09/09/68	Islington	10/09/86	Sheffield United	0+3	+1		1	4			
				Loan	26/02/88	Doncaster Rovers	2							
				£35000	25/03/88	Rotherham United	71+13	5+2	4+1	4+2	27	1	2	1
				£110000	01/08/91	Sheffield United	4+6	+2	+1		1			
				Loan	09/01/92	Grimsby Town	10				3			
				£85000	13/08/92	Grimsby Town	151+5	10+1	8	2	57	3	2	1
				£700000	23/05/97	Charlton Athletic	40	2	2	2	23	1	1	3

THE MANAGER
ALAN CURBISHLEY

Date of Birth . . . . 8th November 1957.
Place of Birth . . . . Forest Gate.
Date of Appointment . . . . . 20th July 1991 as joint manager, June 1995 as sole.

PREVIOUS CLUBS
As Manager . . . . None.
As Coach . . . . None.
As a Player . . . West Ham, Aston Villa, Brighton, Birmingham, Charlton Athletic.

HONOURS
As a Manager
Charlton Athletic: Promotion to the Carling Premiership via play-offs, 1997-98.

As a Player
International: 2 u21, 10 Youth and 18 Schoolboy caps for England.

THE VALLEY
Floyd Road, Charlton, London SE7 8BL

Capacity ....20,000.

First game ....v Summerstown (Sth Suburban Lge) 13.9.19.
First Lge game...v Exeter City (Div 3(S) 27.8.21.
First floodlit game ....Rotherham Utd (Div 2) 20.9.61.

ATTENDANCES
Highest..75,031 v Aston Villa, FA Cup, 12.2.1938.
Lowest...1,452 v Pisa, Anglo Italian Cup, 22.12.93)
OTHER GROUNDS.......Siemens Meadow 1906-07. Woolwich Common1907-08. Pound Park 1908-13.
.... Horn Lane 1913-19. The Valley 1919-23. The Mount 1923-24. The Valley 1924-85.
....Selhurst Park 1985-91. Upton Park 1991-92. The Valley 1992-

HOW TO GET TO THE GROUND

By Road
From M25 take junction 2 (A2 London bound) and follow until road becomes A102 (M). Take the turning marked 'Woolwich Ferry' and turn right along A206 Woolwich Road. This route takes you into Charlton.

Visitors Parking
Visiting coaches located in Anchor and Hope LAne, five minutes walk from ground. Also street parking.

By Rail
Charlton Station (British Rail main line) can be reached from Charing Cross, Waterloo (East) or London Bridge and is two minutes from the ground.

Nearest Railway Station
Charlton.

USEFUL TELEPHONE NUMBERS

Club switchboard 0181 333 4000
Club fax number 0181 333 4001
Club shop 0181 333 4035
Ticket Office .. 0181 333 4010 (fax 333 4011)

Marketing Department....... 0181 333 4020
Internet address.. www.charlton-athletic.co.uk
Clubcall 0891 12 11 46*
*Calls cost 50p per minute at all times. Call costings correct at time of going to press.

MATCHDAY PROGRAMME

Programme Editor ....Rick Everitt.

Number of pages....................56.

Price ....£2.00.

Subscriptions....................Contact the club.

Local Newspapers
Kentish Times, South East London Mercury
..........South London Press, News Shopper
...........................Greenwich Comet Leader
.......................Kent Messenger, Kent Today.

Local Radio Stations
....................Capital Gold, Millenium Radio.

MATCHDAY TICKET PRICES
SEE 'USEFUL TELEPHONE NUMBERS' ABOVE FOR TICKET OFFICE NUMBER.

CHELSEA
(The Blues)
F.A. CARLING PREMIERSHIP
SPONSORED BY: AUTOGLASS

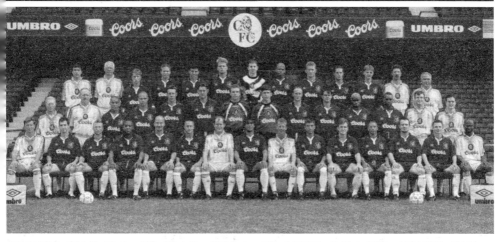

Back Row L-R: Dave Collyer (Youth Development Officer), Bernie Dixson (Youth Development Officer), Chris McCann, Paul Hughes, Neil Clement, Jakob Kjeldbjerg, Nick Colgan, Michael Duberry, Erland Johnsen, Scott Minto, Mark Nicholls, Bob Orsborn (Kit Manager), Ted Dale (Youth Team manager). **Middle Row:** George Price (Reserve Team Physio), Mick McGiven (Reserve Team Manager), Mark Stein, Andy Myers, Craig Burley, David Lee, Dmitri Kharine, Kevin Hitchcock, Frank Leboeuf, Steve Clarke, Frank Sinclair, David Rocastle, Mike Banks (Physiotherapist), Terry Byrne (Assistant Physiotherapist). **Front Row:** Eddie Niedzwiecki (Goal keeper Coach), Gavin Peacock, Dan Petrescu, Eddie Newton, Gianluca Vialli, Dennis Wise, Gwyn Williams (Assistant Manager), Ruud Gullit (Player / Manager), Graham Rix (First Team Coach), Roberto Di Matteo, Mark Huges, Terry Phelan, John Spencer, Jody Morris, Ade Mafe (Fitness / Conditioning Coach).

<table>
<tr><td>

CHELSEA
FORMED IN 1905
TURNED PROFESSIONAL IN 1905
LTD COMPANY IN 1905

CHAIRMAN: K W Bates

DIRECTORS
C Hutchinson (Managing), Yvonne Todd.
SECRETARY
Keith Lacy
COMMERCIAL MANAGER
Carole Phair

MANAGER: Gianluca Vialli
ASSISTANT MANAGER: Gwyn Williams
FIRST TEAM COACH: Graham Rix
RESERVE TEAM MANAGER
Mick McGiven
YOUTH TEAM COACH
Jim Duffy
PHYSIOTHERAPIST
Mike Banks

STATISTICIAN FOR THE DIRECTORY
Ron Hockings

</td><td>

Arsenal were not the only London club to complete a double last season as Chelsea added to their recent haul of silverware, the Coca-Cola League Cup and the European Cup Winners Cup.

The club could, however, have finished empty handed as the dramatic sacking of Ruud Gullit shocked both the Football World and the Chelsea players and questions were asked to whether the season, that was showing so much promise, would just fold and fade away.

A successor was named almost straight away, Vialli would now be the new player/manager and his first task would be to reverse a semi-final first leg 1-2 defeat against Arsenal in order to qualify for the final. They did, 3-1, and Vialli was on his way to winning his first piece of silverware as Chelsea manager, not bad for a newcomer!

In the ECWC however, Vialli would have to negotiate the Quarter finals and Semi finals and so all eyes were watching to see if he had what it takes, or was he just riding on the back of Gullit's dynasty. He proved the doubters wrong by seeing Chelsea through to the final with aggregate scores of 5-2 v. Real Betis (QF) and 4-2 v. Vicenza (SF). In the final itself Chelsea won their second title of the season when Zola came off the bench to score the only goal of the game against german side VFB Stuttgart.

A final League position of fourth will, it is hoped, be improved upon and with the signings of Casiraghi, Laudrup, Ferrer and World Cup winner Desailly, added to an already strong continental team, the 'Blues' will be one of the favourites. However, it will be interesting to see if such a cosmopolitan team can maintain any sort of consistency needed to even challenge for the title. They will though, be a good bet for retaining their ECWC title and maybe getting to Wembley at least once this season.

</td></tr>
</table>

CHELSEA

Carling Prem.   :4th   FA CUP: 3rd Round   LC CUP: Winners   ECWC: Winners

M	DATE	COMP.	VEN	OPPONENTS	RESULT	H/T	LP	GOAL SCORERS/GOAL TIMES	ATT.
1	A 03	CS	H	Manchester United	D 1-1	0-0		Hughes 52	73636
2	09	CP	A	Coventry City	L 2-3	1-1	14	Sinclair 39, Flo 71	(22686)
3	24	CP	A	Barnsley	W 6-0	3-0	11	Petrescu 25, Poyet 37, Vialli 43, 57, 64, 81	(18170)
4	27	CP	A	Wimbledon	W 2-0	0-0	6	Di Matteo 60, Petrescu 63	(22237)
5	30	CP	H	Southampton	W 4-2	4-1	4	Petrescu 7, Leboeff 30, Hughes 31, Wise 34	30008
6	S 13	CP	A	Crystal Palace	W 3-0	2-0	3	Hughes 20, Leboeff 26 (pen), Le Saux 89	(26186)
7	18	ECWC 1/1	H	Slovan Bratislava	W 2-0	1-0		di Matteo 5, Granville 80	23,067
8	21	CP	H	Arsenal	L 2-3	1-1	5	Poyet 40, Zola 60	33012
9	24	CP	A	Manchester United	D 2-2	1-1	5	Hughes 67, Berg 25 (OG)	(55163)
10	27	CP	H	Newcastle United	W 1-0	0-0	4	Poyet 75	31563
11	O 02	ECWC 1/2	A	Slovan Bratislava	W 2-0	1-0		Vialli 27, di Matteo	(15000)
12	05	CP	A	Liverpool	L 2-4	1-2	5	Zola 22, Poyet 85 (pen)	(36647)
13	15	CC 3	H	Blackburn Rovers	D 1-1	0-0		Di Matteo 60	18671
14	18	CP	H	Leicester City	W 1-0	0-0	4	Leboeff 86	33356
15	23	ECWC 2/1	A	Tromso	L 2-3	0-2		Vialli 86, 90	(6438)
16	26	CP	A	Bolton Wanderers	L 0-1	0-0	4		(24080)
17	N 01	CP	A	Aston Villa	W 2-0	1-0	4	Hughes 38, Flo 82	(39372)
18	06	ECWC 2/2	H	Tromso	W 7-1	3-1		Petrescu 13,86, Vialli 24,60,75, Zola 43, Leboeff 55(pen)	29362
19	09	CP	H	West Ham United	W 2-1	0-0	4	Zola 81, Ferdinand 56 (OG)	34382
20	19	CC 4	H	Southampton	W 2-1	0-0		Flo 61, Morris 118	20968
21	22	CP	A	Blackburn Rovers	L 0-1	0-1	4		(27683)
22	26	CP	H	Everton	W 2-0	0-0	3	Wise 80 (pen), Zola 90 (pen)	34148
23	29	CP	H	Derby County	W 4-0	2-0	2	Zola 11, 62, 76, Hughes 34	34544
24	D 06	CP	A	Tottenham Hotspur	W 6-1	1-1	2	Flo 39, 62, 89, Di Matteo 47, Petrescu 59, Nicholls 77	(28476)
25	13	CP	H	Leeds United	D 0-0	0-0	3		34690
26	20	CP	A	Sheffield Wednesday	W 4-1	1-0	3	Petrescu 30, Vialli 56, Leboeff 65 (pen), Flo 84	(28334)
27	26	CP	H	Wimbledon	D 1-1	1-1	3	Vialli 8	34100
28	29	CP	A	Southampton	L 0-1	0-1	3		(15231)
29	J 04	FAC 3	H	Manchester United	L 3-5	0-3		Le Saux 77, Vialli 83, 87	34792
30	07	CC QF	A	Ipswich Town	D 2-2	2-1		Flo 32, Le Saux 45	(22088)
31	10	CP	A	Coventry City	W 3-1	0-1	2	Nicholls 65, 70, Di Matteo 77	34647
32	18	CP	A	Everton	L 1-3	1-1	3	Flo 37	(32355)
33	28	CC SF1	A	Arsenal	L 1-2	0-1		Hughes 69	(38114)
34	31	CP	H	Barnsley	W 2-0	1-0	3	Vialli 22, Hughes 47	34442
35	F 08	CP	A	Arsenal	L 0-2	0-2	3		(38083)
36	18	CC SF2	H	Arsenal	W 3-1	1-0		Hughes 11, Di Matteo 50, Petrescu 53	34330
37	28	CP	H	Manchester United	L 0-1	0-1	5		34511
38	M 05	ECWC QF1	A	Real Betis	W 2-1	2-0		Flo 8, 12	(0)
39	08	CP	H	Aston Villa	L 0-1	0-0	5		33018
40	11	CP	H	Crystal Palace	W 6-2	3-1	5	Vialli 14, 43, Zola 16, Wise 85, Flo 88, 90	31917
41	14	CP	A	West Ham United	L 1-2	0-0	5	Charvet 52	(25829)
42	19	ECWC QF2	H	Real Betis	W 3-1	1-1		Sinclair 29, Di Matteo 49, Zola 90	32300
43	21	CP	H	Leicester City	L 0-2	0-1	5		(21335)
44	29	CC F	N	Middlesbrough	W 2-0	0-0		Sinclair 95, Di Matteo 107	77698
45	A 02	ECWC SF1	A	Vicenza	L 0-1	0-1			(24000)
46	05	CP	A	Derby County	W 1-0	1-0	5	Hughes 37	(30062)
47	08	CP	A	Leeds United	L 1-3	1-2	6	Charvet 11	(37276)
48	11	CP	H	Tottenham Hotspur	W 2-0	0-0	4	Flo 75, Vialli 88	34149
49	16	ECWC SF2	H	Vicenza	W 3-1	1-1		Poyet 35, Zola 51, Hughes 76	33810
50	19	CP	H	Sheffield Wednesday	W 1-0	1-0	4	Leboeff 22 (pen)	29075
51	25	CP	H	Liverpool	W 4-1	1-1	3	Hughes 10, 75, Clarke 69, Flo 70	34639
52	29	CP	H	Blackburn Rovers	L 0-1	0-0	3		33311
53	M 02	CP	A	Newcastle United	L 1-3	0-2	4	Di Matteo 78	(36710)
54	10	CP	H	Bolton Wanderers	W 2-0	0-0	4	Vialli 76, Morris 90	34845
55	13	ECWC F	N	VfB Stuttgart	W 1-0	0-0		Zola 71	30216

Best Home League Attendance: 34845 V Bolton Wanderers   Smallest :29075 V Sheffield Wednesday   Average :33387

Goal Scorers:

CP	(71)	Flo 11, Vialli 11, Hughes 9, Zola 8, Leboeff 5, Petrescu 5, Di Matteo 4, Poyet 4, Nicholls 3, Wise 3, Charvet 2, Clarke 1, Le Saux 1, Morris 1, Sinclair 1, Opponents 2
CC	(11)	Di Matteo 3, Flo 2, Hughes 2, Le Saux 1, Morris 1, Petrescu 1, Sinclair 1
FAC	(3)	Vialli 2, Le Saux 1
ECWC	(22)	Vialli 6, Zola 4, Di Matteo 3, Flo 2, Petrescu 2, Granville 1, Hughes 1, Leboeff 1, Poyet 1, Sinclair 1

1997-98

(D) Babayaro	(F) Charvet	(D) Clarke	(M) Crittenden	(G) De Goey	(M) Di Matteo	(D) Duberry	(F) Flo	(M) Granville	(M) Gullit (Dil)	(M) Harley	(G) Hitchcock	(F) Hughes M	(M) Hughes P	(G) Kharine	(D) Lambourde	(D) Le Saux	(D) Leboeuf	(D) Lee	(M) Morris	(D) Myers	(M) Newton	(F) Nicholls	(D) Petrescu	(M) Poyet	(D) Sinclair	(F) Vialli	(F) Wise	(F) Zola	Referee	#
	X	X	X				X	S				S	X2	S			X						X1		S	S1	X	X	P. Jones	1
	X	X	X2				S1	S					X1			X	X				S2				X	X	X	S	X	X	P.A. Durkin	2
	X	X	X				S1	S3				S	S				X					X		S2	X	X	X	X	X	G Poll	3
	X	X	X	X	X							S	S				X				S		S	X	X	X	X	X	M J Bodenham	4
	S3	X	X	X	S							S	X			X	X					S1	X	X	S2	X	X	X	A B Wilkie	5
	X	S	X	X	S							S	X	X		X	X					X	X		S	X	X	S	G R Ashby	6
	X	X	S	X	S	X	S					S	S	X			X				S		X	X	X	X	X	X		7
	X	X	X	S3								S	S2	X		X	X				S	S1	X	X	X	X	X	DJ Gallagher	8
	X			S1			S					S	X	X		X	X				X	S	X	X	S	X	X	X	G S Willard	9
	X	X	X									S	X2	X		X	X				X	S	X	X	S1	X	X	M A Riley	10
S3	S	X	X		X	S1						S	S			X	X1	X				S2	X2	X3	X	X	S			11
S	X	X	X		S2		S1					S	X			X	X				X	X	X	S	X	X	X	D R Elleray	12
X	X		X			X	X					X	X				X	S1			X	X		S2	X		K W Burge	13	
X	X	X	X		X		S1					S	S2		S	X	X				X		X	X	S3	X	X	U D Rennie	14
X	X	X	X		S	X2						S2		S		X1				S1	X	S	X	X	X	X		15
X	X	X			X	S	S1					S	X			X		S	X	X	X	X	X		P Jones	16	
X	S2	X	S1	S3	S							S	X			X		X	X	X	X	X		X	S W Dunn	17	
X	S3	X	X2	S1	S							S	S		S2	X		X	X3	S	X		X	X1	X	X		18
X	X	X	S				S2					S	X			X		X	X	S1	X		S	X	X	X	G P Barber	19
S2	X	X		X	X	X						X	S3			X	S1	X			X			X	X	D R Elleray	20	
X	X	X	X		S1	S2						S	X			X		X	S	X	X	S	X	X	X	S J Lodge	21	
X	X	S	X	X	X	S3	S1					S	S2			X	X				X	X	X	X	X	N S Barry	22	
X		S2	X	X	S1							S	X1		S	X	X				X	S	X	S1	X2	U D Rennie	23	
X1		X	X	X	X							X	X			X	S1	X	X	X	X	D J Gallagher	24				
		S2	X	X	X							X	X			X	X1	X2	X	S1	X	X	G Poll	25				
	S2	X	X	S1	S						S	S	S	X	X	X2	X	X1	G P Barber	26							
	S1	X	X	X	X	S				S		S	X	X	S	X	X1	X2	X	S2	G S Willard	27					
	X	X	X	S1	X2		S	X	X3		X		S	S2	X1	X	S3	X	M J Bodenham	28						
	X	X	X	X2			S	X	S	S	X	X		S1	X1	X	S2	X	S J Lodge	29						
S2	X	X	X	X3	X	S1		S3		X	X	X		X1		X2		X	P A Durkin	30					
	X	X	X	S	X1	S2	S	S	S	X	X	X		S1			X	X2	M D Reed	31					
	X	X		X1		S2	S	X	S	X	X		X	S	X	X2	S1	A B Wilkie	32						
S1	X	X	X	X2	X		X	X		X	X1	X3	S3	X	M J Bodenham	33									
X	X	X	X	S		S	X		X	X	X1	S1	X	S2	X	X2	S	J T Winter	34						
X		X	X	S3	S1	S	X	S	X	X	X3	X1	X2	X	S2	D J Gallagher	35							
	X	X	X	S	S	X		X	X	S1	X	X1	X	X	G Poll	36									
	X	X	S1	S	X	X	S	X	X	S	S	X	X1	X	S W Dunn	37								
S	X	X	X2	S	S2	S	S	X	X	S1	X	X	S2	X	X1	A Ouzounov	38							
S2		X	X1	X	X	S	S	X	X2	X	X	X	S1	S J Lodge	39									
S	X	S1	X	S	S3	S2	X3	X	X	X2	X1	X	M A Riley	40										
X	S	X	X	X	X	X1	X	S	S1	M J Bodenham	41												
	X	X	X	S	S	S	S1	X	S	S	X	X1	X	X	X	B Heynemann	42							
	X	X	S1	S	X	X	S	X	X	S	S	X	X1	P A Durkin	43									
S1	X	X	X	S2	S	X2	X	X	X	X1	X	X	X	P Jones	44								
X	X	X	X	S	S	S	S	X	X	S1	S	X	X	X1	Manuel Diaz Vega	45							
S2	X2	X	X1	X	X3	X	X	S	X	S3	S1	X	J T Winter	46									
X		X	S2	S	X	S3	S1	X	X	X3	X1	S	X	X2	D R Elleray	47							
	X	X	X	X	X1	S	X	X	X2	S2	X	S1	X	X	S	P A Durkin	48						
S1	X	X	X	S	S2	S	X	X	X2	S3	X1	S	X	X	X3	Batta M	49						
X	X	X2	X	X1	X	S3	X	X3	S1	S	X	S2	G S Willard	50								
S2	X	X	S1	S	X3	X	S	X	S	X3	X2	X	X1	G R Ashby	51							
S1	X	X	X1	S	X	X	S3	X	X3	S	X1	X	S1	P E Alcock	52								
X	X	X	S1	X	S	X1	S3	X1	S	X3	X	S1	X	K W Burge	53								
X	X	X	S2	X3	X	S	X	S	X	X	X1	S1	S3	X2	A B Wilkie	54							
S	X	X	X	X	X1	X	S	S	X	S	S	S2	X	X2	X	X	S1	Stefano Braschi	55			

8	7	22		28	28	23	16	9		3		25	5	10	5	26	32	1	9	11	17	8	31	11	20	14	26	23	CP Appearances
4	4	2		2		18	4	6				4	4		2				3	1	1	11		3	2	7		4	CP Sub Appearances
1+1	0+1	4+2	1	4	4	3	3+1	3	3+1		2	3+3			3	4	4	0+2	1	1	3+1	2	3		4+1	2+1	4	4	CC Appearances
		1		1	1	1	1		1			1									0+1					0+1	1	1	FAC Appearances
2+1	0+1	7+1		10	9	6	3+2	4+1				1+3	1		1+2	3	10		2+1	1+2	6+1	0+2	7+1	5	6	8+1	10	8+1	ECWC Appearances

Also Played: (D) Clement S(1). (G) Colgan S(2). (M) Hampshire S1(13). (F) Sheerin

CHELSEA

CLUB RECORDS

BIGGEST VICTORIES
League: 7-0 v Lincoln City, Division 2, 29.10.1910.
7-0 v Port Vale, Division 2, 3.3.1906.
9-2 v Glossop N.E., Division 2, 1.9.1906.
7-0 v Portsmouth, Division 2, 21.5.1963.
7-0 v Walsall (a), Division 2, 4.2.1989.
F.A. Cup: 9-1 v Worksop, 1st Round, 31.1.1908.
League Cup: 7-0 v Doncaster Rovers, 3rd Round, 16.11.1960.
Europe: 13-0 v Jeunesse Hautcharge, ECWC, 29.9.1971.

BIGGEST DEFEATS
League: 1-8 v Wolverhampton W., Division 1, 26.9.1953.
0-7 v Leeds United, Division 1, 7.10.1967.
0-7 v Nottingham Forest, Division 1, 20.4.1991
F.A. Cup: 0-6 v Sheffield Wednesday, 2nd Round replay, 5.2.1913.
1-7 v Crystal Palace, 3rd Round, 16.11.1960.
League Cup: 2-6 v Stoke City, 3rd Round, 22.10.1974.
Europe: 0-5 v Barcelona, Semi-Final EUFA, 25.5.1966.

MOST POINTS
3 points a win: 99, Division 2, 1988-89 (Division 2 record, 46 games).
2 points a win: 57, Division 2, 1906-07.

MOST GOALS SCORED
98, Division 1, 1960-61.
Greaves 41, Tindall 16, Tambling 9, Brabrook 8, Livesey 8, Blunstone 5, Sillett 2, Anderton 1, Bradbury 1, Bridges 1, Brooks 1, Gibbs 1, Mortimore 1, Harrison 1, opponents 2.

MOST GOALS CONCEDED
100, Division 1, 1960-61.

MOST FIRST CLASS MATCHES IN A SEASON
60 - 1965-66 (League 42, FA Cup 6, Fairs Cup 12).
60 - 1970-71 (League 42, FA Cup 3, League Cup 3, Charity Shield 1, ECWC 10).

MOST LEAGUE WINS
29, Division 2, 1988-89.

MOST LEAGUE DRAWS
18, Division 1, 1922-23.

MOST LEAGUE DEFEATS
27, Division 1, 1978-79.

INDIVIDUAL CLUB RECORDS

MOST GOALS IN A SEASON
Jimmy Greaves: 43 goals in 1960-61 (League 41, League Cup 2).

MOST GOALS IN A MATCH
6. George Hilsdon v Worksop, FA Cup (9-1), 11.1.1908.

OLDEST PLAYER
Dick Spence, 39 years 1 month, 1947-48.
Graham Rix made his Chelsea debut on 15.09.1994 (ECWC) aged 37 years 11 months, he made his League debut on 14.05.1995.

YOUNGEST PLAYER
Ian Hamilton, 16 years 4 months, 1966-67.

MOST CAPPED PLAYER
Glen Hoddle (England) 53.

BEST PERFORMANCES

League: 1988-89: Matches Played 46, Won 29, Drawn 12, Lost 3, Goals for 96, Goals against 50. Points 99. First in Division 2.
Highest Position: 1954-55, 1st in Division 1.
F.A. Cup: 1969-70, 1996-97 winners.
Most Recent Success: 1996-97 winners: 3rd Round WBA (H) 3-0; 4th Round Liverpool (H) 4-2; 5th Round Leicester (A) 2-2, 1-0; Quarter Final Portsmouth (A) 4-1; Semi-Final Wimbledon 3-0; Final Middlesbrough 2-0.
League Cup: 1964-65, 1997-98 winners.
Most Recent Success: 1997-98: 3rd Rnd Blackburn (H) 1-1*, 4th Rnd Southampton (H) 2-1, 5th Rnd (A) 2-2*, Semi-final Arsenal (A) 1-2, (H) 3-1, Final Middlesbrough 2-0.
Europe: ECWC - 1970-71, 1997-98 winners.
Most Recent Success: 1997-98: 1st Rnd Slovan Bratislava (H) 2-0 (A) 2-0, 2nd Rnd Tromso (A) 2-3, (H) 7-1, Quarter-Final Real Betis (A) 1-2, (H) 3-1. Semi-Final Vicenza (A) 0-1, (H) 3-1, Final Stuttgart (Stockholm) 1-0.

ADDITIONAL INFORMATION
PREVIOUS NAMES
None.
PREVIOUS LEAGUES
None.

Club colours:Royal blue with white & amber sleeve trim and white & amber collar, royal blue with white and amber trim shorts and white with royal blue turnover socks.
Change colours: All white with royal blue/yellow trim.

Reserve League: Avon Insurance Combination.

DIVISIONAL RECORD

	Played	Won	Drawn	Lost	For	Against	Points
Division 1/P	2,600	916	618	996	4,264	4,058	2,710
Division 2	786	383	202	201	1,323	887	1,018
Total	3,386	1,299	890	1,197	5,587	4,945	3,728

RECORDS AND STATISTICS

COMPETITIONS

Div 1/P	Div.2	ECWC	UEFA	A/Scot
1907-10	1905-07	1970-71	1965-66	1975-76
1912-24	1910-12	1971-72	1968-69	1976-77
1930-62	1924-30	1994-95		1977-78
1963-75	1962-63	1997-98		
1977-79	1975-77			
1984-87	1979-84			
1989-	1988-89			

HONOURS

Div 1	Div.2	FA Cup	Lge Cup	ECWC	C/Shld
1954-55	1983-84	1970	1965	1971	1955
	1988-89	1997	*1998*	*1998*	FMC
					1986
					1990

MOST GOALS IN A CAREER
Bobby Tambling - 202 (1958-69)

Year	League	FA Cup	Lge Cup	EUFA
1958-59	1	-	-	-
1959-60	1	-	-	-
1960-61	9	-	3	-
1961-62	20	2	-	-
1962-63	35	2	-	-
1963-64	17	2	-	-
1964-65	15	4	6	-
1965-66	16	5	-	2
1966-67	21	6	1	-
1967-68	12	3	-	-
1968-69	17	1	-	2
Total	164	25	10	3

Current leading goalscorer: Dennis Wise - 64 (1990-98)

MOST APPEARANCES
Ron Harris 791+12 (1961-80)

Year	League	FA Cup	Lge Cup	ECWC	EUFA	A/Scott
1961-62	3					
1962-63	7					
1963-64	41	3	1			
1964-65	42	5	6			
1965-66	36	6		10		
1966-67	42	7	3			
1967-68	40	5	1			
1968-69	40	5	3		4	
1969-70	30	8	3			
1970-71	38	3	4	9		
1971-72	41	3	9	4		
1972-73	42	3	7			
1973-74	36	2	1			
1974-75	42	2	4			
1975-76	38+2	4	1			3
1976-77	15+4	2	0+1			2
1977-78	37	4	1			2+1
1978-79	38+2	1	1			
1979-80	38+1	1	1+1			
	646+9	64	46+2	13	14	7+1

RECORD TRANSFER FEE RECEIVED

Amount	Club	Player	Date
£2,500,000	Q.P.R.	John Spencer	11/96
£2,200,000	Tottenham H.	Gordon Durie	8/91
£1,700,000	Leeds United	Tony Dorigo	6/91
£925,000	Everton	Pat Nevin	7/88

RECORD TRANSFER FEE PAID

Amount	Club	Player	Date
£5,400,000	Lazio	Pierluigi Casiraghi	07/98
£4,900,000	Lazio	Roberto Di Matteo	07/96
£2,500,000	Strasbourg	Franck Leboeff	07/96
£2,300,000	Watford	Paul Furlong	5/94

MANAGERS

Name	Seasons	Best	Worst
J T Robertson	1905-06	3(2)	3(2)
David Calderhead	1907-33	0(1)	9(2)
Leslie Knighton	1933-39	8(1)	20(1)
Billy Birrell	1939-52	13(1)	19(1)
Ted Drake	1952-62	1(1)	22(1)
Tommy Docherty	1962-67	3(1)	2(2)
Dave Sexton	1967-74	3(1)	17(1)
Ron Stuart	1974-75	21(1)	21(1)
Eddie McCreadie	1975-77	2(2)	11(2)
Ken Shellitto	1977-78	16(1)	16(1)
Danny Blanchflower	1978-79	22(1)	22(1)
Geoff Hurst	1979-81	4(2)	12(2)
John Neal	1981-85	1(2)	18(2)
John Hollins	1985-88	6(1)	18(1)
Bobby Campbell	1988-91	5(1)	1(2)
Ian Porterfield	1991-93		
David Webb (Trial)	1993	11(P)	11(P)
Glenn Hoddle	1993-96	10(P)	11(P)
Ruud Gullit	1996-98	6(P)	6(P)
Gianluca Vialli	1998-	4(P)	4(P)

LONGEST LEAGUE RUNS

of undefeated matches:	27 (29.10.1988 - 15.4.1989)	of league matches w/out a win:	21 (3.11.1987 - 2.4.1988)
of undefeated home matches:	34 (28.4.1910 - 24.2.1912)	of undefeated away matches:	13 (5.11.1988 - 8.4.1989)
without home win:	11 (30.3.1974 - 28.9.1974)	without an away win:	22 (1.3.1952 - 14.3.1953)
of league wins:	8 (5.2.27 - 21.3.27 & 15.3.89 - 8.4.89)	of home wins:	13 (12.11.1910 - 2.9.1911)
of league defeats:	7 (1.11.1952 - 20.12.1952)	of away wins:	7 (4.2.1989 - 8.4.1989)

CHELSEA

PLAYERS NAME / Honours	Ht	Wt	Birthdate	Birthplace / Transfers	Contract Date	Clubs	APPEARANCES				GOALS			
							League	L/Cup	FA Cup	Other	Lge	L/C	FAC	Oth
G O A L K E E P E R														
De Goey Eduard F	6.6	15.4	20/12/66	Holland		Feyenoord								
Dutch Int. Dutch Lge'93. Dutch Cup 92'94'95				£2250000	10/07/97	Chelsea	28	4	1	10				
LC'98. ECWC'98														
Hitchcock Kevin	6.1	12.2	05/10/62	Canning Town		Barking								
AMC'87. FAC'97. LC'98. ECWC'98				£15000	04/08/83	Nottingham Forest								
					01/02/84	Mansfield Town	182	12	10	20				
				£250000	25/03/88	Chelsea	90+3	12	14	13				
Kharine Dmitri	6.2	13.9	16/08/68	Moscow		CSKA Moscow								
CIS. USSR. Russian Int. Olympic G.Medal'88.				£200000	22/12/92	Chelsea	117	8	12	4				
D E F E N C E														
Babayaro Celestine	5.7	10.04	29/08/78	Nigeria		Anderlecht								
Nigerian Int. Belgium Lge'95. Cup '95 Olympic gold'96				£2250000	20/06/97	Chelsea	8	1+1		2+1				
Broad Stephen			10/06/80	Epsom		Chelsea (T)								
Clarke Steve	5.9	11.1	29/08/63	Saltcoats		St.Mirren	151	21	19	6	6		1	
S:6,B.3,u21.8,Y. SLgeXI.1. Div.2'89. FAC'97.				£422000	19/01/87	Chelsea	321+9	24+2	34+2	28+1	7	1	1	1
LC'98. ECWC'98.														
Clement Neil	6	12.9	03/10/78	Reading	06/10/95	Chelsea (T)	1							
E: Y, S.														
Duberry Michael	6.1	12.13	14/10/75	Enfield	01/08/93	Chelsea	59+2	5	10	6	1		2	
E: u21.3. LC'98. ECWC'98.				Loan	29/09/95	Bournemouth	7			1				
Ferrer Albert				Barcelona										
Spanish Int.				£2200000	09/06/98	Chelsea								
Lambourde Bernard	6.2	12.2	11/05/71	Guadeloupe		Bordeaux								
				£1500000	10/07/98	Chelsea	5+2	3		1+2				
Le Saux Graeme	5.1	11.2	17/10/68	Harrow		St. Pauls (Jersey)								
E:20,B.2,u21.4. Prem'95. LC'98.				Free	09/12/87	Chelsea	77+13	7+6	7+1	8+1	8	1		
					25/03/93	Blackburn Rovers	127+2	10	8	6+1	7			
				£5000000	08/08/97	Chelsea	26	4	1	3	1	1	1	
Leboeff Frank	6	12	22/01/68	Paris		Strasbourg								
French Int. World Cup winner'98. FAC'97				£2500000	12/07/96	Chelsea	58	6	8	10	11		1	1
LC'98. ECWC'98.														
Lee David	6.3	13.12	26/11/69	Kingswood	01/07/88	Chelsea	119+32	13+7	10+4	6+2	11	1		1
E: u21.10,Y.1. Div.2'89.				Loan	30/01/92	Reading	5				5			
				Loan	12/08/94	Portsmouth	4+1							
Myers Andrew	5.8	9.1	03/11/73	Hounslow	25/07/91	Chelsea	73+10	2+1	9+1	4+2	2			
E: u21.4,Y.12,S.3. FAC'97. ECWC'98.														
Petrescu Dan	5.10	11.7	22/12/67	Bucharest		Genoa								
Romanian Int. Rom.Div.1'85'86'87'88. Rom.FAC'85'87'88.						Foggia								
FAC'97. LC'98. ECWC'98.						Steaua Bucharest								
				£1250000	06/08/94	Sheffield Wed	20+9	2	+2		3			
				£2300000	18/11/95	Chelsea	87+2	5	14	7+1	10	2	1	2
Terry John G			07/12/80	London		Chelsea (T)								
M I D F I E L D														
Crittenden Nicholas J	5.8	10.7	11/11/78	Bracknell	09/07/97	Chelsea	0+2	1						
Desailly Marcel				AC Milan										
French Int. World Cup Winner'98.				£4600000	10/06/98	Chelsea								
Di Matteo Roberto	5.10	12	22/01/68	Switzerland		Lazio								
Italian Int. FAC'97. LC'98. ECWC'98.				£4900000	17/07/96	Chelsea	61+3	7	8	9	11	3	2	3
Hampshire Steven G	5.10	10.9	17/10/79	Edinburgh	09/07/97	Chelsea		0+1						
Harley Jon	5.9	10.3	26/09/79	Maidstone	31/05/97	Chelsea (T)	3							
Hughes John Paul	6	12.6	19/04/76	Hammersmith	01/07/94	Chelsea (T)	13+8		1		3			
Morris Jody	5.5	10.2	22/12/78	London	08/01/96	Chelsea (T)	15+10	3		2+1	1	2		
E: u21.3, Y, S. ECWC'98.														
Newton Edward	5.11	11.2	13/12/71	Hammersmith	17/05/90	Chelsea	138+20	15+2	16+2	11+1	8	1	1	
E: u21.2,Y. FAC'97. LC'98.				Loan	23/01/92	Cardiff City	18				4			
Poyet Gustavo	6.1	13.01	15/11/67	Montevideo (Uruguay)		Real Zaragoza								
Uruguay Int. ECWC'98.				Free	15/07/97	Chelsea	11+3			5	4			1
Richardson Jay			14/11/79	Keston		Chelsea (T)								
Slatter Daniel			15/11/80	Cardiff		Chelsea (T)								

42

F O R W A R D

Player / Notes	Ht	Wt	DOB	Birthplace	Club	St1	St2	St3	St4	St5	St6	St7	St8
Casiraghi Pierluigi					Lazio								
Italian Int.				£5400000 29/05/98	Chelsea								
Flo Tore Andre	6.4	13.7	29/08/78	Norway	Brann Bergen								
Norweigen Int. LC'98. ECWC'98.				£300000 04/05/97	Chelsea	16+18	3+1	1	3+2	11	2		2
Laudrup Brian					Glasgow Rangers								
Danish Int. Scottish Prem title, Cup & LC				Free 08/06/98	Chelsea								
Nicholls Mark	5.10		30/05/77		01/07/95 Chelsea	11+16	2+2	1	0+2	3			
				Loan 15/12/95	Chertsey								
Sheerin Joseph E	6.1	13	08/11/77	Hammersmith 27/03/97	Chelsea	0+1							
Vialli Gianluca	5.10	13.5	07/09/64	Cremona	Sampdoria	333				140			
Italian Int. EC'96. FAC'97 . ECWC'98.					Juventus	137				25			
				Free 10/07/96	Chelsea	37+12	3+1	1+4	8+1	20		4	6
Wise Dennis F	5.6	9.5	15/12/66	Kensington	Southampton								
E:12, B.3,u21.1. FAC'88'97. LC'98. ECWC'98.				Free 28/03/85	Wimbledon	127+8	14	11	5	26	3		
				£1600000 03/07/90	Chelsea	237+7	27	25	20	46	6	6	3
Zola Gianfranco	5.6	10.10	05/07/66	Italy	Parma								
Italian Int. FAC'97. LC'98. ECWC"98.				£4500000 15/11/96	Chelsea	45+5	4	8	8+1	16		4	4

ADDITIONAL CONTRACT PLAYERS

Player	Birthplace	Club									
Forssell Mikeal	Iceland	HUK Helsinki									
	Free 01/07/98	Chelsea									
Percassi Luca	Italy	Atalanta									
	Free 01/07/98	Chelsea									

THE MANAGER
GIANLUCA VIALLI

Date of Birth . . . . 7th September 1964.
Place of Birth . . . . Cremona.
Date of Appointment . . . . March 1998.

PREVIOUS CLUBS
As Manager . . . . None.
As Coach . . . . None.
As a Player . . . . Sampdoria, Juventus.

HONOURS
As a Manager
Chelsea: ECWC 1997/98. League Cup 1997/98.

As a Player
Sampdoria: Serie A Championship.
Juventus: European Cup 1996.
Chelsea: FA Cup 1996/97. ECWC 1997/98.
Italy: Full caps.

STAMFORD BRIDGE
Fulham Road, London SW6 1HS

Capacity...34,000 (under construction).

First game..v Liverpool (friendly) 4-0, 4.9.1905.
First floodlit game..v Sparta, 19.3.1951.
Internationals ....England v Scotland, 1913. v Wales, 1929. v Austria, 1932.

ATTENDANCES
Highest...82,905 v Arsenal, Division 1, 12.10.1935.
Lowest...4,767 v Plymouth, Simod Cup, 9.11.1988.

OTHER GROUNDS...None.

HOW TO GET TO THE GROUND

From the North and East
Follow Central London signs from A1/M1 to Hyde Park Corner. Then Guildford (A3) signs to Knightsbridge (A4). AFter one mile turn left into Fulham Road.

From the South
Take A3 or A4. Then A219 to cross Putney Bridge and follow West End signs (A304) to join A308 into Fulham Road.

From the West
Take M4 then A4 to Central London. Then follow signs for West minster (A3220). After three quarters of a mile turn right at crossroads into Fulham Road.

Car Parking: Parking is available at Stamford Bridge Stadium, phone club for more details - 0171 565 1488.

Bus Routes: Numbers 14 and 211 stop outside Stamford Bridge. Nos 11, 28, 295 and C4 stop near Fulham Broadway Station (Harwood Road) and No 22 stops in Kings Road (parallel to Fulham Road).

Nearest Tube Station: Fulham Broadway (District Line).

USEFUL TELEPHONE NUMBERS

Club switchboard. 0171 385 5545

Club fax number 0171 381 4831

Club shop 0171 565 1490

Ticket Office 0171 386 7799

Marketing department 0171 915 1905

Internet address: . . . . . . www.chelseaafc.co.uk

Clubcall. 0891 12 11 59*

*Calls cost 50p per minute at all times.Call costings correct at time of going to press.

MATCHDAY PROGRAMME

Programme Editor . . . . Neil Barnett.

Number of pages . . . . 64.

Price . . . . £2.50.

Subscriptions. . . . . Apply to club

Local Newspapers
. . . . Evening Stanard
. . . . Fulham Chronicle, Fulham Times
. . . . Kensington & Chelsea Times.

Local Radio Stations
. . . . Capital Gold (1548AM)
. . . . LNR (1152AM/97.3FM)
. . . . Capital Radio (95.8FM)*
. . . . GLR (BBC) 1458AM/94.9FM.
*exclusive independent radio commentary contract for Chelsea matches.

MATCHDAY TICKET PRICES

Categories	A	B
East Stand		
Upper Tier	£25	£18
Middle Tier	£50	£50
Matthew Harding Stand		
Upper Tier		Season tickets only
Lower Tier	£21	£16
Shed End Stand		
LowerTier		Season tickets only
UpperTier (non members)	£22	£17
West Stand (uncovered seating)	£21	£16
Visitors	£21	£21
Family Section	£24	£20
Add. Juv/Unaccompanied Juv	£9	£7

COVENTRY CITY
(The Sky Blues)
F.A. CARLING PREMIERSHIP
SPONSORED BY: SUBARU/ISUZU

1998-99 - Back Row (L-R): Liam Daish, Gary Breen, Steve Orgizovic, Magnus Hedman, Phillipe Clement, Paul Williams.
Middle Row: Garry Pendrey (coach), Jim Blyth (goalkeeping coach), Willie Boland, Roland Nilsson, Marcus Hall, Jean-Guy Wallemme, Simon Haworth, Richard Shaw, Trevor Peake (Reserve team manager), Stuart Collie (Physio).
Front Row: Ian Brightwell, Paul Telfer, Gavin Strachan, Trond Soltvedt, Gary McAllister, Gordon Strachan, Dion Dublin, George Boateng, David Burrows, Noel Whelan, Darren Huckerby.

COVENTRY CITY
FORMED IN 1883
TURNED PROFESSIONAL IN 1893
LTD COMPANY IN 1907

PRESIDENT: Eric Grove
CHAIRMAN: Bryan A Richardson
DEPUTY CHAIRMAN: Mike McGinnity
DIRECTORS
J F W Reason, A M Jepson,
D A Higgs, Miss B M Price
SECRETARY
Graham Hover (01203 234 000)

MANAGER: Gordon Strachan OBE
1ST TEAM COACH: Garry Pendrey
RESERVE TEAM COACH: Trevor Peake
ACADEMY DIRECTOR
Richard Money
DIRECTOR OF YOUTH FOOTBALL
Trevor Gould
PHYSIOTHERAPIST
Stuart Collie

STATISTICIAN FOR THE DIRECTORY
Jim Brown

In the final analysis, season 1997-98 will probably be remembered not, for once, another fantastic fight to avoid relegation, but for the teams heroics in the FA Cup and, up to a point, their challenge for a European place in the Carling Premiership. Indeed if it were not for a slow start, during which time they drew seven of their opening 13 Premier League matches, the Sky Blues could have booked a ticket to Europe before the the end of the season. However, as we all know football does not always go to plan and had Gordon Strachan known that the club would embark on a record breaking run of unbeaten matches he and players would not have given the points away so easily earlier on in the season.

The players had hinted at what may come with a fantastic Christmas holiday victory over Manchester United at Highfield Road (3-2), and not content with this they then went to Anfield and dumped Liverpool out of the FA Cup (3-1). After a little hiccup at Chelsea (losing 1-3) the Sky Blues' run of 13 games (in League and Cup) without defeat started with a controversial draw (2-2) with Arsenal on 17th January and ended at home to arch rivals Aston Villa (1-2) on 11th April - that defeat being one of only two recorded at Highfield Road all season. However, the Coventry fans were for once not as upset about being beaten by the Villa as they would normally have been, as Gordon Strachan had managed to do what no other manager had done in the history of the club, beaten Aston Villa at Villa Park. It is a memory that will stay with many Sky Blues' fans for the rest of their lives and maybe substituted for missing out on the FA Cup final itself. It also ment that Viorel Moldovan, a club record signing of £3.25 million, will always be remembered for being the player that scored 'that goal' on St Valentines Day 1998, the day we beat the Villa. (Incidentally received a record £4 million for Moldovan on his departure after only 6 months with the club).

The moment that seemed to dramatically change the fortunes of the club came in the Quarter-Finals of the Cup when Coventry entertained Sheffield United. A 1-1 draw was recorded at Highfield Road, and the players seem to be giving out an air of complacency, after all they had beaten Liverpool, Derby and Aston Villa to get to this point so Sheffield United would be a walk over! Unfortunately in the replay the Sky Blues took an early lead and were guilty of not converting several clear cut chances during the game, chances that would surely have been taken had they thought they were under more pressure. A wonder goal in the last minute of the match squared the tie and with no goals added in extra-time the match was decided after a penalty shoot-out that the Sky Blues did not win.

This seemed to knock the wind out of the Sky Blues' 'sails' and they went back to the form with which they started the season. Had the team still been on a high maybe some of the six draws recorded in their last nine games might have been converted into draws and the Sky Blues' would packing their bags and flying into Europe.

Gordon Strachan has proven himself to be one of the most talented 'young' managers in the game and with the summer signings helping to strengthen what is already the strongest and most talented squad Coventry have had for long time, the future looks good. You never know the club might have another season where the word relegation never gets a mention.

COVENTRY CITY

M	DATE	COMP.	VEN	OPPONENTS	RESULT	H/T	LP	GOAL SCORERS/GOAL TIMES	ATT.
1	A 09	CP	H	Chelsea	W 3-2	1-1	1	Dublin 41, 82, 88	22686
2	11	CP	A	Arsenal	L 0-2	0-1	9		(37324)
3	23	CP	H	Bolton Wanderers	D 2-2	2-0	10	Telfer 8, Huckerby 20	16633
4	27	CP	H	West Ham United	D 1-1	1-0	12	Huckerby 38	18289
5	30	CP	A	Manchester United	L 0-3	0-1	12		(55074)
6	S 13	CP	H	Southampton	W 1-0	0-0	8	Soltvedt 65	18659
7	16	CC 2/1	A	**Blackpool**	**L 0-1**	**0-0**			**(5884)**
8	20	CP	A	Sheffield Wednesday	D 0-0	0-0	11		(21087)
9	24	CP	H	Crystal Palace	D 1-1	1-1	11	Dublin 8	15900
10	28	CP	A	Blackburn Rovers	D 0-0	0-0	12		(19086)
11	O 01	CC 2/2	H	**Blackpool**	**W 3-1**	**0-1**		**McAllister 61, 89 (pen), Dublin 70**	**9565**
12	04	CP	H	Leeds United	D 0-0	0-0	12		17770
13	15	CC 3	H	**Everton**	**W 4-1**	**2-1**		**Hall 6, Salako 33, 59, Haworth 62**	**10087**
14	20	CP	A	Barnsley	L 0-2	0-1	15		(17463)
15	25	CP	H	Everton	D 0-0	0-0	15		18760
16	N 01	CP	A	Wimbledon	W 2-1	2-1	12	Huckerby 16, Dublin 22	(11201)
17	08	CP	H	Newcastle United	D 2-2	1-1	10	Dublin 4, 82	22679
18	18	CC 4	A	**Arsenal**	**L 0-1**	**0-0**			**(30199)**
19	22	CP	A	Derby County	L 1-3	0-3	12	Huckerby 71	(29351)
20	29	CP	H	Leicester City	L 0-2	0-1	15		18309
21	D 06	CP	A	Aston Villa	L 0-3	0-1	16		(33250)
22	13	CP	H	Tottenham Hotspur	W 4-0	1-0	14	Huckerby 42, 84, Breen 63, Hall 87	19499
23	20	CP	A	Liverpool	L 0-1	0-1	16		(39707)
24	26	CP	A	West Ham United	L 0-1	0-1	17		(22477)
25	28	CP	H	Manchester United	W 3-2	1-1	13	Whelan 12, Dublin 86 (pen), Huckerby 87	23054
26	J 03	FAC 3	A	**Liverpool**	**W 3-1**	**1-1**		**Huckerby 45, Dublin 62, Telfer 87**	**(33888)**
27	10	CP	A	Chelsea	L 1-3	1-0	16	Telfer 30	(34647)
28	16	CP	H	Arsenal	D 2-2	1-0	15	Whelan 21, Dublin 66 (pen)	22864
29	24	FAC 4	H	**Derby County**	**W 2-0**	**2-0**		**Dublin 38, 45**	**22824**
30	31	CP	A	Bolton Wanderers	W 5-1	1-1	13	Whelan 25, Huckerby 57, 65, Dublin 73, 79	(25000)
31	F 06	CP	H	Sheffield Wednesday	W 1-0	0-0	12	Dublin 74 (pen)	18375
32	14	FAC 5	A	**Aston Villa**	**W 1-0**	**0-0**		**Moldovan 72**	**(36979)**
33	18	CP	A	Southampton	W 2-1	2-0	10	Whelan 14, Huckerby 29	(15091)
34	21	CP	H	Barnsley	W 1-0	0-0	10	Dublin 89 (pen)	20265
35	28	CP	A	Crystal Palace	W 3-0	2-0	9	Telfer 1, Moldovan 40, Dublin 77	(21810)
36	M 07	FAC QF	H	**Sheffield United**	**D 1-1**	**1-1**		**Dublin 32 (pen)**	**23084**
37	14	CP	A	Newcastle United	D 0-0	0-0	9		(36767)
38	17	FAC QFR	A	**Sheffield United**	**D 1-1**	**1-0**		**Telfer 10**	**(29034)**
39	28	CP	H	Derby County	W 1-0	1-0	9	Huckerby 44	18705
40	A 04	CP	A	Leicester City	D 1-1	0-0	10	Whelan 80	(21137)
41	11	CP	H	Aston Villa	L 1-2	0-1	10	Whelan 59	22792
42	13	CP	A	Tottenham Hotspur	D 1-1	0-0	10	Dublin 86	(33463)
43	19	CP	H	Liverpool	D 1-1	0-1	11	Dublin 47 (pen)	22721
44	25	CP	A	Leeds United	D 3-3	2-2	10	Huckerby 20, 34, 62	(36522)
45	29	CP	H	Wimbledon	D 0-0	0-0	11		17968
46	M 02	CP	H	Blackburn Rovers	W 2-0	2-0	11	Dublin 19 (pen), Boateng 34	18794
47	10	CP	A	Everton	D 1-1	0-1	11	Dublin 89	(40109)

Best Home League Attendance: 23054 V Manchester United   Smallest :15900 V Crystal Palace   Average :19722

Goal Scorers:

CP	(46)	Dublin 18, Huckerby 14, Whelan 6, Telfer 3, Boateng 1, Breen 1, Hall 1, Moldovan 1, Soltvedt 1
CC	(7)	McAllister 2, Salako 2, Dublin 1, Hall 1, Haworth 1
FAC	(8)	Dublin 4, Telfer 2, Huckerby 1, Moldovan 1

(M) Boateng	(M) Boland	(D) Breen	(D) Burrows	(F) Dublin	(F) Ducros	(D) Hall	(F) Haworth	(G) Hedman	(G) Howie	(F) Huckerby	(M) Johansen	(F) Lightbourne	(M) McAllister	(F) Moldovan	(D) Nilsson	(F) O'Neill	(G) Ogrizovic	(D) Prenderville	(M) Richardson	(F) Salako	(D) Shaw	(M) Shilton	(M) Soltvedt	(M) Strachan	(M) Telfer	(F) Whelan	(D) Williams	(M) Willis	Referee	No.
	S2	X	X	X		S		S		X		S1	X				X			S	X	X	X		X		X	X	P.A. Durkin	1
	S2	X	X	X		S		S		X		S1	X				X			S	X	X	X		X		X	X	K W Burge	2
	S1	X	X	X		S		S		X	S	S					X			X	X	X	X		X		X	X	M A Riley	3
	S1	X	X	X		S		S		X		S2			S	S	X			X	X	X	X		X		X	X	N S Barry	4
		X	X		X		X	S	S	X			X				X	X	X	X	X	X	S		X		X	X	G R Ashby	5
	S		X	X		S		S		X	S	S	X				X			X	X	X	S		X		X	X	U D Rennie	6
		S2	X			S1		S				X	X	X		X		X			X	X	X		X		X	X	T Heilbron	7
	S1	S	X	S	X	S		S					S	X		X			X	X	X	X		X		X	X	G S Willard	8
	S1	X	X	X	X		S					S2	X		X		X			X	X	S		X		X	X	G P Barber	9
	X	X	X		X		S	X		S2	X		X	S1			X			S	X	S		X			S	P Jones	10
X	X	X	X	S2	X			X		X			X		X			X	S1	S			X	M D Reed	11
	X	X	X	S2		S1	S			S			X	X	X		X			X	X	X	S		X	S	K =	A B Wilkie	12
	S1	X	X		S	X	X				X	X	X		X		X			X	X	S		X			X	S W Dunn	13
	X	X	X		X	X	S				S1	S	X		X		X			X	X	S	S		S		X	P E Alcock	14
	S		X		X	X	S			X	S1	S1	X		X		X			X	X	X	S		X		X	S J Lodge	15
	S		X		X	X	S	S		X	S	X		X		X			S	X	X	S		X		X	U D Rennie	16
	S	X	X		X	S1	S	X	S	X		X		X		X			X	S	S	X		X		P A Durkin	17
	S	X	X		X	X		S1		X		X		X		X			X	S	X	X		X	G R Ashby	18
	S2	X	X		X	X	S		S1		S	X		X		X			X	S	X		X	D R Elleray	19
X2		X		X	S2	S	X			S	X1	X	S	X		X			X	S1	X	X	M J Bodenham	20
	X	X	X	S1	S2	S	X2				X	S	X		X		X	S3	X3	X1		G P Barber	21
	X	X	X	X	S	X	X		X1		X	S2	S		X		S1	S	X	X2		S W Dunn	22
X			X	S2	X	X2	X			X	S	S	S		X		X1	S1	X	X	P E Alcock	23
X	S		X		X	X		S1		X	X1	S		X	X	S	S	X	X	X	G Poll	24
X1	S1		X	X	X2		X	X		S			X	S	S2	X	X	X	X	N S Barry	25
X	S	X	X		X	S	X		X		S		X	S	S	X	X	X	X	M A Riley	26
	X	X	X		S	X	X			S1		S	X1	S	S	X	S	S	X	X	M D Reed	27
X		X	X	X		X	X			S	X		S	S	X	S	S	X	X	X	S J Lodge	28
X3		X	X	X	S1	X	X2		S2	X	S	S	X	S3	X	X1	M J Bodenham	29
X3	S	X	X	X	S2	X	S	X1	S1	X		S	X2	X	S3	X	X	D J Gallagher	30
X	S	X	X	X	X	S	X		S	X		S	X	X1	S1	X	G R Ashby	31
X	S2	X	X	X	X	S	X	X	S	S1	X		S	X1	X	X2	G S Willard	32
	S1	X	X	X	X	S	X	S	X	X	S	X		X1	S	X	P E Alcock	33
X	X	X	X	S1	S	X	X	X		S	X2	S2	X	X	A B Wilkie	34
X	S	X	X	X	S	X	X	X	X		X1	S1	X	X	S	D R Elleray	35
X	X	X	X	S2	S	X	X2	X	X	S	S1	X1	X	X	S W Dunn	36
X	X	X	X	S1	S	X	X1	X	X	S	X	X2	X2	X	S	P Jones	37
X	X	X	X	S2	S	X	X2	X	X	S	X1	S1	X	X	S	S W Dunn	38
X	X	X	X	S	X	S	X	X	X	S	X	S	X	X	S	K W Burge	39
X	S	X	X	S	X	S	X	X	X	S	X	S	X	X	S	G P Barber	40
X1	X	X	X	S1	S	X	S2	X	X	X	X2	S	X	X	S	D J Gallagher	41
	S3	X	X	X	X2	S	S1	X1	X	X	S2	X3	X	X	X	M A Riley	42
X1	X	X	X	X	S	X	S	X	X	X	S	X	X	X	S1	N S Barry	43
	X	X	X	X1	S	X	S	X	X	X	X	S	X	X	S1	M D Reed	44
	X	X	X	S	X	S	X	X	S1	X	X1	S	X	X	S	J T Winter	45
X2	S2	X	X	S	X	X1	S	X	X	S	X	X	X3	X	S	S J Lodge	46
X	S	X1	X	X	S3	S2	X	X2	X	S	X	X	X3	X	S1	P E Alcock	47
14	**8**	**30**	**33**	**36**	**1**	**20**	**4**	**14**		**32**	**1**	**14**	**5**	**32**	**2**	**24**		**3**	**11**	**33**	**2**	**26**	**2**	**33**	**21**	**17**			CP Appearances	
	11				2	5	6			2	2	6		5		2				4	7				3				CP Sub Appearances	
1+1	3+1	4	2	0+1	3+1	2			0+1	1	3	4		3	1	4			2	4	1+1		2		4			CC Appearances	
5	0+1	5	5	5		2+2	0+1	3		5			2+2	4		2			3	3+1	2+2	4	4	1				FAC Appearances	

Also Played: (D) Borrows S(5). (M) Eustace S(43).

COVENTRY CITY

CLUB RECORDS

BIGGEST VICTORIES
League: 9-0 v Bristol City, Division 3(S), 28.4.1934.
F.A. Cup: 7-0 v Scunthorpe United, 1st Round, 24.11.1934.
League Cup: 7-2 v Chester City, 2nd Round, 9.10.1985.
5-0 v Watford, 5th Round replay, 9.12.1980.
5-0 v Sunderland 5th Round replay, 24.1.1990.
Europe: 4-1 v Trakia Plovdiv, 1st Round (UEFA) 16.9.1970.

BIGGEST DEFEATS
League: 2-10 v Norwich, Division 3(S), 15.3.1930.
1-9 v Millwall, Division 3(S), 19.11.1927.
F.A. Cup: 2-11 v Berwick Rangers, 2.11.1901. (Qualifying Round)
League Cup: 1-8 v Leicester City (h), 1.12.1964.
Europe: (UEFA) 1-6 v Bayern Munich, 20.10.1970.

MOST POINTS
3 points a win: 63, Division 1, 1986-87.
2 points a win: 60, Division 4, 1958-59, Division 3, 1963-64.

MOST GOALS SCORED
108, Division 3(S), 1931-32.
Bourton 49, Lauderdale 19, Lake 14, Shepperd 7, White 6, Holmes 5, Cull 3, Baker, Bowden, Heinmann, Johnson, Opponents.

MOST GOALS CONCEDED
97, Division 3(S) 1935-36; Division 4, 1958-59.

MOST FIRST CLASS MATCHES IN A SEASON
57, 1962-63 (League 46, FA Cup 9, League Cup 2).

MOST LEAGUE WINS
24, Division 3(S), 1935-36; Division 4, 1958-59.

MOST LEAGUE DRAWS
17, Division 3, 1962-63.

MOST LEAGUE DEFEATS
22, Division 2, 1919-20; Division 2, 1924-25; Division 3(S), 1927-28; Division 2, 1951-52; Division 1, 1984-85.

INDIVIDUAL CLUB RECORDS

MOST GOALS IN A SEASON
Clarrie Bourton: 50 goals in 1931-32 (League 49, FAC 1).
Previous holder: F.Herbert 27 (1926-27).

MOST GOALS IN A MATCH
5. C Bourton v Bournemouth, 6-1 (h), Division 3(S), 17.10.1931.
5. A Bacon v Gillingham, 7-3 (a), Division 3(S), 30.12.1933.
5. C Regis v Chester City, 7-2 (h), League Cup, 9.10.1985.

OLDEST PLAYER
Alf Wood, 44 years 207 days v Plymouth, FAC 2nd Rnd, 7.12.1958.

YOUNGEST PLAYER
Brian Hill, 16 years 281 days v Gillingham, Div.3 (S), 30.4.58.

MOST CAPPED PLAYER
Peter Ndlovu (Zimbabwe) 25.

BEST PERFORMANCES

League: 1966-67: Matches Played 42, Won 23, Drawn 13, Lost 6, Goals for 74, Goals against 43, Points 59. First in Division 2.
Highest Position: 1969-70: 6th Division 1.

F.A. Cup: 1986-87: 3rd Round Bolton Wanderers 3-0 (h); 4th Round Manchester United 1-0 (a); 5th Stoke City 1-0 (a); 6th Round Sheffield Wednesday 3-1 (a); Semi-Final Leeds United 3-2; Final Tottenham Hotspur 3-2.

League Cup: Semi-finalists in 1980-81.
Most recent success: 1989-90: 2nd Round Grimsby Town 1-3,3-0; 3rd round QPR 1-0; 4th round Manchester City 1-0; 5th Round Sunderland 0-0,5-0; Semi-Final Nottingham Forest 1-2,0-0.

Europe: (UEFA) 1970-71: 1st Round Trakia Plovdiv 4-1,2-0; 2nd Round Bayern Munich 1-6,2-1.

DIVISIONAL RECORD

	Played	Won	Drawn	Lost	For	Against	Points
Division 1/P	1,276	399	369	508	1,482	1,787	1,380
Division 2	756	279	186	291	1,050	1,099	744
Division 3	230	93	66	71	403	347	252
Division 3(S)	696	282	158	256	1,278	1,102	722
Division 3(N)	42	16	6	20	73	82	38
Division 4	46	24	12	10	84	47	60
Total	**3,046**	**1,093**	**797**	**1,156**	**4,370**	**4,464**	**3,196**

ADDITIONAL INFORMATION
PREVIOUS NAMES
Singers FC, 1883-98.

PREVIOUS LEAGUES
Southern League, Birmingham & District League.

Club Colours: Sky blue with navy blue and white thick stripes, sky blue shorts with white trim, sky blue socks.
Change colours: Yellow and dark blue striped shirt, dark blue shorts and socks with yellow trim.

Reserves League: Pontins Central League Division 1.

RECORDS AND STATISTICS

COMPETITIONS

Div 1/P	Div.2	Div.3	Div.3(S)	Div.4	Texaco
1967-	1919-25	1959-64	1926-36	1958-59	1971-72
	1936-52		1952-58		1972-73
	1964-67				1973-74
			Div.3(N)		UEFA
			1925-26		1970-71

HONOURS

Div.2	Div.3	Div.3(S)	FA Cup
1966-67	1963-64	1935-36	1987

MOST APPEARANCES

Steve Ogrizovic - 596 (1984 - 98)

Year	League	FA Cup	League Cup	Others
1984-85	42	2	2	-
1985-86	42	1	4	-
1986-87*	42	6	5	-
1987-88	40	2	3	-
1988-89	38	1	3	-
1989-90	37	1	7	-
1990-91	37	4	5	-
1991-92	38	2	3	-
1992-93	33	1	2	-
1993-94	33	1	3	-
1994-95	33	4	3	-
1995-96	25	3	1	-
1996-97	38	4	4	-
1997-98	24	2	4	-
	502	34	49	11

*1 goal scored.

MOST GOALS IN A CAREER

C Bourton - 181 (1931-37)

Year	League	FA Cup
1931-32	49	1
1932-33	40	3
1933-34	25	
1934-35	26	3
1935-36	23	2
1936-37	9	
Total	172	9

Current leading goalscorer - Dion Dublin - 68 (09.94-98)

RECORD TRANSFER FEE RECEIVED

Amount	Club	Player	Date
£4,000,000	Fenerbahce	Viorel Moldovan	07/98
£3,750,000	Liverpool	Phil Babb	8/94
£1,500,000	Blackburn Rovers	Kevin Gallacher	3/93
£365,000	Portland Timbers	Gary Collier	3/80

RECORD TRANSFER FEE PAID

Amount	Club	Player	Date
£3,250,000	Grasshopper Z.	Viorel Moldovan	01/98
£3,000,000	Leeds United	Gary McAllister	7/96
£2,000,000	Leeds United	Noel Whelan	12/95
£1,950,000	Manchester Utd	Dion Dublin	9/94

MANAGERS

Name	Seasons	Best	Worst
H Pollitt	1920-21	20 (2)	20 (2)
A Evans	1921-25	18 (2)	22 (2)
J Kerr	1926-28	15 (3S)	20 (3S)
J McIntyre	1928-31	6 (3S)	14 (3S)
H Storer	1931-45	4 (2)	12 (3S)
R Bayliss	1946-47	8 (2)	8 (2)
W Frith	1947-49	10 (2)	16 (2)
H Storer	1949-54	7 (2)	14 (3S)
J Fairbrother	1954-55	9 (3S)	14 (3S)
C Elliott		9 (3S)	9 (3S)
J Carver	1955-56	9 (3S)	9 (3S)
G Rayner			
H Warren	1957-58	8 (3S)	19 (3S)
W Frith	1958-62	4 (3)	2 (4)
J Hill	1962-68	20 (1)	14 (3)
N Cantwell	1968-72	6 (1)	20 (1)
R Dennison	1972		
J Mercer	1972-74	16 (1)	19 (1)
G Milne	1974-81	7 (1)	19 (1)
D Sexton	1981-83	14 (1)	19 (1)
R Gould	1983-84	18 (1)	19 (1)
D Mackay	1984-86	17 (1)	18 (1)
G Curtis/J Sillett	1986-87	10 (1)	18 (1)
J Sillett	1987-90	7 (1)	12 (1)
T Butcher	1990-92	16 (1)	16 (1)
D Howe	1992	19 (1)	19 (1)
R Gould	1992-93	16 (1/P)	16 (1/P)
P Neal	1993-95	11 (P)	11 (P)
R Atkinson	1995-96	16 (P)	16 (P)
G Strachan	1996-	11 (P)	17 (P)

LONGEST LEAGUE RUNS

of undefeated matches: 25 (26.11.1966 - 13.5.1967)	**of league matches w/out a win:** 19 (30.8.1919 - 20.12.1919)
of undefeated home matches: 19 (11.4.1925 - 13.3.1926)	**of undefeated away matches:** 12 (19.11.1966 - 19.8.1967)
without home win: 10 (30.8.1919 - 20.12.1919 & 1.1.92 - 18.4.92)	**without an away win:** 28 (5.1.1924 - 4.4.1925)
of league wins: 6 (20.4.1954 - 28.8.1954 & 24.4.1964 - 1.9.1964)	**of home wins:** 11 (18.10.1952 - 28.2.1953)
of league defeats: 9 (30.8.1919 - 4.10.1919)	**of away wins:** 4 (24.5.1963 - 14.9.1963 & 19.8.1992 - 5.9.1992)

COVENTRY CITY

PLAYERS NAME / Honours	Ht	Wt	Birthdate	Birthplace / Transfers	Contract Date	Clubs	League	L/Cup	FA Cup	Other	Lge	L/C	FAC	Oth
G O A L K E E P E R														
Hedman Magnus C	6.3		19/03/73	Stockholm		Solna AIK								
Swedish Int.				£500000	24/07/97	Coventry City	14		3					
Kirkland Christopher	6.3	11.7	02/05/81	Leicester		Coventry City (T)								
Ogrizovic Steve	6.3	14.7	12/09/57	Mansfield	28/07/77	Chesterfield	16	2						
FAC'87. FLgeXl.1.				£70000	18/11/77	Liverpool	4			1				
				£70000	11/08/82	Shrewsbury Town	84	7	5					
				£82000	22/06/84	Coventry City	502	49	34	11	1			
Scope Tynan	6.2	13.9	30/07/79	Sydney		Coventry City (T)								
D E F E N C E														
Breen Gary	6.1	12	12/12/73	London		Charlton Athletic								
Ei: 15, u21.9.				Free	06/03/91	Maidstone	19							
				Free	02/07/92	Gillingham	45+6	4	5	1				
				£70000	05/08/94	Peterborough United	43+1	2	2	3	1			1
					09/02/96	Birmingham City	37+3	4	1		2			
				£2500000	01/02/97	Coventry City	38+1	3+1	5		1			
Brightwell Ian	5.1	11.7	09/04/68	Lutterworth	07/05/86	Manchester City	285+36	29+2	19+4	4+3	18		1	
E: u21.4, S, Y.3				Free	19/06/98	Coventry City								
Burrows David	5.8	11	25/10/68	Dudley	08/11/86	W.B.A.	37+9	3+1	2	1	1			
E: B.3,u21.7. CS'89'90. Div.1'90. FAC'92. FlgeXl.				£550000	20/10/88	Liverpool	135	16	16+1	14	3			
					17/09/93	West Ham United	25	3	3		1	1		
					06/09/94	Everton	19	2	2					
				£1100000	02/03/95	Coventry City	72+1	6	6					
Burrows Mark	6.3	12.8	14/08/80	Kettering		Coventry City (T)								
Clement Philippe	6.2		22/03/74	Antwerp		Racing Genk								
Belgium Int.				£625000	26/03/98	Coventry City								
Colwell Richard P	5.9	11.2	02/09/79	Wordsley		Coventry City (T)								
Daish Liam	6.2	13.5	23/09/68	Portsmouth	29/09/86	Portsmouth	1			1+1				
Ei:5,u21.5. Div.3'91. Div.2'95. AMC'95.				Free	11/07/88	Cambridge United	138+1	11	17	15	5			3
				£50000	10/01/94	Birmingham City	56	3	5	7	3	1		
				£1500000	24/02/96	Coventry City	31	3			2	1		
Donlevy Andrew	5.11	10.12	13/04/81	Hong Kong		Coventry City (T)								
Hall Marcus	6.1	12.02	24/04/76	Coventry	01/07/94	Coventry City	56+12	9+1	7+2		1	1		
E: B.1, u21.8.														
Mooney Gerard A	5.9	11	28/08/80	Glasgow		Coventry City (T)								
Nilsson Roland N J	6	11.6	27/11/63	Helsingborg		IFK Gothenburg								
Swedish Int.				£375000	08/12/89	Sheffield Wed	151	16	15	3+1	2	1		
					01/08/94	Helsingborgs								
				£200000	29/07/97	Coventry City	32	3	4					
Prenderville Barry	6	12.8	16/10/76	Dublin		Coventry City								
Shaw Richard	5.9	11.5	11/09/68	Brentford	04/09/86	Crystal Palace	178+14	24+2	18	12+1	3			
FMC'91. Div.1'94.				Loan	14/12/89	Hull City	4							
				£650000	17/11/95	Coventry City	89	7	10					
Willimas Jamie L	5.9	12	03/01/80	Bedworth		Coventry City (T)								
Williams Paul D	5.11	12	26/03/71	Burton	13/07/89	Derby County	153+7	10+2	8	14+1	25	2	3	2
E: u21.6.				Loan	09/11/89	Lincoln City	3		2	1				
				£1000000	06/08/95	Coventry City	75+8	10	6		4	1		
M I D F I E L D														
Barnett Christopher J	5.11		20/12/78	Derby	15/05/97	Coventry City								
Boateng George	5.9		05/09/75	Nkawkaw, Ghana		Feyenoord								
Dutch u21 Int.				£250000	19/12/97	Coventry City	14		5		1			
Boland Willie	5.9	10.9	06/08/75	Ennis (Eire)	04/11/92	Coventry City	43+20	5+1	0+1					
Ei: B.1, u21.11,Y, S.														
Devaney Martin	5.1		01/06/80	Cheltenham	04/06/97	Coventry City								
Eustace John	5.1	11.12	03/11/79	Solihull	04/11/96	Coventry City								
McAllister Gary	6.1	11.5	25/12/64	Motherwell		Motherwell	52+7	3+1	7		6		2	
S: 56, B.2, u21.1; SDiv1'85;. Div1'92				£125000	15/08/85	Leicester City	199+2	14+1	5	4	46	3	2	
				£1000000	02/07/90	Leeds United	230+1	26	24	14	31	4	6	4
				£3000000	26/07/96	Coventry City	52	8	4		6	3		
Quinn Barry S	6	12.2	09/05/79	Dublin	31/05/97	Coventry City								
World Youth Cup'98. (Captain)														
Shilton Sam	5.1	10	21/07/78	Nottingham		Plymouth Argyle	1+1		0+1					
						Coventry City	2							
Soltvedt Trond Egil	6.1	0	15/02/67	Voss (Norway)		Rosenborg								
Norway Int.				£500000	24/07/97	Coventry City	26+4	1+1	3+1		1			
Strachan Gavin D	5.1	11.7	23/12/78	Aberdeen	31/05/97	Coventry City	2+7		2+2					
S: U21														
Telfer Paul	5.9	10.2	21/10/71	Edinburgh	07/11/88	Luton Town	91	3	10	2	10		2	1
S: B.2, u21.3.				£1150000	26/06/95	Coventry City	95+3	10	11		4	2	3	
Wallemme Jean-Guy	6		10/08/67	Naubeuge, France		Lens								
French Championship'98				£750000	06/06/98	Coventry City								
F O R W A R D														
Dublin Dion	6	12.4	22/04/69	Leicester	24/03/88	Norwich City								
E: 3. Div.3'91. CS'94.				Free	02/08/88	Cambridge United	133+23	8+2	21	14+1	52	5	11	5
				£1000000	07/08/92	Manchester United	4+8	1+1	1+1	0+1	2	1		

	ht	wt	born	from	date	club	App1	App2	App3	App4	G1	G2	G3	G4
Dublin Dion continued				£1950000	09/09/94	Coventry City	134+1	9+2	13		58	3	7	
Ducros Andrew	5.4	9.8	16/09/77	Evesham		Coventry City	2+6	0+1						
E: Y.														
Eribenne Chukwunyeaka	5.10	11.12	02/11/80	London		Coventry City (T)								
Faulconbridge Craig M.	6.1	0	20/04/78	Nuneaton	05/07/96	Coventry City								
				Loan	01/04/98	Dunfirmline								
Hall Paul	5.9	10.2	7/3/72	Manchester	7/9/90	Torquay United	77+16	7	4+1	5+1	1		2	1
Jamiacan Int.				£70000	3/25/93	Portsmouth	149+40	10+3	6+1	6+2	37	1	2	2
				£300000	07/08/98	Coventry City								
Haworth Simon O	6.1	13.6	03/01/68	Cardiff	07/08/95	Cardiff City	27+10	4	0+1	4	9			1
W: 1, u21.3, Y.				£500000	04/06/97	Coventry City	4+6	2	0+1		.	1		
Huckerby Darren	5.11	10.8	23/04/76	Nottingham	14/07/94	Lincoln City	20+8	2		1	5			2
E: B.1, u21.4.				£500000	10/11/95	Newcastle United	0+1		0+1					
				Loan	05/09/96	Millwall	6				3			
				£1000000	23/11/96	Coventry City	53+6	0+1	9		19		3	
O'Neill Michael	5.11	10.1	05/07/69	Portadown	01/08/87	Newcastle United	48				15			
NI: 31, B.1, u23.1, u21.1, Y, S.					01/08/89	Dundee United	64				11			
					01/08/93	Hibernian	69				13			
				£300000	26/07/96	Coventry City	3+2	1						
				Loan	22/01/98	Aberdeen	4+1		0+1					
				Loan	02/03/98	Reading	9				1			
Whelan Noel	6.2	11.3	30/12/74	Leeds	05/03/93	Leeds United	25+15	3	2		7	1		
E: u21.2, Y. FAYC'93.				£2000000	16/12/95	Coventry City	76+1	4	11		20		3	

THE MANAGER
GORDON STRACHAN OBE

Date of Birth . . . . 9th February 1957.
Place of Birth . . . . Edinburgh.
Date of Appointment . . . . November 1996.

PREVIOUS CLUBS
As Manager. . . . . None.
Assistant Manager/Coach. . . . . Coventry.
As a Player . . . . Dundee, Aberdeen, Manchester Utd, Leeds Utd, Coventry.

HONOURS
As a Manager
None.

As a Player
Aberdeen: Scottish Premier Division Championship 1980, 1984. Scottish Cup 1982, 1983, 1984.
ECWC 1983. ESC 1983.
Manchester United: FA Cup 1985.
Leeds United: Division 2 (now Div.1) championship 1990. Division 1 (now Carling Premiership) 1992.
Scotland: 50 full caps, 1 U21 and Youth.

HIGHFIELD ROAD

King Richard Street, Coventry CV2 4FW

Capacity...23,662.

First game ....v Shrewsbury Town 9.9.1899
First floodlit game ....v Queen of the South, Friendly, 21.10.1953.
ATTENDANCES
Highest ....51,455 v Wolves, Div 2, 29.4.1967.
Lowest...1,086 v Millwall, FMC, 15.10.1985.

OTHER GROUNDS.................Binley Road 1883-87, Stoke Road 1887-99, Highfield Road since 1899.

HOW TO GET TO THE GROUND

From the North and South
Exit the M6 at junction 2, take the A4600 and follow the signs for the City Centre. Cross the roundabout keeping along Ansty Road (A4600). It bears left, and you come to another roundabout. Take right exit and continue for a quarter-of-a-mile. Turn right into Swan Lane. Coventry F.C. is directly ahead of you.

From the East
Exit the M69 at its junction with the M6 and then follow the directions given above.

From the West
Exit the M40 at junction 15 and proceed along the A46 (dual carriageway) for approximately 10 miles until you reach the island, cross the island and continue until you reach the next island. At this point turn first left onto the B4110 signposted "Stoke", follow this road across all sets of traffic lights until you reach a large island, take the third exit off this and then take the first left, continue to the end of the road and then turn left into Walsgrave Road and immediately right into Swan Lane.

USEFUL TELEPHONE NUMBERS

Club switchboard 01203 234 000
Club fax number........................01203 234 099
Club shop 01203 234 030
Ticket Office.......01203 234 020 (fax 234 023)

Marketing Department 01203 234 010
Internet address.......................www.ccfc.co.uk
Clubcall 0891 12 11 66*
*Calls cost 50p per minute at all times. Call costings correct at time of going to press.

MATCHDAY PROGRAMME

Number of pages....................................48.

Price ....£2.00.

Subscriptions ....Please apply to the club.

Local Newspapers
.......................Coventry Evening Telegraph.

Local Radio Stations
.....................BBC Coventry & Warwickshire
....Kix'96, Mercia FM.

MATCHDAY TICKET PRICES

Main Stand .... Adults - £23.00.
.... Juv & OAP - £11.50.
M&B Stand .... Adults - £20.00.
.... Juv & OAP - £10.00.
Comtel East Stand .... Adults - £20.00.
.... Juv & OAP - £10.00.
McDonalds Family Stand .... Adults - £17.00.
.... Juv & OAP - £8.50.
Co-Op Bank West Terrace .... Adults - £17.00.
.... Juv & OAP - £8.50.
J.S.B. Area .... £6.00.
Visitors .... Adults - £20.00.
.... Juv & OAP - £10.50*.
*Concession not available on Matchday.
Student discount of £3.00 applies to West Terrace tickets for Premier League matches until midday on matchday on production of a valid N.U.S. Card.
JSB priced tickets are subject to availability.

DERBY COUNTY
(The Rams)
F.A. CARLING PREMIERSHIP
SPONSORED BY: PUMA

1997-98 - Back Row L-R: Gordon Guthrie (Asst. Physio), Dane Farrell (Fitness Coach), Gary Rowett, Paulo Wanchope, Matt Carbon, Dean Yates, Darryl Powell, Ashley Ward, Christian Dailly, Jacob Laursen, Eric Steele (GK Coach), Billy McEwan (Reserve Team Coach). **Middle Row:** Steve McLaren (First Team Coach), Wayne Sutton, Stefano Eranio, Lee Carsley, Jonathan Hunt, Russell Hoult, Mart Poom, Ron Willems, Aljosa Asanovic, Paul Trollope, Peter Melville (Physio). **Bottom Row:** Francesco Baiano, Chris Powell, Mauricio Solis, Igor Stimac, Jim Smith (Manager), Robin van der Laan, Paul Simpson, Dean Sturridge, Sean Flynn (now W.B.A.). **Seated:** Chris Boden, Nick Wright, Rob Kozluk, Kevin Cooper (now Stockport).

DERBY COUNTY
FORMED IN 1884
TURNED PROFESSIONAL IN 1884
LTD COMPANY IN 1896

CHAIRMAN: L V Pickering
VICE-CHAIRMAN: P Gadsby

DIRECTORS
J N Kirkland BSc, CEng, MICE,
S Webb
CHIEF EXECUTIVE
Keith Loring (
SECRETARY
Keith Pearson (01332 667503)
COMMERCIAL MANAGER
Colin Tunnicliffe

MANAGER: Jim Smith
FIRST TEAM COACH: Steve McLaren

YOUTH TEAM MANAGER
Richie Williams
PHYSIOTHERAPIST
Peter Melville

STATISTICIAN FOR THE DIRECTORY
Vacant - phone 01203 234017 if interested

Under Jim Smith's shrewd management, the Rams did exceedingly well in the Carling Premiership in 1997-98 and certainly caused a few eyebrows to be raised with their style of play and overall performances both at home (the new Pride Stadium) and on their travels. No-one, in truth (except perhaps the most ardent of the club's supporters) believed that the Rams would be challenging strongly for a top six or seven finish and a place in next season's UEFA Cup competition. Smith himself had said publicly that tenth would be a satisfying position - but at the end of the day, after some splendid displays, Derby County celebrated the first season at their new home by finishing a very creditable ninth, missing a UEFA Cup place by just a whisker - one win in fact!

Smith assembled a highly efficient and talented outfit at Derby - one which, on it's day, could match the best in the Carling Premiership. They came unstuck occasionally but for long spells they were strong and resilient at home and positive and workmanlike away.

Indeed, it was not until February that the Rams lost their first home game - beaten 1-0 by Aston Villa - and At that stage of the season they were lying in sixth position, two points behind Arsenal (5th) and only eight adrift of second-placed Blackburn Rovers.

However, a run of disappointing results over the next few weeks saw them slip down the ladder and unfortunately not enough points could be mustered at the death to ensure a UEFA Cup place - but it wasn't for the want of trying.

Manager Smith's multi-foreign team was full of adventurous and competitive players who gave as good as they got throughout the campaign. One of their stars was the lanky and highly-rated Costa Rican Paolo Wanchope, who despite is awkward style, caused defenders all sorts of problems. The Italian duo of Stefano Eranio and Francesco Baiano both performed competently as did Scottish international Christian Dailly, the two Powells, Chris and Darryl and goalkeeper Mart Poom and skipper Jacob Laursen. Jamaican World Cup star Deon Burton found it difficult to get a regular place in the side, but he will be one to watch out for this coming season when one feels that, given the breaks, Derby County could again be bidding for a top six finish.

Tony Matthews.

Derby County

M	DATE	COMP.	VEN	OPPONENTS	RESULT	H/T	LP	GOAL SCORERS/GOAL TIMES	ATT.
1	A 09	CP	A	Blackburn Rovers	L 0-1	0-1	20		(23557)
2	23	CP	A	Tottenham Hotspur	L 0-1	0-1	18		(25886)
3	30	CP	H	Barnsley	W 1-0	1-0	16	Eranio 43 (pen)	27232
4	S 13	CP	H	Everton	W 3-1	2-1	10	Hunt 23, Powell C 33, Sturridge 66	27828
5	16	CC 2/1	A	**Southend United**	**W 1-0**	**1-0**		**Wanchope 43**	**(4011)**
6	20	CP	A	Aston Villa	L 1-2	1-0	15	Baiano 15	(35444)
7	24	CP	A	Sheffield Wednesday	W 5-2	3-2	12	Baiano 8, 48, Laursen 26, Wanchope 33, Burton 74	(22391)
8	27	CP	H	Southampton	W 4-0	0-0	8	Eranio 75 (pen), Wanchope 79, Baiano 82, Carsley 83	25625
9	O 01	CC 2/2	H	**Southend United**	**W 5-0**	**1-0**		**Rowett 43, 57, Wanchope 60, Sturridge 64, Trollope 83**	**18490**
10	06	CP	A	Leicester City	W 2-1	1-0	6	Baiano 21, 62	(19585)
11	15	CC 3	A	**Tottenham Hotspur**	**W 2-1**	**1-1**		**Wanchope 26, 70**	**(20390)**
12	18	CP	H	Manchester United	D 2-2	2-0	7	Baiano 23, Wanchope 38	30014
13	22	CP	H	Wimbledon	D 1-1	0-0	6	Baiano 53	28595
14	25	CP	A	Liverpool	L 0-4	0-1	7		(38017)
15	N 01	CP	H	Arsenal	W 3-0	0-0	6	Wanchope 46, 65, Sturridge 82	30004
16	08	CP	A	Leeds United	L 3-4	3-2	8	Sturridge 4, 11, Asanovic 33 (pen)	(33572)
17	18	CC 4	H	**Newcastle United**	**L 0-1**	**0-0**			**27364**
18	22	CP	H	Coventry City	W 3-1	3-0	5	Baiano 3, Eranio 30 (pen), Wanchope 39	29351
19	29	CP	A	Chelsea	L 0-4	0-2	8		(34544)
20	D 06	CP	H	West Ham United	W 2-0	1-0	7	Sturridge 49, Miklosko 10 (OG)	29300
21	14	CP	A	Bolton Wanderers	D 3-3	0-0	7	Eranio 54, Baiano 64, 68	(23037)
22	17	CP	A	Newcastle United	D 0-0	0-0	7		(36289)
23	20	CP	H	Crystal Palace	D 0-0	0-0	7		26590
24	26	CP	H	Newcastle United	W 1-0	1-0	7	Eranio 4 (pen)	30232
25	28	CP	A	Barnsley	L 0-1	0-0	7		(18686)
26	J 03	FAC 3	H	**Southampton**	**W 2-0**	**0-0**		**Baiano 68 (pen), Powell C 73**	**27992**
27	11	CP	H	Blackburn Rovers	W 3-1	2-0	6	Sturridge 15, 41, Wanchope 88	27823
28	17	CP	A	Wimbledon	D 0-0	0-0	6		(13031)
29	24	FAC 4	A	**Coventry City**	**L 0-2**	**0-2**			**(22824)**
30	31	CP	H	Tottenham Hotspur	W 2-1	1-0	6	Sturridge 25, Wanchope 76	30187
31	F 06	CP	A	Aston Villa	L 0-1	0-0	6		30251
32	14	CP	A	Everton	W 2-1	1-0	6	Stimac 21, Wanchope 50	(34876)
33	21	CP	A	Manchester United	L 0-2	0-1	6		(55170)
34	28	CP	H	Sheffield Wednesday	W 3-0	1-0	6	Wanchope 3, 49, Rowett 67	30203
35	M 15	CP	H	Leeds United	L 0-5	0-3	7		30217
36	28	CP	A	Coventry City	L 0-1	0-1	7		(18705)
37	A 05	CP	H	Chelsea	L 0-1	0-1	8		30062
38	11	CP	A	West Ham United	D 0-0	0-0	9		(25155)
39	13	CP	H	Bolton Wanderers	W 4-0	4-0	7	Wanchope 27, Burton 37, 40, Baiano 45	29126
40	18	CP	A	Crystal Palace	L 1-3	0-0	9	Bohinen 85	(18101)
41	26	CP	H	Leicester City	L 0-4	0-4	10		29855
42	29	CP	A	Arsenal	L 0-1	0-1	10		(38121)
43	M 02	CP	A	Southampton	W 2-0	0-0	9	Dailly 50, Sturridge 88	(15202)
44	10	CP	H	Liverpool	W 1-0	0-0	9	Wanchope 63	30492

Best Home League Attendance: 30492 V Liverpool　　　　Smallest :25625 V Southampton　　　　Average :29105

Goal Scorers:

CP	(52)	Wanchope 13, Baiano 12, Sturridge 9, Eranio 5, Burton 3, Asanovic 1, Bohinen 1, Carsley 1, Dailly 1, Hunt 1, Laursen 1, Powell C1, Rowett 1, Stimac 1, Opponents 1
CC	(8)	Wanchope 4, Rowett 2, Sturridge 1, Trollope 1
FAC	(2)	Baiano 1, Powell C1

(M) Asanovic	(F) Baiano	(M) Bohinen	(F) Burton	(D) Carbon	(D) Carsley	(M) Dailly	(M) Delap	(M) Elliott	(F) Eranio	(G) Hoult	(F) Hunt	(M) Kozluk	(D) Laursen	(G) Poom	(D) Powell C	(F) Powell D	(M) Rowett	(M) Simpson	(F) Solis	(D) Stimac	(F) Sturridge	(M) Trollope	(M) Van der Laan	(M) Wanchope	(F) Ward	(M) Willems	(D) Yates		
		S3	X3	X	X			X	S		X		X	X	X	S2	S	X1		X			X2			S1		D.R. Elleray	1
			X		X	X		X	S		X		X	X	X	S2	S			S3	X	S1	X		X			M J Bodenham	2
S	X			X	X		X	S		X			X	X	X		S1			X	S3	S2	X		X			P A Durkan	3
X	X			X	X		X	S		X			X	X	S3	X	S			X	X	S2	S1					M A Riley	4
				X		X		S	X1	X			X	X	X2	X	S1			X	S2	X	X					P E Alcock	5
S1	X		S2		X	X		X	S		X		X	X	X					X	X	S	S3					J T Winter	6
	X		X		X	X		X	S		S1		X	X	X		X		S		X	S	S	X				M D Reed	7
	X		X		X	X		X	S		S		X	X	X		X		S			S1	S	X				K W Burge	8
X					X		X		X	S2		X		X		X	S3	X		X		X	S1	X				M J Brandwood	9
	X1		X		X	X		X	S				X	X	X		X	S		X	S2	S1	S3	X				G R Ashby	10
			X		X	X		S			S1	X		X	X		X		S2	X	X	X	X	X				D J Gallagher	11
	X		S1		X	X			S		S2	S	X	X	X		X			S		X	X	X				G Poll	12
X	X		S1		X	X			S		S	S	X	X	X	S2	X					X	X	X				U D Rennie	13
	X		X	S		X			S		S	S1	X	X	X	X	S		X		S2	X		X				G S Willard	14
	X		S2	X	X				S		S	S1	X	X	X	X	X			X		S3		X				P E Alcock	15
X	X			X	X	X			S		S3	S1	X	X	X	X	X				X	S2				S		N S Barry	16
	X			X	X			X	S		X		X	X	X	S	X		S1		X			X				M J Bodenham	17
	X		S		X	X		X	S		S2	X	X	X	X	X	S1			S		X		X				D R Elleray	18
	X3		S1		X	X		X	S		S3	X		X	X	X	S2			S		X		X1		X2		U D Rennie	19
	X2		S		X	X	X1	S	S1	X			X	X	X	S2	X			X		X		X		S		A B Wilkie	20
	X		S1		X	X		X	S	S	X2		X	X	X	X				X		X		X1		S		U D Rennie	21
	X3		X2		X		X	X	S	S2			X	X	X	X	S		X1			S1		X	S3	X		K W Burge	22
	X		X2		X		X1	X	S	S			S	X	X	X	X		X			X		X	S2	S1		M J Bodenham	23
	X2		S3		X		X1	S		S			S	X	X	X	X		X	X3		X		X	S2	X		M D Reed	24
	S2		S3	S1	X			X	S				X1	X	X2	X	X		S		X			X3	X	X		G P Barber	25
	X2		X	S	X		S1		S	S	X		X	X	X	X1	X			X				X		S2	X	G R Ashby	26
	X		S2	S				X1	S		X	X	X	X	X	X				X		X2		X		S1	X	G Poll	27
	X		X				S		X	X	S	X	X	X	X		X			X		X		X		X	X	P Jones	28
	X1		X3		X2	S3		X	S	S		X	X	X	X	S2			X			X		X		S1	X	M J Bodenham	29
	X2		S		X	S		X	S			X	X	X	X	X1	S1			X		X		X		S2	X	G S Willard	30
	X2				X	X	S		S			X	X	X	X	S2	X		S	X	S	X		X		S1	X1	P E Alcock	31
				X	X	X	S	X	S		S		X	X	X	S1	X			X		X		X		X1		G W Dunn	32
	X			X	X	X	X1	S	X	S		S	X		X	X	S	X		X		X		X		S1		M D Reed	33
	X		X2		X1	X	S2		X		S1		X		X	X	S	X		X		X		X		S		A B Wilkie	34
	X		X		X	X	S3		X1	S	S1		X3	X	S2	X	X2			X		X		X		S		S J Lodge	35
	X3		X	S1	X	X			X	S		X		X	X1	S2		S3	X2			X		X				K W Burge	36
	X2	X3		S2	X	X	X		X			S1	X	S	X		X		S3		X			X		S		J T Winter	37
	S2		X		S1	X	X	X		X		S			X	X				X		X	X1		S	X2		G P Barber	38
	X		X3				X	X2		X		S1	X	S	X	S	S		X		S1		S3	X	X			D J Gallagher	39
	S1		X	X3		X	X2						S2	S	X			X		X		S3		X1	X			P E Alcock	40
	X2		X		S3	X	X	X	S2	S					X	X	X3				S1			X1	X			G S Willard	41
		X2	S1		X	X	X	X					S		X	X	X1		X		S2		X		S	X		N S Barry	42
	X		X		X	X	X						S		X	X			X		X2		X		S2	X3		M A Riley	43
	X	X2		S1		X	X	X					S		X	X			X		S		X		S	X1		S J Lodge	44
3	30	9	12	3	34	30	10	3	22	2	7	6	27	36	35	12	32	1	3	22	24	4	7	30	2	3	8	CP Appearances	
1	3	17	1		3				12	3	1		2	11	3		6				6	6	3	2	1	7	1	CP Sub Appearances	
1			2	4		2	1	1	2+2	2		2	3	4	1		4				4	2+1	2+1	4				CC Appearances	
2		2		2	0+1		0+1	1				1	1	2	2	2	1+1				2			2		0+2	2	FAC Appearances	

Also Played: (M) Bridge-Wilkinson S(27,28,32). (M) Knight S(34,36,40). (M) Smith S(28).

DERBY COUNTY

CLUB RECORDS

BIGGEST VICTORIES
League: 9-0 v Wolverhampton Wanderers, 10.1.1891.
9-0 v Sheffield Wednesday, Division 1, 2.1.1899.
F.A. Cup: 8-1 v Barnsley, 1st Round, 30.1.1897.
League Cup: 7-0 v Southend, 2nd Round 2nd leg, 7.10.1992.
Europe: (UEFA) 12-0 v Finns Harps, 3rd Round, 15.9.1976.

BIGGEST DEFEATS
League: 0-8 v Blackburn Rovers, Division 1, 3.1.1891.
0-8 v Sunderland, Division 1, 1.9.1894.
F.A. Cup: 2-11 v Everton, 1st Round, 18.1.1890.
League Cup: 0-5 v Southampton, 8.10.1974.
0-5 v West Ham United, 3rd Round, 1.11.1988.
Europe: (UEFA) 1-5 v Real Madrid, 2nd Round, 5.11.1975.

MOST POINTS
3 points a win: 84, Division 3, 1985-86. Division 2, 1986-87.
2 points a win: 63, Division 3(N) 1955-56 & 1956-57, Division 2 1968-69.

MOST GOALS SCORED
111, Division 3(N), 1956-57.
Straw 37, Woodhead 14, Ryan 12, Brown 9, Parry 7, Crowshaw 6, Buchanan 5, Barrowcliffe 4, Ackerman 4, Mays 4, Powell 1, Pye 1, Davies 1, Wyer 1, Opponents 5.

MOST GOALS CONCEDED
90, Division 1, 1936-37.

MOST FIRST CLASS MATCHES IN A SEASON
64 - 1992-93 (League 46, FA Cup 5, League Cup 4, Anglo-Italian 9).

MOST LEAGUE WINS
28, Division 3(N), 1955-56.

MOST LEAGUE DRAWS
19, Division 1, 1976-77. Division 2, 1982-83.

MOST LEAGUE DEFEATS

INDIVIDUAL CLUB RECORDS

26, Division 2, 1954-55.
MOST GOALS IN A SEASON
Jack Bowers: 39 goals in 1930-31 (League 37, FAC 2).

MOST GOALS IN A MATCH
6. Steve Bloomer v Sheffield Wednesday, Division 1, 2.1.1899.

OLDEST PLAYER
Peter Shilton, 42 years 164 days v Watford, Division 2, 29.2.1992.

YOUNGEST PLAYER
Steve Powell, 16 years 33 days v Arsenal, Division 1, 23.10.1971.

BEST PERFORMANCES

MOST CAPPED PLAYER
Peter Shilton (England) 34.
League: 1956-57: Matches played 46, Won 26, Drawn 11, Lost 9, Goals for 111, Goals against 53, Points 63. First in Division 3(N).
Highest Position: Division 1 Champions 1971-72, 1974-75.
F.A. Cup: 1945-46: 3rd Round Luton Town 6-0,3-0; 4th Round West Bromwich Albion 1-0,3-1; 5th Round Brighton & H.A. 4-1,6-0; 6th Round Aston Villa 4-3,1-1; Semi-Final Birmingham City 1-1,4-0; Final Charlton 4-1.
League Cup: 1967-68: 2nd Round Hartlepool United 4-0; 3rd Round Birmingham City 3-1; 4th Round Lincoln City 1-1,3-1; 5th Round Darlington 5-4; Semi-Final Leeds United 0-1,2-3.
Europe: (European Cup) 1972-73: 1st Round Zelj Znicars 2-0,2-1; 2nd Round Benefica 3-0,0-0; 3rd Round Spartak Trnava 0-1,2-0; Semi-Final Juventus 1-3,0-0.

ADDITIONAL INFORMATION
PREVIOUS NAMES
None.

PREVIOUS LEAGUES
None.

Club colours: White shirts with black sleeves, gold piping, black shorts, white socks.
Change colours: Reserves League: Pontins Central League Division 1.

DIVISIONAL RECORD

	Played	Won	Drawn	Lost	For	Against	Points
Division 1/P	2,278	865	535	878	3,590	3,597	2,337
Division 2/1	1,466	597	362	506	2,230	2,084	1,714
Division 3	92	42	28	22	145	95	154
Division 3(N)	92	54	18	20	221	108	126
Total	**3,928**	**1,558**	**943**	**1,427**	**6,263**	**5,866**	**4,331**

RECORDS AND STATISTICS

COMPETITIONS

Div.1/P	Div.2/1	Div.3	Div.3(N)	Euro C	Texaco
1889-07	1907-12	1984-86	1955-57	1972-73	1971-72
1912-14	1914-15			1975-76	
1919-21	1921-26				Wat C
1926-53	1953-54			UEFA	1970
1969-80	1957-69			1974-75	
1987-91	1980-84			1976-77	
1996-	1986-87				
	1991-96				

HONOURS

Div.1	Div.2	Div 3(N)	FAC	Texaco
1971-72	1911-12	1956-57	1945-46	1971-72
1974-75	1914-15			
	1968-69		Wat C	C/S'Ld
	1986-87		1970	1975

MOST APPEARANCES
KEVIN HECTOR 581+8 (1966-82)

Year	League	FA Cup	Lge Cup	Other
1966-67	30	1		
1967-68	41	1	7	
1968-69	41	1	8	
1969-70	41	4	6	
1970-71	42	3	3	
1971-72	42	5	2	6
1972-73	41	5	3	8
1973-74	42	4	3	
1974-75	38	2	2	6
1975-76	29+3	2	2	4
1976-77	28+1	4	2	3
1977-78	11		2	
1980-81	25	2		
1981-82	27+4		2	
	478+8	34	42	27

MOST GOALS IN A CAREER
STEVE BLOOMER - 331 (1892-1914)

Year	League	FA Cup
1892-93	11	
1893-94	19	
1894-95	10	
1895-96	22	5
1896-97	24	7
1897-98	15	5
1898-99	24	6
1899-1900	19	
1900-01	24	
1901-02	15	3
1902-03	12	1
1903-04	20	5
1904-05	13	
1905-06	12	
1910-11	20	4
1911-12	18	1
1912-13	13	1
1913-14	2	
Total	293	38

Current leading goalscorer: Dean Sturridge - 45 (07/91-98)

RECORD TRANSFER FEE RECEIVED

Amount	Club	Player	Date
£2,900,000	Liverpool	Dean Saunders	7/91
£2,200,000	Liverpool	Mark Wright	6/91
£800,000	Millwall	Paul Goddard	12/89
£525,000	Aston Villa	Nigel Callaghan	2/89

RECORD TRANSFER FEE PAID

Amount	Club	Player	Date
£2,500,000	Notts County	Craig Short	9/92
£1,300,000	Notts County	Tommy Johnson	3/92
£1,200,000	Crystal Palace	Marco Gabbiadini	1/92
£1,000,000	Oxford United	Dean Saunders	10/88

MANAGERS

Name	Seasons	Best	Worst
Harry Newbould	1896-06	3(1)	15(1)
Jimmy Methvan	1906-22	7(1)	14(2)
Cecil Potter	1922-25	3(2)	14(2)
George Jobey	1925-41	2(1)	3(2)
Ted Magner	1941-46		
Stuart McMillan	1946-53	3(1)	22(1)
Jack Barker	1953-55	18(2)	22(2)
Harry Storer	1955-62	7(2)	2(3S)
Tim Ward	1962-67	8(2)	18(2)
Brian Clough	1967-73	1(1)	18(2)
Dave Mackay	1973-76	1(1)	4(1)
Colin Murphy	1976-77	15(1)	15(1)
Tommy Docherty	1977-79	12(1)	19(1)
Colin Addison	1979-81	19(1)	6(2)
John Newman	1981-83	13(2)	16(2)
Peter Taylor	1982-84	20(2)	20(2)
Arthur Cox	1984-93	5(1)	7(2)
Roy McFarland	1993-95	6(2/1)	6(2/1)
Jim Smith	1995-	12 (P)	2 (1)

LONGEST LEAGUE RUNS

of undefeated matches:	22 (8.3.1969 - 25.10.1969)	of league matches w/out a win:	20 (1.12.1990 - 4.5.1991)
of undefeated home matches:	23 (5.10.1929 - 11.10.1930)	of undefeated away matches:	13 (18.1.1969 - 27.9.1969)
without home win:	9 (24.11.1990 - 4.5.1991)	without an away win:	33 (1.9.1919 - 2.4.1921)
of league wins:	9 (15.3.1969 - 9.8.1969)	of home wins:	12 (23.10.1971 - 1.4.1972)
of league defeats:	8 (3.4.1965 - 15.9.1965 & 12.12.87 - 10.2.88)	of away wins:	7 (3.10.1992 - 20.12.1992)

DERBY COUNTY

PLAYERS NAME Honours	Ht	Wt	Birthdate	Birthplace Transfers	Contract Date	Clubs	APPEARANCES				GOALS			
							League	L/Cup	FA Cup	Other	Lge	L/C	FAC	Oth
G O A L K E E P E R														
Hoult Russell	6.4	13.2	22/11/72	Leicester	28/03/91	Leicester City	10	3		1				
				Loan	27/08/91	Lincoln City	2	1						
				Loan	22/07/93	Kettering Town								
				Loan	03/11/93	Bolton Wanderers	3+1							
				£200000	22/07/95	Derby County	88+2	5	4					
Knight Richard	6.1	14	03/08/79	Burton		Burton Albion								
					25/06/97	Derby County								
Poom Mart	6.4	13.07	03/02/72	Estonia		FC Wil								
Estonian Int.				£200000	04/08/94	Portsmouth	4	3						
					09/05/96	Tallin SC								
				£500000	26/03/97	Derby County	40	3	2					
D E F E N C E														
Carbonari Horacio				Argentina		Rosario Central								
				£2700000	24/05/98	Derby County								
Carsley Lee K	5.11	11.11	28/04/74	Birmingham	31/05/94	Derby County	102+14	8+2	7	3	4			
Ei: u21.1.														
Elliott Steven W	6.1	13.12	29/10/78	Derby	31/05/97	Derby County (T)	3	2	0+1					
Kozluk Robert	5.7	10.12	05/08/77	Mansfield	31/05/97	Derby County (T)	6+3	2	1					
Laursen Jacob	5.11	12	06/10/71	Denmark		Silkeborg								
Danish Int.				£500000	17/07/96	Derby County	62+2	4	3		2			
Schnoor Stefan				Germany		Hamburg								
				Free	23/06/98	Derby County								
Stimac Igor	6.2	13	06/09/67	Croatia		Hadjuk Split								
Croation Int.				£1500000	01/11/95	Derby County	70	1	4		3			
M I D F I E L D														
Bohinen Lars	5.11	12.02	08/09/66	Vados		Ferencvaros								
Norwegian Int.				£450000	05/11/93	Nottingham Forest	52+5	6+1	2		7		1	
				£700000	14/10/95	Blackburn Rovers	40+18	3+2	2+1		7	1	1	
				£1450000	27/03/98	Derby County	9				1			
Bridge -Wilkinson Marc	5.6	10.8	16/03/79	Coventry	31/05/97	Derby County (T)								
Dailly Christian	5.10	10.11	23/10/73	Dundee	01/08/90	Dundee United	11+33	9	10+2	8+1	18	1		1
S: 3, B.1, u21.3, Y, S.				£500000	12/08/96	Derby County	61+5	6	4+1		4			
Delap Rory	6	11.11	06/07/76	Coldfield	18/07/94	Carlisle United	42+25	4+1	0+3	12+2	7			
Ei: u21.3. AMC'97.				£500000	06/02/98	Derby County	10+3							
McDonald Jamie			29/01/80	Luton	31/05/97	Derby County (T)								
Murphy Leroy A			21/12/77	Derby	04/07/97	Derby County (T)								
Porter Daniel J			23/01/79	Portsmouth	02/06/97	Derby County (T)								
Powell Darryl	6	12.3	15/11/71	Lambeth	22/12/88	Portsmouth	49+49	6+3	8	9+5	11			4
Jamaican Int.				£750000	27/07/95	Derby County	76+17	3+1	5		6			
Radzki Lee M			14/11/78	Mansfield	31/05/97	Derby County (T)								
Rowett Gary	6	12	06/03/74	Bromsgrove	10/09/91	Cambridge United	51+12	7	5+2	5	9	1		2
				£200000	21/05/94	Everton	0+2							
				£300000	20/07/95	Derby County	101+4	8	5+2		3			
Willems Ron	6.1	12.5	20/09/66	Epe		Grasshoppers-Zurich								
				£300000	01/08/95	Derby County	41+18	2	4+2		13	1	2	

Name			DOB	From	Fee	Date	Club								
Baiano Francesco	5.6	10.7	24/02/68	Naples			Fiorentina								
					£650000	01/08/97	Derby County	30+3	1	2		12		1	
Burton Deon	5.8	10.1	25/10/76	Reading		15/02/94	Portsmouth	30+11	1+2	0+1		9			
Jamaican Int.						24/12/96	Cardiff City								
						21/02/97	Portsmouth	12+9	2	0+1		1	2	1	
					£1000000	01/08/97	Derby County	12+17	1	2		3			
Eranio Stefano	5.10	12	29/12/68	Genoa			AC Milan								
					Free	15/07/97	Derby County	23	1	1		5			
Hunt Jonathan	5.10	12.3	02/11/71	Camden			Barnet	12+21	1	0+1	6+2				1
Div.2'95. AMC'95.					Free	20/07/93	Southend United	36+6	0+2	1	6+1	6			
					£50000	16/09/94	Birmingham City	67+10	10+5	3+1	8	18	2	1	4
						23/05/97	Derby County	7+12	2+2			1			
Sturridge Dean C	5.7	10.1	26/07/73	Birmingham	01/07/91		Derby County	102+20	5+1	3	2+1	41	2	2	
Wanchope Pablo	6.4	12	31/07/76	Costa Rica			CS Heridiano								
Costa Rican Int.					£600000	27/03/97	Derby County	32+5	4	2		14	4		

THE MANAGER
JIM SMITH

Date of Birth . . . . 17th November 1940.
Place of Birth . . . . Sheffield.
Date of Appointment . . . . August 1995.

PREVIOUS CLUBS
As Manager . . . . Boston Utd, Colchester Utd, Blackburn Rovers,
. . . . Birmingham City, Oxford Utd, Q.P.R., Newcaslte Utd, Portsmouth.
As Coach . . . . Middlesbrough.
As a Player . . . . Sheffield Utd, Aldershot, Halifax Town, Lincoln City,
. . . . Boston Utd, Colchester Utd.

HONOURS
As a Manager
Colchester Utd: Promotion to Division 3, 1974.
Birmingham City: Promotion to Division 1, 1980.
Oxford United: Division 3 Championship, 1984. Division 2 Championship, 1985.
Derby County: Promotion to the Carling Premiership 1995-96.

As a Player
None.

PRIDE PARK STADIUM
Derby DE24 AXL

Capacity ....30,000.

First game ....v Barnsley, Premiership 30.8.1997.
First floodlit game..
Internationals ....None.

ATTENDANCES
Highest ....30,492 v Liverpool. Premiership, 10.5.1998.

OTHER GROUNDS...Race Course Ground 1884-95. Baseball Ground since 1895.

HOW TO GET TO THE GROUND

From the North
Approaching on the M1 take the exit at Junction 25 onto the A52. After approximately 5 miles and after passing under the bridge, take the left exit to the new Pride Park Stadium.

From East, South and West
Approaching on the M1 take the exit at Junction 24 and get onto the A6. After approximately 6 miles cross the A5111 and at the next round-about take the right exit for the new Pride Park Stadium.

Car Parking: Parking within walking distance of the stadium.

Nearest Railway Station
Derby Midland (-1332 32051)
Ramsline Halt (Specials only)

USEFUL TELEPHONE NUMBERS

Club switchboard 01332 667 503
Club fax number.......................01332 667 519
Ticket Office.............................01332 209 209

Clubcall 0891 12 11 87*
*Calls cost 50p per minute at all times. Call costings correct at time of going to press.

MATCHDAY PROGRAMME

Programme Editor ....J Fearn.

Number of pages....................................48.

Price ....£1.50.

Subscriptions......................£55 per season.

Local Newspapers
............................Derby Evening Telegraph.

Local Radio Stations
..BBC Radio Derby, Ram FM (Commercial).

MATCHDAY TICKET PRICES

East Stand. . . . . £12/£18/£20

West Stand . . . . £18/£20/£23

South Stand £18

EVERTON
(The Toffeemen)
F.A. CARLING PREMIERSHIP
SPONSORED BY: ONE 2 ONE

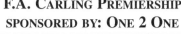

1997-98 - Back Row L-R: Phil Jevons, Slaven Bilic, Graham Allen, Claus Thomsen, Paul Gerrard, Neville Southall, John O'Toole, Joe Parkinson, Andy Hinchcliffe, Richard Dunne, Gareth Farrelly. **Middle Row:** Jimmy Martin, Adrian Heath, John Hills, Michael Branch, John O'Connor, Gavin McCann, Craig Short, John Oster, Mark Quayle, Nick Barmby, Viv Busby, Les Helm. **Front Row:** Tony Grant, Graham Stuart, Gary Speed, Terry Phelan, Earl Barrett, Howard Kendall, Dave Watson, Michael Ball, David Unsworth, Duncan Ferguson, Chris Lane.

EVERTON
FORMED IN 1878
TURNED PROFESSIONAL IN 1885
LTD COMPANY IN 1892

CHAIRMAN: Peter R Johnson
DIRECTORS
Sir Desmond Pitcher (Vice-Chairman),
B C Finch, K M Tamlin,
A Abercromby, Dr D Marsh, Lord
Grantchester,
Sir Phillip Carter, CBE, W Kenwright
SECRETARY
Michael Dunford
COMMERCIAL MANAGER
Andrew Watson

MANAGER: Walter Smith OBE
ASSISTANT MANAGER: Archie Knox

PHYSIOTHERAPIST
A Jones

STATISTICIAN FOR THE DIRECTORY
Vacant (Phone 01203 234017 if interested)

Last season was not a happy one for the Merseysiders. The Blues struggled painfully at times and, in fact, during the course of the campaign, won just nine Carling Premiership matches, only retaining their top Division status thanks to a last-match home draw with Coventry City.

The team and manager Howard Kendall first came under any sort of pressure from the fans (and the media) halfway through the season when the Merseysiders nosedived into the bottom three of the Carling Premiership. Results picked up a little around Christmas time and the New Year, but after going out of the F.A. Cup to Newcastle, failing with a £7 million bid for Manchester City's Georgiou Kinkladze, losing the services of midfielder Gary Speed to Newcastle and winning the 'Manager of the Month' award for for the 15th time in his 19-year managerial career, Kendall himself suddenly found that things weren't doing according to plan at Goodison Park!

Once into February it looked as though things were improving and that safety was in sight with Everton lying a relatively comfortable 15th in the table, five points clear of third-from-bottom Crystal Palace. But then results began to take a turn for the worse....and with ten matches remaining Everton - having played more games than most of their fellow strugglers - knew they were in danger of losing their top League status for the first time since 1954. It was all tense stuff out on the park and with 32 games played, Everton had amassed just 34 points, leaving them in 17th position, only three points clear of the relegation trap-door.

A much-needed 2-0 home win over Leeds helped ease the situation, but two dour draws at Wimbledon and Leicester and a 3-1 defeat at the hands of Sheffield Wednesday quickly followed and at this juncture Nationwide League soccer looked on the cards! With two games left it was touch and go between Everton and Bolton s to who would be relegated - but at the end of the day, lady luck shone her light over Goodison Park and Howard Kendall's men survived by the skin of their teeth despite a 4-0 thrashing at Highbury!

Tony Matthews.

EVERTON

M	DATE	COMP.	VEN	OPPONENTS	RESULT	H/T	LP	GOAL SCORERS/GOAL TIMES	ATT.
1	A 09	CP	H	Crystal Palace	L 1-2	0-1	16	Ferguson 85	35716
2	23	CP	H	West Ham United	W 2-1	0-1	11	Speed 67, Stuart 83	34356
3	27	CP	H	Manchester United	L 0-2	0-1	15		40079
4	S 01	CP	A	Bolton Wanderers	D 0-0	0-0	14		(23131)
5	13	CP	A	Derby County	L 1-3	1-2	18	Stuart 28	(27828)
6	16	CC 2/1	A	**Scunthorpe United**	W 1-0	1-0		**Farrelly 36**	**(7145)**
7	20	CP	H	Barnsley	W 4-2	2-1	13	Speed 12, 77 (pen), Cadamarteri 42, Oster 84	32659
8	24	CP	A	Newcastle United	L 0-1	0-0	16		(36705)
9	27	CP	H	Arsenal	D 2-2	0-2	16	Ball 49, Cadamarteri 56	35457
10	O 01	CC 2/2	H	**Scunthorpe United**	W 5-0	2-0		**Stuart 11, Oster 23, Barmby 66, 67, Cadamarteri 69**	11562
11	04	CP	A	Sheffield Wednesday	L 1-3	0-0	18	Cadamarteri 84	(24486)
12	15	CC 3	A	**Coventry City**	L 1-4	1-2		**Barmby 16**	**(10087)**
13	18	CP	H	Liverpool	W 2-0	1-0	15	Cadamarteri 75, Ruddock 45 (OG)	40112
14	25	CP	A	Coventry City	D 0-0	0-0	16		(18760)
15	N 02	CP	H	Southampton	L 0-2	0-1	17		29565
16	08	CP	A	Blackburn Rovers	L 2-3	1-1	17	Speed 7, Ferguson 55	(25397)
17	22	CP	A	Aston Villa	L 1-2	1-1	20	Speed 11 (pen)	(36389)
18	26	CP	A	Chelsea	L 0-2	0-0	20		(34148)
19	29	CP	H	Tottenham Hotspur	L 0-2	0-0	20		36670
20	D 06	CP	A	Leeds United	D 0-0	0-0	19		(34869)
21	13	CP	H	Wimbledon	D 0-0	0-0	19		28533
22	20	CP	A	Leicester City	W 1-0	0-0	19	Speed 89 (pen)	(20628)
23	26	CP	A	Manchester United	L 0-2	0-2	19		(55167)
24	28	CP	H	Bolton Wanderers	W 3-2	2-2	18	Ferguson 17, 41, 67	37149
25	J 04	FAC 3	H	**Newcastle United**	L 0-1	0-0			20885
26	10	CP	A	Crystal Palace	W 3-1	3-1	15	Barmby 3, Ferguson 12, Madar 34	(23311)
27	18	CP	H	Chelsea	W 3-1	1-1	13	Speed 39, Ferguson 62, Duberry 82 (OG)	32355
28	31	CP	A	West Ham United	D 2-2	1-1	14	Barmby 25, Madar 58	(25905)
29	F 07	CP	A	Barnsley	D 2-2	1-1	15	Ferguson 40, Grant 50	(18672)
30	14	CP	H	Derby County	L 1-2	0-1	16	Thomsen 85	34876
31	23	CP	A	Liverpool	D 1-1	0-0	16	Ferguson 58	(44501)
32	28	CP	H	Newcastle United	D 0-0	0-0	16		37972
33	M 07	CP	A	Southampton	L 1-2	0-0	16	Tiler 89	(15102)
34	14	CP	H	Blackburn Rovers	W 1-0	0-0	16	Madar 62	33423
35	28	CP	H	Aston Villa	L 1-4	1-1	17	Madar 38	36471
36	A 04	CP	A	Tottenham Hotspur	D 1-1	1-0	17	Madar 24	(35624)
37	11	CP	H	Leeds United	W 2-0	2-0	15	Hutchison 10, Ferguson 38	37099
38	13	CP	A	Wimbledon	D 0-0	0-0	16		(15131)
39	18	CP	H	Leicester City	D 1-1	1-1	16	Madar 2	33642
40	25	CP	H	Sheffield Wednesday	L 1-3	0-2	17	Ferguson 72	35497
41	M 03	CP	A	Arsenal	L 0-4	0-2	18		(38269)
42	10	CP	H	Coventry City	D 1-1	1-0	17	Farrelly 6	40109

Best Home League Attendance: 40112 V Liverpool   Smallest :28533 V Wimbledon   Average :35355

Goal Scorers:

CP	(41)	Ferguson 11, Speed 7, Madar 6, Cadamarteri 4, Barmby 2, Stuart 2, Ball 1, Farrelly 1, Grant 1, Hutchison 1, Oster 1, Thomsen 1, Tiler 1, Opponents 2
CC	(7)	Barmby 3, Cadamarteri 1, Farrelly 1, Oster 1, Stuart 1
FAC	(0)	

(D) Allen	(D) Ball	(F) Barmby	(D) Barrett	(F) Beagrie	(D) Bilic	(F) Cadamarteri	(M) Farrelly	(F) Ferguson	(G) Gerrard	(M) Grant	(D) Hinchcliffe	(F) Hutchison	(F) Madar	(M) McCann	(G) Myhre	(D) O'Kane	(F) Oster	(D) Phelan	(D) Short	(G) Southall	(F) Speed	(F) Stuart	(D) Thomas	(M) Thomsen	(D) Tiler	(M) Ward	(D) Watson	(D) Williamson		
	S2	S	X		X	X	S								X	X	S3		X		X	X	X		X		X		S.W. Dunn	1
		X	X		X	X	X								X		S1		X	S2	X	X	S				X	X	P Jones	2
		X	X		X	S	X	S							X		S3		X	X	X	X	S2				X	X	K W Burge	3
		X			X	S	X	S					S2		X		X		S1	X	X	X					X	X	S J Lodge	4
	S2		X		X	S1	S	X	S	X	S	X			X		X		X	X	X	X						X	M A Riley	5
			X		S1	X	X	X			X			S	X		X		X	S	X	X					X	X	M D Reed	6
S	X	S	X		X	X	S1	X			X				S2		X		X	S	X	X					X	X	G R Ashby	7
S1	X	X	X		X		S2	X		X	X		S3		X		X			S	X	X					X		G Poll	8
X		X	X		X		X	X					S1		X	X		X		S	X	X	S		S		X		A B Wilkie	9
X	S2		X		X		S	X			X				X	S1			X	X	X	X					X		D J Gallagher	10
X	S1	S	X		X		X	X			X				X	X		S	S2	X	X	X					X	X	P A Durkin	11
S1	**X**	**S**	**X**		S2		X	X			X				X		X		X	X	X	X					X	X	S W Dunn	12
S2	S	X			X		X	S			X		S1		X	S			X	X	X	X					X	X	M D Reed	13
	S1	S			X		X	S			X		S		X		X		X	X	X	X					X	X	S J Lodge	14
S		X			X		X				X				X	S1			X	X	X	X					X	X	A B Wilkie	15
		X	X		X	S2	X				X				S1	X			X	X	X	X					S	X	P E Alcock	16
S	X	X	X		X	S3	X				X				S1	X			X	X	X	X					X		U D Rennie	17
S1	X		X		X	S2	X				X				S3	X			X	X	X	X	S		X		X		N S Barry	18
S	X		X		X	S3	X1	X					S2		S1	X2	X3		X	X					X	X	X		P Jones	19
S	X		S		X	S	X				X				X			S	X	X			X		X	X	X		P A Durkin	20
S	X	S2	X		X		X	S			X				S1			X	X	X			X		X2		X	X1	G R Ashby	21
S1	X	X	X		X		X	S			X				X1				X	X		S			X		X		J T Winter	22
S2	X3	X	X2		X		X	S			X				X				X	X		S3	S	X1			X	X1	U D Rennie	23
S	X	S			X	X	X	X			S				X1				X	X	X		X	S1	X		X		K W Burge	24
S	**X**	**X**			X	X	X	S	X		X				S1				X	X	X			X1	X		X		M J Bodenham	25
	X	X			X	S2	S1	X	X	S	X1				S			X	X	X				S3	X		X		G P Barber	26
X	X	X			X	S	S1	X	X	S	X	X1			X			S	X2	X				S2	X		X		A B Wilkie	27
S1	X	X			X	S3	X	X		S	X1				S	S1		S		X	X			X			X	X	M D Reed	28
S	X	X1			X	S2	X	X		S	X2				X	X3	S3		X	X			S1	X		X	X	M J Bodenham	29
S	X				S3	S1	X	X	X		X2				X	X3		X2	X	X	S2			X	X		X		S W Dunn	30
	X				X1	X	X	S			X2	S2			X	S1	S		X	S	X	X		X	X		X		P Jones	31
S2	X				X	X	X	S			X	X1			X	S1			X		X	X		X	X?	S			M A Riley	32
S	X	X			X	X1	X	S			X	X	X	A	X			X		X			X		X		X		D R Elleray	33
S	X	X1			X2	S1	X			X	X	X	S	X	X3			X		X			X		X		X		G S Willard	34
	X	X	S1		S2	X2	X	S			X	X	S	X	X1	X3			X		X			X			X		N S Barry	35
	X	X	S		S	S	X	X			X1	X	X	X	X			X		X			X			X			A B Wilkie	36
	X	X2	X	S		S2	X1	S		X	X	X	S	X	X			X		X				X			X		U D Rennie	37
	X	X3	X2	S		S2	X	S		X	X	X1	X	X	X3			X		X				X			X		K W Burge	38
S	X		X2	S1		S	X	X	X3	X1	X	X	X	X	S3			X		X			X			X			S J Lodge	39
X1	X	X	S1	X		S	X	X	X	S1	X	X	X3	S3	X			X			X3			X	S3				G P Barber	40
	X	X	X1	X2		S2	X	X		X	S1	S	X3	S3	X			X			X			X		X		G R Ashby	41
	X	X	S	S	S1	X2	X	S			X	X1	S2	X	X			X			X			X		X		P E Alcock	42
2	21	26	12	4	22	15	18	28	4	7	15	11	15	5	22	12	16	8	27	12	21	14	6	2	19	8	25	15	CP Appearances	
3	4	4	1	2	2	11	8	1			2		2		6	1	15	1	4				1		6		1		CP Sub Appearances	
	1+1	1+1			3	1+2	1	2	2	1	3						3	0+1	2	1	3	3	1				3	2	CC Appearances	
	1	1				1	1	1		1							0+1					1	1	1					FAC Appearances	

Also Played: (M) Branch S1(1,3), S(2), S3(4,16), X(5), S2(15). (D) Dunne X(24,25,36), S(28,33,34,37), S3(35). (D) Hills S(25). (M) Jeffers S(21,22,24), S1(23). (M) Jevons S(14,22,25,32,33). (M) O'Connor S(8,9,14,15), S2(17). (G) O'Toole S(15,16,17,18). (F) Spencer X(34,35,37), S1(36,38). S2(39).

EVERTON

CLUB RECORDS

BIGGEST VICTORIES
League: 8-0 v Stoke City, Division 1, 2.11.1889.
9-1 v Manchester City, Division 1, 3.9.1906.
9-1 v Plymouth Argyle, Division 2, 27.12.1930.
8-0 v Southampton, Division 1, 20.11.1971.
F.A. Cup: 11-2 v Derby County, 1st Round, 18.1.1890.
League Cup: 8-0 v Wimbledon, 2nd Round, 24.8.1978.
Europe: (UEFA) 5-0 v Finn Harps, 1st Round 1st leg, 12.9.1978.
5-0 v Finn Harps, 1st Round 2nd leg, 26.9.1978.

BIGGEST DEFEATS
League: 0-7 v Sunderland, Division 1, 26.12.1934.
0-7 v Wolverhampton Wndrs., Division 1, 22.2.1939.
0-7 v Portsmouth, Division 1, 10.9.1949.
F.A. Cup: 0-6 v Crystal Palace (h), 1st Round, 7.1.1922.
League Cup: No more than 3 goal difference.
Europe: (UEFA) 0-3 v Ujpest Dozsa, 2nd Round 1st leg, 3.11.1965.

MOST POINTS
3 points a win: 90, Division 1, 1984-85 (Division 1 record)
2 points a win: 66, Division 1, 1969-70.

MOST GOALS SCORED
121, Division 1, 1930-31.
Dean 39, Down 14, Critchley 13, Johnson 13, Stein 11, White 10, Martin 7, Rigby 4, Griffith 3, Gee 2, Wilkinson 2, McPherson 1, McLure 1, Opponents 1.

MOST GOALS CONCEDED
92, Division 1, 1929-30.

MOST FIRST CLASS MATCHES IN A SEASON
63 - 1984-85 (League 42, FA Cup 7, League Cup 4, Charity Shield 1, ECWC 9).
63 - 1985-86 (League 42, FA Cup 7, League Cup 5, Charity Shield 1, Screen Super Cup 8).

MOST LEAGUE WINS
29, Division 1, 1969-70.

MOST LEAGUE DRAWS
18, Division 1, 1925-26, 1971-72, 1974-75.

MOST LEAGUE DEFEATS
22, Division 1, 1950-51, 1993-94.

INDIVIDUAL CLUB RECORDS

MOST GOALS IN A SEASON
William 'Dixie' Dean: 63 goals in 1927-28 (League 60, FAC 3).
Previous holder: B Freeman 38 (1908-09).

MOST GOALS IN A MATCH
6. Jack Southworth v West Bromwich Albion, 7-1, Division 1, 30.12.1893.

OLDEST PLAYER
Ted Sager, 42 years, 1953.

YOUNGEST PLAYER
Joe Royle, 16 years, 1966.

MOST CAPPED PLAYER
Neville Southall (Wales) 85.

BEST PERFORMANCES

League: 1969-70: Matches played 42, Won 29, Drawn 8, Lost 5, Goals for 72, Goals against 34, Points 72. 1st Division 1.
Highest Position: Division 1 Champions nine times.
F.A. Cup: Winners in 1905-06, 1932-33, 1965-66, 1983-84.
Most Recent success: 1994-95: 3rd Round Derby County 1-0; 4th Round Bristol City 1-0; 5th Round Norwich City 5-0; 6th Round Newcastle United 1-0; Semi-Final Tottenham Hotspur 4-1; Final Manchester United 1-0.
League Cup: 1976-77: 2nd Round Cambridge United 3-0; 3rd Round Stockport County 1-0; 4th Round Coventry City 3-0; 5th Round Manchester United 3-0; Semi-Final Bolton Wanderers 1-1,1-0; Final Aston Villa 1-1,2-3.
Europe: (ECWC) 1984-85: 1st Round University of Dublin 0-0,1-0; 2nd Round Inter Bratislav 1-0,3-0; 3rd Round Fortuna S 3-0,2-0; Semi-Final Bayern Munich 0-0,3-1; Final Rapid Vienna 3-1.

ADDITIONAL INFORMATION
Previous Names
None.
Previous Leagues
None.

Club colours: Blue & white trim shirts, white shorts, blue socks.
Change colours:

Reserves League: Pontins Central League Premier Division.

DIVISIONAL RECORD

	Played	Won	Drawn	Lost	For	Against	Points
Division 1/P	3,720	1,534	907	1,279	5,958	5,270	4,256
Division 2	168	77	45	46	348	257	199
Total	3,888	1,611	952	1,325	6,306	5,527	4,455

RECORDS AND STATISTICS

COMPETITIONS

Div 1/P	Div.2	Euro C	ECWC	UEFA	Texaco
1888-30	1930-31	1963-64	1966-67	1962-63	1973-74
1931-51	1951-54	1970-71	1984-85	1964-65	
1954-			1995-96	1965-66	
				1975-76	
				1978-79	
				1979-80	

HONOURS

Div 1/P	Div.2	FA Cup	ECWC	C/Sh'ld
1890-91	1930-31	1906	1984-85	1928
1914-15		1933		1932
1927-28		1966		1963
1931-32		1984		1970
1938-39		1995		1984
1962-63				1985
1969-70				1986
1984-85				1987
1986-87				

MOST APPEARANCES

NEVILLE SOUTHALL 736 (1981-97)

Year	League	FA Cup	Lge Cup	Europe	FMC	CT	CS
1981-82	26	1					
1982-83	17		2	-	-	-	-
1983-84	35	8	11	-	-	-	-
1984-85	42	7	4	9	-	-	1
1985-86	32	5	5		6	-	1
1986-87	31	3	3	-	2	-	-
1987-88	32	8	7		1		
1988-89	38	8	5	-	3	1	-
1989-90	38	7	4				
1990-91	38	6	3	-	6	-	-
1991-92	42	2	4	-	2	-	-
1992-93	40	1	6	-	-	-	-
1993-94	42	2	3	-	-	-	-
1994-95	41	6	2	-	-	-	-
1995-96	38	4	2	4	-	-	1
1996-97	34	2	2	-	-	-	-
Totoals	566	70	63	13	20	1	3

MOST GOALS IN A CAREER

WILLIAM DEAN - 377 (1924-38)

Year	League	FA Cup
1924-25	2	
1925-26	32	1
1926-27	21	3
1927-28	60	3
1928-29	26	
1929-30	23	2
1930-31	39	9
1931-32	45	1
1932-33	24	5
1933-34	9	
1934-35	26	1
1935-36	17	
1936-37	24	3
1937-38	1	
Total	349	28

Current leading goalscorer: Duncan Ferguson - 38 (10.94-98)

RECORD TRANSFER FEE RECEIVED

Amount	Club	Player	Date
£8,000,000	Fiorentina	Andrei Kanchelskis	01/97
£2,800,000	Barcelona	Gary Lineker	6/86
£2,500,000	Arsenal	Martin Keown	1/93
£1,500,000	Glasgow Rangers	Trevor Steven	6/89

MANAGERS

Name	Seasons	Best	Worst
Theo Kelly	1939-48	1(1)	14 (1)
Cliff Britton	1948-56	11 (1)	16 (2)
Ian Buchan	1956-58	15 (1)	16 (1)
John Carey	1958-61	5 (1)	16 (1)
Harry Catterick	1961-73	1 (1)	17 (1)
Billy Bingham	1973-77	4 (1)	11(1)
Steve Burtenshaw	1977		
Gordon Lee	1977-81	3 (1)	19 (1)
Howard Kendall	1981-87	1 (1)	8 (1)
Colin Harvey	1987-90	4 (1)	8 (1)
Howard Kendall	1990-94	9 (1)	13 (1/P)
Mike Walker	1994	22 (P)	22 (P)
Joe Royle	1994-97	6 (P)	15 (P)
Howard Kendall	1997-98	17 (P)	17 (P)
Walter Smith	1998-		

RECORD TRANSFER FEE PAID

Amount	Club	Player	Date
£5,750,000	Middlesbrough	Nick Barmby	11/97
£5,000,000	Manchester Utd	Andrei Kanchelskis	8/95
£4,000,000	Glasgow Rangers	Duncan Ferguson	12/94
£3,500,000	Leeds Utd	Gary Speed	7/96

LONGEST LEAGUE RUNS

of undefeated matches:	20 (29.4.1978 - 16.12.1978)	of league matches w/out a win:	14 (6.3.1937 - 4.9.1937)
of undefeated home matches:	39 (6.9.1961 - 7.9.1963)	of undefeated away matches:	11 (21.4.1908 - 27.9.1909)
without home win:	12 (14.9.1957 - 22.3.1958)	without an away win:	35 (19.9.1970 - 8.4.1972)
of league wins:	12 (27.3.1894 - 6.10.1894)	of home wins:	15 (4.10.1930 - 4.4.1931)
of league defeats: 6 (5.3.30-12.4.30, 29.3.58-19.4.58, 4.11.72-9.12.72, 26.12.96-29.1.97)		of away wins:	6 (2.9.1908 - 14.11.1908)

PLAYERS NAME / Honours	Ht	Wt	Birthdate	Birthplace / Transfers	Contract Date	Clubs	League	L/Cup	FA Cup	Other	Lge	L/C	FAC	Oth
G O A L K E E P E R														
Delany Dean			15/09/80	Dublin		Everton								
Gerrard Paul W	6.2	13.1	22/01/73	Heywood	02/11/91	Oldham Athletic	118+1	7	7	1				
E: u21.18.				£1500000	02/08/96	Everton	8+1	2						
Myhre Thomas	6.4	13.12	16/10/73	Sarpsborg, Norway		Viking Stavanger								
Norway Int.				£800000	28/11/97	Everton	22		1					
D E F E N C E														
Ball Michael	5.10	11.2	02/10/79	Liverpool	17/10/96	Everton (T)	23+7	1+1	1		1			
E: Y.														
Bilic Slaven	6.2	13.8	11/09/68	Croatia		Karlsruhe								
Croatian Int. (3rd in WC'98)				£1300000	04/02/96	West Ham United	48	5	1		2	1		
				£4500000	16/07/97	Everton	22+2	3						
Dunne Richard	6.2	15	21/09/79	Dublin	08/10/96	Everton (T)	8+2		2					
Ei: Y.S.														
Eaton Adam P			02/05/80	Wigan	02/06/97	Everton (T)								
Farley Adam J			12/01/80	Liverpool		Everton (T)								
Materazzi Marco				Italy		Perugia								
				£2800000	15/07/98	Everton								
O'Kane John A	5.1	11.5	15/11/74	Nottingham	29/01/93	Manchester United	0+1	2+1	1	1				
FAYC'92. Div.2'97.				Loan	25/10/96	Bury	2+2				2			
				Loan	16/01/97	Bury Town	9		1		1			
				£250000	30/01/98	Everton	12							
Phelan Terry	5.8	10	16/03/67	Manchester	03/08/84	Leeds United	12+2	3		2				
Ei:37,B.2,u23.1,u21.1,Y. FAC'88.				Free	30/07/86	Swansea City	45	4	5	3				
				£100000	29/07/87	Wimbledon	155+4	13+2	16	8	1		2	
				£2500000	25/08/92	Manchester City	93+1	10	8	1			1	
				£900000	15/11/95	Chelsea	13+2		8					
				£850000	01/01/97	Everton	23+1	0+1	1					
Regan Carl A			09/09/80	Liverpool	01/07/97	Everton (T)								
Short Craig J	6	11.4	25/06/68	Bridlington		Pickering								
E: S.				Free	15/10/87	Scarborough	61+2	6	2	7	7			1
				£100000	27/07/89	Notts County	128	6	8	16	6	1	1	2
				£2500000	18/09/92	Derby County	118	11	7	7	9		4	
				£2400000	18/07/95	Everton	68+9	5	4	3	4			
Thomas Tony	5.11	12.5	12/07/71	Liverpool	01/02/89	Tranmere Rovers	254+3	23+1	7	26	12	1		1
LDC'90				£400000	01/08/97	Everton	6+1	1	1					
Tiler Carl	6.4	13	11/01/70	Sheffield	02/08/88	Barnsley	67+4	4	4+1	3+1	3			
E: u21.13.				£1400000	30/05/91	Nottingham Forest	67+2	10+1	6	1	1			
				Loan	18/11/94	Swindon Town	2							
				£750000	28/10/95	Aston Villa	10+1	1	2		1			
					27/03/97	Sheffield United	23	5		3	2			
				Swap	28/11/97	Everton	19		1		1			
Unsworth David G	6	13	16/10/73	Chorley	25/06/92	Everton	108+8	5+2	7	4	11			1
E:1, u21.7, y.14. FAC'95.				£1000000	18/08/97	West Ham United	32	5	4		2			
				£3000000	23/07/98	Aston Villa								
				£3000000	31/07/98	Everton								
Watson David	5.11	11.12	20/11/61	Liverpool	25/05/79	Liverpool								
E:12,u21.7. UEFAu21'84. LC'85.				£100000	29/11/80	Norwich City	212	21	18		11	3	1	
Div2'86.Div1'87.CS'87'95FAC'95				£900000	22/08/86	Everton	392+3	38	44	16+1	23	6	5	3
M I D F I E L D														
Allen Graham	6.1	12	08/04/77	Bolton	01/08/94	Everton	2+4							
John Collins	5.7	10.7	31/01/68	Galashiels, Scotland		Hibernian								
S:52. SFAC'95. French Championship'97.						Celtic								
						Monaco								
				£2500000	27/07/98	Everton								
Dacourt Oliver				Strasborg										
				£3800000	27/07/98	Everton								
Dempsey Gary W			15/01/81	Wexford		Everton (T)								
Farrelly Gareth	6	12.07	28/08/75	Dublin		Home Farm								
Ei:5,B.1, u21.8, Y, S.					21/09/92	Aston Villa	2+6	0+1						
				Loan	21/03/95	Rotherham United	9+1				2			
				£700000	09/07/97	Everton	18+8	1	1		1	1		
Grant Anthony J	5.1	10.2	14/11/74	Liverpool	08/07/93	Everton	30+13	4	1+3	2+2	2			1
CS'95.				Loan	18/01/96	Swindon Town	3				1			
Hutchison Don	6.2	11.08	09/05/71	Gateshead	20/03/90	Hartlepool United	19+5	1+1	2	1	3			
S: B.1				£175000	27/11/90	Liverpool	33+12	7+1	1+2	3+1	7	2		1
				£1500000	30/08/94	West Ham United	22+1	3	0+1		9	2		

Name	Ht	Wt	DOB	From / Fee	Date	Club	App	FAC	LC	Oth	Gls			
Hutchinson continued....				£1200000	11/01/96	Sheffield United	70+8	3+2	5	2+1	5		1	
				£5000000	26/02/98	Everton	11				1			
Jevons Phillip			01/08/79	Liverpool	31/05/97	Everton (T)								
McCann Gavin P	5.11	11	10/01/78	Blackpool	11/05/97	Everton (T)	5+6							
McKay Matthew P	6	12	21/01/81	Warrington		Chester City (T)	3+2							
				£500000	27/03/98	Everton								
O'Brien Michael G			25/09/80	Liverpool		Everton (T)								
Parkinson Joseph S	5.8	12.2	11/06/71	Eccles	01/04/89	Wigan Athletic	115+4	11	9	8	6	1		
FAC'95. CS'95.				£35000	01/07/93	Bournemouth	30	4	4	1	1	1		
				£250000	24/03/94	Everton	88+2	5	9	3	3		1	
Poppleton David J			19/12/79	Doncaster	04/07/97	Everton (T)								
Ward Mitchum	5.8	10.7	19/06/71	Sheffield	01/07/89	Sheffield United	135+19	8+3	7+2	5+1	11	2	2	1
				Loan	01/11/90	Crewe Alexandra	4		1	2	1		1	
				Swap	28/11/97	Everton	8							
Williamson Daniel	5.11	12.3	05/12/73	Newham	03/07/92	West Ham United	47+4	0+2	5		5			
				Loan	04/02/93	Farnborough								
				Loan	08/10/93	Doncaster Rovers	10+3		2	1	1		2	
				Swap	18/08/97	Everton	15	2						

F O R W A R D

Name	Ht	Wt	DOB	From / Fee	Date	Club	App	FAC	LC	Oth	Gls			
Barmby Nick	5.6	11	11/02/74	Hull	09/04/91	Tottenham Hotspur	81+6	7+1	12+1		20	2	5	
E: 10, B.2, u23.3. Y.8,S.				£5250000	08/08/95	Middlesbrough	42	4	3		8	1	1	
					02/11/96	Everton	48+7	1+1	3		6	3	1	
Branch Michael	5.10	11.7	18/10/78	Liverpool	24/10/95	Everton (T)	15+18		1		3			
E: u21.2.														
Cadamarteri Daniel	5.7	11.2	12/10/79	Bradford	15/10/96	Everton (T)	15+12	1+2	1		4	1		
Ferguson Duncan	6.4	14.6	27/12/71	Stirling	01/02/90	Dundee United	75+2	2+1	8		28	2	6	
S:7, B, u21.7. SL'94. SLC'94.FAC'95.				£4000000	20/07/93	Glasgow Rangers	35	1+1	0+3	1	5			
				£4400000	04/10/94	Everton	98+6	4	8+1		34		4	
Jeffers Francis	5.10	10.7	25/01/81	Liverpool	01/07/97	Everton (T)	0+1							
E: Y.														
Madar Mickael	6.1	12.6	08/05/68	Paris		Dep La Coruna								
				Free	31/12/97	Everton	15+2				5			
Milligan Jamie			03/01/80	Blackpool	13/06/97	Everton (T)								
Oster John	5.9	10.8	08/12/78	Boston	11/07/96	Grimsby Town	21+3		0+1		3		1	
W: u21.4, Y.				£1500000	21/07/97	Everton	16+15	3	0+1		1	1		
Spencer John	5.7	9.1	11/09/70	Glasgow		Glasgow Rangers	7+6	?		1+1	2			1
S:14 u21 3, Y				Loan	04/03/89	Grennock Morton	4				1			
				£450000	01/08/92	Chelsea	75+28	5+4	16+4	4+1	36	2	4	1
				£2500000	22/11/96	Q.P.R.	47+1	1	6		22		2	
				Loan	27/03/98	Everton	3+3							
						Everton								

THE MANAGER
WALTER SMITH

Date of Birth . . . .
Place of Birth . . . .
Date of Appointment . . . . June 1998.

PREVIOUS CLUBS
As Manager . . . . Glasgow Rangers.
As Coach . . . . Dundee United.
As a Player . . . . Glasgow Rangers.

HONOURS
As a Manager
Glasgow Rangers: Scottish League Championship. Scottish Cup, Scottish League Cup.

As a Player

GOODISON PARK
Liverpool L4 4EL

Capacity ....40,200.
First game..v Bolton Wanderers, Division 1, 2.9.1892.
First floodlit game ....v Liverpool, 9.10.1957.
ATTENDANCES
Highest ....78,299 v Liverpool, Division 1, 18.9.1948.
Lowest...2,079 v WBA, 23.2.1899.
Internationals ....England v Scotland 1895, 1911.v Ireland 1907, 1924, 1928, 1935, 1947, 1953, 1973.
....v Eire 1949, v Portugal 1951, Poland 1966.
..Brazil v Bulgaria 1966, v Hungary 1966, Portugal 1966. Portugal v North Korea 1966. W.Germany v Russia 1966.
....Ireland v Wales 1973.

OTHER GROUNDS ....Stanley Park 1878-82, Priory Road 1882-84,
....Anfield Road 1884-92, Goodison Park 1892-

HOW TO GET TO THE GROUND

From the North
Use motorway M6 until junction 28 then follow signs Liverpool on A58 then A580 and forward into Walton Hall Avenue for Everton FC.

From the East, and South
Use motorway M6 then M62 until end of motorway then turn right A5058 into Queens Drive. In 3.7 miles turn left A580 into Walton Hall Avenue for Everton FC.

From the West
Use Mersey Tunnel into Liverpool City Centre, then follow signs to Preston (A580) into Walton Hall Avenue for Everton FC.

Car Parking
Extensive parking is available on site at the corner of Prior and Utting Avenue.

Nearest Railway Station
Liverpool (Lime Street) 0151 709 9696.

HOW TO GET TO THE GROUND

Club switchboard 0151 330 2200	Marketing Department....... 0151 330 2400
Club fax number 0151 286 9112	Internet address .... www.evertonfc.com
Club shop 0151 330 2333	Clubcall 0891 12 11 99*
Ticket Office. . 0151 330 2300 (Fax 286 9119)	*Calls cost 50p per minute at all times. Call costings correct at time of going to press.

MATCHDAY PROGRAMME

Programme Editor............ F Tobin.

Number of pages .... 48.

Price .... £1.70.

Subscriptions
.... £58 UK. (For overseas apply to club).

Local Newspapers
..... Liverpool Daily Post, Liverpool Echo.

Local Radio Stations
.... Radio Merseyside, Radio City.

MATCHDAY TICKET PRICES

	Adults	Juv.	Sen.Cit
Main Stand	£18	-	-
Upper Bullens	£17	-	-
Park End Stand	£16	-	-
Top Balcony	£15	£7	-
Family Enclosure	£15	£7	£9
Paddock	£15	-	-
Lower Bullens	£15	£7	£9
Gwladys Stand	£15	-	£9
Gwladys Terrace Seating	£13	£7	-
Visitors			
Upper Bullens	£17	-	-
Lower Bullens	£15	£10	£10

LEEDS UNITED
(The Whites)
F.A. CARLING PREMIERSHIP
SPONSORED BY: PACKARD BELL

Unfortunately Leeds United were unable to supply us with a team photograph for this year's publication

LEEDS UNITED
FORMED IN 1919 (As United)
TURNED PROFESSIONAL IN 1919
LTD COMPANY IN 1920
PRESIDENT: Rt Hon Earl of Harewood
CHAIRMAN: Peter Risdale
VICE-CHAIRMAN: P J Gilman
DIRECTORS
Jeremy Fenn (managing)
Rayner Barker MCIT, MBIM,
William Fotherby, Alec Hudson,
Jack Marjason, Peter McCormick,
Leslie Silver OBE
SECRETARY
Nigel Pleasants (01132 2266000)
COMMERCIAL MANAGER
K Hanvey (01132 266124)
MANAGER: George Graham
ASSISTANT MANAGER: David O'Leary
COACHES
Eddie Gray, David Williams, John Dungworth
YOUTH DEVELOPMENT OFFICER
John Bilton
PHYSIOTHERAPIST
D Swift

STATISTICIAN FOR THE DIRECTORY
Mark Evans

After the successful fight against relegation the previous season, 1997/98 was looked on with more optimism.

Indeed, manager George Graham was extremely busy in the close season, signing no fewer than five players - defender, David Robertson, midfielders Bruno Riberio, David Hopkin and Alfie Haaland, and striker, the flamboyantly named, Jimmy Floyd-Hasselbaink. To make-way for the newcomers, the manager sold, Yeboah, Deane, Rush, Dorigo, Palmer and cancelled the contract of Swedish "wonder boy" Tomas Brolin.

Unfortunately, in pre-season Lee Sharpe suffered a cruciate ligament injury which resulted in him missing the whole season. But the side began the season in a more adventurous fashion, and soon began to settle down, indeed from November 4th, after coming back from 0-3 down to defeat Derby County 4-3, they maintained a position around the UEFA Cup qualifying positions.

The Coca-Cola Cup brought about a disappointing defeat to Reading in Round 4, while the FA Cup brought an even bigger disappointment at the hands of Wolves in Round 6, at Elland Road.

The Carling Premiership though brought about a vast improvement, including two four goal victories over Blackburn Rovers, and as well as the above victory over Derby, the side produced an exhilarating performance in the 5-0 win at Pride PArk. After a draw with Wimbledon on the last day of the season, a final position of fifth was attained, and European football will return to Elland Road once again.

Of the new boys, Jimmy Hasselbaink finished the season with 22 goals and a place in the Dutch World Cup squad, Alfie Haaland got better with each game and Bruno Riberio, bought as a squad player, but went straight into the side and produced many consistent performances. But perhaps the most pleasing feature was the introduction of some members of the clubs successful youth set-up, notably Lee Matthews and Stephen McPhail, but the player to make the biggest impact was young Australian, Harry Kewell. Surely a player with a big future in the game.

George Graham will have set-out his plans for success and the club has witnessed a remarkable change around in his time at the club, and the supporters can now genuinely believe that with a little more quality and George at the helm, the good days will return.

On a sad note the 1997/98 season saw the passing away of one of Leeds United's favourite sons: Billy Bremner. With him he takes many wonderful memories.

Mark Evans

LEEDS UNITED

Carling Prem.   :5th   FA CUP: 6th Round   LC CUP: 4th Round

M	DATE	COMP.	VEN	OPPONENTS	RESULT	H/T	LP	GOAL SCORERS/GOAL TIMES	ATT.
1	A 09	CP	H	Arsenal	D 1-1	1-1	8	Hasselbank 42	37993
2	12	CP	A	Sheffield Wednesday	W 3-1	2-0	5	Wallace 7, 62, Ribeiro 36	(31520)
3	23	CP	H	Crystal Palace	L 0-2	0-1	9		29076
4	26	CP	H	Liverpool	L 0-2	0-1	11		39775
5	30	CP	A	Aston Villa	L 0-1	0-0	14		(39027)
6	S 14	CP	A	Blackburn Rovers	W 4-3	4-3	9	Wallace 3, 17, Molenaar 6, Hopkin 23	(21956)
7	17	CC 2/1	H	Bristol City	W 3-1	1-0		Wetherall 20, Hasselbank 70 (pen), Ribeiro 90	8806
8	20	CP	H	Leicester City	L 0-1	0-1	14		29620
9	24	CP	A	Southampton	W 2-0	1-0	8	Molenaar 36, Wallace 55	(15102)
10	27	CP	H	Manchester United	W 1-0	1-0	6	Wetherall 34	39952
11	30	CC 2/2	A	Bristol City	L 1-2	1-1		Hasselbank 8	(10857)
12	O 04	CP	A	Coventry City	D 0-0	0-0	7		(17770)
13	15	CC 3	A	Stoke City	W 3-1	0-0		Kewell 69, Wallace 93, 105	(16203)
14	18	CP	H	Newcastle United	W 4-1	3-0	6	Ribeiro 30, Kewell 38, Wetherall 47, Beresford 43 (OG)	39834
15	25	CP	A	Wimbledon	L 0-1	0-1	8		(15718)
16	N 01	CP	A	Tottenham Hotspur	W 1-0	1-0	7	Wallace 19	(26441)
17	08	CP	H	Derby County	W 4-3	2-3	4	Wallace 37, Kewell 40, Hasselbank 82 (pen), Bowyer 90	33572
18	18	CC 4	H	Reading	L 2-3	1-1		Wetherall 16, Bowyer 54	15069
19	23	CP	A	West Ham United	W 3-1	0-0	4	Hasselbank 76, 90, Haaland 88	30031
20	29	CP	A	Barnsley	W 3-2	1-2	4	Haaland 35, Wallace 72, Lilley 82	(18690)
21	D 06	CP	H	Everton	D 0-0	0-0	5		34869
22	13	CP	A	Chelsea	D 0-0	0-0	4		(34690)
23	20	CP	H	Bolton Wanderers	W 2-0	0-0	4	Ribeiro 68, Hasselbank 81	31163
24	26	CP	A	Liverpool	L 1-3	0-0	5	Haaland 85	(43854)
25	28	CP	H	Aston Villa	D 1-1	0-0	5	Hasselbank 79	36287
26	J 03	FAC 3	H	Oxford United	W 4-0	2-0		Radebe 17, Hasselbank 45 (pen), Kewell 71, 72	20568
27	10	CP	A	Arsenal	L 1-2	0-0	6	Hasselbank 69	(38018)
28	17	CP	H	Sheffield Wednesday	L 1-2	0-0	7	, Pembridge 63 (OG)	33166
29	24	FAC 4	H	Grimsby Town	W 2-0	1-0		Molenaar 45, Hasselbank 79	29598
30	31	CP	A	Crystal Palace	W 2-0	2-0	7	Wallace 7, Hasselbank 13	(25248)
31	F 06	CP	A	Leicester City	L 0-1	0-1	7		(21244)
32	14	FAC 5	H	Birmingham City	W 3-2	2-0		Wallace 5, Hasselbank 28, 87	35463
33	22	CP	A	Newcastle United	D 1-1	0-0	7	Wallace 83	(36511)
34	28	CP	H	Southampton	L 0-1	0-0	7		28791
35	M 04	CP	H	Tottenham Hotspur	W 1-0	1-0	7	Kewell 45	31394
36	07	FAC QF	H	Wolverhampton Wand	L 0-1	0-0			39902
37	11	CP	H	Blackburn Rovers	W 4-0	0-0	7	Bowyer 48, Hasselbank 53, Haaland 56, 89	32933
38	15	CP	A	Derby County	W 5-0	3-0	6	Halle 32, Bowyer 42, Kewell 60, Hasselbank 72, Laursen 8 (OG)	(30217)
39	30	CP	A	West Ham United	L 0-3	0-2	6		(24107)
40	A 04	CP	H	Barnsley	W 2-1	1-1	5	Hasselbank 20, Moses 80 (OG)	37749
41	08	CP	H	Chelsea	W 3-1	2-1	4	Hasselbank 7, 47, Wetherall 22	37276
42	11	CP	A	Everton	L 0-2	0-2	5		(37099)
43	18	CP	A	Bolton Wanderers	W 3-2	2-0	4	Haaland 17, Halle 34, Hasselbank 86	(25000)
44	25	CP	H	Coventry City	D 3-3	2-2	5	Hasselbank 16, 28, Kewell 75	36522
45	M 04	CP	A	Manchester United	L 0-3	0-2	5		(55167)
46	10	CP	H	Wimbledon	D 1-1	0-0	5	Haaland 82	38172

Best Home League Attendance: 39952 V Manchester United   Smallest :28791 V Southampton   Average :34641

Goal Scorers:

CP	(57)	Hasselbank 16, Wallace 10, Haaland 7, Kewell 5, Bowyer 3, Ribeiro 3, Wetherall 3, Halle 2, Molenaar 2, Hopkin 1, Lilley 1, Opponents 4
CC	(9)	Hasselbank 2, Wallace 2, Wetherall 2, Bowyer 1, Kewell 1, Ribeiro 1
FAC	(9)	Hasselbank 4, Kewell 2, Molenaar 1, Radebe 1, Wallace 1

(G) Beeney	(M) Bowyer	(F) Gray	(M) Haaland	(D) Halle	(D) Harte	(F) Hasselbank	(F) Hiden	(M) Hopkin	(D) Jackson	(M) Jones	(D) Kelly	(F) Kewell	(F) Laurent	(F) Lilley	(G) Martyn	(M) Matthews	(D) Maybury	(M) McPhail	(D) Molenaar	(D) Radebe	(F) Ribeiro	(M) Robertson	(M) Robinson	(F) Shepherd	(F) Wallace	(D) Wetherall		
S	X		S2	X		X		X			X	S1		S	X				S	X	X	X			X	X	D.J. Gallagher	1
S	X		S2	X		X		X			X	S	S	S1	X				X		X	X			X	X	P A Durkin	2
S	X		S2	X		X		X			X	S3		S	X				X	S1	X	X			X	X	U D Rennie	3
S	S		X	X		X		X			X	S		S	X				X	X	X	X			X	S	A B Wilkie	4
S	S		X	S1		X		X			X	X		S2	X				S	X	X	X			X	X	P Jones	5
S	S		S	X		X		X			X	X		S2	X				X	X	S1	X			X	X	S W Dunn	6
S			S	X	X	X		X			X	X			X				X	X	S1	X			X	X	G Poll	7
S	X		X	X	S	X			X	S1		S3	X				S2	X	X	X			X	X		X	K W Burge	8
S	S1		X	X	S	S		X			X	X		S	X				X		X				X	X	S J Lodge	9
S	S		X	X		S		X			X	X		S	X				S1	X	X	X			X	X	M J Bodenham	10
S	X		X	S1		X		X			X			S2	X				X	X		X			X	X	N S Barry	11
S	S	S	X	X	S	X		X			X			S1	X				X		X				X	X	A B Wilkie	12
	S2	X	X			X		X	X	S1	X		S	X	X	X				X	X				X	X	P Jones	13
S	S1	X	X	S		X		X	X	S	X		S	X				X		X	X				X	X	D R Elleray	14
S	X	X	X			X	S		X	S2	X	S1	S	X	X	X				X	X				X	X	G P Barber	15
S	S		S	S		X		X	X	X			X	X	S				X	X				X	X		K W Burge	16
S	S1		X	S2		X	X	X			X	S	S	X	X				X	X				X	X		N S Barry	17
	X	S	X	X				X			S2	X		X	S1	X	X	X				X	X				G P Barber	18
	X	X	S	X		X				S	X	S	S	X	X	X	X	S				X	X				G R Ashby	19
S	X	X	X		X		S	S3	X	S1	S2	X	X	X				X	X				X	X				M D Reed	20
S	X1	X	X	S1		X	X		S	X	S	X	X	X				X	X				X	X				P A Durkin	21
S	S	X	X	X1		X	S1	X	S	S	X	X	X				X	X				X	X					G Poll	22
S	S1	X	X	X1		X	S	S	X	S	X	X	X				X	X				X	X					A B Wilkie	23
S	S	X	X	X	X	S	S	X	X	X	X	X				X	X				X	X						S J Lodge	24
S	X	S	X	S	X	S1	X	S	X	X	X1	X	X	X				X	X								D J Gallagher	25
S3	X3	S	X	S2	X2	S	X	X	S1	X	X	X	S	X	X	X	X1	X									M D Reed	26
S	X2	X1	X	S	S2	X	X	S3	X	S1	X	X	X3	X													G R Ashby	27
X	S	S2	X	X	X	X	S3	X1	X2	X	X3	X	S	S1	X												M J Bodenham	28
S	X	X	X	S	X	X	S	X	S	X	X	X	X	X													G P Barber	29
S	S	S1	S	X2	X	X	X	S2	X1	X	X	X	X1	X													U D Rennie	30
S	S	X	X	X	X	X	S	S1	S2	X2	X	X1	X														N S Barry	31
S	X	X	X	S1	X	X	X	S	X1	X	S	X	X	S	X	X											D J Gallagher	32
S	X	X	S	S	X	X	X	S1	X	S	A	X	X														G S Willard	33
S	A	X	X	X	X	S	S	X	S1	X1	S	X	A	X													K W Burge	34
S	X	X	X1	X	X	S	S	X	S1	X	S2	X	X2														P E Alcock	35
S	X	X	X	X	X	S	S1	X	X	X	X1	X	S														P A Durkin	36
S	X	S	X	X	X	S	X	X1	X	S	S	X	S														D R Elleray	37
S	X	X	X	X	X	S	X	X1	X	S	S1	X	X	S													S J Lodge	38
S	X1	X	X	X	X	X	X	S	X1	X	S1	X	S1														A B Wilkie	39
S	X	X	X	X	S	X	X	S	S1	X	X1	S															K W Burge	40
S	X	S1	X	X	X	S	X	X	S	X1	X	X															D R Elleray	41
X	S1	X	X	X	X	S	X2	S2	X1	X1	S	S	X														U D Rennie	42
S	X	X	X	X	X	S	S	X	X	S	S	X	S	X													J T Winter	43
S	X	X	X2	X	X	S1	X	X	S	S	S2	X1	X														M D Reed	44
S	X	X	X2	X	X1	S1	S	X	X	S	X	S2	S	X	X												G S Willard	45
S	X	X	X	X	S1	S3	X	X1	S2	X	X3	S	X2	X													S W Dunn	46
1	21		26	31	12	30	11	22			34	26			37		9		18	26	26	24			29	33	CP Appearances	
	4	6	2		3		3	1				3		13		3	3	4	4	1	1	2			2	1	CP Sub Appearances	
2+1		3	2+1		3		4				3	2		0+3	4		1		2+1	4	2+1	4			4	4	CC Appearances	
0+1	3		2	3	1+2	4	1	1			3+1	4		0+1	4		2		3	2	3	1			4	3	FAC Appearances	

LEEDS UNITED

CLUB RECORDS

BIGGEST VICTORIES:
League: 8-0 v Leicester City, Division 1, 7.4.1934.
F.A. Cup: 8-1 v Crystal Palace, 3rd Round, 11.1.1930.
7-0 v Leeds Steelworks, Preliminary Round, 25.9.1920.
League Cup: 5-1 v Mansfield Town, 2nd Round, 26.9.1963.
4-0 v Chesterfield, 2nd Round, 23.11.1960.
4-0 v Burnley, 2nd Round, 6.9.1972.
4-0 v Colchester, 3rd Round, 26.11.1977.
4-0 v York City, 2nd Round, 6.10.1987.
Europe: 10-0 v Lyn Oslo, European Cup 1st Round 1st leg, 17.9.1969.

BIGGEST DEFEATS
League: 1-8 v Stoke City, Division 1, 27.8.1934.
F.A. Cup: 2-7 v Middlesbrough, 3rd Round 2nd leg, 4.9.1979.
League Cup: 0-7 v Arsenal, 2nd Round 2nd leg, 4.9.1979.
0-7 v West Ham United, 4th Round, 7.11.1966.
Europe: 0-4 v Lierse, 1st Round, 2nd leg UEFA, 29.9.1971.

MOST POINTS
3 points a win: 85, Division 2, 1989-90.
2 points a win: 67, Division 1, 1968-69.

MOST GOALS SCORED
98, Division 2, 1927-28.
Jennings 21, White 21, Keetley 18, Wainscoat 18, Mitchell 8, Turnbull 8, Armand 2, Hart 1, Townsley 1.

MOST GOALS CONCEDED
92, Division 1, 1959-60.

MOST FIRST CLASS MATCHES IN A SEASON
66- 1967-68 (League 42, FA Cup 5, League Cup 7, UEFA 12).

MOST LEAGUE WINS
27, Division 1, 1968-69, Division 1, 1970-71.

MOST LEAGUE DRAWS
21, Division 2, 1982-83.

MOST LEAGUE DEFEATS
30, Division 1, 1946-47.

INDIVIDUAL CLUB RECORDS

MOST GOALS IN A SEASON
John Charles: 43 goals in 1953-54 (League 42, FA Cup 1).

MOST GOALS IN A MATCH
5. Gordon Hodgson v Leicester City, 8-2, Division 1, 1.10.1938.

OLDEST PLAYER
Peter Lorimer, 38 years 317 days v Barnsley, 27.10.1985.

YOUNGEST PLAYER
Peter Lorimer, 15 years 289 days v Southampton, 29.9.1962.

MOST CAPPED PLAYER
Billy Bremmner (Scotland) 54.

BEST PERFORMANCES

League: 1968-69: Matches played 42, Won 27, Drawn 13, Lost 2, Goals for 66, Goals against 27, Points 67, 1st in Division 1.
Highest Position: Division 1 Champions 1968-69, 1973-74, 1991-92.
F.A. Cup: 1971-72: 3rd Round Bristol Rovers 4-1; 4th Round Liverpool 0-0,2-0; 5th Round Cardiff City 2-0; 6th Round Tottenham Hotspur 2-1; Semi-Final Birmingham City 3-0; Final Arsenal 1-0.
League Cup: 1967-68: 2nd Round Luton 3-1; 3rd Round Bury 3-0; 4th Round Sunderland 2-0; 5th Round Stoke City 2-0; Semi-Final Derby County 1-0, 3-2; Final Arsenal 1-0.
Europe: UEFA Cup winners in 1967-68.
Most recent success: 1970-71: 1st Round Sarpsborg 1-0,5-0; 2nd Round Dynamo Dresden 1-0,1-2; 3rd Round Sparta Prague 6-0,3-2; 4th Round Vitoria Setubul 2-1,1-1; Semi-Final Liverpool 1-0,0-0; Final Juventus 2-2,1-1 (Leeds won on away goals).

ADDITIONAL INFORMATION
PREVIOUS NAMES
Leeds United were formed in October 1919 after Leeds City (formed 1904) had been suspended 'sine die' by the F.A. earlier that same month.

PREVIOUS LEAGUES
Leeds City: West Yorkshire League 1904-05 prior to becoming a Football League club.
Leeds United: Gained admission to the Midland League in November 1919 and the first team competed in this League prior to gaining Football League status in the summer of 1920.

DIVISIONAL RECORD

	Played	Won	Drawn	Lost	For	Against	Points
Division 1/P	1,832	747	470	615	2,744	2,491	2,105
Division 2	1,144	483	309	1,731	1,731	1,451	1,369
Total	3,256	1,230	779	967	4,475	3,942	3,474

Club colours: All white with blue & yellow trim.

Change colours: All yellow with blue & white trim.

Reserves League: Pontins Central League Division 1.

RECORDS AND STATISTICS

COMPETITIONS

Div 1/P	Div.2	Euro C	ECWC	UEFA
1924-27	1920-24	1969-70	1972-73	1965-66
1928-31	1927-28	1974-75		1966-67
1932-47	1931-32	1992-93		1967-68
1956-60	1947-56			1968-69
1964-82	1960-64			1970-71
1990-				1971-72
				1973-74
				1979-80
				1995-96

HONOURS

Div.1	Div.2	FA Cup	Lge Cup	UEFA	C/S'ld
1968-69	1923-24	1972	1967-68	1967-68	1969
1973-74	1963-64			1970-71	1974
1991-92	1989-90				1992

MOST GOALS IN A CAREER
Peter Lorimer - 238 (1962-79 & 1983-85)

Year	League	FA Cup	Lge Cup	Europe
1965-66	13	3		3
1966-67	9	2	2	1
1967-68	17	2	4	8
1968-69	8	1		3
1969-70	14	2		3
1970-71	12	2		5
1971-72	23	3	2	1
1972-73	15	3	3	2
1973-74	12	2		
1974-75	9		3	4
1975-76	10		1	
1976-77	3			
1977-78	6		3	
1983-84	4			
1984-85	9		1	
1985-86	4			
Total	168	20	19	30

(plus 1 in the Charity Shield 1985-86)

Current leading goalscorer - Jerrel Hasselbaink - 22 (07/97-98)

MOST APPEARANCES
Jack Charlton 772 (1952-73)

Year	League	FA Cup	Lge Cup	Europe
1952-53	1			
1953-54				
1954-55	1			
1955-56	34	1		
1956-57	21	1		
1957-58	40	1		
1958-59	39	1		
1959-60	41	1		
1960-61	41	1	4	
1961-62	34	2	3	
1962-63	38	3	1	
1963-64	25		2	
1964-65	39	8	2	
1965-66	40	2	1	11
1966-67	29	6	4	7
1967-68	34	4	5	11
1968-69	41	2	2	7
1969-70	32	9	2	7
1970-71	40	4	1	10
1071-72	41	5	4	
1972-73	18	1	4	2
	629	52	35	55

Includes 1 Charity Shield appearance 1969-70.

RECORD TRANSFER FEE RECEIVED

Amount	Club	Player	Date
£3,500,000	Everton	Gary Speed	06/96
£3,000,000	Coventry	Gary McAllister	07/96
£2,700,000	Blackburn Rovers	David Batty	10/93
£2,000,000	Coventry City	Noel Whelan	12/95

RECORD TRANSFER FEE PAID

Amount	Club	Player	Date
£4,500,000	Manchester United	Lee Sharpe	08/96
£4,250,000	Parma	Tomas Brolin	12/95
£3,400,000	Eintrach Frankfurt	Tony Yeboah	1/95
£3,250,000	Crystal Palace	David Hopkin	07/97

MANAGERS

Name	Seasons	Best	Worst
Arthur Fairclough	1920-27	18(1)	14(2)
Dick Ray	1927-35	5(1)	2(2)
Billy Hampson	1935-47	9(1)	22(1)
Willis Edwards	1947-48	18(2)	18(2)
Frank Buckley	1948-53	5(2)	15(2)
Raich Carter	1953-58	8(1)	10(2)
Bill Lambton	1958-59	15(1)	15(1)
Jack Taylor	1959-61	21(1)	14(2)
Don Revie	1961-74	1(1)	19(2)
Brian Clough	1974		
Jimmy Armfield	1974-78	5(1)	10(1)
Jock Stein	1978		
Jimmy Adamson	1978-80	5(1)	11(1)
Allan Clarke	1980-82	9(1)	20(1)
Eddie Gray	1982-85	7(2)	10(2)
Billy Bremner	1985-88	4(2)	14(2)
Howard Wilkinson	1988-96	1(1/P)	10(2)
George Graham	1996-	5(P)	11(P)

LONGEST LEAGUE RUNS

of undefeated matches:	34 (26.10.1968 - 26.8.1969)	of league matches w/out a win:	17 (1.2.1947 - 26.5.1947)
of undefeated home matches:	39 (14.8.1968 - 28.2.1970)	of undefeated away matches:	17 (2.11.1968 - 26.8.1969)
without home win:	10 (6.2.1982 - 12.5.1982)	without an away win:	27 (29.4.1938 - 30.8.1947)
of league wins:	9 (26.9.1931 - 21.11.1931)	of home wins:	13 (23.11.1968 - 9.8.1969)
of league defeats:	6 (26.4.1947 - 26.5.1947)	of away wins:	8 (1.10.1963 - 21.12.1963)

LEEDS UNITED

PLAYERS NAME Honours	Ht	Wt	Birthdate	Birthplace Transfers	Contract Date	Clubs	League	L/Cup	FA Cup	Other	Lge	L/C	FAC	Oth
G O A L K E E P E R														
Beeney Mark R	6.4	14.7	30/12/67	Tunbridge Wells	17/08/85	Gillingham	2	1						
E: S-P 1; GMVC'89				Free	31/01/87	Maidstone	50	3	11	6				
				Loan	22/03/90	Aldershot	7							
				£30000	28/03/91	Brighton & H.A.	68+1	6	7	6				
				£350000	20/04/93	Leeds United	35	3	4+1					
Martyn Anthony Nigel	6.2	13.1	11/08/66	St.Austell		St.Blazey								
E:7,B.6,u21.11. Div.3'90. FMC'91. Div.1'94.				Free	06/08/87	Bristol Rovers	101	6	6	11				
				£1000000	21/11/89	Crystal Palace	272	36	22	19				
				£2000000	26/07/96	Leeds United	74	7	8					
Robinson Paul W			15/10/79	Beverley	31/05/97	Leeds United (T)								
D E F E N C E														
Doyle Kevin	5.11	11.10	13.10.80	Wexford		Leeds United (T)								
Evans Gareth J	6	11.7	15/02/81	Leeds		Leeds United (T)								
Evans Kevin	6.2	12.9	16/12/80	Carmarthen		Leeds United (T)								
Granville Daniel	5.11	12.5	19/01/75	Islington	19/05/93	Cambridge United	145+22	1+4	0+5	9+2	7			
E: u21.2. ECWC'98.				Loan	12/01/94	Saffron Walden								
				£300000	21/03/97	Chelsea	12+6	3		4+1				1
				£1600000	19/06/98	Leeds United								
Halle Gunner	5.11	11.2	11/08/65	Oslo		Lilestrom (Sweden)								
Norweigen In.				£280000	15/02/91	Oldham Athletic	185+7	16	7	3	17	2	2	
				£400000	13/12/96	Leeds United	51+2	2+1	6		2			
Harte Ian P	5.9	11	31/08/77	Drogheda	15/12/95	Leeds United	24+6	2+2	2+2		2	1		
Ei: 18, u21.3.														
Hiden Martin	6.1	11.6	11/03/73	Stainz		Rapid Vienna								
				£1300000	25/02/98	Leeds United	11		1					
Jackson Mark G	5.11	11.3	30/09/77	Barnsley	01/07/95	Leeds United	11+8		4					
E: Y.														
Kelly Garry	5.9	10	09/07/74	Drogheda		Home Farm								
Ei: 28, u21.5, Y, S.					24/09/91	Leeds United	186+4	18+1	19	7+1	2			
Lynch Damian			31/07/79	Dublin	20/09/96	Leeds United (T)								
Maybury Alan	5.11	11.7	08/08/78	Dublin	17/08/95	Leeds United	10+3	1	2					
Ei: 1, B.1, u21.3, Y.														
Molenaar Robert	6.2	14.4	27/02/69	Holland		FC Volenham								
				£1000000	11/01/97	Leeds United	30+4	2+1	5		3		1	
Radebe Lucas	6	11.8	12/04/69	Johannesberg		Kaizer Chiefs								
South African Int.				£250000	05/09/94	Leeds United	73+11	6+3	9+2				1	
Robertson David	5.11	12.10	17/10/68	Aberdeen		Glasgow Rangers								
S: 3, B.1, u21.7.				£500000	23/05/97	Leeds United	24+2	4	1					
Wetherall David	6.2	13.8	14/03/71	Sheffield	01/07/89	Sheffield Wed								
E: S; Su19.3				£125000	15/07/91	Leeds United	174+7	19+1	17+3	4	12	2	3	
Woodgate Jonathan S			22/01/80		31/05/97	Leeds United (T)								
M I D F I E L D														
Bowyer Lee	5.9	9.11	03/01/77	London	13/04/94	Charlton Athletic	5	0+1						
E: u21.9, Y.				£2600000	05/07/96	Leeds United	53+4	2+1	7		9	1	2	
Boyle Wesley	5.8	10.1	30/03/79	Portadown	26/04/96	Leeds United (T)	0+1							
NI: Y.S. FAYC'97.														
Dixon Kevin R	5.10	12.11	27/06/80	Easington	10/07/97	Leeds United (T)								
Donnelly Paul			31/08/79	Dublin	17/09/96	Leeds United (T)								
Gray Andy	6.1	12	15/11/77	Harrogate	01/07/95	Leeds United (T)	13+9	3+1	0+2					
S: Y.														
Haaland Alf I R	5.1	12	23/11/72	Norway		Ferencvaros								
Norweigen Int.					25/01/94	Nottingham Forest	66+9	2+5	5+1	2+3	7			
				£1600000	17/07/97	Leeds United	26+6	3	2		7			
Hopkin David	6	13	21/08/70	Greenock		Grennock Morton	33+15	2	2					
S: 4, B.1.				£300000	25/09/92	Chelsea	14+11		3+2					
				£800000	29/07/95	Crystal Palace	79+4	6	3	4	21	6		2
					23/07/97	Leeds United	22+3	4	1		1			
Jones Matthew	5.11	11.5	01/09/80	Llanelli		Leeds United (T)								
Kewell Harry	5.11	11.10	22/09/78	Australia	23/12/95	Leeds United	28+4	2	4		5	1	2	
Australian Int. FAYC'97.														
Knarvik Tommy			01/11/79	Bergen		Skjerjard								
					31/05/97	Leeds United								
Lagan Brian	5.5	9.10	03/10/80	N Ireland		Leeds United (T)								
McPhail Stephen	5.10	12	09/12/79	London	31/05/97	Leeds United	0+4							
FAYC'97.														
Quinn Andrew			01/09/79	Halifax	17/09/96	Leeds United								
Ribeiro Bruno	5.9	12.3	22/10/75	Setubal		Vitoria Setubal								
				£500000	18/07/97	Leeds United	28+1	2+1	3		3	1		
Watson David S	5.10	12.10	22/09/80	Strabane		Leeds United (T)								
Wright Andrew			21/10/78	Leeds	26/10/95	Leeds United (T)								

O R W A R D														
eeney Warren J	5.9	10.6	17/01/81	Belfast		Leeds United (T)								
ackworth Anthony	6.2	13.3	19/05/80	Durham	23/05/97	Leeds United (T)								
asselbank Jimmy	6.2	13.5	27/03/72	Paramaribo		Boavista								
utch Int.				£2000000	18/07/97	Leeds United	30+3	3	4		16	2	4	
illey Derek	5.10	12.7	09/02/74	Paisley	13/08/91	Morton								
: Y.				£500000	27/03/97	Leeds United	4+15	0+3	0+1		1			
atthews Lee J	6.3	12.6	16/01/79	Middlesbrough	15/02/96	Leeds United (T)	0+3	0+1						
: Y.														
harpe Lee S	5.11	11.4	27/05/71	Halesowen	31/05/88	Torquay United	9+5			2+3	3			
:8, B1, u21.8; ECWC'91; LC'92.				£185000	10/06/88	Manchester United	160+32	15+8	22+7	18+2	21	9	3	3
'rem'93'94'96; FAC'94'96				£4000000	14/08/96	Leeds United	26	3	0+1		5	1		
hepherd Paul	5.8	10.3	17/11/77	Leeds	15/09/95	Leeds United (T)	1							
: Y.														
mith Alan	5.9	10.6	28/10/80	Wakefield		Leeds United (T)								

THE MANAGER
GEORGE GRAHAM

Date of Birth . . . . 30th November 1944.
Place of Birth . . . . Bargeddie.
Date of Appointment . . . . September 1996.

PREVIOUS CLUBS
As Manager . . . . Millwall, Arsenal.
As Assistant . . . . Crystal Palace.
As a Player . . . . Aston Villa, Chelsea, Arsenal, Manchester United, Portsmouth,
. . . . Crystal Palace.

HONOURS
As a Manager
Millwall: Football League Trophy Winners.
Arsenal: League Championship 1989, 1991. F.A.Cup Winners 1993.
League Cup Winners 1987, 1993. ECWC Winners 1994.
As a Player
Chelsea: League Cup Winners 1965.
Arsenal: League Champions 1971. F.A.Cup Winners 1971. Inter-Cities Fairs Cup winners 1970.
International: 12 full caps & 2 U23 caps for Scotland.

ELLAND ROAD
Leeds, West Yorkshire LS11 0ES

Capacity 38,950

First game ....1920.
First floodlit game ....v Hibernian, 9.11.1953.

ATTENDANCES
Highest ....57,892 v Sunderland FA Cup 5th Round replay, 15.3.1967.
Lowest ....2,274 v Sheffield United, AMC, 16.10.1985.

OTHER GROUNDS ....None.

HOW TO GET TO THE GROUND

From the North
Use A58 or A61 into Leeds City Centre, then follow signs to motorway (M621) to join motorway. In 1.6 miles leave motorway and at round-about join A643 into Elland Road for Leeds United FC.
From the East
Use A63 or A64 into Leeds city centre, then follow signs to motorway (M621) to join motorway. Then as above.
From the South
Use motorway (M1) then M621 until junction with A643, leave motorway and at roundabout join A643 into Elland Road for Leeds United FC.
From the West
Use motorway (M62) then M621 until junction with A643. Leave motorway and at roundabout join A643 into Elland Road for Leeds United.

Car Parking
Wesley Street Corner has park for 1,000 cars (approx), one minute walk from ground.
Nearest Railway Station
Leeds City (01532 448 133)

USEFUL TELEPHONE NUMBERS

Club switchboard. 0113 226 6000
Club fax number 0113 226 6050
Club shop 0113 225 1100
Ticket office . . 0113 226 1000 (fax 226 6055)

Marketing department 0113 226 1155
Internet address . . . . www.lufc.co.uk
Clubcall 0891 12 11 80*
*Calls cost 50p at all times. Call costings correct at time of going to press.

MATCHDAY PROGRAMME

Programme Editor . . . . J Wray.

Number of pages . . . . 52.

Price. . . . . £2.

Subscriptions . . . . £60 UK.

Local Newspapers. . . . .
. . . Yorkshire Post, Yorkshire Evening Post,
. . . . Bradford Telegraph & Argus.

Local Radio Stations
. . . BBC Radio Leeds, Radio Aire (Leeds),
. . . . Pulse Radio (Bradford).

MATCHDAY TICKET PRICES

Categories	Standrad	Premier
West Stand 'B'.	£16.	£19
South Stand	£16.	£19
North Stand.	£16.	£19
North West/East corner.	£17.50	£22.50
Family Stand.	£16.50	£21
East Stand upper	£20.	£25
West Stand Paddock	£22.	£25
West Stand Upper.	£22.	£25

LEICESTER CITY
(The Foxes)
F.A. CARLING PREMIERSHIP
SPONSORED BY: WALKERS CRISPS

998-99 - **Back Row L-R:** David Nish (Academy Director), Steve Sims (Yth. Dev. Officer), John Rudkin (Academy Asst. Director 8-16yrs), Emile Heskey, Garry Parker, Gerry Taggart, ·gguy Arphexad, Kasey Keller, John Hodges, Spencer Prior, Matt Elliott, Steve Walsh, Gary Neil, Alan Smith (Physio), Mick Yeoman (Physio), Ian Andrews (Academy Physio). **Middle Row:** Seamus McDonagh (Goalkeeping coach), Nev Hamilton (Academy Asst. Director 16-19yrs), Paul McAndrew (Kit manager), Bob Walls (Asst. Kit Manager), Lee Allen, ·ontus Kaamark, Lawrie Dudfield, Paul Emerson, Tommy Goodwin, Scott Taylor, Steve Guppy, Graham Fenton, Ross Mitchell, John Robertson (Asst. Manager), Steve Walford (First Team ·oach), Paul Franklin (Reserve Team Coach), Jim Melrose (Chief Scout). **Front Row:** Tony Cottee, Tim McCann, Steve Wenlock, Sam McMahon, Stuart Wilson, Muzzy Isset, Robbie ·vage, John Elsom (Chairman), Martin O'Neill (Manager), Stuart Campbell, Neil Lennon, Theo Zagorakis, Ian Marshall, Martin Fox, Stef Oakes, Rob Ullathorne.

LEICESTER CITY
FORMED IN 1884
TURNED PROFESSIONAL IN 1888
LTD COMPANY IN 1897
PLC IN 1997

PRESIDENT: T W Shipman
CHAIRMAN: J M Elsom FCA
CHEIF EXECUTIVE: Barrie Pierpoint
FINANCE DIRECTOR &
COMPANY SECRETARY S A Kind ACCA
DIRECTOR P H Smith

FOOTBALL SECRETARY
Ian Silvester
FOOTBALL PRESS OFFICER
Paul Mace

MANAGER: Martin O'Neill
ASSISTANT MANAGER: John Robertson
FIRST TEAM COACH: Steve Walford
RESERVE TEAM MANAGER: Paul Franklin
ACADEMY DIRECTOR: David Nish
PHYSIOTHERAPISTS
Alan Smith & Mick Yeomans

STATISTICIAN FOR THE DIRECTORY
Dave Smith

The previous season was always going to be a hard act to follow, and the bare facts showed that City finished one place lower in the table than in 1997 and also failed to land any silverware. However, everyone associated with the club agreed that this was indeed a season of progress, with six more points being secured despite the drop in final placing.

In fact, City got off to a flying start in the face of a very tough run of opening fixtures and only for a matter of a few days did they ever drop below halfway in the table throughout the entire campaign. Interest was maintained right up to the final day, with the team still possessing a mathematical chance of qualifying for Europe through their league placing.

Highlights of the season were wins at both Anfield and Old Trafford, a comprehensive demolition of Derby at Pride Park in front of the live television cameras and a thrilling draw at home to Arsenal, where three of the six goals came in stoppage time. The club's first European campaign for 36 years faltered on the same stumbling block as that of 1961, Atletico Madrid, but not before the Foxes had given the Spanish giants quite a scare that was only effectively relieved when Garry Parker was red carded for the heinous crime of taking a free kick too quickly! In fact, generally, the cup competitions did not bring any cheer this time but the league performance more than compensated.

Individually, Muzzy Izzet stole the honours, being voted 'Player of the Season' and also winning the 'Goal of the Season' award for his last minute equaliser against Crystal Palace in December. Matt Elliott became a fully fledged Scottish international, whilst Lennon (N.Ireland), Savage (Wales), Kaamark (Sweden), Keller (USA) and Zagorakis (Greece) all added to their full international reputations in a cosmopolitan line up. Also honoured were Heskey and Guppy (England B) and Campbell (Scotland Under-21) as the squad finally earned some recognition for their efforts. Frenchman Pegguy Arphexad proved a more than able deputy for Keller when called upon and the host nation must indeed be blessed if they have three better 'keepers to include in their World Cup squad. Young Stuart Wilson continued to show immense promise whilst Rob Ullathorne was welcomed back after a year out with a broken ankle. Only Scott Taylor missed out, injuring ligaments during the pre-season build up, and having to sit out the entire campaign.

The other major talking point around Leicester was the news that the club intend to leave Filbert Street for a new stadium for the millenium. Anticipation was running high in the city as details were eagerly awaited at the season's closure. All in all it was another year of triumph for Martin O'Neill, who will undoubtedly set even more formidable targets next time around.

Dave Smith.

LEICESTER CITY

Carling Prem.	:10th	FA CUP: 4th Round	LC CUP: 3rd Round	UEFA Cup: 1st Round

M	DATE	COMP.	VEN	OPPONENTS	RESULT	H/T	LP	GOAL SCORERS/GOAL TIMES	ATT.
1	A 09	CP	H	Aston Villa	W 1-0	1-0	6	Marshall 37	20304
2	12	CP	A	Liverpool	W 2-1	1-0	4	Elliot 2, Fenton 83	(35007)
3	23	CP	H	Manchester United	D 0-0	0-0	4		21221
4	27	CP	H	Arsenal	D 3-3	0-1	4	Heskey 84, Elliot 89, Walsh 90	21089
5	30	CP	A	Sheffield Wednesday	L 0-1	0-0	6		(24851)
6	S 13	CP	H	Tottenham Hotspur	W 3-0	0-0	5	Walsh 55, Guppy 68, Heskey 77	20683
7	16	UEFA 1/1	A	Athletico Madrid	L 1-2	1-0		Marshall 12	(23000)
8	20	CP	A	Leeds United	W 1-0	1-0	3	Walsh 32	(29620)
9	24	CP	H	Blackburn Rovers	D 1-1	1-1	4	Izzet 43	19921
10	27	CP	A	Barnsley	W 2-0	0-0	3	Marshall 55, Fenton 63	(18660)
11	30	UEFA 1/2	H	Athletico Madrid	L 0-2	0-0			20776
12	O 06	CP	A	Derby County	L 1-2	0-1	4	Elliot 67	19585
13	14	CC 3	A	Grimsby Town	L 1-3	1-0		Marshall 17	(7738)
14	18	CP	A	Chelsea	L 0-1	1-0	5		(33356)
15	27	CP	H	West Ham United	W 2-1	1-0	4	Heskey 16, Marshall 82	20201
16	N 01	CP	A	Newcastle United	D 3-3	2-2	5	Marshall 12, 31, Elliot 54	(36574)
17	10	CP	H	Wimbledon	L 0-1	0-0	7		18553
18	22	CP	H	Bolton Wanderers	D 0-0	0-0	6		20464
19	29	CP	A	Coventry City	W 2-0	1-0	6	Fenton 32, Elliot 74	(18309)
20	D 06	CP	H	Crystal Palace	D 1-1	0-1	6	Izzet 90	19191
21	13	CP	A	Southampton	L 1-2	0-1	7	Savage 84	(15121)
22	20	CP	H	Everton	L 0-1	0-0	8		20628
23	26	CP	A	Arsenal	L 1-2	0-1	9	Lennon 77	(38023)
24	28	CP	H	Sheffield Wednesday	D 1-1	1-0	9	Guppy 28	20800
25	J 03	FAC 3	H	Northampton Town	W 4-0	2-0		Marshall 17, Parker 25 (pen), Savage 53, Cottee 57	20608
26	10	CP	A	Aston Villa	D 1-1	0-0	9	Parker 53 (pen)	(36429)
27	17	CP	A	Liverpool	D 0-0	0-0	9		21633
28	24	FAC 4	A	Crystal Palace	L 0-3	0-1			(15489)
29	31	CP	A	Manchester United	W 1-0	1-0	9	Cottee 28	(55156)
30	F 06	CP	H	Leeds United	W 1-0	1-0	9	Parker 44 (pen)	21244
31	14	CP	A	Tottenham Hotspur	D 1-1	1-0	9	Cottee 34	(28355)
32	28	CP	A	Blackburn Rovers	L 3-5	0-3	10	Wilson 72, Izzet 79, Ullathorne 81	(24854)
33	M 14	CP	A	Wimbledon	L 1-2	0-1	12	Savage 57	(13229)
34	21	CP	H	Chelsea	W 2-0	1-0	9	Heskey 2, 89	21335
35	28	CP	A	Bolton Wanderers	L 0-2	0-0	12		(25000)
36	A 04	CP	H	Coventry City	D 1-1	0-0	12	Wilson 78	21137
37	11	CP	A	Crystal Palace	W 3-0	1-0	10	Heskey 44, 60, Elliot 74	(18771)
38	14	CP	H	Southampton	D 3-3	1-2	10	Lennon 18, Elliot 52, Parker 90 (pen)	20708
39	18	CP	A	Everton	D 1-1	1-1	10	Marshall 38	(33642)
40	26	CP	A	Derby County	W 4-0	4-0	9	Heskey 2, 9, Izzet 3, Marshall 15	(29855)
41	29	CP	H	Newcastle United	D 0-0	0-0	9		21699
42	M 02	CP	H	Barnsley	W 1-0	0-0	8	Zagorakis 57	21293
43	10	CP	A	West Ham United	L 3-4	0-2	10	Cottee 60, 83, Heskey 66	(25781)

Best Home League Attendance: 21699 V Newcastle United   **Smallest :18553 V Wimbledon**   **Average :20615**

Goal Scorers:
CP	(51)	Heskey 10, Elliot 7, Marshall 7, Cottee 4, Izzet 4, Fenton 3, Parker 3, Walsh 3, Guppy 2, Lennon 2, Savage 2, Wilson 2, Ullathorne 1, Zagorakis 1
CC	(1)	Marshall 1
FAC	(4)	Cottee 1, Marshall 1, Parker 1, Savage 1
UEFA	(1)	Marshall 1

78

(D) Andrews	(G) Arphexad	(G) Campbell	(M) Carlstrand	(F) Claridge	(F) Cottee	(D) Elliot	(F) Fenton	(F) Guppy	(F) Heskey	(M) Izzet	(D) Kaamark	(G) Keller	(D) Lennon	(F) Marshall	(M) McMahon	(M) Oakes	(M) Parker	(D) Prior	(F) Savage	(D) Ullathorne	(D) Walsh	(D) Watts	(M) Whitlow	(M) Wilson	(M) Zagorakis		Referee	No
S		X	S2		X		S	X	X	X	X	X	X	X			S	X	S1		X						S J Lodge	1
S		X			X	S2	X	X	X	X	X	X	X				S	X	S1		X						J T Winter	2
S		X	S2		X		S	X	X	X	X	X	X	X			S	X	S1		X						D J Gallagher	3
S			X	S2	X	S1	X	X	X	X	X	X					S3	X	X		X		S				G P Barber	4
S			X	S3	X	S1	X	X	X	X	X	X					S2	X	X		X		S				P E Alcock	5
S		S	S1	S3	X	S2	X	X	X	X	X	X	X				X	X			X						A B Wilkie	6
S	S		S2	S	S1	X	X	X	X	X	X	X	X2				X1	X	S		X		S				R Olsen	7
S	S2			S	X	S1	X	X	X	X	X	X	X				X	X	S		X						K W Burge	8
S		S		S2	X	X	X	X	X	X	X	X	X				X	X	S1		X						N S Barry	9
S		S		S2	S1	X	X	X	X	X	X	X	X				X	X						S			G Poll	10
S		S		S2	X	S3	X	X	X	X	X	X	X	X3			X	X2	S1			X1		S			Harrel Remi	11
	S	S3			X	X	S2	X	X	X	X	X	X				X	X	S1			S					G R Ashby	12
	S	X			X	X	X	X				X	X	X	S2				X		X	X		S1			M A Riley	13
S	X	X			X	S	S2	X	X	X	X	X						X	X			S1	S				U D Rennie	14
S	X	S2			X	S	X	X	X	X	X	X					S1	X	X								M D Reed	15
S	X	S			X	S	X	S2	X	X	X	X					X	X	S1								G S Willard	16
	X	S			X		X	S	X	X	X	X	X				X	X	S2	S1							M A Riley	17
	S	S			X		X	S1	X		X	X	X	X			X	X	S		X		S1				G P Barber	18
	S	S			X		X	X	X		X	X	X	X			X	X		X	S		S				M J Bodenham	19
	S	X3		X2		X	X			X	X	X	X		S3	S		X	X1		X	S2		S1			U D Rennie	20
	S			S2		X	X1	X	X	X	X	X					S	X2	X		X	S		S1			S J Lodge	21
	S			S1		X	X1	X	X	X	X2	X	X				S	X	X		X	S		S2			J T Winter	22
S	X1	X2	S2		S	X	X	X	X	X	X	X					S1		X	X				S			D R Elleray	23
S		S2	S	X		X	X	X	X	X	X	X2					X	S1	X		X1			S			G Poll	24
S		S	S1	X	S2	X3	X	X2	X	X	X	X1					X	X	X					S3			A B Wilkie	25
S			S1	X	S	X	X	X	X	X	X	X1					X	S	X		X			S			M A Riley	26
S			S1	X	S	X	X1	X	X	X	X	X					X	S	X		X			S			S W Dunn	27
S			S1	X	S	X	X	X	X1	X	X	X2					X	S	X		X			S2			P E Alcock	28
S	S2		X3	X	S	X	X	X	X	X	X						X2	S1	X		X1			S3			G R Ashby	29
S	S		X	X	S	X	X	X	X	X	X						X	X	X1				S	S1			N S Barry	30
S	X	S		X	X	S	X	X	X	X	X						X1	X	X				S	S1			S J Lodge	31
	S	S		X2	X	S	X	X		X	X						X1	X	X			S2	X				N S Barry	32
	S	S	X			S	X	X	X		X	X	X2				X	X1			S1		32	X			M A Riley	33
S	X	S3		X2	X	S2	X	X	X	X3		X					X	X1			S1		S	X			P A Durkin	34
S			S	X1	X	S1	X		X	X	X2						X	X	X		S		S1	X1			U D Rennie	35
S			X1	X	S1	X	X	X	X	X		X					S	X2	S				S2	X			G P Barber	36
S				X3	X	X	X	X	X	X	S3						S1	X	X2		S		S2	X			A B Wilkie	37
S				X2	X	X	X	X	X	X	S2						X	X3	S1		S3		S	X1			G Poll	38
S		S1		X	S	X	X	X	X	X	X						X		X				S	X1			S J Lodge	39
S			S1	X	S3	X2	X	X	X	X	X						X	S2	X1				S	X3			G S Willard	40
S			S2	X	S	X	X	X	X	X	X2						X	S1	X				S	X1			M J Bodenham	41
S	S		X1	X	S1	X	X	X	S	X	X						X		X				S	X			J Gallagher	42
S			S2	X	S	X	X	X	X	X	X3					S1		X		X2		S3	X1			U D Rennie	43

6	6		10	7	37	9	37	35	36	35	32	37	22				15	28	28	3	23				12		CP Appearances	
	5	7	12		14								2	1			7	2	7	3	3	3		11	2		CP Sub Appearances	
		1			1	1	1	1	1				1	1	0+1				1		1	1	1		0+1		CC Appearances	
			0+2	2	0+1	2	2	2	2	2	2	2		2	1	2		2	1	2				0+2			FAC Appearances	
0+1	0+1		2	0+2	2	2	2	2	2	2	2		2	2	0+1		2	2	0+1		1	1					UEFA Appearances	

Also Played: (G) Andrews S(41,47). Lenhart S1(9).

LEICESTER CITY

BIGGEST VICTORIES
League: 10-0 v Portsmouth (h) Division 1, 20.10.1928.
F.A. Cup: 13-0 v Notts Olympic (h), 1st Qual. Round, 13.10.1894.
7-0 v Crook Town (h) 3rd Round, 9.1.1932.
League Cup: 8-1 v Coventry City (a) 5th Round, 1.12.1964.
Europe: 4-1 v Glenavon (a) 1st Round, 13.9.1961.

BIGGEST DEFEATS
League: 0-12 v Nottingham Forest (a) Division 1, 21.4.1909.
F.A. Cup: 0-5 v Manchester City (a) 3rd Round replay, 17.1.1997.
League Cup: 1-7 v Sheffield Wednesday (a) 3rd Round,
27.10.1992.
Europe: 0-2 v Atletico Madrid (a) 2nd Round, 15.11.1961.

MOST POINTS
3 points a win: 77, Division 2, 1991-92.
2 points a win: 61, Division 2, 1956-57.

MOST GOALS SCORED
109, Division 2, 1956-57.

MOST GOALS CONCEDED
112, Division 1, 1957-58.

MOST FIRST CLASS MATCHES IN A SEASON
61 - 1991-92 (League 46, FA Cup 2, League Cup 4, Zenith Data 6,
Play-offs 3).

MOST LEAGUE WINS
25, Division 2, 1956-57.

MOST LEAGUE DRAWS
19, Division 1, 1975-76.

MOST LEAGUE DEFEATS
25, Division 1/Premiership, 1977-78, 1994-95.

MOST GOALS IN A SEASON
Arthur Rowley: 44 goals in 1956-57 (League 44, 5 pens).

MOST GOALS IN A MATCH
6. John Duncan v Port Vale, 7-0, Division 2, 25.12.1924.
6. Arthur Chandler v Portsmouth, 10-0, Division 1, 20.10.1928.

OLDEST PLAYER
Joe Calvert, 40 years 313 days, v Southampton (A) 13.12.1947.

YOUNGEST PLAYER
Dave Buchanan, 16 years 192 days, v Oldham Ath. (H) 1.1.1979.

MOST CAPPED PLAYER
John O'Neill (Northern Ireland) 39.

League: 1956-57: Matches played 42, Won 25, Drawn 11, Lost 6,
Goals for 109, Goals against 67, Points 61. First in Division 2.
Highest Position: 1928-29: 2nd in Division 1.
F.A. Cup: Runners-up in 1948-49, 1960-61, 1962-63, 1968-69.
Most recent success: 1968-69: 3rd Round Barnsley 1-1,2-1; 4th
Round Millwall 1-0; 5th Round Liverpool 0-0,1-0; 6th Round
Mansfield Town 1-0; Semi-Final West Bromwich Albion 1-0; Final
Manchester City 0-1.
League Cup: Winners 1963-64
Most Recent success: Winners 1996-97
2nd Round Scarborough 2-0 (A), 2-1 (H);
3rd Round York City 2-0 (A); 4th Round Manchester United 2-0 (H);
5th Round Ipswich Town 1-0 (H); Semi-Final Wimbledon 0-0 (H),
1-1 (A); Final Middlesbrough 1-1 (aet), 1-0 (aet).
Europe: (ECWC) 1961-62: 1st Round Glenavon 4-1,3-1; Atletico
Madrid 1-1,0-2.

ADDITIONAL INFORMATION
PREVIOUS NAMES
Leicester Fosse 1884-1919.

PREVIOUS LEAGUES
Midland League.

Club colours: Royal blue shirts, white shorts, royal blue socks.
Change colours: White shirts, royal blue shorts, white socks.

Reserves League: Pontins Central League Premier Division.

DIVISIONAL RECORD

	Played	Won	Drawn	Lost	For	Against	Points
Division 1/P	1,710	551	446	717	2,584	2,966	1,626
Division 2/1	2,074	854	514	706	3,312	2,933	2,401
Total	3,784	1,404	959	1,423	5,896	5,899	4,027

RECORDS AND STATISTICS

COMPETITIONS

Div 1/P	Div.2/1	ECWC	Texaco	A/Scot
1908-09	1894-08	1961-62	1972-73	1975-76
1925-35	1909-25		1973-74	
1937-39	1935-37	**UEFA**		**A/Italian**
1954-55	1939-54	1997-98		1971-72
1957-69	1955-57			1992-93
1971-78	1969-71			1993-94
1980-81	1978-80			
1983-87	1981-83			
1994-95	1987-94			
	1995-			

HONOURS

Div.2	League Cup	C/Shield
1924-25	1963-64	1971
1936-37	1996-97	
1953-54		
1956-57		
1970-71		
1979-80		

MOST APPEARANCES

Graham Cross 596+3

Year	League	FA Cup	Lge Cup	Europe
1960-61	1			
1961-62	6			2
1962-63	29	6	2	
1963-64	39	1	6	
1964-65	35	5	9	
1965-66	38	4	1	
1966-67	41	1	3	
1967-68	29	6	1	
1968-69	37	8	2	
1969-70	42	5	6	
1970-71	42	6	5	
1971-72	39	3	1	
1972-73	38	2	1	
1973-74	40	7	1	
1974-75	38+2	5	2	
1975-76	1+1			
	495+3	59	40	2

MOST GOALS IN A CAREER

Arthur Chandler - 273 (1923-34)

Year	League	FA Cup
1923-24	24	
1924-25	32	6
1925-26	26	
1926-27	28	1
1927-28	34	
1928-29	34	
1929-30	32	
1930-31	18	
1931-32	12	2
1932-33	4	
1933-34	6	5
1934-35	9	
Total	**259**	**14**

Current leading goalscorer: Steve Walsh - 58 (1986-98)

RECORD TRANSFER FEE RECEIVED

Amount	Club	Player	Date
£3,250,000	Aston Villa	Mark Draper	07/95
£1,500,000	Wolves	Steve Corica	02/96
£1,500,000	Aston Villa	Julian Joachim	02/96
£1,350,000	Derby County	Paul Kitson	03/92

RECORD TRANSFER FEE PAID

Amount	Club	Player	Date
£1,600,000	Oxford United	Matt Elliott	01/97
£1.25m+£0.5m	Notts County	Mark Draper	07/94+07/95
£1,200,000	Birmingham City	Steve Claridge	03/96
£1,000,000	Norwich City	Mark Robins	01/95

MANAGERS

Name	Seasons	Best	Worst
Peter Hodge	1919-26	17(1)	14(2)
Willie Orr	1926-32	2(1)	19(1)
Peter Hodge	1932-34	17(1)	19(1)
Arthur Lochhead	1934-36	21(1)	6(2)
Frank Womack	1936-39	16(1)	1(2)
Tom Bromilow	1939-45		
Tom Mather	1945-46		
John Duncan	1946-49	9(2)	19(2)
Norman Bullock	1949-55	21(1)	15(2)
David Halliday	1955-58	18(1)	5(2)
Matt Gillies	1959-68	4(1)	14(1)
Frank O'Farrell	1968-71	21(1)	3(2)
Jimmy Bloomfield	1971-77	7(1)	18(1)
Frank McLintock	1977-78	22(1)	22(1)
Jock Wallace	1978-82	21(1)	17(2)
Gordon Milne	1982-86	15(1)	3(2)
Bryan Hamilton	1986-87	20(1)	13(2)
David Pleat	1987-91	13(2)	22(2)
Gordon Lee	1991	22(2)	22(2)
Brian Little	1991-94	4(2/1)	6(2/1)
Mark McGhee	1994-95	21(P)	21(P)
Martin O'Neill	1995-	9(P)	5(1)

LONGEST LEAGUE RUNS

of undefeated matches:	19 (6.2.1971 - 18.8.1971)	of league matches w/out a win:	18 (12.4.1975 - 1.11.1975)
of undefeated home matches:	40 (12.2.1898 - 17.4.1900)	of undefeated away matches:	10 (27.2.1971 - 14.8.1971)
without home win:	9 (3.12.1994 - 1.4.1995)	without an away win:	23 (19.11.1988 - 4.11.1989)
of league wins:	7 (15.2.08-28.3.08, 24.1.25-17.3.25)	of home wins:	13 (3.9.1906 - 29.12.1906)
	(26.12.62-9.3.1963, 28.2.93-27.3.93)		
of league defeats:	7 (28.11.1931 - 16.1.1932, 28.8.1990 - 29.9.1990)	of away wins:	4 (13.3.1971 - 12.4.1971)

LEICESTER CITY

PLAYERS NAME Honours	Ht	Wt	Birthdate	Birthplace Transfers	Contract Date	Clubs	League	L/Cup	FA Cup	Other	Lge	L/C	FAC	Oth
G O A L K E E P E R														
Arphexad Pegguy M	6.2	13.7	18/05/73	Guadeloupe		Lens								
French u21 Int.				Free	20/08/97	Leicester City	6							
Hodges John K						Leicester City (T)								
Keller Kasey	5.11	11.13	27/11/69	Washington (USA)		Portland University								
USA Int.				Free	20/02/92	Millwall	176	14	8	4				
					17/08/96	Leicester City	63	9	6	2				
D E F E N C E														
Branston Guy	6	13.4	09/01/79	Leicester	03/07/97	Leicester City (T)								
				Loan	09/02/98	Colchester United	12		1	1				
Elliot Matthew S	6.3	13.6	01/11/68	Wandsworth		Epsom & Ewell								
S: 3.				£5000	09/09/88	Charlton Athletic		1						
				£10000	23/03/89	Torquay United	123+1	9	9	16	15	2	2	1
				£50000	26/03/92	Scunthorpe United	61	6	2	8	8			
				£150000	05/11/93	Oxford United	148	16	11	6	21	1	2	
				£1600000	17/01/97	Leicester City	16		2		4			
				£750000	23/02/96	Leicester City	86+1	8	4	5	9	1		
Emerson Paul G	6.1	12	29/08/78	Newtonards	03/07/97	Leicester City (T)								
Fox Martin R	5.8	11	21/04/79	Sutton-in-Ash'	21/02/97	Leicester City (T)								
Kaamark Pontus S	5.11	12.7	05/04/69	Sweden		Gothenburg								
Swedish Int. LC'97.				£840000	02/11/95	Leicester City	45+1	4	4	2				
Prior Spencer	6.3	12.1	22/04/71	Southend	22/05/89	Southend United	135	9	5	7	3			1
LC'97				£200000	24/06/93	Norwich City	67+7	10+1	0+2	2	1	1		
				£600000	01/08/96	Leicester City	61+3	7	5	2				
Sinclair Frank	5.8	11.2	03/12/71	Lambeth	17/05/90	Chelsea	163+6	17	18	13	7	1	1	3
Jamiacan Int. FAC'97. LC'98.				Loan	12/12/91	W.B.A.	6				1			
				£2000000	01/08/98	Leicester City								
Taggart Gerald	6.1	13.4	18/10/70	Belfast	01/07/89	Manchester City	10+2			1	1			
NI:45, u23.2, u21.1,Y. Div.1'97.				£75000	10/01/90	Barnsley	168+3	11	14	6	13		2	1
				£1500000	01/08/95	Bolton Wanderers	68+1	8	4		4	1		
				Free	01/07/98	Leicester City								
Ullathorne Robert	5.8	10.7	11/10/71	Wakefield	06/07/90	Norwich City	86+8	10+2	7+1	1	7	1		
E: Y1				£600000	18/02/97	Leicester City	3+3	1			1			
Walsh Steven	6.2	11.1	03/11/64	Preston	11/09/82	Wigan Athletic	123+3	7	6	10+2	4			
FRT'85. LC'97.				£100000	24/06/86	Leicester City	330+5	32	12	23	50	3	1	4
M I D F I E L D														
Allen Lewis S	5.10	12	12/03/79	Islington		Leicester City (T)								
Brennan Karl A			19/03/81	Leicester		Leicester City (T)								
Campbell Stuart P	5.10	10.8	09/12/77	Corby	16/08/96	Leicester City	10+11	1+2	2					
LC'97.														
Guppy Stephen	5.11	10.1	29/03/69	Winchester		Wycombe W.	41	4	8	10	8		2	
E: B1, u21.1. S-P.1. GMVC'93. FAT'91'93				£15000	02/08/94	Newcastle United								
				£225000	25/11/94	Port Vale	102+3	7	8	7+1	12			1
				£850000	01/03/97	Leicester City	49+1	1	2	2	2			
Izzet Mustafa	5.10	10.3	31/10/74	Mile End	01/08/93	Chelsea								
LC'97.				£650000	05/07/96	Leicester City	78+2	8	5	5	8	1		
Lennon Neil	5.9	11.06	25/06/71	Lurgan, N.I.	26/06/89	Manchester City	1							
NI: 21, B1, u23.1, u21.2. LC'97.				Free	09/08/90	Crewe Alexandra	117+5	4+1	11	12+1	13		1	
				£750000	23/02/96	Leicester City	86+1	8	4	5	4	1		
Mitchell Ross J	5.11	10.13	24/08/78	Halifax	03/07/97	Leicester City (T)								
Parker Garry S	5.8	11	07/09/65	Oxford	05/05/83	Luton Town	31+11	1+3	6+2		3	1		
E: B, u21.6, u19.3, Y1; LC'89'90'94'97; SC'89				£72000	21/02/86	Hull City	82+2	5	4	2	8			
				£260000	24/03/88	Nottingham Forest	93+4	22+1	16	9	17	4	5	3
				£650000	29/11/91	Aston Villa	79+2	8	10		11		1	
				£550000	10/02/95	Leicester City	87+20	13	9	4+1	10	1	2	2
Oakes Stefan T	5.11	12.4	06/09/78	Leicester	03/07/97	Leicester City (T)								
Taylor Scott D	5.10	10	28/11/70	Portsmouth	22/06/89	Reading	164+43	7+5	11+2	12+4	24	1	3	1
Div.2'94. LC'97.				£500000	12/07/95	Leicester City	59+5	7+3	2+1	3	6			
Thomas Danny			01/05/81	Leamington S.		Nottingham F. (T)								
						Leicester City (T)								
Wilson Stuart K	5.8	9.12	16/09/77	Leicester	04/07/96	Leicester City (T)	0+13	0+1	0+3		3			
Zagorakis Theo	5.9	11.8	27/10/71	Kavala (Greece)		PAOK Salonika								
Greek Int.				£750000	06/02/98	Leicester City	12+2				1			

Player														
Cottee Tony	5.8	11.5	7/11/65	West Ham	9/1/82	West Ham United	203+9	19	24	1	92	14	11	1
E: 7, u21.8, Y.3				£2300000	8/2/88	Everton	158+23	19+4	15+6	11+2	72	11	4	12
				£300000	9/7/94	West Ham United	64+4	8	5		22	4	1	
				Free	5/31/97	Selangor								
				£500000	8/14/97	Leicester City	7+12	1	0+2	0+1	4		1	
				Loan	11/14/97	Birmingham City	2				1			
Dudfield Lawrie G	6	12.4	07/05/80	London	06/06/97	Leicester City (T)								
Fenton Graham	5.10	11.03	22/05/74	Wallsend	13/02/92	Aston Villa	16+13	2+3			3			
E: u21.1. LC'94'96.				Loan	10/01/94	W.B.A.	7				3			
				£1500000	08/11/95	Blackburn Rovers	9+18	0+2	0+1		7			
				£1000000	01/08/97	Leicester City	9+14	1	0+1	0+2	3			
Heskey Emile	6.1	13	11/01/78	Leicester	03/10/95	Leicester City	89+10	9+2	5	5	27	2		
E: B.1, u21.11, Y. LC'97.														
Jaffa Graeme	5.6	9.8	08/05/79	Falkirk	03/07/97	Leicester City (T)								
Marshall Ian P	6.1	12.12	20/03/66	Liverpool	23/03/84	Everton	9+6	1+1			7	1	1	
Div2'91; CS'86				£100000	24/03/86	Oldham Athletic	165+5	17	14	2+1	36		3	1
				£750000	09/08/93	Ipswich Town	79+5	4	9		32	3	3	
				£850000	31/08/96	Leicester City	41+11	1	5	2	15	1	3	1
Neil Gary D C	6	12.10	16/08/78	Glasgow	03/07/97	Leicester City (T)								
Savage Robert	6	10.1	18/10/74	Wrexham	05/07/93	Manchester United								
W: Y,S. FAYC'92.				Free	22/07/94	Crewe Alexandra	74+3	5	5	8	10	5		1
				£400000	23/07/97	Leicester City	28+7	1	2	0+1	2		1	

THE MANAGER
MARTIN O'NEILL

Date of Birth . . . . 1st March 1952.
Place of Birth . . . . Kilrea, Northern Ireland.
Date of Appointment . . . . December 1995.

PREVIOUS CLUBS
As Manager . . . . . . Grantham, Shepshed Charterhouse, Wycombe Wanderers,
. . . . Norwich City.
As Coach. . . . . None.
As a Player . . . . . . Distillery, Nottingham Forest, Norwich City, Manchester City,
. . . . Norwich City, Notts County.

HONOURS
As a Manager
Wycombe: FA Trophy 1991, 1993. Bob Lord Trophy 1992. GMVC champions & promoted to the Football League 1993. Promotion to Division Two via the play-offs 1994.
Leicester City: Promotion to the Carling Premiership via the play-offs 1995/96. League Cup 1996/97.

As a Player
Irish Cup 1971. Division 1 championship 1978. League Cup 1978, 1979. European Cup 1980. Promotion to Division 1 1977, 1982.   **Northern Ireland:** 64 full caps.

FILBERT STREET
Leicester LE2 7FL

Capacity ....21,500 (may increase with addition of extra seats)

First game...v Nottingham Forest 'A' (F) 7.11.1891.
First floodlit game..v Borussia Dortmund (F) 23.10.1957.

ATTENDANCES
Highest...47,298 v Spurs, FAC 5th Rnd, 18.2.1928.
Lowest ....3,440 v Huddersfield, Simod 1st Rnd, 10.11.1987. (Post WW1)

OTHER GROUNDS ....Fosse Road/Racecourse 1884-85. Victoria Park 1885-87.
....Belgrave Road 1887-88. Victoria Park 1888-89. Mill Lane 1889-91.
.... Aylestone Road 1891. Filbert Street 1891-

HOW TO GET TO THE GROUND

From the North
Use motorway (M1) until junction 22 or A46/A607 into Leicester city centre. Follow signs to Rugby into Almond Road, then at end turn right into Aylestone Road. Shortly turn left into Walnut Street, then turn left into Filbert Street for Leicester City FC.

From the East
Use A47 into Leicester city centre. Follow signs to Rugby into Almond Road, then at end turn right into Aylestone Road. Shortly turn left into Walnut Street, then turn left into Filbert Street for Leicester City FC.

From the South
Use M1 or M69 until junction 21, then A46 (sign posted Leicester). Under railway bridge and in 0.2 miles turn right into Upperton Road, then turn right into Filbert Street for Leicester City FC.

From the West
Use motorway M69 or A50 into Leicester City centre and follow signs to Rugby into Almond Road, then at end turn left into Aylestone Road. Shortly turn left into Walnut Street, then left into Filbert Street for Leicester City FC.

Car Parking: Parking adjacent to stadium for season ticket holders only. Street parking is available and there is also a public car park five minutes walk from the ground.
Nearest Railway Station: Leicester (0116 248 1000)

USEFUL TELEPHONE NUMBERS

Club switchboard......................0116 291 5000
Club fax number.......................0116 247 0585
Club shop.................................0116 291 5253
Ticket Office............................0116 291 5232

Marketing Department 0116 291 5052
Internet address ....www.lcfc.co.uk
Clubcall 0891 12 11 85*

*Calls cost 50p per minute all times. Call costings correct at time of going to press.

MATCHDAY PROGRAMME
Programme Editor....... Andrew Bubeer.

Number of pages .... 56 (full colour).

Price........................... £2.

Local Newspapers
Leicester Mercury, Leicester Herald & Post,
.... Melton Times, Coalville Times.

Local Radio Stations
... Leicester Sound, BBC Radio Leicester.

MATCHDAY TICKET PRICES

Executive Tier.................. Adult £24.50 - Juv/SC £12.50

Carling Centre .... £22.50 - £11.50

Carling Wing .... £19.50 - £10.00

Carling Members .... £16.00 - N/A

Carling Family .... £16.00 - £8.00

North Family .... £15.00 - £7.50

South Upper .... £18.00 - £9.00

South Lower............................... £15.00 - N/A

East (Block V) .... £15.00 - £7.50

Supporters Club Corner.................... £15.00 - £7.50

LIVERPOOL
(The Reds or Pool)
F.A. CARLING PREMIERSHIP
SPONSORED BY: CARLSBERG

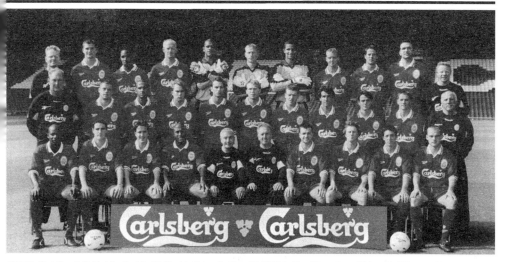

1997-98 - Back Row L-R: Mark Leather (physio), Dominic Matteo, Paul Ince, Mark Wright, Tony Warner, Jorgen Nielsen, David James, Rob Jones, Jamie Redknapp, Neil Ruddock, Sammy Lee (Reserve Team Coach). **Middle Row:** Joe Corrigan (Goalkeeping coach), Jamie Carragher, Phil Babb, Jason McAteer, Patrik Berger, Bjorn Tore Kvarme, Stig Inge Bjornebye, Karlheinz Riedle, David Thompson, Michael Owen, Ronnie Moran (Chief Coach). **Front Row:** Michael Thomas, Mark Kennedy, Oyvind Leonhardsen, John Barnes, Roy Evans (Manager), Doug Livermore (Asst. Manager), Steve Harkness, Steve McManaman, Robbie Fowler, Danny Murphy.

LIVERPOOL
FORMED IN 1892
TURNED PROFESSIONAL IN 1892
LTD COMPANY IN 1892

HON VICE-PRESIDENT
H E Roberts, W D Corkish FCA,
CHAIRMAN: D R Moores
VICE-CHAIRMAN/CHIEF EXECUTIVE
P B Robinson
DIRECTORS
J T Cross, N White, FSCA, T D Smith,
T W Saunders, K E B Clayton FCA,
D M A Chestnutt, R N Parry
SECRETARY
B Morrison
COMMERCIAL MANAGER
M L Turner
MANAGER: Roy Evans & Gerard Houllier
ASSISTANT MANAGER: Doug Livermore
RESERVE TEAM MANAGER
Sammy Lee
YOUTH TEAM MANAGER
H McAuley
PHYSIOTHERAPIST
Mark Leather
STATISTICIAN FOR THE DIRECTORY
Brian Pead (0181 302 6446 Tel/Fax)

Once again, hopes were high for Liverpool as the season got underway, particularly when a new goalscoring sensation, Michael Owen, scored from the spot on the opening day with all the assurance of an old pro with many seasons under his belt. But a home defeat in their first match at Anfield was the prelude to another season of immense promise and potential which culminated in such intense disappointment.

With three games gone, Liverpool were in sixteenth position, and while that position did not really seem to be accurate, it was clearly evident that there were terrible problems in defence, particularly with the centre-backs. David James was again in enigmatic form - one moment brilliant, and in the next abysmal. Inconsistency, however, did not lie entirely at his door, for the whole Liverpool side failed to fulfil their true potential. Chelsea were beaten in some style with a Berger hat-trick in early October, but as the season progressed stories emanated from Anfield that he wanted to return to his native Czechoslovakia. A home defeat against Manchester United finally ended any realistic hopes of a Liverpool championship, but there was always the FA Cup to fight for, wasn't there? Coventry - at Anfield - thought otherwise, winning 3-1 dramatically but deserved.

There was supposed to be some respite from all this unfulfilled potential in the Coca-Cola Cup, until Middlesbrough snatched an early two-goal lead at the Riverside, and summarily dismissed the Reds from the competition.

In Europe, Liverpool enjoyed some success against Glasgow Celtic, but slipped up against Strasboug, losing unnecessarily 0-3, when a single goal defeat would have secured passage into the next round. The same old problems kept recurring like a broken record, when Liverpool's tradition was to break records in a positive manner.

That left, once again, only a UEFA Cup spot to play for. Liverpool, who once reigned supreme as perennial champions of England and Europe, now knew what it was like to suffer the fate of other clubs with little to play for as Spring blossomed into our consciousness.

On Valentine's Day, Owen worked his way into the hearts of Liverpool fans with a face-saving hat-trick against Sheffield Wednesday. It was a love affair which was to continue to grow as the season wore on. In April, he scored a brilliant goal against Manchester United at Old Trafford, which robbed the champions of two vital points - it was as good as victory and Owen, despite being sent off just a few minutes later, wrote himself into Anfield folklore for eternity.

New Champions Arsenal were beaten 4-0 at Anfield with a less than experienced side, but it was but a brief encounter with any sort of success.

Liverpool have much work to do if they are to regain the championship crown which they once thought of as their own. The defence in particular needs immediate attention, but the real problem appears to lie in the fact that the biggest stars on the world stage no longer look upon Anfield as the Mecca of football - that epithet belongs to a large extent down the M62, sad as it is to report. But with French football at its zenith, perhaps the appointment of the technical genius Gerard Houllier will marry significantly with the old traditions represented by Shankley's protege, Roy Evans, in order to take the club into the technological age of the 21st century from its humble working-class roots in the Victorian age.

BRIAN PEAD
TEL & FAX 0181 302 6446

LIVERPOOL

					FA CUP: 3rd Round		LC CUP: Semi Final		UEFA: 2nd Round	

M	DATE	COMP.	VEN	OPPONENTS	RESULT	H/T	LP	GOAL SCORERS/GOAL TIMES	ATT.
1	A 09	CP	A	Wimbledon	D 1-1	0-0	9	Owen 72 (pen)	(26106)
2	12	CP	H	Leicester City	L 1-2	0-1	13	Ince 84	35007
3	23	CP	A	Blackburn Rovers	D 1-1	0-0	15	Owen 53	(30187)
4	26	CP	A	Leeds United	W 2-0	1-0	8	McManaman 23, Riedle 75	(39775)
5	S 13	CP	H	Sheffield Wednesday	W 2-1	0-0	7	Ince 55, Thomas 68	34705
6	16	UEFA 1/1	A	Celtic	D 2-2	1-0		Owen 6, McManaman 89	(50000)
7	20	CP	A	Southampton	D 1-1	1-0	7	Riedle 37	(15252)
8	22	CP	H	Aston Villa	W 3-0	0-0	6	Fowler 56 (pen), McManaman 79, Riedle 90	34843
9	27	CP	A	West Ham United	L 1-2	0-1	9	Fowler 52	(25908)
10	30	UEFA 1/2	H	Celtic	D 0-0	0-0			38205
11	O 05	CP	H	Chelsea	W 4-2	2-1	6	Berger 20, 35, 57, Fowler 64	36647
12	15	CC 3	A	West Bromwich Albion	W 2-0	0-0		Berger 52, Fowler 88	(21986)
13	18	CP	A	Everton	L 0-2	0-1	9		(40112)
14	21	UEFA 2/1	A	Strasbourg	L 0-3	0-1			(18813)
15	25	CP	H	Derby County	W 4-0	1-0	5	Fowler 27, 84, Leonhardsen 65, McManaman 88	38017
16	N 01	CP	A	Bolton Wanderers	D 1-1	1-0	8	Fowler 1	(25000)
17	04	UEFA 2/2	H	Strasbourg	W 2-0	0-0		Fowler 63 (pen), Riedle 84	32,426
18	08	CP	H	Tottenham Hotspur	W 4-0	0-0	7	McManaman 48, Leonhardsen 50, Redknapp 65, Owen 86	38006
19	18	CC 4	H	Grimsby Town	W 3-0	2-0		Owen 28, 44 (pen), 57	28515
20	22	CP	H	Barnsley	L 0-1	0-1	8		41011
21	30	CP	A	Arsenal	W 1-0	0-0	7	McManaman 56	(38094)
22	D 06	CP	H	Manchester United	L 1-3	0-0	8	Fowler 60 (pen)	41027
23	13	CP	A	Crystal Palace	W 3-0	1-0	6	McManaman 39, Owen 55, Leonhardsen 61	(25790)
24	20	CP	H	Coventry City	W 1-0	1-0	5	Owen 14	39707
25	26	CP	H	Leeds United	W 3-1	0-0	4	Owen 46, Fowler 79, 83	43854
26	28	CP	A	Newcastle United	W 2-1	2-1	4	McManaman 31, 43	(36718)
27	J 03	FAC 3	H	Coventry City	L 1-3	1-1		Redknapp 7	33888
28	07	CC QF	A	Newcastle United	W 2-0	0-0		Owen 95, Fowler 103	(33207)
29	10	CP	H	Wimbledon	W 2-0	0-0	4	Redknapp 72, 84	38011
30	17	CP	A	Leicester City	D 0-0	0-0	4		(21633)
31	20	CP	H	Newcastle United	W 1-0	1-0	3	Owen 17	42791
32	27	CC SF1	H	Middlesbrough	W 2-1	1-1		Redknapp 31, Fowler 82	33438
33	31	CP	H	Blackburn Rovers	D 0-0	0-0	4		43890
34	F 06	CP	H	Southampton	L 2-3	1-1	4	Owen 24, 90	43550
35	14	CP	A	Sheffield Wednesday	D 3-3	1-1	3	Owen 27, 73, 78	(35405)
36	18	CC SF2	A	Middlesbrough	L 0-2	0-2			(29828)
37	23	CP	H	Everton	D 1-1	0-0	3	Ince 66	44501
38	28	CP	A	Aston Villa	L 1-2	1-1	4	Owen 5 (pen)	(39377)
39	M 07	CP	H	Bolton Wanderers	W 2-1	0-1	3	Ince 58, Owen 65	44532
40	14	CP	A	Tottenham Hotspur	D 3-3	1-1	3	McManaman 20, 88, Ince 63	(30245)
41	28	CP	H	Barnsley	W 3-2	1-1	3	Riedle 44, 59, McManaman 90	(18684)
42	A 10	CP	A	Manchester United	D 1-1	1-1	3	Owen 36	(55171)
43	13	CP	H	Crystal Palace	W 2-1	1-0	3	Leonhardsen 29, Thompson 85	43007
44	19	CP	A	Coventry City	D 1-1	1-0	3	Owen 33	(22721)
45	25	CP	A	Chelsea	L 1-4	1-1	4	Riedle 45	(34639)
46	M 02	CP	H	West Ham United	W 5-0	4-0	3	Owen 4, McAteer 21, 25, Leonhardsen 45, Ince 61	44414
47	06	CP	H	Arsenal	W 4-0	3-0	3	Ince 28, 30, Owen 40, Leonhardsen 86	44417
48	10	CP	A	Derby County	L 0-1	0-0	3		(30492)

Best Home League Attendance: 44532 V Bolton Wanderers   **Smallest :34705 V Sheffield Wednesday**   **Average :40628**

Goal Scorers:

CP	(68)	Owen 18, McManaman 11, Fowler 9, Ince 8, Leonhardsen 6, Riedle 6, Berger 3, Redknapp 3, McAteer 2, Thomas 1, Thompson 1
CC	(9)	Owen 4, Fowler 3, Berger 1, Redknapp 1
FAC	(1)	Redknapp 1
UEFA	(4)	Fowler 1, McManaman 1, Owen 1, Riedle 1

(D) Babb	(F) Berger	(D) Bjorneby	(M) Carragher	(F) Fowler	(G) Friedel	(M) Gudnason	(D) Harkness	(M) Ince	(G) James	(D) Jones	(F) Kennedy	(D) Kvarne	(M) Leonhardsen	(D) Matteo	(M) McAteer	(F) McManaman	(M) Murphy	(G) Nielsen	(F) Owen	(M) Redknapp	(F) Riedle	(M) Rizzo	(D) Roberts	(D) Ruddock	(M) Thomas	(M) Thompson	(G) Warner	(D) Wright	Referee	No
X		X					S1	X	X	X					S3	X	S2		X		X				X	X		X	G.S. Willard	1
X		X	S3				X	X	X	X				S2		X	S1		X		X			X	S	S		X	J T Winter	2
S	S1	X					X	X	X	X		X			S	X	S		X		X			X		S		X	S J Lodge	3
S	S1	X					X	X	X	X		X			S	X			X		X			X		S		X	A B Wilkie	4
	S2	X					X	X	X	X		X		S1	S3	X	S		X		X			X		S		X	G Poll	5
S	S	X	S				X	X	X	S	X	X	S	X	S	X	S		X		X			X		S		X	A Grasino	6
S2	X	S	S					X	X		X	X	X		X				X		X			X		S		X	P Jones	7
X	X	X	X	X				X		S	X			X	X	X			X		S2	S		X	S1	S			M J Bodenham	8
X	X	X	X	X				X	X		X			S1	X	S1	S	X	S3		X			X	S				D J Gallagher	9
X	X	X	X	X1			S	X	X	X	S	X			S	X	S	S	X	S1				S					Edger Steinborn	10
X	X	X	X	X			S	X	X	X		S1	X		S1	X		S	S	X				X					D R Elleray	11
	X	X	X	X			S2		X			X	S1		X	X			S	X		X	X						A B Wilkie	12
	X	X		X			S	X	X			X	S2		X	X		S	S1	X		X	X					S	M D Reed	13
	X		X				X	X	X	S		X	X	S	X	X	S	S	S1	X			X1	S				S	M Pereira	14
	X		X				X	X	X			X	X	X		X	S	S	X	S			S		S			G S Willard	15
S	X		X				S	X	X	X		X	X	X	X	X	X		S	X	S1								D J Gallagher	16
S2	X2		X				S	X	X	X1		X	X	X	S	X	S	X	X	S1		S							Pedersen	17
S3	X		X				S	X	X	X		X	X	S2	X		S	S1	X	X									S J Lodge	18
S1	X						S	X1	X	X		X	X	X	S	X			X	X	X								J E Pearce	19
X	X	S					S		X	X		X	X	X	X	S1	S		X1	X									J T Winter	20
S	S	X	X					X	X	X	X	X	X	X	S	S1	S	X1	X	X									G Poll	21
S	S1	X2	X	X			S		X	X1	X	X	X	X		S	X	X	S2										D R Elleray	22
S1	S2	X	X				X1	S	X		X	X2	X	X	X	S		S	X	X	S								N S Barry	23
S	S	S	X	X			X		X			X	X	X	X	X		S	X	X	S								P E Alcock	24
S	S2		S2	X1	S		X	X2	X			X	X	X	X	X			X	X2	S1								S J Lodge	25
S	S		S1	X1	S		X	X	X			X	X	X	X	X		S	X	X	S								G R Ashby	26
S	S1		S	S	X		X	X	X			X2	X1	X	X	X	S2		X	X									M A Riley	27
X			S	X	S		X	X	X			X	X	X	X		X1	X	S1										D J Gallagher	28
X	S1		S	X	S		X	X	X	S		X1	X	X	X	S		X	X										M J Bodenham	29
X	S1		S	X	S		X	X	X	S		X	X	X	S	X1	X												S W Dunn	30
X	S		S	X	S		X	X	X	S		X	X	X		X	X	S											G P Barber	31
X			S	X	S	X1	X	X				X	X	X	X	X	X	X	S1										G S Willard	32
X	S1		X	X		X		X	X	S2		X	X	X2	X1	S	S	X	3										P A Durkin	33
X	S2		X1	X		X	X	X	X		S	X2	X	X	S1		S		S									S	J T Winter	34
S2	S		X	X	S		X	X	X	X1	X2	X	X	X	S		X	S	S1										M D Reed	35
X2	X	X	X	X			X	X	X	X		S1	X1	X		X	S2		X										P A Durkin	36
S			X	X1	X		X	X	X	X		X	X	S1	X	X	X	S				S				S			P Jones	37
S2	X	X		X			X	X	S	X1		S	X2		X	S1	X		X	S				X					G Poll	38
	X	S		X			X	X	S	X	S1	X	X	X		X	X	X1						S					K W Burge	39
S2		X	X1		X		X	X	X	X		S	X2	X		X	S	X	X							S1			U D Rennie	40
X		S	S		X		X	X	X	X		S	X1	X		X	S1	X	X	X									G S Willard	41
X	S1		S		X		X	X	X	S		X	X	X1	X	X			X	X				S					G Poll	42
X	S		S		X		X1	X	X	S		S1	X	X	X2	X	X		X						S2				G P Barber	43
X	S	X	S		X			X	X	S		X	X	X	X	X		X	X1	S1									N S Barry	44
X	S1	X	S		X			X	X	S		X2	X	S3	X	X1				X3					S2				G R Ashby	45
X	S	X	X		X	S	X	X	S			X	X		S		X	X	S				S						J T Winter	46
X		X	X		X	S	X	X	S			X		X1	X	S2		X	X2	S		S1							A B Wilkie	47
X	X	X	X		X	S	X		S			X			S	X	X		X	X		S		X					S J Lodge	48
18	6	24	17	19	11		24	31	27	20		22	27	24	15	36	6		34	20	18			2	10	1		6	CP Appearances	
1	16	1	3	1			1			1	1	1	1	2	6		10		2		7				1	4			CP Sub Appearances	
2	2+1	3	2	1			3+1	4	5	2		2	3+2	4	3	5			4	3	2+3				1	1			CC Appearances	
	0+1		1				1	1	1	1		1	1	1	1	0+1			1		1				1	1			FAC Appearances	
1	1+1	4	1	3			1	4	4	3		4	2	2	1	4			3+1	2	1+2				1	1		1	UEFA Appearances	

Also Played: (M) Barnes S(1). (M) Williams S(48).

LIVERPOOL

CLUB RECORDS

BIGGEST VICTORIES
League: 10-1 v Rotherham United, Division 2, 18.2.1896.
9-0 v Crystal Palace, Division 1, 12.9.1989.
6-1 v Crystal Palace, Premiership, 20.8.1994.
F.A. Cup: 8-0 v Swansea City, 3rd Round replay, 9.1.1990.
League Cup: 10-0 v Fulham, 2nd Round 1st leg, 23.9.1986.
Europe: 11-0 v Stromsgodset Gwc, ECWC, 17.9.1974.

BIGGEST DEFEATS
League: 1-9 v Birmingham City, Division 2, 11.12.1954.
0-8 v Huddersfield Town, Division 1, 10.11.1934.
F.A. Cup: 0-5 v Bolton Wanderers, 4th Round, 1945-46.
League Cup: 1-4 v West Ham, 4th Round, 30.11.1988.
Europe: (UEFA) 1-5 v Ajax, 2nd Round, 7.12.1966.

MOST POINTS
3 points a win: 90, Division 1, 1987-88 (equalled record).
2 points a win: 68, Division 1, 1978-79 (Division 1 record).

MOST GOALS SCORED
106, 1895-96.
Allan 25, Ross 23, Becton 17, Bradshaw 12, Geary 11, McVean 7, McQue 5, Hannah 3, Wilkie 1, Bull 1, McCartney 1.

MOST GOALS CONCEDED
97, Division 1, 1953-54.

MOST FIRST CLASS MATCHES IN A SEASON
67 - 1983-84 (League 42, FA Cup 2, League Cup 13, Charity Shield 1, European Cup 9).

MOST LEAGUE WINS
30, Division 1, 1978-79.

MOST LEAGUE DRAWS
19, Division 1, 1951-52.

MOST LEAGUE DEFEATS
23, Division 1, 1953-54.

INDIVIDUAL CLUB RECORDS

MOST GOALS IN A SEASON
Ian Rush: 47 goals in 1983-84 (League 32, FA Cup 2, League Cup 8, European Cup 5).

MOST GOALS IN A MATCH
5. Andy McGuigan v Stoke City (h) 7-0, Division 1, 4.1.1902.
5. John Evans v Bristol Rovers (h) 5-3, Division 2, 15.9.1954.
5. Ian Rush v Luton Town (h) 6-0, Division 1, 29.10.1983.
5. Robbie Fowler v Fulham (h) 5-0, League Cup 2nd Rnd, 5.10.93.

OLDEST PLAYER
Kenny Dalglish, 39 years 58 days v Derby County, 1.5.1990.

YOUNGEST PLAYER
Phil Charnock, ECWC, 16.09.92.

MOST CAPPED PLAYER
Ian Rush (Wales) 59.
Emlyn Hughes (England) 59.

BEST PERFORMANCES

League: 1978-79: Matches played 42, Won 30, Drawn 8, Lost 4, Goals for 85, Goals against 16, Points 68. First in Division 1.
Highest Position: Division 1 champions 18 times.
F.A. Cup: Winners in 1964-65, 1973-74, 1985-86, 1988-89.
Most recent success: 1991-92: 3rd Round Crewe Alexandra 4-0; 4th Round Bristol Rovers 1-1,2-1; 5th Round Ipswich Town 0-0,3-2; 6th Round Aston Villa 1-0; Semi-Final Portsmouth 1-1,0-0 (won 3-1 on penalties); Final Sunderland 2-0.
League Cup: Winners in 1980-81, 1981-82, 1982-83, 1983-84.
Most recent success: 1994-95: 2nd Round Burnley 2-0,4-1; 3rd Round Stoke City 2-1; 4th Round Blackburn Rovers 3-1; 5th Round Arsenal 1-0; Semi-Final Crystal Palace 1-0,1-0; Final Bolton Wanderers 2-1.
Europe: European Cup winners in 1976-77, 1977-78, 1980-81. Most recent success: 1983-84: 1st Round Odense 1-0,5-0; 2nd Round Athletico Bilbao 0-0,1-0; 3rd round Benfica 1-0,4-1; Semi-Final Dynamo Bucharest 1-0,2-1; Final Roma 1-1 (Won on pens). UEFA Cup winners in 1972-73.
Most recent success: 1975-76: 1st round Hibernian 0-1,3-1; 2nd Round Real Sociedad 3-1,6-0; 3rd Round Slask Wroclaw 2-1,3-0; 4th Round Dynamo Dresden 0-0,2-1; Semi-Final Barcelona 1-0,1-1; Final Bruges 3-2,1-1.

DIVISIONAL RECORD

	Played	Won	Drawn	Lost	For	Against	Points
Division 1/P	3,336	1,518	833	985	5,480	4,216	4,233
Division 2	428	243	82	103	977	571	568
Total	**3,764**	**1,742**	**915**	**1,088**	**6,457**	**4,787**	**4,801**

ADDITIONAL INFORMATION
PREVIOUS NAMES
None.
PREVIOUS LEAGUES
Lancashire League.

Club Colours: All red with white trim.
Change Colours: All white with red trim.

Reserves League: Pontins Central League Premier Division.

RECORDS AND STATISTICS

COMPETITIONS

Div 1/P	Div.2	Euro C	ECWC	UEFA	Sup.C	WCC
1894-95	1893-94	1964-65	1965-66	1967-68	1977	1981
1894-04	1895-96	1966-67	1971-72	1968-69	1978	1984
1905-54	1904-05	1973-74	1974-75	1969-70		
1962-	1954-62	1976-77	1992-93	1970-71		Sc Sp
		1977-78	1996-97	1972-73		Sup C
		1978-79		1975-76		1986
		1979-80		1991-92		
		1980-81		1995-96		
		1981-82				
		1982-83				
		1983-84				
		1984-85				

HONOURS

Div 1	Div.2	FAC	Lge C	Euro C	UEFA	C/Sh'd
1900-01	1893-94	1964-65	1980-81	1976-77	1972-73	1964
1905-06	1895-96	1973-74	1981-82	1977-78	1975-76	1965
1921-22	1904-05	1985-86	1982-83	1980-81		1966
1922-23	1961-62	1988-89	1983-84	1983-84		1974
1946-47		1991-92	1994-95		ESC	1976
1963-64					1977	1977
1965-66				Sc Sp		1979
1972-73				Sup C		1980
1975-76				1986		1982
1976-77						1986
1978-79						1988
1979-80						1989
1981-82						
1982-83						
1983-84						
1985-86						
1987-88						
1989-90						

MOST APPEARANCES

Ian Callaghan 845+5 (1959-78)

Year	League	FA Cup	Lge Cup	Europe
1959-60	4			
1960-61	3		2	
1961-62	24	5		
1962-63	37	6		
1963-64	42	5		
1964-65	37	8		9
1965-66	42	1		9
1966-67	40	4		5
1967-68	41	9	2	6
1968-69	42	4	3	2
1969-70	41	6	2	3+1
1970-71	21+1	4	1	5
1971-72	41	3	3	4
1972-73	42	4	8	12
1973-74	42	9	6	4
1974-75	41	2	3	4
1975-76	40	2	3	12
1976-77	32+1	4+1	2	7
1977-78	25+1	1	7	5
	637+3	77+1	42	87+1

MOST GOALS IN A CAREER

Ian Rush - 344 (1980-87/1988-96)

Year	League	FA Cup	Lge Cup	Europe	Other
1980-81					
1981-82	17	3	8	2	
1982-83	24	2	2	2	1
1983-84	32	2	8	5	
1984-85	14	7		5	
1985-86	22	6	3		2
1986-87	30		4		6
1988-89	7	3	1		
1989-90	18	6	2		
1990-91	16	5	5		
1991-92	3	1	3	1	
1992-93	14	1	1	5	1
1993-94	14	1	4		
1994-95	12	1	5		
1995-96	5	1	1		
Total	228	39	47	20	10

Current leading goalscorer: Robbie Fowler - 129 (1992-98)
Previous Holder: Roger Hunt - 285 (1959-70) Lge 245, FAC 18, Lge C 5, Europe 17

RECORD TRANSFER FEE RECEIVED

Amount	Club	Player	Date
£7,000,000	Aston Villa	Stan Collymore	05/97
£3,200,000	Juventus	Ian Rush	6/87
£650,000	Sampdoria	Graham Souness	6/84
£500,000	S V Hamburg	Kevin Keegan	6/77

RECORD TRANSFER FEE PAID

Amount	Club	Player	Date
£8,500,000	Nottingham Forest	Stan Collymore	07/95
£3,600,000	Coventry City	Phil Babb	09/94
£3,250,000	Borussia Dortmund	Patrik Berger	07/96
£2,900,000	Derby County	Dean Saunders	7/91

MANAGERS

Name	Seasons	Best	Worst
John McKenna	1892-96	16(1)	1(2)
Tom Watson	1896-15	1(1)	1(2)
Dave Ashworth	1920-23	1(1)	4(1)
Matt McQueen	1923-28	4(1)	16(1)
George Patterson	1928-36	7(1)	18(1)
George Kay	1936-51	1(1)	19(1)
Don Welsh	1951-56	9(1)	11(1)
Phil Taylor	1956-59	3(2)	4(2)
Bill Shankly	1959-74	1(1)	3(2)
Bob Paisley	1974-83	1(1)	5(1)
Joe Fagan	1983-85	1(1)	2(1)
Kenny Dalglish	1985-91	1(1)	2(1)
Graeme Souness	1991-94	6(P)	6(P)
Roy Evans	1994-	3(P)	4(P)

LONGEST LEAGUE RUNS

of undefeated matches:	31 (4.5.1987 - 16.3.1988)	of league matches w/out a win:	14 (5.12.1953 - 3.4.1954)
of undefeated home matches:	63 (25.2.1978 - 31.1.1981)	of undefeated away matches:	16 (2.9.1893-3.9.94, 9.5.87-16.3.88)
without home win:	10 (13.10.1951 - 22.3.1952)	without an away win:	24 (21.2.1953 - 7.4.1954)
of league wins:	12 (21.4.1990 - 6.10.1990)	of home wins:	21 (29.1.1972 - 30.12.1972)
of league defeats:	9 (29.4.1899 - 14.10.1899)	away wins:	6 (24.9.1904-19.11.1904, 31.12.04-11.3.05, 27.2.82-24.4.82)

LIVERPOOL

PLAYERS NAME Honours	Ht	Wt	Birthdate	Birthplace Transfers	Contract Date	Clubs	League	L/Cup	FA Cup	Other	Lge	L/C	FAC	Oth
G O A L K E E P E R														
Friedel Brad	6.3	14.7	18/05/71	USA		Columbus Crew								
USA Int.				£1000000	23/12/97	Liverpool	11							
James David B	6.5	15	01/08/70	Welwyn Gard.	01/07/88	Watford	89	6	2	1				
E:1, B.1,u21.10;FAYC'89;LC'95				£1000000	06/07/92	Liverpool	187+1	22	17	17				
Nielsen Jorgen T	6	13	06/05/71	Nykobing	31/05/97	Liverpool								
				Loan		Ikast (Denmark)								
Warner Anthony R	6.4	13.9	11/05/74	Liverpool	01/01/94	Liverpool								
				Loan	05/11/97	Swindon Town	2							
D E F E N C E														
Babb Philip A	6	11.7	30/11/70	Lambeth	24/04/89	Millwall								
Ei:25, B.1; LC'95;				Free	10/08/90	Bradford City	73+7	5+1	3	3+1	14			
				£500000	21/07/92	Coventry City	70+7	5	2		3	1		
				£3600000	01/09/94	Liverpool	100+3	16	11	9+1	1			
Bjorneby Stig I	5.1	11.9	11/12/69	Rosenborg (Norway)		Rosenborg								
Norwegian Int. LC'95				£600000	18/12/92	Liverpool	112+4	14	9+2	12	2			2
Harkness Steven	5.1	10.11	27/08/71	Carlisle	23/03/89	Carlisle United	12+1							
E: Y.13				£75000	17/07/89	Liverpool	86+10	11+3	4	12+2	2	1		
				Loan	24/09/93	Huddersfield Town	5		1					
				Loan	03/02/95	Southend United	6							
Heggem Vegard						Rosenborg								
				£3500000	21/07/98	Liverpool								
Jones Eifion P			28/09/80	Llanrug		Liverpool (T)								
Jones Robert M	5.11	11	05/11/71	Wrexham	20/12/88	Crewe Alexandra	59+16	9	0+3	3	2			
W: S; E:8, Y2, u21.2; FAC'92. LC'95 £300000				04/10/91	Liverpool	182	21+1	27	7					
Kvarne Bjorn	6.1	12.4	17/07/72	Trondheim		Rosenborg								
				Free	17/01/97	Liverpool	37+1	2	2	4				
Matteo Dominic	6.1	11.8	28/04/74	Dumfries	27/05/92	Liverpool	64+11	9	4+1	9				
E: B.1, u21.4, Y1.														
Murphy Neil A			19/05/80	Liverpool		Liverpool (T)								
O'Mara Paul			23/11/80	Dublin		Liverpool (T)								
Roberts Gareth W	5.8	11	06/02/78	Wrexham	31/05/97	Liverpool (T)								
Staunton Steve	5.11	11.2	19/01/69	Dundalk		Dundalk								
Ei:74,u21.4. Div.1'90. FAC'89. CS'89. LC'94'96.				£20000	02/09/86	Liverpool	55+10	6+2	14+2	1		4	1	1
				Loan	13/11/87	Bradford City	7+1	2		1				
				£1100000	07/08/91	Aston Villa	205+3	17+2	19+1	15+1	16	1	1	
				Free	02/07/98	Liverpool								
Wright Mark	6.3	12.11	01/08/63	Dorchester	26/08/80	Oxford United	8+2		1					
E: 45, u21.4; FAC'92; FLgXi.1				£80000	25/03/82	Southampton	170	25	17	10	7	2	1	1
				£760000	27/08/87	Derby County	144	15	5	7	10			
				£2200000	15/07/91	Liverpool	156+2	14+2	18	18	5	1		1
Wright Stephen J			08/02/80	Liverpool		Liverpool (T)								
M I D F I E L D														
Carragher Jamie	6	12	28/01/78	Bootle	16/08/96	Liverpool (T)	18+4	2+1		1	1			
E: B.2, u21.11, Yth.														
Cassidy Jamie	5.9	10.07	21/11/77	Liverpool	01/08/95	Liverpool (T)								
Culshaw Thomas A	5.10	12.2	10/10/78	Liverpool	31/05/97	Liverpool (T)								
Doherty Kevin			18/04/80	Dublin		Liverpool (T)								
Gerrard Steven G			30/05/80	Whiston		Liverpool (T)								
Ince Paul E C	5.1	11.7	21/10/67	Ilford	18/07/85	West Ham United	66+6	9	8+2	4	7	3	1	1
E: 43, B.1, u21.2, Y.3. FAC'90. CS'90.				£1000000	14/09/89	Manchester United	200+3	23+1	24+1	18	25	2	1	
ECWC'91. ESC'91. LC'92.				£8000000	01/07/95	Inter Milan								
				£4200000	22/07/97	Liverpool	31	4	1	4	8			
Leonhardsen Oyvind	5.1	11.02	17/08/70	Norway		Rosenborg								
Norwegian International				Loan	01/10/94	Wimbledon	18+2		3		4		1	
				£660000	01/08/95	Wimbledon	55+1	7+2	14		9	1	1	
				£4000000	03/06/97	Liverpool	27+1	3+2	1	2	6			
McAteer Jason	5.1	10.5	18/06/71	Birkenhead		Marine								
Ei: 25, B.1.				22/01/92	Bolton Wanderers	105+5	11	11	8+1	8	2	3	2	
				£4500000	06/09/95	Liverpool	78+9	10+1	10	9	3		3	
Maxwell Layton J	5.8	11	03/10/79	St Asaph	17/07/97	Liverpool (T)								
Murphy Daniel B	5.9	10.8	18/03/77	Chester	21/03/94	Crewe Alexandra	110+24	7	7	15+2	27		4	4
E: u21.2, Y.S.				£1500000	17/07/97	Liverpool	6+10		0+1					
Partridge Richard J			12/09/80	Dublin		Liverpool (T)								

90

	Ht	Wt	DOB	From/Fee	Signed	Club								
Redknapp Jamie F	5.11	11.8	25/06/73	Barton	27/06/90	Bournemouth	6+7	3	3	2				
E: 8, B.1, u21.19, Y2, S. LC'95				£350000	15/01/91	Liverpool	154+23	25	15+1	15+4	19	5	2	1
Thompson David A	5.7	10	12/09/77	Birkenhead	01/08/94	Liverpool	1+6				1			
E: u21.2, Y. FAYC'96.				Loan	21/11/97	Swindon Town	10							
Williams Daniel I	6.1	13	12/07/97	Wrexham	14/05/97	Liverpool (T)								
F O R W A R D														
Berger Patrik	6.2	12.6	10/11/73	Prague		Borussia M'Gladbach								
Czech Int.				£3250000	15/08/96	Liverpool	19+26	5+1	1+2	7+1	9	2		2
Byrne Niall P	5.8	11	03/09/79	Dublin	31/05/97	Liverpool (T)								
Dundee Sean						Karlsruhe								
				£2000000	06/06/98	Liverpool								
Fowler Robert B	5.8	10.3	09/04/75	Liverpool	23/04/92	Liverpool	156+4	25	17	13+1	92	20	9	8
E: 6, B.1, u21.8. EUFAY'93. LC'95.														
Gudnason Haukua			08/09/78	Keflavik		Keflavik								
				£500000	01/12/97	Liverpool								
McManaman Steve	5.11	10.2	11/02/72	Bootle	19/02/90	Liverpool	233+11	32+1	28+1	27	42	10	5	4
E:22, u21.7; Y2. FAC'92. LC'95.														
Newby John P	6	12	28/11/78	Warrington	23/05/97	Liverpool (T)								
Owen Michael	5.9	10.4	14/12/79	Chester	27/03/97	Liverpool	35+3	4		3+1	19	4		1
E: 9, u21.1, Y, S.														
Riedle Karlheinz	5.11	12	16/09/65	Weiler		B. Dortmund								
German Int. WC'90. EC'97.				£1600000	01/08/97	Liverpool	18+7	2+3	1	1+2	6			1

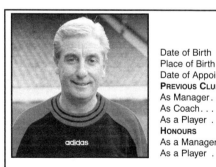

THE MANAGERS
ROY EVANS

Date of Birth . . . . 5th June 1948.
Place of Birth . . . . Bootle.
Date of Appointment . . . . January 1994.
PREVIOUS CLUBS
As Manager. . . . . None.
As Coach. . . . . Liverpool.
As a Player . . . . Liverpool.
HONOURS
As a Manager: . . . . League Cup 1994/95.
As a Player . . . . England Schools.

GERARD HOULLIER

Date of Appointment . . . . July 1998.
Former French International Coach.

ANFIELD
Anfield Road, Liverpool L4 0TH

Capacity ....45,362.

First game ....v Rotherham, 1.9.1892.
First floodlit game ....v Everton, 30.10.1957.
Internationals ....England v Ireland 1899, 1926. v Wales 1905, 1922, 1931.
.... Wales v Scotland 1977. **Euro'96:** Italy v Russia 10.6.96. Italy v Czech Republic 14.6.96.
....Czech Republic v Russia 19.6.96. France v Holland 22.6.96 (QF).
ATTENDANCES
Highest ....61,905 v Wolves, FA Cup 4th Round, 2.2.1952.
Lowest ....1,000 v Loughborough, Division 2, 7.12.1895.

OTHER GROUNDS...None.

HOW TO GET TO THE GROUND

From the North: Use motorway (M6) until junction 28, then follow signs to Liverpool on A58 and forward into Walton Hall Avenue past Stanley Park and turn left into Anfield Road for Liverpool FC.

From the East and South: Use motorway M6 then M62 until end of motorway, then turn right (A5058 into Queens Drive. In 3 miles turn left into Utting Avenue. In 1 mile turn right into Anfield Road for Liverpool FC.

From the West: Use Mersey tunnel into Liverpool City Centre, then follow signs to Preston (A580) into Walton Hall Avenue, then on nearside of Stanley Park turn right into Anfield Road for Liverpool FC.

Car Parking: Limited street parking. Mainly privately-owned car park in Priory Road (5 minutes walk from ground).

Nearest Railway Station: Kirkdale or Lime Street (0151 709 9696)

USEFUL TELEPHONE NUMBERS

Club switchboard 0151 263 2361
Club fax number.......................0151 260 8813
Ticket Office Telephone no...........0151 260 8680.
(Office hours only)

Internet addressCurrently under construction.
Clubcall 0891 12 11 84*
*Calls cost 50p per minute at all times.
Call costings correct at time of going to press.

MATCHDAY PROGRAMME

Programme Editor..........................I Cotton.

Number of pages.....................................50.

Price ....£2.

Subscriptions ....Apply to club.

Local Newspapers
..........Liverpool Daily Post, Liverpool Echo.

Local Radio Stations
.....................Radio Merseyside, Radio City.

MATCHDAY TICKET PRICES

Main, Centenary, Paddock and
Anfield Road Stands £20

Kop Grandstand £18

Family (1+1) - Andfield Rd Stand £30.00

Family (1+1) - Kop Grandstand. £27.00

MANCHESTER UNITED
(The Red Devils)
F.A. CARLING PREMIERSHIP
SPONSORED BY: SHARP

1997-98 - Back Row L-R: Michael Appleton (now P.N.E.), Philip Mulryne, Brian McClair, Nicky Butt, Andy Cole, Chris Casper, Phil Neville, Ryan Giggs, John O'Kane, Gary Neville. Middle Row: Albert Morgan (Kit manager), David Beckham, Jordi Cruyff, Teddy Sheringham, Raimond van der Gouw, Peter Schmeichel, Gary Pallister, Ronny Johnsen, David May, David Fevre (Physio). Fron Row: Terry Cooke, Karel Poborsky, Ole Gunnar Solskjaer, Graeme Tomlinson, Alex Ferguson (Manager), Roy Keane, Brian Kidd (Asst. Manager), Michael Clegg, Denis Irwin, Ben Thornley, Paul Scholes.

MANCHESTER UNITED
FORMED IN 1878
TURNED PROFESSIONAL IN 1885
LTD COMPANY IN 1907

CHAIRMAN: C M Edwards

DIRECTORS
J M Edelson, Sir Bobby Charlton CBE,
E M Watkins, R L Olive,

SECRETARY
Kenneth R Merrett (0161 872 1661/2)
COMMERCIAL MANAGER
Danny McGregor (0161 872 3488)

MANAGER: Alex Ferguson OBE
ASSISTANT MANAGER: Brian Kidd

RESERVE TEAM MANAGER
Jimmy Ryan
YOUTH TEAM MANAGER
Eric Harrison
PHYSIOTHERAPIST
David Fevre

STATISTICIAN FOR THE DIRECTORY
Vacant - call 01203 234017 if interested

When the 1997-98 season commenced, bookies up and down the country, firmly believed that Manchester United were a good bet to emulate Huddersfield Town (1920s), Arsenal (1930s) and Liverpool (1980s) by recording a hat-trick of top Division championship triumphs - and at the turn of the year, with 20 games completed, they held a six point lead over Blackburn Rovers - and were well on course to do just that.

Come March and that third successive title looked there for the taking. The Reds - playing now to regular full houses of around 55,000 at Old Trafford, found themselves a massive 11 points clear of Rovers, with Arsenal a further two points adrift in third place, but the Gunners did have three games in hand.

But then things started to go wrong for Alex Ferguson's man. After been dumped out of the Champions League (beaten by AS Monaco), slowly but surely they saw Arsenal gradually claw themselves back into contention, and when the Londoners won their crucial six-point Carling Premiership game at Old Trafford on 14 March (1-0), even the staunchest United supporter knew at that juncture, it wasn't going to be their year. Indeed, from their remaining 10 Carling Premiership matches, United collected just 18 points, while Arsenal amassed a total of 31 from their last 23 encounters - and duly leap-frogged over Ferguson's side to take their first League title in seven years and tin doing so denied the Reds a third successive Carling Premiership victory. Injuries to key players (including Roy Keane for most of the campaign and then Ryan Giggs) coupled with the inevitable suspensions, no doubt disrupted United's team formation considerably - although manager Ferguson did not use this as an excuse. However, team morale certainly suffered following dismissals from the F.A. Cup and then the European Champions League, but at the end of the day it was perhaps United's home form (14 points dropped all season and a lack of goals late on being the key factors) which let them down - and this allowed Arsenal to complete the coveted League and Cup double.

Tony Matthews.

MANCHESTER UNITED

Carling Prem. :2nd   FA CUP: 5th Round   LC CUP: 3rd Round   European Cup: Quarter-finals

M	DATE	COMP.	VEN	OPPONENTS	RESULT	H/T	LP	GOAL SCORERS/GOAL TIMES	ATT.
1	A 03	CS	A	Chelsea	D 1-1	0-0		Johnsen 58	(73636)
2	10	CP	A	Tottenham Hotspur	W 2-0	0-0	1	Butt 82, Vega 83 (OG)	(26359)
3	12	CP	H	Southampton	W 1-0	0-0	2	Beckham 78	55008
4	23	CP	A	Leicester City	D 0-0	0-0	3		(21221)
5	27	CP	A	Everton	W 2-0	1-0	2	Beckham 29, Sheringham 51	(40079)
6	30	CP	H	Coventry City	W 3-0	1-0	2	Cole 1, Keane 72, Poborsky 89	55074
7	S 13	CP	H	West Ham United	W 2-1	1-1	1	Keane 21, Scholes 76	55068
8	17	EC GB	A	Kosice	W 3-0	1-0		Irwin 31, Berg 61, Cole 88	
9	20	CP	A	Bolton Wanderers	D 0-0	0-0	1		(25000)
10	24	CP	H	Chelsea	D 2-2	1-1	2	Scholes 35, Solskjaer 86	55163
11	27	CP	A	Leeds United	L 0-1	0-1	2		(39952)
12	O 01	EC GB	H	Juventus	W 3-2	1-1		Sheringham 38, Scholes 69, Giggs 90	53,428
13	04	CP	H	Crystal Palace	W 2-0	2-0	2	Sheringham 17, Hreidarsson 29 (OG)	55143
14	14	CC 3	A	Ipswich Town	L 0-2	0-2			(22173)
15	18	CP	A	Derby County	D 2-2	0-2	3	Sheringham 51, Cole 83	(30014)
16	22	EC GB	H	Feyenoord	W 2-1	1-0		Scholes 31, Irwin 72 (pen)	53,188
17	25	CP	H	Barnsley	W 7-0	4-0	1	Cole 17, 18, 44, Giggs 42, 56, Scholes 58, Poborsky 79	55142
18	N 01	CP	H	Sheffield Wednesday	W 6-1	4-0	1	Sheringham 13, 62, Cole 19, 38, Solskjaer 40, 74	55259
19	05	EC GB	A	Feyenoord	W 3-1	2-0		Cole 31,44,74	(51000)
20	09	CP	A	Arsenal	L 2-3	2-2	1	Sheringham 32, 41	(38203)
21	22	CP	A	Wimbledon	W 5-2	0-0	1	Butt 47, Beckham 66, 74, Scholes 80, Cole 85	(26309)
22	27	EC GB	H	Kosice	W 3-0	1-0		Cole 39, Faktor 85 (OG), Sheringham 90	53535
23	30	CP	H	Blackburn Rovers	W 4-0	1-0	1	Solskjaer 17, 53, Kenna 85 (OG)	55175
24	D 06	CP	A	Liverpool	W 3-1	0-0	1	Cole 51, 74, Beckham 70	(41027)
25	10	EC GB	A	Juventus	L 0-1	0-0			(0)
26	15	CP	H	Aston Villa	W 1-0	0-0	1	Giggs 51	55151
27	21	CP	A	Newcastle United	W 1-0	0-0	1	Cole 67	(36767)
28	26	CP	H	Everton	W 2-0	2-0	1	Berg 14, Cole 34	55167
29	28	CP	A	Coventry City	L 2-3	1-1	1	Solskjaer 30, Sheringham 47	(23054)
30	J 04	FAC 3	A	Chelsea	W 5-3	3-0		Beckham 23, 28, Cole 45, 65, Sheringham 73	(34792)
31	10	CP	H	Tottenham Hotspur	W 2-0	1-0	1	Giggs 44, 67	55281
32	19	CP	A	Southampton	L 0-1	0-1	1		(15241)
33	24	FAC 4	H	Walsall	W 5-1	2-0		Cole 10, 66, Solskjaer 38, 69, Johnsen 73	54669
34	31	CP	H	Leicester City	L 0-1	0-1	1		55156
35	F 06	CP	H	Bolton Wanderers	D 1-1	0-0	1	Cole 84	55156
36	15	FAC 5	H	Barnsley	D 1-1	1-1		Sheringham 42	54669
37	18	CP	A	Aston Villa	W 2-0	0-0	1	Beckham 82, Giggs 89	(39372)
38	21	CP	H	Derby County	W 2-0	1-0	1	Giggs 19, Irwin 71 (pen)	55170
39	25	FAC 5R	A	Barnsley	L 2-3	0-2		Sheringham 56, Cole 82	(18655)
40	28	CP	A	Chelsea	W 1-0	1-0	1	Neville 31	(34511)
41	M 04	EC QF1	A	Monaco	D 0-0	0-0			(15000)
42	07	CP	A	Sheffield Wednesday	L 0-2	0-1	1		(39427)
43	11	CP	H	West Ham United	D 1-1	0-1	1	Scholes 65	(25892)
44	14	CP	H	Arsenal	L 0-1	0-0	1		55174
45	18	EC QF2	H	Monaco	D 1-1	0-1		Solskjaer 53	53683
46	28	CP	H	Wimbledon	W 2-0	0-0	1	Johnsen 83, Scholes 90	55306
47	A 06	CP	A	Blackburn Rovers	W 3-1	0-1	1	Cole 56, Scholes 73, Beckham 90	(30547)
48	10	CP	H	Liverpool	D 1-1	1-1	1	Johnsen 12	55171
49	18	CP	H	Newcastle United	D 1-1	1-1	2	Beckham 37	55194
50	27	CP	A	Crystal Palace	W 3-0	2-0	2	Scholes 6, Butt 21, Cole 84	(26180)
51	M 04	CP	H	Leeds United	W 3-0	2-0	2	Giggs 6, Irwin 31 (pen), Beckham 59	55167
52	10	CP	A	Barnsley	W 2-0	1-0	2	Cole 5, Sheringham 76	(18694)

Best Home League Attendance: 55306 V Wimbledon   **Smallest :55008 V Southampton**   Average :55164

Goal Scorers:

CP	(73)	Cole 16, Beckham 9, Sheringham 9, Giggs 8, Scholes 8, Solskjaer 6, Butt 3, Irwin 2, Johnsen 2, Keane 2, Poborsky 2, Berg 1, Neville 1, Opponents 4
CC	(0)	
FAC	(13)	Cole 5, Sheringham 3, Beckham 2, Solskjaer 2, Johnsen 1
EC	(15)	Cole 5, Irwin 2, Scholes 2, Sheringham2, Berg 1, Giggs 1, Solskjaer 1, Opponents 1

(M) Beckham	(D) Berg	(M) Brown	(F) Butt	(D) Clegg	(F) Cole	(F) Cruyff	(D) Curtis	(F) Giggs	(D) Irwin	(D) Johnsen	(M) Keane	(D) May	(F) McClair	(F) Mulryne	(D) Neville G	(D) Neville P	(F) Nevland	(D) Pallister	(G) Pilkington	(F) Poborsky	(G) Schmeichel	(F) Scholes	(D) Sheringham	(D) Solskjaer	(M) Thornley	(F) Twiss	(G) Van Der Gouw	Referee	
S1		X		X		X1	X	X	X		S				S	X		X			S	X	X	X1		S		P. Jones	1
S1		X			X		X	X	X	X					S	X		X			S	X	X	X			S	G Poll	2
S2	S1	X			X		X	X	X	X					S	X		X			S	X	X	X			S	G P Barber	3
X	X	X			X		X	X		X		S	S	X	S			X				X	S1	X			S	D J Gallagher	4
X	X	X		S1			X	X		X		S		X	S			X				S	X	X			S	K W Burge	5
X	X	X		X		S	X	S2		X		S		X	S			X			S1	X		X			S	G R Ashby	6
X	X	X	S	S			X	X		X		S2		X	X			X			S1	X	X				S	D R Elleray	7
X1	X		X	S	X			X		X		S1	S	X	X	X		S			X	X	X	S		S	S		8
X	X	X		X			X			X		S		X	S1			X			X	X	X		S2	S	S	P A Durkin	9
X	X	X		X			X	S3	X	S	X			X				X			X	X	X	S2	S1		S	G S Willard	10
X	X						X	S1	X	X				X	S3			X			X	X	X		S2		S	M J Bodenham	11
X	X	X1	S		S	X	X	X		S	S			X	S2			X				X	S1	X	X2		S		12
X	X		X			X	S2	X		S	S			X	X			X			S1	X	X	X			S	S J Lodge	13
				X	X	X		S2	X		X	X	X		X	S3					X		S1			X	X	P E Alcock	14
X	X		X	S2			X	X	S1			S		X	S3			X			X	X	X	X			S	G Poll	15
X		X	X1	S	S	X	X			S				X	X			X			S	X	X	X	S1	S	S		16
X		X	X	S3	X	X				S				X	X			X			S1	X	X	X				M A Riley	17
X	X	X	X		S3					S2	S	X	X		X			X			S1	X	X	X				G R Ashby	18
X	X		X3			X	X1							X	X	S1		X			S2	X	X2	X	S3		S		19
X	X		X			X				S1				X	X	X		X			S	X	X	X	S		S	M J Bodenham	20
S1	X		X		S	X		X						X	X			X			S	X	X	S			S	P A Durkin	21
X	S3	X1	X		S	X2	X							X	X3			X			S2	X	X	S1	S	S	S		22
X	X	X1	S	X		X		S1		S3				X	X			X2			S2	X		X3	X		S	A B Wilkie	23
X	X	X		X		X				X				X	X			X			S	S	X	X	S		S	D R Elleray	24
X	X		S	S1		S	X		X					X	S2	S		X			X	X2		X	X1	S	S	Not Known	25
X	S	X		X		S		X				X			X	X		X			X	S	X	X	X1		S	P A Durkin	26
X	S	X		X		S	X							X	S2			X	S		X	X1	X2	S1				P Jones	27
X1	X		X		S3	S		X						X	S2		X3	X2	X	S1		X	X					U D Rennie	28
X	X	S2		X		S1	X			X1				X	S	S					X	X	X	X2				N S Barry	29
X	S	X	S			X	X	X		S				X	X			X			X	X1	X	S1				S J Lodge	30
X	S	S	S			X	X	X		S				X	X			X			S	X	X	X				P E Alcock	31
X	X	X1		X		X	X	X		S1				X	X2	S	S2	X	S			X		X				M A Riley	32
X	X		S1	X		3	X1	X		X	S3	S	X	S2				X	X3		X	X	X	S1		X	X2	P A Durkin	33
X	S1		X			X	X	X1		S				X	S3			X	S		X	X2	S2	X			S	G R Ashby	34
X	S1		S	X		X	X			S				X	X			X			X	X	X1	X		S	S	S J Lodge	35
S1	X		X		S2		X	X	X1					X3		S3	S1	X2	X		X		X				S	M A Riley	36
X	X	X	S1	X	S		X	X		X1					X	S1	S	X			X		X				S	M J Bodenham	37
X	X	X	S1	X2	S2	X3	X1			S3					X			X			X		X				S	M D Reed	38
X		X3	X			S2			X	X2				X	X	X1		X			X		S1			S3	S	M A Riley	39
X	S1		X			X	X							X	X	X1		X			X	X	S	S			S	S W Dunn	40
X	X		S	X			X1	X		S	S1			X	X			X			X	X	S	S			S	M D Vega	41
X	X		X	X3	S2			X1		S3				X	X2		S			S1	X	S	X				X	P Jones	42
X	X	X2		X3	S2		X			X	X1			X	X2						X		X	S3	S1		S	G S Willard	43
X			X	X1		X	X3	S3	S	X	X2				X	X		X			X	X	S2	S1			S	A B Wilkie	44
X	S1	X	S2	X		S	X	X		S	S			X1	X		S				X2	X	X	S			X	Helmut Krug	45
X	X		X2	S			X	X		X	S2			X	X						X		X1	S1			X	D J Gallagher	46
X		S1	X			X	X	X		S				X	X			X			X	X	S	X1	S		X	G R Ashby	47
X	S	X		X		X1	X	X2		S2				X	X3			X			X	X	S3		S1		S	G Poll	48
X	S	X2	S	X		X	X			X				X3	X			X			X1	S2	X	S3			S1	U D Rennie	49
X	S	X	S1	X		X	X1			X				X	X			X			X	X	X	S	S		X	P Jones	50
X	S	S2	X			X	X1			X2	S3	S	X	S1	X						X	X3					X	G S Willard	51
	X	X	X1	X		X	X						X		X			X								S	X	P Durkin	52
34	23	1	31	1	31	3	3	28	23	18	9	7	2	1	34	24		33	2	3	32	28	28	15			4	CP Appearances	
3	4	1	2	2	2	2	5	1	2	4		2	11			6	1			7		3	3	7	5		1	CP Sub Appearances	
				1	1	1		0+1	1		1	1	1		1	0+1		1			1		0+1			1	1	CC Appearances	
3+1	2		1		2+1	3	0+1		2	3+1	3		1		3	0+1	2+1	3	2+1	3		4	2	2+1	1+1	2	0+1	FAC Appearances	
8+1	5+2		8	0+1	7+1	0+1		6	7	6	2		0+3		8	6+2		7			2+2	8	7+1	8	3+3		1	EC Appearances	

Also Played: (D) Casper S(36,38,39,41,43,45). (G) Culkin S(29,52). (M) Greening S(52). (D) Higginbottom S1(52). (F) Notman S(52), (D) Wallwork S2(17).

MANCHESTER UNITED

CLUB RECORDS

BIGGEST VICTORIES
League: 10-1 v Wolverhampton Wanderers, Division 2, 15.10.1892.
9-0 v Walsall, Division 2, 3.4.1895.
9-0 v Darwen, Division 2, 24.12,1898.
9-0 v Ipswich Town, Premiership, 4.3.95.
F.A. Cup: 8-0 v Yeovil Town, 5th Round, 12.2.1949.
League Cup: 7-2 v Newcastle United, 4th Round, 1976-77.
5-0 v Tranmere Rovers, 2nd Round, 1976-77.
5-0 v Rotherham United, 2nd Round, 12.10.1988.
5-0 v Hull City, 2nd Round, 23.9.1987.
Europe: 10-0 v Anderlecht, European Cup, 26.9.1956.
BIGGEST DEFEATS
League: 0-7 v Wolverhampton Wanderers, Division 2, 26.12.1931.
0-7 v Aston Villa, Division 1, 27.12.1930.
0-7 v Blackburn Rovers, Division 1, 10.4.1926.
F.A. Cup: 1-7 v Burnley, 1st Round, 1901
0-6 v Sheffield Wednesday, 2nd Round, 1904.
League Cup: 1-5 v Blackpool, 2nd Round, 1966-67.
0-4 v Manchester City, 4th Round, 12.11.1975.
Europe: (ECWC) 0-5 v Sporting Lisbon, Quarter-final, 18.3.1964.

MOST POINTS
3 points a win: 92, Premiership, 1993-94 (Divisional record).
2 points a win: 64, Division 1, 1956-57.
MOST GOALS SCORED
103, Division 1, 1956-57, 1958-59.
Whelen 26, Taylor 22, Viollet 16, Charlton 10, Berry 8, Pegg 6,
Edwards 5, Webster 3, Dawson 3, Scanlon 2, Colman 1, Opponents
1.
(58-59) Charlton 29, Violet 21, Scanlon 16, Bradley 12, Goodwin 6,
Webster 5, Dawson 4, Quixall 4, Cope 2, McGuinness 1, Pearson 1,
Opponents 2.
MOST GOALS CONCEDED
115, Division 1, 1930-31.

MOST FIRST CLASS MATCHES IN A SEASON
63 - 1993-94 (League 42, FA Cup 7, League Cup 9, European Cup
4, Charity Shield 1).

MOST LEAGUE WINS
28, Division 2, 1905-06, Division 1, 1956-57.

MOST LEAGUE DRAWS
18, Division 1, 1980-81.

MOST LEAGUE DEFEATS
27, Division 1, 1930-31.

INDIVIDUAL CLUB RECORDS

INDIVIDUAL CLUB RECORDS
MOST GOALS IN A SEASON
Denis Law: 46 goals in 1963-64 (League 30, FA Cup 10, ECWC 6).

MOST GOALS IN A MATCH
6. Joe Cassidy v Walsall Town Swifts, 9-0, Division 2, 3.4.1895.
6. Harold Halse v Swindon Town, 8-4, Charity Shield, 1911.
6. George Best v Northampton Town (a), 8-2, FA Cup 5th Round,
7.2.1970.

OLDEST PLAYER
Billy Meredith, 46 years 285 days v Derby County, 7.5.1921.

YOUNGEST PLAYER
Duncan Edwards, 16 years 182 days v Cardiff City, 4.4.1953.

MOST CAPPED PLAYER
Bobby Charlton (England) 106.
(England's top goal scorer with 49).

BEST PERFORMANCES

League: 1956-57: Matches played 42, Won 28, Drawn 8, Lost 6,
Goals for 103, Goals against 54, Points 64. First in Division 1.
Highest Position: Division 1/Premiership champions on
11 occasions.
F.A. Cup: Winners in 1908-09,1947-48, 1962-63, 1976-77, 1982-83,
1984-85, 1989-90, 1993-94.
1995-96: 3rd Round Sunderland 2-2, 2-1; 4th Round Readng 3-0;
5th Round Manchester City 2-1; 6th Round Southampton 2-0;
Semi-final Chelsea 2-1; Final Liverpool 1-0.
League Cup: 1991-92: 2nd Round Cambridge United 3-0,1-1, 3rd
round Portsmouth 3-1; 4th Round Oldham Athletic 2-0; 5th Round
Leeds United 3-1; Semi-Final Middlesbrough 0-0,2-1; Final
Nottingham Forest 1-0.
Europe: (European Cup) 1967-68: 1st Round Hibernians Valletta 4-
0,0-0; 2nd Round Sarajevo 0-0,2-1; 3rd Round Gornik Zabrze 2-0,0-
1; Semi-final Real Madrid 1-0,3-3; Final Benfica 4-1 aet.
(ECWC) 1990-91: 1st Round Pecsi Munkas 2-1,1-0; 2nd Round
Wrexham 3-0,2-0; 3rd Round Montpellier 1-1,2-0; Semi-final Legia
Warsaw 3-1,1-1; Final Barcelona 2-1.

DIVISIONAL RECORD

	Played	Won	Drawn	Lost	For	Against	Points
Division 1/P	2,980	1,308	764	908	4,969	4,077	3,731
Division 2	816	406	168	242	1,433	966	980
Total	3,796	1,714	932	1,150	6,402	5,043	4,711

ADDITIONAL INFORMATION
PREVIOUS NAMES
Newton Heath 1878-1902.

PREVIOUS LEAGUES
Football Alliance.

Club colours: Red shirts with black collar, white shorts, black
socks.
Change colours: White shirts, white shorts & black socks.

Reserves League: Pontins Central League Premier Division.

COMPETITIONS

Div.1/P	Div.2	Euro C	ECWC	UEFA	C/Shield	
1892-94	1894-06	1956-57	1963-64	1964-65	1908	1985
1906-22	1922-25	1957-58	1977-78	1976-77	1911	1990
1925-31	1931-36	1965-66	1983-84	1980-81	1952	1993
1936-37	1937-38	1967-68	1990-91	1982-83	1956	1994
1938-74	1974-75	1968-69	1991-92	1984-85	1957	1996
1975-		1993-94		1992-93	1965	1997
		1994-95		1995-96	1967	Wat C
		1996-97			1977	1970
		1997-98			1983	1971

HONOURS

Div.1/P	Div.2	FA Cup	Lge Cup	Euro C	C/Shield
1907-08	1935-36	1908-09	1991-92	1967-68	1908
1910-11	1974-75	1947-48			1911
1951-52		1962-63			1952
1955-56		1976-77		ECWC	1956
1956-57		1982-83		1991	1957
1964-65		1984-85			1965*
1966-67		1989-90			1977*
1992-93		1993-94		ESC	1983
1993-94		1995-96		1991	1990*
1995-96					1993
1996-97					1994
					1996
					*shared

MOST APPEARANCES

Bobby Charlton 756 (1956-73)

Year	League	FA Cup	Lge Cup	Europe
1956-57	14	2		1
1957-58	21	8		2
1958-59	38	1		
1959-60	37	3		
1960-61	39	3		
1961-62	37	7		
1962-63	28	6		
1963-64	40	7		6
1964-65	41	7		11
1965-66	38	7		8
1966-67	42	2		
1967-68	41	2		9
1968-69	32	6		8
1969-70	40	9	8	
1970-71	42	2	6	
1971-72	40	7	6	
1972-73	34+2	1	4	
	604+2	80	24	45

Includes 3 Charity Shield (1963-64, 1965-66 & 1907-08)

RECORD TRANSFER FEE RECEIVED

Amount	Club	Player	Date
£7,000,000	Inter Milan	Paul Ince	07/95
£5,000,000	Everton	Andrei Kanchelskis	08/95
£2,500,000	Barcelona	Mark Hughes	06/86
£1,500,000	Chelsea	Mark Hughes	06/95
£1,500,000	AC Milan	Ray Wilkins	06/84

RECORD TRANSFER FEE PAID

Amount	Club	Player	Date
£10,750,000	PSV Eindhoven	Jaap Stam	05/98
£7,000,000	Newcastle Utd	Andy Cole	01/95
£3,750,000	Nott'm Forest	Roy Keane	07/93
£3,500,000	Slavia Prague	Karel Poborsky	07/96

MOST GOALS IN A CAREER

Bobby Charlton - 248 (1956-73))

Year	League	FA Cup	Lge Cup	Europe
1956-57	10	1		1
1957-58	8	5		3
1958-59	29			
1959-60	17	3		
1960-61	21			
1961-62	8	2		
1962-63	7	2		
1963-64	9	2		4
1964-65	10			8
1965-66	16			2
1966-67	12			
1967-68	15	1		2
1968-69	5			2
1969-70	12	1	1	
1970-71	5		3	
1971-72	8	2	2	
1972-73	6		1	
Total	198	19	7	22

Includes 2 goals in the Charity Shield.

Current leading goalscorer: Ryan Giggs - 65 (12/90-98)

MANAGERS

Name	Seasons	Best	Worst
E Magnall	1903-12	1(1) x2	3(2)
J R Robson	1914-21	12(1)	18(1)
J Chapman	1921-26	9(1)	14(2)
C Hilditch	1926-27	15(1)	15(1)
H Bamlett	1927-31	12(1)	22(1)
W Crickner	1931-32	12(1)	12(1)
A Scott Duncan	1932-37	21(1)	20(2)
M Busby	1945-69	1(1) x5	19(1)
J Murphy	1958		
W McGuinness	1969-70	8(1)	8(1)
M Busby	1970-71	8(1)	8(1)
F O'Farrell	1971-72	8(1)	8(1)
T Docherty	1972-77	3(1)	1(2)
D Sexton	1977-81	2(1)	10(1)
R Atkinson	1981-86	3(1)	8(1)
A. Ferguson	1986-	1(P) x4	13(1)

LONGEST LEAGUE RUNS

of undefeated matches:	26 (21.1.1956 - 20.10.1956)	of league matches w/out a win:	16 (19.3.1930 - 25.10.1930)
of undefeated home matches:	37 (27.4.1966 - 27.3.1968)	of undefeated away matches:	14 (21.1.1956 - 20.10.1956)
without home win:7 (30.3.1920 - 6.9.1920, 19.4.1930 - 1.10.1930)			
(9.12.1933 - 3.3.1934, 22.2.1958 - 21.4.1958, 5.2.1978 - 29.3.1978)		without an away win:	26 (15.2.1930 - 3.4.1931)
of league wins:	14 (8.10.1904 - 1.2.1905)	of home wins:	18 (15.10.1904 - 30.4.1905)
of league defeats:	14 (26.4.1930 - 25.10.1930)	of away wins:	7 (5.4.1993 - 28.8.1993)

MANCHESTER UNITED

PLAYERS NAME Honours	Ht	Wt	Birthdate	Birthplace Transfers	Contract Date	Clubs	League	L/Cup	FA Cup	Other	Lge	L/C	FAC	Oth
G O A L K E E P E R														
Culkin Nicholas	6.2	12.13	7/6/78	York		York City								
				£250000	9/25/95	Manchester United								
Gibson Paul R	6.2	13.4	11/1/76	Sheffield	7/1/95	Manchester United								
Schmeichel Peter B	6.4	13.6	11/18/68	Glodstone (Den)		Brondby								
Den: ; Den FAC'89; Div1'87'88 '89; ESC'91;				£550000	8/12/91	Manchester United	258	17	33	34		1		
EuroC'92 LC'92. PREM'93'94'96'97 FAC'94'96. CS'93'94'96'97.														
Van Der Gouw Raimond	6.3	13.7	3/24/63	Oldenzaal (Holland)		Vitesse Arnham								
					7/1/96	Manchester United	6+1	3		2				
D E F E N C E														
Berg Henning	6	11.9	9/1/69	Edsvill		Lillestrom (Swe)								
Norwegian Int. Prem'95.				£400000	1/26/93	Blackburn Rovers	154+5	16	10	9	4			
				£5000000	8/12/97	Manchester United	23+4		2	5+2	1			1
Casper Christopher M	6	10.7	4/28/75	Burnley	2/3/93	Manchester Utd (T)	0+2	3	1	0+1				
E: Y.8; FAYC'92; UEFA Yth'93				Loan	2/11/96	Bournemouth								
Clegg Michael J	5.8	11.8	7/3/77	Thameside	8/1/95	Manchester Utd (T)	4+3	1	3+1	0+1				
Curtis John C	5.9	11.3	9/3/78	Nuneaton	10/23/95	Manchester Utd (T)	3+5	1						
Ford Ryan	5.9	10.2	9/3/78	Worksop	7/1/97	Manchester Utd (T)								
Higginbottom Danny	6	11.8	12/29/78	Manchester	7/1/97	Manchester Utd (T)	0+1							
Irwin Joseph Dennis	5.8	10.1	10/31/65	Cork	11/3/83	Leeds United	72	5	3	2	1			
Ei: 28, B.1, u21.3, Y, S.				Free	5/22/86	Oldham Athletic	166+1	19	13	5	4	3		
CS'90. ECWC'91; ESC'91; LC'92;FAC'96.				£625000	6/20/90	Manchester United	274+6	28+3	35+1	33	17		6	
PREM'96'97														
Johnsen Jean Ronny	6.3	13.1	6/10/69	Sandefjord (Norway)		Besiktas								
Norway: PREM'97.				£1200000	7/10/96	Manchester United	44+9	1	5	14	2		1	1
May David	6	11.4	6/24/70	Oldham	6/16/88	Blackburn Rovers	123	12+1	10	5	3	2	1	
FAC'96. PREM'97.				£1400000	7/1/94	Manchester United	61+12	5	5	13+1	5	1		1
Neville Philip J	5.11	12	1/21/77	Bury	6/1/94	Manchester United	59+12	3+1	10+1	9+2	1			
E: 12, u21.7, Y, S. FAYC'95; FAC'96; Prem'96'97														
Neville Gary A	5.11	11.7	2/18/75	Bury	1/29/93	Manchester United	112+4	4+1	14+2	16+4	1			
E: 30, Y8; FAYC'92; UEFA Yth'93; FAC'96 Prem'96'97														
Stam Jaap				Holland		PSV Eindhoven								
Dutch Int.				£10750000	5/6/98	Manchester United								
Wallwork Ronald	5.9	12.9	9/10/77	Manchester	3/17/95	Manchester United	0+1							
E: Y				Loan	12/22/97	Carlisle United	10				1			
				Loan	3/19/98	Stockport County	7							
M I D F I E L D														
Beckham David R J	5.11	10.7	5/2/75	Leytonstone	1/29/93	Manchester United	95+15	5+1	9+2	18+1	24		4	4
E: 18. u21.9, Y.4; FAYC'92; FAC'96; Prem'97				Loan	2/28/95	Preston North End	4+1				2			
Brown Wesley	6.1	12.2	3/16/79	Manchester	11/4/96	Manchester Utd (T)	1+1							
Evans Wayne A	5.9	9.12	23/10/80	Carmarthen		Manchester Utd (T)								
Greening Jonathan	6	11.3	02/01/79	Scarborough	3/15/97	York City	5+20	0+1			2			
				£1000000	3/25/98	Manchester Utd (T)								
Keane Roy M	5.11	11.3	8/10/71	Cork		Cobh Ramblers								
Ei: u21.4, Y; FMC'92; CS'93'96'97. FAC'94'96				£10000	8/12/90	Nottingham Forest	114	37	18	5	22	6	3	2
Prem'94'96;'97				£3750000	7/22/93	Manchester United	116+5	9+2	22+1	18	17		1	4
Stewart Michael J			26/02/81	Edinburgh		Manchester Utd (T)								
Teather Paul	5.11	11.2	12/26/77	Rotherham	12/29/94	Manchester Utd (T)								
E: Y				Loan	12/19/97	Bournemouth	5+5							
Wellens Richard P	5.9	10.7	3/26/80	Manchester	5/12/97	Manchester United								
F O R W A R D														
Blomqvist Jesper				Sweden		Parma								
Swedish Int.				£4400000	722/98	Manchester United								
Butt Nicholas	5.9	10.1	1/21/77	Manchester	1/29/93	Manchester United	97+18	3	11+2	24+2	11		1	1
E: 6, u21.7, Y.7; ESFAu.15; FAYC'92 UEFA Yth'93; CS'96'97. FAC'96; Prem'96'97														
Cole Andrew	5.11	11.2	10/15/71	Nottingham	10/18/89	Arsenal	0+1			0+1				
E: 2, B.1, u21.8, Y.20, S. Div1'93. FAC'96. Prem'96				Loan	9/5/91	Fulham	13		2		3			1
				Loan	3/12/92	Bristol City	12				8			
				£500000	7/21/92	Bristol City	29	3	1	4	12	4		1
				£1750000	2/12/93	Newcastle United	69+1	7	4	3	55	8	1	4
				£7000000	1/12/95	Manchester United	89+15	2	12+1	10+4	45		7	6
Cooke Terence J	5.7	9.09	8/5/76	Marston Green	8/1/94	Manchester United	1+3	1+2		0+1		1		
				Loan	1/29/96	Sunderland								
				Loan	11/29/96	Birmingham City	1+3							

Player	Ht	Wt	DOB	Birthplace	Fee/Date	Club								
Cruyff Jordi	6.1	11	2/9/74	Amsterdam		Barcelona								
					£1300000	8/8/96	Manchester United	14+7	2	0+1	3+1	3		
Giggs Ryan J	5.11	10.9	11/29/73	Cardiff	12/1/90	Manchester United	216+18	16+4	29+2	23+2	50	6	5	4
W:21, u21.1, Y; ESFAu.15; ESC'91; LC'92; FAYC'92; Prem'93'94'96'97. CS'93'94'96'97. FAC'94'96.														
Healy David J	5.8	10.9	05/08/79	Downpatrick		Manchester Utd (T)								
Mulryne Philip P	5.8	10.4	1/1/78	Belfast	3/17/95	Manchester United	1	1	0+1					
Nevland Erik	5.9	11.2	11/10/77	Stavanger		Viking Stavanger								
Norway Int.					7/15/97	Manchester United	0+1	0+1	2+1					
Notman Alexander M	5.7	11.5	12/10/79	Edinburgh	12/17/96	Manchester United								
Scholes Paul	5.6	10.8	11/16/74	Salford	1/29/93	Manchester United	66+31	6+1	5+4	9+8	26	5	3	1
E: 11, Y4; UEFA Yth'93; FAC'96; Prem'96'97														
Sheringham Teddy	5.11	10.9	10/29/61	Walthamstow	1/19/84	Millwall	205+15	16+1	12	11+2	93	8	5	5
E: 35, u21.1, Y.11. Div2'88.FMC'92. CS'97.					Loan	2/1/85	Solihull	4+1			1			
					£2000000	7/23/91	Nottingham Forest	42	10	4	6	14	5	2	2
					£2100000	8/28/92	Tottenham Hotspur	163+3	14	17		75	10	13	
						7/1/97	Manchester United	28+3		2+1	5	9		3	1
Solskjaer Ole Gunnar	5.11	11.8	2/26/73	Kristiansund (Norway)		Molde								
Norway Int. Prem'97.					£1500000	7/29/96	Manchester United	40+14		1+4	10+3	24		2	2
Thorrington John G	5.7	10.5	17/10/79	Johannesburg		US College								
							Manchester United								
Twiss Michael J.	5.11	12.1	12/26/77	Salford	7/1/96	Manchester Utd (T)			0+1					
		On a 1 year loan with Sheffield United 7/1/98													
Wilson Mark A	5.11	12.1	2/9/79	Scunthorpe	2/9/96	Manchester Utd (T)								
					Loan	2/23/98	Wrexham	12+1				4			
Wood Jamie	5.11	12.3	9/21/78	Salford	7/1/97	Manchester Utd (T)								

MANAGER
ALEX FERGUSON

Date of Birth .... 31st December 1941.
Place of Birth .... Govan, Glasgow.
Date of Appointment .... 5th November 1986.

PREVIOUS CLUBS
As Manager .... East Stirling, St Mirren, Aberdeen.
Alex was appointed caretaker manager of Scotland in 1985 on the death of Jock Stein until Andy Roxburgh was made manager in July 1986.
As Coach... None.
As a Player...................... Rangers, Queens Park, Dunfermline.

HONOURS
As a Manager
Aberdeen: Scottish Champions 1980, 1984, 1985. Scottish Cup Winners 1982, 1983, 1984, 1986. Scottish League Cup 1986. ECWC 1983.
Manchester United: FA Cup 1990,1994, 1996. ECWC 1991. Super Cup 1991. League Cup 1992. Carling Premier League Champions 1992-93, 1993-94, 1995-96, 1996-97. Charity Shield 1994, 1994, 1996.

As a Player
None.

OLD TRAFFORD
Manchester M16 0RA

Capacity ....55,000.

First game ....v Liverpool, 19.2.1910.
First floodlit game ....v Bolton Wanderers, 25.03.1957.

ATTENDANCES
Highest ....76,962 Wolves v Grimsby, FA Cup Semi-final, 25.3.1939.
Lowest ....Not Known.

OTHER GROUNDS ....North Road, Monsall Road 1880-1893,Bank Street 1883-1910,
.... Old Trafford 1910-1941, Maine Road 1941-49, Old Trafford 1949-

HOW TO GET TO THE GROUND

From the North
Use motorway M61 then M63 until junction 4. Leave motorway and follow signs to Manchester A5081. In 2.5 miles turn right into Sir Matt Busby Way, then turn right into United Road for Manchester United FC.

From the East
Use motorway M62 until junction 17 then A56 into Manchester. Follow signs South then Chester into Chester Road. In 2 miles turn right into Sir Matt Busby Way, then turn left into United Road for Manchester United FC.

From the South
Use motorway M6 until junction 19 then follow signs to Stockport A556 then Altrincham A56. From Altrincham follow signs to Manchester. In 6 miles turn left into Sir Matt Busby Way, then turn left into United Road for Manchester United FC.

From the West
Use motorway M62 then M63 and route from north or as route from south.

Car Parking: Several large parks. Lancashire County Cricket Ground, Talbot Road and Great Stone Road (1,200).
Nearest Railway Station: Manchester Piccadilly (0161 832 8353). Nearest Metrolink Station: Old Trafford.

USEFUL TELEPONE NUMBERS

Club switchboard 0161 872 1661/930 1968
Megastore 0161 848 8181
Ticket Office..............................0161 872 0199
Marketing Department 0161 872 3488

Clubcall 0891 12 11 61*
*Calls cost 50p per minute at all times.
Call costings correct at time of going to press.

MATCHDAY PROGRAMME

Programme Editor. . . . . Cliff Butler.

Number of pages . . . . 48.

Price . . . . £2.00.

Subscriptions . . . . Apply to club.

Local Newspapers
. Manchester Evening News, Sunday Pink.

Local Radio Stations
. BBC Radio Manchester, Piccadilly Radio.
. Manchester Utd Radio (Match Days only) .
. . . . 1413 AM. .

MATCHDAY TICKET PRICES

Phone ticket office for availabilty.

MIDDLESBROUGH
(The Boro)
F.A. CARLING PREMIERSHIP
SPONSORED BY: CELLNET

1997-98 Back Row L-R: Derek Whyte, Paul Merson, Fabio Moreira, Mark Schwarzer, Ben Roberts, Gary Walsh, Gianluca Festa, Fabrizio Ravanelli, Alan White. **Middle Row:** John Pickering first team coach), David Geddis (youth team coach), Gordon McQueen (reserve team coach), Bob Ward (senior physio), Steve Baker, Paul Connor, Robbie Mustoe, Steve Vickers, Mikkel Beck, Philip Stamp, Chris Freestone, Craig Liddle, Mark Summerbell, Craig Harrison, Michael Cummins, Andrew Campbell, Vladimir Kinder, Kenny Wharton (youth coach), Ron Bone (youth dev. officer), Alex Smith (kit manager). **Front Row:** Gary Henderson (physio), David French (masseur), Craig Hignett, Curtis Fleming, Viv Anderson (asst. manager), Nigel Pearson, Bryan Robson (manager), Clayton Blackmore, Alan Moore, Stan Nixon (youth tech. director), John Emmett (fitness coach).

MIDDLESBROUGH
FORMED IN 1876
TURNED PROFESSIONAL IN 1889,
then Amateur 1892, professional again 1899

CHAIRMAN: S Gibson

DIRECTOR
G Cooke
CHIEF EXECUTIVE
K Lamb, F.C.A.
HEAD OF MARKETING
J Knox

MANAGER: Bryan Robson
ASSISTANT MANAGER: Viv Anderson
FIRST TEAM COACH: Gordon McQueen
RESERVE TEAM MANAGER
David Geddis
PHYSIOTHERAPIST
Bob Ward

STATISTICIAN FOR THE DIRECTORY
David Grey/Nigel Ball

Middlesbrough began the 1997/98 season with just one ambition - to regain the Carling Premiership place that many felt had been unjustly lost at the end of the previous season. The expected mass exodus following relegation did not occur; the only significant departure being that of Juninho. This was counterbalanced by the arrival of Paul Merson, who was eventually to be the club's player of the season.

The line-up that started the campaign was therefore little changed from the previous year. Even Ravanelli played the first two games, although a last minute winner in an unconvincing opening day win over Charlton was his only contribution before being transferred to Marseille.

After a shaky start to the season, things soon improved and by December Boro were top of the league and had reached the quarter-finals of the Coca-Cola Cup.

It was then that Emerson, who until then had been having a very good season, staged another of his famed disappearing acts. This time the club decided that enough was enough and sold him to Tenerife very quickly.

The team hardly noticed his departure and went from strength to strength. Particularly impressive was the defeat of Liverpool over two legs in the Coca-Cola Cup to reach a third Wembley final in under a year. Unfortunately, this resulted in another defeat, but a much better performance than in the previous year's FA Cup Final gives hope that Boro's first major trophy can't be too far away.

It was at this point that Bryan Robson made four signings in quick succession, obviously feeling that he needed more attacking options, with Branca, Armstrong, Ricard and Gascoigne all joining the club.

These signings coincided with a slip in league position, falling out of the promotion places for the first time in four months. This spell included successive defeats of 0-4 against Forest and 0-5 against Queens Park Rangers. However, the team quickly recovered and five wins in the last six games were enough to see off the strong challenge from Sunderland and Charlton for second place. On an occasion that had echoes of 1966/67, a home victory over Oxford on the last day of the season was needed to secure promotion. In one of those strange footballing coincidences, Boro won by the same 4-1 scoreline as thirty-one years earlier. The final day was particularly poignant for club captain, Nigel Pearson, a rock in the heart of the defence for four seasons, whose constant knee problems had forced him to announce his retirement.

And now to 1998/99. This year's aim must surely be to consolidate, and ensure that Premiership status is retained. To do this, the squad needs a few additions, particularly in defence, but Bryan Robson surely has this in hand. A season of mid-table obscurity could be welcomed by the fans, who need time to get their breath back after the excitement of the last few years.

David Grey/Nigel Ball.

MIDDLESBROUGH

Division 1   :2nd   FA CUP: 4th Round   LC CUP: Runners Up

M	DATE	COMP.	VEN	OPPONENTS	RESULT	H/T	LP	GOAL SCORERS/GOAL TIMES	ATT.
1	A 09	FL	H	Charlton Athletic	W 2-1	0-1	5	Festa 80, Ravanelli 90	22414
2	23	FL	H	Stoke City	L 0-1	0-0	17		30122
3	30	FL	A	Tranmere Rovers	W 2-0	1-0	10	Mustoe 25, Beck 54	(12095)
4	S 02	FL	A	Stockport County	D 1-1	1-0	10	Merson 6	(8257)
5	13	FL	A	Bradford City	D 2-2	1-1	12	Kinder 42, Ormerod 77	(17767)
6	16	CC 2/1	H	Barnet	W 1-0	0-0		Freestone 56	9611
7	20	FL	H	Birmingham City	W 3-1	3-0	10	Kinder 22, Beck 40, Emerson 43	30125
8	23	CC 2/2	A	Barnet	W 2-0	1-0		Beck 45, Merson 67 (pen)	(3968)
9	28	FL	A	Sunderland	W 2-1	0-0	8	Emerson 67, Mustoe 78	(34819)
10	O 05	FL	H	Sheffield United	L 1-2	1-1	10	Beck 19	30000
11	15	CC 3	H	Sunderland	W 2-0	0-0		Campbell 58, Hignett 90	26451
12	18	FL	A	Crewe Alexandra	D 1-1	0-0	13	Townsend 48	(5759)
13	21	FL	A	Oxford United	W 4-1	1-0	8	Emerson 36, Mustoe 79, Fleming 81, Merson 90	(8306)
14	25	FL	H	Port Vale	W 2-1	1-0	7	Merson 10 (pen), 68 (pen)	30096
15	28	FL	H	Huddersfield Town	W 3-0	2-0	3	Merson 13, Beck 18, 57	29965
16	N 01	FL	A	Wolverhampton Wand	L 0-1	0-0	6		(26896)
17	05	FL	H	Portsmouth	D 1-1	0-0	6	Townsend 65	29724
18	08	FL	H	Queens Park Rangers	W 3-0	2-0	4	Beck 22, Merson 37, Ormerod 90	30067
19	15	FL	A	Norwich City	W 3-1	1-1	4	Beck 39, Merson 52, Ormerod 55	(16011)
20	18	CC 4	H	Bolton Wanderers	W 2-1	1-1		Summerbell 39, Hignett 115	22801
21	22	FL	A	Swindon Town	W 2-1	1-1	2	Merson 22, Emerson 75	(15228)
22	26	FL	H	Nottingham Forest	D 0-0	0-0	3		30143
23	29	FL	H	West Bromwich Albion	W 1-0	1-0	2	Beck 34	30164
24	D 02	FL	A	Ipswich Town	D 1-1	1-0	2	Merson 33	(13619)
25	06	FL	A	Bury	W 1-0	0-0	1	Beck 59	(8016)
26	13	FL	H	Reading	W 4-0	0-0	1	Hignett 77, 90, Beck 79, 85	29876
27	20	FL	A	Manchester City	L 0-2	0-2	1		(28097)
28	26	FL	A	Huddersfield Town	W 1-0	0-0	2	, Gray 75 (OG)	(18820)
29	28	FL	H	Stockport County	W 3-1	1-1	2	Hignett 10, Beck 65, 88	30166
30	J 03	FAC 3	A	Queens Park Rangers	D 2-2	1-1		Hignett 33, Mustoe 63	(13379)
31	06	CC QF	A	Reading	W 1-0	0-0		Hignett 89	(13072)
32	10	FL	A	Charlton Athletic	L 0-3	0-2	2		(15742)
33	13	FAC 3R	H	Queens Park Rangers	W 2-0	0-0		Campbell 54, Mustoe 59	21817
34	17	FL	A	Ipswich Town	D 1-1	0-0	2	Pearson 63	30081
35	24	FAC 4	H	Arsenal	L 1-2	0-2		Merson 62	28264
36	27	CC SF1	A	Liverpool	L 1-2	1-1		Merson 29	(33438)
37	F 01	FL	A	Stoke City	W 2-1	1-1	2	Pearson 17, Moreno 81	(13242)
38	04	FL	H	Tranmere Rovers	W 3-0	2-0	1	Hignett 31, Merson 38, 65	29540
39	06	FL	A	Birmingham City	D 1-1	1-1	2	Festa 38	(20634)
40	14	FL	H	Bradford City	W 1-0	0-0	1	Hignett 49	30165
41	18	CC SF2	H	Liverpool	W 2-0	2-0		Merson 2 (pen), Branca 4	29828
42	21	FL	H	Sunderland	W 3-1	1-0	1	Branca 31, 68, Armstrong 87	30227
43	25	FL	H	Crewe Alexandra	W 1-0	0-0	1	Maddison 80	29936
44	M 01	FL	A	Nottingham Forest	L 0-4	0-0	2		(25286)
45	04	FL	A	Queens Park Rangers	L 0-5	0-4	2		(11580)
46	11	FL	H	Swindon Town	W 6-0	2-0	1	Branca 16, 88, Maddison 22, 55, Armstrong 50, 73	29581
47	14	FL	A	Portsmouth	D 0-0	0-0	2		(17003)
48	22	FL	H	Norwich City	W 3-0	1-0	2	Maddison 22, Armstrong 71, Beck 90	30040
49	29	CC F	A	Chelsea	L 0-2	0-0			(77698)
50	A 04	FL	A	West Bromwich Albion	L 1-2	0-1	3	Branca 76	(20620)
51	07	FL	A	Sheffield United	L 0-1	0-0	4		(18421)
52	11	FL	H	Bury	W 4-0	1-0	4	Ricard 29, Branca 63, 73, 83	30218
53	13	FL	A	Reading	W 1-0	1-0	4	Branca 8	(14501)
54	17	FL	H	Manchester City	W 1-0	1-0	2	Armstrong 44	30182
55	24	FL	A	Port Vale	W 1-0	0-0	2	Merson 2	(12096)
56	29	FL	H	Wolverhampton Wand	D 1-1	1-1	2	Ricard 12	29878
57	M 03	FL	H	Oxford United	W 4-1	0-0	2	Armstrong 47, 48, Hignett 57, 63	30228

Best Home League Attendance: 30228 V Oxford United   Smallest :22414 V Charlton Athletic   Average :29693

Goal Scorers:

FL	(77)	Beck 14, Merson 12, Branca 9, Armstrong 7, Hignett 7, Emerson 4, Maddison 4, Mustoe 3, Ormerod 3, Festa 2, Kinder 2, Pearson 2, Ricard 2, Townsend 2, Fleming 1, Moreno 1, Ravanelli 1, Opponents 1
CC	(11)	Hignett 3, Merson 3, Beck 1, Branca 1, Campbell 1, Freestone 1, Summerbell 1
FAC	(5)	Mustoe 2, Campbell 1, Hignett 1, Merson 1

(F) Armstrong	(M) Baker	(F) Beck	(F) Branca	(F) Campbell	(M) Emerson	(D) Festa	(D) Fleming	(F) Freestone	(M) Gascoigne	(D) Harrison	(M) Hignett	(D) Kinder	(M) Liddle	(M) Maddison	(F) Merson	(M) Moreno	(M) Mustoe	(M) Ormerod	(D) Pearson	(F) Ricard	(G) Roberts	(G) Schwarzer	(M) Stamp	(M) Summerbell	(M) Thomas	(M) Townsend	(D) Vickers	(D) Whyte	Match
	X			X	X	X					S1	X	S		X		X					X		S2				X	A.R. Leake 1
	S1				X	X	S2				X			X	X		X					X		X			X	S	P W Barnes 2
	X			X	X	X	S					X	S1		X		X					X		X		S2	X		P R Richards 3
	X			X	X	X	S					X	S		X		X					X		X		S1	X		S J Baines 4
	S1		X		X		X	S				X	X		X		X	X				X			S	X	X		G Singh 5
	X		X	X	X	X	X					X	S1		X		X					X			S		X		E Lomas 6
	X				S2	X	X			S1		X	S3		X		X	X	X			X					X	X	R D Furnandiz 7
X	X		S1		X	X		S		X		X			X		X				S	X					X		B Knight 8
	X				X	X	X					X	S		X		X	X	X		S	X					X		P Rejer 9
	X				X	X	X	S				X	S		X		X	S1	X		X	X					X		C R Wilkes 10
	X		X	X	X	X	S2			X	S1				X		X				X	X	S				X	X	K A Leach 11
	S2		X	X	X	X					S1	X			X		X	X				X					X	S	J A Kirkby 12
	X			X	X	X	S				X	X			X		X	S2	X			X					X	S1	A Bates 13
X	X			X		X		S			X	X			X		X					X		S1			X	X	S W Mathieson 14
X	X			X		X		S			X	X			X		S1					X		X			X		E K Wolstenholme 15
	X			X		X	X			X	X	S1			X	X					S	X		X		X		X	M E Pierce 16
	X			S2	X	X	X				X				X	X					S	X		S		X	S1	A R Leake 17
S	X	X		X	X	X					X				X	X					S1	X		S		X		X	J P Robinson 18
X	X	S		X	X	X					S1	X			X	X					X	X		S		X		X	S W Mathieson 19
S2		X		X	X	X					X	X			X	X					S1	X		X	X	X	X	X	S J Lodge 20
	X			X	X	X	S				X	X			X	X					X	X		S		X	X	S1	G Cain 21
	X			X	X	X	S			S2	X	X			X	X					S1	X		X		X	X		D Laws 22
	X	S		X	X2	X	X				X	X	X1		X						X	X		S2		X	X	S1	K M Lynch 23
	X	S		X	X	X	X			X1		X2									S2	X		X		X	X	S1	M Fletcher 24
	X			X	X	X					X	X			X	S	X	X				X		S		X	X		W C Burns 25
S1	X			X	X	X					X				X	S2		X1			X	X2	S3	X3				X	C J Foy 26
	X				X	X	X2	X3			X	S3	S1		X		X		X	X1		X	S2		M C Bailey 27
	X1				X	X					X	X2	S2	X1	X		X		X	X		X	X		S	B Coddington 28
	X				X	X					X	X	X		X		X		X	X		X	X		S	D Pugh 29
S	S1		S			S	X	X	S			X	S		X		X				X	X1		X	X	P A Durkin 30
	X	S		X		S	X	X			X	X	S		X	X	S	X			X	X	X	G Cain 31
	X2				S2	X	X	S1	X		X	X3	X	S3	X			X1	X	R J Harris 32
	S	X	X		X		X	X	S	X	X	3	X	A		X			X	X	P A Durkin 33
	X	X1	X		X	X	X	X	X	S	X	X		X		X	S1	M L Dean 34
S1	S	X1	X	X	S2	S	X	X	X	X	X2		X	S		X	X	M A Riley 35
X	X	S		S1	X1	X	X	X	S	X	X		X	X	G S Willard 36
X	S2	X1	X	X	X	S1	X	S	X2	X	S2	X	X	X	P R Richards 37
	X	X	X	S1	X	X	S	X2	X1	X	S2	X	X	X	J A Kirkby 38
X1	X		S1	X	X	X	X	X	X	S1	X	X	X	M E Pierce 39
X1	X	X	X	X	S2	X	S1	X2	X	X	A N Butler 40
S1	X	X	X	S	X1	X	X	X	S	X	X	X	X	P A Durkin 41
S1	S2	X	X	S3	X1	X	X	X	X	X3	X2	X	R D Furnandiz 42
S2	X2	X	X	X	X	S1	X	X	X	X1	P Rejer 43
S2	S	X1	X	X	X2	X	X	X	S1	X	X3	X	X	E K Wolstenholme 44
S3	S2	X	X	X2	S1	X	X1	X3	X	X	A P D'Urso 45
X	S1	X	X	S	X	S2	X	X3	X1	X2	X	X	S J Baines 46
X	S	X	X	S	X	X	X	X	X	X	X	K M Lynch 47
X	S2	X2	X1	X	X	S1	S	X	X	X	X	F G Stretton 48
	S2	X	S	X	X	X2	X	X	X1	X	X	P Jones 49
	X2	X	S2	X	X	S1	X3	X	S3	X	X1	X	D Pugh 50
X	S	X1	X	S	X	X	X	X	X2	X	E Lomas 51
X	X	X	X	S1	S2	X	X	X	X1	X	P S Danson 52
X2	X	X	X1	X	S1	S3	X3	X	X	S2	X	B Knight 53
X	X1	X	X2	S3	X	X	X	X	S1	X	A G Wiley 54
	X	S	X	X	X	X	X	X	S1	X	X	C R Wilkes 55
	X	S	X	X	X	S1	X1	X	X	X	X	X	M C Bailey 56
X1	S	X	X	X	S	X	X	X	X1	X	X	P R Richards 57
7	5	31	11	5	21	38	28		7	16	28	25	2	16	45	1	31	8	29	4	6	35	8	7	10	35	30	4	FL Appearances
4	1	8		2		3	2		4	8	1	4	6		4	1	10		5			2	4		2	3	4	FL Sub Appearances
2+2	6+1	2	3+1	4	7	2	1+1	+1	3+1	4+1	5	1+1	4	7		7	2+1	4	1	1	7	1		6	6	CC Appearances
0+1	0+1		2		2	2			1+1	1	1	3	2	3	2		3	1		3	1		3	3	FAC Appearances

Also Played: (G) Beresford X(46,47,48). (D) Blackmore X(1), S2(54), S(55,56). (G) Dibble X(44,45). (M) Fabio S(20,33). (F) Moore X(2,3,4), S2(6), S1(9). (F) Ravanelli X(1,2). (D) Stockdale X(33,38). (M) Swalwell X(31). (M) Trevor S(14,15).

MIDDLESBROUGH

CLUB RECORDS

BIGGEST VICTORIES
League: 9-0 v Brighton & H.A., Division 2, 23.8.1958.
F.A. Cup: 11-0 v Scarborough, Qual. Round, 1890-91.
9-3 v Goole Town, 3rd Round, 1914-15.
League Cup: 7-0 v Hereford United, 2nd Round 1st leg, 18.09.96.

BIGGEST DEFEATS
League: 0-9 v Blackburn Rovers, Division 2, 6.11.1954.
F.A. Cup: 1-6 v Southampton, 3rd Round, 1905-06.
1-6 v Sheffield Wednesday, 2nd Round, 1894-95.
1-6 v Wolverhampton Wanderers, 3rd Round, 1936-37.
League Cup: 0-4 v Manchester City, Semi-final, 21.1.1976.

MOST POINTS
3 points a win: 94, division 3, 1986-87.
2 points a win: 65, Division 2, 1973-74.

MOST GOALS SCORED
122, Division 2, 1926-27.
Camsell 59, Pease 23, Birrell 16, Williams 9, Carr 6, McClelland 5, McKay 1, Ashman 1, J.Williams 1, Opponents 1.

MOST GOALS CONCEDED
91, Division 1, 1953-54.

MOST FIRST CLASS MATCHES IN A SEASON
60 - 1991-92 (League 46, FA Cup 4, League Cup 8, Zenith Data Cup 2).

MOST LEAGUE WINS
28, Division 3, 1986-87.

MOST LEAGUE DRAWS
19, Division 2, 1924-25.

MOST LEAGUE DEFEATS
27, Division 1, 1923-24.

INDIVIDUAL CLUB RECORDS

MOST GOALS IN A SEASON
George Camsell: 64 goals in 1926-27 (League 59, FA Cup 5).
(English record and League goals (59) is a Division 2 record)

MOST GOALS IN A MATCH
5. Andy Wilson v Nottingham Forest, 6.10.1923.
5. George Camsell v Manchester City 5-3 (a), 25.12.1926.
5. George Camsell v Aston Villa 7-2 (a), 9.9.1935.
5. Brian Clough v Brighton & H.A. 9-0, Division 2, 22.8.1958.

OLDEST PLAYER
Bryan Robson, 38 years, 360 days v Notts County, FAC, 6.1.96.

YOUNGEST PLAYER
Sam Lawrie, 16 years 323 days v Arsenal, Division 1, 3.11.51.
Stephen Bell, 16 years 323 days v Southampton, Division 1, 30.1.1982.

MOST CAPPED PLAYER
Wilf Mannion (England) 26, 1946-51.

BEST PERFORMANCES

League: 1986-87: Matches played 46, Won 28, Drawn 11, Lost 8, Goals for 67, Goals against 30, Points 94. Second in Division 3.
Highest Position: Third in Division 1, 1913-14.
F.A. Cup: 6th round in 1935-36, 1946-47, 1969-70, 1976-77.
Most recent success: 1980-81: 3rd Round Swansea City 5-0; 4th Round West Bromwich Albion 1-0; 5th Round Barnsley 2-1; 6th Round Wolverhampton Wanderers 1-1,1-3.
League Cup: Finalists 1996-97.
Most recent success: 1997-98 finalists: 2nd Round Barnet 1-0, 3-0 3rd Round Sunderland 2-0; 4th Round Bolton W. 2-1(aet); 5th Round Reading 1-0; Semi-Final Liverpool 1-2, 2-0; Final Chelsea 0-2 (aet).

ADDITIONAL INFORMATION
PREVIOUS NAMES
None.

PREVIOUS LEAGUES
Northern League 1889-1899.

Club colours: Red shirts/white trim, white shorts with red trim, red socks.
Change colours: White & sky blue stripes.

Reserves League: Pontins Central League Premier Division.

DIVISIONAL RECORD

	Played	Won	Drawn	Lost	For	Against	Points
Division 1/P	1,982	685	478	819	2,918	3,157	1,894
Division 2/1	1,556	651	377	528	2,466	2,094	1,870
Division 3	92	51	19	22	154	94	149
Total	**3,630**	**1,487**	**874**	**1,369**	**5,538**	**6,345**	**3,913**

RECORDS AND STATISTICS

COMPETITIONS

Division 1/P	Division 2/1	Division 3
1902-24	1899-02	1966-67
1927-28	1924-27	1986-87
1929-54	1928-29	
1974-82	1954-66	
1988-89	1967-74	
1992-93	1982-86	
1995-97	1987-88	
1998-	1989-92	
	1993-95	
	1997-98	

HONOURS

Division 2/1	Anglo/Scot	Amateur Cup
1926-27	1975-76	1895
1928-29		1898
1973-74		
1994-95		

MOST APPEARANCES

Tim Williamson 602 (1902-23)

Year	League	FA Cup
1901-02	2	
1902-03	16	
1903-04	34	4
1904-05	33	2
1905-06	34	5
1906-07	38	2
1907-08	37	1
1908-09	38	1
1909-10	38	2
1910-11	36	4
1911-12	36	4
1912-13	37	4
1913-14	29	1
1914-15	20	2
1919-20	37	2
1920-21	42	1
1921-22	26	1
1922-23	30	3
	563	30

MOST GOALS IN A CAREER

George Camsell - 345 (1925-39)

Year	League	FA Cup
1925-26	3	
1926-27	59	4
1927-28	33	4
1928-29	30	3
1929-30	29	2
1930-31	32	
1931-32	20	
1932-33	17	1
1933-34	23	1
1934-35	14	
1935-36	28	4
1936-37	18	
1937-38	9	1
1938-39	10	
Total	325	20

Current leading goalscorer: Robbie Mustoe - 27 (1990-98)

MANAGERS

Name	Seasons	Best	Worst
Peter McWilliam	1927-34	7(1)	1(2)
Wilf Gillow	1934-44	4(1)	20(1)
David Jack	1944-52	6(1)	19(1)
Walter Rowley	1952-54	13(1)	21(1)
Bob Dennison	1954-63	4(2)	14(2)
Raich Carter	1963-66	10(2)	21(2)
Stan Anderson	1966-73	4(2)	2(3)
Jack Charlton	1973-77	7(1)	1(2)
John Neal	1977-81	9(1)	14(1)
Bobby Murdoch	1981-82	22(1)	22(1)
Malcolm Allison	1982-84	16(2)	17(2)
Willie Maddren	1984-86	19(2)	21(2)
Bruce Rioch	1986-90	18(1)	2(3)
Colin Todd	1990-91	7(2)	21(2)
Lennie Lawrence	1991-94	21(1/P)	9(2/1)
Bryan Robson	1994-	12(P)	2(1)

RECORD TRANSFER FEE RECEIVED

Amount	Club	Player	Date
£12,500,000	Atletico Madrid	Juninho	07/97
£5,750,000	Everton	Nick Barmby	10/96
£5,500,000	Marseille	Fabrizio Ravanelli	09/97
£4,000,000	Tenerife	Emerson	01/98

RECORD TRANSFER FEE PAID

Amount	Club	Player	Date
£7,000,000	Juventus	Fabrizio Ravanelli	07/96
£5,250,000	Tottenham H.	Nick Barmby	08/95
£5,000,000	Arsenal	Paul Merson	08/97
£4,750,000	Sao Paulo	Juninho	10/95

LONGEST LEAGUE RUNS

of undefeated matches:	24 (8.9.1973 - 9.1.1974)	of league matches w/out a win:	19 (3.10.1981 - 6.3.1982)
of undefeated home matches:	27 (8.2.1935 - 10.4.1937)	of undefeated away matches:	14 (14.4.1973 - 12.1.1974)
without home win:	10 (10.11.1984 - 2.3.1985)	without an away win:	33 (7.3.1903 - 7.9.1907)
of league wins:	9 (16.2.1974 - 6.4.1974)	of home wins:	11 (22.11.1913 - 22.4.1914)
of league defeats:	8 (25.8.1954 - 2.10.1954 & 26.12.95 - 17.2.96)	of away wins:	5 (18.2.1974 - 30.3.1974, 21.3.1987 - 9.5.1987)

MIDDLESBROUGH

PLAYERS NAME Honours	Ht	Wt	Birthdate	Birthplace Transfers	Contract Date	Clubs	League	L/Cup	FA Cup	Other	Lge	L/C	FAC	Oth
G O A L K E E P E R														
Beresford Marlon	6.1	12.6	9/2/69	Lincoln	9/23/87	Sheffield Wednesday								
				Loan	8/25/89	Bury	1							
				Loan	9/27/90	Northampton Town	13			2				
				Loan	2/28/91	Crewe Alexandra	3							
				Loan	8/15/91	Northampton Town	15							
					8/28/92	Burnley	240	18	19	11				
				£500000	3/10/98	Middlesbrough	3							
Roberts Ben J	6	12.6	6/22/75	Bishop Auck.	3/24/93	Middlesbrough	6	1		1				
				Loan	10/19/95	Hartlepool United								
				Loan	12/8/95	Wycombe Wanderers								
				Loan	8/27/96	Bradford City	2							
Schwarzer Mark	6.4	13.6	10/6/72	Sydney	11/22/96	Bradford City	13		3					
				£1500000	2/26/97	Middlesbrough	42	10	3					
D E F E N C E														
Baker Steven R	5.10	11.11	9/8/78	Pontefract	7/25/97	Middlesbrough	5+1	2+2	0+1					
Blackmore Clayton G W: 38,u21.3,Y,S. FAC'90. CS'90 ECWC'91. ESC'91. Prem'93.	5.9	11.3	9/23/64	Neath Free Loan	9/28/82 7/11/94 11/1/96	Manchester United Middlesbrough Bristol City	150+36 45+7 5	23+2 3+2	15+6 4+1	19 1	19 4 1	3	1	4
Festa Gianluca	6	12.8	3/12/69	Cagliari £2700000	1/18/97	Inter Milan Middlesbrough	50	11	7		3		1	
Fleming Curtis Ei: 1, u21.5, u23.1. Ei: Div.1'90.	5.8	11.4	10/8/68	Manchester £50000	8/16/91	St.Patricks Middlesbrough	170+14	17+2	12+1	7+1	2	1		
Gavin Jason J			3/14/80	Dublin	5/31/97	Middlesbrough								
Gordon Dean D E: u21.13. Div.1'94.	6	13.4	2/10/73	Croydon £900000	7/4/91 7/1/98	Crystal Palace Middlesbrough	181+20	16+3	14+1	5+1	20	2	1	
Harrison Craig	6	11.13	11/10/77	Gateshead	7/4/96	Middlesbrough	16+4	3+1	2					
Kinder Vladimir Int. Czech	5.11	13	3/9/69	Czechoslovakia £2700000	1/18/97	Slough Middlesbrough	29+3	6	3+1		3			
Pallister Gary E: 22, B9, FLgXI.1; FAC'90; CS'90'93; ECWC'91 ESC'91; FAC'96 Prem'96'97	6.4	13	6/30/65	Ramsgate Free Loan £2300000 £2500000	11/7/84 10/18/85 8/29/89 7/8/98	Billingham Town Middlesbrough Darlington Manchester United Middlesbrough	156 7 313+3	10 36	10 38	13 41+1	5 12	1	1	1
Stockdale Robert		11.30/79		Redcar	1/12/98	Middlesbrough	1		1					
Vickers Stephen LDC'90. Div.1'95.	6.3	12	10/13/67	Bishop Auckland £700000	9/11/85 12/3/93	Spennymoor Utd Tranmere Rovers Middlesbrough	310+1 155+7	20+1 20+1	19 15+1	36 2	11 7	5 2	3	1
M I D F I E L D														
Cronin Gary P			3/16/79	Dublin		Middlesbrough								
Cummins Michael	6	11.12	6/1/78	Dublin		Middlesbrough								
Gascoigne Paul E: 57, B.4, u21.13, Y. FAYC'85. FAC'91. SPrem'96'97.	5.10	11.7	5/27/67	Gateshead £2000000 £5500000 £4300000 £3450000	5/13/85 7/18/88 5/1/92 7/10/95 3/27/98	Newcastle Utd (A) Tottenham Hotspur Lazio Glasgow Rangers Middlesbrough	83+9 91+1 64+10 7	8 14+1 7 0+1	4 6 7+1	2+1 14	21 19 30	1 8 4	3 6 3	2
Lombardi Gustavo				Argentina Loan	7/1/98	River Plate Middlesbrough								
Maddison Neil	5.9	11.8	10/2/69	Darlington £250000	4/14/88 10/31/97	Southampton Middlesbrough	148+19 16+6	9+5 4	8+5 3	1	19 4			
Mustoe Robbie	5.11	11.6	8/28/68	Witney £375000	7/2/86 7/5/90	Oxford United Middlesbrough	78+13 230+11	2 39+1	2 20	3 12+1	10 18	7	2	1
O'Brien Ronald			1/15/79	Dublin	7/28/97	Middlesbrough (T)								
O'Loughlin John A			1/31/79	Letterkenny		Middlesbrough								
Ormerod Anthony	5.10	11.8	3/31/79	Middlesbrough	7/9/96	Middlesbrough (T)	8+10	2+1	2		3			
Stamp Philip L	5.9	11.9	12/12/75	Middlesbrough	2/4/93	Middlesbrough	42+15	9+2	5+3	5+1	3	1	1	
Summerbell Mark	5.8	10.6	10/30/76	Durham		Middlesbrough (T)	7+7	1					1	
Swalwell Andrew			3/29/79	Middlesbrough	7/9/96	Middlesbrough (T)		1						

106

	Ht	Wt	DOB	Birthplace	Fee	Date	Club								
Townsend Andy	5.11	12.7	7/23/63	Maidstone			Welling								
Ei:70,B.1. LC'94'96.					£13500		Weymouth		1						
					£35000	1/15/85	Southampton	77+6	7+1	2+3	3+2	5			
					£300000	8/31/88	Norwich City	66+5	3+1	10	3	8		2	
					£1200000	7/5/90	Chelsea	110	17	7	4	12	7		
					£2100000	7/26/93	Aston Villa	133+1	20	12	10	8	2		1
					£500000	8/29/97	Middlesbrough	35+2	6	3					
Trevor Kris A			5/15/79	South Sheilds		7/25/97	Middlesbrough (T)								
F O R W A R D															
Armstrong Alun	6.1	11.13	2/22/75	Gateshead		10/1/93	Newcastle United								
					£50000	6/23/94	Stockport County	151+8	22	10+1	2	48	8	5	
					£1500000	2/20/98	Middlesbrough	8+3				7			
Beck Mikkel	6.2	12.9	5/12/73	Denmark			Fortuna Koln								
Int. Danish					Free	7/1/96	Middlesbrough	53+10	11+2	5+2		19	5	2	
Branca Marco	6	11.7	1/6/65	Grosseto			Inter Milan								
					£1000000	2/17/98	Middlesbrough	11	2			9	1		
Burdock Gary			3/9/80	Dublin		7/25/97	Middlesbrough (T)								
Campbell Andrew			4/18/79	Middlesbrough		7/4/96	Middlesbrough	6+6	3+1	2			1	1	
Connor Paul			1/12/79	Bishop Auckland		7/9/96	Middlesbrough								
					Loan	2/5/98	Hartlepool United	4+1							
Merson Paul	5.1	11.9	3/20/68	Harlesdon		2/1/85	Arsenal	289+38	38+2	28+3	27+2	78	10	4	7
E:19,B.4,u21.4,Y. CT'89. Div.1'89'91. LC'93.					Loan	1/22/87	Brentford	6+1			1+1				
FAC'93. ECWC'94.					£4500000	8/6/97	Middlesbrough	45	7	3		12	3	1	
Moore Alan	5.1	10.7	11/25/74	Dublin		12/5/91	Middlesbrough	93+19	8+6	2+2	3+1	14	1	2	
Ei: 1, u21.3, Y. Div.1'95															
Reeve Christopher J			10/1/79	Darlington		7/25/97	Middlesbrough (T)								
Ricard Hamilton	6.2	14.5	1/12/74	Colombia			Deportivo Cali.								
Columbian Int.					£2000000	2/27/98	Middlesbrough	4+5	1			2			

THE MANAGER
BRYAN ROBSON

Date of Birth . . . . 11th January 1957.
Place of Birth . . . . Witton Gilbert.
Date of Appointment . . . . May 1994.

PREVIOUS CLUBS
As a Manager. . . . . None.
As Coach. . . . . None.
As a Player. . . . . West Bromwich Albion, Manchester United.

HONOURS
As a Manager
Middlesbrough: Division 1 championship 1994-95. Promotion to Carling Premiership via 2nd place 1997-98.

As a Player
Manchester United: Carling Premiership championship 1992-93, 1993-94. FA Cup 1983, 1985, 1990. ECWC 1991.
Charity Shield 1983. Flg. XI.3.
International: 90 full caps, 7 U21, 3 'B' and Youth for England. (Currently England first team Coach).

CELLNET RIVERSIDE STADIUM
Middlesbrough, Cleveland, TS3 6RS

Capacity..35,000.

First game...v Chelsea (2-0), Premier League, 26.08.1995.
First floodlit game ....v Southampton (0-0), Premier League, 12.09.1995.
ATTENDANCES
Highest ....30,228 v Oxford United, 03.05.98.
Lowest...9,611 v Barnet, Leageu Cup, 16.09.97.

OTHER GROUNDS ....Old Archery Ground 1876-79. Breckon HIll Road 1879-80.
....Linthorpe Road 1880-1903. Ayresome Park 1903-1995.

HOW TO GET TO THE GROUND

From the North & South
Use A19 (sign posted Middlesbrough) until its junction with A66. Continue along A66 through Middlesbrough. At the first roundabout turn left. Cross the railway for Middlesbrough FC.

From the West
Use A66 through Middlesbrough. At the first roundabout turn left. Cross the railway for MIddlesbrough FC.

USEFUL TELEPHONE NUMBERS

Club switchboard 01642 877 700
Club fax number........................01642 877 840
Club shop 01642 877 720
Ticket Office.......01642 877 745 (fax 877 843)

Marketing Department 01642 877 700
Boro Livewire 0891 42 42 00*
*Calls cost 50p per minute at all times.
Call costings correct at time of going to press.

MATCHDAY PROGRAMME
Programme Editor ....Mark Hooper.

Number of pages.....................................48.

Price ....£2.00.

Subscriptions ....Apply to the club.

Local Newspapers
................Evening Gazette, Northern Echo,
....Hartlepool Mail.

Local Radio Stations
........................BBC Radio Cleveland, TFM,
....Century Radio.

MATCHDAY TICKET PRICES
South Stand (Home/Visitors)
Adults.................................. £20.00
Concessions........................... £10.00

All other areas sold to season ticket holders.

NEWCASTLE UNITED
(The Magpies)
F.A. CARLING PREMIERSHIP
SPONSORED BY: NEWCASTLE BREWERIES LTD

1998-99 - **Back Row** left to right: Keith Gillespie, Paul Talbot, Bjarnis Gudjonsson, Carl Serrant, Peter Keen, Lionel Perez, Steve Harper, Shay Given, Stuart Elliott, David Beharral, George Geogiadis, Terry Berghall **Third Row** left to right: Roddie Macdonald (Club Doctor), Derek Wright (Physio), Stephen Glass, Patrick Kelly, Paul Barrett, Jamie McClen, David Burt, Andy Griffin, Garry Brady, Temur Ketsbaia, Aaron Hughes, Paul Dalglish, Terry Gennoe (Goalkeeping Coach) **Second Row** left to right: Paul Winsper (Fitness Coach), Ralf Keidel, Paul Robinson, Paul Arnison, Andreas Andersson, Nolberto Solano, Nikos Dabizas, Alessandro Pistone, Steve Howay, Philippe Albert, Laurent Charvet, John Barnes, Dietmar Hamann, Alan Irvine (Coach) **Front Row**, left to right: Paul Ferris (Assistant Physio), Des Hamilton, Gary Speed, Warren Barton, Steve Watson, Robert Lee, Kenny Dalglish (no longer with club), Terry McDermott (no longer with club), Alan Shearer, Stephane Guivarc'h, Stuart Pearce, David Batty, Tommy Craig (Coach)

NEWCASTLE UNITED
FORMED IN 1892
TURNED PROFESSIONAL IN 1892
LTD COMPANY IN 1895
PLC IN 1996

CHAIRMAN: D Cassidy
DIRECTORS
Freddie Fletcher (Chief Exec.),
Russell Jones, A Wilson

MANAGER: Kenny Dalglish
ASSISTANT MANAGER: Terry McDermott
COACHES: Alan Irvine
YOUTH TEAM COACH: John Carver
PHYSIOTHERAPIST
Derek Wright/Paul Ferris

STATISTICIAN FOR THE DIRECTORY
Dave Graham & David Stewart

Having finished an excellent second in the Carling Premiership in 1996-97. Newcastle United - with Kenny Dalglish still in charge and England striker Alan Shearer in the line-up - were expected to be among the front runners again. Sadly it was not to be.....and in the end the 1997-98 campaign turned out to be a rather disappointing one for all concerned at St. James Park, especially the team, who only staved off the threat of relegation late on and then lost to Arsenal in the F.A. Cup Final at Wembley.

A lot was expected of Shearer, but unfortunately he was an absentee for two-thirds of the campaign with injury problems and the lack of goalscoring power was there for all to see.

The Colombian international Faustino Asprilla did his best, as did Temur Ketsbaia and Keith Gillespie, but when Asprilla left, the goals dried up even more.

United were never really in with a chance of Carling Premiership glory, especially with Shearer missing from their line-up. And with other key players suffering with injury and serving suspensions, there was a distinct lack of continuity within the side.

Manager Dalglish tried all sorts of formations and permutations, but he was frustrated with not having enough strikers available - and to be truthful, the United defence wasn't all that secure at times!

However, to compensate for some very disappointing Carling Premiership performances, certainly away from home, United did give it a go in the European Champions League, and their exciting win over Barcelona (thanks to a fine Asprilla hat-trick) helped ease the pain somewhat. And when the F.A. Cup came round, again United seem to show more enthusiasm and fight and quickly put their mediocre League form behind them as they made steady headway through to Wembley, although they did have a nervy encounter with the minnows of Stevenage Borough.

But at the end of the day, there was nothing to show for their efforts in terms of winning trophies.....one consolation, however, was that this season the diehard Magpies' supporters will see their team competing in the European Cup Winners Cup competition, thanks to Arsenal's double success!

Tony Matthews.

NEWCASTLE UNITED

		Carling Prem. :13th		FA CUP: Runners Up			LC CUP: 6th Round	European Cup; 3rd in Group C	

M	DATE	COMP.	VEN	OPPONENTS	RESULT	H/T	LP	GOAL SCORERS/GOAL TIMES	ATT.
1	A 09	CP	H	Sheffield Wednesday	W 2-1	1-1	4	Asprilla 2, 71	36711
2	13	EC 2Q1/1	H	Croatia Zagreb	W 2-1	1-0		Beresford 21, Beresford 71	34465
3	23	CP	H	Aston Villa	W 1-0	1-0	6	Beresford 12	36783
4	27	EC 2Q1/2	A	Croatia Zagreb	D 2-2*	1-0		Asprilla 44 (pen), Ketsbaia 119	(34000)
5	S 13	CP	H	Wimbledon	L 1-3	1-1	11	Barton 31	36526
6	17	EC GC	H	Barcelona	W 3-2	2-0		Asprilla 21,(pen), 30,49	35274
7	20	CP	A	West Ham United	W 1-0	1-0	8	Barnes 43	(25884)
8	24	CP	H	Everton	W 1-0	0-0	7	Lee 87	36705
9	27	CP	A	Chelsea	L 0-1	0-0	10		(31563)
10	O 01	EC GC	A	Dinamo Kiev	D 2-2	0-2		Beresford 78, Golovko 84 (OG)	(100000)
11	04	CP	H	Tottenham Hotspur	W 1-0	0-0	6	Barton 88	36709
12	15	CC 3	H	Hull City	W 2-0	0-0		Hamilton 47, Rush 83	35856
13	18	CP	A	Leeds United	L 1-4	0-3	10	Gillespie 62	(39834)
14	22	EC GC	A	PSV Eindhoven	L 0-1	0-1			(29200)
15	25	CP	H	Blackburn Rovers	D 1-1	1-0	10	Gillespie 27	36716
16	N 01	CP	H	Leicester City	D 3-3	2-2	9	Barnes 4 (pen), Tomasson 45, Beresford 90	36574
17	05	EC GC	H	PSV Eindhoven	L 0-1	0-2			35214
18	08	CP	A	Coventry City	D 2-2	1-1	9	Barnes 31, Lee 87	(22679)
19	18	CC 4	A	Derby County	W 1-0	0-0		Tomasson 71	(27364)
20	22	CP	H	Southampton	W 2-1	0-1	9	Barnes 54, 75	36759
21	26	EC GC	A	Barcelona	L 0-1	0-1			25000
22	29	CP	A	Crystal Palace	W 2-1	1-0	7	Ketsbaia 45, Tomasson 64	(26085)
23	D 01	CP	A	Bolton Wanderers	L 0-1	0-1	8		(24494)
24	06	CP	H	Arsenal	L 0-1	0-1	9		36751
25	10	EC GC	H	Dinamo Kiev	W 2-0	2-0		Barnes 10, Pearce 21	33694
26	13	CP	A	Barnsley	D 2-2	1-1	9	Gillespie 44, 49	(18687)
27	17	CP	H	Derby County	D 0-0	0-0	9		36289
28	21	CP	H	Manchester United	L 0-1	0-0	9		36767
29	26	CP	A	Derby County	L 0-1	0-1	10		(30232)
30	28	CP	H	Liverpool	L 1-2	1-2	11	Watson 16	36718
31	J 04	FAC 3	A	Everton	W 1-0	0-0		Rush 68	(20885)
32	07	CC QF	H	Liverpool	L 0-2	0-0			33207
33	10	CP	A	Sheffield Wednesday	L 1-2	1-1	11	Tomasson 20	(29446)
34	17	CP	H	Bolton Wanderers	W 2-1	1-0	10	Barnes 6, Ketsbaia 90	36767
35	20	CP	A	Liverpool	L 0-1	0-1	10		(42791)
36	25	FAC 4	H	Stevenage Borough	D 1-1	1-1		Shearer 3	(8040)
37	F 01	CP	A	Aston Villa	W 1-0	0-0	10	Batty 58	(38266)
38	04	FAC 4R	H	Stevenage Borough	W 2-1	1-0		Shearer 15, 66	36705
39	06	CP	H	West Ham United	L 0-1	0-1	10		36736
40	14	FAC 5	H	Tranmere Rovers	W 1-0	1-0		Shearer 22	36675
41	22	CP	H	Leeds United	D 1-1	0-0	13	Hughes 85	36511
42	28	CP	A	Everton	D 0-0	0-0	12		(37972)
43	M 08	FAC QF	H	Barnsley	W 3-1	2-0		Ketsbaia 17, Speed 27, Batty 90	36695
44	14	CP	H	Coventry City	D 0-0	0-0	15		36767
45	18	CP	H	Crystal Palace	L 1-2	0-2	15	Shearer 77	36565
46	28	CP	A	Southampton	L 1-2	0-0	15	Lee 46	(15251)
47	31	CP	A	Wimbledon	D 0-0	0-0	15		(15478)
48	A 05	FAC SF	A	Sheffield United	W 1-0	0-0		Shearer 59	(53452)
49	11	CP	A	Arsenal	L 1-3	0-1	16	Barton 79	(38102)
50	13	CP	H	Barnsley	W 2-1	1-0	15	Andersson 40, Shearer 86	36534
51	18	CP	A	Manchester United	D 1-1	1-1	15	Andersson 11	(55194)
52	25	CP	A	Tottenham Hotspur	L 0-2	0-1	15		(35847)
53	29	CP	A	Leicester City	D 0-0	0-0	15		(21699)
54	M 02	CP	H	Chelsea	W 3-1	2-0	13	Dabizas 38, Lee 42, Speed 58	36710
55	10	CP	A	Blackburn Rovers	L 0-1	0-0	13		(29300)
56	16	FAC F	N	Arsenal	L 0-2	0-1			(79183)

Best Home League Attendance: 36783 V Aston Villa | Smallest :36289 V Derby County | Average :36663

Goal Scorers:

CP	(35)	Barnes 6, Gillespie 4, Lee 4, Barton 3, Tomasson 3, Andersson 2, Asprilla 2, Beresford 2, Ketsbaia 2, Shearer 2, Batty 1, Dabizas 1, Hughes 1, Speed 1, Watson 1
CC	(3)	Hamilton 1, Rush 1, Tomasson 1
FAC	(9)	Shearer 5, Batty 1, Ketsbaia 1, Rush 1, Speed 1
EC	(11)	Asprilla 4, Beresford 3, Barnes 1, Ketsaia 1, Pearce 1, Opponents 1

*AET

(D) Albert	(F) Andersson	(F) Asprilla	(M) Barnes	(D) Barton	(M) Batty	(D) Beresford	(M) Crawford	(M) Dabizas	(D) Elliott	(F) Gillespie	(G) Given	(M) Griffin	(M) Hamilton	(G) Hislop	(D) Howey	(D) Hughes	(M) Keidel	(F) Ketsbaia	(F) Lee	(D) Peacock	(D) Pearce	(D) Pistone	(F) Rush	(F) Shearer	(F) Speed	(G) Smicek	(F) Tomasson	(D) Watson	Referee	#
X		X		X	X									S					X	X		X	X			S	X	X	P. Jones	1
X1		X		X	X	S				S2	X			S1	S				X	X		X	X			S	X2	X		2
X			S1	X	X			S	X	X			S	S					X	X		X	X	X			S2	X	G S Willard	3
X		X		X	X	X1	S		S	S1	X			S2	S				S3	X		X2	X			S	X3	X		4
X	S1	X	X		X					X	X		S		S				S1	X	S		X	X			X	X	M D Reed	5
X	X	X1	X	X	X					X	X			S	S				S1	X	S2			S		S	X2	X		6
X	X	X	X	X	X					X	X		S	S1					S	X	X					S	X	X	S W Dunn	7
X	X	X	S1	X	S3					X	X		S	S						X	X		X	S2			X	X	G Poll	8
X		X	X	X	X			S2	X	S	S	S3		S1					X	X		X	X				X	X	M A Riley	9
X	X2	X	X	X				X	X	S	S	S	S	S1	X1	X			S		X					S2	X		10
S		X	X	X				S	X	X	S	X		X		X			X		X					X	X	M J Bodenham	11
X		X	X		X			X	X	X	S		X	X		X			X		X					X	S1	K M Lynch	12
S		X	X	X	X			S2	X	S	X		X	X	X	S		S1	X	X		X				S1	X	D R Elleray	13
S2		S	X2	X	X1			X	X	S	X	X	S	S1	X	X			X		X				X	X	P A Durkin	14
X		X		X	X			X	S	X	S2	S		X	S1			X	X	X			X	X	X	J T Winter	15
X		X	X	X	X	S		X	S1	X	S	X	X	X		S2			X	X	G S Willard	16
X	X	X		X	S		X	X	X	S	X	S	S	X	X	X	X		17
X	X	S1	X	X	X		X	S	S	S	X	X	X	S	X	P A Durkin	18
X	X	X	X	X	X		S1	X	S	S2	X	X	X	M J Bodenham	19
X	X	S	S	S	S	X	X	X	S	X	X	S	S	X	X	X	D J Gallagher	20
X2	X	X	S	S	X	X	S2	X	X1	S1	S	X	X	21
S	X1	X	S	X	X	X	X	S1	X	X	X	S	S	X	X	X	M A Riley	22
S	S1	X	S	X	S	X1	X	X	X	X	X	X	N S Barry	23
S1	X1	X	X	X	S	S	S	S2	X	X	X	X2	S W Dunn	24
X	X2	X	X	S	X	S	S	X	S1	S2	X	X	X	X1	S	S	X	H Krug	25
X	X1	X	X	X	S	S	X	S	X	X	X	X	S1	X	P E Alcock	26
X	X1	X	S	X	X	S	S	X	S	X	X	S1	X	X	K W Burge	27
X1	X	X	S1	X	X2	X	S	X	S2	X	X	S	S	X	P Jones	28
S2	S3	X	X	X	S	X	X3	S	S1	S	X	X1	X2	X	M D Reed	29
X	X	X1	X	X	X	X	S1	X	S	X	X	X	S	X	G R Ashby	30
X1	X2	X	X	S	X	X	S2	S	X	X	X	X	S1	S	X	M J Bodenham	31
X1	X	X	X	X2	S	X	S	X2	X	X	X	S1	X	D J Gallagher	32
X	X1	X	S	X	S	X2	X	X	3	S1	X	X	X	X	S2	X	X	D R Elleray	33
X1	X	X	X	S	X	S	X	S2	X	X	X	S	X2	X	G Poll	34
X1	X	X2	X	S	X	S	S2	X	X	S	S1	X	G P Barber	35
S1	X2	X	X1	X	S	X	X	S2	X	X	X	S	X	S	X	P Jones	36
S	X1	X	X	X	S	X	X	S	X	X	X	S1	X	S J Lodge	37
X	S1	X	S3	X	S	X	X3	S2	X	X	X	S	X	X2	X1	P Jones	38
S	X	X	X	X	X1	S	X	X	X	X	X	S	X	S1	U D Rennie	39
S2	X	X	X	S	X	S1	X	S	X	X	S	X	X2	X1	G R Ashby	40
S1	X	S	X	X1	X	S	X	X1	S1	X	X	X	S	G S Willard	41
X	X	S	X	X1	X	S	S1	X	X	X	X	S	M A Riley	42
X	X	S	X	X	X	S	S	X	X	X	S	X	X	S	N S Barry	43
X2	X	S	S2	X	S1	X	S	X	X	X	X1	X	X	X	S	P Jones	44
X2	S2	X	X	X	X	X	S	X1	X3	X	S1	X	X	S3	S J Lodge	45
S	X	X	X2	X	S1	X	S2	X1	X	X	S	S	X	G P Barber	46
X	S	S	S1	X	S2	X	X2	X	X	X1	X	X	X	S	X	N S Barry	47
X	X1	X	X	X	X	X	S	S	S1	X	X	S	X	S	G Poll	48
X	S2	X2	X	X	X	X	X1	S	S1	X	X	X	S	S	G S Willard	49
X	X2	S	X	X	X	X1	X	S	S1	X	X	X	S	S2	S W Dunn	50
X	X1	X	X	X	S	S1	X	X	X	X	S	S	X	U D Rennie	51
X1	X	S	X	X	X	S1	X	S	S	S2	X	X	X	X	J T Winter	52
S	S	X	X	X	S	S	X	X	X	X	X	X	S	M J Bodenham	53
X2	S2	X	X	X	X	S3	X1	X	X3	X	X	X	S	S1	K W Burge	54
X	S1	X1	X	X	X	X	S2	X	X	X	S	X	X	D R Elleray	55
S	S1	S3	X2	X	X	S	X	X3	X	X1	X	X	X	S2	P A Durkin	56
21	**10**	**8**	**22**	**17**	**32**	**17**		**10**		**25**	**24**	**4**		**7**	**13**	**11**	**4**	**16**	**26**	**19**	**25**	**28**	**6**	**15**	**13**	**1**	**17**	**27**	CP Appearances	
2	2	2	4	6		1		1		4			5		3			15	2	1			4	2		6	2		CP Sub Appearances	
3			3	2	2	3				2			1+1	3	1	1		1+1	2	2+1		1	2			2+1	2+1		CC Appearances	
3+1	2+1	1	3+2	4+1	6	2+1		2		5	4		1	3	5	0+1		2+4	6	1	7	5	0+1	6	4		2	3+1	FAC Appearances	
7+1		5	5	5	7	7		4		5+2	6		2	2	1+2	0+2		3+5	6	4+1	3+1	5	1			6+1	8		EC Appearances	

111

NEWCASTLE UNITED

CLUB RECORDS

BIGGEST VICTORIES
League: 13-0 v Newport County, Division 2, 5.10.1946 (joint record).
F.A. Cup: 9-0 v Southport, 4th Round, 1.2.1932.
League Cup: 7-1 v Notts County (A), 2nd Round, 5.10.1993.
Europe: 5-0 v Antwerp (A), (UEFA) 1st Round 1st leg, 13.9.1994. (2nd leg United won 5-2, 27.9.1994)

BIGGEST DEFEATS
League: 0-9 v Burton Wanderers, Division 2, 15.4.1895.
F.A. Cup: 1-7 v Aston Villa, 2nd Round, 16.2.1895.
League Cup: 2-7 v Manchester United, 4th Round, 27.10.1976.
Europe: 0-3 v AS Monaco (UEFA) Quarter-final, 18.03.97

MOST POINTS
3 points a win: 96, Division 1, 1992-93 (46 games).
2 points a win: 57, Division 2, 1964-65.

MOST GOALS SCORED
98, Division 1, 1951-52.
G.Robledo 33, Milburn 25, Mitchell 9, Foulkes 6, Davies 5, Hannah 5, Duncan 3, Keeble 3, Prior 2, Walker 2, Brennan 1, Crowe 1, Harvey 1, Taylor 1, Opponents 1.

MOST GOALS CONCEDED
109, Division 1, 1960-61.

MOST FIRST CLASS MATCHES IN A SEASON
63 - 1973-74 (League 42, FAC 10, Lge Cup 3, Texaco Cup 8).

MOST LEAGUE WINS
29, Division 1, 1992-93.

MOST LEAGUE DRAWS
17, Division 2, 1990-91.

MOST LEAGUE DEFEATS
26, Division 1, 1977-78.

INDIVIDUAL CLUB RECORDS

MOST GOALS IN A SEASON
Andy Cole: 41 goals in 1993-94 (League 34, FA Cup 1, League Cup 6).

MOST GOALS IN A MATCH
6. L Shackleton v Newport, Division 2, 13-0, 5.10.1946.

OLDEST PLAYER
William Hampson, 44 years 225 days v Birmingham City, Division 1, 9.4.1927.

YOUNGEST PLAYER
Stephen Watson, 16 years 223 days v Wolverhampton Wders., Division 2, 10.11.1990.

MOST CAPPED PLAYER
Alf McMichael (Northern Ireland) 40.

BEST PERFORMANCES

League: 1992-93: Matches played 46, Won 29, Drawn 9, LOst 8, Goals for 92, Goals against 38, Points 96. First in Division 2/1.
Highest Position: Division 1 champions four times.
F.A. Cup: Winners in 1909-10, 1923-24, 1931-32, 1950-51, 1951-52, 1954-55.
Most recent success: 1954-55: 3rd Round Plymouth 1-0; 4th Round Brentford 3-2; 5th Round Nottingham Forest 1-1,2-2,2-1; 6th Round Huddersfield 1-1,2-0; Semi-final York City 1-1,2-0; Final Manchester City 3-1.
League Cup: 1975-76: 2nd Round Southport 6-0; 3rd Round Bristol Rovers 1-1,2-0; 4th Round Queens Park Rangers 3-1; 5th Round Notts County 1-0; Semi-final Tottenham 0-1,3-1; Final Manchester City 1-2.
Europe: (UEFA) 1968-69: 1st Round Feyenoord 4-0,0-2; 2nd Round Sporting Lisbon 1-1,1-0; 3rd Round Real Zaragossa 2-3,2-1; 4th Round Vittoria Setubal 5-1,1-3; Semi-final Rangers 0-0,2-0; Final Ujpest Dozsa 3-0,3-2.

DIVISIONAL RECORD

	Played	Won	Drawn	Lost	For	Against	Points
Division 1/P	2,742	1,088	654	996	4,278	3,983	2,990
Division 2/1	1,046	481	218	347	1,798	1,438	1,318
Total	**3,788**	**1,569**	**872**	**1,347**	**6,076**	**5,421**	**4,308**

ADDITIONAL INFORMATION
PREVIOUS NAMES
Newcastle East End 1882-92.

PREVIOUS LEAGUES
Northern League.

Club colours: Black/white striped shirts, black shorts, black socks/white tops.

Change colours: Dark blue with gold trim.

Youth League: Northern Intermediate League.

RECORDS AND STATISTICS

COMPETITIONS

Div 1/P	Div.2/1	UEFA	A/Ital	A/Scot	Texaco
898-1934	1893-98	1968-69	1972-73	1975-76	1971-72
1948-61	1934-48	1969-70		1976-77	1972-73
1965-78	1961-65	1970-71			1973-74
1984-89	1978-84	1977-78			1974-75
1993-	1989-93	1994-95			
		1996-97			

HONOURS

Div.1	Div 2/1	FAC	UEFA	A/Ital	C/Shield
1904-05	1964-65	1909-10	1968-69	1972-73	1907
1906-07	1992-93	1923-24			1909
1908-09		1931-32		Texaco	
1926-27		1950-51		1973-74	
		1951-52		1974-75	
		1954-55			

MOST APPEARANCES

Jim Lawrence 496 (1904-22)

Year	League	FA Cup
1904-05	29	8
1905-06	33	8
1906-07	33	1
1907-08	38	6
1908-09	38	7
1909-10	34	8
1910-11	36	8
1911-12	27	
1912-13	34	8
1913-14	21	
1914-15	31	5
1919-20	20	1
1920-21	42	4
1921-22	16	
	432	64

MOST GOALS IN A CAREER

Jackie Milburn - 200 (1946-57)

Year	League	FA Cup
1945-46		2
1946-47	7	1
1947-48	20	
1948-49	19	
1949-50	18	3
1950-51	17	8
1951-52	25	3
1952-53	5	
1953-54	16	2
1954-55	19	2
1955-56	19	2
1956-57	12	
Total	177	23

Current leading goalscorer: Robert Lee - 54 (1992-98)

RECORD TRANSFER FEE RECEIVED

Amount	Club	Player	Date
£7,000,000*	Manchester Utd	Andy Cole	01/95
£6,000,000	Tottenham	Les Ferdinand	07/97
£6,000,000	Tottenham	David Ginola	07/97
£2,500,000	Sunderland	Lee Clark	06/97

*Included Keith Gillespie signing for Newcastle (valued at £1m)

RECORD TRANSFER FEE PAID

Amount	Club	Player	Date
£15,000,000	Blackburn Rovers	Alan Shearer	07/97
£7,500,000	Parma	Faustino Asprilla	02/96
£6,000,000	Q.P.R.	Les Ferdinand	06/95
£4,500,000	Inter Milan	Alessandro Pistone	07/97
£4,000,000	Wimbledon	Warren Barton	06/95
£3,500,000	Blackburn	David Batty	03/96

MANAGERS

Name	Seasons	Best	Worst
A Cunningham	1930-35	5(1)	6(2)
T Mather	1935-39	4(2)	19(2)
S Seymour	1939-47	5(2)	5(2)
G Martin	1947-50	*3(1)	2(2)
S Seymour	1950-54	4(1)	16(1)
D Livingstone	1954-56	*5(1)	8(1)
C Mitten	1958-61	8(1)	21(1)
N Smith	1961-62	11(2)	11(2)
J Harvey	1962-75	7(1)	8(2)
G Lee	1975-77	*7(1)	15(1)
R Dinnis	1977	5(1)	*22(1)
W McGarry	1977-80	21(1)	*22(2)
A Cox	1980-84	*3(2)	11(2)
J Charlton	1984-85	14(1)	14(1)
W McFaul	1985-88	11(1)	*19(1)
J Smith	1988-91	20(1)	*11(2)
O Ardiles	1991-92	11(2)	*23(2)
K Keegan	1992-97	2 (P)	20 (2)
K Dalglish	1997-	2 (P)	13 (P)

*Indicates position when manager left club.

LONGEST LEAGUE RUNS

of undefeated matches:	14 (22.4.1950 - 30.9.1950)	of league matches w/out a win:	21 (14.1.1978 - 23.8.1978)
of undefeated home matches:	31 (9.12.1905 - 12.10.1907)	of undefeated away matches:	10 (16.11.1907 - 23.3.1908)
without home win:	12 (28.12.1977 - 26.8.1978)	without an away win:	18 (4.9.1984 - 20.4.1985)
of league wins:	13 (25.4.1992 - 18.10.1992)	of home wins:	20 (24.4.1906 - 1.4.1907)
of league defeats:	10 (23.8.1977 - 15.10.1977)	of away wins:	6 (2.5.1992 - 18.10.1992)

NEWCASTLE UNITED

PLAYERS NAME / Honours	Ht	Wt	Birthdate	Birthplace / Transfers	Contract Date	Clubs	League	L/Cup	FA Cup	Other	Lge	L/C	FAC	Oth
G O A L K E E P E R														
Given Shay Ei: 17, u21.5, Y.	6.2	13.4	4/20/76	Lifford		Celtic								
				Loan	8/1/94	Swindon Town								
					8/1/94	Blackburn Rovers	2	0+1						
				Loan	8/4/95	Swindon Town								
				Loan	1/19/96	Sunderland								
					7/14/97	Newcastle United	24		4					
Harper Stephen	6.2	13	3/14/75	Easington		Seaham Red Star								
				Free	7/5/93	Newcastle United								
				Loan	9/18/95	Bradford City								
				Loan	8/29/97	Hartlepool United	15							
				Loan	12/18/97	Huddersfield Town	24		2					
Keen Peter	6	11.10	11/16/76	Middlesbrough	3/25/96	Newcastle United								
Perez Lionel	5.11	13.4	4/24/67	France		Bordeaux (France)								
				£200000	8/21/96	Sunderland	74+1	2	4	3				
				Free	5/18/98	Newcastle United								
Reed Matthew W	5.10	11.10	4/7/80	Stanford-Le-Hope	7/11/97	Newcastle Utd (T)								
D E F E N C E														
Albert Phillippe Belgian International	6.3	13.7	8/10/67	Bouillon (Belg)		Anderlecht								
				£2650000	8/12/94	Newcastle United	84+6	11+1	7+1	13+1	8	2	1	1
Arnison Paul S	5.9		9/18/77	Hartlepool	3/1/96	Newcastle United								
Barton Warren E: 2, B.2	6	11	3/19/69	Stoke Newington		Leyton Orient								
						Leytonstone Ilford								
				£10000	7/28/89	Maidstone	41+1	0+2	3	7			1	
				£300000	6/7/90	Wimbledon	178+2	16	11	2	10	1		
				£4000000	8/1/95	Newcastle United	61+11	8	7+2	4+2	4	1		
Beharall David	6	11.7	3/8/79	Newcastle	7/4/97	Newcastle Utd (T)								
Caldwell Stephen	6	11.5	9/12/80	Stirling		Newcastle United								
Charvet Laurent ECWC'98	5.10	12.3	5/8/73	Beziers, France		Cannes								
				Loan	1/22/98	Chelsea	7+4	0+1		0+1	2			
				£500000	7/16/98	Newcastle United								
Dabizas Nikolaos	6	11.11	8/3/73	Amypeo		Olympiakos								
				£2000000	3/13/98	Newcastle United	10+1		2		1			
Elliott Stuart	5.11		8/27/77	Hendon	8/28/95	Newcastle United	2							
				Loan	2/28/97	Hull City	3							
				Loan	2/20/98	Swindon Town	1+1							
Griffin Andrew	5.8	10.10	3/17/79	Wigan	9/5/96	Stoke City	51+5	4+1	2		2			
				£1500000	1/30/98	Newcastle United	4							
Howey Stephen N E:1, Div1'93	6.2	10.9	10/26/71	Sunderland	12/11/89	Newcastle United	146+21	14+2	16+2	9	6	1		
Hughes Aaron W	6	11.2	11/8/79	Maghera Felt	2/28/97	Newcastle United	4	1	0+1	0+1	1			
Kelly Paddy	6	11.7	4/26/78	Kirkcaldy		Celtic								
				Free	8/1/97	Newcastle United								
				Loan	3/26/98	Reading	3							
Macklin Gareth	5.8	10.6	8/27/80	Belfast		Newcastle Utd (T)								
Pearce Stuart E: 76, u21.1; LC'89'90; FMC'89'92	5.11	13	4/24/62	Hammersmith		Wealdstone			2					
				£25000	10/20/83	Coventry City	52		2		4			
				£200000	6/3/85	Nottingham Forest	401	60	37	24	63	10	9	6
				Free	7/21/97	Newcastle United	25		7	1				
Pistone Alessandro	5.11	12.1	7/27/75	Milan		Inter Milan								
				£4300000	7/31/97	Newcastle United	28	1	5	5				
Talbot Paul M	5.10	10.9	8/11/79	Gateshead	7/4/97	Newcastle Utd (T)								
Watson Stephen C E: B.1, u21.12, u19.11, u18.4	6	12.7	4/1/74	North Shields	4/6/91	Newcastle United	152+29	10+6	13+4	17+4	12	1		1
M I D F I E L D														
Barnes John C B E: 73, u21.3; FAYC'82; Div1'88'90; CS'88'90'90; FAC'89	5.11	11.1	9/7/63	Jamaica		Sudbury Court								
				Free	7/14/81	Watford	232+1	21	31	7	66	7	11	
				£900000	6/19/87	Liverpool	309+4	26	51	16	83	3	16	5
				Free	8/14/97	Newcastle United	22+4	3	3+2	1	6			
Barrett Paul	5.9	10.11	4/13/78	Newcastle	6/20/96	Newcastle United								
Batty David E: 35, B.5, u21.7, Y.2. Div2'90. Div1'92.	5.8	12	12/2/68	Leeds	8/3/87	Leeds United	201+10	17	12	17	4			
				£2750000	10/26/93	Blackburn Rovers	30+1	2	4					
				£3750000	3/2/96	Newcastle United	75	4	9	15	3		1	
Brady Gary	5.10	10.9	9/7/76	Glasgow		Tottenham H. (T)								
				Free	7/1/98	Newcastle United								
Burt David C	5.9	10.11	2/5/78	Newcastle	5/23/97	Newcastle Utd (T)								
Coppinger James	5.7	10.3	1/10/81	Middlesbrough		Newcastle United								
Georgiadis George				Greece		Panathinaikos								
				£420000	6/1/98	Newcastle United								
Gudjonsson Bjarni				Akranes										
				£500000	7/14/97	Newcastle United								
Hamilton Derick	5.7	10.12	7/6/65	Bradford	6/1/94	Bradford City	66+22	6	6	4+1	5	1		2
					3/27/97	Newcastle United	7+5	1+1	1			1		
Hamann Dietmar						Bayern Munich								
				£5500000	8/1/98	Newcastle United								
Keidel Ralf	5.8	10.12	3/6/77	Wurzburg		Schweinfurt								

Name														
					1/9/98	Newcastle United								
McClen James D	5.8	10.7	5/13/79	Newcastle	7/4/97	Newcastle Utd (T)								
Serrant Carl	6	11.2	9/12/75	Bradford	7/22/94	Oldham Athletic	84+6	7	6	3	1		1	
E: B.1, u21.2, Y.				£500000	7/7/98	Newcastle United								
Solano Norberto				Puru		Boca Juniors								
				£2500000	8/1/98	Newcastle United								
F O R W A R D														
Andersson Andreas	6.1	12.1	4/10/74	Stockholm		AC Milan								
Swedish Int.				£3600000	1/29/98	Newcastle United	10+2		2+1		2			
Burghall Terence R	6	11.6	9/25/78	Liverpool		Liverpool								
				Free	5/6/97	Newcastle United								
Broadbent David	5.9	10.6	9/26.79	Pembury	7/11/97	Newcastle Utd (T)								
Dalglish Paul	5.9	10	2/18/77	Glasgow		Celtic								
					8/14/96	Liverpool								
				Loan	11/21/97	Bury	1+11		1					
				Free	11/21/97	Newcastle United								
Glass Stephen						Aberdeen								
				Free	7/1/98	Newcastle United								
Gillespie Keith R	5.11	10.11	2/18/75	Bangor	2/3/93	Manchester United	3+6	3			1			
				£1000000	1/10/95	Newcastle United	88+16	7	9+1	7+2	11	1	2	
Guivarc'h Stephane				France		Auzerre								
French Int. WC'98.				£3500000	6/19/98	Newcastle United								
Ketsbaia Timour	5.8	10.12	3/18/68	Gale		AEK Athens								
				Free	7/10/97	Newcastle United	16+15	1+1	2+4	0+1	2		1	
Knight Paul	5.7	10.7	10/16/80	Dublin		Newcastle Utd (T)								
Lee Robert M	5.11	11.6	2/1/66	West Ham		Hornchurch								
E: 2, B.1, u21.2; Div1'93				Free	7/12/83	Charlton Athletic	274+24	16+3	14	10+2	59	1	2	3
				£700000	9/22/92	Newcastle United	206+3	15	20	13	43	3	4	4
McMahon David	6.1	11.5	1/17/81	Dublin		Newcastle Utd (T)								
Robinson Paul D	5.10	10.12	11/20/78	Sunderland	7/14/97	Darlington	7+19	0+1	2+4	0+1	3		1	
				£250000	3/27/98	Newcastle United								
Shearer Alan	5.11	11.3	8/13/70	Newcastle	4/14/88	Southampton	105+13	16+2	11+3	8	23	11	4	5
E: 17,B.1,u21.12,Y.S. Prem'95.				£3600000	7/24/92	Blackburn Rovers	132+6	16	8	9	112	14	2	2
				£15000000	8/1/96	Newcastle United	46+2	1	9	5	27	1	6	1
Speed Gary A.	5.11	10.12	9/8/69	Mancot	6/13/88	Leeds United	231+17	25+1	21	14+3	39	5	11	2
				£4000000	7/1/96	Everton	58	4	2		16	1	1	
				£5500000	2/5/98	Newcastle United	13		4		1		1	
Woodcock Chris J	5.7	10.8	5/7/80	Bradford	7/11/97	Newcastle Utd (T)								

MANAGER
KENNY DALGLISH

Date of Birth . . . . 4th March 1951.
Place of Birth . . . . Glasgow.
Date of Appointment . . . . January 1997.

PREVIOUS CLUBS
As Manager . . . . Liverpool, Blackburn Rovers.
As Coach . . . . None.
As a Player . . . . Celtic, Liverpool.

HONOURS
As a Manager
Liverpool: Division 1 Championship 1986, 1988, 1990. FA Cup Winners 1986, 1989.
Blackburn Rovers: Carling Premiership Champions 1995.
As a Player
Celtic: Scottish Lge Championship 1972'73'74'77. SFA Cup 1972'74'75'77. SLge Cup 1975.
Liverpool: League championship 1979'80'82'83'84'86. FA Cup1986. Lge Cup 1981'82'83'84.
European Cup 1978'81.
International: 102+ full caps and 4 U23 for Scotland.

ST. JAMES PARK
Newcastle-upon-Tyne NE1 4ST

Capacity 36,806

First game ....v Celtic, 3.9.1892.
First floodlit game ....v Celtic, 25.2.1953.

ATTENDANCES
Highest..68,386 v Chelsea, Division 1, 3.9.1930.
Lowest...1,000 v Walsall T S, Div.2, 10.3.1894.

OTHER GROUNDS......................................Chillingham Road, South Byker 1882-86, Heaton 1886-1892. St. James Park 1892-

HOW TO GET TO THE GROUND

From the North
Use A1 into Newcastle then follow sign Hexham into Percy Street, then turn right into Leazes Park Road (or turn left then right into St James' Street) for Newcastle United FC.

From the South
Use A1, A68 and then A6127, cross River Tyne and at roundabout take 1st exit into Mosley Street. One-way keep to left hand lane into Neville Street. At end turn right into Clayton Street for Newgate Street. Then turn left into Leazes Park Road (one-way) turn left then right into St James' Street for Newcastle United FC.

From the West
Use A69 (sign posted Newcastle) enter city centre then turn left into Clayton Street for Newgate Street. Then turn into Leazes Park Road (one-way) turn left then right into St James' Street for Newcastle United FC.

Car Parking: Parking on the north side of the ground. Also street parking is permitted.
Nearest Railway Station: Central Station (0191 232 6262).

USEFUL TELEPHONE NUMBERS

Club switchboard 0191 201 8400
Club fax number 0191 201 8600
Club shops 0191 201 8426
Ticket Office . . 0191 261 1571 (fax 201 8609)

Marketing Department. 0191 201 8422
Internet address .... www.nufc.co.uk
Clubcall 0891 12 11 90*
*Calls cost 50 per minute at all times. Call costings correct at time of going to press.

MATCHDAY PROGRAMME

Programme Editor .... Tony Hardisty.

Number of pages .... 52.

Price........................ £2.

Subscriptions . . Telephone: 0191 4871116.

Local Newspapers
. . Newcastle Chronicle, Newcastle Journal,
.... Sunday Sun, Northern Echo,
.... South Shields Gazette.

Local Radio Stations
Metro Radio, Radio Newcastle, Radio Tees,
.... Century Radio.

MATCHDAY TICKET PRICES

	Adults	Juveniles
Milburn Stand		
Centre sections	£27.50	£16.00
Centre sections Row A	£25.50	£14.00
Wing sections	£24.00	£14.00
Wing sections Row A	£22.00	£12.00
Platinum Club	£30.00	
Paddock	£26.50	£15.00
East Stand		
Upper section	£26.50	£15.00
Family enclosure	£16.50	£7.00
East Paddock	£19.00	£11.50
Sir John Hall Stand	£23.00	£13.00
Disabled	£9.00	£6.50
Exhibition Stand	£23.00	£13.00
Disabled	£9.00	£6.50

NOTTINGHAM FOREST
(The Reds)
F.A. CARLING PREMIERSHIP
SPONSORED BY: PINNACLE

997-98 - **Back Row L-R:** Steve Stone, Colin Cooper, Paul McGregor, Kevin Campbell, Andy Johnson, Geoff Thomas, Paul Smith, Chris Allen, Thierry Bonalair. **Middle Row:** Liam O'Kane (coach), Des Lyttle, Steve Chettle, Marco Pascola, Mark Crossley, Alan Peuls, Chris Bart-Williams, Alan Rogers, ohn Haselden (physio), Mike Kelly (coach). **Front Row:** Ian Woan, Scot Gemmill, David Phillips, Bobby Houghton (Asst. manager), Dave Bassett manager), Pierre Van Hooijdonk, Dean Saunders, Ian Moore.

NOTTINGHAM FOREST
FORMED IN 1865
TURNED PROFESSIONAL IN 1889
LTD COMPANY IN 1982

CHAIRMAN: I I Korn

DIRECTORS
P Soar (Deputy Chairman/Chief Exec),
R A Fairhall, R W Dove, P Markman,
T H Farr, K J Eggleston.
SECRETARY
Paul White (0115 952 6000)
COMMERCIAL DIRECTOR
D Clayton

MANAGER: Dave Bassett
ASSISTANT MANAGER: Micky Adams

PHYSIOTHERAPIST
John Haselden

STATISTICIAN FOR THE DIRECTORY
Vacant

Nottingham Forest - back in the Carling Premiership after just a year's absence - were never out of the top three in the First Division all season, and in the end deserved to be champions.

They played some excellent football - at home and away - and in Dutch international Pierre Van Hoijdonk, they had by far the best striker outside the Carling Premiership! (He top-scored with a total of 34 - only two short of Wally Ardron's club record of 36, set way back in 1950-51.

Manager Dave Bassett was, without doubt, twice a very happy man, when promotion was gained and then the First Division championship was clinched, and now is aim is to consolidate Forest in the top flight in 1998-99.

Promotion was made certain with a 1-0 home win over relegated Reading in the penultimate match of the season, Chris Bart-Williams the lucky man, who grabbed that precious goal. But it was what went on before which guaranteed Forest their place back with the elite.

From the word go they played some smart attacking football with their two main strikers Hoijdonk and Kevin Campbell both in tip-top form. Colin Cooper and Steve Chettle formed a solid back-bone at the heart of the defence while full-backs Des Lyttle, and Alan Rogers, midfielders Scot Gemmill, Steve Woan, Steve Stone, Andy Johnson and Bart-Williams, among others performed splendidly in front of veteran goalkeeper Dave Beasant.

Forest were confident in everything they did. They had a few off-days, losing eight matches in all (only three at home) but generally speaking they were the best team in the First Division and hopefully they will be able to acquire a mid-table position this term in the Carling Premiership. They don't want to have to battle to stay out of trouble on this occasion - not after their exploits of 1997!

Manager Bassett is confident he can produce the goods at The City Ground and he has already admitted that he will require some extra squad members, but he's an experienced campaigner and will certainly do his upmost to ensure that Forest stay in the top flight of English football.

Tony Matthews.

NOTTINGHAM FOREST

Division 1   :1st   FA CUP: 3rd Round   LC CUP: 2nd Round

M	DATE	COMP.	VEN	OPPONENTS	RESULT	H/T	LP	GOAL SCORERS/GOAL TIMES	ATT.
1	A 09	FL	A	Port Vale	W 1-0	1-0	8	Campbell 39	(12533)
2	11	CC 1/1	A	Doncaster Rovers	W 8-0	3-0		Thomas 11, Saunders 15, 78, Hjelde 30, 55, Van Hooijdonk 47, 83, Allen 86	(4547)
3	15	FL 0	H	Norwich City	W 4-1	1-1		Van Hooijdonk 22, Thomas 57, 61, Campbell 59	16524
4	23	FL	A	Oxford United	W 1-0	0-0	1	Bart-Williams 71	(9486)
5	27	CC 1/2	H	Doncaster Rovers	W 2-1	1-0		Guinan 6, Van Hooijdonk 58	9908
6	30	FL	H	Queens Park Rangers	W 4-0	1-0		Van Hooijdonk 44, 48, 87, Saunders 80	18804
7	S 03	FL	H	Manchester City	L 1-3	0-1	2	Campbell 81	23681
8	07	FL	A	Swindon Town	D 0-0	0-0			(13051)
9	13	FL	A	Sheffield United	L 0-1	0-0	5		(24536)
10	17	CC 2/1	H	Walsall	L 0-1	0-0			7841
11	20	FL	H	Portsmouth	W 1-0	1-0	1	Van Hooijdonk 34	17292
12	24	CC 2/2	A	Walsall	D 2-2	0-0		Van Hooijdonk 48, Armstrong 92	(6037)
13	27	FL	H	Stoke City	W 1-0	0-0	1	Campbell 67	19018
14	O 03	FL	A	Huddersfield Town	W 2-0	0-0	1	Cooper 67, Saunders 73	(11258)
15	18	FL	H	Tranmere Rovers	D 2-2	2-1	1	Van Hooijdonk 18, Gemmill 42	17009
16	21	FL	H	West Bromwich Albion	W 1-0	0-0	1	Campbell 75	19243
17	24	FL	A	Reading	D 3-3	1-1	1	Van Hooijdonk 3, 48 (pen), Campbell 64	(12610)
18	N 01	FL	H	Crewe Alexandra	W 3-1	1-1	1	Campbell 9, Van Hooijdonk 54, 86	18268
19	04	FL	A	Bury	L 0-2	0-1	1		(6137)
20	08	FL	A	Sunderland	D 1-1	1-1	2	Hjelde 24	(33160)
21	15	FL	H	Birmingham City	W 1-0	1-0	1	Campbell 17	19610
22	22	FL	H	Charlton Athletic	W 5-2	1-0	1	Van Hooijdonk 21, 50, 56, Woan 76, Campbell 83	18532
23	26	FL	A	Middlesbrough	D 0-0	0-0	1		(30143)
24	29	FL	A	Ipswich Town	W 1-0	0-0	1	Campbell 65	(17580)
25	D 06	FL	H	Bradford City	D 2-2	1-0	2	Cooper 14, Bonnalair 63	17943
26	14	FL	A	Wolverhampton Wand	L 1-2	0-1	2	Johnson A 84	(24635)
27	20	FL	H	Stockport County	W 2-1	0-1	2	Van Hooijdonk 81 (pen), Stone 86	16701
28	26	FL	H	Swindon Town	W 3-0	3-0	1	Campbell 11, 23, Johnson 30	26500
29	28	FL	A	Manchester City	W 3-2	1-0	1	Van Hooijdonk 31 (pen), 55 (pen), Campbell 51	(31839)
30	J 03	FAC 3	A	Charlton Athletic	L 1-4	0-2		Van Hooijdonk 56	(13827)
31	10	FL	H	Port Vale	W 2-1	1-1	1	Van Hooijdonk 27, 82	17639
32	17	FL	A	Norwich City	L 0-1	0-0	1		(17059)
33	24	FL	A	Queens Park Rangers	W 1-0	0-0	1	Cooper 85	(13220)
34	31	FL	H	Oxford United	L 1-3	1-1	1	Van Hooijdonk 27 (pen)	18392
35	F 06	FL	A	Portsmouth	W 1-0	0-0	1	Chettle 52	(15033)
36	17	FL	H	Huddersfield Town	W 3-0	1-0	1	Van Hooijdonk 36, 81, Bonnalair 69	18231
37	21	FL	A	Stoke City	D 1-1	0-1	2	Moore 87	(16899)
38	24	FL	A	Tranmere Rovers	D 0-0	0-0	2		(7377)
39	M 01	FL	H	Middlesbrough	W 4-0	0-0	1	Van Hooijdonk 53, 85 (pen), Campbell 55, Cooper 75	25286
40	04	FL	H	Sunderland	L 0-3	0-1	1		29009
41	07	FL	A	Crewe Alexandra	W 4-1	4-1	1	Bart-Williams 10, Campbell 15, 25, 30	(5759)
42	14	FL	H	Bury	W 3-0	0-0	1	Van Hooijdonk 69, Rogers 82, Armstrong 63 (OG)	18846
43	21	FL	A	Birmingham City	W 2-1	0-0	1	Van Hooijdonk 84, 88	(24663)
44	28	FL	A	Charlton Athletic	L 2-4	1-1	1	Campbell 16, 90	(15815)
45	A 01	FL	H	Sheffield United	W 3-0	2-0	1	Thomas 21, Campbell 28, 83	21512
46	05	FL	H	Ipswich Town	W 2-1	0-0	1	Cooper 53, Van Hooijdonk 57	22292
47	11	FL	A	Bradford City	W 3-0	1-0	1	Campbell 38, Gemmill 62, Bart-Williams 82	(17248)
48	13	FL	H	Wolverhampton Wand	W 3-0	2-0	1	Johnson 33, Van Hooijdonk 40, Campbell 90	22863
49	18	FL	A	Stockport County	D 2-2	1-0	1	Van Hooijdonk 26, Johnson 67	(9892)
50	26	FL	H	Reading	W 1-0	0-0	1	Bart-Williams 88	29302
51	M 03	FL	A	West Bromwich Albion	D 1-1	1-0	1	Stone 18	(23013)

Best Home League Attendance: 29302 V Reading   Smallest :16524 V Norwich City   Average :20543

Goal Scorers:
FL   (82)   Van Hooijdonk 29, Campbell 23, Cooper 5, Bart-Williams 4, Johnson A 4, Thomas 3, Bonnalair 2, Gemmill 2, Saunders 2, Stone 2,
Chettle 1, Hjelde 1, Moore 1, Rogers 1, Woan 1, Opponents 1

CC   (12)   Van Hooijdonk 4, Hjelde 2, Saunders 2, Allen 1, Armstrong 1, Guinan 1, Thomas 1
FAC   (1)   Van Hooijdonk 1

(F) Allen	(M) Armstrong	(M) Barr-Williams	(G) Beasant	(M) Bonnalair	(F) Campbell	(D) Chettle	(D) Cooper	(G) Fettis	(M) Gemmill	(F) Guinan	(D) Harewood	(M) Hjelde	(M) Howe	(M) Johnson A	(M) Johnson D	(D) Lyttle	(F) Moore	(G) Pascolo	(M) Phillips	(D) Rogers	(F) Saunders	(M) Smith	(M) Stone	(D) Thom	(D) Thomas	(F) Van Hooijdonk	(D) Warner	(F) Woan	Referee	#
			X	X	X				S1				X		X			X		X	S2			X		X	X		P.R. Richards	1
X	S2		X		X				X				X			X	S3	X	S1	X	X					X	X		T Heilbron	2
	S			X	X	X			X				X		S1		X			X	S2		X			X	X		J A Kirkby	3
X	S	S1	X	X					X		S2		X		X		X			X						X	X		E K Wolstenholme	4
X	X	X						X		X			X	X		X	S2			X				X		X	S3	S1	P Taylor	5
	S	X	X	X		X			X				X		S		X	S		X	X					X	X		M J Brandwood	6
	S	X		X	X	X			X				X		S1		X	S2	X	X	X			X					C T Finch	7
	S2	X	X	S	X	X			X				X			X				X	X					X	S1		R J Harris	8
	S	X	X	S1	X	X			X				X			X				X	S2					X	X		E Lomas	9
	S2	X	X		X	X			X	S			X		X			X	X	S1						X			A R Leake	10
	X	X		X	X	X	X		X	S			X	S1			X			X	X	S				X			A G Wiley	11
X	X	X		X	X	X	X		X	S			S1			X				X	X	S				X			G Cain	12
	X	X		X	X	X	X		X	S			S1			X				X	X	S				X			M Fletcher	13
	X	X		X	X	X	X		X	S			S1			X				X	X	S				X			S W Mathieson	14
	X	X		X	X	X	X		X	S	X		S			X				X			S1		X			X	B Knight	15
	X	X		X	X	X	X		X	S	X		S2			X				X			S1		X			X	D Pugh	16
X	X	X		X	X	X	X		X	S			S			X				X			X		X			X	M J Brandwood	17
X	X	X		X	X	X	X		X		S1					X	S			X			X		X			S	T Heilbron	18
	X	X		X	X	X	X		X				X			X	S	S		X			X		X			S1	J P Robinson	19
	X	X		X	X	X	X		X				X			X	S	S		X			X		X			S	J A Kirkby	20
S1	X	X		X	X	X	X		X				X			X	S			X			X		X			S2	P S Danson	21
S	S1	X		X	X	X	X		X				X			X	S			X			X		X			X	C J Foy	22
	X	X		X	X	X	X		X				X			X	S	S		X			X		X			S	D Laws	23
	X	X		X	X	X	X		X				X			X	S	S		X			X		X			S	R Pearson	24
S2		X	S1	X	X	X			X	S		X				X1				X			X		X			X2	R J Harris	25
S1		X		X	X	X	X		X			X1		S3		X2	S2	X		X3					X			X	M C Bailey	26
S3		X		S2		X	X		X	X1				X2		S1	X			X3			X		X			X	W C Burns	27
S1		X	S2	X	X	X			X1				X			X	S3			X			X3		X			X2	G Laws	28
S2		X	S1	X	X	X				S		X2		X			X			X			X		X			X1	A G Wiley	29
X1		X	X	X	X	X			X	S		X	S			X	X	S		X					S	S1		R Pearson	30
S1		X	S		X	X1	X		X				X	S		X	S			X			X		X				A P D'Urso	31
S		X	X2	X	X	X			X				X	S2		X				X				S1	X			X1	M F Pierce	32
S2		X	X	X	X	X	X2						X		S					X				S1	X			X1	K A Leach	33
S1		X	X1	X	X				X	X2		X	S2	S						X			X	X				M J Jones	34
S		X	X	X	X				X	X	X	S					X			X			X	X				C R Wilkes	35
S3		X	X	X	X				X1	X	X	S2					X3			X			X	S1	X2				T Heilbron	36
S1	S2	X	X	X	X1	X			X			X3	X2	X	X				X					S3					D Pugh	37
S	X	X	X	X			X	X1	S			X	X	X	X				X					S1					E Lomas	38
	X	X	X	X	X				X	S			X						X			X1		S	X				E K Wolstenholme	39
	X	X	S1	X	X	X			X			S		X	X2	X1			X					S2	X				M C Bailey	40
S2	X	X	X	X3	X				X1			X		S1			S3			X			X		X			X2	M Fletcher	41
S	X	X	X	X	X				X1			X		S1	S2				X			X2		X				P Taylor	42
S	X	X	X	X	X	X			X1			S		X2					X			X		S2	X		S1		S W Mathieson	43
S	X	X	X	X	X	X			X1			S		X					X			X		X	X		S1		K M Lynch	44
S2	X3	X	X	X	X				X			S1		X1					X2			X1	X		S3	X		G Cain	45
S	X	X	X	X	X	X			X			S1		X1					X			X		X	X		S	W C Burns	46
S	X	X	X	X2	X	X1			X			S1		X			S		X			X		X			S2	R Pearson	47
S	X	X	X	X	X1	X			X			X		X					X			X		X			S1	P R Richards	48
S	X	X	X	X1	X				X			X		X			S		X			X		X			S1	P S Danson	49
	X	X	X	X2	X1	X			X			S1		X			S		X			X		X			S2	G B Frankland	50
	X	X	X		X	X	X1			X	X	S2	X2			S			X			X		X			S1	D Orr	51
1	4	30	41	24	42	45	35		43	1	1	23		24	5	35	2	5		46	6		27	13	41			12	FL Appearances	
	14	3		7					1	1	5		10	1		8					3		2	7	1			9	FL Sub Appearances	
2	2+2	3	2	1	2	3	1	1	3	1		2	1	2+1		4	0+2	1	1+1	4	2+1		1	1	4	0+1	0+1		CC Appearances	
1		1	1	1	1	1	1		1			1				1	1			1					0+1				FAC Appearances	

Also Played: (F) McGregor S(35,48).

NOTTINGHAM FOREST

CLUB RECORDS

BIGGEST VICTORIES
League: 12-0 v Leicester City, Division 1, 12.4.1909 (Joint Division 1 record).
F.A. Cup: 14-0 v Clapton, 1st round, 17.1.1891 (a).
League Cup: 7-0 v Bury, 3rd Round 23.9.1980.
Europe: 5-1 v AEK Athens 2nd Round (Euro Cup), 15.11.1978.
4-0 v Eintracht Frankfurt, 1st Round (UEFA), 17.10.1967.

BIGGEST DEFEATS
League: 1-9 v Blackburn Rovers, Division 2, 10.4.1937.
0-8 v West Bromwich Albion, Division 1, 16.4.1900.
0-8 v Leeds City, Division 2, 29.11.1913.
0-8 v Birmingham City, Division 2, 10.3.1920.
0-8 v Burnley, Division 1, 21.11.1959.
F.A. Cup: 0-5 v Southampton, 6th Round, 1962-63.
League Cup: 0-4 v Manchester United, 5th Round, 19.1.1983.
Europe: 1-5 v Valencia, 1st Round, 14.10.1961.

MOST POINTS
3 points a win: 83, Division 1, 1993-94.
2 points a win: 70, Division 3(S), 1950-51 (Division 3(S) record).

MOST GOALS SCORED
110, Division 3(S), 1950-51.
Ardon 36, Capel 23, Collindridge 16, Johnson 15, Scott 9, Leverton 6, Gager 2, Love 1, Burkitt 1, Opponents 1.

MOST GOALS CONCEDED
90, Division 2, 1936-37.

MOST FIRST CLASS MATCHES IN A SEASON
65 - 1979-80 (League 42, FA Cup 2, League Cup 10, European Cup 9, European Super Cup 2).

MOST LEAGUE WINS
30, Division 3(S), 1950-51.

MOST LEAGUE DRAWS
18, Division 1, 1969-70 & 1978-79.

MOST LEAGUE DEFEATS
25, Division 1, 1971-72.

INDIVIDUAL CLUB RECORDS

MOST GOALS IN A SEASON
Wally Ardron: 36 goals in 1950-51 (All League).

MOST GOALS IN A MATCH
5. A Higgins v Clapton (a) 14-0, FA Cup 1st Round, 17.1.1891.

OLDEST PLAYER
Sam Hardy, 41 v Newcastle United, 4.10.1924.

YOUNGEST PLAYER
S J Burke, 16 years 22 days v Ayr United, Anglo-Scot Cup.

MOST CAPPED PLAYER
Stuart Pearce (England) 70.

BEST PERFORMANCES

League: 1950-51: Matches played 46, Won 30, Drawn 10, Lost 6, Goals for 110, Goals against 40, Points 70. First in Division 3(S).
Highest Position: Champions of Division 1, 1977-78.

F.A. Cup: Winners in 1897-98.
Most recent success: 1958-59: 3rd Round 2-2,3-0; 4th Round Grimsby Town 4-1; 5th Round Birmingham 1-1 (2); 6th Round Bolton Wanderers 2-1; Semi-final Aston Villa 1-0; Final Luton Town 2-1.

League Cup: Winners in 1977-78, 1978-79, 1988-89.
Most recent success: 1989-90: 2nd Round Huddersfield Town 1-1,3-3; 3rd Round Crystal Palace 0-0,5-0; 4th Round Everton 1-0; 5th Round Spurs 2-2,3-2; Semi-final Coventry City 2-1,0-0; Final Oldham Athletic 1-0.

Europe: (European Cup) Winners in 1978-79.
Most recent success: 1979-80: 1st Round Oester Vakjo 2-0,1-0; 2nd Round Agres Pitesti 2-1,2-0; 3rd Round Dynamo Berlin 0-1,3-1; Semi-final Real Madrid 2-0,0-1; Final S V Hamburg 1-0.

DIVISIONAL RECORD

	Played	Won	Drawn	Lost	For	Against	Points
Division 1/P	2,140	793	540	806	3,034	3,104	2,374
Division 2/1	1,584	599	394	600	2,414	2,353	1,643
Division 3(S)	88	50	19	19	177	79	119
Total	**3,812**	**1,442**	**953**	**1,417**	**5,625**	**5,536**	**4,136**

ADDITIONAL INFORMATION
PREVIOUS NAMES
None.

PREVIOUS LEAGUES
Football Alliance.

Club colours: Red shirts, white shorts, red socks.

Change colours: Yellow shirts with blue & red trim, blue shorts with red & yellow trim.

Reserves League: Pontins Central League Division 1.

RECORDS AND STATISTICS

COMPETITIONS

Div 1/P	Div.2/1	Div. 3(S)	Euro C	UEFA	Sup C
1892-06	1906-07	1949-51	1978-79	1961-62	1970-80
1907-11	1911-22		1979-80	1967-68	1980-81
1922-25	1925-49		1980-81	1983-84	
1957-72	1951-57			1984-85	Texaco
1977-93	1972-77	W.C.C.		1995-96	1970-71
1994-97	1993-94	1982			
1998-	1997-98				A/Scot
					1976-77

HONOURS

Div.1	Div.2/1	Div.3(S)	FAC	Lge C	Euro C	A/Scot
1977-78	1906-07	1950-51	1898	1977-78	1978-79	1976-77
	1921-22		1959	1978-79	1979-80	
	1997-98			1988-89		Sup C
			C/S'ld	1989-90	Sim. C.	1979-80
			1978		1988-89	
					1991-92	

MOST APPEARANCES
Bobby McKinlay 681+3 (1951-70)

Year	League	FA Cup	Lge Cup	Europe
1951-52	1	1		
1952-53	3			
1953-54	1			
1954-55	37	6		
1955-56	39	1		
1956-57	39	5		
1957-58	40	3		
1958-59	39	9		
1959-60	42	2		
1960-61	42	1	3	
1961-62	42	2	3	2
1962-63	42	7		
1963-64	42	2		
1964-65	42	3		
1965-66	41	1		
1966-67	42	7	2	
1967-68	42	2	2	4
1968-69	30+2	1	1	
1969-70	5+1			
	611+3	53	11	6

MOST GOALS IN A CAREER
Grenville Morris - 225 (1898-1913)

Year	League	FA Cup
1898-99	7	8
1899-1900	8	3
1900-01	14	1
1901-02	7	2
1902-03	24	2
1903-04	12	2
1904-05	12	1
1905-06	19	3
1906-07	21	1
1907-08	7	
1908-09	12	
1909-10	19	1
1910-11	11	1
1911-12	10	
1912-13	16	1
Total	199	26

Current leading goalscorer: Ian Woan - 40 (1990-98)

RECORD TRANSFER FEE RECEIVED

Amount	Club	Player	Date
£8,500,000	Liverpool	Stan Collymore	07/95
£2,100,000	Tottenham H	Teddy Sheringham	9/92
£1,500,000	Sampdoria	Des Walker	5/92
£1,500,000	Manchester Utd	Neil Webb	7/89

RECORD TRANSFER FEE PAID

Amount	Club	Player	Date
£2,500,000	Arsenal	Kevin Campbell	7/95
£2,500,000	Foggia	Bryan Roy	8/94
£2,200,000	Southend United	Stan Collymore	7/93
£2,000,000	Millwall	Teddy Sheringham	7/91

MANAGERS

Name	Seasons	Best	Worst
Harry Radford	1889-97	7(1)	13(1)
Harry Haslam	1897-09	4(1)	1(2)
F W Earp	1909-12	14(1)	15(2)
Bob Masters	1912-25	20(1)	20(2)
Jack Baynes	1925-29	5(2)	17(2)
Stan Hardy	1930-31	17(2)	17(2)
Noel Watson	1931-36	5(2)	19(2)
Harold Wightman	1936-39	18(2)	20(2)
Billy Walker	1939-60	10(1)	4(3S)
Andy Beattie	1960-63	9(1)	19(1)
John Carey	1963-68	2(1)	18(1)
Matt Gillies	1969-72	15(1)	21(1)
Dave Mackay	1972-73	14(2)	14(1)
Allan Brown	1973-75	7(2)	16(2)
Brian Clough	1975-93	1(1)	8(2)
Frank Clark	1993-97	3(P)	2(1)
Stuart Pearce	1996-97	20 (P)	20 (P)
Dave Bassett	1996-97	20 (P)	20 (P)

LONGEST LEAGUE RUNS

of undefeated matches:	42 (26.11.1977 - 25.11.1978)	of league matches w/out a win:	16 (8.2.1913 - 18.10.1913)
of undefeated home matches:	51 (27.4.1977 - 17.11.1979)	of undefeated away matches:	21 (3.12.1977 - 9.12.1978)
without home win:	10 (20.11.1909 - 9.4.1910)	without an away win:	37 (25.1.1913 - 23.1.1915)
of league wins: 7 (24.12.1892 - 25.2.1893, 29.8.1921 - 1.10.1921)		of home wins:	12 (23.2.1980 - 20.9.1980)
of league defeats:	14 (8.2.1913 - 18.11.1913)	of away wins:	5 (5.4.1983 - 29.8.1983, 31.12.1988 - 25.3.1989)
			(21.11.1993 - 16.01.1994)

NOTTINGHAM FOREST

PLAYERS NAME Honours	Ht	Wt	Birthdate	Birthplace Transfers	Contract Date	Clubs	League	L/Cup	FA Cup	Other	Lge	L/C	FAC	Oth
G O A L K E E P E R														
Beasant Dave	6.3	13	3/20/59	Willesden		Edgware Town								
E: 2, B.7. Div4'83. Div2'89. FAC'88. ZDC'90				£1000	8/7/79	Wimbledon	340	21	27	3				
DIV1 97/98				£800000	6/13/88	Newcastle United	20	2	2	1				
				£735000	1/14/89	Chelsea	133	11	5	8				
				Loan	10/24/92	Grimsby Town	6							
				Loan	1/12/93	Wolverhampton W.	4		1					
				£300000	11/4/93	Southampton	85+2	8	9					
					8/28/97	Nottingham Forest	41	2	1					
Crossley Mark G	6	15	6/16/69	Barnsley	7/2/87	Nottingham Forest	271	34	32	18				
E: u21.3				Loan	2/20/98	Millwall	13							
Goodlad Mark	6	13.2	9/9/79	Barnsley	10/2/96	Nottingham Forest								
Pascola Marco	6.2	14.4	5/5/66	Sion, Switzerland		Cagliari								
Swiss Int.				£750000	8/1/97	Nottingham Forest	5	1						
D E F E N C E														
Chettle Stephen	6.1	13.3	9/27/68	Nottingham	8/28/86	Nottingham Forest	357+14	42+3	35+1	21+2	8	1	1	1
E: u21.12; LC'90; FMC'89'92. DIV1 97/98														
Cooper Richard A	5.9	11	9/27/79	Nottingham	5/31/97	Nottingham Forest	8		1					
Cooper Colin T	5.8	9.4	2/28/67	Sedgefield	7/17/84	Middlesbrough	188+5	18	13	19+1	6			2
E: u21.8. DIV1 97/98				£300000	7/25/91	Millwall	77	6	2	2	6			
				£1700000	6/21/93	Nottingham Forest	172+1	14	11	7	20	2	1	
Doig Chris R	6.2	12.6	2/13/81	Dumfries		Nottingham F. (T)								
Edwards Christian	6.3	11.7	11/23/75	Caerphilly	7/20/94	Swansea City	112+2	5	4	7+1	4			
				£175000	3/26/98	Nottingham Forest								
Follett Richard	5.9	10.2	8/29/79	Leamington	9/9/96	Nottingham Forest								
Harewood Marlon	6.1	10	8/25/79	Hampstead	9/9/96	Nottingham Forest	1							
Higgins Paul K	5.7	10.2	1/6/81	Ilkeston		Nottingham F. (T)								
Hjelde Jon O	6.2	13.7	4/30/72	Levanger		Rosenborg								
DIV1 97/98				£600000	8/8/97	Nottingham Forest	23+5	2	1		1	2		
Howarth Paul	5.6	10.1	11/21/80	Nottingham		Nottingham F. (T)								
Jerkan Nikola	6.4	14.3	12/8/64	Croatia		Real Oviedo								
				£1000000	7/26/96	Nottingham Forest	14							
Lyttle Desmond	5.9	12	9/24/71	Wolverhampton	1/9/90	Leicester City								
DIV1 97/98					8/1/91	Worcester City								
				£12500	7/9/92	Swansea City								
				£375000	7/27/93	Nottingham Forest	173+3	18	15	8	3			
Rogers Alan	5.1	11.8	1/3/77	Liverpool	7/1/95	Tranmere Rovers	53+4	1	1		2			
DIV1 97/98					7/4/97	Nottingham Forest	45	4	1		1			
Thom Stuart	6.2	11.8	12/27/76	Dewsbury	1/11/94	Nottingham Forest			1					
				Loan	12/24/97	Mansfield Town	5							
M I D F I E L D														
Armstrong S Craig	5.11	12.04	5/23/75	South Shields	6/2/92	Nottingham Forest	5+14	2+2	1		1	1		
				Loan	12/29/94	Burnley	4							
				Loan	1/5/96	Bristol Rovers								
				Loan	10/18/96	Gillingham	10	2						
				Loan	1/24/97	Watford								
				Loan	3/14/97	Watford	15							
Bart-Williams Chris	5.8	11	6/16/74	Sierra Leone	7/18/91	Leyton Orient	34+2	4		2	2			
E: B.1, Y.12, u21.8. DIV1 97/98				£275000	11/21/91	Sheffield Wednesday	95+25	14+2	8+5	4	4	3	1	1
				£2500000	7/1/95	Nottingham Forest	79+3	8	9	7+1	5			
Bonnalair Thierry	5.9	10.8	6/14/66	Paris		Neuchatel Xamax								
DIV1 97/98				Free	7/17/97	Nottingham Forest	24+7	1	1		2			
Burns John	5.8	10.08	12/4/77	Dublin	8/1/94	Nottingham Forest								
Cowling Lee	5.8	9.04	9/22/77	Doncaster	8/1/94	Nottingham Forest								
Dawson Andrew	5.9	10.2	10/20/78	Northallerton	10/31/95	Nottingham Forest								
Edds Gareth J	5.11	10.12	2/3/81	Sydney		Nottingham F (T)								
Finnigan John	5.8	10.05	3/29/76	Wakefield	8/1/92	Nottingham Forest								
				Loan	3/26/98	Lincoln City	6							
Fitchett Scott	5.8	9.6	1/20/79	Manchester	2/23/96	Nottingham Forest								
Gemmill Scot	5.1	11	1/2/71	Paisley	1/5/90	Nottingham Forest	211+14	27+2	18+2	13+1	21	3	1	4
S: 13, B.2, u21.4; FMC'92. DIV1 97/98														
Gough Steven	5.11	11.10	6/16/80	Burton		Nottingham F. (T)								
Hodgson Richard	5.11	11.4	10/1/79	Sunderland	10/8/96	Nottingham Forest								
Johnson Andrew J	6	11.6	5/2/74	Bristol	3/4/92	Norwich City	56+10	6+1	2		13	2		
E: Y1. DIV1 97/98					7/3/97	Nottingham Forest	24+9	2+1			3			
Melton Stephen	5.11	10.11	10/3/78	Lincoln	10/9/95	Nottingham Forest								
Merino Carlos A	5.8	10	3/15/80	Bilbao		Urdaneta								
						Nottingham Forest								
Stone Steve B	5.9	11.3	8/20/91	Gateshead	5/20/89	Nottingham Forest	163+4	10+1	10	10	20			2
DIV1 97/98														
Thomas Geoff	6.1	12	8/5/64	Manchester	8/13/82	Rochdale	10+1			0+1	1			
E: 9, B.3. FMC'91. DIV1 97/98				Free	3/22/84	Crewe Alexandra	120+5	8	2	2+1	21			
				£50000	6/8/87	Crystal Palace	192+3	24	13+1	15+1	26	3	2	4
				£800000	6/18/93	Wolverhampton W.	35+1	1	1	6	8			
				Free	7/10/97	Nottingham Forest	13+7	1			3	1		

F O R W A R D													
Allen Chris A	5.11 12.2	11/18/72	Oxford	5/14/91	Oxford United	110+40	11+2	5+5	5+3	12	4	1	
			Loan	2/24/96	Nottingham Forest								
				7/3/96	Nottingham Forest		1						
			Loan	11/28/97	Luton Town	15	1			1			
Darcheville Jean-Claude			France		Rennes								
			Loan	6/1/98	Nottingham Forest								
Freedman Doug	5.9 11	1/21/74	Glasgow	5/15/92	QPR								
S: B.1, u21.8, S.			Free	7/26/94	Barnet	42	4	2	2	24	5		
			£800000	9/8/95	Crystal Palace	72+19	3+1	2+1	3+2	31	1		2
			Swap	10/21/97	Wolverhampton W.	25+4		5+1		10		2	
			£950000	8/1/98	Nottingham Forest								
Freeman David	5.11 10.13	11/25/97	Dublin	5/31/97	Nottingham Forest								
Guinan Steve	6.1 12.12	12/24/75	Birmingham	8/1/92	Nottingham Forest	2+4	1			1			
			Loan	12/14/95	Darlington								
			Loan	3/27/97	Burnley	0+6							
			Loan	3/19/98	Crewe Alexandra	3							
Macari Jonathan	5.9 11.4	12/15/79	Stoke	5/31/97	Nottingham Forest								
McGregor Paul A	5.1 10.4	12/17/74	Liverpool	12/13/91	Nottingham Forest	7+23		0+3	0+3	3			1
Moore Ian	5.11 12	8/26/76	Liverpool	7/6/94	Tranmere Rovers	27+12	3+2	1		9	1		
E: u21, Y			Loan	9/13/96	Bradford City	6							
				3/15/97	Nottingham Forest	3+12	0+2	1		1			
Van Hooijdonk Pierre	6.4 13.5	11/29/69	Holland		Torino								
Dutch Int. DIV1 97/98			£1200000	1/7/95	Celtic	63+3	5+1	10	5+2	46	3	9	
Refused to play for Forest in 1998/99			£4500000	3/11/97	Nottingham Forest	49+1	4	0+1		30	4	1	
Woan Ian S	5.1 12.4	12/14/67	Heswall		Runcorn								
DIV1 97/98			£80000	3/14/90	Nottingham Forest	189+20	15+3	20+1	13	31	1	6	2

MANAGER
DAVE BASSETT

Date of Birth . . . . May 1997.
Place of Birth . . . . Wembley.
Date of Appointment . . . . 21st January 1996.

PREVIOUS CLUBS
As Manager . . . . Wimbledon, Watford, Sheffield United, Crystal Palace.
As Coach . . . . Wimbledon.
As a Player . . . . . . Walton & Hersham, Wimbledon, Hendon, Chelsea, Watford.

HONOURS
As a Manager
Wimbledon: Promotion to Div.3 1981. Div.4 Championship 1983. Promotion to Div.2 1984. Promotion to Div.1 1986.
Sheffield United: Promotion to Div.2 1989. Promotion to Div.1 1990.
Nottingham Forest: Division 1 championship 1997-98.

As a Player
Amateur Cup Winners Medal 1973.

CITY GROUND
City Road, Nottingham NG2 5FJ

Capacity ....30,602.

First game ....v Blackburn Rovers, 0-1, 3.9.1898.
First floodlit game ....v Gillingham, 11.9.1961.
Internationals ....England v Wales, 1909.

ATTENDANCES
Highest ....44,946 v Manchester Utd, Div.1, 28.10.1967.
Lowest ....2,624 v WBA, 30.3.1904.

OTHER GROUNDS ....Forest Racecourse 1865-79. The Meadows 1879-80. Trent Bridge 1880-82.
.... Parkside Lenton 1882-85. Gregory Lenton 1885-90. Town Ground 1890-98. City Ground 1898-

HOW TO GET TO THE GROUND

From the North
Use motorway (M1) until junction 26, leave motorway and follow signs into Nottingham A610. Follow signs to Melton Mowbray, Trent Bridge A606. Cross river and turn left into Radcliffe Road, then turn left into Colwick Road for Nottingham Forest FC.
From the East
Use A52 sign posted Nottingham, into West Bridgford, then turn left into Colwick Road for Nottingham Forest FC.
From the South
Use motorway (M1) until junction 24, leave motorway and follow signs to Nottingham (South) to Trent Bridge, turn right into Radcliffe Road, then turn left into Colwick Road for Nottingham Forest FC.
From the West
USe A52 into Nottingham, then follow signs to Melton Mowbray, Trent Bridge A606, cross river and turn left into Radcliffe Road, then turn left into Colwick Road for Nottingham Forest FC.

Car Parking: Street Parking only.
Nearest Railway Station: Nottingham Midland (0345 484 950).

USEFUL TELEPHONE NUMBERS

Club switchboard......................0115 982 4444
Club fax number.......................0115 982 4455
Club shop..................................0115 952 6026
Ticket Office 0115 982 4444 Ex.4371

Marketing Department....0115 952 4444 Ex.4314
Clubcall 0891 12 11 74*
*Calls cost 50p per minute at all times.
Call costings correct at time of going to press.

MATCHDAY PROGRAMME
Programme Editor ....John Lawson.

Number of pages.....................................32.

Price ....£1.50.

Subscriptions ....Apply to club.

Local Newspapers..
Nottingham Evening Post, Derby Telegraph.

Local Radio Stations
...................Radio Nottingham, Radio Trent.

MATCHDAY TICKET PRICES
Prices range between £17.00 - £28.00
Phone the ticket office for further details

SHEFFIELD WEDNESDAY
(The Owls)
F.A. CARLING PREMIERSHIP
SPONSORED BY: SANDERSON ELECTRONICS PLC

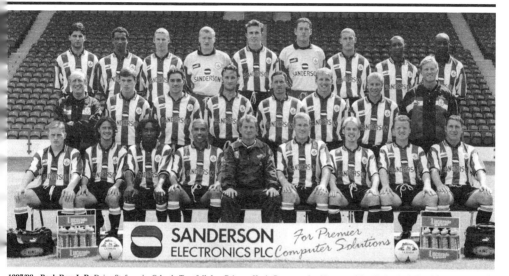

1997/98 - Back Row L-R: Dejan Stefanovic, Orlando Trustfull, Lee Briscoe, Kevin Pressman, Jon Newsome, Matt Clarke, Andy Booth, Wayne Collins, O'Neill Donaldson. **Middle Row:** Peter Shreeves (asst. manager), Ian Nolan, Guy Whittingham, Scott Oakes, Patrick Blondeau, Ritchie Humphreys, Adem Poric, David Galley (physio). **Front Row:** Mark Pembridge, Benito Carbone, Regi Blinker, Des Walker, David Pleat (manager), Peter Atherton, Graham Hyde, Steve Nicol, David Hirst.

SHEFFIELD WEDNESDAY
FORMED IN 1867
TURNED PROFESSIONAL IN 1887
LTD COMPANY IN 1899

CHAIRMAN: D G Richards
DIRECTORS
K T Addy (Vice-Chairman),
G K Hulley, R M Grierson FCA,
J Ashton MP, G Thorpe, H E Culley
SECRETARY
Graham Mackrell 0114 221212
COMMERCIAL MANAGER
Sean O'Toole

MANAGER: Danny Wilson
ASSISTANT MANAGER: Peter Shreeves

RESERVE TEAM MANAGER
Bobby Smith
YOUTH TEAM MANAGER
Albert Phelan
PHYSIOTHERAPIST
Dave Galley

STATISTICIAN FOR THE DIRECTORY
Michael Renshaw

A disappointing season for Wednesday, with not a lot shown to give hope for next time round. The really frightening thought is that it could have been even worse, with relegation on the cards in the first third of the season.

David Pleat failed to build on the reasonable form the 'Owls' showed the previous season and the two major signings he made were hit and miss. Patrick Blondeau came from France with a good reputation but the international full-back looked ill at ease on his few outings. He was later sold to French club Auxerre by new boss Ron Atkinson. The other big signing, Paolo Di Canio from Celtic, was a big hit with his flair, skill and great goals. If only he could learn to curb his temper tantrums he would become a truly great player.

When David Pleat was sacked, after a 6-1 defeat at Old Trafford, coach Peter Shreeves took over for the 5-0 victory at home against Bolton.

Then Ron Atkinson came back to Hillsborough as manager to the end of the season, with his brief to make sure relegation was avoided.

Morale within the club and it's supporters immediately emerged from the depths it had sunk to under the old regime, however, there are still a few fans who find it hard to forgive Mr Atkinson for his sudden departure a few years ago.

He got to work on organising the team and giving it some self belief. He found a way, eventually, of playing the two star Italians together to the benefit of the team. Results improved and a steady, if unspectacular climb away from the bottom of the table took place. Poor away form meant that the team never got more than a few points away from safety. Indeed it took a rare away win at Everton with just three matches to go which meant they survived in the Premier.

The side lacks a real creator in midfield, and have had problems in defence, shipping in goals, despite the good form of 'keeper Kevin Pressman.

To sum up, the 'Owls' need two or three major signings for next season to stand any chance of competing for even a European Place. The decision taken by the board not to renew Ron Atkinson's contract came as a bit of a shock to Ron and the supporters. The big test now for the Owls' leadership is who will they appoint to take on the job of managing the Owls, and converting them into a club challenging for honours. Only time will tell if they get it right or not!

Mick Renshaw.

SHEFFIELD WEDNESDAY

Carling Prem.	:16th			FA CUP: 4th Round				LC CUP: 2nd Round	

M	DATE	COMP.	VEN	OPPONENTS	RESULT	H/T	LP	GOAL SCORERS/GOAL TIMES	ATT.
1	A 09	CP	A	Newcastle United	L 1-2	1-1	17	Carbone 7	(36711)
2	12	CP	H	Leeds United	L 1-3	0-2	18	Hyde 70	31520
3	23	CP	A	Wimbledon	D 1-1	0-1	16	Di Canio 74	(11503)
4	25	CP	A	Blackburn Rovers	L 2-7	1-5	17	Carbone 7, 46	(19618)
5	30	CP	H	Leicester City	W 1-0	0-0	15	Carbone 55	24851
6	S 13	CP	A	Liverpool	L 1-2	0-0	19	Collins 81	(34705)
7	17	CC 2/1	A	**Grimsby Town**	**L 0-2**	**0-1**			**(6429)**
8	20	CP	H	Coventry City	D 0-0	0-0	19		21087
9	24	CP	H	Derby County	L 2-5	2-3	19	Di Canio 5, Carbone 13 (pen)	22391
10	27	CP	A	Aston Villa	D 2-2	2-1	18	Collins 25, Whittingham 42	(32044)
11	O 01	CC 2/2	H	**Grimsby Town**	**W 3-2**	**1-0**		**Di Canio 64, 88, Davison 16 (OG)**	**11120**
12	04	CP	H	Everton	W 3-1	0-0	16	Carbone 78, 82 (pen), Di Canio 89	24486
13	19	CP	A	Tottenham Hotspur	L 2-3	0-3	17	Collins 71, Di Canio 84	(25097)
14	25	CP	H	Crystal Palace	L 1-3	0-1	18	Collins 57	22072
15	N 01	CP	A	Manchester United	L 1-6	0-4	20	Whittingham 68	(55259)
16	08	CP	H	Bolton Wanderers	W 5-0	5-0	19	Di Canio 20, Whittingham 26, Booth 28, 33, 44	25027
17	22	CP	H	Arsenal	W 2-0	1-0	16	Booth 42, Whittingham 86	34373
18	29	CP	A	Southampton	W 3-2	1-0	14	Atherton 27, Collins 68, Di Canio 84	(15244)
19	D 08	CP	H	Barnsley	W 2-1	1-1	13	Stefanovic 19, Di Canio 88	29086
20	13	CP	A	West Ham United	L 0-1	0-0	13		(24344)
21	20	CP	H	Chelsea	L 1-4	0-1	14	Pembridge 71	28334
22	26	CP	H	Blackburn Rovers	D 0-0	0-0	14		33502
23	28	CP	A	Leicester City	D 1-1	0-1	15	Booth 85	(20800)
24	J 03	FAC 3	A	**Watford**	**D 1-1**	**0-0**		**Alexandersson 63**	**(18306)**
25	10	CP	H	Newcastle United	W 2-1	1-1	12	Di Canio 1, Newsome 51	29446
26	14	FAC 3R	H	**Watford**	**D 0-0***	**0-0**		**Sheffield Wed. won 5-3 on penalties**	**18707**
27	17	CP	A	Leeds United	W 2-1	0-0	11	Newsome 51, Booth 83	(33166)
28	26	FAC 4	H	Blackburn Rovers	L 0-3	0-2	11		15940
29	31	CP	H	Wimbledon	D 1-1	1-1	10	Pembridge 14	22655
30	F 06	CP	A	Coventry City	L 0-1	0-0	14		(18375)
31	14	CP	H	Liverpool	D 3-3	1-1	12	Carbone 7, Di Canio 63, Hinchcliffe 69	35405
32	21	CP	H	Tottenham Hotspur	W 1-0	1-0	12	Di Canio 33	29871
33	28	CP	A	Derby County	L 0-3	0-1	13		(30203)
34	M 07	CP	H	Manchester United	W 2-0	1-0	12	Atherton 26, Di Canio 88	39427
35	14	CP	A	Bolton Wanderers	L 2-3	1-1	13	Booth 28, Atherton 58	(24847)
36	28	CP	A	Arsenal	L 0-1	0-1	13		(38087)
37	A 04	CP	H	Southampton	W 1-0	0-0	13	Carbone 79	29677
38	11	CP	A	Barnsley	L 1-2	0-0	14	Stefanovic 86	(18692)
39	13	CP	H	West Ham United	D 1-1	0-1	14	Magilton 59	28036
40	19	CP	A	Chelsea	L 0-1	0-1	14		(29075)
41	25	CP	A	Everton	W 3-1	2-0	13	Pembridge 5, 38, Di Canio 90	(35497)
42	M 02	CP	H	Aston Villa	L 1-3	0-2	14	Sanetti 88	34177
43	10	CP	A	Crystal Palace	L 0-1	0-0	16		(16876)

Best Home League Attendance: 39427 V Manchester United	Smallest :15940 V Blackburn Rovers	Average :28068

Goal Scorers:

CP	(52)	Di Canio 12, Carbone 9, Booth 7, Collins 5, Pembridge 4, Whittingham 4, Atherton 3, Newsome 2, Stefanovic 2, Hinchcliffe 1, Hyde 1, Magilton 1, Sanetti 1
CC	(3)	Di Canio 2, Opponents 1
FAC	(1)	Alexandersson 1

*AET

(M) Alexandersson	(D) Atherton	(D) Barrett	(M) Blondeau	(F) Booth	(F) Briscoe	(F) Carbone	(G) Clarke	(M) Collins	(F) Di Canio	(F) Donaldson	(D) Hinchcliffe	(F) Hirst	(F) Humphreys	(M) Hyde	(M) Magilton	(F) Mayrleb	(D) Newsome	(D) Nicol	(D) Nolan	(F) Oakes	(M) Pembridge	(M) Poric	(G) Pressman	(F) Rudi	(D) Stefanovic	(M) Thome	(D) Walker	(F) Whittingham		
X	X			X	S	S1	S2	X			S	X						X		X			X		X		X	X	P. Jones	1
X	X	X		X	S	X	X	S3				X	S2								X	S1			X		X	S	P A Durkin	2
X	X	X		X	S	S1	X					X			X	S	X	S	X	X	X			X		X	S	A B Wilkie	3
X	X	X		X	S	S2	X			S3		X	X	X	X	X	X	X	S		X			X		X	X	J T Winter	4
X			S2	X	S	S1	X					X	X	X	X	X	X			S	X			X		X	S3	P E Alcock	5
X			S1		S	S2	X		X			X			X	X	X		X		X		S		X		X	X	G Poll	6
X			S1		S	X	X						X	X	S	X		X		X			X		X		X	X	M Fletcher	7
X		X		S	X	X	S3	X			S2		X	X	X	X	S3		X		X			X		X	X	G S Willard	8
		X		X	X	X	X					X			X		S	X	S	X	S1			X		X	X	M D Reed	9
				X	X	X	X					X			X		S	X	S	X	S1			X		X	X	N S Barry	10
				X	X	X	X				S2		X			X		X	S1	X			X		X	X	K W Burge	11
			S1	X	S	X	X				S2		X			X	X	X	S3	X			X		X	X	P A Durkin	12
				X	X	S1	X		S3			X			X		X		X		X		X	X	X	S2		J T Winter	13
				X	X	X	X		S2			X			X		X	S3	X	S1	X			X		X	X	D J Gallagher	14
			S		X	X	X				S2		X			X	S1		X	S3	X			X		X	X	G R Ashby	15
	X	S3	X		S	S	X	S1				S2		X	X	X		X		X			X	X	X	X	X	M D Reed	16
	X	S	X	S1	S	X					S2	S		X	X	X		X		X			X	X	X	X	X	K W Burge	17
	X	X2		S2	S	S1	X				S	S	X1		X			X		X			X	X	X	X	X	S W Dunn	18
	S	X	X1	S	X	X					S	S1	S		X			X		X		X	X	X	X	X	G S Willard	19
S		X3	S2	S	X	X			S3	X1		X			X		X		S1		X	X	X	X	X2		M A Riley	20
S1		X	S3	S	X1	X3			S	S1		X			X		X		X		X	X	X	X1	X		G P Barber	21
X	X	X	X2	S	S1				S	S		X			X		X		X		X2	X1	X	X	S2		J T Winter	22
X	X	X	S	X	S2'3				S3	S1		X			X		X	X2	X1	X	X	X1	X	X	S		G Poll	23
X	X	X1	X	S	X				S1	S		X		X	S	X		X		X	X	X	X	X	S		G S Willard	24
X	X	S2	X	S	X2				S1	X1		X		X	S	X		X		X	X	S	X				D R Elleray	25
X2	X	X	S	X					S1	S		X		X	S2	X		X		X	X	X1	S				G S Willard	26
X1	X	X	S	X	X2				S2	X3	S3	X		X		X		X		X	X	S	X	X	S1		M J Bodenham	27
X		X	X2	S	X			X	S1		S	S2	X2	X	S	X		X		X	X	S	X	X1			J T Winter	28
X1	X	X	X2	S	X			X	S		S	S2	S3	X	S	X		X1		X	X		X	S1			A B Wilkie	29
	X	X	S	X	X			X	X3	S3	S2	X		X		X2		X		X	X1		X	S1			G R Ashby	30
	X	S	X	S	X			X	X1	S1	S	X		X	X2		X1	S1	X3	X	X	S3	X				M D Reed	31
	X	X	S1	X	S			X3	X1	S2	S3	X		X			S	X2	X1	X	X		X				A B Wilkie	33
	X	X	X	S	X			X2	X		S		X1	S	S		S2	X1		X	X		X		X	S1	M J Bodenham	32
	X	X	X	S	X			X	S			X	X1		X2		S2	X	X1	X	X		X		X	S1	P Jones	34
	X	X	X	S	X			X			S	X1		X2		X1	S1	X3	X	X	S3	X		X		G Poll	35
	X	X	X	X1	S			X			S1	S		X2		X1	X	X	S	X	X	S2	S W Dunn			36
	X	X	X	X1	S			X			S	S		X1		X	X	X	S	X	X	X	P Jones			37
		X	X	S2	S			X			S1	S		S	X2		X	X	X	X	X	X	P E Alcock			38
	X	X	X	X	S			X		S		X		S1		S1	X	X1	X	X	X	X	N S Barry			39
	X	X2	X	X	S			X		S2		S1		X	X1	X	X	X	S	X	X	X	G S Willard			40
	X		X	S1	S			X	S	X1	X1	S		X		X		X	X	X	X	X	G P Barber			41
	X3		S	S	X			X		X	S3	X		S2		S1	X1	X	X1	X	S1	M J Bodenham			42
	X	X		S	X1			X				X		S1	X	X	X	X	S	M D Reed					43

5	27	10	5	21	3	28	2	8	34	1	15	3	2	14	13		25	4	27		31		36	19	19	6	38	17	CP Appearances	
1			1	2	4	5	1	11	1	4		3	5	8	7	3		3			4	3	4	3	1			11	CP Sub Appearances	
	1		1+1	1		2	2					0+1		2	1		2		1		2	0+1	2		1		2	2	CC Appearances	
2	3					3			0+3	1	1		3		3	0+2	3		3	3							3	1	FAC Appearances	

Also played: (M) Agogo S3(1).(M) Clough S(6,8,10), X(7,9). (G) Grobbelaar S(9,10,14,15). (M) Quinn S2(41). (F) Sanetti S2(42), X(43) (M) Sedloski S1(35), X(36,37), X1(38).

SHEFFIELD WEDNESDAY

CLUB RECORDS

BIGGEST VICTORIES
League: 9-1 v Birmingham, Division 1, 13.12.1930
8-0 v Sunderland, Division 1, 26.12.1911
F.A. Cup: 12-0 v Halliwell, Round 1, 17.1.1891
League Cup: 8-0 v Aldershot (a), Round 2, 3.10.1989
Europe: 8-1 v Spora Luxembourg, UEFA Cup Rnd 1 1st leg,
16.9.1992

BIGGEST DEFEATS
League: 0-10 v Aston Villa, Division 1, 5.10.1912
F.A. Cup: 0-5 v Wolves, Round 3, 2.3.1889
1-6 v Blackburn Rovers, Final, 29.3.1890
0-5 v Everton (h), Round 3 replay, 27.1.1988
League Cup: 2-8 v Queens Park R., Round 2, 1973-74
Europe: No more than 2 goals

MOST POINTS
3 points a win: 88, Division 2, 1983-84
2 points a win: 62, Division 2, 1958-59

MOST GOALS
106, 1958-59 (Division 2).
Shiner 28, Froggatt 26, Fantham 12, Wilkinson 12, Finney 11, Curtis
5, J McAnearney 3, Kay 3, Quixall 2, Ellis 1, T McAnearney 1,
Young 1, og 1.

MOST LEAGUE GOALS CONCEDED
100, Division 1, 1954-55

MOST FIRST CLASS MATCHES IN A SEASON
61 (46 League, 4 FA Cup, 10 League Cup, 1 ZDS) 1990-91

MOST LEAGUE WINS
28, Division 2, 1958-59

MOST LEAGUE DRAWS
19, Division 3, 1978-79

MOST LEAGUE DEFEATS
26, Division 1, 1919-20; Division 2, 1974-75

INDIVIDUAL CLUB RECORDS

MOST GOALS IN A MATCH
6. Douglas Hunt v Norwich, Division 2, 19.11.1938 (7-0)

MOST GOALS IN A SEASON
Derek Dooley 47, (46 League, 1 FAC) 1951-52.
5 goals once=5; 4 goals twice=8; 3 goals 3 times=9; 2 goals 9
times=18; 1 goal 7 times=7
Previous holder: J Trotter, 37 League (1925-26 & 1926-27).

OLDEST PLAYER
Tom Brittleton 41 years v Oldham, 1.5.1920.

YOUNGEST PLAYER
Peter Fox 15 years 269 days, 31.3.1973

MOST CAPPED PLAYER
Nigel Worthington (N. Ireland) 50

BEST PERFORMANCES

League: 1958-59: Matches played 42, Won 28, Drawn 6, Lost 8,
Goals for 106, Goals against 48, Points 62. 1st in Division 2

Highest: 1st in Division 1

F.A. Cup: 1895-96: 1st rnd. Southampton 3-2; 2nd rnd. Sunderland
2-1; 3rd rnd. Everton 4-0; Semi-Final Bolton 3-1; Final Wolves 2-1.
1906-07: 3rd rnd. Wolves 3-2; 4th rnd. Southampton 1-1, 3-1; 5th
rnd. Sunderland 0-0, 1-0; 5th rnd. Liverpool 1-0; Semi-Final Arsenal
1-0; Final Everton 2-1.
1934-35: 3rd rnd. Oldham 3-1; 4th rnd. Wolves 2-1; 5th rnd. Norwich
City 1-0;6th rnd. Arsenal 2-1; Semi-Final Burnley 3-0; Final West
Bromwich A. 4-2.

League Cup: 1990-91: 2nd rnd. Brentford 2-1, 2-1; 3rd rnd. Swindon
0-0, 1-0; 4th rnd. Derby Co. 1-1, 2-1; 5th rnd. Coventry City 1-0;
Semi-Final Chelsea 2-0, 3-1; Final Manchester Utd 1-0

EUFA: 1963-64: 1st rnd. Olympique Lyonnais 2-4, 5-2; 2nd rnd. AS
Roma 4-0, 0-1;Q/Final Barcelona 3-2, 0-2.

DIVISIONAL RECORD

	Played	Won	Drawn	Lost	For	Against	Points
Division 1/P	2,506	959	598	943	3,892	3,908	2,704
Division 2	1,088	460	281	347	1,693	1,401	1,285
Division 3	230	83	76	71	297	266	242
Total	3,826	1,502	955	1,367	5,890	5,574	4,231

ADDITIONAL INFORMATION
Previous Name
The Wednesday 1867-1929

Previous League
Football Alliance

Club colours: Blue & white striped shirts, blue shorts, blue socks.
Change colours: Yellow shirts, navy shorts.

Reserves League: Pontins Central League Division 1.

RECORDS AND STATISTICS

COMPETITIONS

Div 1/P	Div.2	Div.3	UEFA
1892-99	1899-1900	1975-80	1961-62
1900-20	1920-26		1963-64
1926-37	1937-50		1992-93
1950-51	1951-52		
1952-55	1955-56		
1956-58	1958-59		
1959-70	1970-75		
1984-90	1980-84		
1991-	1990-91		

HONOURS

Div 1/P	Div.2	FA Cup	League Cup
1902-03	1899-1900	1896	1991
1903-04	1925-26	1907	
1928-29	1951-52	1935	**C/Shield**
1929-30	1955-56		1935
	1958-59		

MOST APPEARANCES

ANDREW WILSON 546 (1900-20)

Year	League	FA Cup
1900-01	31	1
1901-02	25	1
1902-03	34	2
1903-04	29	3
1904-05	30	3
1905-06	35	5
1906-07	35	7
1907-08	34	1
1908-09	37	4
1909-10	30	2
1910-11	38	1
1911-12	37	2
1912-13	37	4
1913-14	31	5
1914-15	38	3
1919-20	1	
	502	44

MOST GOALS IN A CAREER

ANDREW WILSON - 216 (1900-20)

Year	League	FA Cup
1900-01	13	
1901-02	9	
1902-03	12	
1903-04	10	2
1904-05	15	2
1905-06	16	2
1906-07	17	4
1907-08	19	
1908-09	18	3
1909-10	12	
1910-11	9	1
1911-12	12	
1912-13	9	2
1913-14	15	
1914-15	13	1
Total	**199**	**17**

Current leading goalscorer: Guy Whittingham - 25 (12.94-98)

RECORD TRANSFER FEE RECEIVED

Amount	Club	Player	Date
£2,750,000	Blackburn Rov.	Paul Warhurst	8/93
£1,700,000	Real Sociedad	Dalian Atkinson	8/90
£800,000	Glasgow Rangers	Mel Sterland	3/89
£600,000	Arsenal	Brain Marwood	3/88

RECORD TRANSFER FEE PAID

Amount	Club	Player	Date
£4,500,000	Celtic	Paolo Di Canio	08/97
£3,000,000	Inter Milan	Benito Carbone	10/96
£2,750,000	Sampdoria	Des Walker	8/93
£2,750,000	Q.P.R.	Andy Sinton	8/93

MANAGERS

Name	Seasons	Best	Worst
Rob Brown	1920-23	1(1)	14(2)
Bill Walker	1933-37	3(2)	22(2)
Jim McMullen	1937-42	3(2)	17(2)
Eric Taylor	1942-58	14(1)	20(2)
Harry Catterick	1958-61	2(1)	5(1)
Vic Buckingham	1961-64	6(1)	6(1)
Alan Brown	1964-67	8(1)	17(1)
Jack Marshall	1967-68	19(1)	19(1)
Tom McAnearney	1968-69	15(1)	15(1)
Danny Williams	1969-71	22(1)	15(1)
Derek Dooley	1971-74	10(2)	19(2)
Steve Burtenshaw	1974-75	22(2)	20(3)
Len Ashurst	1975-77	8(3)	14(3)
Jack Charlton	1977-83	4(2)	18(3)
Howard Wilkinson	1983-88	5(1)	2(2)
Peter Eustace	1989		
Ron Atkinson	1989-91	18(1)	3(2)
Trevor Francis	1991-95	3(1)	7(1/P)
David Pleat	1995-98	7 (P)	15 (P)
Ron Atkinson	1998	16 (P)	16 (P)
Danny Wilson	1998-		

LONGEST LEAGUE RUNS

of undefeated matches:	19 (3.12.1960 - 17.4.1961)	of league matches w/out a win:	20 (7.1.54-17.3.55, 11.1.75-6.9.75)
of undefeated home matches:	31 (13.12.1902 - 29.10.1904)	of undefeated away matches:	11 (6.11.1979 - 12.4.1980)
without home win:	13 (7.2.1974 - 6.9.1975)	without an away win:	35 (28.12.1974 - 16.10.1976)
of league wins:	9 (14.11.1903 - 16.1.1904)	of home wins:	19 (2.9.1899 - 6.10.1900)
of league defeats:	7 (7.1.1893 - 25.3.1893)	of away wins:	6 (28.4.1990 - 6.10.1990)

SHEFFIELD WEDNESDAY

PLAYERS NAME Honours	Ht	Wt	Birthdate	Birthplace Transfers	Contract Date	Clubs	APPEARANCES League	L/Cup	FA Cup	Other	GOALS Lge	L/C	FAC	Oth
G O A L K E E P E R														
Clarke Matt	6.3	11.7	11/3/73	Sheffield	7/28/92	Rotherham United	83+1		3	3				
				£300000	7/11/96	Sheffield Wed.	2+2							
Jones Stuart			10/24/77	Bristol		Weston-Super-Mare								
				£20000	3/26/98	Sheffield Wed.								
Pressman Kevin	6.1	14.2	11/6/67	Fareham	11/7/85	Sheffield Wed.	233	29	14	4				
E: B.1, u21.1, u19.3, Y.6, S				Loan	3/10/92	Stoke City	4			2				
Woodward Jonathan J			6/16/79	Sheffield		Sheffield Wed. (T)								
D E F E N C E														
Atherton Peter	5.11	12.3	4/6/70	Orrell	2/12/88	Wigan Athletic	145+4	8	7	12+1	1			
E: u21.1, S				£300000	8/23/91	Coventry City	113+1	4	2					
				£800000	6/1/94	Sheffield Wed.	132	11	10		6			
Barrett Earl D	5.11	11.2	4/28/67	Rochdale	4/26/85	Manchester City	2+1	1						
E:3,B.4,u21.4. Div.2'91. FLgeXI.1. LC'94. CS'95.				Loan	3/1/86	Chester City	12							
				£35000	11/24/87	Oldham Athletic	181+2	20	14	4	7	1	1	
				£1700000	2/25/92	Aston Villa	118+1	15	9	7	1	1		
				£1700000	1/30/95	Everton	73+1	4	2	3				
				Loan	1/16/98	Sheffield United	5							
				Free	2/27/98	Sheffield Wed.	10							
Billington David J	5.8	10.2	10/15/80	Oxford		Peterborough United	2+3	1+1						
				£50000	5/31/97	Sheffield Wed.								
Cobian Juan				Argentina		Boca Juniors								
					8/1/98	Sheffield Wed.								
Hinchcliffe Andrew G	5.11	12.1	2/5/69	Manchester	6/17/86	Manchester City	107+5	11	12	4	8	1	1	1
E: 6, u21.1, Y.7. FAC'95. CS'95.				£800000	7/17/90	Everton	170+12	21+2	12+2	8	7	1	1	
				£3000000	1/30/98	Sheffield Wed.	15				1			
Geary Derek P			6/19/80	Dublin		Sheffield Wed. (T)								
Newsome Jon	6.2	13.11	9/6/70	Sheffield	7/1/89	Sheffield Wed.	6+1	3						
Div1'92				£150000	6/11/91	Leeds United	62+14	3	3+1	5	3			
				£1000000	6/30/94	Norwich City	35	4	4		3			
				£1600000	3/16/96	Sheffield Wed.	44	2	5		4			
Nolan Ian	6	11.1	7/9/70	Liverpool	8/31/88	Preston North End								
				Free	8/1/89	Northwich Victoria			2					
					8/1/90	Marine								
				£100000	8/2/91	Tranmere Rovers	87+1	10	7	9	1	1		
				£1500000	8/1/94	Sheffield Wed.	135+1	12	10	3	1			
Sedloski Goce	6.1	13.3	4/10/74	Macedonia		Hajduk Split								
Macedonian Int.				£750000	2/27/98	Sheffield Wed.	3+1							
Stefanovic Dejan	6.2	13.2	10/28/74	Yugoslavia		RS Belgrade								
				£2000000	12/22/95	Sheffield Wed.	51+4	2	2		4			
Thome Emerson A	6.1	13.4	3/30/72	Brazil		Benfica								
				Free	3/23/97	Sheffield Wed.	6							
Walker Des	5.11	11.9	11/26/65	Hackney	12/2/83	Nottingham Forest	259+5	40	27	14	1			
E: 59, u21.7. LC'89'90. FMC'89'92				£1500000	8/1/92	Sampdoria								
				£2700000	7/22/93	Sheffield Wed.	191	17	14					
M I D F I E L D														
Agogo Manual	5.9	11.7	8/1/79	Accra	10/8/96	Sheffield Wed.	0+1							
Alexandersson Niclas	6.2	11.7	12/29/71	Halmstad		Gothenburg								
				£750000	12/9/97	Sheffield Wed.	5+1		2				1	
Brennan Dean J G			6/17/80	Dublin		Sheffield Wed. (T)								
Haslam Steven			9/6/79	Sheffield	9/12/96	Sheffield Wed. (T)								
Holmes Peter J			11/18/80	B.Auckland		Sheffield Wed. (T)								
Hyde Graham	5.7	11.7	11/10/70	Doncaster	5/17/88	Sheffield Wed. (T)	124+45	17+3	13+5	4	11	2	2	1
Jonk Wim				Holland		PSV Eindhoven								
Dutch Int.				£2500000	8/1/98	Sheffield Wed.								
Kotylo Krystof Jan	5.11	11.2	9/28/77	Sheffield	7/11/96	Liverpool								
Magilton Jim	5.11	12.7	5/6/69	Belfast	5/14/86	Liverpool								
NI: 39, u23.2, u21.1, Y, S.				£100000	10/3/90	Oxford United	150	9	8	6	34	1	4	3
				£600000	2/11/94	Southampton	124+6	11+2	12		13	1	3	
				£1000000	9/10/97	Sheffield Wed.	13+8	2	1		1			
Nicholson Kevin J			10/2/80	Derby		Sheffield Wed. (T)								
Rudi Petter	6.3	12.10	9/17/73	Norway		Molde								
Norway Int.				£800000	10/17/97	Sheffield Wed.	20+3		2					

F O R W A R D

Name				From	Date	Club								
Booth Andy	6	10.8	3/17/73	Huddersfield	7/1/92	Huddersfield Town	66+14	6+1	4	12+1	38		1	4
				£2700000	7/8/96	Sheffield Wed.	53+5	2	6		17		3	
Briscoe Lee	5.11	10.9	9/30/75	Pontefract	5/22/94	Sheffield Wed.	37+9	2+1						
				Loan	2/27/98	Manchester City	3				1			
Carbone Benito	5.6	10.1	8/14/71	Bagnara		Inter Milan								
				£3000000	10/18/96	Sheffield Wed.	53+6	1	3		15			
Di Canio Paulo	5.9	11.9	7/9/68	Rome		AC Milan								
						Celtic	25+1	2	6	2+1	12	3		
				£3000000	8/1/97	Sheffield Wed.	35+1	2	2		12	2		
Humphreys Ritchie J	5.11	11.3	11/30/77	Sheffield	2/8/96	Sheffield Wed.	17+25	1+2	3+3		3		2	
McKeever Mark	5.9	11.8	11/16/78	Derry		Peterborough Utd	2+1	1						
NI: Y.				£500000	4/15/97	Sheffield Wed.								
Oakes Scott J	5.11	9.12	8/5/72	Leicester	5/9/90	Leicester City	1+2							
E: u21.1					10/22/91	Luton Town	136+37	3+3	12+2	3+3	27	1	5	1
					8/1/96		7+17	0+1	0+1		1			
Platts Mark	5.8	11.12	5/23/79	Sheffield	10/16/96	Sheffield Wed.								
Quinn Alan	5.9	10.6	6/13/79	Dublin	4/24/98	Sheffield Wed.	0+1							
Sanetti Francesco	6.1	12.6	1/11/79	Rome		Genoa								
				Free	4/30/98	Sheffield Wed.	1+1				1			
Whittingham Guy	5.11	11.12	11/10/64	Evesham		Oxford City								
LC'94						Waterlooville								
						Yeovil Town								
				Free	6/9/89	Portsmouth	149+11	7+2	7+3	9	88	3	10	3
				£1200000	8/1/93	Aston Villa	13+5	2		1	3			
				Loan	2/28/94	Wolverhampton W.	13		1		8			
				£700000	12/21/94	Sheffield Wed.	90+22	7+1	6+1		22	2	1	

THE MANAGER
DANNY WILSON

Date of Birth . . . . 1st January 1960.
Place of Birth . . . . Wigan.
Date of Appointment . . . . July 1998.

PREVIOUS CLUBS
As Manager . . . . Barnsley.
As Coach. . . . . Barnet.
As a Player . . . . Wigan Athletic, Bury, Chesterfield, Nottingham Forest,
. . . . Brighton & H.A., Luton Town and Sheffield Wednesday.

HONOURS
As a Manager
Barnsley: Promotion to the Carling Premiership 1996/97.

As a Player
Luton Town: League Cup runner-up 1988.
Sheffield Wednesday: League Cup winner 1991
International: 25 full caps for Northern Ireland.

HILLSBOROUGH
Sheffield S6 1SW

Capacity 39,859

First game ....v Chesterfield, Div 2, 5-1, 2.9.1899.
First floodlit game ....v International XI, 9.3.1955.
Internationals...England v Scotland 1920, v France 1962.
...................W.Germany v Switzerland & v Uruguay 1966. Switzerland v Spain & v Argentina 1966.
...N.Ireland v Bulgaria 1974 **Euro'96:** Denmark v Portugal, Croatia v Denmark, Turkey v Denmark.
ATTENDANCES
Highest ....72,841 v Man. City, FAC 5th Rnd, 17.2.1934.
Lowest ....2,500 v Everton, 5.4.1902.
OTHER GROUNDS: .... Highfields 1867-69. Myrtle Rd 1869-77.
........Sheaf Close 1877-87. Olive Grove 1887-99. Owlerton (changed to Hillsborough 1912) 1899-

HOW TO GET TO THE GROUND

From the North
Use motorway (M1) until junction 34, leave motorway and follow signs to Sheffield (A6109). in 1.5 miles at roundabout take 3rd exit (A6102). In 3.2 miles take right hand lane for turning into Herries Road South for Sheffield Wednesday FC.
From East and South
Use A57 from motorway M1 (junction 33) then at roundabout junction with Ring Road take 3rd exit (A6102) into Prince of Wales Road. At junction with Sheffield Road take left then first right into Jansen Street, then straight forward to rejoin A6102 and then as for the north.
From the West
Use A57 (sign posted Sheffield) then turn left A6101. In 3.8 miles at 'T' junction turn left A61 into Penistone Road for Sheffield Wednesday FC.

Car Parking: Street parking is available.
Nearest Railway Station: Sheffield (01142 726 411).

USEFUL TELEPHONE NUMBERS

Club switchboard. 0114 221 2121
Club fax number 0114 221 2122
Club Shop 0114 221 2345
Ticket Office 0114 221 2401

Marketing Department. 0114 221 2333
Internet address. . . . . www.swfc.co.uk
Clubcall 0891 12 11 86*
*Calls cost 50p per minute at all times. Call costings correct at time of going to press.

MATCHDAY PROGRAMME

Programme Editor . . . . Roger Oldfield.

Number of pages. 52

Price. . . . . £2.

Subscriptions . . . . Apply to club.

Local Newspapers
. . . . Sheffield Newspapers Ltd. (The Star).

Local Radio Stations
. . . . . BBC Radio Sheffield, Radio Hallam.

MATCHDAY TICKET PRICES

. . . . Premier Category/Standard

North & South Centre . . . . £14-£21

Concession . . . . £9-£12

Kop & West Lower . . . . £10-£15

Concession . . . . £7-£10

West Upper. . . . . £13-£18

Concession £9

Family Enclosure £12

Concession £7

SOUTHAMPTON
(The Saints)
F.A. CARLING PREMIERSHIP
SPONSORED BY: SANDERSON ELECTRONICS

1998-99 - Back Row (L-R): Lee Todd, John Beresford, David Hughes, Matthew Oakley, Richard Dryden, Steve Basham, James Beattie, Andy Williams, Stig Johansen. **Middle Row:** Jim Joyce (Physio), Stuart Ripley, David Hirst, Claus Lundervam, Carlton Palmer, Paul Jones, Neil Moss, Kenneth Monkou, David Howells, Scott Marshall, Egil Ostenstad, Malcolm Taylor. **Front Row:** Mark Hughes, Matthew Le Tissier, Stuart Gray (Res. team Manager), David Jones (Manager), Rupert Lowe (Chairman), Terry Cooper (Asst. Manager), John Sainty (Asst. Manager), Jason Dodd, Francis Benali.

SOUTHAMPTON
FORMED IN 1885
TURNED PROFESSIONAL IN 1894
LTD COMPANY IN 1897

PRESIDENT: John Corbett
VICE-PRESIDENT: E T Bates
CHAIRMAN: R J G Lowe
DIRECTORS
K St J Wiseman,
F G L Askham, A E Cowen, I L Gordon,
B D H Hunt (Vice-chairman),
M R Richards FCA
SECRETARY
Brian Truscott (01703 220 505)
COMMERCIAL MANAGER
John O'Sullivan
MANAGER: David Jones
ASSISTANT MANAGERS:
John Sainty/Terry Cooper
RESERVE TEAM MANAGER
Stuart Gray
YOUTH TEAM MANAGER
Joe Jakub
PHYSIOTHERAPIST
Jim Joyce & Don Taylor
STATISTICIAN FOR THE DIRECTORY
John Mason

At last a season of no managerial changes and no mention of the dreaded drop down to Division One, the 'Saints' fans for once could now smile and look forward to a brighter future.

Things were not so rosie however, come October. Only one victory had been recorded, at Crystal Palace, and added to a draw against Liverpool gave Southampton only four points and a League position of bottom - did I say no mention of the dreaded drop!

October was, thankfully, to be the turning point, a run of four wins out of five took them off the bottom, out of the relegation zone and up to 13th. This was further consolidated with a solid Christmas and New Year programme that saw them take 12 points out of a possible 18. This included the 1-0 victory of Manchester United, the third win against United at the Dell in consecutive seasons, this was followed up two matches later with a 3-2 win over Liverpool at Anfield. Defeat against Coventry followed before the 'Saints' won three on the bounce to give them their highest position of the season - 10th.

Indifferent form during April and May saw the club settle in 12th place eight points above the first relegation spot. A mini-run took them to the fourth round of the Coca-Cola Cup where they went out to eventual winners Chelsea (1-2) but the FA Cup never got off the ground after a third round defeat at Derby (0-2) saw them exit at the first hurdle.

Dave Jones has brought in a lot of experienced players such as Mark Hughes, Stuart Ripley and David Howells over the summer and has created quite an impressive squad. One major departure was Kevin Davies, who went for a club record £7,250,000 to Blackburn Rovers.

If the 'old' can mix with the new down at the Dell then Southampton could have another relegation free season.

SOUTHAMPTON

Carling Prem.	:12th		FA CUP: 3rd Round				LC CUP: 4th Round	

M	DATE	COMP.	VEN	OPPONENTS	RESULT	H/T	LP	GOAL SCORERS/GOAL TIMES	ATT.
1	A 09	CP	H	Bolton Wanderers	L 0-1	0-1	18		15206
2	12	CP	A	Manchester United	L 0-1	0-0	17		(55008)
3	23	CP	H	Arsenal	L 1-3	1-1	19	Maddison 25	15246
4	27	CP	H	Crystal Palace	W 1-0	0-0	16	Davies 57	15032
5	30	CP	A	Chelsea	L 2-4	1-4	18	Davies 25, Monkou 59	(30008)
6	S 13	CP	A	Coventry City	L 0-1	0-0	20		(18659)
7	17	CC 2/1	H	Brentford	W 3-1	1-0		Monkou 37, Davies 60, Evans 69	8004
8	20	CP	H	Liverpool	D 1-1	0-1	20	Davies 48	15252
9	24	CP	H	Leeds United	L 0-2	0-1	20		15102
10	27	CP	A	Derby County	L 0-4	0-0	20		(25625)
11	30	CC 2/2	A	Brentford	W 2-0	2-0		Le Tissier 31, 44	(3957)
12	O 04	CP	H	West Ham United	W 3-0	0-0	19	Ostenstad 54, Davies 65, Dodd 69	15212
13	14	CC 3	A	Barnsley	W 2-1	1-1		Le Tissier 15, Davies 88	(9019)
14	18	CP	A	Blackburn Rovers	L 0-1	0-1	19		(24130)
15	25	CP	H	Tottenham Hotspur	W 3-2	0-1	17	Hirst 67, 79, Vega 54 (OG)	15255
16	N 02	CP	A	Everton	W 2-0	1-0	16	Le Tissier 24, Davies 54	(29565)
17	08	CP	H	Barnsley	W 4-1	3-1	14	Le Tissier 2, Palmer 5, Davies 35, Hirst 53	15018
18	19	CC 4	A	Chelsea	L 1-2	0-0		Davies 52	(20968)
19	22	CP	A	Newcastle United	L 1-2	1-0	15	Davies 6	(36759)
20	29	CP	H	Sheffield Wednesday	L 2-3	0-1	16	Hirst 47, Palmer 55	15244
21	D 07	CP	A	Wimbledon	L 0-1	0-1	17		(12009)
22	13	CP	H	Leicester City	W 2-1	1-0	16	Le Tissier 1, Benali 53	15121
23	20	CP	A	Aston Villa	D 1-1	0-0	15	Ostenstad 72	(29343)
24	26	CP	A	Crystal Palace	D 1-1	1-1	15	Oakley 39	(22853)
25	29	CP	H	Chelsea	W 1-0	1-0	13	Davies 16	15231
26	J 03	FAC 3	A	Derby County	L 0-2	0-0			(27992)
27	10	CP	A	Bolton Wanderers	D 0-0	0-0	13		(23333)
28	19	CP	H	Manchester United	W 1-0	1-0	12	Davies 3	15241
29	31	CP	A	Arsenal	L 0-3	0-0	12		(38056)
30	F 06	CP	A	Liverpool	W 3-2	1-1	11	Hirst 8 (pen), 90, Ostenstad 85	(43550)
31	18	CP	H	Coventry City	L 1-2	0-2	12	Le Tissier 79 (pen)	15091
32	21	CP	H	Blackburn Rovers	W 3-0	1-0	11	Ostenstad 19, 88, Hirst 75	15162
33	28	CP	A	Leeds United	W 1-0	0-0	11	Hirst 54	(28791)
34	M 07	CP	H	Everton	W 2-1	0-0	11	Le Tissier 69 (pen), Ostenstad 86	15102
35	14	CP	A	Barnsley	L 3-4	2-3	10	Ostenstad 25, Le Tissier 41, 71	(18368)
36	28	CP	H	Newcastle United	W 2-1	0-0	10	Le Tissier 85 (pen), Pearce 68 (OG)	15251
37	A 04	CP	A	Sheffield Wednesday	L 0-1	0-1	10		(29677)
38	11	CP	H	Wimbledon	L 0-1	0-1	12		14815
39	14	CP	A	Leicester City	D 3-3	2-1	12	Ostenstad 17, 27, Hirst 49	(20708)
40	18	CP	H	Aston Villa	L 1-2	1-1	12	Le Tissier 19	15238
41	25	CP	A	West Ham United	W 4-2	1-1	11	Le Tissier 39, Ostenstad 63, 85, Palmer 79	(25878)
42	M 02	CP	H	Derby County	L 0-2	0-0	12		15202
43	10	CP	A	Tottenham Hotspur	D 1-1	1-1	12	Le Tissier 21	(35995)

Best Home League Attendance: 15255 V Tottenham Hotspur   Smallest :14815 V Wimbledon   Average :15159

Goal Scorers:

CP	(50)	Le Tissier 11, Ostenstad 11, Davies 9, Hirst 9, Palmer 3, Benali 1, Dodd 1, Maddison 1, Monkou 1, Oakley 1, Opponents 2
CC	(8)	Davies 3, Le Tissier 3, Evans 1, Monkou 1
FAC	(0)	

1997-98

(F) Basham	(D) Benali	(D) Beresford	(D) Charlton	(F) Davies	(D) Dodd	(D) Dryden	(F) Evans	(M) Gibbens	(F) Hirst	(M) Hughes	(M) Johansen	(G) Jones	(F) Le Tissier	(D) Lundekvam	(M) Maddison	(M) Magilton	(D) Monkou	(G) Moss	(D) Neilson	(M) Oakley	(F) Ostenstad	(M) Palmer	(M) Richardson	(M) Slater	(D) Spedding	(G) Taylor	(D) Todd	(F) Williams	Referee	#
	S		S1		X	X			S1		X				X	X	X		X		X	X			X	S	X	X	M.J. Bodenham	1
X			S			S1			X	X					X	X	X		X	X	X				X	S	X	S3	G P Barber	2
X			X	X		S3			S2	S1	X				X	X	X		S	X	X			X	S	S	X		D R Elleray	3
X			X	X		S1			X	X	X				X	X	X	S2						X	S	X	S		J T Winter	4
X			X	X		S1			X	S	X				X	X	X	S2		X				X	S	S3	A B Wilkie		5
			S1	X		X			X	S2	X			X	S		X	S3	X	X		X			S	X	U D Rennie		6
	X	S1	X		X				X	X			X	S		X	X	X		X				X	G S Willard		7
X			X	X		X			S	X	X	S	X		X	X	X		X				S	S2	P Jones		8
X			X	X		X			S	X		X	S1	X	X	X		X			S	S	X	S J Lodge		9
X			X	X	X	X			S2	X	X		X	S	X		X		X	X		S	S	S1	K W Burge		10
	S2	X	X	X				S	X	X	X		X	X		X	X		X	S1	P Taylor		11
S1	X	X	X			X	X	X		X		X	S2	X	X	S3	M A Riley		12
S3	X	X	X	S1			X	X	X		X	X	X	X	X	S2	J T Winter		13
X	X	X	X		X	S	X	X	X		X	S2	X	X	X	S	S1	S1	G S Willard		14
X	S2	X	X		X	S	X	X	X		X	X	X	S3	S	S1	N S Barry		15
S3	X	S	X	X		X	X	X	X		X	S2	X	X	S1	S	A B Wilkie		16
S2	X	X	X		X	X	X	X		X	X	X	S1	S	S	S	G R Ashby		17
X	X	X		X	S3	X	X	X	X		X	X	X	S1	S2	D R Elleray		18
S3	X	X	X		X	S	X	X	X		S1	X	X	X2	S2	D J Gallagher		19
S2	X	X	S	X1		X	S	X	X1	X	X	S1	X2	S	S W Dunn		20
X	X	X	S	X	S	X	X1	X	X	S	X	S1	X	X2	S2	M D Reed		21
X	X	X1	X	X	S	X	X	X	X	X	X1	S2	X3	S J Lodge		22
X	X1	X	X	S	X	X	X	X	X	S1	X	X	S	D R Elleray		23
X	S1	X	X	S	X	X2	X	X	S	X3	X1	X	X	S3	S2	P E Alcock		24
X	X	X	X1	S	X	X2	X	X	S	X	S1	X	X	S	S2	M J Bodenham		25
X	X	S	X1	X2	X	X	X	S	X	S1	X	X	S2	G R Ashby		26
X	X	X	X1	X	S	X	X	S	X	X2	X	S1	S	S2	G S Willard		27
X	X1	X	S	X	X	X2	X	X	S	X1	X	X3	S2	S3	M A Riley		28
X	S	X	S2	S	X	S	X1	X	X	S	X	X	X2	X	S1	P Jones		29
X	X2	S2	X	X	X	S	X3	X	S	X1	S3	X	X	X1	J T Winter		30
X	S	X	S3	X	S1	X	X	S	X	X	X3	S2	X2	X1	P E Alcock		31
X	X	X	X	S1	X	X	X	S	X	X	X1	S	S	U D Rennie		32
X	X	X	X	X3	S1	X	X2	X1	S	X	X	S2	S	S3	K W Burge		33
X	X	X	S1	X	X1	X	X	X	S	X	X	S	S	S	D R Elleray		34
X	X	X	S	X	S	X	X	X	S	X	X	X1	S	S1	G R Ashby		35
S2	X	X	X	X	S	S	S	X	X2	X	X1	X	X	S1	G P Barber		36
X	X	S1	X	X	S	X	X	X	S	S	X2	S2	P Jones		37
X3	X	S1	X	X	S	X1	X	X	X	S3	S	X	X1	S1	M D Reed		38
S	X	X	X	X	X	S1	X	X1	S1	S	X	X	S	G Poll		39
S2	X	X	X	X1	X2	S	X	X	S	X	X	X	S	S1	A B Wilkie		40
S1	X	X	X	X1	X	X	X	S	X	X	X	S	D J Gallagher		41
S1	X	X	X2	X1	X	X	X	S	X	X	X	S	S2	M A Riley		42
S3	X	X2	X1	X	S	X3	X	X	X	S	X	X	S2	P Jones		43
32	10	2	20	36	11	6	2	28	6	3	38	25	31	5	30	3	32	21	26	25	3	4		9	3				CP Appearances	
9	1		1	5		2	4		8	3		1		1	2		5	1	8		3	8	3		1	17	CP Sub Appearances	
2+1		1+1	3+1	3	1	2+1		1	1+1	4	3	4		3	2	4	1	3	4	0+1	0+1	1	1+2	CC Appearances	
1		1	1		1	1	1	1	1	1	1	0+1	1	1	FAC Appearances	

Also played:(M) Bowen X(6), S1(8), S2(9). (G) Flahavan S(19,20,22,23). (M) Robinson S2(2), S(4,22,23).(M) Van Gobbel S3(1), X(2). (M) Warner S(41,42), S1(43).

SOUTHAMPTON

CLUB RECORDS

BIGGEST VICTORIES
League: 8-0 v Northampton, Division 3S, 24.12.1921
F.A. Cup: 7-1 v Ipswich Town, Round 3, 7.1.1961
6-0 v Luton Town, Round 4, 8.2.1995
League Cup: 5-0 v Derby County, Round 3, 8.10.1974
5-0 v Wrexham, Round 2, 28.8.1979
5-0 v Rochdale, Round 2, 25.9.1990
Europe (UEFA): 5-1 v Vittoria G, Round 2, 12.11.1969
(ECWC): 4-0 v Marseilles, Round 1, 15.9.1976

BIGGEST DEFEATS
League: 0-8 v Tottenham Hotspur, Division 2, 28.3.1936.
0-8 v Everton, Division 1, 20.11.1971.
F.A. Cup: 0-5 v Manchester City, Round 2, 5.2.1910.
League Cup: 1-7 v Watford, Round 2, 2.9.1980.
Europe: No more than 2 goal defeat.

MOST POINTS
3 points a win: 77, Division 1, 1983-84.
2 points a win: 61, Division 3S, 1921-22, Division 3 1959-60.

MOST GOALS
112, 1957-58 (Division 3S).
Reeves 31, Roper 18, Hoskins 18, Paine 12, Clifton 7, Mulgrew 8, Sydenham 4, Page 4, Walker 3, McGowan 2, Traynor 2, McLaughlin 1, og 2.

MOST FIRST CLASS MATCHES IN A SEASON
61 (42 League, 7 FA Cup, 6 League Cup, 6 ZDS) 1991-92

MOST LEAGUE GOALS CONCEDED
92, Division 1, 1966-67

MOST LEAGUE WINS
26, Division 3, 1959-60

MOST LEAGUE DRAWS
18, Division 2, 1924-25; Division 1/P, 1972-73, 1994-95.

MOST LEAGUE DEFEATS
23, Division 1, 1971-72, 1993-94

INDIVIDUAL CLUB RECORDS

MOST GOALS IN A SEASON
Derek Reeves 45 (League 39, FAC 6) 1959-60.
4 goals twice=8; 3 goals twice=6; 2 goals 3 times=6; 1 goal 25 times=25.
Previous holder: C Wayman 32 (1948-49).

MOST GOALS IN A MATCH
5. Charlie Wayman v Leicester, Div 2, 23.10.1948 (6-0)
5. Derek Reeves v Leeds (LC4) 5.12.1960 (5-4)

OLDEST PLAYER
Peter Shilton, 37 years 233 days v Coventry (Div 1) 9.5.1987.

YOUNGEST PLAYER
Danny Wallace 16 years 313 days v Manchester Utd (Div 1) 29.11.1980.

MOST CAPPED PLAYER
Peter Shilton (England) 49

BEST PERFORMANCES

League: 1921-22: Matches played 42, Won 23, Drawn 15, Lost 4, Goals for 68, Goals against 21, Points 61. 1st in Division 3S.
Highest: 1983-84: 2nd in Division 1.

F.A. Cup: 1975-76 (Div 2): 3rd rnd. Aston Villa 1-1, 2-1; 4th rnd. Blackpool 3-1; 5th rnd. West Bromwich Albion 1-1, 4-0; 6th rnd. Bradford City 1-0; Semi-final Crystal Palace 2-0; Final Manchester United 1-0.

League Cup: 1978-79 (Div 1): 2nd rnd. Birmingham City 5-2; 3rd rnd. Derby County 1-0; 4th rnd. Reading 0-0 2-0; 5th rnd. Manchester City 2-1; Semi-final Leeds United 2-2, 1-0; Final Nottingham Forest 2-3.

Europe (ECWC): 1976-77 (Div 2): 1st rnd. Marseille 4-0, 1-2; 2nd rnd Carrick R.5-2, 4-1; 3rd rnd. Anderlecht 0-2, 2-1.
(UEFA): 1969-70: 1st rnd. Rosenburg 0-1, 2-0; 2nd rnd. Vittoria Guimariers 3-3,5-1; 3rd rnd. Newcastle 0-0, 1-1.

DIVISIONAL RECORD

	Played	Won	Drawn	Lost	For	Against	Points
Division 1/P	1,150	384	318	448	1,567	1,695	1,320
Division 2	1,428	559	353	516	2,221	2,140	1,471
Division 3	92	43	20	29	194	155	106
Division 3(S)	314	150	77	87	562	368	377
Total	2,984	1,136	757	1,062	4,549	4,358	3,274

ADDITIONAL INFORMATION
Previous Name
Southampton St. Mary's

Previous League
Southern League

Club colours: Red & white striped shirts, black shorts, white socks.
Change colours:

Reserves League: Avon Insurance Football Combination.

RECORDS AND STATISTICS

COMPETITIONS

Div 1/P	Div.2	Div.3	Div.3(S)	UEFA	ECWC
1966-74	1922-53	1920-21	1921-22	1969-70	1976-77
1978-	1960-66	1958-60	1953-58	1971-72	
	1974-78			1981-82	
				1982-83	TEXACO
				1984-85	1974-75

HONOURS

DIVISION 3	DIVISION 3(S)	FA CUP
1959-60	1921-22	1975-76

MOST APPEARANCES

TERRY PAINE 805+4 (1956-74)

YEAR	LEAGUE	FA CUP	LGE CUP	EUROPE
1956-57	9			
1957-58	44	2		
1958-59	46	3		
1959-60	46	6		
1960-61	42	2	7	
1961-62	41	2	2	
1962-63	42	7	3	
1963-64	41	1	1	
1964-65	42	2	2	
1965-66	40	1	2	
1966-67	42	3	3	
1967-68	41	4	1	
1968-69	42	4	4	
1969-70	36	3	2	6
1970-71	41	4	1	
1971-72	37+3	2	2	2
1972-73	36+1	1	4	
1973-74	41	4	3	
	709+4	**51**	**37**	**8**

MOST GOALS IN A CAREER

MIKE CHANNON - 227 (19966-77 & 1979-82)

YEAR	LEAGUE	FA CUP	LGE CUP	EUROPE
1965-66	1			
1966-67				
1967-68	7	1		
1968-69	8	1	3	
1969-70	15	2	1	3
1970-71	18	1	1	
1971-72	14	1		1
1972-73	16		2	
1973-74	21	1	1	
1974-75	20	1	3	
1975-76	20	5		
1976-77	17	2	1	4
1979-80	10	1		
1980-81	10			
1981-82	8			1
Total	**185**	**16**	**12**	**9**

(Plus 5 in the Texaco Cup - 1974-75)

Current leading goalscorer: Matthew Le Tissier 198 (1986-98)

RECORD TRANSFER FEE RECEIVED

AMOUNT	CLUB	PLAYER	DATE
£7,250,000	Blackburn Rov.	Kevin Davies	01/06
£3,600,000	Blackburn Rov.	Alan Shearer	07/92
£1,600,000	Leeds United	Rodney Wallace	07/91
£1,200,000	Manchester Utd	Danny Wallace	09/89

RECORD TRANSFER FEE PAID

AMOUNT	CLUB	PLAYER	DATE
£2,000,000	Sheffield Wed.	David Hirst	10/97
£1,300,000	Galatasaray	Ulrich Van Gobbel	10/96
£1,200,000	Chelsea	Neil Shipperley	01/95
£1,000,000	Swindon Town	Alan McLoughlin	12/90

MANAGERS

NAME	SEASONS	BEST	WORST
George Swift	1911-12		
James McIntyre	1919-24	5(2)	2(3S)
Arthur Chadwick	1925-31	4(2)	17(2)
G Kay	1931-36	12(2)	19(2)
George Goss	1936-37	19(2)	19(2)
T Parker	1937-War	15(2)	18(2)
W Dodgin (Snr)	War-1949	3(2)	14(2)
Sid Cann	1949-51	13(2)	21(2)
George Roughton	1952-55	3(2)	6(3)
Ted Bates	1955-73	7(1)	14(3)
Lawrie McMenemy	1973-85	2(1)	13(2)
Chris Nicholl	1985-91	7(1)	14(1)
Ian Branfoot	1991-94	16(1)	18(1/P)
Alan Ball	1994-95	10(P)	18(P)
Dave Merrington	1995-96	17(P)	17(P)
Graeme Souness	1996-97	16(P)	16(P)
David Jones	1997-	12 (P)	12 (P)

LONGEST LEAGUE RUNS

of undefeated matches:	19 (5.9.1921 - 14.1.1922)	of league matches w/out a win:	20 (30.8.1969 - 17.1.1970)
of undefeated home matches:	31 (22.1.1921 - 28.8.1922)	of undefeated away matches:	9 (19.11.77-29.3.78, 17.9.49-21.1.50)
without home win:	10 (6.9.1969 - 17.1.1970)	without an away win:	33 (22.4.1933 - 25.12.1934)
of league wins:	6 (5.9.1964 - 13.10.1964, 3.3.1992 - 8.4.1992)	of home wins:	11 (10.10.1959 - 19.3.1960)
of league defeats:	5 (7.5.1927 - 10.9.1927, 12.1.1957 - 25.2.1957)	of away wins:	3 (On 10 different occasions)
	(30.12.1967 - 10.2.1968, 31.12.1988 - 11.2.1989, Twice in 1993)		

SOUTHAMPTON

PLAYERS NAME Honours	Ht	Wt	Birthdate	Birthplace Transfers	Contract Date	Clubs	League	L/Cup	FA Cup	Other	Lge	L/C	FAC	Oth
							APPEARANCES				**GOALS**			
G O A L K E E P E R														
Bevan Scott	6.5	16.1	9/16/79	Southampton		Southampton (T)								
Jones Paul S	6.3	14.8	3/18/67	Chirk		Kidderminster H.								
				£40000	7/23/91	Wolverhampton W.	33	2	5	4				
				£60000	7/25/96	Stockport County								
					7/28/97	Southampton	38	4	1					
Moss Neil	6.1	12.11	5/10/75	New Milton	1/29/93	Bournemouth	14+1	1	0+1					
				£250000	12/20/95	Southampton	2	2						
D E F E N C E														
Benali Francis	5.9	11	12/30/68	Southampton	1/5/87	Southampton	224+28	19+7	20	3+1	1			
Beresford John E: B.1, Y.10, u19.3, S; Div1'93	5.6	10.12	9/4/66	Sheffield	9/16/83	Manchester City								
				Free	8/4/86	Barnsley	79+9	5+2	5		5	2	1	
				£300000	3/23/89	Portsmouth	102+5	12	11	2	8	2		
				£650000	7/2/92	Newcastle United	176+3	17	17+1	10+1	3		1	
				£1500000	2/5/98	Southampton	10							
Collins Christopher P	6	12.7	9/26/79	Chatham		Southampton (T)								
Dodd Jason E: u21.8	5.11	11.1	11/2/70	Bath		Bath City			0+1					
				£50000	3/15/89	Southampton	214+16	27+1	22	5	7		1	
Dryden Richard Div.4'90.	6	12	6/14/69	Stroud	7/14/87	Bristol Rovers	12+1	2+1	+2	2				
				Loan	9/22/88	Exeter City	6							
					3/8/89	Exeter City	86	7	2	4	13	2		
				£250000	8/9/91	Notts County	30+1	1+1	2+1	2	1			
				Loan	11/18/92	Plymouth Argyle	5			1				
				£165000	3/19/93	Birmingham City	45	4	1					
				£200000	12/16/94	Bristol City	32+5	4	1+1	3	1			
				£150000	8/6/96	Southampton	39+3	6			1	3		
Jenkins Stephen M	6.1	13	1/2/80	Bristol		Southampton (T)								
Lundekvam Claus	6.3	12.1	2/22/73	Norway		SK Brann (Norway)								
					9/1/96	Southampton	58+1	10+1	1					
Marshall Scott S: u21.5,Y,S.	6.1	12.5	01/05/73	Islington	18/03/91	Arsenal	19+5	1+1			1			
				Loan	03/12/93	Rotherham United	10			1	1			
				Loan	25/08/94	Sheffield United	17							
				Free	14/07/98	Southampton								
Monk Garry	5.11	11.13	3/6/79	Bedford		Torquay United								
					5/23/97	Southampton								
Monkou Kenneth Holland: u21. ZDC'90	6	12.9	11/29/64	Surinam		Feyenoord								
				£100000	3/2/89	Chelsea	92+2	12	3	10	2			
				£750000	8/21/92	Southampton	168+8	17+1	14		9	2	1	
Todd Lee	5.5	10.3	3/7/72	Hartlepool		Hartlepool United								
				Free	7/23/90	Stockport County	214+13	24+2	17	24+1	2			2
					7/28/97	Southampton	8+1	1						
Warner Philip	5.10	11.7	2/2/79	Southampton	5/23/97	Southampton (T)	0+1							
M I D F I E L D														
Artzeni Allessandro				Italy		Fiorentina								
				Loan	7/1/98	Southampton								
Blake Dean J F	5.8	10.1	2/20/80	Southampton		Southampton (T)								
Gibbens Kevin	5.10	12.13	11/4/79	Southampton	3/27/98	Southampton (T)	2							
Howells David E: u19.2, Y.8. FLgXI.1. FAC'91. CS'91	5.11	11.1	12/15/67	Guildford	1/28/85	Tottenham Hotspur	238+39	26+5	18+4	7	22	4	1	
				Free	5/18/98	Southampton								
Hughes David W: u21.1. E: u19.4, S	5.9	11	12/30/72	St Albans	7/2/91	Southampton	15+27	3+1	1+5		3		1	
Oakley Matthew	5.11	11	8/17/77	Peterborough	8/1/94	Southampton	60+12	10+1	3+2		4		1	
Palmer Carlton L E: 18, B.5, u21.4	6.2	11.1	12/5/65	Rowley Regis	12/21/84	West Bromwich Albion	114+7	7+1	4	6	4	1		
				£750000	2/23/89	Sheffield Wednesday	204+1	31	18	8+1	14	3		1
				£2600000	6/30/94	Leeds United	101+2	12	11	4	5		1	1
					9/26/97	Southampton	26	3	1		3			
Pelanti Simone				Italy		Fiorentina								
				Loan	7/1/98	Southampton								
F O R W A R D														
Basham Steven	5.11	11.3	12/2/77	Southampton	6/1/96	Southampton	1+14							
				Loan	2/5/98	Wrexham	4+1							
Beattie James	6.1	12	2/27/78	Lancaster	8/1/94	Blackburn Rovers (T)	1+3	2	0+1					
				£1000000	7/10/98	Southampton								
Bradley Shayne	5.11	13.2	12/8/79	Gloucester		Southampton (T)								
Bridge Wayne M	5.10	11.11	8/5/80	Southampton		Southampton (T)								
Davies Kevin	6	12.12	3/26/77	Sheffield	4/18/94	Chesterfield	113+15	6+2	10	9+2	22	1	6	1
				5/14/97	Southampton	20+5	3+1	1		9	3		
Hirst David E: 3, B.3, u21.7, u19.3, Y.8. LC'91	5.11	12.5	12/7/67	Cudworth	11/8/85	Barnsley	26+2	1			9			
				£200000	8/11/86	Sheffield Wednesday	261+33	26+9	12+7	8	106	11	6	5
				£2000000	10/17/97	Southampton	28		1		9			

Name														
Hughes Mark	5.9	11.2	01/11/63	Wrexham	05/11/80	Manchester United	85+4	5+1	10	14+2	37	4	4	2
W:66,u21.5,Y.ECWC'91'98. ESC'91. LC'92'98.				£2500000	01/07/86	Barcelona	28				4			
Prem'93'94. FAC'85'90'94'97. CS'93'94.				Loan		Bayern Munich	18				6			
				£1500000	20/07/88	Manchester United	251+5	32	34+1	27+1	82	12	13	8
				£1500000	01/06/95	Chelsea	88+7	7+3	13+1	1+3	25	3	9	2
				£650000	11/07/98	Southampton								
James Kevin S	5.8	10.5	3/26/80	Merthyr		Southampton (T)								
Johansen Stig	5.9	12.5	6/13/72	Norway		Bodoo Glimt								
				£550000	8/1/97	Southampton	3+3	1+1						
				Loan	2/13/98	Bristol City	2+1							
Le Tissier Matthew	6	11.1	10/14/68	Guernsey	10/17/86	Southampton	346+36	38+6	30+1	11+1	151	26	12	9
E: 8, B.6, u19.2, Y.1. FLgXI.1														
Ostenstad Egil	5.11	13	1/2/72	Haugesund		Viking Stavanger								
Int. Norwegian				£900000	10/3/96	Southampton	50+8	7	1+1		21	3	1	
Paul Mark						Kings Lynn								
				£75000	7/10/98									
Ripley Stuart	5.11	12.6	20/11/67	Middlesbrough	23/12/85	Middlesbrough	210+39	21+2	17+1	20+1	26	3	1	1
E:1,u21.8,Y.4. Prem'95.				Loan	18/02/86	Bolton Wanderers	5			0+1	1			
				£1300000	20/07/92	Blackburn Rovers	172+15	18	14	8+1	13		3	
				£1500000	07/07/98	Southampton								
Sarli Cosimo				Italy		Torino								
				Loan	7/1/98	Southampton								
Williams Andrew P	5.11	10.1	10/8/77	Bristol	5/31/97	Southampton	3+17	1+2	0+1					

THE MANAGER
DAVID JONES

Date of Birth . . . . 17th August 1956.
Place of Birth . . . . Liverpool.
Date of Appointment . . . . 23rd June 1997.

PREVIOUS CLUBS
As Manager . . . . Stockport County.
As Asst.Man/Coach: . . . . Morecambe, Stockport County.
As a Player . . . . Everton, Coventry City, Seiko FC (Hong Kong),
. . . . P.N.E., Morecambe.

HONOURS
As a Manager
Stockport County: Promotion to Division 1 1996/97 via 2nd place in Division 2.
As a Player
England: 1 under-21 cap plus Youth caps.

THE DELL
Milton Road, Southampton SO9 4XX

Capacity 15,280

First game...v Brighton, Sth League, 3.9.1898.
First floodlit game..v Bournemouth, 31.10.1950.

ATTENDANCES
Highest ....531,044 v Manchester Utd, Div.1., 08.10.1969.
Lowest ....1,875 v Port Vale, Division 2, 30.3.1936.

OTHER GROUNDS ....Antelope Ground 1885-1897. County Cricket Ground 1897-98. The Dell 1898-

HOW TO GET TO THE GROUND

From the North
Use A33, sign posted Southampton, via The Avenue, then turn right into Northlands Road and at the end turn right into Archers Road for Southampton FC.

From the East
Use motorway M27 then A334 and follow signs to Southampton A3024. The follow signs to The West into Commercial Road then turn right into Hill Lane and take first turning right into Milton Road for Southampton FC.

From the West
Use M27 then A35 and follow signs to Southampton city centre A3024. Turn left over central station bridge, right into Fourpost Hill, then turn left into Hill Lane and take first turning right into Milton Road for Southampton FC.

Car Parking: Street parking and nearby municipal parks.
Nearest Railway Station: Southampton Central (01703 229 393).

USEFUL TELEPHONE NUMBERS

Club switchboard 01703 220 505
Club fax number........................01703 330 360
Club shop 01703 236 400
Ticket Office.....01703 228 575(recorded message)

Marketing Department 01703 331 417
Internet address ....www.soton.ac.uk/~saints'.
Clubcall 0891 12 11 78*
*Calls cost 50p at all times. Call costings correct at time of going to press.

MATCHDAY PROGRAMME

Programme Editor.............Mr John Hughes.

Number of pages.....................................52.

Price ....£2.00.

Subscriptions ....Apply to club.

Local Newspapers
.............The Daily Echo, Portsmouth News,
...................................Hampshire Chronicle.

Local Radio Stations
.............................Radio Solent, Power FM.

MATCHDAY TICKET PRICES

East/West Centre	£22 .00
Wings	£20.00
Lower Tier	£18.00
Juv.	£8.00
Milton Road	£20.00
Juv.	£8.00
Archers Road	£20.00
Juv.	£8.00
Family Centre	£17.00
Juv.	£8.00
Visitors	£20.00/£18.00

TOTTENHAM HOTSPUR
(Spurs)
F.A. CARLING PREMIERSHIP
SPONSORED BY: HEWLETT PACKARD

Tottenham Hotspur 1998/1999

TOTTENHAM HOTSPUR
FORMED IN 1882
TURNED PROFESSIONAL IN 1895
LTD COMPANY IN 1898

CLUB PRESIDENT: W E Nicholson OBE
CLUB VICE-PRESIDENT: N Soloman
DIRECTORS (EXECUTIVE)
CHAIRMAN: Alan M Sugar
CHIEF EXECUTIVE: C M Littner
FINANCE DIRECTOR: J Sedgwick
(NON-EXECUTIVE
A G Berry (Deputy-Chairman), D A Alexiou,
I Yawetz, C T Sandy,
COMPANY SECRETARY
J Ireland (0181365 5023)
CLUB SECRETARY
Peter Barnes (0181 365 5000)
COMMERCIAL MANAGER
Mike Rollo (0181 365 5010)
DIRECTOR OF FOOTBALL: David Pleat
MANAGER: Christian Gross
ASSISTANT MANAGER: Chris Houghton
RESERVE TEAM MANAGER: Bob Arber
PHYSIOTHERAPIST: Tony Lenaghan
STATISTICIAN FOR THE DIRECTORY
Vacant (call 01203 234017 if interested)

Many people say that the German superstar Jurgen Klinsmann came back to save Spurs from relegation......that may well be so - for Spurs were in deep trouble when he came back to White Hart Lane and in the end, the North Londoners stayed up with four points to spare.

When Klinsmann was signed - for the second time - at the turn of the year, Spurs were struggling. They were deep in relegation trouble, had only Barnsley below them in the Carling Premiership and there was a lack of cohesion and total commitment within the team. Manager Christian Gross, who had taken over the reins from Gerry Francis in November, revealed that Klinsmann would remain at the club until the end of the season, but would not comment about any future plans he or the Spurs' chairman, Alan Sugar, had up their sleeves to keep the German World Cup star at the club after that.

Prior to January, Spurs had performed well below par out on the field which certainly annoyed their long-suffering fans, considering what a talented line-up they could field from time to time with the likes of Walker, Calderwood, Campbell, Nielsen, Vega, Scales, Ginola, Ferdinand, Berti, Sinton, Fox and Wilson. Injuries to key players like Darren Anderton and Chris Armstrong didn't help matters and Chelsea's 6-1 win at White Hart Lane in early December was a bitter pill to swallow. That was a crushing defeat and at that point Spurs looked a poor side, relegation candidates for all to see.

After 22 games had been played Spurs were next to bottom with a meagre 20 points; after 30 games had gone they had mustered only 31 but had climbed out of the bottom three, although they had played a game more than their fellow strugglers.

From mid-March to mid April the atmosphere surrounding Tottenham Hotspur Football Club was mighty tense. As the matches were ticked off, it became more and more uneasy and with five games to go Spurs were 17th in the table, still in deep trouble, having 35 points to their credit, one more than Bolton and Barnsley who were immediately below them.

Successive draws against Coventry and Barnsley didn't do the heart much good, but a vital 2-0 home win over Newcastle certainly eased the pressure. And with two games to go Spurs needed at least one win to be safe - and that came in some style - a 6-2 thrashing of Wimbledon at Selhurst Park, hot-shot and saviour Klinsmann grabbing a fourtimer!

What lies ahead? Spurs never seem to have two seasons the same...and one expects them to be at least a mid-table team this time round.....if they aren't, then Chairman Mr. Sugar may not be so sweet!!   Tony Matthews.

TOTTENHAM HOTSPUR

Carling Prem.　:14th　　　FA CUP: 4th Round　　　LC CUP: 3rd Round

M	DATE	COMP.	VEN	OPPONENTS	RESULT	H/T	LP	GOAL SCORERS/GOAL TIMES	ATT.
1	A 10	CP	H	Manchester United	L	0-2	0-0	20		26359
2	12	CP	A	West Ham United	L	1-2	0-1	19	Ferdinand 81	(25354)
3	23	CP	H	Derby County	W	1-0	1-0	13	Calderwood 45	25886
4	27	CP	H	Aston Villa	W	3-2	1-1	9	Ferdinand 5, 66, Fox 77	26317
5	30	CP	A	Arsenal	D	0-0	0-0	7		(38102)
6	S 13	CP	A	Leicester City	L	0-3	0-0	9		(20683)
7	17	CC 2/1	H	Carlisle United	W	3-2	1-2		Fenn 1, Fox 73, Mahorn 78	19255
8	20	CP	H	Blackburn Rovers	D	0-0	0-0	12		26573
9	23	CP	A	Bolton Wanderers	D	1-1	0-1	11	Armstrong 71	(23433)
10	27	CP	H	Wimbledon	D	0-0	0-0	13		26261
11	30	CC 2/2	A	Carlisle United	W	2-0	1-0		Ginola 43 (pen), Armstrong 51	(13571)
12	O 04	CP	A	Newcastle United	L	0-1	0-0	14		(36709)
13	15	CC 3	H	Derby County	L	1-2	1-1		Ginola 21	20390
14	19	CP	H	Sheffield Wednesday	W	3-2	3-0	11	Dominguez 6, Armstrong 39, Ginola 45	25097
15	25	CP	A	Southampton	L	2-3	1-0	14	Dominguez 41, Ginola 64	(15255)
16	N 01	CP	H	Leeds United	L	0-1	0-1	15		26441
17	08	CP	A	Liverpool	L	0-4	0-0	16		(38006)
18	24	CP	H	Crystal Palace	L	0-1	0-0	17		25634
19	29	CP	A	Everton	W	2-0	0-0	17	Vega 71, Ginola 75	(36670)
20	D 06	CP	H	Chelsea	L	1-6	1-1	18	Vega 43	28476
21	13	CP	A	Coventry City	L	0-4	0-1	18		(19499)
22	20	CP	H	Barnsley	W	3-0	3-0	18	Nielsen 5, Ginola 11, 17	28232
23	26	CP	A	Aston Villa	L	1-4	0-1	18	Calderwood 59	(38644)
24	28	CP	A	Arsenal	D	1-1	1-1	19	Nielsen 28	29610
25	J 05	FAC 3	H	Fulham	W	3-1	2-0		Clemence 19, Calderwood 27, Taylor 61 (OG)	27909
26	10	CP	A	Manchester United	L	0-2	0-1	19		(55281)
27	17	CP	H	West Ham United	W	1-0	1-0	18	Klinsmann 7	30284
28	24	FAC 4	H	Barnsley	D	1-1	1-0		Campbell 29	28722
29	31	CP	A	Derby County	L	1-2	0-1	18	Fox 46	(30187)
30	F 04	FAC 4R	A	Barnsley	L	1-3	0-0		Ginola 72	(18220)
31	06	CP	A	Blackburn Rovers	W	3-0	1-0	17	Berti 37, Armstrong 89, Fox 90	(30388)
32	14	CP	H	Leicester City	D	1-1	0-1	17	Calderwood 51	28355
33	21	CP	A	Sheffield Wednesday	L	0-1	0-1	17		(29871)
34	M 01	CP	H	Bolton Wanderers	W	1-0	1-0	17	Nielsen 45	29032
35	04	CP	A	Leeds United	L	0-1	0-1	17		(31394)
36	14	CP	H	Liverpool	D	3-3	1-1	17	Klinsmann 12, Ginola 48, Vega 80	30245
37	28	CP	A	Crystal Palace	W	3-1	0-0	16	Berti 55, Ginola 72, Klinsmann 77	(26116)
38	A 04	CP	H	Everton	D	1-1	0-0	16	Armstrong 73	35624
39	11	CP	A	Chelsea	L	0-2	0-0	17		(34149)
40	13	CP	H	Coventry City	D	1-1	0-0	17	Berti 68	33463
41	18	CP	A	Barnsley	D	1-1	0-1	17	Calderwood 47	(18692)
42	25	CP	H	Newcastle United	W	2-0	1-0	16	Klinsmann 31, Ferdinand 72	35847
43	M 02	CP	A	Wimbledon	W	6-2	2-2	15	Ferdinand 17, Klinsmann 41, 54, 58, 60, Saib 79	(25820)
44	10	CP	H	Southampton	D	1-1	1-1	14	Klinsmann 27	35995

Best Home League Attendance: 35995 V Southampton　　　　Smallest :25097 V Sheffield Wednesday　　　Average :29144

Goal Scorers:
CP	(44)	Klinsmann 9, Ginola 6, Armstrong 5, Ferdinand 5, Calderwood 4, Berti 3, Fox 3, Nielsen 3, Vega 3, Dominguez 2, Saib 1
CC	(6)	Ginola 2, Armstrong 1, Fenn 1, Fox 1, Mahorn 1
FAC	(5)	Calderwood 1, Campbell 1, Clemence 1, Ginola 1, Opponents 1

Allen	Anderton	Armstrong	Baardsen	Berti	Brady	Calderwood	Campbell	Carr	Clemence	Dominguez	Edinburgh	Fenn	Ferdinand	Fox	Ginola	Grodas	Howells	Iversen	Klinsmann	Mabbutt	Mahorn	Nielsen	Saib	Scales	Sinton	Vega	Walker	Wilson	Referee	#
		S				S	X	X	X				X	S	X		X	X	X			X		S	S1	X	X	X	G Poll	1
		S				S	X	X	S1				X	S	X		X	X	X			X			S2	X	X	X	S J Lodge	2
		S				S		X	X	S1	X		X	S	X		X	X	X	S		S2				X	X	X	M J Bodenham	3
		S				S		X	X	X			X	S2	X		X	X	X	S1		S1				X	X	X	M A Riley	4
		S					X	X	X	S1	X		X		X		X	X	X	S3		S2				X	X	X	G S Willard	5
	S1	S				S	X	X	X	X			X	S	X		X			X		X		X		X		X	A B Wilkie	6
						S	X	S	X	X	X	X	X	X			X	X		X		X	S1	X		X		X	G R Ashby	7
		S				S	X	X	X	X			X	X			X	X		X		X		X	S	S1	X	X	G P Barber	8
	S1	S				X	X	X	X	X			X	X			X	X		X		X	S			S2	X	S	U D Rennie	9
	X	S				S	X	X	X				X	X	X		X			X		X	S1	S	S	X	X	X	P A Durkin	10
	X	S				X	X	X	X	S1			X	X	X		X			S					X	X	X	J T Winter	11
	X	S				X	X	X	X	S1			X	X	X		X			X		X		S		S2	X	X	M J Bodenham	12
	X					S1	X	X					X	X	S		X	X	X	X			S			X	X	X	D J Gallagher	13
S3	X	S				S2	X	X					X	X	S1		X	X	X	X			S			X	X	X	J T Winter	14
S2	X	S				S1	X	X					X	X	S3		X	X	X	X			S			X	X	X	N S Barry	15
S3	X	S				S	X	S1					X	X			X	X	X	X	S2	X				X	X	X	K W Burge	16
X	X	S1	S				X	X					X	S3	X		S	X	X	X		X			S2	X	X	X	S J Lodge	17
S3	X		S				X	X	X	S	X		X		X		X			X				S2		X	S1	X	P A Durkin	18
S	S2	S				X	X1	X					X3	X	X			S3				X2		S1	X	X	X	X	P Jones	19
S3	S2	S				X		X		S1			X	X	X					S		X2	X3	X1	X	X		X	D J Gallagher	20
S	X1	S				X		X	S3		S2		X	X	X			S1		X		X			X3		X	X2	S W Dunn	21
	X2	S				X	X	X	S3	S2			X1	X	X3			S1		S		X			X		X	X2	M D Reed	22
S2	S3					X	X	X	S1	S			X	X			X			X	X3	X			X1		X	X2	A B Wilkie	23
		S				X	X	X	X	S1			X1	X2			S2	X	S	X		S			X	X	X	M A Riley	24
		S2		X		X	X	X	X	X				X1			X	S	S1					X	X2		G P Barber	25
		X	X	S2		X	X	X	X1	X			X2				X	S	S				S1	X		P E Alcock	26
		X	X	S3		X1	X	X		S2			X3	X2		S1	X	S					X	X	X	D R Elleray	27
		X	X	S		S1	X	X	S				X1	X	X		S	X				X	X	X	G R Ashby	28
		X	X			S	X	X	S	S2			X	X	X		S1	X					X1	X	X2	G S Willard	29
	S2	X	X2	S3		S	X	X					X	X	X		S1		X3					X	X1	G R Ashby	30
	S2	X	X	S3		S	X	S1					X2	X	X	S	X			X1				X	X3	G P Barber	31
	X	X	X	S2	X2	X	X			S	S1		X	X	S				S		X			X	X1	S J Lodge	32
	X	X	X1	S1	X	X	X		S2	X2			X	X	S		X			X						M J Bodenham	33
	X1		X	S2	X	S	X						X2	X3	S	S1	X	S		X	S3				X	P Jones	34
	X	X2	S2	S	X	X				S3			X	X	S	X1		X		X	S1			X	X3	P E Alcock	35
	X1	X	S2	S	X	X							X	X2	S	S1	X	S		X				X	X	U D Rennie	36
	X3	S	X	S2	X	X1		S3					X2			S1		X		S		X		X	X	X	M D Reed	37
	X	S	X2	S1	X	X3	S						X	X		S3	X			X	S2			X	X	X1	A B Wilkie	38
S3	X1	S	X3	S2	X	X			S1	X			X	X			X2			X	X	S		X	X	P A Durkin	39
S	X2	X		S1	X	X			S2	X	X	S		X			X			X1		S		X	X	M A Riley	40
S2	S1	S	X		X	X	X	S		X2	X		X			X1		X		S		X	X	M J Bodenham	41
X1	S	S	X		X	X	X			X	X		X			X			S1	S		X	X	J T Winter	42
X	S1	X			X	X	X	S		X1	X2		X	S		X		S2	S		X	X	G P Barber	43
X	S	X1			X2	X	X			X	X	X	S		X	S2	X	S1	S		X	P Jones	44

1	7	13	9	17		21	34	37	12	8	13		19	32	34		14	8	15	8	2	21	3	9	14	22	29	16	CP Appearances	
3	8	6			9	5		1	5	10	3	4	2				6	5		3		4	6	1	5	3			CP Sub Appearances	
		2			1+1	3	2	2	2+1	2	1	1	3	3			1			1		0+1	1		2	1	2	3	CC Appearances	
	0+1	2+1	2		1+1	1+1	3	3	2	1			2	2	3		1			0+1		3			1	3	1	3	FAC Appearances	

Also played:(D) Arber S(5,6). (G) Brown S(26,27,28), S(30). (M) Clapham S(4,25). (M) Gain S(33). (M) Hill S(25).

TOTTENHAM HOTSPUR

CLUB RECORDS

BIGGEST VICTORIES
League: 9-0 v Bristol Rovers, Division 2, 22.10.1977
F.A. Cup: 13-2 v Crewe Alexandra, Round 4, 3.2.1960
League Cup: 5-0 v West Brom. Alb, Round 3, 28.10.1970
7-2 v Doncaster Rovers, Round 5, 3.12.1975
5-0 v Birmingham City, Round 3, 1986-87
5-0 v West Ham United, Round 5, 2.2.1987
5-0 v Hartlepool Utd, Round 1, 26.9.1990
Europe (UEFA): 9-0 v Keflavic, Round 1, 28.9.1971
BIGGEST DEFEATS
League: 0-7 v Liverpool, Division 1, 2.9.1979
F.A. Cup: 0-5 v Stoke City, Round 1, 1.2.1896
1-6 v Huddersfield, Round 6, 3.3.1928
League Cup: 0-4 v Middlesbrough (h), Round 2, 1974-75
Europe 0(UEFA): 1-4 v Bayern Munich, Round 2, 3.11.1982
1-4 v Manchester Utd, Cup Winners Cup Round 2, 10.12.1963

MOST POINTS
3 points a win: 77, Division 1, 1984-85
2 points a win: 70, Division 2, 1919-1920 (Div 2 record)

MOST GOALS
115, 1960-61 (Division 1)
Smith 28, Allen 22, Jones 15, White 13, Dyson 12, Blanchflower 6,
Medwin 5,Norman 4, Mackay 4, Saul 3, Baker 1, og 2

MOST FIRST CLASS MATCHES IN A SEASON
68 (42 League, 5 FA Cup, 7 League Cup, 12 UEFA Cup, 2 Anglos-
Ital. Cup WinnersCup) 1971-72

MOST LEAGUE GOALS CONCEDED
95, Division 1958-59

MOST LEAGUE WINS
32, Division 2, 1919-20
MOST LEAGUE DRAWS
17, Division 1, 1968-69
MOST LEAGUE DEFEATS
22, Division 1, 1934-35

INDIVIDUAL CLUB RECORDS

MOST GOALS IN A MATCH
5. Ted Harper v Reading, Division 2, 30.8.1930 (7-1)
5. Alf Stokes v Birmingham, Division 1, 18.9.1957 (7-1)
5. Les Allen v Crewe Alex., FAC Round 4, 3.2.1960 (13-2)
5. Bobby Smith v Aston Villa, Division 1, 29.3.1958 (6-2)
5. V Woodwood v West Ham Utd, 1904-05
Jack Rowley netted 7 in war-time games
MOST GOALS IN A SEASON
Clive Allen 49 (League 33, League Cup 12, FAC 4) 1986-87
3 goals 3 times=9; 2 goals 9 times=18; 1 goal 22 times=22
League Goals Only: Jimmy Greaves 37, Div 1, 1962-63

OLDEST PLAYER
Jimmy Cantrell, 40 years 349 days v Birmingham, 24.4.1923
YOUNGEST PLAYER
Ally Dick, 16 years 301 days v Manchester City, 20.2.1982
MOST CAPPED PLAYER
Pat Jennings (Northern Ireland) 74

BEST PERFORMANCES

League: 1919-20: Matches played 42, Won 32, Drawn 6, Lost 4,
Goals for 102,against 32, Points 70. Division 2 Champions.
Highest: 1950-51, 1960-61: Division 1 Champions.

F.A. Cup: 1900-01: 1st rnd. Preston North End 1-1, 4-2; 2nd rnd.
Bury 2-1; 3rd rnd. Reading 1-1, 3-0; Semi-final West Bromwich
Albion 4-0; Final SheffieldUnited 2-2, 3-1
1920-21: 1st rnd. Bristol Rov. 6-2; 2nd rnd. Bradford City 4-0; 3rd
rnd.Southend 4-1; Semi-final Preston N E 2-1; Final Wolverhampton
Wndrs 1-0
1960-61: 3rd rnd. Charlton Athletic 3-2; 4th rnd. Crewe Alexandra 5-
1; 5th rnd.Aston Villa 2-0; 6th rnd. Sunderland 1-1, 5-0; Semi-final
Burnley 3-0; Final Leicester 2-0
1961-62: 3rd rnd. Birmingham City 3-3, 4-2; 4th rnd. Plymouth 5-1;
5th rnd.West Brom. Alb 4-2; 6th rnd. Aston Villa 2-0; Semi-final
Manchester United 3-1;Final Burnley 3-1
1966-67: 3rd rnd. Millwall 0-0, 1-0; 4th rnd. Portsmouth 3-1; 5th rnd.
Bristol City 2-0; 6th rnd. Birmingham City 0-0, 6-0; Semi-final
Nottingham Forest 2-1;Final Chelsea 2-1
1980-81: 3rd rnd. Queens Park Rangers 0-0, 3-1; 4th rnd. Hull City
2-0; 5th rnd. Coventry City 3-1; 6th rnd. Exeter City 2-0; Semi-final
Wolverhampton W.2-2, 3-0; Final Manchester City 1-1, 3-2
1981-82: 3rd rnd. Arsenal 1-0; 4th rnd. Leeds United 1-0; 5th rnd.
Aston Villa1-0; 6th rnd. Chelsea 3-2; Semi-final Leicester City 2-0;
Final Queens Park Rangers 1-1, 1-0
1990-91: 3rd rnd. Blackpool 1-0; 4th rnd. Oxford Utd 4-2; 5th rnd.
Portsmouth2-1; 6-1 rnd. Notts County 2-1; Semi-Final Arsenal 3-1;
Final Nottingham Forest2-1

League Cup: 1970-71: 2nd rnd. Swansea City 3-0; 3rd rnd.
Sheffield United 2-1;4th rnd. West Bromwich Albion 5-0; 5th rnd.
Coventry 4-1; Semi-final BristolCity 1-1, 2-0; Final Aston Villa 2-0
1972-73: 2nd rnd. Huddersfield 2-1; 3rd rnd Middlesbrough 1-1, 0-0,
2-1; 4thrnd Millwall 2-0; 5th rnd. Liverpool 1-1, 3-1; Semi-final
Wolverhampton W. 2-1,2-2; Final Norwich 1-0

ECWC: 1962-63: 2nd rnd. Rangers 3-2, 5-2; 3rd rnd Slovan Bratisl.
0-2, 6-0;Semi-final OFK Belgrade 2-1, 3-1; Final Athletico Madrid 5-
1
UEFA: 1971-72: 1st rnd. Keflavic 6-1, 9-0; 2nd rnd. Nantes 0-0, 1-0;
3rd rnd.Rapid Bucharest 3-0, 2-0; 4th rnd. UT Arad 2-0,
1-1; Semi-final AC Milan 2-1, 1-1; Final Wolverhampton W. 2-1, 1-1
1983-84: 1st rnd. Drogheda 6-0, 8-0; 2nd rnd. Feyenoord 4-2, 2-0;
3rd rnd.Bayern Munich 0-1, 2-0; 4th rnd. FK Austria 2-0, 2-2; Semi-
final Hadj. Split 1-2, 1-0; Final Anderlecht 1-1, 1-1, won on pens

DIVISIONAL RECORD

	Played	Won	Drawn	Lost	For	Against	Points
Division 1/P	2,596	1,047	631	918	4,130	3,769	3,000
Division 2	668	311	172	185	1,253	851	794
Total	3,264	1,358	803	1,103	5,390	4,620	3,794

ADDITIONAL INFORMATION
Previous Name
Hotspur F.C. 1882-84

Previous League
None.

Club colours: White shirts, navy shorts, navy socks.
Change colours: Navy shirts.

Reserves League: Avon Insurance Football Combination.

RECORDS AND STATISTICS

COMPETITIONS

Div 1/P	Div.2	Euro C	ECWC	UEFA	Texaco
1909-15	1908-09	1961-62	1962-63	1971-72	1970-71
1920-28	1915-20		1963-64	1972-73	
1933-35	1928-33		1967-68	1973-74	
1950-77	1935-50		1981-82	1983-84	
1978-	1977-78		1982-83	1984-85	
			1991-92		

HONOURS

Div 1/P	Div.2	FAC	ECWC	Lge C	C/S'Ld
1950-51	1919-20	1900-01	1962-63	1970-71	1920
1960-61	1949-50	1920-21		1972-73	1951
		1960-61			1961
		1961-62	UEFA		1962
		1966-67	1971-72		1967
		1980-81	1983-84		1981
		1981-82			1992
		1990-91			shared

MOST APPEARANCES

Steve Perryman 860+4 (1969-86)

Year	League	FA Cup	Lge Cup	Europe
1969-70	21	4		
1970-71	42	5	6	
1971-72	40	5	6	12
1972-73	41	3	10	10
1973-74	40	1	1	12
1974-75	42	2	1	
1975-76	40	2	6	
1976-77	42	1	2	
1977-78	42	2	2	
1978-79	42	7	2	
1979-80	40	6	2	
1980-81	42	9	6	
1981-82	42	7	8	8
1982-83	32+1	3	2	2+1
1983-84	41	4	3	9
1984-85	42	3	5	8
1985-86	22+1	5	4	
	653+2	69	66	61+1

Including 1+1 Charity Shield, 10 Others.

MOST GOALS IN A CAREER

Jimmy Greaves - 266 (161-70)

Year	League	FA Cup	Lge Cup	Europe
1961-62	21	9		
1962-63	37			5
1963-64	35			1
1964-65	29	4		
1965-66	15	3		
1966-67	25	6		
1967-68	23	3		3
1968-69	27	4	5	
1969-70	8	3		
Total	220	32	5	9

Current leading goalscorer: Chris Armstrong - 34 (08/95-98)

RECORD TRANSFER FEE RECEIVED

Amount	Club	Player	Date
£5,500,000	Lazio	Paul Gascoigne	7/91
£5,250,000	Middlesbrough	Nick Barmby	8/95
£4,500,000	Marseille	Chris Waddle	6/89
£2,800,000	Barcelona	Gica Popescu	5/95
£1,500,000	Rangers	Richard Gough	9/87
£1,500,000	Barcelona	Steve Archibald	7/84

RECORD TRANSFER FEE PAID

Amount	Club	Player	Date
£6,000,000	Newcaslte Utd	Les Ferdinand	07/97
£4,500,000	Crystal Palace	Chris Armstrong	6/95
£2,900,000	PSV Eindhoven	Gica Popescu	9/94
£2,600,000	Steaua Bucharest	Ilie Dumetrescu	8/94
£2,200,000	Chelsea	Gordon Durie	8/91

MANAGERS

Name	Seasons	Best	Worst
Frank Brettall	1895-88		
John Cameron	1898		
Fred Kirkham	1898-07		
Pete McWilliam	1907-08		
Billy Minter	1927-30	21(2)	12(2)
Percy Smith	1930-35	3(1)	8(2)
Jack Tresadern	1935-38	5(2)	10(2)
Pete McWilliam	1938-45	8(2)	8(2)
Arthur Turner	1942-46		
Joe Hulme	1945-49	5(2)	8(2)
Arthur Rowe	1949-55	1(1)	1(2)
Jim Anderson	1955-58	2(1)	18(1)
Bill Nicholson	1958-74	1(1)	11(1)
Terry Neill	1974-76	9(1)	19(1)
Keith Burkinshaw	1976-84	4(1)	3(2)
Peter Shreeves	1984-86	3(1)	10(1)
David Pleat	1986-87	3(1)	3(1)
Terry Venables	1987-91	3(1)	13(1)
Peter Shreeves	1991-92	15(1)	15(1)
Doug Livermore	1992-93	8(1/P)	8(1/P)
Ossie Ardiles	1993-94	15(P)	15(P)
Gerry Francis	1994-97	7(P)	10(P)
Christian Gross	1997-	14 (P)	14 (P)

LONGEST LEAGUE RUNS

of undefeated matches:	22 (31.8.1949 - 31.12.1949)	of league matches w/out a win:	16 (29.12.1934 - 13.4.1935)
of undefeated home matches:	33 (2.1.1932 - 23.9.1933)	of undefeated away matches:	16 (10.11.1984 - 21.8.1985)
without home win:	14 (23.10.1993 - 4.4.1994)	without an away win:	22 (25.2.1928 - 16.3.1929)
of league wins:	13 (23.4.1960 - 1.10.1960)	of home wins:	14)24.1.1987 - 3.10.1987)
of league defeats:	7 (1.1.94-27.2.94, 1.10.55-29.10.55)	of away wins:	10 (15.4.1960 - 29.10.1960)
	(18.2.75-22.3.75)		

TOTTENHAM HOTSPUR

PLAYERS NAME Honours	Ht	Wt	Birthdate	Birthplace Transfers	Contract Date	Clubs	League	L/Cup	FA Cup	Other	Lge	L/C	FAC	Oth
G O A L K E E P E R														
Baardsen Espen	6.5	13.13	12/7/77	USA	7/16/96	Tottenham Hotspur	11+1		2+1					
Y. USA:														
Brown Simon J	6.2	15.1	12/3/76	Chelmsford	7/1/95	Tottenham Hotspur								
				Loan	12/19/97	Lincoln City	1							
Segers Hans	5.11	12.12	10/30/61	Eindhoven		PSV Eindhoven								
				£50000	8/14/84	Nottingham Forest	58	4	5					
				Loan	2/13/87	Stoke City	1							
				Loan	11/19/87	Sheffield United	10			1				
Loan 3/1/88 Dunfermline				£180000	9/28/88	Wimbledon	265+2	26	22	7				
				Free	8/30/96	Wolverhampton W.	11		2					
				Free	7/1/98	Tottenham Hotspur								
Walker Ian	6.1	11.9	10/31/71	Watford	12/4/89	Tottenham Hotspur	191+1	16	16	2				
E: 3, B.1, u21.9, Y.17. FAYC'90. CS'91				Loan	8/31/90	Oxford United	2	1						
D E F E N C E														
Arber Mark	6.1	11.9	10/9/77	South Africa	3/27/96	Tottenham Hotspur								
Calderwood Colin	6	12	1/20/65	Stranraer	3/19/82	Mansfield Town	97+3	3+4	6	7	1		1	
S: 29, S. Div4'86				£30000	7/1/85	Swindon Town	328+2	35	17	32	20		1	
				£1250000	7/22/93	Tottenham Hotspur	141+10	14+1	15+1		6		1	
Campbell Sol	6.1	12.1	9/18/74	Newham	9/23/92	Tottenham Hotspur	159+9	17	14+2		2	2	1	
E: 20, B.1, u21.11, Y, S. UEFA Y'93														
Carr Stephen	5.9	12.02	8/29/76	Dublin	8/1/93	Tottenham Hotspur	61+3	5	4					
Ei: u21.12.														
D'Arcy Ross	6		12.2	3/21/78	Balbriggan	7/1/95	Tottenham Hotspur								
Edinburgh Justin	5.9	11.6	12/18/69	Brentwood	8/5/88	Southend United	36+1	2+1	2	4+1				1
FAC'91. CS'91				£150000	7/30/90	Tottenham Hotspur	169+20	19+4	22	3	1			
Scales John R	6.2	12.7	7/4/66	Harrogate		Leeds United								
E: 3, B1: FAC'88; LC'95.				Free	7/11/85	Bristol Rovers	68+4	3	6	3+1	2			
				£70000	7/16/87	Wimbledon	235+5	18+1	20+1	7+1	11			
				£3500000	9/2/94	Liverpool	65	10	14	4+1	2	3		
				£2600000	12/11/96	Tottenham Hotspur	19+3	2						
Tramezzani Paolo				Italy		Piacenza								
				£1350000	76/29/98	Tottenham Hotspur								
Vega Ramon	6.3	13	6/14/71	Zurich		Cagliari								
Int. Swiss				£3700000	1/11/97	Tottenham Hotspur	30+3	2	3		4			
Wilson Clive	5.7	9.1	11/13/61	Manchester	12/8/79	Manchester City	107+2	10	2	5	9	2		
Div2'89				Loan	9/16/82	Chester City	21				2			
				£250000	3/19/87	Chelsea	68+13	3+3	4	10+2	5			
				£450000	7/4/90	QPR	170+2	16	8	2+1	12	1	1	
				Free	8/1/95	Tottenham Hotspur	67+3	7	7+1		1		1	
M I D F I E L D														
Berti Nicola	6.1	12.2	4/14/67	Parma		Inter Milan								
Italian Int.				Free	1/9/98	Tottenham Hotspur	17		2		3			
Clemence Stephen N	5.11	11.7	3/31/78	Liverpool		Tottenham Hotspur	12+5	2	2				1	
Gain Peter	6.1	11	11/11/76	Hammersmith	7/1/95	Tottenham H. (T)								
Gower Mark			10/5/78	Edmonton	5/31/97	Tottenham H. (T)								
Kersey Lee D			8/12/79	Harlow	7/3/97	Tottenham H. (T)								
Marriott Alan			9/3/78	Bedford	7/3/97	Tottenham H. (T)								
Nielsen Allan	5.8	11.2	3/13/71	Esbjerg	1/1/00	Brondby								
Int. Danish				£1650000	7/23/96	Tottenham Hotspur	49+5	3+1	1		9			
Saib Moussa	5.9	11.8	3/6/69	Algeria		Valencia								
Algerian Int.				£2300000	2/27/98	Tottenham Hotspur	3+6				1			
Sinton Andy	5.7	10.7	3/19/66	Newcastle	4/13/83	Cambridge United	90+3	6	3	2	13	1		1
E: 12, B.3, S. FLgXI.1				£2750000	8/19/83	Sheffield Wednesday	47+3	10	4		3			
				£25000	12/13/85	Brentford	149	8	11	14	28	3	1	2
				£350000	3/23/89	QPR	160	14	13	3	22		2	1
				£1500000	1/23/96	Tottenham Hotspur	54+7	3	2		6			
Vaughan Wayne S			2/18/80	Barking	7/15/97	Tottenham H. (T)								
Webb Simon	5.11	12.3	1/19/78	Castle Bar										
Young Luke Paul			7/19/79	Harlow	7/3/97	Tottenham H. (T)								
F O R W A R D														
Allen Rory	5.11	11.2	10/17/77	Beckenham	3/28/96	Tottenham Hotspur	10+6	2+1	1		2	2		
				Loan	3/26/98	Luton Town	7				6			
Anderton Darren	6	11.7	3/3/72	Southampton	2/5/90	Portsmouth	53+9	3+2	7+1	2	7	1	5	
E: 22, B.1, u21.12, Y.1.				£1750000	6/3/92	Tottenham Hotspur	130+16	13	13+1		22	4	2	
Armstrong Chris	6	11	6/19/71	Newcastle		Llay Welfare								
E: B.1. Div1.94				Free	3/3/89	Wrexham	40+20	2+1	+1	5+1	13			3
				£50000	8/16/91	Millwall	11+17	3+1	+1	+1	5	2		
				£1000000	9/1/92	Crystal Palace	118	8	8	2	46	6	5	1
				£4500000	8/1/95	Tottenham Hotspur	61+6	8	6+1		25	5	4	
Bunn James T.			1/12/78	Tottenham	8/14/96	Tottenham Hotspur								
u21. Norwegian														

	Ht	Wt	DOB	From	Fee	Date	Club								
Dominguez Jose Manuel M	5.3	10	2/16/74	Lisbon, Portugal			Benfica								
Portuguese Int.					£180000	3/9/94	Birmingham City	15+10	1+2	2+1	2+2	3			1
					£1800000	8/1/95	Sporting Lisbon								
					£1600000	8/12/97	Tottenham Hotspur	8+10	2+1	1		2			
Fenn Neale M C	5.11	11.2	1/18/77	Edmonton		7/1/95	Tottenham Hotspur	0+8	1	1			1		
u21.1, Y. Ei:					Loan	1/30/98	Leyton Orient	3							
					Loan	3/26/98	Norwich City	6+1				1			
Ferdinand Les	5.11	13.5	12/18/66	Acton			Hayes								
E: 17, B.1. Turkish FAC'89					£15000	3/12/87	QPR	152+11	11+2	6+1	1	60	7	3	
					Loan	3/24/88	Brentford	3							
					Loan	8/1/88	Besiktas								
					£6000000	8/1/95	Newcastle United	67+1	6	4+1	5	41	3	2	4
					£6000000	8/5/97	Tottenham Hotspur	19+2	1	2		5			
Fox Ruel Adrian	5.6	10	1/14/68	Ipswich		1/20/86	Norwich City	148+4	13+3	11+4	12+4	22	3		
E: B.1					£2250000	2/2/94	Newcastle United	54	2	5	1	12	1		1
					£4200000	10/6/95	Tottenham Hotspur	76+6	6+1	8		10	1		
Ginola David	6	13	1/25/67	Gossin			Toulon								
French Int.							Racing Paris								
							Brest								
							Paris St Germain								
					£2500000	7/6/95	Newcastle United	54+4	6	4	7+1	6			1
					£2000000	7/18/97	Tottenham Hotspur	34	3	3		6	2	1	
Iversen Steffen	6.1	11.2	11/10/76	Oslo		1/1/00	Rosenborg								
u21. Norweigen					£2600000	12/7/96	Tottenham Hotspur	24+5				6			
McVeigh Paul	5.6	10.5	12/6/77	Belfast		7/10/96	Tottenham Hotspur	2+1				1			
Y. NI:															

THE MANAGER
CHRISTIAN GROSS

Date of Appointment. . . . . 19th November 1997.

PREVIOUS CLUBS
As Manager. . . . . Grasshopper Zurich.

WHITE HART LANE

748 High Road, Tottenham, London N17 0AP

Capacity 33,083

First game..v Notts County (Friendly), 4-1, 4.9.1899.
Internationals ....England v France 1935, Germany 1935,
....Czechoslovakia 1937, v Italy 1949.

ATTENDANCES
Highest...75,038 v Sunderland, FAC 6th Rnd, 5.3.1938.
Lowest ....5,000 v Sunderland, Division 1, 19.12.1914.

OTHER GROUNDS.............Tottenham Marshes, 1882-1885. Northumberland Park 1885-1898. White Hart Lane 1898-

HOW TO GET TO THE GROUND

From all directions
Use A406 North Circular Road to Edmonton then at traffic signals follow signs to Tottenham A1010 into Fore Street for Tottenham Hotspur FC.

Car Parking: No street parking within a quarter-of-a-mile radius of the ground.

Nearest Railway Station: White Hart Lane (from Liverpool Street, Central London).
Northumberland Park (Liverpool Street).

Underground Stations: Manor House (Piccadilly Line) & Seven Sisters (Victoria Line)
Both stations change to bus routes 259, 279, 359 (Sundays only). Also 149 from Seven Sisters.

USEFUL TELEPHONE NUMBERS

Club switchboard 0181 365 5000
Club fax number.......................0181 365 5005
Ticket Office............................0181 365 5050
Marketing Department 0181 365 5010

Spursline...................................0891 33 55 55*
*Calls cost 50p per minute at all times. Call costings correct at time of going to press.

MATCHDAY PROGRAMME

Programme Editor ....John Fennelly.

Number of pages.....................48.

Price ....£2.00.

Subscriptions ....Apply to club.

Local Newspapers
..........................Waltham Forest Guardian,
.... North London News.

Local Radio Stations
London News Radio, Greater London Radio,
....Capital Radio.

MATCHDAY TICKET PRICES

West Stand

Upper Tier ....£30/£35

Lower Tier ....£24/£29

East Stand

Upper Tier .... £25/£29

Lower Tier ....£21/£24

South Stand

Upper Tier ....£22/£25

Lower Tier ....£18/£21

WEST HAM UNITED
(The Hammers)
F.A. CARLING PREMIERSHIP
SPONSORED BY: DR MARTINS

Unfortunately West Ham United were unable to supply us with a team photograph for this year's publication

WEST HAM UNITED
FORMED IN 1895
TURNED PROFESSIONAL IN 1900
LTD COMPANY IN 1900

CHAIRMAN: Terence W Brown
VICE-CHAIRMAN: Martin W Cearns
DIRECTORS
Charles Warner, P Storrie, N Igoe, P Aldridge
SECRETARY
Neil Harrison
COMMERCIAL MANAGER
Mrs Sue Page (0181 548 2777)

MANAGER: Harry Redknapp
ASSISTANT MANAGER: Frank Lampard

COACH
Roger Cross & Tony Carr
PHYSIOTHERAPIST
John Green, BSC (Hons), MCSP, SRP

STATISTICIAN FOR THE DIRECTORY
John Northcutt & John Helliar

Although West Ham finished in 8th position, their best ever in the Carling Premiership, it was disappointing as they missed out on a UEFA place by one point. The Israeli midfielder Eyal Berkovic had been bought for £1.75 million and it was hoped he would create chances for Hartson and Kitson to score.

West Ham kicked off the season in fine style with wins over Barnsley and Spurs but slipped up with visits to Everton and Manchester United. A flurry of transfer activity took place in September when young Danny Williamson went to Everton in a swap for David Unsworth. Marc Rieper, the Danish defender joined Celtic while Northern Ireland winger Michael Hughes went to Wimbledon. In their place West Ham paid Blackburn £2.3 million for defender Ian Pearce and QPR £1.2 million for the services of midfielder Andy Impey.

In the League Cup Huddersfield were beaten 3-1 on aggregate with Hartson claiming a hat-trick. The big Welshman was on top form as he scored two more in the next round in a 3-0 win over Aston Villa.

The away form was coursing concern with defeats at Leicester, Chelsea and Leeds. Paul Kitson was absent with a groin injury which prompted manager Redknapp to buy the French forward Samassi Abou from Cannes.

Rio Ferdinand was having an excellent season and was rewarded with his first England cap against Cameroon in November. A splendid hat-trick from Frank Lampard saw Walsall beaten in the League Cup. There was joy at Christmas with wins against Sheffield Wednesday and Wimbledon.

The FA Cup brought non-League Emley to Upton Park. The Yorkshire club did themselves proud after narrowly losing 2-1. A few days later Arsenal were the opponents in the League Cup quarter finals. Unfortunately two defensive errors saw the Gunners progress with a 2-1 win. In the 4th round of FA Cup a wonder goal from Kinkladze had given Manchester City hope, but the Hammers held out and Lomas scored the winner against his old club.

A deal arranged with QPR when the Irish pair Rowland and Dowie were exchanged for Trevor Sinclair. The exciting winger had a splendid debut against Everton scoring twice in the 2-2 draw. In the FA Cup Blackburn were tough opponents and after a 1-1 draw at Upton Park the replay saw the teams level after extra-time. A tense penalty shoot out brought joy when first Forrest saved from Hendry and Loams scored for West Ham. In the quarter-finals the Hammer travelled to Highbury and did well to force a 1-1 draw. The replay however was a huge disappointment as once again West Ham faced a penalty shoot out only this time they weren't so lucky.

West Ham were chasing a UEFA spot and after a brilliant 3-0 victory against Leeds and a 2-1 win over Blackburn they were now in 6h place. Unfortunately the defence were in generous mood in the remaining four games when they conceded 15 goals, and a UEFA place was lost.

JOHN NORTHCUTT

WEST HAM UNITED

Carling Prem.   :8th   **FA CUP: 6th Round**   **LC CUP: 6th Round**

M	DATE	COMP.	VEN	OPPONENTS	RESULT	H/T	LP	GOAL SCORERS/GOAL TIMES	ATT.
1	A 09	CP	A	Barnsley	W 2-1	0-1	3	Hartson 56, Lampard 77	(18667)
2	12	CP	H	Tottenham Hotspur	W 2-1	1-0	3	Hartson 3, Berkovic 70	25354
3	23	CP	A	Everton	L 1-2	1-0	7	, Watson 23 (OG)	(34356)
4	27	CP	A	Coventry City	D 1-1	0-1	5	Kitson 64	(18289)
5	30	CP	H	Wimbledon	W 3-1	0-0	3	Hartson 47, Rieper 54, Berkovic 55	24516
6	S 13	CP	A	Manchester United	L 1-2	1-1	6	Hartson 14	(55068)
7	16	CC 2/1	A	Huddersfield Town	L 0-1	0-0			(8525)
8	20	CP	H	Newcastle United	L 0-1	0-1	6		25884
9	24	CP	A	Arsenal	L 0-4	0-4	10		(38012)
10	27	CP	H	Liverpool	W 2-1	1-0	7	Hartson 14, Berkovic 64	25908
11	29	CC 1/1	H	Huddersfield Town	W 3-0	2-0		Hartson 31, 45, 77	16137
12	O 04	CP	A	Southampton	L 0-3	0-0	9		(15212)
13	15	CC 3	H	Aston Villa	W 3-0	2-0		Hartson 7, 80, Lampard 15	20360
14	18	CP	H	Bolton Wanderers	W 3-0	0-0	8	Berkovic 69, Hartson 78, 89	24864
15	27	CP	A	Leicester City	L 1-2	1-1	11	Berkovic 58	20201
16	N 09	CP	A	Chelsea	L 1-2	0-0	14	Hartson 84 (pen)	(34382)
17	19	CC 4	H	Walsall	W 4-1	2-1		Lampard 15, 72, 73, Hartson 16	17463
18	23	CP	A	Leeds United	L 1-3	0-0	15	Lampard 65	(30031)
19	29	CP	H	Aston Villa	W 2-1	1-0	12	Hartson 18, 47	24976
20	D 03	CP	H	Crystal Palace	W 4-1	2-1	10	Hartson 30, Berkovic 45, Unsworth 47, Lomas 71	23335
21	06	CP	A	Derby County	L 0-2	0-1	10		(29300)
22	13	CP	H	Sheffield Wednesday	W 1-0	0-0	10	Kitson 69	24344
23	20	CP	A	Blackburn Rovers	L 0-3	0-1	10		(21653)
24	26	CP	H	Coventry City	W 1-0	1-0	8	Kitson 69	22477
25	28	CP	A	Wimbledon	W 2-1	1-0	8	Kitson 54, Kimble 30 (OG)	(22087)
26	J 03	FAC 3	H	Emley	W 2-1	1-0		Lampard 3, Hartson 80	18629
27	06	CC QF	H	Arsenal	L 1-2	0-1		Abou 75	24770
28	10	CP	H	Barnsley	W 6-0	2-0	7	Lampard 5, Abou 28, 52, Moncur 57, Hartson 65, Lazaridis 89	23714
29	17	CP	A	Tottenham Hotspur	L 0-1	0-1	8		(30284)
30	25	FAC 4	A	Manchester City	W 2-1	1-0		Berkovic 28, Lomas 76	(26495)
31	31	CP	H	Everton	D 2-2	1-1	8	Sinclair 9, 47	25905
32	F 06	CP	A	Newcastle United	W 1-0	1-0	8	Lazaridis 17	(36736)
33	14	FAC 5	H	Blackburn Rovers	D 2-2	2-1		Kitson 25, Berkovic 43	25729
34	21	CP	A	Bolton Wanderers	D 1-1	0-0	8	Sinclair 66	(25000)
35	25	FAC 5R	A	Blackburn Rovers	D 1-1	0-0		Hartson 103	(21972)
36	M 02	CP	H	Arsenal	D 0-0	0-0	7		25717
37	08	FAC QF	A	Arsenal	D 1-1	1-1		Pearce 12	(38077)
38	11	CP	H	Manchester United	D 1-1	1-0	8	Sinclair 6	25892
39	14	CP	H	Chelsea	W 2-1	0-0	8	Sinclair 67, Unsworth 73	25829
40	17	FAC QFR	H	Arsenal	D 1-1	0-1		Hartson 83	25859
41	30	CP	H	Leeds United	W 3-0	2-0	7	Hartson 7, Abou 22, Pearce 68	24107
42	A 04	CP	A	Aston Villa	L 0-2	0-0	7		(39372)
43	11	CP	H	Derby County	D 0-0	0-0	7		25155
44	13	CP	A	Sheffield Wednesday	D 1-1	1-0	8	Berkovic 7	(28036)
45	18	CP	H	Blackburn Rovers	W 2-1	2-1	7	Hartson 6, 26	24733
46	25	CP	H	Southampton	L 2-4	1-1	7	Sinclair 41, Lomas 82	25878
47	M 02	CP	A	Liverpool	L 0-5	0-4	10		(44414)
48	05	CP	A	Crystal Palace	D 3-3	1-1	9	Omoyimni 68, 89, Curcic 4 (OG)	(19129)
49	10	CP	H	Leicester City	W 4-3	2-0	8	Lampard 15, Abou 30, 74, Sinclair 65	25781

Best Home League Attendance: 25908 V Liverpool   **Smallest :22477 V Coventry City**   **Average :24967**

Goal Scorers:

CP	(56)	Hartson 15, Berkovic 7, Sinclair 7, Abou 5, Kitson 4, Lampard 4, Lazaridis 2, Lomas 2, Omoyimni 2, Unsworth 2, Moncur 1, Pearce 1, Rieper 1, Opponents 3
CC	(11)	Hartson 6, Lampard 4, Abou 1
FAC	(9)	Hartson 3, Berkovic 2, Kitson 1, Lampard 1, Lomas 1, Pearce 1

150

	Abou	Alves	Berkovic	Bishop	Breacker	Coyne	Dowie	Ferdinand	Forrest	Hartson	Hodges	Hughes	Impey	Kitson	Lama	Lampard	Lazaridis	Lomas	Mean	Miklosko	Moncur	Omoyinmi	Pearce	Potts	Rieper	Rowland	Sealey	Sinclair	Unsworth	Referee	#
			X2	X1		S	X	S	X			X		X3		S2	S1	X		X	X			X	X					A. B. Wilkie	1
			X		X	S2	X		X	S3		X		S1		S1	X	X		X	X			S	X		S	S		S J Lodge	2
			X		X	S3	X	S	X	S1		X		S2		X	X			X	X			S	X				X	P Jones	3
			X		X	S1	X	S	X	S		X		S		X	X	X		X	X			S	X				X	N S Barry	4
		X	S		X	X	X	S	X	S				S		X	X	X		X	X			S	X				X	G Poll	5
			X		X	S	X		X	X		X		X		S1		X		X	X			X			S	S	X	D R Elleray	6
		X	X		X	S1	X		X	X		X		X		X		X		X				X			S	S	X	C R Wilkes	7
		X	S	X		X	X	S	X	S1				X		X		X		X			X	S2					X	S W Dunn	8
			X	X	S	X	X	S	X	S				X		X	X			X	S1			S					X	P E Alcock	9
		X	S	X		X	X	S	X			X		X		X		X		X				X			S		X	D J Gallagher	10
		X	S	X		X	X	S	X			X		X		X		X		X	X		X	S1					X	M J Bodenham	11
		X	X		X	X	S	X			X		X		X		X			X			S	X	S				X	M A Riley	12
		X	S2	X		X	X	X	X			X		X		X		X		X			X	S1		S		X	S J Lodge	13
		X	S		S	X	X	X	X	S				X		X		X		X			X	X	S		S	X	G R Ashby	14
		X	S		X	X	X	X	X			X		X		X		X		X		S	X	X	S		S	X	M D Reed	15
S2		X	S		S	X	X	X	X			X		X		X		X		X			X	S1		X	S	X	G P Barber	16
X		X	X		S	X	X	X	X			X		X		X		X	S	X			S					X	D Orr	17
X	S	X		X	S2	X	X	S	X			X		X		X		X		X	S1	X	X					X	G R Ashby	18
X1	S1	X		X	S	X	X	S					X		X	S	X		X	X		X					X	P E Alcock	19
X2	S2	X		X	S	X	X	S					X1		X		X		X	S		X	S		S1	S	X	D R Elleray	20
S1	S2	X	X1		X	X	S			S		X	X2		X	X	X		X	S		X	S				S	A B Wilkie	21
S2	S	X	S1		X	X	X			X1	X2		X		X		X		X	S		X	S		X	S	X	M A Riley	22
S1	S	X	S		S	X	X	X			X	X1	X		X		X		X	S		X	S		X	S	X	G R Ashby	23
S	S	X1			X	X	X			X	X	X	X	X	X				X	S1		S			X	X	G Poll	24
S	S			X		X	X	X			X	X	X	X	X				X	S		S			X	X	P A Durkin	25
S1	S	X	X1		S	X	X	X			X		X	S	X	S			X	X						S	X	J T Winter	26
S2		X			S	X	X	X			X	X2	S	X	S				X1	X		S1					X	G P Barber	27
X	S2	X2	S		X	X	X	X	X1					S	X	S				X	S						X	N S Barry	28
X		X2	S		S1	X	X	X	S2					S	X	X1			X	X	S						X	D R Elleray	29
X2		X	S		S2	X	X						S	X	X	X			X	X							X1	D J Gallagher	30
		X	S	X	S	X	X	X	S1				X	X	X	X	S		X	X						S	X1	M D Reed	31
		S1		X	X	X	X	S	X2	X1		S		X	X	X	S			X	S2				X		X	U D Rennie	32
		X	X1		X	X	X	S2	X	X2	S		X	X	X	S		S		X	S1							P Jones	33
		X	S	X		X	X	X	S	X			X	X	X	S		X		X	S					X	X	P E Alcock	34
S1		X1	S	S		X	X	X			X		X	X	X			X		X	S						X	P Jones	35
S		X	S	X1		X	X			X		X	X	X	X			X	X	S1					X	X	P A Durkin	36
X		X1	S		S	X			S1		X		X	X	X	X		S		X	X					S	M D Reed	37
X		X	X	S		S	X		S	X		X1		X	X	X			X	X					X	X	G S Willard	38
X		X	X	S		X	X		S			X1		X	X	X			X	X					X	X	M J Bodenham	39
X		X	S		X	S	X	S2			X	X	X	X	S	S1		X1	X2						X	X	M D Reed	40
X2		X1	S		X	X			X			X		X	S1	X	S2	X	X1						X	X	A B Wilkie	41
S1	S			X	X	X		S	X	X	X			X		S2	S	X3	S3						X	X	S W Dunn	42
S1	X2			X	X	X		X	X	X	X			X		S2	S	X3	S3	X2	S2	X			X	X	G P Barber	43
X1	X			X	X	X		X	X	X	X			X	S	S1	X	S							X	X	N S Barry	44
S	X1			X	X	X	S		X	X	X			X			X						X	S1		X	X	P A Durkin	45
X	X			X	S		S	X	X	X	X		S1			X	X1								X	X	D J Gallagher	46
S1	X1			X	S			X3	X	X	X		X	X	S3	X2	S2	X						X	X	J T Winter	47
X1	X			S		S			X	X	X	X	X	S	S1	X								X	X	G Poll	48
X	X1			X	S	S			X	X	X	X	S1			X	X							X	X	U D Rennie	49
12		34	3	18		7	35	13	32		2	19	12	12	27	27	33		13	17	1	30	14	5	6		14	31	CP Appearances	
7	4	1	1		5				2	3			1		4	1		3		3					9			1	CP Sub Appearances	
1+1	5	0+1	4	2+1	5	3	5		1	3	2		5	1	4		2	1		3			3+1		0+2			5	CC Appearances	
3+2	6		2+1	0+1	6	4	5		0+3		3	2	2		6	6	5		2+1	6					4+1			4	FAC Appearances	

Also played:(M) Alexander S(15). (M) Berthe S(45,46,47,48,49).(G) Finn S(36). (M) Keith S(49). (M) Moore S(10,14), S1(12). (D) Terrier S3(31), S(6,19).

WEST HAM UNITED

CLUB RECORDS

BIGGEST VICTORIES
League: 8-0 v Rotherham United, Division 2, 8.3.1958
8-0 v Sunderland, Division 1, 19.10.1968
F.A. Cup: 6-0 v Bury, Round 2, 1919-20
6-0 v Arsenal, Round 3, 1945-46
League Cup: 10-0 v Bury, Round 2, 25.10.1984
Europe: No more than 4 goals

BIGGEST DEFEATS
League: 0-7 v Sheffield Wednesday, Division 1, 28.11.1959
0-7 v Everton, Division 1, 22.10.1927
0-7 v Barnsley, Division 2, 1.9.1919
F.A. Cup: 0-5 v Aston Villa, Round 2, 1912-13
0-5 v Tottenham Hotspur, Round 3, 1925-26
1-6 v Queens Park Rangers, Round 4 replay, 28.1.1978
League Cup: 0-6 v Oldham Athletic, Semi-Final, 14.2.1990
Europe 0(ECWC): No more than 3 goals

MOST POINTS
3 points a win: 88, Division 1, 1992-93
2 points a win: 66, Division 2, 1980-81

MOST GOALS
101, 1957-58, Division 2.
Dick 21, Keeble 19, Dare 14, Smith 11, Musgrove 9, Bond 8,
Cantwell 4, Malcolm3, Lewis 3, Newman 2, Grice 2, Landsowne 2,
Allison 2, og 2.

MOST LEAGUE GOALS CONCEDED
107 Division 1, 1931-32

MOST FIRST CLASS MATCHES IN A SEASON
62 (42 League, 4 FA Cup, 10 League Cup, 6 European Cup
Winners Cup) 1965-66

MOST LEAGUE WINS
28, Division 2, 1980-81

MOST LEAGUE DRAWS
18, Division 1, 1968-69

MOST LEAGUE DEFEATS
23, Division 1, 1931-32

INDIVIDUAL CLUB RECORDS

MOST GOALS IN A MATCH
6. Geoff Hurst v Sunderland, 8-0, Division 1, 19.10.1968
6. Vic Watson v Leeds United, 8-2, Division 1, 9.2.1929

MOST GOALS IN A SEASON
Vic Watson 50 (League 42, FAC 8) 1929-30.
4 goals once=4; 3 goals 3 times=9; 2 goals 8 times=16; 1 goal 21
times=21.
Previous holder: Vic Watson 34, 1926-27

OLDEST PLAYER
Billy Bonds 41 years 225 days v Southampton (Div 1), 30.4.1988

YOUNGEST PLAYER
Neil Finn, 17 years 3 days v Manchester City (Prem) 1.1.1996.

MOST CAPPED PLAYER
Bobby Moore (England) 108

BEST PERFORMANCES

League: 1980-81: Matches played 42, Won 28, Drawn 10, Lost 4,
Goals for 79.Goals against 29, Points 66. First in Division 2.

Highest: 1985-86: Third in Division 1.

F.A. Cup: 1963-64: 3rd rnd. Charlton Athletic 3-0; 4th rnd. Orient 1-
1, 3-0;5th rnd. Swindon Town 3-1; 6th rnd. Burnley 3-2; Semi-final
Manchester United3-1; Final Preston North End 3-2.
1974-75: 3rd rnd. Southampton 2-1; 4th rnd. Swindon Town 1-1, 2-1;
5th rnd.Queens Park Rangers 2-1; 6th rnd. Arsenal 2-0; Semi-final
Ipswich Town 0-0, 2-1; Final Fulham 2-0.
1979-80: 3rd rnd. West Bromwich Albion 1-1, 2-1; 4th rnd. Orient 3-
2; 5th rnd.Swansea City 2-0; 6th rnd. Aston Villa 1-0; Semi-final
Everton 1-1, 2-1; Final Arsenal 1-0.

League Cup: 1965-66: 2nd rnd. Bristol Rovers 3-3, 3-2; 3rd rnd.
Mansfield Town4-0; 4th rnd. Rotherham United 2-1; 5th rnd. Grimsby
Town 2-2, 1-0; Semi-final Cardiff City 5-2, 5-1; Final West Bromwich
Albion 2-1, 1-4.

Europe (ECWC): 1964-65: 1st rnd. La Gantoise 1-0, 1-1; 2nd rnd.
Sparta Prague2-0, 1-2; 3rd rnd. Lausanne 2-1, 4-3; Semi-final Real
Zaragoza 2-1, 1-1; Final Munich 1860 2-0.

DIVISIONAL RECORD

	Played	Won	Drawn	Lost	For	Against	Points
Division 1/P	1,788	615	441	732	2,656	2,877	1,869
Division 2/1	1,230	537	300	393	1,958	1,622	1,444
Total	**3,018**	**1,152**	**741**	**1,125**	**4,614**	**4,499**	**3,313**

ADDITIONAL INFORMATION
Previous Name
Thames Ironworks 1895-1900

Previous League
Southern League

Club colours: Claret shirts with sky blue side panels & trim, white
shorts & socks with blue trim.
Change colours: White shirts, shorts & socks with claret & blue
piping.

Reserves League: Avon Insurance Football Combination.

RECORDS AND STATISTICS

COMPETITIONS

Div 1/P	Div.2/1	ECWC	Watney	A/Ital
1923-32	1919-23	1964-65	1973	1975
1958-78	1932-58	1965-66		1992-93
1981-89	1978-81	1975-76	Texaco	
1919-92	1989-91	1980-81	1974-75	
1993-	1992-93			

HONOURS

Div.2	FA Cup	C/Shield	ECWC
1957-58	1963-64	1964	1964-65
1980-81	1974-75		
	1979-80		

MOST APPEARANCES

Billy Bonds 781+12 (1967-88)

Year	League	FA Cup	Lge Cup	ECWC
1967-68	37	3	2	
1968-69	42	3	2	
1969-70	42	1	2	
1970-71	37	1	2	
1971-72	42	4	10	
1972-73	39	2	2	
1973-74	40	2	1	
1974-75	31	8	3	
1975-76	17+1		5	9
1976-77	41	2	3	
1977-78	29	3		
1978-79	39	1	1	
1979-80	34	5	9	
1980-81	41	3	8	6
1981-82	29	2	4	
1982-83	34	1	4	
1983-84	27	0+1	2	
1984-85	19+3		4	
1985-86				
1986-87	13+4	3+1	1+2	
1987-88	22	2		
	655+8	46+2	65+2	15

MOST GOALS IN A CAREER

Vic Watson - 326 (1920-35)

Year	League	FA Cup
1920-21	2	
1921-22	12	1
1922-23	22	5
1923-24	3	
1924-25	22	1
1925-26	20	
1926-27	34	3
1927-28	16	
1928-29	29	1
1929-30	42	8
1930-31	14	
1931-32	23	2
1932-33	23	4
1933-34	26	3
1934-35	10	
Total	298	28

Current leading goalscorer: Julian Dicks - 50 (1988-93, 1994-98)

RECORD TRANSFER FEE RECEIVED

Amount	Club	Player	Date
£4,250,000	Everton	Slaven Bilic	05/97
£2,000,000	Everton	Tony Cottee	7/88
£850,000	Celtic	Frank McAvennie	10/87
£800,000	Manchester Utd	Paul Ince	9/89

RECORD TRANSFER FEE PAID

Amount	Club	Player	Date
£3,200,000	Arsenal	John Hartson	02/97
£2,400,000	Espanol	Florin Raducioiu	7/96
£1,600,000	Tottenham	Ilie Dumitrescu	2/96
£1,500,000	Liverpool	Don Hutchison	8/94

MANAGERS

Name	Seasons	Best	Worst
Syd King	1902-32	7 (1)	7 (2)
Charlie Paynter	1932-50	4 (2)	20 (2)
Ted Fenton	1950-61	6 (1)	16 (1)
Ron Greenwood	1961-77	6 (1)	20 (1)
John Lyall	1977-89	3 (1)	7 (2)
Lou Macari	1989-90		
Billy Bonds	1990-94	13 (P)	7 (2)
Harry Redknapp	1994-	8 (P)	14 (P)

LONGEST LEAGUE RUNS

of undefeated matches:	27 (27.12.1980 - 10.10.1981)	of league matches w/out a win:	17 (31.1.1976 - 21.8.1976)
of undefeated home matches:	27 (30.8.1980 - 21.11.1981)	of undefeated away matches:	13 (10.1.1981 - 3.10.1981)
without home win:	13 (29.10.1988 - 15.4.1989)	without an away win:	31 (12.12.1931 - 14.3.1933)
of league wins:	9 (19.10.1985 - 14.12.1985)	of home wins:	16 (30.8.1980 - 7.3.1981)
of league defeats:	9 (28.3.1932 - 29.8.1932)	of away wins:	5 (16.12.22-15.2.23, 26.12.35-15.3.36, 5.10.85-7.12.85)

WEST HAM UNITED							APPEARANCES				GOALS			
PLAYERS NAME Honours	Ht	Wt	Birthdate	Birthplace Transfers	Contract Date	Clubs	League	L/Cup	FA Cup	Other	Lge	L/C	FAC	Oth
G O A L K E E P E R														
Forrest Craig L	6.4	14.4	9/20/67	Vancouver	8/31/85	Ipswich Town	263	21	14	14				
Can; Div2'92				Loan	3/1/88	Colchester United	11							
				Loan	3/26/97	Chelsea	2+1							
					7/23/97	West Ham United	13	2	4					
Hislop Shaka	6.6	12	2/22/69	London	9/9/92	Reading	104	10	3	9				
E: u21.1. Div2'94				£1575000	8/10/95	Newcastle United	53	8	6	3				
				Free	7/6/98	West Ham United								
Miklosko Ludek	6.5	14	12/9/61	Ostrava		Banik Ostrava								
				£300000	2/19/90	West Ham United	314	25	25	8				
Sealey Les	6	11.6	9/29/57	Bethnal Green	3/1/76	Coventry City	158	11	9					
FAC'90. ECWC'91. CS'90				£100000	8/3/83	Luton Town	207	21	28	3				
				Loan	10/5/84	Plymouth Argyle	6							
				Loan	3/21/90	Manchester United	2		1					
				Free	6/6/90	Manchester United	31	8	3	9				
				Free	7/19/91	Aston Villa	18		4	2				
				Loan	3/25/92	Coventry City	2							
				Loan	10/2/92	Birmingham City	12			3				
				Free	1/6/93	Manchester United		1	+1					
				Free	7/18/94	Blackpool	7	2						
				Free	11/28/94	West Ham United	1+1							
				Free	7/6/96	Leyton Orient	11	2						
				Free	11/29/96	West Ham United	1+1							
				Loan	3/26/98	Bury								
D E F E N C E														
Breacker Tim	6	12.6	7/2/65	Bicester	5/15/83	Luton Town	204+6	22+2	21	7	3			
E: u21.2. LC'88				£600000	10/12/90	West Ham United	227+10	20	26+1	7	8			
Coyne Christopher	6.1	13.1	12/20/78	Brisbane		Perth SC								
					1/13/96	West Ham United								
Dicks Julian	5.7	11.7	12/11/68	Bristol	4/12/86	Birmingham City	83+6	5+1	5	2	1			
E: u21.4, B.2				£300000	3/25/88	West Ham United	159	19	14	11	29	5	2	4
				£1500000	9/17/93	Liverpool	24	3	1		3			
				£1000000	10/20/94	West Ham United	95	10	7		21	3		
Ferdinand Rio G	6.2	12	11/7/78	Peckham	11/27/95	West Ham United	46+5	5+1	7		2			
E: 3, u21.4, Y.				Loan	11/8/96	Bournemouth	10							
Hall Richard	6.1	12.8	3/14/72	Ipswich	3/20/90	Scunthorpe United	22	2	3	4	3			
E: u21.11				£200000	2/13/91	Southampton	89+7	7+1	10	3	11		2	
					7/19/96	West Ham United	7							
Henry Anthony F			9/13/79	London	6/6/97	West Ham Utd (T)								
Keith Joseph R			10/1/78	London	7/9/97	West Ham Utd (T)								
Margas Javier				Chile		D. Catolica								
				£2000000	7/30/98	West Ham United								
Potts Steve	5.8	10.5	5/7/67	Hartford (USA)	5/11/84	West Ham United	334+21	34+2	39+1	14+1	1			
E: Y.11														
Ruddock Neil	6.2	12	09/05/68	Wandsworth	03/03/86	Millwall				3+1				1
E: 1, B.1, Y6, u21.4, u19.5. LC'95.				£50000	14/04/86	Tottenham Hotspur	7+2		1+1				1	
				£250000	13/02/89	Southampton	100+7	14+1	10	6	9	1	3	
				£750000	29/07/92	Tottenham Hotspur	38	4	5		3			
				£2500000	22/07/93	Liverpool	111+4	19+1	11	5+1	11	1		
				Loan		QPR	7							
					7/30/98	West Ham United								
M I D F I E L D														
Berkovic Eyal	5.7	10.2	4/2/72			Maccasi Tel Aviv								
				£1500000	10/11/96	Southampton	26+2	4+1	1		4	1		
					7/30/97	West Ham United	34+1	5	6		7		1	
Etherington Craig			9/16/79	Essex	7/9/97	West Ham Utd (T)								
Impey Andrew	5.8	10.6	9/30/71	Hammersmith		Yeading								
E: u21.1 FAV'90.				£35000	6/14/90	QPR	177+9	15+1	7+3	0+2	13	3	1	1
				£1000000	9/26/97	West Ham United	19	3	3					
Keller Marcus				Germany		Karlsruhe								
				Free	5/5/98	West Ham United								
Lampard Frank	5.1	12.4	6/21/78	Romford	7/1/95	West Ham United	30+16	6+1	7		4	4	1	
Lomas Stephen	6	11.1	1/18/74	Hanover (Ger)	1/22/91	Manchester City	102+9	16	10+1		8	1	1	
NI: 26, B.1, Y, S.				£1600000	3/27/97	West Ham United	40	4	5		2		1	
Mean Scott	5.11	11.11	12/13/73	Crawley	8/10/92	Bournemouth	52+22	7+1	2+1	4	9			
				Loan	3/28/96	West Ham United								
					11/11/96	West Ham United	+3							
				Loan	3/27/97	Bournemouth								
Moncur John	5.7	9.1	9/22/66	Stepney	8/22/84	Tottenham Hotspur	10+11	1+2			1			
					9/25/86	Doncaster Rovers	4							
				Loan	3/27/87	Cambridge United	3+1							

154

	Ht	Wt	DOB	From/Fee	Date	Club								
Moncur continued...				Loan	3/22/89	Portsmouth	7							
				Loan	10/19/89	Brentford	5			1	1			
				Loan	10/24/91	Ipswich Town	5+1							
				£80000	3/30/92	Swindon Town	53+5	4	1	4	5			1
				£900000	8/24/94	West Ham United	92+5	11	6+1		5	2	1	
Omoyimni Emmanuel	5.8	10	12/28/77	Nigeria	8/1/94	West Ham United	1+5				2			
				Loan	9/30/96	Bournemouth	5+2							
				Loan	2/27/98	Dundee United								
Pearce Ian	6.1	12.4	5/7/74	Bury St.Ed.	8/1/91	Chelsea	0+4			0+1				
E: Y.10. Prem'95.				£300000	10/4/93	Blackburn Rovers	43+19	4+4	1+2	6+1	1	1	1	
				£1000000	9/19/97	West Ham United	30	3	6		1		1	
F O R W A R D														
Abou Samassi	6	12.8	8/4/73	Ivory Coast		Cannes								
				£300000	11/8/97	West Ham United	12+7	1+1	3+2		5	1		
Boylan Lee M	5.6	11.2	9/2/78	Chelmsford	5/3/97	West Ham United	0+1							
Y. Ei:														
Hartson John	6.1	14.6	4/5/75	Swansea	12/19/92	Luton Town	21+13	+1	2+3	2	6		1	
W:15, u21.9, Y.				£2500000	1/13/95	Arsenal	43+10	2+4	2+1	8+1	14	1	1	1
				£3200000	2/14/97	West Ham United	43	5	5		20	6	4	
Hodges Lee Leslie	5.4	9.06	3/2/78	Newham	8/1/94	West Ham United	+2		+3					
				Loan	9/13/96	Exeter City	16+1							
				Loan	2/28/97	Leyton Orient	3							
Kitson Paul	5.11	10.12	1/9/71	Peterlee	12/15/88	Leicester City	39+11	5	1+1	5	6	3	1	1
E: u21.7. FLg u18.1				£1300000	3/11/92	Derby County	105	7	5	13+1	36	3	1	9
				£2250000	9/24/94	Newcastle United	26+10	3+1	6+1	+1	10	1	3	
				£2300000	2/10/97	West Ham United	26+1	2	2		12		1	
Lazaridis Stan	5.9	12	8/16/72	Perth		West Adelaide								
Int. Austrlian				£300000	8/1/95	West Ham United	42+12	5+1	7+1		3			
Sinclair Trevor	5.1	11.2	3/2/73	Dulwich	8/21/90	Blackpool	84+28	8	6+1	8+5	15			1
E: B.1, u21.14, Y.1, S				£600000	8/12/93	QPR	162+5	13	10		16	3	2	
				£2300000	1/30/98	West Ham United	14				7			
Wright Ian	5.1	11	03/11/63	Woolwich		Greenwich Boro								
E:31,B.3. FMC'91. LC'93. FAC'93'98. Prem'98				Free	02/08/85	Crystal Palace	206+19	19	9+2	19+3	90	9	3	16
				£2500000	24/09/91	Arsenal	212+9	29	16	22	128	29	12	16
					14/07/98	West Ham United								
ADDITIONAL CONTRACT PLAYERS														
Alexander Gary G					10/26/97	West Ham United (T								

THE MANAGER
HARRY REDKNAPP

Date of Birth . . . . 2nd March 1947.
Place of Birth . . . . Poplar.
Date of Appointment . . . . 10th August 1994.

PREVIOUS CLUBS
As Manager . . . . Bournemouth.
As Coach. . . . . None.
As a Player. . . . . West Ham United, Bournemouth, Brentford.

HONOURS
As a Manager
Bournemouth: Division 3 champions 1987.

As a Player
None.

UPTON PARK
Green Street, London E13 9AZ

Capacity ....25,985.

First game..v Millwall, Sth Lge, 1.9.1904.
First floodlit game ....v Tottenham Hotspur, 16.4.1953.

ATTENDANCES
Highest ....42,322 v Tottenham, Div.1, 17.10.1970.
Lowest ....4,500 v Doncaster, Div.2, 24.2.1955.

OTHER GROUNDS...............Memorial Recreation Ground, Canning Town 1900-04. Upton Park 1904-

HOW TO GET TO THE GROUND

From the North and West
Take North Circular (A406) to A124 (East Ham), then on Barking Road for approx 1.5 miles until you approach traffic lights on crossroads. Turn right into Green Street, ground is on right hand side.

From the East
Use A13, sign posted London, then at crossroads turn right (A117). In 0.9 miles at crossroads turn left (A124). In 0.6 miles turn right into Green Street for West Ham United FC.

From the South
Use Blackwall Tunnel and A13 to Canning Town, then follow signs East Ham (A124). In 1.7 miles turn left into Green Street for West Ham United FC.

Car Parking: Ample side-street parking available.
Nearest Railway Station: Upton Park (District Line Tube).

USEFUL TELEPHONE NUMBERS

Club switchboard 0181 548 2748
Club fax number........................0181 548 2758
Club shop 0181 548 2722
Ticket Office..............................0181 548 2700

Marketing Department 0181 548 2777
Internet address ......www.westhamunited.co.uk
Clubcall 0891 12 11 65*
*Calls cost 50p per minute at all times. Call costings correct at time of going to press.

MATCHDAY PROGRAMME

Programme Editor .... Peter Stewart.

Number of pages .... 48.

Price......................... £2.

Subscriptions .... Apply to club.

Local Newspapers
.... Stratford Express, Ilford Recorder.

Local Radio Stations
.... Essex Radio.

MATCHDAY TICKET PRICES

West Stand
Upper Tier................................. £14-£31
Lower Tier................................. £14-£24

East Stand
Upper Tier................................. £14-£31
Lower Tier................................. £14-£31

Bobby Moore Stand
Upper .... £14-£23
Lower .... £11-£19

Centenary Stand
Upper.................................... £18
Lower (Visitors) .... £11-£20

WIMBLEDON
(The Crazy Gang)
F.A. CARLING PREMIERSHIP
SPONSORED BY: ELONEX

1998-99 Back Row: Marcus Gayle, Carl Cort, Neil Sullivan, Mick Harford (Coach), Paul Heald, Dean Blackwell, Ben Thatcher.
Middle Row: Stuart Murdoch (G/K Coach), David Kemp (Coach), Duncan Jupp, Mark Kennedy, Efan Ekoku, Jon Goodman, Carl Leaburn, Andy Roberts, Damien Francis, Brian McAllister, Andy Clarke, Steve Allen (Physio). **Front Row:** Jason Euell, Chris Perry, Stewart Castledine, Kenny Cunningham, Robbie Earle, Joe Kinnear (Manager), Neal Ardley, Michael Hughes, Alan Kimble, Peter Fear, Ceri Hughes. **Inset:** Lawrie Sanchez (Coach)

WIMBLEDON
FORMED IN 1889
TURNED PROFESSIONAL IN 1964
LTD COMPANY IN 1964

PARTNER/GOVERNOR
S G N Hammam. Partners: Kjell Inge Rokke,
Bjorn Rune Gjelsten.
CHAIRMAN: S G Reed
DEPUTY-CHAIRMAN: J H Lelliott
DIRECTORS
P E Cork, PR Lloyd Cooper,
N N Hamman, P. Miller, Jan-Peter Storetvedt
CHIEF EXECUTIVE
David Barnard
SECRETARY
Steve Rooke (0181 771 2233)
MARKETING MANAGER
Sharon Sillitoe
PR & MEDIA MANAGER: Reg Davis
MANAGER: Joe Kinnear
COACHES: Mick Harford, David Kemp &
Lawrie Sanchez.
YOUTH TEAM MANAGER
Ernie Tippett
PHYSIOTHERAPIST
Steve Allen

1997-98 was not one of Wimbledon's best seasons in the top flight - in fact it was their worst in terms of performances! And in fact they only managed to wrestle themselves away from the claws of relegation just after the Easter programme.

It is acceptable now to see Wimbledon playing no-nonsense football, performing with very few stars, doing the simple things and gaining results. But this last season things didn't go according to how manager Joe Kinnear had planned.

They began nervously and after half-a-dozen games had been completed, found themselves positioned third from bottom.

There was, however, some improved performances and results got better over the next two months and come mid-November the Dons had risen to 10th place, just eight points behind champions-to-be Arsenal; who were third!

But then a series of disappointing scorelines saw the Dons fall from grace, gradually slithering down the ladder and at the turn of the year they were down to 14th place, only four points clear of relegation trouble.

But manager Kinnear never doubted his players' talents and commitment, and with some gritty, determined displays, Wimbledon battled on willingly, so much so that going into the last quarter of their Carling Premiership programme they were still a some trouble but had now six points to spare over the relegation candidates.

Hardman Vinny Jones departed company (transferred to Q.P.R.) but his absence didn't effect Wimbledon's competitive performances and they ended the season reasonably well, despite a 6-2 home whipping by neighbours Spurs.

A final position of 15th (one lower than their previous 'worst' in the top flight) was just about what Wimbledon's form of 1997-98 deserved. They certainly had their ups and downs, at home and away, but as always the players came out fighting and if manager Kinnear can hold on to his senior players, namely Neil Sullivan, Dean Blackwell, Chris Perry (who had a terrific season), Jamaica's Robbie Earle and Marcus Gayle, the Norwegian World Cup star Staale Solbakken (signed for £250,000 from Lillestrom), Carl Cort, a fit again Efan Ekoku and Neal Ardley, and add perhaps a couple of experienced professionals to this squad, then 1998-99 should be a far better campaign than the last one for the 'Wombles of Wimbledon'.

Tony Matthews.

WIMBLEDON

Carling Prem.	:15th			FA CUP: 5th Round			LC CUP: 3rd Round			

M	DATE	COMP.	VEN	OPPONENTS	RESULT	H/T	LP	GOAL SCORERS/GOAL TIMES	ATT.
1	A 09	CP	H	Liverpool	D 1-1	0-0	10	Gayle 56	26106
2	23	CP	H	Sheffield Wednesday	D 1-1	1-0	14	Euell 17	11503
3	27	CP	H	Chelsea	L 0-2	0-0	17		22237
4	30	CP	A	West Ham United	L 1-3	0-0	20	Ekoku 80	(24516)
5	S 13	CP	A	Newcastle United	W 3-1	1-1	15	Cort 1, Perry 58, Ekoku 75	(36526)
6	16	CC 2/1	H	Millwall	W 5-1	2-1		Cort 24 (pen), 80, Clarke 44, Euell 56, Castledine 86	6949
7	20	CP	H	Crystal Palace	L 0-1	0-0	18		16747
8	23	CP	H	Barnsley	W 4-1	0-1	13	Cort 49, Earle 64, Hughes C 67, Ekoku 83	7976
9	27	CP	A	Tottenham Hotspur	D 0-0	0-0	15		(26261)
10	O 01	CC 2/2	A	Millwall	W 4-1	2-0		Euell 22, 43, Castledine 47, Gayle 50	(3591)
11	04	CP	H	Blackburn Rovers	L 0-1	0-1	15		15600
12	14	CC 3	A	Bolton Wanderers	L 0-2	0-0			(9875)
13	18	CP	A	Aston Villa	W 2-1	1-1	12	Earle 39, Cort 62	(32087)
14	22	CP	A	Derby County	D 1-1	0-0	11	, Rowett 70 (OG)	(28595)
15	25	CP	H	Leeds United	W 1-0	0-0	9	Ardley 29	15718
16	N 01	CP	H	Coventry City	L 1-2	1-2	10	Cort 27	11201
17	10	CP	A	Leicester City	W 1-0	0-0	9	Gayle 50	(18553)
18	22	CP	H	Manchester United	L 2-5	0-0	10	Ardley 67, Hughes 70	26309
19	29	CP	A	Bolton Wanderers	L 0-1	0-0	11		(22703)
20	D 07	CP	H	Southampton	W 1-0	1-0	10	Earle 17	12009
21	13	CP	A	Everton	D 0-0	0-0	11		(28533)
22	26	CP	A	Chelsea	D 1-1	1-1	12	Hughes 28	(34100)
23	28	CP	H	West Ham United	L 1-2	0-1	12	Solbakken 89	22087
24	J 4	FAC 3	H	Wrexham	D 0-0	0-0			6349
25	10	CP	A	Liverpool	L 0-2	0-0	14		(38011)
26	13	FAC 3R	A	Wrexham	W 3-2	3-1		Hughes 17, 26, Gayle 35	(9539)
27	17	CP	H	Derby County	D 0-0	0-0	14		13031
28	24	FAC 4	A	Huddersfield Town	W 1-0	0-0		Ardley 61	(14533)
29	31	CP	A	Sheffield Wednesday	D 1-1	1-1	16	Hughes 21	(22655)
30	F 09	CP	A	Crystal Palace	W 3-0	0-0	15	Leaburn 47, 51, Euell 57	(14410)
31	14	FAC 5	H	Wolverhampton Wand	D 1-1	1-0		Euell 15	15332
32	21	CP	H	Aston Villa	W 2-1	2-1	13	Euell 10, Leaburn 38	13131
33	25	FAC 5R	A	Wolverhampton Wand	L 1-2	0-0		Jones 48	(25112)
34	28	CP	A	Barnsley	L 1-2	0-1	15	Euell 72	(17102)
35	M 11	CP	H	Arsenal	L 0-1	0-1	15		22291
36	14	CP	H	Leicester City	W 2-1	1-0	14	Roberts 14, Hughes 61	13229
37	28	CP	A	Manchester United	L 0-2	0-0	14		(55306)
38	31	CP	H	Newcastle United	D 0-0	0-0	14		15478
39	A 04	CP	H	Bolton Wanderers	D 0-0	0-0	14		11356
40	11	CP	A	Southampton	W 1-0	1-0	13	Leaburn 38	(14815)
41	13	CP	H	Everton	D 0-0	0-0	13		15131
42	18	CP	A	Arsenal	L 0-5	0-3	13		(38024)
43	25	CP	A	Blackburn Rovers	D 0-0	0-0	14		(24848)
44	29	CP	A	Coventry City	D 0-0	0-0	14		(17968)
45	M 02	CP	H	Tottenham Hotspur	L 2-6	2-2	16	Fear 21, 29	25820
46	10	CP	A	Leeds United	D 1-1	0-0	15	Ekoku 88	(38172)

Best Home League Attendance: 26309 V Manchester United   **Smallest :7976 V Barnsley**   **Average :16682**

Goal Scorers:

CP	(34)	Cort 4, Ekoku 4, Euell 4, Hughes M 4, Leaburn 4, Earle 3, Ardley 2, Fear 2, Gayle 2, Hughes C 1, Perry 1, Roberts 1, Solbakken 1, Opponents 1
CC	(9)	Euell 3, Castledine 2, Cort 2, Clarke 1, Gayle 1
FAC	(6)	Hughes M 2, Ardley 1, Euell 1, Gayle 1, Jones 1

1997-98

(F) Ardley	(D) Blackwell	(M) Castledine	(F) Clarke	(F) Cort	(D) Cunningham	(M) Earle	(F) Ekoku	(F) Euell	(M) Fear	(M) Francis	(F) Gayle	(G) Heald	(F) Holdsworth	(F) Hughes M	(M) Hughes C	(M) Jones	(D) Jupp	(F) Kennedy	(D) Kimble	(F) Leaburn	(D) McAllister	(D) Perry	(D) Reeves	(M) Roberts	(M) Solbakken	(G) Sullivan	(D) Thatcher	Referee	#
X	X	S3	S2		X	X	X				X		S	X		S1	X		X			X				X	S	G.S. Willard	1
X	X		S1		X	X	S2	X			X		S	X		S3	X		X			X				X	S	A B Wilkie	2
X	X		S1		X	X	X	S2			X		S	X		S		S	X		X	X				X		M J Bodenham	3
X	X		S3		X	X	S2	X			S1		S	X		S		X	X		X	X				X		G Poll	4
X	X	S1	S		X			X	S			X		S	X	X			X			X				X	S2	M D Reed	5
		X	X	X	X		X				S3	X	S2		X	S1	X			X	X						X	K W Burge	6
	X	X	S3	X	X	S	X				X	S	S2		X	X			X			X				X	S1	P E Alcock	7
	X		S		X	X	X	X			S	S	S		X	X			X			X				X	S1	J T Winter	8
	X				X	X	X	S2			S	S	S	S	X	X	X		X			X				X	S1	P A Durkin	9
		X	X		X			S1	X	X	X	X			X							X	S2			S	X	S W Dunn	10
X	X			X	X			S2			S1	S		X	X	X			X			S				X	S	D J Gallagher	11
		X	S1	S2	X	X	X				X					X			S3		X	X				X	X	N S Barry	12
S1	X		X	X	X	X					S	S		X	X	X			S		S	X				X	X	K W Burge	13
S1	X	S		X	X	X					S	S		X	X	X			S2		X					X	X	U D Rennie	14
X	X	S	S		X	X					S1	S			X	X	X				S	X				X	X	G P Barber	15
S3	X		S2	X	X	X					S1	S			X	X	X				S	X				X	X	U D Rennie	16
X	X		S	X							X	S		X	X	X	X	S				X		S	S	X	X	M A Riley	17
X	X		S2	X	X	S3					X	S		X	X	X			S			X		S1		X	X	P A Durkin	18
X	X		S	X	X	S					X	S		X	X	X			S			X		S		X	X	J T Winter	19
X	X		S	X1	X						X2	S		X		S2	S	S1				X				X	X	M D Reed	20
X	X	S	S1	X1	X						X2	S		X		S2						X			S	X	X	G R Ashby	21
X	X	S	S	S1	X						X1	S		X		X	S					X			S	X	X	G S Willard	22
X	X	S2	S1	X	X						X1	S		X	S	X2						X			S	X	X	P A Durkin	23
X		S2	X3	X	X						S3			X	X	S1			X			X			X1	X	X2		24
X	X		S2	X1	X						X2	S		X		X			X		S1	X				S	X	M J Bodenham	25
X	X		S	X1	X	X	S1				X	S		X	S	X			X			X				S	X	S W Dunn	26
X	X		S	X1	X						X1	S		X	S	X			X			X				S	X	P Jones	27
X	X	S1	S3	X	X	X1			S		X3	S		X		X2			X			X			S2	X		D R Elleray	28
X	X	X	S		X						S1	S		X					X	X		X	S		S	X		A B Wilkie	29
X2	X	S2	S1	S							X1			X		X			X	X		X	S		X	X	X	K W Burge	30
X	X	S	S1	X1							X	X		S		X	X		S			X	S			X	X	U D Rennie	31
X	X		S	S2							X	X		X2	S				X	X1		X	S	S1	X	X	X	G R Ashby	32
X	X	S1	S3	S2							X3	X2		X	S				X	X1		X	S			X	X	U D Rennie	33
X	X	X1		S	X						X	S1		X		X			X			X	S			X	X	G P Barber	34
X	X		S3	X							X3		S	S1		X			X	X1	S2	X			X	X	X2	D J Gallagher	35
X	X		S		X	X					X	S		X	S				X		X	X	S	X		X	X	M A Riley	36
X		S	S	X	X				S		X	S1	S	X					X		X	X	S	X		X	X	D J Gallagher	37
X	X		S	S	X	X					X	S		X	S				X		X	X		X		X	X	N S Barry	38
X1	X	S1		X	X		X1	S3			S1	S		X	S				X	X3		X		X		X	X	M J Bodenham	39
X	X		S	X	X						X1	S		X	S1				X			X	S	X		X	X	M D Reed	40
X	X		S1						S2		X		S	X	X2				X1			S		X		X	X	K W Burge	41
X2	X3		X	S1	X						X3	S		X	X1				S			S3	X		X	X	X	P Jones	42
X	X1			X	X						S	S		X2					S			X	X		X	X	X	G Poll	43
X	X1				X	X			S2	X2	S3	S		S	S				X3	X	X	S1	X		X	X	X	J T Winter	44
									S	X1	X	S	S2	S		X		S3			X3	X	X2	X		X	X	G P Barber	45
X									S1	X1	X	S			S			S			X	X	X	X	X	X	X	S W Dunn	46
31	35	3	1	16	32	20	11	14	5		21		4	29	13	22	3	4	23	15	4	35		12	4	38	23	CP Appearances	
3		3	13	6		2	5	5	3	2	9		1		4	2			2	1	3			2			3	CP Sub Appearances	
		3	2+1	1+1	3	1	1+1	3	1		2+1		2	0+1		2	1+1	1		0+1		2	3	0+1		1	3	CC Appearances	
5	4	1+2	0+4	4+1	3	3	0+1	2	2		3+1			4		2	3+1	2		3			5		1+1	5	3	FAC Appearances	

WIMBLEDON

CLUB RECORDS

BIGGEST VICTORIES
League: 6-0 v Newport County, Division 3, 3.9.1983
F.A. Cup: 7-2 v Windsor & Eton, Rnd 1, 22.11.1980
League Cup: 5-0 v Blackburn, Round 1, 24.9.1985

BIGGEST DEFEATS
League: 1-7 v Aston Villa (A), Premier League, 11.2.95.
1-6 v Carlisle Utd., Division 2, 23.3.1985
1-6 v Gillingham, Division 2, 13.2.1982
1-6 v Newcastle Utd (A), Premier League, 21.10.95.
F.A. Cup: 0-6 v Fulham, Rnd 1 replay, 1930-31
League Cup: 0-8 v Everton, Round 2, 29.8.1978

MOST POINTS
3 points a win: 98, Division 4, 1982-83.
2 points a win: 61, Division 4, 1978-79.

MOST GOALS
97, 1983-84, Division 3
Cork 28, Hodges 16, Evans 12, Fishender 8, Ketteridge 7, Downes 4, Park 4, Morris 3, Peters 3, Smith 3, Thomas 3, Hatter 2, Galliers 1, Winterburn 1, og2.

MOST LEAGUE GOALS CONCEDED
81, Division 3, 1979-80

MOST FIRST CLASS MATCHES IN A SEASON
56 (46 League, 2 FA Cup, 2 League Cup, 6 Football League Group Cup) 1981-82

MOST LEAGUE WINS
29, Division 4, 1982-83

MOST LEAGUE DRAWS
16, Division 1, 1977-78, 1989-90

MOST LEAGUE DEFEATS
22, Division 3, 1979-80

INDIVIDUAL CLUB RECORDS

MOST GOALS IN A MATCH
4. Alan Cork v Torquay United, Division 4, 28.2.1979 (4-1).

MOST GOALS IN A SEASON
Alan Cork 33, (League 29, FAC 2, Lge C 2) 1983-84
3 goals once=3; 2 goals 6 times=12; 1 goal 17 times=17

OLDEST PLAYER
Dave Donaldson, 37 years 4 months. v Hartlepool (Div 4) 9.2.1979.

YOUNGEST PLAYER
Kevin Gage 17 years 15 days v Bury (Div 4), 2.5.1981.

MOST CAPPED PLAYER
Kenny Cinningham (Eire) 13.

BEST PERFORMANCES

League: 1982-83: Matches played 46, Won 29, Drawn 11, Lost 6, Goals for 95, Goals against 45, Points 98. First in Division 4.

Highest: 1986-87, 1993-94: 6th in Division 1.

F.A. Cup: 1987-88: 3rd rnd. West Bromwich Albion 4-1 (h); 4th rnd. MansfieldTown 2-1 (a); 5th rnd. Newcastle United 3-1 (a); 6th rnd. Watford 2-1 (a); Semi-final Luton Town 2-1; Final Liverpool 1-0.

League Cup: 1993-94: 5th Round

ADDITIONAL INFORMATION
Previous Name
Wimbledon Old Centrals 1889-1905

Previous Leagues
Isthmian League, Southern League

Club colours: Dark blue with yellow trim.

Change colours: Red with black trim.

DIVISIONAL RECORD

	Played	Won	Drawn	Lost	For	Against	Points
Division 1/P	478	169	147	162	616	617	654
Division 2	84	37	23	24	129	113	134
Division 3	138	50	34	54	210	232	174
Division 4	184	91	47	46	304	204	258
Total	884	347	251	286	1,259	1,166	1,220

RECORDS AND STATISTICS

COMPETITIONS

Div.1/P	Div.2	Div.3	Div.4
1986-	1984-86	1979-80	1977-79
		1981-82	1980-81
		1983-84	1982-83

HONOURS

Division 4	FA Cup
1982-83	1988

MOST GOALS IN A CAREER

	Alan Cork - 167 (1977-92)		
Year	League	FA Cup	Lge Cup
1977-78	4		
1978-79	22	2	1
1979-80	12		1
1980-81	23	2	1
1981-82			
1982-83	5		
1983-84	29	2	2
1984-85	11		
1985-86	11		4
1986-87	5		2
1987-88	9	1	2
1988-89	2		
1989-90	5		
1990-91	5	1	
1991-92	2		
Total	145	8	14

Current leading goalscorer: Efangwu Ekoku - 35 (1994-98)

MOST APPEARANCES

	Alan Cork 414+96 (1977-92)			
Year	League	FA Cup	Lge Cup	Others
1977-78	17			
1978-79	45	5	3	
1979-80	41+1	5	5	
1980-81	41	5	4	
1981-82	6		2	
1982-83	7			
1983-84	41+1	2	5	1
1984-85	26+2	5	1	
1985-86	36+2	1	3	
1986-87	22+8	0+3	1	
1987-88	28+6	5+1	2+1	0+1
1988-89	9+16	1+1	2+2	0+1
1989-90	12+19	0+1	0+1	1+1
1990-91	9+16	1+1	1+1	1+0
1991-92	12+7		0+2	0+1
	352+78	30+7	29+7	3+4

RECORD TRANSFER FEE RECEIVED

Amount	Club	Player	Date
£4,000,000	Newcastle Utd	Warren Barton	06/95
£3,750,000	Liverpool	Oyvind Leonhardsen	00/07
£3,500,000	Bolton	Dean Holdsworth	10/97
£3,500,000	Liverpool	John Scales	08/94

MANAGERS

Name	Seasons	Best	Worst
Allen Batsford	1977-78	13(4)	13(3)
Dario Gradi	1978-81	22(3)	4(4)
Dave Bassett	1981-87	6(1)	1(4)
Bobby Gould	1987-90	7(1)	12(1)
Ray Harford	1990-91	7(1)	7(1)
Peter Withe	1991-92		
Joe Kinnear	1992-	6 (P)	15 (P)

RECORD TRANSFER FEE PAID

Amount	Club	Player	Date
£2,000,000	Liverpool	Mark Kennedy	03/98
£2,000,000	Crystal Palace	Andy Roberts	03/98
£1,600,000	West Ham	Michael Hughes	09/97
£1,600,000	Millwall	Ben Thatcher	07/96

LONGEST LEAGUE RUNS

of undefeated matches:	22 (15.1.1983 - 14.5.1983)	of league matches w/out a win:	14 (23.2.1980 - 15.4.1980 16.9.95 - 26.12.95)
of undefeated home matches:	21 (22.1.1983 - 3.12.1983)	of undefeated away matches:	12 (22.1.1983 - 27.8.1983)
without home win:	9 (23.9.95 - 20.1.96)	without an away win:	11 (5.4.1989-30.9.1989, 14.9.1991-25.2.1992)
of league wins:	7 (9.4.1983 - 7.5.1983)	of home wins:	8 (9.4.1983 - 17.9.1983, 8.4.1978 - 14.10.1978)
of league defeats:	7 (16.9.95 - 6.11.95, 4.9.96 - 19.10.97)	of away wins:	3 (23.12.78-28.2.79, 31.3.84-14.4.84, 10.4.91-20.4.91)

WIMBLEDON

PLAYERS NAME Honours	Ht	Wt	Birthdate	Birthplace Transfers	Contract Date	Clubs	League	L/Cup	FA Cup	Other	Lge	L/C	FAC	Oth
G O A L K E E P E R														
Heald Paul A	6.2	12.5	9/20/68	Wath on Dearne	6/30/87	Sheffield United								
					12/2/88	Leyton Orient	176	13	9	21				
					3/10/92	Coventry City	2							
				Loan	3/24/94	Swindon Town	1+1							
				£125000	7/25/95	Wimbledon	20+1	5						
Murphy Brendan	5.11	11.12	8/19/75	Wexford		Bradford City								
				Free	9/26/94	Wimbledon								
Sullivan Neil S: 3	6	12.1	2/24/70	Sutton	7/26/88	Wimbledon	105+1	8	19					
				Loan	5/1/92	Crystal Palace	1							
D E F E N C E														
Blackwell Dean E: u21.6	6.1	12.1	12/5/69	Camden	7/7/88	Wimbledon	132+22	11	20+1	1	1			
				Loan	3/15/90	Plymouth Argyle	5+2							
Cunningham Ken Ei: u21.4, B.1	5.11	11.2	6/28/71	Dublin		Tolka Rov								
					9/18/89	Millwall	132+4	10	1	5+1	1		1	
				£650000	11/9/94	Wimbledon	127+2	12	21					
Futcher Andrew	5.7	10.07	2/10/78	Enfield	8/1/94	Wimbledon								
Hawkins Peter S	6	11.4	9/18/78	Maidstone	5/31/97	Wimbledon								
Hodges Danny	6	12.7	9/14/76	Greenwich	1/1/00	Wimbledon								
Jupp Duncan A	6	12.12	1/25/75	Haslemere	7/12/93	Fulham	101+4	10+2	9+1	9+1	2		1	1
					8/25/96	Wimbledon	9	2	2+2					
Kimble Alan Div3'91	5.11	12.4	8/6/66	Dagenham	8/8/84	Charlton Athletic	6							
				Loan	8/23/85	Exeter City	1	1						
				Free	8/22/86	Cambridge United	295+4	23+1	29	22	24		1	
				£175000	7/27/93	Wimbledon	122+5	14+1	19					
McAllister Brian	5.11	12.5	11/30/70	Glasgow	3/1/89	Wimbledon	74+11	7+1	5+3	1				
				Loan	12/5/90	Plymouth Argyle	7+1							
				Loan	3/8/96	Crewe Alexandra								
Pearce Andy	6.6	14.6	4/20/66	Bradford-on-Avon		Halesowen Town								
				£15000	5/14/90	Coventry City	68+3	6	3	1	4			
				£500000	6/24/93	Sheffield Wednesday	63+3	10+1	6+1		3		1	
				£600000	11/22/95	Wimbledon	7+1		1+2					
Perry Chris	5.8	10.8	4/20/70	Surrey	7/2/91	Wimbledon	122+9	14	21		2		1	
Thatcher Ben	5.11	11.1	11/30/75	Swindon	6/8/92	Millwall	46+2	4	5	1	1			
				£1900000	7/5/96	Wimbledon	32+3	3	2					
M I D F I E L D														
Castledine Stewart	6.1	12.13	1/22/73	Wandsworth	7/2/91	Wimbledon	17+10	4	2+3		4	3		
				Loan	8/25/95	Wycombe Wanderers								
Earle Robbie Jamaican Int.	5.9	10.1	1/27/65	N'castle-u-Lyme	7/5/82	Port Vale	284+10	21+2	20+1	18+1	77	4	4	5
				£775000	7/19/91	Wimbledon	222+2	21	30	1	51	5	7	1
Fear Peter E: u21.3	5.11	11.7	9/10/73	Sutton	7/2/92	Wimbledon	51+19	8+2	4		3	1		
Francis Damien J	6.1	10.7	2/27/79	London	5/31/97	Wimbledon	+2							
Hughes Ceri M W: 8, B.2, Y	5.9	11.6	2/26/71	Pontypridd	7/1/89	Luton Town	157+18	13	12	4	16	1	2	
					7/4/97	Wimbledon	13+4	2	1		1			
Odlum Gary M	5.11	11.4	10/19/78	Beckenham	5/31/97	Wimbledon								
Roberts Andrew J	5.11	11.5	3/20/74	Dartford	10/29/91	Millwall	132+6	12	7	4	5	2		1
				£2520000	6/1/95	Crystal Palace	106+2	7+1	8	6	2			1
				£1200000	3/10/98	Wimbledon	12				1			
F O R W A R D														
Ardley Neal E: u21.10	5.11	11.9	9/1/72	Epsom	7/29/91	Wimbledon	122+16	13+3	17+2		10	2	1	
Clarke Andrew E: S-P.2. GMVC'91	5.11	11.7	7/22/67	Islington		Barnet			5+1				1	
				£250000	2/21/91	Wimbledon	74+96	13+12	9+7		17	4	2	

Player	Ht	Wt	DOB	From	Date	Club	App Lge	App FLC	App FAC	App Oth	Gls Lge	Gls FLC	Gls FAC	Gls Oth
Cort Carl	6.4	12.7	11/1/77	Southwark	6/7/96	Wimbledon	16+7	1+1	3+1		4	2		
				Loan	2/3/97	Lincoln City	5+1				1			
Ekoku Efangwu	6.1	12	6/8/67	Manchester		Sutton United			1					
Nigerian Int.				£100000	5/11/90	Bournemouth	43+19	+2	5+2	3+1	21		2	2
				£500000	3/26/93	Norwich City	21+10	2	1+1	3	15	1		1
				£900000	10/14/94	Wimbledon	90+10	7+1	16+1		31	1	3	
Euell Jason	6.2	12.7	2/6/77	London		Wimbledon	22+13	4	3+5		8	3	1	
Gayle Marcus	6.1	12.9	9/27/70	Hammersmith	7/6/89	Brentford	118+38	6+3	6+2	14+6	22		2	2
E: Y.1. Jamaican Int. Div3'92				£250000	3/24/94	Wimbledon	108+25	13+1	15+2		17	5	3	
Goodman Jon	6	12.3	8/2/71	Walthamstow		West Ham United								
				Free		Bromley								
				£50000	8/20/90	Millwall	97+20	5+4	5+1	3	27			
				£650000	11/9/94	Wimbledon	28+31	1+1	3+4		11		3	
Hinds Leigh M	5.8	10.7	8/17/78	Beckenham	5/31/97	Wimbledon								
Hughes Michael E	5.6	10.8	8/2/71	Larne	8/17/88	Manchester City	25+1	5	1	1	1			
				£450000	4/1/92	Strasbourg								
				Loan	11/29/94	West Ham United	15+2		2		2			
				Free	7/4/96	West Ham United	61+5	7	5		3		1	
				£800000	9/25/97	Wimbledon	29		3		4		2	
Kennedy Mark	5.11	11.9	5/15/76	Dublin	5/6/92	Millwall	37+6	6+1	3+1		9	2	1	
Ei: 18, u21.7, Y5, S.				£1500000	3/21/95	Liverpool	5+11	0+2	0+2	0+2				
				Loan	1/27/98	QPR	8				2			
				£1750000	3/27/98	Wimbledon	4							
Leaburn Carl	6.3	13	3/30/69	Lewisham	4/22/87	Charlton Athletic	276+46	19	19+2	9+5	53	5	4	4
E: Y1,u.19.				Loan	3/22/90	Northampton Town	9							
				£000000	1/0/08	Wimbledon	15+1				4			
O'Connor Richard	5.9	10.7	8/30/78	Wandsworth	6/7/96	Wimbledon								
Renner Victor D	6	11.2	4/18/79	Sierra Leone		Wimbledon (T)								

The Manager
Joe Kinnear

Date of Birth .... 27th December 1946.
Place of Birth .... Dublin.
Date of Appointment .... January 1991.

Previous Clubs
As Manager .... Doncaster.
As Reserve Team Manager .... Wimbledon.
As a Player .... Tottenham Hotspur, Brighton & Hove Albion.

Honours
As a Manager
5 Managers' Manager Awards - Managers' Manager of 1994-95.

As a Player
Tottenham: FA Cup winner 1967. League Cup winner 1970/71, 1971/72. UEFA Cup winner 1972/73.
International: 26 full caps for Eire.

SELHURST PARK
London SE25 6PY

Capacity 26,309

First game ....v Sheffield Wed., Division 2, 30.8.1924.
First floodlit game ....v Chelsea, 28.9.1953.
ATTENDANCES
Highest ....30,115 v Manchester Utd, Prem, 9.5.1993.
Lowest ....2,151 v Hereford, Lge Cup, 5.9.1993.

PREVIOUS GROUNDS...Plough Lane

HOW TO GET TO THE GROUND

From the North
From motorway (M1) or A1, use A406 North Circular Road to Chiswick. Follow signs South Circular Road (A205) to Wandsworth. Then use A3 to A214 and follow signs to Streatham. Join A23. In 1 mile turn left (B273). At the end turn left into High Street then forward into Whitehorse Lane for Crystal Palace FC.
From the East
Use A232 (sign posted Croydon) to Shirley then join A215 (sign posted Norwood). In 2.2 miles turn left (B266) into Whitehouse Lane.
From the South
Use A23 (sign posted London) then follow signs Crystal Palace (B266) via Thornton Heath into Whitehorse Lane.
From the West
Use motorway (M4) to Chiswick then route from North or A232 (sign posted Croydon) to Beddington, then follow signs London A23. After, follow signs Crystal Palace (B266) via Thornton Heath into Whitehorse Lane.

Car Parking: Sainsbury's car park (468 spaces) on first come first served basis. Street parking is also available.
Nearest Railway Station: Thornton Heath/Norwood Junction/Selhurst.

USEFUL TELEPHONE NUMBERS

Club switchboard 0181 771 2233
Club fax number 0181 768 0640
Club shop 0181 768 6100
Ticket Office 0181 771 8841

Marketing Department. 0181 771 2233
Internet address . . . . www.wimbledonfc.co.uk
Clubcall 0891 12 11 75*
*Calls cost 50p per minute at all times. Call costings correct at time of going to press.

MATCHDAY PROGRAMME

Programme Editor.......................Reg Davis.

Number of pages.....................................48.

Price ....£2.

Subscriptions
........Home matches £55 including postage.
.... Home & away £110 including postage.

Local Newspapers
.Wimbledon Guardian, South London Press
...............Wimbledon News, Surrey Comet.

Local Radio Stations
....Capital Radio.

MATCHDAY TICKET PRICES

Whitehorse Lane Stand . . . . £10.00/£20.00; £8.00/£14.00

Concessions . . . . £10.00/£20.00; £6.00/£12.00

Main Stand. . . . . £8.00/£14.00; £12.00/£22.00

Concessions . . . . £6.00/£12.00; £10.00/£20.00

Holmesdale Road . . . . £8.00/£14.00

Concessions . . . . £6.00/£12.00

Arthur Wait Stand (Visitors) . . . . £10.00/£20.00

NATIONWIDE
EAGUE DIVISION 1

...1998-99

DIVISION ONE
1997-98

FINAL LEAGUE TABLE

		P	W	D	L	F	A	Pts
1	Nottingham Forest (Prem)	46	28	10	8	82	42	94
2	Middlesbrough (Prem)	46	27	10	9	77	41	91
3	Sunderland (Prem)	46	26	12	8	86	50	90
4	Charlton Athletic (+11) - *Play-off winners*	46	26	10	10	80	49	88
5	Ipswich Town (-1)	46	23	14	9	77	43	83
6	Sheffield United (-1)	46	19	17	10	69	54	74
7	Birmingham City (+3)	46	19	17	10	60	35	74
8	Stockport County (Div.2)	46	19	8	19	71	69	65
9	Wolverhampton W. (-6)	46	18	11	17	57	53	65
10	West Bromwich Albion (+6)	46	16	13	17	50	56	61
11	Crewe Alexandra (Div.2)	46	18	5	23	58	65	59
12	Oxford United (+5)	46	16	10	20	60	64	58
13	Bradford City (+8)	46	14	15	17	46	59	57
14	Tranmere Rovers (-3)	46	14	14	18	54	57	56
15	Norwich City (-2)	46	14	13	19	52	69	55
16	Huddersfield Town (+4)	46	14	11	21	50	72	53
17	Bury (Div.2)	46	11	19	16	42	58	52
18	Swindon Town (+1)	46	14	10	22	42	73	52
19	Port Vale (-11)	46	13	10	23	56	66	49
20	Portsmouth (-13)	46	13	10	23	51	63	49
21	Queens Park Rangers (-12)	46	10	19	17	51	63	49
22	Manchester City (-8)	46	12	12	22	56	57	48
23	Stoke City (-11)	46	11	13	22	44	74	46
24	Reading (-6)	46	11	9	26	39	78	42

The figure in brackets denotes the number of places lost or gained on the club's 1996-97 final position.

NATIONWIDE LEAGUE DIVISION ONE - 1998-99

BARNSLEY
(The Tykes)
F.A. CARLING PREMIERSHIP
SPONSORED BY: ORA ELECTRONICS

1997-98 - Back Row L-R: Paul Smith (Physio), Sean McClare, Shane Hulson, Chris Morgan, Paul Wilkinson, Tony Bullock, Lars Leese, David Watson, Steve Davis, Mark Hume, Paul Bagshaw, Darren Sheridan, Mick Tarmey (Physio). **Middle Row:** Eric Winstanley (First team coach), Dean Jones, Rory Prendergast, Luke Beckett, Jonathan Perry, Carl Rose, Andy Gregory, Danny Shenton, Arjan De Zeeuw, Eric Tinkler, Laurens Ten Heuvel, Adrian Moses, Neil Thompson, Norman Rimmington (kit manager), Malcolm Shotton (Reserve Team manager). **Front Row:** Peter Shirtliff (Player/coach), Clint Marcelle, Andrew Liddell, Nicky Eaden, Martin Bullock, Neil Redfearn, Danny Wilson (Manager), Matty Appleby, John Hendrie, Jovo Bosancic, Ales Krizan, Georgi Hristov, Colin Walker (Youth team coach).

BARNSLEY
FORMED IN 1887
TURNED PROFESSIONAL IN 1888
LTD COMPANY IN 1899

PRESIDENT: Arthur Raynor
CHAIRMAN: John Dennis
VICE-CHAIRMAN: Barry Taylor
DIRECTORS:
Michael Hall, Christopher Harrison,
Michael Hayselden, John Kelly, Ian Potter.

GENERAL MANAGER/SECRETARY:
Michael Spinks
SALES & MARKETING MANAGER
G Barlow

MANAGER: John Hendrie
FIRST TEAM COACH: Eric Winstanley
RESERVE TEAM COACH: Malcolm Shotton

YOUTH TEAM COACH
Colin Walker

PHYSIOTHERAPIST
Michael Tarmey & Paul Smith

CLUB STATISTICIAN FOR THE DIRECTORY
Ian Sawyer

After a valiant attempt - especially towards the end of their 38-match programme - Barnsley bid farewell to the Carling Premiership and duly returned to the Nationwide League, having spent just one season with the big boys - their first in fact in the club's 110 year history. It was a terrific experience, nevertheless, for the Yorkshire club and already the bookies have marked them down as potential promotion candidates to make a swift return to the top flight....and manager Danny Wilson is confident that the Tykes will again be a force to be reckoned with in the First Division, just like they were two years ago.

There is no doubt that Barnsley found it mighty tough in the Carling Premiership last season, certainly over the first three months or so and then towards the end. After ten matches they were already propping up the table with only six points in the bank and 28 goals conceded. Just past the halfway stage in the season (20 matches fulfiled) the Tykes were still last of the pile, having accumulated 15 points out of a possible 60 and at this juncture, even the staunchest of fans knew that staying up was going to be very difficult. And that's how it turned out despite the signing of striker Jan-Aage Fjortoft from Sheffield United for £800,000 and some battling League performances during the second half of the campaign when they also defeated Manchester United in the F.A. Cup. Barnsley even climbed off the bottom and they got within striking distance of the safety zone but it was too tough a task. And sadly for all associated with the famous Oakwell club, Barnsley mustered a mere 10 points from their last ten matches and at the end of the day were five adrift of 17th placed Everton, who survived with a last-match draw.

Obviously manager Wilson and his players were all bitterly disappointed men at the end of the season along with the team's supporters, but Wilson himself knows that the experience gained by playing against the likes of Arsenal, Liverpool, Manchester United and Newcastle among others will stand the team in good stead for the months ahead. Barnsley played some good, smart football at times - both at home and away - but a string of defeats (some of them heavy) early on in the proceedings made it a difficult task when it came to the crunch in late April and May.

Tony Matthews.

BARNSLEY

Carling Prem.   :19th   FA CUP: 6th Round   LC CUP: 3rd Round

M	DATE	COMP.	VEN	OPPONENTS	RESULT		H/T	LP	GOAL SCORERS/GOAL TIMES	ATT.
1	A 09	CP	H	West Ham United	L	1-2	1-0	15	Redfern 9	18667
2	12	CP	A	Crystal Palace	W	1-0	0-0	10	Redfern 56	(21547)
3	24	CP	H	Chelsea	L	0-6	0-3	14		18170
4	27	CP	H	Bolton Wanderers	W	2-1	1-1	10	Tinkler 12, Hristov 47	18661
5	30	CP	A	Derby County	L	0-1	0-1	10		(27232)
6	S 13	CP	H	Aston Villa	L	0-3	0-1	14		18649
7	16	CC 2/1	A	Chesterfield	W	2-1	0-0		Redfern 87 (pen), Ward 90	(6318)
8	20	CP	A	Everton	L	2-4	1-2	17	Redfern 32, Barnard 78	(32659)
9	23	CP	A	Wimbledon	L	1-4	1-0	18	Tinkler 41	(7976)
10	27	CP	H	Leicester City	L	0-2	0-0	19		18660
11	30	CC 2/2	H	Chesterfield	W	4-1	2-0		Liddell 37, Redfern 44, Sheridan 55, Hristov 84	8417
12	O 04	CP	A	Arsenal	L	0-5	0-3	20		(38049)
13	14	CC 3	H	Southampton	L	1-2	1-1		Liddell 26	9019
14	20	CP	H	Coventry City	W	2-0	1-0	18	Ward 11, Redfern 66 (pen)	17463
15	25	CP	A	Manchester United	L	0-7	0-4	19		(55142)
16	N 01	CP	H	Blackburn Rovers	D	1-1	0-1	19	Bosancic 79	18665
17	08	CP	A	Southampton	L	1-4	1-3	20	Bosancic 37 (pen)	(15018)
18	22	CP	A	Liverpool	W	1-0	1-0	19	Ward 35	(41011)
19	29	CP	H	Leeds United	L	2-3	2-1	19	Liddell 8, Ward 28	18690
20	D 08	CP	A	Sheffield Wednesday	L	1-2	1-1	20	Redfern 29	(29086)
21	13	CP	H	Newcastle United	D	2-2	1-1	20	Redfern 9, Hendrie 75	18687
22	20	CP	A	Tottenham Hotspur	L	0-3	0-3	20		(28232)
23	26	CP	A	Bolton Wanderers	D	1-1	1-1	20	Hristov 20	(25000)
24	28	CP	H	Derby County	W	1-0	0-0	20	Ward 67	18686
25	J 03	FAC 3	H	Bolton Wanderers	W	1-0	1-0		Barnard 26	15042
26	10	CP	A	West Ham United	L	0-6	0-2	20		(23714)
27	17	CP	H	Crystal Palace	W	1-0	1-0	20	Ward 26	17819
28	24	FAC 4	A	Tottenham Hotspur	D	1-1	0-1		Redfern 58 (pen)	(28722)
29	31	CP	A	Chelsea	L	0-2	0-1	20		(34442)
30	F 04	FAC 4R	H	Tottenham Hotspur	W	3-1	0-0		Ward 51, Redfern 58, Barnard 88	18220
31	07	CP	H	Everton	D	2-2	1-1	20	Fjortoft 24, Barnard 63	18672
32	15	FAC 5	A	Manchester United	D	1-1	1-1		Hendrie 38	(54700)
33	21	CP	A	Coventry City	L	0-1	0-0	20		(20265)
34	25	FAC 5R	H	Manchester United	W	3-2	2-0		Hendrie 9, Jones 45, 65	18655
35	28	CP	H	Wimbledon	W	2-1	1-0	18	Fjortoft 25, 63	17102
36	M 08	FAC QF	A	Newcastle United	L	1-3	0-2		Liddell 57	(36695)
37	11	CP	A	Aston Villa	W	1-0	1-0	18	Ward 17	(29519)
38	14	CP	H	Southampton	W	4-3	3-2	18	Ward 17, Jones 32, Fjortoft 42, Redfern 56 (pen)	18368
39	28	CP	H	Liverpool	L	2-3	1-1	18	Redfern 37, 85 (pen)	18684
40	31	CP	A	Blackburn Rovers	L	1-2	0-1	18	Hristov 68	(24179)
41	A 04	CP	A	Leeds United	L	1-2	1-1	19	Hristov 44	(37749)
42	11	CP	H	Sheffield Wednesday	W	2-1	0-0	19	Ward 65, Fjortoft 71	18692
43	13	CP	A	Newcastle United	L	1-2	0-1	19	Fjortoft 50	(36534)
44	18	CP	H	Tottenham Hotspur	D	1-1	1-0	18	Redfern 19	18692
45	25	CP	H	Arsenal	L	0-2	0-1	19		18691
46	M 02	CP	A	Leicester City	L	0-1	0-0	19		(21293)
47	10	CP	H	Manchester United	L	0-2	0-1	19		18694

Best Home League Attendance: 18694 V Manchester United   Smallest :17102 V Wimbledon   Average :18443

Goal Scorers:
CP	(37)	Redfern 10, Ward 8, Fjortoft 6, Hristov 4, Barnard 2, Bosancic 2, Tinkler 2, Hendrie 1, Jones 1, Liddell 1
CC	(7)	Liddell 2, Redfern 2, Hristov 1, Sheridan 1, Ward 1
FAC	(10)	Barnard 2, Hendrie 2, Jones 2, Redfern 2, Liddell 1, Ward 1

(D) Appleby	(M) Barnard	(D) Bosancic	(G) Bullock	(M) Bullock	(D) Dezeeuw	(D) Eaden	(F) Fjortoft	(F) Hendrie	(F) Hristov	(D) Jones	(D) Krizan	(G) Leese	(F) Liddell	(F) Marcelle	(F) Markstedt	(M) McClare	(D) Morgan	(D) Moses	(F) Redfern	(M) Sheridan	(D) Shirtliff	(M) Ten Heuvel	(M) Thompson	(M) Tinkler	(F) Ward	(G) Watson	(F) Wilkinson	
	X		X3	X	X			X	S2			S	S3	S1						X	X	S	X1		X		X2	A. B .Wilkie 1
X	X	S	X	X	X			X	S			S	S	S						X	X	X			X	X		N S Barry 2
S	X		X	X	X			X	S2			S	S3	S1						X	X	X			X	X	X	G Poll 3
X	X		S2	X	X			X	X			S1	S3	X						X	X	S			X	X	S	D J Gallagher 4
X	X		S	S	X	X		S2	X				X	X	X					X	X	S1			X		S3	P A Durkan 5
X	X		S2	X	X			X					X	X						X	X	S1	S3		X	X		G P Barber 6
S1	X		S		X			X		X	X			X						X	X	X	S2		X	X		P S Danson 7
X	X		S3	X				S1		S	S	X	S2							X	X	X			X	X	X	G R Ashby 8
X	X		X	X				S2		X	S	X	S1			S				X	X	X			X		X	J T Winter 9
X	X		S1	X				S		X	X	X	S2							X	X	X		S	X	S	S	G Poll 10
X	X		S1	X				S2		X	X	X	S3							X	X	X			X	X		U D Rennie 11
	X		S1	X	S2			S3		X	S	X	S							X	X	X		X	X	X	X	P Jones 12
S	X		X	X	X			S1		X		X	S2							X	X	X		X		X	X	J T Winter 13
	X	S	X	X	X			S1		X	S	X	S							S2	X	X		X		X	X	P E Alcock 14
	X	S3	X	X	X		S1	X		X	S		S							S2	X	X		X		X	X	M A Riley 15
S3	X		X	X	S1			X	X		X	S	S2	S						X	X	X			X		X	G Poll 16
S3	X		X	X	X			X		X	S	X	S							X		S1	X	S2	X		X	G R Ashby 17
S1	X	S	X	X	X			S2	S			X	X		X					X	X				X	X	S	J T Winter 18
S2	X	X	X	X	X			S	S3			X	X		X					S1	X	X			X	X	S	M D Reed 19
X2	X	X	S2		X			S1	S		X	X	X1							X	X	X				X	S	G S Willard 20
X3	X	X1	S3		X			S2	S		X	X	X2							X	X	S1			X	X	S	P E Alcock 21
X	X		S2	X	X			S	S1			X	X2		X1					X	X	S			X	X	X	M D Reed 22
S	X		S	X	X			S1	X1		S	S2	X2	S						X	X	X			X	X	X	S W Dunn 23
S	X	S	S2	X	X			X1				S1	X2	S						X	X	X			X	X	X	G P Barber 24
S	X	S	S1	X	X		S	X2				S2	X1							X	X	X			X	X	X	D R Elleray 25
X1	X	S		X			S3	X3		X2		S	S1	S2			X			X	X	X			X	X	S	N S Barry 26
	X	S	S		X	X1		S		S		S1	X	X			X			X	X	X			X	X	X	M D Reed 27
	X	S1	S	X	X	X2				S	S2	X					S	X	X	X			X1		X	X		G R Ashby 28
X	X		X3	X	X	X2	S2	S			S	S3					S1	X	X1	X					X	X		J T Winter 29
X	X		X	X	X	X	S	S		S	S				S		X	X	X				S	X	X		G R Ashby 30
X	X		X	X	X	X1	S1	S2				S	S	X2	X	X				S	X	X		M J Bodenham 31
S1		X		X	X1		X2			X	S	S2	S				X	X	X				S	X	X		M A Riley 32
S		X		X2		X	X1	S1	S3	X			S2					X	X	X3				S	X	X		A B Wilkie 33
X2	X	X	X3				X1	S	X			S1	S3	X			X	X	S2				S	X	X		M A Riley 34
	X	X2	S		X	X				S	S	X	X1		X	X	X	S2				S1	X	X		G P Barber 35
	X		S1	X2	X			S2	S	S	X	X1				X	X	X	X				S	X	X		N S Barry 36
	X2		X		X	X1		S	X	S	S1	S				X	X	X	X				S2	X	X		P Jones 37
	X		X	X	X	S2	X2	S	S	S		X				X	X	X				S3	X1	X		G R Ashby 38
X	X	S3	X1		X	X2		S2	X		S	S1	X3		S	X	X	X					X		G S Willard 39
S	X	X	X1		X			X	X3		S	S3	S1'2		X	X	X	S2					X	X		M D Reed 40
	X	X	X1	S	S	S2		X	X2			S				X	X	X					X	X		K W Burge 41
S		X	X	X	S1	X1	X	S	S	S				X	X	X					X	X		P E Alcock 42
	X		X3	X	X	X2	S2	S	X	X1			S3			X	X	X			S1		X	X		S W Dunn 43
S	X		X	X	X	S1		X1		S	S	S2				X	X				X2	X	X		M J Bodenham 44
	X	S2	X	X	X	X3	S3		X			S	X1			X	X				X2	S1	X		M A Riley 45
	X	S1	S2	X	X	X3			X2		S	S3	X			X	X	S			X1	X	X		J Gallagher 46
X1	X	S	X		S1	S2		X2	X			S	S			X	X	X				X	X		P Durkin 47
13	33	13		23	26	32	12	7	11	12	12	8	13	9	6		10	32	37	20	4		3	21	28	30	3	CP Appearances
2	2	4		10		3	3	13	12			1	13	11	1		1	3		6	1			4	1		1	CP Sub Appearances
1+1	3			1+1	2	2		1+2		3	2	2	0+2				2	3	3	1	0+1		2	3	1			CC Appearances
1+1	5	3+1		3+2	5	5		4	1+1	1	1		1+4	3+1	1		3	6	6	3+1			2	6	6			FAC Appearances

BARNSLEY

BIGGEST VICTORIES
League: 9-0 v Loughborough Town, Division 2, 28.1.1899.
9-0 v Accrington Stanley, Division 3N, 3.2.1934 (a).
F.A. Cup: 8-0 v Leeds City, Qualifying Rnd, 3.11.1894.
League Cup: 6-0 v Peterborough, Round 1, 15.9.1981.

BIGGEST DEFEATS
League: 0-9 v Notts County, Division 2, 19.11.1927.
F.A. Cup: 1-8 v Derby County, Round 1, 30.1.1897.
League Cup: No defeat by more than 3 goals.

MOST POINTS
3 points a win: 80, Division 1, 1996-97.
2 points a win: 67, Division 3N, 1938-39.

MOST GOALS SCORED
118 Division 3(N), 1933-34.

MOST GOALS CONCEDED
108, Division 2, 1952-53.

MOST FIRST CLASS MATCHES IN A SEASON
58 - 1960-61 (46 League, 10 FA Cup, 2 League Cup).

MOST LEAGUE WINS
30, Division 3(N), 1938-39.
30, Division 3(N), 1954-55.

MOST LEAGUE DRAWS
18, Division 3, 1971-72.

MOST LEAGUE DEFEATS
29, Division 2, 1952-53.

MOST GOALS IN A SEASON
Cecil McCormack: 34 - 1950-51 (League 33, FAC 1).

MOST GOALS IN A MATCH
5, F.Eaton v South Shields, 6-1, Division 3(N), 9.4.1927.
5, P.Cunningham v Darlington, 6-2, Division 3(N), 4.2.1933.
5, B.Asquith v Darlington, 7-1, Division 3(N), 12.11.1938.
5, C.McCormack v Luton, 6-1, Division 2, 9.9.1950.

OLDEST PLAYER
Beaumont Asquith, 37 years 3 months v Coventry City, 19.11.1927.

YOUNGEST PLAYER
Glyn Riley, 16 years 171 days v Torquay United, 11.1.1975.

MOST CAPPED PLAYER
Gerry Taggart (Northern Ireland) 24 caps.

League: 1938-39: Matches played 42, Won 30, Drawn 7, Lost 5, Goals for 94, Goals against 34, Points 67. First in Division 3(N).
Highest Position: 1914-15, 1921-22, Third Division 2.
F.A. Cup: 1911-12: 3rd Rnd. Birmingham City 0-0,3-1; 4th Rnd. Leicester City 1-0; Bolton Wanderers 2-1; 6th Rnd. Bradford City 0-0,0-0,0-3,0-0; Semi-Final Swindon Town 0-0, 1-0; Final West Bromwich Albion 0-0,1-0.
League Cup: 1981-82: 1st Rnd. Peterborough United 3-2,6-0; 2nd Rnd. Swansea City 2-0,2-3; 3rd Rnd. Brighton & Hove Albion 4-1; 4th Rnd. Manchester City 1-0; 5th Rnd. Liverpool 0-0,1-3.

ADDITIONAL INFORMATION
PREVIOUS NAMES
Barnsley St.Peters.
PREVIOUS LEAGUES
Midland.

Club Colours: Red shirts, white shorts, red & white hooped socks.
Change Colours:

Reserves League: Pontins League Division 2.
Youth League: Northern Intermediate League.

	Played	Won	Drawn	Lost	For	Against	Points
DIVISIONAL RECORD							
Premiership	38	10	5	23	37	61	40
Division 2/1	2,504	871	622	1,011	3,471	3,905	2,629
Division 3	552	183	159	210	736	838	525
Division 3N	218	130	38	50	467	278	298
Division 4	460	177	127	156	628	555	481
Total	**3,772**	**1,371**	**951**	**1,436**	**5,334**	**5,637**	**3,973**

RECORDS AND STATISTICS

COMPETITIONS

PREM.	DIV.2/1	DIV.3	DIV.3(N)	DIV.4
1997-98	1898-32	1959-65	1932-34	1965-68
	1934-38	1968-72	1938-39	1972-79
	1939-53	1979-81	1953-55	
	1955-59			
	1981-97			
	1998-			

HONOURS

DIV.3(N)	FA CUP
1933-34	1911-12
1938-39	
1954-55	

MOST APPEARANCES

BARRY MURPHY 564 (1962-78)

YEAR	LEAGUE	FA CUP	LGE CUP
1962-63	21		2
1963-64	4		1
1964-65	22	1	1
1965-66	7+3		2
1966-67	14		
1967-68	46	1	1
1968-69	46	6	3
1969-70	46	4	1
1970-71	45	4	1
1971-72	46	3	3
1972-73	42	2	2
1973-74	10+1		2
1974-75	35	1	1
1975-76	36+1		2
1976-77	46	2	4
1977-78	43	2	3
	509+5	26	29

MOST GOALS IN A CAREER

ERNIE HINE - 130 (1921-26 & 1934-38)

YEAR	LEAGUE	FA CUP
1921-22	12	1
1922-23	23	1
1923-24	19	
1924-25	15	
1925-26	12	
1934-35	9	
1935-36	14	5
1936-37	13	
1937-38	6	
Total	123	7

Current top goalscorer: Andy Liddell - 38 (07.91-98)

RECORD TRANSFER FEE RECEIVED

AMOUNT	CLUB	PLAYER	DATE
£1,500,000	Nott'm Forest	Carl Tiler	5/91
£750,000	Nott'm Forest	David Currie	1/90
£350,000	Huddersfield	Andy Payton	7/96
£300,000	Portsmouth	John Beresford	3/89

RECORD TRANSFER FEE PAID

AMOUNT	CLUB	PLAYER	DATE
£1,500,000	Gjorgi Hristou	Partizan Belgrade	07/97
£250,000	Oldham Athletic	David Currie	9/91
£200,000	Aston Villa	Gareth Williams	8/91
£180,000	Burnley	Steve Davies	7/91

MANAGERS

NAME	SEASONS	BEST	WORST
John McCartney	1901-04	8(2)	11(2)
Arthur Fairclough	1904-12	6(2)	19(2)
John Hastie	1912-14	4(2)	5(2)
Harry Lewis	1914-19	3(2)	13(2)
Peter Sant	1919-26	3(2)	16(2)
John Commins	1926-29	11(2)	16(2)
Arthur Fairclough	1929-30	17(2)	17(2)
Brough Fletcher	1930-37	14(2)	8(3N)
Angus Seed	1937-53	9(2)	1(3N)
Tim Ward	1953-60	16(2)	17(3N)
John Steel	1960-71	7(3)	18(4)
John McSeventy	1971-72	22(3)	22(3)
John Steel	1972-73	14(4)	14(4)
Jim Iley	1973-78	6(4)	13(4)
Allan Clarke	1978-80	11(3)	4(4)
Norman Hunter	1980-84	6(2)	2(3)
Bobby Collins	1984-85	11(2)	11(2)
Alan Clarke	1985-89	7(2)	14(2)
Mel Machin	1989-93	8(2)	19(2)
Viv Anderson (P)	1993-94	18(1/2)	18(1/2)
Danny Wilson (P)	1994-98	19 (P)	10 (1)
John Hendrie (P)	1998-		
			(P) Player-manager.

LONGEST LEAGUE RUNS

of undefeated matches:	21 (1.10.1933 - 5.5.1934)	of league matches w/out a win:	26 (13.12.52 - 29.8.53)
of undefeated home matches:	36 (6.2.1933 - 24.11.1934)	of undefeated away matches:	10 (27.12.1938 - 15.4.1939)
without home win:	11 (6.12.1952 - 24.9.1953)	without an away win:	29 (14.3.1908 - 19.11.1910)
of league wins:	10 (5.2.1955 - 23.4.1955)	of home wins:	12 (3.10.1914 - 8.3.1915)
of league defeats:	9 (14.3.1953 - 25.4.1953)	of away wins:	5 (27.12.1938 - 25.2.1939)

PLAYERS NAME Honours	Ht	Wt	Birthdate	Birthplace Transfers	Contract Date	Clubs	League	L/Cup	FA Cup	Other	Lge	L/C	FAC	Oth
G O A L K E E P E R														
Bullock Antony B	6.1	13.8	2/18/72	Warrington		Leek Town								
						Barnsley								
Leese Lars	6.5	14.5	8/18/69	Germany		Bayer Leverkusen								
				£250000	7/23/97	Barnsley	8+1	2						
Watson David N	6	12	11/10/73	Barnsley	7/4/92	Barnsley	172	14	11	1				
E: u21.5,Y.8.														
D E F E N C E														
Appleby Matthew W	5.11	11	4/16/72	Middlesbrough	5/4/90	Newcastle United	18+2	2+1	2	2+2				
				Loan	11/25/93	Darlington	10		1	1				
				Free	6/15/94	Darlington	77+2	2	4	8	7			3
				£250000	7/16/96	Barnsley	48+2	5+1	2+1					
Barnard Darren Sean	5.10	12	11/30/71	Germany		Wokingham Town								
E: S. W: 1.				£50000	7/25/90	Chelsea	18+11	1+1	1+1		2			
				Loan	11/18/94	Reading	3+1							
				£175000	10/6/95	Bristol City	77+1	4	6	6	15	1		1
				£750000	8/8/97	Barnsley	33+2	3	5		2		2	
Bassinder Gavin D	6	12.2	9/24/79	Mexborough	5/31/97	Barnsley (T)								
Cross Matthew	5.6	12.3	3/25/80	Bury	5/31/97	Barnsley (T)								
Dezeeuw Arjan	6.1	13.11	4/16/70	Holland		Telstar								
				£250000	11/1/95	Barnsley	99	6	9		3			
Eaden Nicholas	5.11	11.3	12/12/72	Sheffield	6/4/91	Barnsley	205+6	12+1	14	2	8			
Jones Scott	5.11	11.06	5/1/75	Sheffield	2/1/94	Barnsley	27+6		1+2		1		2	
Krizan Ales	5.11	13.4	7/25/71	Slovenia		Maribor Branik								
				£500000	7/30/97	Barnsley	12	3	1					
Morgan Christopher P	5.11	11.11	2/13/78	Barnsley	5/10/97	Barnsley	10+1		3					
Moses Adrian	6.1	12.5	5/4/75	Doncaster	7/2/93	Barnsley	81+10	4	10		3			
M I D F I E L D														
Bullock Martin	5.5	10.07	3/5/75	Derby		Eastwood Town								
				£15000	9/4/93	Barnsley	72+57	4+3	4+6	1	1		1	
Gregory Andrew	5.8	10.9	10/8/76	Barnsley		Barnsley (T)								
McClare Sean P	5.9	10.13	1/12/78	Rotherham	5/10/97	Barnsley (T)								
Richardson Kevin	5.7	11.7	12/4/62	Newcastle	12/8/80	Everton (A)	95+14	10+3	13	7+2	16	3	1	
E: 1. FAC'84. CS'84. Div.1'85'89. ECWC'85. LC'94.				£225000	9/4/86	Watford	39	3	7	1	2			
				£200000	8/26/87	Arsenal	88+8	13+3	9	3	5	2	1	
				£750000	7/1/90	Real Sociedad								
				£450000	8/6/91	Aston Villa	142+1	15	12	10	13	3		
				£300000	2/16/95	Coventry City	74+3	8	7			1		
				£150000	9/10/97	Southampton	25+3	4	1					
				£300000	7/1/98	Barnsley								
Sheridan Darren	5.6	10.12	12/8/67	Manchester		Winsford United		1						
				£10000	8/12/93	Barnsley	133+12	7+1	7+2	1+1	4	1		
Tinkler Eric	6.2	12.8	7/30/70	Capetown		Cagliari								
South African Int.				£650000	7/23/97	Barnsley	21+4	2	2		2			
Van Der Laan Robin	6	13.8	9/5/68	Schiedam		Wageningen								
				£80000	2/21/91	Port Vale	154+22	11+1	9+1	11+1	24	1	1	1
				£675000	8/2/95	Derby County	61+4	6+2	3+1		8		3	
				£500000	7/1/98	Barnsley								
F O R W A R D														
Bagshaw Paul J	5.7	12.2	5/29/79	Sheffield	5/31/97	Barnsley (T)								
Fjortoft Jan A	6	12.8	1/10/67	Aalesund, Norway		Rapid Vienna								
				£500000	7/29/93	Swindon Town	62+10	9	3	1	27	9	2	
				£1300000	3/31/95	Middlesbrough	37+4	7	0+2		10	2	1	
				£700000	1/31/97	Sheffield United	29+4	3+1	1+1	3	19	1	2	1
				£800000	1/16/98	Barnsley	12+3				6			
Hendrie John G	5.7	11.12	10/24/63	Lennoxtown	5/18/81	Coventry City	15+8	2			2			
S: Y. Div.3'85. Div.2'90.Div.1'95.				Loan	1/10/84	Hereford United	6							
				Free	7/2/84	Bradford City	173	17	11	11	46	3	6	4
				£500000	6/17/88	Newcastle United	34	2	4	3	4	1		
				£600000	6/20/89	Leeds United	22+5	1	1	2	5			
				£550000	7/5/90	Middlesbrough	181+11	22+2	10+2	6	44	6	2	4
				£200000	10/11/96	Barnsley	43+13		6		16		3	
Hristov Georgi	5.10	11.5	1/30/76	Macedonia		Patizan Belgrade								
Macedonian Int.				£1500000	7/23/97	Barnsley	11+12	1+2	1+1		4	1		

Liddell Andrew	5.8	10.5	6/28/73	Leeds	7/6/91	Barnsley	139+51	10+1	5+7	2+1	34	3	1	
;: u21.11														
Marcelle Clinton	5.4	10	11/9/68	Trinidad		Felgueiras								
					8/8/96	Barnsley	35+25	3+3	5+1		8		1	
Marksedt Peter	5.11	13.10	1/11/72	Vasteras (Sweden)		Vasteras SK								
				£250000	11/21/97	Barnsley	6+1		1					
Rose Karl	5.8	10.8	10/12/78	Barnsley		Barnsley								
Ward Ashley A	6.1	12.4	11/24/70	Manchester	8/5/89	Manchester City	0+1		0+2					
				Loan	1/10/91	Wrexham	4			1	2			
				£80000	7/30/91	Leicester City	2+8	2+1	0+1	0+1				
				Loan	11/21/92	Blackpool	2				1			
				£80000	12/1/92	Crewe Alexandra	58+3	4	2	7	25	2	4	5
				£500000	12/8/94	Norwich City	25				8			
				£1000000	3/19/96	Derby County	32+8	1+1	2		9		1	
				£1000000	9/5/97	Barnsley	28+1	3	6		8	1	1	

ADDITIONAL CONTRACT PLAYERS

Heckingbottom Marc		5/31/97	Barnsley (T)
Kennedy Paul J		5/31/97	Barnsley (T)
Smith Andrew A		5/31/97	Barnsley (T)
Taylor David J		5/31/97	Barnsley (T)
Wood James		5/31/97	Barnsley (T)

THE MANAGER
JOHN HENDRIE (PLAYER MANAGER)

Date of Birth . . . . 24th October 1963.
Place of Birth . . . . Lennoxtown.
Date of Appointment . . . . July 1998.

PREVIOUS CLUBS
As Manager . . . . None.
As Coach . . . . None.
As a Player . . . . Coventry City, Hereford Utd (Loan), Bradford City, Newcastle Utd,
. . . . Leeds Utd, Middlesbrough, Barnsley.

HONOURS
As a Manager
None.
As a Player

Bradford City: Division 3 Championship 1985.
Leeds United: Division 2 Championship 1990.
Middlesbrough: Division 1 Championship 1995.
International: Scottish Youth.

Oakwell Ground

Grove Street, Barnsley, South Yorkshire S71 1ET

Capacity . . . . .19006 (All seater).
First game . . . . .v Gawber (Friendly) 15.10.1887 (0-0).
First floodlit game . . . . .v Bolton W. (Friendly) 23.1.1962.

ATTENDANCES
Highest . . . . .40,255 v Stoke City, FA Cup 5th Rnd, 15.2.1936.
Lowest . . . . .1,627 v Grimsby Town, Anglo Italian Cup, 14.9.93.

HOW TO GET TO THE GROUND

From The North
M1 to J37. Take A628 towards Barnsley and follow signs for Football Ground.

From The South
M1 to J37. Proceed as above.

From The East
A635 towards Barnsley and follow signs for Football Ground.

From The West
A628 towards Barnsley and shortly after crossing M1 Jnt 37 follow signs for Football Ground.

Car Parking: Official car parks for 1,200 vehicles adjacent to ground. Cost £1. Visitors use Queens Ground car park.
Railway Station: Barnsley 01742 26411.

USEFUL TELEPHONE NUMBERS

Club switchboard .01226 211 211
Ticket Office 01226 295 353
Marketing Department 01226 211 211

Clubcall 0891 12 11 52*
*Calls cost 50p at all times.
Call costings correct at time of going to press.

MATCHDAY PROGRAMME

Programme Editor .Keith Lodge

Number of pages 32

Price . . . .

Subscriptions . . . . .Apply to club.

Local Newspapers
. . . . .Barnsley Chronicle (weekly),
. . . . .Barnsley Star (Daily)
. . . . .Yorkshire Post, Yorkshire on Sunday.

Local Radio Stations
. . . . .Radio Sheffield, Hallam FM.

MATCHDAY TICKET PRICES (97/98)

East Stand Upper Tier £12.50
OAP/Juveniles £6.50
East Stand Lower Tier £11
OAP/Juveniles £6
The Ora Stand £10.50
OAP/Juveniles £6

Visiting Supporters
West Stand Upper Tier £12.50
West Stand Lower Tier £11
Spion Kop £10.50

BIRMINGHAM CITY
(The Blues)
NATIONWIDE LEAGUE DIVISION 1
SPONSORED BY: AUTO-WINDSCREENS

1998/99 Back Row L-R: Neil McDiarmid (Physio), Paul Furlong, Dele Adebola, Chris Holland, Kevin Poole, Ian Bennett, Darren Purse, Michael Johnson, Martin O'Connor, Ian Bowyer (Reserve team Manager). **Middle Row:** Arvel Lowe (Fitness coach), Steve Robinson, Bryan Hughes, Peter Ndlovu, Nicky Forster, Jerry Gill, Jon Bass, Martin Grainger, Frank Barlow (Assistant Manager). **Front Row:** Tony Hey, Jon McCarthy, Simon Charlton, Trevor Francis (Manager), Mick Mills (Assistant Manager), Gary Ablett, Darren Wassall, Chris Marsden.

BIRMINGHAM CITY
FORMED IN 1875
TURNED PROFESSIONAL IN 1885
LTD COMPANY IN 1888

CHAIRMAN: J F Wiseman
Managing Director: Karren Brady

DIRECTORS:
D Sullivan, A Jones, D Gold, B Gold, R Gold,
H Brandman
SECRETARY: Alan G Jones, BA, MBA
COMMERCIAL MANAGER
Allan Robson

MANAGER: Trevor Francis
ASSISTANT: Mick Mills & Frank Barlow

RESERVE TEAM MANAGER
Ian Bowyer
DIRECTOR OF YOUTH COACHING
Brian Estick
PHYSIOTHERAPIST
Neil McDiamond

CLUB STATISTICIAN FOR THE DIRECTORY
Dave Drage

If only Birmingham had maintained their opening form. If they had they would not only have easily qualified for the play-offs, but might well have made a strong challenge for an automatic promotion spot.

They shot out of the Division One 'blocks' with 12 points taken from their opening five matches, but then only won once in their next 14 games, giving them a position of 14th. A good run during December and January placed them back in the top ten, but they were always chasing and couldn't quite get back into the top six to give them a chance of promotion.

The Coca-Cola Cup saw them comfortably through the 1st round, 4-0, v. Gillingham, and the 2nd round, 5-3, v. Stockport County, but they were no match for Premiership title challengers Arsenal, going out 1-4. The FA Cup also ended at the hands of a Premier League club but not until Crewe had been beaten in the 3rd round, 2-1, and Stockport, again, in the 4th round, 2-1. The 'Blues' travelled to Elland Road for the 5th round and put up a good performance to narrowly go out 2-3, Hasselbaink scoring the winner three minutes from time.

Birmingham have had a superb pre-season, claiming the scalps of a few Premiership sides along the way. Now they have to take that form into Division One, maintain it and then maybe they can look forward to taking on the Premiership boys again in 1999/2000, only this time for points.

BIRMINGHAM CITY

Division 1 :6th   **FA CUP: 5th Round**   **LC CUP: 3rd Round**

M	DATE	COMP.	VEN	OPPONENTS	RESULT	H/T	LP	GOAL SCORERS/GOAL TIMES	ATT.
1	A 09	FL	H	Stoke City	W 2-0	1-0	6	Devlin 33, Ndlovu 87	20608
2	12	CC 1/1	A	Gillingham	W 1-0	0-0		Francis 85	(5246)
3	23	FL	H	Reading	W 3-0	1-0	6	Devlin 38, Bruce 81, Ndlovu 88	16495
4	26	CC 1/2	H	Gillingham	W 3-0	0-0		Furlong 68, Devlin 75, Ndlovu 78	7921
5	29	FL	A	Stockport County	D 2-2	0-1	3	Devlin 68, Francis 73	(6260)
6	S 02	FL	A	Tranmere Rovers	W 3-0	2-0	3	Hughes 11, Furlong 44, Ndlovu 64	(6620)
7	09	FL	A	Huddersfield Town	W 1-0	0-0	1	Furlong 69	(9477)
8	14	FL	H	Sunderland	L 0-1	0-0	1		17478
9	17	CC 2/1	H	Stockport County	W 4-1	1-0		Hughes 40, Robinson 51, Devlin 77 (pen), 87	4900
10	20	FL	A	Middlesbrough	L 1-3	0-3	4	Furlong 50	(30125)
11	23	CC 2/2	A	Stockport County	L 1-2	0-1		Furlong 70 (pen)	(2074)
12	27	FL	A	Sheffield United	D 0-0	0-0	4		(20553)
13	O 04	FL	H	Crewe Alexandra	L 0-1	0-0	7		16548
14	12	FL	H	Wolverhampton Wand	W 1-0	1-0	3	Marsden 8	17822
15	14	CC 3	A	Arsenal	L 1-4	1-0		Hey 20	(27097)
16	18	FL	A	Bury	L 1-2	0-2	7	Grainger 90	(5700)
17	22	FL	A	Charlton Athletic	D 1-1	0-0	8	Devlin 83	(10072)
18	25	FL	H	Oxford United	D 0-0	0-0	11		16352
19	28	FL	H	Ipswich Town	D 1-1	0-1	9	Bruce 80	16778
20	N 01	FL	A	Queens Park Rangers	D 1-1	1-1	9	Furlong 42	(12715)
21	04	FL	H	Bradford City	D 0-0	0-0	10		14552
22	08	FL	H	Norwich City	L 1-2	1-2	13	Devlin 27	16464
23	15	FL	A	Nottingham Forest	L 0-1	0-1	14		(19610)
24	23	FL	A	West Bromwich Albion	L 0-1	0-0	14		(18444)
25	29	FL	H	Portsmouth	W 2-1	1-1	14	Furlong 36, 73	17738
26	D 06	FL	A	Port Vale	W 1-0	1-0	10	Cottee 19	(7509)
27	13	FL	H	Manchester City	W 2-1	0-0	10	Forster 89, O'Connor 90	21014
28	20	FL	A	Swindon Town	D 1-1	1-1	10	Forster 22	(10334)
29	26	FL	A	Ipswich Town	W 1-0	0-0	10	, Cundy 83 (OG)	(17459)
30	28	FL	H	Tranmere Rovers	D 0-0	0-0	10		19533
31	J 03	FAC 3	A	Crewe Alexandra	W 2-1	1-1		Furlong 22 (pen), 55	(4607)
32	10	FL	A	Stoke City	W 7-0	3-0	8	Hughes 4, 9, Forster 26, Furlong 50, 69, 87, McCarthy 56	(14940)
33	17	FL	H	Huddersfield Town	D 0-0	0-0	8		17850
34	24	FAC 4	H	Stockport County	W 2-1	1-0		Hughes 31, 84	15882
35	27	FL	H	Stockport County	W 4-1	3-0	7	Furlong 7, 31, 89, McCarthy 16	17118
36	31	FL	A	Reading	L 0-2	0-0	9		(10315)
37	F 06	FL	H	Middlesbrough	D 1-1	1-1	9	McCarthy 3	20634
38	14	FAC 5	A	Leeds United	L 2-3	0-2		Ablett 63, Ndlovu 81	(35463)
39	17	FL	A	Crewe Alexandra	W 2-0	2-0	8	Adebola 42, Hughes 45	(5559)
40	22	FL	H	Sheffield United	W 2-0	1-0	7	Grainger 31, Johnson 66	17965
41	25	FL	H	Bury	L 1-3	0-1	8	Johnson 89	20021
42	28	FL	A	Wolverhampton Wand	W 3-1	1-1	8	Ndlovu 35, 78 (pen), Adebola 71	(25591)
43	M 04	FL	A	Norwich City	D 3-3	2-0	8	Ndlovu 12, 88, Adebola 44	(9819)
44	07	FL	H	Queens Park Rangers	W 1-0	1-0	6	Adebola 16	18298
45	10	FL	A	Sunderland	D 1-1	0-0	5	Adebola 51	(37602)
46	14	FL	A	Bradford City	D 0-0	0-0	7		(16392)
47	21	FL	H	Nottingham Forest	L 1-2	0-0	7	Ndlovu 61 (pen)	24663
48	28	FL	H	West Bromwich Albion	W 1-0	0-0	7	Johnson 89	23260
49	A 04	FL	A	Portsmouth	D 1-1	0-0	7	Adebola 84	(14591)
50	11	FL	A	Port Vale	D 1-1	0-0	7	Ndlovu 86	17193
51	13	FL	A	Manchester City	W 1-0	0-0	7	Adebola 90	(29569)
52	18	FL	H	Swindon Town	W 3-0	2-0	7	Furlong 9, 34 (pen), Hughes 82	17016
53	25	FL	A	Oxford United	W 2-0	0-0	6	Furlong 85, Ford 73 (OG)	(8818)
54	M 03	FL	H	Charlton Athletic	D 0-0	0-0	6		25877

Best Home League Attendance: 25877 V Charlton Athletic   **Smallest :14552 V Bradford City**   **Average :18751**

Goal Scorers:

FL	(60)	Furlong 15, Ndlovu 9, Adebola 7, Devlin 5, Hughes 5, Forster 3, Johnson 3, McCarthy 3, Bruce 2, Grainger 2, Cottee 1, Francis 1, Marsden 1, O'Connor 1, Opponents 2
CC	(10)	Devlin 3, Furlong 2, Francis 1, Hey 1, Hughes 1, Ndlovu 1, Robinson 1
FAC	(6)	Furlong 2, Hughes 2, Ablett 1, Ndlovu 1

(D) Ablett	(F) Adebola	(D) Bass	(G) Bennett	(D) Bruce	(D) Charlton	(F) Cottee	(F) Devlin	(F) Forinton	(F) Forster	(F) Francis	(F) Furlong	(D) Gill	(D) Grainger	(M) Hey	(M) Holland	(F) Hughes	(D) Johnson	(M) Marsden	(M) McCarthy	(F) Ndlovu	(M) O'Connor	(G) Poole	(D) Purse	(D) Rea	(M) Robinson	(D) Wassall		Official	#
X			X	X			X			S3			X	X	S2	X	S1			X	X				X	X		E.K. Wolstenholme	1
X		X	X				X			S1	X		S2			X	X			X	X	S			X	X		M C Bailey	2
X			X	X			X			S2	X		X	X	S3	X	S1			X	X					X		E Lomas	3
X		X	X				X			S2	X		X	X	X	X	S1			X		S				X		F G Stretton	4
X	S	X	X				S1			S2	X		X			X	X			X	X				X	X		A R Leake	5
X		X	X				X			S1	X		X	X	S2	X	S3			X	X					X		G B Frankland	6
X		X	X				X			S2	X		X	X	S1	X	S			X	X					X		D Laws	7
X		X	X				X			S2	X		X	S3	X	S1		X	X	X						X	J A Kirkby	8
X	X	X					X			S1	X		X	X	X	S2			X		S				X	X	A N Butler	9
X		X	X				X			S2	X		X	X	S3	X	S1	X	X	S1						X	R D Furnandiz	10
X	X	X					X			S1	X		X		X	S2		X	X	S				X	X	R J Harris	11
X		X	X				S3			S1	X		X	X	X	S2			X						X		T Heilbron	12
X		X	X				S1			X			X	X	S	S	X	X	X	X						X	D Laws	13
X	X	X					X				X	S2	X	S	X	S	X	X	S1	X							M J Brandwood	14
X	S3	X	X				X			S2			X	X	X	S1		X	X					X	X		U D Rennie	15
X		X	X				X			S2			X	X		S1	X	X	X	X				S3	X		D Pugh	16
X		X					S1		X	S3			X		S2	X	X	X	X					X	X		C R Wilkes	17
X		X	X				S2		X	S1			X	X	X	S	S	X	X						X		G Cain	18
X		X	X	X			X		S1	X			X		S	X	X	X	X						X		M C Bailey	19
X		X	X				S1		X		X		X		S	X	X	X	S					X	X	S J Baines	20
X		X	X				X		S2		X		X			S1	X	X	X	X					X		M E Pierce	21
X		X	X				X			S2	X		X		X	X	X	X	S						S1		R Pearson	22
X		X	X		S1	X					X		X		S3	S2	X	X			X				X	X	P S Danson	23
X		X	X	X		S2					X		X		S	X	X	X	S1						X		S G Bennett	24
X		X	X	X	X1	S1					X		X2	X	X	X	X	S2				S			X		S W Mathieson	25
X		X	X	X	S2	X1	S1				X		X2	X	X	X	X	S3							X		E Lomas	26
X	X1	X	X	X		X3		S3	S2				X	S1		X	X2	X							X		A P D'Urso	27
X		X	X	X	X2		X	S2			S1		X		X	S	X							X1			R Styles	28
X		X	X	X			X	S2			S1		X1	S		X	X2	X							X		R D Furnandiz	29
X		X	X	X			X1	S2	X2				X	S3	X3	X	S1								X		M R Halsey	30
X		X	X				X2	S2	X		X		X1	S1	X	X	S	X	S	X	S				S		J A Kirkby	31
X	X		X1	X			X2	S	X				X	S1	X	X	S2	X									T Heilbron	32
X	X3	X	X				X2	S3	X				X	S2	X	X	S1	X1									M J Jones	33
X	X2	X	X				X	S2	X1		X3		X	S	X	X	S1	X	S				S3				G S Willard	34
X		X	X1				X2	S2	X		X		X	S1	X	X	S							X			P Taylor	35
X		X	X3				X2		X		X		S3	X1	X	X	S2							X			P Rejer	36
X	S1	X	X	X2			X1		X		X		X3	S2	X	X	S3	X						X			M E Pierce	37
X		X	X	X		S1	S	X1			X2		S	X	S2	X	X	X	S								D J Gallagher	38
	X3	X	X1	X			S3				X	S2	X2	X	X	X	X					S1					C J Foy	39
	X	X	X	X			S2				X	X1	X3	X	X2	X	X	X				S3		S1			B Knight	40
X	X1	X		X3			S3				X2		X	S1	S2	X	X	X				X					M C Bailey	41
X	X		X	X			S3				S2		X1	X	X	X3	X2					S1			X		G Cain	42
X	X		X	X			S1				S		X	X	X	X1	X				S		X				A Bates	43
S	X	X	X	X			S2				S1		X1	X	X	X2	X										R J Harris	44
S	X	X	X	X			S				X		S1	X	X	X1	X										K M Lynch	45
S	X	X	X	X			S1				X2		S2	X	X	X1	X										F G Stretton	46
S1	X	X	X	X			S2				X		S3	X	X2	X3	X1										S W Mathieson	47
S3	X	X	X	X		S2	X2				S1		X	X	X1		X										R Pearson	48
X	X	X		X			S3				X2		X	X1	X2	X					X	S1					A P D'Urso	49
S	X	X	X	X			S2	S1			X1		X	X2	X												G Cain	50
	X	X1	X	X			S3				X2		X	X	X	X3	X				S1	S2					T Heilbron	51
	X		X	X3	X		S2		X2	X			X	X	X	X					S3	S1					W C Burns	52
	X		X	X	X				X	X2			X3	X	X	X	S3	X1			S2	S1					R Styles	53
	X		X	X			S3		X3	X1			S2	X	X	X2	X	X			X	S1					R J Harris	54
34	16	30	45	40	23	4	13		12	2	24	3	27	8	2	34	22	31	41	29	32	1	2		17	14	FL Appearances	
2	1					1	1	9	1	16	18	1	6	1	8	6	16	1		10	1		6		8		FL Sub Appearances	
5		3+1	5	2			5			0+5	4		4+1	2	3	4	1+4			5	3				4	5	CC Appearances	
3		3	3	3	1		0+1		3	0+2	2		3			3	0+2	2	3	1+1	3					0+1	FAC Appearances	

BIRMINGHAM CITY

CLUB RECORDS

BIGGEST VICTORIES
League: 12-0 v Walsall Town Swifts, Division 2, 17.12.1892.
12-0 v Doncaster Rovers, Division 2, 1.4.1903.
F.A. Cup: 10-0 v Druids, 9.11.1889.
League Cup: 6-0 v Manchester City, 11.12.1962.
Europe: 5-0 v Boldklub Copenhag, 7.12.1960.

BIGGEST DEFEATS
League: 1-9 v Sheffield Wednesday, Division 1, 13.12.1930.
1-9 v Blackburn Rovers, Division 1, 5.1.1895.
0-8 v Derby County, Division 1, 30.11.1895.
0-8 v Newcastle United, Division 1, 23.11.1907.
0-8 v Preston North End, Division 1, 1.2.1958.
F.A. Cup: 0-6 v Wednesbury O.B., Qualifying Rnd., 17.10.1881.
0-6 v Tottenham Hotspur, 6th Rnd., 12.4.1967.
League Cup: 0-5 v Tottenham Hotspur, 3rd Rnd., 29.10.1986.
Europe: (Fairs) 1-4 v Barcelona, Final, 4.5.1960.
2-5 v RCD Espanol 1st Rnd 1st leg, 11.11.61.

MOST POINTS
3 points a win: 89, Division 2, 1994-95.
2 points a win: 59, Division 2, 1947-48.

MOST GOALS SCORED
103, Division 2, 1893-94.
Mobley 24, Wheldon 22, Walton 16, Hands 14, Hallam 9, Jenkyns 6, Izon 4, Lee 3, Jolley 2, Pumfrey, Devey, Jackson 1 each.

MOST GOALS CONCEDED
96, Division 1, 1964-65.

MOST FIRST CLASS MATCHES IN A SEASON
63 - 1994-95 (46 League, 5 FA Cup, 4 League Cup, 8 AMC)

MOST LEAGUE WINS
27, Division 2, 1979-80.

MOST LEAGUE DRAWS
18, Division 1, 1937-38 & Division 2, 1971-72.

MOST LEAGUE DEFEATS
29, Division 1, 1985-86.

INDIVIDUAL CLUB RECORDS

MOST GOALS IN A SEASON
Walter Abbott 42 - 1898-99 (League 34, FAC 8).
5 goals once; 3 goals 5 times; 2 goals 7 times, 1 goal 8 times.

MOST GOALS IN A MATCH
5, Walter Abbott v Darwen (h), 8-0, Division 2, 26.11.1898.
5, John McMillan & R McRoberts v Blackpool (h), 10-1, Division 2, 2.3.1901.
5, Ben Green v Middlesbrough (h), 7-0, Division 1, 26.12.1905.
5, Jimmy Windridge v Glossop (h), 11-1, Division 2, 23.1.1915.

OLDEST PLAYER
Dennis Jennings, 40 years 190 days, 6.5.1950.

YOUNGEST PLAYER
Trevor Francis, 16 years 7 months v Cardiff City, 5.9.1970.

MOST CAPPED PLAYER
Malcolm Page (Wales) 28, 1971-79.
Harry Hibbs (For England), 25, 1951-54.

BEST PERFORMANCES

League: First in Division 2 - 1947-48: Matches played 42, Won 22, Drawn 15, Lost 5, Goals for 55, Goals against 24, Points 59.
Highest Position: 6th in Division 1, 1955-56.

F.A. Cup: Winners in 1930-31 v West Bromwich Albion, 1-2.
Most Recent Success: (1955-56) 3rd Rnd. Torquay United 7-1 (a); 4th Rnd. Leyton Orient 4-0 (a); 5th Rnd. West Bromwich Albion 1-0 (a); 6th Rnd. Arsenal 3-1 (a); Semi Final Sunderland 3-0 (n); Final Manchester City 1-3.
League Cup: (1962-63) 2nd Rnd. Doncaster Rovers 5-0; 3rd Rnd. Barrow 1-1 (a), 5-1 (h); 4th Rnd. Notts County 3-2 (h); 5th Rnd. Manchester City 6-0 (h); Semi-Final Bury 1-1 (a), 3-2(h); Final Aston Villa 0-0(a),3-1(h).
Europe: (Fairs Cup) Runners-up in 1958-60 v Barcelona, 0-0(h),1-4(a).
Most Recent Success: (1960-61) 1st Rnd. Ujpest Dozsa 3-2(h),2-1(a); 2nd Rnd. Boldklub Copenhagen 4-4(a),5-0(h); Semi-Final Inter Milan 2-1(a),2-1(h); Final A.S.Roma 2-2(h),0-2(a).
Auto Windscreen Shield: Winners 1994-95.

DIVISIONAL RECORD

	Played	Won	Drawn	Lost	For	Against	Points
Division 1	2,040	651	501	888	2,776	3,296	1,845
Division 2/1	1,622	709	393	528	2,621	2,106	1,943
Division 3/2	184	82	55	47	258	197	310
Total	3,846	1,442	949	1,463	5,655	5,599	4,098

ADDITIONAL INFORMATION
Previous Names: Small Heath Alliance (1875-88); Small Heath (1888-1905).
Previous League: Football Alliance.

Club Colours: Royal blue shirts, white shorts, blue stockings.
Change colours:

Reserves League: Pontins Central League Premier Division.

RECORDS AND STATISTICS

COMPETITIONS

Div 1/P	Div.2/1	Div.3/2
1894-96	1892-94	1989-92
1901-02	1896-1901	1994-95
1903-08	1902-03	
1921-39	1908-21	**Fairs Cup**
1948-50	1939-48	1955-58
1955-65	1950-55	1958-60
1972-79	1965-72	1960-61
1980-84	1979-80	1961-62
1985-86	1984-85	
	1992-94	
	1995-	

HONOURS

Div.2	Div.3/2	League Cup	A.M. Cup
1892-93	1994-95	1962-63	1990-91
1920-21			1994-95
1947-48			
1954-55			

MOST GOALS IN A CAREER

Joe Bradford - 267 (1920-35)

Year	League	FA Cup
1920-21	1	
1921-22	10	
1922-23	18	1
1923-24	24	
1924-25	11	
1925-26	26	1
1926-27	22	1
1927-28	29	3
1928-29	22	2
1929-30	23	
1930-31	14	8
1931-32	26	2
1932-33	14	
1933-34	5	
1934-35	4	
Total	249	18

Current Top goalscorer - Paul Furlong - 31 (07.96-98)

MOST APPEARANCES

Gil Merick 551 (1945-60)

Year	League	FA Cup	Europe
1945-46		8	
1946-47	41	4	
1947-48	36		
1948-49	41	2	
1949-50	42	1	
1950-51	42	6	
1951-52	41	2	
1952-53	35	7	
1953-54	38	2	
1954-55	27	4	
1955-56	38	6	2
1956-57	40	7	2
1957-58	28	1	3
1958-59	34	6	2
1060 60	?		1
	485	56	10

MANAGERS

Name	Seasons	Best	Worst
Bob McRoberts	1910-15	3(2)	20(2)
Bill Beer	1923-27	8(1)	17(1)
Les Knighton	1928-33	9(1)	15(1)
George Liddell	1933-39	12(1)	20(1)
Willie Camkin	1939-45		
Ted Goodier	1945		
Harry Storer	1945-48	1(2)	3(2)
Bob Brocklebank	1949-54	17(1)	6(2)
Arthur Turner	1954-58	6(1)	1(2)
Albert Beasley	1958-60	9(2)	19(2)
Gil Merrick	1960-64	17(2)	20(2)
Joe Mallett	1964-65	22(2)	22(2)
Stan Cullis	1965-70	4(2)	18(2)
Fred Goodwin	1970-75	10(1)	9(2)
Willie Bell	1975-77	13(2)	19(2)
Sir Alf Ramsey	1977-78	11(1)	11(1)
Jim Smith	1978-82	13(1)	3(2)
Ron Saunders	1982-86	17(1)	2(2)
John Bond	1986-87	19(2)	19(2)
Gary Pendry	1987-89	19(2)	12(3)
Dave Mackay	1989-90	7(3)	7(3)
Lou Macari	1991		
Terry Cooper	1991-94	19(2/1)	2(3)
Barry Fry	1994-96	22(1)	22(1)
Trevor Francis	1996-	7 (1)	10 (1)

RECORD TRANSFER FEE RECEIVED

Amount	Club	Player	Date
£2,500,000	Coventry City	Gary Breen	1/97
£1,180,000	Nottingham Forest	Trevor Francis	2/79
£550,000	Coventry City	Liam Daish	2/96
£500,000	Leicester City	Steve Claridge	3/96

RECORD TRANSFER FEE PAID

Amount	Club	Player	Date
£1,500,000	Chelsea	Paul Furlong	7/96
£800,000	Stockport County	Kevin Francis	1/95
£800,000	Southend Utd	Ricky Otto	12/94
£750,000	Blackburn Rovers	Mike Newell	7/96

LONGEST LEAGUE RUNS

of undefeated matches:	20 (1994-95)	of league matches w/out a win:	17 (1985-86)
of undefeated home matches:	36 (1970-72)	of undefeated away matches:	15 (1947-48)
without home win:	11 (1962-63)	without an away win:	32 (1980-82)
of league wins:	13 (1892-93)	of home wins:	17 (1902-03)
of league defeats:	8 (1978-79, 1985)	of away wins:	9 (1897)

BIRMINGHAM CITY

PLAYERS NAME Honours	Ht	Wt	Birthdate	Birthplace Transfers	Contract Date	Clubs	League	L/Cup	FA Cup	Other	Lge	L/C	FAC	Oth
APPEARANCES / GOALS							APPEARANCES				GOALS			
G O A L K E E P E R														
Bennett Ian M	6	12	10/10/70	Worksop		QPR								
Div.2'95. AMC'95.				Free	3/20/91	Newcastle United								
				Free	3/22/91	Peterborough Utd	72	10	3	4				
				£325000	12/17/93	Birmingham City	177	21	13	10				
Poole Kevin	5.1	11.11	7/21/63	Bromsgrove	6/26/81	Aston Villa	28	2	1	1				
CC 96/97				Loan	11/8/84	Northampton Town	3							
					8/27/87	Middlesbrough	34	4	2	2				
				Loan	3/27/91	Hartlepool United	12							
				£40000	7/30/91	Leicester City	164	9	8	12				
				Free	8/4/97	Birmingham City	1							
D E F E N C E														
Ablett Gary	6	11.4	11/19/65	Liverpool	11/19/83	Liverpool	103+6	10+1	16+2	9	1			
CS 1988 Div.1 1988 FAC 1989 CS 1990				Loan	1/25/85	Derby County	3+3			2				
Div.1 1990 CS 1995 FAC 1995			Loan	9/10/86	Hull City	5								
				£750000	1/14/92	Everton	128	12	12	4	5		1	
				Loan	3/1/96	Sheffield United	12							
					8/15/96	Birmingham City	72+5	7	6		1		1	
Bass Jon	6	12.02	7/1/76	Weston-S-M.	6/27/94	Birmingham City	37+2	3	4					
				Loan	10/11/96	Carlisle United	3							
Charlton Simon	5.7	11.1	10/25/71	Huddersfield	7/1/89	Huddersfield Town	121+3	9	10	14	1	1		
E: S				£250000	6/8/93	Southampton	104+9	8+4	8+1		2	1		
				Loan	12/5/97	Birmingham City	4+1							
				£250000	1/7/98	Birmingham City	19		1					
Dyson James G	6.2	12	4/20/79	Wordsley	7/1/97	Birmingham City (T)								
Gardner Lee D			5/18/78	Doncaster	10/22/97	Birmingham City (T)								
Gill Jeremy M	5.8	11	9/8/70	Clevedon		Leyton Orient								
E: SP.1						Yeovil Town								
				£25000	7/14/97	Birmingham City	3							
Grainger Martin	5.1	11.7	8/23/72	Enfield	7/28/92	Colchester United	37+9	3	3+2	3	7			1
				£60000	10/21/93	Brentford	67+1	2	4	5	9		1	2
				£400000	3/25/96	Birmingham City	56+8	4+1	5		5			
Johnson Michael O	5.11	11	7/4/73	Nottingham	7/9/91	Notts County	102+5	9	4	15+1				
				£225000	9/1/95	Birmingham City	80+24	6+6	2+3	3	3			
Purse Darren J	6	12.4	2/14/77	London	2/22/94	Leyton Orient	85+8	4	2	14+1	6			4
					8/1/96	Oxford United	27+1	6	1		4	2		
				£600000	2/16/98	Birmingham City	2+6							
Rea Simon	6.1	13	9/20/76	Coventry	8/1/94	Birmingham City	2+1			1+1				
				Loan	11/13/95	Kettering Town								
Wassall Darren P	5.11	12.3	6/27/68	Birmingham	6/1/86	Nottingham Forest	17+10	6+2	3+1	4+2				1
FMC'92				Loan	10/23/87	Hereford United	5		1	1				
				Loan	3/2/89	Bury	7				1			
				£600000	6/15/92	Derby County	91+8	9	4	11				
				Loan	9/11/96	Manchester City	13+1	2						
				Loan	3/27/97	Birmingham City	8							
					5/17/97	Birmingham City	14	5						
M I D F I E L D														
Hey Antoine	5.9	11.7	9/19/70		7/16/97	Birmingham City	8+1	2					1	
Marsden Chris	5.11	10.12	03/01/69	Sheffield	06/01/87	Sheffield United	13+3	1		1	1			
					15/07/88	Huddersfield Town	113+8	15+1	6+2	10	9			
				Loan	02/11/93	Coventry City	5+2							
				£150000	11/01/94	Wolverhampton W.	8		3					
				£250000	15/11/94	Notts County	7		1					1
				£700000	16/02/96	Stockport County	63+2	13	4	4	3			1
				£500000	10/9/97	Birmingham City	31+1	2			1			
McCarthy Jon	5.9	11.5	18/08/70	Middlesbrough	07/11/87	Hartlepool United	0+1							
NI: 7, B.2				Free	01/08/88	Shepshed Albion								
				Free	22/03/90	York City	198+1	8	11	15	31	1	3	3
				£450000	01/08/95	Port Vale	93+1	10	7	8	12	2	1	2
				£1850000	9/11/97	Birmingham City	41		3		3			

O'Connor Martin	5.8	10.8	12/10/67			Bromsgrove Rovers								
SLP'92.				£25000	6/26/92	Crystal Palace	2			1+1				
				Loan	3/24/93	Walsall	10		2		1			1
				£40000	2/14/94	Walsall	53	4	5	1	12	1	1	
					7/5/96	Peterborough United	18	4	2		3			
					11/29/96	Birmingham City	56+1	3	3		5			
Robinson Steven	5.4	10.11	1/17/75	Nottingham	6/9/93	Birmingham City	28+12	4	0+1	1		1		
				Loan	12/15/95	Kidderminster H.								
				Loan	3/15/96	Peterborough United								
Tait Paul	6.1	10	7/31/71	Sutton C'dfield	8/2/88	Birmingham City	134+35	12+2	6+2	13+6	14			4
Div.2'95. AMC'95.				Loan	12/24/97	Northampton Town	2+1							
F O R W A R D														
Adebola Bamberdele	6.3	12.6	6/23/75	Liverpool	6/21/93	Crewe Alexandra	97+27	3+3	8+2	9+1	39	2	3	2
				Loan	2/2/94	Northwich Victoria								
				£1000000	2/5/98	Birmingham City	16+1				7			
Barnes Steve	5.4	10.5	1/5/76	Harrow		Welling								
				£75000	10/9/95	Birmingham City	0+3	0+1		0+1	1			
				Loan	1/23/98	Brighton & H.A.	12							
Forinton Howard L	5.11	11.4	9/18/75	Boston		Yeovil Town								
				£75000	7/14/97	Birmingham City	0+1							
Forster Nicholas	5.9	11.5	9/8/73	Caterham		Shrewsbury Town								
						Gillingham	54+13	3+2	6		24	2		
				£100000	6/17/94	Brentford	108+1	11	8	6+1	39	3	1	3
				£700000	1/31/97	Birmingham City	16+19		3		6			
Furlong Paul A	6	11.8	10/1/68	Wood Green		Enfield				4				1
E: SP.5. FAT'88.				£130000	7/31/91	Coventry City	27+10	4	1+1	1	4	1		
				£250000	7/24/92	Watford	79	7	2	2	37	3	4	
				£2300000	5/26/94	Chelsea	44+20	3+1	5+4	7	13		1	3
				£1500000	7/16/96	Birmingham City	61+7	8	4		25	3	3	
Hughes Bryan	5.9	10	6/19/76	Liverpool		Wrexham	72+23	2	13+3	14	12		7	3
					3/12/97	Birmingham City	44+7	3	3		5		1	2
Johnson Andrew			2/10/81	Bedford	8/7/97	Birmingham City (T)								

MANAGER
TREVOR FRANCIS

Date of Birth .... 19th April 1954.
Place of Birth .... Plymouth.
Date of Appointment .... May 1996.

PREVIOUS CLUBS
As Manager .... Queens Park Rangers, Sheffield Wednesday.
As Coach .... None.
As a Player . Birmingham City, Nottingham Forest, Manchester City, Sampdoria,
.... Atlanta (USA), Glasgow Rangers, QPR, Sheffield Wednesday.

HONOURS
As a Manager
None.

As a Player
Nottingham Forest: European Cup.
Glasgow Rangers: Premier League 1987.
England: 52 Full appearances.

St. Andrews Ground

Small Heath, Birmingham B9 4NH

Capacity ....25,899 (All seater).
First game ....v Middlesbrough, 26.12.1906.
First floodlit game...v Borussia Dortmund (F), 31.10.1956.

ATTENDANCES
Highest ....66,844 v Everton ,FA Cup 5th Round, 11.2.1939.
Lowest ....1,500 v Chesterfield, Division 2, 17.4.1909.

HOW TO GET TO THE GROUND

From North and East: M6 to J6, A38 (M). Branch left, first exit from roundabouts. A45 along Dartmouth Middleway. Left into St. Andrews Road for ground.

From South: M5 to J4, or A435 or A41 into Birmingham. A45 to Coventry Road then left into St. Andrews Road for ground.

From West: A456, A41 then A45 into Coventry Road, left into St. Andrews Road for ground.

Car Parking
Car parks in Coventry Road and Cattell Road. £2 per car on match days.

Nearest Railway Station
Buses from Birmingham New Street or Snow Hill, or walk from Bordesley Station from Birmingham Moor Street.

USEFUL TELEPHONE NUMBERS

Club switchboard 0121 772 0101
Club fax number 0121 766 7866
Club shop .... 0121 772 0101 Ext. 8
Ticket Office............. 0121 773 3803

Marketing Department . . 0121 772 0101 Ext.7
Clubcall 0891 12 11 88*

*Calls cost 50p per minute at all times. Call costings correct at time of going to press.

MATCHDAY PROGRAMME

Programme Editor............... Peter Lewis

Number of pages 48

Price £1.70

Subscriptions................. Apply to club.

Local Newspapers
. . Birmingham Post & Evening Mail, Sports Argus.
.... Express & Star, Sporting Star.

Local Radio Stations
.... BBC Radio W.M. & BRMB.

MATCHDAY TICKET PRICES

MATCH B...................................... £11
Main Stand.................................... £13
Spoin Kop.................................... £14
Family.. £10
Juveniles/OAP £6

Match A - add a £1 to all prices.

BOLTON WANDERERS
(The Trotters)
NATIONWIDE LEAGUE DIVISION 1
SPONSORED BY: REEBOK

1998-99 - Back Row L-R: Hasney Aljofree, Jimmy Phillips, Dean Holdsworth, Per Frandsen, Keith Branagan, Jussie Jaaskelainen, Gavin Ward, Greg Strong, Neil Cox, Mike Whitlow. **Middle Row:** Mark Fish, Andy Todd, Robbie Elliott, Claus Jensen, Bob Taylor, Nicky Spooner, Arnar Gunnlaugsson, Scott Taylor, Peter Beardsley. **Front Row:** Michael Johansen, Nathan Blake, Phil Brown (coach), Colin Todd (Manager), Gudni Bergsson, Scott Sellers.

BOLTON WANDERERS
FORMED IN 1874
TURNED PROFESSIONAL IN 1880
LTD COMPANY IN 1895

PRESIDENT: Nat Lofthouse OBE
CHAIRMAN: G Hargreaves
DIRECTORS
G Ball, G Seymour, G Warburton,
W B Warburton, P Carside, B Scowcroft

SECRETARY/Chief Executive
D McBain (01204 389 200)
COMMERCIAL MANAGER
T Holland

MANAGER: Colin Todd
COACH: Phil Brown
RESERVE TEAM MANAGER
Steve Carroll
YOUTH TEAM MANAGER
Dean Crombie
PHYSIOTHERAPIST
Ewan Simpson

CLUB STATISTICIAN FOR THE DIRECTORY
Simon Marland

O nce again the Carling Premiership proved to great a challenge for Bolton Wanderers, only this time it wasn't until the last day of the season that their fate was sealed, indeed they went into the final fixture a place above the relegation zone.

Having scored 100 goals and won 98 points from their 46 games in Division One in 1996/97, it appeared that Bolton were certainly to good for the Division and so would maybe fair a little better in the Carling Premiership this time around. This was backed up with a 1-0 win over Southampton on the opening day, followed by a draw at Coventry City. However, they did not record another win until October 26th against Chelsea, the team who would later determine the future of the Wanderers. Back-to-back wins in early December saw them reach their highest position since the second game of the season - 14th, but by January they were back in the bottom three.

There they stayed until the last match of the season. A 5-2 win at Crystal Palace had seen them swap places with Everton and so if they could match the 'Toffeemen's' result on the last day of the season Bolton would stay up. Bolton, as mentioned, went to Chelsea who had the final of the ECWC coming up on the following Wednesday and Everton had to play tough to beat Coventry City. At half-time the scores read: Chelsea 0-0 Bolton; Everton 1-0 Coventry. A mix up in the Bolton defence lead to a Vialli goal and relegation looked certain. However, a Coventry equaliser suddenly increased the tension at Stamford Bridge as the Chelsea supporters were cheering on Bolton and actually booing their players when in possession. The hope was short lived as Jody Morris, almost regretfully, scored a second for Chelsea and Everton not Bolton stayed up.

If Bolton bounce straight back up again this season they might well have grounds to put in a claim for an intermediate Division to be created for those clubs who are too strong for Division One but do not quite have the resources for the Carling Premiership!

BOLTON WANDERERS

	Carling Prem.	:18th		FA CUP: 3rd Round				LC CUP: 4th Round	

M	DATE	COMP.	VEN	OPPONENTS	RESULT	H/T	LP	GOAL SCORERS/GOAL TIMES	ATT.
1	A 09	CP	A	Southampton	W 1-0	1-0	7	Blake 42	(15206)
2	23	CP	A	Coventry City	D 2-2	0-2	8	Blake 69, 76	(16633)
3	27	CP	A	Barnsley	L 1-2	1-1	13	Beardsley 31	(18661)
4	S 01	CP	H	Everton	D 0-0	0-0	12		23131
5	13	CP	A	Arsenal	L 1-4	1-3	16	Thompson 13	(38138)
6	16	CC 2/1	A	**Leyton Orient**	W 3-1	2-1		**Todd 13, Frandsen 20, McGinlay 79**	**(4128)**
7	20	CP	H	Manchester United	D 0-0	0-0	16		25000
8	23	CP	H	Tottenham Hotspur	D 1-1	1-0	16	Thompson 20	23433
9	27	CP	A	Crystal Palace	D 2-2	1-2	17	Beardsley 36, Johansen 66	(17134)
10	30	CC 2/2	H	**Leyton Orient**	D 4-4	2-2		**Blake 7, 35, McGinlay 63 (pen), Gunnlaugsson 65**	6444
11	O 04	CP	H	Aston Villa	L 0-1	0-1	17		24196
12	14	CC 3	H	**Wimbledon**	W 2-0	0-0		**Pollock 91, McAllister 94 (OG)**	9875
13	18	CP	A	West Ham United	L 0-3	0-0	18		(24864)
14	26	CP	H	Chelsea	W 1-0	0-0	17	Holdsworth 72	24080
15	N 01	CP	H	Liverpool	D 1-1	0-1	17	Blake 84	25000
16	08	CP	A	Sheffield Wednesday	L 0-5	0-5	18		(25027)
17	18	CC 4	A	**Middlesbrough**	L 1-2	1-1		**Thompson 33**	**(22801)**
18	22	CP	A	Leicester City	D 0-0	0-0	18		(20464)
19	29	CP	H	Wimbledon	W 1-0	0-0	18	Blake 90	22703
20	D 01	CP	H	Newcastle United	W 1-0	1-0	13	Blake 22	24494
21	06	CP	A	Blackburn Rovers	L 1-3	0-2	14	Frandsen 83	(25503)
22	14	CP	H	Derby County	D 3-3	0-0	16	Thompson 50, Blake 72, Pollock 77	23037
23	20	CP	A	Leeds United	L 0-2	0-0	17		(31163)
24	26	CP	H	Barnsley	D 1-1	1-1	16	Bergsson 38	25000
25	28	CP	A	Everton	L 2-3	2-2	17	Bergsson 42, Sellars 43	(37149)
26	J 03	FAC 3	A	**Barnsley**	L 0-1	0-1			**(15042)**
27	10	CP	H	Southampton	D 0-0	0-0	18		23333
28	17	CP	A	Newcastle United	L 1-2	0-1	19	Blake 72	(36767)
29	31	CP	H	Coventry City	L 1-5	1-1	19	Sellars 22	25000
30	F 06	CP	A	Manchester United	D 1-1	0-0	19	Taylor 59	(55156)
31	21	CP	H	West Ham United	D 1-1	0-0	18	Blake 86	25000
32	M 01	CP	A	Tottenham Hotspur	L 0-1	0-1	19		(29032)
33	07	CP	A	Liverpool	L 1-2	1-0	19	Thompson 7	(44532)
34	14	CP	H	Sheffield Wednesday	W 3-2	1-1	19	Frandsen 31, Blake 53, Thompson 69 (pen)	24847
35	28	CP	H	Leicester City	W 2-0	0-0	19	Thompson 52, 90	25000
36	31	CP	H	Arsenal	L 0-1	0-0	19		25000
37	A 04	CP	A	Wimbledon	D 0-0	0-0	18		(11356)
38	11	CP	H	Blackburn Rovers	W 2-1	1-0	18	Holdsworth 20, Taylor 67	25000
39	13	CP	A	Derby County	L 0-4	0-4	18		(29126)
40	18	CP	H	Leeds United	L 2-3	0-2	19	Thompson 57, Fish 90	25000
41	25	CP	A	Aston Villa	W 3-1	2-0	18	Cox 18, Taylor 41, Blake 83	(38392)
42	M 02	CP	H	Crystal Palace	W 5-2	3-2	17	Blake 6, Fish 20, Phillips 30, Thompson 74, Holdsworth 79	24449
43	10	CP	A	Chelsea	L 0-2	0-0	18		(34845)

Best Home League Attendance: 25000 V Barnsley   **Smallest :22703 V Wimbledon**   Average :24353

Goal Scorers:

CP	(41)	Blake 12, Thompson 9, Holdsworth 3, Taylor 3, Beardsley 2, Bergsson 2, Fish 2, Frandsen 2, Sellars 2, Cox 1, Johansen 1, Phillips 1, Pollock 1
CC	(10)	Blake 2, McGinlay 2, Frandsen 1, Gunnlaugsson 1, Pollock 1, Thompson 1, Todd 1, Opponents 1
FAC	(0)	

(D) Aljofree	(F) Beardsley	(M) Bergsson	(F) Blake	(G) Branagan	(F) Carr	(D) Cox	(D) Elliott	(D) Fairclough	(D) Fish	(D) Frandsen	(M) Giallanza	(F) Gunnlaugsson	(F) Holdsworth	(M) Johansen	(D) McAnespie	(F) McGinlay	(D) Phillips	(M) Pollock	(F) Salako	(M) Sellars	(M) Sheridan	(D) Strong	(D) Taggart	(F) Taylor	(M) Thompson	(D) Todd	(G) Ward	(M) Whitlow		
		X	X	X		X	X			X		S			S	S	X	S	X		X			X		X			M.J. Bodenham	1
	S2	X	X	X		X	X			X					S		X	S1	X		X			X		X	S	S	M A Riley	2
	X	X	X	X			X			X				S1	S	S2	X	X		X			X		X	X	S	S	D J Gallagher	3
	X	X	X	X			X			X				S2	S1	S3	X	X		X			X		X	X	S	S	S J Lodge	4
	X	X	X	X			X			X		S2			S	X		X	X		X			X		X	S1	S	N S Barry	5
		X	X	X						X				S1	X	X	S2	X		X		X		X		X	X	S	G P Barber	6
	S1	X	X	X					X	X					S	S	X		X		X			X		X	S	S	X	P A Durkin	7
	X	X	X	X					X	X				S	S	S		X		X			X		X	X	S	X	U D Rennie	8
	X	X	X	X						X		S		S1	S		S	X		X			X		X	X	S	X	D R Elleray	9
	X		X							X		S1		X	X	S2	X	X		X			S3		X	X	X	X	G B Frankland	10
	X		X							X		S1	X		S	X	S	X		X					X	X	X	X	G Poll	11
	X	X		X						X		S1			X	S	X		X					X		X	X	X	X	N S Barry	12
	X	X	X	X						X		S	X	S1		S2	X	X		X					X	X		X	G R Ashby	13
S	X	X	X	X					X	X		S	X	S		X	X		X		S1		X		X			S	P Jones	14
S	X	X	X	X	X	S2				X		S	X	S	S1	X	S	X		X					X		S	X	D J Gallagher	15
	S	X	X	X		S2				X		X	X	S	X	X	S		X					S1		X	S	X	M D Reed	16
	X	X	X							X	X	S2		S1				X		X				X		X	S	X	S J Lodge	17
	S	X	X	X		S				X	X	S1	X	S		S		X		X				X		X	S	X	G P Barber	18
	S	X	X	X						X	X	S1	X	S		S		X		X				X1	X			X	J T Winter	19
	S	X	X		X2					X	X	S		S	S	S		X		X				X		X	S	X	N S Barry	20
	S	X	X	X	X2					X	X	S1	X1			S		X		X			S		X	X	S2	X	M A Riley	21
X2	X	X			S	S		X		X		S1			S2			X		X		X1			X	X	X		U D Rennie	22
X	X	X		S1	S	X			X	X		S		X1			X	X		X					X	X	S	S	A B Wilkie	23
X	X	X			S	S3			X2	X		S1		X1			X			X			S2		X	X	X	S	S W Dunn	24
X1	X	X		S2	X		X	X2		X		S1		S3			S	X		X					X	X	X	X	K W Burge	25
S2	X	X			S1		S	X	X		X		S				X2			X				X	X	X	X	X1	D R Elleray	26
	S	X	X	X	X					X		S1			X	X1		X1		X				X	X	X	S		G S Willard	27
S	X		X	X	S	X			X	X		S1			S		X	X		X			X1		X	S			G Poll	28
	S1		X	X		X		X	X				S2			S		X	X1	X		X		X2	X	X	S		D J Gallagher	29
		X	X	X		X			X	X			S1	S			X		X	S			X1	X	X	S	S		S J Lodge	30
		X	X	X		X1		X		S1	X	X			S	X		S			S		S	X	X	S	S		P E Alcock	31
	X	X	X		X		X2	X		S1	X	S2			X	X1			S	S		S	X	X	X		S		P Jones	32
	X	X	X		X			X	X	X		S	S			S				X		S			X	X	S		K W Burge	33
S	X	X	X		X		S	X			S	S				X			X					X	X	S	S		G Poll	34
	X	X	X		X		S	X	X	S		X1	S2		X		S1		X				X	X	S	S		U D Rennie	35
	X	X	X		X			X	X2	S		X	S2		X2		S1		X			S2		X	X	X1	S		K W Burge	36
	X	X	X		X		X	X2	S		X1	S			X			S2		X			S1	X	X	S	S		M J Bodenham	37
X	X	X	X		X		X	X		X1					S		X	X	S	S1	X	S		X	X	S			M A Riley	38
X	S3	X	X1		X		X2	X3	X	S				S		S2		X		X	X	S	X	X	X	S1			D J Gallagher	39
	X	X	X		X		X	X	S2			S			X1		S1	X2		S	X		X3	X					J T Winter	40
	X	X	X		X		S2	X2	X1	S3			S1			X		S		X		X	X3	X					D R Elleray	41
	X2	X	X		X			X	X		S1	S3			X		S2			X3		X1	X	S					N S Barry	42
	X2	X	X		X				X	S1			S2			X		S3		X3		X1	X1	X	S				A B Wilkie	43
2	14	34	35	34		20	4	10	22	38		2	17	4	1	4	21	25		22	12		14	10	33	23	4	13	CP Appearances	
3	1			5	1		1				3	13	3	12	1	3	1	1	7				1	2		2	2		CP Sub Appearances	
0+1	1	1			0+1			1	1		0+3	1+2	2	2+1	1+1	4		3		1+1	1		4	4	1	3			CC Appearances	
									1	1								1					1	1	1	1	1	1	FAC Appearances	

Also Played: (D) Coleman S(13). (G) Jaaskelainen S(22,23,24,25,26,40,41,43,43).

185

BOLTON WANDERERS

CLUB RECORDS

BIGGEST VICTORIES
League: 8-0 v Barnsley, Division 2, 6.10.1934.
F.A. Cup: 13-0 v Sheffield United, Round 2, 1.2.1890.
League Cup: 6-1 v Tottenham Hotspur, Round 4, 27.11.1996.

BIGGEST DEFEATS
League: 0-7 v Burnley, Division 1, 1.3.1890.
0-7 v Sheffield Wednesday, Division 1, 1.3.1915.
0-7 v Manchester City, Division 1, 21.3.1936.
F.A. Cup: 1-9 v Preston North End, Round 2, 10.12.1887.
League Cup: 0-6 v Chelsea, Round 4 Replay, 8.11.1971.

MOST POINTS
3 points a win: 98, Division 1, 1996-97.
2 points a win: 61, Division 3, 1972-73.

MOST GOALS SCORED
100, 1996-97, Division 1.
McGinlay 24, Blake 21, Thompson 11, Sellars 8, Fairclough 6,
Frandsen 5, Johansen 5, Pollock 4, Bergsson 3, Taggart 3,
Lee 2, Paatelainen 2, Sheridan 2, Green 1, Taylor 1, Opponents 2.

MOST GOALS CONCEDED
92, Division 1, 1932-33.

MOST FIRST CLASS MATCHES IN A SEASON
64 - (league 46, FA Cup 8, League Cup 4, Anglo Italian 6) 1993/94.

MOST LEAGUE WINS
28, Division 1, 1996-97.

MOST LEAGUE DRAWS
17, Division 3, 1991-92.

MOST LEAGUE DEFEATS
25, Division 2, 1970-71.
25, Premiership, 1995-96.

INDIVIDUAL CLUB RECORDS

MOST GOALS IN A SEASON
Joe Smith - 38, 1920-21 (League 38).

MOST GOALS IN A MATCH
5, J.Cassidy v Sheffield United, 13-0, FA Cup, 1.2.1890.
5, T.Caldwell v Walsall, 8-1, Division 3, 10.9.1983.

OLDEST PLAYER
Peter Shilton, 45 years 239 days v Wolves, 14.5.1995.

YOUNGEST PLAYER
Ray Parry, 15 years 267 days v Wolverhampton Wanderers,
13.10.1951.

MOST CAPPED PLAYER
Nat Lofthouse (England) 33.

BEST PERFORMANCES

League: 1st in Division One 1996/97.
P 46 **W** 28 **D** 14 **L** 4 **F** 100 **A** 53 **Pts** 98
Highest Position: 3rd Division 1, 1891-92, 1920-21, 1924-25.

F.A. Cup: Winners in 1922-23 v West Ham United, 2-0.
Winners in 1925-26 v Manchester City, 1-0.
Winners in 1928-29 v Portsmouth, 2-0.
Most Recent Success: (1957-58) 3rd Rnd. Preston North End (a)
3-0; 4th Rnd. York City (a) 0-0, (h) 3-0; 5th Rnd. Stoke City (h) 3-1;
6th Rnd. Wolverhampton W. (h) 2-1; Semi-Final Blackburn Rovers 2-
1; Final Manchester United 2-0.

League Cup: (1994-95) 2nd Round Ipswich (A) 3-0, (H) 1-0,
3rd Round Sheffield Utd (A) 2-1, 4th Round West Ham (A) 3-1,
5th Round Norwich (H) 1-0, Semi-Final Swindon (A) 1-2, (H) 3-1,
Final Liverpool 1-2.

ADDITIONAL INFORMATION
PREVIOUS NAME
Christ Church FC 1874-1877.
PREVIOUS LEAGUES
None.

Club Colours: White shirts with red & blue trim, navy blue shorts,
red socks.
Change Colours: All yellow.

Reserves League: Pontins Central League Division 1.
'A' Team: Lancashire League Division 1.

DIVISIONAL RECORD							
	Played	Won	Drawn	Lost	For	Against	Points
Division 1/P	2,384	885	531	968	3,661	3,854	2,318
Division 2/1	1,033	445	255	333	1,608	1,270	1,229
Division 3/2	513	201	137	175	672	598	692
Division 4	46	22	12	12	66	42	78
Total	3,976	1,553	935	1,488	6,007	5,764	4,317

RECORDS AND STATISTICS

COMPETITIONS

Div 1/P	Div.2/1	Div.3/2	Div.4
1888-99	1899-1900	1971-73	1987-88
1900-03	1903-05	1983-87	
1905-08	1908-09	1988-93	
1909-10	1910-11		
1911-33	1933-35		
1935-64	1964-71		
1978-80	1973-78		
1995-96	1980-83		
1997-98	1993-95		
	1996-97		
	1998-		

HONOURS

Div.2/1	Div.3	FA Cup	AMC (SVT)
1908-09	1972-73	1922-23	1988-89
1977-78		1925-26	
1996-97		1928-29	
		1957-58	

MOST APPEARANCES

Edie Hopkinson 578 (1956-70)

Year	League	FA Cup	Lge Cup
1956-57	42	1	
1957-58	33	7	
1958-59	39	6	
1959-60	26	3	
1960-61	42	3	5
1961-62	42	1	2
1962-63	39	1	1
1963-64	31	4	1
1964-65	40	3	1
1965-66	42	3	2
1966-67	41	3	1
1967-68	40	1	3
1968-69	42	2	1
1969-70	20		4
	519	**38**	**21**

MOST GOALS IN A CAREER

Nat Lofthouse - 290 (1945-61)

Year	League	FA Cup	Lge Cup	Others
1945-46		2		
1946-47	18	3		
1947-48	18			
1948-49	7	1		
1949-50	10	3		
1950-51	21	1		
1951-52	18			
1952-53	22	8		
1953-54	17	1		
1954-55	15			
1955-56	32	1		
1956-57	28			
1957-58	17	3		
1958-59	29	4		
1959-60				
1960-61	3		3	
Total	**255**	**27**	**3**	**5**

Current leading goalscorer: Nathan Blake - 40 (1995-98)

RECORD TRANSFER FEE RECEIVED

Amount	Club	Player	Date
£4,500,000	Aston Villa	Alan Thompson	06/98
£4,500,000	Liverpool	Jason McAteer	9/95
£3,500,000	Celtic	Alan Stubbs	6/96
£550,000	Celtic	Andy Walker	6/94

RECORD TRANSFER FEE PAID

Amount	Club	Player	Date
£3,750,000	Wimbledon	Dean Holdsworth	10/97
£2,500,000	Newcastle United	Robbie Elliott	07/97
£1,500,000	Partizan Belgrade	Sasa Cursic	10/95
£1,500,000	Barnsley	Gerry Taggart	8/95

MANAGERS

Name	Seasons	Best	Worst
John Somerville	1908-10	19(1)	1(2)
Will Settle	1910-15	4(1)	2(2)
Tom Mather	1915-19		
Charles Foweraker	1919-44	3(1)	3(2)
Walter Rowley	1944-50	14(1)	18(1)
Bill Ridding	1951-68	4(1)	12(2)
Nat Lofthouse (x3)	1968-71	12(2)	22(2)
Jimmy McIlroy	1970		
Jimmy Meadows	1971		
Jimmy Armfield	1971-74	11(2)	7(3)
Ian Greaves	1974-80	17(1)	10(2)
Stan Anderson	1980-81	18(2)	18(2)
George Mulhall	1981-82	19(2)	19(2)
John McGovern	1982-85	22(2)	19(3)
Charles Wright	1985	17(3)	17(3)
Phil Neal	1985-92	4(3)	3(4)
Bruce Rioch	1992-95	3(2/1)	2(3/2)
Roy McFarland/Colin Todd	1995		
Colin Todd	1995-	18 (P)	1 (1)

LONGEST LEAGUE RUNS

of undefeated matches:	23 (13.10.1990 - 9.3.1991)	of league matches w/out a win:	26 (7.4.1902 - 10.1.1903)
of undefeated home matches:	27 (24.4.1920 - 24.9.1921)	of undefeated away matches:	11 (10.12.1904 - 21.4.1905)
without home win:	11 (19.4.1902 - 10.1.1903)	without an away win:	36 (25.9.1948 - 2.9.1950)
of league wins:	11 (5.11.1904 - 2.1.1905)	of home wins:	17 (11.10.1924 - 25.4.1925)
of league defeats:	11 (7.4.1902 - 18.10.1902)	of away wins:	5 (10.12.1904 - 18.3.1905)

BOLTON WANDERERS

PLAYERS NAME Honours	Ht	Wt	Birthdate	Birthplace Transfers	Contract Date	Clubs	League	L/Cup	FA Cup	Other	Lge	L/C	FAC	Oth
G O A L K E E P E R														
Branagan Keith	6	11	7/10/66	Fulham	8/4/83	Cambridge United	110	12	6	6				
DIV1 96/97				£100000	3/25/88	Millwall	46	1	5	1				
				Loan	11/24/89	Brentford	2			1				
				Loan	10/1/91	Gillingham	1							
				Free	7/3/92	Bolton Wanderers	200	29	9	7	1			
Glennon Matthew W	6.2	13.11	10/8/78	Stockport	7/3/97	Bolton W. (T)								
Jaaskelainen Jussi	6.4	12.10	4/17/75	Vaasa		VPS (Finland)								
				£100000	11/14/97	Bolton Wanderers								
Ward Gavin J	6.2	12.12	6/30/70	Sutton Coldfield		Aston Villa								
Div.3'93. WFAC'93.				Free	9/26/88	Shrewsbury Town								
				Free	9/18/89	WBA								
				Free	10/5/89	Cardiff City	58+1		1	7				
				£175000	7/16/93	Leicester City	38	3	+1	4				
				£175000	7/13/95	Bradford City								
				£300000	3/29/96	Bolton Wanderers	19+3	2	4					
D E F E N C E														
Aljofree Hasney	6	12.1	7/11/78	Manchester	5/31/97	Bolton Wanderers	2							
Cox Neil J	6	12.1	10/8/71	Scunthorpe	3/20/90	Scunthorpe United	17		4	4+1	1			
E: u21.6. LC'94.				£400000	2/12/91	Aston Villa	26+16	5+2	4+2	2	3		1	
				£1000000	7/19/94	Middlesbrough	102+3	14+1	5	2	3		1	
					5/27/97	Bolton Wanderers	20+1		+1		1			
Elliott Robert J	5.11	11.6	12/25/73	Newcastle	4/3/91	Newcastle United	69+8	5	7+2	5+1	9			
E: Y1					7/2/97	Bolton Wanderers	4							
Fish Mark Anthony	6.2	12.7	3/14/74	Capetown		Lazio								
South African Int.				£2500000	9/16/97	Bolton Wanderers	22	1	1		2			
Frandsen Per	5.8	12.6	2/6/70	Denmark		F C Copenhagen								
DIV1 96/97				£1250000	8/2/96	Bolton Wanderers	77+1	8+1	3+1		7	1		
Gardner Ricardo						Harbour View								
Jamaican Int.				£1000000	7/1/98	Bolton Wanderers								
Holden Dean T J			9/15/79	Salford		Bolton W. (T)								
Phillips James	6	12	2/8/66	Bolton	8/1/83	Bolton Wanderers	103+5	8	7	14	2			
DIV1 96/97				£95000	3/27/87	Glasgow Rangers	19+6	4		4				
				£110000	8/26/88	Oxford United	79	3	4	2	6			1
				£250000	3/15/90	Middlesbrough	139	16	10	5	6			2
				£250000	7/20/93	Bolton Wanderers	181+2	23+1	10	9	2			2
Spooner Nicky	5.11	11	6/5/71	Manchester	7/12/89	Bolton Wanderers	22+1	2	3	0+1	2			
Strong Greg	6.2	11.12	9/5/75	Bolton	10/1/92	Wigan Athletic (T)	28+7	5	1	3+1	3			
E: Y, S.					9/10/95	Bolton Wanderers	0+1	1+1						
				Loan	11/21/97	Blackpool	11		1	1	1			
Todd Andrew J J	5.9	10.6	9/21/74	Derby	3/6/92	Middlesbrough	7+1	1+1		5				
				Loan	2/27/95	Swindon Town	13							
				£250000	8/1/95	Bolton Wanderers	38+14	7+5	1		2	1		
M I D F I E L D														
Bergsson Gudni	5.11	10.7	7/21/65	Reykjavik		Valur (Iceland)								
Icelandic Int. CS'91.DIV1 96/97				£100000	12/15/88	Tottenham Hotspur	51+20	4+2	2+2	5+1	3			
				£65000	5/21/95	Bolton Wanderers	106+4	12+1	3	3	9			
Doherty Martin A	6.1	12.2	10/17/78	Urmston	7/3/97	Bolton W. (T)								
Johansen Michael B	5.6	10.5	7/22/72	Golstrup		F C Copenhagen								
DIV1 96/97				£1250000	8/2/96	Bolton Wanderers	28+21	4+2	1+1		6			
Sellars Scott	5.8	10	11/27/65	Sheffield	7/25/83	Leeds United	72+4	4	4	2	12	1		1
DIV1 96/97				£20000	7/28/86	Blackburn Rovers	194+8	12	11	20	35	3	1	2
				£800000	7/1/92	Leeds United	6+1	1+1		1				
				£700000	3/9/93	Newcastle United	54+1	4+1	3	4	5	1		1
				£750000	12/7/95	Bolton Wanderers	84+1	6+1	4		13			
Smith Gordon			12/18/80	Glasgow		Bolton W. (T)								
Whitlow Michael W	6.1	11.6	1/13/68	Northwich		Witton Albion								
CC 96/97				£10000	11/11/88	Leeds United	62+15	4+1	1+4	9	4			
				£250000	3/27/92	Leicester City	141+6	12	6	16	6	1		
				£600000	9/19/97	Bolton Wanderers	13	3	1					
F O R W A R D														
Beardsley Peter A	5.8	11.7	1/18/61	Newcastle	8/9/79	Carlisle United	93+11	6+1	15		22		7	
E:59, B2; FLg.1; Div1'88'90;FAC'89; CS'88'89'90				£275000	4/1/82	Vancouver Wh'caps								
				£300000	9/9/82	Manchester United		1						
				Free	3/1/83	Vancouver Wh'caps								
				£150000	9/23/83	Newcastle United	146+1	10	6	1	61			
				£1900000	7/24/87	Liverpool	120+11	13+1	22+3	5	46	1	11	1
				£1000000	8/5/91	Everton	81	8	4	2	25	5	1	1
				£1400000	7/16/93	Newcastle United	126+3	11	11	11	47	4	3	4
				£450000	8/20/97	Bolton Wanderers	14+3	3	0+1		2			
				Loan	2/17/98	Manchester City	5+1							
				Loan	3/26/98	Fulham	8		1	1	1			1

Name	Ht	Wt	DOB	From	Date	Club								
Blake Nathan	6	12.8	1/27/72	Cardiff		Chelsea								
DIV1 96/97				Free	8/20/90	Cardiff City	113+18	6+2	10	13+2	35		4	1
				£300000	2/17/94	Sheffield United	35+12	2+1	1	1	22	1		
				£1200000	12/23/95	Bolton Wanderers	91+4	8	6		31	5	2	
Buggie Lee D			2/11/81	Bury		Bolton W. (T)								
Gudjohnsen Eidur						PSV Eindhoven								
Icelandic Int.				Free	7/1/98	Bolton Wanderers								
Gunnlaugsson Arnar	6	11.10	3/6/73	Iscland		Akranes								
Icelandic Int.				£100000	8/1/97	Bolton Wanderers	2+13	0+3	1				1	
Holdsworth Dean	5.11	11.13	11/8/86	Walthamstow	11/12/86	Watford	2+14			0+4	3			
E: B.1. Div3'92				Loan	2/11/88	Carlisle United	4				1			
				Loan	3/18/88	Port Vale	6				2			
				Loan	8/25/88	Swansea City	4+1				1			
				Loan	10/13/88	Brentford	2+5				1			
				£125000	9/29/89	Brentford	106+4	7+1	6	12+2	53	6	7	9
				£720000	7/20/92	Wimbledon	148+21	16+3	13+7		58	11	7	
				£3500000	10/3/97	Bolton Wanderers	17+3				3			
Potter Lee	5.11	12.10	9/3/78	Salford	7/3/97	Bolton W. (T)								
Taylor Bob	5.1	11.9	03/02/67	Horden		Horden								
				Free	27/03/88	Leeds United	33+9	5+1	1	4+1	9	3		1
				£175000	23/03/89	Bristol City	96+10	6+1	9+1	3	50	2	5	1
				£300000	31/01/92	W.B.A.	211+27	16	6+2	16+3	96	6	3	8
				Loan	1/8/98	Bolton Wanderers	10+2				3			
				Free	7/1/98	Bolton Wanderers								
Taylor Scott James	5.11	11.04	5/5/76	Chertsey		Staines								
				£15000	2/8/95	Millwall	1+5							
				£150000	3/29/96	Bolton Wanderers	5+10	0+3	1		1	1	1	
				Loan	3/26/98	Blackpool	3+2				1			
Xiourouppa Costas			9/11/79	Dudley	9/17/96	Bolton Wanderers								

THE MANAGER
COLIN TODD

Date of Birth . . . . 12th December 1948.
Place of Birth. . . . . Chester-le-Street.
Date of Appointment . . . . January 1995.

PREVIOUS CLUBS
As Manager. . . . . Whitley Bay, Middlesbrough.
As Assistant. . . . . Middlesbrough, Bolton Wanderers.
As a Player . . . . Sunderland, Derby County, Everton, Birmingham City,
. . . . Nottingham Forest, Oxford Utd, Vancouver Whitecaps, Luton.

HONOURS
As a Manager
Bolton: Division One Championship 1996/97.

As a Player
Sunderland: FA Youth Cup 1967.
Derby County: Division 1 championship 1972, 1975.
England: 27 full, 14 u23 & Youth caps.　　　　**FLgeXI:** 3 caps.

The Reebok Stadium

Burnden Way, Lostock, Bolton BL6 6JW

Capacity . . . . .25,000.
First game . . . . .v Everton, 01/09/97, Premiership.
First floodlit game . . . . .v Everton, 01/09/97, Premiership.

ATTENDANCES
Highest . . . . .25,000 v Manchester United 20/09/97.
Lowest . . . . .6,444 v Leyton Orient, LC 2nd rnd 2nd leg, 30/09/97.

OTHER GROUNDS . . . . .Pikes Lane, Burnden Park.

HOW TO GET TO THE GROUND

From all directions:
Use M61.
Exit at junction 6 - signposted A6027 Horwich.
Follow Horwich and ground is visable from slip road.

Nearest Railway Station:
Bolton (01204 528216).

USEFUL TELEPHONE NUMBERS

Club switchboard .01204 673 673
Club fax number. .01204 673 773
Club shop 01204 673 500
Ticket Office. . . . . . .01204 673 601 (fax 673 773)

Marketing Department 01204 673 770
INternet address . . . . .www.boltonfc.co.uk
Clubcall 0891 12 11 64*

*Calls cost 50p per minute at all times. Call costings correct at time of going to press.

MATCHDAY PROGRAMME

Programme Editor . . . . .Simon Marland.

Number of pages . . . . .36 (A4 size).

Price . . . .£2.

Subscriptions. . . . .£50 (All home matches).

Local Newspapers
. . . . .Bolton Evening News.

Local Radio Stations
. . . . .Piccadilly Radio, G.M.R.

MATCHDAY TICKET PRICES

West & East Stand Upper Tier
Adult £19.00
Seniors £13.00
Juveniles. £11.00

West & East Stand Lower Tier
Adult £17.00
Seniors £12.00
Juveniles. £9.00

South - Upper Tier
Adult £17.00
Seniors £12.00
Juveniles. £9.00

South Lower Tier
Adult £14.00
Seniors £11.00
Juveniles. £9.00

North Lower Tier
Adult £14.00
Seniors £11.00
Juveniles. £9.00

BRADFORD CITY AFC
(The Bantams)
NATIONWIDE LEAGUE DIVISION 1
SPONSORED BY: JCT 600

1998-99 - Back Row L-R: Robbie Blake, Edinho, John McGinlay, Nigel Pepper, Daniel Verity, Stephen Wright, David Donaldson. **Middle Row:** Ron Futcher (Yth. Dev. Officer), Gareth Grant, Mark Bower, Paul Bolland, Andrew O'Brien, Gary Walsh, Darren Moore, Mark Prudhoe, Robert Steiner, Ashley West wood, John Dreyer, Craig Ramage, Alan Jackson (Kit manager). **Front Row:** Steve Smith (Yth team manager), Jamie Lawrence, Gareth Whalley, Wayne Jacobs, Chris Hutchings (Assistant Manager), Paul Jewell (Manager), Stuart McCall, Peter Beagrie, Gordon Watson, Steve Redmond (Physio).

BRADFORD CITY AFC
FORMED IN 1903
TURNED PROFESSIONAL IN 1903
LTD COMPANY IN 1983

CHAIRMAN: G Richmond
VICE-CHAIRMAN: D Thompson

DIRECTORS
T Goddard, FCCA, MrsE Richmond,
D Richmond, S A Harvey
ASSOCIATE DIRECTORS
A Biggin, M Scott, E Smith, M Smith,
H Williams

SECRETARY
Jon Pollard

COMMERCIAL MANAGER
Allan Gilliver

MANAGER: Paul Jewell
ASSISTANT MANAGER: Chris Hutchings

YOUTH TEAM MANAGER
Steve Smith

PHYSIOTHERAPIST
Steve Redmond

STATISTICIAN FOR THE DIRECTORY
Terry Frost

Is it really only two year son from the play-off success at Wembley, and only 12 months since Bradford City secured their hard-earned Division One status with a victory against Queens Park Rangers, at Valley Parade, in the final game of the season?

No such drama this time round for the home side (finishing their last seasonal fixture with four teenagers in the team) - although, ironically, final day visitors Portsmouth won 3-1 to preserve new manager Alan Ball's side from relegation.

The defeat did represent, however, the Bantams' fourth reversal in their last five League fixtures and, with just two goals scored and 14 conceded in that depressing run, Bradford City finished the season in their lowest placing of the campaign.

Despite the disappointing season finale, the positive aspects have seen a year of consolidation (with six home-bred youngsters signing professional contracts), a fourth successive season of progress in terms of League position, and the club enjoying the largest percentage crowd increase in the whole of the Football League (from an average of 5,000 to 15,000). Add to that the fact that the Youth Team carried off the last-ever Northern Intermediate League Cup (and finished third in the League), and you cannot help but share in the optimism abounding the city in terms of further progress next term.

After all, there is the return of the supporters' hero, Stuart McCall, from Glasgow Rangers, after 10 years exile from Bradford City, a club record expenditure on new players including £1.3 million signing Isiah Rankin, from Arsenal's reserves and £1 million strike partner, Lee Mills from Port Vale - the Bantam's first six-figure signing - and the continued off-the-field commercial successes initially generated by the business acumen of go-ahead chairman, Geoffrey Richmond.

On the reverse side of the coin there were early exits from both the domestic knock-out competitions - 3-2 on aggregate against near-neighbours Huddersfield Town in the Coca-Cola Cup and 2-0 at Maine Road against relegated Manchester City in the FA Cup - and a miserable goal-per-game return from the 46 League fixtures. In addition, the club's disciplinary record saw referees brandish eight red cards (a record shared only with Gillingham) and administer 63 bookings.

If new Manager Paul Jewell, at 34 on e of the youngest Football League bosses, is to win over his doubters (given the torrid end of season from which saw only 4 wins from 16 matches - himself only gaining 6 wins from 21 in charge), then these latter statistics must be adequately addressed.

Rest assured, everyone at Valley Parade will be totally committed to realising their collective dream of Premiership football. Let's hope it is sooner rather than later! TERRY FROST

BRADFORD CITY

Division 1		:13th		FA CUP: 3rd Round				LC CUP: 1st Round		

M	DATE	COMP.	VEN	OPPONENTS	RESULT	H/T	LP	GOAL SCORERS/GOAL TIMES	ATT.
1	A 09	FL	H	Stockport County	W 2-1	1-0	3	Edhino 24, Steiner 74	14312
2	12	CC 1/1	A	Huddersfield Town	L 1-2	1-2		Steiner 16	(8720)
3	15	FL	H	Stoke City	D 0-0	0-0	5		13823
4	23	FL	H	Ipswich Town	W 2-1	1-0	4	Steiner 10, Cundy 52 (OG)	13913
5	26	CC 1/2	H	Huddersfield Town	D 1-1	1-0		Edhino 6	8065
6	30	FL	A	Reading	W 3-0	2-0	3	Lawrence 9, Pepper 16, 66	(7163)
7	S 02	FL	A	Huddersfield Town	W 2-1	1-0	1	Edhino 18, Blake 67	(13159)
8	05	FL	H	Sunderland	L 0-4	0-4	1		16484
9	13	FL	H	Middlesbrough	D 2-2	1-1	2	Steiner 15, Edhino 62	17767
10	21	FL	A	Charlton Athletic	L 1-4	1-3	5	Edhino 11	(11583)
11	27	FL	A	Oxford United	D 0-0	0-0	5		(6468)
12	O 04	FL	H	Wolverhampton Wand	W 2-0	2-0	2	Steiner 35, Kulcsar 41	15236
13	18	FL	A	Port Vale	D 0-0	0-0	5		(7148)
14	21	FL	A	Portsmouth	D 1-1	1-0	6	Edhino 40	(6827)
15	25	FL	H	Crewe Alexandra	W 1-0	0-0	4	Edhino 75	15333
16	N 01	FL	H	West Bromwich Albion	D 0-0	0-0	7		16212
17	04	FL	A	Birmingham City	D 0-0	0-0	7		(14552)
18	08	FL	A	Swindon Town	L 0-1	0-1	10		(10029)
19	15	FL	H	Tranmere Rovers	L 0-1	0-0	12		16494
20	18	FL	H	Sheffield United	D 1-1	0-0	11	McGinlay 70	16127
21	22	FL	A	Manchester City	L 0-1	0-0	13		(29746)
22	29	FL	H	Norwich City	W 2-1	1-0	10	Steiner 13, 47	16637
23	D 06	FL	A	Nottingham Forest	D 2-2	0-1	11	Steiner 73, Pepper 90	(17943)
24	13	FL	H	Bury	W 1-0	1-0	11	McGinlay 25	15812
25	21	FL	A	Queens Park Rangers	L 0-1	0-1	11		(8853)
26	26	FL	A	Sunderland	L 0-2	0-1	11		(40055)
27	28	FL	H	Huddersfield Town	D 1-1	1-1	11	Blake 10	17842
28	J 03	FAC 3	A	Manchester City	L 0-2	0-2			(23686)
29	10	FL	A	Stockport County	W 2-1	2-0	11	Jacobs 32, Blake 43	(8460)
30	16	FL	A	Stoke City	L 1-2	1-2	11	McGinlay 21	(10459)
31	24	FL	H	Swindon Town	D 1-1	1-0	11	Edhino 24	15130
32	27	FL	H	Reading	W 4-1	2-1	10	Lawrence 23, Edhino 32, 68, Blake 62	13021
33	31	FL	A	Ipswich Town	L 1-2	0-0	11	Blake 56	(11864)
34	F 06	FL	H	Charlton Athletic	W 1-0	1-0	11	Blake 18	14851
35	14	FL	A	Middlesbrough	L 0-1	0-0	11		(30165)
36	18	FL	A	Wolverhampton Wand	L 1-2	0-1	12	Blake 58	(21510)
37	21	FL	H	Oxford United	D 0-0	0-0	12		14190
38	24	FL	H	Port Vale	W 2-1	1-1	11	Melville 35, Pepper 58	13293
39	28	FL	A	Sheffield United	L 1-2	0-1	11	Steiner 85	(17848)
40	M 07	FL	A	West Bromwich Albion	D 1-1	0-1	11	Steiner 39	(13281)
41	14	FL	H	Birmingham City	D 0-0	0-0	12		16392
42	21	FL	A	Tranmere Rovers	L 1-3	1-0	13	Youds 20	(9463)
43	28	FL	H	Manchester City	W 2-1	1-0	11	Pepper 49, Edhino 66	17099
44	A 04	FL	A	Norwich City	W 3-2	1-0	11	Jacobs 41, Lawrence 46, Blake 47 (pen)	(13260)
45	11	FL	H	Nottingham Forest	L 0-3	0-1	12		17248
46	13	FL	A	Bury	L 0-2	0-1	12		(6570)
47	19	FL	H	Queens Park Rangers	D 1-1	1-0	12	Steiner 18	14871
48	25	FL	A	Crewe Alexandra	L 0-5	0-4	13		(5054)
49	M 03	FL	H	Portsmouth	L 1-3	0-1	13	Ramage 86	15890

Best Home League Attendance: 17842 V Huddersfield Town   **Smallest :13021 V Reading**   **Average :15539**

Goal Scorers:

FL	(46)	Edhino 10, Steiner 10, Blake 8, Pepper 5, Lawrence 3, McGinlay 3, Jacobs 2, Kulcsar 1, Melville 1, Ramage 1, Youds 1, Opponents 1
CC	(2)	Edhino 1, Steiner 1
FAC	(0)	

Beagrie (F)	Blake (F)	Bolland (M)	Davies (M)	Dreyer (D)	Edghino (M)	Jacobs (D)	Kulcsar (M)	Lawrence (F)	McAnespie (D)	McGinlay (M)	Melville (D)	Midgley (F)	Moore (D)	Murray (F)	O'Brien (D)	O'Kane (D)	Pepper (M)	Prudhoe (G)	Ramage (M)	Sepp (M)	Sinnott (D)	Small (D)	Steiner (F)	Sundgot (F)	Walsh (G)	Wilder (D)	Youds (D)	Zabica (G)	Referee	
S1	X			X	X	X	X							X			X	X				S2	S			X	X		D. Pugh	1
X	S1			X	X	X								X	S		X	X	S				X			X	X		W C Burns	2
X	S3			X	X	X								X			X	X	S2				X	S1		X	X		T Heilbron	3
X	S1			X	X	X								X			X	X	S2				X	S2		X	X		T Jones	4
X	S2			X	X	X								X			X		S1				X	S3		X	X	X	M J Brandwood	5
X	S1			X	X	X	S2	X						X			X		S3				X			X	X	X	C R Wilkes	6
X	S1			X	X	X	S2	X						X			X		S3				X			X	X	X	R Pearson	7
X	S1			X	X	X	S3	X						X			X		S2				X			X	X	X	M Fletcher	8
X	S			X	X	X		X						X			S	X	X				X	S		X	X		G Singh	9
X	X			X	X	X		X						X	S3		S1	X	X							S2	X	X	A R Leake	10
X				S2	X	X	X							X	S				X				X	S1	X	X	X		A P D'Urso	11
X	S2				X	X	X	S1						X	X				X				X	S	X	X	X		G Laws	12
				X	X	X	X	X						X	S2			X					X	S3	X	S1	X		P S Danson	13
X	S				X	X	X	S1						X	X			X	S				X			X	X	X	S G Bennett	14
X				S3	X	X	X	S2						X	X			X	S1				X			X	X	X	R D Furnandiz	15
X	S				X	X	X	S1						X	X		X	S	X				X			X		X	W C Burns	16
X				X	X	X	X2							X	X1	S	X		X				S1			X	S2	X	M E Pierce	17
X				S	X	X	X			X				X	S1		X		X				S2			X		X	A N Butler	18
X	S3			X	X		X	S1		X				X	X		X						S2			X	X	X	T Heilbron	19
X	S			X			X			X				X	S1		X						S		X	X		X	E K Wolstenholme	20
X				X	X		X	X		X				X	S2	S3	X	X					S1			X		X	F G Stretton	21
S	S			X			X	X		X				X	X	S	X	X					X			X		X	P R Richards	22
S1				X	S2		X	X		X2				X	X	X1			X				X			X	S3	X	R J Harris	23
X2	S3			X3	S1		X	X		X1		X			X		X		S2				X			X	X	X	G B Frankland	24
X	S3				S1			X2		X3				X	X		X		S2			X1	X			X	X	X	S W Mathieson	25
X3	S1			X			X			S3				X	X		X		X1		X	X2	X	S2		X		X	P Rejer	26
X	X						X	X		S1				X	X		X					X1	X			X	X	X	J A Kirkby	27
X	X				X		X2			S1		S2		X	X		X	S		S			X			X	X1	X	G P Barber	28
X	X	S1			X		X			X1	S			X	X				X				X	S		X	X		M S Pike	29
X	X	S2			S1	X		X1		X				X	X		X					X2	S			X	X		R Pearson	30
	X	S2			X1	X		X3				S3	X2	X	X		X						S1			X	X	X	C J Foy	31
	X	S			X2	X		X				S1		X	X		X		X1				S2			X	X	X	G Laws	32
S3	X	S2			X1	X		X						X	X		X		X2				S1		X	X3	X		R Styles	33
X	X				X1	X		X				S		S1	X		X		X				S			X	X		D Pugh	34
X	X2	X1	S		X	X		X			X			X	X						S1		S2			X	X		A N Butler	35
X	X	S			X1	X		X		S1				X	X								S			X	X	X	A P D'Urso	36
X	X				X2	X		X1		S2	X			X	X			S1							X	X	X		T Jones	37
X	X2				S2	X		X			X			S1	X		X		X	S					X	X	X1		W C Burns	38
X	X				X1	X		X2			X			S	S2		X		X				S1			X	X	X	R D Furnandiz	39
X	X				S1	X		X						X	S	S	X		X				X1			X	X	X	J P Robinson	40
X3	X1				X			X		S1				S2	X		X	X	X2	S3			X			X	X	X	F G Stretton	41
	X	S1	S3		X			X3						X1	X		X	X	X2	S2			X			X	X		P R Richards	42
	X	S	S2		S1	X		X	X1						X				X		X	X	X2			X			E K Wolstenholme	43
	X	S1	X1		X	X2		X	X			X			X				S	X	S	X				X			P Taylor	44
	X	S			X	X		X	X					X	S	X		X				X			X	X		R Pearson	45
	X	S2			X1	X		X	X					S1	X		X1		X2	X3			X2			X			K A Leach	46
	X		S		X	X		X	X					S1	X		X1		X				X2			X			C J Foy	47
	X	S2	S3		X3	X		X	X					X2	X				X				X1			X			D Orr	48
	S2	X			X	X					X2			X	X				X3	S1									G Cain	49
31	23	2	1		15	34	36	14	38	7	12	6		18	29	23	7	31	8	24		7	5	26		35	31	38 3	FL Appearances	
3	11	8	3	2	7		3	5		5		2		9	3		1		8	3				11	5		4		FL Sub Appearances	
2	0+2			2	2	2		2						2			2	1	0+1				2	0+1		2	2	1	CC Appearances	
1	1				1		1		0+1		0+1		1	1		1			1				1		1	1	1		FAC Appearances	

Also Played: (M) Bower S2(44), X(46), S3(49). (M) Donaldson S(27). (M) Grant S2(47), S1(48), X1(49). (M) McLean S(28).(M) Verity S(45), S3(46).

BRADFORD CITY

CLUB RECORDS

BIGGEST VICTORIES
League: 11-1 v Rotherham United, Division 3(N), 25.8.1928.
FA Cup: 11-3 v Walker Celtic, FA Cup 1st Rnd. Replay, 1.12.1937.
League Cup: 4-0 v Rochdale, 2nd Rnd. 27.10.1982.

BIGGEST DEFEATS
League: 0-8 v Manchester City, Division 2, 7.5.1927.
1-9 v Colchester United, Division 4, 30.12.1961.
FA Cup: 1-6 v Newcastle United, 3rd Rnd, 7.3.1963.
0-5 v Burnley, 5th Rnd (Replay), 23.2.1960.
0-5 v Tottenham, 3rd Rnd (Replay), 7.1.1970.
League Cup: 1-7 v Aston Villa, 5th Rnd, 23.11.1964.

MOST POINTS
3 points a win: 94, Division 3, 1984-85.
2 points a win: 63, Division 3(N), 1928-29.

MOST GOALS SCORED
128, 1928-29 (Division 3(N))
Whitehurst 24, Moon 15, Edmunds 11, Scriven 10, Cairns 9, Cochrane 9, Bauld 8, Bedford 8, Randall 8, Moore 7, Barkas 5, White 4, Burkinshaw 4, Harvey 2, Mitchell 1, Russell 1, Opponents 2.

INDIVIDUAL CLUB RECORDS

MOST GOALS IN A SEASON
David Layne - 36 (League 34, FA Cup 2) Div 4, 1961-62.

MOST GOALS IN A MATCH
Albert Whitehurst - 7 v Tranmere Rovers, 8-0, Div 3(N), 6.3.1929.

MOST GOALS IN A CAREER
Robert Campbell - 143 (Lge 121, FAC 5, Lge Cup 11, Others 6).

MOST APPEARANCES
Cyril 'Cec' Podd 1970-84 (Lge 494+8, FAC 30, Lge C 33+1, Others 8)
Total: 574

OLDEST PLAYER
Tommy Cairns, 41 years 7 days v Bradford P.A., 7.11.1931.

YOUNGEST PLAYER
Robert Cullingford, 16 years 141 days v Mansfield Town, 22.4.1970.

MOST CAPPED PLAYER
Harry Hampton (Northern Ireland) 9.
Evelyn Lintott (England) 4.

BEST PERFORMANCES

League: 1984-85: **P** 46 **W** 28 **D** 10 **L** 8 **F** 77 **A** 45 **Pts** 94. First in Division 3.

Highest: 5th in Division 1, 1910-11.

F.A. Cup: Winners in 1911.
1st Rnd. New Brompton 1-0. 2nd Rnd. Norwich City 2-1. 3rd Rnd. Grimsby Town 1-0. 4th Rnd. Burnley 1-0. Semi-Final Blackburn Rovers 3-0.
Final Newcastle United 0-0, 1-0.

League Cup: 5th Round, 1964-65, 1987-88, 1988-89.

ADDITIONAL INFORMATION
Previous Names: None

Previous League: None (One of only two clubs to gain admission to Football League without playing a senior fixture - Chelsea being the other).

Club Colours: Amber/claret stripes, black shorts, black with claret & amber topped socks.
Change Colours:

Reserves League: Pontins Central League Division 2.

RECORDS AND STATISTICS

COMPETITIONS

Div.1/P	Div.2/1	Div.3/2	Div.3(N)	Div.4
1908-22	1903-08	1958-61	1927-29	1961-69
	1922-27	1969-72	1937-58	1972-77
	1929-37	1977-78		1978-82
	1985-90	1982-85		
	1996-	1990-96		

MOST APPEARANCES

CECIL PODD - 565+9 (1970-84)

YEAR	LEAGUE	FA CUP	LGE CUP	OTHERS
1970-71	19	3		
1971-72	9+1		2	
1972-73	40+1	4	1	
1973-74	36+1	2	1	
1974-75	44	1	2	
1975-76	45	6	2	
1976-77	43	2	1	
1977-78	34+3	1	1	
1978-79	39	2	3+1	
1979-80	37+2	2	4	
1980-81	35		4	
1981-82	46	1	6	4
1982-83	37	4	4	2
1983-84	30	2	2	2
	494+8	30	33+1	8
Previous holder: Ian Cooper - 493 (1965-77)				

RECORD TRANSFER FEE RECEIVED

AMOUNT	CLUB	PLAYER	DATE
£1.850,000	Wolves	Dean Richards	05/95
£875,000	Everton	Stuart McCall	06/88
£250,000	Newcastle United	Peter Jackson	10/86
£70,000	Derby County	Bobby Campbell	08/83

RECORD TRANSFER FEE PAID

AMOUNT	CLUB	PLAYER	DATE
£600,000	Crewe	Gareth Whalley	07/98
£500,000	Norrkoping	Robert Steiner	07/97
£500,000	Southampton	Gordon Watson	01/97
£300,000	Darlington	Robert Blake	03/97
£300,000	Bristol Rovers	John Taylor	06/88

HONOURS

DIVISION 2	DIVISION 3	DIVISION 3(N)	FA CUP	DIVISION 3(N) C.
1907-08	1984-85	1928-29	1911	1938-39

MOST GOALS IN A CAREER

BOBBY CAMPBELL - 143 (1979-86)

YEAR	LEAGUE	FA CUP	LGE CUP	OTHERS
1979-80	8			
1980-81	19		3	
1981-82	24		3	2
1982-83	25	2	3	3
1983-84	9			1
1984-85	23	3		
1985-86	10		2	
1986-87	3			
	121	5	11	6
Current leading goalscorer: Paul Jewell - 67 (07.88-98)				

MANAGERS

NAME	SEASONS	BEST	WORST
R.Campbell	1903-05	8 (2)	10 (2)
P.O'Rourke	1905-21	5 (1)	11 (2)
D.Menzies	1921-26	21 (1)	18 (2)
C.Veitch	1926-28	22 (2)	6 (3N)
P O'Rourke	1928-30	18 (2)	1 (3N)
J Peart	1930-35	6 (2)	11 (2)
R.Ray	1935-38	12 (2)	21 (2)
F.Westgarth	1938-43	3 (3N)	14 (3N)
R.Sharp (Hon.)	1943-46	-	-
J.Barker	1946-47	-	-
J.Milburn	1947-48	5 (3N)	14 (3N)
D.Steele	1948-52	7 (3N)	22 (3N)
A.Harris (Hon.)	1952	-	-
I.Powell	1952-55	5 (3N)	16 (3N)
P.Jackson Snr.	1955-61	3 (3N)	22 (3)
R.Brocklebank	1961-64	5 (4)	23 (4)
W.Harris	1965-66	-	19 (4)
W.Watson	1966-68	11 (4)	23 (4)
G.Hair	1968	5 (4)	-
J.Wheeler	1968-71	10 (3)	4 (4)
B.Edwards	1971-75	24 (3)	8 (4)
R.Kennedy	1975-78	4 (4)	17 (4)
J.Napier	1978	-	22 (3)
G.Mulhall	1978-81	5 (4)	15 (4)
R.McFarland	1981-82	2 (4)	-
T.Cherry	1982-87	13 (2)	12 (3)
T.Dolan	1987-89	4 (2)	10 (2)
T.Yorath	1989-90	14 (2)	-
J.Docherty	1990-91	23 (2)	8 (3)
F.Stapleton	1991-94	7 (2)	16 (3)
Chris Kamara	1995-98	21 (1)	6 (2)
Paul Jewell	1998-	13 (1)	13 (1)

LONGEST LEAGUE RUNS

of undefeated matches:	21 (1968-69)	of league matches w/out a win:	16 (1948-49)
of undefeated home matches:	25 (1975-78)	of undefeated away matches:	10 (1968-69)
without home win:	10 (1962-64)	without an away win:	29 (1925-27)
of league wins:	10 (1983-84)	of home wins:	9 (1952-53, 1961-64)
of league defeats:	8 (1932-33)	of away wins:	5 (1928-29, 1981-82, 1984-85)

BRADFORD CITY

PLAYERS NAME Honours	Ht	Wt	Birthdate	Birthplace Transfers	Contract Date	Clubs	League	L/Cup	FA Cup	Other	Lge	L/C	FAC	Oth
G O A L K E E P E R														
Prudhoe Mark	6	13	11/11/63	Washington	9/11/81	Sunderland	7							
GMVC'90. Div4'91. FLgXl				Loan	11/4/83	Hartlepool United	3							
				£22000	9/24/84	Birmingham City	1	4						
				£22000	2/27/86	Walsall	26	4	1					
				Loan	12/11/86	Doncaster Rovers	5							
				Loan	3/26/87	Grimsby Town	8							
				Loan	8/29/87	Hartlepool United	13							
				Loan	11/6/87	Bristol City	3			2				
				£10000	12/11/87	Carlisle United	34	2						
				£10000	3/16/89	Darlington	146	8	9	6				
				£120000	6/24/93	Stoke City	82	6+1	5	7				
				Loan	9/30/94	Peterborough United	6							
				Loan	11/29/94	Liverpool								
				Loan	2/14/97	York City	2							
					7/16/97	Bradford City	8	1						
Walsh Gary	6.3	14	3/21/68	Wigan	4/25/85	Manchester United	49+1	7		6				
E: u21.2. ECWC'91. ESC'91.FAC'94.				Loan	8/11/88	Airdrie	3	1						
				Loan	11/19/93	Oldham Athletic	6							
				£250000	8/11/95	Middlesbrough	43	9	4					
				£300000	9/26/97	Bradford City	34	1	1					
D E F E N C E														
Bower Mark J	5.10	10.11	1/23/80	Bradford	3/28/98	Bradford City (T)	1+2							
Dreyer John B	6	11.6	6/11/63	Alnwick		Wallingford								
					1/8/85	Oxford United	57+3	10+1	2	3	2			
				Loan	12/13/85	Torquay United	5							
				Loan	3/27/88	Fulham	12		2					
				£140000	6/27/88	Luton Town	212+2	13	14	8	14	1		
				Free	7/15/94	Stoke City	32+18	5	1	4+1	3			1
				Loan	3/23/95	Bolton Wanderers	1+1			1+1				
				£25000	11/7/96	Bradford City	42+3	2	3		1		3	
Jacobs Wayne	5.9	10.2	2/3/69	Sheffield	1/3/87	Sheffield Wednesday	5+1	3		1				
				£27000	3/25/88	Hull City	127+2	7	8	6	4			
				Free	8/5/93	Rotherham United	40+2	4	1	2	2			
				Free	8/5/94	Bradford City	139+2	11	8	5	6		2	
Moore Darren	6.2	12	4/22/74	Birmingham	11/18/92	Torquay United	102+1	6	7	8	7		1	2
				£62500	7/19/95	Doncaster Rovers	77	4	1	2	7			1
					6/18/97	Bradford City	17	1						
O'Brien Andrew	6.3	11.9	6/29/79	Harrogate	10/4/96	Bradford City	41+7		4		2		1	
Todd Lee	5.5	10.3	07/03/72	Hartlepool		Hartlepool United								
				Free	23/07/90	Stockport County	214+11	24+2	17	32+1	2		2	
				£500000	28/07/97	Southampton	9+1	1						
				£250000	7/1/98	Bradford City								
Verity Daniel R	5.11	10.12	4/19/80	Bradford	3/28/98	Bradford City (T)	0+1							
Westwood Ashley	6	11.3	31/08/76	Bridgnorth	01/07/94	Manchester United								
E: Y. FAYC'95.				£40000	28/07/95	Crewe Alexandra	93+5	8	9	10	9		2	
				£150000	7/1/98	Bradford City								
M I D F I E L D														
Bolland Paul G	5.10	10.12	12/23/79	Bradford	1/9/98	Bradford City (T)	2+8							
Donaldson David	5.7	9.8	12/17/78	Gravesend	7/1/97	Bradford City (T)								
McCall Stuart	5.6	10.2	6/10/66	Leeds	6/14/82	Bradford City (A)	235+3	16	12	12+1	37	3	3	3
Scottish Int. Div.3'85.				£850000	6/15/88	Everton	99+4	11	16+2	8+1	5	1	3	
via Glasgow Rangers				£300000	7/1/98	Bradford City								
Patterson Andrew			11/26/80	Kirkaldy		Bradford City								
Pepper Nigel	5.1	10.3	4/25/68	Rotherham	4/26/86	Rotherham United	35+10	1	1+1	3+3	1	1		
				Free	7/18/90	York City	223+13	16+2	12	14+1	40	3	2	
					2/28/97	Bradford City	41+1	3	1		10			
Ramage Craig	5.9	11.8	3/30/70	Derby	7/20/88	Derby County	33+9	6+1	3+1	0+3	4	2	1	
E: u21.2				Loan	2/16/89	Wigan Athletic	10			0+1	2			
				£90000	2/21/94	Watford	99+5	8+1	7		27	2		
				Loan	2/10/97	Peterborough United	7							
					6/24/97	Bradford City	24+8	0+1			1			
Whalley Gareth	5.1	11.6	19/12/73	Manchester	29/07/92	Crewe Alexandra	174+6	10+1	15+1	24	9	1	4	3
E: S.				£600000	7/1/98	Bradford City								
F O R W A R D														
Beagrie Peter	5.8	9.1	11/28/65	Middlesbrough	9/10/83	Middlesbrough	24+8	1		1+1	2			
E: B.2, u21.2				£35000	8/16/86	Sheffield United	81+3	5	5	4	11			
				£210000	6/29/88	Stoke City	54	4	3		7		1	
				£750000	11/2/89	Everton	88+26	7+2	7+2	5+1	12	3		1
				Loan	9/26/91	Sunderland	5				1			
				£1000000	3/24/94	Manchester City	46+6	8	4+1		3	1	1	
					7/2/97	Bradford City	30+3	3	1					
				Loan	3/26/98	Everton	4+2							

Player	Ht	Wt	DOB	Fee	Date	Club								
lake Robert J	5.11	12	3/4/76	Middlesbrough	7/1/94	Darlington	54+14	4+2	3+1	3	20	1		1
					3/27/97	Bradford City	26+13	+2	1		8			
avies Lawrence	6.1	11.11	9/3/77	Abergavenny	8/19/96	Leeds United (T)								
				Free	6/1/97	Bradford City	1+3							
				Loan	12/1/97	Darlington	2							
rant Gareth M	5.9	10.4	9/6/80	Leeds	4/17/98	Bradford City(T)	1+2							
ewell Paul	5.8	10.8	9/28/64	Liverpool	9/30/82	Liverpool								
MC'85.				£15000	12/20/84	Wigan Athletic	117+20	5+2	9	14+4	35		5	7
				£80000	7/21/88	Bradford City	217+52	16+1	12+1	8+1	57	6	3	1
				Loan	8/16/95	Grimsby Town								
awrence James H	5.1	12.3	3/8/70	Balham		Cowes								
C 96/97					10/15/93	Sunderland	2+2	+1						
				£20000	3/17/94	Doncaster Rovers	16+9	2	1	3	3			
				£175000	1/6/95	Leicester City	22+26	2+4	1+1		1	1		
				£50000	6/9/97	Bradford City	37+5	3	1		3			
lcGinlay John	5.9	11.6	4/8/64	Inverness		Yeovil Town				5			2	
;9,B.1. Isth Lge Prem'88.DIV1 96/97						Elgin				1			1	
					2/22/89	Shrewsbury Town	58+2	4	1	3	27		2	2
				£175000	7/11/90	Bury	16+9	1	1	1+1	9			
				£80000	1/21/91	Millwall	27+7	2+1	2	2	10			1
				£125000	9/30/92	Bolton Wanderers	180+12	23+2	16+1	11	87	14	10	7
				£625000	11/6/97	Bradford City	11+5	1	0+1		2	1		
teiner Robert H	6.2	13.5	6/20/73	Finsprong (Sweden)		Norrkoping								
				Loan	10/31/96	Bradford City	14+1		1		4		1	
				£500000	7/3/97	Bradford City	26+10	2	1		14	1	1	
Vatson Gordon	6	12.9	3/20/71	Sidcup	4/5/89	Charlton Athletic	20+11	2	+1	1+1	7	1		
;: u21.2				£250000	2/20/91	Sheffield Wed.	29+27	6+5	5+2	2+2	15	3	2	1
				£1200000	3/17/95	Southampton	36+15	6+2	5		8	4	1	
				£500000	1/17/97	Bradford City	3				1			

ADDITIONAL CONTRACT PLAYERS

Player	Ht	Wt	DOB	Fee	Date	Club								
Wright Stephen						Glasgow Rangers								
				Free	7/1/98	Bradford City								

THE MANAGER
PAUL JEWELL

Date of Birth . . . . 28th September 1964.
Place of Birth . . . . Liverpool.
Date of Appointment . . . . January 1998.

PREVIOUS CLUBS
As Manager . . . . None.
As Coach . . . . Bradford City.
As a Player . . . . Liverpool, Wigan Athletic, Bradford City, Grimsby (Loan).

HONOURS
As a Manager
None.
. . . .
As a Player
Wigan Athletic: Associate Members Cup 1985.

VALLEY PARADE

Valley Parade, Bradford, West Yorkshire BD8 7DY

Capacity 18,018

First game ....v Gainsborough Trin., Div 2 5.9.1903
First floodlit game ....v Hull City, 20.12.1954

ATTENDANCES
Highest ....39,146 v Burnley, FAC 4th Rnd, 11.3.1911
Lowest ....1,179 v Hartlepool United, AMC, 22.2.1984

HOW TO GET TO THE GROUND

From the North
A650 to Bradford. Join Ring Road, A6036. Turn left into Valley Parade for ground.

From the South and West
M62 and M606 to Bradford. Fourth exit from roundabout to A6036 Ring Road.
Left at crossroads A650, left into Valley Parade.

From East
A647 to Bradford. Right at crossroads, A6036. Left at crossroads A650.
Left into Valley Parade.

USEFUL TELEPHONE NUMBERS

Club switchboard 01274 773 355

Club fax number 01274 773 356

Club Shop 01274 770 012

Ticket Office 01274 770 022

Marketing Department. 01274 773 355

e-mail .... bradfordcityfc @ compuserve.com
Website under contructiion.

MATCHDAY PROGRAMME

Programme Editor .... Jon Pollard.

Number of pages 40

Price £1.80

Subscriptions .... £40 per season

Local Newspapers
...... Telegraph and Argus, Bradford Star
Local Radio Stations ....
.... The Pulse 97.5 & 102.5 FM
.... BBC Radio Leeds (388 MW)
.... Magic 828 (362 MW)

MATCHDAY TICKET PRICES

Sunwin Stand £13
.... OAP/Juv £7
Allied Colloids Stand £13
.... OAP/Juv £7
Diamond Seal Kop £9
.... OAP/Juv £5
Family Packages
Allied Colloids Stand A & B block or Sunwin stand F block
1 Adult & 1 Junior £13
1 Adult & 2 Junior £16
2 Adult & 1 Junior £26
2 Adult & 2 Junior £29
Extra Adult £13
Extra Junior £6
Senior Citizen £7
Only one application per household. Senior Cit. prices are for additional
applicants only and cannot replace Adults in family packages.

BRISTOL CITY
(The Robins)
NATIONWIDE LEAGUE DIVISION 1
SPONSORED BY: SANDERSON COMPUTER RECRUITMENT

1998-99 - **Back Row L-R:** Carl Hutchiings, Scott Murray, Matthew Hale, Tony Sharpe, Paul Tisdale, Tommy Doherty, Mickey Bell, Dwayne Plummer, Greg Goodridge, Gary Owers (now with Notts County), Jim Brennan, Louis Carey. **Middle Row:** Dr Dasgupta, Brian Tinnion, Steve Torpey, Julian Watts, Mark Shail, Steve Phillips, Keith Welsh, Stuart Naylor, Sean Dyche, Ade Akinbiyi, Shaun Taylor, Rob Edwards, Tony Fawthrop (chief scout). **Front Row:** Buster Footman (Physio), Kevin Langan, Matt Hewlett, Soren Andersen, John Clapp (Director), John Ward (Manager), Scott Davidson (Executive Chairman), Terry Connor (First team coach), John Laycock (Vice-chairman), Colin Cramb, Adam Locke, Matt Stowell, Mike Gibson (Goalkeeping coach).

BRISTOL CITY
FORMED IN 1894
TURNED PROFESSIONAL IN 1897
LTD COMPANY IN 1897

CHAIRMAN: Scott Davidson

DIRECTORS
John Clapp, Bob Neale, Keith Dawe,
Stephen Lansdown, J Laycock, A Gooch
GENERAL MANAGER
Ian Wilson
COMMERCIAL MANAGER
Shaun Parker

MANAGER: John Ward
FIRST TEAM COACH: Terry Connor

PHYSIOTHERAPIST
Buster Footman

STATISTICIANS FOR THE DIRECTORY
David Woods & David Peacey

Hindsight is a wonderful thin. If those voicing their concerns at City's plight in early October had had the benefit of seeing how the season would subsequently unfold then their concerns would have eased somewhat. (Modesty forbids the suggestion that they had only to read in last year's summary that 'they should be there of thereabouts come next Spring' come to that!) Defeat at Priestfield Stadium on 4 October saw City in 19th position - to the pessimist, a relegation place, to the optimist, a game in hand on all but two clubs in the Division, a chance - should that game be won - of being on the fringe of the promotion places!

Quite simply, that game was the season's watershed for the club as it was then to enjoy an unbeaten run of 15 games, (13 won), that saw them comfortably into second spot by the turn of the year and, effectively, in a two-horse race with Watford as to the destination of the championship. One win in the final five games saw the championship slip away, Watford under Graham Taylor (a long-standing friend and colleague of City boss John Ward), clinched the title by just three points. For City, the consolation was the successful blend of established players (Tinnion, Taylor, Welch); newcomers (Locke, Bell) and youngsters (Carey and Doherty) to the extent that a hard-core of 13 players topped 30 appearances each, the side having a settled look to it and, as the season developed, an air of confidence and belief too.

Ward considers this achievement to be his best to date but is keen to emphasise the team effort, from all connected with the club, to get this club, any club come to that, where they are. He certainly hasn't lacked backing from the board as emphasised close-season in signings such as Ade Akinbiyi and Tony Thorpe - they'll certainly be competing for the main striking roles with Colin Cramb and Steve Torpey (both brought to the club for the previous campaign) goals having come from several sources last term but with Shaun Goater (top scorer with 18 goals) moving to Manchester City (ironic that the clubs have 'swapped' divisions for this season) it'll be interesting to see what the best combination is.

Into the unknown then in '98/99. Bolton, Palace, Sunderland, Sheffield United, Birmingham...City'll do well to consolidate but mid-table isn't beyond them. An improvement in cup form, (out at the early stages of all three competitions entered in '97/98), wouldn't go amiss and it's not that the playing surface doesn't compliment their fluent play, groundsman Steve Drew bettering the previous season's 'highly commended' by picking up the groundsman of the year for Division Two this time around.

Hindsight is a wonderful thing. Brilliant support last season - but some may need reminding that patience is a virtue...

DAVE PEACEY.

BRISTOL CITY

Division 2	:2nd			FA CUP: 2nd Round		LC CUP: 2nd Round		AWS: Southern Quarter-Final

M	DATE	COMP.	VEN	OPPONENTS	RESULT	H/T	LP	GOAL SCORERS/GOAL TIMES	ATT.
1	A 09	FL	A	Grimsby Town	D 1-1	1-0	14	Torpey 27	(6220)
2	12	CC 1/1	H	**Bristol Rovers**	D 0-0	0-0			9341
3	15	FL	H	Blackpool	W 2-0	0-0	6	Cramb 48, Goater 87	9043
4	23	FL	A	Northampton Town	L 1-2	1-2	11	Cramb 5	(6217)
5	26	CC 1/2	A	**Bristol Rovers**	W 2-1	0-0		**Taylor 59, Bent 118**	(5872)
6	30	FL	H	Wigan Athletic	W 3-0	3-0	7	Goater 26, 37, 39 (pen)	9255
7	S 02	FL	H	Fulham	L 0-2	0-1	11		10293
8	13	FL	A	Wrexham	L 1-2	0-1	18	Goater 68	(3251)
9	17	CC 2/1	A	**Leeds United**	L 1-3	0-1		**Goater 77**	(8806)
10	20	FL	H	Bournemouth	D 1-1	1-0	19	Goater 26	8330
11	27	FL	H	Luton Town	W 3-0	3-0	15	Bell 5 (pen), Torpey 27, 31	8509
12	30	CC 2/2	H	**Leeds United**	W 2-1	1-1		**Goodridge 41, Taylor 61**	10857
13	O 04	FL	A	Gillingham	L 0-2	0-2	19		(6277)
14	11	FL	A	Southend United	W 2-0	1-0	15	Bell 34, Hails 56 (OG)	(3273)
15	17	FL	H	York City	W 2-1	0-1	6	Cramb 68, Torpey 82	9568
16	21	FL	H	Preston North End	W 2-1	0-0	7	Bell 64 (pen), Goodridge 89	9039
17	25	FL	A	Walsall	D 0-0	0-0	7		(4618)
18	29	FL	A	Millwall	W 2-0	1-0	3	Torpey 9, Locke 54	(7026)
19	N 01	FL	H	Oldham Athletic	W 1-0	0-0	2	Bell 61 (pen)	10221
20	04	FL	A	Bristol Rovers	W 2-1	1-0	2	Goater 27, 49	(7552)
21	08	FL	A	Brentford	W 4-1	2-0	2	Torpey 31, Goater 32, 67, Doherty 77	(6183)
22	15	FAC 1	H	**Millwall**	W 1-0	1-0		**Taylor 24**	8413
23	18	FL	H	Plymouth Argyle	W 2-1	2-0	2	Bell 33, 34	10867
24	22	FL	H	Wycombe Wanderers	W 3-1	1-0	2	Hewlett 38, 59, Torpey 67	11129
25	29	FL	A	Carlisle United	W 3-0	1-0	2	Goater 19, 53, Goodridge 59	(5044)
26	D 02	FL	H	Burnley	W 3-1	0-1	2	Goodridge 48, 83, Bell 71 (pen)	11136
27	07	FAC 2	A	**Bournemouth**	L 1-3	0-1		**Cramb 81**	(5687)
28	13	FL	A	Watford	D 1-1	0-0	2	Goater 53	(16072)
29	20	FL	H	Chesterfield	W 1-0	1-0	2	Bell 13 (pen)	11792
30	26	FL	H	Millwall	W 4-1	2-0	2	Cramb 10, Edwards 17, Tinnion 59, Taylor 68	16128
31	28	FL	A	Fulham	L 0-1	0-0	2		(13273)
32	J 10	FL	H	Grimsby Town	W 4-1	3-0	1	Cramb 1, 39, Taylor 5, Goater 47	12567
33	13	AWS S2	H	**Millwall**	W 1-0	1-0		**Locke 15**	2557
34	17	FL	A	Wigan Athletic	W 3-0	2-0	1	Doherty 3, Tinnion 23, Goater 71	(5078)
35	24	FL	H	Northampton Town	D 0-0	0-0	2		14753
36	27	AWS SQF	A	**Bournemouth**	L 0-1	0-0			(2124)
37	31	FL	H	Wrexham	D 1-1	1-0	2	Goater 5	11741
38	F 03	FL	A	Blackpool	D 2-2	0-0	2	Hewlett 66, 76	(3724)
39	06	FL	A	Bournemouth	L 0-1	0-1	2		(6623)
40	14	FL	H	Gillingham	L 0-2	0-0	2		11781
41	21	FL	A	Luton Town	D 0-0	0-0	2		(6405)
42	24	FL	A	York City	W 1-0	0-0	2	Bell 64 (pen)	(3770)
43	28	FL	H	Southend United	W 1-0	1-0	2	Cramb 44	12049
44	M 03	FL	H	Brentford	D 2-2	0-1	2	Torpey 55, Cockerill 61 (OG)	10398
45	14	FL	H	Bristol Rovers	W 2-0	1-0	1	Bell 34 (pen), Goater 59	17086
46	21	FL	A	Plymouth Argyle	L 0-2	0-0	2		(7622)
47	28	FL	A	Wycombe Wanderers	W 2-1	1-0	2	Cramb 41, 84	(6326)
48	31	FL	A	Oldham Athletic	W 2-1	0-1	1	Goodridge 52, Roberts 53	(4543)
49	A 04	FL	H	Carlisle United	W 1-0	0-0	1	Goodridge 53	12578
50	11	FL	A	Burnley	L 0-1	0-1	1		(10600)
51	13	FL	H	Watford	D 1-1	0-0	1	Edwards 68	19141
52	18	FL	A	Chesterfield	L 0-1	0-1	1		(5085)
53	25	FL	H	Walsall	W 2-1	1-1	1	Owers 3, Tinnion 80	15059
54	M 02	FL	A	Preston North End	L 1-2	1-2	2	McCarthy 9	(12067)

Best Home League Attendance: 19141 V Watford	Smallest :8330 V Bournemouth	Average :11846

Goal Scorers:

FL	(69)	Goater 17, Bell 10, Cramb 9, Torpey 8, Goodridge 6, Hewlett 4, Tinnion 3, Doherty 2, Edwards 2, Taylor 2, Locke 1, McCarthy 1, Owers 1, Roberts 1, Opponents 2
CC	(5)	Taylor 2, Bent 1, Goater 1, Goodridge 1
FAC	(2)	Cramb 1, Taylor 1
AWS	(1)	Locke 1

1997-98

(F) Barclay	(F) Bell	(F) Bent	(M) Brennan	(D) Carey	(F) Cramb	(M) Doherty	(D) Dyche	(M) Edwards	(F) Goater	(F) Goodridge	(M) Hewlett	(M) Johansen	(M) Jordan	(M) Langan	(M) Locke	(F) McCarthy	(F) Murray	(G) Naylor	(M) Owers	(M) Paterson	(D) Plummer	(M) Roberts	(D) Shail	(D) Taylor	(D) Tinnion	(M) Tisdale	(F) Torpey	(G) Welch		
S2	X			X	S1		X	X		X								X	X					X	X	S	X	X	G.B. Frankland	1
S	X	S2			X		X	X		X					X				X	X				X	X	S1		X	G Cain	2
S	X	S1		X	X		X	X		X					X				X	X				X	X	S2		X	G Singh	3
	X	S3		X	X		X	X		X									X	X				X	X	S2	S1	X	P Taylor	4
	X	S1	S2	X			X	X		X					X				X	X				X	X	S		X	P Rejer	5
S3	X			X	X		X	X		X				S1					X	X				X	X	S2		X	M E Pierce	6
S2	X			X	X		X	X		X					S1				X	X				X	X	S		X	R J Harris	7
	X		S1	X			X	X	S3	X									X	X				X	X	X	S2	X	A Bates	8
	X		X	S	S			X	S1	X	X								X	X				X	X	X	X	X	G Poll	9
	X		X	S			X	X	S	X									X	S				X	X	X	X	X	M Fletcher	10
S1	X			S	X	S2		X		X					X				X					X	X		X	X	E Lomas	11
S1	X		S		X	X	X		X						X				X		S			X	X		X	X	N S Barry	12
	X			X	X	X	S1	X	S						X				X		S		S	X	X		X	X	A P D'Urso	13
	X		S	X	X			S1							X				X		S2		X	X	X		X	X	D Orr	14
	X				X	X	X	S2		S1	S				X				X				X	X	X		X	X	M R Halsey	15
S	X			S	X	X	X	X		X					X	S			X					X	X		X	X	R Styles	16
	X			S	X	X	X	X	S1	X	S2				X				X					X	X		X	X	C J Foy	17
	X			X	X		X	X	S	X	X				X					S				X	X		X	X	F G Stretton	18
	X			X	X	S2	X	X	S1	S	X				X									X	X		X	X	D R Crick	19
		X	X	S1	S	X	X	X	X						X									X	X		X	X	M C Bailey	20
	X		S	X	S	S1	X	X	X						X									X	X		X	X	P S Danson	21
	X		S	X	S	X		X	X	X				S1	X				S					X	X	S	X	X	M Fletcher	22
	X	S1	X	S	X		X	X	X					S2	X									X	X		X	X	A G Wiley	23
	X		X	X	S2	X		X	X	X				S1	X								S	X	X		X	X	M K Lynch	24
S3	X	S1	X	X	X2		S2	X	X3	X					X									X	X1			X	M S Pike	25
S1	X	X	X	X1	X		X	X	X					S	X									X	X	S		X	A Bates	26
S2	X	X1	X	X		X	X	X		S	X			S	X				S				X	S1	X2			X	M R Halsey	27
S	X		X	X1	X	S1	X	X	X						X	S								X	X			X	B Knight	28
	X		X	X1	S		X	X	X2	X					X	S1			S2					X	X			X	A P D'Urso	29
	X		X	X	X		X	X2	X1						X	S1			S					X	X		S2	X	R J Harris	30
	X		X	X	X1										X2	S1			S					X	X		S2	X	J P Robinson	31
	X		X	X	X2		X	X3	X	S2					X1	S1								X	X		S3	X	E K Wolstenholme	32
	X		X	S2			X1	X2		S1					X		X		X					X	X	X		X	(blank)	33
	X		X	X2	X		X	X	X1	S1					X				X		S			X	X		S2	X	D Laws	34
	X		X	X1	X			X	X	X					S				X		S			X	X		S1	X	D J Hine	35
	X		X	X	X			S2	S1	X					X1		X	X2						X	X	X		X	(blank)	36
	X		X	X2	X1		X	X	X	S1					X		S							X	X		S2	X	P S Danson	37
	X		X	X1	S		X	X	X	S1					X		S							X	X		S1	X	G B Frankland	38
S1	X		X				X	X	X1	X					S1		S							X	X		X1	X	P Rejer	39
	X						X	X	X	X	X1				X2		S2		X	S				X	X		S1	X	A R Hall	40
	X		X	S2			X	X	X1	X	X2				X		S1							X	X		S	X	K A Leach	41
	X		X	S2			X	X2		X1	S				X		X		S1					X	X		X	X	B Coddington	42
	X	S	X	X2	X1		X	X						S2	X		X		S1					X	X		X	X	R Styles	43
	X	S	X	X1	S		X	S1		X	X			S2	X		X2							X	X		X1	X	M J Brandwood	44
	X		X	S1	S		X	X	S2	X					X		X2							X	X2		X1	X	E Lomas	45
S2	X	S	X	X	S1		X1	X							X		X							X	X2		X	X	M Fletcher	46
	X		X	X3	S1			X2	X1						X	X	S2		X			S3		X	X		X	X	R D Furnandiz	47
	X1	X	X3	S1				X	X						X	S3		X	S2		X2			X	X		X	X	D Pugh	48
	X		X	X1	S2			X	X						X	X2		X	S	S1				X	X		X	X	M E Pierce	49
	X		X	X	S1		S		X	X1					X	X2	S2		X					X	X		X	X	A N Butler	50
	X		X	X2		S1		X3	S2						X	X	S3		X					X1	X		X	X	A G Wiley	51
	X		X	X2	X	S	X	S	X						X	X	S2		X	S1				X	X			X1	R Pearson	52
	X		X	X1	X			X2	S2		S				X	X	S1	X	X	X				X					S W Mathieson	53
	S	X	X2	X			X	X	S2						X	X1	S1	X	X					X					C J Foy	54
44		4	37	34	22	10	34	28	28	27	2				35	7	10	2	20	7		1	2	43	44	2	19	44	FL Appearances	
8		2		2	1	6	8	1	3	5	3	7	1		3	2			13					2			3	10	FL Sub Appearances	
0+1	4	0+2	1+1	2	1	3	3	1+1	3				3				4	3				4	4	1+1	2					CC Appearances	
0+1	2		1	2	1	1	1	2	2	1	0+1	2			2	1+1	1	1	2										FAC Appearances	
2		2	1+1	1	1+1	0+1	1+1	2	2	2	2	2	2	2															AWS Appearances	

BRISTOL CITY

BIGGEST VICTORIES
League: 9-0 v Aldershot, Division 3(S), 28.12.1946.
F.A. Cup: 11-0 v Chichester City, Round 1, 5.11.1960.
League Cup: 4-0 v Rotherham United, Round 2, 15.9.1970.
4-0 v Peterborough United, Round 3, 2.10.1979.
5-1 v Cardiff City, Round 1 2nd Leg, 25.8.92.

BIGGEST DEFEATS
League: 0-9 v Coventry City, Division 3(S), 28.4.1934.
F.A. Cup: 0-5 v Preston North End, Round 5 replay, 25.2.1935.
0-5 v Brentford, Round 4, 2nd leg, 31.1.1946.
1-6 v Sunderland, Round 4, 25.1.1964.
League Cup: 0-5 v Everton, Round 2, 13.9.1967.
1-6 v West Ham United, Round 2, 2nd leg, 9.10.1984.
1-6 v Sunderland, Round 2, 2nd leg, 8.10.1990.

MOST POINTS
3 points a win: 91, Division 3, 1989-90.
2 points a win: 70, Division 3(S), 1954-55.

MOST GOALS SCORED
104, Division 3(S), 1926-27.

MOST GOALS CONCEDED
97, Division 2, 1959-60.

MOST FIRST CLASS MATCHES IN A SEASON
64 (League 46, FA Cup 6, Lge Cup 9, AMC 3) 1988-89.

MOST LEAGUE WINS
30, Division 2, 1905-06; Division 3(S), 1954-55.

MOST LEAGUE DRAWS
17, Division 2, 1919-20, 1965-66; Division 4, 1982-83.

MOST LEAGUE DEFEATS
26, Division 2, 1959-60.

MOST GOALS IN A SEASON
Don Clark: 41 goals in 1946-47 (League 36, FAC 5).

MOST GOALS IN A MATCH
6. 'Tot' Walsh v Gillingham, Division 3(S), 15.1.1927 (9-4).

OLDEST PLAYER
Terry Cooper, 40 years 86 days, 6.10.1984.

YOUNGEST PLAYER
Nyrere Kelly, 16 years 8 months, 16.10.1982.

MOST CAPPED PLAYER
Billy Wedlock (England) 26.

League: Champions of Division 2, 1905-06.
Highest Position: Runners-up in Division 1, 1906-07.
F.A. Cup: Runners-up in 1908-09.
League Cup: Semi-Finals in 1970-71, 1988-89.

ADDITIONAL INFORMATION
PREVIOUS NAMES
Bristol South End 1894-97. Amalgamated with Bedminster 1900.

PREVIOUS LEAGUES
Southern League 1897-1901.

Club colours: Red shirts, white shorts, red and white socks.
Change Colours: Yellow shirts, green shorts, red socks.

Reserves League: None.
Youth League: South East Counties League.

DIVISIONAL RECORD

	Played	Won	Drawn	Lost	For	Against	Points
Division 1	358	114	94	150	428	510	322
Division 2/1	1648	590	421	637	2217	2346	1675
Division 3/2	690	301	173	216	1085	866	965
Division 3 (S)	860	374	209	277	1411	1207	957
Division 4	92	37	27	28	129	114	138
Total	3,648	1,416	924	1,308	5,270	5,043	4,042

RECORDS AND STATISTICS

COMPETITIONS

Div.1	Div.2/1	Div 3/2	Div.3 (S)	Div.4
1906-11	1901-06	1960-65	1922-23	1982-84
1976-80	1911-22	1981-22	1924-27	
	1923-24	1984-90	1932-55	
	1927-32	1995-98		
	1955-60			
	1965-76			
	1980-81			
	1990-95			
	1998-			

HONOURS

Div.2	Div.3(S)	Ang/Scot	AMC	Welsh Cup
1905-06	1922-23	1977-78	1985-86	1933-34
	1926-27			
	1954-55			

MOST GOALS IN A CAREER

John Atyeo - 350 (1951-66)

Year	League	FA Cup	Lge Cup	Others
1951-52	12	2	-	-
1952-53	11	-	-	-
1953-54	22	3	-	-
1954-55	28	-	-	-
1955-56	30	1	-	-
1956-57	23	5	-	-
1957-58	23	2	-	-
1958-59	26	-	-	-
1959-60	16	1	-	-
1960-61	19	7	3	-
1961-62	26	3	-	-
1962-63	16	2	-	-
1963-64	21	4	2	-
1964-65	23	-	-	-
1965-66	19	-	-	-
Total	**315**	**30**	**5**	**-**

Current leading goalscorer: Mark Tinnion - 19 (03/93-98)

MOST APPEARANCES

John Atyeo - 643 (1951-66)

Year	League	FA Cup	Lge Cup	Others
1951-52	44	2	-	-
1952-53	33	-	-	-
1953-54	45	3	-	-
1954-55	46	1	-	-
1955-56	39	1	-	-
1956-57	37	3	-	-
1957-58	42	4	-	-
1958-59	40	3	-	-
1959-60	42	1	-	-
1960-61	37	5	3	-
1961-62	42	5	1	-
1962-63	30	3	1	-
1963-64	46	5	1	-
1964-65	38	4	-	-
1965-66	35	1	-	-
Total	**596**	**41**	**6**	**-**

RECORD TRANSFER FEE RECEIVED

Amount	Club	Player	Date
£1,750,000	Newcastle Utd	Andy Cole	03/93
£600,000	Norwich City	Rob Newman	07/91
£325,000	Coventry City	Gary Collier	08/79
£110,000	Chelsea	Chris Garland	09/71

RECORD TRANSFER FEE PAID

Amount	Club	Player	Date
£1,200,000	Gillingham	Ade Akinbiyi	05/98
£500,000	Arsenal	Andy Cole	07/92
£250,000	Everton	Ray Atteveld	03/92
£250,000	Celtic	J Dziekanowski	01/92

MANAGERS

Name (since 1946)	Seasons	Best	Worst
Sam Hollis	1901-05	4 (2)	6 (2)
Harry Thickett	1905-10	2 (1)	1 (2)
Frank Bacon*	1910-11		
Sam Hollis	1911-13	10 (1)	16 (?)
George Hedley	1913-15	8 (2)	13 (2)
Jack Hamilton*	1915-19	1st	W.War
Joe Palmer	1920-21	3 (2)	8 (2)
A Annan/C Hancock*	1921		
Alex Raisbeck	1921-29	12 (2)	1 (3S)
Joe Bradshaw	1929-32	16 (2)	22 (2)
Bob Hewison	1932-38	2 (3S)	19 (3S)
Clarrie Bourton*	1938-39	8 (3S)	8 (3S)
Bob Hewison	1940-49	3 (3S)	16 (3S)
Bob Wright	1949-50	15 (3S)	15 (3S)
Pat Beasley	1950-58	11 (2)	15 (3S)
J Seed/L Bardsley*	1958		
Peter Doherty	1958-60	10 (2)	22 (2)
Les Bardsley*	1960		
Fred Ford	1960-67	5 (2)	14 (3)
Les Bardsley*	1967		
Alan Dicks	1967-80	13 (1)	19 (2)
T Collins/K Wimshurst*	1980		
Bob Houghton	1980-82	21 (2)	23 (3)
R Hodgson/G Sharpe*	1982		
Terry Cooper	1982-88	5 (3)	14 (4)
Joe Jordan	1988-90	2 (3)	11 (3)
Jimmy Lumsden	1990-92	9 (2)	9 (2)
Aizle'd/Osman/Shelton*	1992		
Denis Smith	1992-93	17 (2)	17 (2)
Russell Osman	1993-94	15 (2/1)	15 (2/1)
Joe Jordan	1994-97	23 (1)	13 (2)
John Ward	1997-	2 (2)	5 (2)

LONGEST LEAGUE RUNS

of undefeated matches:	24 (9.9.1905 -10.2.1906)	of league matches w/out a win:	15 (29.4.1933 - 4.11.1933)
of undefeated home matches:	25 (24.10.1953 - 27.11.1954)	of undefeated away matches:	21 (16.9.1905 - 22.9.1906)
without home win:	10 (17.10.1931 - 5.3.1932)	without an away win:	23 (8.10.1932 - 28.10.1933)
of league wins:	14 (9.9.1905 - 2.12.1905)	of home wins:	12 (24.4.1926 - 29.1.1927)
of league defeats:	7 (5.9.1931- 3.10.1931 & 3.10.1970 - 7.11.71)	of away wins:	6 (16.9.1905 - 25.11.1905)

BRISTOL CITY

PLAYERS NAME Honours	Ht	Wt	Birthdate	Birthplace Transfers	Contract Date	Clubs	League	L/Cup	FA Cup	Other	Lge	L/C	FAC	Oth
G O A L K E E P E R														
Naylor Stuart	6.4	11.3	12/6/62	Wetherby	6/19/80	Lincoln City	49	4	2	6				
				Loan	2/23/83	Peterborough United	8							
				£100000	2/18/86	W.B.A.	354+1	22	13	20				
					8/13/96	Bristol City	36	4	4					
Phillips Steven J	6.1	11.10	5/6/78	Bath		Paulton Rovers								
					5/31/97	Bristol City								
Welch Keith	6.2	12.5	10/3/68	Bolton		Bolton Wanderers								
				Free	3/3/87	Rochdale	205	12	10	12				
				£200000	7/25/91	Bristol City	250	16	13	11				
D E F E N C E														
Carey Louis	5.11	11.1	1/22/77	Bristol	7/3/95	Bristol City	98+4	4+1	8	1+2				
Dyche Sean	6	11.7	6/28/71	Kettering	5/20/89	Nottingham Forest								
				Free	2/1/90	Chesterfield	219+12	9	13	16	8		1	
					7/9/97	Bristol City	10+1	1						
Jordan Andrew J			12/14/79	Manchester	4/24/98	Bristol City (T)								
Plummer Dwayne J	6.3	11.6	10/12/76											
Shail Mark	6.1	13.03	10/15/66	Sweden		Worcester City			2					
E: SP.1.				£5000		Yeovil Town			8					
				£45000	3/25/93	Bristol City	96+7	5+1	10	4	4		1	
Taylor Shaun	6.1	12.8	2/26/63	Plymouth	1/1/00	Bideford								
Div.4'90. Div.2'96. DIV2 95/96				Free	12/10/86	Exeter City	200	12	9	12	17			
				£200000	7/26/91	Swindon Town	213	22	14	10	30	2		1
				£100000	9/6/96	Bristol City	71	4	5	1	3	2	1	
Tinnion Mark	5.11	11.5	2/23/68	Stanley	2/26/86	Newcastle United	30+2	5		1+1	2			
				£150000	3/9/89	Bradford City	137+8	12	9	7+1	22	1	4	2
				£180000	3/23/93	Bristol City	185+8	12	13+2	2+2	16		3	
Watts Julian	6.3	13.7	3/17/71	Sheffield	7/10/90	Rotherham United	17+3	1	4	2	1			
LC'97.				£80000	3/13/92	Sheffield Wed.	12+4	1		1	1			
				Loan	12/18/92	Shrewsbury Town	9			1				
				£210000	3/29/97	Leicester City	31+7	6+1	2+1	4	1			
				Loan	8/29/97	Crewe Alexandra	5							
				Loan	2/5/98	Huddersfield Town	8							
				Free	7/1/98	Bristol City								
M I D F I E L D														
Brennan Jim	5.9	11.06	5/8/77	Canada		Sora Lazio								
				Free	10/5/94	Bristol City	11+3		1					
Doherty Thomas E	5.8	9.13	3/17/79	Bristol		Bristol City	22+8	1	1+1		2			
Edwards Robert	6	11.1	7/1/73	Kendal	4/10/90	Carlisle United	48	4	1	2+1	5			
W: B.2,u21.9,Y.				£135000	3/27/91	Bristol City	169+24	15+1	13+2	10+1	5	1		2
Hale Matthew J	5.6	10	2/2/79	Bristol	7/8/97	Bristol City (T)								
Hewlett Matthew	6.2	10.11	2/25/76	Bristol	8/12/93	Bristol City	97+12	8+1	3+1	2	8		2	
E: Y.				Loan	12/30/94	Bath City								
Hutchings Carl	5.11	11	9/24/74	Hammersmith	7/12/93	Brentford	144+18	9+1	11+1	11+3	7			
				£130000	7/1/98	Bristol City								
Langan Kevin	5.11	11.2	4/7/78	Jersey	5/31/97	Bristol City	0+3		0+1					
Locke Adam S	5.11	12.7	8/20/70	Croydon	6/21/88	Crystal Palace								
				Free	8/6/90	Southend United	56+17	5	2+1	6+1	3			
				Loan	10/8/93	Colchester United	4			1				
					9/23/94	Colchester United	64+14	5+1	5	4+2	8			
					7/8/97	Bristol City	36+2	3	2		1			
Muntasser Jehad	5.11	12.5	7/26/78	Tripoli	7/9/97	Arsenal		0+1						
				Free	2/27/98	Bristol City								
Tisdale Paul	5.9	10.9	1/14/73	Malta	6/5/91	Southampton	5+11	0+1	0+1		1			
E: u18.3, SFA				Loan	3/12/92	Northampton Town	5							
				Loan	11/29/96	Huddersfield Town	1							
				Free	6/2/97	Bristol City	2+3	1+1	1					
				Loan	12/19/97	Exeter City	10				1			
F O R W A R D														
Akinbiyi Adeola P	6.1	12	10/10/74	Hackney	2/5/93	Norwich City	22+26	2+3	1+2	0+1	3	2		
				Loan	1/21/94	Hereford United	3+1				2			
				Loan	11/24/94	Brighton & H.A.	7				4			
				£250000	1/13/97	Gillingham	63	2	2		28		1	
				£1200000	7/1/98	Bristol City								

204

Name	Ht	Wt	DOB	From	Fee	Date	Club								
Andersen Soren				Denmark			Aalborg BK								
					£410000	7/1/98	Bristol City								
Bell Michael	5.8	10.4	11/15/71	Newcastle		7/1/90	Northampton Town	133+20	7+1	5	9+2	10		1	1
						10/21/94	Wycombe W.	117+1	5	9	2+1	6		2	
						7/9/97	Bristol City	44	4	2		10			
Brown Aaron W			3/14/80	Bristol			Bristol City (T)								
Cramb Colin	6	11.09	6/23/74	Lanark		8/1/90	Hamilton Acad.	48				10			
						8/1/93	Southampton	1							
						8/1/94	Falkirk	8				1			
						2/1/95	Hearts	6				1			
						12/15/95	Doncaster Rovers	59+2	2	1		25	1	1	1
						7/11/97	Bristol City	32+6	2	1		9		1	
Goodridge Greg	5.6	10	2/10/75	Barbados			Lambada WI								
Barbados International					Free	3/24/94	Torquay United	32+6	4	2+1	3+1	4	1		1
					£100000	8/9/95	Q.P.R.	0+7	0+1	0+1		1			
						8/16/96	Bristol City	47+12	4+1	5+1	0+1	12	1	1	
Murray Scott	5.11	11	5/26/74	Aberdeen		8/1/93	Aston Villa	4							
					£150000	12/10/97	Bristol City	10+13							
Thorpe Anthony	5.9	12	4/10/74	Leicester		8/18/92	Luton Town	91+22	5+4	5+2	3+2	46	5	2	1
					£800000	2/27/98	Fulham	5+8			1+1	3			
					£1000000	7/1/98	Bristol City								
Torpey Stephen	6.3	13.3	12/8/70	Islington		2/14/89	Millwall	3+4	0+1						
AMC'94.					£70000	11/21/90	Bradford City	86+10	6	2	8	22		6	
					£80000	8/3/93	Swansea City	150+11	9+2	10	16+2	44	2	5	6
						8/8/97	Bristol City	19+10	2	1		8			

ADDITIONAL CONTRACT PLAYERS

Name	Ht	Wt	DOB	From	Fee	Date	Club								
Stowell Matt							Slough Town								
					£15000	7/1/98	Bristol City								

THE MANAGER
JOHN WARD

Date of Birth . . . . 1951.
Place of Birth. . . . . Lincoln.
Date of Appointment. . . . . March 1997.

PREVIOUS CLUBS
As Manager . . . . York City, Bristol Rovers.
As Assistant/Coach . . . . Watford, Aston Villa.
As a Player . . . . Lincoln City, Watford, Grimsby Town, Lincoln City

HONOURS
As a Manager
Bristol City: Promotion to Division 1, 1997-98.
. . . .
As a Player
None.

ASHTON GATE
Bristol BS3 2EJ

Capacity ....20,832.

First game...v Bolton W. 3.9.1904.
First floodlit game...v Wolves 27.1.1953.

ATTENDANCES
Highest ....43,335 v P.N.E. FA Cup 5th Rnd, 16.2.1935.
N.B. Over 50,000 were judged to be in the ground on 30.1.1935 for the FA Cup 4th Rnd replay v Portsmouth, when the gates were rushed and the crowd broke in. Official paid attendance was given as 42,885.
Lowest...1,515 v Oxford United, Anglo Italian Cup, 7.9.1993.

OTHER GROUNDS........St John's Lane 1894-1904, Bedminster's Ashton Gate (14 matches) 1900-01.

HOW TO GET TO THE GROUND

From the North and West
Use motorway (M5) until junction 16. Leave motorway and follow signs to Bristol (A38). Follow signs to City Centre then follow signs to Taunton (A38). In 1.2 miles cross Cumberland Basin swing bridge, then branch left into Winterstoke Road for Bristol City FC.

From the East
Use motorway (M4), then M32 and follow signs to the City Centre, then follow signs to Taunton A38. In 1.2 miles cross Cumberland Basin swing bridge, then branch left into Winterstoke Road for Bristol City FC.

From the South
Use motorway (M5) until junction 18. Leave motorway and follow signs to Bristol (A4) along Portway then turn right and follow signs to Taunton over Cumberland Basin swing bridge, then branch left into Winterstoke Road for Bristol City FC.
To use the Bristol City FC park and ride scheme follow AA signs to 'Bristol City car park', which is in Anchor Road.

Car Parking: There is limited street parking around ground.
Nearest Railway Station: Temple Meads (01272 294 255).

USEFUL TELEPHONE NUMBERS

Club switchboard. 0117 963 0630
Club fax number 0117 963 0700
Club shop 0117 963 0637
Ticket Office 0117 966 6666

Marketing Department. 0117 963 0600
Internet address . . . . www.bcfc.co.uk
Clubcall 0898 12 11 76*
*Calls cost 50p per minute at all times. Call costings correct at time of going to press.

MATCHDAY PROGRAMME

Programme Editor . . . . . Steve Henderson.

Number of pages . . . . . 40 - A4 (Saturday).
. . . . 16-24 - A4 (Midweek).

Price. . . . . £2.00 (Saturday).
. . . . £1.00 (Midweek).

Subscriptions . . . . Apply to club.

Local Newspapers
Bristol Evening Post, Western Daily Press,
. . . . Green'un, Sunday Independent.

Local Radio Stations
. . . . Radio Bristol, GWR/Brunel Radio,
. . . . Galaxy Radio.

MATCHDAY TICKET PRICES

	MEMBERS	NON-MEM.
Atyeo Stand	£10	£11
S.Cit & Students/Juv	£7/£5	£8/£6
Evening Post Dolman Stand	£12	£13
S.Cit & Students/Juv	£9/£2	£10/£3
GWR fm Family Enclosure	£12	£13
S.Cit & Students/Juv	£9/£2	£10/£3
Brunel Ford Williams Stand	£12	£13
S.Cit & Students/Juv	£9/£5	£10/£6
Platinum Seating	£17	£18
S.Cit & Students/Juv	£12/£7	£13/£8

BURY
(The Shakers)
NATIONWIDE LEAGUE DIVISION 1
SPONSORED BY: BIRTHDAYS (RON WOOD GREETING CARDS LTD)

1990-99 - Back Row L-R: Steve Redmond, Peter Swan, Chris Swailes, Chris Lucketti, Andy Preece, Brian Linighan, Andy Woodward. **Middle Row:** Ron Reid (Asst. Manager), Tony Ellis, Tony Battersby (now Lincoln), Laurent D'Jaffo, Dean Kiely, Gary Hoggeth. Gordon Armstrong, Nigel Jemson, Nick Daws, Alan Raw (Physio). **Front Row:** Dean West, Rob Matthews, Dean Barrick, Neil Warnock (Manager), Terry Robinson (Chairman), Lennie Johnrose, Tony Rigby, Mark Patterson.

BURY
FORMED IN 1885
TURNED PROFESSIONAL IN 1885
LTD COMPANY IN 1897

CHAIRMAN: T Robinson
VICE-CHAIRMAN
Canon J R Smith, MA
DIRECTORS
J Smith, C H Eaves FCA, F Mason
SECRETARY
Mr J Heap
COMMERCIAL MANAGER
N Neville

MANAGER: Neil Warnock
ASSISTANT MANAGER: Ron Reid

PHYSIOTHERAPIST
Alan Raw

STATISTICIAN FOR THE DIRECTORY
& OFFICIAL CLUB HISTORIAN
Peter Cullen

Having come up as champions of Division Two the previous season, an opening run of eight games with only one defeat gave them an encouraging start and maybe promoted thoughts of gaining a play-off place.

However, Division One is fast gaining a reputation of being one of the toughest Divisions in the country and Bury had recorded only two wins by Boxing Day and were now sitting in the relegation zone. It wasn't until February 25th when they entertained Birmingham City that their form took a change for the better. Birmingham were beaten 3-1 followed by a 1-0 over Swindon, a 1-1 draw v. Portsmouth and a 1-0 over Norwich. This little run took them out of the drop zone and was just enough to keep them the right side of relegation for the rest of the season.

There was little to cheer in the cup competitions either as a 2nd round defeat against Sunderland ended any Coca-Cola Cup interest, whilst in the FA Cup Sheffield United were the victors, albeit in a replay, in the 3rd round.

With Neil Warnock joining Bury as manager in the Summer hopes are high that he can produce a team that can finish in the top half of the table. Whether they will be strong enough for a play-off position remains to be seen, as long as there is no mention of relegation then the fans will be happy.

BURY

Division 1	:17th		FA CUP: 3rd Round			LC CUP: 2nd Round		

M	DATE	COMP.	VEN	OPPONENTS	RESULT	H/T	LP	GOAL SCORERS/GOAL TIMES	ATT.
1	A 09	FL	H	Reading	D 1-1	0-1	11	Armstrong 51	5065
2	12	CC 1/1	A	Crewe Alexandra	W 3-2	2-2		Armstrong 30, Jepson 34 (pen), Johnson 49	(2618)
3	15	FL	A	Stockport County	D 0-0	0-0	14		(7260)
4	23	FL	H	Charlton Athletic	D 0-0	0-0	18		4657
5	26	CC 1/2	H	Crewe Alexandra	D 3-3	2-2		Andy Gray 33, Johnson 35, Battersby 113 (pen)	3296
6	30	FL	A	Wolverhampton Wand	L 2-4	1-2	19	Battersby 19, Johnson 61	(21141)
7	S 02	FL	A	Crewe Alexandra	W 2-1	1-1	13	Johnson 13, Swan 63	(4447)
8	07	FL	H	Tranmere Rovers	W 1-0	1-0	7	Swan 41	5073
9	12	FL	H	Manchester City	D 1-1	0-0	6	Johnson 65	11216
10	16	CC 2/1	A	Sunderland	L 1-2	1-1		Daws 42	(18775)
11	20	FL	A	Port Vale	D 1-1	0-1	12	Swan 82	(6781)
12	23	CC 2/2	H	Sunderland	L 1-2	0-2		Johnson 65	3928
13	27	FL	H	West Bromwich Albion	L 1-3	0-2	14	Lucketti 90	6439
14	O 04	FL	A	Stoke City	L 2-3	0-0	17	Swan 70, Andy Gray 85 (pen)	(11760)
15	11	FL	A	Swindon Town	L 1-3	1-2	18	Battersby 41	(7640)
16	18	FL	H	Birmingham City	W 2-1	2-0	16	Johnson 19, Swan 27	5700
17	21	FL	H	Queens Park Rangers	D 1-1	0-0	16	Battersby 57	4602
18	25	FL	A	Ipswich Town	L 0-2	0-0	16		(10478)
19	N 01	FL	A	Norwich City	D 2-2	1-2	15	Battersby 40, Johnrose 90	(14419)
20	04	FL	H	Nottingham Forest	W 2-0	1-0	15	Swan 15, Johnson 63	6137
21	08	FL	H	Portsmouth	L 0-2	0-0	15		5065
22	15	FL	A	Oxford United	D 1-1	1-1	15	Swailes 43	(5811)
23	22	FL	H	Sunderland	D 1-1	1-1	17	Lucketti 9	7790
24	29	FL	A	Huddersfield Town	L 0-2	0-1	17		(11929)
25	D 06	FL	H	Middlesbrough	L 0-1	0-0	20		8016
26	13	FL	A	Bradford City	L 0-1	0-1	22		(15812)
27	20	FL	H	Sheffield United	D 1-1	1-0	22	Johnrose 18	6012
28	26	FL	A	Tranmere Rovers	D 0-0	0-0	24		(9146)
29	28	FL	H	Crewe Alexandra	D 1-1	0-0	23	Patterson 62	5661
30	J 03	FAC 3	A	Sheffield United	D 1-1	1-0		Andy Gray 7	(14009)
31	10	FL	A	Reading	D 1-1	0-1	23	Gray 87	(7499)
32	13	FAC 3R	H	Sheffield United	L 1-2	0-0		Andy Gray 84	4920
33	18	FL	H	Stockport County	L 0-1	0-1	23		5699
34	27	FL	H	Wolverhampton Wand	L 1-3	1-1	23	Battersby 42	6134
35	31	FL	A	Charlton Athletic	D 0-0	0-0	23		(15312)
36	F 06	FL	H	Port Vale	D 2-2	1-2	23	Battersby 30, Ellis 60	5285
37	14	FL	A	Manchester City	W 1-0	0-0	23	Butler 52	(28885)
38	17	FL	H	Stoke City	D 0-0	0-0	22		5802
39	21	FL	A	West Bromwich Albion	D 1-1	0-1	23	Ellis 57	(15840)
40	25	FL	A	Birmingham City	W 3-1	1-0	21	Rigby 32, Patterson 53, Ellis 75	(20021)
41	28	FL	H	Swindon Town	W 1-0	1-0	18	Daws 39	5002
42	M 03	FL	A	Portsmouth	D 1-1	1-0	19	Johnrose 21	(12462)
43	07	FL	H	Norwich City	W 1-0	0-0	17	Jemson 60 (pen)	5154
44	14	FL	A	Nottingham Forest	L 0-3	0-0	18		(18846)
45	21	FL	H	Oxford United	W 1-0	0-0	17	Ellis 68	5159
46	28	FL	A	Sunderland	L 1-2	1-1	17	Small 28	(37425)
47	A 04	FL	H	Huddersfield Town	D 2-2	1-1	17	Butler 33, Ellis 46	8042
48	11	FL	A	Middlesbrough	L 0-4	0-1	20		(30218)
49	13	FL	H	Bradford City	W 2-0	1-0	18	Ellis 40, Daws 53	6570
50	18	FL	A	Sheffield United	L 0-3	0-1	18		(16056)
51	25	FL	H	Ipswich Town	L 0-1	0-0	19		7830
52	M 03	FL	A	Queens Park Rangers	W 1-0	1-0	17	Armstrong 22	(15210)

Best Home League Attendance: 11216 V Manchester City   Smallest :4602 V Queens Park Rangers   Average :6179

Goal Scorers:

FL	(42)	Battersby 6, Ellis 6, Swan 6, Johnson 5, Johnrose 3, Armstrong 2, Butler 2, Daws 2,Lucketti 2, Patterson 2, Andrew Gray 1, Andy Gray 1, Jemson 1, Rigby 1, Small 1, Swailes 1
CC	(8)	Johnson 3, Armstrong 1, Battersby 1, Daws 1, Andy Gray 1, Jepson 1
FAC	(2)	Andy Gray 2

1997-98

(M) Armstrong	(M) Barrass	(F) Battersby	(F) Butler	(D) Dalglish	(F) Daws	(M) Daws	(F) Ellis	(F) Gray Andrew	(M) Gray Andy	(M) Hughes	(F) Jemson	(F) Jepson	(M) Johnrose	(F) Johnson	(G) Kiely	(D) Linighan	(D) Lucketti	(F) Matthews	(D) Morgan	(M) Patterson	(D) Peake	(M) Randall	(M) Rigby	(D) Small	(M) Swailes	(D) Swan	(D) West	(D) Woodward	Referee	No.
S1		X	X		X			X			X	X	X	X		X						S3				S2	X		T. Heilbron	1
X		X	X		X			X	S3	X	X	X	X	X		X						S2				S1	X		A G Wiley	2
X		X	X		X			X	S		X	X	X	X		X						S2				S1	X		K A Leach	3
X			X		X			X	S		X	X	X	X		X						S				X	X	S	G B Frankland	4
X	S1	X	X		X			X	S2		X	X	X	X		X						S3				X	X		R Pearson	5
X		X	X		X			X	S3		S2	X	X	X		X						S1				X	X		G Cain	6
X		X	X		X			X	X		S2	X	X	X		X						S				X		S1	M J Brandwood	7
X		X	X		X			X	X		S2	X	X	X		X						S1				X		S	R D Furnandiz	8
X		X	X		X			X	X		S2	X	X	X		X						S				X		S1	P R Richards	9
X	S	X	X		X				X		X	X	X	X	S2	X						X						S1	F G Stretton	10
X		X	X		X			X	X		S2	X	X	X	X	S	X					S1				X		X	T Jones	11
X	S2	X	X		X			X	X		X	X	X	X	S3	X						S1						X	K M Lynch	12
S		X	X		X			X	X		X	X	X	X		X		X				S1				X		S2	B Coddington	13
		X	X		X			X	X		X	X	X	X		X		X				S1				X		S2	C J Foy	14
		X	X		X			X	X		X	X	X	X		X		X		S1			S2			X		S3	S J Baines	15
		X	X		X			X	X		X	X	X	X		X		X		S			S2			X		S1	D Pugh	16
		X	X		X			X	X		X	X	X	X		X		X		S1			S2			X		S	A N Butler	17
		X	X		X			X	X		X	X	X	X	S	X				X	S2	S1				X		X	A P D'Urso	18
S3		X	X		X			X	X		S2	X	X	X		X				X						S1		X	J A Kirkby	19
S2		X	X		X			X	X		S1	X	X	X		X				X						X		X	J P Robinson	20
X		X	X		X			X	X		S3	X	X	X		X				X	S2	S1				X		X	D Laws	21
X		X	X		X				X		X		X	X		X				S	S1	S2	X		X	X		X	P Taylor	22
X		X	X	S1	X				X		X	X	X	X		X					X	S	X		X	X		S2	G Singh	23
X		X2	X	S2	X				X		X	X	X	X		X				X1	S3		X		X	X		S1	G Laws	24
X		X1	X	S2	X		S1		X		X	X	X	X		X				S			X		X	X		X2	W C Burns	25
X			X	S2	X	X	X				X	X	X	X		X				S1	S3		X2	X				X1	G B Frankland	26
X		X1	X	X	X	X	X				S	X	X	X		X						X						X	M J Brandwood	27
X		X	X	S	X	S	X1				X	X	X	X		X			X			X						S1	R Pearson	28
X	X1		S1	X	X	X	X				X	X	X	X		X				X2	S		X					S2	G Cain	29
X	X		X1	X		X					S1	X		X	X	S	X		X	X	S	S			X			X	D Orr	30
X	X2		X		X	S2	X				S1	X		X	X		X			X1								S	M E Pierce	31
X	X	X		X		X					S1	X		X	S	X				S	S	S2	X2	X		X1			D J Gallagher	32
X	S2	X		X	X2	X					X1		X		X				X			S1			S			X	R D Furnandiz	33
	X2	X	S2	X	X	X					X		X		X						S1	X		X1		X		S	K M Lynch	34
	X2	X	X	X	X						X		X		X	S3				S1	S2	X		X1		X			A G Wiley	35
S1	X2	X	S	X		X			X		X		X		X	S2	X1			X		X				X			B Coddington	36
X	S2	X		X	X2				X1		X		X		X	S3		X		S2	X	S1				X			T Heilbron	37
X	X2	X		X					X3	X1			X		X	S3		X		S2	X	S1				X			J P Robinson	38
X		X	S2	X		X2					X		X		X	S1		X		X	X	S3	X1			X			M L Dean	39
X		X	S3	X	X2				X1		X		X		X	S1		X		X	X	S2							M C Bailey	40
X	S1	X	S2	X					X1		X		X		X	X2		X		X	X					S			M Fletcher	41
X	S1	X	S	X					X		X		X		X	X1		X		X	X					S			S G Bennett	42
X	S3	X		X	S2				X3	X1			X		X	X2		X		X	X					S1			R Pearson	43
X	S1		S3	X	X				X3				X		X	X1		X2	X	X	S2		X			X			P Taylor	44
X	S3			X	X3				X2		X		X		X	S1		X1	X	X	S2						S1		G Singh	45
X		X		X	X				X2		X		X		X	X3	X1	S3	X	S2			S1				S1		A N Butler	46
X		X	X	X	X				S1		X		X		X	X2		S2	X	X1		S				X	S		S W Mathieson	47
X1		X	X2	X					S2		X		X		X	X3		S1	X	S3		X				X			P S Danson	48
X	S		X	X					S		X		X		X	X		S	X	X			X2						K A Leach	49
X	S1	X		X	X				S		X		X		X	X1		S2	X	X			X2						S J Baines	50
X		X		X	X				S3		X		X		X	X2		S2	X1	S1			X3					X	G Laws	51
X	S2	X		X	X2				S1		X		X		X	X3		S3	X	X1			X1					X	A G Wiley	52
33	28	43	1	46	21	4	21	12	11	7	44	17	44	46	9	5	18	3	2	8	18	12	26	4				20	FL Appearances	
4	9		11		1	2	1	1	4	9						6		3	13	16	1					11		12	FL Sub Appearances	
3	0+1	3+1	4		4			3	2+2		4	4	4	4	0+2	4			1+3				1+1	2				1+1	CC Appearances	
2		2	1	1	2				2		0+2	2		2		2				1			0+1		2	1		2	FAC Appearances	

Also Played: (M) Forrest S(30). (F) Pugh X(1).

BURY

CLUB RECORDS

BIGGEST VICTORIES
League: 8-0 v Tranmere Rovers, Division 3, 10.1.1970
(Bury have scored eight goals four times in the League).
F.A. Cup: 12-1 v Stockton, 1st Round, 2.2.1897.
League Cup: 5-1 v Brighton, 1st Round, 12.9.1961
Others:

BIGGEST DEFEATS
League: 0-8 v Sheffield United, Division 1, 6.4.1896.
0-8 v Swindon Town, Division 3, 8.12.1979.
F.A.Cup:
League Cup: 0-10 v West Ham United, Round 2,
25.10.1983.
Others:

MOST POINTS
3 points a win: 84, Division 4, 1984-85.
2 points a win: 68, Division 3, 1960-61.

MOST GOALS SCORED
108, Division 3, 1960-61.

MOST GOALS CONCEDED
99, Division 1, 1928-29.

MOST FIRST CLASS MATCHES IN A SEASON
63, 1980-81 (46 League, 5 League Cup, 5 FA Cup, 7
Anglo/Scottish).

MOST LEAGUE WINS
30, 1960-61.

MOST LEAGUE DRAWS
20, 1978-79.

MOST LEAGUE DEFEATS
25, 1956-57, 1966-67.

INDIVIDUAL CLUB RECORDS

MOST GOALS IN A SEASON
Craig Madden: 43 goals in 1981-82 (League 35, FA Cup
4, League Cup 3, Group Cup 1)

MOST GOALS IN A MATCH
5. Ray Pointer v Rotherham United, 6-1, Division 2,
2.10.1965.
5. Eddie Quigley v Millwall (h), 5-2, Division 2, 15.2.1947.

OLDEST PLAYER
Stan Pearson, 38 years, 241 days.

YOUNGEST PLAYER
Brian Williams, 16 years 133 days, 18.3.1972.

MOST CAPPED PLAYER
Bill Gorman (Eire) 11.

BEST PERFORMANCES

League: 4th in Division 1, 1925-26.
F.A. Cup: Winners in 1900, 1903.
League Cup: Semi-Final 1963.

ADDITIONAL INFORMATION
PREVIOUS NAMES
None.

PREVIOUS LEAGUE
Lancashire League 1890-1894.

Club Colours: White shirts, royal blue shorts, royal blue
socks.
Change colours: Royal blue shirts, white shorts, blue &
white socks.

Reserves League: Pontins League (Division Three)

DIVISIONAL RECORD

	Played	Won	Drawn	Lost	For	Against	Points
Division 1/P	804	279	180	345	1,176	1,340	738
Division 2/1	1576	591	335	650	2,361	2,512	1,528
Division 3/2	966	370	256	340	1,371	1,225	1,131
Division 4	540	230	151	159	831	635	767
Total	**3,886**	**1,470**	**922**	**1,494**	**5,739**	**5,712**	**4,164**

RECORDS AND STATISTICS

COMPETITIONS

Div.1/P	Div.2/1	Div.3/2	Div.4
1894-1911	1894	1956-60	1970-73
1923-28	1911-23	1966-67	1979-84
	1928-56	1968-70	1991-96
	1960-66	1973-79	
	1967-68	1984-91	
	1997-	1996-97	

HONOURS

Div. 2\1	Div. 3/2	FA Cup
1894-95	1960-61	1900
	1996-97	1903

MOST APPEARANCES

Norman Bullock - 539 (1920-35)

Year	League	FA Cup	Lge Cup	Others
1920-21	24	1	-	-
1921-22	18	-	-	-
1922-23	40	4	-	-
1923-24	24	-	-	-
1924-25	36	1	-	-
1925-26	41	2	-	-
1926-27	37	1	-	-
1927-28	35	3	-	-
1928-29	37	3	-	-
1929-30	35	2	-	-
1930-31	42	3	-	-
1931-32	38	4	-	-
1932-33	39	3	-	-
1933-34	35	4	-	-
1934-35	25	2	-	-
Totals	506	33	-	-

MOST GOALS IN A CAREER

Craig Madden - 153 (1977-86)

Year	League	FA Cup	Lge Cup	Others
1978-79	1	-	-	-
1979-80	10	2	-	-
1980-81	10	-	-	2
1981-82	35	4	3	1
1982-83	20	-	1	-
1983-84	17	1	2	-
1984-85	22	1	1	1
1985-86	14	3	3	-
Totals	129	11	10	4

Current leading goalscorer: Lennie Johnrose - 25 (12.93-98)

MANAGERS

Name (since 1946)	Seasons	Best	Worst
Norman Bullock	1946-49	12 (2)	20 (2)
John McNeil	1950-53	17 (2)	20 (2)
Dave Russell	1953-61	13 (2)	4 (3N)
Bob Stokoe	1961-65	8 (2)	18 (2)
Bert Head	1965	19 (?)	19 (2)
Les Shannon	1966-69	21 (2)	2 (3)
Jack Marshall	1969	-	-
Les Hart	1969-70	19 (3)	19 (3)
Colin McDonald	1970	-	-
Tommy McAnearney	1970-72	22 (3)	9 (4)
Allan Brown	1972-73	12 (4)	12 (4)
Bobby Smith	1974-77	7 (3)	4 (4)
Bob Stokoe	1977	15 (3)	15 (3)
Dave Hatton	1978-79	19 (3)	19 (3)
Dave Connor	1979	21 (3)	21 (3)
Jim Iley	1980-84	5 (4)	15 (4)
Martin Dobson	1984-89	13 (3)	4 (4)
Sam Ellis	1989-90	5 (3)	5 (3)
Mike Walsh	1990-95	7 (3)	13 (4/3)
Stan Ternent	1995-98	1 (2)	3 (3)
Neil Warnock	1998-		

RECORD TRANSFER FEE RECEIVED

Amount	Club	Player	Date
£1,100,000	Ipswich Town	David Johnson	11/97
£400,000	Southampton	David Lee	08/91

RECORD TRANSFER FEE PAID

Amount	Club	Player	Date
£200,000	Ipswich Town	Chris Swailes	11/97
£175,000	Shrewsbury	John McGinlay	06/90

LONGEST LEAGUE RUNS

of undefeated matches:	18 (1961)	of league matches w/out a win:	19 (1911)
of undefeated home matches:	25 (1967-68, 03.04.95-)	of undefeated away matches:	8 (1961)
without home win:	13 (1937, 1978)	without an away win:	42 (1910-1912)
of league wins:	9 (1960)	of home wins:	15 (1894-95)
of league defeats:	6 (1953, 1967)	of away wins:	6 (1960)

BURY

PLAYERS NAME Honours	Ht	Wt	Birthdate	Birthplace Transfers	Contract Date	Clubs	League	L/Cup	FA Cup	Other	Lge	L/C	FAC	Oth
							APPEARANCES				**GOALS**			
G O A L K E E P E R														
Kiely Dean	6.1	11.8	10/10/70	Salford	10/30/87	Coventry City								
E: Y.4.DIV2 96/97					3/9/90	York City	210	9	4	16				
				Free	8/15/96	Bury	90	8	3					
D E F E N C E														
Barrass Matthew	5.11	12	2/28/80	Bury	9/15/97	Bury (T)		0+1						
Barrick Dean	5.7	11.7	30/09/69	Hemsworth	07/05/88	Sheffield Wed.	11				2			
DIV3 95/96				£50000	14/02/91	Rotherham United	96+3	6	8	5	7			1
				£50000	11/08/93	Cambridge United	90+1	7	7	6	3	1	1	
					9/11/95	Preston North End	98+11	7+1	5	6	1	1		
				Free	7/1/98	Bury								
Foster John	5.11	11.2	9/19/73	Manchester	7/15/92	Manchester City	17+2	2+1	2+1					
				Free	3/26/98	Carlisle United	7							
				Free	7/1/98	Bury								
Linighan Brian	6	10.3	11/2/73	Hartlepool	7/16/92	Sheffield Wed.	1	1	1					
				Free	7/2/97	Bury		0+2						
Lucketti Chris	6	12.1	9/28/71	Littleborough		Rochdale	1							
DIV2 96/97				Free	8/23/90	Stockport County								
				Free	7/12/91	Halifax Town	73+5	2	2	4	2	1		
				£50000	10/1/93	Bury	234+1	16	11	14	8		1	1
Redmond Stephen	5.1	11.2	11/2/67	Liverpool	12/3/84	Manchester City	231+4	24	17	11	7			
E: u21.14. Y. FAYC'86.				£300000	7/10/92	Oldham Athletic	195+10	20	10+2	1+1	4			
				Free	7/1/98	Bury								
Swailes Christopher W	6.1	12.11	10/11/70	Gateshead	5/23/89	Ipswich Town								
FA Vase'93				£10000	3/28/91	Peterborough Utd								
				£8000	9/1/91	Boston United								
					8/1/92	Kettering Town								
					8/1/93	Bridlington								
				Free	10/27/93	Doncaster Rovers	49	2	1	2		1		
				£150000	3/23/95	Ipswich Town	34+3	3		2	1			
				£200000	11/14/97	Bury	12+1		2		1			
Swailes Daniel	6.3	12.6	4/1/79	Bolton	8/1/96	Bury (T)								
Swan Peter	6.2	14.12	9/28/66	Leeds	8/6/84	Leeds United	43+6	3	3	1+2	11	2		
				£200000	3/23/89	Hull City	76+4	2+3	2	1	24	1		
				£300000	8/16/91	Port Vale	105+6	6	9	12	6		1	1
				£300000	7/22/94	Plymouth Argyle	24+3	2	2		2	1		
				£200000	8/10/95	Burnley	47+2	2	2	4	7			
					8/8/97	Bury	27+11	1+1	1		6			
West Dean	5.1	11.07	12/5/72	Morley	8/17/91	Lincoln City	86+25	9	6	6+2	19	1	1	1
DIV2 96/97				Loan	8/27/93	Boston United								
					9/28/95	Bury	82+5	6	2	1+1	5			
Woodward Andrew	5.1	10.12	9/23/73	Stockport	7/29/92	Crewe Alexandra	9+11	2		+3				
DIV2 96/97					3/13/95	Bury	46+18	1+2	2	3				
M I D F I E L D														
Armstrong Gordon I	6	11.1	7/15/67	Newcastle	7/10/85	Sunderland	331+18	25+4	19	18+1	50	3	4	4
DIV2 96/97				Loan	8/24/95	Bristol City	6							
				Loan	1/5/96	Northampton Town	4		1		1			
					7/16/96	Bury	48+20	5	2+1		4	1		
Crossland Mark D	5.11	12.2	12/14/78	Tameside	5/31/97	Bury (T)								
Daws Nicholas	5.11	13.2	3/15/70	Manchester		Altrincham		2+1						
DIV2 96/97				£10000	8/13/92	Bury	255+17	18+3	12	10+2	10	2		
Forrest Martyn	5.10	12.2	1/2/79	Bury	8/1/96	Bury (T)								
Johnrose Lennie	5.1	11.5	11/29/69	Preston	6/16/88	Blackburn Rovers	20+22	2+1	+3	2	11	1		
DIV2 96/97					1/21/92	Preston North End	1+2				1			
				£50000	2/28/92	Hartlepool United	59+7	5+1	5	5	11	4	1	
					12/7/93	Bury	188+6	14+2	7	7	23		1	1
Patterson Mark A	5.6	10.1	5/24/65	Darwen	5/1/83	Blackburn Rovers	89+12	4	3+1	2+4	20	1		
FMC'87				£20000	6/15/88	Preston North End	54+1	4+1	4	7	19			
				£80000	2/1/90	Bury	42	2	1	4	10			
				£65000	1/10/91	Bolton Wanderers	146+7	11+3	17	9	10	1	1	
				£300000	12/22/95	Sheffield United	72+2	9	3		4			
				Loan	3/27/97	Southend United	4							
				£125000	12/11/97	Bury	18		1		2			
Rigby Tony	5.7	10.8	8/10/72	Ormskirk	5/16/90	Crewe Alexandra								
					8/1/91	Lancaster City								
					8/1/92	Burscough								
				Free	1/6/93	Bury	128+38	6+1	3+1	10	23	1		
				Loan	2/14/97	Scarborough	5				1			
F O R W A R D														
Battersby Tony	6	12.09	8/30/75	Doncaster	7/5/93	Sheffield United			2+1					1
				Loan	3/23/95	Southend United	6+2				1			
				£200000	1/8/96	Notts County	20+19	1	+2	4	8			
				Loan	3/3/97	Bury	9+2				2			
					5/22/97	Bury	28+9	3+1	2		8	1		
D'Jaffo Laurent						Ayr United								
				Free	7/1/98	Bury								

Ellis Tony 5.11 11 10/20/64 Salford

Fee	Date	Club								
		Northwich Victoria								
Free	8/22/86	Oldham Athletic	5+3	1		1				
£23000	10/6/87	Preston North End	80+6	3	5	11+1	26			5
£250000	12/20/89	Stoke City	66+11	5+1	1+4	3+2	19	1		
£50000	8/14/92	Preston North End	70+2	4	6	6	48	2	3	3
£165000	7/25/94	Blackpool	138+6	10+1	7	6	55	6	1	1
£70000	12/11/97	Bury	20+1				5			

Jemson Nigel 5.1 11.1 8/10/69 Hutton
E: u21.1. LC'90. AMC'96.

Fee	Date	Club								
Hutton	7/6/87	Preston North End	28+4		2	5+1	8		1	5
£150000	3/24/88	Nottingham Forest	45+2	9	3+1	1	13	4	3	
Loan	12/3/88	Bolton Wanderers	4+1							
Loan	3/15/89	Preston North End	6+3			2	2			1
£800000	9/17/91	Sheffield Wed.	26+25	3+4	3+3	2+2	9	1		1
Loan	9/10/93	Grimsby Town	6			1	1			
£300000	9/8/94	Notts County	5+6	1+1		1	1	1		
Loan	1/13/95	Watford	3+1							
Loan	4/25/95	Coventry City								
Loan	2/15/96	Rotherham United								
£60000	7/10/96	Oxford United	67	12	2		26	6		
£100000	2/5/98	Bury	11+4				1			

Matthews Robert 6 12.5 10/14/70 Slough
E: u18.3, S. DIV2 96/97.

Fee	Date	Club								
Free	3/26/92	Notts County	12+13		1+2	1+1	8			
£80000	3/3/95	Luton Town	6+5							
	9/8/95	York City	14+3			1		3	1	
	1/12/96	Bury	42+16	1+3	1		9			

Preece Andy 6.1 12 3/27/67 Evesham
via Worcester City 8/89

Fee	Date	Club								
		Evesham								
Free	8/31/88	Northampton Town	0+1	0+1		0+1				
Free	3/22/90	Wrexham	44+7	5+1	1	5	7	1	2	1
£10000	12/18/91	Stockport County	89+8	2+1	7	12+2	42		3	9
£350000	6/23/94	Crystal Palace	17+3	4+2	2+3		4	1		
£200000	7/5/95	Blackpool	114+12	8+2	2+3	12	35	1	2	2
Free	7/1/98	Bury								

THE MANAGER
NEIL WARNOCK

Date of Birth . . . . 1st December 1948.
Place of Birth . . . . Sheffield.
Date of Appointment . . . . June 1998.

PREVIOUS CLUBS
As Manager . . . . .Gainsborough Trinity, Burton Albion, Scarborough, Notts Co.
. . . . Huddersfield, Plymouth Argyle.
As a Player . . . . Chesterfield, Rotherham, Hartlepool, Scunthorpe,
. . . . Aldershot, Barnsley, York, Crewe.

HONOURS
As a Manager
Scarborough: GMVC'87.
Notts County: Promotion to Div.2.

As a Player
None.

GIGG LANE
Bury, Lancashire, BL9 9HR

Capacity ....11,340.

First game ....Accrington v Church, 18.6.1885.
First floodlit game ....v Wolverhampton Wanderers, 3-1, 6.10.1953.

ATTENDANCES
Highest...35,000 v Bolton Wanderers FA Cup 3rd Round, 9.1.1960.
Lowest ....416 v Tranmere Rovers, AMC, 26.2.1986.

OTHER GROUNDS ....None.

HOW TO GET TO THE GROUND

From the North
Exit the M60 Motorway (recently re-named M60 from M62 on this stretch) at junction 18 onto M66 (s/p Bury). Leave M66 at junction 2 (A58), keep left at exit roundabout onto A58 (s/p Bury). After 0.5 miles turn left at traffice lights into Heywood Street. After 0.5 miles fork left on bend into Parkhills Road. At mini roundabout take first exit into Market Street. At give-way, turn right into Gigg Lane.

From the East, South and West
Use motorway M60 (formerly M62) until junction 17. Leave motorway and follow signs to Bury (A56). In 3.1 miles, having gone through six sets of traffic lights, turn right into Gigg Lane for Bury FC. (facing Manchester Road playing fields on left).

Car Parking
Ample side-street parking is available.

Nearest Railway Station (Metro-link trains only - no rail service)
Bury Metro Interchange.

USEFUL TELEPHONE NUMBERS

Club switchboard 0161 764 4881
Club fax number......................0161 764 5521
Club shop 0161 705 2144
Ticket Office.....0161 705 21 44 (fax 763 3103

Marketing Department0161 764 4881 (fax 762 9620)
Internet address (unofficial)....www.buryfc.crgatlons.co.uk
Clubcall 0898 12 11 97*
*Calls cost 50p per minute at all times. Call costings correct at time of going to press.

MATCHDAY PROGRAMME

Programme Editor.........................P Cullen.

Number of pages.....................................48.

Price ....£1.80.

Subscriptions ....Apply to club.

Local Newspapers
..............Bury Times, Bolton Evening News,
.........................Manchester Evening News.

Local Radio Stations
...............................Piccadilly Radio, G.M.R.

MATCHDAY TICKET PRICES

Seats
Adults................................... £14.00
Juniors/Senior Citizens £8.00

Terrace
Adults................................... £12.00
Juniors/Senior Citizens £12.00

CREWE ALEXANDRA
(The Railwaymen)
NATIONWIDE LEAGUE DIVISION 1
SPONSORED BY: LC CHARLES

1998/99 - Back Row L-R: Terry McPhillips (Asst. Yth Coach), David Wright, David Whittaker, Mark Foran, Matthew Wicks, David Walton, Steve Anthrobus, Chris Lightfoot, Neil Baker (Asst. Manager). **Middle Row:** Eddie Edwards (Physio), Kevin Street, Gareth Chadwick, Mike Williamson, Richard Norris, Colin Webster, Jason Kearton, Phil Charnock, Lee Unsworth, Peter Morse, Peter Smith, Steve Macauley, John Fleet (Kit man.). **Front Row:** Colin Little, Neil Critchley, Shaun Smith, James Collins, Dario Gradi MBE (Manager), Marcus Bignot, Kenny Lunt, Mark Rivers, Jermaine Wright.

CREWE ALEXANDRA
FORMED IN 1877
TURNED PROFESSIONAL IN 1893
LTD COMPANY IN 1892

PRESIDENT: N Rowlinson
CHAIRMAN: E J Bowler MPS
VICE-CHAIRMAN
N Hassall FCCA
DIRECTORS
J McMillan, D Rowlinson, R Clayton,
D Gradi, N Rowlinson.
SECRETARY
Mrs Gill Palin (01270) 213 014)
MARKETING MANAGER
Alison Bowler

MANAGER: Dario Gradi MBE
ASSISTANT MANAGER: Neil Baker
RESERVE TEAM MANAGER
Neil Baker
YOUTH TEAM MANAGER
Steve Holland
PHYSIOTHERAPIST
Bernadette Oakes & Eddie Edwards
STATISTICIAN FOR THE DIRECTORY
Harold Finch

Following promotion via the Play offs at Wembley to go into Division One, there were many pundits who were forecasting a quick relegation, especially after the departure of Danny Murphy to Liverpool and Rob Savage to Leicester City. Early results, especially those at home did little to ally those fears but gradually the team settled down and the results improved.

The turning point of the season came in January 1998, although going out of the FA Cup at the third round stage they were to remain unbeaten in League fixtures. That group of results meant that manager, Dario Gradi was to receive the 'Manager of the Month' award. In addition, in the New Years honours list, Dario was awarded the MBE making it a real month to remember.

February 1998 saw the departure of the clubs leading scorer, Dele Adebola to Birmingham City in a £1 million deal and for a short time the goals became harder to find than when Dele had been present.

With a safety target of 50 points normally sufficient to retain a place in Division One, that target was achieved by the end of March following an away win at Stockport. Three further wins in the last six games enabled the club to finish the season in a very respectable 11th place in the league table.

Despite having to cope without defensive stalwart Steve Macauley for the whole of the season through injury and also Gareth Whalley and Ashley Westwood for long spells, the side matured as the season progressed.

Out of the youth team came Kenny Lunt and Kevin Street to play their part in the teams progress and with David Wright, Peter Smith and James Collins also tasting first team action, hope for the future look bright. Seth Johnson established a regular place in the England under 18 side and is definitely one for the future.

A key signing during the season was Dave Walton from Shrewsbury Town for an initial fee of £500,000 a new club record, he was later followed by Mark Foran from Peterborough United and Jermaine Wright who also played their part.

With the new stand projected for the end of the 1998/99 season, the careful planning made by the club is coming to fruition. Other than the senior side, the youth side reached the quarter final stage of the FA Youth Cup, amongst their victims, Sunderland, Manchester City and Spurs.   HAROLD FINCH.

CREWE ALEXANDRA

Division 1		:11th		FA CUP: 3rd Round			LC CUP: 1st Round	

M	DATE	COMP.	VEN	OPPONENTS	RESULT	H/T	LP	GOAL SCORERS/GOAL TIMES	ATT.
1	A 09	FL	A	Swindon Town	L 0-2	0-1	23		(8334)
2	12	CC 1/1	H	**Bury**	**L 2-3**	**2-2**		**Lunt 7, Smith 41**	**2618**
3	15	FL	H	West Bromwich Albion	L 2-3	1-1	21	Adebola 35, Rivers 63	5234
4	23	FL	A	Norwich City	W 2-0	1-0	13	Rivers 29, Smith 60	(11821)
5	26	CC 1/2	A	**Bury**	**D 3-3**	**2-2**		**Rivers 21, Smith 37, Butler 89 (OG)**	**(3296)**
6	S 02	FL	H	Bury	L 1-2	1-1	20	Smith 43 (pen)	4447
7	13	FL	A	Portsmouth	W 3-2	1-0	19	Rivers 1, Anthrobus 57, Adebola 85	(9505)
8	16	FL	H	Port Vale	L 0-1	0-0	19		5519
9	20	FL	H	Queens Park Rangers	L 2-3	0-2	21	Lunt 53, Adebola 76	5348
10	27	FL	H	Tranmere Rovers	W 2-1	1-0	18	Anthrobus 27, Street 89	4845
11	O 04	FL	A	Birmingham City	W 1-0	0-0	16	Rivers 58	(16548)
12	11	FL	A	Reading	D 3-3	3-2	13	Little 19, Adebola 30, Westwood 12	(6685)
13	18	FL	H	Middlesbrough	D 1-1	0-0	15	Adebola 55	5759
14	21	FL	H	Ipswich Town	D 0-0	0-0	15		4730
15	25	FL	A	Bradford City	L 0-1	0-0	15		(15333)
16	29	FL	A	Manchester City	L 0-1	0-1	15		(27384)
17	N 01	FL	A	Nottingham Forest	L 1-3	1-1	17	Little 15	(18268)
18	04	FL	H	Wolverhampton Wand	L 0-2	0-1	19		5743
19	08	FL	H	Oxford United	W 2-1	2-1	17	Westwood 31, Anthrobus 41	4524
20	15	FL	A	Charlton Athletic	L 2-3	1-2	18	Street 44, Smith 66	(14091)
21	22	FL	H	Stockport County	L 0-1	0-1	19		5231
22	29	FL	A	Sheffield United	L 0-1	0-0	22		(16973)
23	D 06	FL	H	Huddersfield Town	L 2-5	1-2	23	Charnock 41, Adebola 47	4861
24	13	FL	A	Stoke City	W 2-0	1-0	20	Smith 11, Little 75	(14623)
25	20	FL	H	Sunderland	L 0-3	0-2	23		5404
26	26	FL	H	Manchester City	W 1-0	1-0	19	Holsgrove 19	5759
27	28	FL	A	Bury	D 1-1	0-0	19	Adebola 81	(5661)
28	J 03	FAC 3	H	**Birmingham City**	**L 1-2**	**1-1**		**Rivers 31**	**4607**
29	11	FL	H	Swindon Town	W 2-0	0-0	17	Little 46, Street 84	4176
30	17	FL	A	West Bromwich Albion	W 1-0	1-0	17	Little 22	(15257)
31	24	FL	A	Port Vale	W 3-2	3-1	13	Smith 2 (pen), Whalley 33, Foran 41	(10571)
32	31	FL	H	Norwich City	W 1-0	0-0	14	Fuglestad 61 (OG)	5559
33	F 06	FL	A	Queens Park Rangers	L 2-3	0-1	14	Anthrobus 62, Johnson 72	(13429)
34	14	FL	H	Portsmouth	W 3-1	0-0	14	Little 48, Garvey 58, Lunt 72	5114
35	17	FL	H	Birmingham City	L 0-2	0-2	14		5559
36	21	FL	A	Tranmere Rovers	W 3-0	1-0	13	Rivers 45, Little 64, 70	(7534)
37	25	FL	A	Middlesbrough	L 0-1	0-0	13		(29936)
38	28	FL	H	Reading	W 1-0	0-0	12	Rivers 10	5202
39	M 03	FL	A	Oxford United	D 0-0	0-0	11		(6069)
40	07	FL	H	Nottingham Forest	L 1-4	1-4	12	Little 29	5759
41	14	FL	A	Wolverhampton Wand	L 0-1	0-1	14		(24272)
42	21	FL	H	Charlton Athletic	L 0-3	0-2	14		5252
43	28	FL	A	Stockport County	W 1-0	0-0	14	Smith 89 (pen)	(8370)
44	A 11	FL	A	Huddersfield Town	L 0-2	0-2	15		(11263)
45	13	FL	H	Stoke City	W 2-0	1-0	13	Westwood 16, Lightfoot 48	5759
46	18	FL	A	Sunderland	L 1-2	1-2	14	Charnock 31	(40441)
47	25	FL	H	Bradford City	W 5-0	4-0	12	Anthrobus 20, Street 25, Little 29, 39, 65	5054
48	30	FL	H	Sheffield United	W 2-1	0-0	11	Little 80, Anthrobus 82	5759
49	M 03	FL	A	Ipswich Town	L 2-3	1-1	11	Charnock 40, Garvey 60	(19105)

Best Home League Attendance: 5759 V Stoke City					Smallest :4176 V Swindon Town			Average :5243	

Goal Scorers:

FL	(58)	Little 13, Adebola 7, Anthrobus 6, Rivers 6, Smith 6, Street 4, Charnock 3, Westwood 3, Garvey 2, Lunt 2, Foran 1, Holsgrove 1, Johnson 1, Lightfoot 1, Whalley 1, Opponents 1
CC	(5)	Smith 2, Lunt 1, Rivers 1, Opponents 1
FAC	(1)	Rivers 1

(F) Adebola	(F) Anthrobus	(G) Bankole	(D) Bignott	(M) Charnock	(M) Collins	(D) Foran	(F) Garvey	(F) Guinan	(M) Holsgrove	(D) Johnson	(G) Kearton	(D) Lightfoot	(F) Little	(M) Lunt	(F) Moralee	(D) Pope	(D) Rivers	(D) Smith S	(F) Smith P	(M) Street	(M) Tierney	(D) Unsworth	(M) Walton	(M) Watts	(D) Westwood	(M) Whalley	(F) Wright J	(M) Wright D	
X			X				S2			X	X	X			X	S3	S1	X	X			X			X		X		G. Singh 1
X			X				S2			X	X	S1	X	X	S3		X	X				X			X				A G Wiley 2
X	S2		X				X			X	X	X			X	X	S	S	S	S		X			X				A R Leake 3
X	S2		X				S1			X	X		X	X		X	X	X	X						X	X		S3	D Orr 4
S2	X	X		X	S1		S3			X			X		X	X		X	X						X	X			R Pearson 5
X	S3		X	X						X	X				S1	X		X	X			S2		X	X				M J Brandwood 6
X	X		X	X						X	X	S2	S1	X			X	X	S3			X	X		X				P Taylor 7
X	X		X	X	S1					X	X	S	X	X			X	X		S2		X	X		X				K A Leach 8
X	X		X	X	S					X	X		S1	X			X	X				X		X	X	S			C J Foy 9
X	X		X	X						X	X		S1	X			X	X		S1		X		X	X	S3			P S Danson 10
X	X		X	X						S1	X		S	X		S	X	X				X			X	X			D Laws 11
X	X		X	X						X			X	X		S	X	X	S1	S2		X			X				R Styles 12
X	X		X	X						X	X		S1	X		S2	X	X		S3		X			X				J A Kirkby 13
X	X		X	X						X	X		S1	X		S	X	X		S		X			X				G B Frankland 14
X	X		X	X	S					X	X			X		S2	X			S1		X	X		X				R D Furnandiz 15
X	S1		X	X						X	X			X			X	X		S2		S	X		X				K M Lynch 16
X	X		X	X						X	X		X	X			X	X	S	S1	S	X	X		X				T Heilbron 17
	X		X	X						X	X		X	X			S	X	S1	X		S	X	X	X				A P D'Urso 18
	X		X	X						X	X		X	X		S1	S	X		X		S2	X		X				E Lomas 19
S1	X		X	X						X	X		X	X			X	X		X		S2	X		X				M E Pierce 20
X			X	X					X	X	X				S2	S1	S3	X		X		X	X						C R Wilkes 21
X			X	X					X	X2	X		S2			X1	X	S1		X		X	X						M R Halsey 22
X			X	X					X2	X1	X		S3	S1	S2	X	X	X		X3		X							D Orr 23
X1			X	X			X	S2	X	X	X		S1	X2		X	X	X		X		X							A G Wiley 24
X			X	X			X	S2	X2	X	X		S1	X		X	X	X		X1		X			S				A N Butler 25
X			X	X			X	S	S2	X2	X1		X	S		X	X	X1		X		S1	S	X	X				G Cain 27
X		S	X	X				S		X	X	X		X	S		X	X		S	S	X	X						J A Kirkby 28
X			X	X			S			S2	X	X		X			X1	X		S1		X		X		X	X2		A R Leake 29
X			X	X1		S2				X	X		X	X		S1		X		S		X		X2	X				R J Harris 30
X	S		X					X		X	X		X2	X		X1	X			S1		S2	X		X				P R Richards 31
X	S		X		S	X1				X	X	S1	X	X		X	X			X	X	X						M L Dean 32
	X2		X		X		X			X	X	S2	X	X					S	S1		X1	X			X			M C Bailey 33
	X		X1			X				X	X	X	X	X			X	X		S1		X	X			X			R Pearson 34
	X		X			X1				X	X	X	X	X			X	X		S1		X	X			X			C J Foy 35
	X		X							X	X	S3	S1	X	X3		X2	X		S2		X	X		X	X1		E K Wolstenholme 36
	X		X							X1	X	S2	X	X2	S		X	X		S1		X	X		X				P Rejer 37
X3	X		X							X	X	X2	S2	S3		X1	X			S1		X	X		X				K M Lynch 38
	X		X							X	X	X1	X	S1	S			X		S		X	X		X	X			M E Pierce 39
X2	X		X							X	X	S	X	X	S2		X			S1	X1	X	X		X				M Fletcher 40
X1			X	X2						X	X	S	X	S			X	S1		X		X	X		X				G B Frankland 41
	S		X	X		X		X		X	X		X	X		S1			S	X		X		X		X1			W C Burns 42
			X	X		X		X1		X	X		X	X				X2	X			X		X	S1				T Heilbron 43
			X	X1		S3		X2		X	X		X	X			X3	X		S1	S2		X		X	X			A R Leake 44
X2			X							X	X	X	X				S3	X		X3	S2	S1		X1	X				R J Harris 45
	X		X	X		X1	X			X	X	S1	X2	S3			X			X			X			X3	S2		J P Robinson 46
	X	X		X		X					X		X1	X2	S2		S2	X		X2		X	X					S1	D Orr 47
X	X	X	X			S	X			X			X1	S1			X	S	X			X	X						P Rejer 48
X	X	X2	X		X3	X				X								S1	X	X1		X					S2	S3	R D Furnandiz 49
26	27	3	42	33		10	8	3	7	39	43	7	29	29	3	2	31	43	1	15	1	31	27	5	19	18	3		FL Appearances
1	3			1	2	5				1	1		6	11	12	6	4	4		5	17	3	5		2		2	3	FL Sub Appearances
1+1	1	1	2	0+1		0+2				2	1	1+1	1	2	1+1		2	2				1			2	1			CC Appearances
1			1	1						1	1	1	1		1			1				1	1						FAC Appearances

Also Played: (M) Foster S(35). (D) Pemberton X(1,2).

CREWE ALEXANDRA

CLUB RECORDS

BIGGEST VICTORIES
League: 8-0 v Rotherham United, Division 3(N), 1.10.1932.
F.A. Cup: 7-1 v Gresley Rovers, 1st Round, 12.11.1994.
5-0 v Druids, 1st Round, 1887-88.
5-0 v Billingham Synthonia 1st Round, 1948-49.
6-1 v Wrexham, 1st Round, 14.11.1992.
6-1 v Accrington Stanley, 2nd Round, 5.12.1992.
AMC: 6-0 v Chester City (a), 2nd Round, 29.11.1994.

BIGGEST DEFEATS
League: 1-11 v Lincoln City, Division 3(N), 29.9.1951.
F.A. Cup: 2-13 v Tottenham Hotspur, 4th Round replay, 3.2.1960.

MOST POINTS
3 points a win: 83, Division 2, 1994-95
2 points a win: 59, Division 4, 1962-63.

MOST GOALS SCORED
95, Division 3(N), 1931-32.

MOST LEAGUE GOALS CONCEDED
110.

MOST LEAGUE WINS
25.

MOST LEAGUE DRAWS
18.

MOST LEAGUE DEFEATS
31.

INDIVIDUAL CLUB RECORDS

MOST GOALS IN A SEASON
Terry Harkin: 35 goals in 1964-65, Division 4.

MOST GOALS IN A MATCH
5. Tony Naylor v Colchester United, 7-1, Division 3, 24.4.1993.

OLDEST PLAYER
Kenny Swain, 39 years 281 days v Maidstone, 5.11.1991.

YOUNGEST PLAYER
Steve Walters, 16 years 119 days v Peterborough United, 6.5.1988.

MOST CAPPED PLAYER
Bill Lewis (Wales) 12.
J.H.Pearson (England) 1.

BEST PERFORMANCES

BEST PERFORMANCES
League: 10th Division 2, 1892-93.
F.A. Cup: Semi-Final 1888.
League Cup: 3rd Round 1960-61, 1974-75, 1975-76, 1978-79, 1992-93.
Welsh Cup: Winners (2).

ADDITIONAL INFORMATION
PREVIOUS NAMES
None.

PREVIOUS LEAGUES
Central League.

Club colours: Red shirts, white shorts with red trim.
Change colours: White shirts with navy trim.

Reserves & 'A' Team League: Lancashire League.

DIVISIONAL RECORD

	Played	Won	Drawn	Lost	For	Against	Points
Division 2/1	156	38	22	96	198	405	116
Division 3/2	322	121	71	130	378	410	410
Division 4/3	1,458	505	377	576	1,914	2,107	2,297
Division 3 (N)	1,282	453	273	556	1,933	2.230	1,179
Total	3,218	1,117	743	1,348	4,423	5,152	3,957

RECORDS AND STATISTICS

COMPETITIONS

DIV.2/1	DIV.3/2	DIV 3(N)	DIV.4/3
1892-96	1962-63	1921-58	1958-62
1997-	1967-68		1963-67
	1988-90		1968-88
	1993-97		1990-93

HONOURS

WELSH CUP
1936
1937

MOST APPEARANCES

TOMMY LOWRY - 482 (1966-78)

YEAR	LEAGUE	FA CUP	LGE CUP	OTHERS
1966-67	21	-	-	-
1967-68	45	1	2	-
1968-69	36	3	3	-
1969-70	31	2	1	-
1970-71	44	3	2	-
1971-72	46	1	1	1
1972-73	40	3	1	-
1973-74	42	2	2	-
1974-75	43	2	4	-
1975-76	41	1	5	-
1976-77	45	3	2	-
1977-78	2	-	1	-
Total	436	21	24	1

MOST GOALS IN A CAREER

HERBERT SWINDELLS - 132 (1928-37)

YEAR	LEAGUE	FA CUP	LGE CUP	OTHERS
1928-29	5	-	-	-
1929-30	4	-	-	-
1930-31	11	-	-	-
1931-32	21	1	-	-
1932-33	14	2	-	-
1933-34	14	-	-	-
1934-35	19	-	-	-
1935-36	21	1	-	-
1936-37	17	2	-	-
Total	126	6	-	-

Current leading goalscorer: Gareth Smith - 37 (12.91-98)

RECORD TRANSFER FEE RECEIVED

AMOUNT	CLUB	PLAYER	DATE
£1,500,000*	Liverpool	Danny Murphy	07/97
£750,000	Leicester City	Neil Lennon	02/96

*Fee could rise to £3,000,000 after appearances.

RECORD TRANSFER FEE PAID

AMOUNT	CLUB	PLAYER	DATE
£500,000	Shrewsbury	Dave Walton	10/97
£80,000	Leicester City	Ashley Ward	12/92
£80,000	Barnsley	Darren Foreman	03/90

MANAGERS

NAME (SINCE 1946)	SEASONS	BEST	WORST
George Lillycrop (Trainer)	1938-44	8	-
Frank Hill (Player/Manager)	1944-48	8	12
Arthur Turnor	1948-51	7	16
Harry Catterick (Player/Manager)	1951-53	10	16
Ralph Ward	1953-55	16	24
Maurice Lindley	1956-57	-	24
W. Cook	1957-58	-	-
Harry Ware	1958-60	9	18
Jimmy McGuigan	1960-64	3	22
Ernie Tagg	1964-71	4	23
Dennis Viollet	1971	-	-
Jimmy Melia	1972-74	21	24
Ernie Tagg	1974-75	18	-
Harry Gregg	1975-78	12	16
Warwick Rimmer	1978-79	-	24
Tony Waddington	1979-81	18	24
Arfon Griffiths	1981-82	-	24
Peter Morris	1982-83	-	23
Dario Gradi	1983-	11 (2/1)	17

LONGEST LEAGUE RUNS

of undefeated matches:	14 (1990)	of league matches w/out a win:	30 (1956-57)
of undefeated home matches:	28 (1967-68)	of undefeated away matches:	7 (1966-67, 1990, 1993)
without home win:	15 (1979)	without an away win:	56 (1955-57)
of league wins:	7 (1928-29, 1986)	of home wins:	16 (1938)
of league defeats:	10 (1923, 1957-58, 1979)	of away wins:	5 (1986)

CREWE ALEXANDRA

PLAYERS NAME Honours	Ht	Wt	Birthdate	Birthplace Transfers	Contract Date	Clubs	League	L/Cup	FA Cup	Other	Lge	L/C	FAC	Oth
G O A L K E E P E R														
Kearton Jason B	6.1	11.1	7/9/69	Ipswich (Aus)		Brisbane Lions								
				Free	10/31/88	Everton	3+3	1	1					
				Loan	8/13/91	Stoke City	16			1				
				Loan	1/9/92	Blackpool	14							
				Loan	1/20/95	Notts County	10			2				
				Loan	3/21/96	Preston North End								
				Free	11/5/96	Crewe Alexandra	73	1	5	6				
D E F E N C E														
Bignott Marcus	5.9	11	8/22/74	Birmingham		Kidderminster H.								
				£175000	8/29/97	Crewe Alexandra	42		1					
Foran Mark	6.4	13.12	10/30/73	Aldershot	11/3/90	Millwall								
				Loan	8/1/92	Slough		1						
				£25000	8/28/93	Sheffield United	4	1		+1	1			
				Loan	8/26/94	Rotherham United	3							
				Loan	9/13/95	Wycombe W.	5	2						
					2/8/96	Peterborough Utd	22+3		1	1	1			
				Loan	1/22/97	Lincoln City	1+1							
				Loan	3/3/97	Oldham Athletic	+1							
				£45000	12/12/97	Crewe Alexandra	9+2			1				
Johnson Seth A Y. E:	5.11	10.7	3/12/79	Birmingham	9/20/96	Crewe Alexandra	47+4	2	1	0+3	2			
Lightfoot Chris	6.1	12	4/1/70	Penketh	7/11/88	Chester City	263+14	15+2	16+2	14+2	32	1	1	5
				£87500	7/13/95	Wigan Athletic								
				£50000	3/22/96	Crewe Alexandra	27+15	1+1	1+1	2+2	2		1	
Macauley Steven R FAVC'86.	6.1	12	3/4/69	Lytham	8/1/86	Fleetwood Town				1				
					11/5/87	Manchester City								
				£25000	3/24/92	Crewe Alexandra	157+4	12	12	18	21		1	3
Smith Gareth Shaun	5.1	11	4/9/71	Leeds	7/1/89	Halifax Town	6+1			1				
				Free	8/1/90	Emley								
				Free	12/31/91	Crewe Alexandra	214+19	6+1	12+2	18+1	29	2	3	3
Unsworth Lee P	5.11	11.2	2/25/73	Eccles		Ashton								
					2/17/94	Crewe Alexandra	74+18	5+1	4+1	6+2		1	1	
Walton David Div.3'94.	6.2	13.4	10/04/73	Bedlington		Ashington								
				Free	15/05/91	Sheffield United								
					05/11/93	Shrewsbury Town	127+1	7	10	11	10		1	1
				£500000	10/20/97	Crewe Alexandra	27		1					
Wicks Matthew	6.2	13.5	08/09/78	Reading		Manchester United								
					23/01/96	Arsenal								
				£100000	7/1/98	Crewe Alexandra								
Wright David	5.11	10.8	5/1/80	Warrington	6/18/97	Crewe Alexandra (T)	0+3							
M I D F I E L D														
Charnock Philip A	5.1	11.3	2/14/75	Southport	5/27/92	Liverpool		1		0+1				
				Loan	2/9/96	Blackpool								
				Loan	9/30/96	Crewe Alexandra	6+4							
				Free	12/6/96	Crewe Alexandra	47+3	2	3	3	3			
Collins James I	5.8	10	5/28/79	Liverpool	5/31/97	Crewe Alexandra (T)	0+1	0+1						
Critchley Neil			10/18/78	Crewe	7/4/97	Crewe Alexandra (T)								
Lunt Kenny V	5.10	10	11/20/79	Runcorn	6/12/97	Crewe Alexandra (T)	29+12	2			2	1		
Morse Peter R			3/5/79	Stoke	8/19/97	Crewe Alexandra (T)								
Norris Richard B			1/5/78	Birkenhead		Marine								
					2/14/97	Crewe Alexandra								
Whittaker David A			8/13/78	Stockport	7/9/97	Crewe Alexandra (T)								
Williamson Michael P			12/29/78	Liverpool	7/9/97	Crewe Alexandra								

F O R W A R D													
Anthrobus Steve	6.2	12.13	11/10/68	Lewisham	8/4/86	Millwall	19+2	3		1	4		
				Loan	2/9/90	Southend United							
				£150000	2/16/90	Wimbledon	27+1	1	2				
				Loan	1/21/94	Peterborough United							
				Loan	8/26/94	Chester City	7						
				£25000	8/1/95	Shrewsbury Town	60+12	4+1	5+3	5+1	16		1	
					3/24/97	Crewe Alexandra	37+3	1			6		
Jack Rodney A	5.7	10.7	9/28/72	Jamaica		Lambada WI							
				Free	10/10/95	Torquay United	80+5	6	6	5	24	1		3
				£500000	7/1/98	Crewe Alexandra							
Little Colin C	5.11	11	11/4/72	Wythenshaw		Hyde United							
						Crewe Alexandra	28+10	1	1		13		
Lovelock Andy						Southam United							
				Free	7/1/98	Crewe Alexandra							
Rivers Mark A	5.10	11	11/26/75	Crewe	5/6/94	Crewe Alexandra (T)	76+17	4+1	8	5+2	22	1	3	3
Smith Peter L Y. E:	5.11	10.8	9/18/78	Rhuddlan	3/15/97	Crewe Alexandra	1+5						
Street Kevin	5.10	10.8	11/25/77	Crewe	5/31/97	Crewe Alexandra (T)	15+17				4		
Wright Jermaine	5.9	10.13	10/21/75	Greenwich	11/27/92	Millwall							
				£60000	12/29/94	Wolverhampton W.	4+15	1+3		0+1		1	
				Loan	3/1/96	Doncaster Rovers							
				£25000	2/27/98	Crewe Alexandra	3+2						
ADDITIONAL CONTRACT PLAYERS													
Foster Stephen J					2/16/98	Crewe Alexandra (T)							
Hay Danny						Perth Glory							
				£60000	7/1/98	Crewe Alexandra							
Welsby Kevin J					2/16/98	Crewe Alexandra (T)							

THE MANAGER
DARIO GRADI

Date of Birth . . . . 8th July 1941.
Place of Birth. . . . . Milan.
Date of Appointment . . . . May 1993.

PREVIOUS CLUBS
As Manager. . . . . .Wimbledon, Crystal Palace.
As Assistant . . . . Chelsea, Derby County, Wimbledon, Orient (Youth Team).
As a Player . . . . Sutton United.

HONOURS
As a Manager
Wimbledon: Promotion to Division 3, 1978-79.
Crewe: Promotion to Division 3, 1989-90. Promotion to Division 2, 1993-94.
Promotion to Division 1, via the play-offs, 1996-97.

As a Player
England Semi-Professional.

GRESTY ROAD

Crewe, Cheshire CW2 6EB

Capacity 6,000

First game...v Basford, 1877.
First floodlit game ....v All Stars XI, 29.10.1958.

ATTENDANCES
Highest ....20,000 v Tottenham, FA Cup 4th Round, 30.1.1960.
Lowest ....994 v Stockport, AMC, 14.1.1986.

OTHER GROUNDS..Earle Street, Edleston Road, Nantwich Road.

HOW TO GET TO THE GROUND

From the North
Use motorway (M6) until junction 17 and follow signs to Crewe (A534). At Crewe roundabout follow signs to Chester into Nantwich Road. Then take next turning on left into Gresty Road for Crewe Alexandra FC.

From the East and South
Use A52 then A5020 (sign posted Crewe), then at Crewe roundabout follow signs to Chester into Nantwich Road. Then take next turning on left into Gresty Road for Crewe Alexandra FC.

From the West
Use A534 (sign posted Crewe) and immediately before Crewe Railway Station turn right into Gresty Road for Crewe Alexandra FC.

Nearest Railway Station
Crewe (5mins) 01270 255 245)

USEFUL TELEPHONE NUMBERS

Club switchboard 01270 213 014
Club fax number 01270 216 320
Club shop .... 01270 213 014 Ext. 101
Ticket Office... 01270 252 610 (fax 216 320)

Marketing Department01270 213 014 Ext. 113
Club Call 0891 12 16 47*
*Calls cost 50p per minute at all times.
Call costings correct at time of going to press.

MATCHDAY PROGRAMME

Programme Editor................Robert Wilson.

Number of pages....................................36.

Price ....£2.00.

Local Newspapers
.............Crewe Chronicle, Crewe Guardian,
............................Evening Sentinel, Hanley.

Local Radio Stations
................................Radio Stoke (94.6 FM),
...................Signal Radio 102.6 & 96.9 FM.

MATCHDAY TICKET PRICES

Ringways Stand	£13
Juv/OAP	£10/£6
Family Stand	£13
Juv/OAP	£10/£6
South Stand	£13
Juv/OAP	£10/£6
Paddock	£11
Juv/OAP	£8/£6
Gresty Road Visitors Stand	£13
Juv/OAP	£10/£6

CRYSTAL PALACE
(The Eagles)
NATIONWIDE LEAGUE DIVISION 1
SPONSORED BY: TDK

1997-98 - Back Row L-R: Steve Kember (reserve team manager), Sagi Burton, Andy Linighan, David Tuttle, Carlo Nash, Gareth Ormshaw, Kevin Miller, Hermann Hreidarsson, Neil Emblen, George Ndah, Gary Sadler (physio).
Middle Row: Ray Wilkins (coach), Danny Boxall, Jamie Fullarton, Kevin Muscat, Neil Shipperley, Carl Veart, Paul Warhurst, Gareth Davies, Ray Lewington (first team coach). **Front Row:** Dougie Freedman, Dean Gordon, Marc Edworthy, Andy Roberts (captain), Steve Coppell (manager), Attilio Lombardo, Simon Rodger, Bruce Dyer, Leon McKenzie.

CRYSTAL PALACE
FORMED IN 1905
TURNED PROFESSIONAL IN 1905
LTD COMPANY IN 1905

CHAIRMAN: M Goldberg
DIRECTORS
P Alexander (Managing), R Anderson,
P Barnes, S Coppell, L Grimes,
S Hume-Kendall, J McAvoy, P Morley CBE,
V Murphy, G Wilder
SECRETARY
Mike Hurst
PUBLIC RELATIONS MANAGER
Terry Byfield

MANAGER: Terry Venables
ASSISTANT MANAGERS
Terry Fenwick

PHYSIOTHERAPIST
Gary Sadler MCSP/SRP

STATISTICIAN FOR THE DIRECTORY
Mike Purkiss

Again, another return to the Carling Premiership League became a disaster resulting in relegation as bottom club, this after starting with an away win at Everton on the opening day of the season. Our away record was good, yet at Selhurst Park nothing went right, and we went into the record books as the worst home start of a season. Our first win being recorded not until mid April (15 League games) beating Arsenal's record of March 1913. A last minute winner on the last day of the term gave us two wins, saving us from equalling the record of one home win of a season held by several clubs.

In the cups we had three home wins, with 3-0 victory over Leicester City (Bruce Dyer scoring the only hat-trick of the season) before the eventual Cup winners, Arsenal, knocked us out, after a draw at Highbury.

Another club record of only 15 goals scored at home was set, with Neil Shipperley top scorer with seven (also scoring two in a match against West Ham which was abandoned due to floodlight failure).

The middle part of the term saw a run of 15 games without a win until our visit to Newcastle United in March saw three points in a match. Our club record signing was made when the French u21, Valerien Ismael, came from Strasburg for £2,750,000 in January. Kevin Miller was also a record buy as a goalkeeper beating Nigel Martyn's previous best, and Kevin had the honour of being the only ever-present this term, and Marc Edworthy took the 'Player of the Year' award, both players of English origin.

We now look forward to the Mark Goldberg and Terry Venables partnership, which will hopeful bring us promotion again in 1999.

Mike Purkiss.

CRYSTAL PALACE

Carling Prem.	:20th			FA CUP: 5th Round			LC CUP: 2nd Round		

M	DATE	COMP.	VEN	OPPONENTS	RESULT	H/T	LP	GOAL SCORERS/GOAL TIMES	ATT.
1	A 09	CP	A	Everton	W 2-1	1-0	2	Lombardo 34, Dyer 62 (pen)	(35716)
2	12	CP	H	Barnsley	L 0-1	0-0	9		21547
3	23	CP	A	Leeds United	W 2-0	1-0	5	Warhurst 22, Lombardo 51	(29076)
4	27	CP	A	Southampton	L 0-1	0-0	8		(15032)
5	30	CP	H	Blackburn Rovers	L 1-2	0-2	9	Dyer 51	20849
6	S 13	CP	H	Chelsea	L 0-3	0-2	13		26186
7	16	CC 2/1	A	**Hull City**	L 0-1	0-1			(9323)
8	20	CP	A	Wimbledon	W 1-0	0-0	10	Lombardo 79	(16747)
9	24	CP	A	Coventry City	D 1-1	1-1	9	Fullarton 9	(15900)
10	27	CP	H	Bolton Wanderers	D 2-2	2-1	11	Warhurst 9, Gordon 19	17134
11	30	CC 2/2	H	**Hull City**	W 2-1	0-1		**Veart 56, Ndah 77**	6407
12	O 04	CP	A	Manchester United	L 0-2	0-2	13		(55143)
13	18	CP	H	Arsenal	D 0-0	0-0	14		26180
14	25	CP	A	Sheffield Wednesday	W 3-1	1-0	12	Hreidarsson 27, Rodger 52, Shipperley 60	(22072)
15	N 08	CP	H	Aston Villa	D 1-1	1-0	12	Shipperley 42	21097
16	24	CP	A	Tottenham Hotspur	W 1-0	0-0	10	Shipperley 57	(25634)
17	29	CP	H	Newcastle United	L 1-2	0-1	10	Shipperley 66	26085
18	D 03	CP	A	West Ham United	L 1-4	1-2	12	Shipperley 41	(23335)
19	06	CP	A	Leicester City	D 1-1	1-0	12	Padovano 43	(19191)
20	13	CP	H	Liverpool	L 0-3	0-1	15		25790
21	20	CP	A	Derby County	D 0-0	0-0	13		(26590)
22	26	CP	H	Southampton	D 1-1	0-1	13	Shipperley 61	22853
23	28	CP	A	Blackburn Rovers	D 2-2	1-1	14	Dyer 11, Warhurst 48	(23872)
24	J 03	FAC 3	H	**Scunthorpe United**	W 2-0	1-0		**Emblen 44, 87**	11624
25	10	CP	H	Everton	L 1-3	1-3	17	Dyer 16	23311
26	17	CP	A	Barnsley	L 0-1	0-1	17		(17819)
27	24	FAC 4	H	**Leicester City**	W 3-0	1-0		**Dyer 32, 62, 66**	15489
28	31	CP	H	Leeds United	L 0-2	0-2	17		25248
29	F 09	CP	H	Wimbledon	L 0-3	0-0	18		14410
30	15	FAC 5	A	**Arsenal**	D 0-0	0-0			(37164)
31	21	CP	A	Arsenal	L 0-1	0-0	19		(38094)
32	25	FAC 5R	H	**Arsenal**	L 1-2	1-2		**Dyer 35**	15674
33	28	CP	H	Coventry City	L 0-3	0-2	20		21810
34	M 11	CP	A	Chelsea	L 2-6	1-3	20	Hreidarsson 7, Bent 87	(31917)
35	14	CP	A	Aston Villa	L 1-3	0-3	20	Jansen 62	(33781)
36	18	CP	A	Newcastle United	W 2-1	2-0	20	Lombardo 14, Jansen 23	(36565)
37	28	CP	H	Tottenham Hotspur	L 1-3	0-0	20	Shipperley 82	26116
38	A 11	CP	A	Leicester City	L 0-3	0-1	20		18771
39	13	CP	A	Liverpool	L 1-2	0-1	20	Bent 72	(43007)
40	18	CP	H	Derby County	W 3-1	0-0	20	Jansen 73, Curcic 80, Bent 90	18101
41	27	CP	H	Manchester United	L 0-3	0-2	20		26180
42	M 02	CP	A	Bolton Wanderers	L 2-5	2-3	20	Gordon 8, Bent 16	(24449)
43	05	CP	H	West Ham United	D 3-3	1-1	20	Bent 44, Rodger 48, Lombardo 63	19129
44	10	CP	H	Sheffield Wednesday	W 1-0	0-0	20	Morrison 90	16876

Best Home League Attendance: 26186 V Chelsea	**Smallest :14410 V Wimbledon**	**Average :21983**

Goal Scorers:

CP	(37)	Shipperley 7, Bent 5, Lombardo 5, Dyer 4, Jansen 3, Warhurst 3, Gordon 2, Hreidarsson 2, Rodger 2, Curcic 1, Fullarton 1, Morrison 1, Padovano 1
CC	(2)	Ndah 1, Veart 1
FAC	(6)	Dyer 4, Emblen 2

(F) Bent	(F) Brolin	(F) Curcic	(M) Dyer	(D) Edworthy	(D) Emblen	(F) Freedman	(M) Fullarton	(F) Ginty	(M) Gordon	(M) Hreidarsson	(F) Ismael	(F) Jansen	(D) Linighan	(F) Lombardo	(F) McKenzie	(G) Miller	(M) Muscat	(G) Nash	(F) Padovano	(D) Quinn	(M) Roberts	(D) Rodger	(F) Shipperley	(M) Smith	(D) Tuttle	(F) Veart	(F) Warhurst	(M) Zohar	Referee	No.
		X	X				S1		X		S		X	X		X	X	S			X	X	S2		X		S2	X	S.W. Dunn	1
		X	X				S1		X		S		X	X		X	X	S			X	X	S2		X		S	X	N S Barry	2
		X	X	S1			S3		X		S		X	X		X	X	S			X	X	S2		X			X	U D Rennie	3
		X	X	S1					X		S		X	X		X	X	S			X	X	S2		X			X	J T Winter	4
		X	X	S1		S			X		S2		X	X		X	X	S			X	X	S3		X			X	K W Burge	5
		X		X	S1		X		X		S		X	X		X	X	S			X		X		X	S3		S2	G R Ashby	6
	S2			X			X	X	X		X		X			X	X	S			X		X		X	S1	X		**A B Wilkie**	**7**
		X	S2				S1		X		X		X	X		X	X	S			X		S3		X		X	S	P E Alcock	8
		X					X	X	X		X		X	X	S2	X	X	S		S	X		X			S1		S	G P Barber	9
		X					X	X	X		X		X	X		X	X	S	S2		X		S1			S3	S	S	D R Elleray	10
		X			S2		X		X		X			X		X						S3	X			X	X	X	**P A Durkin**	**11**
		X			S1		X		X		X			X		X	S				X	X	S				X	S2	S J Lodge	12
	S		X					X	X		X			X		X					X		X		X		X	S	S W Dunn	13
		X	X		S2				X		X					X			S		S	X	X	X	X			S	D J Gallagher	14
		X	X		S1				X		X			X		X		S			S	X	X	X	S			J T Winter	15
		X	X						X		X			X		X		S	X		X	X	X			S1	X	S	P A Durkin	16
		X1			S3				X		X					X		S	X3		X2	X	X	S1		S	X	S2	M A Riley	17
		X	X		X		S		X		X					X		S	S1			X	X	X1		S	X	X	D R Elleray	18
		X	X2		S1		S	X	X		X					X		S	X1			X	X			X	X	X	U D Rennie	19
		X	S1		X		S2	X	X		X					X		S	X1	S		X	X				X	S	N S Barry	20
	S1		X		X		X	X	X		X					X		S	S			X	X				X	X1	M J Bodenham	21
	X		S		X1	X	X	X			X					X		S	S			X	X2				X	S2	P E Alcock	22
	X1		X		X	X	X		X		X				S1	X		S	S			X	X				X		P Jones	23
		X	X	X			S1	X	X		X					X		S			S	X	X		X2			X1	**D J Gallagher**	**24**
S2	X		X	X	X1		X	S	X	X						X		S			X	X2					X		G P Barber	25
X	X		X	X			X	S1	X	X1						X		S			X	X					X		M D Reed	26
		X	X	X			X	X	X	X						X		S			X	X					X		**P E Alcock**	**27**
X	X		X	X	S		S		X	S	X					X		S			X	X					X		U D Rennie	28
X2	X		X	X	S		S2	X	X	X1	X					X		S			X	S1					X		K W Burge	29
	X		X	X	S		X		X	X	X					S					X	X			X	S			**M J Bodenham**	**30**
S1	X		X2	X			X		X	X	X					S					X	X			X1	S2			J T Winter	31
	X3		X	X	S2		X	S	X	X	X	X	S3			S1					X2	X			X1				**M J Bodenham**	**32**
S2	X3		X2	X			X	X	X	X	X	S3	S3			S					X	X1			X				D R Elleray	33
S3	X		X1	X2			X		X	X	X	S1	S	S2		X		S			X				X3				M A Riley	34
X3	X		X	X1			X		X	X	X	S2	S	S3		X		S			S1	X2			X				G P Barber	35
X1	X		X				X	X3	X	X	S3	X	X	S	X3	X		S			X2	X			X				S J Lodge	36
S	X2	X1	X				X		X	S1	X	S1	X			X		S	S1		X	S3			X				M D Reed	37
S3		S1	S2	X			X		X	S	X		X			X		S	X1			X	X			X		X3	A B Wilkie	38
X	X2		S2	X			X1		X	X	X	S				X		S	S			X	X			X			G P Barber	39
S2	X	X		X			X		X	X	X	X2	X	S1		X		S	S1			X	X			X			P E Alcock	40
X	X1	X	S2	X			S1		X	S3	X	S3	X		X3	X		S			X2	X			X		S		P Jones	41
X		X	S				X		X	X		X	X1			X		S			X	S	S1		X		X		N S Barry	42
X	X2		X				S2		X	X	X1		X	S	X	X		S			X	X2	X		S1		X		G Poll	43
X	X1		X						X	X			X	X	X		S	S	X	X2				X			X		M D Reed	44

10	13	6	21	33	8	2	19	2	36	26	13	5	26	21		38	9		8		25	27	17	16	8	1	22	2	CP Appearances	
6		2	3	1	5	5	6	3	1	4		3			3	3		2	1		2	9	2	1	5		4		CP Sub Appearance	
		0+1	1		1+1	1		2		2		2	2			1	1				1	0+1	2		1		1		CC Appearances	
	3		4	4	1+1		3	0+1	4	4	3		2+1		0+1	4					4	3		4			1		FAC Appearances	

Also Played: (M) Billio S2(36,37), X2(38.(D) Boxall S1(25), X (11), S(26,27,2844). (M) Bonetti S2(13), S1(14). (D) Burton-Goodwin X(21), S1(22), S(23), S2(24).(D) Davies S(16,18), S2(19). (F) Folan S(30,43), S1(44). (F) Martin S(27). (F) Morrison S2(44). (F) Ndah S1(11,13), X(12,14), S(15). (G) Ormshaw S(12,13,14). (D) Pitcher S(23). (M) Thomson S(21,24,26).

CRYSTAL PALACE

CLUB RECORDS

BIGGEST VICTORIES
League: 9-0 v Barrow, Division 4, 10.10.1959.
F.A. Cup: 7-0 v Luton Town, 3rd Round, 16.1.1929.
League Cup: 8-0 v Southend, 2nd Round, 25.9.1990.

BIGGEST DEFEATS
League: 0-9 v Liverpool, Division 1, 12.9.1989.
F.A. Cup: 0-9 v Burnley, 2nd Round replay, 1908-09.
League Cup: 0-5 v Nottingham Forest, 3rd Round replay, 1.11.89.

MOST POINTS
3 points a win: 90, Division 1, 1993-94.
2 points a win: 64, Division 4, 1960-61.

MOST GOALS SCORED
110, Division 4, 1960-61.
Byrne 30, Summersby 25, Heckman 14, Woan 13, Gavin 8,
Petchley 7, Uphill 6, Barnett 2, Lunnis 1, McNicholl 1, Noakes 1,
Opponents 2.

MOST GOALS CONCEDED
86, Division 3(S), 1953-54.

MOST FIRST CLASS MATCHES IN A SEASON
59 - 1988-89 (League 46, FA Cup 1, League Cup 3, Simod Cup 5,
Play-offs 4).

MOST LEAGUE WINS
29, Division 4, 1960-61.

MOST LEAGUE DRAWS
19, Division 2, 1978-79.

MOST LEAGUE DEFEATS
29, Division 1, 1980-81.

INDIVIDUAL CLUB RECORDS

MOST GOALS IN A SEASON
Peter Simpson: 54 goals in 1930-31 (League 46, FA Cup 8).
Previous holder: P.A.Cherrett, 32 goals in 1926-27.

MOST GOALS IN A MATCH
6. Peter Simpson v Exeter, 7-2, Division 3(S), 4.10.1930.

OLDEST PLAYER
Wally Betteridge, 41 (Debut - Player/coach), 27.10.1928 (0-8).

YOUNGEST PLAYER
Phil Hoadley, 16 years 3 months, 27.4.1968.

MOST CAPPED PLAYER
Eric Young (Wales) 19.

BEST PERFORMANCES

League: 1960-61: Matches played 46, Won 29, Drawn 6, Lost 11,
Goals for 110, Goals against 69, Points 64. 2nd in Division 4.
Highest Position: 1990-91, 3rd in Division 1.
F.A. Cup: 1989-90: 3rd Round Portsmouth 2-1; 4th Round
Huddersfield Town 4-0; 5th Round Rochdale 1-0; 6th Round
Cambridge 1-0; Semi-Final Liverpool 4-3; Final Manchester United
3-3 aet, replay 0-1.
League Cup: 1992-93: 2nd Round Lincoln City (a) 3-1, (h) 1-1; 3rd
Round Southampton (a) 2-0; 4th Round Liverpool (a) 1-1, (h) 2-1
aet; 5th Round Chelsea (h) 3-1; Semi-Final Arsenal (h) 1-3, (a) 0-2.

ADDITIONAL INFORMATION
PREVIOUS NAMES
None.

PREVIOUS LEAGUES
Southern League.

Club colours: Red and blue shirts, red shorts with blue & white
trim.
Change colours:
Reserves League: Neville Ovenden Football Combination.

DIVISIONAL RECORD

	Played	Won	Drawn	Lost	For	Against	Points
Division 1/P	492	130	144	218	505	730	481
Division 2/1	984	377	269	338	1,271	1,189	1,221
Division 3	276	113	86	77	419	332	312
Division 3(S)	1,166	438	292	436	1,831	1,853	1,168
Division 4	138	68	30	40	284	204	166
Total	3,056	1,126	821	1,109	4,310	4,308	3,348

COMPETITIONS

Div .1/P	Div.2/1	Div.3	Div.3(S)	Div.4
1969-73	1921-25	1920-21	1925-58	1958-61
1979-81	1964-69			
1989-93	1973-74			Texaco
1994-95	1976-79			1972-73
1997-98	1981-89			
	1993-94			
	1995-97			
	1998-			

HONOURS

Div. 2/1	Div. 3	FMC
1978-79	1920-21	1991
1993-94		

MOST APPEARANCES

JIM CANNON 665 + 4 (1972-86)

Year	League	FA Cup	Lge Cup	Others
1972-73	3			
1973-74	13+1		1	
1974-75	34+2	2	0+1	
1975-76	40	8	2	
1976-77	46	6	3	
1977-78	39	1	4	
1978-79	41	4	4	
1979-80	42	3	3	
1980-81	33	1	4	
1981-82	42	5	4	
1982-83	41	4	5	
1983-84	30	2	2	
1984-85	40	2	2	
1985-86	42	1	4	1
1986-87	42	2	4	1
1987-88	40	1	1	1
	568+3	42	43+1	3

MOST GOALS IN A CAREER

PETER SIMPSON - 166 (1929-34)

Year	League	FA Cup
1929-30	36	1
1930-31	46	8
1931-32	24	1
1932-33	14	1
1933-34	20	1
1934-35	14	
Total	154	12

Current leading goalscorer: Bruce Dyer - 41 (03.94-98)

MANAGERS

Name	Seasons	Best	Worst
John Robson	1905-07	1(2)	19(1)
Eddie Goodman	1907-25	14(2)	1(3S)
Alec Maley	1925-27	6(3S)	13(3S)
Fred Maven	1927-30	2(3S)	9(3S)
Jack Tresadern	1930-35	2(3S)	12(3S)
Tom Bromilow	1935-36	6(3S)	6(3S)
R.S. Moyse	1936	14(3S)	14(3S)
Tom Bromilow	1937-39	2(3S)	7(3S)
George Irwin	1939-47	13(3S)	22(3S)
Jack Butler	1947-40	2(3S)	3(3S)
Ron Rooke	1949-50	3(3S)	3(3S)
F Dawes/C Slade	1950-51	24(3S)	24(3S)
Laurie Scott	1951-54	13(3S)	22(3S)
Cyril Spiers	1954-58	14(3S)	23(3S)
George Smith	1958-60	7(4)	8(4)
Arthur Rowe	1960-63	11(3)	2(4)
Dick Graham	1963-66	7(2)	2(3)
Arthur Rowe (Acting)	1966		
Bert Head	1966-72	18(1)	11(2)
Malcolm Allison	1972-76	21(1)	5(3)
Terry Venables	1976-80	13(1)	3(3)
Ernie Walley	1980	20(1)	22(1)
Malcolm Allison	1980-81	22(10	22(1)
Dario Gradi	1981	22(1)	15(2)
Steve Kember	1981-82	15(2)	15(2)
Alan Mullery	1982-84	15(2)	18(2)
Steve Coppell	1984-93	3(1)	15(2)
Alan Smith	1993-95	1(1)	1(1)
Dave Bassett	1996-97	3(1)	3(1)
Steve Coppell	1997-98	6 (1)	6 (1)
Attillio Lombardo (caretaker)	1998	20(P)	20(P)
Terry Venables	1998-		

RECORD TRANSFER FEE RECEIVED

Amount	Club	Player	Date
£4,500,000	Tottenham H.	Chris Armstrong	06/95
£2,500,000	Arsenal	Ian Wright	9/91
£1,350,000	Arsenal	Kenny Sansom	8/80
£400,000	Derby County	Dave Swindlehurst	4/80

RECORD TRANSFER FEE PAID

Amount	Club	Player	Date
£2,750,000	RC Strasbourg	Valerien Ismael	1/98
£2,300,000	Millwall	Andy Roberts	7/95
£1,800,000	Sunderland	Marco Gabbiadini	9/91
£1,350,000	Bristol Rovers	Nigel Martin	11/89

LONGEST LEAGUE RUNS

of undefeated matches:	18 (1.3.1969 - 16.8.1969)	of league matches w/out a win:	20 (24.2.1962 - 13.10.1962)
of undefeated home matches:	32 (28.2.1930 - 8.10.1932)	of undefeated away matches:	10 (22.12.1928 -1.4.1929,
			26.12.1968 - 10.8.1969, 16.8.1975 - 6.12.1975, 18.11.78 - 3.4.79).
without home win:	11 (14.4.1973 - 17.11.1973)	without an away win:	31 (15.3.1980 - 3.10.1981).
of league wins:	8 (9.2.1991 - 26.3.1921)	of home wins:	12 (19.12.1925 - 28.8.1926).
of league defeats:	8 (18.41925 - 19.9.1925)	of away wins:	4 (1931-32, 1932-33 & 1975-76)

CRYSTAL PALACE

PLAYERS NAME / Honours	Ht	Wt	Birthdate	Birthplace / Transfers	Contract Date	Clubs	League	L/Cup	FA Cup	Other	Lge	L/C	FAC	Oth
G O A L K E E P E R														
Digby Fraser	6.1	12.12	23/04/67	Sheffield	4/25/85	Manchester United								
E: u21.5, u19.1, Y.7, S.Div.2'96.				£32000	9/25/86	Swindon Town	417	33	21	33+1				
				Free	7/1/98	Crystal Palace								
Kendall Lee M			1/8/81	Newport		Crystal Palace (T)								
Miller Kevin	6.1	13	3/15/69	Falmouth		Newquay								
Div4'90				Free	3/9/89	Exeter City	163	7	12	18				
				£250000	5/14/93	Birmingham City	24	4		2				
				£250000	8/1/94	Watford	128	10	10					
					7/21/97	Crystal Palace	38	2	4					
Ormshaw Gareth D	6	11.7	7/8/79	Durban		Ramsey Town								
					5/31/97	Crystal Palace								
D E F E N C E														
Austin Dean	5.11	11.11	26/04/70	Hemel Hempstead		St.Albans								
				£12000	22/03/90	Southend United	96	4	2	7	2	1		
				£375000	04/06/92	Tottenham Hotspur	117+7	7+2	16+1					
				Free	7/1/98	Crystal Palace								
Burton-Goodwin Osagyefo	6.2	13.6	11/25/77	Birmingham	8/30/96	Crystal Palace	1+1		0+1					
Edworthy Marc	5.7	9.6	12/24/72	Barnstaple	3/30/91	Plymouth Argyle	52+17	5+2	5+2	2+2	1			
				£350000	6/1/95	Crystal Palace	119+4	8	8	6		1		
Hibburt James	5.11	11.7	10/30/79	Ashford	11/2/96	Crystal Palace								
Hreidarsson Hermann	6.1	12.12	7/11/74	Iceland		IBV								
					8/1/97	Crystal Palace	26+4	2	4		2			
Ismael Valerien	6.2	13.1	9/28/75	Strasbourg		Strasbourg								
				£2750000	1/16/98	Crystal Palace	13		3					
Linighan Andy	6.3	12.6	6/18/62	Hartlepool	9/19/80	Hartlepool United	110	7+1	8	1	4	1		1
E: B.4. LC'93. FAC'93. ECWC'94				£200000	5/15/84	Leeds United	66	6	2	2	3	1		
				£65000	1/17/86	Oldham Athletic	87	8	3	4	6	2		
				£350000	3/4/88	Norwich City	86	6	10	4	8			
				£1250000	7/4/90	Arsenal	101+17	13+1	12+2	9+1	5	1	1	1
				£150000	1/27/97	Crystal Palace	45	2	2+1	3	2			
Mullins Hayden	5.11	10.7	3/27/79	Reading		Crystal Palace								
Rodger Simon L	5.9	10.13	10/3/71	Shoreham		Bognor Regis								
Div.1'94.				£1000	7/2/90	Crystal Palace	133+21	15+1	5+3	5+2	7			
				Loan	10/28/96	Manchester City	8				1			
				Loan	2/14/97	Stoke City	5							
Smith James Anthony	5.7	10.8	9/17/74	Birmingham	6/7/93	Wolves (T)	71+6	10+1	2	4				1
					10/22/97	Crystal Palace	16+2		4					
Tuttle David	6.1	12	2/6/72	Reading	2/8/90	Tottenham Hotspur	10+3	3+1		1				1
				Loan	1/21/93	Peterborough United	7							
				£350000	8/1/93	Sheffield United	37	1	1					
				£300000	3/8/96	Crystal Palace	56+2	4	1	5	3			
Woozley David J	6	12.10	12/6/79	Berkshire		Crystal Palace (T)								
M I D F I E L D														
Dyer Bruce A	6	10.9	4/13/75	Ilford	4/19/93	Watford	29+2	4	1	2	6	2		1
E: u21.6. Div.1'94.				£1100000	3/10/94	Crystal Palace	90+31	7+2	7+1	3+2	34	1	6	
Frampton Andrew J K			9/3/79	Wimbledon	5/31/97	Crystal Palace (T)								
Fullarton Jamie	5.9	10.9	7/20/74	Bellshill	6/13/91	St Mirren								
					7/1/96	Bastia								
				Free	8/1/97	Crystal Palace	19+6	2	3		1			
Graham Gareth L	5.7	10.7	12/6/78	Belfast	5/31/97	Crystal Palace								
Rizzo Nicholas	5.10	12	6/9/79	Sydney	9/26/96	Liverpool								
				Free	7/1/98	Crystal Palace								
F O R W A R D														
Bent Marcus	6.2	12.4	5/19/78	Hammersmith	7/21/95	Brentford (T)	56+14	7	8	5+1	8	1	3	1
				£150000	1/8/98	Crystal Palace	10+6				5			
Curcic Sasa	5.9	10.7	2/14/72	Yugoslavia		Patizan Belgrade								
				£1500000	10/28/95	Bolton Wanderers	28	3	2		4	1	2	
				£4000000	8/23/96	Aston Villa	20+9	1+1	2				1	
				£1000000	3/26/98	Crystal Palace	6+2				1			
Folan Anthony	6	11	9/18/78	Lewisham	9/20/96	Crystal Palace	0+1							

Name				From	Date	Club								
Harris Jason	6.1	11.2	11/24/76	Sutton	6/14/96	Crystal Palace								
Loan					11/22/96	Bristol Rovers	5+1				2			1
Jansen Matt	5.11	10.13	10/20/77	Carlisle		Carlisle United	26+16	4+1	1+3		10	3		
MC 96/97				£1000000	2/27/98	Crystal Palace	5+3				3			
Lombardo Attilio	5.11	11.7	1/6/66	St Maria		Juventus								
alian Int. EC'96				£1600000	8/8/97	Crystal Palace	21+3				5			
Martin Andrew P	6	10.1	2/28/80	Cardiff	2/28/97	Crystal Palace								
McKenzie Leon M	5.11	11.2	5/14/72	Croydon	10/7/95	Crystal Palace (T)	8+28	4	1+4		2	1		
Loan					10/3/97	Fulham	1+2							
Morrison Clinton H	5.11	10	5/14/79	Tooting	5/31/97	Crystal Palace	0+1				1			
Padovano Michele	5.10	10.10	8/28/66	Turin		Juventus								
alian Int.				£1700000	11/18/97	Crystal Palace	8+2				1			
Shipperley Neil	5.11	13.2	10/30/74	Chatham	9/24/92	Chelsea	20+7	2+1	3		5	1	1	
: u21.4				£1250000	1/8/95	Southampton	65+1	5+1	10		13	2	5	
				£100000	10/25/96	Crystal Palace	34+9	2	1		14			
Warhurst Paul	6.1	12.1	9/26/69	Stockport	7/1/88	Manchester City								
E: u21.8. Prem'95.				£10000	10/27/88	Oldham Athletic	60+7	8	5+4	2	2			
				£750000	1/17/91	Sheffield Wednesday	60+6	9	7+1	5	6	4	5	3
				£2700000	8/17/93	Blackburn Rovers	30+27	6+2	2+1	4+2	4			
					7/31/97	Crystal Palace	22	1	1		3			

ADDITIONAL CONTRACT PLAYERS

Name	From	Date	Club
Amsalem David			Beiter Jerusalem
	£800000	7/1/98	Crystal Palace
Ledesma Cristian			Argentinos Juniors
	£1000000	7/1/98	Crystal Palace
Rodriguez Pablo			Argentinos Juniors
	£1000000	7/1/98	Crystal Palace

MANAGER
TERRY VENABLES

Date of Birth . . . . 6th January 1943.
Place of Birth . . . . Bethnal Green.
Date of Appointment . . . . June 1998.

PREVIOUS CLUBS
As Manager . . . . Crystal Palace, QPR, Barcelona, Tottenham.
As International Manager . . . . England, Australia.
As Coach . . . . Crystal Palace.
As a Player . . . . Chelsea, Tottenham, QPR, Crystal Palace.

HONOURS
As a Manager
Crystal Palace: Promotion to Division 2 - 1976. Division 2 championship 1979.
Barcelona: Spanish Leageu winners. European Cup finalists.
England: Euro'96 semi-finalists.

As a Player
Chelsea: League Cup 1965. **Tottenham:** FA Cup 1967. Football League representative.
International: Played at every level for England, culminating in 2 full caps.

SELHURST PARK

London SE25 6PU

Capacity 26,500

First game ....v Sheffield Wed., Division 2, 30.8.1924.
First floodlit game ....v Chelsea, 28.9.1953.
ATTENDANCES
Highest ....51,482 v Burnley, Division 2, 5.5.1979.
Lowest ....2,207 v Brighton, FMC, 16.10.1985.

OTHER GROUNDS ....Crystal Palace 1905-15. Herne Hill 1915-18. The Nest 1918-24.
.... Selhurst Park 1924-

HOW TO GET TO THE GROUND

From the North
From motorway (M1) or A1, use A406 North Circular Road to Chiswick. Follow signs South Circular Road (A205) to Wandsworth. Then use A3 to A214 and follow signs to Streatham. Join A23. In 1 mile turn left (B273). At the end turn left into High Street then forward into Whitehorse Lane for Crystal Palace FC.
From the East
Use A232 (sign posted Croydon) to Shirley then join A215 (sign posted Norwood). In 2.2 miles turn left (B266) into Whitehouse Lane.
From the South
Use A23 (sign posted London) then follow signs Crystal Palace (B266) via Thornton Heath into Whitehorse Lane.
From the West
Use motorway (M4) to Chiswick then route from North or A232 (sign posted Croydon) to Beddington, then follow signs London A23. After, follow signs Crystal Palace (B266) via Thornton Heath into Whitehorse Lane.

Car Parking: Club car park (468 spaces) on first come first served basis. Street parking is also available.
Nearest Railway Station: Thornton Heath/Norwood Junction/Selhurst.

USEFUL TELEPHONE NUMBERS

Club switchboard 0181 768 6000
Club fax number 0181 771 5311
Club shop 0181 768 6100
Ticket office 0181 771 8841

Marketing department 0181 768 6000
Internet address .... www.cpfc.co.uk
Clubcall. 0891 400 333*
*Calls cost 50p per minute at all times. Call costings correct at time of going to press.

MATCHDAY PROGRAMME

Programme Editors
.... Pete King & James Coome.

Number of pages .... 56.

Price. .... £2.

Subscriptions .... £54 (inland) Home only.

Local Newspapers
.... Croydon Advertiser
.... South London Press.

Local Radio Stations
.... G.L.R., Capital Gold.

MATCHDAY TICKET PRICES (97-98)

	CAT A	CAT B
DIRECTORS BOX		
Executive Lounge/Steve Coppell Lounge	£30	£28
Senior Citizens/U16s	£20	£18
Junior Eagles	£18	£15
MAIN STAND		
Stanley Stephenson/Players/Glaziers Lounge	£25	£23
Senior Citizens/U16s (all Lounges)	£15	£14
Junior Eagles (all Lounges)	£13	£12
ARTHUR WAIT STAND		
Adult	£20	£18
Senior Citizens/U16s	£12	£11
Junior Eagles	£10	£9
WHITEHOUSE LANE STAND		
Adult	£16	£14
Senior Citizens/U16s	£9	£8
Junior Eagles	£7	£6
HOLMESDALE STAND		
Adult	£16-£20	£14-£19
Senior Citizens/U16s	£9	£8
Junior Eagles	£7	£6
FAMILY AREA - MAIN STAND (BLOCKS A & J)		
Palace Club Member	£16	£14
Senior Citizens/U16s	£9	£8
Junior Eagles	£6	£5

GRIMSBY TOWN
(The Mariners)
NATIONWIDE LEAGUE DIVISION 1
SPONSORED BY: DIXON MOTORS PLC

1998-99 - Back Row L-R: Jack Lester, Wayne Burnett, Steve Livingstone (now St Johnstone), Mark Lever, Andy Love, Darren Wrack (now Wasall), Aidan Davison, Tony Gallimore, Peter Handyside, Richard Smith, Paul Groves. **Middle Row:** Mike Bielby (Kit Manager), Lee Nogan, Daryl Clare, Tommy Widdrington, Kevin Donovan, Steve Croudson, Kingsley Black, John McDermott, Jim Dobbin, David Smith, Paul Mitchell (Physio). **Front Row:** Matthew Bloomer, Matthew Oswin, Andrew Oakes, Alan Buckley (Manager), John Cockerill (Assistant Manager), Adam Buckley, Danny Butterfield, Ben Chapman.

GRIMSBY TOWN
FORMED IN 1878
TURNED PROFESSIONAL IN 1890
LTD COMPANY IN 1890

LIFE PRESIDENT
T J Lindley
CHAIRMAN: W H Carr
VICE-CHAIRMAN: T Aspinall
DIRECTORS
C T Aspinall, J Teanby, M Rouse, S Bygott
CHIEF EXECUTIVE
Ian Fleming (01472 697 111)
COMMERCIAL MANAGER
Tony Richardson

MANAGER: Alan Buckley
ASSISTANT MANAGER: John Cockerill
YOUTH TEAM MANAGER
Ian Knight
PHYSIOTHERAPIST
Paul Mitchell

STATISTICIAN FOR THE DIRECTORY
Les Triggs

How can one in a couple of paragraphs summarise the most astounding season in the 120 year history of the club. A marathon programme of 68 games culminating in two Wembley victories bringing both the Auto Windscreens Shield and an immediate return to First Division football back to Blundell Park.

Following the disappointment of relegation, the return of Alan Buckley as manager was not welcomed with universal acclaim and scepticism seemed justified as Buckley sought to rebuild the team and it was not until the 7th league game that the Mariners recorded their first 2nd Division win.

Despite disappointing league results hope was rekindled as first Sheffield Wednesday and then Leicester City were ousted from the Coca-Cola Cup. Hopes of further progress were, alas, dashed by a Michael Owen hatrick at Anfield.

By now a gradual improvement in league form saw the side gradually pull away from the relegation zone, but it was not until an undefeated run in December saw them climb from mid-table into fourth position that possibility of promotion arose.

A brief prospect of further giant killing after a 3-0 ousting of Norwich from the FA Cup faded with a 0-2 defeat at Elland Road in the Fourth Round.

Whilst Watford and Bristol Rovers pulled ahead of the pack in the second division. The Mariners attentions were somewhat diverted from league matters by progress in the much maligned Auto Windscreens Shield as the prospects of a first ever Wembley appearance. This goal achieved with a 2-0 second leg victory at Burnley. Fortunately a combination of pre Wembley jitters and the strain on player as the programme reached 60 matches was reflected elsewhere and despite winning only one of the next eight league games the Mariners remained in 3rd position.

The rest as they say is history two visits to 'the field of dreams' in five weeks, two 62,000+ attendances and two wins to bring an euphoric end to a truly remarkable season.

It is possibly unfair to pick out any individual player, but Aidan Davison behind a solid defence with Mark Lever and Peter Handyside in his best season yet commanding the centre were unbreached on 35 occasions. Kevin Donovan's 21 goals, including the vital one that clinched promotion made him 'player of the year'. And late signing Wayne Burnett commanded midfield to prove the final piece in Buckley's promotion scheme.

From the ever fertile youth programme Daryl Clare established himself in the senior squad and in the Eire U21 side and defender Danny Butterfield made the occasional senior appearance and was selected for England at U18 level.

There is little doubt that the current squad can do well in the first division although some are attracting interest from higher spheres, but the continuing ground capacity of under 9,000 remains a problem. Talks about a new ground have gone on long enough, it is time for deeds.

Les Triggs.

GRIMSBY TOWN

Division 2   :3rd   **FA CUP: 4th Round**   **LC CUP: 4th Round**   **AWS: Winners**

M	DATE	COMP.	VEN	OPPONENTS	RESULT	H/T	LP	GOAL SCORERS/GOAL TIMES	ATT.
1	A 09	FL	H	Bristol City	D 1-1	0-1	9	Widdrington 74	6220
2	12	CC 1/1	A	Oldham Athletic	L 0-1	0-0			(5656)
3	15	FL	A	Plymouth Argyle	D 2-2	0-2	14	Donovan 66 (pen), Nogan 73	(6002)
4	23	FL	H	Wrexham	D 0-0	0-0	20		4404
5	26	CC 1/2	H	Oldham Athletic	W 5-0	3-0		Lester 3, 6, 11, Livingstone 56, Donovan 79	5078
6	30	FL	A	Brentford	L 1-3	0-2	21	Nogan 66	(3875)
7	S 02	FL	A	Preston North End	L 0-2	0-0	23		(9489)
8	09	FL	H	York City	D 0-0	0-0	23		5308
9	13	FL	A	Fulham	W 2-0	1-0	20	Livingstone 22, 88	(6874)
10	17	CC 2/1	H	Sheffield Wednesday	W 2-0	1-0		Groves 17, Livingstone 51	6429
11	20	FL	H	Millwall	L 0-1	0-0	21		4267
12	27	FL	A	Bournemouth	W 1-0	0-0	20	Groves 57	(3712)
13	O 01	CC 2/2	A	Sheffield Wednesday	L 2-3	0-1		Nogan 46, Groves 48	(11120)
14	04	FL	H	Wigan Athletic	W 2-1	1-0	15	Donovan 1 (pen), 78 (pen)	4623
15	11	FL	A	Northampton Town	W 1-0	1-0	12	Donovan 44	4778
16	14	CC 3	H	Leicester City	W 3-1	0-1		Jobling 68, Livingstone 72, 77	7738
17	18	FL	A	Blackpool	D 2-2	1-1	14	Nogan 7, Donovan 85 (pen)	(5234)
18	21	FL	A	Oldham Athletic	L 0-2	0-0	16		(4152)
19	25	FL	H	Watford	L 0-1	0-1	17		5699
20	N 01	FL	H	Southend United	W 5-1	3-0	13	Nogan 4, 61, Lester 16, Groves 19, Widdrington 52	4501
21	04	FL	A	Walsall	D 0-0	0-0	13		(2599)
22	08	FL	A	Chesterfield	L 0-1	0-0	15		(5004)
23	15	FAC 1	A	Shrewsbury Town	D 1-1	1-0		Southall 15	(3193)
24	18	CC 4	A	Liverpool	L 0-3	0-2			(28515)
25	22	FL	H	Burnley	W 4-1	1-1	15	Groves 18, Widdrington 58, Lester 72, Nogan 77	4829
26	25	FAC 1R	H	Shrewsbury Town	W 4-0	2-0		Nogan 29, Lester 72, Jobling 89, Herbert 45 (OG)	3242
27	29	FL	A	Gillingham	W 2-0	1-0	13	Jobling 35, Black 76	(4855)
28	D 02	FL	H	Wycombe Wanderers	D 0-0	0-0	14		4160
29	06	FAC 2	H	Chesterfield	D 2-2	2-0		Rodger 8, Nogan 31	4762
30	09	AWS N1	A	Chesterfield	W 1-0	0-0		Nogan 71	(1128)
31	12	FL	A	Bristol Rovers	W 4-0	2-0	7	Gallimore 23, Livingstone 26, 84, Donovan 82	(4801)
32	16	FAC 2R	A	Chesterfield	W 2-0	1-0		Lester 22, Groves 79	(4553)
33	20	FL	H	Carlisle United	W 1-0	0-0	7	McDermott 56	6222
34	26	FL	A	York City	D 0-0	0-0	7		(7093)
35	28	FL	H	Preston North End	W 3-1	3-0	4	Donovan 10, 36, Black 19	6725
36	J 03	FAC 3	H	Norwich City	W 3-0	1-0		McDermott 25, Woods 47, Donovan 76	8161
37	10	FL	A	Bristol City	L 1-4	0-3	6	Groves 82	(12567)
38	13	AWS N2	H	Hull City	W 1-0	1-0		Butterfield 16	4778
39	17	FL	A	Brentford	W 4-0	2-0	5	Groves 10, Smith 18, Donovan 59, Clare 85	4624
40	24	FAC 4	A	Leeds United	L 0-2	0-1			(29598)
41	27	AWS NQF	A	Scunthorpe United	W 2-0	0-0		Groves 85, Burnett 90	(4596)
42	31	FL	H	Fulham	D 1-1	0-0	7	Burnett 88	6785
43	F 06	FL	A	Millwall	W 1-0	1-0	6	Livingstone 23	(6020)
44	14	FL	A	Wigan Athletic	W 2-0	0-0	5	Nogan 51, Donovan 86	(3548)
45	17	AWS NSF	H	Blackpool	W 1-0	0-0		Burnett 77	8027
46	21	FL	H	Bournemouth	W 2-1	0-1	4	Groves 78, O'Neill 65 (OG)	5456
47	24	FL	H	Blackpool	W 1-0	0-0	3	Clare 59	4924
48	28	FL	A	Northampton Town	L 1-2	1-0	4	Donovan 17	(6932)
49	M 03	FL	A	Chesterfield	D 0-0	0-0	3		4940
50	07	FL	A	Southend United	W 1-0	0-0	3	Clare 58	(4829)
51	10	AWS NF1	H	Burnley	D 1-1	0-1		Groves 78	6064
52	14	FL	H	Walsall	W 3-0	1-0	3	Nogan 58, Donovan 67, 89	4916
53	17	AWS NF2	A	Burnley	W 2-0	1-0		Nogan 10, Donovan 57	(10257)
54	21	FL	A	Luton Town	D 2-2	0-4	4	Gallimore 53, Donovan 63	(5700)
55	24	FL	A	Plymouth Argyle	W 1-0	0-0	3	Groves 79	4661
56	28	FL	A	Burnley	L 1-2	1-1	3	Lester 16	(8256)
57	31	FL	A	Wrexham	D 0-0	0-0	3		(5421)
58	A 04	FL	H	Gillingham	D 0-0	0-0	3		5190
59	07	FL	H	Luton Town	L 0-1	0-0	3		4455
60	10	FL	A	Wycombe Wanderers	D 1-1	0-1	3	Lester 90	(5846)
61	13	FL	H	Bristol Rovers	L 1-2	1-2	4	Donovan 12 (pen)	5484
62	19	AWS F	N	Bournemouth	W 2-1*	0-1		Glass 75 (OG), Burnett 112 (golden goal)	(62432)
63	21	FL	A	Carlisle United	W 1-0	1-0	3	Donovan 27 (pen)	(3956)
64	25	FL	A	Watford	D 0-0	0-0	3		(14002)
65	M 02	FL	H	Oldham Athletic	L 0-2	0-0	3		8054
66	09	PO SF1	A	Fulham	D 1-1	0-1		Donovan 80	(13954)
67	13	PO SF2	H	Fulham	W 1-0	0-0		Donovan 18	8689
68	24	PO F	H	Northampton Town	W 1-0	1-0		Donovan 18	62988

Best Home League Attendance: 8054 V Oldham Athletic   Smallest :4160 V Wycombe Wanderers   Average :5271

Goal Scorers:

FL	(55)	Donovan 16, Nogan 8, Groves 7, Livingstone 5, Lester 4, Clare 3, Widdrington 3, Black 2, Gallimore 2, Burnett 1, Jobling 1, McDermott 1, Smith 1, Opponents 1
CC	(12)	Livingstone 4, Lester 3, Groves 2, Donovan 1, Jobling 1, Nogan 1
FAC	(12)	Lester 2, Nogan 2, Donovan 1, Groves 1, Jobling 1, McDermott 1, Rodger 1, Southall 1, Woods 1, Opponents 1
AWS	(10)	Burnett 3, Groves 2, Nogan 2, Butterfield 1, Donovan 1, Opponents 1
PO	(2)	Donovan 2

*Extra-time

232

Black	Burnett	Butterfield	Clare	Davison	Dobbin	Donovan	Fickling	Gallimore	Gilbert	Groves	Handyside	Holsgrove	Jobling	Lester	Lever	Livingstone	McDermott	Nogan	Pearcey	Rodger	Smith	Southall	Widdrington	Woods	Wrack	Referee	#
X			X	X	X		X	X					S1		X	X	X	X			S			X	S2	G.B. Frankland	1
X			X	X	X	X	X						S2		X	X	X	X		S3			X	S1		P R Richards	2
			X	X	X	X	X	X					S1	S2	X	X	X	X			X			S		M C Bailey	3
			X	X	S	X	X	X					X	X	X	S1	X	X		X	S					R D Furnandiz	4
			X	X	X		X	X	X				X	X	S1	X	X			X	S2	S3				D Laws	5
			X	X	X		S3	X	X	X			X	X	X	S2	X	X		X	S1					B Coddington	6
S2			X	X			X	X	X				X	X	X	X	X			X	S1	S3				A Bates	7
S1	X			X	X	X	X	X				S3	S2	X	X		X	X		X						S W Mathieson	8
X	X			X	S	S	X	X	X			S1	X	X	S2	X	X									R Styles	9
X				X	X	X	X	X			S	S1	X	X	X	X			X	S						M Fletcher	10
X				X	X	X	X	X				S1	X	X	X	X	X			S3	S2					T Heilbron	11
X			X	X	X	X	X	X				X	X	X	X	S1				S2	S					P Taylor	12
X				X	X	X	X	X	S		S1	X	X	X	X				X	S						K W Burge	13
X			X	X	X	X	X	S1			X	X	S2	X	X					X	S3					P Rejer	14
X	X			X	X	X	X	S2	S1		S3		X	X	X	X				X						F G Stretton	15
X	X		X	X	X	X	X	S1	X		S2		X	X	X	X				X	S					M A Riley	16
X				X	X	X	X	S1	X	S2	X		X	X	X	X				X						M S Pike	17
X				X	X	X	X	S2	X	S1	X		X	X	X	X				X	S3					C J Foy	18
X			X	X	X	X	X	S			X	X	S2	X	X					X	S1					M D Messias	19
X		S2		X	X	X	X	S1	X		X	X	X	X	X					X	S3					M L Dean	20
X		S3	X	X	X	X	X	S2	X		X	S1	X	X	X					X						T Jones	21
X				X	X	X	X	S2	X	X	X	S1	X	X	X					S3						A R Leake	22
X		S	X	X	X	X	X	S		S1	X	X	S	X	X				X	S						U D Rennie	23
X		X	X	X	X	X	X	S3	X	X	S1	X	X	X					S1	X						J E Pearce	24
X		X	X	X	X	X	X	S2	X	S1	X	X	X				X	S	S	X						A N Butler	25
X	S	S2		X	X	X	X	X	X	S1	X	X	X	S3												U D Rennie	26
X	S		X	X	X	X	X	X	X	X1	S1	X	X													D Orr	27
X1		S3	X	X	X	X	X	X	X2	S1	X	X	X3	S2												B Coddington	28
	S	S2	X	X	X	X	X	X1	S1	X	X	S	X	X2					S							D Pugh	29
	S1	S3	X	X	X	X	X	S2	X3	X	X2	X1	X														30
	S3	S2	X	X	X	X	X	X	X3	S1	X	X1	X2						X							S G Bennett	31
	S	S1	X	X	X	X	X	X1	X	S	X	S	X	X					S							D Pugh	32
S1	S2	X2	X	X	X	X	X	X	S	X	X	X	X1													M J Jones	33
X	S	S1	X	X	X	X	X1	S	X	X	X	X														J P Robinson	34
Y	S1	X3	X	X	X	X	S3	S2	X	X	X2	X1														D Laws	35
X	S2	X3	X	X2	X	X	X	S3	X	X1	Y					S1	S								M C Bailey	36
X	S1	X2	X	X	X	X	X	X	X	X1							S2								E K Wolstenholme	37
X	X2	X	X		X	X	X	X1									X3	S3								38
S1	X2	X	X	X3	X	S3	X	X	X			X	S2	X1												A Bates	39
X	S	S1	X	X	X	X1	X	X	X	S	S	X							S							G P Barber	40
X1	X	X2	X	X	X	S1	S2	X	X	X																	41
S2	X	S1	X	X	X1	X	X	S3	X2	X3	X	X														G Cain	42
S2	X	X	X	X	X	X	X	S1	X2	X1	X	X	S1	X												S W Mathieson	43
S	X	X	X	X	X	X	S	S1	X	X	X1	X														M Fletcher	44
X	X	X	X	X	S1	X1	X	X	X	X																	45
S2	X	S3	X	X	X	X	X	S1	X1	X	X	X3	X2													K M Lynch	46
X	X	S	S1	X	X	X	X	X	X	X1								S								S J Baines	47
X2	X	S1	X	S	X	X	S2	X	S1	X	X	X	X1										S2			B Knight	48
X2	X	X	X	X	X	X	S1	X	X	X1	S															F G Stretton	49
X2	X	X	X	X	S	X	X	S	X	X	X	X1	X													G Singh	50
S2	X	X	X	X1	X	S1	S3	X2	X	X3	X																51
S2	X	X1	X	X2	X	X	S3	S1	X	X3	X															B Coddington	52
	X	X	X	X	X	X	X	X	X	X																	53
S	X	S	X	X	X	X	X	X	S1	X1	X															A R Hall	54
S1	X	S	X1	X	X	X	S2	X2	X																	P R Richards	55
X1	S2	X2	X	X	X	X	S	X3	X	S3	X															J A Kirkby	56
X	X	S1	S	X	X	X1	X	S1	X	X																E Lomas	57
S2	X	S1	X	X	X	X	X	X1	X2																	G B Frankland	58
S2	X	X	X	S3	X	X	X2	X3					X1	S1												R Pearson	59
S1	X	X	X	S	X1	X	S	X	X	X																A P D'Urso	60
S2	X3	S1	X	X1	X	X	X	S	X	X2																C J Foy	61
S1	X	X3	X	X1	X	S2	X	S3	X	X2																	62
X	X	S1	X	S	X	S	X1	X	X	X																K M Lynch	63
S3	X	X	X3	X	X	S1	X	X1	X	X2																A N Butler	64
S2	X	S1	X	X1	X	X3	S3	X2	X	X																P Rejer	65
S3	X	S2	X	X	X	X	S1	X3	X1	X	X2															T Heilbron	66
S2	X	X	X1	X	X	S	X	S1	X	X2												X2				C R Wilkes	67
S2	X	X	X1	X	X	X	S	X1	S1	X	X2															T Heilbron	68
24	20	4	8	42	1	46	34	5	46	40	3	17	27	37	28	40	33	4	10	17	4	15	1			FL Appearances	
15	1	3	14		1		1		1		2	7	13	13	1	13	1	3	1	1	6	9	1			FL Sub Appearances	
5		1		5		6		5	1	6	6	1+3	3+2	5	3+3	6	1	1+1		1	1+1	5+1	0+2			CC Appearances	
4	0+1	1+4		6		6		6	6		5	4	1+1	2+3	6	4		5		1+1	2	0+1				FAC Appearances	
2+2	5	1+1	4+1	7		6		7		7	6+1	2+2	4+1	6	4+1	7	5		1	4		1	1	0+1		AWS Appearances	
0+3	3		0+1	3		3		3	3	3	0+1	3	3	0+2	3	3		3			3					PO Appearances	

Also played: Bloomer S1(38). Chapman S2(38).

GRIMSBY TOWN

CLUB RECORDS

BIGGEST VICTORIES
League: 9-2 v Darwen, Division 2, 15.4.1899.
7-0 v v Bristol Rovers (a), Division 2, 1957-58.
F.A. Cup: 10-0 v Boston, 2nd Round, 24.10.1981.
League Cup: 6-1 v Rotherham United, 2nd Round, 6.11.1984.
BIGGEST DEFEATS
League: 1-9 v Arsenal, Division 1, 28.1.1931.
F.A. Cup: 1-9 v Phoenix Bessemer, 2nd Round, 25.11.1982.
League Cup: 0-6 v Burnley, 2nd Round, 10.9.1968.
MOST POINTS
3 points a win: 83, Division 3, 1990-91.
2 points a win: 68, Division 3(N), 1955-56.
MOST GOALS SCORED
103, Division 2, 1933-34.
Glover 42, Craven 18, jennings 13, Bestall 11, Holmes 7, Kelly 3, Dyson 3, Ponting 2, Moralee 2, Dodds 1, Lewis 1.
MOST GOALS CONCEDED
111, Division 1, 1947-48.
MOST FIRST CLASS MATCHES IN A SEASON
59 - 1979-80 (League 46, FA Cup 4, League Cup 9).
MOST LEAGUE WINS
31, Division 3(N), 1955-56.
MOST LEAGUE DRAWS
20, Division 1, 1993-94.
MOST LEAGUE DEFEATS
28, Division 1, 1947-48.
BEST PERFORMANCES
League: 1925-26: Matches Played 42, Won 26, Drawn 9, Lost 7, Goals for 93, Goals against 40, Points 61. First in Division 3(N).
Highest Position: 5th Division 1, 1934-35.
F.A. Cup: Semi-finalists 1935-36, 1938-39.
League Cup: 5th Round 1979-80, 1984-85.

INDIVIDUAL CLUB RECORDS

MOST GOALS IN A SEASON
Pat Glover: 43 goals in 1933-34 (League 42, FA Cup 1).

MOST GOALS IN A MATCH
6. Tommy McCairns v Leicester Fosse, Division 2, 11.4.1896.

OLDEST PLAYER
George Tweedy, 40 years 84 days v York City, 3.4.1953.

YOUNGEST PLAYER
Tony Ford, 16 years 143 days (Sub) v Walsall, 4.10.1975.

MOST CAPPED PLAYER
Pat Glover (Wales) 7.

PREVIOUS MANAGERS

ADDITIONAL INFORMATION
PREVIOUS NAMES
Grimsby Pelham.

PREVIOUS LEAGUES
Football Alliance; Midland League (1910).

Club colours: Black & white striped shirts, black shorts and white socks.
Change colours: Blue shirts.

Reserves League: Pontins Central League.
Youth: Midland Purity League..

DIVISIONAL RECORD

	Played	Won	Drawn	Lost	For	Against	Points
Division 1	488	167	97	224	756	940	431
Division 2/1	1,840	676	413	751	2,763	2,933	1,934
Division 3/2	736	291	185	260	1,031	950	822
Division 3 (S)	42	15	9	18	49	59	39
Division 3 (N)	432	200	85	147	672	534	485
Division 4	368	155	92	121	520	460	441
Total	3,906	1,504	881	1,521	5,791	5,876	4,152

RECORDS AND STATISTICS

COMPETITIONS

Div.1	Div.2/1	Div.2/3	Div.3(N)	Div.4
1901-03	1892-01	1920-21	1921-26	1968-72
1929-32	1903-10	1959-62	1951-56	1977-79
1934-48	1911-20	1964-68		1988-90
	1926-29	1972-77		
	1932-34	1979-80		
	1948-51	1987-88		
	1956-59	1990-91		
	1962-64	1997-98		
	1980-87			
	1991-97			
	1998-			

HONOURS

Div.2	Div.3(N)	Div.3	Div.4	AMC
1900-01	1925-26	1979-80	1971-72	1997-98
1933-34	1955-56			

MOST GOALS IN A CAREER

Pat Glover - 197 (1930-39)

Year	League	FA Cup	Lge Cup	Others
1930-31	2	-	-	-
1931-32	12	4	-	-
1932-33	22	2	-	-
1933-34	42	1	-	-
1934-35	34	2	-	-
1935-36	31	4	-	-
1936-37	29	4	-	-
1937-38	4	-	-	-
1938-39	4	-	-	-
Total	180	17	-	-

Current leading goalscorer: Paul Groves - 44
(08.92-06.96 + 07.97-98)

MOST APPEARANCES

Keith Jobling - 493 (1953-66)

Year	League	FA Cup	Lge Cup	Others
1953-54	9	-	-	-
1954-55	6	1	-	-
1956-57	6	-	-	-
1957-58	13	-	-	-
1958-59	42	3	-	-
1959-60	42	2	-	-
1960-61	36	1	1	-
1961-62	46	1	1	-
1962-63	41	1	1	-
1963-64	41	1	1	-
1964-65	46	4	2	-
1965-66	42	6	5	-
1966-67	21	2	4	-
1967-68	18	1	-	-
1968-69	41	1	4	-
Total	450	24	19	-

MANAGERS

Name	Seasons	Best	Worst
Hayden Price	1920		
George Fraser	1921-24	3 (3N)	14 (3N)
Wilf Gillow	1924-32	13 (1)	12 (3N)
Frank Womack	1932-36	5 (1)	13 (2)
Charles Spencer	1937-51	16 (1)	22 (2)
Bill Shankly	1951-54	2 (3N)	17 (3N)
Bill Walsh	1954-55	17 (3N)	23 (3N)
Allenby Chilton	1955-59	13 (2)	23 (3N)
Tim Ward	1960-62	2 (3)	6 (3)
Tom Johnston	1962-64	19 (2)	21 (2)
Jimmy McGuigan	1964-67	10 (3)	17 (3)
Don McEvoy	1967-68	22 (3)	22 (3)
Bill Harvey	1968-69	22 (3)	23 (4)
Bobby Kennedy	1969-71	16 (4)	23 (4)
Lawrie McMenemy	1971-73	9 (3)	19 (4)
Ron Ashman	1973-75	6 (3)	16 (3)
Tommy Casey	1975-76	16 (3)	18 (3)
John Newman	1977-79	2 (4)	6 (4)
George Kerr	1979-82	7 (2)	1 (3)
Dave Booth	1982-85	5 (2)	19 (2)
Mick Lyons	1985-87	15 (2)	21 (2)
Bobby Roberts	1987-88	22 (3)	22 (3)
Alan Buckley	1988-94	9 (2/1)	9 (4)
Brian Laws	1994-96	10 (1)	10 (1)
Kenny Swain	1996-97	-	-
Alan Buckley	1997-	3 (2)	3 (2)

RECORD TRANSFER FEE RECEIVED

Amount	Club	Player	Date
£1,500,000	Everton	John Oster	07/97
£1,000,000	Blackburn Rovers	Gary Croft	03/96
£650,000	Sunderland	Shaun Cunnington	07/92
£600,000	West Brom	Paul Groves	05/96

RECORD TRANSFER FEE PAID

Amount	Club	Player	Date
£300,000	Southampton	Tommy Wriddrington	07/96
£180,000	Carlisle United	Tony Gallimore	03/96
£140,000	Chelsea	Steve Livingstone	10/93
£135,000	Luton Town	Graham Rodger	01/92

LONGEST LEAGUE RUNS

of undefeated matches:	19 (16.2.1980 - 30.8.1980)	of league matches w/out a win:	18 (10.10.1981 - 16.3.1982)
of undefeated home matches:	33 (8.10.1974 - 28.2.1976)	of undefeated away matches:	9 (23.2.80-30.8.80, 19.11.83-10.3.84)
without home win:	12 (27.9.1947 - 17.3.1948)	without an away win:	23 (2.10.1982 - 28.10.1983)
of league wins:	11 (19.1.1952 - 29.3.1952)	of home wins:	17 (9.3.1894 - 28.3.1895)
of league defeats:	9 (30.11.1907 - 18.1.1908)	of away wins:	5 (26.1.1952 - 22.3.1952)

PLAYERS NAME Honours	Ht	Wt	Birthdate	Birthplace Transfers	Contract Date	Clubs	League	L/Cup	FA Cup	Other	Lge	L/C	FAC	Oth
G O A L K E E P E R														
Davison Aidan	6.1	13.2	5/11/68	Sedgefield		Spennymoor Utd								
						Billingham Synth.		1						
					3/25/88	Notts County	1							
				£6000	10/7/89	Bury								
				Free	8/14/91	Millwall	34	3	3	2				
				£25000	7/26/93	Bolton Wanderers	35+2		8	4				
				Loan	10/9/96	Ipswich Town								
					3/14/97	Bradford City	10							
				Free	5/31/97	Free Players								
				Free	7/16/97	Grimsby Town	42	5	6	3				
Love Andrew M	6.1	13.12	3/28/79	Grimsby	3/1/97	Grimsby Town	3							
D E F E N C E														
Bloomer Matthew B	6.1	13	11/3/78	Grimsby	7/3/97	Grimsby Town (T)								
Butterfield Daniel P	5.9	11.8	11/21/79	Boston	8/7/97	Grimsby Town (T)	4+3	1	0+1					
Chapman Ben	5.7	10.12	3/2/79	Scunthorpe	7/11/97	Grimsby Town (T)								
Handyside Peter D S: u21.5.	6.1	12.3	7/31/74	Dumfries	11/21/92	Grimsby Town	134+6	13	10	7	1			
Lever Mark	6.3	12.8	3/29/70	Beverley	8/9/88	Grimsby Town	293+9	20+1	15+2	12	8			
McDermott John	5.7	10	2/3/69	Middlesbrough	6/1/87	Grimsby Town	359+15	24+1	26+1	14	7		1	
Smith Richard	6	12.1	10/3/70	Lutterworth	8/15/96	Grimsby Town	15+2	1	1		1			
M I D F I E L D														
Buckley Adam C			8/2/79	Nottingham	8/7/97	Grimsby Town (T)								
Burnett Wayne	6	12.6	9/4/71	Lambeth	11/13/89	Leyton Orient	34+6	3+1	3+1	4	1	1		
				£90000	8/19/92	Blackburn Rovers								
					8/9/93	Plymouth Argyle	61+9	3	8	3+1	3			
				£150000	9/17/96	Huddersfield Town	43+6	6	1+1			1		
				Loan	1/9/98	Grimsby Town	6+1				1			
				£100000	2/27/98	Grimsby Town	14			3	1			
Coldicott Stacy	5.1	11.8	20/04/74	Redditch	04/03/92	W.B.A.	64+40	8+1	2+2	7+3	3		1	
				Loan	30/08/96	Cardiff City	6							
				£125000	7/1/98	Grimsby Town								
Donovan Kevin	5.9	11	12/17/71	Halifax	10/11/89	Huddersfield Town	11+9	1+1	1	4	1		2	
				Loan	2/13/92	Halifax Town	6							
				£25000	10/1/92	WBA	139+28	9+2	7+1	15+1	19	6	3	4
					7/29/97	Grimsby Town	45	6	6	3	16	1	1	2
Gallimore Anthony	5.11	11.3	2/21/72	Crewe	7/11/90	Stoke City	6+5							
				Loan	10/3/91	Carlisle United	8							
				Loan	2/26/92	Carlisle United	8							
				Loan	3/25/93	Carlisle United	8				1			
				£15000	7/13/93	Carlisle United	80	6	7	17	6	1		1
				£125000	3/28/96	Grimsby Town	80+6	7	7	3	4			
Groves Paul	5.11	11.5	2/28/66	Derby	10/1/86	Burton Albion			2+1					
				£12000	4/18/88	Leicester City	7+9	1	0+1	0+1	1	1		
				Loan	8/20/89	Lincoln City	8	2			1			
				£60000	1/25/90	Blackpool	106+1	6	9	13	21	1	4	3
				£125000	8/12/92	Grimsby Town	137+1	8+1	7	4	28	2	1	1
				£600000	6/16/96	WBA	27+1	2	1		4	1		
					7/17/97	Grimsby Town	46	6	6	3	7	2	1	
Smith David E: u21.10	5.8	10.2	3/29/68	Stonehouse	7/7/86	Coventry City	144+10	17	6	4+1	19			
				Loan	1/6/93	Bournemouth	1							
					3/12/93	Birmingham City	35+3	4	0+1	1	3			
				£90000	1/31/94	WBA	82+20	4+2	1+3	4+1	2			
				£200000	1/16/98	Grimsby Town	14			3				
Widdrington Tommy	5.8	11.1	10/1/71	Newcastle	5/10/90	Southampton	67+8	3+1	11		3			
				Loan	9/12/91	Wigan Athletic	5+1	2						
					7/10/96	Grimsby Town	56+7	7+1	3		7			

FORWARD

Player	Ht	Wt	DOB	From	Date	Club								
Black Kingsley	5.8	10.11	6/22/68	Luton	7/7/86	Luton Town	123+4	16+2	5+1	3+2	25	1	2	1
NI: 30, u21.1, B, S; LC'88; FMC'92. AMC'98				£1500000	9/2/91	Nottingham Forest	80+18	19+1	4	4+2	14	5		
				Loan	3/2/95	Sheffield United	8+3				2			
				Loan	9/29/95	Millwall								
				Free	8/15/96	Grimsby Town	43+20	7	5	2+5	2			1
Clare Daryl	5.9	12	8/1/78	Jersey	12/9/95	Grimsby Town	8+15	0+1	1+4	0+1	3			
Ei: U21.1.														
Lester Jack W	5.1	11.2	10/8/75	Sheffield	7/8/94	Grimsby Town	44+30	3+4	5+1	3	9	3	2	
				Loan	9/20/96	Doncaster Rovers	5+6				1			
Livingstone Stephen	6.1	12.7	9/8/69	Middlesbrough	7/16/86	Coventry City	17+14	8+2		0+1	5	10		
				£450000	1/17/91	Blackburn Rovers	25+5	2	1		10		1	
				£350000	3/23/93	Chelsea	0+1							
				Loan	9/3/93	Port Vale	4+1							
				£140000	10/29/93	Grimsby Town	140+32	7+4	6+5	0+2	33	4	2	
Nogan Lee	5.1	11	5/21/69	Cardiff	3/25/87	Oxford United	57+7	4+1	2+1	4+1	10		1	1
W: 1, B.1, u21.1				Loan	3/25/87	Brentford	10+1				2			
				Loan	9/17/87	Southend United	6	2		1	1			1
				£350000	12/12/91	Watford	97+8	5+2	2	1+2	26	3	1	
				Loan	3/17/94	Southend United	4+1							
				£250000	1/13/95	Reading	71+20	5+1	2	3	26	1	2	
				Loan	2/14/97	Notts County	6							
					7/23/97	Grimsby Town	33+3	6	4	3	8	1	2	

THE MANAGER
ALAN BUCKLEY

Date of Birth . . . . 20th April 1951.
Place of Birth . . . . Eastwood.
Date of Appointment . . . . October 1995.

PREVIOUS CLUBS
As Manager . . . . Walsall, Kettering Town, Grimsby Town, WBA.
As Coach . . . .
As a Player . . . . Nottingham Forest, Walsall, Birmingham, Walsall.

HONOURS
As a Manager
Grimsby Town: Promotion to Division 3, 1990. Promotion to Division 2, 1991.
Promotion to Division 1, 1998. AMC winners 1998.

As a Player
None.

BLUNDELL PARK

Cleethorpes, North East Lincolnshire DN35 7PY

Capacity 8,870

First game ....v Luton Town, 3-3, 2.9.1899.
First floodlit game ....v Gainsborough T, 9.3.1953.

ATTENDANCES
Highest ....31,657 v Wolves, FA Cup 5th Rnd, 20.2.1937.
Lowest ....970 v Scunthorpe Utd, AMC, 15.12.1987.

OTHER GROUNDS ....None.

HOW TO GET TO THE GROUND

From the North and West
Use motorway (M18) then A180, sign posted Grimsby, then follow signs to Cleethorpes A1098.

From the South
Use A1 then A16 and follow signs to Cleethorpes and at roundabout take first exit into Grimsby Road A1098 for Grimsby Town FC.

Car Parking
Street parking available.

Nearest Railway Station
Cleethorpes, Grimsby (01472 353 556).

USEFUL TELEPHONE NUMBERS

Club switchboard.....................01472 697 111
Club fax number.......................01472 693 665
Club shop ....01472 697 111 Ext. 136
Marketing Department...............01472 697 111

Internet address ....www.gtfc.co.uk
Hotline......................................0891 55 58 55*
*Calls cost 50p per minute at all times.Call costings correct at time of going to press.

MATCHDAY PROGRAMME

Programme Editor ....Timothy Harvey.

Number of pages.....................................40.

Price ....£1.70.

Subscriptions ....Apply to club.

Local Newspapers
........................Grimsby Evening Telegraph,
..............Sports Telegraph, Grimsby Target.

Local Radio Stations
.................Radio Humberside, Viking Radio.

MATCHDAY TICKET PRICES

Upper John Smith's Stand & Main Stand

Adults £12

Children - all seats. £5

OAP's - all seats £6

Pontoon End & Lower John Smith's

Adults . . . . £10 (with Mariners Discount Card)

. . . . £12 without Card (Apply to club for Card)

HUDDERSFIELD TOWN
(The Terriers)
NATIONWIDE LEAGUE DIVISION 1
SPONSORED BY: PANASONIC

1998-99 - Back Row: Gerry Murphy (Yth. Dev. Manager), Ryan Crossley, Simon Baldry, Chris Hurst, Sam Collins, Wayne Allison, Marcus Browning, Steve Jenkins, Paul Dalton, Darren Edmondson, Paul Scott, Robin Wray (Yth team Manager). **Middle Row:** Jeff Lee (Chief Scout), Delroy Facey, Ian Lawson, Kevin Gray, Paul Cuss, Nico Vaesen, Steve Francis, Grant Johnson, Sean Hessey, Paul Barnes, John Dickens (Physio), Dave Buckby (Yth. team Physio). **Front Row:** Terry Yorath (1st team Coach), David Beresford, Barry Horne, Andy Morrison, Lee Richardson, Marcus Stewart, Peter Jackson (Manager), Rob Edwards, Jonathan Dyson, Dave Phillips, Tom Cowan, Ben Thornley, Terry Dolan (Reserve team Coach).

HUDDERSFIELD TOWN
FORMED IN 1908
TURNED PROFESSIONAL IN 1908
LTD COMPANY IN 1908

PRESIDENT: Lawrence Batley OBE
CHAIRMAN: J M Asquith
DIRECTORS
D A Taylor(Vice-chairman), E R Whiteley,
D G Headey
SECRETARY
A D Sykes (01484 420 335)
COMMERCIAL MANAGER
Alan Stevenson

MANAGER: Peter Jackson
ASSISTENT MANAGER: Terry Yorath
RESERVE TEAM MANAGER
Terry Dolan
YOUTH DEVELOPMENT OFFICER
Gerry Murphy
YOUTH TEAM MANAGER
Robin Wray
PHYSIOTHERAPIST
John Dickens

STATISTICIAN FOR THE DIRECTORY
Richard Stead

After last season's war of attrition due to injury problems, Huddersfield were made many favourites for relegation in 1997-98.

This seemed even more evident when during the close season, not one single player was added to bolster the squad.

By the end of September, local rivals, Bradford City were beaten in the Coca-Cola Cup and Premiership West Ham United were defeated 1-0 on home soil, before Two were disposed of in a televised return leg. However one glance at the league table showed them rooted to the bottom without a win.

October opened with the Sky television cameras at the McAlpine Stadium for the defeat against champions elect Nottingham Forest, now with the season in turmoil it culminated in the dismissal of manager Brian Horton. Within the day the Terriers had appointed former Captain Peter Jackson and former Wales boss Terry Yorath as his no.2.

After an initial baptism of fire, the season really kick started in November with a first league win recorded at the 15th attempt, winning 3-1 against Stoke City, a first league win since March and only the fourth since New Years Day. November also witnessed a Sky televised win against Manchester City ten years to the day that a club record 1-10 defeat was recorded on the same ground.

As the New Year approached Town had set the highest stadium attendance for a league match against Middlesbrough - 18,820 and they had recorded their first successful penalty in 20 months - only the second to be awarded in that period.

Big steps had been taken by the end of January, the highest league win recorded, a 5-1 win against Oxford United. They also remained unbeaten in the league and finally climbed out of the relegation zone for the first time in the season, only a 4th round FA Cup exit by Wimbledon dampening any spirits.

Five games in six games, mostly against promotion elect sides saw them slip dangerously back into the relegation mire, but a season adopted as the 'GREAT ESCAPE' was finally completed with five wins in eight games to confirm division one status. The last being a 1-0 victory over West Bromwich Albion. April also saw a stadium record for a reserve fixture, 5,012. The reason being, a little matter of the former captain and now manager finally hanging up his boots after 772 senior appearances, even managing to score a penalty - a nice touch to bow out of playing with the club that has most endeared to him.

Much credit must go to the rookie manager and the widely experienced No.2 for guiding them to safety when all seemed lost. A record of 37 players were used in all, surpassing the previous record set only last season as the battle for consistency was sought. With some shrewd dealings on the transfer market made, among them the loan signing of Newcastle' goalkeeper Steve Harper and £800,000 spent on Swindon Town's big front man Wayne Allison, also the signings of experienced Barry Horne and David Phillips, the great escape was completed with some skilful displays.

With further signings promised next season and the commitment of the management duo, it promises to be a season to look forward to.

RICHARD STEAD.

HUDDERSFIELD TOWN

Division 1   **:16th**   **FA CUP: 4th Round**   **LC CUP: 2nd Round**

M	DATE	COMP.	VEN	OPPONENTS	RESULT	H/T	LP	GOAL SCORERS/GOAL TIMES	ATT.
1	A 09	FL	A	Oxford United	L 0-2	0-0	24		(7085)
2	12	CC 1/1	H	Bradford City	W 2-1	2-1		Payton 5, Dreyer 45 (OG)	8720
3	23	FL	A	Swindon Town	D 1-1	1-1	22	Stewart 43	(7683)
4	26	CC 1/2	A	Bradford City	D 1-1	0-1		Burnett 77	(8065)
5	30	FL	H	Sheffield United	D 0-0	0-0	23		14268
6	S 02	FL	H	Bradford City	L 1-2	0-1	23	Stewart 75	13159
7	09	FL	H	Birmingham City	L 0-1	0-0	23		9477
8	13	FL	H	Ipswich Town	D 2-2	1-0	24	Jenkins 41, Dyer 88	9313
9	16	CC 2/1	H	West Ham United	W 1-0	0-0		Dyer 75	8525
10	20	FL	A	Stockport County	L 0-3	0-2	24		(6995)
11	27	FL	A	Wolverhampton Wand	L 1-1	0-0	24	Stewart 32	(21723)
12	29	CC 2/2	A	West Ham United	L 0-3	0-2			(16137)
13	O 03	FL	H	Nottingham Forest	L 0-2	0-0	24		11258
14	14	FL	H	Charlton Athletic	L 0-3	0-1	24		9596
15	18	FL	A	Sunderland	L 1-3	1-1	24	Dalton 45	(24782)
16	21	FL	A	Port Vale	L 1-4	0-1	24	Stewart 86	(5244)
17	25	FL	H	Portsmouth	D 1-1	0-1	24	Dalton 80	8985
18	28	FL	A	Middlesbrough	L 0-3	0-2	24		(29965)
19	N 01	FL	H	Stoke City	W 3-1	0-0	24	Richardson 46, Stewart 79, Dalton 90	10916
20	04	FL	A	Tranmere Rovers	L 0-1	0-1	24		(5127)
21	07	FL	A	Manchester City	W 1-0	0-0	24	Edwards 76	(24425)
22	15	FL	H	Reading	W 1-0	0-0	24	Dalton 74	12617
23	22	FL	A	Queens Park Rangers	L 1-2	0-1	24	Morrison 88	(16066)
24	29	FL	H	Bury	W 2-0	1-0	23	Dalton 6, 83	11929
25	D 06	FL	A	Crewe Alexandra	W 5-2	2-1	22	Stewart 24, 70, Dalton 40, 83 (pen), Allison 89	(4861)
26	13	FL	H	Norwich City	L 1-3	0-2	24	Stewart 58	11436
27	20	FL	A	West Bromwich Albion	W 2-0	0-0	20	Dalton 51, 72	(14619)
28	26	FL	H	Middlesbrough	L 0-1	0-0	23		18820
29	28	FL	A	Bradford City	D 1-1	1-1	22	Dalton 34	(17842)
30	J 10	FL	A	Oxford United	W 5-1	3-0	19	Phillips 29, Stewart 41, 55, Allison 59, Gray 21 (OG)	10378
31	13	FAC 3	A	Bournemouth	W 1-0	1-0		Stewart 16	(7385)
32	17	FL	A	Birmingham City	D 0-0	0-0	19		(17850)
33	24	FAC 4	H	Wimbledon	L 0-1	0-0			14533
34	27	FL	A	Sheffield United	D 1-1	1-1	20	Dalton 24	(16535)
35	31	FL	H	Swindon Town	D 0-0	0-0	19		10028
36	F 06	FL	H	Stockport County	W 1-0	0-0	18	Allison 53	11121
37	14	FL	A	Ipswich Town	L 1-5	1-1	19	Stewart 37	(10509)
38	17	FL	A	Nottingham Forest	L 0-3	0-1	20		(18231)
39	21	FL	H	Wolverhampton Wand	W 1-0	0-0	18	Dyson 90	12633
40	24	FL	H	Sunderland	L 2-3	0-3	19	Allison 50, Phillips 58	14615
41	28	FL	A	Charlton Athletic	L 0-1	0-0	22		(12908)
42	M 03	FL	H	Manchester City	L 1-3	1-2	22	Dalton 37	15694
43	07	FL	A	Stoke City	W 2-1	2-0	21	Barnes 15, Stewart 18	(12594)
44	14	FL	H	Tranmere Rovers	W 3-0	1-0	17	Allison 10, Stewart 56, Hill 77 (OG)	10844
45	21	FL	A	Reading	W 2-0	0-0	15	Stewart 73, 88	(8593)
46	28	FL	H	Queens Park Rangers	D 1-1	0-0	15	Gray 59	13681
47	A 04	FL	A	Bury	D 2-2	1-1	15	Richardson 34 (pen), 70	(8042)
48	11	FL	H	Crewe Alexandra	W 2-0	2-0	14	Allison 42, Johnson 44	11263
49	13	FL	A	Norwich City	L 0-5	0-2	16		(16550)
50	18	FL	H	West Bromwich Albion	W 1-0	1-0	13	Baldry 11	11704
51	25	FL	A	Portsmouth	L 0-3	0-1	14		(14013)
52	M 03	FL	H	Port Vale	L 0-4	0-2	16		15610

Best Home League Attendance: 18820 V Middlesbrough   **Smallest :8985 V Portsmouth**   **Average :12145**

Goal Scorers:

FL	(50)	Stewart 15, Dalton 13, Allison 6, Richardson 3, Phillips 2, Baldry 1, Barnes 1, Dyer 1, Dyson 1, Edwards 1, Gray 1, Jenkins 1, Johnson 1, Morrison 1, Opponents 2
CC	(4)	Burnett 1, Dyer 1, Payton 1, Opponents 1
FAC	(1)	Stewart 1

(F) Allison	(F) Baldry	(F) Barnes	(G) Bartram	(M) Beresford	(F) Browning	(M) Burnett	(D) Collins	(M) Dalton	(F) Dyer	(D) Dyson	(D) Edmondson	(F) Edwards	(G) Francis	(M) Gray	(G) Harper	(M) Horne	(D) Jenkins	(M) Johnson	(F) Lawson	(M) Makel	(M) Martin	(D) Morrison	(F) Payton	(F) Phillips	(M) Richardson	(D) Ryan	(F) Stewart	(D) Watts		
			X		X			X		X	X	X								X				X	X	X		X	X	M.R. Halsey	1
			X		X			X		X	X	X				X				X				X	X	X		X	X	W C Burns	2
	S1		X	X	S2	X			X	X		X	X	S		X				X				X	X			X	X	A G Wiley	3
	X		S	X	X			X	X		X	S	X			X				X				X	X			X	X	M J Brandwood	4
	X			X	X			X	X		S1	X	X			X		S3		X				X	X			X	X	F G Stretton	5
	X		S2	X	X			X	X		X	X				X		S1		X	S3			X	X			X	X	R Pearson	6
	X		S3	X	X			X	X		S1	X	X			X				X		X	X				X		D Laws	7
	X		X			X	S2	S3	X	S1		X				X				X	X	X					X		D Pugh	8
	S1			X		X	X	X	X		X	X	X			X		S	X	X				X			X	C R Wilkes	9
			S1		X		X	X	X	X	S2	X	X			X				X				X	X		X	X	G Cain	10
				X		S1		S2	X	X	S3	X	X			X				X	X	X					X		R J Harris	11
			S2	X		X			X	X1	X	X				X		S1	X2	X	X						X	M J Bodenham	12
	X			X	S	S1	X	X	X	S2		X				X				X	X						X	S W Mathieson	13
				X	S2	X		S1	X	S	X	X	X			X				X	X				X	X	M Fletcher	14
		X		S1	X	X	X	X	X		X	S				S2				X				X	X	T Jones	15
		X		S2	X	X	X	X	X		X	S3	X	X		S1				X				X	X	M C Bailey	16
	X	X		S		X		X	S1		X	X	X			S2				X	X	X	J P Robinson	17
	X	X		S2		X		X	S1		X	X	X			S				X	X	X	E K Wolstenholme	18
	X			S		X	S	X	X	X		X	X			S1				X	X	X	K M Lynch	19
	X			S2	S	X	S1	X		X		X	X			X				X	X	X	A Bates	20
	X			S		X		X	X		X	X				S1				X	X	X	G B Frankland	21
X		X		S		X	X	X	X		X	X	X	X	S1	S2		X		X		W C Burns	22
X		X		S2		X	X	X	X		X	X	X		X	S1		X		X		R Styles	23
X		X		S		X	X	S1	X		X	X				X	S	X		X1	G Laws	24
X		X		S		X	X1		X		X	X		S	X	X	S1	X	D Orr	25
X		X		X		X	X2	S2	X		X	X1			X1	X	S1	X	A R Leake	26
X			S1	X2	S	X		X	X	X	X		X1	X	S2	X	C R Wilkes	27
X			S		X		X	X	X	X2	X	S1	S2		X1	X	B Coddington	28
X			X		S1	X	X	X	X	X1	X		S	X	S2	X2	J A Kirkby	29
X			X1		X		X	X	X	X2	S1	S		X	S2	X	C J Foy	30
X			X2		X	S	S	S	X	X	X	X1	S1	X	X	S2	X	P Rejer	31
X	S1		X1		X		S		X	X	X	X		X	X	S	X	M J Jones	32
X			X1		X	S3	S1	S	X	X	X	X	X2	S	X3	X	32	X	D P Elleray	33
X			X1		X		X		X	X	X	X1	S3	S2	X	X	S1	M Fletcher	34
X					X		X		X2	X	X1	X	S3	S2	X	X	S1	E K Wolstenholme	35
X	S1				X		X	X	X		X	X	X		X	X1	X	A R Hall	36
X	S1				X1		X2		X	X	X	X	X		X	X	M E Pierce	37
X	S				S1	S		X	X	X	X	X		X	X1	X	T Heilbron	38
X	S1				X		X	S	X	X	X	X		X	X1	X	R Pearson	39
X	X1				X		X	S2	S	X	X2	X		X	S1	X	C J Foy	40
X	S	X			S1		X1	X	X2	X		X	X		X	S2	X	M J Brandwood	41
X	X		S1		X2		X1	X2	X		X	X		X	X	S2	X	G Cain	42
X	S1	X1		X	S			S2	X	X	X			X	X2	X	X	E Lomas	43
X		X	X1		X	S1		X	X	X		X		X	X	X	P Taylor	44
X	X2		X1		X		X	X	X		X	S	X	X	X	P R Richards	45
X	X1		X	X		X	X	X	X	S	X	S1	X	X	X	S W Mathieson	46
X	S1	X	X1	X2	X		X	X	X	S2	X		X	X	X	A R Leake	47
X	X1		X2	X		X	X	X	S2	X		X	X	X	S G Bennett	48
X				X	S		X	X	X	X1		X	X	X	X1	A P D'Urso	49
X	X1			X	S1	X	X	X	X	S		X	X	X	S1	M Fletcher	50
X1	X		X	X	X		X	X	X2	S1		X	X3	X	F G Stretton	51
X1		X	X3	S3		X	X	X2	X		S1	X	X	X	F G Stretton	52
27	8	11	12	5	10	11	9	26	8	35	15	26	9	34	24	29	28	28	3	10	2	22	4	29	16	10	38	8	FL Appearances	
3	4		3	4	4	1	5	4	1	4	11	1		1	1	1	15	3	1	1		5		3					FL Sub Appearances	
1+1			1	1	3+1	1	1	3	2	4	2	2			4		0+1	4	1	3	2			2	4				CC Appearances	
1					2		2	0+1	0+1	2	2	2	2	2	2		0+1			2	2		0+2		4				FAC Appearances	

Also played: (F) Facey S(2), S2(7,52). X(8). (M) Heary X(1,52), S2(2), S3(51).(M) Hessey S(44), S2(45). (M) Hurst S2(5,9), S3(10), X(11). (M) Midwood S1(1). (M) Murphy S(23). (M) Nielsen S1(45,48), S3(51), S(46,47,49,50).(G) O'Connor S(1,12), S1(2), X(13). (D) Smith S(36,44), S2(37,42), X(38,39,40,41). (M) Williams S(4).

HUDDERSFIELD TOWN

CLUB RECORDS

BIGGEST VICTORIES
League: 10-1 v Blackpool, Division 1, 13.12.1930.
F.A. Cup: 7-0 v Lincoln United, 1st Round, 16.11.1991.
7-1 v Chesterfield (a), 3rd Round, 12.1.1929.

BIGGEST DEFEATS
League: 1-10 v Manchester City, Division 2, 7.11.1987.
F.A. Cup: 0-6 v Sunderland, 3rd Round, 1949-50.

MOST POINTS
3 points a win: 82, Division 3, 1982-83.
2 points a win: 66, Division 4, 1979-80.

MOST GOALS SCORED
101, Division 4, 1979-80.

MOST GOALS CONCEDED
100, Division 2, 1987-88.

MOST FIRST CLASS MATCHES IN A SEASON
61 - 1993-94 (League 46, Lge Cup 4, AMC 8, FA Cup 3)
61 - 1992-93 (League 46, Lge Cup 4, AMC 5, FA Cup 6)
61 - 1991-92 (League 46, Lge Cup 5, AMC 5, FA Cup 3, P/Off 2)

MOST LEAGUE WINS
28, Division 2, 1919-20.

MOST LEAGUE DRAWS
17, Division 1, 1926-27. Division 2, 1972-73.

MOST LEAGUE DEFEATS
28, Division 2, 1987-88.

INDIVIDUAL CLUB RECORDS

MOST GOALS IN A SEASON
Dave Mangnall: 42 goals in 1931-32 (League 33, FA Cup 9).

MOST GOALS IN A MATCH
5. D Mangnall v Derby County (h), 6-0, Division 1, 21.11.1931.
5. A P Lythgoe v Blackburn Rovers (h), 6-0, Division 1, 13.4.1935.

OLDEST PLAYER
W H Smith, 39 years, 1934.

YOUNGEST PLAYER
Dennis Law, 15 years 10 months, 1956.

MOST CAPPED PLAYER
Jimmy Nicholson (Northern Ireland) 31.
Ray Wilson (England) 30.

BEST PERFORMANCES

League: Champions of Division 1 (3).

F.A. Cup: Winners (1).
League Cup: Semi-Final 1967-68.

PREVIOUS NAMES
None.

PREVIOUS LEAGUES
Midland League.

Club colours: Blue & white striped shirts, white shorts, blue & white hoop on turnover socks.
Change colours: Cream shirts with horizontal blue stripe & blue sleeves, cream shorts with blue trim, blue & cream striped socks.

Reserves League: Pontins Central League.
Youth League: Northern Intermediate League.

DIVISIONAL RECORD

	Played	Won	Drawn	Lost	For	Against	Points
Division 1	1,306	497	329	480	1,935	1,912	1,340
Division 2/1	1,254	477	321	456	1,766	1,684	1,381
Division 3/2	552	217	148	187	753	674	750
Division 4	230	100	64	66	337	246	264
Total	3,342	1,291	862	1,189	4,791	4,516	3,735

RECORDS AND STATISTICS

COMPETITIONS

Div.1	Div.2/1	Div.3/2	Div.4
1919-51	1910-19	1972-74	1974-79
1952-55	1951-52	1979-82	
1969-71	1955-69	1987-88	
	1971-72	1987-95	
	1995-		

HONOURS

Div.1	Div.2	Div.4	FA Cup
1923-24	1969-70	1979-80	1922
1924-25			
1925-26			

Huddersfield were the first, of only three clubs, to win the Championship three years in succession.

MOST APPEARANCES

W H Smith 574 (1913-34)

Year	League	FA Cup
1913-14	4	
1914-15	24	1
1915-16		
1916-17		
1917-18		
1918-19		
1919-20	39	5
1920-21	33	2
1921-22	40	9
1922-23	35	5
1923-24	39	3
1924-25	41	1
1925-26	28	2
1926-27	39	1
1927-28	38	8
1928-29	32	6
1929-30	33	5
1930-31	30	
1931-32	31	4
1932-33	17	
1933-34	18	1
1934-35		
	521	53

MOST GOALS IN A CAREER

George Brown - 159 (1921-29)

Year	League	FA Cup
1921-22	4	
1922-23	6	
1923-24	8	
1924-25	20	
1925-26	35	
1926-27	27	1
1927-28	27	8
1928-29	15	8
Total	142	17

Current top goalscorer: Marcus Stewart 28 (15.08.96 - 05.98)

MANAGERS

Name	Seasons	Best	Worst
F Walker	1908-10	5(ML)	16 (NEL)
D Pudan	1910-12	13(2)	17(2)
A Fairclough	1912-19	8(2)	13(2)
A Langley	1919-21	17(1)	2(2)
H Chapman	1921-25	1(1)	14(1)
O Potter	1925-26	1(1)	1(1)
J Chaplin	1926-29	2(1)	16(1)
C Stephenson	1929-42	2(1)	19(1)
T Magner	1942-43	5(FLNRS)	8(FLNRS)
D Steele	1943-47	15(1)	20(1)
G Stephenson	1947-52	15(1)	21(1)
A Beatie	1952-56	3(1)	12(2)
W Shankly	1956-60	6(2)	14(2)
E Boot	1960-64	6(2)	12(2)
T Johnston	1964-68	6(2)	14(2)
I Greaves	1968-74	15(1)	10(3)
R Collins	1974-75	24(3)	24(3)
T Johnston	1975-77	5(4)	9(4)
J Haselden	1977-78	11(4)	11(4)
M Buxton	1978-86	12(2)	9(4)
S Smith	1986-87	17(2)	17(2)
M MacDonald	1987-88	23(2)	23(2)
E Hand	1988-92	8(3)	14(3)
I Ross	1992-93	3(3)	15(3)
Neil Warnock	1993-95	1(2)	11(2)
Brian Horton	1995-97	8(1)	20(1)
Peter Jackson	1997-	16 (1)	16 (1)

ML= Midland League. NEL= North Eastern League.
FLNRS= Football League, North Regional Section.

RECORD TRANSFER FEE RECEIVED

Amount	Club	Player	Date
£2,700,000	Sheffield Wed.	Andy Booth	07.96
£375,000	Southampton	Simon Charlton	6/93
£300,000	Leicester City	Iwan Roberts	10/93
£250,000	Reading	Craig Maskell	8/90
£250,000	Swindon	Duncan Shearer	6/88

RECORD TRANSFER FEE PAID

Amount	Club	Player	Date
£1,200,000	Bristol Rovers	Marcus Stewart	7/96
£500,000	Blackpool	Andy Morrison	7/96
£350,000	Barnsley	Andy Payton	7/96
£325,000	Bradford City	Lee Duxbury	12/94

LONGEST LEAGUE RUNS

of undefeated matches:	27 (1924-25)	of league matches w/out a win:	22 (1971-72)
of undefeated home matches:	28 (1982-83)	of undefeated away matches:	18 (1924-25)
without home win:	11 (1971-72)	without an away win:	31 (1936-37)
of league wins:	11 (1919-21)	of home wins:	11 (1925-26)
of league defeats:	7 (1913-14, 1955-56)	of away wins:	5 (1924-25)

HUDDERSFIELD TOWN

PLAYERS NAME Honours	Ht	Wt	Birthdate	Birthplace Transfers	Contract Date	Clubs	League	L/Cup	FA Cup	Other	Lge	L/C	FAC	Oth
G O A L K E E P E R														
Cuss Paul M	6.1	13.5	4/19/74	Huddersfield	7/19/97	Huddersfield Town								
Francis Stephen S	5.11	11.5	5/29/64	Billericay	8/24/82	Chelsea	71	6	10	1				
E: Y2; FMC'86'88				£20000	2/27/87	Reading	216	15	15	13				
				£150000	8/1/93	Huddersfield Town	184	20	9	12				
Vasen Nico						Eendracht Aalst								
				£80000	7/1/98	Huddersfield Town								
D E F E N C E														
Brennan Damien			8/30/80	Dublin		Huddersfield Town								
Collins Sam J	6.2	13.5	6/5/77	Pontefract	7/6/94	Huddersfield Town	12+3	3+1						
Cowan Thomas	5.8	10.8	8/28/69	Bellshill		Clydebank	16			2	2			
					2/1/89	Glasgow Rangers	8+4		+1	2				
				£350000	8/1/91	Sheffield United	45	5	2	1				
				Loan	10/1/93	Stoke City	14	1		3				
				£150000	3/24/94	Huddersfield Town	132	13	7	6	7	1	1	
Dyson Jonathan P	6.1	12	3/23/72	Mirfield	12/29/90	Huddersfield Town	124+16	14+2	7	7+4	3			
Edmondson Darren	6	12.2	11/4/71	Coniston	7/17/90	Carlisle United	204+9	15	15	20	9	1	3	3
					4/3/97	Huddersfield Town	24+4	2	0+1					
Jenkins Steve R	5.1	10.9	7/16/72	Merthyr	7/1/90	Swansea City	140+10	10+1	10+1	25	1			
W: u21.2, Y.AGT'94				£275000	11/3/95	Huddersfield Town	93+1	9	8		2			
Morrison Andrew C	5.11	12	7/30/70	Inverness	7/6/88	Plymouth Argyle	105+8	10+1	6	2+1	6	1		
				£500000	8/5/93	Blackburn Rovers	1+4		1					
				Free	12/9/94	Blackpool	47		2	3	3			
					8/15/96	Huddersfield Town	32+2	5	2		2			
Phillips David O	5.1	11.2	7/29/63	Wegburg (Ger)	8/3/81	Plymouth Albion	65+8	2+1	12+1	4	15	1		
W: 52, u21.4, Y4; FAC'87				£65000	8/23/84	Manchester City	81	8	5	5	13			3
				£150000	6/5/86	Coventry City	93+7	8	9	5+1	8		1	2
				£525000	7/31/89	Norwich City	152	12	14	8	17		1	1
					8/20/93	Nottingham Forest	37+7	5+1	6+2	3				
				Free	11/14/97	Huddersfield Town	29		2		2			
M I D F I E L D														
Beresford David	5.8	10.09	11/11/76	Middlesbrough	7/22/94	Oldham Athletic	31+32	3+3	0+1	2	2			
					3/27/97	Huddersfield Town	11+3	1			1			
Dalton Paul	5.11	12	4/25/67	Middlesbrough		Brandon United								
FLgXl.1				£35000	5/3/88	Manchester United								
				£20000	3/4/89	Hartlepool United	140+11	10	7	9	37	2	1	3
				£275000	6/11/92	Plymouth Argyle	93+5	5	7	6	25	2	5	
				£125000	8/11/95	Huddersfield Town	71+17	6+2	6		22	1		
Gray Kevin J	6	13	1/7/72	Sheffield	7/1/90	Mansfield Town	129+12	8	6+1	12+2	3	1		2
				£20000	7/18/94	Huddersfield Town	112+4	7	6	3	2			
Heary Thomas M	5.9	11.3	2/14/79	Dublin	9/17/96	Huddersfield Town	4+4	0+1	1					
Hessey Sean	5.10	12.6	9/19/78	Whiston		Liverpool (T)								
				Free	9/15/97	Leeds United								
				Free	12/24/97	Wigan Athletic								
				Free	3/13/98	Huddersfield Town	0+1							
Horne Barry	5.1	12.3	5/18/62	St.Asaph		Rhyl								
W:49. WFAC'86. FAC'95. CS'95.				Free	6/26/84	Wrexham	136	10	7	15	17	1	2	3
				£60000	7/17/87	Portsmouth	66+4	3	6		7			
				£700000	3/22/89	Southampton	111+1	15+2	15	7	6	3	3	1
				£675000	7/1/92	Everton	118+5	12+1	11+1	3	3			
				7/19/96	Birmingham City	33	4	3					
				10/13/97	Huddersfield Town	29+1		2					
Hurst Christopher Mark	5.11	11.6	10/3/73	Barnsley		Emley								
				£30000	8/29/97	Huddersfield Town	1+2	0+1						
Johnson Ian G	5.11	10.8		Dundee United										
u21.6. S:				£90000	11/14/97	Huddersfield Town								
Richardson Lee J	5.11	11	3/12/69	Halifax	7/6/87	Halifax Town	43+13	4	4+2	6	2			
				£175000	2/9/89	Watford	40+1	1+1	1		1			
				£250000	8/15/90	Blackburn Rovers	50+12	1		2+2	3			
					9/16/92	Aberdeen	59+5	2+2	9	3	6	1	2	1
				£300000	8/12/94	Oldham Athletic	82+6	6	3	4	21	2		
				Loan	8/14/97	Stockport County	4+2							
				£65000	10/23/97	Huddersfield Town	16+5		0+2		3			

Player	Ht	Wt	DOB	Fee/Type	Date	Club								
Thornley Benjamin L	5.9	10.9	21/04/75	Bury	29/01/93	Manchester United	1+8	4	1					
: u21.3, S; ESFAu15; FAYC'92				Loan	06/11/95	Stockport County	8+2			1	1			
				Loan	22/02/96	Huddersfield Town	12				2			
				£175000	7/1/98	Huddersfield Town								
F O R W A R D														
Allison Wayne	6.1	13.5	10/16/68	Huddersfield	7/6/87	Halifax Town	74+10	3	4+1	8+1	21	2	2	3
Div.2'96.				£250000	7/26/89	Watford	6+1							
				£300000	8/9/90	Bristol City	112+46	4+5	9+1	6+2	35	2	5	3
				£475000	7/22/95	Swindon Town	97+3	9	7	3	31	3	2	
				£800000	11/11/97	Huddersfield Town	27		1		6			
Baldry Simon	5.1	11	2/12/76	Huddersfield	7/14/94	Huddersfield Town	31+21	3+2		1+2	3			1
Barnes Paul	5.1	12.09	11/16/67	Leicester	11/16/85	Notts County	36+17		0+1	4+6	14			5
				£30000	3/23/90	Stoke City	10+14	0+2		3+1	3			2
				Loan	11/8/90	Chesterfield	1		1				1	
				£50000	7/15/92	York City	117+1	5	4	11	61			2
				£350000	3/4/96	Birmingham City	13				6			
				£400000	9/6/96	Burnley	61+2	5	4		30	1		
				Swap	1/16/98	Huddersfield Town	11+4				1			
Browning Marcus	6.1	13	4/22/71	Bristol	7/1/89	Bristol Rovers	152+22	7+3	8	12+3	13		1	3
				Loan	9/18/92	Hereford United	7				5			
					2/18/97	Huddersfield Town	22+4	1						
Edwards Robert	5.8	11.7	2/23/70	Manchester	7/11/88	Crewe Alexandra	81+42	5	8+5	7+8	29	1	3	5
				£150000	3/8/96	Huddersfield Town	64+17	5+1	2+1		11	1	1	
Facey Delroy M	6	13	4/22/80	Huddersfield	3/15/97	Huddersfield Town	2+4							
Lawson Ian J	5.11	10.05	11/4/71	Huddersfield	1/27/95	Huddersfield Town	11+25	1+3	1+1		3			
Stewart Marcus	5.1	10.3	11/7/72	Bristol	7/18/91	Bristol Rovers	137+34	11	7+1	16+1	57	5	3	14
E: S.				£1200000	8/15/96	Huddersfield Town	57+4	8	3		23	4	1	

THE MANAGER
PETER JACKSON

Date of Birth . . . . 6th April 1961.
Place of Birth . . . . Bradford.
Date of Appointment . . . . October 1997.

PREVIOUS CLUBS
As Manager . . . . None.
As Coach . . . . None.
As a Player . . . . . . Bradford City, Newcastle United, Bradford City, Huddersfield.

HONOURS
As a Manager
None.

As a Player
Bradford City: Division 3 Championship 1985.

THE ALFRED MCALPINE STADIUM
Huddersfield, West Yorkshire HD1 6PX

Capacity 19,600

First game..v Wycombe W., Div 2. 8/94.
First floodlit game ....As above.

ATTENDANCES
Highest...18,775 v Birmingham City, Division 2, 06.05.95, (1-2).
Lowest ....4,183 v York City, AMC, 18.10.94, (3-0).

OTHER GROUNDS...Leeds Road

HOW TO GET TO THE GROUND

From the East and M1 (Junction 38)
Use A642, sign posted Huddersfield, into town centre, then follow signs Leeds (A62) into Leeds Road, turn right down Bradley Mills Road for Huddersfield Town FC.

From the South
Use A616 (sign posted Huddersfield) into town centre, then follow signs Leeds (A62) into Leeds Road, turn right down Bradley Mills Road for Huddersfield Town FC.

From the West
Use motorway M62 until junction 23 then A640 or A62 into Leeds Road, turn right down Bradley Mills Road for Huddersfield Town FC.

Car Parking: Parking for 1,400 cars.

Nearest Railway Station: Huddersfield (01484 531 226).

USEFUL TELEPHONE NUMBERS

Club switchboard 01484 484 100
Club fax number 01484 484 101
Club shop 01484 484 144
Ticket Office.............01484 484 123

Marketing Department.......01484 484 140
Internet address... www.huddersfield-town.co.uk
Clubcall 0891 12 16 35*
*Calls cost 50p per minute at all times. Call costings correct at time of going to press.

MATCHDAY PROGRAMME

Programme Editor ...... Alan Stevenson.

Number of pages .... 40.

Price .... £1.80.

Subscriptions .... Apply to club.

Local Newspapers
.... Huddersfield Examiner.

Local Radio Stations
.... Radio Leeds, The Pulse.

MATCHDAY TICKET PRICES

John Smith Stand
Adults.................................... £12.00
Juv/OAP.................................. £6.00

Lawrence Batley Lower
Adults.................................... £13.50
Juv/OAP.................................. £7.00

Lawrence Batley Upper
Adults.................................... £15.00
Juv/OAP.................................. £8.00

Panasonic Stand Upper
Adults.................................... £12.00
Juv/OAP.................................. £6.00

IPSWICH TOWN
(The Blues or The Town)
NATIONWIDE LEAGUE DIVISION 1
SPONSORED BY: GREENE KING

1998-99 - Back Row L-R: John Kennedy, Wayne Brown, David Theobold, David Williams (physio), Stuart Niven, Neil Midgley, Chris Keeble. **Middle Row:** Stewart Houston (first team coach), Mark Burgess, Marco Holster, Mauricio Taricco, James Scowcroft, Danny Sonner, Colin Stewart, Richard Wright, Lee Bracey, Adam Tanner, Richard Naylor, Sean Friars, Terry Bowes, Paul Mason, Dale Roberts (asst. manager). **Front Row:** Jamie Clapham, Matt Holland, David Johnson, Jason Cundy, Tony Mowbray, George Burley (manager), Mick Stockwell, Mark Venus, Alex Mathie, Kieron Dyer, Bobby Petta.

IPSWICH TOWN
FORMED IN 1887
TURNED PROFESSIONAL IN 1936
LTD COMPANY IN 1936

CHAIRMAN: David R Sheepshanks
DIRECTORS
Roger J Finbow, Philip W Hope-Cobbold,
John Kerr MBE, John S Kerridge,
Richard J Moore,

SECRETARY
David Rose (01473 219 211)
SALES & PROMOTIONS MANAGER
Mike Noye (01473 400540)

MANAGER: George Burley
ASSISTANT MANAGER: Dale Roberts

RESERVE TEAM COACH
Bryan Klug
YOUTH TEAM COACH
Paul Goddard
PHYSIOTHERAPIST
Dave Williams

STATISTICIAN FOR THE DIRECTORY
Paul Voller

After a rather mediocre start to the season, George Burley's team came on strongly after January and finished their League programme in style, clinching a play-off spot after losing only once in their last 20 matches.

When they met Charlton in the play-off semi-final, they were bang in form, but for the second season running, they missed out on a Wembley appearance, and a possible Premiership place, by losing twice to the 'Addicks'.

Several players who had appeared in the play-offs v. Sheffield United a year earlier were in action against Charlton and they were devastated after failing again to reach Wembley.

At the end of the day there can only be one winner to every competition. Most of Ipswich's displays in the second half of 1997-98 were superb. After 23 matches had been completed they had 27 points (six wins, nine draws). But from their last 23 fixtures they ran up a staggering 56 (out of a possible 69) to finish eight points short of an automatic promotion place. One can reflect on that poor start to the season which cost Ipswich dearly at the end, but there's no doubt that the scoring technique of Andy Johnson, went a long way in taking the Portman Road club into the play-offs. Argentinian Mauricio Taricco also had a fine season, as did the evergreen Mick Stockwell, young goalkeeper Richard Wright, defenders Jason Cundy and Adam Tanner, strikers Alex Mathie and James Scowcrift, and Kieron Dyer and Bobby Petta.

Manager Burley is now hoping his players can continue where they left off before they met Charlton in the play-offs!.

Tony Matthews.

IPSWICH TOWN

Division 1   :5th   FA CUP: 4th Round   LC CUP: 6th Round

M	DATE	COMP.	VEN	OPPONENTS	RESULT	H/T	LP	GOAL SCORERS/GOAL TIMES	ATT.
1	A 09	FL	A	Queens Park Rangers	D	0-0	0-0	13		(17614)
2	12	CC 1/1	A	Charlton Athletic	W	1-0	1-0		Venus 15	(6598)
3	23	FL	A	Bradford City	L	1-2	0-1	21	Dyer 74	(13913)
4	26	CC 1/2	H	Charlton Athletic	W	3-1	2-0		Stein 30, Scowcroft 61, Brown 45 (OG)	10989
5	30	FL	H	West Bromwich Albion	D	1-1	1-0	22	Stein 40	13508
6	S 02	FL	H	Swindon Town	W	2-1	1-1	14	Venus 35, Sonner 82	11246
7	13	FL	A	Huddersfield Town	D	2-2	0-1	20	Dyer 90, Edmondson 65 (OG)	(9313)
8	16	CC 2/1	H	Torquay United	D	1-1	0-1		Stockwell 89	8031
9	20	FL	H	Stoke City	L	2-3	0-2	22	Scowcroft 47, Holland 66	10665
10	23	CC 2/2	A	Torquay United	W	3-0	1-0		Holland 22, 61, Dyer 90	(3598)
11	26	FL	A	Norwich City	L	1-2	0-1	22	Stein 74	(18911)
12	O 04	FL	H	Manchester City	W	1-0	0-0	22	Mathie 62	14322
13	14	CC 3	H	Manchester United	W	2-0	2-0		Mathie 13, Taricco 44	22173
14	18	FL	A	Oxford United	L	0-1	0-0	22		(7594)
15	21	FL	A	Crewe Alexandra	D	0-0	0-0	22		(4730)
16	25	FL	H	Bury	W	2-0	0-0	20	Tanner 79 (pen), Dozzell 85	10478
17	28	FL	A	Birmingham City	D	1-1	1-0	20	Holland 34	(16778)
18	N 01	FL	A	Charlton Athletic	L	0-3	0-2	21		(12627)
19	04	FL	H	Stockport County	L	0-2	0-0	22		8938
20	09	FL	H	Sheffield United	D	2-2	0-1	21	Legg 51, Gregory 88	9695
21	15	FL	A	Wolverhampton Wand	D	1-1	1-1	21	Johnson 44	(21937)
22	18	CC 4	A	Oxford United	W	2-1	0-0		Dozzell 63, Mowbray 93	(5723)
23	22	FL	A	Reading	W	4-0	2-0	18	Holland 26, Johnson 30, Scowcroft 49, Naylor 87	(9400)
24	29	FL	H	Nottingham Forest	L	0-1	0-0	20		17580
25	D 02	FL	H	Middlesbrough	D	1-1	0-1	21	Johnson 90	13619
26	06	FL	A	Tranmere Rovers	D	1-1	1-0	19	Johnson 27	(5720)
27	13	FL	H	Portsmouth	W	2-0	1-0	16	Cundy 30, Johnson 68	11641
28	20	FL	A	Port Vale	W	3-1	3-0	14	Mathie 10, 22, Johnson 43	(5784)
29	26	FL	H	Birmingham City	L	0-1	0-0	16		17459
30	28	FL	A	Swindon Town	W	2-0	0-0	13	Johnson 49 (pen), Petta 79	(10609)
31	J 03	FAC 3	A	Bristol Rovers	D	1-1	0-1		Stockwell 71	(8610)
32	07	CC QF	H	Chelsea	D	2-2	1-2		Taricco 45, Mathie 61	22088
33	10	FL	H	Queens Park Rangers	D	0-0	0-0	14		12672
34	13	FAC 3R	H	Bristol Rovers	W	1-0	1-0		Johnson 43	11362
35	17	FL	A	Middlesbrough	D	1-1	0-0	15	Johnson 77	(30081)
36	24	FAC 4	H	Sheffield United	D	1-1	1-0		Johnson 45	14654
37	27	FL	A	West Bromwich Albion	W	3-2	0-0	13	Holland 57, Scowcroft 75, Cundy 89	(12403)
38	31	FL	H	Bradford City	W	2-1	0-0	13	Mathie 71, 86	11864
39	F 03	FAC 4R	A	Sheffield United	L	0-1	0-1		Holland 78	(14144)
40	06	FL	A	Stoke City	D	1-1	0-1	13	Holland 78	(11416)
41	14	FL	H	Huddersfield Town	W	5-1	1-1	12	Holland 42, Johnson 53, 61, Mathie 68, Naylor 89	10509
42	18	FL	A	Manchester City	W	2-1	0-1	11	Petta 83, Dyer 90	(27156)
43	21	FL	H	Norwich City	W	5-0	3-0	9	Mathie 2, 27, 42, Petta 55, 80	21858
44	24	FL	H	Oxford United	W	5-2	3-1	7	Mathie 28, Johnson 34, 38, 85, Holland 55	11824
45	28	FL	A	Sunderland	D	2-2	2-1	8	Petta 10, Dyer 28	(35114)
46	M 03	FL	A	Sheffield United	W	1-0	1-0	7	Holland 18	(14120)
47	07	FL	H	Charlton Athletic	W	3-1	0-1	5	Stockwell 53, Cundy 76, Johnson 87	19831
48	14	FL	A	Stockport County	W	1-0	0-0	5	Johnson 55	(8939)
49	21	FL	H	Wolverhampton Wand	W	3-0	1-0	5	Johnson 3, Holland 56, Scowcroft 73	21510
50	28	FL	H	Reading	W	1-0	1-0	5	Scowcroft 39	19075
51	A 05	FL	A	Nottingham Forest	L	1-2	0-0	5	Scowcroft 46	(22292)
52	11	FL	H	Tranmere Rovers	D	0-0	0-0	6		18039
53	13	FL	A	Portsmouth	W	1-0	1-0	5	Johnson 8	(15040)
54	18	FL	H	Port Vale	W	5-1	3-0	5	Johnson 4, 58, Petta 27, 29, Mathie 56	16205
55	25	FL	A	Bury	W	1-0	0-0	5	Stockwell 74	(7830)
56	28	FL	H	Sunderland	W	2-0	0-0	5	Holland 47, Mathie 60	20902
57	M 03	FL	H	Crewe Alexandra	W	3-2	1-1	5	Johnson 33, Stockwell 53, Mathie 54	19105
58	10	PO SF1	H	Charlton Athletic	L	0-1	0-1			21681
59	13	PO SF2	A	Charlton Athletic	L	0-1	0-1			(15585)

Best Home League Attendance: 21858 V Norwich City   Smallest :8938 V Stockport County   Average :14893

Goal Scorers:

FL	(77)	Johnson 20, Mathie 13, Holland 10, Petta 7, Scowcroft 6, Dyer 4, Cundy 3, Stockwell 3, Naylor 2, Stein 2, Dozzell 1, Gregory 1, Legg 1, Sonner 1, Tanner 1, Venus 1, Opponents 1
CC	(14)	Holland 2, Mathie 2, Taricco 2, Dozzell 1, Dyer 1, Mowbray 1, Scowcroft 1, Stein 1, Stockwell 1, Venus 1, Opponents 1
FAC	(3)	Johnson 2, Stockwell 1
PO	(0)	

(G) Bracey	(D) Brown	(M) Clapham	(D) Cundy	(M) Dozzell	(M) Dyer	(D) Gregory	(M) Holland	(F) Johnson	(M) Kerslake	(M) Legg	(M) Mason	(F) Mathie	(M) Milton	(D) Mowbray	(F) Naylor	(F) Petta	(F) Scowcroft	(M) Sonner	(F) Stein	(M) Stockwell	(D) Swailes	(M) Tanner	(D) Taricco	(F) Uhlenbeek	(D) Venus	(M) Whyte	(M) Williams	(G) Wright	Referee	#
			X		X	S3	X				X		S1			X	X			X	S2		X		X		X	X	C.R. Wilkes	1
S		X		X	S1	X		X								X	X			X	S		X		X		X	X	D Orr	2
S		X		X			S1						S2			X	X		X	X			X		X		X	X	T Jones	3
S		X		X			S2						X				X	S1	X	X			X		X		X	X	S G Bennett	4
S		X		X			S1						X				X		X	X	X		X		X		X	X	M R Halsey	5
		X		X		S						S2	X1			X2	S1		X	X	X	X	X		X		X	X	P Taylor	6
		X		X								X	S	S	S1		X		X	X	X		X		X		X	X	D Pugh	7
S		X		X			S1					S2	X	X	X	X		X	X			X		X		X	X	S J Baines	8
	S1		X		X		S					S	X	X	X	X		X	X	X		X		X		X	X	B Knight	9
S		X		X		X			X	S1	S	X	X		X	X		X	X					X		X	X	A G Wiley	10
		X		X		S2	S1	S	X	X	X		X		X	X		S1	X			X	X	M J Brandwood	11
		X	X	X	X	X		X	X	S2	X	X		S	X	S1	X	X	M C Bailey	12
S		X	X	X		X	X	S1	X	X	S2	X	X	X	X	P E Alcock	13
	X	X	X	X	S	X	S1	X	S2	X	X	X	X	A G Wiley	14
	X	X	X	S	X	S	X	X	X	S	X	X	X	G B Frankland	15
	X	X	X	S2	X	S	X	S1	X	X	X	X	A P D'Urso	16
	X	X	X	S2	X	S3	X	S1	X	X	X	X	M C Bailey	17
	X	X	X	X	X	S3	S2	X	S1	X	X	X	X	X	P Rejer	18
	X	S1	X	S2	X	X	X	X	X	S	X	X	X	X	S G Bennett	19
	X	X	X	S2	X	X	S	X	S1	X	X	X	X	M E Pierce	20
	X	X	S1	X	X	X	S2	S	X	X	X	J A Kirkby	21
S		X	X	X	S1	X	X	X	S	X	X	X	X	S W Mathieson	22
	X	X	X	X	X	S2	S1	X	S2	X	X	X	X	A R Leake	23
	X	X	X1	X	S	S	S1	X	X	X	X	R Pearson	24
	X	X	X1	S3	X3	X2	S1	X	X	S2	X	X	M Fletcher	25
	X	X	X	S	S1	X	X	S	X	X	X	X	G Singh	26
	X	X1	X	S3	S1	X1	X3	S2	X	X	X	X	K Leach	27
	X	X	X	X3	S1	X1	X2	X	X	X	X	T Heilbron	28
	X	X	X	X	S1	S	X	S	X	X1	X	X	X	R D Furnandiz	29
	S	X1	X	S1	X	X	X	X	X	X	X	X	D Orr	30
S		X	X	X2	S2	X	S	X1	X	S	S1	X	X	M R Halsey	31
S	X	X	X	X1	X	S1	X	X	S2	X	X2	X	X	P A Durkin	32
	X	X	X	S2	S1	X	X2	X1	S	X	X	W C Burns	33
S	X	X	S	S	X	X	X	X	X	X	X	X	M R Halsey	34
X1	X	X	S1	X	X	X	X	X	X	X	M L Dean	35
S	X	X	S	S	X	X	S	X	X	X	X	X	X	A B Wilkie	36
X1	X	X	S	S	S1	X	S1	X2	X	X3	X	M D Messias	37
X1	X	X	S2	S3	X	S1	S1	X	X	X	R Styles	38
S	X	X	X2	S2	S	S1	X	S3	X	X1	X	X	X3	X	A B Wilkie	39
	X	X	S2	X	X	X3	X	X	X1	X2	X	M S Pike	40
X1	X	X	X2	S2	S3	X3	X	S1	X	G B Frankland	41
X1	X	X	X2	S2	S1	S	X	X	C R Wilkes	43
	X	X	X	X	X1	X	S1	S2	X3	X	X	S	X	P S Danson	44
	X	X	X	X2	X1	S2	X1	S1	X	S	X	M J Jones	45
	X	X	X	X1	X	X2	S1	S2	X	S	X	A G Wiley	46
	X	X	X	X1	X	S1	X	S	S	X	P R Richards	47
	X	X	X	X1	X	S1	X	S	X	S	X	J A Kirkby	48
	X	X2	X	X1	X	X3	S1	X	S3	X	B Knight	49
	X	X	X1	X	S2	X	X2	S1	X	X	X	B Coddington	50
	X	X	X	X	S2	X2	X1	X	S	X	S1	X	W C Burns	51
	X	X	X1	S1	X2	X3	X	S2	X	S3	X	M C Bailey	52
	X	X	X	X2	X1	X	S2	X	S1	X	M J Brandwood	53
	X	X	X2	X3	S2	S3	X	S1	X1	X	X	P Taylor	54
	X	X	X	X2	X1	S1	S2	X	S	X	X	G Laws	55
	X	X2	X	X1	X	X3	S3	S1	X	S3	X	X	K A Leach	56
	X	X	X	X3	X	S3	S1	X1	X1	S1	X	X	R D Furnandiz	57
X1	X	X	X	X	X2	S2	S	X	S1	X	X	M Fletcher	58
S	X	X	X	X2	X	S2	S1	X1	X	X	X	E K Wolstenholme	59
1	22	40	8	41	2	46	30		2	6		1	25	7	23	28	19	6	6	46	3	14	41	6	12	2	23	46	FL Appearances	
	1			6			1		5			12	13	2	5	4	12	17	1			2	4		5	2			FL Sub Appearances	
	6	2	7	0+2	7		1+1	1	1	3+2	1+1	4	3+2	5	1+1	3+1	6	1	0+1	6		5		7	7	CC Appearances	
	3		2	4	4		0+2	2	3+1	0+1	4	3+1	4	2	1		4	4	FAC Appearances	
	1	2	2	2	2	2	2	0+2	0+1	2	2	1+1	2	2	PO Appearances	

Also played: (M) Keeble S3(28), (M) Kennedy S2(28), S(36).(M) Tully S(10).

IPSWICH TOWN

CLUB RECORDS

BIGGEST VICTORIES
League: 7-0 v Portsmouth, Division 2, 7.11.1964.
7-0 v Southampton, Division 1, 2.2.1974.
7-0 v West Bromwich Albion, Division 1, 6.11.1976.
F.A. Cup: 11-0 v Cromer, 3rd Qualifying Round, 31.10.1936.
League Cup: 5-0 v Northampton, 2nd Round, 30.8.1977
6-1 v Swindon, 4th Round, 26.11.1985.
Europe: 10-0 v Floriana, 25.9.1962.

BIGGEST DEFEATS
League: 0-9 v Manchester Utd, 4.3.95.
1-10 v Fulham, Division 1, 16.12.1983.
F.A. Cup: 1-7 v Southampton, 3rd Round, 2.2.1974.
League Cup: 0-4 v Arsenal, 2nd Round, 9.9.1971.
2-6 v Aston Villa, 4th Round, 30.11.1988.
Europe: 0-4 v Bruges, 2nd Round, 5.11.1975.

MOST POINTS
3 points a win: 84, Division 2, 1991-92.
2 points a win: 64, Division 3(S), 1953-54, 1955-56.

MOST GOALS SCORED
106, Division 3(S), 1955-56.
Parker 30, Garneys 19, Grant 16, Reed 12, Blackman 8, McLuckie 6, Elsworthy 3, Leadbetter 4, Acres 2, Brown 2, Myles 1, Snell 1, Opponents 2.

MOST GOALS CONCEDED
121, Division 1, 1963-64.

MOST FIRST CLASS MATCHES IN A SEASON
66 - 1980-81 (League 42, FA Cup 7, League Cup 5, UEFA Cup 12).

MOST LEAGUE WINS
27, Division 3(S), 1953-54.

MOST LEAGUE DRAWS
18, Division 2, 1990-91.

MOST LEAGUE DEFEATS
29, Premiership 1994-95.

INDIVIDUAL CLUB RECORDS

MOST GOALS IN A SEASON
Ted Phillips: 46 goals in 1956-57 (League 41, FA Cup 5).

MOST GOALS IN A MATCH
5. Ray Crawford v Florina, 10-0, European Cup, 25.9.1962.
5. Alan Brazil v Southampton, 5-2, Division 1, 16.2.1982.

OLDEST PLAYER
Mick Burns, 43 years 219 days v Gateshead, FA Cup, 12.1.1952.

YOUNGEST PLAYER
Jason Dozzell, 16 years 56 days v Coventry, 4.2.1984.

MOST CAPPED PLAYER
Allan Hunter (Northern Ireland) 47.

BEST PERFORMANCES

League: 1955-56: Matches played 46, Won 25, Drawn 14, Lost 7, Goals for 106, Goals against 64, Points 64. Third in Division 3(S).
Highest Position: First in Division 1, 1961-62.
F.A. Cup: 1977-78: 3rd Round Cardiff City 2-0; 4th Round Hartlepool United 4-1; 5th Round Bristol Rovers 2-2,3-0; 6th Round Millwall 6-1; Semi-final W.B.A. 3-1; Final Arsenal 1-0.
League Cup: Semi-finalists in 1981-82.
Most recent success: 1984-85: 2nd Round Derby County 4-2,1-1; 3rd Round Newcastle United 1-1,2-1; 4th Round Oxford United 2-1; 5th Round Q.P.R. 0-0,2-1; Semi-final Norwich City 1-0,0-2.
Europe: (UEFA) 1980-81: 1st Round Aris Salonika 5-1,1-3; 2nd Round Bohemians 0-2,3-0; 3rd Round Widzew Lodz 5-0,0-1; 4th Round St. Ettiene 4-1,3-1; Semi-final Cologne 1-0,1-0; Final AZ67 Alkmaar 3-0,2-4.

DIVISIONAL RECORD

	Played	Won	Drawn	Lost	For	Against	Points
Division 1/P	1,008	373	250	385	1,344	1,392	1,104
Division 2/1	786	334	211	247	1,258	1,094	1,043
Division 3(S)	486	214	112	160	806	695	540
Total	2,280	921	563	790	3,408	3,181	2,687

ADDITIONAL INFORMATION
PREVIOUS NAMES
None.

PREVIOUS LEAGUES
Southern League.

Club colours: Royal blue shirts with white sleeves, white shorts with blue trim.
Change colours:

Reserves League
Avon Insurance Football Combination.

RECORDS AND STATISTICS

COMPETITIONS

Div 1/P	Div.2/1	Div.3(S)	Euro C	UEFA	ECWC
1961-64	1954-55	1938-54	1962-63	1973-74	1978-79
1968-86	1957-61	1955-57		1974-75	
1992-95	1964-68			1975-76	Texaco
	1986-92			1977-78	1972-73
	1995-			1979-80	
				1980-81	
				1981-82	
				1982-83	

HONOURS

Div.1	Div.2	Div.3(S)	FA Cup	UEFA
1961-62	1960-61	1953-54	1977-78	1980-81
	1967-68	1956-57		Texaco
	1991-92			1972-73

MOST GOALS IN A CAREER
Ray Crawford - 227 (1958-69)

Year	League	FA Cup	Lge Cup	Europe
1958-59	25	1		
1959-60	18			
1960-61	40			
1961-62	33	1	3	
1962-63	25			8
1963-64	2			
1965-66	8			
1966-67	21	3	1	
1967-68	16		5	
1968-69	16		1	
Total	204	5	10	8

Current top goalscorer - Michael Stockwell - 38 (12.82-98)

MOST APPEARANCES
Mick Mills 737+4 (1966-82)

Year	League	FA Cup	Lge Cup	Europe
1965-66	2			
1966-67	21+1	1	2	
1967-68	9+1	1	1+1	
1968-69	35+1	1		
1969-70	40	1	3	
1970-71	42	6	2	
1971-72	35	2	1	
1972-73	42	2	2	
1973-74	42	3	4	8
1974-75	42	9	5	
1975-76	42	3	1	4
1976-77	37	3	2	
1977-78	34	7	2	5
1978-79	42	5	1	6
1979-80	37	4	2	3
1980-81	33	6	5	10
1981-82	42	3	8	2
1982-83	11		2	2
	588+3	57	43+1	40

Plus 8 Texaco Cup 1972-73 & 1 Charity Shield 1978-79.

MANAGERS

Name	Seasons	Best	Worst
Michael O'Brien	1936-37		
Adam Scott Duncan	1937-55	1(1)	3(3S)
Alf Ramsey	1955-63	1(1)	3(3S)
Jackie Milburn	1963-64	22(1)	22(1)
Bill McGarry	1964-68	1(2)	15(2)
Bobby Robson	1968-82	2(1)	19(1)
Bobby Ferguson	1982-87	9(1)	5(2)
John Duncan	1987-90	8(2)	9(2)
John Lyall	1990-95	1(2)	14(2)
George Burley	1995-	20(P)	5(1)

RECORD TRANSFER FEE RECEIVED

Amount	Club	Player	Date
£1,750,000	Tottenham H	Jason Dozzell	8/93
£800,000	Sheffield Utd	Brian Gayle	9/91
£750,000	Glasgow Rangers	Terry Butcher	8/86
£500,000	Tottenham H	Alan Brazil	3/83

RECORD TRANSFER FEE PAID

Amount	Club	Player	Date
£1,100,000	Bury	David Johnson	11/97
£1,000,000	Tottenham Hotspur	Steve Sedgley	6/94
£750,000	Oldham Athletic	Ian Marshall	8/93
£650,000	Derby County	Geriant Williams	5/92

LONGEST LEAGUE RUNS

of undefeated matches:	23 (8.12.1979 - 26.4.1980)	of league matches w/out a win:	21 (28.8.1963 - 20.12.1963)
of undefeated home matches:	33 (27.10.1979 - 28.3.1981)	of undefeated away matches:	11 (15.12.1979 - 18.4.1980)
without home win:	9 (24.8.1963 - 28.12.1963)	without an away win:	27 (10.5.1963 - 29.9.1964)
of league wins:	8 (19.8.1953 - 16.9.1953)	of home wins:	14 (19.9.1956 - 9.3.1957)
of league defeats:	10 (9.9.1954 - 16.10.1954)	of away wins:	5 (10.9.1976 - 27.12.1976)

PLAYERS NAME / Honours	Ht	Wt	Birthdate	Birthplace Transfers	Contract Date	Clubs	APPEARANCES League	L/Cup	FA Cup	Other	GOALS Lge	L/C	FAC	Oth
G O A L K E E P E R														
Bracey Lee	6.1	12.8	9/11/68	Barking	7/6/87	West Ham United								
WFAC'91.				Free	8/27/88	Swansea City	99	8	11	10				
				£47500	10/17/91	Halifax Town	73	2	1	2				
				£20000	8/23/93	Bury	86+2	7	2	3				
				Loan	3/14/97	Ipswich Town								
					8/5/97	Ipswich Town								
Wright Richard I	6.2	13	11/5/77	Ipswich	1/2/95	Ipswich Town	112	13	8	6				
E: U21.8, Y, S.														
D E F E N C E														
Brown Wayne L	6	12.6	8/20/77	Barking	9/30/96	Chester City	2		0+1					
					3/7/97	Ipswich Town	1							
Mowbray Tony	6.1	13	11/22/63	Saltburn		Middlesbrough								
E: B						Celtic								
				£300000	10/6/95	Ipswich Town	50+2	5	6	3	2	1		1
Taricco Mauricio	5.9	11.7	3/10/73	Buenos Aires		Argentinos Jnrs.								
				£175000	9/9/94	Ipswich Town	118+3	14	8	7	3	2		
Venus Mark	6	11.8	4/6/67	Hartlepool										
Div3'89				Free	9/6/85	Leicester City	58+3	3	2	2+1	1			
				£40000	3/23/88	Wolverhampton W.	271+17	17+1	15+1	17	7	1		2
					3/22/91	Hartlepool United	4			0+1				
					7/18/97	Ipswich Town	12+2	5	1	2	1	1		
M I D F I E L D														
Burgess Mark Paul	5.11	11.9	2/3/79	Ipswich	6/2/97	Ipswich Town								
Clapham James R	5.9	10.11	12/7/75	Lincoln		Tottenham Hotspur	0+1							
				Loan	1/29/97	Leyton Orient	6							
				Loan	3/27/97	Bristol Rovers	4+1							
				Loan	1/9/98	Ipswich Town	12							
				£300000	3/13/98	Ipswich Town	10			1				
Dyer Kieron	5.7	9.7	12/29/78	Ipswich	12/3/96	Ipswich Town	43+11	7	3	3+1	4	1		
Y. E:														
Friars Sean	5.9	11	5/15/79	Derry	5/31/97	Liverpool (T)								
				Free	7/1/98	Ipswich Town								
Holland Matthew	5.9	11.4	4/11/74	Bury	7/3/92	West Ham United								
				Loan	10/21/94	Bournemouth								
				£150000	11/18/94	Bournemouth	97+7	6	3	2	17			
					7/31/97	Ipswich Town	46	7	4	2	10	2		
Keeble Chris	5.11	10.7	9/17/78	Colchester	6/2/97	Ipswich Town	0+1							
Kennedy John N	5.9	10.3	8/19/78	Cambridge	6/2/97	Ipswich Town	0+1							
Mason Paul D	5.8	12.1	9/3/63	Liverpool		Everton								
SLC'90; SFAC'90				Free		F.C. Groningen								
				£200000	8/1/88	Aberdeen	138+20	13+2	11+1	7	27	8	1	1
				£400000	6/18/93	Aberdeen	103+10	10	4+3	4	25	4	3	3
Midgley Neil	5.11	11.3	10/21/78	Cambridge	6/2/97	Ipswich Town								
Niven Stuart	5.11	12.8	12/24/78	Glasgow	9/23/96	Ipswich Town	2							
Sonner Daniel James	5.11	12.8	1/9/72	Wigan	8/15/96	Ipswich Town	28+23	6+2	1+1	+1	3	1		
Stockwell Michael T	5.6	10.3	2/14/65	Chelmsford	12/17/82	Ipswich Town	420+21	36+4	26+3	22+2	31	4	2	2
Div2'92														
Tanner Adam D	6	12.1	10/25/73	Maldon	7/13/92	Ipswich Town	36+18	1+1	5+1	3+1	7			1
Theobald David J	6.3	11.6	12/15/78	Cambridge	6/2/97	Ipswich Town								

FORWARD

	Ht	Wt	DOB	From / Fee	Date	Club								
Johnson David A	5.6	12.03	8/15/76	Kingston		Manchester United								
DIV2 96/97				Free	7/5/95	Bury	73+24	8+3	2+1	1+1	18	4		
				£800000	11/14/97	Ipswich Town	30+1		4	2	20		2	
Holster Marco						Heracles								
				Free	7/1/98	Ipswich Town								
Mathie Alexander	5.1	10.7	12/20/68	Bathgate	5/15/87	Celtic	7+4		1	+1				
				£100000	8/1/91	Grennock Morton	73+1	2	5	7	31	1	3	9
				Loan	3/30/93	Port Vale	+3							
				£285000	7/30/93	Newcastle United	3+22	2+2			4			
				£500000	2/24/95	Ipswich Town	88+13	9+2	2+2	6	37	7		1
Naylor Richard	6.1	13.7	2/28/77	Leeds	9/27/96	Ipswich Town	19+13	1+2	+1		6	1		
Petta Bobby	5.7	11.3	8/6/74	Rotterdam	8/15/96	Ipswich Town	29+9	4+2	3+1	2	7			
Scowcroft James B	6.1	12.2	10/25/73	Bury St. Edmunds	7/1/94	Ipswich Town	72+23	11+1	7	3+4	17	2		1

ADDITIONAL CONTRACT PLAYERS

				From / Fee	Date	Club								
Bowes Terry						Arsenal (T)								
				Free	7/1/98	Ipswich Town								

THE MANAGER
GEORGE BURLEY

Date of Birth . . . . 3rd June 1956.
Place of Birth. . . . . Cumnock.
Date of Appointment . . . . December 1994.

PREVIOUS CLUBS
As Manager . . . . Aye United, Colchester United.
As Coach . . . . Motherwell, twice.
As a Player . . . . Ipswich Town, Sunderland, Gillingham.

HONOURS
As a Manager
None.

As a Player
Ipswich Town: FA Cup 1978, UEFA 1981.
International: 11 full caps, 2 U23, 5 U21, Y, S for Scotland.

PORTMAN GROUND
Ipswich, Suffolk IP1 2DA

Capacity 22,600

First game ....v V Beccles Caxton,
....Suffolk Challenge Cup, 7-1, 2.3.1889.
First floodlit game...v Arsenal, Friendly, 16.2.1960.

ATTENDANCES
Highest ....38,010 v Leeds Utd, FAC 6th Rnd, 8.3.1975.
Lowest...3,116 v Leyton Orient, 25.3.1953.

OTHER GROUNDS...None.

HOW TO GET TO THE GROUND

From the North and West
Use A45 sign posted to Ipswich West.
Proceed straight through Constable County Hotel traffic lights.
At the second set of traffic lights turn right into West End Road.
The ground is 400 metres along on the left.

From the South:
Follow signs for Ipswich West, then proceed as above.

Car Parking: Large parks in Portman Road, Portman's Walk & West End Road.

Nearest Railway Station: Ipswich (01473 57373)

USEFUL TELEPHONE NUMBERS

Club switchboard 01473 400 500
Club fax number........................01473 400 040
Club shop 01473 400 501
Ticket Office.............................01473 400 555

Marketing Department 01473 400 523
Internet Address ....www.itfc.co.uk
Clubcall 0839 66 44 88*
*Calls cost 50p per minute at all times Call costings correct at time of going to press.

MATCHDAY PROGRAMME

Programme Controller ....Tim Barnett.

Number of pages...

Price ....£2.

Subscriptions ....Apply to club.

Local Newspapers
......East Anglian Daily Times, Evening Star.

Local Radio Stations ....
SGR FM, Saxon Radio, BBC Radio Suffolk.

MATCHDAY TICKET PRICES (97/98)

Adults . . . . £12, £15, £18.
Juniors . . . . £6.
Senior Citizens . . . . £8.

NORWICH CITY
(The Canaries)
NATIONWIDE LEAGUE DIVISION 1
SPONSORED BY: COLMAN'S OF NORWICH

1998-99 - Back Row L-R: Alex Allen, Victor Segura, Craig Fleming, Chris Llewellyn, Adrian Coote, Kevin Scott, Drewe Broughton, Keith O'Neill, Iwan Roberts, Lee Marshall. **Middle Row:** Tim Sheppard (Physio), Darren Kenton, Shaun Carey, Erik Fuglestad, Andy Marshall, Matt Jackson, Robert Green, Daryl Sutch, Bradley Andrews, Darel Russell, Dave Carolan (Sports Scientist). **Front Row:** Che Wilson, Mike Milligan, Neil Adams, Darren Eadie, Bruce Rioch (Manager), Bryan Hamilton (Director of Football), Craig Bellamy, Peter Grant, Adrian Forbes, Tommy Henderson.

NORWICH CITY
FORMED IN 1902
TURNED PROFESSIONAL IN 1905
LTD COMPANY IN 1905

CHAIRMAN: B W Lockwood
DIRECTORS
R J Munby (Vice-Chairman),
R Cooper, M M Foulger, B J Skipper,
Delia Smith, E M S Wynn Jones
CHIEF EXECUTIVE: G Bennett
SECRETARY
Andrew Neville (01603 760 760)

MANAGER: Bruce Rioch
DIRECTOR OF FOOTBALL: Brian Hamilton
RESERVE TEAM MANAGER
Steve Foley
YOUTH TEAM MANAGER
Keith Webb
PHYSIOTHERAPIST
Tim Sheppard MCSP, SRP

STATISTICIAN FOR THE DIRECTORY
John Brock

The Canaries struggled through most of the 1997-98 season and offered little to cheer their supporters. They made a terrible start when they lost their first three League games and occupied bottom place in the table. Matters were made worse when they were knocked out of the Coca-Cola Cup at the first hurdle by Barnet, from two divisions below. Already the pre-season optimistic hopes of promotion seemed very distant.

Nevertheless the club ended August by moving off the bottom of the table with a hard-fought win at Sunderland's new Stadium of Light. Other highpoints in the first half of the season included the club's first away win over Manchester City for thirty-three years and a home win over neighbours Ipswich Town. There was, however, no consistency, and the Canaries were unable to mount a serious challenge on the play-off places.

The new year began disastrously with heavy defeats at Grimsby Town in the F.A. Cup (another early cup exit at the hands of a club from a lower division) and at Wolverhampton Wanderers. These two shocking results were followed by two unexpected home wins against promotion-chasing Nottingham Forest and Sunderland. But these two good results were followed by a run of fourteen games without a win, which took the club to the brink of the relegation places. To make matters worse this run included an embarrassing 5-0 defeat at Ipswich Town.

One of the Canaries' main failings was their shortage of goals. Yet just when things were getting desperate towards the end of the season, they completed their home programme with two successive 5-0 wins. And an away win on the last day of the season left the club in a relatively healthy fifteenth place.

Undoubtedly the club suffered from a high number of injuries. Darren Eadie and Keith O'Neill - two of the most promising players - were out for a long time. Nevertheless this allowed some of the youngsters to shine: most notably Craig Bellamy, who ended up as the leading goal-scorer, and Chris Llwellyn.

Despite the poor season, it still came as a surprise when the Board dispensed with manager Mike Walker's services. Besides the manager, other familiar faces that will not be present at Carrow Road next season include Bryan Gunn, Robert Fleck, John Polston and Rob Newman, all great servants of the club.

John D Brock.

NORWICH CITY

Division 1	:15th		FA CUP: 3rd Round				LC CUP: 1st Round		

M	DATE	COMP.	VEN	OPPONENTS	RESULT	H/T	LP	GOAL SCORERS/GOAL TIMES	ATT.
1	A 09	FL	H	Wolverhampton Wand	L 0-2	0-1	22		17230
2	12	CC 1/1	H	Barnet	W 2-1	2-1		Roberts 13, Adams 38	5429
3	15	FL 0	A	Nottingham Forest	L 1-4	1-1	23	O'Neil 7	(16524)
4	23	FL	H	Crewe Alexandra	L 0-2	0-1	24		11821
5	26	CC 1/2	A	Barnet	L 1-3	0-0		Roberts 46	(2846)
6	30	FL	H	Sunderland	W 1-0	0-0	20	Sutch 75	(29204)
7	S 02	FL	A	Portsmouth	D 1-1	0-0	17	Adams 89 (pen)	(10577)
8	13	FL	H	Port Vale	W 1-0	0-0	16	Fleck 58	11269
9	17	FL	H	Charlton Athletic	L 0-4	0-3	16		10157
10	20	FL	A	Manchester City	W 2-1	1-1	15	Adams 37, Coote 63	(27258)
11	26	FL	H	Ipswich Town	W 2-1	1-0	10	Eadie 9, Cundy 60 (OG)	18911
12	O 04	FL	A	Tranmere Rovers	L 0-2	0-1	16		(6674)
13	18	FL	H	Stockport County	D 1-1	0-1	17	Eadie 73	12689
14	21	FL	H	Reading	D 0-0	0-0	17		17781
15	25	FL	A	Swindon Town	L 0-1	0-0	17		(9256)
16	N 01	FL	H	Bury	D 2-2	2-1	16	Bellamy 2, Adams 23	14419
17	04	FL	A	West Bromwich Albion	L 0-1	0-0	17		(13949)
18	08	FL	A	Birmingham City	W 2-1	2-1	16	Forbes 23, 36	(16464)
19	15	FL	H	Middlesbrough	L 1-3	1-1	16	Roberts 32	16011
20	22	FL	H	Oxford United	W 2-1	1-0	15	Fleck 31, Bellamy 61	11241
21	29	FL	A	Bradford City	L 1-2	0-1	15	Bellamy 75	(16637)
22	D 03	FL	A	Queens Park Rangers	D 1-1	0-0	15	Forbes 51	(10141)
23	06	FL	H	Sheffield United	W 2-1	0-0	15	Fuglestad 84, Vonk 61 (OG)	11745
24	13	FL	A	Huddersfield Town	W 3-1	2-0	12	Forbes 3, Bellamy 40, Grant 90	(11436)
25	20	FL	H	Stoke City	D 0-0	0-0	12		12265
26	26	FL	A	Charlton Athletic	L 1-2	0-0	13	Bellamy 79 (pen)	(14472)
27	30	FL	H	Portsmouth	W 2-0	1-0	11	Jackson 14, Bellamy 65	16441
28	J 03	FAC 3	A	Grimsby Town	L 0-3	0-1			(8161)
29	10	FL	A	Wolverhampton Wand	L 0-5	0-4	12		(23073)
30	17	FL	H	Nottingham Forest	W 1-0	0-0	11	Roberts 47	17059
31	28	FL	H	Sunderland	W 2-1	1-0	12	Eadie 33, Craddock 62 (OG)	15940
32	31	FL	A	Crewe Alexandra	L 0-1	0-0	12		(5559)
33	F 06	FL	H	Manchester City	D 0-0	0-0	12		15274
34	14	FL	H	Port Vale	D 2-2	0-1	13	Grant 64, Jackson 68	(6664)
35	18	FL	H	Tranmere Rovers	L 0-2	0-0	13		12105
36	21	FL	A	Ipswich Town	L 0-5	0-3	14		(21858)
37	24	FL	A	Stockport County	D 2-2	0-1	14	Grant 46, Coote 89	(7471)
38	28	FL	H	Queens Park Rangers	D 0-0	0-0	14		12730
39	M 04	FL	H	Birmingham City	D 3-3	0-2	14	Bellamy 47, 68, Llewellyn 58	9819
40	07	FL	A	Bury	L 0-1	0-0	15		(5154)
41	14	FL	H	West Bromwich Albion	D 1-1	1-0	15	Bellamy 5	19069
42	22	FL	A	Middlesbrough	L 0-3	0-1	16		(30040)
43	28	FL	A	Oxford United	L 0-2	0-0	18		(7869)
44	A 04	FL	H	Bradford City	L 2-3	0-1	20	Llewellyn 64, Bellamy 89	13260
45	11	FL	A	Sheffield United	D 2-2	0-2	19	Bellamy 73, Llewellyn 78	(16915)
46	13	FL	H	Huddersfield Town	W 5-0	2-0	17	Fleming 12, Adams 30 (pen), Roberts 57, 67, Fuglestad 90	16550
47	18	FL	A	Stoke City	L 0-2	0-1	17		(13098)
48	25	FL	H	Swindon Town	W 5-0	2-0	15	Llewellyn 16, Jackson 34, Roberts 51, Bellamy 68, Fenn 76	18443
49	M 03	FL	A	Reading	W 1-0	0-0	15	Bellamy 57	(14817)

Best Home League Attendance: 19069 V West Bromwich Albion   **Smallest :9819 V Birmingham City**   **Average :14445**

Goal Scorers:

FL   (52)   Bellamy 13, Roberts 5, Adams 4, Forbes 4, Llewellyn 4, Eadie 3, Grant 3, Jackson 3, Coote 2, Fleck 2, Fuglestad 2, Fenn 1, Fleming 1, O'Neil 1, Sutch 1, Opponents 3

CC   (3)   Roberts 2, Adams 1

FAC   (0)

(F) Adams	(M) Bellamy	(F) Bradshaw	(M) Carey	(M) Coote	(M) Eadie	(F) Fenn	(F) Fleck	(D) Fleming	(F) Forbes	(D) Fuglestad	(M) Grant	(G) Gunn	(D) Jackson	(M) Kenton	(M) Llewellyn	(G) Marshall A	(M) Marshall L	(M) Milligan	(M) Mills	(D) Newman	(M) O'Neil	(D) Polston	(F) Roberts	(M) Russell	(D) Scott	(M) Segura	(M) Simpson	(M) Sutch		
X	S1				X		S2	X								X				X	X	X	X	X		S	S	X	M C Bailey	1
X	X	X		S			X	X							S	X					S1	X	X	X	X	X	X	X	C T Finch	2
X	S1	X			X		S									X					S2	X	X	X	X	X	X		J A Kirkby	3
X					X		X		S2		X					X		X	X	X	X	X	X		S	S1			D Orr	4
X					X		X		S		X					X		X		X	S1	X	X		S	S		X	M Fletcher	5
X					X		X			X			X	S2		X				X	S1	X	X		S	X		X	R D Furnandiz	6
X					X		X			X			X	S2		X				X	S1	X	X	S3	X			X	B Knight	7
X	S2			S1			X	S	X		X		X			X				X		X		X	X			X	S J Baines	8
X	S1			X			X	S2	X		X		X		S	X		X		X		X		X				X	A P D'Urso	9
X	X			X			X	X	X1		X		X			X				S3	S2	S1		X				X	A N Butler	10
X	S1			S2	X		X		X		X		X			X		X		S				X				X	M J Brandwood	11
X				S1	X		X		X		X		X	S2		X		X	X									X	E K Wolstenholme	12
X	X			S2	X		X	X	X		X		X			X				S3				X			S1	X	P Taylor	13
X	X			S1			X		X		X		X			X			X	S	S2			X			X	X	F G Stretton	14
X	X			S1			X		X		X		X			X			X	S2	S3			X			X	X	M R Halsey	15
X	X			X			X		X		X		X			X	X	X		S				X		S2		X	J A Kirkby	16
X	X			X			X		X		X		X			X	X	X		S3			S2	X		S1		X	D Laws	17
X				S			X		X				S	X		X	X	X		X			X	X		X	S1	X	R Pearson	18
X	S2						X		X	S3	X		X			X		X	S1	X			X	X	X	X		X	S W Mathieson	19
X	X						X		X	X			X	S		X		X		S	X		X	X	X	X			B Coddington	20
X1	X						X		S1	X			X	S		X		X		S			X	X	X	X		X	P R Richards	21
X	X						X		S1	X			X	S		X		X		S			X	X	X	X		X1	P Rejer	22
X	X		S				X				X		X	S		X				S	X		X	X	X	X		X	S G Bennett	23
X	X		S2				X1		X2		X	S1	X	S		X							X	X	X	X		X	A R Leake	24
	X	X1					S	X	X	X			X			X		S	X		S1		X	X	X	X			R J Harris	25
	X	S					S	X	X	X			X			X		X	X		S1	X1		X	X	X			P S Danson	26
	X	S				S1	S	X1	X	X			X			X		X	X		X		X	X	X	X			K M Lynch	27
X	S				X2	X		X	X				S	S2	X		X	X		X				X	X1		S1		M C Bailey	28
	X	X1				S2			X	X	X	X	S	S1				X			X		X	X2				X	D Pugh	29
			X	X			X	X	X	X	X	X	S								S	X		X				X	M E Pierce	30
			X	X		S		X	X2	X	X	X	S				X1	S2				X				S1		X	M J Brandwood	31
X			X	X		S	X	X	X	X	X	X						S			X				S			X	M L Dean	32
X				X	X1		S		S1	X2	X		X					S2			X				X			X	B Knight	33
X				X			S1	X		X			X	X2	S2	X		S			X			X1				X	A G Wiley	34
X	S1		X	X			X2	X			X1		X	S3	S2	X		X3						X				X	D R Crick	35
	X	X					X3	X	X1		X		X	S2	S1	X		S3									X2	X	C R Wilkes	36
	X	S1		X			X	X1		X			X	X	X	X	S		S					X				X	J P Robinson	37
	X	S1	X1				S2	X	X2		X		X	X	X	X	S							X				X	G Singh	38
X	X	S2					X2	X	X		X		X	S1	X	X		S						X			X1	X	A Bates	39
X	X	S3					X2	X	X1		X3		X	X	X	X	S1	S2										X	R Pearson	40
X	X						X2	X	X1	X3			X	X	S3	X	S1					S2						X	P S Danson	41
X	X						S	X	X	S1	X		X	X1		X											S	X	F G Stretton	42
X	X	X1			S1		X		X2	X			X			X	S					S2	X					X	K A Leach	43
X	X			S1	X		X		X	X1			X			X	X	S				S	S					X	P Taylor	44
X	X	S		X	X		X		X		X		X			X	X	S				S	S		X			X	K M Lynch	45
X	X			X2	X		X1		X	S			X	X		X	X					X		S1	S2			X	S G Bennett	46
X	X		S2		X1			X3	S1		X		X			X					S3	X		X	X2			X	G Cain	47
X	X2	S1	S2		X			X		X			X	X3	X		X1				S3	X		X				X	T Heilbron	48
X	X	X			X1			X			X		X	X	S		S2	X2	S1	X								X	T Jones	49
30	30	1	11	11	18	6	23	20	28	23	33	4	39	7	10	42	2	20	11	10	5	7	29		22	22	2	40	FL Appearances	
6		3	12	1	1	4	2	5	1	2		2	4	5		2		9	4	4	5	2	1		2	3	4		FL Sub Appearances	
2	1	1			1		2	1		1			1			2		1		1+1	0+1	2	2		1	2		2	CC Appearances	
1					1		1	1		1			0+1	1		1		1		1			1		1	1		0+1	FAC Appearances	

Also Played: (F) Broughton S1(16). (M) Hilton S(30).

NORWICH CITY

BIGGEST VICTORIES
League: 10-2 v Coventry City, Division 3(S), 15.3.1930.
8-0 v Walsall, Division 3(S), 29.12.1951.
F.A. Cup: 8-0 v Sutton United, 4th Round, 28.1.1989.
League Cup: 7-1 v Halifax Town, 4th Round, 27.11.1963.
Europe: 3-0 v Vitesse Arnhem, UEFA Cup 1st Rnd 1st Leg, (H) 15.09.93.

BIGGEST DEFEATS
League: 0-7 v Walsall, Division 3(S), 13.9.1930.
0-7 v Sheffield Wednesday, Division 2, 19.11.1938.
F.A. Cup: 0-6 v Luton Town, 2nd Round, 10.12.1927.
0-6 v Manchester City, 4th Round, 24.1.1981.
League Cup: 1-6 v Manchester City, 2nd Round 2nd replay, 29.9.1975.
Europe: 0-1 v Inter Milan, UEFA Cup 3rd Rnd both legs, (H) 24.11.93 & (A) 08.12.93.

MOST POINTS
3 points a win: 84, Division 2, 1985-86.
2 points a win: 64, Division 3(S), 1950-51.

MOST GOALS SCORED
99, Division 3(S), 1952-53.
Ackerman 20, Gavin 20, Johnston 15, Summers 10, Ashman 9, Kinsey 7, McCrohan 7, Rattray 5, Adams 3, Coxon 2, Opponents 1.

MOST GOALS CONCEDED
100, Division 3(S), 1946-47.

MOST FIRST CLASS MATCHES IN A SEASON
60 - 1972-73 (League 42, FA Cup 3, League Cup 7, Texaco Cup 8).

MOST LEAGUE WINS
26, Division 3(S), 1951-52.

MOST LEAGUE DRAWS
23, Division 1, 1978-79.

MOST LEAGUE DEFEATS
24, Division 3(S), 1930-31 & 1946-47. Division 2, 1938-39.

MOST GOALS IN A SEASON
Ralph Hunt: 31 goals in 1955-56, Division 3(S).

MOST GOALS IN A MATCH
5. Roy Hollis v Walsall, Division 3(S), 29.12.1951.
5. T Hunt v Coventry City, 10-2, Division 3(S), 15.3.1930.

OLDEST PLAYER
Albert Sturgess, 42 years 249 days v Millwall Athletic, Division 3(S), 14.2.1925.

YOUNGEST PLAYER
Ian Davies, 17 years 29 days (sub) v Birmingham City, Division 1, 27.4.1974.

MOST CAPPED PLAYER
Mark Bowen (Wales) 35.

League: 1950-51: Matches played 46, Won 25, Drawn 14, Lost 7, Goals for 82, Goals against 45, Points 64. Second in Division 3(S).
Highest Position: 3rd in Premier League, 1992-93.
F.A. Cup: Semi-finalists 1958-59, 1988-89.
Most recent success: 1991-92: 3rd Round Barnsley 1-0; 4th Round Millwall 2-1; 5th Round Notts County 3-0, 6th Round Southampton 0-0,2-1 (aet); Semi-final Sunderland 0-1.
League Cup: Winners in 1961-62.
Most recent success: 1984-85: 2nd Round Preston North End 3-3, 6-1; 3rd Round Aldershot 0-0, 4-0; 4th Round Notts County 3-0; 5th Round Grimsby Town 1-0; Semi-final Ipswich Town 0-1,2-0; Final Sunderland 1-0.
Europe: 1993-94: 1st Round Vitesse Arnhem 3-0, 0-0, 2nd Round Bayern Munich 2-1,1-1, 3rd Round Inter Milan 0-1, 0-1.

ADDITIONAL INFORMATION
PREVIOUS NAMES
None.

PREVIOUS LEAGUES
Southern League.

Club colours: All yellow with green trim.
Change colours: All green with yellow trim.

Reserves League: Avon Insurance Football Combination.

DIVISIONAL RECORD

	Played	Won	Drawn	Lost	For	Against	Points
Division 1/P	826	257	251	318	970	1,177	930
Division 2/1	978	374	249	355	1,405	1,370	1,089
Division 3	92	46	24	22	171	116	116
Division 3(S)	1,124	423	291	410	1,779	1,725	1,137
Total	3,020	1,100	815	1,088	4,325	4,398	3,272

RECORDS AND STATISTICS

COMPETITIONS

Div 1/P	Div.2	Div.3	Div.3(S)	A/Scot	Texaco
1972-74	1934-39	1958-60	1920-34	1975-76	1972-73
1975-81	1960-72		1939-58	1976-77	1973-74
1982-85	1974-75			1977-78	1974-75
1986-95	1981-82		**UEFA**	1978-79	
	1985-86		1993-94		
	1995-				

MOST APPEARANCES

Kevin Keelan 680 (1963-80)

Year	League	FA Cup	Lge Cup	Others
1963-64	16		1	
1964-65	23	1		
1965-66	42	4	1	
1966-67	39	3	1	
1967-68	30	3	3	
1968-69	32	1	3	
1969-70	33		1	
1970-71	38	1	4	
1971-72	42	1	5	
1972-73	42	3	7	7
1973-74	42	1	7	4
1974-75	38	1	9	3
1975-76	42	5	3	3
1976-77	38	1	2	3
1977-78	26	2	1	1
1978-79	22	1	3	
1979-80	26	3	6	
	571	31	57	21

RECORD TRANSFER FEE RECEIVED

Amount	Club	Player	Date
£5,000,000	Blackburn Rovers	Chris Sutton	7/94
£2,250,000	Newcastle Utd	Ruel Fox	2/94
£2,100,000	Chelsea	Robert Fleck	8/92
£1,200,000	Glasgow Rangers	Dale Gordon	11/91
£1,200,000	Chelsea	Andy Townsend	7/90
£1,200,000	Arsenal	Andy Linighan	7/90

RECORD TRANSFER FEE PAID

Amount	Club	Player	Date
£1,000,000	Leeds United	Jon Newsome	6/94
£925,000	Port Vale	Darren Beckford	6/91
£700,000	Derby County	Paul Blades	7/90
£580,000	Glasgow Rangers	Robert Fleck	12/87

HONOURS

Division 2	Division 3(S)	League Cup
1971-72	1933-34	1961-62
1985-86		1984-85

MOST GOALS IN A CAREER

John Gavin - 132 (1949-58)

Year	League	FA Cup
1949-50	1	
1950-51	17	1
1951-52	19	1
1952-53	20	
1953-54	13	1
1954-55	6	
1955-56	13	2
1956-57	16	
1957-58	17	5
Total	122	10

Current leading goalscorer: Darren Eadie - 34 (02.93-98)

MANAGERS

A Turner 1902-05, J Bowman 1905-07, J McEwen 1907-09,
A Turner 1909-10, J Stansfield 1910-15, F Buckley 1919-20,
C O'Hagan 1920.

Name	Seasons	Best	Worst
A Gosnell	1921-26	11(3S)	18(3S)
J Stansfield	1926	-	-
C Potter	1926-29	16(3S)	17(3S)
J Kerr	1929-33	3(3S)	22(3S)
T Parker	1933-37	11(2)	1(3S)
H Young	1937-00	11(2)	14(2)
A Jewell	1939	21(2)	21(2)
R Young	1939-45	-	-
D Lochhead	1945-46	-	-
C Spiers	1946-47	21(3S)	21(3S)
D Lochhead	1947-50	10(3S)	21(3S)
N Low	1950-55	2(3S)	11(3S)
T Parker	1955-57	7(3S)	24(3S)
A Macauley	1957-61	4(2)	8(3S)
W Reid	1961-62	17(2)	17(2)
G Swindin	1962	-	-
R Ashman	1962-66	6(2)	17(2)
L Morgan	1966-69	9(2)	13(2)
R Saunders	1969-73	20(1)	11(2)
J Bond	1973-80	10(1)	3(2)
K Brown	1980-87	5(1)	3(2)
D Stringer	1987-92	4(1)	18(1)
Mike Walker	1992-94	3(P)	3(P)
John Deehan	1994-95	12(P)	20(P)
Martin O'Neill	1995	-	-
Gary Megson	1995-96	16(2/1)	16(2/1)
Mike Walker	1996-98	13(1)	15(1)
Bruce Rioch	1998-		

LONGEST LEAGUE RUNS

of undefeated matches:	20 (31.8.1950 - 11.1.1951)	of league matches w/out a win:	25 (22.9.1956 - 2.3.1957)
of undefeated home matches:	31 (21.8.1971 - 2.12.1972)	of undefeated away matches:	12 (14.9.1985 - 8.3.1986)
without home win:	12 (29.9.1956 - 2.3.1957)	without an away win:	41 (3.9.1977 - 18.8.1979)
of league wins:	10 (23.11.1985 - 1.2.1986)	of home wins:	12 (15.3.1952 - 4.10.1952)
of league defeats: 7 (4.9.1935 - 5.10.1935, 12.1.1957 - 2.3.1957)		of away wins:	5 (3.9.1988 - 19.11.1988)
(1.4.1995 - 14.5.1995)			

NORWICH CITY

PLAYERS NAME Honours	Ht	Wt	Birthdate	Birthplace Transfers	Contract Date	Clubs	League	L/Cup	FA Cup	Other	Lge	L/C	FAC	Oth
G O A L K E E P E R														
Green Robert P	6.2	12.7	1/18/80	Chertsey	7/3/97	Norwich City								
Marshall Andrew J	6.2	12.7	4/14/75	Bury	7/6/93	Norwich City	69+1	4	3+1					
				Loan	9/9/96	Bournemouth	11							
				Loan	11/21/96	Gillingham	5	1						
D E F E N C E														
Allen Alexander	6.2	12.6	2/10/80	Doncaster	2/19/97	Norwich City								
Fleming Craig	6	11.7	10/6/71	Halifax	3/21/90	Halifax Town	56+1	4	3	3+2				
				£80000	8/15/91	Oldham Athletic	157+6	12+1	11	4	1			
					6/30/97	Norwich City	20+2	1	1		1			
Fuglestad Erik	5.11	11.3	8/13/74	Randaberg	1/1/00	Viking Stavanger								
				Free	11/8/97	Norwich City	23+1		1		2			
Jackson Matthew A	6	12.12	10/19/71	Leeds	7/4/90	Luton Town	7+2	2		0+1				
E: u21.10, u19.5, S. FAC'95. CS'95.				Loan	3/27/91	Preston North End	3+1		1					
				£600000	10/18/93	Everton	132+6	9	14	4	6			
				Loan	3/26/96	Charlton Athletic								
				Loan	8/20/96	QPR	5							
				Loan	10/31/96	Birmingham City	10							
				£450000	12/24/96	Norwich City	58+2		2		5			
M I D F I E L D														
Bellamy Craig	5.8	10.5	7/13/79	Cardiff	1/20/97	Norwich City	30+9	1	1		13			
u21.4, Y, S. W:														
Carey Shaun P	5.9	10.06	5/13/76	Kettering	7/1/94	Norwich City	24+11	2+2	1+1					
Coote Adrian	6.3	11.9	9/30/78	Great Yarmouth	7/3/97	Norwich City	11+11				2			
u21, u17. NI:														
Eadie Darren M	5.8	10.6	6/10/75	Chippenham	2/5/93	Norwich City	119+13	18+1	6+1	1+1	31	2	1	
E: u21.7, Y2														
Grant Peter	5.9	10.3	8/30/65	Bellshill		Celtic								
u21. S: 2, B,				£150000	8/22/97	Norwich City	32+2	1	1		3			
Kenton Darren E	5.9	11.6	9/13/78	Wandsworth	7/3/97	Norwich City	8+4							
Llewellyn Chris M	5.11	11.6	8/29/79	Swansea	5/31/97	Norwich City	10+5		0+1		4			
Marshall Lee	5.9	9.12	8/1/75	Nottingham		Enfield								
				Free	4/25/97	Norwich City	5+2							
Milligan Michael J	5.8	11	2/20/67	Manchester	3/2/85	Oldham Athletic	161+1	19+1	12	4	17	1	1	
Ei:1, B1, u21.1				£1000000	8/24/90	Everton	16+1	0+1	1	4+1	1			1
				£600000	7/17/91	Oldham Athletic	117	11	9	1	6	1		1
				£850000	6/27/94	Norwich City	101+8	11	6		5			
O'Neil Keith P	6.1	11	2/16/76	Dublin	7/1/94	Norwich City	39+14	6+2	3		8			
Russell Darel F R	5.10	11.1	10/22/80	Ilford	11/27/97	Norwich City	0+1							
Segura Abascal Victor	5.11	11.9	3/30/73	Zaragoza		Ileida								
Int. Spanish				Free	8/4/97	Norwich City	22+3	2	1					
Sutch Daryl	5.11	10.12	9/11/71	Beccles	7/6/90	Norwich City	131+33	11+3	6+3	2+3	7			
E: u21.4, Y2														
Wilson Che C	5.9	11.5	1/17/79	Ely	7/3/97	Norwich City								

O R W A R D														
dams Neil J	5.8	10.8	11/23/65	Stoke	7/1/85	Stoke City	31+1	3	1	3	4			
: u21.1; Div1'87; CS'86; Div2'91				£150000	7/7/86	Everton	17+3	4+1		5+1		1		
				Loan	1/11/89	Oldham Athletic	9							
				£100000	6/21/89	Oldham Athletic	93+36	13+2	10+2	1+1	23	1	2	
				£250000	2/17/94	Norwich City	149+15	14+1	6		22	4	1	
roughton Drewe O	6.3	12	10/25/78	Hitchin	3/15/97	Norwich City	3+6				1			
orbes Adrian	5.7	11	1/23/79	London	8/30/96	Norwich City	31+11		1		4			
: E:														
loberts Iwan	6.3	12.6	6/26/68	Bangor	7/4/86	Watford	40+23	6+2	1+6	5	9	3		
V: 4, Y				£275000	8/2/90	Huddersfield Town	141+1	13+1	12	14	51	6	4	8
				£100000	11/25/93	Leicester City	58+5	15	3		9		2	
				£1000000	7/4/96	Wolverhampton W.	23+8	2	0+1	2	12			
				£900000	7/8/97	Norwich City	29+2	2			5	2		

THE MANAGER
BRUCE RIOCH

Date of Birth . . . . 6th September 1947.
Place of Birth . . . . Aldershot.
Date of Appointment . . . . 12th June 1998.

PREVIOUS CLUBS
As Manager . . . . Millwall, Middlesbrough, Bolton, Arsenal.
As Player/Manager . . . . Torquay United.
As assistant manager . . . . Queens Park Rangers.
As a Player . . . . Luton, Aston Villa, Derby, Everton, Derby,
. . . . Torquay, BIrmingham (loan), Sheffield United.

HONOURS
As a Manager
Middlesbrough: uPromotion to Div.2 1987, Promotion to Dov.1 1988.
Bolton: Promotion to Div.1 1993. Promotion to Premiership 1995.

As a Player
Derby: Division 1 Championship 1974-75.
International: 24 full caps for Scotland.

CARROW ROAD
Norwich NR1 1JE

Capacity 21,994

First game ....v West Ham, Div.2, 31.8.1935.
First floodlit game ....v Sunderland, 17.10.1956.

ATTENDANCES
Highest ....43,984 v Leicester City, FAC 6th Rnd, 30.3.1963.
Lowest ....1,801 v Northampton, FLT, 14.8.1982.

OTHER GROUNDS ....Newmarket Road 1902-08.The Nest, Rosary Road 1908-35.
....Carrow Road 1935-

HOW TO GET TO THE GROUND

From the North
Use the A47 to Norwich. Appropriate exit and further directions are clearly signposted.

From the East
Use the A47 to Norwich. Appropriate exit and further directions are clearly signposted.

From the South and West
Approach Norwich on the A11 or A140. Join the A47 (direction Great Yarmouth) just outside Norwcih. Appropriate exit and further directions are clealy signposted.

Car Parking Numerous private parks nearby. Multistory parks in Malt House Road and St Andrews Street. Street parking nearby in Rose Lane, Carrow Hill and side streets of King Street. Coaches must park at Lower Clarence Road Car Park.

Nearest Railway Station Norwich (01603 -1603 632 055)

USEFUL TELEPHONE NUMBERS

Club switchboard 01603 760 760
Club fax number 01603 613 886
Club shop 01603 218 711
Ticket Office 01603 761 661

Marketing Department....... 01603 218 712
Internet address........ www.ecn.co.uk/ncfc
Clubcall 0891 12 11 44*
*Calls cost 50p per minute at all times. Call costings correct at time of going to press.

MATCHDAY PROGRAMME

Programme Editor .... Kevan Platt.

Number of pages .... 48.

Price......................... £2.

Subscriptions
Home only....... £60 (UK), £75 (Europe)
.... £90 (Outside Europe)
Home & away .. £120 (UK), £150 (Europe)
.... £180 (Outside Europe)

Local Newspapers
.... Eastern Counties Newspapers.

Local Radio Stations
.... Radio Norfolk, Radio Broadland.

MATCHDAY TICKET PRICES

	GRADE OF MATCH	ADULT	CONCESSION	U16	U12
Family Area's	A	£17	£11	£5	£1
	B	£11	£6	£3	£1
	C	£4	£1	£1	£1
Norwich & Peterborough Stand	A	£18	£11	N/A	£4
South Stand, Barclay Stand	B	£12	£7	N/A	£3
Wensum & Thorpe Areas	C	£5	£1	N/A	£1
(anywhere except family/lounges/premium)					
Castle & Cathedral	A	£23	N/A	N/A	N/A
Lounges	B	£17	N/A	N/A	N/A
	C	£5	N/A	N/A	N/A
City & County	A	£20	N/A	N/A	N/A
Lounges	B	£15	N/A	N/A	N/A
	C	£5	N/A	N/A	N/A
Geoffrey Watling City Stand	A	£19	N/A	N/A	N/A
Centre seats	B	£14	N/A	N/A	N/A
(Seats 75 - 140, Rows A-G)	C	£5	N/A	N/A	N/A
International Cavery &	A	£60	£60	£60	£60
Exec. viewing lounge	B	£45	£45	£45	£45
These seats include 3 course meal,	C	£35	£35	£35	£35
programme & half-time tea & coffee					

OXFORD UNITED
(The U's)
NATIONWIDE LEAGUE DIVISION 1
SPONSORED BY: UNIPART

1998/99 - Back Row L-R: Mickey Lewis (Yth team coach), Mark Harrison (Asst. Manager), John Clinkard (Physio), Ken Ridley (Kit man.) **3rd Row:** Peter Rhoades-Brown (Football in teh Comm.), Rob Folland, Dean Windass, Phil Gilchrist, Martin Gray, Andrew Rose, Paul Powell, Mark Jones (Soccer course director). **2nd Row:** Phil Whitehead, Tony Wright, Joey Deauchamp, Christophe Remy, Simon Weatherstone, Jamie Cook, Steve Davis, David Smith, Danny Hill, Elliott Jackson. **Front Row:** Phil Whelan, Brian Wilsterman, Simon Marsh, Andy Thomson, Malcolm Shotton (Manager), Les Robinson, Nicky Banger, Kevin Francis, Matt Murphy.

OXFORD UNITED
FORMED IN 1893
TURNED PROFESSIONAL IN 1949
LTD COMPANY IN 1949

PRESIDENT: The Duke of Marlborough
CHAIRMAN: K Cox
DIRECTORS
G Coppock, N Harris
SECRETARY
Mick Brown (01865 761503)
MARKETING
Trevor Baxter

MANAGER: Malcolm Shotton
ASSISTANT MANAGER: Mark Harrison
RESERVE/YOUTH TEAM MANAGER
Mickey Lewis
PHYSIOTHERAPIST
John Clinkard

STATISTICIAN FOR THE DIRECTORY
Roy Grant

Once again United's season was one of two halves with this time the team having a good second half which saw them rise to a final position of 12th. The past season's improvement came about after the appointment of new manager Malcolm Shotton, the fans favourite for the post and a former captain in the Oxford hey days of the mid 1980s. With little money to work with, he was forced to sell leading scorer Nigel Jemson (£100,000) and defender Darren Purse (£800,000) but was allowed to sign defender Steve Davis, from his former club Barnsley, and big Kevin Francis who came from Birmingham as part of the Purse deal. They soon settled into the side, gelling well with what was often a young side alongside established pros.

The season had not started well two wins in eight, and with the club's financial position dire it was not long before talented midfielder Bobby Ford had to be sold, for a giveaway price, to keep the club afloat at Christmas. The team had dropped to 22nd and looked set for a relegation battle. Smith left for West Brom and his assistant Malcolm Crosby took over the reigns for a spell before Shotton took over (Crosby joining Smith at Albion). The new manager enjoyed a great start winning seven out of 11 (including a 3-1 success at Champions Forest) and saw his first managerial charges rise up the table. The successes came from hard work and graft and goals from the talented Joey Beauchamp, who had an inspired season, top scoring with 19 goals and Francis who was an instant hit. Youngsters Paul Powell, Jamie Cook, Simon Weatherstone and Simon Marsh (who went on to win England U21 honours) were allowed long runs, those, plus Wales U21 player Tony Wright, Rob Folland and Andy Rose, more teenagers given their debuts look set to be United's future.

The team had a good run in the Coca-Cola reaching round four before going down to Ipswich however the FA Cup again saw them knocked out at the first stage after going down at Leeds when a money boosting cup run was required.

The playing future looks bright, some chopping and changing is to be expected in the summer but the clubs main priority must be the proposed new stadium which must see work restarted to completion before terrace exemption runs out next August.

ROY GRANT

OXFORD UNITED

Division 1   :12th   FA CUP: 3rd Round   LC CUP: 4th Round

M	DATE	COMP.	VEN	OPPONENTS	RESULT	H/T	LP	GOAL SCORERS/GOAL TIMES	ATT.
1	A 09	FL	H	Huddersfield Town	W 2-0	0-0	1	Jemson 69 (pen), Aldridge 77	7085
2	12	CC 1/1	H	Plymouth Argyle	W 2-0	1-0		Purse 25, Logan 78 (OG)	5083
3	15	FL	A	Charlton Athletic	L 2-3	0-1	9	Purse 85, Jemson 89 (pen)	(10230)
4	23	FL	H	Nottingham Forest	L 0-1	0-0	14		9486
5	26	CC 1/2	A	Plymouth Argyle	W 5-3	0-2		Beauchamp 47, 88, Jemson 48, Purse 64, Murphy 74	(3037)
6	30	FL	A	Portsmouth	L 1-2	1-1	15	Ford B 36	(10209)
7	S 02	FL	A	Sunderland	L 1-3	1-2	19	Angel 19	(27643)
8	07	FL	H	Wolverhampton Wand	W 3-0	2-0	14	Beauchamp 17, 71, Ford B 23	6921
9	13	FL	A	Reading	L 1-2	1-1	17	Jemson 2	(9003)
10	16	CC 2/1	H	York City	W 4-1	0-1		Robinson 53, Aldridge 62, Beauchamp 77, 81	2923
11	20	FL	H	Sheffield United	L 2-4	1-2	19	Jemson 25, 76	7514
12	23	CC 2/2	A	York City	W 2-1	0-0		Aldridge 88, Banger 90	(1555)
13	27	FL	H	Bradford City	D 0-0	0-0	21		6468
14	O 04	FL	A	West Bromwich Albion	W 2-1	1-1	19	Banger 13, Purse 53	(15819)
15	11	FL	A	Stockport County	L 2-3	0-0	19	Purse 84, Aldridge 88	(7333)
16	14	CC 3	H	Tranmere Rovers	D 1-1	0-1		Beauchamp 76	3878
17	18	FL	H	Ipswich Town	W 1-0	0-0	18	Smith 64	7594
18	21	FL	H	Middlesbrough	L 1-4	0-1	18	Purse 51	8306
19	25	FL	A	Birmingham City	D 0-0	0-0	18		(16352)
20	N 01	FL	H	Manchester City	D 0-0	0-0	18		8592
21	04	FL	A	Stoke City	D 0-0	0-0	16		(8423)
22	08	FL	A	Crewe Alexandra	L 1-2	1-2	19	Ford M 14	(4524)
23	15	FL	H	Bury	D 1-1	1-1	20	Banger 30	5811
24	18	CC 4	H	Ipswich Town	L 1-2	0-0		Beauchamp 66	5723
25	22	FL	A	Norwich City	L 1-2	0-1	22	Powell 81	(11241)
26	29	FL	H	Port Vale	W 2-0	1-0	19	Beauchamp 32, Jemson 57	5762
27	D 06	FL	A	Swindon Town	L 1-4	1-1	21	Ford M 24	(10902)
28	12	FL	H	Queens Park Rangers	W 3-1	2-1	17	Jemson 3, Beauchamp 36, 49	6664
29	20	FL	A	Tranmere Rovers	W 2-0	0-0	16	Massey 54, Robinson 87	(5181)
30	26	FL	A	Wolverhampton Wand	L 0-1	0-1	17		(26238)
31	28	FL	H	Sunderland	D 1-1	1-1	17	Jemson 27 (pen)	8659
32	J 03	FAC 3	A	Leeds United	L 0-4	0-2			(20568)
33	10	FL	A	Huddersfield Town	L 1-5	0-3	18	73	(10378)
34	17	FL	H	Charlton Athletic	L 1-2	1-0	20	Jemson 6	7234
35	24	FL	H	Portsmouth	W 1-0	0-0	18	Beauchamp 90	7402
36	31	FL	A	Nottingham Forest	W 3-1	1-1	16	Beauchamp 9, 49, Weatherstone 90	(18392)
37	F 06	FL	A	Sheffield United	L 0-1	0-1	17		(16881)
38	17	FL	H	West Bromwich Albion	W 2-1	1-0	16	Gilchrist 15, Francis 81	9412
39	21	FL	A	Bradford City	D 0-0	0-0	16		(14190)
40	24	FL	A	Ipswich Town	L 2-5	1-3	17	Francis 10, Donaldson 59 (pen)	(11824)
41	28	FL	H	Stockport County	W 3-0	1-0	15	Davis 5, Donaldson 65, Francis 80	6650
42	M 03	FL	H	Crewe Alexandra	D 0-0	0-0	15		6069
43	07	FL	A	Manchester City	W 2-0	1-0	14	Beauchamp 44, Cook 81	(28720)
44	14	FL	H	Stoke City	W 5-1	1-0	13	Murphy 45, 61, Francis 65, 68, Beauchamp 87	7300
45	17	FL	H	Reading	W 3-0	1-0	11	Beauchamp 44, 70, Gray 77	8103
46	21	FL	A	Bury	L 0-1	0-0	12		(5159)
47	28	FL	H	Norwich City	W 2-0	0-0	10	Francis 64, Beauchamp 80 (pen)	7869
48	A 04	FL	A	Port Vale	L 0-3	0-2	12		(6524)
49	11	FL	H	Swindon Town	W 2-1	2-0	10	Francis 28, Gilchrist 37	8005
50	14	FL	A	Queens Park Rangers	D 1-1	1-0	10	Davis 24	(12859)
51	18	FL	H	Tranmere Rovers	D 1-1	1-0	10	Cook 22	6489
52	25	FL	H	Birmingham City	L 0-2	0-0	11		8818
53	M 03	FL	A	Middlesbrough	L 1-4	0-0	12	Banger 70	(30228)

Best Home League Attendance: 9486 V Nottingham Forest   Smallest :5762 V Port Vale   Average :7488

Goal Scorers:

FL   (60)   Beauchamp 13, Jemson 9, Francis 7,Purse 4, Banger 3, Aldridge 2, Cook 2, Davis 2, Donaldson 2, Ford B 2, Ford M 2, Gilchrist 2, Gray 2, Murphy 2, Angel 1, Massey 1, Powell 1, Robinson 1, Smith 1, Weatherstone 1

CC   (15)   Beauchamp 6, Aldridge 2, Purse 2, Banger 1, Jemson 1, Murphy 1, Robinson 1, Opponents 1

FAC   (0)

(F) Aldridge	(F) Angel	(F) Banger	(M) Beauchamp	(M) Cook	(D) Davis	(F) Donaldson	(D) Ford	(M) Ford	(F) Francis	(D) Gilchrist	(M) Gray	(G) Jackson	(F) Jemson	(F) Marsh	(M) Massey	(M) Murphy	(D) Powell	(D) Purse	(M) Remy	(D) Robinson	(M) Rose	(M) Smith	(G) Van Heusden	(F) Weatherstone	(D) Whelan	(G) Whitehead	(M) Wilsterman	(M) Wright	
S1	S2	X	X				X	X		X			X						S2	X	X		X				X	X	M.R. Halsey 1
S1		X	X				X	X		X			X				S			X	X	X	X				X	S	P S Danson 2
S2		X	X				X	X		X	S1		X		X					X		X	X				X	S	C T Finch 3
	S1		X	S2			X			X				X	X		X		X	X	X	X	X					X	E K Wolstenholme 4
X	S1		X				X			X			X	X	X	S	S2		X	X	X	X					X	X	M E Pierce 5
S2	X		X				X			X			X			X	S3	X	X	X	X		X			S1	X	X	S W Mathieson 6
S2	X	X	X				X		S3	X			X				S1			X	X	X		X			X	X	A R Leake 7
X	X		X	S3			X			X	S1		X			S2				X		X		X			X	X	C R Wilkes 8
X	X	S2	X				X		X	X	X	X	X		S3					X		X		X			S1		S G Bennett 9
X	S1	X	X				X		X	X	X	X	S						X		X		X			S			M C Bailey 10
X	X	S2	X				X		X	X	X	X	S3						X		X		X			S1			M J Brandwood 11
S3	S1	X	X				X		X	X	X	X	X	X	S2					X		X		X					D Laws 12
S1	S2	X	X		X	X	S3		X										X	X	X	X	X	X		X			A P D'Urso 13
X	S2	X	X				X		X					S		X	X	X	X	X		X	X	X			S1		T Jones 14
X	S1	X	X				X	S2	X					S3					X	X	X		X					X	R D Furnandiz 15
X	X	X	X				X		X	X	S			S1			X	X	X		X	X						X	J A Kirkby 16
X	X	X	X				X							S1	S	X		X	X	X		X				X		A G Wiley 17
X	X	X	X				X		S1					S3	S2	X	X		X	X		X				X		A Bates 18
S2	X		X				X		X	S1				X	S3			X	X		X	X				X		G Cain 19
S1	S	X	X		X	X	X		X		X			S2			X		X		X	X				X		D Orr 20
S2	S	X	X		X	X	X		X		X			S1			X		X		X	X				X		R Pearson 21
S3		X	X		X	X	X	X		X			X	S2	S1		X		X	X				X		E Lomas 22
		X	X		X	X	X	S	X			X	S1	S2		X		X	X				X		P Taylor 23
		X	X		X	X	X	X		X			X	S2	S1	X		X		X	X		S			S W Mathieson 24
	X	X			X	X	X	X		X		X	X	S1	S2		X		X		X				S	B Coddington 25
X3	S3	S1	X			X					X2		X1	S2		X		X		X			X	X	M Fletcher 26
X	S2		X				X		S1	X2	X		X	S3			X		X3		X			X	X1	F G Stretton 27
X1		S1		X			X		X	X	X		X			X	S2	X2		X		X			X		T Heilbron 28
X	S		X				X		X	X	X		X			X	S	X		X			X	S	S J Baines 29
X1	S1		X				X		X	X	X		X2			X	S2	X		X3		X			X	S3	P R Richards 30
X1	S		X	S1			X		X	X	X		X			X		X		X		X			X	S	A R Leake 31
	S1		X	S2		X3				X	X	S	X2	X1		X	X	S3	X		X			X	S	M D Reed 32
		X	S2					X	X	X	X		X	X	X	X1		X2		S		X	S1	C J Foy 33
S1		X	X1					X			X	S2	X	X2	X3		X		X		X			X	S3	A N Butler 34
	S3		X					X	X	X	X1	X3	X2		X		X		X			X	S1	F G Stretton 35
		X	X2		X1		X	X	X	X3		S3		X		X		X	S1		X	X	X	M J Jones 36
S2		X	S1		X2		X	X	X			S3	X	X		X		X3		X	X1	T Heilbron 37
	S1		X		X2	X3	X	X	X	X			X1		X		X		S2	X	S3	P Taylor 38
	S1		X		X2	X1	X	X	X			X		S	X		S2	X	X	S	T Jones 39
		X	S1	X	X2	X	X	X			X1		X		X		S2	X	X	S	P S Danson 40
		X	S	X	X	X1	X	X		X				X		X		S	X	S1	B Coddington 41
	S1	X	X			X	X	X	X	X2	S2		X		X		X1	X	S	M E Pierce 42
		X	X2	X		X	X	X	X	X1		S1	X		X		X	S2	X	S	W C Burns 43
S1	X	X2	X			X	X	X	X1	S2		X		X		X	S	B Knight 44
S3	X	X1	X2		X3	X	X	X	X	X		X		X		X	S2	M Fletcher 45
S2	X	X1	X		X	X	X	X	X2	S1		X		X		X	S	G Singh 46
S2	X	S1	X		X	X	X	X	X2	X1	S	X		X		X	K A Leach 47
S1	X	X1	X		X	X	X	X	X1		X	S3	S1		X	K M Lynch 48
S1	X1	X1	X		X	X	X	X	X		X	S		S2		X	S W Mathieson 49
	X	X2	S1	X		X	X1	X		X	X		X	S	S2	S1		X	C R Wilkes 50
X1		X	X		X	X	X		X	X		X	S	X2	S1		X	S2	M R Halsey 51
S1	X	S2	X		X	X		X	X1	X2		S1	X		X	R Styles 52
S2	X	S3	X		X3	X	X		X	X2	X1	S1	X		X	P R Richards 53
13	9	18	44	9	15	6	22	17	15	35	28	3	24	13	14	15	11	27	13	46		43	11	2	6	32	15		FL Appearances
11	13	10		11				1		4	3		1	3	14	10	1	3			1	1	9	2			9	1	FL Sub Appearances
3+2	2+2	4+1	6			2	6		5	1	3	5	2	0+1	+3	0+1	6	4	6		6	2		1	1	1	CC Appearances
0+1		1	0+1		1			1	1	1		1		1		1	1	0+1	1		1			1		FAC Appearances

Also Played: (M) Folland S(16), S2(17,36). (F) Stevens S3(4).

OXFORD UNITED

CLUB RECORDS

BIGGEST VICTORIES
League: 7-0 v Barrow,Division 4, 19.12.1964.
F.A. Cup: 9-1 v Dorchester Town, 1st Rnd, 11.11.1995.
League Cup: 6-0 v Gillingham, Rnd 2, 24.9.1986.

BIGGEST DEFEAT
League: 0-6 v Liverpool, Div. 1, 22.3.1986.
F.A. Cup: by 4 goals on three occasions.
League Cup: 0-5 v Nottingham Forest, 4.10.78.

MOST LEAGUE POINTS
(3pts for win) 95, Div 3, 1983-84
(2pts for win) 61, Div 4,1964-65

MOST GOALS SCORED
91, Division 3, 1983-84.
Biggins 19, Hebberd 11, Vinter 11, Lawrence 9, Thomas 7, Aldridge 4, McDonald 4, Rhodes-Brown 4, Briggs 3, Brock 3, Whatmore 3, Opponents 3, Jones 2, Shotton 1.
MOST GOALS CONCEDED
80, Division 1, 1985-86; Division 1, 1987-88.

MOST FIRST CLASS MATCHES IN A SEASON
65, 1983-84 (46 League, 7 FA Cup, 11 League Cup, 1 AMC).

MOST LEAGUE WINS
28 (from 46), Division 3, 1983-84. 25 (from 42) Division 2, 1984-85.

MOST LEAGUE DRAWS
19, Division 2, 1990-91.

MOST LEAGUE DEFEATS
22, Division 2, 1989-90; Division 2, 1991-92.

INDIVIDUAL CLUB RECORDS

MOST GOALS IN A SEASON
John Aldridge 34 (League 30, FAC 1,League Cup 3) 1984-85.
3 goals twice = 6; 2 goals 8 times = 16; 1 goal 12 times = 12.

MOST GOALS IN A MATCH
4, Tony Jones v Newport County (5-1), Div.4, 22.9.1962.
4, Arthur Longbottom v Darlington (5-0), Div.4, 26.10.1963.
4, Bill Calder v Walsall (6-1), League Cup 1st Rnd. replay, 7.9.1964.
4, John Aldridge v Gillingham (6-0), League Cup 2nd Rnd., 24.9.1986.
4, Richard Hill v Walsall (a) (5-1), Div.2, 26.12.1988.
4, John Durnin v Luton Town (4-0), Div.1, 14.11.1992.

OLDEST PLAYER IN A LEAGUE MATCH
Colin Todd, 35 years 4 months.

YOUNGEST PLAYER IN A LEAGUE MATCH
Jason Seacole, 16 years 5 months

MOST CAPPED PLAYER
Jim Magilton (N. Ireland) 18

BEST PERFORMANCES

League: Div3 1983-84: **P** 46 **W** 28 **D** 11 **L** 7 **F** 91 **A** 50 **Pts** 95.
Div 2 1984-85: **P** 42 **W** 25 **D** 9 **L** 8 **F** 84 **A** 36 **Pts** 84.
(The only team to win succesive championships of Div.3 & 2.)
Highest: 18th Div 1 1983-84 & 1986-87.
FA Cup: 6th Rnd. 1963-64
League Cup: Winners in 1985-86, v Q.P.R. (3-0).

ADDITIONAL INFORMATION
Previous League: Southern League
Previous Names: Headington United (until 1960)

Club colours: Yellow shirts navy trim, navy shorts, navy socks with yellow trim.

Change colours: All white.

Reserves League: Avon Insurance Football Combination.

DIVISIONAL RECORD

	Played	Won	Drawn	Lost	For	Against	Points
Division 1/P	124	27	38	59	150	229	119
Division 2/1	746	245	201	300	889	973	831
Division 3/2	598	236	171	191	826	711	757
Division 4/3	138	50	43	45	216	178	143
Total	**1,606**	**558**	**453**	**595**	**2,099**	**2,091**	**1,850**

RECORDS AND STATISTICS

COMPETITIONS

Div.1/P	Div.2/1	Div.3/2	Div.4
1985-88	1968-76	1965-68	1962-65
	1984-85	1976-84	1965-70
	1988-94	1994-96	
	1996-		

HONOURS

Division 2	Division 3	Lge Cup
1984-85	1967-68	1985-86
	1983-84	

MOST APPEARANCES

John Shuker 529+5 (1962-77)

Year	League	FA Cup	Lge Cup	Ang/Ital
1962-63	18			
1963-64	12	4		
1964-65	11			
1965-66	33+1	2	1	
1966-67	24+2	3	1	
1967-68	36+1	3	2	
1968-69	34	2	1	
1969-70	34	2	5	
1970-71	42	5	2	
1971-72	41	1	3	
1972-73	36	2	3	3
1973-74	41	1	1	
1974-75	32	1	1	
1975-76	40	1	3	
1976-77	29+1	2	1	
	473+5	29	24	3

Previous holder: Ron Atkinson 425+1 (1962-71)

MOST GOALS IN A CAREER

John Aldridge 90 (1983-87)

Year	League	FA Cup	Lge Cup	FMC
1983-84	4			
1984-85	30	1	3	
1985-86	23	1	5	2
1986-87	15		6	
	72	2	14	2

Current leading goalscorer: Joey Beauchamp - 59 (1989-91, 10.95-98)

RECORD TRANSFER FEE RECEIVED

Amount	Club	Player	Date
£1,600,000	Leicester City	Matt Elliott	01/97
£1,100,000	Derby County	Dean Saunders	10/88
£825,000	Liverpool	Ray Houghton	10/87
£750,000	Liverpool	John Aldridge	1/87

RECORD TRANSFER FEE PAID

Amount	Club	Player	Date
£285,000	Gillingham	Colin Grenall	2/88
£275,000	Swansea	Andrew Melville	7/90*
£250,000	Liverpool	John Durnin	2/89
£200,000	Man. City	Paul Simpson	10/88

*League Tribunal ordered further sums to Swansea City on sale in 8/93 of Andrew Melville to Sunderland. These figures have not been disclosed.

MANAGERS

Name	Seasons	Best	Worst
A Turner	1959-69	22(2)	18(4)
R Saunders	1969	20(2)	20(2)
G Summers	1969-75	8(2)	17(2)
M Brown	1975-79	20(2)	18(3)
W Asprey	1979-80	17(3)	17(3)
R Barry (caretaker)	1980	-	-
I Greaves	1980-82	5(3)	14(3)
J Smith	1982-85	1(2)	5(3)
M Evans	1985-88	18(1)	18(1)
M Lawrenson	1988	21(1)	8(2)
B Horton	1988-93	10(2)	21(2)
Denis Smith	1993-97	17 (1)	7 (2)
M. Crosby (caretaker)	1997-98	-	-
Malcolm Shotton	1998-	12 (1)	12 (1)

LONGEST LEAGUE RUNS

of undefeated matches:	20 (17.3.1984 - 29.9.1984)	of league matches w/out a win:	27 (14.11.1987 - 27.8.1988)
of undefeated home matches:	20 (3.10.1964 - 25.8.1965)	of undefeated away matches:	12 (28.2.1984 - 22.9.1984)
without home win:	13 (21.11.1987 - 2.5.1988)	without an away win:	24 (14.9.1974 - 27.9.1975)
of league wins:	6 (14.1.67-26.2.67, 16.3.68-6.4.68, 4.12.82-3.1.83)	of home wins:	10 (15.9.1984 - 29.12.1984)
of league defeats:	7 (4.5.1991 - 7.9.1991)	of away wins:	4 (4.12.1982 - 3.1.1983, 7.5.1984 - 22.9.1984)

OXFORD UNITED

PLAYERS NAME Honours	Ht	Wt	Birthdate	Birthplace Transfers	Contract Date	Clubs	League	L/Cup	FA Cup	Other	Lge	L/C	FAC	Oth
G O A L K E E P E R														
Jackson Elliot	6.1	13	8/27/79	Swindon	7/2/96	Oxford United	6	3						
Whitehead Philip M	6.3	13.7	12/17/69	Halifax	7/1/88	Halifax Town	42	2	4	4				
				£60000	3/9/90	Barnsley	16							
				Loan	3/7/91	Halifax Town	9							
				Loan	11/29/91	Scunthorpe United	8			2				
				Loan	9/4/92	Scunthorpe United	8	2						
				Loan	11/19/92	Bradford City	6			4				
				£75000	11/1/93	Oxford United	185	13	13	3				
D E F E N C E														
Gilchrist Philip A	6		11.12 8/25/73	Stockton-on-T	12/5/90	Nottingham Forest								
				Free	1/10/92	Middlesbrough								
				Free	11/27/92	Hartlepool United	77+5	4+1	4	5				
				£100000	2/17/95	Oxford United	132+3	14	7	3	8			
Powell Paul						Oxford United	12+12	0+1	1	0+2	1			
Robinson Leslie	5.8	11.1	3/1/67	Shirebrook		Chesterfield								
				Free	10/6/84	Mansfield Town	11+4			1				
					11/27/86	Stockport County	67	2	4	4	3			
				£10000	3/24/88	Doncaster Rovers	82	4	5	5	12		1	1
				£150000	3/19/90	Oxford United	287+5	31	14+1	10	3	3		
Rose Andrew M	5.9	10.3	8/9/78	Ascot	7/2/97	Oxford United (T)	0+1							
Whelan Phil E: u21.4.	6.4	14.1	3/7/72	Stockport	7/2/90	Ipswich Town	64+5	6+1	2+1	1	2			
				£300000	4/12/95	Middlesbrough	18+4	5	3		1			
				Free	7/18/97	Oxford United	6+2	1						
M I D F I E L D														
Beauchamp Joey FLge.u18.1.	5.11	11.1	3/13/71	Oxford	5/16/89	Oxford United	117+7	6+1	8	5+1	20	2	3	
				Loan	10/30/91	Swansea City	5		1		2			
				£1000000	6/22/94	West Ham United								
				£850000	6/22/94	Swindon Town	38+4	7+1	2	4	3			
				£300000	10/12/95	Oxford United	104+16	14	4+2	0+2	27	6	1	
Cook James S	5.11	10.9	8/2/79	Oxford	7/2/97	Oxford United (T)	9+11		0+1		2			
Gray Martin D	5.9	10.11	8/17/71	Stockton	2/1/90	Sunderland	42+15	5+1	0+2	3+1	1			
				Loan	1/9/91	Solihull	3+2			1				
				Loan	10/20/95	Fulham								
				£100000	3/28/96	Oxford United	74+6	8	2		4			
Hill Danny E: U21.4, Y, S.	5.9	11.03	01/10/74	Enfield	09/09/92	Tottenham Hotspur	4+6	0+2						
				Loan	24/11/95	Birmingham City	5	2						
				Loan	15/02/96	Watford	1							
				Loan	2/19/98	Cardiff City	7							
				Free	7/1/98	Oxford United								
Lewis Michael E: Y.7.	5.6	10.6	2/15/65	Birmingham	2/18/82	WBA	22+2	4+1	4					
				£25000	11/16/84	Derby County	37+6	2	0+1	4	1			
					8/25/88	Oxford United	276+24	15+2	12+1	11+1	7			
Murphy Matthew S	5.11	11.5	8/20/71	Northampton		Corby								
				£20000	2/12/93	Oxford United	52+64	2+8	2+3	3+3	17	2		3
				Loan	12/12/97	Scunthorpe United	1+2							
Remy Christophe	5.9	12.1	8/6/71		7/25/97	Oxford United	13+3	4						
Smith David C	5.8	11.2	12/26/70	Liverpool	7/4/89	Norwich City	13+5		2+1	1+1				
				£100000	7/5/94	Oxford United	170+2	22	9	7	2	1		
Wilsterman Brian H	6.1	12.8	11/19/66	Surinam		Beerschot								
				£200000	2/28/97	Oxford United	16+9	1						
Wright Anthony A	5.7	10.11	9/1/79	Swansea	4/17/98	Oxford United (T)	0+1							

O R W A R D														
anger Nicholas L	5.8	10.6	2/25/71	Southampton	4/25/89	Southampton	18+37	2+2	0+2	1	8	3		
				£250000	10/4/94	Oldham Athletic	44+20	6	2+1	0+1	10	1		
				Free	7/25/97	Oxford United	17+10	4+1			3	1		
olland Robert W	5.9	10.13	9/16/79	Swansea	10/12/97	Oxford United (T)	0+2							
rancis Kevin	6.7	15.08	12/6/67	Birmingham		Mile Oak Rovers								
iv.2'95. AMC'95.				Free	2/2/89	Derby County	0+10	1+2	1+2	0+1			1	
				£45000	2/21/91	Stockport County	131+4	8	9	25	76	4	6	18
				£800000	1/20/95	Birmingham City	32+39	6+5	3+3	4	13	5	2	1
				£100000	2/16/98	Oxford United	15				7			
Iarsh Simon T	5.11	11.2	1/29/77	Ealing	11/22/94	Oxford United	29+6	4+2	2	2	1			
homson Andy	5.1	10.07	01/04/71	Motherwell		Queen of the South								
				£250000	04/07/94	Southend United	87+35	4+1	3+2	1+2	28			
				Free	7/1/98	Oxford United								
Veatherstone Simon	5.11	11	1/26/80	Reading	3/27/97	Oxford United	2+10				1			
Vindass Dean	5.9	12.3	4/1/69	Hull		North Ferriby Utd								
					10/24/91	Hull City	173+3	11	7	12	57	4		3
					10/95	Aberdeen								
				£475000	7/10/98	Oxford United								

THE MANAGER
MALCOLM SHOTTON

Date of Birth . . . . 16th February 1957.
Place of Birth. . . . . Newcastle upon Tyne.
Date of Appointment . . . . 26th January 1998.

PREVIOUS CLUBS
As Manager. . . . . None.
As Coach . . . . Ayr United, Barnsley.
As a Player . . . . Leicester City, Nuneaton Borough, Oxford United, Portsmouth,
. . . . Huddersfield, Barnsley, Hull City, Ayr United, Barnsley.

HONOURS
As a Manager
None.

As a Player
Oxford United: League Cup 1986. Division 3(2) 1984. Division 2(1) 1985.

MANOR GROUND
London Road, Headington, Oxford OX3 7RS

Capacity..9,572
Standing..6,769
Seating..2,803

First game..1.10.1898
First floodlit game..v Banbury, 18.12.1950(first club to stage a floodlit game)
ATTENDANCES
Highest..22,750 v Preston North End, FA Cup 6th Round, 29.2.1964.
Lowest ....1,055 v Portsmouth, ZDS Cup, 12.12.1990.

OTHER GROUNDS..None.

HOW TO GET TO THE GROUND

From the North: From North (M40) leave at junction 9. Follow signs for A34 to Oxford. Take slip road A44 marked Witney, Woodstock. At roundabout take first exit (Pear Tree). Follow to next roundabout A44 junction with A40 Woodstock Road, take second exit marked A40 London. Down to next roundabout (Banbury Road), take second exit on to Northern by-pass. Cars should take next left turn at slip road marked New Marston half-a-mile and JR Hospital 1 mile. (Coaches should follow diversions to avoid weak bridge, next roundabout A40, Green Road, take fifth exit, follow signs for A40 junction with (B4105) Marston). Down to mini-roundabout turn left. Straight up Headley Way, coaches should take second junction right marked Franklin Road which leads into coach park.

From South: A34 by-pass to junction A44 Pear Tree. Follow directions as North.

From the East: Cars and coaches should follow coach diversion directions as from Green Road roundabout.

From the West: Take A34 following signs to M40. Take exit A44 marked Woodstock, take third exit Pear Tree, follow as North.

Car Parking: Street parking near ground. Take care for matchday parking restrictions.
Nearest Railway Station: Oxford (01865 722 333)

HOW TO GET TO THE GROUND

Club switchboard 01865 761 503
Club fax number 01865 741 820
Club shop 01865 761 503
Ticket Office............ 01865 761 503

Marketing Department 01865 761503
Internet address .... http:www.oufc.co.uk
Clubline.............. 0891 44 00 55*

*Calls cost 50p per minute at all times. Call costings correct at time of going to press.

MATCHDAY PROGRAMME

Programme Editor .... Ian Davies.

Number of pages .... 28 full colour.

Price .... £1.70.

Subscriptions .... Apply to club.

Local Newspapers
.... Oxford Mail, Oxford Times.

Local Radio Stations
.... Thames Valley FM, Fox FM.

MATCHDAY TICKET PRICES

	NON MEMBERS PRICE	MEMBERS IN ADVANCE
Terrace		
Adult	£11.00	£9.50
Under 16/Over 65	£6.50	£5.50
Seats		
Adult	£14.00	£12.50
Under 16/Over 65	£9.50	£8.00
Covered Family Seats		
Adult	£12.00	£10.50
Over 65	£7.50	£6.00
Under 16	£6.50	£5.00
Uncovered Family Seats		
Adult	£11.00	£9.50
Over 65	£7.00	£5.50
Under 16	£6.00	£4.50
Manor Executive Club Seats		
Adult	£25.00	£17.00
Under 16/Over 65	£16.00	£11.00

PORT VALE
(The Valiants)
NATIONWIDE LEAGUE DIVISION 1
SPONSORED BY: TUNSTALL ASSURANCE LTD.

1998/99 - Back Row (L R): Allen Tankard, Liam Burns, Neil Aspin, Mark Snijders, Rogier Koordes, Anthony Gardner, George O'Callaghan, Lee Mills, Dave Barnet, Michael Walsh, Stewart Talbot. **Middle Row:** Alan Rankin (Physio), Jim Cooper (Comm. Officer), Gareth Ainsworth, Richard Eyre, Paul Musselwhite, Kevin Pilkington, Jan Jansson, Martin Foyle, Mark Grew (Yth. team coach), Stan Nicholls (Kit Man.). **Front Row:** Matthew Carragher, Tony Naylor, Brian McGlinchey, Bill Dearden (1st team coach), John rudge (Manager), Ian Bogie, Wayne Corden, John MqQuade.

PORT VALE
FORMED IN 1876
TURNED PROFESSIONAL IN 1885
LTD COMPANY IN 1911

PRESIDENT: J Burgess
CHAIRMAN: W T Bell, L.A.E., MIMI

DIRECTORS
I McPherson, A Belfield,
S Plant (Associate Director)
SECRETARY
F W Lodey (01782 814134)
MARKETING MANAGER
N Hughes (01782 835524)

MANAGER: John Rudge
ASSISTANT MANAGER: Bill Dearden

YOUTH TEAM MANAGER
Mark Grew
PHYSIOTHERAPIST
R Carter

STATISTICIAN FOR THE DIRECTORY
Philip Sherwin

A season that took Vale supporters through the full range of emotions began with high hopes and ended with the elation of avoiding relegation on the last day of the campaign.

Pre-season optimism took an early dent with just one win from the opening six games, including an embarrassing Coca-Cola exit against York City, but then matters began to improve. The arrival of club record signing Gareth Ainsworth, to replace the transferred Jon McCarthy, gave the club a lift and by early November the team occupied eighh place after successive away wins at Manchester City and Tranmere.

Unfortunately the wheels then came off somewhat co-incidentally when defensive king-pin Neil Aspin was missing through injury. Seven successive league defeats, the clubs worst run since 1957, and a run of only one goal scored in eight games plunged them to the fringe of the relegation zone. To add to their woes they faced a daunting prospect in the FA Cup with a visit to Arsenal in the Third Round but the return of Aspin helped to trigger off an inspired performance that yielded a goalless draw.

The replay also ended all square after extra-time, 1-1, and after being ahead in the penalty shoot-out Vale succumbed 4-3, but in the knowledge that they took the double winners-elect all the way.

The throwing away of a 2-0 lead at fellow strugglers Bury kept the alarm bells ringing and by the end of February they had fallen to the bottom of the table. A goalless draw against local rivals Stoke City (next to bottom) and a home defeat by Tranmere Rovers seemed to confirm that the writing was on the wall. But then hope sprang eternal.

Victory over Reading and Manchester City inspired confidence and the arrival of Ray Graydon as coach helped behind the scenes. Dave Barnett also came on loan from Dunfermline to help shore up the defence and a 3-0 win over Oxford United meant that the escape was almost complete. Unfortunately three successive defeats meant that nothing less than victory in the final game at Huddersfield would save them from the trapdoor. As it turned out an early goal paved the way for a 4-0 victory, the team's fourth successive victory at the McAlpine Stadium, and everyone can now look forward to a fifth consecutive season at this level for the first time since the 1930s.

Gareth Ainsworth was a runaway winner of the Supporters 'Player of the Year' award and although not finishing as top scorer for the first time (Lee Mills took that honour) Tony Naylor won Sky TVs Nationwide 'goal of the season' award for his strike against Sunderland.

The imminent completion of the new stand on the Lorne Street side of the ground should enable Vale Park to have an all seater capacity of around 23,000.

Phil Sherwin.

PORT VALE

Division 1   :19th   FA CUP: 3rd Round   LC CUP: 1st Round

M	DATE	COMP.	VEN	OPPONENTS	RESULT	H/T	LP	GOAL SCORERS/GOAL TIMES	ATT.
1	A 09	FL	H	Nottingham Forest	L 0-1	0-1	21		12533
2	12	CC 1/1	H	York City	L 1-2	1-1		Mills 24	2749
3	15	FL	A	Portsmouth	L 1-3	1-2	22	Talbot 43	(10605)
4	23	FL	H	Sunderland	W 3-1	2-0	15	Mills 2, Naylor 39, 72	8290
5	26	CC 1/2	A	York City	D 1-1	0-1		Mills 89	(3195)
6	S 03	FL	A	Wolverhampton Wand	D 1-1	0-0	18	Foyle 82	(21524)
7	09	FL	H	Stockport County	W 2-1	2-1	11	Mills 1, 36	6615
8	13	FL	A	Norwich City	L 0-1	0-0	15		(11269)
9	16	FL	A	Crewe Alexandra	W 1-0	0-0	9	Mills 55	(5519)
10	20	FL	H	Bury	D 1-1	1-0	11	Ainsworth 7	6781
11	27	FL	H	Queens Park Rangers	W 2-0	2-0	8	Snijders 17, Naylor 20	7197
12	O 04	FL	A	Swindon Town	L 2-4	1-0	9	Glover 36, Foyle 86	(8048)
13	12	FL	A	Stoke City	L 1-2	1-2	11	Naylor 21	(20125)
14	18	FL	H	Bradford City	D 0-0	0-0	14		7148
15	21	FL	H	Huddersfield Town	W 4-1	1-0	7	Talbot 47, Ainsworth 73, Naylor 83, Horne 26 (OG)	5244
16	25	FL	A	Middlesbrough	L 1-2	0-1	13	Foyle 90	(30096)
17	N 01	FL	H	Reading	D 0-0	0-0	14		6569
18	04	FL	A	Manchester City	W 3-2	2-2	11	Snijders 17, Talbot 45, Naylor 50	(24554)
19	08	FL	A	Tranmere Rovers	W 2-1	1-0	7	Naylor 14, 66	(7063)
20	15	FL	H	West Bromwich Albion	L 1-2	0-0	11	Mills 48	11124
21	22	FL	H	Sheffield United	D 0-0	0-0	9		8017
22	29	FL	A	Oxford United	L 0-2	0-1	12		(5762)
23	D 06	FL	H	Birmingham City	L 0-1	0-1	13		7509
24	13	FL	A	Charlton Athletic	L 0-1	0-0	14		(11077)
25	20	FL	H	Ipswich Town	L 1-3	0-3	17	Foyle 50	5784
26	26	FL	A	Stockport County	L 0-3	0-0	18		(10003)
27	28	FL	H	Wolverhampton Wand	L 0-2	0-1	18		10898
28	J 03	FAC 3	A	Arsenal	D 0-0	0-0			(37471)
29	10	FL	A	Nottingham Forest	L 1-2	1-1	20	Mills 17	(17639)
30	14	FAC 3R	H	Arsenal	D 1-1	0-0		Corden 112	14964
31	17	FL	H	Portsmouth	W 2-1	1-1	18	Talbot 29, Mills 56	6028
32	24	FL	H	Crewe Alexandra	L 2-3	1-3	19	Naylor 1, Porter 74 (pen)	10571
33	31	FL	A	Sunderland	L 2-4	1-3	20	Talbot 36, Jansson 90	(39258)
34	F 06	FL	A	Bury	D 2-2	2-1	20	Mills 10, Bogie 17	(5285)
35	14	FL	H	Norwich City	D 2-2	1-0	21	Mills 34, 85	6664
36	17	FL	H	Swindon Town	L 0-1	0-1	21		5925
37	21	FL	A	Queens Park Rangers	W 1-0	1-0	21	Mills 24	(14198)
38	24	FL	A	Bradford City	L 1-2	1-1	21	Foyle 28	(13293)
39	M 01	FL	H	Stoke City	D 0-0	0-0	24		13853
40	04	FL	H	Tranmere Rovers	L 0-1	0-0	24		5465
41	07	FL	A	Reading	W 3-0	2-0	23	Mills 6, Talbot 19, Jansson 82	(7139)
42	14	FL	H	Manchester City	W 2-1	1-0	19	Foyle 13, Ainsworth 73	13122
43	21	FL	A	West Bromwich Albion	D 2-2	0-1	20	Jansson 69, Foyle 90	(14242)
44	28	FL	A	Sheffield United	L 1-2	0-0	20	Corden 90	(15860)
45	A 04	FL	H	Oxford United	W 3-0	2-0	18	Naylor 42, Mills 42, Ainsworth 84	6524
46	11	FL	A	Birmingham City	D 1-1	0-0	17	Ainsworth 58	(17193)
47	13	FL	H	Charlton Athletic	L 0-1	0-0	19		9973
48	18	FL	A	Ipswich Town	L 1-5	0-3	20	Barnett 65	(16205)
49	24	FL	H	Middlesbrough	L 0-1	0-1	20		12096
50	M 03	FL	A	Huddersfield Town	W 4-0	2-0	19	Foyle 2, Jansson 24, 60, Mills 79	(15610)

Best Home League Attendance: 13853 V Stoke City   Smallest :5244 V Huddersfield Town   Average :8432

Goal Scorers:

FL	(56)	Mills 14, Naylor 10, Foyle 8, Talbot 6, Ainsworth 5, Jansson 5, Snijders 2, Barnett 1, Bogie 1, Corden 1, Glover 1, Porter 1, Opponents 1
CC	(2)	Mills 2
FAC	(1)	Corden 1

	(M) Ainsworth	(D) Aspin	(D) Barnett	(D) Beesley	(M) Bogie	(M) Burns	(D) Carragher	(M) Corden	(M) Eyre	(F) Foyle	(D) Glover	(D) Griffiths	(D) Hill	(M) Jansson	(M) Koordes	(D) Mahorn	(M) McCarthy	(F) Mills	(G) Musselwhite	(F) Naylor	(M) Porter	(D) Snijders	(D) Stokes	(M) Talbot	(D) Tankard	(G) Van Heusden	Player	No
		X						X		S2	X		X	S1			X	X	X	X	X		S	S	X	X	P.R. Richards	1
		X						X		S1	X		X	X			X	X	X	X	S1			X	X	S	A R Leake	2
			S					X			X		X	X	X		X	X		S1	X		S2	X	X		R J Harris	3
		X	S1					X		S3	X		X				X	X	X	X	X		S2	X	X		A P D'Urso	4
		X			X			X		S1			X	S2			X	X	X	X			X	X	X	S	B Coddington	5
		X						X		S2			X	S1			X	X	X	X			S	X	X		A N Butler	6
		X	S					X					X	S1			X	X	X	S	X	X		X	X		G Laws	7
	S1	X	S					X					X	X			X	X	X	X	X	S		X	X		S J Baines	8
	X	X	X					X					X	S2			X	X	X	S	S1	X		X	X		K A Leach	9
	X	X	X		S			X					X	S			X	X	X	X	S			X	X		T Jones	10
	X	X	X					X		S2			X	S3	X			X	X	X	S1	X	S3	X	X		K Wolstenholme	11
	X	X	X					S2		S3	X			X		X		X	X	X	S1	X		X	X		S G Bennett	12
	X	X	S3					S1		S2			X			X		X	X	X	S1	X		X	X		C R Wilkes	13
	X	X	X		X		S	S2						S			X	X	X	X	S1	X		X	X		P S Danson	14
	X	X	X		X		X	S						S			X	X	X	X	X			X	X		M C Bailey	15
	X	X	X		X		X	S2						S1	S3			X	X	X	X			X	X		S W Mathieson	16
	X	X	X		X		X	X						S2				X	X	S1	S	X		X	X		G Cain	17
	X	X	S1		X		X	S2						X			S3	X	X	X	X			X	X		M J Brandwood	18
	X	X	X		X		S					S1	X	X			S2	X	X	X	S1			X			K M Lynch	19
	X	X			X		S3	S2						X	X			X	X	X	S1	X		X	X		R D Furnandiz	20
	X	X	X		X		S3	S1						X				X	X	X	S2	X		X	X		D Pugh	21
	X	X1	X		X		X2	S2					S1	S				X	X	X2	X			X	X		M Fletcher	22
	X1		X		X		X2	X		X		X					X	X	X	S1	X		X	X	X		E Lomas	23
	X		X		X1	S	S	X		X		X	S1				X	X	X	X	X		X	X	X		M R Halsey	24
	X		X		X	S3	X			S2		X2					X	X	S1	X1	X		X	X	X3		T Heilbron	25
	X		X	X		S2	X			X	X1	X2				S		X	X	S1	X		X	X		F G Stretton	26
	X		X	X		X2	S1			X	X1	X						X	X	X1	X	S		X	X		P Taylor	27
	X	X			X		X	S1	S		X	S		X	S		S	X	X1	X	X			X	X	S	P E Alcock	28
	S1	X		X	X3		S3	S2			X						X	X	X2	X	X1			X	X		A P D'Urso	29
	X	X			X		X	S2	S		X						S1	X1	X1	X	X	S	X2	X	X	S	N S Barry	30
	X	X		S	X		X	S1			X			X				X	X1	X	X		S	X	X		M C Bailey	31
	X	X		X	S3		X3	S2	S1	X							X2	X	X	X	X	X1		X			P R Richards	32
	X	X			X2	S1	X	X3		X		X1		S3			S2	X	X	X	X			X			M S Pike	33
	X	X			X		X	S		S		X1					X	X	X	X	X				X		B Coddington	34
	X	X3			X1			S1		S2	S3	X		X			X	X	X2	X	X			X			A G Wiley	35
	X				S3		X	S		X2	X		X	X3				X		S2	X	X		X1	X	X	M D Messias	36
	X				S		S	X	S	X	X		X	X			X		X	S	X			X	X	X	A N Butler	37
	X2				S1		X	S3		X	X		X	X3			X		S2	X	X		X1	X	X		W C Burns	38
	X				X		X	S		X	X		X	X			X2		S2	X	S1		X1	X	X		P Rejer	39
	X				X		X2	S1		X	X		X	X1			X		S2	X	S			X	X		A R Leake	40
	X				X		X	S		X1	X		X	X			X		S1	X	S2			X			M R Halsey	41
	X	S2			X		X	S1		X	X		X	X			X1	X		X			S	X			R D Furnandiz	42
		X			X		X1	S1		X	X		X	X	X2	X	S	S2	X	X				X	X		T Heilbron	43
	X	X			X		X	S2		X	X		X	X			X	X	S3	S1		X2	X1				S G Bennett	44
	X	X			X	X	S			X			X		S		X	X	X	S1			X1	X			K M Lynch	45
	X	X			X	X	S			S2	X		X1				X	X	X2	S			X	X			G Cain	46
	X	X			X	X1	S1			S2	X		X				X	X	X2	S			X	X			E K Wolstenholme	47
	X	X			X	S		S1		S1	X		X	X2			X	X	X1	S2			X	X			P Taylor	48
	X	X			X	S		X		S2	X1		X	X			X	X	S2	X1			X	X2			C R Wilkes	49
	X	X			X	S		X		X	X		X	X			X	X	S	S1			X1	X			F G Stretton	50
FL Appearances	38	26	8	5	32		26	19		19	21	3	25	22	9		4	39	41	28	28	22	5	42	39	5		
FL Sub Appearances	2		1		6	1		14	1	20	4		2	11	1	1		3		10	13	2	3					
CC Appearances		2			1			2		0+2	1		2	1+1			2	2	2	2	0+1		1	2	2			
FAC Appearances	2	2			2			2		0+2			2					0+1	2	2	2			2	2			

273

PORT VALE

BIGGEST VICTORIES
League: 9-1 v Chesterfield, Division 2, 24.9.1932
8-0 v Gateshead, Division 4, 26.12.1958
F.A. Cup: 8-2 v Alfreton (a), 6th Qual. Rnd, 13.12.1924.
League Cup: 5-1 v Wrexham, Rnd 1, 13.9.1983

BIGGEST DEFEATS
League: 0-10 v Sheffield United, Division 2, 10.12.1892
0-10 v Notts County, Division 2, 26.2.1895
F.A. Cup: 0-7 v Small Heath, 5th Qual. Round, 10.12.1898
League Cup: 0-4 v Northampton Town, Rnd 1, 2.9.1987

MOST POINTS
3 points a win: 89, Division 2, 1992-93
2 points a win: 69, Division 3N, 1953-54

MOST GOALS
110, 1958-59 (Division 4)
Steele 23, Wilkinson 21, Barnett 20, Poole 17, Cunliffe 14, Jackson 8, Kinsey3, Hall 2, Sproson 1, og 1.

MOST LEAGUE GOALS CONCEDED
106, Division 2, 1935-36

MOST GOALS IN A SEASON
Wilf Kirkham (1926-27) 38 League, 3 FA Cup, Total 41

MOST FIRST CLASS MATCHES IN A SEASON
62, 1995-96 (46 League, 6 FA Cup, 2 League Cup, 8 Anglo/Italian).

MOST LEAGUE WINS
30, Division 3N, 1929-30

MOST LEAGUE DRAWS
20, Division 3, 1977-78

MOST LEAGUE DEFEATS
28, Division 2, 1956-57
MOST GOALS IN A MATCH

6. Stewart Littlewood v Chesterfield, Division 2, 24.9.1932 (9-1)

OLDEST PLAYER
Tom Holford, 46 yrs 68 days, 5.4.1924

YOUNGEST PLAYER
Malcolm McKenzie, 15yrs 347 days, 12.4.1965

MOST CAPPED PLAYER
Sammy Morgan (Northern Ireland) 7
League: 1953-54: Matches played 46, Won 26, Drawn 17, Lost 3,

Goals for 74,Goals against 21, Points 69. 1st in Division 3N.

Highest: 5th Division 2, 1930-31.

F.A. Cup: 1953-54: 1st rnd. Darlington 3-1; 2nd rnd. Southport 1-1, 2-0; 3rd rnd. Queens Park Rangers 1-0; 4th rnd. Cardiff City 2-0; 5th rnd. Blackpool 2-0; 6th rnd. Leyton Orient 1-0; Semi-Final West Bromwich Albion 1-2.

League Cup: 1991-92: 1st rnd. Bye, 2nd rnd. Notts County 2-1, 2-3; 3rd rnd.Liverpool 2-2, 1-4.
1996-97: 1st rnd. Crewe 1-0, 5-1. 2nd rnd. Carlisle 1-0, 2-2.
3rd rnd. Oxford 0-0, 0-2.
2nd rnd. 1960-61; 1962-63; 1963-64; 1967-68; 1972-73; 1981-82; 1983-84; 1984-85; 1985-86; 1986-87; 1988-89; 1989-90; 1990-91; 1994-95.

ADDITIONAL INFORMATION
Previous Leagues: Midland League
Previous Name: Burslem Port Vale 1884-1909

Club colours: White shirts, black shorts.
Change colours: All yellow with black trim.

Reserves League: Pontins Central League Division 1
Youth League: Midland Melville Youth League.

DIVISIONAL RECORD							
	Played	Won	Drawn	Lost	For	Against	Points
Division 2/1	1,236	517	345	674	2,112	2,561	1,479
Division 3/2	920	336	255	329	1,240	1,237	1,047
Division 3(N)	218	105	66	47	367	230	276
Division 3(S)	348	122	89	137	458	460	333
Division 4	598	220	185	193	802	715	704
Total	**3,620**	**1,300**	**940**	**1,380**	**4,979**	**5,203**	**3,839**
(Excluding Leeds City results 1919-20)							

RECORDS AND STATISTICS

COMPETITIONS

Div.2/1	Div.3(N)	Div.3(S)	Div.3/2	Div.4
1892-96	1929-30	1938-52	1959-65	1958-59
1898-07	1936-38	1957-58	1970-78	1965-70
1919-29	1952-54		1983-84	1978-83
1930-36			1986-89	1984-86
1954-57			1992-94	
1989-92				
1994-				

HONOURS

Division 3(N)	Division 4	AGT
1929-30	1958-59	1992-93
1953-54		

MOST APPEARANCES

Roy Sproson 831+5 (1950-72)

Year	League	FA Cup	Lge Cup
1950-51	10		
1951-52	28		
1952053	45	2	
1953-54	45	8	
1954-55	42	3	
1955-56	42	2	
1956-57	39	2	
1957-58	37	3	
1958-59	21	1	
1959-60	41	6	
1960-61	43	3	3
1961-62	46	7	1
1962-63	42	4	1
1963-64	46	5	1
1964-65	45	2	1
1965-66	28+2	4	
1966-67	30+1	2	1
1967-68	32	1	1
1968-69	41+1	5	
1969-70	46	5	1
1970-71	5+1		1
1971-72	1		
	755+5	65	11

MOST GOALS IN A CAREER

Wilf Kirkham - 164 (1923-29 & 1931-33)

Year	League	FA Cup
1923-24	7	
1924-25	26	7
1925-26	35	
1926-27	38	3
1927-28	13	1
1928-29	15	
1931-32	4	
1932-33	15	
Total	153	11

Current leading goalscorer: Martin Foyle - 92 (1991-98)

MANAGERS

Name	Seasons	Best	Worst
T Clare	1905-06	17(2)	17(2)
S Gleaves	1906-07	16(2)	16(2)
A Walker	1911-13		
H Myatt	1913-14		
T Holford	1914-17		
J Cameron	1918-19		
J Schofield	1919-29	8(2)	21(2)
T Morgan	1929-32	5(2)	1(3N)
T Holford	1932-36	8(2)	21(2)
W Cresswell	1936-37	11(3N)	11(3N)
T Morgan	1937-39	15(3N)	18(3S)
W Frith	1944-46		
G Hodgson	1946-51	8(3S)	13(3S)
I Powell	1951		
F Steele	1951-57	12(2)	13(3S)
N Low	1957-62	7(3)	15(3S)
F Steele	1962-65	3(3)	22(3)
J Mudie	1965-67	13(4)	19(4)
S Matthews	1967-68	18(4)	18(4)
G Lee	1968-74	6(3)	13(4)
R Sproson	1974-77	6(3)	19(3)
C Harper	1977		
R Smith	1977-78	21(3)	21(3)
D Butler	1978-79	16(4)	16(4)
A Bloor	1979		
J McGrath	1979-83	23(3)	20(4)
J Rudge	1983-	8(1)	12(4)

RECORD TRANSFER FEE RECEIVED

Amount	Club	Player	Date
£1,500,000	Birmingham	Jon McCarthy	09/97
£1,000,000	Sheffield Wed.	Ian Taylor	08/94
£925,000	Norwich City	Darren Beckford	6/91
£350,000	Charlton Athletic	Andy Jones	8/87

RECORD TRANSFER FEE PAID

Amount	Club	Player	Date
£500,000	Lincoln City	Gareth Ainsworth	09/97
£450,000	York City	Jon McCarthy	07/95
£375,000	Oxford United	Martin Foyle	6/91
£200,000	Middlesbrough	Dean Glover	2/89

LONGEST LEAGUE RUNS

of undefeated matches:	19 (5.5.1969 - 8.11.1969)	of league matches w/out a win:	17 (7.12.1991 - 21.03.1992)
of undefeated home matches:	43 (20.12.1952 - 18.9.1954)	of undefeated away matches:	12 (16.9.1953 - 9.1.1954)
without home win:	13 (28.3.1978 - 21.10.1978)	without an away win:	24 (2.12.1893 - 23.3.1895)
of league wins:	8 (8.4.1893 - 30.9.1893)	of home wins:	12 (9.2.1952 - 8.9.1952, 31.8.1953 - 25.12.1953)
of league defeats:	9 (9.3.1957 - 20.4.1957)	of away wins:	5 (20.3.1993 - 24.4.1993)

PORT VALE

PLAYERS NAME Honours	Ht	Wt	Birthdate	Birthplace Transfers	Contract Date	Clubs	League	L/Cup	FA Cup	Other	Lge	L/C	FAC	Oth
G O A L K E E P E R														
Musselwhite Paul	6.2	12.9	12/22/68	Portsmouth	12/1/86	Portsmouth								
AGT'93				Free	3/21/88	Scunthorpe United	132	11	7	13				
				£20000	7/30/92	Port Vale	244	12	20	19				
Pilkington Kevin W	6	12	08/03/74	Hitchin	06/07/92	Manchester United	4+2	1	1					
ESFAu18.1; FAYC'92				Loan	02/02/96	Rochdale	6							
				Loan	22/01/97	Rotherham United	17							
				Free	7/1/98	Port Vale								
D E F E N C E														
Aspin Neil	6	12.8	4/12/65	Gateshead	10/6/82	Leeds United	203+4	9	17	11	5	1		
AGT'93				£200000	7/28/89	Port Vale	315+3	19	23	18	3			
Burns Liam	6.1	12.9	10/30/78	Belfadt	7/9/97	Port Vale (T)	0+1							
Carragher Matthew	5.9	10.7	1/14/76	Liverpool	11/25/93	Wigan Athletic	102+17	6+1	10+1	7+1		1	2	
DIV3 96/97				Free	7/3/97	Port Vale	25							
Snijders Mark W	6.1	13.12	3/12/72	Alkmaar		AZ Alkmaar								
				Free	9/8/97	Port Vale	22+2		2		2			
Tankard Allen	5.11	11.7	5/21/69	Fleet	5/27/87	Southampton	5			2				
				Free	7/4/88	Wigan Athletic	205+4	15	13	20	4	1		
				£87500	7/26/93	Port Vale	163+5	16	13	8+1	2		1	
Walsh Michael	6	12.4	8/5/77	Rotherham	8/1/94	Scunthorpe United	94+9	4	9	5	1			
				£100000	7/1/98	Port Vale								
M I D F I E L D														
Ainsworth Gareth	5.11	12.5	5/10/73	Blackburn	9/12/97	Port Vale	37+2		2		5			
Bogie Ian	5.7	10.2	12/6/67	Newcastle	12/18/85	Newcastle United	7+7	0+1	1+2	3				1
					2/9/89	Preston North End	67+12	3+1	3	4+1	12			
				£145000	8/16/91	Millwall	44+7	1	2	3	1			
				£50000	3/23/93	Port Vale	94+16	7	7+2	8	7	1	2	
				£100000	10/14/93	Leyton Orient	62+3	2	2	8+1	5			
Corden S Wayne	5.9	10.6	11/1/75	Leek	7/20/94	Port Vale	26+21	3	2		1		1	
Eyre Richard P	5.11	11.7	9/15/76	Poynton	7/1/95	Port Vale	0+1							
Jansson Jan	5.11	11.2	1/26/68	Kalmar		Norrkoping								
				Loan	11/4/96	Port Vale	10+1		1		1			
					7/16/97	Port Vale	22+11	1+1			6			
Koordes Rogier	6.1	12.11	6/13/72	Holland	2/14/97	Port Vale	16+7							
McGlinchey Brian	5.7	10.2	10/26/77	Derry		Manchester City (T)								
				Free	7/1/98	Port Vale								
Talbot Stewart	6	13	6/14/73	Birmingham	8/10/94	Port Vale	76+21	2+3	4+1	2+3	10			1
F O R W A R D														
Beadle Peter	6.1	11.12	5/13/72	London	5/5/90	Gillingham	42+25	2+4	1+1	1	14	2		
				£300000	6/4/92	Tottenham Hotspur								
				Loan	3/25/93	Bournemouth	9				2			
				Loan	3/4/94	Southend United	8				1			
					9/12/94	Watford	9+11				1			
				£30000	11/17/95	Bristol Rovers	97+10	2+1	5	5	39		2	1
				£300000	7/1/98	Port Vale								
Foyle Martin	5.11	11.2	5/2/63	Salisbury	8/13/80	Southampton	6+6	0+2			1	2		
AGT'93				£10000	8/3/84	Solihull	98	10	8	6	35	5	5	
				£140000	3/26/87	Oxford United	120+6	16	5	3+1	36	4	3	1
				£375000	6/25/91	Port Vale	182+56	17+3	13+4	13+3	67	7	9	9

276

Name					Fee	Date	Club								
Mills R Lee	6.1	12.11	7/10/70	Mexborough			Stocksbridge								
						12/9/92	Wolverhampton W.	12+13	1	3+1	3	2		1	1
					£400000	2/24/95	Derby County	16				7			
					£200000	8/1/95	Port Vale	82+28	7+3	0+3	6	35	5		4
Naylor Tony	5.5	9	3/29/67	Manchester			Droylsden								
					£20000	3/22/90	Crewe Alexandra	104+18	7+2	9	12	45	5	6	9
					£150000	7/16/94	Port Vale	126+26	9	9	5+1	47	4	1	3
ADDITIONAL CONTRACT PLAYERS															
Barnett Dave							Dunfermline								
					Free	7/1/98	Port Vale								
McQuade John							Hamilton Ac.								
					Free	7/1/98	Port Vale								

THE MANAGER
JOHN RUDGE

Date of Birth . . . . 21st October 1944.
Place of Birth . . . . Wolverhampton.
Date of Appointment . . . . December 1983.

PREVIOUS CLUBS
As Manager. . . . . None.
As Coach . . . . Torquay United.
As a Player . . . . Huddersfield Town, Carlisle United, Torquay United,
. . . . Bristol Rovers, Bournemouth.

HONOURS
As a Manager
Port Vale: Promotion to Division 3, 1986. Promotion to Division 2, 1989. AGT Winners 1993. Promotion to Division 1, 1994.

As a Player
Bristol Rovers: Promotion to Division 2, 1974.

VALE PARK
Hamil Road, Burslem, Stoke-on-Trent ST6 1AW

Capacity 22,356
Seating 17,616

First game ....v Newport Co., Div.3(S), 24.8.1950.
First floodlit game ....v WBA (Friendly), 24.9.1958.

ATTENDANCES
Highest...49,768 v Aston Villa, FAc 5th Rnd, 20.2.1960.
Lowest..994 v Hereford Utd, AMC, 22.12.1986.

OTHER GROUNDS ....Limekiln Lane 1876-81. Westport 1881-84. Moorland Road 1884-86.
.... Athletic Ground 1886-1913. Recreation Ground 1913-1950. Vale Park 1950-

HOW TO GET TO THE GROUND

From the North
Use motorway (M6) until junction 16 then join A500, sign posted Stoke. In 5.9 miles branch left and at roundabout take 1st exit A527. In 0.4 miles turn right B5051 into Newcastle Street and at end over crossroads into Moorland Road. Shortly turn left into Hamil Road for Port Vale FC.

From the East
Use A50 or A52 into Stoke-on-Trent then follow signs to Burslem A50 into Waterloo Road. At Burslem crossroads turn right into Moorland Road. Shortly turn left into Hamil Road for Port Vale FC.

From the South and West
Use motorway (M6) until junction 15 then A5006 and A500. In 6.3 miles branch left and at roundabout take 3rd exit A527. In 0.4 miles turn right B5051 into Newcastle Street and at end over crossroads into Moorland Road. Shortly turn left into Hamil Road for Port Vale FC.

Car Parking: (Ample) behind the Railway Stand, on Hamil Road car park and streets.
Nearest Railway Station: Longport, Stoke-on-Trent (0345 484950)

USEFUL TELEPHONE NUMBERS

Club switchboard 01782 814 134
Club Fax number.......... 01782 834 981
Club Shop.............. 01782 833 545
Ticket Office............. 01782 814 134

Marketing Department....... 01782 835 524
Internet address .... www.port-vale.co.uk
Clubcall 0891 12 16 36*
*Calls cost 50p per minute at all times. Call costings correct at time of going to press.

MATCHDAY PROGRAMME

Programme Editor .... Neil Hughes.

Number of pages .... 48.

Price .... £1.80.

Subscriptions .... Apply to club.

Local Newspapers
.... The Sentinel, The Green'Un.

Local Radio Stations
.... Radio Stoke, Signal Radio.

MATCHDAY TICKET PRICES

Mizuno Stand............................. £12.50
Juv/OAP.............................. £6.50/£9.50
Railway Paddock £11.50
Juv/OAP.............................. £6/£8.50
Sentinal Stand £11.50
Juv/OAP.............................. £6/£8.50
Family Stand............................. £11
Juv/OAP................................. £5/£8
Terraces .... Lome Street £10
Juv/OAP................................. £5/£7

Visiting Supporters .... Caudwell End £13

PORTSMOUTH
(The Pompey)
NATIONWIDE LEAGUE DIVISION 1
SPONSORED BY: KJC MOBILE PHONES

1997-98 - Back Row L-R: Deon Burton (now Derby), Jimmy Carter, Ashkan Karimzadeh, Mark Thompson, Hamilton Thorp, Keith Waldon (Asst. manager), Andy Thomson, Martin Hinshelwood (Youth manager), Mathias Svensson, Martin Allen, Nathan Jukes, Alan McLoughlin, Fitzroy Simpson.
Middle Row: Gordon Neave (Kit manager), Neil Sillett (physio), Danny Hinshelwood, Gavin Rees, Jon Hawley, Aaron Flahavan, Alan Knight, Russell Perrett, John Durnin, Adam Williams, Ian McDonald (Reserve manager), Shaun North (Youth coach), **Front Row:** Sam Igoe, Andy Cook, Paul Hall, Robbie Pethick, David Waterman, Adrian Whitbread, Terry Fenwick (Manager), David Hillier, Scott Bundy, Lee Russell, Robert Simpson, Andy Awford, Andy Turner.

PORTSMOUTH
FORMED IN 1898
TURNED PROFESSIONAL IN 1898
LTD COMPANY IN 1898

CHAIRMAN: Martin Gregory

DIRECTORS
B A V Henson FCA,
G P Hinkinson, F E Dinenage

SECRETARY
P A Weld (01705 731 204)
COMMERCIAL MANAGER
Julie Baker

MANAGER: Alan Ball
FIRST TEAM COACH: Kevin Bond
RESERVE TEAM COACH:
Neil McNab
YOUTH TEAM COACH:
Martin Allen

PHYSIOTHERAPIST
Jonathan Trigg

STATISTICIAN FOR THE DIRECTORY
Peter Macey

Unsettling matters of the field play gave Portsmouth little hope of achieving anything of any note during the 1997/98 season. Terry Venables eventually sold his stake in the club and Terry Fenwick was also destined to leave the club, leaving the players to pick up the pieces on the field.

Old favourite, Alan Ball, was appointed manager in January, and set about the task of getting Portsmouth off the bottom of Division One and in to the safety zone. It took a few games for things to improve but a run of seven unbeaten games (including four consecutive wins), during February and March, lifted Portsmouth out of the relegation places.

However, a return to indifferent form in the latter stages of the season meant that Portsmouth had to win the final game of the season, or they would risk being relegated. Thankfully for the Portsmouth fans they recorded a fine 3-1 win over Bradford to keep hold of their Division One status for another season.

With a pre-season behind them Alan Ball will be hoping to create his own team that will hopeful not have any of the distractions off the field, as they did in 1997/98.

PORTSMOUTH

Division 1	:20th			FA CUP: 3rd Round			LC CUP: 1st Round	

M	DATE	COMP.	VEN	OPPONENTS	RESULT	H/T	LP	GOAL SCORERS/GOAL TIMES	ATT.
1	A 09	FL	A	Manchester City	D 2-2	1-1	10	Aloisi 5, Hall 80	(30474)
2	12	CC 1/1	A	**Peterborough United**	D 2-2	2-1		**Thorp 7, Hillier 24**	**(3613)**
3	15	FL	H	Port Vale	W 3-1	2-1	4	Aloisi 24, Svensson 38, 47	10605
4	23	FL	A	Sheffield United	L 1-2	0-2	7	Perrett 57	(15895)
5	26	CC 1/2	H	**Peterborough United**	L 1-2	1-1		**Svensson 36**	**6395**
6	30	FL	H	Oxford United	W 2-1	1-1	7	Aloisi 3, Svensson 66	10209
7	S 02	FL	H	Norwich City	D 1-1	0-0	6	Turner 66	10577
8	13	FL	H	Crewe Alexandra	L 2-3	0-1	11	Aloisi 70, 73	9505
9	20	FL	A	Nottingham Forest	L 0-1	0-1	16		(17292)
10	24	FL	A	Queens Park Rangers	L 0-1	0-1	16		(12620)
11	27	FL	H	Reading	L 0-2	0-1	19		9593
12	O 04	FL	A	Stockport County	L 1-3	0-2	23	Aloisi 73	(7824)
13	18	FL	H	West Bromwich Albion	L 2-3	0-1	23	McLoughlin 78, Foster 85	9158
14	21	FL	H	Bradford City	D 1-1	1-1	23	McLoughlin 17	6827
15	25	FL	A	Huddersfield Town	D 1-1	1-0	23	Igoe 38	(8985)
16	31	FL	H	Swindon Town	L 0-1	0-1	23		8707
17	N 05	FL	A	Middlesbrough	D 1-1	0-0	23	Igoe 85	(29724)
18	08	FL	A	Bury	W 2-0	0-0	22	Aloisi 53, Durnin 90	(5065)
19	15	FL	H	Sunderland	L 1-4	1-3	23	Aloisi 7	10702
20	29	FL	A	Birmingham City	L 1-2	1-1	24	Hall 35	(17738)
21	D 06	FL	H	Stoke City	W 2-0	2-0	24	Aloisi 31, Svensson 43	7072
22	09	FL	H	Wolverhampton Wand	W 3-2	1-0	21	Durnin 14, 47, Hillier 74	8042
23	13	FL	A	Ipswich Town	L 0-2	0-1	23		(11641)
24	20	FL	H	Charlton Athletic	L 0-2	0-1	24		8581
25	26	FL	A	Queens Park Rangers	W 3-1	1-1	21	Pethick 35, McLoughlin 62 (pen), Hall 80	12314
26	30	FL	A	Norwich City	L 0-2	0-1	24		(16441)
27	J 03	FAC 3	H	**Aston Villa**	D 2-2	2-1		**Foster 6, 38**	**16013**
28	10	FL	H	Manchester City	L 0-3	0-1	24		13512
29	14	FAC 3R	A	**Aston Villa**	L 0-1	0-1			**(23355)**
30	17	FL	A	Port Vale	L 1-2	1-1	24	Durnin 36	(6028)
31	24	FL	A	Oxford United	L 0-1	0-0	24		(7402)
32	31	FL	H	Sheffield United	D 1-1	1-1	24	Foster 18	12003
33	F 06	FL	H	Nottingham Forest	L 0-1	0-0	24		15033
34	14	FL	A	Crewe Alexandra	L 1-3	0-0	24	Aloisi 80	(5114)
35	17	FL	H	Stockport County	W 1-0	1-0	24	Claridge 14	8622
36	21	FL	A	Reading	W 1-0	0-0	24	Whitbread 83	(9928)
37	24	FL	A	West Bromwich Albion	W 3-0	2-0	22	Hillier 12, Claridge 33, McLoughlin 86	(12757)
38	28	FL	H	Tranmere Rovers	W 1-0	1-0	20	Aloisi 37	12250
39	M 03	FL	H	Bury	D 1-1	0-1	20	Aloisi 68	12462
40	07	FL	A	Swindon Town	W 1-0	0-0	18	Durnin 89	(9100)
41	14	FL	H	Middlesbrough	D 0-0	0-0	20		17003
42	21	FL	A	Sunderland	L 1-2	0-1	21	Hall 70	(38134)
43	29	FL	A	Wolverhampton Wand	L 0-2	0-1	21		(20718)
44	A 04	FL	H	Birmingham City	D 1-1	0-0	22	Thomson 90	14591
45	07	FL	A	Tranmere Rovers	D 2-2	1-1	22	Durnin 21, Hall 81	(8020)
46	11	FL	A	Stoke City	L 1-2	0-0	22	Durnin 69	(15569)
47	13	FL	H	Ipswich Town	L 0-1	0-1	22		15040
48	18	FL	A	Charlton Athletic	L 0-1	0-0	23		(14082)
49	25	FL	H	Huddersfield Town	W 3-0	1-0	21	Pethick 27, Thomson 60, Durnin 70	14013
50	M 03	FL	A	Bradford City	W 3-1	1-0	20	Durnin 35, 73, Igoe 64	(15890)

Best Home League Attendance: 17003 V Middlesbrough					**Smallest :6827 V Bradford City**		**Average :11149**	

Goal Scorers:

FL	(51)	Aloisi 12, Durnin 10, Hall 5, McLoughlin 4, Svensson 4, Igoe 3, Claridge 2, Foster 2, Hillier 2, Pethick 2, Thomson 2, Perrett 1, Turner 1, Whitbread 1
CC	(3)	Hillier 1, Svensson 1, Thorp 1
FAC	(2)	Foster 2

1997-98

(M) Allen	(M) Aloisi	(D) Awford	(F) Carter	(F) Claridge	(F) Durnin	(M) Enes	(G) Flahavan	(M) Foster	(F) Hall	(F) Harries	(M) Hillier	(M) Igoe	(G) Knight	(M) McLoughlin	(D) Perrett	(D) Pethick	(M) Robinson	(D) Russell	(F) Simpson F	(M) Simpson R	(F) Svensson	(D) Thomson	(M) Thorp	(F) Turner	(D) Vlachos	(D) Waterman	(D) Whitbread		
	X	S3					X				X	X	X	X	S1						X		X	X	S2		X	X	D Laws	1
	X	X	S		X			X			X	X		X		S1							X	X	S	X	X	F G Stretton	2
	X			X			X	X			X	X		X		S	X	X				X	X	S1	S	X	X	R J Harris	3
	X	S			X			X			X	X		X		X			X		X	X	S1	S2		X	X	R Pearson	4
	X				X			X			X	X		X	X	X	S2	X	X	X	X	S1	S3			X	C R Wilkes	5
X	X	S			S1			X			X		X	X	X	X			X	S2	X		X	C R Wilkes	6			
X	X				S1			X			X		X	X	X	X				S2	X		S	X	S W Mathieson	6		
X	X				S1			X			X		X	X	X	X				S2	X		S	X	B Knight	7		
S3	X				S1			X			X		X	X	X	X					X	S2	X	P Taylor	8			
	X				X		X	S2	X		X	X		X	X	X					S	X	S1	X	A G Wiley	9		
	X	X		X			X			X	X		X	X	X	X	S2				S1		X	M R Halsey	10			
	X	S3			X		X			X	X		X	S1	X	X	X				S2		X	M C Bailey	11			
	X	X	S1		X			X	S2	X		X	X	X			X	X		X	S	P R Richards	12				
	X	X			X	X	X	X			X		X	S1	X	S	S	X			X	S2		X	S J Baines	13		
	X	S1			S	X	X			X	X	X	X	X	X		S	X			X	S2		X	S G Bennett	14		
	X	X		S	S	X	X			X	X	X	X	X		S	X			X			X	J P Robinson	15			
	X	X	S1		X	X	S	X	X	S2	X	X	X	X			X				X	P S Danson	16				
	X	S3		X	S1		X	X	S2	X	X	X	X	X				X		X	A R Leake	17					
	X			X	S		S1	X	X	X	X	X	X				X	X	S	X	D Laws	18					
	X			X	S2		S1	X	X	S3	X	X	X	X			X	X	S	X	A P D'Urso	19				
X1	X				X		X3	S3	X	X	S1	X	X	X2	S2	X		X	S W Mathieson	20								
	X2	X		S2		X1	X	X	S1	X	X	X	X	X		S	X	P Rejer	21									
	X	X		X2	X	S1	X	X	S	X	X	X1	S2	X	D Orr	22											
	X1	X		X	X2	X2	X	X	X	X3	X	X	S1	S3	X	K Leach	23									
S2	X	X		X	X1	S1	X	X	X2	X	X	X	S	A Bates	24											
X1	X	S1		X	X2	S2	X	X	S	X	X	X	X	M J Brandwood	25										
X3	X	S3	S2		X	X	S1	X	X	X	X	X1	X2	K M Lynch	26										
X2	X	S2		S	X X	S S1	X	X	X	X	X1	X	S	U D Rennie	27									
	X	S2	S1		X	X	X1	X	X	X	X	X	S	P Taylor	28										
	X	S2		X	S X1	X	S	X	X	X	X2	S1	X	S	X	U D Rennie	29								
S2	X	S1		X	X2	X	X	S	X	X	X	X	X1	X	M C Bailey	30									
S1	X	X	X		S	X	X	X	X	X	X1	X	F G Stretton	31											
	X	X	X	X		X	X1	X	S	X	S1	X	X	M R Halsey	32										
S2	X	X	X2	S	X	X1	S1	X	X	X	X	C R Wilkes	33												
S2	X	X	X1		X	S1	X	X	X	X2	X	R Pearson	34												
S1	X2	X	X		X	X	X	X	S2	X	X	B Knight	35												
S2	X	X2	X		X	X1	X3	X	X	S3	S1	X	X	A G Wiley	36									
S1	X2	X	S		X	X1	X	X	X	S2	X	X	X	E K Wolstenholme	37									
S3	X2	X		X		X	S2	X3	X1	X	X	S1	X	X	R J Harris	38								
S	X	X	X		X	S1	X	X	X X1	S	X	X	X	S G Bennett	39									
S	X1	X	X	S1	X	X	X	X	S	X	X	X	K A Leach	40										
S2	X3	X	S3		X	S1	X2	X	X	X1	X	X	X	K M Lynch	41									
S1	X	S2		X	X	X	X	X	X1	X2	X	D Pugh	42											
S3	X	X	S1	X	X2	X1	X	X3	S2	X	X	T Jones	43											
X	X1	X	X2	X		X	X	X	X S2	S1	X	S	X	A P D'Urso	44									
S	X	X	X	X	S1	X	X1	X	X	X	S	X	W C Burns	45										
S2	X2	X	X3	X	S1	X	X1	X	X	S3	X	X	R D Furnandiz	46										
S	X2	X	X	S1	X		X	X	X	X S2	X1	X	M J Brandwood	47									
X1	X	X	X	S1	X2	X	X	S2	X	X	S	X	J A Kirkby	48										
S1	X	S	X	X	S	X	X	X	X	X1	X	M Fletcher	49											
S	S	X	X	X	X	X	X	X	X	X	G Cain	50												
4	33	36	6	10	23	1	26	13	22		30	21	20	34	15	43	15	8	17		17	34		12	15	11	38	FL Appearances	
10	5	3	4		11	4		3	7	1		10		3	1	1			2		2	9	1	7	4		4	FL Sub Appearances	
	2	1			1			2		1		2	1		1	1+1		0+1	1		1	2	1+1	0+1		1	2	CC Appearances	
	1	2	0+1		1+1			2	2		1	2	2		2	1		1	1		1+1	2		1		1	1	FAC Appearances	

Also Played: (D) Cook Andy X(12). (M) Cook Aaron S (32),X1(35). (D) Hinshelwood S(31). (M) Wright S(12).

PORTSMOUTH

CLUB RECORDS

BIGGEST VICTORIES
League: 9-1 v Notts County, Division 2, 9.4.1927
F.A. Cup: 7-0 v Stockport (h), Rnd 3, 8.1.1949
League Cup: 5-0 v Rotherham United Rnd 2, 5.10.1993

BIGGEST DEFEATS
League: 0-10 v Leicester City, Division 1, 20.10.1928
F.A. Cup: 0-5 v Everton, Round 1, 1902-03
0-5 v Tottenham H, Round 3, 16.1.1937
0-5 v Blackburn Rov, Rnd 1 2nd Replay, 1899-90
League Cup: 0-5 v Queens Park Rangers, Round 2, 6.10.1981

MOST POINTS
3 points a win: 91, Division 3, 1982-83
2 points a win: 65, Division 3, 1961-62

MOST GOALS
91, 1979-80 (Division 4)
Garwood 17, Laidlaw 16, Hemmerman 13, Brisley 12, Rogers 9, Gregory 5, Ashworth 4, Aizelwood 2, Bryant 2, Perrin 2, Davey 1, McLaughlin 1, Purdie 1, Todd 1, Showers 1, og 4

MOST LEAGUE GOALS CONCEDED
112, Division 1, 1958-59

MOST FIRST CLASS MATCHES IN A SEASON
61 (46 League, 2 FA Cup, 7 League Cup, 6 Anglo Italian) 1993-94

MOST LEAGUE WINS
27, Division 3, 1961-62; Division 3, 1982-83

MOST LEAGUE DRAWS
19, Division 3, 1981-82

MOST LEAGUE DEFEATS
27, Division 1, 1958-59

INDIVIDUAL CLUB RECORDS

MOST GOALS IN A MATCH
5. Alf Strange v Gillingham, Division 3, 27.1.1923 (6-1)
5. Peter Harris v Aston Villa, Division 1, 3.9.1958 (5-2)
(Peter Harris's 5th goal was his 200th league & cup goal for Portsmouth)

MOST GOALS IN A SEASON
Guy Whittingham 47 (Lge 42, Lg Cup 2, Anglo-Ital 3) 1992-93
4 goals once=4, 3 goals three times=9, 2 goals 6 times=12, 1 goal 22 times=22
Previous holder: Billy Haines (Lge 40, FAC 3) 1926-27

OLDEST PLAYER
Jimmy Dickinson MBE, 40 exactly v Northampton, 24.4.1965

YOUNGEST PLAYER
Clive Green, 16 years 259 days v Wrexham, 21.8.1976
(also youngest goalscorer when 16 yrs 280 days v Lincoln City, 11.9.1976)

MOST CAPPED PLAYER
Jimmy Dickenson (England) 48

BEST PERFORMANCES

League: 1961-62: Matches played 46, Won 27, Drawn 11, Lost 8, Goals for 87, Goals against 47, Points 65. 1st in Division 3.
Highest: 1948-49, 1949-50: 1st in Division 1.

F.A. Cup: 1938-39: 3rd rnd. Lincoln 4-0; 4th rnd. West Bromwich Albion 2-0; 5th rnd. West Ham United 2-0; 6th rnd. Preston North End 1-0; Semi-final Huddersfield 2-1; Final Wolves 4-1.

League Cup: 1960-61: 2nd rnd. Coventry 2-0; 3rd rnd. Manchester City 2-0; 4th rnd. Chelsea 1-0; 5th rnd. Rotherham 0-3. 1993-94: 5th rnd.
1993-94: 2nd rnd. Rotherham 0-0, 5-0; 3rd rnd. Swindon 2-0; 4th rnd. Peterborough 0-0, 1-0; 5th rnd. Manchester Utd 2-2, 0-1.

ADDITIONAL INFORMATION
Previous League: Southern League.

Club colours: Royal blue shirts with white trim, white shorts, red socks.
Change colours:

Reserves League: Avon Insurance Football Combination.

DIVISIONAL RECORD

	Played	Won	Drawn	Lost	For	Against	Points
Division 1	1,090	405	257	428	1,729	1,828	1,074
Division 2/1	1,426	513	373	553	1,996	2,056	1,615
Division 3	318	120	95	103	412	379	376
Division 3(S)	126	61	36	29	207	121	158
Division 4	92	44	24	24	153	97	112
Total	**3,052**	**1,143**	**785**	**1,137**	**4,497**	**4,481**	**3,335**

RECORDS AND STATISTICS

COMPETITIONS

Div.1	Div.2/1	Div.3	Div.3(S)	Div.4
1927-59	1924-27	1920-21	1921-24	1978-80
1987-88	1959-61	1961-62		
	1962-76	1976-78		
	1983-87	1980-83		
	1988-			

HONOURS

Div.1	Div.3	Div.3(S)	FA Cup	C/Shield
1948-49	1961-62	1923-24	1938-39	1949
1949-50	1982-83			

MOST APPEARANCES

Jimmy Dickinson 829 (1946-65)

Year	League	FA Cup	Lge Cup	C/Shield
1946-47	40	2		
1947-48	42	2		
1948-49	41	5		
1949-50	40	5		1
1950-51	41	1		
1951-52	40	4		
1952-53	40	2		
1953-54	40	7		
1954-55	25			
1955-56	39	2		
1956-57	42	2		
1957-58	42	2		
1958-59	39	4		
1959-60	42	1		
1960-61	40	1	4	
1961-62	46	1	4	
1962-63	42	5	3	
1963-64	42	1	2	
1964-65	41	2	2	
	764	49	15	1

MOST GOALS IN A CAREER

Peter Harris - 208 (1946-60)

Year	League	FA Cup
1946-47	1	
1947-48	13	1
1948-49	17	5
1949-50	16	1
1950-51	5	
1951-52	9	1
1952-53	23	
1953-54	20	4
1954-55	23	
1955-56	23	1
1956-57	12	2
1957-58	18	
1958-59	13	
1959-60	1	
Total	193	15

Current leading goalscorer: Alan McCloughlin - 53 (1992-98)

MANAGERS

Name	Seasons	Best	Worst
Since joining the League			
John McCartney	1920-27	2(2)	12(3S)
John Tinn	1927-47	4(1)	20(1)
J R Jackson	1947-52	1(1)	8(1)
Eddie Lever	1952-58	3(1)	20(1)
Freddie Cox	1958-61	22(1)	21(2)
Bill Thompson	1961		
George Smith	1961-70	5(2)	1(3)
Ron Tindall	1970-73	16(2)	17(2)
John Mortimore	1973-74	15(2)	15(2)
Ron Tindall	1974		
Ian St John	1974-77	17(2)	20(3)
Jimmy Dickinson	1977-79	24(3)	7(4)
Frank Burrows	1979-82	6(3)	4(4)
Bobby Campbell	1982-84	16(2)	1(3)
Alan Ball	1984-89	20(1)	4(2)
John Gregory	1989-90		
Frank Burrows	1990-91		
Jim Smith	1991-95	3(2/1)	17(2/1)
Terry Fenwick	1995-98	7(1)	21(1)
Alan Ball	1998-		

RECORD TRANSFER FEE RECEIVED

Amount	Club	Player	Date
£3,500,000	Manchester C.	Lee Bradbury	08/97
£1,700,000	Tottenham H.	Darren Anderton	6/92
£1,000,000	Inter Milan	Mark Hateley	6/84
£130,000	Brighton & H.A.	Steve Foster	6/79

RECORD TRANSFER FEE PAID

Amount	Club	Player	Date
£650,000	Celtic	Gerry Creaney	1/94
£450,000	Q.P.R.	Colin Clarke	5/90
£315,000	Aston Villa	Warren Aspinall	8/88
£300,000	Barnsley	John Beresford	3/89

LONGEST LEAGUE RUNS

of undefeated matches:	15 (18.4.1924 - 18.10.1924)	of league matches w/out a win:	25 (22.1.1958 - 17.10.1959)
of undefeated home matches:	32 (3.1.1948 - 27.8.1949)	of undefeated away matches:	14 (1.3.1924 - 18.10.1924)
without home win:	16 (6.2.1958 - 17.10.1959)	without an away win:	24 (26.1.1938 - 11.3.1939)
of league wins:	7 (19.4.1980-30.8.1980, 22.1.1983-1.4.1983)	of home wins:	14 (13.9.1986 - 28.2.1987)
of league defeats:	9 (22.11.1959-17.1.1960, 21.3.1959-29.8.1959)	of away wins:	6 (1.4.1980 - 30.8.1980)
	(3.11.1963 - 22.12.1963, 21.10.1975 - 6.12.1975)		

PORTSMOUTH

PLAYERS NAME / Honours	Ht	Wt	Birthdate	Birthplace / Transfers	Contract Date	Clubs	League	L/Cup	FA Cup	Other	Lge	L/C	FAC	Oth
G O A L K E E P E R														
Flahavan Aaron	6.1	12.1	12/15/75	Southampton	2/15/94	Portsmouth	50	6	0+1					
Knight Alan	6.1	13.1	7/3/61	Balham	3/12/79	Portsmouth	663	49	40	21				
E: u21.2, Y.3, Div3'83														
D E F E N C E														
Awford Andrew	5.9	11.9	7/14/72	Worcester	7/24/89	Portsmouth	229+6	23	15	12	1			
E: u21.9, Y.13														
Cook Aaron	6.1	11.4	12/6/79	Caerphilly	1/30/98	Portsmouth	1							
Hinshelwood Danny	5.9	10.11	12/4/75	Bromley	8/1/92	Nottingham Forest								
E: Y					2/28/96	Portsmouth	5							
				Loan	3/3/97	Torquay United	7+2							
Perrett Russell	6.3	13.2	6/18/73	Barton-on-Sea		Lymington AFC								
					10/2/95	Portsmouth	54+3	3	4		2			
Pethick Robert	5.1	11.7	9/8/70	Tavistock		Plymouth Argyle								
						Weymouth								
				£30000	10/1/93	Portsmouth	154+26	12+3	8	3+1	2			
Russell Lee	5.11	11.4	9/3/69	Southampton	7/12/88	Portsmouth	103+20	8+2	4+2	5+2	3			
				Loan	9/9/94	Bournemouth	3							
Thorgersen Thomas						Brondy								
				£100000	7/1/98	Portsmouth								
Thomson Andrew	6.3	14.12	3/28/74	Swindon	5/1/93	Swindon Town	21+1	5		3		1		
				£75000	12/29/95	Portsmouth	69+8	2	4+1		3			
Vlachos Michail	5.11	12.10	9/20/67	Athens		AEK Athens								
Greek Int.				Loan	1/30/98	Portsmouth	15							
Waterman David G	5.11	12	5/16/77	Guernsey	8/1/96	Portsmouth	10+8	1	1					
Whitbread Adrian	6.2	11.8	10/22/71	Epping	11/13/89	Leyton Orient	125	10+1	11	8	2		1	
				£500000	7/29/93	Swindon Town	34+1		2		1			
				£650000	8/17/94	West Ham United	3+8	2+1	1					
				Loan	11/9/95	Portsmouth	13							
				£200000	10/24/96	Portsmouth	62	2	2		1			
M I D F I E L D														
Allen Martin	5.1	11	8/14/65	Reading	5/27/83	QPR	128+8	15+3	9	2	16	1	1	1
E: u21.2, u19.3, Y				£675000	8/24/89	West Ham United	160+27	15+3	14	10	25	5	4	
				Loan	9/11/95	Portsmouth								
				£500000	2/22/96	Portsmouth	34+12				4			
Aloisi John	6	12.13	2/5/76	Australia		Cremonese								
Australian Int.				£300000	8/8/97	Portsmouth	33+5	2	1		12			
Hillier David	5.1	11.6	12/18/69	Blackheath	2/11/88	Arsenal	82+22	13+2	13+2	5+4	2			
E: u21.1, FAYC'88. Div.1'91.				£200000	11/4/96	Portsmouth	52	2	3		4	1	1	
Igoe Samuel	5.6	10.8	9/30/75	Spelthorne	2/15/94	Portsmouth (T)	47+47	4+3	0+3		5			
Jukes Nathan B	5.11	11.13	4/10/79	Worcester	7/4/97	Portsmouth (T)								
McLoughlin Alan	5.8	10	4/20/67	Manchester	4/25/85	Manchester United								
Ei: 16, B.2				Free	8/15/86	Swindon Town	101+5	11+3	4+2	10	18	5		1
				Loan	3/13/87	Torquay United	21+3				4			
				£1000000	12/13/90	Southampton	22+2	0+1	4	1	1			
				Loan	9/30/91	Aston Villa				1				
				£400000	2/17/92	Portsmouth	239+11	21	12+1	9	43	3	6	1
Robinson Matt	5.1	10.8	12/23/74	Exeter	7/1/93	Southampton	2+10		1+2					
				£50000	2/20/98	Portsmouth	15							
Simpson Robert A	5.11	11.6	3/3/76	Luton	5/31/97	Portsmouth	3+2							
Soley Steve				Liverpool		Leek Town								
				£30000	7/1/98	Portsmouth								
F O R W A R D														
Durnin John	5.1	11.4	8/18/65	Bootle		Waterloo Dock								
				Free	3/29/86	Liverpool		1+1						
				Loan	10/20/88	WBA	5				2			
				£225000	2/10/89	Oxford United	140+21	7	7	4+1	44	1	1	1
				£200000	7/15/93	Portsmouth	100+52	10+1	5+1	4+2	24	2		
Kyzeridis Nicos						Paniliakos								
				£100000	7/1/98	Portsmouth								

Simpson Fitzroy	5.6	10.4	2/26/70	Trowbridge	7/6/88	Swindon Town	78+27	15+2	2+1	3+2	9	1	
				£500000	3/6/92	Manchester City	58+13	5+1	4+1		4		
				£200000	8/17/95	Portsmouth	81+6	6	5		8		
Turner Andy	5.9	10.4	3/28/75	Woolwich	4/8/92	Tottenham Hotspur	8+12	0+2	0+1		3	1	
Ei: u21.2				Loan	8/26/94	Wycombe Wanderers	3+1						
				Loan	11/28/95	Huddersfield Town	2+3				1		
				Loan	3/28/96	Southend United	4+2						
				£250000	9/3/96	Portsmouth	34+6	2+2	1		3		
ADDITIONAL CONTRACT PLAYERS													
Wright David S					10/3/97	Portsmouth (T)							

THE MANAGER
ALAN BALL

Date of Birth . . . . 12th May 1945.
Place of Birth . . . . Farnworth.
Date of Appointment . . . . January 1998.

PREVIOUS CLUBS
As Manager . . . . Blackpool. Vancouver Whitecaps (as player/amanager),
. . . . Portsmouth, Stoke City, Exeter City, Southampton, Manchester City.
As Coach . . . . Bristol Rovers, Portsmouth.
As a Player. Blackpool, Everton, Arsenal, Southampton (twice), Bristol Rovers.

HONOURS
As a Manager
Portsmouth: Promotion to Division 1, 1987.

As a Player
Everton: Division 1 Championship, 1970
International: 72 full caps and 8 u23 for England. World Cup Winner 1966.

FRATTON PARK
57 Frogmore Road, Portsmouth PO4 8RA

Capacity ....19,179.

First game ....v Southampton (Friendly) 2-0, 6.9.1899.
First floodlit game ....v Newcastle, 2.3.1953.
Second Set ....v Burnley, 10.10.1962.

ATTENDANCES
Highest ....51,385 v Derby County, FAC 6th Rnd, 20.2.1949.
Lowest ....2,499 v Wimbledon, Z.Data 1st Rnd, 5.12.1989.

OTHER GROUNDS ....None.

HOW TO GET TO THE GROUND

From the North and West
Use motorway (M27) and (M275) and at end at roundabout take 2nd exit and in 0.2 miles, at 'T' junction turn right (A2047) into London Road.
In 1.3 miles over railway bridge and turn left into Goldsmith Avenue. In 0.6 miles turn left into Frogmore Road for Portsmouth FC.

From the East
Use A27 then follow signs to Southsea (A2030). In 3 miles at roundabout turn left (A288). Then turn right into Priory Crescent then take next turning right into Carisbrooke Road for Portsmouth FC.

Car Parking: Side-street parking only.

Nearest Railway Station: Fratton (by Fratton Park), Portsmouth 01705 825 711)

USEFUL TELEPHONE NUMBERS

Club switchboard 01705 731 204
Club fax number.......................01705 734 129
Ticket Office.............................01705 618 777
Marketing Department 01705 731 204

Clubcall 0898 12 11 82*
*Calls cost 50p per minute at all times.
Call costings correct at time of going to press.

MATCHDAY PROGRAMME

Programme Editor (97/98) ....Julie Baker.

Number of pages (97/98) ....40.

Price (97/98).....................................£1.50.

Subscriptions................Available from Club.

Local Newspapers
.........................Portsmouth Evening News.

Local Radio Stations
............................Ocean F.M., Radio Solent.

MATCHDAY TICKET PRICES (97/98)

South Stand
A Section (Adults/Concessions) .... £14/£9
B Section .... £16/£10
C Section .... £16/£10
Enclosure................................. £11/£6

North Stand
E Section .... £12/£7
F Section .... £14/£8
G Section .... £12/£7
Lower.................................... £11/£5
Family Section .... £11/£4

QUEENS PARK RANGERS
(The Rangers or The R's)
NATIONWIDE LEAGUE DIVISION 1
SPONSORED BY: ERICSSON

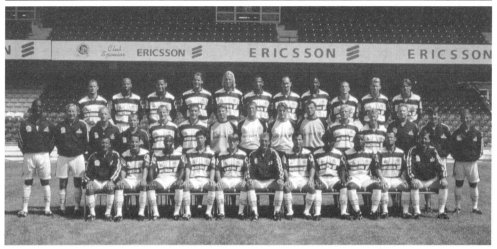

1997-98 - Back Row L-R: Trevor Challis, Lee Charles, Nigel Quashie, Chris Plummer, Karl Ready, Michael Mahoney-Johnson, Stephen Morrow, Steve Slade, Paul Murray, Kevin Gallen, Paul Bruce. **Middle Row:** bob Oteng (Kit manager), Steve Burtenshaw (Chief Scout), Mark Browse (Physio), Craig Hamilton (Masseur), Mike Sheron, Mark Perry, Paul Hart, Richard Hurst, Tony Roberts, Lee Harper, Steve Yates, Simon Barker, Brian Morris (Physio), Warren Neill (Youth manager), Gary Micklewhite (Youth coach). **Front Row:** John Hollins (Reserve manager), Matthew Rose, Danny Maddix, Matthew Brazier, Mark Graham, Stewart Houston (Manager), Gavin Peacock, Rufus Brevett, Trevor Sinclair, John Spencer, Bruce Rioch (Asst. manager).

QUEENS PARK RANGERS
FORMED IN 1885
TURNED PROFESSIONAL IN 1898
LTD COMPANY IN 1899

CHAIRMAN: C Wright
CHIEF EXECUTIVE: C Berlin
DIRECTORS
N G G Blackburn, Sir Terence Burns,
N R A Butterfield, P D Ellis, P A Hart
A J Hedges, C J C Levison
ASSOCIATE DIRECTORS
A Ingham (club), A Ellis (club),
K Westcott (sponsor).
SECRETARY
Miss S F Marson
SALES & MARKETING EXECUTIVE
Brian Rowe (0181 743 0262)

MANAGER: Ray Harford
PLAYER/COACH: Vinnie Jones
RESERVE TEAM COACH
Iain Dowie
PHYSIOTHERAPIST
Brian Morris BA HA

STATISTICIAN FOR THE DIRECTORY
Andy Shute

Three managers, 32 players used, of whom twelve made their debuts, and you can possibly see why QPR had the sort of season they had!

After narrowly missing out on the play-offs last season, it was hoped that Rangers would be challenging for one of the two automatic promotion spots, or at the very least a play-off place. The season started well, and after a 1-0 win versus Portsmouth in the eighth game of the season Rangers moved into second place. However, that was the end of the good times, eight games and one win later and the management team of Stewart Houston and Bruce Rioch parted company with QPR. John Hollins took over as a caretaker boss for five games (1 win, 2 draws) before Ray Harford was appointed manager, arriving from West Bromwich Albion.

A 1-0 victory followed in his first game in charge against Bradford City in mid-December, but this was Rangers' only victory until a 3-2 success in February against Crewe. By this stage QPR had slid down the League to 15th and were now involved in another relegation battle.

A surprising 5-0 victory over promotion candidates Middlesbrough kept Rangers out of the bottom three, though this was only their third win in 17 games under Ray Harford's command. Four new signings were made on or near deadline day at the end of March; Baraclough (Notts County), Scully Man. City, Vinnie Jones as player-coach (Wimbledon) and Ruddock (loan from Liverpool). These players came into the Rangers side to earn six draws from the last seven games of the season and secure Rangers' Division One status.

QPR were knocked out of both cup competitions at the first stage, by Wolves in the two legged Coca-Cola Cup, and by Middlesbrough after a replay in the FA Cup.

Twelve players made their debuts for QPR this season and only twice did QPR keep the same line-up for two consecutive League games, which may go someway to explain the inconsistency, though it has to be said that for the second half of the season their results were consistent; draw or defeat!!

Andy Shute.

QUEENS PARK RANGERS

Division 1   :21st   FA CUP: 3rd Round   LC CUP: 1st Round

M	DATE	COMP.	VEN	OPPONENTS	RESULT	H/T	LP	GOAL SCORERS/GOAL TIMES	ATT.
1	A 09	FL	H	Ipswich Town	D 0-0	0-0	14		17614
2	12	CC 1/1	H	Wolverhampton Wand	L 0-2	0-1			8355
3	15	FL	A	Tranmere Rovers	L 1-2	0-1	16	Peacock 90	(7467)
4	23	FL	H	Stockport County	W 2-1	1-1	10	Sinclair 23, 56	11108
5	27	CC 1/2	A	Wolverhampton Wand	W 2-1	1-0		Peacock 36, Murray 66	(18398)
6	30	FL	A	Nottingham Forest	L 0-4	0-1	12		(18804)
7	S 02	FL	A	Reading	W 2-1	0-1	11	Spencer 70, Swales 71 (OG)	(10203)
8	13	FL	H	West Bromwich Albion	W 2-0	1-0	9	Sheron 15, Peacock 76	14399
9	20	FL	A	Crewe Alexandra	W 3-2	2-0	8	Spencer 4, Maddix 8, Sinclair 47	(5348)
10	24	FL	H	Portsmouth	W 1-0	1-0	2	Spencer 44	12620
11	27	FL	A	Port Vale	L 0-2	0-2	3		(7197)
12	O 04	FL	H	Charlton Athletic	L 2-4	1-2	6	Sheron 25, 79	14825
13	18	FL	A	Sheffield United	D 2-2	0-1	9	Murray 58, Morrow 90	(18006)
14	21	FL	A	Bury	D 1-1	0-0	10	Spencer 83	(4602)
15	26	FL	H	Manchester City	W 2-0	2-0	8	Ready 13, Peacock 34 (pen)	14451
16	N 01	FL	H	Birmingham City	D 1-1	1-1	8	Barker 36	12715
17	05	FL	A	Swindon Town	L 1-3	1-0	13	Peacock 14	(10132)
18	08	FL	A	Middlesbrough	L 0-3	0-2	14		(30067)
19	15	FL	H	Stoke City	D 1-1	0-1	13	Barker 60 (pen)	11920
20	22	FL	H	Huddersfield Town	W 2-1	1-0	10	Quashie 26, 79	16066
21	29	FL	A	Wolverhampton Wand	L 2-3	0-1	11	Sheron 60, Peacock 85	(23645)
22	D 03	FL	A	Norwich City	D 1-1	0-0	11	Peacock 71	10141
23	06	FL	H	Sunderland	L 0-1	0-0	12		15266
24	12	FL	A	Oxford United	L 1-3	1-2	12	Peacock 19	(6664)
25	21	FL	H	Bradford City	W 1-0	1-0	12	Peacock 28 (pen)	8853
26	26	FL	A	Portsmouth	L 1-3	1-1	12	Sheron 31	(12314)
27	28	FL	H	Reading	D 1-1	1-0	12	Spencer 16	13015
28	J 03	FAC 3	H	Middlesbrough	D 2-2	1-1		Spencer 5, Gallen 75	13379
29	10	FL	A	Ipswich Town	D 0-0	0-0	13		(12672)
30	13	FAC 3R	A	Middlesbrough	L 0-0	0-0			(21817)
31	17	FL	H	Tranmere Rovers	D 0-0	0-0	13		12033
32	24	FL	A	Nottingham Forest	L 0-1	0-0	14		13220
33	31	FL	A	Stockport County	L 0-2	0-1	17		(7958)
34	F 06	FL	H	Crewe Alexandra	W 3-2	1-0	15	Kennedy 43, 59, Ready 78	13429
35	14	FL	A	West Bromwich Albion	D 1-1	1-0	15	Dowie 26	(19143)
36	17	FL	A	Charlton Athletic	D 1-1	1-1	15	Peacock 22 (pen)	(15555)
37	21	FL	H	Port Vale	L 0-1	0-1	15		14198
38	25	FL	H	Sheffield United	D 2-2	1-1	15	Sheron 4, Ready 54	9560
39	28	FL	A	Norwich City	D 0-0	0-0	16		(12730)
40	M 04	FL	H	Middlesbrough	W 5-0	4-0	15	Bruce 37, Gallen 39, Sheron 45, 54, Vickers 32 (OG)	11580
41	07	FL	A	Birmingham City	L 0-1	0-1	16		(18298)
42	14	FL	H	Swindon Town	L 1-2	1-2	16	Quashie 8	13486
43	21	FL	A	Stoke City	L 1-2	0-1	18	Barker 89 (pen)	(11051)
44	28	FL	A	Huddersfield Town	D 1-1	0-0	19	Jones 55	(13681)
45	A 01	FL	H	Wolverhampton Wand	D 0-0	0-0	17		12337
46	10	FL	A	Sunderland	D 2-2	0-1	17	Sheron 75, 83	(40014)
47	14	FL	H	Oxford United	D 1-1	0-1	19	Gallen 81	12859
48	19	FL	A	Bradford City	D 1-1	0-1	19	Gallen 48	(14871)
49	25	FL	A	Manchester City	D 2-2	2-1	18	Sheron 8, Pollock 21 (OG)	(32040)
50	M 03	FL	H	Bury	L 0-1	0-1	21		15210

Best Home League Attendance: 17614 V Ipswich Town   Smallest :8853 V Bradford City   Average :13083

Goal Scorers:

FL	(51)	Sheron 11, Peacock 9, Spencer 5, Barker 3, Gallen 3, Quashie 3, Ready 3, Sinclair 3, Kennedy 2, Bruce 1, Dowie 1, Jones 1, Maddix 1, Morrow 1, Murray 1, Opponents 3
CC	(2)	Murray 1, Peacock 1
FAC	(2)	Gallen 1, Spencer 1

(F) Baraclough	(D) Bardsley	(M) Barker	(D) Brazier	(D) Brevett	(F) Dowie	(F) Gallen	(G) Harper	(M) Heinola	(M) Jones	(F) Kennedy	(M) Kulcsar	(D) Maddix	(M) Morrow	(M) Murray	(M) Peacock	(D) Perry	(M) Quashie	(D) Ready	(G) Roberts	(M) Rose	(M) Rowland	(D) Ruddock	(F) Scully	(M) Sheron	(M) Sinclair	(F) Slade	(F) Spencer	(D) Yates		
		X	X	X		X						X	X	X	X		S1			X					S2	S3	X		C.R. Wilkes	1
		X	S3	X		X						X	X	X	X					X					X	S1	X		A P D'Urso	2
		X	S2	X		X						X	X	X	X					X					X	S1	X		S W Mathieson	3
		X	X	X		X						X	X	X	X			S2		X					X	S1	X	S3	P S Danson	4
		X		X		S1	X					X	X	X	X			S		X					X	X		S	J A Kirkby	5
		X		X		S1	X					X	X	X	X					X					X	X	S2	S3	M J Brandwood	6
	S		X			X						X	X	X	X	S	X			X					X	X	S	X	M Fletcher	7
	S		X			X						X	X	X	X		X	S1		X					X	X	S	X	M E Pierce	8
	S		X			X						X	X	X	X		X	X							X	X	S1	X	C J Foy	9
	S		X			X						X	X	X	X		X	X	S1						X	X	S	X	M R Halsey	10
	S2		X			X						X	X	X	X		X	X		X					X	X	S1	X	K Wolstenholme	11
	S2		X			X						X	X	X	X		X	S		X					X	X	S1	X	P Taylor	12
	X		X			X						X	X	X	X			X		X				X	S1	S3	X	S2	K M Lynch	13
	X		X			X						X	X	X	X			X		S				X	X	S	X	X	A N Butler	14
	S1		X			X						X	X	X	X			X		X				X	X	S3	X	S2	R J Harris	15
	X		X			S1	X					X	X		X			S	X					X	X		X	S2	S J Baines	16
	X	X				X	X					X	X		X			S3	X		X				X	X	S1		S2	D Pugh	17
	X	X				X						X	X		X		X	S	X					X	X	S1		S	J P Robinson	18
	X	X										S		X	X	X	S1	X	X					X	X		X	X	M C Bailey	19
	X	X	S1										S	X	X	X	X	X	X					X	X			X	R Styles	20
	X	X	S1										X	X	X		X	X	X					X	X	S		X1	B Coddington	21
	X1	X	S1								X	X	X		X	X	X						X	X		S		P Rejer	22
	X	S1									S	X	X1	X	X	X							X1	X		X	X	M E Pierce	23
	S	S2	X2								S1		X	X1	X	X	X	X						X	X		X	X	T Heilbron	24
		X		S1					X1	X		S2	X	S	X	X	X						X2	X		X	X	S W Mathieson	25
	S	X		S1						X			X	X	S	X	X	X						X	X		X1	X	M J Brandwood	26
	S		X	S						X			X	X	S	X	X							X	X		X	X	B Knight	27
	S		X	S2	S					X			X	X	S	X	X	X						X2	X	S1	X1	X	P A Durkin	28
	S		X	S					X	S			X	X	X	X	X							X	X		X1	X	W C Burns	29
	S	X3		S1	X								X	X	X	X	X							X2	X	S2	X1	X	P A Durkin	30
	X2	X		X	X	S						X	X	X		X	X						X1		S1		X	A R Hall	31
	X1	X		X2	X	S2						X	X	X		X	X								S1	X	X	K A Leach	32
	S		X		X	S		X				X	X1	X		X	X			X					S1		X	X	M Fletcher	33
		X	X2	X	S	X	S1					X	X1	X		X	X			X				S2			X	M C Bailey	34
	S		X	X1	X	S	X	X				X	X	X		X			X			S1				X	C J Foy	35
	X1		X	S2	X	S1		X				X	X	X		X			X			X2				D Orr	36
	X2		X	X1	X		X					X	X	X	S3		X			X				S2			X3	A N Butler	37
X			X2	S2	X		X	X			X1	X	X	S		X			X				X			S1	P Taylor	38
X			X	S	X	S2		X	X2	X			X1			X			X				X			S1	G Singh	39
X			X2	X	S3	X	X					X		X1	X3	X			X				S2		X	A P D'Urso	40
X			X	X	S2		X	S2	X2		X			X			X			X			S1		X3	R J Harris	41
X2			X	X	S2	X	X				X1		X	X		X			X			S3		X	A N Butler	42
X		X		X1	S1	X	S3		X2	X				X			X		X	X	X	X	S2		X3	A R Leake	43
X	X	X		S1	X1	X	S	X			S		X	X				X	X	X	X				A A Kirkby	44
X	X	S		S1	X1	X	S	X		X1			X	X				X	X	X	X		X		J A Kirkby	45
X	X			X2	X	X1	X			S		X	X	S2	X	X	X	S1		B Coddington	46
X	X			X	X	S2	X	X1	S		X2	X	X	X	X	S1		C R Wilkes	47
X	X			X	X	S	X	X1		X	X	S	X	X	X	S1		C J Foy	48
X	X			X	S2	X		S3	X		S1	X2	X1	X3	X	K A Leach	49
X	X			X	X	S2	X2		X	X	X	S	X1	X		X	S1	A G Wiley	50
8	12	20	8	20	9	19	36		7	8	11	23	31	31	38	6	30	38	10	13	7	7	7	36	24	3	22	21	FL Appearances	
	3	3	3	2	8		10			1	2		1	1	2	3	1		3				4	2	19	1	9	FL Sub Appearances	
	2	0+1	2		1	2				1	2	2	2	2		2	2	1			2	2	1+1	1	CC Appearances	
		2		0+2	1					1	1	2	2	2		2	2	2		0+2	2	2	FAC Appearances	

Also Played: (F) Bruce S3(30), S2(31), S(32), S1(37,40,42), X1(41). (F) Charles S(19). (F) Graham S2(2), S(3). (F) Mahoney-Johnson S(20,22), S2(23). (D) Plummer S(21). (G) Sommer S(30).

QUEENS PARK RANGERS

CLUB RECORDS

BIGGEST VICTORIES
League: 8-0 v Merthyr, Division 3S, 9.3.1929
F.A. Cup: 8-1 v Bristol Rovers (a), Round 1, 27.11.1937
7-0 v Barry Town, Round 1, 1961-62
League Cup: 8-1 Crewe, Round 2, 3.10.1983
Europe (UEFA): 7-0 v Brann Bergen, Round 1, 29-9-1976

BIGGEST DEFEATS
League: 1-8 v Mansfield, Division 3, 15.3.1965
1-8 v Manchester United, Division 1, 19.3.1969
0-7 v Southend United, Division 3S, 7.4.1928
0-7 v Coventry City, Division 3S, 4.3.1933
0-7 v Torquay United, Division 3S, 22.4.1935
0-7 v Barnsley, Division 2, 4.11.1950
F.A. Cup: 0-5 v Huddersfield, Round 4, 23.1.1932
0-5 v Derby County, Round 6, 12.3.1948
0-5 v Huddersfield (h), Round 3, 1948-49
1-6 v Burnley, Round 3, 1961-62
1-6 v Hereford, Round 2, 1957-58
League Cup: 0-4 v Reading, Round 2, 23.9.1964
0-4 v Newcastle, Round 2, 8.10.1974
Europe (UEFA): 0-4 v Partizan Belgrade, 7.11.1984

MOST POINTS
3 points a win: 85, Division 2, 1982-83
2 points a win: 67, Division 3, 1966-67

MOST GOALS
111, Division 3, 1961-62.
Bedford 36, Evans 19, Lazarus 12, Towers 12, McClelland 11, Angell 6, Collins 6, Barber 4, Keen 2, Francis 1, og 2.

MOST LEAGUE GOALS CONCEDED
95, Division 1, 1968-69

MOST FIRST CLASS MATCHES IN A SEASON
59 (42 League, 2 FA Cup, 7 League Cup, 8 UEFA Cup) 1976-77

MOST LEAGUE WINS
26, Div 3S, 1947-48; Div 3, 1966-67; Div 2, 1982-83

MOST LEAGUE DRAWS
18, Division 1, 1991-92

MOST LEAGUE DEFEATS
28, Division 1, 1968-69

INDIVIDUAL CLUB RECORDS

MOST GOALS IN A SEASON
Rodney Marsh, 44 (League 30, FAC 3, League Cup 11) 1966-67.
(League Only) George Goddard, 37, Div 3S, 1929-30

MOST GOALS IN A MATCH
5. Alan Wilks v Oxford, Round 3, League Cup, 10.10.1967.

OLDEST PLAYER
Jimmy Langley, 38 years 96 days.

YOUNGEST PLAYER
Frank Sibley, 15 years 274 days.

MOST CAPPED PLAYER
Alan McDonald (Northern Ireland) 51

BEST PERFORMANCES

League: 1966-67: Matches played 46, Won 26, Drawn 15, Lost 5, Goals for 103,Goals against 38, Points 67. First in Division 3

Highest: 1975-76: 2nd in Division 1.

F.A. Cup: 1981-82: 3rd rnd. Middlesbrough 1-1, 3-2; 4th rnd. Blackpool 0-0, 5-1; 5th rnd. Grimsby 3-1; 6th rnd. Crystal Palace 1-0; Semi-final West Bromwich Albion 1-0; Final Tottenham 1-1, 0-1.

League Cup: 1966-67: 1st rnd. Colchester 5-0; 2nd rnd. Aldershot 1-1, 2-0; 3rnd. Swansea 2-1; 4th rnd. Leicester 4-2; 5th rnd. Carlisle 2-1; Semi-final Birmingham 4-1, 3-1; Final West Bromwich Albion 3-2.

UEFA Cup: 1976-77: 1st rnd. Brann Bergen 4-0, 7-0; 2nd rnd. Slovan Bratislava 3-2, 5-2; 3rd rnd FC Cologne 3-0, 1-4; 4th rnd. AEK Athens 3-0, 0-3.

ADDITIONAL INFORMATION
Previous Name: St. Judes 1885-87

Previous League: Southern League

Club colours: Blue and white shirts, white shorts, white socks.

Change colours: All red.

Reserves League: Avon Insurance Football Combination.

DIVISIONAL RECORD

	Played	Won	Drawn	Lost	For	Against	Points
Division 1/P	822	277	223	322	1,028	1,111	969
Division 2/1	638	261	172	205	924	794	769
Division 3	414	188	98	128	782	601	474
Division 3(S)	1,158	466	276	416	1,781	1,692	1,208
Total	**3,032**	**1,192**	**769**	**1,071**	**4,515**	**4,198**	**3,320**

RECORDS AND STATISTICS

COMPETITIONS

Div 1/P	Div.2/1	Div.3	Div.3(S)	UEFA
1968-69	1948-52	1958-67	1920-48	1976-77
1973-79	1967-68		1952-58	1984-85
1983-96	1969-73			
	1979-83			
	1996-			

HONOURS

Div.2	Div.3	Div.3(S)	League Cup
1982-83	1966-67	1947-48	1966-67

MOST GOALS IN A CAREER

George Goddard - 186 (1926-33)

Year	League	FA Cup
1926-27	22	
1927-28	26	
1928-29	36	1
1929-30	37	2
1930-31	24	4
1931-32	17	2
1932-33	12	3
Total	**174**	**12**

Current leading goalscorer: Kevin Gallen - 28 (09.92-98)

MOST APPEARANCES

Tony Ingham 548 (1950-63)

Year	League	FA Cup	Lge Cup
1950-51	24		
1951-52	17		
1952-53	43	3	
1953-54	40	4	
1954-55	38	3	
1955-56	41	1	
1956-57	46	3	
1957-58	46	3	
1958-59	46	2	
1959-60	46	3	
1960-61	46	2	2
1961-62	40	4	2
1962-63	41	2	
	514	**30**	**4**

RECORD TRANSFER FEE RECEIVED

Amount	Club	Player	Date
£6,000,000	Newcastle Utd	Les Ferdinand	06/95
£2,700,000	Newcastle Utd	Darren Peacock	03/94
£2,700,000	Sheffield Wed.	Andy Sinton	08/93
£1,700,000	Manchester Utd	Paul Parker	07/91

RECORD TRANSFER FEE PAID

Amount	Club	Player	Date
£2,750,000	Stoke City	Mike Sheron	08/97
£2,500,000	Chelsea	John Spencer	11/96
£1,500,000	Glasgow Rangers	Mark Hateley	09/95
£1,250,000	Borussia Dortmund	Ned Zelic	07/95

MANAGERS

Name	Seasons	Best	Worst
James Cowan	1907-13		
James Howie	1919-20		
Ned Liddell	1920-25	3(3S)	22(3S)
Bob Hewison	1925-31	3(3S)	22(3S)
John Browman	1931		
Archie Mitchell	1931-33	13(3S)	16(3S)
Mitchell O'Brien	1933-35	4(3S)	13(3S)
Billy Birrell	1935-39	3(3S)	9(3S)
Ted Vizard	1939-44		
Dave Mangall	1944-52	13(2)	3(3S)
Jack Taylor	1952-59	10(3)	21(3S)
Alex Stock	1959-68	2(2)	15(3)
Tommy Docherty	1968		
Les Allen	1969-71	22(1)	11(2)
Gordon Jago	1971-74	4(1)	8(2)
Dave Sexton	1974-77	2(1)	14(1)
Frank Sibley	1977-78	19(1)	19(1)
Steve Burtenshaw	1978-79	20(1)	20(1)
Tommy Docherty	1979-80	5(2)	5(2)
Terry Venables	1980-84	5(1)	8(2)
Alan Mullery	1984		
Frank Sibley	1984-85	19(1)	19(1)
Jim Smith	1985-88	5(1)	16(1)
P Shreeve (Caretaker)	1988-89		
Trevor Francis	1989-90	9(1)	9(1)
Don Howe	1990-91	12(1)	12(1)
Gerry Francis	1991-94	5(1/P)	11(1)
Ray Wilkins	1994-96	8(P)	19(P)
Stewart Houston	1996-97	9(1)	9(1)
Ray Harford	1997-	21 (1)	21 (1)

LONGEST LEAGUE RUNS

of undefeated matches:	20 (19.11.1966 - 11.4.1967)	of league matches w/out a win:	20 (23.11.1968 - 12.4.1969)
of undefeated home matches:	25 (18.11.1972 - 5.2.1974)	of undefeated away matches:	17 (27.8.1966 - 11.4.1967)
without home win:	10 (23.11.1968 - 10.4.1969)	without an away win:	22 (27.12.1954-26.12.1955, 11.5.69-13.9.70
of league wins:	8 (7.11.1931 - 28.12.1931)	of home wins:	11 (26.12.1972 - 28.4.1973)
of league defeats:	9 (15.2.1969 - 12.4.1969)	of away wins:	7 (2.4.1927 - 4.9.1927)

QUEENS PARK RANGERS

PLAYERS NAME Honours	Ht	Wt	Birthdate	Birthplace Transfers	Contract Date	Clubs	League	L/Cup	FA Cup	Other	Lge	L/C	FAC	Oth
G O A L K E E P E R														
Bankole Ademola	6.3	13	9/9/69	Nigeria	11/30/95	Doncaster Rovers								
				Free	12/27/95	Leyton Orient								
				Free	9/25/96	Crewe Alexandra	6	1						
				£50000	7/1/98	QPR								
Harper Lee C	6.1	13	10/30/71	Chelsea		Sittingbourne								
				£150000	6/16/94	Arsenal	1							
					7/10/97	QPR	35	2	1					
Hurst Richard	6	12	12/23/76	Hammersmith	8/1/94	QPR								
D E F E N C E														
Heinola Anti	5.7	10.5	3/20/73	Helsinki		Heracles								
				£100000	1/15/98	QPR	0+10							
McFlynn Terry M			3/27/81	Magherafelt	5/11/98	QPR (T)								
Maddix Daniel	5.11	11.7	10/11/67	Ashford	7/25/85	Tottenham Hotspur								
				Loan	11/1/86	Southend United	2							
				Free	7/23/87	QPR	204+33	19	21+2	2+3	8	2	2	
Ord Richard	6.2	12.8	03/03/70	Murton	14/07/87	Sunderland	223+20	17+5	11+1	5+2	7		1	
E: u21.3 DIV.1'96.				Loan	22/02/90	York City	3							
				£65000	7/1/98	QPR								
Owen Karl	5.11	12.8	10/12/79	Coventry	10/15/96	QPR								
Perry Mark J	5.11	11.3	10/19/78	Perivale	10/26/95	QPR	8+2	2			1			
Plummer Chris E: S	6.3	11.06	10/12/76	Hounslow	7/1/94	QPR	4+2	2						
Ready Karl W: B.2, u21.5	6.1	12.2	8/14/72	Neath	8/13/90	QPR	115+14	4+2	7		6	1		
Rose Matthew	5.11	11.1	9/24/75	Dartford	8/1/94	Arsenal	2+3							
					5/20/97	QPR	13+3	2						
Whittle David L	5.11	12.7	12/2/78	Waterford	5/31/97	QPR								
Yates Steve Div3'90	5.11	11	1/29/70	Bristol	7/1/88	Bristol Rovers	196+1	9	11	21				
				£650000	8/16/93	QPR	116+11	5	7		2			
M I D F I E L D														
Currie Michael J			10/19/79	Westminster		QPR (T)								
Jeanne Leon C			11/17/80	Cardiff		QPR (T)								
Jones Vinnie FAC'88. Div2'90	6	11.12	1/5/65	Watford		Wealdstone								
				£10000	11/20/86	Wimbledon	77	6+2	11+2	3	9		1	
				£650000	6/20/89	Leeds United	44+2	2	1	4	5			
				£700000	9/13/90	Sheffield United	35	4	1	1	2			
				£575000	8/30/91	Chelsea	42	1	4	5	4		1	2
				£700000	9/10/92	Wimbledon	171+6	21+1	21		12	2	1	
				£500000	3/26/98	QPR	7				1			
Kulcsar George Australian Int.	6.1	13.8	8/12/67	Budapest		Antwerp								
				£100000	3/7/97	Bradford City	22+3				1			
				£250000	12/19/97	QPR	11+1							
Morrow Steve NI:17,u21.3,Y.S. FAYC'88.LC'93. ECWC'94.	6	11.3	7/2/70	Belfast	5/5/88	Arsenal	39+23	7+4	5+2	1+4	1	2		
				Loan	1/16/91	Reading	10							
				Loan	8/14/91	Watford	7+1		1					
				Loan	10/30/91	Reading	3							
				Loan	3/4/92	Barnet	1							
					3/27/97	QPR	36	2	1		2			
Murray Paul	5.8	10.5	8/31/76	Carlisle	6/14/94	Carlisle United	27+14	2	1	6+1				
				£300000	3/8/96	QPR	48+6	3	5		5	1		
Quashie Nigel	5.9	11	7/20/78	Nunhead	8/1/95	QPR	50+7	0+1	4		3		2	
Rowland Keith NI: Y. SLP'91. FLg u18.1	5.11	10	9/1/71	Portadown	10/2/89	Bournemouth	65+7	5	8	3	2			
				Loan	8/1/90	Farnborough			1					
				Loan	1/8/93	Coventry City	0+2							
				£110000	8/6/93	West Ham United	63+17	3+2	5+1		1			
				Swap	1/29/98	QPR	7							
F O R W A R D														
Baraclough Ian E: FLge u18.1. DIV3 97/98.	6.1	11.1	12/4/70	Leicester	12/15/88	Leicester City			1	0+1				
				Loan	3/22/90	Wigan Athletic	8+1				2			
				Loan	12/21/90	Grimsby Town	1+3							
				Free	8/13/91	Grimsby Town	1							
				Free	8/21/92	Lincoln City	68+5	7	4	7	10	1		
				Free	6/6/94	Mansfield Town	36	5	4	3	3			
				£150000	10/13/95	Notts County	106+3	5+1	8	3	10	1		
				£50000	3/19/98	QPR	8							
Bruce Paul M	5.11	12.1	2/18/78	London	5/31/96	QPR	1+4		0+1		1			
Dowie Iain NI: 25, u21.1	6.1	12.12	1/9/65	Hatfield		Hendon								
				£30000	12/14/88	Luton Town	53+13	3+1	1+2	5	15			4
				Loan	9/13/89	Fulham	5				1			
				£480000	3/22/91	West Ham United	12				4			
				£500000	9/3/91	Southampton	115+7	8+3	6	4	30	1	1	
				£400000	1/13/95	Crystal Palace	15		6		4		4	
				£125000	9/7/95	West Ham United	59+10	10+1	3+1		8	2	1	
				Swap	1/29/98	QPR	9+2				1			

292

Name	Ht	Wt	DOB	Birthplace	Date	Club							
allen Kevin	6	12	9/21/75	Chiswick	9/22/92	QPR	78+18	4+1	4+2		24	2	2
: Y.11, S. UEFA Y'93													
raham Richard	5.7	10	8/5/79	Newry	8/9/96	QPR	2	2					
raham Mark	5.7	10	10/24/74	Newry	5/26/93	QPR	14+2	0+1	2				
II: Y, S													
angley Richard B	5.11	11.4	12/27/79	London	5/31/97	QPR							
opez Rik A	5.11	11.4	12/25/79	Northwick Pk	5/31/97	QPR							
usardi Mario	5.9	10.2	9/27/79	Islington	5/31/97	QPR							
ahoney-Johnson Michael	5.1	11	11/6/76	Paddington	8/1/94	QPR	0+1						
				Loan	8/30/96	Wycombe W.	2+2				2		
				Loan	2/13/98	Brighton & H.A.	3+1						
urser Wayne M	5.11	12	4/13/80	Basildon	5/31/97	QPR							
cully Anthony D T	5.7	11.12	6/12/76	Dublin	12/2/93	Crystal Palace	0+3						
				Loan	10/14/94	Bournemouth	6+4			2			
				Loan	1/5/96	Cardiff City	13+1						
					8/12/97	Manchester City	1+8						
				Loan	1/27/98	Stoke City	7						
				£155000	3/17/98	QPR	6						
heron Michael N	5.9	11.3	1/11/72	Liverpool	7/5/90	Manchester City	82+18	9+1	5+3	1	24	1	3
E: u21.16													
				Loan	3/28/91	Bury	1+4			2	1		
				£1000000	8/26/94	Norwich City	17+4	4	4		1	1	2
					11/13/95	Stoke City	61+5	4	1	2	34	5	
					7/1/97	QPR	35+4		2		11		
lade Steve	5.11	10.1	10/6/75	Romford	7/1/94	Tottenham Hotspur							
				£350000	7/8/96	QPR	14+24	1+1	0+2		4		
				Loan	2/13/97	Brentford	4						

THE MANAGER
RAY HARFORD

Date of Birth. . . . . 1st June 1945.
Place of Birth. . . . . Halifax.
Date of Appointment . . . . February 1997.

PREVIOUS CLUBS
As Manager . . . . Fulham, Luton, Wimbledon, Blackburn, WBA.
As Coach/Assistant . . . . Fulham, Luton, Wimbledon, Blackburn.
As a Player. . . . Charlton Ath., Exeter, Lincoln, Mansfield, Port Vale, Colchester.

HONOURS
As a Manager
Luton: League Cup winners 1988, runners-up 1989. Simod Cup runners-up 1988
Blackburn: Premiership Champions 1995 (As Assistant Manager).

As a Player
None.

RANGERS STADIUM
South Africa Road, Shepherds Bush, London W12 7PA

Capacity 19,148
First game...v West Ham Utd, FA Cup, 8.9.1917.
First floodlit game ....v Arsenal, 5.10.1953.
2nd Set...v Colchester, 23.8.1966.

ATTENDANCES
Highest ....35,353 v Leeds Utd, Div.1, 12.1.1974.
Lowest ....3,245 v Coventry City, Div 3, 22.5.1963.

OTHER GROUNDS .... Welfords Field 1885-89. London Scottish Ground, Brondesbury Home Farm,
........Kensall Rise Green Gun Club, Wormwood Scrubs, Kilburn C.C. 1889-99, Kensal Rise 1899-1901, Latimer Rd,
....Knotting Hill 1901-04, Agriculture Soc, Park Royal 1904-07, Park Royal Ground 1907-17.
..... Loftus Road 1917-31, White City 1931-33, Loftus Road 1933-62. White City 1962-63. South Africa Road 1963-

HOW TO GET TO THE GROUND

From the North: Use motorway (M1) and A406 North Circular Road as for Neasden. In 0.7 miles turn left then join A404, sign posted Harlesden, then follow signs Hammersmith and turn right in to White City Road then turn left into South Africa Road for Q.P.R..

From the East: Use A12, A406 then A503 then join Ring Road and follow signs Oxford to join A40 (M). In 2 miles branch left (sign posted The West) to join M41. At roundabout take 3rd exit (A40) then join A4020, sign posted Acton. In 0.3 miles turn right into Loftus Road for Q.P.R. FC.

From the South: Use A206, A3 to cross Putney Bridge and follow signs Hammersmith. Follow signs Oxford (A219) to Shepherds Bush then join A4020, sign posted Acton. In 0.3 miles turn right into Loftus Road for Q.P.R. FC.

From the West: Use motorway (M4) to Chiswick then A315 and A402 to Shepherds Bush, then join A4020 sign posted Acton. In 0.3 miles turn right into Loftus Road for Q.P.R. FC.

Car Parking: Limited side-street parking available.
Nearest Railway Station: Shepherds Bush (Tube), White City (Central Line)

USEFUL TELEPHONE NUMBERS

Club switchboard 0181 743 0262
Club fax number.......................0181 749 0994
Club shop 0181 749 6862
Ticket Office............................0181 749 7798

Marketing Department 0181 740 2514
Clubcall 0891 12 11 62*
*Calls cost 50p per minute at all times.
Call costings correct at time of going to press.

MATCHDAY PROGRAMME

Programme Editor (97/98)....Sheila Marson.

Number of pages (97/98) ....36.

Price (97/98)..................................£1.50.

Subscriptions ....Please apply to club.

Local Newspapers
...Shepherds Bush Gazette, Acton Gazette.

Local Radio Stations
....Capital Radio.

MATCHDAY TICKET PRICES (97/98)

South Africa Road. £17

Juv/OAP £9

Ellerslie Road £15

Juv/OAP £8

Loftus Road Upper Level (Members only) £12

Juv/OAP £6

Lower Level (Members). £14

Juv/OAP £7

Paddocks £12

Juv/OAP £6

School Upper £15

Juv/OAP £8

School Lower £13

Juv/OAP £7

SHEFFIELD UNITED
(The Blades)
NATIONWIDE LEAGUE DIVISION 1
SPONSORED BY: WARDS BREWERY LTD

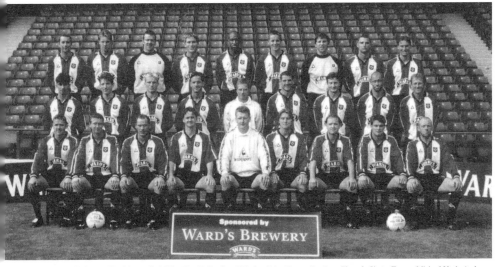

1997-98 Back Row L-R: Don Hutchinson, Carl Tiler, Alan Kelly, Gareth Taylor, Brian Deane, Jan Aage Fjortoft, Simon Tracey, Michael Vonk, Andy Scott. **Middle Row:** Vassilis Borbokis, Chris Short, Roger Nilsen, David Holdsworth, Willie Donachie, David White, Petr Katchouro, Paul McGrath, Nicky Marker. **Front Row:** Nick Henry, Mark Beard, Dane Whitehouse, Andy Walker, Nigel Spackman, Wayne Quinn, John Ebbrell, Mitch Ward, Mark Patterson.

SHEFFIELD UNITED
FORMED IN 1889
TURNED PROFESSIONAL IN 1889
LTD COMPANY IN 1899

VICE-CHAIRMAN: F Pye

DIRECTORS
F Pye, B Proctor, K McCabe,
S White

SECRETARY
David Capper (0114 221 5757)
COMMERCIAL MANAGER
Andy Daykin

PLAYER/MANAGER:
Steve Bruce

YOUTH TEAM MANAGER
Russell Slade & Steve Myles
PHYSIOTHERAPIST
Denis Pettitt

STATISTICIAN FOR THE DIRECTORY
Andrew Treherne

In another eventful season, and against all the odds, the club almost achieved the dream of promotion and the FA Cup. However, the semi final stages were the eventual finishing point in both competitions.

The season stared off os full of promise. With Nigel Spackman installed in the Manager's chair, Paul McGrath performing to international standard in defence, and the returning hero Brian Deane up front, the club began the season with a convincing victory over Sunderland in the opening match of the season. The unbeaten league run continued until the away defeat at West Bromwich Albion on 25th October, at which time the team were 6th in the table. The next away game brought a 1-0 victory at Reading with the 6000th League goal scored by Mark Patterson. This was to be the final league away win of the season, probably the main reason for the ultimate failure to achieve promotion: only the impressive home form kept the team in the hunt.

The match at Port Vale brought a season ending for Dane Whitehouse, and by this time Wayne Quinn and Paul McGrath had also succumbed to knee injuries. This was the beginning of the disruption to the team due to injuries and transfer policy: the latter ultimately leading to the resignation of manager Spackman, who felt he could no longer continue when his players were being sold from under him. The disruption came at the time when United were still in fifth place and preparing for a crucial sixth round cup tie at Coventry. Unsurprisingly, the next match brought the first home defeat of the season by Ipswich Town. In order to attempt a degree of continuity, Steve Thompson, one of the coaching staff, was appointed as caretaker manager until the end of the season.

Then followed the most dramatic period of the season. A creditable draw at Coventry, which followed victories over Bury, Ipswich, and Reading, saw a replay in which only one minute remained when David Holdsworth, a towering influence throughout the season, volleyed an equaliser. With no further goals in extra time, a penalty shoot out ensued in which Alan Kelly made three incredible saves and the winning penalty was walloped home by youngster Quinn. This gave United a semi final against Newcastle United and the prospect of two Wembley trips at the end of the season. Despite a creditable performance, however, ace predator Alan Shearer made sure the first part of the double was gone.

After this the team regrouped for one last push for a play off: by this stage automatic promotion was a distant hope. The team had games in hand due to the Cup run and international call ups, but this meant that four games needed to be played in the last week of the season. With no further goals in extra time, a penalty shoot out ensued in which Alan Kelly made three incredible saves and the winning penalty was walloped home by youngster Quinn. A last minute equaliser at Tranmere by Paul Devlin proved to be the point that booked a two leg semi final against Sunderland. A slender 2-1 lead from the first leg proved insufficient as a partisan crowd saw Sunderland score twice to end the United Wembley dream.

With the prospect of another close season managerial change, it remains to be seen if the Blades can sustain the challenge to attain the play-offs for the third season running, or even the prize of automatic promotion.

ANDREW TREHERNE.

SHEFFIELD UNITED

Division 1   :6th   FA CUP: Semi Final   LC CUP: 4th Round

M	DATE	COMP.	VEN	OPPONENTS	RESULT	H/T	LP	GOAL SCORERS/GOAL TIMES	ATT.
1	A 10	FL	H	Sunderland	W 2-0	2-0	5	Fjortoft 33, Borbokis 43	17324
2	12	CC 1/1	A	Wrexham	D 1-1	0-0		Borbokis 63	(3644)
3	15	FL	A	Wolverhampton Wand	D 0-0	0-0	6		(23102)
4	23	FL	H	Portsmouth	W 2-1	2-0	3	Fjortoft 3, 15	15895
5	26	CC 1/2	H	Wrexham	W 3-1	1-1		Deane 28, Whitehouse 74, Fjortoft 82	7181
6	30	FL	A	Huddersfield Town	D 0-0	0-0	6		(14268)
7	S 13	FL	H	Nottingham Forest	W 1-0	0-0	7	Taylor 78	24536
8	16	CC 2/1	A	Watford	D 1-1	1-0		Scott 18	(7154)
9	20	FL	A	Oxford United	W 4-2	2-1	6	Deane 1, Fjortoft 39 (pen), Holdsworth 67, Whitehouse 80	(7514)
10	23	CC 2/2	H	Watford	W 4-0	1-0		Whitehouse 49, 80, Deane 56, Day 18 (OG)	7511
11	27	FL	H	Birmingham City	D 0-0	0-0	7		20553
12	O 05	FL	A	Middlesbrough	W 2-1	1-1	5	Deane 23, Whitehouse 59	(30000)
13	14	CC 3	A	Walsall	L 1-2	0-0		Borbokis 49	(8239)
14	18	FL	H	Queens Park Rangers	D 2-2	1-0	6	Deane 31, Marcello 73	18006
15	21	FL	H	Stockport County	W 5-1	2-1	2	Whitehouse 6, Fjortoft 21, 49, 90, Deane 55	16241
16	25	FL	A	West Bromwich Albion	L 0-2	0-1	6		(17311)
17	N 01	FL	H	Tranmere Rovers	W 2-1	0-0	4	Tiler 83, Taylor 85	16578
18	04	FL	A	Reading	W 1-0	0-0	2	Patterson 51	(8132)
19	09	FL	A	Ipswich Town	D 2-2	1-0	4	Taylor 8, Ward 79	(9695)
20	15	FL	H	Manchester City	D 1-1	1-0	5	Deane 21	23780
21	18	FL	A	Bradford City	D 1-1	1-0		Deane 62	(16712)
22	22	FL	A	Port Vale	D 0-0	0-0	5		(8017)
23	29	FL	H	Crewe Alexandra	W 1-0	0-0	5	Fjortoft 47	16973
24	D 02	FL	H	Stoke City	W 3-2	0-1	5	Taylor 46, Fjortoft 64, Deane 80	14347
25	06	FL	A	Norwich City	L 1-2	0-0	5	Deane 51	(11745)
26	09	FL	A	Charlton Athletic	L 1-2	0-1	5	Marker 88	(9868)
27	13	FL	H	Swindon Town	W 2-1	1-1	3	Holdsworth 45, Saunders 81	18115
28	20	FL	A	Bury	D 1-1	0-1	4	Deane 79	(6012)
29	26	FL	A	Stoke City	D 2-2	0-0	5	Taylor 59, Deane 90	(19723)
30	28	FL	H	Charlton Athletic	W 4-1	2-0	3	Taylor 8, Saunders 32, Deane 57, Marker 64	18677
31	J 03	FAC 3	H	Bury	D 1-1	0-1		Fjortoft 65	14009
32	10	FL	A	Sunderland	L 2-4	1-1	5	Saunders 17, Taylor 82	(36391)
33	13	FAC 3R	A	Bury	W 2-1	0-0		Saunders 48, Fjortoft 71	(4920)
34	17	FL	H	Wolverhampton Wand	W 1-0	1-0	5	Marcello 39	22144
35	24	FAC 4	A	Ipswich Town	D 1-1	0-1		Saunders 81 (pen)	(14654)
36	27	FL	H	Huddersfield Town	D 1-1	1-1	4	Saunders 28	16535
37	31	FL	A	Portsmouth	D 1-1	1-1	5	, Knight 31 (OG)	(12003)
38	F 03	FAC 4R	H	Ipswich Town	W 1-0	1-0		Hutchison 13 (pen)	14144
39	06	FL	H	Oxford United	W 1-0	1-0	4	Ford 43	16881
40	13	FAC 5	H	Reading	W 1-0	0-0		Sandford 87	17845
41	22	FL	A	Birmingham City	L 0-2	0-1	5		(17965)
42	25	FL	A	Queens Park Rangers	D 2-2	1-1	5	Saunders 8, Stuart 69	(9560)
43	28	FL	H	Bradford City	W 2-1	1-0	5	Taylor 34, 79	17848
44	M 03	FL	H	Ipswich Town	L 0-1	0-1	5		14120
45	07	FAC QFR	A	Coventry City	D 1-1	1-1	7	Marcello 45	(23084)
46	14	FL	H	Reading	W 4-0	1-0	6	Stuart 44, Marcello 46, Taylor 54, Quinn 90	15473
47	17	FAC QFR	H	Coventry City	D 1-1*	0-1		Holdsworth 89 (Sheff. Utd won 3-1 on penalties)	29034
48	21	FL	A	Manchester City	D 0-0	0-0	6		(28496)
49	28	FL	H	Port Vale	W 2-1	0-0	6	Marcello 83, Saunders 89	15860
50	A 01	FL	A	Nottingham Forest	L 0-3	0-2	6		(21512)
51	05	FAC SF	H	Newcastle United	L 0-1	0-0			53452
52	07	FL	H	Middlesbrough	W 1-0	0-0	5	Saunders 52	18421
53	11	FL	H	Norwich City	D 2-2	2-0	5	Stuart 29, Borbokis 35	16915
54	13	FL	A	Swindon Town	D 1-1	0-1	6	Marcello 81	(5956)
55	18	FL	H	Bury	W 3-0	1-0	6	Stuart 29, Saunders 76, 85	16056
56	25	FL	H	West Bromwich Albion	L 2-4	1-1	7	Stuart 9 (pen), Marcello 69	21248
57	28	FL	A	Tranmere Rovers	D 3-3	0-1	6	Quinn 52, Saunders 78, Devlin 90	(7526)
58	30	FL	A	Crewe Alexandra	L 1-2	0-0	6	Hamilton 89	(5759)
59	M 03	FL	A	Stockport County	L 0-1	0-0	6		(9683)
60	10	PO SF1	H	Sunderland	W 2-1	0-1		Marcello 56, Borbokis 75	23800
61	13	PO SF2	A	Sunderland	L 0-2	0-2			(40092)

Best Home League Attendance: 24536 V Nottingham Forest   Smallest :14120 V Ipswich Town   Average :17936

Goal Scorers:
FL	(69)	Deane 11, Saunders 10, Taylor 10, Fjortoft 9, Marcello 6, Stuart 5, Whitehouse 3, Borbokis 2, Holdsworth 2, Marker 2, Quinn 2, Devlin 1, Ford 1, Hamilton 1, Patterson 1, Tiler 1, Ward 1, Opponents 1
CC	(10)	Whitehouse 3, Deane 2, Borbokis 2, Fjortoft 1, Scott 1, Opponents 1
FAC	(8)	Fjortoft 2, Saunders 2, Holdsworth 1, Hutchison 1, Marcello 1, Sandford 1
PO	(2)	Borbokis 1, Marcello 1

*AET

(M) Borbokis	(F) Deane	(M) Dellas	(D) Derry	(F) Devlin	(F) Fjortoft	(M) Ford	(M) Hamilton	(D) Holdsworth	(F) Hutchison	(F) Katchouro	(G) Kelly	(M) Marcello	(D) Marker	(D) McGarth	(M) Morris	(D) Nilsen	(M) Patterson	(M) Quinn	(D) Sandford	(F) Saunders	(D) Short	(F) Stuart	(F) Taylor	(D) Tiler	(G) Tracey	(M) Whitehouse	(D) Wilder	(M) Woodhouse	Referee
X	X			X		X					S1		X	X		S2	X	X				X	X		X		X		G Cain 1
X	X			X		X							X	X		S1	X	X				S2	X	X	X		X		E Wolstenholme 2
X	X		S			X			X	X			X	X		X	X						X	X	X		X		P S Danson 3
X	X					X			X	S1			X	X		X	X						X	X	X		X		R Pearson 4
X	X			X		X			X	S	S1		X			X	X					S2	X		X		X		G B Frankland 5
X	X			X		X			X	S	S1		X			X	X					S2	X	X	X		X		F G Stretton 6
X				X		X			X				X			X	X	S1	X			S2	X	X	X		X		E Lomas 7
X						X	S1	X	X				X	X	X						X	X		X		X			M E Pierce 8
X	X			X					X	S1			X	X		S2	X	X					X	X	X		X		M J Brandwood 9
X	X					X	S	X					X			X	X	X			S1		X	X	X		X		G Singh 10
X	X					X	S	X					X	X		X	X					S1	X	X	X		X		T Heilbron 11
X						X	S	X					X	X		X	X						X	X	X		X		C R Wilkes 12
X	X		S1			X		X	X				X	X		X	X						X	X	X		X		E Lomas 13
X	X					X	S		X		S1	X	X			X	X						X	X	X		X		K M Lynch 14
X	X					X	S3		X	X	S1	X	X			X	X						X	X	X		X		D Laws 15
X						X	S	S2	X	X	X	X	X			X	X						X	X	X		X		D Orr 16
X	X					X		X	X			S2	X			X	X	X				S1	X	X	X		X		A R Leake 17
X	X					S		X	X			S	X	X		X	X						X	X	X		X		P S Danson 18
X	X					S		X	X			S	X	X		X	X						X	X	X		X		M E Pierce 19
X	X					S2		X	X			S		X		S1	X						X	X	X		X		P Rejer 20
X	X					X		X	X			S		X	S		X						X	X	X		X		E K Wolstenholme 21
X	X					S		X	X			S2	X			X	S1						X	X	X		X		D Pugh 22
X3	X	X		X2	S3		X	X					X			X	X1					X	S2	X				S1	M R Halsey 23
X	X	X		X	S3		X2						X			X1	X3					X	S2	X		X		S1	G B Frankland 24
X	X		X1	X		X				S			X						X		X	S1		X		X		X	S G Bennett 25
X	X		S2	X	S3			X					X			X1				X		X2				X		S1	M C Bailey 26
X	X		X1	X		X	S		X				X			X				X		X2	S1			X		S2	T Jones 27
	X		X1	X		X	S	X	X	S			X			X				X		X	X		X		X	M J Brandwood 28
X1	X		S	X			S1	S2	X	X			X			X				X		X	X		X		X2	S W Mathieson 29
X1	X2		S	X		X	S2	X	X				X			X				X		S1	X		X			G Laws 30
X	X		S1	X		X	X	S2	X				X			X				X		S	X1				X2	D Orr 31
X	X		S		X		X	X					X			X				X		X	S1					P R Richards 32
X2			X	X	X	S		S					X			X				X		X	X1	X				D J Gallagher 33
			X		X	X	X2	X				S1	X1			X						X	X					W C Burns 34
		X1		X		X		X		X	X	S1			X	X	X						X					A B Wilkie 35
		X		X	X2	X1	X			X	S2		X			X	X					X			X			M Fletcher 36
		X	S1	X	X	S		X					X	X	X							X			X			M R Halsey 37
		X		X	X	S	S	X1	X		X	S1	X	X	X1	X	S1						X					A B Wilkie 38
		S2		X	X	X	S1	X		X2			X	X	X	X1	X						X					T Heilbron 39
X				X	X	X	S2	X	S1	X			X	X2		X1	X	X					X					N S Barry 40
X1		S1		X		X		S3	X	S2	X			X2	X			X3											B Knight 41
X1		X		X		X			X				X			X	X			X	S1								P Taylor 42
X2		X		X		X			X		S	X		S2	X		X1	X	X		S								R D Furnandiz 43
X1		X2		X		X			X			X	X	X		X													A G Wiley 44
X	S			X		X			S2	X	X2	X		X	X1	X	X						S					S W Dunn 45
X			X	S1	X		S2	X	X1	X			X	X	X3	X2												C J Foy 46
X	S2			X		X		S1	X	X3	X2		S3	X		X	X	X1		X		S							S W Dunn 47
X2	S1	X	S2	X			X	X3			X	X	X1	S3	X													R Pearson 48
	S2	S3		X2	X3		X	X			X	X	X3	X	X1	S2				X	X							G Bennett 49
	X	X	S1	S3	X		X2	X1			X	X3	X	S2	X	X												G Cain 50
X	S2			X		X	S3	X	X1	X2		X	X	X3	S	X	S1	S										G Poll 51
X	S		S1	X		X	X2	X	S		X	X	X1	X	X2													E Lomas 52
X	S2	S1		X	X2	X	S	X	S		X	X	X1															K M Lynch 53
	S2	S1	X	X2	X		S	X	X	X1	X	X	X							X								D Pugh 54
X	X		S1	X		X		X	X	X	X	X											S1					S J Baines 55
X	X2	S1		X		X	X	X1	X		X	X			X	X2												M E Pierce 56
	S	X		X			S1	X1	S2	X2	S3	X1	X	X	X			X				X2						T Heilbron 57
X		X		X	S2	X2	X1	S1	X	X	X	X	X3		X			X		X								P Rejer 58
X		X		X	X2	X1	S1	X	X	S2	X		X	X														C R Wilkes 59
X	S	X	X	X	X		S1	X	S	X	X	X	X1	X													C R Wilkes 60
X	S2		X	X2	X	X3	X1	S3	X	X	X	X	S1													X	M E Pierce 61
36	24	5	8	4	15	20	8	40	14	6	19	12	43	12		18	17	28	15	23	5	27	13	17	27	17	7	4	FL Appearances
	4		4	6	2	3			4	10		9			5	4	1		1		1	15				1	5		FL Sub Appearances
5	4			2+1			5	0+1	3+1	1		4	2	1+1	5	5			0+1		1+2	5	4	5					CC Appearances
6	1	0+2		1+1	8		8	4	4+1	8	0+2	2	4+1	6	6	4	6	5+2	2		0+1	1		2		1		FAC Appearances
1		0+1		2		2	2	2		1+1	2	0+1		2	2	0+1	1		2		1							PO Appearances

Also Played: (D) Beard S(3,31,32,36,37,38,40,47), S2(8,33,34). X(35). S1(44,45). (D) Barrett X(34,36,37,39,41). (M) Burley S(4). (M) Cullen S1(36), S(37), S3(46). (M) Davies S(35). (G) Dibble S(1). (M) George S(31,33,35). (M) Hawes S(2). (M) Henry S(25), X3(26). (D) Lee X(29,30,34), X1(32). (M) Lehtinen S(35). (M) Ludlam S(35,45). (M) O'Connor S(42,56,59), S2(43), S1(58). (F) Rush X(42,43,44,48). (F) Scott S1(3,12), X7,8,10), S3(9), S2(11), S(13). (D) Vonk X(25,26,27). (F) Walker S3(7), S(8,10). (D) White S2(4), X(5). (M) Ward S2(12,15). S(13,14,18). S1(19), X(20,21,22).

SHEFFIELD UNITED

CLUB RECORDS

BIGGEST VICTORIES
League: 10-0 v Port Vale (a), Div 2, 10.12.1892 (The only time a club has scored 10 Lge goals away from home)
10-0 v Burnley, Division 1, 19.1.1929
(Most goals) 11-2 v Cardiff City, 1.1.1926
F.A. Cup: 5-0 v Corinthians, Round 1, 10.1.1925
5-0 v Newcastle, Round 1, 10.1.1914
5-0 v Barrow, Round 3, 7.1.1956
League Cup: 4-0 v Fulham, Round 1, 25.9.1961
5-1 v Grimsby, Round 2, 26.10.1982
5-1 v Rotherham United, Round 1, 3.9.1985

BIGGEST DEFEATS
League: 1-8 v Arsenal, Division 1, 12.4.1930
2-9 v Arsenal, Division 1, 24.12.1932
3-10 v Middlesbrough, Division 1, 18.11.1933
0-7 v Tottenham Hotspur, Division 2, 12.11.1949
F.A. Cup: 0-13 v Bolton Wanderers, Round 2, 1.2.1890
League Cup: 0-5 v West Ham United, Round 5, 17.11.1971

MOST POINTS
3 points a win: 96, Division 4, 1981-82
2 points a win: 60, Division 2, 1952-53

MOST GOALS
102, Division 1, 1925-26.
Johnson 23, Tunstall 20, Boyle 13, Gillespie 12, Menlove 12, Mercer 8, Partridge 6, Hoyland 3, Roxborough 1, Waugh 1, Longworth 1, Grew 1, og 1.

MOST FIRST CLASS MATCHES IN A SEASON
61 (46 League, 7 FA Cup, 5 League Cup, 3 Sherpa Van Trophy) 1988-89

MOST LEAGUE GOALS CONCEDED
101, Division 1, 1933-34

MOST LEAGUE WINS
27, Division 4, 1981-82

MOST LEAGUE DRAWS
18, Division 1, 1920-21, Premier Division 1993-94

MOST LEAGUE DEFEATS
26, Division 1, 1975-76

INDIVIDUAL CLUB RECORDS

MOST GOALS IN A SEASON
Jimmy Dunne 46 (League 41, FAC 5) 1930-31
4 goals once=4; 3 goals 5 times=15; 2 goals 4 times=8; 1 goal 19 times=19.
Previous holder: Jimmy Dunne 36, 1928-29.

MOST GOALS IN A MATCH
5. Harry Hammond v Bootle, 8-3, Division 2, 26.11.1892
5. Harry Johnson v West Ham Utd, 6-2, Division 1, 26.12.1927

OLDEST PLAYER
Jimmy Hagan, 39 years 236 days v Derby County, 14.9.1957

YOUNGEST PLAYER
Steve Hawes, 17 years 47 days v WBA 2.9.96.

MOST CAPPED PLAYER
Billy Gillespie (Northern Ireland) 25

BEST PERFORMANCES

League: 1981-82: Matches played 46, Won 27, Drawn 15, Lost 4, Goals for 94, Goals against 41, Points 96. First in Division 4.
Highest: Division 1 Champions.
F.A. Cup: 1898-99: 1st rnd. Burnley 2-2, 2-0; 2nd rnd. Preston North End 2-2,2-1; 3rd rnd. Notts County 1-0; Semi-final Liverpool 2-2, 4-4, 1-0; Final Derby 4-1.
1901-02: 1st rnd. Northampton 2-0; 2nd rnd. Bolton Wanderers 2-1; 3rd rnd. Newcastle Utd. 1-1, 2-1; Semi-final Derby County 1-1, 1-1, 1-0; Final Southampton 1-1, 2-1.
1914-15: 3rd rnd. Blackpool 2-1; 4th rnd. Liverpool 1-0; 5th rnd. Bradford 1-0; 6th rnd. Oldham 0-0, 3-0; Semi-final Bolton Wanderers 2-1; Final Chelsea 3-0.
1924-25: 3rd rnd. Corinthians 5-0; 4th rnd. Sheffield Wednesday 3-2; 5th rnd.Everton 2-0; 6th rnd. West Bromwich Albion 2-0; Semi-final Southampton 2-0;Final Cardiff 1-0.
League Cup: 1961-62: 1st rnd. Fulham 1-1, 4-0; 2nd rnd. Newcastle 2-2, 2-0; 3rd rnd. Portsmouth 1-0; 4th rnd. Bye; 5th rnd Blackpool 0-0, 0-2.
1966-67: 1st rnd. Bye; 2nd rnd. Sunderland 1-1, 1-0; 3rd rnd. Burnley 2-0; 4th rnd. Walsall 2-1; 5th rnd. Birmingham 2-3.
1971-72: 1st rnd. Bye; 2nd rnd. Fulham 3-0; 3rd rnd. York City 3-2; 4th rnd.Arsenal 0-0, 2-0; 5th rnd. West Ham United 0-5.

DIVISIONAL RECORD							
	Played	Won	Drawn	Lost	For	Against	Points
Division 1/P	2,318	861	552	905	3,499	3,707	2,325
Division 2/1	1,262	549	322	391	2,089	1,665	1,509
Division 3	230	100	49	81	366	300	317
Division 4	46	27	15	4	94	41	96
Total	3,856	1,537	938	1,381	6,048	5,713	4,309

ADDITIONAL INFORMATION
Club colours: Red/white striped shirts, black shorts, red/black socks.
Change colours: All white.

Reserves League
Pontins League Division 2

RECORDS AND STATISTICS

COMPETITIONS

Div 1/P	Div.2/1	Div.3	Div.4	Texaco	Watney
1893-1934	1892-93	1979-81	1981-82	1972-73	1970
1945-49	1934-39	1982-84		1973-74	1972
1953-56	1949-53	1988-89		1974-75	
1961-68	1956-61				A/Scot
1971-76	1968-71				1975-76
1990-94	1976-79			A/Ital	1977-78
	1984-88			1994-95	1978-79
	1989-90				1979-80
	1994-				1980-81

HONOURS

Div.1	Div.2	Div.4	FA Cup
1897-98	1952-53	1981-82	1899
			1902
			1915
			1925

MOST APPEARANCES

Joe Shaw 689 (1948-66)

Year	League	FA Cup	Lge Cup
1948-49	19		
1949-50	37	3	
1950-51	36		
1951-52	39	5	
1952-53	42	3	
1953-54	35	2	
1954-55	41	1	
1955-56	19		
1956-57	30	1	
1957-58	41	4	
1958-59	41	6	
1959-60	39	3	
1960-61	42	7	1
1961-62	37	5	5
1962-63	40	3	1
1963-64	41	3	
1964-65	25	3	
1965-66	27	2	
	631	51	7

MOST GOALS IN A CAREER

J Johnson - 223 (1919-31)

Year	League	FA Cup
1919-20	12	1
1920-21	12	
1921-22	17	
1922-23	17	1
1923-24	15	
1924-25	16	5
1925-26	23	1
1926-27	23	1
1927-28	33	9
1928-29	33	
1929-30	3	
1930-31	1	
Total	205	18

Current leading goalscorer: Dane Whitehouse - 44 (1989-97)

MANAGERS

Name	Seasons	Best	Worst
J Wolstinholm	1898-99	16(1)	16(1)
J Nicholson	1899-32	2(1)	20(1)
J Davison	1932-52	6(1)	11(2)
R Freeman	1952-54	13(1)	1(2)
J Mercer	1954-59	22(1)	7(2)
J Harris	1959-68	5(1)	4(2)
A Rowley	1968-69	9(2)	9(2)
J Harris	1969-73	10(1)	6(2)
K Furphy	1973-76	6(1)	13(1)
J Sirrell	1976-78	22(1)	11(2)
C Coldwell	1978	12(2)	12(2)
H Haslam	1978-81	20(2)	12(3)
M Peters	1981	21(3)	21(3)
I Porterfield	1981-86	7(2)	1(4)
B McEwan	1986-88	9(2)	9(2)
Dave Bassett	1988-95	9(1)	2(3)
Howard Kendall	1995-97	5(1)	9(1)
N Spackman (Caretaker)	1997-98	6 (1)	6 (1)
S Thompson (Caretaker)	1998	6 (1)	6 (1)
Steve Bruce	1998-		

RECORD TRANSFER FEE RECEIVED

Amount	Club	Player	Date
£2,700,000	Leeds United	Brian Deane	7/93
£1,750,000*	Bolton Wanderers	Nathan Blake	12/95
£750,000	Notts County	Tony Agana	11/91
£575,000	Chelsea	Vinny Jones	9/91

*Included Mark Patterson coming to United.

RECORD TRANSFER FEE PAID

Amount	Club	Player	Date
£1,500,000	Leeds United	Brian Deane	07/97
£1,000,000*	West Ham	Don Hutchinson	12/95
£700,000	Ipswich Town	Brain Gayle	9/91
£650,000	Leeds United	Vinny Jones	9/90

*Could increase to £1.2m after so many appearances.

LONGEST LEAGUE RUNS

of undefeated matches:	22 (2.9.1899 - 20.1.1900)	of league matches w/out a win:	19 (27.9.1975 - 14.2.1976)
of undefeated home matches:	27 (31.8.1936 - 6.11.1937)	of undefeated away matches:	11 (3.12.1892 - 30.10.1893)
without home win:	10 (26.3.1949 - 22.10.1949)	without an away win:	20 (19.4.1975 - 14.4.1976)
of league wins:	8 (6.2.1893-12.4.1893, 5.9.1903-31.10.1903)	of home wins:	11 (30.4.1960 - 3.12.1960)
	(1.2.1958 - 5.4.1958, 14.9.1960 - 22.10.1960)		
of league defeats:	7 (19.8.1975 - 23.9.1975)	of away wins:	6 (10.12.1891 - 12.4.1892)

PLAYERS NAME / Honours	Ht	Wt	Birthdate	Birthplace / Transfers	Contract Date	Clubs	League	L/Cup	FA Cup	Other	Lge	L/C	FAC	Oth
G O A L K E E P E R														
Kelly Alan	6.2	12.5	8/11/68	Preston	9/25/85	Preston North End	142	1	8	13				
Ei: 3, u23.1, u21.1, Y				£150000	7/24/92	Sheffield United	190+3	12	17	2				
Tracey Simon	6	12	12/9/67	Woolwich	2/3/86	Wimbledon	1			1				
				£7500	10/19/88	Sheffield United	183+2	11	14	10				
				Loan	10/28/94	Manchester City	3							
				Loan	1/3/95	Norwich City	1		2					
				Loan	8/4/95	Nottingham Forest								
				Loan	11/2/95	Wimbledon								
D E F E N C E														
Borbokis Vassilios	5.11	12	2/10/69	Serres		AEK Athens								
				£900000	7/9/97	Sheffield United	35	6	6	1	3	2		1
Bruce Steve	6	12.6	12/31/60	Corbridge	10/27/78	Gillingham	203+2	15	14		29	6	1	
E: B1, Y8; Div2'86; LC'85'92; FAC'90; ECW				£125000	8/24/84	Norwich City	141	20	9	10	14	5	1	
Prem'93'94'96;				£800000	12/18/87	Manchester United	279	31+1	36	30+2	35	6	3	7
				Free	6/1/96	Birmingham City	70+2	6	6		2		1	
				£200000	7/1/98	Sheffield United								
Cullen David J	6	12	1/10/73	Durham	9/16/91	Doncaster Rovers	8+1	2+1	0+1	1		1		
via Spennymoor, Morpeth				Free	3/27/97	Hartlepool United	33+1	2	1	2	12			
				£250000	1/26/98	Sheffield United	0+2							
Dellas Traianos	6.4	15	1/31/76	Salonika	8/26/97	Sheffield United (T)	5+4		0+2	0+1				
Derry Shaun	5.10	10.13	12/6/77	Nottingham	4/13/96	Notts County	76+3	4+1	6+1	3	4		1	
DIV3 97/98				£500000	1/26/98	Sheffield United	8+4							
Holdsworth David	6.1	12.4	11/8/68	Walthamstow	11/8/86	Watford	249+9	20	14+1	8+2	10	2	1	
E: u21.1, Y.6				£500000	10/7/96	Sheffield United	76	6	9	5	3		1	
Marker Nick	6	12.11	5/3/65	Budleigh Salt.	5/4/83	Exeter City	196+6	11	8	8	3	1		3
				£95000	10/31/87	Plymouth Argyle	201+1	15	9	7	13	3	1	1
				£500000	9/23/92	Blackburn Rovers	41+13	3+1	4+1	1+1	1			
					7/25/97	Sheffield United	41	4	8	2	2			
Nilsen Roger	5.9	11.8	8/8/69	Norway		Viking Stavanger								
Norwegian International				£550000	11/2/93	Sheffield United	142+6	7+1	9+2	2+1				
Sandford Lee	6.1	12.2	4/22/68	Basingstoke	12/4/85	Portsmouth	66+6	11	4	2+1	1			
E: Y, S. AGT'92. Div2'93				£140000	12/22/89	Stoke City	209+3	16	14	27	8		2	4
				£500000	7/5/96	Sheffield United	40+5	3	7	3+1	2		1	
Wilder Chris	5.11	10.1	9/23/67	Stockbridge	9/26/85	Southampton								
				Free	8/20/86	Sheffield United	89+4	8+1	7	3	1			
				Loan	11/2/89	Walsall	4		1	2				
				Loan	10/12/90	Charlton Athletic	2							
				Loan	11/28/91	Charlton Athletic	1							
				Loan	2/27/92	Leyton Orient	16			1	1			
				£50000	7/30/92	Rotherham United	111+4	7	15+2	5+1	10		1	
				£130000	1/2/96	Notts County	46	2	4					
					3/27/97	Bradford City	34+6	3	1					
				£150000	3/26/98	Sheffield United	7+1			1				
M I D F I E L D														
Bettney Christopher J	5.11	10.1	10/27/77	Chesterfield		Sheffield United	0+1							
Davies Kevin John	5.11	12	11/15/78	Sheffield	6/3/97	Sheffield United (T)								
Ebbrell John K	5.7	9.12	10/1/69	Bromborough	11/7/86	Everton	207+10	17	20	9+2	13	1	3	2
E: B.1, u21.14, Y.4, S. GMAFS. FAC'95. CS'95.					3/3/97	Sheffield United	1							
Ford Robert J	5.8	11	9/22/74	Bristol	10/6/92	Oxford United	104+11	14+2	9	7	7	1	2	1
				£400000	11/28/97	Sheffield United	20+3		8	2	1			
Hamilton Ian	5.9	11.3	12/14/67	Stevenage	12/24/85	Southampton								
					3/29/88	Cambridge United	23+1	1	2	2	1			
					12/23/88	Scunthorpe United	139+6	6	6+1	14+1	18			3
				£170000	6/19/92	WBA	228+11	13+2	10+1	14+2	23	1	1	3
					3/26/98	Sheffield United	8			2	1			
Henry Nicholas I	5.6	10.8	2/21/69	Liverpool	7/6/87	Oldham Athletic	264+9	30+4	21	5	19	3		
					3/6/97	Sheffield United	10			2				
Lehtinen Ville	5.10	11.7	12/17/78	Tampere		HJK Helsinki								
				£50000	1/14/98	Sheffield United								
Ludlam Ryan	6	12.6	5/12/79	Carlisle	6/12/97	Sheffield United (T)	0+5		0+2	0+1				
Morris Lee	5.10	10.7	4/30/80	Blackpool	12/22/97	Sheffield United (T)								
O'Connor Jonathan	5.1	11.03	10/29/76	Darlington	10/28/93	Everton	3+2							
E: Y.14, S.				Swap	2/23/98	Sheffield United	0+2							
Quinn Wayne	5.1	11.7	11/19/76	Cornwall	12/6/94	Sheffield United	28	5	4+1	2	2			
Whitehouse Dane	5.9	10.12	10/14/70	Sheffield	7/1/89	Sheffield United	204+27	20+1	14+3	6	38	8	2	2
FLg u18.1														
Woodhouse Curtis	5.8	11	4/17/80	Driffield	8/8/97	Sheffield United (T)	4+5		1					
F O R W A R D														
Devlin Paul J	5.8	10.1	4/14/72	Birmingham	11/1/90	Stafford Rangers			0+1					
				£40000	2/22/92	Notts County	106+9	9+1	5	14+1	19	1	1	4
				£250000	3/1/96	Birmingham City	59+15	8+1	3+1		28	4	2	
				£200000	3/13/98	Sheffield United	4+6			2	1			
Katchouro Petr	5.11	11.5	8/2/72	Belarus		Dinamo Minsk								
				Belarus Int	7/11/96	Sheffield United	34+22	5+3	2+6	3	12	1		1

Name			DOB	From	Fee	Date	Club									
Marcello Cipriano D S	6	13.8	10/11/69	Brazil			Dep Aleves									
					£400000	10/6/97	Sheffield United	12+9		5+1	1+1	6		1	1
aunders Dean	5.8	10.6	6/21/64	Swansea		6/24/82	Swansea City	42+7	2+1	1	1+1	12			
J: 49. FAC'92. FLC'94.					Loan	3/29/85	Cardiff City	3+1							
					Free	8/7/85	Brighton & H.A.	66+6	4	7	3	21		5	
					£60000	3/12/87	Oxford United	57+2	9+1	2	2	22	8	2	1
					£1000000	10/28/88	Derby County	106	12	6	7	42	10		5
					£2900000	7/19/91	Liverpool	42	5	8	6	11	2	2	10
					£2300000	9/10/92	Aston Villa	111+1	15	9	8	37	7	4	1
						7/1/95	Galatasaray								
					£1500000	7/16/96	Nottingham Forest	38+2	5+1	2		5	2	2	
					Free	12/5/97	Sheffield United	23+1		6	2	10		2	
tuart Graham C	5.8	11.6	10/24/70	Tooting		6/15/89	Chelsea	70+17	11	5+2	3+2	14	2	1	1
:: u21.5, Y.5, S. FAC'95.					£850000	8/19/93	Everton	96+12	6	7+1	2+1	19	2	3	1
						11/28/97	Sheffield United	27+1		6	0+1	5			
aylor Gareth K	6.2	12.05	2/25/73	Weston-s-Mare			Southampton								
					Free	7/29/91	Bristol Rovers	24+16	0+1	1+1	5	12			
					£1250000	9/27/95	Crystal Palace	9+1				3			
						3/8/96	Sheffield United	47+22	5+2	5+2	1+2	23	1		
ADDITIONAL CONTRACT PLAYERS															
Burley Adam G						2/12/98	Sheffield United (T)								
Twiss Michael (Forw')	5.10	12.1	12/26/77	Salford		7/1/96	Manchester Utd (T)								
					Loan (1Year)	7/1/98	Sheffield United								

PLAYER/MANAGER
STEVE BRUCE

Date of Birth . . . . 31st December 1960.
Place of Birth . . . . Corbridge, Northumberland.
Date of Appointment . . . . June 1998.

PREVIOUS CLUBS
As Manager . . . . None.
As a Player . . . . Gillingham, Norwich City, Manchester United
. . . . Birmingham City.

HONOURS
As a Manager
None.

As a Player
Norwich City: League Cup 1985. Division Two Championship 1986.
Manchester United: Premiership 1993'94'96. FA Cup 1990'94. League Cup 1992.
ECWC 1991. European Super Cup 1991.
International: 1 England 'B' cap and Youth . . . .

BRAMALL LANE GROUND
Sheffield S2 4SU

Capacity..30,370.

First game...Sheffield Club v Hallam (Charity Match), 0-0, 28.12.1862.
As Sheffield Utd... v Birmingham St Georges (friendly) 0-4, 28.9.1889.
First floodlit game..v Rotherham, 16.3.1954.

ATTENDANCES
Highest...68,287 v Leeds United, FAC 5th Rnd, 15.1.1936.
Lowest..1,500 v Bootle, Division 1, 10.9.1892.

OTHER GROUNDS...None.

HOW TO GET TO THE GROUND

From the North
Use motorway M1 until junction 34. Leave motorway and follow signs, Sheffield (A6109). In 3.4 miles turn left and shortly at roundabout take 4th exit into Sheaf Street. Then at 2nd roundabout take 5th exit into St Mary's Road (sign posted Bakewell). In half-a-mile left into Bramall Lane for Sheffield United FC.
From the East and South
Use (A57) from motorway M1 (junction 31 or 33) then at roundabout take 3rd exit into Sheaf Street. Then at 2nd roundabout take 5th exit in St Mary's Road and proceed as above.
From the West
Use A57, sign posted Sheffield, and at roundabout take 4th exit A6134 into Upper Hanover Street. Then at 2nd roundabout take 3rd exit into Bramall Lane.

Car Parking: The ground is five minutes away from car parks in the City Centre. Side-street parking is ample.
Nearest Railway Station: Sheffield Midland (0114 272 6411).

USEFUL TELEPHONE NUMBERS

Club switchboard. 0114 221 5757
Club fax number 0114 272 3030
Club shop 0114 221 3132
Ticket Office 0114 221 3122

Marketing Department. 0114 221 3108
Internet address . . . . www.sufc.co.uk
Clubcall. 0891 888 650*
*Calls cost 50p per minute at all times. Call costings correct at time of going to press.

MATCHDAY PROGRAMME

Programme Editor. . . . . Andy Pack

Number of pages . . . . 48.

Price . . . . £1.80.

Subscriptions . . . . Apply to club.

Local Newspapers
. . . . Sheffield Newspaper Ltd
. . . . (The Star, Sheffield Telegraph)

Local Radio Stations
. . . . . BBC Radio Sheffield, Radio Hallam.

MATCHDAY TICKET PRICES (97/98)

Laver Stand £16

Juv/OAP. £8

Kop £10

Juv/OAP. £7

John Street Stand £16

Juv/OAP. £8

Family Enclosure £11

Juv/OAP. £5

STOCKPORT COUNTY
(The Hatters)
NATIONWIDE LEAGUE DIVISION 1
SPONSORED BY: ROBINSON BEST BITTER

1998-99 Back Row L-R: Francis Vaughan, Ian Moore, Stephen Grant, Aaron Wilbraham, Martin McIntosh, Brett Angell, Wayne Phillips. **Middle Row:** Dave Moss (Res. team manager), Sean Connelly, James Flood, Graham Branch, Carlo Nash, Eric Nixon, David Fish, Ian gray, James Gannon, Colin Woodthorpe, Sean Mannion, Rodger Wylde (Physio). **Front Row:** Austin Speight (Centre of Excellence Director), Craig Madden (Yth Team Manager), Simon Travis, Paul Cook, Mike Flynn, Mike Phelan (Asst. Manager), Gary Megson (Manager), Chris Byrne, Tony Dinning, Kevin Cooper, John Bishop (Kit manager), Harry McNally (Chief scout).

STOCKPORT COUNTY
FORMED IN 1883
TURNED PROFESSIONAL IN 1891
LTD COMPANY IN 1908

CHAIRMAN: Brendon Elwood
VICE-CHAIRMAN
Grahame White
DIRECTORS
Mike Baker, Michael H Rains, Brian Taylor,
David Jolley
SECRETARY
Gary Glendenning BA A.C.C.A.
COMMERCIAL MANAGER
John Rutter

MANAGER: Gary Megson
ASSISTANT MANAGER: Mike Phelan
RESERVE TEAM MANAGER
Dave Moss
YOUTH TEAM MANAGER
Simon Travis
PHYSIOTHERAPIST
Rodger Wylde

STATISTICIAN FOR THE DIRECTORY
Ian Watts & Stuart Brennan

Stockport County's first season back in Division One in over sixty years, started slowly and by mid September, having played seven League games, they had only recorded three points and were second from bottom.

However, form improved from that point on as come December they had played another 13 matches winning nine, drawing two and losing only two. This placed the club in seventh place, their highest of the season.

The club maintained form good enough to only see them leave the top ten once, but they could never quite step up the extra gear needed to challenge for a play-off place.

The Cup competitions both ended after only two rounds. In the Coca-Cola Cup Mansfield Town proved to be difficult opponents with the Third Division club winning the first leg 4-2. In the second leg Stockport did enough, just, to win through winning the match 6-3, and the tie 8-7 on aggregate. In the second round fellow Division One side, Birmingham City, went through 5-3 on aggregate. The FA Cup also ended with Birmingham City knocking out the 'Hatters' 2-1 after Preston North End had been disposed of in the third round.

Having lost his striking partner, Alun Armstrong - sold to Middlesbrough - Brett Angel finished up as top goalscorer with 25 goals in all competitions, Brett was so nearly the only ever-present too, missing just one League match.

Stockport will hoping that this season with a better start they can gain the vital points, that last season they missed out on, to claim a play-off place.

STOCKPORT COUNTY

Division 1   :8th   FA CUP: 4th Round   LC CUP: 2nd Round

M	DATE	COMP.	VEN	OPPONENTS	RESULT	H/T	LP	GOAL SCORERS/GOAL TIMES	ATT.
1	A 09	FL	A	Bradford City	L 1-2	0-1	15	Durkan 68	(14312)
2	12	CC 1/1	A	Mansfield Town	L 2-4	1-2		Angell 36, Woodthorpe 75	(2170)
3	15	FL	H	Bury	D 0-0	0-0	18		7260
4	23	FL	A	Queens Park Rangers	L 1-2	1-1	20	Armstrong 28	(11108)
5	26	CC 1/2	H	Mansfield Town	W 6-3	2-1		Dinning 28, Angell 45, Flynn 66, Armstrong 70, Mutch 88, Cooper 90	2840
6	29	FL	H	Birmingham City	D 2-2	1-0	13	Armstrong 6, Angell 48	6260
7	S 02	FL	H	Middlesbrough	D 1-1	0-1	15	Connelly 60	8257
8	09	FL	A	Port Vale	L 1-2	1-2	19	Dinning 43 (pen)	(6615)
9	13	FL	A	Stoke City	L 1-2	0-1	21	Mutch 48	(11743)
10	17	CC 2/1	A	Birmingham City	L 1-4	0-1		Angell 89	(4900)
11	20	FL	H	Huddersfield Town	W 3-0	2-0	17	Angell 6, 18, Armstrong 63	6995
12	23	CC 2/2	H	Birmingham City	W 2-1	1-0		Armstrong 37, Mutch 87	2074
13	27	FL	A	Charlton Athletic	W 3-1	0-1	16	Armstrong 69, Angell 72, Rufus 78 (OG)	(12083)
14	O 04	FL	H	Portsmouth	W 3-1	2-0	12	Angell 45, 90, Cook 7 (OG)	7824
15	11	FL	H	Oxford United	W 3-2	0-0	6	Angell 47, Dinning 71, Armstrong 75	7333
16	18	FL	A	Norwich City	D 1-1	1-0	8	Angell 34	(12689)
17	21	FL	A	Sheffield United	L 1-5	1-2	12	McIntosh 23	(16241)
18	25	FL	H	Wolverhampton Wand	W 1-0	1-0	9	Cook 20	9804
19	N 01	FL	H	Sunderland	D 1-1	0-0	11	Gannon 79	9473
20	04	FL	A	Ipswich Town	W 2-0	0-0	8	Angell 70, 81	(8938)
21	08	FL	A	Reading	L 0-1	0-1	11		(7444)
22	15	FL	H	Swindon Town	W 4-2	2-1	7	Cook 8, McIntosh 33, Armstrong 79, 87	7694
23	22	FL	A	Crewe Alexandra	W 1-0	1-0	6	Cooper 23	(5231)
24	29	FL	H	Manchester City	W 3-1	3-0	6	Cook 6, Armstrong 8, Angell 30	11351
25	D 06	FL	A	West Bromwich Albion	L 2-3	0-1	6	Armstrong 60, Bryne 90	(13597)
26	13	FL	H	Tranmere Rovers	W 3-1	1-1	7	Bryne 45, Cooper 47, Angell 90	7903
27	20	FL	A	Nottingham Forest	L 1-2	1-0	8	Armstrong 15	(16701)
28	26	FL	H	Port Vale	W 3-0	0-0	7	Travis 66, 80, Bennett 71	10003
29	28	FL	A	Middlesbrough	L 1-3	1-1	8	Flynn 30	(30166)
30	J 03	FAC 3	A	Preston North End	W 2-1	1-0		Angell 30, 48	(12180)
31	10	FL	H	Bradford City	L 1-2	0-2	9	Armstrong 84	8460
32	18	FL	A	Bury	W 1-0	1-0	7	Angell 15	(5699)
33	24	FAC 4	A	Birmingham City	L 1-2	0-1		Armstrong 66	(15882)
34	27	FL	A	Birmingham City	L 1-4	0-3	8	Connelly 79	(17118)
35	31	FL	H	Queens Park Rangers	W 2-0	1-0	7	Armstrong 14, Dinning 58 (pen)	7958
36	F 06	FL	A	Huddersfield Town	L 0-1	0-0	8		(11121)
37	14	FL	H	Stoke City	W 1-0	0-0	7	Grant 82	8701
38	17	FL	A	Portsmouth	L 0-1	0-1	7		(8622)
39	21	FL	H	Charlton Athletic	W 3-0	1-0	6	Cooper 12, 53, Mutch 66	7705
40	24	FL	H	Norwich City	D 2-2	1-0	6	Dinning 19, Grant 46	7471
41	28	FL	A	Oxford United	L 0-3	0-1	7		(6650)
42	M 03	FL	H	Reading	W 5-1	4-0	6	Bryne 10, 32, Angell 11, 70, Grant 23	6148
43	07	FL	A	Sunderland	L 1-4	0-1	8	Angell 61	(34870)
44	14	FL	H	Ipswich Town	L 0-1	0-0	8		8939
45	21	FL	A	Swindon Town	D 1-1	0-0	8	Woodthorpe 86	(6684)
46	28	FL	H	Crewe Alexandra	L 0-1	0-0	8		8370
47	A 04	FL	A	Manchester City	L 1-4	1-3	9	Wilbraham 6	(31855)
48	11	FL	H	West Bromwich Albion	W 2-1	1-1	9	Cooper 25 (pen), Bryne 68	7943
49	13	FL	A	Tranmere Rovers	L 0-3	0-2	9		(8070)
50	18	FL	H	Nottingham Forest	D 2-2	1-1	9	Angell 29, 67	9892
51	25	FL	A	Wolverhampton Wand	W 4-3	1-2	9	Cooper 40 (pen), 83 (pen), Bryne 57, 87	(22452)
52	M 03	FL	H	Sheffield United	W 1-0	0-0	8	Cooper 62	9683

Best Home League Attendance: 11351 V Manchester City   Smallest :6148 V Reading   Average :8237

Goal Scorers:

FL	(71)	Angell 18, Armstrong 12, Cooper 8, Bryne 7, Dinning 4, Cook 3, Grant 3, Connelly 2, McIntosh 2, Mutch 2, Travis 2, Bennett 1, Durkan 1, Flynn 1, Gannon 1, Wilbraham 1, Woodthorpe 1, Opponents 2
CC	(11)	Angell 3, Armstrong 2, Mutch 2, Cooper 1, Dinning 1, Flynn 1, Woodthorpe 1
FAC	(3)	Angell 2, Armstrong 1

	(F) Angell	(F) Armstrong	(D) Bennett	(D) Bound	(M) Bryne	(F) Cavaco	(D) Connelly	(M) Cook	(M) Cooper	(D) Dinning	(M) Durkan	(M) Flynn	(D) Gannon	(M) Grant	(G) Gray	(M) Kalogeracos	(M) Marsden	(M) McGoldrick	(M) McIntosh	(F) Mutch	(G) Nash	(G) Nixon	(M) Phillips	(F) Richardson	(D) Searle	(D) Travis	(F) Wallwork	(D) Wilbraham	(M) Woodthorpe		
	X	X	X			X		X	S	X	X	X			X	S1	X					S2			X					D. Pugh	1
	X	X	X			X		X	S1	X	X	X		X	S	X						S2			S1	S			X	J P Robinson	2
	X	X	X			X		S3	S1	X	X	X		X	S2	X						S2			X				X	K A Leach	3
	X	X	X			X		S2	X	S	X	X		X	X	X			S1						X				X	P S Danson	4
	X	X	X			X		X	S1	S2	X	X		X	X	X			S3		X		X		X				X	A R Leake	5
	X	X	X			X		S	X	S				X		X	X	S1			X	X		X	X				X	S J Baines	6
	X	X	X			X		S1	X				S2	X		X	X	S3			X	X		X	X				X	G Laws	7
	X		X			X		X		X		X	S2	X		X	X	X			S1	S		X	X				X	B Coddington	8
	X		X			X		X	X	S1	X			X		X	X	X			S	S2		S	S2				X	A N Butler	9
	X	X	X			X		X	X		X			X		X	S				S1	S		S	S				X	G Cain	10
	X	X	X			X		X	X		X			X		X	S1				S	S		S	S				X	R J Harris	11
	X	X		S		X		X	X		X			X		X	S	S1	X			X		X					X	J A Kirkby	12
	X	X				X		X	X		X			X		X	S	S1	X			S		X					X	P R Richards	13
	X	X	X	S		X		X	X		X			S		X	S1		X			X		X					X	R D Furnandiz	14
	X	X	X	S		X		X	X		X			X		S2	S1		X			X		X					X	P Taylor	15
	X	X	X	S		X		X	X		X			X		X	S1		X			X		S	S				X	D Laws	16
	X	X	X			X	X	X	X		X			X		X	S1	S	X			S		X					X	R Pearson	17
	X	X	X			X	X	X	X		X			X		X	S	S	X			S		S					X	A G Wiley	18
	X	X	X			X	X	X			X			X		X	S		X			S1	S		X				X	S G Bennett	19
	X	X	X			X	X	X			X			X		S2			X			X		S1	S3				X	M R Halsey	20
	X	X	X	S		X		X	X		X			X		S2			X			X		S1						M J Brandwood	21
	X	X		S2		X		X	X	S1	X			X		X	S3		X			X		X						C R Wilkes	22
	X	X		S1		X	X1	S	X		X			X		X		S	X			X		X						E K Wolstenholme	23
	X	X	X			X	X1	S2	S1		X			X		X2		S3	X			X3								M C Bailey	24
	X	X	X1			X		X2	S		X			X		X		S1	X			X		S	S2					M Fletcher	25
	X	X	X1					S3	X	X3	X			X		X			X			X		X1	X				S1	W C Burns	26
	X	X	X1			X		X	S		X			X		X			X			X		X	S1				S	F G Stretton	27
	X	X	X3			X		S1	X		X2	S2		X		X			X			X		X1	S3				X	D Pugh	28
	X	X	X			X		X	X	S	X			X		X		S	X			X		S	X					M D Messias	29
	X	X	X			X		X	X	S1	X1			X		X		S	X			X		X	S					M S Pike	30
	X	X	X	S2		X	X1	X2	S3		X	X				X			X			X		X	S1					R D Furnandiz	31
	X	X	X	S1	X1	X3	X	S2		X	X					X			X2	S3		X		X2	S3			S		G S Willard	32
	X	X	X3	S2		X	X	S1		X	X2					X			X			X		X1	S3					P Taylor	33
	X	X		X1		X	X	S1	X	S	X					X			X			X		X	S					M Fletcher	34
		X		X		X		S3	X	X1	X							S1			X2	X3							S2	A R Hall	35
	X			X3		X	X2	X		X	X	S1						X1		X	S3			S2					X	G Laws	36
	X			X3	S1	X	X	X2	X		X	X1	X				S1	X	S2		S								X	B Knight	37
	X			S		X	X	X2	X		X2		S2	X1			X	S1	X	X									X	G B Frankland	38
	X			S		X	X	X2	X		X	S2	X1				S1		X	X									X	J P Robinson	39
	X			S1		X	X	X3	X		X	S3	X2				S2		X	X1									X	B Coddington	40
	X2			X		X	X		X1		X	X	X				S2	S	X	X		S							X	T Jones	41
	X			X		X	X		X1		X	X	X2				S2	S	X	X		S1							X	E K Wolstenholme	42
	X			S1		X	X	X			X	X1					X	S	S	X	X2		X1	S2					X	J A Kirkby	43
	X			X	S1	X					X	X1					X	S	S	X	X		X			X			X	D Orr	44
	X			X	S1	X					X	X			X		S3		X	X2		X1		X	X		S2	X3	T Heilbron	45
	X			X	X	S1					X	S		X	X		X		X	S			X1	X		X			R J Harris	46
	X			X	X	X					X	S1					X		X			S	S	X1	X		A Bates	47	
	X2		X1			X					X	S1					X		X			X		S2	S	X1	X2		A N Butler	48	
	X			X	X	X					X	S2	S				X	S1		X	X1		X2					P S Danson	49	
	X			X	X3	X					X	S2					X	S3	S1		X	X2	X1				R D Furnandiz	50	
	X			X	X2	S					X	S1					X	X			X		X	X1	S2		C R Wilkes	51	
																															52

Also Played: (M) Aunger S1(28).

FL Appearances: 45 | 29 | 27 | | 21 | | 45 | 25 | 30 | 24 | 5 | 34 | 31 | 9 | 3 | | 10 | 2 | 38 | 2 | | 43 | 7 | 4 | 27 | 3 | 7 | 6 | 29

FL Sub: | | | 5 | 2 | | | 8 | 6 | 2 | | 5 | 7 | | 2 | | | 18 | 8 | | | | 6 | 2 | 4 | 10 | | 1 | 3

Appearances: 4 | 3 | 4 | 1+1 | | 4 | 3+1 | 3+1 | 1+1 | 2 | | 4 | 2 | | 1 | 4 | | | 2 | 1+2 | | 2 | | | 2 | | 2 | 0+1 | | 4

CC Appearances: 2 | 2 | 2 | 1+1 | | 2 | 1 | 2 | 1+1 | | | 1 | 2 | | | | | | 2 | | | 2 | | | 2 | | 2 | 0+1 | |

FAC Appearances

STOCKPORT COUNTY

CLUB RECORDS

BIGGEST VICTORIES
League: 13-0 v Halifax Town, Div 3(N), 6.1.1934.
(Joint League record victory)
FA Cup: 7-0 v Wrexham (h) 3rd Qualifying Round, 4.23.2893.
League Cup: 5-2 v Sheffield United (a) 2nd Round 2nd Leg, 24.09.1959.
Others: 4-0 v Rochdale, 1st Round AMC, 30.11.1993.

BIGGEST DEFEATS
League: 1-8 v Chesterfield, Div 2, 19.4.1902.
0-7 v Burton Utd, Div 2, 10.10.1903.
0-7 v Bristol City, Div 2, 20.1.1906.
0-7 v Fulham, Div 2, 8.3.1913. 0-7 v Port Vale, Div 3N, 10.4.1954.
0-7 v Aldershot, Div 4, 22.2.1964. 0-7 v Hull City, Div 4, 29.1.1983.
FA Cup: 0-7 v Portsmouth, 3rd Round, 8.1.1949.
1-8 v Bury, 2nd Qualifying Round, 29.10.1892.
League Cup: 0-7 v Crystal Palace, 2nd Round 2nd leg, 4.9.1979.
0-7 v Sheffield Wednesday, 2nd Round 2nd leg, 6.10.1986
(at Manchester City)
Others: 1-5 v Burnley, 1st Round 1st Leg AMC, 24.1.1984.

MOST LEAGUE POINTS
3 points a win: 85, Division 2, 1993-94.
2 points a win: 64, Division 4, 1966-67.

MOST GOALS SCORED
115, 1933-34, Division 3 (N) (42 games).
Lythgoe 46, Stevenson 16, Downes 15, Foulkes 13, Hill 8,
Vincent 7, Humpish 5, Robinson 4, Wilkins 1, og 1.

MOST LEAGUE GOALS CONCEDED
97, Division 2, 1925-26.

MOST FIRST CLASS MATCHES IN A SEASON
67 - 1996-97 (League 46, FA Cup 4, Coca-Cola Cup 11, AMC 6).

MOST LEAGUE WINS
28, Division 3(N), 1928-29 & 1929-30.

MOST LEAGUE DRAWS
21, Division 3, 1988-89.

MOST LEAGUE DEFEATS
29, Division 4, 1964-65 & 1969-70.

INDIVIDUAL CLUB RECORDS

MOST GOALS IN A SEASON
Alf Lythgoe: 47 in 1933-34 (League 46 + FA Cup 1).

MOST GOALS IN A MATCH
5. Joe Smith v Southport (h), 6-3, Div 3(N),7.1.1928.
5. Joe Smith v Lincoln City (h), 7-3, Div 3(N), 15.9.1928.
5. F Newton v Nelson, 6-1, Div 3(N), 21.9.1929.
5. Alf Lythgoe v Southport, 6-1, Div 3(N), 25.8.1934.
5. W McNaughton v Mansfield Town, 6-1, Div 3(N), 14.12.1935.
5. Jack Connor v Workington (h), 6-0, Div 3(N), 8.11.1952.
5. Jack Connor v Carlisle United (h), 8-1, Div 3(N), 7.4.1956.

OLDEST PLAYER IN A LEAGUE MATCH
Alec Hard 40 years 47 days, v Crewe Alexandra (h), 25.12.1951.

YOUNGEST PLAYER IN A LEAGUE MATCH
Steve Massey 16 years 337 days, Darlington (h) (sub), 28.02.1975.

MOST CAPPED PLAYER
Martin Nash (Canada) 3.
1997 v El Salvador, Jamaica & Costa Rica

BEST PERFORMANCES

Highest Position: 8th in Division 1, 1997/98.
FA Cup: 5th Round in 1934-35.
Most recent success: 1949-50: 1st rnd. Billingham SR (h) 3-0;
2nd rnd. Nott'm Forest (h) 2-0; 3rd rnd. Barnsley (h) 3-0;
4th rnd. Hull City (h) 0-0, (a) 2-0; 5th rnd. Liverpool (h) 1-2.
League Cup: 1996-97: 1st rnd. Chesterfield (h) 2-1, (a) 2-1;
2nd rnd. Sheffield Utd (h) 2-1, (a) 5-2; 3rd rnd. Blackburn (a) 1-0;
4th rnd. West Ham Utd (a) 1-1, (h) 2-1; 5th rnd. Southampton (h) 2-2,
(a) 2-1; Semi-final Middlesbrough (h) 0-2, (a) 1-0.
Others: AMC finalists 1991-92.
Most recent success: 1992-93: Group. Chesterfield (a) 3-0,
Chester City (h) 2-0; 1st rnd. Hartlepool Utd (h) 1-0;
2nd rnd. Bradford City (a) 4-3; 3rd rnd. Chesterfield (h) 2-1;
Semi-final Wigan Ath. (a) 1-2, (h) 2-0;
Final Port Vale (Wembley) 1-2.

DIVISIONAL RECORD

	Played	Won	Drawn	Lost	For	Against	Points
Division 2/1	852	257	194	405	1,018	1,446	725*
Division 3/2	460	180	116	164	642	592	602
Division 3(N)	1,076	515	230	331	2,027	1,444	1,258
Division 4	1,329	438	352	542	1,600	1,896	1,380
Total	3,717	1,390	892	1,442	5,287	5,378	3,967

*Two points deducted: 1926-27.

ADDITIONAL INFORMATION
Previous Name: Heaton Norris Rovers 1883-88;
Heaton Norris 1888-90
Previous League: The Combination 1891-94;
Lancashire League 1894-1900; Lancashire Combination 1904-05

Club colours: Blue and white striped shirt, blue shorts & blue socks.
Change colours:
Reserves League: Pontins League Division Three.

RECORDS AND STATISTICS

COMPETITIONS

Div.2/1	Div.3/2	Div.3(N)	Div.4
1900-04	1958-59	1921-22	1959-67
1905-21	1967-70	1926-37	1970-91
1922-26	1991-97	1938-58	
1937-38			
1997-			

HONOURS

Div. 3(N)	Div. 4	Div 3(N) Cup
1921-22	1966-67	1934-35
1936-37		

MOST GOALS IN A CAREER

Jack Connor - 139 (1951-56)

Year	League	FA Cup	Lge Cup	Others
1951-52	15	-	-	-
1952-53	26	4	-	-
1953-54	31	3	-	-
1954-55	30	-	-	-
1955-56	30	-	-	-
Totals	132	7	-	-

Current leading goalscorer: Jim Gannon - 66 (03.90-98)

MOST APPEARANCES

Andy Thorpe - 548+7 (1978-86, 1987-92)

Year	League	FA Cup	Lge Cup	Others
1977-78	4	-	-	-
1978-79	38	1	3	-
1979-80	36	-	4	-
1980-81	37+1	2	2	-
1981-82	46	2	2	-
1982-83	45+1	1	2	-
1983-84	45	1	4	1
1984-85	31	1	4	1
1985-86	30	-	2	2
1987-88	20	1	-	-
1988-89	41	1	2	2
1989-90	38+2	2	4	5
1990-91	40	1	1+1	2
1991-92	33+1	1	2	5+1
Totals	484+5	14	32+1	15+1

MANAGERS

Name	Seasons	Best	Worst
George Ellis	-1896	-	-
Fred Stewart	1896-11	10 (3)	-
Sam Ormerod	1903-04	17 (2)	-
Fred Stewart	1904-11	10 (2)	-
Harry P Lewis	1911-14	12 (2)	19 (2)
David Ashworth	1914-19	14 (2)	-
Albert Williams	1919-24	13 (2)	1 (3N)
Fred Scotchbrook	1924-26	-	-
Lincoln Hyde	1926-31	2 (3N)	7 (3N)
Andrew Wilson	1932-33	3 (3N)	-
Fred Westgarth	1933-36	3 (3N)	7 (3N)
Bob Kelly	1936-38	-	-
Bob Marshall	1939-49	4 (3N)	17 (3N)
Andy Beattie	1949-52	3 (3N)	10 (3N)
Dick Duckworth	1952-56	7 (3N)	-
Willie Moir	1956-60	5 (3N)	21 (3)
Reg Flewin	1960-63	-	19 (4)
Trevor Porteous	1963-65	-	24 (4)
Bert Trautmann	1965	-	-
Eddie Quigley	1965-66	-	-
Jimmy Meadows	1966-69	9 (3)	1 (4)
Walter Galbraith	1969-70	-	24 (3)
Matt Woods	1970-71	11 (4)	-
Steve Fleet (acting)	1971-72	-	-
Brian Doyle	1972-74	11 (4)	24 (4)
Jimmy Meadows	1974-75	20 (4)	-
Roy Chapman	1975-76	21 (4)	-
Eddie Quigley	1976-77	-	-
Alan Thompson	1977-78	-	-
Mike Summerbee	1978-79	-	-
Jimmy McGuigan	1979-82	-	20 (4)
Eric Webster	1982-85	12 (4)	22 (4)
Colin Murphy	1985	-	-
Les Chapman	1985-86	-	-
Jimmy Melia	1986	-	-
Colin Murphy	1986-87	-	-
Asa Hartford	1987-89	20 (4)	-
Danny Bergara	1989-95	4 (2)	3 (4)
David Jones	1995-97	2 (2)	9 (2)
Gary Megson	1997-	8 (1)	8 (1)

Only seasons where a Manager was in charge throughout are included in the best and worst seaons.

RECORD TRANSFER FEE RECEIVED

Amount	Club	Player	Date
£1,600,000	Middlesbrough	Alun Armstrong	02/98
£800,000	Birmingham City	Kevin Francis	01/95
£350,000	Q.P.R.	Andy Preece	06/94
£250,000	W.B.A.	Paul A Williams	03/91

RECORD TRANSFER FEE PAID

Amount	Club	Player	Date
£250,000	Tranmere Rovers	Paul Cook	10/97
£150,000	P.N.E.	Mike Flynn*	03/93
£70,000	Sheffield United	Jim Gannon*	03/90
£70,000	Halifax Town	Neil Matthews	

LONGEST LEAGUE RUNS

of undefeated matches:	18 (1933)	of league matches w/out a win:	15 (1989)
of undefeated home matches:	48 (1927-29)	of undefeated away matches:	8 (1921-22, 1929, 1929-30)
without home win:	12 (1986)	without an away win:	37 (1901-03)
of league wins:	8 (1927-28)	of home wins:	13 (1928-29, 1930)
of league defeats:	9 (1908-09)	of away wins:	7 (1951)

STOCKPORT COUNTY

PLAYERS NAME Honours	Ht	Wt	Birthdate	Birthplace Transfers	Contract Date	Clubs	League	L/Cup	FA Cup	Other	Lge	L/C	FAC	Oth
G O A L K E E P E R														
Gray Ian J	6.2	12	2/25/75	Manchester	7/16/93	Oldham Athletic								
				Loan	11/18/94	Rochdale	12			3				
				£20000	7/17/95	Rochdale	66	4	5	3				
					7/30/97	Stockport County	3	2						
Nash Carlo J	6.5	14.1	9/13/73	Bolton		Cliftonville								
				£35000	9/20/96	Crystal Palace	21	1		3				
				Free	7/1/98	Stockport County								
Nixon Eric AMC'90	6.4	14.3	10/4/62	Manchester		Cuzon Ashton								
				£1000	12/10/83	Manchester City	58	8	10	8				
				Loan	8/29/86	Wolverhampton W.	16							
				Loan	11/28/86	Bradford City	3							
				Loan	12/23/86	Southampton	4							
				Loan	1/23/87	Carlisle United	18							
				£60000	3/24/88	Tranmere Rovers	341	34	19	45+1				
				Loan	1/9/96	Reading	1							
				Loan	2/5/96	Blackpool	20			2				
				Loan	9/13/96	Bradford City	12							
				£100000	8/28/97	Stockport County	43	2	2					
D E F E N C E														
Bennett Thomas	5.11	11.8	12/12/69	Falkirk	12/16/87	Aston Villa								
				Free	7/5/88	Wolverhampton W.	103+12	73+1	4+2	3				
				£75000	6/1/95	Stockport County	93	20	9		5	2		
Connelly Sean	5.1	11.1	6/26/70	Sheffield		Hallam								
				Free	8/12/92	Stockport County	206+5	24	12+1	8	2	1		
Dinning Tony	6.2	12.11	4/12/75	Wallsend	10/1/93	Newcastle United								
				Free	6/23/94	Stockport County	75+25	7+5	1+7	2	8	1		1
Gannon James	6.2	12.6	9/7/68	Southwark		Dundalk								
					4/27/89	Sheffield United								
				Loan	2/22/90	Halifax Town	2							
				£40000	3/7/90	Stockport County	301+14	31+2	17	31+2	52	4	1	9
				Loan	1/14/94	Notts County	2							
McIntosh Martin	6.2	12	3/19/71	East Kilbride		Hamilton Acc.								
				£80000	9/1/97	Stockport County	38	2	2		2			
Woodthorpe Colin J	5.11	11.8	1/13/69	Ellesmere Port	8/23/86	Chester City (T)	154+1	10	8+1	18	6			1
				£175000	8/17/90	Norwich City	36+7	0+2	6	1+1	1			
				£400000	7/20/94	Aberdeen	43+5	5+1	4	5+2	1	1		
				£200000	7/24/97	Stockport County	29+3	4			1	1		
M I D F I E L D														
Byrne Chris T	5.9	10.4	2/9/75	Liverpool		Macclesfield Town								
					6/11/97	Sunderland	4+4	1+1						
				£200000	11/21/97	Stockport County	21+5		1+1		7			
Cook Paul	5.11	10.1	2/22/67	Liverpool		Marine								
					7/20/84	Wigan Athletic	77+6	4	6+1	5+1	14			1
				£73000	5/23/88	Norwich City	3+3			1+1				
				£250000	11/1/89	Wolverhampton W.	191+2	7	5+2	6+1	19	1		1
				£500000	8/18/94	Coventry City	33+1	3	3		3			
				£250000	3/29/96	Tranmere Rovers	54+6	8	1		4			
				£250000	10/24/97	Stockport County	25		1		3			
Cooper Kevin L	5.6	10.7	2/8/75	Derby	5/31/94	Derby County	0+2	0+1		0+1				
				Loan	3/24/97	Stockport County	11+1				3			
					8/8/97	Stockport County	30+8	3+1	2		11	1		
Flynn Michael E: u19.2.	6	11	2/23/69	Oldham	2/7/87	Oldham Athletic	37+3	1+1	1	2	1			
				£100000	12/22/88	Norwich City								
				£125000	12/4/89	Preston North End	134+2	6	6+1	13	7		1	
				£125000	3/25/93	Stockport County	224+1	24	14	12	12	2	1	
Mannion Sean			3/3/80	Dublin		Stella Maris								
				Free	2/27/98	Stockport County								
Phillips Wayne W: B.2.	5.10	11.2	12/15/70	Bangor	8/23/89	Wrexham (T)	184+23	17+1	12+2	18+6	16		1	1
				Loan	2/13/98	Stockport County	7+6							
				£400000	7/1/98	Stockport County								
Vaughan Francis H			9/8/79	Salford		Stockport County (T)								
F O R W A R D														
Angell Brett	6.2	12.8	6/20/68	Marlborough	8/1/86	Portsmouth								
					8/1/87	Cheltenham Town		1				1		
				£40000	2/19/88	Derby County								
				£33000	10/20/88	Stockport County	60+10	3	3	8	28		1	4
				£100000	8/2/90	Southend United	109+6	7+1	3	9+1	47	4	2	10
				£500000	1/17/94	Everton	16+4	0+1			1			
				£600000	3/23/95	Sunderland	10	1				1		
				Loan	1/30/96	Sheffield United	6				2			
				Loan	3/28/96	WBA	0+3							
				£120000	8/19/96	Stockport County	75+4	12+2	5	4+1	33	6	3	1

Name	Ht	Wt	DOB	Fee/From	Date	Club						
Branch Graham	6.2	13	12/02/72	Liverpool		Heswell						
				Free	02/07/91	Tranmere Rovers	55+47	4+8	1+2	2+1	10	1
				Loan	20/11/92	Bury	3+1			1	1	
				Loan	12/24/97	Wigan Athletic	2+1					
				Free	7/1/98	Stockport County						
Grant Stephen	5.10	11.7	4/14/77	Birr		Athlone						
EI: u21.2.				Free	8/10/95	Sunderland						
				Free	5/31/97	Shamrock Rovers						
				£30000	9/1/97	Stockport County	9+7				3	
Moore Ian	5.11	12	26/08/76	Liverpool	06/07/94	Tranmere Rovers	41+17	3+2	1+1	0+1	12	1
E: u21.7, Y				Loan	13/09/96	Bradford City	6					
				£1000000	15/03/97	Nottingham Forest	3+12	0+2	1		1	
				Loan	9/26/97	West Ham United	0+1					
				£800000	7/1/98	Stockport County						
Travis Simon Chris	5.10	11	3/22/77	Preston		Torquay (T)	4+4	1	1			
via Holywell Town				£10000	9/14/97	Stockport County	3+10	0+1	0+1		2	
Wilbraham Aaron T	6.3	12.4	10/21/79	Knutsford	3/26/98	Stockport County (T)	6+1				1	

THE MANAGER
GARY MEGSON

Date of Birth . . . . 2nd May 1959.
Place of Birth . . . . Manchester.
Date of Appointment . . . . July 1997.

PREVIOUS CLUBS
As Manager . . . . .Blackpool.
As Assistant . . . . Norwich City.
As a Player . . . . Plymouth, Everton, Sheffield Wed., Nott'm Forest,
. . . . Newcastle Utd, Sheffield Wed., Manchester City, Norwich City.

HONOURS
As a Manager
None.

As a Player
Eire: 1 full cap, 1 'B' cap and 1 U21 cap.

EDGELEY PARK

Hardcastle Road, Edgeley, Stockport,Cheshire SK3 9DD

Capacity 12,140

First game..v Gainsborough Trinity 1-1, Div.2, 13.09.02.
First floodlit game ....v Fortuna '54 Geleen (Neth) 0-3, 16.10.56

ATTENDANCES
Highest ....27,833 v Liverpool, FAC 5th Rnd, 11.2.1950.
Lowest..1,000 v Carlisle Utd, AMC, 8.12.1986.

OTHER GROUNDS ....Heaton Norris Rec. Ground 1883-84,
.Heaton Norris W'derers Cricket Ground 1884-85, Chorlton's Farm 1885-87, Wilkes' Field 1887-89,
....Green Lane 1899-1902.

HOW TO GET TO THE GROUND

From the North, South and West
Use motorway (M63) until junction 11, sign posted Cheadle (A560). At roundabout follow A560 to Stockport and in 0.3 miles turn right at lights, sign posted Stockport County FC). In 1 mile turn right into Caroline Street for Stockport County FC.

From the East
Use A6 into Stockport Town centre and turn left into Greek Street, opposite the Town Hall. At roundabout go straight over and into Mercian Way and in 0.2 miles left into Caroline Street for Stockport County FC.

Car Parking
Limited street parking around the ground with pay-and-display car parks off Mercian Way.
Nearest Railway Station
Stockport Edgeley - short walk to the ground.
Leave station by left hand entrance, cross road at top of station approach, walk left onto Mercian Way, the ground is then on your left.

USEFUL TELEPHONE NUMBERS

Club switchboard 0161 286 8888
Club fax number 0161 286 8900
Club shop 0161 286 8899
Ticket office 0161 286 8888

Marketing Department. 0161 286 8901
Clubcall 0891 12 16 38*
*Calls cost 50p per minute at all times.
Call costings correct at time of going to press.

MATCHDAY PROGRAMME

Programme Editor (97/98). . . . Steve Bellis.

Number of pages (97/98) . . . . 56.

Price (97/98) . . . . £1.50.

Subscriptions . . . . £40 inc. postage.

Local Newspapers
. . . . Stockport Express Advertiser,

Local Radio Stations
. . . Radio Piccadilly, G.M.R., Signal Radio.

MATCHDAY TICKET PRICES (97/98)

Main Stand	£14
OAP	£7
Juniors	£5
Cheadle Stand	£12
OAP	£7
Juniors	£5
Vernon Stand	£12
OAP.	£7
Juniors	£5

SUNDERLAND
(The Rokerites)
NATIONWIDE LEAGUE DIVISION 1
SPONSORED BY: VAUX

1997-98 Back Row L-R: Kevin Phillips, Paul Heckingbottom, Michael Bridges, Jan Eriksson, Niall Quinn, Richard Ord, Jody Craddock, Darren Holloway, Lee Clark, Michael Gray. **Middle Row:** Kim Heiselberg, John Mullin, Chris Makin, Lionel Perez, Tony Coton, Edwin Zoetebier, Sam Aiston, Andy Melville, Gareth Hall. **Front Row:** Darren Williams, Craig Russell, Martin Smith, Steve Agnew, Alex Rae, Kevin Ball, Martin Scott, Chris Byrne, Alan Johnston, Paul Bracewell.

SUNDERLAND
FORMED IN 1879
TURNED PROFESSIONAL IN 1886
LTD COMPANY IN 1906

CHAIRMAN: R S Murray
DIRECTORS
J M Fickling (Vice-Chairman),
G McDonnell (Commercial),
D C Stonehouse (Finance)
SECRETARY
Mark Blackbourne
MARKETING & COMMERCIAL
DEVELOPMENT MANAGER
Grahame McDonnell

MANAGER: Peter Reid
ASSISTANT MANAGER: Bobby Saxton
YOUTH TEAM COACH
Bryan 'Pop' Robson

STATISTICIAN FOR THE DIRECTORY
Eddie Brennan

Although followers of Sunderland Football Club are used to seasons full of rollercoaster emotions, this past campaign will take some beating. The team bagged the most away wins in Division One, racked up 90 points, scored 101 goals in all competitions, yet missed promotion due to a single missed penalty in a sudden death Wembley shoot-out. Harsh does not seem a strong enough adjective.

Despite the ultimate disappointment of missing out on an instant return to the Premiership, last season was arguably one of the most exciting and at times, most enjoyable in the club's recent history. The first match in the new 'Stadium of Light' saw Sunderland defeat Manchester City 3-1 in front of nearly 40,000 fans and portents for the season looked good. Although the team were languishing in 13th place by October giving few indications of the fireworks to come, the next three months saw Sunderland embark on a 17 game unbeaten run that propelled them to fourth in the table.

The team was by then, almost unrecognisable from the relegated outfit of seven month earlier. Record signing Lee Clark providing much needed midfield creativity alongside the now established Alex Rae, whilst another summer purchase, striker Kevin Phillips from Watford, couldn't stop scoring, striking up a lucrative partnership with revitalised Niall Quinn. The side's attacking prowess was further enhanced by the signing of Nicky Summerbee from Manchester City in November who, in tamdem with fellow winger Allan Johnston, created numerous goalscoring opportunities. Injuries had forced manager Peter Reid to assemble a young and relatively inexperienced defence, two of whom, Darren Holloway and Darren Williams, went on to gain selection to the England B squad.

By the end of January, the race for the automatic promotion slots appeared to be between the three relegated sides from the previous term and Sunderland's impressive 3-0 win away at leaders Forest lifted them into the top two for the first time. A bad slip-up at this stage by either Sunderland, Forest or Middlesbrough was likely to prove costly and, unfortunately for the Wearsiders, it was they who made it. A squandered two-goal lead at home to relegation haunted Q.P.R. in April, coupled with defeat at Ipswich in the season's penultimate game, allowed the Teesider's to snatch second place, condemning Sunderland to the play-offs.

Having seen off Sheffield United over two legs, Sunderland faced Charlton at Wembley. Defensive naivete' was in evidence as, having led three times, Sunderland were forced to settle for a heart-stopping 4-4 draw, during which Phillips notched his 35th goal of the season, breaking Brian Clough's 36-year-old record. So to penalties and heartbreak for Michael Gray, one of the campaign's top performers, who was the unlucky man after 13 spot kicks had been successfully converted.

One hopes that the players will be able to lift themselves after such a shattering end to a season that had promised so much. The play-offs themselves have never been particularly kind to Sunderland and but for a poor start last term, they would have undoubtedly avoided the end of season lottery and won an automatic promotion place. This will be the number one priority for the forthcoming campaign.

EDDIE BRENNAN

SUNDERLAND

Division 1   :3rd   FA CUP: 4th Round   LC CUP: 3rd Round

M	DATE	COMP.	VEN	OPPONENTS	RESULT	H/T	LP	GOAL SCORERS/GOAL TIMES	ATT.
1	A 10	FL	A	Sheffield United	L 0-2	0-2	21		(17324)
2	15	FL	H	Manchester City	W 3-1	1-0	10	Quinn 17, Phillips 83, Clark 90	38894
3	23	FL	A	Port Vale	L 1-3	0-2	16	Phillips 76	(8290)
4	30	FL	H	Norwich City	L 0-1	0-0	18		29204
5	S 02	FL	H	Oxford United	W 3-1	2-1	12	Phillips 40, Makin 44, Melville 58	27643
6	05	FL	A	Bradford City	W 4-0	4-0	6	Gray 5, Clark 31, Phillips 34, Johnston 37	(16484)
7	14	FL	A	Birmingham City	W 1-0	0-0	6	Gray 72	(17478)
8	16	CC 2/1	H	Bury	W 2-1	1-1		Williams 44, Bridges 55	18775
9	20	FL	H	Wolverhampton Wand	D 1-1	1-1	7	Smith 17	32983
10	23	CC 2/2	A	Bury	W 2-1	2-0		Smith 11, Rae 32	(3928)
11	28	FL	H	Middlesbrough	L 1-2	0-0	11	Ball 90	34819
12	O 04	FL	A	Reading	L 0-4	0-2	13		(10795)
13	15	CC 3	A	Middlesbrough	L 0-2	0-0			(26451)
14	18	FL	H	Huddersfield Town	W 3-1	1-1	11	Smith 40, Bridges 68, Clark 74	24782
15	21	FL	H	Swindon Town	D 0-0	0-0	13		27553
16	25	FL	A	Stoke City	W 2-1	1-0	10	Clark 40, 70	(14587)
17	N 01	FL	A	Stockport County	D 1-1	0-0	12	Clark 90	(9473)
18	04	FL	H	Charlton Athletic	D 0-0	0-0	12		25455
19	08	FL	H	Nottingham Forest	D 1-1	1-1	12	Phillips 2	33160
20	15	FL	A	Portsmouth	W 4-1	3-1	8	Quinn 11, Clark 14, Johnston 33, Summerbee 65	(10702)
21	22	FL	A	Bury	D 1-1	1-1	8	Phillips 31	(7790)
22	29	FL	H	Tranmere Rovers	W 3-0	3-0	8	Clark 12, 15, Phillips 43	26674
23	D 06	FL	A	Queens Park Rangers	W 1-0	0-0	7	Quinn 85	(15266)
24	13	FL	H	West Bromwich Albion	W 2-0	1-0	8	Phillips 40, Johnston 53	29231
25	20	FL	A	Crewe Alexandra	W 3-0	2-0	6	Phillips 1, Summerbee 37, Quinn 82	(5404)
26	26	FL	H	Bradford City	W 2-0	1-0	4	Phillips 11, Johnston 58	40055
27	28	FL	A	Oxford United	D 1-1	1-1	5	Phillips 14	(8659)
28	J 03	FAC 3	A	Rotherham United	W 5-1	1-0		Phillips 14 (pen), 55, 71, 75, Quinn 85	(11500)
29	10	FL	A	Sheffield United	W 4-2	1-1	4	Quinn 21, Rae 66, Phillips 81, 90	36391
30	17	FL	A	Manchester City	W 1-0	0-0	4	Phillips 55	(31715)
31	24	FAC 4	A	Tranmere Rovers	L 0-1	0-0			(14055)
32	28	FL	A	Norwich City	L 1-2	0-1	4	Clark 84	(15940)
33	31	FL	H	Port Vale	W 4-2	3-1	3	Johnston 11, Phillips 13, Quinn 20, Carragher 86 (OG)	39258
34	F 06	FL	A	Wolverhampton Wand	W 1-0	0-0	3	Ball 88	(27502)
35	17	FL	H	Reading	W 4-1	2-0	3	Quinn 21, Rae 22, Phillips 46, 61	40579
36	21	FL	A	Middlesbrough	L 1-3	0-1	3		(30227)
37	24	FL	A	Huddersfield Town	W 3-2	1-0	3	Johnston 16, 23, 39 (pen)	(14615)
38	28	FL	H	Ipswich Town	D 2-2	1-2	3	Williams 13, Phillips 50	35114
39	M 04	FL	A	Nottingham Forest	W 3-0	1-0	3	Rae 32, Johnston 66, Phillips 80	(29009)
40	07	FL	H	Stockport County	W 4-1	1-0	2	Quinn 41, 54, 64, Phillips 86	34870
41	10	FL	H	Birmingham City	D 1-1	0-0	2	Johnston 90	37602
42	15	FL	A	Charlton Athletic	D 1-1	1-0	3	Phillips 36	(15355)
43	21	FL	H	Portsmouth	W 2-1	1-0	2	Phillips 16, Johnston 84	38134
44	28	FL	H	Bury	W 2-1	1-1	2	Clark 43, Phillips 70 (pen)	37425
45	A 03	FL	A	Tranmere Rovers	W 2-0	2-0	2	Phillips 6, Summerbee 12	(14116)
46	10	FL	H	Queens Park Rangers	D 2-2	1-0	2	Quinn 28, 55	40014
47	13	FL	A	West Bromwich Albion	D 3-3	2-2	2	Quinn 17, 50, Phillips 27	(20181)
48	18	FL	A	Crewe Alexandra	W 2-1	2-1	2	Ball 5, Clark 23	40441
49	25	FL	H	Stoke City	W 3-0	1-0	2	Williams 6, Phillips 54	41214
50	28	FL	A	Ipswich Town	L 0-2	0-0	2		(20902)
51	M 03	FL	A	Swindon Town	W 2-1	2-0	3	Phillips 21, 44	(14868)
52	10	PO SF1	A	Sheffield United	L 1-2	1-0		Ball 17	(23800)
53	13	PO SF2	H	Sheffield United	W 2-0	2-0		Phillips 38, Marker 21 (OG)	40092
54	25	PO F	A	Charlton Athletic	D 4-4	0-1		Quinn 50, 74, Phillips 58, Summerbee 99	(77739)

Best Home League Attendance: 41214 V Stoke City   Smallest :24782 V Huddersfield Town   Average :34413

Goal Scorers:

FL	(86)	Phillips 29, Quinn 14, Clark 13, Johnston 11, Ball 3, Rae 3, Summerbee 3, Gray 2, Smith 2, Williams 2, Bridges 1, Makin 1, Melville 1, Opponents 1
CC	(4)	Bridges 1, Rae 1, Smith 1, Williams 1
FAC	(5)	Phillips 4, Quinn 1
PO	(7)	Phillips 2, Quinn 2, Ball 1, Summerbee 1, Opponents 1

1997-98

	(M) Agnew	(F) Aiston	(D) Ball	(M) Bracewell	(F) Bridges	(M) Byrne	(M) Clark	(D) Craddock	(F) Dichio	(D) Gray	(D) Hall	(D) Holloway	(F) Johnston	(M) Lumsden	(M) Makin	(D) Melville	(F) Mullin	(D) Ord	(G) Perez	(F) Phillips	(F) Quinn	(M) Rae	(F) Russell	(D) Scott	(F) Smith	(D) Summerbee	(G) Weaver	(M) Williams	(M) Zoetebier	Referee	#
	X		X		S1	S2	X		X						X	X		X	X		X	X		X	X				S	G Cain	1
	X	S2	X			X	X		X						X	X		X	X	X	X	X	X						S1	E K Wolstenholme	2
			X	X		X	X	S	X						X	X	S2	X	X	X	X	X			S1				A P D'Urso	3
	X	S1	X			S2	X		X				S		X	X		X	X	X	X	X		X						R D Furnandiz	4
		X				S1	X		X						X	X	X	X	X	X	X	X	S2		S				S	A R Leake	5
		X	S2			X	X	S	X				X		X	X	S1	X	X	X			X	X				X		M Fletcher	6
		X	S			X	X		X				X	X	S1	X	X	X	X	X		S2		X				X		J A Kirkby	7
	S		X	X	X		X		X	S		X		X			X		S1	X	X		X	X				X		F G Stretton	8
			X		X	S2	X		X				X		X			X		S	S1	X	X					X		W C Burns	9
	X		S2	X	X	S	X		X				X			X		X	S1	X	X		X					X	X	K M Lynch	10
			X		S	S	X		X				X	S1		X	X	X	X	X		S2		X	X			X		P Rejer	11
			X			S	X		X		X	X	X	X	X		S1	X	S2		X	X		X	X			X		M J Brandwood	12
		X		X	S2	X	X		X			X		S	X			X		X	X	S1		X	X			X		K A Leach	13
		X		S1	X	X	X		X			S2		X			X		X	X			X	X						T Jones	14
		X		X	S	X	X		X		S	X	S	X			X		X	X				S1			X		S W Mathieson	15
		X		X	X	X	X		X		X	X		X			S2		X	X		S1	S1	X			X		S J Baines	16
			X	X		Wiley X	X		X		X	X		S			S		X	X		S2	S1	X			X		A G Wiley	17
			X	S	X	X	X		X		X	X		S		S	S		X	X		X		X			X		G Cain	18
			X	S	X	X	X		X		X	X		S			S		X	X	S1	X		X			X		J A Kirkby	19
			S		X	X	X		X		X	X				S			X	X	X	X		X	S1		X		A P D'Urso	20
			S		X	X	X	S1	X		X	X		X		S2			X	X	X	X		X			X		G Singh	21
			S		X	X	X		X		X	S	S	X		S			X	X	X	X		X			X		J P Robinson	22
			S		X	X	X		X		X	S	S	X		S			X	X	X	X		S	X		X		M E Pierce	23
			S		X	X	X		X		X	X		S		S			X	X	X	X		S	X		X		B Coddington	24
					X	X	X		X		X	X1		S		S		S	X	X	X	X		S1	X		X		A N Butler	25
					X	X	X		X		X	X1		S		S			S	X	X	X		S1	X		X		P Rejer	26
					X	X	X		X		X	X1		S					S	X	X	X		S1	X		X		A R Leake	27
			X		X		X		X		X	X		S		S	S	X	X	X	X		S	X		X		S	E Lomas	28
			X		X		X		X		X	X		S		S	S		X	X	X	X		S	X		X		P R Richards	29
			S			X	X		X		X	X		S1					X	X	X	X		S	X		X1		M D Messias	30
			S			X	X		X		X	X		X				S	S	X	X	X		S	X	S		M D Reed	31
			S			X	X	S1	X		X	S		X		X			X	X	X1	X			X		X		M J Brandwood	32
			X			X	X		X		X		X	X		S		S1	X	X	X				X		X1		M J Pike	33
			X			X	X	S1	X	X		X		X1			S	S	X	X	X						X		R J Harris	34
			X			X	X	S1	X	S	X	X		S			S		X	X	X	X1			X				J A Kirkby	35
			S			X	X	S1	X		X	X1		X				S	X	X	X			X		X1			R D Furnandiz	36
			S1			X	X	S2	X		X	X		X			S		X	X	X2	X			X1				C J Foy	37
			S1			X	X	X	X		X	X		X		S			X	X	X			X1			X		M J Jones	38
			X			X	X	S1	X		X	X		S					X	X	X			S			X		M C Bailey	39
			X			X	X	S1	X		X	X		S				X1	X	X	X			S1			X		E K Wolstenholme	40
			X			X	X	X1	X		X	X2		X		S			X	X	X			S2			X		K M Lynch	41
			X			X	X1	S2	X		X	X		X		S1			X	X	X2	X			S		X		C R Wilkes	42
			X			X		S1	X		X	X		X				S	X	X	X1	X2			S2		X		D Pugh	43
			X			X		S	X	S	X	X		X				S	X	X	X				S		X		A N Butler	44
			X			X		S	S	X	S	X	X	X				S	X	X	X				X		X		A G Wiley	45
			X			X		S	S	X		X	X		X					X	X	X			S		X		B Coddington	46
			X			X2	S1	S3	X		X	X1		X			S		X	X	X3	S2			X		X		E Lomas	47
			X			X	X	S	X		X	X		X			S		X	X	X				X		X		J P Robinson	48
			X		S		X		X		X	X		X					X	X	X1	S			X		X		T Jones	49
			X1			X	X	S2	X		X			X2			X		X	X	X			S1			X		K A Leach	50
			X		S1		X	X	X1	X		X			X		X			S	X	X			S		X		J E Pearce	51
			X		S		X	X	X		X			X2	X		X1		S1	X	X			S2		X		C R Wilkes	52
			X			X	X	S1	X		X			X		X			S	X	X1	X		S		X		X	M E Pierce	53
			X			X3	X	S2	X		X			X1	X		S1			X	X2	X	S3			X		X	E K Wolstenholme	54
FL Appearances	3	1	29	6	4	46	31	2	44	1	32	38	1	23	10	1	13	46	42	33	24		8	11	22			35		FL Appearances	
FL Sub Appearances		2	2	1	3	4		1	11		1	2		2		5	1		1	2	5	3		5	3			1		FL Sub Appearances	
CC Appearances	1	2+1	2	2	1+1	1	3		3			2		3				1		1+1	2+1	3	1+1		3			3	2	CC Appearances	
FAC Appearances						2	2		2		2	2		2				2	2	2	2			2	1					FAC Appearances	
PO Appearances		3				3	3		1+2		2	2		3	3		1+1		0+1	3	3	2	0+2			3		3	3	PO Appearances	

SUNDERLAND

CLUB RECORDS

BIGGEST VICTORIES
League: 9-1 v Newcastle, Division 1, 5.12.1908
8-0 v Derby County, Division 1, 1.9.1894
F.A. Cup: 11-1 v Fairfield, Round 1, 2.2.1895
League Cup: 7-1 v Oldham Athletic, Round 2, 24.9.1962

BIGGEST DEFEATS
League: 0-8 v Sheffield Wednesday, Division 1, 26.12.1911
0-8 v West Ham Utd, Division 1, 19.10.1968
0-8 v Watford, Division 1, 25.9.1982
F.A. Cup: 2-7 v Aston Villa, Round 4, 27.1.1934
0-5 v Arsenal, Round 2, 1905-06
0-5 v Liverpool, Round 1 replay, 1921-22
0-5 v Tottenham Hotspur, Round 6 replay, 1960-61
League Cup: 0-6 v Derby County, Round 3, 31.10.1990

MOST POINTS
3 points a win: 93, Division 3, 1987-88
2 points a win: 61, Division 2, 1963-64

MOST GOALS
109, Division 1, 1935-36
Carter 31, Gurney 31, Gallagher 19, Davis 10, Conner 6, Duns 5, Goddard 2,Hornby 2, Thompson 1, McNab 1, og 1.

MOST LEAGUE GOALS CONCEDED
97, Division 1, 1957-58

MOST FIRST CLASS MATCHES IN A SEASON
59 (46 League, 1 FA Cup, 8 League Cup, 1 Zenith, 3 Play-Offs) 1989-90

MOST LEAGUE WINS
27, Division 3, 1987-88

MOST LEAGUE DRAWS
18, Division 1, 1954-55, Division 2/1 1994-95

MOST LEAGUE DEFEATS
22, Division 1, 1956-57; Division 1, 1969-70; Division 1, 1984-85; Division2/1 1992-93

INDIVIDUAL CLUB RECORDS

MOST GOALS IN A MATCH
5. C Buchan v Liverpool, 7.12.1919 (7-0)
5. R Gurney v Bolton W., 7.12.1935 (7-2)
5. D Sharkey v Norwich, 20.2.1962 (7-1)

MOST GOALS IN A SEASON
Dave Halliday 43, 1928-29
4 goals once=4, 3 goals twice=6, 2 goals ten times=20, 1 goal 13 times=13

OLDEST PLAYER
Bryan `Pop' Robson, 38 years 128 days v Leicester, 12.5.1984

YOUNGEST PLAYER
Derek Forster, 15 years 184 days v Leicester, 22.8.1964

MOST CAPPED PLAYER
Martin Harvey (Northern Ireland) 34

BEST PERFORMANCES

League: 1963-64: Matches played 42, Won 25, Drawn 11, Lost 6, Goals for 87,Goals against 37, Points 61. 2nd in Division 2.

Highest: First in Division 1.

F.A. Cup: 1936-37: 3rd rnd. Southampton (A) 3-2; 4th rnd. Luton Town (A) 2-2,(H) 3-1; 5th rnd. Swansea (H) 3-0; 6th rnd. Wolverhampton W. 1-1 (A), 2-2 (H),4-0 (N); Semi-final Millwall 2-1; Final Preston North End 3-1.
1972-73: 3rd rnd. Notts County 1-1 (A), 2-0 (H); 4th rnd. Reading 1-1 (H), 3-1(A); 5th rnd. Manchester City 2-2 (A), 3-1 (H); 6th rnd. Luton 2-0 (H); Semi-final Arsenal 2-1; Final Leeds 1-0.

League Cup: 1984-85: 2nd rnd. Crystal Palace 2-1 (H), 0-0 (A); 3rd rnd.Nottingham Forest 1-1 (A), 1-0 (H); 4th rnd. Tottenham Hotspur 0-0 (H), 2-1(A); 5th rnd. Watford 1-0; Semi-final Chelsea 2-0 (H), 3-2 (A); Final Norwich 0-1.

Europe (ECWC): 1973-74: 1st rnd. VASAS Budapest 2-0 (A), 1-0 (H); 2nd rnd. Sporting Lisbon 2-1 (H), 0-2 (A).

DIVISIONAL RECORD

	Played	Won	Drawn	Lost	For	Against	Points
Division 1/P	2,770	1,117	631	1,022	4,566	4,270	2,929
Division 2/1	1,082	447	303	332	1,592	1,320	1,365
Division 3	46	27	12	7	92	48	93
Total	3,898	1,591	934	1,361	6,250	5,638	4,387

ADDITIONAL INFORMATION
Previous Names
Sunderland & District Teachers' Association F.C. 1879-80.

Previous League
Northumberland & District Football Association 1880-90.

Club colours: Red and white striped shirts, black shorts, red socks with white band.
Change colours:

Reserves League: Pontins Central League Division 2

RECORDS AND STATISTICS

COMPETITIONS

Div.1/P	Div.2/1	Div.3	ECWC
1890-58	1958-64	1987-88	1973-74
1964-70	1970-76		
1976-77	1977-80		
1980-85	1985-87		
1990-91	1988-90		
1996-97	1991-96		
	1997-		

HONOURS

Div.1	Div.2/1	Div.3	FA Cup
1891-92	1975-76	1987-88	1937
1892-93	1995/96		1973
1894-95			
1901-02			
1912-13			
1935-36			

MOST APPEARANCES

Jim Montgomery 611+12 (1961-77)

Year	League	FA Cup	Lge Cup	Others
1961-62	12		1	
1962-63	42	4	7	
1963-64	42	6	1	
1964-65	9			
1965-66	29	1	2	
1966-67	42	5	2	
1967-68	39	2	3	
1968-69	42	1	1	
1969-70	41	1	1	4
1970-71	42	1	1	
1971-72	31	3	1	4
1972-73	41	9	1	
1973-74	41	2	4	4
1974-75	40	1	1	
1975-76	38	5	1	
1976-77	6		4	
	537	41	33	12

MOST GOALS IN A CAREER

R Gurney - 228 (1925-39)

Year	League	FA Cup
1925-26	4	
1926-27	7	
1927-28	4	
1929-30	15	2
1930-31	31	2
1931-32	16	
1932-33	15	7
1933-34	21	1
1934-35	30	4
1935-36	31	
1936-37	20	6
1937-38	9	1
1938-39	2	
Total	205	23

Current leading goalscorer: Kevin Phillips - 34 (07.97-98)

RECORD TRANSFER FEE RECEIVED

Amount	Club	Player	Date
£1,800,000	Crystal Palace	Marco Gabbiadini	09/91
£275,000	Sheffield Wed.	Mark Proctor	09/87
£275,000	Manchester Utd	Chris Turner	07/85
£275,000	Everton	Paul Bracewell	04/84

RECORD TRANSFER FEE PAID

Amount	Club	Player	Date
£2,500,000	Newcastle Utd	Lee Clark	06/97
£1,300,000	Man. City	Niall Quinn	08/96
£1,000,000	Millwall	Alex Rae	05/96
£1,000,000	Wolves	David Kelly	08/95

MANAGERS

Name	Seasons	Best	Worst
Tom Watson	1890-96	1(1)	7(1)
Robert Campbell	1896-99	2(1)	15(1)
Alex Mackie	1899-05	1(1)	6(1)
Robert Kyle	1905-28	1(1)	16(1)
Johnny Cochrane	1928-39	1(1)	16(1)
William Murray	1939-57	3(1)	20(1)
Alan Brown	1957-64	21(1)	16(2)
George Hardwick	1964-65	15(1)	15(1)
Ian McColl	1965-68	15(1)	19(1)
Alan Brown	1968-72	17(1)	16(2)
Bob Stokoe	1972-76	1(2)	6(2)
Jimmy Adamson	1976-78	20(1)	6(2)
Billy Elliott	1978-79	4(2)	4(2)
Ken Knighton	1979-81	17(1)	2(2)
Alan Durban	1981-84	13(1)	19(1)
Len Ashurst	1984-85	21(1)	21(1)
Lawrie McMenemy	1985-87	18(2)	20(2)
Denis Smith	1987-91	19(1)	1(3)
Malcolm Crosby	1991-93	18(2)	18(2)
Terry Butcher	1993	21(2/1)	21(2/1)
Mick Buxton	1993-95	12(1)	12(1)
Peter Reid	1995-	18(P)	20(1)

LONGEST LEAGUE RUNS

of undefeated matches:	16 (11.11.1922 - 24.2.1923)	of league matches w/out a win:	14 (16.4.1985 - 14.9.1985)
of undefeated home matches:	44 (18.10.1890 - 6.12.1893)	of undefeated away matches:	14 25.11.1978 - 18.8.1979)
without home win:	12 (5.9.1981 - 27.2.1982)	without an away win:	28 (15.11.1952 - 2.1.1954)
of league wins:	13 (14.11.1891 - 22.4.1892)	of home wins:	19 (10.1.1891 - 16.4.1892)
of league defeats:	9 (23.11.1976 - 15.1.1977)	of away wins:	5 (1891-92, 1892, 1912-13, 1963)

SUNDERLAND

PLAYERS NAME Honours	Ht	Wt	Birthdate	Birthplace Transfers	Contract Date	Clubs	League	L/Cup	FA Cup	Other	Lge	L/C	FAC	Oth
G O A L K E E P E R														
Coton Tony	6.2	13.07	5/19/61	Tamworth	1/1/00	Mile Oak Rovers								
E: B.1				Free	10/13/78	Birmingham City	94	10	10					
				£300000	9/27/84	Watford	233	18	32	8				
				£1000000	7/20/90	Manchester City	162+1	16	12	3				
				£500000	1/23/96	Manchester United								
				£350000	7/18/96	Sunderland	10	2						
Shannon Greg	6.1	11.4	2/15/81	Maghreafelt		Maghera Colts								
				Free	2/27/98	Sunderland (T)								
Sorensen Thomas						OB Odense								
				£500000	7/1/98	Sunderland								
Weaver Luke D	6.2	13.2	6/26/79	Woolwich	11/1/96	Leyton Orient	9		1					
				£250000	1/9/98	Sunderland								
D E F E N C E														
Ball Kevin	5.9	11.6	11/12/64	Hastings		Coventry City (T)								
				Free	10/6/82	Portsmouth	96+9	8+1	8	6	4			
DIV1 95/96				£350000	7/16/90	Sunderland	279+5	19+2	15	7	19	3		2
Butler Paul J	6.3	13	11/2/72	Manchester	7/5/91	Rochdale	151+7	8+1	6+2	12+1	10			
DIV2 96/97				£100000	8/23/96	Bury	83+1	8	2	3	4			1
				£600000	7/1/98	Sunderland								
Craddock Jody	6	11.1	7/25/75	Bromsgrove		Christchurch								
				Free	8/13/93	Cambridge United	273+9	6	9	7	7	1		
				Loan	10/4/93	Woking								
					8/4/97	Sunderland	31+1	3	2	3				
Dickman Elliott	5.9	9.8	10/11/78	Hexham	5/31/97	Sunderland								
Gray Michael	5.7	10.8	8/3/74	Sunderland	7/1/92	Sunderland	167+19	11+3	7+1	2	12		1	
DIV1 95/96														
Harrison Gerald R	5.11	12.12	4/15/72	Lambeth	12/18/89	Watford	6+3			1				
				Free	7/23/91	Bristol City	24+13	2+2	1	4+1	1			
				Loan	1/24/92	Cardiff City	10			1				
				Loan	11/19/93	Hereford United	6	1		1				
				Free	3/24/94	Huddersfield Town								
				Free	8/5/94	Burnley	116+8	5+1	6+2	7+1	3			
				Free	7/1/98	Sunderland								
Heckingbottom Paul	5.11	12	7/17/77	Barnsley		Manchester United								
				Free	7/14/95	Sunderland								
				Loan	10/17/97	Scarborough	28+1			1				
Holloway Darren	5.10	12.6	10/3/77	Bishop Auck.		Sunderland (T)	32		2	3				
E: u21.1.				Loan	8/29/97	Carlisle United	5							
Maley Mark	5.9	12.3	1/26/81	Newcastle		Sunderland (T)								
Melville Andrew	6.1	12.6	11/29/68	Swansea	7/25/86	Swansea City	165+10	10	14+1	13	22		5	2
W: 20, B.1, u21.2. WFAC'89 DIV1 95/96				£275000	7/23/90	Oxford United	135	12	6	6	13	1		1
					8/9/93	Sunderland	160	12+1	9	2	12			
				Loan	2/13/98	Bradford City	6				1			
Scott Martin	5.9	11	1/7/68	Sheffield	1/10/86	Rotherham United	93+1	11	7+2	7	3	2		2
Div4'89 DIV1 95/96				£200000	12/5/90	Bristol City	171	10	10	8	14	1		1
				£750000	12/23/94	Sunderland	91	7	5		7	1		
Summerbee Nicholas	5.8	11.8	8/26/71	Altrincham	7/20/89	Swindon Town	89+23	9+1	2+4	7	6	3		1
E: B.1, u21.3				£1500000	6/24/94	Manchester City	119+12	11+2	12		6	2	2	
				£1000000	11/14/97	Sunderland	22+3		2	3	3			1
M I D F I E L D														
Clark Lee	5.8	11.7	10/27/72	Wallsend	12/9/89	Newcastle United	154+42	17	14+2	7+5	23		3	1
E: u21.11, Y6; Div1'93					6/7/97	Sunderland	46	1	2	3	12			
Duke David			11/7/78	Inverness		Redby								
				Free	7/3/97	Sunderland								
Lumsdon Christopher	5.7	10.3	12/15/79	Newcastle	7/3/97	Sunderland (T)	1							
Makin Christopher	5.1	10.6	5/8/73	Manchester	11/2/91	Oldham Athletic	93+1	7	11	1+1	4			
				Loan	8/28/92	Wigan Athletic	14+1				2			
				Free	8/5/97	Sunderland	23+2	3	1	1+1	1			
Rae Alex	5.8	11.8	9/30/69	Glasgow		Falkirk	71+12	5	2+1		20	1		
S: u21.9				£100000	8/20/90	Millwall	168+13	11+2	11	10	50		4	1
				£750000	7/1/96	Sunderland	35+15	3+1	2	+2	5	2		
Thirlwell Paul	5.11	11.4	2/13/79	Newcastle	5/31/97	Sunderland								

Player	Ht	Wt	DOB	From	Date	To	Lg	FAC	LC	Oth	Lg G	FAC G	LC G	Oth G
Wainwright Neil	6	11.5	11/4/77	Warrington	3/27/97	Wrexham	7+4		1		3			
				£100000	7/1/98	Sunderland								
Williams Darren	5.11	11.11	4/28/77	Middlesbro'		York City	16+4	4+1	1	3			1	
				£50000	10/18/96	Sunderland	45+2	3	2+1	3	4	1		

F O R W A R D

Player	Ht	Wt	DOB	From	Date	To	Lg	FAC	LC	Oth	Lg G	FAC G	LC G	Oth G
Aiston Sam	6.1	12.1	11/21/76	Newcastle		Newcastle United								
Div.1'96. E: S.				Free	7/14/95	Sunderland	5+15	0+1	0+2					
				Loan	2/21/97	Chester City	14	1		2				
Beavers Paul M	6.3	13.5	10/2/78	Blackpool	5/31/97	Sunderland								
Bridges Michael	6.1	10.11	8/5/78	North Shields	11/9/95	Sunderland	18+30	3+1	2		8	1		
u21.1. E:														
Dichio Daniel	6.2	11	10/19/74	Hammersmith	5/17/93	QPR	56+18	6	2+3		21	3		
E: Y,S				Loan	2/18/94	Welling								
				Loan	3/24/94	Barnet	9				2			
					5/31/97	Sampdoria								
				£750000	1/28/98	Sunderland	2+11			1+2				
Johnston Allan	5.7	9.7	12/14/73	Glasgow	6/23/90	Hearts	46+38	3+2	4+1		12	2		
u21.3. S:					7/1/96	Rennes								
				£550000	4/5/97	Sunderland	41+4	2	2	3	12			
Mullin John	6	11.5	8/11/75	Bury	8/11/75	Burnley	7+11		2		2			
				£40000	8/12/95	Sunderland	15+11	1	2+1		2			
				Loan	2/13/98	Preston North End	4+3							
				Loan	3/26/98	Burnley	6							
Phillips Kevin	5.7	11	7/25/73	Hitchin		Baldock Town								
				£10000	12/19/94	Watford	54+5	2	2		24	1		
					7/15/97	Sunderland	42+1		2	3	28		4	2
Proctor Michael A	5.11	12.7	10/3/80	Sunderland		Sunderland (T)								
Quinn Niall	6.4	12.4	10/6/66	Dublin	11/30/83	Arsenal	59+8	14+2	8+2	+1	14	4	2	
Ei: 42, B.1, u23.1, u21.5,Y. LC'87				£800000	3/21/90	Manchester City	183+20	20+2	13+3	3	65	6	4	1
					8/17/96	Sunderland	41+6	1	2	2	16	1	1	2
Smith Martin	5.11	12	11/13/74	Sunderland	9/6/92	Sunderland	85+24	6+4	7+2		22	1	1	
E: S														

THE MANAGER
PETER REID

Date of Birth . . . . 20th June 1956.
Place of Birth . . . . Liverpool.
Date of Appointment . . . . March 1995.

PREVIOUS CLUBS
As Manager . . . . Manchester City.
As Coach . . . . None.
As a Player . . . . Bolton Wanderers, Everton, Q.P.R, Manchester City,
. . . . Southampton, Notts County, Bury.

HONOURS
As a Manager
Sunderland: Division 1 Champions 1995-96. Manager fo the Year 1995-96.

As a Player
Division 1 championship 1985, 1987. Division 2 championship 1978. FA Cup 1984. ECWC 1985.
P.F.A. Player of the Year 1985. CS 1984, 1985, 1987.
International: 13 full caps and 6 under-21 caps for England.

SUNDERLAND STADIUM OF LIGHT
Stadium Park, Sunderland SR5 1SU

Capacity..42,000
First game...v Ajax (Friendly), 0-0, 30.07.97.

ATTENDANCES
Highest...41,214 v Stoke City (League), 3-0, 25.04.98.
Lowest...18,775 v Bury (League Cup), 2-1, 16.09.98.

OTHER GROUNDS..............Blue House Field, Groves Field, Horatio Street, ABBS Field, Roker Park.

HOW TO GET TO THE GROUND

Exit the A1 at the A690 Durham/Sunderland exit. After approx. 4 miles turn left onto the A19 (signposted Tyne Tunnel), Keep in the left lane and take the slip road signposted Washington/Sunderland onto the bridge over the River Wear.
Turn right onto the A1231 (signposted Washington/Sunderland) stay on this road going straight through 4 roundabouts in to Sunderland. continue straight through 3 sets of traffic lights and the stadium car park is on the right about half a mile past the traffic lights.

USEFUL TELEPHONE NUMBERS

Club switchboard 0191 551 5000
Club fax number 0191 551 5123
Club shop 0191 551 5050
Ticket Office . 0191 551 5151 (Fax 551 5150)

Marketing Department....... 0191 551 5555
Internet address .... www.sunderland-afc.com
Clubcall................ 0898 12 11 40*
*Calls cost 50p per minute at all times. Call costings correct at time of going to press.

MATCHDAY PROGRAMME

Programme Editor......... Rob Mason.

Number of pages .... 48.

Price .... £1.50.

Subscriptions .... Apply to club.

Local Newspapers...................
.... Journal/Chronicle/Sunday Sun
...... Sunderland Echo, Northern Echo
.... Sunderland & Washington Times
.... Shields Gazette.

Local Radio Stations
.... Metro Radio, Radio Tees
.... Radio Newcastle, Sun City 103.4.

MATCHDAY TICKET PRICES

West Stand Centre........................ £19.00
West Stand Wings £17.00
West Stand Wings (Junior) £15.00

McEwans Stand Centre £19.00
McEwans Stand Wings.................... £17.00
McEwans Stand Wings (Junior) £15.00

Premier Concourse Centre.................. £22.00
Premier Concourse Wings £17.00
Premier Concourse Wings (Junior) £15.00

North Stand £15.00

Metro FM Stand £17.00
Metro FM Stand (Junior)................... £15.00

Corner Adult........................... £15.00
Corner Junior.......................... £5.00
Corner Concession....................... £11.00

McDonalds Family Enc. Adult £11.00
McDonalds Family Enc. Junior £5.00

SWINDON TOWN
(The Robins)
NATIONWIDE LEAGUE DIVISION 1
SPONSORED BY: NATIONWIDE BUILDING SOCIETY

SWINDON TOWN F.C.

1997-98 - Back Row L-R: Wayne Allison, Mark Seagraves, Fraser Digby, Steve Mildenhall, Frank Talia, Steve Finney, Kevin Watson. **Middle Row:** Alan McDonald, Mark Walters, Craig Taylor, Gary Elkins, Mark Robinson, Scott Leitch, Ian Culverhouse, Frederic Darras, Alex Finlayson. **2nd Front Row:** Lee Collins, Peter Holcroft, Phil King, Darren Bullock, Wayne O'Sullivan, Ty Gooden, Steve Cowe. **Front Row:** Jason Drysdale, Jonathan Trigg (physio), Ross MacLaren (reserve team coach), Steve McMahon (manager), Mike Walsh (1st team coach), Les O'Neill (chief scout), Alex Smith.

SWINDON TOWN
FORMED IN 1879
TURNED PROFESSIONAL IN 1894
LTD COMPANY IN 1894

PRESIDENT: C Green
CHAIRMAN: Rikki Hunt (Director of Football)
VICE-CHAIRMAN
Cliff Puffett
DIRECTORS
Peter Archer, Willie Carson (Associate),
Peter Goodwin CBE, Mike Spearman,
Sir Seton Wills Bt.
CHEIF EXECUTIVE/SECRETARY
Steve Jones
SALES & MARKETING
M Stevens

MANAGER: Steve McMahon
ASSISTANT MANAGER: Mike Walsh
RESERVE TEAM MANAGER
Ross MacLaren
YOUTH TEAM MANAGER
Thomas Wheeldon
PHYSIOTHERAPIST
Jonathan Trigg
STATISTICIAN FOR THE DIRECTORY
Chris Thompson

Promotion candidates to relegation possibles best describes the sought of season Swindon Town had in 1997/98. Early November and Steve McMahon's men record a 1-0 win over Bradford City and head the Division One table, come the last day of the season and a 1-2 defeat at the hands of Sunderland sees the club finish in 18th place, only four points clear of the relegation zone.

It's not easy to say what went wrong, which in some ways must irritate Steve McMahon even more, at least if you can see the problems you can try and fix them! It would seem that it was all down to confidence within the players. During the early season the players were on a high and use to the winning ways, but after a three match run of defeats, ironically following their above mentioned match against Bradford that saw them go top, their confidence level dropped and the team got into losing ways that saw them slide down the table.

A third round exit out of the FA Cup at the hands of non-League Stevenage Borough, at home, did not help moral either. The Coca-Cola Cup was also ended at the first hurdle, this time Second Division Watford being the victors, 3-1 on aggregate.

McMahon will be hoping he and the players can rediscover the form that saw them challenging not only for a play-off place but for automatic promotion last season, and will not want to see a continuation of their end of season form, as a bad start could see them leave Division One via the wrong exit!

SWINDON TOWN

Division 1   :17th   FA CUP: 3rd Round   LC CUP: 1st Round

M	DATE	COMP.	VEN	OPPONENTS	RESULT	H/T	LP	GOAL SCORERS/GOAL TIMES	ATT.
1	A 09	FL	H	Crewe Alexandra	W 2-0	1-0	4	Allison 43, Finney 88 (pen)	8334
2	12	CC 1/1	H	Watford	L 0-2	0-1			6271
3	15	FL	A	Reading	W 1-0	1-0	3	Hay 17	(9338)
4	23	FL	H	Huddersfield Town	D 1-1	1-1	2	Hay 20	7683
5	26	CC 1/2	A	Watford	D 1-1	0-1		Leitch 57	(7712)
6	30	FL	A	Stoke City	W 2-1	0-1	4	Allison 78, Hay 80	(23000)
7	S 02	FL	A	Ipswich Town	L 1-2	1-1	5	Allison 22	(11246)
8	07	FL	H	Nottingham Forest	D 0-0	0-0	5		13051
9	13	FL	H	Tranmere Rovers	W 2-1	1-1	3	Walters 13, Casper 64	6811
10	20	FL	A	West Bromwich Albion	D 0-0	0-0	2		(16237)
11	27	FL	A	Manchester City	L 0-6	0-3	6		(26646)
12	O 04	FL	H	Port Vale	W 4-2	0-1	3	Hay 49, 81, 86, Taylor 67	8048
13	11	FL	H	Bury	W 3-1	2-1	2	Hay 4, 14, Gooden 79	7640
14	18	FL	A	Wolverhampton Wand	L 1-3	1-1	2	Hay 24 (pen)	(21794)
15	21	FL	A	Sunderland	D 0-0	0-0	3		(27553)
16	25	FL	H	Norwich City	W 1-0	0-0	2	Hay 84	9256
17	31	FL	A	Portsmouth	W 1-0	1-0	1	Hay 23	(8707)
18	N 05	FL	H	Queens Park Rangers	W 3-1	0-1	1	Walters 66, Taylor 84, Hay 87	10132
19	08	FL	H	Bradford City	W 1-0	1-0	1	Cowe 24	10029
20	15	FL	A	Stockport County	L 2-4	1-2	2	Hay 20, Leitch 85	(7694)
21	22	FL	H	Middlesbrough	L 1-2	1-1	3	Ndah 12	15228
22	28	FL	A	Charlton Athletic	L 0-3	0-2	4		(13769)
23	D 06	FL	H	Oxford United	W 4-1	1-1	4	Walters 34 (pen), Finney 56, Gooden 86, Wilsterman 24 (OG)	10902
24	13	FL	A	Sheffield United	L 1-2	1-1	6	Finney 24	(18115)
25	20	FL	H	Birmingham City	D 1-1	1-1	7	Finney 11	10334
26	26	FL	A	Nottingham Forest	L 0-3	0-3	9		(26500)
27	28	FL	H	Ipswich Town	L 0-2	0-0	9		10609
28	J 03	FAC 3	H	Stevenage Borough	L 1-2	1-1		Walters 5	9422
29	11	FL	A	Crewe Alexandra	L 0-2	0-0	10		(4176)
30	17	FL	H	Reading	L 0-2	0-2	10		9500
31	24	FL	A	Bradford City	D 1-1	0-1	10	Hay 90	(15130)
32	28	FL	H	Stoke City	W 1-0	0-0	9	Robinson 71	6683
33	31	FL	A	Huddersfield Town	D 0-0	0-0	10		(10028)
34	F 06	FL	H	West Bromwich Albion	L 0-2	0-1	10		9861
35	10	FL	A	Tranmere Rovers	L 0-3	0-2	10		(5288)
36	17	FL	H	Port Vale	W 1-0	1-0	10	Collins 4	(5925)
37	21	FL	H	Manchester City	L 1-3	0-1	11	Cowe 71	12280
38	28	FL	A	Bury	L 0-1	0-1	13		(5002)
39	M 07	FL	H	Portsmouth	L 0-1	0-0	13		9100
40	11	FL	A	Middlesbrough	L 0-6	0-2	13		(29581)
41	14	FL	A	Queens Park Rangers	W 2-1	2-1	11	Walters 16 (pen), Onuora 45	(13486)
42	18	FL	H	Wolverhampton Wand	D 0-0	0-0	12		7770
43	21	FL	H	Stockport County	D 1-1	0-0	11	McDonald 77	6684
44	A 04	FL	H	Charlton Athletic	L 0-1	0-0	13		7845
45	11	FL	A	Oxford United	L 1-2	0-2	13	Ndah 64 (pen)	(8005)
46	13	FL	H	Sheffield United	D 1-1	1-0	14	Walters 33	5956
47	18	FL	A	Birmingham City	L 0-3	0-2	16		(17016)
48	25	FL	A	Norwich City	L 0-5	0-2	17		(18443)
49	M 03	FL	H	Sunderland	L 1-2	0-2	17	Walters 86	14868

Best Home League Attendance: 15228 V Middlesbrough   Smallest :5956 V Sheffield United   Average :9505

Goal Scorers:
FL	(42)	Hay 14, Walters 6, Finney 4, Allison 3, Cowe 2, Gooden 2, Ndah 2, Taylor 2, Casper 1, Collins 1, Leitch 1, McDonald 1, Onuora 1, Robinson 1, Opponents 1
CC	(1)	Leitch 1
FAC	(1)	Walters 1

320

(F) Allison	(D) Borrows	(M) Bullock	(M) Casper	(M) Collins	(M) Cowe	(M) Cuervo	(D) Culverhouse	(D) Darras	(M) Davis	(G) Digby	(D) Drysdale	(F) Finney	(M) Gooden	(M) Hay	(M) Howe	(M) Kerslake	(F) Leitch	(D) McDonald	(F) Ndah	(M) Onuora	(M) Robinson	(D) Seagraves	(D) Smith	(G) Talia	(M) Taylor	(M) Thompson	(F) Walters	(M) Watson	Referee	#
X	S1				X		X			X	X		S2	X	X			X	X			X	X				S		G. Singh	1
X			S2	X		X				X	X	X	X					X	X			X	X				S1	S	M Fletcher	2
X	S3				X		X			X	X	S1	X	X				X	X			X	X				S2		A P D'Urso	3
X	X		S2	X		X				X	X		X	X				X	X				X				X	S	A G Wiley	4
X	S			S	X		X			X		X	X	X				X	X			X		X			X		B Knight	5
X	S1				X		X			X	X	X	X	X				X	X			X	S2				X		G B Frankland	6
X	S1			S	X		X			X	X	X	X	X			X1		X			X	S2				X		P Taylor	7
X	X	X	X				X			X	X	S	X	X				X									X	S	R J Harris	8
X	X	X	X				X			X	X	X	S2	X	X			X					S				X	S1	M C Bailey	9
X	X	X	X	S	X		X			X	X	X	X	X				X				S	X						F G Stretton	10
X	X	X	X		X		X			X	S3		X	S2				X	X			X					S1		R Pearson	11
X	X		S2	S			S1			X	X		X	X				X	X				X		X	X	X		S G Bennett	12
X	X	S1	X	S						X	S2		X	X				X	X				X		X	X	X		S J Baines	13
X	X	X	X	S		X				X			X	X				X					X		X		X		C J Foy	14
X	X	X	X	X	S		X			X			X	X				X					X		X	S1	X	X	S W Mathieson	15
X	X	X	X		S		X			X			X	X					S1			X			X	X	X	X	M R Halsey	16
X	X	X	X		S		X			X			X	X				X					X		X	X	X	X	P S Danson	17
X	X	X			X		X	S1	X				X	X				X					X		X	X	X	X	D Pugh	18
	X			X		X		S		X		X		X	X			X	X				X		X				A N Butler	19
	X			X		X				S	S1	X	X	X				X	X		S2		X		X	X	X	X	M J Brandwood	20
	X				S					X	X	X	X	X		X	X	X	X			X		X	X	S1	X		G Cain	21
X	S1		S2	S3						X	X	X	X	X				X	X			X		X	X		X		A P D'Urso	22
X	X1		X	S1	X					X		X	X	X				X	X			X		S2	X	X2			F G Stretton	23
X	X	X	S		X1					X		X	X	X				X	X			S1	X	S					T Jones	24
X	X	S1		S3		X				X	X2	X	S2			X	X3		X			X	X	X1					R Styles	25
X1		X			X	S1	X2	X	S2	X			X	X				X				X	S	X	S				G Laws	26
	S2			X	X1	X		S3	X	X		X	X	X	X2	X	X		X			S1	X	X3					D Orr	27
	X			X		X	S1	S2	X	X			X	X				X				X	X1	X2					S W Mathieson	28
X	X1		X	S1	S			X	S2	X	X		X	X		X2	X		X			X							A R Leake	29
X	X2	S1		X	S		X	X	X	X	X	X	X		X1		X				X					S2		E Lomas	30
X		X	S1	X1			X	X	X	X	X	S	S2				X			S	X					C J Foy	31
X		X	S	X			X1	X		X	X	S1	S		X			X				X	X				A R Hall	32
X		X	S	S2			X1	X2	X	X	X	X	S		X			X		X				F K Wolstenholme	33
X		X	S2	X1	S3		X		X	X3	X2	X	X				X				X			S1	M R Halsey	34
X		X	S3	X2	X1		X	X		X3	X	X				X				X		S1	S2	P S Danson	35
X	X	S2	S1		X3	X1	X	X2	X			X				X				X		S3	M D Messias	36
X	X	S1		X1	X3	X	X	S3	X			X				X				X	S2	B Coddington	37
X	X	S	S2		X1	X	X2	X			X				X	X	X	S1	M Fletcher	38
X	X	X	X		X	X	S	S	X			X			X	X	X	K A Leach	39
X	X	S		X	S	X	X	S	X	X	S	X			X	X	S J Baines	40
X	X	X	S		X	X	S2	X	X	X	X2	X			X1	A N Butler	41
X	X	X	S	X	X	X	X	S	X	X1	X2	X	S			X	A R Leake	42
X	X	X	S1	X	X	S	X	X	X	X	X1		X	D Orr	43
X	X	X	X	S2	X	X1	X	X2		X	S1	R D Furnandiz	44
X	X	X1	S	S1	X	X	X	X	X	S		X	S3	X3	S W Mathieson	45
X	X	X1	S2	S3	X	X	X2	S1	X3	X		X	X	D Pugh	46
X	X	S1	X	X	X	S	X1	X2	X	X	T Heilbron	47
X	X2	X	X1	X	X	S1	X	X	X	X	S2	J E Pearce	49

16	40	26	8	22	8	14	9	12	5	38	11	17	38	30	9	10	25	30	14	6	26	5	2	2	28	10	25	13	FL Appearances	
	5	1	4	9	9	2	2	1			3	6	1	6	1			1	3			1		3		4	9	5	FL Sub Appearances	
2			0+1	2			2			2	1	2	1	2	1			2	2			1	2		1	2	1+1	1	CC Appearances	
			1		1			1		1	0+1	0+1	1	1				1	1			1		1	1	1	FAC Appearances	

Also Played: (D) Elkins S(5,16,17). (D) Elliott X2(37), S1(41).(M) Hulbert S1(14), S(15,17,28). (D) King S(38). (M) Lowe S(6). (F) McA eavey S(80< S2(48). (M) McMahon S1(4). (M) Meechan S(14), S(18,19,28).(G) Mildenhall X(17,32,33,37). S(28). (D) Pattimore S2(18), S1(19). (G) Warner X(19, 0), S(21).

SWINDON TOWN

BIGGEST VICTORIES
League: 9-1 v Luton Town, Division 3S, 28.4.1921
8-0 v Newport County, Div 3S, 26.12.1938
8-0 v Bury, Division 3, 8.12.1979
F.A. Cup: 10-1 v Farnham United Breweries FC (a), Round 1, 28.11.1925
League Cup: 6-0 v Torquay United (a), Rnd 2 1st leg 23.9.1992

BIGGEST DEFEATS
League: 0-9 v Torquay United, Division 3S, 8.3.1952
F.A. Cup: 1-10 v Manchester City, Round 2, 29.1.1930
League Cup: 0-5 v Notts County, Round 3, 1962-63
0-5 v Liverpool, Round 3, 1980-81

MOST POINTS
3 points a win: 102, Division 4, 1985-86 (League record)
2 points a win: 64, Division 3, 1968-69

MOST GOALS
100, 1926-27, Division 3S.
Morris 47, Eddelston 11, Thom 8, Wall 7, Petrie 6, Denyer 5, Dickinson 3, Flood 3, Jeffries 3, Archer 1, Weston 1, Brown 1, Bailey 1, Johnson 1, Daniel 1, og1.

MOST LEAGUE GOALS CONCEDED
105, Division 3S, 1932-33

MOST FIRST CLASS MATCHES IN A SEASON
64 (46 League, 4 FA Cup, 4 League Cup, 5 Freight Rover Trophy, 5 Play-offs)1986-87

MOST LEAGUE WINS: 32, Division 4, 1985-86

MOST LEAGUE DRAWS: 17, Division 3, 1967-68

MOST LEAGUE DEFEATS: 25, Division 3S, 1956-57

MOST GOALS IN A MATCH
5. Harry Morris v Queens Park Rangers, 18.12.1927, Div 3S (6-2).
5. v Norwich City, 26.4.1930, Div 3S (5-1).
5. Keith East v Mansfield, 20.11.1965, Div 3. (6-2).

MOST GOALS IN A SEASON
Harry Morris 48, (47 League, 1 FA Cup) 1926-27.
5 goals once=5; 4 goals once=4; 3 goals 3 times=9; 2 goals 5 times=10; 1 goal 20 times=20.

OLDEST PLAYER
Alex Ferguson 43 years 103 days, v Bristol City (Div. 3S), 15.11.1947.

YOUNGEST PLAYER
Paul Rideout, 16 years 107 days v Hull (Div 3), 29.11.1980).

MOST CAPPED PLAYER
Rod Thomas (Wales) 30

League: 1985-86: Matches played 46, Won 32, Drawn 6, Lost 8, Goals for 82,Goals against 43, Points 102. First in Division 4.
Highest: 1989-90: 4th Division 2.
F.A. Cup: 1989-90: 4th rnd. Crystal Palace 3-1; 2nd rnd. Burnley 2-0; 3rd rnd.Tottenham Hotspur 3-2; 4th rnd. Manchester City 2-0; Semi-Final Newcastle Utd. 0-2.
1912: 1st rnd. Sutton 5-0; 2nd rnd. Notts County 2-0; 3rd rnd. West Ham United1-1, 4-0; 4th rnd. Everton 2-1; Semi-Final Barnsley 0-0, 0-1.
League Cup: 1968-69: 1st rnd. Torquay 2-1; 2nd rnd. Bradford City 1-1;4-3; 3rd rnd. Coventry City 2-2, 3-0; 4th rnd. Derby County 0-0, 1-0; Semi-Final Burnley 2-1; Final Arsenal 3-1.

ADDITIONAL INFORMATION
Previous Name: None.

Previous League: Southern League.

Club colours: Red shirts, shorts & socks with white & green trim.

Change colours:

Reserves League: Avon Insurance Combination Division 1.

DIVISIONAL RECORD

	Played	Won	Drawn	Lost	For	Against	Points
Premier	42	5	15	22	47	100	30
Division 2/1	706	240	196	270	943	1,003	824
Division 3/2	874	358	237	279	1,315	1,101	1,016
Division 3(S)	1,334	491	333	510	2,058	2,130	1,315
Division 4	184	87	39	58	263	211	300
Total	**3,140**	**1,181**	**820**	**1,139**	**4,605**	**4,545**	**3,485**

RECORDS AND STATISTICS

COMPETITIONS

Div.1/P	Div.2/1	Div.3/2	Div.3(S)	Div.4
1993-94	1963-65	1920-21	1921-58	1982-86
	1969-74	1958-63		
	1987-93	1965-69		
	1994-95	1974-82		
	1996-	1986-87		
		1995-96		

HONOURS

Division 2	Division 4	League Cup	Anglo/Ital
1995-96	1985-86	1968-69	1970

MOST GOALS IN A CAREER

Harry Morris 230 (1926-33)

Year	League	FA Cup
1926-27	47	1
1927-28	38	6
1928-29	27	5
1929-30	28	1
1930-31	35	
1931-32	29	
1932-33	12	1
Total	**216**	**14**

Current leading goalscorer: Mark Walters - 15 (07.96-98)

MOST APPEARANCES

John Trollope 886+3 (1960-81)

Year	League	FA Cup	Lge Cup	Other
1960-61	44	3	3	
1961-62	46	2	3	
1962-63	46	4	2	
1963-64	42	3	4	
1964-65	42	1	1	
1965-66	46	3	1	
1966-67	46	8	5	
1967-68	46	4	2	
1968-69	19+1	1	2	
1969-70	42	4	2	7
1970-71	39	2	3	4
1971-72	42	1	1	
1972-73	34	2	1	
1973-74	36	2	3	
1974-75	46	5	1	
1975-76	46	5	4	
1976-77	35	7		
1977-78	40	4	6	
1978-79	16+2		2	
1979-80				
1980-81	14			
	767+3	61	47	11

MANAGERS

As secretary, Sam Allen took control of team matters between 1902-1948. However, a team manager was appointed in 1933.

Name	Seasons	Best	Worst
Ted Vizard	1933-39	8(3S)	19(3S)
Neil Harris	1939		
Louis Page	1945-53	4(3S)	18(3S)
Maurice Lindley	1953-58	4(3S)	24(3S)
Bert Head	1958-65	14(2)	16(3)
Danny Williams	1965-69	2(3)	10(3)
Fred Ford	1969-71	5(2)	12(2)
Dave Mackay	1971-72	11(2)	11(2)
Les Allen	1977-74	11(2)	22(2)
Danny Williams	1974-78	4(3)	19(3)
Bob Smith	1978-80	5(3)	10(3)
John Trollope	1980-83	17(3)	8(4)
Ken Beamish	1983-84	17(4)	17(4)
Lou Macari	1984-89	12(2)	8(4)
Osvaldo Ardiles	1989-91	4(2)	
Glenn Hoddle	1991-93	5(2/1)	8(2)
John Gorman	1993-94	22(P)	
Steve McMahon	1994-	18 (1)	1(2)

RECORD TRANSFER FEE RECEIVED

Amount	Club	Player	Date
£1,500,000	Manchester City	Kevin Horlock	1/97
£1,300,000	Middlesbrough	Jan Aage Fjortoft	3/95
£1,250,000	Tottenham	Colin Calderwood	8/93
£1,150,000	Manchester City	Nicky Summerbee	6/94

RECORD TRANSFER FEE PAID

Amount	Club	Player	Date
£850,000	West Ham	Joey Beauchamp	6/94
£600,000	Newcastle	Mark Robinson	7/94
£500,000	Leyton Orient	Adrian Whitbread	7/93
£500,000	Rapid Veienna	Jan Aage Fjortoft	7/93

LONGEST LEAGUE RUNS

of undefeated matches:	22 (12.1.1986 - 23.8.1986)	of league matches w/out a win:	9 (17.4.1993 - 20.11.1993)
of undefeated home matches:	26 (24.2.1968 - 29.3.1969)	of undefeated away matches:	13 (18.1.1986 - 6.9.1986)
without home win:	10 (28.2.56-15.9.56, 17.4.93-20.11.93)	without an away win:	30 (25.11.1972 - 15.4.1974)
of league wins:	8 (2.1.26-27.3.26, 12.1.86-15.3.86)	of home wins:	14 (26.8.1985 - 15.3.1986)
of league defeats:	6 (1967, 3.5.8.1980 - 6.9.1980)	of away wins:	6 (18.1.1986 - 8.3.1986.

SWINDON TOWN

PLAYERS NAME Honours	Ht	Wt	Birthdate	Birthplace Transfers	Contract Date	Clubs	League	L/Cup	FA Cup	Other	Lge	L/C	FAC	Oth
G O A L K E E P E R														
Glass James R	6.1	11.1	01/08/73	Epsom	04/07/91	Crystal Palace (T)								
				Loan	2/10/95	Portsmouth	3							
				Loan	12/21/95	Gillingham								
				Loan	1/31/96	Burnley								
				Free	08/03/96	Bournemouth	94	4	4	7				
				Free	7/1/98	Swindon Town								
Mildenhall Stephen	6.4	12.1	5/13/78	Swindon		Swindon Town	4+1	2						
Talia Frank Div.2'96.	6.1	13.6	7/20/72	Melbourne		Sunshine George								
				Free	8/28/92	Blackburn Rovers								
				Loan	12/29/92	Hartlepool United	14		1					
				Loan	9/8/95	Swindon Town								
				£150000	11/10/95	Swindon Town	32	6		1				
D E F E N C E														
Borrows Brian E: B.1.	5.11	10.12	12/20/60	Liverpool	4/23/80	Everton	27	2						
				£10000	3/24/83	Bolton Wanderers	95	7	4	4				
				£82000	6/6/85	Coventry City	396+13	42	26	10+1	11	1	1	
				Loan	9/17/93	Bristol City	6							
				Loan	9/5/97	Swindon Town	15							
				Free	11/14/97	Swindon Town	25							
Davis Sol S	5.7	11	9/4/79	Cheltenham	4/10/98	Swindon Town (T)	5+1							
Hall Gareth D W: 9, u21.1. Div2'89. ZDC'90 DIV.1'96.	5.8	10.07	20/03/69	Croydon	25/04/86	Chelsea	115+16	12+1	6	10+4	3			1
				£300000	19/01/96	Sunderland	41+7	3	2					
				Loan	10/3/97	Brentford	6							
				Free	7/1/98	Swindon Town								
King Phil E: B.1.	5.8	11.9	12/28/67	Bristol	1/7/85	Exeter City	24+3	1		1+2				
				£3000	7/14/86	Torquay United	24	2	1	2	3			
				£155000	6/2/87	Swindon Town	112+4	11	5	13	4			
				£400000	11/30/89	Sheffield Wed.	124+5	17	9	4	2			
				Loan	10/22/93	Notts County	6			2				
				£250000	8/1/94	Aston Villa	13+3	3		4				
				Loan	10/30/95	WBA	4			1				
				Free	3/26/97	Swindon Town	5							
				Loan	10/20/97	Blackpool	6							
McDonald Alan E: Y1	6.2	12.7	10/12/63	Belfast	8/12/81	QPR	395+8	44	33	5	13	2	2	
				Loan	3/24/83	Charlton Athletic	9							
				Free	7/7/97	Swindon Town	30+3	2	1		1			
Reeves Alan	6	12	19/11/67	Birkenhead		Heswell								
					9/20/88	Norwich City								
				Loan	2/9/89	Gillingham	18							
				£10000	8/18/89	Chester City	31+9	1+1	3	3	2			
				Free	7/2/91	Rochdale	119+2	12	6	5	9	1		
				£300000	9/6/94	Wimbledon	52+5	2+2	8		4			
				Free	7/1/98	Swindon Town								
Taylor Craig	6.1	12.3	1/24/74	Plymouth		Dorchester								
					9/3/96	Swindon Town	27+4	0+1	1		1			
Willis Adam	6.1	12.2	9/21/76	Nuneaton		Coventry City (T)								
				Free	4/22/98	Swindon Town								
M I D F I E L D														
Bullock Darren J	5.8	12.4	2/12/69	Worcester		Nuneaton Borough								
				£55000	11/19/93	Huddersfield Town	127+1	11	8	9	16	1	2	1
					2/21/97	Swindon Town	38+6				1			
Collins Lee	5.8	10.8	2/3/74	Bellshill		Albion Rovers								
				£15000	11/15/95	Swindon Town	28+8		3	1	1			
Cowe Steve	5.7	10.2	9/29/74	Gloucester	8/1/93	Aston Villa								
				£100000	3/28/96	Swindon Town	39+26	3+2	1		9			
Cuervo Philippe	5.11	12.6	8/13/69	Calais		St Etienne								
				Free	8/8/97	Swindon Town	14+9	2						
Gooden Ty Div.2'96.	5.8	12.6	10/23/72	Canvey Island	Free	Arsenal								
				Free		Wycombe Wanderers								
				Free	1/31/94	Swindon Town	74+24	4+1	4+1	3+1	8	1		
Howe Stephen R	5.7	10.04	11/6/73	Annisford	8/1/92	Nottingham Forest	4+6	1		1+1	2			
				Loan	1/17/97	Ipswich Town	2+1	1						
				£30000	1/16/98	Swindon Town	9+1							
Hulbert Robin J Y, S. E:	5.9	10.5	3/14/80	Plymouth	9/24/96	Swindon Town	0+1	0+1						
Kerslake David E: u21.1, u19.4, Y.27, S	5.8	11	6/19/66	Stepney	6/1/83	QPR	38+20	6+2	2+2	2+2	6	4		
				£110000	11/24/89	Swindon Town	133+2	12	8	10	1			
				£500000	3/11/93	Leeds United	8							
				£450000	9/24/93	Tottenham Hotspur	34+3	5	1+1					

Name	Ht	Wt	DOB	From	Date	Club								
...erslake continued....				Loan	11/22/96	Swindon Town	8							
				Free	5/31/97	Charlton Athletic								
				Free	8/16/97	Ipswich Town	2+5	1+1						
				Loan	12/12/97	Wycombe W.	9+1							
				Free	3/10/98	Swindon Town	10							
nuora Ifem	6	11.1	7/28/67	Glasgow	7/28/89	Huddersfield Town	115+50	10+6	12+3	13+3	30	4	3	3
				Free	7/20/94	Mansfield Town	17+11		0+1	1	8			
				Free	8/16/96	Gillingham	53+9	6	4		23	1	2	
				£120000	3/13/98	Swindon Town	6				1			
Robinson Mark	5.9	10.6	11/21/68	Rochdale	1/10/87	WBA	2	0+1						
Div.2'96.				Free	6/23/87	Barnsley	117+20	7+2	7+1	3+2	6			1
				£450000	3/9/93	Newcastle United	14+11		1					
				£600000	7/22/94	Swindon Town	155+1	15	10	6+1	3			
Watson Kevin E	6	12.6	1/3/74	Hackney	5/15/92	Tottenham Hotspur	4+1	1+1	0+1			1		
				Loan	3/24/94	Brentford	2+1							
				Loan	12/2/94	Bristol City	1+1							
				Loan	7/15/96	Barnet	13							
					8/15/96	Swindon Town	31+15	1+1	1+1		1			

F O R W A R D

Name	Ht	Wt	DOB	From	Date	Club								
Hay Christopher	6	12.5	8/28/74	Glasgow		Celtic								
					8/6/97	Swindon Town	30+5	1	1		14			
Leitch Donald S	5.8	11.1	10/6/69	Motherwell		Hearts								
					7/28/96	Swindon Town	68+1	7	1		1	2		
McAreavey Paul			12/3/80	Belfast	9/4/97	Swindon Town	0+1							
Meechan Alexander T	5.10	10.10	1/29/80	Plymouth	10/17/97	Swindon Town (T)	0+1							
Ndah George E	6.1	10	12/23/74	Dulwich	8/10/92	Crystal Palace	28+38	3+5	2	4+1	7	2		
E: Y.3.				Loan	10/13/95	Bournemouth	12			1	2			
				Loan	8/29/97	Gillingham	4							
				£500000	11/21/97	Swindon Town	14		1		2			
Walters Mark E	5.9	11.5	6/2/64	Birmingham	5/18/82	Aston Villa	168+13	20+1	11+1	7+3	39	6	1	2
E: 1, B.1, u21.9, Y, S. FAYC'80, ESC'82.				£500000	12/31/87	Glasgow Rangers	101+5	13	14	10	32	11	6	2
SPD'89'90'91. SLC'89'91. FAC'92.				£1250000	8/13/91	Liverpool	58+36	10+2	6+3	8+1	14	4		1
				Loan	3/24/94	Stoke City	9				2			
				Free	1/18/96	Southampton	4+1		4					
				Free	7/30/96	Swindon Town	49+12	5+1	2		13	1	1	

THE MANAGER
STEVE McMAHON

Date of Birth . . . . 29th August 1979.
Place of Birth . . . . Liverpool.
Date of Appointment . . . . November 1994.

PREVIOUS CLUBS
As Manager . . . . None.
As Asst.Man/Coach . . . . None.
As a player . . . . Everton, Aston Villa, Liverpool, Manchester City, Swindon.

HONOURS
As a Manager
Swindon: Division 2 Championship 1995/96.

As a Player
Liverpool: Division 1 championship 1986, 1988, 1990. FA Cup 1986, 1989.
Charity Shield 1986,1988,1989. Super Cup 1986.

COUNTY GROUND
County Road, Swindon SN1 2ED

Capacity 15,728

First game ....v Old St Stephens, 13.5.1893.
First floodlit game ....v Bristol City, 02.04.1951.

ATTENDANCES
Highest ....32,000 v Arsenal, FA Cup, 15.1.1972. 29,106 v Watford, Division 3, 29.3.1969.
Lowest ....1,681 v Darlington, Division 4, 17.4.1984.

OTHER GROUNDS ....Bradford's Field, Globe Field, The Croft (1884-1895)

HOW TO GET TO THE GROUND

From all directions
Two miles towards Town Centre from M4, junction 15.

Car Parking
Town centre car parks. No off street parking.

Nearest Railway Station
Swindon (01793 536 804) 10-15 minutes walk.

USEFUL TELEPHONE NUMBERS

Club switchboard 01793 430 430
Club fax number 01793 536 170
Club Shop 01793 423 030
Ticket Office .. 01793 529 000 (Fax 431 887)

Marketing Department. 01793 532 121
Clubcall 0891 12 16 40*
*Calls cost 50p per minute at all times.
Call costings correct at time of going to press.

MATCHDAY PROGRAMME

Programme Editor .... Jason Harris.

Number of pages .... 48.

Price .... £1.50.

Subscriptions .... £50.

Local Newspapers
Wiltshire Newspapers (Evening Advertiser),
.... Western Daily Press.

Local Radio Stations
.... GWR, BBC Wiltshire Sound.

MATCHDAY TICKET PRICES (97/98)

Rover Family Stand
Adults: £11.50 .... Concessions/Juniors: £6
Family Tickets (1+1): £11 .... Additional juniors: £1

Wheelchair Enclosures
Includes one helper £5.50

North Stand & Intel Stand - Enclosure/wings
Adults: £12.50. .... Concessions/Juniors: £7.50

North Stand & Intel Stand - Intermediate Block
Adults: £14 .... Concessions/Juniors: £8

North Stand & Intel Stand - Centre Block
Adults: £15 .... Concessions/Juniors: £8.50

TRANMERE ROVERS
(The Rovers)
NATIONWIDE LEAGUE DIVISION 1
SPONSORED BY: WIRRAL BOROUGH COUNCIL

1998-99 - Back Row L-R: Tommy Holmes, Richard Hinds, Dave Challinor, Mauro Pereira, Clint Hill, Liam O'Brien, John McGreal, Gary Jones, Micky Mellon, Kenny Irons, John Morrissey. **Middle Row:** Ray Mathias (Now at Wigan), Warwick Rimmer (Yth. dev. Officer), Andy Moran, Alan Morgan, Kevin McIntyre, Steve Simonsen, Andy Parkinson, Danny Coyne, Dirk Hebel, Gareth Powell, Neil Gibson, Steve Frail, George Santos, Barry Crowe, Mick Horton (Club Secretary), Kevin Sheedy (Asst. Manager). **Front Row:** Steve Mungall (Centre of Excellence Manager), Dave Philpotts (Chief scout/coach), Jaon Koumas, Ryan Williams, David Kelly (Team captain), John Aldridge (Manager), Lee Jones, Andy Thompson, Alan Mahon, Les Parry (Physio), John McMahon (Yth. team coach).

TRANMERE ROVERS
FORMED IN 1885
TURNED PROFESSIONAL IN 1912
LTD COMPANY IN 1912

PRESIDENT: H B Thomas
CHAIRMAN: Frank Corfe
DIRECTORS
F Williams, A J Adams,
J Holsgrove, H Jones, C N Wilson
SECRETARY
Mick Horton
COMMERCIAL MANAGER
Janet Ratcliffe (0151 608 0371)

DIRECTOR OF FOOTBALL: John King
MANAGER: John Aldridge
ASSISTANT MANAGER: Kevin Sheedy

YOUTH TEAM COACH
John McMahon
PHYSIOTHERAPIST
Les Parry

STATISTICIAN FOR THE DIRECTORY
Peter Bishop

During the mid-Nineties, Tranmere Rovers reached the play-offs in three successive seasons and yet, for two of the last three campaigns, the club has flirted with the relegation zone. So what has changed? Not a lot at Prenton Park, rather it's the division which has changed dramatically with an influx of big, well supported clubs, many of whom have top flight experience and think nothing of splashing out two or three million on one player.

In contrast, Tranmere, as one of the division's 'poor relations' scrape around looking for bargains. Despite banking in excess of £3 million from the transfers of Ian Moore, Alan Rogers, Pat Nevin and Eric Nixon, boss John Aldridge was able to shell out only a fraction on Lee Jones (£100,000), David Kelly (£350,000), and Ryan Williams (£70,000) plus four free transfers. Despite such a modest investment by current first division standards, Rovers started the season well with Lee Jones and Kelly forming a potent partnership, which contributed to the season's best victory, 6-0 versus Reading at home, in late September. But with Kelly and Lee Jones suffering a succession of injuries, the team struggled to score and in consequence plummeted down the table to go into the Christmas period in 22nd place. The loss of experienced defenders Gary Stevens and Andy Thorn (to a career ending injury) didn't help matters as Aldridge was forced to blood youngsters like Clint Hill, Andy Parkinson, Alan Morgan, Dave Challinor and 'keeper Steve Simonsen, who proved such a success he ended the season in the England U21 side. The youngsters however did not let the side down and, when they went seven games without defeat, the foundations for recovery were laid and after a few nervous moments consolidated their position to finish 14th and well clear of danger.

In the Coca-Cola Cup, Rovers went out on penalties away at Oxford in the 3rd round, however they fared much better in the FA Cup. A difficult away tie at Non-League Hereford in the 3rd round was successfully negotiated (3-0) and Sunderland beaten 1-0 at Prenton Park to end their 22 game unbeaten record, in Round 4, to set up a big pay-day against Shearer and Co. at Newcastle. Indeed, it was Shearer's goal that proved decisive.

The season ended with John Aldridge appearing for the last time as a player, against Wolves, and fittingly he signed-off with two goals to take his tally to 174 for Rovers and 474 overall. He also became the club's oldest player in a League match at 39 years and 229 days.

Peter Bishop.

TRANMERE ROVERS

Division 1   :14th   FA CUP: 5th Round   LC CUP: 3rd Round

M	DATE	COMP.	VEN	OPPONENTS	RESULT	H/T	LP	GOAL SCORERS/GOAL TIMES	ATT.
1	A 09	FL	A	West Bromwich Albion	L 1-2	0-2	17	Kelly 75	(16727)
2	12	CC 1/1	H	Hartlepool United	W 3-1	0-1		Jones L 57, Morrissey 69, Kelly 89	3878
3	15	FL	H	Queens Park Rangers	W 2-1	1-0	11	Kelly 39, Jones L 72	7467
4	22	FL	A	Manchester City	D 1-1	0-0	5	Jones L 61	(26336)
5	26	CC 1/2	A	Hartlepool United	L 1-2	1-1		O'Brien 45	(1626)
6	30	FL	H	Middlesbrough	L 0-2	0-1	11		12095
7	S 02	FL	H	Birmingham City	L 0-3	0-2	16		6620
8	07	FL	A	Bury	L 0-1	0-1	20		(5073)
9	13	FL	A	Swindon Town	L 1-2	1-1	22	Jones L 43	(6811)
10	16	CC 2/1	A	Notts County	W 2-0	1-0		Jones G 31, Kelly 61	(1779)
11	20	FL	H	Reading	W 6-0	5-0	18	Morrissey 3, Kelly 10, 41, Jones L 20, Jones G 38, Thompson 59	5565
12	23	CC 2/2	H	Notts County	L 0-1	0-1			3287
13	27	FL	A	Crewe Alexandra	L 1-2	0-1	20	Stevens 60	(4845)
14	O 04	FL	A	Norwich City	W 2-0	1-0	18	Kelly 12, Jones L 68	6674
15	14	CC 3	A	Oxford United	D 1-1	1-0		Kelly 34	(3878)
16	18	FL	A	Nottingham Forest	D 2-2	1-2	20	Jones L 4, Thompson 60	(17009)
17	22	FL	A	Wolverhampton Wand	L 1-2	0-2	20	Jones G 65	(20841)
18	25	FL	H	Charlton Athletic	D 2-2	1-0	21	Branch 12, Jones L 60	5911
19	N 01	FL	A	Sheffield United	L 1-2	0-0	22	Kelly 69	(16578)
20	04	FL	H	Huddersfield Town	W 1-0	1-0	18	Irons 3	5127
21	08	FL	H	Port Vale	L 1-2	0-1	20	Irons 51	7063
22	15	FL	A	Bradford City	W 1-0	0-0	17	Aldridge 60	(16494)
23	22	FL	H	Stoke City	W 3-1	1-1	16	Jones L 9, Aldridge 66, O'Brien 86	8009
24	29	FL	A	Sunderland	L 0-3	0-3	16		(26674)
25	D 06	FL	H	Ipswich Town	D 1-1	0-1	17	Jones L 73	5720
26	13	FL	A	Stockport County	L 1-3	1-1	19	Aldridge 33	(7903)
27	20	FL	H	Oxford United	L 0-2	0-0	21		5181
28	26	FL	H	Bury	D 0-0	0-0	22		9146
29	28	FL	A	Birmingham City	D 0-0	0-0	21		(19533)
30	J 09	FL	A	West Bromwich Albion	D 0-0	0-0	20		8058
31	13	FAC 3	A	Hereford United	W 3-0	1-0		Jones G 14, 53, Hill 59	(7473)
32	17	FL	A	Queens Park Rangers	D 0-0	0-0	22		(12033)
33	24	FAC 4	H	Sunderland	W 1-0	0-0		Parkinson 77	14055
34	31	FL	H	Manchester City	D 0-0	0-0	22		12830
35	F 04	FL	A	Middlesbrough	L 0-3	0-2	22		(29540)
36	06	FL	A	Reading	W 3-1	1-0	22	Irons 10, Kelly 65, Branch 72	(7069)
37	10	FL	H	Swindon Town	W 3-0	2-0	18	Thompson 35, Branch 39, Morrissey 73	5288
38	14	FAC 5	A	Newcastle United	L 0-1	0-1			(36675)
39	18	FL	A	Norwich City	W 2-0	0-0	17	O'Brien 66, Kelly 75	(12105)
40	21	FL	H	Crewe Alexandra	L 0-3	0-1	17		7534
41	24	FL	H	Nottingham Forest	D 0-0	0-0	18		7377
42	28	FL	A	Portsmouth	L 0-1	0-1	19		(12250)
43	M 04	FL	A	Port Vale	W 1-0	0-0	17	Kelly 47	(5465)
44	14	FL	A	Huddersfield Town	L 0-3	0-1	21		(10844)
45	21	FL	H	Bradford City	W 3-1	0-1	19	Irons 57, Jones G 65, Kelly 81	9463
46	28	FL	A	Stoke City	W 3-0	2-0	16	Jones G 26, Mellon 39, Kelly 60	(16692)
47	A 03	FL	H	Sunderland	L 0-2	0-2	16		14116
48	07	FL	H	Portsmouth	D 2-2	1-1	16	Jones G 14, Challinor 53	8020
49	11	FL	A	Ipswich Town	D 0-0	0-0	16		(18039)
50	13	FL	H	Stockport County	W 3-0	2-0	15	Jones G 7, 42, Mellon 51	8070
51	18	FL	A	Oxford United	D 1-1	0-1	15	Mahon 69	(6489)
52	25	FL	A	Charlton Athletic	L 0-2	0-1	16		(15393)
53	28	FL	H	Sheffield United	D 3-3	1-0	14	O'Brien 10, Jones G 64, Parkinson 66	7526
54	M 03	FL	H	Wolverhampton Wand	W 2-1	1-0	14	Aldridge 34, 75	11144

Best Home League Attendance: 14116 V Sunderland   Smallest :5127 V Huddersfield Town   Average :8000

Goal Scorers:

FL	(54)	Kelly 11, Jones L 9, Jones G 8, Aldridge 5, Irons 4, Branch 3, O'Brien 3, Thompson 3, Mellon 2, Morrissey 2, Challinor 1, Mahon 1, Parkinson 1, Stevens 1
CC	(7)	Kelly 3, Jones G 1, Jones L 1, Morrissey 1, O'Brien 1
FAC	(4)	Jones G 2, Hill 1, Parkinson 1

(F) Aldridge	(F) Branch	(D) Challinor	(M) Cook	(G) Coyne	(D) Frail	(M) Hebel	(D) Hill	(M) Irons	(F) Jones L	(F) Jones G	(F) Kelly	(F) Koumas	(D) Kubicki	(M) Mahon	(D) McGreal	(M) McIntyre	(M) Mellon	(M) Morgan	(F) Morrissey	(M) O'Brien	(F) Parkinson	(M) Powell	(G) Simonsen	(D) Stevens	(D) Thompson	(D) Thorn	Player	No
S2	X		X	X				S3	X	X	X				X				S1	X				X	X	X	P. Taylor	1
S			X	X				S1	X	X	X				X			S2	X	X				X	X	X	B Coddington	2
S2	S1		X	X				S3	X	X	X				X				X	X				X	X	X	S W Mathieson	3
S	S2		X	X				S1	X	X	X				X				X	X				X	X	X	M J Brandwood	4
S	S2		X	X				S1	X	X	X				X				X	X				X	X	X	A R Leake	5
S1	S3		X	X				S2	X	X	X				X				X	X				X	X	X	P R Richards	6
S1	X	X	X	X				S2	X	X								X	S	X				X	X	X	G B Frankland	7
	X	S2	X	X				X	X	X					X			X	S3	S1				X	X	X	R D Furnandiz	8
S	S1		X	X				S	X	X	X				X				X	X				X	X	X	M C Bailey	9
	S2		X	X				S3	X	X	X			S1	X				X	X				X	X	X	S G Bennett	10
	S3	X	X	X					X	X	X			S1	X			S2	X					X	X	X	D Laws	11
	S1	X	X	X					X	X	X			S2	X			S3	X	X				X	X	X	R Pearson	12
S	X	X	X	X				S2	X	X	X			S1	X			S1	X					X	X	X	P S Danson	13
S3	X	X		X				X	X	X				S2	X			S1	X					X	X		E K Wolstenholme	14
	X	X		X				X	X	X	X			S1	X			S	X	S2				X	X		J A Kirkby	15
	S1	X		X		X		X	X	X	X			X		S2		X	S					X	X		B Knight	16
	X	X		X				X	X	X				X		S		X	X	S1	S2			X	X		E Lomas	17
S	X	X		X				X	X	X				S2		S1		X	X					X	X		A G Wiley	18
	X	X		X				X	X	X	X			X		S1	S							X	X	X	A R Leake	19
	X	S		X				X	X	X	X			X		X		S						X	X	X	A Bates	20
	X	S2		X				X	X	X	X			S1		X		X	S3					X	X	X	K M Lynch	21
X	X	S						X	X					S1	X		X		S2	X			X	X	X	X	T Heilbron	22
X								X	X	S2	X			S3	X		X		S1	X			X	X	X	X	G Laws	23
X1	S2							X3	X	S3	X			X	X		X		S1	X			X	X	X	X2	J P Robinson	24
S1	X							X	X2	S	X			S2	X		X		X	X			X	X1			G Singh	25
X	X				S			X	X	X				S	X		X	X	X1	S1			X	X			M Fletcher	26
S2		S1						X	X	X	X			X		X2	X	X		X			X		X	X	S J Baines	27
		S						X1	X	X	X			X		X		S1	X	S			X	X	X	X	R Pearson	28
								X	X	X	X			X		X	X	S	X	S			X		X	X	M R Halsey	29
X1								X		S2	X			X		X	X	S	X	S1			X	X2	X	X	D Laws	30
S	X		S				S1	X		X	X			S3	X		X3		S2	X	X2		X		X	X1	R J Harris	31
X1	X						X	V		X				X	X	S		X		S	X	S1		X	X	X	A R Hall	32
S	X		S				X	X		X	X			S	X	S	X	X	S	X	X		X		X		M D Reed	33
	S2	X		X					X2	X				S3	X		X3	X1	S1	X	X		X		X		C R Wilkes	34
	S1	X		X3				X		X2	X			X			X	S3	S2	X	X1		X		X		J A Kirkby	35
	X	X		X		X		X		S2	X			X2		S1		X	X1	X			X		X		K A Leach	36
	X2	X		X1		X		X		S3	X			X		S1		X	X3	S2			X		X		P S Danson	37
X1	X							X	X2	S3	X			S	X		S2	X	X	X3	S1	S	X		X		G R Ashby	38
	X							X	X	S2	X			S	X		S1	X1	X	X	X2		X		X		D R Crick	39
	X							X	X	S1	X	X	S		X	S	X		X	X1			X		X		E K Wolstenholme	40
	S1	X						X	X	X	X1				X	S	X		X	X			X		X		E Lomas	41
	X	X		S1				X2		X	X			S3		X	X1	X		X			X		X		R J Harris	42
	X2	X						X	S2	X	X		X			S1	S	X1	X				X		X		A R Leake	43
	X	X		X	X				X3					X	S3	X		S1	X1	X2	S2		X		X		G Laws	44
	X							X	X1	X	X		X	S3	X		S2	X2	X3	S1			X		X		P R Richards	45
	X							X	X	X	X	X1	X		X		S1	X	X	S			X		X		M Fletcher	46
	X			S	X1	X2	X		X				X		S1		X	X	S2				X		X		A G Wiley	47
	X			S1	X	X2	X		X				X		X		X	S1	X	X			X		X		W C Burns	48
	X			X	X	S2	X2		X				X	S	X		X1	S1	X				X		X		M C Bailey	49
	X			S	X		X		X				X	S1	X		X	S2	X	X1	X2		X		X		A N Butler	50
	X			X1	X		X		X				X	S2	X		X	X	S2				X		X		M R Halsey	51
	X			X	X1	S2	X		X				X	X2	X		X	S1	X	X			X		X		P Rejer	52
	X			X2	S1	X1	X		X				X	S2	X		X	S	X	X			X		X		T Heilbron	53
X				S3				X	X2	S1	X		X3		X		X		X1	S2	X		X		X		K M Lynch	54
7	16	28	9	16	4		13	36	29	37	28		12	3	42		24	14	27	37	8		30	25	44	17	FL Appearances	9
7	9	4			2		1	7	5	6	1			15		2	9	5	10	3		10					FL Sub Appearances	
1+3	2	4	5				1+3	5	5	4		0+3	5		0+2	4+1			5	5	3	1					CC Appearances	
1	3			2+1	2		2+1	3		0+1	3		2+1	1+1	3	2+1		3		3	1						FAC Appearances	

329

TRANMERE ROVERS

CLUB RECORDS

BIGGEST VICTORIES
League: 11-1 v Durham City, Div 3N, 7.1.1928
13-4 v Oldham, Div 3N, 26.12.1935
F.A. Cup: 13-0 v Oswestry, 10.10.1914
League Cup: 5-1 v Oxford Utd, Rnd 2, 21.9.1993

BIGGEST DEFEATS
League: 2-9 v Q.P.R., Div 3, 3.12.1960
0-8 v Grimsby Town, Div 3N, 14.9.1925
0-8 v Bradford City, Div 3N, 6.3.1929
0-8 v Lincoln City, Div 3N, 21.4.1930
0-8 v Bury, Div 3, 10.1.1970
F.A. Cup: 1-9 v Tottenham, Rnd 3 replay, 14.1.1953
League Cup: 0-6 v Q.P.R., Rnd 3, 23.9.1969
0-6 v West Ham Utd, Rnd 2, 11.9.1974

MOST POINTS
3 points a win: 80, Division 4, 1988-89, Div 3, 1989-90
2 points a win: 60, Division 4, 1964-65

MOST GOALS
111, Division 3N, 1930-31
J Kennedy 34, Dixon 32, Watts 27, Meston 8, Urmson 7, Barton 1, Lewis 1, og 1

MOST LEAGUE GOALS CONCEDED
115, Division 3, 1960-61

MOST FIRST CLASS MATCHES IN A SEASON
65 (46 League, 1 FA Cup, 7 League Cup, 8 Leyland Daf, 3 Play-Offs) 1989-90

MOST LEAGUE WINS
27, Division 4, 1964-65

MOST LEAGUE DRAWS
22, Division 3, 1970-71

MOST LEAGUE DEFEATS
31, Division 2, 1938-39

INDIVIDUAL CLUB RECORDS

MOST GOALS IN A MATCH
9. Robert `Bunny' Bell v Oldham Athletic, 26.12.1935

MOST GOALS IN A SEASON
Robert `Bunny' Bell 40 (League 35, FA Cup 5,) 1933-34
4 goals twice=8; 3 goals 4 times=12; 1 goal 12 times=12. Total 40
John Aldridge 40 (League 22, Lge Cup 8, FA Cup 3, AMC 7) 1991-92
3 goals 4 times=12; 2 goals 5 times=10, 1 goal 18 times=18. Total 40

OLDEST PLAYER
George Payne, 39 years 202 days, Div 3, 11.3.1961

YOUNGEST PLAYER
William `Dixie' Dean, 16 years 355 days, Div 3N, 12.1.1924

MOST CAPPED PLAYER
John Aldridge (Eire) 30

BEST PERFORMANCES

League: 1992-93: Matches Played 46, Won 23, Drawn 10, Lost 13, Goals for 72, Goals against 56, Points 79.
Fourth in Division 1

Highest: 4th Division 1, 1992-93

F.A. Cup: 1967-68: 1st rnd. Rochdale (h) 5-1; 2nd rnd. Bradford P.A. (a) 3-2; 3rd rnd. Huddersfield (h) 2-1; 4th rnd. Coventry City 1-1, 2-0; 5th rnd. Everton (a) 0-2

League Cup: 1993-94: 2nd Rnd. Oxford United 5-1, 1-1; 3rd Rnd. Grimsby 4-1; 4th Rnd. Oldham Ath. 3-0; 5th Rnd. Nottingham F. 1-1, 2-0; Semi-Final Aston Villa 3-1, 1-3 (lost 5-4 on pens).

DIVISIONAL RECORD

	Played	Won	Drawn	Lost	For	Against	Points
Division 2/1	364	131	98	135	484	495	485
Division 3	736	242	213	281	980	1,028	743
Division 3(N)	1,240	506	255	479	2,073	1,987	1,267
Division 4	780	318	185	277	1,179	1,057	955
Total	3,120	1,197	751	1,172	4,716	4,567	3,450

ADDITIONAL INFORMATION
Previous Name
Belmont 1884-85

Previous League
Central League 1919-21

Club colours: All white shirts, blue shorts, blue/white socks.
Change colours: Claret & sky blue shirts, shorts & socks.

Reserves League: Pontins Central League Division 1.
Youth League: Lancashire League Divisions 1 & 2.

RECORDS AND STATISTICS

COMPETITIONS

Div.2/1	Div.3(N)	Div.3	Div.4
1938-39	1921-38	1958-61	1961-67
1991-	1939-58	1967-75	1975-76
		1976-79	1979-89
		1989-91	

HONOURS

Division 3(N)	Leyland Daf	Welsh Cup
1937-38	1990	1934-35

MOST APPEARANCES

Ray Mathias 626+11 (1967-84)

Year	League	FA Cup	Lge Cup
1967-68	13		
1968-69	26	1	5
1969-70	20+4		
1970-71	46	3	3
1971-72	46	7	3
1972-73	45	2	1
1973-74	38+1	2	3
1974-75	40	1	3
1975-76	46	1	2
1976-77	46	1	3
1977-78	46	2	2
1978-79	45	3	2
1979-80	38+4	3	4
1980-81	37	3	4
1981-82	1		1
1982-83	16		3
1983-84	6+1	1	
1984-85	2		
	557+10	29+1	40

MOST GOALS IN A CAREER

Ian Muir -180 (1985-95)

Year	League	FA Cup	Lge Cup	Others
1985-86	14	1		
1986-87	20	3		2
1987-88	27	2		
1988-89	21	5	2	1
1989-90	23		4	8
1990-91	13			8
1991-92	5			
1992-93	2			
1993-94	9			
1994-95	7	3		
Total	141	14	6	19

Current leading goalscorer: John Morrissey - 63 (10.85-98)

MANAGERS

Name	Seasons	Best	Worst
Bert Cooke	1912-35	4(3N)	21(3N)
Jack Carr	1935-36	3(3N)	3(3N)
Jim Knowles	1936-39	22(2)	19(3N)
Bill Ridding	1939-45		
Ernie Blackburn	1946-55	4(3N)	19(3N)
Noel Kelly	1955-57	16(3N)	23(3N)
Peter Farrall	1957-60	7(3)	20(3)
Walter Galbraith	1961	21(3)	21(3)
Dave Russell	1961-69	7(3)	15(4)
Jackie Wright	1969-72	16(3)	20(3)
Ron Yeats	1972-75	10(3)	22(3)
John King	1975-80	12(3)	15(4)
Bryan Hamilton	1980-85	6(4)	21(4)
Frank Worthington	1985-87	19(4)	20(4)
Ronnie Moore	1987		
John King	1987-96	4(2/1)	20(4)
John Aldridge	1996-	11(1)	14 (1)

RECORD TRANSFER FEE RECEIVED

Amount	Club	Player	Date
£2,000,000	Nott'm Forest	Alan Rogers	08/97
£1,500,000	Sheffield Wed.	Ian Nolan	08/94
£750,000	Middlesbrough	Steve Vickers	11/93
£120,000	Cardiff City	Ronnie Moore	2/79

RECORD TRANSFER FEE PAID

Amount	Club	Player	Date
£500,000	Aston Villa	Shaun Teale	8/95
£350,000	Glasgow Rangers	Gary Stevens	10/94
£350,000	Glasgow Celtic	Tommy Coyne	3/93
£300,000	Everton	Pat Nevin	8/92

LONGEST LEAGUE RUNS

of undefeated matches:	18 (16.3.1970 - 4.9.1970)	of league matches w/out a win:	15 (19.2.1979 - 18.4.1979)
of undefeated home matches:	26 (24.10.1988 - 10.11.1989)	of undefeated away matches:	10 (27.12.1983 - 21.4.1984)
without home win:	11 (19.2.1979 - 9.5.1979)	without an away win:	35 (19.11.1977 - 14.4.1979)
of league wins:	9 (9.2.1990 - 19.3.1990)	of home wins:	18 (22.8.1964 - 28.3.1965)
of league defeats:	8 (29.10.1938 - 17.12.1938)	of away wins:	4 (17.2.1990 - 17.3.1990)

TRANMERE ROVERS

PLAYERS NAME Honours	Ht	Wt	Birthdate	Birthplace Transfers	Contract Date	Clubs	League	L/Cup	FA Cup	Other	Lge	L/C	FAC	Oth
G O A L K E E P E R														
Coyne Daniel	5.11	12.7	8/27/73	Prestatyn	5/8/92	Tranmere Rovers	93+1	13	1	2				
W: full, u21.2, S, Y														
Simonsen Steven	6.3	13.2	4/3/79	South Shields	10/9/96	Tranmere Rovers (T)	30		3					
E: u21.														
D E F E N C E														
Challinor David	6.1	12	10/2/75	Chester	7/18/94	Tranmere Rovers	32+5	2	3		1			
Frail Stephen	5.11	12.3	8/10/69	Glasgow		Hearts								
				£90000	1/30/98	Tranmere Rovers	4+2							
Hill Clinton S	6	11.6	10/19/78	Liverpool	7/9/97	Tranmere Rovers	13+1		2+1				1	
Holmes Thomas M	6	12.8	9/1/79	Bebington		Tranmere Rovers								
McGreal John	5.11	10.11	8/2/72	Liverpool	7/30/90	Tranmere Rovers	157+2	15+1	7	5+1	1			
Santos Georges						Toulon								
				Free	7/1/98	Tranmere Rovers								
Thompson Andy	5.4	10.6	11/9/67	Cannock	11/16/85	WBA	18+6	0+1	2	1+1	1			
Div4'88. Div3'89. SVT'88				£35000	11/21/86	Wolverhampton W.	356+20	22	20	33	43		1	1
				Free	7/5/97	Tranmere Rovers	44	5	3		3			
M I D F I E L D														
Gibson Neil D	5.11	10.8	10/11/79	St Asaph		Tranmere Rovers (T)								
Hebel Dirk J	5.11	12.1	11/24/72	Cologne		Bursapor (Turkey)								
					12/12/97	Tranmere Rovers								
Irons Kenneth	5.9	11	11/4/70	Liverpool	11/9/89	Tranmere Rovers	270+37	19+7	13+2	28+3	39	4	3	3
Mahon Alan	5.11	11.5		Dublin	4/19/95	Tranmere Rovers	17+28	0+5	0+1		3			
Ei: u21.3, S.														
Mauro	6.1	12.12	6/16/76	Portugal		Casapia								
					6/1/98	Tranmere Rovers								
McIntyre Kevin	5.11	12	12/23/77	Liverpool	11/6/96	Tranmere Rovers	0+2							
Mellon Michael	5.8	11.3	3/18/72	Paisley	12/6/89	Bristol City	26+9	3	1+1	5+3	1			
				£75000	2/11/93	WBA	38+7	3+2	0+1	6	6			1
				£50000	11/23/94	Blackpool	123+1	9	4	5	14	1		1
				£300000	10/31/97	Tranmere Rovers	24+9		2+1		2			
Morgan Alan	5.11	11	11/2/73	Aberystwyth	5/8/92	Tranmere Rovers	15+10	0+2	2		1			
O'Brien Liam	6.1	11.1	9/5/64	Dublin		Shamrock Rovers								
Ei: 11, Y. Ei Lge'84'85'86. Ei Cup'85'86. Div1'93				£60000	10/14/86	Manchester United	16+15	1+2	+2		2			
				£250000	11/15/88	Newcastle United	131+20	9	12+2	9+2	19	1	1	1
				£300000	1/21/94	Tranmere Rovers	151+7	15+1	7+1	5+1	10	1	1	
Williams Ryan N	5.4	9.1	8/31/78	Mansfield	1/1/00	Mansfield Town	4+12	2	0+1					
				Free	8/8/97	Tranmere Rovers								
F O R W A R D														
Jones Gary S	6.3	14	5/11/75	Chester	7/5/93	Tranmere Rovers	75+46	9+2	4+2	1+1	20	3	2	
Jones Phillip L	5.9	10.5	5/29/73	Wrexham	7/5/91	Wrexham	24+15	2	1+2	4+1	9		1	2
W: u21.8 (6 gls, record scorer for Wales u21)				£300000	3/12/92	Liverpool	0+2	0+1						
				Loan	9/3/93	Crewe Alexandra	4+4				1			
				Loan	3/27/97	Tranmere Rovers	8				5			
					6/3/97	Tranmere Rovers	29+5	5			9	1		

Player				Fee	Date	Club	1	2	3	4	5	6	7	8
Kelly David	5.11	11.3	11/25/65	Birmingham		Alvechurch								
Ei: 17, B.2, u23.1, u21.3 Div1 '93					12/21/83	Walsall	115+32	11+1	12+2	14+3	63	4	3	10
				£600000	8/1/88	West Ham United	29+12	11+3	6	2+1	7	5		2
				£300000	3/22/90	Leicester City	83+3	6	1	2	22	2		1
				£250000	12/4/91	Newcastle United	70	4	5	4	35	2	1	1
				£750000	6/23/93	Wolverhampton W.	73+5	5	11	4	26	2	6	2
				£900000	9/19/95	Sunderland	32+2	2+1	3		2			
					8/5/97	Tranmere Rovers	28+1	4	3		11	3		
Koumas Jason	5.11	11	9/25/79	Wrexham	2/20/98	Tranmere Rovers								
Moran Andrew J	5.11	11.3	10/7/79	Wigan		Tranmere Rovers								
Morrissey John	5.8	11.9	3/8/65	Liverpool	3/10/83	Everton	1		0+1					
E: Y.2				Free	8/2/85	Wolverhampton W.	5+5	1			1			
				£8000	10/2/85	Tranmere Rovers	390+54	38+2	28+2	39+3	50	2	5	6
Parkinson Andrew J	5.8	10.12	5/27/79	Liverpool		Liverpool								
					5/31/97	Tranmere Rovers	8+10		2+1		1		1	
ADDITIONAL CONTRACT PLAYERS														
Powell Gareth F					2/13/98	Tranmere Rovers (T)								

THE MANAGER
JOHN ALDRIDGE

Date of Birth . . . . 18th September 1958.
Place of Birth . . . . Liverpool.
Date of Appointment . . . . March 1996.

PREVIOUS CLUBS
As Manager . . . . None.
As Coach . . . . None.
As a Player . . . . Newport Co., Oxford Utd, Liverpool, Real Sociedad.

HONOURS
As a Manager
None.

As a Player
Newport County: Welsh FA Cup 1980.
Oxford United: League Div.2 1985. League Cup 1986.
Liverpool: League Div.1 1988. CS 1988. FA Cup 1989.
Eire: 69 full caps.

PRENTON PARK
Prenton Road West, Birkenhead, Merseyside L42 9PN

Capacity...16,789 (all seater)

First game...v Lancaster, 8-0, 9.3.1912.
First floodlit game ....v Rochdale, 2-1, 29.9.1958.

ATTENDANCES
Highest...24,424 v Stoke City, FAC 4th Rnd, 5.2.1972.
Lowest...937 v Halifax, AMC, 20.2.1984.

OTHER GROUNDS ..Steeles Field 1884-87. Ravenshaws Field (later renamed Prenton Park) 1887-1912.

HOW TO GET TO THE GROUND

From the North
Use Mersey Tunnel and motorway M53 until junction 3. Leave motorway and at roundabout take 1st exit (A552). In 1.3 miles at Half-way House crossroads turn right (B5151) then turn left into Prenton Road West for Tranmere Rovers FC.

From the South
Use motorway M53 until junction 4, leave motorway and at roundabout take 4th exit B5151. In 2.5 miles turn right into Prenton Road West for Tranmere Rovers FC.
Away supporters should use the Kop end of the ground. Entrance from main car park.

Car Parking: No car parking available at ground on match days, except for visiting coaches. Car park tickets cost £50 for season.

Nearest Railway Station: Hamilton Square, Rock Ferry (1 mile). Liverpool Lime Street (Main Line).

USEFUL TELEPHONE NUMBERS

Club switchboard 0151 608 4194
Club fax number.......................0151 608 4385
Club shop 0151 608 0438
Ticket Office............................0151 609 0137

Marketing Department ....0151 608 0371 (fax 608 4724)
Internet address www.merseyworld.com/rovers
Clubcall 0891 12 16 46*
*Calls cost 50p per minute at all times. Call costings correct at time of going to press.

MATCHDAY PROGRAMME

Programme Editor..................Peter Bishop.

Number of pages.....................................40.

Price ....£1.60.

Subscriptions ....Details available from Club.

Local Newspapers
...Liverpool Daily Post & Echo, Wirral News,
....Wirral Globe.

Local Radio Stations
...............................BBC Radio Merseyside,
.............City Gold and City FM (Radio City),
................................MFM (Marcher Sound).

MATCHDAY TICKET PRICES

This season all matches will be graded either A, B or C.
Category A matches will cost £14.00
Category B...£12.00
Category C...£10.00

Concessions will be given if concessions are offered at the away grounds and will be:
Under-16s £5.00
Senior Citizens..£7.00

WATFORD
(The Hornets)
NATIONWIDE LEAGUE DIVISION 1
SPONSORED BY: CTX COMPUTER PRODUCTS

1998/99- Back Row L-R: Chris Cummins (Yth. Academy Asst.), Kirk Wheeler (Football in the Com.), Colin Pluck, Steve Palmer, Keith Millen, Grant Cornock, Jason Lee, Darren Ward, Dean Yates, James Panayi, Tommy Mooney, Daniel Grieves, Rob Smith (Football in the Com.), Jimmy Gilligan (Yth. Academy Asst.).**Middle Row:** Gary Johnson (Yth. Academy Director), Tom Walley (Coach), Richard Johnson, Micah Hyde, Ronny Rosenthal, Robert Page, Allan Smart, Alec Chamberlain, Chris Day, Gifton Noel-Williams, Alon Hazan, Johann Gudmundsson, Michael Ngonge, David Perpetuini, Paul Rastrick (Physio), Ken Barry (Kit manager). **Front Row:** Shay Connolly (Yth Academy Physio), Nigel Gibbs, Stuart Slater, Mark Boyce, Nathan Lowndes, Darren Bazeley, Oliver Squires, Kenny Jackett (First team coach), Graham Taylor (General manager), Luther Blissett (Coach), Paul Robinson, Clint Easton, Nick Wright, Wayne Andrews, Tommy Smith, Peter Kennedy, Luke Anthony (Yth Academy Physio).

WATFORD
FORMED IN 1891
TURNED PROFESSIONAL IN 1897
LTD COMPANY IN 1909

JOINT LIFE PRESIDENTS
Elton John CBE & Geoff Smith
CHAIRMAN: Elton John CBE
DIRECTORS
Brian Anderson, Charles Lisack,
David Meller, Haig Oundjian
SECRETARY
John Alexander
HEAD OF SALES & MARKETING
Mark Devlin

GENERAL MANAGER: Graham Taylor
FIRST TEAM COACH: Kenny Jackett
COACH: Luther Blissett, Tom Walley
YOUTH ACADEMY DIRECTOR
Gary Johnson
PHYSIOTHERAPIST
Paul Rastrick
STATISTICIAN FOR THE DIRECTORY
Audrey Adams

Winning the Second Division Championship halted ten years of slow but inexorable decline at Watford. It also represented a personal triumph for Graham Taylor, back in charge of team affairs twenty years after he first came to the club. After the heartaches at Lancaster Gate and Molineaux, Taylor might have been forgiven for staying in the background, but he had the courage to put himself back in the firing line and the outcome was his fourth promotion success with Watford. It was good to have the old Taylor bounce and smile restored; the man himself suddenly looked ten years younger!

The team was very much in the Taylor mould: fit, highly disciplined and hard-working, though the lack of a prolific goalscorer was a drawback. The departure of Kevin Phillips, Kevin Miller and david Connolly during the summer robbed the club of three of its best players. Taylor bought six replacements, leaving himself change from one million pounds. Of these, winger Peter Kennedy proved an unqualified success, finishing leading scorer and winning a place in the PFA divisional team. Micah Hyde was also influential, helping his midfield partner Richard Johnson to his best-ever season, while Ronnie Rosenthal, with his Premiership pedigree and know-how, proved an inspired free transfer signing.

However, it was Alec Chamberlain, the much-travelled goalkeeper, who was justly voted the 'Player of the Season' and joined Kennedy in the PFA team after a string of impressive performances and an ever-present record in League matches. Utility player Steve Palmer managed to start a League match wearing every shirt from 1 to 14 during the course of the season, a unique achievement, while Nigel Gibbs, enjoying his first promotion after 14 years at Vicarage Road, celebrated with a rare goal at Oldham, his first away goal for ten years!

With 50 points in the bag by Christmas, Watford went off the boil in February and March but had built up a big enough lead to clinch promotion on Easter Monday, appropriately enough at Ashton Gate. The Championship followed on the last day of the season at Fulham. Despite these successes, the undoubted highlight of the whole campaign was the 4-0 success at Luton, Watford's first win against the traditional enemy for 11 years which was celebrated long and hard. FA Cup hopes ended in a penalty shoot-out at Hillsborough. Off the pitch, Elton John received a standing ovation when he attended Vicarage Road the day after singing at Princess Diana's funeral; the subsequent award of a knighthood in the New Years' honours list was widely welcomed. The Watford chairman also reached the West End through the medium of the hit play "Elton John's Glasses", the bitter-sweet story of a sad Watford obsessive.

It was significant that with things going well on the pitch, the biggest controversy of the season concerned the decision to drop the "Z Cars" theme that had heralded the teams coming on to the pitch since 1963. Watford are not over-endowed with traditions, and it seemed a pity.

The season ended with an open bus parade shared with the Saracens, Watford's rugby-playing tenants who won the Tetley's Cup for the first time. With ground-sharing here to stay, the pitch is being relaid during the summer, and a youth academy has been set up with a further eye to the future. Going all the back up to the Premiership may be an unrealistic ambition: but with Taylor and John reunited at Vicarage Road, anything is possible.

AUDREY ADAMS

WATFORD

Division 2	:1st			FA CUP: 3rd Round				LC CUP: 2nd Round	AWS: Southern Round 1	

M	DATE	COMP.	VEN	OPPONENTS	RESULT	H/T	LP	GOAL SCORERS/GOAL TIMES	ATT.
1	A 09	FL	H	Burnley	W 1-0	1-0	7	Lee 30	11155
2	12	CC 1/1	A	Swindon Town	W 2-0	1-0		Noel-Williams 12, Rosenthal 63	(6271)
3	15	FL	A	Carlisle United	W 2-0	0-0	2	Kennedy 59, Johnson 78	(7395)
4	23	FL	H	Brentford	W 3-1	2-0	1	Millen 3, Melvang 10, Johnson 89	10125
5	26	CC 1/2	H	Swindon Town	D 1-1	1-0		Hyde 15	7712
6	30	FL	A	Preston North End	L 0-2	0-1	2		(11042)
7	S 02	FL	A	Plymouth Argyle	W 1-0	0-0	1	Noel-Williams 71	(5141)
8	07	FL	H	Wycombe Wanderers	W 2-1	1-0	1	Hyde 5, Lee 61	12100
9	13	FL	H	Chesterfield	W 2-1	1-0	1	Rosenthal 44, Lee 61	11204
10	16	CC 2/1	H	Sheffield United	D 1-1	0-1		Kennedy 88	7154
11	20	FL	A	Gillingham	D 2-2	0-1	1	Rosenthal 49 (pen), Johnson 72	(7780)
12	23	CC 2/2	A	Sheffield United	L 0-4	0-1			(7511)
13	27	FL	H	York City	D 1-1	0-1	1	Lee 71	13812
14	O 04	FL	A	Luton Town	W 4-0	4-0	1	Johnson 5, Thomas 18, Kennedy 26, 28	(9041)
15	14	FL	A	Bristol Rovers	W 2-1	0-0	1	Kennedy 62, Rosenthal 80 (pen)	(8110)
16	18	FL	H	Millwall	L 0-1	0-1	1		12530
17	21	FL	H	Fulham	W 2-0	1-0	1	Rosenthal 41, Robinson 87	11486
18	25	FL	A	Grimsby Town	W 1-0	1-0	1	Rosenthal 1	(5699)
19	N 01	FL	H	Blackpool	W 4-1	1-0	1	Lee 35, 52, Johnson 63, Rosenthal 69	9723
20	04	FL	A	Southend United	W 3-0	2-0	1	Kennedy 14, 37, 67	(4001)
21	08	FL	A	Walsall	D 0-0	0-0	1		(5077)
22	15	FAC 1	A	Barnet	W 2-1	0-1		Rosenthal 61, 67	(4040)
23	18	FL	H	Oldham Athletic	W 2-1	1-0	1	Thomas 4, Mooney 82	
24	22	FL	A	Northampton Town	W 1-0	0-0	1	Kennedy 57	(7372)
25	29	FL	H	Wigan Athletic	W 2-1	2-1	1	Thomas 11, Mooney 45	9455
26	D 02	FL	A	Wrexham	D 1-1	0-0	1	Rosenthal 72	(3702)
27	06	FAC 2	A	Torquay United	D 1-1	1-1		Noel-Williams 20	(3416)
28	09	AWS S1	A	Fulham	L 0-1	0-0			(3364)
29	13	FL	H	Bristol City	D 1-1	0-0	1	Noel-Williams 84	16072
30	16	FAC 2R	H	Torquay United	W 2-1	0-0		Noel-Williams 91, 108	5848
31	20	FL	A	Bournemouth	W 1-0	0-0	1	Kennedy 57	(6081)
32	26	FL	A	Wycombe Wanderers	D 0-0	0-0	1		(8090)
33	28	FL	H	Plymouth Argyle	D 1-1	0-0	1	Mooney 89	11594
34	J 03	FAC 3	H	Sheffield Wednesday	D 1-1	0-0		Kennedy 64	18306
35	10	FL	A	Burnley	L 0-2	0-2	2		(9551)
36	14	FAC 3R	A	Sheffield Wednesday	D 0-0*	0-0		(Sheffield Wed. won 5-3 on penalties)	(18707)
37	17	FL	H	Preston North End	W 3-1	2-0	2	Kennedy 16, 60, Hyde 27	10182
38	24	FL	A	Brentford	W 2-1	1-1	1	Mooney 7, Johnson 71	(6969)
39	31	FL	A	Chesterfield	W 1-0	0-0	1	Noel-Williams 87	(5975)
40	F 08	FL	H	Gillingham	L 0-2	0-1	1		10498
41	14	FL	H	Luton Town	D 1-1	0-0	1	Robinson 51	15182
42	21	FL	A	York City	D 1-1	0-1	1	Palmer 90	(4890)
43	25	FL	A	Millwall	D 1-1	0-1	1	Mooney 49	(7126)
44	28	FL	H	Bristol Rovers	W 3-2	2-0	1	Noel-Williams 17, Rosenthal 23, Mooney 87	12186
45	M 03	FL	H	Walsall	L 1-2	0-1	1	Noel-Williams 56	8096
46	07	FL	A	Blackpool	D 1-1	0-0	1	Bazeley 53	(5237)
47	14	FL	H	Southend United	D 1-1	1-0	2	Hyde 44	10750
48	17	FL	H	Carlisle United	W 2-1	1-0	1	Palmer 4, Bazeley 58	7274
49	21	FL	A	Oldham Athletic	D 2-2	1-0	1	Bazeley 7, Gibbs 61	(5744)
50	28	FL	H	Northampton Town	D 1-1	0-0	1	Johnson 56	14268
51	A 04	FL	A	Wigan Athletic	L 2-3	0-3	2	Foley 54, Hyde 80	(4262)
52	11	FL	H	Wrexham	W 1-0	1-0	2	Lee 9	12340
53	13	FL	A	Bristol City	D 1-1	0-0	2	Lee 64	(19141)
54	25	FL	H	Grimsby Town	D 0-0	0-0	2		14002
55	28	FL	H	Bournemouth	W 2-1	0-1	2	Lee 47, Noel-Williams 68	12834
56	M 02	FL	A	Fulham	W 2-1	1-0	1	Noel-Williams 33, Lee 71	(17114)

Best Home League Attendance: 16072 V Bristol City		Smallest :7274 V Carlisle United	Average :11168

Goal Scorers:

FL	(67)	Kennedy 11, Lee 10, Rosenthal 8, Johnson 7, Noel-Williams 7, Mooney 6, Hyde 4, Bazeley 3, Thomas 3, Palmer 2, Robinson 2, Foley 1, Gibbs 1, Melvang 1, Millen 1, Opponents 1
CC	(4)	Hyde 1, Kennedy 1, Noel-Williams 1, Rosenthal 1
FAC	(6)	Noel-Williams 3, Rosenthal 2, Kennedy 1
AWS	(0)	

*AET

(F) Andrews	(F) Bazeley	(G) Chamberlain	(G) Day	(M) Easton	(M) Foley	(D) Gibbs	(F) Hazan	(D) Hyde	(F) Johnson	(F) Kennedy	(F) Lee	(F) Lowndes	(D) Melvang	(D) Millen	(D) Mooney	(F) Noel-Williams	(D) Page	(M) Palmer	(D) Pluck	(D) Robinson	(D) Rooney	(F) Rosenthal	(F) Slater	(M) Smith	(M) Talboys	(F) Thomas	(D) Ward	Referee	
		X		X			X	X	X	X				X	X	X	X	S					X			S	S	P.S. Danson	1
	X	S		X			X	X	X	X				X	X	X	X	S				S1	X					M Fletcher	2
	X			X			X	X	X	X				X	X	X	X	S1				S2	X		S3			D Pugh	3
S2	X						X	X	X				X	X	X	X	X	S1				X	X		S	X		S G Bennett	4
S2	X	S					X	X	X				X	X	X	X	X	S1				X	X					B Knight	5
S3	X			X			X	X	X					X	X	X	X					X	X		S2	S1		J A Kirkby	6
	X		S				X	X	X	X		X		X	X	X	X					X	S	S				A P D'Urso	7
	X	S2		S1			X	X	X	X		X		X	X	X	X					X						P Rejer	8
S	X	S		X			X	X	X	X				X	X	X	X					X	S					S W Mathieson	9
S1	X	S	S		X		X	X	X	X				X	X	X	X					X						M E Pierce	10
	X	S	S2				X	X	X	X		X		X	X	X	X	X				X	S1					R Styles	11
	S	X	S1	X			X	X	X	X				X	S	X	X					X	X					G Singh	12
	X			X			X	X	X	X				X	X	X	X	S1				X	S2			S		A G Wiley	13
	X	S		X			X	X	X					X	X	S1	X	X		S		X	X			X		T Heilbron	14
S	X			S			X	X	X					X	X	X	X	X				X	X			X		M L Dean	15
	X			X			X	X	X	X				X	X	S1	X	S2				X	X			S3		A N Butler	16
	X	X	S				X	X		X				X	X	X	X	S				X	X	S				K M Lynch	17
	X	X	S				X	X		X				X	X	X	X	S1		X		X	X	S				M D Messias	18
	X	X	S1				X	X		X				X	X	X	X	S3				X				S2		G Singh	19
	X	S		X			X	X	X					X	X	X	X	X				X				S1		R D Furnandiz	20
	X	S		X			X	X	X					X	X	X	X	X				S				S1		P R Richards	21
	X	S	S		X		X	X	X	X				X	X	X	X	S				X	S			S1		G S Willard	22
	X	S		X			X	X	X					X	X	X	X	X				S2	X		S1			A R Hall	23
	X	S		X			X	X	X					X	X	X	X	X				S	X		S	S	X	J P Robinson	24
	X	S		X			X	X	X					X	X	X	X	X				S	X			X		A Bates	25
	X	S		S1			X	X	X					X	X	X	X1	X				S2	X			X2		D Laws	26
	X	S	S		X		X	X	X		S1		X	X	X1	X	S2	X		S		X				X2		G R Ashby	27
		X	X						X	X								X	X	X	X					X1	S1		28
	X	S	S		X		X	X	X	X				X	X	X	X	S		X1		S						B Knight	29
	X	S	S		X		X	X	X	X	S		X	X	X	X1	X	S2					S1					G R Ashby	30
	X	S		X			X	X	X	X	S		X	X	X	X	X	X										E Lomas	31
	X	S					X	X	X	X	S		X	X	X	X	X	S										J E Pearce	32
	X	S		X			X	X	X	X	S1		X	X	X	X	X	S		X1								S G Bennett	33
	X	S	X		X		X	X	X	X	X1		X	X		X	S		S	S					S1			G S Willard	34
	X	X1		X			X	X	X	X	X2		X	X	S1		X	S2								S		R Pearson	35
	X	S	S		X		X	X	X	X	S		X	X	X1	X	X			X					S1	S		G S Willard	36
	X			X	X1		X	X	X	X			X	X		X	S1								S	S		S J Baines	37
	X			X	X2		X	X	X	X			X	X		X	X1	S1							S2	S		M Fletcher	38
	X			X			X	X	X		S		X	X	S1	X	X								X1	S		T Jones	39
	X			X			X	X	X	X2			X	X	X1	X	S1								S2	S		R D Furnandiz	40
	X			X			X	X		X	S		X	X	S1	X	X					X1				S		J A Kirkby	41
	X	S2		X			X	X3	X		S3		X	X		X	S1	X2		X	X1							G Cain	42
	X	S	S1	X			X	X		X1			X	X		X	S1	X2		X	X1							K M Lynch	43
S1	X	X1	X2	X			X						X	X	X	X	X				X	S2			S			K A Leach	44
S2	X	X1	X2	X									X	X	X3	X	X				X	S1			S3			J P Robinson	45
X	X	X		X	S		X		X				X	X	X	X	S				X1	S						M S Pike	46
X3	X	X1		X		X	X2	S3	S1	X	X	X	X				S2											D R Crick	47
X1	X	X	S1	X			X		X	X	X	S	X				X	S										F G Stretton	48
X	X	X1	S1	X	S1		X		X	X	X	S	X				X1											M D Messias	49
	X		S2	X1	S1	X	X2	X		X	X		X		X		S	X										C R Wilkes	50
X	X	S		S1	X	X	X3		X2	X	S3		X		X1		X											P Rejer	51
X	X	S1		X	X3	X	X1	X2		X	X	S2		X		S3												R Styles	52
X	X	S		X	X1		X	X2		X	X	S1	X	X		S												A G Wiley	53
X	X	S1		X	X	X1		X2		X	X	S2		X		S												A N Butler	54
S	X	X					X	X	X	X		X2		X	X	S2		S1										A R Hall	55
S	X	X			S1	X	X	X	X			X	X	X2		X1	S2											W C Burns	56
	14	46		8	2	34	7	40	42	34	35	1	4	38	45	27	41	32	1	14		24	9			8		FL Appearances	
2	2		4	6	4	3				1	3						11	9		8		1	5	1	2	8		FL Sub Appearances	
0+2		3	1	0+1		3		4	4	4	3		1	2	4	3	4	2+1		3+1	3					8		CC Appearances	
	5		1		5		5	5	5	4	1+1		4	5	4	4	3+1	1+1		2		0+1		1+3				FAC Appearances	
	1	1							1	1				1	1	1	1	1				1				0+1		AWS Appearances	

Also Played: Grieves X(28). Ljung X(28).

WATFORD

BIGGEST VICTORIES
League: 8-0 v Sunderland, Division 1, 25.9.1982
F.A. Cup: 10-1 v Lowestoft, Round 1, 27.11.1927
League Cup: 8-0 v Darlington, Round 2, 6.10.1987
Europe: 3-0 v Kaiserslauten, Round 1, 28.9.1983

BIGGEST DEFEATS
League: 1-8 v Crystal Palace, Division 4, 23.9.1959
1-8 v Aberdare, Division 3S, 2.1.1926
0-7 v Port Vale, Division 3S, 15.9.1947
F.A. Cup: 0-10 v Wolverhampton W., Round 1, 13.12.1912
League Cup: 0-5 v Coventry City, Round 1, 9.12.1980
1-6 v Blackburn Rovers, Round 4, 9.12.1992
Europe: 0-4 v Sparta Prague, UEFA 3, 1983-84

MOST POINTS
3 points a win: 88, Division 2, 1997-98
2 points a win: 71, Division 4, 1977-78

MOST GOALS
92, 1959-60 (Division 4).
Holton 42, Uphill 29, Hartle 6, Benning 5, Gregory 3, Bunce 3,
Walter 2, Chung1, og 1.

MOST LEAGUE GOALS CONCEDED
89, Division 3S, 1925-26

MOST FIRST CLASS MATCHES IN A SEASON
60 (46 League, 6 FA Cup, 2 League Cup, 4 Simod Cup, 2 Play-Offs)
1988-89

MOST LEAGUE WINS
30, Division 4, 1977-78

MOST LEAGUE DRAWS
19, Division 2, 1996/97.

MOST LEAGUE DEFEATS
28, Division 2, 1971-72

MOST GOALS IN A SEASON
Cliff Holton, 48 (42 League, 6 FA Cup), 1959-60
MOST GOALS IN A MATCH
5, Eddie Mummery v Newport County (8-2), Div 3(S), 5.1.1924
MOST APPEARANCES
Luther Blissett: 443+52 (1975-92 - 3 spells). 369+46 League,
32+2 FA Cup, 41+3 League Cup, 1+1 FMC.
OLDEST PLAYER
Jim McLaren 41 years, 172 days v. Crystal Palace 31.12.1938.
YOUNGEST PLAYER
Keith Mercer 16 years 125 days v. Tranmere Rovers 16.02.1973.
MOST CAPPED PLAYER
John Barnes (England) 31 & Kenny Jackett (Wales) 31

League: 2nd in Division 1, 1982-83.
F.A. Cup: Runners-up 1983-84. Lost 0-2 v Everton.
League Cup: Semi-finals 1978-79, v Nottingham Forest 0-0, 1-3.
Europe (UEFA): 3rd Round 1983-84. Lost 2-3, 0-4 v Sparta Prague.

ADDITIONAL INFORMATION
Previous Names
Watford Rovers until 1891 or amalgamation of West Herts & Watford
St. Marys in1898

Previous Leagues
Southern League

Club colours: Yellow shirts with red sleeves, black collar and cuffs.
Red shorts, red socks with yellow top s and two black hoops.

Change colours: Blue and silver striped shirts with red pinstripes.
Blue shorts. Blue socks with red tops and two red hoops.

Reserves League: Avon Insurance Football Combination.

DIVISIONAL RECORD							
	Played	Won	Drawn	Lost	For	Against	Points
Division 1	250	93	58	99	386	372	337
Division 2/1	620	199	176	245	736	807	722
Division 3/2	690	281	197	210	998	845	801
Division 3(S)	1,334	488	333	513	1,972	2,029	1,309
Division 4	230	110	51	69	387	296	271
Total	**3,124**	**1,171**	**817**	**1,136**	**4,479**	**4,349**	**3,440**

RECORDS AND STATISTICS

COMPETITIONS

Div.1	Div.2/1	Div.3/2	Div.3(S)	Div.4	UEFA
1982-88	1969-72	1920-21	1921-58	1958-60	1983-84
	1979-82	1960-69		1975-78	
	1988-96	1972-75			
	1998-	1978-79			
		1996-98			

HONOURS

Division 3/2	Division 4	Division 3(S) Cup
1968-69	1977-78	1936-37
1997-98		(shared)

MOST APPEARANCES

Luther Blissett - 440+52 (1975-92 - 3 spells)

Year	League	FA Cup	Lge Cup	Others
1975-76	1+2	-	-	-
1976-77	1+3	-	-	-
1977-78	17+16	-	-	-
1978-79	40+1	1	6+1	-
1979-80	40+2	4	2	-
1980-81	42	3	8	-
1981-82	40	3	6	-
1982-83	41	4	3	-
1984-85	38+3	5	5	-
1985-86	20+3	-	3	-
1986-87	35	5	1	1
1987-88	17+8	4+2	1+2	-
1988-89	3	-	1	-
1991-92	34+8	1	4	0+1
Total	**369+46**	**30+2**	**40+3**	**1+1**

MOST GOALS IN A CAREER

Luther Blissett - 180 (1975-92 - 3 spells)

Year	League	FA Cup	Lge Cup	Others
1975-76	1	-	-	-
1976-77	-	-	-	-
1977-78	6	-	-	-
1978-79	21	-	7	-
1979-80	10	1	-	-
1980-81	11	-	2	-
1981-82	19	-	3	-
1982-83	27	2	1	-
1984-85	21	6	1	-
1985-86	7	-	1	-
1986-87	11	4	-	-
1987-88	4	-	-	-
1988-89	1	-	-	-
1991-92	9	2	1	-
Total	**148**	**15**	**17**	**-**

Current leading goalscorer: Thomas Mooney - 31 (03/94-98)

RECORD TRANSFER FEE RECEIVED

Amount	Club	Player	Date
£2,300,000	Chelsea	Paul Furlong	05/94
£1,250,000	Crystal Palace	Bruce Dyer	03/94
£1,000,000	Liverpool	David James	06/92
£1,000,000	Aston Villa	Gary Penrice	03/91
£1,000,000	Manchester City	Tony Coton	07/90

RECORD TRANSFER FEE PAID

Amount	Club	Player	Date
£550,000	AC Milan	Luther Blissett	08/84
£500,000	Bristol Rovers	Gary Penrice	11/89
£425,000	Millwall	Jamie Moralee	07/94
£300,000	Charlton Ath.	Joe McLaughlin	08/90

MANAGERS

Name (since 1946)	Seasons	Best	Worst
John Goodhall	1903-10		
Harry Kent	1910-26	6 (3S)	20 3(S)
Fred Pagnam	1926-29	8 (3S)	21 (3S)
Neil McBain	1929-37	4 (3S)	16 (3S)
Bill Findlay	1937-47		
Jack Bray	1947-48	15 (3S)	15 (3S)
Eddie Hapgood	1948-50	6 (3S)	17 (3S)
Ron Gray	1950-51	23 (3S)	23 (3S)
Hayden Green	1951-52	21 (3S)	21 (3S)
Len Goulden	1952-55	4 (3S)	10 (3S)
John Paton	1955-56	21 (3S)	21 (3S)
Len Goulden	1956		
Neil McBain	1956-59	11 (3S)	15 (4)
Ron Burgess	1959-63	4 (3)	4 (4)
Bill McGarry	1963-64	3 (3)	3 (3)
Ken Furphy	1964-71	18 (2)	12 (3)
George Kirby	1971-73	22 (2)	19 (3)
Mike Keen	1973-77	7 (3)	8 (4)
Graham Taylor	1977-87	2 (1)	1 (4)
Dave Bassett	1987-88		
Steve Harrison	1988-90	20 (1)	4 (2)
Colin Lee	1990	15 (2)	15 (2)
Steve Perryman	1990-93	10 (2)	20 (2)
Glenn Roeder	1993-96	7 (1/2)	7 (1/2)
Kenny Jackett	1996-97		
Graham Taylor	1997-	1 (2)	1(2)

LONGEST LEAGUE RUNS

of undefeated matches: 23 (1.10.96 - 4.3.97)	of league matches w/out a win: 19 (27.11.1971 - 8.4.1972)
of undefeated home matches: 27 (15.10.1963 - 19.12.1964)	of undefeated away matches: 12 (17.3.1977 - 16.9.1978)
without home win: 9 (14.12.1971-15.4.1972, 25.8.1990-1.12.1990)	without an away win: 32 (17.4.1971 25.11.1972)
of league wins: 7 (17.11.34-29.12.34, 26.12.77-28.1.78)	of home wins: 8 (29.8.31-21.11.31, 3.11.34-2.2.35, 6.9.77-12.11.77)
of league defeats: 9 (26.12.1972 - 27.2.1973)	of away wins: 5 (25.4.1981 - 22.9.1981)

WATFORD

PLAYERS NAME Honours	Ht	Wt	Birthdate	Birthplace Transfers	Contract Date	Clubs	APPEARANCES League	L/Cup	FA Cup	Other	GOALS Lge	L/C	FAC	Oth
G O A L K E E P E R														
Chamberlain Alec	6.2	11.11	6/20/64	March		Ramsey Town								
DIV2 97/98					7/27/81	Ipswich Town								
				Free	8/3/82	Colchester United	188	11	10	12				
				£80000	7/28/87	Everton								
				Loan	11/1/87	Tranmere Rovers	15							
				£150000	7/27/88	Luton Town	138	7	7	7				
				Free	7/8/93	Sunderland	60+1	5	6	1				
				Loan	3/23/95	Liverpool								
Day Chris	6.2	12.4	7/28/75	Waltham Cross	4/16/93	Tottenham Hotspur								
E: Y. UEFA Y'93					8/6/96	Crystal Palace	24	2	2					
					7/16/97	Watford		1						
D E F E N C E														
Gibbs Nigel	5.7	11.11	11/20/65	St.Albans	11/23/83	Watford	361+12	22	39+1	13	5	2		
DIV2 97/98														
Hyde Micah A	5.9	10.5	11/10/74	Newham	5/19/93	Cambridge United	149+30	3	9+2	6+1	25			
DIV2 97/98					7/18/97	Watford	40	4	5		4	1		
Millen Keith	6.1	12	9/26/66	Croydon	8/7/84	Brentford	301+4	26	18	30+1	17	2	1	
Div3'92. DIV2 97/98					3/22/94	Watford	153+1		14		9		4	
Page Robert	6	11.8	9/3/74	Llwynypia	4/19/93	Watford	100+5	8	9+1					
DIV2 97/98														
Pluck Colin I	6	12.1	9/6/78	London	5/31/97	Watford	1							
Robinson Paul P	5.9	12.11	12/14/78	Watford	2/13/97	Watford	22+11		3+2		2			
DIV2 97/98														
Ward Darren P	6.3	12.1	9/13/78	Kenton		Watford								
Yates Dean	6.1	11	10/26/67	Leicester	6/14/85	Notts County	291+2	20	20	32	33			4
E: u21.5				£350000	1/26/95	Derby County	65+3	3	3		3			
				Free	7/13/98	Watford								
M I D F I E L D														
Easton Clint J	5.11	10.4	10/1/77	Barking	10/14/96	Watford	25+4	0+1	3		1			
Grieves Daniel L	5.9	10.7	9/21/78	Watford	5/31/97	Watford								
Gudmundsson J-hann	5.9	13	12/7/77	Reykjavik		Keflavik								
					3/26/98	Watford								
Johnson Richard M	5.11	11.4	4/27/74	Newcastle (Aus)	5/11/92	Watford	143+20	12+1	11+1	0+1	13	1		
DIV2 97/98														
Palmer Steve	6.1	12.13	3/31/68	Brighton		Cambridge University								
Div2'92. DIV2 97/98				Free	8/1/89	Ipswich Town	82+24	3	8+3	3+2	2		1	
				£135000	9/28/95	Watford	107+10	8+1	7+1		4			
Perpetuini David P	5.8	10	9/26/79	Hitchin	7/3/97	Watford (T)								
Smith Thomas W	5.8	10	5/22/80	H.Hempstead	10/21/97	Watford (T)	0+1		0+1					
Squires Oliver H	5.11	12.3	9/15/80	Harrow		Watford (T)								
F O R W A R D														
Andrews Wayne M	5.9	11.4	1/25/77	Paddington										
Bazeley Darren	5.11	10.9	10/5/72	Northampton	5/6/91	Watford	153+49	12+4	11+1	3+1	19	2	3	
DIV2 97/98														
Hazan Alon	6	13.8	9/14/67	Ashdod		I Hashdod (Israel)								
				£200000	1/13/98	Watford	7+3							
Kennedy Peter H J	5.11	11.11	9/10/73	Lurgan	8/27/96	Notts County	20+2	1	2				1	
DIV2 97/98				7/17/97	Watford	34	4	5		11	1	1		
Lee Jason	6.3	13.8	5/9/71	Forest Gate	6/2/89	Charlton Athletic	0+1			0+2				
DIV2 97/98				Loan	2/6/91	Stockport County	2							
				£35000	3/1/91	Lincoln City	86+7	6	2+1	4	21		1	
					8/6/93	Southend United	18+6	1	1	5+3	3			3
				£200000	3/4/94	Nottingham Forest	41+35	4+2	0+5	4+2	14	1		
				Loan	2/5/97	Charlton Athletic	7+1				3			
				Loan	3/27/97	Grimsby Town	2+5				2			
					6/7/97	Watford	35+1	3	4		10			
Lowndes Nathan P	5.11	10.04	6/2/77	Salford	8/1/94	Leeds United								
				£40000	10/3/95	Watford	1+6	0+1	1+2					
Mooney Thomas	5.11	12.6	8/11/71	Middlesbrough	11/23/88	Aston Villa								
Flg u18.1 DIV2 97/98				Free	8/1/90	Scarborough	96+11	11+2	3	6	29	8		2
				£100000	7/12/93	Southend United	9+5	1+1		2+3	5			
				Loan	3/17/94	Watford	10				2			
					7/21/94	Watford	143+8	15	10+1		27	1	1	

Name			DOB	From	Date	Club								
gonge Michel						Samsunspor (Turkey)								
				Free	7/1/98	Watford								
oel-Williams Gifton R	6.1	14.6	1/21/80	Islington	10/18/96	Watford	34+23	3	6		9	1	4	
IV2 97/98														
osenthal Ronny	5.11	12	10/11/63	Haifa (Israel)		Maccabi Haifa								
srael. CS'90. DIV2 97/98						FC Bruge								
						Standard Liege								
				Loan	3/22/90	Liverpool	5+3							
				£1000000	6/29/90	Liverpool	27+39	2+7	5+3	2+4	21	1		
				£250000	1/26/94	Tottenham Hotspur	55+32	3	7+2		8	1	2	
				Free	8/12/97	Watford	24+1	3+1	2		8	1	2	
later Stuart I	5.7	10.5	3/27/69	Sudbury	4/2/87	West Ham United	134+7	16+1	16	5	11	2	3	2
: B2, u21.3				£1500000	8/14/92	Celtic	40+4	3+2	3	4	3			
				£750000	9/30/93	Ipswich Town	33+11	4	1	2+2	3			
					11/28/96	Watford	22+8	3	3		1			
mart Allan	6.2	12.7	7/8/74	Perth		Caledonian								
				£15000	11/22/94	Preston North End	17+4		2	1+1	6		1	
				Loan	11/21/95	Carlisle United	3+1							
				Loan	9/13/96	Northampton Town								
					10/8/96	Carlisle United	16	1			5			
				£75000	7/1/98	Watford								
homas David J	5.11	11.7	9/26/75	Caerphilly	7/25/94	Swansea City	36+20	2	0+1	3+3	10			2
				Free	7/23/97	Watford	8+8		1+3		3			
Wright Nicholas J	5.11	11.02	10/15/75	Derby	7/12/94	Derby County								
				Loan	11/28/97	Carlisle United	13				3			
				£35000	2/27/98	Carlisle United	12				3			
				£100000	7/198	Watford								

THE MANAGER
GRAHAM TAYLOR

Date of Birth . . . . 15th September 1944.

Place of Birth. . . . . Worksop.

Date of Appointment . . . . 2nd May 1997.

PREVIOUS CLUBS

As Manager. . . . . .Lincoln, Watford, Aston Villa, England, Wolves.

As a Player . . . . Grimsby, Lincoln.

HONOURS

As a Manager

Lincoln City: Division 4 Championship 1976.
Watford: Division 2 Championship 1998.

As a Player
None.

VICARAGE ROAD STADIUM
Watford WD1 8ER

Capacity 22,000

First game..v Millwall, Div 3(S), 0-0, 30.8.1922.
First floodlit game..v Luton Town, Friendly, October 1953.

ATTENDANCES
Highest ....34,099 v Manchester Utd, FAC, 3.2.1969.
Lowest ....1,700 v Southend, ZDS Cup, 2.10.1991.

OTHER GROUNDS ....Cassio Road 1899-1922. Vicarage Road 1922-

HOW TO GET TO THE GROUND

From the North: Exit M1 at junction 5 and take second exit off roundabout, A41, signposted Harrow. Continue short distance to next roundabout and take third exit to Hartspring Lane. Follow this road through a set of traffic lights and continue straight ahead (now Aldenham Road to another roundabout. Go straight over (second exit) still following Aldenham Road, to next traffic lights. When through the lights, move into right-hand lane (marked Watford) and follow one-way system around to Bushey Station, then moving into left-hand lane. Turn left under Bushey Arches, into Eastbury Road. At traffic lights, turn right into Deacons Hill and continue to next traffic lights, turning left into Cardiff Road for visitors' entrance to stadium/coach park.
From the South: Exit M1 at junction 5 and take first exit off roundabout, A41 signposted Harrow (then as North).
From the East: Exit M25 at junction 21A and join the M1 at junction 6. Exit at junction 5 (then as North).
From the West: Exit M25 at junction 19 and take third exit off roundabout, A411 (Hempstead Road), signposted Watford. Continue for approximately two miles and at roundabout go straight across (right-hand lane) to next roundabout, then take third exit into Rickmansworth Road. Take second turning on the left into Cassio Road. Continue through traffic lights, to Merton Road and straight on to Wiggenhall Road. At traffic lights, turn right into Cardiff Road (as North).
Car Parking: No public parking available at ground. There are several multi-story parks in the town centre.
Nearest Railway Station: Watford Junction or Watford High Street (01923 245 001) or Watford Halt. For Bus details phone 0345 788788 - 'Network Watford'.

USEFUL TELEPHONE NUMBERS

Club switchboard 01923 496 000
Club fax number 01923 496 001
Club shop 01923 496 005
Ticket Office 01923 496 010

Marketing Department. 01923 496 291
Internet address........ www.watfordfc.com
Hornets' Hotline 0891 10 4 10 4*
*Calls cost 50p per minute at all times. Call costings correct at time of going to press.

MATCHDAY PROGRAMME

Programme Editors ...... Andrew French.

Number of pages .... 40.

Price .... £2.00.

Subscriptions .... Apply to club.

Local Newspapers.................
...... Watford Observer, Watford Review
.... St Albans Herald and Post
.... Watford Free Observer
.... London Evening Standard.

Local Radio Stations
..... Chiltern Radio, G.L.R., Capital Radio
.... BBC Three Counties Radio.

MATCHDAY TICKET PRICES

Rous Stand - Upper tier

Adults...	£16
Category 'A' matches	£20

Vicarage Road End, Rookery End, East and Lower Rous Stands

Adults...	£14
Child aged 15 & under	£10
Senior Citizen	£10
Students (Members only)	£10

Family Areas - East and Lower Rous Stands

1st Parent...	£14
2nd Parent	£10
Senior Citizen	£10
Child aged 13-15	£8
12 & Under	£5

Wheelchair Areas - subject to space

Chairbound..	£6
Helper..	£12

WEST BROMWICH ALBION
(The Throstles, 'Baggies' or 'Albion')
NATIONWIDE LEAGUE DIVISION 1
SPONSORED BY: WEST BROMWICH BUILDING SOCIETY

Unfortunately West Bromwich Albion were unable to supply us with a team photograph for this year's publication

WEST BROMWICH ALBION PLC
FORMED IN 1878-79
TURNED PROFESSIONAL IN 1885
LTD COMPANY IN 1891 **PLC** in 1996

PRESIDENT: Sir F A Millichip
VICE-PRESIDENT: J Silk
CHAIRMAN: A B Hale
DIRECTORS
J D Wile (Chief Executive),
J W Brandrick, B Hurst,
B McGing (Financial),
C M Stapleton (Vice-chairman),
P Thompson
SECRETARY
Dr. John Evans (0121 525 8888)
COMMERCIAL EXECUTIVE
Tom Cardall

MANAGER: Denis Smith
FIEST TEAM COACH: Malcolm Crosby
COACHES: Cyrille Regis & Richard O'Kelly
PHYSIOTHERAPIST
Paul Mitchell

HAWTHORNS CURATOR &
STATISTICIAN FOR THE DIRECTORY
Tony Matthews

For Albion, the 1997-98 season was one of two completely different halves! From August to December, under manager Ray Harford, the Baggies held a top six placing.

But following Harford's sudden 'transfer' to Q.P.R. and the arrival of Denis Smith from Oxford United, Albion's fortunes dipped and they slipped slowly out of the promotion race, eventually finishing 10th, ending the campaign well with good wins over Sheffield United and Middlesbrough and creditable draws against both Sunderland & Nottingham Forest.

Albion topped the League in early September and were hardly ever out of the top four until late December, but once into the New Year their form became spasmodic. Confidence seemed to drain away and although they kept in touch with the leaders until mid-February, there was no way they were going to make the play-offs.

It must be said that Albion scrambled a series of home wins to keep up with the leaders before Christmas, and their away form, at times, was very poor. Indeed, Albion suffered some bad defeats, including a 5-0 walloping at Charlton. But they did 'double up' over arch rivals Wolves and did well against several of the better placed clubs.

It was a pity that they performed so poorly against those in the lower regions. Relegated Manchester City completed the double over the Baggies; Stoke claimed two draws and Reading won at Elm Park.

Injuries to key players didn't help, and Albion's two bosses fielded 35 different defensive formations during the season.

On the bright side, though, £200,000 signing Lee Hughes from Kidderminster finished his first season in top-class football with 14 goals, sharing top spot with Andy Hunt. Record signing Kevin Kilbane played in 50 first-class matches , while Richard Sneekes had 49 outings, goalkeeper Alan Miller 47 and striker Andy Hunt 44.

Milestones during 1997-98 included 300 club appearances for Daryl Burgess, 200 League games for Andy Hunt and 250 first team outings for Paul Raven and Bob Taylor. Richard Sneekes topped the 100 League appearance mark on the last day of the season v. Nottingham Forest which also produced Albion's biggest home gate of the campaign (23,013).

Attendances were good and the average League gate at The Hawthorns was 16,639 - up by more than 1,500 on 1996-97.

Tony Matthews.

WEST BROMWICH ALBION

Division 1		:10th		FA CUP: 4th Round		LC CUP: 3rd Round		

M	DATE	COMP.	VEN	OPPONENTS	RESULT	H/T	LP	GOAL SCORERS/GOAL TIMES	ATT.
1	A 09	FL	H	Tranmere Rovers	W 2-1	2-0	2	Kilbane 37, Hunt 38	16727
2	12	CC 1/1	A	**Cambridge United**	D 1-1	1-0		**Peschisolido 5**	(3520)
3	15	FL	A	Crewe Alexandra	W 3-2	1-1	2	Hunt 25 (pen), Hughes 85, 90	(5234)
4	24	FL	A	Wolverhampton Wand	W 1-0	1-0	2	, Curle 16 (OG)	21511
5	27	CC 1/2	H	**Cambridge United**	W 2-1	0-1		**Hunt 85, Sneekes 102 (pen)**	10264
6	30	FL	A	Ipswich Town	D 1-1	0-1	2	Sneekes 58	(13508)
7	S 03	FL	A	Stoke City	D 0-0	0-0	4		(17500)
8	07	FL	H	Reading	W 1-0	0-0	1	Hunt 79	15966
9	13	FL	A	Queens Park Rangers	L 0-2	0-1	4		(14399)
10	16	CC 2/1	A	**Luton Town**	D 1-1	1-1		**Taylor 35**	(3437)
11	20	FL	H	Swindon Town	D 0-0	0-0	3		16237
12	23	CC 2/2	H	**Luton Town**	W 4-2	1-1		**Raven 40, McDermott 52, Peschisolido 67, 88**	7227
13	27	FL	A	Bury	W 3-1	2-0	2	Peschisolido 10, 45, 60	(6439)
14	O 04	FL	H	Oxford United	L 1-2	1-1	4	Hunt 7	15819
15	15	CC 3	H	**Liverpool**	L 0-2	0-0			21986
16	18	FL	A	Portsmouth	W 3-2	1-0	3	Mardon 7, Hunt 49, 51	(9158)
17	21	FL	A	Nottingham Forest	L 0-1	0-0	4		(19243)
18	25	FL	H	Sheffield United	W 2-0	1-0	3	Hunt 7, Hughes 87	17311
19	N 01	FL	A	Bradford City	D 0-0	0-0	5		(16212)
20	04	FL	H	Norwich City	W 1-0	0-0	4	Hughes 85	13949
21	08	FL	H	Charlton Athletic	W 1-0	1-0	3	Hunt 35	16124
22	15	FL	A	Port Vale	W 2-1	0-0	3	Hunt 57, Hamilton 68	(11124)
23	23	FL	H	Birmingham City	W 1-0	0-0	2	Sneekes 82	18444
24	29	FL	A	Middlesbrough	L 0-1	0-1	3		(30164)
25	D 02	FL	H	Manchester City	L 0-1	0-0	4		17904
26	06	FL	H	Stockport County	W 3-2	1-0	3	Sneekes 17, Hughes 78, Hunt 85	13597
27	13	FL	A	Sunderland	L 0-1	0-1	4		(29231)
28	20	FL	H	Huddersfield Town	L 0-2	0-0	5		14619
29	26	FL	A	Reading	L 1-2	0-2	6	Kilbane 77	(10154)
30	28	FL	H	Stoke City	D 1-1	0-0	7	Hunt 62	17690
31	J 09	FL	A	Tranmere Rovers	D 0-0	0-0	7		(8058)
32	13	FAC 3	H	**Stoke City**	W 3-1	2-0		**Sneekes 28, 32, Kilbane 78**	17598
33	17	FL	H	Crewe Alexandra	L 0-1	0-1	7		15257
34	24	FAC 4	A	**Aston Villa**	L 0-4	0-1			(39372)
35	27	FL	H	Ipswich Town	L 2-3	0-0	9	Murphy 69, Flynn 72	12403
36	31	FL	A	Wolverhampton Wand	L 1-0	0-0	8	Hunt 72	(28244)
37	F 06	FL	A	Swindon Town	W 2-0	1-0	7	Carbon 40, Evans 81	(9861)
38	14	FL	H	Queens Park Rangers	D 1-1	0-1	6	Hughes 75	19143
39	17	FL	A	Oxford United	L 1-2	0-1	6	Taylor 63	(9412)
40	21	FL	H	Bury	D 1-1	1-0	8	Hughes 44	15840
41	24	FL	H	Portsmouth	L 0-3	0-2	10		12757
42	28	FL	A	Manchester City	L 0-1	0-1	10		(28460)
43	M 03	FL	A	Charlton Athletic	L 0-5	0-1	10		(10893)
44	07	FL	H	Bradford City	D 1-1	0-1	10	Burgess 90	13281
45	14	FL	A	Norwich City	D 1-1	0-1	10	Hughes 51	(19069)
46	21	FL	H	Port Vale	D 2-2	1-0	10	Flynn 24, Taylor 83	14242
47	28	FL	A	Birmingham City	L 0-1	0-0	11		(23260)
48	A 04	FL	H	Middlesbrough	W 2-1	1-0	10	Quinn 22 (pen), 47	20620
49	11	FL	A	Stockport County	L 1-2	1-1	11	Hughes 20	(7943)
50	13	FL	H	Sunderland	D 3-3	2-2	10	Hughes 1, 89, Kilbane 11	20181
51	18	FL	A	Huddersfield Town	L 0-1	0-1	11		(11704)
52	25	FL	A	Sheffield United	W 4-2	1-1	10	Hunt 30, Hughes 65, 78, Kilbane 72	(21248)
53	M 03	FL	H	Nottingham Forest	D 1-1	0-1	10	Hughes 89 (pen)	23013

Best Home League Attendance: 23013 V Nottingham Forest		**Smallest :12403 V Ipswich Town**		**Average :16636**

Goal Scorers:

FL	(50)	Hughes 14, Hunt 13, Kilbane 4, Peschisolido 3, Sneekes 3, Flynn 2, Quinn 2, Taylor 2, Burgess 1, Carbon 1, Evans 1, Hamilton 1, Mardon 1, Murphy 1, Opponents 1
CC	(8)	Peschisolido 3, Hunt 1, McDermott 1, Raven 1, Sneekes 1, Taylor 1
FAC	(3)	Sneekes 2, Kilbane 1

1997-98

	(D) Beesley	(D) Burgess	(M) Butler	(D) Carbon	(F) Carr	(M) Coldicott	(D) Dobson	(F) Evans	(M) Flynn	(D) Hamilton	(D) Holmes	(F) Hughes	(F) Hunt	(D) Kilbane	(D) Mardon	(M) McDermott	(G) Miller	(D) Murphy	(D) Nicholson	(D) Nicol	(F) Peschisolido	(D) Potter	(M) Quailey	(F) Quinn	(M) Raven	(M) Smith	(M) Sneekes	(F) Taylor	(D) Van Blerk	Player	
			X			S3			X	S1		S2	X	X	X	X	X	X	X		X					X				P. Taylor	1
			X				S		X	S1			X	X	X	X	X	X	X		X					X				G B Frankland	2
			X						X	S2	X	S1	X	X	X		X	X	X		X					X	S3			A R Leake	3
			X					S	X	S2	X	S1	X	X		X	X		X		X				X	X				T Heilbron	4
			X			S3			X	S2	X	S1	X	X	X		X		X		X					X	X			A N Butler	5
			X			S3			X	S2	X		X	X	X		X		X							X	S1	X	X	M R Halsey	6
	X	X					S		X	S2	X		X		X		X		X							X	X	X	X	E Lomas	7
	X	X					S		X	S2	X		X		X		X		X							X	X	X		P S Danson	8
	X	X				S3			X	S1	X		X		X	S2	X		X							X	X	X		M E Pierce	9
	X					X		S		X	X		X	X		X	X	S	X							X	X	X	X	E K Wolstenholme	10
	X					S2	S		X	X			X	X		X	X	X			S1					X	X	X	X	F G Stretton	11
	X						S		X	X			X	X		X	X	X			S1					X	X	X	X	P R Richards	12
	X					S	S		X	X			X	X		X	X	X			X					X	X	X		B Coddington	13
	X					S1	S		X	X			X	X		S2	X	X			X					X	X	X		T Jones	14
	X	S3					S1		X	X	X	X	S2		X		X		X							X	X	X	X	A B Wilkie	15
	X	S1					S		X	X	X	X	S2	X	X		X		X							X	X			S J Baines	16
	X	X		X		S1			X	X		X	S2	X	X		X		S3							X	X			D Pugh	17
	X	X				S2	S		X	X		X	S1	X	X		X									X	X			D Orr	18
	X	X				S2	S3		X	X		X	S1	X	X		X									X	X			W C Burns	19
		X				S2	X		X	X		X	S1	X	X		X									X	X			D Laws	20
	X	X				S2			X	X		X	X	X	X		X									X	X			S J Baines	21
	X	X				X	S1		X	X	X	S	X	X		X										X	X	S		R D Furnandiz	22
	X	X				S	S		X	X		X	X	X	X		X									X	X			S G Bennett	23
	X	X				X	S	S2		X	X2	S1	X	X		X										X	X1			K M Lynch	24
	X	X				X	S	S1		X	X2	S2	X	X		X										X	X1			J A Kirkby	25
	X	X					X	X2	S1	X	S2	X	X3		X		X									S3	X1			M C Bailey	26
	X	X					X		X1		S1	X	X	X		X		X								S	X2	S2		B Coddington	27
	X	X				X3	S3		X		S1	X	X2	X	X		X									S2	X	X1		C R Wilkes	28
	X	X2					X		X		S1	X	X	X	X3	X	X									X	X			A P D'Urso	29
	X	X				S1	S	S2		X1		X	X		X		X									X	X			P S Danson	30
	S	X					X	S2	S1	X	X	X2	X1		X		X	X								X				D Laws	31
	S	S1					X	X1	S	X	X	X	X		X		X	X	X					S		X				P Jones	32
	S	X2					X	S2	X1		S1	X	X		X		X	X								X				R J Harris	33
	S	X2				S3	X	S2	S1	X3	X	X1	X		X		X	X								X				N S Barry	34
		S1	X				S	S	X1	X	X	X	X		X		X	X								X1				M D Messias	35
	X	X				S1	S	S2		X	X	X2	X		X		X	X								X1				S W Mathieson	36
	X	X		X1		S	S	S1		X	X	X	X1		X		X	X								X		S1		M R Halsey	37
		X		X1		S	S			X	X	X	X	X		X	X									X		S1		C J Foy	38
	S	X2	X	S1		S2			X	X	X1		X		X		X	X								X		X		P Taylor	39
	S	X2	X			S2			X	X			X		X		X	X						S1		X1	X		M L Dean	40
	X	X		S2	S1				X	X2	X1		X	X		X	X				X		X					X	E K Wolstenholme	41
	X	X	X			X2			S3	X3			X		X		X				X	S1	X1					X	A N Butler	42
	X	X2	X	S3		X			S1	X			X3				X				X		X					X	R Styles	43
	X		X1	S		X2			X	X		X					X				X	S2						X	J P Robinson	44
X	X								X	X1	X		X			X			X				X2			X	S2	X	P S Danson	45
X		S1	X						X	X1			X	X3		X			X				X2			X	S2	X	T Heilbron	46
X	X		X			S2			X2				X1	X		X	X		X			S	S1	X		X		X	R Pearson	47
X			X			S1			X			X1	X2	X		X	X		X							X	S2	X	D Pugh	48
X			X			S		S		X		X	X1	X		S	X		X							X	S1	X	A Bates	49
X1			X			S			X			X	X2	X		S1	X		X							X	S2	X	E Lomas	50
X		X1				S			X			X	X2	X		X	X		S1	X2						X	S2	X	A P D'Urso	51
	X					S			X			X2	X	X3		X	X		X			S2	S3			X	S1	X	M E Pierce	52
X1			X			S			X1				X				S1	X		X			S1	X		X		X	D Orr	53
8	27	31	16	1	7	6	2	30	29	30	18	38	42	18	13	41	14	16	9	6	4		12	8	18	37	11	8	FL Appearances	
	3		3	15	5	8	5	8			19		1				3			2	1	5	1		4	5	4		FL Sub Appearances	
3	2+1		1	0+2	4	3+2	3	0+2	4	5	2	2	4	1	2		3+1			4	3	5	3						CC Appearances	
	1+1		0+1	2	1+1	0+1	2	2	2	2	2	2	2	2	2					2	2	2				2			FAC Appearances	

Also Played: (M) Adamson X(49,50,51). (G) Crichton S(32,34), X(52,53). (M) Gilbert S2(43,43), S1(44), S3(46). (G) Spink S(2,10,12), X(5). (M) Thomas S1(7,8) X(9).

WEST BROMWICH ALBION

CLUB RECORDS

BIGGEST VICTORIES
League: 12-0 v Darwen, Division 1, 4.4.1892 (League Record)
F.A. Cup: 10-1 v Chatham, Round 3, 2.3.1889.
League Cup: 6-1 v Coventry City, Round 4, 10.11.1965; v Aston Villa, Round 2,14.9.1966
Europe (UEFA): 4-0 v Dynamo Bucharest, Round 2, 27.11.1968

BIGGEST DEFEATS
League: 3-10 v Stoke City, Division 1, 4.2.1937.
F.A. Cup: 0-5 v Leeds United, Round 4, 18.2.1967
League Cup: 0-5 v Tottenham Hotspur, Round 4, 28.10.1970
1-6 v Nottingham Forest, Round 2, 6.10.1982
Europe: No more than 3 goals.

MOST POINTS
3 points a win: 85, Division 2, 1992-93
2 points a win: 60, Division 1, 1919-20

MOST GOALS
105, Division 2 1929-30
Cookson 33, Glidden 20, Carter 19, Wood 7, Cresswell 6, Evans 5, Shaw 4, Boston 3, Edwards 3, W.G. Richardson 2, Fitton 1, og 2.

MOST LEAGUE GOALS CONCEDED
98, Division 1, 1936-37

MOST FIRST CLASS MATCHES IN A SEASON
59 (42 League, 6 FA Cup, 3 League Cup, 8 UEFA Cup) 1978-79

MOST LEAGUE WINS: 28, Division 1, 1919-20

MOST LEAGUE DRAWS: 19, Division 1, 1979-80

MOST LEAGUE DEFEATS: 26, Division 1, 1985-86

INDIVIDUAL CLUB RECORDS

MOST GOALS IN A MATCH
6, Jimmy Cookson v Blackpool, Div 2, 17.9.1927

MOST GOALS IN A SEASON
'W.G.' Richardson 40 (League 39, FA Cup 1) 1935-36
4 goals twice=8, 3 goals twice=6, 2 goals 5 times=10, 1 goal 17 times=17

OLDEST PLAYER
George Baddeley, 39 years, 345 days v Sheffield Wed. 18.04.1914

YOUNGEST PLAYER
Charlie Wilson, 16 years, 73 days v Oldham (Div 1), 1.10.1921
(Frank Hodgetts was 16 yrs 26 days when he played for Albion v Notts County in a wartime game on 26.10.1940)

BEST PERFORMANCES

League: 1919-20: Matches played 42, Won 28, Drawn 4, Lost 10, Goals for 104,Goals against 47, Points 60. (Champions)

F.A. Cup: 1887-88: 1st rnd. Wednesbury O.A. (a) 7-1; 2nd rnd. Mitchell St,George (a) 1-0; 3rd rnd. Wolves (h) 2-0; 4th rnd. bye; 5th rnd. Stoke City (h)4-1. 6th rnd. Old Carthusians (h) 4-2; Semi-Final, Derby Junction 3-0; Final Preston North End, 2-1
1891-92: 3rd rnd. Old Westminsters (a) 3-2; 4th rnd. Blackburn Rovers (h) 3-1;5th rnd. Sheffield Weds. (h) 2-1; Semi-Final Nottingham Forest 1-1, 1-1, 6-2;Final Aston Villa 3-0
1930-31: 3rd rnd. Charlton Athletic (h) 2-2, (a) 1-1, (n) 3-1; 4th rnd.Tottenham Hotspur (h) 1-0; 5th rnd. Portsmouth (a) 1-0; 6th rnd. Wolves (h) 1-1, (a) 2-1; Semi-Final Everton, 1-0; Final Birmingham 2-1
1953-54: 3rd rnd. Chelsea (h) 1-0; 4th rnd. Rotherham United (h) 4-0; 5th rnd.Newcastle United (h) 3-2; 6th rnd. Tottenham Hotspur (h) 3-0; Semi-Final Port Vale, 2-1; Final Preston North End, 3-2
1967-68: 3rd rnd. Colchester (a) 1-1, (h) 4-0; 4th rnd. Southampton (h) 1-1,(a) 3-2; 5th rnd. Portsmouth (a) 2-1; 6th rnd. Liverpool (h) 0-0, (a) 1-1, (n)2-1; Semi-Final Birmingham City, 2-0; Final Everton, 1-0

League Cup: 1965-66: 2nd rnd. Walsall (h) 3-1; 3rd rnd. Leeds United (a) 4-2;4th rnd. Coventry City (a) 1-1, (h) 6-1; 5th rnd. Aston Villa (h) 3-1; Semi-Final Peterborough United (h) 2-1, (a) 4-2; Final West Ham United (a) 1-2, (h)4-1

Europe (UEFA): 1978-79: 1st rnd. Galatasary, 3-1, 3-1; 2nd rnd. Sporting Braga,2-0, 1-0. 3rd rnd. Valencia, 1-1, 2-0; 4th rnd. Red Star, 0-1, 1-1.

ADDITIONAL INFORMATION
In 1956-57 Albion played 42 First Division games. They won 14, drew 14,and lost 14 for a total of 42 points and finished halfway in the table (11th)

Previous Name
West Bromwich Strollers 1878-80
Previous League:
None

Club colours: Navy blue/white striped shirts, white shorts, white socks.
Change colours: Red shirts, navy blue sleeves, navy blue shorts, red & blue ringed socks.

Reserves League
Pontins Central League Division 2.

DIVISIONAL RECORD

	Played	Won	Drawn	Lost	For	Against	Points
Division 1	2,652	988	637	1,027	4,134	4,224	2,673
Division 2/1	1,212	508	301	403	1,924	1,569	1,457
Division 3/2	92	44	24	24	152	103	156
Total	3,956	1,540	962	1,454	6,210	5,896	4,285

RECORDS AND STATISTICS

COMPETITIONS

Div.1	Div.2/1	Div.3.2	ECWC	FMC	Texaco	A/Scot
1888-01	1901-02	1991-93	1968-69	1986	1970-71	1975-76
1902-04	1904-11			1987	1972-73	1976-77
1911-27	1927-31		EUFA	1988	1974-75	A/Ital.
1931-38	1938-49		1966-67	SC	Watney C	1969-70
1949-73	1973-76		1978-79	1988-89	1971-72	1970-71
1976-86	1986-91		1979-80	ZC		1994-95
	1993-		1981-82	1989-91	AGT	1995-96
					1991-92	T/Cal
						1977-78
						1978-79

HONOURS

Div.1	Div.2	FAC	Lge Cup	C/Shield
1919-20	1901-02	1887-88	1965-66	1920
	1910-11	1891-92		1954
		1930-31		
		1953-54		
		1967-68		

MOST GOALS IN A CAREER

Tony Brown - 261 (1963-80)

Year	League	FA Cup	Lge Cup	Europe
1963-64	5			
1964-65	9			
1965-66	17		10	
1966-67	14	1	1	3
1967-68	11	4		
1968-69	17	2	1	3
1969-70	10	1	2	
1970-71	28	2		
1971-72	17	1		
1972-73	12	1	1	
1973-74	19	4		
1974-75	12	1		
1975-76	8	4		
1976-77	8			
1977-78	19	3	1	
1978-79	10	2	1	2
1979-80	2	1	1	
Total	**218**	**27**	**18**	**8**

Current leading goalscorer: Richard Sneekes - 24 (03.96-98)

MOST APPEARANCES

Tony Brown 704+16 (1963-80)

Year	League	FA Cup	Lge Cup	Europe	Other
1963-64	13				
1964-65	17				
1965-66	35	1	9		
1966-67	31	2	4	3	
1967-68	35	10	1		
1968-69	42	4	2	6	1
1969-70	40	1	8+1		4
1970-71	42	4	2		6
1971-72	40	1	1		3
1972-73	38+1	5	3		4
1973-74	41	4	2		
1974-75	32+2	3	2		3
1975-76	37+3	4	1		1
1976-77	36+1	2	3		3
1977-78	41	6	2		1
1978-79	29+2	6	1	5+1	2
1979-80	12+4	0+1	5	2	
	561+13	**53+1**	**46+1**	**16+1**	**28**

MANAGERS

Name	Seasons	Best	Worst
Thomas Foster	1885-87	5(1)	6(1)
Louis Ford	1887-90	5(1)	6(1)
W. Pierre Dix	1890-92	12(1)	12(1)
Henry Jackson	1892-94	8(1)	8(1)
E Stephenson	1894-95	13(1)	13(1)
Clement Keys	1895		
Frank Heaven	1896-02	7(1)	1(1)
Fred Everiss	1902-48	1(1)	11(2)
Jack Smith	1948-52	14(1)	3(2)
Jesse Carver	1952-53	4(1)	4(1)
Vic Buckingham	1953-59	2(1)	17(1)
Gordon Clark	1959-61	4(1)	10(1)
Archie Macauley	1961-63	9(1)	14(1)
Jimmy Hagan	1963-67	6(1)	14(1)
Alan Ashman	1967-71	8(1)	18(1)
Don Howe	1971-75	16(1)	16(2)
Johnny Giles	1975-77	7(1)	3(2)
Ronnie Allen	1977		
Ron Atkinson	1978-81	3(1)	10(1)
Ronnie Allen	1981-82	17(1)	17(1)
Ron Wylie	1982-84	11(1)	17(1)
Johnny Giles	1984-85	12(1)	12(1)
Nobby Stiles	1985		
Ron Saunders	1986-87	22(1)	22(1)
Ron Atkinson	1987-88	20(2)	20(2)
Brain Talbot	1988-91	9(2)	9(2)
Bobby Gould	1991-92	7(3)	7(3)
Ossie Ardiles	1992-93	4(3/2)	4(3/2)
Keith Burkinshaw	1993-94	21(1/2)	21(1/2)
Alan Buckley	1994-97	19(1)	19(1)
Ray Harford	1997		
Dennis Smith	1997-	10 (1)	10 (1)

RECORD TRANSFER FEE RECEIVED

Amount	Club	Player	Date
£1,500,000	Manchester Utd	Bryan Robson	10/81
£995,000	Real Madrid	Laurie Cunningham	6/79
£225,000	Manchester City	Asa Hartford	6/79
£75,000	Norwich City	Colin Suggett	2/73

RECORD TRANSFER FEE PAID

Amount	Club	Player	Date
£1,250,000	P.N.E.	Kevin Kilbane	06/97
£748,000	Manchester City	Peter Barnes	7/79
£516,000	Middlesbrough	David Mills	1/79
£138,000	Rangers	Willlie Johnson	12/72

LONGEST LEAGUE RUNS

of undefeated matches:	17 (23.11.1901 - 29.3.1902)	of league matches w/out a win:	14 (28.10.95 - 3.2.96)
of undefeated home matches:	19 (2.9.01-11.10.02, 7.9.08-6.9.09)	of undefeated away matches:	11 (23.4.57-14.12.57, 26.1.80-13.9.80)
without home win:	9 (2.5.21-26.11.21, 21.8.71-11.12.71)	without an away win:	27 (27.12.1969 - 12.4.1971)
of league wins:	11 (5.4.1930 - 8.9.1930)	of home wins:	11 (20.10.1906 - 1.4.1907)
of league defeats:	11 (28.10.95 - 26.11.95)	of away wins:	7 (22.4.1953 - 31.10.1953)

WEST BROMWICH ALBION

PLAYERS NAME Honours	Ht	Wt	Birthdate	Birthplace Transfers	Contract Date	Clubs	League	L/Cup	FA Cup	Other	Lge	L/C	FAC	Oth
G O A L K E E P E R														
Adamson Chris	5.11	11	11/4/78	Ashington	7/2/97	WBA (T)	3							
Miller Alan	6.3	14.6	3/29/70	Epping	5/5/88	Arsenal (T)	6+2							
E: u21.4, S. FAYC'88. ECWC'94. Div.1'95.				Loan	11/24/88	Plymouth Argyle	13		2					
				Loan	8/15/91	WBA	3							
				Loan	12/19/91	Birmingham City	15			1				
				£500000	8/12/94	Middlesbrough	57	3	2	2				
				Loan	1/28/97	Grimsby Town	3							
				£400000	2/28/97	WBA	53	4	2					
D E F E N C E														
Burgess Daryl	5.11	12.3	1/24/71	Birmingham	7/1/89	WBA	278+5	16+2	8	14	9	3		
Carbon Matthew P	6.2	12.4	6/8/75	Nottingham	4/13/93	Lincoln City	40+3	3	3	2+2	7	1		
u21.4. E:				£400000	3/8/96	Derby County	11+8	1	0+1					
				£800000	1/26/98	WBA	16				1			
Dobson Tony	6.1	12.1	2/5/69	Coventry	7/7/86	Coventry City	51+3	5+3		0+1	1			
E: u21.4				£300000	1/17/91	Blackburn Rovers	36+5	5	2	1				
				£150000	9/22/93	Portsmouth	48+5	6	1+1	4	2			1
				Loan	12/15/94	Oxford United	5							
				Loan	1/29/96	Peterborough Utd	4							
				Free	8/8/97	WBA	6+4	0+2	2					
Holmes Paul	5.11	11	2/18/68	Stocksbridge	2/24/86	Doncaster Rovers	42+5		3+1	1	1		1	
				£6000	8/12/88	Torquay United	127+11	9	9+2	13+3	4			
				£40000	6/5/92	Birmingham City	12		1					
				£100000	3/19/93	Everton	21	4	1	0+2				
				Loan	1/12/96	WBA								
				£80000	2/15/96	WBA	85+1	5	3	3	1			
Kilbane Kevin D	6	13	10/21/74	Preston		Cambridge United								
u21.2. Ei: 2,					8/1/93	Preston North End	39+8	4		1+1	3			
					6/12/97	WBA	42+1	5	2		4		1	
Mardon Paul	6	12	9/14/69	Bristol	1/29/88	Bristol City	29+13	3+3		1		1		
1. W:				Loan	9/13/90	Doncaster Rovers	3							
				£115000	8/16/91	Birmingham City	54+10	11+1	1	3				
				£40000	11/18/93	WBA	113+7	8	3	2	3			
Murphy Shaun P	6	12	11/5/70	Sydney (Aus)		Perth Italia (Aus)								
					9/4/92	Notts County	100+9	5+2	6	12+1	5			2
				£500000	12/27/96	WBA	30+4	1	2		3			
Potter Graham	5.11	11	5/20/75	Solihull	7/1/92	Birmingham City	23+2		1	6	2			
Y. E: u21.2				Loan	9/17/93	Wycombe W.	2+1	1		1				
				£75000	12/20/93	Stoke City	41+4	2+1	4	5	1			
					7/23/96	Southampton	2+6	1+1						
					2/14/97	WBA	6+5							
Van Blerk Jason C	6.1	13	3/16/68	Sydney		Go Ahead Eagles								
22. Australia:				£300000	9/8/94	Millwall	68+5	5	6+1		2			
				Free	8/9/97	Manchester City	10+9	0+1	0+1					
				£50000	3/13/98	WBA	8							
M I D F I E L D														
Bortolazzi Mario	5.10	11.3	1/10/65	Verona		Genoa								
				Free	8/11/98	WBA								
Butler Peter J	5.9	11.1	8/27/66	Halifax	8/21/84	Huddersfield Town	0+5							
				Loan	1/24/86	Cambridge United	14			1	1			
				Free	7/8/86	Bury	9+2	2	1			1		
				Free	12/10/86	Cambridge United	55	4	2	2	9			
				£75000	2/12/88	Southend United	135+7	12	2	11	9	1		2
				Loan	3/24/92	Huddersfield Town	7							
				£125000	8/12/92	West Ham United	70	4	3	1	3			
				£350000	10/4/94	Notts County	20	2	2	3				
				Loan	1/30/96	Grimsby Town	3							
				£175000	3/28/96	WBA	52+8	2+1	1+2					
Flynn Sean M	5.7	11.2	3/13/68	Birmingham		Halesowen Town				5+2				
				£20000	12/3/91	Coventry City	90+7	5	3		9	1		
				£225000	6/1/95	Derby County	39+20	3	3		3			
				Loan	3/27/97	Stoke City	5							
					8/8/97	WBA	30+5	4	0+1		2			

McDermott Andrew	5.9	11.3	3/24/77	Australia		IOS Australia								
					8/4/95	QPR	6				2			
					3/27/97	WBA	19	2				1		
Maresca Enzo	5.10	11.4	2/10/80	Salerno		Cagliari								
				Free	7/9/98	WBA								
Quailey Brian	6.1	13.11	3/21/78	Leicester	1/12/98	WBA	0+5							
Raven Paul	6	12.3	7/28/70	Salisbury	6/6/88	Doncaster Rovers	52	2	5	2	4			
ESFA U18.4				£100000	3/23/89	WBA	216+4	16	8	15	14	1	3	1
				Loan	11/27/91	Doncaster Rovers	7							
Sneekes Richard	5.11	12.2	10/30/68	Amsterdam		Ajax								
u21, Y. Dutch:						Fortuna Sittard								
				£200000	8/12/94	Bolton Wanderers	37+1	7+1	1		6	1	1	
				£400000	3/11/96	WBA	92+8	7	3		21	1	2	
F O R W A R D														
Angel Mark	5.8	11.01	8/23/75	Newcastle	12/31/93	Sunderland								
				Free	8/9/95	Oxford United	40+33	4+4	4+2	2+1	4			1
				Free	7/1/98	WBA								
Evans Michael	6	11.5	1/11/73	Plymouth	3/30/91	Plymouth Argyle	131+33	8+1	10+2	7	39		3	2
1. Ei:					3/4/97	Southampton	14+8	2+1			4	1		
				£750000	10/24/97	WBA	2+8		1+1		1			
Hughes Lee	5.10	11.6	5/22/76	Birmingham		Kidderminster								
E: SP. FA. XI.				£250000	5/19/97	WBA	18+19	0+2	2		14			
Quinn Stephen J	6.2	11.11	12/15/74	Coventry		Birmingham City	1+3							
u21.1. NI: 13,				£25000	7/5/93	Blackpool	164+28	11+5	3+3	7+2	44	6	4	2
				Loan	3/4/94	Stockport County	0+1							
				£500000	2/20/98	WBA	12+1				2			

THE MANAGER
DENNIS SMITH

Date of Birth . . . . 19th November 1947.
Place of Birth . . . . Stoke.
Date of Appointment . . . . December 1997.

PREVIOUS CLUBS
As Manager . . . . York City, Sunderland Bristol City, Oxford United.
As Coach/Assistant . . . . None.
As a Player . . . . Stoke City, York City.

HONOURS
As a Manager
York City: Division 4 champions 1984.
Sunderland: Promotion to Division 1, 1990.
Oxford United: Promotion to Division 1, 1996.

As a Player
Stoke City: League Cup 1972.

THE HAWTHORNS
Halfords Lane, West Bromwich B71 4LF

Capacity...25,296 (all seater)

First game..v Derby County, 1-1, 3.9.1900.
First floodlit game...v Chelsea, Div.1, 1-1, 18.9.1957)
Internationals ....England v N.Ireland 1922, v Belgium 1924, v Wales 1945.

ATTENDANCES
Highest...64,815 v Arsenal, FAC 6th Rnd, 6.3.1937.
Lowest ....405 v Derby County, Div 1, 29.11.1890.
OTHER GROUNDS ....Coopers Hill 1878. Dartmouth Park 1879-81.Bunns Field 1881-82.
.... Four Acres (Dartmouth CC) 1882-85.Stoney Lane 1885-1900. The Hawthorns 1900-

HOW TO GET TO THE GROUND

From all directions
Use motorway (M5) until junction 1.
Leave motorway and follow local signs on matchdays to ground. Signs for Hawthorne Station Park & Ride are useful!.

Car Parking
Car parks of Halfords Lane and Middlemore Road, street parking in some areas within 10 minutes walk of ground.

Nearest Railway Station
Rolfe St. Smethwick (One and a quarter miles).
Hawthorns Halt (400 yards).

USEFUL TELEPHONE NUMBERS

Club switchboard 0121 525 8888
Club fax number.......................0121 525 8888
Ticket Office.............................0121 553 5472
Marketing Department 0121 525 8888

Clubcall 0898 12 11 93*
*Calls cost 50p per minute at all times.
Call costings correct at time of going to press.

MATCHDAY PROGRAMME

Programme Editor ....Andy Exley/Club.

Number of pages.....................................40.

Price ....£1.80.

Subscriptions ....Apply to club.

Local Newspapers
...............................Sandwell Evening Mail,
.... Birmingham Post & Evening Mail,
.... Express & Star,
.......................Sports Argus, Sporting Star,
.... Sunday Mercury.

Local Radio Stations
....BRMB Radio, Radio WM, Beacon Radio,
......................Mercia Sound, W.A.B. Radio.

MATCHDAY TICKET PRICES (97/98)

Halford Lane Centre	£17
Concessions	£10
Halford Lane Wings	£16
Concessions	£9.50
WBBS Centre	£14
Concessions	£8
WBBS Wings	£14
Concessions	£8
BRE/SME/Paddock	£12
Concessions	£6.50

WOLVERHAMPTON WANDERERS
(Wolves)
NATIONWIDE LEAGUE DIVISION 1
SPONSORED BY: GOODYEAR

Unfortunately Wolverhampton Wanderers were unable to supply us with a team photograph for this year's publication

WOLVERHAMPTON WANDERERS
FORMED IN 1877
TURNED PROFESSIONAL IN 1888
LTD COMPANY IN 1892

PRESIDENT: Sir Jack Hayward
CHAIRMAN: Sir Jack Hayward
DIRECTORS
Jack Harris, John Harris,Rachel Heyhoe Flint,
Rick Hayward
SECRETARY
Richard Skirrow
COMMERCIAL DIRECTOR
David Clayton

MANAGER: Mark McGhee
ASSISTANT MANAGER: Colin Lee
COACH: Mike Hickmen

PHYSIOTHERAPISTS
Barry Holmes
STATISTICIAN FOR THE DIRECTORY
Vacant

Wolverhampton Wanderers have been in the same Division now for nine years and last season they never really looked promotion material despite pushing for a top six place all the way through the campaign. Inconsistency was their downfall and their home form at times left a lot to be desired. Indeed, Wolves had 24 points taken off them at Molineux, winning only 13 of their 23 matches - fewer than any of the top six clubs. Goalscoring too was a problem at times, especially with ace marksman Steve Bull an absentee for long periods. In their First Division programme Wolves mustered 57 goals - with just 15 coming on their travels when they registered five wins and five draws.

Occasionally they put in some solid performances under manager Mark McGhee but so often they produced a poor display and in the end finished well off the pace, down in ninth position, nine points off a play-off spot.

The gates at Molineux were superb once more - averaging over 24,000 (CHECK) - but for the first time in five years there was a turnout of under 20,000 (v. Reading) and this could be the sign of the things to come if results are not forthcoming this season.

Goalkeeper Mike Stowell was the only ever-present in the Wolves side. He had a fine season, along with young superstar Robbie Keane, who graduated to the full international arena with the Republic of Ireland after some superb performances as a goalscoring midfielder. New recruits Kevin Muscat and Dougie Freedman (both signed from Crystal Palace), Steve Froggatt and Simon Osborn plus youngster Chris Westwood all did well

On reflection, manager McGhee - who had his critics - had several injury problems to contend with which obviously caused him a lot of concern when selecting his side. Defenders Keith Curle, Dean Richards, Steve Sedgley and Adrian Williams each spent time in the treatment room, as did 'Bully,' fellow striker Don Goodman and Tony Daley, who has been forced to retire.

Wolves are - say their fans - a Premiership club, but they still have to get there. No club has a divine right to be where they are. They have to earn that status whatever Division they play in. Promotion has to be won and relegation avoided before the prizes are handed out - and Wolves are finding it hard going these days, even to make the play-offs.

Tony Matthews.

WOLVERHAMPTON WAND

Division 1	:9th			FA CUP: Semi Final			LC CUP: 3rd Round	

M	DATE	COMP.	VEN	OPPONENTS	RESULT	H/T	LP	GOAL SCORERS/GOAL TIMES	ATT.
1	A 09	FL	A	Norwich City	W 2-0	1-0	7	Keane 34, 64	(17230)
2	12	CC 1/1	A	Queens Park Rangers	W 2-0	1-0		Froggatt 13, Paatelainen 85	(8355)
3	15	FL	H	Sheffield United	D 0-0	0-0	7		23102
4	24	FL	A	West Bromwich Albion	L 0-1	0-1	11		(21511)
5	27	CC 1/2	H	Queens Park Rangers	L 1-2	0-1		Ferguson 62	18398
6	30	FL	A	Bury	W 4-2	2-1	9	Keane 5, 86, Bull 42, 51	21141
7	S 03	FL	H	Port Vale	D 1-1	0-0	7	Bull 74	21524
8	07	FL	A	Oxford United	L 0-3	0-2	9		(6921)
9	13	FL	H	Charlton Athletic	W 3-1	3-0	6	Bull 9, 33, Froggatt 27	22683
10	16	CC 2/1	A	Fulham	W 1-0	1-0		San Juan 33	(5933)
11	20	FL	A	Sunderland	D 1-1	1-1	9	, Melville 34 (OG)	(32983)
12	24	CC 2/2	H	Fulham	W 1-0	0-0		Goodman 90	17862
13	27	FL	H	Huddersfield Town	D 1-1	1-1	11	Bull 1	21723
14	O 04	FL	A	Bradford City	L 0-2	0-2	14		(15236)
15	12	FL	A	Birmingham City	L 0-1	0-1	15		(17822)
16	14	CC 3	A	Reading	L 2-4	1-2		Bull 44, 58	(11080)
17	18	FL	H	Swindon Town	W 3-1	1-1	12	Freedman 12, Curle 78, Simpson 80	21794
18	22	FL	H	Tranmere Rovers	W 2-1	2-0	9	Robinson 15, Freedman 17	20841
19	25	FL	A	Stockport County	L 0-1	0-1	12		(9804)
20	N 01	FL	H	Middlesbrough	W 1-0	0-0	10	Keane 82	26896
21	04	FL	A	Crewe Alexandra	W 2-0	1-0	6	Freedman 14, Muscat 63	(5743)
22	08	FL	A	Stoke City	L 0-3	0-2	8		(18490)
23	15	FL	H	Ipswich Town	D 1-1	1-1	9	Keane 27	21937
24	29	FL	H	Queens Park Rangers	W 3-2	1-0	9	Osborn 44, Goodman 66, 76	23645
25	D 06	FL	A	Manchester City	W 1-0	1-0	9	, Symons 42 (OG)	(28999)
26	09	FL	A	Portsmouth	L 2-3	0-1	9	Westwood 76, Froggatt 87	(8042)
27	14	FL	H	Nottingham Forest	W 2-1	1-0	9	Freedman 20, Robinson 66	24635
28	20	FL	A	Reading	D 0-0	0-0	9		(11715)
29	26	FL	H	Oxford United	W 1-0	1-0	8	Goodman 18	26238
30	28	FL	A	Port Vale	W 2-0	1-0	6	Muscat 45, Freedman 87	(10898)
31	J 10	FL	H	Norwich City	W 5-0	4-0	6	Keane 22, Goodman 24, Freedman 43, 44, 77	23073
32	14	FAC 3	A	Darlington	W 4-0	1-0		Freedman 18, Paatelainen 66, 90, Ferguson 90	(5018)
33	17	FL	A	Sheffield United	L 0-1	0-1	6		(22144)
34	24	FAC 4	A	Charlton Athletic	D 1-1	1-0		Richards 48	(15540)
35	27	FL	A	Bury	W 3-1	1-1	6	Keane 21, Simpson 54, 61	(6134)
36	31	FL	H	West Bromwich Albion	L 0-1	0-0	6		28244
37	F 03	FAC 4R	H	Charlton Athletic	W 3-0	1-0		Curle 31 (pen), Naylor 48, Paatelainen 66	20429
38	06	FL	A	Sunderland	L 0-1	0-0	6		27502
39	14	FAC 5	A	Wimbledon	D 1-1	0-1		Paatelainen 69	(15332)
40	18	FL	H	Bradford City	W 2-1	1-0	6	Robinson 43, Bull 89	21510
41	21	FL	A	Huddersfield Town	L 0-1	0-0	7		(12633)
42	25	FAC 5R	H	Wimbledon	W 2-1	0-0		Robinson 63, Freedman 85	25112
43	28	FL	H	Birmingham City	L 1-3	1-1	9	Freedman 14	25591
44	M 04	FL	A	Stoke City	D 1-1	1-0	9	Freedman 22	21058
45	07	FAC QF	A	Leeds United	W 1-0	0-0		Goodman 82	(39902)
46	14	FL	H	Crewe Alexandra	W 1-0	0-0	9	Keane 35	24272
47	18	FL	A	Swindon Town	D 0-0	0-0	8		(7770)
48	21	FL	A	Ipswich Town	L 0-3	0-1	9		(21510)
49	29	FL	H	Portsmouth	W 2-0	1-0	8	Goodman 45, Osborn 90	20718
50	A 01	FL	A	Queens Park Rangers	D 0-0	0-0	8		(12337)
51	05	FAC SF	H	Arsenal	L 0-1	0-1			39372
52	07	FL	A	Charlton Athletic	L 0-1	0-1	8		(13743)
53	11	FL	H	Manchester City	D 2-2	1-1	8	Simpson 85, Margetson 34 (OG)	24458
54	13	FL	A	Nottingham Forest	L 0-3	0-2	8		(22863)
55	18	FL	H	Reading	W 3-1	1-1	8	Muscat 9, Goodman 69, 90	19785
56	25	FL	H	Stockport County	L 3-4	2-1	8	Keane 5, 59, Atkins 45	22452
57	29	FL	A	Middlesbrough	D 1-1	1-1	8	Atkins 10	(29878)
58	M 03	FL	A	Tranmere Rovers	L 1-2	0-1	9	Goodman 51	(11144)

Best Home League Attendance: 28244 V West Bromwich Albion	Smallest :19785 V Reading	Average :23253

Goal Scorers:

FL	(57)	Keane 11, Freedman 10, Goodman 8, Bull 7, Simpson 4, Muscat 3, Robinson 3, Atkins 2, Froggatt 2, Osborn 2, Curle 1, Westwood 1, Opponents 3
CC	(7)	Bull 2, Ferguson 1, Froggatt 1, Goodman 1, Paatelainen 1, San Juan 1
FAC	(12)	Paatelainen 4, Freedman 2, Curle 1, Ferguson 1, Goodman 1, Naylor 1, Richards 1, Robinson 1

(D) Atkins	(F) Bull	(F) Claridge	(D) Curle	(F) Daley	(D) Emblen	(M) Ferguson	(M) Foley	(F) Freedman	(M) Froggatt	(F) Goodman	(M) Keane	(D) Kubicki	(D) Muscat	(D) Naylor	(M) Osborn	(F) Paatelainen	(D) Richards	(M) Robinson	(F) San Juan	(M) Sedgley	(G) Segers	(M) Simpson	(M) Slater	(F) Smith	(G) Stowell	(D) Westwood	(D) Williams	(F) Wright J		
X	X	X			X		X	X	X	X								S		X				X	X	S			M C Bailey	1
X	X	X			X		X	X	X	X							S1	S		X				X	X				A P D'Urso	2
X	X	X			X		X	X	X	X							S2			X				X	X	S		S1	P S Danson	3
X	X	X			X		X	X	X	X							S1	S		X				X	X	S			T Heilbron	4
X	X				X		X	X	S	X							X			X		X		X	X	S		S	J A Kirkby	5
X	X				X	S	X	X	X	X							S			X				X	X			S1	G Cain	6
X	X				X		X		X	X								X		X				X	X	S		S1	A N Butler	7
X	X				X		X		X	X							S2	X		X				X	X	S		S1	C R Wilkes	8
X	X				X	S	X		X	X							X	X		X				X	X	S		S1	K M Lynch	9
X	X				X	S2	X		X	X							X	X	S1	X				X	X	S		S	M R Halsey	10
X	X				X			S	X	X							X	X	X					X	X	S1	X		W C Burns	11
X	X				X	S		S2	X	X							X	X	X					X	X	S1	X		S W Mathieson	12
	X	X			X	S2		S1	X	X							X	X	X					X	X	S		X	R J Harris	13
X	X	X			X	S		X	X	X							S1	S	X					X	X	S		X	G Laws	14
X	X	X			X	S2			X			X						S1	X		X			X	X	S		X	M J Brandwood	15
X	X	X			X	S2			S1			X					X	X	X			X		X	X	S		X	C R Wilkes	16
X	X	X			X	S2	X		X	X		S1					X			X				X	X			X	C J Foy	17
X	X	X			X	X	X		S	X		S					X			X				X	X			X	E Lomas	18
X	X	X			X	S1	X	X		S	X						X			X				X	X			X	R Pearson	19
S	X	X			X	X	X		X	X	X	S					X			X				X	X			X	M E Pierce	20
S	X	X			X	X		X	X	X	X	S					X			X				X	X			X	A P D'Urso	21
S	X	X			X	X		X	X	X	X	S1					X			X				X	X			X	E K Wolstenholme	22
X		X			X	X		X	X			X			S1	S2		X			X			X	X	X	X		J A Kirkby	23
X		X			X	S1		X2	X	X					X1	S2				X				X	X	X	X		B Coddington	24
X		X			X	S		X	X	X		X			X	S1				X			S	X	X	X			C R Wilkes	25
X		X			X	S1		X	X	X	X3	X1			X2	S3				X		S2		X	X				D Orr	26
X		X			X	S1		X	X1	X					X	S		X		X				X	X			S	M C Bailey	27
X		X			X	S1		X	X	X1					X	S		X		X		S		X	X	S			S G Bennett	28
X		X	S			X1	X	X		X	S1			X	X	S		X		X				X		X			P R Richards	29
X		X	S			X	X	X1	X2				X	X	S1	X	S2			X				X		X			P Taylor	30
X		X	S3		X		X	X	X2	X3		X	X1	S2	X	S1				X				X		X			D Pugh	31
X		X	S2		X		X	X	X1	S		X	S	S1	X	X2		X	S					X					G Cain	32
X2		X	S1		X		X	X1	X	X3		X		S3	X	S2		X						X		X			W C Burns	33
X		X	S		S		X	X	X	S		X	X	X	X			X	X	S		X		X					G Poll	34
S1		X					X	X	X	X1			X		X	S		X	X			X		X		X			K M Lynch	35
S1		X					X	X1	X	X2			X		X	S		X	X			X		X		X			S W Mathieson	36
S1		X	S		X		X		X2	S		X	X		X	X1		X		X		S2		X		X			G Poll	37
S		X			X		X		X	X		X	X		X	X		X						X		X			R J Harris	38
X		X	S				S1	X		X		X	X2	X	X		X1	X		X				X				S2	U D Rennie	39
X	S1	X					X		X1			X	X2	X	X			X						X				S	A P D'Urso	40
X	S1	X					X1			S		X	X	X	X			X		S		X	S	X					R Pearson	41
X	S3	X					X		X2			X	X	X	X			X	X1	S1		X		X				S2	U D Rennie	42
X	S2	X					X		X2		X1		X	X	X			X	X			S1		X		S			G Cain	43
X	X	X					X2		X1			S1	X	S2	X	X			X	X								E K Wolstenholme	44
S	X1	X					X		S1	X	X	X	X	X					X	S		X	S			X		P A Durkin	45
S	S2	X					X2	X1	X	X		X	X	X	X			X		X	S1					X		G B Frankland	46
S	S1	X					X1	X	X	S		X	X	X	X			X								X		A R Leake	47
S2	X						S3	X		S1			X2	X3	X1	X				X						X		B Knight	48
	S1	X	X		X			X	X1	S3		X						X2	X	S2	X3			X				T Jones	49
	X1	X			X			S1	X		S2		X		X2		X	S		X	X			X				J A Kirkby	50
	S1	X	X					X	X1	S3		X3	S		X	X2		X	X	X	X	S2		S			X	S J Lodge	51
	X	S			X			S2	X	X2		X	X1	X3					X	X	X	S1	S3				X	F G Stretton	52
	X	S			X		S1	S	X	X		X1					X		X	X	X			X				M R Halsey	53
	X1	S	X		S			S1	X	X			X					X		X	X					X		P R Richards	54
S2	X	X3	X						X	S3			X	X	X				X2		X	X		X	X1			T Heilbron	55
X	X	X	X2		X				X	X		X	X	X						S1			X	X1	S2			R D Furnandiz	56
X	S		X		X	S			S1	X	X1		X	X	X								X			X		M C Bailey	57
X	X1	S3	X		X	X2			S1	X			X	X		X					S2		X3		X			K M Lynch	58
30	**24**	**4**	**40**		**6**	**22**	**1**	**25**	**31**	**29**	**34**	**12**	**22**	**14**	**23**	**10**	**13**	**27**	**4**	**18**	**11**	**23**	**4**	**11**	**35**	**3**	**20**		FL Appearances	
4	7	1		2	1	4	4	2	1	4			2	2	1	13		5		1		5	2			1		4	FL Sub Appearances	
5	5		2			0+2		3	2+1	3+1	4		2	2	1		4+1		1		5	2		5	1+1	2			CC Appearances	
4+1	1+2	1	7	0+1	2		5+1	3	6	1+2		5	3	4+1	7	7		6	2	2+2	0+1			5			2+2		FAC Appearances	

Also played: (M) Coleman X(7,8,9), S1(11). (M) Corica S(17,18), S2(19). (F) Crowe S(1,8,39), S1(7). (M) Diaz S(2,7), X(8). (F) Gilkes X(23,24), X1(25). (M) Murray S(37,39,42,44). (M) Roberts S(45). (M) Wright S X(48,49,53).

353

WOLVERHAMPTON WANDERERS

CLUB RECORDS

BIGGEST VICTORIES
League: 10-1 v Leicester City, Division 1, 15.4.1938
9-0 v Fulham, Division 1, 16.9.1959
F.A. Cup: 14-0 v Crosswells Brewery, Rnd 2, 13.11.1886
League Cup: 6-1 v Shrewsbury, Rnd 2, 24.9.1991
Europe: 5-0 v F K Austria, 30.11.1960

BIGGEST DEFEATS
League: 1-10 v Newton Heath, Division 1, 15.10.1892
0-9 v Derby County, Division 1, 10.1.1891
F.A. Cup: 0-6 v Rotherham Utd, Rnd 1, 16.11.1985
League Cup: 0-5 v Fulham, Rnd 3, 5.10.1966
0-5 v Sunderland, Rnd 2 replay, 27.10.1982
Europe: 0-4 v Barcelona, European Cup Q-Final, 2.10.1960

MOST POINTS
3 points a win: 92, Division 3, 1988-89
2 points a win: 64, Division 1, 1957-58

MOST GOALS
115, Division 2, 1931-32.
Hartill 30, Bottrill 21, Phillips 18, Deacon 13, Lowton 9, Baraclough 7,Buttery 6, Hollingworth 4, Crook 2, Martin 1, Redfern 1, Richards 1, Smalley 1,og 1.

MOST FIRST CLASS MATCHES IN A SEASON
61 (46 League, 3 FA Cup, 4 League Cup, 8 Sherpa Van Trophy) 1987-88

MOST LEAGUE GOALS CONCEDED
99, Division 1, 1905-06

MOST LEAGUE WINS
28, Division 1, 1957-58; Division 1, 1958-59

MOST LEAGUE DRAWS
19, Division 2, 1990-91

MOST LEAGUE DEFEATS
25, Division 1, 1964-65; Division 1, 1983-84; Division 2, 1984-85; Division3, 1985-86

INDIVIDUAL CLUB RECORDS

MOST GOALS IN A MATCH
5. J Brodie v Stoke, 8-0, FA Cup 3, 22.2.1890
5. J Butcher v Accrington, 5-3, Div 1, 19.11.1892
5. T Phillipson v Bradford City, 7-2, Div 2, 25.12.1926
5. W Hartill v Notts County, 5-1, Div 2, 12.10.1929
5. W Hartill v Aston Villa, 5-2, Div 1, 3.9.1934

MOST GOALS IN A SEASON
Steve Bull, 52, 1987-88.
League 34, FA Cup 3, League Cup 3, SVT 12.
League only: D Westcott 38, 1946-47

OLDEST PLAYER
Lawrie Madden 37 yrs 222 days v Derby County, 8.5.1993

YOUNGEST PLAYER
Jimmy Mullen, 16 years 43 days v Leeds United, 18.2.1939
Wartime: Cameron Buchanan, 14 yrs 57 days v W.B.A., 26.9.1942

MOST CAPPED PLAYER
Billy Wright, 105 for England

BEST PERFORMANCES

Wolverhampton are the only League Club to have been Champions of all Four Divisions: Div 1, 1954, 1958, 1959; Div 2, 1932, 1977; Div 3N 1924; Div 3,1989; Div 4, 1988

League: 1957-58: Played 42, Won 28, Drawn 8, Lost 6, Goals For 103, Goals Against 47, Points 64. First in Division One

Highest: Division One Champions 3 times

F.A. Cup: 1892-93: 1st rnd. Bolton Wanderers 1-1, 2-1; 2nd rnd. Middlesbrough 2-1; 3rd rnd. Darwen 5-0; Semi-Final Blackburn Rovers 2-1; Final Everton 1-0
1907-08: 1st rnd. Bradford City 1-1, 1-0; 2nd rnd. Bury 2-0; 3rd rnd. Swindon Town 2-0; 4th rnd. Stoke City 1-0; Semi-Final Southampton 2-0; Final Newcastle United 3-1
1948-49: 3rd rnd. Chesterfield 6-0, 4th rnd. Sheffield Utd 3-0; Liverpool 3-1;6th rnd. West Bromwich Albion 1-0; Semi-Final Manchester United 1-1, 1-0; Final Leicester City 3-1
1959-60: 3rd rnd. Newcastle United 2-2, 4-2; 4th rnd Charlton Athletic 2-1; 5th Luton Town 4-1; 6th rnd. Leicester City 2-1; Semi-Final Aston Villa 1-0; Final Blackburn Rovers 3-0

League Cup: 1973-74: 2nd rnd. Halifax Town 3-0; 3rd rnd. Tranmere Rovers 1-1,2-1; 4th rnd. Exeter City 5-1; 5th rnd. Liverpool 1-0; Semi-Final Norwich City 1-1, 1-0; Final Manchester City 2-1
1979-80: 2nd rnd. Burnley 1-1, 2-0; 3rd rnd. Crystal Palace 2-1; 4th rnd. Queens Park Rangers 1-1, 1-0; 5th rnd. Grimsby Town 0-0, 1-1, 2-0; Semi-Final Swindon Town 1-2, 3-1; Final Nottingham Forest 1-0

UEFA Cup: 1971-72: 1st rnd. Academica 3-0, 4-1; 2nd rnd. Den Haag 3-1, 4-0; 3rd rnd. Carl Zeiss 1-0, 3-0; Quarter-Final Juventus 1-1, 2-1; Semi-Final Ferencvaros 2-2, 2-1; Final Tottenham Hotspur 1-2, 1-1

ADDITIONAL INFORMATION
Previous Name: None.
Previous League: None.

Club colours: Gold shirts, black shorts, gold socks.

Change colours:

Reserves League: Pontins Central League Division 1.

DIVISIONAL RECORD

	Played	Won	Drawn	Lost	For	Against	Points
Division 1	2,270	911	506	853	3,874	3,671	2,344
Division 2/1	1,470	588	343	539	2,286	2,061	1,703
Division 3	92	37	24	31	153	147	135
Division 3(N)	42	24	15	3	76	27	63
Division 4	92	51	16	25	151	93	169
Total	3,966	1,611	904	1,451	6,530	5,999	4,414

RECORDS AND STATISTICS

COMPETITIONS

Div.1	Div.2/1	Div.3N	Euro C	Texaco	Watney	C/Sld
1888-06	1906-23	1923-24	1958-59	1970-71	1972-73	1949-50
1932-65	1924-32		1959-60	1972-73		1954-55
1967-76	1965-67	Div.3	ECWC		F/SVT	1958-59
1977-82	1976-77	1985-86	1960-61	A/Ital	1985-86	1959-60
1983-84	1982-83	1988-89	UEFA	1969-70	1986-87	1960-61
	1984-85		1971-72		1987-88	
	1989-	Div.4	1973-74		1988-89	
		1986-88	1974-75			
			1980-81			

HONOURS

Div.1	Div.2	Div.3	Div.4	FAC	Lge C	C/S/sld
1953-54	1931-32	1923-24	1987-88	1892-93	1973-74	1949-50*
1957-58	1976-77	1988-89		1907-08	1979-80	1954-55*
1958-59				1948-49		1959-60
				1959-60		1960-61*

*Shared

Also won the Texaco Cup - 1970-71 & SVT 1987-88

MOST APPEARANCES

DEREK PARKIN 607+2 (167-82)

Year	League	FA Cup	Lge Cup	Europe
1967-68	15			
1968-69	42	2	3	
1969-70	42	1	3	
1970-71	39	2	1	
1971-72	32	2	1	7
1972-73	18	3		
1973-74	39	3	6	4
1974-75	41	1	1	2
1975-76	30	6	3	
1976-77	42	5	1	
1977-78	38	3	1	
1978-79	42	7	1	
1979-80	40	3	11	
1980-81	19+1	6+1	1	2
1981-82	21	1	2	
	500+1	45+1	35	15

Includes 7 Texaco Cup 70-71, 4 Anglo-Itl 69-70, 1 Watney C. 72-70.

MOST GOALS IN A CAREER

STEVE BULL - 300 (1986-98)

Year	League	FA Cup	Lge Cup	Others
1986-87	15			4
1987-88	34	3	3	12
1988-89	37	-	2	11
1989-90	24	1	2	-
1990-91	26	-	-	1
1991-92	20	-	3	-
1992-93	16	1	1	1
1993-94	14	-	-	1
1994-95	16	-	2	1
1995-96	15	2	-	-
1996-97	23	-	-	-
1997-98	7	2	-	-
Total	247	9	13	31

RECORD TRANSFER FEE RECEIVED

Amount	Club	Player	Date
£1,125,000	Manchester City	Steve Daley	9/79
£240,000	Arsenal	Alan Sunderland	11/77
£100,000	Liverpool	Alun Evans	6/68

MANAGERS

Name	Seasons	Best	Worst
Jack Addenbrooke	1885-1922	3(1)	19(2)
George Jobey	1922-24	22(2)	1(3)
Albert Hoskins	1924-26	4(2)	6(2)
Fred Scotchbrook	1926-27	15(2)	15(2)
Major Frank Buckley	1927-44	2(1)	17(2)
Ted Vizard	1944-48	3(1)	5(1)
Stan Cullis	1948-64	1(1)	18(1)
Andy Beattie	1964-65	21(1)	21(1)
Ronnie Allen	1965-68	17(1)	6(2)
Bill McGarry	1968-76	4(1)	20(1)
Sammy Chung	1976-78	15(1)	1(2)
John Barnwell	1978-81	6(1)	18(1)
Ian Greaves	1982		
Graham Hawkins	1982-84	22(1)	2(2)
Tommy Docherty	1984-85	22(2)	22(2)
Sammy Chapman	1985		
Bill McGarry	1985		
Sammy Chapman	1985-86	23(3)	23(3)
Brian Little	1986		
Graham Turner	1986-94	10(2)	4(4)
Graham Taylor	1994-95	4(1)	4(1)
Mark McGhee	1995-	3(1)	20(1)

RECORD TRANSFER FEE PAID

Amount	Club	Player	Date
£1,300,000	Bradford City	Dean Richards	5/95
£1,250,000	Aston Villa	Tony Daley	5/94
£1,150,000	Aston Villa	Andy Gray	9/80
£185,000	Hull City	Peter Daniel	3/78

LONGEST LEAGUE RUNS

of undefeated matches:	20 (24.11.1923 - 5.4.1924)	of league matches w/out a win:	19 (1.12.1984 - 6.4.1985)
of undefeated home matches:	27 (24.3.1923 - 6.9.1924)	of undefeated away matches:	11 (5.9.1953 - 2.1.1954)
without home win:	13 (17.11.1984 - 27.4.1985)	without an away win:	32 (4.3.1922 - 6.10.1923)
of league wins:	8 (13.3.1915-17.4.1915, 4.2.1967-28.3.1967)	of home wins:	14 (7.3.1953 - 28.11.1953)
	(14.3.1987 - 20.4.1987, 15.10.1988 - 26.11.1988)		
of league defeats:	8 (5.12.1981 - 13.2.1982)	of away wins:	5 (1.1.38-26.2.38, 20.8.62-22.9.62, 9.2.80-7.4.80)

WOLVERHAMPTON WAND

PLAYERS NAME / Honours	Ht	Wt	Birthdate	Birthplace / Transfers	Contract Date	Clubs	League	L/Cup	FA Cup	Other	Lge	L/C	FAC	Oth
G O A L K E E P E R														
Bray Justin R			11/1/79	Gt Yarmouth	7/26/97	Wolverhampton (T)								
Stowell Michael	6.2	11.1	4/19/65	Preston		Leyland Motors								
				Free	2/14/85	Preston North End								
				Free	12/12/85	Everton				1				
				Loan	9/3/87	Chester City	14			2				
				Loan	12/24/87	York City	6							
				Loan	2/2/88	Manchester City	14	1						
				Loan	10/21/88	Port Vale	7			1				
				Loan	3/17/89	Wolverhampton W.	7							
				Loan	2/8/90	Preston North End	2							
				£250000	6/28/90	Wolverhampton W.	312	23	19	11				
D E F E N C E														
Atkins Mark	6	12.5	8/14/68	Doncaster	7/9/86	Scunthorpe United	45+5	3+1	5	6+1	2			
E: S				£45000	6/16/88	Blackburn Rovers	224+29	20+4	11+3	16+1	34	4		1
				£1000000	9/21/95	Wolverhampton W.	100+11	12	9+1	2	8	2		1
Curle Keith	6	12	11/14/63	Bristol	11/20/81	Bristol Rovers	21+11	3	1		4			
E: 3, B.4. FRT'86. SC'88. FLgXI.1				£5000	11/4/83	Torquay United	16		1	1	5	1		
				£10000	3/3/84	Bristol City	113+8	7+1	5	14+1	1			
				£150000	10/23/87	Reading	40	8		5				
				£500000	10/21/88	Wimbledon	91+2	7	5	6	3			1
				£2500000	8/14/91	Manchester City	171	18	14	1	11	2		
					8/1/96	Wolverhampton W.	60+1	2	7	2	3		1	
Emblen Neil	6.1	12.07	6/19/71	Bromley		Tonbridge								
						Sittingbourne								
				£175000	11/8/93	Millwall	12		1					
				£600000	7/14/94	Wolverhampton W.	80+8	2+2	7+2	2+1	9	1		
				£2000000	8/21/97	Crystal Palace	8+5		1+1				2	
				£900000	3/26/98	Wolverhampton W.	6+1							
Green Ryan M			10/20/80	Cardiff		Wolverhampton (T)								
Hackett Stephen J			9/17/80	Dublin		Wolverhampton (T)								
Naylor Lee M	5.8	11.8	3/19/80	Bloxwich	10/10/97	Wolverhampton (T)	14+2	1	3				1	
Richards Dean	6	12	6/9/74	Bradford	7/10/92	Bradford City	52+4	4	3	2+2	3			
				£1850000	6/30/95	Wolverhampton W.	68+3	7	8		2		1	
Williams Adrian	6.2	12.6	8/16/71	Reading	1/28/97	Wolverhampton W.	24	2	2+2	2				1
W: 1. Div2'94														
M I D F I E L D														
Andrews Keith J			9/13/80	Dublin		Wolverhampton (T)								
Corica Steve	5.8	10.11	3/24/73	Australia		Marconi								
Int. Austrlian				£100000	8/11/95	Leicester City								
				£1100000	2/16/96	Wolverhampton W.	49+4	2	1		2			
Crowe Seamie M M			11/18/80	Galway		Wolverhampton (T)								
Dixon Alan			10/9/79	Dublin	10/12/96	Wolverhampton (T)								
Ferguson Darren	5.11	10.9	2/9/72	Glasgow	7/11/90	Manchester United	20+7	2+1						
S: u21.8, Y. Prem'93				£250000	1/13/94	Wolverhampton W.	92+20	13	9+1	6	4	2	3	
Froggatt Stephen	5.11	11	3/9/73	Lincoln	1/26/91	Aston Villa	30+5	1+1	5+2		2		1	
E: u21.2				£1000000	7/11/94	Wolverhampton W.	91+7	8	3		7	2		
Jones Mark A			9/7/79	Walsall	9/14/96	Wolverhampton (T)								
Murray Matthew W			5/2/81	Solihull	2/2/98	Wolverhampton W.								
Muscat Kevin	6	12.8	8/7/73	Crawley		South Melbourne								
				£35000	8/16/96	Crystal Palace	51+2	4	2	2	2	1		
				Swap	10/21/97	Wolverhampton W.	22+2		5		3			
Osborn Simon	5.11	11.4	1/19/72	Croydon	1/3/90	Crystal Palace	47+8	11	2	1+3	4	1		
				£90000	8/17/94	Reading	31+1	4		3	5			
				£1100000	7/7/95	QPR								
				£1000000	12/22/95	Wolverhampton W.	74+3	1	8	2	9	1		
Robinson Carl P	5.11	12.1	10/13/76	Llandrindod	1/1/00	Wolverhampton W.	28+6	4	7		3		1	
u21.6, Y. W:				Loan	3/28/96	Shrewsbury Town								
Sedgley Stephen P	6.1	12.6	5/26/68	Enfield	6/2/86	Coventry City	81+3	9	2+2	5+1	3	2		
E: u21.11; FAC'91; CS'91				£750000	7/28/89	Tottenham Hotspur	147+17	24+3	12+1	5+3	8	1	1	
				£1000000	6/15/94	Ipswich Town	105	10	5	5	15	2		1
					7/12/97	Wolverhampton W.	18+1	2	6					
Simms Gordon H			3/23/81	Larne		Wolverhampton (T)								
Simpson Paul D	5.6	11.3	7/26/66	Carlisle	8/4/83	Manchester City	99+22	10+1	10+2	8+3	18	2	4	
E: u21.5, Y2				£200000	10/31/88	Oxford United	138+6	10	9	5	43	3	2	2
				£500000	2/2/92	Derby County	135+51	12+3	4+4	14+2	48	6	1	2
				Loan	12/6/96	Sheffield United	2+3							
				£75000	11/13/97	Wolverhampton W.	23+5		2+2		4			
F O R W A R D														
Bull Steve	5.11	11.4	3/28/65	Tipton		Tipton Town								
E: 13, B.5, u21.5. Div4'88. Div3'89. SVT'88				Free	8/24/85	WBA	2+2	2		1+2	2	1		
				£35000	11/21/86	Wolverhampton W.	448+9	30+1	18+2	33+1	246	15	7	32
Claridge Steve	5.11	11.08	4/10/66	Portsmouth		Portsmouth								
Div.3'91. Div.2'95. AWS'95. CC 96/97					11/30/84	Bournemouth	3+4		1		1			
				£10000	10/1/85	Weymouth								
				£14000	10/13/88	Solihull	58+4	2+1	6	5	19		1	2

Player	H	W	DOB	Birthplace	Fee	Date	Club								
Claridge continued...					£75000	2/8/90	Cambridge United	56+23	2+4	1	6+3	28	2		1
					£160000	7/17/92	Luton Town	15+1	2			2	2	3	1
					£195000	11/20/92	Cambridge United	53	4	4	3	18	3		
					£350000	1/7/94	Birmingham City	58+2	3	5	7	20	1		4
					£1200000	3/1/96	Leicester City	52+10	8	3	3	16	2		1
					Loan	1/23/98	Portsmouth	10				2			
					£350000	3/26/98	Wolverhampton W.	4+1			1				
Crowe Glen	5.11	12.13	12/25/77	Dublin		1/1/01	Wolverhampton W.	6+4				1			
u21.1, Y. E:					Loan	2/21/97	Exeter City	10				5			
					Loan	10/24/97	Cardiff City	7+1			1	1			
Foley Dominic	6.1	12.8	7/7/76	Cork			Wolverhampton W.	2+12	0+2	0+1	0+2	1			
					Loan	2/24/98	Watford	2+6				1			
Gilkes Michael	5.8	10.1	7/20/65	Hackney			Leicester City								
FMC'88. FLgXl'88. Div2'94					Free	7/10/84	Reading	348+45	25+7	31+2	26+2	43	6	1	2
					Loan	1/28/92	Chelsea	0+1			0+1				
					Loan	3/4/92	Southampton	4+2							
						3/27/97	Wolverhampton W.	8				1			
Keane Robert D	5.9	11.7	7/8/80	Dublin		7/26/97	Wolverhampton (T)	34+4	3+1	1+1		11			
Lamey Nathan J			10/14/80	Leeds			Wolverhampton (T)								
Paatelainen Mixu	6	13.11	2/3/67	Helsinki			Valkeakosken Haka								
Finnish Int.						10/1/87	Dundee United	101+32	8+2	20+1	2+1	34	5	2	1
						3/31/92	Aberdeen	53+22	6	7+1	3	23	3	1	1
					£300000	7/29/94	Bolton Wanderers	58+11	8+1	1+1	3	15	2		1
						8/8/97	Wolverhampton W.	10+13	4+1	4+1				1	4

THE MANAGER
MARK MCGHEE

Date of Birth . . . . 25th May 1957.
Place of Birth . . . . Glasgow.
Date of Appointment . . . . December 1995.

PREVIOUS CLUBS
As Manager . . . . Reading, Leicester City.
As Coach. . . . . None.
As a Player. . . Bristol City (A), Morton, Newcastle Utd, Aberdeen, SV Hamburg,
. . . . Celtic, Newcastle Utd, Reading (player-manager).

HONOURS
As a Manager
Reading: Division 2 champions 1993-94.

As a Player
Scottish League Chapions 1980, 1984, 1986, 1988. Scottish Cup 1982, 1983, 1984, 1988, 1989.
ECWC 1983.
Scotland: 4 full caps and 1 u21 cap.

MOLINEUX STADIUM
Waterloo Road, Wolverhampton WV1 4QR

Capacity 28,500

First game ....v Aston Villa, 2.9.1889.
First floodlit game ....v South Africa XI, 30.9.1953.

ATTENDANCES
Highest...61,315 v Liverpool, FA. Cup 5th Rnd, 11.2.1939.
Lowest ....900 v Notts County, Div.1, 17.10.1891.

OTHER GROUNDS ....Goldthorn Hill 1877-79, John Harper's Field 1877-81, Dudley Road 1881-89.

HOW TO GET TO THE GROUND

From the North
Use motorway M6 until junction 12, leave motorway and follow signs to Wolverhampton (A5) then A449 and at roundabout take 2nd exit into Waterloo Road, then turn left in Molineux Street for Wolverhampton Wanderers FC.
From the East
Use motorway M6 until junction 10, leave motorway and follow signs to Wolverhampton 9A454). Then at crossroads turn right into Stafford Street. In 0.2 miles turn left into Ring Road. Then at next crossroads turn right into Waterloo Road and shortly turn right into Molineux Street for Wolverhampton Wanderers FC.
From the South
Use motorway M5 until junction 12, leave motorway and follow signs to Wolverhampton (A4123) turn right then shortly turn left into Ring Road. In 1 mile turn left into Waterloo Road and shortly turn right into Molineux Street for Wolverhampton Wanderers FC.
From the West
Use A454, sign posted Wolverhampton, and at roundabout turn left into Ring Road, then left into Molineux Street for Wolverhampton FC.

Car Parking: Available around 'The West Park', in side streets and at the rear of the North Bank.

Nearest Railway Station: Wolverhampton (01902 595 451)

USEFUL TELEPHONE NUMBERS

Club switchboard 01902 655 000
Club fax number........................01902 687 006
Ticket Office...............................01902 653653

Clubcall 0891 12 11 03*
*Calls cost 50p per minute at all times.
Call costings correct at time of going to press.

MATCHDAY PROGRAMME

Programme Editor (97/98)Lorraine Hennessy.

Number of pages (97/98) ....48.

Price (97/98)......................................£1.50.

Subscriptions................Please contact club.

Local Newspapers
......................Express & Star, Evening Mail,
....Sporting Star.

Local Radio Stations
...............Beacon Radio, BRMB, Radio WM.

MATCHDAY TICKET PRICES (97/98)
Adults . . . . £12 - £17
Juniors/OAP/Students. . . . . £8.50 - £11

Jack Harris/Stand Cullis £12

John Ireland Stand Upper. £15

Billy Wright £17

NATIONWIDE
LEAGUE DIVISION 2

...1998-99

DIVISION TWO
1997-98

FINAL LEAGUE TABLE

		P	W	D	L	F	A	Pts
1	Watford (+12)	46	24	16	6	67	41	88
2	Bristol City (+3)	46	25	10	11	69	39	85
3	Grimsby Town (Div.1) - *Play-off winners*	46	19	15	12	55	37	72
4	Northampton Town (Div.3)	46	18	17	11	52	37	71
5	Bristol Rovers (+12)	46	20	10	16	70	64	70
6	Fulham (Div.3)	46	20	10	16	60	43	70
7	Wrexham (+1)	46	18	16	12	55	51	70
8	Gillingham (+3)	46	19	13	14	52	47	70
9	Bournemouth (+7)	46	18	12	16	57	52	66
10	Chesterfield (-)	46	16	17	13	46	44	65
11	Wigan Athletic (Div.3)	46	17	11	18	64	66	62
12	Blackpool (-5)	46	17	11	18	59	67	62
13	Oldham Athletic (Div.1)	46	15	16	15	62	54	61
14	Wycombe Wanderers (+4)	46	14	18	14	51	53	60
15	Preston North End (-)	46	15	14	17	56	56	59
16	York City (+4)	46	14	17	15	52	58	59
17	Luton Town (-14)	46	14	15	17	60	64	57
18	Millwall (-4)	46	14	13	19	43	54	55
19	Walsall (-7)	46	14	12	20	43	52	54
20	Burnley (-11)	46	13	13	20	55	65	52
21	Brentford (-17)	46	11	17	18	50	71	50
22	Plymouth Argyle (-3)	46	12	13	21	55	70	49
23	Carlisle United (Div.3)	46	12	8	26	57	73	44
24	Southend United (Div.1)	46	11	10	25	47	79	43

The figure in brackets denotes the number of places lost or gained on the club's 1996-97 final position.

BLACKPOOL
(The Seasiders)
NATIONWIDE LEAGUE DIVISION 2
SPONSORED BY: TELEWEST COMMUNICATIONS

1998/99 Back Row L-R: Paul Kelly (Physio), David Bardsley, John Hills, Jamie Skroch, Gary Brabin, Marvin Bryan, Brett Ormerod, David Jones, Steve Longworth, Michael Davies (Reserve team manager). **Middle Row:** Jack Chapman (Chief scout), Anton Rogan, Ian Hughes, Mike Conroy, Steve Banks, Phil Barnes, Clarke Carlisle, Chris Malkin, Jason Jarrett, Alan Crawford (Youth Team manager). **Front Row:** Scott Garvey, Martin Aldridge, Tony Butler, Nigel Worthington (Manager), Mick Henshaw (Asst. Manager), Phil Clarkson, Jason Blunt, Junior Bent.

BLACKPOOL
FORMED IN 1887
TURNED PROFESSIONAL IN 1887
LTD COMPANY IN 1896

HON VICE PRESIDENTS: R P Gibrail,
J Armfield, K Chadwick,
Sir Stanley Matthews, W Beaumont
CHAIRMAN: Mrs V Oyston
DIRECTORS:
Mrs G Bridge (Managing),
M Joyce, C Muir OBE,
G Warburton (Commercial Director)
SECRETARY: Carol Banks
(01253 404 331)
COMMERCIAL MANAGER
Frank Layton

MANAGER: Nigel Worthington
ASSISTANT MANAGER: Mike Hennigan
RESERVE TEAM MANAGER
Michael Davies
YOUTH TEAM MANAGER
Alan Crawford
PHYSIOTHERAPIST
Paul Kelly

CLUB STATISTICIAN FOR THE DIRECTORY
& OFFICIAL CLUB STATISTICIAN
Roger Harrison

Blackpool had a chance of making the play-offs at one stage but defeats at Easter put the hopes to bed. New manager Nigel Worthington made a few changes in personnel during the season. James Quinn, Tony Ellis and Micky Mellon left and at the end of the season David Linighan, Andy Preece and Jason Lydiate were among the names released.

Phil Clarkson nicknamed 'the Ghost' was top scorer from midfield and newcomers during the campaign were Junior Bent, Ian Hughes and John Hills. The Coco-Cola Cup pitted us against Manchester City and we triumphed on penalties at Maine Road. The Second Round was against Premier side Coventry City who were beaten 1-0 at Bloomfield Road and we increased this to 2-0 in the first half at Highfield Road but eventually lost 2-3 on aggregate.

In the FA Cup we narrowly defeated Blyth Spartans 4-3. In the Second Round we lost 1-2 at Oldham Athletic.

During the summer David Bardsley returned to his original club, and Jason Blunt (Leeds United), Steve Bushell (York City) and Steve Garvey (Crewe Alex.) were free transfers in. Lee Philpott and Mark Bonner, who were offered new terms, departed to Lincoln City and Cardiff City respectively, whilst a late signing was Martin Aldridge a free transfer from Oxford United.

Roger Harrison.

BLACKPOOL

Division 2   :12th   FA CUP: 2nd Round   LC CUP: 2nd Round   AWS: Northern Semi-Final

M	DATE	COMP.	VEN	OPPONENTS	RESULT	H/T	LP	GOAL SCORERS/GOAL TIMES	ATT.
1	A 09	FL	H	Luton Town	W 1-0	1-0	6	Lydiate 11	6547
2	12	CC 1/1	H	Manchester City	W 1-0	0-0		Preece 73	8084
3	15	FL	A	Bristol City	L 0-2	0-0	13		(9043)
4	23	FL	H	Wycombe Wanderers	L 2-4	1-2	19	Quinn 23, Brabin 89	4733
5	26	CC 1/2	A	Manchester City	L 0-1	0-0			(12563)
6	30	FL	A	Bournemouth	L 0-2	0-1	22		(4196)
7	S 02	FL	A	Wrexham	W 4-3	0-2	14	Ellis 62, 69, 76, Bonner 82	(3762)
8	07	FL	H	Carlisle United	W 2-1	1-0	8	Ellis 19, Carlisle 90	7259
9	13	FL	A	Wigan Athletic	L 0-3	0-0	14		(5517)
10	16	CC 2/1	H	Coventry City	W 1-0	0-0		Linighan 76	5884
11	20	FL	H	Oldham Athletic	D 2-2	1-1	14	Quinn 42, Philpott 53	7174
12	27	FL	H	Southend United	W 3-0	1-0	7	Bonner 12, Ellis 80, Clarkson 88	4542
13	O 01	CC 2/2	A	Coventry City	L 1-3	1-0		Linighan 36	(9565)
14	04	FL	A	Millwall	L 1-2	0-0	13	Ellis 86	(7042)
15	11	FL	A	Fulham	L 0-1	0-1	17		(7761)
16	18	FL	H	Grimsby Town	D 2-2	1-1	17	Quinn 44, Ellis 77	5234
17	21	FL	H	Chesterfield	W 2-1	1-0	13	Clarkson 42, Quinn 47 (pen)	3682
18	25	FL	A	Bristol Rovers	W 3-0	1-0	9	Bonner 30, Clarkson 48, Preece 53	(6183)
19	N 01	FL	A	Watford	L 1-4	0-1	12	Preece 73	(9723)
20	04	FL	H	Northampton Town	D 1-1	1-0	11	Clarkson 37	3685
21	08	FL	H	Burnley	W 2-1	1-1	10	Clarkson 41, Preece 74	7429
22	15	FAC 1	H	Blyth Spartans	W 4-3	1-2		Preece 4, Linighan 59, Clarkson 71, 89	4814
23	18	FL	A	Gillingham	D 1-1	0-1	10	Ellis 90	(5045)
24	22	FL	H	York City	W 1-0	0-0	8	Strong 68	4508
25	29	FL	A	Walsall	L 1-2	1-0	9	Clarkson 35	(3933)
26	D 02	FL	H	Plymouth Argyle	D 0-0	0-0	9		3281
27	06	FAC 2	A	Oldham Athletic	L 1-2	0-0		Ellis 83	(6590)
28	13	FL	A	Brentford	L 1-3	1-1	11	Preece 4	(3725)
29	20	FL	H	Preston North End	W 2-1	2-0	9	Preece 21, Philpott 37	8342
30	26	FL	A	Carlisle United	D 1-1	0-1	11	Ormerod 52	(8010)
31	28	FL	H	Wrexham	L 1-2	1-0	12	Ormerod 17	5424
32	J 10	FL	A	Luton Town	L 0-3	0-1	14		(5574)
33	13	AWS N2	H	York City	D 1-1	0-1		Clarkson 87 (Blackpool won 10-9 on penalties)	1105
34	17	FL	H	Bournemouth	W 1-0	1-0	12	Clarkson 19	4550
35	24	FL	A	Wycombe Wanderers	L 1-2	1-1	14	Preece 20	(5073)
36	27	AWS NQF	H	Wigan Athletic	W 1-0	1-0		Preece 15	1687
37	31	FL	H	Wigan Athletic	L 0-2	0-2	15		5288
38	F 03	FL	H	Bristol City	D 2-2	0-0	14	Preece 54, Bent 88	3724
39	06	FL	A	Oldham Athletic	W 1-0	0-0	12	Bent 55	(6576)
40	14	FL	H	Millwall	W 3-0	3-0	11	Bryan 9, Malkin 19, Preece 39	4455
41	17	AWS NSF	A	Grimsby Town	L 0-1	0-0			(8027)
42	21	FL	A	Southend United	L 1-2	0-2	12	Brabin 49	(3340)
43	24	FL	A	Grimsby Town	L 0-1	0-0	12		(4924)
44	28	FL	H	Fulham	W 2-1	0-1	12	Preece 77, Clarkson 85	5183
45	M 07	FL	H	Watford	D 1-1	0-0	12	Clarkson 88	5237
46	14	FL	A	Northampton Town	L 0-2	0-1	15		(6586)
47	21	FL	H	Gillingham	W 2-1	0-0	13	Malkin 73, Clarkson 83	4165
48	28	FL	A	York City	D 1-1	1-0	11	Preece 5	(3650)
49	A 04	FL	H	Walsall	W 1-0	0-0	11	Preece 48	4451
50	07	FL	A	Burnley	W 2-1	1-1	8	Clarkson 44, Bent 51	(13413)
51	11	FL	A	Plymouth Argyle	L 1-3	1-0	10	, Heathcote 28 (OG)	(5655)
52	13	FL	H	Brentford	L 1-2	0-2	10	Taylor 81	3926
53	18	FL	A	Preston North End	D 3-3	2-1	11	Clarkson 3, 65, Hills 45	(13500)
54	25	FL	H	Bristol Rovers	W 1-0	0-0	12	Brabin 68	7057
55	M 02	FL	A	Chesterfield	D 1-1	0-0	12	Carlisle 86	(4462)

Best Home League Attendance: 8342 V Preston North End   Smallest :3281 V Plymouth Argyle   Average :5212

Goal Scorers:

FL	(59)	Clarkson 13, Preece 11, Ellis 8, Quinn 4, Bent 3, Bonner 3, Brabin 3, Carlisle 2, Malkin 2, Ormerod 2, Philpott 2, Bryan 1, Hills 1, Lydiate 1, Strong 1, Taylor 1, Opponents 1
CC	(3)	Linighan 2, Preece 1
FAC	(5)	Clarkson 2, Ellis 1, Linighan 1, Preece 1
AWS	(2)	Clarkson 1, Preece 1

(G) Banks	(M) Bent	(M) Bonner	(M) Brabin	(M) Bradshaw	(F) Bryan	(M) Butler	(F) Carlisle	(M) Clarkson	(F) Conroy	(M) Dixon	(F) Ellis	(F) Greenacre	(D) Hills	(M) Hughes	(D) King	(D) Linighan	(M) Longworth	(D) Lydiate	(F) Malkin	(M) Mellon	(M) Ormerod	(M) Philpott	(F) Preece	(F) Quinn	(M) Reed	(M) Strong	(F) Taylor	(M) Worthington		
X		X	X	X	X	S	X												X			X	X	X				S	S.W. Mathieson	1
X		X	X	X	X	X										S		X	S1			X	X	X					T Jones	2
X		X	X	X	X	X										S1		X	X			X	X	X					G Singh	3
X		X	X	X	X	X										S1		X	S3	S2		X	X	X					B Coddington	4
X		X	X		X	X					S3				X			S1	S2	X		X1	X						D Pugh	5
X	S1	X	X		X	X	S	X			X							X	S2	X		X							A P D'Urso	6
X	X	X		X	X	X	X		X		X							S	X	S1		X						X	C J Foy	7
X	X	X	S1		X	X	X	X			X							S	X	S2		X						X	W C Burns	8
X	X	X		X	X	X	X		X		X							X		X	S2	X	S1						A R Leake	9
X		X		X	X	S	S		X		X				X			X	X	S1	X	X	X	X					T Heilbron	10
X	S2	X		X	X		S1	S			X							X		X		X	X	X					R Pearson	11
X	X	X		X	X			S2			X				X			X		X		X	X	S3				S1	D Laws	12
X		X		X	X		X				X				X			X	X	S	X	X	X	S					M D Reed	13
X	S1	X		X	X		X				X				X			X		X		X	X					S2	M E Pierce	14
X	S	X			X		S	S1			X				X			X		X		X	X	X				X	K A Leach	15
X	S2	X			X			S1			X				X			X		X		X	X	X				X	M S Pike	16
X	S	X	S		X	X		X			X			X	X			X		X		X	X					S1	G Laws	17
X	S2	X	S3		X	X		X			X			X	X			X		X		X	X					S1	B Knight	18
X	S1	X	S		X	X		X			X			X	X			X		X		X	X						G Singh	19
X	S	X	S		X	X		X			X			X	X					X		S	X	X					K M Lynch	20
X	S	X	S1		X	X		X			X			X						S		X	X	X					M J Brandwood	21
X	X	X	S			X		X		X	X			X	S2	X			S1	X	X								M L Dean	22
X	X	X	X			X		X	S2		X			X				X		X		S	X	S1					M Fletcher	23
X	X	X	S			X		X			X			X				X				S1	X	X			X		S J Baines	24
X	X	X	S			X		X			X			X				X	S1			X2	X1			X		S2	M J Jones	25
X	X1	X	S1		X	X		X			X			X				X		S	X2	S2	X			X			C J Foy	26
X	X1	X	X		X	X	S	X			X			X				X		S1		S	X			S			G B Frankland	27
X	S1				X	X		X			X			X		X			S	X		X2	X		S2	X			A R Hall	28
X	X1				X	X		X			X			X		S3			X2	S1	X2	X		S2	X			R Pearson	29
X	X				X	X		X			X			X		S		X1	S1	X		X			S	X		D Laws	30
X	S1	X			X	X		X			X			X				X		X		X	X1		S	X		M D Messias	31
X	S2	X			X	X		S1	X		X			X2		X1	S	X				X	X	X					R Styles	32
X	X				X	X		X			X			X		X				X	S1	X	X		X1					33
X	X	X1			X	X		X	X			X							S2	X		X2		X		S1			S W Mathieson	34
X	X		X1		X		X	X			X				X				X	S2		X2		X			X		A N Butler	35
X	X2		S2		X		X	X			X				X				X	S1	X1		X			X				36
X	X	X	S2		X	S	X2	X			X				X				X	S1		X1		X			X		T Heilbron	37
X	X	X	S		X	X		X			X			X	S			X1				S1	X			X			G B Frankland	38
X	X	X			X	X		X			X			X	S1			X				S	X	S2		X2			A R Leake	39
X	X2	X	S1		X	X		X			X			X				X1				S	X	S2					D Pugh	40
X	X	X	S1		X	X		X			X		X	X				X1				X2		X	S2					41
X	X	X2	S2		X	X		X			X			X	X			X1	X			S1		X				S2	P S Danson	42
X		X		X	X	X		X			X			X	X			X1	X			S1		X			S	S J Baines	43
X	S2		X3	X	S3	X		X			X			X	X			X1	X2			S1	X					M L Dean	44
X	X		X		X	S	X						S1	X	X			X		X1	S		X					M S Pike	45
X	S1	X		X	X	S	X						X2	X				X		X1	S2		X					M J Jones	46
X	X	X			X	X	S	X					X1	X	X	X		S		S1			X					J A Kirkby	47
X	X2	X1			X	X		X					S1	X	X							S		X			S2	P S Danson	48
X	X				X	X		X		X			S	X	X							S		X			S	G Cain	49
X	X		X		X	X		X	X1				X	X					S			S		X			S1	K M Lynch	50
X		X		X	X		X	X					X	X1				S1				S2	X				S	B Knight	51
X		X	S1		X1	X	X	S					X	X	X							X		X			X	T Jones	52
X	X1		S1		X	X	S	X	S2				X	X								X		X			X2	P Rejer	53
X	S		X		X	X	X	S					X	X								X		X			X	F G Stretton	54
X			X		X	X	X	X	X2				X	X					S1		X1			X				K A Leach	55

45	25	32	15	6	43	37	8	42	5	6	18	2	19	20	6	26		22	13	9	5	27	42	11		11	3	4	FL Appearances	
	11		9				3	3	1		2		1			3	2	1	7	1	4	8	2	3	3		2	5	FL Sub Appearances	
4		4	2	3	4	2		3			2+1			3		3+1	0+3	3				3	3	4	3				CC Appearances	
2	2	1		1	2		2		2	2	2				1	0+1	0+1		0+1	2	1								FAC Appearances	
3	3	1	0+2		3	2	1			2	3			1		0+1		3	0+1	3	0+1	1	1						AWS Appearances	

Also Played: (G) Barnes S(16,22,27), X(51). (M) Bridges S(34). (F) Carden S(3). (M) Foster X1(28). (M) Haddow S(3), S1 35). (M) Nowland S(42,43), S2(55). (M) Robinson S(9, 54). (D) Rogan X(5,6). (M) Russell S(2,3). (M) Thompson S(14,35,43,55), X(54).

CLUB RECORDS

BIGGEST VICTORIES
League: 8-4 v Charlton Athletic, Division 1, 27.9.1952.
7-0 v Reading, Division 2, 10.11.1928.
7-0 v Preston North End, Division 1, 1.5.1948.
7-0 v Sunderland, Division 1, 13.10.1957.
Most Goals Scored in a Cup Tie: 10-0 v Lanerossi, Anglo-Italian Cup, 10.6.1972.

BIGGEST DEFEATS
League: 1-10 v Small Heath, Division 2, 2.3.1901.
1-10 v Huddersfield Town, Division 1, 13.12.1930.
In a Cup Competition: 0-6 v Barnsley, FA Cup Round 1 Replay, 1909-10.

MOST POINTS
3 points a win: 86, Division 4, 1984-85.
2 points a win: 58, Division 2, 1929-30, 1967-68.

BEST PERFORMANCES
League: 2nd Division 1, 1955-56.
F.A. Cup: Winners in 1953.
League Cup: Semi-Final 1962.

HONOURS
Division 2 Champions 1929-30.
FA Cup Winners 1953.
Anglo-Italian Cup Winners 1971.

LEAGUE CAREER
Elected to Div 2 1896, Failed to gain re-election 1899, Re-elected to Div 2 1900, Promoted to Div 1 1929-30, Relegated to Div 2 1932-33, Promoted to Div 1 1936-37, Relegated to Div 2 1966-67, Promoted to Div 1 1969-70, Relegated to Div 2 1970-71, Relegated to Div 3 1977-78, Relegated to Div 4 1980-81, Promoted to Div 3 1984-85, Relegated to Div 4 1989-90, Promoted to Div 3 1991-92 (Now Div 2).

INDIVIDUAL CLUB RECORDS

MOST GOALS IN A SEASON
Jimmy Hampson - 46, Division 2,1929-30 (League 45, FA Cup 1).

MOST GOALS IN A MATCH
5, Jimmy Hampson v Reading, Division 2, 10.11.1928.
5, Jimmy McIntosh v Preston North End, Division 1, 01.05.1948.

OLDEST PLAYER
Sir Stanley Matthews, 46.

YOUNGEST PLAYER (In a League match)
Trevor Sinclair, 16 years 170 days v Wigan Athletic, 19.8.1989.

MOST CAPPED PLAYER
Jimmy Armfield (England) 43.

PREVIOUS MANAGERS

Since 1946: Joe Smith, Ron Stuart, Stan Mortensen, Les Shannon, Jimmy Meadows, Bob Stokoe, Harry Potts, Allan Brown, Jimmy Meadows, Bob Stokoe, Stan Ternent, Alan Ball (jnr), Allan Brown, Sam Ellis, Jimmy Mullen, Graham Carr, Billy Ayre, Sam Allardyce, Gary Megson.

ADDITIONAL INFORMATION
PREVIOUS NAME
In 1899 South Shore amalgamated with Blackpool who had been formed when Blackpool St John disbanded in 1887.

PREVIOUS LEAGUE
Lancashire League.

Club colours: All Tangerine.

Change colours: All royal blue.

Reserves League: Pontins Central League Div 2.
Youth League: Lancashire League.

LONGEST LEAGUE RUNS

of undefeated matches:	17 (1968)	of league matches w/out a win:	19 (1970-71)
of undefeated home matches:	24 (1990-91)	of undefeated away matches:	10 (1973-74)
without home win:	16 (1966-67)	without an away win:	41 (1907-09)
of league wins:	9 (1936-37)	of home wins:	15 (1990-91)
of league defeats:	8 (1898-99)	of away wins:	6 (1936-37)

THE MANAGER

Nigel Worthington . . . . appointed in July 1997.

PREVIOUS CLUBS
As a Manager. . . . . None.
As an Assistant/Coach . . . . None.
As a Player. . . . . Ballymena, Notts County, Sheffield Wednesday, Leeds United, Stoke City.

HONOURS
As a Manager . . . . None.
As a Player. . . . . **Ballymena:** UC 1981, IC 1981. **Sheffield Wednesday:** League Cup 1991.
International Honours. . . . . 64 full caps and 1 Youth cap for Northern Ireland.

BLACKPOOL

PLAYERS NAME Honours	Ht	Wt	Birthdate	Birthplace Transfers	Contract Date	Clubs	League	L/Cup	FA Cup	Other	Lge	L/C	FAC	Oth
G O A L K E E P E R														
Banks Steve	5.11	12.4	2/9/72	Hillingdon	3/24/90	West Ham United				1				
				Loan	3/25/93	Gillingham								
				Free	6/24/93	Gillingham	67		7	2				
				£60000	8/18/95	Blackpool	114	9	7	4				
Barnes Phillip K	6.1	11.1	3/2/79	Sheffield	6/25/97	Rotherham United	2							
					7/18/97	Blackpool	1							
D E F E N C E														
Bardsley David E: 2, Y.2	5.1	10	11/09/64	Manchester	05/11/82	Blackpool	45	2+1	2					
				£150000	23/11/83	Watford	97+3	6	13+1	1	7	1	1	
				£265000	18/09/87	Oxford United	74	12	5	3	7			
				£500000	15/09/89	Q.P.R.	252+1	20	19	3	4	1		1
				Free	7/1/98	Blackpool								
Butler Philip Anthony	6.2	12	9/28/72	Stockport	5/13/91	Gillingham (T)	142+6	12	12+1	5+1	5			1
				£225000	8/15/96	Blackpool	78+1	5	3	4				1
Carlisle Clarke James	6.1	12.7	10/14/79	Preston	8/8/97	Blackpool (T)	8+3				2			
Hills John D	5.8	10.8	4/21/78	Blackpool	10/27/95	Blackpool								
				Loan	1/30/97	Swansea City	11							
					4/5/97	Everton	1+3							
				Loan	1/16/98	Blackpool	8							
				£75000	2/27/98	Blackpool	11							
Rogan Anthony Gerard P NI: 18. SPD'88. SC'88'89.	6	13	3/25/66	Belfast		Celtic	115+12	12+1	18	8	4		1	
				£350000	10/4/91	Sunderland	45+1	1	8	2	1			
					8/9/93	Oxford United	56+2	4	4	2	3			
				Free	8/11/95	Millwall	30+6	1	2	1	8			
				Free	8/7/97	Blackpool	1	1						
Thompson Philip P	5.11	12	4/1/81	Blackpool	10/3/97	Blackpool (T)	1							
M I D F I E L D														
Bent Junior Anthony	5.6	10.9	3/1/70	Huddersfield	8/28/97	Blackpool	24+11		2		3			
Blunt Jason E: Y.	5.9	10.10	8/16/77	Penzance	1/1/95	Leeds United (T)	2+2	0+1						
				Free	7/1/98	Blackpool								
Bonner Mark	5.11	10.1	6/7/74	Ormskirk	6/18/92	Blackpool	156+22	15+3	11	8+3	14			1
Brabin Gary E: SP.	5.11	14.8	12/9/70	Liverpool	12/14/89	Stockport County	1+1			1+1				
					8/1/90	Gateshead								
					8/1/91	Runcorn								
				£45000	7/26/94	Doncaster Rovers	27+1	2	1	2	8			
				£125000	3/29/96	Bury	5							
					8/15/96	Blackpool	14+9	2	1		3			
Bushall Stephen	5.7	10.5	28/12/72	Manchester	25/02/91	York City	156+18	8+1	5	11+2	10	2		1
				Free	7/1/98	Blackpool								
Clarkson Philip I	5.11	10.8	11/13/68	Garstang		Fleetwood Town			1					
				£22500	10/15/91	Crewe Alexandra	75+18	6+1	3+1	6+5	27	1	2	1
					3/13/96	Scunthorpe United	48+3	2	2		19	1	2	
				£80000	2/4/97	Blackpool	59+3	3	2		18		2	
Hughes Ian W: u21.11. DIV2 96/97	5.11	10.9	8/2/64	Bangor	11/19/91	Bury	167+25	15+3	7+2	16+3	1			
				£200000	12/10/97	Blackpool	20+1							
Jones David J	5.7	9.10	11/17/78	Goole		Goole Town								
				Free		Blackpool								
Worthington Nigel NI: 50. Y1; UC'81; IC'81;LC'91	5.11	12.6	11/4/61	Ballymena		Ballymena	67							
				£100000	7/1/81	Notts County	62+5	11	4		4			
				£125000	2/6/84	Sheffield Wednesday	334+4	41	29	9	12	1		1
				£250000	7/4/94	Leeds United	21+6	2	3+1		1			
				Free	7/17/96	Stoke City	12	3					1	
				Free	7/10/97	Blackpool	4+5							
F O R W A R D														
Aldridge Martin J	5.11	11.4	06/12/74	Northampton	8/27/93	Northampton Town	50+20	1+2	1+1	5	17		1	4
				Loan	12/9/95	Dagenham & Red.								
				Free	12/22/95	Oxford United	46+26	8+4	2+2		19	3		
				Free	7/1/98	Blackpool								
Bent Junior	5.5	10.6	3/1/70	Huddersfield	12/9/87	Huddersfield Town	25+11	1	3+1	4	6		1	
				Loan	11/30/89	Burnley	2				3			
				£30000	3/22/90	Bristol City	141+41	10+3	12+3	5+3	20	1	2	
				Loan	3/26/92	Stoke City	1							
				Loan	10/28/96	Shrewsbury Town	3							
					8/29/97	Blackpool								
Bryan Marvin	6	12.2	8/2/75	Paddington	8/17/92	QPR								
				Loan	12/8/94	Doncaster Rovers	5				1			
				Free	8/10/95	Blackpool	121+2	8+2	5	6	3			
Conroy Michael Div.4'92.	6	11	12/31/65	Glasgow		Coventry City								
				Free	8/1/84	Clydebank	92+22	4+1	5+2		38			
					12/1/87	St.Mirren	9+1		+1		1			
				£50000	9/28/88	Reading	65+12	3+2	8+2	2+2	7		1	
				£35000	7/16/91	Burnley	76+1	4	9+1	7+1	30	1	4	4
				£85000	8/20/93	Preston North End	50+7	2+1	7	2+3	22		2	
				£75000	8/9/95	Fulham	88+6	11	5+1	4	32	6	3	1
				£50000	3/26/98	Blackpool	5+1							
Garvey Stephen H	5.9	10.9	22/11/73	Stalybridge	25/10/91	Crewe Alexandra	68+40	6+7	3+4	8+3	8	2	2	1
				Free	7/1/98	Blackpool								
Longworth Steven P	5.9	11	2/6/80	Leyland	11/14/97	Blackpool (T)	0+2		0+1					
Malkin Chris LCD'90	6.3	12	6/4/67	Hoylake		Stork AFC								
				Free	7/27/87	Tranmere Rovers	184+48	20+5	9+4	26+7	59	6	2	8
				£400000	7/13/95	Millwall	46+6	5	2		14	1	1	
					10/11/96	Blackpool	21+14	0+3	2+1		4			
Nowland Adam C	5.11	11.6	7/6/81	Preston	2/20/98	Blackpool (T)	0+1							
Ormerod Brett R	5.11	11.4	10/18/76	Blackburn		Accrington Stanley								
					3/21/97	Blackpool	4+8		0+1		2			
ADDITIONAL CONTRACT PLAYERS														
Robinson Philip D					9/12/97	Blackpool (T)								

Bloomfield Road

Blackpool, Lancashire FY1 6JJ

Capacity . . . . .11,047.
Covered Standing . . . . .3,500.
Seating . . . . .3,036.
First game . . . .(League) v Gainsborough Town, 1-1, 8.9.1900.
First floodlit game . . . . .v Hearts, 2-1, 13.10.1958.

ATTENDANCES
Highest . . . . .38,098 v Wolves, Division 1, 17.9.1955.
Lowest . . . . .1,228 v Rochdale, Sherpa Van Trophy, 6.12.1988.

HOW TO GET TO THE GROUND

From the North, East and South
Leave M6 Motorway at junction 32 and follow signs to Blackpool M55. At end of motorway the ground is immediately on the right hand side of the Municipal Car Park.

Car Parking
Parking for 1,000 cars. Street Parking also available.

Nearest Railway Station
Blackpool North (01772 594 39).

USEFUL TELEPHONE NUMBERS

Club switchboard 01253 405 331
Club fax number 01253 405 011
Club shop 01253 405 331
Ticket Office 01253 404 331

Marketing Department. 01253 405 331
Internet address . wwwcyberscape.net/users/bfc/
Tangerine Call 0891 12 16 48*
*Calls cost 50p per minute at all times. Call costings correct at time of going to press.

MATCHDAY PROGRAMME

Programme Editor
. . . . . . Geoff Warburton & Roger Harrison

Number of pages. 40

Price. £1.70

Subscriptions£60 for all home programmes.

Local Newspapers
. . . . Blackpool Evening Gazette.

Local Radio Stations
. . . . . . Red Rose Radio, Radio Lancashire
. . . . Radio Wave.

MATCHDAY TICKET PRICES

South & West Paddocks
Adult £10.00
Senior Citizen £5.00
Junior (Under 16). £5.00
East Paddock
Adult £10.00
Senior Citizen £5.00
Junior (Under 16). £5.00
West Stand (Reserved Box)
Adult £12.00
Senior Citizen £8.50
Junior (Under 16). £7.50
All Other Seats (South & West Stand)
Adult £12.00
Senior Citizen £7.50
Junior (Under 16). £6.50
Executive Box
All seats standard price £24.00
West Stand and Family Block
1 Adult 1 Junior. £15.00
1 Adult 2 Junior. £18.00
2 Adult 1 Junior. £27.00
2 Adult 2 Junior. £30.00

AFC BOURNEMOUTH
(The Cherries)
NATIONWIDE LEAGUE DIVISION 2
SPONSORED BY: SEWARD ROVER - MG

1997-98 Back Row L-R: Eddie Howe, Antony griffin, Owen Coll, Dave Wells, Jimmy Glass, Steve Fletcher, Rob Murray, Franck Rolling.
Middle Row: Sean O'Driscoll (Youth Team Manager), Juston Harrington, Russell Beardsmore, Leo Cotterell, John Williams (Assistant Manager), Jamie Vincent, John O'Neill, Neil Young, Steve Hardwick (Physio).
Front Row: James Hayter, Mike Dean, Jamie Jenkins, Steve Robinson, Mel Machin (Manager), Ian Cox, John Bailey, Mark Rawlinson, David Town.

AFC BOURNEMOUTH
FORMED IN 1899
TURNED PROFESSIONAL IN 1912
LTD COMPANY IN 1914

PRESIDENT: P W Hayward
CHAIRMAN: T S Watkins
DIRECTORS
K R Dando, A H Kaye, M A Jones,
SECRETARY
Keith MacAllster
CORPORATE MANAGER
Miss D Edwards
COMMERCIAL MANAGER
Terry Lovell

MANAGER: Mel Machin
ASSISTANT MANAGER: John Williams
RESERVE TEAM MANAGER
John Williams
YOUTH TEAM MANAGER
Sean O'Driscoll
PHYSIOTHERAPIST
Steve Hardwick

STATISTICIAN FOR THE DIRECTORY
Andy Shute

This season was not about the league, or the FA Cup, or the Coca-Cola League Cup - all that mattered in the end was the Auto Windscreens Shield in which Bournemouth made it all the way to the final, and a visit to Wembley for the first time in their 99 year history.

Victories over Leyton Orient (2-0), Bristol City (1-0), Luton Town (1-0), set up a Southern Area Final against Walsall. A 2-0 away win in the first leg, had everyone convinced that Bournemouth were at Wembley. The second leg produced one of the most exciting and nerve-wrecking nights ever seen at Dean Court. Half-time 0-0, but two early goals in the second half from Walsall made the scores level on aggregate. Bournemouth then scored through an own-goal, before Walsall scored again in the 81st minute to put them ahead on away goals. All seemed lost until six minutes from the end when frenchman, Frank Rolling, scored to send Bournemouth to Wembley and spark off a pitch celebration at the end to remember for a longtime.

The final itself against Grimsby Town was a superb day out for all involved with Bournemouth - around 30,000 Bournemouth fans made the trip to Wembley (where are they on a normal Saturday?). John Bailey put Bournemouth ahead, but Grimsby scored late on to send the match to sudden death extra-time. AFCB had a couple of half-chances but Grimsby scored and it was all over, a 1-2 defeat.

As for the league campaign, Bournemouth topped the table after four league games, but from then on their results were inconsistent, and AFCB were always on the verge of the play-off places, but never quite fulfiling their potential.

In the other two "minor"(!) cup competitions Bournemouth lost to Torquay in the Coca-Cola Cup, and lost to Huddersfield, after beating Heybridge and Bristol City in the FA Cup.

ANDY SHUTE

BOURNEMOUTH

Division 2	:9th			FA CUP: 3rd Round		LC CUP: 1st Round	AWS: Runners-up

M	DATE	COMP.	VEN	OPPONENTS	RESULT	H/T	LP	GOAL SCORERS/GOAL TIMES	ATT.
1	A 09	FL	A	Northampton Town	W 2-0	0-0	5	Vincent 69, Fletcher 75	(6384)
2	12	CC 1/1	H	Torquay United	L 0-1	0-1			3215
3	15	FL	H	Wigan Athletic	W 1-0	0-0	1	Rolling 89	3799
4	23	FL	A	Oldham Athletic	L 1-2	0-1	6	Robinson 62	(4986)
5	26	CC 1/2	A	Torquay United	D 1-1	1-0		Rolling 25	(2278)
6	30	FL	H	Blackpool	W 2-0	1-0	1	Tomlinson 31, Robinson 80	4196
7	S 02	FL	H	Bristol Rovers	D 1-1	1-1	5	Robinson 20 (pen)	5550
8	05	FL	A	Gillingham	L 1-2	1-0	5	Fletcher 44	(5168)
9	13	FL	H	Luton Town	D 1-1	0-1	6	O'Neill 83	4561
10	20	FL	A	Bristol City	D 1-1	0-1	7	Robinson 83	(8330)
11	27	FL	H	Grimsby Town	L 0-1	0-0	11		3712
12	O 04	FL	A	Chesterfield	D 1-1	1-0	14	Rolling 14	(4482)
13	11	FL	A	Preston North End	W 1-0	0-0	10	Warren 72	(8531)
14	18	FL	H	Fulham	W 2-1	1-0	4	Cox 17, 65	7606
15	21	FL	H	Millwall	D 0-0	0-0	8		4752
16	25	FL	A	Burnley	D 2-2	0-1	8	Howe 59, Vincent 68	(9501)
17	N 01	FL	H	Brentford	D 0-0	0-0	7		4772
18	04	FL	A	Wrexham	L 1-2	0-2	9	Warren 89	(2462)
19	08	FL	A	Plymouth Argyle	L 0-3	0-2	12		(5067)
20	15	FAC 1	H	Heybridge Swifts	W 3-0	1-0		Beardsmore 3, Robinson 58, 66	3385
21	18	FL	H	Southend United	W 2-1	1-1	11	Fletcher 44, Warren 48	3019
22	22	FL	H	Carlisle United	W 3-2	2-1	9	Fletcher 6, Beardsmore 35, O'Neill 64	3709
23	29	FL	A	Wycombe Wanderers	D 1-1	0-0	8	Robinson 77 (pen)	(4340)
24	D 02	FL	H	York City	D 0-0	0-0	8		3365
25	07	FAC 2	H	Bristol City	W 3-1	1-0		O'Neill 79, Fletcher 89, Carey 13 (OG)	5687
26	13	FL	A	Walsall	L 1-2	0-0	10	Robinson 72	(3548)
27	20	FL	H	Watford	L 0-1	0-0	15		6081
28	26	FL	H	Gillingham	W 4-0	1-0	12	Jones 15, 88, Robinson 53, Young 78	5672
29	28	FL	A	Bristol Rovers	L 3-5	1-4	13	Jones 9, Cox 74, Robinson 84 (pen)	(7256)
30	J 10	FL	H	Northampton Town	W 3-0	0-0	11	Jones 63, Fletcher 78, Young 83	4257
31	13	FAC 3	H	Huddersfield Town	L 0-1	0-1			7385
32	17	FL	A	Blackpool	L 0-1	0-1	13		(4550)
33	20	AWS S2	H	Leyton Orient	W 2-0	0-0		Jones 47, Robinson 87 (pen)	1732
34	24	FL	H	Oldham Athletic	D 0-0	0-0	12		4079
35	27	AWS SQF	H	Bristol City	W 1-0	0-0		Vincent 80	2124
36	31	FL	A	Luton Town	W 2-1	1-0	9	Brissett 10, Fletcher 58	(5466)
37	F 06	FL	H	Bristol City	W 1-0	1-0	8	Fletcher 41	6623
38	14	FL	H	Chesterfield	W 2-0	2-0	8	Warren 13, 41	4271
39	17	AWS SSF	H	Luton Town	W 1-0	0-0		Rolling 86	5367
40	21	FL	A	Grimsby Town	L 1-2	1-0	9	Warren 24	(5456)
41	24	FL	A	Fulham	W 1-0	1-0	8	Robinson 38	(7708)
42	28	FL	H	Preston North End	L 0-2	0-2	10		5009
43	M 03	FL	H	Plymouth Argyle	D 3-3	1-2	9	Fletcher 17, 89, Vincent 80	3545
44	07	FL	A	Brentford	L 2-3	2-2	9	Rolling 36, 42	(4973)
45	10	AWS SF1	A	Walsall	W 2-0	2-0		Rolling 13, Bearsmore 30	(6017)
46	14	FL	H	Wrexham	L 0-1	0-0	10		5512
47	17	AWS SF2	H	Walsall	L 2-3	0-0		Evans 55 (og), Rolling 82	8972
48	21	FL	A	Southend United	L 3-5	0-0	12	Stein 58, Bailey 75, Fletcher 90	(4823)
49	28	FL	A	Carlisle United	W 1-0	1-0	10	Stein 22	(4951)
50	A 04	FL	H	Wycombe Wanderers	D 0-0	0-0	10		4271
51	07	FL	A	Wigan Athletic	L 0-1	0-0	11		(2798)
52	11	FL	A	York City	W 1-0	1-0	11	O'Neill 33	(2840)
53	14	FL	H	Walsall	W 1-0	0-0	9	Fletcher 71	3404
54	19	AWS F	N	Grimsby Town	L 1-2	1-0		Bailey 31	62432
55	25	FL	H	Burnley	W 2-1	0-0	10	Robinson 56, Fletcher 62	6527
56	28	FL	A	Watford	L 1-2	1-0	10	Stein 13	(12834)
57	M 02	FL	A	Millwall	W 2-1	2-1	9	Stein 45, Witter 11 (OG)	(7872)

Best Home League Attendance: 7606 V Fulham   Smallest :3019 V Southend United   Average :4708

Goal Scorers:

FL	(57)	Fletcher 12, Robinson 10, Warren 6, Jones 4, Rolling 4, Stein 4, Cox 3, O'Neill 3, Vincent 3, Young 2, Bailey 1, Beardsmore 1, Brissett 1, Howe 1, Tomlinson 1, Opponents 1
CC	(1)	Rolling 1
FAC	(6)	Robinson 2, Beardsmore 1, Fletcher 1, O'Neill 1, Opponents 1
AWS	(8)	Rolling 3, Bailey 1, Beardsmore 1, Jones 1, Robinson 1, Vincent 1

1997-98

(F) Bailey	(M) Beardsmore	(F) Brissett	(F) Cox	(M) Dean	(F) Fletcher S	(M) Fletcher C	(G) Glass	(M) Griffin	(F) Harrington	(F) Hayter	(D) Howe	(F) Jones	(F) Murray	(F) O'Neill	(M) Rawlinson	(F) Robinson	(D) Rolling	(F) Stein	(M) Teather	(M) Tomlinson	(F) Town	(D) Vincent	(M) Warren	(G) Wells	(D) Young		
X	X	S	X		X		X				S			X	X	X	X			S1		X			X	E. Lomas	1
X		S1	X		X		X				X			S3	X	X	X				S2	X			X	R D Furnandiz	2
X		S1	X		X		X		S2	S	X			X	X	X	X					X			X	A N Butler	3
X	S	S1	X		X		X			S				X	X	X	X					X			X	G Laws	4
X	X	S1	X		X		X		S3		S2			X	X	X	X					X			X	R J Harris	5
X	X	S1	X				X			S		S	S	X	X	X	X			X		X			X	A P D'Urso	6
X	X	S2	X				X			S1		S3		X	X	X	X			X		X			X	R Styles	7
	X		X		X		X		S	S		S1		X	X	X	X			X1		X			X	S G Bennett	8
X	X		X		X		X		S	S1		S2		X		X	X			X		X			X	C R Wilkes	9
X	X	S1	X		X		X			X		S	S2	X		X				X		X			X	M Fletcher	10
X	X	S2	X		X		X		S	S1				X	X	X				X		X			X	P Taylor	11
X	X	S1	X		X		X		S	S2				X	X	X						X			X	A Bates	12
X	X	S	X		X		X		S	X				S	X	X						X	X		X	J P Robinson	13
X	X	S	X		X		X		S	X				S1	X	X						X	X		X	F G Stretton	14
	X	S1	X		X		X		S	X				X	X	X						X	X	S	X	D Orr	15
	X	S2	X		X		X		S	X				X	X	S1						X	X		X	M L Dean	16
	X	X	X		X		X			X				S2	S1	S3	X	X				X	X		X	B Coddington	17
	X	X	X		X		X		S	X				S2	S1	X	X					X	X		X	M D Messias	18
	X	S1	X	S2	X		X			X				X	X	X	S3					X	X		X	F Taylor	19
	X	S	X		X		X		S1	X		S	X	X	X	S2				X	X	S	X	S G Bennett	20
	X		X		X		X		X	X				X	S1	X	S		S	X	X		X	D R Crick	21
	X		X		X		X		X	X				X	S1	X	S		S2	X	X		X	M J Brandwood	22
	X		X		X		X		X1	X				X	S	X	S		S1	X	X		X	P S Danson	23
S1	X		X		X		X		X1	X				X		X			S2	X	X2		X	R J Harris	24
X	X1	S	X		X		X		S	X				X	S1	X			S	X	X	S	X	M R Halsey	25
X			X	S	X		X		X	X		S1		X	X1	X	S				X	X		X	C R Wilkes	26
X			X	S	X		X		S2	X			X1	X		S1	X2				X	X		X	E Lomas	27
		X	X2		X		X		S2	X	X		X1	X		S1	X1				X	X		X	A Bates	28
		S2	X3		X		X		S1	X	X		X1	X2		S3					X	X		X	C J Foy	29
		X	X		X	S	S		X	X	X		X	X		S	X				X	X		X	M C Bailey	30
S2		X	X		X		X1	S	X		S3	X2		X	S1					X3	X	S	X	P Rejer	31
32	S1	X	X		X		X		S3		X	X1	X2		X						X3		X	S W Mathieson	32
		S2	X	X1	X		X			X	X2	S1		X		X				X	X	X				33
X	X1	X	X		X		X		S	X	X		X		X		S			X	S1	X			A P D'Urso	34
X	X2	X	X		X		X		S2	X			X		X		S1			X	X1	X			35
X	X1	X	X		X		X		S	S			X		X		S1			X	X	X		R D Furnandiz	36
X	X1	X	X		X		X		S	S			X		X	X	S1			X	X	X		P Rejer	37
X	X2	X	X		X		X		S1				X	S3	X	X	S2			X1	X	X		M R Halsey	38
X		X	X		X		X						X	X	X	X					X	X			39
X	X2	X	X		X	S2	X		S3				X3	X1	X	X	S1				X	X		K M Lynch	40
X	X1	X	X		X		X		S1	S2			X		X	X	S				X	X		K A Leach	41
X	X2	X	X		X		X			S1			X1		X	X		S2	X	X		X	P Taylor	42
X		X	X	S3	X		X		S1				X2		X	X	X1	S2	X3			X		A N Butler	43
X	S3	X	X		X		X		S2				X2		X	X	X	S1		X	X1	X		B Coddington	44
X	X	X	X		X		X		S1				X1		X	X	X				X	X		45
X3	X	S3	X		X		X		S2				X1	S1	X	X	X			X2		X		G Singh	46
X	X	X	X		X		X		S1				X1		X	X	X				X	X		47
X	X	S3	X3		X		X		X				S2	S1	X	X2	X			X1		X		A Bates	48
	X	S	X	X	X		X		X				S	S	X	X					X	X		M L Dean	49
	X3	X	X	X1	X		X		X				S2	X2	X	X			S1	S3				M Fletcher	50
X2	X	X	S		X		X		X				S2		X	X1	X		S1	X				D Pugh	51
X	S1	X	X		X		X		X				X	S	S	X				X	X1	X		G Singh	52
X3	X	S1	X	S3	X		X		X				S2		X		X1			X	X2	X		P S Danson	53
X	X1	S2	X		X		X		X				S1		X		X			X	X2	X		54
X	X	S1	X	S	X		X		X				S2		X	X2				X1	X			D R Crick	55
X	X1	S3	X	S1	X		X		X					X	X1	X				X	X		S1	A R Hall	56
X2	X	S1	X		X		X		X				S2		X		X			S	X1	X		S W Mathieson	57
30	**28**	**13**	**46**	**3**	**42**	**0**	**46**	**4**			**31**	**5**	**34**	**16**	**45**	**26**	**11**	**5**	**6**		**43**	**29**			**43**	FL Appearances	
2	1	18		5		1		4	5	9	4	9	9	4	5	1	7	1		1	1					FL Sub Appearances	
2	1	0+2	2		2		2		0+1		1+1		0+1	2	2	2	2			0+1	2				2	CC Appearances	
1+1	2	1	3		3		3		1+1		3		0+1	3	1+1	3	0+2				3	3			3	FAC Appearances	
5	3	2+2	6	1	6		6		0+1	3+2	1	4+2	1	6	3	1+1					5	4			6	AWS Appearances	

AFC BOURNEMOUTH RECORDS AND STATISTICS

CLUB RECORDS

BIGGEST VICTORIES
League: 7-0 v Swindon Town, Division 3(S), 22.9.1956.
Most Goals Scored in a Cup Tie: 11-0 v Margate, FA Cup, 20.11.1971.

BIGGEST DEFEATS
League: 0-9 v Lincoln City, Division 3, 1.12.1982.
Most Goals conceded in a Cup Tie: 0-7 v Burnley, FA Cup 3rd Round Replay, 1965-66.
0-7 v Sheffield Wednesday, FA Cup 4th Round, 1931-32.

MOST POINTS
3 points a win: 97, Division 3, 1986-87.
2 points a win: 62, Division 3, 1971-72.

RECORD TRANSFER FEE RECEIVED
£800,000 from Everton for Joe Parkinson, March 1994.

RECORD TRANSFER FEE PAID
£300,000 to Manchester City for Paul Moulden, July 1989.

BEST PERFORMANCES
League: 12th Division 2, 1988-89.
FA Cup: 6th Round, 1956-57.
League Cup: 4th Round, 1961-62, 1963-64.

HONOURS
Division 3 Champions 1986-87.
Associate Members Cup 1983-84.

LEAGUE CAREER
Elected to Div.3(S) 1923, Transferred to Div.3 1957-58, Relegated to Div.4 1969-70, Promoted to Div.3 1970-71, Relegated to Div.4 1974-75, Promoted to Div.3 1981-82, Promoted to Div.2 1986-87, Relegated to Div.3 (now Div.2) 1989-90.

INDIVIDUAL CLUB RECORDS

MOST GOALS IN A SEASON
Ted MacDougall - 49, 1970-71 (League 42, FA Cup 7).

MOST GOALS IN A MATCH
Ted MacDougall - 9 v Margate, FA Cup 1st Rnd. (11-0) 20.11.1971 (All time FA Cup record).

OLDEST PLAYER
Harry Kinghorn, 48 years v Brentford, 11.3.1929.

YOUNGEST PLAYER
Jimmy White, 15 years v Brentford, 30.4.1958.

MOST CAPPED PLAYER
Gerry Peyton (Eire) 7.

PREVIOUS MANAGERS

Harry Kinghorn 1920-25, Leslie Knighton 1925-28, Frank Richards 1928-30, Billy Birrell 1930-35, Bob Crompton 1935-36, Charles Bell 1936-39, Harry Kinghorn 1939-47, Harry Lowe 1947-50, Jack Bruton 1950-56, Freddie Cox 1956-58, Don Welsh 1958-61, Bill McGarry 1961-63, Reg Flewin 1963-65, Freddie Cox 1965-70, John Bond 1970-73, Trevor Hartley 1973-75, John Benson 1975-79, Alec Stock 1979-80, Dave Webb 1980-82, Don Megson 1982, Harry Redknapp 1983-92, Tony Pullis 1992-94.

ADDITIONAL INFORMATION
Previous League: Southern League.

Previous Names: Boscombe St Johns 1899.
Boscombe FC 1899-1923. Bournemouth & Boscombe AFC 1923-72.

Club colours: Red & black striped shirts, white shorts & white socks.

Change colours: Yellow & blue halves shirts blue shorts & socks.

Reserves League: Avon Insurance League Division 1.

LONGEST LEAGUE RUNS

of undefeated matches:	18 (1982)	of league matches w/out a win:	14 (1973-74)
of undefeated home matches:	33 (1962-63)	of undefeated away matches:	13 (1961)
without home win:	10 (1931-32)	without an away win:	26 (1976-77)
of league wins:	7 (1970)	of home wins:	12 (1968, 1971)
of league defeats:	7 (1955)	of away wins:	5 (1948)

THE MANAGER

MEL MACHIN . . . . appointed September 1994.

PREVIOUS CLUBS
As Manager . . . . Manchester City, Barnsley.
As Asst.Man/Coach . . . . Norwich City.
As a player . . . . Port Vale, Gillingham, Bournemouth, Norwich City.

HONOURS
As a Manager . . . . None.
As a Player . . . . None.

BOURNEMOUTH | APPEARANCES | GOALS

PLAYERS NAME / Honours	Ht	Wt	Birthdate	Birthplace / Transfers	Contract Date	Clubs	League	L/Cup	FA Cup	Other	Lge	L/C	FAC	Oth
G O A L K E E P E R														
Colgan Nick	6.1	13.6	9/19/73	Drogheda	10/1/92	Chelsea (T)	1							
Ei: B.1, u21.9, Y, S.				Loan	10/16/97	Brentford	5							
				Loan	2/27/98	Reading	5							
				Free	7/1/98	Bournemouth								
Ovendale Mark J	6.2	13.2	11/22/73	Leicester		Wisbech Town								
				Free	8/15/94	Northampton Town	6			2				
via Barry Town				£30000	5/14/98	Bournemouth								
D E F E N C E														
Howe Eddie	5.9	11.2	11/29/77	Newport IW	7/4/96	Bournemouth (T)	42+16	1+1	3	3+2	1			
E: u21.2.														
Hughes Richard	5.9	9.12	6/25/79	Glasgow		Atlanta								
				Free	01/08/97	Arsenal								
				£20000	8/1/98	Bournmouth								
Griffin Anthony R	5.11	11.2	3/22/79	Bournemouth	4/26/97	Bournemouth (T)	1							
Jenkins Jamie	5.8	10.7	1/1/79	Pontypool	7/10/97	Bournemouth (T)								
Rolling Franck	6.1	14	8/23/68	Colmar (France)		Ayr United								
				£100000	6/1/95	Leicester City	18	4	0+1					
					8/8/97	Bournemouth	26+4	2	0+2		4	1		
Tindall Jason	6.1	11.10	11/15/77	Mile End		Charlton Ath. (T)								
				Free	7/1/98	Bournemouth								
Vincent Jamie R	5.11	11.6	6/18/75	London	7/13/93	Crystal Palace	19+6	2+1	1			1		
					8/30/96	Bournemouth	71+2	2+1	4		3			
Young Neil	5.8	10.5	8/31/73	Harlow	8/17/91	Tottenham Hotspur								
				Free	10/11/94	Bournemouth	159+1	7	9	4	2			
M I D F I E L D														
Bailey John	5.8	10.8	5/6/69	Lambeth		Enfield								
				£40000	8/5/95	Bournemouth	106+10	6+1	5+1	8+1	6			1
Beardsmore Russell	5.6	9	9/28/68	Wigan	10/2/86	Manchester United	30+26	3+1	4+4	2+5	4			
E: u21.5. ESC'91.				Loan	12/19/91	Blackburn Rovers	1+1							
				Free	6/29/93	Bournemouth	167+11	14	9	5	4		1	
Berthe Mohamed			9/12/72	Guyana		Gaz Ajaccio								
						West Ham United								
				Free	7/1/98	Bournemouth								
Dean Michael	5.9	11.1	3/9/78	Weymouth		Bournemouth	17+8		1					
Fletcher Carl N	5.10	11.7	4/7/80	Surrey Heath	2/20/98	Bournemouth (T)	2+1							
Rawlinson Mark	5.8	11.11	6/9/75	Bolton	7/5/93	Manchester United								
				Free	7/1/95	Bournemouth	41+27	2+1	2+1	1	2			
F O R W A R D														
Cox Ian G	6	12.2	3/25/71	Croydon		Crystal Palace								
						Whyteleafe								
						Carshalton Athletic								
				£35000	3/8/94	Crystal Palace	1+10		1+1					
				Free	3/28/96	Bournemouth	97	4	4		11			
Fletcher Steven	6	12.1	6/26/72	Hartlepool	8/23/90	Hartlepool United	19+13	0+2	1+2	2+2	4	1		1
				£30000	7/28/92	Bournemouth	173+15	15	8	3	36	2	1	
Hayter James E	5.9	10.13	4/9/79	Newport	3/27/97	Bournemouth (T)	0+7							
Robinson Stephen	5.8	10.7	12/10/74	Lisburn	1/27/93	Tottenham Hotspur	1+1							
NI: B, u21.6,Y,S.				Free	10/20/94	Bournemouth	144+13	6	8+1	4	30		3	1
Stein Mark	5.6	11.10	1/29/66	Capetown	1/31/84	Luton Town (T)	41+13	4+1	9	3	19		3	1
E: Y. LC'88. AMC'92. Div.2'93.				Loan	1/29/86	Aldershot	2				1			
				£300000	8/26/88	QPR	20+13	4	2+1	4	4	2	1	
					9/15/89	Oxford United	72+10	4	2+1	3	18			
				£100000	9/15/91	Stoke City	94	8	4	17	50	8		10
				£1500000	10/28/93	Chelsea	46+4	0+1	9	2+1	21		2	2
				Loan	11/22/96	Stoke City	11				4			
				Loan	8/22/97	Ipswich Town	6+1	3+1			2	1		
				Loan	3/4/98	Bournemouth	11			3	4			
				Free	7/1/98	Bournemouth								
Town David	5.8	11.7	12/9/76	Bournemouth	7/14/94	Bournemouth	1/+23	0+4		0+1	2			
Warren Christer	5.1	11.3	10/10/74	Bournemouth		Cheltenham Town								
				£40000	31/03/95	Southampton	1+7	1						
				Loan	11/10/96	Brighton & H.A.	3							
				Loan	06/03/97	Fulham	8+3				1			
				£50000	10/8/97	Bournemouth	29+1		3	4	6			

DEAN COURT GROUND
Bournemouth, Dorset BH7 7AF

Capacity ....11,000.

First game ....In the League - 01.09.1923.
First floodlit game ....v Northampton 27.09.1961.

ATTENDANCES
Highest ....28,799 v Manchester United, FA Cup 6th Round, 02.03.1957.
Lowest ....1,218 v Reading, Autoglass Trophy, 05.01.1993.

OTHER GROUNDS......................................Castleman Road, Pokedown 1899-1910. Dean Court 1910-

HOW TO GET TO THE GROUND

From the North and East
A338 to roundabout junction with A3060. Take second exit, then first from next roundabout into Littledown Avenue. Turn right into Thistlebarrow Road for Dean Court.

From the West
A3049 to Bournemouth. In 2 miles after, lights at Wallisdown, turn left into Talbot Road. Take first exit from roundabout into Queens Park South Drive, then second exit from next roundabout into Littledown Avenue. Turn right into Thistle Road for Dean Court.

Car Parking: Parking for 1,500 cars.

Nearest Railway Station: Bournemouth. Tel: 01202 558 216.

USEFUL TELEPHONE NUMBERS

Club switchboard 01202 395 381
Ticket Office 01202 395 381
Marketing department 01202 395 381

Clubcall 0891 12 11 63*
*Calls cost 50p per minute at all times.
Call costings correct at time of going to press.

MATCHDAY PROGRAMME

Programme Editor (97/98)Mike Cunningham.

Number of pages (97/98) ....40.

Price (97/98)......................................£1.50.

Subscriptions (97/98) ....£43.

Local Newspapers
....Evening Echo.

Local Radio Stations
.....Two Counties Radio, BBC Radio Solent.

MATCHDAY TICKET PRICES (1997/98)
Adults . . . . £7 - £15
Juniors. . . . . £3 - £9

1883

BRISTOL ROVERS
(The Pirates or The Gas)
NATIONWIDE LEAGUE DIVISION 2
SPONSORED BY: COWLIN CONSTRUCTION

1998-99 - Back Row (L-R): Lee Zabek, Trevor Challis, Jamie Shore, Barry Hayles, Mark Smith, Geraint Bater, JAmie Cureton, Frankie Bennett, Robert Trees, Luke Basford. **Middle Row:** Roger Brinsford (Secretary) Roy Dolling (Yth. Dev. Manager), Steve Foster, Rob Claridge, Peter BEadle (now Port Vale), Andy Collett, Tom White, Lee Jones, MAecus Andreasson, Andy Tillson, James French, Josh Low, Phil Kite (Physio), Toni Watloa (Company Secretary). **Front Row:** Rod Wesson (Director of Yth), John Gingell (Fitness coach), Ron Craig (Director), Ian Holloway (Player/manager), Geoff Dunford (Vice-Chairman), Gary Penrice (player/coach), Barry Bradshaw (Director), Ray Kendall (Kit manager), Phil Bater (Director of Yth. Football).

BRISTOL ROVERS
FORMED IN 1883
TURNED PROFESSIONAL IN 1897
LTD COMPANY IN 1896

PRESIDENT: Marquis of Worcester
CHAIRMAN: Denis M H Dunford
DIRECTORS
R Craig, G H M Dunford (Vice-chairman)
V B Stokes, R Andrews, C Jelf, B Bradshaw
SECRETARY
Roger Brinsford
COMMERCIAL MANAGER
Graham Bowen (0117 986 9999)

MANAGER: Ian Holloway
PLAYER-COACH: Gary Penrice
DIRECTOR OF YOUTH FOOTBALL
Phil Bater
PHYSIOTHERAPIST
Phil Kite

STATISTICIAN FOR THE DIRECTORY
Mike Jay

So close, yet so far....that was the sorry end to the 1997-98 season for Bristol Rovers, who would have given everything to be playing alongside their arch rivals Bristol City in the First Division this season.

As it is, they will have to spend another campaign in Division Two after failing to overcome Northampton Town in the play-off semi-final which resulted in them missing out on a Wembley showdown with Grimsby Town and possible promotion at the end of the day.

Throughout 1997-98, the Pirates were always challenging for a top six place and they achieved this reasonably comfortably with a total of 70 points to finish in fifth place.

Only promoted Watford and Bristol City recorded more League wins than Rovers' 20, and, in fact, no team scored more goals than the 70 claimed by Rovers, who on the other hand lost 16, more or equal than any of the other teams finishing in the top 10.

But then once into the play-offs they were confident of winning through to Wembley after claiming a 2-0 first-leg advantage. But in the return fixture at Sixfields, the Cobblers bounced back in style and over-ran the Pirates to go through 3-2 on aggregate - much to the disappointment of player-manager Ian Holloway, his players and the team's supporters.

Barry Hayles top-scored for Rovers with 25 goals (including one in the play-off semi-final) and there is no doubt that he had a fine season, being watched by several Premiership and First Division club scouts on numerous occasions.

Rovers' boss Ian Holloway will certainly want to hold onto Hayles and hopefully build around the strong, former Stevenage Borough striker ......and then push on again towards his goal - that of winning promotion to the First Division.

Tony Matthews.

BRISTOL ROVERS

Division 2   :5th   FA CUP: 3rd Round   LC CUP: 1st Round   AWS: Southern Quarter-finals

M	DATE	COMP.	VEN	OPPONENTS	RESULT	H/T	LP	GOAL SCORERS/GOAL TIMES	ATT.
1	A 09	FL	H	Plymouth Argyle	D 1-1	1-0	10	Hayles 41	7386
2	12	CC 1/1	A	Bristol City	D 0-0	0-0			(9341)
3	13	FL	H	Gillingham	L 1-2	0-0	10	Hayles 52	6572
4	15	FL	A	York City	W 1-0	0-0	4	Hayles 56	(3307)
5	23	FL	H	Carlisle United	W 3-1	2-1	3	Bennett 9, Hayles 20, Penrice 46	6044
6	26	CC 1/2	H	Bristol City	L 1-2	0-0		Alsop 48	5872
7	30	FL	A	Burnley	D 0-0	0-0	4		(9887)
8	S 02	FL	A	Bournemouth	D 1-1	1-1	7	Cureton 29 (pen)	(5550)
9	09	FL	H	Walsall	W 2-0	1-0	4	Ramasut 21, Hayles 65	6225
10	20	FL	A	Chesterfield	D 0-0	0-0	5		(5309)
11	27	FL	A	Oldham Athletic	D 4-4	3-3	5	Beadle 29, 33, Hayles 45, Cureton 86 (pen)	(5990)
12	O 04	FL	H	Wrexham	W 1-0	0-0	3	Ramasut 55	6829
13	14	FL	H	Watford	L 1-2	0-0	5	Penrice 83	8110
14	18	FL	A	Wycombe Wanderers	L 0-1	0-0	10		(5836)
15	21	FL	A	Brentford	W 3-2	2-1	6	Hayles 12, 71, Beadle 17	(3967)
16	25	FL	H	Blackpool	L 0-3	0-1	10		6183
17	N 01	FL	A	Northampton Town	D 1-1	0-0	9	Cureton 79	(7264)
18	04	FL	H	Bristol City	L 1-2	0-1	12	Tilson 85	7552
19	08	FL	H	Fulham	L 2-3	0-1	14	Penrice 61, 78	6166
20	14	FAC 1	H	Gillingham	D 2-2	1-1		Alsop 19, Holloway 87	4825
21	18	FL	A	Preston North End	W 2-1	1-0	12	Penrice 10, Alsop 57	(7798)
22	22	FL	A	Southend United	D 1-1	0-1	13	Beadle 85	(3653)
23	25	FAC 1R	A	Gillingham	W 2-0	2-0		Hayles 14, Penrice 28	(4459)
24	29	FL	H	Millwall	W 2-1	1-0	10	Beadle 10, Hayles 80	5542
25	D 02	FL	A	Wigan Athletic	L 0-3	0-1	11		(2738)
26	06	FAC 2	A	Wisbech	W 2-0	0-0		Beadle 52, Hayles 78	(3593)
27	08	AWS S1	H	Cambridge United	W 1-0	0-0		Cureton 46	2386
28	12	FL	H	Grimsby Town	L 0-4	0-2	12		4801
29	20	FL	A	Luton Town	W 4-2	4-2	10	Cureton 12, Hayles 21, 37, Beadle 31	(5266)
30	26	FL	A	Walsall	W 1-0	0-0	8	Beadle 48	(6634)
31	28	FL	A	Bournemouth	W 5-3	4-1	5	Beadle 15, 26, 43, Hayles 28, 75	7256
32	J 03	FAC 3	H	Ipswich Town	D 1-1	1-0		Beadle 36	8610
33	10	FL	A	Plymouth Argyle	W 2-1	2-0	3	Cureton 23, Hayles 27	6850
34	13	FAC 3R	A	Ipswich Town	L 0-1	0-1			(11362)
35	14	AWS S2	A	Exeter City	W 2-1	2-0		Bennett 19, Tillson 45	(1851)
36	17	FL	H	Burnley	W 1-0	0-0	3	Cureton 50	7208
37	24	FL	H	Carlisle United	L 1-3	0-2	4	Cureton 55	(5725)
38	28	AWS SQF	H	Walsall	L 0-1	0-0			4165
39	31	FL	A	Gillingham	D 1-1	1-1	5	Cureton 38 (pen)	(5593)
40	F 06	FL	H	Chesterfield	W 3-1	1-1	4	Bennett 13, Cureton 68, 89	5481
41	14	FL	A	Wrexham	L 0-1	0-1	7		(3716)
42	21	FL	H	Oldham Athletic	W 3-1	2-0	6	Hayles 43, 79, Ramasut 44	5789
43	24	FL	H	Wycombe Wanderers	W 3-1	0-0	4	Hayles 51, Beadle 58, Ramasut 81	5805
44	28	FL	A	Watford	L 2-3	0-2	5	White 51, Cureton 81	(12186)
45	M 03	FL	A	Fulham	L 0-1	0-0	7		(6878)
46	07	FL	H	Northampton Town	L 0-2	0-1	8		6535
47	10	FL	H	York City	L 1-2	0-1	8	Ramasut 52	4289
48	14	FL	A	Bristol City	L 0-2	0-1	8		(17086)
49	21	FL	H	Preston North End	D 2-2	0-1	8	Cureton 71, Hayles 75	5278
50	27	FL	H	Southend United	W 2-0	0-0	8	Tillson 62, Hayles 75	5323
51	A 04	FL	A	Millwall	D 1-1	0-0	8	Zabek 88	(5635)
52	10	FL	H	Wigan Athletic	W 5-0	3-0		Hayles 25, Ramasut 31, Beadle 45, 51, 56	6038
53	13	FL	A	Grimsby Town	W 2-1	2-1	7	Hayles 39, 42	(5484)
54	18	FL	H	Luton Town	W 2-1	2-0	5	Beadle 5, Tilson 32	8038
55	25	FL	A	Blackpool	L 0-1	0-0	7		(7057)
56	M 02	FL	H	Brentford	W 2-1	0-0	5	Cureton 51, Hayles 84	9043
57	10	PO SF1	H	Northampton Town	W 3-1	2-0		Beadle 30, Bennett 37, Hayles 46	9173
58	13	PO SF2	A	Northampton Town	L 0-3	0-1			(7501)

Best Home League Attendance: 9043 V Brentford   Smallest :4289 V York City   Average :6462

Goal Scorers:

FL	(70)	Hayles 23, Beadle 15, Cureton 13, Ramasut 6, Penrice 5, Tilson 3, Bennett 2, Alsop 1, White 1, Zabek 1
CC	(1)	Alsop 1
FAC	(7)	Beadle 2, Hayles 2, Alsop 1, Holloway 1, Penrice 1
AWS	(3)	Bennett 1, Cureton 1, Tillson 1
PO	(3)	Beadle 1, Bennett 1, Hayles 1

(F) Alsop	(M) Basford	(F) Beadle	(F) Bennett	(G) Collett	(F) Cureton	(M) Foster	(F) French	(D) Gayle	(D) Hayfield	(M) Hayles	(G) Higgs	(M) Holloway	(G) Jones	(M) Lockwood	(F) Low	(F) Parmenter	(F) Penrice	(D) Perry	(D) Power	(D) Pritchard	(F) Ramasut	(M) Skinner	(M) Smith	(D) Tilson	(D) White	(M) Whyte	(M) Zabek		
X		S3		X	X	S1		X		X		X						X	X	X			S2	X				M. Fletcher	1
X	X	S1	X	X	X		X			X	S	X						X	X						X	S		G Cain	2
S2	X	S1	X	X				X		X		X						X	X	X	X				X	S		P S Danson	3
X	S	X	X	X			X			X		X						X	X		S1				X	X		G B Frankland	4
X		S1	X	X			X			X		X						X	X		S				X	X		G Singh	5
X		S1	X	X	X		X			X	S	X		S2				X	X	X				X				P Rejer	6
X		X	X	X		S		X		X		X						X	X		X	S1		X				T Heilbron	7
X		S1	X	X		S		X		X		X						X	X		S2				X			R Styles	8
S		X	X	X				X		X		X			S			X	X		X			X	S			M E Pierce	9
S		X	S1	X				X		X		X						X	X	X				X			S	D Pugh	10
S		X	S1	X				X		X	X	X	X					X	X					X				A Bates	11
S		X	S1	X	X			X		X		X						X	X					X		S2		J A Kirkby	12
X		X	X	X			X		X		X			S	S1			X	X	S				X				M L Dean	13
X		X	X	X	S1		X		X		X				X			X	X	S				X		S		A R Leake	14
S		X	S	X	S		X		X		X				X			X	X		X			X				M R Halsey	15
S3		X	S1	X			X		X		X			X	S2			X	X		X			X				B Knight	16
S		X	S1	X	X		X		X		X			X	S			X		X				X				S W Mathieson	17
S2		X	X	X	X	X	X		X		X			X	S			X		X				X	S1			M C Bailey	18
X		X	X	X	S		S		X		X			X				X	X	S1				X	X			M J Jones	19
X		X	S	X	S2		X		X	S	X			X	S1			X		X				X	X		S	G Singh	20
X		X	S1	X		S		X		X		X	X	S2			X							X	X			B Coddington	21
X	S1	X	X			X		X		X		X	X	S3	X	S2		X						X	X			M Fletcher	22
S		X	X	S	S1		X	X	S	X		X		X	X			X	X					X	X			G Singh	23
S1		X	X	S			X		X		X		S2	X	X2	X1		X						X	X			A R Hall	24
S3		X	X			X1	X		X		S2		X2	X	S1	X3		X		X				X	X			K M Lynch	25
S		X	X	S			X	X	S	X		X		X	X			X	X					X	X			A P D'Urso	26
S3	X	X		X				S3	X	X		S2	X	X2		X		X				X1	S1						27
S2	X	X		X	S1			X1	X		S3		X	X3		X2			X				X	X				S G Bennett	28
S	S1	X	X	X	X			X	X		X		X		X			X			X1		X					D Orr	29
S		X	X	X1	X			S1	X		X		X		X			X	X		X	S		X				D R Crick	30
S2	S1	X		X	X			S	X2		X1		X		X			X						X				C J Foy	31
	S	X	S1	X	X	X		S	X	S	X		X		X			X			X1			S	X			M R Halsey	32
		X	S1	X	X3	X		X			X		X2		X			X			X1		33	X		S?		G Singh	33
		X	S2	X	X2			S3	X	S	X		X		X			X	S1		X1	X3		X			X	M R Halsey	34
X1	X	S1	X	X			X		X	S2			X	X2								X	X			X			35
X1	X	S1	X	X	X			S2	X2		X		X		X			X	X					X		S		R Styles	36
X1	X	S1	X	X	X			S2	X		X		X2					X	X					X	S1	S		T Heilbron	37
	X	X1		X	X				X	X	X		X		X			X	X					X	S1				38
X		S2		X	X			X1	X2	X	X		S1		S			X						X			X	J P Robinson	39
X2	X	X3		X	X			S3	X	X	X							S1	X		S2			X			X1	D R Crick	40
		X3		X	X			X	X	X			S1					X	X1	S1	X			X	S3		X1	S W Mathieson	41
		X1		X	X			S1	X	X								X2		X	X	X	X2	X	S		S2	M E Pierce	42
		X		X	X			S	X	X	S1							X1		X	X	X	X	X	S2			M J Jones	43
		X		X	X			S	X	X	S2							X2		X	X	X1	X	X	S1			K A Leach	44
		X		X	X			S	X	X	X				S2					X	X	X1		X	X2	S1		R J Harris	45
		X	X2	X	X			S	X		X	X			S2			X	X		X1			X			S1	P Rejer	46
		X		X	X	X		S1	X		X				S			X	X	X1		X			X		S	A Bates	47
		X	S1	X	X			S2	X		X				X1			X	X2	X	X			X	S			E Lomas	48
		X	S	X	X			X1	X		X				X			X	X	X	S1			X	S			A P D'Urso	49
		X		X2	X			S1	X		X	X			X			X	X	X	X1			X	S2				51
		X	S1	X	X			S	X		X	X	S		X			X	X	X	X1			X			X	P S Danson	51
		X	S	X	X			S	X	X	X				X			S		X	X			X			X	S J Baines	52
		X	S	X	X			X		X	X	X			S			S	S	X	X			X			X	C J Foy	53
		X	S	X	X			X		X	X	X			S			S	S	X	X			X			X	A R Leake	54
		X	S	X	X			X		X	X	X1			S1			S1	S	X	X			X			X	F G Stretton	55
		X	S2	X2	X			S1	X		X				X			X	S	X	X1			X			X	D Pugh	56
		X	X1		X			S1	X		X	X			X			X	S	S2	X	X2		X			X	R J Harris	57
		X	X2		X			S2	X		X	X			X			X	S	S1	X	X1		X			X	M Fletcher	58
10	5	36	8	30	39	32	2	16	9	45	8	34	8	22	6	1	38	24	9	32	25	4	32	22	9			FL Appearances	
7	2	4	11		4	2	1	9				5			2	4	3	2	1	1	6			1	2	4	4	FL Sub Appearances	
2		1+1	1+1	2	2	1		2		2		2		0+1			2	2		1			2					CC Appearances	
1		4	0+2	5	2	3	0+2	3+1	5		3		5	2+1		5	2+1		5	2			3	5				FAC Appearances	
2	3	2+1	1	1	2	2		1	1+2	2	2		2+1	2	1	1	2		1	2			1+1	1	0+1	1		AWS Appearances	
		2	2		2			0+2	2			2		2	2				0+2	2	2			2			2	PO Appearances	

BRISTOL ROVERS   RECORDS AND STATISTICS

CLUB RECORDS

BIGGEST VICTORIES
League: 7-0 v Swansea City, Division 2, 2.10.1954.
7-0 v Brighton & Hove Albion, Division 3(S), 29.11.1952.
7-0 v Shrewsbury Town, Division 3, 21.3.1964.
F.A. Cup: 6-0 v Merthyr Tydfil, Round 1, 14.11.1987.

BIGGEST DEFEATS
League: 0-12 v Luton Town, Division 3(S), 13.4.1936.
F.A. Cup: 1-8 v Queens Park Rangers, 27.11.1937.

MOST POINTS
3 points a win: 93, Division 3, 1989-90.
2 points a win: 64, Division 3(S), 1952-53.

MOST GOALS SCORED
92, Division 3(S), 1952-53.

RECORD TRANSFER FEE RECEIVED
£1,400,000 from Huddersfield for Marcus Stewart, July 1996.

RECORD TRANSFER FEE PAID
£370,000 to Queens Park Rangers for Andy Tillson, November 1992.

BEST PERFORMANCES
League: 6th in Division 2, 1955-56, 1958-59.
Highest Position:
F.A. Cup: 6th Round 1950-51, 1957-58.
League Cup: 5th Round, 1970-71, 1971-72.

HONOURS
Division 3 South Cup 1934-35.
Champions of Division 3(S), 1952-53.
Champions of Division 3, 1989-90.

LEAGUE CAREER
Original members of Div 3 1920, Transferred to Div 3 South 1921, Div 2 1952-53, Div 3 1961-62, Div 2 1973-74, Div 3 1980-81, Div 2 (now Div 1) 1989-90, Div 2 1992-93.

INDIVIDUAL CLUB RECORDS

MOST GOALS IN A SEASON
Alfie Biggs: 37 goals in 1963-64 (League 30, FA Cup 1, League Cup 6).

MOST GOALS IN A MATCH
6. Jack Jones v Weymouth, FA Cup, 15-1, 17.11.1900.

OLDEST PLAYER
Jack Evans, 39 years, 9.4.1928.

YOUNGEST PLAYER
Ronnie Dix, 15 years 180 days v Norwich City, 3.3.1928.
(Youngest player to score in the Football League, in his second match).

MOST CAPPED PLAYER
Neil Slatter (Wales) 10, 1983-85.
Geoff Bradford (England) 1, 1955.

PREVIOUS MANAGERS

1899-1920 Alf Homer; 1920-21 Ben Hall; 1921-26 Andrew Wilson; 1926-29 Joe Palmer; 1929-30 David McLean; 1930-36 Albert Prince Cox; 1936-37 Percy Smith; 1938-49 Brough Fletcher; 1950-68 Bert Tann; 1968-69 Fred Ford; 1969-72 Bill Dodgin; 1972-77 Don Megson; 1977-79 Bobby Campbell; 1979-80 Harold Jarman; 1980-81 Terry Cooper; 1981-83 Bobby Gould; 1983-85 David Williams; 1985-87 Bobby Gould, 1987-91 Gerry Francis; 1991 Martin Dobson; 1991-92 Dennis Rofe; 1992-93 Malcolm Allison, 1993-96 John Ward.

ADDITIONAL INFORMATION
Previous Names: Black Arabs, Eastville Rovers.
Previous Leagues: Southern League.

Club colours: Blue & white quartered shirts, white shorts, blue socks.
Change colours: Yellow shirts, black shorts & socks.

Reserves League: Avon Insurance Football Combination.
'A' Team: South East Counties League Div.2.

LONGEST LEAGUE RUNS

of undefeated matches:	32 (1973-74)	of league matches w/out a win:	20 (1980-81)
of undefeated home matches:	34 (1989-90)	of undefeated away matches:	17 (1973-74)
without home win:	10 (1980-81)	without an away win:	23 (1980-81)
of league wins:	12 (1952-53)	of home wins:	10 (1934-35)
of league defeats:	8 (1961-62)	of away wins:	5 (1952-53, 1964)

THE MANAGER

IAN HOLLOWAY . . . . appointed May 1996.

PREVIOUS CLUBS
As Manager . . . . None.
As Asst.Man/Coach . . . . None.
As a player . . . . Bristol Rovers, Wimbledon, Brentford, Torquay (Loan), Bristol Rovers, QPR.

HONOURS
As a Manager . . . . None.
As a Player. . . . . **Bristol Rovers:** Division 3 championship medal 1990.

BRISTOL ROVERS

PLAYERS NAME Honours	Ht	Wt	Birthdate	Birthplace Transfers	Contract Date	Clubs	League	L/Cup	FA Cup	Other	Lge	L/C	FAC	Oth
G O A L K E E P E R														
Collett Andrew A	5.11	11.3	10/28/73	Stockton	3/6/92	Middlesbrough	2			3				
				Loan	10/18/94	Bristol Rovers								
				£10000	3/23/95	Bristol Rovers	104	4	7	6				
Jones Lee	6.3	14.4	8/9/70	Pontypridd		AFC Porth								
				£7500	3/24/94	Swansea City	9	+1		1				
				Swap	3/6/98	Bristol Rovers	7			2				
Kite Philip E: Y.5,S.	6.1	14.7	10/26/62	Bristol	10/31/80	Bristol Rovers	96	12	8	2				
				£50000	8/16/84	Southampton	4			1				
				Loan	3/27/86	Middlesbrough	2							
				Free	2/7/87	Gillingham	70	5	4	10				
				£20000	8/16/89	Bournemouth	7	1						
				£25000	8/10/90	Sheffield United	11	5	1	1				
				Loan	11/21/91	Mansfield Town	11			1				
				Loan	9/9/92	Plymouth Argyle	2							
				Loan	10/24/92	Rotherham United	1							
				Loan	11/27/92	Crewe Alexandra	5		1	2				
				Loan	3/25/93	Stockport County	5							
				Free	7/1/93	Cardiff City	17+1	2	+1	2				
				Free	8/11/94	Bristol City	5+1	2						
					8/5/96	Bristol Rovers								
D E F E N C E														
Basford Luke W B	5.6	8.5	1/6/80	Croydon	8/14/97	Bristol Rovers (T)	5+2			3				
Challis Trevor E: u21.1,Y.2, S	5.7	10	23/10/75	Paddington	01/07/94	Q.P.R.	12+1		2					
				Free	7/1/98	Bristol Rovers								
Foster Stephen	6.1	12	12/3/74	Mansfield		Woking								
				£150000	5/23/97	Bristol Rovers	31+2	1	3	4				
Pritchard David	5.7	11.4	5/27/72	Wolverhampton		WBA	1+4							
					8/1/92	Telford United				2				
				£15000	2/25/94	Bristol Rovers	123+1	7	10	8				
Tilson Andrew	6.2	12.7	6/30/66	Huntingdon		Kettering Town								
				Free	7/14/88	Grimsby Town	104+1	8	10	5	6			
				£400000	12/21/90	QPR	27+2	2		1	2			
				Loan	9/15/92	Grimsby Town	4			1				
				£370000	11/7/92	Bristol Rovers	188+2	12	10	15	7	1		1
White Thomas	5.11	12.02	1/26/76	Bristol	7/13/94	Bristol Rovers	44+4		5	+1	1			
M I D F I E L D														
Hayles Barry	5.9	13	5/17/72	Lambeth		Stevenage Borough								
				£250000	6/4/97	Bristol Rovers	43	2	5	2	22		2	1
Holloway Ian S	5.7	9.12	3/12/63	Kingswood	3/18/81	Bristol Rovers	104+7	10	8	5	14	1	2	
				£35000	7/18/85	Wimbledon	19	3	1		2			
				£25000	3/12/86	Brentford	27+3	2	3	+1	2			
				Loan	1/30/87	Torquay United	5							
				£10000	8/21/87	Bristol Rovers	179	5	10	20	26		1	3
				£230000	8/12/91	QPR	130+17	12+1	7+1	1+1	4		1	
					8/5/96	Bristol Rovers	62+7	4	4		1		1	
Shore James A	5.9	10.9	9/1/77	Bristol		Norwich City (T)								
				Free	7/1/98	Bristol Rovers								
Zabek Lee K	6	12	10/13/78	Bristol		Bristol Rovers	9+5			2	1			
F O R W A R D														
Bennett Frank	5.7	11.8	1/3/69	Birmingham		Halesowen Town								
				£7500	2/24/93	Southampton	5+14	1+2	+1		1			
				Loan	10/28/96	Shrewsbury Town					1			
					11/29/96	Bristol Rovers	14+15	1+1	+2	2	3			1
Low Joshua	6.1	12	2/15/79	Bristol		Bristol Rovers	6+7	+2	2+1					
Meaker Michael W: B.1, u21.2	5.11	11.5	18/08/71	Greenford	07/02/90	Q.P.R.	14+12	1	1	0+1	1	1		
				Loan	20/11/91	Plymouth Argyle	4			1				
				£550000	19/07/95	Reading	46+21	3	0+3		2	1		
				Free	7/1/98	Bristol Rovers								
Penrice Gary	5.8	11.1	3/23/64	Bristol		Mangotsfield								
				Free	11/6/84	Bristol Rovers	186+2	11	11	13+2	53	3	7	2
				£500000	11/14/89	Watford	41+4		4	1	17		1	1
				£1000000	3/8/91	Aston Villa	14+6				1			
				£625000	10/29/91	QPR	46+14	4+1	2+1	1	17	1	1	
				£300000	11/15/95	Watford	26+13	2+1	1		2			
				Free	7/18/97	Bristol Rovers	37+2	2	5	2	5		1	
Ramasut Maham W Tom	5.9	10.1	8/30/77	Cardiff	7/28/95	Norwich City								
				Free	9/4/96	Bristol Rovers	29+12		3	2	6			
ADDITIONAL CONTRACT PLAYERS														
Andreasson Marcus						Osters IF								
				Free	17/1/98	Bristol Rovers								
Smith Mark J W					12/19/97	Bristol Rovers								
Trees Robert						Manchester Utd (T)								
				Free	17/1/98	Bristol Rovers								

THE MEMORIAL GROUND
Filton Avenue, Horfield, Bristol BS7 0AQ

Capacity ....10,000.
Covered Standing ....
Seated..

First game..v Carlisle United, Football League, 12.08.95.
First floodlit game ....v Gillingham, League Cup 1st Rnd 2nd Leg, 23.08.95.

ATTENDANCES
Highest...9,173, v Northampton (Play-off semi-final, 1st leg), 10.05.98.
Lowest...3,513, v Chesterfield, Football League, 23.03.96.

OTHER GROUNDS ....Eastville. Twerton Park.

HOW TO GET TO THE GROUND

From all directions:
M5,
M4,
M32,
Off at junction 2,
around the roundabout,
turn off into Muller Road,
pass 6 sets of traffic lights (2 pedestrian),
turn left into Filton Avenue at 6th set of lights.

USEFUL TELEPHONE NUMBERS

Club switchboard. 0117 977 2000
Club fax number 0117 977 3888
Club shop 0117 924 7474/961 1772
Ticket Office. . 0117 924 3200 (Fax 924 4454)

Marketing Department. 0117 924 7474
Clubcall 0891 66 44 22*
*Calls cost 50p per minute at all times.
Call costings correct at time of going to press.

MATCHDAY PROGRAMME

Programme Editor . . . . . . Keith Brookman.

Price . . . . £2.00.

Subscriptions. . . . . Apply to club

Local Newspapers
. Western Daily Press, Bristol Evening Post
. . . . Bath Evening Chronicle
. . . . Sunday Independent
. . . . Kingswood/North Avon Gazette

Local Radio Stations
. . . . Radio Bristol, GWR Radio.

MATCHDAY TICKET PRICES

Centenary Stand
Adults. £14.00
Juniors/Senior Citizens £10.00
Y/Pirate £7.50
WEST STAND - WING
Adults. £14.00
Juniors/Senior Citizens £10.00
Y/Pirate £7.50
WEST STAND - CENTRAL
Adults. £17.00
Juniors/Senior Citizens £17.00
Y/Pirate £17.00
TERRACING
Adults. £10.00
Juniors/Senior Citizens £6.00
Y/Pirate £4.50

BURNLEY
(The Clarets)
NATIONWIDE LEAGUE DIVISION 2
SPONSORED BY: P3 COMPUTERS

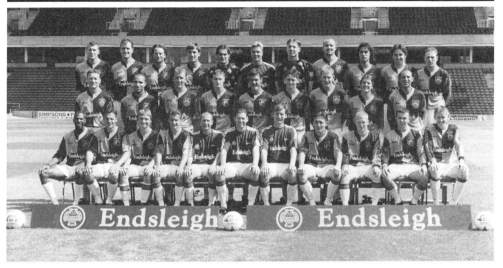

1997-98 - **Back Row** L-R: Glen Little, Ian Helliwell, Vince Overson, Mark Winstanley, Marlon Beresford, Chris Woods, Craig Mawson, Steve Blatherwick, Marco Gentile, Ian Duerden, Phil Eastwood. **Middle Row:** Nigel Gleghorn, Gerry Harrison, Jamie Hoyland, Andy Cooke, Richard Huxford, Colin Carr-Lawton, Paul Smith, Mark Ford, Damian Matthew. **Front Row:** Michael Williams, Paul Barnes, Chris Brass, Chris Vinicombe, Gordon Cowans (reserve team coach), Chris Waddle (manager), Glen Roeder (asst. manager), David Eyers, Jason Heffernan, Paul Weller, Garth West.

BURNLEY
FORMED IN 1882
TURNED PROFESSIONAL IN 1883
LTD COMPANY IN 1897¹

CHAIRMAN: F J Teasdale
VICE-CHAIRMAN
Dr R D Iven MRCS(Eng), LRCOP (Lond), MRCGP
DIRECTORS
R B Blakeborough, C Holt
B M Rothwell, JP
SECRETARY
John W Howarth F.A.A.I. 01282 700000
COMMERCIAL MANAGER
Peter Davis

MANAGER: Stan Ternant
RESERVE TEAM MANAGER
Gordon Cowans
YOUTH TEAM MANAGER
Terry Pashley/Alan Harper
PHYSIOTHERAPIST
A Jones

STATISTICIAN FOR THE DIRECTORY
Wallace Chadwick

The season started, as they so often do at Turf Moor, with high hopes. The appointment of Chris Waddle as manager seemed a bold and ambitious move, and along with a back-up team of Glenn Roeder, Gordon Cowans and Chris Woods, all seemed well set for the side to build on the promise of the previous season and hopefully get out of the Second Division..

It soon became clear that it wasn't going to be so straightforward. Waddles new signings were intended primarily to bolster the defence, and only three goals conceded in the first six League games might have seemed a good start but for the fact that the "goals for" column at the same stage read 'nil'. The team had still to win after ten League outings, by which time Stoke had humiliated them 4-0 at Turf Moor to ensure a continuation of the club's dismal recent record in the Coca-Cola Cup.

League form did improve sufficiently in November for Burnley to move out of the bottom four but a new low was reached when Rotherham outplayed the Clarets to record a 3-0 first round replay victory at Turf Moor in the FA Cup. By the beginning of January, more bad results in the League saw them back in bottom spot.

Waddle maintained that results were not reflecting the team's efforts, but most supporters saw little evidence of that view until a turnabout in January beginning with probably the season's best performance, a 2-0 win against leaders Watford which was actually more emphatic than the score. Five straight wins followed soon after, including an astonishing 7-2 thrashing of York. The transformation coincided with a change from 5-3-2 (or was it 3-5-2?) to 4-4-2 and the introduction of wingers to the side...given Waddle's record as a player, it was surprising that the change took so long to implement.

The Auto Windscreens Shield brought some light relief from the continuing relegation struggle, with Burnley reaching the Northern final before bowing to Grimsby's superior skills. In the League, however, another bad run sent the side back to the bottom by the end of March, with a difficult run-in seemingly leaving little hope. Against all the odds, Burnley beat four of the top six teams in their remaining games, leaving matters to be settled in a do-or-die final game against fellow strugglers Plymouth. They survived in front of a crowd of nearly 19,000, proof again of the enormous potential of this under-achieving club.

There were few real playing successes of 1997/98, but Glen Little, whose belated introduction to the side sparked the January revival, was a revelation with his unorthodox wing-play; Andy Payton continued to do what he has done throughout his career, score goals, and he proved an ideal partner for the still-improving Andy Cooke; Neil Moore was generally solid at the back; and Gerry Harrison, probably the most consistent player of the campaign, was a rock in defence and a threat on the break. But, Payton and Moore apart, Waddle's signings were generally a disappointment, and changes in personnel and tactics far too frequent.

Waddle is now departed, and at the time of writing it seems likely that Burnley will change course and go for an experienced manager who knows his way around the lower divisions. But with a possible takeover on the way and the prospect of serious money to spend, nothing is certain at the moment. What is most likely is that 1998/99 will be a lot different from 1997/98, and what is most necessary is a considerable improvement.

Wallace Chadwick.

BURNLEY

Division 2	:20th			FA CUP: 1st Round			LC CUP: 2nd Round	AWS: Northern Final	

M	DATE	COMP.	VEN	OPPONENTS	RESULT	H/T	LP	GOAL SCORERS/GOAL TIMES	ATT.
1	A 09	FL	A	Watford	L 0-1	0-1	21		(11155)
2	12	CC 1/1	A	Lincoln City	D 1-1	0-1		Howey 77	(3010)
3	15	FL	H	Gillingham	D 0-0	0-0	21		11811
4	23	FL	A	Southend United	L 0-1	0-1	24		(4218)
5	26	CC 1/2	H	Lincoln City	W 2-1	2-1		Cooke 1, Eyres 17 (pen)	4644
6	30	FL	H	Bristol Rovers	D 0-0	0-0	23		9887
7	S 02	FL	H	Oldham Athletic	D 0-0	0-0	24		11189
8	07	FL	A	Chesterfield	L 0-1	0-1	24		(7406)
9	13	FL	A	York City	L 1-3	1-0	24	Barnes 11	(5424)
10	16	CC 2/1	H	Stoke City	L 0-4	0-1			4175
11	20	FL	A	Preston North End	D 1-1	0-1	24	Cooke 80	13809
12	24	CC 2/2	A	Stoke City	L 0-2	0-1			(6041)
13	27	FL	A	Brentford	L 1-2	0-1	24	Ford 57	(4548)
14	O 04	FL	H	Wycombe Wanderers	D 2-2	1-1	24	Creaney 3, 73	9057
15	11	FL	H	Carlisle United	W 3-1	1-0	24	Barnes 18, Creaney 67, 71	10687
16	18	FL	A	Wrexham	D 0-0	0-0	24		(5132)
17	21	FL	A	Plymouth Argyle	D 2-2	1-1	24	Eyres 7 (pen), Creaney 56	(3006)
18	25	FL	H	Bournemouth	D 2-2	1-0	23	Waddle 45, Creaney 65	9501
19	N 01	FL	H	Walsall	W 2-1	1-0	22	Barnes 27, Cooke 80	9292
20	04	FL	A	Luton Town	W 3-2	1-2	18	Williams 24, Creaney 61, Barnes 66	(5315)
21	08	FL	A	Blackpool	L 1-2	1-0	20	Creaney 14	(7429)
22	15	FAC 1	A	Rotherham United	D 3-3	2-2		Cooke 24, Moore 37, Weller 55	(5709)
23	18	FL	H	Millwall	L 1-2	1-1	20	Cooke 29	8834
24	22	FL	A	Grimsby Town	L 1-4	1-1	21	Weller 16	(4829)
25	25	FAC 1R	H	Rotherham United	L 0-3	0-1			3118
26	29	FL	H	Northampton Town	W 2-1	0-0	19	Moore 76, Barnes 82	8369
27	D 02	FL	A	Bristol City	L 1-3	1-0	22	Barnes 29	(11136)
28	13	FL	H	Wigan Athletic	L 0-2	0-2	23		9520
29	19	FL	A	Fulham	L 0-1	0-0	23		(5096)
30	26	FL	H	Chesterfield	D 0-0	0-0	23		10861
31	J 03	FL	A	Gillingham	L 0-2	0-1	24		(5886)
32	10	FL	H	Watford	W 2-0	2-0	24	Cooke 14, 35	9551
33	17	FL	A	Bristol Rovers	L 0-1	0-0	24		(7208)
34	24	FL	H	Southend United	W 1-0	1-0	24	Payton 44	9386
35	27	AWS N2	H	Notts County	W 2-0	0-0			0
36	31	FL	H	York City	W 7-2	2-1	21	Moore 40, Brass 46, Cooke 49, 58, 88, Payton 82, Barras 44 (OG)	9975
37	F 03	AWS NQF	H	Carlisle United	W 4-1	0-0			0
38	06	FL	A	Preston North End	W 3-2	0-1	19	Payton 48, Cooke 57, Moore 90	(12263)
39	14	FL	A	Wycombe Wanderers	L 1-2	0-1	19	Cooke 88	(5926)
40	17	AWS NSF	H	Preston North End	W 1-0	0-0			0
41	21	FL	H	Brentford	D 1-1	0-0	20	Little 78	10097
42	24	FL	A	Wrexham	L 1-2	1-1	22	Cooke 30	8576
43	28	FL	A	Carlisle United	L 1-2	1-2	22	Cooke 50	(7192)
44	M 07	FL	A	Walsall	D 0-0	0-0	23		(5212)
45	10	AWS NF1	A	Grimsby Town	D 0-0	0-0			(0)
46	14	FL	H	Luton Town	D 1-1	0-0	23	Payton 61	9656
47	17	AWS NF2	H	Grimsby Town	D 0-0	0-0			0
48	21	FL	A	Millwall	L 0-1	0-1	24		(7582)
49	28	FL	H	Grimsby Town	W 2-1	1-1	24	Little 12, Payton 80	8256
50	A 04	FL	A	Northampton Town	W 1-0	1-0	22	Payton 16	(7264)
51	07	FL	H	Blackpool	L 1-2	1-1	22	Payton 13	13413
52	11	FL	H	Bristol City	W 1-0	1-0	22	Payton 7 (pen)	10600
53	13	FL	A	Wigan Athletic	L 1-5	0-2	22	Little 87	(4926)
54	18	FL	H	Fulham	W 2-1	1-1	22	Cooke 2, Payton 83	9745
55	25	FL	A	Bournemouth	L 1-2	0-0	22	Matthew 72 (pen)	(6527)
56	28	FL	A	Oldham Athletic	D 3-3	3-1	22	Cooke 26, Weller 32, Little 38	(9781)
57	M 02	FL	H	Plymouth Argyle	W 2-1	2-1	20	Cooke 12, 41	18811

Best Home League Attendance: 18811 V Plymouth Argyle   Smallest :8256 V Grimsby Town   Average :10473

Goal Scorers:

FL	(55)	Cooke 16, Payton 9, Creaney 8, Barnes 6, Little 4, Moore 3, Weller 2, Brass 1, Eyres 1, Ford 1, Matthew 1, Waddle 1, Williams 1, Opponents 1
CC	(3)	Cooke 1, Eyres 1, Howey 1
FAC	(3)	Cooke 1, Moore 1, Weller 1
AWS	(8)	Payton 3, Cooke 2, Henderson 1, Little 1, Vinnicombe 1

	(F) Barnes	(G) Beresford	(D) Blatherwick	(D) Brass	(F) Cooke	(M) Cowans	(M) Creaney	(F) Eastwood	(F) Eyres	(M) Ford	(M) Harrison	(M) Henderson	(M) Howey	(M) Hoyland	(D) Huxford	(M) Kiwomya	(M) Little	(M) Matthew	(M) Moore	(F) Mullin	(F) Payton	(M) Robertson	(F) Smith P	(D) Vinnicombe	(F) Waddle	(F) Weller	(M) Williams	(D) Winstanley	(G) Woods	Referee	
1	X	X	X	X				X	X	X					S2	X			S1						X		X	X	S	P.S. Danson	1
2	X	X	X	X				X	X		X		X		X			S1						X	S		X	X	X	S J Baines	2
3	X	X	X	X				X	X		X		X		X			S3						X	S2	S1	X	X		G Laws	3
4	X	X	X	X	X			X	X		X		X		X			S1							S2	X	X	X	X	M R Halsey	4
5	X	X	X	S	X				X				X		X			X						S	X	X		X		C J Foy	5
6	X	X	X	S						S1			X		X			X	S2							X	X		X	T Heilbron	6
7	S1	X	X	X				X	X		X		X			X		X	S2					S		X	X		X	J P Robinson	7
8	X	X	X	X				X	X		X		X				S	X	S		S1					X	X			D Laws	8
9	X	X	X	X	X			X	X		X		X				S1	S2	X	S						X	X			R D Furnandiz	9
10	X	X	X	X				X	X		X		X				S2	X	X					S1		S1	X	X		J A Kirkby	10
11		X		X	X	X		X			X		X			S3		S2	X	X					X	X	S1			E K Wolstenholme	11
12		X		X	X	X	X	X			X		X						X						X	X				A P D'Urso	12
13	X	X		X		S1	X		X	X	X		X						X						X	X				R Styles	13
14	X	X		X		S3	X		X	X	X		X						X						X	X	S1	S	X	D Pugh	14
15	X	X		X	S2		X		X	X	X		X						X						X	X	S1	S	X	A G Wiley	15
16	X	X		X	S3		X		X	X	X		X						X						X	X	S2	S1		G Cain	16
17	X	X		X	S		X		X	X	X		X						X						X	X	S1	S		P Rejer	17
18	X	X		X	S2		X			X		X					S		X						X	X	S1	S		M L Dean	18
19	X	X	S3	X	S1	X	X							X						X					S2	X	X	X		E Lomas	19
20	X	X	S	X	X	X	X							X						X					S1	X	X	X		B Knight	20
21	X	X	S1	X	S2	X	X							X						X					S	X	X	X		M J Brandwood	21
22	X	X	S2	X	X	X						S	S3	X					X						S1	X	X	X	S	F G Stretton	22
23	X	X	S2	X	X	X						S	S1	X					X						X	X	X	X		M S Pike	23
24			X	X	X	X						S1	S						X						X	X	X	X		A N Butler	24
25	X	X	X	X	X	X						S1	S2	X					X						S	X	X	X	S	F G Stretton	25
26	X	X	X	X	S1	S						X	X	X2					X			S2			X	X	X	X1		M D Messias	26
27	X	X	X	X	S2	S						X	X	X					X			S1			X2	X1	X	X		A Bates	27
28	X	X	X1	X	X							X	X	X					X			S1			S2	X2	X	X	S	P R Richards	28
29	X	X		X	X							X	X	X						X					S	X	X	X1		P S Danson	29
30	X	X		X	X							X	X	X						S1	X				S2	X2	S		X1	T Heilbron	30
31	X	X		X	X							X3	X	X						S2	X				S1	X1	S3		X2	S G Bennett	31
32	X		S1	X							X	X			S				X	X	X				X		X1		X	R Pearson	32
33	X		S	X							X	X			S2					X2	X1	X		X	S1		X		X	R Styles	33
34	X		S2	X1							X	X			S					X	X	X		X	S1		X	X2	X	P Rejer	34
35	X	X									X1				X				X					X	X	X	S1		X		35
36	X	X		X							X				S1				X	X	X				X	X		S	X1	E Lomas	36
37	X	X	S1	X							X	X	S2		X					X	X2		X	X				X1			37
38	X	X	S2	X							X	S1			S				X	X	X			X1	X			X	X	F G Stretton	38
39	X	S2	X	X							X	S1			S				X	X	X			X1	X			S	X	S J Baines	39
40	X	X	X	X						S3	X1	S2			S1				X	X3	X		X2	X				X		40
41			X	X							S1	X	S			S				X	X1	X		X	X			X		M J Jones	41
42			X	X							S1	X	S			X1				X	X2	X		X			S2	X		T Heilbron	42
43	X	S2	X	X							X2	X	S1		S2				X	X	X			X1			X2	X		S W Mathieson	43
44				X	X				S1		X	X		S		S				X	X	X			S1		X1	X	X	G Laws	44
45				X	X						X	X			S1					X	X2	X		X1	S2		X	X	X		45
46				X	X						X	X1	S	S1						X	X	X		S2	X2			X	X	M L Dean	46
47				X	X						X			S1						X	X	X1	X	X			X	X	X		47
48				X	X						X	X	S1	S2	S					X			X1	X	X	X		X	X2	M J Brandwood	48
49				X	X						X	X	S3		S1		X3			X	X	X		X2	S2	X1		X	X	J A Kirkby	49
50				X	X						X	X	S		S					X	X	X		X	S	X		X	X	A R Hall	50
51				X	X						X1	X			S					X	X	X		X	S	X		X	X	K M Lynch	51
52			S3		X						X			S2			X3	X	X	X1			S1	X2			X	X	X	A N Butler	52
53			S2	X							X	X	S1		X				X2	X	X	X1		X2				X	X	J P Robinson	53
54			S2	X							X	X		S			X2	X	X	X1			S1				X	X	X	D Pugh	54
55				X	X				S1		X	X			S				X	X	X			X1			X	X	X	D R Crick	55
56				X	X				S2		X	X			S1				X	X1	X		X2				X	X	X	W C Burns	56
57				X	X						X	X		S	S				X	X	X			S			X	X	X	P Taylor	57
	23	34	13	37	26	5	9	1	13	32	33		21	2	4	1	19	21	38	6	19	8	8	20	26	31	13	27	12	FL Appearances	
	1		7	3	8	1	1	2		4	1	7	2	7		2	4	6	2		3	6	3	5	7	1				FL Sub Appearances	
	3	4	3	3	2	1		1		4	2		3		2+1		0+2	3+1	2			2		2+1	2+1	2	2	2		CC Appearances	
	2	2	1+1	2	2	2				0+1	0+2		2						2					0+1	1	2	2	2		FAC Appearances	
	3	3	3+1	5						4+1	3		0+3	0+1	2+1				3		2	4		5	3+1	3	3+1		2	1 4 2	AWS Appearances	

Also Played: (F) Carr-Lawton S2(24), S(25). (F) Duerden X(6). (M) Gentile X(12). (M) Gleghorn S(5), X(6). (G) Parks S(56). Smith C S1(8). (M) Robertson S(32).

BURNLEY

RECORDS AND STATISTICS

CLUB RECORDS

BIGGEST VICTORIES
League: 9-0 v Darwen, Division 1, 9.1.1892.
F.A. Cup: 9-0 v Crystal Palace, 2nd Round, 10.2.1909.
9-0 v New Brighton, 4th Round, 26.1.1957.
9-0 v Penrith, 1st Round (a), 17.11.1984.
League Cup: 6-0 v Grimsby Town, 2nd Round, 10.9.1968.
BIGGEST DEFEATS
League: 0-10 v Aston Villa, Division 1, 29.8.1925.
0-10 v Sheffield United, Division 1, 19.1.1929.
F.A. Cup: 0-11 v Darwen Old Wanderers, 1st Round, 17.10.1885.
League Cup: 0-4 v Peterborough, 5th Round, 17.11.1965.
0-4 v Leeds United, 2nd Round, 6.9.1972.
0-4 v West Ham, 2nd Round, 2.9.1980.
0-4 v Manchester United, 2nd Round, 26.9.1984.
MOST POINTS
3 points a win: 83, Division 4, 1991-92.
2 points a win: 62, Division 2, 1972-73.
MOST GOALS SCORED: 102, Division 1, 1960-61.
MOST GOALS CONCEDED: 108, Division 1, 1925-26.
MOST FIRST CLASS MATCHES IN A SEASON
62 - 1960-61 (League 42, FA Cup 7, League Cup 8, European Cup 4, Charity Shield 1).
MOST LEAGUE WINS: 25, Division 4, 1991-92.
MOST LEAGUE DRAWS: 17, Division 3, 1981-82.
MOST LEAGUE DEFEATS: 23, Division 1, 1975-76.
BEST PERFORMANCES
League: 1972-73: Played 42, Won 24, Drawn 14, Lost 4, Goals for 72, Against 35, Points 62. Champions of Division 2.
Highest Position: Champions of Division 1 - 1920-21, 1959-60.
F.A. Cup: 1913-14: 1st Round South Shields 3-1; 2nd Round Derby County 3-2; 3rd Round Bolton Wanderers 3-0; 4th Round Sunderland 0-0,2-1; Semi-Final Sheffield United 0-0,1-0; Final Liverpool 1-0.
League Cup: Semi-Final in 1960-61, 1968-69.
1982-83: 1st Round Bury 5-3,3-1; 2nd Round Middlesbrough 3-2,1-1; 3rd Round Coventry 2-1; 4th Round Birmingham City 3-2; 5th Round Tottenham 4-1; Semi-Final Liverpool 0-3,1-0.
Europe: European Cup: 1960-61, 2nd Round Reims 2-0,2-3; 3rd Round Hamburg 3-1,1-4.
European Fairs Cup: 1966-67, 1st Round V.F.B.Stuttgart 1-1,2-0;

2nd Round Lausanne-Sports 3-1,5-0; 3rd Round Napoli 3-0,0-0; 4th Round Eintracht Frankfurt 1-1,1-2.
HONOURS: Champions of Division 1, 1920-21, 1959-60.
Champions of Division 2, 1897-98, 1972-73.
Champions of Division 3, 1982-83.Champions of Division 4, 91-92.
FA Cup winners in 1913-14.
Charity Shield winners in 1960-61, shared in 1973-74.
LEAGUE CAREER: Div 1 88-97, Div 2 97-98, Div 1 98-00, Div 2 00-13, Div 1 13-30, Div 2 30-47, Div 1 47-71, Div 2 71-73, Div 1 73-76, Div 2 76-80, Div 3 80-82, Div 2 82-83, Div 3 83-85, Div 4 85-92, Div 3/2 92-94, Div 2/1 94-95, Div.3/2 1995-

INDIVIDUAL CLUB RECORDS

MOST GOALS IN A SEASON
Jimmy Robson: 37 goals in 1960-61 (League 25, FA Cup 5, Lge Cup 4, EC 3).
Willie Irvine: 37 goals in 1965-66 (League 29, FAC 5, Lge Cup 3).
MOST GOALS IN A MATCH
6. Louis Page v Birmingham City (a), Division 1, 10.4.1926.
OLDEST PLAYER
Jerry Dawson, 40 years 282 days, (Christmas Day 1928).
YOUNGEST PLAYER
Tommy Lawton, 16 years 174 days, 28.3.1936.
MOST CAPPED PLAYER
Jimmy McIlroy (Northern Ireland) 51. Bob Kelly (England) 11.

PREVIOUS MANAGERS

Arthur Sutcliffe 1893-96; Harry Bradshaw 1896-99; Ernest Mangnall 1900-03; Spen Whittaker 1903-10; John Haworth 1910-24; Albert Pickles 1925-32; Tom Bromilow 1932-35; Alf Boland 1935-40; Cliff Britton 1945-48; Frank Hill 1948-54; Alan Brown 1954-57; Billy Dougall 1957-58; Harry Potts 1958-70; Jimmy Adamson 1970-76; Joe Brown 1976-77; Harry Potts 1977-79; Brian Miller 1979-83; Frank Casper 1983; John Bond 1983-84; John Benson 1984-85; Martin Buchan 1985; Tommy Cavanagh 1985-86; Brian Miller 1986-89; Frank Casper 1989-91, Jimmy Mullen 1991-96, Adrian Heath 1996-97. Chris Waddle 1997-98.
ADDITIONAL INFORMATION
Previous Name: Burnley Rovers 1881-82.
Club colours: Claret shirts with light blue sleeves, white shorts & socks.
Reserves League: Pontins Central League Division 2.

LONGEST LEAGUE RUNS

of undefeated matches:	30 (1920-21)	of league matches w/out a win:	24 (1979)
of undefeated home matches:	34 (1911-13)	of undefeated away matches:	15 (1972-73)
without home win:	11 (1979)	without an away win:	31 (1901-03)
of league wins:	10 (1912-13)	of home wins:	17 (1920-21)
of league defeats:	8 (1889-90,1895, 1995)	of away wins:	7 (1991-92)

THE MANAGER

STAN TERNENT . . . . June 1998.

PREVIOUS CLUBS
As Manager . . . . Blackpool, Hull City, Bury.
As Asst.Man/Coach . . . . Bradford, Crystal Palace, Chelsea, Bury.
As a player . . . . Burnley, Carlisle, Sunderland.

HONOURS
As a Manager . . . . **Bury:** Promotion to Division 2, 1995-96. Division 2 champions, 1996-97.
As a Player . . . . **Carlisle United:** Promotion to Division 1, 1973-74.

BURNLEY

PLAYERS NAME Honours	Ht	Wt	Birthdate	Birthplace Transfers	Contract Date	Clubs	League	L/Cup	FA Cup	Other	Lge	L/C	FAC	Oth
G O A L K E E P E R														
Mawson Craig J			5/16/79	Keighley	7/30/97	Burnley (T)								
Parks Tony	5.10	11.5	1/28/63	Hackney	9/22/80	Tottenham (A)	37	1	5	5				
				Loan	10/1/86	Oxford United	5							
				Loan	9/1/87	Gillingham	2							
				£60000	8/24/88	Brentford	71	7	8	5				
				Free	2/27/91	Fulham	2							
				Free	8/15/91	West Ham United	6		3					
				Free	8/21/92	Stoke City	2	1						
Free 10/14/92 Falkirk				Free	9/6/96	Blackpool								
				Free	8/13/97	Burnley								
				Loan	2/13/98	Doncaster Rovers	6							
D E F E N C E														
Blatherwick Steven S	6.1	12.12	9/20/73	Nottingham	8/1/92	Nottingham Forest	10	2	1					
				Loan	8/1/93	Wycombe W.	2							
				Loan	9/11/95	Hereford United								
				Loan	3/27/97	Reading	6+1							
					7/17/97	Burnley	13+7	3	1+1					
Brass Christopher	5.9	11.08	7/24/75	Easington		Burnley	83+10	5+1	4+1	2	1			
				Loan	10/14/94	Torquay United	7		2	1				
Howey Lee Mathew	6.2	13.9	4/1/69	Sunderland	10/2/86	Ipswich Town (T)								
via Blyth Spartans & Bishop Auckland				Free	3/25/93	Sunderland	39+30	1+4	2+4	0+1	8	2	1	
				£200000	8/11/97	Burnley	21+2	3	2	0+1		1		
Morgan Steve	5.11	12	9/19/68	Oldham	8/12/86	Blackpool	135+9	13	16	10+1	10	2	1	1
Div.3'97. E: u19.2.				£115000	7/16/90	Plymouth Argyle	120+1	7	6	5	6			
				£150000	7/14/93	Coventry City	65+3	5	5		2	3		
				Loan	3/1/96	Bristol Rovers	6			2				
				Free	8/15/96	Wigan Athletic	32+4	2	1		2			
				Free	7/1/98	Burnley								
West Gareth	6.1	11.1	8/1/78		6/1/96	Burnley								
Winstanley Mark	6.1	12.7	1/22/68	St Helens	7/22/86	Bolton Wanderers	215+5	19+1	19	26	3			3
					8/5/94	Burnley	150+1	13	8	4	5			
M I D F I E L D														
Ford Mark	5.7	9.3	10/10/75	Pontefract	3/5/93	Leeds United	26+2	7	5	0+1	1			
E: Y.5; FAYC'93				Free	7/18/97	Burnley	32+4	2	0+1		1			
Little Glen	6.3	13	10/15/75	Wimbledon		Glentoran								
					11/29/96	Burnley	24+8	0+2	1+1	0+1	4			
Moore Neil	6.1	12.9	9/21/72	Liverpool	8/29/97	Burnley	38+2	2	2		3		1	
Robertson Mark W	03.9	12.4	4/6/77	Sydney		Marconi								
				Free	1/16/98	Burnley	8+3			3+1				
Smith Carl P	5.8	11	1/15/79	Sheffield		Burnley (T)								
Williams Michael A	5.11	11.6	11/21/69	Bradford		Maltby MW								
				Free	2/13/91	Sheffield Wed	16+7	3+2		1	1			
				Loan	12/18/92	Halifax Town	9				1			
				Loan	10/18/96	Huddersfield Town	2							
				Loan	3/27/97	Peterborough Utd	6							
				Free	7/16/97	Burnley	13+1	2	2		1			
F O R W A R D														
Carr-Lawton Colin	5.11	11.7	9/5/78	South Shields	9/23/96	Burnley	+1							
Cooke Andrew	6	12	1/2/74	Shrewsbury		Newtown								
					5/1/95	Burnley	55+33	3+2	3+2	2+2	34	2	1	
Eastwood Philip	5.11	12.2	4/6/78	Blackburn	6/1/96	Burnley	1+2							
				Loan	2/27/98	Telford United								
Eyres David	5.11	11	2/26/64	Liverpool		Rhyl								
				£10000	8/15/89	Blackpool	147+11	11+1	11	13+2	38	1	2	4
				£90000	7/29/93	Burnley	163+4	14	12	7	37	6	7	3
Henderson Kevin	5.11	13.2	6/8/74	Ashington		Morpeth Town								
					2/5/98	Burnley	0+7							
Jepson Ronald F	6.1	13.2	12/05/63	Stoke		Nantwich Town								
Div.2'97.				Free	23/03/89	Port Vale	12+10	1+1	1+1					
				Loan	25/01/90	Peterborough United	18				5			
				£80000	12/02/91	Preston North End	36+2	2		3	8			4
				£60000	29/07/92	Exeter City	50+3	6	3	4	21	2	1	1
				£80000	07/12/93	Huddersfield Town	95+12	6+1	4	6	31	2	3	1
				Free	01/08/97	Bury	31+16	7	0+3	1+1	9			2
				£30000	1/16/98	Oldham Athletic	9				4			
				Free	7/1/98	Burnley								
Payton Andy	5.9	10.6	10/3/67	Whalley	7/29/85	Hull City	116+28	9+2	8	3	55	2		
				£750000	11/22/91	Middlesbrough	8+11		1+3		3			
					8/14/92	Celtic	20+18	3+2	1+1	3	15	5		
				£100000	11/25/93	Barnsley	99+8	7	6+1		41	3	1	
				Free	8/15/96	Huddersfield Town	42+1	7	2		17	3		
				Swap	1/16/98	Burnley	19			5	9			3
Smith Ian Paul	6	13.3	1/22/76	Easington	8/1/95	Burnley	41+20	1+1	3+1		4			
Weller Paul	5.8	10.13	3/6/75	Brighton	8/1/93	Burnley	77+17	4+2	4+1	2	5		1	

TURF MOOR
Brunshaw Road, Burnley, Lancs BB10 4BX

Capacity ....22,546.

First game..v Rawtemstall, 17.02.1883.
First floodlit game ....v Blackburn (friendly), .12.1957.

ATTENDANCES
Highest ....54,775 v Huddersfield Town, FA Cup Round 3, 23.2.1924.
Lowest ....1,138 v Darlington, AMC, 13.3.1986.

OTHER GROUNDS ....None.

HOW TO GET TO THE GROUND

From the North
Follow signs to Burnley (A56) into Town Centre, at roundabout take first exit into Yorkshire Street, shortly over crossroads into Brunshaw Road.
From the East:
Follow signs Burnley (A646) then join A671 enter town centre by Todmorden Road and at the end turn right at crossroads into Brunshaw Road.
From the South:
(or use route from west). Use M62, M66 and A56 signposted Burnley into town centre, then at roundabout take 3rd exit in Yorkshire Street, shortly at crossroads forward into Brunshaw Road.
From the West and South:
Use M6 to junction 31, then Blackburn bypass and A679 into Burnley town centre and at roundabout take third exit into Yorkshire Street, shortly over crossroads into Brunshaw Road.

Car Parking: Parks in Church Street and Fulledge Recreation Ground for approx 500 vehicles each (chargeable). Both are five minutes walk from ground.
Nearest Railway Station: Burnley Central.

USEFUL TELEPHONE NUMBERS

Club switchboard 01282 700 000
Club fax number 01282 700 014
Club shop 01282 700 016
Ticket Office............. 01282 700 010

Marketing Department. 01282 700 007
Internet address .... www.clarets.co.uk
Clubcall 0891 12 11 53*
*Calls cost 50p per minute at all times. Call costings correct at time of going to press.

MATCHDAY PROGRAMME

Programme Editor .... Paul Agnew.

Number of pages .... 48.

Price.......................£1.50.

Subscriptions .... Apply to club.

Local Newspapers
.... Lancashire Evening Telegraph
.... Burnley Express.

Local Radio Stations
..... Radio Lancashire, Red Rose Radio.

MATCHDAY TICKET PRICES

Endsleigh Stand (Visitors) .... £12.

Concessions .... £6.

Bob Lord .... £12.

Concessions .... £6.

North Stand.......................... £14/£12.

Concessions .... £7/£6.

East Stand .... £10/£9.

Concessions .... £4.50.

CHESTERFIELD
(The Spireites)
NATIONWIDE LEAGUE DIVISION 2
SPONSORED BY: KENNING CAR VAN & TRUCK RENTAL (HOME)
GK FORD MOTOR GROUP (AWAY)

1997-98 - Back Row L-R: James Lomas, Tony Lormor, Andy Leaning, Billy Mercer, Darren Carr, Jamie Hewitt
Middle Row: Adrian Shaw (Youth Dev. Officer), Iain Dunn, Mark Williams, Steve Wilkinson, Ian Breckin, Andrew Morris, Steve Gaughan, Chris Beaumont, Roger Willis, Lee Rogers, Dave Rushbury.
Front Row: Mark Jules, Ton Curtis, Chris Perkins, Kevin Randall (Asst. Manager), John Duncan (Manager), Jonathan Howard, Paul Holland, Marcus Ebdon.

CHESTERFIELD
FORMED IN 1866
TURNED PROFESSIONAL IN 1891
LTD COMPANY IN 1871

PRESIDENT
His Grace The Duke of Devonshire MC,DL,JP

CHAIRMAN: J Norton-Lea
VICE-CHAIRMAN: B W Hubbard
DIRECTOR: R F Pepper, Mike Warner
SECRETARY/GENERAL MANAGER
Phil Hough
COMMERCIAL MANAGER
Jim Brown

MANAGER: John Duncan
ASSISTANT MANAGER: Kevin Randall

PHYSIOTHERAPIST
Dave Rushbury

STATISTICIAN FOR THE DIRECTORY
Richard West

Following the departure of Kevin Davies to Southampton, Chesterfield knew at the outset that goalscoring could be a problem for them during 1997-98 - and so it proved!

In 1996-97 with Davies in their attack alongside Howard, they netted only 42 League goals....in 1997-98 they managed just four more and finished 10th in the final table with 65 points, five adrift of Fulham who took th3e final play-off spot.

One might reflect and say that had Davies stayed with the 'Spireites' for another twelve months things may have been different. As it was, he went on to score well at The Dell and is now ready to do business with Blackburn Rovers.

Chesterfield certainly missed his presence in attack and they found it difficult at times to finish off teams after taking the lead. They battled on well though and were perhaps unlucky not to get closer than they did to a top six finish.

Realistically, Chesterfield drew far too many matches - seventeen in total, including 10 away from home. They were beaten only three times at The Recreation Ground, yet ran up just three victories on their travels. Scoring goals, has mentioned earlier, was a major problem for the team - just 15 were recorded in 23 away games and this clearly proves a point. Manager John Duncan who has now been in charge at the club for over five years. tried all he could to remedy this during the season, all to no avail.

Let's hope that a goalscorer comes along to give Chesterfield the boost they require to set them up for a promotion challenge this time round.

Tony Matthews.

CHESTERFIELD

Division 2		:10th		FA CUP: 2nd Round		LC CUP: 2nd Round	AWS: Northern Round 1	

M	DATE	COMP.	VEN	OPPONENTS	RESULT	H/T	LP	GOAL SCORERS/GOAL TIMES	ATT.
1	A 09	FL	H	Walsall	W 3-1	1-0	3	Willis 8, Perkins 81, Lormor 85	5193
2	12	CC 1/1	A	Wigan Athletic	W 2-1	0-0		Willis 67, 82	(3413)
3	15	FL	A	Brentford	D 0-0	0-0	5		(4000)
4	23	FL	H	Preston North End	W 3-2	3-0	4	Ebdon 31, Jules 35, Hewitt 41	6288
5	26	CC 1/2	H	Wigan Athletic	W 1-0	0-0		Lormor 78	4076
6	30	FL	A	Plymouth Argyle	D 1-1	0-1	3	Lormor 85 (pen)	(5284)
7	S 02	FL	A	York City	W 1-0	1-0	2	Morris 42	(3284)
8	07	FL	H	Burnley	W 1-0	1-0	2	Lormor 3	7406
9	13	FL	A	Watford	L 1-2	0-1	2	Willis 81	(11204)
10	16	CC 2/1	H	Barnsley	L 1-2	0-0		Lormor 58 (pen)	6318
11	20	FL	H	Bristol Rovers	D 0-0	0-0	3		5309
12	27	FL	A	Wrexham	D 0-0	0-0	3		(3921)
13	30	CC 2/2	A	Barnsley	L 1-4	0-2		Lormor 59 (pen)	(8417)
14	O 04	FL	H	Bournemouth	D 1-1	0-1	4	Carr 77	4482
15	11	FL	H	Wigan Athletic	L 2-3	1-1	7	Lormor 11, Wilkinson 57	4673
16	18	FL	A	Oldham Athletic	L 0-2	0-0	12		(5777)
17	21	FL	A	Blackpool	L 1-2	0-1	14	Curtis 61	(3682)
18	25	FL	H	Wycombe Wanderers	W 1-0	0-0	11	Holland 48	4119
19	N 01	FL	A	Fulham	D 1-1	0-1	10	Holland 53	(7998)
20	04	FL	H	Gillingham	D 1-1	0-0	10	Wilkinson 47	3420
21	08	FL	H	Grimsby Town	W 1-0	0-0	9	Reeves 77	5004
22	15	FAC 1	H	Northwich Victoria	W 1-0	1-0		Reeves 6	5327
23	18	FL	A	Carlisle United	W 2-0	0-0	6	Ebdon 47, Beaumont 90	(3591)
24	22	FL	A	Millwall	D 1-1	0-0	6	Perkins 68	(6556)
25	29	FL	H	Southend United	W 1-0	0-0	4	Willis 57	4101
26	D 02	FL	A	Northampton Town	D 0-0	0-0	4		(4824)
27	06	FAC 2	A	Grimsby Town	D 2-2	0-2		Willis 52, Breckin 72	(4762)
28	09	AWS N1	H	Grimsby Town	L 0-1	0-0			1128
29	13	FL	H	Luton Town	D 0-0	0-0	4		4358
30	16	FAC 2R	H	Grimsby Town	L 0-2	0-1			4553
31	20	FL	A	Bristol City	L 0-1	0-1	8		(11792)
32	26	FL	A	Burnley	D 0-0	0-0	8		(10861)
33	28	FL	H	York City	D 1-1	0-0	9	Reeves 57	5320
34	J 03	FL	H	Brentford	D 0-0	0-0	7		4049
35	10	FL	A	Walsall	L 2-3	1-0	10	Reeves 2, Howard 90	(4042)
36	17	FL	H	Plymouth Argyle	W 2-1	1-1	8	Wilkinson 12, 47	3879
37	24	FL	A	Preston North End	D 0-0	0-0	8		(8233)
38	31	FL	H	Watford	L 0-1	0-0	8		5975
39	F 06	FL	A	Bristol Rovers	L 1-3	1-1	11	Wilkinson 42	(5481)
40	14	FL	A	Bournemouth	L 0-2	0-2	13		(4271)
41	21	FL	H	Wrexham	W 3-1	2-0	11	Howard 12, 45, Reeves 64	3919
42	24	FL	H	Oldham Athletic	W 2-1	1-0	11	Howard 44, Williams 63	4077
43	28	FL	A	Wigan Athletic	L 1-2	1-2	11	Wilkinson 7	(3017)
44	M 03	FL	A	Grimsby Town	D 0-0	0-0	11		(4940)
45	07	FL	H	Fulham	L 0-2	0-0	11		5129
46	14	FL	A	Gillingham	L 0-1	0-0	14		(5672)
47	21	FL	H	Carlisle United	W 2-1	0-1	10	Willis 54, Holland 82	3967
48	28	FL	H	Millwall	W 3-1	2-0	9	Willis 20, 55, Howard 22	3952
49	A 03	FL	A	Southend United	W 2-0	1-0	8	Reeves 25, Willis 88	(5425)
50	11	FL	H	Northampton Town	W 2-1	0-1	8	Breckin 48, Williams 71	5064
51	14	FL	A	Luton Town	L 0-3	0-1	10		(5884)
52	18	FL	H	Bristol City	W 1-0	0-0	9	Williams 44	5085
53	25	FL	A	Wycombe Wanderers	D 1-1	1-1	9	Willis 19	(5113)
54	M 02	FL	H	Blackpool	D 1-1	0-0	10	Howard 49	4462

Best Home League Attendance: 7406 V Burnley	**Smallest :3420 V Gillingham**	**Average :4749**

Goal Scorers:

FL	(46)	Willis 8, Howard 6, Wilkinson 6, Reeves 5, Lormor 4, Holland 3, Williams 3, Ebdon 2, Perkins 2, Beaumont 1, Breckin 1, Carr 1, Curtis 1, Hewitt 1, Jules 1, Morris 1
CC	(5)	Lormor 3, Willis 2
FAC	(3)	Breckin 1, Reeves 1, Willis 1
AWS	(0)	

1997-98

(F) Beaumont	(D) Breckin	(D) Carr	(F) Creaney	(M) Curtis	(F) Dunn	(M) Ebdon	(D) Garvey	(M) Gaughen	(G) Gayle	(D) Hewitt	(M) Holland	(F) Howard	(F) Jackson	(F) Jules	(G) Leaning	(M) Lenagh	(M) Lomas	(F) Lormor	(G) Mercer	(M) Misse-Misse	(F) Morris	(M) Pearce	(D) Perkins	(M) Reeves	(D) Rogers	(F) Wilkinson	(D) Williams	(F) Willis		
		X		X	S1	X		X		X	X			S2			X	X				X				S3	X	X	T. Jones	1
X	X	S		X	S	X				X	X			S			X	X				X					X	X	C J Foy	2
X	S1	X		X	S	X				X	X			S			X	X				X					X	X	C R Wilkes	3
	S	X		X		X				X	X			X			X	X			S1	X			S	S	X	X	P Rejer	4
S1		X		X		X				X	X			X			X	X			S	X				S	X	X	J P Robinson	5
S3	S1	X		X		X				X	X		S2	X			X	X		X		X					X		K A Leach	6
S1	X			X	S	X				X	X			X			X	X		X		X					X		G Cain	7
X1	X			X				S		X	X	S1	S	X			X	X		X		X					X		D Laws	8
S1	X			X				S		X	X	X		X			X	X		X		X				S2	X	X	S W Mathieson	9
X	X			X	S			S		X	X	X		X			X	X				X				S	X	X	P S Danson	10
X	X			X	S2					X	X3	X		S1			X	X				X				S3	X	X	D Pugh	11
S	X			X		X				X	X			X			S	X				X				S1	X	X	G Singh	12
X	X			X		S		S1		X	X		X		S2	X		X				X				X	X		U D Rennie	13
	X	S2		X	S1	X				X				X			X3	X				X				X	X	X	A Bates	14
X	X			X	S1	X				X			S2	X			X	X				X			S	X	X	A R Hall	15
X	X			X		X	S1			X		S		S	S	X	X	X				X		X	X	X	X		M J Jones	16
X	X			X		X	X	X		X		X		S1		S2						X		X		X	X		G Laws	17
X	X			X		S2	X	X	X	X	X	S1		S			X					X				X	X		M S Pike	18
X	X				X	S	X	X	X	X	S1			X								X			S	X	X	X	C J Foy	19
X	X				X	S	X	X	X	X	S1			X								X			S	X	X	X	M L Dean	20
X	X				X	S	X	X	X	X				X								X		S	X	S	X	X	A R Leake	21
X	X			S1	X			X	X	X	X	S2	X	X								S	X	S	X	X	X		N S Barry	22
X	X			S	X			X	X	X	X			X							X1	X	S	S1	X	X			M D Messias	23
X	X			S	X			X	X	X	X			X								X		S	S	X	X	S1	P Rejer	24
X	X	S		S	X			X	X	X	X			X								X		S	X1	X	S1		A G Wiley	25
X	X	S			X			X	X	X	X			X								X		S	X	X	X		E K Wolstenholme	26
X	X	S2			S	X			X	X	X			X1	X	S		S				X			X2	X	S1		D Pugh	27
	X		S3	X	X3								X	X	S2	X		X				S1	X		X	X1	X2			28
X	X			S	S	X			X	X				X	S	S		X				X			X	X	X	X	J P Robinson	29
X1	X			S	S	X			X	X				X	S	S		X				X	S1		X	X	X	X	D Pugh	30
X	X			S1		X			X	X				X1		S		X				X			X2	X	S2		A P D'Urso	31
X	X			X		X				X	X	X1				S		X				X	X		S	X	S1		T Heilbron	32
X	X			X	S	X				X	X1	X						X				X	X		S	X	S1		G B Frankland	33
X	X	X2		X		X3				X	S3	X1						X				X	X		X	S2	X	S1	G Laws	34
X2	X	S2		X		X3				X1	X	X		S1				X				X			X	X	X	S3	P S Danson	35
X	X	X1	X	S		X				X	X							X		S		X			X	X	X	S1	K M Lynch	36
S	X	X1	X			X				X	X	S2						X				X			X2	X	S1	C R Wilkes	37
S1	X			X	S3	X1				X	X	X						X				X	X2	X	X	X	S2	T Jones	38
X3	X			X	S3					X	X1	X						X				X	X2	X	S1	X	S2	D R Crick	39
X1	X			X	S1					X	X2	X						X				X	X	S	X	X	S2	M R Halsey	40
X1	X			X	S	S1				X		X		X	S			X				X			X	X	X		M J Brandwood	41
X1	X			X	S					X		X		X	S			X				X			X	X	X	S1	G Singh	42
X	X			X2	S					X	S2	X		X1				X				X			X	X	X	S	W C Burns	43
X	X			X						X	S1	X		X	S			X				X1	X		X	X	S	F G Stretton	44
X1	X			X						X	X	X		X	S1			X			S	X		S	X	X		A P D'Urso	45
X3	X	X				X				X	X	X		S1	S3		X	X1				X	X		X2		S2	M Fletcher	46
S	S	X		X						X	X	X		X				X				X	X		S	X	X	P Rejer	47
S1	X			X						X	X	X		X	S			X				X			S	X	X	C J Foy	48
S2	X			S1		X1				X	X2	X		X				X				X			S	X	X	M J Jones	49
S	X			X		X				X	X			X	X			X				X			S	X	X	E K Wolstenholme	50
S1	X	X		X						X	X			X	X1			X				X			X	X	X	M C Bailey	51
X	S1	X1		X						X	X			X			S	S2		X		X			X2	X	X	R Pearson	52
X	X			X	S1					X		X1				S2	X2	X				X	X3		X	X		P R Richards	53
X	X1	S1		X	S					X		X			S2	X2	X				X	X		X	X		K A Leach	54

32	40	8	3	34		29	2	2	5	44	32	30		29	5	2	11	36	1	3		43	26	2	24	44	19		FL Appearances	
/	3	2	1	2	6	4	1			3	5	3		4	3	2	2			1					1	6		15	FL Sub Appearances	
3+1	3	1		4		2			0+1	4	3	2		0+1	3			4	4			3			1	4	3		CC Appearances	
3	3	0+1			0+1	3				3	3	2		0+1	3	2			1			2	1+1		3	3	1+1		FAC Appearances	
		1		0+1	1	1				1	1	0+1		1		1		1			0+1	1			1	1	1	1	AWS Appearances	

Also Played: (D) Allardyce S3(53). (M) Brown S(22). (M) Leach S(51).

CHESTERFIELD   RECORDS AND STATISTICS

CLUB RECORDS

BIGGEST VICTORIES
League: 10-0 v Glossop, Division 2, 17.1.1903.
F.A. Cup: 5-0 v Wath Athletic (a), 1st Round, 1925-26.
League Cup: 5-0 v Mansfield (a), 1st Round, 1971-72.
5-0 v Scunthorpe United, 1st Round replay, 1972-73.

BIGGEST DEFEATS
League: 0-10 v Gillingham (a), Division 3, 5.9.1987.
F.A. Cup: 1-8 v West Ham United, 1st Round, 1913-14.
0-7 v Burnley, 3rd Round, 1956-57.

MOST POINTS
3 points a win: 91, Division 4, 1984-85.
2 points a win: 64, Division 4, 1969-70.

MOST GOALS SCORED
102, Division 3(N), 1930-31.

RECORD TRANSFER FEE RECEIVED
£200,000 from Wolves for Alan Birch, August 1981.

RECORD TRANSFER FEE PAID
£150,000 to Carlisle United for Phil Bonnyman, March 1980.

BEST PERFORMANCES
League: 4th Division 2, 1946-47.
F.A. Cup: Semi-Final - Middlesbrough 3-3, 0-3 - 1996-97.
League Cup: 4th Round 1964-65.

HONOURS
Champions Division 3(N) 1930-31, 1935-36.
Champions Division 4, 1969-70, 1984-85.
Anglo-Scottish Cup winners 1980-81.

LEAGUE CAREER
Elected to Div 2 1899, Failed re-election 1908-09, Re-elected to Div 3(N) 1921-22, Div 2 1930-31, Div 3(N) 1932-33, Div 2 1935-36, Div £(N) 1950-51, Transferred to Div 3 1958, Div 4 1960-61, Div 3 1969-70, Div 4 1982-83, Div 3 1984-85, Div 4 (now Div 3) 1988-89, Div 2 1994-95.

INDIVIDUAL CLUB RECORDS

MOST GOALS IN A SEASON
Jimmy Cookson: 46 goals in 1925-26 (League 44, FA Cup 2).

MOST GOALS IN A MATCH
No player has ever scored more than 4 goals in a match, but this feat has been achieved on 19 occasions.

OLDEST PLAYER
Billy Kidd, 40 years 232 days v Southampton, Division 2, 20.9.1947.

YOUNGEST PLAYER
Dennis Thompson, 16 years 160 days v Notts County, Division 2, 26.12.1950.

MOST CAPPED PLAYER
Walter McMillan (Northern Ireland) 4.

PREVIOUS MANAGERS

1945-49 Bob Brocklebank; 1949-52 Bob Marshall; 1952-58 Ted Davison; 1958-62 Dugald Livingstone; 1962-67 Tony McShane; 1967-73 Jimmy McGuigan; 1973-76 Joe Shaw; 1976-80 Arthur Cox; 1980-83 Frank Barlow; 1983-87 John Duncan; 1987-88 Kevin Randall; 1988-91 Paul Hart; 1991-93 Chris McMenemy.

ADDITIONAL INFORMATION
PREVIOUS NAMES
Chesterfield Municipal until 1915, Chesterfield Town 1919-22.

PREVIOUS LEAGUES
Midland League.

Club colours: Royal blue & blue striped shirts with white & red trim, blue shorts with white trim, blue socks.

Reserves League: Pontins League.

LONGEST LEAGUE RUNS

of undefeated matches:	21 (1994-95)	of league matches w/out a win:	16 (1960-61, 1983)
of undefeated home matches:	27 (1925-26)	of undefeated away matches:	12 (1994-95)
without home win:	9 (1963)	without an away win:	26 (1907-08)
of league wins:	10 (1933)	of home wins:	17 (1929-30)
of league defeats:	9 (1960)	of away wins:	6 (1933)

THE MANAGER

JOHN DUNCAN . . . . appointed February 1993.

PREVIOUS CLUBS
As Manager . . . . Hartlepool United, Chesterfield, Ipswich Town.
As Player Manager . . . . Scunthorpe United.
As a player . . . . Dundee, Tottenham Hotspur, Derby County, Scunthorpe United.

HONOURS
As a Manager . . . . Chesterfield: Division 4 Champions 1985. Promotion to Division 2 via the play-offs 1995.
As a Player . . . . Scottish Football League.

CHESTERFIELD

PLAYERS NAME Honours	Ht	Wt	Birthdate	Birthplace Transfers	Contract Date	Clubs	League	L/Cup	FA Cup	Other	Lge	L/C	FAC	Oth
G O A L K E E P E R														
Leaning Andrew J	6	13	5/18/63	Howden		Rowntree Mac.								
				Free	7/1/85	York City	69	4	8	5				
				Free	5/28/87	Sheffield United	21	2	2					
				£12000	9/27/88	Bristol City	75	5	7	2				
				Free	3/24/94	Lincoln City	36	6	3	2				
					10/4/96	Chesterfield	14		2					
Mercer Billy	6.1	11	5/22/69	Liverpool	8/21/87	Liverpool								
					2/16/89	Rotherham United	104	12	12	10				
				£75000	10/12/94	Sheffield United	3							
				Loan	3/21/95	Nottingham Forest								
				£100000	12/12/95	Chesterfield	105	6	9	4				
D E F E N C E														
Breckin Ian AWS 95/96	6.1	12.9	2/24/75	Rotherham	11/1/93	Rotherham United	130+2	6	5	10	5			
					7/24/97	Chesterfield	40+3	3	3		1		1	
Carr Darren	6.2	13	9/4/68	Bristol	8/20/86	Bristol Rovers	26+4	2+2	3	2				
					10/30/87	Newport County	9							
				£8000	3/10/88	Sheffield United	12+1	1	3+1	1	1			
				£35000	9/18/90	Crewe Alexandra	96+8	8	12	10	5		2	
				£30000	7/21/93	Chesterfield	84+2	9	6+3	7	4			
Hewitt Jamie	5.11	10.8	5/17/68	Chesterfield	4/22/86	Chesterfield	240+9	10	8+1	11+2	14	1		
				Free	8/1/92	Doncaster Rovers	32+1	3+1	1	3		1		
					10/8/93	Chesterfield	169+7	11	13	9	9		1	
Lenagh Steven M	6.3	13.9	3/21/79	Durham		Sheffield Wed. (T)								
				Free	2/20/98	Chesterfield	0+3			0+1				
Perkins Chris	5.11	10.9	1/9/74	Nottingham	11/19/92	Mansfield Town	3+5			0+1				
				Free	7/15/94	Chesterfield	104+10	5+1	12	6+3	2	1		
Williams Mark S Div.3'94.	6	13	9/28/70	Hyde		Newtown								
				Free	3/27/92	Shrewsbury Town	98+6	7+1	6	6	3			1
				£20000	8/7/95	Chesterfield	126	7	12	5	9		1	
M I D F I E L D														
Curtis Tommy	5.8	11.4	3/1/73	Exeter	7/1/91	Derby County								
				Free	8/12/93	Chesterfield	193+4	15	13	10	10	1	1	
Ebdon Marcus W: u21.2, Y.	5.9	11	10/17/70	Pontypool	8/16/89	Everton								
				Free	7/15/91	Peterborough United	136+11	14+2	12+3	11+1	15	1		
					3/21/97	Chesterfield	39+5	2	3		3			
Holland Paul	5.11	12.1	7/8/73	Lincoln	7/4/91	Mansfield Town	149	11	7	9	25		3	
					6/1/95	Sheffield United								
				£200000	1/5/96	Chesterfield	71+4	5	10	1	8			
Lomas James	5.11	10.9	10/18/77	Chesterfield										
Pearce Alexander G	5.9	10.9	5/26/80	Bolton	3/6/98	Chesterfield (T)								
F O R W A R D														
Beaumont Chris	5.11	11.7	12/5/65	Sheffield		Denaby United								
				Free	7/21/88	Rochdale	31+3	0+1	2	2	7	1	1	
				£0000	7/21/89	Stockport County	238+20	14+3	15	32+2	39	3	1	6
					8/15/96	Chesterfield	61+11	5+1	6+2	1	2	1		
Carss Tony	5.10	12	3/31/76	Alnwick		Bradford City (T)								
				Free	8/29/94	Blackburn Rovers								
				Free	8/11/95	Darlington	33+24	5	2+1	4	2	1		
				Free	7/28/97	Cardiff City	36+6	2	5+1	1	1			
				Free	7/1/98	Chesterfield								
Dunn Iain G W E:u19.4	5.11	11.7	4/1/70	Howden	7/7/88	York City	46+31	3+1	3+1	1+3	11			
				Free	8/14/91	Chesterfield	8+5			1				
					8/1/92	Scarborough								
				Free	9/29/92	Peterborough Utd				0+1				
				Free	10/1/92	Scarborough								
				Free	11/1/92	Goole Town								
				Free	12/4/92	Huddersfield Town	62+57	6+3	6+3	11+7	14	3	3	9
				Loan	9/20/96	Scunthorpe United	4							
					2/28/97	Chesterfield	10+7		0+2					
Howard Jonathan	5.11	11.7	10/7/71	Sheffield	7/10/90	Rotherham United	25+11	0+1	4	3+1	5		2	
					12/9/94	Chesterfield	71+38	5	10+1	5+3	18		2	2
Jules Mark	5.11	11.1	9/5/71	Bradford	7/3/90	Bradford City	0+1							
				Free	8/14/91	Scarborough	57+20	6+4	1+1	6	16	2		4
				£40000	5/21/93	Chesterfield	135+26	10+7	12+2	7	4	2		
Reeves David	6	11.7	19/11/67	Birkenhead	06/08/86	Sheffield Wednesday	8+9	1+1	1+1	+1	2	1		
				Loan	17/12/86	Scunthorpe United	3+1				2			
				Loan	01/10/87	Scunthorpe United	6				4			
				Loan	20/11/87	Burnley	16			2	8			1
				£80000	17/08/89	Bolton Wanderers	111+23	14+1	8+5	9+2	30	1	5	7
				£80000	25/03/93	Notts County	9+4	1			2			
					01/10/93	Carlisle United	127	9	9	23	49	5	4	6
				Free	08/10/96	Preston North End	45+2	3+1	2	1	12	3	3	
					11/6/97	Chesterfield	26		1+1		5		1	
Wilkinson Stephen J DIV3 95/96	5.11	10.9	9/1/68	Lincoln	9/6/86	Leicester City	5+4		1		1			
				Loan	9/8/88	Crewe Alexandra	3+2				2			
				£80000	10/2/89	Mansfield Town	214+18	13+1	10+1	17	83	4	2	1
				£90000	6/12/95	Preston North End	44+8	4	2	2	13	4	1	
					7/11/97	Chesterfield	24+6	1	3		6			
Willis Roger C	6.2	12	6/17/67	Sheffield	7/20/89	Grimsby Town	1+8	0+1						
				£10000	8/1/90	Barnet	39+5	2	5+1	1+4	13		3	1
				£175000	10/6/92	Watford	30+6		1		2			
				£150000	12/31/93	Birmingham City	11+5		+1		5			
				£100000	9/16/94	Southend United	30+1				7			
					8/13/96	Peterborough Utd	33+6	3	5+1		6			
					7/8/97	Chesterfield	19+15	3	1+1		7	2	1	

RECREATION GROUND
Saltergate, Chesterfield S40 4SX

Capacity 11,308
Seating 2,608

First game ....v Lincoln City, 9.9.1899.
First floodlit game ....v Lincoln City, 23.10.1967.

Attendances
Highest...30,968 v Newcastle United, Division 2, 7.4.1939.
Lowest..1,053 v Burnley, AMC, 21.1.1986.

Other Grounds ....None.

HOW TO GET TO THE GROUND

From the North
Use motorway (M1) until junction 30, then follow signs to Chesterfield (A619). In town centre follow signs to Old Brampton into Saltergate for Chesterfield FC.

From East and South
Follow signs to Chesterfield (A617) into town centre then follow signs to Old Brampton into Saltergate for Chesterfield FC.

From the West
Follow signs to Chesterfield (A619) then at roundabout take first exit into Foljambe Road at the end turn right into Saltergate for Chesterfield FC.

Car Parking: Street parking near ground allowed. Car parks 0.5 miles from ground in Saltergate.
Nearest Railway Station: Chesterfield (01246 74371)

USEFUL TELEPHONE NUMBERS

Club switchboard 01246 209 765
Club fax number.......................01246 556 799
Ticket office 01246 209 765
Marketing Department 01246 231 535

Spireites Hotline......................0891 55 58 18*
*Calls cost 50p per minute at all times.
Call costings correct at time of going to press.

MATCHDAY PROGRAMME

Programme Editor (97/98) ....K Barson.

Number of pages (97/98) ....36.

Price (97/98).....................................£1.60.

Subscriptions ....Apply to club.

Local Newspapers
.................Derbyshire Times, Sheffield Star,
....Chesterfield Star.

Local Radio Stations
...........Radio Hallam, Radio BBC Sheffield.

MATCHDAY TICKET PRICES (1997/98)

Centre Stand. £10
Juv/OAP £5

Wing Stand. £9
Juv/OAP £5

Terraces £8
Juv/OAP £4

Away - standing £8
Away - seated. £9

COLCHESTER UNITED
(The U's)
NATIONWIDE LEAGUE DIVISION 2
SPONSORED BY: GUARDIAN DIRECT/ASHBYS

554000 (((•—•))) EAST COAST **CABLE** (((•—•))) EAST COAST **CABLE** ((•—

1998/99 - Back Row L-R: Paul Abrahams, Tony Lock, Karl Duguid, Joel Rogers, David Gregory, Neil Gregory, Geraint Williams.
Middle Row: Adrian Webster (Yth. Dev.), Micky Cook (Director of Yth.), Brian Owen (Physio), Simon Betts, Aaron Skelton, Ian Wiles, Carl Emberson, Tamer Fernandes, Steve Forbes, Richard Wilkins, Tony Adcock, Steve Bradshaw (F.I.C.), Paul Dyer (Res. Team Manager), Geoff Harrop (Asst. Director of Yth.). **Front Row:** Sponsor, Joe Dunne, Paul Buckle, David Greene, Mark Sale, Steve Wignall (Manager), David Rainford, Nicky Haydon, Ian Hathaway, Scott Stamps, Sponsor.

COLCHESTER UNITED
FORMED IN 1937
TURNED PROFESSIONAL IN 1937
LTD COMPANY IN 1937

CHAIRMAN: Gordon Parker
VICE-CHAIRMAN
Peter Heard
DIRECTORS
Peter Powell, John Worsp,
Steve Gage (Managing Director)
SECRETARY
Marie Partner
MARKETING MANAGER
John Schultz
COMMERCIAL MANAGER
Brian Wheeler
MANAGER: Steve Wignall
ASSISTANT MANAGER: Steve Whitton
RESERVE TEAM MANAGER
Paul Dyer
YOUTH TEAM MANAGER
Micky Cook
PHYSIOTHERAPIST
Brian Owen

STATISTICIAN FOR THE DIRECTORY
Vacant

Colchester United crowned a terrific second-half to the 1997098 season by winning the Third Division play-off final at the home of English football - Wembley Stadium - when they beat Torquay United 1-0, thanks to a first-half penalty converted by David Gregory.

Throughout the first half of the campaign the 'U's' played some neat and tidy football, at home and away, but after Christmas they played even better - and a lot of people, not connected with the club, agreed that promotion was well deserved. Under the guidance of manager Steve Wignall, the players responded magnificently, even when the odds were stacked against them with injuries and suspensions disrupting team selection and were always in contention from February onwards,
The 'U's' had started brightly enough, winning four and drawing two of their opening eight matches.

Surprisingly, after a dozen games had been completed they had slipped down the Division to 13th. They continued to find it hard going and at the halfway stage in the proceedings had fallen an extra place to a disturbing 14th, having obtained a mere 31 points out of a possible 69.

Towards the end of January performances started to perk up and slowly but surely the team forced it's way up towards the play-off zone. At the end of February (with 35 games played) the 'U's' were ninth - well in touch with the clubs immediately above them. Going into the final stretch, Colchester buckled down and from their last six matches they secured 13 points to finish fourth, just one point away from an automatic promotion place.

But that disappointment of just missing out was soon forgotten at Wembley where around 15,000 supporters cheered the team's triumph over Torquay to clinch a place in Division Two.

Tony Matthews.

COLCHESTER UNITED

| Division 3 | | :4th | | FA CUP: 2nd Round | | | LC CUP: 1st Round | | AWS: Southern Round 1 |

M	DATE	COMP.	VEN	OPPONENTS	RESULT	H/T	LP	GOAL SCORERS/GOAL TIMES	ATT.
1	A 09	FL	H	Darlington	W 2-1	1-0	4	Abrahams 32, Buckle 58 (pen)	2958
2	12	CC 1/1	H	Luton Town	L 0-1	0-0			2840
3	15	FL	A	Hartlepool United	L 2-3	1-1	8	Buckle 37 (pen), Abrahams 60	(2174)
4	22	FL	H	Barnet	D 1-1	0-0	5	Wilkins 73	3286
5	26	CC 1/2	A	Luton Town	D 1-1	0-1		Hathaway 52	(2816)
6	30	FL	A	Torquay United	D 1-1	0-0	14	Wilkins 65	(2081)
7	S 02	FL	A	Cambridge United	L 1-4	1-1	17	Gregory D 37	(3264)
8	08	FL	H	Brighton & H.A.	W 3-1	1-0	11	Greene 4, 57 Abrahams 49	3081
9	12	FL	H	Scarborough	W 1-0	0-0	5	Lock 87	2756
10	20	FL	A	Swansea City	W 1-0	0-0	6	Greene 48	(3414)
11	27	FL	H	Exeter City	L 1-2	0-1	9	Abrahams 53	3175
12	O 04	FL	A	Mansfield Town	D 1-1	1-1	9	Greene 12	(2341)
13	11	FL	A	Peterborough United	L 2-3	1-0	11	Rankin 32, Adcock 82	(6277)
14	18	FL	H	Shrewsbury Town	D 1-1	0-1	13	Skelton 52	2977
15	21	FL	H	Doncaster Rovers	W 2-1	2-1	9	Sale 5, Skelton 7	2588
16	25	FL	A	Leyton Orient	W 2-0	1-0	7	Adcock 4, Forbes 77	(4592)
17	31	FL	H	Scunthorpe United	D 3-3	3-0	7	Rankin 1, Buckle 32, Sale 39	3134
18	N 04	FL	A	Macclesfield Town	D 0-0	0-0	8		(1577)
19	08	FL	A	Rochdale	L 1-2	0-1	12	Duguid 60	(1702)
20	15	FAC 1	A	Brentford	D 2-2	1-1		Sale 37, Gregory D 87	(2899)
21	18	FL	H	Notts County	W 2-0	0-0	10	Sale 67, Rankin 86	2643
22	22	FL	H	Lincoln City	L 0-1	0-0	12		2932
23	25	FAC 1R	H	Brentford	D 0-0*	0-0		Colchester won 4-2 on penalties	3613
24	29	FL	A	Rotherham United	L 2-3	0-1	13	Skelton 48, Sale 61	(3259)
25	D 06	FAC 2	H	Hereford United	D 1-1	1-0		Gregory D 10	3558
26	09	AWS S1	A	Leyton Orient	L 0-1	0-0			(933)
27	13	FL	A	Hull City	L 1-3	0-0	15	Adcock 89	3896
28	16	FAC 2R	A	Hereford United	D 1-1*	0-0		Forbes 47 (Hereford won 5-4 on penalties	(3725)
29	19	FL	H	Chester City	W 2-0	1-0	13	Adcock 13, Duguid 76	1897
30	26	FL	A	Brighton & H.A.	D 4-4	3-0	14	Rankin 15, 29, Adcock 24, Stamps 74	(2647)
31	29	FL	H	Cambridge United	W 3-2	1-1	13	Wilkins 45, 48, Skelton 67	4518
32	J 03	FL	H	Hartlepool United	L 1-2	0-1	13	Buckle 82	2885
33	10	FL	A	Darlington	L 2-4	0-1	13	Gregory N 68, 79	(2170)
34	16	FL	H	Torquay United	W 1-0	0-0	11	Lock 86	2776
35	20	FL	H	Cardiff City	W 2-1	0-0	11	Gregory N 70, Buckle 80	1949
36	24	FL	A	Barnet	L 2-3	2-1	13	Skelton 4, Wilkins 83	(2471)
37	31	FL	A	Scarborough	D 1-1	0-0	13	Whitton 46	(2219)
38	F 06	FL	H	Swansea City	L 1-2	1-0	13	Gregory N 29	2789
39	13	FL	H	Mansfield Town	W 2-0	1-0	12	Lock 30, Gregory D 68	2320
40	21	FL	A	Exeter City	W 1-0	0-0	11	Lock 69	(3346)
41	24	FL	A	Shrewsbury Town	W 2-0	1-0	10	Gregory N 7, Gregory D 68	(1972)
42	27	FL	H	Peterborough United	W 1-0	0-0	7	Branston 61	4117
43	M 03	FL	H	Rochdale	D 0-0	0-0	9		2112
44	07	FL	A	Scunthorpe United	L 0-1	0-1	10		(2143)
45	14	FL	H	Macclesfield Town	W 5-1	1-1	7	Sale 35, 57, Skelton 77, Abrahams 80, Lock 87	2760
46	21	FL	A	Notts County	D 0-0	0-0	8		(6284)
47	28	FL	A	Lincoln City	W 1-0	1-0	7	Dunne 29	(4040)
48	A 03	FL	H	Rotherham United	W 2-1	1-1	6	Skelton 12, Sale 56	3824
49	11	FL	A	Cardiff City	W 2-0	0-0	6	Abrahams 47, Gregory D 59	(2809)
50	13	FL	H	Hull City	W 4-3	2-1	4	Gregory D 6, Lock 14, Dunne 78, Duguid 90	4700
51	18	FL	A	Chester City	L 1-3	0-3	4	Abraham 74	(1780)
52	25	FL	H	Leyton Orient	D 1-1	1-1	5	Gregory N 45	6220
53	M 02	FL	A	Doncaster Rovers	W 1-0	0-0	4	Gregory N 57	(3572)
54	10	PO SF1	A	Barnet	L 0-1	0-0			(3858)
55	13	PO SF2	H	Barnet	W 3-1	1-1		Gregory N 11, 95, Greene 65	5863
56	22	PO F	N	Torquay United	W 1-0	1-0		Gregory D 23 (pen)	19486

Best Home League Attendance: 6220 V Leyton Orient   **Smallest :1897 V Chester City**   **Average :3148**

Goal Scorers:

FL	(72)	Abrahams 7, Gregory N 7, Sale 7, Skelton 7, Lock 6, Adcock 5, Buckle 5, Gregory D 5, Rankin 5, Wilkins 5, Greene 4, Duguid 3, Dunne 2, Branston 1, Forbes 1, Stamps 1, Whitton 1
CC	(1)	Hathaway 1
FAC	(4)	Gregory D 2, Forbes 1, Sale 1
AWS	(0)	
PO	(4)	Gregory N 2, Greene 1 Gregory D 1	*AET

(F) Abrahams	(F) Adcock	(D) Betts	(M) Branston	(M) Brolin	(M) Brown	(M) Buckle	(D) Cawley	(F) Duguid	(F) Dunne	(G) Emberson	(M) Forbes	(D) Greene	(D) Gregory	(F) Gregory	(F) Hathaway	(M) Haydon	(M) Lock	(M) Newell	(M) Rainford	(F) Rankin	(F) Sale	(M) Skelton	(F) Stamps	(F) Whitton	(M) Wilkins	Name	No
X	S2					X	X			X	S1	X	X		X		S				X	X	X		X	B. Knight	1
X	S2					X	X			X	S1	X	X		X		S3				X	X	X		X	S G Bennett	2
X	S2					X	X			X	S1	X	X		X		S3				X	X	X		X	J P Robinson	3
X	S3					X	X			X	S2	X	X		X		S1				X	X	X		X	M C Bailey	4
X	S1					X	X			X	X	X	X		X		S2				X		X	S	X	D Orr	5
X	S					X	X			X	X	X	X		X	X	S				X		X	S	X	D R Crick	6
X	X3					X1	X			X	X2	X	X				S2	S3			X		X		X	F G Stretton	7
X	X					X	X			X	X	X	X				S2	S1			X		X		X	J A Kirkby	8
X	X					X	X			X	X	X	X		S2	S	S1				X		X		X	A G Wiley	9
X	X					X	X			X	X	X	X		S		S2				X		X	S1	X	S W Mathieson	10
X	S1					X	X			X		X	X				S2			X	X	X	X	S	X	A N Butler	11
X	S					X	X			X		X	X				S			X	X	X	X	S1	X	K M Lynch	12
S2	X						X	S1		X		X					S			X	X	X	X	X	X	P Taylor	13
S2	X			S1	X	X	S3			X	X						X			X	X	X	X	X		R J Harris	14
X	X			S	X	X	S1			X	X		X				X	S			X	X	X		X	A P D'Urso	15
S1	X		S		X	X				X	X	X				S2	X				X	X				A Bates	16
	X		S1		X	X				X	X	X					S3			X	X	X	X	S2		R D Furnandiz	17
	X		S		S2	X	S1			X	X	X					S2			X	X	X	X	X		C J Foy	18
	X		S			X	X	S1		X	X	X					S2			X	X	X	X			T Heilbron	19
S2	S3					X	X	S1	X	X3	X	X		S				S		X	X2	X	X	X1		B Knight	20
X	S					X	X	X	X	S1	X	X		S2						X	X		X	X		R Styles	21
X	S2	X				X	X	X	X	X	X	X		S1						X	X	S		X		R Pearson	22
X1	X2	X				X	X	X	X	X	X	X		S1	S	S2	S			X	S3			X3		B Knight	23
S	X					X	X	X	X	X	S	X	X				X			S1	X	X1		X		W C Burns	24
X1	X			X		X	X	X	S	X3	X		X2	S3	S1	S				X	X	S2				K M Lynch	25
X2						X1	X	S3	X	X	S1		X			X	S2		X3	X	X	X					26
X						S1	X		X	X	X3	X				S2	X	S3			X	X2		X1		M J Jones	27
X	S2					S	X	S1	X	X	X	X				X1	S3	S			X	X2		X3		M A Cooper	28
X						S	X	S1	X1	X	X	X					S		X		X	X		X		M E Pierce	29
X						S1	X	S2	X	X	X2	X							X	S	X1	X		X		M D Haxby	30
X						X	X1	X		X		X				S2	S1			X2	X	S	X	X		P Rejer	31
X1						S3	X		X	X		X2	X			S2	S1			X	X	Y3	X			A G Wiley	32
						X	X		X	S1	X	S3	X		X	S2			X	X2	X3	X1	X			S W Mathieson	33
						X	X1		X	X	X	S1	X		X	S2			X	X	X2	S	X			F G Stretton	34
						X		S2	X	X	X	X				X2	S3			X3	X1	X	S1	X		M C Bailey	35
						X3	X		X	X2	X	X				S1	S2			X	X	X1	S3	X		P S Danson	36
S	S						S	X	X	X	X	X				X				X	X			X		D Laws	37
						S3		S1	X	X	X	X	X				X1	S2			X2	X		X3	X	J A Kirkby	38
		X	X			X		S2		X	X1	X2	X		X						S1			X	X	J P Robinson	39
S	X	X				X		S		X	X	X					X			S	X	X		X		A Bates	40
S1	X	X				X		S2		X	X	X				X1				S	X	X		X		C R Wilkes	41
X	X	X				X		S2	X	X2	X	X1					X			S	X	X		X		D R Crick	42
X	X	X				X			X	X				S1	S	X		S	X1	X			X			S J Baines	43
X2	X	X				X			X	X				X1	S1	X	X		S	S2	X			X		K M Lynch	44
S1		X				X		X1	X	X	X3	X		S3	S2	X2				X	X			X		S G Bennett	45
X1		X				X		S1	X	X	S2	X		S3	X				X2	X3			X			E Lomas	46
S2		X	X			X		S	X1	X	S1	X				X2				X	X			X		M J Brandwood	47
S2		X	X			X		S	X	X		X				X1				X2	X			X		R Styles	48
S1		X	X1			X		S3	X	X		X	S1			X3				X2	X			X		M Fletcher	49
S1		X	X			X		S3	X	X	X1	S2				X3				X2	X			X		P Taylor	50
S1		X	X			X2		S3	X	X		X				X				X3	X1			X		P R Richards	51
X3		X	X			X		S2	X	X	S3	X1	X			X				X2	S1			X		A R Hall	52
X2		X				X		S2	X	X	S3	X				S1				X1	X			X3		T Heilbron	53
S		X	X			X		S	X	X	X	X	X1			S1				X	X					E K Wolstenholme	54
X1		X				X		S2	X	X	X3	X	X2			S1				X	S3		X			T Heilbron	55
S		X				X		S2	X	X	X	X	X1			S1				X	X2		X			M Fletcher	56
16	19	16	12			33	27	6	22	46	25	38	42	12	5	9	14			10	38	37	26	15	37	FL Appearances	
9	6			2		5		15	3		10			2	3	7	8	18			1	1	2		6	FL Sub Appearances	
2	0+2					2	2			2	1+1	2	2		2		0+2				2	1	2		2	CC Appearances	
1+1	3+1	2+1				1	3	3+1	3+1	4	2	4	4	1+1	1+1	0+3				3	3+1	2+1	2		2	FAC Appearances	
	1					1	1	0+1	1	1	0+1	1			1	0+1				1	1	1				AWS Appearances	
1		3	1			3		0+2	3	3	3	3	3	3		1	0+3				3	2+1			2	PO Appearances	

393

COLCHESTER UNITED   RECORDS AND STATISTICS

CLUB RECORDS

BIGGEST VICTORIES
League: 9-1 v Bradford City, Division 4, 30.12.1961.
F.A. Cup: 7-0 v Yeovil Town, 2nd Round, 1958.

BIGGEST DEFEATS
League: 0-8 v Leyton Orient, 15.10.1988.

MOST POINTS
3 points a win: 81, Division 4,1982-83.
2 points a win: 60, Division 4, 1973-74.

RECORD TRANSFER FEE RECEIVED
£120,000 from Wimbledon for P McGee, February 1989.

RECORD TRANSFER FEE PAID
£45,000 to Sporting Lochern for D Tempest, August 1987.

BEST PERFORMANCES
League: 3rd Division 3(S), 1956-57.
Highest Position:
F.A. Cup: 6th Round (shared record for Division 4) 1970-71.
League Cup: 5th Round 1974-75.

HONOURS
GMVC winners 1991-92.
FA Trophy winners 1991-92.

LEAGUE CAREER
Elected to Div.3(S) 1950, Transferred to Div.3 1958, Relegated to Div.4 1960-61, Promoted to Div.3 1961-62, Relegated to Div.4 1964-65, Promoted to Div.3 1965-66, relegated to Div.4 1967-68, Promoted to Div.3 1973-74, Relegated to Div.4 1975-76, Promoted to Div.3 1976-77, relegated to Div.4 1980-81, Relegated to GM Vauxhall Conference 1989-90, Promoted to Div 3 (Old 4) 1991-92.

INDIVIDUAL CLUB RECORDS

MOST GOALS IN A SEASON
Bobby Hunt: 38 goals in 1961-62 (League 37, FA Cup 1).

MOST GOALS IN A MATCH
No one has scored more than four.

OLDEST PLAYER
Benny Fenton, 39 years 6 months.

YOUNGEST PLAYER
Lindsay Smith, 16 years 218 days v Grimsby Town, 24.4.1971.

MOST CAPPED PLAYER
None.

PREVIOUS MANAGERS

(Since joining the Football League)
Ted Fenton; Jimmy Allen, Jack Butler, Benny Fenton, Neil Franklin, Dick Graham, Jim Smith, Bobby Roberts, Allan Hunter, Cyril Lea, Jock Wallace, Mick Mills, Ian Atkins, Roy McDonough, George Burley.

ADDITIONAL INFORMATION
PREVIOUS NAMES
None.

PREVIOUS LEAGUES
Southern League; Alliance Premier (Vauxhall Conference).

Club Colours: Royal blue & white striped shirts, royal blue shorts, white socks.

Reserves League: Springheath Print Capital League.

LONGEST LEAGUE RUNS

of undefeated matches:	20 (1956-57)	of league matches w/out a win:	20 (1968)
of undefeated home matches:	27 (1956-57)	of undefeated away matches:	9 (1956-57)
without home win:	11 (1958)	without an away win:	19 (1950-51, 1959-60)
of league wins:	7 (1968-69)	of home wins:	13 (1976-77)
of league defeats:	8 (1954)	of away wins:	5 (1981, 1987)

THE MANAGER

STEVE WIGNALL. . . . . appointed January 1995.

PREVIOUS CLUBS
As Manager. . . . . Aldershot.
As Asst.Man/Coach. . . . .
As a player . . . . Doncaster Rovers, Colchester United, Brentford, Aldershot.

HONOURS
As a Manager . . . . None.
As a Player . . . . None.

COLCHESTER UNITED

PLAYERS NAME Honours	Ht	Wt	Birthdate	Birthplace Transfers	Contract Date	Clubs	League	L/Cup	FA Cup	Other	Lge	L/C	FAC	Oth
G O A L K E E P E R														
Emberson Carl W	6.1	12.5	7/13/73	Epsom	5/4/91	Millwall				1				
				Loan	12/17/92	Colchester United	13							
				Free	7/6/94	Colchester United	141+1	7	7	8				
Fernandes Tamer H	6.2	13.8	12/7/74	London	7/12/93	Brentford (T)	13+3	1	2	1+2				
E: Y.				Loan	10/12/93	Wealdstone								
				Loan		Peterborough Utd								
				Free	1997/98	Colchester United								
D E F E N C E														
Branston Guy	6	13.4	1/9/79	Leicester	7/3/97	Leicester City (T)								
				Loan	2/9/98	Colchester United	12		1		1			
				Free	7/1/98	Colchester United								
Greene David M	6.2	11.1	10/26/73	Luton	9/3/91	Luton Town	18+1	2	1	+1				
E: u21.5				Loan	11/23/95	Colchester United	14			2	1			
				Loan	3/1/96	Brentford	11							
				Free	8/15/96	Colchester United	37	2	4	3	4			1
Gregory David	5.11	11.6	1/23/70	Colchester	3/31/87	Ipswich Town	16+16	3+2	1	3+2	2			4
				Loan	1/9/95	Hereford United	2			1				
				Free	7/4/95	Peterborough United								
				Free	12/8/95	Colchester United	81+11	3+1	5	2	6		2	3
M I D F I E L D														
Buckle Paul	5.7	10.1	12/16/70	Hatfield	7/1/89	Brentford	42+15	5+1	3+1	6+5	1			
				Free	2/3/94	Torquay United	46+2	4	3	3	5			
				Free	11/3/95	Exeter City	22		1	2	2			
				Free	11/28/96	Colchester United	57+5	2	1	9	5			3
Forbes Steven D	6.2	12.6	12/24/75	London		Sittingbourne								
				£45000	7/11/94	Millwall	+5	+1						
					3/14/97	Colchester United	25+10	1+1	2	3	2		1	
Goss Jeremy	5.9	10.9	5/11/65	Cyprus	3/23/83	Norwich City (T)	155+33	14+3	14+4	15	13	3		6
W: 7. FAYC'83.				via Hearts										
				Free	3/26/98	Colchester United								
Haydon Nicholas	5.11	11.7	8/10/78	Barking	1/1/00	Colchester United	9+9		1+1		1			
Lock Anthony C	5.11	11	9/3/76	Harlow	4/18/95	Colchester United	14+26	+2	+3	+3	8			
				Loan	3/15/96	Chelmsford								
Rainford David J	6	11.11	4/21/79	Stepney	7/3/97	Colchester Utd (T)								
Skelton Aaron	5.11	11.05	11/22/74	Welwyn G.C.	5/31/94	Luton Town	5+3	+1	2	1				
				Free	7/3/97	Colchester United	37+2	1	3+1	2+1	7			
Wilkins Richard J	6	11.6	5/28/65	Lambeth		Haverhill Rovers								
Div.3'91.				Free	11/20/86	Colchester United	150+2	6	7+2	9+3	34	4		3
				£65000	7/25/90	Cambridge United	79+2	6	8+1	9	7			
				Free	7/20/94	Hereford United	76+1	6	6	8	5			2
					8/26/96	Colchester United	77	5	3	8	7		1	
Williams David Geraint	5.7	10.6	05/01/62	Treorchy	12/01/80	Bristol Rovers	138+3	14	9+2	5	8		2	
W: 13, u21.2, Y: Div2'87				£40000	29/03/85	Derby County	276+1	26+1	17	11	9	1		
				£650000	01/07/92	Ipswich Town	217	24+1	18	4	3			
				Free	7/1/98	Colchester United								
F O R W A R D														
Abrahams Paul	5.8	10.6	10/31/73	Colchester	8/11/92	Colchester United	30+25	2+3	4	3	8		2	2
				£30000	3/9/94	Brentford	26+9	1+2		1	8			
				Loan	1/5/96	Colchester United								
				£20000	10/21/96	Colchester United	29+11		1	2	9			
Duguid Karl	5.11	11	21/3/78	Hitchin	7/16/96	Colchester Utd (T)	23+34	0+2	3+2	1+5	7			
Gregory Neil R	6	11.1	10/7/72	Ndola (Zambia)	2/21/92	Ipswich Town	7+18	2+1	+1	3+2	2			2
				Loan	2/3/94	Chesterfield	2+1				1			
				Loan	3/3/95	Scunthorpe United	10				7			
				Loan	11/22/96	Torquay United	5							
				Loan	11/27/97	Peterborough United	2+1				1			
				Loan	1/2/98	Colchester United	10				5			
				£50000	3/26/98	Colchester United	2+3			3	5			
Hathaway Ian	5.8	10.6	8/22/68	Wordsley		Bedworth								
				£8000	2/8/89	Mansfield Town	21+23	1+1	1	3+1	2			1
					3/22/91	Rotherham United	5+8			+1	1			
				Free	7/30/93	Torquay United	115+26	9+1	9+1	4+3	14	1	2	1
				Loan	4/9/96	Chesterfield								
				Free	7/3/97	Colchester United	5+7	2	1+1		1			
Sale Mark	6.5	13.8	2/27/72	Burton-on-Trent	7/10/90	Stoke City	+2							
				Free	7/31/91	Cambridge United								
					3/26/92	Birmingham City	11+10	2		3+1	1			2
				£10000	3/5/93	Torquay United	30+14	1	2	3+1	8		1	
				£20000	7/26/94	Preston North End	10+3	1+1	+1	4	6			
				Free	7/31/95	Mansfield Town	36+9	4	2	1	12	1		
					3/10/97	Colchester United	48+1	2	3	3	10		1	
Stamps Scott	5.11	11	3/20/75	Birmingham	7/6/93	Torquay United	81+6	5	2	1+1	5			1
					3/26/97	Colchester United	33+1	2	2+1	2	1			
ADDITIONAL CONTRACT PLAYERS														
Heuvel Arafath						Veendam								
				Free	7/1/98	Colchester United								

LAYER ROAD GROUND
Colchester, Essex CO2 7JJ

Capacity 7,556

First game..Not known.
First floodlit game ....Not known.

ATTENDANCES
Highest ....19,073 v Reading, FA Cup Round 1, 27.11.1948.
Lowest...Not known.

OTHER GROUNDS..None.

HOW TO GET TO THE GROUND

From the North
Follow signs in Colchester on A133/B1508 or A12, then follow signs to Layer B1026 into Layer Road for Colchester United FC.

From the East
Follow signs into Colchester on A604 or A133 then follow signs to Layer B1026 into Layer Road for Colchester United FC.

From the South and West
Follow signs into Colchester on A604 or A12 then follow signs to Layer B1026 into Layer Road for Colchester United FC.

Car Parking
Street parking only.

Nearest Railway Station
Colchester North (01206 564 777)

USEFUL TELPHONE NUMBERS

Club switchboard 01206 508 800
Club fax number 01206 508 803
Club shop 01206 561 180
Ticket Office 01206 574 042

Clubcall.................................0891 73 73 00*
Calls cost 50p per minute at all times.*
Call costings correct at time of going to press.

MATCHDAY PROGRAMME

Programme Editor (97/98). . Brian Wheeler.

Number of pages (97/98) . . . . 40.

Price (97/98) . . . . £1.50.

Subscriptions . . . . Apply to club.

Local Newspapers . . . .
. . . . . Evening Gazette (Mon-Fri evenings),
East Anglian Daily Times (Mon-Fri mornings),
. Essex County Standard (weekly-Fridays).

Local Radio Stations
. . . . SGR FM (Colchester),
. . . Essex Radio (Southend & Chelmsford)
. . . . 257 MW.

MATCHDAY TICKET PRICES (97/98)

Terraces £7
Juniors. £4.50

Family Enclosure. £6
Juniors. £2.50

Seats £9
Juniors £6

FULHAM
(The Cottagers)
NATIONWIDE LEAGUE DIVISION 2
SPONSORED BY: DEMON INTERNET

1998-99 - Back Row L-R: Chris Smith (Physio), Ryan Palmer, Alan Neilson, Paul Trollope, Andy Arnott, Paul Moody, Kit Symons, Shaun Maher, Ian McGuckin, Matthew Lawrence, Sean Davis. **Middle Row:** Malcolm Martin (Asst. Physio), Alex Court (Exercise Physiologist), Paul Peschisolido, Rufus Brevett, Ian Selley, Luke Cornwall, Andre Arendse, Maik Taylor, Rod McAree, Simon Morgan, Steve MacAnespie, Gus Uhlenbeek, John Marshall (Youth Team coach), Alan Bevan (Kit manager). **Front Row:** Neil Smith, Rob Scott, Wayne Collins, Chris Coleman, Paul Bracewell (Player coach), Kevin Keegan (Chief Operating Officer), Frank Sibley (Asst. Manager), Matthew Brazier, Paul Brooker, John Salako, Steve Hayward.

FULHAM
FORMED IN 1879
TURNED PROFESSIONAL IN 1898
LTD COMPANY IN 1903

CHAIRMAN: M Al Fayed
DIRECTORS
W F Muddyman (Vice-Chairman),
A M Muddyman, M Griffiths,
S H Benson
SECRETARY
Etain McKinney
MARKETING DIRECTOR
Mrs Annie Bassett

GENERAL MANAGER: Ian Branfoot
MANAGER: Kevin Keegan
ASSISTANT MANAGER: Frank Sibley
PLAYER COACH: Paul Bracewell

YOUTH MANAGER
John Marshall
PHYSIOTHERAPIST
Chris Smith Grad. Dip. Phys. MCSP.

STATISTICIAN FOR THE DIRECTORY
Dennis Turner

Fulham fans will look back on 1997/98 season and wonder what went wrong and why. Going from easy play-off candidates to actually only just qualifying on goals scored is something all involved at Fulham were not expecting, and having claimed a play-off spot they then lost out in the first stages.

With a squad that is quickly resembling that of a Division One side, or even a Premiership side, it was maybe too presumptuous to expect Fulham to 'walk' the Division, after all bringing in big signings does not always guarantee you success.

However, the play-offs may well have turned out differently had they not gone into them off-form. With three games of the season remaining Fulham sat in third place with a play-off place assured, so it seemed, but they were to gain no more points as all three were lost. This in turn saw Ray Wilkins dismissed as manager and Kevin Keegan taking over for the play-offs. But the damage had been done and Fulham lost 1-2 on aggregate against eventual promotion winners Grimsby Town.

The FA Cup brought a glamour tie against London rivals Tottenham Hotspur, live on Sky. Losing 1-3 the 'Cottagers' put up a better show than the score-line suggests. The Coca-Cola Cup saw them defeat Wycombe in the first round (6-5 on aggregate, 4-4 in the second leg) but lose out to Wolves in the second round after two 0-1 defeats.

With Kevin Keegan at the helm the Fulham fans can look forward to some good football that should see them at least qualify for the play-offs. However, in a Division that's tough to get of as it is, the addition of Manchester City and Stoke City will make things even tougher.

FULHAM

Division 2   :6th   FA CUP: 3rd Round   LC CUP: 2nd Round   AWS: Southern Quarter-finals

M	DATE	COMP.	VEN	OPPONENTS	RESULT	H/T	LP	GOAL SCORERS/GOAL TIMES	ATT.
1	A 09	FL	H	Wrexham	W 1-0	1-0	8	Conroy 39	8789
2	12	CC 1/1	A	Wycombe Wanderers	W 2-1	1-1		Newhouse 28, Conroy 72	(4360)
3	15	FL	A	Walsall	D 1-1	0-0	8	, Keister 53 (OG)	(4418)
4	23	FL	H	Luton Town	D 0-0	0-0	7		8142
5	26	CC 1/2	H	Wycombe Wanderers	D 4-4	3-1		Newhouse 5, 41, Carpenter 24, Conroy 65	5055
6	30	FL	A	Wycombe Wanderers	L 0-2	0-1	12		(6278)
7	S 02	FL	A	Bristol City	W 2-0	1-0	10	Newhouse 14, Carpenter 79	(10293)
8	09	FL	H	Plymouth Argyle	W 2-0	0-0	7	Moody 57, 77	8961
9	13	FL	H	Grimsby Town	L 0-2	0-1	9		6874
10	16	CC 2/1	H	Wolverhampton Wand	L 0-1	0-1			5933
11	20	FL	A	Southend United	L 0-1	0-1	11		(5026)
12	24	CC 2/2	A	Wolverhampton Wand	L 0-1	0-0			(17862)
13	27	FL	A	Wigan Athletic	L 1-2	1-1	18	Hayward 19	(4951)
14	O 04	FL	H	Oldham Athletic	W 3-1	1-0	10	Moody 11, 53, Sinnott 64 (OG)	8805
15	11	FL	H	Blackpool	W 1-0	1-0	8	Conroy 35	7761
16	18	FL	A	Bournemouth	L 1-2	0-1	13	, Vincent 72 (OG)	(7606)
17	21	FL	A	Watford	L 0-2	0-1	15		(11486)
18	25	FL	H	Northampton Town	D 1-1	1-0	16	Peschisolido 45	9848
19	N 01	FL	H	Chesterfield	D 1-1	1-0	17	Blake 39	7998
20	04	FL	A	Millwall	D 1-1	0-0	15	Peschisolido 54	(10291)
21	08	FL	A	Bristol Rovers	W 3-2	1-0	11	Carpenter 37, Scott 83, 89	(6166)
22	16	FAC 1	A	Margate	W 2-1	1-1		Carpenter 21, Scott 76	(5100)
23	18	FL	H	York City	D 1-1	0-1	13	Peschisolido 57	5521
24	21	FL	H	Gillingham	W 3-0	1-0	8	Peschisolido 10, 86, Watson 60	8274
25	29	FL	A	Preston North End	L 1-3	1-1	14	Scott 6	(9723)
26	D 02	FL	H	Brentford	D 1-1	0-1	13	Peschisolido 66	10767
27	06	FAC 2	H	Southend United	W 1-0	0-0		Blake 57 (pen)	8537
28	09	AWS S1	H	Watford	W 1-0	1-0		Moody 18	3364
29	13	FL	A	Carlisle United	L 0-2	0-0	15		(4574)
30	19	FL	H	Burnley	W 1-0	0-0	10	Cullip 85	5096
31	26	FL	A	Plymouth Argyle	W 4-1	1-1	10	Moody 18, 80, Hayward 63, Trollope 75	(9469)
32	28	FL	H	Bristol City	W 1-0	0-0	6	Moody 55	13273
33	J 05	FAC 3	A	Tottenham Hotspur	L 1-3	0-2		Smith 54	(27909)
34	10	FL	A	Wrexham	W 3-0	1-0	4	Moody 38, Peschisolido 56, Trollope 85	(5338)
35	13	AWS S1	H	Wycombe Wanderers	W 3-1	1-1		Thomas 2, 87, Freeman 88	4319
36	17	FL	H	Wycombe Wanderers	D 0-0	0-0	6		10468
37	24	FL	A	Luton Town	W 4-1	2-1	3	Moody 1, 36, 55 (pen), Hayward 61	(8366)
38	27	AWS SQF	H	Luton Town	L 1-2	0-1		Lightbourne 62	5103
39	31	FL	A	Grimsby Town	D 1-1	0-0	4	Lightbourne 56	(6785)
40	F 06	FL	H	Southend United	W 2-0	1-0	3	Peschisolido 25, Lightbourne 55	9122
41	14	FL	A	Oldham Athletic	L 0-1	0-0	6		(6063)
42	21	FL	H	Wigan Athletic	W 2-0	0-0	5	Hayward 56, Peschisolido 89	7791
43	24	FL	H	Bournemouth	L 0-1	0-1	6		7708
44	28	FL	A	Blackpool	L 1-2	1-0	6	Coleman 24	(5183)
45	M 03	FL	H	Bristol Rovers	W 1-0	0-0	5	Thorpe 75	6878
46	07	FL	A	Chesterfield	W 2-0	0-0	5	Morgan 50, Blake 76	(5129)
47	14	FL	H	Millwall	L 1-2	1-0	5	Thorpe 26	12316
48	21	FL	A	York City	W 1-0	0-0	6	Peschisolido 75	(4871)
49	28	FL	A	Gillingham	L 0-2	0-1	6		(10507)
50	A 04	FL	H	Preston North End	W 2-1	0-1	5	Brazier 68, Collins 77	8814
51	07	FL	H	Walsall	D 1-1	0-1	5	Trollope 86	6733
52	11	FL	A	Brentford	W 2-0	1-0	4	Moody 21, 77	(10510)
53	13	FL	H	Carlisle United	W 5-0	2-0	3	Peschisolido 9, 42, 56, Moody 72 (pen), Thorpe 75	9243
54	18	FL	A	Burnley	L 1-2	1-1	3	Moody 35	(9745)
55	25	FL	A	Northampton Town	L 0-1	0-1	4		(7443)
56	M 02	FL	H	Watford	L 1-2	0-1	6	Beardsley 61	17114
57	09	PO SF1	H	Grimsby Town	D 1-1	1-0		Beardsley 45 (pen)	13954
58	13	PO SF2	A	Grimsby Town	L 0-1	0-0			(8689)

Best Home League Attendance: 17114 V Watford   Smallest :5096 V Burnley   Average :8969

Goal Scorers:
FL	(60)	Moody 15, Peschisolido 13, Hayward 4, Scott 3, Thorpe 3, Trollope 3, Blake 2, Carpenter 2, Conroy 2, Lightbourne 2, Beardsley 1, Brazier 1, Coleman 1, Collins 1, Cullip 1, Morgan 1, Newhouse 1, Watson 1, Opponents 3
CC	(6)	Newhouse 3, Conroy 2, Carpenter 1
FAC	(4)	Blake 1, Carpenter 1, Scott 1, Smith 1
AWS	(5)	Thomas 2, Freeman 1, Lightbourne 1, Moody 1
PO	(1)	Beardsley 1

Appearance grid — column headers (left to right): (M) Arendse, (F) Beardsley, (F) Blake, (M) Bracewell, (D) Brevett, (M) Brooker, (M) Carpenter, (M) Cockerill, (D) Coleman, (M) Collins, (F) Conroy, (M) Cullip, (M) Hayward, (D) Herrera, (M) Lawrence, (D) McAnespie, (F) Moody, (D) Morgan, (D) Neilson, (F) Newhouse, (F) Peschisolido, (F) Scott, (D) Smith, (G) Taylor, (D) Thomas, (F) Thorpe, (M) Trollope, (G) Walton, (D) Watson

Are	Bea	Bla	Brc	Brv	Bro	Car	Coc	Col	Cln	Con	Cul	Hay	Her	Law	McA	Moo	Mor	Nei	New	Pes	Sco	Smi	Tay	Tho	Thp	Tro	Wal	Wat	Referee	No
		X			X	S2					X	X	X	X		S3	X		X		S1	X					X	X	A.P. D'Urso	1
						X	X				X	X	X	X	X	S3	X		X		S1	X					X		P Rejer	2
			S3			X	X				X	X	X	X	X		X		X		S2	X					X		F G Stretton	3
			X			X	S2				X	X	X	X			X		X		S1	X					X		M E Pierce	4
					X	X	S3				X	X	X	X			X			X1	S2	X					X		C T Finch	5
	X		S3	S1	X						X	X	X	X	X	S2	X		X			X					X		E Lomas	6
	X		S3	S1	X						X	X	X	X	X		X		X		S2	X					X		R J Harris	7
	X		X	S3	S2						X	X	X	X	X		X		X		S1	X					X		S J Baines	8
	X		X		S						X	X	X	X	X		X		X		S2	X		S1			X		R Styles	9
X			S2		X						X	X	X	X	X		X		X		S1	X		S					M R Halsey	10
X					X				S2			X	X	X			X		S3		X	X		S1					P Taylor	11
X			X	X							X	X	X	X	X		X		X		S1	S2							S W Mathieson	12
X			X	X							X	X	X	X	X		X					S2	S1						R D Furnandiz	13
X	X		X	X							X	X	X	X			X					X							G Fingh	14
	X	X			X						X	X	X	X			X				S1	X					X		K A Leach	15
	X	X			S2						X	X	X	X		S3	X					X					X		F G Stretton	16
		X			S						X	X	X	X			X				S1	X					X		K M Lynch	17
		X			S1							X	X	X			X			X	S	X					X	S2	M Fletcher	18
		X			X	S			S			X	X	X			X			X	X	X					X	S	C J Foy	19
X		X			X	S						X	X	X			X			X	S1	X						S2	C R Wilkes	20
X		X			X							X	X	X			X			X	S1	X		S				S2	M J Jones	21
X	X	X			X					S	S	X	X				X			X	X	X	X	S		S	X	X	R Styles	22
	X	X			X					S1	S2	X	X				X			X	X	X	X				X		S G Bennett	23
	X	X			X					X	X	X	X				S			X	X	X	X				X		R J Harris	24
	X	X			X					X	X	X		S1			X			X	X	X	X	S		S	X1		E Lomas	25
	S	X			S					X1				X			X			X	X	X	X		X				S J Baines	26
	X	X			S					X	S2	X		X1	S1		X			X	X2	X	X		X	S	S	B Knight	27
					X				X1		X		X	S1	X		X			X	X	X2	X	S2	X			X		28
		X3			S3			X			X		X	X2	S2	S1	X			X	X1	X	X					X	W C Burns	29
		X3			X2			X			S3	X	X	X1	S1	X			X	X	X	X	S2						P S Danson	30
		X			X			S			X		X	X			X			X	X	X	X	S				X	M Fletcher	31
		X			S2			S			X	X1	X				X			X	X	X	S					X	J P Robinson	32
	S	X			S			S			X	X	X	X	S		X			X	X	X	X		X	X	S	X	G P Barber	33
	S	X2			S2						X	X	X	X			X			X1	X	X	X					X	A G Wiley	34
		X		X							X	X	X	X			X				X2		X				X			35
	S	X						X			X		X	X			X			X1	X	X	X				X		C R Wilkes	36
	S	X						X	S1		X		X	X			X			X1	X	X	X				X		S W Mathieson	37
	X	X			X	X		X	X			X	X							S2		X				X			38
		X3	X	S				X	S1		X		X	X1		S				X	X	X				X		G Cain	39
		X	X	S2				X	S1	S			X	X		X2			X	X	X	X				X		A Bates	40
		X	X	S				S	S	S		S1	X	X		X1			X	X	X	X				X		R D Furnandiz	41
	S	X	X	X1		X3		X	X		X			X		X				X	X	X				X		A R Hall	42
	S3	X	X		X3			X	X		X			X		X2			X	X	X	S2			X1			K A Leach	43
	S1	X	X		S			X			X		X1			X			X	X	X2	X				X	M L Dean	44
X	X	X	X		X			X1		S2	X			S		X			X	X	X2	X					R J Harris	45
	X	X	X		X			X			X	X	S		X	S		X	X	X			X	X	A P D'Urso	46
	X1	X	X		S			X			X	X	S		X		X	X			X	X	M E Pierce	47
	X	X1	X		S			X			X		S2	X	X	X2			X	X	M S Pike	48
	X	X		S3				X			X		X2	X1	S2	X3		P Taylor	49
	X	X						X	X		S	X2	X	S1	S2	X1		M J Brandwood	50
	X	X						X2		S	X1	X	X	S1	S2		A N Butler	51
	X	X3	X					X2	X	X1	X	S1	S2		D Orr	52
	X	X	X					X1	X	X2	X	S2	S3		R Styles	53
	X	X	X					X		S	X	X2	X	S2	S1		D Pugh	54
	X2	X	X					X	X		X	X1	X	S1	S		C J Foy	55
	X	X	X					X	X	S	X2	X1	X	S2	S1		W C Burns	56
X3	S2	X	X					X2	X	X	X	X1	S3	X	S1	X	T Heilbron	57
	S	X	X	S1				X	X1	X	X	X	X	S	X	X	X	C R Wilkes	58

Totals

FL Appearances	6, 8, 24, 36, 11, 4, 15, 5, 26, 10, 10, 18, 32, 26, 43, 2, 27, 18, 17, 7, 32, 6, 42, 28, 5, 19, 12, 4
FL Sub Appearances	2, 5, 9, 3, 3, 1, 3, 3, 2, 6, 1, 1, 11, 2, 4, 8, 5
CC Appearances	2, 1+1, 4, 2+1, 3, 4, 4, 4, 2+1, 4, 3+1, 0+4, 3, 2
FAC Appearances	1, 2, 3, 1, 1, 1+1, 3, 2, 1, 1+1, 1, 2, 3, 2, 3, 2, 2
AWS Appearances	2, 2, 2, 1, 1, 2, 1, 3, 2+1, 1, 2+1, 1, 1, 2+1, 1, 2
PO Appearances	1, 0+1, 2, 2, 0+1, 2, 2, 1, 2, 2, 0+1, 1, 1+1, 2

Also played:(M) Aggrey S(22,24), (F) Arnott S1(35,38,43), S(42), (D) Brazier S1(48,49,53), X(50,51), X(52), S(52), S2(55), X(54), (F) Cusack X(10,11), S3(12,15), S(13,14),(F) Freeman S1(16,34,36,45,47), X(35), S2(37,44), X2(38) S(46). (F) Lightbourne X(36,338,39), X2(37), X1(40),(M) McAtee S2(2,35), X(3,5), S(4,14), X(12,13),(M) McKenzie S1(14), S(15), X(16), S(17) Maher X1(35,38),(M) Selley X(16,17,18).

FULHAM RECORDS AND STATISTICS

CLUB RECORDS

BIGGEST VICTORIES
League: 10-1 v Ipswich Town, Division 1, 26.9.1963.
10-2 v Torquay United, Division 3, 10.9.1931.
F.A. Cup: 7-0 v Swansea, 1st Round, 11.11.1995.

BIGGEST DEFEATS
League: 0-9 v Wolverhampton Wanderers, Division 1, 16.9.1959.
League Cup: 0-10 v Liverpool, 2nd Round, 23.9.1986.

MOST POINTS
3 points a win: 87, Division 3, 1996-97.
2 points a win: 60, Division 2, 1958-59. Division 3, 1970-71.

MOST GOALS SCORED
111, Division 3(S), 1931-32.

RECORD TRANSFER FEE RECEIVED
£333,333 from Liverpool for Money, May 1980.

RECORD TRANSFER FEE PAID
£2,100,000 to Blackburn for Chris Coleman, December 1997.

BEST PERFORMANCES
League: 10th Division 1, 1959-60.
F.A. Cup: Runners-up 1974-75.
League Cup: 5th Round 1967-68, 1970-71.

HONOURS
Champions of Division 3(S) 1931-32.
Champions Division 2, 1948-49.

LEAGUE CAREER
Elected to Div 2 1907, Div 3(S) 1927-28, Div 2 1931-32, Div 1 1948-49, Div 2 1951-52, Div 1 1958-59, Div 2 1967-68, Div 3 1968-69, Div 2 1970-71, Div 3 1979-80, Div 2 1981-82, Div 3 (now Div 2) 1985-86, Div 3 1993-94. Div 2 1997-98.

INDIVIDUAL CLUB RECORDS

MOST GOALS IN A SEASON
Frank Newton: 43, Division 3(S), 1931-32.

MOST GOALS IN A MATCH
6. Ronnie Rooke v Bury, 6-0, FA Cup 3rd Round, 7.1.1939.

OLDEST PLAYER
Jimmy Sharpe, 40 years, April 1920 (Played in an emergency and scored his only goal for the club many years after officially retiring!)

YOUNGEST PLAYER
Tony Mahoney, 16 years, 1976.

MOST CAPPED PLAYER
Johnny Haynes (England) 56.

PREVIOUS MANAGERS

1904-09 Harry Bradshaw, 1909-24 Phil Kelso, 1924-26 Andy Ducat, 1926-29 Joe Bradshaw, 1929-31 Ned Liddell, 1931-34 James McIntyre, 1934-35 Jimmy Hogan, 1935 Joe Edelston (acting), 1935-48 Jack Peart, 1948-49 Frank Osborne, 1949-53 Bill Dodgin, 1956-58 Dug Livingstone, 1958-64 Bedford Jezzard, 1964-65 Arthur Stevens (acting), 1965-68 Vic Buckingham, 1968 Bobby Robson, 1968 Johnny Haynes (acting), 1968-72 Bill Dodgin (jnr), 1972-76 Alec Stock, 1976-80 Bobby Campbell, 1980-84 Malcolm MacDonald, 1984-86 Ray Harford, 1986-90 Ray Lewington, 1990-91 Alan Dicks, 1991 Ray Lewington (caretaker), 1991-94 Don Mackay, 1994-96 Ian Branfoot. Micky Adams 1996-97. Ray Wilkins 1997-98.

ADDITIONAL INFORMATION
PREVIOUS NAMES
Fulham St Andrews 1879-98.
PREVIOUS LEAGUES
Southern League.
Club colours: White shirts with black band, black shorts with white trim.

Reserves League: Capital League.
Youth League: South East Counties.

LONGEST LEAGUE RUNS

of undefeated matches:	15 (1957, 1970)	of league matches w/out a win:	15 (1950)
of undefeated home matches:	28 (1921-22)	of undefeated away matches:	9 (1958, 1970)
without home win:	9 (8.5.1993 - 6.11.1993)	without an away win:	31 (1964-66)
of league wins:	8 (1963)	of home wins:	12 (1959)
of league defeats:	11 (1961-62)	of away wins:	5 (1966, 1981)

THE MANAGER

Kevin Keegan . . . . appointed May 1998.

PREVIOUS CLUBS
As Manager. . . . . Newcastle United.
As Asst.Man/Coach . . . . None.
As a player . . . . Scunthorpe, Liverpool, SV Hamburg, Southampton, Newcastle United.

HONOURS
As a Manager. . . . . **Newcastle:** Division 1 championship 1992-93.
As a Player . . . . **Liverpool:** Division 1 championship (3 times). FA Cup, European Cup (twice), UEFA Cup (twice).
. . . . **International:** 63 full caps and 5 u23 for England.

FULHAM

PLAYERS NAME / Honours	Ht	Wt	Birthdate	Birthplace / Transfers	Contract Date	Clubs	League	L/Cup	FA Cup	Other	Lge	L/C	FAC	Oth
G O A L K E E P E R														
Arendse Andre South African Int.	6.4	11.5	6/27/67	Capetown	8/7/97	Capetown Spurs Fulham	6	2	1					
Taylor Maik S Army Rep. BHLP.	6.5	13.8	11/8/63	Germany Free £500000 £700000	7/13/95 1/1/97 11/17/97	Farnborough Basingstoke Town Barnet Southampton Fulham	70 18 28	5	6	2				
D E F E N C E														
Brazier Matthew	5.8	10.07	7/2/76	Leytonstone £65000	7/1/94 3/20/98	QPR Fulham	36+13 3+4	3+2	3		2 1	1		
Brevett Rufus	5.8	11	9/24/69	Derby £250000 £375000	7/8/88 2/15/91 1/28/98	Doncaster Rovers QPR Fulham	106+3 141+11 11	5 9+1	4 8	10+1	3 1			
Coleman Chris W:4,u21.10,Y,S. WC'89'91. Div.1'94.	6.2	14.06	6/10/70	Swansea Free £275000 £2800000 £2100000	9/1/87 7/19/91 12/16/95 12/1/97	Manchester City Swansea City Crystal Palace Blackburn Rovers Fulham	159+1 126+11 27+1 26	8 20+2 2	13 8 2 1	15 2	2 13 2	2	1 1	
McAnespie Stephen	5.9	10.7	2/1/72	Kilmarnock £900000 £100000 Loan	8/1/93 9/30/95 11/28/97 3/26/98	Vasterhauringe Raith Bolton Wanderers Fulham Bradford City	37 19+5 2+2 7	6	1					
McGuckin Thomas Ian	6.2	12.2	4/24/73		6/20/91 6/13/97	Hartlepool United Fulham	147+5	13+1	6	6	9	1		
Maher Shaun P	6.2	12.3	6/10/78	Dublin										
Morgan Simon C E: u21.2.	5.1	11.7	9/5/68	Birmingham £100000	11/15/84 10/12/90	Leicester City Fulham	147+13 283+5	14 22	4+1 14	3 17	3 42	1 1	1	4
Neilson Alan B W: 3, B.2, u21.7.	5.11	12.4	9/26/72	Wegburg (Ger) £500000 £250000	2/11/91 8/1/95 11/28/97	Newcastle United Southampton Fulham	35+7 41+13 16	4 7	4 1+1 2	4	1			
Smith Neil J FAYC'90.	5.7	11.1	9/30/71	Lambeth £40000	7/24/90 10/17/91 7/3/97	Tottenham Hotspur Gillingham Fulham	191+9 42+2	10 3	17 3	7+1 +1	10	1	2 1	2
Symons Kit W: 27, B.1, u21.2, Y	6.1	10.1	08/03/71	Basingstoke £1200000 Free	30/12/88 17/08/95 7/1/98	Portsmouth Manchester City Fulham	180 124	19 6	10 9	13+1	10 4			1
M I D F I E L D														
Bracewell Paul E: 3, u21.13. CS'84'85. Div1'85'93'96. ECWC'85. UEFA'84.	5.8	10.9	7/19/62	Heswell £250000 £425000 £250000 £250000 £100000 £75000	2/6/80 7/1/83 5/25/84 8/23/89 6/16/92 8/1/95 10/10/97	Stoke City Sunderland Everton Sunderland Newcastle United Sunderland Fulham	123+6 38 95 112+1 67+9 76+1 36	6 4 11 9 3+1 8	6 2 19+2 10 6+2 3 3	17+2 6 2 2 2	5 4 7 2 3 	1 2 1	1	
Brooker Paul	5.8	10	11/25/76	Hammersmith	6/12/97	Fulham	4+29	1+2	+1	1+1	2	1		
Collins Wayne A	6	12	3/4/69	Manchester £10000 £400000	7/29/93 8/1/96 1/23/98	Winsford United Crewe Alexandra Sheffield Wednesday Fulham	103+15 16+16 10+3	5 2	8+1 1	14+1 2	14 6 1	1		2
Davis Sean	5.11	12	9/20/79	Clapham	10/14/96	Fulham	+1							
Hayward Steve E: Y.13. FLge u18.1.	5.1	11.7	9/8/71	Pelsall £100000	9/17/88 3/13/95 6/23/97	Derby County Carlisle United Fulham	12+11 87+2 32+3	+2 6 4	1 4 1+1	2+4 8 1	1 13 4	1	1	
Lawrence Matthew	5.1		6/19/74	Northampton	2/7/97	Grays Athletic Wycombe Wanderers Fulham	13+3 56+1	4 4	1 2	2	1			
McAree Rodney	5.7	10.1	8/10/74	Dungannon Free Free	8/21/91 7/26/94 12/29/95	Liverpool Bristol City Fulham	4+2 22+6	2 2+2		+1	3			
Selley Ian E: u21.3,S. LC'93. FAC'93. ECWC'94.	5.9	10.1	6/14/74	Chertsey Loan £500000	5/6/92 12/3/96 10/17/97	Arsenal Southend United Fulham	35+6 3+1 3	5+1	3	8+2				2
Trollope Paul J	6	12.2	6/3/72	Swindon Free Loan £100000 Loan Loan £600000	12/23/89 3/26/92 12/16/94 1/19/95 8/30/96 10/11/96 11/28/97	Swindon Town Torquay United Derby County Derby County Grimsby Town Crystal Palace Fulham	85+3 4+1 43+17 6+1 +1 19+5	5+1 3+2	3 3+1	6+1 2	12 1 4 1 3	1 1		
F O R W A R D														
Arnott Andy	6.1	12	10/18/73	Chatham Free	5/13/91 1/25/96 6/19/97	Gillingham Leyton Orient Fulham	40+22 46+3 +1	2+3 2	10+2 2	3+1	12 6	1		
Moody Paul	6.3	12.6	6/13/67	Portsmouth £4000 £50000 Loan £60000	7/15/91 12/9/92 2/19/94 7/17/97	Fareham Waterlooville Southampton Reading Oxford United Fulham	7+5 97+35 27+5	1 9+4 2+1	0+1 7+1 1+1	1 3 1	1 49 15	4	5	3
Peschisolido Paolo Canadian Int.	5.4	10.5	5/25/71	Canada £25000 £400000 £400000 £1100000	11/11/92 8/1/94 3/29/96 9/2/96 10/24/97	Toronto BI (Canada) Birmingham City Stoke City Birmingham City WBA Fulham	37+6 39+1 7+2 5+2 32	2 3 3+1 2	0+1 2 2	1+1 3+1 2	16 13 1 3 18	1 2 3		
Salako John E:5. FMC'91. Div.1'94.	5.1	11	2/11/69	Nigeria Loan £1500000 Free Free	11/3/86 8/14/89 8/1/95 3/26/98 5/18/98	Crystal Palace Swansea City Coventry City Bolton Wanderers Fulham	172+43 13 68+4 0+7	19+5 9	20 2 4	11+3	23 3 4	5 3	4 1	2 1
Scott Robert	6.1	11.1	8/15/73	Epsom £20000 Loan £30000	8/1/93 3/22/95 1/10/96	Sutton United Sheffield United Scarborough Fulham	0+1 8 61+18	0+1 3+5	3	2 0+1	3 17	1	1	1
Uhlenbeek Guss	5.9	12.5	20/08/70	Paramaribo £100000 Free	11/08/95 7/1/98	SV Tops Ipswich Town Fulham	77+12	5+3	4+3	7+1	4			

CRAVEN COTTAGE
Stevenage Road, Fulham, London SW6 6HH

Capacity ....19,250 (For away fans 4,000)

First game...v Minerva, 5-0, Middx Snr Cup, 10.10.1896.
First floodlit game...v Sheffield Wednesday, 4-1,
....League, September 1962.

ATTENDANCES
Highest...49,335 v Millwall, Div 2, 8.10.1938.
Lowest ....1,108 v Gillingham, Autoglass Trophy, 28.11.1991.

OTHER GROUNDS ....None as a professional club.

HOW TO GET TO THE GROUND

From the North
Use motorway (M1) sign posted London then take North Circular Road (A406), sign posted West to Neasden, follow signs to Harlesden (A404), then Hammersmith (A219) and at Broadway follow sign to Fulham and in 1 mile turn right into Harbord Street and at end turn left for Fulham FC.
From the East & South
Use South Circular Road (A205) and take sign to Putney Bridge (A219). Cross bridge and follow sign to Hammersmith and in 0.5 miles turn left into Bishops Park Road and at end turn right for Fulham FC.
From the West
Use motorway (M4) then A4 and in 2 miles branch left, sign posted, other routes into Hammersmith Broadway, follow sign Fulham (A219) and in 1 mile turn right into Harbord Street and at end turn left for Fulham FC.
Car parking: Ample in adjacent streets.
Nearest Railway Station: Putney. **Nearest Tube Stations:** Putney Bridge or Hammersmith.

USEFUL TELEPHONE NUMBERS

Club switchboard 0171 384 4700
Club fax number.......................0171 384 4715
Ticket Office............................0171 384 4710

Marketing Department 0171 384 4744
Internet address ....www.fulham/c.co.uk
Clubcall 0891 44 00 44*
*Calls cost 50p per minute at all times. Call costings correct at time of going to press.

MATCHDAY PROGRAMME

Programme Editor.....................Mike Lewis.

Number of pages....................................40.

Price ....£2.

Subscriptions ....Apply to club.

Local Newspapers
....Fulham Chronicle,
.... Hammersmith & Fulham Gazette, .
........................Wandsworth Borough News. .

Local Radio Stations
................................Greater London Radio,
................................Capital & Capital Gold.

MATCHDAY TICKET PRICES
Seats £14.00
Juv/OAP. £7.00

Terraces £10.00
Juv/OAP. £5.00

GILLINGHAM
(The Gills)
NATIONWIDE LEAGUE DIVISION 2
SPONSORED BY: KOOL

1997-98 - Back Row L-R: Wayne Jones (physio), Paul Smith, Sam Tydeman, Leo Fortune-West, Roland Edge, Ian Chapman, Kevin Bremner (youth manager), **2nd row from back:** Tony Pulis (manager), Neil Masters, Siomn Ratcliffe, Guy Butters, Richard Green, Jim Stannard, Steve Butler, Glen Thomas, Adrian Pennock, Matthew Bryant, Lindsay Parsons (asst. manager). **3rd row from back:** Lennie Piper, Mark O'Connor, Dennis Bailey, Andy Hessenthaler, Paul Scally (chairman & chief exec.), Mick Galloway, Ade Akinbiyi, James Pinnock, Steve Norman. **Front Row:** Youth team: Barry Sinclair, Danny Bovis, Paul Hobbs, Jim Corbett, Richard Radbourne, Tommy Osborne.

GILLINGHAM
FORMED IN 1893
TURNED PROFESSIONAL IN 1894
LTD COMPANY IN 1893

CHAIRMAN/CHIEF EXECUTIVE
Paul Scally

DIRECTORS
P Spokes FCCA
SECRETARY
Gwen Poynter
COMMERCIAL MANAGER
Mike Sullivan

MANAGER: Tony Pulis
ASSISTANT MANAGER: Lindsay Parsons
YOUTH TEAM MANAGER
Kevin Bremner

PHYSIOTHERAPIST
Wayne Jones

STATISTICIAN FOR THE DIRECTORY
Roger Triggs

But for a bad couple of months leading up to Christmas, Gillingham would have qualified for at least a play-off spot, and may even have challenged Bristol City and Watford. As it was the 'Gills' lost out on a play-off place on goals scored!

A 2-1 win over Plymouth Argyle on October 25th had seen Gillingham go third, but they did not record another win until December 29th - 11 games later. They then played out the rest of the season losing only four times and but for a 0-0 draw on the last day of the season, would have qualified for the promotion play-offs.

The FA Cup brought little to cheer about as Bristol Rovers won through, after a replay, in the first round and the the 'Gills' fared no better in the Coca-Cola Cup as they suffered a first round exit against Birmingham (0-4 on aggregate).

The club will be hoping that they can start the new season as they finished last year, and hope that they can avoid the sought of bad run that cost them the chance of promotion. The Division though has had two major players added to its ranks this year, in the form of Manchester City and Stoke City, so it will not be an easy task.

GILLINGHAM

Division 2   :8th   FA CUP: 1st Round   LC CUP: 1st Round   AWS: Southern Round 1

M	DATE	COMP.	VEN	OPPONENTS	RESULT	H/T	LP	GOAL SCORERS/GOAL TIMES	ATT.
1	A 09	FL	H	Preston North End	D 0-0	0-0	15		6562
2	12	CC 1/1	H	Birmingham City	L 0-1	0-0			5246
3	13	FL	A	Bristol Rovers	W 2-1	0-0	1	Butler 77, Akinbiyi 80	(6572)
4	15	FL	A	Burnley	D 0-0	0-0	3		(11811)
5	23	FL	H	Walsall	W 2-1	0-0	2	Smith 49, Akinbiyi 68	5083
6	26	CC 1/2	A	Birmingham City	L 0-3	0-0			(7921)
7	30	FL	A	York City	L 1-2	0-0	5	Bailey 84	(2853)
8	S 02	FL	A	Brentford	L 0-2	0-0	9		(4903)
9	05	FL	H	Bournemouth	W 2-1	0-1	3	Butters 48 (pen), Butler 76	5168
10	20	FL	H	Watford	D 2-2	1-0	9	Butters 36, Butler 58	7780
11	27	FL	A	Carlisle United	L 1-2	0-0	12	Butters 90 (pen)	(5063)
12	O 04	FL	A	Bristol City	W 2-0	2-0	7	Akinbiyi 6, 44	6277
13	11	FL	H	Wycombe Wanderers	W 1-0	0-0	4	Akinbiyi 78	5545
14	18	FL	A	Northampton Town	L 1-2	0-2	6	Akinbiyi 53	(7191)
15	21	FL	A	Wigan Athletic	W 4-1	1-0	4	Akinbiyi 31, Ratcliffe 47, Butler 71 (pen), Fortune-West 79	(3214)
16	25	FL	H	Plymouth Argyle	W 2-1	1-1	3	Akinbiyi 32, Fortune-West 87	6679
17	N 01	FL	H	Millwall	L 1-3	0-1	5	Fortune-West 67	8383
18	04	FL	A	Chesterfield	D 1-1	0-0	5	Akinbiyi 73	(3420)
19	07	FL	A	Oldham Athletic	L 1-3	0-2	6	Butters 49	(5338)
20	14	FAC 1	A	Bristol Rovers	D 2-2	1-1		Onuora 42, Akinbiyi 82	(4825)
21	18	FL	H	Blackpool	D 1-1	1-0	6	Butters 32	5045
22	21	FL	A	Fulham	L 0-3	0-1	9		(8274)
23	25	FAC 1R	H	Bristol Rovers	L 0-2	0-2			4459
24	29	FL	H	Grimsby Town	L 0-2	0-1	15		4855
25	D 02	FL	H	Luton Town	D 2-2	1-1	15	Akinbiyi 26, 56	(4408)
26	09	AWS S1	H	Peterborough United	L 0-1	0-0			905
27	13	FL	H	Southend United	L 1-2	1-0	16	Southall 4	4744
28	20	FL	A	Wrexham	D 0-0	0-0	17		(2834)
29	26	FL	A	Bournemouth	L 0-4	0-1	17		(5672)
30	29	FL	H	Brentford	W 3-1	2-0	15	Akinbiyi 45, 80, Aspinall 10 (OG)	5908
31	J 03	FL	H	Burnley	W 2-0	1-0	11	Butler 10, Smith 68	5886
32	10	FL	A	Preston North End	W 3-1	2-0	8	Butters 7, Galloway 45, Onuora 51	(7776)
33	17	FL	H	York City	D 0-0	0-0	9		5891
34	31	FL	H	Bristol Rovers	D 1-1	1-1	10	Onuora 1	5593
35	F 08	FL	A	Watford	W 2-0	1-0	9	Akinbiyi 20, 90	(10498)
36	14	FL	A	Bristol City	W 2-0	0-0	9	Corbett 48, Southall 71	(11781)
37	21	FL	A	Carlisle United	W 1-0	0-0	8	Butler 71	6270
38	24	FL	H	Northampton Town	W 1-0	0-0	7	Butters 69 (pen)	6463
39	28	FL	A	Wycombe Wanderers	L 0-1	0-1	7		(5583)
40	M 03	FL	H	Oldham Athletic	W 2-1	1-0	6	Akinbiyi 50, Kelly 35 (OG)	5254
41	07	FL	H	Millwall	L 0-1	0-0	6		(8241)
42	14	FL	H	Chesterfield	W 1-0	0-0	6	Corbett 83	5672
43	21	FL	A	Blackpool	L 1-2	0-0	7	Fortune-West 88	(4165)
44	28	FL	H	Fulham	W 2-0	1-0	7	Akinbiyi 32, 90	10507
45	31	FL	A	Walsall	L 0-1	0-0	7		(3117)
46	A 04	FL	A	Grimsby Town	D 0-0	0-0	7		(5190)
47	11	FL	H	Luton Town	W 2-1	1-1	6	Akinbiyi 29, 49	6846
48	13	FL	A	Southend United	D 0-0	0-0	6		(6151)
49	18	FL	H	Wrexham	D 1-1	1-1	7	Akinbiyi 44	7869
50	25	FL	A	Plymouth Argyle	W 1-0	0-0	6	Smith 90	(7941)
51	M 02	FL	H	Wigan Athletic	D 0-0	0-0	8		10361

Best Home League Attendance: 10507 V Fulham   Smallest :4744 V Southend United   Average :6463

Goal Scorers:

FL	(52)	Akinbiyi 21, Butters 7, Butler 6, Fortune-West 4, Smith 3, Corbett 2, Onuora 2, Southall 2, Bailey 1, Galloway 1, Ratcliffe 1, Opponents 2
CC	(0)	
FAC	(2)	Akinbiyi 1, Onuora 1
AWS	(0)	

(F) Akinbiyi	(D) Ashby	(F) Bailey	(G) Bartram	(D) Bryant	(F) Butler	(D) Butters	(F) Corbett	(F) Fortune-West	(M) Galloway	(D) Green	(M) Hessenthaler	(D) Masters	(D) Moss	(M) Ndah	(F) O'Connor	(M) Onuora	(D) Patterson	(D) Pennock	(F) Pinnock	(M) Piper	(G) Pollitt	(D) Ratcliffe	(M) Smith	(F) Southall	(G) Stannard	(F) Statham	(D) Thomas	(G) Walton		
X	X	S1		X	X	X			S2	X	S3	X	X	X								X	X						S.J. Baines	1
X	S		X	X	X			S1	X	X	X		X		X							X	X				S		M C Bailey	2
X	X	S1		X	X	X			S2	X	S	X		X	S							X	X			X			P S Danson	3
X	X			X	X	X	S3	S2			S1	X	X	X								X	X						G Laws	4
X	X			X	X	X		S2			S1	X		X	X				S3			X	X			X			R J Harris	5
X	X			X	X	X	S3		X		S1	X		X							S2	X	X						F G Stretton	6
X	X	S1		X	X	X			X		X	S	X		X	S						X	X			X			E Wolstenholme	7
X	X	X		X	S1	X			X		X	S	X		X	X					S	X	X			X			M E Pierce	8
X	X	X		S	X	X			X		S1	X		X	X						S	X	X			X			S G Bennett	9
X	X	S3		X	X	X		S2	S1	X	X	X		X	X							X	X						R Styles	10
X	X	S		X	X	X		S2		X	X	X		X	X				S				X						K M Lynch	11
X	X			X	X	X	X	S2	S1	X		X			X	S3						X	X						A P D'Urso	12
X	X	S1		X	X		S	S2	X	X	X											X	X	X	X				M R Halsey	13
X	X			X			S	X	X	X									S	S		X	X	X	X				G Singh	14
X	X	X		X			S1	X	X	X									S	S		X	X	X	X				W C Burns	15
X	X	X		X			S2	X	X	X						S1	S					X	X	X	X				A N Butler	16
X	X			S2			X	X	X	X						X	X	S				S1	X	X	X				B Knight	17
X	X			S2	X		X	S1	X	X						X	X	X				S3	X	X	X				M L Dean	18
X	X	S1		S2	X	X			S	X	X					X	X						X	X	X	X			T Jones	19
X	X			S	X	X		S	X	X	X					X	X					S1	X	X	X	X			G Singh	20
X	X			S1	X	X		S	X		X					S2	X					X	X	X	X				M Fletcher	21
X	X	X		X	S2	X		S	X		X					X	X					S1	X	X	X				R J Harris	22
X	X			X	X	X		S1	S2		X					X	X	S				S3	X	X	X	X			G Singh	23
X	X	X1		S2	S1	X2			X		X		X			X							S	X	X	X			D Orr	24
X	X			X	S		S		X1	S1	X	X				X						X	X	X	X	X			P Taylor	25
S2	X			X	X		S1			S3	X3	X1				X						X	X2	X	X	X				26
X	X			X	S3				X1	S2	X	X				X1	X2				X		X	X		S1			F G Stretton	27
X					S	X	S		X	X	X					X				X	S1	X	X					X1	E K Wolstenholme	28
X				S1	S3	X			S2	X2	X3	X				X		X		X	X1	X	X						A Bates	29
X	X			S1	X	X			X		X	X1				S		X		X		X	X		X				R Styles	30
X	X			X	X	X			X	S						S	X1	X		X		X	X		S1				S G Bennett	31
	X			X	X	X	X	3	3	X	X					X					X		X	X		X			M J Brandwood	32
	X			X	X	X	S1	X	X1	X						X						X	X	X	S				A G Wiley	33
X3	X			S1	X	X	S2	S3	X	X2	X					X1						X	X	X					J P Robinson	34
X	X			S2	X1	X	S3		X2		X					S1	X	X				X	X3					X	R D Furnandiz	35
X	X			S1	X2	X	X		X1		X					S2	X	X				S3	X	X					A R Hall	36
X	X			S1	X	X1			S2	X	S					X2	X	X				X	X	X					D R Crick	37
X	X			X	X	X			X1	X	X					S1	X	X				S	X	X					M R Halsey	38
X	X			X	X	X			X1	X	X					S1	X	X				S	X	X	X				M C Bailey	39
X	X			S2	X2	X			S1		X1					X	X	X				X	X	X					P S Danson	40
X	X			S3	X2	X3	S1		S2		X1					X	X	X				X	X	X					C R Wilkes	41
X	X			X1	X		S2	S3	S2	S1	X	X3				X	X					X	X		X				M Fletcher	42
X	X			X	X	X1		X	S1	X	S					X	X					S	X	X					J A Kirkby	43
X	X			X	X	S1		X1	X	X	S					X	X					X	X			S			P Taylor	44
X	X			X	X	S1		S2	X2	X1	X					X	X					X	X						K M Lynch	45
X	X			X	X	S1		S	S	X						X	X					X	X1			X			G B Frankland	46
X3	X			X	X2			S1	S3	X						X	X					X	X1			S2			F G Stretton	47
X	X			X	X			X	S1	X	X					X	X					X	X1	S					D Orr	48
X	X			X	X2		S1	S2	X	X						X	X					X	X1						A N Butler	49
X	X1			X	X	S1		X3		X	X2	X				X	X	S3				X			S2				M J Brandwood	50
X				X	X1	S3			X	X3	X2	X	X	X		X						X	S2		S1				A Bates	51
44	43	7	9	25	30	31	8	5	32	17	42	11	10	4		16	23	20			6	16	46	22	20	16	2	1	FL Appearances	
		6		10	13		8	15	7	8						6			1	1			5		1		4	1	FL Sub Appearances	
2	1			2	2	2	0+1	2	1+1	2		2		1					0+1			2	2						CC Appearances	
2	2			1	2	2		0+1	1+1	2						2	2					0+2	2			2	2		FAC Appearances	
0+1	1			1	1		0+1		0+1	1	1					1							1	1	1	1	1		AWS Appearances	

Also played:(M) Chapman X(6). (M) Edge S(32).

405

GILLINGHAM

RECORDS AND STATISTICS

CLUB RECORDS

BIGGEST VICTORIES
League: 10-0 v Chesterfield, Division 3, 5.9.1987 (Div. 3 record).
F.A. Cup: 10-1 v Gorleston (h), 1st Round, 16.11.1957.

BIGGEST DEFEATS
League: 0-8 v Luton Town, Division 3(S), 14.4.1929.
League Cup: 0-6 v Oxford United, 2nd Round, 24.9.1986.

MOST POINTS
3 points a win: 83, Division 3, 1984-85.
2 points a win: 62, Division 4, 1973-74.

RECORD TRANSFER FEE RECEIVED
£1,200,000 from Bristol City for Ade Akinbiyi, May 1998.

RECORD TRANSFER FEE PAID
£250,000 to Norwich City for Adeola Akinbiyi, January 1997.

MOST GOALS IN A SEASON
Ernie Morgan: 33 goals in 1954-55 (League 31, FA Cup 2).

BEST PERFORMANCES
League: 4th Division 3, 1978-79, 1984-85.
F.A. Cup: 5th Round 1969-70.
League Cup: 4th Round 1963-64, 1996-97.

HONOURS
Champions of Division 4, 1963-64.

LEAGUE CAREER
Original members of Div 3 1920, Transferred to Div 3(S) 1921, Failed to gain re-election 1938, Southern League 1938-44, Kent League 1944-46, Southern League 1946-50, Re-elected to Div 3(S) 1950, Transferred to Div 4 1958, Div 3 1964-65, Div 4 1971-72, Div 3 1974-75, Div 4 (now Div 3) 1988-89, Div 2 1995-96.

INDIVIDUAL CLUB RECORDS

MOST GOALS IN A MATCH
6. Fred Cheesmur v Merthyr Town (h), 6-0, Division 3(S), 26.4.1930.

OLDEST PLAYER
John Simpson, 39 years 137 days.

YOUNGEST PLAYER
Billy Hughes, 15 years 275 days v Southend, 13.4.1976.

MOST CAPPED PLAYER
Tony Cascarino (Eire) 3.

PREVIOUS MANAGERS

(Since 1920)
1920-23 John McMillian, 1923-26 Harry Curtis, 1926-30 Albert Hoskins, 1930-32 Dick Hendrie, 1932-37 Fred Mavern, 1937-38 Alan Ure, 1938-39 Bill Harvey, 1939-58 Archie Clark, 1958-62 Harry Barratt, 1962-66 Freddie Cox, 1966-71 Basil Hayward, 1971-74 Andy Nelson, 1974-75 Len Ashurst, 1975-81 Gerry Summers, 1981-87 Keith Peacock, Paul Taylor 1987-88, 1988-89 Keith Burkinshaw, 1989-92 Damien Richardson, 1992-93 Glenn Roeder, 1993-95 Mike Flanagan, Neil Smillie 1995.

ADDITIONAL INFORMATION
PREVIOUS NAMES
New Brompton 1893-1913.

PREVIOUS LEAGUES
Southern League, Kent League.

Club colours: Blue and black stripped shirts, black shorts with blue trim.
Change colours: Red and black.

Reserves League: Capital League.
Youth League: South East Counties.

LONGEST LEAGUE RUNS

of undefeated matches:	20 (1973-74)	of league matches w/out a win:	15 (1972)
of undefeated home matches:	48 (1963-65)	of undefeated away matches:	10 (1973-74)
without home win:	9 (1961)	without an away win:	28 (21.3.1992 - 18.9.1993)
of league wins:	7 (1954-55)	of home wins:	10 (1963)
of league defeats:	10 (1988-89)	of away wins:	4 (1953-1981)

Missing seasons in 'away without a win', between 1938-50, was when they were a non-League club.

THE MANAGER

TONY PULIS . . . . appointed July 1995.

PREVIOUS CLUBS
As Manager. . . . . Bournemouth.
As Asst.Man/Coach . . . . Bournemouth.
As a player . . . . Bristol Rovers, Happy Valley (Hong Kong), Bristol Rovers, Newport County, Bournemouth,
. . . . Gillingham, Bournemouth.

HONOURS
As a Manager . . . . Promotion to Division 2, 1995-96.
As a Player . . . . Newport County: Division 3 Championship 1987.

GILLINGHAM

PLAYERS NAME Honours	Ht	Wt	Birthdate	Birthplace Transfers	Contract Date	Clubs	League	L/Cup	FA Cup	Other	Lge	L/C	FAC	Oth
G O A L K E E P E R														
Bartram Vince	6.2	13.4	8/7/68	Birmingham	8/17/85	Wolves (T)	5	2	3					
				Loan	10/27/89	Blackpool	9			2				
				£65000	7/24/91	Bournemouth	132	10	14	6				
				£400000	8/10/94	Arsenal	11	0+1						
				Loan	10/17/97	Huddersfield Town	12							
				Free	3/20/98	Gillingham	9							
D E F E N C E														
Ashby Barry FAYC'89.	6.2	13.2	11/21/70	Brent	12/1/88	Watford	101+13	6	4	2+1	3			
					3/22/94	Brentford	119+2	11	9	8+1	4		1	
					8/8/97	Gillingham	41	1	2					
Bryant Matthew	6.1	12.4	9/21/70	Bristol	7/1/89	Bristol City	201+2	9+1	11	9	7			
				Loan	8/24/90	Walsall	13	4						
				Free	8/7/96	Gillingham	62+11	8	3					
Butters Guy E: u21.3	6.3	13	10/30/69	Hillingdon	8/5/88	Tottenham Hotspur	34+1	2+1	1		1			
				Loan	1/13/90	Southend United	16			2	3			
				£375000	9/28/90	Portsmouth	148+6	16+1	7	7+2	6	1		
				Loan	11/4/94	Oxford United	3			1	1			
					10/18/96	Gillingham	58	2	5		7			
Edge Roland	5.9	11.6	11/25/78	Gillingham	5/31/97	Gillingham (T)								
Green Richard E	6	12.8	11/22/67	Wolverhampton	7/19/86	Shrewsbury Town	120+5	11	5	5	5	1		1
				Free	10/25/90	Swindon Town								
				Free	3/6/92	Gillingham	206+10	12+1	16	6	16		1	
Masters Neil	6.1	13.3	5/25/72	Ballymena	8/31/90	Bournemouth	37+1	4	5+2	2	2	1	1	
				£600000	12/22/93	Wolverhampton W.	10+2							
				Free	5/15/97	Gillingham	11							
Patterson Mark	5.1	11.5	9/13/68	Leeds	6/30/86	Carlisle United	19+3	4			1			
				£60000	11/10/87	Derby County	41+10	5+2	4	5+1	3			2
				£85000	7/23/93	Plymouth Argyle	130+3	3	8	9	3			
				£150000	10/30/97	Gillingham	23		2					
Pennock Adrian	5.11	12.1	3/27/71	Ipswich	7/4/89	Norwich City	1							
				£30000	8/14/92	Bournemouth	130+1	9	12	8	9		1	
					10/2/96	Gillingham	46	1	2		3			
Ratcliffe Simon E: u19.3, Y.1, S. Div.3'92.	5.11	11.9	2/8/67	Urmston	2/13/85	Manchester United								
				£40000	6/16/87	Norwich City	6+3	2						
				£100000	1/13/89	Brentford	197+17	13+3	9+1	23+2	16			2
				Free	8/4/95	Gillingham	100+5	11	5+2		10	2	1	
Williams Paul R C	5.6	10.7	9/11/69	Leicester	7/1/88	Leicester City								
					7/5/89	Stockport County	61+9	3	4	7+5	4			1
				£150000	8/12/93	Coventry City	8+6	3+1	1					
				Loan	11/19/93	WBA	5							
				Loan	3/17/95	Huddersfield Town	9		1					
				£50000	8/10/95	Plymouth Argyle	131	6	8	4	4			1
				Free	7/1/98	Gillingham								
M I D F I E L D														
Galloway Michael A	5.11	11.5	10/13/74	Nottingham	6/15/93	Notts County	17+4	2	+2	3				
				Loan	3/27/97	Gillingham	6+2				1			
					0/8/9?	Gillingham	32+7	2	1+1		2			
Hessenthaler Andrew E: S-P.1. 1LP'91	5.7	11	8/17/65	Dartford		Dagenham & Red.	5					1		
				£65000	9/12/91	Watford	195	13	5	4	12	1	2	
				Free	8/7/96	Gillingham	79	9	5		8			
Saunders Mark	5.10	11.6	23/07/71	Reading		Tiverton								
				Free	22/08/95	Plymouth Argyle	60+12	1+1	2+3	2	11			
				Free	7/1/98	Gillingham								
Smith Paul W SLP'93. (while on loan with Dover)	5.11	13.7	9/18/71	Lenham	3/16/90	Southend United	18+2			0+1	1			
				Free	8/6/93	Brentford	159	12	12	13	11	1	3	2
				Free	7/3/97	Gillingham	31	1			3			
Statham Brian E: u21.3,u19.2. Div.3'92.	5.8	11.6	21/05/69	Zimbabwe	03/08/87	Tottenham Hotspur	20+4	2	0+1					
				Loan	28/03/91	Reading	8							
				Loan	20/11/91	Bournemouth	2			1				
				£70000	16/01/92	Brentford	148+18	12	6	22	1		1	
				£10000	8/22/97	Gillingham	16+4	2		1				
F O R W A R D														
Butler Steve E: S.P.3. GMVC'89.	6.2	13	1/27/62	Birmingham		Wokingham Town								
						Windsor			1					
				Free	12/19/84	Brentford	18+3		2	3				
				Free	8/1/86	Maidstone	76	4	18	10	41	3	7	
				£150000	3/13/91	Watford	40+22	4+3	1	2+1	9			
				Loan	12/18/92	Bournemouth	1							
				£75000	12/23/92	Cambridge United	91+2	4+1	5	3	41		4	
				£100000	12/15/95	Gillingham	63+24	3	4		18	1		
Hodge John AMC'94.	5.6	10	01/04/69	Skelmersdale	01/01/00	Falmouth Town								
				Free	12/09/91	Exeter City	57+8	3	2	8+2	10	1		1
				£20000	14/07/93	Swansea City	87+25	6+2	6	13+4	10	3		
				Free	27/09/96	Walsall	67+9	5	7+1	5+2	12		2	
				Free	7/1/98	Gillingham								
O'Connor Mark Div.3'87.	5.7	10.2	3/10/63	Southend	6/1/80	QPR	2+1							
				Loan	10/7/83	Exeter City	38	2		3	1	1	1	1
				£20000	8/13/84	Bristol Rovers	79+1	8	7	4	10	1	1	1
				£25000	3/27/86	Bournemouth	115+13	5+3	7	4+1	12			
				£70000	12/15/89	Gillingham	107+9	8	7+1	6+2	8			1
				Free	7/5/93	Bournemouth	56+2	7+1	4	1	3			
				Free	8/4/95	Gillingham	35+4	4	4		1			
Pinnock James	5.9	11.5	8/1/78	Dartford	5/31/97	Gillingham	0+3							
Southall Nicholas	5.1	11.4	1/28/72	Stockton	1/1/00	Darlington								
				Free	2/21/91	Hartlepool United	118+20	6+1	4+4	6+2	24	3		
				£40000	7/12/95	Grimsby Town	55+17	3+3	4+3		6	1	2	
				Free	12/29/97	Gillingham	22+1				2			
Taylor Robert	6	11.6	4/30/71	Norwich	3/26/90	Norwich City								
				Loan	3/28/91	Leyton Orient	0+3							
					8/31/91	Birmingham City								
				Free	10/21/91	Leyton Orient	54+19	1+1	2+1	2+1	20			
				£100000	3/24/94	Brentford	172+1	16	10	10	56	6	8	3
				£500000	7/1/98	Gillingham								

PRIESTFIELD STADIUM
Redfern Avenue, Gillingham, Kent ME7 4DD

Capacity 10,422
Covered Standing 4,823
Seating..1,225

First game ....v Woolwich Arsenal, Friendly, 2.9.1893.
First floodlit game ....v Bury, Lge Cup, 25.9.1963.

ATTENDANCES
Highest ....23,002 v Q.P.R., FA Cup 3rd Rnd, 10.1.1948.
Lowest ....963 v Colchester, AMC, 23.1.1985.

OTHER GROUNDS...None.

HOW TO GET TO THE GROUND

Use motorway (M2) until junction 4.
Leave motorway and follow signs to Gillingham.
Straight over two roundabouts, at 3rd roundabout turn left (A2).
In 500 yards straight over roundabout.
Traffic lights in 200 yards Woodlands Road.
Go straight over until next traffic lights.
Stadium on left.
One block street parking.

Nearest Railway Station
Gillingham (10 minutes walk from ground).

USEFUL TELEPHONE NUMBERS

Club switchboard 01634 576 828
.... 01634 851 462/01634 851 854
Club fax number 01634 850 986
Ticket Office .... as for switchboard

Commercial sales team 01634 281 267
Clubcall 0891 33 22 11*
*Calls cost 50p per minute at all times.
Call costings correct at time of going to press.

MATCHDAY PROGRAMME

Programme Editor .... Matt Davison.

Number of pages .... 48.

Price .... £1.80.

Subscriptions .... Yes.

Local Newspapers
. Kent Today, Medway News and Standard.

Local Radio Stations
.... BBC Radio Kent, Invicta Radio.

MATCHDAY TICKET PRICES

NEW STAND
Gold club (inc. matchday prog) £16.00
Silver club
Adult £13.00
Senior Citizen £11.00
Juvenile £7.50
Bronze club
Adult £11.00
Senior Citizen £9.00
Juvenile £6.00
MAIN STAND
Enclosure
Adult £12.00
Senior Citizen £10.00
Juvenile £7.00
Terrace
Adult £9.50
Senior Citizen £7.50
Juvenile £4.50

LINCOLN CITY
(The Red Imps)
NATIONWIDE LEAGUE DIVISION 2
SPONSORED BY: ALSTOM

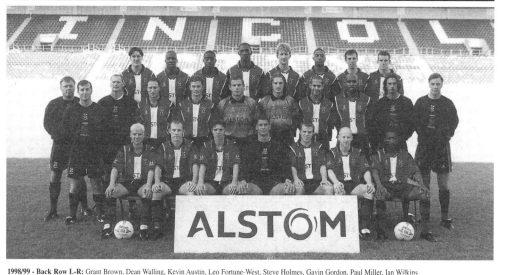

1998/99 - Back Row L-R: Grant Brown, Dean Walling, Kevin Austin, Leo Fortune-West, Steve Holmes, Gavin Gordon, Paul Miller, Ian Wilkins
Middle Row: Wally Downs (Coach), Michael Cain (Kit Man.), Phil Stant (Asst. Manager), Lee Philpott, Jason Perry, John Vaughan, Barry Richardson, Lee Thorpe, Colin Alcide, Michael Wait (Asst. Physio), Keith Oakes (Physio).
Front Row: John finnigan, Jon Whitney, Craig Stones, Shane Westley (Manager), Paul Smith, Stuart Bimson, Terry Fleming.

LINCOLN CITY
FORMED IN 1884
TURNED PROFESSIONAL IN 1885
LTD COMPANY IN 1895

PRESIDENT: H Dove
CHAIRMAN: K J Reames
VICE-CHAIRMAN
G R Davey
DIRECTORS
H C Sills, J Hicks, N Woolsey, P Jackson
SECRETARY
G R Davey
COMMERCIAL MANAGER
G R Davey

MANAGER: Shane Westley
ASSISTANT MANAGER: Phil Stant
COACH: Wally Downs

PHYSIOTHERAPIST
Keith Oakes

STATISTICIAN FOR THE DIRECTORY
Ian Nannestad

On the very last day of the Nationwide League season (Sunday 3 May) in front of a near full-house at Sincil bank, Lincoln City beat Brighton 2-1 to clinch promotion to the Second Division - and what joyous scenes there were around this quaint old ground with manager Shane Westley, who had taken over the reins from John Beck in the New Year, as delighted as anyone at the success he and his players had achieved.

Not everyone's favourites to be in the promotion frame when the season commenced, the 'Imps' made a slow start, winning four and losing three of their opening eight matches.

After roughly a third of the season had been completed (16 matches played) they had climbed into the leading group and were pushing Peterborough, Notts County and Exeter strongly at the top.

At the turn of the year (25 games completed) the industrious 'Imps' were well placed. They were still in third spot and were playing some delightful football. But then they started to slip up - only temporarily one should add, losing 3-1 and 5-3 at home to Chester City and Notts County respectively and drawing 2-2 at Scarborough. But they got back on track quickly with a narrow victory over Hull City and from then on all things went basically according to plan, although they did lose a crucial game at the time away to Torquay (3-2)..

With under two months of the season to go and 10 matches remaining, the 'Imps' with 55 points in their locker, were in ninth place - two wins off a play-off spot and still had it all to do. But from their remaining fixtures they pocketed a massive 20 points and took that automatic promotion spot after a superb late burst.
Now for the Division One!

* Interesting point: three 'Imps' players - Barry Richardson,, Jason Barrett and Lee Thorpe - were put on misconduct charges after an on-pitch brawl during their game with Macclesfield in March.

Tony Matthews.

409

LINCOLN CITY

Division 3	:3rd			FA CUP: 2nd Round			LC CUP: 1st Round	AWS: Northern Round 1	

M	DATE	COMP.	VEN	OPPONENTS	RESULT	H/T	LP	GOAL SCORERS/GOAL TIMES	ATT.
1	A 09	FL	A	Chester City	L 0-2	0-0	22		(2478)
2	12	CC 1/1	H	Burnley	D 1-1	1-0		Stant 39	3010
3	15	FL	H	Shrewsbury Town	W 1-0	0-0	18	Miller 53	3019
4	23	FL	A	Notts County	W 2-1	1-0	7	Alcide 26, Stant 76	5707
5	26	CC 1/2	A	Burnley	L 1-2	1-2		Ainsworth 26	(4644)
6	30	FL	H	Scarborough	D 3-3	2-1	9	Ainsworth 35, 42, 70	3162
7	S 02	FL	H	Mansfield Town	L 0-2	0-1	11		3539
8	10	FL	A	Rotherham United	L 1-3	0-0	16	Miller 88	(2871)
9	13	FL	A	Hull City	W 2-0	1-0	13	Thorpe 23, Fleming 76	(4736)
10	20	FL	H	Cardiff City	W 1-0	1-0	11	Thorpe 5	3130
11	27	FL	A	Barnet	D 0-0	0-0	11		(1734)
12	O 04	FL	H	Cambridge United	D 0-0	0-0	11		3397
13	11	FL	H	Torquay United	D 1-1	0-1	8	Fleming 48	2462
14	18	FL	A	Scunthorpe United	W 1-0	0-0	6	Walling 72	(4152)
15	22	FL	A	Brighton & H.A.	W 1-0	0-0	4	Thorpe 64	(1036)
16	25	FL	H	Darlington	W 3-1	3-0	4	Thorpe 1, 44, Whitney 33	3384
17	N 01	FL	H	Leyton Orient	W 1-0	0-0	4	Walling 59	4129
18	04	FL	A	Rochdale	D 0-0	0-0	4		(1337)
19	08	FL	A	Swansea City	D 0-0	0-0	4		(2871)
20	15	FAC 1	H	Gainsborough T.	D 1-1	1-0		Walling 15	6014
21	18	FL	H	Doncaster Rovers	W 2-1	1-0	4	Walling 14, Holmes 66	2957
22	22	FL	A	Colchester United	W 1-0	0-0	1	Gordon 61	(2932)
23	25	FAC 1R	A	Gainsborough T.	W 3-2	3-2		Walling 15, 17, Whitney 18	(5726)
24	29	FL	H	Macclesfield Town	D 1-1	0-1	1	Gordon 59	3402
25	D 02	FL	A	Exeter City	W 2-1	0-1	1	Thorpe 47, Brown S 80	(4224)
26	06	FAC 2	H	Emley	D 2-2	1-1		Fleming 12, 90	3729
27	09	AWS N1	A	Wigan Athletic	L 0-2	0-0			(1467)
28	13	FL	H	Hartlepool United	D 1-1	1-0	2	, Cullen 14 (OG)	2849
29	17	FAC 2R	A	Emley	D 3-3	0-0		Whitney 64, Alcide 69, Hone 115	(4891)
30	20	FL	A	Peterborough United	L 1-5	1-4	3	Thorpe 2	(8771)
31	26	FL	H	Rotherham United	L 0-1	0-0	3		6350
32	28	FL	A	Mansfield Town	D 2-2	0-1	3	Alcide 55, Smith 83	(3449)
33	J 01	FL	H	Chester City	L 1-3	0-2	6	Brown S 48	2913
34	17	FL	A	Scarborough	D 2-2	1-0	7	Thorpe 10, Walling 90	(2905)
35	24	FL	H	Notts County	L 3-5	0-3	11	Smith 48, Hone 52, Brown S 64	5911
36	31	FL	H	Hull City	W 1-0	0-0	9	Walling 21	4067
37	F 06	FL	A	Cardiff City	W 1-0	0-0	8	Alcide 51	(2896)
38	13	FL	A	Cambridge United	D 1-1	0-1	7	Alcide 57	(3891)
39	21	FL	H	Barnet	W 2-0	0-0	6	Hone 54, Gordon 89	2945
40	24	FL	H	Scunthorpe United	D 1-1	1-0	6	Alcide 20	3407
41	28	FL	A	Torquay United	L 2-3	1-2	8	Thorpe 41, Alcide 67	(3540)
42	M 03	FL	H	Swansea City	D 1-1	0-0	8	Thorpe 80	2281
43	07	FL	A	Leyton Orient	L 0-1	0-1	9		(4745)
44	14	FL	H	Rochdale	W 2-0	1-0	6	Thorpe 14, Alcide 82	2992
45	21	FL	A	Doncaster Rovers	W 4-2	2-2	6	Stant 8, Thorpe 10, Martin 72, Alcide 84	(2357)
46	24	FL	A	Shrewsbury Town	W 2-0	1-0	6	Alcide 13, Thorpe 73	(1877)
47	28	FL	H	Colchester United	L 0-1	0-1	6		4040
48	A 04	FL	A	Macclesfield Town	L 0-1	0-0	7		(3278)
49	13	FL	A	Hartlepool United	D 1-1	1-1	8	Alcide 30	(1997)
50	18	FL	H	Peterborough United	W 3-0	3-0	7	Alcide 2, 44, Smith 6	6748
51	21	FL	H	Exeter City	W 2-1	1-0	4	Holmes 30, 80	4284
52	25	FL	A	Darlington	D 2-2	1-1	4	Holmes 21 (pen), Bailey 90	(3160)
53	M 02	FL	H	Brighton & H.A.	W 2-1	0-0	3	Fleming 55, Thorpe 58	9890

Best Home League Attendance: 9890 V Brighton & H.A.	Smallest :2281 V Swansea City	Average :3968	

Goal Scorers:

FL	(60)	Thorpe 14, Alcide 12, Walling 5, Holmes 4, Ainsworth 3, Brown 3, Fleming 3, Gordon 3, Smith 3, Hone 2, Miller 2, Stant 2, Martin 1, Bailey 1, Miller 1, Whitney 1, Opponents 1
CC	(2)	Ainsworth 1, Stant 1
FAC	(9)	Walling 3, Fleming 2, Whitney 2, Alcide 1, Hone 1
AWS	(0)	

(F) Ainsworth	(M) Alcide	(D) Austin	(F) Bailey	(F) Barnett	(D) Bimson	(D) Brown G	(F) Brown Steve	(D) Chandler	(M) Finnigan	(F) Flash	(D) Fleming	(M) Gordon	(M) Harris	(D) Holmes	(D) Hone	(F) Martin	(F) Miller	(F) Regis	(G) Richardson	(D) Robertson	(M) Smith	(F) Stant	(M) Stones	(F) Thorpe	(G) Vaughan	(M) Walling	(D) Whitney	(M) Wilkins		
X		X		X			S				X			X	X		X		X		X	X	X		X				A.R. Hall	1
X		X		X			S				X			X	X		X		X	S	X	X	X		X				S J Baines	2
X		X		X			S1				X		S	X	X		X		X	S2	X	X			X				M L Dean	3
X	X	X		X			S				S		S	X	X		X		X		X	X	X		X				P R Richards	4
X	X			X			S	X		S1				X	X		X		X	S	X	X			X				C J Foy	5
X	X	X		X			S				S		S	X	X		X		X		X	X			X				T Jones	6
X	X	X		X			S				S	S1	X	X			X		X		X	X			X				M D Messias	7
X	X	X		X	S		S1				X				X		X		X		X	X	X		X				D Pugh	8
	X	X		X	S		X				X				X		X		X	S1	X	X			X	S			W C Burns	9
	X		X	S2			X	X	S		X				X		X		X	X	X	X		X	X	S1			G Laws	10
	X	X		S			S1			X		X		X	X		X		X	S	X		X	X					J P Robinson	12
	X	X	S	X			X			X	X		X		S2		X	S1	X		X	X							G B Frankland	13
	X	X		S				S1	X		X		X	X	S	X	X	S	X	X	X			X	X				E K Wolstenholme	14
	X	X		S2		S1	X			X	X	X	S1	X	X		X	X		X		X	X				R J Harris	15
	X	X		S3		S2	X			X	X	X	S1	X	X		X	X		X		X	X				A R Leake	16
	X	X		S1			X				X		X	S2	X	X	S3	S2	X	X			X	X			M R Halsey	17
	X	X		X			X				X	X	X	X	S1	X	X	S3	S2		S	S	X	X			F G Stretton	18
	X	X		X			X	S1			X	X	X	X		S	S	X	X	S		X	X			C J Foy	19
	X		X	S	S2				X	X	X	X	X	S		X	S1	X	S	X	X	X		M D Reed	20
	X	X		S1				X	X	X	X	S		S	S	X		X	X			G Cain	21
	X	X		S				X	X	X	X		X	S	S	X		X	X		R Pearson	22
	X	X	S	S			X	X	X	X	X	S		X	S	X	S	X	X		M D Reed	23
	X	X	S	S1			X	X2			X	X1	S2	X			X	X	X2	P Rejer	24
	X	X	S2	S1			X	X1		X	S	X	X	X		X	X2	M J Brandwood	25
S1	X	X	S3	X2			X	X		X	X	S	S2	X3	S	X	X1	T Heilbron	26
S3	X	X	S2	S1			X3	X1	X	X	X	X2	X	X	X		27
S1	X	X		S2			X	X1	X		X2	S	X	X	X	S W Mathieson	28
S1	X	X	S	X2			X	X1	X	X	X	S	S2	S	X	X	X	T Heilbron	29
X	X2			S3			X	X1	X	S2	X3	S1	X	X	X	G Laws	30
S1	X			X2			X	X1	X	S	X	S2	X	X	X	M S Pike	31
S2	X	X		X2			X	X1	X	X	S1	S	X	X	X	A P D'Urso	32
X2	X	X	S1	S2			X	3	X		X1	X	X	X	K A Leach	33
X	X	X	X	X2			X		S1	S2	X1	X	X	X	S3	J A Kirkby	34
S	X	X	S	S1			X	X1	X	X		X	X	X	W C Burns	35
S1	X	X	X2	X			X		X	S	X1	S2	X	X	G B Frankland	36
X	X			S1			X		X	X	X1		X	X	D Orr	37
X	X			X			X		X	X	S	S	X	X	P S Danson	38
X1	X		X	X			S1	X	X	X	S	S	X	T Heilbron	39
X	X		X1	X			S	X	X	X	S1	X	X	G Laws	40
X	X		S	X		X	S	X	X	S	X	X	S G Bennett	41
X	X		X2	X1	S1		X	S2	X	X	S3	X	X	M J Jones	42
X3	X		S1	X	X1		X	S3	X	S2	X2	X	A Bates	43
X	X		X1	X	S1		X		X	X	X	S	X	X	A R Hall	44
X	X			X			S	X	S1	X	X1	X	X	X	X	E K Wolstenholme	45
X	X			X			X	X	X	S	S	X	X	S J Baines	46
X	X	S1		X			X	X1	X2	S2	X	X	X	S	M J Brandwood	47
X	X	X1	X	X		X	X	X	S	X	S1	X	X	E Lomas	48
X	X	X	X	X		X	X	X	S1	X	S	X1	X	X	M L Dean	49
X	X	S1	X	X		X	X	S	S	X1	X	X	X	B Coddington	50
X	X	S	X	X		X	X1	X	S1	X	X	X	S	P Taylor	51
X	X	S2	X	X		X	X	X2	S	X	X	X1	S1	M S Pike	52
X	X	S1	X	X		X	X	X	S	S	X	X1	X	R Pearson	53
6	25	46	1	33	7	15	16		6	2	40	9		46	22	26	20	15	17	10	44	19	35	42	1				FL Appearances	
4		4		5		15			3		4	1		2	7	4	2	4	5				2	1				FL Sub Appearances	
2	1	1		2				1		1+1			2	2		2		2		2	2	2	2				CC Appearances	
	0+2	4		4	0+1	2+1				4	4		4	3	4		2+2	1+1	4		4	4				FAC Appearances	
	0+1	1		1	0+1	0+1					1		1	1	1			1	1	1	1	1				AWS Appearances	

Also played:(G) Brown Simon X(30).

CLUB RECORDS

BIGGEST VICTORIES
League: 11-1 v Crewe Alexandra, Division 3(N), 29.9.1951.
F.A. Cup: 13-0 v Peterborough (a), 1st Qualifying Round, 12.10.1895.
8-1 v Bromley, 2nd Round, 10.12.1938.
BIGGEST DEFEATS
League: 3-11 v Manchester City, Division 2, 23.3.1895.
0-8 v Notts County, Division 2, 23.1.1897.
0-8 v Preston North End, Division 2, 28.12.1901.
1-9 v Wigan Borough, Division 3(N), 3.3.1923.
0-8 v Stoke City, Division 2, 23.2.1957.
F.A. Cup: 0-5 v Grimsby Town, 4th Qualifying Round, 10.12.1892.
0-5 v Stoke City, 1st Round, 11.01.1907.
League Cup: 0-5 v Leicester City, 3rd Round, 05.10.1966.
Others: 2-7 v Doncaster Rovers, Division 3(N) Cup Round 1, 28.10.1937.

MOST POINTS: 3 points a win: 77, Division 3, 1981-82.
2 points a win: 74, Division 4, 1975-76.
MOST GOALS SCORED: 121, Division 3(N), 1951-52.
RECORD TRANSFER FEE RECEIVED
£400,000 + appearance payment from Newcastle Utd for Darren Huckerby, November 1995.
RECORD TRANSFER FEE PAID
£63,000 to Leicester City for Grant Brown, January 1990.
BEST PERFORMANCES
League: 5th Division 2, 1901-02.
F.A. Cup: Equivalent 5th Round 1886-87, 18889-90, 1901-02.
League Cup: 4th Round 1967-68.
HONOURS
Champions of Division 3(N), 1931-32, 1947-48, 1951-52.
Champions of Division 4, 1975-76. Champions of GMVC 1987-88.
LEAGUE CAREER: Original members of Div 2 1892, Not re-elected to Div 2 1908, re-elected Div 2 1909, Not re-elected 1911, Re-elected Div 2 1912, Not re-elected 1920, Re-elected Div 3(N) 1921, Div 2 1931-32, Div 3(N) 1933-34, Div 2 1947-48, Div 3(N) 1948-49, Div 2 1951-52, Div 3 1960-61, Div 4 1961-62, Div 3 1975-76, Div 4 1978-79, Div 3 1980-81, Div 4 1985-86, GMVC 1986-87, Div (now Div 3) 1987-88.

INDIVIDUAL CLUB RECORDS

MOST GOALS IN A SEASON
Allan Hall: 42 goals in 1931-32, Division 3(N).

MOST GOALS IN A MATCH
6. Andy Graver v Crewe Alexandra (h) 11-1, Division 3(N), 29.9.1951.
6. Frank Keetley v Halifax Town (h) 9-1, Division 3(N), 16.1.1932.

OLDEST PLAYER
John Burridge, 42 years 57 days v Rochdale, Division 3, 29.1.1994.

YOUNGEST PLAYER
Shane Nicholson, 16 years 112 days, League Cup v Charlton, 23.9.1986.

MOST CAPPED PLAYER
David Pugh (Wales) 3.
George Moulson (Eire) 3.

PREVIOUS MANAGERS

(since 1947)
Bill Anderson 1947-64; Con Moulson (coach) 1965; Roy Chapman (player/coach) 1965-66; Ron Gray 1966-70; Bert Loxley 1970-71; David Herd 1971-72; Graham Taylor 1972-77; George Kerr 1977; Willie Bell 1977-78; Colin Murphy 1978-85; John Pickering 1985; George Kerr 1985-87; Peter Daniel (caretaker) 1987; Colin Murphy 1987-90; Alan Clarke 1990; Steve Thompson 1990-93; Keith Alexander 1993-94, Sam Ellis 1994-95.

ADDITIONAL INFORMATION
PREVIOUS NAMES
None.
PREVIOUS LEAGUES
None.
Club colours: red and white striped shirts, black shorts with red trim, red socks with black & white trim.
Change colours: Blue shirts yellow trim, blue shorts, blue socks.
Reserves League: Pontins League.
Youth League: (Juniors) Midland Purity Youth League.

LONGEST LEAGUE RUNS

of undefeated matches:	18 (1980)	of league matches w/out a win:	19 (1978)
of undefeated home matches:	35 (1975-76)	of undefeated away matches:	12 (1980)
without home win:	11 (1978-79)	without an away win:	35 (1896-98)
of league wins:	10 (1930)	of home wins:	14 (1982)
of league defeats:	12 (1896-97)	of away wins:	5 (1968, 1975, 1989, 1992)

THE MANAGER

SHANE WESTLEY . . . . appointed January 1998.

PREVIOUS CLUBS
As Manager . . . . None.
As Asst.Man/Coach . . . . Lincoln City.
As a player . . . . Charlton Ath., Southend, Wolves, Brentford, Southend (Loan), Lincoln City.

HONOURS
As a Manager . . . . **Lincoln City:** Promotion to Division 2, 1997/98.
As a Player . . . . None.

LINCOLN CITY

PLAYERS NAME Honours	Ht	Wt	Birthdate	Birthplace Transfers	Contract Date	Clubs	League	L/Cup	FA Cup	Other	Lge	L/C	FAC	Oth
G O A L K E E P E R														
Richardson Barry	6.1	12.1	8/5/69	Wallsend	5/20/88	Sunderland								
					3/21/89	Scunthorpe United								
				Free	8/3/89	Scarborough	30	1		1				
				Free	6/16/91	Stockport County								
				Free	9/10/91	Northampton Town	96	4	5	8				
				£20000	7/25/94	Preston North End	17	2	3	1				
				£20000	10/20/95	Lincoln City	92	4	5					
Vaughan John	5.11	13.1	6/26/64	Isleworth	6/30/82	West Ham United								
				Loan	3/11/85	Charlton Athletic	6							
				Loan	9/5/85	Bristol Rovers	6							
				Loan	10/23/85	Wrexham	4							
				Loan	3/4/86	Bristol City	2							
				£12500	8/21/86	Fulham	44	4	4	3				
				Loan	1/21/88	Bristol City	3							
				Free	6/6/88	Cambridge United	178	13	24	16				
				Free	8/5/93	Charlton Athletic	5+1		2	1+1				
				Free	7/26/94	Preston North End	65+1	2	2	5				
					8/2/96	Lincoln City	29	3						
				Loan	2/3/97	Colchester United	5							
D E F E N C E														
Austin Kevin	5.9	10.12	2/12/73	London	1/1/00	Saffron Walden								
				£1000	8/19/93	Leyton Orient	101+9	4	6	7	3	1		
				Free	8/15/96	Lincoln City	88	6	4		1			
Brown Grant A	6	11.12	11/19/69	Sunderland	7/1/88	Leicester City	14	2						
				£63000	8/20/88	Lincoln City	303+1	17	10	15	12	1		2
Fleming Terry	5.9	10.09	1/5/73	Marston Green	7/2/91	Coventry City	8+5	+1						
				Free	8/3/93	Northampton Town	26+5	2	+1	+1	1			
				Free	7/18/94	Preston North End	20+7	2	+1	3+1	2			
					12/7/95	Lincoln City	94+5	6+1	4		4	1	2	
Holmes Steve	6.2	13	1/13/71	Middlesbrough	7/17/89	Lincoln City								
					1/1/90	Gainsborough T.								
					1/1/92	Guisborough T.								
				£10000	3/14/94	Preston North End	5		3	3	1			
				Loan	3/31/94	Bromsgrove Rovers								
				Loan	3/10/95	Hartlepool United	5				2			
				£30000	3/15/96	Lincoln City	96+1	6	4	2	12	2		
Perry Jason W: 1, B.2, u21.3, Y, S.	5.11	10.4	02/04/70	Newport	28/08/87	Cardiff City	278+3	22	14+1	20+1	5			
				Free	03/07/97	Bristol Rovers	24+1	2	2+1	2				
				Free	7/1/98	Lincoln City								
Walling Dean FAV'91. Div.3'95. AMC'97. Free 01/08/90 Guiseley. via Franklin	6	10.8	17/04/69	Leeds		Leeds United								
				Free	30/07/87	Rochdale	43+22	3	0+1	1+1	8			
				Free	01/07/91	Carlisle United	230+6	18	14+1	35	21	3	1	5
				£75000	9/30/97	Lincoln City	35	4			5		3	
Whitney Jonathan D	5.11	12.3	12/23/70	Nantwich	1/1/00	Wigan Athletic								
					1/1/01	Skelmersdale Utd								
				Free	1/1/02	Winsford United			1					
				£10000	10/21/93	Huddersfield Town	14			4				
				Loan	3/17/95	Wigan Athletic	12							
					8/1/95	Lincoln City	82+3	6	5	3	4	1	2	
Wilkins Ian J			4/3/80	Lincoln	9/19/97	Lincoln City (T)	1+1							
M I D F I E L D														
Alcide Colin	6.2	13.11	4/14/72	Huddersfield	1/1/00	Emley								
				£15000	12/5/95	Lincoln City	84+13	4+2	+2	1	25	2	1	
Philpott Lee Div.3'91.	5.9	11.8	2/21/70	Hackney	7/17/86	Peterborough United	1+3		+1	+2				
					5/31/89	Cambridge United	118+16	10	19	15	17	1	3	2
				£350000	11/24/92	Leicester City	56+13	2+1	4+1	4+1	3			
				£75000	3/22/96	Blackpool	51+20	5	4	0+2	5	1		
				Free	7/1/98	Lincoln City								
Reeson Nicholas D			5/5/80	Boston		Lincoln City (T)								
Smith Paul A	5.11	11.7	1/25/76	Hastings		Hastings Town								
				£50000	1/13/95	Nottingham Forest								
				£30000	10/17/97	Lincoln City	15+2		1		3			
Stones Craig	5.11	11.2	5/31/80	Scunthorpe	3/15/97	Lincoln City	10+7		1+1					
F O R W A R D														
Barnett Jason V	5.9	10.1	4/21/76	Shrewsbury	7/4/94	Wolverhampton W.								
				£5000	10/26/95	Lincoln City	91+8	4	5	3	2			
Finnigan John	5.8	10.05	29/03/76	Wakefield	01/08/92	Nottingham Forest								
				£50000	7/1/98	Lincoln City								
Gordon Kenyatta G	6.1	12	6/24/79	Manchester	7/3/96	Hull City (T)	22+16	1+4		1+1	9	1		
				£30000	11/7/97	Lincoln City	9+4		4	1	3			
Fortune-West Leo						Stevenage Borough								
				Free	7/12/95	Gillingham	48+19	3+1	3+1		18	2	2	
				Loan	3/27/97	Leyton Orient	1+4							
				Free	7/1/98	Lincoln City								
Miller Paul	6	11	1/31/68	Woking	1/1/00	Wimbledon								
					1/1/01	Wealdstone								

SINCIL BANK
Lincoln LN5 8LD

Capacity 10,918

ATTENDANCES
Highest ....23,196 v Derby County, League Cup 4th Round, 15.11.1967.
Lowest ....1,003 v Scunthorpe, AMC, 25.11.1986.

OTHER GROUNDS ....None.

HOW TO GET TO THE GROUND

From the North, East and West
Use A15, A57, A46 or A158 into Lincoln City centre then follow Newark (A46) in High Street, left into Scorer Street and right into Cross Street for Lincoln City FC.

From South
Use A1 then A46 (sign posted Lincoln) then following signs city centre into High Street and turn right into Scorer Street and right again into Cross Street for Lincoln City FC.

Car Parking
Club Car Park £2, plus street parking available.

Nearest Railway Station
Lincoln Central (01522 539502).

USEFUL TELEPHONE NUMBERS

Club switchboard......................01522 880 011
Club fax number.......................01522 880 020
Ticket Office.............................01522 522224

Impsline...................................0891 66 46 66*
Calls cost 50p per minute at all times.
*Call costings correct at time of going to press.

MATCHDAY PROGRAMME

Programme Editor (97/98) .....David Teague.

Number of pages (97/98) ....32.

Price (97/98)......................................£1.50.

Subscriptions (97/98) ....£45.

Local Newspapers
...........Lincolnshire Echo, Lincoln Standard.

Local Radio Stations
..............BBC Radio Lincolnshire, Lincs FM.

MATCHDAY TICKET PRICES (97/98)

St Andrews Stand
Adult £10
Juv/OAP £8
Family 1+1 . . . . £13
1+2 - £16. . . . . 1+3 - £19
Stacey West Stand (Covered seating or standing)
Adult. £8
Juv/OAP £6
Family 1+1 . . . . £8
1+2 - £11.50. . . . . 1+3 - £15
Linpave Stand (inc. visitors) £10
Juv/OAP £8
South Park Stand
Adult. £8
OAP £6
E.G.T. Family Stand: Family 1+1 . . . . £11
1+2 - £4. . . . . 1+3 - £17

LUTON TOWN
(The Hatters)
NATIONWIDE LEAGUE DIVISION 2
SPONSORED BY: UNIVERSAL SALVAGE AUCTIONS

1997-98 - Back Row L-R: Robert Kean, Sean Evers, Stuart Douglas, Steve Augustine, Andrew Barr, Paul McLaren, Simon Davies, Gary Doherty, Matthew Spring, Ian Jones, Andrew Fotiadis, Richard Harvey, Dwight Marshall. **Standing:** Bob Bird (financial controller), Cherry Newbery (club secretary), Clive Goodyear (physio), Paul Lowe (youth dev. officer), Wayne Turner (first team coach), Paul showler, David Oldfield, Mitchell Thomas, Nathan Abbey, Ian Feuer, Kelvin Davis, Marvin Johnson, Chris Willmott, Graham Alexander, John Moore (youth team coach), Trevor Peake (reserve team manager), Kathy Leather (commercial manager), Les Shannon (scouting co-ordinator). **Seated:** Liam George, Tony Thorpe, Steve Davis, Nigel Terry (director), David Kohler (chairman), Lennie Lawrence (manager), Cliff Bassett (director), Chris Green (director), Gary Waddock, Julian James, Terry Sweeney. **Front Row:** Jimmy Cox, Russell Lawes, Stuart Fraser, Darren Howe, James Ayres, Daniel Tate, Nick Webb, Emerson Boyce, Moses Jerry, Michael McIndoe, Andre Scarlett, Delroy McKoy.

LUTON TOWN
FORMED IN 1885
TURNED PROFESSIONAL IN 1890
LTD COMPANY IN 1897

CHAIRMAN: D A Kohler B.Sc(Hons) ARICS

DIRECTORS
C Green, C Bassett, N Terry
SECRETARY
Cherry Newbery
COMMERCIAL MANAGER
Kathy Leather

MANAGER: Lennie Lawrence
FIRST TEAM COACH: John Moore

YOUTH TEAM MANAGER
John Moore
PHYSIOTHERAPIST
Clive Goodyear

STATISTICIAN FOR THE DIRECTORY
Vacant - phone 01203 234017 if interested.

Luton Town's manager Lennie Lawrence was a very relieved man after his players saved themselves from the threat of relegation with a 1-1 draw at Brentford in their penultimate League game of the season. It had been a nervous last third to the campaign for the former Charlton and Middlesbrough boss with his players continuously treading on the edge of the relegation trap-door since 31 January when they lost at home to AFC Bournemouth. For three months or so the results of both Luton and the teams close by, were monitored daily by Lawrence and just prior to seeing safety achieved he looked very stern and cautious, struggling to raise a smile. But smile he did when the Hatters knew they were safe and destined to spend at least one season in the Second Division.

Luton, relegated from the First Division in 1996, were looking odds on at one stage to go straight through into the Third, but under Lawrence's shrewd managership they battled on bravely and eventually avoided the dreaded drop by finishing, as it turned out, in 17th place with a total of 57 points, seven clear of relegated Brentford (21st).

Their overall form left a lot to be desired. They struggled at home, winning only seven and losing nine of their 23 matches. Away from Kenilworth Road they did better than expected, attaining 29 points, one more than at home!

Scoring goals was sometimes a problem - sixty obtained all told (35 at home, 25 away)....and when Tony Thorpe - the Hatters' top marksman in 1996-97 - was sold to Fulham for £800,000 in February (at a crucial time in the season) some supporters weren't too pleased. But at the end of the day Luton Town survived to fight on again in Division Two and who knows what might happen over the next eight months.

Tony Matthews.

LUTON TOWN

Division 2   :17th   FA CUP: 1st Round   LC CUP: 2nd Round   AWS: Southern Semi-Final

M	DATE	COMP.	VEN	OPPONENTS	RESULT	H/T	LP	GOAL SCORERS/GOAL TIMES	ATT.
1	A 09	FL	A	Blackpool	L	0-1	0-1	24		(6547)
2	12	CC 1/1	A	Colchester United	W	1-0	0-0		Thorpe 88	(2840)
3	18	FL	H	Southend United	W	1-0	0-0	14	Douglas 75	5140
4	23	FL	A	Fulham	D	0-0	0-0	15		(8142)
5	26	CC 1/2	H	Colchester United	D	1-1	1-0		Thorpe 34	2816
6	30	FL	H	Oldham Athletic	D	1-1	0-0	13	Thorpe 60	5404
7	S 02	FL	H	Millwall	L	0-2	0-0	16		5781
8	09	FL	A	Northampton Town	L	0-1	0-1	18		(7246)
9	13	FL	A	Bournemouth	D	1-1	1-0	21	Marshall 43	(4561)
10	16	CC 2/1	H	West Bromwich Albion	D	1-1	1-1		Douglas 24	3437
11	20	FL	H	Wrexham	L	2-5	1-2	23	Davis 41, Gray 50	5241
12	23	CC 2/2	A	West Bromwich Albion	L	2-4	1-1		Davis 37, Thorpe 74	(7227)
13	27	FL	A	Bristol City	L	0-3	0-3	23		(8509)
14	O 04	FL	H	Watford	L	0-4	0-3	23		9041
15	11	FL	H	Plymouth Argyle	W	3-0	1-0	23	Thorpe 35, 58, Davies 83	4931
16	18	FL	A	Wigan Athletic	D	1-1	0-0	22	Oldfield 68	(4466)
17	21	FL	A	Carlisle United	W	1-0	0-0	21	White 87	(4341)
18	25	FL	H	Brentford	W	2-0	1-0	18	Alexander 19, Thorpe 59	5972
19	N 01	FL	A	Wycombe Wanderers	D	2-2	1-1	18	Oldfield 45, Thorpe 74	(6219)
20	04	FL	H	Burnley	L	2-3	2-1	19	Alexander 33, 35	5315
21	08	FL	H	Preston North End	L	1-3	1-2	22	Thorpe 25	5767
22	15	FAC 1	H	Torquay United	L	0-1	0-0			3446
23	22	FL	H	Walsall	L	0-1	0-0	23		4726
24	29	FL	A	York City	W	2-1	1-0	20	Alexander 12, Thorpe 72	(3636)
25	D 02	FL	H	Gillingham	D	2-2	1-1	21	Davis 25, Thorpe 77	4408
26	13	FL	A	Chesterfield	D	0-0	0-0	22		(4358)
27	20	FL	H	Bristol Rovers	L	2-4	2-4	22	Allen C 8, Oldfield 25	5266
28	26	FL	A	Northampton Town	D	2-2	0-2	22	Oldfield 67, Thorpe 85	8035
29	28	FL	A	Millwall	W	2-0	0-0	20	Davis 89, Thorpe 90	(7461)
30	J 03	FL	A	Southend United	W	2-1	1-1	19	Alexander 2, 61	(5056)
31	10	FL	H	Blackpool	W	3-0	1-0	18	Thorpe 32, 73, 75	5574
32	13	AWS S2	H	Brentford	W	2-1	0-0		Thorpe 52, Oldfield 81	4319
33	17	FL	A	Oldham Athletic	L	1-2	0-0	18	Alexander 79	(6057)
34	24	FL	H	Fulham	L	1-4	1-2	19	Thorpe 44	8366
35	27	AWS SQF	A	Fulham	W	2-1	1-0		Marshall 21, Thorpe 90	(5103)
36	31	FL	H	Bournemouth	L	1-2	0-1	19	Johnson 71	5466
37	F 06	FL	A	Wrexham	L	1-2	0-0	20	Davis 89	(3527)
38	14	FL	A	Watford	D	1-1	0-0	20	Johnson 80	(15182)
39	17	AWS SSF	A	Bournemouth	L	0-1	0-0			(5367)
40	21	FL	H	Bristol City	D	0-0	0-0	21		6405
41	24	FL	H	Wigan Athletic	D	1-1	1-1	20	Oldfield 28	4403
42	28	FL	A	Plymouth Argyle	W	2-0	0-0	19	Fotiadis 79, Evers 88	(4846)
43	M 03	FL	A	Preston North End	L	0-1	0-0	20		(6992)
44	07	FL	A	Wycombe Wanderers	D	0-0	0-0	21		6114
45	14	FL	A	Burnley	D	1-1	0-0	21	Thomas 80	(9656)
46	21	FL	H	Grimsby Town	D	2-2	0-0	23	Evers 66, Davis 85	5700
47	28	FL	A	Walsall	W	3-2	1-0	21	Oldfield 35, Allen R 58, Marshall 73	(3922)
48	A 04	FL	H	York City	W	3-0	2-0	19	Alexander 35 (pen), Oldfield 45, Gray 85	5541
49	07	FL	A	Grimsby Town	W	1-0	0-0	17	Allen R 53	(4455)
50	11	FL	A	Gillingham	L	1-2	1-1	19	Allen R 45	(6846)
51	14	FL	H	Chesterfield	W	3-0	1-0	17	Williams 23 (OG), Allen R 48, Oldfield 63,	5884
52	18	FL	A	Bristol Rovers	L	1-2	0-2	19	Oldfield 75	(8038)
53	25	FL	A	Brentford	D	2-2	1-1	18	Marshall 13, Allen R 59	(6598)
54	M 02	FL	H	Carlisle United	W	3-2	1-0	17	Evers 25, Oldfield 84 , Allen 90,	6729

Best Home League Attendance: 9041 V Watford   **Smallest :4403 V Wigan Athletic**   **Average :5879**

Goal Scorers:

FL	(60)	Thorpe 14, Oldfield 10, Alexander 8, Allen R 6, Davis 5, Evers 3, Marshall 3, Gray 2, Johnson 2, Allen C 1, Davies 1, Douglas 1, Fotiadis 1, Thomas 1, White 1, Opponents 2
CC	(5)	Thorpe 3, Davis 1, Douglas 1
FAC	(0)	
AWS	(4)	Thorpe 2, Marshall 1, Oldfield 1

(D) Alexander	(F) Allen C	(F) Allen R	(M) Davies	(D) Davis S	(G) Davis K	(G) Dibble	(M) Doherty	(F) Douglas	(M) Evers	(G) Feuer	(F) Fotiadis	(M) Fraser	(F) George	(M) Gray	(D) Harvey	(D) James	(D) Johnson	(F) Marshall	(D) McGowan	(D) McLaren	(M) Oldfield	(D) Patterson	(D) Small	(M) Spring	(D) Thomas	(F) Thorpe	(M) Waddock	(M) White	Player	No
X			X	X				S1	S	X					S		X			X	X				X	X	X		S.W. Mathieson	1
X			X	X			X	S	X						S1		X			X	X				X	X	X		S G Bennett	2
X			X	X				S1		X	X				S	X	X	X		S2					X	X	X		C J Foy	3
X			X	X	X			X							S3	X	X	X	S2	S1	X				X		X		M E Pierce	4
			X	X				S1	S						X	X	X	X		X	X				X	X	X		D Orr	5
			X	X	X			S1							X	X	X	S2	X	X				X	X	X		A N Butler	6
X			X	X			S3	S2	S1						X	X	X	X	X	X					X	X		R D Furnandiz	7
		S1	X	X			S2	X	S1						X	X	X	X	X	X		X				X		R J Harris	8
		X	X	X			S2	X	S1						X	X	X	X	X	X		X				X		C R Wilkes	9
X		S1	X		X	S	X	X					S2		X		X	X		X	X					X		E K Wolstenholme	10
			X		X		X	S1					X	X			X	X	X	X	X		X		S2		X	P Rejer	11
		X	X		X	S	X	X					S2	X	X			X	X					S1	X		X	P R Richards	12
		X		X				X				X	X					X	X	X	X		X	S1	X	X	X	E Lomas	13
		X2		X			S2				X	X	S1		X1	X	X		X	S	X	X	X	X	X	T Heilbron	14
X		S1		X		X		S2					S	X			X	X		X	X	X	X	X	X	X	D R Crick	15
X		S2	X	X	S				X		X			S1		X	X	X	X	X			X	X	X	J A Kirkby	16
X		S	X	X				X			X		S2	X	X		X			X	X	X	S1	X	X	G Cain	17
X		S	X	X				X			X	S1	S2		X	X	X	X	X	X	X	X	X	C R Wilkes	18
X		S	X	X	S		X		X	X			X	X	X	X	X	X	X	X	S	M J Brandwood	19
X		S	X	X	S1		X	X	X	X	X	X	X	X	X	X	B Knight	20
X		S3	X	S1		X	X	X	S2	X	X	X	X	X	X	C R Wilkes	21
X		S1	S	S3	S	X	X	X	X	X	X	S2	X	X	X	X	P A Durkin	22
X		X	S1	X	X	S	X	X	X	X	S2	X	X	X	X	M R Halsey	23
X	X	S	X	X	S	X	X	X	S	X	X	X	X	D Pugh	24
X	X	S	X	X	S2	X	X	X	X	S1	X	X2	X1	P Taylor	25
X	X	S	X	S1	X	S	X1	X	X	X	X	X	X	J P Robinson	26
X	X	S2	X	X1	X	S1	X2	X	X	X	X	S	X	D Orr	27
X1	X	S	X	X	S1	X	X	S	X	X	X	C R Wilkes	28
X	X	S	X	S	X	X	S	X	X	X	A Bates	29
X	X	S	X	S	X	X	S	X	X	X	B Knight	30
X	X	S	X	S	S	X	X	X	X	X	X	R Styles	31
X2	X	X	X	X	X	S1	X	X	X	X1	S2	X	32
X	X	S1	X	S	X	S2	X	X1	X	X2	X	T Heilbron	33
X	X	S1	X	S	X	S	X	X	X	X	X1	S W Mathieson	34
X	X	X	X	X	X2	X1	X	X	S2	S1	35
X	X2	S3	X	X	S2	X	X	S1	X1	X	X	X3	R D Furnandiz	36
X	X	S	X	X	S	X	X	X	S1	X	X1	T Jones	37
X	X2	S3	X	S2	X	X3	S1	X	X	X	X1	X	J A Kirkby	38
X	X	X1	X	X	S1	X	X	X	X	X	X	39
X	X1	X	X	X2	S1	X	S2	X	X	X	X	S	X	K A Leach	40
X	S	X	X	X	S1	X	X1	X	X	S	X	S G Bennett	41
X	S	X	X	S2	X	S1	X	X1	X	X	A P D'Urso	42
X	S2	X2	X	X3	X	S1	X	X1	X	S3	X	B Coddington	43
X	S2	X	X	X	S1	X	X1	X	X2	X	S	M E Pierce	44
S1	X	X	X	X2	X	X	S2	X	X1	S	M L Dean	45
X	S	S	X	X	S1	X	X1	X	X	X	X	X	S	A R Hall	46
X	X	S	X	X	S2	S1	X	X	X1	X2	X	X	X	W C Burns	47
X	X	X2	X	X	S1	X	X1	X	X	X	X	S	S2	D R Crick	48
X	S	X	X	S3	S2	S1	X	X2	X	X1	X	X	X	R Pearson	49
X	X	X	X	S3	S1	S2	X1	X2	X	X	X3	F G Stretton	50
X	X1	X	X	S1	X	X	X	X	X2	X	S2	S	M C Bailey	51
X	X	X	X	S2	X	X1	X2	X	S3	X3	S1	A R Leake	52
X	X	X	X	S2	S1	X	X1	X2	X	S3	X	X	M R Halsey	53
X	X	X	X	S3	S1	X	X1	X	X2	X	X	S2	X3	J P Robinson	54
39	14	7	8	38	32	1	1	5	14	13	5	1	1	14	5	23	13	19	6	41	45	23	15	6	27	27	36	26	FL Appearances	
	12							9	12	9				10			3	1	1	10	2				6	1	1	2	FL Sub Appearances	
2		3+1	4		2			3+1	2		1		0+2	1	2+1		1			3	2	4	4		2	2+1	4	1	CC Appearances	
1		0+1						0+1			1	1		1			1	1		1	1	0+1		1	1	1	1	1	FAC Appearances	
2	3		3	2	1			3	2		0+1	0+1	1				2			2	3	3			2	1+1	0+2	3	AWS Appearances	

Also Played: (M) Abbey X(5). (M) Kean S(2), S2(13). (M) Omogbehin S(13). (D) Peake S3(11), (F) Showler S(5), S3(6).

CLUB RECORDS

BIGGEST VICTORIES
League: 12-0 v Bristol Rovers, Division 3 (S), 13.4.1936 (Divisional record).
F.A. Cup: 9-0 v Clapton, 1st Round, 30.11.1927.
League Cup: 7-2 v Mansfield, 2nd Round, 3.10.1989.
BIGGEST DEFEATS
League: 0-9 v Birmingham City, Division 2, 12.11.1898.
F.A. Cup: 0-7 v Crystal Palace, 1st Round, 16.1.1929.
League Cup: 1-5 v Everton, 3rd Round, 1968-69.
MOST POINTS
3 points a win: 88, Division 2, 1981-82.
2 points a win: 66, Division 4, 1967-68.
MOST GOALS SCORED
103, 1936-37.
Payne 55, Stephenson 17, Ball 8, Dawes 8, Roberts 8, Rich 2, Finlayson 2, Fellowes 1, Hancock 1, Hodge 1.
MOST GOALS CONCEDED
95, Division 2, 1898-99.
MOST FIRST CLASS MATCHES IN A SEASON
58 - 1987-88 (League 40, FA Cup 6, League Cup 8, Simod Cup 4).
MOST LEAGUE WINS
27, Division 3(S), 1936-37, Division 4, 1967-68.
MOST LEAGUE DRAWS
21, Division 2/1, 1992-93.
MOST LEAGUE DEFEATS
24, Division 2, 1962-63, Division 3, 1964-65.
RECORD TRANSFER FEE RECEIVED
£2,500,000 from Arsenal for John Hartson, January 1995.
RECORD TRANSFER FEE PAID
£650,000 to Odense for Lars Elstrup, August 1989.
BEST PERFORMANCES
League: 7th in Division 1, 1986-87.
F.A. Cup: Runners-up 1958-59. Lost 1-2 v Nottingham Forest.
League Cup: Winners 1987-88. Won 3-2 v Arsenal.

INDIVIDUAL CLUB RECORDS

MOST GOALS IN A CAREER
Gordon Turner: 265 (1949-64). 243 League, 18 FA Cup, 4 Lge Cup.
MOST GOALS IN A SEASON
Joe Payne: 58 goals in 1936-37 (League 55, FA Cup 3).
MOST GOALS IN A MATCH
10. Joe Payne v Bristol Rovers, 12-0, Division 3(S), 13.4.1936 (League record).
MOST APPEARANCES
Bob Morton: 550 (1948-64). 495 League, 48 FA Cup, 7 Lge Cup.
OLDEST PLAYER
Trevor Peake, 39 years, 17 days, 27.2.96.
YOUNGEST PLAYER
Mike O'Hara, 16 years, 32 days, 1.10.1960.
MOST CAPPED PLAYER
Mal Donaghy (Northern Ireland) 58.

PREVIOUS MANAGERS

George Thomson 1925-27, John McCartney 1927-29, George Kay 1929-31, Harold Wightman 1931-35, Edwin Liddell 1935-38, Neil McBain 1938-39, George Martin 1939-47, Dally Duncan 1947-58, Syd Owen 1959-60, Sam Bartram 1960-62) Jack Crompton 1962, Bill Harvey 1962-64, George Martin 1964-66) Allan Brown 1966-68, Alec Stock 1968-72, Harry Haslam 1972-78 David Pleat 1978-86, John Moore 1986-87, Ray Harford 1987-90) Jim Ryan 1990-91, David Pleat 1991-95, Terry Westley 1995.
ADDITIONAL INFORMATION
PREVIOUS NAMES
None.
PREVIOUS LEAGUES
United League, Southern League.
Club colours: White shirts with blue shoulders, blue horts with white trim.
Change colours: Orange shirts and shorts.
Reserves League: Neville Ovenden Football Combination.

COMPETITIONS

Div.1	Div.2/1	Div.3/2	Div.3(S)	Div.4	Texaco
1955-60	1897-1900	1920-21	1921-37	1965-68	1974-75
1974-75	1937-55	1963-65			
1982-92	1960-63	1968-70			Wat Cup
	1970-74	1996-			1971
	1975-82				
	1992-96				

HONOURS

Div.2	Div.3(S)	Div.4	Leagues Cup
1981-82	1936-37	1967-68	1987-88

LONGEST LEAGUE RUNS

of undefeated matches:	19 (13.1.68-27.4.68, 7.4.69-11.10.69)	of league matches w/out a win:	16 (1964)
of undefeated home matches:	39 (24.1.1925 - 30.4.1927)	of undefeated away matches:	10 (20.4.1981 - 14.11.1981)
without home win:	10 (26.10.64-25.1.65, 16.9.72-6.1.73)	without an away win:	32 (26.11.1898 - 28.4.1900)
of league wins:	9 (22.1.1977 - 8.3.1977)	of home wins:	15 (1.4.1967 - 26.12.1967)
of league defeats:	8 (11.11.1899 - 6.1.1900)	of away wins:	5 (2.5.1981 - 3.10.1981)

THE MANAGER

LENNIE LAWRENCE . . . . appointed December 1995.
PREVIOUS CLUBS
As Manager . . . . Plymouth (caretaker), Charlton, Middlesbrough, Bradford.
As Asst.Man/Coach . . . . Plymouth, Lincoln City.
As a player . . . . Croydon, Carshalton Athletic, Sutton United.
HONOURS As a Manager . . . . Charlton Athletic: Division 2 runners-up 1985-86.
As Asst. Manager . . . . Promotion to Division 3 1980-81.

LUTON TOWN							APPEARANCES				GOALS			
PLAYERS NAME Honours	Ht	Wt	Birthdate	Birthplace Transfers	Contract Date	Clubs	League	L/Cup	FA Cup	Other	Lge	L/C	FAC	Oth
G O A L K E E P E R														
Abbey Nathanael	6.1	11.13	7/11/78	Islington	5/2/96	Luton Town (T)		1						
				Loan	2/27/98	Woking								
Davis Kelvin G	6.1	13.2	9/29/76	Bedford	7/1/94	Luton Town	50	1		4	1	1		
				Loan	9/16/94	Torquay United	2	1		1				
D E F E N C E														
Alexander Graham	5.1	11.1	10/10/71	Coventry	3/20/90	Scunthorpe United	111+8	9+1	8	11+2	14	2		2
				£100000	7/8/95	Luton Town	117+3	9	5+1	3+1	10			
Boyce Emmerson O	5.11	11.7	9/24/79	Aylesbury		Luton Town (T)								
Davis Stephen M Div4'92	6.2	12.8	10/30/68	Hexham	7/6/87	Southampton	5+1							
				Loan	11/21/89	Burnley	7+2							
				Loan	3/28/91	Notts County	6+2							
				£60000	8/17/91	Burnley	119	6	14	13	15	2	1	
				£750000	7/13/95	Luton Town	113+2	11	4	6	14			1
Fraser Stuart T	5.9	11	1/9/80	Edinburgh	4/2/98	Luton Town (T)	1							
James Julian C	5.1	11.11	3/22/70	Tring	7/1/88	Luton Town	261+20	16+1	22+1	11+1	13	1		
E; u21.2				Loan	9/12/91	Preston North End	6							
Johnson Marvin A	5.11	11.6	10/29/68	Wembley	11/12/86	Luton Town	244+14	18+2	12+1	11	6	1	1	
McGowan Gavin FAYC'94.	5.8	11.10	1/16/76	Blackheath	7/1/94	Arsenal (T)	3+3		1					
				Loan	3/27/97	Luton Town	2							
				Loan	7/11/97	Luton Town	6+2							
				Free	7/1/98	Luton Town								
McLaren Paul	6	12.06	11/17/76	Wycombe	5/31/94	Luton Town (T)	63+17	4+1	2	5	1			
Thomas Mitchell A E: B1, u21.3, Y3	6	12	10/2/64	Luton	8/27/82	Luton Town	106+1	5	18					
				£233000	7/7/86	Tottenham Hotspur	136+21	28+1	12		6	1	1	
				£525000	8/7/91	West Ham United	37+1	5	4	2	3			
					8/27/92	Luton Town	106+1	5	18		1			
				Free	11/12/93	Luton Town	141+9	9	7	2+1	4			
Wilmott Christopher A	6.2	11.5	9/30/77	Bedford		Luton Town								
M I D F I E L D														
Augustine Steve K	6	13.7	12/13/78	Hammersmith	7/2/97	Luton Town (T)								
Davies Simon I FAYC'92	5.11	11.8	4/23/74	Winsford	7/6/92	Manchester United	4+7	4+2		2+1				i
				Loan	12/17/00	Exeter City	5+1		1		1			
				Loan	10/29/96	Huddersfield Town	3							
					8/5/97	Luton Town	8+11	3+1	0+1		1			
Evers Sean A	5.9	9.11	10/10/77	Hitchin	6/1/95	Luton Town	16+9	2			3			
McIndoe Michael	5.8	11	12/2/79	Edinburgh		Luton Town (T)								
Spring Matthew J	5.11	11.7	11/17/79	Harlow	7/2/97	Luton Town (T)	6+6		1					
White Alan	6.1	13.2	3/22/76	Darlington	7/8/94	Middlesbrough				1				
				£40000	9/22/97	Luton Town	26+2	1	1		1			
F O R W A R D														
Cox James D	5.6	10.7	4/11/80	Gloucester	5/8/98	Luton Town (T)								
Doherty Gary M	6.1	13	1/31/80	Donegal	7/2/97	Luton Town (T)	1+9		0+1					
Douglas Stuart	5.8	11.5	4/9/78	London										
Fotiadis Andrew	5.11	11.7	9/6/77	Hitchin	8/15/96	Luton Town	14+18	0+2	1+1	1+1	4			
George Liam B	5.9	11.4	2/2/79	Luton	5/31/97	Luton Town	1	0+2						
Gray Philip	5.10	12.5	10/2/68	Belfast	8/21/86	Tottenham (T)	4+5		0+1					
				Loan	1/17/90	Barnsley	3		1					
				Loan	11/8/90	Fulham	3			2				1
				£275000	8/16/91	54+5	4	2	2	22	3	1		
				£800000	7/19/93	Sunderland	108+7	9	8	2	34	4	3	
via Nancy 07/96. Fortuna Sittard				£400000	9/19/97	Luton Town	14+3	1		0+1	2			
Showler Paul E: SP.2. NPL'90. NPLD1'89.	5.11	11.9	10/10/66	Doncaster		Sheffield Wed.								
						Bentley Vics.								
						Goole Town								
						Colne Dynamoes								
						Altrincham			1					
				Free	8/15/91	Barnet	69+2	2	3+1	7	12		1	
				Free	8/4/93	Bradford City	72+16	8+1	6	4+1	15	5	2	
					8/19/96	Luton Town	20+3	3+1	4	1	5			
ADDITIONAL CONTRACT PLAYERS														
Bacque Herve						Monaco								
				Free	7/1/98	Luton Town								
Lough Lee						Ashford Town								
				Free	7/1/98	Luton Town								

KENILWORTH ROAD

1 Maple Road, Luton, Beds LU4 8AW

Capacity ....9,970 (All seater)

First game..v Plymouth, 4.9.1905.
First floodlit game ....v Fenerbahce, 7.10.1957.
ATTENDANCES
Highest...30,069 v Blackpool, FA Cup 6th Round replay, 4.3.1959.
Lowest...1,823 v Southend, Anglo Italian Cup, 5.9.1993.

OTHER GROUNDS ....Excelsior Dallow Lane 1885-97, Dunstable Road 1897-05,
....Kenilworth Road 1905-

HOW TO GET TO THE GROUND

From the North and West
Use motorway (M1) until junction 11 then follow signs to Luton A505 into Dunstable Road. Forward through one-way system and then turn right into Kenilworth Road for Luton Town FC.

From the South and East
Use motorway (M1) until junction 10 or A6/A612 into Luton Town centre, then follow signs to Dunstable into Dunstable Road A505. Under railway bridge then turn left into Kenilworth Road for Luton Town FC.

Car Parking
Street parking near ground only available.

Nearest Railway Station
Luton Midland Road (01582 27612).

USEFUL TELEPHONE NUMBERS

Club switchboard......................01582 411 622

Ticket Office............................01582 416 976

Clubcall 0891 12 11 23*
*Calls cost 50p per minute at all times.
Call costings correct at time of going to press.

MATCHDAY PROGRAMME

Programme Editor (97/98).......Simon Oxley.

Number of pages (97/98) ....48.

Price (97/98)....................................£1.50.

Subscriptions ....Apply to club.

Local Newspapers.....................................
...............................Luton News, The Herald,
....Luton on Sunday.

Local Radio Stations
.........Chiltern Radio, Three Counties Radio.

MATCHDAY TICKET PRICES (97/98)

	14 days before match	less than 14 days
Main Stand A&E	£14.50	£15.50
Juv/OAP	£7.50	£8
Block F	£11.50	£12.50
Juv/OAP	£5.50	£6
Block G	£7.50	£8
Juv/OAP	£5	£5.50
Main Stand C&G	£11.50	£12.50
Juv/OAP	£5.50	£6
Restricted View B,H&J	£7.50	£8
Juv/OAP	£5	£5.50
Kenilworth Upper tier	£11.50	£12.50
Juv/OAP	£5.50	£6
Kenilworth Lower Tier	£11.50	£12.50
Juv/OAP	£5.50	£6
New Stand	£14.50	£15.50
Juv/OAP	£7.50	£8

MACCLESFIELD TOWN
(Silkmen)
NATIONWDIE LEAGUE DIVISION 2
SPONSORED BY: BODYCOTE

Back Row L-R: Peter Davenport (Coach), Darren Lonergan, Leroy Chambers, Dominic Barclay, Efetobore Sodje, Martin McDonald, Steve Payne, Steve Wade (Physio). **2nd Row:** Goeff Lutley (res. Team Manager), Steve Wood, greg Brown, Rae Ingram, Phil Morgan, Ryan Price, Glynn Clyde, Richard Landon, Neil Sorvel, Steve Hitchen, Eric Campbell (Asst. Physio). **3rd Row:** Keiron Durkan, Stuart Whittaker, Graeme Tomlinson, Steve Brown, Gil Prescott (Asst. Manager), Sammy McIlroy (Manager), Neil Howarth, Ben Sedgemore, John Askey, Darren Tinson. **Front Row:** Andy Wright, Mike Lomax, Peter Griffiths, Brad Pates, Phil Cain, Chris Leonard, Paul O'Neill, Matt Buckley.

MACCLESFIELD TOWN
FORMED IN 1874
TURNED PROFESSIONAL IN 1997
CHAIRMAN: A Cash
DIRECTORS
R Higginbotham, J Brooks,
E Ashley, C Garlick, H Armstrong, R Flowers,
J Chesworth
SECRETARY
Colin Garlick
COMMERCIAL MANAGER
Jackie Birks

MANAGER: Sammy McIlroy
ASSISTANT MANAGER: Gil Prescot
RESERVE TEAM MANAGER: Goeff Lutley

PHYSIOTHERAPIST
Steve Wade

STATISTICIAN FOR THE DIRECTORY
Vacant

What a magnificent season it was for Macclesfield Town. Managed by the former Manchester United, Manchester City and Northern Ireland midfielder Sammy McIlroy, the Moss Rose club gained promotion from Division Three in their very first campaign as a Nationwide League club - and they were the only club in the country to remain unbeaten at home throughout the League season.

Twelve years earlier a mere 130 fans had seen Macclesfield play Kings Lynn in a Northern Premier League match. In April 1997, just over 3,000 supporters attended the home game with Bromsgrove Rovers when a 4-0 victory secured the Vauxhall Conference championship, and then on 25 April 1998, a full house of almost 6,000 packed into Moss Rose to see 'Macca's' men clinch promotion to the Second Division after beating Chester City 3-2.

It was a fairytale come true for several supporters, but Town boss McIlroy sincerely believed his side was good enough to challenge for promotion even before a ball was kicked in the Third Division - and how right he was!

Starting off with a hard-earned but deserved 2-1 home win over Torquay, Macclesfield were never really out of the leading group although at times their position didn't suggest that - and early on in the campaign they even headed the table.

After 12 games had been completed they were fourth on 20 points, seven behind top-dogs Peterborough United. At the turn of the year - with 24 matches completed, amazingly the 'Silkmen' with a Nigerian cult hero in their ranks (Effie Sodje) found themselves way down the Division in 12th spot, but only four points adrift of the play-offs. After 32 games had gone by, McIlroy's marauders were in third spot, having accumulated 19 points out of a possible 24. And they never looked back after that, racing on towards the finishing line and amassing 27 more points in the process to finish up with a total of 82, ensuring them the runners-up spot behind Notts County (99 points).

On 6 December 1997 Macclesfield were well and truly hammered 7-0 at HOME by Walsall in the F.A. Cup. Who would have thought that five months later Sammy McIlroy and his merry men would be celebrating promotion at the very first attempt! Bring on Manchester City.........

Tony Matthews.

MACCLESFIELD TOWN

Division 3		:2nd		FA CUP: 2nd Round			LC CUP: 1st Round	AWS: Northern Round 2	

M	DATE	COMP.	VEN	OPPONENTS	RESULT	H/T	LP	GOAL SCORERS/GOAL TIMES	ATT.
1	A 09	FL	H	Torquay United	W 2-1	1-1	5	Sodje 7, Landon 56	3379
2	12	CC 1/1	H	Hull City	D 0-0	0-0			2249
3	15	FL	A	Brighton & H.A.	D 1-1	1-0	5	Landon 38	(2336)
4	23	FL	H	Doncaster Rovers	W 3-0	1-0	1	Askey 72, Landon 89 (pen), Brookes 44 (OG)	2635
5	26	CC 1/2	A	Hull City	L 1-2	1-1	5	Mason 42	(3300)
6	30	FL	A	Hartlepool United	D 0-0	0-0	4		(2283)
7	S 02	FL	A	Rochdale	L 0-2	0-0	10		(2197)
8	05	FL	H	Darlington	W 2-1	0-1	4	Power 50, 88	2459
9	13	FL	H	Swansea City	W 3-0	1-0	3	Gardiner 42, Peel 63, Askey 66	2479
10	20	FL	A	Scarborough	L 1-2	1-1	7	Peel 38	(2256)
11	27	FL	H	Peterborough United	D 1-1	0-0	6	Landon 87 (pen)	3079
12	O 04	FL	A	Leyton Orient	D 1-1	0-1	7	Landon 90	(4522)
13	11	FL	A	Notts County	D 1-1	0-1	6	Wood 74	(4871)
14	18	FL	H	Mansfield Town	W 1-0	0-0	4	Cooper 59	3277
15	21	FL	H	Exeter City	D 2-2	0-2	5	Whittaker 69, Cooper 73	2286
16	25	FL	A	Chester City	D 1-1	0-0	8	Landon 51	(3245)
17	N 01	FL	A	Rotherham United	L 0-1	0-0	10		(3649)
18	04	FL	H	Colchester United	D 0-0	0-0	12		1577
19	08	FL	H	Cambridge United	W 3-1	2-0	7	Gardiner 21, Power 23, 88	2337
20	15	FAC 1	A	Hartlepool United	W 4-2	0-0		Wood 49, 81, Whittaker 71, 88	(3165)
21	18	FL	A	Shrewsbury Town	L 3-4	2-1	11	Wood 39, Power 74, Griffiths 35 (OG)	(2600)
22	22	FL	H	Hull City	W 2-0	1-0	8	Peel 37, Landon 87	2508
23	29	FL	A	Lincoln City	D 1-1	1-0	10	Whittaker 14	(3402)
24	D 06	FAC 2	H	Walsall	L 0-7	0-2			3566
25	13	FL	A	Barnet	L 1-3	0-0	13	Wood 68	(1710)
26	20	FL	H	Cardiff City	W 1-0	0-0	12	Wood 85	2398
27	26	FL	A	Darlington	L 0-2	0-0	12	Askey 90, Devos 48 (OG)	(3449)
28	28	FL	H	Rochdale	W 1-0	0-0	12	Howarth 52 (pen)	2666
29	J 10	FL	A	Torquay United	L 0-2	0-1	12		(2428)
30	13	AWS N2	H	Preston North End	L 0-1	0-0			1618
31	17	FL	H	Hartlepool United	W 2-1	0-0	12	Chambers 52, Wood 72	2334
32	20	FL	H	Scunthorpe United	W 2-0	2-0	8	Chambers 7, 37	1450
33	24	FL	A	Doncaster Rovers	W 3-0	1-0	7	Sorvel 10, Wood 54, 81	(1707)
34	27	FL	H	Brighton & H.A.	W 1-0	0-0	5	Whittaker 53	2024
35	31	FL	A	Swansea City	D 1-1	1-1	5	Howarth 8	(3293)
36	F 06	FL	H	Scarborough	W 3-1	3-0	4	Askey 14, Wood 15, Howarth 44	2488
37	14	FL	H	Leyton Orient	W 1-0	1-0	3	McDonald 14	2725
38	21	FL	A	Peterborough United	W 1-0	0-0	2	Askey 70	(6224)
39	24	FL	A	Mansfield Town	L 0-1	0-0	3		(2683)
40	28	FL	H	Notts County	W 2-0	0-0	3	Askey 50, Wood 70	5122
41	M 03	FL	A	Cambridge United	D 0-0	0-0	3		(2012)
42	07	FL	H	Rotherham United	D 0-0	0-0	3		3156
43	14	FL	A	Colchester United	L 1-5	1-1	5	Whittaker 37	(2760)
44	21	FL	H	Shrewsbury Town	W 2-1	0-0	3	Chambers 49, Wood 81	3013
45	28	FL	A	Hull City	D 0-0	0-0	3		(3677)
46	A 04	FL	H	Lincoln City	W 1-0	0-0	3	Wood 88	3278
47	11	FL	A	Scunthorpe United	L 0-1	0-1	3		(2949)
48	13	FL	H	Barnet	W 2-0	2-0	2	Sodje 10, Power 25	4171
49	18	FL	A	Cardiff City	W 2-1	0-1	2	Sodje 58, Sorvel 79	(2497)
50	25	FL	H	Chester City	W 3-2	1-0	2	Wood 14, Sorvel 49, Power 59	5982
51	M 02	FL	A	Exeter City	W 3-1	1-0	2	Wood 12, Davenport 51, Philliskirk 59	(4499)

Best Home League Attendance: 5982 V Chester City			Smallest :1450 V Scunthorpe United	Average :2905

Goal Scorers:

FL	(63)	Wood 13, Landon 7, Power 7, Askey 6, Chambers 4, Whittaker 4, Howarth 3, Peel 3, Sodje 3, Sorvel 3, Cooper 2, Gardiner 2, Davenport 1, McDonald 1, Philliskirk 1, Opponents 3
CC	(1)	Mason 1
FAC	(4)	Whittaker 2, Wood 2
AWS	(0)	

(M) Askey	(M) Brown	(F) Chambers	(M) Cooper	(F) Davenport	(M) Durkan	(D) Edey	(D) Gardiner	(M) Hitchen	(D) Howarth	(D) Ingram	(M) Irving	(F) Landon	(F) Mason	(M) McDonald	(M) Mitchell	(D) Payne	(F) Peel	(F) Philliskirk	(F) Power	(G) Price	(D) Rose	(M) Sedgemore	(D) Sodje	(M) Sorvel	(D) Tinson	(F) Whittaker	(M) Wood	Player	No
X			S2					X					X1	X		S	X2		S1	X	X		X	X	X		X	W.C. Burns	1
X			S					X					X	X		X	X		S1	X	X		X	X	X	X	X	A K Leach	2
X			S					X					X	X		S	X		S1	X	X		X	X	X		X	P Taylor	3
X			S					X					X	X		S2	X		S1	X	X		X	X	X		X	M D Messias	4
X			S					X					X	X		S1	X		S2	X	X		X	X	X		X	S J Baines	5
X			S					X					X	X		S2	X		S1	X	X		X	X	X		X	M S Pike	6
X2			S					X					S2	X		S1	X		X	X	X		X	X1	X		X	D Laws	7
S1								S	X					S2		X	X	X	X	X	X		X	X	X		X	A R Leake	8
S2								X	S1	X				S3		X	X	X	X	X	X		X	X	X		X	A R Hall	9
X				S1				X	X	X				S2	S3			X		X	X	X		X	X	X		X	J P Robinson	10
X		X						S	X	X				S1	S			X		X1	X	X		X	X	X			M J Jones	11
X		X						S1	X	X				S3				X		X	X		X	X	X	S2	X	D R Crick	12
X		X						X		X	S							S		X	X	S	X	X	X	X	X	K M Lynch	13
X		X						X		X	S1	S2						X	S3	X	X	X	X	X	X	X	X	G Laws	14
X		X						X		X	X	S						S1		X	X	X	X	X	X	X	X	P S Danson	15
X		X						S		X	X	S1			X			S2		X	X		X	X	X	X	X	E K Wolstenholme	16
		X						S		X	X	X			X	S1		S2	X		X	X	X	X	X	X	X	A N Butler	17
		X						X		S	X	X			X	S2		S1	X		X	X	X	X	X	X	X	C J Foy	18
								X	S2	S		S1			X	X		X	X	X	X		X	X	X	X	X	B Coddington	19
		X						S	S1	S		S2	X	X		X	X		X	X	X		X	X	X	X	X	G Laws	20
		X						S	S1	S2		X	X			X	X		X	X	X		X	X	X	X	X	D Pugh	21
		S						X	S2	S1			X	X		X	X		X	X	X		X	X	X	X	X	P R Richards	22
		S						X	S1				X	X	X2		X		X	X	X		X	X	X	X	X2	P Rejer	23
		S						X	S1	S2	S3		X1	X	X		X		X2	X	X		X	X	X	X	X3	A R Leake	24
X			S					X	S1		X			X1		X	X	S	X	X	X		X	X	X		X	D Orr	25
X			X					X	X1	S		X		X	S1		X	X	S2		X	X		X	X			S	F G Stretton	26
X			X					X	X2	S		X		X	S2		X	X	S1		X	X1		X	X			X	B Knight	27
X	X		X1					X	X				S	S1	X		X		X	X	S		X	X			X	M L Dean	28
X3	X	X	S3					X	X				S2	X1			X		X2	X	S1		X	X			X	C R Wilkes	29
X1		X						X	X				S2	X	X		X		X2	X		X	S1	1		X			30
X		X						S	X				S	X	X		X		X		X	X	X	X	X		G Singh	31
X1		X						S	X				S	X	X		X	S1	X		X	X	X	A	X	X	T Heilbron	32
X1		X			S2			X2	S				X	X	A		S1		X	X	X	X	X	X	X	M C Bailey	33
X	X1							X					X	X			S1		X	X	X	X	X	X	X	E Lomas	34
X		X			S			X					S	X	X		S		X	X	X	X	X	X	X	A P D'Urso	35
X1		X			S			X					S	X	X		X		S1	X	X	X	X	X	X	M J Brandwood	36
X1		X			S			X					X	X	S1	S2		X	X	X	X	X2	X		G B Frankland	37
X		X			S			X					X	X		S	S		X	X	X	X	X	X	G Laws	38
X	X1		S					S					X	X		X	S1	X	X	X	X	X	X	P R Richards	39
X	X1		S					S					X	X		S1	X	X	X	X	X	X	X	P R Richards	40
X1	X2		S					X					X	X		S2	S1	X	X	X	X	X	X	M D Messias	41
X2	S	X1						X					X			X	S2	S1	X	X	X	X	A R Leake	42
X	S	X1						X					X			X	S2	S1	X	X	X2	X	S G Bennett	43
X		X						S	X				X	S1		X	X	S	X	X1	X	J P Robinson	44
X	X2		X1					S	X				X	S2	X	X	S1	X	X	X	T Jones	45
X3	S1							S2	X			X1	X			X	X	S3	X	X2	X	E Lomas	46
X								S3	X			X3	X		S2		X	X	S1	X	X2	X1	A R Hall	47
X1	S1		S2					X					X			X3	X	X	S3	X	X2	X	G Singh	48
X2	S2		X1	S				X					X			X	X	X	X	S1	X	R Styles	49
X1	S1		S2					S	X				X			X	S1	X	X	X2	X	J A Kirkby	50
X1		X3		S2				X					S3			X	S1	X	X	X	X2	X	X	M R Halsey	51

37	2	17	8	2	2	9	7	1	38	5	6	6	7	22	2	39	10	1	21	46	15	5	41	41	44	29	42	FL Appearances	
2		4		2	2	4		1		3		3	11	5		4			4		9	17		4		4	2	FL Sub Appearances	
2									2				2	2		0+2	2		0+2	2	2		2	2	2		2	CC Appearances	
								1				1	0+2	0+1	0+1		1+1	2	2		2	2	2		2	2	2	2 1	FAC Appearances	
1	1							1				1	0+1		1		1		1	1		1	0+1		1	1		AWS Appearances	

Also Played: (G) Clyde S(20,24). (M) Kirk S1(40).

CLUB RECORDS

BIGGEST VICTORIES
League: N/A at the time of going to press.
F.A. Cup:
Other: 15-0 v Chester St. Marys - Cheshire Senior Cup 2nd Rnd 16.02.1886.

BIGGEST DEFEATS
League: N/A at the time of going to press.
F.A. Cup:
Other: 13-1 v Tranmere Rovers Reserves 03.05.1929.

MOST POINTS
3 points a win: N/A at the time of going to press.
2 points a win:

MOST GOALS SCORED IN A SEASON
N/A at the time of going to press.

RECORD TRANSFER FEE RECEIVED
£50,000 for Mike Lake from Sheffield United - 1988.

RECORD TRANSFER FEE PAID
£30,000 to Stevenage Boro' for Efetobore Sodje, August 1997.

BEST PERFORMANCES
League: N/A at the time of going to press.
F.A. Cup: N/A at the time of going to press.

HONOURS
GMVC Champions 1994/95, 1996/97. FA Trophy Winners 1970, 1996. Bob Lord Trophy (GMVC Lge Cup) Winners 1994. NPL Challenge Cup Winners 1986. Presidents Cup Winners 1986. Cheshire Senior Cup Winners 16 times. Cheshire County League Champions 6 times. Staffs Senior Cup Winners 1993/94. Championship Shield 1996.

LEAGUE CAREER
Promoted to Division 3 in 1996/97.

INDIVIDUAL CLUB RECORDS

MOST GOALS IN A SEASON
N/A at the time of going to press.

MOST GOALS IN A MATCH
N/A at the time of going to press.

OLDEST PLAYER
N/A at the time of going to press.

YOUNGEST PLAYER
N/A at the time of going to press.

MOST CAPPED PLAYER
N/A at the time of going to press.

PREVIOUS MANAGERS

ADDITIONAL INFORMATION
PREVIOUS NAMES
None

PREVIOUS LEAGUES
Manchester League, Cheshire League, Northern Premier League, GM Vauxhall Conference.

Club colours: Blue & white.
Change colours: White shirts & socks, blue shorts.

Reserves League
North West Alliance League.

LONGEST LEAGUE RUNS (N/A at the time of going to press)

of undefeated matches:	of league matches w/out a win:
of undefeated home matches:	of undefeated away matches:
without home win:	without an away win:
of league wins:	of home wins:
of league defeats:	of away wins:

THE MANAGER

SAMMY MCILROY . . . . appointed Summer 1993

PREVIOUS CLUBS
As Manager . . . . Northwich Victoria, Ashton United.
As Player/Coach. . . . . Bury, Preston North End.
As a player . . . . Manchester United, Stoke City, Manchester City, Bury, Preston.

HONOURS
As a Manager . . Macclesfield Town: Bob Lord Trophy 1993. GMVC Champions 1994/95, 1996/97. FA Trophy 1996.
. . . . Promotion to Division 2, 1997-98.
As a Player . . . . Manchester United: FA Cup 1977.
International: . . . . 88 full caps for Northern Ireland.

MACCLESFIELD TOWN

PLAYERS NAME Honours	Ht	Wt	Birthdate	Birthplace Transfers	Contract Date	Clubs	League	L/Cup	FA Cup	Other	Lge	L/C	FAC	Oth
G O A L K E E P E R														
Morgan Phillip J	6.1	13	18/12/74	Stoke-on-Trent	01/07/93	Ipswich Town (T)	1							
E: Y, S				Free	06/07/95	Stoke City								
				Loan	06/10/95	Macclesfield Town								
				Loan	14/10/96	Chesterfield	2							
				Free	7/1/98	Macclesfield Town								
Price Ryan	6.4	14	3/13/70	Stafford		Stafford Rangers								
E: SP.3.						Bolton Wanderers								
				£20000	8/9/94	Birmingham City				1				
					8/5/97	Macclesfield Town	46	2	2					
D E F E N C E														
Clyde Glynn	6.4	11.13	3/26/76	Limavady	5/31/97	Barnsley								
					8/8/97	Macclesfield Town								
Howarth Neil	6.2	12.12	11/15/71	Bolton	7/2/90	Burnley (T)	0+1							
E: SP.2. GMVC'95'97. FAT'96.				Free	9/3/93	Macclesfield Town	38+3	2	1		3			
Ingram Rae	5.11	11.7	06/12/74	Manchester	09/07/93	Manchester City	18+5	1	4					
				Loan	3/19/98	Macclesfield Town	5							
				Free	7/1/98	Macclesfield Town								
Payne Steve	5.11	12.5	8/1/75	Castleford	7/12/93	Huddersfield (T)								
				Free	12/23/94	Macclesfield Town	39	2	2					
Sodje Efetobore	6.1	12	10/5/72	Greenwich		Stevenage Borough								
GMVC'96.				£30000	7/11/97	Macclesfield Town	41	2	2		3			
Tinson Darren	6	12.12	11/15/71	Birmingham		Northwich Victoria								
GMVC'97.				£10000	7/30/97	Macclesfield Town	40	2	2					
M I D F I E L D														
Askey John	6	12.2	11/4/64	Stoke	1987	Macclesfield Town	37+2	2			6			
Brown Greg J	5.10	11.6	7/31/78	Manchester	6/20/96	Chester City	1+3		0+1	0+1				
				Free	12/23/97	Macclesfield Town	2							
Durkan Keiran	5.11	10.05	12/1/73	Chester	7/16/92	Wrexham	37+5	2	3+1	14	3		2	1
				£75000	2/16/96	Stockport County	52+12	10+1	4		4		3	
					3/25/98	Macclesfield Town	2+1							
Hitchen Steven J	5.8	11.4	11/28/76	Salford	7/4/95	Blackburn R (T)								
				Free	7/11/97	Macclesfield Town	1+1							
McDonald Martin	6	11.7	12/4/73		8/2/96	Doncaster Rovers	48	4	2		4			
					12/9/97	Macclesfield Town	22				1			
Sedgemore Ben	5.11	13.11	8/5/75	Wolverhampton	5/17/93	Birmingham City								
				Loan	12/22/94	Northampton Town	1							
				Free	1/10/96	Peterborough Utd	13+4		1					
					8/1/96	Mansfield Town	58+9	1	2+1		6			
				£25000	3/19/98	Macclesfield Town	5							
Sorvel Neil	6	12.9	3/2/73	Widnes	7/31/91	Crewe Alex. (T)	5+4		1+1	4				
GMVC'95'97. FAT'96.				Free	8/21/92	Macclesfield Town	41+4	2	2	0+1	3			
Wood Steve	5.9	10.10	6/23/63	Manchester	7/14/97	Macclesfield Town	42	2	1		13		2	
F O R W A R D														
Barclay Dominic	5.10	11.9	9/5/76	Bristol	8/1/93	Bristol City	2+10	0+1	0+1					
				Free	7/1/98	Macclesfield Town								
Brown Steve	6	12.7	12/6/73	Southend	7/10/92	Southend United (T)	10		0+1	1	2			
				Free	7/5/93	Scunthorpe United								
				Free	8/27/93	Colchester United	56+6	2	5	4	17		1	1
					3/22/95	Gillingham	8+1				2			
				£20000	10/6/95	Lincoln City	47+25	0+3	3+1	3+1	8			1
Chambers Leroy D	5.11	12	10/25/72	Sheffield	6/13/91	Sheffield Wed. (T)								
				Free	8/11/95	Chester City	29+4	2		1				
via Boston United.				£6000	12/21/98	Macclesfield Town	17+2			1	3			
Davenport Peter	5.11	11.3	3/24/61	Birkenhead	1/5/82	Nottingham Forest	114+4	10	7+1	10+1	54	1	1	2
B.1. E: 1.				£750000	3/12/86	Manchester United	73+19	8+2	2+2		22	4		
				£750000	11/3/88	Middlesbrough	53+6	2	4	7+1	7			1
				£350000	7/19/90	Sunderland	72+27	5+2	9+1	14+1	15	1	2	
				Free	7/1/93	Airdrie	35+3	3	3+2		9	1		
				Free	8/16/94	St Johnston	12+10	3	0+1	2	4			1
				Free	5/23/95	Stockport County	3+3				1			
					1/1/99	Southport								
					2/1/99	Macclesfield Town	2+2				1			
Landon Richard	6.3	13.5	3/22/70	Worthing		Bedworth								
				£30000	1/26/94	Plymouth Argyle	21+9	0+1	0+1	2	12			
				£30000	8/3/95	Stockport County	7+6	0+1	0+1		4			
				Loan	1/24/97	Macclesfield Town								
				Loan	3/3/97	Rotherham United	7+1							
					7/11/97	Macclesfield Town	6+11	2	0+1		7			
				Loan	2/27/98	Hednesford Town								
Ohandjianian Demis	5.8	10.1	5/1/78	Manchester	2/14/97	Doncaster Rovers	0+1							
					3/1/97	Macclesfield Town								
Tomlinson Graeme	5.9	11.7	10/12/75	Keighley	01/01/00	Bradford City	12+5		0+1		6			
				£100000	12/07/94	Manchester United		0+2						
				Loan	22/03/96	Luton Town	1+6							
				Loan	8/8/97	Bournemouth	6+1				1			
				Loan	3/26/98	Millwall	2+1				1			
				Free	7/1/98	Macclesfield Town								
Whittaker Stuart	5.7	8.11	1/2/75	Liverpool		Liverpool								
				Free	5/14/93	Bolton Wanderers	2+1	0+1						
				Loan	8/30/96	Wigan Athletic	2+1							
				Free	8/8/97	Macclesfield Town	29+2		2		4		2	
ADDITIONAL CONTRACT PLAYERS														
Gee Daniel					5/3/97	Macclesfield Town								
Lomax Michael						Blackburn R. (T)								
				Free	7/1/98	Macclesfield Town								
Wright Andrew						Sunderland (T)								
				Free	7/1/98	Macclesfield Town								

MOSS ROSE
London Road, Macclesfield, Cheshire SK11 7SP

Capacity...6,028
Standing..4,975
Seating..1,053

First game (In the League) ....v Torquay United, (2-1), 09.08.97.
First floodlit game..v Hull City, Lge Cup, (0-0), 12.08.97.

ATTENDANCES
Highest ....9,008 v Winsford Utd, Cheshire Senior Cup 2nd Rnd, 04.02.48.
Lowest...

OTHER GROUNDS...1874-1891 Rostron Field.

HOW TO GET TO THE GROUND

From the North
Leave the M6 at junction 19, follow A537 to Macclesfield. Follow signs for the Town Centre and then the A523 to Leek. Ground is approximately 1 mile on the right.

From the South
Exit M6 at junction 17, follow A534 to Congleton, then A536 to Macclesfield. When coming into Macclesfield you pass the Rising Sun on the left, quarter of a mile further on the right had side is a Texaco Garage, turn right into Moss Lane follow this lane which brings you round the back of the ground.

Car Parking
Street parking.

Nearest Railway Station
Macclesfield 1.5 miles away.

USEFUL TELEPHONE NUMBERS

Club switchboard 01625 264 686
Club fax number.......................01625 264 692
Marketing Department 01625 264 693
Ticket Office 01625 264 686

Clubcall 0891 88 44 82*
*Calls cost 50p per minute at all times.
Call costings correct at time of ging to press.

MATCHDAY PROGRAMME

Programme Editor ....Chris Pugsley.

Number of pages....................................36.

Price ....£1.50.

Subscriptions ....Aply to club.

Local Newspapers.....Macclesfield Express,
.........................Manchester Evening News,
.................Manchester Evening News Pink.

Local Radio Stations
..................GMR (BBC), BBC Radio Stoke,
....................Piccadilly Radio, Signal Radio.

MATCHDAY TICKET PRICES (97/98)

MainStand . . . . £9/£6

Main Stand Terrace. . . . . £7/£5

Star Lane Stand . . . . £7/£5

Star Lane Terrace (covered) . . . . £8/£5

Moss Lane Terrace. . . . . £7/£5

Visitors Section

Estate Road Terrace (covered) . . . . £8/£5

Corner Paddock . . . . £8/£5

MANCHESTER CITY
(City or The Blues)
NATIONWIDE LEAGUE DIVISION 2
SPONSORED BY: BROTHER

Back Row (L-R): Asa Hartford (Coach), Richard Money (Coach), Ronnie Evans (Reserves Coach), Uwe Rosler, Eddie McGoldrick, Steve Lomas (now West Ham), Alan Kernaghan, Tommy Wright, Martyn Margetson, Lee Crooks, Paul Beesley, Chris Greenacre, Nick Summerbee, Rae Ingram, Roy Bailey (Physio), Alex Stepney (Goalkeeping Coach). **Front Row:** Ian Brightwell, Peter Beagrie (now Bradford City), Richard Edghill, Georgiou Kinkladze, Scott Hiley, Paul Dickov, Frank Clark (Manager), Kit Symons, Alan Hill (Assistant Manager), Neil Heaney, Kevin Horlock, Jeff Whitley, John Foster, Michael Brown, Martin Phillips.

MANCHESTER CITY
FORMED IN 1887
TURNED PROFESSIONAL IN 1887
LTD COMPANY IN 1894

CHAIRMAN: D A Bernstein
CHIEF EXECUTIVE: Michael Turner
DIRECTORS
J Wardle, D Tueart, M Turner,
A Lewis, A Thomas,
SECRETARY
Bernard Halford (0161 224 5000)
COMMERCIAL MANAGER
Geoff Durbin (0161 224 5000)

MANAGER: Joe Royle
ASSISTANT MANAGER: Alan Hill
1ST TEAM COACH: Willie Donachie
& Asa Hartford
YOUTH COACH
Neil McNabr
PHYSIOTHERAPIST
Roy Bailey

STATISTICIAN FOR THE DIRECTORY
Dennis Chapman

Six seasons ago, a strong attacking team with players showing flair and determination was the scene at Maine Road. Since then season by season it has become progressively poor. Three seasons at the bottom end of the Premiership; relegation to the First Division where everyone thought the club would bounce back, but on slipping through this league over two seasons and now starting the 1998-99 season in unknown territory - Division Two.

The pattern was set for failure after the first five games, won 1, drawn 2, lost 2, so the struggle started in August and continued throughout the season. The best run (!) being 2 wins together against West Bromwich Albion and Huddersfield Town.

New signings Bradbury, Vaughan and Wiekens arrived, and with the regular seniors from the previous season, the team looked capable of having a successful season. Bradbury with a high price tag around his neck could not get going. He showed early that he would be an asset, but goals dried up. Lee scored only 2 goals in the first 11 league and Coca-Cola Cup games. He then went down with a back injury after playing in an u21 game in Italy which kept him out for four months.

The warning signals became evident during October when City played six league games, scoring only one goal. Prior to this, the first embarrassment was being dumped out of the Coca-Cola Cup by Blackpool after City lost in a penalty shoot out at home.

The regular sequence of win one league game then lose one continued throughout the first half of the season. New debuts came into the team but still no set pattern of consistency could be found. The last of the teams natural senior wingers, Nicky Summerbee, left to go to Sunderland in exchange for Craig Russell, leaving the team with no wide players, so the style of play became cramped in midfield and no scope to change the pattern.

The problems and concern for the future continued through January and February. A brief flurry in the FA Cup where City produced an excellent display against West Ham United in the 4th Round. The team matched the Hammers skills but lost by the odd goal of three. Kinkladze produced a gem of a goal running through their defence avoiding tackles to place the ball in the net.

By now the spirit appeared to be rock bottom. There had to be some immediate action. This happened in mid February when Frank Clark was relieved of his position. Joe Royle and Willie Donachie were brought in, who brought in Beardsley and Briscoe on loan straight away. This had a steadying influence, but the results still did not come. After the end of their loan period both players were not retained. In mid March Joe Royle signed four new players, Jobson (Oldham), Pollock (Bolton), Goater (Bristol City) and Ian Bishop returning from West Ham United after eight and half seasons away. As it happened too late and relegation became reality.

City would have had avoided relegation on the last day if the results had gone as they hoped. Funnily enough, the team recorded its best win of the season winning 5-2 at Stoke City, but both Port Vale and Portsmouth won their games and stayed up.

The final sad item was the departure of Kinkladze and Rosler. Former manager Frank Clark persisted with them, but their form became disappointing. Joe Royle on his arrival axed Kinkladze after two games where it was apparent Geo had lost interest in playing for the club even though he (Geo) insisted he wished to remain. Both have now gone elsewhere - Rosler back to Germany, Kinkladze to Holland. **Dennis Chapman.**

MANCHESTER CITY

Division 1 :22th **FA CUP: 4th Round** **LC CUP: 1st Round**

M	DATE	COMP.	VEN	OPPONENTS	RESULT	H/T	LP	GOAL SCORERS/GOAL TIMES	ATT.
1	A 09	FL	H	Portsmouth	D 2-2	1-1	9	Rosler 16, Wiekens 55	30474
2	12	CC 1/1	A	**Blackpool**	L 0-1	0-0			(8084)
3	15	FL	A	Sunderland	L 1-3	0-1	15	Kinkladze 75 (pen)	(38894)
4	22	FL	H	Tranmere Rovers	D 1-1	0-0	14	Horlock 46	26336
5	26	CC 1/2	H	**Blackpool**	W 1-0	0-0		Horlock 88	12563
6	30	FL	A	Charlton Athletic	L 1-2	1-0	21	Wiekens 20	(14009)
7	S 03	FL	A	Nottingham Forest	W 3-1	1-0	14	Brannan 19, 70, Dickov 88	(23681)
8	12	FL	A	Bury	D 1-1	0-0	15	Morley 81	(11216)
9	20	FL	H	Norwich City	L 1-2	1-1	20	Bradbury 26	27258
10	27	FL	H	Swindon Town	W 6-0	3-0	17	Kinkladze 6, Horlock 37, Dickov 49, 60, Bradbury 80, Casper 16 (OG)	26646
11	O 04	FL	A	Ipswich Town	L 0-1	0-0	21		(14322)
12	18	FL	H	Reading	D 0-0	0-0	21		26488
13	22	FL	H	Stoke City	L 0-1	0-0	21		25333
14	26	FL	A	Queens Park Rangers	L 0-2	0-2	22		(14451)
15	29	FL	H	Crewe Alexandra	W 1-0	1-0	21	Greenacre 44	27384
16	N 01	FL	A	Oxford United	D 0-0	0-0	20		(8592)
17	04	FL	H	Port Vale	L 2-3	2-2	21	Wiekens 15, Dickov 41	24554
18	07	FL	H	Huddersfield Town	L 0-1	0-0	21		24425
19	15	FL	A	Sheffield United	D 1-1	0-1	22	Horlock 90	(23780)
20	22	FL	H	Bradford City	W 1-0	0-0	21	Vaughan 90	29746
21	29	FL	A	Stockport County	L 1-3	0-3	21	Brannan 49	(11351)
22	D 02	FL	A	West Bromwich Albion	W 1-0	0-0	17	Dickov 55	(17904)
23	06	FL	H	Wolverhampton Wand	L 0-1	0-1	18		28999
24	13	FL	A	Birmingham City	L 1-2	0-0	21	Shelia 88	(21014)
25	20	FL	H	Middlesbrough	W 2-0	2-0	19	Rosler 51 (pen), Dickov 31	28097
26	26	FL	A	Crewe Alexandra	L 0-1	0-1	20		(5759)
27	28	FL	A	Nottingham Forest	L 2-3	0-1	20	Shelia 56, Dickov 77	31839
28	J 03	FAC 3	H	**Bradford City**	W 2-0	2-0		**Rosler 36, Brown 42**	23686
29	10	FL	A	Portsmouth	W 3-0	1-0	17	Russell 44, Kinkladze 51, Rosler 89	(13512)
30	17	FL	H	Sunderland	L 0-1	0-0	21		31715
31	25	FAC 4	H	**West Ham United**	L 1-2	0-1		**Kinkladze 59**	26495
32	28	FL	H	Charlton Athletic	D 2-2	1-0	21	Dickov 7 (pen), Symons 88	24058
33	31	FL	A	Tranmere Rovers	D 0-0	0-0	21		(12830)
34	F 06	FL	A	Norwich City	D 0-0	0-0	21		(15274)
35	14	FL	H	Bury	L 0-1	0-0	22		28885
36	18	FL	H	Ipswich Town	L 1-2	1-0	23	Symons 5	27156
37	21	FL	A	Swindon Town	W 3-1	1-0	22	Rosler 22, 77, Bradbury 83	(12280)
38	24	FL	A	Reading	L 0-3	0-2	23		(11513)
39	28	FL	H	West Bromwich Albion	W 1-0	1-0	21	Rosler 43	28460
40	M 03	FL	A	Huddersfield Town	W 3-1	2-1	17	Wiekens 9, Briscoe 45, Tskhadadze 65	(15694)
41	07	FL	H	Oxford United	L 0-2	0-1	20		28720
42	14	FL	A	Port Vale	L 1-2	0-1	22	Wiekens 61	(13122)
43	21	FL	H	Sheffield United	D 0-0	0-0	22		28496
44	28	FL	A	Bradford City	L 1-2	1-0	22	Whitley Jeff 24	(17099)
45	A 04	FL	H	Stockport County	W 4-1	3-1	21	Goater 5, Jobson 32, Bradbury 37, 57	31855
46	11	FL	A	Wolverhampton Wand	D 2-2	1-1	21	Pollock 13, Horlock 64	(24458)
47	13	FL	H	Birmingham City	L 0-1	0-0	21		29569
48	17	FL	A	Middlesbrough	L 0-1	0-1	21		(30182)
49	25	FL	H	Queens Park Rangers	D 2-2	1-2	23	Kinkladze 1, Bradbury 48	32040
50	M 03	FL	A	Stoke City	W 5-2	1-0	22	Goater 32, 71, Dickov 49, Bradbury 64, Horlock 90	(28000)

Best Home League Attendance: 32040 V Queens Park Rangers **Smallest :24058 V Charlton Athletic** **Average :28197**

Goal Scorers:

FL	(56)	Dickov 9, Bradbury 7, Rosler 6, Horlock 5, Wiekens 5, Kinkladze 4, Brannan 3, Goater 3, Shelia 2, Symons 2, Briscoe 1, Greenacre 1, Jobson 1, Morley 1, Pollock 1, Russell 1, Tskhadadze 1, Vaughan 1, Whitley Jeff 1, Opponents 1
CC	(1)	Horlock 1
FAC	(3)	Brown 1, Kinkladze 1, Rosler 1

(D) Beesley	(F) Bradbury	(D) Branman	(M) Brightwell	(F) Briscoe	(M) Brown	(M) Conlan	(F) Dickov	(D) Edghill	(F) Goater	(D) Horlock	(F) Kinkladze	(G) Margetson	(M) McGoldrick	(M) Pollock	(F) Rosler	(F) Russell	(F) Scully	(M) Shelia	(D) Summerbee	(D) Symons	(D) Tskhadadze	(D) Van Blerk	(D) Vaughan	(G) Weaver	(D) Whitley Jeff	(M) Whitley Jim	(M) Wiekens	(G) Wright	Referee	No.
X	X	X					S2		X	X	X				X				S1	X			X					X	D Laws	1
	X	X	X						X	X	X	S			X					X					X			X	**T Jones**	**2**
	X	X	X						X	X	X				X				S2	X	S1	X	S					X	E K Wolstenholme	3
X	X	X	X						X	X	X	S			X				S1	X	S	X						X	M J Brandwood	4
	X	X	X				S2		X	X	X			S1	X				X	X	S3	X						X	**D Pugh**	**5**
	X	X	X				S			X		X	X		X		S1		X	X		X	S					X	R J Harris	6
	X	X	X				S1	X	X	X	X	X	X		X				X	X		X	S					X	C T Finch	7
S	X	X						X	X	X	X	X			X		S1		X	X		X						X	P R Richards	8
	X	X	X				S2		X	X	X				X		S	S1	X	X		X						X	A N Butler	9
X	X	X	X			S1	X	X	X	X	X	X			X				S2	X		X	S					X	R Pearson	10
X	X	X	X				X	X	X	X	X				X				S2	X		X						X	M C Bailey	11
	X	X					S		X	X	X	X	S1		X				S2	X		X						X	K A Leach	12
	X	X				S2	X	X	X	X	X	X	X						S1	X		X						S	A R Leake	13
	X	X	X				X	X	X	X	X	X	X							X			S				S1	X	R J Harris	14
	X				X	S3	X	X	X	X						S2			X	X		S1	X		X	X	X	X	K M Lynch	15
	X				X		X	X	X							S			X	X		X	X		X	X	X	X	D Orr	16
	X				S	X	X	X	X						X				X	X		X			X	X	X	X	M J Brandwood	17
	X	S1			S2	X	X	X	X						X			S3	X			X	X		X	X		X	G B Frankland	18
	X				S1	S2	X	X	X	X	X				X			S	X			X			X			X	P Rejer	19
	X				S1		X	X	X	X	X				X				X			S			X			X	F G Stretton	20
	X				S1		X	X	X	X	X	X1			X				X						X			X	E K Wolstenholme	21
	X				X		X	X	X	X		X1	X2		S2	X		S	X		S	X		S1	X			X	J A Kirkby	22
	X				X		X	X	X	X					X		S1		X	X		X	X		X1	X	X	X	C R Wilkes	23
	X		S1		X1		X	X	X	X					X		X		X	X		S	X		S	X	S	X	A P D'Urso	24
	X	X			X		X	X	X	X					X				X	X		X			S			X	M C Bailey	25
	X	S2			X1		X	X	X	X					X				X	X		X2	S1		X	X		X	T Jones	26
	X	X2			X		X	X	X	X					X				X	X		S2	X		X1		X	X	A G Wiley	27
X	**X**	**X**			**X2**			**X**		**X**	**S**		**X**	**X3**	**S**	**X**		**X**	**S2**			**X**	**S1**	**X1**	**X**	**G P Barber**	**28**
	S		X	X	X		X			X	X			X	X			X	X		X	S		X	S		X	P Taylor	29
	S2	X	X	S1	X		X1			X	X			X1		X3	S3				X2			X	X	M D Messias	30
S	S	X	X		X	X	S			X	X			X	X	S		X	X		X			S		X	**D J Gallagher**	**31**
S3		X	X	X2	X		X			X3	X1			X	X				S1	X		X			X	P R Richards	32
X1		X	X		X		X			X	X			X	X2				S1	S			X	C R Wilkes	33
S	X		X1		X		X2			X	X			X	X		S2		S1		X	B Knight	34
S1	X		X1		S2		X			X	X			X	X	X			S	X2		X	T Heilbron	35
S2	S3		X		X		X1			X	X			X	X				X	X	X	G B Frankland	36
S3	X	X		X			X2			X	S1			X	X			S3	X1	X	S1	X	B Coddington	37
X	X3	X	X	S2			X	S1			X	X			S3	X1	X	X	A Bates	38
S1	X	X	X	X			X	S			X	S		X	X1	X	X	A N Butler	39
X1	X	X2	S				X	S1		X	X	S2	X	X	G Cain	40
X2	X3	S3	S2				X	S1	X1		X	X	X	W C Burns	41
X2	S2	S1	X	X	X	S3		X	X	X	X	R D Furnandiz	42
X1	S2	S1	X	X	X	X	X2	X	R Pearson	43
S3	X	X	X	X	X	X3	S2	X	X2	X	X	S1	E K Wolstenholme	44
X	X	X	S	X	X	S	S	X	X	X	R J Harris	45
X2	S1	X	X	X	X	X3	S2	S3	X	X	X	M R Halsey	46
X3	S2	S1	X	X	X	X	S3	X	X	X	T Heilbron	47
X	S3	X2	X	X	X	S1	X	X1	X	X	A G Wiley	48
X	X3	S1	X	X1	X2	S3	X	X	X	K A Leach	49
X	S1	X3	X	X2	X	S2	X	X	S3	X1	X	X	M C Bailey	50
4	23	27	19	5	18	1	21	36	7	25	29	28	6	8	23	17	1	12	4	42	10	10	19	14	17		35	18	FL Appearances	
3	4	5	2		8	6	9				1		1			6	7	8		5			9		3	2	2		FL Sub Appearances	
2	2	2	0+1				2		2	2			0+1		2					2		1	0+1				2	2	CC Appearances	
	1	2	2				2		1	2	2				2					2		2	0+1	2	1+1		1	2	FAC Appearances	

Also Played: (F) Beardsley X2(36,38), S2(37), X(39,40,41). (M) Bishop X1(44,46,47), X(45), S2(48,49).(M) Crooks S (16,23,31), S2(32), X(33,34,35), S1(36).(F) Greenacre S2(14), X(15,16), S(21,33), S3(28). (D) Jobson X(42,43,44,45,46), X2(47). (F) Creaney X(19). (F) Heaney X(12,13), X3(42), S(43).(G) Jackson X(6). (F) Kelly S(17), X(18). (D) Kernaghan X(2,3), S(4). (M) Lever S(2). (D) Morley S(1,2), X(8), S1(16,17).

CLUB RECORDS

BIGGEST VICTORIES
League: 10-0 v Darwen, Division 2, 18.2.1899.
F.A. Cup: 10-1 v Swindon Town, 4th Round (Replay), 29.1.1930.
9-0 v Gateshead, 3rd Round (Replay), 18.1.1933.
League Cup: 6-0 v Scunthorpe United, 2nd Round, 10.9.1974.
6-0 v Torquay United, 2nd Round, 25.10.1983.
Europe: 5-0 v S K Lierse, 2nd Round, 26.11.1969.
BIGGEST DEFEATS
League: 0-8 v Burton Wanderers, Division 2, 26.12.1894.
1-9 v Everton, Division 1, 3.9.1906.
0-8 v Wolverhampton Wndrs, Division 1, 23.12.1933.
F.A. Cup: 0-6 v Preston North End, 30.1.1897.
2-8 v Bradford Park Avenue (h), 4th Round, 30.1.1946.
League Cup: 0-6 v Birmingham City, 5th Round, 11.12.1962.
Europe: No more than two goals. (4 games)
MOST POINTS
3 points a win: 82, Division 2, 1988-89.
2 points a win: 62, Division 2, 1946-47.
MOST GOALS SCORED
108, Division 2, 1926-27.
Johnson 25, Hicks 21, Roberts 14, W Cowan 11, Austin 10, Barrass 7, Broadhurst 7, Bell 4, McMullan 3, S Cowan 2, Gibson 2, Pringle 1, Opponents 1.
MOST GOALS CONCEDED
102, Division 1, 1962-63.
MOST FIRST CLASS MATCHES IN A SEASON
62 - 1969-70 (League 42, FA Cup 2, League Cup 7, Charity Shield 1, ECWC 10).
MOST LEAGUE WINS
26, Division 2, 1946-47. Division 1, 1967-68.
MOST LEAGUE DRAWS
18, Premiership, 1993-94.
MOST LEAGUE DEFEATS
22, Division 1, 1958-59, Division 1, 1959-60.
RECORD TRANSFER FEE RECEIVED
£4,925,000 from Ajax for Georgi Kinkladze, May 1998.
RECORD TRANSFER FEE PAID
£3,000,000 to Portsmouth, for Lee Bradbury, July 1997.
BEST PERFORMANCES
League: 1902-03: Matches played 34, Won 25, Drawn 4, Lost 5, Goals for 95, Goals against 29, Points 54. First in Division 2.
Highest Position: Champions of Division 1, 1936-37, 1967-68.

Best Performances continued...
F.A. Cup: Winners in 1903-04, 1933-34, 1955-56.
Most Recent success: 1968-69: 3rd Round Luton Town 1-0; 4th Round Newcastle United 0-0,2-0; 5th Round Blackburn Rovers 4-1; 6th Round Tottenham Hotspur 1-0; Semi-final Everton 1-0; Final Leicester City 1-0.
League Cup: Winners in 1969-70.
Most recent success: 1975-76: 2nd Round Norwich City 1-1,2-2,6-1; 3rd Round Nottingham Forest 2-1; 4th Round Manchester United 4-0; 5th Round Mansfield Town 4-2; Semi-final Middlesbrough 0-1,4-0; Final Newcastle United 2-1.
Europe: ECWC 1969-70: 1st Round Athletico Bilbao 3-3,3-0; 2nd Round Lierse 3-0,5-0; 3rd Round Academica Coimbra 0-0,1-0; Semi-final Schalke 04 0-1,5-1; Final Gornik Zabrze 2-1.

INDIVIDUAL CLUB RECORDS

MOST GOALS IN A SEASON
Tom Johnson: 38 goals in 1928-29 (Division 1).
Previous holder: F Roberts 31.
MOST GOALS IN A MATCH
5. Tom Johnson v Everton (a), 6-2, Division 1, 15.9.1928.
5. R.S. Marshall v Swindon Town, 10-1, FA Cup 4th Rnd (replay), 29.1.1930.
5. George Smith v Newport, 5-1, Division 2, 14.6.1947.
OLDEST PLAYER
Billy Meredith, 49 years 245 days v Newcastle United, FA Cup semi-final, 29.3.1924.
YOUNGEST PLAYER
Glyn Pardoe, 15 years 314 days v Birmingham City, Division 1, 11.4.1962.
MOST CAPPED PLAYER
Colin Bell (England) 48.

PREVIOUS MANAGERS

L Furniss1892-93. J Parlby 1893-95. S Ormrod1895-02. T Maley 1902-06. H W Newbould1906-12. E Magnell 1912-24. D Ashworth 1924-25. P Hodge1926-32. W Wild1932-46. S Cowan 1946-47. J Thompson1947-50. L McDowell 1950-63. G Poyser 1963-65. J Mercer OBE1965-7. M Allison 1971-73 . J Hart 1973. R Saunders 1973-74.T Book 1974-79. M Allison 1979-80. J Bond 1980-83. J Benson 1983. W McNeill MBE 1983-86. J Frizzell1986-87. M Machin. 1987-89. H Kendall 1989-90. P Reid 1990-93. B Horton1993-95. A Ball 1995-96. Frank Clark 1996-98
ADDITIONAL INFORMATION
PREVIOUS NAMES: Ardwick F.C. 1887-95 (an amalgamation of West Gorton and Gorton Athletic).
PREVIOUS LEAGUES: Football Alliance.
Club colours: Lazer blue shirts, white shorts.

COMPETITIONS

Div 1/P	Div.2/1	Div.3/2	Euro C	ECWC	UEFA	Texaco
1899-02	1892-93	1998-	1968-69	1969-70	1972-73	1971-72
1903-09	1902-03			1970-71	1976-77	1974-75
1910-26	1909-10	FMC			1977-78	
1928-38	1926-28	1985-86			1978-79	A/Ital
1947-50	1936-47	1986-87				1970-71
1951-63	1950-51	1987-88				
1966-83	1963-66	1988-89				A/Scot
1985-87	1983-85	1989-90				1975-76
1989-96	1987-89	1990-91				
	1996-98	1991-93				

HONOURS

Div.1	Div.2	FA Cup	Lge Cup	ECWC
1936-37	1898-99	1903-04	1969-70	1969-70
1967-68	1902-03	1933-34	1975-76	
	1909-10	1955-56		C/Sh'd
	1927-28	1968-69		1937
	1946-47			1968
	1965-66			1972

LONGEST LEAGUE RUNS

of undefeated matches:	22 (16.11.46-19.4.47, 26.12.36-1.5.37)		of league matches w/out a win:	17 (26.12.1979 - 7.4.1980)
of undefeated home matches:	41 (25.12.1919 - 19.11.1921)		of undefeated away matches:	12 (23.11.1946 - 14.5.1947)
without home win:	9 (26.12.1979 - 7.4.1980)		without an away win:	34 (11.2.1986 - 17.10.1987)
of league wins:	9 (13.4.1912 - 28.9.1912)		of home wins:	16 (13.11.1920 - 27.8.1921)
of league defeats:	8 (23.08.95 - 14.10.95)		of away wins:	6 (7.3.1903 - 26.9.1903)

THE MANAGER

Joe Royle . . . . appointed February 1998.
Previous Clubs as a Manager: Oldham, Everton. . . . . **As a Player:** Everton, Man. City, Bristol City, Norwich City.
Honours
As a Manager: **Oldham:** Division 2 champions 1990-91. **Everton:** FA Cup winners 1994-95.
As a Player: **Everton:** League Championship 1970. **Man. City:** League Cup winners 1976. **England:** 6 full & 10 u23.

MANCHESTER CITY

PLAYERS NAME Honours	Ht	Wt	Birthdate	Birthplace Transfers	Contract Date	Clubs	League	L/Cup	FA Cup	Other	Lge	L/C	FAC	Oth
G O A L K E E P E R														
Brown Michael	5.9	11.7	11/6/70	Stranraer	6/3/97	Manchester City	3+1							
Weaver Nicholas J	6.3	13.1	3/2/79	Sheffield	5/31/97	Manchester City								
Wright Thomas J	6.1	13.5	8/29/63	Belfast	1/1/00	Linfield								
NI: 22, u21.1; Div1'93				£30000	1/27/88	Newcastle United	72+1	6	4	1				
Loan 2/14/91 Hull City 6 Lge Apps				£450000	9/24/93	Nottingham Forest	11	2						
				Loan	10/4/96	Reading	17							
Loan 1/17/97 Manchester City 5 Lge Apps					3/3/97	Manchester City	26		2					
D E F E N C E														
Beesley Paul	6.1	11.5	7/21/65	Liverpool	1/1/00	Marine								
				Free	9/22/84	Wigan Athletic	153+2	13	6	11	3			
				£175000	10/20/89	Leyton Orient	32		1	2	1			1
				£300000	7/10/90	Sheffield United	162+6	12+1	9+2	3	5		1	1
				£250000	8/2/95	Leeds United	19+3	5+1	5	2+2				
				£600000	2/7/97	Manchester City	10+3							
Loan 12/24/97 Port Vale 5 Lge Apps				Loan	3/13/98	WBA	8							
Brannan Gerald	6	13.3	1/15/72	Prescot	7/3/90	Tranmere Rovers	227+11	26	10+1	26+1	20	4		1
					3/12/97	Manchester City	38+5	2	1		4			
Edghill Richard	5.8	10.6	9/23/74	Oldham	7/15/92	Manchester City	85	10	2					
E: B.1, u21.2														
Fenton Nicholas L	5.11	10.2	11/23/79	Preston	5/31/97	Manchester City								
Fenton Anthony B	5.11	10.4	11/23/79	Preston	5/31/97	Manchester City								
Hiley Scott	5.9	10.4	9/27/68	Plymouth	8/4/86	Exeter City	205+5	17	14	16+2	12			
Div4'90. Div2'95				£100000	3/12/93	Birmingham City	44	6	1	1				
				£250000	4/1/96	Manchester City	4+5							
Holmes Shaun N	0	0	12/27/80	Derry		Manchester City (T)								
Horlock Kevin	6	12	11/1/72	Bexley	7/1/91	West Ham United								
NI: 2, B.1. Div2'96.				Free	8/27/92	Swindon Town	151+12	15+2	12	5+2	22	1	3	
				£1500000	1/31/97	Manchester City	43	2			9	1		
Jobson Richard I	6.1	13.05	5/9/63	Holderness	1/1/00	Burton Albion								
E: B.2; Div2'91				£22000	11/5/82	Watford	26+2	2	+1	5+1	4			
				£40000	2/7/85	Hull City	219+2	12	13	9	17	1		
				£460000	8/30/90	Oldham Athletic	176+1	13	13	2	10	1		
				£1000000	10/26/95	Leeds United	22	2	1		1			
Loan 1/23/98 Southend United 8 Lge Apps 1gl.				Free	3/12/98	Manchester City	6				1			
Morley David T	6.2	12.7	9/25/77	St Helens	1/3/96	Manchester City	1+2				1			
					3/14/98	Ayr United								
Rimmer Stephen A	6.3	13.2	5/23/79	Liverpool	5/29/96	Manchester City								
Shelia Murtaz	6.2	13.6	3/25/69	Georgia		Vladikavkaz								
Georgian Int.				£400000	11/26/97	Manchester City	12		2		2			
Tskhadadze Kakhaber	6.2	12.7	9/7/68	Georgia		Al Vladikavkaz								
eorgian Int.				£300000	1/30/98	Manchester City	10				1			
Vaughan Anthony J	6.1	11.02	10/11/75	Manchester	7/1/94	Ipswich Town	56+10	4+1	2	4	3			
E: S				7/7/97	Manchester City	19	2			1			
Whitley Jeffrey	5.8	10	4/14/75	Zambia	2/19/96	Manchester City	19+8		2		2			
M I D F I E L D														
Bailey Alan	6	12	11/1/78	Manchester	7/3/97	Manchester City								
Bishop Ian	5.9	10.12	5/29/65	Liverpool	5/24/83	Everton	+1							
E: B.1				Loan	3/22/84	Crewe Alexandra	4							
				£15000	10/11/84	Carlisle United	131+1	8	5	4	14	1	1	
				£35000	7/14/88	Bournemouth	44	4	5	4	2			
				£465000	8/2/89	Manchester City	18+1	4		1	2	1		
				£500000	12/28/89	West Ham United	241+14	21+1	22+1	4+1	12	1	3	1
				Free	3/26/98	Manchester City	4+2							
Brown Michael D	5.7	10.06	1/25/77	Hartlepool	8/1/94	Manchester City	38+16	1+3	8				1	
				Loan	3/27/97	Hartlepool United	6				1			
Crooks Lee	6.1	11.1	1/14/78	Wakefield	8/1/94	Manchester City	11+9	+1	2					
Mason Gary	5.8	10.1	10/15/79	Edinburgh	10/21/96	Manchester City								
Morley Neil T	5.8	10.2	11/16/78	Warrington	1/3/96	Manchester City								
Pollock Jamie	6	11.2	2/16/74	Stockton	12/18/91	Middlesbrough	144+11	17+2	13+1	4+1	18	1	1	
E: Y.8. Div.1'95'97					11/22/96	Bolton Wanderers	43+3	4+1	4		5	1	2	
				£1000000	3/19/98	Manchester City	8				1			
Porteous Andrew G	5.11	10.11	9/13/79	Edinburgh	9/24/96	Nottingham Forest								
				Free	12/5/97	Manchester City								
Whitley James	5.9	11	4/14/75	Zambia	8/1/94	Manchester City	17+2		1+1					
Wiekens Gerard	6.1	13	2/25/73	Holland		SC Veendam								
				£500000	7/10/97	Manchester City	35+2	2	1		5			
F O R W A R D														
Bradbury Lee	6	12.7	7/3/75	Isle of Wight	10/3/95	Portsmouth	42+13	1+2	3		16		1	
				Loan	1/2/96	Exeter City	14				5			
					8/1/97	Manchester City	23+4	2			7			
Clough Nigel	5.9	11.8	3/19/66	Sunderland		Heanor Town								
E: 14, B.3, u21.15; LC'89'90;FMC'89'92; FLgXI.1				Free	9/15/84	Nottingham Forest	307+4	46	28	11+3	101	22	6	1
				£2275000	6/7/93	Liverpool	29+10	3	2		7	2		
				£1500000	1/24/96	Manchester City	32+5	2	3		4		1	
				Loan	12/21/96	Nottingham Forest	9+3				1			
Conlan Barry J	6.3	13.7	10/1/78	Drogheda	8/14/97	Manchester City	1+6							
Ei: u21.1.				Loan	2/27/98	Plymouth Argyle	13				2			
Dickov Paul	5.6	11.5	11/1/72	Livingston	12/28/90	Arsenal	6+15	2+2			3	3		
S: u21.5,Y,S. ECWC'94.				Loan	10/8/93	Luton Town	8+7				1			
Loan 3/23/94 Brighton & H.A. 8 Lge Apps 5gls.					8/23/96	Manchester City	44+13	2+1	2+1		13			
Goater Leonardo Shaun	5.11	11.4	2/25/70	Bermuda		Manchester United								
Bermuda Int. AWS '95/96				Free	10/25/89	Rotherham United	169+40	13+4	12+3	15+5	70	4	7	5
				Loan	11/12/93	Notts County	1							
					8/15/96	Bristol City	28+5	3	2		17	1		
				£500000	3/26/98	Manchester City	7				3			
Greenacre Christopher	5.11	12.8	12/23/77	Halifax	7/1/95	Manchester City	2+5		+1		1			
				Loan	3/6/98	Blackpool	2+2							
Heaney Neil	5.9	11.1	11/3/71	Middlesbrough	11/14/89	Arsenal	4+3	+1						
E: u21.6, Y.3. FAYC'88				Loan	1/3/91	Hartlepool United	2+1							
				Loan	1/9/92	Cambridge United	9+4		1		2			
				£300000	3/22/94	Southampton	42+19	4+2	6		5		2	
				£750000	11/27/96	Manchester City	13+5		2		1		1	
Loan 3/24/98 Charlton Athletic				Loan	4/6/98	Charlton Athletic	4+1			3				
Kavelashvila Mikhail	6	12.1	7/22/71	Georgia		Spartak Vladikavkaz								
Georgian Int.				£1400000	3/28/96	Manchester City	9+19	0+1			3			
Kelly Raymond	5.11	12	12/29/76	Athlone		Athlone								
				£30000	8/1/94	Manchester City	1							
Phillips Martin J	5.11	12.8	3/13/76	Exeter	7/4/94	Exeter City	25+14	1+1	1+2	0+5	2			
				£500000	11/25/95	Manchester City	3+12	0+1			1			
Loan 1/5/98 Scunthorpe United 2+1 Lge Apps				Loan	3/10/98	Exeter City	7+1							
Russell Craig	5.1	12	2/4/74	South Shields	7/1/92	Sunderland	103+47	7+6	6+3	2+4	31	1	2	
DIV1 95/96				£1000000	11/14/97	Manchester City	17+7		2		1			
ADDITIONAL CONTRACT PLAYERS														
Tiatto Danny						FC Baden								
				£300000	7/1/98	Manchester City								

MAINE ROAD
Moss Side, Manchester M14 7WN

Capacity ....31,458.

First game ....v Sheffield Utd, 2-1, 25.8.1923.
First floodlit game ....v Hearts, 14.10.1953.

ATTENDANCES
Highest ....84,569 v Stoke City, FA Cup 6th Round, 3.3.1934 (record outside London).
Lowest..4,029 v Leeds United, FMC, 14.10.1985.

OTHER GROUNDS ....Clowes Street 1880-81; Kirkmanshulme C.C. 1881-82; Queens Road 1882-84;
.............................Pink Bank Lane 1884-85; Bulls Head Ground, Reddish Lane 1885-87; Hyde Road 1887-1923;
.... Maine Road 1923-

HOW TO GET TO THE GROUND

From the North: Use motorway M61 then M63 until junction 9. Leave motorway and follow signs Manchester A5103. In 2.8 miles at crossroads turn right in Claremont Road. In 0.4 miles turn right into Maine Road for Manchester City FC.

From the East: Use motorway M61 until junction 17 then A56 into Manchester. Follow signs to Manchester Airport then turn left to join motorway A57(M). Follow signs to Birmingham to join A5103. Then in 1.3 miles turn left into Claremont Road. In 0.4 miles turn right into Maine Road for Manchester City.

From the South: Use motorway M6 until junction 19 then A556 and M56 until junction 3. Keep forward A5103 sign posted Manchester. In 2.8 miles at crossroads turn right into Claremont Road. In 0.4 miles turn right into Maine Road for Manchester City FC.

From the West: Use motorway M62 then M63 and route as from north. Or use M56 route as from south.

Car Parking: Kippax Street car park holds 400 vehicles (approx). Some street parking is permitted, parking at local schools.
Nearest Railway Station: Manchester Piccadilly (0161 832 8353).

USEFUL TELEPHONE NUMBERS

Club switchboard 0161 224 5000
Club fax number.......................0161 248 8449
Ticket Office..............................0161 226 2224

Clubcall 0891 12 11 91*
*Calls cost 50p per minute at all times.
Call costings correct at time of going to press.

MATCHDAY PROGRAMME

Programme Editor (97/98) .....Mike Beddow.

Number of pages (97/98) ....48.

Price (97/98)......................................£1.80.

Subscriptions ....Apply to the club.

Local Newspapers
...Manchester Evening News, Football Pink.

Local Radio Stations
.........................GMR Talk, Piccadilly Radio.

MATCHDAY TICKET PRICES (97/98)

Main Stand
Blocks B, C. £17
Other Blocks £16
Block G (OAP only). £5
North Stand £11
Juv/OAP £7
Blocks K,L (Juv/OAP) £6
Platt Lane Stand
Main Section. £12
JD Sports Famiy Enclosure £10
Juv/OAP £6
Kippax Stand
Upper Tier. £15
Lower Tier. £13

MILLWALL
(The Lions)
NATIONWIDE LEAGUE DIVISION 2
SPONSORED BY: LIVETV

1997-98 Back Row L-R: Steve Aris, Dave Savage, Alan McLeary, Brian Law, Tony Witter, Damian Webber, Keith Stevens, Scott Fitzgerald, Paul Sturgess, Danny Hockton. **Middle Row:** Gill Chapman (Reserve Physio), Kenny Brown, Ricky Newman, Graham Robertson, Tim Carter, James Connor, David Nurse, Dean Canoville, Lee McRobert, Bobby Bowry, Gerry Docherty (Physio). **Front Row:** Marc Bircham, Lucas Neill, Jason Dair, Paul Hartley, Kevin O'Callaghan (no longer with the club), Billy Bonds (Manager), Pat Holland (Asst. Manager), Maurice Doyle, Brendan Markey, Gerard Lavin, Paul Allen.

MILLWALL
FORMED IN 1885
TURNED PROFESSIONAL IN 1893
LTD COMPANY IN 1894

LIFE PRESIDENT
R I Burr
CHAIRMAN: T Paphitis
DIRECTORS
R Burr, P Mead, S Ring, D Woodward,
D Sullivan
SECRETARY
Y Haines
MARKETING MANAGER

MANAGER: Keith Stevens
ASSISTANT MANAGER: Alan McLeary
RESERVE TEAM MANAGER
Steve Gritt
YOUTH DEVELOPMENT OFFICER
Bob Pearson
PHYSIOTHERAPIST
Gerry Docherty

STATISTICIAN FOR THE DIRECTORY
Millwall FC Museum

After surviving the financial crisis by the skin of their teeth, new chairman Theo Phaphitis installed Billy Bonds as the Lions new manager. Bonds signed on some very experienced players and had an excellent start to the new campaign with a 3-0 win over Brentford. Things looked very rosy up to December, then as in the past two seasons injuries to key players such as promising youngsters Richard Sadlier, Lucas Neill, along with McLeary and Stevens et al. Also some poor performances saw Millwall's slow down the table until we were relying on other club's results for safety from relegation.

A club record of 38 players were used during the season as the manager was forced to frequently shuffle the team around.

The cups offered no respite either, an humiliating defeat at the hands of Wimbledon in the Coca-Cola, after a nail biting exciting win over Northampton on penalties (2-0), in which saw Tim Carter make two excellent saves and the evergreen Kenny Brown score the winner, summed up neatly the ups and downs Millwall suffered.

Further injuries to new signings, Stuart Nethercott, who was in great form alongside Brian Law - he damaged a shoulder in the best game of the season at Fulham. Then the injury to Andy Gray, still a dynamic force in midfield, just when it seemed a recovery could be made was a further kick in the teeth.

Paul Shaw from Arsenal finished as leading goalscorer mainly through brilliant shots around the penalty box. Goals were scarce no more than one being scored at the Den since the 2-1 defeat of Oldham in early October.

Keith Stevens reached 550 appearances for Millwall on 28/12/97. The club also passed the 3,500 points mark in the 1-0 win over Wycombe Wanderers in December.

Billy Bonds released 10 players at the season's end in May and then the news broke that he himself was leaving the Den.

Richard Lindsay - Millwall FC Museum.

MILLWALL

Division 2   :18th   FA CUP: 1st Round   LC CUP: 2nd Round   AWS: Southern Round 2

M	DATE	COMP.	VEN	OPPONENTS	RESULT	H/T	LP	GOAL SCORERS/GOAL TIMES	ATT.
1	A 09	FL	H	Brentford	W 3-0	1-0	4	Sadlier 50, Grant 61, Bates 22 (OG)	8951
2	12	CC 1/1	A	Northampton Town	L 1-2	1-0		Grant 33	(3773)
3	15	FL	A	Preston North End	L 1-2	1-1	11	Sadlier 5	(11486)
4	23	FL	H	York City	L 2-3	1-1	16	Grant 21, 71	6583
5	27	CC 1/2	H	Northampton Town	W 2-1	0-0		Hockton 51, 61	4364
6	S 02	FL	A	Luton Town	W 2-0	0-0	13	Law 68, Hockton 72	(5781)
7	13	FL	H	Southend United	W 3-1	0-1	13	Newman 54, Sadlier 68, Hockton 90	8606
8	16	CC 2/1	A	Wimbledon	L 1-5	1-2		Savage 16	(6949)
9	20	FL	A	Grimsby Town	W 1-0	0-0	6	Wilkinson 79	(4267)
10	27	FL	A	Northampton Town	L 0-2	0-0	10		(6578)
11	O 01	CC 2/2	H	Wimbledon	L 1-4	0-2		Shaw 90 (pen)	3591
12	04	FL	H	Blackpool	W 2-1	0-0	6	Wilkinson 49, Grant 65	7042
13	11	FL	H	Oldham Athletic	W 2-1	0-1	3	Law 58, Black 67	7906
14	18	FL	A	Watford	W 1-0	1-0	3	Shaw 36	(12530)
15	21	FL	A	Bournemouth	D 0-0	0-0	3		(4752)
16	25	FL	H	Wigan Athletic	D 1-1	0-0	4	Bowry 90	7986
17	29	FL	H	Bristol City	L 0-2	0-1	5		7026
18	N 01	FL	A	Gillingham	W 3-1	1-0	4	Black 34, Shaw 83, Wilkinson 89	(8383)
19	04	FL	H	Fulham	D 1-1	0-0	4	Shaw 84	10291
20	08	FL	H	Carlisle United	D 1-1	1-0	4	Law 3	6959
21	15	FAC 1	A	Bristol City	L 0-1	0-1			(8413)
22	18	FL	A	Burnley	W 2-1	1-1	3	Bowry 2, Savage 62	(8834)
23	22	FL	H	Chesterfield	D 1-1	0-0	3	Shaw 61	6556
24	29	FL	A	Bristol Rovers	L 1-2	0-1	3	Shaw 60	(5542)
25	D 03	FL	H	Walsall	L 0-1	0-0	5		4647
26	09	AWS S1	A	Cardiff City	W 2-0	1-0		Shaw 37, Grant 65	(1219)
27	13	FL	A	Plymouth Argyle	L 0-3	0-2	6		(4460)
28	20	FL	H	Wycombe Wanderers	W 1-0	0-0	4	Shaw 48	6092
29	26	FL	A	Bristol City	L 1-4	0-2	6	Veart 52	(16128)
30	28	FL	H	Luton Town	L 0-2	0-0	10		7461
31	J 10	FL	A	Brentford	L 1-2	1-1	12	Grant 20	(5529)
32	13	AWS S2	A	Bristol City	L 0-1	0-1		Locke 15	(2557)
33	17	FL	H	Wrexham	L 0-1	0-0	15		5550
34	24	FL	A	York City	W 3-2	0-1	11	Grant 47, Shaw 64, 90	(3508)
35	31	FL	A	Southend United	D 0-0	0-0	11		(5705)
36	F 06	FL	H	Grimsby Town	L 0-1	0-1	14		6020
37	14	FL	A	Blackpool	L 0-3	0-3	15		(4455)
38	21	FL	H	Northampton Town	D 0-0	0-0	15		6007
39	25	FL	H	Watford	D 1-1	1-0	14	Shaw 26	7126
40	28	FL	A	Oldham Athletic	D 1-1	0-0	15	, McNiven 67 (OG)	(4805)
41	M 03	FL	A	Carlisle United	L 0-1	0-0	16		(5217)
42	07	FL	H	Gillingham	W 1-0	0-0	15	Law 47	8241
43	14	FL	A	Fulham	W 2-1	0-1	13	Shaw 48, Gray 77	(12316)
44	17	FL	A	Wrexham	L 0-1	0-1	13		(4167)
45	21	FL	H	Burnley	W 1-0	1-0	9	Grant 21	7582
46	25	FL	H	Preston North End	L 0-1	0-1	9		5888
47	28	FL	A	Chesterfield	L 1-3	0-2	13	Tomlinson 60	(3952)
48	A 04	FL	H	Bristol Rovers	D 1-1	0-0	13	Shaw 89	5635
49	11	FL	A	Walsall	L 0-2	0-1	16		(3307)
50	13	FL	H	Plymouth Argyle	D 1-1	1-1	18	Hockton 4	5496
51	18	FL	A	Wycombe Wanderers	D 0-0	0-0	18		(5371)
52	24	FL	A	Wigan Athletic	D 0-0	0-0	16		(4045)
53	M 02	FL	H	Bournemouth	L 1-2	1-2	18	Grant 24 (pen)	7872

Best Home League Attendance: 10291 V Fulham   **Smallest :4647 V Walsall**   **Average :7023**

Goal Scorers:

FL	(43)	Shaw 11, Grant 8, Law 4, Hockton 3, Sadlier 3, Wilkinson 3, Black 2, Bowry 2, Gray 1, Newman 1, Savage 1, Tomlinson 1, Veart 1, Opponents 2
CC	(5)	Hockton 2, Grant 1, Savage 1, Shaw 1
FAC	(0)	
AWS	(3)	Grant 1, Locke 1, Shaw 1

1997-98

(M) Allen	(D) Bircham	(M) Black	(M) Bowry	(D) Brown	(G) Carter	(G) Crossley	(M) Doyle	(D) Fitzgerald	(M) Grant	(M) Gray	(F) Hockton	(M) Lavin	(D) Law	(D) McLeary	(M) McRobert	(M) Neill	(D) Nethercott	(M) Newman	(M) Ryan	(M) Sadlier	(F) Savage	(M) Shaw	(G) Spink	(D) Stevens	(D) Sturgess	(F) Veart	(F) Wilkinson	(D) Witter	Player	#
X			X	X			X	X			S2		X	X				X			X	X			X				R.J. Harris	1
X			X	X			X	X			S		X					X			X	X			X			X	J Kirkby	2
X		S1	X	X			X	X					X	X				X			X	X			X			S	T Jones	3
X	S3	S2	X	X			X	X	S1				X	X				X			X	X			X				K A Leach	4
X	S		X	X	X				X				X	X				X				X			X				M R Halsey	5
X	S		X	X	X		S1		X				X					X				X			X				R D Furnandiz	6
X			X	X	X			S2	X				X	X				X		S1	X				X				C T Finch	7
X	S		X	X	X		S		X				X	X				X			X	X			X				K W Burge	8
X	S		X	X	X						S1		X	X				X			X	X			X			X	T Heilbron	9
X			X	X				S1			S		X	X				X			X	X	X		X			X	S J Baines	10
	S		X						X		S1							X			X		X		X	X		X	S W Dunn	11
X		X	X	X			S1				S3		X	X				X				X	X		S2			X	M E Pierce	12
X		X	X	X			S	S	X				X	X				X			S1	X	X					X	M Fletcher	13
X		X	X	X			S2	S	X				X	X				X			S1	X	X					X	A N Butler	14
X		X	X	X			S2	S	X				X	X				X			S1	X	X					X	D Orr	15
X		X	X	X			S	S	X1				X	X				X				X	X					X	M C Bailey	16
X		X	X	X			S	S	S		S2		X	X				X			S1	X	X					X	F G Stretton	17
S	X	X	X	X			S	S					X	X				X				X	X		X			X	B Knight	18
S	X	X	X	X	X		S	S			S1		X	X				X				X	X		X			X	C R Wilkes	19
S2		X	X				S				S1		X	X				X				X	X		X			X	A P D'Urso	20
X1	S2		X	X			X3	S	S3		S1		X	X				X				X			X		X2	X	M Fletcher	21
	X		X	X			S	S	S1		S		X	X				X				X	X		X		X	X	M S Pike	22
S1	X		X	X									X	X				X				X	X		X	X		X	P Rejer	23
	X2		X				X	S1	S3				X		X1		S2	X				X	X	X	X3			X	A R Hall	24
X1	S		X				X	X	S2				X			S1		X				X	X	X	X		X2		R Styles	25
S3	X	X1	X				X	X	X				S1		X	X3				X	X2	X	S2							26
S2	X1	X2	X				X		X3							S3		S1			X	X	X		X			X	P S Danson	27
S1			X				X		X2				X				X				X1	X	X		S1	X	X2		G Singh	28
S			X				X		X				S		X1			X			X	X	X		S1	X			R J Harris	29
S1			X				X		X				X				S				X	X	X	X		X	X1		A Bates	30
X	S		X				S		X				S1					X			X	X	X			X		X1	A N Butler	31
X	X		X1				S3	X	X3		X2		X					X			X	X			S1	X2	X			32
X		X	X	X	X		S3	X2	X1		X		X					X				X		S2	X	S1	X		D Orr	33
X		X	X	X						X1		X	S			X		X				X			S	S1	X		T Jones	34
X		X	X	X					X			X				X		X	X			X		S		S			K A Leach	35
X		X	X	X					X1	S2			X			X2		X	X			X		S		S1			S W Mathieson	36
S		X	X	X				S1	X1	S2			X			X		X				X			X	X2		X	D Pugh	37
		X	X	X			X	S2		S			S1			X	X1	X	X		X2	X						X	A P D'Urso	38
		X	X	X			X	S		S			X			X	X	X	X		X	X						X	K M Lynch	39
		X	X	X			S3	S2		X3	S1		X				X	X1			X	X					X2		R Pearson	40
S2		X	X	X			S				X1		S1			X	X	X			X2	X					X		G B Frankland	41
		X	X1	X			X	S1					X			X	X	X			X	X						S	C R Wilkes	42
S3		X	X	X			S2	X		X3	X		X2			X1		X				X						S1	M E Pierce	43
S		X	X	X			X	X				S						X			X	X	X1			S1		X	R D Furnandiz	44
		X	X	X			S1	X		X1			X					X			X	S	X			S		X	M J Brandwood	45
		X1	X	X			S1	X		X3			X					X			X1	S1	X			S3		X	C R Wilkes	46
		X	X	X			S			X		X	X		S1			X					X1	X1		S1		X	C J Foy	47
		X	X	X			S			X			S1	X		X	S2	X				X						X	P S Danson	48
X		X	X	X			X1			X								X			X2	X	S2			S1		X	M L Dean	49
X2		X	X	X						X			X3	S2	X			X1			X	S1				X		X	S J Baines	50
S		X	X				X	X		X2	X1		X					X			S2	X	X			S1		X	F G Stretton	51
		X	X				X	X		X1			X				S				X	X	X	S		S1		X	M D Messias	52
		X	X				X	X		X		S3			X2								X			S1		X	S W Mathieson	53
21	3	13	41	44	12	13	8	16	31	12	10	4	40	19	4	3	10	35	16	3	24	40	21	3	12	7	22	10	FL Appearances	
7	1		2				12	2	8		16	3			1	3				1	7				2	1	8	1	FL Sub Appearances	
3			2	4	3		1	1	3		2+1		3	2				4			1	3	2		4		1	2	CC Appearances	
1	0+1		1	1				0+1			0+1		1	1				1			1				1		1		FAC Appearances	
1+1	2	1		2			1+1	2	2		0+2		2			1		1			1	2	2			0+1	0+1	1	AWS Appearances	

Also Played: (M) Cahill X(53). (D) Cook X(31,33), X3(53). (M) Dair S(5). (M) Harris X2(48), S3(50), X1(53). (M) Nurse S(2,21), X(11). (M) Reid S(35), S2(53). (M) Robertson S(1,11), S2(3). (M) Roche S1(1), X(11). (F) Tomlinson X(47), X1(48), S2(49). (D) Webber S(2,6,7,8,9), S1(5), S2(10), X(11).

MILLWALL

CLUB RECORDS

BIGGEST VICTORIES
League: 9-1 v Torquay United, Division 3(S), 29.8.1927.
9-1 v Coventry City, Division 3(S) 19.11.1927.
F.A. Cup: 7-0 v Gateshead, 2nd Round, 12.12.1936.
League Cup: 5-1 v Northampton, 3rd Round replay, 16.10.1967.
BIGGEST DEFEATS
League: 1-8 v Plymouth, Division 2, 16.1.1932.
F.A. Cup: 1-9 v Aston Villa, 4th Round, 28.1.1946.
League Cup: 1-7 v Chelsea, 1st Round, 10.10.1960.
MOST POINTS
3 points a win: 90, Division 3, 1984-85.
2 points a win: 65, Division 3(S), 1927-28 & Division 3, 1965-66.
MOST GOALS SCORED
127, Division 3(S) (Record), 1927-28.
MOST GOALS CONCEDED
100, Division 3(S), 1955-56.
MOST FIRST CLASS MATCHES IN A SEASON
61 - 1984-85 (League 46, FA Cup 7, League Cup 4, Freight Rover Trophy 4).
MOST LEAGUE WINS: 30, Division 3(S), 1927-28.
MOST LEAGUE DRAWS
18, Division 3(S), 1921-22; Division 3(S), 1922-23.
MOST LEAGUE DEFEATS
26, Division 3(S), 1957-58.
RECORD TRANSFER FEE RECEIVED
£2,300,000 from Liverpool for Mark Kennedy, March 1995.
£2,300,000 from Crystal Palace for Andy Roberts, July 1995.
RECORD TRANSFER FEE PAID
£800,000 for Paul Goddard from Derby County, December 1989.
BEST PERFORMANCES
League: 10th in Division 1, 1988-89.
F.A.Cup: Semi-finals in 1899-00, 1902-03, 1936-37.
League Cup: 5th Round in 1973-74, 1976-77, 1994-95.

INDIVIDUAL CLUB RECORDS

MOST GOALS IN A CAREER
Teddy Sheringham: 111 (1983-91). 93 League, 5 FA Cup, 8 Lge Cup
5 Others.
MOST GOALS IN A SEASON
Richard Parker: 38 goals in 1926-27 (League 37, FA Cup 1).
Peter Burridge: 38 goals in 1960-61 (League 35, FA Cup 2, League Cup 1).
E.Sheringham: 38 goals in 1990-91 (Lge 33, FA Cup 2,Lge Cup 2, FMC 1).
MOST GOALS IN A MATCH
5. Richard Parker v Norwich City, 6-1, Division 3(S), 28.8.1926.
MOST APPEARANCES
Barry Kitchener: 589+7 (1966-82). 518+5 League, 29+2 FA Cup, 42 Lge Cup.
OLDEST PLAYER
Jack Fort, 41 years 8 months.
YOUNGEST PLAYER
David Mehmet, 16 years 5 months.
MOST CAPPED PLAYER

PREVIOUS MANAGERS

Eamonn Dunphy (Eire) 23.
F B Kidd 1894-99, E R Stopher 1899-1900, G A Saunders 1900-11, H Lipsham 1911-18, R Hunter 1918-33, W McCracken 1933-36, C Hewitt 1936-40, W Voisey 1940-44, J Cook 1944-48, C Hewitt 1948-56, R Gray 1956-58, J Seed 1958-59, J Smith 1959-61 R Gray 1961-63, W Gray 1963-66, B Fenton1966-74, G Jago1974-77 G Petchley 1978-80, P Anderson 1980-82, G Graham 1982-86, I Docherty 1986-90, B Rioch 1990-92, M McCarthy 1992-96, J Nicholl 1996-97, J Docherty 1997. B Bonds 1997-98.

ADDITIONAL INFORMATION
PREVIOUS NAMES
Millwall Rovers 1885. Millwall Athletic 1889.
PREVIOUS LEAGUES
United, London, Western Leagues. Southern District Combination. Southern League.
Club colours: Blue shirts, white shorts, blue socks.

COMPETITIONS

Dɪᴠ.1/P	Dɪᴠ.2/1	Dɪᴠ.3/2	Dɪᴠ.3(S)	Dɪᴠ.4
1988-90	1928-34	1962-64	1920-28	1958-62
	1938-48	1965-66	1934-38	1964-65
	1966-75	1975-76	1948-58	
	1976-79	1979-85		
	1985-88	1996-		**FLT**
	1990-96			1982-83

HONOURS

Dɪᴠ.2	Dɪᴠ.3(S)	Dɪᴠ 3(S) KO	Dɪᴠ.4	FLT
1987-88	1927-28	1936-37	1961-62	1982-83
	1937-38			

LONGEST LEAGUE RUNS

of undefeated matches:	19 (27.4.1959 - 7.11.1959)	of league matches w/out a win:	20 (26.12.1989 - 5.5.1990)
of undefeated home matches:	59 (20.4.1964 - 14.1.1967)	of undefeated away matches:	10 (5.3.21 -7.9.21, 13.2.88-15.10.88)
without home win:	9 (1.1.1990 - 1.9.1990)	without an away win:	26 (7.11.1979 - 26.12.1980)
of league wins:	10 (10.3.1928 - 26.4.1928)	of home wins:	13 (15.12.1923 - 30.8.1924)
of league defeats:	11 (10.4.1929 - 21.9.1929)	of away wins:	5 (17.3.1928 - 25.4.1928)

THE MANAGER

Keith Stevens . . . . appointed May 1998.

PREVIOUS CLUBS
As Manager . . . . None.
As Asst.Man/Coach . . . . Millwall.
As a player . . . . Millwall.

HONOURS
As a Manager . . . . None.
As a Player . . . . Division 2 championship 1988. FLT 1983.

MILLWALL

PLAYERS NAME Honours	Ht	Wt	Birthdate	Birthplace Transfers	Contract Date	Clubs	League	L/Cup	FA Cup	Other	Lge	L/C	FAC	Oth
G O A L K E E P E R														
Roberts Anthony	6.1	12.4	04/08/69	Holyhead	24/07/87	Q.P.R.	122	10	10+1	2				
W: 2, B.2, u21.2, Y				Free	7/1/98	Millwall								
Smith Philip A			12/14/79	Wembley		Millwall (T)								
Spink Nigel	6.2	14.6	8/8/58	Chelmsford		Chelmsford								
E: 1, B.2. EC'82. ESC'82. LC'94. FLgXI				£4000	1/1/77	Aston Villa	357+2	45	28	25+1				
				Free	1/31/96	WBA	19	2		2				
				£50000	9/26/97	Millwall	21		1					
D E F E N C E														
Bircham Marc	5.11	10.12	5/11/78	Wembley	5/22/96	Millwall	8+1		+1					
Brown Kenny J	5.8	11.6	7/11/67	Upminster	7/10/85	Norwich City	24+1			3				
				Free	8/10/88	Plymouth Argyle	126	9	6	3	4			
				£175000	8/2/91	West Ham United	56+8	2+1	7+2	2+2	5		1	
				Loan	9/7/95	Huddersfield Town	5							
				Loan	10/27/95	Reading	12	3			1			
				Loan	3/1/96	Southend United	6							
				Loan	3/28/96	Crystal Palace	5+1			3	2			1
				Loan	9/9/96	Reading	5							
				£75000	12/27/96	Birmingham City	21	2						
					7/31/97	Millwall	44	4	1					
Cook Andy	5.9	10.12	8/10/69	Romsey	7/6/87	Southampton	11+5	4	1	1	1			
				£50000	9/13/91	Exeter City	70	2	7	6	1		1	1
				£125000	7/23/93	Swansea City	54+8	2	3	9+1				2
				£35000	12/20/96	Portsmouth	7+2							
				£50000	1/8/98	Millwall	2							
Cort Leon			9/11/79	Southwark		Dulwich Hamlet								
				Free	1/22/98	Millwall								
Fitzgerald Scott	6	12.2	8/13/69	Westminster	7/13/89	Wimbledon	95+11	13	5	1	1			
Ei: B.1, u21.2				Loan	11/23/95	Sheffield United	6							
				Loan	10/11/96	Millwall	7							
					7/17/97	Millwall	16+3	1						
Law Brian	6.2	11.12	1/1/70	Merthyr Tydfil	8/15/87	QPR	19+1	2+1	3	1				
W: 1, u21.1, Y. S				£134000	12/23/94	Wolverhampton W.	26+4	1+1	7		1			
				Free	7/21/97	Millwall	40	3	1		4			
McLeary Alan	5.1	10.9	10/6/64	Lambeth	10/12/81	Millwall	289+18	16+1	24+1	22+1	5		2	2
E: B.2,u21.1,Y.6. AMC'83. Div.2'88.				Loan	7/23/92	Sheffield United	3							
				Loan	10/16/92	Wimbledon	4	2						
				Free	5/27/93	Charlton Athletic	44	2	5	3	2			
				Free	7/31/95	Bristol City	31+3	5						
					2/21/97	Millwall	34		2	1				
Nethercott Stuart	5.9	12.4	3/21/73	Ilford	8/17/91	Tottenham Hotspur	31+23		5+3				1	
				Loan	9/5/91	Maidstone	13+1			1				
				Loan	2/13/92	Barnet	3							
				Loan	1/22/98	Millwall	3							
				Free	3/26/98	Millwall	10							
Ryan Robert P	5.11	11.05	5/16/77	Dublin		Belvedere								
				Free	7/26/94	Huddersfield Town	12+2	2						
				£10000	1/30/98	Millwall	16							
Sturgess Paul C	5.11	12.5	8/4/75	Dartford	7/1/93	Charlton Athletic	66+8	6+1	1	5				
				Free	7/2/97	Millwall	12+4	4	1					
M I D F I E L D														
Bowry Robert	5.8	10	5/19/71	Hampstead	8/8/90	QPR								
Div1'94				Free	4/4/92	Crystal Palace	23+9	7	1		1			
				£220000	7/5/95	Millwall	191+3	7	5		5			
Cahill Timothy	5.10	10.11	12/6/79	Sydney		Sydney United								
				Free	7/31/97	Millwall	1							
Gray Andrew A	5.11	13.3	2/22/64	Lambeth		Dulwich Hamlet								
				£2000	11/8/84	Crystal Palace	91+7	9+1	3	0+1	27	2		
				£150000	11/25/87	Aston Villa	34+3	3	3+1	0+2	4	1	1	
				£425000	2/2/89	QPR	11				2			
				£500000	8/18/89	Crystal Palace	87+3	15	11	14	12	4	2	4
				£900000	2/27/92	Tottenham Hotspur	23+10				2			
via Marbella				Loan	12/23/92	Swindon Town	3							
via Falkirk 12/22/95				Free	7/22/97	Bury	21	3	2		1	1	2	
					1/21/98	Millwall	12				1			
Lavin Gerard	5.8	10.8	2/5/74	Corby	5/11/92	Watford	105+5	9	6	2+1	3	1		
				£400000	11/23/95	Millwall	29+6		2+1					
Neill Lucas E	5.9	11.1	1/1/70	Sydney		Sydney	43+14	1+1	2		3			
u21 Int. Australian														
Newman Richard A	5.9	10.7	8/5/70	Guildford	1/22/88	Crystal Palace	43+5	5	5+2	2	3			
Div1'94				Loan	2/28/92	Maidstone	9+1				1			
				£500000	7/19/95	Millwall	108+4	9	5		5			
Reid Steven J	5.11	11.10	3/10/81	Kingston	1/30/98	Millwall (T)	0+1							
Roche Stephen M	5.11	11.2	10/2/78	Dublin		Millwall	4+4	1						
Y,S. Ei:														
Sadlier Richard	6.2	12.1	1/14/79	Dublin	8/14/96	Millwall	10+4	1			3			
F O R W A R D														
Canoville Dean	6.1	11.1	11/30/78	Perivale	12/6/95	Millwall	0+2							
Carter Jimmy	5.1	10.4	09/11/65	Hammersmith	15/11/83	Crystal Palace								
Div2'88				Free	30/09/85	Q.P.R.								
				£15000	12/03/87	Millwall	99+11	6+1	6+1	5+1	11		2	
				£800000	10/01/91	Liverpool	2+3		2	0+1				
				£500000	08/10/91	Arsenal	18+7	1	2+1		2			
				Loan	23/03/94	Oxford United	8+1							
				Free	06/07/95	Portsmouth	60+12	5+1	0+2		5	1		
				Free	7/1/98	Millwall								
Grant Kim T.	5.10	10.12	9/25/72	Ghana		Charlton Ath. (T)	74+49	3+9	8+5	5+2	18	1	5	1
Ghana INt.				£250000	3/15/96	Luton Town	18+17	4	0+2	2+1	5	2		1
					8/7/97	Millwall	31+8	3		2	8	1		1
Harris Neil	5.11	12.8	7/12/77	Orsett	3/26/98	Millwall	2+1							
Hockton Danny J	5.11	11.11	2/7/79	Barking	10/1/96	Millwall	10+17	2+1	+1		3	2		
McDougald David	5.11	10.12	12/01/75	Texas	12/07/93	Tottenham Hotspur								
E: S.					12/05/94	Brighton & H.A.	70+7	7	4	6	14	2	3	3
				Loan	10/04/96	Chesterfield	9							
					23/08/96	Rotherham United	13+4		1		2			
				Free	7/1/98	Millwall								
Savage David P T	6.2	12.7	7/30/73	Dublin		Longford Town (Eire)								
Ei: u21.2				£15000	5/27/94	Millwall	103+26	11	6+2		6	2	2	
Shaw Paul	5.11	12.4	9/4/73	Burnham	9/18/91	Arsenal	1+11		+1		2			
E: Y.1.				Loan	3/23/95	Burnley	8+1				4			
				Loan	8/11/95	Cardiff City	6							
				Loan	10/20/95	Peterborough Utd	12		2		5			
				£250000	0/15/97	Millwall	40	2			11	1		

ADDITIONAL CONTRACT PLAYERS

| Stuart Jamie | | | | | 7/1/98 | Millwall | | | | | | | | |

437

THE NEW DEN
Zampa Road, London SE16 3LN

Capacity..20,146 (All seater)

First game..v Sporting Lisbon, 1-2, 4.8.1993.
First floodlit game..As above.

ATTENDANCES
Highest...20,093 v Arsenal, FA Cup 3rd Round, 10.1.1994.
Lowest..2,795 v Colchester United, AWS 1996/97.

OTHER GROUNDS...........................Glengall Road 1885-86. Back of Lord Nelson 1886-90. East Ferry Road 1890-01.
....North Greenwich 1901-10. The Den 1910-93. The New Den 1993-

HOW TO GET TO THE GROUND

From the North: From motorway M1 and A1 follow signs London A1 then City, then follow signs to Shoreditch, Whitechapel. Then follow signs to Ring Road, Dover to cross Tower Bridge. In 1.8 miles at roundabout turn left into Old Kent Road, turn left before Railway Bridge (Ilderton Road). Take 7th right for new stadium.

From the East: Use A2 sign posted London. At New Cross follow signs, City, Westminster, into Kendar Street and at end turn left. Turn right at next traffic lights (Ilderton Road) and then take 7th right for new stadium.

From the South and West: Use A2 sign posted London. At New Cross follow signs, City, Westminster, into Kendar Street and at end turn left. Turn right at next traffic lights (Ilderton Road) and then take 7th right for new stadium.

Car Parking: Street parking.

Nearest Railway Station: New Cross Gate BR & tube, New Cross BR & Tube, South Bermondsey BR (Away) and Surrey Quays tube.

USEFUL TELEPHONE NUMBERS

Club switchboard 0171 232 1222
Club fax number.......................0171 231 3663
Club shop 0171 231 9845
Ticket Office.............................0171 231 9999

Clubcall 0891 40 03 00*
*Calls cost 50p per minute at all times.
Call costings correct at time of going to press.

MATCHDAY PROGRAMME

Programme Editor (97/98).Deano Standing.

Number of pages (97/98) ....40.

Price (97/98)....................................£1.70.

Subscription service ....Yes.

Local Newspapers
..................................South London Press,
.......................South East London Mercury,
....Southwark News.

Local Radio Stations
....Capital Radio.

MATCHDAY TICKET PRICES (97/98)
West Stand Upper Tier £16
Juv/OAP..................................£5/£8

West Stand Lower Tier £14
Juv/OAP..................................£5/£7

East Stand Upper Tier.........................£15
Juv/OAP..............................£5/£7.50

East Stand Lower Tier.........................£12
Juv/OAP..................................£5/£6

South Stand Upper & Lower £10
Juv/OAP....................................£5

Family Enclosure.............................£11
Juv/OAP...............................£3/£4.50
Additional Junior Lion within a family.............£3

NORTHAMPTON TOWN
(The Cobblers)
NATIONWIDE LEAGUE DIVISION 2
SPONSORED BY: NATIONWIDE BUILDING SOCIETY

1998-99 - Back Row L-R: Denis Casey (Physio), Colin Hill, Chris Freestone, Gary Hughes, Michael Warner, Sean Parrish, Tony Godden (Coach). **Middle Row:** Kevin Broadhurst (Yth. Coach), Charlie Bishop, Dean Peer, Chris Lee, Billy Turley, Duncan Spedding, Andy Woodman, Carl Heggs, James Hunt, David Seal, Garry Thompson (Reserve Team Coach). **Front Row:** Ian Atkins (Manager), Damian Matthew, John Frain, Roy Hunter, Ali Gibb, Ray Warburton, Carlo Corazzin, Ian Clarkson, Kevin Wilson (Assistant Manager).   **Photo by: Pete Norton.**

NORTHAMPTON TOWN
FORMED IN 1897
TURNED PROFESSIONAL IN 1897
LTD COMPANY IN 1922

PRESIDENT: R Church
CHAIRMAN: B J Ward
DIRECTORS
B Hancock, D Kerr, B Lomax, C Smith,
B Stonhill (Vice-chairman),
M A Church, B W Collins
SECRETARY
Rebecca Kerr
COMMERCIAL MANAGER
Bob Gorrill

MANAGER: Ian Atkins
ASSISTANT MANAGER: Kevin Wilson
RESERVE TEAM MANAGER
Garry Thompson
YOUTH TEAM MANAGER
Kevin Broadhurst
PHYSIOTHERAPIST
Dennis Casey

**STATISTICIAN FOR THE DIRECTORY
& OFFICIAL CLUB HISTORIAN**
Frank Grande

Manager Ian Atkins did not let the grass grow under his feet, or wallow in the glory of the Wembley play off victory over Swansea. To start the new season in Division Two, he revamped the forward line allowing Neil Grayson (Hereford), and Mark Cooper (Welling) to move on and filling their places with Carl Heggs, who had played against Northampton for Swansea in the play off final, and David Seal, a £90,000 record buy from Bristol City. After defeat at Bournemouth, in the opening game of the season, the club went nine league games before tasting defeat again, and sat comfortably near the top of the table.

The team was basically that of last season, with the addition of David Brightwell (Blackpool), in defence, Paul Conway (Carlisle) in midfield and Kevin Wilson (Walsall) up front as player/coach.

Despite losing both key midfielders, Parrish and Hunter, during the season, through injury, the club still maintained its high position, it also saw another 'star' emerge in the form of James Hunt, a midfielder who was released by Notts County, in the close season.

Manager Atkins, bolstered the defence in mid season, firstly with Northern Ireland International Colin Hill, who had returned from Sweden, and then paid out £20,000 for Charlie Bishop from Wigan. The final piece of the jigsaw saw Chris Freestone a striker,join from Middlesbrough, first on loan and then in a £70,000 deal, he was followed by the experienced Jason Dozzell, on a non contract basis.

A bad run in April saw the club fall out of the play offs, but they pulled themselves back with an away win at Plymouth, and a 1-0 victory over fellow promotion rivals Fulham, clinching a play off spot with a 0-0 draw at York.

Bristol Rovers won the first leg of the semi 3-1 and looked to be coasting, but in the second leg, in front of a capacity crowd at Sixfields, Northampton won 3-0, with skipper Warburton fittingly heading in the winning goal 13 minutes from time.

This time there was no fairy tale at Wembley, Grimsby won by the only goal of the game, and the 41,000 supporters, who had come to watch Northampton, resigned themselves to another season in Division Two.

The club were involved in penalty shoot outs in all three cup competitions, ironically for the first time in their history, they went out to Millwall in the Coca-Cola, but beat Basingstoke in the FA Cup, and Plymouth in the Auto Windscreens.

FRANK GRANDE

439

NORTHAMPTON TOWN

Division 2   :4th   FA CUP: 3rd Round   LC CUP: 1st Round   AWS: Southern Quarter-finals

M	DATE	COMP.	VEN	OPPONENTS	RESULT		H/T	LP	GOAL SCORERS/GOAL TIMES	ATT.
1	A 09	FL	H	Bournemouth	L	0-2	0-0	20		6384
2	12	CC 1/1	H	Millwall	W	2-1	0-1		Gayle 60, Seal 65	3773
3	15	FL	A	Wycombe Wanderers	D	0-0	0-0	20		(5130)
4	23	FL	H	Bristol City	W	2-1	2-1	14	Seal 23, Gayle 45	6217
5	27	CC 1/2	A	Millwall	L	1-2	0-0		Gayle 90	(4364)
6	30	FL	A	Carlisle United	W	2-0	2-0	10	Seal 16, 34	(6307)
7	S 02	FL	A	Walsall	W	2-0	1-0	6	Seal 30, Gayle 80	(4435)
8	09	FL	H	Luton Town	W	1-0	1-0	3	Parrish 1	7246
9	13	FL	A	Oldham Athletic	D	2-2	1-2	3	Seal 1, Hunter 64 (pen)	(5829)
10	20	FL	H	Wigan Athletic	W	1-0	0-0	2	Seal 54	6570
11	27	FL	H	Millwall	W	2-0	0-0	2	Sampson 53, Hunter 65 (pen)	6578
12	O 04	FL	A	Southend United	D	0-0	0-0	2		(4300)
13	11	FL	A	Grimsby Town	L	0-1	0-1	2		(4778)
14	18	FL	H	Gillingham	W	2-1	2-0	2	Gayle 35, Heggs 39	7191
15	21	FL	H	York City	D	1-1	1-0	2	Hunter 6 (pen)	6059
16	25	FL	A	Fulham	D	1-1	0-1	2	Gayle 50	(9848)
17	N 01	FL	H	Bristol Rovers	D	1-1	0-0	3	Gayle 58	7264
18	04	FL	A	Blackpool	D	1-1	0-1	3	Sampson 75	(3685)
19	08	FL	A	Wrexham	L	0-1	0-0	5		(3768)
20	15	FAC 1	A	Exeter City	D	1-1	1-1		Hunter 36	(4605)
21	18	FL	H	Brentford	W	4-0	4-0	4	Heggs 4, Gayle 10, Seal 40, 43	5277
22	22	FL	H	Watford	L	0-1	0-0	4		7372
23	25	FAC 1R	H	Exeter City	W	2-1	1-1		Hunter 10, Heggs 86	5259
24	29	FL	A	Burnley	L	1-2	0-0	6	Gibb 50	(8369)
25	D 02	FL	H	Chesterfield	D	0-0	0-0	6		4824
26	06	FAC 2	H	Basingstoke Town	D	1-1	1-0		Seal 39	5881
27	09	AWS S1	H	Plymouth Argyle	W	1-0	0-0		Heggs 82 (Northampton won 5-3 on penalties)	2631
28	13	FL	A	Preston North End	L	0-1	0-0	7		(7448)
29	16	FAC 2R	A	Basingstoke Town	D	0-0	0-0			(4933)
30	20	FL	H	Plymouth Argyle	W	2-1	0-1	5	Freestone 66, 71	5546
31	26	FL	A	Luton Town	D	2-2	2-0	4	Dozzell 7 (pen), White 12 (OG)	(8035)
32	28	FL	H	Walsall	W	3-2	1-1	3	Seal 31, Freestone 48, Dozzell 54	7094
33	J 03	FAC 3	A	Leicester City	L	0-4	0-2			(20608)
34	10	FL	A	Bournemouth	L	0-3	0-0	5		(4257)
35	13	AWS S2	H	Torquay United	W	5-1	1-0		Freestone 28,64, Frain 51, Heggs 67, 80	2845
36	17	FL	H	Carlisle United	W	2-1	0-1	4	Heggs 54, Dozzell 77	6327
37	24	FL	A	Bristol City	D	0-0	0-0	5		(14753)
38	27	AWS SQF	A	Peterborough United	L	1-2	1-1		Sampson 24	(5516)
39	31	FL	H	Oldham Athletic	D	0-0	0-0	6		6559
40	F 06	FL	A	Wigan Athletic	D	1-1	0-0	7	Freestone 68	(3579)
41	10	FL	H	Wycombe Wanderers	W	2-0	0-0	4	Seal 59 (pen), Freestone 69	5302
42	14	FL	H	Southend United	W	3-1	2-1	3	Freestone 30, Brightwell 42, Frain 56	6147
43	21	FL	A	Millwall	D	0-0	0-0	3		(6007)
44	24	FL	A	Gillingham	L	0-1	0-0	5		(6463)
45	28	FL	H	Grimsby Town	W	2-1	0-1	3	Seal 59, Gleghorn 64	6932
46	M 03	FL	H	Wrexham	L	0-1	0-1	4		5183
47	07	FL	A	Bristol Rovers	W	2-0	1-0	4	Freestone 34, Dozzell 61 (pen)	(6535)
48	14	FL	A	Blackpool	W	2-0	1-0	4	Freestone 27, Heggs 73	6586
49	21	FL	A	Brentford	D	0-0	0-0	5		(5746)
50	28	FL	A	Watford	D	1-1	0-0	5	Peer 83	(14268)
51	A 04	FL	H	Burnley	L	0-1	0-1	6		7264
52	11	FL	A	Chesterfield	L	1-2	1-0	7	Clarkson 9	(5064)
53	13	FL	H	Preston North End	D	2-2	1-0	7	Sampson 78, Seal 82	5664
54	18	FL	A	Plymouth Argyle	W	3-1	1-1	5	Freestone 8, 47, 90	(6389)
55	25	FL	H	Fulham	W	1-0	0-0	5	Peer 58	7443
56	M 02	FL	A	York City	D	0-0	0-0	4		(6688)
57	10	PO SF1	A	Bristol Rovers	L	1-3	0-2		Gayle 74	(9173)
58	13	PO SF2	H	Bristol Rovers	W	3-0	1-0		Heggs 34, Clarkson 61, Warburton 77	7501
59	24	PO F	N	Grimsby Town	L	0-1	0-1			(62988)

Best Home League Attendance: 7443 V Fulham   Smallest :4824 V Chesterfield   Average :6393

Goal Scorers:

FL	(52)	Seal 12, Freestone 11, Gayle 6, Dozzell 4, Heggs 4, Hunter 3, Sampson 3, Peer 2, Brightwell 1, Clarkson 1, Frain 1, Gibb 1, Gleghorn 1, Parrish 1, Opponents 1
CC	(3)	Gayle 2, Seal 1
FAC	(4)	Hunter 2, Heggs 1, Seal 1
AWS	(7)	Heggs 3, Freestone 2, Frain 1, Sampson 1
PO	(4)	Clarkson 1, Gayle 1, Heggs 1, Warburton 1

(M) Bishop	(D) Brightwell	(D) Clarkson	(F) Conway	(M) Dozzell	(M) Frain	(F) Freestone	(F) Gayle	(M) Gibb	(M) Gleghorn	(M) Heggs	(M) Hill	(M) Hunt	(M) Hunter	(M) Lee	(M) Parrish	(M) Peer	(M) Potter	(D) Rennie	(D) Sampson	(F) Seal	(M) Tait	(G) Turley	(F) Van Dullemen	(D) Warburton	(M) Warner	(M) West	(F) Wilson	(G) Woodman		
	X	X		X	X		S2			X			X	X	X				X	S1		S3		X				X	1	E. Lomas
	X	X		X	S1		S3			X			X	X	X				X	X		S2		X				X	2	J Kirkby
	X	X	X		X		S			S1			X	S		X			X	X				X				X	3	B Knight
	X	X	X		X		S			S2			X			X	S1		X	X				X				X	4	P Taylor
	X	X		X	X		S2			S1			X			X	S		X	X				X				X	5	M R Halsey
	X	S2		X	X		S			S1			X			X	X		X	X				X				X	6	R Pearson
	X	X		X	X		S			S1			X			X	X		X	X				X		S2		X	7	T Heilbron
	X	X		X	X		S			S			X			X	X		X	X				X		S1		X	8	R J Harris
	X	X		X	X		S			S1			X			X	X		X	X1				X		S2		X	9	G B Frankland
	X	X		X	X		S			X			X			X		S1	X1	X				X	S			X	10	P S Danson
	X	X		X	X		S2			X			X			X		X	X1	X				X	S			X	11	S J Baines
	X	X		X			S2			S1			X			X	X		X	X				X	X	S		X	12	A N Butler
	X	X		X	X		S3			S1			X	X	X	X	S2		X	X				X				X	13	F G Stretton
	X	X		X	X		S2			X			X			X		S1	X	X				X		S3		X	14	G Singh
	X	X		X	X		S2			X		S1	X	S		X	X		X	X				X				X	15	M J Brandwood
	X	X		X	X		S1			S3		S2	X			X	X		X	X				X				X	16	M Fletcher
	X	X		X	X		S1			X		S	X	S		X	X		X	X				X			S	X	17	S W Mathieson
	X	X		X	X		S2			X			X	S3		X	S1	X	X	X				X				X	18	K M Lynch
	X	X		X	X		S1			S2		S3	X			X			X	X				X	X			X	19	G Laws
	X	X		X	S1		X			S	X	S2	X			X	X	X	X	S				X		S		X	20	K M Lynch
	X	X		X	X		S1			X			X			X	S2	X		X	X				X		S3			21	M E Pierce
		X		X			S1		X		X	X	X	X	X				X	X				X	S	S2		X	22	J P Robinson
	X	X		X	S1		X			X			X	X	X				X	X	S	S	S	X	S	S2		X	23	K M Lynch
	X	X2		X			X	X		X	X		X					X1	S1					X	S2	S		X	24	M D Messias
	X	X		X	X		S2			X	X	X2	X					X1						X	S	S1		X	25	E K Wolstenholme
	X	X		X	X1	X				X	X	S1	X						X	S		X	S		X	S	S		X	26	A N Butler
		X		X	S3	X3	X			S2	X1	X	X			X				X	X		X	X2						27	
X	X	X			S1	X	S2			X	X	X	X	X				X2		X1						S			X	28	M S Pike
	X	X		X	X	X2				X	X	X1	X			X			S1		S			S2		S		X	29	D Orr
X2	X	X		X			S2			X3	X	S1	X1			X			S3										X	30	D Pugh
	X	X	X2	X	X1						X	X	X			X			S	S1				S2				X	31	C R Wilkes
	X	X	X3	X	S1	X2				S2	X		X			X			X1	X				S3				X	32	R D Furnandiz
X3	X	X		X	X	X2	S1			32	X1	S3	X		X				S		S			X		S2		X	33	A B Wilkie
	X	X		X3	X	X2	S2	X		S1	X		X			X1				S3	X							X	34	M C Bailey
		X		X	X	X				X1		X	X	X	X				X					X		S1			35	
		X	X	X2	S1					X1	X	X	X	S2	X				X	X				X	X			X	36	B Coddington
	X			X	X	S1				X	X	X							X	S				X	X			X	37	D J Hine
	X			X2	X	X	S2	X			X1	X			X3				X	S3		X		X	S1				38	
	X	X		X	X	X	S1	S			X	X	X			S			X	X1				X				X	39	D Orr
	X	X		X	X	X2	S			X	X	X1							X	S2				X		S1		X	40	R Pearson
	X	X		X	X1	X				S2	X	X							X	X2				X	S3	S1		X	41	G Cain
	X				X	X		S2		X									X	X2				X	X1	S1		X	42	A R Leake
	X	X		X2	X	X	S2	S		X									X	X1				X		S1		X	43	A P D'Urso
	X1	X2		X3	X	X	S2	S1		X									X	S3				X				X	44	M R Halsey
X2		X1		S2	X	X	S1	X		X									X	X3				X	S3			X	45	B Knight
	S			X2	X	X	S1	S		X			X	S2					X	X1				X				X	46	D R Crick
X		X		X2	X	X3	S2	S3	S1	X1	X								X					X				X	47	P Rejer
X		X		X2	X	X1	S2	S1		X3	X	S3							X					X				X	48	M J Jones
	X	X		X1	X	X	S2	S	X1	X2									X					X				X	49	A G Wiley
	X2	X3		S1	X	X		S3	S2	X	X								X					X			X1	X	50	C R Wilkes
	X	S2		X	X		S1	X2	X	X3	S3								X					X				X	51	A R Hall
X		X		S	X	X	S1			X	X	X							X					X1				X	52	E K Wolstenholme
		X		X1	X	X2	S1			X	X3	X							S3					X		S2		X	53	M Fletcher
X		X		S	X	X	S1			X	X	X							X	X1				X			S	X	54	K A Leach
		X		X	X	S1	S			X	X	X							X	X1				X			S	X	55	C J Foy
	S3	X1		X3	X	X	S2	S1		X	X	X							X	X2				X				X	56	A N Butler
X1		X		X2	X	X	S2			X3	X							S1		X	S3				X				X	57	R J Harris
	S1	X			X	X1	X	S		X	X	X							X	S				X				X	58	M Fletcher
	X			S	X	X	X1	S2		X	X2	X							X	S1				X				X	59	T Heilbron
7	34	42	2	18	45	23	26	6	3	21	27	14	28	3	12	26	4	3	39	30	2			39	3	1	1	46		FL Appearances
1				1	3		9	28	5	12		7		3		4		2		7	1		1			7	1	8		FL Sub Appearances
2	2	1		2			1+1	0+2		1+1			2		1	2			2	2				0+1	2					CC Appearances
1	5	5	1	5	1		4	2+3		4+1	3	1+2	5	1+1		4			1	2	2+1			3	0+1		0+1	5		FAC Appearances
	2	1		2	3	2+1	1+1			2	1+1	3	3	1		1	1+1			2+1				2	0+2			3		AWS Appearances
1	0+1	3		1	3	3	3	0+2		2	3	3		2+1					2+1	0+2				3				3		PO Appearances

Also Played: (D) Colkin S1(27), S(29,36), X(35). (D) Drysdale X1(51). (M) Ten Heuvel S(42).

NORTHAMPTON TOWN   RECORDS AND STATISTICS

CLUB RECORDS

BIGGEST VICTORIES
League: 10-0 v Walsall, Division 3(S), 5.11.1927.
F.A. Cup: 10-0 v Sutton, 7.12.1907.
League Cup: 8-0 v Brighton, 1.11.1966.

BIGGEST DEFEATS
League: 0-10 v Bournemouth, Division 3(S), 2.9.1939.
F.A. Cup: 2-8 v Manchester United (h), 5th Round, 7.2.1970.
League Cup: 0-5 v Fulham, 13.10.1965. 0-5 v Ipswich, 30.8.1977.
0-5 v Orient, 20.8.1991.

MOST POINTS
3 points a win: 99, Division 4, 1986-87.
2 points a win: 68, Division 4, 1975-76.

MOST GOALS SCORED
109, Division 3(S), 1952-53, Division 3, 1962-63.

RECORD TRANSFER FEE RECEIVED
£265,000 from Watford for Richard Hill, March 1987.

RECORD TRANSFER FEE PAID
£90,000 to Bristol City for David Seal, 11 August 1997.

BEST PERFORMANCES
League: 21st Division 1, 1965-66.
F.A. Cup: 5th Round 1911-12, 1933-34, 1949-50, 1969-70.
League Cup: 5th Round 1964-65, 1966-67.

HONOURS
Champions Division 3, 1962-63.
Champions Division 4, 1986-87.

LEAGUE CAREER
Original members of Division 3 1920, Transferred to Div 3(S) 1921,
Div 4 1957-58, Div 3 1960-61, Div 2 1962-63, Div 1 1964-65, Div 2
1965-66, Div 3 1966-67, Div 4 1968-69, Div 3 1975-76, Div 4 1976-
77, Div 3 1986-87, Div 4 (now Div 3) 1989-90, Div 2 1997-98.

INDIVIDUAL CLUB RECORDS

MOST GOALS IN A SEASON
Cliff Holton: 39 goals in 1961-62 (League 36, FA Cup 3).

MOST GOALS IN A MATCH
5. R Hoten v Crystal Palace (h) 8-1, Division 3(S), 27.10.1928.
5. A Dawes v Lloyds Bank (h) 8-1, FA Cup 1st Round, 26.11.1932.

OLDEST PLAYER
E Lloyd-Davies, 42 years, 1919.

YOUNGEST PLAYER
Adrian Mann, 16 years 297 days v Bury, 5.5.1984.

MOST CAPPED PLAYER
E Lloyd-Davies (Wales) 12.

PREVIOUS MANAGERS

1903-12 Herbert Chapman, 1912-13 Walter Bull, 1913-19 Fred
Lessons, 1920-25 Bob Hewison, 1925-31 Jack Tresadern, 1931-36
Jack English Snr., 1936-37 Sid Puddlefoot, 1937-War Warney
Cresswell, War-1949 Tom Smith, 1949-55 Bob Dennison, 1955-59
Dave Smith, 1959-63 Dave Bowen, 1963 Jack Jennings (caretaker),
1963-67 Dave Bowen, 1967-68 Tony Marchi, 1968-69 Ron Flowers,
1969-72 Dave Bowen, 1972-73 Bill Baxter, 1973-76 Bill Dodgin,
1976-77 Pat Crerand, 1977 Committee*, 1977-78 John Petts, 1978-
79 Mike Keen, 1979-80 Clive Walker, 1980-81 Bill Dodgin, 1981-84
Clive Walker, 1984-85 Tony Barton, 1985-90 Graham Carr, 1990-92
Theo Foley, 1992-93 Phil Chard, 1993- 94 John Barnwell.
*Committee: 1 director, 1 coach, 2 senior players.

ADDITIONAL INFORMATION
PREVIOUS NAMES
None.
PREVIOUS LEAGUES
Northants League, Midland League and Southern League.
Club colours: Claret shirts, with white shoulders, white shorts,
claret socks.
Change colours: White shirts with claret shoulders, claret shorts,
white socks
Youth Team League: Midland Melville Youth League.

LONGEST LEAGUE RUNS

of undefeated matches:	21 (1986-87)	of league matches w/out a win:	18 (1969)
of undefeated home matches:	29 (1932-33, 1975-76)	of undefeated away matches:	12 (1986-87)
without home win:	11 (1989-90)	without an away win:	33 (1921-23)
of league wins:	8 (1960)	of home wins:	12 (1927)
of league defeats:	8 (1935)	of away wins:	5 (1978)

THE MANAGER

IAN ATKINS . . . . appointed January 1995.

PREVIOUS CLUBS
As Manager . . . . Colchester United (player-manager), Cambridge United (player-manager), Doncaster Rovers.
As Asst.Man/Coach . . . . Birmingham City.
As a player . . . . Shrewsbury Town, Sunderland, Everton, Ipswich Town, Birmingham.

HONOURS
As a Manager . . . . **Birmingham:** Promotion. **Northampton:** Promotion to Division 2 1996/97.
As a Player . . . . **Everton:** Div.1 champions, ECWC winner. **Shrewsbury:** Promotion from Div.4, Div.3 champions.

NORTHAMPTON TOWN

PLAYERS NAME Honours	Ht	Wt	Birthdate	Birthplace Transfers	Contract Date	Clubs	League	L/Cup	FA Cup	Other	Lge	L/C	FAC	Oth
G O A L K E E P E R														
Newell Paul C	6.1	14.7	2/23/69	Woolwich	6/17/87	Southen Utd (T)	15		2	1				
				£5000	8/6/90	Leyton Orient	61	3	3	4				
Loan 8/12/92 Colchester Utd 14 Lge, 2 LC apps				Free	7/26/94	Barnet	16		1					
via 9/5/97 Colchester United				Free	1/29/96	Darlington	41	4	2	4				
				Free	2/27/98	Northampton Town								
Turley Billy			7/15/73			Evesham								
				Free	6/1/95	Northampton Town	3							
				Loan	2/5/98	Leyton Orient	14							
Woodman Andrew	6.1	12.4	8/11/71	Camberwell	7/1/89	Crystal Palace								
				Free	7/4/94	Exeter City	6	1	1	2				
				Free	3/10/95	Northampton Town	145	8	8	10				
D E F E N C E														
Bishop Darren C DIV3 96/97	6	13.7	2/16/68	Nottingham		Stoke City (T)								
				Free	4/17/86	Watford								
				Free	8/10/87	Bury	104+10	5	4	12+1	6		1	
				£50000	7/24/91	Barnsley	124+6	11+1	9	5	1			
				Loan	1/12/96	Preston North End	4							
				Loan	3/28/96	Burnley	9							
				£20000	8/15/96	Wigan Athletic	27+1	1		2				
					12/12/97	Northampton Town	7		1	1				
Clarkson Ian	5.11	11.8	12/4/70	Solihull	12/15/88	Birmingham City	125+11	12	5+1	17+1				
				£40000	9/13/93	Stoke City	72+3	6	5	8+2				
					8/2/96	Northampton Town	87	6	6	6	1			1
Hill Colin F via Maritimo 7/86.	6	12.11	11/12/63	Uxbridge	8/7/81	Arsenal (T)	46	4	1		1			
				Free	10/30/87	Colchester United	64+5	2	7	3+1			2	
				£85000	8/1/89	Sheffield United	77+5	5	10+2	3	1			
				£200000	3/26/92	Leicester City	140+5	10+2	8	9+1		1		
				Free	7/1/97	Trelleborg								
				Free	11/7/97	Northampton Town	27		3	6				
Sampson Ian	6.2	12.8	11/14/68	Wakefield		Goole Town								
					11/13/90	Sunderland	13+4	1	0+2	0+1	1			
				Loan	12/8/93	Northampton Town	8							
				Free	8/5/94	Northampton Town	154+3	10	4	11	14			1
Spedding Duncan	6.1	11.1	07/09/77	Camberley	31/05/97	Southampton (T)	4+3	0+1						
				£60000	7/1/98	Northampton Town								
Warburton Raymond	6	11.5	10/7/67	Rotherham	10/5/85	Rotherham United	3+1		2	2				
				Free	8/8/89	York City	86+4	8	6	7	9	1	1	
				£35000	2/4/94	Northampton Town	174	6	7	13	11		1	3
M I D F I E L D														
Gibb Alistair	5.9	10.08	2/17/76	Salisbury	7/1/94	Norwich City								
				Loan	9/22/95	Northampton Town								
				£15000	2/5/96	Northampton Town	24+50	3+3	2+3	2+3	4			
Hunt James	5.8	10.3	12/17/76	Derby	7/15/94	Notts County	15+4		0+1	0+2	1			
				Free	8/7/97	Northampton Town	14+7		1+2	3				
Hunter Roy	5.9	10.12	10/29/73	Middlesbrough	3/4/92	WBA			4+1	1				
				Free	6/1/95	Northampton Town	80+17	6	8	7	9		2	1
Matthew Damian E: u21.9. Div.1'94.	5.11	10.1	9/23/70	Islington	6/13/89	Chelsea	13+8	5		1				
				Loan	9/25/92	Luton Town	3+2				1			
				£150000	2/11/94	Crystal Palace	17+7	2+1	1		1			
				Loan	1/12/96	Bristol Rovers								
				Loan	0/13/96	Burnley	21+6	3+1			1			
				Free	7/1/98	Northampton Town								
Parrish Sean	5.9	10	3/14/72	Wrexham	7/12/90	Shrewsbury Town	1+2	1		3				1
				Free	8/1/91	Telford United			4					
				£20000	5/28/94	Doncaster Rovers	40+2	2	1	1	5			
				Free	8/2/96	Northampton Town	48+2	5	1	3	9			1
Peer Dean AMC'91.	6.2	11.5	8/8/69	Stourbridge	7/9/87	Birmingham City	106+14	14+1	2+1	11+1	8	3		1
				Loan	12/18/92	Mansfield Town	10			1				
				Free	11/16/93	Walsall	41+4	2	4+2	3	8			
				Free	6/1/95	Northampton Town	70+23	3+2	6	6+3	4	1		
Warner Michael	5.9	10.10	1/17/74	Harrogate		Tamworth								
					6/1/95	Northampton Town	4+15		0+2					
				Loan	2/16/96	Telford United								
F O R W A R D														
Corazzin Carlo	5.9	12.5	12/25/71	Canada		Vancouver								
				£20000	12/10/93	Cambridge United	73+1	2	4	3	29			2
				£150000	3/28/96	Plymouth Argyle	58+13	2+1	2+2	+1	23		1	
				Free	7/1/98	Northampton Town								
Freestone Christopher	5.11	11.7	9/4/71	Nottingham		Arnold								
				£10000	12/2/94	Middlesbrough	2+6	1+1	0+1		1	1		
				Loan	4/3/97	Carlisle United	3+2				2			
				£75000	12/12/97	Northampton Town	22+2		1	3	11			
Heggs Carl	6	11.1	11/10/70	Leicester		Leicester United								
					22/08/91	W.B.A.	13+27	2	0+1	6+3	3			1
				Loan	27/01/95	Bristol Rovers	2+3				1			
				£60000	01/06/95	Swansea City	33+13	2	2	4+1	7			1
				£40000	8/1/97	Northampton Town	21+12	1+1	4+1	3+1	4		1	3
Lee Christian	6.2	11.7	10/8/76	Aylesbury		Doncaster Rovers								
				Free	7/13/95	Northampton Town	16+24	2	2+3	3+2	7	2		
Seal David	5.11	12.4	1/26/72	Sydney (Aus)		Eendracht Aalst(Bel)								
				£80000	10/5/94	Bristol City	24+27	4+1	1+1	2+1	10	3		1
					6/11/97	Northampton Town	29+7	1	2+1	+2	12	1	1	
Wilkinson Paul E: u21.4; CS'86; Div1'87	6	11.9	10/30/69	Louth	11/8/82	Grimsby Town	69+2	10	4+2		27	5	1	
				£250000	3/28/85	Everton	19+12	3+1	3	6+2	6	7	1	1
				£200000	3/26/87	Nottingham Forest	32+2	3	4+1	1	5	1	2	
				£300000	8/16/88	Watford	133+1	4	8+1	8	52	1		3
				£550000	8/16/91	Middlesbrough	159+4	16	11	5+1	53	8	5	4
				Loan	10/26/95	Oldham Athletic	4		1		1			1
				Loan	12/1/95	Watford	4							
				Loan	3/28/96	Luton Town	3							
				Free	7/19/96	Barnsley	48+1	4	2		9	2		
				£100000	9/18/97	Millwall	22+8	1	1	1	3			
				Free	7/1/98	Northampton Town								
Wilson Kevin J NI: 42. Div.2'89. FMC'90.	5.7	10.7	4/18/61	Banbury		Banbury United								
				£20000	12/21/79	Derby County	106+16	8+3	8		30	8	3	
				£100000	1/5/85	Ipswich Town	94+4	8	10	7	34	8	3	4
				£335000	6/25/87	Chelsea	124+28	10+2	7+1	14+5	42	4	1	8
				£225000	3/27/92	Notts County	58+11	3+1	2	5+1	3			
				Loan	1/13/94	Bradford City	5							
				Free	8/2/94	Walsall	123+1	8	13	5	37	3	7	1
					7/14/97	Northampton Town	1+8		0+1					

443

SIXFIELDS
Upton Way, Northampton NN5 5QA

Capacity..7,653.

First game ....v Barnet, Division 3, 15.10.1994.
First floodlit game ....v Barnet, AMC, 1.11.1994.

ATTENDANCES
Highest ....7,478 v Arsenal, Testimonial, 14.08.96.
Lowest..2,109 v Plymouth Argyle, AMC, 07.11.95.

OTHER GROUNDS ....County Ground 1897-94.

HOW TO GET TO THE GROUND
From the North and West
M1 to junction 16. Take A45 (signposted Northampton/Duston). After approx. 3.25 miles there is a roundabout; take the fourth exit onto Upton Way for the ground.

From the South
M1 to junction 15a, then A43 (signposted Northampton) to A45 Northampton Ring Road. Bear left (signposted Daventry) at second roundabout, then take first exit into Upton Way and the ground is immediately on the left.

From the East
Either A43 or A428 to A45. Once on the A45, follow signs for Daventry until you pass the Rugby Ground (Franklin Gardens). At the second roundabout after this, take the first exit into Upton Way for the ground.

Car Parking: There is on-site parking at Sixfields with six overflow car parks to take the strain on busy days.
Nearest Railway Station: Castle Station (01908 370 883 - Milton Keynes Enqs.)

USEFUL TELEPHONE NUMBERS

Club switchboard 01604 757 773
Club fax number..........01604 751 613
Club Shop...............01604 759 456
Ticket Office.............01604 588 338

Marketing Department 01604 757 773 Ext.213
Internet address ....www.NTFC.co.uk
Clubcall 0839 66 44 77*
*Calls cost 50p per minute at all times. Call costings correct at time of going to press.

MATCHDAY PROGRAMME

Programme Editor ....Mike Berry.

Number of pages ....48.

Price ....£1.80.

Subscriptions ....Apply to club.

Local Newspapers
.. Chronicle and Echo, Evening Telegraph,
...................Northants Post.

Local Radio Stations
.... Northants Radio, Radio Northampton.

MATCHDAY TICKET PRICES

West Stand

Upper	£13.50
Concessions	£9.50
Lower	£12.50
Concessions	£8.50

East Stand

Adult	£11.50
Concessions	£6.00
Family Tandem	£14.50
Family Tricycle	£17.50
Family Two+Two	£29.00

North Stand

Adult	£10.50
Concessions	£7.50
Wheelchair	£6.00
Carer/Companion	£6.00

NOTTS COUNTY
(The Magpies)
NATIONWIDE LEAGUE DIVISION 2
SPONSORED BY: SAPA LTD

1997-98 - Back Row L-R: Paul Mitchell, Gary Martindale, Craig Dudley, Gary Jones, Ian Baraclough, Phil Robinson, Mark Robson, Steve Finnan.
Middle Row: Roger Cleary (Physio), Shaun Cunnington, Ian Hendon, James Lindley, Andrew Norwood, Shaun Derry, Ian Richardson, Alan Young (Youth Manager)
Front Row: Dean Randall, Gary Strodder, Matt Redmile, Mark Smith (Asst. Manager), Sam Allardyce (Manager), Devon White, Graeme Hogg, Sean Farrell.

NOTTS COUNTY
FORMED IN 1862 (Oldest League Club)
TURNED PROFESSIONAL IN 1885
LTD COMPANY IN 1890

CHAIRMAN: D C Pavis
VICE-CHAIRMAN
J Mounteney
DIRECTORS
W Barrowcliffe, G Davey (Managing),
Mrs V Pavis,
M Youdell MBE
SECRETARY
Ian Moat
COMMERCIAL MANGER
Clair Finnigan
MANAGER: Sam Allardyce
ASSISTANT MANAGER: Mark Smith

YOUTH TEAM MANAGER
Gary Brazil
PHYSIOTHERAPIST
Roger Cleary

STATISTICIAN FOR THE DIRECTORY
Ian Moat

Notts County became the first team since Jack Charlton's Middlesbrough back in season 1973-74, to clinch promotion during the month of March. The 'Magpies' actually made sure of the Third Division championship when defeating Leyton Orient by a goal to nil in front of their home fans on 28 March - this after an amazing run of results which saw them amass 53 points out a possible 60.

Managed by Sam Allardyce, the former defensive journeyman who starred with so many different clubs during the 1960s and '70s, assembled a very resilient squad at Meadow Lane and there is no doubt that County were by far the best team in the Third Division, losing only five games out of the 46 played, two at home. They scored 82 League goals and finished with a massive haul of 99 points. No team in the country in any Division including the Premiership - won more away games that County (15) and indeed, their three away defeats was equalled only by Watford.

Staring off with a 2-1 win over Rochdale, County were on top of the table as September gave way to October and at the turn of the year they were still on top of the pile with 50 points already in the bank from 25 matches.

Into February, with 30 games played, and ace striker Gary Jones in cracking form (he ended up with 28 goals to his credit - the Division's top marksman) the 'flying' Magpies were well on their way to glory, leading second-placed Peterborough United by 13 points (65-52). And when they had completed their 40th League game (on 28 March) the promotion celebrations started in earnest.

Notts County are back - and now they will be striving to close the gap between themselves and their arch rivals Forest by quickly gaining promotion to the First Division. Play it again Sam!

Tony Matthews.

NOTTS COUNTY

Division 3		:1st			FA CUP: 2nd Round			LC CUP: 2nd Round	AWS: Northern Round 2

M	DATE	COMP.	VEN	OPPONENTS	RESULT	H/T	LP	GOAL SCORERS/GOAL TIMES	ATT.
1	A 09	FL	H	Rochdale	W 2-1	1-0	6	Robson 45 (pen), Redmile 88	4173
2	12	CC 1/1	A	Darlington	D 1-1	1-1		White 3	(2189)
3	15	FL	A	Hull City	W 3-0	1-0	1	Redmile 31, White 71, Jones 73	(7412)
4	23	FL	H	Lincoln City	L 1-2	0-1	4	White 63	5707
5	26	CC 1/2	H	Darlington	W 2-1	1-0		Baraclough 25 (pen), Hendon 103	1925
6	30	FL	A	Cardiff City	D 1-1	1-1	7	Finnan 9	(6191)
7	S 02	FL	A	Hartlepool United	D 1-1	0-0	8	Baraclough 52 (pen)	(2010)
8	07	FL	H	Scunthorpe United	W 2-1	1-0	5	Redmile 6, Derry 86	5009
9	13	FL	H	Mansfield Town	W 1-0	1-0	2	Martindale 24	6706
10	16	CC 2/1	H	Tranmere Rovers	L 0-2	0-1			1779
11	20	FL	A	Shrewsbury Town	W 2-1	0-0	2	Jones 71, Finnan 82	(2532)
12	23	CC 2/2	A	Tranmere Rovers	W 1-0	1-0		Dudley 43	(3287)
13	27	FL	A	Scarborough	W 2-1	1-1	1	Baraclough 3 (pen), Farrell 75	(2751)
14	O 04	FL	H	Darlington	D 1-1	1-1	2	Dudley 3	4428
15	11	FL	H	Macclesfield Town	D 1-1	1-0	3	Richardson 43	4871
16	18	FL	A	Swansea City	W 2-1	0-1	3	Jones 57, Jackson 77	(3668)
17	21	FL	A	Rotherham United	D 1-1	1-0	3	Farrell 40	(3161)
18	25	FL	H	Cambridge United	W 1-0	0-0	2	Jones 49	4279
19	N 01	FL	A	Barnet	W 2-1	0-0	1	Baraclough 64, Derry 82	(2530)
20	04	FL	H	Chester City	L 1-2	0-0	2	Strodder 60	3104
21	08	FL	H	Exeter City	D 1-1	0-0	2	Strodder 56	5107
22	16	FAC 1	H	Colwyn Bay	W 2-0	0-0		Hogg 59, Richardson 67	3074
23	18	FL	A	Colchester United	L 0-2	0-0	3		(2643)
24	22	FL	A	Leyton Orient	D 1-1	0-0	4	Farrell 67	(4372)
25	29	FL	H	Peterborough United	D 2-2	2-1	4	Jones 27, Robson 39	8006
26	D 03	FL	A	Brighton & H.A.	W 1-0	1-0	3	Farrell 7	(1279)
27	06	FAC 2	A	Preston North End	D 2-2	1-1		Derry 84	(7583)
28	13	FL	H	Doncaster Rovers	W 5-2	3-1	1	Baraclough 2, 8 (pen), Finnan 74, Farrell 85, Utley 22 (OG)	4024
29	16	FAC 2R	H	Preston North End	L 1-2	0-0		Farrell 51	3052
30	20	FL	A	Torquay United	W 2-0	1-0	1	Farrell 9, 72	(2536)
31	26	FL	A	Scunthorpe United	W 2-1	1-1	1	Jones 6, 48	(4781)
32	28	FL	H	Hartlepool United	W 2-0	1-0	1	Farrell 13, 87	6073
33	J 10	FL	A	Rochdale	W 2-1	0-0	1	Jones 68, Robinson 72	(2387)
34	17	FL	H	Cardiff City	W 3-1	1-1	1	Robinson 21, Jones 76, 79	6448
35	20	FL	H	Hull City	W 1-0	0-0	1	Richardson 55	4017
36	24	FL	A	Lincoln City	W 5-3	3-0	1	Farrell 5, 72, Baraclough 25, Strodder 35, Jones 62	(5911)
37	27	AWS N2	A	Burnley	L 0-2	0-0			(2442)
38	31	FL	A	Mansfield Town	W 2-0	2-0	1	Jones 16, 31	(6786)
39	F 06	FL	H	Shrewsbury Town	D 1-1	0-1	1	Jones 90	5789
40	14	FL	A	Darlington	W 2-0	2-0	1	Jones 16, Finnan 24	(2781)
41	21	FL	H	Scarborough	W 1-0	1-0	1	Farrell 6	5645
42	24	FL	H	Swansea City	W 2-1	2-1	1	Jones 11, 41	4484
43	28	FL	A	Macclesfield Town	L 0-2	0-0	1		(5122)
44	M 03	FL	A	Exeter City	W 5-2	3-1	1	Robson 7, Farrell 10, 35, Jones 48, 77	(2966)
45	07	FL	H	Barnet	W 2-0	1-0	1	Jones 33, Hughes 85	6180
46	14	FL	A	Chester City	W 1-0	0-0	1	Jones 85	(2753)
47	21	FL	H	Colchester United	D 0-0	0-0	1		6284
48	28	FL	H	Leyton Orient	W 1-0	0-0	1	Robson 50	8383
49	A 03	FL	A	Peterborough United	L 0-1	0-0	1		(6498)
50	11	FL	H	Brighton & H.A.	D 2-2	0-1	1	Hughes 61, Jones 75	5344
51	13	FL	A	Doncaster Rovers	W 2-1	0-0	1	Strodder 56, Finnan 64	(2485)
52	18	FL	H	Torquay United	W 3-0	1-0	1	Pearce 1, Jones 74, 78	5183
53	25	FL	A	Cambridge United	D 2-2	1-2	1	Jones 26, 75	(4009)
54	M 02	FL	H	Rotherham United	W 5-2	1-1	1	Jones 30, 73, Pearce 50, Farrell 75, Robinson 89	12430

Best Home League Attendance: 12430 V Rotherham United	Smallest :3104 V Chester City	Average :5725

Goal Scorers:

FL	(82)	Jones 28, Farrell 15, Baraclough 6, Finnan 5, Robson 4, Strodder 4, Redmile 3, Robinson 3, Derry 2, Hughes 2, Pearce 2, Richardson 2, White 2, Dudley 1, Jackson 1, Martindale 1, Opponents 1
CC	(4)	Baraclough 1, Dudley 1, Hendon 1, White 1
FAC	(4)	Derry 1, Farrell 1, Hogg 1, Richardson 1
AWS	(0)	

1997-98

(F) Baraclough	(M) Cunnington	(D) Derry	(M) Diuk	(F) Dudley	(F) Dyer	(F) Farrell	(F) Finnan	(D) Hendon	(F) Hogg	(M) Hughes	(M) Jackson	(F) Jones	(F) Kiwomya	(F) Lormor	(F) Martindale	(D) Mitchell	(M) Otto	(D) Pearce	(G) Pollitt	(M) Poric	(D) Redmile	(M) Richardson	(M) Robinson	(F) Robson	(F) Stevens	(D) Strodder	(G) Ward	(F) White		
S1	X		X3			X	X				X							X1			X	S2	X2	X		X	X	S3	M.D.Messias	1
S1	X	X	S			X	X				X							X			X	S	X	X		X	X	X	A W Mathieson	2
S2	X	X	S			X	X				X							X			X	S1	X	X		X	X	X	B Coddington	3
X			S1			X	X	X			X				S2			X	S		X	X	X				X	X	P R Richards	4
X			S1			X	X	X			X				S2	S		X			X	X				X	X	X	E Lomas	5
X	S2	S				X	X	X			X1				S1			X			X	X	X			X	X	X2	R Styles	6
X	S	X				X	X	X			X				S			X			X	S1	X			X	X	X	G Laws	7
X	S	X	S1			X	S				X				X	X	X				X		X			X	X	X	D R Crick	8
X		X	S3			X	X		S2		X				X	X	X				X		X			X	X	S1	G Cain	9
X	S2	S3	S1			X	X				X				X	X	X				X		X			X	X	X	S G Bennett	10
X	X	X	S2			X	X		S1		X				X			X			X	S3					X	X	A R Hall	11
X	X	X		X	X	X	X	S1		X				S2				X			X	X			S3		X		R Pearson	12
X		X	X	S1		X	X				X				S			X			X	X	S2			X	X	X	C J Foy	13
X		X	X	S1	X	X				X				S2		S			X			X	X			X	X	X	A G Wiley	14
X		X	X	S1	S2	X				X				S3		X	X			X		X				X	X		K M Lynch	15
X		X	S			X	X	X			X				S2			S1			X	X		X			X	X	P Rejer	16
X		X	S			X	X	X			X				S1			X				X	X				X	X	J P Robinson	17
X		X	S			X	X	X			X				X			X				X	S2	X			X	X	G Singh	18
X		X				X	X	X			X				X			X				X	S2	X			X	X	C R Wilkes	19
X		X				X	X	X			X				X			X				X	S2	X			X	X	P Taylor	20
X		X	X			X	X	X			S2							X			S1	X	X	X1			X	X	M S Pike	21
	S3		X			X	X	X		S	S1				X				X	X	X	X				X	X		T Jones	22
X		X				X	X	X		X	X				S2			X			X	S1	S	X			X	X	R Styles	23
X		X				X	X	X		S1	X				X			X			X	S	X2				X	X	M C Bailey	24
X		X	S1		X	X1	X				X				S			X			X	S2	X2				X	X	M J Brandwood	25
X		X	S2		X1	X	X				S				S1			X			X	X	X2				X	X	S G Bennett	26
X	S	X	S2			X	X			S3	X2				X3			S1	S		X	X1	X				X	X	P S Danson	27
X3		X				X2	X		X		S3				S2			X			X	S1	X1				X	X	E Lomas	28
X		X	S2			X3	X	X			X2				S3			X			X	S	S1	X1			X	X	P S Danson	29
X		X		X3	X	X				X1	S2				S1			X			X	S3	X2				X	X	M Fletcher	30
X1		X		X3	X	X				X	S				S2			X			X	S1	X2				X	X	D Pugh	31
X	S	X				X	X	X			X	S			S			S1			X		X				X	X	M J Jones	32
X	S	X				X	X	X			X	S			S1			X			X	X	X					X	A R Hall	33
X	S2	X				X	X	X1			X				S			X			X	X	X2					X	G B Frankland	34
X	S	X				X	X	X			X				S			X			X	X	X			X	X	X	E K Wolstenholme	35
X		X				X1	X				X	S			S1			X			X	X	X	S		X	X		W C Burns	36
X3	X		S3								X		X		X	X1		X			X2	X	X				X			37
X						X	X	X1	S1		X							S3			X2	X	X				X	X	R Pearson	38
X			S2			X	X	X1	S1		X				S			S			X	X	X				X	X	K M Lynch	39
X	S1		S			X1	X	X			X				S			X			X	X	X				X	X	A Bates	40
X	S1					X2	X	X			S3				X		S2	X3			X1	X	X				X	X	S J Baines	41
X	X					X2	X	X1			X				S2	S1					X	X	X	S			X	X	M L Dean	42
X			S1			X	X				X1	S2				X			X			X	X1	S1				X	P R Richards	43
X			S2	X	X	X				X			X2		S1	S2	S				X	X1	X				X	X	C R Wilkes	44
X				X	X2	X	X				X				S2	S					X	X	X1	S1			X	X	T Jones	45
X				X	X2	X	X				X	S3	X3	S2				X	X			X	X	S1		S1	X		T Heilbron	46
	S1					X	X1	X	X	X1	S3	X3	S1					X			X	X				X	X	E Lomas	47
						X	X2	X	X	X	S2						X		S1	S	X	X1				X	X	G Singh	48
				X	X1	X	X			X2	X1	X				S		X			S2	X	X				X	X	D Orr	49
			S2	X		X				X	X2	X				S		X1	X			X	S1				X	X	D R Crick	50
	S2		S1	X		X				X	X1	X				S		X			X	X2	X				X	X	M D Messias	51
	S2		S1	X		X				X	X1	X				S3		X			X	X2	X				X	X	M Fletcher	52
			S2			X	X	X2			X	S3	X					X			X1	X3			S1		X	X	J P Robinson	53
	S			S	X	X				X	S1	X						X			X1	X		X			X	X	B Knight	54
36	3	27	5	10	32	41	38	4	12	4	43		2	5		4	37	2	3		32	25	30	26		37	44	4	FL Appearances	
2	6	1	1	12	3	3			3	11	1		2	5	17	1		1		1	2	5	10	2		2		2	FL Sub Appearances	
3+1	1+1	2+1	0+1	1+1		1	4	4	1+1						2+1		1+1		2	3	4	2	2		0+1	3	4	3	CC Appearances	
2		1+2		1+2	2	3	2+1	1	0+1	2+1							1+1			2+1		3	1	2+1	3		3	3	FAC Appearances	
1	1	0+1					1	1							1		1		1		1	1	1	1		1	1	1	AWS Appearances	

Also Played: Henshaw S1(37), (M) Jones S(18,19,20). (M) Lindley S(22,29). Randall S2(37).

CLUB RECORDS

BIGGEST VICTORIES
League: 10-0 v Port Vale, Division 2, 26.2.1895.
11-1 v Newport County, 15.1.1949.
F.A. Cup: 15-0 v Thornhill (no Rotherham), 1st Round, 24.10.1885.
League Cup: 5-0 v Mansfield, 30.8.1988.
5-0 v Swindon Town, 17.10.1962.
BIGGEST DEFEATS
League: 1-9 v Blackburn Rovers, Division 1, 16.11.1889.
1-9 v Aston Villa, Division 3(S), 29.9.1930.
1-9 v portsmouth, Division 2, 9.4.1927.
0-8 v West Bromwich Albion, Division 1, 25.10.1919.
0-8 v Newcastle United, Division 1, 26.10.1901.
F.A. Cup: 1-8 v Newcastle united, 3rd Round, 8.1.1927.
League Cup: 1-7 v Newcastle United (h), 2nd Round, 5.10.1993.
MOST POINTS: 3 points a win: 99, Division 3, 1997-98.
2 points a win: 69, Division 4, 1970-71.
MOST GOALS SCORED: 107, Division 4, 1959-60.
Newsham 24, Forrest 19, Bircumshaw 17, Roby 11, Joyce 10, Withers 8, Hateley 8, Horobin 7, Carver 2, Opponents 1.
MOST GOALS CONCEDED: 97, Division 2, 1934-35.
MOST FIRST CLASS MATCHES IN A SEASON
62 - 1993-94 (League 46, FA Cup 3, League Cup 4, Anglo/Italian 9).
MOST LEAGUE WINS: 30, Division 4, 1970-71.
MOST LEAGUE DRAWS: 18, Division 4, 1968-69.
MOST LEAGUE DEFEATS: 28, Division 3, 1963-64.

BEST PERFORMANCES
League: 1970-71: Matches played 46, Won 30, Drawn 9, Lost 7, Goals for 89, Goals against 36, Points 69. First in Division 4.
Highest Position: 3rd in Division 1, 1890-91, 1900-01.
F.A. Cup: 1893-94: 1st Round Burnley (h) 1-0; 2nd Round Burton (a) 2-1; 3rd round Nottingham Forest (a) 1-1 (h) 4-1; Semi-final Blackburn Rovers 1-0; Final Bolton Wanderers 4-1.
League Cup: 5th Round in 1963-64, 1972-73.
Most recent success: 1975-76: 2nd Round Sunderland (h) 2-1; 3rd Round Leeds United (a) 1-0; 4th Round Everton (a) 2-2, (h) 2-0; 5th Round Newcastle United (a) 0-1.
HONOURS: Division 2 Champions 1896-97, 1913-14, 1922-23.
Division 3(S) Champions 1930-31, 1949-50.
Division 4 Champions 1970-71. FA Cup 1893-94.
Anglo-Italian Cup winners in 1994-95. Runners-up 1993-94.
Division 3 Champions 1997-98.
LEAGUE CAREER: Founder member of Football League 1988, Div 2 1892-93, Div 1 1896-97, Div 2 1912-13, Div 1 1913-14, Div 2 1919-20, Div 1 1922-23, Div 2 1925-26, Div 3(S) 1929-30, Div 2 1930-31, Div 3(S) 1934-35, Div 2 1949-50, Div 3 1957-58, Div 4 1958-59, Div 3 1959-60, Div 4 1963-64, Div 3 1970-71, Div 2 1972-73, Div 1 1980-81, Div 2 1983-84, Div 3 1984-85, Div 2 (now Div 1) 1989-90, Div 2 1994-95. Div 3 1997-98. Div 2 1998-

INDIVIDUAL CLUB RECORDS

MOST GOALS IN A SEASON
Tom Keetley: 41 goals in 1930-31 (League 39, FA Cup 2).

MOST GOALS IN A MATCH
9. Harry Curshaw v Wednesbury Strollers, FA Cup 2nd Round replay, 10.12.1881.

OLDEST PLAYER: Albert Iremonger, 41 years 320 days.

YOUNGEST PLAYER: Tony Bircumshaw, 16 years 54 days.

MOST CAPPED PLAYER
Kevin Wilson (Northern Ireland) 13.
Harry Curshaw (England) 8.

RECORD TRANSFER FEE RECEIVED
£2,500,000 from Derby County for Craig Short, 9/92.

RECORD TRANSFER FEE PAID
£750,000 for Tony Agana from Sheffield United, 11/91.

PREVIOUS MANAGERS

Albert Fisher 1913-27, Horace Henshall 1927-34, Charles Jones 1934, David Platt 1934, Percy Smith 1935-36; Jim McMullen 1936-37, Harry Parkes 1938-39, Tony Towe 1939-42, Frank Womack 1942-43, Frank Buckley 1944-46, Arthur Strolley 1946-49, Eric Houghton 1949-53, George Dryser 1953-57, Tommy Lawton 1957-58, Frank Hill 1958-61, Tim Coleman 1961-63, Eddie Lowe 1963-65, Tim Coleman 1965-66, Jack Burkitt 1966-67, Andy Beattie 1967, Bill Gray 1967-68, Jack Wheeler 1968-69, Jimmy Sirrell 1969-75, Ronnie Fenton 1975-77, Jimmy Sirrell 1977-82, Howard Wilkinson 1982-83, Larry Lloyd 1983-84, Ritchie Barker 1984-85, Jimmy Sirrell 1985-87, John Barnwell 1987-88, Neil Warnock 1988-92, Mick Walker 1992-94, Howard Kendal 1995, Colin Murphy & Steve Thompson 1995-97.

ADDITIONAL INFORMATION
PREVIOUS NAMES: None.
PREVIOUS LEAGUES: None.

Club colours: Black and white striped shirts, black shorts, black socks.
Change colours:

Reserves League: Pontins Central League Division 1.
Youth League: Melville Youth League.

LONGEST LEAGUE RUNS

of undefeated matches:	19 (26.4.1930 - 6.12.1930)	of league matches w/out a win:	18 (26.11.1904 - 8.4.1905)
of undefeated home matches:	25 (17.8.1970 - 14.8.1971)	of undefeated away matches:	10 (24.7.1971 - 30.10.1971)
without home win: 13 (3.12.1904 - 23.9.1905, 24.11.79 - 26.4.80)		without an away win:	24 (23.12.1933 - 30.1.1935)
of league wins:	8 (17.1.1914 - 14.3.1914)	of home wins:	14 (17.9.1959 - 13.2.1960)
of league defeats:	7 (1888-89, 1912, 1933, 1983)	of away wins:	5 (15.9.1896 - 31.10.1896)

THE MANAGER

SAM ALLARDYCE . . . . appointed January 1997.
PREVIOUS CLUBS
As Manager . . . . Limerick, Blackpool.
As Asst.Man/Coach . . . . Preston North End (caretaker/Youth team coach).
As a player . . . . Bolton Wanderers, Sunderland, Millwall, Tampa Bay, Coventry City, Huddersfield Town,
. . . . Bolton Wanderers, Preston North End, West Bromwich Albion.

HONOURS
As a Manager . . . . **Notts County:** Division 3 Championship 1997-98.
As a Player . . . . Division 2 Championship 1978, FLT 1983.

NOTTS COUNTY

PLAYERS NAME Honours	Ht	Wt	Birthdate	Birthplace Transfers	Contract Date	Clubs	League	L/Cup	FA Cup	Other	Lge	L/C	FAC	Oth
G O A L K E E P E R														
Ward Darren	5.11	12.9	5/11/74	Mansfield	7/27/92	Mansfield Town	81	5	5	6				
DIV3 97/98				£150000	7/11/95	Notts County	128	10	10	7				
D E F E N C E														
Billy Chris	6	10.9	1/2/73	Huddersfield	7/1/91	Huddersfield Town	46+11	5+1	3	9+1	2			
					8/10/95	Plymouth Argyle	108+11	5	8	2	8		1	
				Free	7/1/98	Notts County								
Fairclough Chris	5.11	11.2	12/04/64	Nottingham	12/10/81	Nottingham Forest	102+5	9+1	6	9+2	1	1		
E: B.1, u21.7. Div.2'90. Div.1'92. CS'92. Div.1'97.				£387000	03/07/87	Tottenham Hotspur	60	7	3		5			
				£500000	23/03/89	Leeds United	189+6	17+2	14+1	14	21	2		
				£500000	04/07/95	Bolton Wanderers	89+1	11	5		8			
				Free	7/1/98	Notts County								
Hendon Ian M	6	12	12/5/71	Ilford	12/20/89	Tottenham Hotspur	+4	1		0+2				
E: u21.7, Y.19. FAYC'90. CS'91DIV3 97/98				Loan	1/16/92	Portsmouth	1+3							
				Loan	3/26/92	Leyton Orient	5+1							
				Loan	3/17/93	Barnsley	6							
				£50000	8/9/93	Leyton Orient	129+1	8	7	11	5			1
				Loan	3/23/95	Birmingham City	4							
					2/24/97	Notts County	50	4	2+1		1			
Liburd Richard	5.9	11.1	9/26/73	Nottingham		Eastwood Town								
				£20000	3/25/93	Middlesbrough	41	4	2	5	1			
				£200000	7/21/94	Bradford City	74+3	6+2	2+2	2	3			
				Free	2/27/98	Carlisle United	9							
				Free	7/1/98	Notts County								
Pearce Dennis	5.9	11	9/10/74	Wolverhampton	6/7/93	Aston Villa								
DIV3 97/98					7/3/95	Wolverhampton W.	7+2	1	1					
				Free	7/18/97	Notts County	37+1	3	2+1		2			
Redmile Matthew	6.4	12.11	11/12/76	Nottingham	1/1/00	Notts County	55+2	4	6	1	5			
DIV3 97/98														
Strodder Gary	6.1	11.4	4/1/65	Cleckheaton	4/8/83	Lincoln City	122+10	7+1	2+1	5+1	6			
DIV3 97/98					3/20/87	West Ham United	59+6	8	4+2	2	2			
				£190000	8/22/90	WBA	123+17	8+1	7	10	8		1	
				£145000	7/14/95	Notts County	108+2	8	8	6	9			
M I D F I E L D														
Marshall Ben	6	12	9/5/79	Sutton	7/16/97	Notts County (T)								
Murray Shaun	5.8	11.2	12/7/70	Newcastle	12/10/87	Tottneham (T)								
E: Y, S.				£100000	6/12/89	Portsmouth	21+13	2+1	1+3	2+2	1	1		
					11/1/93	Scarborough	29		2	2	5			
				£200000	8/11/94	Bradford City	105+25	7+2	4+2	4	8	1		2
				Free	7/1/98	Notts County								
Owers Gary	5.11	11.1	10/3/68	Newcastle	10/8/86	Sunderland	241+8	25+1	10+2	11+1	24	1		1
Div.3'88. FLgeXI.1.				£300000	12/23/94	Bristol City	121+5	9	9	9	9	1		2
				£15000	7/1/98	Notts County								
Richardson Ian	5.11	11.1	10/22/70	Barking	1/1/00	Dagenham & Red.								
DIV3 97/98				£60000	8/23/95	Birmingham City	3+4	3+1	2	1+2				
				£200000	3/22/96	Notts County	56+7	4	1	3	3		1	
Tierney Francis	5.1	11	10/09/75	Liverpool	3/22/93	Crewe Alexandra (T)	57+30	6	1+4	5+6	10			3
E: Y.				Free	7/1/00	Notts County								
F O R W A R D														
Darby Duane	5.11	11.2	17/10/73	Birmingham	03/07/92	Torquay United	60+48	4+3	1+4	5+3	26	1		2
				£60000	7/19/95	Doncaster Rovers	8+9	2	0+1	1+1	4			
					27/03/96	Hull City	75+3	5	4	4	27	1	6	2
				Free	7/1/98	Notts County								
Dudley Craig M	5.11	11.4	9/12/79	Ollerton	3/1/97	Notts County	11+16	1+1	1+2		3	1		
Dyer Alexander C	6.1	12	11/14/65		8/13/97	Huddersfield Town	8+4	3			1	1		
				Free	3/2/98	Notts County								
					5/18/98	Outside'98								
					5/19/98	Notts County	10							
Farrell Sean	6.1	12.8	2/28/69	Watford	3/5/87	Luton Town	14+11		2+1	1+2	1		1	2
DIV3 97/98				Loan	3/1/88	Colchester United	4+5				1			
				Loan	9/13/91	Northampton Town	4				1			
				£100000	12/19/91	Fulham	93+1	5+1	2	8	31	3	1	3
				£120000	8/5/94	Peterborough Utd	49+17	4+2	4+1	3+1	20	1	3	1
					10/14/96	Notts County	42+7	1	5		16	1		
Finnan Steve	5.9	10.9	4/20/76	Kent	1/1/00	Woking								
DIV3 97/98				£100000	8/1/95	Birmingham City	8+5	2+2		2+1	1			
				Loan	3/5/96	Notts County								
					11/1/96	Notts County	59+8	4	7		5			
Jackson Justin J	5.11	11.2	12/10/74	Manchester		Woking								
					9/26/97	Notts County	4+11		0+1		1			
Jones Gary	6.1	12.9	4/6/69	Huddersfield	1/1/00	Rossington Main								
DIV3 97/98				Free	1/26/89	Doncaster Rovers	10+10	1			2			
				£8500	11/1/89	Grantham								
				£17500	1/1/90	Kettering Town								
				£3000	8/1/91	Boston United								
				£25000	6/3/93	Southend United	33+14	1	1	4+1	14			2
				Loan	8/16/93	Dagenham & Red.	0+4			+1	2			
				Loan	9/17/93	Lincoln City				+1				
				£140000	3/1/96	Notts County	80+9	3+1	4+1	1+1	36	1	1	
Robson Mark A	5.7	10.2	5/22/69	Newham	12/17/86	Exeter City	26		2	2	7			
DIV3 97/98				£50000	7/17/87	Tottenham Hotspur	3+5	1						
				Loan	3/24/88	Reading	5+2							
				Loan	10/5/89	Watford	1							
				Loan	12/22/89	Plymouth Argyle	7							
				Loan	1/3/92	Exeter City	7+1			3	1			1
				Free	14/2/92	West Ham United	42+8	2	2	4+1	8		1	
				£125000	11/17/93	Charlton Athletic	80+24	4+2	10	2	9		2	
				Free	6/23/97	Notts County	25+3	1	3		4			
Quayle Mark	5.9	10.2	10/2/78	Liverpool		Everton (T)								
				Free	7/1/98	Notts County								
ADDITIONAL CONTRACT PLAYERS														
Beattie Darren						Moraban (Australia)								
				Free	7/1/98	Notts County								
Henshaw Terrence R					2/27/98	Notts County (T)								
Lindley James E					11/14/97	Notts County (T)								

MEADOW LANE
Nottingham NG2 3HJ

Capacity ....20,300.

First game..v Nottingham Forest, September 1910.
First floodlit game ....v Derby County, 23.3.1953, 1-1, Att: 20,193.

ATTENDANCES
Highest ....47,310 v York City, FACup 6th Round, 10.3.1955.
Lowest...1,616 v Peterborough United, FMC, 12.12.1989.

OTHER GROUNDS ....Park Hallow. Meadows Cricket Ground. Beeston Cricket Ground.
....Castle Cricket Ground. Trent Bridge Cricket Ground.

HOW TO GET TO THE GROUND

From the North
Use motorway (M1) until junction 26, leave motorway and follow signs into Nottingham A610. Follow signs to Melton Mowbray, Trent Bridge A606. On nearside of River Trent turn left into Meadow Lane for Notts County FC.

From the East
Use A52 sign posted Nottingham to Trent Bridge, cross River and then turn right into Meadow Lane for Notts County FC.

From the South
Use motorway (M1) until junction 24, leave motorway and follow signs to NOttingham (South) to Trent Bridge, cross river and then right into Meadow Lane for Notts County FC.

From the West
Use A52 into Nottingham, then follow signs to Melton Mowbray, Trent Bridge A606 on nearside of River Trent turn left into Meadow Lane for Notts County FC.

Car Parking: Limited street parking near ground but ample space in the City of Nottingham Corporation car park only 20 minutes walk.
Nearest Railway Station: Nottingham Midland (all enquiries to Derby Station 01332 32051)

USEFUL TELEPHONE NUMBERS

Club switchboard. 0115 952 9000
Club fax number 0115 955 3994
Club shop 0115 955 7205
Ticket Office 0115 955 7210

Marketing Department. 0115 955 7220
Clubcall 0891 88 86 84*
*Calls cost 50p per minute at all times.
Call costings correct at time of going to press.

MATCHDAY PROGRAMME

Programme Editor. . . . . Terry Bowles.

Number of pages . . . . 40.

Price . . . . £1.50.

Subscriptions . . . . Apply to club.

Local Newspapers
. . . . Nottingham Evening Post.

Local Radio Stations
. . . . Radio Nottingham, Radio Trent.

MATCHDAY TICKET PRICES

Derek Pavis Stand

Adults	£15.00
Juniors	£7.50
Senior Citizens	£10.00

Blocks B & C

Adults	£13.00
Juniors	£7.00
Senior Citizens	£9.00

Jimmy Sirrel Stand - Block Y & Unreserved Block Z
Family Stand

Adults	£11.00
Juniors	£5.50
Senior Citizens	£6.00
1 Adult & 1 Child	£16.00

OLDHAM ATHLETIC
(The Latics)
NATIONWIDE LEAGUE DIVISION 2
SPONSORED BY: SLUMBERLAND

1997-98 - Back Row (L-R): Steve Redmond, Richard Graham, Doug Hodgson, Shaun Garnet, Ian Ormondroyd, Lee Sinnott, Sean McCarthy, Barrie Hart, Carl Serrant. **Middle Row:** Bill Urmson (chief youth coach), Toddy Orlygsson, Mark Allott, Matthew Rush, Ian Ironside, Gary Kelly, Andrew Holt, Lloyd Richardson, David McNiven, Alex Moreno (physio). **Front Row:** Andy Ritchie (player coach), Scott McNiven, Stuart Barlow, Lee Duxbury, Neil Warnock (manager), Paul reid, Paul Rickers, Andrew Hughes, Ron Reid (asst. manager).

OLDHAM ATHLETIC
FORMED IN 1895
TURNED PROFESSIONAL IN 1899
LTD COMPANY IN 1906

PRESIDENT: R Schofield
CHAIRMAN: I H Stott

DIRECTORS
D A Brierley (Vice-Chairman),
G T Butterworth, P Chadwick, J C Slevin,
D R Taylor, N Holden
SECRETARY
J T Cale (0161 624 4972)
COMMERCIAL MANAGER
Alan Hardy (0161 624 0966)

MANAGER: Andy Ritchie
COACH
Bill Urmson
PHYSIOTHERAPIST
Alexis Moreno

STATISTICIAN FOR THE DIRECTORY
Gordon A Lawton

At the turn of the year (3 January) Oldham Athletic were lying eighth in the table and looked a good bet for a play-off spot in Division Two. They had accumulated 36 points from their 24 games and were only one win away from third-placed Northampton Town. manager Neil Warnock had his team playing well and with a game in hand it seemed as if the Latics would be there or thereabouts come May if they could maintain any sort of consistency. But then it all went wrong.

Over the next ten weeks - up to mid-March - Oldham fulfiled another twelve matches but earned only 12 points. They had slipped down to twelfth spot and the confidence within the team had disappeared. There was a lack of cohesion throughout the ranks, determination was lacking and there was a distinct lack of fire-power up front. Goals had been flowing early on - 38 from the first 24 League games - but from the next 12 only 10 were obtained and promotion had disappeared. Warnock left the club after 15 months in charge, being replaced by former player Andy Ritchie, initially on a caretaker basis, before he was given the job on a full-time basis in May.

At the end of the season Oldham had to be satisfied with thirteenth place in the table - 61 points in the bank out of a possible 138. Surprisingly they finished 11 points clear of relegation, yet only nine short of a play-off place!

Their away form let them down badly - only two wins recorded all season. They performed well in front of their own supporters (13 victories and seven draws) with some players, including £2 million-rated defender Carl Serrant, who gained England 'B' honours and centre-back Richard Graham (until he was injured) doing sterling work. But gaining promotion is all about consistency and unfortunately the Latics didn't have that in their locker during the second half of 1997-98. Perhaps better things will be forthcoming this time round.

Tony Matthews.

OLDHAM ATHLETIC

Division 2	:13th			FA CUP: 3rd Round			LC CUP: 1st Round		AWS: Northern Round 1

M	DATE	COMP.	VEN	OPPONENTS	RESULT	H/T	LP	GOAL SCORERS/GOAL TIMES	ATT.
1	A 09	FL	H	York City	W 3-1	1-0	2	Garnett 11, Barlow 46, Reid 90	6474
2	12	CC 1/1	H	Grimsby Town	W 1-0	0-0		Ritchie 76	5656
3	15	FL	A	Wrexham	L 1-3	0-2	10	McCarthy 54	(4429)
4	23	FL	H	Bournemouth	W 2-1	1-0	5	McCarthy 17, 75	4986
5	26	CC 1/2	A	Grimsby Town	L 0-5	0-3			(5078)
6	30	FL	A	Luton Town	D 1-1	0-0	8	Barlow 54	(5404)
7	S 02	FL	A	Burnley	D 0-0	0-0	8		(11189)
8	09	FL	H	Preston North End	W 1-0	0-0	5	Wright 76	8732
9	13	FL	H	Northampton Town	D 2-2	2-1	4	Graham 12, McNiven S 35	5829
10	20	FL	A	Blackpool	D 2-2	1-1	4	Barlow 43, 68	(7174)
11	27	FL	H	Bristol Rovers	D 4-4	3-3	4	Barlow 7, 22, McCarthy 24, Garnett 58	5990
12	O 04	FL	A	Fulham	L 1-3	0-1	4	Hodgson 71	(8805)
13	11	FL	A	Millwall	L 1-2	1-0	13	Hodgson 25	(7906)
14	18	FL	H	Chesterfield	W 2-0	0-0	7	Ritchie 61, Barlow 72	5777
15	21	FL	H	Grimsby Town	W 2-0	0-0	5	Wright 48, Duxbury 90	4152
16	25	FL	A	Southend United	D 1-1	1-1	5	Barlow 34	(3595)
17	N 01	FL	A	Bristol City	L 0-1	0-0	8		(10221)
18	04	FL	H	Wigan Athletic	W 3-1	2-1	7	McCarthy 5, 62, Graham 24	5446
19	07	FL	H	Gillingham	W 3-1	2-0	4	Reid 25 (pen), 54, Barlow 37	5338
20	15	FAC 1	H	Mansfield Town	D 1-1	1-0		McCarthy 14	5253
21	18	FL	A	Watford	L 1-2	0-1	7	Duxbury 57	(0)
22	22	FL	H	Brentford	D 1-1	0-0	7	McCarthy 66	5012
23	25	FAC 1R	A	Mansfield Town	W 1-0	1-0		Serrant 43	(4097)
24	29	FL	A	Plymouth Argyle	W 2-0	1-0	5	Rickers 90, Mauge 9 (OG)	(5452)
25	D 02	FL	H	Carlisle United	W 3-1	2-1	3	Rickers 43, Barlow 45, Duxbury 49	4449
26	06	FAC 2	H	Blackpool	W 2-1	0-0		Graham 58, Barlow 81	6590
27	09	AWS N1	A	Carlisle United	L 0-1	0-0			(1518)
28	13	FL	A	Wycombe Wanderers	L 1-2	0-0	3	Barlow 72	(5327)
29	19	FL	H	Walsall	D 0-0	0-0	3		4677
30	26	FL	A	Preston North End	D 1-1	1-0	3	Hodgson 32	(13441)
31	J 03	FAC 3	A	Cardiff City	L 0-1	0-1			(6635)
32	10	FL	A	York City	D 0-0	0-0	7		(4454)
33	17	FL	H	Luton Town	W 2-1	0-0	7	Graham 54, 65	6057
34	24	FL	A	Bournemouth	D 0-0	0-0	6		(4079)
35	27	FL	H	Wrexham	W 3-0	2-0	3	Rickers 30, Duxbury 45, Ritchie 84	4680
36	31	FL	A	Northampton Town	D 0-0	0-0	3		(6559)
37	F 06	FL	H	Blackpool	L 0-1	0-0	5		6576
38	14	FL	H	Fulham	W 1-0	0-0	4	Duxbury 82	6063
39	21	FL	A	Bristol Rovers	L 1-3	0-2	7	Starbuck 60 (pen)	(5789)
40	24	FL	A	Chesterfield	L 1-2	0-1	9	Garnett 82	(4077)
41	28	FL	H	Millwall	D 1-1	0-0	9	Barlow 56	4805
42	M 03	FL	A	Gillingham	L 1-2	1-1	10	Holt 27	(5254)
43	14	FL	A	Wigan Athletic	L 0-1	0-0	12		(4277)
44	21	FL	H	Watford	D 2-2	0-1	11	Littlejohn 53, Allott 90	5744
45	28	FL	A	Brentford	L 1-2	0-2	14	Reid 67	(4547)
46	31	FL	H	Bristol City	L 1-2	1-0	14	Rush 23	4543
47	A 04	FL	H	Plymouth Argyle	W 2-0	1-0	12	Littlejohn 42, 53	4244
48	11	FL	A	Carlisle United	L 1-3	1-2	12	Hodgson 41	(4594)
49	13	FL	H	Wycombe Wanderers	L 0-1	0-0	16		4305
50	18	FL	A	Walsall	D 0-0	0-0	16		(3562)
51	25	FL	H	Southend United	W 2-0	0-0	14	Jepson 67, McNiven D 87	4485
52	28	FL	H	Burnley	D 3-3	1-3	13	Jepson 27, Rickers 76, Allott 77	9781
53	M 02	FL	A	Grimsby Town	W 2-0	0-0	13	Jepson 66, 70	(8054)

Best Home League Attendance: 9781 V Burnley | Smallest :4152 V Grimsby Town | Average :5572

Goal Scorers:

FL	(62)	Barlow 12, McCarthy 7, Duxbury 5, Graham 4, Hodgson 4, Jepson 4, Reid 4, Rickers 4, Garnett 3, Littlejohn 3, Allott 2, Ritchie 2,
		Wright 2, Holt 1, McNiven D 1, McNiven S 1, Rush 1, Starbuck 1, Opponents 1
CC	(1)	Ritchie 1
FAC	(4)	Barlow 1, Graham 1, McCarthy 1, Serrant 1
AWS	(0)	

(M) Allott	(F) Barlow	(D) Boxall	(F) Duxbury	(D) Garnett	(M) Graham	(M) Hodgson	(D) Holt	(M) Hughes	(D) Innes	(F) Jepson	(G) Kelly	(M) Littlejohn	(F) McCarthy	(D) McNiven D	(F) McNiven S	(M) Orlygsson	(G) Pollitt	(D) Redmond	(M) Reid	(M) Rickers	(F) Ritchie	(M) Rush	(D) Serrant	(D) Sinnott	(F) Starbuck	(M) Thompson	(M) Tipton	(D) Wright	Referee	
S	X		X	X		X					X		X		S	X		X	X	X	S		X						C.T. Finch	1
S	X	X	X		S2						X				S1	X		X	X	X	X		X	X					P R Richards	2
S2	X		X	X	X	S1						X		X		S	X		X	X				X	X				A G Wiley	3
X	X		X	X	X	S3		S2			X		X		S1			X		X	X			X	X				G Laws	4
S2	X		X	X	X	S1		X					X			X			X	X				X	S				D Laws	5
S	X		X	X	X	X							X			X		X	X	X			X	X				S1	A N Butler	6
S	X		X	X	X				X				S1			X		X	X	X			X	X				S	J P Robinson	7
S	X		X	X	S				S1				X			X		X	X	X			X	X				X	G Cain	8
S2	X			X	X				S				X		X	X	S1	X	X	X			X	X				X	G B Frankland	9
	X		X	X	S								X		S1	X	X	X	X	S2			X	X				X	R Pearson	10
	X	S1	X	X	S3								X			X	X	X	X	S2			X	X				X	A Bates	11
	X		X	X	X			S2					X		X	X			S1				X	X				X	G Fingh	12
	X		X	X	S2								X	S1	X	X	X	X					X	X				M Fletcher	13
	X		X	X	S3									X	X	X	X	X	S2	S1	X		X	X				M J Jones	14
	X		X	X								S1			X	X	X	X	S	S	X	S2					X	C J Foy	15
	X		X	X	S2						X		S1		X	X	X	X	S		X						X	R Styles	16
	X		X	X	S3						X		X		X	X	X	X	S1	X	X						S2	D R Crick	17
X	X		X	X	S2						X		X		X	X	X	X	S1	X	S						X	E K Wolstenholme	18
S	X		X	X	S1						X		X		X	X	X	X			X		S				X	T Jones	19
S3	X	X	X		X		S1	S		X			X			X			X	X		S2	X				X	M A Riley	20
S2	X	X	X	X	X		S						X			X		X		X		S1	X					A R Hall	21
S1	X	X	X	X			S2						X			X			X	X			X				X	M S Pike	22
X	S1		X	X	X		S			X		X	X		X			X	X	X			X				S	M A Riley	23
S	X	X	S	X	X		S			X						X	X	X	X	X			X					B Knight	24
S1	X	X1	X	S	X	X		S2				X					X	X	X	X2			X					D Pugh	25
X2	X1		X	S	X		S			X			X		S1			X	X	X	X	S2	X					G B Frankland	26
X		X	X3	X	X		X1	X		X			X		X				S1'2						S2					27
S1	X		S2	X	X						X			X1				X	X	X	X2		X					P Taylor	28
X	X	X		X	X					X		S1	S					X	X	X1	S							G Laws	29
S2	X		X	X2		X1				X			X	S1				X	X	X				X				K M Lynch	30
S1	X2		X3	X	X	X	S			X			X			X		X	X1	S3	S2							M E Pierce	31
	X	X	X	X			S					S1	X2			X	X	X	X1	S2		X				X		R D Furnandiz	32
S	X1		X	X				X	X			S1	S2			X	X	X		X2				X				T Heilbron	33
X1	S1		X	X					X	X			S			X	X	X		X				X	X			A P D'Urso	34
	X		X	X						X			S	X			X	X	X	X			S	X	S			E K Wolstenholme	35
	S		X	X		X				X			S1	X			X	X	X	X1	X		S	X				D Orr	36
	X	X3	X	X					X	X			X				X2	X	S2	X1			S1		S3			A R Leake	37
	X	X	X	X					X1	X			X				X	X	X	X			S1	X	S			R D Furnandiz	38
	X	X	X							X			X				X	X2	X	X1			X	X				M E Pierce	39
S1		X	X	X1						X		X3	X	X			S1	X	S3				X	X	X1			G Singh	40
	X2	X	X	X	S	X				X		S1	S2				X	X		X				X1				R Pearson	41
	X	X	X	X1	X	S				X	X		S1				X	X		S1				X1				P S Danson	42
S	X2	X	X	X		S1				X	X	X	S2				X	X		X				X				P R Richards	43
S2	X	X	X		X				X1	X	X		X				X	X	S1	X2		S3						M D Messias	44
X3	X	X	X	S1	X				X	X			S2			X2	X	X	S3	X1								B Knight	45
S2	X	X	X	X	X				X	X1			X3			S3	X	X	X2				X			S1		D Pugh	46
S1	X	X	X	X2	S2				X	X1			X	S			X	X	X				X					M S Pike	47
S2	X1	X	X	S1	X				X	X3			S3	X	X				X	X2	X							J A Kirkby	48
X3	X	X2	X	S2					X	X			S3	X	X		X	X1		X								G Cain	49
X	X	X1	X	X		S2		X2					S	X	X	X	X	S1		X								S G Bennett	50
X	X		X	X2	S3		X3				S1	S2	X1	X	X	X	X		X									M L Dean	51
X3	X1		X	X	S3					X2	S1		X	X	X	X	X		X									W C Burns	52
X		S2	X	X	S3		X3	X2		S1	X	X	X		X											1		P Rejer	53

10	31	18	37	32	34	22	7	1	2	9	26	5	16	2	25	8	16	32	44	35	10	11	30	11	7	8	1	10	FL Appearances	
12	1		1	2	6	7	9	2			9	6	7	3		2		5	5	5		2	2				2	2	FL Sub Appearances	
0+1	2		2	2	1	0+2		1			1		1		1+1	1		2	2	1		2	1					1	CC Appearances	
2+2	3+1		4	2	3	3	1	0+1			4		3		3+1			3	4	4	1+1	0+3	3					1	FAC Appearances	
1		1	1	1	1			1	1		1		1		1							0+1				0+1		1	AWS Appearances	

Also Played: (M) Clitheroe S1(49), S2(52), X1(53). (G) Grobbelaar S(31), X(50,51,52,53). (M) Hotte S2(39). (G) Ironside X(5). (M) Johnson S(26). (F) Kyratzoglou S3(13). (M) Miskelly S(20,23). (F) Ormondroyd S2(6). Robinson S3(27). (M) Salt S(22,23,28,38), X(27), X1(43).

OLDHAM ATHLETIC

CLUB RECORDS

BIGGEST VICTORIES
League: 11-0 v Southport, Division 4, 26.12.1962
F.A. Cup: 11-1 v Lytham, Round 1, 18.11.1925
League Cup: 7-0 v Scarborough, Round 3, 25.10.1989
BIGGEST DEFEATS
League: 4-13 v Tranmere Rovers, Division 3N, 26.12.1935
0-9 v Hull City, Division 3N, 5.4.1958
F.A. Cup: 0-6 v Huddersfield Town, Round 3, 13.1.1932
0-6 v Tottenham H, Round 3, 14.1.1933 (h)
League Cup: 1-7 v Sunderland, Round 2, 24.9.1962
MOST POINTS
3 points a win: 88, Division 2, 1990-91
2 points a win: 62, Division 3, 1973-74
MOST GOALS
95, 1962-63, Division 4.
Lister 30, Whittaker 17, Colquhoun 13, Ledger 8, Frizzell 5,
Johnstone 5, Bowie5, Williams 5, McCall 4, og 3
MOST LEAGUE GOALS CONCEDED
95, Division 2, 1934-35
MOST FIRST CLASS MATCHES IN A SEASON
65 (46 League, 9 FA Cup, 9 League Cup, 1 Zenith Data) 1989-90
MOST LEAGUE WINS
25, Division 3, 1973-74
25, Division 2, 1990-91
MOST LEAGUE DRAWS
21, Division 2, 1988-89
MOST LEAGUE DEFEATS
26, Division 2, 1934-35; Division 4, 1958-59; Division 4, 1959-60
RECORD TRANSFER FEE RECEIVED
£1,700,000 from Aston Villa for Earl Barrett, February 1992.
RECORD TRANSFER FEE PAID
£700,000 for Ian Olney from Aston Villa, May 1992.
BEST PERFORMANCES
League: 1990-91 - 1st in Division 2.
P 46 **W** 25 **D** 13 **L** 8 **F** 83 **A** 53 **Pts** 88.
Highest: 1914-15: Second in Division 1
F.A. Cup: Semi-Finals 1912-13, 1989-90, 1993-94.
League Cup: Finalists 1989-90.

INDIVIDUAL CLUB RECORDS

MOST GOALS IN A SEASON
Tom Davis 35 (League 33, FAC 2) Div 3N, 1936-37
3 goals four times=12, 2 goals 3 times=6, 1 goal 17 times
Previous holder: W Walsh 32 (1935-36)
MOST GOALS IN A MATCH
7. Eric Gemmill v Chester, Division 3N, 19.1.1953 (11-2)
7. Bert Lister v Southport, Division 4, 26.12.1962
Frank Bunn scored 6 goals against Scarborough, Lge Cup,
25.10.1989, thus setting a record for the competition
OLDEST PLAYER
Bobby Collins, 42 years, 63 days v Rochdale 20.04.1973.
YOUNGEST PLAYER
Eddie Hopkinson, 16 years, 76 days v Crewe Alexandra 12.01.1952
MOST CAPPED PLAYER
Gunnar Halle 53 (Norway)

PREVIOUS MANAGERS

David Ashworth 1906-14, Herbert Bamlett 1914-21,
Charles Roberts 1921-22 David Ashworth 1923-24,
Robert Mellor 1924-27, Andrew Wilson 1927-32,
Robert Mellor 1932-33, Jim McMullen 1933-34,
Robert Mellor 1934-35, Frank Womack 1945-47,
Bill Wooton 1947-50, George Hardwick 1950-56,
Ted Goodier 1956-58, Norman Dodgin 1958-60,
Danny McLennan 1960, Jack Rowley 1960-63,
Les McDowell 1963-65, Gordon Hurst 1965-66,
Jimmy McIlroy 1966-68, Jack Rowley 1968-69,
Jimmy Frizzell 1970-82, Joe Royle1982-94, Graham Sharp1994-97,

ADDITIONAL INFORMATION
PREVIOUS NAME
Pine Villa
PREVIOUS LEAGUE
Lancashire League

Club colours: Royal blue with white sided shirts and shorts..
Change colours: White shirts, claret shorts, claret socks.

Reserves League: Pontins Central League Division 1.

COMPETITIONS

Div 1/P	Div.2/1	Div.3	Div.3(N)	Div.4	Texaco	A/Scot
1910-23	1907-10	1963-69	1935-53	1958-63	1974-75	1977-78
1991-94	1923-35	1971-74	1954-58	1969-71		1978-79
	1953-54					1979-80
	1974-91					1980-81
	1994-					

HONOURS

Division 2	Division 3	Division 3(N)
1990-91	1973-74	1952-53

LONGEST LEAGUE RUNS

of undefeated matches:	20 (1.5.1990 - 10.11.1990)	of league matches w/out a win:	17 (4.9.1920 - 18.12.1920)
of undefeated home matches:	28 (3.2.23-18.4.24, 14.1.89-28.3.90)	of undefeated away matches:	11 (14.4.1973 - 10.11.1973)
without home win:	9 (4.9.1920 - 18.12.1920)	without an away win:	31 (24.4.1974 - 15.11.1975)
of league wins:	10 (12.1.1974 - 12.3.1974)	of home wins:	14 (11.1.1903 - 25.11.1903)
of league defeats:	8 (27.12.32-18.2.33, 15.12.34-2.2.35)	of away wins:	5 (12.1.1974 - 5.3.1974)

THE MANAGER
ANDY RITCHIE . . . . appointed May 1998.

PREVIOUS CLUBS
As Manager . . . . None.
As Asst.Man/Coach . . . . None.
As a player . . . . Manchester Utd, Brighton, Leeds Utd, Oldham, Scarborough, Oldham.

HONOURS
As a Manager . . . . None.
As a Player . . . . **Oldham:** Division 2 championship, 1991.
International . . . . 1 u21 cap plus youth and schools' caps.

OLDHAM ATHLETIC

Player	Ht	Wt	DOB	Birthplace	Fee/Type	Date	Club								
GOALKEEPER															
Miskelly David T			9/3/79	Ards		7/1/97	Oldham Athletic (T)								
DEFENCE															
Earnshaw Mark W			11/11/78	Leeds		7/1/97	Oldham Athletic (T)								
Barnett Shaun	6.2	13.1	11/22/69	Wallasey		6/15/88	Tranmere Rov. (T)								
					Loan	10/1/92	Chester City	9							
					Loan	12/11/92	Preston NE	10			1	2			
					Loan	2/26/93	Wigan Athletic	13			1				
					£200000	3/11/96	Swansea City	15	2						
					£150000	9/19/96	Oldham Athletic	54+3	2	3	1	4			
Holt Andrew	6.1	11.11	5/21/78	Manchester		3/27/97	Oldham Athletic (T)	7+7		1		1			
Innes Mark	5.10	12.1	9/27/78	Bellshill		5/31/97	Oldham Athletic (T)	2+2							
McNiven David J	5.11	10.6	5/27/78	Leeds		9/16/96	Oldham Athletic (T)	5+11	0+1	0+1		1			
Salt Phillip T	5.11	11.9	3/2/79	Huddersfield		7/1/97	Oldham Athletic (T)	1							
Selfe Oliver			10/1/79	Warrington		7/1/97	Oldham Athletic (T)								
Sinnott Lee E: u21.1, Y.4.	6.1	11.9	7/12/65	Pelsall		11/16/82	Walsall	40	3	4		2			
					£100000	9/15/83	Watford	71+7	6	11		2			
					£130000	7/23/87	Bradford City	173	19	9	12	6		1	
					£300000	8/8/91	Crystal Palace	53+2	9+1	1	2				
						12/9/93	Bradford City	34	2	2	2	1			
					£105000	12/23/94	Huddersfield Town	85+2	6	4	3	1			
						7/3/97	Oldham Athletic	10+2	1						
					Loan	3/26/98	Bradford City	7							
MIDFIELD															
Allott Mark S	6	10.12	3/16/78	Manchester		10/11/96	Oldham Athletic	10+17	0+1	2+2		3			
Graham Richard E	6.2	12.1	11/28/74	Dewsbury		7/16/93	Oldham Athletic	113+8	9	9	1	8		1	
Hodgson Doug	6.2	13.1	2/27/69	Frankston (Aus)			Heidelberg Alex								
					£30000	7/22/94	Sheffield United	24+6	3+1	2+1	1	1			
					Loan	10/17/96	Burnley	1							
						2/28/97	Oldham Athletic	32+7	0+2	3		4			
Hotte Mark S	5.11	11.1	9/27/78	Bradford		7/1/97	Oldham Athletic (T)	0+1							
Littlejohn Adrian E: S.	5.9	10.5	9/26/70	Wolverhampton			WBA								
					Free	5/24/89	Walsall	26+18	2+1	1+1	4+1	1			
					Free	8/6/91	Sheffield United	44+25	5+1	3+2	1	12		1	1
					£100000	7/22/95	Plymouth Argyle	101+10	6	6+2	3	30		3	
					Swap	3/20/98	Oldham Athletic	5				3			
Murphy Gerrard P			12/19/78	Manchester		5/31/97	Oldham Athletic (T)								
Orlygsson Thorvaldur	5.11	10.13	8/2/66	Odense			KA Akureyri								
					£175000	12/9/89	Nottingham Forest	31+6	5+1	1	0+1	?	?		
					Free	8/5/93	Stoke City	00+0	?	6	6	16	1	1	1
					£180000	12/22/95	Oldham Athletic	46+8	5+1	3+1	1				
Reid Paul R	5.9	10.8	1/19/68	Oldbury		1/9/86	Leicester City	140+22	13	5+1	6+2	21	4		
					Loan	3/19/92	Bradford City	7							
					£25000	7/27/92	Bradford City	80+2	3	3	5	15	2		1
					£70000	5/20/94	Huddersfield Town	69+7	9	5+1	1	6	1		
						3/27/97	Oldham Athletic	53	2	4		5			
Rickers Paul S	5.1	11	5/9/75	Leeds		7/16/93	Oldham Athletic	105+6	6	6+1	1+2	9			
Rush Matthew	5.11	12.1	8/6/71	Hackney		3/24/90	West Ham United	29+19	4		2+1	5			
					Loan	3/12/93	Cambridge United	4+6							
					Loan	1/10/94	Swansea City	13		4					
					£330000	8/18/95	Norwich City	0+3							
					Loan	10/28/96	Northampton Town								
					Loan	12/24/96	Northampton Town	13				3			
						3/27/97	Oldham Athletic	17+7			0+3	3			
Swan Iain			10/16/79	Glasgow		7/21/97	Oldham Athletic (T)								
FORWARD															
Clitheroe Lee J	5.10	10.4	11/18/78	Chorley		7/1/97	Oldham Athletic (T)	1+2							
Duxbury Lee	5.8	11	10/7/69	Keighley		7/4/88	Bradford City	204+5	18+1	11	13	25	1		
					Loan	1/18/90	Rochdale	9+1			1				
					£250000	12/23/94	Huddersfield Town	26			3	2			
					£135000	11/15/95	Bradford City	63	2	5	3	7			
						3/7/97	Oldham Athletic	47+2	2	4		6			
McCarthy Sean C	6.1	11.7	9/12/67	Bridgend			Bridgend Town								
						10/22/85	Swansea City	76+15	4+1	5+2	9+1	25	3	4	6
					£50000	8/18/88	Plymouth Argyle	67+3	7	3	+1	19	5	1	1
					£250000	7/4/90	Bradford City	127+4	10+2	8	8+1	60	10	2	7
					£500000	12/3/93	Oldham Athletic	117+23	10	6+1	3	42	2	1	1
					Loan	3/26/98	Bristol City	7				1			
McNiven Scott			7/8/72	Leeds		9/27/94	Oldham Athletic (T)	49+10	4+1	5	3	1			
Ritchie Andy E: u21.1, Y.4, S. Div.2'91.	5.1	11.1	11/28/60	Manchester		12/5/77	Manchester United	26+7	3+2	3+1		13			
					£500000	10/17/80	Brighton & H.A.	82+7	3+1	9		23	1	2	
					£150000	3/25/83	Leeds United	127+9	11	9	2+1	40	3	1	
					£50000	8/14/87	Oldham Athletic	187+30	18+2	8+2	3	83	18	4	
					Free	8/3/95	Scarborough	59+9	4	4		17	1	1	
						2/21/97	Oldham Athletic	13+11	1	1+1		2	1		
Tipton Matthew J	5.10	10.7	6/26/80	Bangor		7/1/97	Oldham Athletic (T)	1+2							
Whitehall Steve	5.1	11	08/12/68	Bromborough			Southport								
					£20000	23/07/91	Rochdale	212+26	10+3	13+2	15+1	75	4	3	10
					£20000	8/8/97	Mansfield Town	42+1	2	2	2	24		1	1
					£50000	7/1/98	Oldham Athletic								

BOUNDARY PARK

Oldham, Lancashire OL1 2PA

Capacity..13,599

First game..v Colne (Lancs. Comb), 1.9.1906.
First floodlit game ....v Burnley, 1961-62.

ATTENDANCES
Highest ....47,671 v Sheffield Wednesday, FA Cup 4th Round, 25.1.1930.
Lowest...1,841 v WBA, Simod Cup, 10.11.1987.

OTHER GROUNDS..Sheepfoot Lane 1895-1905. Boundary Park 1905-
.... (In 1986 En Tout Cas Sporturf laid an artificial surface, new grass was laid in 1991)

HOW TO GET TO THE GROUND

From North, East, South and West
Use motorway M62 until junction 20, then A627 to junction A664.
Leave motorway and at roundabout take 1st exit onto Broadway.
1st right off Broadway into Hilbre Avenue, which leads to car park.

Car Parking
Parking for 1,200 cars on site adjacent to ground.

Nearest Railway Station
Werneth.

USEFUL TELEPHONE NUMBERS

Club switchboard 0161 624 4972

Club fax number.......................0161 652 6501

Club shop 0161 652 0966

Ticket Office.............................0161 624 4972

Marketing Department 0161 627 1802

Internet address ....www.u-net.com/latics/

Clubcall 0891 12 11 42*

*Calls cost 50p per minute at all times. Call costings correct at time of going to press.

MATCHDAY PROGRAMME

Programme Editor..............Gordon Lawton.

Number of pages.....................................48.

Price ....£1.60.

Subscriptions ....Apply to club.

Local Newspapers
....Oldham Chronicle,
Manchester Evening News (Saturday Pink),
....Oldham Advertiser.

Local Radio Stations
............Radio Piccadilly, Radio Manchester,
...............................Radio Cavell (Hospital),
.... Key 103, Sunset Radio, Radio Latics.

MATCHDAY TICKET PRICES

Adults . . . . £7.50 - £13.00
Concessions . . . . £5.00 - £8.00

PRESTON NORTH END
(The Lillywhites)
NATIONWIDE LEAGUE DIVISION 2
SPONSORED BY: BAXI

Unfortunately Preston North End were unable to supply us with a team photograph for this year's publication

PRESTON NORTH END
FORMED IN 1881
TURNED PROFESSIONAL IN 1885
LTD COMPANY IN 1893

PRESIDENT: Tom Finney, OBE,CBE,JP
VICE-PRESIDENT: T C Nicholson, JP,FCIOB
CHAIRMAN: Bryan Gray
SECRETARY: Peter Church
DIRECTORS
Vice Chairmen: Keith Leeming
Malcolm Woodhouse
Chief Executive: Peter Church
Tony Scholes (Finance)
D Shaw, David Taylor
COMMERCIAL MANAGER
Steve White

MANAGER: David Moyes
FIRST TEAM COACH: Kelham O'Hanlon

YOUTH TEAM MANAGER
Neil McDonald
PHYSIOTHERAPIST
Mick Rathbone

STATISTICIAN FOR THE DIRECTORY
Lawrence Bland

Another disappointing season, frustrating for supporters, who harboured expectations of possible promotion. Even with the transfer of Kevin Kilbane to West Bromwich Albion for a record package of £1.25m, some good signings were made pre-season, including Gary Parkinson from Burnley and a trio of young Manchester United starlets, one of whom, Michael Appleton cost half a million, a club record.

The season began well, with three wins in the first five games, with wins over Watford and Grimsby Town, we were in 4th place, and even in mid-October after winning a televised Friday night game at Carlisle we were third. Then it all started going wrong! The goals dried up, games were lost by the odd goal, often to struggling sides at home, the team seemed to lose confidence at times. The fans did, criticism poured in for the chairman, manager, coach, in fact everything from the pitch to the match programme had its critics. It wasn't a 'happy ship' at times. The side continued to fail to play to its potential, and after the home defeat by Gillingham on January 10th, manager Gary Peters resigned. There was much media speculation about the appointment of Ian Rush as player-manager, they continued all season! Many thought an experienced manager was called for, but North End followed recent tradition and promoted the assistant manager, in this case David Moyes to the full manager's job.

It may prove a good choice. Gary Peters was offered the job as manager of North End's school of excellence, which he surprisingly excepted. Coach Steve Harrison later moved to Aston Villa. Results took some time to improve, beginning with a win at Bournemouth of February 28th, with the season finishing with only two defeats in the last 13 games, lifting the side out of any relegation danger.

In the cups, we lost the final of the pre-season Isle of Man Festival, 1-0 to Wrexham. The Coca-Cola Cup saw both legs won against Rotherham United in Round One. We even beat Premiership Blackburn Rovers 1-0, unfortunately we had already lost the first leg 6-0, a record League Cup defeat. In the FA Cup, we beat both top and bottom of Division 3, in the opening rounds, before losing to Stockport County. A good run in the Auto Windscreens Shield looked on, but we lost at Burnley in the Northern semi-final.

The highlight of the season was a knighthood for club President Tom Finney, at long last! In July 1998, the new £3m, 6,100 seater, north stand will open, the Bill Shankly Kop, which increases the capacity of Deepdale to 21,588. Player of the season was Sean Gregan, player's player of the season was Lee Ashcroft, the Supporter's Club choice was Teuvo Moilanan. Young player of the season was Jonathan Macken.

The Reserves had a good first season in the Premier Division of the Pontin's League, avoiding relegation, with the visit of Manchester United Reserves in March attracting a gate of 9,072.

Lawrence Bland.

PRESTON NORTH END

Division 2   :15th   FA CUP: 3rd Round   LC CUP: 2nd Round   AWS: Northern Semi-finals

M	DATE	COMP.	VEN	OPPONENTS	RESULT	H/T	LP	GOAL SCORERS/GOAL TIMES	ATT.
1	A 09	FL	A	Gillingham	D 0-0	0-0	16		(6562)
2	12	CC 1/1	A	Rotherham United	W 3-1	0-0		Macken 53, Reeves 59, 60	(2901)
3	15	FL	H	Millwall	W 2-1	1-1	7	Macken 43, Ashcroft 51	11486
4	23	FL	A	Chesterfield	L 2-3	0-3	10	Rankine 63, Barrick 88	(6288)
5	26	CC 1/2	H	Rotherham United	W 2-0	0-0		Reeves 52, Macken 70	9441
6	30	FL	H	Watford	W 2-0	1-0	9	Nogan 38, 67	11042
7	S 02	FL	H	Grimsby Town	W 2-0	0-0	4	Reeves 67, Ashcroft 74	9489
8	09	FL	A	Oldham Athletic	L 0-1	0-0	9		(8732)
9	13	FL	H	Walsall	D 0-0	0-0	7		9092
10	17	CC 2/1	A	Blackburn Rovers	L 0-6	0-2			(22564)
11	20	FL	A	Burnley	D 1-1	1-0	8	Nogan 20	(13809)
12	27	FL	A	Wycombe Wanderers	D 0-0	0-0	8		(4838)
13	30	CC 2/2	H	Blackburn Rovers	W 1-0	1-0		Barrick 15	11472
14	O 04	FL	H	Brentford	W 2-1	0-1	5	Ashcroft 50, Murdock 84	8804
15	11	FL	H	Bournemouth	L 0-1	0-0	11		8531
16	17	FL	A	Carlisle United	W 2-0	1-0	3	Parkinson 22, Ashcroft 46	(6541)
17	21	FL	A	Bristol City	L 1-2	0-0	10	, Dyche 68 (OG)	(9039)
18	25	FL	H	Wrexham	L 0-1	0-0	13		9098
19	N 01	FL	H	Plymouth Argyle	L 0-1	0-0	16		8405
20	04	FL	A	York City	L 0-1	0-0	17		(3370)
21	08	FL	A	Luton Town	W 3-1	2-1	13	Lormor 16, Eyres 45, Ashcroft 87	(5767)
22	15	FAC 1	H	Doncaster Rovers	W 3-2	0-1		Gregan 56, 65, Eyres 63	7953
23	18	FL	H	Bristol Rovers	L 1-2	0-1	14	Jackson 53	7798
24	22	FL	A	Wigan Athletic	W 4-1	1-0	14	Cartwright 21, 53, Ashcroft 71, Kidd 74	(5649)
25	29	FL	A	Fulham	W 3-1	1-1	12	Ashcroft 11, 69 (pen), 83	9723
26	D 02	FL	A	Southend United	L 2-3	2-3	12	Lormor 6, 11	(2307)
27	06	FAC 2	H	Notts County	D 2-2	1-1		Parkinson 22, Ashcroft 71	7583
28	09	AWS N1	H	Darlington	W 3-2	1-0		Appleton 28, Eyres 61, 110	2703
29	13	FL	H	Northampton Town	W 1-0	0-0	8	Macken 56	7448
30	16	FAC 2R	A	Notts County	W 2-1	0-0		Moyes 89, Eyres 96	(3052)
31	20	FL	A	Blackpool	L 1-2	0-2	11	Holt 51	(8342)
32	26	FL	H	Oldham Athletic	D 1-1	0-1	13	Holt 51	13441
33	28	FL	A	Grimsby Town	L 1-3	0-3	14	Gregan 89	(6725)
34	J 03	FAC 3	H	Stockport County	L 1-2	0-1		Ashcroft 71 (pen)	12180
35	10	FL	H	Gillingham	L 1-3	0-2	17	Gregan 76	7776
36	13	AWS N2	A	Macclesfield Town	W 1-0	0-0		Cartwright 48	(1618)
37	17	FL	A	Watford	L 1-3	0-2	17	Parkinson 55	(10182)
38	24	FL	H	Chesterfield	D 0-0	0-0	17		8233
39	27	AWS NQF	H	Mansfield Town	W 1-0	1-0		Nogan 39	3609
40	31	FL	A	Walsall	D 1-1	0-0	18	Nogan 89 (pen)	(5377)
41	F 06	FL	A	Burnley	L 2-3	1-0	18	Nogan 34, Jackson 61	12263
42	14	FL	A	Brentford	D 0-0	0-0	18		(4952)
43	17	AWS NSF	A	Burnley	L 0-1	0-1			(10079)
44	21	FL	H	Wycombe Wanderers	D 1-1	0-0	18	Macken 64	7665
45	24	FL	H	Carlisle United	L 0-3	0-2	18		8985
46	28	FL	A	Bournemouth	W 2-0	2-0	17	Davey 16, Appleton 22	(5009)
47	M 03	FL	H	Luton Town	W 1-0	0-0	15	Kidd 64	6992
48	07	FL	A	Plymouth Argyle	L 0-2	0-1	17		(4201)
49	14	FL	H	York City	W 3-2	0-1	16	Eyres 47, Appleton 82, Parkinson 87	7664
50	21	FL	A	Bristol Rovers	D 2-2	1-0	16	Davey 23, Ashcroft 83	(5278)
51	25	FL	A	Millwall	W 1-0	1-0	16	Ashcroft 33	(5888)
52	28	FL	H	Wigan Athletic	D 1-1	1-0	16	Ashcroft 33	10171
53	A 04	FL	A	Fulham	L 1-2	0-0	16	Macken 33	(8814)
54	11	FL	H	Southend United	W 1-0	0-0	13	Parkinson 63	8096
55	13	FL	A	Northampton Town	D 2-2	1-0	14	Ashcroft 45, Macken 90	(5664)
56	18	FL	H	Blackpool	D 3-3	1-2	14	Eyres 23, Parkinson 50, Macken 60	13500
57	25	FL	A	Wrexham	D 0-0	0-0	16		(7302)
58	M 02	FL	H	Bristol City	W 2-1	2-1	15	Ashcroft 5, Eyres 10	12067

Best Home League Attendance: 13500 V Blackpool   **Smallest :6992 V Luton Town**   **Average :9468**

Goal Scorers:

FL	(56)	Ashcroft 14, Macken 6, Nogan 5, Parkinson 5, Eyres 4, Lormor 3, Appleton 2, Cartwright 2, Davey 2, Gregan 2, Holt 2, Jackson 2, Kidd 2, Barrick 1, Murdock 1, Rankine 1, Reeves 1, Opponents 1
CC	(6)	Reeves 3, Macken 2, Barrick 1
FAC	(8)	Ashcroft 2, Eyres 2, Gregan 2, Moyes 1, Parkinson 1
AWS	(5)	Eyres 2, Appleton 1, Cartwright 1, Nogan 1

1997-98

(M) Appleton	(F) Ashcroft	(M) Atkinson	(M) Barrick	(M) Cartwright	(D) Darby	(F) Davey	(F) Eyres	(D) Gregan	(F) Holt	(D) Jackson	(D) Kidd	(F) Lormor	(G) Lucas	(F) Macken	(M) McKenna	(G) Moilanen	(D) Moyes	(F) Mullin	(D) Murdock	(F) Nogan	(M) O'Hanlon	(D) Parkinson	(F) Rankine	(F) Reeves	(M) Sissoko	(D) Sparrow		
	X		S	X	S		X		X	X		X		X		X		X	X	S1		X	X	X			S.J. Baines	1
S2	X		S1	X			X		X	X		X		X		X		X	X	S3		X	X	X			G Laws	2
S2	X		S1	X			X		X	X		X		X		X		X	X	S		X	X	X			T Jones	3
S1	X		X	X	S3		X		X	X		X		X		X				S2		X	X	X			P Rejer	4
X	X		X	X	S2		S		X	X		X		S1		X			X			X	X	X			K A Leach	5
X	X		X	X	S2		S		X	X		X		S1		X			X			X	X	X			J A Kirkby	6
X	X		X	X	S2	S1			X	X		X		S		X			X			X	X	X			A Bates	7
X	X		X	X	S				X	X		X		S1		X	S		X			X	X	X			G Cain	8
X	X		X	X	S				X		X	S2		S1		X			X			X	X	X			G Laws	9
	X	S	X	X	X				X	X		X		S1		X	S					X	X	X			S J Lodge	10
S1	X		X	X					X	X		X		S		X			S			X	X	X			E K Wolstenholme	11
X	X	S2	X		S				X	X		X		X		X			X			X	X	S1			S G Bennett	12
X	X		X	S2			X	S1	X	X		X		X		X			X			X	X	S3			M A Riley	13
X	X		X	S2			X	S1	X	X						X			X			X	X				M J Jones	14
X	X	S1	X	X			X		X	X			X			X			S2			X	X				J P Robinson	15
X	X		X	X	S				S	X						X	X		X		S	X	X	X			G B Frankland	16
X	X		X	X	S				S	X						X	X		X		S	X	X	X			R Styles	17
X	X	X		X	S2					X		S1				X			X			X	X	X			W C Burns	18
	X		S1	X		X	S2	S3		X		X				X	X		X			X	X				A R Hall	19
S2	X		X				X	S3		X		X				X	X		X			X	X				G Singh	20
X	X		X	S	S		X		X	X	X			S1		X			X			X	X				C R Wilkes	21
X	X		X	S2			X	X	S	X	X	X	S	S		X			S1			X	X				M D Messias	22
X	X	S1		S			X	S2	X	X	X					X			X			X	X				B Coddington	23
X	X		X	X	S1			S1	X	X						X			S			X	X				A G Wiley	24
X	X1		X	X			X	S1	X	X						X			S		S	X	X				E Lomas	25
X	X		X	X1			X	S1	X	X	S					X			S			X	X				M R Halsey	26
X	X		X	X1			X	S	X	X	X	X		S1					S		S	X					P S Danson	27
X	X		X	S2			X	X		X	X	X1	X	S1					X2			X						28
X			X				X	X	S1	X	X			X1	X	X			S		S	X					M S Pike	29
X			X				X		S1	X	X1	X2		X3		X	S2			S3	S	X	S				P S Danson	30
X		X3	S1	X1			X		S2	X	X2			X		X	S3					X					R Pearson	31
X		X1	X	S2			X		X	X	S1		S3	X3		X	X		X		X?	X					K M Lynch	32
X		X1	X		S1		X		X		X		S3			X	X1		X				S1	S2			D Laws	33
X	X1	S		S2			X		S1	X	X	S	S	X		X						X2	X				M D Messias	34
X		S	S1	X1			X		X2	X		X		X					X	S2		X					M J Brandwood	35
		X	X				X		X	S1		X		X	X				X1			X	X					36
S		X1					X		X	X		X		X	X	S1			S			X	X				S J Baines	37
S			X				X		X	X		X	X1	X	S1				S			X	X				C R Wilkes	38
		X	X				X		X	X		X	X1	S1					X			X	X					39
S2			X				X	X2		X		X		S1	X1				X			X	X				B Knight	40
S1	X		X				X	X1	X			X		X	S				S			X	X				F G Stretton	41
X	X		S1	X			S	S2		X		X1				X		X2	X			X					P Rejer	42
X	X		X	X					X					S1		X			X		X	X1	X					43
X	X		X	X					S			X		S1		X		X1	X		X1	X		S1			M D Messias	44
X	X1		X	X3	S3	S1			X					S2		X	X	X2				X		X			A N Butler	45
X	X1			S			X		X	X		X				X	S1		X			X	S	X1			P Taylor	46
X	X			S			X		X	X		X				X	S2		X			X	S	X2			B Coddington	47
X	X		S1				X		X	X		X1				X	S2		X			X	S	X2			D Orr	48
X	X		X	S		X2	X		X			X				X	X1		X			X		S2			R Pearson	49
X	X		S	S1			X		X			X		X2		X			X	S2		X	X1				A P D'Urso	50
X	X2		S1	S3			X		X			X	X1	X3		X			X	S2		X					C R Wilkes	51
X	X		S2	S1			X		X2					X1		X		S	X	S		X	X	S1			E Lomas	52
X1	X		X	S1			X		X			S2		X2		X	S		X			X	X				M J Brandwood	53
	X		X	S2			X		X			X2		X	S1	X			X			X		X1			G B Frankland	54
	X		X	S1			X1	X2						X	X	X			X	S2		X	X				M Fletcher	55
	X		X				X	X1	S					X	X	X	X		X	S1		X	X				P Rejer	56
S1	X		X				X	X1	X			X		X	X	S			S			X	X		X		K M Lynch	57
S	X		X				X	X	X			X		X	X	X			S			X	X		S		C J Foy	58
31	37	1	29	24	6	17	26	33	4	39	32	9	6	20	4	40	8	4	27	14		44	34	12	4	1	FL Appearances	
7		2	4	12	6	1	2	2	10	1	1	3		9	1		1	3		8		1	1	1	3		FL Sub Appearances	
2+1	4		3+1	3+1	1+1			3		0+2	4	4		2+2		4			2	1+1		4	4	3+1			CC Appearances	
4	3		3	0+1	3		4	4	0+1	4	4	3	1	2+1	3	0+1			1+1	0+1		4	2				FAC Appearances	
2	2		3	3	0+1	2	3	3	0+1	4	3	3	3	0+3		1		1	2	3		4	2				AWS Appearances	

PRESTON NORTH END   RECORDS AND STATISTICS

CLUB RECORDS

RECORD LEAGUE VICTORY
10-0 v Stoke City (h), Div 1, 14.9.1889
Most Goals Scored in a Cup Tie
26-0 v Hyde, FA Cup 1st Round, 15.10.1887

RECORD LEAGUE DEFEAT
0-7 v Blackpool (h), Div 1, 1.5.1948   0-7 v Nottingham Forest (a),
Div 2, 9.4.1927
Record Cup Defeat
0-6 v Charlton Athletic, FA Cup Round 5, 1945-46
0-6 v Blackburn Rovers, Leageu Cup Round 2 1st leg, 17.09.97.

MOST LEAGUE POINTS
(2pts for win) 61, Div 4, 1970-71
(3pts for win) 90 1986-87

MOST LEAGUE GOALS
100 Div 2, 1927-28 100 Div 1, 1957-58.

RECORD TRANSFER FEE RECEIVED
£900,000* for Kevin Kilbane from West Bromwich Albion, July 1997.
*rising to £1.25 million after appearances.

RECORD TRANSFER FEE PAID
£500,000 for Michael Appleton from Manchester United, August'97.

BEST PERFORMANCES
League: Champions Div 1 (2) FA Cup: Winners (2)
League Cup: 4th Round 1963, 1966, 1972, 1981
HONOURS: Champions Div 1 *1888-89 (first winners), 1889-90
Champions Div 2,1903-04, 1912-13, 1950-51 Champions Div 3
1970-71. Champions Div 3 1995-96. FA Cup Winners *1889,1938
*League and FA Cup Double

LEAGUE CAREER
Original Members of Football League 1888   Relegated to Div
21900-01   Promoted to Div 1 1903-04
Relegated to Div 2 1911-12   Promoted to Div 1 1912-13
Relegated to Div 21913-14   Promoted to Div 1 1914-15
Relegated to Div 2 1924-25   Promoted to Div 1 1933-34
Relegated to Div 21948-49   Promoted to Div 1 1950-51
Relegated to Div 2 1960-61   Relegated to Div 3 1969-70
Promoted to Div 21970-71   Relegated to Div 3 1973-74
Promoted to Div 2 1977-78   Relegated to Div 3 1980-81
Relegated to Div 41984-85   Promoted to Div 3 (now Div 2) 1986-87
Relegated to Div 4/3 1992-93 Promoted to Div 2 1995-96.

INDIVIDUAL CLUB RECORDS

MOST APPEARANCES FOR CLUB
Alan Kelly (1961-75): League 447+Cup games 65 Total512

MOST CAPPED PLAYER: TOM FINNEY, 76 ENGLAND
Record Goalscorer in a Match: Jimmy Ross, 8 v Hyde (h), 26-0, 1st
Round FA Cup,15.10.1887

RECORD LEAGUE GOALSCORER IN A SEASON
Ted Harper 37, Div 2, 1932-33 In All Competitions: Ted Harper 37
(League 37) 1932-33

RECORD LEAGUE GOALSCORER IN A CAREER
Tom Finney 187 In All Competitions: Tom Finney 210 (League 187
+ FA Cup 23) 1946-60.

OLDEST PLAYER IN A LEAGUE MATCH
Bob Kelly 40 years 50 days, 5.1.1935 v Everton(h)

YOUNGEST PLAYER IN A LEAGUE MATCH
Steve Doyle, 16 years 166 days, 15.11.1974 v Tranmere Rovers (a)

PREVIOUS MANAGERS

1919 V Hayes   1924 T Lawrence   1925 F Richards
1927 A Gibson   1931-32 L Hyde   1932-36 No Manager
1936-37 T Muirhead   1937-49 No Manager   1949-53 W Scott
1953-54 Scot Symon   1954-56 F Hill   1956-61 C Britton
1961-68 J Milne   1968-70 R Seith   1970-73 A Ball (Snr)
1973 F Lord (Caretaker)   1973-75 R Charlton   1975-77 H Catterick
1977-81 N Stiles   1981 T Docherty   1981-83 G Lee
1983-85 A Kelly   1985 T Booth   1986 B Kidd
1986 J Clark (Caretaker)   J McGrath 1986-90 L Chapman
1990-92 S Allardyce (Caretaker) 1992-94 John Beck. 1994-98 Gary
Peters
ADDITIONAL INFORMATION
Club colours: White shirts, navy blue shorts & white socks.
Change colours: Red shirts with navy trim, red shorts, navy & red
hooped socks. **3rd Strip:** Royal blue with luminous yellow trim.
Reserves League: Pontins League Prem. **Youth:** Lancs Lge Div 1.

LONGEST LEAGUE RUNS

of undefeated matches:	23 (1888-89)	of league matches w/out a win:	15 (1923)
of undefeated home matches:	31 (1903-04)	of undefeated away matches:	11 (1888-89)
without home win:	9 (1965-66)	without an away win:	33 (1897-99)
of league wins:	14 (1950-51 - joint League record)	of home wins:	20 (1891-92)
of league defeats:	8 (1983, 1984)	of away wins:	8 (1950-51)

THE MANAGER

DAVID MOYES . . . . appointed January 1998.

PREVIOUS CLUBS
As Manager. . . . . None.
As Asst.Man/Coach. . . . . Preston North End.
As a player . . . . Celtic, Cambridge Utd, Bristol City, Shrewsbury Town.

HONOURS
As a Manager . . . . None.
As a Player . . . . None.

PRESTON NORTH END

PLAYERS NAME Honours	Ht	Wt	Birthdate	Birthplace Transfers	Contract Date	Clubs	League	L/Cup	FA Cup	Other	Lge	L/C	FAC	Oth
G O A L K E E P E R														
Lucas David A	6	11.4	11/23/77	Chapletown	12/24/92	Preston North End	9	1	1					
Y. E:				Loan	12/12/95	Darlington	6							
				Loan	10/3/96	Darlington	1							
				Loan	12/23/96	Scunthorpe United	6			2				
Moilanen Tuevo	6.5	12.6	12/12/73	Oulu		F.F.Jaro								
				£50000	12/5/95	Preston North End	46	5	3					
				Loan	12/12/96	Scarborough	4							
				Loan	1/17/97	Darlington	16							
D E F E N C E														
Darby Julian	6	11.4	10/3/67	Bolton	7/22/86	Bolton Wanderers	258+12	25	19	31+1	36	8	3	5
E: S. SVT'89				£150000	10/28/93	Coventry City	25+1		1		5			
				£250000	11/23/95	WBA	32+7		2	4	1			
					6/12/97	Preston North End	6+6	1+1	2+1					
				Loan	3/26/98	Rotherham United	3							
Gregan Sean M	6.2	12.5	3/29/74	Guisborough	12/20/91	Darlington	129+7	8	7	10+1	4			1
				£300000	11/29/96	Preston North End	54+2	3	4		3		2	
Jackson Michael	5.11	11.9	12/4/73	Chester	7/29/92	Crewe Alexandra	5	1	1	2				
E: Y.2,S. DIV2 96/97				Free	8/13/93	Bury	154+2	10	3	9	13	1		
					3/26/97	Preston North End	46+1	4	4		2			
Kidd Ryan	5.11	10	10/6/71	Radcliffe	7/12/90	Port Vale	1	+2		+1				
DIV3 95/96				Free	7/15/92	Preston North End	166+14	12+1	10	7+1	6	1		1
Moyes David	6.1	11.5	4/25/63	Blythswood		Celtic	19+5	8+1		2+1				
E: Y.2,S.DIV3 95/96				Free	10/28/83	Cambridge United	79	3	1	3	1			
				£10000	10/10/85	Bristol City	83	6	5	15	6			
				£30000	10/30/87	Shrewsbury Town	91+5	4	3	5	11		1	
					8/1/90	Dunfermline	105	7	5		13		1	
					8/1/93	Hamilton Acad.	5							
					8/1/95	Preston North End	142+1	5	10+1	13	14	1	2	1
Murdock Colin J	6.1	12	7/2/75	Ballymena	7/21/92	Manchester United								
NI: Y.4, S					5/23/97	Preston North End	27	2	1+1		1			
Parkinson Gary	5.1	11.6	1/10/68	Thornaby		Everton								
				Free	1/17/86	Middlesbrough	194+8	20	17	19	5	1	1	
				Loan	10/10/92	Southend United	6							
				Free	3/2/00	Bolton Wanderers	1+2			4				
				£80000	1/27/94	Burnley	134+1	12	9	5	4			1
					5/30/97	Preston North End	44+1	4	4		5		1	
M I D F I E L D														
Appleton Michael A	5.9	11.13	12/4/75	Salford	8/1/94	Manchester United		1+1						
				Loan	9/15/95	Lincoln City								
				Loan	1/17/97	Grimsby Town	10				3			
				£500000	8/8/97	Preston North End	31+7	2+1	4		2			
Cartwright Lee	5.8	10.6	9/19/72	Rossendale	7/30/91	Preston North End	198+34	10+1	12+2	10+4	16	2	1	
DIV3 95/96														
McKenna Paul	5.7	11.13	10/20/77	Chorley	1/1/96	Preston North End	9+2				1			
F O R W A R D														
Ashcroft Lee	5.1	11	9/7/72	Preston	7/16/91	Preston North End	78+13	3	5	6+2	13			1
E: u21.1				£225000	8/1/93	WBA	66+24	2+3	3+1	8+3	17		1	
				Loan	3/28/96	Notts County								
				Loan	9/5/96	Preston North End	7				3			
					11/8/96	Preston North End	56+1	4	4		17		2	
Davey Simon	5.1	11.2	10/1/70	Swansea	7/3/89	Swansea City	37+12	1	1+2	2+3	4		1	
WFAC'91. DIV3 95/96				Free	8/5/92	Carlisle United	105	10	7	15	18	1	2	2
				£75000	2/23/94	Preston North End	97+8	4	2+1	5	21	1		
Eyres David	0	0			10/29/97	Preston North End	26+2		4		4		2	
Holt Michael	5.11	11.6	7/28/77	Burnley		Blackburn Rovers								
					8/16/96	Preston North End	11+21	2+1	1+2		5	1		
Macken Jonathan P.	5.1	12.1	9/7/77	Manchester	7/1/96	Manchester United								
					7/31/97	Preston North End	20+9	2+2	2+1		6	2		
Morgan Mark P	6	11.3	10/23/78	Belfast	5/31/97	Preston North End(T)								
Nogan Kurt	5.1	11.1	9/9/70	Cardiff	7/11/89	Luton Town	17+16	1+3		1+1	3	1		
W: u21.2.				Free	9/30/92	Peterborough Utd				0+1				
				Free	10/17/92	Brighton & H.A.	71	4	4+1	5	42	2	4	
				£300000	2/24/95	Burnley	86+5	8	2	4	33	5		4
					3/13/97	Preston North End	19+10	1+1			5			
Rankine S Mark	5.1	11.8	9/30/69	Doncaster	7/4/88	Doncaster Rovers	160+4	8+1	8	14	20	1	2	2
				£70000	1/31/92	Wolverhampton W.	112+20	9+1	14+2	7+2	1			
					9/16/96	Preston North End	53+5	6	3		1			

461

SIR TOM FINNEY WAY

Deepdale, Preston, Lancashire PR1 6RU

Capacity..21,588.
Seating 9,000
First game..v Eagley (F) 0-1, 5.10.1878.
First floodlit game.........................v Bolton W., Lancs Senior Cup 1st Rnd, 3-0, Att: 12,000, 21.10.53.

ATTENDANCES
Highest..42,684 v Arsenal, Div 1, 23.4.1938.
Lowest ....751 v Bury, AMC, 29.1.1986.

OTHER GROUNDS ....None.

HOW TO GET TO THE GROUND

From the North
Use motorway (M6) then M55 until junction 1, leave motorway and follow signs to Preston A6. In 1.9 miles at crossroads turn left A5085 into Blackpool Road. In 0.8 miles turn right A6063 into Deepdale for Preston North End FC.

From the East and South
Use motorway (M6) until junction 31, leave motorway and follow signs Preston A59. In 1 mile at roundabout take 2nd exit into Blackpool Road. In 1.3 miles turn left A6063 into Deepdale for Preston North End FC.

From the West
Use motorway (M55) until junction 1, leave motorway and follow signs Preston A6. In 1.9 miles at crossroads turn left A5085 into Blackpool Road. In 0.8 miles turn right (A6063) into Deepdale for Preston North End FC.

Car Parking: Club park on Deepdale Road (West Stand) side of ground for 500 vehicles. Limited off-street parking Cost (match-days): £1.00.

Nearest Railway Station: Preston (01772 59439)

USEFUL TELEPHONE NUMBERS

Club switchboard 01772 902 020
Club fax number.......................01772 653 266
Club shop 01772 902 041
Ticket Office.............................01772 902 000

Marketing Department 01772 902 020
Internet address ....www.prestonnorthend.co.uk
P.N.E. Clubcall........................0891 66 02 20*

*Calls cost 50p per minute at all times. Call costings correct at time of going to press.

MATCHDAY PROGRAMME

Programme Editor.....................John Booth.

Number of pages......................................40.

Price ....£1.80.

Subscriptions ....Apply to club.

Local Newspapers
............................Lancashire Evening Post.

Local Radio Stations
...........Red Rose Radio, Radio Lancashire.

MATCHDAY TICKET PRICES

Sir Tom Finney Stand £13.00
Concessions. £8.00

Sir Tom Finney Stand Family Area £12.00
Concessions. £3.00

Bill Shankly Kop £13.00
Concessions. £8.00

Town End. £9.50
Concessions. £5.50

Pavillion Paddock South £10.00
Concessions. £6.00

Pavillion Stand £12.00
Concessions. £6.00

READING
(The Royals)
NATIONWIDE LEAGUE DIVISION 2
SPONSORED BY: AUTOTRADER (SHIRTS)

1998-99 - Back Row (L-R): Mass Sarr, Neville Roach, Paul Bryson, Keith McPherson, Andy Bernal, Lee Hodges, Grant Smith, Jason Bowen, Andy Legg, Martin Williams, Steve Swales, Ross Harrison. **Middle Row:** Alan Pardew (Reserve team manager), Ron Grant (Kit manager), Jason Bristow, John Polston, Phil Parkinson, Jimmy Crawford, Carl Asaba, Scott Howie, Nicky Hammond, Barry Hunter, Jim McIntyre, Stuart Gray, Linvoy Primus, Gareth Davies, Pat Bonner (Assistant Manager), Steve Kean (First team coach). **Front Row:** John Stephenson (Director of Youth Football), Paul Turner (Physio), Byron Glasgow, Martyn Booty, Robert Fleck, Grant Brobnei, Tommy Burns (Manager), James Lambert, Graeme Murty, Ray Houghton, Mark Reilly, Jordon Norris, Paul Bell (Assistant Physio), Kevin Dillon (Youth team manager).

READING
FORMED IN 1871
TURNED PROFESSIONAL IN 1895
LTD COMPANY IN 1895

CHAIRMAN: J Madejski
CHEIF EXECUTIVE: Nigel Howe
DIRECTOR
I Wood-Smith
SECRETARY
Andrea Barker
COMMERCIAL MANAGER
Kevin Girdler

MANAGER: Tommy Burns
ASSISTANT MANAGER: Pat Bonner

RESERVE TEAM MANAGER:
Alan Parden
DIRECTOR OF YOUTH FOOTBALL
John Stephenson
PHYSIOTHERAPIST
Paul Turner

STATISTICIAN FOR THE DIRECTORY
David Downs

For the first time in their league history Reading finished bottom of a division. Relegation to Division Two was bad enough but the fact that it could have been avoided with a little more foresight increased the frustration felt by the club's loyal supporters.

The appointment of a manager to replace Mick Gooding and Jimmy Quinn was delayed until three weeks before the start of the season. The new arrival Terry Bullivant from Barnet, had little time to assemble or train a squad and early season results confirmed that the team lacked motivation and organisation. Reading were in and around the relegation places from September onwards but despite rumblings in the local press and among the fans the board professed their faith in the manager and his players and the situation was allowed to continue. Bullivant looked to be out of his depth but a brief revival around Christmas time, highlighted by a 2-0 victory at Swindon, took Royals up to fourteenth, their highest placing of the campaign.

The cup competitions provided a rare boost too. Reading reached round five of the Coca-Cola Cup to equal a club record before losing very unluckily at home to Middlesbrough, and also round five of the FA Cup, a stage they last achieved in 1935. That cup run included a replay win over a plucky non-League Cheltenham Town, and a penalty shootout victory against Cardiff City when goalie Nick Hammond performed heroics as, despite injury, he saved three spot-kicks.

After the cups it was back to the fight for survival in Division One. Loan players came and went, the line-up and playing formation were altered, but basically the team just wasn't good enough to stay up. If everyone had shown the spirit of Hammond, skipper Phil Parkinson or centre-backs Linvoy Primus and Andy Bernal, there might have been a chance but it was not to be. Bullivant eventually left after a humiliating 3-0 defeat at local rivals Oxford United, when disgruntled fans staged a sit-down protest in front of the team coach.

Tommy Burns arrived from Newcastle United as his replacement and signed seven players days after his appointment, but it was too late. Reading had lost thirteen of their last fourteen matches and relegation became a virtual formality. If only Burns had been given the job a month earlier he might just have been able to keep the Royals in Division One.

Compounding the sadness felt by the supporters was the closure of Elm Park, the home of Reading FC for 102 years. The final game against Norwich City attracted a season's best gate of 14,817, but even that occasion was marred by an uninspired display by the team.

The move to the all-seater, palatial Madejski Stadium took place in August 1998. The first game resulted in a 3-0 victory over Luton Town. Perhaps Burns is on his way to finding a team to match its home. Up the Royals!

David Downs.

READING

Division 1	:24th			FA CUP: 5th Round				LC CUP: 6th Round	

M	DATE	COMP.	VEN	OPPONENTS	RESULT	H/T	LP	GOAL SCORERS/GOAL TIMES	ATT.
1	A 09	FL	A	Bury	D 1-1	1-0	12	Swales 12	(5065)
2	12	CC 1/1	H	**Swansea City**	W 2-0	0-0		Lambert 58, Roach 76	4829
3	15	FL	H	Swindon Town	L 0-1	0-1	17		9338
4	23	FL	A	Birmingham City	L 0-3	0-1	23		(16495)
5	26	CC 1/2	A	**Swansea City**	D 1-1	0-0		Asaba 54	(3333)
6	30	FL	H	Bradford City	L 0-3	0-2	24		7163
7	S 02	FL	H	Queens Park Rangers	L 1-2	1-0	24	Hodges 10	10203
8	07	FL	A	West Bromwich Albion	L 0-1	0-0	24		(15966)
9	13	FL	H	Oxford United	W 2-1	1-1	23	Asaba 21, Hodges 61	9003
10	16	CC 2/1	H	**Peterborough United**	D 0-0	0-0			5138
11	20	FL	A	Tranmere Rovers	L 0-6	0-5	23		(5565)
12	23	CC 2/2	A	**Peterborough United**	W 2-0	0-0		Asaba 51, Williams 70	(6067)
13	27	FL	A	Portsmouth	W 2-0	1-0	22	Hodges 15, Williams 88	(9593)
14	O 04	FL	H	Sunderland	W 4-0	2-0	20	Asaba 16, 26, Williams 60, Lambert 64	10795
15	11	FL	H	Crewe Alexandra	D 3-3	2-3	17	Asaba 35, 59, Westwood 42 (OG)	6685
16	14	CC 3	H	**Wolverhampton Wand**	W 4-2	2-1		Parkinson 35, Meaker 47, McPherson 55, Williams 33 (OG)	11080
17	18	FL	A	Manchester City	D 0-0	0-0	19		(26488)
18	21	FL	A	Norwich City	D 0-0	0-0	19		(17781)
19	24	FL	H	Nottingham Forest	D 3-3	0-1	18	Williams 57 (pen), Lambert 73, Primus 80	12610
20	N 01	FL	A	Port Vale	D 0-0	0-0	19		(6569)
21	04	FL	H	Sheffield United	L 0-1	0-0	20		8132
22	08	FL	H	Stockport County	W 1-0	1-0	18	Morley 42 (pen)	7444
23	15	FL	A	Huddersfield Town	L 0-1	0-0	19		(12617)
24	18	CC 4	A	**Leeds United**	W 3-2	1-1		Asaba 9, Williams 66, Morley 85	(15069)
25	22	FL	H	Ipswich Town	L 0-4	0-2	21		9400
26	29	FL	A	Stoke City	W 2-1	1-0	18	Morley 32 (pen), 59	(11103)
27	D 06	FL	H	Charlton Athletic	W 2-0	2-0	16	Hodges 9, Morley 36 (pen)	8076
28	13	FL	A	Middlesbrough	L 0-4	0-0	17		(29876)
29	20	FL	H	Wolverhampton Wand	D 0-0	0-0	18		11715
30	26	FL	H	West Bromwich Albion	W 2-1	2-0	15	Williams 27, McDermott 1 (OG)	10154
31	28	FL	A	Queens Park Rangers	D 1-1	0-1	16	Morley 64	(13015)
32	J 06	CC QF	H	**Middlesbrough**	L 0-1	0-0			13072
33	10	FL	H	Bury	D 1-1	1-0	15	, Lucketti 29 (OG)	7499
34	13	FAC 3	A	**Cheltenham Town**	D 1-1	0-1		Morley 71	(6000)
35	17	FL	A	Swindon Town	W 2-0	2-0	14	Lovell 9, Lambert 14	(9500)
36	20	FAC 3R	H	**Cheltenham Town**	W 2-1	1-0		Morley 38, Booty 72	9686
37	24	FAC 4	A	**Cardiff City**	D 1-1	0-0		Asaba 56	(10174)
38	27	FL	A	Bradford City	L 1-4	1-2	16	Asaba 2	(13021)
39	31	FL	H	Birmingham City	W 2-0	0-0	15	Hodges 74, Asaba 83	10315
40	F 03	FAC 4R	H	**Cardiff City**	D 1-1	0-1		Morley 56	11808
41	06	FL	H	Tranmere Rovers	L 1-3	0-1	16	Williams 75	7069
42	13	FAC 5	A	**Sheffield United**	L 0-1	0-0			(17845)
43	17	FL	A	Sunderland	L 1-4	0-2	17	Bowen 53	(40579)
44	21	FL	H	Portsmouth	L 0-1	0-0	19		9928
45	24	FL	H	Manchester City	W 3-0	2-0	15	Hodges 8, Houghton 29, Asaba 90	11513
46	28	FL	A	Crewe Alexandra	L 0-1	0-1	17		(5202)
47	M 03	FL	A	Stockport County	L 1-5	0-4	18	Williams 80 (pen)	(6148)
48	07	FL	H	Port Vale	L 0-3	0-2	22		7139
49	14	FL	A	Sheffield United	L 0-4	0-1	23		(15473)
50	17	FL	A	Oxford United	L 0-3	0-1	23		(8103)
51	21	FL	H	Huddersfield Town	L 0-2	0-0	24		8593
52	28	FL	A	Ipswich Town	L 0-1	0-1	24		(19075)
53	A 04	FL	H	Stoke City	W 2-0	1-0	23	O'Neill 32, Meaker 48	10448
54	10	FL	A	Charlton Athletic	L 0-3	0-2	23		(14220)
55	13	FL	A	Middlesbrough	L 0-1	0-1	24		14501
56	18	FL	A	Wolverhampton Wand	L 1-3	1-1	24	Brayson 45	(19785)
57	26	FL	A	Nottingham Forest	L 0-1	0-0	24		(29302)
58	M 03	FL	H	Norwich City	L 0-1	0-0	24		14817

Best Home League Attendance: 14817 V Norwich City   **Smallest :6685 V Crewe Alexandra**   **Average :9676**

Goal Scorers:

FL	(39)	Asaba 8, Hodges 6, Williams 6, Morley 5, Lambert 3, Bowen 1, Brayson 1, Houghton 1, Lovell 1, Meaker 1, O'Neill 1, Primus 1, Swales 1, Opponents 3
CC	(12)	Asaba 3, Williams 2, Lambert 1, McPherson 1, Meaker 1, Morley 1, Parkinson 1, Roach 1, Opponents 1
FAC	(5)	Morley 3, Asaba 1, Booty 1

(F) Asaba	(D) Bernal	(D) Bodin	(D) Booty	(M) Bowen	(M) Caskey	(M) Crawford	(D) Davies	(M) Gray	(G) Hammond	(M) Hodges	(M) Houghton	(G) Howie	(F) Lambert	(M) Legg	(M) Lovell	(G) Mautone	(M) McIntyre	(D) McPherson	(M) Meaker	(F) Morley	(F) O'Neill	(M) Parkinson	(D) Primus	(F) Roach	(D) Swales	(D) Thorp	(D) Wdowczyk	(M) Williams	Referee	#
X	X		X							X	X		X		X	S							X	S2	X			X	T. Heilbron	1
X	X		X							X	X		X		X	S							X	S1	X			X	P Taylor	2
X	X		X								X		X		X	S			S3				X	S1	X			X	A P D'Urso	3
X	X	S1	X								X		X		X	S							X	S2	S			X	E Lomas	4
X	X	X	X								X		X		X	X			X				X	S2	S			S1	G Singh	5
X	X		X								X		X		X	X			X			S2	X					S1	C R Wilkes	6
X	X		X								X		X		X	X			X				X	S1	S		S	S	M Fletcher	7
X	X										X		X		X	X			X			X	X	S1	S			S	P S Danson	8
X	X										X		X		X				X			X	X	S2	S1				S G Bennett	9
X	X	S1								X	S3		X		X				X			X	X	X	X			S2	P Rejer	10
X	X										X		X		X				X			X	X	S	S2			S1	D Laws	11
X	X									X	X		X		X				X			X	X	S1	X		S	X	R D Furnandiz	12
X	X									X	X		X			X			X			X	X	S	S		S	X	M C Bailey	13
X	X												X			X			X			X	X	S	S2		S1	X	M J Brandwood	14
X	X				X								X			X			X			X	X	S	X		S1	X	R Styles	15
X	X				S2					X			X			X			X			X	X	S1	X		S3	X	C R Wilkes	16
X	X				S								X			X			X			X	X	S	X		S1	X	K A Leach	17
		S	S	X									X			X			X			X	X	S	X		S	X	F G Stretton	18
		S	S	X									X			X			X			X	X	S1	X		S	X	M J Brandwood	19
		S		X				X								X		S1	X			X	X		X		S	X	G Cain	20
		S		X				X								X			X			X	X		X		S	X	P S Danson	21
X	X			X				X		S1			X					X	X			X	X		X		S		M R Halsey	22
X	X		S		X			X	S1				X					X	X			X	X		X			X	W C Burns	23
X	X		S		X			X	S1	X		S						X	X			X	X		X			X	G P Barber	24
X	X		S2		X			X	S1	X								X	X			X	X	S	X			X	A R Leake	25
X3			X	S2			X	S1	X	X1							X		X			X	X		X	S3		X2	T Jones	26
X			X	S1			X	X2		X1		S2					X		X			X	X	S	X		S	X	S W Mathieson	27
X			X	S1		X	X	X		X1		S					X		X			X	X	S	X		S	X	C J Foy	28
X	X	X		S		X	X	X2		X		S1				X1		X				X		X			S2	X	S G Bennett	29
X2	X	S	X	S1		X	X	X		X		X1		S2				X				X		X				X	A P D'Urso	30
X	X	S	S1	X		X	X	X				X1						X					X		X			X	B Knight	31
X	X		X	S1	S		X	X		X						X			X	X				X	S		X1	G Cain	32
X	X	X	X	X		X	X	X			X		S			S		S	X			X	X		X	S		M E Pierce	33
	X	X	S2	X		X	X2		X1				S1	X							X	X	S			K A Leach	34
	X	X	X		S	X	X1	S1	X	X2			S2	X				X	X			X	S1		E Lomas	35
X	X	X	X	S	X1	X	X2	S2	X		X		S	X			X	X	X	S1		K A Leach	36
X2	X	X	X	X3		X	X1	X		X		S				S3		X			X	X	S		X1	S J Lodge	37
X	X	X2	X		X	X	X1	X1	S				S			X		X			X	X	S2		G Laws	38
X	X	X	X	X	X	S1	X	S2			X2		X			X	X	X	S		X1	P Rejer	39
X	X	X	X	X	S1	X	S			S	X	X			X	X	S	X1	S J Lodge	40
X1	X	X	X	X2	X	S1	S	S	X	X	X		S1	K A Leach	41
X1	X	X	X	X	X	S	S	S	X	X	X	S1	N S Barry	42
X	X	X	X	X	X	S	S	X	X	X	X1	J A Kirkby	43
X	X	X	X	S	X	X	S1	S	X	X	X	X1	A G Wiley	44
X	X	X	X1	X	X1	X	S1	S	X	X	X	X	A Bates	45
X1	X	X	X	X	X	X	X	S	X	S	X	K M Lynch	46
X	X	X	S1	X1	X	X	X	X	S	X	T Jones	47
X2	X	X3	X	X	X	S2	S1	X	S3	X1	M R Halsey	48
X	S	S	X	S1	X	X	X	X	X	X1	C J Foy	49
X	S	X	S1	X	X	X1	X	X	X	M Fletcher	50
X	S1	X	X	X	X2	X	X1	S	X	X	S2	X	P Taylor	51
X	S1	X	X1	X	X	X2	X1	X	X	X	B Coddington	52
S1	X	X	X	X	X	X	X2	X1	X	X	F G Stretton	53
X	X	X	X	X	X1	X2	S1	S3	X	X	M E Pierce	54
X	X	S3	X	X	X	X2	X1	S2	X1	X3	B Knight	55
X	X	X	X	X	X	X1	S1	X		S	T Heilbron	56
X	X	X	X	X	X1	X2	X	X	S	G B Frankland	57
X	X	X	X	S2	X	X2	X	X	S	T Jones	58

31	34	3	24	11	19	4	17	7	18	20	20	7	33	10	8	14	6	24	16	17	9	36	36		26		3	25	FL Appearances	
1		1	1	3	4	1	1			4	5		1		7				5	6	1			8	5	3	3	3	FL Sub Appearances	
7	6	1	4+1	0+1	1+1		1			2	5+1		5+1	6		5			6	3	2		5	6	1+4	6	1+1	4+2	CC Appearances	
3	5	1	5	5	0+1		3			4	4+1		2+2	3		0+2	5		1		5		0+1	1+1	FAC Appearances	

Also Played: (M) Ashdown S(40,42). (G) Bibbo S(31,34,36,37), X(41,42,43). (F) Brayson S2(52,54,57), X(55,56) S1(58). (G) Colgan X(46,47,48,49,50). (F) Fleck X(52,58), S2(53), X3(54), S1(57). (M) Glasgow S2(3,15),12,21,23,34), X(20). (F) Holsgrove S1(1), S2(2), X(3), S(8). (M) Kelly X(52,55), X1(58). (M) Robins X(6,7,8,9,11). (D) Sandford X (8,9,11,13,14). (M) Smith S(9).

CLUB RECORDS

BIGGEST VICTORIES
League: 10-2 v Crystal Palace, Division 3S, 4.9.1946
F.A. Cup: 8-3 v Corinthians, Rnd.1, 1935-36
6-0 v Leyton, Round 2, 1925/26
League Cup: 4-0 v QPR, Round 2, 23.9.1964
5-1 v Southend United, Round 2, 1965/66
5-1 v Oxford United, Round 1, 1979/80
BIGGEST DEFEATS
League: 1-8 v Burnley, Division 2, 13.9.1930
F.A. Cup: 0-18 v Preston North End, Round 1, 27.1.1894
League Cup: 0-5 v Leicester City, Round 2, 1966/67
0-5 v Watford, Round 2, 1977/78
MOST POINTS
3 points a win: 94, Division 3, 1985-86
2 points a win: 65, Division 4, 1978-79
MOST GOALS
112, 1951-52 (Division 3S)
Blackman 39, Bainbridge 18, Lewis 15, Edelston 14, Henley 10, Simpson 8, Owens4, Brice 2, Brooks 1, 1og.
MOST FIRST CLASS MATCHES IN A SEASON
60 (46 league + 10 FA Cup + 4 Lge Cup) 1989-90
MOST LEAGUE GOALS CONCEDED
96, Division 2, 1930-31
MOST LEAGUE WINS
29, Division 3, 1985-86
MOST LEAGUE DRAWS
19, Division 4, 1973-74
Division 3, 1989-90
MOST LEAGUE DEFEATS
24, Division 2, 1930-31
Division 3, 1976-77
RECORD TRANSFER FEE RECEIVED
£1,575,000 from Newcastle Utd for Shaka Hislop, August 1995.
RECORD TRANSFER FEE PAID
£700,000 to Tottenham for Darren Caskey, February 1996.
BEST PERFORMANCES
League: 1985-86: Matches played 46, Won 29, Drawn 7, Lost 10, Goals for 67,Goals against 51, Points 94. 1st in Division 3.
Highest: 2nd, Division 1, 1994-95.

Best Performances continued...
F.A. Cup: 1926-27: 1st rnd. Weymouth 4-4, 5-0; 2nd rnd. Southend, 3-2; 3rd rnd.Manchester United, 1-1,2-2,2-1; 4th rnd. Portsmouth, 3-1; 5th rnd. Brentford,1-0; 6th rnd, Swansea, 3-1; Semi-Final, Cardiff City, 0-3.
League Cup: 1965-66: 1st rnd, Port Vale, 2-2, 1-0; 2nd rnd, Southend, 5-1; 3rd rnd, Derby County, 1-1, 2-0; 4th rnd, Cardiff City 1-5.
1978-79: 1st rnd, Gillingham, 3-1, 2-1; 2nd rnd, Wolves, 1-0; 3rd rnd,Rotherham, 2-2, 1-0, 4th rnd, Southampton, 0-0, 0-2.
1995-96: 2nd rnd, WBA H1-1,A4-2. 3rd rnd, Bury H2-1.
4th rnd, Southampton H2-1. 5th rnd, Leeds A1-2.

INDIVIDUAL CLUB RECORDS

MOST GOALS IN A MATCH
6. Arthur Bacon v Stoke City, Division 2, 3.4.1931 (7-3)
MOST GOALS IN A SEASON
Trevor Senior, 36 League, 1 FA Cup, 4 Lge Cup, Total 41 (1983-84)
3 goals 2 times = 6, 2 goals 10 times = 20, 1 goal 15 times = 15.
Previous holder: Ronnie Blackman, 40 (39 league, 1 FA Cup) 1951-52.
OLDEST PLAYER
Beaumont Ratcliffe, 39 years 336 days v Northampton Town, 1947-48
YOUNGEST PLAYER
S Hetkze, 16 years 184 days v Darlington, 4.12.71
MOST CAPPED PLAYER
Jimmy Quinn (Northern Ireland) 17

PREVIOUS MANAGERS

Harry Matthews 1902-22. Arthur Chadwick 1923-25.
Angus Wylie 1926-31. Joe Smith 1931-35. Billy Butler 1935-39.
John Cochrane 1939. Joe Edelston 1939-47. Ted Drake 1947-52.
Jack Smith 1952-55. Harry Johnson 1955-63. Roy Bentley1963-69.
Jack Mansell 1969-72. Charlie Hurley 1972-77. Maurice Evans 1977-84. Ian Branfoot 1984-89. Ian Porterfield1989-91.
Mark McGhee 1991-94. M Gooding & J Quinn1994-97.
Terry Bullivant 1997-98.

ADDITIONAL INFORMATION
Previous League: Southern League
Club colours: Royal Blue & white hooped shirts, white shorts and socks. **Change colours:Toro** red & white shirts, toro red shorts and toro red & white socks.
Reserves League: Capital League. **Youth League:** S E Counties, Allied Counties Youth League.

COMPETITIONS

Div.2/1	Div.3.2	Div.3(S)	Div.4	Watney C.
1926-31	1958-71	1920-26	1971-76	1970
1986-88	1976-77	1931-58	1977-79	
1994-98	1979-83		1983-84	
	1984-86			
	1986-94			
	1998-			

HONOURS

Div.3/2	Div.3(S)	Div.4	Div.3(S) Cup
1985-86	1925-26	1978-79	1937-38
1993-94			**Simod Cup**
			1987-88

LONGEST LEAGUE RUNS

of undefeated matches:	19 (1973)	of league matches w/out a win:	14 (1927)
of undefeated home matches:	55 (1933-36)	of undefeated away matches:	11 (1985)
without home win:	8 (1954, 1991)	without an away win:	21 (1952-53)
of league wins:	13 (1985, record for start of a season)	of home wins:	19 (1931-32)
of league defeats:	6 (1971)	of away wins:	7 (1951-52, 1985)

THE MANAGER

Tommy Burns . . . . appointed March 1998.
Previous Clubs
As Manager: Kilmarnock, Celtic. As Assitant/Coach: Celtic, Kilmarnock.
As a Player. . . . . Celtic, Kilmarnock.
Honours
As a Manager: None.
As a Player: Scottish League championship, Scottish Cup and Scottish League Cup. 8 full caps for Scotland.

READING

PLAYERS NAME / Honours	Ht	Wt	Birthdate	Birthplace / Transfers	Contract Date	Clubs	APPEARANCES League	L/Cup	FA Cup	Other	GOALS Lge	L/C	FAC	Oth
G O A L K E E P E R														
Hammond Nicky	6	11.13	9/7/67	Hornchurch	7/12/85	Arsenal								
				Loan	8/23/86	Bristol Rovers	3							
				Free	7/1/87	Swindon Town	65+2	11	10	6				
				£40000	8/14/95	Plymouth Argyle	4	2		1				
				Loan	12/13/95	Reading								
				£40000	1/9/96	Reading	24	2	5					
Howie Scott	6.2	13.7	1/4/72	Glasgow		Clyde								
S: u21.5.				£300000	8/12/93	Norwich City	1+1							
				£300000	10/13/94	Motherwell								
				Loan	1/28/98	Coventry City								
				£30000	3/26/98	Reading	7							
Mautone Steve	6.1	13.2	8/10/70	Australia		Canberra Cosmos								
				£30000	3/29/96	West Ham United	1	2						
				Loan	9/6/96	Crewe Alexandra	3							
				Loan	2/17/97	Reading	7							
					3/27/97	Reading	22	5						
D E F E N C E														
Bernal Andrew	5.1	12.5	7/16/66	Canberra (Aus)		Sporting Gijon								
Aus: 21				Free	9/24/87	Ipswich Town	4+5			0+2				
					8/1/90	Sydney Olympic								
				£30000	7/26/94	Reading	142	14+1	9	3	2			
Booty Martyn J	5.8	11.2	5/30/71	Kirby Muxloe	5/30/89	Coventry City	4+1	2	2					
				Free	10/7/93	Crewe Alexandra	74+1	2	5	11	3			
				£75000	1/18/96	Reading	55+1	6+1	7		1		1	
Bristow Jason P			4/23/80	Basingstoke	5/7/98	Reading (T)								
Davies Gareth M	5.1	11.3	12/11/73	Hereford	4/10/92	Hereford United	91+4	5+2	4	5	2			
W: u21.7.				£120000	7/1/95	Crystal Palace	17+3		2		2			
					2/21/97	Cardiff City	6				2			
					3/29/97	Crystal Palace	5+2			1				
				£175000	12/12/97	Reading	17+1	1	3					
Gray Stuart	5.11	11.2	Hallogate	12/12/73		Celtic								
				£100000	3/26/98	Reading	7							
Hunter Barry	6.4	12	11/18/68	Coleraine	1/1/00	Crusaders								
				£50000	8/20/93	Wrexham	58+2	4	5	13	1			1
				£400000	7/9/96	Reading	26+1	1	1		2			
McPherson Keith	5.11	11	9/11/63	Greenwich	9/12/81	West Ham United	1							
FAYC'81. Div4'87. Div2'94				Loan	9/30/85	Cambridge United	11				1			
				£15000	1/23/86	Northampton Town	182	9	12	13	8	1		
					8/24/90	Reading	251+5	19+1	11+1	20+1	9	1		
Polston John D	5.11	11.3	10/06/68	Walthamstow	16/07/85	Tottenham Hotspur	17+7	3+1						
E: Y6				£250000	24/07/90	Norwich City	200+15	20+1	17+1	9	8	2	1	1
				Free	7/1/98	Reading								
Primus Linvoy Stephen	6	14	9/14/73	Forest Gate	8/14/92	Charlton Ath (T)	4	0+1		0+1				
				Free	7/18/94	Barnet	127	9+1	8	4	7		1	
				£400000	8/2/97	Reading	36	6	1		1			
Swales Steve	5.8	10	12/26/73	Whitby	8/3/92	Scarborough	51+3		5	3				
				£70000	7/13/95	Reading	33+10	5+1	6		1			
M I D F I E L D														
Bowen Jason	5.6	8.11	8/24/72	Merthyr Tydfil	7/1/90	Swansea City	93+31	6+1	9+2	15+3	26	2	1	8
W:1,u21.5,Y. AMC'94.				£275000	7/24/95	Birmingham City	34+13	4+6	1+4	2	7	2		2
				£200000	12/24/97	Reading	11+3	0+1	5		1			
Brebner Grant I	5.10	11.11	06/12/77	Edinburgh	17/03/95	Manchester United								
				Loan	1/9/98	Cambridge United	6				1			
Loan 2/26/98 Hibernian 9 SLge Apps 1 gl.				£300000	7/1/98	Reading								
Caskey Darren	5.8	10.7	8/21/74	Basildon	3/6/92	Tottenham Hotspur	17+12	3+1	3+1		4	1		
E: S, Y.15. UEFA Y'93				Loan	10/27/95	Watford								
				£700000	2/1/96	Reading	58+13	2+1	2+1		2		1	
Crawford James	5.11	11.06	5/1/73	Dublin		Bohemians								
					8/1/94	Newcastle United	0+2	0+1						
				Loan	9/27/96	Rotherham United	11							
Loan 2/27/98 Dundee United				£50000	3/26/98	Reading	4+1							
Glasgow Byron	5.6	10.11	2/18/79	London	8/27/96	Reading	3+4		0+1					
Hodges Lee Leslie	6	12.1	9/4/73	Epping	2/29/92	Tottenham H. (T)	0+4							
E: Y.				Loan	2/26/93	Plymouth Argyle	6+1				2			
Loan 12/31/93 Wycombe 2+2 Lge, 1 FAC, 1Oth				Free	5/31/94	Barnet	94+11	6+1	6+1	3+1	26		4	
				£100000	8/2/97	Reading	20+4	5+1	4+1		6			
Houghton Raymond J	5.7	10.1	1/9/62	Glasgow	7/5/79	West Ham United	0+1							
Ei:69. LC'86'94. Div.1'88'90. CS'88'90. FAC'89'92.				Free	7/7/82	Fulham	129	12	4		16	2	3	
				£147000	9/13/85	Oxford United	83	13	3	6	10	3		1
				£825000	10/19/87	Liverpool	147+6	14	26+1	8	28	3	4	3
				£900000	7/28/92	Aston Villa	83+12	11+2	7	4+2	6	2	2	1
				£300000	3/23/95	Crystal Palace	69+3	6	4	4	7			1
				Free	7/18/97	Reading	20+5	5+1	2+2		1			
Legg Andy	5.8	10.7	7/28/66	Neath		Britton Ferry								
WFAC'89'91.					8/12/88	Swansea City	155+8	9+1	16	15+3	29		4	5
				£275000	7/23/93	Notts County	61+3	7	4+1	10	5			4
				£250000	3/1/96	Birmingham City	31+14	3+1	2+1		5			
				Loan	1/3/97	Ipswich Town	6	1			1			
				£75000	2/20/98	Reading	10							
McIntyre Jim	5.11	12	5/24/72	Alexandria		Kilmarnock								
				£420000	3/26/98	Reading	6							
Murty Graeme	5.11	11.2	11/13/74	Middlesbro'	3/23/93	York City	106+12	10	5	4+1	7	2		
				£700000	7/7/98	Reading								
Parkinson Phil	6	11.6	12/1/67	Chorley	12/7/85	Southampton								
Div2'94				£12000	3/8/88	Bury	133+12	6+1	4	13	5		1	1
				£37500	7/10/92	Reading	192+23	20+1	13	4+2	7	2	1	
Williams Martin	5.9	11.12	7/12/73	Luton		Leicester City								
				Free	9/13/91	Luton Town	12+28	1	+1	2+1	2			
				Free	7/13/95	Reading	45+12	5+3	1+1		8	2		
F O R W A R D														
Asaba Carl	6.2	13	1/28/73	London		Dulwich Hamlet								
					8/9/94	Brentford	49+5	5	4	4	25			2
				Loan	2/16/95	Colchester United	9+3				2			
					8/7/97	Reading	30+1	7	3		8	3	1	
Brayson Paul	5.4	10.10	9/16/77	Newcastle	8/1/95	Newcastle United		0+1						
				Loan	1/30/97	Swansea City	11				5			
				£100000	3/26/98	Reading	2+4				1			
Fleck Robert	5.1	10.3	8/11/65	Glasgow		Glasgow Rangers	61+24	3+5	1+1	3+4	29	2		3
S: 4, u21.7,Y. SPD'87.SLC'87'88				£580000	12/17/87	Norwich City	130+13	13	16+2	7	40	11	11	4
				£2100000	8/13/92	Chelsea	35+5	7	1		3	1		
Loan 11/1/93 Partick Thistle 1+1 SLge Apps 1gl				Loan	12/17/93	Bolton Wanderers	6+1			1	1			
Loan 1/12/95 Bristol City 10 Lge Apps 1gl				£650000	9/29/95	Norwich City	93+10	9+2	3		16	2		
				£50000	3/26/98	Reading	3+2							
Harrison Ross			12/28/79	Leamington S.	5/2/98	Reading (T)								
Lambert James	5.7	10.4	9/14/73	Henley	7/3/92	Reading	75+48	8+3	9+2	2+3	16	2	1	1
Roach Neville	5.11	11	9/29/78	Reading	3/27/97	Reading	2+8	1+4			1	1		
ADITIONAL CONTRACT PLAYERS														
Ashdown Jamie L					2/2/98	Reading (T)								
Sarr Mass						Hadjuk Split								
				£158000	7/7/98	Reading								
Reilly Mark						Kilmarnock								
				Free	7/1/98	Reading								

MADEJSKI STADIUM
Reading RG2 0FL

Capacity ....25,000 all seater.

First game..v Luton Town, Football League, 22.08.98.
First floodlit game ....Not yet played at the time of going to press.

ATTENDANCES
Highest...Not yet know at time of going to press.
Lowest..Not yet know at time of going to press.

OTHER GROUNDS...........Reading Recreation Ground 1871. Reading CC 1882. Coley Park 1882-89.
....Caversham CC 1889-96. Elm Park 1896-98.

HOW TO GET TO THE GROUND

From all directions
The Madejski Stadium is literally five minutes from junction 11 of the M4.

Car Parking: Parking for 1,800 cars but check with club to confirm availabilty.

Nearest Railway Station: Reading (01734 595 911) and bus or Reading West.

USEFUL TELEPHONE NUMBERS

Club switchboard. 0118 968 1100
Club fax number 0118 968 1101
Ticket Office. . 0118 968 1000 (Fax 968 1001)
Megastore 0118 968 1234

Marketing Department. 0118 968 1300
Internet address . . . . www.readingfc.co.uk
Clubcall 0891 12 10 00*
*Calls cost 50p per minute at all times. Call costings correct at time of going to press.

MATCHDAY PROGRAMME

Programme Editor. . . . . Andi Jenkins.

Number of pages . . . . 56.

Price . . . . £2.00.

Subscriptions . . . . Contact supporters club.

Local Newspapers
  Reading Evening Post, Reading Chronicle.

Local Radio Stations
  . . . . . BBC Thames Valley FM, Radio 210.

MATCHDAY TICKET PRICES

	Pre Match Sale	Match Day Sale
West Upper Stand		
. . . .	£18.00	£20.00
West Lower/North/East		
Adults	£12.00	£14.00
Concessions	£7.00	£8.00
Young Royals	£6.00	£6.00
Disabled	£6.00	£7.00

STOKE CITY
(The Potters)
NATIONWIDE LEAGUE DIVISION 2
SPONSORED BY: BRITANNIA

1998-99 - Back Row L-R: Dave Kevan, Paul Stewart, Neil Mackenzie, Steve Tweed, Justin Whittle, Kyle Lightbourne, Brian Small, Chris Short, David Oldfield, Peter Thorne. Rob Ryles, **Middle Row:** Allan Evans, Richard Burgess, Jamie Cartwright, Robert Heath, Clive Clarke, Carl Muggleton, Stuart Fraser, Ashley Wooliscroft, James O'Connor, Jamie Godbold, Stephen Taaffe, Ian Cranson. **Front Row:** Ray Wallace, Stephen Woods, Matthew Bullock, Graham Kavanagh, Larus Sigurdsson, Tony McAndrew, Brian Little (Manager), Phil Robinson, Kevin Keen, Richard Forsyth, Dean Crowe, Simon Sturridge.

STOKE CITY
FORMED IN 1868
TURNED PROFESSIONAL IN 1885
LTD COMPANY IN 1908

PRESIDENT: Sir Stanley Matthews
CHAIRMAN: P Coates

DIRECTORS
K A Humphreys (Vice-Chairman)
D J Edwards, P E Doona B.A. (Hons.) FCA,
SECRETARY
M J Potts (01782 413 511)

MANAGER: Brian Little
ASSISTANT MANAGER: Tony McAndrew
BACK ROOM STAFF
Dave Kevan
Rob Ryles
Allan Evans
Ian Cranson

STATISTICIAN FOR THE DIRECTORY
Wade Martin

One of the most forgettable seasons in the club's 130 year history.

The season started with both anguish and joy. The joy came from moving to the new all-seater and modern Britannia Stadium a joint venture between the club, the local authority and the St Modwen Property Group. Whilst the stadium had its fair share of teething problems not least to do with access, ticketing and a Safety Certificate that arrived only in the nick of time, it was applauded by the overwhelming majority of Stoke fans who had been brought up to worship at the Victoria Ground. Whilst clearly not as atmospheric as their previous home it was a project that all involved with should take great pride.

The rest of a dreadful season covers the anguish. It started with a delay by the board in announcing a new manager to succeed the popular Lou Macari. After an interminable delay they appointed Macari's number 2 Chic Bates. The immensely affable Bates must have realised he was not first choice and so must have the players. The initial results were moderate but the decline set in November and December and culminated in the ultimate humiliation - a 7-0 home defeat by Birmingham City.

Bates and the players escaped the early dismay of the fans who preferred to target their wrath at a board who had been unable or unwilling to commit funds to the transfer market to improve a side that had not proved good enough in the previous campaign. The scenes that followed the Birmingham fiasco did not put anyone in a good light and led to the CHairman standing down - the club operated for some months apparently without one! There was insufficient communication between the board and fans and without doubt the move to a new stadium put the club under immense financial pressure.

After a short period and a victory Bates was replaced by Chris Kamara. Kamara a former fans favourite sadly promised too much and delivered nothing. His appointment was later acknowledged to be a mistake by the board but few fans at the time voice any thought of the disaster that were to befall the club.

If body language is any guide the players quickly lost faith in Kamara and his apparent policy of having a revolving door of players who were neither good enough nor committed enough. Apparently training was poorly executed and it was a blessed relief when Kamara was relieved of his duties. Bates' number two Alan Durban succeeded him in a last desperate effort to avoid relegation. The record book shows he failed although his record albeit short was better than his predecessors.

I suppose an objective assessor might say that the club deserved to be relegated for so mishandling affairs, even if this fan can't.

WADE MARTIN.

469

STOKE CITY

Division 1   :23rd   FA CUP: 3rd Round   LC CUP: 3rd Round

M	DATE	COMP.	VEN	OPPONENTS	RESULT	H/T	LP	GOAL SCORERS/GOAL TIMES	ATT.
1	A 09	FL	A	Birmingham City	L 0-2	0-1	18		(20608)
2	12	CC 1/1	A	Rochdale	W 3-1	1-1		Kavanagh 26, Thorne 67, Forsyth 74	(2509)
3	15	FL	A	Bradford City	D 0-0	0-0	19		(13823)
4	23	FL	A	Middlesbrough	W 1-0	0-0	12	Stewart 59	(30122)
5	27	CC 1/2	H	Rochdale	D 1-1	0-0		Kavanagh 85	12768
6	30	FL	H	Swindon Town	L 1-2	1-0	13	Forsyth 34	23000
7	S 03	FL	H	West Bromwich Albion	D 0-0	0-0	16		17500
8	13	FL	H	Stockport County	W 2-1	1-0	13	Wallace 28, Thorne 50	11743
9	16	CC 2/1	A	Burnley	W 4-0	1-0		Thorne 37, 62, Kavanagh 68, 81	(4175)
10	20	FL	A	Ipswich Town	W 3-2	2-0	13	Thorne 12, 32, Stewart 54	(10665)
11	24	CC 2/2	H	Burnley	W 2-0	1-0		Keen 36, Thorne 72	6041
12	27	FL	A	Nottingham Forest	L 0-1	0-0	15		(19018)
13	O 04	FL	H	Bury	W 3-2	0-0	11	Andrade 63, Forsyth 69, Thorne 73	11760
14	12	FL	H	Port Vale	W 2-1	2-1	7	Forsyth 5, Keen 34	20125
15	15	CC 3	H	Leeds United	L 1-3	0-0		Kavanagh 66 (pen)	16203
16	19	FL	A	Charlton Athletic	D 1-1	0-0	8	Wallace 51	(12345)
17	22	FL	A	Manchester City	W 1-0	0-0	6	Wallace 63	(25333)
18	25	FL	H	Sunderland	L 1-2	0-1	8	Stewart 81	14587
19	N 01	FL	A	Huddersfield Town	L 1-3	0-0	13	Griffin 78	(10916)
20	04	FL	H	Oxford United	D 0-0	0-0	14		8423
21	08	FL	H	Wolverhampton Wand	W 3-0	2-0	9	Kavanagh 7, 22 (pen), Forsyth 58	18490
22	15	FL	A	Queens Park Rangers	D 1-1	1-0	10	Forsyth 4	(11920)
23	22	FL	A	Tranmere Rovers	L 1-3	1-1	11	Kavanagh 35 (pen)	(8009)
24	29	FL	H	Reading	L 1-2	0-1	13	Thorne 81	11103
25	D 02	FL	A	Sheffield United	L 2-3	1-0	13	Thorne 8, 63	(14347)
26	06	FL	A	Portsmouth	L 0-2	0-2	14		(7072)
27	13	FL	H	Crewe Alexandra	L 0-2	0-1	15		14623
28	20	FL	A	Norwich City	D 0-0	0-0	15		(12265)
29	26	FL	H	Sheffield United	D 2-2	0-0	14	Forsyth 66, Thorne 86	19723
30	28	FL	A	West Bromwich Albion	D 1-1	0-0	15	Thorne 47	(17690)
31	J 10	FL	H	Birmingham City	L 0-7	0-3	16		14940
32	13	FAC 3	A	West Bromwich Albion	L 1-3	0-2		Gabbiadini 61	(17598)
33	16	FL	H	Bradford City	W 2-1	2-1	14	Forsyth 35 (pen), Thorne 42	10459
34	28	FL	A	Swindon Town	L 0-1	0-0	17		(6683)
35	F 01	FL	H	Middlesbrough	L 1-2	1-1	18	Kavanagh 36 (pen)	13242
36	06	FL	H	Ipswich Town	D 1-1	1-0	19	Holsgrove 15	11416
37	14	FL	A	Stockport County	L 0-1	0-0	20		(8701)
38	17	FL	A	Bury	D 0-0	0-0	18		(5802)
39	21	FL	H	Nottingham Forest	D 1-1	1-0	20	Crowe 32	16899
40	25	FL	H	Charlton Athletic	L 1-2	1-1	20	Kavanagh 42	10027
41	M 01	FL	A	Port Vale	D 0-0	0-0	23		(13853)
42	04	FL	A	Wolverhampton Wand	D 1-1	0-1	22	Crowe 89	(21058)
43	07	FL	H	Huddersfield Town	L 1-2	0-2	24	Tiatto 90	12594
44	14	FL	A	Oxford United	L 1-5	0-1	24	Crowe 69	(7300)
45	21	FL	H	Queens Park Rangers	W 2-1	1-0	23	Crowe 51, Dowie 21 (OG)	11051
46	28	FL	H	Tranmere Rovers	L 0-3	0-2	23		16692
47	A 04	FL	A	Reading	L 0-2	0-1	24		(10448)
48	11	FL	H	Portsmouth	W 2-1	0-0	23	Pickering 78, Lightbourne 90	15569
49	13	FL	A	Crewe Alexandra	L 0-2	0-1	23		(5759)
50	18	FL	H	Norwich City	W 2-0	1-0	21	Sigurdsson 19, Lightbourne 50	13098
51	25	FL	A	Sunderland	L 0-3	0-1	22		(41214)
52	M 03	FL	H	Manchester City	L 2-5	0-1	23	Thorne 63, 86	28000

Best Home League Attendance: 28000 V Manchester City   Smallest :8423 V Oxford United   Average :15003

Goal Scorers:

FL	(44)	Thorne 12, Forsyth 7, Kavanagh 5, Crowe 4, Stewart 3, Wallace 3, Lightbourne 2, Andrade 1, Griffin 1, Holsgrove 1, Keen 1, Pickering 1, Sigurdsson 1, Tiatto 1, Opponents 1
CC	(11)	Kavanagh 5, Thorne 4, Forsyth 1, Keen 1
FAC	(1)	Gabbiadini 1

(M) Andrade	(M) Crowe	(F) Donaldson	(M) Forsyth	(F) Gabbiadini	(M) Griffin	(M) Heath	(M) Holsgrove	(M) Kavanagh	(M) Keen	(F) Lightbourne	(M) Macari	(M) Mackenzie	(D) McKinlay	(M) McMahon	(D) McNally	(G) Muggleton	(M) Nyamah	(D) Pickering	(F) Scully	(M) Sigurdsson	(M) Sobiech	(G) Southall	(M) Stewart	(F) Thorne	(M) Tiatto	(D) Tweed	(D) Wallace	(D) Whittle	
			X					X	X						S	X	X	X		X			X	X		S	X	X	E.K. Wolstenholme 1
			X					X	X						S2	X	X	X		X			X	X		X	X	S	D Pugh 2
S			X					X	X						S	X	X	X		X			X	X		X	X	S	T Heilbron 3
S2			X		X			X	X						S1	X		X		X			X	X		X	X	S	P W Barnes 4
			X		X			X	X							X		X		X			X	X		X	X	S2	S W Mathieson 5
S1			X		X			X	X						S	X		X		X			X	X		X	X	X	G B Frankland 6
S1			X		X			X	X							X	S	X					X	X		X	X	X	E Lomas 7
S1			X		X			X	X							X		X		X			X	X		X	X	S	B Coddington 8
X			X		X			X	X					S2		S	X	X		X				X		X	X	S1	J A Kirkby 9
			X		X			X	X					S	S	X	X	X		X			X	X		X	X	S	B Knight 10
	X		X					S3	X					X	X	X	X	X		X				X		X	X	S2	A P D'Urso 11
	S1		X1	X				X	X					S2	X2	X		X		X				X		X	X	S	M Fletcher 12
X			X		X			X	X					S	S1	X		X		X				X		X	X	S	C J Foy 13
X	S1		X		X			X	X					S		X		X		X			X			X	X	S	C R Wilkes 14
X	S2		X		X			X	X						X	X	S1	X						X		X	X	S3	P Jones 15
X			X		X			X	X		S1	S			X	X		X						X		X	X	S2	R D Furnandiz 16
			X		X			X	X			S			X	X	S1	X					X	X		X	X	S	A R Leake 17
			X		X			X	X					S	X	X		X					X	X		X	X	S	S J Baines 18
S1			X		X			X	X					S2	S	X		X					X	X		X	X		K M Lynch 19
S1			X		X			X	X					S1		X		X					X	X		X	X	S	R Pearson 20
S1			X		X			X	X							X		X					X	X		X	X	S	E K Wolstenholme 21
S			X		X			X	X						S	X	X	X					X	X		X	X		M C Bailey 22
S			X		X			X	X			S			S1	X		X					X	X		X	X		G Laws 23
X1			X		X			X	X							X		X					X2	X	S1	X		S	T Jones 24
			X		X			X	X				S	X	S1	X		X						X	X1	X		S	G B Frankland 25
			X		X			X	X				S	X1	S1	X		X						X		X		S	P Rejer 26
S			X		X1			X	X					X	X	X		X					X	X	S1	X		S	A G Wiley 27
			X		X			X	X					X	S	X		X					X	X		X		S	R J Harris 28
			X	S1	X			X	X					X		X		X					X1	X2	S2	X		S	S W Mathieson 29
			X	S2	X			X	X					X1		X		X					X2	X		X	S1	S3	P S Danson 30
			X	S2	X			X	X					X		X	X1	X					X2	X		X	S1	S	T Heilbron 31
			X	X				X	X					S	S	X	S	X		X			X	S1		X1	X	X	P Jones 32
			X	X1	X			X	X					S	S1	X		X		S			X	X		X	X	X	R Pearson 33
			S1				X	X1	X						S2	S	X	X	X	X2			X			X	X	X	A R Hall 34
			S1				X	X	X					X	X	S		X	X	X				S	X1	X	X	X	P R Richards 35
			S1				X	X2	X		S2	X	X1		X	X		X	X	X				S		X	X	X	M S Pike 36
			X1				X	X	X		S3	S1	X2	X3	X	X		X	X	X				S2		X	X	X	G Laws 37
	X							X	X	S					S1	X		X	X	X			X	S		X	X	X	J P Robinson 38
	X							X	X1	S2	X			S1		X		X	X2	X			X			X	X	X	D Pugh 39
	X						S	X	X1	X	X					X		X2	X				S1	X	S2	X	X	X	R D Furnandiz 40
	S1		X				S	X	X							X		X	X	X		X	X	X	X1	X	X	X	P Rejer 41
	S1		X				S	X2	X		X			S2				X1		X			X	X		X	X	X	E K Wolstenholme 42
	S1		X				S	X	X	S3	X3						X1		X	X	X		X	X		X	X	X	E Lomas 43
	S2	X	X		S1			X	X2							X		X	X	X			X	X	X1	X	X	S	B Knight 44
	X	X2	X					X	X	S1					X			X	X	X	X	X1			S2	X		A R Leake 45
	X		X					X1	X3	S2	S1			X				X	X	X	X	X		X2	S1	X	X	X	M Fletcher 46
	X		X					X1	X3	S2	S1			X				X	X	X		X		X	S3	X2		S3	F G Stretton 47
X3		X2					S2	X	X	S1				X				X	X1	X		X	X		X1		X	S3	R D Furnandiz 48
X			X					X2	X	X	S2			X			X1	X	X	X		X			X	X	S	R J Harris 49
X			X				X	S	X	X1						X	X	X				S1	X	S	X	X	X	G Cain 50
X		X3	X					X	S1	X	X2					X	X	X				S2	X1	X	X	S3	T Jones 51	
			X					X	S	X	X	X1				X	X	X				X	X		X	X	X	M C Bailey 52
4	10	2	37	2	23	4	11	44	37	9		7	3	7	3	34	9	42	7	43	3	12	22	33	11	35	36	15	FL Appearances
8	6		6		2	1		3	4	3	5				10	1			1					3	4	3	3	5	FL Sub Appearances
2	1+1		4		4			4+1	5		1+1				2+1		5	1+1	5	5			2	4	5	5	0+4		CC Appearances
					1	1	1								1								1	0+1	1	1	1		FAC Appearances

Also played: (F) Carruthers S1(19), S2(20). (M) Crowe S(51).

CLUB RECORDS

BIGGEST VICTORIES
League: 9-0 v Plymouth Argyle,Division 2, 17.12.1960
F.A. Cup: 7-1 v Burnley, Round 2, 20.2.1896
League Cup: 6-2 v Chelsea, Round 2, 22.10.1974
Europe: 3-1 v Kaiserslautern, UEFA Cup, 1972-73
BIGGEST DEFEATS
League: 0-10 v Preston North End, Division 1, 4.2.1937
F.A. Cup: 0-7 v Leicester City, 14.11.1910
League Cup: No more than 3 goals
Europe: 0-4 v Kaiserslautern, UEFA Cup 1972-73
MOST POINTS
3 points a win: 93, Division 3/2, 1992-93
2 points a win: 63, Division 3N, 1926-27
MOST GOALS
92, Division 3N, 1926-27
Wilson 25, Davies 14, Eyres 12, Bussey 8, Williams 6, Archibald 6, Johnson 5,Armitage 5, Williams 5, Watkin 3, Cull 1, Beswick 1, Opponents 1
MOST LEAGUE GOALS CONCEDED
91, Division 1, 1984-85
MOST FIRST CLASS MATCHES IN A SEASON
67 (42 League, 9 FA Cup, 12 League Cup, 4 Texaco Cup) 1971-72
MOST LEAGUE WINS
27, Division 3(N), 1926-27
27, Division 3/2, 1992-93
MOST LEAGUE DRAWS
19, Division 2, 1989-90
MOST LEAGUE DEFEATS
31, Division 1, 1984-85
RECORD TRANSFER FEE RECEIVED
£2,500,000 from Q.P.R.for Mike Sheron, June 1997.
RECORD TRANSFER FEE PAID
£450,000 to Sheffield Wed for Ian Cranston, July 1989.
BEST PERFORMANCES
League: 1926-27: Matches played 42, Won 27, Drawn 9, Lost 6, Goals for 92,Goals against 40, Points 63. 1st in Division 3N
Highest: Fourth in Division 1, 1935-36 & 1946-47
F.A. Cup: 1898-99: 3rd rnd. Sheffield Wednesday (a) 2-2, (h) 2-0; 4th rnd.Birmingham City (h) 2-2, (a) 2-1; 5th rnd. Tottenham H (h) 4-1; Semi-final Derby County 1-3

1970-71: 3rd rnd. Millwall 2-1; 4th rnd. Huddersfield 3-3, 0-0, 1-0; 5th rnd.Ipswich Town 0-0 1-0; 6th rnd. Hull City 3-2; Semi-final Arsenal 2-2, 0-2
1971-72: 3rd rnd. Chesterfield 2-1; 4th rnd. Tranmere Rov 2-2, 2-0; 5th rnd.Hull City 4-1; 6th rnd. Manchester Utd 1-1, 2-1; Semi-final Arsenal 1-1, 1-2
League Cup: 1971-72: 2nd rnd. Southport 2-1; 3rd rnd. Oxford

INDIVIDUAL CLUB RECORDS

United 1-1, 1-0;4th rnd. Manchester Utd 1-1, 0-0, 2-1; 5th rnd. Bristol Rov 4-2; Semi-final West Ham Utd, 1-2, 1-0, 0-0, 3-2; Final Chelsea 2-1.
MOST GOALS IN A MATCH
7. Neville Coleman v Lincoln, Div 2, 23.2.1957
MOST GOALS IN A SEASON
Charles Wilson, 38, (32 League, 6 FA Cup) 1927-28
3 goals twice=6, 2 goals seven times=14, 1 goal 18 times=18
OLDEST PLAYER
Sir Stanley Matthews, 50 years 5 days v Fulham, 6.2.1965
YOUNGEST PLAYER
Peter Bullock, 16 years 163 days v Swansea, 19.4.1958
MOST CAPPED PLAYER
Gordon Banks (England) 36
ADDITIONAL INFORMATION
Previous Name: Stoke Ramblers, Stoke-upon-Trent, Stoke.
Previous League: Southern League; Birmingham League; Football Alliance
Club colours: Red and white striped shirts, white shorts, red & white socks.
Change colours: Green & black striped shirts, black shorts, green & black socks.
Reserves League: Pontins Central League Premier Division.

PREVIOUS MANAGERS

Tom Slaney 1874-83. Walt Cox 1883-84. Harry Lockett 1884-90. Joe Bradshaw 1890-92. Arthur Reeves 1892-95. William Rowley 1895-97. H Austerberry 1897-08. A J Barker 1908-14. Peter Hodge 1914-15. Joe Schofield 1915-19. Arthur Shallcross 1919-23. John Rutherford 1923. Tom Mather 1923-25. Bob McGory 1935-52. Frank Taylor 1952-60. Tony Waddington 1960-77. George Eastham 1977-78. Alan A'Court 1978. Alan Durban 1978-81.Ritchie Barker 1981-83. Bill Asprey 1984-85. Mick Mills 1985-89. Alan Ball 1989-91. Lou Macari 1991-93. Joe Jordan 1993-94. Lou Macari 1994-97. Chic Bates 1997-98. Chris Kamara 1998. Alan Durban 1998*. *Caretaker.

COMPETITIONS

Div.1	Div.2/1	Div.3/2	Div.3(N)
1888-90	1890-91	1890-93	1926-27
1891-1907	1907-08	1998-	
1922-23	1919-22		
1933-53	1923-26		
1963-77	1927-33		
1979-86	1953-63		
	1977-79		
	1986-90		
	1993-98		

HONOURS

Div.2	Div.3/2	Div.3(N)	Lge Cup	Watney
1932-33	1992-93	1926-27	1971-72	1973
1962-63				AMC
				1991-92

LONGEST LEAGUE RUNS

of undefeated matches:	25 (5.9.1992 - 20.2.1993)	of league matches w/out a win:	7 (15.9.1984 - 22.12.1984)
of undefeated home matches:	23 (15.12.1973 - 21.12.1974)	of undefeated away matches:	12 (12.9.1992 - 30.1.1993)
without home win:	9 (15.4.1963 - 30.11.1963)	without an away win:	30 (16.1.1897 - 18.12.1899)
of league wins:	7 (2.9.1905 - 23.9.1905, 4.4.1947 - 26.5.1947)	of home wins:	11 (30.3.1895 - 21.12.1895)
of league defeats:	11 (6.4.1985 - 17.8.1985)	of away wins:	5 (14.1.1922 - 11.3.1922, 4.4.1947 - 26.5.1947)

THE MANAGER

Brian Little . . . . appointed 13th May 1998
PREVIOUS CLUBS
As Manager: Darlington, Wolves, Leicester, Aston Villa. **As Assistant Manager/Coach:** Wolves. **As a player:** Aston Villa.
HONOURS as Manager
Darlington: GM Vuaxhall Conference 1989-90. Division Four Championship 1990-91.
Leicester: Promotion to Premiership 1993-94. **Aston Villa:** League Cup 1995-96.

STOKE CITY

PLAYERS NAME / Honours	Ht	Wt	Birthdate	Birthplace / Transfers	Contract Date	Clubs	League	L/Cup	FA Cup	Other	Lge	L/C	FAC	Oth
G O A L K E E P E R														
Fraser Stuart J	6	12.1	8/1/78	Cheltenham	7/3/97	Stoke City								
Muggleton Carl E:u21.1	6	11.13	9/13/68	Leicester	9/17/86	Leicester City	46		3	5				
				Loan	9/10/87	Chesterfield	17			2				
				Loan	2/1/88	Blackpool	2							
				Loan	10/28/88	Hartlepool United	8			2				
				Loan	3/1/90	Stockport County	4							
				Loan	8/13/93	Stoke City	6	1		2				
				£150000	1/11/94	Celtic	12		1					
				£200000	7/21/94	Stoke City	96	12	1	4				
				Loan	11/1/95	Rotherham United								
				Loan	3/28/96	Sheffield United	4							
Southall Neville	6.1	12.2	9/16/58	Llandudno		Winsford United								
						Bangor City								
				£6000	6/14/80	Bury	39		5					
				£150000	7/13/81	Everton	578	65	70	37				
				Loan	1/27/83	Port Vale	9							
				Loan	12/24/97	Southend United	9							
				Loan	2/27/98	Stoke City	4							
				Free	3/17/98	Stoke City	7							
D E F E N C E														
Clarke Clive	5.11	12.3	1/14/80	Dublin	5/31/97	Stoke City								
Pickering Ally	5.9	10.8	6/22/67	Manchester		Buxton								
				£18500	2/2/90	Rotherham United	87+1	6	9	7	2			
				£110000	10/27/93	Coventry City	54+11	5+1	4				1	
				£200000	8/15/96	Stoke City	81+1	9	2		1			
Small Bryan E: u21, Y.	5.9	11.09	11/15/71	Birmingham	7/9/90	Aston Villa	31+5	2	2+1	4				
				Loan	9/9/94	Birmingham City	3							
				Free	3/20/96	Bolton Wanderers	11+1	1	3					
				Loan	9/8/97	Luton Town	15							
				Loan	12/19/97	Bradford City	5							
				Loan	1/30/98	Bury	7							
				Loan	3/2/98	Bury	11							
				Free	7/1/98	Stoke City								
Short Chris AIC'95.	5.1	12.02	09/05/70	Munster		Pickering								
				Free	11/07/88	Scarborough	42+1	5	1	3+1	1			
				£100000	05/09/90	Notts County	77+15	5	4+1	7	2		1	
				Loan	23/12/94	Huddersfield Town	6			1				
					29/12/95	Sheffield United	40+4	3+1	7	1+1				
				Free		Stoke City								
Sigurdsson Kristjan O	5.11	11.11	10/7/80	Akureyri		KA Akureyri								
				Free	12/9/97	Stoke City								
Sigurdsson Larus Icelandic Int. u21, Y.	6	11.5	6/4/73	Iceland		Iceland								
				£150000	10/21/94	Stoke City	155+2	11	4+1	4	2			
Tweed Steven S: B, u21.	6.3	13.2	8/9/72	Edinburgh via Ionikos		Hibernian								
				Free	8/8/97	Stoke City	35+3	5	1					
Wallace Ray E:u21.4	5.6	10.2	10/2/69	Greenwich	4/21/88	Southampton	33+2	8	2	2				
				£100000	7/8/91	Leeds United	5+2							
				Loan	3/20/92	Swansea City	2							
				Loan	3/11/94	Reading	3							
				Free	8/12/94	Stoke City	140+7	12	5	11	12			1
					12/16/94	Hull City	7							
Whittle Justin	6.1	12.12	3/18/71	Derby		Celtic								
				Free	10/20/94	Stoke City	56+8	2+4	2	2				
M I D F I E L D														
Bullock Matthew	5.8	11	11/1/80	Stoke	11/21/97	Stoke City (T)								
Cartwright James	5.6	9.6	10/11/79	Lichfield	11/6/96	Stoke City								
Crowe Dean	5.5	11.3	6/6/79	Stockport	9/5/96	Stoke City	9+6	1+1			4			
Forsyth Richard	5.11	12.12	10/3/70	Dudley		Kidderminster H.								
				£50000	7/13/95	Birmingham City	12+13	7+2	2	3	2			
					8/15/96	Stoke City	76	7	2		15	1		
Heath Robert	5.8	10	8/31/78	Stoke	5/31/97	Stoke City	4+2							
Keen Kevin E: Y.10,S	5.6	10.3	2/25/67	Amersham		West Ham United	187+32	21+1	15+7	14+2	21	5	1	3
				£600000	7/7/93	Wolverhampton W.	37+5	2+1	5	4	7		1	1
				£300000	10/19/94	Stoke City	84+26	9+2	3	2	7	1		
Mackenzie Neil D	6.2	12.5	4/15/76	Birmingham	10/25/96	Stoke City	11+21	1+1	0+1					
Nyamah Kofi	5.11	11.7	6/20/75	Islington	5/19/93	Cambridge United	9+14	0+2	3+1	4	2			1
				Free	7/1/95	Kettering Town								
				£25000	2/14/97	Stoke City	9+7	1+1						
O'Connor James	5.7	10.4	9/1/79	Dublin	9/5/96	Stoke City								
Oldfield David E:u21.1	6	12.2	30/05/68	Perth (Aus)	16/05/86	Luton Town	21+8	4+2	0+1	2+1	4	2		2
				£600000	14/03/89	Manchester City	18+8	2+1		0+1	6	2		1
				£150000	12/01/90	Leicester City	155+19	10+1	6	11+3	25	1	2	2
				Loan	24/02/95	Millwall								
				£150000	21/07/95	Luton Town	99+18	11	2	7+2	18	2		4
				Free	7/1/98	Stoke City								
Robinson Phillip Div.4'88. Div.3'89. AMC'88'91.DIV3 97/98	5.9	10.1	1/6/67	Stafford	1/8/85	Aston Villa	2+1				1			
				£5000	7/3/87	Wolverhampton W.	63+8	6	3	8+2	8	1		
				£67500	8/18/89	Notts County	65+1	6	1+1	9+1	5	1		
				Loan	3/18/91	Birmingham City	9			2+1				
					9/1/92	Huddersfield Town	74+1	4	8	8	4		1	
					12/9/94	Chesterfield	60+1	1	2	8	17			4
Loan 12/30/94 Telford United					8/15/96	Notts County	63+14	4	6+1		5		1	
				Free	7/1/98	Stoke City								
Scheuber Stuart M			4/3/81	Rhuddlan	5/13/98	Stoke City (T)								
Stewart Paul E: 3, B5, u21.1, Y2; FAC'91;CS'91; Div1'94	5.11	12.4	10/7/64	Manchester	10/13/81	Blackpool	188+13	11	7	6	56	3	2	1
				£200000	3/19/87	Manchester City	51	4	6	2	26	2	1	1
				£1700000	6/21/88	Tottenham Hotspur	126	23	9	9	28	7	2	2
				£2300000	7/29/92	Liverpool	28+4	6	1	3	1			2
				Loan	1/24/94	Crystal Palace	18				3			
				Loan	9/2/94	Wolverhampton W.	5+3			2	2			
				Loan	3/5/96	Sunderland	31+5	3			5			
					7/1/97	Stoke City	22	2	1		3			
Loan 2/8/95 Burnley 6 Lge App.														
Taaffe Steven	5.5	9	9/10/79	Stoke	9/12/96	Stoke City	0+3							
Woods Stephen J	5.11	11.13	12/15/76	Davenham		Davenham	0+1							
				Loan	3/26/98	Plymouth Argyle	4+1							
Woolliscroft Ashley D	5.11	11.2	12/15/76	Davenham	5/31/97	Stoke City								
F O R W A R D														
Burgess Richard	5.8	11	8/18/78	Bromsgrove	7/5/96	Aston Villa (T)								
					5/17/97	Stoke City								
Godbold Jamie T	5.4	9	11/10/80	Great Yarmouth	5/31/97	Stoke City								
Holsgrove Paul via Wokingham Town via Hercules	6.11	11.1	8/26/69	Wellington	2/9/87	Aldershot	0+3		1					
				£25000	1/1/91	Luton Town	1+1							
				Free	8/13/92	Millwall	3+8	0+1	0+1	2				
				Free	8/10/94	Reading	62+6	8+2	5		6	1		
					11/21/97	Crewe Alexandra	7+1		1		1			
				Free	1/27/98	Stoke City	11+1				1			
Lightbourne Kyle Bermuda Int.	6.2	11	9/29/08	Bermuda	12/11/92	Scarborough	11+8	1		0+1	3			
				Free	9/17/93	Walsall	157+7	8	16+2	6	65	2	12	6
				£500000	7/18/97	Coventry City	1+6	3			2			
				Free		Fulham	4				2			
				£500000	2/20/98	Stoke City	9+4				2			
Sturridge Simon AMC'91	5.5	10.7	12/9/69	Birmingham	7/8/88	Birmingham City	129+21	10+4	8	14	30	1	2	5
					9/24/93	Stoke City	42+26	2+1	3+3	7+3	14		1	
Thorne Peter Div.2'96.	6	12.3	6/21/73	Manchester	6/20/91	Blackburn Rovers	10+1							
				Loan	3/11/94	Wigan Athletic								
				£200000	1/18/95	Swindon Town	65+12	5+1	4+2	1+1	27	4		1
					7/25/97	Stoke City	32+3	4	0+1		12	4		

BRITANNIA STADIUM
Stanley Matthews Way, Stoke-on-Trent, Staffordshire ST4 4EG

Capacity 28,000

First game..v Coventry City (Friendly) 2-0, 30th July 1997.
First floodlit game ....As above.

ATTENDANCES
Highest ....28,000 v Manchester City (Lge) 2-5, 3rd May 1998.
Lowest ....8,423 v Oxford United (Lge) 0-0, 4th November 1997.

OTHER GROUNDS..Sweeting Fields 1875-78. Victoria Ground 1878-1997.

HOW TO GET TO THE GROUND

From the North, West and South
M6 to J15. Take the A500 to Stoke-on-Trent then the A50 to Derby/Uttoxeter (the Britannia Stadium will be signposted at this point and visable on the skyline to the right). Once on the A50 you have to drive past the stadium on the right to the first exit and come back down the westbound carriageway of the A50 to get to the stadium.

From the East
A50 all the way to Stoke-on-Trent. Stadium to the left.

Car Parking: Matchday parking is available for supporters on the South car park, access from Trentham Road only.

Nearest Railway Station: Stoke (01782 411 411).

USEFUL TELEPHONE NUMBERS

Club switchboard 01782 592 222
Club fax number 01782 592 221
Club shop 01782 592 244
Ticket Office .. 01782 592 200 (Fax 592 201)

Marketing Department...... 01782 592 211
Clubcall 0891 12 10 40*
*Calls cost 50p per minute at all times.
Call costings correct at time of going to press.

MATCHDAY PROGRAMME

Programme Editor .... Tony Tams.

Number of pages .... 48.

Price .... £1.50.

Subscriptions..... £42 UK, £50 Overseas.

Local Newspapers
The Sentinel, North Staffordshire Advertiser.

Local Radio Stations
.... BBC Radio Stoke, Signal Radio.

MATCHDAY TICKET PRICES

Main Stand (Upper)
Adults £16
U17/OAP................................... £9

Main Stand (Lower)
Adults £15
U17/OAP................................... £8

North Stand
Adults £11
U17/OAP................................... £7

East Stand
Adults £14
U17/OAP................................... £8

Family Stand
Adults £11
U17/OAP................................... £6
U13..................................... £3

WALSALL
(The Saddlers)
NATIONWIDE LEAGUE DIVISION 2
SPONSORED BY: BANKS'S

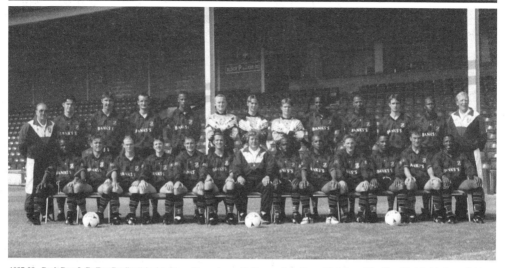

1997-98 - Back Row L-R: Tom Bradley (physio), Darren Rogers (now with Stevenage), Ian Roper, Mark Perry, Clive Platt, Mark Smith, Danny Naisbitt, James Walker, Michael Ricketts, John Williams (now with Exeter City) Stuart Ryder, Mark Blake, Eric McManus (youth dev. officer).
Front Row: John Keister, Wayne Evans, Dean Keates, Gary Porter, John Hodge, Adrian Viveash, Jan Sorensen (manager), Roger Boli, Louie Donowa, Wayne Thomas, Andy Watson, Derek Mountfield (coach), Darren Beckford.

WALSALL
FORMED IN 1888
TURNED PROFESSIONAL IN 1888
LTD COMPANY IN 1921

CHAIRMAN:
DIRECTORS
K R Whalley, M N Lloyd, C Welch,
R Tisdale, S A Josebury
SECRETARY
Roy Whalley (01922 22791)
COMMERCIAL MANAGER
Roy Whalley

MANAGER: Ray Graydon

YOUTH TEAM COACH
Eric McManus
PHYSIOTHERAPIST
Tom Bradley

STATISTICIAN FOR THE DIRECTORY
Mervyn Sargeant

Early season interest centred on the unknown new manager, Jan Sorenson, and the arrival of two French players in August - Roger Boli and Jean-Francois Peron, following the sale of the previous season's topscorer Kyle Lightbourne. Disappointingly only one of the first seven league games was won, and the end of September saw the club two from bottom of the table. All was not doom and gloom however, both Boli and Peron were proving to be good signings and with Boli and his strike partner Andy Watson scoring regularly, hope remained. In the Coca-Cola cup both Nottingham Forest and Sheffield United were beaten, before a fourth round defeat at West Ham. On the back of these performances league results began to improve and Walsall were reasonably well placed in twelfth position at Christmas. With Macclesfield Town being beaten 7-0 away in the FA Cup second round, 1998 was looked forward to with anticipation.

It all went wrong again after an FA Cup fourth round defeat at Manchester United. Despite some good football from the Saddlers, they were never really in with a chance and United ran out 5-1 winners. Cup form was continued in the Auto-Windscreen Shield, with progress being made to the Southern Area Final. Dreams of a first ever Wembley appearance were then dashed by a two-leg defeat to Bournemouth. Following the Manchester United game, only three of the next fifteen league games were won. Andy Watson's season finished in February due to injury, and Roger Boli's might just as well have done, as after going on the transfer list, he appeared to lose all interest in playing. Desperate loan signings were made to try and turn things around. Eydelie and Tholot were brought in from Sion in Switzerland, but neither made any real impact. In addition Gijsbert Bos signed on loan from Rotherham, but never featured in a first team game!

Four of the last five league games were lost, but thanks to other teams' results relegation was avoided.

Transfer listed Jean-Francois Peron had a superb season, and quite rightly won the 'player of the year' award, and the emergence of Dean Keates in midfield was a big plus for the season. Jan Sorenson not surprisingly paid the price for poor league form and was dismissed. His successor, Ray Graydon, is in his first managerial role, and has a lot to do to turn things around. A lot of supporters are very unhappy at the club's apparent lack of investment in the playing side. Large fees have been received in recent years for the sale of Houghton, O'Connor and Lightbourne, with very little being spent on transfer fees for new signings. Fan unrest in March led to the resignation of Chairman Jeff Bonsor, and the club being put up for sale. With no new owners as yet, an inexperienced manager, some of Walsall's better players wanting to leave, and the recent track record of not paying transfer fees for new signings it is difficult to look forward to 1998/99 with any optimism.

MERVYN SARGEANT.

WALSALL

Division 2   :19th   FA CUP: 4th Round   LC CUP: 4th Round   AWS: Southern Final

M	DATE	COMP.	VEN	OPPONENTS	RESULT	H/T	LP	GOAL SCORERS/GOAL TIMES	ATT.
1	A 09	FL	A	Chesterfield	L 1-3	0-1	19	Platt 78	(5193)
2	12	CC 1/1	H	Exeter City	W 2-0	0-0		Platt 58, Boli 72	2321
3	15	FL	H	Fulham	D 1-1	0-0	16	Mountfield 87	4418
4	23	FL	A	Gillingham	L 1-2	0-0	21	Boli 89	(5083)
5	26	CC 1/2	A	Exeter City	W 1-0	0-0		Boli 50	(2467)
6	30	FL	H	Southend United	W 3-1	2-1	14	Boli 11, 25, 90	3304
7	S 02	FL	H	Northampton Town	L 0-2	0-1	17		4435
8	09	FL	A	Bristol Rovers	L 0-2	0-1	20		(6225)
9	13	FL	A	Preston North End	D 0-0	0-0	22		(9092)
10	17	CC 2/1	A	Nottingham Forest	W 1-0	0-0		Skinner 53	(7841)
11	20	FL	H	York City	W 2-0	0-0	20	Boli 49, Hodge 80	2972
12	24	CC 2/2	H	Nottingham Forest	D 2-2	0-0		Watson 113, 115	6037
13	27	FL	A	Plymouth Argyle	L 1-2	1-1	22	Boli 31	(6207)
14	O 04	FL	H	Carlisle United	W 3-1	1-0	20	Boli 16, 60, Watson 74	3957
15	11	FL	H	Wrexham	W 3-0	2-0	14	Boli 16, Hodge 18 (pen), Watson 82	4042
16	14	CC 3	H	Sheffield United	W 2-1	0-0		Watson 56, Tiler 88 (OG)	8239
17	18	FL	A	Brentford	L 0-3	0-0	18		(4874)
18	21	FL	A	Wycombe Wanderers	L 2-4	2-3	19	Viveash 29, Watson 39	(3884)
19	25	FL	H	Bristol City	D 0-0	0-0	20		4618
20	N 01	FL	A	Burnley	L 1-2	0-1	20	Viveash 79	(9292)
21	04	FL	H	Grimsby Town	D 0-0	0-0	21		2599
22	08	FL	H	Watford	D 0-0	0-0	21		5077
23	15	FAC 1	H	Lincoln United	W 2-0	1-0		Watson 35, Boli 90	3279
24	19	CC 4	A	West Ham United	L 1-4	1-2		Watson 45	(17463)
25	22	FL	A	Luton Town	W 1-0	0-0	18	Hodge 60	(4726)
26	29	FL	H	Blackpool	W 2-1	0-1	16	Watson 64, Boli 86	3933
27	D 03	FL	A	Millwall	W 1-0	0-0	16	Keates 78	(4647)
28	06	FAC 2	H	Macclesfield Town	W 7-0	2-0		Boli 21, 57 (pen), Hodge 34 (pen), 90, Viveash 47, Porter 73, 85	(3566)
29	09	AWS S1	A	Barnet	W 2-1	1-0		Blake 38, Boli 57	(754)
30	13	FL	H	Bournemouth	W 2-1	0-0	13	Boli 60, Hodge 66	3548
31	19	FL	A	Oldham Athletic	D 0-0	0-0	14		(4677)
32	26	FL	H	Bristol Rovers	L 0-1	0-0	15		6634
33	28	FL	A	Northampton Town	L 2-3	1-1	16	Porter 40, Hodge 61	(7094)
34	J 10	FL	A	Chesterfield	W 3-2	0-1	15	Watson 79, 82, Reeves 55 (OG)	4042
35	13	FAC 3	A	Peterborough United	W 2-0	1-0		Watson 43, 73	(12809)
36	17	FL	A	Southend United	W 1-0	0-0	14	Watson 53	(3310)
37	20	AWS S2	H	Brighton & H.A.	W 5-0	2-0		Watson 18, Boli 38,83, Keates 52, Allan 80 (OG)	2562
38	24	FAC 4	A	Manchester United	L 1-5	0-2		Boli 72	(54669)
39	28	AWS SQF	A	Bristol Rovers	W 1-0	0-0		Boli 91 (Golden goal)	(4165)
40	31	FL	H	Preston North End	D 1-1	0-0	14	Hodge 90 (pen)	5377
41	F 06	FL	H	York City	L 0-1	0-1	15		(2959)
42	14	FL	A	Carlisle United	D 1-1	0-0	16	Hodge 47	(4530)
43	17	AWS SSF	A	Peterborough United	W 2-1	0-0		Boli 80, Ricketts 81	(4199)
44	21	FL	A	Plymouth Argyle	L 0-1	0-1	16		4612
45	24	FL	H	Brentford	D 0-0	0-0	16		3166
46	28	FL	A	Wrexham	L 1-2	1-2	18	Ricketts 44	(3622)
47	M 03	FL	A	Watford	W 2-1	1-0	17	Tholot 9, Blake 72	(8096)
48	07	FL	H	Burnley	D 0-0	0-0	16		5212
49	10	AWS SF1	H	Bournemouth	L 0-2	0-2			6017
50	14	FL	A	Grimsby Town	L 0-3	0-0	18		(4916)
51	17	AWS SF2	A	Bournemouth	W 3-2	0-0		Thomas 47, Boli 53, Tholot 80	(8972)
52	21	FL	H	Wigan Athletic	W 1-0	0-0	17	Peron 57	3169
53	28	FL	H	Luton Town	L 2-3	0-1	17	Viveash 52, Tholot 74	3922
54	31	FL	H	Gillingham	W 1-0	0-0	17	Evans 71	3117
55	A 04	FL	A	Blackpool	L 0-1	0-0	17		(4451)
56	07	FL	A	Fulham	D 1-1	1-0	18	Boli 30	(6733)
57	11	FL	H	Millwall	W 2-0	1-0	14	Tholot 1, Hodge 59 (pen)	3307
58	14	FL	A	Bournemouth	L 0-1	0-0	18		(3404)
59	18	FL	H	Oldham Athletic	D 0-0	0-0	17		3562
60	21	FL	A	Wigan Athletic	L 0-2	0-0	17		(2725)
61	25	FL	A	Bristol City	L 1-2	1-1	19	Tholot 23	(15059)
62	M 02	FL	H	Wycombe Wanderers	L 0-1	0-1	19		4412

Best Home League Attendance: 6634 V Bristol Rovers	Smallest :2599 V Grimsby Town	Average :4062

Goal Scorers:

FL	(43)	Boli 12, Hodge 8, Watson 7, Tholot 4, Viveash 3, Blake 1, Evans 1, Keates 1, Mountfield 1, Peron 1, Platt 1, Porter 1, Ricketts 1, Opponents 1
CC	(9)	Watson 4, Boli 2, Platt 1, Skinner 1, Opponents 1
FAC	(12)	Boli 4, Watson 3, Hodge 2, Porter 2, Viveash 1
AWS	(13)	Boli 6, Blake 1, Keates 1, Ricketts 1, Tholot 1, Thomas 1, Watson 1, Opponents 1

476

(D) Blake	(D) Boli	(F) Donowa	(D) Evans	(D) Eydelie	(M) Gadsby	(F) Hodge	(M) Keates	(M) Keister	(F) Marsh	(D) Mountfield	(M) Naisbitt	(M) Peron	(F) Platt	(M) Porter	(F) Ricketts	(D) Rogers	(D) Roper	(D) Ryder	(M) Skinner	(F) Tholot	(M) Thomas	(D) Viveash	(G) Walker	(M) Watson	(F) Williams		Player	No.
	X	X	X			X	S	X		S			X	X			X					X	X		S1		T. Jones	1
S	X	X	X			X	X	X		X			X	X				S				X	X		S		T Bates	2
	X	X	X			X	X	X		X			X	X				S				X	X	S1			F G Stretton	3
S	X	S1	X			X	X	X		X		X	X	X								X	X	S2			R J Harris	4
X	X	S	X			S	S1	X		X			X	X			X					X	X	X			R Styles	5
X	X		X			S		X				X	S1	X	S	X	X					X	X	X			D Pugh	6
X	X	X	X			S2						X	S1	X	S3	X	X					X	X	X			T Heilbron	7
X	X	X	X			X	S1		X			X	X			X	S					X	X	S2			M E Pierce	8
	X		X			X	X		X			X	X		S1	X	S	X	S			X	X	X			G Laws	9
	X		X			X	X		X			X	S	X		X	S2	X	S1			X	X	X			A R Leake	10
	X		X			X	X					X	S1	X		X	S	X	S			X	X	X			C R Wilkes	11
	X		X			X	X		X			X	S2	S3		X	S1	X				X	X	X			G Cain	12
	X		X			X	X2		X			X	S1	S2	X1		S	X				X	X	X			M R Halsey	13
	X		X			X	X		X	X		X	S	S1			S	X				X	X	X			S J Baines	14
	X		X			X	X		X	X		X	S	S			S	X				X	X	X			B Coddington	15
	X		X			X	X		X	X		X	S	S			S	X				X	X	X			E Lomas	16
S1	X		X			X			X	X		X	S2	X			S	X				X	X	X			A P D'Urso	17
X	X		X			S2			X	X		X	S3				S1	X				X	X	X			D R Crick	18
S	X		X			X			X	X		X	X		S1		S	X				X	X	X			C J Foy	19
S	X		X			X			X	X		X	X		S1		S	X				X	X	X			E Lomas	20
S2	X		X			X			X	X		S	X		S1		X	X				X	X	X			T Jones	21
	X	X	X				X	X	X	S		X			S	X	X					X	X	S1			P R Richards	22
	X		X			S2	X	X	X	S1	S	S	X			S	X		X	S		X	X	X			A Bates	23
	X		X			X	X	X2	X1	X		X			X		S2	S1			S		X	X	X		D Orr	24
S	X		X			X	X		X	X		X			X		X	S1			S		X	X	X		M R Halsey	25
S	X		X			X	X1		X	X		X			X		X	S1			S		X	X	X		M J Jones	26
S1	X		X			X1	X		X	X		X			X		S				S		X	X	X		R Styles	27
S	X1		X			X	X			X	S	X	S	S	S2	X	S1				X		X	X	X2		A R Leake	28
S2	X		X1			X	X			X			X	S1	X2	X					X		X	X				29
X	X					X	X1	X	X	X		X				S1		S	S			X	X	X			C R Wilkes	30
X	X					X	X	X	X	X		X		S		S	S	X					X	X			G Laws	31
X	X		S			X	X	X1	X	X		X			S1		S	X				X	X	X			D R Crick	32
S1	X		X			X	X	S	X			X			X		S	X				X	X1	X			R D Furnandiz	33
S	X		X			X	X		X1			X	S	X			S1					X	X	X			P S Danson	34
S1	X		X			X	X		X	X		S	X1	S	X		S	S				X	X	X			W C Burns	35
X	X		X			X	X		X	X1			S	X			S1					X	X	X			S B Bennett	36
S2	X		X			X	X2		X	X1			S3	X			S1					X	X	X3				37
S1	X		X			X	X		X	X		S	X1	S	X	S		S				X	X	X			P A Durkin	38
	X		X			X	X		X				X		X				X	X			X	X				39
S2	X		X			X	X		X	X1			X	S	X2			S1				X	X	X			B Knight	40
X	X		X			X1	X2		X	S		X				S1		X			S2	X	X	X			C J Foy	41
X	X1		X			X	X		X			X				S1	X	S			S	X	X	X			E Lomas	42
X	X		X			X1	X		X			X		S1		X						X	X	X				43
X1	X		X			X	X	S	X	S		X	S1		X		X					X	X				F G Stretton	44
X	X		X			X	X	S	X			X	X		S		X	S				X	X				M D Messias	45
X	X		X			X	X		X			X1	X		S1		X	S		S		X	X				M S Pike	46
X	X1		X	X			X	S1	S	S			S		X		X			X		X	X				J P Robinson	47
X1	X		X	X		X			X				S	S1	X		X	S		X		X	X				G Laws	48
	X		X	X			X		X1				S1	X	X	X1	X		X	X		X	X	X				49
X			X	X1		X	X			S1			X	X	S3		X			X3	S1	X1	X				B Coddington	50
	X		X			S1	X					X1	X	X	X1		X				X	X	X				51
	X		X	S			X		X			X	X1	X	X		X		S1	S	X	X				M J Jones	52
S	X		X	S2			X2					X	X1	X	S1		X				X	X	X1				W C Burns	53
S1			X	X		X1	X	S	X	X		X			X		X				X		X				K M Lynch	54
S	X		X	X1		X		S1	X	X		X			X	S2	X				X		X				G Cain	55
	X1		X	X		S2			X	X		X			X1		S		X2		X	X					A N Butler	56
S	X		X	X		X			X	X		X			S		S				S	X	X				M L Dean	57
S	X		X	X		X			X	X1		X			X		X	S			X	X	X				P S Danson	58
S	X		X	X		X			X	X2	S	X1			X		S2				X	X	X				S G Bennett	59
S	X		X	X		S2			X			X			X	S1		X	X1		X	X2	X				G B Frankland	60
	X		X	S		X	X		X				S1	X	X		X	S		X	X1	X1	X				S W Mathieson	61
S2		X	S	S1		X	X			X			X	X			X			X	X2	X1	X				S J Baines	62
16	41	5	43	10		35	32	11	36	26		38	12	25	6	4	18	11	10	13	3	42	46	23			FL Appearances	
7	1		1	1	1	4	1	2	1				8	4	18		3	2		1	2			4	1		FL Sub Appearances	
1	6	1	6			5	5+1	3	2	6		5	1+1	2+2	0+1	2	0+2	1	3			0+1	6	6	5		CC Appearances	
0+2	4		4			3+1	4	1	4	2+1		4	0+1	3	1+1		1					4	4	4			FAC Appearances	
1+2	6		6	1		5+1	5		5	1		5	1+3	5	3+1		4+1	3		1+1	1	4	6	3			AWS Appearances	

Also Played: (F) Beckford S(2). (F) Bos S(54).

CLUB RECORDS

RECORD LEAGUE VICTORY
10-0 v Darwen,Div 2, 4.3.1899
Most Goals Scored in a First Class Cup Tie: 6-1 v Leytonstone (a),
Round 1,30.11.1946   6-1 v Margate, Round 1, 24.11.1955

RECORD LEAGUE DEFEAT
0-12 v Small Heath, Div 2, 17.12.1892   0-12 v Darwen,Div 2,
26.12.1896
Record Cup Defeat: 0-6 v Wednesday Town, FA Cup Round 2,
1883-84   0-6 v West Bromwich Albion, FA Cup Rnd 1 replay, 1899-
1900   0-6 v Aston Villa, FA Cup Round 1, 1911-12

MOST LEAGUE POINTS
(3pts for win) 83, Div 3, 1994-95.
(2pts for win) 65, Div4, 1959-60

MOST LEAGUE GOALS
102, Division 4, 1959-60

RECORD TRANSFER FEE RECEIVED
£600,000 from West Ham United for David Kelly, August 1988

RECORD TRANSFER FEE PAID
£175,000 to Birmingham City for Alan Buckley, June1979

BEST PERFORMANCES
League: 6th Div 2 1898-99
FA Cup: 5th Round 1939, 1975,1978 and last sixteen 1889
League Cup: Semi-Final 1983-84

HONOURS
Champions Div 4 1959-60

LEAGUE CAREER
Elected to Div 2 1892   Failed to gain re-election 1895
Rejoined Div 2 1896 Failed re-election 1901   Elected as original
members of Div 3N 1921   Transferred to Div 3S 1927
Transferred to Div 3N 1931   Transferred to Div 3S 1936
Joined Div 4 1958   Promoted to Div 3 1959-60
Promoted to Div 2 1960-61   Relegated to Div 3 1962-63
Relegated to Div 41978-79   Promoted to Div 3 1979-80
Promoted to Div 2 1987-88   Relegated to Div 3 1988-89
Relegated to Div 4(now Div 3) 1989-90 Promoted to Div 2 1994-95

INDIVIDUAL CLUB RECORDS

MOST APPEARANCES FOR CLUB
Colin Harrison (1964-82): League 452+15 + FA Cup 36+ League
Cup 19 Total 507+15 subs
Most Capped Player: Mick Kearns 15, Eire   For England: None
RECORD GOALSCORER IN A MATCH
Johnny Devlin 5 v Torquay United (h), 7-1, Div3S, 1.9.1949   Gilbert
Alsop 5 v Carlisle Utd (a), 6-1, Div 3N, 2.2.1935   W.Evans 5 v
Mansfield Town, 7-0, Div 3N, 5.10.1935
RECORD LEAGUE GOALSCORER IN A SEASON
Gilbert Alsop 40, Div 3N, 1933-34, 1934-35 In All Competitions:
Gilbert Alsop 44 (League 40 + FA Cup 4) 1934-35
RECORD LEAGUE GOALSCORER IN A CAREER
Tony Richards 184, 1954-63   In All Competitions: Alan Buckley 204
(League 174 + Cups 30) 1973-84
OLDEST PLAYER IN A LEAGUE MATCH
Des Bremner 37 years 240 days v Bristol City, 5.5.1990
YOUNGEST PLAYER IN A LEAGUE MATCH
Geoff Morriss 16 years 218 days v Scunthorpe, 14.9.1965

PREVIOUS MANAGERS

1921-26 J Burchell   1926-27 D Ashworth   1927-28 J Torrance
1928-29 J Kerr   1929-30 S Scholey   1930-32 P O'Rourke   1932-34
W Slade   1934-37 Andy Wilson   T Lowes 1937-44   1944-51 Harry
Hibbs   1951-52 G McPhee   1952-53 Brough Fletcher   1953-56
Frank Buckley   1956-57 John Love   1957-64 Bill Moore   1964 Alf
Wood   1964-68 Ray Shaw   1968 Dick Graham   1968-69 Ron Lewin
1969-72 Bob Moore   1972-73 John Smith   1973 Jim McEwan   1973
Ronnie Allen   1973-77 Doug Fraser   1977-78 Dave Mackay   1978
Alan Buckley   1978Alan Ashman   1978 Frank Sibley   1978-81 Alan
Buckley   1981-82 Neil Martin   1982-86 Alan Buckley   1986-88
Tommy Coackley   1988-89 Ray Train   1989-90 John Barnwell   1990
Paul Taylor   1990-94 Kenny Hibbitt   1994-95. Jan Sorensen 1997-98.

ADDITIONAL INFORMATION
Previous Name: Walsall Swifts (1877) and Walsall Town (1879)
amalgamated and played as Walsall Town Swifts until 1895
Club Colours: Red shirts and shorts with black trim.
Change Colours:

Reserves League: Pontins League **Youth Team:** Melville Midland Lge

LONGEST LEAGUE RUNS

of undefeated matches:	21 (1979-80)	of league matches w/out a win:	18 (1988-89)
of undefeated home matches:	26 (1960-61)	of undefeated away matches:	13 (1979-80)
without home win:	10 (1988-89, 1989-90)	without an away win:	29 (1953-54)
of league wins:	7 (1933-34)	of home wins:	9 (1973)
of league defeats:	15 (1988-89)	of away wins:	6 (24.4.1993 - 18.9.1993)

THE MANAGER

RAY GRAYDON . . . . appointed June 1998.

PREVIOUS CLUBS
As Manager. . . . . None.
As Asst.Man/Coach . . . . None.
As a player . . . . Bristol Rovers, Aston Villa, Coventry City, Washington (USA), Oxford Utd.

HONOURS
As a Manager . . . . None.
As a Player. . . . . England Youth.

WALSALL							APPEARANCES				GOALS			
PLAYERS NAME Honours	Ht	Wt	Birthdate	Birthplace Transfers	Contract Date	Clubs	League	L/Cup	FA Cup	Other	Lge	L/C	FAC	Oth
G O A L K E E P E R														
Larkin James T	6	13.7	10/23/75	Canada	1/16/98	Cambridge United	1							
				Free	3/20/98	Walsall								
Naisbitt Daniel J	6.1	11.13	11/21/78	Bishop Auck.	7/5/97	Walsall (T)								
Walker James	5.11	11.8	7/9/73	Nottingham	7/9/91	Notts County								
				Free	8/4/93	Walsall	141+1	10	15	3				
D E F E N C E														
Brissett Jason	5.11	11.1	9/7/74	Wanstead		Arsenal								
				Free	6/14/93	Peterborough United	27+8	5+1	2+1	3+1		1	1	1
				Free	12/23/94	Bournemouth	96+28	5+2	4	3	8			2
				Free	7/1/98	Walsall								
Evans Duncan W	5.10	12	8/25/71	Welshpool		Walsall								
Eydelie Jean			2/3/66	Angouleme		Sion F.C.								
				Loan	3/2/98	Walsall	10+1							
Gadsby Matthew J	6	11.3	9/6/79	Sutton C'fld	5/1/98	Walsall (T)	0+1							
Roper Ian	6.4	14	6/20/77	Nuneaton	5/15/95	Walsall	26+11	+2	2+1	1				
Viveash Adrian	6.1	11.9	9/30/69	Swindon	7/14/88	Swindon Town	51+3	6+1	+1	2	3			
				Loan	1/4/93	Reading	5			1				1
				Loan	1/20/95	Reading	6							
				Loan	8/10/95	Barnsley	2							
				Free	11/13/95	Walsall	118	8	13	3	12		2	1
M I D F I E L D														
Keates Dean	5.5	10.3	6/30/78	Walsall	9/27/96	Walsall	31+2	5+1	4		1			
Keister John Sierra Leonne Int.	5.8	11	11/11/70	Walsall	9/18/93	Walsall	76+27	3	10+2	2+2	2			
Peron Jean F	5.8	10.10	10/11/65	France		Lens								
				Free	8/24/97	Walsall	38	5	4	5	1			
Porter Gary E: u21.12, Y.13. FAYC'82	5.6	10.6	3/6/66	Sunderland	3/6/84	Watford	362+38	30+2	25+2	12+1	17	5	3	2
				Free	7/25/97	Walsall	25+4	2+1	3		1		2	
Thomas Wayne	6.0	12.2	8/28/78	Walsall	10/11/96	Walsall	17+7	+1	2					
Watson Andrew WFAC'91.	5.9	11.2	4/1/67	Leeds										
				Free	8/23/88	Halifax Town	75+8	5+1	6	7	15	2	1	1
				£40000	7/31/90	Swansea City	9+5	+1		1+1	1			
				£30000	9/19/91	Carlisle United	55+1	4	3	1	22	1	1	1
				£55000	2/5/93	Blackpool	88+27	6	3+2	7+1	23	5		1
				£60000	9/4/96	Walsall	45+18	5	4+3		12	4	3	
F O R W A R D														
Davis Neil	5.8	11	8/15/73	Redditch		Redditch United								
				£25000	8/1/91	Aston Villa (T)	0+2		0+1					
				Loan	10/25/96	Wycombe W.	13			1				
				Free	7/1/98	Walsall								
Marsh Chris	6	12.1	1/14/70	Sedgley	7/11/88	Walsall	231+32	13+2	24+1	14+1	11		4	
Platt Clive	6.4	13	10/27/77	Wolverhampton		Walsall	12+13	1+2	0+1		3	1		
Rammell Andrew	5.1	11.7	10/02/67	Nuneaton		Atherstone			0+1					
				£40000	26/09/89	Manchester United								
				£100000	14/09/90	Barnsley	138+27	10+2	11+1	8	40		4	1
					22/02/96	Southend United	50+19	3+3	2+1	1	13	1		
				Free	7/1/98	Walsall								
Ricketts Michael	6.3	13.1	12/4/78	Birmingham		Walsall	8+27	0+2	1+1		3			
Tholot Didier	5.9	11.6	4/2/64	France		Sion F.C.								
				Loan	3/2/98	Walsall	13+1			1+1	4			1
Wrack Darren	5.9	11.1	05/05/76	Cleethorpes	12/07/94	Derby County	2+7	0+3	0+1					
					15/08/96	Grimsby Town	5+8			0+1	1			
				Loan	17/02/97	Shrewsbury Town	3+1			1				
				Free	7/1/98	Walsall								
ADDITIONAL CONTRACT PLAYERS														
Pointon Neil						Hearts								
				Free	7/1/98	Walsall								

BESCOT STADIUM
Bescot Crescent, Walsall WS1 4SA

Capacity 9,000
Seating 6,700

First game ....v Aston Villa, Friendly, 18.8.1991.
First floodlit game ....v Cambridge Utd, Lge Cup, 28.8.1991.

ATTENDANCES
Highest ....10,628, England 'B' v Switzerland, 20.5.1991.
Lowest ....1,837 v Mansfield Town, AMC Rnd 1, 8.12.1992.

OTHER GROUNDS ....Fellows Park.

HOW TO GET TO THE GROUND

From the North
Use A461, sign posted Walsall, then join A4148 Broadway North around Ring Road. Turn left at traffic lights into Bescot Crescent, ground on left.

From the East, South and West
Use motorway M6 until junction 9, leave motorway and follow signs Walsall A461, then turn right A4148 into Broadway West. Turn right at first set of traffic lights into Bescot Crescent Stadium on left.

Car Parking: Car park for 1,200 vehicles at ground.

Nearest Railway Station: Bescot Stadium Station 70 yards from Ground.

USEFUL TELEPHONE NUMBERS

Club switchboard 01922 622 791
Club fax number 01922 613 202
Club shop 01922 613 356
Ticket Office 01922 651 400

Marketing Department. 01922 651 412
Internet address .... www.saddlers.co.uk
Official Clubcall. 0891 55 58 00*

*Calls cost 50p per minuteat all times. Call costings correct at time of going to press.

MATCHDAY PROGRAMME

Programme Editor ....Don Stanton.

Number of pages.....................................32.

Price ....£1.50.

Subscriptions ....Apply to club shop.

Local Newspapers
.....................Express & Star, Sporting Star
.........................Birmingham Evening Mail
.Birmingham Post & Mail, Walsall Observer.

Local Radio Stations
....BBC Radio West Midlands, BRMB Radio
....Beacon Radio.

MATCHDAY TICKET PRICES

Gilbert Alsop Terrace. .... Advanced £8.50/Matchday £9

Juv/OAP. .... £6/£7

H.L.Fellows Stand Centre .... £12/£13

Juv/OAP Block J,K,Q,R, only .... £8/£9

Bank's Family Stand

Family Area (1 adult & 1 child) .... £11/£12

Adults. .... £11/£12

Juv. .... £2/£2

Senior Citizens &Students .... £8/£8

William Sharp Stand £12

Juv £8

Swifts Club £20

Reserve Games £2

Juniors & Senior Citizens £1

WIGAN ATHLETIC
(The Latics)
NATIONWIDE LEAGUE DIVISION 2
SPONSORED BY: JJB SPORTS

1997-98 - Back Row L-R: Tony Black, David Lowe, Charlie Bishop, Ian Kilford, Pat Gibbon, Niel Fitchenry, Gavin Johnson, Brendan O'Connell.
Middle Row: Simon Farnworth, Steve Morgan, Graeme Jones, Lee Butler, Andy Saville, Roy Carroll, Paul Rogers, Scott Green, John Bensom.
Front Row: Paul warne, David Lee, Kevin Sharp, John deehan, Colin Greenall, Roberto Martinez, Graham Lancashire.

WIGAN ATHLETIC
FORMED IN 1932
TURNED PROFESSIONAL IN 1932
LTD COMPANY IN 1932

PRESIDENT: S Jackson
CHAIRMAN: Dave Whelan
DIRECTORS
B Ashcroft, D Sharpe (Vice-chairman),
J Winstanley, P Williams
CHIEF EXECUTIVE/SECRETARY
Mrs Brenda Spencer

MANAGER: Ray Mathias
ASSISTANT MANAGER: John Benson
YOUTH DEVELOPMENT OFFICER
David Crompton MSc, BSc (Econ), BA
YOUTH TEAM COACH: Alex Cribley
PHYSIOTHERAPIST
Simon Farnworth
FOOTBALL C0-ORDINATOR: Frank Lord

STATISTICIAN FOR THE DIRECTORY
Geoffrey Lea

As champions of Division Three last year Wigan Athletic came up on a high hoping for equally exciting times during the 1997/98 season, and with an opening day 5-2 victory of Wycombe Wanderers it looked as though the good times would continue.

However, only one point was picked up in their next four games and reality soon hit home. Finding it difficult to find any form the 'Latics' hit a season's low, 21st place, after a 1-2 defeat by Watford. This was the catalyst for a rival and three wins were strung together to lift back out of the relegation zone. Enough was achieved to keep them out of the drop zone without really pulling clear until April when they started a run of eight games, winning five, drawing two and losing only one to finish the season in a creditable and safe 11th.

The Coca-Cola cup was over after the first round after an aggregate score of 1-3 was recorded against Chesterfield, whilst in the FA Cup wins over Carlisle (1-0), and York (2-1) earned them a third round tie with Premiership outfit Blackburn. The Premier team proved a little to strong for Wigan, but the 'Latics' did leave Ewood Park before scoring twice against them, final score 2-4.

Under the new management of Ray Mathias, Wigan will be hoping to spend most of the season in top half of the table, but whether they strong enough to challenge for a play-off place remains to be seen, as a strong Division has got stronger this season with addition of a couple of larger relegated Division One clubs.

WIGAN ATHLETIC

Division 2   :11th   FA CUP: 3rd Round   LC CUP: 1st Round   AWS: Northern Quarter-Final

M	DATE	COMP.	VEN	OPPONENTS	RESULT	H/T	LP	GOAL SCORERS/GOAL TIMES	ATT.
1	A 09	FL	H	Wycombe Wanderers	W 5-2	4-0	1	O'Connell 5, 27, 90, Green 28, Kilford 42	4706
2	12	CC 1/1	H	Chesterfield	L 1-2	0-0		Lee 50	3413
3	15	FL	A	Bournemouth	L 0-1	0-0	9		(3799)
4	23	FL	H	Plymouth Argyle	D 1-1	1-0	9	Lowe 25	3761
5	26	CC 1/2	A	Chesterfield	L 0-1	0-0			(4076)
6	30	FL	A	Bristol City	L 0-3	0-3	15		(9255)
7	S 02	FL	A	Carlisle United	L 0-1	0-0	18		(5352)
8	08	FL	H	Wrexham	W 3-2	1-0	12	O'Connell 36, Lowe 72, Jones 78 (pen)	3872
9	13	FL	H	Blackpool	W 3-0	0-0	11	Johnson 48, Lowe 62, 82	5517
10	20	FL	A	Northampton Town	L 0-1	0-0	13		(6570)
11	27	FL	H	Fulham	W 2-1	1-1	6	Johnson 26, Greenall 89	4951
12	O 04	FL	A	Grimsby Town	L 1-2	0-1	12	Lowe 51	(4623)
13	11	FL	A	Chesterfield	W 3-2	1-1	9	O'Connell 13, Greenall 62, Lowe 67	(4673)
14	18	FL	H	Luton Town	D 1-1	0-0	8	Jones 72 (pen)	4466
15	21	FL	H	Gillingham	L 1-4	0-1	12	Lee 69	3214
16	25	FL	A	Millwall	D 1-1	0-0	14	Jones 86	(7986)
17	N 01	FL	H	York City	D 1-1	0-0	14	Greenall 90	3701
18	04	FL	A	Oldham Athletic	L 1-3	1-2	16	Lowe 14	(5446)
19	08	FL	A	Southend United	L 0-1	0-0	17		(2716)
20	15	FAC 1	A	Carlisle United	W 1-0	1-0		Jones 40	(5182)
21	22	FL	H	Preston North End	L 1-4	0-1	19	Kilford 59	5649
22	29	FL	A	Watford	L 1-2	1-2	21	Jones 10	(9455)
23	D 02	FL	H	Bristol Rovers	W 3-0	1-0	18	Kilford 20, Lowe 78, 85	2738
24	06	FAC 2	H	York City	W 2-1	0-0		Martinez 69, Lee 88	4021
25	09	AWS N1	H	Lincoln City	W 2-0	0-0		Jones 73, 89 (pen)	1467
26	13	FL	A	Burnley	W 2-0	2-0	18	Lee 13, Jones 44	(9520)
27	20	FL	H	Brentford	W 4-0	2-0	16	Lowe 24, Smeets 34, 82, Kilford 88	3301
28	26	FL	A	Wrexham	D 2-2	1-1	16	Smeets 22, Kilford 71	(4577)
29	28	FL	H	Carlisle United	L 0-2	0-1	17		4511
30	J 03	FAC 3	A	Blackburn Rovers	L 2-4	0-2		Lee 62, Lowe 68	(22402)
31	10	FL	A	Wycombe Wanderers	W 2-1	1-0	16	Martinez 20, Lee 81	(5549)
32	13	AWS N2	H	Rotherham United	W 3-0	1-0		Jones 19,58, Lowe 90	1495
33	17	FL	H	Bristol City	L 0-3	0-2	16		5078
34	24	FL	A	Plymouth Argyle	L 2-3	2-0	18	Kilford 37, Lee 41	(4345)
35	27	AWS NQF	A	Blackpool	L 0-1	0-0			(1687)
36	31	FL	A	Blackpool	W 2-0	2-0	16	Warne 8, Lydiate 15 (OG)	(5288)
37	F 06	FL	H	Northampton Town	D 1-1	0-0	16	Morgan 61	3579
38	14	FL	H	Grimsby Town	L 0-2	0-0	17		3548
39	21	FL	A	Fulham	L 0-2	0-0	17		(7791)
40	24	FL	A	Luton Town	D 1-1	1-1	17	Jones 16	(4403)
41	28	FL	H	Chesterfield	W 2-1	2-1	16	Lowe 16, Jones 37 (pen)	3017
42	M 07	FL	A	York City	D 2-2	1-0	18	Greenall 45, Jones 72	(3536)
43	14	FL	H	Oldham Athletic	W 1-0	0-0	17	Kilford 64	4277
44	17	FL	H	Southend United	L 1-3	0-2	17	Lowe 84	2616
45	21	FL	A	Walsall	L 0-1	0-0	18		(3169)
46	28	FL	A	Preston North End	D 1-1	0-1	18	Lowe 57	(10171)
47	A 04	FL	H	Watford	W 3-2	3-0	18	Barlow 12, Lowe 25, Kilford 40	4262
48	07	FL	H	Bournemouth	W 1-0	0-0	14	Lee 80	2798
49	10	FL	A	Bristol Rovers	L 0-5	0-3	15		(6038)
50	13	FL	H	Burnley	W 5-1	2-0	13	Barlow 31, Lowe 43, 87, Warne 77, Kilford 80	4926
51	18	FL	A	Brentford	W 2-0	0-0	12	Bradshaw 54 (pen), Kilford 68	(4480)
52	21	FL	H	Walsall	W 2-0	0-0	10	Barlow 47, Jones 69	2725
53	24	FL	H	Millwall	D 0-0	0-0	10		4045
54	M 02	FL	A	Gillingham	D 0-0	0-0	11		(10361)

Best Home League Attendance: 5649 V Preston North End   Smallest :2616 V Southend United   Average :3968

Goal Scorers:

FL	(64)	Lowe 16, Kilford 10, Jones 9, Lee 5, O'Connell 5, Greenall 4, Barlow 3, Smeets 3, Johnson 2, Warne 2, Bradshaw 1, Green 1, Martinez 1, Morgan 1, Opponents 1
CC	(1)	Lee 1
FAC	(5)	Lee 2, Jones 1, Lowe 1, Martinez 1
AWS	(5)	Jones 4, Lowe 1

(F) Barlow	(M) Bishop	(F) Black	(F) Bradshaw	(F) Branch	(F) Broughton	(G) Butler	(G) Carroll	(M) Fitzhenry	(M) Green	(D) Greenall	(D) Johnson	(F) Jones	(M) Kilford	(F) Lancashire	(M) Lee	(F) Lowe	(M) Martinez	(D) McGibbon	(D) Morgan	(F) Mustoe	(D) Newman	(F) O'Connell	(M) Rogers	(F) Saville	(M) Sharp	(M) Smeets	(M) Warne	(M) Whitworth		
X	S					X			X	X	X				X	X	X				S1		X	X	X				J.A. Kirkby	1
S	S2					X			X	X	X				X	S1	X	X					X	X	X				C J Foy	2
		S2			X	X			S3	X	X				X	S1	X	X					X	X	X				A N Butler	3
					S1	X			S	X	X	X			X	X	X						X	X	X		S		D Laws	4
						X			X	X	X	X	X	S3	X	X	X	X				X	X	S1	S2				J P Robinson	5
						X			X	X	X	X			X	X	X	X				X		S1	S3		S2		M E Pierce	6
					S2	X			X	X	X	X			X		X	X					X	X	S1	X		S	S W Mathieson	7
					S1	X			X	X	X	X	X	S	S	X	X	X					X	X	X				T Heilbron	8
						X			X	X	X	X			S	X	X	X	X				X	S1	S2	X			A R Leake	9
						X		S	X	X	X	X			X	X	S2	X					X	X	S1	X			P S Danson	10
						X			X	X	X	X			X	X	X	X					X	S2	S1	X		S	R D Furnandiz	11
						X			X	X	S1	X			X	X	X	X					X	S	X	X	X	S2	P Rejer	12
X						X			X	X	S	X			X	X	X						X	S1	S	X	X		A R Hall	13
X	X					X				X	S1	X			X	X	X	X	S3				X		X	X		S2	M D Messias	14
X	X					X				X	X				X	X	X	S					X	X	S	X	S1		W C Burns	15
X	X					X				X		X	X		X	X	S	X					X		X	S	S		M C Bailey	16
	X					X				X	X	S	X		X	X	S2	X					X		X	S1			M J Jones	17
X	X					X				X	X				X	S		X	X				X		X	S1	S2		E K Wolstenholme	18
X	X					X				X	X		S2			S1	X	X				X	X		X	S3			K A Leach	19
	X					X	S		X	X	X	X			X	X	X	S	X				S		X	S	S		R Pearson	20
	X					X			X	X	X	X			X	X	X	X					X	X	X	S			A G Wiley	21
		X1				X			X	X	X				X	X	S	X	X				X	S1	X	S2			A Bates	22
						X			X	X	X				X	X	X	X2					X	S2	X1	S1	S		K M Lynch	23
					S	X			X	X	X	X1	X		X	X	X	X					X	S	S1	S	S		M J Brandwood	24
X						X			X1	X2		X	S1		X	X3	S2	X	X				X		X		S3			25
	S1					X			X	X		X2	X1		X	X	X	X					X		X	S	S2		P R Richards	26
						X	X	S1	X	X					X2	X3		X1	X				X		X	X	S2		J P Robinson	27
			S1			X	S	S	X	X					X	X1		X	X				X		X2	S1	S2		M L Dean	28
			X2			X			X	X3					X	X		S3	X	X			X		X1	S1	S2		T Jones	29
					S	X			X	X		X1			X	S1		X	X	X			X		S	X	S		N S Barry	30
	X					X1			X	X					S1	X	X	X	X				X		S	X2	S2		M R Halsey	31
						X			X		X		X		X	X	X	X		X	S1		X		X	X1				32
		X3				X			X1	X					X	X	X	X2	X				X		S2	S1	S3		D Laws	33
			X1			X			X	X		X			X	S	X	X					X2		X	S2	S1		P Taylor	34
						X			X	X		X	X		X1	X	X	X							X	X	S1			35
	X					X		S	X	X		X	X		X	S	X	X							X	X	X		T Heilbron	36
	X					X			X	X	S		X		X	X	X	X		X		S			S1	X1	X		R Pearson	37
	X					X			X		X2	X			X	X	X	X		X					S1	S2	S		M Fletcher	38
	X					X			X		X		X		X	S1	X1	X	X	S			X		S		X		A R Hall	39
	X					X1			X	X		X	X		X2	S	X	X					S2		X		S1		S G Bennett	40
	X					X			X	X		X	X		X2	X	X	S1	X				S		X		S2		W C Burns	41
						X			X	X		X	X		X	X	S1	X	X1				X		X	S	S		F G Stretton	42
	X					X			X	X		X	X		X	X	X	X					X	X1	S	S	S1		P R Richards	43
	X					X			X1	X	X2	X			X	X	S2	X					X		X		S1	S	S W Mathieson	44
	X					X			X	X1		X	X		S2	X		X2	S				X		X		S1	X	M J Jones	45
X2	X					X			X1			X	S1		X	X	X	S	X		X		X			S2			E Lomas	46
X1	X					X			X			X	S1		X	X	S	X		X		X							P Rejer	47
X2	X					X			S1			X			X	X	X	X1		X		X				S2			D Pugh	48
X	X					X			X2			X1	X3		X	X		X		X		X			S3	S2	S2		S J Baines	49
X1	X					X			X			X			X	S1		X		X		X			X1	S1	S	S	J P Robinson	50
X1	X					X			X			X3			X	X	X2	S3		X		X			S2	S1			M S Pike	51
X2						X		X2	X	X					X	X1	X	X		X		X					S1	S2	S2	G B Frankland	52
X1	X					X			X	S	X	S2			X	X	X2	X		X		X				S1		M D Messias	53
X1	X					X			X	S	X	S1			X	X	X	X		X		X			S			A Bates	54
9	7		27	2	1	17	29	1	37	39	18	28	29		41	42	26	32	13		8	17	32		33	10	3	1	FL Appearances	
	1		1	1	3			2	1			2	5	1	1	2	1		7	3				6	5	4	13	22	3	FL Sub Appearances
		0+1				1	1		2	2	2	1	1+1	0+1	2	2	1	2					2	2	0+1	1+1			CC Appearances
		1				1	2		3	2	3	2	3		3	2+1	2	3	1				1	1	1+1	1			FAC Appearances
	1					1	2	1	2	3		3	1+1		3	2+1	1	3	0+1			2			2	3	0+2		AWS Appearances

Also played:(D) Bruno X1(38). (M) Crompton S(36). (F) Diaz S2(27), S(47,48), X(49).(G) Farnworth S(30). (M) Woods X(19).

WIGAN ATHLETIC RECORDS AND STATISTICS

CLUB RECORDS

RECORD LEAGUE VICTORY
7-1 v Scarborough (h) Div.3, 11.03.1997.
7-2 v Scunthorpe Utd, (a), Div 4, 12.3.1982 5-0 v Peterborough
Utd, (h), Div 4, 19.1.1982 5-0 v Swansea City, (h), Div 3,
18.1.1986 6-1 v Swansea City (a),Div 3,6.4.1991
Most Goals Scored in a Cup Tie: 6-0 v Carlisle United, FA Cup Rnd
1, 24.11.1934 6-0 v Rochdale, Freight Rover Trophy (Northern
Section), 28.1.1986

RECORD LEAGUE DEFEAT
0-5 v Bristol Rovers, Div 3, 26.2.1983 1-6 v Bristol Rovers, Div 3,
3.3.1990
Record Cup Defeat: 0-5 v Chelsea (h), FA Cup Round 3 replay,
26.1.1985

MOST LEAGUE POINTS
(3pts a win) 91, Div 4, 1981-82
(2pts a win) 55, Div 4,1978-79, 1979-80

MOST LEAGUE GOALS
84, Div 3, 1996-97.

RECORD TRANSFER FEE RECEIVED
£350,000 from Coventry City for Peter Atherton, August 1991

RECORD TRANSFER FEE PAID
£350,000 to Hull City for Roy Carroll, April 1997.

BEST PERFORMANCES
League: 4th Div 3 1985-86 & 1986-87
FA Cup: 6th Round1986-87
League Cup: 4th Round 1981-82

HONOURS
Freight Rover Trophy 1985.
Division 3 Champions 1996/97.

LEAGUE CAREER
Elected to Div 4 1978 Promoted to Div 3 (now Div 2) 1982
Relegated to Div 3 1992-93 Promoted to Div 2 1996/97.

INDIVIDUAL CLUB RECORDS

MOST APPEARANCES FOR CLUB
Kevin Langley (1982-86 & 1990-1994): League 307+10 +FA Cup
27+1 + League Cup 21 + Other Competitions 27 Total 382+11 sub
MOST CAPPED PLAYER
None
RECORD GOALSCORER IN A MATCH
Paul Jewell 4 v Aldershot, Div 3, 1.3.1988
RECORD LEAGUE GOALSCORER IN A SEASON
Graeme Jones: 31, Div 3 1996/97.
In all competitions: Graeme Jones - 33 (31 Lge, 1 Lge Cup, 1 AMC)
RECORD LEAGUE GOALSCORER IN A CAREER
Peter Houghton 62, 1978-83 In All Competitions: Peter Houghton
68 (League 62 + FA Cup 3 + League Cup 3)

OLDEST PLAYER IN A LEAGUE MATCH
Joe Jakub, 38 years, 76 days v Exeter City, Division 3, 21.2.95.
YOUNGEST PLAYER IN A LEAGUE MATCH
Steve Nugent, 16 years 132 days v Leyton Orient, Division 3,
16.9.1989

PREVIOUS MANAGERS

Charlie Spencer 1932-37 Jimmy Milne 1946-47 Bob Pryde 1949-52
Ted Goodier 1952-54 Walter Crook 1954-55 Ron Suart 1955-56
Billy Cooke 1956 Sam Barkas 1957 Trevor Hitchen 1957-58
Malcom Barrass 1958-59 Jimmy Shirley 1959 Pat Murphy 1959-60
Allenby Chilton 1960 Johnny Ball 1961-63 Allan Brown 1963-66 Alf
Craig 1966-67 Harry Leyland 1967-68 Alan Saunders 1968 Ian
McNeill 1968-70 Gordon Milne 1970-72 Les Rigby 1972-74 Brian
Tiler 1974-76 Ian McNeill 1976-81 Larry Lloyd 1981-83 Harry
McNally 1983-85 Bryan Hamilton 1985-86 Ray Mathias 1986-89
Bryan Hamilton 1989-91 Dave Philpotts 1991-93, Kenny Swain 1993-94
Graham Barrow 1994-95. John Deehan 1995-98.

ADDITIONAL INFORMATION
Previous Name: None.
Previous League: Lancashire Combination, Cheshire League,
Northern Premier.
Club Colours: Blue shirts and shorts with white trim.
Change Colours: White shirts with green trim, white shorts.
Reserves League: Pontins League Division Three.

LONGEST LEAGUE RUNS

of undefeated matches:	21 (1981-82)	of league matches w/out a win:	14 (1989)
of undefeated home matches:	25 (1985-86)	of undefeated away matches:	11 (1986)
without home win:	6 (1988, 1989)	without an away win:	15 (1988)
of league wins:	6 (1986, 1993)	of home wins:	8 (1978-79)
of league defeats:	7 (1993)	of away wins:	4 (1987, 1988)

THE MANAGER

Ray Mathias. . . . . .appointed August 1998.
PREVIOUS CLUBS
As Manager . . . .
As Asst.Man/Coach . . . .
As a player. . . . . Tranmere Rovers.
HONOURS
As a Manager . . . . None.
As a Player . . . . None.

WIGAN ATHLETIC

PLAYERS NAME / Honours	Ht	Wt	Birthdate	Birthplace / Transfers	Contract Date	Clubs	League	L/Cup	FA Cup	Other	Lge	L/C	FAC	Oth
G O A L K E E P E R														
Carroll Roy	6.2	11.9	9/30/77	Enniskillen		Hull City	46	2	1					
					5/31/97	Wigan Athletic	29	1	2					
Naylor Roy	6	12	9/15/78	Liverpool	6/13/97	Liverpool (T)								
				Free	7/1/98	Wigan Athletic (NC)								
D E F E N C E														
Fitzhenry Neil	6	12	9/24/78	Bilinge	10/25/96	Wigan Athletic (T)	1+2							
Green Scott	5.11	11.12	1/15/70	Walsall	7/20/88	Derby County								
				£50000	3/17/90	Bolton Wanderers	166+54	19+4	20+3	16+4	24	1	4	
					6/28/97	Wigan Athletic	36+1	2	3		1			
Griffiths Gareth	6.4	14	10/04/70	Winsford		Rhyl								
				£1000	08/02/93	Port Vale	90+4	8	7	7	4		1	
				Loan	10/31/97	Shrewsbury Town	6							
				Free	7/1/98	Wigan Athletic								
Lee David M DIV1 96/97	5.7	10	11/5/67	Blackburn	8/8/86	Bury	203+5	15	6	19+1	35	1		4
				£350000	8/27/91	Southampton	11+9		+1	1+1				
				£300000	11/2/92	Bolton Wanderers	124+31	19+1	13+2	8+1	17	2		
					7/18/97	Wigan Athletic	41+2	2	3		5	1	2	
McGibbon Patrick C G NI: 6, B.4, U21.1, S.	6.2	13.12	9/6/73	Lurgan		Portadown								
				£100000	8/1/92	Manchester United								
				Loan	9/20/96	Swansea City	1							
				£250000	8/1/97	Wigan Athletic	42+3	2	3	1				
Sharp Kevin E: Y,S. UEFA Yth'93. FAYC'93.DIV3 96/97	5.9	10.7	9/19/74	Canada		Auxerre (France)								
				£60000	10/20/92	Leeds United	11+5							
				£100000	11/30/95	Wigan Athletic	83+9	2+1	3+1		8			
M I D F I E L D														
Jenkinson Leigh	6	12.2	7/9/69	Thorne	6/15/87	Hull City (T)	95+35	7+2	6+1	9+2	13			1
				Loan	9/13/90	Rotherham United	5+2							
				£300000	3/12/93	Coventry City	22+10	0+1	3		1			
				Loan	11/1/93	Birmingham City	2+1							
				Free	8/1/95	St. Johnstone								
				Free	7/1/98	Wigan Athletic								
Kilford Ian DIV3 96/97	5.11	10.5	10/6/73	Bristol	4/3/91	Nottingham Forest	0+1							
					12/23/93	Wigan Athletic	113+20	6+1	6+2	5	29		1	1
Martinez Roberto DIV3 96/97	5.11	11.12	7/13/73	Balaguer	Free	7/26/93	CF Balaguer (Spain)								
						Wigan Athletic	105+12	5	7	2	14	1	4	
Porter Andy AGT'93	5.9	11.2	17/09/68	Macclesfield	29/06/87	Port Vale	313+44	22+1	20+4	26+2	22		3	1
				Free	7/1/98	Wigan Athletic								
Rogers Paul A E: SP.6. IPL'85'86. DIV3 96/97	6	12.05	3/21/65	Portsmouth		Sutton United								
				£35000	1/29/92	Sheffield United	107+2	7	4	1	10	1		
					12/29/95	Notts County	21+1		1	4	2		1	
				Loan	12/13/96	Wigan Athletic	7+2				3			
					3/7/97	Wigan Athletic	43+6	2	1		3			
F O R W A R D														
Barlow Stuart	5.11	11	7/16/68	Liverpool	6/6/90	Everton	24+44	3+4	4+3		10	1	2	
				Loan	1/10/92	Rotherham United				+1				
				£350000	11/20/95	Oldham Athletic	78+14	5+1	6+1	1	31		1	
				£45000	3/26/98	Wigan Athletic	9				3			
Bradshaw Carl E: Y4	6	11	10/2/68	Sheffield	8/23/86	Sheffield Wednesday	16+16	2+2	6+1	1	4		3	
				Loan	8/24/86	Barnsley	6							
				£50000	9/30/88	Manchester City	1+4		0+1	0+1				
				£50000	9/7/89	Sheffield United	122+25	10+1	12+1	4	8	2	3	
				£50000	7/28/94	Norwich City	55+10	6+1	2		2	1		
				Free	10/6/97	Wigan Athletic	27+1		1		1			
Jones Graeme A NPL Div.1'93. FA Vase'93. Div.3'97	6	12.12	3/13/70	Gateshead		Bridlington								
				£10000	8/2/93	Doncaster Rovers	81+11	4+1	2+1	5	27	1	2	1
					8/23/96	Wigan Athletic	28+5	1	3		9		1	
Lowe David A E: u21.2, Y.7. AMC'85.DIV3 96/97 Div.2'92.	5.11	11.4	8/30/65	Liverpool	6/1/83	Wigan Athletic	179+9	8	16+1	18	40		4	9
				£80000	6/26/87	Ipswich Town	121+13	10	3	10+2	37	2		6
				Loan	3/19/92	Port Vale	8+1				2			
				£250000	7/13/92	Leicester City	47+19	0+3	1+2	3	19	1		
				Loan	2/18/94	Port Vale	18+1				5			
				£125000	3/28/96	Wigan Athletic	77+10	4	3+1		25		1	
Smeets Jorg			5/11/70	Bussum		Heracles								
				£100000	10/3/97	Wigan Athletic	10+13		1		3			
Warne Paul	5.9	11.2	5/8/73	Norwich		Wroxham								
				£25000	7/30/97	Wigan Athletic	3+22				2			
ADDITIONAL CONTRACT PLAYERS														
Crompton Paul A					1/30/98	Wigan Athletic (T)								
Mills Leon						Manchester Utd (T)								
				Free	7/1/98	Wigan Athletic								

SPRINGFIELD PARK
Wigan, Lancashire WN6 7BA

Capacity..7,097
Covered Standing 2,967
Seating..1,109

First game (As Wigan Ath.) ....5,106 v Port Vale Reserves. Cheshire Lge.
First ever game..Wigan County v Burton Swifts, 1.9.1897.
ATTENDANCES
Highest ....27,526 v Hereford Utd, FA Cup 2nd Rnd.,2.12.1953.
....*(Record for two non-League clubs outside of Wembley)*
Lowest ....983 v Bury, AMC, 19.10.1993.

OTHER GROUND...None.

HOW TO GET TO THE GROUND

From the North: Exit M6 at junction 27 and turn left at end of slip road. Turn right at T-junction, signposted Shevington. After 1 mile turn left into Old Lane (signed B5375 Standish Lower Ground). The road winds through countryside for approx. 2 miles. Go straight on at cross roads (you can see floodlights ahead). After 0.75 miles, turn left at traffic lights into Springfield Road, take second left (First Avenue) into ground.
From the South & West: Exit M6 at junction 25. At end of slip road (approx. 1 mile) turn left, signposted Wigan A49. Follow signs for Wigan A49 for 1.8 miles to complex junction (Homestyle warehouse is ahead of you). Turn left at traffic lights into Robin Park Road. Go straight on for 1 mile to crossroads, then turn right. After 0.75 miles, turn left at traffic lights into Springfield Road. Take second left (First Avenue) into ground.
From the East: Exit M61 at junction 6 (signposted Chorley, Horwich A6027) and take first exit at roundabout. NB: do not exit at junction 5 which is signposted Wigan. At next roundabout, take first left (signposted Westhoughton A6, Wigan B5238) into Chorley Road. After 0.3 miles turn right (signposted Wigan B5238). After 1.8 miles turn left at Aspull War Memorial (signposted Wigan B5238). After 2.2 miles just after *Earl of Balcarres pub* turn right at traffic lights (Central Park, Wigan RLFC, is now facing you). Turn left at lights and get in right hand lane. Go straight through three sets of lights until Morrisons is on left hand side, BBC North on right hand side, and the college ahead and to the right (building has a large wheel on wall). Turn right as lights into Parsons Walk, thus passing the college on your left. Follow this road for 0.7 miles tosecond setof traffic lights. Turn right into Springfield Road, then second left (First Avenue) into ground.
Car Parking: Parking in nearby side streets.
Nearest Railway Station: Wigan Wallgate or Wigan Northwestern (01942 242 231)

USEFUL TELEPHONE NUMBERS

Club switchboard 01942 244 433
Club fax number 01942 494654
Club shop 01942 243 067
Ticket Office 01942 244 433

Marketing - Elaine Mitchingon 01942 243 067
Clubcall 0891 12 16 55*
*Calls cost 50p per minute at all times.
Call costings correct at time of going to press.

MATCHDAY PROGRAMME

Programme Editor . . . . Geoff Lea.

Number of pages . . . . 32.

Price . . . . £1.80.

Subscriptions . . . . £45 inc. P&P.

Local Newspapers
 . . . . Wigan Observer, Wigan Evening Post
 . . . . Wigan Reporter.

Local Radio Stations
 . . . . Piccadilly Gold, BBC GMR
 . . . . . . Red Rose Gold, Wish FM, City FM.

MATCHDAY TICKET PRICES

Phoenix Stand

Adults £10

Juv/OAP £6

Cable North West Family Stand

Adults £10

U16. . . . . £5

Terraces

Adult £7.50

U16/OAP. £4

WREXHAM
(The Robins)
NATIONWIDE LEAGUE DIVISION 2
SPONSORED BY: CARLSBERG TETLEY

1998-99 Back Row L-R: Dave Brammer, Dean Spink, Andy Marriott, Mark Cartwright, David Walsh, Mark McGregor, Karl Connolly.
Standing: Steve Cooper, Andy Griffiths, Tony Humes, Brian Carey, Dave Ridler, Paul Mazzarella, Jake Edwards, Deryn Brace, Robin Gibson, Mel Pejic (Physio). **Sitting:** Craig Skinner, Kevin Russell, Neil Roberts, Peter Ward, Joey Jones (Coach), Brian Flynn (Manager), Kevin Reeves (Assistant Manager), Martyn Chalk, Gareth Owen, Steve Thomas, Phil Hardy.

WREXHAM
FORMED IN 1872
TURNED PROFESSIONAL IN 1912
LTD COMPANY IN 1912

PRESIDENT: F Tomlinson
CHAIRMAN: W P Griffiths
VICE-CHAIRMAN
B Williams
DIRECTORS
Mrs B Derosa, C Griffiths, P Griffiths,
S F Mackreth, D Rhodes, C G Paletta
SECRETARY
D Rhodes (01978 262 129)
COMMERCIAL MANAGER
Alan Thomas (01978 352 536)

MANAGER: Brian Flynn
ASSISTANT MANAGER: Kevin Reeves
COACHES: Joey Jones & Ian Rush
YOUTH DEVELOPMENT OFFICER
Cliff Sear
PHYSIOTHERAPIST
Mel Pejic

STATISTICIAN FOR THE DIRECTORY
Gareth M Davies

'Deja Vue' would be the words on the lips of the majority of Racecourse fans following the latest successful fight against promotion !

The most recent disappointment saw Wrexham accumulate just seven points out of 24 in the run up to the promotion play-off's. This time around the club were in the most promising position to date to make the end of season scramble for the extra promotion place. However, an inexplicable loss of form by the players at a vital stage of the season once again proved the stumbling block in the continuing quest for First Division football.

'Consistent inconsistency' and the lack of a regular goalscorer up front was their eventual undoing. This has now become an annual occurrence which hardly instills confidence in the supporters who must be congratulated for their patience!

Brian Flynn and his erstwhile staff have worked wonders in securing the club a comfortable position in the Second Division since their promotion in 1992/93, but it seems progress is hampered by financial restrictions, and a seemingly lack of ambition by the club in failure to press home advantages.

The town itself is developing apace, business wise, and one hopes the Directors will do their utmost to attract more sponsorship at the Racecourse, as marketing is of the utmost importance in this day and age.

The commercial and administration staff are doing their bit and must be encouraged from the top. The attendances have remained low and this reflects a certain 'no confidence' feeling among the 'floating fans', although the loyal 3,500 - 4,000 are among the most loyal, and the 'away' support the envy of many.

On the plus side, two young products of the clubs' successful youth policy, who featured strongly during the campaign, were local boy Neil Roberts, who plays up front, and flanker Neil Wainwright, although the latter has now sadly left the club to join Sunderland.

Following the failure to reach the play-offs, there was speculation that Brian Flynn was about to leave Wrexham for pastures new, but this failed to materialise and he remains committed in his attempt to take the club into a higher standard of football.

The general feeling among the 'Robins' supporters is that the team needs two or three quality signings to make a 'serious assault' on a promotion place (easier said than done with the 'Bosman Rule' now in force) with a striker of scoring ability essential. This in a league which will be even more competitive with the addition of Manchester City and Stoke to it's ranks.

GARETH M DAVIES.

WREXHAM

Division 2   :6th   FA CUP: 3rd Round   LC CUP: 1st Round   AWS: Northern Round 2

M	DATE	COMP.	VEN	OPPONENTS	RESULT	H/T	LP	GOAL SCORERS/GOAL TIMES	ATT.
1	A 09	FL	A	Fulham	L 0-1	0-1	23		(8789)
2	12	CC 1/1	H	Sheffield United	D 1-1	0-0		Connolly 67	3644
3	15	FL	H	Oldham Athletic	W 3-1	2-0	12	Jones 8, Carey 44, Ward 77	4429
4	23	FL	A	Grimsby Town	D 0-0	0-0	12		(4404)
5	26	CC 1/2	A	Sheffield United	L 1-3	1-1		Spink 21	(7181)
6	S 02	FL	H	Blackpool	L 3-4	2-0	19	Owen 22, Phillips 39, Spink 51	3762
7	08	FL	A	Wigan Athletic	L 2-3	0-1	19	Spink 57, 83	(3872)
8	13	FL	H	Bristol City	W 2-1	1-0	16	Spink 13, Watkin 60	3251
9	20	FL	A	Luton Town	W 5-2	2-1	12	Brammer 11, Connolly 26, 63, 73, Skinner 62 (pen)	(5241)
10	27	FL	H	Chesterfield	D 0-0	0-0	14		3921
11	O 04	FL	A	Bristol Rovers	L 0-1	0-0	17		(6829)
12	11	FL	A	Walsall	L 0-3	0-2	19		(4042)
13	18	FL	H	Burnley	D 0-0	0-0	20		5132
14	21	FL	H	Southend United	W 3-1	0-1	17	McGregor 60, Kelly 65, Connolly 87 (pen)	2039
15	25	FL	A	Preston North End	W 1-0	0-0	15	Chalk 50	(9098)
16	N 01	FL	A	Carlisle United	D 2-2	2-2	15	Roberts 20, 33	(4464)
17	04	FL	H	Bournemouth	W 2-1	2-0	8	Roberts 12, Spink 15	2462
18	08	FL	A	Northampton Town	W 1-0	0-0	7	Roberts 48	3768
19	15	FAC 1	A	Rochdale	W 2-0	0-0		Roberts 56, Connolly 65	(3956)
20	18	FL	A	Wycombe Wanderers	D 0-0	0-0	9		(3635)
21	22	FL	H	Plymouth Argyle	D 1-1	0-0	10	Ward 71	3641
22	29	FL	A	Brentford	D 1-1	0-0	11	Owen 62	(3748)
23	D 02	FL	H	Watford	D 1-1	0-0	10	McGregor 90	3702
24	05	FAC 2	A	Chester City	W 2-0	2-0		Connolly 38, 45	(5224)
25	13	FL	A	York City	L 0-1	0-0	12		(2871)
26	20	FL	H	Gillingham	D 0-0	0-0	13		2834
27	26	FL	H	Wigan Athletic	D 2-2	1-1	14	Owen 39, Connolly 65	4577
28	28	FL	A	Blackpool	W 2-1	0-1	11	Owen 85, Wainwright 88	(5424)
29	J 4	FAC 3	A	Wimbledon	D 0-0	0-0			(6349)
30	10	FL	H	Fulham	L 0-3	0-1	13		5338
31	13	FAC 3R	H	Wimbledon	L 2-3	1-3		Connolly 7, 46	9539
32	17	FL	A	Millwall	W 1-0	0-0	11	Wainwright 75	(5550)
33	20	AWS N2	A	Mansfield Town	L 0-1	0-0			(1325)
34	27	FL	A	Oldham Athletic	L 0-3	0-2	13		(4680)
35	31	FL	A	Bristol City	D 1-1	0-1	13	Roberts 48	(11741)
36	F 06	FL	H	Luton Town	W 2-1	0-0	10	Brammer 66, Roberts 88	3527
37	14	FL	H	Bristol Rovers	W 1-0	1-0	10	Owen 26	3716
38	21	FL	A	Chesterfield	L 1-3	0-2	10	Owen 76	(3919)
39	24	FL	A	Burnley	W 2-1	1-1	10	Roberts 11, Wilson 64	(8576)
40	28	FL	H	Walsall	W 2-1	2-1	8	Brammer 6, Wainwright 29	3622
41	M 03	FL	A	Northampton Town	W 1-0	1-0	8	Spink 39	(5183)
42	07	FL	H	Carlisle United	D 2-2	1-1	7	Ward 45, Connolly 78	4242
43	14	FL	A	Bournemouth	W 1-0	0-0	7	Owen 53	(5512)
44	17	FL	H	Millwall	W 1-0	1-0	5	Roberts 6	4167
45	21	FL	H	Wycombe Wanderers	W 2-0	1-0	3	Brammer 90, Kavanagh 42 (OG)	4290
46	28	FL	A	Plymouth Argyle	L 0-2	0-1	4		(4759)
47	31	FL	H	Grimsby Town	D 0-0	0-0	4		5421
48	A 04	FL	H	Brentford	D 2-2	0-1	4	Wilson 60, Ward 63	4132
49	11	FL	A	Watford	L 0-1	0-1	5		(12340)
50	13	FL	H	York City	L 1-2	0-0	5	Wilson 65	5231
51	18	FL	A	Gillingham	D 1-1	1-1	6	Wilson 16	(7869)
52	25	FL	H	Preston North End	D 0-0	0-0	7		7302
53	M 02	FL	A	Southend United	W 3-1	1-1	6	Ward 43, 86, Connolly 72	(4220)

Best Home League Attendance: 7302 V Preston North End   Smallest :2039 V Southend United   Average :4109

Goal Scorers:

FL	(55)	Roberts 8, Connolly 7, Owen 7, Spink 6, Ward 6, Brammer 4, Wilson 4, Wainwright 3, McGregor 2, Carey 1, Chalk 1, Jones 1, Kelly 1, Phillips 1, Skinner 1, Watkin 1, Opponents 1
CC	(2)	Connolly 1, Spink 1
FAC	(6)	Connolly 5, Roberts 1
AWS	(0)	

(F) Basham	(D) Brace	(M) Brammer	(D) Carey	(G) Cartwright	(F) Chalk	(F) Connolly	(M) Cross	(M) Griffiths	(D) Hardy	(D) Humes	(D) Jones	(F) Kelly	(G) Marriott	(D) McGregor	(M) Owen	(M) Phillips	(D) Ridler	(F) Roberts	(F) Russell	(F) Skinner	(M) Spink	(M) Thomas	(F) Wainwright	(M) Ward	(F) Watkin	(D) Williams	(F) Wilson	Opponent / No.
	X	S1	X		X	X					X			X	X		X		S	X	X			X	S2			A.P. D'Urso 1
	X	S	X		S	X					X			X	X	X				X	X	X		X	S1			E Wolstenholme 2
	X	S1	X		S	X					X			X	X		X			X	X	X		X	S			A G Wiley 3
	X	X	X	S	S1	X					X			X	X	S	X			X	X			X				R D Furnandiz 4
	X	X	X		S1	X	S				X			X	X	S	X			X	X			X				G B Frankland 5
	X	X	X		S1	X	X				S	X		X	X	X	X			X	X	S		X				C J Foy 6
	X	X	X		X	X	X				S	X		X	X	X	X				X	S			S			T Heilbron 7
	X	X			X		X	X	S1		X			X	X	X				X	X			S		S2		A Bates 8
	X	X			X		X				X			X	X	X				S	X	X		S	S1			P Rejer 9
	X	X			X		X				X			X	X	X	S3	S1	X	X			S2					G Singh 10
	X	X			X		X	X	X	X	X			X	X	X	S	S1		X			S2					J A Kirkby 11
	X	X	X		X	X					X	X	S	S1	X	X	S2			X				X				B Coddington 12
	X	X			S2	X					X	X	S	X	X	X	S1			X				X				G Cain 13
	X	X			S	X					X	X	S	X	X	X	S			X				X				A R Hall 14
	X	X			S1	X					X	X	S	X	X	X	S2			X				X				W C Burns 15
	X	X				X					X	X	S	X	X	X	S1		X	S2	X			X				J P Robinson 16
	X	X			S						X	X	S1	X	X	X			X	X	X	X	S		X				M D Messias 17
	X	X			S						X	X	X		X		S	X	X	X	X	S		X				G Laws 18
			S	S1	X	S	S	X	X	X		X		X	X	X	X		X		S	X						A R Hall 19
			S1	X	S	S	X	X	X	X		X		X	X	X		X		S	X							P R Richards 20
			S1	X	X	X	X	X	X	X		S	X	X	X	S2	X		X									G B Frankland 21
		X	X	X	X		X	X1		X	S1	X	S	X	X	X		S	X				X					F G Stretton 22
		X	X1	X	X		S			X	X	X	X	X	X		S1			X								D Laws 23
		X1	S	X	X2	X		S1		X	X	X	X	X	S2	X		X		S	X							S J Baines 24
		X		X	X	X2		S		X	X	X	S2	X	S1	X		X1		X								A N Butler 25
		X		X	X	X	X			X	X	X	X2	S2	S	S1	X		X1		X							E K Wolstenholme 26
		X	X1	X		X	X3			X	X	X			S3	S2	X	S1	X2		X							M L Dean 27
S	S1	X		X		X				X	X	X		X	X	X2	X			S2	X1							M D Messias 28
		X		X		X				X	X	X		X	X1	X	X	S1		X								29
		X		S2	X		X				X	X		X	X	S1	X		X1	X	X2							A G Wiley 30
S	S	X	S	S1	X		X				X	X	X	X	X		S		X	X1								J W Dunn 31
S	X	X		S	X		X				X	X	X	X	X		S		X	X								D Orr 32
X1	X			X2	X		X				X	X	X	S3	S2		S1	X	S1	X	X3							33
S	X	X		S2	X		X				X	X	X	X2	X	X1			S1	X								E K Wolstenholme 34
S	X	X			X1		X				X	X	X	X	X		S1	X	S									P S Danson 35
S2	X	X				X					X	X	X	X		X1	X2	S1	X									T Jones 36
X	X	X	X	X			S				X	X	X		S	S	X	X										S W Mathieson 37
X2	X	X	X	X	X1		S3				X	X	X3	X		S1	S2	X										M J Brandwood 38
X2	X	X	X	X1			S				X	X	X	X	S2		X	X					S1					T Heilbron 39
X	X1	X				S1				X	X	X	X	S2		X2	X		S									M S Pike 40
	X	X	S	S	X	S				X	X	X	X	X	X	X		X				X					X	D R Crick 41
	S	X	S1	X	S				X	X	X	X	X	X1	X		S	X				X					X	S J Baines 42
	S2	X	S1	X1	X				X	X	X	X	X	S	X	S1	X2	X				X		X	X2	G Singh 43
	X	X	S2	X	X				X	X1	X	S	X	S	X		X			X		X	X	R D Furnandiz 44
	X	X	S1	X1	X				X	X	X	S	X	S	X	S2	X1			X		X	X	G B Frankland 45
	X	X		X	X		X		S1	X	X	S	X	S	X2			X			X	R J Harris 46
	X	X		X	X2	S	X	S1	X	X	S2	X		X			X1	E Lomas 47
	X	X	X		X	S2	X	S1	X	X		X2		X1	S	X	C J Foy 48
	X	X	X	S1	X	S3	X	X2	X3	S2	X1	X	R Styles 49
	X	X	X1	S2	X	X3	S3	X	X	X	S1	X2	X	A Bates 50
	X		X	X	X	X	X	X	S	X	S	X	X	S	X	A N Butler 51
X	X2	X	X1	X	X	X	S2	X	X	S1	X	X	K M Lynch 52
	X1	X	X2	S3	X	X	X	X	S1	X3	X	S2	X	X	J A Kirkby 53
4	8	29	43	4	15	31	2		34	22	12	5	42	41	36	14	18	29	11	16	33		7	35	3		12	FL Appearances
1		4			11	4					2	2	5			1	4	6	2	5	5		9	3		4	2	3		1	FL Sub Appearances
	2	1	2	0+1	2				2		2	2	2		2		1	2	2		2		0+1	CC Appearances
		3	1+2	4	4			1	1+1		4	3	4	2	4	3+1	1	4	FAC Appearances
	1	1	1		1			1	1	1	0+1	1	0+1	0+1	1	1	1	AWS Appearances

Also Played: (M) Gardner S3(34). (D) Thomas S(56).

CLUB RECORDS

RECORD LEAGUE VICTORY
10-1 v Hartlepool, Div 4, 3.3.1962
Most Goals Scored in a Cup Tie: 11-1 v New Brighton (h), Div 3N Cup, 1933-34
RECORD LEAGUE DEFEAT
0-9 v Brentford, Div 3, 15.10.1963
Record Cup Defeat: 1-9 v Wolverhampton Wanderers, FA Cup Rnd 3, 1930-31
MOST LEAGUE POINTS
(2pts for win) 61, Div 4, 1969-70, Div 3, 1977-78
(3pts for win) 80 Div 3, 1992-93
MOST LEAGUE GOALS
106, Div 3N, 1932-33

RECORD TRANSFER FEE PAID
£210,000 to Liverpool for Joey Jones, Oct 1978
RECORD TRANSFER FEE RECEIVED
£800,000 from Birmingham City for Brian Hughes, March 1997.

BEST PERFORMANCES
League: 15th Div 2, 1978-79
FA Cup: 6th Round 1973-74,1977-78
League Cup: 5th Round 1961, 1978   Welsh Cup: Winners (23), Runners-up (22). This is a record number of victories and appearances in the Final
European Cup Winners Cup: Quarter-Final 1975-76
European Competitions entered
European Cup Winners Cup: 1972-73, 1975-76,1978-79, 1979-80, 1984-85, 1986-87, 1990-91
HONOURS
Div 3 Champions 1977-78   Welsh Cup Winners (23)
Welsh Cup Runners-Up (22)

LEAGUE CAREER
Original members of Div 3N 1921   Transferred to Div 3 1958
Relegated to Div 4 1959-60 Promoted to Div 3 1961-62
Relegated to Div 4 1963-64 Promoted to Div 31969-70
Promoted to Div 2 1977-78   Relegated to Div 3 1981-82
Relegated to Div 4 1982-83 (now Div 3) Promoted to Div 2 1992-93

INDIVIDUAL CLUB RECORDS

MOST APPEARANCES FOR CLUB
Arfon Griffiths (1959-61 & 1962-79) Total 586+6 subs (not including Cup ties)
MOST CAPPED PLAYER
Joey Jones (Wales) 29   0For England: None
RECORD GOALSCORER IN A MATCH
A Livingstone 7 v Tranmere Rovers, Wartime Football League North, 25.10.1943   T Bamford 6 v New Brighton (h), 11-1, Div3N Cup, 1933-34   T H Lewis 5 v Crewe Alexandra (h) 7-0, Div 3N, 20.9.1930   T Bamford 5 v Carlisle United (h) 8-1, Div 3N, 17.3.1934
RECORD LEAGUE GOALSCORER IN A SEASON
Tommy Bamford, 44, Div 3N, 1933-34
RECORD LEAGUE GOALSCORER IN A CAREER
Tommy Bamford, 175, 1929-35
OLDEST PLAYER IN A LEAGUE MATCH
W. Lot Jones 46 years, 1921-22
YOUNGEST PLAYER IN A LEAGUE MATCH
Ken Roberts 15 years 158 days v Bradford Park Avenue, 1.9.1951
Ken shares this record with Albert Geldard (Bradford P.A.) as the two youngest players to play in the Football League.

PREVIOUS MANAGERS

1924-26 Charles Hewitt   1929-31 Jack Baynes   R Burkinshaw Dec 1931-Jan 1932   1932-36 Ernest Blackburn   Captain Logan 1937-38   1939-42Tommy Morgan   1942-49 Tom W Williams   C Lloyd March-May 1949   1949-50 Leslie J McDowall   1951-54 Peter Jackson   1954-57 Clifford Lloyd   1957-59 John Love   1960-61 Billy Morris   1961-65 Ken Barnes   1965-66 Billy Morris   1966-67Jack Rowley   1967 Cliff Lloyd   1967-8 Alvan Williams   1968-77 John Neal   1977-81 Arfon Griffiths   1981-82 Mel Sutton   1982-85 Bobby Roberts   Dixie McNeil 1985-89   Brian Flynn 1989-

ADDITIONAL INFORMATION
Previous Names: Wrexham Athletic 1881-82.
Wrexham Olympic 1884-88.
Previous Leagues: The Combination, Birmingham League

Club colours: Red shirts white trim, white shorts, red socks with white tops.
Change colours: Old gold with blue trimmed shirts, blue shorts, blue with old gold trimmed socks.
Reserves League: Pontins Central League Division 2.

LONGEST LEAGUE RUNS

of undefeated matches:	16 (1966)	of league matches w/out a win:	14 (1923-24, 1950)
of undefeated home matches:	38 (1969-70)	of undefeated away matches:	9 (1992-93)
without home win:	10 (1980-81)	without an away win:	31 (1982-83)
of league wins:	7 (1961, 1978)	of home wins:	13 (19832-33)
of league defeats:	9 (1963)	of away wins:	7 (1961)

THE MANAGER

BRIAN FLYNN . . . . appointed November 1989.

PREVIOUS CLUBS
As Manager . . . . None.
As Asst.Man/Coach . . . . None.
As a player . . . . Burnley, Leeds Utd, Cardiff City, Doncaster Rovers, Bury, Limerick, Doncaster Rovers.

HONOURS
As a Manager . . . . Promotion to Division 2, 1992-93.
As a Player . . . . 66 full caps, 2 U23 and Schools honours for Wales.

WREXHAM

PLAYERS NAME / Honours	Ht	Wt	Birthdate	Birthplace / Transfers	Contract Date	Clubs	League	L/Cup	FA Cup	Other	Lge	L/C	FAC	Oth
G O A L K E E P E R														
Cartwright Mark	6.1	12.5	1/13/73	Chester		York City								
				Free	8/17/91	Stockport County								
					3/5/94	Wrexham	7		1					
Marriott Andrew	6.1	13.3	10/11/70	Sutton-in-Ashfield	10/22/88	Arsenal								
E: u21.1, Y.2,S. FLge u18.1.Div.4'92. FMC'92.				£50000	6/20/89	Nottingham Forest	11	1		1				
				Loan	9/6/89	West Bromwich Albion		3						
				Loan	12/29/89	Blackburn Rovers	2							
				Loan	3/21/90	Colchester United	10							
				Loan	8/29/91	Burnley	15			2				
				£200000	10/8/93	Wrexham	213	10	21	19				
Walsh David	6.1	12	4/29/79	Wrexham		Wrexham (T)								
D E F E N C E														
Brace Deryn	5.9	10.8	3/15/75	Haverfordwest 7/6/93		Norwich City								
W: u21.5, Y.				Free	4/28/94	Wrexham	60+4	5	5	5	2			
Carey Brian P	6.3	13.9	5/31/68	Cork		Cork City								
EI: 3, u21.1				£100000	9/2/89	Manchester United								
				Loan	1/17/91	Wrexham	3							
				Loan	12/24/91	Wrexham	13	3	3	1				
				£250000	7/16/93	Leicester City	51+7	3	0+1	4	1			
				£100000	7/8/96	Wrexham	81	4	12	2	1			
Hardy Phil	5.11	10.2	4/9/73	Ellesmere Port	11/24/90	Wrexham	264+1	16	26	31				
E: u21.3.														
Humes Tony	5.11	11	3/19/66	Blyth	5/26/83	Ipswich Town	107+13	6	4	10	10		1	1
				£40000	3/27/92	Wrexham	180+6	7	19	13	8		1	
Jones Phillip B					3/27/97	Wrexham (T)								
McGregor Mark	5.11	10.5	2/16/77	Chester		Wrexham	106+7	3	12+1	3	4			
Ridler David G	6.1	12.2	3/12/76	Liverpool		Wrexham	25+6		3					
M I D F I E L D														
Brammer David	5.9	11	2/28/75	Bromborough 7/2/93		Wrexham	87+15	5+1	3+2	5+2	10			
Griffiths Andrew	5.11	12	11/21/78	Wirral	11/14/97	Wrexham (T)								
Owen Gareth	5.11	11.4	10/21/71	Chester	7/6/90	Wrexham	210+44	7+1	19+4	28+1	28			
W: u21.8.														
Roberts Stephen W			2/24/80	Wrexham		Wrexham (T)								
Thomas Stephen	5.10	11.12	6/23/79	Hartlepool	9/1/97	Wrexham (T)								
Ward Peter	5.11	11.7	10/15/64	Durham		Chester-Le-Street								
					1/7/87	Huddersfield Town	24+13	1+1	2	1	2			
				Free	7/20/89	Rochdale	83+1	5	7	5	10		1	
					6/6/91	Stockport County	140+2	8	7	26	10	1		6
				Free	6/1/95	Wrexham	91+3	5	16	1	13		1	1
F O R W A R D														
Chalk Martyn	5.6	10	8/30/69	Louth		Louth United								
				£10000	1/23/90	Derby County	4+3		3	+1	1		1	
				£40000	6/30/94	Stockport County	24+9	3	1	1+1	6	1		
					8/1/95	Wrexham	68+20	2+1	7+2		6			
Connolly Karl	6.1	12.6	2/9/70	Prescot	5/8/91	Wrexham	259+14	18	27	23+1	68	3	10	5
Roberts Paul	5.11	11.9	7/29/77	Bangor	5/31/97	Wrexham								
Roberts Neil W	5.11	11.1	4/7/78	Wrexham		Wrexham	29+6		2+2		8		1	
Rush Ian	6	12.6	20/10/61	St Asaph	9/25/79	Chester City	33+1		5		14		3	
W: 73 (24 Gls - Int. Record), u21.2, S.				£300000	5/1/80	Liverpool	182	38	22	31+1	109	21	20	17
Div.1'82'83'84'86'90; LC'81'82'83'84'95.				£3200000	7/1/86	Juventus								
FAC'86'89'92. EC'84.				Loan	7/1/86	Liverpool	42	9	3	3	30	4		6
				£2800000	8/23/88	Liverpool	223+22	30	30+6	16+1	90	23	19	7
				Free	5/1/96	Leeds United	34+2	2	2+2		3			
				Free	8/15/97	Newcastle United	6+4	2	0+1	1		1	1	
				Loan	2/24/98	Sheffield United	4							
				Free	7/1/98	Wrexham								
Russell Kevin J	5.8	10.1	12/6/66	Brighton		Brighton & H.A.								
E: Y.6. Div.2'93.				£10000	7/17/87	Wrexham	84	4	4	8	43	1		3
				Free	10/9/87	Portsmouth	3+1	+1	+1	1+1	1			
				£175000	6/20/89	Leicester City	24+19	+1	1	5	10			2
				Loan	9/6/90	Peterborough United	7			3				
				Loan	1/17/91	Cardiff City	3							
				Loan	11/7/91	Hereford United	3		1	2				
				Loan	1/2/92	Stoke City	5		1					
				£95000	7/16/92	Stoke City	30+10	3	2	4+1	5			1
				£150000	6/28/93	Burnley	26+2	4	4	1	6	1		1
				£125000	3/3/94	Bournemouth	17				1			
				£60000	2/24/95	Notts County	9+2							
				£60000	6/1/95	Wrexham	84+12	4	9+2	2	7	1	3	
Skinner Craig	5.11	11	10/21/70	Heywood	6/13/89	Blackburn Rovers	11+5	+1	1	3				1
					8/21/92	Plymouth Argyle	42+11	4	5+2	3+1	3		1	
				£50000	6/1/95	Wrexham	58+17	3+1	7+1	2	8	1		
Spink Dean	6.1	13.6	22/01/67	Birmingham		Halesowen Town			1					
Div.3'94.				£30000	01/07/89	Aston Villa								
				Loan	20/11/89	Scarborough	3		1	2				
				Loan	01/02/90	Bury	6			1				
				£75000	15/03/90	Shrewsbury Town	244+29	22+2	18+2	19+2	53	1	6	3
				£65000	7/15/97	Wrexham	33+3	2	1+1	1	6	1		

RACECOURSE GROUND
Mold Road, Wrexham, Clwyd, LL11 2AN

Capacity..11,500
Covered Standing...6,500
Seating...5,026

First game ....v Past & Present Grove Park School, 19.10.1872.
First floodlit game..v Swindon Town (h), Div.3, 30.09.1959.

ATTENDANCES
Highest ....34,445 v Manchester United, FA Cup 4th Round, 26.1.1991.
Lowest...627 v Mansfield Town, AMC Preliminary Round, 15.10.1991.
OTHER GROUNDS............................... Rhosddu Recreation Ground 1880-83. Grosvenor Road 1884.

HOW TO GET TO THE GROUND

From the North and West
Use A483 and Wrexham bypass until junction with A541, then branch left and at roundabout follow signs to Wrexham into Mold Road for Wrexham FC.

From the East and South
Follow signs into Wrexham on A543 or A525 then follow signs A541 into Mold Road for Wrexham FC.

Car Parking: Parking at St Marks, Bodhyfryd Square, Eagles Meadow, Old Guild Hall, Hill Street, Holt Street and Town Hall (Hill Street.

Nearest Railway Station: Wrexham General.

USEFUL TELEPHONE NUMBERS

Club switchboard 01978 262 129
Club fax number 01978 357 821
Club shop 01978 352 536
Ticket Office............. 01978 262 129

Marketing Department .... as for shop.
Clubcall 0891 12 16 42*
*Calls cost 50p per minute at all times.
Call costings correct at time of going to press.

MATCHDAY PROGRAMME

Programme Editor
.... David Roberts & Geraint Parry

Number of pages .... 32.

Price .... £1.80.

Subscriptions .... Apply to club.

Local Newspapers
.... Wrexham Evening Leader, Daily Post
Wrexham Weekly Leader, Shropshire Star.

Local Radio Stations
.. Radio City, Marcher Sound, Radio Clwyd
.. BBC Radio Wales, B.B.C. Radio Cymru.

MATCHDAY TICKET PRICES

Executive Box............................. £15.00

Yale Centre (reserved) £12.00
Yale Wings (unreserved)
Adult £11.00
Juniors/Senior Citizens..................... £7.00

Standing
Adult £9.00
Juniors/Senior Citizens..................... £5.00

Family Tickets (stand)
1 adult 1 junior.......................... £14.00
1 adult 2 juniors £17.00

WYCOMBE WANDERERS
(The Chairboys)
NATIONWIDE LEAGUE DIVISION 2
SPONSORED BY: MIZUNO

1998/99 - Back Row L-R: Terry Evans (Yth team physio), Michael Simpson, Paul McCarthy, David Carroll, Martin Taylor, Keith Scott, John Cornforth, Dannie Bulman, David Jones (Physio). **Middle Row:** Jeff Lamb, Steve Brown, Keith Drown, Keith Ryan, Lee Holsgrove, Mick Forsyth, Adrian Cole (Yth Dev. Officer), Nicky Mohan, Andrew Baird, Alan Beeton, Gary Wraight, Aaron Patton. **Front Row:** Jason Kavanagh, Maurice Harkin, Jason Cousins, Wayne Turner (no longer with the club), Neil Smillie (Manager), Gary Goodchild (Yth team manager), Mark Stallard, Steve McGavin, Paul Read.

WYCOMBE WANDERERS
FORMED IN 1884
TURNED PROFESSIONAL IN 1974
LTD COMPANY IN 1980

PATRON: J Adams
PRESIDENT: M E Seymour
CHAIRMAN: I L Beeks
DIRECTORS
G Cox, B R Lee, A Parry, G Peart,
G Richards, A Thibault
SECRETARY
John Reardon
COMMERCIAL MANAGER
Mark Austin, BA

MANAGER: Neil Smillie

YOUTH TEAM MANAGER
Gary Goodchild
PHYSIOTHERAPIST
Dave Jones

STATISTICIAN FOR THE DIRECTORY
Vacant phone 01203 234017 if interested

Wycombe Wanderers had a moderate 1997-98 season, finishing 14th in the table with 60 points, 10 clear of relegation and 10 short of a play-off spot.

During the first half of the campaign, with John Gregory in charge, the 'Chairboys' didn't produce the goods as expected. They failed to press home their advantage in several matches and a lack of goalscoring power was there for all to see.

Defensively they looked solid, while the midfield was competitive and creative. But up front, the goals were few and far between and in fact only 30 were scored in the opening 24 matches.

In late December Wycombe were hovering on the brink of the relegation zone, having chalked up just 27 points out of a possible 72. They were, in fact, only four better off than Luton Town who were fourth from bottom and in the drop-zone.

But when Gregory left Adams Park to take over at the club he used to play for Aston Villa, the 'Chairboys' picked up their game under new boss Neil Smillie, the former Brighton & Hove Albion player, who had been promoted from youth team manager, and gradually climbed the table.

Goalkeeper Martin Taylor had a fine season between the posts, while defenders Nicky Mohan and Paul McCarthy put in some sterling performances, along with left-back Micky Forsyth until he was injured late on. Dave Carroll and Steve Brown both grafted hard and long in midfield while up front there were spirited displays on a regular basis from Mark Stallard and Steve McGavin. Nothing fancy comes from Wycombe. They play competitively, always giving 100 per-cent out on the field and give their opponents plenty to think about.

Wycombe Wanderers - a Football League club for only six years - finished sixth in the Second Division in 1994-95; they came 12th in 1995-96 and claimed 18th spot in 1996-97. They have improved considerably on that latter placing and now this coming year will be looking to challenge strongly for a play-off place at least - and they could do just that if they can retain the services of their key players.

Tony Matthews.

WYCOMBE WANDERERS

Division 2   :14th   FA CUP: 1st Round   LC CUP: 1st Round   AWS: Southern Round 2

M	DATE	COMP.	VEN	OPPONENTS	RESULT	H/T	LP	GOAL SCORERS/GOAL TIMES	ATT.
1	A 09	FL	A	Wigan Athletic	L 2-5	0-4	17	Scott 66, 69	(4706)
2	12	CC 1/1	H	Fulham	L 1-2	1-1		Read 42	4360
3	15	FL	H	Northampton Town	D 0-0	0-0	17		5130
4	23	FL	A	Blackpool	W 4-2	2-1	8	Stallard 36, 50, Kavanagh 38, Cornforth 62	(4733)
5	26	CC 1/2	A	Fulham	D 4-4	1-3		Ryan 30, Scott 49, 81, Harkin 61	(5055)
6	30	FL	H	Fulham	W 2-0	1-0	6	Cornforth 8, Stallard 60	6278
7	S 02	FL	H	Southend United	W 4-1	2-1	3	Stallard 10, 90, Cornforth 44, Read 59	4528
8	07	FL	A	Watford	L 1-2	0-1	4	Read 69	(12100)
9	13	FL	H	Carlisle United	L 1-4	1-2	10	Cornforth 11	6018
10	19	FL	A	Brentford	D 1-1	1-1	6	Stallard 3	(3695)
11	27	FL	H	Preston North End	D 0-0	0-0	9		4838
12	O 04	FL	A	Burnley	D 2-2	1-1	11	Cornforth 13 (pen), Scott 54	(9057)
13	11	FL	A	Gillingham	L 0-1	0-0	16		(5545)
14	18	FL	H	Bristol Rovers	W 1-0	0-0	15	Stallard 71	5836
15	21	FL	H	Walsall	W 4-2	3-2	9	Stallard 11, 22, 47, Read 27	3884
16	25	FL	A	Chesterfield	L 0-1	0-0	12		(4119)
17	N 01	FL	H	Luton Town	D 2-2	1-1	11	Stallard 12, McGavin 62	6219
18	04	FL	A	Plymouth Argyle	L 2-4	1-2	14	Scott 52, Collins 5 (OG)	(2993)
19	08	FL	A	York City	L 0-2	0-1	16		(3343)
20	15	FAC 1	H	Basingstoke Town	D 2-2	1-0		Cornforth 16, 61 (pen)	3932
21	18	FL	H	Wrexham	D 0-0	0-0	15		3635
22	22	FL	A	Bristol City	L 1-3	0-1	16	Scott 82 (pen)	(11129)
23	25	FAC 1R	A	Basingstoke Town	D 2-2*	1-1		McGavin 17, 74 (Wycombe lost 5-4 on penalties)	(5085)
24	29	FL	H	Bournemouth	D 1-1	0-0	16	Stallard 52	4340
25	D 02	FL	A	Grimsby Town	D 0-0	0-0	16		(4160)
26	09	AWS S1	A	Southend United	W 1-0	1-0		Stallard 43	(1577)
27	13	FL	H	Oldham Athletic	W 2-1	0-0	17	Scott 53, McGavin 83	5327
28	20	FL	A	Millwall	L 0-1	0-0	18		(6092)
29	26	FL	H	Watford	D 0-0	0-0	18		8090
30	28	FL	A	Southend United	W 2-1	1-0	15	Scott 6, 84	(5162)
31	J 10	FL	H	Wigan Athletic	L 1-2	0-1	19	Brown 89	5549
32	13	AWS S2	A	Fulham	L 1-3	1-1		Harkin 38	(4319)
33	17	FL	A	Fulham	D 0-0	0-0	19		(10468)
34	24	FL	H	Blackpool	W 2-1	1-1	16	Harkin 8, Stallard 67	5073
35	31	FL	A	Carlisle United	D 0-0	0-0	17		(6220)
36	F 06	FL	H	Brentford	D 0-0	0-0	17		6328
37	10	FL	A	Northampton Town	L 0-2	0-0	17		(5302)
38	14	FL	H	Burnley	W 2-1	1-0	14	Brown 32, McCarthy 57	5926
39	21	FL	A	Preston North End	D 1-1	0-0	14	Brown 60	(7665)
40	24	FL	A	Bristol Rovers	L 1-3	0-0	14	Scott 71	(5805)
41	28	FL	H	Gillingham	W 1-0	1-0	14	Ryan 29	5583
42	M 03	FL	H	York City	W 1-0	0-0	13	Ryan 71	3768
43	07	FL	A	Luton Town	D 0-0	0-0	14		(6114)
44	14	FL	H	Plymouth Argyle	W 5-1	1-1	9	Ryan 23, Scott 47, Stallard 52, 75, Carroll 83	5508
45	21	FL	A	Wrexham	L 0-2	0-1	14		(4290)
46	28	FL	H	Bristol City	L 1-2	0-1	15	Harkin 57	6326
47	A 04	FL	A	Bournemouth	D 0-0	0-0	14		(4271)
48	10	FL	H	Grimsby Town	D 1-1	1-0	13	Scott 17	5846
49	13	FL	A	Oldham Athletic	W 1-0	0-0	12	Stallard 66	(4305)
50	18	FL	H	Millwall	D 0-0	0-0	13		5371
51	25	FL	H	Chesterfield	D 1-1	1-1	15	Stallard 26	5113
52	M 02	FL	A	Walsall	W 1-0	1-0	14	Read 18	(4412)

Best Home League Attendance: 8090 V Watford   Smallest :3635 V Wrexham   Average :5414

Goal Scorers:

FL	(51)	Stallard 17, Scott 11, Cornforth 5, Read 4, Brown 3, Ryan 3, Harkin 2, McGavin 2, Carroll 1, Kavanagh 1, McCarthy 1, Opponents 1
CC	(5)	Scott 2, Harkin 1, Read 1, Ryan 1
FAC	(4)	Cornforth 2, McGavin 2
AWS	(2)	Harkin 1, Stallard 1

*AET

1997-98

(M) Baird	(M) Beeton	(D) Bodin	(M) Brown	(M) Carroll	(M) Comforth	(D) Cousins	(D) Forsyth	(M) Harkin	(M) Hodson	(D) Kavanagh	(M) Kenslake	(D) Mahon	(D) McCarthy	(F) McGavin	(G) Parkin	(M) Patton	(F) Read	(M) Ryan	(F) Scott	(M) Simpson	(F) Stallard	(G) Taylor	(M) Wraight			Referee	No.
S3		X	X	S1		X				X			X	X	S2	X	X	X	X	X						J.A. Kirkby	1
	S		X	X	X	X	S1			X			X	X	X	S	X	X	X							P Rejer	2
		X	X	X		X	S	S		X			X	X	S1		X	X	X	X						B Knight	3
X					S1	X	X	X		S3			X	X	S2	X	X	X	X	X						B Coddington	4
		S1	X	X		X	X			X			X	S2	X	X	X	X	S3	X						C T Finch	5
X		X		X		X	S2			X			X	X	S1		X	S3	X	X						E Lomas	6
X		X	S3	X		X	X			X			X	X	S1		X	S2	X	X						K A Leach	7
X		X	S	X		X	S2			X			X	X	X		X	S1	X	X						P Rejer	8
X		X	S2	X	S1		X			X			X	X	X		X	S3	X	X						F G Stretton	9
	X	X	S1	X	X			X					X	X	S	X	X	S	X	X						M C Bailey	10
	X	X	X	X	X	S2	S3			X			X	X	X	S1	X	X		X						S G Bennett	11
	X	X	X	X	X	X	S			S1			X	S2	X	X		X	X	X						D Pugh	12
	X	X	X	X	S	X	S1		X			X			X	X	S	X	X						M R Halsey	13
	X	X	X	X	S3	X	S2			X		X		X	X	X		X	X						A R Leake	14
S3		X	X	X		X	S1			X			X	X	X		S2	X	X						D R Crick	15
S		X	X		X	X	S2			X			X	X	X		S1	X	X						M S Pike	16
		X	X	X	X	S2				X	X	S	X	X	X		X	S1	X	X						M J Brandwood	17
		X		X	X			X		S1	X	S	S2	X	X	X	X	X						R Styles	18
S1		X		X		S2				X	X	X	X	X	S	X	X	X	X						M L Dean	19
S2		X	X	X		X	S	X		X			X	X	X	X	S1	X	X		X	S				P E Alcock	20
X		X		X	X	S2				X	S1	X		X	X	X	S3	X						P R Richards	21
X		X		X2	X		S1			X		X	S2	X	X1	X	X	S	X						K M Lynch	22
X		X		X	X	X	S		S1		X	X	X	S	S3	X	X	S2	X						G P Barber	23
		X		X	X	X	S			X		X	X	X	S	S	X	X	X						P S Danson	24
S		X	X		X	X	S			X	X	X	X	X	X	S	X	X	X						B Coddington	25
		X	X		X1	X	X			X			X	X2	X	S2		X	X	S1							26
		X	X		S	X	S1	X	X			X	X	X	X	S	X1	X						P Taylor	27
		X	X		S1	X	S2	X1	X			X	X	X2	X	X	S	X						G Singh	28
		X	X		X	S	X	X	S	X	X	X	X	X	S	X						J E Pearce	29
		X	X		X	S2	X	X	S	X	X2	X	X	X	X1	X						R J Harris	30
		X	X	S2		S1	X	X	X		X1	X	S	X	X	X2					M R Halsey	31
	X	X2	S2		X		X	X1	X		X	X	X	Y	X	X	S1						32
		X	X	S		X		X		X			X	X	X	X	S				C R Wilkes	33
S		X	S		X	X		Y	X	S	X		X	X	X	X						A N Butler	34
X			S1	32	X1	X		X		X	X	X2	S	X	X	X	X						C J Foy	35
	X	S	S		X	X		X	X		X	S1	X	X1	X	X						S G Bennett	36
	X	S2	S		X	X		X	X	X2	S1	X	X1	X	X						G Cain	37
S		X	X		X	S1		X	X	X	S2	X	X1	X2	X						S J Baines	38
	X	X		X	S1	X	S	X	X	X	X	X	X1	X						M D Messias	39
	X3	X		X	S1	X	S2	X	X2	X1	X	X	S3	X						M J Jones	40
S		X	X		X	S	X	X	X	X	X	X	X1	X						M C Bailey	41
	X	X	S	X	S1	X	X	X	X	X	X	S1	X						A R Hall	42
	X	X	X	S	S1	X	X	X	X	X	X	S1	X						M E Pierce	43
S2		X	X	X	X	X2	X	X3	S1	X	X1	S3	X	X						A G Wiley	44
S1		X	X	S	X1	X	X	X2	S2	X	X1	X	X						G B Frankland	45
X		X	X2	X	S1	X	X1	S2	X	X	S	X						R D Furnandiz	46
X		X	X	X	X	S	X	S	X	X	X	X						M Fletcher	47
S	X	X	X	S	X	X	X	S	X	X	X	X						A P D'Urso	48
S	X	X	X	X	X	X	X	X	X	S	X						G Cain	49
	X	X1	X	S1	X	X	S	X	X	X	X	S	X						F G Stretton	50
S3	X	X	X	S2	X	X2	X	X	S1	X1	X3	X						P R Richards	51
S2	X	X	X3	X	X1	X	X	S3	X	X	S1	X2	X						S J Baines	52
	15	5	40	35	18	25	25	13	43	9	33	28	35	1		14	40	28	10	43	45	1				FL Appearances	
2	5		4	6	4			22		2	1		3	2		14		1	11							FL Sub Appearances	
		1+1	2	2		2	1+1	2				2	1+1		2	1	1	2	1+1	2						CC Appearances	
1+1		1	1	2	1	1	1+1	2		2	1	2		1+1	2	2	0+2	2								FAC Appearances	
	2	2	0+1	1	1	2		2	1	1	1	2		2	0+1	1	2	2	0+2							AWS Appearances	

WYCOMBE WANDERERS RECORDS AND STATISTICS

CLUB RECORDS

RECORD LEAGUE VICTORY
4-0 v Scarborough (h), Division 3, 2.11.1993
Most Goals Scored in a Cup Tie: 15-1 v Witney Town (h), FA Cup
Prelim Rnd replay,14.9.1955
(First Class) 5-0 v Hitchin Town (a), Second Round, 3.12.1994.
RECORD LEAGUE DEFEAT
2-5 v Colchester United (h) Division 3, 18.9.1993; 0-3 v Mansfield
Town, Division 3, 12.2.1994. 1-4 v Stockport (a) Div.2 24.9.94. 1-4 v
Wrexham (a) Div.2, 1.11.94. 0-3 v Mansfield (a) Div.3, 12.2.94.
0-3 v Birmingham (h) Div.2, 18.3.95.
Record Cup Defeat: 0-8 v Reading (h), FA Cup 1st Qualifying Rnd,
28.10.1899 (First Class) 1-5 v Watford (a), FA Cup 2nd Rnd,
5.12.1959

MOST LEAGUE POINTS
(3pts for win) 78, Division 2 1994-95

MOST LEAGUE GOALS
67, Division 3 1993-94

RECORD TRANSFER FEE RECEIVED
£375,000 from Swindon for Keith Scott, November 1993
RECORD TRANSFER FEE PAID
£140,000 to Birmingham City for Steve McGavin, March 1995.

BEST PERFORMANCES
League: 6th Division 2 1994-95
FA Cup: 3rd Round 1974-75,1985-86, 1993-94
League Cup: 2nd Round 1993-94

HONOURS: Third Division Play-off Winners 1993-94; GM Vauxhall
Conference Champions 1992-93; F.A. Amateur Cup Winners 1930-
31; F.A. Trophy Winners1990-91, 1992-93; Isthmian League
Champions 1955-56, 1956-57, 1970-71, 1971-72, 1973-74, 1974-
75, 1982-83, 1986-87; Spartan League Champions 1919-20,1920-
21; Bob Lord Trophy Winners 1991-92; Anglo-Italian Trophy
Winners1975-76; Conference Shield Winners 1991-92, 1992-93,
1993-94; Hitachi(League) Cup Winners 1984-85; Berks & Bucks
Senior Cup Winners 24 times

LEAGUE CAREER
Promoted to Division 3 1992-93   Promoted to Division 2 1993-94

INDIVIDUAL CLUB RECORDS

MOST APPEARANCES FOR CLUB
Paul Hyde 59 (1993-94)
MOST CAPPED PLAYER
(England Semi-Pro.) Larry Pritchard 26 (1970-74)
RECORD LEAGUE GOALSCORER IN A SEASON
Miquel DeSouza: 20 (1995-96) 18 League 2 League Cup.
RECORD LEAGUE GOALSCORER IN A CAREER
20 - Somon Garner (13 League, 3 FAC, 4 Others) 1993-95.
20 - Miquel DeSouza (18 League 2 League Cup) 1995-96.
MOST GOALS IN A MATCH
3 - Simon Garner v Hitchin Town (a), FAC 2nd Rnd, 3.12.1994.
3 - Miquel DeSouza v Bradford (a) 2.9.95, Bradford (h) 26.3.96.

OLDEST PLAYER IN A LEAGUE MATCH
Cyrille Regis, 37 years 86 days v Leyton Orient (a) Div.2, 6.5.1995.
YOUNGEST PLAYER IN A LEAGUE MATCH
Anthony Clark, 18 years 29 days v Leyton Orient (a) Div.2, 6.5.1995.

PREVIOUS MANAGERS

First coach appointed 1951: (Coaches) 1951-52 James McCormack
1952-61 Sid Cann 1961-62 Graham Adams 1962-64 Don Welsh
1964-68 Barry Darvill (Managers): 1969-76 Brian Lee 1976-77
Ted Powell 1977-78 John Reardon 1978-80 Andy Williams
1980-84 Mike Keen 1984-86 Paul Bence 1986-87 Alan Gane
1987-88 Peter Suddaby 1988-90 Jim Kelman 1990-95 Martin
O'Neill, 1995-96 Alan Smith. 1996-98 John Gregory.

ADDITIONAL INFORMATION
Previous League: 1896-1908 Southern Div 2; 1898-99 Bucks &
Contiguous Counties;1901-03 Berks & Bucks Senior; 1908-14 Great
Western Suburban; 1919-21 Spartan;1921-85 Isthmian; 1985-86
Gola; 1986-87 Vauxhall-Opel; 1987-93 GM Vauxhall Conference
Club Colours: Sky & navy striped quarters, sky shorts.
Change Colours:

Reserves League: Springheath Print Capital League
Youth: South East Counties Division Two

LONGEST LEAGUE RUNS

of undefeated matches:	14 (19.8.95 - 26.11.95)	of league matches w/out a win:	8 (21.2.1995 - 25.3.1995)
of undefeated home matches:	11 (1.10.1994 - 4.3.1995)	of undefeated away matches:	9 (14.8.1993 - 27.11.1993)
without home win: 3 (19.4.94-7.5.94, 26.12.95-4.2.95,4.3.95-25.3.95)		without an away win:	9 (11.2.1995 - 19.4.1995)
of league wins:	4 (3.1.1994-25-1.1994, 26.2.1994-19.3.1994)	of home wins:	6 (2.11.1993 - 25.1.1994)
of league defeats:	3 (29.1.1994 - 19.2.1994)	of away wins:	3 (31.8.1993 - 2.10.1993, 26.2.1994 - 19.3.1994)

THE MANAGER

NEIL SMILLIE . . . . appointed February 1998.

PREVIOUS CLUBS
As Manager . . . . None
As Asst.Man/Coach. . . . . Wycombe Wanderers.
As a player . . . . Crystal Palace, Brentford, Brighton, Watford, Reading, Brentford.

HONOURS
As a Manager . . . . None.
As a Player . . . . None.

WYCOMBE WANDERERS

PLAYERS NAME Honours	Ht	Wt	Birthdate	Birthplace Transfers	Contract Date	Clubs	League	L/Cup	FA Cup	Other	Lge	L/C	FAC	Oth
G O A L K E E P E R														
Taylor Martin J	5.11	12.4	12/9/66	Tamworth		Mile Oak Rovers								
					7/2/86	Derby County	97	7	5	11				
				Loan	9/23/87	Carlisle United	10	1	1	2				
				Loan	12/17/87	Scunthorpe United	8							
				Loan	9/20/96	Crewe Alexandra	6							
				Loan	3/27/97	Wycombe W.	4							
				Free	6/14/97	Wycombe W.	45	2	2					
D E F E N C E														
Baird Andrew C	5.10	12.6	1/18/79	East Kilbride	4/9/98	Wycombe W. (T)	0+2							
Beeton Alan	5.11	11	10/4/78	Watford	7/1/97	Wycombe W. (T)	15+5		1+1					
Cousins Jason	6	11.8	10/4/70	Hayes	7/13/89	Brentford	20+1	3		2+2				
GMVC'93. FAT'93.				Free	7/1/91	Wycombe W.	167+7	12	19	12	4	1		
Forsyth Michael E	5.11	12.2	3/20/66	Liverpool	11/16/83	WBA	28+1	1	2	1				
E: B.1, u21.1, Y.8. Div.2'87.				£25000	3/28/86	Derby County	323+1	36	15+1	29	8	1		
				£200000	2/23/95	Notts County	7							
				Loan	9/27/96	Hereford United	11							
				£25000	12/6/96	Wycombe W.	47+1	2	2		2			
Holsgrove Lee	6.2	12.5	12/13/79	Wendover	5/31/97	Millwall (T)								
				Free	3/24/98	Wycombe W.								
Mohan Nicholas	6	11.1	10/6/70	Middlesbrough	11/18/87	Middlesbrough	93+6	11	9	11	4			
				Loan	9/26/92	Hull City	5				1			
				£330000	7/7/94	Leicester City	23	2	1					
				£225000	7/13/95	Bradford City	83	8	5	5	4			
				Loan	8/14/97	Wycombe W.	6							
				£75000	8/14/97	Wycombe W.	27		2	1				
McCarthy Paul J	5.11	13.5	8/4/71	Cork	8/15/96	Wycombe W.	63+6	6	5		1	1		
M I D F I E L D														
Brown Stephen	5.11	10.12	7/6/66	Northampton	8/11/83	Northampton Town	14+1				3			
				Free	8/1/84	Irthlingborough D.								
				Free	7/21/89	Northampton Town	145+13	10	12	10+1	19	1	2	1
				£40000	2/9/94	Wycombe W.	193+9	12+2	11+1	3+1	16			
Carroll Dave	6	12	9/20/66	Paisley		Ruislip Manor								
E: S. GMVC'93. FAT'91'93.				£6000	7/1/88	Wycombe W.	163+5	13	19	10	25		4	3
Cornforth John	6.1	12.8	10/7/67	Whitley Bay	10/11/85	Sunderland	21+11	0+1		1+3	2			
Div.3'88. AMC'94.				Loan	11/6/86	Doncaster Rovers	6+1			2	3			
				Loan	11/23/89	Shrewsbury Town	3			2				
				Loan	1/11/90	Lincoln City	9				1			
				£50000	8/2/91	Swansea City	130+2	12	14	19	14		1	1
				£350000	3/26/96	Birmingham City	8							
				£50000	12/6/96	Wycombe W.	26+8	2	2		5		2	
				Loan	2/13/98	Peterborough Utd	3+1							
Patton Aaron A	5.6	12.1	2/27/79	London	7/1/97	Wycombe W. (T)	0+1							
Ryan Keith	6	11.7	6/25/70	Northampton		Wycombe W.	124+5	7	8+3	10+1	12	2	3	
GMVC'93. FAT'91'93.						Berkhamsted								
Wraight Gary P	5.6	11.7	3/5/79	Epping	7/1/97	Wycombe W. (T)	1							
F O R W A R D														
Harkin Maurice	5.10	11.11	8/16/79	Derry	2/14/97	Wycombe W. (T)	13+26	1+1	1+2	2	2	1		1
McGavin Steve	5.11	10.1	1/24/69	North Walsham		Sudbury Town								
GMVC'92. FAT'92.						Ipswich Town								
				£10000	7/28/92	Colchester United	55+3	2	6	4	17	2		
				£150000	1/7/94	Birmingham City	6+2				1			
				£175000	3/20/95	Wycombe W.	100+13	4+2	6+1	1+1	14		3	
Read Paul C	5.11	12.6	9/25/73	Harlow	1/11/91	Arsenal								
S. E:				Loan	3/10/95	Leyton Orient	11		1					
				Loan	10/6/95	Southend United	3+1		1		1			
				£35000	1/17/97	Wycombe W.	20+20	2	1+1		8	1		
Scott Keith	6.3	13.4	6/10/67	London		Hinckley United								
GMVC'93. FAT'91'93				Free		Leicester United								
				Free	3/22/90	Lincoln City	7+9	0+1		1+1	2			
				£30000	7/5/93	Wycombe W.	15	4	8	10	10	2	1	2
				£300000	11/18/93	Swindon Town	43+8	5		3	12	3		1
				£300000	12/30/94	Stoke City	16+2		2		3		1	
					11/11/95	Norwich City	10+15	0+2	0+2		5			
				Loan	2/16/96	Bournemouth								
				Loan	2/7/97	Watford	6				1			
				Loan	3/27/97	Wycombe W.	8				3			
					7/2/97	Wycombe W.	28+1	1	2		14	2		
Stallard Mark	6	12.04	10/24/74	Derby	11/6/91	Derby County	16+8	1+1	2+2	3	2	1		1
				Loan	9/23/94	Fulham								
					1/18/96	Bradford City	31+11	2	0+1	3	10	1		2
				Loan	2/14/97	Preston North End	3				1			
					3/7/97	Wycombe W.	54	1+1			21			
Vinnicombe Christopher	5.9	10.4	10/20/70	Exeter	7/1/89	Exeter City	35+4	5		2	1	1		
E: u21.12.				£150000	11/3/89	Glasgow Rangers	14+9	1	1+1		1			
				£200000	6/30/94	Burnley	90+5	9	2	4	3			
				Free	7/1/98	Wycombe W.								
ADITIONAL CONTRACT PLAYERS														
Bulman Dannie						Ashford Town								
				£10000	7/1/98	Wycombe W.								
Westhead Mark						Telford United								
				Free	7/1/98	Wycombe W.								

ADAMS PARK
Hillbottom Road, High Wycombe, Buckinghamshire HP12 4HJ

Capacity 10,000
Covered Standing 2,198
Seating..7,802

First game...9.8.1990 v Nottingham Forest, friendly.
First floodlit game ....As above.

ATTENDANCES
Highest ....9,007 v West Ham, FAC 3rd Rnd, 7.1.95.
Lowest ....2,323 v Barnet, AMC 1st Rnd, 28.9.1993.

OTHER GROUNDS ....Loakes Park, Daws Hill Park, Spring Gardens, The Rye.

HOW TO GET TO THE GROUND

From all Directions
Exit M40 at junction 4 and take A4010 John Hall Way, sign posted Aylesbury. Cross over three mini roundabouts into New Road, continue down hill to two mini roundabouts at bottom. Turn sharp left at first into Lane End Road and turn right at next mini roundabout into Hillbottom Road. Continue through industrial Estate to Adams Park at end.
From Town Centre
Take A40 west, sign posted Aylesbury, after 1.5 miles turn left after second set of traffic lights into Chapel Lane. Turn right and right again at mini roundabouts into Lane End Road (then as above).

Car Parking: Club car park (340 spaces) or on adjacent Industrial Estate (some charging).

Nearest Railway Station: High Wycombe (01494 441 561)
London Marylebone to Birmingham Snow Hill Line - 2.9 miles from ground.
Special buses depart station at 1.55pm and 2.25pm Saturdays, 6.35pm and 7.05pm midweek, returning 10 minutes after the match.

USEFUL TELEPHONE NUMBERS

Club switchboard 01494 472 100
Club fax number 01494 527 633
Club shop 01494 450 957
Ticket Office 01494 441 118

Marketing Department.. 01494 472 100 - Mark Austin.
'Ringing the Blues' 0891 446 855*
*Calls cost 50p per minute at all times.
Call costings correct at time of going to press.

MATCHDAY PROGRAMME

Programme Editor .... Adrian Wood

Number of pages .... 44.

Price .... £1.80.

Subscriptions .... Apply to club.

Local Newspapers
.... Bucks Free Press
.... Wycombe/South Bucks Star.

Local Radio Stations
.... Chiltern Radio (Dunstable)
.... Radio 210 (Reading)
.... Radio Berkshire (Reading)
.... Eleven Seventy Am (High Wycombe).

MATCHDAY TICKET PRICES

Amersham &Wycombe College Stand £14.00

VP's £25.00

OAP/Juniors.................................. £13.00/£12.00

Servispak Stand (Upper) .... £10.00-£14.00

OAP/Juniors .... £9.00-£13.00/£8.00-£12.00

Bucks Free Press Family Enclosure................ £10.00

OAP/Juniors.................................. £8.00/£6.00

AXA Equity & Law Stand Terrace £9.00

YORK CITY
(The Minster Men)
NATIONWIDE LEAGUE DIVISION 2
SPONSORED BY: PORTAKABIN LTD

York City - 1998/99

YORK CITY
FORMED IN 1922
TURNED PROFESSIONAL IN 1922
LTD COMPANY IN 1922

CHAIRMAN: D M Craig OBE, JP, BSc, FICE
DIRECTORS
J E H Quickfall, F.C.A.
E B Swallow, C Webb
SECRETARY
Keith Usher (01904 624 47)
COMMERCIAL MANAGER
Mrs Maureen Leslie (01904 645 941)

MANAGER: Alan Little
FIRST TEAM COACH: Derek Bell
YOUTH TEAM MANAGER
Paul Stancliffe
PHYSIOTHERAPIST
Jeff Miller

STATISTICIAN FOR THE DIRECTORY
David Batters

Although avoiding the last gasp scramble to escape relegation, as in the two previous campaigns, 1997/98 was however another season of under achievement for York City and the final position of 16th in Division Two was disappointing. It was a season of two halves. In mid November they were third in the table and at Christmas were well poised to make a strong promotion challenge. In the New Year, however, their form dipped especially at home - 8 of the first 11 games at Bootham Crescent were won but only 1 of the last 12! In the final analysis, vital away wins in the closing weeks notably at high flying Bristol Rovers and Wrexham kept them away from the danger zone. Overall away form was good with only eight defeats on their travels, but failure to convert some of the ten draws into victories checked their progress especially in mid term.

The chief problem was the lack of scoring power. Leading marksman Rodney Rowe notched 16 goals but after mid November only found the net in one league game when he scored twice in a defeat at Preston in March. Gary Bull again lost his scoring touch and top scorer from the previous season Neil Tolson missed much of the campaign due to injury. Prodigal son Marco Gabbiadini returned to the club in February over ten years after leaving Bootham Crescent, but beset by injuries he was unable to make an impact and was released at the end of the season. The defence was sound and newcomers Barry Jones, ex-Wrexham, and Neil Thompson, ex-Barnsley, fitted in well. Midfielder Steve Bushall was "Clubman of the Year" and Andy McMillan passed 450 senior games for the club. The ever popular right back is now in City's all time appearance list and 1998/99 will be his testimonial season.

Average league attendances of 3,850 were the highest for four years. There was no joy in the cup competitions with defeat at Blackpool in the Auto Windscreen Shield following a marathon penalty shoot out (9 - 10).

Departures during the season saw long serving central-defender Steve Tutill move to Darlington and popular winger Paul Stephenson to Hartlepool. In March highly rated young forward Jonathan Greening was signed by Manchester United for an initial fee believed to be in the region of £500,000 rising to a possible £2 million.

1998/99 will be City's 6th successive season out of the basement league equalling a club record set in the 1970s. For the club to amount a serious promotion challenge Alan Little, now the 4th longest serving manager in City's history, has at the top of his shopping list an experienced proven goalscorer and a left winger.   **DAVID BATTERS.**

YORK CITY

Division 2   :16th   FA CUP: 2nd Round   LC CUP: 2nd Round   AWS: Northern Round 2

M	DATE	COMP.	VEN	OPPONENTS	RESULT		H/T	LP	GOAL SCORERS/GOAL TIMES	ATT.
1	A 09	FL	A	Oldham Athletic	L	1-3	0-1	18	Bushall 64	(6474)
2	12	CC 1/1	A	Port Vale	W	2-1	1-1		Bull 32, Bushall 90	(2749)
3	15	FL	H	Bristol Rovers	L	0-1	0-0	23		3307
4	23	FL	A	Millwall	W	3-2	1-1	17	Tinkler 45, Pouton 62, Stephenson 87	(6583)
5	26	CC 1/2	H	Port Vale	D	1-1	1-0		Barras 37	3195
6	30	FL	H	Gillingham	W	2-1	0-0	11	Rowe 60, Greening 88	2853
7	S 02	FL	H	Chesterfield	L	0-1	0-1	15		3284
8	09	FL	A	Grimsby Town	D	0-0	0-0	16		(5308)
9	13	FL	H	Burnley	W	3-1	0-1	12	Davis 62, Rowe 64, Tolson 81	5424
10	16	CC 2/1	A	Oxford United	L	1-4	1-0		Rowe 43	(2923)
11	20	FL	A	Walsall	L	0-2	0-0	16		(2972)
12	23	CC 2/2	H	Oxford United	L	1-2	0-0		Murty 63	1555
13	27	FL	A	Watford	D	1-1	1-0	17	Tolson 33	(13812)
14	O 04	FL	H	Plymouth Argyle	W	1-0	1-0	9	Rowe 8	2894
15	11	FL	H	Brentford	W	3-1	1-0	6	Stephenson 17, Tinkler 51, Murty 66	2831
16	17	FL	A	Bristol City	L	1-2	1-0	8	Rowe 37	(9568)
17	21	FL	A	Northampton Town	D	1-1	0-1	11	Rowe 48	(6059)
18	25	FL	H	Carlisle United	W	4-3	1-2	6	Rowe 14, Stephenson 81, 84, Bushall 86	3700
19	N 01	FL	A	Wigan Athletic	D	1-1	0-0	6	Rowe 76	(3701)
20	04	FL	H	Preston North End	W	1-0	0-0	6	Tinkler 61	3370
21	08	FL	A	Wycombe Wanderers	W	2-0	1-0	3	Barras 45 (pen), Rowe 55	3343
22	15	FAC 1	A	Southport	W	4-0	1-0		Rowe 18, 68, Pouton 75, Player 69 (OG)	(3952)
23	18	FL	A	Fulham	D	1-1	1-0	5	Barras 20 (pen)	(5521)
24	22	FL	A	Blackpool	L	0-1	0-0	5		(4508)
25	29	FL	H	Luton Town	L	1-2	0-1	7	Cresswell 87	3636
26	D 02	FL	A	Bournemouth	D	0-0	0-0	7		(3365)
27	06	FAC 2	A	Wigan Athletic	L	1-2	0-0		Rowe 82	(4021)
28	13	FL	H	Wrexham	W	1-0	0-0	5	Barras 62	2871
29	19	FL	A	Southend United	D	4-4	2-2	4	Pouton 22, 66, Barras 45 (pen), Tinkler 88	(3215)
30	26	FL	H	Grimsby Town	D	0-0	0-0	5		7093
31	28	FL	A	Chesterfield	D	1-1	0-0	8	Greening 90	(5320)
32	J 10	FL	H	Oldham Athletic	D	0-0	0-0	9		4454
33	13	AWS N2	A	Blackpool	L	1-0	1-1		Rowe 23	(1105)
34	17	FL	A	Gillingham	D	0-0	0-0	10		5891
35	24	FL	H	Millwall	L	2-3	1-0	10	Stephenson 11, Bull 87	3508
36	31	FL	A	Burnley	L	2-7	1-2	12	Pouton 35, 76	(9975)
37	F 06	FL	H	Walsall	W	1-0	1-0	9	Tinkler 27	2959
38	14	FL	A	Plymouth Argyle	D	0-0	0-0	12		(4382)
39	21	FL	H	Watford	D	1-1	1-0	13	Barras 24 (pen)	4890
40	24	FL	H	Bristol City	L	0-1	0-0	13		3770
41	28	FL	A	Brentford	W	2-1	0-0	13	Gabbiadini 50, Jones 70	(4490)
42	M 03	FL	A	Wycombe Wanderers	L	0-1	0-0	14		(3768)
43	07	FL	H	Wigan Athletic	D	2-2	0-1	13	Thompson 46, McGibbon 53 (OG)	3536
44	10	FL	A	Bristol Rovers	W	2-1	1-0	10	Jones 50, Cresswell 72	(4289)
45	14	FL	A	Preston North End	L	2-3	1-0	11	Rowe 2, 77	(7664)
46	21	FL	H	Fulham	L	0-1	0-0	15		4871
47	28	FL	H	Blackpool	D	1-1	0-1	12	Cresswell 90	3650
48	A 04	FL	A	Luton Town	L	0-3	0-2	15		(5541)
49	11	FL	H	Bournemouth	L	0-1	0-1	18		2840
50	13	FL	A	Wrexham	W	2-1	0-0	15	Thompson 67 (pen), Cresswell 81	(5231)
51	18	FL	H	Southend United	D	1-1	0-0	15	Tolson 74	2850
52	25	FL	A	Carlisle United	W	2-1	0-1	13	Pouton 62, McMillan 84	(3897)
53	M 02	FL	H	Northampton Town	D	0-0	0-0	16		6688

Best Home League Attendance: 7093 V Grimsby Town   Smallest :2831 V Brentford   Average :3853

Goal Scorers:

FL	(52)	Rowe 10, Barras 6, Pouton 5, Stephenson 5, Tinkler 5, Cresswell 4, Tolson 3, Bushall 2, Greening 2, Jones 2, Thompson 2, Bull 1, Davis 1, Gabbiadini 1, McMillan 1, Murty 1, Opponents 1
CC	(5)	Barras 1, Bull 1, Bushall 1, Murty 1, Rowe 1
FAC	(5)	Rowe 3, Pouton 1, Opponents 1
AWS	(1)	Rowe 1

1997-98

(M) Alderson	(D) Atkinson	(D) Barras	(F) Bull	(M) Campbell	(F) Cresswell	(M) Davis	(F) Gabbiadini	(M) Greening	(D) Hall	(D) Himsworth	(D) Jones	(M) Jordan	(D) McMillan	(M) Murty	(M) Norris	(M) Pouton	(F) Reed	(M) Rennison	(F) Rowe	(F) Rush	(G) Samways	(F) Stephenson	(M) Thompson	(M) Tinkler	(F) Tolson	(D) Tutill	(G) Warrington	Referee	No
	X	X	X					S			S	X		X		X					S1		X	X	X	X	X	C.T. Finch	1
	X	X	X	X1				X			S	X		X		X			X2		X	S1	X	X	S2	X		A R Leake	2
	X	X	X	X				X			S1	X		X		X			X	S3	X	S2	X		X		X	G B Frankland	3
	X	S2	X		S1			X			S	X		X	X			X1	X2	X	X	X		X			K A Leach	4
S	X	X	X		S1		S2	X				X		X	X	X		X	X	X			X				B Coddington	5
S3	X	X	X		S1		S2	X				X		X	X	X		X	X	X		X	X				E Wolstenholme	6
S		S	X	X			X	X				X	S1	X	X	X		X	X	X		X	X				G Cain	7
	X		X	X		X		X			S	X	X	X	X	S2	S	X		X	X		X	X		S1		S W Mathieson	8
	X	S1	X		X			X				X	X	S2	S		X		X	X		X	X	X		R D Furnandiz	9
	X	S1	X					X			S	X	X	X	S		X		X	X		X	X	X		M C Bailey	10
	X	S	X		X			X				X	X	S2		X	S1	X		X	X		X	X		C R Wilkes	11
S	X	X	X					X			S	X	X	S1	X		X		X	X		X	X		D Laws	12
S	X	S1	X					X			X	X	X	X	X		X	S	X	X		X	X		A G Wiley	13
	X	S1	X					X	S2	S		X	X	X	X		X		X	X		X	X		R Pearson	14
	X	S2	X				S1	X	S3	X	X	X	X		X		X		X	X		X	X		P R Richards	15
	X	S	X				S	X	S	X	X	X	X		X		X		X	X		X	X		M R Halsey	16
	X	X	X				S	X	S	X	X	X	X		X		X		X	X		X	S		M J Brandwood	17
	X	X	X				S1	X	S3	X	X	X	X		X		X		X	X		X	S2		D Laws	18
	X	X	X				S	X	S1	S	X	X	X		X		X		X	X		X	X		M J Jones	19
	X	X	X				S	X	S	S1	X	X	X		X		X		X	X		X	X		G Singh	20
	X	X	X				S2	X	S3	S1	X	X	X		X		X		X	X		X	X		M L Dean	21
S3	X	X	X	S2			X	S1	S		X	X	X		X		X		X	X		X	X	S	B Coddington	22
S	X	X	X	S1			X	X	S		X	X	X		X	X	X		X	X		X			S G Bennett	23
S2	X		X	X		S1	X	S		X	X	X		X	X	X		X	X		X			S J Baines	24
X	X	X1	X	S1		S		S		X	X	X		X		X		X		X	X	D Pugh	25
S	X	S1	X	X			S		X	X	X	X1		X		X		X	X	R J Harris	26
S	X	S1	X	X1		S		X	S2	X	S	X2	X		X		X	X	M J Brandwood	27
	X	S2	X	X2		S3	X	X	S1		X	X	X1	X3		X		X	X	A N Butler	28
	X	S2	X	X		S1	X	X1	X	S	X	X	X2		X		X	X	P Taylor	29
	X	S		X		S	X	X	X	S	X	X	X		S	X	X	J P Robinson	30
	X		X2		S2	X	X1	X	S1		X	X	S	X	X	G B Frankland	31
	X	S	X	X1		S1	X	X		X	X	S	X		X	X	R D Furnandiz	32
S2	S1		X	X		X	X	X	X1	X	X	X2		X	X		33
	X	X	X	X		S	X	X	X	S1	X	X	X		X1	X	A G Wiley	34
	X	S2	X	X1		S1	X	X	X3	S3	X	X2	X	X	T Jones	35
X	X	X	X		S1		S2	X	S3	X	X	X1	X2	X	E Lomas	36
	X	X1	X		S1	X	X	X	S1	X	S	X	X1	X	C J Foy	37
	X	X	X		S2	X1	X3	X	S3	X2	S1	X	X	X	M L Dean	38
	X	X	X		X	X	S	X	X	S	S	X	X	G Cain	39
	X	X1	X	S		S1	X	S	X	X	X1	X	X	B Coddington	40
	X	X		X	S1	X	S	X	S	X1	X	X	C R Wilkes	41
	X	X		X	X	X	S	X	X	S	S	X	X	X	A R Hall	42
	X	X		X2	S2	X	S	X	X	S1	X	X	X	X1	F G Stretton	43
	X		X	S	X	S	X	X	X	S	X	S	A Bates	44
	X1	X	X2	S2	X	S3	X	X3	X	X	X	X	S1	R Pearson	45
	X	X	X1	X	S	X	X	X	X	X	S1	M S Pike	46
	X	X	S2	X2	X	X	X	X	X1	X	X	S1	P S Danson	47
	S	X	X2	S2	X	X	X	X	X	X1	X	X	S1	X	D R Crick	48
X3	X	X	S1	S2	X	X2	X	X	S3	X	X	X1	G Singh	49
	S	X	X	X	S	X	X	X	X	X	X	X	A Bates	50
	S	X	X	X1	X	X	X	X	S1	X	X	X	G Laws	51
	X2	X1	X	S2	X	X	X	X	X	X	X	S1	X	E K Wolstenholme	52
S2	X		X	X	X	X	S1	X	X1	S	X2	X	X	X	A N Butler	53
3	38	18	40	1	18	2	5	5	31	9	23	6	30	32	37	21	1	38	1	29	34	12	43	10	2	17		FL Appearances	
1	2		9		8		2	15		1	6				10		2		4	1		3	2		1	6		FL Sub Appearances	
	4	3+1	4	1	0+1		0+1	4			4	2	3+1	2		3		4	3+1	4	2+1	1		CC Appearances	
0+1	2	1+1	2		1+1			1		1+1	1		0+1	2	2	2		1	2		2		1	FAC Appearances	
0+1	0+1		1		1			1	1	1		0+1	1	1	1	1		1	1			1	AWS Appearances	

Also Played: (M) Dawson S(46,47). (M) Garrett S(51).

501

YORK CITY

RECORDS AND STATISTICS

CLUB RECORDS

RECORD LEAGUE VICTORY
9-1 v Southport,Div 3N, 2.2.1957
Most Goals Scored in a Cup Tie: 7-1 v Horsforth (h), Prelim. Round
FA Cup,1924-25 7-1 v Stockton Malleable (h), FA Cup 3rd
Qualifying Round, 1927-28 7-1 v Stockton (h), FA Cup 1st
Qualifying Round, 1928-29 6-0 v South Shields(a), FA Cup 1st
Round, 1968-69
7-1 v Hartlepool Utd (h), Leyland Daf Cup,1989-90.
RECORD LEAGUE DEFEAT
0-12 v Chester, Div 3N, 1.2.1936
Record Cup Defeat: 0-7 v Liverpool, FA Cup Round 5 replay,
20.2.1985

MOST LEAGUE POINTS
(3pts a win) 101, Div 4, 1983-84
(2pts a win) 62, Div 4,1964-65

MOST LEAGUE GOALS
96, Div 4, 1983-84

RECORD TRANSFER FEE RECEIVED
£450,000 from Port Vale for Jon McCarthy, August 1995.

RECORD TRANSFER FEE PAID
£140,000 for Adrian Randall from Burnley, December 1995.

BEST PERFORMANCES
League: 15th Div 2, 1974-75
FA Cup: Semi-final Replay,1954-55 (as a Third Division club)
League Cup: 5th Round, 1961-2
HONOURS
Champions Div 4, 1983-84

LEAGUE CAREER
Elected to Div 3N 1929 Transferred to Div 4 1958 Promoted to
Div 3 1958-59
Relegated to Div 4 1959-60 Promoted to Div 3 1964-65
Relegated to Div 41965-66 Promoted to Div 3 1970-71
Promoted to Div 2 1973-74 Relegated to Div 3 1975-76
Relegated to Div 41976-77 Promoted to Div 3 1983-84
Relegated to Div 4 (now Div 3) 1987-88 Promoted to Div 2 1992-93
MOST APPEARANCES FOR CLUB

INDIVIDUAL CLUB RECORDS

Barry Jackson (1958-70): League 481 + FA Cup 35 +League Cup
22 Total 538

MOST CAPPED PLAYER
Peter Scott, 7 Northern Ireland   For England: None

RECORD GOALSCORER IN A MATCH
Alf Patrick 5 v Rotherham United, 6-1, Div 3,20.11.1948
RECORD LEAGUE GOALSCORER IN A SEASON
Bill Fenton, 31, Div 3N, 1951-52   Arthur Bottom 1954-55 and 1955-
56, Div 3N   In All Competitions: Arthur Bottom, 39(League 31, FA
Cup 8) 1954-55
RECORD LEAGUE GOALSCORER IN A CAREER
Norman Wilkinson, 127, 1954-66   In All Competitions: Norman
Wilkinson, 143, (League 127, FA Cup 16) 1954-66

OLDEST PLAYER IN A LEAGUE MATCH
Matt Middleton, 42 years 6 months, May 1950
YOUNGEST PLAYER IN A LEAGUE MATCH
Reg Stockill, 15 years 6 months, Aug 1929

PREVIOUS MANAGERS

1929-30 John Collier   1930-33 G W Sherrington   1933-37John
Collier   1937-50 Tom Mitchell   1950-52 Dick Duckworth   1952-53
Charlie Spencer   1953-54 Jim McCormick   1956-60 Sam Bartram
1960-67 Tom Lockie   1967-68 Joe Shaw   1968-75 Tom Johnston
1975-77 Wilf McGuinness   1977-80Charlie Wright   1980-81 Barry
Lyons   1982-87 Denis Smith   1987-88 Bobby Saxton   1988-91
John Bird   1991-93 John Ward

ADDITIONAL INFORMATION
Previous League: Midland League

Club Colours: All red with black and white trim.
Change Colours:

Reserves League: Pontins Central League Div 2
`A' Team: Northern Intermediate League

LONGEST LEAGUE RUNS

of undefeated matches:	21(1973-74)	of league matches w/out a win:	17 (May-Oct 1987)
of undefeated home matches:	32 (1970-71)	of undefeated away matches:	10 (1973-74)
without home win:	12 (1981-82)	without an away win:	38 (Sept 1986 - Mar 1988)
of league wins:	7 (1964)	of home wins:	14 (1964-65)
of league defeats:	8 (1966)	of away wins:	5 (1983, 1984)

THE MANAGER

ALAN LITTLE . . . . appointed March 1993.

PREVIOUS CLUBS
As Manager . . . . York City (Caretaker).
As Asst.Man/Coach . . . . Hartlepool United (C), York City (A.M.).
As a player . . . . Aston Villa, Southend United, Barnsley, Doncaster Rovers, Torquay United,
. . . . Halifax Town, Hartlepool United.

HONOURS
As a Manager . . . . Promotion to Division 2, 1992-93 (via the play-offs).
As a Player . . . . None.

YORK CITY

PLAYERS NAME / Honours	Ht	Wt	Birthdate	Birthplace Transfers	Contract Date	Clubs	APPEARANCES League	L/Cup	FA Cup	Other	GOALS Lge	L/C	FAC	Oth
G O A L K E E P E R														
Warrington Andrew	6.3	12.13	6/10/76	Sheffield	6/11/94	York City	51	6	2+1	2				
D E F E N C E														
Barras Tony	6	12.3	3/29/71	Billingham	7/6/89	Hartlepool United	9+3	2	1	1				
				Free	7/23/90	Stockport County	94+5	2	7	19+1	5			
				Loan	2/25/94	Rotherham United	5				1			
					7/18/94	York City	144+4	16	9	5+1	11	2	1	1
Hall Wayne	5.8	10.2	10/25/68	Rotherham	12/19/88	Darlington								
				Free	1/1/89	Hatfield Main								
				Free	3/15/89	York City	288+16	21+1	11+1	19	8		1	1
Himsworth Gary	5.7	9.1	12/19/69	Pickering	1/27/88	York City	74+14	5		5+2	8			
				Free	12/5/90	Scarborough	83+9	7+2	1+1	6+1	6	1		
				Free	7/16/93	Darlington	60+6	3+1	3	6	5			4
				£25000	2/16/96	York City	49+8	4	5+1		3		1	
Jones Barry WFAC'95.	6	12.1	6/30/70	Liverpool		Prescot Cables								
					1/19/89	Liverpool				0+1				
				Free	7/10/92	Wrexham	184+11	14+1	11+2	21+1	5	1		
				£35000	1/21/98	York City	23				2			
McMillan Andy	5.11	10.13	6/22/68	South Africa	10/17/87	York City	377+12	25	16	23	5			
Rennison Graham L	6	12.8	10/2/78	York	4/3/98	York City (T)	1							
M I D F I E L D														
Agnew Steve DIV1 95/96	5.9	10.6	11/9/65	Shipley	11/10/83	Barnsley	185+9	13	20	6+1	29	3	4	
				£700000	6/25/91	Blackburn Rovers	2	2						
				Loan	11/21/92	Portsmouth	3+2							
				£250000	2/9/93	Leicester City	52+4	4+1	2	2	4			
				£250000	1/12/95	Sunderland	56+7	4	2+1		9		1	
				Free	7/7/98	York City								
Jordan Scott	5.11	11.2	7/19/75	Newcastle	10/21/92	York City	63+31	4+1	2+2	3+4	5	1		
Pouton Alan	6	12.2	2/1/77	Newcastle		Newcastle United								
					11/7/95	Oxford United								
					12/8/95	York City	55+8	3+1	5	2	6		1	
Sharples John B	6	11.3	1/26/73	Bury		Ayr United								
					3/28/96	York City	38	3	1		1			
Thompson Neil E: SP.	5.10	12.8	10/2/63	Beverley		Nottingham (T)								
				Free	11/28/81	Hull City	29+2							
				Free	8/1/83	Scarborough	87	8	4	9	15	1		1
				£100000	6/9/89	Ipswich Town	199+7	14+1	17	8	19	1	1	2
				Free	6/10/96	Barnsley	27	4	1		5			
				Loan	12/24/97	Oldham Athletic	8							
				Loan	3/2/98	York City	12				2			
				Free	5/11/98	York City					2			
Tinkler Mark E: S, Y.7; UEFA Yth'93; FAYC'93	6	11.4	10/24/74	Bishop Auckland	11/29/91	Leeds United	14+11	1		0+1				
					3/25/97	York City	52+1	4	2		6			
F O R W A R D														
Cresswell Richard	5.11	11.7	9/20/77	Bridlington		York City	36+22	1+3	1+2	1	5			
				Loan	3/27/97	Mansfield Town	5				1			
Prendergast Rory	5.8	12	4/6/78	Pontefract		Rochdale								
						Barnsley								
				Free	7/1/98	York City								
Reed Martin J	6.1	11.7	1/10/78	Scarborough	10/25/96	York City	23+1	2	2					
Rowe Rodney C	5.8	12.8	7/30/75	Huddersfield	7/12/93	Huddersfield Town	14+20	+2	6+1	3	2		2	1
				Loan	8/11/94	Scarborough	10+4	4			1	1		
				Loan	3/20/95	Bury	1+2							
					2/18/97	York City	47+4	3	2		13	1	3	
Tolson Neil	6.2	12.4	10/25/73	Walsall	12/17/91	Walsall	3+6		+1	1+2	1	1		
				£150000	3/24/92	Oldham Athletic	+3							
					12/2/93	Bradford City	32+31	1+4	3+1	2+2	12	1	1	3
					8/15/96	York City	9+6	2			3			
Woods Neil S	6	12.11	30/07/66	Bradford	31/08/83	Doncaster Rovers	55+10	4	5	5+2	16	1	2	3
				£120000	22/12/86	Glasgow Rangers	0+3							
				£120000	03/08/87	Ipswich Town	15+12		4		5			1
					01/03/90	Bradford City	13+1				2			
				£82000	23/08/90	Grimsby Town	175+51	11+3	8+2	8	42	2	3	1
				Loan	11/6/97	Wigan Athletic	1							
				Loan	1/19/98	Scunthorpe United	2							
				Loan	2/16/98	Mansfield Town	5+1							
				Free	7/1/98	York City								
ADDITIONAL CONTRACT PLAYERS														
Dawson Andrew S					3/20/98	York City (T)								
Garrett Martin B					4/17/98	York City (T)								
Norris Michael					12/5/97	York City (T)								

BOOTHAM CRESCENT
York YO3 7AQ

Capacity 9,534
Covered Standing 5,865
Seating 3,669

First game ....v Stockport County, 1932.
First floodlit game ....v Q.P.R., September 1959.

ATTENDANCES
Highest...28,123 v Huddersfield, FAC 6th Rnd, 5.3.1938.
Lowest..957 v Carlisle Utd, AMC Prelim Rnd, 22.10.1991.
OTHER GROUNDS ....Fulfordgate 1922-32.

HOW TO GET TO THE GROUND

From the North
Use A1 then A59, sign posted York. Cross railway bridge and in 1.9 miles turn left into Water End. At end turn right A19, sign posted City Centre. In 0.4 miles turn left into Bootham Crescent for York City FC.

From the East
Use A1079 into York City centre and follow signs for Thirsk (A19) into Bootham. Cross railway bridge and then take 2nd turning on right into Bootham Crescent for York City FC.

From the South
Use A64. Turn left onto by-pass and follow signs for Thirsk (A19). Then turn left sign posted York and then take left into Bootham Crescent for York City FC.

From the West
Use B1224, sign posted York into city centre and follow signs to Thirsk (A19) into Bootham. Cross railway bridge and then take 2nd turning on right into Bootham Crescent for York City FC.

Car Parking: Ample parking in side streets. **Nearest Railway Station:** York (01904 642 155)

USEFUL TELEPHONE NUMBERS

Club switchboard 01904 624 447
Club fax number 01904 631 457
Club shop 01904 645 941
Ticket Office . . 01904 624 447 (Fax 631 457)

Marketing Department 01904 645 941
Clubcall 0891 66 45 45*
*Calls cost 50p per minute at all times.
Call costings correct at time of going to press.

MATCHDAY PROGRAMME

Programme Editor . . . . James Richardson.

Number of pages . . . . 36.

Price . . . . £1.80.

Subscriptions . . . . Apply to club.

Local Newspapers
. . . . Yorkshire Evening Press.

Local Radio Stations
. . . . BBC Radio York & Minster FM.

MATCHDAY TICKET PRICES

Main Stand and Enclosure £11.00
Juv/OAP. £7.00

Popular Stand. £9.00
Juv/OAP. £6.00

Ground. £8.00
Juv/OAP. £5.00
Popular Stand transfer. £1

Enclosure. £11.00
Juv/OAP. £7.00
(Only obtainable from Ticket Office)

Family Stand (max. 3 children) £8.50
Child £5.00

NATIONWIDE
LEAGUE DIVISION 3

...1998-99

DIVISION THREE
1997-98

FINAL LEAGUE TABLE

		P	W	D	L	F	A	Pts
1	Notts County (Div.2)	46	29	12	5	82	43	99
2	Macclesfield Town (GMVC)	46	23	13	10	63	44	82
3	Lincoln City (+6)	46	20	15	11	60	51	75
4	Colchester United (+4) - *Play-off winners*	46	21	11	14	72	60	74
5	Torquay United (+16)	46	21	11	14	68	59	74
6	Scarborough (+6)	46	19	15	12	67	58	72
7	Barnet (+8)	46	19	13	14	61	51	70
8	Scunthorpe United (+5)	46	19	12	15	56	52	69
9	Rotherham United (Div.2)	46	16	19	11	67	61	67
10	Peterborough United (Div.2)	46	18	13	15	63	51	67
11	Leyton Orient (+5)	46	19	12	15	62	47	66
12	Mansfield Town (-1)	46	16	17	13	64	55	65
13	Shrewsbury Town (Div.2)	46	16	13	17	61	62	61
14	Chester City (-8)	46	17	10	19	60	61	61
15	Exeter City (+7)	46	15	15	16	68	63	60
16	Cambridge United (-6)	46	14	18	14	63	57	60
17	Hartlepool United (+3)	46	12	23	11	61	53	59
18	Rochdale (-4)	46	17	7	22	56	55	58
19	Darlington (-1)	46	14	12	20	56	72	54
20	Swansea City (-15)	46	13	11	22	49	62	50
21	Cardiff City (-14)	46	9	23	14	48	52	50
22	Hull City (-5)	46	11	8	27	56	83	41
23	Brighton & Hove Albion (-)	46	6	17	23	38	66	35
24	Doncaster Rovers (-5)	46	4	8	34	30	113	20

The figure in brackets denotes the number of places lost or gained on the clubs 1996-97 final position.

BARNET
(The Bees)
NATIONWIDE LEAGUE DIVISION 3
SPONSORED BY: LOADED

1997/98 - Back Row (L-R): Lee Howarth, Danny Mills, Tarkan Mustafa, Lee harrison, Warren Goodhind, Billy Manuel, Jon Ford
Middle Row: Tony Kleanthous (chairman), Kieren Adams, Ken Charlery, Michael Basham, Micky Tomlinson, Sean Devine, Matt Brady, David McDonald, Paul Wilson, Michael Harle, Dean samuels, John Barnett (director). **Front Row:** Phil Simpson, Gary Andreson (physio), Kevin Rattray, John Still (manager), Sam Stockley, Micky Halsall (asst. manager), Udo Onwere.

BARNET
FORMED IN 1888
TURNED PROFESSIONAL IN 1965

CHAIRMAN: A A Kleanthous

DIRECTORS:
D J Buchler FCA, J Barnett

CLUB SECRETARY: D Stanley

COMMERCIAL MANAGER
C Leggatt

MANAGER: John Still
ASSISTANT MANAGER: Mick Halsall

YOUTH TEAM MANAGER
Terry Harvey

PHYSIOTHERAPIST
Gary Gilbert-Anderson

Barnet came so close to winning promotion - and to lose in the play-offs to Colchester United was a bitter disappointment for everyone at Underhill. From the word go manager John Still got his players working together as a unit. Performances were determined rather than brilliant, but the consistency was there for all to see.

After the first quarter of the campaign, the 'Bees' found themselves in ninth position with 18 points.

At the halfway mark (with 23 matches completed) they had accumulated 35 points and had climbed up to seventh place, nine points behind the leaders, Notts County.

At this stage of the season unfortunately the goals were not going in as planned and, in fact, over the next ten matches, the 'Bees' scored only another 13 times, but they weren't losing - and they actually climbed to second place at one point.

Holding onto fifth spot, just four points behind second-placed Macclesfield and just two behind Torquay United, who were in the last automatic promotion place, barnet entered the last phase of the season in a confident mood.

It was all about consistency at this juncture and everyone at Underhill, from the players, all of the management and the diehard fans - remember Barnet are one of the poorest supported teams in the Nationwide League incidentally - knew that promotion was now well within their sights.

But the run proved difficult and from their remaining 13 matches, the 'Bees' collected just 16 points - losing their last two games - and in the end they had to settle for seventh place, just sneaking a play-off spot by one point from Scunthorpe United. They missed automatic promotion by five points (two wins would have done it).

Manager Still was obviously disappointed and even more so after his team had been beaten by Colchester over two-legs in the play-off semi-final. But he believes that Barnet can figure again this season, given the breaks, and if he can hold on to his star striker Sean Devine.....and this time round he will be aiming for the championship - and why not!

Tony Matthews.

BARNET

Division 3	:7th		FA CUP: 1st Round		LC CUP: 2nd Round			AWS: Southern Round 1	
M	DATE	COMP.	VEN	OPPONENTS	RESULT	H/T	LP	GOAL SCORERS/GOAL TIMES	ATT.
1	A 09	FL	A	Swansea City	L 0-1	0-0	20		(6800)
2	12	CC 1/1	H	Leyton Orient	D 1-1	0-1		Thompson-Minton 77 (pen)	1073
1	A 09	FL	A	Rotherham United	W 3-2	1-1	1	Harle 3, Charlery 82, Devine 84	(4220)
2	12	CC 1/1	A	Norwich City	L 1-2	1-2		, Polston 35 (OG)	(5429)
3	15	FL	H	Exeter City	L 1-2	0-2	7	Charlery 60	3137
4	22	FL	A	Colchester United	D 1-1	0-0	4	Howarth 59	(3286)
5	26	CC 1/2	H	Norwich City	W 3-1	0-0		Heald 68, Devine 69, 80	2846
6	30	FL	H	Chester City	W 2-1	0-0	5	Wilson 75 (pen), Devine 76	1790
7	S 02	FL	H	Swansea City	W 2-0	2-0	4	Charlery 8, Wilson 42 (pen)	1946
8	07	FL	A	Peterborough United	L 1-5	0-2	8	Samuels 59	(7243)
9	13	FL	A	Cambridge United	W 3-1	1-0	6	Charlery 40, Devine 73, Heald 80	(3395)
10	16	CC 2/1	A	Middlesbrough	L 0-1	0-0			(9611)
11	20	FL	H	Scunthorpe United	L 0-1	0-1	9		1951
12	23	CC 2/2	H	Middlesbrough	L 0-2	0-1			3968
13	27	FL	H	Lincoln City	D 0-0	0-0	8		1734
14	O 04	FL	A	Cardiff City	D 1-1	0-1	8	Charlery 49	(3938)
15	11	FL	A	Shrewsbury Town	L 0-2	0-1	13		(2112)
16	18	FL	H	Hull City	W 2-0	1-0	9	Howarth 30, McGleish 62	2315
17	21	FL	H	Rochdale	W 3-1	1-0	4	Harle 39, Heald 48, Samuels 84	1310
18	25	FL	A	Mansfield Town	W 2-1	1-1	5	McGleish 18, Wilson 60 (pen)	(2340)
19	N 01	FL	H	Notts County	L 1-2	0-0	6	McGleish 60	2530
20	05	FL	A	Brighton & H.A.	W 3-0	1-0	5	Searle 44, Wilson 57, Howarth 76	(1025)
21	08	FL	A	Doncaster Rovers	D 1-1	1-0	5	Charlery 38	2015
22	15	FAC 1	H	Watford	L 1-2	1-0		Charlery 9	4040
23	18	FL	H	Torquay United	D 3-3	1-1	6	McGleish 29, Devine 59, 66	1246
24	22	FL	A	Hartlepool United	L 0-2	0-1	7		(2225)
25	29	FL	H	Darlington	W 2-0	2-0	6	McGleish 10, Devine 24	1726
26	D 02	FL	A	Leyton Orient	L 0-2	0-1	7		(2598)
27	09	AWS S1	H	Walsall	L 1-2	0-0		Wilson 89	754
28	13	FL	H	Macclesfield Town	W 3-1	0-0	4	Searle 56, Adams 70, Devine 84	1710
29	19	FL	A	Scarborough	L 0-1	0-1	6		(1714)
30	26	FL	H	Peterborough United	W 2-0	0-0	6	Simpson 57, Devine 79	3449
31	28	FL	A	Swansea City	W 2-0	1-0	5	McGleish 32, Simpson 90	(3987)
32	J 10	FL	H	Rotherham United	D 0-0	0-0	5		2558
33	17	FL	A	Chester City	W 1-0	0-0	4	Devine 51	(2479)
34	20	FL	A	Exeter City	D 0-0	0-0	4		(3697)
35	24	FL	H	Colchester United	W 3-2	1-2	3	Devine 44, 62, McGleish 60	2471
36	31	FL	H	Cambridge United	W 2-0	1-0	3	Heald 29, Simpson 63	2455
37	F 04	FL	H	Scunthorpe United	D 1-1	0-0	2	McGleish 73	(2313)
38	14	FL	H	Cardiff City	D 2-2	1-2	4	Wilson 43 (pen), McGleish 69	2406
39	21	FL	A	Lincoln City	L 0-2	0-0	5		(2945)
40	24	FL	A	Hull City	W 2-0	1-0	4	McGleish 24, Samuels 85	(3296)
41	28	FL	H	Shrewsbury Town	D 1-1	1-1	4	McGleish 16	2322
42	M 03	FL	A	Doncaster Rovers	W 2-0	0-0	4	Basham 51, McGleish 59	(739)
43	07	FL	A	Notts County	L 0-2	0-1	4		(6180)
44	14	FL	A	Brighton & H.A.	W 2-0	1-0	3	Simpson 7, Howarth 71	2845
45	21	FL	A	Torquay United	D 0-0	0-0	4		(4020)
46	28	FL	H	Hartlepool United	D 1-1	1-1	4	Devine 5	2344
47	A 04	FL	A	Darlington	W 3-2	2-0	4	Devine 10, 30, 87	(1880)
48	11	FL	H	Leyton Orient	L 1-2	0-0	4	Goodhind 55	3437
49	13	FL	A	Macclesfield Town	L 0-2	0-2	6		(4171)
50	18	FL	H	Scarborough	D 1-1	1-1	6	Devine 15	2353
51	25	FL	H	Mansfield Town	L 0-1	0-0	7		2797
52	M 02	FL	A	Rochdale	L 1-2	0-2	7	McGleish 90	(2102)
53	10	PO SF1	H	Colchester United	W 1-0	0-0		Heald 48	3858
54	13	PO SF2	A	Colchester United	L 1-3	1-1		Goodhind 40	(5863)

Best Home League Attendance: 3449 V Peterborough United   Smallest :1246 V Torquay United   Average :2298

GOAL SCORERS:

FL	(61)	Devine 16, McGleish 13, Charlery 6, Wilson 5, Howarth 4, Simpson 4, Heald 3, Samuels 3, Harle 2, Searle 2, Adams 1, Basham 1, Goodhind 1
CC	(4)	Devine 2, Heald 1, Opponents 1
FAC	(1)	Charlery 1
AWS	(1)	Wilson 1
PO	(2)	Goodhind 1, Heald 1

(M) Adams	(D) Basham	(F) Charlery	(M) Coggon	(M) De Vito	(F) Devine	(D) Doolan	(D) Ford	(D) Goodhind	(D) Harle	(G) Harrison	(D) Heald	(D) Howarth	(D) Manuel	(M) McDonald	(F) McGleish	(M) Mills	(M) Mustafa	(M) Onwere	(F) Samuels	(D) Sawyers	(M) Searle	(M) Simpson	(D) Stockley	(D) Wilson			
	X				X		X	S1	X	X		X	X	X		X		X	S			X	S2		M L Dean	1
	X				X		X	X	X	X	X	X	X	X	S2	X			S2			X	S1		C T Finch	2
	X				X		X	X	X	X	X	X	X		X	S2	S1		S1		S3	X			D R Crick	3
	X				X		X	S2	X	X	X	X	X		X	S3	S1				X	X	X		M C Bailey	4
	X				X		X	S2	X	X	X	X			X	S1	S3				X	X	X		M Fletcher	5
	X				X		X	S1	X	X	X	X	X		X	S2	S3				X	X	X		A G Wiley	6
	X				X			X	X	X	X		X			S1	X	X	S	S	X	X	X		S G Bennett	7
	X				X			X	S1	X	X	X			X	X	S3	S2			X	X	S		J P Robinson	8
	X				X		X	X	X	X	X	X	S			X	S1				X	X	S		A P D'Urso	9
	X				X		X	X	X	X	X	X	S			X	S1				X	X	S		E Lomas	10
	X				X		X	X	X	X	X	X	S2			X	S1				X	X			M E Pierce	11
	X				X		X	X	X	X	X	X	S2			X	S1				X	X	S		B Knight	12
	X				X		X		X	X	X	X	X		X	S3	X	S2			X	X	S1		D Orr	13
	X						X	S1	X	X	X	X	S2	X	X		X	S3		X		X	X		P S Danson	14
	X						X	X	X	X	X	X	S3	X		S1	X	S2		X		X	X		M D Messias	15
S1	X						X	X	X	X	X	X	S	X		S		S2		X		X	X		M J Brandwood	16
S1	X						X	S3	X	X	X	X	X	X				S2		X		X	X		B Coddington	17
S1	X				S2		X		X	X	X	X	X	X				S	S1	X		X	X		P Rejer	18
X	X				S2		X		X	X	X	X	X	X			S	S1		X		X	X	X1	C R Wilkes	19
X	X						X	S	X	X	X	X	X	S	X		S			X		X	X		A N Butler	20
X	X						X	X	X	X	X	X	S	X			S			X		X	X		R Styles	21
	S	X	S				X	S	X	X	X	X	X	X			S1	S2		X		X	X		G S Willard	22
					X		X	S	X	X	X	X	X	X			S1	S2		X		X	X		A Bates	23
					X		X	X	X	X	X	X	S			X	S1			X		X	S		R D Furnandiz	24
					X		X	X3	X	X	X	X	S2	X1	S1	X		X2		X	S3				G Singh	25
	S1				X		X1	S2	X	X	X	X	S	X		X2		X		X	X				A P D'Urso	26
X	X				X			X		X	X	X	S1	S2		X	X	X	X	X	S3				??	27
S2	X	S3			X			S1	X	X	X1	X	X2	X3			X			X	X	X			D Orr	28
X	X1				X		S	X	X2	X		X	S2	X			X	S1	X	X					K M Lynch	29
X					X			X	X	X	X	X	S1	X2	S3		X	X	X1	S1					B Knight	30
S1	X				X			X	X	X	X	X	S2	X	S		X1	X		S	X				K A Leach	31
X					X			X	X	X	X	X	S	X	3		X	X	S	X					P Rejer	32
	X1	32			X	X	X	X	X	X	X	X	X2			S	X	S1	X						C J Foy	33
	S2				X	X	S	X	X	X	X	X	X2			S1	X1	X	X						M Fletcher	34
	S				X	X	S	X	X	X	X	X	X			S	X	X	X						P S Danson	35
	S1				X	X	S	X	X	X	X	X	X1			S	X	X	X						M E Pierce	36
X1	S1				X	X	X	X	X	X	X	X			X	S		S2	X2	X	X3				W C Burns	37
S3	S1				X	X	X1	X	X	X	X	X		S2	X2	X	X1								R Styles	38
X	X				S1	X	S	X2	X	X	X		S2	X	X	X1									T Heilbron	39
X					X1	X	S3	X	X	X	X	X		S1	S2	X2	X	X3							S W Mathieson	40
X	S2				X	X	S	X1	X	X	X		S1	X			X	X2							A R Hall	41
X	S3				X3	X	X	X	X	X	X2		S2	X1	S1		X								R Pearson	42
X	S2				X2	X	X1	X	X	X	X		S1	X3	S3		X								T Jones	43
X					X3	X	S1	X	X	X	X	S2		S3	X	X1	X2								M C Bailey	44
X					X	X	S2	X	X	X	X		S	X1	X2	X	S1								G Cain	45
X1	S1				X	X	S	X	X	X	X		S2	X2	X	X									J P Robinson	46
X	S3				X	X	S1	X	X	X	X3	S2	X1	X2	X	X									S J Baines	47
X	S1				X	X	X1	X	X	X	S	X2	S2	X	X										C R Wilkes	48
X1	S2				X	X	S3	X3	X	X	X	X2	S1	X	X										G Singh	49
X2					X	X	S2	X1	X	X	X	S1	S	X	X	X									M J Jones	50
S2			S2	X	X	X	X	X	X	X1	S1	X2	X	X2											B Knight	51
S1			S	X	X		X	X	X	X	X	X	S2	X1	X2										P S Danson	52
X	S1				X	X	X	X	S2	X1	X1	S	X2	X	X										E K Wolstenholme	53
X	X				X	X	X	X	S3	X2	S2	X1	S1	X	X3										T Heilbron	54
4	19	18			37	17	19	22	42	46	42	45	10	1	37	5	2	11		1	26	27	40	34	FL Appearances	
7	1	14		1	3			13	1				7			1	9	6	21		4	4	1	5	FL Sub Appearances	
		4			4		4	3+1	3	4	4	4	2+1	0+1				1	0+1	2+1	0+3		3	4	CC Appearances	1+1
		1					1		1	1	1	1	1			1					1		1	1	FAC Appearances	
1	1		1		1		1			1	0+1		0+1			1			1	1	1	1	0+1		AWS Appearances	
2	1+1		1		2	2	2	2	2	0+2		2				0+1		2	1+1	2	1				PO Appearances	

509

BARNET

RECORDS AND STATISTICS

CLUB RECORDS

SINCE JOINING THE FOOTBALL LEAGUE
RECORD LEAGUE VICTORY
6-0 v Lincoln City (away), Division 4.9.1992.
Most Goals scored in a Cup tie: 9-0 v Wealdstone, FAC, 1961-62
First Class Cup tie: 6-3 v Brentford, AMC, 17.12.1991.
5-0 v Tiverton Town, FA Cup 1st Round, 16.11.1992.

RECORD LEAGUE DEFEAT
1-5 v York City (h), Division 3, 13.3.1993.

RECORD TRANSFER FEE RECEIVED
£800,000 from Crystal Palace for Dougie Freedman, 1995.

RECORD TRANSFER FEE PAID
£130,000 to Peterborough fro Greg Heald, August 1997.

BEST PERFORMANCES
League: 3rd in Division 4/3, 1992-93.
FA Cup: 3rd Round in 1964-65, 1970-71, 1972-73, 1981-82, 1990-91(As a non-League club) 1991-92, 1993-94 (As a League club).
League Cup: 2nd Round in 1993-94, 1994-95.

HONOURS SINCE JOINING THE FOOTBALL LEAGUE
None.

LEAGUE CAREER
Promoted to Division 4/3 1990-91, Promoted to Division 2 1992-93.

MOST APPEARANCES

INDIVIDUAL CLUB RECORDS

Gary Bull - 106 (1989-93): League 83, FA Cup 11, League Cup 4, AMC 6, Play-offs 2.

MOST CAPPED PLAYER
No Barnet player has won a full cap.

RECORD GOALSCORER IN A MATCH
4 - Douglas Freedman v Rochdale, 6-2, 13.9.95.
4 - Lee Hodges v Rochdale, 8.4.96.

RECORD LEAGUE GOALSCORER IN A SEASON
Gary Bull 20, 1991-92.
In All Competitions: Mark Carter - 32 (1991-92): League 19, FA Cup 5, League Cup 2, AMC 5, Play-offs 1.

RECORD LEAGUE GOALSCORER IN A CAREER
Gary Bull - 37 (1991-93).
In All Competitions: Mark Carter - 47 (1991-93): League 31, FA Cup 6, League Cup 2, Others 8.

PREVIOUS MANAGERS

(Since 1946): Lester Finch, George Wheeler, Dexter Adams, Tommy Coleman, Gerry Ward, Gordon Ferry, Brian Kelly, Bill Meadows, Barry Fry, Roger Thompson, Don McAllister, Barry Fry, Gary Phillips.

ADDITIONAL INFORMATION
Previous Leagues: Olympian, London Athenian, Southern, Alliance, Gola, GM Vauxhall Conference.
Previous Name: Barnet Alston F.C.

Club colours: Amber shirts with black stripes, black shorts, black socks.
Change colours: All blue.

Reserves League: Springheath Print Capital League.

LONGEST LEAGUE RUNS

of undefeated matches:	12 (1992-93)	of league matches w/out a win:	6 (1993)
of undefeated home matches:	16 (1992-93)	of undefeated away matches:	5 (1992-93)
without home win:	2 (1993)	without an away win:	9 (1991-92)
of league wins:	5 (1993)	of home wins:	8 (1991)
of league defeats:	3 (1992, 1993)	of away wins:	2 (1991, 3 TIMES 1993)

THE MANAGER
John Still . . . . appointed in June 1997.

PREVIOUS CLUBS
As a Manager . . . . None.
As an Asst.Man/Coach . . . . Lincoln City.
As a player . . . . Leyton Orient.

HONOURS
As a Manager . . . . None.
As a Player . . . . None.

BARNET

PLAYERS NAME Honours	Ht	Wt	Birthdate	Birthplace Transfers	Contract Date	Clubs	APPEARANCES League	L/Cup	FA Cup	Other	GOALS Lge	L/C	FAC	Oth
G O A L K E E P E R														
Harrison Lee D	6.2	11	9/12/71	Billericay	7/3/90	Charlton Athletic								
				Loan	11/18/91	Fulham				1				
				Loan	3/24/92	Gillingham	2							
				Loan	12/18/92	Fulham				1				
				Free	7/15/93	Fulham	11+1		1	5				
					1/13/97	Barnet	67	4	1	2				
D E F E N C E														
Basham Michael	5.11	11	9/27/73	Barking	7/3/92	West Ham United								
				Loan	11/18/93	Colchester United	1							
				Free	3/24/94	Swansea City	18		5	8				
				Free	12/18/95	Peterborough United	17+2	1	0+1		1			
				Free	8/5/97	Barnet	19+1			2	1			
Doolan John	6.1	12.1	5/7/74	Liverpool	6/1/92	Everton								
				Free	9/2/94	Mansfield Town	128+3	8	7	3+1	10	1	2	1
				£60000	1/13/98	Barnet	17							
Goodhind Warren E	5.11	11.2	8/16/77	South Africa	7/3/96	Barnet	23+15	3+2	1	2	1			1
Harle Michael J L	5.11	11.12	10/31/72	Lewisham	7/1/89	Gillingham	1+1				1			
					8/1/92	Sittingbourne								
				£50000	8/1/93	Millwall	12+8	1+1	1		1			
				Loan	12/8/95	Bury								
					7/16/97	Barnet	42+1	3	1	2	2			
Heald Greg J	6.1	12.8	9/26/71	London		Enfield								
				£20000	7/8/94	Peterborough United	101+4	8	8+1	8	6			
					8/8/97	Barnet	42	4	1	2	3	1		1
Manuel Billy Div.3'92	5.8	12	6/28/69	Hackney	7/28/87	Tottenham Hotspur								
					2/10/89	Gillingham	74+13	2	3	5	5			
				£60000	6/14/91	Brentford	83+11	7+1	4	8+2	1	1		
				Free	9/16/94	Peterborough United								
				Free	10/28/94	Cambridge United	10		2					
				Free	2/28/95	Peterborough United	27	4	1+1	2	2	3		
				Free	1/26/96	Gillingham	9+12		1	1				
				Free	7/18/97	Barnet	10+7	2+1	1	0+2				
Sawyers Robert	5.10	11.3	11/20/78	Dudley	5/1/98	Barnet	1							
Stockley Sam	6	12	9/5/77	Tiverton	9/6/96	Southampton								
				Free	12/31/96	Barnet	61+1	4	1	2				
Wilson Paul R GMVC'91.	5.9	10.11	9/26/64	Forest Gate		Billericay Town								
						Barking								
					3/1/88	Barnet	229+16	11+1	23+1	9+2	25	1		
M I D F I E L D														
Adams Kieran	5.11	11.6	10/20/77	St.Ives	8/1/94	Barnet	9+11	0+1			1			
Coggon Simon J					3/27/97	Barnet (T)	1							
Currie Darren	5.9	11.07	11/29/74	Hampstead	7/2/93	West Ham United								
				Loan	9/5/94	Shrewsbury Town	10+2				2			
				Loan	2/3/95	Shrewsbury Town	5							
				£70000	2/7/96	Shrewsbury Town	46+20	2+1	3		8	1		
				Free	3/26/98	Plymouth Argyle	5+2							
				Free	7/1/98	Barnet								
Mustafa Tarkan	5.10	11.7	8/28/73	London	8/5/97	Barnet	2+9	0+1						
Onwere Udo	6	11.7	11/9/71	Hammersmith	7/11/90	Fulham	66+19	4+2	1+1	9	7			
				Free	8/12/94	Lincoln City	40+3	5	1	4	4			1
				Free	8/1/96	Dover Athletic								
				Free	9/14/96	Blackpool	5+4	1	1					
				Free	8/5/97	Barnet	11+6	2+1	0+1					
Searle Stevie	5.10	11.2	3/7/77	Lambeth	8/1/97	Barnet	26+4		1	2	2			
Simpson Phillip	5.8	11.12	10/19/69	Lambeth		Stevenage Borough								
					8/2/96	Barnet	36+4	3		1+1	4			
F O R W A R D														
Brady Matthew	6	10.4	10/27/77	London	5/1/95	Barnet	2+9							
Charlery Ken	6.1	13.03	11/28/64	Stepney		Fisher Athletic			1					
						Beckton								
						Basildon								
				£35000	3/1/89	Maidstone	41+18	1+3	+3	5+4	11	1		
				£20000	3/28/91	Peterborough United	45+6	10	3	11	19	5	1	7
				£350000	10/16/92	Watford	45+3	3	1	+1	13			
				£150000	12/16/93	Peterborough United	70	2	2+1	2	24		3	1
				£350000	7/4/95	Birmingham City								
				Loan	2/9/96	Peterborough United	54+1	4	6	1	12	1	6	
					3/25/97	Stockport County	9+1							
					8/7/97	Barnet	18+14	4	1	1+1	6		1	
Devine Sean	6	13	9/6/72	Lewisham		Famagusta								
				£10000	9/1/95	Barnet	102+4	8	5	3	46	3	5	
De Vito Claudio	6.1	12.2	7/21/78	Peterborough		Northampton T. (T)								
				Free	3/26/98	Barnet	0+1							
McGleish Scott	5.10	11.7	2/10/74	Barnet		Edgware Town								
				Free	5/24/94	Charlton Athletic	0+6							
				Loan	3/10/95	Leyton Orient	4+2			1	1			1
				Free	7/4/95	Peterborough Utd	3+10	0+1	0+1	3+1				2
				Loan	2/23/96	Colchester United	10+5			2	6			
				Loan	9/2/96	Cambridge United	10	1			7			
				£50000	11/22/96	Leyton Orient	36	3	1	1	7	1		
				£70000	10/1/97	Barnet	37		1	2+1	13			
Samuels Dean	6.2	11.1	3/29/73	Hackney		Boreham Wood								
					12/24/97	Barnet	12+25	0+3	0+1	0+1	4			

Underhill Stadium
Barnet Lane, Herts EN5 2BE

Capacity. 3,887

First game . . . . v Crystal Palace, 7.9.1907 (London Lge).

ATTENDANCES
Highest. . . . . 11,026 v Wycombe W., FA Amateur Cup
. . . . 4th Round, 1951-52.
Lowest. . . . . 248 v Milton Keynes City,Southern League
. . . . First Division North, 1975-76.

HOW TO GET TO THE GROUND

From North, South, East and West
Use M1 then M25, turn off at junction 23. Follow signs for Barnet (A100). Ground is located at the foot of Barnet Hill, behind the Old Red Lion Public House.

Car Parking
Surrounding roads under police control or HIgh Barnet underground station car park.

Nearest Railway Station
High Barnet (LT Northern Line) New Barnet (British Rail).

USEFUL TELEPHONE NUMBERS

Club switchboard 0181 441 6932
Club fax number. 0181 447 0655
Club shop 0181 440 0725
Ticket Office. 0181 449 6325

Marketing Department 0181 441 6932
Clubcall 0891 12 15 44*
*Calls cost 50p per minute at all times.
Call costings correct at time of going to press.

MATCHDAY PROGRAMME

Programme Editor . . . . .D Bracegirdle.

Number of pages. 32

Price £1.50

Subscriptions . . . . .Apply to club

Local Newspapers
Barnet & Finchley Press, Barnet Advertiser, Barnet Independent, Barnet Borough Times, ...Hendon & Finchley Times.

Local Radio Stations
. . . . . . .LBC, Capital, Chiltern, Three Counties.

MATCHDAY TICKET PRICES

Main Stand . . . . £12 (Concessions £6)

Family Stand £10 (£5)

East Terrace £7 (£3.50)

North & West Terrace . . . . £5 (Free)

South Stand £8

BRENTFORD
(The Bees)
NATIONWIDE LEAGUE DIVISION 3
SPONSORED BY: GMB

Unfortunately Brentford were unable to supply us with a team photograph for this year's publication

BRENTFORD
FORMED IN 1889
TURNED PROFESSIONAL IN 1899
LTD COMPANY IN 1901

PRESIDENT: W Wheatley
CHAIRMAN: Ron Noades

SECRETARY
Polly Kates
MARKETING MANAGER
Peter Gilham

MANAGER: Ron Noades
ASSISTANT MANAGER: Kevin Lock

YOUTH TEAM MANAGER
Bob Booker
PHYSIOTHERAPIST
Roy Johnson

STATISTICIAN FOR THE DIRECTORY
Frank Coumbe

After failing to win promotion to Division One in 1996/97, having been in a strong position all season, the Bees' fans were entitled to see another promotion push in 1997/98. What they got, however, was a season of struggle that culminated with relegation after a last day defeat at Bristol Rovers.

Manager David Webb spent the summer with his colleagues negotiating to buy the club. This he achieved a week before the season commenced but, in the meantime, he hadn't been negotiating with out of contract players and Paul Smith, Barry Ashby and Brian Statham moved to Gillingham for tribunal determined fees and Carl Asaba was sold to Reading. The Bees started the campaign with a very light weight side and were well beaten by Millwall.

Before the next match Webb appointed Eddie May and Clive Walker as the new management team. Under this combination Brentford secured some good home points but were continually beaten on their travels. Following defeat at home to Carlisle in November, which saw the Bees slip into the bottom four, May and Walker were sacked by Webb. The fans had every sympathy for Eddie May. Webb had blocked a number of potential signings he'd wanted to make and had never given him a fair chance.

Micky Adams was immediately installed as new manager and his first game, a 4-1 home defeat to Bristol City, saw Brentford fall to bottom of the division. He adopted a more defensive formation as he attempted to stem the number of goals conceded by the team.

The Bees' fans, disappointed at the Way their club was being pulled apart, set up an 'Independent Supporters Association' whose main aim was to remove David Webb from the club by peaceful demonstrations. They were true to their word. Regular chants of "we want Webby out" were sung at matches but there wasn't a hint of trouble. Webb ignored the wishes of the fans, in fact he didn't even turn up for home matches.

The Bees finally got out of the bottom four after a win at Carlisle in March but were sucked back a month later. A draw against Luton in the penultimate game again pulled them out before that last day reverse relegated them.

In the League Cup Shrewsbury were beaten 6-4 on aggregate before Southampton knocked the Bees out (1-5). The FA Cup saw defeat on penalties to Colchester while there was instant dismissal by Luton in the AWS (1-2).

In a season when a record 38 players were used few came out with much credit. Robert Taylor had a superb first two thirds of the season scoring 16 goals, most of them spectacular, but only managed two more in the rest of the campaign while versatile Carl Hutchings improved as the season wore on to such an extent that he was clearly the best player in the team. Old 'war-horse' Glenn Cockerill and Graeme Hogg also deserve a mention for their performances and attitude.

As the season closed there were very strong rumours that Ron Noades was going to buy Webb out. Is this a good or bad move for Brentford? I don't know but let's hope things get better.   Frank Coumbe.

BRENTFORD

Division 2		:21st		FA CUP: 1st Round		LC CUP: 2nd Round		AWS: Southern Round 2	

M	DATE	COMP.	VEN	OPPONENTS	RESULT	H/T	LP	GOAL SCORERS/GOAL TIMES	ATT.
1	A 09	FL	A	Millwall	L 0-3	0-1	22		(8951)
2	12	CC 1/1	H	**Shrewsbury Town**	D 1-1	0-0		Denys 65	2040
3	15	FL	H	Chesterfield	D 0-0	0-0	22		4000
4	23	FL	A	Watford	L 1-3	0-2	23	Taylor 76 (pen)	(10125)
5	26	CC 1/2	A	**Shrewsbury Town**	W 5-3	3-0		Rapley 15, 80, Taylor 30, 75, Bent 38	(2136)
6	30	FL	H	Grimsby Town	W 3-1	2-0	17	Rapley 12, Taylor 25, 71	3875
7	S 02	FL	H	Gillingham	W 2-0	0-0	12	Bent 73, Taylor 79 (pen)	4903
8	05	FL	A	Southend United	L 1-3	1-3	12	Rapley 2	(3458)
9	13	FL	A	Plymouth Argyle	D 0-0	0-0	15		(4394)
10	17	CC 2/1	A	**Southampton**	L 1-3	0-1		Taylor 65	(8004)
11	19	FL	H	Wycombe Wanderers	D 1-1	1-1	15	Taylor 31	3695
12	27	FL	H	Burnley	W 2-1	1-0	13	Hutchings 2, Rapley 89	4548
13	30	CC 2/2	H	**Southampton**	L 0-2	0-2			3957
14	O 04	FL	A	Preston North End	L 1-2	1-0	16	Bent 35	(8804)
15	11	FL	A	York City	L 1-3	0-1	18	Taylor 75	(2831)
16	18	FL	H	Walsall	W 3-0	0-0	16	Taylor 49, Denys 56, Bent 90	4874
17	21	FL	H	Bristol Rovers	L 2-3	1-2	18	Bent 7, Rapley 46	3967
18	25	FL	A	Luton Town	L 0-2	0-1	19		(5972)
19	N 01	FL	A	Bournemouth	D 0-0	0-0	19		(4772)
20	04	FL	H	Carlisle United	L 0-1	0-1	22		3424
21	08	FL	H	Bristol City	L 1-4	0-2	24	Reina 84	6183
22	15	FAC 1	H	**Colchester United**	D 2-2	1-1		Taylor 9, 55	2899
23	18	FL	A	Northampton Town	L 0-4	0-4	24		(5277)
24	22	FL	A	Oldham Athletic	D 1-1	0-0	22	Scott 80	(5012)
25	25	FAC 1R	A	**Colchester United**	D 0-0*	0-0		(Colchester won 4-2 on pens.	(3613)
26	29	FL	H	Wrexham	D 1-1	0-0	23	Aspinall 80	3748
27	D 02	FL	A	Fulham	D 1-1	1-0	23	Gleghorn 35	(10767)
28	13	FL	H	Blackpool	W 3-1	1-1	21	Taylor 32, Townley 62, 78	3725
29	20	FL	A	Wigan Athletic	L 0-4	0-2	21		(3301)
30	26	FL	H	Southend United	D 1-1	1-0	21	Taylor 42	5341
31	29	FL	A	Gillingham	L 1-3	0-2	22	Taylor 81	(5908)
32	J 03	FL	A	Chesterfield	D 0-0	0-0	22		(4049)
33	10	FL	H	Millwall	W 2-1	1-1	21	Taylor 44, Aspinall 59	5529
34	13	AWS S2	A	**Luton Town**	L 1-2	0-0		Townley 90	(3106)
35	17	FL	A	Grimsby Town	L 0-4	0-2	21		(4624)
36	24	FL	H	Watford	L 1-2	1-1	23	Rapley 21	6969
37	31	FL	H	Plymouth Argyle	W 3-1	0-1	22	Bates 62, Scott 66, Hogg 88	4783
38	F 06	FL	A	Wycombe Wanderers	D 0-0	0-0	22		(6328)
39	14	FL	H	Preston North End	D 0-0	0-0	22		4952
40	21	FL	A	Burnley	D 1-1	0-0	22	Taylor 49	(10097)
41	24	FL	A	Walsall	D 0-0	0-0	24		(3166)
42	28	FL	H	York City	L 1-2	0-0	24	McGhee 75	4490
43	M 03	FL	A	Bristol City	D 2-2	1-2	22	Bryan 44, Rapley 79	(10398)
44	07	FL	H	Bournemouth	W 3-2	2-2	22	Hutchings 3, Bryan 44, Rapley 81	4973
45	14	FL	A	Carlisle United	W 2-1	0-1	20	Hogg 62, Scott 72	(6021)
46	21	FL	H	Northampton Town	D 0-0	0-0	20		5746
47	28	FL	H	Oldham Athletic	W 2-1	2-0	20	Scott 38, Taylor 44	4547
48	A 04	FL	A	Wrexham	D 2-2	1-0	20	Rapley 9, Hutchings 68	(4132)
49	11	FL	H	Fulham	L 0-2	0-1	21		10510
50	13	FL	A	Blackpool	W 2-1	2-0	21	Hutchings 3, Aspinall 13 (pen)	(3926)
51	18	FL	H	Wigan Athletic	L 0-2	0-0	21		4480
52	25	FL	H	Luton Town	D 2-2	1-1	20	Scott 22, Hutchings 80	6598
53	M 02	FL	A	Bristol Rovers	L 1-2	0-0	21	Rapley 79	(9043)

Best Home League Attendance: 10510 V Fulham	**Smallest :3424 V Carlisle United**	**Average :5037**

Goal Scorers:

FL	(50)	Taylor 13, Rapley 9, Hutchings 5, Scott 5, Bent 4, Aspinall 3, Bryan 2, Hogg 2, Townley 2, Bates 1, Denys 1, Gleghorn 1, McGhee 1, Reina 1
CC	(7)	Taylor 3, Rapley 2, Bent 1, Denys 1
FAC	(2)	Taylor 2
AWS	(1)	Townley 1

*AET

514

(D) Anderson	(F) Aspinall	(M) Barrowcliff	(D) Bates	(M) Benstead	(F) Bent	(M) Bryan	(M) Canham	(M) Cockerill	(M) Cullip	(G) Dearden	(F) Dennis	(M) Denys	(D) Gleghorn	(M) Hall	(F) Hogg	(D) Hurdle	(M) Hutchings	(F) McGhee	(F) McPherson	(M) Oatway	(F) Rapley	(F) Reina	(F) Scott	(F) Taylor	(M) Thompson	(M) Townley	(D) Watson	(M) Wormull		
X		X	X	S	X		S			X		S1				X	X	X						X				X	R.J. Harris	1
X		X	X	S		S1				X		X				X	X	X			S2			X				X	G Singh	2
X		X	X	S	X		X			X		X				X	X				S1			X				X	C R Wilkes	3
X		X	X	S	X		X			X		X				X	X		X		S1			X				S	S G Bennett	4
X		X	X	S	X		X			X		X				X	X				X			X				S2	A Bates	5
X		X	X	S	X		X			X		X				X	X			X		X		X				S	B Coddington	6
X		X	X	S	X		X			X		X				X	X			X		X		X				S	M E Pierce	7
X		X	X	S	X		X			X		X				X	X			X		X		X				S1	B Knight	8
X		X	X	S	X	S1				X		X				X	X			X		X		X					M J Brandwood	9
X	X	X	X	S	X	S	X			X		X				X	X			X		X		X					G S Willard	10
X		X	X	S	X		S			X		X				X	X	S1			X			X		X			M C Bailey	11
X		X	X	S	X		S2			X		X				X	X	S1			X			X		X			R Styles	12
X		X	X	S	X		S2			X		X				X	X	X			X	S1		X		X			P Taylor	13
X		X	X	S	X					X			X			X	X	S1		X	X	S2		X		X			M J Jones	14
X		X	X	X	X					X		S2	X			X	X	S1		X	X	S1		S					P R Richards	15
X		X	X	S	X	S2				X		X				X	X			X	X			X		X			A P D'Urso	16
X		X	X	S	X	S2				X		X				X	X	S1		X	X			X		X			M R Halsey	17
X		X	X	S	X		S1			X		X				X	X			X	X			X		S			J A Kirkby	18
X		X	X	S	X		S			X			X			S	X	X		X	X			X		X			B Coddington	19
X		X	X	S	X		S2			S		S1				X	X	X			X	X		X		X			P Rejer	20
X		X	X	X				X		X		S1				X	X	X			X			X		X		S	P S Danson	21
		X			X	S	S2	X		X		S				X	X	X			X	S1	X	X		X			B Knight	22
	S1	X			X		X	X		X		S3	X			X	X	X			X	S2	X	X		X			M E Pierce	23
X	S3	X				X		X		X			X			X	X		S1	X	S2	X		X		X			M S Pike	24
X		X	S		X	X		X		X		X				S2	X	X	X	X	S	X		X		X			B Knight	25
X	S2	X		X1			X2			X		X				X	S3	X	X3	S1		X		X				X	F G Stretton	26
X	X			S1	S2		X1			X		X				X	X	X	X			X2		X		X			S J Baines	27
X	S2			S1	S3					X		X				X	X	X	X2			X	X1		X		X	X3	A R Hall	28
X	S2			S1			X1			X		X				X	X3	X2	X		S3			X		X		X	J P Robinson	29
X	S1			S2						X		X				X	X3	X			X2	X		X	X1		X		C J Foy	30
X	X1	X		S2		S3		X	S1		X2					X				X3		X	X	X	X		X		R Styles	31
X		X		S		X		X		X		X		X			X			S		X	X	X	X		X		G Laws	32
X					X			X	S	X2	X		X1				X			S2		X	X	X	X		X	S1	A N Butler	33
X								X	S3	X	X						X			X		X	X	X	X		X			34
X					X1			X		S2	X						X	S3		X	S1		X2	X		X3	X	X	A Bates	35
X					S	X				S			X		X	X	S			X	X		X	X				X	M Fletcher	36
		X			X2	X			S2				X		X	X	S1		X3		X	X						X1	M C Bailey	37
		X			S1	X			S				X		X	X	X	X	X1	S2		X2	X					X	S G Bennett	38
X		X		S	X								X		X	X2	X1		S1		X	X						X	P Rejer	39
X		X			S								X		X	X	S1		X	X1	X							X	M J Jones	40
X		X			S		X	X					X		X	X			S1	X	X1	X						X	M D Messias	41
X		X			S1	S3	X3	X	X				X		X	X			X1	X2	X	S2						X	C R Wilkes	42
X		X			X1	S3	X3	X	X				X		X	X			X2	S2	X		S1					X	M J Brandwood	43
X		X			X1	S2	X	X					X	X2			X2			S3	X	S1		X3				X	B Coddington	44
X		X			S2	X3	X	X					X	X1		X2	S3		S1	X	X							X	A R Leake	45
X		X			S2	X1	X	X					X	X					X	X3	S1	X2						X	A G Wiley	46
		X			X	X1	X	X					X	X	S1				X2	X3			S2		X			X	B Knight	47
		X			X	X1	X	X					X	X	X				X2	X3			S2		X			X	C J Foy	48
X		X			S3	S2	X3	X	X				X2		X	X	S1			X	X	X1						X	D Orr	49
X		X			S1		X	X					X		X	X			S2	X	X1		X					X	T Jones	50
X		X			S1		X1	X	S2				X		X	X	S			X		X		X				X	M S Pike	51
X1		X				X3	X	X	S3				X		X	X			S1	S2	X		X2		X			X	M R Halsey	52
X		X3				X2	X	X	S1				X		X	X			S2	S3	X	X						X	D Pugh	53
17	24	5	40	1	19	2	10	23	13	35		12	11	6	17	17	43	19	7	30	23	2	24	39	6	15	25	3	FL Appearances	
	6			5	9	11			5	7							10	2	3	14	4	2	1	2	1			2	FL Sub Appearances	
4		3	4		3	2+2			4			4				4	4	2		3+1	0+1		4					1+1	CC Appearances	
	2	2		2	0+1	0+1	2		2							1+1	2	2	1	2	0+1	2		1				1	FAC Appearances	
	1				1			1	0+1	1	1									1			1	1	1			1	AWS Appearances	

Also Played: Adams S1(34). (M) Blaney S(47), S1(48), X(50,52), X2(51), X1(53). (M) Clark S3(34,37,46,48), S2(39), S(40,41). (G) Colgan X(16,17,18,19,20). (G) Fernandes S(22). (M) Goddard-Crawley S1(5,10), S(6,7,8,9). (M) Myall X(19,20), S(21,25). (F) Omigie S2(3). (G) Pollitt X(36,37,38,39,40). (M) Spencer X(1,2).

CLUB RECORDS

BIGGEST VICTORIES
League: 9-0 v Wrexham, Division 3, 15.10.1963.
F.A. Cup: 7-0 v Windsor & Eton (a), 1st Round, 20.11.1982.

BIGGEST DEFEATS
League: 0-7 v Swansea City, Division 3(S), 8.11.1924.
0-7 v Walsall, Division 3, 19.1.1957.
F.A. Cup: 1-7 v Manchester United, 3rd Round, 1927-28.

MOST POINTS
3 points a win: 85, Division 2, 1994-95.
2 points a win: 62, Division 3(S), 1932-33.
62, Division 4, 1962-63.

MOST GOALS SCORED
98, Division 4, 1962-63.

RECORD TRANSFER FEE RECEIVED
£800,000 from Reading for Carl Asaba, August 1997.

RECORD TRANSFER FEE PAID
£275,000 to Chelsea for Joe Allon, November 1992.

BEST PERFORMANCES
League: 5th in Division 1, 1935-36.
F.A. Cup: 6th Round, 1938, 1946, 1949, 1989.
League Cup: 4th Round, 1982-83.

HONOURS
Champions Division 3(S), 1932-33.
Champions Division 2, 1934-35.
Champions Division 4, 1962-63.
Champions Division 3, 1991-92.

LEAGUE CAREER
Founder Members of Division 3, 1920.
Division 3(S) 1921-33, Div 2 1932-33, Div 1 1934-35, Div 2 1946-47, Div 3(S) 1953-54, Div 4 1961-62, Div 3 1962-63, Div 4 1965-66, Div 3 1971-72, Div 4 1972,73, Div 3 1977-78, Div 2 (now Div 1) 1991-92, Div 2 1992-98. Div 3 1998-

INDIVIDUAL CLUB RECORDS

MOST GOALS IN A SEASON
Jack Holliday: 39 goals in 1932-33. (League 38, FA Cup 1).

MOST GOALS IN A MATCH
5. Jack Holliday v Luton Town, Division 3 (S), (a) 28.1.1933 (5-5).
5. Billy Scott v Barnsley, Division 2, (h) 15.12.1934 (8-1).
5. Peter McKennan v Bury, Division 2, (h) 18.2.1949 (8-2).

OLDEST PLAYER
Dai Hopkins, 39 years 7 months 13 days, 26.5.1947.

YOUNGEST PLAYER
Danis Salman, 15 years 8 months 3days, 15.11.1975.

MOST CAPPED PLAYER
Dai Hopkins (Wales) 12.
Billy Scott & Leslie Smith (England) 1.

PREVIOUS MANAGERS

(Since 1945)
Harry Curtis (Sec./Manager) 1926-49; A.H.'Jackie'Gibbons (Sec./Man.) 1949-52; Jim Bain 1952-53; Tommy Lawton (players/manager) 1953; Bill Dodgin (Senior) 1953-57; Malcolm MacDonald 1957-65; Tommy Cavanagh 1965-66; Billy Gray 1966-67; Jimmy Sirrel 1967-69; Frank Blunstone 1969-73; Mike Everitt 1973-75; John Docherty 1975-76; Bill Dodgin (Junior) 1976-80; Fred Callaghan 1980-84; Frank McLintock 1984-87; Steve Perryman 1987-90; Phil Holder 1990-93; Eddie May 1997; Micky Adams 97-98

ADDITIONAL INFORMATION
PREVIOUS NAMES
None.
PREVIOUS LEAGUES
Southern League.
Club colours: Red & white striped shirts, black shorts, black socks with red/white turnover.
Change colours: Blue & yellow shirts, blue shorts.
Reserves League: Springheath Print Capital League.
Youth League: South East Counties.

LONGEST LEAGUE RUNS

of undefeated matches:	16 (1932, 1967)	of league matches w/out a win:	16 (1994)
of undefeated home matches:	24 (1934-35)	of undefeated away matches:	11 (1993)
without home win:	11 (1947)	without an away win:	21 (1965-66)
of league wins:	9 (1932)	of home wins:	21 (1929-30)
of league defeats:	9 (1925,1928)	of away wins:	5 (1956, 1981)

Brentford won all 21 home games in 1929-30, they also played 44 away League games without a draw between 1923-25.

THE MANAGER

RON NOADES . . . . appointed in June 1998.

PREVIOUS CLUBS
As Manager . . . . None.
As Assistant/Coach . . . . None.
As a player . . . . None.

HONOURS
As a Manager . . . . None.
As a Player . . . . None.

BRENTFORD

PLAYERS NAME Honours	Ht	Wt	Birthdate	Birthplace Transfers	Contract Date	Clubs	APPEARANCES League	L/Cup	FA Cup	Other	GOALS Lge	L/C	FAC	Oth
G O A L K E E P E R														
Dearden Kevin	5.11	12.8	3/8/70	Luton	8/5/88	Tottenham Hotspur	0+1	1						
				Loan	3/9/89	Cambridge United	15							
				Loan	8/31/89	Hartlepool United	10							
				Loan	3/23/90	Swindon Town	1							
				Loan	8/24/90	Peterborough United	7							
				Loan	1/10/91	Hull City	3							
				Loan	8/16/91	Rochdale	2							
				Loan	3/19/92	Birmingham City	12							
				Free	9/30/93	Brentford	198	16	12	14				
Pearcey Jason	6.1	13.12	7/23/71	Leamington	7/18/89	Mansfield Town (T)	77	5	2	7				
				£10000	11/15/94	Grimsby Town	49	3	1					
				Free	7/1/98	Brentford								
D E F E N C E														
Anderson Ijah	5.8	10.6	12/30/75	Hackney		Tottenham Hotspur								
					8/2/94	Southend United								
					7/31/95	Brentford	88	10	3+2	4+1	3	1		
Bates Jamie Div.3'92.	6.1	13	2/24/68	Croydon	6/1/87	Brentford	372+20	33+3	17+1	38	17	2	1	1
Boxall Danny J	5.8	10.05	8/24/77	Croydon	8/1/94	Crystal Palace	5+3	1+1						
				Loan	11/21/97	Oldham Athletic	5		1					
				Loan	2/27/98	Oldham Athletic	12							
				Free	7/1/98	Brentford								
Cullip Daniel	6.1	12.7	9/17/76	Bracknell	8/15/96	Fulham	41+9	8	2	1	2			
				£75000	2/20/98	Brentford	13							
Quinn Robert	5.11	11.02	11/8/76	Sidcup	8/1/94	Crystal Palace	18+5	2+1		2+1	1	1		
				£40000	7/1/98	Brentford								
Townley Leon	6.2	13.6	2/16/76	Loughton	7/1/94	Tottenham H. (T)								
				£50000	9/18/97	Brentford	15+1	1	1	1	2		1	
Watson Paul D	5.8	10.1	1/4/75	Hastings	12/8/92	Gillingham	57+5	4	6	5+3	2			
					8/15/96	Fulham	43	3	1	1	3	1		
				£50000	12/12/97	Brentford	25							
M I D F I E L D														
Clark Dean W			3/31/80	Hillingdon		Brentford (T)								
Cockerill Glen	5.1	12.4	8/25/59	Grimsby	11/1/76	Lincoln City	65+6	2	2		10			
				£11000	12/6/79	Swindon Town	23+3	3						
				£40000	8/12/81	Lincoln City	114+1	16	7	1	25	1		
				£125000	3/23/84	Sheffield United	62	6	1		10	1		
				£225000	10/17/85	Southampton	272+15	35+2	20+2	12	32	5	2	
				Free	12/10/93	Leyton Orient	89+1	4	3	10	7	1		
				Free	8/23/96	Fulham	31+8	5+1	1		1			
					11/7/97	Brentford	23		2					
Oatway Anthony	5.7	10.10	11/28/73	Hammersmith	8/4/94	Cardiff City	29+3	2	1+1	3+1		1		
				Free	12/28/95	Torquay United	65+2	3	1		1			
					8/19/97	Brentford	30+3		2					
Thompson Niall	6	12	4/16/74	Birmingham	7/16/92	Crystal Palace (J)								
				Free	11/4/94	Colchester United	5+8	0+1						
						Zulte VV								
				Free	2/27/98	Brentford	6+2							
F O R W A R D														
Aspinall Warren E: Y. AMC'85'97.	5.9	12.8	9/13/67	Wigan	8/31/85	Wigan Athletic (T)	21+12	1	2+3	1+5	10		2	2
				£150000	2/4/86	Everton	0+7	0+1		0+2				
				Loan	2/6/86	Wigan Athletic	18		2		12			2
				£300000	2/19/87	Aston Villa	40+4	4	1+1		14	2		
				£315000	8/26/88	Portsmouth	97+35	8+3	4+5	6+1	21	3	2	2
				Loan	8/27/93	Bournemouth	4+2				1			
				Loan	10/14/93	Swansea City	5			1				
				£20000	12/31/93	Bournemouth	26+1	4	1	1	8			
				Free	3/8/95	Carlisle United	99+8	8	6	10+1	12	3		1
				£50000	11/21/97	Brentford	24			1	3			
Bryan Derek K	5.10	11.5	10/11/74	London		Hampton								
				£50000	8/28/97	Brentford	2+9		0+1		2			
Dennis Kevin	5.11	12	12/14/76	Isington		Arsenal								
					8/15/96	Brentford	11+9	2		1				
Denys Ryan H	5.6	11.2	8/16/78	Brentford	7/1/97	Brentford (T)	10+6	2			1	1		
				Loan	2/27/98	Yeovil Town								
Freeman Darren	5.11	13	8/22/73	Brighton		Horsham								
				Free	1/31/95	Gillingham	4+8		0+1	2				1
				£15000	7/4/96	Fulham	32+1	2		3	9			1
				Free	6/1/98	Brentford								
McGhee David	5.11	11.04	6/19/76	Sussex	7/15/94	Brentford	120+24	9+2	11	6+1	11	1	1	
Rapley Kevin J	5.9	10.8	9/21/77	Reading	3/27/97	Brentford	24+15	3+1	0+1		9	2		
Scott Andrew	6.1	11.5	8/2/72	Epsom		Sutton United								
				£50000	12/1/92	Sheffield United	39+36	5	2+1	3+1	6	2		3
				Loan	10/18/96	Chesterfield	4+1				3			
				Loan	3/21/97	Bury	2+6							
					11/21/97	Brentford	24+2		1		5			
ADDITIONAL CONTRACT PLAYERS														
Owusu Lloyd						Slough Town								
				£25000	7/1/98	Brentford								
Powell Darren						Hampton								
				£15000	7/1/98	Brentford								

GRIFFIN PARK
Braemar Road, Brentford, Middx, TW8 0NT

Capacity 13,800
Covered Standing 1,800
Seating 9,300

First game ....v Plymouth Argyle, 1.9.1904.
First floodlit game ....v Chelsea, 5.10.1954.

ATTENDANCES
Highest ....39,626 v Preston North End, FA Cup 6th Rnd, 5.3.1938.
Lowest ....1,110 v Swindon Town, AMC, 6.1.1987.

OTHER GROUNDS ....None.

HOW TO GET TO THE GROUND

From the North:
Use M1 or A1 then A406 North Circular Road to Chiswick then follow signs for the South Circular Road. In 0.3 miles turn right A315 (S.P. Brentford). In 0.5 miles turn right into Ealing Road for Brentford FC.
From the East:
Use either A406 North Circular Road then as above or South Circular Road A205. Cross Kew Bridge and turn left A315 (S.P. Brentford). In 0.5 miles turn right into Ealing Road for Brentford FC.
From the South:
Use A240/A3/M3 or A316 to junction with South Circular Road. A205. Cross Kew Bridge and turn left A315 (S.P. Brentford). In 0.5 miles turn right into Ealing Road for Brentford FC.
From the West:
Use M4 until junction 1, leave Motorway and follow signs for South Circular Road. In 0.3 miles turn right A315 (S.P. Brentford). In 0.5 miles turn right into Ealing Road for Brentford FC. Alternative use M25/M4.
Car Parking: Street parking available.
Nearest Railway Station: Brentford or South Ealing (Tube), Piccadilly Line.

USEFUL TELEPHONE NUMBERS

Club switchboard 0181 847 2511
Ticket Office 0181 847 2511
Marketing Department 0181 847 2511

Clubcall 0891 12 11 08*
*Calls cost 50p per minute at all times.
Call costings correct at time of going to press.

MATCHDAY PROGRAMME

Programme Editor ....Peter Gilham.

Number of pages ....32.

Price ....£1.50.

Subscriptions ....£55.

Local Newspapers
Brentford & Chiswick Times, Ealing Gazette,
....Middlesex Chronicle, Hounslow Informer, .
.....................................Weekend Recorder.

Local Radio Stations
.....................................Capital Gold, GLR.

MATCHDAY TICKET PRICES

A Block . . . . £10 (Juv/OAP £5)

E Block . . . . £13 (Juv/OAP £10.20)

B Block . . . . £11.50 (Juv/OAP £8.70)

D Block . . . . £14 (Juv/OAP £11.20)

Terraces (Home & away) . . . . £8 (Juv/OAP £5)

Away End Seats . . . . £13 (Juv/OAP £10)

BRIGHTON & HOVE ALBION
(The Seagulls)
NATIONWIDE LEAGUE DIVISION 3
SPONSORED BY: DONATELLO

1997/98 - Back Row L-R: John Jackson (youth dev. officer), Robbie reinelt, Ross McNally, Peter Smith, Mark Morris, John Humphrey, Stuart Tuck, Malcolm Stuart (physio). **Middle Row:** Kerry Mayo, Craig Maskell, James Rowlands, Mark Ormerod, Stuart Storer, Ross Johnson, Nicky Rust, derek Allan, denny Mundee, Paul Armstrong, **Front Row.** Jack Riddell (kit man), Gary Hobson, Ian Baird, Paul McDonald, Steve Gritt (manager), Jeff Minton, Eric Saul, John Westcott, Jeff Wood (asst. manager).

BRIGHTON & HOVE ALBION
FORMED IN 1900
TURNED PROFESSIONAL IN 1901
LTD COMPANY IN 1904

CHAIRMAN: RKnight
DIRECTORS
R Foulkner, M Perry, R Pinnock
Sir John Smith

GENERAL MANAGER: Nick Rowe
SECRETARY: Derek Allan

MANAGER: Brian Horton
ASSISTANT MANAGER: Jeff Wood

YOUTH TEAM MANAGER
Dean Wilkins
DIRECTOR OF YOUTH: Martin Hinshelwood
PHYSIOTHERAPIST
Malcolm Stuart

STATISTICIAN FOR THE DIRECTORY
James Millen

For the second consecutive season Brighton finished 91st in the Football League and once again it was the off the field problems that dominated the season. Even before the season had got underway the club were rocked with the threat of expulsion from the League after a delay in paying a £500,000 bond. This was a guarantee to safeguard the club's future whilst they were playing at Gillingham. Fortunately, the club survived a vote at an E.G.M. of the Football League to throw them out. However, when the season began the club was still in turmoil with Bill Archer still stalling over the signing of the change of ownership of the club and it wasn't until early September that Dick Knight finally became chairman.

The club's problems were made all the worse by having to play home matches at Gillingham, therefore it was not unsurprising that it was nine games before Brighton won their first game, at home to Rochdale. This was, however, to be only one of six wins all season. A number of all time lows were suffered by the club; including their smallest ever league gate - 1,025 against Barnet, fewest number of wins in a season and managing to go twelve home games without a win. Manager Steve Gritt wasn't helped by having to off-load his top wage earners at the end of November to keep the club's running costs down.

The cup competitions failed to provide any respite either; a 3-1 defeat on aggregate by Leyton Orient in the Coca-Cola Cup, was followed by Hereford gaining some small revenge for the loss of their league status with a 2-1 win in the First Round of the FA Cup. Whilst Walsall ended their AWS aspirations by thumping them 5-0.

The most incredible game of the season was the Boxing Day clash with Colchester. At half-time Brighton looked doomed being 3-0 down, but they mounted a second half fightback to grab an amazing 4-4 draw which included a hat-trick from on-loan Paul Emblem.

A second Fans United match was held, this time against the club suffering just as many troubles - Doncaster Rovers. The match was titled the 'Love-in', but the game failed to live up to expectations and Brighton were unable to repeat last season's success and were forced to settle for a goalless draw.

Shortly afterwards, Steve Gritt was dismissed as manager and was replaced by former club skipper Brian Horton. The team's performances improved enough to ensure that they weren't involved in another end of season relegation dogfight.

Brighton made two unsuccessful attempts to move away from Gillingham. Initially to Millwall and then to Woking, both were doomed to failure and the club and fans were stuck with the trip to Gillingham for home games. The club's directors instead turned their attention to obtaining a temporary home within the Brighton area. The athletics stadium at Withdean was the club's favoured site, however their application to play here met with strong opposition from the local residents.

The supporters organised a massive 'Bring Home The Albion' campaign with the aid of banners, posters and ribbons which were displayed all round the county of Sussex, a move which was heavily backed by the local newspaper. The fans also began an appeal for a People's Player, a number of events were organised including a sponsored walk along the seafront in Brighton & Hove.

Finally, in early June the club and its supporters had something to celebrate after the council gave the club planning permission to Play at Withdean Stadium for the next three years, whilst a permanent site is found.

James Millen.

BRIGHTON & H.A.

Division 3	:23th			FA CUP: 1st Round			LC CUP: 1st Round	

M	DATE	COMP.	VEN	OPPONENTS	RESULT	H/T	LP	GOAL SCORERS/GOAL TIMES	ATT.
1	A 09	FL	A	Swansea City	L 0-1	0-0	20		(6800)
2	12	CC 1/1	H	Leyton Orient	D 1-1	0-1		Thompson-Minton 77 (pen)	1073
3	15	FL	H	Macclesfield Town	D 1-1	0-1	19	McDonald 63	2336
4	22	FL	A	Scarborough	L 1-2	1-1	19	Mayo 25	(2505)
5	26	CC 1/2	A	Leyton Orient	L 1-3	1-1		Maskell 23	(3690)
6	30	FL	H	Leyton Orient	L 0-1	0-0	22		2285
7	S 03	FL	H	Peterborough United	D 2-2	1-1	22	Mayo 14, Maskell 55	1215
8	08	FL	A	Colchester United	L 1-3	0-1	22	Baird 47	(3081)
9	13	FL	H	Darlington	D 0-0	0-0	22		1803
10	20	FL	A	Torquay United	L 0-3	0-2	23		(2110)
11	27	FL	H	Rochdale	W 2-1	1-1	22	Morris 16, Tuck 73	1544
12	O 04	FL	A	Doncaster Rovers	W 3-1	1-0	21	Allan 38, Maskell 66, Pemberton 85 (OG)	(2351)
13	11	FL	A	Chester City	L 0-2	0-1	21		(2402)
14	18	FL	H	Exeter City	L 1-3	0-1	22	Reinelt 79	2210
15	22	FL	H	Lincoln City	L 0-1	0-0	23		1036
16	25	FL	A	Hull City	D 0-0	0-0	23		(5686)
17	N 01	FL	A	Hartlepool United	D 0-0	0-0	23		(2561)
18	05	FL	H	Barnet	L 0-3	0-1	23		1025
19	08	FL	H	Rotherham United	L 1-2	0-1	23	Storer 86	1950
20	15	FAC 1	A	Hereford United	L 1-2	0-0		Storer 61	(5787)
21	18	FL	A	Cambridge United	D 1-1	0-1	23	Emblen 73	(2370)
22	22	FL	H	Cardiff City	L 0-1	0-1	23		2086
23	29	FL	A	Scunthorpe United	W 2-0	0-0	23	Storer 47, Ryan 68	(3187)
24	D 03	FL	H	Notts County	L 0-1	0-1	23		1279
25	13	FL	A	Mansfield Town	D 1-1	0-1	23	Thompson-Minton 83	(2197)
26	20	FL	H	Shrewsbury Town	D 0-0	0-0	23		1917
27	26	FL	H	Colchester United	D 4-4	0-3	23	Emblen 47, 62, 67, Thompson-Minton 87 (pen)	2647
28	28	FL	A	Peterborough United	W 2-1	1-0	23	Thompson-Minton 21, Reinelt 54	(8221)
29	J 10	FL	A	Swansea City	L 0-1	0-1	23		2997
30	17	FL	A	Leyton Orient	L 1-3	0-0	23	Reinelt 53	(6591)
31	20	AWS S2	A	Walsall	L 0-5	0-0			
32	24	FL	H	Scarborough	D 1-1	1-0	23	Smith 31	1988
33	27	FL	A	Macclesfield Town	L 0-1	0-0	23		(2024)
34	31	FL	A	Darlington	L 0-1	0-0	23		(2487)
35	F 06	FL	H	Torquay United	L 1-4	1-1	23	Smith 24	2083
36	14	FL	H	Doncaster Rovers	D 0-0	0-0	23		6339
37	21	FL	A	Rochdale	L 0-2	0-1	23		(1865)
38	24	FL	A	Exeter City	L 1-2	1-1	23	Ansah 33	(2754)
39	28	FL	H	Chester City	W 3-2	2-1	23	Mayo 30, 60, Ansah 42	2510
40	M 03	FL	A	Rotherham United	D 0-0	0-0	23		(3724)
41	07	FL	H	Hartlepool United	D 0-0	0-0	23		2811
42	14	FL	A	Barnet	L 0-2	0-1	23		(2845)
43	21	FL	H	Cambridge United	L 0-2	0-2	23		2746
44	28	FL	A	Cardiff City	D 0-0	0-0	23		(3509)
45	A 04	FL	H	Scunthorpe United	W 2-1	1-0	23	Thompson-Minton 29, 87 (pen)	2141
46	11	FL	A	Notts County	D 2-2	1-0	23	Mayo 20, 70	(5344)
47	13	FL	H	Mansfield Town	D 1-1	1-0	23	Reinelt 33	2704
48	18	FL	A	Shrewsbury Town	L 1-2	1-0	23	Thompson-Minton 29	(2728)
49	25	FL	H	Hull City	D 2-2	1-0	23	Ansah 32, Barker 54	3888
50	M 02	FL	A	Lincoln City	L 1-2	0-0	23	Barker 90	(9890)

Best Home League Attendance: 6339 V Doncaster Rovers		Smallest :1025 V Barnet		Average :2328

Goal Scorers:

FL	(38)	Mayo 6, Thompson-Minton 6, Emblen 4, Reinelt 4, Ansah 3, Barker 2, Maskell 2, Smith 2, Storer 2, Allan 1, Baird 1, McDonald 1, Morris 1, Ryan 1, Tuck 1, Opponents 1
CC	(2)	Maskell 1, Thompson-Minton 1
FAC	(1)	Storer 1
AWS	(0)	

1997-98

	(D) Allan	(M) Ansah	(M) Armstrong	(M) Atkinson	(M) Baird	(M) Barker	(M) Barnes	(M) Emblen	(F) Gislason	(M) Hilton	(D) Hobson	(D) Humphreys	(F) Linger	(F) Mahoney-Johnson	(F) Maskell	(M) Mayo	(F) McDonald	(D) Morris	(G) Ormerod	(M) Reinelt	(G) Rust	(M) Saul	(D) Smith	(F) Storer	(F) Thomas	(M) Thompson-Minton	(D) Tuck	(M) Westcott	(M) Yorke-Johnson		
	S	S									X	X			X	X	X		X	X			X					S1		A G Wiley	1
		S									X	X			X	X	X	X	X	S			X	X				S1		B Knight	2
	S		S2								X	X			X	X	X	X	X	X			X					S1		P Taylor	3
	S2	S									X	X			X	X	X		X	X			X	X				S1		A N Butler	4
											X	X			X	X	X		X	X		S1	X		X			S2	X	P S Danson	5
	S			X							X	X			X	X	X		X	S1			X		X			S2	X	M C Bailey	6
		S2		X							X	X			X	X			X	X		S1	X	X				S	X	M R Halsey	7
	S	X1		X							X				X2	X	S1	X	X	X			X	X				S2	X	J A Kirkby	8
	X		X									S			X	X	S2	X	X	X			X	X			X	S1	X	D R Crick	9
	X		S2	X											S3	X	X	X	X	X			X	X		S1		X	X	D Orr	10
	X	X	X					X							X	X			X	X	S			S1	X	X	X	X	S	S W Mathieson	11
	X	X	X					X							X	X	S1		X	X	S		S2		X	X	X	X	S	F G Stretton	12
	X		X			X		X							X	X			X	X	S		S1		X	X	X	X	S	M S Pike	13
	X	X	X			X		S	X						X	X			X	X	S1			X	X		X	X	S	S G Bennett	14
	X							S	X		X				X	X			X	X	S			X	X		X	X	X	R J Harris	15
	X							S	X		X				X	X	S		X	X	S			X	X		X	X	X	E Lomas	16
	X	S						X	S1						X	X	S	X	X	X			X				X	X	X	E. K. Wolstenholme	17
	X	S1			X	X		X			X				X	X	S2	X	X	X			X				X	X	X	A N Butler	18
	X	S1			X	X		X							X	S2	X	X				S3	X			X	X	X	M Fletcher	19
	X	S1	S			X									X	X	X		X		S	X	X	X	X	X	X	X	S	G R Ashby	20
	X	X	S		X											X			X	X	X	X	X	X	X	X	X	S2	X	W C Burns	21
	X	S1	X		X														X	X	X	X	X	X	X	X	S2	X	A P D'Urso	22
		S			X		S								X		X		X	X	X	X	X	X	X	X	X1		J Leech	23
		S			X		S1								X	X	X1		X	X	X	X	X	X	X	X		S G Bennett	24
		S	X		X		X								X				X	X	S1	X	X	X	X	X2		X1	M L Dean	25
		S		X	X		X		X					X2					X	S2	X	X1	X	X	X	S1		R D Furnandiz	26
		S		X	X		X		X					X				X	S	X	X	X	X	X1	X		M D Haxby	27
	S3			X	X		X		X					X				S1	X	X	X1	X	X	X2	X		A R Hall	28
		S2	S1		X	X		X		X1				X				X	X	X	S	X	X	X2	X		F G Stretton	29
	X		S		X	X		X						X				X	X	X		X	X	X1	S1	X		J P Robinson	30
	X	X	X		X			X						X				X	X	X		X	X	X	S	S	X	S3	(—)	31
	X			X	X	X		X						X				X	S	X		X	X	S	X	S	X	D Orr	32
	X1			X3	X	X			S1		X2			X				X	X	X		X	S2	S3	X	X	E Lomas	33
				X2	X	X			X					X				X	X	X1		X	X	S2	X1	X2	X	B Coddington	34
		S3		X3	X			X		S1				X				X	X	S2		X	X1	X2	X	S J Baines	35
				S1	X		X	X						X				X1	X	X		X	X	S	S	S	X	P Taylor	36
	S1				X		X	X3	X2					X				X1	X	X		X	X	S3	S2	X	P R Richards	37
	X			S	X	X					X			X		X		S	X	X	X	X1	X	X	X	A G Wiley	38
	X	S		S	X	X					X			X		X		S	X	X		X	X	X	X	P S Danson	39
	X	S		S	X	X	X				X			X		X		S	X	X		X2		X	M R Halsey	40
	X1	S2	X		X			X	X	S1				X		X		S	X	X		X2		X	B Knight	41
	S	S1	X		X		X	X	X2					X		X		S2	X	X		X1		X	M C Bailey	42
	S1	X	X		X		X1	X	S					X		X			X2	X		S2		X	C R Wilkes	43
	S2	X	X			X1	X							X		X	S1		X	S	X2	X		X	A Bates	44
	X1	X	X	X		S3	X				X2			X		X			X	X		X	X	S1	A N Butler	45
		X	X	X		X1	X2	X			X			X		X	X	S	X		X	X1		X	D R Crick	46
		X	X	X		X	X	X			X			X		X			X	S	X	X	X	X	B Coddington	47
	S1	X	X	X		X		X			X			X		X	X1		X	X		X	X	X	G Singh	48
	X	X	X	X		X	X2				X			S1		X	S2		X	X1		X	X	S G Bennett	49
	X	X	X1		X			X						X		X	S2		S1	X2	X		X	R Pearson	50
17	7	12	9	9	15	12	14	7	4	30	11	17	3	15	43	7	15	30	25	16	25	33	7	32	19	19	35		FL Appearances	
2	7	8		1			1	3	1	1	1	1	4		7	4	2	4		3	15								FL Sub Appearances	
						2	2		2	2	2	1	2	2		0+1	2		2		0+2	1							CC Appearances	
				1			1	1	1		1	1		1	1	1	1		1	0+1									FAC Appearances	
1	0+1	1		1			1		0+1		1		1	1			1		1	0+1									AWS Appearances	

Also Played: (D) Andrews X(44,50), S2(45), S(47,48,49). (M) McNally S(30), S2(31) S1(34), X(35). (M) Packham S(20). (F) Ryan X(22), S1(23), S(24) S2(25,28). (M) Streeter S1(46,47). (M) Woolsey S2(46), S(47,48), X(49), S3(50).

BRIGHTON & H.A.   RECORDS AND STATISTICS

CLUB RECORDS

BIGGEST VICTORIES
League: 9-1 v Newport, Division 3(S), 18.4.1951.
9-1 v Southend, Division 3, 27.11.1965.
F.A. Cup: 12-0 v Shoreham, 1.10.1932.
10-1 v Wisbech, FA Cup Round 1, 13.11.1965.

BIGGEST DEFEATS
League: 0-9 v Middlesbrough, Division 2, 23.8.1958.
League Cup: 0-8 v Northampton, 4th Round replay, 1.11.1966.

MOST POINTS
3 points a win: 84, Division 3, 1987-88.
2 points a win: 65, Division 3(S), 1955-56 & Division 3, 1971-72.

MOST GOALS SCORED
112, Division 3, 1955-56.

RECORD TRANSFER FEE RECEIVED
£900,000 from Liverpool for Mark Lawrenson, August 1981.

RECORD TRANSFER FEE PAID
£500,000 to Manchester United for Andy Ritchie, October 1980.

BEST PERFORMANCES
League: 13th Division 1, 1981-82.
F.A. Cup: Runners-up 1982-83. **League Cup:** 5th Round 1978-79.

HONOURS
Charity Shield Winners 1910. Champions Division 3(S) 1957-58.
Champions Division 4, 1964-65.

LEAGUE CAREER
Original members of Division 3 1920, Div 3(S) 1921, Div 2 1957-58,
Div 3 1961-62, Div 4 1962-63, Div 3 1964-65, Div 2 1971-72, Div 3
1972-73, Div 2 1976-77, Div 1 1978-79, Div 2 1982-83, Div 3 1986-
87, Div 2 1987-88, Div 3 (now Div 2) 1991-92, Div 3 1996-97.

INDIVIDUAL CLUB RECORDS

MOST GOALS IN A SEASON
Peter Ward: 36 goals in 1976-77 (League 32, FA Cup 1, League
Cup 3)

MOST GOALS IN A MATCH
6. Arthur Attwood v Shoreham, 12-0, FA Cup, 1.10.1932.

OLDEST PLAYER
Jimmy Case, 41 years 165 days, 31.10.95.

YOUNGEST PLAYER
Simon Fox, 16 years 238 days v Fulham, Div 2, 23.4.1994.

MOST CAPPED PLAYER
Steve Penney (Northern Ireland) 17.

PREVIOUS MANAGERS

(Since 1945) Charles Webb 1919-47; Tommy Cook 1947; Don
Welsh 1947-51; Billy Lane 1951-61; George Curtis 1961-63; Archie
Macauley 1963-68; Freddie Goodwin 1968-70; Pat Saward 1970-73;
Brian Clough 1973-74; Peter Taylor 1974-76; Alan Mullery 1976-81;
Mike Bailey 1981-82; Jimmy Melia 1982-83; Chris Cattlin 1983-86;
Alan Mullery 1986-87; Barry Lloyd 1987-93; Liam Brady 1993-95;
Jimmy Case 1995-96. Steve Gritt 1996-98.

ADDITIONAL INFORMATION
PREVIOUS NAMES
Brighton United 1898-1900.
Brighton & Hove Rangers 1900-1901.
PREVIOUS LEAGUES
Southern League.
Club colours: Blue & white striped shirts, blue shorts, white socks.
Change colours: All red.
Reserves League: Avon Insurance Football Combination.
Youth: South Eastern Counties League Division Two.

LONGEST LEAGUE RUNS

of undefeated matches:	16 (1930-31)	of league matches w/out a win:	15 (1947-48, 1972-73)
of undefeated home matches:	27 (1975-76)	of undefeated away matches:	9 (1938)
without home win:	12 (1997-98)	without an away win:	21 (1982-83)
of league wins:	9 (1926)	of home wins:	14 (1955-56. 1975-76)
of league defeats:	12 (1972-73)	of away wins:	4 (1926, 1936 twice)

THE MANAGER

BRIAN HORTON . . . . appointed February 1998.

PREVIOUS CLUBS
As Manager . . . . Hull City, Manchester City, Huddersfield Town.
As Asst.Man/Coach. . . . . Oxford United.
As a player. . . . . Walsall, Hednesford Town, Port Vale, Brighton, Luton Town, Hull City.

HONOURS
As a Manager. . . . . **Hull City:** Promotion to Division 2.
As a Player . . . . **Brighton:** Promotions to 2nd & 1st Divisions. **Luton:** Promotion to 1st Division.

BRIGHTON & H.A.

PLAYERS NAME / Honours	Ht	Wt	Birthdate	Birthplace / Transfers	Contract Date	Clubs	League	L/Cup	FA Cup	Other	Lge	L/C	FAC	Oth
G O A L K E E P E R														
Ormerod Mark	6	11.05	2/5/76	Bournemouth	7/21/94	Brighton & H.A.	51	2						
Walton Mark	6.2	14.7	6/1/69	Merthyr Tydfil	2/21/87	Luton Town								
				£15000	11/5/87	Colchester United	40	3	8	5				
				£75000	8/15/89	Norwich City	22	1	5					
				Loan	8/27/93	Wrexham	6							
				Free	1/27/94	Dundee United								
				Free	3/2/94	Bolton Wanderers	3							
				Free	9/9/94	Wrexham								
					8/9/96	Fulham	41	5		1				
				Loan	2/5/98	Gillingham	1							
				Loan	3/26/98	Norwich City								
				£25000	7/1/98	Brighton & HA								
D E F E N C E														
Allan Derek	6	10.13	12/24/74	Irvine		Aye United	5							
				£70000	3/16/93	Southampton	0+1							
				Free	6/14/96	Brighton & H.A.	55+2	2	1	1	1			
Andrews Benjamin P	6	12.10	11/18/80	Burton	3/26/98	Brighton & H.A. (T)	2+1							
Culverhouse Ian	5.10	11.2	9/22/64	B. Stortford	9/24/82	Tottenham H. (A)	1+1							
				£50000	10/8/85	Norwich City	295+1	23	28	22	1			
				£250000	12/9/94	Swindon Town	95+2	9	10	1				1
				Free	8/1/98	Brighton & H.A.								
Hobson Gary	6.1	12.1	11/12/71	Hull	7/17/91	Hull City	107+6	10	1+1	4				
					3/27/96	Brighton & H.A.	74+4	4	3	1	1			
Smith Peter J	6.1	12.7	7/12/69	Stone		Alma Swanley								
				Free	8/8/94	Brighton & H.A.	114+11	8+2	6	5+1	5		1	
Thomas Glen	6.1	13.3	10/6/67	Hackney	10/9/85	Fulham	246+5	21	8	14+1	6			
				Free	11/4/94	Peterborough Utd	6+2		0+1	2				
				Free	3/23/95	Barnet	22+1	2		1				
				£30000	1/15/96	Gillingham	20+8		1	1				
				Free	7/1/98	Brighton & H.A.								
Tuck Stuart	5.9	10.8	10/1/74	Brighton	7/9/93	Brighton & H.A.	76+15	6	2	4+1	1			
Yorke-Johnson Ross	6	12.4	1/2/76	Brighton	7/22/94	Brighton & H.A.	54+3	1	2	3				
M I D F I E L D														
Armstrong Paul G	5.10	10.3	10/5/78	Dublin	7/11/97	Brighton & H.A. (T)	12+8			1				
Bennett Mickey	5.11	11.11	7/27/69	Camberwell	4/27/87	Charlton Athletic (A)	24+11	4	1	6+1	2			
				£250000	1/9/90	Wimbledon	12+6	1+1	0+1	1+1	2			
				£60000	7/14/92	Brentford	40+6	4+1	1	6+1	4			
				Free	3/24/94	Charlton Athletic	19+5		1		1			
				Free	8/14/96	Millwall	1+1							
				Free	8/14/96	Cardiff City	5+9	2	1+1	0+1	1			
via Cambridge City 12.96 (Free)				Free	12/8/97	Leyton Orient	1+1			1				
Loan Cambridge City 03.98-05.98				Loan	7/1/98	Brighton & H.A.								
Hart Gary						Stansted								
				£1000	7/1/98	Brighton & H.A.								
Mayo Kerry	5.1	11.7	9/21/77	Cuckfield	8/6/96	Brighton & H.A.	65+3	2	1+1	1	6			
Mills Danny	6	11.8	2/13/75	Sidcup	7/1/93	Charlton Athletic (T)				0+2				
				Free	9/29/95	Barnet	10+17	1	1+2	0+1				
				Free	7/1/98	Brighton & H.A.								
Thompson-Minton Jeffrey	5.6	11.1	12/28/73	Hackney	1/11/92	Tottenham Hotspur	2	0+1			1			
				Free	7/25/94	Brighton & H.A.	106+2	8	6	4	14	1		
Woolsey Jeff	5.11	12.3	11/8/77	Upminster	7/4/96	Arsenal (T)								
				Free	5/31/97	Q.P.R.								
				Free	3/25/98	Brighton & H.A.	1+2							
Wormull Simon	5.10	12.3	12/1/76	Crawley	7/1/95	Tottenham H. (T)								
				Free	7/14/97	Brentford	3+2	1+1		1				
				Free	3/25/98	Brighton & H.A.	17+2			1				
F O R W A R D														
Ansah Andrew	5.10	11.1	3/19/69	Lewisham		Dorking								
				Free	3/21/89	Brentford	3+5	0+1						
				Free	3/29/90	Southend United	141+16	7+2	4	7+3	33			5
				Loan	11/4/94	Brentford	2+1		2	1				1
				Loan	11/15/95	Brentford	6		1	1				
				Free	3/15/96	Peterborough Utd	0+2			1				
				Free	3/28/96	Gillingham	0+2							
				Free	12/19/96	Leyton Orient	0+2							
via Hayes, Heybridge Swifts				Free	11/7/97	Brighton & H.A.	7+7		0+1	1	3			
Barker Richard	6	13.5	5/30/75	Sheffield	7/27/93	Sheffield Wed. (T)								
E: Y, S.		via Linfield		Loan	9/29/95	Doncaster Rovers	5+1			0+1				
				Loan	12/19/97	Brighton & H.A.	15+2			1	2			
					8/1/98	Brighton & H.A.								
Browne Stafford						Hastings Town								
				Free	7/1/98	Brighton & H.A.								
Moralee Jamie	5.11	11	12/2/71	Wandsworth	7/3/90	Crystal Palace (T)	2+4							
				Free	9/3/92	Millwall	56+11	3+1	1	3+1	19	1		
				£450000	7/13/94	Watford	40+9	6+1	5		7			
				Free	8/8/96	Crewe Alexandra	10+6	1+1	2					
				Free	7/1/98	Brighton & H.A.								
Ryan John	5.8	11.06	12/7/75		8/1/96	Brighton & H.A.	1+3				1			
Storer Stuart	5.11	11.8	1/16/67	Rugby	8/23/83	Mansfield Town	0+1							
AMC'89.					8/1/84	VS Rugby								
				Free	1/10/85	Birmingham City	5+3	1						
					3/6/87	Everton								
				Loan	7/23/87	Wigan Athletic	9+3	4						
				£25000	12/24/87	Bolton Wanderers	95+28	9+2	7+3	16+5	12		2	1
				£25000	3/25/93	Exeter City	54	4	3	2	6	1	1	1
				£15000	3/2/95	Brighton & H.A.	100+18	5+1	4+1	3	11		1	1
Streeter Terry S	6.1	13	10/26/78	Brighton	4/10/98	Brighton & H.A. (T)	0+2							
Westcott John P J	5.6	10.4	5/31/79	Eastbourne	7/11/97	Brighton & H.A. (T)	19+14	0+2	1					
ADDITIONAL CONTRACT PLAYERS														
Packham William J					11/7/97	Brighton & H.A. (T)								

ADMINISTRATION OFFICE
118 Queens Road, Brighton, East Sussex BN1 3XG

GROUND - THE PRIESTFIELD STADIUM*
(Gillingham Football Club)
Redfern Avenue, Gillingham, Kent, ME7 4DD
*Brighton will be sharing with Gillingham until the end of Ocotber 1998 at which time the club will then play its football at Withdean Stadium, Tongdean Lane, Brighton.

HOW TO GET TO THE GROUND

Use motorway (M2) and leave at junction 4, then follow signs to Gillingham. Straight over two roundabouts, then turn left at third roundabout (A2).
In 500 yards straight over roundabout. Straight over traffic lights in about 200 yards at Woodlands Road. Stadium is on the left at next set of traffic lights.

Car Parking
One block of street parking.

Nearest Railway Station
Preston Park - approx. 5 minutes walk.

Park & Ride
In operation on match days - cars to be parked at either Brighton University or Mill Road. Buses will then ferry supporters to the ground.

USEFUL TELEPHONE NUMBERS

Administration Office 01273 778 855
Administration fax number 01273 321 095
Ticket Information....................0891 800 600*

Albion Clubline........................0891 44 00 66*
*Calls cost 50p per minute at all times.
Call costings correct at time of going to press.

MATCHDAY PROGRAMME

Programme Editor
........Gareth Roberts (Bishops Printers Ltd).

Number of pages....................................32.

Price ....£1.30.

Subscriptions ....Apply to club.

Local Newspapers
....Evening Argus.

Local Radio Stations
....................BBC Southern Counties Radio,
..............Southern FM, South Coast Radio.

MATCHDAY TICKET PRICES

North Stand (Home) .... £14.00 (Covered)

North Stand (Away)................... £12.00 (Uncovered)

South Stand Centre .... £12.00 (Uncovered)

South Stand Sides .... £12.00 (Uncovered)

Address as for Administration Office above.

CAMBRIDGE UNITED
(The U's)
NATIONWIDE LEAGUE DIVISION 3
SPONSORED BY: C & R WINDOWS

997/98 - Back Row (L-R): Paul Wilson, Marc Joseph, Jamie Campbell, Dave Thompson, John Taylor, Ian ashbee, Paul Wanless.
Middle Row: Michael Kyd, Adie Hayes, Ben Chenery, Shaun Marshall, Scott Barrett, Trevor Benjamin, Jamie Barnwell, Ken Steggles (physio).
Front Row: David Williamson, Jason Rees, David Preece (player coach), Roy McFarland (manager), Billy Beall, Adam Wilde, Matthew Joseph.

CAMBRIDGE UNITED
FORMED IN 1919
TURNED PROFESSIONAL IN 1946
LTD COMPANY IN 1948

CHAIRMAN: R H Smart
VICE-CHAIRMA: R F Hunt
DIRECTORS
G G Harwood, J S Howard,
G P Lowe, R T Summerfield.
SECRETARY
Steve Greenall (01223 566 500)
COMMERCIAL MANAGER
David Smith

MANAGER: Roy McFarland

PLAYER/COACH: David Preece

YOUTH TEAM MANAGER
David Batch
PHYSIOTHERAPIST
Ken Steggles

STATISTICIAN FOR THE DIRECTORY
Colin Faiers

Another confusing and frustrating season for followers of Cambridge United - after just six games and by early September, they were top of the Division Three table but then a disastrous run of 14 games without a win saw them drop down the table to 19th place my mid November before the run was halted with an FA Cup win. After that some patchy form but some stronger form in the run in to the season's end gave hope for the coming season.

The close season of 1997 saw Micah Hyde and Jody Craddock leave for fees which at least guaranteed financial stability for the season ahead. Roy MacFarland was also afforded the luxury of some cash to dip into the transfer market and spent wisely with the purchase of Martin Butler from Walsall for what will prove to be a bargain fee of £22,500. Other new arrivals were defender Ben Chenery from Luton Town, defender Jamie Campbell from Barnet and midfielder Jason Rees from Portsmouth. Opening game defeat against Scarborough was then followed by an encouraging draw in the Coca-Cola Cup against West Bromwich Albion and then four wins in the next five league games to leave United on top of the table albeit for just 48 hours. The rot then set in with a home defeat by Barnet and was followed by a series of frustrating defeats and draws.

The turning point was on November 25 in the FA Cup first round replay at home to Plymouth. 2-0 down at half-time, the introduction of substitute Trevor Benjamin was the catalyst for a revival with two goals in three minutes forcing the match into extra time with a Paul Wilson penalty securing a win which was promptly followed up by a league victory against Hartlepool four days later. Hopes were running high but December saw disappointment with a local derby at Peterborough, no joy in the Auto Windscreen Trophy at Bristol Rovers and a second round FA Cup replay defeat in a bad tempered and controversial tie at Stevenage. The team did regain some credit with a Boxing Day win against Orient but once the team found the start of a new year to be less than successful with five games in January producing just 2 points.

Form then picked up in February - TV cameras at the first two games. BBC TV for a Nick Hornby omnibus saw the team defeat Doncaster Rovers 2-1 and the Sky cameras witnessing a 1-1 draw against Lincoln City managed by ex United manager John Beck. Two defeats in the last twelve games which included victory against Peterborough United and a creditable draw against champions Notts County left the faithful ever expectant for the season ahead.

Martin Butler justified his transfer fee by finishing as leading scorer with 13 goals closely followed by Michael Kyd with 12 and the ever reliable John Taylor with 10, now the second highest goal scorer in the club's history. Jamie Campbell was ever present whilst Paul Wanless made a clean sweep of the fans player of the year awards.

More good news in the close season with the transfer of former U Danny Granville from Chelsea to Leeds producing a healthy and unexpected transfer bonus to keep the finances stable. The youth set up continues to be strong and is a constant source of new blood and with the reserves now in the Combination, there should be the back up to ride injuries that have affected small squads in the past.

COLIN FAIERS.

CAMBRIDGE UNITED

Division 3		:16th		FA CUP: 2nd Round			LC CUP: 1st Round		AWS: Southern Round 1

M	DATE	COMP.	VEN	OPPONENTS	RESULT	H/T	LP	GOAL SCORERS/GOAL TIMES	ATT.
1	A 09	FL	A	Scarborough	L 0-1	0-0	19		(2225)
2	12	CC 1/1	H	West Bromwich Albion	D 1-1	0-1		Kyd 67	3520
3	15	FL	H	Rotherham United	W 2-1	0-0	11	Kyd 46, Taylor 82	2725
4	23	FL	A	Chester City	D 1-1	1-0	14	Kyd 7	(2167)
5	27	CC 1/2	A	West Bromwich Albion	L 1-2	1-0		Butler 13	(10264)
6	30	FL	H	Shrewsbury Town	W 4-3	1-1	6	Wanless 10, 61, Butler 57, Kyd 71	2585
7	S 02	FL	H	Colchester United	W 4-1	1-1	3	Butler 6, 47, Taylor 62, 69	3264
8	05	FL	A	Leyton Orient	W 2-0	1-0	1	Kyd 34, Foster 77	(4638)
9	13	FL	H	Barnet	L 1-3	0-1	5	Taylor 84	3395
10	20	FL	A	Doncaster Rovers	D 0-0	0-0	5		(1258)
11	27	FL	H	Cardiff City	D 2-2	0-1	5	Barnwell-Edinboro 50, 79	2728
12	O 04	FL	A	Lincoln City	D 0-0	0-0	5		(3397)
13	11	FL	A	Mansfield Town	L 2-3	1-2	7	Finney 35, Wanless 76	(2239)
14	18	FL	H	Rochdale	D 1-1	1-0	10	Finney 16	2703
15	21	FL	H	Hull City	L 0-1	0-0	14		2388
16	25	FL	A	Notts County	L 0-1	0-0	15		(4279)
17	N 01	FL	H	Torquay United	D 1-1	1-0	14	Butler 24	2314
18	04	FL	A	Scunthorpe United	D 3-3	2-0	15	Wilson 10, Butler 17, Wanless 76	(2417)
19	08	FL	A	Macclesfield Town	L 1-3	0-2	18	Campbell 60	(2337)
20	15	FAC 1	A	Plymouth Argyle	D 0-0	0-0			(4793)
21	18	FL	H	Brighton & H.A.	D 1-1	1-0	18	Wilson 23	2370
22	22	FL	A	Darlington	D 1-1	1-1	19	Taylor 7	(2221)
23	25	FAC 1R	H	Plymouth Argyle	W 3-2	0-2		Beall 74, Benjamin 77, Wilson 95 (pen)	3139
24	29	FL	H	Hartlepool United	W 2-0	1-0	17	Kyd 2, Campbell 47	2513
25	D 02	FL	A	Peterborough United	L 0-1	0-0	17		(10791)
26	06	FAC 2	H	Stevenage Borough	D 1-1	0-1		Butler 83	4847
27	08	AWS S1	A	Bristol Rovers	L 0-1	0-0			(2386)
28	12	FL	H	Exeter City	W 2-1	1-1	14	Taylor 16, 79	2224
29	15	FAC 2R	A	Stevenage Borough	L 1-2	1-1		Butler 17	(4886)
30	20	FL	A	Swansea City	D 1-1	0-1	15	Wilson 59 (pen)	(2605)
31	26	FL	H	Leyton Orient	W 1-0	0-0	15	Wanless 47	4808
32	29	FL	A	Colchester United	L 2-3	1-1	15	Barnwell-Edinboro 6, 68	(4518)
33	J 10	FL	H	Scarborough	L 2-3	1-1	16	Brebner 21, Wilson 54	2636
34	17	FL	A	Shrewsbury Town	D 1-1	1-1	16	10	(2210)
35	24	FL	H	Chester City	L 1-2	0-0	16	Wilson 81 (pen)	2473
36	27	FL	A	Rotherham United	D 2-2	0-0	16	Kyd 59, Chenery 71	(3096)
37	31	FL	A	Barnet	L 0-2	0-1	16		(2455)
38	F 07	FL	H	Doncaster Rovers	W 2-1	0-1	16	Taylor 54, Wanless 82	2478
39	13	FL	H	Lincoln City	D 1-1	1-0	16	Chenery 25	3891
40	21	FL	A	Cardiff City	D 0-0	0-0	18		(2681)
41	24	FL	A	Rochdale	L 0-2	0-1	20		(1192)
42	28	FL	H	Mansfield Town	W 2-0	0-0	17	Charles 71, Ashbee 78	2303
43	M 03	FL	H	Macclesfield Town	D 0-0	0-0	18		2012
44	07	FL	A	Torquay United	W 3-0	1-0	17	Kyd 42, Benjamin 55, Wanless 79	(3809)
45	14	FL	A	Scunthorpe United	D 2-2	2-0	17	Benjamin 24, 41	2423
46	21	FL	A	Brighton & H.A.	W 2-0	2-0	16	Kyd 30, Benjamin 37	(2746)
47	28	FL	A	Darlington	W 1-0	0-0	18	Taylor 90	2649
48	A 04	FL	A	Hartlepool United	D 3-3	1-1	14	Butler 17, 54, Wanless 53	(1867)
49	11	FL	H	Peterborough United	W 1-0	0-0	14	Kyd 81	5445
50	13	FL	A	Exeter City	L 0-1	0-1	15		(3527)
51	18	FL	H	Swansea City	W 4-1	2-1	15	Butler 17, 38, Kyd 56, 81	2336
52	25	FL	H	Notts County	D 2-2	2-1	15	Butler 19, Beall 29	4009
53	M 02	FL	A	Hull City	L 0-1	0-1	16		(4930)

Best Home League Attendance: 5445 V Peterborough United	**Smallest :2012 V Macclesfield Town** Average :2899

Goal Scorers:

FL	(63)	Kyd 11, Butler 10, Taylor 10, Wanless 8, Wilson 5, Barnwell-Edinboro 4, Benjamin 4, Campbell 2, Chenery 2, Finney 2, Ashbee 1, Beall 1, Brebner 1, Charles 1, Foster 1
CC	(2)	Butler 1, Kyd 1
FAC	(5)	Butler 2, Beall 1, Benjamin 1, Wilson 1
AWS	(0)	

(D) Ashbee	(F) Barwell-Edinboro	(G) Barrett	(F) Beall	(F) Benjamin	(M) Brebner	(F) Butler	(M) Campbell	(F) Charles	(D) Chenery	(D) Duncan	(M) Finney	(D) Foster	(M) Hayes	(D) Joseph Matt	(D) Joseph Marc	(M) Kyd	(G) Larkin	(G) Marshall	(M) McCammon	(M) Preece	(M) Rees	(F) Rodosthenous	(F) Taylor	(M) Wanless	(D) Wilde	(D) Williamson	(D) Wilson	(M) Youngs		
		X		X		X	X		X			X		X	X2					X	X1		S1	X		S2	X		M.S.Pike	1
		X	S2	X		X	X		X			X		X	X					X			S1	X	X		X		G B Frankland	2
		X		X		X	X		X			X		X	X					X	X		S1	X		S2	X		G Cain	3
		X		X		X	X		X			X	S	S	X					X	X		S1	X		S	X		S J Baines	4
		X		X	S3	X	X		X			X		X	S2	X				S2	X		S1	X	X	X	X		A N Butler	5
		X		X		X	X		X			X		X	S3	X				S1	X		X	X		X	X	S2	M Fletcher	6
		X		X		X	X		X			X		S	X	X				S1	X		X	X			X		F G Stretton	7
		X		X		X	X		X			X		S	X	X				S1	X		X	X		S1	X		M J Brandwood	8
		X		X		X	X		X			X		S	X	X				S2	X		X	X		S1	X		A P D'Urso	9
	S1	X		X		X	X		X			X		S	X	X				X			S2	X	X	X	X		M J Jones	10
	X	X		S2			X		X			X	S1		X	X				X	X		X	X			X	S	D R Crick	11
	X	X	S	S1		X	X						X	X	S	S				X			X	X			X		J P Robinson	12
		X		S1		X1	X			X	X	X	S2	X	X					X3	X2	S3	X				X		A R Leake	13
	S1			X		X	X			X	X	S	X	X						X	S	S	X				X		D Orr	14
	S1			X		X	X			X	X	S	S	X				X		S2	X		X	X			X		B Knight	15
			S3	X		X	X			X	X	S2	X	X	X			X		X			S1	X			X		G Singh	16
		X	S	X		X	X			S1	X	X	X	X	X					X			S	X			X		S G Bennett	17
		X	S1	X		X	X			S2	X	X	X	X	X					X			S	X			X		E Lomas	18
X		X	S3	X		X	X			S2	X	X	X	X	X					X			S1	X			X		B Coddington	19
X		X	X	X	S	X	X		X			X		X	X			S		X	S		S1	X			X		R J Harris	20
X		X	X	X		X	X		X			X		X	X					X	S		S1	X			X		W C Burns	21
X		X	X	S2		X	X		X			X		S						X	S1		X	X			X		E K Wolstenholme	22
X		X	X	S1		S2	X		X			X		X	X			S		X	S		X	X			X		R J Harris	23
X		X	X	X		S	X		X			X		X	X					S			X	X			X		P Taylor	24
X		X	X	X		S1	X		X			X		X	X					S			X1	X			X		A N Butler	25
X		X	X	X		S1	X		X2			X		X	X			S	S2	S			X	X			X		B Coddington	26
X	S1	X		X		X	X			X	X			X	X				X2	S3	X	X3			X			X1		27
X		X	X	X		X	X		X1			X		S1	S					S			X	X			X		J A Kirkby	28
X	S3	X	X	X		X	X		X			X1		S1	S2	S			S			X2	X			X3		B Coddington	29
X		X	X3	X1		X	X		X2			X		S3	S1					S			S2	X			X		A R Hall	30
X		X	S	X		X	X		X			X		S	X					S			X	X			X		K A Leach	31
X	X	X	S2			X			X1		X3			S3	X					X	S1	X2					X		P Rejer	32
X	X	X	X	X	X		X2				X3			S2	S1					S3	X1						X		D R Crick	33
	X	X	S1	X		X			X2	S2				X	X1					X						S	X		T Jones	34
X	S1	X	X1	X		X				X				X	X					S			X	X			X	S	S G bennett	35
		X	X			C	J	Foy	X	X		X		X	X					S1			S	X1			X	S	C J Foy	36
	X	X	X			X	X		X	X				X	X2					S			S1	X		X1	S2	M E Pierce	37
	S1	X		X			X			X				S2	X	X				X2			X	X		S	X1	G Singh	38
X2	X	X		S1			X	X	X	X		S			X	X				X			X1	X	S2			P S Danson	39
X	X	X	S1	S			X	X	X	X					X	X				X2				X1	S2		S	E Lomas	40
X	X1	X	X	S1			X	X	X						X	X				X2			X	S2			S	F G Stretton	41
X	X	X	S1	S			X	X	X						X	X				X			X1				S	M E Pierce	42
X	X1	X	X	S1			X	X	X					S	X	X				X				X			S	M D Messias	43
X	S	X	X	X			X	X	X					S	X	X				X				X			S	A N Butler	44
X		X	X	X		S2	X	X1	X	X				X	X2					S			S1	X			X		A P D'Urso	45
X		X	X	X		S1	X	X1	X	X				S	X					S			S1	X			S		C R Wilkes	46
X		X1	X	X			X	X	X						X	X				S			S1	X			S		M R Halsey	47
X		X1	X	X			X	X		X					X	X2				S1			S2	X			S		T Jones	48
X	S	X1	X	X			X	X	X						X	X				X			S1	X			S		W C Burns	49
X		X1	X	X			X	X	X						X	X							S1	X			S		D R Crick	50
X		X1	X	X			X	X	X1						X	X			S1				S	X2			X		M L Dean	51
X		X1	X	X			X	X	X						X	X				S			S1	X			S		J P Robinson	52
X3		X	X1	X			X	X							X	X2			S2					X			S	S3	G Singh	53

27	11	43	25	16	6	28	46	7	36	18	4	26	5	5	37	36	1	2		15	17		19	42		2	31	1	FL Appearances	
	5		5	9		3				1	3		3	2	4	2			2	7	3	2	15		2	4		3	FL Sub Appearances	
		2		0+2		2	2		2			2		0+1	2	2						2	0+2	2		2	2		CC Appearances	
4	0+1	4	4	2+1		2+2	4		4			4		0+1	3+1				0+1	2			3+1	4			4		FAC Appearances	
1	0+1	1		1		1	1				1	1			0+1				1	0+1	1	1	1			1	1		AWS Appearances	

Also Played: (M) Moore S(50), S2(51). (M) Murphy S(1,2,3). (M) Smith S1(53).

CAMBRIDGE UNITED   RECORDS AND STATISTICS

CLUB RECORDS

BIGGEST VICTORIES
League: 6-0 v Darlington, Division 4, 18.9.1971.
6-0 v Hartlepool United, Division 4, 11.2.1989.
7-2 v Cardiff City (a) Division 2, 30.4.1994.
F.A. Cup: 5-1 v Bristol City, 5th Round 2nd replay, 27.2.1990.

BIGGEST DEFEATS
League: 0-6 v Aldershot (a) Division 3, 13.4.1974.
0-6 v Darlington (a), Division 4, 28.9.1974.
0-6 v Chelsea (a), Division 2, 15.1.1983.
League Cup: 0-5 v Colchester United, 1st Round, 1970-71.
0-5 v Derby County, Round 2, 4.10.1989.

MOST POINTS
3 points a win: 86, Division 3, 1990-91.
2 points a win: 65, Division 4, 1976-77.

MOST GOALS SCORED
87, Division 4, 1976-77.

RECORD TRANSFER FEE RECEIVED
£1,000,000 from Manchester United for Dion Dublin, August 1992.

RECORD TRANSFER FEE PAID
£195,000 to Luton Town for Steve Claridge, November 1992.

BEST PERFORMANCES
League: 5th in Division 2, 1991-92.
F.A. Cup: 6th Round 1989-90, 1990-91.
League Cup: 5th Round, 1992-93.

HONOURS
Champions of Division 4, 1976-77.
Champions of Division 3, 1990-91.

LEAGUE CAREER
Elected to Div 4 1970, P. Div 3 1972-73, R. Div 4 1973-74, P. Div 3 1976-77, P. Div 2 1977-78, R. Div 3 1983-84, R. Div 4 1984-85, P. Div 3 1989-90, P. Div 2 (now Div 1) 1990-91, R. Div 2 1992-93, R. Div 3 1994-95.

INDIVIDUAL CLUB RECORDS

MOST GOALS IN A SEASON
David Crown: 27 goals in 1985-86 (League 24, FA Cup 1, Freight Rover Trophy 2).

MOST GOALS IN A MATCH
5. Steve Butler v Exeter City, Division 2, 4.4.1994.

OLDEST PLAYER
John Ryan, 37 years 134 days v Derby County, 1.12.1984.

YOUNGEST PLAYER
Andy Sinton, 16 years 228 days v Wolverhampton W., 2.11.1982.

MOST CAPPED PLAYER
Tom Finney (Northern Ireland) 7.

PREVIOUS MANAGERS

(Since 1951)
Bill Whittaker 1951-55; Gerald Williams 1955; Bert Johnson 1955-59; Bill Craig 1959; Alan Moore (was player coach from 1959-60) 1960-63; Roy Kirk (caretaker) 1963-64; Roy Kirk 1964-66; Matt Wynn (caretaker) 1966-67; Bill Leivers 1967-74; Ray Freeman (caretaker) 1974; Ron Atkinson 1974-78; John Docherty 1978-83; John Ryan 1984-85; John Cozens (caretaker) 1984-85; Ken Shellito 1985-86; Chris Turner 1986-90; John Beck 1990-92; Gary Johnson (caretaker) 1992; Ian Atkins 1992-93; Gary Johnson 1993-95, Tommy Taylor 1995-96.

ADDITIONAL INFORMATION
PREVIOUS NAMES
Abbey United until 1951.
PREVIOUS LEAGUES
Southern League.
Club Colours: Yellow with balck trimmed shirts, black shorts.
Change colours:

Reserves League: Springheath Print Capital League.
Youth League: South East Counties.

LONGEST LEAGUE RUNS

of undefeated matches:	14 (1972)	of league matches w/out a win:	31 (1983-84. A League Record)
of undefeated home matches:	22 (1977-78)	of undefeated away matches:	12 (1990)
without home win:	16 (1983-84. A League Record)	without an away win:	32 (1981-83)
of league wins:	7 (1977)	of home wins:	10 (1977-78)
of league defeats:	7 (1983, 1984, 1984-85, 1985)	of away wins:	4 (20.3.1994 - 30.4.1994)

Cambridge United played 12 successive home league games without conceding a goal in 1982-83.

THE MANAGER

ROY MCFARLAND . . . . appointed November 1996.

PREVIOUS CLUBS
As Manager . . . . Derby County, Bolton Wanderers.
As Asst.Man/Coach . . . . Derby County.
As a player . . . . Tranmere Rovers, Derby County, Bradford, Derby County..

HONOURS
As a Manager . . . . None.
As a Player . . . . **Derby Co.:** Div.1 1972, 1975. Div.2 1969. **England:** 28 full caps & 5 u23.

CAMBRIDGE UNITED							APPEARANCES				GOALS			
PLAYERS NAME / Honours	Ht	Wt	Birthdate	Birthplace / Transfers	Contract Date	Clubs	League	L/Cup	FA Cup	Other	Lge	L/C	FAC	Oth
G O A L K E E P E R														
Barrett Scott	6	12.11	4/2/63	Ilkeston		Ilkeston Town								
GMVC'92. FAT'92.					9/27/84	Wolverhampton W.	30	1	1	3				
				£10000	7/24/87	Stoke City	51	2	3	4				
				Loan	1/10/90	Colchester United	13							
				Loan	3/22/90	Stockport County	10			2				
					8/1/91	Colchester United				5				
				Free	8/14/92	Gillingham	47	5	4	2				
				Free	8/2/95	Cambridge United	149	8	8	2				
Marshall Shaun A	6.1	12.12	10/3/78	Fakenham	10/18/96	Cambridge United	3							
Van Heusden Arjan	6.3	13.12	12/11/72	Alphen (Holland)		Noordwijk								
				£4500	8/15/94	Port Vale	27	4		2				
				Loan	9/26/97	Oxford United	11	2						
				Free	7/1/98	Cambridge United								
D E F E N C E														
Ashbee Ian	6.1	12.1	9/6/76	Birmingham	11/9/94	Derby County	1							
				Free	12/13/96	Cambridge United	42+2		4		1			
Chenery Benjamin R	6.1	11.5	1/28/77	Ipswich	3/7/95	Luton Town	2		1					
				Free	7/3/97	Cambridge United	36	2	4		2			
Duncan Andrew	5.11	13.4	10/20/77	Hexham	7/1/96	Manchester United								
				Loan	1/9/98	Cambridge United	13+1							
					4/7/98	Cambridge United	5							
Joseph Marc	6.1	12.9	11/10/76	Leicester										
McAvoy Lawrence D			9/7/79	Lambeth	5/14/98	Cambridge Utd (T)								
Wilde Adam	5.11	11.8	5/22/79	Southampton	8/30/96	Cambridge United	0+3							
M I D F I E L D														
Armstrong Dean P			9/7/79	Chiswick	5/14/98	Cambridge United								
Campbell Jamie	6.1	11.3	10/21/72	Birmingham	7/1/91	Luton Town	10+26	1	1+3	1+2	1			
				Loan	11/25/94	Mansfield Town	3		2		1			
				Loan	3/10/95	Cambridge United	12							
				Free	7/11/95	Barnet	48+14	3+3	4+1		5	1	1	
					8/8/97	Cambridge United	45	2	4		2			
Kyd Michael	5.8	12.1	5/21/77	Hackney		Cambridge United	77+41	4+2	5+3	2+2	23	1	1	
				Loan	11/17/95	Bishop Stortford								
Mustoe Neil J	5.9	12.10	11/5/76	Gloucester	7/1/95	Manchester Utd (T)								
					1/7/98	Wigan Athletic				0+1				
				Free	7/1/98	Cambridge United								
Preece David	5.6	11.05	5/28/63	Bridgnorth	7/22/80	Walsall	107+4	18	6	1	5	5	1	
				£150000	12/6/84	Luton Town	328+8	23	27	8+1	21	3	2	1
				Free	8/11/95	Derby County	10+3	2			1			
				Loan	11/24/95	Birmingham City								
				Loan	3/21/96	Swindon Town								
				Free	9/6/96	Cambridge United	34+13	3+1	0+1					
Russell Alex	5.9	11.7	3/17/73	Crosby		Burscough								
				£4000	7/11/94	Rochdale	83+19	5	1+1	2+3	14	1		
				Free	7/1/98	Cambridge United								
Smith Thomas E	5.9	10.1	11/25/77	Northampton	5/3/95	Manchester United								
				Free	4/27/98	Cambridge United	0+1							
Wanless Paul	6.1	13.4	12/14/73	Banbury	12/3/91	Oxford United	9+13	0+3		1+1		1		
				Free	7/7/95	Lincoln City	7+1			2				
				Loan	1/25/96	Woking								
				Loan	4/11/96	Cambridge United								
				Free	8/15/96	Cambridge United	83+3	3	5	1	12			
Webb Darren L			10/24/79	Brighton	5/14/98	Cambridge Utd (T)								
F O R W A R D														
Beall Matthew	5.8	10.11	12/4/77	Enfield	3/28/96	Cambridge Utd (T)	73+8	2	6	0+1	7		2	
Benjamin Trevor	6.2	13.2	2/8/79	Kettering	2/21/97	Cambridge Utd (T)	17+20	0+3	2+1	5		1		
Butler Martin	5.11	11.3	9/15/74	Wordsley	5/24/93	Walsall	43+31	2+1	2+5	2+2	8		2	2
					8/8/97	Cambridge United	28+3	2	2+2		10	1	2	
Cockrill Darren P			2/28/80	Gt. Yarmouth	5/14/98	Cambridge Utd (T)								
McCammon Mark J	6.5	14.5	8/7/78	Barnet		Cambridge City								
					12/5/97	Cambridge United	0+2		0+1	1				
Taylor John P	6.1	12.2	10/24/64	Norwich	12/17/82	Colchester United								
Div3'91					8/1/85	Sudbury Town								
					8/24/88	Cambridge United	139+21	9+2	21	12+2	46	2	10	2
					3/28/92	Bristol Rovers	91+4	4	3	5	44	1		
				£300000	7/5/94	Bradford City								
				£200000	3/23/96	Luton Town	27+10	2		1	3			1
				Loan	9/27/96	Lincoln City	5				2			
				Loan	11/8/96	Colchester United	8		1		5			
				Free	1/10/97	Cambridge United	37+17	0+2	3+1		14			
Youngs Thomas A	5.9	10.4	08/31/79	Bury St. Ed.	7/3/97	Cambridge Utd (T)	1+3			1				

ABBEY STADIUM
Newmarket Road, Cambridge CB5 8LN

Capacity 9.667
Covered Standing 6,425
Seating 3,242

First game...v University Press, Friendly, 31.8.1932.
First floodlit game...v Great Yarmouth, East Anglian Cup, 21.10.57.

ATTENDANCES
Highest ....14,000 v Chelsea (friendly), 1.5.1970.
Lowest ....857 v Colchester United, AMC 24.11.1987.

OTHER GROUNDS ....None.

HOW TO GET TO THE GROUND

From the North
Use A1 and A14 signposted to Cambridge, then follow signs for Newmarket. Leave A14 to join B1047 to Cambridge. Turn right into Newmarket Road for Cambridge United FC.

From the East
Follow signs A14 to Cambridge, use A1303 to Cambridge, then follow signs for Newmarket Road for Cambridge United FC.

From the South
Use A10 or M11, follow signs for A14 to Newmarket. Leave A14 to join B1047 to Cambridge, turn right into Newmarket Road for Cambridge United FC.

From the West
Follow signs A428 to Cambridge, then A14 to Newmarket and as for North.

Car Parking: Limited parking at main entrance. Off-street parking permitted. Also at Coldhams Common for visitors.

Nearest Railway Station: Cambridge (01223 311 999)

USEFUL TELEPHONE NUMBERS

Club switchboard 01223 566 500
Club fax number 01223 566 502
Club shop 01223 566 503
Ticket Office............. 01223 566 500

Marketing Department....... 01223 566 503
Clubcall 0891 55 58 85*
*Calls cost 50p per minute at all times.
Call costings correct at time of going to press.

MATCHDAY PROGRAMME

Programme Editor ...... Andrew Pincher.

Number of pages .... 36.

Price .... £1.70.

Subscriptions .... Apply to club.

Local Newspapers
.... Cambridge Evening News.

Local Radio Stations
.... BBC Radio Cambridgeshire, Q103,
.... Chiltern Radio.

MATCHDAY TICKET PRICES

Main Stand

Adults................................. £12.00

Juv/OAP/Students £6.00

Terraces

Adults..................................... £8

Juv/OAP/Students............................ £5

Family Enclosure

Adults..................................... £8

Juv/OAP/Student............................. £5

CARDIFF CITY
(The Bluebirds)
NATIONWIDE LEAGUE DIVISION 3
SPONSORED BY:

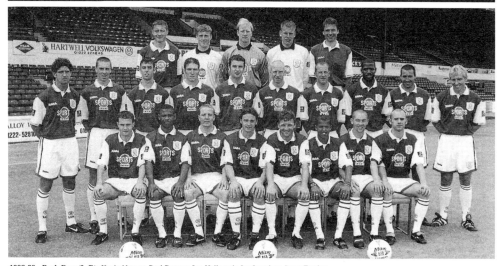

1998-99 - Back Row (L-R): Kevin Nugent, Paul Buttery, Jon Hallworth, Ian Loveless, Jason Fowler.
Middle Row: Lee Phillips, Graham Mitchell, Mark Delaney, Scott Young, Lee Jarman, Andy Saville, Jeff eckhardt, John Williams, Mike Ford, Richard Carpenter.
Front Row: Mark Bonner, Nathan Cadette, Gareth Stoker, Craig Middleton, David Penny, Robert Earnshaw, Christian Roberts, Wayne O'Sullivan.

CARDIFF CITY
FORMED IN 1899
TURNED PROFESSIONAL IN 1910
LTD COMPANY IN 1910

CHAIRMAN: Samesh Kumar
DIRECTORS
Joan Hill (Chief Executive)
Rodney East, P Guy, R Phillips, S Borley
D Temme

SECRETARY
Ceri Whitehead

DIRECTOR OF FOOTBALL: Kenny Hebbitt
MANAGER: Frank Burrows

PHYSIO
Jimmy Goodfellow

STATISTICIAN FOR THE DIRECTORY
Vacant - phone 01203 234 017 if interested

After having failed in the 1996-97 play-offs, Cardiff City were hoping for at least a repeat performance in terms of a League placing in 1997-98, but it was not to be, and, in truth, the 'Bluebirds' had a very disappointing campaign, finishing fourth from bottom of the Third Division after winning just nine of their 46 League games (only Brighton and relegated Doncaster Rovers recorded fewer victories).

Yet things began so brightly with successive wins in their first two matches. And it was three wins and three draws from their opening six fixtures.

But then things started to go wrong for manager Russell Osman and coach Kenny Hibbitt. After 10 matches had been completed the 'Bluebirds' were still on three wins and had slipped down to eighth from bottom - ten points adrift of the leaders Peterborough. Already dumped out of the Coca-Cola Cup in the first round by Southend, but still in the F.A. Cup after wins over Slough Town and Hendon, Cardiff struggled through to the New Year when they found themselves slowly slipping down the table, well away from that last play-off spot of seventh.

Another F.A. Cup win - 1-0 over Oldham - was followed by more poor League results and after going out of that competition (to Reading) Cardiff's season simply fizzled out completely. They even brought back former manager Frank Burrows in a bid to boost things up at Niniuan Park but nothing changed and when the curtain came down, one reflected on a very poor season all round for the famous old Welsh club. "It can only get better" said one ardent supporter and that's a fact which everyone associated with the 'Bluebirds' will be hoping to put right as soon as possible.

Tony Matthews.

CARDIFF CITY

Division 3	:21st			FA CUP: 4th Round			LC CUP: 1st Round	AWS: Southern Round 1	

M	DATE	COMP.	VEN	OPPONENTS	RESULT	H/T	LP	GOAL SCORERS/GOAL TIMES	ATT.
1	A 09	FL	A	Leyton Orient	W 1-0	0-0	10	Dale 62	(5414)
2	12	CC 1/1	H	**Southend United**	D 1-1	1-1		Rollo 89	2804
3	23	FL	A	Mansfield Town	W 2-1	1-0	6	Partridge 7, Greenacre 68	(2743)
4	26	CC 1/2	A	**Southend United**	L 1-3	0-2		Fowler 61	(3002)
5	30	FL	H	Notts County	D 1-1	1-1	11	Young 37	6191
6	S 02	FL	H	Shrewsbury Town	D 2-2	0-1	9	Partridge 56, O'Sullivan 79	4271
7	09	FL	A	Exeter City	D 1-1	0-0	11	Fowler 73	(4843)
8	13	FL	H	Rochdale	W 2-1	1-1	8	White 39, Eckhardt 87	4306
9	16	FL	H	Chester City	L 0-2	0-2	9		3949
10	20	FL	A	Lincoln City	L 0-1	0-1	12		(3130)
11	27	FL	A	Cambridge United	D 2-2	1-0	13	Greenacre 31, Eckhardt 90	(2728)
12	O 04	FL	H	Barnet	D 1-1	1-0	14	Eckhardt 22	3938
13	18	FL	A	Rotherham United	D 1-1	1-1	17	Penney 20 (pen)	(3197)
14	21	FL	A	Darlington	D 0-0	0-0	17		(2278)
15	25	FL	H	Hartlepool United	D 1-1	0-1	16	Crowe 74	3383
16	N 02	FL	H	Swansea City	L 0-1	0-1	17		6459
17	04	FL	A	Doncaster Rovers	D 1-1	0-0	18	Saville 59	(1004)
18	08	FL	A	Torquay United	D 1-1	0-0	19	Stoker 69	2797
19	11	FL	H	Scunthorpe United	D 0-0	0-0	18		2340
20	15	FAC 1	A	Slough Town	D 1-1	0-1		O'Sullivan 16	(2262)
21	18	FL	H	Hull City	W 2-1	2-0	15	Saville 2, Penney 19	2504
22	22	FL	A	Brighton & H.A.	W 1-0	1-0	14	Allan 20 (OG)	(2086)
23	25	FAC 1R	H	Slough Town	W 3-2*	1-1		Dale 22, Saville 55, White 114	2343
24	29	FL	H	Scarborough	D 1-1	0-1	14	Dale 69	2593
25	D 06	FAC 2	H	**Hendon**	W 3-1	3-0		Dale 21, 45, Saville 41	2578
26	09	AWS S1	H	**Millwall**	L 0-2	0-0			1219
27	13	FL	H	Peterborough United	D 0-0	0-0	14		3401
28	20	FL	A	Macclesfield Town	L 0-1	0-0	16		(2398)
29	26	FL	H	Exeter City	D 1-1	1-0	17	Dale 10	6623
30	28	FL	A	Shrewsbury Town	L 2-3	0-1	18	Fowler 69, Young 78	(3238)
31	J 03	FAC 3	H	**Oldham Athletic**	W 1-0	1-0		Fowler 18	6635
32	10	FL	A	Leyton Orient	W 1-0	1-0	15	Penney 19 (pen)	4335
33	17	FL	A	Notts County	L 1-3	1-1	17	Harris 31	(6448)
34	20	FL	A	Colchester United	L 1-2	0-0	17	Dale 85	(1949)
35	24	FAC 4	H	**Reading**	D 1-1	0-0		Nugent 47	10174
36	27	FL	A	Chester City	D 0-0	0-0	17		(1757)
37	31	FL	A	Rochdale	D 0-0	0-0	17		(1445)
38	F 03	FAC 4R	A	**Reading**	D 1-1	1-0		Dale 40 (Lost 4-3 on penalties)	(11808)
39	06	FL	H	Lincoln City	L 0-1	0-0	19		2896
40	14	FL	A	Barnet	D 2-2	2-1	20	Saville 4, Fowler 16	(2406)
41	17	FL	H	Mansfield Town	W 4-1	1-0	16	Saville 42 (pen), Fowler 46, Carss 53, Penney 78	2451
42	21	FL	H	Cambridge United	D 0-0	0-0	17		2681
43	24	FL	H	Rotherham United	D 2-2	1-1	16	Saville 17, White 68	2731
44	28	FL	H	Scunthorpe United	D 3-3	1-2	18	Saville 29, 52, 88	(2135)
45	M 03	FL	A	Torquay United	L 0-1	0-1	19		(3358)
46	08	FL	A	Swansea City	D 1-1	0-0	19	Fowler 58	(5621)
47	14	FL	H	Doncaster Rovers	W 7-1	2-0	19	Saville 27, 84, O'Sullivan 45, Roberts 55, Beech 68, Penney 77, Young 78	2931
48	21	FL	A	Hull City	W 1-0	0-0	17	Roberts 57	(3408)
49	28	FL	H	Brighton & H.A.	D 0-0	0-0	17		3509
50	A 03	FL	A	Scarborough	L 1-3	0-3	18	Saville 51	(2905)
51	11	FL	H	Colchester United	L 0-2	0-0	20		2809
52	13	FL	A	Peterborough United	L 0-2	0-0	21		(4756)
53	18	FL	H	Macclesfield Town	L 1-2	1-0	21	Roberts 25	2497
54	25	FL	A	Hartlepool United	L 0-2	0-1	21		(2817)
55	M 02	FL	H	Darlington	D 0-0	0-0	21		2610

Best Home League Attendance: 6623 V Exeter City Smallest :2340 V Scunthorpe United Average :3574

Goal Scorers:

FL	(48)	Saville 11, Fowler 5, Penney 5, Dale 4, Eckhardt 3, Roberts 3, Young 3, Greenacre 2, O'Sullivan 2, Partridge 2, White 2, Beech 1, Carss 1, Crowe 1, Harris 1, Stoker 1, Opponents 1
CC	(2)	Fowler 1, Rollo 1
FAC	(10)	Dale 4, Saville 2, Fowler 1, O'Sullivan 1, Nugent 1, White 1
AWS	(0)	

*AET

(M) Beech	(M) Cadette	(M) Carss	(M) Crowe	(F) Dale	(M) Earnshaw	(D) Eckhardt	(G) Elliott	(M) Fowler	(F) Greenacre	(G) Hallworth	(M) Harris	(M) Hill	(D) Jarman	(D) Lloyd	(F) Middleton	(F) Nugent	(M) O'Sullivan	(F) Partridge	(M) Paterson	(M) Penney	(D) Phillips	(M) Roberts	(F) Rollo	(M) Saville	(M) Stoker	(F) White	(F) Young	(G) Zois	Referee	No.
X	X		X					X		X	X	X		X	S	X	X			X					S2	S1	X		B Coddington	1
X	X							X		X	X	X		X	S3	X	X		X					S2		S1	X	X	R J Harris	2
X	X							X	X	X	X	X		X	S	X		S1	X		X				X	S2			M S Pike	3
X	X							X		X	X	X	S2	S3	X		S1	X		X					X	X	X		M c Bailey	4
X	X				S			X	X	X	X	X	S1		X		X	X	X						X	S2	X		R Styles	5
X	X				S			X	X	X	X	X		X		S	X	X						X1	S1	X		D Pugh	6
X					S2			X1	X	X	X	X		X		S3	X	X	X2					S1	X2	X		A G Wiley	7
X	S				S2			X	X	X	X	X		X		X	X			S1				X	X	X		M J Jones	8
X	S1							X	X	X	X	X	S	S	X1		X	X						X	X	X		M J Brandwood	9
X	X							X	X	X	X	X	S3		S1	X	X2							X	S2	X		G Laws	10
X	X			X	S1			X	X	X	X	X	S3		X	S2								X	X	X		D R Crick	11
X	X							X	X	X	X	X		X		S1	X							S3	S2	X		P S Danson	12
X	X							X	X	X	X	X		X	S1		X	S	X					S	X			S W Mathieson	13
X	X							X	X	X	X	X		X		X	X	X	S	X				S	X1			R D Furnandiz	14
X	X	X	S1					X	X	X			S	X	X	X	X	X						S					K A Leach	15
X	X	X						X	X	X			X	X	S1	X				X	S2	S3	X						R J Harris	16
X	S2	X	S3					X	X	X			X	X	S1	X				X	X				X				S J Baines	17
X	S	X	S1					X	X	X			X	X		X	X	X		X	X				S				A R Hall	18
X	S2	X	S1					X	X	X			X	X	X	X	X		X	X				S				P Rejer	19
X	S1		X		S	X		X	X				X	X	X	X		S	S	X1	S	X						S W Dunn	20
X	X	X	S1					X	X				X	X	X	X		S	S	S								A N Butler	21
X	X	X	S1		X			X	X				X	X	X	X		S	X	S2	X							A P D'Urso	22
X	X	X3			X			S	X	S1			X	X2	X	S2	X	S	S3	X1								D J Gallagher	23
X	X	S2	X					X1	S1	X			X	X2	X	X		S											C R Wilkes	24
X1	X	X		S				X	X2	S1			X	X	X	X3	S2	X	S3	S	X								P Taylor	25
	X	X		S2	X			X					X	X2	X	S1	X	X	X											26
X	X	X						X	X	S	X	X	S	S	X	X	X		S	X1	S	X							A Bates	27
X	X	X3						X	X	S2	X2	X	X1	X	S1	S3	X												F G Stretton	28
X	X	X		X				X	X	S	X	X	S	X	X	X	S	S	X										S B Bennett	29
X	X	X		X2				X	X	S	X1	X	X	X	S1	S2	X												G Singh	30
X	X	X		S2	S	X1		X	X	X	S	X2	S	X	S1		X									X			M E Pierce	31
X	X	X		S	X1			X	X	X	S2	X	X	X2	S1		X									X			M J Jones	32
X	X2	X	X3	X	X			X	X	S2	X1	X	X			S3	X		S1	X									G B Frankland	33
X	X1	A	X1	X	X1		S1	X	X	X	S	S	X	X1	S	S	X		S1	X									M C Bailey	34
X	X	X	X	S			X	X1	S	S	X	S1	S	X															S J Lodge	35
X	X		X					X	X	X	X	X1	X	X	S	X	X			S	S1	X							B Coddington	36
X1	X	X						X	X	X	X	X	S	X	X	S		X	S	X	S	X							W C Burns	37
X	X	X	X1	S3				X	X	X	S1	X	X3	X	X	X	S2	S	X2										S J Lodge	38
X	X		X1					X	X	X	X	X2	X	S1	S2	X	X	S2											D Orr	39
X	X	X2						X	X	X	S	X	X1	S1	X	S1	X2												R Styles	40
X	X	S1	X2					X	X	X	X	X	S2	S	X1	X2													D Pugh	41
X	X2	X1	X		X	X		X	X	S2	X	S3	X	S1	X														E Lomas	42
X	X		X1					X	X	X	S1	S	X	S	X	X	S	X	X									X	G Cain	43
X	X		X					X	X	X	X	S	X	S	S	X	X	S											A R Leake	44
X	X1		X					X	X	X	X	S	X	S	S1	X	X1												P Taylor	45
X	S1							X	X	X	S	X	X	X	S1	X	S1	X1											M J Brandwood	46
X1	S1							X	X	X	S	X	X	X	X2	X	S2	X											M R Halsey	47
X	X	S1		X				X	X	X	X	S	X	X1	X	X											X		S J Baines	48
X	X	S1	S2	X				X	X	X	S	X2	X	X1	X											X			A Bates	49
X3	S1	X	X2		X1			X	X	X	X	X	X	S3	S2	X		X								X			R Pearson	50
X	S3	X1	X2	S1				X	X	X	X	X	X3	S2	X											X			M Fletcher	51
X	S1	X	X3	S3				X	X	X	X1	X	X	S	X2	X										X2			M J Jones	52
X	S1	X1	S2					X	X	X3	X	S3	X	X	X	X2										X			R Styles	53
X	S1		S2					X	X	X3	X	S3	X	X2	X	X1	X												W C Burns	54
X2	S2							X	X	X	X	X	X	X	X	X	S1		X1	S									S G Bennett	55
46	36	7	16		19	2		38	11	43	38	7	18		28	2	40	15	5	32	7	5	3	32	12	12	31	1	FL Appearances	
	4	6	1	9	5	2	1								5	2	5	2	3	7	2	1	6	2	1	8	17		FL Sub Appearances	
2		2						2		2	2	1+1	0+2	2	1	0+1	2		1			0+1		1+1	2	2			CC Appearances	
6	5+1		6		2+1	1	3+1	5	6	0+3		6	2	5	2		6			0+2	4+1	1+3	0+1	6					FAC Appearances	
	1	1		0+1	1					1					1	1		0+1		1			1	1	1	1		AWS Appearances	

Also Played: (D) Harriott X1(26). (M) Parnell S(44). (F) Philliskirk S(14).

CARDIFF CITY

RECORDS AND STATISTICS

CLUB RECORDS

BIGGEST VICTORIES
League: 7-0 v Burnley, Division 1, 1.9.1928.
9-2 v Thames, Division 3(S), 6.2.1932.
7-0 v Barnsley, Division 2, 7.12.1957.
F.A. Cup: 8-0 v Enfield 1st Round, 1931-32.
(Scored 16 in a Welsh Cup tie, 20.1.1961)
Europe: 8-0 v P.O.Larnaca (Cyprus), ECWC 1st Round, 1970-71.
BIGGEST DEFEATS
League: 2-11 v Sheffield United, Division 1, 1.1.1926.
0-9 v Preston North End, Division 2, 7.5.1966.
F.A. Cup: 1-6 v Aston Villa, 3rd Round, 1928-29.
0-5 v Charlton Athletic, 3rd Round, 1937-38.
MOST POINTS
3 points a win: 86, Division 3, 1982-83.
2 points a win: 66, Division 3(S), 1946-47.
MOST GOALS SCORED: 93, Division 3(S), 1946-47.
RECORD TRANSFER FEE RECEIVED
£300,000 for Nathan Blake from Sheffield United, February 1994.
RECORD TRANSFER FEE PAID
£200,000 to San Jose Earthquakes for Godfrey Ingram, Sept 1982.
BEST PERFORMANCES
League: Runners-up Division 1, 1923-24.
Highest Position: 2nd Division 1, 1923-24.
F.A. Cup: Winners in 1926-27.
League Cup: Semi-Finals in 1965-66.
Welsh Cup: Winners 22 times.
Europe: (ECWC) Semi-Finals in 1967-68
HONOURS
Champions of Division 3(S), 1946-47.
Champions of Division 3, 1992-93.
FA Cup winners in 1926-27.
Charity Shield winners in 1927.
Welsh Cup winners 22 times.
LEAGUE CAREER
Elected to Div 2 1920, Div 1 1920-21, Div 2 1928-29, Div 3(S) 1930-31, Div 2 1946-47, Div 1 1951-52, Div 2 1956-57, Div 1 1959-60, Div 2 1961-62, Div 3 1974-75, Div 2 1975-76, Div 3 1981-82, Div 2 1982-83, Div 3 1984-85, Div 4 1985-86, Div 3 1987-88, Div 4 (now Div 3) 1989-90, Div 2 1992-93, Div 3 1994-95

INDIVIDUAL CLUB RECORDS

MOST GOALS IN A SEASON
John Toshack: 31 goals in 1968-69 (League 22, Cup ties 9).

MOST GOALS IN A MATCH
6. Derek Tapscott v Knighton Town (Welsh FA Cup) 20.01.61.

OLDEST PLAYER
George Latham, 42 v Blackburn Rovers, Division 1, 2.1.1922.

YOUNGEST PLAYER
John Toshack, 16 v Leyton Orient, Division 2, 13.11.1965.

MOST CAPPED PLAYER
Alf Sherwood (Wales) 39.

PREVIOUS MANAGERS

Davy McDougall 1910-11; Fred Stewart 1911-33; Bartley Wilson 1933-34; B Watts Jones 1934-37; Bill Jennings 1937-39; Cyril Spiers 1939-46; Billy McCandless 1946-48; Cyril Spiers 1948-54; Trevor Morris 1954-58; Bill Jones 1958-62; George Swindin 1962-64; Jimmy Schoular 1964-73; Frank O'Farrell 1973-74; Jimmy Andrews 1974-78; Richie Morgan 1978-81; Graham Williams 1981-82; Len Ashurst 1982-84; Jimmy Goodfellow & Jimmy Mullen (caretakers) 1984; Alan Durban 1984-86; Frank Burrows 1986-89; Len Ashurst 1989-91; Eddie May 1991-94; Terry Yorath 1994-95; Eddie May 1995. Kenny Hibbitt 1995-96. Russell Osman 1996-98.

ADDITIONAL INFORMATION
PREVIOUS NAMES
Riverside FC (1899-1908) amalgamated with Riverside Albion (1902). Cardiff City from 1908.

PREVIOUS LEAGUES
Southern League. Cardiff & District F.L. South Wales League.

Club colours: Blue with white sleeved shirts, white shorts with blue trim.
Change colours: Yellow shirts, black shorts.
Reserves League: Neville Ovenden Football Combination.

LONGEST LEAGUE RUNS

of undefeated matches:	21 (1946-47)	of league matches w/out a win:	15 (1936-37)
of undefeated home matches:	27 (1939/46/47)	of undefeated away matches:	10 (1946-47)
without home win:	10 (1986-87)	without an away win:	44 (1971-73)
of league wins:	9 (1946)	of home wins:	9 (1922-23, 1951-52)
of league defeats:	7 (1933)	of away wins:	7 (1993)

MANAGER

FRANK BURROWS . . . . appointed February 1998.

PREVIOUS CLUBS
As Manager . . . . Portsmouth, Cardiff City.
As Asst.Man/Coach . . . . Portsmouth, Swindon, Sunderland.
As a player . . . . Raith Rovers, Scunthorpe, Swindon, Mansfield (Loan).

HONOURS
As a Manager . . . . None.
As a Player . . . . **Swindon:** League Cup Winners 1969.

CARDIFF CITY

PLAYERS NAME Honours	Ht	Wt	Birthdate	Birthplace Transfers	Contract Date	Clubs	League	L/Cup	FA Cup	Other	Lge	L/C	FAC	Oth
G O A L K E E P E R														
Hallworth Jonathan G	6.2	13.1	10/26/65	Stockport	5/25/83	Ipswich Town	45	4	1	6				
				Loan	1/1/85	Bristol Rovers	2			1				
				£75000	2/3/89	Oldham Athletic	171+2	20	20	3				
				Free	8/6/97	Cardiff City	42	2	4					
D E F E N C E														
Delaney Mark						Caernarvon								
				Free	7/1/98	Cardiff City								
Eckhardt Jeff	6	11.7	10/7/65	Sheffield	8/23/84	Sheffield United	73+1	7	2	5	2			
				£50000	11/20/87	Fulham	245+4	13	5+1	15	25			3
				£50000	7/21/94	Stockport County	56+6	6+2	5	1	7	1	4	
					8/23/96	Cardiff City	53+3	1	4+1	2	7			
Ford Michael P WFAC'88.	6	11.6	09/02/66	Bristol	11/02/84	Leicester City								
				Free	01/08/84	Consett								
				Free	19/09/84	Cardiff City	144+1	6	9	7	13			
				£150000	10/06/88	Oxford United	273+16	27+1	12+1	8	16	2	1	1
				Free	7/1/98	Cardiff City								
Jarman Lee	6.3	13.2	12/16/77	Cardiff										
Mitchell Graham						Raith Rovers								
				Free	7/1/98	Cardiff City								
Phillips Lee	6.1	11.9	3/18/79	Aberdare	11/4/96	Cardiff City	9+2							
M I D F I E L D														
Bonner Mark	5.10	11	6/7/74	Ormskirk	6/18/92	Blackpool	156+22	15+3	11	10+3	14			1
				Free	7/1/98	Cardiff City								
Cadette Nathan D W: Y.	5.10	11.1	1/6/80	Cardiff	4/2/98	Cardiff City (T)	0+4							
Carpenter Richard	6	12	30/09/72	Sheerness	13/05/91	Gillingham	107+15	2+1	9+1	7	4			1
				£25000	26/09/96	Fulham	49+9	4	2	2	7	1	1	
				£35000	7/1/98	Cardiff City								
Fowler Jason	6	11.12	8/20/74	Bristol	7/8/93	Bristol City	16+9	1+2		1+1				
					8/15/96	Cardiff City	75	4	4+1	2	10	1	1	1
O'Sullivan Wayne Div.2'96.	5.11	11.2	2/25/74	Cyprus	5/1/93	Swindon Town	64+24	11	1+3	2+2	3	1	1	
					8/22/97	Cardiff City	40+3	0+1	3		2			
Parnell Blake L					2/27/98	Cardiff City (T)								
Penney David M Weslh Cup'91.	5.10	12	8/22/97	Wakefield		Pontefract Collieries								
				£1500	9/26/85	Derby County	6+13	2+3	1	1+3		1	1	1
				£175000	6/23/89	Oxford United	76+34	10+1	2+2	3+1	15		1	
				Loan	3/28/91	Swansea City	12				3			
				£20000	3/24/94	Swansea City	112+17	5+1	7	14	20	2	1	
				£20000	7/24/97	Cardiff City	02+2	1	6		5			
Stoker Gareth	5.9	10.1	2/22/73	Bishop Auckland		Leeds United								
				Free	9/13/91	Hull City	24+6	3	2+1	0+2	2			
					3/16/95	Hereford United	65+5	5+1	3+1	5+1	6		1	1
					1/29/97	Cardiff City	29+1	1+1	0+3	1+1	4			
F O R W A R D														
Earnshaw Robert	5.8	10.10	4/6/81	Zambia	3/26/98	Cardiff City (T)	0+5			0+1				
Middleton Craig	5.11	10.13	9/10/70	Nuneaton	5/30/89	Coventry City	2+1	1						
				Free	7/20/93	Cambridge United	169+10	9	2	2	34			
				Free	9/2/96	Cardiff City	68+6	2+1	6	2	4		1	
Nugent Kevin P	6.1	13.03	4/10/69	Edmonton	7/8/87	Leyton Orient	86+8	9+3	9	9+1	19	6	3	1
				£200000	3/23/92	Plymouth Argyle	120+5	9	10	4+3	31	2	3	
				£75000	9/29/95	Bristol City	47+22	2+2	3+2	2	14		1	
				Free	8/4/97	Cardiff City	2+2	1	2				1	
Roberts Christian J W: Y.	5.10	12.8	10/22/79	Cardiff	9/12/97	Cardiff City (T)	5+6				3			
Saville Andy DIV3 96/97	6	12	12/12/64	Hull	23/08/83	Hull City	74+27	18	3+2	4+2	18	1	1	
				£100000	23/03/89	Walsall	28+10	2		1+1	5			
				£80000	09/03/90	Barnsley	71+11	5+1	2+1	4	21			1
				£60000	13/03/92	Hartlepool United	37	4	4	3	13	1	5	1
				£155000	22/03/93	Birmingham City	51+8	4	1	1	17	1		
				Loan	30/12/94	Burnley	3+1		1		1			
				£100000	28/07/95	Preston North End	56	6	2	2	30			1
				£125000	25/10/96	Wigan Athletic	17+8	0+1	1	1	4			
				£75000	10/31/97	Cardiff City	32+1		4+1		11		2	
Williams John	6.1	13.12	5/11/68	Birmingham		Cradley Town								
				£5000	8/19/91	Swansea City	36+3	2+1	3	1	11			
				£250000	7/1/92	Coventry City	66+14	4	2		11			
				Loan	10/7/94	Notts County	3+2				2			
				Loan	12/23/94	Stoke City	1+3							
				Loan	2/3/95	Swansea City	6+1				2			
				£150000	9/15/95	Wycombe W.	34+18	4+1	5	2	8	2	4	
				Free	2/14/97	Hereford United	8+3				3			
				Free	7/21/97	Walsall	0+1							
				Free	8/29/97	Exeter City	16+20				4			
				Free	7/1/98	Cardiff City								
Young Scott	6.1	12	1/14/76	Pontypridd	7/4/90	Cardiff City	117+14	6+1	8	9+3	4			1

ADDITIONAL CONTRACT PLAYERS

Semus Kelly						ICD, Dublin								
				Free	7/1/98	Cardiff City								

NINIAN PARK
Sloper Road, Cardiff CF1 8SX

Capacity ....14,660.

First game ....v Ton Pentre, Southern Lge Div 2, 24.9.1910.
First floodlit game..v Grasshoppers Zurich
....(Friendly) 5.10.1960.

ATTENDANCES
Highest....................61,566 Wales v England, 14.10.1961. 57,893 v Arsenal, Division 1, 22.4.1953.
Lowest...............1,006 v Swansea City, AMC, 28.1.1986. 581 v Taffs Well, Welsh Cup, 25.11.1986.

OTHER GROUNDS: .... None.

HOW TO GET TO THE GROUND

From the North
Follow signs to Cardiff (A470) until junction with Cardiff bypass. At roundabout take 3rd exit A48 (sign posted Port Talbot). In 2 miles at roundabout take 1st exit (A4161) into Cowbridge Road . In half a mile turn right along Lansdowne Road. At end at crossroads turn right (A4055) into Leckwith Road. In 0.2 miles turn left into Sloper Road to Cardiff City FC.

From the East
Use motorway (M4), then A48 into Cardiff bypass. Follow Port Talbot then in 2 miles at roundabout take first exit A4161 into Cowbridge Road. In half a mile turn right along Lansdowne Road. At end at crossroads turn right (A4055) into Leckwith Road. In 0.2 miles turn left into Sloper Road for Cardiff City FC.

From the West
Use the M4 and leave at junction 33, taking the A4232 (traffic from the A48 can also join the A4232 at the Culverhouse Cross junction). Leave the A4232 at the exit the City Centre, B4267 for Cardiff City FC.

Car Parking: (Shared with the Leckwith athletic stadium) across the road from Ninian Park.
Nearest Railway Station: Cardiff Central (01222 228 000)

USEFUL TELEPHONE NUMBERS

Club switchboard 01222 398 636
Club fax number 01222 341 148
Ticket Office 01222 398 636

Bluebirds Hotline . . . 0891 12 11 71*
*Calls cost 50p per minute at all times.
Call costings correct at time of going to press.

MATCHDAY PROGRAMME

Programme Editor....................Kathy Shea.

Number of pages.....................32.

Price ....£1.50.

Subscriptions ....Apply to the club.

Local Newspapers
................South Wales Echo, Western Mail.

Local Radio Stations
........BBC Radio Wales, Red Dragon Radio,
......................................BBC Radio Cymru.

MATCHDAY TICKET PRICES

Grandstand C&D............................ £12
Juv/OAP £7

Grandstand elsewhere....................... £10
Juv/OAP £6

Ground £8
Juv/OAP £4

CARLISLE UNITED
(The Cumbrians)
NATIONWIDE LEAGUE DIVISION 3
SPONSORED BY: EDDIE STOBART LIMITED

CARLISLE
UNITED

1998/99 - Back Row L-R: Andrew Douglas, Gareth McAlindon, Kevin Sandwith, Rob Bowman, Mark Thustan, Tony Hopper, Eddie Harrison, Richard Prokas, **Standing:** Scott Thornthwaite, Phil Hetjerington, Neil Dalton (Physio), Paul Boertien, Stuart Whitehead, Scott Paterson, Michael Swann, Paul Heritage, Tony Caig, Barry Clark, David Brightwell, Will Varty, Scott Dobie, David Heslop (Asst. Yth Coach), Paul Antony, Barry Stevens. **Seated:** Graham Anthony, Jeff Thorpe, Dariusz Kubicki, Ian Stevens, John Halpin (coach), Michael Kulghton)Director of football), David Wilkes (coach), Billy Barr (club captain), Steve Finney, Damon Searle, Andy Couzens. **Front Row:** Adam Thwaites, James Heath, Alan Hodgson, Paul Ballentyne, John Heggie, Paul reid, Gavin Skelton, Michael Irving, Jon-Karl Benson, John Hore.

CARLISLE UNITED
FORMED IN 1904
TURNED PROFESSIONAL IN
LTD COMPANY IN 1921

CHAIRMAN & CHIEF EXECUTIVE
Michael Knighton
DIRECTORS
M Knighton, B Chaytow (Vice-Chairman),
A Dowbeck, R McKnight, H A Jenkins,
J T T Fuller
SECRETARY
Angela Ritchie
COMMERCIAL MANAGER
M Hudson
DIRECTOR OF FOOTBALL
Michael Knighton
COACHES
David Wilkes & John Halpin

PHYSIOTHERAPIST
Neil Dalton
STATISTICIAN FOR THE DIRECTORY
Bill Rodger

Carlisle United had a poor 1997-98 season. They finished next to bottom of the Second Division and were duly relegated with a very disappointing record of only 12 wins and eight draws from their 46 matches.

In truth - and the supporters know this - at no stage during the season did they ever look like getting out of relegation trouble!

They hovered on the brink from the word go and although occasionally they looked as if they might climb away from the danger zone, within a matter of days they were back in trouble.

They were in the bottom three after the first month; then after manager Mervyn Day was dismissed, they squeezed up to 20th after 11 games (being only one win better off than Burnley) and at the turn of the year found themselves in 23rd spot with only six wins under their belt from 25 starts.

Things didn't improve all that much and come mid-February - with Michael Knighton in charge of team affairs, the writing was on the wall for the Cumbrians, who were now in deep trouble with just 31 points to their credit (from 31 matches).

The team couldn't string together a decent run of results and as the games were slowly ticked by, it became increasingly difficult for them to win matches. Indeed, after beating Wrexham 2-0 away on 29th December, Carlisle managed only six more successes in their remaining 21 fixtures, including a run of four victories from nine early in the New Year. It came as no surprise to a lot of people when relegation finally came following a 2-1 home defeat by York City in late April.

During the season, Rory Delap was sold to Derby County for £500,000; efforts were made to entice Peter Beardsley back to Brunton Park; five French players were given trials at the club early in the campaign and referee Jeff Winter was struck in the face by a boiled sweet during a Coca-Cola Cup clash with Spurs (which Carlisle lost over two legs).

Things will have to be sorted out quickly at Brunton Park. Carlisle have some useful players and the support is there if the team is playing well. It's not going to be easy getting out of the Third Division, but everyone associated with the Cumbrian club believe that promotion can be achieved at the first attempt and the bookies have already given generous odds on United doing just that in 1998-99.

Tony Matthews.

CARLISLE UNITED

Division 2		:23th		FA CUP: 1st Round			LC CUP: 2nd Round		AWS: Northern Quarter-finals	

M	DATE	COMP.	VEN	OPPONENTS	RESULT	H/T	LP	GOAL SCORERS/GOAL TIMES	ATT.
1	A 09	FL	A	Southend United	D 1-1	0-1	12	Smart 51	(4507)
2	12	CC 1/1	A	Chester City	W 2-1	1-0		Smart 32, Jansen 52	(2367)
3	15	FL	H	Watford	L 0-2	0-0	18		7395
4	23	FL	A	Bristol Rovers	L 1-3	1-2	22	Jansen 38	(6044)
5	26	CC 1/2	H	Chester City	W 3-0	2-0		Walling 21, Jansen 38, 70	4208
6	30	FL	H	Northampton Town	L 0-2	0-2	24		6307
7	S 02	FL	H	Wigan Athletic	W 1-0	0-0	22	McAlindon 90	5352
8	07	FL	A	Blackpool	L 1-2	0-1	22	Archdeacon 89 (pen)	(7259)
9	13	FL	A	Wycombe Wanderers	W 4-1	2-1	19	Couzens 5, Jansen 39, 90, Archdeacon 77 (pen)	(6018)
10	17	CC 2/1	A	Tottenham Hotspur	L 2-3	2-1		Couzens 40, Aspinall 45	(19255)
11	20	FL	H	Plymouth Argyle	D 2-2	2-1	18	Jansen 3, 45	5667
12	27	FL	H	Gillingham	W 2-1	0-0	16	Archdeacon 48, Pounewatchy 63	5063
13	30	CC 2/2	H	Tottenham Hotspur	L 0-2	0-1			13571
14	O 04	FL	A	Walsall	L 1-3	0-1	18	Archdeacon 82 (pen)	(3957)
15	11	FL	A	Burnley	L 1-3	0-1	20	Couzens 83	(10687)
16	17	FL	H	Preston North End	L 0-2	0-1	20		6541
17	21	FL	H	Luton Town	L 0-1	0-0	22		4341
18	25	FL	A	York City	L 3-4	2-1	22	Pounewatchy 25, Barr 35, McAlindon 78	(3700)
19	N 01	FL	A	Wrexham	D 2-2	2-2	24	Stevens 12, Bowman 16	4464
20	04	FL	A	Brentford	W 1-0	1-0	23	Jansen 45	(3424)
21	08	FL	A	Millwall	D 1-1	0-1	23	Jansen 85	(6959)
22	15	FAC 1	H	Wigan Athletic	L 0-1	0-1			5182
23	18	FL	H	Chesterfield	L 0-2	0-0	23		3591
24	22	FL	A	Bournemouth	L 2-3	1-2	24	Barr 24, Stevens 61	(3709)
25	29	FL	H	Bristol City	L 0-3	0-1	24		5044
26	D 02	FL	A	Oldham Athletic	L 1-3	1-2	24	Anthony 9	(4449)
27	09	AWS N1	H	Oldham Athletic	W 1-0*	0-0		McAlindon 99	1518
28	13	FL	H	Fulham	W 2-0	0-0	24	Stevens 60, 83	4574
29	20	FL	A	Grimsby Town	L 0-1	0-0	24		(6222)
30	26	FL	H	Blackpool	D 1-1	1-0	24	Stevens 15	8010
31	28	FL	A	Wigan Athletic	W 2-0	1-0	22	Stevens 4, McAlindon 88	(4511)
32	J 6	AWS N2	H	Rochdale	W 6-1	0-0		Anthony 23, Pounewatchy 38, Stevens 42,51, Wright 73,78	2350
33	10	FL	H	Southend United	W 5-0	1-0	22	Wright 42, Jansen 52, 65, Stevens 81, Wallwork 85	5389
34	17	FL	A	Northampton Town	L 1-2	1-0	22	Stevens 37	(6327)
35	24	FL	H	Bristol Rovers	W 3-1	2-0	20	Stevens 3, 44, 87	5725
36	31	FL	H	Wycombe Wanderers	D 0-0	0-0	20		6220
37	F 03	AWS NQF	A	Burnley	L 1-4	0-0		Prokas 55	(4573)
38	06	FL	A	Plymouth Argyle	L 1-2	0-1	23	Stevens 51 (pen)	(4540)
39	14	FL	H	Walsall	D 1-1	0-0	23	Varty 89	4530
40	21	FL	A	Gillingham	L 0-1	0-0	23		(6270)
41	24	FL	A	Preston North End	W 3-0	2-0	21	Barr 10, Wright 26, 62	(8985)
42	28	FL	H	Burnley	W 2-1	1-0	20	Stevens 18, Smart 81	7192
43	M 03	FL	H	Millwall	W 1-0	0-0	19	Smart 51	5217
44	07	FL	A	Wrexham	D 2-2	1-1	19	Wright 37, Stevens 83	(4242)
45	14	FL	H	Brentford	L 1-2	1-0	19	Stevens 39	6021
46	17	FL	A	Watford	L 1-2	0-1	19	Stevens 68	(7274)
47	21	FL	A	Chesterfield	L 1-2	1-0	21	Smart 40	(3967)
48	28	FL	H	Bournemouth	L 0-1	0-1	22		4951
49	A 04	FL	A	Bristol City	L 0-1	0-0	23		(12578)
50	11	FL	H	Oldham Athletic	W 3-1	2-1	23	Stevens 7, Anthony 12, Smart 88	4594
51	13	FL	A	Fulham	L 0-5	0-2	23		(9243)
52	21	FL	H	Grimsby Town	L 0-1	0-1	23		3956
53	25	FL	H	York City	L 1-2	1-0	23	Smart 37	3897
54	M 02	FL	A	Luton Town	L 2-3	0-1	23	Anthony 52, Wright 82	(6729)

Best Home League Attendance: 8010 V Blackpool   Smallest :3591 V Chesterfield   Average :5393

Goal Scorers:

FL	(56)	Stevens 17, Jansen 9, Smart 6, Wright 5, Archdeacon 4, Anthony 3, Barr 3, McAlindon 3, Couzens 2, Pounewatchy 2, Bowman 1, Varty 1, Wallwork 1
CC	(7)	Jansen 3, Aspinall 1, Couzens 1, Smart 1, Walling 1
FAC	(0)	
AWS	(8)	Stevens 2, Wright 2, Anthony 1, McAlindon 1, Pounewatchy 1, Prokas 1

*AET

(M) Anthony	(F) Archdeacon	(F) Aspinall	(M) Barr	(D) Boertien	(M) Bowman	(G) Caig	(D) Couzens	(M) Delap	(F) Dobie	(D) Foster	(M) Harrison	(D) Holloway	(M) Hopper	(D) Hoyland	(F) Jansen	(D) Liburd	(F) McAlindon	(M) Milligan	(D) Pounewatchy	(M) Prokas	(M) Sandwith	(F) Smart	(F) Stevens	(M) Thorpe	(D) Varty	(F) Walling	(D) Wallwork	(F) Wright		
	X	X	X			X		X							S1		S			X	X		X		S2	X	X		S.G. Bennett	1
	X	X	X			X		X	S1						X		S	S		X			X		X	X	X	X	E Lomas	2
	X	X	X			X		X	S2						X		S	S1		X			X		X	X	X	X	D Pugh	3
	X	X	X	S		X	X		S2						X		S1	X		X					X	X	X		G Singh	4
	X	X	X	S3		X	X		S1						X		X	S2	X						X	X			G Laws	5
	X	X	X			X	X		X		S2				X		S1	S	X	X					X	X			R Pearson	6
	X	X	X			X	X			X	X				X	S	X	S	S						X	X			S W Mathieson	7
	X	X	X			X	X			X	X				X	S1	S	X	S						X	X			W C Burns	8
	X	X	X			X	X		S1	X					X	X	S	X	X	S					X				F G Stretton	9
	X	X	X	S		X	X	S1	X						X	X	S	X	X						X				G R Ashby	10
	X	X	X	S		X	X		X						X		X	X	X		S2				X				P R Richards	11
	X	X	X	S		X	X			X					X		X	X	X	S					X				K M Lynch	12
	X	X	X	S1	S	X	X	S2	X						X		X	X	X						X				J T Winter	13
	X	X	X	X		X	X	S1							X		X	X	X	S2					X				S J Baines	14
	X	X	S	X	X	X									X	X	S	X	X				S1		X				A G Wiley	15
	X	X		X	X	S1		X		X					X	S3		X					S2		X				G B Frankland	16
	X	X	X	X	X	X		X		X					X	S2	S	X					S1		X				G Cain	17
	X	X	S	X	X	X			S						X	X	S1	X					X		X				D Laws	18
	X	X	S2	X	X	X			S1						X	X	S	X					X		X				J P Robinson	19
	X	X	X		X	X	S2	S							X	X	S1	X					X		X				P Rejer	20
	X	X	X		X	X	S1	S							X	X	S	X					X		X				A P D'Urso	21
	X	X	X		X	X	S2		S1						X	X	S	X	X				X		X				R Pearson	22
	X	X	X		X	X1	X		X						X	S2	S	X					X		X				M D Messias	23
		X	X		X	S		X	X1		S	X			S1		S1	X	X				X					X	M J Brandwood	24
X		X	X		X	S		X	X1		S	X			S1		S1	X	X				X					X	M S Pike	25
X2		X	X	S	X	S2		X	X1	X	X				S1			X					X					X	D Pugh	26
X		X	X		X	S		X	S2		X	X3			S3	X1	X			X2			X					X		27
X		X	X1		X	S	S1	S		X	X							X					X		X			X	W C Burns	28
X		X			X		X	S		X1	X	X			S			X				X	S1	X				X	M J Jones	29
X		X			X	S	X			X	X						S	X					X	S		X	X	X	D Laws	30
		X	X1	X	X		S			S1	X			X	S2	X						X2	X		X	X	X	I Jones	31
X2		X			X	S2	X1			S1	X	X3		S3	X							X	X	X	X	X	X	X		32
X		X			X	S	X				X				S	X	S					X	X	X	X	X	X	D Laws	33
X		X			X	S	X	S1							X1	X	S					X	X	X	X	X	X	B Coddington	34
X		X			X	S	X				X				S1	X	S2			X	X2	X	X	X1	T Heilbron	35
X			S	X	S	X1					X				X1	X	X					X	X	X			X		C J Foy	36
X					X1	X	S1	X	X							X	X	X				X	X	X			X		37
X		X			X	S			X					S2		X	X	X1		X	X2	X	X		A G Wiley	38
X2		X		S	X	S2		S1			X				X1		X			X		X		E Lomas	39
X		X			X	S	S1				X					S		X		X	X		X	X	D R Crick	40
X2		X			X	S2	S1				X						X	X1	X		X	X	A N Butler	41
X		X		S	X	S	S				X	X					X	X	X	X	X	S W Mathieson	42
X		X			X	X	S1				X		X				X	X	X1	X	X	G B Frankland	43
X		X			X	S1	S2				X		X				X	X2	X	S	X	X1	S J Baines	44
X3		X			X	S3	S2				S1		X1				X	X	X	X	X2	X	A R Leake	45
X		X			X	X		S			X		S				X	X	X	X	X	X	F G Stretton	46
X		X	S1	X	X	S				S					X	X	X	X1	X	X	P Rejer	47
X		X1			X	S1		X		X			S			X	X	X	X	S1	X	M L Dean	48
X		X			X	S1	X	S		X1		X	X	X	X	X	X	M E Pierce	49
X		X			X	S	S	X		X		X	X	X	X	X	J A Kirkby	50
X		X			X	X		X			S	S1	X	X	X	X1	X	X	R Styles	51
		X	X1	X	S1	X		X	X	X	X	S	X	X	X	K M Lynch	52
X		X			X2	X	X1	X	S2	S1	X	X	X	X	X	E K Wolstenholme	53
X		X			X	X	X	X	S	X	X	X	X	X	J P Robinson	54

25	18	18	39	8	6	46	18	8	9	7	6	5	16	5	22	9	16	2	39	33	2	16	33	12	43	6	10	25	FL Appearances	
	1	1				9	1	14		4		3		1			12	5		1	1			4	2	1			FL Sub Appearances	
4	4	4	0+2		4	3	1	0+4		2				4		3	0+1	3	4		1		1	4	2		CC Appearances	
1	1	1	1		1			0+1				0+1		1		1	1		1			1	1		FAC Appearances	
3			2	1	1	3	0+3	2	1+1			1+1		2		1+2	1	2	2		3	1	3	2	2	AWS Appearances	

Also Played: (M) Croci X(16). (G) Dixon S(22). (M) Gray S1(38), S(54). (M) Hughes X1(48), S(49,51,53). (M) Pagnal X1(40), S(41). (F) Peacock X(1), S1(12). (M) Sanowity S(24). (M) Skelton S (52,54).

539

CARLISLE UNITED

RECORDS AND STATISTICS

CLUB RECORDS

BIGGEST VICTORIES
League: 8-0 v Hartlepool United, Division 3(N), 1.9.1928.
8-0 v Scunthorpe United, Division 3(N), 25.12.1952.
F.A. Cup: 6-1 v Billingham Synthonia, Round 1, 1.17.1956.

BIGGEST DEFEATS
League: 1-11 v Hull City, Division 3(N), 14.1.1939.
F.A. Cup: 0-5 v West Ham United, !st Round replay, 1909-10.
1-6 v Wigan Athletic, 1st Round, 1934-35.
1-6 v Bradford City, 1st Round, 1951-52.
0-5 v Bristol City, 4th Round replay, 28.1.1981.

MOST POINTS
3 points a win: 80, Division 3, 1981-82.
2 points a win: 62, Division 3(N), 1950-51.

RECORD TRANSFER FEE RECEIVED
£1,500,000 from Crystal Palace for Matt Jansen, February 1998.

RECORD TRANSFER FEE PAID
£121,000 to Notts County for David Reeves, October 1993.

BEST PERFORMANCES
League: 22nd in Division 1, 1974-75.
F.A. Cup: 6th Round, 1974-75.
League Cup: Semi-Finals in 1969-70.

HONOURS
Champions of Division 3, 1964-65, 1994-95.

LEAGUE CAREER
Elected to Div 3N 1928, Transferred to Div 4 1958, Div 3 1961-62, Div 4 1962-63, Div 3 1963-64, Div 2 1964-65, Div 1 1973-74, Div 2 1974-75, Div 3 1976-77, Div 2 1981-82, Div 3 1985-86, Div 4 (now Div 3) 1986-87, Div 2 1994-95. Div 3 1995-96, Div 2 1996-97. Div 3 1997-98.
MOST GOALS IN A SEASON

INDIVIDUAL CLUB RECORDS

Hugh McIlmoyle: 44 goals in 1963-64 (League 39, League Cup 5).

MOST GOALS IN A MATCH
5. H.Mills v Halifax Town, Division 3(N), 11.9.1937.
5. Jim Whitehouse v Scunthorpe United, 8-0, Division 3(N), 25.12.1952.

OLDEST PLAYER
Bryan 'Pop' Robson, 39 years 321 days v Shrewsbury Town, 28.9.1985.

YOUNGEST PLAYER
Rory Delap, 16 years 306 days v Scarborough, 8.5.1993.

MOST CAPPED PLAYER
Eric Welsh (Northern Ireland) 4.
W.Clark; Ivor Broadis; Bill Shankly; Fred Emery; Andy Beattie; Ivor

PREVIOUS MANAGERS

Powell; Alan Ashman; Tim Ward; Bob Stokoe; Ian MacFarlane; Alan Ashman; Dick Young; Bobby Moncur; Martin Harvey; B.S.Robson; Bob Stokoe; Harry Gregg; Aidan McCaffery, Mick Wadsworth.

ADDITIONAL INFORMATION
PREVIOUS NAMES
Shaddongate United.

PREVIOUS LEAGUES
North Eastern League.

Club colours: Royal blue with white collar, red trim and red and white hoops on sleeves.
Change colours: All gold with green, red & white trim.

Reserves League: Midland Senior League.

'A' Team: Lancashire League Division 2.

LONGEST LEAGUE RUNS

of undefeated matches:	15 (1950-51, 1983-84)	of league matches w/out a win:	14 (1935)
of undefeated home matches:	22 (1950-51)	of undefeated away matches:	12 (1950-51)
without home win:	8 (1954, 1991-92)	without an away win:	20 (1970-71)
of league wins:	6 (1937, 1981-82)	of home wins:	7 (1930-35)
of league defeats:	8 (1935)	of away wins:	4 (1964-65)

MANAGER

MICHAEL KNIGHTON . . . . Appointed September 1997.

PREVIOUS CLUBS
As Manager . . . . None.
As Asst.Man/Coach . . . . None.
As a player. . . . . None.

HONOURS
As a Manager . . . . None.
As a Player . . . . None.

CARLISLE UNITED

PLAYERS NAME Honours	Ht	Wt	Birthdate	Birthplace Transfers	Contract Date	Clubs	APPEARANCES				GOALS			
							League	L/Cup	FA Cup	Other	Lge	L/C	FAC	Oth
G O A L K E E P E R														
Craig Anthony	6.1	12	4/11/74	Whitehaven	7/10/92	Carlisle United	185	14	12	17				
Heritage Paul	6.2	12.11	4/17/79	Sheffield		Sheffield United (T)								
				Free		Barnsley								
				Free	7/1/98	Carlisle United								
D E F E N C E														
Boertien Paul	5.11	11	1/20/79	Haltwhistle	5/31/97	Carlisle United	8+1	+2	1					
Bowman Rob	6.1	12.4	11/21/75	Durham	11/20/92	Leeds United (T)	4+3	0+1		1				
				Free	2/21/97	Rotherham United	13							
				Free	9/14/97	Carlisle United	6+1			1	1			
Brightwell David	6.1	13.05	1/7/71	Lutterworth	4/11/88	Manchester City	35+8	2+1	5+2		1		1	
				Loan	3/22/91	Chester City	6							
				Loan	8/11/95	Lincoln City								
				Loan	9/11/95	Stoke City								
				£30000	12/29/95	Bradford City	23+1		1	2				
				Loan	12/12/96	Blackpool	1+1							
				Free	7/18/97	Northampton Town	34+1	2	5	+1	1			
				Free	7/7/98	Carlisle United								
Couzens Andrew J FAYC'93.	5.11	11.11	6/4/75	Shipley	3/5/93	Leeds United	17+11	4+1		+2	1	1		
					7/21/97	Carlisle United	18+9	3			2	1		
Kubicki Darisz Polish Int. Div.1'96.	5.1	11.7	06/06/63	Warsaw		Legia Warsaw								
				£200000	28/08/91	Aston Villa	24+1	3	4+1	1				
				£100000	04/03/94	Sunderland	135+1	7	7					
				Free	08/08/97	Wolverhampton W.	12	4						
				Loan	3/3/98	Tranmere Rovers	12							
				Free	7/1/98	Carlisle United								
Patterson Scott	5.11	12.10	5/13/72	Aberdeen		Cove Rangers								
				£15000	3/19/92	Liverpool								
				Free	7/4/94	Bristol City	40+10	6	2	3	1			
				Loan	11/7/97	Cardiff City	5							
					7/1/98	Carlisle United								
Searle Damon P Div.3'93. W: B.1, u21.7, Y. WFAC'93.	5.11	10.5	10/26/71	Cardiff	8/20/90	Cardiff City	233+2	9	13	29	3	1		
					8/15/96	Stockport County	33+4	2	2					
					7/7/98	Carlisle United								
Varty John W 97 AMC'	6	12.4	10/1/76	Workington		Carlisle United	74+3	8	3	6+1	1			
M I D F I E L D														
Anthony Graham John	5.7	9.7	8/9/75	South Shields	7/7/93	Sheffield United	0+3	1		2				
				Loan	3/1/96	Scarborough								
					3/26/97	Swindon Town	3							
				Free	8/14/97	Plymouth Argyle	4	1						
				Free	11/26/97	Carlisle United	25				3			
Barr William J	5.11	10.8	1/21/69	Halifax	7/6/88	Halifax Town	178+18	8+1	11+1	14+3	13	2	2	
				Free	6/17/94	Crewe Alexandra	70+12	2	4	6+1	6			
				Free	7/21/97	Carlisle United	39	4	1		3			
Hopper Tony	5.11	11.07	5/31/76	Carlisle	7/18/94	Carlisle United	35+20		2+1	1	1			
Prokas Richard	5.8	11.4	1/22/76	Penrith	7/18/94	Carlisle United	97+9	7+1	5	12+1	2			
Sandwith Kevin	5.11	12.5	4/30/78	Workington	10/18/96	Carlisle United	2+1							
Skelton Gavin R					4/20/98	Carlisle United (T)								
Thorpe Jeffery	5.1	12.8	11/17/72	Cockermouth	7/2/91	Carlisle United	100+63	7+3	4+2	8+12	7			1
F O R W A R D														
Dobie Robert S	6.1	11.12	10/10/78	Workington	4/29/97	Carlisle United	9+16	0+4	0+1		1			
Finney Stephen K Div.2'96.	5.1	12	31/10/73	Hexham	02/05/92	Preston North End	1+5		0+1	1+1	1			
				Free	12/02/93	Manchester City	1		1					
				Free	01/08/95	Swindon Town	47+26	6+1	2+5	2+1	18	1	2	1
				Loan	10/10/97	Cambridge United	4+3			2				
				Free	7/1/98	Carlisle United								
McAlindon Gareth 97 AMC'	5.9	11.1	4/6/77	Hexham		Newcastle United								
				Free	7/10/95	Carlisle United	19+24	3	1+1	0+2	4		1	
Stevens Ian AMC'89.	5.9	12	10/21/66	Malta	11/22/84	Preston North End	9+2		1		2			
				Free	10/27/86	Stockport County	1+1		0+1	0+1				
					12/1/86	Lancaster City								
				Free	3/25/87	Bolton Wanderers	26+21	1+2	4	3+1	7		2	
				Free	7/3/91	Bury	100+10	3+1	2+2	7+1	38			3
				£20000	8/1/94	Shrewsbury Town	94+17	2+1	4+2	8+2	37		2	11
				Free	5/7/97	Carlisle United	33+4		1		17			
Whitehead Stuart	5.11	12.4	17/07/76	Bromsgrove		Bromsgrove								
					01/08/96	Bolton Wanderers								
				Free	7/1/98	Carlisle United								

BRUNTON PARK
Warwick Road, Carlisle, Cumbria CA1 1LL

Capacity..10,925 at present.
By Christmas the capacity will rise to 17,300, and eventually the stadium will accomadate for 28,000 all seated spectators.

First game...Not known.
First floodlit game ....Not known.

ATTENDANCES
Highest ....27,500 v Birmingham City, FA Cup 3rd Round, 5.1.1957
.... & Middlesbrough, FA Cup 5th Round, 7.2.1970.
Lowest ....859 v Hartlepool, AMC 1st Round, 15.12.1992.

OTHER GROUNDS: .... None.

HOW TO GET TO THE GROUND

From the North, East, South
Use Motorway M6 until junction 43. Leave motorway and follow signs to Carlisle (A69) into Warwick Road for Carlisle United FC.

From the West
Follow signs into Carlisle then forward (A69) along Warwick Road for Carlisle United FC.

Car Parking
Car park for 1,500 vehicles next to ground. Entrance in St Aidan's Road. 50p cars, 32.00 coaches. Limited street parking permitted.

Nearest Railway Station
Carlisle Citadel (01228 4471)

Club switchboard 01228 526 237
Club fax number 01228 526 237
Club shop 01228 524 014
Ticket Office. 01228 526 237

Marketing Department. 01228 524 014
Internet address . . . . www.carlisleunited.co.uk
Clubcall 0891 12 16 32*
*Calls cost 50p per minute at all times. Call costings correct at time of going to press.

MATCHDAY PROGRAMME

Programme Editor
. . . . . . Mark M Knighton and Paul Newton.

Number of pages . . . . 40.

Price . . . . £1.60.

Subscriptions . . . . Apply to club.

Local Newspapers
. . . . Cumbrian Newspapers.

Local Radio Stations
. . . . BBC Radio Cumbria, CFM Radio.

MATCHDAY TICKET PRICES

East Stand
Adults. £11.00
Concessions. £6.00
Additional children £3.00

C Stand (Adults only) £11.00

Platinum Stand
Adults. £10.00
Concessions. £6.00

A Stand (Adults) £10.00

B Stand (Adults) £10.00

Family Stand
Adults. £10.00
Concessions. £6.00

Warwick Road & Paddock
Adults. £8.00
Concessions. £5.00

CHESTER CITY
(The Blues)
NATIONWIDE LEAGUE DIVISION 3
SPONSORED BY: SAUNDERS HONDA

Back Row L-R: Craig Warrington, Philip Clench, Matty Woods, Nick Richardson, Spencer Whelan, Andy Milner, John Jones, Gary Bennet, Chris Priest.
Middle Row: Stuart Walker, John Murphy, Julian Alsford, Ronnie Sinclair, David Flitcroft, Wayne Brown, Shawn Reid, Rod Thomas, Dave Fogg.
Front Row: Ryan Dobson, Rod McDonald, Neil Fisher, Gary Shelton, Iain Jenkins, Kevin Ratcliffe, Stuart Rimmer, Ross Davidson, Martin Giles.

CHESTER CITY
FORMED IN 1884
TURNED PROFESSIONAL IN 1902
LTD COMPANY IN 1909

PATRON: Duke of Westminster

CHAIRMAN: M.S Guterman

SECRETARY
D E Barber J.P. Amitd

GENERAL MANAGER: W Wingrove
MANAGER: Kevin Ratcliffe
PLAYER COACH: Gary Shelton

YOUTH TEAM MANAGER
David Fogg

PHYSIOTHERAPIST
Stuart Walker

STATISTICIAN FOR THE DIRECTORY
John Martin

Chester were keen to improve on last season's play-off semi-final and an opening win over Lincoln City was the positive start they were after. The early season form was patchy, winning three on the bounce but then losing two, but fourth position was achieved during October.

Chester maintained enough good form to keep them in touch with the play-offs up until February but only three victories in the final months of the season saw the club drop out of contention and finally settle in fourteenth place.

There was little to cheer in the Cup competitions either as both the Coca-Cola Cup and FA Cup were left early on. A first round defeat against Carlisle United (5-1 on aggregate) ended the Coca-Cola Cup competition whilst a second round defeat against Wrexham (0-2) saw the 'Blues' go out of the FA Cup, after a first round win over Winsford United (2-1).

This season Kevin Ratcliffe will want to make sure they can maintain enough good form to once again challenge for a play-off spot and not fade away as they did last year.

CHESTER CITY

Division 3 :14th FA CUP: 2nd Round LC CUP: 1st Round AWS: Northern Round 1

M	DATE	COMP.	VEN	OPPONENTS	RESULT	H/T	LP	GOAL SCORERS/GOAL TIMES	ATT.
1	A 09	FL	H	Lincoln City	W 2-0	0-0	3	Flitcroft 74, Bennett 85	2478
2	12	CC 1/1	H	Carlisle United	L 1-2	0-1		Woods 73	2367
3	23	FL	H	Cambridge United	D 1-1	0-1	15	Bennett 68	2167
4	26	CC 1/2	A	Carlisle United	L 0-3	0-2			(4208)
5	30	FL	A	Barnet	L 1-2	0-0	17	Simpson 61 (OG)	(1790)
6	S 02	FL	A	Scunthorpe United	L 1-2	1-0	21	Bennett 23	(2633)
7	05	FL	H	Hull City	W 1-0	1-0	15	Bennett 41	2271
8	13	FL	H	Shrewsbury Town	W 2-0	1-0	14	Bennett 21, 65	2853
9	16	FL	A	Cardiff City	W 2-0	2-0	7	Alsford 11, Bennett 32 (pen)	(3949)
10	20	FL	A	Mansfield Town	L 1-4	1-3	10	Davidson 18 (pen)	(2183)
11	27	FL	A	Rotherham United	L 2-4	0-3	12	Alsford 68, Priest 74	(3061)
12	O 04	FL	H	Hartlepool United	W 3-1	2-1	6	Whelan 34, Bennett 38, Murphy 73	2163
13	11	FL	H	Brighton & H.A.	W 2-0	1-0	4	Bennett 39, 50	2402
14	18	FL	A	Torquay United	L 1-3	0-3	5	Richardson 90	(2047)
15	21	FL	A	Scarborough	L 1-4	0-2	8	Thomas 47	(1451)
16	25	FL	H	Macclesfield Town	D 1-1	0-0	11	Priest 78	3245
17	N 01	FL	H	Rochdale	W 4-0	1-0	8	McDonald 10, Bennett 69, Rimmer 72, 80	2431
18	04	FL	A	Notts County	W 2-1	0-0	5	McDonald 61, Bennett 87	(3104)
19	08	FL	A	Leyton Orient	L 0-1	0-1	6		(3894)
20	15	FAC 1	H	Winsford United	W 2-1	0-1	9	Richardson 53, Priest 75	3885
21	18	FL	H	Peterborough United	D 0-0	0-0	9		2612
22	26	FL	H	Swansea City	W 2-0	1-0	7	Flitcroft 33 (pen), Thomas 53	1510
23	29	FL	H	Exeter City	D 1-1	0-1	8	Rimmer 66	2288
24	D 02	FL	A	Doncaster Rovers	L 1-2	1-1	9	Jones 13	(864)
25	05	FAC 2	H	Wrexham	L 0-2	0-2			5224
26	09	AWS N1	A	Scunthorpe United	L 1-2	0-0		Flitcroft 75 (pen)	(813)
27	13	FL	H	Darlington	W 2-1	0-0	7	McDonald 74, Alsford 80	1812
28	19	FL	A	Colchester United	L 0-2	0-1	8		(1897)
29	26	FL	A	Hull City	L 0-1	0-0	10	Whelan 82, Thomas 87	(4808)
30	28	FL	H	Scunthorpe United	W 1-0	0-0	10	Priest 63	2263
31	J 10	FL	A	Lincoln City	W 3-1	2-0	10	Priest 37, Jenkins 44, Rimmer 73	(2913)
32	17	FL	H	Barnet	L 0-1	0-0	10		2479
33	24	FL	A	Cambridge United	W 2-1	0-0	9	Rimmer 53, McDonald 90	(2473)
34	27	FL	H	Cardiff City	D 0-0	0-0	9		1757
35	31	FL	A	Shrewsbury Town	D 1-1	0-1	10	Woods 70	(3002)
36	F 06	FL	H	Mansfield Town	L 0-1	0-0	11		2055
37	14	FL	A	Hartlepool United	D 0-0	0-0	11		(2186)
38	21	FL	H	Rotherham United	W 4-0	0-0	9	Murphy 47, Alsford 50, Priest 71, 87	2432
39	24	FL	H	Torquay United	L 1-3	0-2	12	Woods 46	2163
40	28	FL	A	Brighton & H.A.	L 2-3	1-2	12	Flitcroft 9, Murphy 78	(2510)
41	M 03	FL	H	Leyton Orient	D 1-1	0-1	11	Richardson 65	1650
42	07	FL	A	Rochdale	D 1-1	0-0	11	Murphy 85	(1955)
43	14	FL	H	Notts County	L 0-1	0-0	14		2753
44	21	FL	A	Peterborough United	L 1-2	1-1	15	McDonald 43	(4817)
45	28	FL	A	Swansea City	L 0-2	0-1	16		(2500)
46	A 04	FL	A	Exeter City	L 0-5	0-3	17		(2965)
47	11	FL	H	Doncaster Rovers	W 2-1	2-1	16	Flitcroft 7 (pen), Rimmer 35	1593
48	13	FL	A	Darlington	L 0-1	0-0	17		(1901)
49	18	FL	H	Colchester United	W 3-1	3-0	16	Whelan 19, Fisher 34, Rimmer 36	1780
50	25	FL	A	Macclesfield Town	L 2-3	0-1	17	Whelan 52, Thomas 79	(5982)
51	M 02	FL	H	Scarborough	D 1-1	0-0	14	Rimmer 86	2719

Best Home League Attendance: 3245 V Macclesfield Town Smallest :1510 V Swansea City Average :2255

Goal Scorers:

FL	(60)	Bennett 12, Rimmer 8, Priest 6, McDonald 5, Alsford 4, Flitcroft 4, Murphy 4, Thomas 4, Whelan 4, Richardson 2, Woods 2, Davidson 1, Fisher 1, Jenkins 1, Jones 1, Opponents 1
CC	(1)	Woods 1
FAC	(2)	Priest 1, Richardson 1
AWS	(1)	Flitcroft 1

1997-98

(D) Alsford	(F) Bennett	(M) Brown	(D) Davidson	(M) Dobson	(M) Fisher	(M) Flitcroft	(M) Giles	(D) Jenkins	(M) Jones	(F) McDonald	(M) McKay	(F) Milner	(M) Moss	(F) Murphy	(M) Priest	(M) Richardson	(F) Rimmer	(M) Shelton G	(M) Shelton A	(G) Sinclair	(F) Thomas	(D) Whelan	(D) Woods	(M) Wright	Player	No.
X	X		X		X	X		X					S		S2		X	X			X	X	X	S1	A.R. Hall	1
X	X		X		X	X		X				S2		S		X	X			X	X	X	S1		E Lomas	2
X	X		X		X	X		X			S1		X		S		X			X	X	X	S2		S J Baines	3
X	X		X		X	X		X				X		S1	S3		X			X	X	X	S2		G Laws	4
X	X		X		X	X		X				X			S	X	X			X	S	X	S1		A G Wiley	5
X	X		X		X	X		X				X			S2	X	X			X	S3	X	S1		B Coddington	6
X	X		X		X	X		X				X			S	X	S2			X	S1	X	X		T Jones	7
X	X		X		X	X		X				X			S2	X	S1			X	S	X	X		A N Butler	8
X	X		X		X	X		X	S2						X	X	S1			X	S3	X	X		M J Brandwood	9
X	X	S	X		X	X		X	S	X					X	X				X	S1	X			M R Halsey	10
X	X	S	X		X	X		X		X			S2		X	X				X	S1	X			M D Messias	11
X	X		X		S1	X		X		S3				X	X	X	S2			X	X	X			G Cain	12
X	X1				X	X			S	S2			X	X	X	S1	X		X	X2	X				M S Pike	13
X	X				S3	X		X		S2			X	X	X	S1	X		X	X	X				R Styles	14
X	X			S	X	X		X			S1		X	X	X	S2			X	X	X				J A Kirkby	15
X	X			S	X	X		X			X		X	X	X	S1			X	X	X				E K Wolstenholme	16
X	X	X		X	X		X	S2	X				X	X	X	S1			X						M Fletcher	17
X	X	X		X		X	X	X		X			S1	X	X	X1	S		S						P Taylor	18
X	X	X		X		X	X	X		X			S1	X	X	X	S		S2						R J Harris	19
X	X	X			X	X	S	X		X			S2	X	X	X		S	X	X					S J Lodge	20
X	X	X			X	X	S	X		S1			S	X	X	X			X	X					G Laws	21
X	X	X	S		X	X		X		S2	S1			X	X			X	X						P R Richards	22
X	X	X	S		X	X		X	X	S	S			X	X			X	X						D Laws	23
X		X	X			X	S	X	X	X			X	X	S	S		X	X						A R Leake	24
X	X	X	S1		X1	X	S	X	S1	S			X	X	X1		S	X	X						S J Baines	25
X		X	X		X	X		X	X				X1	X				X					S1			26
X		X	X	X1	X2		X	X	S1	S2			X	X			X	X				S			P Rejer	27
X	X		X			X		X	S	X				X	X			X	X1	X	S1	S			M E Pierce	28
X	X		X			X	S	X	S2	X1				X	X			X	S1	X	X2				K A Leach	29
X	X		X		S1	X		X	S					X	X			X	X1	X	S				F G Stretton	30
X	X		X1			X		X	S					X	X			X	S1	X	X				K A Leach	31
X	X			X	X1		X			S1	S2		S	X	X	X			X	X	X2				C J Foy	32
X	X				X	X		X		X	S			X	X	X			X	S	X				S G bennett	33
X	X1				X	X	X			S	S			S1	X	X			X	X	X				B Coddington	34
X	X				X	S	X		X1				S	X	X			X	S1	X	X				A Bates	35
X	X1				X	X	X		S	X2			S1	X	X			X	X2	X					G B Frankland	36
X			X		S		X		S	X			X	X	X	X	X	X	S	X		X			E K Wolstenholme	37
X	S1		X2		S2		X			X			X	X		X1	S	X	X	X	X				J P Robinson	38
X	S3		X		S1	S2	X1			X2			X	X		X3		X	X	X	X				M S Pike	39
X	S2		X		X1	X				S			X	X		X2		X	S1	X	X				P S Danson	40
X	X		X		S1	X		X					X	X		X	S		X	X1	S	X			P Rejer	41
X	X				X	X	S	X		X	X		X	X			S		X	X		X			R D Furnandiz	42
X	X				X	X		X	S	X			X	X			S	S	X	X		X			T Heilbron	43
X	X1		X			X		X		X	X		X	X			S2	X	S1	X	S				K M Lynch	44
	X1		X		X	X	X			S1	X2		X	X			S2	S	X	X	X				D R Crick	45
	X		X		X	X		X					X	X		X	X2	S	X	S1	X	X1	S2		B Knight	46
	X1	X		X	X	S							X	X	X	X	S	X	X	X	S1				M J Brandwood	47
	S1	X		X	X	S2							X	X	X	X	S	X2	X	X	X1				A R Leake	48
	X1	X		X2	X	X	S1					S	X	X	X	X	S2	X	X	X	X				P R Richards	49
		X			X	X	X	S					X	X	X	X	S	S1	X	X	X1				J A Kirkby	50
		X		X1	X	X	S						X	X	X	X	S1	X	X	X	S				M Fletcher	51
39	37	13	24	6	29	43	8	34	2	21	3	1	19	37	41	26	3			33	25	35	24	3	FL Appearances	
	4				6	1	2		5	10	2		8		3	8		2			13	5	2		FL Sub Appearances	
2	2		2		2	2		2		1			0+2	0+1		2	1			2	2	2	0+2		CC Appearances	
2	2	2	0+1		2	2		2	0+1	1			0+1	2	1+1					2	2				FAC Appearances	
1		1	1		1	1		1	1					1	1	1						1	0+1		AWS Appearances	

CHESTER CITY   RECORDS AND STATISTICS

CLUB RECORDS

BIGGEST VICTORIES
League: 12-0 v York City, Division 3(N), 1.2.1936.
F.A. Cup: 6-1 v Darlington, 1st Round, 25.11.1933.
5-0 v Crewe Alexandra, 1st Round, 1964-65.
5-0 v Runcorn (a), 1st Round replay, 28.11.1978.

BIGGEST DEFEATS
League: 0-9 v Barrow, Division 3(N), 10.2.1934.
2-11 v Oldham Athletic, Division 3(N), 19.1.1952.
F.A. Cup: 0-7 v Blackburn Rovers, 2nd Round, 1890-91.
League Cup: 2-9 v Leyton Orient, 3rd Round, 1962-63.

MOST POINTS
3 points a win: 84, Division 4, 1985-86.
2 points a win: 57, Division 4, 1974-75.

MOST GOALS SCORED
119, Division 4, 1964-65.
(in this season 4 players scored 20 goals or more, the only occasion this has ever happened in the Football League. The 119 goals were shared between just 8 players).

RECORD TRANSFER FEE RECEIVED
£300,000 from Liverpool for Ian Rush, May 1980.

RECORD TRANSFER FEE PAID
£94,000 to Barnsley for Stuart Rimmer, August 1991.

BEST PERFORMANCES
League: 5th Division 3, 1977-78.
F.A. Cup: 5th Round replay, 1976-77, 1979-80.
League Cup: Semi-Final 1974-75. Welsh Cup: Winners (3).

HONOURS
Division 3(N) Cup winners 1935-36, 1936-37.
Debenhams Cup winners 1977. Welsh Cup winners (3).

LEAGUE CAREER
Elected to Div 3(N) 1931, Div 4 1957-58, Div 3 1974-75, Div 4 1981-82, Div 3 (now Div 2) 1985-86, Div 3 1992-93.

INDIVIDUAL CLUB RECORDS

MOST GOALS IN A SEASON
Dick Yates: 44 goals in 1946-47 (League 36, Others 8).

MOST GOALS IN A MATCH
5. T.Jennings v Walsall, 5-1, Division 3(N), 30.1.1932.
5. Barry Jepson, York City, 9-2, Division 4, 8.2.1958.

OLDEST PLAYER
Graham Barrow, 39 years 234 days v P.N.E., Division 3, 2.4.1994.

YOUNGEST PLAYER
Aidan Newhouse, 15 years 350 days v Bury, 7.5.1988.

MOST CAPPED PLAYER
Bill Lewis (Wales) 7.

PREVIOUS MANAGERS

1930-36 Charles Hewitt; 1936-38 Alex Raisbeck, 1938-53 Frank Brown; 1953-56 Louis Page; 1956-59 John Harris; 1959-61 Stan Pearson; 1961-63 Bill Lambton; 1963-68 Peter Hauser; 1968-76 Ken Roberts; 1976-82 Alan Oakes; 1982 Cliff Sear*; 1982-83 John Sainty*; 1983-85 John McGrath; 1985-92 Harry McNally; Graham Barrow* 1992-94; Mike Pejic 1994-95; Derek Mann* 1995.
*Includes period as caretaker manager.

ADDITIONAL INFORMATION
PREVIOUS NAMES
Chester until 1983.

PREVIOUS LEAGUES
Cheshire League.

Club colours: Blue & white striped shirts, blue shorts, white socks.
Change colours: Claret & white.

Reserves League: Lancashire League, Pontins League.

LONGEST LEAGUE RUNS

of undefeated matches:	18 (1934-35)	of league matches w/out a win:	26 (1961-62)
of undefeated home matches:	27 (1973-75)	of undefeated away matches:	12 (1939-46)
without home win:	13 (1961-62)	without an away win:	29 (1971-72, 1977-78)
of league wins:	8 (1934, 1936, 1978)	of home wins:	10 (1932, 1963-64)
of league defeats:	9 (7.4.1993 - 21.8.1993)	of away wins:	4 (1934, 1936)

THE MANAGER

KEVIN RATCLIFFE . . . . appointed April 1995

PREVIOUS CLUBS
As Manager. . . . . None.
As Asst.Man/Coach . . . . None.
As a player. . . . . Everton, Dundee, Cardiff City, Derby County, Chester City.

HONOURS
As a Manager . . . . None.
As a Player . . . . Division 1 championship 1985, 1987. FA Cup 1984. ECWC 1985.
. . . . Charity Shield 1984, 1985, 1986,1987. Division 3 championship 1993.
International . . . . 56 full caps, 2 U21, Youth and Schoolboy level for Wales.

CHESTER CITY

PLAYERS NAME / Honours	Ht	Wt	Birthdate	Birthplace / Transfers	Contract Date	Clubs	League	L/Cup	FA Cup	Other	Lge	L/C	FAC	Oth
APPEARANCES / GOALS														
G O A L K E E P E R														
Brown Wayne	6.1	11.12	1/14/77	Southampton	7/3/95	Bristol City	1							
via Weston-S-Mare (Free - 8/96)				Free	9/30/96	Chester City	15		2	1				
Cutler Neil A	6.1	12	03/09/76	Birmingham	06/09/93	W.B.A.								
E: S				Loan	09/12/94	Cheltenham Town								
Loan 03/02/95 Cheltenham Town				Loan	28/10/95	Coventry City								
Loan 09/12/95 Tamworth				Loan	27/03/96	Chester City	1							
					15/08/96	Crewe Alexandra								
				Loan	30/08/96	Chester City	5							
				Free	7/1/98	Chester City								
D E F E N C E														
Crosby Andrew K	6.2	13	03/03/73	Rotherham	01/01/00	Leeds United								
				Free	04/07/91	Doncaster Rovers	41+10	1+1	2	4+1				1
				Loan	12/10/93	Halifax Town								
				Free	10/12/93	Darlington	179+2	10	11	9	3		1	
				Free	7/1/98	Chester City								
Davidson Ross J	5.1	11.6	11/13/73	Chertsey		Walton & Hersham								
					6/5/93	Sheffield United	1			2				
				Free	3/26/96	Chester City	82	3	2+1	2	4			
Ratcliffe Kevin	5.11	10.2	12/4/62	Mancot	11/18/78	Everton	356+3	46	57	29+1	2			
W: 59, u21.2, Y,S. Div1'85'87. FAC'84.ECWC'85				Loan	8/1/92	Dundee	4	1						
				Free	8/12/93	Cardiff City	25	1		3	1			
				Free	1/20/94	Derby County	6							
				Free	7/19/94	Chester City	23	2	1	2+1				
Whelan Spencer	6.1	11.13	9/17/71	Liverpool		Liverpool								
				Free	4/3/90	Chester City	196+19	11+1	9+3	4+1	8	2		
Woods Matthew	6.1	12.13	9/9/76	Gosport		Everton								
					8/9/96	Chester City	35+17	0+3	3	1+1	3	1		
M I D F I E L D														
Ciench Philip			3/23/79	Chester	7/2/97	Chester City (T)								
Cross Jonathan	5.1	11.4	02/03/75	Wallasey	15/11/92	Wrexham	92+27	4+3	4+1	9+6	12	1	1	1
				Loan	12/2/96	Hereford United	5			1	1			
				Free	7/1/98	Chester City								
Flitcroft David	5.11	12	1/14/74	Bolton	5/2/92	Preston North End	4+4	0+1		0+1	2			
				Loan	9/17/93	Lincoln City	2	0+1						
				Free	12/9/93	Chester City	104+21	6+1	6	5	11			
Priest Chris	5.1	10.1	10/18/73	Leigh	6/1/92	Everton								
				Loan	9/9/94	Chester City								
				Free	1/11/95	Chester City	125+5	3	5	6	22	1		
Richardson Nick	6	12.7	4/11/67	Halifax		Emley								
				Free	11/15/88	Halifax Town	89+12	6+4	2+1	6	17	2	1	1
				£35000	8/13/92	Cardiff City	106+5	7	6	12+2	13			2
				Loan	10/21/94	Wrexham	4				2			
				Loan	12/16/94	Chester City	6				1			
				£22500	8/8/95	Bury								
				£40000	9/7/95	Chester City	86+4	4	3	2	6		1	1
Shelton Andrew M	5.10	12	6/19/80	Sutton C.	4/10/98	Chester City	0+2							
Shelton Gary	5.7	10.12	3/21/58	Nottingham	3/1/76	Walsall	12+12	0+1	2+2				1	
E: u21.1.				£80000	1/18/78	Aston Villa	24	2+1			7	1		
				Loan	3/13/80	Notts County	8							
				£50000	3/25/82	Sheffield Wednesday	195+3	19	23+1	1	18	3	3	
				£150000	7/24/87	Oxford United	60+5	7+1	5	1	1	2		
					8/24/89	Bristol City	149+1	12	9	9	24			3
				Loan	2/11/94	Rochdale	3							
				Free	7/22/94	Chester City	62+7	4	3	2	6			2
Smith Alex P	5.7	9	15/02/76	Liverpool	01/08/94	Everton								
				Free	12/01/96	Swindon Town	17+14				1			
				Free	2/6/98	Huddersfield Town	4+2							
				Free	7/1/98	Chester City								
F O R W A R D														
Beckett Luke	5.11	11.6	11/25/76	Sheffield		Barnsley (T)								
				Free	7/1/98	Chester City								
Bennett Gary M	5.11	11	9/20/63	Kirby		Kirby Town								
AMC'85. WFAC'95.				Free	10/9/84	Wigan Athletic	10+10		1	3+1	3			1
				Free	8/22/85	Chester City	109+17	6+4	8+1	10	36	1	5	5
					11/11/88	Southend United	36+6	4	1	2+1	6	4		
				£20000	3/1/90	Chester City	71+9	8	5	4+1	15	2	1	1
				Free	8/12/92	Wrexham	120+1	17	7	9	77	9	3	9
				£300000	7/13/95	Tranmere Rovers								
				£200000	3/27/96	Preston North End	16+8				5			1
					3/1/97	Wrexham	15		0+1		5			
				£50000	7/21/97	Chester City	37+4	2	2		12			
Jones Jonathan	5.11	11.5	10/27/78	Wrexham	10/27/78	Chester City (T)	5+19		0+1	1+2	2			
Murphy John	6.1	14	10/18/76	Whiston	8/1/94	Chester City	24+31	3+3	0+1	1	8	1		
Thomas Roderick C	5.6	10.6	10/10/70	Brent	5/3/88	Watford	63+21	3+2	0+1	3+1	9			
E: u21.1, Y., S. FAYC'89.				Loan	3/27/92	Gillingham	8		1		1			
				Free	7/12/93	Carlisle United	124+21	11+1	9+4	20	16	3		8
				Free	7/4/97	Chester City	25+13	2	2		4			
Wright Darren	5.6	10	9/7/79	Warrington	12/12/97	Chester City (T)	3+2			0+1				
ADDITIONAL CONTRACT PLAYERS														
Moss Darren M					4/17/98	Chester City (T)								

DEVA STADIUM
Bumpers Lane, Chester, Cheshire

Capacity 6,000
Covered Standing 2,640
Seating..3,094

First game ....v Stockport Co., Lge Cup, 25.8.1992.
First floodlit game ....As above.

ATTENDANCES
Highest ....5,638 v P.N.E., Div 3, 2.4.1994.
Lowest..774 v Rotherham United (AMC) 26.9.1996.

OTHER GROUNDS ....Sealand Road

HOW TO GET TO THE GROUND

From the North
Use motorway (M56), A41 or A56 sign posted to Chester, into Town Centre, then follow signs to Queensferry (A548) onto Sealand Road, turn into Bumpers Lane for Chester City FC.
From the East
Use A54 or A51 sign posted Chester, into Town Centre, then follow signs to Queensferry (A548) into Sealand Road as above.
From the South
Use A41 or A483 sign posted Chester Town Centre, then follow signs to Queensferry (A548) into Sealand Road as above.
From the West
Use A55, A494 or A548 sign posted Chester, then follow signs to Queensferry. Follow signs to Birkenhead (A494), then in 1.2 miles branch left to join the A548 Chester into Sealand Road as above.

Car Parking: Parking at the ground.
Nearest Railway Station: British Rail, Chester (01244 340 170)

USEFUL TELEPHONE NUMBERS

Club switchboard 01244 371 376/371 809
Club fax number......................01244 390 265
Ticket Office.............................01244 371 376
Marketing Department 01244 390 243

Clubcall 0891 12 16 13*
*Calls cost 50p per minute at all times.
Call costings correct at time of going to press.

MATCHDAY PROGRAMME

Programme Editor.........................J Stanley.

Number of pages....................................32.

Price ....£1.50.

Subscriptions ....Apply to club.

Local Newspapers
............Chester Chronicle, Evening Leader.

Local Radio Stations
...Radio Merseyside, Marcher Sound Radio.

MATCHDAY TICKET PRICES

East & West Stands £10
Juv/OAP £5

Terraces. £7.50
Juv/OAP £4

DARLINGTON
(The Quakers)
NATIONWIDE LEAGUE DIVISION 3
SPONSORED BY: DARLINGTON BUILDING SOCIETY

1997-98 - Back Row L-R: Carl Shutt, Darren Roberts, Simon Shaw, Richard Hope, Jason Devos, Lee Turnbull, Kenny Lowe, Michael Oliver, Brian Atkinson. **Middle Row:** Peter Drake (Kit manager), Paul Robinson, Lee Brydon, Loukas Papaconstantinou, Andy Crosby (capt), David Preece, Phil Brumwell, Glenn Naylor, Mark Barnard, Andy Thompson (Groundsman). **Front Row:** Willie Giummarra, Mark Riley (Physio), Gary Bannister (Asst. Director of coaching), David Hodgson (Director of coaching), Captain J Wood (Physical training advisor), Stuart Gibson (Youth team manager), Iain Leckie (Football in the community officer), Neil Tarrant.

DARLINGTON
FORMED IN 1883
TURNED PROFESSIONAL IN 1908
LTD COMPANY IN 1891

PRESIDENT: Alan Noble
CHAIRMAN: B Lowery
DIRECTORS
G Hodgson (Vice-chairman)
M J Peden (Chief Executive)
SECRETARY
Kenneth Lavery

MANAGER: David Hodgson
ASSISTANT MANAGER: Gary Bannister

YOUTH TEAM MANAGER
Stuart Gibson
PHYSIOTHERAPIST
Mark Riley

STATISTICIAN FOR THE DIRECTORY
Frank Tweddle

Sadly 1997-98 was not the greatest of seasons for Darlington who struggled for long periods and eventually finished in 19th position with only 54 points out of a possible 138. Their away form was very poor - only one win, six draws and 13 goals from 23 matches - and this was certainly the key factor as to why the 'Quakers' had such a miserable campaign.

They had finished in exactly the same position in 1996-97 and everyone associated with the Feethams club was hoping for better things this time round. But it was not to be and in the end of proceedings there is no doubt that most of the regular supporters were relieved that summer had arrived!

After 14 matches had been completed Darlington found themselves fourth from bottom having mustered only two wins and six draws for a total of 12 points.

Knocked out of the Coca-Cola Cup at the first hurdle by Notts County, the 'Quakers' were almost dismissed from the F.A. Cup in the opening round by Solihull Borough. They survived and after a hard fought win at Hednesford in the next round, went in with the big boys in January. By this time, though, their League form was suffering. They were fifth from bottom with only 26 points from 23 games and despite a plucky performance against First Division Wolverhampton Wanderers, they were duly knocked out of the Cup 4-0 at Feethams. After that nothing went according to plan out on the park, and from their second set of 23 League games, Darlington secured a pultry 28 more points and ended up in another lowly position.

Tony Matthews.

549

DARLINGTON

Division 3	:19th			FA CUP: 3rd Round			LC CUP: 1st Round		AWS: Northern Round 1

M	DATE	COMP.	VEN	OPPONENTS	RESULT	H/T	LP	GOAL SCORERS/GOAL TIMES	ATT.
1	A 09	FL	A	Colchester United	L 1-2	0-1	18	Oliver 75 (pen)	(2958)
2	12	CC 1/1	H	**Notts County**	D 1-1	1-1		**Roberts 24**	**2189**
3	23	FL	A	Exeter City	L 0-1	0-0	22		(3334)
4	26	CC 1/2	A	**Notts County**	L 1-2	0-1		**Naylor 90**	**(1925)**
5	30	FL	H	Rotherham United	D 1-1	0-0	23	Roberts 69	2613
6	S 02	FL	H	Scarborough	L 1-2	1-2	22	Roberts 36	2417
7	05	FL	A	Macclesfield Town	L 1-2	1-0	23	Roberts 26	(2459)
8	09	FL	H	Swansea City	W 3-2	0-2	21	Roberts 51, Naylor 87, 90	2150
9	13	FL	A	Brighton & H.A.	D 0-0	0-0	21		(1803)
10	20	FL	H	Hartlepool United	D 1-1	1-1	21	Naylor 21	3169
11	27	FL	H	Mansfield Town	D 0-0	0-0	21		2596
12	O 04	FL	A	Notts County	D 1-1	1-1	22	Roberts 2	(4428)
13	11	FL	A	Rochdale	L 0-5	0-2	23		(2134)
14	18	FL	H	Doncaster Rovers	W 5-1	1-1	20	Naylor 42, Devos 50, 70, Shutt 85, Shaw 90	2451
15	21	FL	H	Cardiff City	D 0-0	0-0	20		2278
16	25	FL	A	Lincoln City	L 1-3	0-3	21	Roberts 82	(3384)
17	N 01	FL	H	Hull City	W 4-3	1-1	20	Shaw 9, Dorner 56, Devos 67, Roberts 87	2893
18	04	FL	A	Torquay United	L 1-2	0-1	22	Roberts 67	(1411)
19	08	FL	A	Peterborough United	D 1-1	0-1	21	Roberts 49	(6207)
20	15	FAC 1	H	**Solihull**	D 1-1	1-0		**Naylor 1**	**2318**
21	18	FL	H	Leyton Orient	W 1-0	1-0	20	Dorner 28	1703
22	22	FL	H	Cambridge United	D 1-1	1-1	20	Shutt 6	2221
23	26	FAC 1R	A	**Solihull**	D 3-3	1-1		**Atkinson 44 (pen), Robinson 71, Dorner 89**	**(2000)**
24	29	FL	A	Barnet	L 0-2	0-2	20		(1726)
25	D 06	FAC 2	A	**Hednesford Town**	W 1-0	0-0		**Roberts 49 (pen)**	**(1900)**
26	09	AWS N1	A	**Preston North End**	L 2-3	0-0		**Atkinson 74 (pen), Midgley 85**	**(2703)**
27	13	FL	A	Chester City	L 1-2	0-0	22	Davidson 89 (OG)	(1812)
28	20	FL	H	Scunthorpe United	W 1-0	0-0	20	Crosby 54	2267
29	26	FL	H	Macclesfield Town	W 2-0	0-0	20	Naylor 45, Oliver 55, Dorner 65, 73	3449
30	J 06	FL	A	Scarborough	L 1-2	0-0	20	Atkinson 60	(1751)
31	10	FL	H	Colchester United	W 4-2	1-0	19	Gaughen 40, Roberts 58, Dorner 86, Haydon 84 (OG)	2170
32	14	FAC 3	H	**Wolverhampton Wand**	L 0-4	0-1			**5018**
33	17	FL	A	Rotherham United	L 0-3	0-2	20		(3877)
34	24	FL	H	Exeter City	W 3-2	1-1	17	Dorner 38, Naylor 51, 60	1917
35	27	FL	A	Swansea City	L 0-4	0-2	18		(2128)
36	31	FL	H	Brighton & H.A.	W 1-0	0-0	15	Dorner 52	2487
37	F 06	FL	A	Hartlepool United	D 2-2	0-2	18	Roberts 62, 88	(3212)
38	14	FL	H	Notts County	L 0-2	0-2	18		2781
39	21	FL	A	Mansfield Town	L 0-4	0-0	19		(2071)
40	24	FL	A	Doncaster Rovers	W 2-0	1-0	18	Dorner 41, Robinson 85	(1342)
41	28	FL	H	Rochdale	W 1-0	0-0	16	Robinson 54	2181
42	M 03	FL	H	Peterborough United	W 3-1	1-0	16	Robinson 35, Resch 59, Shutt 85	1939
43	07	FL	A	Hull City	D 1-1	0-0	16	Dorner 33	(3616)
44	14	FL	H	Torquay United	L 1-2	1-1	18	Naylor 21	2386
45	21	FL	A	Leyton Orient	L 0-2	0-1	19		(4752)
46	28	FL	A	Cambridge United	L 0-1	0-0	20		(2649)
47	31	FL	H	Shrewsbury Town	W 3-1	1-1	17	Shutt 35, 85, Ellison 83	1816
48	A 04	FL	H	Barnet	L 2-3	0-2	18	Campbell 46, Dorner 82	1880
49	11	FL	A	Shrewsbury Town	L 0-3	0-0	19		(1942)
50	13	FL	H	Chester City	W 1-0	0-0	18	Ellison 65	1901
51	18	FL	A	Scunthorpe United	L 0-1	0-0	19		(2267)
52	25	FL	H	Lincoln City	D 2-2	1-1	19	Hope 34, Ellison 62	3160
53	M 02	FL	A	Cardiff City	D 0-0	0-0	19		(2610)

Best Home League Attendance: 3449 V Macclesfield Town	**Smallest :1703 V Leyton Orient**	**Average :2384**

Goal Scorers:

FL	(56)	Roberts 12, Dorner 10, Naylor 8, Shutt 5, Devos 3, Ellison 3, Robinson 3, Oliver 2, Shaw 2, Atkinson 1, Campbell 1, Crosby 1, Gaughen 1, Hope 1, Resch 1, Opponents 2
CC	(2)	Naylor 1, Roberts 1
FAC	(5)	Atkinson 1, Dorner 1, Naylor 1, Roberts 1, Robinson 1
AWS	(2)	Atkinson 1, Midgley 1

(M) Atkinson	(D) Barnard	(M) Brumwell	(D) Brydon	(M) Campbell	(D) Crosby	(M) Davey	(D) Devos	(M) Di Lella	(M) Dorner	(M) Ellison	(D) Fickling	(M) Gaughen	(F) Giummarra	(D) Gray	(D) Hope	(M) Liddle	(F) Lowe	(F) Naylor	(M) Oliver	(G) Preece	(D) Resch	(F) Roberts	(F) Robinson	(M) Shaw	(F) Shutt	(M) Turnbull	(D) Tutill	Referee	#
X		S2		X		X									X		X	X	X	X		X	S1	X	X	S3		B. Knight	1
S	X		X		X									X	X		X	X	X	X		X	S		X	S		A W Mathieson	2
X	X			X		X								X	X		S1	S3	X	X		X	S2		X	X		A R Hall	3
X	X			X		X								X	X		X	S3	X	X		X	S1		X	S2		E Lomas	4
X	X			X		X									X	X		X	X	X		X	S1		X	S		M J Jones	5
X	X	S2	X		X									S3	X	X		X	X	X		X			X	S1		E K Wolstenholme	6
X		X	X											S3	X	X2		X	X3	X		X1	X	S2	S1	X		A R Leake	7
X	X	X	X											S3	X	X		X	X	X		X	S2		S1	X		W C Burns	8
	X	X	X			X								S3	X	X		X	X	X		X	S2		S1	X		D R Crick	9
	X	X	X		X	X	S								X		S	X	X	X		X			X	S1		J A Kirkby	10
	X	X	X		X	X							S		X		S2	X	X	X		X			X	S1		M L Dean	11
	X	X	X		X	X	X							S	X		S	X	X	X		X			S1			A G Wiley	12
	X	S1	X		X	X	X								S			X	X	X		X	S2	X	X			T Jones	13
S2	X	S3			X	X	X		X						X		X	X		X			X		X	X		P R Richards	14
S2		S			X	X	X		X						X		X	X	X	X	X	S1		X	X			R D Furnandiz	15
S2	S1	S3			X	X	X		X						X		X	X	X	X	X		X	X	X			A R Leake	16
X	X				X	X	X		X						X		S	S2	X	X	X		X	X	X			D Pugh	17
X	X	S3	S2		X	X			X						X			S1	X	X	X		X	X				K A Leach	18
X	X		X		X	S1			X2						X		S		X	X	X1	X		X		S2		M D Messias	19
X	S	X			X				X						X			X	X	X		X	S2	X	S1	S3		J P Robinson	20
X	X	S1			X		X		X						X			X	X	X		X	S	X	X	X	S		D Laws	21
	X	S			X		X		X		X				X			X	X	X		X	S1	X	X	X		E K Wolstenholme	22
X	X	S2			X		X		X					S			X	X	X	X	S			X	X	X	S1	U D Rennie	23
X	X1	S3			X				X3				X					X2	X	X	S1			X		S2		G Singh	24
X	S	S1	S2		X		X						X					X	X	X1	X	X2		X		S		P R Richards	25
X	X				X		X1						X		X1		X	X2	X		X3	S3	X						26
X	X	S			X		X	S2					X			S1	X	X		X	X1	X						P Rejer	27
X	X	S			X		X	S1					X				X	X	X	X	S		X					M S Pike	28
X	X3	X						S3	X2				X				X1	X	X	X	S1			X		S2		B Knight	29
X2	X	X			X			X3				X1	X				S1	X	X	S2	X	S3	X					A N Butler	30
X	X1	S3		X3	X		X						X				X2	X	X	S1	X	S2	X			S		S W Mathieson	31
X	X	S					X	S1	X				X				X	X	X	X	X1			X				G Cain	32
X	X	S		S	X	S1	X						X		S		X	X	X1	X				X	S1			M J Brandwood	33
X3	X1	S1			X		X						X				X	X2	X	X	S3			X	S2			R Pearson	34
X	X	X					X		X				X				X	X	X	X	S	X		X	S			R Styles	35
X	X	X					X		X				X		S1		X3	X2	X	X1	X	S2	X	S3			G Cain	36
X	X	X1			S		X		X				X				X	X1	X		S1		X	S1			A Bates	37
X	X3	S1			S3			X2					X	X		X	X	X			X	S2		X		M C Bailey	38
X1		X			S3			X					X	X		X	S1	X3		S2	X2		X		A P D'Urso	39
S	X				S			X					X	X		X	X	X1		S1	X		X	X	M D Messias	40
S	X				S			X					X	X		X	X	X	X1	X	S1		X	X	C J Foy	41
S2	X				X			X					X2	X		X	S3	X3	X1	S1		X	X	P Taylor	42
	X1	S						X					X	X		X	S2	X	X2	X	X	S1	X	W C Burns	43
X		X	S2		X			X1					X3	X		X	X	S3	X		X	S1	X2	P S Danson	44
X		X	S		X			S2		X	X1		X	X		X	X	X		X	S1	X2	M R Halsey	45
X3	S3	X		S1				S2	X	X1			X	X		X2	X	X		X	X	T Jones	46
X	S1	X3		X	X			S3	S2	X		X1	X		X2	X	X		X	X	S J Baines	47
X	X		X1	S				X2	X				X	X		S1	X	X		S2	P R Richards	48
X2	S2	X		X				X1	S3	X		X	X		X	X	X		S1	A R Leake	49
S	X	X	S1	X		X			X2	X	X1		X	X		X	X		S2	S W Mathieson	50
	X	X	S	X		X		X	X	S		X	X		X	X	X		S	M S Pike	51
S3	X	S2	X1	X				X	X2	S1		X	X		X3	X	X		S G Bennett	52

29	30	26	11	4	32	10	24		25	4	8	23		6	34	15	5	38	33	45	15	24	7	28	14	4	7	FL Appearances	
3	6	9	4	2	2	1		5	2	4		1	4		2	4	6		2	4	6	2	4	12	3	18	5	FL Sub Appearances	
1	2		1		2	1								2	2		1+1	2	2		2	0+1		2	0+1			CC Appearances	
4	3	0+3	1+1		4		3		3			2		1		4	4	4	1+1	3	2+2	4	1+1	0+2				FAC Appearances	
1	1			1		1			1			1		0+1		1		1	1		1	0+1	1					AWS Appearances	

Also Played: (M) Davies X(26,28)X2(27). (M) Gilmore S(25). (D) Hilton S2(5). (F) Midgley S2(26), X1(28). (M) Papaconstantinou X(11), S(20,23). (M) Stephenson S(32).

CLUB RECORDS

BIGGEST VICTORIES
League: 9-2 v Lincoln City, Division 3(N) 7.1.1928.
F.A. Cup: 7-2 v Evenwood, 1st Round, 17.11.1958.
Freight Rover Trophy: 7-0 v Halifax Town, 3.3.1985.

BIGGEST DEFEATS
League: 0-10 v Doncaster Rovers, Division 4, 25.1.1964.

MOST POINTS
3 points a win: 85, Division 4, 1984-85 (87, GMVC, 1989-90).
2 points a win: 59, Division 4, 1965-66.

RECORD TRANSFER FEE RECEIVED
£250,000 from PNE for Sean Gregan, November 1996.

RECORD TRANSFER FEE PAID
£95,000 to Motherwell for Nick Cusack, January 1992.

BEST PERFORMANCES
League: 15th Division 2, 1925-26.
F.A. Cup: 3rd Round 1910-11, 5th Round 1957-58 (both last 16).
League Cup: 5th Round 1967-68.

HONOURS
Division 3(N) Champions 1924-25.
Division 3(N) Cup 1933-34.
G.M.V.C. Champions 1989-90.
Division 4 Champions 1991.

LEAGUE CAREER
Original member of Div 3(N) 1921, Div 2 1924-25, Div 3(N) 1926-27, Transferred to Div 4 1958, Div 3 1965-66, Div 4 1966-67, Div 3 1984-85, Div 4 1986-87, G.M.V.C. 1988-89, Div 4 1989-90, Div 3 1990-91, Div 4 (now Div 3) 1991-

INDIVIDUAL CLUB RECORDS

MOST GOALS IN A SEASON
David Brown: 39, Division 3(N), 1924-25.

MOST GOALS IN A MATCH
5. Tom Ruddy v South Shields, Division 2, 23.4.1927.
5. Maurice Wellock, Division 3(N), 15.2.1930.

OLDEST PLAYER
Jimmy Case, 39 years 128 days v Wycombe W., Division 3, 23.10.1993.

YOUNGEST PLAYER
Dale Anderson, 16 years 254 days, 4.5.1987.

MOST CAPPED PLAYER
Jason Devos, Canada (3).

PREVIOUS MANAGERS

(Since 1946)
Bill Forrest, George Irwin, Bob Gurney, Dick Duckworth, Eddie Carr, Lol Morgan, Jimmy Greenhalgh, Ray Yeoman, Len Richley, Frank Brennan, Allan Jones, Ralph Brand, Dick Connor, Bill Horner, Peter Madden, Len Walker, Billy Elliott, Cyril Knowles, Paul Ward (Player/manager), David Booth, Brian Little, Frank Gray, Ray Hankin, Alan Murray, Paul Futcher, Eddie Kyle (Caretaker), Jim Platt

ADDITIONAL INFORMATION
PREVIOUS NAMES
None.

PREVIOUS LEAGUES
Northern League, North Eastern League, G.M.Vauxhall League.

Club colours: Black and white shirts, black shorts.
Change colours: All green.

Reserves League: Pontins League.

LONGEST LEAGUE RUNS

of undefeated matches:	17 (1968)	of league matches w/out a win:	19 (1988-89)
of undefeated home matches:	36 (1923-25)	of undefeated away matches:	14 (1968-69
without home win:	18 (1988-89)	without an away win:	36 (1952-54)
of league wins:	5 (1922, 1924, 1975, 1985, 1989 (GMVC)	of home wins:	8 (1923-24, 1924, 1935-36)
of league defeats:	8 1985)	of away wins:	4 (1948) 5 (1989 GMVC)

THE MANAGER (DIRECTOR OF COACHING)

David Hodgson . . . . appointed November 1996.

PREVIOUS CLUBS
As Manager . . . . None.
As Asst.Man/Coach . . . . None.
As a player . . . . Middlesbrough, Liverpool, Sunderland, Norwich, Middlesbrough (Loan),Jerez, ... Sheffield Wed., Metz, Swansea.

HONOURS
As a Manager . . . . None.
As a Player . . . . None.
. . . . **England:** 6 u21 caps.

LAYERS NAME / onours	Ht	Wt	Birthdate	Birthplace Transfers	Contract Date	Clubs	APPEARANCES League	L/Cup	FA Cup	Other	GOALS Lge	L/C	FAC	Oth
O A L K E E P E R														
reece David	6.2	11.11	8/26/76	Sunderland	6/30/94	Sunderland	1							
				Free	7/9/97	Darlington	44	2	4					
amways Mark	6.2	14	11/11/68	Doncaster	8/20/87	Doncaster R. (T)	121	3	4	10				
					3/26/92	Scunthorpe United	180	10	16	16				
				Free	7/18/97	York City	29	4	1					
				Free	7/1/98	Darlington								
tephenson Ashlyn	6.2	11.5	7/6/74	Manchester		Kilkenny								
					12/24/97	Darlington								
E F E N C E														
arnard Mark	6	11.1	11/27/75	Sheffield	7/13/94	Rotherham United								
				Free	9/27/95	Darlington	100+8	7	5	5	3			
ennett Gary E	6.1	12.1	12/4/61	Manchester	9/8/79	Manchester City								
				Free	9/16/81	Cardiff City	85+2	6	3		11	1		
				£65000	7/26/84	Sunderland	362+7	34+1	17+1	21	23	1		1
				Free	11/1/95	Carlisle United	26			5	5			1
				Free	8/2/96	Scarborough	85+2	4+1	4	1	18	3		
				Free	7/1/98	Darlington								
evos Jason	6.4	13.7	1/2/74	Canada	11/29/96	Darlington	31+1	1	4		3			
ope Richard	6.2	12.6	6/22/78	Stockton		Blackburn Rovers								
					2/14/97	Darlington	54+1	2	1		1			
iddle Craig	5.11	12	10/21/71	Chester-Le-Street		Blyth Spartans								
				Free	7/12/94	Middlesbrough	20+5	3+2	2	2				
				Loan	2/20/98	Darlington	15							
				Free	7/1/98	Darlington								
eed Adam	6	12	2/18/75	B. Auckland	7/16/93	Darlington (T)	45+7	1+1	1	3	1			
				£200000	8/9/95	Blackburn Rovers								
				Loan	2/21/97	Darlington	14							
				Loan	12/5/97	Rochdale	10			2				1
				Free	7/1/98	Darlington								
M I D F I E L D														
tkinson Brian	5.11	11.6	1/19/71	Darlington	7/21/89	Sunderland	119+22	8+2	13	2+3	4		2	
E: u21.6				Loan	1/19/96	Carlisle United								
					8/10/96	Darlington	53+8	5	4+1		5		1	
rumwell Philip	5.7	11.2	8/8/75	Darlington	6/30/94	Sunderland								
				Free	8/11/95	Darlington	71+28	5	5+3	3+2	1		2	
ampbell Paul A	6.1	11	1/29/80	Middlesbrough	1/23/98	Darlington (T)	4+2				1			
aughen Steven E	6	13.6	4/14/70	Doncaster		Hatfield Main Colliery								
				Free	1/21/88	Doncaster Rovers	42+25	2+2	4+1	5+1	3			
				Free	7/1/90	Sunderland								
				£10000	1/21/92	Darlington	159+12	8	6	10+1	15		1	
				£30000	8/16/96	Chesterfield	16+4	1+1	0+1	1		1		
					11/21/97	Darlington	23+1		2	1	1			
unt David	5.7	12	3/5/80	Durham	2/21/97	Darlington	0+1							
liver Michael	5.11	12.4	8/2/75	Cleveland	8/19/92	Middlesbrough	0+1							
				£15000	7/7/94	Stockport County	17+5	0+2	2		1			
					8/15/96	Darlington	66+11	6	6		11			
O R W A R D														
orner Mario	5.10	13.2	3/21/70	Baden		Molding								
						Motherwell								
					10/17/97	Darlington	25+2		3		10		1	
abbiadini Marco	5.10	13.4	1/20/68	Nottingham	9/5/85	York City (A)	42+18	4+3		4	14	1		3
E: B.1, Fl.1, u21.2.				£80000	9/23/87	Sunderland	155+2	14	5	9	74	9		4
				£1800000	10/1/91	Crystal Palace	15	6	1	3	5	1		1
				£1000000	1/31/92	Derby County	163+25	13	8+1	16+1	50	7	3	8
Panionios 8.96 (Free)				Loan	10/14/96	Birmingham City	0+2							
				Loan	1/31/97	Oxford United	5				1			
				Free	12/24/97	Stoke City	2+6		1				1	
				Free	2/20/98	York City	5+2				1			
				Free	7/1/98	Darlington								
aylor Glenn	5.11	11.01	8/11/72	Howden	3/5/90	York City	78+32	2+3	4+1	3+4	30		2	
					9/27/96	Darlington	66+11	1+1	6		18	1	2	
oberts Darren	6	12.4	10/12/69	Birmingham		Burton Albion								
				Loan	3/18/94	Hereford United	5+1				5			
				Free	7/18/94	Chesterfield	10+15	3	2	2+5	1	1		3
				Loan	12/30/94	Telford United								
					8/15/96	Darlington	66+6	6	4		28	3	1	
				Loan	2/20/98	Peterborough United	2+1							
hutt Carl	5.11	11.13	10/10/61	Sheffield		Spalding								
Div.1'92. Div.2'90.				Free	5/13/85	Sheffield Wed.	36+4	3	4+1		16	1	4	
				£55000	10/30/87	Bristol City	39+7	5+2	7+1	10+1	10	4	4	4
				£50000	3/23/89	Leeds United	46+33	6+2	10	4+5	17	2	1	4
				£50000	8/23/93	Birmingham City	23+9	3			4			
				Loan	8/11/94	Bradford City								
				£75000	9/9/94	Bradford City	60+27	8+2	3+2	5+2	15	1		1
					3/27/97	Darlington	19+19	2	1+1		7			

FEETHAMS
Darlington, Co.Durham DL1 5JB

Capacity ....8,500.

First game ....1883.
First floodlit game ....v Millwall, 19.9.1960.

ATTENDANCES
Highest...21,023 v Bolton, Lge Cup 3rd Rnd, 14.11.1960.
Lowest ....657 v Halifax, AMC, 3.3.1985.

OTHER GROUNDS ....None.

HOW TO GET TO THE GROUND

From the North
Use motorway (A1M) then A167 sign posted Darlington into town centre, then follow signs to Northallerton into Victoria Road for Darlington FC.

From the East
Use A67 sign posted Darlington into town centre, then follow signs to Northallerton into Victoria Road for Darlington FC.

From the South
Use motorway (A1M) and A66M then A66 sign posted Darlington and at roundabout take the fourth exit into Victoria Road for Darlington FC

From the West
Use A67 sign posted Darlington into town centre and at roundabout take 3rd exit into Victoria Road for Darlington FC.

Car Parking: Adequate space in adjacent side streets.
Nearest railway Station: Darlington (01325 55111)

Club switchboard 01325 240 240
Club fax number.......................01325 381 377
Club Shop.................................01325 242 020
Ticket Office..............................01325 240 240

Marketing Department 01325 240 240
Clubcall 0891 10 15 55*
*Calls cost 50p per minute ct all times.
Call costings correct at time of going to press.

MATCHDAY PROGRAMME

Programme Editor ....Ken Lavery.

Number of pages.....................................28.

Price ....£1.30.

Subscriptions ....Apply to club.

Local Newspapers
...............Northern Echo, Evening Gazette.

Local Radio Stations
...........BBC Radio Cleveland, T.F.M. Radio.

MATCHDAY TICKET PRICES

Seats	£6
Juv/OAP	£3
Terraces	£6
Juv/OAP	£3

EXETER CITY
(The Grecians)
NATIONWIDE LEAGUE DIVISION 3
SPONSORED BY: EXETER FRIENDLY SOCIETY

1998-99 - Back row L-R: Chris Fry, Scott Walker, Chris Holloway, Jon Gittens, Steve Flack, Shaun Gale, Barry McConnell, Jimmy Gardner, Luke Vinnicombe. **Middle Row:** Lee Baddeley, Jon Richardson, Chris Curran, Darran Rowbotham, Danny Potter, Ashley Bayes, John Wilkinson, Gavin Chesterfield, Danny Harris. **Front Row:** Graeme Power, Goeff Breslan, Noel Blake (Asst. Manager), George Kent (Scout), Peter Fox (Manager), Mike Radford (Yth. Dev. Officer) Simon Shakeshaft (Physio), Jason Rees, Billy Clark.

EXETER CITY
FORMED IN 1904
TURNED PROFESSIONAL IN 1908
LTD COMPANY IN 1908

CHAIRMAN: A I Doble
DIRECTORS
M Couch, S Dawe, G Vallance, P Carter,
M Shelbourne
SECRETARY
Margaret Bond (01392 54073)
COMMERCIAL MANAGER
David Bird

MANAGER: Peter Fox
ASSISTANT MANAGER: Noel Blake

YOUTH TEAM MANAGER
Mike Radford

PHYSIO
Simon Shakeshaft

STATISTICIAN FOR THE DIRECTORY
Vacant
(Phone 01203 234017 if interested)

Things were looking distinctively rosy for the 'Grecians' as October gave way to November. Peter Fox's side were lying third in the table behind Peterborough United and Notts County, having amassed 28 points from their opening 14 games. Playing some smart, attacking football and giving very little away, the signs looked good.

Over the next six weeks Exeter maintained their form and when they had fulfilled their 20th League encounter (a 1-1 draw at Chester) they were still in third position with 35 points, two less than Lincoln City who had taken over the leadership.

But then over the next 12 matches the 'Grecians' collected a mere eleven points and slipped right down the table to eleventh, leaving themselves well short of a play-off spot and a massive 23 points behind the table-topping Notts County.

A 1-0 home reverse against Colchester was followed by a narrow defeat at Swansea (2-1) and a 1-1 draw with Peterborough, and at this juncture the play-offs seemed a vast distance away. But Fox somehow got his players back on track and with six games remaining, there was still an outside chance that the 'Grecians' could claw themselves back in contention.

Unfortunately the points-gap was just that fraction too wide to close and despite some better performances, the 'Grecians' missed out, eventually finishing a disappointing 15th with a total of 60 points, 10 short of that final play-off spot.

Tony Matthews.

EXETER CITY

	Division 3	:15th		FA CUP: 1st Round			LC CUP: 1st Round		AWS: Southern Round 2	

M	DATE	COMP.	VEN	OPPONENTS	RESULT	H/T	LP	GOAL SCORERS/GOAL TIMES	ATT.
1	A 09	FL	H	Hartlepool United	D 1-1	0-1	13	Flack 85	3409
2	12	CC 1/1	A	Walsall	L 0-2	0-0			(2321)
3	15	FL	A	Barnet	W 2-1	2-0	4	Flack 15, Birch 43	(3137)
4	23	FL	H	Darlington	W 1-0	0-0	2	Rowbotham 70 (pen)	3334
5	26	CC 1/2	H	Walsall	L 0-1	0-0			2467
6	30	FL	A	Doncaster Rovers	W 1-0	1-0	1	Rowbotham 26	(1186)
7	S 02	FL	A	Torquay United	W 2-1	0-0	1	Rowbotham 47, 84	(4217)
8	09	FL	H	Cardiff City	D 1-1	0-0	1	Flack 90	4843
9	13	FL	A	Leyton Orient	L 0-1	0-1	4		(4040)
10	20	FL	H	Rotherham United	W 3-1	1-0	3	Gardner 22, Gale 60, Braithwaite 74	3420
11	27	FL	A	Colchester United	W 2-1	1-0	2	Rowbotham 34, Flack 56	(3175)
12	O 04	FL	H	Scarborough	D 1-1	1-1	3	Flack 23	4464
13	11	FL	H	Swansea City	W 1-0	1-0	2	Birch 32	3909
14	18	FL	A	Brighton & H.A.	W 3-1	1-0	2	Rowbotham 22, 48 (pen), Gale 66	(2210)
15	21	FL	A	Macclesfield Town	D 2-2	2-0	1	Flack 24, Rowbotham 44	(2286)
16	25	FL	H	Scunthorpe United	L 2-3	1-1	3	Williams 25, 55	4552
17	N 01	FL	H	Peterborough United	D 0-0	0-0	3		5984
18	04	FL	A	Hull City	L 2-3	0-1	3	Flack 66, Gale 90	(3837)
19	08	FL	A	Notts County	D 1-1	1-0	3	Rowbotham 3	(5107)
20	15	FAC 1	H	Northampton Town	D 1-1	1-1		Rowbotham 32	4605
21	18	FL	H	Mansfield Town	W 1-0	1-0	2	Devlin 32	2888
22	22	FL	H	Shrewsbury Town	D 2-2	1-1	3	Rowbotham 1, Flack 69	4041
23	25	FAC 1R	A	Northampton Town	L 1-2	1-1		Clark 43	(5259)
24	29	FL	A	Chester City	D 1-1	1-0	2	Rowbotham 45	(2288)
25	D 02	FL	H	Lincoln City	L 1-2	1-0	3	Williams 11	4224
26	12	FL	A	Cambridge United	L 1-2	1-1	4	Blake 19	(2224)
27	20	FL	H	Rochdale	W 3-0	3-0	4	Tisdale 30, Devlin 38, Richardson 44 (pen)	3378
28	26	FL	A	Cardiff City	D 1-1	0-1	4	Illman 82	(6623)
29	28	FL	H	Torquay United	D 1-1	1-1	6	Rowbotham 12	8350
30	J 6	AWS S2	H	Bristol Rovers	L 1-2	0-0		Illman 56	1851
31	10	FL	A	Hartlepool United	D 1-1	1-0	8	Flack 38	(2507)
32	17	FL	H	Doncaster Rovers	W 5-1	2-0	6	Rowbotham 15, 45, Flack 50, Illman 62, Fry 80	4145
33	20	FL	H	Barnet	D 0-0	0-0	6		3697
34	24	FL	A	Darlington	L 2-3	1-1	6	Flack 44, 81	(1917)
35	31	FL	H	Leyton Orient	D 2-2	1-1	8	Rowbotham 21, Birch 79	4023
36	F 06	FL	A	Rotherham United	L 0-1	0-0	10		(4158)
37	14	FL	A	Scarborough	L 1-4	0-2	10	Rowbotham 62 (pen)	(2078)
38	21	FL	H	Colchester United	L 0-1	0-0	12		3346
39	24	FL	H	Brighton & H.A.	W 2-1	1-1	11	Williams 36, McConnell 90 (pen)	2754
40	28	FL	A	Swansea City	L 1-2	0-0	11	McConnell 87 (pen)	(3323)
41	M 03	FL	H	Notts County	L 2-5	1-3	12	Rowbotham 42, Clark 59	2966
42	07	FL	A	Peterborough United	D 1-1	1-0	13	Clark 32	(4888)
43	14	FL	H	Hull City	W 3-0	2-0	11	McConnell 16, 58, Baddeley 38	3052
44	21	FL	A	Mansfield Town	L 2-3	1-1	11	Richardson 45, Gale 62	(2033)
45	28	FL	A	Shrewsbury Town	D 1-1	0-1	13	Flack 54	(2251)
46	A 04	FL	H	Chester City	W 5-0	3-0	11	Rowbotham 6, McConnell 12, 63, Clark 45, Flack 82	2965
47	13	FL	H	Cambridge United	W 1-0	1-0	11	Birch 13	3527
48	18	FL	A	Rochdale	L 0-3	0-0	12		(1850)
49	21	FL	A	Lincoln City	L 1-2	0-1	12	Rowbotham 64 (pen)	(4284)
50	25	FL	H	Scunthorpe United	L 1-2	1-2	14	Rowbotham 38 (pen)	(2024)
51	M 02	FL	H	Macclesfield Town	L 1-3	0-1	15	Birch 46	4499

Best Home League Attendance: 8350 V Torquay United	Smallest :2754 V Brighton & H.A.	Average :3990

Goal Scorers:

FL	(68)	Rowbotham 20, Flack 14, McConnell 6, Birch 5, Gale 4, Williams 4, Clark 3, Devlin 2, Illman 2, Richardson 2, Baddeley 1, Blake 1, Braithwaite 1 Fry 1, Gardner 1, Tisdale 1
CC	(0)	
FAC	(2)	Clark 1, Rowbotham 1
AWS	(1)	Illman 1

(?) Saddocky	(G) Bayes	(M) Birch	(D) Blake	(F) Braithwaite	(M) Clark	(D) Curran	(M) Cyrus	(M) Devlin	(G) Dungey	(F) Flack	(M) Fry	(D) Gale	(M) Gardner	(F) Ghazghazi	(D) Hare	(M) Harris	(M) Holcroft	(M) Holloway	(F) Illman	(F) McConnell	(M) Medlin	(M) Minett	(F) Phillips	(F) Richardson	(F) Rowbotham	(M) Tisdale	(F) Wilkinson	(F) Williams		
	X			S	X	X				X	S1	X	X	S2	X						X	X		X	X				R.D. Furnandiz	1
	X	X			X	X				X	S1	X	X	S	S						X	X		X	X				T Bates	2
X	X	X		S2	X					X	X	X	X		S1						S3	X		X	X				D R Crick	3
X	X	X	S1		X	S				X	X	X	X	S2								X		X	X				A R Hall	4
	X	X1	X	X3	X	X				X	S2	X2	X		S3							S1		X	X				R Styles	5
S3	X		X		X	X				X	X	X	X				X				S2	X		X	X			S1	J P Robinson	6
S1	X		X		X	X				X	S	X	X				X					X		X	X			S2	C R Wilkes	7
S	X		X		X	X				X	S2	X	X				S2				X			X	X			S1	A G Wiley	8
S	X		X		X	X				X	X	X	X				S2					X		X	X			S1	P Rejer	9
X	X	X	X	S1	X					X	X	X	X		S2							X		X	X			X	G Singh	10
2,3	X	X	X	S1		X2				X	X	X	X		S3							X		X	X			X1	A N Butler	11
X	X	X	X	S2		S1				X	X	X	X		S							X		X	X			X	M Fletcher	12
X	X	X	X	S2		S	S1			X	X	X	X									X		X	X			X	A Bates	13
X	X	X	X			S	X			X	X	X	X								S	S		X	X			X	S G Bennett	14
X	X	S1	X			X				X	X	X	X	S	S							X		X	X			X	P S Danson	15
X	X	X	X	S		S2	S1			X	X	X	X									X		X	X			X	M J Jones	16
X	X	X	X		S	X	X			S1	X	X									S			X	X			X	F G Stretton	17
X	X	X	S3		X	X	X			X	X	S1									S2			X	X			X	S W Mathieson	18
X	X	X	X		X	S	X			X	X	X	S											X	X			S1	M S Pike	19
	X	X	X	S1	X					S	X		X			S		S	S		X	X		X	X				K M Lynch	20
	X	X	X		X	X				X	X		X						S		S1	X		X	X				R J Harris	21
S	X	X	X		X	X				X	S2	X		S1							X			X	X				B Knight	22
X	X	X	X		X	S1				X	X	X	S2								S	S		X	X				K M Lynch	23
X	X	X	X			X	X		X1	S1	X	X	S								X			X	X2			S2	D Laws	24
X	X	X	X			X				S1	X	X2									S	S2		X	X			X1	M J Brandwood	25
X		X	X			X	X	X		X2	X	S1									S	X1		X	X			S2	J A Kirkby	26
	X		X			X	X			X	S2	X	S							S1		X		X	X1	X		X2	D R Crick	27
	X		X			X	X1			X	S2	X	S							S1		X2		X	X			X	S B Bennett	28
	X		X			X	X			S2	X	X	S1	X						X1		X		X	X2	X			M E Pierce	29
S2	X		X2			X				X	S1	X	X3	X						X	S3	X1		X						30
	X		X			X				S1	X	X	X	S1						X1	S			X		X			J P Robinson	31
X	X	X1	X			S2	X			X	S1	X2								X3				X	X	X		S3	P Rejer	32
X	X		X			S	X			X	X	X								X1				X	X	X		S1	M Fletcher	33
X2	X	S2	X			X	X			X	X	X	S							X1				X	X	X		S1	R Pearson	34
X	X	X	S			X	X			X	X		X							X2		S1		X1	X	X		S2	S J Baines	35
X	X	X2	X			X				S1	X		X								S2	S		X	X			X1	M D Messias	36
X	X	X	X3			X1	X			X	X		X		S1						S1	S3		X	X			X1	P R Richards	37
X	X	X	X			X	X			X1	X	X		S2	X						S2	X2			X2			S1	A Bates	38
X	X	X	X				X			X2	X	X1	X	S1				S1			X	X				X			A G Wiley	39
X	X	X	X			X				X1	X3	X		S1				S1			X	S3		X	X			X1	E Lomas	40
X	X	X	X			X						S1			X1			X			X	S		X	X2			S2	C R Wilkes	41
X2	X	X1	X			X	X					S2						X3			X	X3		X	X			S1	R Styles	42
X	X	X	X			X				X		X						X1			X2	S	S1	X	X			S2	R J Harris	44
X	X	X	X			X				S1	X	X						S			X1		X2	X	X			S2	G Laws	45
X	X	X	X			X				X2	S1	S2	X								X2			X	X1			S2	B Knight	46
X	X	X	X			X				X		X						S			X1		X2	X	X	S1		S2	D R Crick	47
X	X	X	X3			X2				X2	X	S2									S3			X	X	X1		S1	G B Frankland	48
X	X	X	X			X1				X1	X	X	S											X	X			S1	P Taylor	49
X	X	X	X3			X				X2	S2	X	X								S1	S3	X1	X	X				M J Jones	50
	X	X			X					S2	X	X2		X				X1			X3			X	X	X		S3	M R Halsey	51
29	45	31	36		31	9	17	31	1	37	16	42	19	1	5		3	4	6	10	11	6	7	41	42	10		16	FL Appearances	
3		2	2	5		4	2			4	12	1	4	8	2		3	2	2	6	9		1		1		1	20	FL Sub Appearances	
2	1	2	1		2	2			2	0+2	2	2		0+1				1		1+1		2	2			CC Appearances				
1	2	2	0+1	2		1+1			1	1	1	1+1					1			2	2			FAC Appearances					
0+1		1		1				1		0+1	1	1	1			1	0+1	1			1		S3	AWS Appearances						

Also Played: (M) Breslan S(39), S1(51).(G) Fox S(20,23).

EXETER CITY   RECORDS AND STATISTICS

CLUB RECORDS

BIGGEST VICTORIES
League: 8-1 v Coventry, Division 3(S) 4.12.1926.
8-1 v Aldershot, Division 3(S) 4.5.1935.
7-0 v Crystal Palace, Division 3(S) 9.1.1954.
F.A. Cup: 9-1 v Aberdare, 1st Round, 26.11.1927.
Other: 11-6 v Crystal Palace, Division 3(S) Cup, 24.1.1934.

BIGGEST DEFEATS
League: 0-9 v Notts County, Division 3(S), 16.10.1948.
0-9 v Northampton Town, Division 3(S), 12.4.1958.
League Cup: 1-8 v Aston Villa, 2nd Round 7.10.1985.

MOST POINTS
3 points a win: 89, Division 4, 1989-90.
2 points a win: 62, Division 4, 1976-77.

MOST GOALS SCORED: 88, Division 3(S), 1932-33.

RECORD TRANSFER FEE RECEIVED
£500,000 from Manchester City for Martin Phillips, November 1995.

RECORD TRANSFER FEE PAID
£10,000 + £5,000 + £125,000 to Bristol Rovers for Richard Dryden, March 1989, May 1989, July 1991.

BEST PERFORMANCES
League: 2nd Division 3(S) 1932-33.
F.A. Cup: 6th Round replay 1930-31.
League Cup: 4th Round.

HONOURS
Champions of Division 4, 1989-90.
Division 3(S) Cup winners 1933-34.

LEAGUE CAREER
Elected to Div 3 1920, Transferred to Div 3(S) 1921, Div 4 1957-58, Div 3 1963-64, Div 4 1965-66, Div 3 1976-77, Div 4 1983-84, Div 3(now Div 2) 1989-90, Div 3 1993-94

INDIVIDUAL CLUB RECORDS

MOST GOALS IN A SEASON
Rod Williams: 37 goals in 1936-37 (League 29, FA Cup 7, Division 3(S) Cup 1).

MOST GOALS IN A MATCH
6. James Bell v Weymouth, 1st Preliminary Rnd., 3.10.1908.
6. Fred Whitlow v Crystal Palace, Division 3(S) Cup, 24.1.1934 (11-6)

YOUNGEST PLAYER
Cliff Bastin, 16 years 31 days v Coventry City, 14.4.1928.

MOST CAPPED PLAYER
Dermot Curtis (Eire) 1.

PREVIOUS MANAGERS

1908-22 Arthur Chadwick, 1923-27 Fred Mavin, 1928-29 David Wilson, 1929-35 Billy McDevitt, 1935-40 Jack English, 1945-52 George Roughton, 1952-53 Norman Kirkman, 1953-57 Norman Dodgin, 1957-58 Bill Thompson, 1958-60 Frank Broome, 1960-62 Glen Wilson, 1962-63 Cyril Spiers, 1963-65 Jack edwards, 1965-66 Ellis Stuttard, 1966-67 Jock Basford, 1967-69 Frank Broome, 1969-76 John Newman, 1977-79 Bobby Saxton, 1979-83 Brian Godfrey, 1983-84 Gerry Francis, 1984-85 Jim iley, 1985-87 Colin Appleton, 1988 John Delve (caretaker), 1988-91 Terry Cooper, 1991-94 Alan Ball.

ADDITIONAL INFORMATION
PREVIOUS NAMES
None.
PREVIOUS LEAGUES
None.

Club colours: Red & white striped shirts, black shorts, red socks.
Change colours: Blue & white striped shirts, blue shorts.
Reserves League: Avon Combination Division 2.
'A' Team: Devon & Exeter Premier.

LONGEST LEAGUE RUNS

of undefeated matches:	13 (1986)	of league matches w/out a win:	18 (1984)
of undefeated home matches:	23 (1989-90)	of undefeated away matches:	8 (1964)
without home win:	9 (1984)	without an away win:	27 (1986-87)
of league wins:	7 (1977)	of home wins:	13 (1932-33)
of league defeats:	7 (1921, 1923, 1925, 1936, 1984)	of away wins:	6 (1977)

THE MANAGER

PETER FOX . . . . appointed June 1995.

PREVIOUS CLUBS
As Manager . . . . None.
As Asst.Man/Coach . . . . None.
As a player. . . . . Sheffield Wednesday, Barnsley, Stoke City.

HONOURS
As a Manager . . . . None.
As a Player . . . . None.

EXETER CITY

PLAYERS NAME Honours	Ht	Wt	Birthdate	Birthplace Transfers	Contract Date	Clubs	League	L/Cup	FA Cup	Other	Lge	L/C	FAC	Oth
G O A L K E E P E R														
Bayes Ashley	6.1	12.9	4/19/72	Lincoln	7/5/90	Brentford	4	5	2	1				
				Free	8/13/93	Torquay United	98	7	9	6				
					7/15/96	Exeter City	86	4	4					
Fox Peter	5.11	12.4	7/5/57	Scunthorpe	6/1/75	Sheffield Wed.	49		3					
AMC'92. Div.2'93.				Loan	12/22/77	Barnsley	1	1						
				£15000	3/4/78	Stoke City	409	32	22	14				
				Free	7/15/93	Exeter City	107+1	7	6	4				
Potter Danny						Colchester United								
				Free	7/1/98	Exeter City								
D E F E N C E														
Baddeley Lee	6.1	12.1	7/12/74	Cardiff	8/13/91	Cardiff City	112+21	4+2	8	23	1			
				Free	2/6/97	Exeter City	36+5		1		1			
Blake Noel	6	13.11	1/12/62	Kingston (Jam)	1/1/00	Sutton Coldfield								
					8/1/79	Aston Villa	4							
Loan 3/1/82 Shrewsbury Town 6 Lge Apps.				£55000	9/15/82	Birmingham City	76	12	8		5			
				£150000	8/24/84	Portsmouth	144	14	10	5	10	1	2	1
				Free	7/4/88	Leeds United	51	4+1	2	4	4			
				£175000	2/9/90	Stoke City	74+1	6	3+1	4+1	3			
Loan 2/27/92 Bradford City 6 Lge Apps.				Free	7/20/92	Bradford City	31+1	2	3	3	3		1	
					12/1/93	Dundee United								
					8/31/95	Exeter City	126+2	5	5		9			
Chesterfield Gavin			8/18/79	Neath	5/20/98	Exeter City (T)								
Curran Chris	5.11	11.9	9/17/71	Birmingham	7/13/90	Torquay United	127+6	12	5	8	3			
				£20000	12/22/95	Plymouth Argyle	27+4	1+1	1	3				
					7/31/97	Exeter City	9	2						
Gale Shaun	6	11.6	10/8/69	Reading	7/12/88	Portsmouth	2+1			0+1				
				Free	7/13/94	Barnet	153+5	12	6	5	6			
					6/16/97	Exeter City	42+1	2	2		4			
Gittens Jon	5.11	12.6	22/01/64	Birmingham		Pagent Rangers								
				£10000	16/10/85	Southampton	18	4	1					
				£40000	22/07/87	Swindon Town	124+2	15+1	9	13+1	6			1
				£400000	28/03/91	Southampton	16+3	4		1				
Loan 19/02/92 Middlesbrough 9+3 Lge Apps.				£200000	27/07/92	Middlesbrough	13	0+1	1					
				Free	09/08/93	Portsmouth	81+2	10	3	3	2			
				Free	05/08/96	Torquay United	78	6	4	5	9			2
				Free	7/1/98	Exeter City								
Power Graeme R	5.9	10.1	07/03/77	Harrow	11/04/95	Q.P.R.								
E: Y.					16/09/96	Bristol Rovers	25+1		1	1+2				
				Free	7/1/98	Exeter City								
Vinnicombe Luke			3/7/80	Paignton	5/20/98	Exeter City (T)								
M I D F I E L D														
Birch Paul	5.6	10.9	11/20/62	Birmingham	7/10/00	Aston Villa	153+20	21+4	9+5	5+2	16	5	3	1
ESC'82. FAYC'80				£400000	2/1/91	Wolverhampton W.	128+14	11+1	2+1	8+1	15	3		1
				Loan	3/7/96	Preston North End	11				2			
					8/15/96	Doncaster Rovers	26+1	2	1		2			
				Free	3/27/97	Exeter City	33+2	1	2		5			
Breslan Geoffrey F	5.8	11	6/4/80	Torbay	2/23/98	Exeter City (T)	0+1							
Clark William R	6	12.4	5/19/67	Christchurch	9/25/84	Bournemouth (T)	4							
					10/16/87	Bristol Rovers	235+13	11+1	8+1	19+2	14			1
				Free	10/30/97	Exeter City	31		2	1	3		1	
Fry Christopher D	5.9	9.6	10/23/69	Cardiff	8/3/88	Cardiff City	22+33	1+2	0+2	0+2	1			
W: S.				Free	8/2/91	Hereford United	76+14	6+2	8+2	6	10		1	
					10/24/93	Colchester United	101+28	3+3	3+1	6+1	16	1		
					7/29/97	Exeter City	16+12	0+2	1		1			
Gardner James F	5.11	10.6	10/26/78	Beckenham	5/31/97	Wimbledon								
					7/30/97	Exeter City	19+4	2	1		1			
Harris Daniel			12/18/79	Exeter	5/20/97	Exeter City (T)								
Holloway Chris D	5.10	11.7	2/5/80	Swansea	11/14/97	Exeter City (T)	4+2							
Rees Jason	5.5	10.2	12/22/69	Aberdare	7/1/88	Luton Town 2	59+23	3+2	2+1	5+1				2
W: 1, B.1, u21.3, Y, S.				Loan	12/23/93	Mansfield Town	15			1				
				Free	7/18/94	Portsmouth	30+13	2+1	0+1		3			
Loan 1/31/97 Exeter City 7 Lge Apps.				Free	8/8/97	Cambridge United	17+3	2		1				
				Free	7/1/98	Exeter City								
Walker Scott			3/17/80	Exeter	5/20/98	Exeter City (T)								
F O R W A R D														
Flack Steve	6.2	14.4	5/29/71	Cambridge	1/1/00	Cambridge City								
				£10000	11/13/95	Cardiff City	6+5				1			
				£10000	9/16/96	Exeter City	57+11	2	3	2+1	18	1		
McConnell Barry	5.11	10.3	1/1/77	Exeter	1/1/00	Exeter City (T)	10+6	1	1		6			
Richardson Jonathan	6	12	8/29/75	Nottingham	7/7/94	Exeter City (T)	168+4	7	7	5	4	1		
Rowbotham Darren	5.10	12.13	10/22/66	Cardiff	11/7/84	Plymouth Argyle (T)	110+8	1	0+3	1+1	2		1	
W: Y.					10/31/87	Exeter City	110+8	11	8	5	47	6	5	1
				£25000	9/13/91	Torquay United	14		3	2	3		1	
				£20000	1/2/92	Birmingham	31+5	0+1		3+1	6			
Loan 12/18/92 Mansfield Town 4 Lge Apps.				Loan	3/25/93	Hereford United	8				2			
				Free	7/6/93	Crewe Alexandra	59+2	3	4	6+2	21	1	3	
				Free	7/28/95	Shrewsbury Town	31+9	3+2	4	1+3	9	2	1	
				Free	10/24/96	Exeter City	67+1	2	4	2	31		2	1
Wilkinson John C	5.9	11	8/24/79	Exeter	5/1/98	Exeter City (T)	0+1							

St. James Park
Well Street, Exeter, Devon EX4 6PX

Capacity 10,570

First game ....Not Known.
First floodlit game ....Not Known.

ATTENDANCES
Highest ....20,984 v Sunderland, FA Cup 6th Round replay, 4.3.1931.
Lowest ....1,515 v Darlington, Division 4, 30.4.1988.

OTHER GROUNDS ....None.

HOW TO GET TO THE GROUND

From the North: Use motorway (M5) until junction 30. Leave motorway and follow signs to City Centre along Sidmouth Road for Heavitree Road, then at roundabout take 4th exit into Western Way and at roundabout take 2nd exit into Old Tiverton Road, then take next turning left into St. James Road for Exeter FC.

From the East: Use A30 sign posted Exeter, into Heavitree Road, then at roundabout take 4th exit into Western Way and at roundabout take 2nd exit into Old Tiverton Road, then take next turning left into St James Road for Exeter FC.

From the South and West: Use A38 and follow signs to the City Centre into Western Way and at roundabout take 3rd exit passing Coach Station, then at next roundabout take 2nd into Old Tiverton Road, and turn left into St James Road for Exeter City FC.

Car Parking: Use City Centre car parks and local street parking.

Nearest Railway Station: Exeter St Davids (01392 33551)

USEFUL TELEPHONE NUMBERS

Club switchboard 01392 254 073
Club fax number......................01392 425 885
Club shop 01392 254 073
Ticket office 01392 254 073

Marketing Department 01392 214 422
Clubcall 0891 44 68 68*
*Calls cost 50p per minute at all times.
Call costings correct at time of going to press.

MATCHDAY PROGRAMME

Programme Editor ....Mike Blackstone

Number of pages....................................48.

Price ....£1.70.

Subscriptions ....Apply to club.

Local Newspapers
...Express & Echo, Western Morning News,
...................................Sunday Independent.

Local Radio Stations
........BBC Radio Devon, The New Devonair.

MATCHDAY TICKET PRICES

Grandstand
Adult £10.00
Concessions... £7.00
Under 16 blocks A and C only £5.00

Cowshed
Adult £8.50
Concessions... £5.00
*Under 16.. £2.00

Big Bank
Adult £8.50
Concessions... £5.00
*Under 16.. £2.00

* +2 free matches for children under 16 ground admissions only.

HALIFAX TOWN
(The Shaymen)
NATIONWIDE LEAGUE DIVISION 3
SPONSORED BY: NATIONWIDE MANUFACTURER: BIEMME

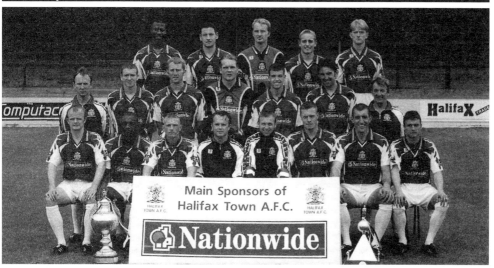

1998-99 - Back Row (L-R): Gareth Hamlet, Paul Stoneman, Lee Martin, Damian Place, Jonathan Brown.
Middle Row: Alan Russell Cox (Physio), Chris Newton, James Stansfield, Tim Carter, Richard Lucas, Ian Dearden, Tommy Gilbert (Team Trainer).
Front Row: Mark Bradshaw, David Yanson, Kevin Hulme, Andy May (Asst. Manager), Kieran O'Regan (Player-manager), Geoff Horsfield, Mark Sertori, Andy Thackeray.

DONCASTER FREE PRESS
FORMED IN 1911
TURNED PROFESSIONAL IN 1885
LTD COMPANY IN 1905 & 1920

CHAIRMAN
JC Stockwell
PRESIDENT
S J Brown
DIRECTORS
D C Greenwood, A Hall, D Cairns, S J Brown, M Hitchen.
SECRETARY
Derek A Newiss
COMMERCIAL MANAGER
David Worthington

PLAYER/MANAGER: Kieran O'Regan
ASSISTANT MANAGER
Andy May
TEAM TRAINER
Tommy Gilbert

PHYSIOTHERAPIST
Alan Russell Cox

STATISTICIAN FOR THE DIRECTORY
Vacant - phone 01203 234017 if interested

Having been in the Football Conference since 1993, Halifax finally regained their football League status in some style, finishing nine points clear of their nearest rivals.

Indeed the 'Shaymen' went top after a 3-1 win over Yeovil on 6th September and only dropped to second place once during the season.

With Cheltenham enjoying a good run in the cup competitions and Rushden & Diamonds getting off to a slow start, Halifax had little to distract their path to Division Three.

The FA Cup saw Halifax getting to the 4th qualifying round where they were knocked out by Gainsborough Trinity. A replay defeat against Slough ended any hopes of reaching Wembley in the FA Trophy and a first round exit of the Spalding Challenge Cup was inflicted on the 'Shaymen' by Stalybridge Celtic.

The team will come up into the Football League and hugely reformed side from the one that were relegated six years ago and could be a very good bet to gain promotion in their first season. If they do, they will be following in the footsteps of Wycombe and Macclesfield who both succeeded in moving up to Division Two in their first season of League Football. This fact is a great testament to the standard of football in the Football Conference and underlines the great season Halifax Town had to achieve promotion.

HALIFAX TOWN

Vauxhall Conference: 1st   **FA CUP: 4th Qual. Round**   **SPALDING CHALLENGE CUP: 1st Round**   **FA TROPHY: 2nd Round**

M	DATE	VEN	COMP.	OPPONENTS	RESULT		ATT.	GOAL SCORERS/GOAL TIMES	LP
1	16.08	A	VC	Hayes	W	2-1	907	Horsfield 30, Lyons 67.	4
2	23.08	A	VC	Slough Town	D	1-1	790	Paterson 74 (pen).	8
3	25.08	A	VC	Southport	D	0-0	1,889		11
4	30.09	H	VC	Welling United	W	1-0	1,011	Paterson 31.	7
5	02.09	A	VC	Telford United	W	3-0	805	Brook 14, Horsfield 34, 47.	2
6	06.09	H	VC	Yeovil Town	W	3-1	1,500	**Horsfield 3** (42, 55, 75).	1
7	16.09	H	VC	Telford United	**W**	**6-1**	1,119	**Horsfield 3** (2, 9, 59), O'Regan 46, Stoneman 48, Hulme 70.	1
8	20.09	A	VC	Farnborough Town	W	2-1	919	Horsfield 45, Brook 62.	1
9	30.09	H	VC	Leek Town	W	2-1	1,329	Paterson 27, Bradshaw 67.	1
10	04.10	H	VC	Kettering Town	W	3-0	1,836	Hulme 28, Bradshaw 43, Thackeray 63.	1
11	18.10	H	VC	Stevenage Borough	W	4-0	2,138	Horsfield 29, 65, Hulme 46, Bradshaw 52 (pen).	1
12	28.10	A	VC	Morecambe	D	1-1	3,914	Horsfield 19.	1
13	01.11	A	VC	Cheltenham Town	L	0-4	2,508		2
14	08.11	H	VC	Kidderminster Harriers	W	2-1	1,799	Paterson 52, Kilcline 77.	2
15	15.11	A	VC	Stalybridge Celtic	W	1-0	1,421	Stoneman 43.	1
16	22.11	H	VC	Hereford United	W	3-0	2,214	**Horsfield 3** (64, 78, 88).	1
17	29.11	A	VC	Woking	D	2-2	3,319	Horsfield 62, Paterson 72 (pen).	1
18	05.12	H	VC	Stalybridge Celtic	W	3-1	2,453	Lyons 34, Horsfield 45, 57.	1
19	09.12	H	VC	Northwich Victoria	W	4-2	2,165	Lyons 59, Bradshaw 70, Paterson 81, 87.	1
20	13.12	A	VC	Leek Town	L	0-2	1,282		1
21	20.12	H	VC	Hednesford Town	D	1-1	3,338	Horsfield 56	1
22	26.12	A	VC	Gateshead	D	2-2	1,239	Paterson 5, Horsfield 7	1
23	29.12	A	VC	Kettering Town	D	1-1	2,276	Philliskirk 49	1
24	01.01	H	VC	Gateshead	W	2-0	3,194	Horsfield 64,77	1
25	17.01	A	VC	Stevenage Borough	W	2-1	2,946	Hulme 59, Philliskirk 89.	1
26	24.01	H	VC	Slough Town	W	1-0	2,098	Horsfield 24.	1
27	07.02	A	VC	Rushden & Diamonds	L	0-4	3,675		1
28	14.02	A	VC	Dover Athletic	W	1-0	1,316	Hulme 2.	1
29	21.02	A	VC	Yeovil Town	W	1-0	2,584	Paterson 45 (pen).	1
30	28.02	H	VC	Farnborough Town	W	1-0	2,352	Horsfield 36.	1
31	07.03	H	VC	Dover Athletic	D	1-1	1,949	Hulme 45.	1
32	14.03	A	VC	Hednesford Town	D	0-0	1,856		1
33	17.03	H	VC	Morecambe	W	5-1	2,507	Bradshaw 34, Thackeray 38, Paterson 46, Kilcline 51, Horsfield 58.	1
34	21.03	H	VC	Rushden & Diamonds	W	2-0	3,951	OG (Wooding) 72, Paterson 85..	1
35	28.03	H	VC	Hayes	D	1-1	2,506	Horsfield 13.	1
36	04.04	H	VC	Woking	W	1-0	2,826	Hulme 22.	1
37	11.04	A	VC	Hereford United	D	0-0	3,304		1
38	13.04	H	VC	Southport	W	4-3	4,701	Paterson 42, Hulme 50, Hanson 82, 84.	1
39	18.04	A	VC	Kidderminster Harriers	W	2-0	3,151	Horsfield 43, Paterson 80.	1
40	20.04	A	VC	Northwich Victoria	L	0-2	2,106		1
41	25.04	H	VC	Cheltenham Town	D	1-1	6,357	Horsfield 41.	1
42	02.05	A	VC	Welling United	**L**	**2-6**	1,344	Horsfield 20, Brook 78.	1

1997/98 CUP COMPETITIONS

F.A. CUP

13.09	H	1Q	Droylsden	W	4-1	799	Brooks 37, 51, Paterson 54, Horsfield 90.
27.09	H	2Q	Leigh RMI	W	4-0	1,103	Paterson 32 (pen), 64, Brook 51, Horsfield 90.
11.10	H	3Q	Ossett Town	W	5-0	1,060	Horsfield 15, Hulme 20, 45, Brook 39, 52.
25.10	A	4Q	Gainsborough Trinity	L	1-2	1,730	Horsfield 33.

F.A. TROPHY

10.01	H	1	Blyth Spartans	W	2-1	1,712	Brook 11, Lyons 90.
31.01	H	2	Slough Town	D	1-1	1,633	Peterson 51.
03.02	A	2 R	Slough Town	L	0-2	876	

SPALDING CHALLENGE CUP

07.10	A	1	Stalybridge Celtic	L	1-3	489	Boardman 85.

RECORDS AND STATISTICS

CLUB RECORDS

BIGGEST VICTORIES
League: 6-0 v Bradford (h), Div.3(N), 02.01.1937
6-0 v Doncaster Rovers (h), Div.4, 02.11.1976.
F.A. Cup: 7-0 v Bishop Auckland (h), 2nd Round replay, 1966.

BIGGEST DEFEATS
League: 0-13 v Stockport County, Div.3(N), 06.01.1934.
Cup: 0-7 v Darlington, AMC, 03.03.1985.

MOST POINTS
3 points a win: 60, Division 4, 1982-83.
2 points a win: 57, Division 4, 1968-69.

MOST GOALS SCORED
83, Division 3(N), 1957-58.

RECORD TRANSFER FEE RECEIVED
£250,000 from Watford for Wayne Allison, August 1989.

RECORD TRANSFER FEE PAID
£50,000 to Hereford United for Ian Juryeff, September 1990.

BEST PERFORMANCES
League: 2nd Division 3(N), 1934-35.
F.A. Cup: 5th Round 1932-33, 1952-53.
League Cup: 4th Round 1964.

HONOURS
None.

LEAGUE CAREER
Original members of Div.3(N) 1921. Transferred to Div.3 1958.
Relegated to Div.4 1962-63. Promoted to Div.3 1968-69.
Relegated to Div.4 1975-76.
Relegated to GM Vauxhall Conference 1992-93.
Promoted to Div.3 1997-98.

INDIVIDUAL CLUB RECORDS

MOST GOALS IN A CAREER
Ernest Dixon, 129, 1922-30.

MOST GOALS IN A SEASON
Albert Valentine - 34, Div.3(N), 1934-35.

MOST GOALS IN A MATCH
5. William Chambers v Hartlepool United, Div.3(N) 07.04.1934 (6-2).
5. Albert Valentine v New Brighton, Div.3(N) 09.03.1935 (6-2).

OLDEST PLAYER

YOUNGEST PLAYER
Paul Willis, 17 years 80 days, 14.04.1987.

MOST CAPPED PLAYER
None.

PREVIOUS MANAGERS

(Since 1946)
Jack Breedon, W Wooton, Jimmy Thompson, Gerald Henry, Bobby Browne, Willie Watson, Billy Burnicle, Harry Hooper, Willie Watson, Vic Metcalfe, Alan Ball (snr), George Kirby, Ray Henderson, George Mulhall, John Quinn, Alan Ball (snr), Jimmy LAwson, George Kirby, Micky Bullock, Mick Jones, Bill Ayre, Jim McCaliog, John McGrath, Peter Wragg, John Bird, John Carroll.

ADDITIONAL INFORMATION
PREVIOUS NAMES
None.

PREVIOUS LEAGUES
North Eastern League. GM Vauxhall Conference.

Club colours: Blue shirts with white trim, white shorts with blue trim.

LONGEST LEAGUE RUNS

of undefeated matches:	17 (1969)	of league matches w/out a win:	22 (1978-79)
of undefeated home matches:	19 (1974-75)	of undefeated away matches:	11 (1970-71)
without home win:	13 (1990)	without an away win:	40 (1950-52)
of league wins:	7 (1964)	of home wins:	8 (1935)
of league defeats:	8 (1946-47)	of away wins:	4 (1927)

THE MANAGER/PLAYER

KIERAN O'REGAN . . . . appointed August 1998.

PREVIOUS CLUBS
As Manager. . . . . None.
As Asst.Man/Coach . . . .
As a player . . . . Brighton, Swindon, Huddresfield, WBA, Halifax.

HONOURS
As a Manager . . . .
As a Player . . . . **Halifax Town:** GM Vauxhall Conference Champions 1997-98.

HALIFAX TOWN

PLAYERS NAME / Honours	Ht	Wt	Birthdate	Birthplace / Transfers	Contract Date	Clubs	APPEARANCES				GOALS			
							League	L/Cup	FA Cup	Other	Lge	L/C	FAC	Oth
G O A L K E E P E R														
Carter Tim / E: Y3	6.2	13.8	05/10/67	Bristol	08/10/85	Bristol Rovers	47	2	2	2				
				Loan	14/12/87	Newport County	1							
				£50000	24/12/87	Sunderland	37	9		4				
				Loan	18/03/88	Carlisle United	4							
				Loan	15/09/88	Bristol City	3							
				Loan	21/11/91	Birmingham City	2	1						
				Free	01/08/92	Hartlepool United	18	4	1	2				
				Free	06/01/94	Millwall	62	5	3	1				
				Free	7/1/98	Halifax Town								
Martin Lee	6	13	9/9/68	Huddersfield	7/1/87	Huddersfield Town	54		4	5				
				Free	7/31/92	Blackpool	98	8	4	7				
				Loan	1/25/96	Bradford City								
						Rochdale								
					1997	Halifax Town								
D E F E N C E														
Bradshaw Mark / E: S.P.	5.11	11	9/7/69	Ashton-U-Lyne		Blackpool								
				Loan		York City	1							
						Halifax Town								
Murphy Jamie	6.1	12.7	2/25/73	Manchester	8/23/90	Blackpool	48+7	4	3	2+3	1	1		
				Free	9/14/95	Doncaster Rovers	46+7	2	1	2				
				Free	7/1/97	Halifax Town								
Setori Mark	6.3	13.4	01/09/67	Manchester	07/02/87	Stockport County	3+1	1						
				Free	01/07/88	Lincoln City	43+7	6	4	5	9		1	2
				£30000	09/02/90	Wrexham	106+4	8+1	6	9+1	3			
				Free	22/07/94	Bury	3+9	1	2+1	1+2	1			1
Loan 01/03/96 Witton Albion				Free	15/08/96	Scunthorpe United	82+1	6	7	4+1	2			
				Free	7/1/98	Halifax Town								
Stoneman Paul	6.1	13	2/26/73	Tynemouth	7/26/91	Blackpool (T)	38+5	5	3	3	1			
				Loan	12/16/94	Colchester United	3			1				
						Halifax Town								
Thackeray Andy / FAYC.	5.9	11	2/13/68	Huddersfield	2/15/86	Manchester City								
				Free	8/1/86	Huddersfield Town	2			0+1				
				£5000	3/27/87	Newport County	53+1	3+1	1	2+1	4			1
				£5000	7/20/88	Wrexham	139+13	10	6	13+2	14	1		
				£15000	7/15/92	Rochdale	161+4	8+1	7+1	10+3	13		1	2
					7/1/97	Halifax Town								
M I D F I E L D														
Brown Jon	5.10	11.3	9/8/66	Barnsley		Denaby United								
				£1500	7/1/90	Exeter City	153+14	9	12+1	14	3		1	
						Halifax Town								
Hulme Kevin	5.10	11.9	12/2/67	Farnworth		Radcliffe Borough								
				£5000	3/16/89	Bury	82+28	4+3	4+1	4+8	21	2	1	2
				Loan	10/26/89	Chester City	4							
				£42500	7/14/93	Doncaster Rovers	33+1	2	1	2	8	1		
				£42500	8/11/94	Bury	24+5	2	2	2				
				Free	9/30/95	Lincoln City	4+1		1	1+1				
						Halifax Town								
O'Regan Kieran	5.8	10.12	11/9/63	Cork		Tramore Athletic								
					4/9/83	Brighton & H.A.	69+17	6+1	3	2+1	2			1
				Free	8/12/87	Swindon Town	23+3	5+1	2+1	3	1			1
					8/4/88	Huddersfield Town	187+12	15+1	16+1	20+1	25	1	3	3
				£25000	7/8/93	West Bromwich A	35+9	3+1	2	3	2			
						Halifax Town								
Place Damian	5.9	10.7	12/31/78	Halifax		Halifax Town (T)								
F O R W A R D														
Butler Peter J	5.9	11.1	27/08/66	Halifax	21/08/84	Huddersfield Town	0+5							
				Loan	24/01/86	Cambridge United	14			1	1			
				Free	08/07/86	Bury	9+2	2	1			1		
				Free	10/12/86	Cambridge United	55	4	2	2	9			
				£75000	12/02/88	Southend United	135+7	12	2	11	9	1		2
				Loan	24/03/92	Huddersfield Town	7							
				£125000	12/08/92	West Ham United	70	4	3	1	3			
				£350000	04/10/94	Notts County	20	2	2	3				
				Loan	30/01/96	Grimsby Town	3							
				£175000	28/03/96	W.B.A.	52+8	2+1	1+2					
				Free	7/1/98	Halifax Town								
Hamlet Gareth	6		1/10/80			Halifax Town (T)								
Hanson David	6	13.7	19/11/68	Huddersfield	19/07/93	Bury	1	2						
				Free	18/08/94	Halifax Town								
via Hednesford Town				£50000	04/10/95	Leyton Orient	26+22	1+1	1+1	2+2	5			
				Loan	16/02/96	Welling								
				Loan	10/03/97	Chesterfield	3			1				
				Free	1/1/98	Halifax Town								
Horsfield Geoff	6		11/1/73	Barnsley	3/26/92	Scarborough (A)	12		1+1	1+1	1			
						Witton Albion								
						Halifax Town								
Newton Chris	6		11/5/79	Leeds		Halifax Town (T)								
Paterson Jamie	5.4	10	26/04/73	Dumfries		Halifax Town								
					01/08/94	Falkirk	4							
					13/10/95	Scunthorpe United	34+20		4+1	2	2		1	
				Free	1997	Halifax Town								

THE SHAY
Halifax, West Yorkshire HX1 2YS

Capacity 5,149
Covered Standing 2,600
Seating...1,878

First game ....v Darlington, 03.09.1921.
First floodlit game ....v Belgrade, 1961.

ATTENDANCES
Highest.................................36,885 v Tottenham Hotspur, FA Cup Round 5, 14.02.1953.
Lowest ....150 v Lincoln City, AMC, 11.02.1986.

OTHER GROUNDS ....None.

HOW TO GET TO THE GROUND

From the North
Take A629 to Halifax Town Centre. Take 2nd exit at roundabout into Broad Street and follow signs for Huddersfield (A629) into Skircoat Road.

From the South, East and West
Exit M62 at junction 24 and follow Halifax (A629) signs to Town centre into Skircoat Road for ground.

Car Parking: Available around the ground.

Nearest Railway Station: Halifax.

HOW TO GET TO THE GROUND

Club switchboard 01422 347 815
Club fax number 01422 353 423
Club shop 01422 353 423

Ticket Office 01422 347 815
Marketing Department. 01422 353 423

MATCHDAY PROGRAMME

Programme Editor. ...... Andrew Pinfield.

Number of pages .... 36.

Price....................... £2.00

Subscriptions .... Apply to club.

Local Newspapers
.... Halifax Courier, Yorkshire Post
.... Telegraph Argus.

Local Radio Stations
.... Pulse Radio, Radio Leeds.

MATCHDAY TICKET PRICES

Seats
Adults.................................... £9.00
Juniors/Senior Citizens...................... £5.00
Under 12s £3.00

Standing
Adults.................................... £8.00
Juniors/Senior/Citizens...................... £4.00
Under 12s £2.00

HARTLEPOOL UNITED
(The Pool)
NATIONWIDE LEAGUE DIVISION 3
SPONSORED BY: CAMERONS BREWERY COMPANY

1998/99 - Back Row (L-R): Paul Moss, Jeff Smith, Michael Dunwell, Tommy Miller, Glen Downey, Denny Ingram, Christopher McDonald, J.D. Briggs, Craig Lake. **Middle Row:** Billy Horner (coach), Gary Hinchley (physio), Chris Beech, Nicky Evans, Mark Nash, Graeme Lee, Steven Howard, Martin Holland, Steven Hutt, Darren Timmons, Martin Pemberton, Paul Stephenson, Paul Baker (player/coach), Tommy Miller (Yth Dev. officer), Mick Smith (Yth team coach). **Front Row:** Stuart Brightwell, Stuart Irvine, Gustavo Di Lella, Mick Tait (Manager), Michael Barron, Brian Honour (coach), Darren Knowles, Ian Clark, Craig Midgley.

HARTLEPOOL UNITED
FORMED IN 1908
TURNED PROFESSIONAL IN 1908
LTD COMPANY IN 1908

VICE-PRESIDENT: R Boyes
CHAIRMAN: Harold Hornsey
DIRECTORS
A Bamford, FRICS, D Jukes
COMMERCIAL EXECUTIVE
Frank Baggs
SECRETARY
Maureen Smith

MANAGER: Mick Tait
COACH: Paul Baker

YOUTH TEAM MANAGER
Billy Horner
Brian Honour (Assistant Youth Team Coach)

PHYSIOTHERAPIST
Gary Hinchley

STATISTICIAN FOR THE DIRECTORY
Gordon Small

Although they finished in the relatively lowly position of 17th place in Division Three, there was some optimism in 1997-98 that Hartlepool were at last back on the right track after a run of five disappointing seasons. For much of the time a promotion play-off position looked to be a real possibility, but unfortunately a dip in form early in the new year resulted in them steadily dropping down the table.

In many ways it was a strange season. Early on Hartlepool United came under the ownership of IOR, a Scottish firm with Scandinavian connections. This seemed to bring some financial stability, and one interesting development was the appearance of a procession of overseas born players who were signed as trialists. Manager Mick Tait was able to assemble a team which was difficult to beat, but in practice it was also a team that did not win enough. They became the draw specialists, eventually sharing the points on no fewer than 23 occasions to equal the all-time Football League record. At home Hartlepool were beaten only once in league games, and but for the 1-0 slip up against Scunthorpe it would have been a clean sweep for the first time in clubís history.

Overall Hartlepool were stronger in defence than in attack, but it was two midfielders who received most of the accolades. Norwegian international Jan Ove Pedersen was rated by many to be the most skilful player at the Vic in years, while strong running Jon Cullen was top goalscorer, was chosen for the PFA Division Three side and then joined Sheffield United for a welcome £250,000. Initially the goalkeeper position was a problem, but Steve Harper had an impressive loan spell, before Martin Hollund was brought in to become the automatic choice. At right back the ever present Darren Knowles was a real battler, while Richard Lucas ably complemented him on the left. Hartlepool were particularly well served in central defence, with Graeme Lee and ëPlayer of the Yearí Michael Barron enhancing their reputations, with captain Russell Bradley an excellent role model, and with Glen Davies also playing his part when required. Utility defender Denny Ingram had his best season yet, midfielder Chris Beech got better as the season progressed, while Ian Clark looked to be a real discovery playing equally well in defence or attack. Of the forwards, Paul Baker played well before his injury, Stephen Halliday struggled to find consistency, but Steve Howard made the best of a difficult job to show that he could yet make his name as a front runner. Gustavo Di Lella, Craig Midgley, Tommy Miller, and Paul Stephenson all came into the side towards the end of the season, and all will be expected to play important roles in 1998-99.

A disagreement behind the scenes at the end of the season saw Mick Tait compelled to resign as manager, but thankfully after a cooling off period he was persuaded to resume. There has been little transfer activity in the close season, but it must be encouraging that seven YTS players have been signed as first year professionals, particularly as Pool will have their Reserves in the Pontins League for the first time. Hartlepool have ambitions to be up with the promotion challengers in 1998-99, but realistically there will need to be some team strengthening. Interestingly this season they are scheduled to make their debut on live television, while a ground sharing deal with West Hartlepool RFC will mean that Premiership football is at last on view at the Victoria Park.

Gordon Small.

567

HARTLEPOOL UNITED

Division 3   :17th   FA CUP: 1st Round   LC CUP: 1st Round   AWS: Northern Round 2

M	DATE	COMP.	VEN	OPPONENTS	RESULT	H/T	LP	GOAL SCORERS/GOAL TIMES	ATT.
1	A 09	FL	A	Exeter City	D 1-1	1-0	12	Cullen 38	(3409)
2	12	CC 1/1	A	**Tranmere Rovers**	**L 1-3**	**1-0**		**Howard 14**	**(3878)**
3	15	FL	H	Colchester United	W 3-2	1-1	3	Baker 2, Allon 55, 62	2174
4	23	FL	A	Rotherham United	L 1-2	0-2	11	Cullen 85	(3086)
5	26	CC 1/2	H	**Tranmere Rovers**	**W 2-1**	**1-1**		**Baker 23, Lee 74**	**1626**
6	30	FL	H	Macclesfield Town	D 0-0	0-0	15		2283
7	S 02	FL	H	Notts County	D 1-1	0-0	14	Howard 67	2010
8	07	FL	A	Scarborough	D 1-1	0-0	12	Cullen 61	(3027)
9	13	FL	H	Torquay United	W 3-0	1-0	12	Baker 45, Cullen 48, Lee 55	1927
10	20	FL	A	Darlington	D 1-1	1-1	14	Cullen 20	(3169)
11	27	FL	H	Shrewsbury Town	W 2-1	2-0	7	Ingram 2 (pen), Cullen 11	2253
12	O 04	FL	A	Chester City	L 1-3	1-2	12	Baker 29	(2163)
13	11	FL	A	Doncaster Rovers	D 2-2	0-1	10	Cullen 83, Lucas 89	(1526)
14	18	FL	H	Leyton Orient	D 2-2	2-1	11	Howard 3, Ingram 32	2108
15	21	FL	H	Peterborough United	W 2-1	1-0	7	Howard 12, 78	1990
16	25	FL	A	Cardiff City	D 1-1	1-0	10	Baker 21	(3383)
17	N 01	FL	H	Brighton & H.A.	D 0-0	0-0	12		2561
18	04	FL	A	Swansea City	W 2-0	1-0	9	Cullen 76, Baker 89	(2949)
19	08	FL	A	Scunthorpe United	D 1-1	0-1	10	Knowles 65	(3272)
20	15	FAC 1	H	**Macclesfield Town**	**L 2-4**	**0-0**		**Beech 53, Pedersen 63**	**3165**
21	18	FL	H	Rochdale	W 2-0	1-0	7	Beech 36, Halliday 67	1666
22	22	FL	H	Barnet	W 2-0	1-0	6	Cullen 25, 76	2225
23	29	FL	A	Cambridge United	L 0-2	0-1	9		(2513)
24	D 02	FL	A	Hull City	D 2-2	1-0	8	Beech 30, Lucas 90	1933
25	09	AWS N1	A	**Shrewsbury Town**	**W 2-1**	**0-0**		**Lee 70, Pederson 85**	**(1130)**
26	13	FL	A	Lincoln City	D 1-1	0-1	9	90	(2849)
27	20	FL	H	Mansfield Town	D 2-2	1-0	8	Halliday 24, Howard 90	2309
28	26	FL	H	Scarborough	W 3-0	1-0	7	Halliday 4, 68, Clark 87	3905
29	28	FL	A	Notts County	L 0-2	0-1	8		(6073)
30	J 03	FL	A	Colchester United	W 2-1	1-0	6	Clark 14, Howard 73	(2885)
31	10	FL	H	Exeter City	D 1-1	0-1	7	Clark 50	2507
32	13	AWS N2	H	**Scunthorpe United**	**L 1-2**	**0-1**		**Lee 70**	**1491**
33	17	FL	A	Macclesfield Town	L 1-2	0-0	8	Cullen 53	(2334)
34	24	FL	H	Rotherham United	D 0-0	0-0	12		2375
35	31	FL	A	Torquay United	L 0-1	0-0	12		(2238)
36	F 06	FL	H	Darlington	D 2-2	2-0	12	Pedersen 15, Clark 42	3212
37	14	FL	H	Chester City	D 0-0	0-0	13		2186
38	21	FL	H	Shrewsbury Town	L 0-1	0-0	13		(2160)
39	24	FL	A	Leyton Orient	L 1-2	1-1	14	Clark 43	(3713)
40	28	FL	H	Doncaster Rovers	W 3-1	1-0	13	Clark 17, Bradley 80, Howard 82	1920
41	M 03	FL	H	Scunthorpe United	L 0-1	0-1	15		1588
42	07	FL	A	Brighton & H.A.	D 0-0	0-0	15		(2811)
43	14	FL	H	Swansea City	W 4-2	1-1	13	Halliday 44, Lee 47, 54, Beech 63	1727
44	21	FL	A	Rochdale	L 1-2	0-0	14	Clark 83	(1395)
45	28	FL	A	Barnet	D 1-1	0-1	15	Midgley 67	(2344)
46	A 04	FL	H	Cambridge United	D 3-3	1-1	15	Miller 3, Di Lella 71, 88	1867
47	11	FL	A	Hull City	L 1-2	1-0	15	Midgley 34	(3343)
48	13	FL	H	Lincoln City	D 1-1	1-1	16	Beech 22	1997
49	18	FL	A	Mansfield Town	D 2-2	2-1	17	Beech 39, 41	(2047)
50	25	FL	H	Cardiff City	W 2-0	1-0	16	Midgley 3, Ingram 54 (pen)	2817
51	M 02	FL	A	Peterborough United	D 0-0	0-0	17		(4727)

Best Home League Attendance: 3905 V Scarborough   Smallest :1588 V Scunthorpe United   Average :2241

Goal Scorers:

FL	(61)	Cullen 12, Clark 7, Howard 7, Beech 6, Baker 5, Halliday 5, Ingram 3, Lee 3, Midgley 3, Allon 2, Di Lella 2, Lucas 2, Bradley 1, Knowles 1, Pedersen 1, Miller 1
CC	(3)	Baker 1, Howard 1, Lee 1
FAC	(2)	Beech 1, Pedersen 1
AWS	(3)	Lee 2, Pederson 1

568

1997-98

	(F) Allon	(F) Baker	(D) Barron	(M) Beech	(D) Bradley	(M) Clark	(F) Connor	(M) Cullen	(D) Davies	(D) Davis	(M) Di Lella	(G) Dobson	(F) Elliott	(F) Halliday	(G) Harper	(G) Holland	(M) Howard	(M) Hutt	(D) Ingram	(F) Irvine	(M) Knowles	(M) Larsen	(D) Lee	(M) Lucas	(F) McDonald	(F) Midgley	(M) Miller	(M) Pedersen	(F) Stephenson	
	X	X	S	X	X			X	X	X				S1			X		X		X		S	X						R.D. Furnandiz 1
	X	X		X	X			X	X	X				S1			X		X		X		S	X				S		B Coddington 2
	X	X	X	X				X	X	X				S1			X		X		X		S	X				S		J P Robinson 3
	X	X	X	X	X			X	X					S2			S3		X		X		S1	X						F G Stretton 4
		X	X		X			X						X	S	X	X		X		X		X	X				S		A R Leake 5
	S1	X	X		X			X					S	X	X		X		X		X		X	X						M S Pike 6
		X	X	X	X			X						X	X		S1		X		X		X	X						G Laws 7
		X	X	X	X			X	S				S2	X	X		S1		X		X		X	X						M L Dean 8
		X	X	X	X			X					S2	X	X		S1		X		X		X	X						M D Messias 9
		X		X	X			X					S3	X	X		S2		X		X		X	X	S1					J A Kirkby 10
		X		X	X			X						S	X		X		X		X		X	X	X		S			T Jones 11
		X		X	X			X	S					X	X		X		X		X		X	X	X			S2		G Cain 12
		X		X	X			X	S1					S2	X		X		X	X	X		X	X			X			D Pugh 13
		X	X	X	X			X	X				S		X		X		X		S1		X	X						W C Burns 14
		S	X	X	X			X	X					X	X		X		X		X		X	X						S J Baines 15
		X		X	X	S		X	X					X	X		X		X		X	S	X	X						K A Leach 16
		X		X	X	S2		X	X				S1	X			X		X		X		X	X					X	E K Wolstenholme 17
		X	S	X	S			X	X					S	X		X		X		X		X	X					X	M Halsey 18
		X	S2	S1	X			X	X					S3	X		X		X		X		X	X					X	A Bates 19
		X	X		S3	X	X		X	X				S1			X			X	X		X	X	X	S			X	G Laws 20
		X	X	X		X	S		X	X					X		X				X	S	X	X					X	K M Lynch 21
		X	X	X		X	S			X					X	X		S	S	X		X	X					X	R D Furnandiz 22
		X	X	X	S2	X2	X			X				X1		X	S1	S			X		X	X					X	P Taylor 23
		X	X	X	X1		X							X		X	S1	S			X		X	X			S	X	X	T Jones 24
		X	X	X			X							X		X	X				X	X	X					X	25
		X	X	X		X	S		X					X		X	X		S				X	X					X	S W Mathieson 26
		X2	X	X1	S		X							X		X			S1		X		S2	X					X	P R Richards 27
		X	X		S1		X							X		X	X1		X		X			X	X		S	X		A R Leake 28
		X	X		S2		X							X2		X	X3		X		X1	S3	S1	X	X			X		M J Jones 29
		X	X	X	X		X									X	X		S		X		X1	X	X1	S		X		A G Wiley 30
			X	X	X1		X							S1		X	X		X		X		X	S	X	X	S	X		J P Robinson 31
		X	X	X	X			X						X1		X	X	X			X	S1	X					X	32
			X	X	X2		X							X1		X	S1		X		X		S2	X	X				X	G Singh 33
		X	X	X	X									S		X	X		X	X	S		X	X	S				X	D Pugh 34
		X		X				X						X1		X	X		S	X	S1		X	X	S				X	A N Butler 35
		X		X	X1	X		X						S1		X	X		X	S	X			X	S				X	G Cain 36
		X		X	X	X	X1		X							X	X		S		S1			X	X	S		X	E K Wolstenholme 37
		X		X	X3	X2		X1								X	X	X		S2		X		X	X			S1		P Rejer 38
		X	X	X	X			X1	S					S1		X	X	X		X	S		X	X				S		R Styles 39
		X	X	X	X		S									X	X	X	S	X			X	X						G Laws 40
		X	X	X3	X	S3		S1						S2		X	X	X2		X			X1	X					X	J A Kirkby 41
		X	X	X				X						S		X	X	X		X			S	X				X		B Knight 42
		X1	X	X				X						S1		X	X		S				X	X	S	X	X		A Bates 43
		X	X	X	S2				X			S1		X		X	S2				X		X2	X		X2	X1		C J Foy 44
		X	X	X	X							S				X	X				S		X	X	S	X	X		J P Robinson 45
		X	X3		X1							S1				X	X		X	S2	X		X	X	S3	X2	X		T Jones 46
		X	S1	X	X			S				X1				X	X		X	S	X		X	X	X1	S		X	X	M D Messias 47
		X	X	X	S			S1								X	X		X	S	X		X1	S		X	X		M L Dean 48
		X	X	X			X	S								X	X		X	S1	X			S		X1	X		C R Wilkes 49
		X	X	X			X	S1						S		X	X		X1	S2				X	X			X2	W C Burns 50
		X	X	X			S		S							X	X		X	S1	X			X1	X			X	A P D'Urso 51
FL Appearances	3	16	32	34	43	19	4	28	18	2	1	1		21	15	28	34	4	35	1	46		35	42	4	9	11	17	3	
FL Sub Appearances	1		1	2	5	1		2		4		4		10		9		1	8			4	2		2		2			
CC Appearances	1	2	1	1			2	1	1		1		1	1+1	0+1			2		2		2		1	2				1	
FAC Appearances		1	1		0+1		1	1				1	0+1	0+1			1		1		1		1	1					1	
AWS Appearances		2	2	2	1		2						2		2	2			2		0+1	2	1						2	

Also played:(M) Cooper S(6,7). (M) Gavin S(11,14), S1(12,15), s3(13). (M) Nash S3(38). (F) Tait S(7,9,20). (F) Walton S(5).

HARTLEPOOL UNITED   RECORDS AND STATISTICS

CLUB RECORDS

BIGGEST VICTORIES
League: 10-1 v Barrow, Division 4, 4.4.1959.
F.A. Cup: 6-0 v North Shields, 1st Round, 30.11.1946.
6-1 v Scarborough, 1st Round, 20.11.1971.
6-3 v Marine, 2nd Round replay, 15.12.1975.

BIGGEST DEFEATS
League: 1-10 v Wrexham, Division 4, 3.3.1962.
F.A. Cup: 0-6 v Manchester City, 3rd Round, 3.1.1976.
Other: 0-8 v Crewe Alexandra, AMC, 17.10.1995.

MOST POINTS
3 points a win: 82, Division 4, 1990-91.
2 points a win: 60, Division 4, 1967-68.

MOST GOALS SCORED
90, Division 3(N) 1956-57.

RECORD TRANSFER FEE RECEIVED
£300,000 from Chelsea for Joe Allon, August 1991.

RECORD TRANSFER FEE PAID
£60,000 to Barnsley for Andy Saville, March 1992.

BEST PERFORMANCES
League: 2nd Division 3(N) 1956-57.
F.A. Cup: 4th Round 1954-55, 1977-78, 1988-89, 1992-93.
League Cup: 4th Round 1974-75.

HONOURS
None.

LEAGUE CAREER
Original members of Div 3(N) 1921, Transferred to Div 4 1958, P. Div 3 1967-68, R. Div 4 1968-69, P. Div 3 (now Div 2) 1990-91.

MOST GOALS IN A SEASON
Joe Allon: 35 goals in 1990-91. (League 28, FA Cup 3, League Cup 2, Leyland Daf 2).

INDIVIDUAL CLUB RECORDS

MOST GOALS IN A MATCH
7. Billy Smith v St Peters Albion (10-1), FA Cup, 17.11.1923.
5. Harry Simmons v Wigan Borough (6-1), Division 3(N), 1.1.1931.
5. Bobby Folland v Oldham Athletic (5-1, Division 3(N), 15.4.1961.

OLDEST PLAYER
Mick Tait, 40 years 173 days, 22.03.1997.

YOUNGEST PLAYER
John McGovern, 16 years 205 days, 21.5.1966.

MOST CAPPED PLAYER
Amby Fogarty (Eire) 1.

PREVIOUS MANAGERS

1908-12 Fred Priest, 1912-13 Percy Humphreys, 1913-20 Jack Manners, 1920-22 Cecil Potter, 1922-24 David Gordon, 1924-27 Jack Manners, 1927-31 Bill Norman, 1931-35 Jackie Carr, 1935-39 Jimmy Hamilton, 1943-57 Fred Westgarth, 1957-59 Ray Middleton, 1959-62 Bill Robinson, 1962-63 Allenby Chilton, 1963-64 Bob Gurney, 1964-65 Alvan Williams, 1965 Geoff Twentyman, 1965-67 Brian Clough, 1967-70 Angus McLean, 1970-71 John Simpson, 1971-74 Len Ashurst, 1974-76 Ken Hale, 1976-83 Billy Horner, 1983 John Duncan, 1983 Mick Docherty, 1983-86 Billy Horner, 1986-88 John Bird, 1988-89 Bobby Moncur, 1989-91 Cyril Knowles, 1991-93 Alan Murray; 1993 Viv Busby, 1993-94 John MacPhail, 1994-95 David McCreery, Keith Houchen 1995-96.

ADDITIONAL INFORMATION
PREVIOUS NAMES
Until 1968 Hartlepool United: 1968-77 Hartlepool.
PREVIOUS LEAGUES
North Eastern League.

Club colours: White with blue trimmed shirts, blue shorts.
Change colours:

Reserves League: Northern Alliance.
Youth League: Northern Intermediate.

LONGEST LEAGUE RUNS

of undefeated matches:	17 (1968)	of league matches w/out a win:	18 (1962-63, 1993)
of undefeated home matches:	27 (1967-68)	of undefeated away matches:	8 (1992)
without home win:	8 (1977, 1984, 1986, 1993)	without an away win:	31 (1937-38)
of league wins:	7 (1956, 1968)	of home wins:	12 (1933, 1951)
of league defeats:	8 (1950, 1993)	of away wins:	4 (1921-22, 1979, 1991)

THE MANAGER

MICK TAIT . . . . appointed November 1996.

PREVIOUS CLUBS
As Manager. . . . . None.
As Asst.Man/Coach. . . . . Hartlepool United.
As a player. . . . . Oxford United. Carlisle, Hull, Portsmouth, Reading, Darlington.

HONOURS
As a Manager . . . . None.
As a Player . . . . None.

HARTLEPOOL UNITED

PLAYERS NAME Honours	Ht	Wt	Birthdate	Birthplace Transfers	Contract Date	Clubs	League	L/Cup	FA Cup	Other	Lge	L/C	FAC	Oth
G O A L K E E P E R														
Hollund Martin	6	12.13	8/11/74	Stord		Brann								
					11/21/97	Hartlepool United	28			2				
Miotto Simon				Australia		Australia								
						Patick Thistle								
				Free	8/1/98	Hartlepool United								
D E F E N C E														
Barron Michael J	5.11	11.3	12/22/74	Salford	2/2/93	Middlesbrough	2+1	1		3+3				
				Loan	9/6/96	Hartlepool United	16							
				Free	7/8/97	Hartlepool United	32+1	1	1					
Downey Glen	6.1	11.13	9/20/78	Newcastle	7/8/97	Hartlepool United								
Ingram Stuart Denevan	5.11	11.8	6/27/76	Sunderland	7/5/94	Hartlepool United	149+5	10+1	5	4	6			
Lee Graeme B	6.2	13.5	5/31/78	Middlesboro'	1/1/00	Hartlepool United	35+2	1	1		3	1		
Miller Thomas W	6	11.8	1/8/79	Easington	7/8/97	Hartlepool Utd (T)	11+2				1			
M I D F I E L D														
Beech Christopher S	5.11	11.4	9/16/74	Blackpool	7/9/93	Blackpool	53+29	4+4	1	3+3	4			2
				Free	8/15/96	Hartlepool United	76+2	3	3	1	14	1	1	
Clark Ian D	5.11	11.7	10/23/74	Stockton	8/11/95	Doncaster Rovers	23+22	1+2	1+1	4	3			1
				Free	10/24/97	Hartlepool United	19+5		0+1	1	7			
Howard Steve	6.1	14.6	5/10/76	Durham		Tow Law Town								
					8/8/95	Hartlepool United	92+21	6	3	2	21	1		2
Hutt Stephen G	6.3	12	2/19/79	Middlesbrough	7/8/97	Hartlepool United	4							
Knowles Darren	5.6	10.1	10/8/70	Sheffield	7/1/89	Sheffield United								
				£3000	9/14/89	Stockport County	51+12	2+4		14+1				
				Free	8/4/93	Scarborough	139+5	11	9	4	2			
					3/27/97	Hartlepool United	53	2	1		1			
Pemberton Martin C	5.11	12.6	01/02/76	Bradford	7/22/94	Oldham Athletic	0+5	0+1		0+1				
				Free	3/20/97	Doncaster Rovers	33+2	0+1			3			
				Free	3/26/98	Scunthorpe United	3+3							
				Free	7/1/98	Hartlepool United								
F O R W A R D														
Baker David P	6.1	13.2	1/5/63	Newcastle	7/1/84	Southampton								
				Free	7/2/85	Carlisle United	66+5	4	3	2+1	11	1		
				Free	7/31/87	Hartlepool United	192+5	12	16	16	67	4	6	5
				£77000	8/1/92	Motherwell								
				£40000	1/7/93	Gillingham	58+4		5	2	16		1	
				£15000	10/1/94	York City	36+12	2+2	3	5+1	18	2		
				£25000	1/19/96	Torquay United	28	2			8	3		
				£15000	10/4/96	Scunthorpe United	20		3		9		5	
					3/27/97	Hartlepool United	22	2			7	1		
Brightwell Stuart	5.6	10.9	31/01/79	Easington	1/31/96	Manchester Utd (T)								
				Free	7/1/98	Hartlepool United								
Di Lella Gustavo	5.8	10.7	10/6/73	Buenos Aires		Blyth Spartans								
				Free	12/2/97	Darlington	0+5							
				Free	2/27/98	Blyth Spartans								
				Free	3/20/98	Hartlepool United	1+4				2			
Irvine Stuart C	5.9	11.1	3/1/79	Hartlepool	11/8/96	Hartlepool United	3+10		0+1	0+1	1			
McDonald Christopher S. S:	6	13	10/14/75	Edinburgh	12/13/93	Arsenal								
				Free	8/31/95	Stoke City								
				Free	8/15/96	Hartlepool United	13+2	2						
Midgley Craig	5.7	11.7	5/24/76	Bradford	8/1/94	Bradford City	0+11		0+4	1	1			
				Loan	12/7/95	Scarborough								
				Loan	12/1/97	Darlington	1							
				£10000	3/13/98	Hartlepool United	9				3			
Nash Marc	5.9	11.7	5/13/78	Newcastle		Benfield Park								
					2/20/98	Hartlepool United	0+1							
Stephenson Paul E: Y.2.	5.11	10	1/2/68	Wallsend	1/2/86	Newcastle United	58+3	3	2	2	1			
				£300000	11/10/88	Millwall	81+17	3	9	8	6	1	2	1
				Loan	11/21/92	Gillingham	12			2	2			
				£30000	3/4/93	Brentford	70	6	1+1	5	2	1		
					8/7/95	York City	91+6	9+2	5	1+1	8			1
				Free	3/20/98	Hartlepool United	3							

TRAINEES: J.D. Briggs, Michael Dunwell, Nicky Evans, Craig Lake, Paul Moss, Jeff Smith, Darren Timmons

THE VICTORIA PARK
Hartlepool, Cleveland TS24 8BZ

Capacity..7,229
Seating..3,466
Terrace..3,263

First game ....v Newcastle Utd Res. (F) 6-0, 2.9.1908.
First floodlit game..v Southend Utd, Div 4, 1-2, 6.1.1967.

ATTENDANCES
Highest ....17,426 v Manchester Utd, FA Cup 3rd round, 18.1.1957.
Lowest..655 v Bradford City, Football League Trophy, 18.8.1982.
....790 v Stockport County, Division 4, 5.5.1984.

OTHER GROUNDS..None.

HOW TO GET TO THE GROUND

From the North
Use A1, A19 then A179, sign posted Hartlepool to Hart. In 2.5 miles at traffic signals forward, then at crossroads turn right into Clarence Road for Hartlepool United FC.

From the South and West
Use A1, A19 and A689 into Hartlepool town centre, then bear right into Clarence Road for Hartlepool United FC.

Car Parking
Side street parking is ample.

Nearest Railway Station
Hartlepool Church Street (01429 274 039).

HOW TO GET TO THE GROUND

Club switchboard 01429 272 584
Club fax number 01429 863 007
Club Shop............... 01429 272 584

Ticket Office.............. 01429 272 584
Marketing Department....... 01429 272 584

MATCHDAY PROGRAMME

Programme Editor .... Mike Challards.

Number of pages .... 32.

Price........................ £1.30

Subscriptions....... Please apply to club.

Local Newspapers
.... Hartlepool Mail, Northern Echo.

Local Radio Stations
.... T.F.M, Radio Cleveland.

MATCHDAY TICKET PRICES

Seats £9
Juv/OAP £6

Terraces £7
Juv/OAP £5

HULL CITY
(The Tigers)
NATIONWIDE LEAGUE DIVISION 3
SPONSORED BY: THE UNIVERSITY OF HULL

1998/99 - Back Row L-R: David Brown, Brian McGinty, Mark Greaves, Rob Dewhurst, Neil Whitworth, Michael Edwards.
Middle Row: Billy Kirkwood (Asst. Manager), Dexter Tucker, Gregor Rioch, Matthew Baker, Steve Wilson, Matt Hocking, Warren Joyce, Mark Hateley (Manager).
Front Row: Richard Peacock, Jon French, Steven Hawes, Sam Sharman, Kevin Gage, David D'Auria, Neil Mann, Lee Ellington.

HULL CITY
FORMED IN 1904
TURNED PROFESSIONAL IN 1904
LTD COMPANY IN 1904

PRESIDENT: T C Waite, FMI, MIRTE
CHAIRMAN: David Lloyd
DIRECTOR
Albert Harrison
SECRETARY
Brian Johnson
COMMERCIAL MANAGER
Frank Killen

MANAGER
Mark Hateley
ASSISTANT MANAGER
Billy Kirkwood
YOUTH TEAM MANAGER
Rod Arnold
PHYSIOTHERAPIST
Keith Warner

STATISTICIAN FOR THE DIRECTORY
Chris Thompson

Mark Hateley's first season in management was, to say the least, tough. Only going higher than 21st once during the season, the fact that Doncaster Rovers were so far off the pace meant that relegation was never an issue.

Never being in a position to challenge for a play-off place and not having the fear of relegation to inspire the players, Hateley's job was made that little bit trickier and Hull never really got any kind of consistency going. A run of three games without defeat was enjoyed before Christmas and only game was lost in the final five matches of the season giving some hope of a change in fortunes.

The main highlight of the season was when they entertained Premiership Crystal Palace in the second round of the Coca-Cola Cup. Having knocked out Macclesfield Town, 2-1 on aggregate, they recorded a 1-0 win at Boothferry Park to take a slight advantage to Selhurst Park. After 90 minutes and extra-time the aggregate scoreline read: Crystal Palace 2, Hull City 2, thus seeing Hull through to the next round on the away goal rule. A trip to Newcastle United in the third round was a nice reward for their efforts against the 'Eagles', but Dalglish's men went through 2-0. The FA Cup however, was forgotten about as soon as it started, as a 0-2 defeat at the hands of non-League Hednesford meant a first round exit.

With a season behind him, Hateley will be hoping he take what he has learnt about the management game, and will be hoping to at least finish in a comfortable mid-table position.

HULL CITY

Division 3   :22th   FA CUP: 1st Round   LC CUP: 3rd Round   AWS: Northern Round 2

M	DATE	COMP.	VEN	OPPONENTS	RESULT	H/T	LP	GOAL SCORERS/GOAL TIMES	ATT.
1	A 09	FL	A	Mansfield Town	L 0-2	0-1	24		(4627)
2	12	CC 1/1	A	Macclesfield Town	D 0-0	0-0			(2249)
3	15	FL	H	Notts County	L 0-3	0-1	24		7412
4	23	FL	A	Peterborough United	L 0-2	0-1	24		(5701)
5	26	CC 1/2	H	Macclesfield Town	W 2-1	1-1		Peacock 14, Joyce 117	3300
6	30	FL	H	Swansea City	W 7-4	2-1	18	Darby 13, 62, 82, Rioch 36, Hodges 54, Mann 69, 73	5198
7	S 02	FL	H	Rotherham United	D 0-0	0-0	20		6127
8	05	FL	A	Chester City	L 0-1	0-1	21		(2271)
9	13	FL	H	Lincoln City	L 0-2	0-1	22		4736
10	16	CC 2/1	H	Crystal Palace	W 1-0	1-0		Darby 22	9323
11	20	FL	A	Rochdale	L 1-2	1-1	22	Lowthorpe 38	(2085)
12	27	FL	A	Scunthorpe United	L 0-2	0-1	23		(4905)
13	30	CC 2/2	A	Crystal Palace	L 1-2	1-0		Wright 30	(6407)
14	O 04	FL	H	Torquay United	D 3-3	1-0	23	Peacock 18, Gordon 66, Greaves 72	5139
15	11	FL	H	Scarborough	W 3-0	2-0	22	Peacock 8, Rocastle 20, Quigley 65	5350
16	15	CC 3	A	Newcastle United	L 0-2	0-0			(35856)
17	18	FL	A	Barnet	L 0-2	0-1	23		(2315)
18	21	FL	A	Cambridge United	W 1-0	0-0	21	Greaves 88	(2388)
19	25	FL	H	Brighton & H.A.	D 0-0	0-0	22		5686
20	N 01	FL	A	Darlington	L 3-4	1-1	22	Joyce 28, Rioch 54, Gordon 81	(2893)
21	04	FL	H	Exeter City	W 3-2	1-0	22	Joyce 5, Ellington 65, 84	3837
22	08	FL	H	Shrewsbury Town	L 1-4	0-2	22	Rioch 76	4758
23	15	FAC 1	H	Hednesford Town	L 0-2	0-1			6091
24	18	FL	A	Cardiff City	L 1-2	0-2	22	Darby 64	(2504)
25	22	FL	A	Macclesfield Town	L 0-2	0-1	22		(2508)
26	29	FL	H	Doncaster Rovers	W 3-0	0-0	22	Rioch 58 (pen), Hocking 83, Gore 48 (OG)	4721
27	D 02	FL	A	Hartlepool United	D 2-2	0-1	22	Joyce 52, Hodges 73	(1933)
28	09	AWS N1	H	Scarborough	W 2-1	1-0		Darby 29, Atkin 49 (OG)	1518
29	13	FL	H	Colchester United	W 3-1	0-0	20	Dewhurst 55, Rioch 58 (pen), Darby 84	3896
30	20	FL	A	Leyton Orient	L 1-2	0-1	21	Wright 86	(4013)
31	26	FL	H	Chester City	W 1-0	0-0	21	Dewhurst 68	4808
32	28	FL	A	Rotherham United	L 4-5	1-2	21	Darby 32, 72, Hodges 66, 69	(5995)
33	J 10	FL	H	Mansfield Town	D 0-0	0-0	21		4440
34	13	AWS N2	A	Grimsby Town	L 0-1	0-1			(4778)
35	17	FL	A	Swansea City	L 0-2	0-1	22		(2899)
36	20	FL	A	Notts County	L 0-1	0-0	22		(4017)
37	24	FL	H	Peterborough United	W 3-1	0-0	20	Joyce 49, Darby 67, 74	4669
38	31	FL	A	Lincoln City	L 0-1	0-1	22		(4067)
39	F 06	FL	H	Rochdale	L 0-2	0-1	22		4031
40	14	FL	A	Torquay United	L 1-5	1-3	22	Bettney 16	(2793)
41	21	FL	H	Scunthorpe United	W 2-1	2-1	22	Dewhurst 15, McGinty 38	4904
42	24	FL	H	Barnet	L 0-2	0-1	22		3296
43	28	FL	A	Scarborough	L 1-2	0-2	22	Boyack 61	(3831)
44	M 03	FL	A	Shrewsbury Town	L 0-2	0-0	22		(1523)
45	07	FL	H	Darlington	D 1-1	0-1	22	Wright 79	3616
46	14	FL	A	Exeter City	L 0-3	0-2	22		(3052)
47	21	FL	H	Cardiff City	L 0-1	0-0	22		3408
48	28	FL	H	Macclesfield Town	D 0-0	0-0	22		3677
49	A 04	FL	A	Doncaster Rovers	L 0-1	0-1	22		(2597)
50	11	FL	H	Hartlepool United	W 2-1	0-1	22	Brown 48, 72	3343
51	13	FL	A	Colchester United	L 3-4	1-2	22	Boyack 24, McGinty 48, Darby 71	(4700)
52	18	FL	H	Leyton Orient	W 3-2	1-0	22	Mann 32, Lowthorpe 46, Boyack 48	3744
53	25	FL	A	Brighton & H.A.	D 2-2	0-1	22	Darby 51, 61	(3888)
54	M 02	FL	H	Cambridge United	W 1-0	1-0	22	Darby 32	4930

Best Home League Attendance: 7412 V Notts County   Smallest :3296 V Barnet   Average :4597

Goal Scorers:

FL	(56)	Darby 13, Rioch 5, Hodges 4, Joyce 4, Boyack 3, Dewhurst 3, Mann 3, Brown D 2, Ellington 2, Gordon 2, Greaves 2, Lowthorpe 2, McGinty 2, Peacock 2, Wright 2, Bettney 1, Hocking 1, Quigley 1, Rocastle 1, Opponents 1
CC	(4)	Darby 1, Joyce 1, Peacock 1, Wright 1
FAC	(0)	
AWS	(2)	Darby 1, Opponents 1

(M) Bettney	(F) Boyack	(D) Brien	(F) Brown D	(F) Darby	(D) Dewhurst	(D) Doncel - Varcarel	(D) Edwards	(M) Ellington	(F) Fewings	(M) Gage	(D) Greaves	(F) Hateley	(M) Hocking	(F) Hodges	(M) Joyce	(F) Lowthorpe	(M) Mann	(D) Maxfield	(M) McGinty	(M) Morley	(M) Peacock	(M) Quigley	(D) Rioch	(F) Rocastle	(M) Thomson	(M) Tucker	(G) Wilson	(D) Wright		
	X			X							S2	X			X		X				X	X	X			X	S	X	M.J. Jones	1
	X	X	X								S	S1			X		X				X	X	X			X	S	X	A K Leach	2
	X	X	X								S	X			X		X				X	X	X			X	S	X	B Coddington	3
	X	X	X	X							S1				X	X	X	S2			X	X	X				S	X	A Bates	4
	X	X	X	X								X	X	S1	S2		X				X	X	X					X	S J Baines	5
	X	X	X	S1									X	X	X		X				X	X	X			S	X	D Laws	6
	X	X	X	S2							X	S1	X	X	X		X				X	X	X			S	X	A R Hall	7
	X	X	X	S1							X		X	X	X		X					X	X			S	X	T Jones	8
	X	X	X			X					X		X	X	X						X	X	X			S	X	W C Burns	9
	X	X	X	X			S1				X	X	X	X	X						X	S2	X			S	X	A B Wilkie	10
	X	X	X	X				S1	S2		X	X	X	X	X						X		X			S	X	M S Pike	11
X	X			X				X	X	X		X	X	X	X						X	S1	X		S		X	X	G B Frankland	12
X	X			X			S3	X	X	X	X		X	X	X						X	S1	X				X	X	P A Durkin	13
X	X			S2				X	X	X	X	X	X	X	X						X		X		S		X	X	M L Dean	14
X								X	X	X	S2	X	X	X	X						X	S1	X	X	S		X	X	R Pearson	15
X	X			S3				X	X	X	X	X	X	X	X						S1	S2	X	X			X	X	K M Lynch	16
X	X							X	X	X	X	X	X	S	X	S3					X	S2	X	X			X		M J Brandwood	17
X	X							X	X	X	X	X	X	S	X							S	X	X			X	X	B Knight	18
X	S1							X	X	X	X	X	X	X	S3						X		X	X			X	X	E Lomas	19
X	S							X	X	X	X	X	X	S1	X	X					X		X				X	X	D Pugh	20
X	X						S1	X		X	X	X	X	X	X	S	S2				X		X				X	X	S W Mathieson	21
	X						X	X	X	X	X	X	X	X	X	S1	S				X	S	X				X	X	F G Stretton	22
	S	X		S1	S2		X	X	X	X	X	X	S	X	X						X		X	S			X	X	D Laws	23
X		X						S2	X	X	X	X	S1	S3	X						X		X	X			X	X	A N Butler	24
S3		X						X	S1	X	X	X	X	X	X	S2					X		X				X	X	P R Richards	25
S2		X						X2	X	X	X	X	S3	S1	X	X1					X	X3					X	X	C J Foy	26
X3		X	X					S1	X	X	X	X	S3	X1	X	X2					S2	X					X		T Jones	27
		X	X				S3	S2	X1		X	X3	X	S1	X		X	X2			X						X			28
X		X	X				S			S		X	X	X	X	X			S			X	X	X			X		M J Jones	29
X		X	X							X2	X	X	X	X	X1	S1			S	X	X						X	S2	B Coddington	30
X		X	X		S					X	X	X	X	X	X1	S1			S1	X	X						X	S	K A Leach	31
X		X	X		X					S1	X	X	X	X	X	X2	S1		X1								X		S J Baines	32
X		X	X						S1	X	X	X	S	X	X				X2				X		S2	X		K M Lynch	33
X		X	X		X					X	X2	X	S2	X		S1		X1								X	X		34
X		X	X		X2			S1	S2	X		X	S	S	X		X								X1	X	X	A R Leake	35
X2		X	X						X		X	S2	X	X3	X1	X	S3							S1	X		E K Wolstenholme	36
X		X	X	X						S		X	X	X			X	X							S	X		A G Wiley	37
X		X	X	X						S		X	X1			X	X	X						S1	X		G B Frankland	38
X		X	X	X	S2							X	X	X2	X	X3		S1							S3	X		G Laws	39
X		X	X	X1							X	X	X1	S3	X		X3		X		S1					X		A P D'Urso	40
X		X1	X		X	S1						X	X		S3		X	X2		X3					S2	X	X	C J Foy	41
X		X	X	X1							X	S2	X		X	S3		X3		X					S1	X	X2	S W Mathieson	42
X	X			X	S	S2					X		X1	X2	S1	X	X							X			D Pugh	43
X	X			X1	S	X	X				S1		X		S2	X	X2									X		M S Pike	44
X	X				X	X2					S2		X1	X	X	S		X	X		S1		X			X		P Taylor	45
X	X				X2	X					S1		X		X		S2	X		X1			X		S	X	X	P Rejer	46
X2	X				X						X	X1	X	S	S2	X	S1	X								X		S J Baines	47
	X	X			X						X		X	S1	X	X1		X		X1						X		G Cain	48
	X	X	S1		S	X					X		X	S2	X	X2	X1								X		K A Leach	49
	X	X3	S1		X	X							X	S3	X1	X2			X						X	S2	M D Messias	50
	X	X2		X	X								X	X1	S2		X	S	X						X	S1	P Taylor	51
	X	X3	X		X						S3		X	X	X1		S2	X2	X						X	S1	E K Wolstenholme	52
	X	X1	X3		X							S3		X	S2	X2		X3							X	S1	S G Bennett	53
	X	X2	X		X						S2		X	X3	S1		X	X1							X	S3	G Singh	54
28	12	14	7	27	24	8	20	4	13	8	17	4	31	13	45	18	20	10	21	5	26	4	38	10	9	1	37	25	FL Appearances	
2	1	2		4	1	3	5	2	8	5		5		5	14	4		3	1	5	1				6			8	FL Sub Appearances	
1	5	3	3	3		0+1	1+2		2	4+1	2	1	3+1		2+1				4+1	1+3	4	1	3		2	5			CC Appearances	
		1							0+1	0+1	1	1		1			2	2	0+2	2		1+1	1		1	1		1	FAC Appearances	
1		2	2		1	0+1	0+1	1					2	2			1			1							2	1	AWS Appearances	

Also played:(F) Brown A S1(1), S(3,9), S3(5), S2(6,8). Dickenson X(4,5,6), S1(9). (F) Gordon S2(12,13,19,20), S1(14,17) S(18). (D) Trevitt X(1,2,3,8,9).(M) Wharton S(37,38,48), X1(39).

HULL CITY

RECORDS AND STATISTICS

CLUB RECORDS

BIGGEST VICTORIES
League: 10-0 v Halifax Town, Division 3(N), 26.12.1930.
11-1 v Carlisle United, Division 3(N), 14.01.1939.
FA Cup: 8-2 v Stalybridge Celtic, 1st Round, 26.11.1932.

BIGGEST DEFEATS
League: 0-8 v Wolverhampton Wndrs, Division 2, 4.11.1911.
FA Cup: 0-5 v Fulham, 3rd Round, 9.1.1960.
League Cup: 0-5 v Lincoln City, 1st Round, 9.8.1980.
0-5 v Manchester United, 2nd Round 1st leg, 23.9.1987.

MOST LEAGUE POINTS
(3pts a win) 90, Division 4, 1982-83.
(2pts for win) 71, Div ision 3, 1965-66.

RECORD TRANSFER FEE RECEIVED
£750,000 from Middlesbrough for Andy Payton, November 1991.
(Installments could take fee to £1,000,000)

RECORD TRANSFER FEE PAID
£200,000 to Leeds United for Peter Swan, March 1989.

BEST PERFORMANCES
League: 3rd Division 2, 1909-10.
FA Cup: Semi-finals 1929-30.
League Cup: 4th Round 1973-74, 1975-76, 1977-78.

HONOURS
Champions of Division 3(N) 1932-33, 1948-49.
Champions of Division 3 1965-66.

LEAGUE CAREER
Elected to Div 2 1905, Div 3(N) 1930-31, Div 2 1933-34, Div 3(N) 1936-37, Div 2 1948-49, Div 3(N) 1956-57, Transferred to Div 3 1958-59, Div 2 1959-60, Div 3 1960-61, Div 2 1966-67, Div 3 1978-79, Div 4 1981-82, Div 3 1983-84, Div 2 1985-86, Div 3 (now Div 2) 1990-91.

INDIVIDUAL CLUB RECORDS

MOST GOALS IN SEASON
Bill McNaughton: 42 goals in 1932-33 (League 39, FA Cup 3)

MOST GOALS IN A MATCH
5. Ken McDonald v Bristol City, 5-1, Division 2, 17.11.1928.
5. Slim Raleigh v Halifax Town, 10-0, Division 3(N), 26.12.1930.

OLDEST PLAYER IN A LEAGUE MATCH
Eddie Burbanks, 40 years 15 days, 16.4.1953.

YOUNGEST PLAYER IN A LEAGUE MATCH
Matthew Edeson, 16 years 63 days v Fulham, 10.10.1992.

MOST CAPPED PLAYER
Terry Neill (Northern Ireland) 15.

PREVIOUS MANAGERS

1905-13 Ambrose Langley, 1913-14 Harry Chapman, 1914-16 Fred G Stringer, 1919-21 David M Menzies, 1921-23 P Lewis, 1923-31 Bill McCracken, 1931-34 Hayden Green, 1934-36 Jack Hill, 1936 David Menzies, 1936-46 Ernie Blackburn, 1946-48 Major Buckley, 1948-51 Raich Carter, 1952-55 Bob Jackson, 1955-61 Bob Brocklebank, 1961-70 Cliff Britton, 1970-74 Terry Neill, 1974-77 John Kaye, 1977-78 Bobby Collins, 1978-79 Ken Houghton, 1980-82 Mike Smith, 1982-84 Colin Appleton, 1984-88 Brian Horton, 1988-89 Eddie Gray, 1990 Colin Appleton, 1990-91 Stan Ternant, 1991-97 Terry Dolan.

ADDITIONAL INFORMATION
Previous League: None.

Previous Names: None.

Club colours: Amber and white striped shirt, black sleeves, black shorts.

Change colours:

Reserves League: Pontins Central League Division 2.

LONGEST LEAGUE RUNS

of undefeated matches:	15 (1964-65, 1983)	of league matches w/out a win:	27 (1990)
of undefeated home matches:	25 (1932-33, 1965-66)	of undefeated away matches:	13 (1948-49)
without home win:	15 (1990)	without an away win:	35 (1979-81)
of league wins:	10 (1948, 1966)	without an away win:	19 (1965-66)
of league defeats:	8 (1934)	of away wins:	5 (Several occasions)

THE MANAGER

MARK HATELEY . . . . appointed July 1997.

PREVIOUS CLUBS
As Manager. . . . . None.
As Coach. . . . . None.
As a player. . . . . Coventry City, Portsmouth, AC Millan, Monaco, Glasgow Rangers, Q.P.R., Leeds Utd (Loan),
. . . . Glasgow Rangers.

HONOURS
As a Manager . . . . None.
As a Player. . . . . 32 full caps, 10 u21 & Youth caps for England.
International: None.

576

LAYERS NAME / onours	Ht	Wt	Birthdate	Birthplace Transfers	Contract Date	Clubs	League	L/Cup	FA Cup	Other	Lge	L/C	FAC	Oth
O A L K E E P E R														
aker Matthew						Hull City (T)								
ilson Stephen L	5.11	10.7	4/24/74	Hull	7/13/92	Hull City	130+1	9	8	7				
E F E N C E														
ewhurst Robert M	6.3	12	9/10/71	Keighley	10/15/90	Blackburn Rovers	13	2		1				
				Loan	12/20/91	Darlington	11		1		1			
				Loan	10/2/92	Huddersfield Town	7							
				Free	11/5/93	Hull City	128+2	8	7	4	13			
dwards Michael	6.1	12	4/25/80	12/23/97	Hull City	20+1			1					
eaves Mark A	6.1	13	1/22/75	Hull	10/4/96	Hull City	40+14	2	2	1	4			
ocking Matthew J	5.11	11.5	1/30/78	Boston	5/16/96	Sheffield United								
				£25000	9/26/97	Hull City	31	2	1	2	1			
orley Ben	5.9	10.1	12/22/80	Hull	12/12/97	Hull City (T)	5+3			1				
och Greg	5.11	10.9	6/24/75			Luton Town								
				Loan		Barnet	3							
				Free	8/11/95	Peterborough United	13+5	2	2+1	2+1				
					8/15/96	Hull City	75+3	6	3	1	6	2		
arman Samuel J	5.11	12.1	11/7/77	Hull		Sheffield Wednesday								
				Free	3/11/97	Hull City	2+2							
hitworth Neil						Kilmarnock								
				Free	7/1/98	Hull City								
I D F I E L D														
Auria David	5.8	11	3/26/70	Swansea	8/2/88	Swansea City	27+18	2+2	1	4	6			
": Y. WFAC'94.					8/22/94	Scarborough	31+3	1+2	3+1	1	7			
				Free	12/6/95	Scunthorpe United	103+4	6	7	4+1	18		1	
				Free	7/1/98	Hull City								
llington Lee S	5.11	11	7/3/80	Bradford		Hull City	4+5	0+1	0+1	0+1	2			
ench Jon	5.10	10.10	9/25/76	Bristol	7/15/95	Bristol Rovers (T)	8+9	0+1	0+3	2+1	1			1
				Free	7/1/98	Hull City								
age Kevin W	5.10	12.11	4/21/64	Chiswick	1/4/82	Wimbledon (A)	135+33	7+2	8+3	0+1	15	1	1	
: Y.				£100000	7/17/87	Aston Villa	113+2	13	9	8	8	3	1	
				£150000	11/15/91	Sheffield United	107+5	6	10+2	1	7			
				Free	3/28/96	Preston North End	20+3		1					
				Free	9/19/97	Hull City	8+2		1					
awes Steven	5.8	11.10	7/17/78	High Wycombe	3/2/96	Sheffield Utd (T)	1+3							
				Loan	9/18/97	Doncater Rovers	7+1							
				Loan	2/20/98	Doncaster Rovers	1+2							
				Free	7/1/98	Hull City								
oyce Warren	5.9	11.11	1/20/65	Oldham	6/23/82	Bolton Wanderers	180+4	14+1	11	11	17	1	1	2
				£35000	10/16/87	Preston North End	170+7	8	6	19	34	2	1	7
				£160000	5/19/92	Plymouth Argyle	28+2	6	2	2	3	1		
				£140000	7/7/93	Burnley	65+5	7	4	8	9	1	1	1
				Loan	1/20/95	Hull City	9							
					8/1/96	Hull City	90	5+1	4	2	9	1		1
ann Neil	5.11	12	11/19/72	Nottingham		Notts County								
				Free	9/6/90	Grimsby Town								
					8/1/91	Spalding United								
					8/1/92	Grantham								
				Free	7/30/93	Hull City	105+31	8+3	5+2	4+2	8		1	1
cGinty Brian	6.1	12.6	12/10/76	East Kilbride	7/1/93	Glasgow Rangers								
					11/28/97	Hull City	21		1+1		2			
eacock Richard J	5.11	11	10/29/72	Sheffield	10/14/93	Hull City	130+29	9+2	7	3+1	19	2	1	
O R W A R D														
rown David A	5.9	12.6	02/10/78	Bolton	20/10/95	Manchester Utd (T)								
				Free	7/1/98	Hull City								
ateley Mark	6.1	11.07	11/7/61	Liverpool	8/1/78	Coventry City	86+6				25			
					8/1/83	Portsmouth	38	4	2		21	2	1	
					8/1/84	AC Milan	66				17			
					8/1/88	Monaco								
					8/1/90	Glasgow Rangers	165				85			
					11/4/95	QPR	10+4	0+1	1		2			
				Loan	8/20/96	Leeds United	5+1							
				Free	3/14/97	Glasgow Rangers								
				Free	7/9/97	Hull City	4+5	4+1						
ucker Dexter C	6.2	12	2/22/79	Pontefract	1/9/98	Hull City (T)	1+6							

BOOTHFERRY PARK
Boothfery Road, Hull, North Humberside HU4 6EU

Capacity 12,996

First game..31st August 1946.
First floodlit game ....19th January 1953.

ATTENDANCES
Highest ....55,019 v Manchester United, FA Cup 6th Round, 26.2.1949.
Lowest ....890 v Doncaster Rovers. AMC, 27.9.1994.

OTHER GROUNDS ....The Boulevard, Dairycoates, Anlaby Road..

HOW TO GET TO THE GROUND

From the North
Use A1 or then A1079, sign posted HUll, into town centre. Hten follow signs to Leeds (A63) into Anlaby Road. At roundabout take first exit into Boothferry Road for HUll City AFC.

From the East
Use motorway (M62) then A63, sign posted Hull, into Boothferry Road for Hull City AFC.

From the South and West
Use motorway (M1), M18 then M62 and A63, sign posted Hull, into Boothferry Road for Hull City AFC.

Car Parking: Limited parking in front of ground.

Nearest Railway Station: Hull Paragon (01482 26033) or Boothferry Halt by the ground.

USEFUL TELEPHONE NUMBERS

Club switchboard .... 01482 327 200   Clubcall 0891 88 86 88*
Club fax number .... 01482 565 752   *Calls cost 50p per minute at all times.
Ticket Office .... 01482 351 119   Call costings correct at time of going to press.

MATCHDAY PROGRAMME

Programme Editor (97/98) ....Rob Smith.

Number of pages (97/98) ....32.

Price (97/98)......................................£1.50.

Subscriptions ....Apply to club.

Local Newspapers................Hull Daily Mail.

Local Radio Stations
...............BBC Radio Humberside (95.5FM, .
....MW1485KHZ)
................................Viking Radio (96.6 FM)

MATCHDAY TICKET PRICES (97/98)

Best Stand	£10
Juv/OAP	£5
Family Stand	£8
Juv/OAP	£4
South Stand	£8
Juv/OAP	£4
Ground	£7
Juv/OAP	£3

LEYTON ORIENT
(The O's)
NATIONWIDE LEAGUE DIVISION 3
SPONSORED BY: MARCHPOLE GROUP

1997/98 - **Back Row L-R:** Roger Joseph, Shaun Howes, Justin Channing, Mark Warren, David Morrison, Daniel Brown, Adve Hanson.
Middle Row: Simon Clark, Colin West, Stuart Hicks, Paul Hyde, Luke Weaver, Lee Shearer, Dean Smith, Tony Richards.
Front Row: Sam Winston, Scott McGleish, Alex Inglethorpe, Dominc Naylor, Martin Ling, Carl Griffiths, Joe Baker.

LEYTON ORIENT
FORMED IN 1881
TURNED PROFESSIONAL IN 1903
LTD COMPANY IN 1906

CHAIRMAN: Barry Hearn
VICE-CHAIRMAN
D L Weinrabe
CHIEF EXECUTIVE: Bernard Goodall
DIRECTORS
S J Dawson, D R Dodd, R P Cousens,
J Goldsmith (Friba), H Linney, V Marsh,
T.Wood

SECRETARY
David Burton (0181 539 2223)
COMMERCIAL MANAGER
F Woolf

MANAGER: Tommy Taylor
RESERVE TEAM COACH
Tommy Cunningham
DIRECTOR OF COACHING: Paul Brush
PHYSIOTHERAPIST
Andy Taylor

STATISTICIAN FOR THE DIRECTORY
Vacant - phone 01203 234017 if interested

After 36 matches had been completed, the 'O's' were still in with a great chance of making the Third Division play-offs. They had 55 points in the bag and were lying in eighth place and had a game in hand over two teams immediately above them (Peterborough United and Rotherham). But the Londoners just couldn't keep things going until the season's end and from their remaining 30 points they could only manage to secure eleven and eventually had to settle for a lowly position of 11th, ten points short of that last promotion spot.

Starting off reasonably well under manager Tommy Taylor, Orient won four, drew one and lost four of their opening nine matches, also knocking Brighton out of the Coca-Cola Cup.

But after 15 matches had been completed, the 'O's' and slipped alarmingly and were sitting in eighteenth position with less than a point a game to show for their efforts. Things weren't going too well at this juncture, but manager Taylor made a few adjustments and over the next two months (10 games played) results improved immeasurably, Orient taking 20 points out of a possible 30 to move up to 11th spot, just one win away from the play-offs.

They continued to maintain their form, only occasionally slipping up when least expected, and as mentioned at the start of this review, with ten matches left they had a good chance of making the play-offs. Even when entering the final straight, with just six matches remaining, the 'O's' still had an outside chance of squeezing into the top seven. Alas, it was not to be and when the final whistle sounded, the 'O's' had to settle for a mid-table finish, despite being a mere four points away from Barnet, who took that last play-off position with 70 points.

Interesting fact - Orient were fined £20,000 by the F.A. for fielding three ineligible players - Mark Warren, Simon Clark and Stuart Hicks - in League games.

Tony Matthews.

LEYTON ORIENT

Division 3   :11th   FA CUP: 1st Round   LC CUP: 2nd Round   AWS: Southern Round 1

M	DATE	COMP.	VEN	OPPONENTS	RESULT	H/T	LP	GOAL SCORERS/GOAL TIMES	ATT.
1	A 09	FL	H	Cardiff City	L	0-1	0-0	21		5414
2	12	CC 1/1	A	Brighton & H.A.	D	1-1	1-0		Griffiths 39	(1073)
3	15	FL	A	Scunthorpe United	L	0-1	0-1	23		(3068)
4	23	FL	H	Rochdale	W	2-0	1-0	20	Smith 1 (pen), 87 (pen)	3463
5	26	CC 1/2	H	Brighton & H.A.	W	3-1	1-1		Griffiths 9, McGleish 73, Baker 90	3690
6	30	FL	A	Brighton & H.A.	W	1-0	0-0	13	Griffiths 66	(2285)
7	S 02	FL	A	Doncaster Rovers	W	4-1	0-1	7	Clark 47, 67, 71, Griffiths 58	(1098)
8	05	FL	H	Cambridge United	L	0-2	0-1	9		4638
9	13	FL	H	Exeter City	W	1-0	1-0	9	Griffiths 21	4040
10	16	CC 2/1	H	Bolton Wanderers	L	1-3	1-2		Inglethorpe 41	4128
11	20	FL	A	Peterborough United	L	0-2	0-2	13		(6629)
12	27	FL	A	Swansea City	D	1-1	0-0	15	Clark 71	(0)
13	30	CC 2/2	A	Bolton Wanderers	D	4-4	2-2		Inglethorpe 6, Griffiths 17, Baker 53, Warren 89	(6444)
14	O 04	FL	H	Macclesfield Town	D	1-1	0-0	15	Griffiths 27	4522
15	11	FL	H	Rotherham United	D	1-1	0-0	16	Griffiths 90	3658
16	18	FL	A	Hartlepool United	D	2-2	1-2	14	Inglethorpe 44, Griffiths 82	(2108)
17	21	FL	A	Torquay United	D	1-1	1-0	15	Harris 6	(1702)
18	25	FL	H	Colchester United	L	0-2	0-1	17		4592
19	N 01	FL	A	Lincoln City	L	0-1	0-0	18		(4129)
20	04	FL	H	Scarborough	W	3-1	2-1	14	Inglethorpe 21, 33, Harris 90	2480
21	08	FL	H	Chester City	W	1-0	1-0	14	Smith 25	3894
22	15	FAC 1	A	Hendon	D	2-2	2-1		Griffiths 5, Smith 33	(2421)
23	18	FL	A	Darlington	L	0-1	0-1	16		(1703)
24	22	FL	A	Notts County	D	1-1	0-0	16	Harris 70	4372
25	25	FAC 1R	H	Hendon	L	0-1	0-0			3355
26	29	FL	A	Mansfield Town	D	0-0	0-0	16		(2086)
27	D 02	FL	H	Barnet	W	2-0	1-0	13	Smith 43, Hanson 90	2598
28	09	AWS S1	H	Colchester United	W	1-0	0-0		Inglethorpe 51	933
29	13	FL	A	Shrewsbury Town	W	2-1	2-0	12	Simpson 21, Smith 38	(2137)
30	20	FL	H	Hull City	W	2-1	1-0		Smith 44, Harris 52	4013
31	26	FL	A	Cambridge United	L	0-1	0-0	11		(4808)
32	28	FL	H	Doncaster Rovers	W	8-0	4-0	11	Griffiths 20, 49, 56, Inglethorpe 39, Smith 42 (pen), Richards 45, 60, Baker 67	4437
33	J 10	FL	A	Cardiff City	L	0-1	0-1	11		(4335)
34	17	FL	H	Brighton & H.A.	W	3-1	0-0	11	Griffiths 55, Simpson 79, 83	6591
35	20	AWS S2	A	Bournemouth	L	0-2	0-0			(1732)
36	24	FL	A	Rochdale	W	2-0	0-0	10	Inglethorpe 64, Griffiths 69	(1774)
37	31	FL	A	Exeter City	D	2-2	1-1	11	Ling 32, Clark 85	(4023)
38	F 06	FL	H	Peterborough United	W	1-0	0-0	9	Baker 83	5991
39	14	FL	A	Macclesfield Town	L	0-1	0-1	9		(2725)
40	21	FL	H	Swansea City	D	2-2	1-1	10	Griffiths 42, Harris 65	4261
41	24	FL	H	Hartlepool United	W	2-1	1-1	9	Joseph 21, Harris 70	3713
42	28	FL	A	Rotherham United	L	1-2	1-0	10	Griffiths 43	(3542)
43	M 03	FL	A	Chester City	D	1-1	1-0	10	Smith 27	(1650)
44	07	FL	H	Lincoln City	W	1-0	0-0	8	Inglethorpe 76	4745
45	14	FL	A	Scarborough	L	0-2	0-1	10		(2655)
46	21	FL	H	Darlington	W	2-0	1-0	10	Naylor 39, Inglethorpe 75	4752
47	28	FL	A	Notts County	L	0-1	0-0	10		(8383)
48	A 04	FL	H	Mansfield Town	D	2-2	1-2	10	Griffiths 43, 69	4081
49	11	FL	A	Barnet	W	2-1	0-0	9	Baker 83, Griffiths 90	(3437)
50	13	FL	H	Shrewsbury Town	L	2-3	1-0	10	Maskell 30, Griffiths 53	4956
51	18	FL	A	Hull City	L	2-3	0-1	12	Inglethorpe 47, Griffiths 52	(3744)
52	21	FL	H	Scunthorpe United	W	1-0	0-0	11	Ling 75	2735
53	25	FL	A	Colchester United	D	1-1	1-1	11	Inglethorpe 45	(6220)
54	M 02	FL	H	Torquay United	W	2-1	2-0	11	Smith 4 (pen), Maskell 24	6545

Best Home League Attendance: 6591 V Brighton & H.A.   Smallest :2480 V Scarborough   Average :4369

Goal Scorers:

FL	(62)	Griffiths 18, Inglethorpe 9, Smith 9, Harris 6, Clark 5, Baker 3, Simpson 3, Ling 2, Maskell 2, Richards 2, Hanson 1, Joseph 1, Naylor 1
CC	(9)	Griffiths 3, Baker 2, Inglethorpe 2, McGleish 1, Warren 1
FAC	(2)	Griffiths 1, Smith 1
AWS	(1)	Inglethorpe 1

Baker	Bennett	Channing	Clark	Colkin	Griffiths	Hanson	Harris	Hicks	Hyde	Inglethorpe	Joseph M	Joseph R	Ling	Linger	MacKenzie	Maskell	McGleish	Naylor	Pitcher	Raynor	Regis	Richards	Richardson	Simpson	Smith	Turley	Warren	West	Referee	No
	X	X			S3		X	X				S1	X			X	X				S2			X		X	X	X	B Coddington	1
S	X		X				X	X				S1	X			X	X				S1			X		X	X	X	B Knight	2
S2	X				S3		X	X				S1	X			X	X				X			X		X	X	X	M D Messias	3
S1		X		X			X	X				X	X			X	X				S2	X		X		X	S3		R Styles	4
S1		X		X			X	X				X	X			X	X				X	S		X		X		S	P S Danson	5
S2		X	S1	X			X	X				X	X			X	X				X			X		X		S	M C Bailey	6
S2		X	S3	X			X	X				X	X			X	X				X			X		X	S1		M S Pike	7
S1		X	X	X			X	X				S	X			X	X				X			X		X	S2		M J Brandwood	8
S3	X	X	X				X	X	X			S1	X			X	X							X			S2		P Rejer	9
	X	X					X	X	X			S	X			X	X				S1			X		X	S		G P Barber	10
	X	X	S	X	S2			X	X			S1	X				X				X			X		X			C T Finch	11
S1	X	X	S2			X	X	X	X			S	X				X							X		X			K A Leach	12
X	S1	X	S3	X		X	X	X	X			S2	X				X							X		X			G B Frankland	13
X	S1	X	S2			X	X	X	X				X		S		X							X		X			D R Crick	14
S1	X	X				X		X	X			S2	X				X							X		X			M E Pierce	15
S1	X	X	S3		X			X	X			X	X		S2		X							X		X			W C Burns	16
X	X	X	X		X			X	X			S2	X	S			X							X		X			G Singh	17
X	X	X	X		X		X	X	X			S	X	S2			X							X		X	S1		A Bates	18
	X	X	S2		X	S1	X	X	X			S	X				X		X					X		X			M R Halsey	19
S	X	X			X	S1	X	X	X			S2	X				X		X					X		X			D Orr	20
S	X	X			X	S1	X	X	X			S2	X				X		X					X		X			R J Harris	21
S	X	X		X	X	X	X	X	X			S2	X	S			X							X		X	S1		G Poll	22
	X	X			X	X	X	X	X			S	X	S			X		X					X		X			D Laws	23
S1	X	X			S	X	X	X	X			X	X	S	X		X							X		X			M C Bailey	24
S2	X	X		X	S3	X	X	X	X			S	X	S1			X							X		X			M J Bodenham	25
X	X	X	S		X	S1	X1	X	X			S	X				X							X		X			R D Furnandiz	26
X2	X	X			X	S1	X1	X	X	S		S2	X				X							X		X			A P D'Urso	27
X	X	X		X1	X1	S2	X2		X			X	X				X						S1	X		X				28
S3	X	X			S2	X1	X		X			S1	X	X			X						X2	X		X			E K Wolstenholme	29
	X			S2	S1	X2	X	X	X			X					X						S	X1	X	X			B Coddington	30
	X			S1	S3	X	X1	X	X3			X	X				X						S2	X2	X	X			K A Leach	31
S2	X	X		X1		X	S1	X	X	X3		X	X				X						X2	S3	X				M J Brandwood	32
	X1	X			X	S2	X	X	X			X	X				X	X			S1			X2		X			M J Jones	33
S1	X2	X			X		X	X	S			X	X				X				X1		X1	S2	X	X			J P Robinson	34
S2	X1	X			X	S1	S3	X				X				X	X				X2		X3	X					35
S	X	X			X	S1		X				X					X				X1			X		X			A R Leake	36
	X2	X			X	S1		X3	X1	X	S3	X					X				S2			X		X			S J Baines	37
S2	S	X			X	S1			X1	X	X2	X					X							X	X	X			M Fletcher	38
S1	S	X			X			X	X	X1	X	X					X				X			X	X	X			G B Frankland	39
S1	S	X			X	S2		X1	X	X		X					X				X2			X	X	X			D Orr	40
S1		X			X2		X	X1	X			X					X				S		S2	X	X				R Styles	41
		S2	X		X2		S3	X	X		X1	S1					X		X3					X	X	X			T Heilbron	42
		S1	X		X		S	X	X			X					X		X1					X	X	X			P Rejer	43
S2		S3	X		X	S1	X2	X	X			X3					X		X1					X	X	X			A Bates	44
S2		S1	X			X	X2	X	X		X1	X					X		S		X		X	X	X			T Jones	45
S		X	X			X2	X	X				X					X		S2		S1	X1	X	X				P S Danson	46
		X	X		X	X1	X	X				X			S1		X		S2		S3	X2	X3	X				G Singh	47
S1		X	X		X	S2	X	X		X2		X				X1	X		S			X	X	X			M R Halsey	48
S1		X	X		X	X	X	X		X		S				X1	X		S2				X	X	X			C R Wilkes	49
S1	X2	X			X	X	X	X				X				X1	X		S2				X	X	X	X		M E Pierce	50
S1	X1		X			X2	X	X		X		X	X		X	X	X		S			S2	X	X	X	X		E K Wolstenholme	51
S2					S1	X	X	X	X	X2	X	X	X				X		X3			X1	X	X				M R Halsey	52
S2		X			X	X		X	X	X	X	X2					X				X1		S1	X				A R Hall	53
S2		X			X2	X		X	X	X	X	X3					X	S1					X1	X				A R Leake	54
4	1	29	39	5	31	4	21	35	28	38	14	13	46	4	7	8	43	1	5	4	10	1	9	43	14	41	2		FL Appearances	
27	1	5		6	2	8	14					12		2	1				5		7		5					5	FL Sub Appearances	
1+1		2+1	3	0+1	4		1	4	4	2		2+1	4		3	4		1+2		4	4			4	4	1			CC Appearances	
0+1		2	2		2	1+1	2	2	2	1		0+1	2	0+1			2				2		2	2	2	0+1			FAC Appearances	
1+1	1	2	1		2	0+2	1+1		1	1	1	1	1		2	1		1	1+1				2	1		1+1			AWS Appearances	

Also played:(M) Brazier S(39). (M) Cooper S3(33), X(35). (F) Fenn X(37,38,39). (M) Hodge X(3). (M) Martin S3(52). (F) Morrison X(1), S(53), S3(54).((D) Shearer S(2). (M) Williams S3(15).

LEYTON ORIENT

CLUB RECORDS

BIGGEST VICTORIES
League: 9-2 v Aldershot, Division 3(S), 10.2.1934.
8-0 v Crystal Palace, Division 3, 12.11.1955.
8-0 v Rochdale, Division 4, 20.10.1987.
8-0 v Colchester United, Division 4, 15.10.1988.
League Cup: 9-2 v Chester, 3rd Round, 15.10.1962.

BIGGEST DEFEATS
League: 1-7 v Torquay United (A) Division 3(S), 16.4.1949.
1-7 v Stoke City (a), Division 2, 7.9.1956, also 0-6 on seven occasions.
F.A. Cup: 0-8 v Aston Villa, 4th Round, 30.1.1929.

MOST POINTS
3 points a win: 75, Division 4, 1988-89.
2 points a win: 66, Division 3, 1955-56.

MOST GOALS SCORED
106, Division 3(S), 1955-56.

RECORD TRANSFER FEE RECEIVED
£600,000 from Notts County for John Chiedozie, August 1981.

RECORD TRANSFER FEE PAID
£175,000 to Wigan Athletic for Paul Beesley, October 1989.

BEST PERFORMANCES
League: 22nd Division 1, 1962-63.
F.A. Cup: Semi-final 1977-78.
League Cup: 5th Round 1963.

HONOURS
Champions of Division 3(S), 1955-56.
Champions of Division 3, 1969-70.

LEAGUE CAREER
Elected to Div 2 1905, Div 3(S) 1928-29, Div 2 1955-56, Div 1961-62, Div 2 1962-63, Div 3 1965-66, Div 2 1969-70, Div 3 1981-82, Div 4 1984-85, Div 3 (now Div 2) 1988-89.

INDIVIDUAL CLUB RECORDS

MOST GOALS IN A SEASON
Tom Johnston: 36 goals in 1957-58 (League 35, FA Cup 1).

MOST GOALS IN A MATCH
5. R Heckman v Lovells Athletic (h), 7-1, 1st Round, 19.8.1955.

OLDEST PLAYER
John Rutherford, 42 years v Portsmouth (h) Division 2, 2.4.1927.

YOUNGEST PLAYER
Chris Bart-Williams, 16 years 232 days v Tranmere Rovers (h), Division 3, 2.2.1991.

MOST CAPPED PLAYER
John Chiedozie (Nigeria) 8.
J Townrow & O Williams (England) 2.

PREVIOUS MANAGERS

S Ormerod 1905-07; W Holmes 1907-22; P Proudfoot 1923-28; A Grimsdell 1929-30; P Proudfoot 1930-31; J Seed 1931-33; D Pratt 1933-35; P Proudfoot 1935-39; W Wright 1939-40; W Hall 1945; W Wright 1945-46; C Hewitt 1946-48; N McBain 1948-49; A Stock 1949-56; L Gore (caretaker) 1956; A Stock 1956-57; L Gore (caretaker)1957-58; A Stock 1958-59; J Carey 1961-63; L Gore (caretaker) 1963; B Fenton 1963-64; L Gore (caretaker) 1964-65; D Sexton 1965; L Gore (caretaker) 1965-66; R Graham 1966-68; J Bloomfield 1968-71; G Petchey 1971; J Bloomfield 1971-81; P Went 1981; K Knighton 1981-83; Frank Clark 1983-91; Peter Eustace 1991-94; John Sitton & Chris Turner 1994, Pat Holland 1995-96.

ADDITIONAL INFORMATION
Previous Names: 1881-86 Glyn Cricket & Football Club, 1886-88 Eagle FC, 1888-98 Orient FC, 1898-1946 Clapton Orient, 1946-67 Leyton Orient, 1967-87 Orient, 1987 Leyton Orient.
Previous Leagues: None.
Club colours: Red and white checked shirt, black shorts with red and white trim.
Change colours:
Reserves League: Capital League. **Youth League:** S.E. Counties.

LONGEST LEAGUE RUNS

of undefeated matches:	14 (1954-55)	of league matches w/out a win:	23 (1962-63)
of undefeated home matches:	25 (1913-14)	of undefeated away matches:	9 (1954-55)
without home win:	14 (1962-63)	without an away win:	34 (1938-47)
of league wins:	10 (1956)	of home wins:	12 (1954)
of league defeats:	8 (1927-28)	of away wins:	6 (1956)

THE MANAGER

TOMMY TAYLOR . . . . appointed November 1996.

PREVIOUS CLUBS
As Manager . . . . None.
As Asst.Man/Coach . . . . None.
As a player . . . . Leyton Orient, West Ham, Leyton Orient, Beerschot (Bel), Charlton.

HONOURS
As a Manager . . . . None.
As a Player . . . . England: 11 u23 caps, Youth & Schools caps.

582

PLAYERS NAME / Honours	Ht	Wt	Birthdate	Birthplace / Transfers	Contract Date	Clubs	League	L/Cup	FA Cup	Other	Lge	L/C	FAC	Oth
G O A L K E E P E R														
Hyde Paul	6.1	15.8	4/7/63	Hayes		Hillingdon Borough								
AT 1993 GMVC 1993						Hayes								
				£15000	7/6/93	Wycombe W.	105	10	13	13				
					8/14/96	Leicester City								
				Loan	2/3/97	Leyton Orient	4							
					3/14/97	Leyton Orient	37	4	2					
MacKenzie Chris N	6	12.6	5/14/72	Northampton		Corby								
				£15000	7/20/94	Hereford United	59+1	1	4	8	1			
				Free	10/17/97	Leyton Orient	4			1				
D E F E N C E														
Clark Simon	6.1	12.6	3/12/67	London		Stevenage Borough								
				Free	5/25/94	Peterborough Utd	101+5	5	12	4+1	4			1
					6/4/97	Leyton Orient	39	3	2		5			
Hicks Stuart	6.1	12.6	5/30/67	Peterborough	8/10/84	Peterborough Utd								
					8/1/85	Wisbech								
				Free	3/24/88	Colchester United	57+7	2	5	5			1	
				Free	8/19/90	Scunthorpe United	67	4	4	8	1		1	
				Free	8/10/92	Doncaster Rovers	36	2	1	2				
					8/27/93	Huddersfield Town	20+2	3	3	1	1			
					3/24/94	Preston North End	3+1			1				1
					2/22/95	Scarborough	81+4	4	4		2			
				Free	8/5/97	Leyton Orient	35	4	2					
Joseph Roger	5.11	11.10	12/24/65	Paddington		Southall								
E: B.2.				Free	10/4/85	Brentford	103+1	7	1	8	2			
				£150000	8/25/88	Wimbledon	155+7	17+2	11+1	6				
				Loan	3/2/95	Millwall	5							
				Free	2/28/97	West Bromwich A.	0+2							
				Free	8/7/97	Leyton Orient	13+12	2+1	0+1	1				
Joseph Matthew N A	5.7	10.2	9/30/72	Bethnal Green	11/17/90	Arsenal								
				Free	12/7/92	Gillingham								
					11/19/93	Cambridge United	319+3	14+1	14	10	14			
				£10000	1/22/98	Leyton Orient	14				1			
Richardson Craig T	5.8	10.3	10/8/79	Newham	8/22/97	Leyton Orient (T)	1							
Smith Dean	6.1	12	3/19/71	West Brom	7/1/89	Walsall	137+5	10	4	10	2			
				£75000	6/17/94	Hereford United	115+1	10	7	10+1	19	3		4
					6/5/97	Leyton Orient	43	4	2		9		1	
Walschaerts Wim						KFC Tilen								
				Free	7/1/98	Leyton Orient								
M I D F I E L D														
Ampadu Kwame	5.10	11.10	12/20/70	Bradford	11/19/88	Arsenal (T)	0+2							
Ei: u21.4, Y. AMC.'94.				Loan	10/31/90	Plymouth Argyle	6			1	1			
				£50000	6/24/91	West Bromwich	27+22	6+1	1	5	4			1
				£15000	2/16/94	Swansea City	128+19	8+1	5+1	16	12	1	1	1
				Free	7/1/98	Leyton Orient								
Brown Daniel			9/12/80	London	5/13/98	Leyton Orient (T)								
F O R W A R D														
Baker Joseph P J	5.8	10.7	4/19/77	London		Charlton Athletic								
				Free	6/1/95	Leyton Orient	23+47	1+3	0+3	0+2	3	2		
Griffiths Carl	5.9	10.6	7/16/71	Oswestry	9/26/88	Shrewsbury Town	110+33	7+4	6	7+3	54	3	2	3
W: B.1, u21.2, Y. FLge u18.1.				£500000	10/29/93	Manchester City	11+7	0+1	2		4			
				£200000	8/17/95	Portsmouth								
				£225000	3/28/96	Peterborough United	6+10	0+2	1+1		2	1	1	
				Loan	10/31/96	Leyton Orient	5				3			
					3/7/97	Leyton Orient	39+2	4	2		21	3	1	
Harris Jason A S	6.1	11.7	11/24/76	Sutton	7/3/95	Crystal Palace	0+2	0+2						
				Loan	11/22/96	Bristol Rovers	5+1			1	2			1
				Loan	8/11/97	Lincoln City	0+1							
				£20000	9/23/97	Leyton Orient	21+14	1	2	1+1	6			
Inglethorpe Alex M	5.11	11	11/14/71	Epsom	7/1/90	Watford	2+10	1+2		1+1	2			1
					5/18/95	Leyton Orient	78+6	4	1+1	1	26	2		
Ling Martin	5.8	10.2	7/15/66	West Ham	1/13/84	Exeter City	109+8	8	4	5	14			
				£25000	7/14/86	Swindon Town	2	1+1						
				£15000	10/16/86	Southend United	126+12	8	7	11+1	31	2	1	3
				Loan	1/24/91	Mansfield Town	3							
				£15000		Swindon Town	132+17	11+1	10+1	12+1	10	1	1	1
					8/15/96	Leyton Orient	83+5	6	4		3			1
Maskell Craig	5.11	11.4	4/10/68	Aldershot	4/15/86	Southampton	2+4				1			
				£20000	5/31/88	Huddersfield Town	86+1	6	8	7	43	4	3	4
				£250000	8/7/90	Reading	60+12	2	5	1	26			
				£225000	7/9/92	Swindon Town	40+7	3+1	2+1	4	21	1		4
				£250000	2/7/94	Southampton	8+8			1	1			
				Loan	12/28/95	Bristol City								
				£40000	3/1/96	Brighton & H.A.	65+1	4	3	1	20	1	1	1
				Free	8/1/97	Hong Kong								
				Free	3/26/98	Leyton Orient	6+1				2			
Morrison David	5.11	12.5	11/30/74	Waltham Forest		Chelmsford								
				£30000	5/12/94	Peterborough United	59+18	4+1	5+3	4+1	12	1		
					3/21/97	Leyton Orient	9+1							
Raynor Paul	6	12.11	4/29/66	Nottingham	4/2/84	Nottingham F (A)	3							
Loan 3/28/85 Bristol Rovers 7+1 Lge Apps				Free	8/15/85	Huddersfield Town	38+12	3	2+1	1	9			
				Free	3/27/87	Swansea City	170+21	11+1	8+1	15+1	27	3	1	3
Loan 10/17/88 Wrexham 6 Lge Apps				Free	3/10/92	Cambridge United	46+3	3	1	2+1	2			1
				£36000	7/23/93	Preston N. E.	72+8	4+1	7	10	9		1	2
					9/12/95	Cambridge United	1+1		2	1				
via Guang Deong				Free	2/27/98	Leyton Orient	4+5							
Richards Tony	6	13.1	9/17/73	Newham	8/14/92	West Ham United								
				Free	8/1/93	Hong Kong								
				Free	8/1/94	Sudbury Town								
				8/10/95	Cambridge United	29+11	2		2	5			
					7/24/97	Leyton Orient	10+7	1+2			2			
Simpson Colin	6.1	11.05	4/30/76	Oxford	7/6/94	Watford	0+1							
				Free	5/31/97	Hendon								
				Free	12/12/97	Leyton Orient	9+5				3			
Warren Mark W	5.9	10.5	11/12/74	Clapton	7/6/92	Leyton Orient	81+8	6	4	1	2	1		
E: Y.2.														

BRISBANE ROAD
Leyton, London E10 5NE

Capacity 18,869
Seating 7,171

First game ....v Cardiff City, 28.8.1937.
First floodlit game ....v Brighton & Hove Albion, 10.9.1959.

ATTENDANCES
Highest...34,345 v West Ham United, FA Cup 4th Round, 25.1.1964.
Lowest...749 v Brentford, AMC, 15.12.1986.

OTHER GROUNDS ....None.

HOW TO GET TO THE GROUND

From the North and West
Use A406 North Circular Road (sign posted Chelmsford) to Edmonton, then in 2.6 miles at roundabout take 3rd exit A112 (sign posted Leyton). Pass Leyton Midland Road Station and in half-a-mile turn right into Windsor Road, then turn left into Brisbane Road for Leyton Stadium.

From the East
Use A12 (sign posted London then City) to Leytonstone and follow signs Hackney into Grove Road. At Leyton cross main road and forward into Ruckholt Road, then turn right then left into Leyton High Road and in 0.2 miles turn left into Buckingham Road then right into Brisbane Road for Leyton Orient FC.

Car Parking: Street parking around the ground.

Nearest Railway Station: Leyton Central.
Nearest Tube Station: Leyton (Central Line).

USEFUL TELEPHONE NUMBERS

Club switchboard. 0181 926 1111
Club fax number 0181 926 1110
Club shop 0181 926 1009
Ticket Office. 0181 926 1111/1008

Marketing Department. 0181 926 1008
Internet address. . . . www.matchroom.com/orient
Clubcall 0891 12 11 50*
*Calls cost 50p per minute at all times. Call costings correct at time of going to press.

MATCHDAY PROGRAMME

Programme Editor . . . . Tim Reder.

Number of pages . . . . 42.

Price . . . . £1.50.

Subscriptions. . . . . Apply to the club shop.

Local Newspapers
. Waltham Forest Guardian, Ilford Recorder
. Hackney Gazette, East London Advertiser
. . . . Stratford Express.

Local Radio Stations
. . . . Radio Goodmayes,
. . . . Whipps Cross Hospital Radio.

MATCHDAY TICKET PRICES

Main Centre
Adults. £13.00
Concessions. £9.00

North/South Wings
Adults. £12.00
Concessions. £8.00

West Stand
Adults. £11.00
Concessions. £7.00

Terrace/Enclosure
Adults. £10.00
Concessions. £6.00

Executive Club
Adults. £27.00
Concessions. £15.00

MANSFIELD TOWN
(The Stags)
NATIONWIDE LEAGUE DIVISION 3
SPONSORED BY:

1997/98 Back Row L-R: Bob Shaw (chief scout), Steve Harper, Michael Sissons, Mark Peters, John Doolan, Stewart Hadley, Darren Clarke, Iyseden Christie, David Kerr, Ivan Hollett (asst. youth team mnager). **Middle Row:** Lee Williams, Steve Whitehall, Ben Sedgemore, Duncan Roberts, Scott Eustace, Stuart Watkiss, Ian Bowling, John Schofield, Leigh Holbrook, John Walker. **Back Row:** Tony Ford (asst manager/youth team coach), Alan Meale (MP for Mansfield), Keith Haslam (chairman), Steve Parkin (manager), Tony Hewson (associate director), Barry Statham (physio).

MANSFIELD TOWN
FORMED IN 1905
TURNED PROFESSIONAL IN 1905
LTD COMPANY IN 1905

CHAIRMAN/CHIEF EXEC: Keith Haslam
DIRECTOR
M Haslam
SECRETARY
Christine Reynolds (01623 23567)
MARKETING MANAGER
Nicola Wilcockson

MANAGER: Steve Parkin
ASSISTANT MANAGER: Tony Ford

YOUTH TEAM MANAGER
Tony Ford

PHYSIOTHERAPIST
Barry Statham

STATISTICIAN FOR THE DIRECTORY
Vacant

Under the leadership of manager Steve Parkin, the 'Stags' had a moderate season, finishing halfway up the table after amassing 65 points from their 46 matches. Beaten only three times at Field Mill, the 'Stags' played well away from home and in total registered 23 points on their travels, but they lacked consistency and perhaps settled for 12th position after a rather mixed set of results. Starting off with a useful 2-0 home win over Hull City, they lost four of their next seven and after 12 fixtures had been completed found themselves in fifteenth spot with only 15 points to show for their efforts.

Iyesden Christie (signed from Coventry City) and Steve Whitehall (who finished up as top scorer with 26 goals) were Mansfield's key players and a lot revolved around Christie in midfield. The rest of the players certainly gave a good account of themselves and the team as a whole was never really overpowered, or indeed, outplayed by another side all season.

At the turn of the year Mansfield were way down the ladder, well away from a play off spot and at this stage in the season were looking for consolidation. One or two new faces were introduced to the team and results fluctuated. As time rolled by the 'Stags' played with more composure, having no worries about relegation and after 40 matches had been completed they were occupying twelfth position with 55 points, still only six away from a play-off spot. But it was too big a gap to claw back and from their last six matches the 'Stags' gained a further 10 points to end up exactly halfway in the Division, having had in some ways a fairly comfortable season.

They are certainly hoping for better things in 1998-99 and could well be one of the dark horses for promotion.

Tony Matthews.

MANSFIELD TOWN

Division 3   :12th   FA CUP: 1st Round   LC CUP: 1st Round   AWS: Northern Quarter-finals

M	DATE	COMP.	VEN	OPPONENTS	RESULT	H/T	LP	GOAL SCORERS/GOAL TIMES	ATT.
1	A 09	FL	H	Hull City	W 2-0	1-0	2	Christie 38, Clarke 54	4627
2	12	CC 1/1	H	**Stockport County**	**W 4-2**	**2-1**		**Christie 44, 46, 48, Gannon 32 (OG)**	**2170**
3	15	FL	A	Rochdale	L 0-2	0-2	13		(2133)
4	23	FL	H	Cardiff City	L 1-2	0-1	19	Doolan 86 (pen)	2743
5	26	CC 1/2	A	**Stockport County**	**L 3-6**	**1-2**		**Christie 14, Doolan 67, Ford 83**	**(2840)**
6	30	FL	H	Scunthorpe United	L 0-1	0-0	21		(3414)
7	S 02	FL	A	Lincoln City	W 2-0	1-0	16	Whitehall 16, Christie 84	(3539)
8	05	FL	H	Doncaster Rovers	D 1-1	1-0	12	Christie 43	2874
9	13	FL	A	Notts County	L 0-1	0-1	19		(6706)
10	20	FL	H	Chester City	W 4-1	3-1	15	Whitehall 26, 38, Ford 28, Christie 85	2183
11	27	FL	A	Darlington	D 0-0	0-0	17		(2596)
12	O 04	FL	A	Colchester United	D 1-1	1-1	18	Whitehall 6	2341
13	11	FL	H	Cambridge United	W 3-2	2-1	14	Christie 11, Whitehall 17, 62	2239
14	18	FL	A	Macclesfield Town	L 0-1	0-0	15		(3277)
15	21	FL	A	Swansea City	W 1-0	0-0	13	Clarke 66	(2589)
16	25	FL	H	Barnet	L 1-2	1-1	14	Hackett 20	2340
17	N 01	FL	A	Shrewsbury Town	L 2-3	1-1	16	Whitehall 43, Christie 88	(2338)
18	04	FL	H	Rotherham United	D 3-3	1-2	16	Whitehall 16, 49, Christie 75	2927
19	08	FL	H	Scarborough	W 3-2	2-2	16	Peacock 30, Whitehall 39, Harper 90 (pen)	2134
20	15	FAC 1	A	**Oldham Athletic**	**D 1-1**	**0-1**		**Whitehall 65**	**(5253)**
21	18	FL	A	Exeter City	L 0-1	0-1	17		(2888)
22	22	FL	A	Peterborough United	D 1-1	0-1	17	Peacock 57	(6202)
23	25	FAC 1R	H	**Oldham Athletic**	**L 0-1**	**0-1**			**4097**
24	29	FL	H	Leyton Orient	D 0-0	0-0	18		2086
25	D 02	FL	A	Torquay United	L 1-2	1-0	18	Peacock 45	(1440)
26	13	FL	H	Brighton & H.A.	D 1-1	1-0	19	Whitehall 1	2197
27	20	FL	A	Hartlepool United	D 2-2	0-1	18	Christie 68, Sedgemore 71	(2309)
28	28	FL	H	Lincoln City	D 2-2	1-0	19	Whitehall 43, 58	3449
29	J 03	FL	H	Rochdale	W 3-0	0-0	17	Williams 71, 78, Whitehall 86	2303
30	07	AWS N2	H	**Wrexham**	**W 1-0**	**0-0**		**Whitehall 78 (pen)**	**1325**
31	10	FL	A	Hull City	D 0-0	0-0	17		(4440)
32	17	FL	H	Scunthorpe United	W 1-0	1-0	14	Kerr 5	2375
33	27	AWS NQF	A	**Preston North End**	**L 0-1**	**0-0**			**(3609)**
34	31	FL	H	Notts County	L 0-2	0-2	16		6786
35	F 03	FL	A	Doncaster Rovers	W 3-0	1-0	15	Eustace 20, Whitehall 49, Harper 64	(1538)
36	06	FL	A	Chester City	W 1-0	0-0	14	Whitehall 55 (pen)	(2055)
37	13	FL	A	Colchester United	L 0-2	0-1	14		(2320)
38	17	FL	A	Cardiff City	L 1-4	0-1	15	Williams 74	(2451)
39	21	FL	H	Darlington	W 4-0	0-0	14	Harper 47, 48, 63, Sedgemore 67	2071
40	24	FL	H	Macclesfield Town	W 1-0	0-0	13	Peters 73	2683
41	28	FL	A	Cambridge United	L 0-2	0-0	14		(2303)
42	M 03	FL	A	Scarborough	D 2-2	0-1	14	Christie 66, Clarke 90	(2019)
43	07	FL	H	Shrewsbury Town	D 1-1	0-1	14	Peacock 48	2219
44	14	FL	A	Rotherham United	D 2-2	2-2	15	Whitehall 13, 28	(4054)
45	21	FL	H	Exeter City	W 3-2	1-1	13	Ford 39, 67, Peters 66	2033
46	28	FL	H	Peterborough United	W 2-0	2-0	12	Whitehall 15, Tallon 45	2760
47	A 04	FL	A	Leyton Orient	D 2-2	2-1	12	Whitehall 9, Clarke 32	(4081)
48	11	FL	H	Torquay United	D 2-2	0-1	13	Whitehall 52, Peacock 75	2282
49	13	FL	A	Brighton & H.A.	D 1-1	0-1	13	Christie 83	(2704)
50	18	FL	H	Hartlepool United	D 2-2	1-2	14	Whitehall 22, 60	2047
51	25	FL	A	Barnet	W 1-0	0-0	12	Whitehall 52 (pen)	(2797)
52	M 02	FL	H	Swansea City	W 1-0	0-0	12	Kerr 52	2867

Best Home League Attendance: 6786 V Notts County   **Smallest :2033 V Exeter City**   **Average :2720**

Goal Scorers:
FL	(64)	Whitehall 24, Christie 10, Harper 5, Peacock 5, Clarke 4, Ford 3, Williams 3, Kerr 2, Peters 2, Sedgemore 2, Doolan 1, Eustace 1, Hackett 1, Tallon 1
CC	(7)	Christie 4, Doolan 1, Ford 1, Opponents 1
FAC	(1)	Whitehall 1
AWS	(1)	Whitehall 1

(G) Bowling	(M) Christie	(M) Clarke	(D) Doolan	(F) Eustace	(M) Ford	(G) Gibson	(D) Hackett	(F) Hadley	(F) Harper	(M) Hassell	(M) Hutchinson	(D) Jones	(M) Kerr	(M) Milner	(M) Peacock	(D) Peters	(M) Schofield	(M) Sedgemore	(M) Sedlan	(M) Sisson	(D) Squires	(D) Tallon	(D) Thom	(M) Walker	(D) Watkiss	(M) Whitehall	(M) Williams	(F) Woods	Referee	
X	X	X	X	X	X				X			X	S				X	S							X	X	S		M.J. Jones	1
X	X		X	X	X				X	S		X	S				X	X							X	X	S		J P Robinson	2
X	X		X	X	X				X			X	S2				X	X							X	X	S1		A Bates	3
X			X	X	X				X			X	S1	S2			X	X				X				X	X		M S Pike	4
X	X	X	X	X	X				X			X	S				X	S							X	X	S		T Jones	5
X	X	X	X	X	X				X			X	S2				X	S1			S				X	X	S		C J Foy	6
X	X	X	X	X	X				X			X					X	S			S				X	X	S		M D Messias	7
X	X	X	X	X	X				X			X			S		X	S1							X	X	S		R Pearson	8
X	X	S1	X	X	X		X		X					S2			X	X							X	X	S3		G Cain	9
X	X	X	X	X	X		X		X	S2				S3			X	X								X	S1		M R Halsey	10
X	X		X	X	X		X		X	X							X	X								X	S		M L Dean	11
X	X		X	X	X		X	S1	X	X							X	X			S					X	S		K M Lynch	12
X	X	X	X	X	X		X	S1	X	S							X	X								X	S		A R Leake	13
X	X1	X	X	X2	X		X		X	S							X	X								X	S2		G Laws	14
	X	X	X	X		X	X		X	X						S1		X	X		S					X	X		M Fletcher	15
	X	X	X	X		X	X	X		X						S1	S	X	X		S					X	X		P Rejer	16
S1			X		X	X		X	X						S2		X	X	X		S					X	X		M C Bailey	17
	S2	X	X	S1	X	X		X	X						S		X	X	X							X	X		A R Hall	18
S1		X	X	X	X	X		X	S						S		X	X	X							X	X		S W Mathieson	19
X2		X	X	X	X			X							S		X	X	X	S1						X	X		M A Riley	20
S1		X	X	X	X	X		X			S				S		X	X	X							X	X		R J Harris	21
S1		X	X	X	X	X		X			S				S		X	X	X							X	X		M E Pierce	22
S1		X	X		X	X		X	S	S	S				S		X	X	X	S	X	S				X	X		M A Riley	23
	X	X	X		X	X		X							S	S	X	X	X	S						X	X		R D Furnandiz	24
S3	S2	X			X	X		X					X2		X	X1	X	S1				X3				X	X		D R Crick	25
S1		X		X2	X		X		X				S		X1		X	S2				X				X	X		M L Dean	26
X	S3	X	X	X	X		X		X1	X			S1		X2			S2				X			X3		X		P R Richards	27
X	S	X		X	X				X1	X			S1		X		S					X	X			X	X		A P D'Urso	28
X2	S			X	X1				X	X			S1		X		X	S2				X	X			X	X		M S Pike	29
X	S2			X1			X		X			X2	X		X		X				X	X	X	S1		X	X			30
X	X				X				X	S		X2	X1		X		S1				X	X	S2		X	X		K M Lynch	31
X	S1	S2	X		X				X			A2	X1		A		A				X	X	S		X	X		E K Wolstenholme	32
X	S1	S2	X2		X				X			X			X		X				X	X			X	X1			33
X	X	S3	S1	X3	X				X			X1			S1		X				X				X	X		R Pearson	34
X	X	S2	X	X2	X				X			S1	S3		X	X	X				X				X3	X1		B Coddington	35
X	X	X	X	X	X				X		S	S	S		X	X	X				X							G B Frankland	36
X	X	X	X	X	X				X			S1	X1		X	X3	X	S3			X2					S2		J P Robinson	37
X	X		X						X1			S2	S	S1	X	X2	X				X				X	X	X	D Pugh	38
X	S		X1		X		X		X			S	S1	X	X	X	X				X				X	X	X1	M C Bailey	39
X	S				X		X		X			S1		X	X	X	X				X				X	X	X1	T Jones	40
X	S3		S1	X	X		X		X			X1	S2	X2	X	X3	X				X					X	X	R D Furnandiz	41
X	X				X		X		X			S	S1	X	X		X				X					X	X	X1	R D Furnandiz	42
X	X1	X2			X		X		X			S	X		X		X				X				S1	X	S2		S G Bennett	43
X	X				X		X		X			S	X	X	X	S	X				X				X	X	X	S	S W Mathieson	44
X	S1				X		X	S	X			S	X1	X	X		X				X			X	X	X	X		R J Harris	45
X	S1				X		X	S	X			S	X1	X	X		X				X			X	X	X	X		A R Leake	46
X	S1				X		X	S	X			S	X	X	X		X				X				X	X	X		M R Halsey	47
X	S1				X		X	S	X			S	X	X	X		X				X1				X	X	X		T Heilbron	48
X	S1				X		X		X			S2	X	X1	X		X				X2				S	X	X		B Coddington	49
X	S2	X2		S1	X		X		X			S	X	X1	X		X				X				X	X	X		C R Wilkes	50
X	X	S2	S1		X		X		X			X2	X	X1	X		X			S	X				X	X	X		B Knight	51
X	X1	S1	X		X				X	X	S	X2		X	X		X		S2		X				X	X	X		G B Frankland	52
33	26	26	24	24	33	13	23		46	8		6	7	1	25	24	44	21			1	26	5		10	42	33	5	FL Appearances	
	13	9		5	1		2			1			11	6	7			7	1	1				1		1	5	1	FL Sub Appearances	
2	2	1	2	2	2				2			2					2	1							2	2			CC Appearances	
2	0+2	1	2	2	2			2	2			2			2	2	2	1+1							2	2			FAC Appearances	
2	0+1	0+1		0+1	2				2				2		2	2	2					2	2	0+1		2	2		AWS Appearances	

Also Played: (D) Holbrook S(3,4). (D) Roberts X(41).

CLUB RECORDS

BIGGEST VICTORIES
League: 9-2 v Rotherham United, Division 3(N), 27.12.1932.
8-1 v Q.P.R., Division 3, 15.3.1965.
7-0 v Scunthorpe United, Division 4, 21.4.1975.
F.A. Cup: 8-0 v Scarborough (a), 1st Round, 22.11.1952.
9-2 v Hounslow, 1st Round replay, 5.11.62.
BIGGEST DEFEATS
League: 1-8 v Walsall, Division 3(N), 19.1.1933.
F.A. Cup: 0-5 v Sheffield Wednesday (a), 3rd Round 10.1.1946.
0-5 v Bristol Rovers (a), 3rd Round, 4.1.1958.
League Cup: 0-5 v Chesterfield (h), 1st Round replay 23.8.1971.
0-5 v Notts County (a) 1st Round, 30.8.1988.
2-7 v Luton Town (a), 2nd Round, 3.10.1989.
MOST POINTS
3 points a win: 81, Division 4, 1985-86.
2 points a win: 68, Division 4, 1974-75.
MOST GOALS SCORED
108, Division 4, 1962-63.

RECORD TRANSFERS FEE RECEIVED
£638,500 from Swindon Town for Colin Calderwood (£27,000 7/85 +
£611,500 8/93 when Calderwood moved on to Tottenham).
RECORD TRANSFER FEE PAID
£80,000 to Leicester City for Steve Wilkinson, Oct 1989 & to Notts
County for Wayne Fairclough, March 1990.

BEST PERFORMANCES
League: 21st Division 2, 1977-78.
F.A. Cup: 6th Round, 1968-69.
League Cup: 5th round 1975-76.
HONOURS
Division 4 champions 1974-75.
Division 3 champions 1976-77.
Freight Rover Trophy winners 1986-87.
LEAGUE CAREER: Elected to Div 3(S) 1931, Transferred to Div
3(N) 1932, Transferred to Div 3(S) 1937, Transferred to Div 3(N)
1947, Transferred to Div 3 1958, Div 4 1959-60, Div 3 1962-63, Div
4 1971-72, Div 3 1974-75, Div 2 1976-77, Div 3 1977-78, Div 4
1979-80, Div 3 1985-86, Div 4 1990-91, Div 3 (now Div 2) 1991-92,
Div 3 1992-93.

INDIVIDUAL CLUB RECORDS

MOST GOALS IN A SEASON
Ted Harston: 58 goals in 1936-37 (League 55, FA Cup 3).

MOST GOALS IN A MATCH
7. Ted Harston v Hartlepool United, Division 3(N), 8-2, 23.1.1937.

OLDEST PLAYER
David Owen 'Dai' Jones, 38 years 207 days v Wrexham (a), Division
3(N), 4.5.1949.

YOUNGEST PLAYER
Cyril Poole, 15 years 351 days v New Brighton (h), Division 3(N),
27.2.1937.

MOST CAPPED PLAYER
John McClelland (Northern Ireland) 6 (38).

PREVIOUS MANAGERS

J Baynes 1922-25; E Davison (player/manager) 1926-27; J Hickling
1928-33; H Martin 1933-35; C Bell 1935; H Wightman 1936;
H Parkes 1936-38; J Poole 1938-44; C Barke 1944-45; R Goodall
1945-49; F Steele 1949-51; S Mercer 1953-56; C Mitten 1956-58;
S Weaver 1958-60; R Carter 1960-63; T Cummings 1963-67;
T Eggleston 1967-70; J Basford 1970-71; D Williams 1971-74;
D Smith 1974-76; P Morris 1976-78; B Bingham 1978-79; M Jones
1979-81; S Boam 1981-83; I Greaves 1983-89; George Foster 1989-
93, A King 1993-96.

ADDITIONAL INFORMATION
PREVIOUS NAMES
Weslyons (1897).
PREVIOUS LEAGUES
Midland League.
Club colours: Amber with royal blue stripe down sides, royal blue collar
Change colours: White shirts with thin blue stripes, short as shirt,
white socks.
Reserves League: Pontins League Division 2.
'A' Team: Midland Purity Youth League.

LONGEST LEAGUE RUNS

of undefeated matches:	20 (1976)	of league matches w/out a win:	12 (1959, 1974, 1979-80)
of undefeated home matches:	38 (1976-77)	of undefeated away matches:	8 (1976, 1991)
without home win:	11 (1959)	without an away win:	37 (1931-33)
of league wins:	7 (1962, 1991)	of home wins:	10 (1949)
of league defeats:	7 (1947)	of away wins:	7 (1976, 1991)

THE MANAGER

STEVE PARKIN . . . . appointed September 1996.

PREVIOUS CLUBS
As Manager. . . . . None.
As Asst.Man/Coach. . . . . Mansfield.
As a player. . . . . Stoke City, West Bromwich Albion, Mansfield.

HONOURS
As a Manager . . . . None.
As a Player . . . . 5 caps for England U21, 6 Youth, & schoolboy caps.

MANSFIELD TOWN

PLAYERS NAME / Honours	Ht	Wt	Birthdate	Birthplace / Transfers	Contract Date	Clubs	League	L/Cup	FA Cup	Other	Lge	L/C	FAC	Oth
G O A L K E E P E R														
Bowling Ian	6.3	13.11	7/27/65	Sheffield		Gainsborough T.								
				Free	10/23/88	Lincoln City	59	3	2	4				
				Loan	8/17/89	Hartlepool United	1							
				Loan	3/25/93	Bradford City	7							
				£27500	7/28/93	Bradford City	29	2	2+1	1				
				Free	8/11/95	Mansfield Town	123	6	6	1				
D E F E N C E														
Hackett Warren J FAYC'90.	6	12.5	12/16/71	Plaistow		Tottenham Hotspur								
				Free	7/3/90	Leyton Orient	74+2	4	8	7	3		1	
				Free	7/26/94	Doncaster Rovers	39	2	1	3				
				£50000	10/20/95	Mansfield Town	89+1	2	5		5			
Parkin Stephen J E: u21.5, Y.6, S.	5.6	10.7	11/7/65	Mansfield	11/12/83	Stoke City	104+9	9	9	6	5			
				£190000	6/16/89	WBA	44+4	3		2+1	2			
				Free	7/16/92	Mansfield Town	84+3	2	5+1	6+1	3		1	
Peters Mark W: B.1, u21.3.	6	11.3	7/6/72	St.Asaph	7/5/90	Manchester City								
				Free	9/2/92	Norwich City								
				Free	8/10/93	Peterborough United	17+2	2		2				
				Free	9/30/94	Mansfield Town	70+1	3	6	5	8			
Ryder Stuart E: u21.3.	6	12.1	06/11/73	Sutton C'field	16/07/92	Walsall	86+15	5+1	9	7+1	5			
				Free	7/1/98	Mansfield Town								
Tallon Gary T	5.10	12.7	Drogheda	9/5/73		Drogheda United								
				£30000	11/27/91	Blackburn Rovers								
				Free	6/20/96	Kilmarnock	4	1	1					
				Loan	3/26/97	Chester City	1							
				Free	12/1/97	Mansfield Town	26			1				
Watkiss Stuart P	6.2	13.7	5/8/66	Wolverhampton	7/13/84	Wolverhampton W.	2							
				Free	2/28/86	Crewe Alexandra	3							
				Free	8/5/93	Walsall	60+2	8	5+1	2	3			
				Free	2/16/96	Hereford United	19			2				
					8/15/96	Mansfield Town	40+1	3	1		1			
M I D F I E L D														
Christie Iyseden	6	12.2	11/14/76	Coventry		Coventry City	0+1	0+1						
				Loan	11/18/96	Bournemouth	3+1							
				Loan	2/7/97	Mansfield Town	7							
					6/10/97	Mansfield Town	26+13	2	+2		10	4		
Clarke Darrell J	5.11	12	12/16/77	Mansfield	7/3/96	Mansfield Town	43+11	1	1+1		6			
Ford Tony	5.9	12.2	5/14/59	Grimsby	5/1/77	Grimsby Town	321+33	31+3	14+4	2	55	4	2	
				£35000	7/8/86	Stoke City	112	8	9	6	13			1
				Loan	3/27/89	Sunderland	8+1				1			
				£145000	3/24/89	WBA	114	7	4	2+1	14			1
				£50000	11/21/91	Grimsby Town	59	1	3		3			
				Loan	9/16/93	Bradford City	5							
				Free	8/1/94	Scunthorpe United	73+3	4	7	4	9	1	1	
					10/25/96	Mansfield Town	57+3	2	2		5	1	1	
Hassell Robert J	5.10	12.6	6/4/80	Derby	11/1/96	Mansfield Town (T)	8+1							
Kerr David W	5.11	11.2	9/6/74	Dumfries	9/10/91	Manchester City	4+2							
				Loan	9/22/95	Mansfield Town	4+1				1			
					8/15/96	Mansfield Town	7+11		1		2			
Schofield John D	5.11	11.3	16/05/65	Barnsley		Gainsborough T.								
				Free	10/11/88	Lincoln City	209+10	11	5+2	12+1	10	2		
				Free	18/11/94	Doncaster Rovers	107+3	4	2	3	12			
				£10000	8/8/97	Mansfield Town	44	2	2	2				
Sedlan Jason M	5.9	11.2	8/5/79	Peterborough	11/24/97	Mansfield Town (T)	0+1							
Sisson Michael	5.9	10	11/24/78	Sutton in Ashfield	1/27/98	Mansfield Town (T)	0+1							
Williams Lee E: Y.1, S.	5.7	11.13	2/3/73		1/26/91	Aston Villa								
				Loan	11/8/92	Shrewsbury Town	2+1		1+1	2			1	
					3/23/94	Peterborough United	83+8	4+1	5+1	7	1		1	
					3/18/97	Tranmere Rovers								
				Free	3/29/97	Mansfield Town	36+7		2		3			
F O R W A R D														
Harper Steve J Div.4'92.	5.11	11.12	2/3/69	Newcastle-u-L.	6/29/87	Port Vale	16+12	1+2		1+1	2			
					3/23/89	Preston North End	57+20	1+1	1+2	6+1	10			1
				Free	7/23/91	Burnley	64+5	1+2	10	8	8		3	
				Free	8/7/93	Doncaster Rovers	56+8	2	3	4	11	1		
				£20000	9/8/95	Mansfield Town	112+3	4	6	2	12		1	
Lormor Anthony	6	11.5	10/29/70	Ashington		Newcastle United	6+2				3			
				£25000	1/29/90	Lincoln City	90+10	1+2	4	6	30	2	2	
				Loan	3/3/94	Halifax Town								
				Free	7/4/94	Peterborough United	2+3		1	1+1				
				Free	12/23/94	Chesterfield	94+13	8	5	6+1	35	4	3	3
				£130000	11/7/97	Preston North End	9+3		3	3	3			
				Loan	2/20/98	Notts County	2+5							
				£20000	7/7/98	Mansfield Town								
Milner Jonathan R	5.9	10.12	3/30/81		8/22/97	Mansfield Town (T)	1+6							
Peacock Lee A	6	12.8	10/9/76	Paisley	3/10/95	Carlisle United (T)	52+24	2+3	4+1	6+4	11		1	
				£150000	10/17/97	Mansfield Town	25+7		2	2	5			

ADDITIONAL CONTRACT PLAYERS

PLAYERS NAME	Ht	Wt	Birthdate	Birthplace / Transfers	Contract Date	Clubs	League	L/Cup	FA Cup	Other	Lge	L/C	FAC	Oth
Hutchinson James A					11/17/97	Mansfield Town (T)								

FIELD MILL GROUND

Quarry Lane, Mansfield, Nottingham NG18 5DA

Capacity 7,033
Covered Standing 1,638
Seating...3,329

First game...v Swindon Town, August 1931.
First floodlit game ....v Cardiff City, (friendly), 5.10.1961.
An experimental match under artificial lights took place at Field Mill on 22.2.1930.
ATTENDANCES
Highest...24,467 v Nott'm Forest, FAC Rnd 3, 10.1.1963.
Lowest ....1,086 v Darlington, AMC, 22.2.1984.

OTHER GROUNDS: ....None.

HOW TO GET TO THE GROUND

From the North
Use motorway M1 until junction 29. Leave motorway and follow signs to Mansfield A617. In 6.3 miles turn right into Rosemary Street B6030. In 1 mile turn right into Quarry Lane for Mansfield Town FC.

From the East
Use A617 to Rainworth. In 3 miles, at crossroads, turn left (B6030) into Windsor Road. At end turn right into Nottingham Road. Shortly turn left into Portland Street, then turn left into Quarry Lane for Mansfield Town FC.

From the South and West
Use motorway M1 until junction 28 then follow signs to Mansfield (A38). In 6.4 miles at crossroads turn right into Belvedere Street (B6030). In 0.4 miles turn right into Quarry Lane for Mansfield Town FC.

Car Parking: Space for 500 cars at the ground.
Nearest Railway Station: Mansfield Alfreton Parkway.

USEFUL TELEPHONE NUMBER

Club switchboard.... 01623 623 567
Club fax number 01623 625 014
Ticket Office........ 01482 351119
Marketing Department 01623 658 070

Clubcall 0891 12 13 11*
*Calls cost 50p per minute at all tmes.
Call costings correct at time of going to press.

MATCHDAY PROGRAMME

Programme Editor (97/98) ....Mick Saxby.

Number of pages (97/98) ....32.

Price (97/98)....................................£1.20.

Subscriptions ....Apply to club.

Local Newspapers
....................................Chronicle Advertiser,
...........................Nottingham Evening Post.

Local Radio Stations
..................Radio Trent, Radio Nottingham.

MATCHDAY TICKET PRICES

Seats £10
Juv/OAP £5

Family Stand. £10
Juv £5

Terraces £8
Juv/OAP £3

PETERBOROUGH UNITED
(The Posh)
NATIONWIDE LEAGUE DIVISION 3
SPONSORED BY: THOMAS COOK GROUP LIMITED

1997/98 - Back Row L-R: Simon Davies, Anders Koogi, Greg Heald, Mark Foran, Mark Tyler, Bart Griemink, Jimmy Quinn, Ashley Neal, David Farrell, Chris McMenamin. **Middle Row:** Gordon Ogbourne (kit man), Neil Lewis, Adrian Boothroyd, Martin Carruthers, Mick Dudley, Andy Edwards, Miquel Deo Souza, Deo Linton, Zeke Rowe, Adam Drury, Niall Inman. **Front Row:** Chris Turner (football co-ordinator), Giuliano Grazioli, Derek Payne, Steve Castle, Barry Fry (manager), Peter Boizot (chairman), Phil Neal (asst. manager), Wayne Bullimore, Chir sCleaver, Scott Houghton, Roy Johnson (physio).

PETERBOROUGH UNITED
FORMED IN 1934
TURNED PROFESSIONAL IN 1934
LTD COMPANY IN 1934

PREIDENT: Peter Boizot, M.B.E.
CHAIRMAN: Peter Boizot
VICE-CHAIRMAN: Roger Terrell
DIRECTORS
Alf Hand, Nigel Hards, Philip Sugar
SECRETARY
Miss Caroline Hand

MANAGER: Barry Fry
ASSISTANT MANAGER: Jimmy Quinn
YOUTH ACADEMY DIRECTOR
Kit Carson
PHYSIOTHERAPIST
Phil McLoughlin

STATISTICIAN FOR THE DIRECTORY
Mick Robinson

Having started out so positively, Posh fans were left wondering what went wrong. Sitting in first place for most of the early months all the good for an automatic promotion place any minor hicups and many they would drop to the play-off zone. But come the end of the season even a play-off place wasn't achieved.

Only one defeat in the opening 12 games was recorded putting them on top of the pile. During November they played six matches and drew every single one and dropped to second. Alternating from second to third over the Christmas period and the early months of the New Year it wasn't until mid February that things started to go wrong. A run of six games without a win saw them drop to eighth and three wins in the last eight meant that Peterborough finished an unbelievable 10th!

Whether it was a lack of concentration or just confidence only Barry Fry will know but he will be confident that he can do the job that they should have completed this year.

PETERBOROUGH UNITED

Division 3		:10th		FA CUP: 3rd Round		LC CUP: 2nd Round		AWS: Southern Semi-final	

M	DATE	COMP.	VEN	OPPONENTS	RESULT	H/T	LP	GOAL SCORERS/GOAL TIMES	ATT.
1	A 09	FL	H	Scunthorpe United	L 0-1	0-0	23		5761
2	12	CC 1/1	H	Portsmouth	D 2-2	1-2		Carruthers 81, Awford 8 (OG)	3613
3	15	FL	A	Doncaster Rovers	W 5-0	1-0	6	Edwards 31, Payne 56, Carruthers 67, 88, Quinn 69	(1920)
4	23	FL	H	Hull City	W 2-0	1-0	3	Carruthers 30, Quinn 88	5701
5	26	CC 1/2	A	Portsmouth	W 2-1	1-1		Farrell 44, Quinn 56	(6395)
6	30	FL	A	Rochdale	W 2-1	1-1	2	Carruthers 13, Farrell 58	(2104)
7	S 03	FL	A	Brighton & H.A.	D 2-2	1-1	4	Carruthers 20, Payne 85	(1215)
8	07	FL	H	Barnet	W 5-1	2-0	1	Quinn 25, 39 (pen), 52, Farrell 56, Carruthers 60	7243
9	13	FL	A	Rotherham United	D 2-2	1-2	1	Carruthers 19, 72	(3859)
10	16	CC 2/1	A	Reading	D 0-0	0-0			(5138)
11	20	FL	H	Leyton Orient	W 2-0	2-0	1	Castle 2, Quinn 21	6629
12	23	CC 2/2	H	Reading	L 0-2	0-0			6067
13	27	FL	A	Macclesfield Town	D 1-1	0-0	4	Houghton 80	(3079)
14	O 04	FL	H	Swansea City	W 3-1	2-0	1	Quinn 19, 35, Houghton 23	5849
15	11	FL	H	Colchester United	W 3-2	0-1	1	Carruthers 54, Houghton 60, Quinn 77	6277
16	18	FL	A	Scarborough	W 3-1	3-0	1	Bullimore 16, Farrell 20, Quinn 27	(2565)
17	21	FL	A	Hartlepool United	L 1-2	0-1	2	Desouza 89	(1990)
18	25	FL	H	Torquay United	W 2-0	1-0	1	Carruthers 38, Quinn 64	6325
19	N 01	FL	A	Exeter City	D 0-0	0-0	2		(5984)
20	04	FL	H	Shrewsbury Town	D 1-1	1-0	1	Houghton 9	4727
21	08	FL	H	Darlington	D 1-1	1-0	1	Quinn 41	6207
22	14	FAC 1	A	Swansea City	W 4-1	2-0		Quinn 27, Castle 34, 70, Carruthers 86	(2821)
23	18	FL	A	Chester City	D 0-0	0-0	1		(2612)
24	22	FL	H	Mansfield Town	D 1-1	1-0	2	Quinn 4	6202
25	29	FL	A	Notts County	D 2-2	1-2	2	Gregory 6, Quinn 58 (pen)	(8006)
26	D 02	FL	H	Cambridge United	W 1-0	0-0	2	Quinn 85	10791
27	06	FAC 2	H	Dagenham & Red.	W 3-2	1-0		Carruthers 21, Quinn 74, 82	5572
28	09	AWS S1	A	Gillingham	W 1-0	0-0		Farrell 55	(905)
29	13	FL	A	Cardiff City	D 0-0	0-0	3		(3401)
30	20	FL	H	Lincoln City	W 5-1	4-1	2	Carruthers 12, 14, Farrell 24, 80, Thorpe 45 (OG)	8771
31	26	FL	A	Barnet	L 0-2	0-0	2		(3449)
32	28	FL	H	Brighton & H.A.	L 1-2	0-1	2	Quinn 85	8221
33	J 06	AWS S2	A	Swansea City	W 2-1	0-0		Houghton 77, Quinn 89	(1179)
34	10	FL	H	Scunthorpe United	W 3-1	2-1	2	Carruthers 18, Bodley 26, Quinn 63	(3584)
35	13	FAC 3	H	Walsall	L 0-2	0-1			12809
36	17	FL	H	Rochdale	W 3-1	2-1	2	Cleaver 24, Quinn 45, 74	5676
37	24	FL	H	Hull City	L 1-3	0-0	2	Edwards 84	(4669)
38	27	AWS SQF	H	Northampton Town	W 2-1	1-1		Castle 7, Edwards 60	5516
39	31	FL	H	Rotherham United	W 1-0	0-0	2	Quinn 65	7165
40	F 06	FL	A	Leyton Orient	L 0-1	0-0	3		(5991)
41	10	FL	H	Doncaster Rovers	L 0-1	0-0	3		4577
42	14	FL	A	Swansea City	W 1-0	0-0	2	Desouza 75	(3737)
43	17	AWS SSF	A	Walsall	L 1-2	0-0		Desouza 57	4199
44	21	FL	H	Macclesfield Town	L 0-1	0-0	4		6224
45	24	FL	H	Scarborough	D 0-0	0-0	5		4208
46	27	FL	A	Colchester United	L 0-1	0-0	5		(4117)
47	M 03	FL	A	Darlington	L 1-3	0-1	6	Desouza 67	(1939)
48	07	FL	H	Exeter City	D 1-1	0-1	6	Cleaver 53	4888
49	14	FL	A	Shrewsbury Town	L 1-4	0-3	8	Carruthers 48	(2421)
50	21	FL	H	Chester City	W 2-1	1-1	7	Carruthers 7, Farrell 56	4817
51	28	FL	A	Mansfield Town	L 0-2	0-2	8		(2760)
52	A 03	FL	H	Notts County	W 1-0	0-0	8	Castle 78	6498
53	11	FL	A	Cambridge United	L 0-1	0-0	8		(5445)
54	13	FL	H	Cardiff City	W 2-0	0-0	7	Castle 48, Inman 67	4756
55	18	FL	H	Lincoln City	L 0-3	0-3	9		(6748)
56	25	FL	A	Torquay United	L 1-3	1-2	9	Green 5	(4472)
57	M 02	FL	H	Hartlepool United	D 0-0	0-0	10		4727

Best Home League Attendance: 10791 V Cambridge United	Smallest :4208 V Scarborough	Average :6184

Goal Scorers:

FL	(63)	Quinn 20, Carruthers 15, Farrell 6, Houghton 4, Castle 3, Desouza 3, Cleaver 2, Edwards 2, Payne 2, Bodley 1, Bullimore 1, Green 1, Gregory 1, Inman 1, Opponents 1
CC	(4)	Carruthers 1, Farrell 1, Quinn 1, Opponents 1
FAC	(7)	Quinn 3, Carruthers 2, Castle 2
AWS	(6)	Castle 1, Desouza 1, Edwards 1, Farrell 1, Houghton 1, Quinnn 1

(D) Bodley	(M) Bullimore	(F) Carruthers	(M) Castle	(F) Cleaver	(M) Cornforth	(M) Davies	(F) Desouza	(D) Drury	(M) Edwards	(M) Etherington	(F) Farrell	(D) Foran	(M) Gill	(M) Green	(F) Gregory	(M) Houghton	(M) Inman	(F) Lewis	(D) Linton	(M) McMenamin	(D) Neal	(M) Payne	(F) Quinn	(D) Rennie	(F) Roberts	(M) Rowe	(G) Tyler	(D) Vickers		
X	S1	S2	X	S3			X		X		X					X		X	X			X	X					X	D. Orr	1
X	S3	S1	X	S2			X		X		X					X		X	X			X	X					X	F G Stretton	2
	S	X	X	S1				X	X		X					S2		X	X	X		X	X					X	A R Hall	3
X	S	X	X	X			X		X		X	S				X		X	X			X	X					X	A Bates	4
X	S	X	X	S			X		X		X					X		X	X			X	X					X	C R Wilkes	5
X	S	X	X	S2			X		X		X		S1			X		X	X			X	X					X	M L Dean	6
X	S2	X1	X2	S3			X3		X		X					S1		X	X			X	X					X	M R Halsey	7
X	S	X	S					S	X		X					X		X	X	X		X	X					X	J P Robinson	8
X	S	X	S						X		X					X		X	X	X		X	X					X	M S Pike	9
X	S1	X	X						X		X	S				X		X	X			X	X					X	P Rejer	10
X	S1	X	S2						X		X	S				X		X	X			X	X					X	C T Finch	11
X	S1	X	S2				S3		X		X					X		X	X			X	X					X	R D Furnandiz	12
X	X	X	X				S2	S	X		X					X		X	S1	X		X	X					X	M J Jones	13
X	X	X	X				S3	S1	X		X					X		X	S2	X		X	X					X	B Knight	14
X	X	X	X				S1		X		X					X		X	X	X		X	X					X	P Taylor	15
X	X	X	X				S1	S	X		X					X		X	X	X		X	X					X	E Lomas	16
X	X	X	X				S1		X		X					X		X	S3	X		S2	X					X	S J Baines	17
X	X	X	X				S2		X		X					X			S1	X		X	X					X	T Heilbron	18
X	X	X	X				S1	S	X		X					X		X	X	X		X	X					X	F G Stretton	19
X	X	X	X				S2		X		X					X		X	X	X		X	X					X	J A Kirkby	20
X	X	X	X				S2	S1	X		X					X2		X1	X	X		X	X					X	M D Messias	21
X	S2	X	X				S		X		X					X		X	S1	X		X	X					X	A G Wiley	22
X	X	X	X				S	S	X		X					X		X	X	X		X	X					X	G Laws	23
X	X	X					S1	S3	X		X					X		X	X	X		X	X			S1		X	M E Pierce	24
	S1	X						X	X		X			X		X	S	X1	X	X		X	X			S		X	M J Brandwood	25
	S3	X						S2	X		X			X	X1			X3	X	X2		X	X			S1		X	A N Butler	26
	S	X	S2					X	X		X			X		X1		X2	X3	S3		X	X			S1		X	R D Furnandiz	27
		X2	X1					X	X		X			X		X		X				S2	X			S1		X		28
	S	X	X					X	X		X			S1		X		S	X	X		X	X			X1		X	A Bates	29
		X	X					X	X		X			S		X1		S1	X			X	X			S2		X	G Laws	30
	X2	X1						X	X		X					X		S1	X3		S3	X	X			S2		X	B Knight	31
		X3	S1	S3				X2	X1		X			S2		X		X	X	X		X	X		X	X		X	A R Hall	32
	X2	S1	S2					X	X		X					X		X1	X			X	X			X		X		33
X		X	S					S1	X		X			X1		X		X	X	X		X	X			X		X	G B Frankland	34
X		X	S					S	X		X			X		X		X	X	X		X	X		S	X		X	W C Burns	35
X		S3	S1					S2	X		X			X2	X1			X	X3			X	X			X		X	M R Halsey	36
X		X1	S2	X		S1		S3	X		X			X3		X		X	X3	X	X2		X			X		X	A G Wiley	37
X		X	X					X	X		X					X		X	X			X	X			X		X		38
X		X	S					X	X		X			S		X1		X	S			X	X			X		X	P Taylor	39
X		X		S				S1	X	X	X			X1	S1			X	X3			X	X2			X		X	M Fletcher	40
X		X1		S3		X		S1	X	X	X			X1	S1			X	X			X	X2			X		X	M L Dean	41
X	S1	S2		S	X	X1	X		X		X							S2	X1			X	X			S3		X	G Singh	42
X	X3		S1			X2		X	X		X					S2		X2	S			S1	X	X		S3		X		43
X		X		X3			X1	X	X		S1			S2		X		X				S3	X1	X2	X			X	G Laws	44
X		X		X1			X1	X	X		X			X2		S2		X				S3	X1	X2	X			X	R J Harris	45
X		X	X1				X	X	X		X			X2		S2		X				X						X S	D R Crick	46
X	S		X	X1	S1		X	X	X		X				S1	X		X				X1					X		C J Foy	47
X		X	X	S			X	X	X		X				S	X		X				X					X		R Styles	48
X		X	X	S1			S2	X1	X		X			X2		S		X				X	X				X		G Cain	49
X1	S	X	X	S			S1	X	X		X					X		X				X	X				X		K M Lynch	50
	S	X	X	S			X	X1	X		X					X		X	S1			X	X				X		A R Leake	51
		X	X				S	X	X		X			S		X	X		X	X		X	X				X		D Orr	52
	X2	X					S3	X1	X		X				S2		X3		X	S1		X	X		X		X		W C Burns	53
S		X	X				S	X	X		X							X	X	X		X	X	X		S	X		M J Jones	54
X	X1	X					S2	X1	X		X					X		X	X		S2		X3	X2	S3		X		B Coddington	55
	S1		X	S2		X2			X	X3			X1	X				X	X		X	X		S3		X	X		A Bates	56
		X		X1					X	X3	S3		X	X2		S1		X	X							X	X		A P D'Urso	57
31	8	37	34	4	3	4	8	24	46	2	40	3	2	2	2	24	4	31	25	25	2	35	40	18	2	3	46	1	FL Appearances	
	7	2	3	10	1	2	16	7			2	1		2	1	6		3	5	3	2	2	2			1	3		FL Sub Appearances	
4		0+3	3+1	4			1+1	1	4		4					3		4	2	2		4	4				4		AWS Appearances	
2		0+1	3	2+1				1	3		3	1				2		3	2+1	2	0+1	3	3			0+1	3		CC Appearances	
2	1	3	2+1	0+2	1	1	4	4	4		4	1			1	1		0+1	2	3		3	3+1	4		0+2	4		FAC Appearances	

Also Played: (M) Evans S(5). (G) Griemink S(22,27,35).(M) Shearer S(15,18,22). (M) Shields S2(57).

593

PETERBOROUGH UNITED RECORDS AND STATISTICS

CLUB RECORDS

BIGGEST VICTORIES
League: 8-1 v Oldham Athletic, Div 4, 26.11.1969; 7-0 v Barrow, Div 4, 9.10.1971.

MOST GOALS SCORED IN A CUP TIE
9-1 v Rushden, 6.10.45.

BIGGEST DEFEAT
League: 0-7 v Tranmere Rovers, Div 4, 29.10.1985

MOST LEAGUE POINTS
(3pts for win) 82, Div 4, 1981-82
(2pts for win) 66, Div 4,1960-61

MOST LEAGUE GOALS
134, Division 4, 1960-61
Bly 52, Hails 21, Smith 17, Emery 15, McNamee 16, Ripley 5, Dunne 1, Raymor 1,og 6.

RECORD TRANSFER FEE RECEIVED
£350,000 from Birmingham for Martin O'Connor, November 1996.

RECORD TRANSFER FEE PAID
£350,000 (set by tribunal) for Martin O'Connor from Walsall, July 1996.

BEST PERFORMANCES
League: 10th Div 1, 1992/93, FA Cup: 6th rnd. 1964-65
League Cup: Semi Final 1965-66

HONOURS
League Division 4 Champions, 1960-61, 1973-74.

LEAGUE CAREER
Elected to Div 4 1960
Promoted to Div 3 1961
Demoted to Div 4 1968
Promoted to Div 3 1974
Relegated to Div 4 1979
Promoted to Div 3 1990
Promoted to Div 1 1992
Relegated to Div 2 1994
Relegated to Div 3 1997

INDIVIDUAL CLUB RECORDS

MOST APPEARANCES
Tommy Robson: League 440+42 + FA Cup 43+2 + League Cup 31+1 +Texaco 3 Total 517+45 (1968-81)

MOST CAPPED PLAYER
A Millington (Wales) 8

RECORD LEAGUE GOALSCORER IN A SEASON
Terry Bly 54 (League 52, FAC 2) 1960-61
4 goals 2 times = 8; 3 goals 5 times = 15; 2 goals 6 times = 12; 1 goal 17times = 17.

RECORD LEAGUE GOALSCORER IN A CAREER
Jim Hall 122 0In All Competitions: JimHall 137 (League 122, FAC 11, Lge Cup 4) 1967-75

OLDEST PLAYER IN A LEAGUE MATCH
Norman Rigby, 38 years 333 days, 21.4.1962.

YOUNGEST PLAYER IN A LEAGUE MATCH
Mark Heeley, 16 years 229 days, 24.4.1976.

PREVIOUS MANAGERS

1934-36 Jock Porter, 1936-37 Fred Taylor, 1937-38 VicPoulter, 1938-48 Sam Haden, 1948-50 Jack Blood, 1950-52 Bob Gurney, 1952-54Jack Fairbrother, 1954-58 George Swindin, 1958-62 Jimmy Hagan, 1962-64 JackFairbrother, 1964-67 Gordon Clark, 1967-69 Norman Rigby, 1969-72 Jim Iley,1972-77 Noel Cantwell, 1977-78 John Barnwell, 1978-79 Billy Hails, 1979-82Peter Morris, 1982-83 Martin Wilkinson, 1983-86 John Wile, 1986-88 NoelCantwell, 1988-89 Mick Jones, 1989-90 Mark Lawrenson, 1990-91 Dave Booth, 1991-93 Chris Turner, 1993-94 Lil Fuccillo, 1994 Chris Turner, 1994 John Still.

ADDITIONAL INFORMATION
Previous League: Midland League.
Previous Names: None
Club colours: Blue shirt, white shorts, blue socks.
Change colours: All red.
Reserves League: Capital League.
Youth League: Midland Intermediate.

LONGEST LEAGUE RUNS

of undefeated matches:	17 (17.12.1960 - 15.4.1961)	of league matches w/out a win:	17 (28.9.1978 - 30.12.1978)
of undefeated home matches:	32 (21.4.1973 - 9.11.1974)	of undefeated away matches:	8 (28.1.69-19.4.69, 19.3.88-10.9.88)
without home win:	9 (1.2.1992 - 14.3.1992)	without an away win:	26 (7.1.1976 - 22.3.1977)
of league wins:	9 (1.2.1992 - 14.3.1992)	of home wins:	15 (3.12.1960 - 28.8.1961)
of league defeats:	5 (26.12.1988 - 21.1.1989)	of away wins:	5 (22.3.1988 - 7.5.1988)

THE MANAGER/DIRECTOR OF FOOTBALL

BARRY FRY . . . . appointed May 1996.

PREVIOUS CLUBS
As Manager . . . . Dunstable, Hillingdon, Bedford T, Maidstone, Barnet, Southend Utd, Birmingham City.
As Asst.Man/Coach . . . . None.
As a player . . . . Manchester Utd, Bolton W., Luton, Leyton Orient, Gravesend & Northfleet, Dunstable.

HONOURS
As a Manager . . . . **Barnet:** GMVC 1990-91. **Birmingham:** Division 2 & AMC 1994-95.
As a Player . . . . **England:** Schoolboys caps.

PETERBOROUGH UNITED

PLAYERS NAME / Honours	Ht	Wt	Birthdate	Birthplace / Transfers	Contract Date	Clubs	League	L/Cup	FA Cup	Other	Lge	L/C	FAC	Oth
G O A L K E E P E R														
Connor Daniel	6.2	12.9	1/31/81	Dublin		Peterborough (T)								
Griemink Bart	6.3	15.4	3/29/72	Holland	11/9/96	Birmingham City	20	3	1	1+1				
					9/9/96	Barnsley								
				£25000	10/9/96	Peterborough Utd	27		4	4				
Tyler Mark	6	12.9	4/2/77	Norwich	12/7/94	Peterborough Utd	53+1	4	3	2				
				Loan	1/25/96	Billericay Town								
D E F E N C E														
Bodley Michael / GMVC'91	5.11	12	9/14/67	Hayes	9/17/85	Chelsea	6	1		1	1			
				£50000	1/12/89	Northampton Town	20			2				
				£15000	10/1/89	Barnet	69	2	10	9	3			
				Free	7/15/93	Southend United	65+1	3	2	4	2			
				Loan	11/23/94	Gillingham	6+1			1				
				Loan	1/23/95	Birmingham City	3							
					8/15/96	Peterborough Utd	62	7	7		1			
Boothroyd Adrian N	5.7	11	2/8/71	Bradford	7/1/89	Huddersfield Town	9+1							
				£30000	6/20/90	Bristol Rovers	10+6	1		+1				
				Free	11/19/92	Hearts	+4		+2				2	
				Free	8/1/94	Mansfield Town	99+3	7	6	5+1	3			
					8/15/96	Peterborough Utd	24+2	2	4+1		1			
Chapple Phil	6.2	13.1	11/26/66	Norwich	7/10/85	Norwich City (A)								
					3/29/88	Cambridge Utd	183+4	11	23	17	19	2	1	
				£100000	8/13/93	Charlton Athletic	128+14	11	9	5	15			
				Free	7/1/98	Peterborough Utd								
Drury Adam	5.9	10.13	8/29/78	Cambridge										
Koogi Anders B	5.10	11.1	9/8/79	Denmark	7/2/97	Peterborough (T)								
Linton Desmond M	6.1	11.13	9/5/71	Birmingham	1/9/90	Leicester City	6+5	+1		1				
					10/22/91	Luton Town	65+17	4+1	9	6	1			
					3/26/97	Peterborough Utd	33+5	2	2+1					
Neal Ashley J	5.11	13.6	12/16/74	Northampton	4/27/93	Liverpool								
				Loan	9/27/96	Brighton & H.A.	8							
				Free	12/13/96	Huddersfield Town								
					3/27/97	Peterborough Utd	6+2		+1					
Rennie David	6	12	8/29/64	Edinburgh	5/18/82	Leicester City	21	2			1			
				£50000	1/17/86	Leeds United	95+6	7	7	4	5	1		1
				£175000	7/31/89	Bristol City	101+3	8	9	5	8			
				£120000	2/20/92	Birmingham City	32+3	1	1	1	4			
				£100000	3/11/93	Coventry City	80+2	6	3+1		3			
				Free	8/2/96	Northampton Town	45+3	4	1	3	3			
				Free	12/1/97	Peterborough Utd	18							
Vickers Ashley J	6.3	12.10	6/14/72	Sheffield		Heybridge Swifts								
				£5000	12/22/97	Peterborough Utd	1							
M I D F I E L D														
Castle Steve	5.11	12.5	5/17/66	Barkingside	5/18/84	Leyton Orient	232+11	15+1	23+1	18+2	55	5	6	
				£195000	6/30/92	Plymouth Argyle	98+3	5	8	6	35	1	1	
				£275000	7/21/95	Birmingham City	16+7	11	1	2	1			1
				Loan	2/15/96	Gillingham								
				Loan	2/3/97	Leyton Orient	4				1			
					5/14/97	Peterborough Utd	34+3	4	2+1		3	2		
Davies Simon	5.9	11.4	10/23/79	Haverfordwest	7/2/97	Peterborough (T)	4+2			1				
Edwards Andrew	6.2	12.7	9/17/71	Epping	4/24/89	Southend United	41+6	5	4	9	2			2
				£400000	7/6/95	Birmingham City	37+3	12	2	4	1	1		1
					11/29/96	Peterborough Utd	70	4	7		2			
Etherington Matthew	5.10	10.1	8/14/81	Truro	4/24/98	Peterborough (T)	2							
Gill Matthew J	5.11	12.2	11/8/80	Norwich	3/26/98	Peterborough (T)	2							
Houghton Scott / E: Y.7,S. FAYC'90.	5.5	11.6	10/22/71		8/24/90	Tottenham Hotspur	0+10	0+2		0+2	2			
				Loan	3/26/91	Ipswich Town	7+1				1			
				Loan	12/17/92	Gillingham	3							
				Loan	2/26/93	Charlton Athletic	6							
				Free	8/10/93	Luton Town	7+9	2+1	0+1	2	1			
				£15000	9/7/94	Walsall	38		5	2	8	1		
					7/5/96	Peterborough Utd	50+12	5+2	7		7	12	1	
Inman Niall	5.8	10.8	2/6/76	Wakefield	2/6/99	Peterborough Utd	5+3	1	0+1		1			
McMenamin Chris	5.11	11.1	12/27/73	Donegal	9/20/96	Coventry City								
				Free	8/8/97	Peterborough Utd	25+3	2	2					
Payne Derek	5.6	10.8	4/26/67	Edgware		Hayes								
				£12000	7/22/91	Barnet	50+1	2	2	3+1	6			
					7/21/94	Watford	33+3	3	2+1		1			
					8/8/96	Peterborough Utd	70+2	7	9		4			
Rowe Ezekiel B	5.11	11.8	10/30/73	Stoke Newington	6/12/92	Chelsea								
				Loan	11/12/93	Barnet	9+1	2			2	1		
				Loan	3/28/96	Brighton & H.A.	9				3			
					8/30/96	Peterborough Utd	13+14	2	3+2		3			
				Loan	2/20/98	Doncaster Rovers	6				2			
Scott Richard	5.9	10.1	29/09/74	Dudley	17/05/93	Birmingham City	11+1	3+1		3				
					22/03/95	Shrewsbury Town	91+14	6	8+1	8+1	18		3	1
					7/1/98	Peterborough Utd								
Shearer Peter / E: SP.1. Div.2'95. AMC'95.	6	11.6	2/4/67	Coventry	2/5/85	Birmingham City	2+2	1			1			
				Free	8/4/86	Rochdale	1	1			2			
					8/1/87	Nuneaton Borough			1					
					8/1/88	Cheltenham Town								
				£7000	3/9/89	Bournemouth	76+9	6	5	2+1	10	1	1	1
				£18000	8/1/92	Birmingham City	22+3	2	2	4	7		2	3
				£75000	1/5/94	Peterborough Utd								
				Free	8/6/97									
F O R W A R D														
Carruthers Martin	5.11	11.9	8/7/72	Nottingham	7/4/90	Aston Villa	2+2		0+1	0+1				
				Loan	10/31/92	Hull City	3				6			
				£300000	7/5/93	Stoke City	60+30	7+3	3+1	10+4	13	1	3	3
					11/18/96	Peterborough Utd	50+3	3+1	6		19	1	4	
Cleaver Christopher W	5.9	11.7	3/24/79	Hitchin	10/28/96	Peterborough Utd	10+17	0+2	0+1	1+2	3			
Desouza Juan / via Yeovil Town, Dorchester, Dagenham & Red.	5.11	11	2/11/70	Newham	7/4/89	Charlton Athletic								
				Free	7/4/89	Bristol City								
				£25000	2/1/94	Birmingham City	5+10	2		1	2			
				Loan	11/25/94	Wycombe W.	1							
				Loan	11/25/94	Bury	2+1				1			
				£100000	2/3/95	Wycombe W.	72+10	8	6	2	28	2	2	
					3/26/97	Peterborough Utd	16+15	1+1			5			
Farrell David	5.11	11.2	11/11/71	Birmingham		Redditch United								
				£45000	1/6/92	Aston Villa	5+1	2						
				Loan	1/25/93	Scunthorpe Utd	4+1			2	1			
				£100000	9/14/95	Wycombe W.	44+16	6	3+2	2	6			
				Free	7/2/97	Peterborough Utd	40+2	4	3		6	1		
Grazioli Giuliano / via Stevenage Boro'	5.11	12	3/23/75	London	10/19/95	Peterborough Utd	2+5	+2	+3		1		1	
				Loan	11/1/95	Yeovil Town								
				Loan	2/10/96	Enfield								
				Free	7/1/98	Peterborough								
Green Francis	5.9	11.6	8/25/80	Nottingham		Ikeston Town								
				£25000	3/2/98	Peterborough Utd	2+2				1			
Lewis Nell A	5.7	10.9	6/28/74	Wolverhampton	7/9/92	Leicester City	41+10	3+1	1	2	1			
				£60000	6/25/97	Peterborough Utd	31+3	4	3					
Martin Jae	5.11	11.10	2/5/76	Hampstead	5/7/93	Southend Utd (T)	1+7	1+1		0+1				
				Loan	9/9/94	Leyton Orient	1+3			1				
				Free	7/1/95	Birmingham Town	1+6			0+2				
					8/21/96	Lincoln City	29+12	5	1	0+1	5	1		
				Free	7/1/98	Peterborough Utd								
Quinn Jimmy M / NI: 46. B.1. Div2'94	6	11.6	11/18/59	Belfast	1/1/00	Oswestry								
				£10000	12/31/81	Swindon Town	34+15	1+1	5+3	1	10		6	2
				£32000	8/15/84	Blackburn Rovers	58+13	6+1	4	2	17	2	3	1
				£50000	12/19/86	Swindon Town	61+3	6	5	10+1	30	8		5
				£210000	6/20/88	Leicester City	13+18	2+1	+1	+1	6			
					3/17/89	Bradford City	35	2		1	13	1		
				£320000	12/30/89	West Ham Utd	34+13	3	4+2		19	1	2	
				£55000	8/5/91	Bournemouth	4+1	5		2	19	2		1
				£55000	7/27/92	Reading	150+33	12+4	9	6+3	71	12	5	6
				Free	7/15/97	Peterborough Utd	40+2	4	3		19	1	3	
Shields Anthony G	5.7	10.10	6/4/80	Londonderry	5/1/98	Peterborough T)	0+1							

595

LONDON ROAD GROUND
Peterborough PE2 8AL

Capacity 15,314

First game .... v Gainsborough, 01.09.34.
First floodlit game .... v Arsenal, 08.02.60.

ATTENDANCES
Highest .... 30,096 v Swansea City, FA Cup 5th Round, 20.2.1965.
Lowest .... 279 v Aldershot, AMC, 17.4.1986.

OTHER GROUNDS: .... None.

HOW TO GET TO THE GROUND

From the North and West
Use A1 then A47 sign posted Peterborough into town centre. Follow signs to Whittlesey and cross river bridge into London Road for Peterborough United FC.

From East
Use A47 into Peterborough town centre and follow signs to Whittlesey and cross river bridge into London Road for Peterborough United FC.

From the South
Use A1 then A15 sign posted Peterborough into London Road for Peterborough United FC.

Car Parking: Ample parking available at ground.

Nearest Railway Station: Peterborough (01733 68181)

USEFUL TELEPHONE NUMBERS

Club switchboard 01733 563 947
Club fax number 01733 557 210
Ticket Office 01733 63947

Clubcall 0891 12 16 54*
*Calls cost 50p per minute at all times.
Call costings correct at time of going to press.

MATCHDAY PROGRAMME

Programme Editor .... Russell Plummer.

Number of pages .... 32.

Price .... £1.50.

Subscriptions .... Please apply to club.

Local Newspapers
.... Herald & Post, Evening Telegraph.

Local Radio Stations
..... Radio Cambridgeshire, Hereward Radio.

MATCHDAY TICKET PRICES

Main Stand £11
Juv/OAP £5.50

Wing Stand/Enclosure £9
Juv/OAP £4.50

Terraces £7
Juv/OAP £3.50

PLYMOUTH ARGYLE
(The Pilgrims)
NATIONWIDE LEAGUE DIVISION 3
SPONSORED BY: ROTOLOK

Founded in 1886

1998-99 - Back Row L-R: Simon Collins, Matthew Parsons, Martin Gritton, James Dungey, Jon Sheffield, Jon Ashton, Lee Phillips, Lee Power. **Middle Row:** John James (Yth. dev. officer), Richard Flash, Jon Beswetherick, Brendan McGovern, Mick Heathcote, Chris Hargreaves, Paul Gibbs, Ronnie Mauge, Kevin Summerfield (Yth team coach). **Front Row:** Earl Jean, Martin Barlow, Kevin Hodges (manager), Steve McCall (Asst. manager), Paul Wotton, Liam Ford.

PLYMOUTH ARGYLE
FORMED IN 1886
TURNED PROFESSIONAL IN 1903
LTD COMPANY IN 1903

PRESIDENT: Sam Rendell
CHAIRMAN: Dan McCauley
DIRECTORS
Peter Bloom (Vice-Chairman), Roy Griggs.
SECRETARY
Roger Matthews (01752 562 561/2/3)
COMMERCIAL MANAGER
Donna Shirley

MANAGER: Kevin Hodges
ASSISTANT MANAGER: Steve McCall
YOUTH TEAM MANAGER
Kevin Summerfield
PHYSIOTHERAPIST
Norman Medhurst

STATISTICIAN FOR THE DIRECTORY
Jonathan Brewer

Having finished 17th the previous year an improvement was hoped for in the new campaign, however this was going to have to be done on a shoestring budget. Mick Jones in his first full season in charge was going to have to scour the market for 'free' signings, loan players and non-contract personnel who could cut the mustard in Division 2.

After weeks of battles all around the country with every player used giving their all, Division 2 status rested on the last game. An away trip to Turf Moor, Burnley. Argyle had plenty of chances to win a very even contest, but as summed up much of the season they came up just short and lost 2-1. In fairness most supporters had resigned themselves to relegation as Argyle had not risen above 18th all year. The cup competitions couldn't be blamed for distracting the league progress. Auto Windscreens, Coca-Cola and FA all ended in first round exits.

The close season saw a lot of the players moving to pastures new. Many of them signing for clubs in the division they had just been relegated from. Another departure was Mick Jones who paid the price of relegation though nobody could ever question his dedication to what many saw as an unenviable task. Jones' successor was Kevin Hodges, a man well known to the Plymouth faithful. The task he has accepted is to repeat the feat performed by Neil Warnock in 1995-96 and take Argyle out of the league's basement at the first time of asking.

JONATHAN BREWER

PLYMOUTH ARGYLE

Division 2 :22th   FA CUP: 1st Round   LC CUP: 1st Round   AWS: Southern Round 1

M	DATE	COMP.	VEN	OPPONENTS	RESULT	H/T	LP	GOAL SCORERS/GOAL TIMES	ATT.
1	A 09	FL	A	Bristol Rovers	D 1-1	0-1	13	Heathcote 58	(7386)
2	12	CC 1/1	A	**Oxford United**	**L 0-2**	**0-1**			**(5083)**
3	15	FL	H	Grimsby Town	D 2-2	2-0	15	Logan 28, Littlejohn 42	6002
4	23	FL	A	Wigan Athletic	D 1-1	0-1	18	Logan 84	(3761)
5	26	CC 1/2	H	**Oxford United**	**L 3-5**	**2-0**		**Wilson 12, Logan 29, Smith 46 (OG)**	**3037**
6	30	FL	H	Chesterfield	D 1-1	1-0	16	Jean 31	5284
7	S 02	FL	H	Watford	L 0-1	0-0	20		5141
8	09	FL	A	Fulham	L 0-2	0-0	21		(8961)
9	13	FL	H	Brentford	D 0-0	0-0	23		4394
10	20	FL	A	Carlisle United	D 2-2	1-2	22	Littlejohn 6, Wilson 74	(5667)
11	27	FL	H	Walsall	W 2-1	1-1	21	Barlow 34, 70	6207
12	O 04	FL	A	York City	L 0-1	0-1	22		(2894)
13	11	FL	A	Luton Town	L 0-3	0-1	22		(4931)
14	18	FL	H	Southend United	L 2-3	2-2	23	Littlejohn 30, Corazzin 31	3430
15	21	FL	H	Burnley	D 2-2	1-1	23	Jean 40, Heathcote 47	3006
16	25	FL	A	Gillingham	L 1-2	1-1	24	Jean 4	(6679)
17	N 01	FL	A	Preston North End	W 1-0	0-0	23	Corazzin 65	(8405)
18	04	FL	H	Wycombe Wanderers	W 4-2	2-1	20	Corazzin 17, 18, Littlejohn 54, Mauge 57	2993
19	08	FL	H	Bournemouth	W 3-0	2-0	18	Jean 10, Littlejohn 15, 84	5067
20	15	FAC 1	H	**Cambridge United**	**D 0-0**	**0-0**			**4793**
21	18	FL	A	Bristol City	L 1-2	0-2	17	Corazzin 83	(10867)
22	22	FL	A	Wrexham	D 1-1	0-0	17	Corazzin 58	(3641)
23	25	FAC 1R	A	**Cambridge United**	**L 2-3**	**2-0**		**Mauge 21, Jean 45**	**(3139)**
24	29	FL	H	Oldham Athletic	L 0-2	0-1	18		5452
25	D 02	FL	A	Blackpool	D 0-0	0-0	20		(3281)
26	09	AWS S1	A	**Northampton Town**	**L 1-1**			**O'Hagan 69 (Northampton won 5-3 on penalties)**	**(2631)**
27	13	FL	H	Millwall	W 3-0	2-0	20	Collins 23, Billy 43, Corazzin 78 (pen)	4460
28	20	FL	A	Northampton Town	L 1-2	1-0	20	Corazzin 45	(5546)
29	26	FL	H	Fulham	L 1-4	1-1	20	Barlow 5	9469
30	28	FL	A	Watford	D 1-1	0-0	21	Saunders 85	(11594)
31	J 10	FL	H	Bristol Rovers	L 1-2	0-2	23	Corazzin 50	6850
32	17	FL	A	Chesterfield	L 1-2	1-1	23	Corazzin 33 (pen)	(3879)
33	24	FL	H	Wigan Athletic	W 3-2	0-2	21	Saunders 52, Barlow 77, Collins 86	4345
34	31	FL	A	Brentford	L 1-3	1-0	23	Corazzin 27	(4783)
35	F 06	FL	H	Carlisle United	W 2-1	1-0	21	Heathcote 45, Corazzin 68	4540
36	14	FL	H	York City	D 0-0	0-0	21		4382
37	21	FL	A	Walsall	W 1-0	1-0	19	Heathcote 15	(4612)
38	24	FL	A	Southend United	L 0-3	0-1	19		(4363)
39	28	FL	H	Luton Town	L 0-2	0-0	19		4846
40	M 03	FL	A	Bournemouth	D 3-3	2-1	21	Saunders 31, Logan 40, Corazzin 89	(3545)
41	07	FL	H	Preston North End	W 2-0	1-0	20	Wotton 36, Conlan 65	4201
42	14	FL	A	Wycombe Wanderers	L 1-5	1-1	22	Corazzin 44	(5508)
43	21	FL	H	Bristol City	W 2-0	0-0	19	Saunders 50, Conlan 77	7622
44	24	FL	A	Grimsby Town	L 0-1	0-0	19		(4661)
45	28	FL	H	Wrexham	W 2-0	1-0	19	Corazzin 31, Saunders 79	4759
46	A 04	FL	A	Oldham Athletic	L 0-2	0-1	21		(4244)
47	11	FL	H	Blackpool	W 3-1	0-1	20	Logan 78, Corazzin 90 (pen), Butler 57 (OG)	5655
48	13	FL	A	Millwall	D 1-1	1-1	20	Corazzin 25	(5496)
49	18	FL	H	Northampton Town	L 1-3	1-1	20	Saunders 45	6389
50	25	FL	H	Gillingham	L 0-1	0-0	21		7941
51	M 02	FL	A	Burnley	L 1-2	1-2	22	Saunders 25	(18811)

Best Home League Attendance: 9469 V Fulham   Smallest :2993 V Wycombe Wanderers   Average :5323

Goal Scorers:

FL	(55)	Corazzin 17, Saunders 7, Littlejohn 6, Barlow 4, Heathcote 4, Jean 4, Logan 4, Collins 2, Conlan 2, Billy 1, Mauge 1, Wilson 1, Wotton 1, Opponents 1
CC	(3)	Logan 1, Wilson 1, Opponents 1
FAC	(2)	Jean 1, Mauge 1
AWS	(1)	O'Hagan 1

1997-98

(M) Anthony	(M) Ashton	(M) Barlow	(D) Beswetherick	(F) Billy	(M) Blackwell	(M) Clayton	(M) Collins	(M) Conlan	(F) Corazzin	(M) Currie	(D) Heathcote	(M) Hodges	(F) Illman	(F) Jean	(M) Littlejohn	(M) Logan	(M) Mauge	(M) O'Hagan	(D) Perkins	(M) Phillips	(M) Rowbotham	(M) Saunders	(G) Sheffield	(F) Starbuck	(D) Williams	(M) Wilson	(M) Woods	(M) Wotton	Referee	No.
X			X				X		X		X			S	S1	X	X					X	X		X	S		X	M. Fletcher	1
X							X		X		X			S	S	X	X1	X				X	X		X	S1		X	P S Danson	2
X			X		S1				X		X			S1	X	X1	X					X	X		X	S		X	M C Bailey	3
X			X						X		X			S	X	X	X	X				X	X		X	S1		X	D Laws	4
X	S2		S	X					X		S1			X	X	X						X	X		X	X		X	M E Pierce	5
X	S		S	X					X		S1			X	X	X						X	X		X	X		X	K A Leach	6
X	S	S1	X						X		S2			X	X	X	X					X	X		X	X		X	A P D'Urso	7
S		X	X				S2		X		X			X	X	X	X					X	X		X	S1		X	S J Baines	8
S		X	X				S		X		S1			X	X	X	X					X	X		X	X		X	M J Brandwood	9
		X	X				S	X	X		S			X	X	X					S1	X	X		X	X		X	P R Richards	10
		X	X				S	X	X		S	S		X	X		X					X	X		X	X		X	M R Halsey	11
		X	X				S	X	X		S	S1		X		X						X	X		X	X		X	R Pearson	12
		X	S	X			X		X		S			X	S1	X						X	X		X	X		X	D R Crick	13
		X	X				X	X	X		S	S1		X		X						X	X		X	S		X	C R Wilkes	14
	S	X	X				X		X		S			X		X						X	X		X	S		X	P Rejer	15
	S3	X					X	X	X		S2			X		X						X	X		X	S1		X	A N Butler	16
	S	X	X				X		X		S			X		X						X	X		X	S		X	A R Hall	17
	S	X	X				X		X		S1			X		X						X	X		X	X		X	R Styles	18
S		X	S	X			X				X	S	X	X		X		X				X	X		X	X		X	F Taylor	19
S	X	X	X	S			X				X	S1		X	X	X		X				X	X		X	X	X	X	R J Harris	20
		X	X				X		X		X		X	X	X	X					S	S1	X		X	S2		X	A G Wiley	21
		X	X				X		X		X		X	X	X	S1					S	X	X		X	S		X	G B Frankland	22
		X	X	S			X		S		X		X	X	X	X					S2	X	X		X	S1		X	R J Harris	23
		X	X				X		X		X		X	X	X	X2	S1				S	S2	X		X			X1	B Knight	24
		X	X				X		X		X		S	X1		S1					X	X	X		X			S	C J Foy	25
		X	X				X		X2		X		S2	X		X1					X	X	X		X			S1		26
	S3	X	X				X		X2		X1	S1		X		X3					X	X	X		X			S2	P S Danson	27
	S	X	X				X		X		X		S1		X1		X				X	X	X		X			S	D Pugh	28
		X	X3				X		X		X		X	S3	S2	X	S1	X2			X	X1	X		X				M Fletcher	29
		X					X		X		X		X	X1	S1	X	S				X	X	X		X			S	S G Bennett	30
		X					X		X		X		X	X1	X		X	S2		S1	X	X	X		X2			S	G Singh	31
	X	S					X		X		X		X	S1	S2	X	X1				X	X	X		X			X2	K M Lynch	32
		X					X		X		X		X	S1	X	S1	X	S			X2	X	X		X				P Taylor	33
		X					X		X		X		X	S3	X	S1	X3				S2	X1	X2	X		X			M C Bailey	34
		X					X		X2		X		X	X1	S2	S					S1	X	X	X		X			A G Wiley	35
		X					X		X		X		X	S	S	X1	S1				X	X	X		X				M L Dean	36
		X					X		X		X		X	S1	X				X1		X	X	X		X		S		F G Stretton	37
	S	X					X		X		X		X	X	S1				X2		X1	X	X		X		S2	M J Brandwood	38
		X				X	X	X	X		X		X	S	S						X1	X	X		X		S1	A P D'Urso	39
		X				X2	X	X	X		X		X	S	S2	S					S1	X	X	X1		X			A N Butler	40
	S	X					X	X	X		X		X	S	S	X					X	X	X		X			X	D Orr	41
X1	S	X					X	X2	X		X		X	S2	S1	X					S1	X	X	X1		X			A G Wiley	42
		X					X	X	X2		X						S			S2	S1	X	X	X	X1			X	M Fletcher	43
	S	X2					X	X			X				X1	S2	S			S1	X	X	X					X	P R Richards	44
		X					X	X2	S1	X						S2			S3	X	X	X	X1		X	X	R J Harris	45
		X				X	X3	X	S1	X				S2					S3	X	X	X	X2	X1		X	X1	M S Pike	46
		X				X2	X	X	X					S2		X	S1		S	X	X	X	X1				B Knight	47
		X2				X1	X	X3						S1		X	S2			X	X	X			S3	X	S J Baines	48
		X				X2	X	X	X					S2		X	S1			X	X3	X	S3		X1	K A Leach	49
		X				X	X1	X	X					S1			S2			X	X	S	X2		X	M J Brandwood	50
	X2					S3	X	X	X					S2			S1			X	X	X3	X1		X	X	P Taylor	51
5		41		41			30	13	38	5	36	9	1		16	27	23	23	5		3	23	34	46	6	39	7	4	31	FL Appearances
	1		2			1	2			2			2	5	20	4	4	8	4		7	2	3		1		4	1	3	FL Sub Appearances
2	0+1		1			1		1		2		2		0+1	1	2	2	1				2		2		2	1+1		2	CC Appearances
	2		2				2				2			0+1	2	2	1	2				0+1	2	2		2	1+1		2	FAC Appearances
	1		1			1				1			1	0+1	1	1	1		1			1	1	1		1			0+1	AWS Appearances

Also Played: (M) Sargent S(20).

CLUB RECORDS

BIGGEST VICTORIES
8-1 v Millwall,Division 2, 16.1.1932 8-1 v Hartlepool U. (a),
Division 2, 7.5.1994 7-0 v Doncaster Rovers, Division 2, 5.9.1936
6-0 v Corby, FA Cup Round 3,22.1.1966

BIGGEST DEFEATS
0-9 v Stoke City, Division 2, 17.12.1960
Record Cup Defeat
1-7 v Tottenham Hotspur, FA Cup Rnd 4, 1966-67 0-6 v West Ham
United, League Cup Rnd 2, 26.9.1962

MOST LEAGUE POINTS
(3pts for win) 87, Division 3, 1986-87
(2pts for win)68, Division 3S, 1929-30

MOST LEAGUE GOALS
107, Division 3S, 1925-26 (42 games) 107, Division 3S,1951-52
(46 games)

RECORD TRANSFER FEE RECEIVED
£750,000 from Southampton for Mickey Evans, 3rd March 1997.

RECORD TRANSFER FEE PAID
£300,000 to Port Vale for Peter Swan, July 1994

BEST PERFORMANCES
League: Third in Div 2 1931-32, 1952-53 FA Cup: Semi-Finalists
1983-84
League Cup: Semi-Finalists 1964-65, 1973-74

HONOURS
Champions Division 3S 1929-30, 1951-52 Champions Division 3
1958-59

LEAGUE CAREER
Founder Members of Division 3 1920 Transferred to Division 3S
1921-22
Promoted to Div 2 1929-30 Relegated to Div 3S 1949-50
Promoted to Div 21951-52 Relegated to Div 3S 1955-56
Transferred to Div 3 1958-59 Promoted to Div 2 1958-59
Relegated to Div 31967-68 Promoted to Div 2 1974-75
Relegated to Div 3 1976-77 Promoted to Div 2 1985-86
Relegated to Div 3/21991-92 Relegated to Div 3 1994/95
Promoted to Div 2 1995-96.

INDIVIDUAL CLUB RECORDS

MOST APPEARANCES FOR CLUB
Kevin Hodges (1978-93): League 502+28, FA Cup 39,League Cup
32+3, Other 9+2 Total 582+33

MOST CAPPED PLAYER
Moses Russell (Wales) 20, 1920-28

RECORD GOALSCORER IN A MATCH
Wilf Carter, 5 v Charlton Athletic, 6-4, Div 2,27.12.1960

RECORD LEAGUE GOALSCORER IN A SEASON
Jack Cock, 32, 1926-27 In All Competitions: Jack Cock, 32 (all
league) 1926-27 W Carter 32 (League 26, FA Cup 6) 1957-58
Tommy Tynan, 32 (League 31, FA Cup 1) 1984-85

RECORD LEAGUE GOALSCORER IN A CAREER
Sam Black, 176, 1924-37 In All Competitions: Sam Black, 185
(League 176, FA Cup 9) 1924-37

OLDEST PLAYER IN A LEAGUE MATCH
Peter Shilton, 44 years 21 days v Burnley Div 2, 9.10.1993.

YOUNGEST PLAYER IN A LEAGUE MATCH
Lee Phillips, 16 years 43 days v Gillingham, 29.10.1996.

PREVIOUS MANAGERS

1903-05 Frank Brettall 1905-06 Bob Jack 1906-07 Will Fullerton
1910-38 Bob Jack 1938-48 Jack Tresadern 1948-55 Jim Rae 1955-60
Jack Rowley 1960-61 George Taylor/ Neil Dougall 1961-63 Ellis Stuttard
1963 Vic Buckingham 1963-64 Andy Beattie 1964-65 Malcolm Allison
1965-68 Derek Ufton 1968-70 Billy Bingham 1970-72 Ellis Stuttard
1972-77 Tony Waiters 1977-78 Mike Kelly 1978 Lennie Lawrence
1978-79 Malcolm Allison 1979-81 Bobby Saxton 1981-83 Bobby
Moncur 1983-84 John Hore 1984-88 Dave Smith 1988-90 Ken Brown
1990-92 David Kemp 1992-95 Peter Shilton, 1995 Steve McCall.
1995-97 Neil warnock. Mike Jones1997-98.

ADDITIONAL INFORMATION
Previous Name: Argyle Athletic Club 1886-1903
Club colours: Green with black band around shirt.
Change colours:

Reserves League: Avon Combination

LONGEST LEAGUE RUNS

of undefeated matches:	22 (1929)	of league matches w/out a win:	13 (1962-63)
of undefeated home matches:	47 (1921-23)	of undefeated away matches:	9 (1929)
without home win:	8 (1989-90)	without an away win:	27 (1975-76)
of league wins:	9 (1930,1986)	of home wins:	17 (1922)
of league defeats:	9 (1947)	of away wins:	6 (1929)

THE MANAGER

KEVIN HODGES. . . . . appointed June 1998.

PREVIOUS CLUBS
As Manager . . . . Torquay United.
As Asst.Man/Coach. . . . . Torquay United.
As a player. . . . . Plymouth Argyle, Torquay United.

HONOURS
As a Manager . . . . None.
As a Player . . . . None.

PLAYERS NAME Honours	Ht	Wt	Birthdate	Birthplace Transfers	Contract Date	Clubs	APPEARANCES League	L/Cup	FA Cup	Other	GOALS Lge	L/C	FAC	Oth
G O A L K E E P E R														
Blackwell Kevin	5.11	12.10	12/21/58	Luton		Barnet								
GMVC'87.					11/1/86	Scarborough	44	11	2	2				
				£15000	11/8/89	Notts County								
				Free	1/15/93	Torquay United	18			2				
				Free	8/5/93	Huddersfield Town	3+2	0+1	1	3				
				Free	8/11/95	Plymouth Argyle	24		3					
Sheffield Jonathan	6	12	2/1/69	Bedworth	2/16/87	Norwich City	1							
				Loan	9/22/89	Solihull	11			1				
				Loan	8/21/90	Solihull	15			1				
				Free	3/18/91	Cambridge United	56	3	4	6				
				Loan	12/23/93	Colchester United	6							
				Loan	1/28/94	Swindon Town	2							
				Loan	9/15/94	Hereford United	8	2						
					7/20/95	Peterborough United	62	8	6	5				
					7/21/97	Plymouth Argyle	46	2	2					
D E F E N C E														
Ashton Jon F	5.11	11.4	8/4/79	Plymouth	7/29/97	Plymouth Argyle (T)		0+1						
Beswetherick Jonathan	5.11	10.3	6/25/71	Barnstaple	9/4/96	Plymouth Argyle	0+2							
Heathcote Micky	6.1	12.7	9/10/65	Kelloe	1/1/00	Spennymoor Utd								
				£15000	8/19/87	Sunderland	6+3			0+1				
				Loan	12/17/87	Halifax Town	7		1		1			
				Loan	1/4/90	York City	3			1				
				£55000	7/12/90	Shrewsbury Town	43+1	6	5	4	6			
				£150000	9/12/91	Cambridge United	123+5	7	5+2	7	13	1	2	2
				£70000	7/27/95	Plymouth Argyle	122+1	6	6	4	8	1	1	
James Anthony	6.3	13.8	6/27/67	Sheffield	1/1/00	Gainsborough T.								
				£20000	8/22/88	Lincoln City	24+5	2		0+1				
				£150000	8/23/89	Leicester City	79+28	6	2	3+1	11			
				Free	7/25/94	Hereford United	35	4	1	5	4			1
					8/15/96	Plymouth Argyle	34	1	3		1			
McCall Steve	5.11	11.3	15/11/60	Carlisle	05/10/78	Ipswich Town	249+1	29	23+1	18+1	7		1	3
				£300000	03/06/87	Sheffield Wednesday	21+8	2+3	1	0+1	2			
				Loan	08/02/90	Carlisle United	6							
				£25000	26/03/92	Plymouth Argyle	90+3	5	6	6	4			
				Free	15/08/96	Torquay United	43+8	3+1		4	2			1
				Free	7/1/98	Plymouth Argyle								
M I D F I E L D														
Barlow Martin	5.7	10.3	6/26/71	Plymouth	7/1/89	Plymouth Argyle	230+31	7+1	12	12+1	19	2		
Collins Simon	5.9	10.5	12/16/73	Pontefract	7/1/92	Huddersfield Town	32+19	4+3	1+4	1+3	3	2		
				Loan	1/14/94	Halifax Town								
					3/6/97	Plymouth Argyle	41+3	1			3			
Flash Richard G	5.9	11.8	08/04/76	Birmingham		Manchester Utd (T)								
via Wolves					21/02/97	Watford	0+1							
				Free	7/1/98	Plymouth Argyle								
Mauge Ron	5.1	10.6	3/10/69	Islington	7/22/87	Charlton Athletic								
				Free	9/21/88	Fulham	47+3	4	1	2	2			
				£40000	7/30/90	Bury	92+15	8+2	8	10+2	10	2	2	
				Loan	9/26/91	Manchester City				0+1				
				£40000	7/22/95	Plymouth Argyle	88+13	4	8	4	10		3	1
Wotton Paul			8/17/77	Plymouth	1/1/00	Plymouth Argyle	42+10	2	4	2	2			1
F O R W A R D														
Gibbs Paul	5.1	11.3	26/10/72	Gorleston		Diss Town								
					06/03/95	Colchester United	39+13		1+1	3	3			
				Free	26/07/97	Torquay United	40+1	4	3	3	7	1	1	1
				Free	7/1/98	Plymouth Argyle								
Hargreaves Chris	5.11	11	5/12/72	Cleethorpes	12/6/89	Grimsby Town	15+36	2+2	1+2	2+4	5	1	1	
				Loan	3/4/93	Scarborough	2+1							
					7/26/93	Hull City	34+15	1	2+1	3+1			1	
				Free	7/13/95	WBA	0+1			0+1				
				Loan	2/19/96	Hereford United	15+2			1				
				Free	7/1/96	Hereford United	42+2	3+1	1	1				
				Free	7/1/98	Plymouth Argyle								
Jean Earl	5.8	11.4	10/9/71	St Lucia	12/6/96	Ipswich Town	0+1							
				Free	1/23/97	Rotherham United	7+11				6			
				Free	8/8/97	Plymouth Argyle	16+20	1	2		4		1	
Phillips Lee P	5.11	12	9/16/80	Penzance	1/9/98	Plymouth Argyle (T)	3+9			0+1				
ADDITIONAL CONTRACT PLAYERS														
Power Lee						Hibernian								
				Free	7/1/98	Plymouth Argyle								

HOME PARK
Plymouth, Devon PL2 3DQ

Capacity 19,700
Covered Standing 7,000
Seating 6,400

First game ....v Northampton T, Sth Lge, 2-0, 5.9.1903.
First floodlit game ....v Exeter, 26.10.1953.

ATTENDANCES
Highest..43,596 v Aston Villa, Division 2, 10.10.1936.
Lowest ....1,875 v Hull, 11.5.1979.

OTHER GROUNDS...None.

HOW TO GET TO THE GROUND

From all directions
Use A38 Plymouth bypass as far as the Tavastock Road (A386).
Then branch left and follow signs to Plymouth (A386).
In 0.7 miles turn right then left (A3041) into Outland Road for Plymouth Argyle FC.

Car Parking
Free car park adjoining ground, space for 1,000 cars.

Nearest Railway Station
Plymouth (01752 21300)

USEFUL TELEPHONE NUMBERS

Club switchboard 01752 562 561
Club fax number 01752 606 167
Club shop 01752 558 292
Ticket Office 01752 562 561/606 167

Marketing Department ... 01752 562 561/606 167
Pilgrimline 0839 44 22 70*
*Calls cost 50p per minute at all times.
Call costings correct at time of going to press.

MATCHDAY PROGRAMME

Programme Editor .... Stephen Hill.

Number of pages .... 40.

Price .... £1.50.

Subscriptions .... Apply to the club.

Local Newspapers
.. Evening Herald, Western Morning News.

Local Radio Stations
.... Plymouth Sound AM (11.52 Kz).

MATCHDAY TICKET PRICES

Grandstand Centre £13
OAP £11

Family Lynhurst Enclosure..................... £10
Juv/OAP £4

Devonport Enclosure.......................... £9
Juv/OAP £4

Away Standing £7.50

ROCHDALE
(The Dale)
NATIONWIDE LEAGUE DIVISION 3
SPONSORED BY: CARCRAFT

1998/99 - Back Row L-R: Keith Hicks (Centre of excellence), Trevor Jones ('A' team Coach), David Hamilton (Yth. Coach), Keith Hill, Glen Robson, Mark Leonard, Neil Edwards, Lance Key, Mark Monington, David Gray, Alan Johnson, David Bywater (Centre of excellence), Joe Hinnigan (1st team coach/physio). **Middle Row:** Gary Jones, Ian Bryson, Dean Stokes, Robie Painter, Graham Barrow (Manager), Graham Lancashire, David Dayliss, Mark Stuart, Paul Sparrow. **Front Row:** Phil Edghill, Mark Bailey, Andy Barlow, Jason Peake, Paul Carden, Andy Farrell.

ROCHDALE
FORMED IN 1907
TURNED PROFESSIONAL IN 1907
LTD COMPANY IN 1910

PRESIDENT: Mrs L Stoney
CHAIRMAN: D F Kilpatrick
DIRECTORS
K Clegg (Managing Director)
J Marsh, G Morris, C Dunphy,
G R Brierley,
SECRETARY
Karen Jagger
MARKETING & SPONSORSHIP MANAGER
Les Duckworth

MANAGER: Graham Barrow
FIRST TEAM COACH
Joe Hinnighan
YOUTH TEAM COACH
David Hamilton
PHYSIOTHERAPIST
Joe Hinnighan

STATISTICIAN FOR THE DIRECTORY
Stephen Birch

The malaise at Spotland continued in 1997-98. Fifty eight league points, although matching the total for the previous season, was only good enough for eighteenth position, a fall of four positions from the previous year and the lowest position for nine years. In recent seasons consistency had been the biggest problem, but 1997-98 saw a change in fortunes with the Dale playing like lions at home, having the second best home record in the division, but lambs on the road. The 15 home wins have only been bettered once in the last 70 years while one has to go back 29 years since the fans saw Rochdale hit more goals at Spotland. However form was left at home. The first five away games and eight of the first nine were lost, the team failing to find the net in 14 of 23 away games - a new club record. Two road wins were recorded - at Hull and Doncaster. Nonetheless the last time Rochdale won at Hull, Clem Attlee was Prime Minister, so the win at Boothferry Park was treasured.

The performance in the cup competitions was even worse with home defeats and first round exits in both the Coca-Cola and FA Cups. Another win at Doncaster in the AWS competition led to a mauling by Carlisle in round 2. But there is no need to pity Dale's debutant goalie on the other end of Carlisle's six goals - Stephen Bywater. He was later sold to West Ham for a club record fee without playing another first team game.

The season had begun optimistically with the club securing its 3000th league point in the first home game of the season (and the 3060th game in all) and the further development of the ground with the erection of the Pearl Street stand. But as the season progressed manager Graham Barrow faced increasing criticism from supporters over team selection and tactics. Robbie Painter was top scorer with 17 league goals, the only one to make double figures, and missed only one league game. There was a modest rise in attendance reflecting the improved home form, but still not enough to break the 2000 per game mark. The season ended on a bright note with 25 points gained from the last 15 games. 1998-99 marks thirty years since the club's one and only promotion. This end of season form will need to be rekindled if Rochdale are to finally end their tenure as the league's longest surviving cellar dwellers.

STEPHEN BIRCH

ROCHDALE

M	DATE	COMP.	VEN	OPPONENTS	RESULT	H/T	LP	GOAL SCORERS/GOAL TIMES	ATT.
1	A 09	FL	A	Notts County	L 1-2	0-1	15	Painter 69	(4173)
2	12	CC 1/1	H	Stoke City	L 1-3	1-1		Painter 32	2509
3	15	FL	H	Mansfield Town	W 2-0	2-0	9	Russell 11, Painter 22	2133
4	23	FL	A	Leyton Orient	L 0-2	0-1	17		(3463)
5	27	CC 1/2	A	Stoke City	D 1-1	0-0		Russell 90	(12768)
6	30	FL	H	Peterborough United	L 1-2	1-1	20	Painter 19	2104
7	S 02	FL	H	Macclesfield Town	W 2-0	0-0	15	Carter 47, Hill 73	2197
8	09	FL	A	Shrewsbury Town	L 0-1	0-0	19		(2410)
9	13	FL	A	Cardiff City	L 1-2	1-1	20	Carter 8 (pen)	(4306)
10	20	FL	H	Hull City	W 2-1	1-1	19	Hill 13, Stuart 78	2085
11	27	FL	A	Brighton & H.A.	L 1-2	1-1	19	Bayliss 35	(1544)
12	O 04	FL	H	Scunthorpe United	W 2-0	1-0	17	Russell 3, Painter 58 (pen)	2087
13	11	FL	H	Darlington	W 5-0	2-0	9	Painter 3 (pen), 71, Lancashire 10, 89, Russell 85	2134
14	18	FL	A	Cambridge United	D 1-1	0-1	12	Gouck 64	(2703)
15	21	FL	A	Barnet	L 1-3	0-1	16	Leonard 60	(1310)
16	25	FL	H	Rotherham United	L 0-1	0-1	18		2267
17	N 01	FL	A	Chester City	L 0-4	0-1	19		(2431)
18	04	FL	H	Lincoln City	D 0-0	0-0	19		1337
19	08	FL	H	Colchester United	W 2-1	1-0	17	Stuart 44, Painter 62 (pen)	1702
20	15	FAC 1	H	Wrexham	L 0-2	0-0			3956
21	18	FL	A	Hartlepool United	L 0-2	0-1	19		(1666)
22	22	FL	A	Doncaster Rovers	W 3-0	1-0	18	Stuart 42, 56, Lancashire 69	(1503)
23	29	FL	H	Torquay United	L 0-1	0-0	19		1729
24	D 06	FL	A	Scarborough	L 0-1	0-1	19		(1705)
25	09	AWS N1	A	Doncaster Rovers	W 1-0	1-0		Reed 39	(580)
26	13	FL	H	Swansea City	W 3-0	2-0	18	Painter 26, 37, Leonard 62	1482
27	20	FL	A	Exeter City	L 0-3	0-3	19		(3378)
28	26	FL	H	Shrewsbury Town	W 3-1	1-1	16	Lancashire 40, Painter 74, Bryson 90	2247
29	28	FL	A	Macclesfield Town	L 0-1	0-0	17		(2666)
30	J 03	FL	A	Mansfield Town	L 0-3	0-0	19		(2303)
31	06	AWS N2	A	Carlisle United	L 1-6	0-0		Stuart 55	(2350)
32	10	FL	H	Notts County	L 1-2	0-0	20	Farrell 81	2387
33	17	FL	A	Peterborough United	L 1-3	1-2	19	Farrell 30	(5676)
34	24	FL	H	Leyton Orient	L 0-2	0-0	21		1774
35	31	FL	H	Cardiff City	D 0-0	0-0	21		1445
36	F 06	FL	A	Hull City	W 2-0	1-0	21	Russell 4, Stuart 64	(4031)
37	14	FL	A	Scunthorpe United	L 0-2	0-1	21		(2284)
38	21	FL	H	Brighton & H.A.	W 2-0	1-0	20	Jones 37, Gouck 54	1865
39	24	FL	H	Cambridge United	W 2-0	1-0	19	Gouck 28, 77	1192
40	28	FL	A	Darlington	L 0-1	0-0	20		(2181)
41	M 03	FL	A	Colchester United	D 0-0	0-0	21		(2112)
42	07	FL	H	Chester City	D 1-1	0-0	19	Lancashire 68	1955
43	14	FL	A	Lincoln City	L 0-2	0-1	21		(2992)
44	21	FL	H	Hartlepool United	W 2-1	0-0	20	Painter 75 (pen), Farrell 89	1395
45	28	FL	H	Doncaster Rovers	W 4-1	2-0	19	Painter 18, 58, Stuart 41, Lancashire 59	1858
46	A 04	FL	A	Torquay United	D 0-0	0-0	20		(2796)
47	11	FL	H	Scarborough	W 4-0	1-0	18	Painter 17, 58, Lancashire 76, Farrell 87	1795
48	13	FL	A	Swansea City	L 0-3	0-0	18		(2854)
49	18	FL	H	Exeter City	W 3-0	0-0	18	Bayliss 50, Lancashire 60, 62	1850
50	25	FL	A	Rotherham United	D 2-2	0-0	18	Jones 31, Painter 43 (pen)	(3463)
51	M 02	FL	H	Barnet	W 2-1	2-0	18	Gouck 22, Painter 45	2102

Best Home League Attendance: 2387 V Notts County   **Smallest :1192 V Cambridge United**   **Average :1875**

Goal Scorers:

FL	(56)	Painter 17, Lancashire 9, Stuart 6, Gouck 5, Farrell 4, Russell 4, Bayliss 2, Carter 2, Hill 2, Jones 2, Leonard 2, Bryson 1
CC	(2)	Painter 1, Russell 1
FAC	(0)	
AWS	(2)	Reed 1, Stuart 1

(M) Atkinson	(M) Bailey	(M) Barlow	(D) Bayliss	(M) Bryson	(G) Bywater	(F) Carden	(F) Carter	(G) Edwards	(M) Farrell	(M) Fensome	(M) Gouck	(M) Gray	(D) Hill	(M) Irwin	(F) Jones	(G) Key	(M) Lancashire	(F) Leonard	(F) Painter	(D) Pender	(D) Reed	(F) Robson	(M) Russell	(D) Scott	(M) Smith	(F) Stuart	Referee	#
	X	X	S2				S3		X2	X	X3		X1			X		X	X				X	S1		X	M.D.Messias	1
	X	X	S		S		X		X	X	X		X			X		X	X						S	X	D Pugh	2
	S1	X	S		S		X		X	X	X		X			X		X	X				X			X	A Bates	3
	S2	X	S				X		X	X	X		X			X		X	X				X		S1	X	R Styles	4
	X		X				S2		X	X	X		X			X		X	X				X	S	S1	X	S W Mathieson	5
	S1	X			S		S2		X	X	X		X			X		X	X				X		X	X	M L Dean	6
	X	X	S				X		X	X	X		X			X		X	X				X	S	S1		D Laws	7
	X	X	X		S		X		X	X	X					X			X				X	S	S1	X	C J Foy	8
	X	X	X				X1		X	X	S		X			X		X	X				X		S1		M J Jones	9
	X	X	X		S		X		X	X	X		X			X		X	X				X	S	S1		M S Pike	10
	X	X1	X		S		X		X	X	X	S	X			X		X	X				X		S1		S W Mathieson	11
	X		X	X			S		X	X	X	S	X			X	X	X	X				X		S1		A R Hall	12
	X	S1	X	X			S		X	X			X			X	X	X	X				X		S		T Jones	13
	X	X	S3				S2		X	X	X		X			X	X	X	X				X			X	D Orr	14
	X	X	S1				S		X	X	X		X			X	X	X	X				X			S2	B Coddington	15
X1	X						S1		X	X	X		X	S		X	X2	X	X				X			S2	G Laws	16
	X		X				S		X	X	X		X	S		X		X	X				X	S	X		M Fletcher	17
	S1	X		X			S		X	X	X	X				X			X	X			X	S		X	F G Stretton	18
	S	X		X			S		X	X	X	X				X			X	X	S		X			X	T Heilbron	19
	S	X	S						X	X	X	X						S	X	X	S		X			X	A R Hall	20
	S1	X	S				X		X	X	X	X			S			X	X	X			X			X	K M Lynch	21
	X	X	X				X			S	S		X					X1	X	X	X		S1			X	P S Danson	22
	X	X1	X	X2			X			S	S1		X					X	X	X	X		S2			X	J A Kirkby	23
	X	X	X				X			X1	X							X2	X	X	X	X	S2		S		S1	D Laws	24
	X	X	X1				X		X	X	X							X	X	X	X					S1			25
X2	X1		X	S2			X		X	X	X							X3	X	X	X	S3				S1	M D Messias	26
X			X2				X	X	X	X1								X	X	X	X		S1	S		S2	D R Crick	27
X3	X2	X	S2				X	X	X	X							S1	X	X	X1	X					S3	A G Wiley	28
X	S	X1	S	X			X	X	X	X				X	X	X	X	X	X			X			S1		M L Dean	29
X3	S1		S2	X2			X	X	X1					X	X	X	X2	X	X			X			S3		M S Pike	30
	X		X	X2	X		X	X	S2								X1	X	X	X	X		S1		X		A R Hall	31
S2	X2	X	X				X	X		X					S	S1	X1	X	X	X						X		32
	X2	X1	X				X	X	S		S1		X		S2			X	X	X			X			X	M R Halsey	33
			X				X	X	S1	X1		X	S	X2				X	X	X	S2	X	X			X	A R Leake	34
	X						X	X	X			X	X	S	X		X	X	X	X1	S	X			S1		W C Burns	35
X	X						X	X	X	X		X		S	S1	X1	X	X				X	S		X		G Laws	36
	X2	X	S1			S	X	X	X	X		X					S2	X	X1			X			X		T Jones	37
	S	X				S	X	X	X	X		X		X			S1	X	X			X1			X		P R Richards	38
	S	X				S	X	X	X	X		X		X			S	X	X			X			X		F G Stretton	39
	S1	X1					X	X	X	X		X		X			S2	X	X		S	X2			X		M D Messias	40
	S1	X1				S	X	X	X	X		X		X			S	X	X			X			X		S J Baines	41
	X	S					X	X	X	X		X		X			X	X	X			S	S		X		R D Furnandiz	42
	X3	X	S1		X1			X	X		X		X2	X			X	X			S2	S3			X		A R Hall	43
	X	X	S	S				X	X		X		X	X1	X		X				S1				X		C J Foy	44
	X	X	S1				X	X	X1	X		X		X2	S	X		X			S2				X		S W Mathieson	45
	X	X			S2		X	X	X	X		X		X1		X2		X			S1				X		G Singh	46
	S1	X	X		S2		X	X	X	X		X		X	S	X2		X1							X		A G Wiley	47
	X	X	X		S1		X	X	X	X1		X		X	S	X		X			S				X		P Rejer	48
	S	X	X		S1		X	X	X	X		X1		S	X	X		X			X				X		G B Frankland	49
	S1	X	X	X2			X	X	X	X	S	X1		X				X				S2			X		R Pearson	50
	S1	X	X		X		X	X	X	X1		X	S	X2			X			S2				X		P S Danson	51
5	24	35	23	12		3	7		27	40	42	36		36	17	19	20	33	45	14	10		26	1	1	30	FL Appearances	
1	9	3	6	3		4	4			2				1				7			7		5	2	2	14	FL Sub Appearances	
2	1	1			1+1		2	2	2		2			2				2	2				1		0+1	2	CC Appearances	
			1	1			1	1	1		1			1				1	1	0+1			1			1	FAC Appearances	
	2		2	2	1		1	2	2	1+1				1				1	2	2	2	2		0+1		1+1	AWS Appearances	

ROCHDALE

RECORDS AND STATISTICS

CLUB RECORDS

RECORD LEAGUE VICTORY
8-1 v Chesterfield, Div 3N, 18.12.1926   7-0 v Walsall,Div 3N,
24.12.1921   7-0 v York City (a), Div 3N, 14.1.1939   7-0 v
Hartlepool,Div 3N, 2.11.1957

RECORD LEAGUE DEFEAT
1-9 v Tranmere Rovers, Div 3N, 25.12.1931   0-8 v Wrexham(a), Div
3, 28.9.1929   0-8 v Leyton Orient (a), Div 4, 20.10.1987
Record Cup Defeat
0-6 v Wigan Athletic, Freight Rover Trophy, 28.1.1986

MOST LEAGUE POINTS
(2pts a win) 62 Div 3N, 1923-24
(3pts a win) 67 Div 4,1991-92

MOST LEAGUE GOALS
105, Div 3N, 1926-27

RECORD TRANSFER FEE RECEIVED
For Stephen Bywater from West Ham - fee determined on appearances at club & international level.

RECORD TRANSFER FEE PAID
£80,000 to Scunthorpe Utd for Andy Flounders, August 1991

BEST PERFORMANCES
League: 9th Div 3, 1969-70   FA Cup: 5th Round, 1989-90
League Cup: Runners-Up 1962 (4th Div Record)

HONOURS
None

LEAGUE CAREER
Elected to Div 3N 1921   Transferred to Div 3 1958
Relegated to Div 4 1958-59   Promoted to Div 3 1968-69
Relegated to Div 4 (now Div 3) 1973-74

INDIVIDUAL CLUB RECORDS

MOST APPEARANCES FOR CLUB
Graham Smith (1966-74): League 316+1, FA Cup 15,League Cup
13 Total 344+1 sub

MOST CAPPED PLAYER
No Rochdale player has won an international cap

RECORD GOALSCORER IN A MATCH
Tommy Tippett 6 v Hartlepool (a), 8-2, Div 3N,21.4.1930

RECORD LEAGUE GOALSCORER IN A SEASON
Albert Whitehurst 44 (1926-27)   In All Competitions: Albert
Whitehurst, 46 (League 44 + FA Cup 2)

RECORD LEAGUE GOALSCORER IN A CAREER
Reg Jenkins 119   In All Competitions: Reg Jenkins 130 (League
119 + FA Cup 5 + League Cup 6) 1964-73

MOST GOALS SCORED IN A FIRST CLASS MATCH
Record League Victory (above)   8-2 v Crook Town (h), 1st Round
FA Cup, 26.11.1927   8-2 v Hartlepool United (a), Div3N, 22.4.1930

OLDEST PLAYER IN A LEAGUE MATCH
Jack Warner (player/manager) 41 years 195 days v Chesterfield, Di
3N, 4.4.1953

PREVIOUS MANAGERS

YOUNGEST PLAYER IN A LEAGUE MATCH
Zac Hughes, 16 years 105 days v Exeter City, Div 4, 19.9.1987
1920-21 William Bradshaw   1921-22 No appointment made   1922-
23 Thomas C Wilson   1923-30 Jack Peart   1930 Harry Martin
(caretaker)   1930-31 William Smith Cameron   1931-32 Vacant
1932-34 Herbert Hopkinson   1934-35 William H Smith   1935-37
Ernest Nixon (caretaker)   1937-38 Sam Jennings   1938-52 Ted
Goodier   1952 Jack Warner   1953-58 Harry Catterick   1958-60
Jack Marshall   1960-67 Tony Collins   1967-68 Bob Stokoe   1968-
70 Len Richley   1970-73 Dick Connor   1973-76 Walter Joyce
1976-77 Brian Green   1977-78 Mike Ferguson   1978-79 Peter
Madden (caretaker)   1979 Doug Collins   1979-83 Peter Madden
1983-84 Jimmy Greenhoff   1984-86 Vic Halom   1986-88Eddie
Gray   1988-89 Danny Bergara   1989-91 Terry Dolan   1991-94
Dave Sutton   1994- Mick Docherty (caretaker).

ADDITIONAL INFORMATION
Club colours: All blue with white trim.

Change colours: Green shirt, black shorts, green socks.

Reserves League: Pontins League.

LONGEST LEAGUE RUNS

of undefeated matches:	20 (1923-24)	of league matches w/out a win:	28 (1931-32)
of undefeated home matches:	34 (1923-25)	of undefeated away matches:	9 (1923-24)
without home win:	16 (1931-32)	without an away win:	37 (1977-78)
of league wins:	8 (1969)	of home wins:	16 (1926-27)
of league defeats:	17 (1931-32)	of away wins:	4 (1923-24, 1926, 1946, 1947, 1969)

THE MANAGER

GRAHAM BARROW . . . . appointed May 1996.

PREVIOUS CLUBS
As Manager . . . . Chester City, Wigan Athletic
As Asst.Man/Coach. . . . . Chester City.
As a player . . . . Altrincham, Wigan Athletic, Chester City.

HONOURS
As a Manager. . . . . Northern Sports Writers Manager of the Year 1993/94.
As a Player . . . . Promoted with both Wigan and Chester. Autoglass Trophy winner.

ROCHDALE

PLAYERS NAME Honours	Ht	Wt	Birthdate	Birthplace Transfers	Contract Date	Clubs	League	L/Cup	FA Cup	Other	Lge	L/C	FAC	Oth
G O A L K E E P E R														
Edwards Neil R	0	0			11/3/97	Rochdale	27		1					
Key Lance	6.2	14	5/13/68	£10000	4/14/90	Sheffield Wednesday			+1					
				Loan	10/12/93	Oldham Athletic	2							
				Loan	1/26/95	Oxford United	6							
				Free	8/6/97	Rochdale	19	2						
D E F E N C E														
Bayliss David	5.8	11	6/8/76	Liverpool	1/1/00	Rochdale	71+10	4	2+1	2	2			
Hill Keith	6	11.3	5/17/69	Bolton	5/9/87	Blackburn Rovers	89+7	6	5+1	3+2	4	1		
					9/23/92	Plymouth Argyle	117+6	7	10	9+1	2			
					8/15/96	Rochdale	77+1	4	2		5			
Johnson Alan K	6	12	2/19/71		4/1/89	Wigan Athletic	163+17	7+2	14+2	14+3	13	1	1	3
					2/15/94	Lincoln City	56+6	2	4	3+1				1
				Free	9/6/96	Rochdale								
Pender John P Ei: u21.1, Y. Div.4'92. DIV3 96/97	6	13.12	11/19/63	Luton	11/8/81	Wolverhampton W.	115+2	5	7		3		1	
				£35000	7/23/85	Charlton Athletic	41	1	1	2				1
				£50000	10/30/87	Bristol City	83	11	8	12	3			
				£70000	10/18/90	Burnley	170	10	19	21	9	1	1	1
				£30000	8/22/95	Wigan Athletic	67+3	2	5	3	1			
				Free	7/23/97	Rochdale	14		+1					
Peake Jason E: Y, S.	5.11	12.10	9/29/71	Leicester	1/9/90	Leicester City	4+4			1+1	1			
				Loan	2/13/92	Hartlepool United	5+1				1			
				Free	8/26/92	Halifax Town	32+1		1	2	1			
					3/23/94	Rochdale	91+4	3	5	7	6		2	1
					7/30/96	Brighton & HA	27+3	2	2	1	1			
				Free	10/8/97	Bury	3+3							
				Free	7/1/98	Rochdale								
Sparrow Paul DIV3 95/96	6.1	11	24/03/75	London	13/07/93	Crystal Palace								
				£20000	14/03/96	Preston North End	20		1	1				
				Free	7/1/98	Rochdale								
Stokes Dean	5.7	10.7	23/05/70	Birmingham		Halesowen Town								
					15/01/93	Port Vale	53+7	1+1	4	5+3				
				Free	7/1/98	Rochdale								
Williams Scott W: u21.5, Y.	6	11	07/08/74	Bangor	02/07/93	Wrexham	26+6	1		2+2				
				Free	7/1/98	Rochdale								
M I D F I E L D														
Bailey Mark	5.8	10.12	8/12/76	Stoke	7/12/94	Stoke City								
					10/10/96	Rochdale	35+11	2	1					
Barlow Andrew Div.2'91.	5.9	11.1	11/24/65	Oldham	7/31/84	Oldham Athletic	243+16	22	19	6	5			
				Free	11/1/93	Bradford City	2							
				Free	7/13/95	Blackpool	76+3	4+2	4	3	2			
				Free	7/5/97	Rochdale	35+3	1	1					
Bryson James Ian DIV3 95/96	5.11	11.11	11/26/62	Kilmarnock	1/1/00	Kilmarnock	194+21	12+7	14+2		40	1	3	
				£40000	8/24/88	Sheffield United	138+17	11+2	18+4	7	36	1	4	3
				£20000	8/12/93	Barnsley	16	2		2	3	1		
				£42500	11/29/93	Preston North End	141+10	6+1	7+1	10	14	1		1
				Free	7/5/97	Rochdale	12+3		1		1			
Farrell Andrew J	5.11	11	10/7/65	Colchester	9/21/83	Colchester United	98+7	9	8	6	5			
				£13000	8/7/87	Burnley	237+20	17+4	19+2	27+3	19	1		3
				£20000	9/22/94	Wigan Athletic	51+3	3	4+1	5	1			1
					8/15/96	Rochdale	75+3	4	3		7			
Gray David	0	0		Check pos	4/24/98	Rochdale								
Lancashire Graham	0	0			10/2/97	Rochdale	20+7				8			
Monington Mark AMC'96.	6.1	13	21/10/70	Bilsthorpe	23/03/89	Burnley	65+19	5	4+1	4+2	5		1	
					28/11/94	Rotherham United	75+4	3	1	4	3			
				Free	7/1/98	Rochdale								
F O R W A R D														
Carden Paul	0	0				Blackpool	0+1		0+1					
				Free	3/3/98	Rochdale	3+4							
Leonard Mark A	5.11	11.1	9/27/62	St. Helens	1/1/00	Witton Albion								
					2/24/82	Everton								
				Loan	3/24/83	Tranmere Rovers	6+1							
				Free	6/1/83	Crewe Alexandra	51+3	4	2	3+1	15	2		
				Free	2/13/85	Stockport County	73	5	1	2	23	2		3
				£40000	9/27/86	Bradford City	120+37	13+5	6+3	6+5	29	6	1	3
					3/27/92	Rochdale	9				1			
				£50000	8/13/92	Preston North End	19+3	2			1			
				Free	8/13/93	Chester City	28+4	2	3	3	9		1	
				Free	10/14/94	Wigan Athletic	60+4	2	6	6	12		2	2
					8/15/96	Rochdale	71	4	2		6			
Robson Glen	5.11	10.1	9/25/77	Sunderland	11/13/96	Rochdale	+10							
Stuart Mark R	5.11	10.11	12/15/66	Chiswick	7/3/84	Charlton Athletic	89+18	7+3	1	9+1	28	2	1	
				£150000	11/4/88	Plymouth Argyle	55+2	4	3	2	11			1
				Loan	3/22/90	Ipswich Town	5							
				£80000	8/3/90	Bradford City	22+7	6	+1	1+1	5	1		
				Free	10/30/92	Huddersfield Town	9+6		2	4	3			1
				Free	7/5/93	Rochdale	157+25	9+1	6	5+3	41	1	1	1
				Loan	8/7/95	Chesterfield								

SPOTLAND
Willbutts Lane, Rochdale OL11 5DS

Capacity...6,448
Covered Standing..3,837
Seating...2,611

First game ....v Oldham Ath., Friendly, 3.9.1907.
First floodlit game ....v St. Mirren, 16.2.1954.

ATTENDANCES
Highest ....24,231 v Notts County, FAC 2nd Rnd, 10.12.1949
Lowest...588 v Cambridge Utd, Div 3, 5.2.1974
(played on a Tuesday afternoon during power cuts)

OTHER GROUNDS...None.

HOW TO GET TO THE GROUND

From all directions
Use motorway M62 until junction 20 then follow signs to Rochdale.
On to A627 (M), at first roundabout keep left and at second go straight ahead signed Blackburn.
At traffic lights after 1 mile go straight ahead into Sandy Lane.
Ground on right after half-a-mile.

Car Parking
Street parking only.

Nearest Railway Station
Rochdale.

USEFUL TELEPHONE NUMBERS

Club switchboard 01706 644 648
Club fax number.......................01706 648 466
Club shop 01706 647 521
Ticket Office.............................01706 644 648

Marketing Department 01706 644 648
Internet address......www.rochdale-football-club.co.uk
Clubcall 0891 55 58 58*
*Calls cost 50p per minute at all times. Call costings correct at time of going to press.

MATCHDAY PROGRAMME
"THE VOICE OF SPOTDALE"

Programme Editor ....Franics Collins &
....Richard Wild.

Number of pages....................................32.

Price ....£1.60.

Subscriptions ....Apply to club.

Local Newspapers
......................................Rochdale Observer
..........................Manchester Evening News.

Local Radio Stations
...........Radio Manchester, Radio Piccadilly.

MATCHDAY TICKET PRICES

Ground £8.00

Juniors/Seniors. £4.00

Main Stand £10.00

Juniors/Seniors. £5.00

W.M.G. Stand £8.00

Juniors/Seniors. £4.00

Family Stand. £8.00

Junior. £1.00

Seniors. £4.00

ROTHERHAM UNITED
(The Merry Millers)
NATIONWIDE LEAGUE DIVISION 3
SPONSORED BY: ONE 2 ONE

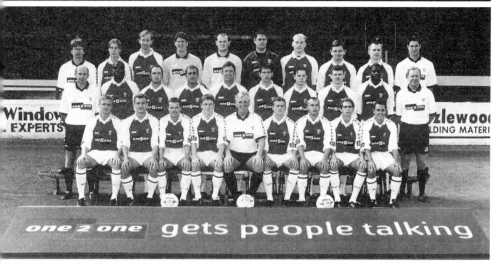

1998-99 - Back Row L-R: Billy Russell (Yth. Coach), Chris Sedgwick, Alan Knill, Mike Pollitt, Paul Pettinger, Bobby Mimms, Gijsbert Bos, Neil Richardson, David Bass, Fraser Foster (Yth. Dev. Officer). **Middle Row:** Ian Bailey (Physio), Vance Warner, Darren Garner, Andy Roscoe, Steve Thompson, Richard Tracey, Paul Dillon, Lee Glover, Jason White, John Breckin (Assistant Manager). **Front Row:** Gary Scott, Gary Martindale, Martin Clark, Chris Beech, Ronnie Moore (Manager), Jamie Ingledow, Trevor Berry, Danny Hudson, Paul Hurst.

ROTHERHAM UNITED
FORMED IN 1884
TURNED PROFESSIONAL IN 1905
LTD COMPANY IN 1920

CHAIRMAN: K F Booth
VICE-CHAIRMAN
R Hull
DIRECTORS
C Luckock, J A Webb
CHEIF EXECUTIVE
P Henson (01709 512434)
COMMERCIAL MANAGER
D Nicholls (01709 512 760)

MANAGER
Ronnie Moore
ASSISTANT MANAGER
John Breckin

YOUTH TEAM COACH
Bill Russell
PHYSIOTHERAPIST
Ian Bailey

STATISTICIAN FOR THE DIRECTORY
Stuart Smith

With the appointment of Ronnie Moore, a former Millmoor favourite, as manager prior to the start of the season, the expectations of some fans for an immediate return to Division 2 were high.

However the shadow of the 1996/97 season will take some lifting and the task of clearing out all the dead wood and the raising or moral, which could not have been lower, will take more than one season. Ronnie in his early weeks, of his first League managerial position, stated that he had a 2 year plan to get the Millers out of 3rd Division, which is probably a realistic target.

Having said all that the 1997/98 season must go down as a season of if's and but's. If we hadn't had 3 players sent off and Bobby Mimms carried off, against a poor Shrewsbury side, perhaps we would not have lost 2-1. If we hadn't had both central defenders taken off with injuries in the very first game against Barnet we would not have lost 3-2, and would have beaten them to the last play-off spot. If we had got more than 2 wins in the fifteen games through February and March, then we would have easily made the play-offs, if not an automatic promotion place. MAybe if Rotherham United had not been hit with so many early season, re-occurring injuries they would have been able to maintain a good quality of consistency and not drawn so many eminately winable games.

All these facts culminated in the Millers having to rely on Barnet losing their last game at Rochdale (which they did) and then winning at, already champions, Notts County. The game 12,500 saw on that last Saturday of the season must go into the 'freaky football' category. 2-1 down with 20 minutes to go and Rotherham started to send defenders permanently forward in an attempt to save the season. An equaliser with 10 minutes to go gave us hope, however the top heavy millers were soon exposed and eventually went down 5-2, and were destined for another season in division 3.

However, this season was measurably better than the previous 2 with several high points to look back on. For me the highlight of the season was Rotherhams first ever live televised match, the 3-0 win away in the FA Cup first round replay against a much fancied Burnley side, run by player/manager Chris Waddle.

We are now looking forward to the second year of Ronnies master plan, and an escape back to Division 2.

STUART SMITH.

609

ROTHERHAM UNITED

Division 3   :10th   FA CUP: 3rd Round   LC CUP: 1st Round   AWS: Northern Round 2

M	DATE	COMP.	VEN	OPPONENTS	RESULT	H/T	LP	GOAL SCORERS/GOAL TIMES	ATT.
1	A 09	FL	H	Barnet	L 2-3	1-1	14	Roscoe 30, Goodwin 61 (pen)	4220
2	12	CC 1/1	H	**Preston North End**	L 1-3	0-0		**Richardson 76**	**2901**
3	15	FL	A	Cambridge United	L 1-2	0-0	20	Bos 51	(2725)
4	23	FL	A	Hartlepool United	W 2-1	2-0	16	Berry 27, Hayward 37	3086
5	26	CC 1/2	A	**Preston North End**	L 0-2	0-0			**(9441)**
6	30	FL	A	Darlington	D 1-1	0-0	16	Glover 75	(2613)
7	S 02	FL	A	Hull City	D 0-0	0-0	18		(6127)
8	10	FL	H	Lincoln City	W 3-1	0-0	13	Roscoe 68, Glover 74, White 80	2871
9	13	FL	H	Peterborough United	D 2-2	2-1	15	White 40, Thompson 44	3859
10	20	FL	A	Exeter City	L 1-3	0-1	17	Bos 88	(3420)
11	27	FL	H	Chester City	W 4-2	3-0	16	White 17, Bos 37, 40, Glover 47	3061
12	O 04	FL	A	Shrewsbury Town	L 1-2	0-1	16	White 89	(2432)
13	11	FL	A	Leyton Orient	D 1-1	0-0	18	White 51	(3658)
14	18	FL	H	Cardiff City	D 1-1	1-1	18	Thompson 3 (pen)	3197
15	21	FL	H	Notts County	D 1-1	0-1	18	Hayward 89	3161
16	25	FL	A	Rochdale	W 1-0	1-0	13	Garner 5	(2267)
17	N 01	FL	H	Macclesfield Town	W 1-0	0-0	11	Hayward 69	3649
18	04	FL	A	Mansfield Town	D 3-3	2-1	13	White 22, Glover 27, Garner 50	(2927)
19	08	FL	A	Brighton & H.A.	W 2-1	1-0	9	Richardson 3, Glover 49	(1950)
20	15	FAC 1	H	**Burnley**	D 3-3	2-2		**Roscoe 17, 65, Knill 35**	**5709**
21	18	FL	H	Scunthorpe United	L 1-3	0-1	13	Roscoe 60	3355
22	22	FL	A	Scarborough	W 2-1	0-1	9	Roscoe 52, Thompson 72	(3317)
23	25	FAC 1R	A	**Burnley**	W 3-0	1-0		**White 10, Berry 68, Garner 89**	**(3118)**
24	29	FL	H	Colchester United	W 3-2	1-0	7	Glover 11, 63, Knill 73	3259
25	D 02	FL	A	Swansea City	D 1-1	0-0	6	Garner 80	(2463)
26	06	FAC 2	H	**Kings Lynn**	W 6-0	0-0		**Glover 48, Richardson 53, Garner 55, Druce 70, Berry 80, Hudson 89**	**5883**
27	13	FL	H	Torquay United	L 0-1	0-0	11		3636
28	19	FL	A	Doncaster Rovers	W 3-0	1-0	5	Roscoe 37 , Glover 69, Taylor 70	(3533)
29	26	FL	A	Lincoln City	W 1-0	0-0	5	White 82	(6350)
30	28	FL	H	Hull City	W 5-4	2-1	5	Glover 21, 49, 54, 62, Taylor 25	5995
31	J 03	FAC 3	H	**Sunderland**	L 1-5	0-1		**Garner 69**	**11500**
32	10	FL	A	Barnet	D 0-0	0-0	4		(2558)
33	17	FL	A	Darlington	W 3-0	2-0	3	Goodwin 5, White 39, 90	3877
34	20	AWS N2	A	**Wigan Athletic**	L 0-3	0-0			**(1495)**
35	24	FL	A	Hartlepool United	D 0-0	0-0	5		(2375)
36	27	FL	H	Cambridge United	D 2-2	0-0	6	Richardson 89, Taylor 90	3096
37	31	FL	A	Peterborough United	L 0-1	0-0	6		(7165)
38	F 06	FL	H	Exeter City	W 1-0	0-0	5	Glover 63	4158
39	14	FL	H	Shrewsbury Town	L 0-1	0-0	6		3603
40	21	FL	A	Chester City	L 0-4	0-0	8		(2432)
41	24	FL	A	Cardiff City	D 2-2	1-1	8	Middleton 111 (OG), Glover 61	(2731)
42	28	FL	H	Leyton Orient	W 2-1	0-1	7	Roscoe 88, Monington 90	3542
43	M 03	FL	H	Brighton & H.A.	D 0-0	0-0	7		3724
44	07	FL	A	Macclesfield Town	D 0-0	0-0	7		(3156)
45	14	FL	H	Mansfield Town	D 2-2	2-2	9	Knill 31, 34	4054
46	21	FL	A	Scunthorpe United	D 1-1	0-0	9	Glover 52	(4011)
47	28	FL	H	Scarborough	D 0-0	0-0	9		3836
48	A 03	FL	A	Colchester United	L 1-2	1-1	9	Martindale 12	(3824)
49	11	FL	H	Swansea City	D 1-1	1-1	10	Martindale 40	2942
50	13	FL	A	Torquay United	W 2-1	1-0	9	White 31, Roscoe 50	(3963)
51	18	FL	H	Doncaster Rovers	W 3-0	0-0	8	Berry 75, 90, White 86	4328
52	25	FL	H	Rochdale	D 2-2	0-2	8	White 68, Glover 90	3463
53	M 02	FL	A	Notts County	L 2-5	1-1	10	White 11, Glover 64	(12430)

Best Home League Attendance: 5995 V Hull City   Smallest :2871 V Lincoln City   Average :3651

Goal Scorers:

FL	(67)	Glover 17, White 13, Roscoe 7, Bos 4, Berry 3, Garner 3, Hayward 3, Knill 3, Taylor 3, Thompson 3, Goodwin 2, Martindale 2, Richardson 2, Monington 1, Opponents 1
CC	(1)	Richardson 1
FAC	(13)	Garner 3, Berry 2, Roscoe 2, Druce 1, Glover 1, Hudson 1, Knill 1, Richardson 1, White 1
AWS	(0)	

1997-98

(M) Bass	(F) Berry	(F) Bos	(D) Browrigg	(M) Clark	(D) Darby	(D) Dillon	(F) Druce	(M) Garner	(F) Glover	(D) Goodwin	(F) Hayward	(M) Hudson	(D) Hurst	(D) Knill	(F) Martindale	(G) Mimms	(D) Mornington	(G) Pettinger	(M) Poric	(D) Richardson	(M) Roscoe	(M) Scott	(F) Sedgwick	(M) Shuttleworth	(M) Taylor	(M) Thompson	(M) Warner	(M) White		
S1	X	S2		X			X		X	X			X	X		X	X				X		S3		X				M L Dean	1
S	X	S1		X		S	X	X					X	X		X			X		X	X				X			G Laws	2
X	X	X	S	X			S2			X	S1		X	X		X			X		X	X				X		X	G Cain	3
X	X	X		X			S	X		S	X		X	X		X			X		X	X	S						F G Stretton	4
X	X	X		X			X	X		S1		S	X	X		X		X		X	X	S2							K A Leach	5
X	X	S2		X			X	X	X	S1			X			X			X	X	X	X	S3						M J Jones	6
X	X	S1		X			X	X	X	S2		X			X			X	X	S								X	A R Hall	7
X	X	S3		X			X	X				X			X			X	X	S2		S1		X		X3			D Pugh	8
X	X	S1		X			S2	X				X	X		X			X	X	S			X	X	X				M S Pike	9
X	X	S2		X			S1	X				X	X		X			S	X			X	X	X					G Singh	10
X	S	X		X				X				S1	X		X			S	X			X	X	X					M D Messias	11
X	S2	X					S1	X				S	X		X			X	X			X	X	X					A R Leake	12
X	S	S		X			X	X				S	X		X		X	X	X			X	X	X					M E Pierce	13
X	X	X		X		X	X				S	S1	S2	X			X			X					X				S W Mathieson	14
S3	X			X		X	X				X		X	S1	X			X		X	X	S2			X				J P Robinson	15
S2	X			X		S1	X				X		X	X		X			X		X	X	S3		X			X	G Laws	16
S	X			X			X	X			X	S1		X		X			X		X	X			X		X	X	A N Butler	17
S2	X			X			X	X			S		S1	X		X			X		X	X			X		X	X	A R Hall	18
S1	X			X			X	X			S		S	X		X			X		X	X			X		X	X	M Fletcher	19
S				X		S	X	X			X	S2	X	X		X			X		S			S1	X		X	X	F G Stretton	20
X				X		S3	X	X			X	S2	S1	X		X			X		X	X			X		X	X	T Jones	21
S				X			X	X			X	S1	S	X	X		X			X		X	X			S		X		T Heilbron	22
S	X			X			X	X			S1	S		X	X		X		S			X	X			X		X	F G Stretton	23
X				X			X	X			S1	S		X			X			X		X	X			X		X1	W C Burns	24
S	X2			X			X	X			S1	X1	S2	X			X			X		X	X			X		X	C R Wilkes	25
S2	X			X		X	X3	X		S1	S	S3	X1			X			X		S	X	X			X		X2	C J Foy	26
X	X			X1		S1	X	X			S		X	S		X			X		X	X	S		X				R Pearson	27
	X	S					X	X	S1			S	X			X			X		X	X			X	X	X	X1	A G Wiley	28
	X	S					X	X	S1			S	X			X			X		X	X			X	X1	X	X	M S Pike	29
	X	S					X	X	X1			S1	X			X			X		X	X			X		X	X	S J Baines	30
	X						S	X	X	S1			X	X		X	S	S		X1	X	X		S		X	X	X	E Lomas	31
	X						S	X	X	X			X	X		X	3		X	X	X	S			X		X		P Rejer	32
	X1						X	X	X				S1	X		X			X		X	X			X	S2	X	X	M J Brandwood	34
							S2		X	S1	S3			X		X	X		X1	X	X			X3	X	X		X2		33
	X	S2					X	X	X			S1		X		X	X		X	X2	S			X2	X1			D Pugh	35
	X	S2					X	X	S1		X			X		X	X		X	X2	S			X	X1			C J Foy	36
	X	S1					X	X				X1	S	X		X	X1		X	S1	X			X	X			P Taylor	37
	X	S				S1	S		X				X		X	X			X	X	X			X	X1			M D Messias	38
	X	X		X		S	X			S1	X	S	X		X	X		X	X1	X				X				M J Jones	39
	X			X		S1	S2	X				X		X	X	X3	X1	X		S3			X	X2	J P Robinson	40
	X			X			S	X			X		X	X1	S	S1			X			S3	X	X	G Cain	41
	X			X			X	X				S	X		X	X		X1	S	X				X3		X2	T Heilbron	42
	X			X			S	X				S	X		X	X		X1	S	X				S1		M R Halsey	43
	X	S3		X1		X3	X2	X			S2		S1			X	X		X				X	A R Leake	44
	X			X		X	S	X	X				S1		X	X	X	X		S	X			X	S W Mathieson	45
	X1				X		X	S1	X	X			S	S2	X	X			X	X			X2	X	K M Lynch	46
	X			X	X		X	X					S	X	X			X1	X2			S2	X	S1	G B Frankland	47
	X2			X	X	S3	X					S1	X	X3			X	X			S2	X1	X	R Styles	48
	X			X1		S1	X2					X	X	X	S		X	X			S2	X	X	T Jones	49
	X			S	X		X				S	X	X	X	X	X	S		X	X			X	X	A P D'Urso	50
	X			S	X		X	S1			S	X	X1	X	X			X	X			X	X	M C Bailey	51
	X2			S	X		X1	X			S1	X	X	S2	X			X	X			X	X	R Pearson	52
	S1			X1	S	X		X	X		S		X	X		X			X	X			X	X	B Knight	53
13	40	6		28	3	14	5	37	36	8	6	6	19	38	7	43	15	3	4	37	43	6			10	32	21	26	FL Appearances	
5	2	10				2	9	3	1	5	7	4		11		1				1	2	1	4			7		1	FL Sub Appearances	
1	2	1+1		2										2	2					2	2		0+1			1			CC Appearances	
0+1	3			3			1	4	4	0+2	1+1	0+2	4	3		4				4	4	1		0+1		3	3	2	FAC Appearances	
				0+1					1	0+1	0+1		1			1			1	1	1	1		1	1	1		1	AWS Appearances	

CLUB RECORDS

RECORD LEAGUE VICTORY
8-0 v Oldham Athletic, Div 3N, 26.5.1947
Record Cup Victory and Most Goals Scored in a Cup Tie
6-0 v Spennymoor United,FA Cup Round 2, 1977-78   6-0 v
Wolverhampton Wanderers, FA Cup Round 1,16.11.1985

RECORD LEAGUE DEFEAT
1-11 v Bradford City, Div 3N, 25.8.1928*
* First match of the season. Rotherham United won their second
match at home!
Record Cup Defeat
0-15 v Notts County, FA Cup Round 1, 24.10.1885

MOST LEAGUE POINTS
(2pts for win) 71, Div 3N, 1950-51
(3pts a win) 82, Div4, 1988-89

MOST LEAGUE GOALS
14, Div 3N, 1946-47

RECORD TRANSFER FEE RECEIVED
£325,000 from Sheffield Wednesday for Matt Clarke, July 1996.
RECORD TRANSFER FEE PAID
£110,000 to Wolves for Paul Blades, July 1995.

BEST PERFORMANCES
League: 3rd Div 2, 1954-55
FA Cup: 5th Round 1952-53,1967-68
League Cup: Finalists 1960-61

HONOURS
Division 3N Champions 1950-51
Division 3 Champions 1980-81
Division 4 Champions1988-89
AMC winners 1995-96.

LEAGUE CAREER
Rotherham Town: Elected to Div 2 1893   Not re-elected to Div 2
1896
Rotherham County: Elected to Div 2 1919   Relegated to Div 3N
1923   Promoted to Div 2 1951   Relegated to Div 3 1968
Relegated to Div 4 1973   Promoted to Div 3 1975   Promoted to
Div 2 1981   Relegated to Div 3 1983
Relegated to Div 4 1988   Promoted to Div 3 1989   Relegated to
Div 4 1991 Promoted to Div 3 (now Div 2) 1992,
Relegated to Div 3 1997.

INDIVIDUAL CLUB RECORDS

MOST APPEARANCES FOR CLUB
Danny Williams (1946-60): 459

MOST CAPPED PLAYER
Shaun Goater, Bermuda (6+), Harold Millership, 6 Wales

RECORD GOALSCORER IN A MATCH
No player has scored more than four goals

RECORD LEAGUE GOALSCORER IN A SEASON
Wally Ardron, 38, Div 3N, 1946-47

RECORD LEAGUE GOALSCORER IN A CAREER
Gladstone Guest, 130, 1946-56

OLDEST PLAYER IN A LEAGUE MATCH
Chris Hutchings, 36 years 175 days v Bradford City, Div.2
27.12.1993

YOUNGEST PLAYER IN A LEAGUE MATCH
Kevin Eley, 16 years 72 days v Scunthorpe (h), 3-0, 15.5.1984

PREVIOUS MANAGERS

(Since 1946): Reg Freeman   Andy Smailes   Tom Johnston   Danny
Williams   Jack Mansell   Tommy Docherty   Jimmy McAnearney
Jimmy McGuigan   Ian Porterfield   Emlyn Hughes   George Kerr
Norman Hunter   Dave Cusack   Billy McEwan   Phil Henson
Archie Gemmil/John McGovern   Danny Bergara

ADDITIONAL INFORMATION
Previous League: Midland League

Previous Names: Thornhill United (1884), Rotherham County
(1905), amalgamated in 1925 with Rotherham Town as Rotherham
United

Club colours: Red and white.

Change colours: Navy /silver.

Reserves League: Pontins Central League Division 2.
Youth League: Northern Intermediate.

LONGEST LEAGUE RUNS

of undefeated matches:	18 (1950-51)	**of league matches w/out a win:**	14 (1934, 1977-78)
of undefeated home matches:	27 (1939-46-47, 1980-81)	**of undefeated away matches:**	16 (1950-51)
without home win:	9 (1983)	**without an away win:**	33 (1894-96-1919 - non-League club)
of league wins:	9 (1982)	**of home wins:**	22 (1939-46-47)
of league defeats:	8 (1956)	**of away wins:**	8 (1948)

THE MANAGER

RONNIE MOORE . . . . appointed June 1997.

PREVIOUS CLUBS
As Manager . . . . Southport.
As Coach. . . . . Tranmere.
As a player . . . . Cardiff, Rotherham, Tranmere.

HONOURS
As a Manager . . . . None.
As a Player . . . . Division 3 championship 1980-81.
International: None.

ROTHERHAM UNITED

PLAYERS NAME / Honours	Ht	Wt	Birthdate	Birthplace / Transfers	Contract Date	Clubs	League	L/Cup	FA Cup	Other	Lge	L/C	FAC	Oth
GOALKEEPER														
Mimms Bobby	6.2	12.1	10/12/63	York	8/5/81	Halifax Town								
				£15000	11/6/81	Rotherham United	83	7	3	1				
				£150000	5/30/85	Everton	29	2	2	4				
				Loan	3/13/86	Notts County	2							
				Loan	12/11/86	Sunderland	4							
				Loan	1/23/87	Blackburn Rovers	6							
				Loan	9/24/87	Manchester City	3							
				£325000	2/25/88	Tottenham Hotspur	37	5	2					
				£250000	12/22/90	Blackburn Rovers	126+2	15	9	4				
				Free	9/6/96	Preston North End	27	2	1					
				Free	8/8/97	Rotherham United	43		4					
Pettinger Paul A	6.1	13.4	10/1/75	Sheffield	10/16/92	Leeds United								
				Loan	8/11/95	Rotherham United								
				Loan	3/28/96	Gillingham								
				Free	8/3/96	Carlisle United								
				Free	8/1/97	Rotherham United	3	2						
Pollitt Michael	6.3	14.1	24/09/72	Farnworth	01/07/90	Manchester United								
via Free 10/07/91 Bury				Free	01/12/92	Lincoln City	57	5	2	4				
				Free	11/08/94	Darlington	40	2	2	3				
				£75000	14/11/95	Notts County	10			2				
Loan 8/26/97 Oldham Ath. 16 Lge Apps				Loan	12/12/97	Gillingham	6							
Loan 1/22/98 Brentford 5 Lge Apps				£75000	2/23/98	Sunderland								
				Free	7/1/98	Rotherham United								
DEFENCE														
Beech Chris	5.10	11.12	11/5/75	Congleton	11/12/92	Manchester City								
E: Y, S.				Free	8/7/97	Cardiff City	46	2	6		1			
				Free	7/1/98	Rotherham United								
Clark Martin A	5.9	10.12	9/12/70	Accrington		Southport								
				Free	6/25/97	Rotherham United	28	2	3					
Dillon Paul	5.9	10.11	10/22/78	Limerick	2/7/97	Rotherham United	25+4				1			
Hurst Paul	5.7	10.4	9/25/74	Sheffield	8/12/93	Rotherham United	87+30	4	7	9+1	4		1	
AWS 95/96														
Knill Alan	6.2	11.7	10/8/64	Slough	10/14/82	Southampton								
W: 1, Y. WFAC'89.				Free	7/13/84	Halifax Town	118	6	6	6	6			
				£15000	8/14/87	Swansea City	89	4	5	7	3			
				£95000	8/18/89	Bury	141+3	7	8	14+1	9		1	1
				Loan	9/24/93	Cardiff City	4							
					11/5/93	Scunthorpe United	131	5	10	6	8			
				Free	7/7/97	Rotherham United	38	2	3		3		1	
Richardson Neil T	5.11	13.5	3/3/68	Sunderland		Brandon United								
AWS 95/96					8/18/89	Rotherham United	164+15	13+1	8+1	10+2	9	1	1	1
				Loan	11/8/96	Exeter City	14							
Scott Gary C	5.8	11.2	2/3/78	Liverpool	10/18/95	Tranmere Rovers (T)								
				Free	8/7/97	Rotherham United	6+1		1		1			
Warner Vance	6	13.2	9/0/74	Leeds	9/11/91	Nottingham F (T)	4+1	1+1						
E: Y.				Loan	2/2/96	Grimsby Town	3							
					9/1/97	Rotherham United	21		3					
MIDFIELD														
Bass David	5.11	12.7	11/29/74	Frimley	7/14/93	Reading	7+4							
				Free	7/1/97	Rotherham United	13+5	1	0+1					
Garner Darren	5.9	12.7	12/10/71	Plymouth		Dorchester								
AWS 95/96				£30000	6/1/95	Rotherham United	98+3	6	5	6	6		3	1
Hudson Danny				Liverpool	8/1/96	Rotherham United	6+4		+2				1	
Roscoe Andrew	5.11	12	6/4/73	Liverpool		Bolton Wanderers								
AWS 95/96				Free	7/17/91		2+1			1+1				
					2/2/95	Rotherham United	157+7	8	6	7	13		2	2
Thompson Stephen J	5.9	11	11/2/64	Oldham	11/4/82	Bolton Wanderers	329+6	27	21	39	49	2	4	2
AMC'89.				£180000		Luton Town	5	2						
					10/22/91	Leicester City	105+3	6	5	11+3	18	2	1	4
				£200000	2/24/95	Burnley	43+6	2			1			
				Free	7/22/97	Rotherham United	32+7	1	3		3			
Tracey Richard S	5.11	10.12	7/9/79	Dewsbury	6/4/97	Sheffield United (T)								
				Free	3/19/98	Rotherham United								
FORWARD														
Berry Trevor	5.7	10.8	8/1/74	Haslemere		Bournemouth								
AWS 95/96					8/1/91	Aston Villa								
				£20000	10/13/95	Rotherham United	92+15	3+1	4+1	7	14		2	1
Bos Gijsbert	6.4	12.7	2/22/73	Spakenburg (Holland)		Fenerbahce								
				£10000	3/19/96	Lincoln City	28+6	5			6	3		
					8/4/97	Rotherham United	6+10	1+1			4			
				Loan	3/26/98	Walsall								
Glover Edward Lee	5.11	12.1	4/24/70	Kettering	5/2/87	Nottingham Forest	61+15	6+5	8+2	4+1	9	2	1	1
S: u21.3, Y. FMC'92				Loan	9/14/89	Leicester City	3+2				1			
				Loan	1/18/90	Barnsley	8		4					
				Loan	9/2/91	Luton Town	1							
				£200000	8/2/94	Port Vale	38+14	5+1	0+2	3+2	7	4		2
				£150000	8/15/96	Rotherham United	51+7	3	5		18		1	
				Loan	3/3/97	Huddersfield Town	11							
Martindale Gary	5.11	11.9	6/24/71	Liverpool		Burscough								
					3/24/94	Bolton Wanderers								
				Free	7/4/95	Peterborough United								
				£175000	3/6/96	Notts County	35+31	3+1	3+1	2+1	13			3
				Loan	2/7/97	Mansfield Town	5				2			
					3/12/98	Rotherham United	7+1				2			
Sedgwick Christopher E	5.11	10.10	4/28/80	Sheffield	8/8/97	Rotherham Utd (T)	0+4	0+1						
White Jason	6.2	12	19/10/71	Meriden	04/07/90	Derby County								
				Free	06/09/91	Scunthorpe United	44+24	1+1	3+3	4+4	16	1	1	1
				Loan	20/08/93	Darlington	4				1			
				Free	10/12/93	Scarborough	60+3	2+1	5	1	20		1	
				£35000	01/06/95	Northampton Town	55+22	1+4	3	5+2	18			
				£25000	9/9/97	Rotherham United	26+1	2	1		12		1	

MILLMOOR GROUND
Rotherham, South Yorkshire S60 1HR

Capacity...11,514
Covered Standing...6,951
Seating..4,573

First game...v Tranmere, 31.8.1925.
First floodlit game....................................v Bristol Rovers, Lge Cup 2nd Rnd, 23.11.1960.

ATTENDANCES
Highest..25,000 v Sheffield Utd, Div.2, 13.12.1952.
Lowest..1,182 v Scarborough, AMC, 27.11.1990.

OTHER GROUNDS...None.

HOW TO GET TO THE GROUND

From the North
Use motorway M1 until junction 34, leave motorway and follow signs to Rotherham (A6109). Cross railway bridge and then turn right into Millmoor Lane for Rotherham United FC.

From the East
Use A630 into Rotherham and then follow signs to Sheffield into Masborough Street, then turn left into Millmoor Lane for Rotherham United FC.

From the South and West
Use motorway M1 until junction 34, leave motorway and follow signs to Rotherham (A6178). At roundabout take 1st exit into Ring Road and at next roundabout 1st exit in Masborough Street (A6109). Take 1st turning left into Millmoor for Rotherham United FC.

Car Parking: There are parks within easy distance of the ground in Kimberworth Road and Main Street.
Nearest Railway Station: Rotherham Central (Town Centre)

USEFUL TELEPHONE NUMBERS

Club Switchboard 01709 512 434
Club fax number 01709 512 762
Club Shop 01709 512 760
Ticket Office 01709 512 434

Marketing Department. 01709 512 760
Internet address. . . . . . . www.themillers.co.uk
Clubcall 0891 66 44 42*
*Calls cost 50p per minute at all times. Call costings correct at time of going to press.

MATCHDAY PROGRAMME

Programme Editor ....
...............Dave Nicholls & Gerry Somerton.

Number of pages.....................................48.

Price ....£1.60.

Subscriptions ....Apply to club.

Local Newspapers
.......................Sheffield Morning Telegraph,
.Sheffield Star (including Saturday special), .
................................Rotherham Advertiser.

Local Radio Stations
..........................Radio Hallam (194 MWs),
.... Radio Sheffield (290 MW).

MATCHDAY TICKET PRICES

Main Stand. £10.00
Juv/OAP. £6.50

Millmoor Lane Stand. £8.00
Juv/OAP. £5.50

Enclosure Stand. £8.50
Juv/OAP. £5.50

Tivoli Terrace £8.00
Juv/OAP. £5.00

Visiting Seats £10.00
Juv/OAP. £6.50

SCARBOROUGH

(The Boro)
NATIONWIDE LEAGUE DIVISION 3
SPONSORED BY: ARNOTT INSURANCE

Scarborough Town 1998/99

SCARBOROUGH
FORMED IN 1879
TURNED PROFESSIONAL IN 1926
LTD COMPANY IN 1933

PRESIDENT & CHIEF EXECUTIVE
J R Birley
CHAIRMAN: J Russell
DIRECTORS
J Russell, T Milton, R Robinson, R Kemp,
R Green, Mrs G Russell
SECRETARY
Mrs Gillian Russell

MANAGER: Mike Wadsworth
ASSISTANT MANAGER: Ray McHale

RESERVE TEAM MANAGER
&
YOUTH TEAM MANAGER
Ray McHale

PHYSIOTHERAPIST
J Murray

It was a case of 'so near yet so far!' for plucky Scarborough who came mightily close to making it into the Second Division after a splendid effort which eventually saw them beaten in the play-off semi-final by the 'seaside' counterparts, Torquay United.

They missed automatic promotion by just three points, taking sixth place in the final league table - but then capitulated against the 'Gulls', losing both legs of their semi-final showdown.

It was a bitter disappointment for manager Mick Wadsworth who knew that two victories in the last two Nationwide League games would bring Scarborough automatic promotion. But they failed to win either of those matches, drawing 0-0 at home with Shrewsbury and then sharing the spoils at Chester (1-1). Those four extra points would have taken 'Boro into third place and into the Second Division.

Staring off tentatively, 'Boro took time to settle into their rhythm and after a dozen games they were situated way down the ladder in 16th position with only 15 points to their name. But over the next 10 games their form picked up considerably and when 1997 gave way to 1998 'Boro had moved up into the top half of the Division, having taken their points tally to 37 from 24 starts.

Wadsworth was able to field a settled side for most of the time and as time rolled by so the results were forthcoming and at the 36-match mark (early March) 'Boro had hauled themselves into the play-offs and were right on course to gain automatic promotion.

They moved themselves up to fourth place with eight games to go and after 40 matches had been completed in-form 'Boro were being strongly tipped to go up with Notts County and either Torquay or Macclesfield. But Barnet, Colchester and Lincoln were pressing them hard at this stage, and in the end the pressure got to Wadsworth's men, who sadly missed the boat. First of all they failed to take maximum points from their last two matches and then allowed Torquay to destroy them in the play-offs.

It was a sad end to an very enjoyable season for the men from the McCain Stadium, especially for 18 year-old Dutchman Martin Schwillens, who became the youngest football club director in the country when he joined the Scarborough Board in January 1998.

Tony Matthews.

SCARBOROUGH

Division 3	:6th			FA CUP: 1st Round			LC CUP: 1st Round		AWS: Northern Round 1

M	DATE	COMP.	VEN	OPPONENTS	RESULT	H/T	LP	GOAL SCORERS/GOAL TIMES	ATT.
1	A 09	FL	H	Cambridge United	W 1-0	0-0	8	Williams 71	2225
2	12	CC 1/1	H	**Scunthorpe United**	L 0-2	0-1			**1907**
3	15	FL	A	Torquay United	L 0-1	0-0	15		(1863)
4	22	FL	H	Brighton & H.A.	W 2-1	1-1	2	Bennett 43, Robinson 60	2505
5	26	CC 1/2	A	**Scunthorpe United**	L 1-2	1-1		**Bennett 6**	**(2145)**
6	30	FL	A	Lincoln City	D 3-3	1-2	8	Brown 21, Bennett 54, Van Der Velden 69	(3162)
7	S 02	FL	A	Darlington	W 2-1	2-1	5	Rockett 12, Bennett 42	(2417)
8	07	FL	H	Hartlepool United	D 1-1	0-0	6	Bennett 66	3027
9	12	FL	A	Colchester United	L 0-1	0-0	7		(2756)
10	20	FL	H	Macclesfield Town	W 2-1	1-1	8	Williams 14, 53	2256
11	27	FL	H	Notts County	L 1-2	1-1	10	Campbell 12	2751
12	O 04	FL	A	Exeter City	D 1-1	1-1	10	Brodie 6	(4464)
13	11	FL	A	Hull City	L 0-3	0-2	15		(5350)
14	18	FL	H	Peterborough United	L 1-3	0-3	16	Brodie 64	2565
15	21	FL	H	Chester City	W 4-1	2-0	12	Robinson 11, Atkin 42, Williams 48, 71	1451
16	25	FL	A	Shrewsbury Town	W 1-0	0-0	9	Bennett 51	(2395)
17	N 01	FL	H	Doncaster Rovers	W 4-0	0-0	5	McElhatton 52, Bennett 67, Williams 76, 87	2345
18	04	FL	A	Leyton Orient	L 1-3	1-2	7	Williams 2	(2480)
19	08	FL	A	Mansfield Town	L 2-3	2-2	11	Robinson 21, Mitchell 35	(2134)
20	15	FAC 1	A	**Scunthorpe United**	L 1-2	0-1		**Robinson 52**	**(3039)**
21	18	FL	H	Swansea City	W 3-2	1-1	8	McElhatton 38, 65, Williams 70	1408
22	22	FL	H	Rotherham United	L 1-2	1-0	10	Mitchell 45	3317
23	29	FL	A	Cardiff City	D 1-1	1-0	11	McElhatton 41	(2593)
24	D 06	FL	H	Rochdale	W 1-0	1-0	9	Campbell 44	1705
25	09	AWS N1	A	**Hull City**	L 1-2	0-0		**Campbell 71**	**(1518)**
26	13	FL	A	Scunthorpe United	W 3-1	2-1	6	Williams 20, 35 (pen), Conway 59	(2535)
27	19	FL	H	Barnet	W 1-0	1-0	4	Brodie 3	1714
28	26	FL	A	Hartlepool United	L 0-3	0-1	8		(3905)
29	J 06	FL	H	Darlington	W 2-1	1-0	7	Williams 43 (pen), Robinson 87	1751
30	10	FL	A	Cambridge United	W 3-2	1-1	3	Bennett 18, Brodie 70, 81	(2636)
31	17	FL	H	Lincoln City	D 2-2	0-1	5	Bennett 54, Campbell 78	2905
32	20	FL	H	Torquay United	W 4-1	1-0	3	Bennett 42, Campbell 55, McElhatton 66, Brodie 81	2467
33	24	FL	A	Brighton & H.A.	D 1-1	0-1	4	Mitchell 86	(1988)
34	31	FL	H	Colchester United	D 1-1	0-0	4	Campbell 84	2219
35	F 06	FL	A	Macclesfield Town	L 1-3	0-3	7	Williams 73 (pen)	(2488)
36	14	FL	H	Exeter City	W 4-1	2-0	6	McElhatton 7, Brodie 35, 53, Williams 57	2078
37	21	FL	A	Notts County	L 0-1	0-1	7		(5645)
38	24	FL	A	Peterborough United	D 0-0	0-0	7		(4208)
39	28	FL	H	Hull City	W 2-1	2-0	5	Brodie 2, Conway 28 (pen)	3831
40	M 03	FL	H	Mansfield Town	D 2-2	1-0	5	Tate 13, Brodie 82	2019
41	10	FL	A	Doncaster Rovers	W 2-1	1-0	5	Campbell 37, Rockett 84	(1129)
42	14	FL	H	Leyton Orient	W 2-0	1-0	4	Williams 36, Campbell 73	2655
43	21	FL	A	Swansea City	D 0-0	0-0	5		(2797)
44	28	FL	A	Rotherham United	D 0-0	0-0	5		(3836)
45	A 03	FL	H	Cardiff City	W 3-1	3-0	3	Worrall 8, 15, Bennett 44	2905
46	11	FL	A	Rochdale	L 0-4	0-1	5		(1795)
47	13	FL	H	Scunthorpe United	D 0-0	0-0	5		3427
48	18	FL	A	Barnet	D 1-1	1-1	5	Bennett 34	(2353)
49	25	FL	H	Shrewsbury Town	D 0-0	0-0	6		3712
50	M 02	FL	A	Chester City	D 1-1	0-0	6	Flitcroft 82 (OG)	(2719)
51	10	PO SF1	H	**Torquay United**	L 1-3	1-1		**Rockett 40**	**5246**
52	13	PO SF2	A	**Torquay United**	L 1-4	1-3		**Rockett 22**	**(5386)**

Best Home League Attendance: 3831 V Hull City	Smallest :1408 V Swansea City	Average :2489

Goal Scorers:

FL	(67)	Williams 15, Brodie 10, Bennett G 9, Campbell 7, McElhatton 6, Robinson 4, Mitchell 3, Bennett T 2, Conway 2, Rockett 2, Worrall 2, Atkin 1, Brown 1, Tate 1, Van Der Velden 1, Opponents 1
CC	(1)	Bennett G 1
FAC	(1)	Robinson 1
AWS	(1)	Campbell 1
PO	(2)	Rockett 2

	(D) Atkin	(D) Bennett G	(M) Bennett T	(F) Bocherski	(F) Brodie	(D) Brown	(G) Buxton	(M) Campbell	(M) Carr	(F) Conway	(M) Dobbin	(G) Elliott	(D) Heckingbottom	(M) Jackson	(D) Kay	(G) Martin	(F) McElhatton	(M) Mitchell	(G) Rhodes	(F) Robinson	(M) Rockett	(M) Russell	(M) Snodin	(D) Sutherland	(M) Tate	(M) Van Der Velden	(M) Williams	(M) Worrall	
M.S.Pike 1	S3	X	S2		X										X	X	X			X			S1	X		X	X	X	
G Laws 2	X	X	S1		X										X	X	X	S3		S2			X	X		X	X	X	
P Rejer 3	X	S1	X		X										X	X	X	S2		X			X	X		X	X	S3	
A N Butler 4	S1	X	X		X										X	X	X			X			X	X		S	X	S2	
P R Richards 5	S1	X	X		X										X	X	X	S3		X			X			X	X	S2	
T Jones 6	X	X	X		X	X									X	X				X			X	S3	S1		X	S2	
E K Wolstenholme 7	S3	X	X		X	X									X	X				X			X	X	S2	S1	X		
M L Dean 8	S	X	X		X	X		S1							X	X				X			X	X	S2	X	X		
A G Wiley 9	S	X	X		X			S1							X	X	S2			X			X	X		X	X		
J P Robinson 10	X		X			X		X							X	X	S2	S1		X			X	X		X	X	S3	
C J Foy 11	X		X		X			X							X	X	S1	S3		S2	X		X	X		X	X		
M Fletcher 12	X	X	X		X			X							X	X	S1			S2	X		X	X	S3		X		
R Pearson 13	X	X	X		X			S1							X	X	X	S2		X			X	X	S3		X		
E Lomas 14	X	X	X		X			S2				X			X	X		X		X			S3	S1			X		
J A Kirkby 15	X	X	X		X			S1				X			X	X		S2		X			X		S3		X		
B Coddington 16	X	X	X		X			S1				X			X	X		S2		X			X	S			X		
G B Frankland 17	X	X	X		X			X				X	X		X	X	S1			X			X		S2		X		
D Orr 18	X	X	X		X			X				X			X	X	S1			X			X		S3		X		
S W Mathieson 19	X	X	X		S1			S2				X			X	X	S1			X			X		S3		X		
A B Wilkie 20	X	X		S	X			S1	S3	S					X	X		X		X			X		S2		X		
M J Jones 21	X	X						X	S2	S						X		X		X			X	X	S1		X		
T Heilbron 22	X	X	S1		X			X	S			X				X		X		X			X		S2		X		
C R Wilkes 23		X	S	S	X				S			X			X		X		X	X	X			X1	S1		X		
D Laws 24	X	X	X1			X2	S					X			X		S1	X		X				S2			X		
25	X	X	X3		S3			X				X			X1	S1	X	X2		X				S2			X		
G Singh 26	X	S			X			X2		X		X			X		S1	X1	X					S2			X		
K M Lynch 27	X				X			X2		X		X			X		X1		X		S1	S3	S2		X3		X		
A R Leake 28	X	S2	S3		X			S1		X		X			X1		X	X2	X	X3					X		X		
A N Butler 29		X	S3		X2			X1		X		X				X	S2	X	S1	X					X3		X		
D R Crick 30		X	S2		X1			X		X		X				X	S2	X	S1	X					X		X		
J A Kirkby 31		X	S2		X			X		X2		X1			X		X	S	X	S1					X		X		
M D Messias 32	S2	X	S1		X			X				X			X	S3	X	X2	X		X1				X3				
D Orr 33	S1	X	S1		X			X				X			X		X2	X							X2		X		
D Laws 34	S1	X	X		X	X		X				X1			X		X2	X					X3	S2		X	S3		
M J Brandwood 35	S1	X	X		X			X1		X					S1		X	X3	X		X1				X	S3			
P R Richards 36		X	S		X					X	X	X			X		S1		X				S2			X2	X2		
S J Baines 37	X	X			X					X3	X	X			X		S2				S3	X		S1		X1	X2		
R J Harris 38	S2	X			X3					X	X	X			X1		S1			X	S3	X2	X				X		
D Pugh 39	S	X			X					X	X	X			X		S1		X1	X	S		X				X		
R D Furnandiz 40	X	X	X2		X			S2		X		X			X		S3		X1				X3		S1				
M L Dean 41	S3	X	X		X3			X2		X		X			X		S2		X				S1			X	X1		
T Jones 42	X	X	X		X3			X2		X		X			X	X1		S1					S3			X	X		
R Styles 43	X	X			X1			S			X	X			X		S1		S				S2			X	X		
G B Frankland 44		X	S		X			X1		X	X				X		S1				X2	S2			X	X		
R Pearson 45		X	S2		X3			X1		X	X				X		S3				X2		S1			X	X		
A G Wiley 46		X	S2		X			X1		X	X2	X			X		S3				X3		S1			X	X		
M S Pike 47	X	X			X2			S1		X		X			X		S2	X1			X	X	S			X	X		
M J Jones 48	X	X	S		X1			S1		X		X			X		X				X		X			X2	X		
B Coddington 49	X	S2			S1				X			X			X2		X2	S3			X	X				X1	X3		
M Fletcher 50	X	X2			X			X3		X		X			X	X1	S3		X				X	X		S1	S2		
M E Pierce 51	S3	X	S1		X			X		X		X			X		S2	X		X2	X3				X1	X		
R J Harris 52	X1		X2		X			X		X		X			X		S2	S3	X		S1	X3			X	X		
FL Appearances	26	40	24		43	4	3	20		13	1		15	28	2	40	17	38	8	11	28	32	33	18	3	5	40	14	
FL Sub Appearances	8	2	10		1			14			1						4	27	8			4	2		2	4	21	3	7	
CC Appearances	1+1	2	1+1		2									2	2	0+2		1+1	1		1	2			2	2	1+1		
FAC Appearances	1	1		1		0+1	0+1							1	1	1		1	1		1	1		1	0+1	1			
AWS Appearances	1	1		0+1		1					1		1	1	0+1	1	1				0+1	1							
PO Appearances	1+1	1	1+1		2			2				2		2	2	0+1	0+2	2			1+1	1		2	2				

CLUB RECORDS

RECORD LEAGUE VICTORY & MOST GOALS SCORED
4-0 v BoltonWanderers, Division 4, 29.8.1987   4-0 v Newport
County (a), Division 4,12.4.19880   4-0 v Doncaster R., Division 3,
23.4.94 5-2 v Torquay Utd,Division 4, 29.9.1988
Most Goals Scored in a First Class Cup Tie
6-0 v Rhyl Athletic, FA Cup Round1, 29.11.1930

RECORD LEAGUE DEFEAT
1-5 v Barnet, Division 4, 8.2.1992
Record Cup Defeat
0-8 v Mansfield Town (h), FA Cup Rnd 1, 22.11.1952

MOST LEAGUE GOALS
67, Division 4, 1988-89

MOST LEAGUE POINTS
(3pts for win) 77, Division 4, 1988-89

RECORD TRANSFER FEE RECEIVED
£350,000 (¨100,000 7/89 + ¨250,000 9/92) from Notts County for
Craig Short

RECORD TRANSFER FEE PAID
£100,000 to Leicester City for Martin Russell,February 1989

BEST PERFORMANCES
League: 5th Division 4, 1988-89 FA Cup: Third Round
(1931,1938, 1976, 1978)   League Cup: Fourth Round, 1992-93

HONOURS
FA Trophy Winners 1973, 1976, 1977 (Record) GM Vauxhall
ConfereneceChampions 1987 Midland League Champions 1930
Scarborough & District LeagueChampions 1946 North Easter
League Champions 1963   Vauxhall Floodlit League Winners 1973,
1975 Northern Premier League Cup Winners 1977 Bob Lord
TrophyWinners 1984 North Eastern Counties League Cup
Winners 1963 East Riding CupWinners (8 times) 1888, 1889,
1891, 1892, 1893, 1897, 1901, 1902 North RidingSenior Cup
Winners 1909, 1929, 1939, 1948, 1956, 1959, 1961, 1962, 1969,
1973,1974, 1977, 1978, 1981, 1982, 1985, 1988 Festival of
Football Winners 1990

INDIVIDUAL CLUB RECORDS

MOST APPEARANCES FOR CLUB
Steve Richards (1987-91): (League 164 + FA Cup 5 +League Cup
15 + Others 12) 0Total 196

MOST CAPPED PLAYER
Kyle Lightbourne, Bermuda

RECORD GOALSCORER IN A MATCH
Darren Foreman 3 v Northampton, Div 3, 10.10.1992(4-2) & Darren
Foreman 3 v York City, Div 3, 19.12.1992 (4-2)

RECORD LEAGUE GOALSCORER IN A SEASON
(Football League only) Darren Foreman 27,Div 4/3, 1992-93
In All Competitions: Darren Foreman, 31 (League 27, Lge Cup 2,
Autoglass 2)1992-93

RECORD LEAGUE GOALSCORER IN A CAREER
(Football League only) Darren Foreman,34, 1991-93
In All Competitions: Darren Foreman 40 (League 34, League Cup
4, Others 2)1991-93

OLDEST PLAYER TO PLAY IN A LEAGUE MATCH
John Burridge, 41 years 338 days v Doncaster Rovers, Division 3,
6.11.1993

YOUNGEST PLAYER IN A LEAGUE MATCH
Lee Harper, v Scunthorpe Utd, Division 3,2.10.1993

PREVIOUS MANAGERS

(Since the war): G Hall H Taylor F Taylor A Bell RHalton C
Robson G Higgins A Smailes E Brown A Frank S Myers
GShaw C Appleton K Houghton C Appleton J McAnearney J
Cottam H Dunn N Warnock R McHale P Chambers B Ayre

ADDITIONAL INFORMATION
Previous Leagues: Northern (1898-1910) Yorkshire Combination
(1910-14) Northern (1914-26) Yorkshire (1926-27) Midland
(1927-40) Scarborough &District (1945-46) Midland (1946-60)
Northern Counties (1960-62) NorthEastern (1962-63) Midland
(1963-68) Northern Premier (1968-79) Alliance Premier (1979-
87) Football League (1987-)
Club colours: White shirts with red & green sleeves, white shorts
with red trim, red socks.
Change colours:
Reserves League: Pontins League.

LONGEST LEAGUE RUNS

of undefeated matches:	9 (1988, 1990, 1990-91)	of league matches w/out a win:	6 (1989)
of undefeated home matches:	13 (1992)	of undefeated away matches:	6 (1.5.1993 - 2.10.1993)
without home win:	13 (23.3.1993 - 16.10.1993)	without an away win:	11 (1990,1992)
of league wins: 3 (x2 1987-88, 1988-89, x2 1989-90, x2 1992-93,94)		of home wins:	6 (1987)
of league defeats:	6 (1989)	of away wins:	3 (1992)

THE MANAGER

MICK WADSWORTH . . . . appointed July 1996.

PREVIOUS CLUBS
As Manager . . . . Carlisle United.
As Asst.Man/Coach . . . . Barnsley, Norwich City.
As a player . . . . Scunthorpe United.

HONOURS
As a Manager . . . . **Carlisle**: Division 3 Champions 1994/95.
As a Player . . . . None.

SCARBOROUGH

PLAYERS NAME Honours	Ht	Wt	Birthdate	Birthplace Transfers	Contract Date	Clubs	League	L/Cup	FA Cup	Other	Lge	L/C	FAC	Oth
							APPEARANCES				GOALS			
G O A L K E E P E R														
Elliott Anthony R	6	12.12	11/30/69	Nuneaton	12/3/86	Birmingham City		1						
				Free	12/22/88	Hereford United	75	5	6	9				
				Free	7/29/92	Huddersfield Town	15	2	3	3				
				Free	6/28/93	Carlisle United	22+1		1	5				
					8/15/96	Cardiff City	38+1	2	1					
				Free	2/13/98	Scarborough	15			2				
D E F E N C E														
Jackson Richard	5.7	9.4	4/18/80	Whitby	10/30/97	Scarborough (T)	2							
Kay John	5.1	11.6	1/29/64	Great Lumley	8/7/81	Arsenal	13+1							
				£25000	7/20/84	Wimbledon	63	3	3	1	2			
				Loan	1/8/85	Middlesbrough	8							
				£22500	7/22/87	Sunderland	196+3	19	12	6				
				Free	8/23/96	Preston North End	7	3						
				Free	9/27/96	Scarborough	74	2	2	2			1	
M I D F I E L D														
Bazelya Eammom M	5.7	9.12	10/25/78	Birmingham	5/31/97	Scarborough								
Bullimore Wayne A E: S. Free 11/10/93 Stockport County	5.1	11.07	12/09/70	Sutton-in-Ash.	16/09/88	Manchester United								
				Free	09/03/91	Barnsley	27+8	2+1	1+1		1			
				Free	19/11/93	Scunthorpe United	51+2	2	5	3	9	1	1	1
				Free	15/12/95	Bradford City	1+1							
				Loan	20/09/96	Doncaster Rovers	4							
				Free	26/03/97	Peterborough Utd	10+11	0+3	0+1	1	1			
				Free	7/1/98	Scarborough								
Campbell Neil A	6.2	13.7	1/26/77	Middlesborough	9/5/97	Scarborough	20+14		0+1	2	7			
Hoyland Jamie E: Y.3.	6	12.8	23/01/66	Sheffield	12/11/83	Manchester City	2	0+1						
				Free	11/07/86	Bury	169+3	14+1	6	12	35	5		2
				£250000	04/07/90	Sheffield United	72+15	3+3	8+2	2	6	1	1	1
				Loan	04/03/94	Bristol City	6							
Loan 14/10/94 Burnley				£130000	08/11/94	Burnley	77+10	5	7	5+1	4			
				Loan	11/20/97	Carlisle United	5							
				Free	7/1/98	Scarborough								
Rockett Jason	5.11	11.5	9/26/69	London	3/25/92	Rotherham United								
				Free	8/4/93	Scarborough	171+1	9	7	5	11			2
Russell Matthew L	5.11	11.5	1/17/78	Dewsbury	9/16/96	Scarborough	1+6							
				Loan	3/26/98	Doncaster Rovers	4+1							
Williams Gareth J	5.1	11.8	3/12/67	Isle of Wight	1/1/00	Gosport Borough								
				£30000	1/9/88	Aston Villa	6+6	0+1	2	0+1				
				£200000	8/6/91	Barnsley	23+11	1	1+1	1+1	6			
				Loan	9/17/92	Hull City	4							
				Loan	8/23/94	Wolverhampton W.								
				Loan	9/6/94	Hull City	16				2			
				Free	9/16/94	Bournemouth	0+1							
				Free	9/27/94	Northampton Town	38+12	2	1+1	5+1	1			
					8/2/96	Scarborough	84+3	5	4	2	25	1		
Worrall Benjamin	5.8	10.06	12/7/75	Swindon	7/8/94	Swindon Town	1+2							
					8/2/96	Scarborough	21+15	2+2		2	3			
F O R W A R D														
Milbourne Ian	5.11	11.2	1/21/79	Hexham	7/4/97	Newcastle Utd (T)								
				Free	7/1/98	Scarborough								
Robinson Spencer L	5.7	11.5	12/29/65	Bradford	1/1/00	Nottingham Forest								
				Free	1/5/84	Huddersfield Town	17+4				2			
				Loan	12/18/85	Tranmere Rovers	4				3			
				£60000	7/8/86	Bury	248+14	17+3	9	24	89	6	1	4
				£130000	7/14/93	Bristol City	31+10	1	5	1	4	1		
				£250000	7/26/94	Burnley	43+20	5	5	0+1	9	2	1	
				Free	8/5/97	Scarborough	28+8	1+1	1	0+2	4		1	
Tate Christopher D.	6	11.10	12/27/77	York	7/17/96	Sunderland								
				Free	8/5/97	Scarborough	3+2		0+1	1+1	1			

THE MCCAIN STADIUM
Seamer Road, Scarborough YO12 4HF

Capacity 5,900
Covered Standing 1,000
Seating..3,500.
Terracing ....1,400.

First game..Not known.
First floodlit game ....Not known.

ATTENDANCES
Highest ....11,162 v Luton Town, FAC 3rd Rnd, 1938.
Lowest ....412 v Scunthorpe Utd, AMC, 27.9.1993.

OTHER GROUNDS..None.

HOW TO GET TO THE GROUND

The ground is situated on the main Scarborough-York Road (A64).
Half-a-mile on left past B&Q going into Town.

Car Parking: In streets around the ground.

Nearest Railway Station: Scarborough Central (2 miles)

USEFUL TELEPHONE NUMBERS

Club switchboard .... 01723 375 094   Club shop................. 01723 375094
Club fax number .... 01723 378 733   Ticket Office.............. 01723 375 094

MATCHDAY PROGRAMME

Programme Editor ....Eric Pickup.

Number of pages.....................................36.

Price ....£1.50.

Subscriptions...£30.

Local Newspapers
..Scarborough Evening News, The Mercury.

Local Radio Stations
..............................Radio York, Y.C.R. Radio.

MATCHDAY TICKET PRICES

Main Stand.............................. £10.50
OAP....................................... £6.50
Junior..................................... £5.00

Family Stand £8.00
OAP....................................... £4.00
Juv. £2.50

SCUNTHORPE UNITED
(The Iron)
NATIONWIDE LEAGUE DIVISION 3
SPONSORED BY: MOTEK

1998/99 • Back Row L R: Lee Marshall, Chris Hope, Tim Clarke, Richard Logan, Tommy Evans, Ashley Fickling, Sean McAuley.
Middle Row: Nigel Adkins (Physio), John Eyre, Russell Wilcox, Jimmy Neil, John Gayle, James Featherstone, Darryn Stamp, Gary Bull, Paul Wilson (Yth Dev. Officer). **Front Row:** Brian Page, Steve housham, ALex Calvo-Garcia, Mark Lillis (Asst. Manager), Brian LAws (Manager), Jamie Forrester, Paul Harsley, Steve Nottingham.

SCUNTHORPE UNITED
FORMED IN 1904
TURNED PROFESSIONAL IN 1912
LTD COMPANY IN 1912

CHAIRMAN: K Wagstaff
VICE-CHAIRMAN
R Garton
DIRECTORS
B Borrill, C Plumtree, B Collen, S Wharton,
J Godfrey
CHIEF EXECUTIVE/SECRETARY
A D Rowing (01724 848 077)

MANAGER: Brian Laws
ASITANT MANAGER: Mark Lillis
YOUTH TEAM MANAGER
Paul Wilson

PHYSIOTHERAPIST
Nigel Adkins

STATISTICIAN FOR THE DIRECTORY
Vacant

The 'Iron' under manager Brian Laws, missed the play-offs by a single point, finishing just behind Barnet in eighth place with a total of 69.

Generally speaking the Glanford Park club had a good season. They played well within themselves for the majority of the campaign, but perhaps lacked that vital ingredient when it came to winning tight matches.

Their end-of-season position in Division Three was, to say the least, annoying - after they came with a terrific late challenge.

With six games remaining the 'Iron' were back in 13th position, six places below the play-off line. But they collected 13 points from their remaining fixtures only to miss out right at the death.

Laws thought at one stage that promotion was out of the question. But as the season progressed and teams began to cancel each other out, the 'Iron' gradually got closer and closer to the leading pack - only to miss out by the narrowest of margins when the final whistle sounded.

Perhaps the lack of strike-power was Scunthorpe's downfall. In their 46 matches they netted a disappointing 56 goals (only four teams in the Division notched fewer - and all finished in the bottom five) and they conceded 52.

The 'Iron' dropped 29 points at Glanford Park, yet on their travels balanced the books to a tee by collecting the same number from creditable eight wins and five hard-fought draws.

Laws will be hoping for the same commitment in 1998-99 which his players showed during the second half of 1997-98 - and if they materialises, then the 'Iron' could well be in line for promotion, certainly a top seven finish.

Tony Matthews.

SCUNTHORPE UNITED

Division 3	:8th			FA CUP: 3rd Round		LC CUP: 2nd Round		AWS: Northern Quarter-final

M	DATE	COMP.	VEN	OPPONENTS	RESULT	H/T	LP	GOAL SCORERS/GOAL TIMES	ATT.
1	A 09	FL	A	Peterborough United	W 1-0	0-0	9	Forrester 62	(5761)
2	12	CC 1/1	A	Scarborough	W 2-0	1-0		Garcia 20, 73	(1907)
3	15	FL	H	Leyton Orient	W 1-0	1-0	2	Forrester 19	3068
4	23	FL	A	Swansea City	L 0-2	0-1	10		(4895)
5	26	CC 1/2	H	Scarborough	W 2-1	1-1		Calva 24, 61	2145
6	30	FL	H	Mansfield Town	W 1-0	0-0	3	Calva 73	3414
7	S 02	FL	H	Chester City	W 2-1	0-1	2	Eyre 72 (pen), 86	2633
8	07	FL	A	Notts County	L 1-2	0-1	4	, Strodder 89 (OG)	(5009)
9	13	FL	H	Doncaster Rovers	D 1-1	1-1	7	Eyre 23	3378
10	16	CC 2/1	H	Everton	L 0-1	0-1			7145
11	20	FL	A	Barnet	W 1-0	1-0	4	Eyre 28 (pen)	(1951)
12	27	FL	H	Hull City	W 2-0	1-0	3	Forrester 4, Calva 60	4905
13	O 01	CC 2/2	A	Everton	L 0-5	0-2			(11562)
14	04	FL	A	Rochdale	L 0-2	0-1	4		(2087)
15	18	FL	H	Lincoln City	L 0-1	0-0	7		4152
16	21	FL	H	Shrewsbury Town	D 1-1	1-1	6	Forrester 20	2303
17	25	FL	A	Exeter City	W 3-2	1-1	6	Walsh 43, Hope 47, D'Auria 82	(4552)
18	31	FL	A	Colchester United	D 3-3	0-3	6	Hope 53, D'Auria 61,63	(3134)
19	N 04	FL	H	Cambridge United	D 3-3	0-2	6	Forrester 59, Eyre 62, D'Auria 67	2417
20	08	FL	H	Hartlepool United	D 1-1	1-0	8	Hope 38	3272
21	11	FL	A	Cardiff City	D 0-0	0-0	6		(2340)
22	15	FAC 1	H	Scarborough	W 2-1	1-0		Wilcox 41, Calva 71	3039
23	18	FL	A	Rotherham United	W 3-1	1-0	5	Eyre 36, 50, Forrester 80	(3355)
24	22	FL	A	Torquay United	W 4-2	2-1	5	Calva 11, 78, D'Auria 45, Wilcox 71	(2152)
25	29	FL	H	Brighton & H.A.	L 0-2	0-0	5		3187
26	D 06	FAC 2	H	Ilkeston Town	D 1-1	0-0		Forrester 76	4187
27	09	AWS N1	H	Chester City	W 2-1	0-0		Eyre 76 (pen), 84 (pen)	813
28	13	FL	H	Scarborough	L 1-3	1-2	10	D'Auria 10	2535
29	17	FAC 2R	A	Ilkeston Town	W 2-1	2-0		Forrester 10, Wilcox 30	(2109)
30	20	FL	A	Darlington	L 0-1	0-0	13		(2267)
31	26	FL	H	Notts County	L 1-2	1-1	13	Hendon 3 (OG)	4781
32	28	FL	A	Chester City	L 0-1	0-0	13		(2263)
33	J 03	FAC 3	A	Crystal Palace	L 0-2	0-1			(11624)
34	06	AWS N2	A	Hartlepool United	W 2-1	1-0		Calva 44, Housham 88	(1491)
35	10	FL	H	Peterborough United	L 1-3	1-2	14	Forrester 23	3584
36	17	FL	A	Mansfield Town	L 0-1	0-1	15		(2375)
37	20	FL	A	Macclesfield Town	L 0-2	0-2	15		(1450)
38	24	FL	H	Swansea City	W 1-0	1-0	14	D'Auria 21	2123
39	27	AWS NQF	H	Grimsby Town	L 0-2	0-0			4596
40	30	FL	A	Doncaster Rovers	W 2-1	1-1	14	D'Auria 23, Housham 82	(2036)
41	F 06	FL	H	Barnet	D 1-1	0-0	15	Walker 51	2313
42	14	FL	H	Rochdale	W 2-0	1-0	14	Regis 16, Eyre 75	2284
43	21	FL	A	Hull City	L 1-2	1-2	15	Regis 36	(4904)
44	24	FL	A	Lincoln City	D 1-1	0-1	15	Forrester 61	(3407)
45	28	FL	H	Cardiff City	D 3-3	2-1	15	Eyre 14 (pen), Forrester 32, Calva 86	2135
46	M 03	FL	A	Hartlepool United	W 1-0	1-0	13	Wilcox 23	(1588)
47	07	FL	H	Colchester United	W 1-0	1-0	12	McAuley 17	2143
48	14	FL	A	Cambridge United	D 2-2	0-2	12	Forrester 52, Stamp 77	(2423)
49	21	FL	H	Rotherham United	D 1-1	0-0	12	Eyre 77	4011
50	28	FL	H	Torquay United	W 2-0	0-0	11	Hope 69, Calva 85	3264
51	A 04	FL	A	Brighton & H.A.	L 1-2	0-1	13	Hope 66	(2141)
52	11	FL	H	Macclesfield Town	W 1-0	1-0	11	D'Auria 9	2949
53	13	FL	A	Scarborough	D 0-0	0-0	12		(3427)
54	18	FL	H	Darlington	W 1-0	0-0	10	Sertori 49	2267
55	21	FL	A	Leyton Orient	L 0-1	0-0	11		(2735)
56	25	FL	H	Exeter City	W 2-1	2-1	11	D'Auria 7, Harsley 43	2024
57	M 02	FL	A	Shrewsbury Town	W 2-0	1-0	8	Marshall 21, Forrester 60	(2704)

Best Home League Attendance: 4905 V Hull City **Smallest :2024 V Exeter City** **Average :3006**

Goal Scorers:

FL	(56)	Forrester 11, D'Auria 10, Eyre 10, Calva 6, Hope 5, Regis 2, Wilcox 2, Harsley 1, Housham 1, Marshall 1, McAuley 1, Sertori 1, Stamp 1, Walker 1, Walsh 1, Opponents 2
CC	(4)	Calva 2, Garcia 2
FAC	(5)	Forrester 2, Wilcox 2, Calva 1
AWS	(4)	Eyre 2, Calva 1, Housham 1

(M) Calvo-Garcia	(G) Clarke	(M) D'Auria	(G) Evans	(M) Eyre	(F) Forrester	(M) Graves	(M) Harsley	(D) Hope	(M) Housham	(M) Laws	(M) Marshall	(D) McAuley	(M) Murphy	(D) Neil	(D) Nottingham	(M) Ormondroyd	(M) Pemberton	(F) Phillips	(F) Regis	(D) Sertori	(M) Shakespeare	(M) Sheldon	(M) Stamp	(M) Stanton	(M) Walker	(D) Walsh	(D) Wilcox	(F) Woods		
X	X	X		X					X	S					X					X	X	S			X	X	X		D. Orr	1
X	X	X		X				X	X	S			X							X		S	S1		X	X	X		G Laws	2
X	X	X	S2	X				X	S1				X							X	X	S			X	X	X		M D Messias	3
X	X	X		S1	X			X				S2	X							X	X	S3			X	X	X		C R Wilkes	4
X	X	X	S	X	X			X	S			X								X		S1			X	X	X		P R Richards	5
X	X	X		X	X			X	S1			X		S2						X	X	S			X	X			C J Foy	6
X	X	X		S1	X			X	X			X		S						X	X	S			X	X			B Coddington	7
X	X	X		S1	X			X	X	S2		X		X		X				X		S			X				D R Crick	8
X	X	X		X	X			X	X	S2		X				X				X		S			X	S1			M L Dean	9
X	X	X		X	X		S	X	X			X		S						X		S			X				M D Reed	10
X	X			X	X		S1	X	X	X	S	X		S						X		X			X				M E Pierce	11
X	X	X		X	X		S	X	X		S1	X								X		X	S2		X				G B Frankland	12
X		X	X	X	X			X	X3	S1	S2	X				S3				X		X1			X		S3		D J Gallagher	13
X	X			X	X2			X	X	S1	S2	X				S3				X		X1			X	X			A R Hall	14
X	X	S2		X	X			X	X		X	X				X				X		S	S1		X	X			E K Wolstenholme	15
X	X	S2		X	X			X	S1	X	X	X								X		S	X		X	X			R Pearson	16
X	X	X		X	X			X			X	X	X				S			X		S	S		X	X			M J Jones	17
S1	X	X		X	X			X			X	X	X							X		S			X	X			R D Furnandiz	18
X	X	X	S	X	X			X	S1	X	X									X		S			X	X			E Lomas	19
X	X	X		X	X			X	X		S									X		S			X	X	X		A Bates	20
X	X	X		X	X			X	X	S1										X		S			X	X	X		P Rejer	21
X	X	X	S	X	X			X	X	S2		S				S1				X		S			X	X	X		A B Wilkie	22
X	X	X		X	X			X	X	S		S1				S				X		S			X	X	X		T Jones	23
X	X	X		X	X			X			S	X				S				X		S				X	X		P Taylor	24
X	X	X		X	X			X		S1	X1	X2				S2				X		S				X	X		J Leech	25
X	X	X	S	X	X			X		S	X1	X2				S2				X		S1				X	X		E K Wolstenholme	26
	X	X		X1	X			X				X				S1				X		X			X	X				27
X	X	X		X	X			X	S1			X	X			S2				X		S			X	X1	X2		G Singh	28
X1	X	X		X	X			X	S1			X		S		S				X		S			X	X	X		E K Wolstenholme	29
X1	X	X		X	X3			X	S1			X	S1			S3				X					X	X	X1		M S Pike	30
S3	X	X3		X	X			X	X			X2		X		S2				X					X	X1	S1		D Pugh	31
S2	X	X		X	X1			X	X			S2	S1	X2		X				X			X2				X		F G Stretton	32
X	X	X		X	X			X	X	S2		S				S1				X		X			X	X2	X1		D J Gallagher	33
X	X	X		X	X1			X	X				X			S1				X		X			X	X				34
X	X1	X		X2				X	X				S			S2	S1			X		X			X	X	X		G B Frankland	35
X	X	S		X	X			X	X1	X2	S2					X	X			X		X			X	X			E K Wolstenholme	36
X	X	S2	S1	X				X	X1							S3	X2			X		X			X	X	X	X3	T Heilbron	37
X		X	X	S1	X			X	X1		X					S				X		X			X	X	X	S	J P Robinson	38
X	X	X		X2	X			X	X			X				S2	X1			X		X			X	X	X			39
X	X	X		S2	X2			X	S1		X					S3				X		X			X1	X	X	X3	P R Richards	40
X	X	X		X	X			X	X	S1						S2	X		X	X		X			X	X1	X	S	W C Burns	41
X	X	X2		X			S2	X1	X							S3			X3	X		X			X	S1	X		T Jones	42
X1	X	X		X2			S1	X		S		X				S2			X	X		X			X		X		C J Foy	43
S	X	X		S1	X		X	X		X		X	S2			X			X1	X		X			X		X2		G Laws	44
S2	X	X		X	X		X	X		X		S1				X3				X		X	S3		X	X			A R Leake	45
X	X	S1		X2	S2		X1	X				X	X	X		S				X		X			X	X	X		J A Kirkby	46
X	X			X	S1		X	X			X1	X				S2				X2	S	S			X	X	X		K M Lynch	47
X2	X			X	X		X				S2	X				X1				X	S	S1			X	X	X		A P D'Urso	48
X	X	X		X1	S		X					S	X			S1						X			X	X	X		K M Lynch	49
X	X	X		X1	X		X					S	X			S	S1					X			X	X	X		M D Messias	50
X	X	X		X1	X		X					X2	X				S1				S2		X2		X		X		A N Butler	51
X	X	X		X3	S2		X2	X				S3					X1			X			S1		X		X		A R Hall	52
X		X	X	X1				X				S2					X2			X		S		S1	X		X		M S Pike	53
X2	X	X	S1	X				X				S2					X1			X			S		X	X	X		S W Mathieson	54
X2	X	X		X1	X			X				S1	X3				S3			X					S2	X	X		M R Halsey	55
X1	X	X		X	X3		S3	X				X1								X					S1	X	X		M J Jones	56
S2	X	X2		X	X3		S1	X				X		X			X1						S3		X	X			R Styles	57
39	41	37	5	33	43		11	46	17	9	12	30	1	6	1	7	3	2	9	40	3		4		38	37	30	2	FL Appearances	
5		4		9	2	3	4		7	5	9	5	2	1		13	3	1		1	1	1		6	1	2	2	1	FL Sub Appearances	
4	3	4	1	3	4			4	3	1+1	3		1			4	1+1				4		0+1		4	2	2+1		CC Appearances	
4	4	4		4	4			4	2+1	0+2	3		1	1		0+3					4		0+1		4	3	4		FAC Appearances	
2	3	3		2+1	3			3	1		1	1		1		0+3					3	1			2	3	3		AWS Appearances	

SCUNTHORPE UNITED RECORDS AND STATISTICS

CLUB RECORDS

RECORD LEAGUE VICTORY
8-1 v LutonTown, Div 3, 24.4.1965
Most Goals Scored in a Cup Tie
9-0 v Boston United, FA Cup 1st Round,21.11.1953

RECORD LEAGUE DEFEAT
0-8 v Carlisle United, Div 3N, 25.12.1952
Record Cup Defeat
0-7 v Coventry City, FA Cup Round 1, 29.11.1934

MOST LEAGUE POINTS
(3pts a win) 83, Div 4, 1982-83
(2pts a win) 66, Div 3N,1957-58

MOST LEAGUE GOALS
88, Div 3N, 1957-58

RECORD TRANSFER FEE RECEIVED
£400,000 from Aston Villa for Neil Cox, February1991

RECORD TRANSFER FEE PAID
£80,000 to York City for Ian Helliwell, August 1991

BEST PERFORMANCES
League: 4th Div 2, 1961-62 FA Cup: 5th Round 1957-58,1969-70
League Cup: Never beyond 3rd Round

HONOURS
Div 3N Champions 1957-58

LEAGUE CAREER
Elected to Div 3N 1950   Promoted to Div 2 1957-58
Relegated to Div 3 1963-64
Relegated to Div 4 1967-68   Promoted to Div 3 1971-72
Relegated to Div 41972-73   Promoted to Div 3 1982-83
Relegated to Div 4 (now Div 3) 1983-84

INDIVIDUAL CLUB RECORDS

MOST APPEARANCES FOR CLUB
Jack Brownsword (1950-65): League 597 + Cup 54 Total 651

MOST CAPPED PLAYER
No Scunthorpe player has won an international cap

RECORD GOALSCORER IN A MATCH:
Barrie Thomas 5 v Luton Town (h), 8-1, Div 3,24.4.1965

RECORD LEAGUE GOALSCORER IN A SEASON
Barrie Thomas 31, Div 2, 1961-62   In AllCompetitions: Barrie Thomas, 31 (all league)

RECORD LEAGUE GOALSCORER IN A CAREER
Steve Cammack 110   In All Competitions: Steve Cammack 120 (League 110, FA Cup 6, League Cup 2, AMC 2) 1979-81 & 1981-86

OLDEST PLAYER IN A LEAGUE MATCH
Jack Brownsword, 41 years, 1965

YOUNGEST PLAYER IN A LEAGUE MATCH
Mike Farrell, 16 years 240 days, 8.11.1975

PREVIOUS MANAGERS

Leslie Jones 1950-51   Bill Corkhill 1951-56   Ron Stuart1956-58   Tony Macshane 1958-59   Bill Lambton (3 days) 1959   Frank Soo 1959-60   Dick Duckworth 1960-64   Freddie Goodwin 1964-67   Ron Ashman 1967-73 Ron Bradley 1973-74   Dickie Rooks 1974-76   Ron Ashman 1976-81   John Duncan1981-83   Allan Clarke 1983-84   Frank Barlow 1984-87   Mick Buxton 1987-91   Bill Green 1991-93   Richard Money 1993-95   Dave Moore 1994-96, Mick Buxton 1996-97.

ADDITIONAL INFORMATION
Previous League: Midland League
Previous Name: Merged with Lindsey United in 1910 to become Scunthorpe and Lindsey United. Dropped the name Lindsey in 1958
Club colours: Sky blue & claret halved shirts, white shorts & socks.
Change colours:
Reserves League: Pontins Central League Div 3.

LONGEST LEAGUE RUNS			
of undefeated matches:	15 (1957-58, 1971-72)	of league matches w/out a win:	14 (1973-74-1974-75)
of undefeated home matches:	21 (1950-51)	of undefeated away matches:	9 (1981-82-1982-83)
without home win:	7 (1963-64, 1972-73, 1989)	without an away win:	30 (1977-78)
of league wins:	6 (1954, 1965)	of home wins:	7 (1984-85, 1987)
of league defeats:	7 (1972-73)	of away wins:	5 (1965-66)

THE MANAGER

Brain Laws . . . . appointed February 1997.

Previous Clubs
As Manager . . . . Grimsby Town.
As Asst.Man/Coach . . . . None.
As a player . . . . Burnley, Huddersfield, Middlesbrough, Nottingham Forest, Grimsby, Darlington, Scunthorpe.

Honours
As a Manager . . . . None.
As a Player . . . . Football League XI. England 'B' cap.

SCUNTHORPE UNITED

PLAYERS NAME / Honours	Ht	Wt	Birthdate	Birthplace / Transfers	Contract Date	Clubs	League	L/Cup	FA Cup	Other	Lge	L/C	FAC	Oth
G O A L K E E P E R														
Clarke Tim	6.3	13.7	9/19/68	Stourbridge		Halesowen Town			1					
				£25000	10/22/90	Coventry City								
				£15000	7/22/91	Huddersfield Town	70	7	6	8				
				Loan	2/12/93	Rochdale	2							
					10/21/93	Shrewsbury Town	30+1	3		1				
				Free	9/28/96	York City	17	1	4					
				Loan	2/21/97	Scunthorpe United	6							
					3/25/97	Scunthorpe United	50	3	4					
Evans Thomas R	6	12	12/31/76	Doncaster	7/3/95	Sheffield United (T)								
				Free	6/14/96	Crystal Palace								
				Free	8/22/97	Scunthorpe United	5	1						
D E F E N C E														
Fickling Ashley	5.1	11	15/11/72	Sheffield	26/07/91	Sheffield United		1						
E: u18.8.				Loan	26/11/92	Darlington	14			1				
				Loan	12/08/93	Darlington	1	1						
				Free	23/03/95	Grimsby Town	26+13	2+1	2+1		2			
				Loan	3/26/98	Darlington	8							
					7/1/98	Scunthorpe United								
Hope Chris	6.1	12.7	11/14/72	Sheffield		Darlington								
				Free	8/23/90	Nottingham Forest								
				£50000	7/5/93	Scunthorpe United	188+8	9	14	8	11		1	
McAuley Sean	6	11.9	6/23/72		7/1/90	Manchester United								
S: u21.1.					4/22/92	St.Johnstone	52+2	3	3					
				Loan	11/4/94	Chesterfield	1		1+1	2	1			
					7/21/95	Hartlepool United	83	6	3	2	1			
					3/26/97	Scunthorpe United	39+5	3	2		1			
Neil James D	5.8	10.05	2/28/74	Bury St.Ed	7/13/94	Grimsby Town	1+1							
				Free	8/7/97	Scunthorpe United	6+1	1						
Nottingham Steven E	6	11.3	6/21/80	Peterborough	5/1/98	Scunthorpe Utd (T)	1							
Stanton Nathan	5.9	11.3	5/6/81	Nottingham	4/10/98	Scunthorpe United	0+1							
E: Y.														
Wilcox Russell	6	11.1	3/25/64	Hemsworth	5/28/80	Doncaster Rovers	1							
E: SP.3. Div.4'87.DIV3 95/96				Free	8/1/81	Frickley Athletic			7				1	
				£15000	6/30/86	Northampton Town	137+1	6	10	8	9			1
				£120000	8/6/90	Hull City	92+8	5	5	5+1	7		1	
				£60000	7/30/93	Doncaster Rovers	77	3	3	3	6	1		
				£60000	9/21/95	Preston North End	62	4	2	1	1		1	
					7/7/97	Scunthorpe United	30+1	2+1	4		2		2	
M I D F I E L D														
Calvo-Garcia Alexander	5.11	11.8	1/1/72	Ordizia		Scunthorpe United	46+11	4	6	3	7	3	1	1
Eyre John R	6.1	11.3	10/9/74	Hull	7/16/93	Oldham Athletic	4+6	0+2			1			
				Loan	12/15/94	Scunthorpe United	9				8			
				£40000	7/4/95	Scunthorpe United	109+14	7	8	2	28	2	1	1
Graves Wayne A	5.8	10.7	9/18/80	Scubthorpe	4/10/98	Scunthorpe Utd (T)	0+3							
Harsley Paul	5.8	11.5	5/29/78	Scunthorpe	7/16/96	Grimsby Town (T)								
				Free	7/5/97	Scunthorpe United	11+4				1			
Housham Steve	5.11	11.7	2/24/76	Gainsborough	12/23/93	Scunthorpe United	73+16	3+1	5+1	2+1	4			1
Logan Richard A	6.1	13.3	5/24/00	Barnsley		Belper Town								
						Gainsborough T.								
				Free	11/15/93	Huddersfield Town	33+10	3	1	9	1			1
				£20000	10/26/95	Plymouth Argyle	67+19	4	2+2	4	12	1		
				Free	7/1/98	Scunthorpe Utd								
Shakespeare Craig R	5.11	12.5	10/26/63	Birmingham	11/5/81	Walsall	276+8	31	22	18	45	6	6	2
				£300000	6/19/89	Sheffield Wed.	15+2	3		0+1	1			
				£275000	2/8/90	WBA	104+8	6	5	5	12	1	2	1
				£115000	7/14/93	Grimsby Town	84+22	6+1	5+3	0+1	10			
				Free	7/5/97	Scunthorpe United	3+1	1+1	0+1					
				Loan	3/26/98	Telford United								
Walker Justin	5.11	11.08	9/6/75	Nottingham	8/1/92	Nottingham Forest								
E: Y				Loan	3/26/97	Scunthorpe United	8+1							
					5/9/97	Scunthorpe United	38+2	4	3		1			
F O R W A R D														
Bull Gary	5.9	11.7	12/06/66	Tipton	15/10/86	Southampton								
GMVC'91.					29/03/88	Cambridge United	13+6	0+1		0+2	4			
					01/03/89	Barnet	83	4	11	8	37	4	3	2
				£2000	21/07/93	Nottingham Forest	4+8	2	0+3		1			
				Loan	9/12/94	Birmingham City	10			2	6			1
				Loan	17/08/95	Brighton & H.A.	10			1	2			2
				Free	29/12/95	Birmingham City	3+3	0+1	0+2	1				1
				Free	04/03/96	York City	66+17	7+2	5+1		11	2		
				Free	7/1/98	Scunthorpe United								
Gayle John	6.4	13.1	30/07/64	Bromsgrove		Burton Albion								
AMVC'91				£30000	01/03/89	Wimbledon	17+3	3			2			
				£175000	21/11/90	Birmingham City	39+5		2	8+1	10			4
				Loan	20/08/93	Walsall	4				1			
				£100000	13/09/93	Coventry City	3	1+2						
				£70000	17/08/94	Burnley	7+7	1+1	1+1		3	1	1	
				£70000	23/01/95	Stoke City	15+11	2	0+1	3+1	4			
				Loan	14/03/96	Gillingham	9				3			
				£25000	10/02/97	Northampton Town	35+13	1+1	4	9+1	7	2		4
				Free	7/1/98	Scunthorpe United								
Featherstone James L	6.2	12.12	11/12/79	Wharfdale		Blackburn R. (J)								
				Free	4/24/98	Scunthorpe United	0+1							
Forrester Jamie	5.6	10.4	11/1/74	Bradford	1/1/00	Auxerre (France)								
				£60000	10/20/92	Leeds United	7+2		1+1		2			
				Loan	9/1/94	Southend United	3+2							
				Loan	3/10/95	Grimsby Town	7+2				1			
				Free	10/17/95	Grimsby Town	27+14		3+1		6		3	
					3/21/97	Scunthorpe United	51+2	4	4		17		2	
Marshall Lee A	5.9	9.12	8/1/75	Nottingham	8/3/92	Nottingham F. (T)								
				Free	3/20/95	Stockport County	1							
				Free	8/24/96	Eastwood Town								
				£5000	6/13/97	Scunthorpe United	12+9	0+1	1	1	1			
Sheldon Gareth	5.11	12	5/8/80	Barnsley	5/1/98	Scunthorpe Utd (T)	0+1							
Stamp Darryn	6.3	12	9/21/78	Beverley		Hessle								
					7/5/97	Scunthorpe United	4+6	0+1			1			

GLANFORD PARK
Doncaster Road, Scunthorpe DN15 8TD

Capacity 9,200
Covered Standing 2,773
Seating 6,427

First game ....v Hereford Utd, League, 27.8.1988.
First floodlit game ....Huddersfield, Lge Cup, 30.8.1988.

ATTENDANCES
Highest ....8,775 v Rotherham, Div 4, 1.5.1989.
Lowest ....859 v Chesterfield, AMC, 18.12.1990.

OTHER GROUNDS..Old Show Ground.

HOW TO GET TO THE GROUND

From all Directions
Use motorway (M18) to junction 5, exit on to M180, at junction 3 exit on to M181, at roundabout take third exit. The ground can clearly be seen on the right as you approach the roundabout.

Car Parking
Club park adjacent to ground for 800 vehicles.
£1 per car.

Nearest Railway Station
Scunthorpe.

USEFUL TELEPHONE NUMBERS

Club switchboard 01724 848 077
Club fax number 01724 857 986
Clubshop................. 01724 848 077
Ticket Office............. 01724 848 077

Marketing Department...... 01724 848 8077
Internet address
..... http://freespace.virgin.net/sufc/scunthorpe-utd.htm
Clubcall 0891 12 16 52*
*Calls cost 50p per minute at all times. Call costings correct at time of going to press.

MATCHDAY PROGRAMME

Programme Editor .... S Sephton.

Number of pages .... 32.

Price .... £1.70.

Subscriptions .... Apply to club.

Local Newspapers
.... Scunthorpe Evening Telegraph.

Local Radio Stations
.... Radio Humberside, Viking Radio.

MATCHDAY TICKET PRICES

Evening Telegraph Stand (seating)
Adult £10.00
Juniors/Senior Citizens..................... £5.50

GMB Stand (seating)
Adult £9.00
Juniors/Senior Citizens..................... £4.50

British Steel Stand (standing)
Adult £7.00
Juniors/Senior Citizens..................... £3.50

Executive Club
Adult £14.50
Juniors/Senior Citizens..................... £10.00

Matchday Special Ticket
Seating in Main Stand, entry to lounge area, 3 course meal in restaurant, coffee at half-time, programme and car parking.
.... £23.00.

SHREWSBURY TOWN
(The Town or Blues)
NATIONWIDE LEAGUE DIVISION 3
SPONSORED BY: TERN HILL COMMUNICATIONS

1998-99 Back Row L-R: Andrew Tretton, Kevin Joblin, Peter Wilding, Devon White, MArk Williams, Brian Gayle, Nathan Blamey, Anthony Briscoe.
Middle Row: Ray Pullen (Physio), Mark Kearney (Asst. Manager), Steve Kerrigan, Paul Edwards, Glyn Thompson, Austin Berkley, Craaig Herbert, Roger Preece (Yth. Coach), Charle Walker (Chief scout). **Front Row:** Kevin Seabury, Dean Craven, Garth Hanmer, Steve JAgicka, Jake King (Manager), Lee Steele, MArtyn Naylor, Paul Evans, Craig Poutney.

SHREWSBURY TOWN
FORMED IN 1886
TURNED PROFESSIONAL IN 1905
LTD COMPANY IN 1936

PRESIDENT: F C G Fry
VICE-PRESIDENT: Dr J Millard Bryson,
G W Nelson, W H Richards
CHAIRMAN: R Wycherley

DIRECTORS
K R Woodhouse,
M J Starkey, A Hopkins
SECRETARY
M J Starkey (01743 360 111)
COMMERCIAL MANAGER
M Thomas (01743 356 316)

MANAGER: Jake King
ASSITANT MANAGER: Mark Kearney
YOUTH COACH: Roger Preece
CHIEF SCOUT
C Walker
PHYSIOTHERAPIST
Ray Pullen

STATISTICIAN FOR THE DIRECTORY
Richard & Nicola Stocken

After relegation in 1997 hopes were high of a rapid return but the task it seems was considerably under estimated. The drastic changes on the field made by new manager Jake King took much longer to work than anyone anticipated. The club wisely set out to balance the budget on modest gates. Following summer departures King could bring in only non League players or free transfers. It was only towards the season's end that the right blend of youth and experience developed. A total of 33 players were used.

Players like top scorer Lee Steele with 13 league goals, Peter Wilding and Gareth Hanmer gradually looked more comfortable as the season unfolded. Steve Kerrigan signed from Scotland, Andrew Tretton from Derby together with experienced Devon White and Brian Gayle all contributed to a second half table climb.

By the end of September out of the Coca-Cola Cup in Round 1 to Brentford, Town were in 20th place with just two wins. Despite an FA Cup replay exit at Grimsby two months later had seen an improvement to 15th, the result of five wins including a first away win in 12 months at Hull and a 4-3 victory over promoted Macclesfield.

A third Round 1 exit to Hartlepool in the AWS in December and 18th spot virtually brought the season to an end, no surprise as King still searched for the right blend on the field.

The lowest point of the season in January was a 0-1 defeat at Doncaster and after a 0-3 defeat at Torquay there followed a marked improvement. Just five defeats in the last 19 games. This included a draw at champions Notts County together with wins at Rotherham, Swansea and a dramatic 3-2 win at Orient. 0-2 down with only 10 men a second-half Lee Steele hat trick secured the points. The final position 13th.

Dreadful gates underline Shrewsbury's problems. Total league gates for 23 games just reached one premiership gate at Old Trafford. The club can only progress through shrewd transfer deals. Manager King has shown early signs of his ability in this area. Many doubted early season signings but they developed well and he certainly maximised assets in the October sale of Dave Walton to Crewe for a club record £700,000. More prized assets may need to be sold to survive. A way of life at Gay Meadow but hopes are realistic that 1999 will see a promotion drive.

RICHARD STOCKEN

SHREWSBURY TOWN

Division 3	:13th			FA CUP: 1st Round				LC CUP: 1st Round			AWS: Northern Round 1

M	DATE	COMP.	VEN	OPPONENTS	RESULT	H/T	LP	GOAL SCORERS/GOAL TIMES	ATT.
1	A 09	FL	H	Doncaster Rovers	W 2-1	1-0	7	Walton 8, Currie 55	3029
2	12	CC 1/1	A	Brentford	D 1-1	0-0		Currie 78	(2040)
3	15	FL	A	Lincoln City	L 0-1	0-0	14		(3019)
4	23	FL	H	Torquay United	L 1-2	0-0	18	Evans 82	2556
5	26	CC 1/2	H	Brentford	L 3-5	0-3		Steele 55, 68, 82 (pen)	2136
6	30	FL	A	Cambridge United	L 3-4	1-1	19	Evans 19, Scott 52, Dempsey 88	(2585)
7	S 02	FL	A	Cardiff City	D 2-2	1-0	19	Berkeley 39, Steele 52	(4271)
8	09	FL	H	Rochdale	W 1-0	0-0	13	Evans 78 (pen)	2410
9	13	FL	A	Chester City	L 0-2	0-1	17		(2853)
10	20	FL	H	Notts County	L 1-2	0-0	20	Blamey 51	2532
11	27	FL	A	Hartlepool United	L 1-2	0-2	20	Evans 78 (pen)	(2253)
12	O 04	FL	A	Rotherham United	W 2-1	1-0	19	White 13, Currie 83 (pen)	2432
13	11	FL	H	Barnet	W 2-0	1-0	19	Steele 29, Currie 76	2112
14	18	FL	A	Colchester United	D 1-1	1-0	19	Seabury 25	(2977)
15	21	FL	A	Scunthorpe United	D 1-1	1-1	19	Currie 39 (pen)	(2303)
16	25	FL	H	Scarborough	L 0-1	0-0	19		2395
17	N 01	FL	H	Mansfield Town	W 3-2	1-1	15	White 43, Scott 66, 78	2338
18	04	FL	A	Peterborough United	D 1-1	0-1	17	White 65	(4727)
19	08	FL	A	Hull City	W 4-1	2-0	15	Steele 17, White 45, 52, Scott 69	(4758)
20	15	FAC 1	H	Grimsby Town	D 1-1	0-1		Herbert 67	3193
21	18	FL	H	Macclesfield Town	W 4-3	1-2	12	White 27, 57, 84, Scott 58	2600
22	22	FL	A	Exeter City	D 2-2	1-1	13	Scott 17, 79	(4041)
23	25	FAC 1R	A	Grimsby Town	L 0-2	0-2			(3242)
24	29	FL	H	Swansea City	L 0-1	0-0	15		2697
25	D 09	AWS N1	H	Hartlepool United	L 1-2	0-0		Wilding 76	1130
26	13	FL	H	Leyton Orient	L 1-2	0-2	17	Steele 90	2137
27	20	FL	A	Brighton & H.A.	D 0-0	0-0	17		(1917)
28	26	FL	A	Rochdale	L 1-3	1-1	18	Wilding 45	(2247)
29	28	FL	H	Cardiff City	W 3-2	1-0	16	Brown 37, White 53, Preece 86	3238
30	J 10	FL	A	Doncaster Rovers	L 0-1	0-0	18		(1116)
31	17	FL	H	Cambridge United	D 1-1	1-1	18	Taylor 1 (OG)	2210
32	24	FL	A	Torquay United	L 0-3	0-2	19		(1996)
33	31	FL	H	Chester City	D 1-1	1-0	19	Steele 7	3002
34	F 06	FL	A	Notts County	D 1-1	1-0	20	Hanmer 16	(5789)
35	14	FL	A	Rotherham United	W 1-0	0-0	17	Steele 62	(3603)
36	21	FL	H	Hartlepool United	W 1-0	0-0	16	Evans 90	2160
37	24	FL	H	Colchester United	L 0-2	0-1	17		1972
38	28	FL	A	Barnet	D 1-1	1-1	19	Tretton 25	(2322)
39	M 03	FL	H	Hull City	W 2-0	0-0	17	Evans 79, Kerrigan 90	1523
40	07	FL	A	Mansfield Town	D 1-1	1-0	18	Seabury 18	(2219)
41	14	FL	H	Peterborough United	W 4-1	3-0	16	White 29, Steele 36, 57, Scott 42	2421
42	21	FL	A	Macclesfield Town	L 1-2	0-0	18	Brown 47	(3013)
43	24	FL	H	Lincoln City	L 0-2	0-1	18		1877
44	28	FL	H	Exeter City	D 1-1	1-0	18	Steele 26	2251
45	31	FL	A	Darlington	L 1-3	1-1	19	Scott 41	(1816)
46	A 04	FL	A	Swansea City	W 1-0	1-0	18	Berkeley 40	(2623)
47	11	FL	H	Darlington	W 3-0	0-0	15	Scott 52, Steele 57, Berkeley 78	1942
48	13	FL	A	Leyton Orient	W 3-2	0-1	14	Steele 55, 67, 82	(4956)
49	18	FL	H	Brighton & H.A.	W 2-1	0-1	13	Kerrigan 83, Jagielka 84	2728
50	25	FL	A	Scarborough	D 0-0	0-0	13		(3712)
51	M 02	FL	H	Scunthorpe United	L 0-2	0-1	13		2704

Best Home League Attendance: 3238 V Cardiff City	Smallest :1523 V Hull City	Average :2403

Goal Scorers:

FL	(61)	Steele 13, Scott 10, White 10, Evans 6, Currie 4, Berkeley 3, Brown 2, Kerrigan 2, Seabury 2, Blamey 1, Dempsey 1, Hanmer 1, Jagielka 1, Preece 1, Tretton 1, Walton 1, Wilding 1, Opponents 1
CC	(4)	Steele 3, Currie 1
FAC	(1)	Herbert 1
AWS	(1)	Wilding 1

(M) Berkeley	(D) Blamey	(F) Brown	(M) Currie	(M) Dempsey	(F) Dudley	(G) Edwards	(M) Evans	(G) Gall	(D) Gayle	(D) Griffiths	(M) Hanmer	(D) Herbert	(M) Jagielka	(F) Kernigan	(M) Naylor	(D) Nwadike	(M) Preece	(D) Scott	(D) Seabury	(M) Steele	(D) Taylor L	(F) Taylor M	(D) Tretton	(D) Walton	(F) Ward	(M) White	(M) Wilding	(F) Williams	Player	
S	X	X	X		X	X	X					X	S1		X				S	X		X		X				X	D R Crick	1
S	X	X	X	X		X	X					X	S2						S1	X		X		X				X	G Singh	2
S	X	X	X	X		X	X					X	S1						S	X		X		X				X	M L Dean	3
S3	X	S1	X	X		X	X					X						S2	X		X				X			X	M J Jones	4
S1		S3			X	X			X	X	X		X	X		X	S2	X	X	X		X						X	A Bates	5
X		S2		S1	X	X			X	X	X		X	X		X	X	X	X	X	S							X	M Fletcher	6
X		X		X		X	X			S	X	X1					X	S	X	X	X				S1				D Pugh	7
X		X		X		X	X			S	X	X					X	S2	X		X				S1		X	X	C J Foy	8
X		X	S1	X		X	X			S	X						X	S2	X		X				X		X	X	A N Butler	9
S2	X	S1	S3	X		X	X				X	X						X	X	X				X				X	A R Hall	10
S2	X		S1			X	X		X		X	X					X	X	S	X				X		X		T Jones	11
S1	X	X				X	X		X		X	X					X	S	S	X				X		X		A R Leake	12
X	X	X	X	S1			S	X	X		X	X					X		S2	X				X		X	X	M D Messias	13
X	X	X	X	S1			S	X	X		X	X					X	X	S	X						X	X	R J Harris	14
X	X	X	X	S2			S3	X	X		X	X					X	S1	X							X	X	R Pearson	15
X	X	X	X	S			S2	X	X		X	X	S1				X	S	X							X	X	B Coddington	16
	X		X		X	X	X	X	X		X	X					X	S2	S1	X				S3	X	X	M C Bailey	17
	S	S	S			X	X		X	X		X	X				X	X	X	X					X	X	J A Kirkby	18
	S	S	S			X	X		X	X		X	X				X	X	X	X					X	X	F G Stretton	19
S	S	S	S		S1	X	X		X	X		X	X				X	X	X	X	X				X	X	U D Rennie	20
	S	S	S			X	X		X	X		X	X				X	X	X	X					X	X	D Pugh	21
	S1	S2	S			X	X		X	X		X	X				X	X	X	X					X	X	B Knight	22
S		X	S		S1	X	X		X	X		X	X				X	X	X	X		X	S		S1	X	X	U D Rennie	23
S2		S3				X	X		X	X		X	X				X2	X	X1			S1		X3	X	X	M L Dean	24
X	X					X	X		X	X		X	X					X		X		X			X	X		25
S1		X			X		X		X			X	S		S	X	X1		X	X		X			X	X	E K Wolstenholme	26
S		X			X		X	X	S1			X	X			X1		X1	X	X			X	X	R D Furnandiz	27
		S2			X		X		X	S1	S3		X	X3	X	X		X2	X			X	X1	A G Wiley	28
X	X1			X			X		X	X	S		X	S		X	S1	S1	X			X	X			X	G Singh	29
X	X		X			X	X	S					X1	S1	X		X	X		X	S2	M Fletcher	30
S1	S1		X	X	X		S		X	X1			X1	X		X	X	X			X	T Jones	31
S1			S1	X	X		X	S		X1		X1	X		X	X	X	X	X		X	R J Harris	32
X		X1		X	X	X	S		S			X	X		X	X	X	X	X		S1	A Bates	33
X			X	X	X	X	S			S		X	X		X	X	X	X	X	X	S	K M Lynch	34
X			X	X	X	X	S		S1			X	X	X1	X2	X	X1	X			X	S2	M J Jones	35
X			X	X	X	X	X		S			X	X	X	X1	X		X1	X		X	S	P Rejer	36
X			X	X	X	X	S1			X	X1	X	X2			X		X	S	S2	C R Wilkes	37
X			X	X	X	X	S	X		X	S	X			X		X	X	S	A R Hall	38
X			X	X	X	X	S	X		X	S	X		X1		X1	X	M S Pike	39
X	S		X	X	X	X	X		X	S	X	S1		X1	X	S G Bennett	40
X	S	X		X	X	X	S			X	X	X		X1	X	S1	G Cain	41
X	S	X1		X	X	X	X	S1		X	X	X		X	X	J P Robinson	42
X		X		X	X	X	S	S1		S	X	X		X1	X	S J Baines	43
X		X1		X	X	X	S	X		S	X	X		S1	X	G Laws	44
X	X3		X	X1	X	X	S2	X		S1	X	X2		X	S3	T Jones	45
X	X		X	X	X	X	S	X		S	X	X		S	X	A R Leake	46
X2	X1		X	X	X	X	S1	X		S2	X	X		S	X	P R Richards	47
X	X1		X	X	X	X	S1	X		S	X	X		S	X	M E Pierce	48
X	X1		X	X	X	X	S1	X		S	X	X		S	X	G Singh	49
X2	X		X	X	X	X	S2			S	X	X	X	X1	X	S1	B Coddington	50
	X2			X	X1	X	X	S1	X3		X	X	X	X	X	S3	R Styles	51
28	9	24	10	8	3	34	37	11	23	6	39	23	4	11	2	1	25	28	35	37	1	17	14	6	3	30	33		FL Appearances	
8		6	6	4	1		2						1	12	3				2	6	4	1		1		3	2	1	FL Sub Appearances	5
0+1		1+1	1	1			2					1	2	1+1		1	0+1		1	1+1	2		2			2	2		CC Appearances	
			1		0+1	2	2					2	2					2	2	2	1	2			0+1	2	2		FAC Appearances	
1		1					1	1				1	1					1	1	1	1					1	1		AWS Appearances	

Also Played: (M) Craven X(51). (G) Germaine X(30).(M) Overson X(10,11), (M) Pountney S2(51).

629

CLUB RECORDS

RECORD LEAGUE VICTORY
7-0 v Swindon Town, Div 3S, 6.5.1955
Most Goals Scored in a League Match
7-2 v Luton Town (a), Div 3, 10.3.1965   7-1 v Blackburn Rovers (h),
Div 3, 2.10.1971   7-4 v Doncaster Rovers, Div 4,1.2.1975
Most Goals Scored in a Cup Tie
11-2 v Marine (h), FA Cup 1st Rnd, 11.11.95.
RECORD LEAGUE DEFEAT
1-8 v Norwich City (h), Div 3S, 13.9.1952   1-8 v Coventry City (a),
Div 3, 22.10.1963   0-7 v Bristol Rovers (a), Div 3, 21.3.1964

MOST LEAGUE GOALS
101, Division 4, 1958-59

MOST LEAGUE POINTS
(3pts for win) 79, Div 3, 1993-94
(2pts for win) 62,Division 4, 1974-75

RECORD TRANSFER FEE RECEIVED
£700,000 from Crewe for Dave Walton, 20.10.97.
RECORD TRANSFER FEE PAID
£100,000 to Aldershot for John Dungworth in November1979.
£100,000 to Southampton for Mark Blake, August 1990

BEST PERFORMANCES
League: 8th Division 2, 1983-84, 1984-85
FA Cup: 6th Round1978-79, 1981-82
League Cup: Semi-Final 1960-61
Welsh Cup: Winners 1891,1938, 1977, 1979, 1984, 1985
HONOURS
Champions Div 3 1978-79, 1993-94
Welsh Cup Winners (6 times)

LEAGUE CAREER
Elected to Div 3N 1950   Reverted to Div 3S 1951   Joined Div4
1958
Promoted to Div 3 1958-59   Relegated to Div 4 1973-74
Promoted to Div 31974-75   Promoted to Div 2 1978-79
Relegated to Div 3 1988-89   Relegated to Div 4 (now Div 3) 1991-
92   Promoted to Div 2 1993-94. Relegated to Div 3 1996-97.

INDIVIDUAL CLUB RECORDS

MOST APPEARANCES FOR CLUB
Colin Griffin 1975-89: League 402+4 + FA Cup 30 +League Cup 25
+ Others 9 Total 466+4 subs

MOST CAPPED PLAYER
Jimmy McLoughlin 5, Northern Ireland & Bernard McNally
5,Northern Ireland For England: None

RECORD GOALSCORER IN A MATCH
Alf Wood 5 v Blackburn Rovers (h), 7-1, Div 3,2.10.1971

RECORD LEAGUE GOALSCORER IN A SEASON
Arthur Rowley 38, Div 3, 1958-59 In All Competitions: Alf Wood
40 (League 35, FA Cup 2, League Cup 3) 1971-72

RECORD LEAGUE GOALSCORER IN A CAREER
Arthur Rowley 152, 1958-65 In All Competitions: Arthur Rowley
167 (League 152, FA Cup 11, League Cup 4) 1958-65

OLDEST PLAYER IN A LEAGUE MATCH
Asa Hartford, 40 years 69 days v Brentford1.1.1991

YOUNGEST PLAYER IN A LEAGUE MATCH
Graham French, 16 years 175 days v Reading (H), 30.09.1961.

PREVIOUS MANAGERS

(Since 1950): 1950-52 Sammy Crooks 1952-54 Walter Rowley
1954-56 Harry Potts 1956-57 John Spuhler 1957-68 Arthur
Rowley 1968-72Harry Gregg 1972-74 Maurice Evans 1974-78
Alan Durban 1978 Ritchie Barker 1978-84 Graham Turner 1984-
87 Chic Bates 1987 Ken Brown 1987-90 Ian McNeil 1990-91
Asa Hartford 1991-93 John Bond Fred Davies 1993-97.
ADDITIONAL INFORMATION
Previous League: Shropshire County Lge, Birmingham League
Midland League
Club colours: Blue shirts, white shorts, blue socks.
Change colours: White & sky blue stripes, black shorts, white
socks.
Reserves League: Pontins League.
'A' Team: Midland Melville Youth Lge.

LONGEST LEAGUE RUNS

of undefeated matches:	16 (30.10.1993 - 26.2.1994)	of league matches w/out a win:	17 (1992)
of undefeated home matches:	31 (1978-79)	of undefeated away matches:	14 (30.10.1993 - 30.4.1994)
without home win:	9 (1992)	without an away win:	22 (02.11.1996 - 08.11.1997)
of league wins:	7 (1955)	of home wins:	8 (1955, 1975)
of league defeats:	7 (1951-52, 1987)	of away wins:	5 (6.11.1993 - 1.1.1994)

THE MANAGER

JAKE KING . . . . appointed May 1997.

PREVIOUS CLUBS
As Manager . . . . Telford United.
As Asst.Man/Coach . . . . Newtown.
As a player. . . . . Shrewsbury, Wrexham, Cardiff.

HONOURS
As a Manager . . . . None.
As a Player . . . . Division 3 Championship, Welsh Cup.

SHREWSBURY TOWN

PLAYERS NAME / Honours	Ht	Wt	Birthdate	Birthplace / Transfers	Contract Date	Clubs	League	L/Cup	FA Cup	Other	Lge	L/C	FAC	Oth
G O A L K E E P E R														
Edwards Paul	5.11	11.5	2/22/65	Liverpool		Leek Town								
Div.3'94.				Free	8/24/88	Crewe Alexandra	29	4	3	4				
				Free	8/6/92	Shrewsbury Town	203	13	15+1	14				
D E F E N C E														
Blamey Nathan	5.11	11	6/10/77	Plymouth		Southampton								
				Free	4/1/97	Shrewsbury Town	15	1			1			
Gayle Brian W	6.1	13.12	3/6/65	Kingston	10/31/84	Wimbledon	76+7	7	8	2	3	1	1	
				£325000	7/6/88	Manchester City	55	8	2	1	3			
				£330000	1/19/90	Ipswich Town	58	3	0+1		4			
				£750000	9/17/91	Sheffield United	115+2	9	11	1	9		1	1
				Free	8/14/96	Exeter City	10	1						
				Free	10/10/96	Rotherham United								
				Loan	3/27/97	Bristol Rovers								
				Free	7/18/97	Bristol Rovers	16	2						
				Free	12/8/97	Shrewsbury Town	23							
Hanmer Gareth C	5.6	10.3	10/12/73	Shrewsbury		Newtown								
				£20000	6/18/96	WBA								
				£10000	7/16/97	Shrewsbury Town	39	1	2	1	1			
Herbert Craig	6	12	11/9/75	Coventry		Torquay United								
				Free	3/18/94	WBA	8	2		1				1
				Free	7/23/97	Shrewsbury Town	23+1	2	2				1	
Jobling Kevin A	5.9	10.11	01/01/68	Sunderland	09/01/86	Leicester City	4+5		0+1	3				2
					19/02/88	Grimsby Town	251+34	13+4	10+3	7+7	10	1	2	
				Loan	10/01/94	Scunthorpe United				1				
				Free	7/1/98	Shrewsbury Town								
Naylor Martin	5.9	10.2	8/2/77	Walsall		Telford United								
				Free	7/2/97	Shrewsbury Town	2	1						
Seabury Kevin	5.9	11.6	11/24/73	Shrewsbury	7/6/92	Shrewsbury Town	121+20	6+2	8	5+1	2	1		
Tretton Andrew T	6.1	12.07	10/9/76	Derby	5/31/94	Derby County								
				Free	5/31/97	Chesterfield								
				Free	12/11/97	Shrewsbury Town	14				1			
Wilding Peter J	0.1	12.12	11/28/68	Shrewsbury		Telford United								
				£10000	6/10/97	Shrewsbury Town	33+1	2	2	1	1			1
M I D F I E L D														
Berkeley Austin	5.9	10.1	1/28/73	Dartford	5/13/91	Gillingham	0+3			0+3				
				Free	5/16/92	Swindon Town	0+1	0+1		3+1				1
				Free	9/5/95	Shrewsbury Town	84+14	4+2	5+1	6	4			
Craven Dean	5.7	10.10	2/17/79	Shrewsbury	7/1/97	WBA (T)								
				Free	3/26/98	Shrewsbury Town	1							
Evans Paul S	5.6	10.8	9/1/74	Oswestry	7/2/93	Shrewsbury Town	146+20	10+2	11+1	7	20	1	2	1
Div.3'94.														
Preece Roger	5.9	10.4	6/9/69	Much Wenlock		Coventry City								
				Free	8/15/86	Wrexham	89+21	2+1	5	8+1	12			1
				Free	8/14/90	Chester City	167+5	10	8	11	4		1	
				Free	7/4/97	Shrewsbury Town	25+2		2		1			
F O R W A R D														
Briscoe Anthony M			8/16/78	Birmingham		Shrewsbury Town	0+1							
Jagielka Stephen	5.8	11.5	3/10/78	Manchester	7/15/96	Stoke City (T)								
				Free	7/30/97	Shrewsbury Town	4+12	1+1			1			
Kerrigan Steven P	6.1	12.4	10/9/72	Bailliston		Aye United								
				£25000	1/21/98	Shrewsbury Town	11+3				2			
Pountney Craig F	5.7	9.10	11/23/79	Bromsgrove	5/1/97	Shrewsbury Town (T)	0+1							
Steele Lee A J	5.8	12.7	12/7/73	Liverpool		Northwich Victoria								
				£30000	7/23/97	Shrewsbury Town	37+1	2	1	1	13	3		
White Devon W	6.3	13.8	3/2/64	Nottingham		Arnold Kingswell								
				Free	12/14/84	Lincoln City	21+8			2+1	4			2
				Free	10/1/86	Boston United								
				Free	8/21/87	Bristol Rovers	190+12	9	10	19	54	2	3	2
				£100000	3/28/92	Cambridge United	157	4	1	1	4	1		1
				£100000	1/26/93	QPR	15+10	1+1			9			
				£100000	12/23/94	Notts County	16+4		2	3	7		1	
				£100000	2/16/96	Watford	26+10	4	2		8		1	
					3/15/97	Notts County	11+3	3			2	1		
				£30000	9/23/97	Shrewsbury Town	30+2		2		10			
Williams Mark	5.11	13.6	12/10/73	Bangor	7/6/92	Shrewsbury T. (T)	0+3							
				Free	3/8/93	Telford United								
				Free	7/2/97	Shrewsbury Town	0+5							

GAY MEADOW
Shrewsbury SY2 6AB

Capacity 8,000
Covered Standing 2,000
Seating 3,500

First game ....v Wolves Res. (Birmingham Lge), 10.9.1910.
First floodlit game ....v Q.P.R., Div.3, 21.11.1959.

ATTENDANCES
Highest ....18,917 v Walsall, Div.3, 26.4.1961.
Lowest ....920 v Torquay Utd, Associate Members Cup, 16.1.1991.

OTHER GROUNDS ....Old Racecourse. Copthorne.

HOW TO GET TO THE GROUND

From the North
Use A49 or A53 and at roundabout take 2nd exit (A5112) into Telford Way. In 0.8 miles at roundabout take 2nd exit. Then at 'T' junction turn right into Abbey Foregate (A458) for Shrewsbury Town FC.
From the East
Use A5 then A458 into Shrewsbury and into Abbey Foregate for Shrewsbury Town FC.
From the South
Use A49 and follow signs Shrewsbury Town centre then at end of Coleham Head turn right in to Abbey Foregate for Shrewsbury Town FC.
From the West
Use A458 then A5 around Shrewsbury Ring Road, Roman Road, then turn left A49 into Hereford Road, and at end of Coleman Head turn right into Abbey Foregate for Shrewsbury Town.

Car Parking: Park adjacent to ground and a public car park five minutes away.
Nearest Railway Station: Shrewsbury (01743 64041)

USEFUL TELEPHONE NUMBERS

Club switchboard 01743 360 111
Club fax number 01743 236 384
Club Shop 01743 356 316
Ticket Office 01743 360 111

Marketing Department. 01743 356 316
Internet address: . www.shrewsburytown.co.uk
Town Talk 0891 12 11 94*

*Calls cost 50p per minute at all times. Call costings correct at time of going to press.

MATCHDAY PROGRAMME

Programme Editor . . . . Don Stanton.

Number of pages . . . . 40.

Price . . . . £1.70.

Subscriptions . . . . . Aply to club for details.

Local Newspapers
. . . Shropshire Star, Shrewsbury Chronicle.

Local Radio Stations
. . . . Radio Shropshire, Beacon Radio.

MATCHDAY TICKET PRICES

Wakeman Stand (members only)
Adults £10
Juv/OAP £6

Centre Stand (members only)
Adults £12
Juv/OAP £12

Family Enclosure (members only)
1 Adult and 1 Child £10.00
Each additional Child £2.00
Each additional adult £12.00
(children must be accompanied by an adult)

Ground
Adults £8.00
Juv/OAP £5.00
(Members only - juniors and senior citizens must hold a membership card to qualify for concessionary admission)

Visiting Supporters
Adults seated/standing . . . . £10.00/£8.00
Juv/OAP seated/standing . . . . £7.00/£5.00

SOUTHEND UNITED
(The Shrimpers)
NATIONWIDE LEAGUE DIVISION 3
SPONSORED BY: PROGRESSIVE PRINTING (UK) LIMITED

1998-99- Back Row L-R: Kevin Maher, Chris Perkins, Leo Roget, Tony Henriksen, Martyn MArgetson, Simon Coleman, Trevor Fitzpatrick, Keith Dublin. **Middle Row:** John Gowens, MArk Beard, Rob Newman, Simon Livett, Andy Harris, Mark Stimson, Julian HAils, Spencer Barham. **Front Row:** Adrian Clarke, David Whyte, Micky Gooding, Alvin Martin, Peter Trevivian, Alex Burns, Nathan Jones.

SOUTHEND UNITED
FORMED IN 1906
TURNED PROFESSIONAL IN 1906
LTD COMPANY IN 1919

PRESIDENT: N J Woodcock
CHAIRMAN: V T Jobson
VICE-CHAIRMAN/CHIEF EXECUTIVE
J W Adams
DIRECTORS
J Bridge, B R Gunner, W R Kelleway,
G King, J Main, R J Osborne,
D M Markscheffel,
MARKETING DIRECTOR
C Wooldridge

MANAGER: Alvin Martin
ASSISTANT MANAGER: Peter Trevivian
YOUTH TEAM MANAGER
Peter Johnson

SPORTS THERAPISTS
John Gowens and Spencer Barham

STATISTICIAN FOR THE DIRECTORY
Dave Goody

For the second season on the bounce Southend United were relegated from the Division from which they started. With the rot setting hard and fast from the 1996/97 demotion they couldn't turn their fortunes around and spent most of the new season in the bottom few places.

With four points from the first three games it look as though life would not to difficult in Division 2, however it turned out that the two clubs, Burnley and Carlisle, from which they had gained the points would also be battling it out at the wrong end of the table.

The Cup competitions gave them little to cheer about either as both the Coca-Cola Cup and FA Cup were over by the second round. Derby County won 6-0 on aggregate in the Coca-Cola Cup and Fulham were the victors in the FA Cup after Cardiff City (4-2 on aggregate) and Woking (2-0 were seen off in the first round of the respective competitions.

Alvin Martin will have learnt alot from his first full season as manager and will be hoping he can take some his experience into the new season and holt the slide of Southend United.

SOUTHEND UNITED

Division 2   :24th   FA CUP: 2nd Round   LC CUP: 2nd Round

M	DATE	COMP.	VEN	OPPONENTS	RESULT		H/T	LP	GOAL SCORERS/GOAL TIMES	ATT.
1	A 09	FL	H	Carlisle United	D	1-1	1-0	11	Boere 25	4507
2	12	CC 1/1	A	Cardiff City	D	1-1	1-0		Byrne 40	(2804)
3	18	FL	A	Luton Town	L	0-1	0-0	20		(5140)
4	23	FL	H	Burnley	W	1-0	1-0	13	Boere 6	4218
5	26	CC 1/2	H	Cardiff City	W	3-1	2-0		Williams 16, 18, Marsh 79	3002
6	30	FL	A	Walsall	L	1-3	1-2	18	Williams 22	(3304)
7	S 02	FL	A	Wycombe Wanderers	L	1-4	1-2	21	Boere 43	(4528)
8	05	FL	H	Brentford	W	3-1	3-1	11	Marsh 3, Boere 25, Clarke 43	3458
9	13	FL	A	Millwall	L	1-3	1-0	17	Boere 19	(8606)
10	16	CC 2/1	H	Derby County	L	0-1	0-1			4011
11	20	FL	H	Fulham	W	1-0	1-0	15	Lewis 16	5026
12	27	FL	A	Blackpool	L	0-3	0-1	19		(4542)
13	O 01	CC 2/2	A	Derby County	L	0-5	0-1			(18490)
14	04	FL	H	Northampton Town	D	0-0	0-0	21		4300
15	11	FL	H	Bristol City	L	0-2	0-1	21		3273
16	18	FL	A	Plymouth Argyle	W	3-2	2-2	19	Clarke 20, N'Diaye 75, Wotton 3 (OG)	(3430)
17	21	FL	A	Wrexham	L	1-3	1-0	20	Rammell 22	(2039)
18	25	FL	H	Oldham Athletic	D	1-1	1-1	21	Coulbault 13	3595
19	N 01	FL	A	Grimsby Town	L	1-5	0-3	21	Coulbault 63	(4501)
20	04	FL	H	Watford	L	0-3	0-2	24		4001
21	08	FL	H	Wigan Athletic	W	1-0	0-0	19	Boere 71	2716
22	15	FAC 1	A	Woking	W	2-0	0-0		Jones 88, Gridelet 90	(4059)
23	18	FL	A	Bournemouth	L	1-2	1-1	19	Dublin 5	(3019)
24	22	FL	H	Bristol Rovers	D	1-1	1-0	20	N'Diaye 40	3653
25	29	FL	A	Chesterfield	L	0-1	0-0	22		(4101)
26	D 02	FL	H	Preston North End	W	3-2	3-2	19	Boere 25 (pen), Gridelet 42, 45	2307
27	06	FAC 2	H	Fulham	L	0-1	0-0			(8537)
28	09	AWS S1	H	Wycombe Wanderers	L	0-1	0-0			1577
29	13	FL	A	Gillingham	W	2-1	0-1	19	Coulbault 89, Boere 90	(4744)
30	19	FL	H	York City	D	4-4	2-2	18	Clarke 28, 42, Dublin 52, 82	3215
31	26	FL	A	Brentford	D	1-1	0-1	19	Coulbault 80	(5341)
32	28	FL	H	Wycombe Wanderers	L	1-2	0-1	19	Thomson 47	5162
33	J 03	FL	H	Luton Town	L	1-2	1-1	20	Thomson 19	5056
34	10	FL	A	Carlisle United	L	0-5	0-1	20		(5389)
35	17	FL	H	Walsall	L	0-1	0-0	20		3310
36	24	FL	A	Burnley	L	0-1	0-1	22		(9386)
37	31	FL	H	Millwall	D	0-0	0-0	24		5705
38	F 06	FL	A	Fulham	L	0-2	0-1	24		(9122)
39	14	FL	A	Northampton Town	L	1-3	1-2	24	Boere 34	(6147)
40	21	FL	H	Blackpool	W	2-1	2-0	24	Dublin 9, Boere 12	3340
41	24	FL	H	Plymouth Argyle	W	3-0	1-0	23	Aldridge 40, Maher 62, Jobson 73	4363
42	28	FL	A	Bristol City	L	0-1	0-1	23		(12049)
43	M 07	FL	H	Grimsby Town	L	0-1	0-0	24		4829
44	14	FL	A	Watford	D	1-1	0-1	24	Thomson 65	(10750)
45	17	FL	A	Wigan Athletic	W	3-1	2-0	23	Thomson 32, Rammell 33, Whyte 87	(2616)
46	21	FL	H	Bournemouth	W	5-3	0-0	22	Boere 59 (pen), 66, Thomson 62, 65, Clarke 88	4823
47	27	FL	A	Bristol Rovers	L	0-2	0-0	23		(5323)
48	A 03	FL	H	Chesterfield	L	0-2	0-1	23		5425
49	11	FL	A	Preston North End	L	0-1	0-0	24		(8096)
50	13	FL	H	Gillingham	D	0-0	0-0	24		6151
51	18	FL	A	York City	D	1-1	1-0	24	Boere 30	(2850)
52	25	FL	A	Oldham Athletic	L	0-2	0-0	24		(4485)
53	M 02	FL	H	Wrexham	L	1-3	1-1	24	Boere 12	4220

Best Home League Attendance: 6151 V Gillingham   Smallest :2307 V Preston North End   Average :4202

Goal Scorers:

FL	(47)	Boere 14, Thomson 6, Clarke 5, Coulbault 4, Dublin 4, Gridelet 2, N'Diaye 2, Rammell 2, Aldridge 1, Jobson 1, Lewis 1, Maher 1, Marsh 1, Whyte 1, Williams 1, Opponents 1
CC	(4)	Williams 2, Byrne 1, Marsh 1
FAC	(2)	Gridelet 1, Jones 1
AWS	(0)	

(F) Aldridge	(M) Allen	(M) Beard	(M) Beeston	(F) Boere	(M) Byrne	(F) Clarke	(D) Coleman	(M) Coulthault	(D) Dublin	(M) Gridelet	(M) Hails	(D) Harris	(D) Jobson	(M) Jones N	(M) Lewis	(M) Maher	(F) Marsh	(M) N'Diaye	(M) Neilsen	(F) Perkins	(F) Rammell	(D) Roget	(G) Royce	(G) Southall	(D) Stimson	(D) Thomson	(M) Whyte	(F) Williams	Player	No.
			X	X	X	S1			X			X		X			X				S2	X	X		X	X			S.G. Bennett	1
			X		X	X			X			X		X			X				S1	X	X		S	X			R J Harris	2
			X	X	X	X			X			X		X			X				S1	X	X		S	X			C J Foy	3
			X	X	X	X			X		S2	X		X			X					X	X			S1		X	M R Halsey	4
			X	X	X	X			X		S2	X		X			X				S1	X	X			S		X	M c Bailey	5
			X	X	X	X			X	S3	S1	X		X							S2	X	X					X	D Pugh	6
			X	X	X	X			X		X	X	S2	X					S1		S	X	X					X	K A Leach	7
			X		S	X			X		X	X	X	X		X			S		S1	X	X					X	B Knight	8
		S	X	X	S1	X			X		X	X	X	X			X				S2	X	X					X	C T Finch	9
			X	X	X	X					X	X	X	X	S2		X				S3	X	X			S1		X	P E Alcock	10
			S3	X	X	X					X	X	X	X	X		X				S2		X					X	P Taylor	11
X				X	X	X					X	X		X	X		X		S	S2	X		X			S1			D Laws	12
X					S	X			X	X	X	X		X	X		X		S	S	X		X			X			M J Brandwood	13
X						X				X	S1	X		X	X		X		S	X	X		X			X			A N Butler	14
X				X	X	X		S2	X	S1	X			X	X		X				X	X		X			S3			D Orr	15
X					X			X	S	X	X			X	X				X		S	X		X			S			C R Wilkes	16
X				X		X		X	S	X	X	X		X	X				X		S1	X		X			S2			A R Hall	17
	X					X		X	X	S2	X			X	X				X		S	X		X			S1			R Styles	18
	X					X		X	X	X	X			X	X1				X		S	X		X			S1			M L Dean	19
	X					X		X	X	X	X			X	S				X		S	X		X			S1			R D Furnandiz	20
	X				S2	X		X	X	X	X			X	X				X			X		X			S1			K A Leach	21
					S1	X		X	X	X	X			X	X				S	S	X		X			X			D J Gallagher	22
	S1		X		X	X		X	X	X	X			X	X		S2		S			X				X			D R Crick	23
S			X		X	X		X	X	X	X			X	X				X			X				S			M Fletcher	24
	X		X		X	S1		X	X	X	X	X1		X					X1		S	X				S1			A G Wiley	25
			X		X	X		X	X	X	X			X	X				X		S	S	X			S1			M R Halsey	26
			X3		X2	X		X	X	X	X			X	S1				X1	S	S	S3	X			X			B Knight	27
	X		X		X	X		X	X					S1	X				X	X	X	X2	X			X1	S2			28
	S		X		X	X		X	X	X	X			X	S				X1	S1		X				X			F G Stretton	29
	S1		X		X	X		X	X	X	X			X					X1	S		X				X			P Taylor	30
	X		X		X	X		X	X	X	X			X					X	S				X	S	S			C J Foy	31
	X				X			X	X	X	X	X	X	X				X2	X1	S			X	S1	S2			R J Harris	32
					X			X	X	X	X	X	X	X	X			X1	S	S		X	X	X			B Knight	33
					X			X	X		X	X	X		X				S	X	S		X	X	X	X	D Laws	34
					X			X	X2	X	X	X	X	X1					S2	S	X		X	X	X	X	S B Bennett	35
			S1		X			X	X2	X	X	X	S	S2	X						X1		X	X	X	P Rejer	36
					X			X	X	X1	X	X	X	X	X	S1	X		S2				X	X	X2	K A Leach	37
					X			X	X	X2	X	X	X	X	X	S2	X		X1				X	X	S1	A Bates	38
					X	X1		S	X	X2	X	X	X	X	S1	X				X		X	X	X	S2	A R Leake	39
					X2		X	X	X	S1	X	X	X1	X				S			X		X			S2	P S Danson	40
X					X1		X3	X	X2	S2	X	X	X	X							S1		X		S3	M J Brandwood	41
X1					X		X2	X	X	X	X	X	X1	X					S		X		S2	S3	R Styles	42
X3					X	S1	X	X	X	X	X	X1	X	X				X2		X		S2	S3	G Singh	43
					X	X	S1	X	X	X	X	S		X	S				X		X		X	X	S	D R Crick	44
			S2		X	X3	X	X	X	X	X1		X				X2		X		X	X	X	S1	S W Mathieson	45
S3					X2	X3	X	X	X	X	X1	X					S2		X		X	X	X	S1	A Bates	46
S1					X	X2	X	X	X1	X	X								X		X	X	X	S2		47
S2					X	X	X	X	X2	X								S		X	S	X	X1	X	M J Jones	48
X					S1	X	X1	X	S	X		X	S				X	S	X	X	X	X	G B Frankland	49
X					X	X	S1	X	X1	X	S				S	X	X	X	X	X	D Orr	50
X			X		X	S2	X2	X	X		X	S1	X		X	X	X1	G Laws	51
X					X	X1	X	X	S	X	S		X	X	S1	M L Dean	52
S2					X	X2	X	X	X	S3	X1	X	S1	X3	X	X	J A Kirkby	53
7	5	6	5	28	9	42	14	30	41	31	41	26	8	33	14	18	9	15	1	3	18	11	37	9	17	16	3	6	FL Appearances	
4		2	1	3	1	3		4		6	3	1		5			2	4	2	8					3	17	5		FL Sub Appearances	
		1	3	2	3	4		3	2	2+1	3		2		4	1+1		4			1+3	3	4			2		1+1	CC Appearances	
			1+1	2		2		2	2	2	2		2	1+1	1		1+1			1			1		2	2			FAC Appearances	
	1				1	1		1	0+1	1	1		1	1	1		1			1		1	0+1			1			AWS Appearances	

Also Played: (M) Fitzpatrick S1(33,35), X(34). (G) Henriksen S(22), S2(27). (M) Jones M S(14,34). (M) Nzamba S1(11). (M) Parris S(1,2,3,4), X(6).

SOUTHEND UNITED   RECORDS AND STATISTICS

CLUB RECORDS

BIGGEST VICTORIES
League: 9-2 v Newport Co., Div 3S, 5.9.1936
7-0 v QPR, Div 3S, 7.4.1928
8-1 v Cardiff City, Div 3S, 20.2.1937
7-0 v Workington, Div 4, 29.3.1968
F.A. Cup: 10-1 v Golders Green, Round 1, 24.11.1934
9-0 v Kings Lynn, Round 1, 16.11.1968
10-1 v Brentwood, Round 2, 7.12.1968
League Cup: 6-1 v Bournemouth, 13.8.1968
BIGGEST DEFEATS
League: 0-8 v Northampton Town, Div 3S, 22.3.1924
1-9 v Brighton, Div 3, 27.11.1965
F.A. Cup: 0-6 v Burnley, Round 2, 30.1.1915
League Cup: 0-8 v Crystal Palace, Rnd 2, 25.9.1990
MOST POINTS
3 points a win: 85, Division 3, 1990-91
2 points a win: 67, Division 4, 1980-81
MOST GOALS
92, Division 3S, 1950-51
Stubbs 19, Wakefield 15, Davies 12, Tippett 12, Grant 12, French 5, Sibley 5,Lawler 4, McAlinden 2, Anderson 1, Butler 1, Woods 1, og 3
MOST LEAGUE GOALS CONCEDED
86, Division 1, 1996/97
MOST FIRST CLASS MATCHES IN A SEASON
57 (46 League, 1 FA Cup, 2 League Cup, 8 Anglo Italian Cup) 1993-94
MOST LEAGUE WINS
30, Division 4, 1980-81
MOST LEAGUE DRAWS
19, Division 4, 1976-77
MOST LEAGUE DEFEATS
26, Division 3, 1965-66
RECORD TRANSFER FEE RECEIVED
£2,200,000 from Nottingham Forest for Stan Collymore, July 1993.
RECORD TRANSFER FEE PAID
£750,000 to Crystal Palace for Stan Collymore, November 1992.
BEST PERFORMANCES
League: 1980-81: Matches Played 46, Won 30, Drawn 7, Lost 9, Goals for 79, Goals against 31, Points 67. First in Division 4
Highest: 12th Division 2, 1991-92

COMPETITIONS

Div.2/1	Div.3(S)	Div.3\2	Div.4/3
1991-97	1921-58	1920-21	1966-72
		1958-66	1976-78
		1972-76	1980-81
		1978-80	1984-87
		1981-84	1989-90
		1987-89	1998-
		1990-91	
		1997-98	

Best performances continued....
F.A. Cup: Last Sixteen: 1920-21, 1926-26, 1951-52, 1975-76.
Most Recent Success: 1992-93: 3rd rnd. Millwall (h) 1-0; 4th rnd. Huddersfield (a) 2-1; 5th rnd. Sheffield Wednesday (a) 0-2
League Cup: Never past Round 3

INDIVIDUAL CLUB RECORDS

MOST GOALS IN A MATCH
5. Jim Shankly v Merthyr Tydfil, 6-0, Div 3S, 1.3.1930
5. H. Johnson v Golders Green, 10-1, FAC Rnd 1, 24.11.1934
5. Billy Best v Brentwood, 10-1, FAC Rnd 2, 7.12.1968

MOST GOALS IN A SEASON
Jim Shankly 35 (League 34, FAC 1) 1928-29
3 goals 2 times=6; 2 goals 6 times=12; 1 goal 17 times=17. Total 35

OLDEST PLAYER
Not known.

YOUNGEST PLAYER
Phil O'Connor, 16 years 76 days, 26.12.1969.

MOST CAPPED PLAYER
George McKenzie (Eire) 9

PREVIOUS MANAGERS

Tom Mather 1920-21; F L Birnie 1921-24; D B Jack 1924-39;
Harry Warren 1946-56; Eddie Perry 1956-60; Frank Broome 1960;
Ted Fenton 1961-65; Alvin Williams 1965-67; Ernie Shepherd 1967-69;
Geoff Hudson 1969-70; Arthur Rowley1970-76; Dave Smith 1976-82;
Peter Morris 1982-84; Bobby Moore 1984-86; David Webb 1986-87;
Dick Bate 1987; Paul Clark 1987-88; Dave Webb 1988-92;
Colin Murphy 1992-93; Barry Fry 1993-94; Peter Taylor 1993-95;
Steve Thompson 1995; Ronnie Whelan 1995-97.

ADDITIONAL INFORMATION
Previous Names
None.
Previous League
Southern League
Club colours: Blue shirts, white shorts, white socks.
Change colours:

Reserves League: Capital League.

HONOURS

DIVISION 4
1980-81

LONGEST LEAGUE RUNS

of undefeated matches:	16 (20.2.1932 - 29.8.1932)	of league matches w/out a win:	7 (31.12.1983 - 14.4.1984)
of undefeated home matches:	32 (16.2.1980 - 1.5.1981)	of undefeated away matches:	9 (4.3.1972 - 29.4.1972)
without home win:	8 (2.10.1948 - 22.1.1949)	without an away win:	27 (13.11.1920 - 4.2.1922)
of league wins: 7 (4.10.1924 - 6.11.1924, 24.4.1990 - 18.9.1990)		of home wins:	18 (4.4.1980 - 9.1.1981)
of league defeats:	6 (29.8.1987 - 19.9.1987)	of away wins:	5 (31.8.1931 - 3.10.1931, 9.4.1991 - 3.9.1991)

THE MANAGER

ALVIN MARTIN . . . . appointed July 1997.
PREVIOUS CLUBS
As Manager: None As Asst.Man/Coach: None As a player: West Ham United, Leyton Orient.
HONOURS
As a Manager: None As a player: **West Ham:** FA Cup 1980. Division 2 Championship 1981. **England:** 17 full caps, 2 B and Youth.

OUTHEND UNITED

O A L K E E P E R

Player	HT	WT	DOB	From/Fee	Date	Club								
enriksen Toni	6.3	13.9	4/25/73	Hammel		Randers Freja								
					10/18/96	Southend United			0+1					
argetson Martyn	6	13.1	08/09/71	Neath	05/07/90	Manchester City	23	0+2	3	1				
/: B.2, u21.7, Y, S				Loan	08/12/93	Bristol Rovers	2+1							
				Loan	23/03/95	Luton Town								
				Free	7/1/98	Southend United								

E F E N C E

Player	HT	WT	DOB	From/Fee	Date	Club								
eard Mark	5.1	10.12	08/10/74	Roehampton	18/03/93	Millwall	32+13	3+1	4		2		1	
				£117000	18/08/95	Sheffield United	22+16	2+1	2+2					
				Loan	10/24/97	Southend United	6+2			1				
				Free	7/1/98	Southend United								
oleman Simon	6	10.8	3/13/68	Worksop	7/29/85	Mansfield Town	96	9	7	7	7			1
				£400000	9/26/89	Middlesbrough	51+4		5	10	2			1
				£300000	8/15/91	Derby County	62+8	5+1	5	12	2			
				£250000	1/20/94	Sheffield Wednesday	10+5	3	2		1			
				£350000	10/5/94	Bolton Wanderers	34	4	2		5			
				Free	2/20/98	Southend United	13							
ublin Keith	5.7	10	1/29/66	H. Wycombe	1/28/84	Chelsea	50+1	6	5	5+1				
				£3500	8/14/87	Brighton & H.A.	132	5	7	7	5		1	
				£275000	7/17/90	Watford	165+3	12	4	6	2			
					7/21/94	Southend United	168+1	9	4	1	9			
arris Andrew D	5.11	11.11	2/26/77	Springs	3/24/94	Liverpool								
					8/15/96	Southend United	70+2	5	2					
ewman Robert N	6.2	12	13/12/63	B'ford on Avon	05/10/81	Bristol City	382+12	29+1	27	33	52	2	2	5
MC'86				£600000	15/07/91	Norwich City	181+24	22+2	13	7	14	2	1	
oan 12/12/97 Motherwell				Loan	3/26/98	Wigan Athletic	8							
				Free	7/1/98	Southend United								
oget Leo Thomas Erl	6.1	12.2	8/1/77	Ilford	7/5/95	Southend United	40+4	3			1			
				Loan	12/1/95	Dover Athletic								
timson Mark	5.11	11	12/27/67	Plaistow	7/15/85	Tottenham Hotspur	1+1							
				Loan	3/15/88	Leyton Orient	10							
				Loan	1/19/89	Gillingham	18							
				£200000	6/16/89	Newcastle United	82+4	5	7	6	2		1	
				Loan	12/10/92	Portsmouth	3+1							
				£100000	7/23/93	Portsmouth	43+1	9	2	3	1	1		
				£25000	3/15/96	Southend United	33+5							

M I D F I E L D

Player	HT	WT	DOB	From/Fee	Date	Club								
ridelet Phil	5.11	12	4/30/67	Hendon		Hendon								
:: S-P4				£25000	9/1/90	Barnet			0+1					
				£175000	9/21/90	Barnsley	3+3		1	1				
				Loan	3/5/93	Rotherham United	9							
				Free	8/1/95	Southend United	148+27	4	4	5	10		1	1
ails Julian	5.9	11	11/20/67	Lincoln		Hemel Hempstead								
					8/29/90	Fulham	99+13	5+1	2	9	12			
				Free	12/2/94	Southend United	129+17	5+2	3		6			
ones Mark			8/4/79	Havering	10/3/97	Southend United (T)	1							
ones Nathan J	5.7	10.12	5/28/73	Rhondda		Merthyr Tydfil								
				£10000	6/30/95	Luton Town								
via Nomincia (Spain)				Free	8/5/97	Southend United	34+5	4	2	0+1			1	
aher Kevin	6	12.5	10/17/76	Ilford	7/1/95	Tottenham (T)								
i: u21.4				Free	1/23/98	Southend United	18			1				
ielsen John	5.8	11.5	4/7/72	Aarhus		Ikast								
				Free	8/2/96	Southend United	18+11	2	1	1	3	1		
hyte David A	5.9	10.7	4/20/71	Greenwich		Greenwich Boro'								
iv.1'94.				Free	2/15/89	Crystal Palace	17+10	5+2	0+1	0+3	4	2		1
				Loan	3/26/92	Charlton Athletic	7+1				2			
				£450000	7/5/94	Charlton Ahtletic	65+20	5+2	3+1	0+2	28	4	1	
				Free	9/19/97	Reading								
				Free	10/31/97	Ipswich Town	2							
				Free	1/22/98	Bristol Rovers	0+4		0+1					
				Free	3/13/98	Southend United	3+5			1				

F O R W A R D

Player	HT	WT	DOB	From/Fee	Date	Club								
Clarke Adrian J	5.1	11	9/28/74	Cambridge	7/6/93	Arsenal	4+3		1+1					
E: Y.1,S.				Loan	3/27/97	Southend United	7							
				Free	7/12/97	Southend United	40+3	4	2		5			
Fitzpatrick Trevor J J	6.1	12.10	2/19/80	Frimley	1/1/98	Southend United	1+2							
Perkins Christopher P	5.11	12.11	3/1/80	Stepney	9/26/97	Southend Utd (T)	3+2		1					

ADDITIONAL CONTRACT PLAYERS

Player				From/Fee	Date	Club								
Burns Alex						SC Heracles								
				Free	7/1/98	Southend United								
Livett Simon						West Ham United								
				Free	1/7/98	Southend United								

ROOTS HALL
Victoria Avenue, Southend-on-Sea SS2 6NQ

Capacity 12,435

First game ....v Norwich City, Div. 3(S) (3-1, 20.08.55. Att: 17,700.
First floodlit game...Not Known.
ATTENDANCES
Highest ....31,033 v Liverpool, FAC 3rd Rnd, 10.1.1979.
Lowest...653 v Northampton, AMC, 13.3.1986.
OTHER GROUNDS..Roots Hall 1909-1919. The Kursaal 1919-1934.
....Southend Stadium 1934-1955. Played at New Writtle Street,Chelmsford in 1940, during the war.

HOW TO GET TO THE GROUND

From the North and East
Use A127, sign posted Southend, and then at roundabout take 3rd exit into Victoria Avenue for Southend United FC.

From the South
Use A13, sign posted Southend, and then turn left into West Road and at end turn left into Victoria Avenue for Southend United FC.

Car Parking: Reserved car park on match days. Ample street parking is available.

Nearest Railway Station: Southend Central (01702 611 811) Prittlewell.

USEFUL TELEPHONE NUMBERS

Club switchboard 01702 304 050
Club fax number 01702 330 164
Club shop 01702 601 351
Ticket Office 01702 304 090

Clubcall...........................0839 66 44 44*
*Calls cost 50 per minute at all times.
Call costings correct at time of going to press.

MATCHDAY PROGRAMME

Programme Editor..............Kevin O'Donnell.

Number of pages.....................................48.

Price ....£1.60.

Subscriptions ....Apply to club.

Local Newspapers
.............Evening Echo, Standard Recorder,
....Yellow Advertiser.

Local Radio Stations
...........................Essex Radio, BBC Essex.

MATCHDAY TICKET PRICES

East Stand
Blue Block* £10.00
Yellow Block £12.00
Red Block. £12.00
Green Block £12.00
Black Block. £10.00
Black junior/OAP/Student** £5.00
South Stand
Upper Tier*** £10.00
Lower Tier*
  Adult £8.00
  Junior/OAP/UB40 Holder £4.00
West Stand
Adult £10.00
Junior/OAP. £5.00
Blocks AA,F
Adult £10.00
Junior/OAP. £5.00
*These sections may not be available for all matches during the season. **Students - 16-19 years old. Must be full time and have Student ID. ***Please note this section may contain supporters using musical instruments during play.

SWANSEA CITY
(The Swans)
NATIONWIDE LEAGUE DIVISION 3
SPONSORED BY: Evening Post

1997/98 - Back Row L-R: Paul Morgan (physio), Gary Jones, Joao Moreira, Kristian O'Leary, Jamie Harris, Jason Price, Ryan Casey, Paul Agnew, Alan Curtis (youth team coach). **Middle Row:** Mike Davenport (physio), Robert King, Mark Clode, Shaun Chapple, Lee Jones Roger Freestone, Christian Edwards, Kwame Ampadu, Damian Lacey, Ron Walton (youth dev. officer). **Front Row:** David O'Gorman, Steve Jones, Jonathan Coates, Billy Ayre (asst. manager), Jan Molby (manager), Keith Walker (capt), Tony Bird, Richard Appleby.

SWANSEA CITY

FORMED IN 1900

TURNED PROFESSIONAL IN 1912

LTD COMPANY IN 1912

PRESIDENT: Ivor Pursey MBE

CHAIRMAN: Steve Hamer

VICE-CHAIRMAN

N J McClure

DIRECTORS

Professor D H Farmer, R G Hamill

CLUB SECRETARY

Miss Vicky Townsend (01792 474114)

MANAGER: John Hollins MBE

ASSISTANT MANAGER: Allan Curtis

YOUTH TEAM MANAGER

Malcolm Elias

PHYSIOTHERAPIST

Mike Davenport

STATISTICIAN FOR THE DIRECTORY

Colin Jones

During a season which saw the Football Club finish in it's lowest position in the Football League since the reelection season of 1974/5, the club, despite a change of ownership at the start of the season was struggling to convince it's supporters that an influx of quality players would be on the agenda as well as the building of a new Stadium.

Despite the loss of quality players in Penney, Thomas, Heggs and Torpey before the start of the season, supporters genuinely felt that the swans would go one better than the previous season and be among the promotion contenders. This fact was underlined when nearly 7,000 fans attended the first home game of the season against Brighton.

By the first week of October however, all hopes of promotion appeared lost, and the Club had sacked both Jan Molby and Billy Ayre, and appointed former Fulham duo Micky Adams and Alan Cork as their replacements.

The Pantomime season had come early to the Vetch Field, because within 14 days Micky Adams resigned, stating that personal reasons, but also hinting at a lack of funding promised for new players was not forthcoming. A month later a League game had to be cancelled at the Vetch Field at short notice because of a lack of a Safety Certificate, through a fault in a back up generator.

The majority of genuine supporters had realised for a number of years that the Club was being run down, but there appeared to be no let up in farcical events emanating from the Football Club, with the distinct possibility of not only entering the League of Wales set up, but to possible extinction.

By this time, press releases from the Chairman Steve Hamer, and the Club's new Chief Executive Peter Day could not convince supporters that any genuine progress was being made at the Club.

Although Jan Molby had made mistakes during his short reign as Player Manager at the Vetch Field, he had nevertheless, encouraged the Swans to play attractive football. With his presence in midfield being a huge asset to the Swans in Division Three, it came as a surprise to supporters that his only league appearance last season came at Peterborough, to be followed by the sack 4 days later.

With Alan Cork accepting the hot seat at the Vetch Field, helped initially by Ian Branfoot, his previous playing record with Wimbledon appeared to be against him as his side were quite wrongly labelled a long ball outfit.inexperienced in management, Cork worked tirelessly to improve the confidence of a team firmly entrenched in the bottom six of the Third Division. Funds were made available to bring in Cusack and Newhouse from Fulham, Bound from Stockport and Alsop from Bristol Rovers. During the season almost £300,000 was invested in new players to the Vetch Field.

As well as lacking a proven goalscorer to put away the half chances, consistency week in, week out proved to be the stumbling block for the Club, as they failed time and time again to kill off the opposition.

With a record 37 players being used in league and cup games, another disappointing statistic for the Club was the record number of 10 dismissals during the season. Tony Bird, in his first season back in LEague Football ended the season top of the goalscoring charts, but he was sent off twice during the season at Notts County and Cambridge United, ironically by the same referee.

A week before the Swans reported back for pre-season training Alan Cork was sacked as Manager. The Club's board of directors issued a statement declaring that over a period of weeks they had lost faith in his style of play, and ability in the transfer market. The impending move to the new Morfa Stadium at the start of the 1999/2000 season would give a new Manager the time to mould the Swans this season into a possible promotion side.

Two days later QPR assistant manager John Hollins was given a 3 year contract and appointed the new Manager of the Swans.

COLIN JONES.

SWANSEA CITY

Division 3   :20th   FA CUP: 1st Round   LC CUP: 1st Round   AWS: Southern Round 2

M	DATE	COMP.	VEN	OPPONENTS	RESULT	H/T	LP	GOAL SCORERS/GOAL TIMES	ATT.
1	A 09	FL	H	Brighton & H.A.	W 1-0	0-0	11	Bird 79	6800
2	12	CC 1/1	A	Reading	L 0-2	0-0			(4829)
3	23	FL	H	Scunthorpe United	W 2-0	1-0	9	Bird 46 (pen), Sertori 11 (OG)	4895
4	26	CC 1/2	H	Reading	D 1-1	0-0		Coates 49	3333
5	30	FL	A	Hull City	L 4-7	1-2	12	Coates 14, Bird 53, Price 65, Dewhurst 77 (OG)	(5198)
6	S 02	FL	A	Barnet	L 0-2	0-2	13		(1946)
7	05	FL	H	Torquay United	W 2-0	0-0	8	O'Gorman 63, Bird 90	4135
8	09	FL	A	Darlington	L 2-3	2-0	9	Bird 13, O'Gorman 35	(2150)
9	13	FL	A	Macclesfield Town	L 0-3	0-1	16		(2479)
10	20	FL	H	Colchester United	L 0-1	0-0	18		3414
11	27	FL	H	Leyton Orient	D 1-1	0-0	18	Bird 58	0
12	O 04	FL	A	Peterborough United	L 1-3	0-2	20	Bird 79	(5849)
13	11	FL	A	Exeter City	L 0-1	0-1	20		(3909)
14	18	FL	H	Notts County	L 1-2	1-1	21	Edwards 5	3668
15	21	FL	H	Mansfield Town	L 0-1	0-0	22		2589
16	24	FL	A	Doncaster Rovers	W 3-0	2-0	20	Bird 9, O'Gorman 12, Lacey 80	(1170)
17	N 02	FL	A	Cardiff City	W 1-0	1-0	20	Walker 11	(6459)
18	04	FL	H	Hartlepool United	L 0-2	0-0	20		2949
19	08	FL	H	Lincoln City	D 0-0	0-0	20		2871
20	14	FAC 1	H	Peterborough United	L 1-4	0-2		Appleby 69	2821
21	18	FL	A	Scarborough	L 2-3	1-1	21	Bird 2, 76	(1408)
22	26	FL	A	Chester City	L 0-2	0-1	21		(1510)
23	29	FL	A	Shrewsbury Town	W 1-0	0-0	21	Coates 73	(2697)
24	D 02	FL	H	Rotherham United	D 1-1	0-0	20	Coates 49	2463
25	13	FL	A	Rochdale	L 0-3	0-2	21		(1482)
26	20	FL	H	Cambridge United	D 1-1	1-0	22	Watkin 11	2605
27	26	FL	A	Torquay United	L 0-2	0-0	22		(2998)
28	28	FL	H	Barnet	L 0-2	0-1	22		3987
29	J 10	FL	A	Brighton & H.A.	W 1-0	1-0	22	Bird 37	(2997)
30	17	FL	H	Hull City	W 2-0	0-0	21	Bird 48, Coates 89	2899
31	20	AWS S2	H	Peterborough United	L 1-2	1-0		Bound 40	1179
32	24	FL	A	Scunthorpe United	L 0-1	0-1	22		(2123)
33	27	FL	H	Darlington	W 4-0	2-0	20	Edwards 13, Alsop 22, Appleby 49, O'Gorman 89	2128
34	31	FL	H	Macclesfield Town	D 1-1	1-1	20	Alsop 10	3293
35	F 06	FL	A	Colchester United	W 2-1	0-1	18	Coates 52, Price 78	(2789)
36	14	FL	H	Peterborough United	L 0-1	0-0	19		3737
37	21	FL	A	Leyton Orient	D 2-2	1-1	21	Coates 33, O'Gorman 76	(4261)
38	24	FL	A	Notts County	L 1-2	1-2	21	Hartfield 19	(4484)
39	28	FL	H	Exeter City	W 2-1	0-0	21	Hartfield 80, Bird 81	3323
40	M 03	FL	A	Lincoln City	D 1-1	0-0	20	Price 69	(2281)
41	08	FL	H	Cardiff City	D 1-1	0-0	20	Coates 84	5621
42	14	FL	A	Hartlepool United	L 2-4	1-1	20	Watkin 11, Walker 49	(1727)
43	21	FL	H	Scarborough	D 0-0	0-0	21		2797
44	28	FL	H	Chester City	W 2-0	1-0	21	Barwood 14, Watkin 87	2500
45	A 04	FL	H	Shrewsbury Town	L 0-1	0-1	21		2623
46	11	FL	A	Rotherham United	D 1-1	1-1	21	Alsop 17	(2942)
47	13	FL	H	Rochdale	W 3-0	0-0	20	Appleby 61, 65, Walker 74	2854
48	18	FL	A	Cambridge United	L 1-4	1-2	20	Bird 22	(2336)
49	25	FL	H	Doncaster Rovers	D 0-0	0-0	20		3661
50	M 02	FL	A	Mansfield Town	L 0-1	0-0	20		(2867)

Best Home League Attendance: 6800 V Brighton & H.A.   Smallest :0 V Leyton Orient   Average :3296

Goal Scorers:

FL	(49)	Bird 14, Coates 7, O'Gorman 5, Alsop 3, Appleby 3, Price 3, Walker 3, Watkin 3, Edwards 2, Hartfield 2, Barwood 1, Lacey 1, Opponents 2
CC	(1)	Coates 1
FAC	(1)	Appleby 1
AWS	(1)	Bound 1

(M) Agnew	(F) Alsop	(F) Ampadu	(D) Appleby	(F) Bird	(D) Bound	(F) Casey	(M) Chappell	(M) Clode	(F) Coates	(M) Cusack	(D) Edwards	(G) Freestone	(D) Harris	(D) Hartfield	(D) Hills	(F) Jenkins	(F) Jones G	(M) Lacey	(M) Mainwearing	(D) Moreira	(M) Newhouse	(M) O'Gorman	(D) O'Leary	(M) Phillips	(M) Price	(F) Puttnam	(M) Walker	(F) Watkin	Referee	No.
	X		X			S	S		X		X		X	X					X		X		X			X	X	X	A G Wiley	1
	X	S1	X				S		X		X	X	X					S2	X		X		X			X	X	X	P Taylor	2
	X	S2	X				S1		X		X	X	X		X	S	X				X					X	X	X	C R Wilkes	3
	X	X	X				S		X		X	X	X	S					S		X		X			X	X	X	G Singh	4
	X	X	X				S		X		X	X	S	X		X					X		X			X	X	X	D Laws	5
	X	X	X				S		X		X	S1	X	S				S			X	X	X	X		X	X	X	S G Bennett	6
	X	X	X				X		X		X	X	S	X	S	S1					X	X	X			X		X	M E Pierce	7
	X	X	X				S		X		X	X	S	X	S	X	X	S			X	X	X			X		X	W C Burns	8
X	X	X	X				S1		X		S2	X	X	S							X		X			X		X	A R Hall	9
X	X	X	X				S		X		X	S2	X	S1				S1			X		X			X		X	S W Mathieson	10
		X	X						X		X	X	S1		S2	X			X		X	S	X		X	X	X	K A Leach	11
X		X	X	S1	X		X		X		X	X	S		X						S	X			X	X	X	B Knight	12
X		S1	X	X	X		X		X		X	X	S2					S3	X				X			X	X	A Bates	13
X		X	X				X		X		X	X	S3							X	S2	X	S1		X	X	X	P Rejer	14
X		X	X				X		X		X	X						S2		X	S1	X	S3	X		X	X	M Fletcher	15
X		X	X				X		X		X	X							S2	X	X	X	S3	S1		X	X	T Jones	16
S		X	X			X	X	X	X	X		X							S		S1	X		X		X	X	X	R J Harris	17
S		X	X			X	X	X	X	X		X						S2		X		X		X		X	X	S1	M Halsey	18
		X	X	S		X	X	X	X	X		X						S1		X		X		X		X	S2	C J Foy	19
	S1	X	X	S		X	X	X	X	X		X						S	S3	X		X		X		X	S2	A G Wiley	20
	X	X	X			S3	X	X	X	X		X						S1		X		X		X		X	S2	M J Jones	21
	X	X	X	X	S	X	X	X	X	X		X						S	X		S					X	S2	P R Richards	22
	X	X	X			X	X	X	X	X	X							S	S	S1		X			X	X1	M L Dean	23
	X	X1	X			X	X	X	X	X	X							S	S	S1		X			X	X	C R Wilkes	24
	X	X	S2	X		X	X	X	X	X	X2									S1	S		X		X1	X	M D Messias	25
	X	X1	S2	X		X	X	X	X	X	X2		S1							S3		X			X	X3	M C Bailey	26
	X	X	X		X2	X	X	X	X	X1	X	X	X						S2	X	S			X	S1	K A Leach	27
S2	X	X	S			X	X	X	X	X2	X	X	X						X1	X				S1	F G Stretton	29
	X	X			X1	X	X	X	X	X	X					S1		X			X	X2	A R Leake	30
		X	X	X		X	S1	X		X		X	X		X			X1	X							31
X		X	X2	X1			X	X	X	X	S		X	X				S1				X	S2	J P Robinson	32
X1		X	X2	X	S		X	X	X	X				X	X			S2	X			X	S1	R Styles	33
X		X	X1	X	S1		X	X	X	X	X2						S2		X		X	S	A P D'Urso	34
X2		X3	X1	X			X	X	X	X	X	S3				S2		X	X2		X	S1	J A Kirkby	35
X		S2	X	X1			X	X	X	X	S					S1	X	X2		X	G Singh	36
	S1	X2	X	X			X3	X	X	X	X1		S3			S2	X	X		X	D Orr	37
X		X	X				X	X	X1	X	X3	S1	S2			X	X2		X	M L Dean	38
		X	X				X	X	X	X	S3	X2		S2	X	X3	E Lomas	39
		X	X				X	X	X	X	X	X2	S		S2	X	X	M J Jones	40
	X1	X	X				X	X	X	X	X3	S2	X2		S1	S3	X	X	M J Brandwood	41
X		X	X				X2	X	X	X	X3	S1	S2		S3	X1	X	X	A Bates	42
X		X	X				X	X	X	X	S	X	S1	S	X	X1	R Styles	43
	X3	X	X	S1			X	X	X	X	X2	X	S3	X	S2	X	D R Crick	44
X		X	S2				X	X3	X	X	X	X1	S3	S1	X	X2	A R Leake	45
X2		X3	S2	X			X1	X	X	X	S1	S3	X	X	X	T Jones	46
X2		X	S1	X			X	X	X	X3	X	S2	S3	X	X	X1	P Rejer	47
	X3	X	X				S1	X	X	X1	X	X	S2	S3	X	X2	M L Dean	48
X		X					X	X	X	X	X3	S2	S1	X	S3	X1	X	X2	D Pugh	49
X3		X	X	S3			X	X		X	X	X1	X	S1	X2	G B Frankland	50

7	12	16	33	35	28	2	3	7	42	32	32	43		22	7	14	3	15	2	5	3	11	25		31	4	39	24	FL Appearances	
	2	2	6		4	1	1	2					6			7	5	6	1		5	23	4	6	3			8	FL Sub Appearances	
	2		1+1	2				2		2	2	0+1				0+1		1	2			2		1	2	2	2		CC Appearances	
0+1	1	1				1	1	1	1				0+1		1				1		1		1			0+1	FAC Appearances	
	1	1		1		0+1	1	1	1	1	1	1		1	1				1	1			1	1		AWS Appearances	

Also played:(M) Barwood S2(3),S1(39), X1(44). (F) Brown S3(30), S1(40). (M) Howard S3(38), X1(39,40). (F) Jones J X(50). (G) Jones L X(9,21). (M) Molby X(11), (M) Munroe S2(50). (D) Trevitt X3(25).

CLUB RECORDS

RECORD LEAGUE VICTORY
8-0 v Hartlepool United, Div 4, 1.4.1978
Most Goals Scored in a Cup Tie: 12-0 v Sliema Wanderers (Malta),
1st rnd 1st leg, European Cup Winners Cup, 15.9.1982
RECORD LEAGUE DEFEAT
1-8 v Fulham, Div 2, 22.1.1938   1-8 v Newcastle United,Div 2,
2.9.1939   0-7 v Tottenham Hotspur, Div 2, 3.12.1932   0-7 v Bristol
Rovers, Div 2, 2.10.1954   0-7 v Workington, Div 3, 4.10.1960
Record Cup Defeat
0-8 v Liverpool, FA Cup Round 3 replay, 9.1.1990   0-8 v Monaco,
ECWC 1st rnd 2nd leg, 1.10.1991
European Competitions entered: European Cup Winners Cup
1961-62, 1966-67, 1981-82, 1982-83, 1983-84, 1989-90, 1991-92
MOST LEAGUE POINTS
(3pts a win) 73, Division 2 1992-93
(2pts a win) 62, Div3S, 1948-49
MOST LEAGUE GOALS
92, Div 4, 1976-77
RECORD TRANSFER FEE RECEIVED
£375,000 from Crystal Palace for Chris Coleman, June 1991 (Fee
paid in installments. Final payment made when Coleman played his
50th game for Palace). £375,000 from Nott'm Forest for Des Lyttle,
July 1993
RECORD TRANSFER FEE PAID
£340,000 to Liverpool for Colin Irwin, Aug 1981
BEST PERFORMANCES
League: 6th Div 1 1981-82
FA Cup: Semi-finals 1926, 1964
League Cup: 4th Round 1964-65, 1976-77
European Cup Winners Cup: 2nd round
Welsh Cup Winners (10)
HONOURS
Champions Div 3S 1924-25, 1948-49   Welsh Cup Winners (10
times) Autoglass Trophy 1993-94
LEAGUE CAREER
Original Members of Div 3 1920   Promoted to Div 2 1924-25
Relegated to Div 3S 1946-47   Promoted to Div 2 1948-49
Relegated to Div 31964-65   Relegated to Div 4 1966-67
Promoted to Div 3 1969-70   Relegated to Div 4 1972-73
Promoted to Div 31977-78   Promoted to Div 2 1978-79
Promoted to Div 1 1980-81   Relegated to Div 2 1982-83
Relegated to Div 31983-84   Relegated to Div 4 1985-86
Promoted to Div 3 (now Div 2) 1987-88   Relegated to Div 3 1995-96

INDIVIDUAL CLUB RECORDS

MOST APPEARANCES FOR CLUB
`Wilfy' Milne (1920-37): League 585 + FA Cup 44 +Welsh Cup 28
Total 657

MOST CAPPED PLAYER
Ivor Allchurch, 42 Wales   For England: None

RECORD GOALSCORER IN A MATCH
Jack Fowler 5 v Charlton Athletic, 6-1 Div 3S,27.9.1924
RECORD LEAGUE GOALSCORER IN A SEASON
Cyril Pearce 35, 1931-32   In All Competitions: Cyril Pearce 39 (Lge
35 + Welsh Cup 4)
RECORD LEAGUE GOALSCORER IN A CAREER
Ivor Allchurch 166 (1949-58 & 1965-68)   In All Competitions: Ivor
Allchurch, 189 (League 166 + FA Cup 9 + League Cup 4+ Welsh
Cup 10)

OLDEST PLAYER IN A LEAGUE MATCH
Tommy Hutchison 43 years 171 days v Southend,12.3.91
YOUNGEST PLAYER IN A LEAGUE MATCH
Nigel Dalling, 15 years 10 months

PREVIOUS MANAGERS

1912-14 Walter Whittaker   1914-15 William Bartlett   1919-26 Joe
Bradshaw   1927-31 James Thompson   1934-39 Neil Harris   1939-
47 Haydn Green   1947-55 Billy McCandless   1955-58 Ron
Burgess   1958-65 Trevor Morris   1965-66 Glyn Davies   1967-69
Billy Lucas   1969-72 Roy Bentley   1972-75 Harry Gregg   1975-78
Harry Griffiths   1978-84 John Toshack   1984 Colin Appleton
1985-86 John Bond   1986-89 Terry Yorath   1989-90 Ian Evans
1990-91 Terry Yorath   1991-95 Frank Burrows.
In addition B Watts-Jones, Joe Sykes, Walter Robins, Doug
Livermore, Wyndham Evans, Les Chappel, Tommy Hutchison,
Bobby Smith and Jimmy Rimmer all acted in a `caretaker' capacity
for short periods. Jan Molby, Alan Cork.

ADDITIONAL INFORMATION
Previous Name: Swansea Town (until Feb 1970)
Previous League: Southern League.
Club Colours: All white.
Change Colours: Orange & white shirts, blue shorts.
Reserves League:

LONGEST LEAGUE RUNS

of undefeated matches:	19 (1970-71)	of league matches w/out a win:	15 (1989)
of undefeated home matches:	28 (1925-27)	of undefeated away matches:	12 (1970-71)
without home win:	9 (1938)	without an away win:	46 (1982-84)
of league wins:	8 (1961)	of home wins:	17 (1948-49)
of league defeats:	9 (1990-91)	of away wins:	4 (1955-56, 1987-88, 1993)

THE MANAGER

JOHN HOLLINS MBE . . . . appointed July 1998.

PREVIOUS CLUBS
As Manager/Assistant . . . . Queens Park Rangers.
As a player. . . . . Chelsea, QPR, Arsenal, Chelsea.

HONOURS
As a Manager . . . . None.
As a Player. . . . . **England:** 'B', u23 and youth caps.

SWANSEA CITY

PLAYERS NAME Honours	Ht	Wt	Birthdate	Birthplace Transfers	Contract Date	Clubs	League	L/Cup	FA Cup	Other	Lge	L/C	FAC	Oth
G O A L K E E P E R														
Freestone Roger	6.2	14.6	8/19/68	Newport	4/2/86	Newport County	13			1				
W: u21.1. Div.2'89. AMC'94.				£95000	3/10/87	Chelsea	42	2	3	6				
				Loan	9/29/89	Swansea City	14			1				
				Loan	3/9/90	Hereford United	8							
				£50000	9/5/91	Swansea City	311+1	18	19	30	3			
Jones Jason A	6.2	12.7	5/10/78	Wrexham		Liverpool (T)								
W: Y.				Free	12/29/97	Swansea City	1							
D E F E N C E														
Appleby Richard D	5.8	10.6	9/18/75	Middlesboro'	8/12/93	Newcastle United				2				
				Free	12/12/95	Ipswich Town	+3			1				
				Free	8/15/96	Swansea City	40+5	3+1	1	1	4		1	
Bound Matthew	6.2	12	11/9/72	Melksham	5/3/91	Southampton	2+3							
				Loan	8/27/93	Hull City	7				1			
				£125000	10/26/94	Stockport County	44	1	3	2	5		1	1
				Loan	9/11/95	Lincoln City								
					11/21/97	Swansea City	28							
Cusack Nicholas J	6	11.13	24/12/65	Maltby		Alvechurch								
					18/06/87	Leicester City	5+11		+1	1+1	1			
				£40000	29/07/88	Peterborough Utd	44	4	4	2	10	1	1	
				£100000	02/08/89	Motherwell	68+9	5	3+1	1+1	17	4	2	1
				£95000	24/01/92	Darlington	21				6			
				£95000	16/07/92	Oxford United	48+11	3	4+2	2+1	10	2	1	
				Loan	24/03/94	Wycombe W.	2+2				1			
				Loan	04/11/94	Fulham								
				Free	06/01/95	Fulham	109+6	6+4	7+1	5+2	14	1	1	3
				£50000	10/30/97	Swansea City	32		1	1				
Howard Michael A	5.6	10.4	12/2/78	Birkenhead	7/9/97	Tranmere (T)								
				Free	2/23/98	Swansea City	2+1							
Jones Steve R	5.11	12.2	12/25/70	Bristol	1/1/00	Swansea City	61+1	2	2	3	1			
Munroe Karl A	6	10.11	9/23/79	Manchester	5/1/98	Swansea City (T)	0+1							
O'Leary Kristian	6	13.4	8/30/77	Port Talbot	1/1/00	Swansea City	32+8	1	2+1		1			
Smith Jason						Tiverton Town								
						Coventry City								
						Tiverton Town								
				£10000	7/1/98	Swansea City								
Thomas Martin R	5.8	10.8	12/09/73	Lymington	19/06/92	Southampton								
				Free	24/03/94	Leyton Orient	5				2			
				Free	21/07/01	Fulham	59+31	6+1	4	7+1	8		1	2
				Free	7/1/98	Swansea City								
M I D F I E L D														
Clode Mark	5.7	10.6	2/24/73	Plymouth	3/30/91	Plymouth Argyle								
AMC'94.				Free	7/23/93	Swansea City	107+10	7+2	6	8	3			
Hartfield Charlie	6	13.8	9/4/71	Lambeth	9/20/89	Arsenal (T)								
				Free	8/6/91	Sheffield United	45+11	2+1	4+1	1	1			
				Loan	2/5/97	Fulham	1+1							
				Free	11/27/97	Swansea City	22			1	2			
Lacey Damian J	5.9	11.3	8/3/77	Bridgend	8/15/96	Swansea City	25+7	2			1			
O'Gorman Dave	5.8	11.10	6/20/72	Chester	7/6/90	Wrexham (T)	8+9		1	1				
				Free	7/1/91	Northwich Victoria								
via Barry Town				£20000	8/8/97	Swansea City	11+23	2		1	5			
Phillips Gareth R	5.8	9.8	7/19/79	Porth	11/8/96	Swansea City	0+7							
Price Jason	6.2	11.5	4/12/77	Aberdare	1/1/00	Aberavon								
				Free	6/1/95	Swansea City	32+4	2	1		3			
Walker Keith	6	11.9	4/17/66	Edinburgh	1/1/00	Stirling Albion	82+9	5	5		16	3	2	
					1/1/01	St.Mirren	41+2	3	1	3	6			
				£80000	11/23/89	Swansea City	261+8	10	21	24	9		1	
F O R W A R D														
Barwood Daniel D	5.9	11	2/25/81	Caerphilly	1/16/98	Swansea City (T)	1+2				1			
Bird Anthony	5.11	11.9	9/1/74		8/4/93	Cardiff City	44+31	8	4+2	12+4	12	2	1	3
				Free	8/8/97	Swansea City	34+6	2	1		14			
Casey Ryan P	6	10.2	1/3/79	Coventry	9/30/96	Swansea City	5+11							
Coates Jonathan	5.8	10.4	6/27/75	Swansea	7/8/93	Swansea City	87+24	4+1	4	5	11	1		
Harris James C	6.2	13.7	6/28/79	Swansea	8/24/97	Swansea City	0+6	0+1						
				Loan	3/1/98	Haverfordwest								
Jenkins Lee D	5.9	10	6/28/79	Pontypool	5/31/97	Swansea City	14+7							
Mainwearing Carl A	6	11.13	3/15/80	Swansea	11/12/97	Swansea City (T)	2+1		0+1					
Newhouse Aidan	6.1	13.5	23/05/72	Wallasey	01/07/89	Chester City	29+15	5+1	0+2	2+3	6			1
E: Y.13				£100000	22/02/90	Wimbledon	7+16	1+1	2	0+1	2			
				Loan	21/01/94	Port Vale	0+2		0+1					
				Loan	02/12/94	Portsmouth	6				1			
				Loan	07/12/95	Torquay United								
				Free	18/06/97	Fulham	7+1	3+1			1	3		
				£30000	10/31/97	Swansea City	3+5		1					
Watkin Stephen	5.10	11.10	6/16/71	Wrexham	7/24/87	Wrexham (T)	167+33	11+3	16+6	17+5	55	4	12	4
				£110000	9/26/97	Swansea City	24+8		0+1		3			

VETCH FIELD
Swansea SA1 3SU

Capacity...16,550
Covered Standing 13,003
Seating..3,547

ATTENDANCES
Highest ....32,796 v Arsenal, FA Cup 4th Round, 17.2.1968.
Lowest ....1,311 v Brentford, Division 4, 26.4.1976.

OTHER GROUNDS..None.

HOW TO GET TO THE GROUND

Five minutes walk from city bus station or take South Wales Transport Co Ltd from High Street General Station to Lowere Oxford Street.
Car parking near ground at Quadrant.

Car Parking
Car park 200 yards from ground in the Kingsway. Covered supervised parking within 75 yards. There is also ample street parking.

Nearest Railway Station
Swansea High Street (01792 467 777)

USEFUL TELEPHONE NUMBERS

Club switchboard......................01792 474 114
Club fax number......................01792 646 120   Clubcall 0891 12 16 39*
Club shop ....01792 462 584   *Calls cost 50p per minute at all times.
Ticket Hotline...........................0845 604 0189   Call costings correct at time of going to press.

MATCHDAY PROGRAMME

Programme Editor
..........................Major Reg Pike, I.S.M, T.D.

Number of pages....................................32.

Price ....£1.50.

Subscriptions
..........Please contact club (01792 462 584)

Local Newspapers
........................Evening Post, Western Mail.

Local Radio Stations
..........Swansea Sound, BBC Radio Wales.

MATCHDAY TICKET PRICES (97/98)

Centre Stand................................£11

Family Stand ....1+1 £14, 1+2 - £16

Wing Stand................................£9
OAP..£6.50

Terraces....................................£7.50
Juv/OAP £4

644

TORQUAY UNITED
(The Gulls)
NATIONWIDE LEAGUE DIVISION 3
SPONSORED BY: WESTWARD DEVELOPMENTS

1997-98 Back Row L-R: Lee Barrow, Jon Gittens, Alex Watson, Andy McFarlane, Jamie Robinson, Wayne Thomas, Paul Mitchell. **Middle Row:** Ian Pearce (Youth team physio), Damien Davey (Physio), 'Charlie' Oatway (now at Brentford), Andy Gurney, Matthew Gregg, Paul Gibbs, Wayne Hockley, Phil Lloyd (Youth coach), Peter Distin (Asst. youth manager). **Front Row:** Leon Hapgood, Rodney Jack, Kevin Hodges (Head coach), Mervyn Benney (Chairman), Steve McCall (Asst. coach/Yth dev. officer), Tony Bedeau, Michael Preston.

TORQUAY UNITED
FORMED IN 1899
TURNED PROFESSIONAL IN 1921
LTD COMPANY IN 1921

CHAIRMAN: M Benney
DIRECTORS
M Bateson, Mrs S Bateson, M Beer
I Hayman, H Kindeleit, B Palk
SECRETARY
Heather Kindeleit (01803 328 666)
COMMERCIAL REP.
Cedric Munslow
ADMINISTRATION
Ann Sandford
TEAM COACH: Wes Saunders

YOUTH TEAM COACH
Steve McCall
PHYSIOTHERAPIST
Damien Davey

STATISTICIAN FOR THE DIRECTORY
John Lovis

Uncertainty over the future ownership of the club, the departure of player-coach Garry Nelson to take up a position with the PFA, a new Chairman whose priority was to cut the club's overdraft; all these factors did little to convince even the most optimistic Gulls fan that this was to be a memorable season. Wrong! Kevin Hodges and his new assistant Steve McCall, who had stepped up to become player-coach, signed on free transfers Paul Gibbs, Andy Gurney, Jamie Robinson, Ken Veysey and Kevin Hill who all proved to be better players than those released.

A fantastic team spirit was created and although it was only an average start to the campaign the signs were there that the players had a desire to improve. Things really took off in the new year when the team managed a club shattering eight successive league wins to take them from mid-table to second place. This coincided with the loan signing of striker Jason Roberts from Wolves whose strength and pace allied o the will-of-the-wisp skills of Rodney Jack gave opposition defences a severe testing.

After Roberts returned to Wolves good results were hard to come by but it seemed that a win over Peterborough on the penultimate Saturday had put them back in the driving seat for automatic promotion. Needing just one point at Leyton Orient to secure the prize nearly three thousand Gulls fans made the trip to Brisbane Road. A needlessly conceded early penalty and a second goal after only 24 minutes made it a nightmare first half. But an Andy McFarlane goals with 13 minutes remaining gave us hope and in a grandstand finish only the width of a post denied Alex Watson the goal which would have taken us up.

So the the play-offs and two magnificent performances against Scarborough made it our third trip to Wembley in the space of nine years. Although the Wembley display against Colchester was below par it took a harshly awarded "ball to hand" penalty to defeat the Gulls who were marginally the better side on the night. Once again the Gulls followers turned out in force; over nine thousand made the journey to the twin towers for a Friday night game which had been moved from the Saturday to accommodate an England friendly.

In the two main cup competitions progress was made to the second round with impressive victories over second division opposition and the FA Cup replay defeat in extra-time at Watford was notable not only for the great team performance but the incredible noise made by United's loyal followers.

Centre-back Jon Gittens deservedly but narrowly won the 'Player of the Year' award from a number of outstanding contenders.

At the time of writing most of the successful squad have signed up for the coming season and, given the same attitude which took the side so far, there is good reason for optimism.

JOHN LOVIS.

TORQUAY UNITED

Division 3		**:5th**		**FA CUP: 2nd Round**		**LC CUP: 2nd Round**	**AWS: Southern Round 2**	

M	DATE	COMP.	VEN	OPPONENTS	RESULT	H/T	LP	GOAL SCORERS/GOAL TIMES	ATT.
1	A 09	FL	A	Macclesfield Town	L 1-2	1-1	16	Gurney 9	(3379)
2	12	CC 1/1	A	**Bournemouth**	W 1-0	1-0		**Gibbs 43 (pen)**	(3215)
3	15	FL	H	Scarborough	W 1-0	0-0	12	Gittens 73	1863
4	23	FL	A	Shrewsbury Town	W 2-1	0-0	5	Jack 57, 64	(2556)
5	26	CC 1/2	H	**Bournemouth**	D 1-1	0-1		**Jack 116**	2278
6	30	FL	H	Colchester United	D 1-1	0-0	10	Gittens 85	2081
7	S 02	FL	H	Exeter City	L 1-2	0-0	12	Gurney 66	4217
8	05	FL	A	Swansea City	L 0-2	0-0	14		(4135)
9	13	FL	A	Hartlepool United	L 0-3	0-1	18		(1927)
10	16	CC 2/1	A	**Ipswich Town**	D 1-1			**McFarlane 1**	(8031)
11	20	FL	H	Brighton & H.A.	W 3-0	2-0	16	Gittens 16, Hapgood 45, Hill 69	2110
12	23	CC 2/2	H	**Ipswich Town**	L 0-3	0-1			3598
13	27	FL	H	Doncaster Rovers	W 2-0	1-0	14	Hill 1, Hapgood 48	1650
14	O 04	FL	A	Hull City	D 3-3	0-1	13	Bedeau 73, Gittens 90, McFarlane 92	(5139)
15	11	FL	A	Lincoln City	D 1-1	1-0	12	Watson 12	(2462)
16	18	FL	H	Chester City	W 3-1	3-0	8	McCall 14, Jack 21, McFarlane 26	2047
17	21	FL	H	Leyton Orient	D 1-1	0-1	10	Gibbs 89	1702
18	25	FL	A	Peterborough United	L 0-2	0-1	12		(6325)
19	N 01	FL	A	Cambridge United	D 1-1	0-1	13	Gibbs 73 (pen)	(2314)
20	04	FL	H	Darlington	W 2-1	1-0	11	Jack 25, Bedeau 52	1411
21	08	FL	A	Cardiff City	D 1-1	0-0	13	McFarlane 51	(2797)
22	15	FAC 1	A	**Luton Town**	W 1-0	0-0		**Gibbs 73 (pen)**	(3446)
23	18	FL	A	Barnet	D 3-3	1-1	14	Gibbs 21 (pen), Jack 57, Gittens 87	(1246)
24	22	FL	H	Scunthorpe United	L 2-4	1-2	15	Gibbs 34, Gurney 79	2152
25	29	FL	A	Rochdale	W 1-0	0-0	12	Jack 49	(1729)
26	D 02	FL	H	Mansfield Town	W 2-1	0-1	10	Gurney 74, Thomas 85	1440
27	06	FAC 2	H	**Watford**	D 1-1	1-1		**Gurney 37**	3416
28	13	FL	A	Rotherham United	W 1-0	0-0	8	Gibbs 59 (pen)	(3636)
29	16	FAC 2R	A	**Watford**	L 1-2	0-0		**Clayton 103**	(5848)
30	20	FL	H	Notts County	L 0-2	0-1	10		2536
31	26	FL	H	Swansea City	W 2-0	0-0	9	Hill 52, Roberts 80	2998
32	28	FL	A	Exeter City	D 1-1	1-1	7	Leadbitter 6	(8350)
33	J 10	FL	H	Macclesfield Town	W 2-0	1-0	9	Mitchell 21, Roberts 60	2428
34	13	AWS S2	A	**Northampton Town**	L 1-5	0-1		**Gittens 73**	(2845)
35	16	FL	A	Colchester United	L 0-1	0-0	9		(2776)
36	20	FL	A	Scarborough	L 1-4	0-1	10	, Heckingbottom 70 (OG)	(2467)
37	24	FL	H	Shrewsbury Town	W 3-0	2-0	8	Gurney 27, Gittens 45, Roberts 61	1996
38	31	FL	H	Hartlepool United	W 1-0	0-0	7	Gibbs 76	2238
39	F 06	FL	A	Brighton & H.A.	W 4-1	1-1	5	Roberts 38, 66, Gurney 52, Jack 90	(2083)
40	14	FL	H	Hull City	W 5-1	3-1	5	Clayton 14, Hill 27, 43, Hapgood 58, Jack 72	2793
41	21	FL	A	Doncaster Rovers	W 1-0	0-0	3	Bedeau 87	(1424)
42	24	FL	A	Chester City	W 3-1	2-0	2	Gurney 13, Roberts 33, Jack 83	(2163)
43	28	FL	H	Lincoln City	W 3-2	2-1	2	Jack 31, Gurney 36, Gibbs 68 (pen)	3540
44	M 03	FL	H	Cardiff City	W 1-0	1-0	2	Hill 45	3358
45	07	FL	A	Cambridge United	L 0-3	0-1	2		3809
46	14	FL	A	Darlington	W 2-1	1-1	2	Bedeau 28, Jack 90	(2386)
47	21	FL	H	Barnet	D 0-0	0-0	2		4020
48	28	FL	A	Scunthorpe United	L 0-2	0-0	2		(3264)
49	A 04	FL	H	Rochdale	D 0-0	0-0	2		2796
50	11	FL	A	Mansfield Town	D 2-2	1-0	2	Hill 43, Gurney 80	(2282)
51	13	FL	H	Rotherham United	L 1-2	0-1	3	Bedeau 67	3963
52	18	FL	A	Notts County	L 0-3	0-1	3		(5183)
53	25	FL	H	Peterborough United	W 3-1	2-1	3	Clayton 16, McFarlane 45, Jack 63	4472
54	M 02	FL	A	Leyton Orient	L 1-2	0-2	5	McFarlane 78	(6545)
55	10	PO SF1	A	**Scarborough**	W 3-1	1-0		**Jack 22, Gittens 50, McFarlane 72**	(5246)
56	13	PO SF2	H	**Scarborough**	W 4-1	3-1		**Jack 6, 7, McCall 38, Gibbs 55**	5386
57	22	PO F	A	**Colchester United**	L 0-1	0-1			(0)

Best Home League Attendance: 4472 V Peterborough United   **Smallest :1411 V Darlington**   Average :2679

Goal Scorers:

FL	(68)	Jack 12, Gurney 9, Gibbs 7, Hill 7, Gittens 6, Roberts 6, Bedeau 5, McFarlane 5, Hapgood 3, Clayton 2, Leadbitter 1, McCall 1, Mitchell 1, Thomas 1, Watson 1, Opponents 1
CC	(3)	Gibbs 1, Jack 1, McFarlane 1
FAC	(3)	Clayton 1, Gibbs 1, Gurney 1
AWS	(1)	Gittens 1
PO	(7)	Jack 3, Gibbs 1, Gittens 1, McCall 1, McFarlane 1

1997-98

(D) Barrow	(F) Bedeau	(M) Clayton	(F) Gibbs	(D) Gittens	(M) Gomm	(G) Gregg	(D) Gurney	(M) Hadley	(M) Hapgood	(M) Hill	(F) Hockley	(F) Jack	(M) Leadbitter	(D) McCall	(M) McFarlane	(M) Mitchell	(M) Newall	(M) Oatway	(F) Partridge	(M) Roberts	(M) Robinson	(M) Smillie	(F) Thomas	(M) Tully	(G) Veysey	(D) Watson	Opponent	No
S	S1		X	X		X	X			S2		X		X	X	X		X			X					X	W.C. Burns	1
S	X		X	X		X	X		S1	X	S	X			X		X				X					X	R D Furnandiz	2
S	X		X	X		X	X			X		X		S2	S1	X		X			X					X	P Rejer	3
S1	S2	X	X	X		X	X			S		X		X	X	X					X					X	M J Jones	4
S	S	X	X	X		X	X			X		X		S1	X	X					X					X	R J Harris	5
S2	S1	X	X	X		X	X			S3		X		X	X	X					X					X	D R Crick	6
S	X	X	X	X		X	X			S	S	X		X	X						X					X	C R Wilkes	7
S	X	X	X	X			X			X		X		X	S1	X					X				X	X	M E Pierce	8
S	S	X	X	X			X			S1		X		X		X					X		X		X	X	M D Messias	9
S1		X	X			X	X			S	X		X	X						X		S2				X	S J Baines	10
	S2	X	X			X	X			S1		X	X	X		X					X		S3			X	D Orr	11
	S1	X	X			X	X			X	X	X		X		X					X		S			X	A G Wiley	12
	X	X	X			X	X			X	X			S	X	S1					X		S			X	B Knight	13
	X	X	X			X	X			X	X			S1	X	S					X		S2			X	M L Dean	14
	X	X	X			X	X			S	X			X	X						X		S	S		X	G B Frankland	15
	S	X	X			X	X			S1	X			X	X						X		S2			X	R Styles	16
	S1	X	X			X	X			S	X			X	X						X		S			X	G Singh	17
	S2	X	X			X	X			S1	X			X	X						X		S			X	T Heilbron	18
	S2	X	X			X	X			S1	X			X	X						X		S			X	S G Bennett	19
	S1	X	X			X	X			S1	X			X	X						X		S			X	K A Leach	20
	S2	X	X			X	X			S1	X			X	X						X		S			X	A R Hall	21
	X	X	X	X	S	X	X			X	X		X						S		X		S	S	S	X	P A Durkin	22
	X	X	X	X		X	X			X	X		X						S		X		S1	S1		X	A Bates	23
	X	X	X	X		X	X			X	X				S2						X		S	S1		X	P Taylor	24
	X	X	X1	X			X			X	X		X	S1							X		S	S	X	X	J A Kirkby	25
X1	X2	X		X			X			X3	X		X	S2							X		S1	S3	X	X	D R Crick	26
	S	X	X	X		S	X			X	X1		X	S1							X		X	S	X	X	G R Ashby	27
	S	X	X	X			X			X	X1		X	S1							X		X	X	X	X	R Pearson	28
S1	X	X	X			S	X			X3	X1		X2	S2			S				X		X	S3	X	X	G R Ashby	29
	S		X				X			X2	X1		X	X			X				S1	X	X	S2	X	X	M Fletcher	30
	S		X				X			S	S		X	X			X				X	X	S	X		X	M C Bailey	31
		X	X			X	X			S	S		X	X							X	X	S	X		X	M E Pierce	32
		X	X	A			S			S	X		X	X			X				X	X	S1	X1	X	X	C R Wilkes	33
S3	X2		X	S1			S2			X	X3		X			X1				Y		X	X	X	X	X		34
	X1						X			S2	S		X				X2				X	X	S1		X	A	F G Stretton	35
S2	X	X				X	X			X1			X	X			S			X2	X		S1		X	X	M D Messias	36
S2	X	X1	X			X				X			X2	X			S1			X3	X		S3		X	X	R J Harris	37
S3	X	X	X			X	X1			X2	X		X3				S2			X	X			S1	X	X	A N Butler	38
	S		X				X			X1	X		X	X	S1		S				X	X			X	X	S J Baines	39
S1	X					X2	X			X	X		X	X			S2			X1	X				X	X	A P D'Urso	40
S2	X	S1	X				X			X1	X2		X	X			S			X	X				X	X	J A Kirkby	41
S	X	X	X				X			S	X		X	X			S			X	X				X	X	M S Pike	42
S1	X	X	X				X			S	X		X1	X			S			X	X				X	X	S G Bennett	43
S1	X	X	X				X			S	X		X2	X1						X	X		S2		X	X	P Taylor	44
X	X	X1	X				X			S	X		X	X2	S1						X		S2		X	X	A N Butler	45
X1	X		X			S	X			S2	S3		X	X	X						X	S	S1	X	X	X	W C Burns	46
X1	X	X3	X				X			S2	S3		X	X3	X2					S2	X		S1	X	X	X	G Cain	47
X1	X	X3	X				X				S3		X	X2	X2					X3	X		X1	X	X	X	M D Messias	48
	X	X					X			S2			X	X2	S3	S1				X3	X		X1	X	X	X	G Singh	49
S	X1	X					X			S			X	X1	X					X	X		X	X	X	X	T Heilbron	50
S1		X	X				X			S	X1		X	X	X					X2	X		S2	X	X	X	A P D'Urso	51
S2	X1	X	X				X			X			X	X1	X3					X2	X		S3		X	X	M Fletcher	52
S2	X1	X	X				X			X			X	S1	X	X2				S	X				X	X	A Bates	53
S1	X	X	X				X			X1			X	S2	X2	X				S	X				X	X	A R Leake	54
S1	X	X	X			X				S			X1	X	X	X2					X		S2		X	X	M E Pierce	55
S2	X	X	X				X			S1			X2	X	X1	X3					X		S3		X	X	R J Harris	56
S1	X	X	X		X	X				S			X	X	X1	X2					X		S2			X	M Fletcher	57
14	41	40	45		19	44		15	31		40	21	20	18	11		2	4	13	46		5	4	27	46		FL Appearances	
2	20	1						7	6		5	7	4	3	1		1	1				16	5				FL Sub Appearances	
0+1	1+1	3	4		4	4		1+1	4		4		1+1	3	2		1			4		0+1				4	CC Appearances	
1+1	3	3	3		1	3		3	3		3	0+2	3							3		2	0+1	2	3		FAC Appearances	
0+1	3	3	3	0+1	1	3		0+1	1		1	1	1			1			1			1	1	1	1		AWS Appearances	
0+3	3	3	3		1	3			0+1		3	3	3							3		0+3	2	3			PO Appearances	

Also Played: (M) Alcock S1(1), S(2). (M) Hapgood S2(50). (M) Hockley S2(42), S3(50). (M) Hodges S1(26). (M) Tucker S3(49).

TORQUAY UNITED   RECORDS AND STATISTICS

CLUB RECORDS

RECORD LEAGUE VICTORY
9-0 v Swindon Town, Div 3S, 8.3.1952
Record Cup Victory and Most Goals Scored in a Cup Tie: 7-1 v
Northampton Town(h), FA Cup 1st Round, 14.11.1959 (all goals
scored by Torquay-born players:Graham Bond (3), Ernie Pym (3),
and Tommy Northcott)
6-0 v Canterbury City, FA Cup Round 1, 1964-65

RECORD LEAGUE DEFEAT
2-10 v Fulham, Div 3S, 7.9.1931   2-10 v Luton Town, Div3S,
2.9.1933   1-9 v Millwall, Div 3S, 29.8.1927
Record Cup Defeat: 0-7 v Southend United, Leyland Daf 5th Q-
Final, 26.02.1991

MOST LEAGUE POINTS
(3pts a win) 77, Div 4, 1987-88
(2pts a win) 60, Div 4,1959-60

MOST LEAGUE GOALS
89, Div 3(S), 1956-57

RECORD TRANSFER FEE RECEIVED
£185,000 from Manchester United for Lee Sharpe, June 1988

RECORD TRANSFER FEE PAID
£60,000 to Dundee for Wes Saunders, July 1990

BEST PERFORMANCES
League: 2nd Div 3S 1956-57
FA Cup: 4th Round 1948-49,1954-55, 1970-71, 1982-83, 1989-90
League Cup: Never past 3rd Round

HONOURS
Sherpa Van Trophy Finalists 1989

LEAGUE CAREER
Elected to Div 3S 1927   Original Members of Division 4 1958
Promoted to Div 3 1960   Relegated to Div 4 1962
Promoted to Div 3 1966   Relegated to Div 4 1972
Promoted to Div 3 1991   Relegated to Div 4/3 1992

INDIVIDUAL CLUB RECORDS

MOST APPEARANCES FOR CLUB
Dennis Lewis (1947-59): League 443 + FA Cup 30 Total473

MOST CAPPED PLAYER
Gregory Goodridge, Barbados International

RECORD GOALSCORER IN A MATCH
Robin Stubbs 5 v Newport County, 8-3, Div 4,19.10.1963

RECORD LEAGUE GOALSCORER IN A SEASON
Sammy Collins, 40, Div 3S, 1955-56   In All Competitions: Sammy
Collins 42 (League 40 + FA Cup 2)

RECORD LEAGUE GOALSCORER IN A CAREER
Sammy Collins 204, 1948-58   In All Competitions: 219 (League
204 + FA Cup 15)

OLDEST PLAYER IN A LEAGUE MATCH
David Webb, 38 years 8 months v Crewe Alexandra, Div 4, 5.1.1985
YOUNGEST PLAYER IN A LEAGUE MATCH
David Byng, 16 years 36 days v Walsall, Div3, 14.8.1993
(Since 1946): John Butler   John McNeil   Bob John   Alex Massie

PREVIOUS MANAGERS

Eric Webber   Frank O'Farrell   Allan Brown   Jack Edwards
Malcolm Musgrove   Frank O'Farrell   Mike Green   Frank O'Farrell
Bruce Rioch   David Webb   John Sims   Stuart Morgan   Cyril
Knowles   David Smith   John Impey   Ivan Golac   Paul Compton,
Don O'Riordan, Eddie May. Kevin Hodges.

ADDITIONAL INFORMATION
Previous League: Southern League
Previous Name: Torquay Town (1910), Amalgamated with
Babbacombe in 1920

Club Colours: Yellow & navy blue stripes, navy shorts, yellow
socks with navy blue top
Change Colours: All white.

LONGEST LEAGUE RUNS

of undefeated matches:	15 (1960, 1990)	of league matches w/out a win:	17 (1938)
of undefeated home matches:	31 (1956-57)	of undefeated away matches:	7 (1976, 1990)
without home win:	11 (1961)	without an away win:	28 (1991-1992)
of league wins:	8 (24.01.98 - 03.03.98)	of home wins:	13 (1966-67)
of league defeats:	8 (1948, 1971)	of away wins:	5 (1959)

TEAM COACH

WES SAUNDERS. . . . . appointed July 1998.

PREVIOUS CLUBS
As Manager. . . . . None.
As Coach. . . . . Torquay.
As a player . . . . Newcastle Utd, Bradford City, Carlisle Utd, Dundee, Torquay.

HONOURS
As a Manager . . . . None.
As a Player . . . . None.

TORQUAY UNITED

PLAYERS NAME Honours	Ht	Wt	Birthdate	Birthplace Transfers	Contract Date	Clubs	League	L/Cup	FA Cup	Other	Lge	L/C	FAC	Oth
G O A L K E E P E R														
Gregg Matthew S	5.11	12	11/30/78	Cheltenham		Torquay United	21	4	1	1				
Veysey Kenneth J	5.10	12.7	6/8/67	Hackney		Dotchester Town								
					9/4/97	Torquay United	27		2	2				
D E F E N C E														
Gurney Andrew	5.7	10.7	1/25/74	Bristol	7/10/92	Bristol Rovers	100+8	7	5	14	9	1		
				Free	7/10/97	Torquay United	44	4	3	3	9		1	
Herrera Roberto	5.7	10.6	12/06/70	Torquay	01/03/88	Q.P.R.	4+2	1+2		1+1				
				Loan	17/03/92	Torquay United	11							
				Loan	24/10/92	Torquay United	5							
				Free	29/10/93	Fulham	143+2	15	13	7+1	1			
				£30000	7/1/98	Torquay United								
Tully Stephen R	5.9	11	2/10/80	Paignton	10/10/97	Torquay United (T)	4+5		0+1					
Watson Alex E: Y.4. CS'89.	6	11.9	4/5/68	Liverpool	5/18/85	Liverpool	3+1	1+1	1+1	1				
				Loan	8/30/90	Derby County	5							
				£150000	1/18/91	Bournemouth	145+6	14	12	5	5	1	1	
				Loan	9/11/95	Gillingham								
				£50000	11/23/95	Torquay United	120	6	6	3	4			
M I D F I E L D														
Clayton Gary E: SP.	5.10	12.8	2/2/63	Sheffield	8/23/86	Doncaster Rovers	34+1	2	3	2	5			
				£10000	7/2/87	Cambridge United	166+13	17+1	9	7	17	3		2
				Loan	1/25/91	Peterborough Utd	4							
				£20000	2/18/94	Huddersfield T.	15+4		0+1	4	1			2
					8/10/95	Plymouth Argyle	32+6	2	2	1	2			
				Free	8/21/97	Torquay United	41	3	3	3	2		1	
Hapgood Leon D	5.6	10	8/7/79	Torbay	5/3/97	Torquay United	15+8	1+1	3		3			
Hodges Kevin	5.8	11.2	6/12/60	Bridport	3/2/78	Plymouth Argyle	502+28	32+3	39	9+2	81		3	2
				Loan	1/21/92	Torquay United	3							
				Free	8/15/96	Torquay United	0+1							
Leadbitter Chris Div.3'91.	5.9	10.6	10/17/67	Middlesbrough	9/4/85	Grimsby Town								
				Free	8/21/86	Hereford United	32+4	2	2	3	1			
				Free	8/2/88	Cambridge United	144+32	16	16+2	11+2	18	3		1
				£25000	8/16/93	Bournemouth	20+7	2+1	3	1				
				Free	7/27/95	Plymouth Argyle	47+6	2	6	4+1			1	1
				Free	11/2/97	Torquay United	21+5		0+2	3	1			
McFarlane Andy AGT'94.	6.3	12.6	11/30/68	Wolverhampton	1/1/00	Cradley Heath								
				£20000	11/20/90	Portsmouth	0+2							
				£20000	8/6/92	Swansea City	33+22	3	0+6	7+5	8	1	3	2
				£15000	8/4/95	Scunthorpe United	48+12	4	2+2	3	19	1	2	2
				£20000	1/10/97	Torquay United	37+4	3		3	8	1		1
McGorry Brian	5.10	12.8	4/16/70	Liverpool		Weymouth								
				£30000	8/13/91	Bournemouth	56+5	7	7+3	5	11		2	1
				£60000	2/10/94	Peterborough Utd	44+8	0+2	2	2	6			
				Free	8/18/95	Wycombe W.	0+4	1		1				
via Hereford United				Free	7/1/98	Torquay United								
Robinson Jamie	6.1	12.3	2/26/72	Liverpool	6/4/90	Liverpool								
				Free	7/17/92	Barnsley	8+1		3					
				Free	1/28/94	Carlisle United	40+3	1+2	2	6+2	3			1
				Free	7/2/97	Torquay United	46	4	3	3				
F O R W A R D														
Bedeau Anthony C	5.9	11.1	3/24/79	Hammersmith		Torquay United	18+27	1+1	1+2	0+3	6			
Hill Kevin	5.8	9.12	3/6/76	Exeter		Torrington								
				Free	8/8/97	Torquay United	31+6	4	3	1+1	7			
Newall Justin J	5.9	11	2/8/80	Germany	9/26/97	Torquay United (T)	0+1							
Partridge Scott	5.9	10.09	10/13/74	Grimsby	7/10/92	Bradford City	0+5	1						
				Free	2/18/94	Bristol City	24+33	3+4	1+3		7	1		
				Loan	10/13/95	Torquay United								
				Loan	1/22/96	Plymouth Argyle								
				Loan	3/8/96	Scarborough								
					2/14/97	Cardiff City	29+8	2	1		2			
					3/26/98	Torquay United	4+1							
Thomas Wayne	5.11	11.1	8/28/78	Walsall		Torquay United	7+32	0+1	2	+3	1			

ADDITIONAL CONTRACT TRANSFERS

Gomm Richard A					11/14/97	Torquay United (T)								
Hadley Shaun L					3/13/98	Torquay United (T)								
Smillie Duncan					3/13/98	Torquay United (T)								

PLAINMOOR GROUND
Torquay, Devon TQ1 3PG

Capacity 6,490
Covered Standing 4,131
Seating 2,359

First game .... (As Torquay Town) v St Austell, 2-0, 03.09.1910.
First floodlit game .... v Birmingham City (F) 2-3, 22.11.1954.

ATTENDANCES
Highest .... 21,908 v Huddersfield, FAC 4th Rnd, 29.1.1955.
Lowest .... 601 v Swansea, AMC, 2.12.1986.
.... 967 v Chester, Division 4, 2.5.1984.

OTHER GROUNDS .... None.

HOW TO GET TO THE GROUND

From the North
Use A38 then A380 to Kingskerswell. In 1 mile at roundabout take 1st exit. In 1 mile turn left (A3022) sign posted Babbacombe. In 0.8 miles turn left then right into Westhill Road and Warbro Road for Torquay United FC.

From the West
Use A380 into Torquay town centre then follow signs to Teignmouth (A379) into Lymington Road, then turn right into Upton Hill, keep forward into Bronshill Road. Take 2nd turning on left into Derwent Road and at end turn right then turn right again into Marnham Road for Torquay United FC.

Car Parking: Street parking. Coaches park at Lymington Road Coach Station.

Nearest Railway Station: Torquay (01752 221 300)

USEFUL TELEPHONE NUMBERS

Club switchboard 01803 328 666
Club fax number 01803 323 976
Club shop 01803 328 666
Ticket Office 01803 328 666

Marketing Department. 01803 328 666
Clubcall 0891 66 45 65*
*Calls cost 50p per minute at all times.
Call costings correct at time of going to press.

MATCHDAY PROGRAMME

Programme Editor....... Dave Wilkinson.

Number of pages .... 30.

Price .... £1.70.

Subscriptions .... Home only £38.

Local Newspapers
.. Herald Express, Western Morning News.

Local Radio Stations
...... BBC Radio Devon, Geminin Radio.

MATCHDAY TICKET PRICES

Popular Side
Adults.................................... £8.00
Senior/Student £5.00
Under-16 .... £4.00

Other Areas
Adult £9.00
Senior/Student £6.00
Under-16 .... £4.00

200 Club Executive Pass £15.00

CLUB INDEX

DEADLINE NEWS

Listed are some of the player movements and managerial changes to have taken place since the Ultimate Football Guide's deadline.

PLAYER'S NAME	FROM	TO	DATE	FEE
T R A N S F E R S				
Armstrong Gordon	Bury	Burnley	August	Free
Beesley Paul	Manchester City	Port Vale	August	Free
Carr Darren	Chesterfield	Gillingham	August	£75,000
Claridge Steve	Wolverhampton Wanderers	Portsmouth	August	undisclosed
Connelly Gordon	Airdrie	York City	August	£70,000
Dailly Christian	Derby County	Blackburn Rovers	August	£5,300,000
Edworthy Marc	Crystal Palace	Coventry City	August	£850,000
Gray Andy	Leeds United	Nottingham Forest	August	£175,000
Grobbelaar Bruce	Chesham United	Bury	September	Non-Contract
Hiley Scott	Manchester City	Southampton	August	Free
Louis-Jean Mattieu	Le Havre	Nottingham Forest	August	£100,000
McCarthy Sean	Oldham Athletic	Plymouth Argyle	August	£20,000
Mills Lee	Port Vale	Bradford City	August	£1,000,000
Phillips Martin	Manchester City	Portsmouth	August	£100,000
Prior Spencer	Leicester City	Derby County	August	£700,000
Quashie Nigel	Queens Park Rangers	Nottingham Forest	August	£3,000,000
Rankin Isaiah	Arsenal	Bradford City	August	£1,300,000
Roberts Jason	Wolverhampton Wanderers	Bristol Rovers	August	£250,000
Swan Peter	Bury	Burnley	August	Free
Yorke Dwight	Aston Villa	Manchester United	August	£12,600,000
L O A N S				
Allen Graham	Everton	Tranmere Rovers	August	
Beardsley Peter	Bolton Wanderers	Fulham	August	
Clarke Andy	Wimbledon	Port Vale	August	
Coyne Chris	West Ham United	Bradford City	August	
de Souza Miguel	Peterborough United	Southend United	August	
Goram Andy	Rangers	Notts County	August	
Mean Scott	West Ham United	Port Vale	August	
Torpey Steve	Bristol City	Notts County	August	
M A N A G E R S - O U T				
Kenny Dalglish	Newcastle United	August		
Christian Gross	Tottenham Hotspur	September		
M A N A G E R S - I N				
Ruud Gullit	Newcastle United	August		
David Pleat (Caretaker)	Tottenham Hotspur	September		

Euro 2000......*the road to the finals*

ENGLAND'S FIXTURES....

Sweden	away	5th September 1998
Bulgaria	home	10th October 1998
Luxemburg	away	14th October 1998
Poland	home	27th March 1999
Sweden	home	5th June 1999
Bulgaria	away	9th June 1999
Luxemburg	home	4th September 1999
Poland	away	8th September 1999

SCOTLAND'S FIXTURES....

Lithuania	away	5th September 1998
Estonia	home	10th October 1998
Faroe Isles	home	14th October 1998
Bosnia	home	27th March 1999
Czech Republic	home	31st MArch 1999
Czech Republic	away	9th June 1999
Bosnia	away	4th September 1999
Estonia	away	8th September 1999
Lithiania	home	9th October 1999

WALES' FIXTURES....

Italy	home	5th September 1998
Denmark	away	10th October 1998
Belarus	home	14th October 1998
Switzerland	away	31st March 1999
Italy	away	5th June 1999
Denmark	home	9th June 1999
Belarus	away	4th September 1999
Switzerland	home	9th October 1999

NORTHERN IRELAND'S FIXTURES....

Turkey	away	5th September 1998
Finland	home	10th October 1998
Moldova	home	18th November 1998
Germany	home	27th March 1999
Turkey	home	4th September 1999
Germany	away	8th September 1999
Finland	away	9th October 1999
Moldova	away	TBC

REPUBLIC OF IRELAND'S FIXTURES....

Croatia	home	5th September 1998
Yugoslavia	home	10th October 1998
Malta	away	14th October 1998
Macedonia	away	27th March 1999
Yugoslavia	away	5th June 1999
Croatia	away	4th September 1999
Malta	home	8th September 1999
Macedonia	home	10th October 1999

FRANCE 1998

ENGLAND'S WORLD CUP MATCH BY MATCH RECORD

Group G final position: 2nd   Round reached in the finals: 2nd Round.

M	DATE	Round	VEN	OPPONENTS	RESULT	H/T	GOAL SCORERS/GOAL TIMES	ATT.
1	J 15	R1 (G)	N	Tunisia	W 2-0	1-0	Shearer 42, Scholes 90	54,587
2	J 22	R1 (G)	N	Romania	L 1-2	0-0	Owen 83	37,000
3	J 26	R1 (G)	N	Columbia	W 2-0	2-0	Anderton 20, Beckham 30	41,000
4	J 30	R2	N	Argentina	D 2-2	2-2	Shearer 10 (pen), Owen 16 (Lost 3-4 on penalties)	36,000

Goal Scorers: (7)   Owen 2, Shearer 2 (1 pen), Anderton 1, Beckham 1, Scholes 1.

SCOTLAND'S WORLD CUP MATCH BY MATCH RECORD

Group A final position: 4th.

M	DATE	Round	VEN	OPPONENTS	RESULT	H/T	GOAL SCORERS/GOAL TIMES	ATT.
1	J 10	R1 (A)	N	Brazil	L 1-2	1-1	Collins 38 (pen)	80,000
2	J 16	R1 (A)	N	Norway	D 1-1	0-0	Burley 66	30,236
3	J 23	R1 (A)	N	Morocco	L 0-3	0-1	-	35,000

Goal Scorers: (2)   Burley 1, Collins 1.

THE 1998 WORLD CUP RESULTS AND SCORERS

Group A

Brazil   2(1) v (1) 1 Scotland
  Sampaio 4   *Collins 38 (pen)*
  Boyd 73 (og)
Morocco   2 (1) v (1) 2 Norway
Hadji 38, Hadda 59   *Chippo 45 (og)*
Scotland   1(0) v (0) 1 Norway
  Burley 66   *Flo. H 46*
Brazil   3(2) v (0) 0 Morocco
  Ronaldo 9   *Flo. H 46*
  Rivaldo 45
  Bebeto 50
Scotland   0(0) v (1)3 Morocco
                          Bassir 22, 85
                          Hadda 47
Brazil   1(0) v (0)2 Norway
  Bebeto 78   *Flo. T 83*
                          Rekdal 89 (pen)

Group B

Italy   2 (1) v (1) 2   Chile
  Vieri 10   *Salas 45, 50*
R. Baggio 85 (pen)
Cameroon 1 (0) v (0) 1   Austria
  Njanka 77   *Polster 90*
Chile   1 (0) v (0) 1   Austria
  Salas 70   *Vastic 90*
Italy   3 (1) v (0) 0 Cameroon
  Di Biagio 8
  Vieri 75, 89
Italy   2 (0) v (0) 1   Austria
  Vieri 49   *Herzog 90 (pen)*
R. Baggio 90
Chile   1 (1) v (0) 1 Cameroon
  Sierra 21   *Mboma 56*

Group C

S. Arabia 0 (0) v (0) 1   Denmark
                          Reiper 68
France   3 (1) v (0) 0 S. Africa
  Dugarry 35
Issa 78 (og), Henry 90

S. Africa   1 (0) v (1) 1   Denmark
  McCarthy 52   *B. Laudrup 13*
France   4 (1) v (0) 0 S. Arabia
  Henry 36, 77
  Trezeguet 68
  Lizarazu 85
France   2 (1) v (1) 1   Denmark
  Djorkaeff 13 (pen) *M. Laudrup 42 (p)*
  Petit 56
S. Africa   2 (1) v (1) 2 S. Arabia
  Bartlett 18, 90 (p) *al-Jaber 45 (pen)*
                          al-Thyniyan 74 (p)

Group D

Paraguay 0 (0) v (0) 0 Bulgaria
Spain   2 (1) v (1) 3   Nigeria
Hierro 21, Raul 47 *Adepoju 24*
                          Lawal 73, Oliseh 78
Nigeria   1 (1) v (0) 0 Bulgaria
  Ikpeba 27
Spain   0 (0) v (0) 0 Paraguay
Spain   6 (2) v (0) 1 Bulgaria
  Hierro 6 (pen)   *Kostadinov 56*
  Luis Enrique 18
  Morientes 53, 81
  Batchov 88 (og)
  Kiko 90
Nigeria   1 (1) v (1) 3 Paraguay
  Oruma 11   *Ayala 1, Benitez 59*
                          Cardozo 86

Group E

S. Korea   1 (1) v (0) 3   Mexico
  Seok-Ju Ha 28   *Palaez 51*
                          Hernandez 75, 84
Holland   0 (0) v (0) 0 Belgium
Belgium   2 (1) v (0) 2   Mexico
  Wilmots 43, 48   *Garcia Aspe 56 (p)*
                          Bianco 63
Holland   5 (2) v (0) 0 S. Korea
Cocu 37, Overmars 41
Bergkamp 71, V.Hooijdonk 79
R de Boer 83

Holland   2 (2) v (0) 2   Mexico
  Cocu 4, R de Boer 19 *Pelaez 51*
                          Hernandez 75
Belgium   1 (1) v (0) 1 S. Korea
  Nilis 7   *Sang-Chul Yoo 71*

Group F

Yugoslavia 1 (0) v (0) 0   Iran
  Mihajlovic 73
Germany   2 (1) v (0) 0   USA
  Moeller 9
  Klinsmann 65
Germany   2 (0) v (1) 2Yugoslavia
  Tarnat 73   *Mijatovic 13*
  Bierhoff 80   *Stojkovic 54*
USA   1 (0) v (1) 2   Iran
  McBridge 87   *Estilli 40*
                          Mahdavikia 84
Germany   2 (0) v (0) 0   Iran
  Bierhoff 50
  Klinsmann 58
USA   0 (0) v (1) 1Yugoslavia
                          Komljenovic 4

Group G

England   2 (1) v (0) 0   Tunisia
  Shearer 42,
  Scholes 90
Romania   1 (1) v (0) 0 Colombia
  Ilie 45
Colombia 1 (0) v (0) 0   Tunisia
  Preciado 83
Romania   2 (0) v (0) 1 England
  Molodovan 47   *Owen 83*
  Petrescu 90
Romania   1 (0) v (1) 1 Tunisia
  Molodovan 72   *Souayah 10 (pen)*
Colombia 0 (0) v (2) 2 England
                          Anderton 20
                          Beckham 30

Group H

Argentina 1(1) v (0) 0   Japan
  Batistuta 28

Jamaica   1 (1) v (1) 3 Croatia
  Earle 45   *Stanic 27*
                          Prosinecki 53
                          Suker 69
Japan   0 (0) v (0) 1 Croatia
                          Suker 77
Argentina 5 (1) v (0) 0 Jamaica
                          Ortega 32, 55
Batistuta 73,79,83 (p)
Argentina 1 (1) v (0) 0   Croatia
                          Pineda 34
Japan   1 (0) v (1) 2 Jamaica
  Nakayama 75   *Whitmore 39,54*

Second Round

Italy   1 (1) v (0) 0   Norway
  Vieri 18
Brazil   4 (3) v (0) 1   Chile
Cesar Sampaio 11,27 *Salas 69*
Ronaldo 45(p), 70
France   1 (0) v (0) 0 Paraguay
Blanc 114 (golden goal)
Denmark   4 (2) v (0) 1 Nigeria
  Moller 3   *Babangida 77*
  B.Laudrup 12
  Sand 59, Helveg 76
Germany   2 (0) v (0) 1   Mexico
  Klinsmann 75   *Hernandez 47*
  Bierhoff 86
Holland   2 (1) v (0) 1Yugoslavia
  Bergkamp 38   *Komljenovic 49*
  Davids 90
Romania   0 (0) v (1) 1 Craotia
                          Suker 45 (pen)
England   2 (2) v (2) 2 Argentina
  Shearer 10 (pen) *Batistuta 6 (pen)*
  Owen 16   *Zanetti 45*
(Argentina win 4-3 on penalties)

(1) Seaman	(2) Campbell	(3) Le Saux	(4) Ince	(5) Adams	(6) Southgate	(7) Beckham	(8) Batty	(9) Shearer	(10) Sheringham	(11) McManaman	(12) Neville (G)	(13) Martyn	(14) Anderton	(15) Merson	(16) Scholes	(17) Lee	(18) Keown	(19) Ferdinand (L)	(20) Owen	(21) Ferdinand (R)	(22) Flowers	REFEREES
X	X	X	X	X	X			X	X	X1			X		X		X		S1			M Okada (Japan)
X	X	X	X1	X		S1		X	X	X2		X		X		X			S2			M Batta (France)
X	X	X	X	X		X	S3		S1	X	X2		X1	S2					X3			B Carter (Mexico)
X	X	X1	X	X	S1	X50	S2	X			X		X2	S3	X3		X					K M Nielsen (Denmark)
4	4	4	4	4	1+1	2+1	2+2	4	2	0+1	3		4	0+1	4	0+1	4	0+1	2+2			**TOTAL APPEARANCES**

(1) Leighton	(2) McNamara	(3) Boyd	(4) Calderwood	(5) Hendry	(6) McKinlay	(7) Gallacher	(8) Burley	(9) Durie	(10) Jackson	(11) Collins	(12) Sullivan	(13) Donnelly	(14) Lambert	(15) Gemmill	(16) Weir	(17) McKinlay (B)	(18) Elliott	(19) Whyte	(20) Booth	(21) Gould	(22) Dailly	REFEREES
X	X	X	X	S2	X	X	X	X	X1	X		X			X		S1				X2	J M Garcia Aranda (Spain)
X	S2	X	X1	X		X	X	X	X2	X		X			X	S1					X	L Vagner (Hungary)
X	X1	X		S1	X	X50	S2	X		X		X			X				S2		X	A M Bujsaim (United Arab Emirates)
3	1+1	3	2	3	0+2	3	3	2+1	2	3		3			1+1	0+1			0+1		3	**TOTAL APPEARANCES**

Quarter-Finals

Italy   0 (0) v (0) 0 France
(France win 4-3 on penalties)

Brazil   3 (3) v (1) 2 Denmark
Bebeto 11 / Jorgensen 2
Rivaldo 26, 60 / B.Laudrup 50

Holland 2 (1) v (1) Argentina
Kluivert 12 / C.Lopez 18
Bergkamp 89

Germany 0 (0) v (1) 3 Croatia
Jarni 45
Vlaovic 80
Suker 85

Semi-Finals

Brazil   1 (0) v (0) 1 Holland
Ronaldo 46 / Kluivert 87
(Brazil win 4-2 on penalties)

France   2 (0) v (0) 1 Croatia
Thuram 47, 70 / Suker 46

Third-Place play off

Holland 1 (1) v (2) 2 Croatia
Zenden 21 / Prosinecki 13
Suker 36

THE FINAL

France   3 (2) v (0) 0 Brazil
Zidane 27, 45, Petit 90

The Teams

France	Brazil
Barthez	Taffarel
Lizarazu	Cafu
Desailly[50]	Aldair
Thuram	Junior Baiano
Leboeuf	Roberto Carlos
Djorkaeff[1]	Cesar Sampaio[1]
Deschamps (c)	Dunga (c)
Zidane	Rivaldo
Petit	Leonardo[2]
Karembeu[2]	Ronaldo
Guivarc'h[3]	Bebeto
Subs:	Subs:
Vieira[1]	Edmundo[1]
Boghossian[2]	Denilson[2]
Dugarry[3]	

ENGLAND'S FOREIGN LEGION

PLAYERS WHO PLAY THEIR FOOTBALL IN ENGLAND AND PLAYED IN THE WORLD CUP FOR OPPOSING COUNTRIES

PLAYER	CLUB	COUNTRY	STAGE REACHED	APPS.	GOALS
Patrick Vieira	Arsenal	France	World Cup winner	2	–
Marcel Desailly	Chelsea*	France	World Cup winner	7	–
Emmanuel Petit	Arsenal	France	World Cup winner	6	2
Frank Leboeuf	Chelsea	France	World Cup winner	3	–
Igor Stimac	Derby County	Croatia	Third-place winners	7	–
Slaven Bilic	Everton	Croatia	Third-place winners	7	–
Jaap Stam	Manchester United*	Holland	Semi-finals	7	–
Dennis Bergkamp	Arsenal	Holland	Semi-finals	7	3
Marc Overmars	Arsenal	Holland	Semi-finals	6	–
Pierre van Hooijdonk	Nottingham Forest	Holland	Semi-finals	3	1
Ed de Goey	Chelsea	Holland	Semi-finals	-	–
Jimmy F. Hasselbaink	Leeds United	Holland	Semi-finals	2	–
Peter Schmeichel	Manchester United	Denmark	Quarter-finals	5	–
Allan Nielsen	Tottenham Hotspur	Denmark	Quarter-finals	5	–
Per Frandsen	Bolton Wanderers	Denmark	Quarter-finals	2	–
Brian Laudrup	Chelsea*	Denmark	Quarter-finals	5	3
Jacob Laursen	Derby County	Denmark	Quarter-finals	1	–
Jugen Kilinsmann	Tottenham	Germany	Quarter-finals	5	3
Roberto Di Matteo	Chelsea	Italy	Quarter-finals	2	–
Frode Grodas	Tottenham Hotspur	Norway	2nd Round	4	–
Gunnar Helle	Leeds United	Norway	2nd Round	1	–
Ronny Johnsen	Manchester United	Norway	2nd Round	4	–
Henning Berg	Manchester United	Norway	2nd Round	4	–
Stig Inge Bjornebye	Liverpool	Norway	2nd Round	4	–
Oyvind Leonhardsen	Liverpool	Norway	2nd Round	3	–
Tore Andre Flo	Chelsea	Norway	2nd Round	4	1
Thomas Myhre	Everton	Norway	2nd Round	-	–
Espen Baardsen	Tottenham Hotspur	Norway	2nd Round	-	–
Egil Ostenstad	Southampton	Norway	2nd Round	1	–
Ole Gunnar Solskjaer	Manchester United	Norway	2nd Round	3	–
Dan Petrescu	Chelsea	Romania	2nd Round	4	1
Viorel Moldovan	Coventry City	Romania	2nd Round	4	2
Colin Calderwood	Tottenham Hotspur	Scotland	Group A	3	–
Colin Hendry	Blackburn Rovers	Scotland	Group A	3	–
Kevin Gallacher	Blackburn Rovers	Scotland	Group A	3	–
Neil Sullivan	Wimbledon	Scotland	Group A	-	–
Scott Gemmill	Nottingham Forest	Scotland	Group A	1	–
Billy McKinlay	Blackburn Rovers	Scotland	Group A	1	–
Matt Elliott	Leicester City	Scotland	Group A	-	–
Christian Dailly	Derby County	Scotland	Group A	3	–
Martin Hiden	Leeds United	Austria	Group B	-	–
Mark Fish	Bolton Wanderers	South Africa	Group C	3	–
Lucas Radebe	Leeds United	South Africa	Group C	3	–
Albert Ferrer	Chelsea*	Spain	Group D	3	–
Brad Friedel	Liverpool	USA	Group F	1	–
Kasey Keller	Leicester City	USA	Group F	1	–
Hamilton Ricard	Middlesbrough	Colombia	Group G	1	–
Fitzroy Simpson	Portsmouth	Jamaica	Group H	3	–
Marcus Gayle	Wimbledon	Jamaica	Group H	3	–
Robbie Earle	Wimbledon	Jamaica	Group H	3	1
Deon Burton	Derby County	Jamaica	Group H	3	–
Frank Sinclair	Chelsea	Jamaica	Group H	3	–
Darryl Powell	Derby County	Jamaica	Group H	2	–
Paul Hall	Portsmouth	Jamaica	Group H	3	–

*Yet to play in England but signed before World Cup Finals.

Printed and bound by Unwin Brothers Ltd.,
The Gresham Press, Old Woking, Surrey GU22 9LH
A Member of the Martins Printing Group